How does **CONTEXT** impact our growth and development?
Do the places, sociocultural environments, and ways in which we were raised influence who we will become and how we will grow and change?

EXPLORE DEVELOPMENT THROUGH THE THEME OF
CONTEXTS

A thoroughly integrated emphasis on the role of context in the lifespan and the diverse forms that context takes (gender, race and ethnicity, socioeconomic status, etc.) helps readers understand the wide range of dynamic influences that shape human development.

Lives in Context and **Cultural Influences on Development** boxes include compelling examples of contextual and cultural influences on development and highlight issues informed by lifespan research including cyberbullying, cultural differences in childbirth, the gender divide in STEM fields, and more.

LIVES IN CONTEXT

The Gender Divide

Gender roles have broadened but women have been slow to reach equal representation in traditionally male-dominated careers in fields such as medicine, law, and science.

Women have entered the workforce in increasing numbers since the 1960s. As generations of women are raised by working mothers and societal perspectives on gender roles have broadened, young women have become interested in careers traditionally held by men. However, women have been slow to reach equal representation in traditionally male-dominated careers in fields such as medicine, law, and science. Careers traditionally held by females, such as nursing, administrative office support, and medical assisting, remain predominantly female—and earn less than traditionally male professions.

Why do few women enter science and other stereotypically masculine careers? We have seen in prior chapters that girls and boys show similar cognitive capacities and that girls tend to show higher levels of achievement on reading and writing tasks. With advancing grade, and particularly entrance to high school, girls' self-esteem tends to decline and they become more uncertain of their academic abilities than do boys (Jacobs, Lanza, Osgood, Eccles, & Wigfield, 2002). During college, many women come to doubt their ability to succeed in male-dominated careers and become more likely to choose non-science majors; or, if they continue in science, they choose socially oriented fields like those in the health professions (Benbow Lubinski, Shea, & Eftekhari-Sanjani, 2000). Prior achievement in math and science is not related to gender gaps in science fields, suggesting that women who choose nonscience majors are not less skilled in these areas (Riegle-Crumb, King, Grodsky, & Muller, 2012).

Young women's ambivalence may be exacerbated by debates raised in recent years regarding whether women's professional success is incompatible with career success. Some studies suggest that parenthood had a negative effect on women's career success, especially when women give birth to their first child at around the same time they enter their careers, whereas men's career success tends to be independent of parenthood (Abele & Spurk, 2011). One study of physicians found that women with children tended to be less advanced in their specialty qualifications, less prone to choose prestigious surgical fields, less likely to have a mentor, and less often aspire to prestigious senior hospital or academic positions (Buddeberg-Fischer et al., 2010). Some conclude that successful women professionals are less likely to have children (Hewlett, 2002).

Whether high-profile traditionally male-dominated careers interfere with women's desires to have children or women who wish to remain childless enter high-power careers is questionable. Regardless, career success and child-rearing can be combined when women have adequate support (Mills, Rindfuss, McDonald, & te Velde, 2011). Experts advise that young women should consider their life plans—what they expect for their professional and personal lives—when planning their futures. There is a need for high school and college programs to help young women develop and achieve high vocational aspirations, set goals to help them achieve their aspirations, and plan ahead to integrate their professional and personal lives.

What Do You Think?

1. Compare the career and family responsibilities that men and women face.
2. From your perspective, is there a gender divide in employment opportunities and barriers? Why or why not? If so, what can be done to reduce gender differences?

CULTURAL INFLUENCES ON DEVELOPMENT

Defining Culture

Cultural influences on development are illustrated by the many ethnic communities that comprise most U.S. cities. What subcultures and neighborhoods can you identify in your community?

A very large and influential part of our context is culture—a set of customs, knowledge, attitudes, and values that are shared by members of a group and are learned early in life through interactions with group members (Holstede, 2001). Most classic theories and research on human development are based on Western samples, and developmental researchers once believed that the processes of human development were universal. Early studies of culture and human development took the form of cross-cultural research, comparing individuals and groups from different cultures to examine how these universal processes worked in different contexts (Gardiner & Kosmitzki, 2010).

In recent decades, we have learned that the cultural context in which individuals live influences development, the timing and expression of many aspects of development (Gardiner & Kosmitzki, 2010). For example, the average age that infants begin to walk varies with cultural context. In Uganda, infants begin to walk at about 10 months of age, in France at about 15 months, and the United States at about 12 months. These differences are influenced by parenting practices that vary by culture. African parents tend to handle infants in ways that stimulate walking, by playing games that allow infants to practice jumping and walking skills (Hopkins & Westra, 1989; Super, 1981). Developmental researchers have argued that because much of the research in

human development has focused on individuals from Western industrialized societies, there is a danger of defining typical development in Western samples as the norm, which can lead to narrow views of human development that do not take into account the variety of contexts in which people live. At the extreme, differences in human development within other cultural groups can be seen as abnormal (Rogoff & Morelli, 1989). Some argue that cross-cultural research that compares the development of people from different cultures in order to understand universals in development is misguided because norms vary by cultural context (Schweder et al., 1998).

There is a growing trend favoring *cultural research*, which examines how culture itself influences development, over cross-cultural research, which simply examines differences across cultures (Schweder et al., 1998). From a cultural research perspective, culture influences our development because it contributes to the context in which we are embedded, transmitting values, attitudes, and beliefs that shape our thoughts, beliefs, and behaviors (Cole, 1999). The shift toward cultural research permits the examination of the multiple cultures that exist within a society. For example, American culture is not homogeneous; many subcultures exist, defined by factors such as ethnicity (e.g., African American, Asian American), religion (e.g., Christian, Muslim), geography (e.g., southern, midwestern), and others, as well as combinations of these factors. Instead of looking for universal similarities in development, cultural research in human development aims to document diversity and understand how the historical and cultural context in which we live influences development throughout our lifetime (Schweder et al., 1998).

What Do You Think?

1. How would you describe American culture? Can you identify aspects of American culture that describe most, if not all, people in the country? Are there aspects of culture in which people or subgroups of people differ?
2. What subcultures can you identify in your own neighborhood, state, or region of the country? What characterizes each of these subcultures?
3. Consider your own experience. With which culture or subculture do you identify? How much of a role do you think your cultural membership has had in your own development?

> *"The material in this textbook was extremely clear and concise. The approach of examining places, environments, and how we were raised was very helpful in explaining the concepts."*
>
> —Emily Bennet, Student Reviewer

EXPLORE DEVELOPMENT THROUGH
APPLICATION

Applying Developmental Science and **Ethical and Policy Applications of Lifespan Development** boxes reflect the increasing relevance and influence of developmental science on issues such as the effectiveness of the federal Head Start program, infant sign language, gender disparities in poverty, the availability of family leave, and whether juvenile criminal offenders should face the death penalty.

"I found the material to be helpful and intriguing. I was easily able to connect and apply the concepts to my life."

—Sarah Crandall, Student Reviewer

"The chapters are organized well and have clear structure to help engage students."

—Kate Vokoun, Instructor, Long Beach City College

APPLYING DEVELOPMENTAL SCIENCE

The Importance of Context in Developmental Science

In its early years, the study of human development was based in laboratory research devoted to uncovering universal aspects of development by stripping away contextual influences (Wertlieb, 2003). This basic research was designed to examine universal processes that apply to all people, such as perceptual development (e.g., what visual skills are infants born with?).

As developmental scientists began to apply their knowledge outside of laboratory settings, however, it became apparent that there are a great many individual differences in development. Developmental scientists have since realized the importance of context. The field of *applied developmental science* has emerged, studying individuals within the contexts in which they live. This approach promotes the ability to understand the diverse range of patterns development takes throughout the life course (Lerner, 2010; Wertlieb, 2003).

Research in human development is now directed toward understanding a variety of social problems and issues of immediate social relevance, such as the capacities of preterm infants, children's ability to provide eyewitness testimony,

adolescent sexual practices, and the impact of disability on the psychological and social adjustment of older adults and their adult children (Fisher, Busch-Rossnagel, Jopp, & Brown, 2013; Lerner, 2012). Applied developmental scientists study and make contributions to social policies on issues that affect children, adolescents, adults, and their families, including environmental quality, health and health care delivery, violence, hunger and poor nutrition, school failure, and pervasive poverty (Tseng, 2012). Developmental scientists seek to enhance the life chances of diverse groups of individuals, families, and communities. Throughout this book, you will be introduced to these and more issues studied by applied developmental scientists.

What Do You Think?

1. Identify three areas that you believe are in need of study or intervention.
2. What challenges do children, adolescents, or adults face that you believe should be studied and addressed?

ETHICAL AND POLICY APPLICATIONS OF LIFESPAN DEVELOPMENT

Same-Sex Marriage and the Law

Same-sex couples share many similarities with heterosexual couples, including longevity and parenting competence (Biblarz & Savci, 2010). However, until the July 2015 Supreme Court decision in *Obergefell v. Hodges*, in many states they were unable to legally marry. Marriage confers health and psychosocial benefits to all couples: same or opposite-sex. Prior to *Obergefell*, same-sex marriage was legal in 36 states and the District of Columbia, but not all states recognized same-sex unions from other states (Pew Research Center, 2015b). *Obergefell v. Hodges* combined four cases challenging states' rights to refuse to recognize or license same-sex marriages, denying couples seek legal rights and protections that come with marriage, such as the right to jointly adopt children.

The interdisciplinary nature of applied developmental science is illustrated by an amicus curiae brief for *Obergefell v. Hodges*, submitted to inform the Supreme Court justices (see http://www.apa.org/about/offices/ogc/amicus/obergefell.pdf). The brief was jointly authored and submitted by more than a dozen professional organizations in psychology, social work, and medicine, including the American Psychological Association (APA), American Medical Association, American Academy of Pediatrics (AAP), National Association of Social Workers, and Association for Marriage and Family Therapy. The amicus brief referred to scientific findings that same-sex relationships are equivalent to heterosexual relationships in essential respects and that there is no scientific basis for concluding that same-sex couples are not fit parents or

that children of same-sex couples are any less psychologically healthy and well-adjusted than children of heterosexual couples. The brief therefore argued that excluding same-sex couples from the institution of marriage denies them social, psychological, and health benefits and is stigmatizing.

With the *Obergefell* ruling, the United States joins the more than a dozen countries with national laws allowing gays and lesbians to marry, including Canada, Finland, Spain, the Netherlands, Argentina, and New Zealand (Pew Research Center, 2015a). In a 2015 survey, nearly two thirds (57%) of Americans said they supported same-sex marriage, compared with 39% who opposed it (Pew Research Center, 2015c). As shown in Figure 14.4, there are large cohort differences such that younger generations express higher levels of support for same-sex marriage, but in recent decades, older generations also have become more supportive of it.

What Do You Think?

1. What role should developmental scientists take in advising courts and policy makers? Do you think they should participate in writing amicus curiae briefs? Why or why not?
2. What might be some of the reasons we see cohort differences in attitudes toward same-sex marriage? Identify contextual factors that might contribute to some of the generational differences we see.

LIFESPAN BRAIN DEVELOPMENT

Brain-Based Education

Effective instruction emphasizes active learning through creative play, artwork, physical activity, and social play.

The brain-based education perspective views learning as multidimensional, including more than academics. Children are encouraged to develop all aspects of their brains, tapping physical, musical, creative, cognitive, and other abilities. According to brain-based educators, the brain changes with experience and is plastic; therefore, everyday experiences such as learning an instrument, role-playing, and learning vocabulary may alter children's brains.

Some brain-based education emphasizes teaching different parts of the brain separately. For example, a common brain-based education instructional strategy is to teach for the left or right lateralized brain. The "left-brain" is said to be the "logical" hemisphere, concerned with language and analysis, while the "right-brain" is said to be the "intuitive" hemisphere concerned with spatial patterns and creativity (Sousa, 2001). Brain-based learning theorists may then encourage teachers to teach specific hemispheres during adapted lessons. To teach to the left hemisphere, teachers have students engage in reading and writing, while right hemisphere-oriented lessons have students create visual representations of concepts (Sousa, 2001).

However, some experts argue that the leap from neurological research to the classroom is large and not supported (Alferink

& Farmer-Dougan, 2010). Like most abilities, language and spatial information are processed differently but simultaneously by the two hemispheres. It is highly improbable, then, that any given lesson, regardless of analytic or spatial type, can stimulate activation of only one hemisphere. Although lateralized, the brain functions as a whole.

For many researchers, the problem of brain-based education is its reliance on the brain itself and in its oversimplification of complex theories and research (Alferink & Farmer-Dougan, 2010; Busso & Pollack, 2014). Although we have learned much, brain research is in its infancy. Researchers do not know enough about how the brain functions and learns to draw direct inferences about teaching (Bruer, 2008). For example, magnetic resonance imaging (MRI) research illuminates patterns of brain activity, but researchers do not yet conclusively know what those patterns mean or if those patterns of brain activity have implications for behavior (Willis, 2007). Using these findings to inform education is premature. Many researchers, therefore, find it problematic to state that teaching strategies should be derived from brain research—at least not yet.

On the positive side, however, brain-based education emphasizes active learning. Teachers who foster active learning encourage students to become engaged and participate in their own learning, such as being creative in artwork, physical activity, and story making (Bruer, 2008). Active learning is an important educational strategy. Active learning is in line with cognitive theory, such as Piaget's, which points to the constructive nature of knowledge, that children must interact with the world and actively construct and modify their schemes. Although many developmental researchers argue that the neurological science behind brain-based education is questionable, the active learning practices that comprise many brain-based learning activities advance children's learning.

What Do You Think?

Identify an advantage and a disadvantage to brain-based education. In your view, should preschools emphasize teaching specifically to the left or right hemisphere?

EXPLORE DEVELOPMENT THROUGH
THE BRAIN

Lifespan Brain Development boxes apply research on neurological development to topics such as the multidimensional "brain-based education" movement, videos that claim to promote precocious infant learning, and how changes in the middle-aged brain relate to behavioral changes typical of individuals in midlife.

"It was very clear and it was a very good read!"

—Elizabeth Strowbridge, Student Reviewer

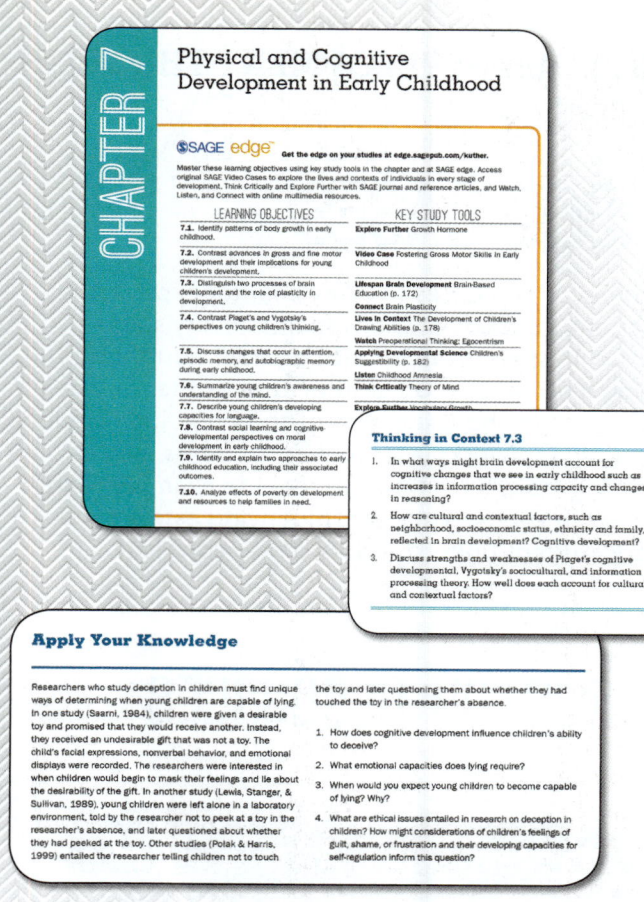

CHAPTER 7

Physical and Cognitive
Development in Early Childhood

EXPLORE DEVELOPMENT THROUGH
HELPFUL LEARNING
AND STUDYING TOOLS

Concept maps that introduce each text section and learning objectives (revisited in chapter-ending summaries) anchor student learning goals while emphasizing key text concepts.

Thinking in Context critical thinking questions at the end of each section and at the end of each boxed feature encourage students to consider and apply theory and research to solve problems.

Chapter-ending **Applying Your Knowledge** case scenarios, followed by in-depth questions, help students apply their understanding of text concepts to particular situations or problems.

"*The video on development by Dr. Kuther was a great example and I see myself showing that video at the very beginning of the course. It is a great example that showcases the importance of the multidisciplinary approach to developmental psychology.*"

—Erikson Neilans, Instructor, University at Buffalo

EXPLORE DEVELOPMENT THROUGH
DR. KUTHER'S
CHALK TALKS

Author Tara Kuther narrates a series of whiteboard-style animations that bring the section-opening concept maps to life. These brief, captivating videos help students learn basic concepts outside the classroom, allowing class time to be spent on active learning, while follow-up questions stimulate critical thinking.

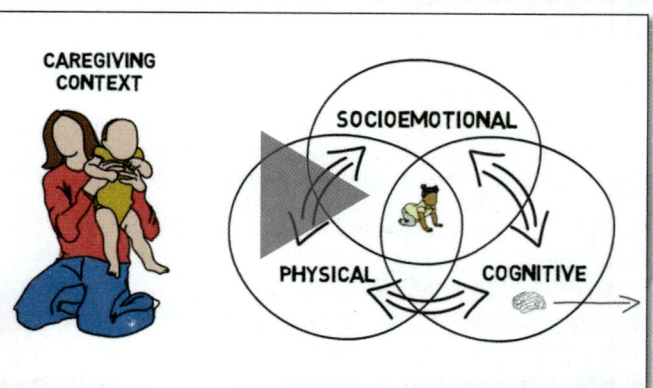

EXPLORE DEVELOPMENT THROUGH
LIVES IN CONTEXT VIDEO CASES

Original Video Cases in every chapter explore the lives and contexts of individuals in every stage of the lifespan, from infancy to older adulthood. Using audio narration, author Tara Kuther guides students beyond the covers of this book into homes, schools, and workplaces to help students master learning objectives through real-life examples and demonstrations, while accompanying assessments track student understanding of key concepts.

EXPLORE DEVELOPMENT THROUGH
ADDITIONAL STUDENT AND INSTRUCTOR RESOURCES

edge.sagepub.com/kuther

SAGE edge offers a robust online environment you can access anytime, anywhere, and features an impressive array of free tools and resources to keep you on the cutting edge of your learning experience.

SAGE edge for Instructors supports your teaching by making it easy to integrate quality content and create a rich learning environment for students.

- **Video and multimedia content** including original demonstrations, interviews, cases, and whiteboard animations to enhance engagement and appeal to students with different learning styles

- **Course Management System integration** to make it easy for student test results and graded assignments to seamlessly flow into instructor gradebooks

- **Test banks built on Bloom's Taxonomy** to provide a diverse range of test items with diploma test generation

- **Sample course syllabi** with suggested models for structuring one's course

- Editable, chapter-specific **PowerPoint® slides** that offer flexibility when creating multimedia lectures

- An **Instructor's Manual** mapped to chapter learning objectives featuring lecture notes, discussion questions, chapter exercises, class assignments, and more

- EXCLUSIVE access to full-text **SAGE journal and reference articles** to expose students to important research and scholarship tied to chapter concepts

SAGE edge for Students provides a personalized approach to help you accomplish your coursework goals in an easy-to-use learning environment.

- Mobile-friendly **eFlashcards** to strengthen understanding of key concepts

- Mobile-friendly practice **quizzes** to encourage self-guided assessment and practice

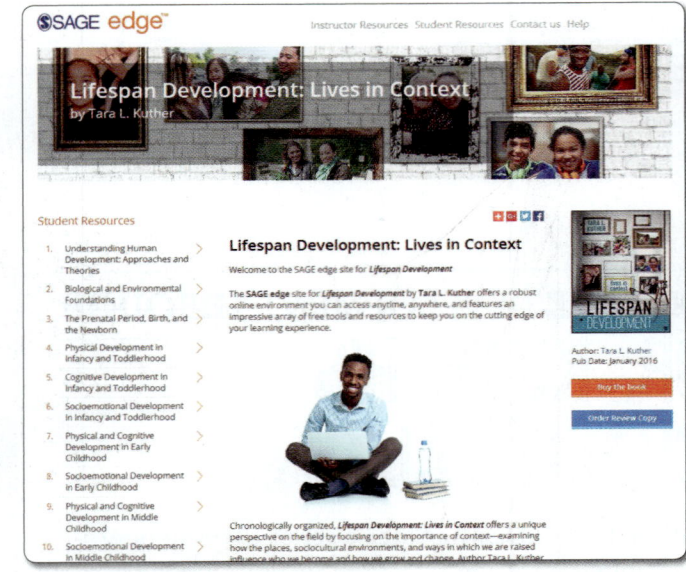

- A complete online **action plan** to track student progress and enhance the learning experience

- **Chapter summaries** with **learning objectives** to reinforce the most important material

- **Video and multimedia content** including original demonstrations, interviews, cases, and whiteboard animations to appeal to students with different learning styles

- **Interactive exercises** and meaningful web links to help students mine internet resources, explore topics, and answer critical-thinking questions

- EXCLUSIVE access to full-text **SAGE journal and reference articles** accompanied by discussion questions to support and expand on chapter concepts

LIFESPAN
DEVELOPMENT

SAGE was founded in 1965 by Sara Miller McCune to support the dissemination of usable knowledge by publishing innovative and high-quality research and teaching content. Today, we publish over 900 journals, including those of more than 400 learned societies, more than 800 new books per year, and a growing range of library products including archives, data, case studies, reports, and video. SAGE remains majority-owned by our founder, and after Sara's lifetime will become owned by a charitable trust that secures our continued independence.

Los Angeles | London | New Delhi | Singapore | Washington DC

LIFESPAN DEVELOPMENT

[LIVES IN CONTEXT]

TARA L. KUTHER
Western Connecticut State University

Los Angeles | London | New Delhi
Singapore | Washington DC

Los Angeles | London | New Delhi
Singapore | Washington DC

FOR INFORMATION:

SAGE Publications, Inc.
2455 Teller Road
Thousand Oaks, California 91320
E-mail: order@sagepub.com

SAGE Publications Ltd.
1 Oliver's Yard
55 City Road
London EC1Y 1SP
United Kingdom

SAGE Publications India Pvt. Ltd.
B 1/I 1 Mohan Cooperative Industrial Area
Mathura Road, New Delhi 110 044
India

SAGE Publications Asia-Pacific Pte. Ltd.
3 Church Street
#10-04 Samsung Hub
Singapore 049483

Printed in the United States of America.

ISBN 978-1-4833-6885-6

Acquisitions Editor: Reid Hester
Editorial Assistant: Morgan Shannon
eLearning Editor: Lucy Berbeo
Development Editor: Nathan Davidson
Production Editor: Olivia Weber-Stenis
Copy Editor: Megan Markanich
Typesetter: C&M Digitals (P) Ltd.
Proofreader: Sally Jaskold
Indexer: Hyde Park Publishing Services
Cover Designer: Gail Buschman
Marketing Manager: Shari Countryman

This book is printed on acid-free paper.

SUSTAINABLE FORESTRY INITIATIVE
Certified Sourcing
www.sfiprogram.org
SFI-00993
THIS LABEL APPLIES TO TEXT STOCK ONLY

16 17 18 19 20 10 9 8 7 6 5 4 3 2 1

BRIEF CONTENTS

CONTENTS

PART I. FOUNDATIONS OF LIFESPAN HUMAN DEVELOPMENT

1

UNDERSTANDING HUMAN DEVELOPMENT: APPROACHES AND THEORIES

2

BIOLOGICAL AND ENVIRONMENTAL FOUNDATIONS

PART III. EARLY CHILDHOOD

7

PHYSICAL AND COGNITIVE DEVELOPMENT IN EARLY CHILDHOOD

8

SOCIOEMOTIONAL DEVELOPMENT IN EARLY CHILDHOOD

PART IV. MIDDLE CHILDHOOD

9

PHYSICAL AND COGNITIVE DEVELOPMENT IN MIDDLE CHILDHOOD

10

SOCIOEMOTIONAL DEVELOPMENT IN MIDDLE CHILDHOOD

LIST OF BOXED FEATURES

PREFACE

Lifespan Development: Lives in Context has its origins in 20-plus years of class discussions about the nature of development in which my students have questioned, challenged, and inspired me. My goal in writing this text is to explain the sophisticated interactions that constitute development in a way that is comprehensive yet concise.

Lifespan Development: Lives in Context focuses on two key themes that promote understanding of how humans develop through the lifespan: the centrality of context and the applied value of developmental science. These two themes are highlighted throughout the text as well as in boxed features. This text also emphasizes cutting-edge research and a student-friendly writing style.

CONTEXTUAL PERSPECTIVE

Development does not occur in a vacuum but is a function of dynamic interactions between individuals, their genetic makeup, and myriad contextual influences. We are all embedded in multiple layers of context, including tangible and intangible circumstances that surround our development, such as family, ethnicity, culture, neighborhood, community, norms, values, and historical events. The contextual approach of *Lifespan Development: Lives in Context* emphasizes understanding the role of context in diversity and the many forms that diversity takes (gender, race and ethnicity, socioeconomic status, etc.). The text emphasizes how the places, sociocultural environments, and ways in which we are raised influence who we become and how we grow and change throughout the lifespan. This theme is infused throughout the text and highlighted specifically in two types of boxed features: Lives in Context and Cultural Influences on Development.

EMPHASIS ON APPLICATION

The field of lifespan developmental science is unique because so much of its content has immediate relevance to our daily lives. Students may wonder this: Do the first three years shape the brain for a lifetime of experiences? Is learning more than one language beneficial to children? Should teens work? Do people's personalities change over their lifetimes? Do adults go through a midlife crisis? How common is dementia in

older adulthood? *Lifespan Development: Lives in Context* engages students by exploring these and many more real-world questions. The emphasis on application is highlighted specifically in two types of boxed features: Applying Developmental Science and Ethical and Policy Applications of Lifespan Development. The Ethical and Policy Applications of Lifespan Development feature reflects the increasing influence of developmental science on issues such as the effectiveness of the federal Head Start program, whether juvenile criminal offenders should face the death penalty, the availability of family leave, the manifestations of workplace age discrimination, and gender disparities in poverty.

CURRENT RESEARCH

The lifespan course comes with the challenge of covering the growing mass of research findings within the confines of a single semester. In writing *Lifespan Development: Lives in Context*, I have sifted through the most current research available, selecting important findings. However, classic theory and research remains an important foundation for today's most exciting scholarly work. I integrate cutting-edge and classic research to present a unified story of what is currently known in developmental psychology. One of the most rapidly growing areas of developmental science research is in neuroscience, and this is reflected in the Lifespan Brain Development boxed feature, which applies research on neurological development to issues such as videos that claim to promote precocious infant learning, the multidimensional "brain-based education" movement, and how changes in the middle-aged brain relate to behavioral changes typical of individuals in midlife.

ACCESSIBLE WRITING STYLE

Having taught at a regional public university for the past 20 years, I write in a style intended to engage undergraduate readers like my own students. This text is intended to help them understand challenging concepts in language that will not overwhelm: I have avoided jargon but maintained the use of professional and research terms that students need to know in order to digest classic and current literature in the lifespan development field.

ORGANIZATION

Lifespan Development: Lives in Context is organized into eighteen chronological chapters that depict the natural unfolding of development over the lifespan from genetic foundations, conception, and birth to older adulthood and the end of life. Chapters are grouped into eight thematic units that represent the major periods in the lifespan.

Part I, Foundations of Lifespan Human Development, includes Chapters 1, 2, and 3. Chapter 1 combines lifespan theory and research design within a single chapter. I chose this streamlined approach because, given limited class time, many instructors do not cover stand-alone research chapters. The streamlined approach combines comprehensive coverage of methods of data collection, research design, developmental designs (such as sequential designs), and ethical issues in research with full coverage of the major theories in developmental psychology. Chapter 2 presents the biological foundations of development, including patterns of genetic inheritance, gene-environment interactions, and epigenetics. Chapter 3 describes prenatal development and birth.

Part II, Infancy and Toddlerhood, comprises three chapters because the rapid and dramatic transformations over the first years of life merit comprehensive discussion of the physical, cognitive, and socioemotional changes in stand-alone chapters (Chapters 4, 5, and 6).

The remaining parts contain two chapters each: physical and cognitive development as well as socioemotional development. Part III covers early childhood; Part IV, middle childhood; Part V, adolescence; Part VI, early adulthood; Part VII, middle adulthood; and Part VIII, late adulthood. The final chapter, Chapter 18: Socioemotional Development in Late Adulthood and the End of Life, also includes material on death and dying and adjustment to bereavement in older adulthood. I chose to include this material within Chapter 18 to reflect the importance of death as a part of life and coping with death as a developmental task of this period in life.

PEDAGOGY

My day-to-day experiences in the classroom have helped me to keep college students' interests and abilities at the forefront. Unlike many textbook authors, I teach four classes each semester at a comprehensive regional public university (and have done so for the past two decades). I have taught an online course more often than not since 2002. My daily exposure to multiple classes and many students helps keep me grounded in the ever-changing concerns and interests of college students. I teach a diverse group of students. Some live on campus but most commute. Most of my students are ages 18 to 24, but my classes also include many so-called nontraditional

students over the age of 24. A growing number are veterans. I have many opportunities to try new examples and activities. I believe that what works in my classroom will be helpful to readers and instructors. I use the pedagogical elements of *Lifespan Development: Lives in Context* in my own classes and modify them based on my experiences.

LEARNING OBJECTIVES AND SUMMARIES

Core learning objectives are listed at the beginning of each chapter. The end-of-chapter summary returns to each learning objective, recapping the key concepts presented in the chapter related to that objective.

CRITICAL THINKING

Thinking in Context: At the end of each main section within the chapter, these critical thinking questions encourage readers to compare concepts, apply theoretical perspectives, and consider applications of research findings presented. In addition, each boxed feature concludes with critical thinking questions that challenge students to assess and evaluate the issues highlighted in that feature. The boxed features are as follows:

- Applying Developmental Science
- Cultural Influences on Development
- Ethical and Policy Applications of Lifespan Development
- Lifespan Brain Development
- Lives in Context

APPLICATION

Applying Your Knowledge: Each chapter closes with a case scenario, followed by in-depth questions that require students to apply their understanding to address a particular situation or problem.

SUPPLEMENTS

ORIGINAL VIDEO

Lifespan Development is accompanied by a robust collection of **Lives in Context Video Cases**, which help students understand key concepts through real-life examples, as well as **Dr. Kuther's Chalk Talks**, a series of whiteboard-style videos carefully crafted to engage students with course content. All can be accessed at the open-access SAGE edge website, **edge.sagepub.com/kuther**, described in more detail below.

FOR INSTRUCTORS

SAGE edge is a robust online environment featuring an impressive array of free tools and resources. Instructors using this book can access customizable PowerPoint slides, along with an extensive test bank built on Bloom's taxonomy that features multiple-choice, true/false, essay and short answer questions for each chapter. The instructor's manual is mapped to learning objectives and features lecture notes, discussion questions, chapter exercises, class assignments and more.

FOR STUDENTS

At the start of each chapter, learning objectives are paired with **Key Study Tools** available at **edge.sagepub.com/kuther** and designed to promote mastery of course material. Students are encouraged to access boxed features and **Video Cases**, **Explore Further** with SAGE's influential handbooks and encyclopedias, and **Think Critically** with articles from award-winning SAGE journals accompanied by discussion questions; they can also **Watch** web clips, **Listen** to podcasts, and **Connect** with web resources. The text can be paired with an Interactive eBook that offers one-click access to these study tools for a seamless learning experience. Students can practice with mobile-friendly **eFlashcards** and take the **Web Quiz** at SAGE edge to find out what they've learned.

ACKNOWLEDGMENTS

This book has benefited from the support of many. I have been very fortunate to work with an exceptionally talented and accommodating team at SAGE. Thanks go to Lucy Berbeo for coordinating the ancillaries and videos that accompany this book, Nathan Davidson for his expertise in design and figures, and Shari Countryman for coordinating marketing. I also thank Lara Parra and Morgan McCardell. Thanks go to Michele Sordi, who expressed interest in this project many years ago. I am indebted to Elsa Peterson for providing timely, comprehensive, and insightful feedback accompanied by clear editorial suggestions that substantially improved the manuscript. Lisa Caya, Erin Harmeyer, Sara Harris, Mark G. Harmon, Daniel McConnell, and Brandy Moore provided invaluable support in constructing ancillaries and videos, for which I am appreciative. I especially thank my editor, Reid Hester, for wise counsel, encouragement, and ardent support.

Thanks go to SAGE family and friends and the faculty and students at California State University, Northridge, who participated in the chapter videos.

I thank my students for asking the questions and engaging in the discussions that inform this book. Finally, I thank my family. My parents, Phil and Irene Kuther, have provided unconditional love and support throughout my own lifespan. I have learned much about development from my stepchildren, Freddy and Julia, and I thank them. Most of all, I am thankful for the support of my husband, Fred, for his patience, encouragement, and unwavering optimism and love throughout this process—and every day.

SAGE wishes to thank the following reviewers for their valuable contributions to the development of this manuscript:

Linda Aulgur, Westminster College, Fulton MO

Diana Lang Baltimore, Iowa State University

David E. Baskind, Delta College

Geralynne A. Berg, Lac Courte Oreilles Ojibwa Community College

Shannon Bert, University of Oklahoma

David M. Biek, Middle Georgia State College

Sandra Broz, Northeast Community College

Kristine A Camacho, Worcester State University

Amy Chanmugam, University of Texas at San Antonio

Michael E. Cox, Ohio Christian University

Gregory Czyszczon, Blue Ridge Community College

Sabrina Des Rosiers, Barry University

Roberta Dihoff, Rowan University

Theresa Garfield Dorel, Texas A&M University San Antonio

Laura Duvall, Cerritos College

Carrie Fitzgerald, Fredonia, State University of New York

Anne Marie Ross Freeman, Rockingham Community College

Wykeshia W. Glass, North Carolina Central University

Jerry Green, Tarrant County College

Erin Harmeyer, University of Wyoming

Elizabeth A. Hennon, University of Evansville

Vivian C. Hsu, Pennsylvania State University–Abington

Nichole L. Huff, NC State University

Kathy Immel, UW-Fox Valley

Keun Kyu Kim, Delaware State University

Pamela J. Lemons, SLCC

Nancy S. Longo, Capella University

Merranda Romero Marin, New Mexico State University

Brandy Moore, Texas A&M University–Texarkana

Robin Musselman, Lehigh Carbon Community College

Jennifer Ortiz Garza, University of Houston–Victoria

Gary Popoli, Stevenson University

Jane Proudlove, Red Deer College

Martha Ravola, Alcorn State University

Fay Roseman, Barry University

Amy G. Sauber, Temple University

Lisa L. Schulz, University of North Texas

Nancy Smuckler, University of Wisconsin–Milwaukee

Rodger Stein, American River Community College

Tara M. Stoppa, Eastern University

Lisa Strout, Rivier University

Michela Tripodi, Kean University

Anna Valcheva, The College of St. Rose

Kathleen Vokoun, Long Beach Community College

John Walsh, Metropolitan State University

Heather M. Whaley, Carson Newman University

ABOUT THE AUTHOR

Tara L. Kuther is professor of psychology at Western Connecticut State University where she has taught courses in child, adolescent, and adult development since 1996. She earned her BA in psychology from Western Connecticut State University and her MA and PhD in developmental psychology at Fordham University. Dr. Kuther's research on moral development, social cognition, and risks to adolescent development has appeared in journals such as *Journal of Adolescence, Journal of Early Adolescence, Addictive Behaviors,* and the *American Journal of Orthopsychiatry.* Dr. Kuther is particularly interested in promoting undergraduate and graduate students' professional development and has authored over a dozen books intended to help students navigate the challenges of pursing undergraduate and graduate degrees in psychology.

Dr. Kuther is fellow of the Society for the Teaching of Psychology (American Psychological Association, Division 2). Her interest in promoting excellence in college teaching has influenced her scholarly and professional activities. Dr. Kuther's work examining ethical issues that arise in higher education and methods of sensitizing students to ethical issues has appeared in journals such as *Teaching of Psychology, College Teaching,* and *Gerontology and Geriatrics Education.* Currently the chair of the Society for Research in Child Development Teaching Committee, Dr. Kuther has also been active in the Society for the Teaching of Psychology as executive committee member, chair of the Task Force on Instructional Research Awards, and chair of the Long-Range Planning Committee.

PART I

Foundations of Lifespan Human Development

Development is a lifelong process. We experience many dynamic changes in biological, cognitive, and socioemotional processes that interact over time. For example, brain development, a biological change, permits more sophisticated thinking, or cognitive development, which influences socioemotional development including how children understand emotions and how they interact with other people.

All throughout life we are embedded in multiple contexts that influence, and are influenced by, us. The specific contexts and the relative importance of each shift over time. In infancy the family context is most pertinent because an infant spends all of its time with its caregivers. As the child develops and enters school, peer and school contexts become increasingly important. In adolescence and adulthood, the work context emerges.

All of the contexts in which we are embedded interact, influencing each other. Interactions at home with parents and siblings influence interactions at school and in the peer group. We are also embedded in a larger neighborhood context, with a more distal influence on us, through factors such as the availability of parks and playgrounds, after-school programs, and feelings of safety. We and our ever-changing contexts are also embedded in a culture that influences our values, attitudes, and beliefs throughout our lives.

Watch at
edge.sagepub.com/kuther

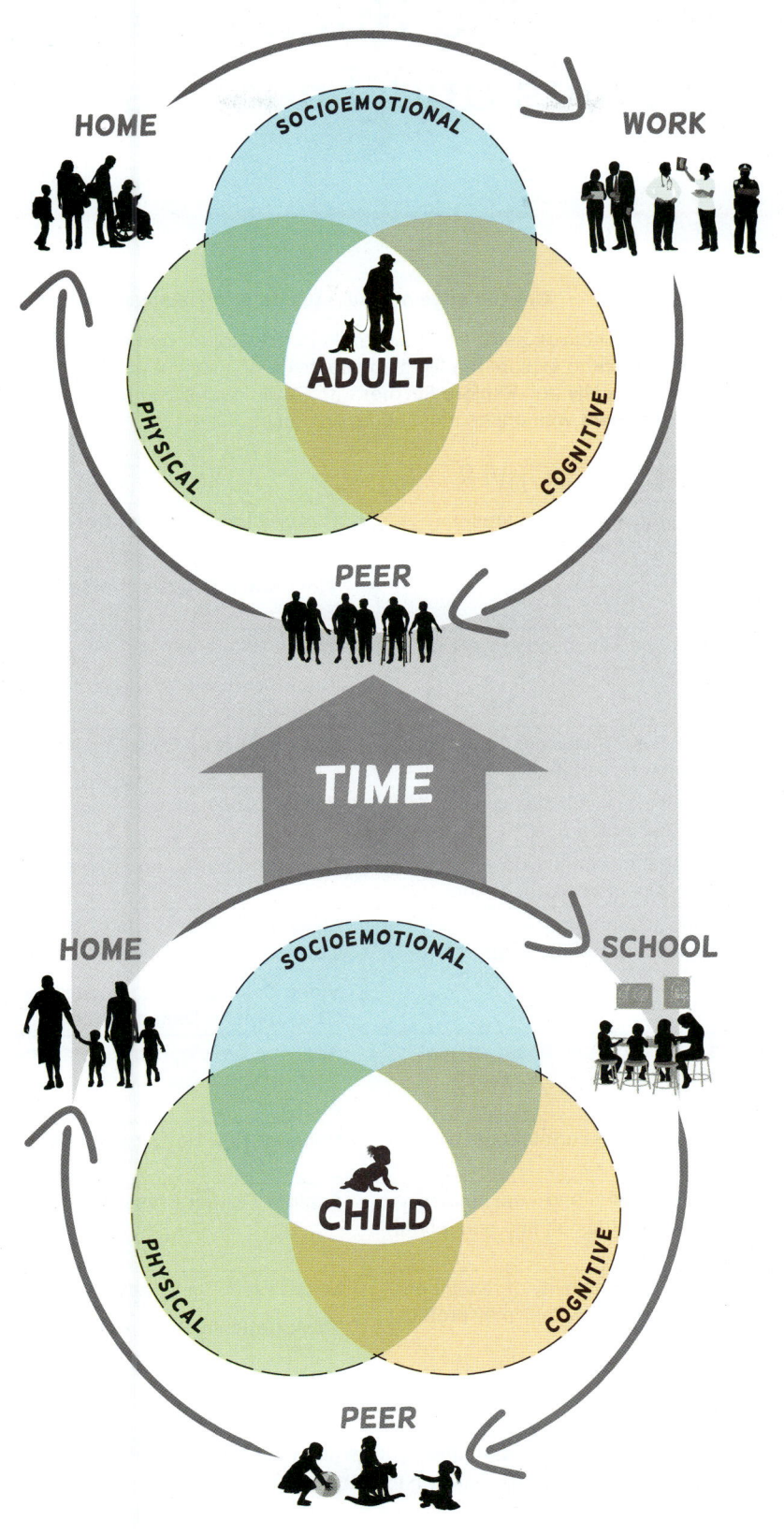

Images: ©iStock.com

CHAPTER 1

Understanding Human Development: Approaches and Theories

$SAGE edge™   **Get the edge on your studies at edge.sagepub.com/kuther.**

Master these learning objectives using key study tools in the chapter and at SAGE edge. Access original SAGE **Video Cases** to explore the lives and contexts of individuals in every stage of development, **Think Critically** and **Explore Further** with SAGE journal and reference articles, and **Watch**, **Listen**, and **Connect** with online multimedia resources.

LEARNING OBJECTIVES	KEY STUDY TOOLS
1.1. Outline five principles of the lifespan developmental perspective.	**Cultural Influences on Development** Defining Culture (p. 8)
	Video Case Context and Development: Large Family
1.2. Explain three theoretical controversies about human development.	**Watch** Nature vs. Nurture Controversy
	Think Critically Nature and Nurture Influence Development
1.3. Differentiate Freud's psychosexual theory from Erikson's psychosocial theory.	**Explore Further** Early Childhood Development
1.4. Distinguish operant and classical conditioning from social learning.	**Watch** Conditioning
1.5. Compare Piaget's cognitive-developmental theory and information processing theory.	**Connect** Information Processing Theory
1.6. Contrast sociocultural systems theories and evolutionary perspectives on development.	**Lives in Context** Sociohistorical Influences on Development (p. 21)
	Video Case Sociohistorical Influences on Development: Desegregation
1.7. Compare self-report and observational methods of collecting information about participants.	**Applying Developmental Science** The Importance of Context in Developmental Science (p. 25)
1.8. Contrast the uses of correlational and experimental research.	**Connect** How Do Correlational Studies Work?
1.9. Assess the strengths and weaknesses of cross-sectional, longitudinal, and sequential research designs.	**Explore Further** Cross-Sectional Design
1.10. Discuss the responsibility of researchers to their participants and how they may protect them from harm.	**Listen** Facebook's Newsfeed Study
	Think Critically Role of Institutional Review Boards

Think back over your lifetime. How have you grown and changed through the years? Do your parents describe you as a happy baby? Were you fussy? Do you remember your first day of kindergarten? What are some of your most vivid childhood memories? Did you begin puberty early, late, or was your development similar to others your age? Were your adolescent years a stressful time? What types of changes do you expect to undergo in your adult years? Where will you live? Will you have a spouse? Will you have children? What career will you choose? How might these life choices and circumstances influence how

Get more out of your study time.

The **SAGE Interactive eBook** provides one-click access to integrated study tools that will enrich your understanding of course content.

▶ **Watch** video clips to learn actively

▣ **Think Critically** with SAGE Journals

▤ **Explore Further** with SAGE Reference

▣ **Connect** with relevant web resources

▣ **Listen** to podcasts for real-world context

you age and your perspective in older adulthood? Will your personality remain the same or change over time? In short, how will you change over the course of your lifespan?

WHAT IS LIFESPAN HUMAN DEVELOPMENT?

This is a book about **lifespan human development**— the ways in which people grow, change, and stay the same throughout their lives, from conception to death. When people use the term *development*, they often mean the transformation from infant to adult. However, development does not end with adulthood. We continue to change in predictable ways throughout our lifetime—even into old age. Developmental scientists study human development. They seek to understand lifetime patterns of change.

How have you grown and changed throughout your life? How have your early experiences influenced your later experiences and who you are today? Table 1.1 illustrates the many phases of life that we progress through from conception to death. Each phase of life may have a different label and set of developmental tasks, but all have value. The changes that we

undergo during infancy influence how we experience later changes, such as those during adolescence and beyond. This is true for all ages in life. Each phase of life is important and accompanied by its own demands and opportunities.

Change is the most obvious indicator of development. The muscle strength and coordination needed to play sports increases over childhood and adolescence, peaks in early adulthood, and begins to decline thereafter, declining more rapidly from middle to late adulthood. Similarly, children's capacity to learn and perform cognitive tasks increases as they progress from infancy through adolescence, and adults typically experience a decline in the speed of cognitive processing. However, there also are ways in which we change little over our lifetimes. Some personality traits, for example, are highly stable over the lifespan, so that we remain largely the "same person" into old age (McCrae, 2002; Roberts & Caspi, 2003; Wortman, Lucas, & Donnellan, 2012).

Lifespan human development can be described by several principles. As discussed in the following sections, development is (1) multidimensional, (2) multidirectional, (3) plastic, (4) influenced by multiple contexts, and (5) multidisciplinary (Baltes, 1997; Baltes & Carstensen, 2003; Baltes, Lindenberger, & Staudinger, 1998).

DEVELOPMENT IS MULTIDIMENSIONAL

Physical changes such as body growth are the most obvious forms of development. Not only do our bodies change but so do our minds, the ways in which we show emotion, and our social relationships. In this way, development is multidimensional: It entails changes in many areas of development, including the physical, the cognitive, and the psychosocial (Baltes et al., 1998; Baltes, 1997; Staudinger & Lindenberger, 2003). **Physical development** refers to body maturation and growth, including body size, proportion, appearance, health, and perceptual abilities. **Cognitive development** refers to the maturation of thought processes and the tools that we use to obtain knowledge, become aware of the world around us, and solve problems. **Socioemotional development** includes changes in personality, emotions, views of oneself, social skills, and interpersonal relationships with

FIGURE 1.1: Multidimensional Nature of Development

Physical
Cognitive
Socioemotional

Advances in physical, cognitive, and socioemotional development interact, permitting children to play sports, learn more efficiently, and develop close friendships.

TABLE 1.1 Ages in Human Development

LIFE STAGE	APPROXIMATE AGE	DESCRIPTION
Prenatal	Conception to birth	Shortly after conception, a single-celled organism grows and multiplies. This is the most rapid period of physical development in the lifespan as basic body structures and organs form and grow. The fetus hears, responds to sensory stimuli (such as the sound of its mother's voice), learns, remembers, and begins the process of adjusting to life after birth.
Infancy and toddlerhood	Birth to 2 years	The newborn is equipped with senses that help it to learn about the world. Environmental influences stimulate the brain to grow more complex, and the child interacts with her environment, shaping it. Physical growth occurs as well as the development of motor, perceptual, and intellectual skills. Children show advances in language comprehension and use, problem solving, self-awareness, and emotional control. They become more independent and interested in interacting with other children and form bonds with parents and others.
Early childhood	2 to 6 years	Children grow steadily over these years of play prior to beginning elementary school. Children's muscles strengthen, and they become better at controlling and coordinating their bodies. Children's bodies become more slender and adultlike in proportions. Memory, language, and imagination improve. Children become more independent and better able to regulate their emotions as well as develop a sense of right and wrong. Children become more aware of their own characteristics and feelings. Family remains children's primary social tie, but other children become more important and new ties to peers are established.
Middle childhood	6 to 11 years	Growth slows, and health tends to be better in middle childhood than at any other time during the lifespan. Strength and athletic ability increase dramatically. Children show improvements in their ability to reason, remember, read, and use arithmetic. As children advance cognitively and gain social experience, they understand themselves and think about moral issues in more complex ways as compared with younger children. As friendships develop, peers and group memberships become more important.
Adolescence	11 to 18 years	Adolescents' bodies grow rapidly. They become physically and sexually mature. Though some immature thinking persists, adolescents can reason in sophisticated and adultlike ways. Adolescents are driven to learn about themselves and begin the process of discovering who they are, apart from their parents. Most adolescents retain good relationships with parents, but peer groups increase in importance. Adolescents and their peers influence each other reciprocally. It is through adolescents' interactions with family and peers that they begin to establish a sense of who they are.
Early adulthood	18 to 40 years	In early adulthood, physical condition peaks and then shows slight declines with time. Lifestyle choices, such as smoking, diet, and physical activity, play a large role in influencing health. As they enter early adulthood, young adults experience a great many changes, such as moving out of the family home, going to college, establishing mature romantic relationships, and beginning careers. The timing of these transitions varies, but most fully enter adult roles by the mid-20s. Young adults' understanding of themselves is complex and shifts as they experience life changes and take on new responsibilities and new roles. Young adults make and carry out decisions regarding career, lifestyle, and intimate relationships. Most young adults join the workforce, marry or establish a long-term bond with a spouse, and become parents.
Middle adulthood	40 to 65 years	In middle adulthood, people begin to notice changes in their vision, hearing, physical stamina, and sexuality. Basic mental abilities, expertise, and practical problem-solving skills peak. Career changes and family transitions require that adults continue to refine their understandings of themselves. Some adults experience burnout and career changes while others enjoy successful leadership positions and increased earning power at the peak of their careers. Stress stems from assisting children to become independent, adapting to an empty nest, and assisting elderly parents with their own health and personal needs.

(Continued)

TABLE 1.1 (Continued)

LIFE STAGE	APPROXIMATE AGE	DESCRIPTION
Late adulthood	65 years and beyond	Most older adults remain healthy and active despite physical declines. Reaction time slows, and most older adults show decline in some aspects of memory and intelligence, but an increase in expertise and wisdom compensates for losses. Most older adult friendships are old friendships, and these tend to be very close and a source of support. At the same time, older adults are less likely to form new friendships than at other times in life. They face adjustments to retirement, confront decreased physical health and strength, cope with personal losses (such as the death of a loved one), think about impending death, and search for meaning in their lives.
Death		Death itself is a process. Regardless of whether it is sudden and unexpected, the result of a lengthy illness, or simply old age, death entails the stopping of heartbeat, circulation, breathing, and brain activity. A person's death causes changes in his or her social context—family members and friends must adjust to and accept the loss.

family and friends. Each of these areas of development overlap and interact. With advances in cognitive development, for example, a child may become better able to take her best friend's point of view, which in turn influences her socioemotional development as she becomes more empathetic and sensitive to her friend's needs and develops a more mature friendship. Figure 1.1 illustrates these three areas of development and how they interact.

DEVELOPMENT IS MULTIDIRECTIONAL

Development is commonly described as a series of improvements in performance and functioning, but in fact development is multidirectional, meaning that it consists of both gains and losses, growth and decline, throughout the lifespan (Baltes et al., 1998; Baltes, 1997; Staudinger & Lindenberger, 2003). For example, we are born with a *stepping reflex*, an innate involuntary response in which infants make steplike movements when held upright over a table, bed, or hard horizontal surface (for more information about reflexes, see Chapter 4). Over the first year of life, infants gain new motor skills, and the stepping reflex disappears (Thelen, Fisher, & Ridley-Johnson, 2002). In contrast, older adults' social networks narrow and they have fewer friends; however, their relationships become more significant and meaningful (Carstensen & Mikels, 2005). Throughout life, there is a shifting balance between gains, improvements in performance (common early in life), and losses, declines in performance (common late in life; Baltes & Carstensen, 2003). At all ages, however, individuals can compensate for losses by improving existing skills and developing new ones (Boker, 2013; Freund & Baltes, 2007). For example, though the speed at which people think tends to slow in older adulthood, increases in knowledge and experience enable older adults to compensate for the loss of speed, so that they generally retain their ability to complete day-to-day tasks and solve everyday problems (Bluck & Gluck, 2004; Hess, Leclerc, Swaim, & Weatherbee, 2009; Margrett, Allaire, Johnson, Daugherty, & Weatherbee,

2010). Outside of our awareness, the brain naturally adapts to a lifetime of sensory experiences in order to portray the world around us efficiently and accurately as we age well into older adulthood (Moran, Symmonds, Dolan, & Friston, 2014).

DEVELOPMENT IS PLASTIC

Development is characterized by **plasticity**: It is malleable or changeable. Frequently, the brain and body can compensate for illness and injury. Children who are injured and experience brain damage may show resilience as other parts of the brain may take on new functions. The plastic nature of human development allows people to modify their traits and capacities throughout life (Baltes et al., 1998; Baltes, 1997; Staudinger & Lindenberger, 2003). For example, older adults who have experienced a decline in balance and muscle strength can regain and improve these capabilities through exercise (Marques et al., 2013; McAuley et al., 2013). Plasticity generally tends to decline as we age, but it does not disappear entirely. For example,

Reuters/Mike Blake

Some plasticity is retained throughout life. Practicing athletic activities can help older adults rebuild muscle and improve balance.

short instruction can enhance the memory capacities of very old adults but less so than younger adults (Singer, Lindenberger, & Baltes, 2003). Thus, memory plasticity is preserved, but to a reduced degree, in very old age.

DEVELOPMENT IS INFLUENCED BY MULTIPLE CONTEXTS

In its simplest terms, **context** refers to where and when a person develops. Context includes aspects of the physical and social environment such as family, neighborhood, country, **culture**, and historical time period. Context also includes intangible factors—characteristics that are not visible to the naked eye, such as values, customs, and ideals. Culture is a particularly important context that influences us, as illustrated in Cultural Influences on Development (p. 8).

In order to understand a given individual's development, we must look to his or her context. For example, consider the context in which you were raised. Where did you grow up? City? Suburb? Rural area? What was your neighborhood like? Were you encouraged to be assertive and actively question the adults around you, or were you expected to be quiet and avoid confrontation? How large a part was religion in your family's life? How did religious values shape your parent's child-rearing practices and your own values? How did your family's economic status affect your development?

An important context that influences our development is the time period in which we live. Some contextual influences are tied to particular historical eras and explain why a generation of people born at the same time, called a **cohort**, are similar in ways that people born at other times are different. History-graded influences include wars, epidemics, and economic shifts such as periods of depression or prosperity (Baltes, 1987). These influences shape our development and our views of the world—and set cohorts apart from one another. Adults who came of age during the Great Depression and World War II are similar in some ways that make them different from later cohorts; for example, they tend to have particularly strong views on the importance of the family, civic mindedness, and social connection (Rogler, 2002). Age-graded influences, those tied to chronological age, such as the age at which the average person enters school, reaches puberty, graduates high school, gets married, or has children, are also shaped by context as the normative age of each of these events has shifted over the last few generations (Baltes, 1987).

What role have larger historical events played in your development? For example, consider Hurricane Sandy of October 2012, the second costliest hurricane in the United States, which affected 24 states, including the entire Eastern Seaboard, with flooding, downed power lines, and many destroyed homes. Other examples of historical events include the terrorist attacks of September 11, 2001, the election of the first African American president of the United States in 2008, and the school shooting in Newtown, Connecticut, in 2012. How have historical events influenced you and those around you? Can you identify ways in which, because of historical events, your cohort may differ from your parents' cohort?

DEVELOPMENT IS MULTIDISCIPLINARY

To say that people are complex is an understatement. Scientists who study lifespan human development attempt to understand people's bodies, minds, and social worlds. The contributions of many disciplines are needed to understand how people grow, think, and interact with their world. Psychologists, sociologists, anthropologists, biologists, neuroscientists, and medical researchers all conduct research that is relevant to understanding aspects of human development. For example, consider cognitive development. Children's performance on cognitive measures, such as problem solving, is influenced by their physical health and nutrition (Anjos et al., 2013), interactions with peers (Fawcett & Garton, 2005), and neurological development (Ullman, Almeida, & Klingberg, 2014)—findings from the fields of medicine, psychology, and neuroscience, respectively. In order to understand how people develop at all periods in life, developmental scientists must combine insights from all of these disciplines.

The field of lifespan human development studies the ways in which people grow, change, and stay the same throughout their lives. Human development is complex. We change in multiple ways, show gains and losses over time, and retain the ability to change over our lifespan. The context in which we live influences who we become. Developmental science incorporates research from multiple disciplines.

Thinking in Context 1.1

1. Describe your own development. In what ways have you changed over your lifetime? What characteristics have remained the same?

2. Lifespan human development is multidimensional, multidirectional, plastic, and influenced by multiple contexts. Consider your own experience, and provide examples from your life that illustrate the multidimensional, multidirectional, and plastic nature of development. How does the context in which you were raised and live influence your development?

3. Compare the historical context in which you, your parents, and your grandparents were raised. How might historical and societal influences have affected your grandparents' development, their worldview, and their child-rearing strategies? What about your parents? How might historical influences affect your own development, worldview, and perspective on parenting?

Defining Culture

Cultural influences on development are illustrated by the many ethnic communities that comprise most U.S. cities. What subcultures and neighborhoods can you identify in your community?

A very large and influential part of our context is culture—a set of customs, knowledge, attitudes, and values that are shared by members of a group and are learned early in life through interactions with group members (Hofstede, 2001). Most classic theories and research on human development are based on Western samples, and developmental researchers once believed that the processes of human development were universal. Early studies of culture and human development took the form of *cross-cultural research*, comparing individuals and groups from different cultures to examine how these universal processes worked in different contexts (Gardiner & Kosmitzki, 2010).

In recent decades, we have learned that the cultural context in which individuals live influences the timing and expression of many aspects of development (Gardiner & Kosmitzki, 2010). For example, the average age that infants begin to walk varies with cultural context. In Uganda, infants begin to walk at about 10 months of age, in France at about 15 months, and the United States at about 12 months. These differences are influenced by parenting practices that vary by culture. African parents tend to handle infants in ways that stimulate walking, by playing games that allow infants to practice jumping and walking skills (Hopkins & Westra, 1989; Super, 1981). Developmental researchers have argued that because much of the research in

human development has focused on individuals from Western industrialized societies, there is a danger of defining typical development in Western samples as the norm, which can lead to narrow views of human development that do not take into account the variety of contexts in which people live. At the extreme, differences in human development within other cultural groups can be seen as abnormal (Rogoff & Morelli, 1989). Some argue that cross-cultural research that compares the development of people from different cultures in order to understand universals in development is misguided because norms vary by cultural context (Schweder et al., 1998).

There is a growing trend favoring *cultural research*, which examines *how* culture itself influences development, over cross-cultural research, which simply examines differences across cultures (Schweder et al., 1998). From a cultural research perspective, culture influences our development because it contributes to the context in which we are embedded, transmitting values, attitudes, and beliefs that shape our thoughts, beliefs, and behaviors (Cole, 1999). The shift toward cultural research permits the examination of the multiple cultures that exist within a society. For example, American culture is not homogenous; many subcultures exist, defined by factors such as ethnicity (e.g., African American, Asian American), religion (e.g., Christian, Muslim), geography (e.g., southern, midwestern), and others, as well as combinations of these factors. Instead of looking for universal similarities in development, cultural research in human development aims to document diversity and understand how the historical and cultural context in which we live influences development throughout our lifetime (Schweder et al., 1998).

What Do You Think?

1. **How would you describe American culture? Can you identify aspects of American culture that describe most, if not all, people in the country? Are there aspects of culture in which people or subgroups of people differ?**

2. **What subcultures can you identify in your own neighborhood, state, or region of the country? What characterizes each of these subcultures?**

3. **Consider your own experience. With which culture or subculture do you identify? How much of a role do you think your cultural membership has had in your own development?**

BASIC ISSUES IN LIFESPAN HUMAN DEVELOPMENT

Developmental scientists agree that people change throughout life and show increases in some capacities and decreases in others from conception to death. Yet, how development proceeds, the specific changes that occur, and the causes of change are debated. Developmental scientists' explanations of

how people grow and change over their lives are influenced by their perspectives on three basic issues, or fundamental questions, about human development:

1. Do people remain largely the same over time or do they change dramatically?

2. What role do people play in their own development— how much are they influenced by their surroundings, and how much do they influence their surroundings?

CONTEXT AND DEVELOPMENT: LARGE FAMILY

Family size is an important context for development. A large family offers unique supports.

Watch the video at edge.sagepub.com/kuther

3. To what extent is development a function of inborn genetic endowments, as compared with the environment in which individuals live?

The following sections examine each of these questions.

CONTINUITIES AND DISCONTINUITIES IN DEVELOPMENT

Do children slowly grow into adults, steadily gain more knowledge and experience, and become better at reasoning? Or do children grow in spurts, showing sudden and large gains in knowledge and reasoning capacities? In other words, in what ways is developmental change **continuous**, characterized by slow and gradual change, or **discontinuous**, characterized by abrupt change? As shown in Figure 1.2, a discontinuous view of development emphasizes sudden transformation in abilities and capacities whereas a continuous view emphasizes the gradual and steady changes that occur. Scientists who argue that development is continuous in nature point to slow and cumulative changes we experience in the amount or degree of skills, such as a child slowly gaining experience, expanding his or her vocabulary, and becoming quicker at problem solving or a middle-aged adult experiencing gradual losses of muscle and strength. The discontinuous view of development describes the changes we experience as large and abrupt, with individuals of various ages dramatically different from one another. For example, puberty quickly transforms children's bodies into more adultlike adolescent

bodies, infants' understanding and capacity for language is fundamentally different from that of school-age children, and children make leaps in their reasoning abilities over the course of childhood (Piek, Dawson, Smith, & Gasson, 2008), such as from believing that inanimate objects such as robotic dogs are alive to understanding that life is a biological process (Gelman & Opfer, 2002).

It was once believed that development was either continuous or discontinuous—that changes were either slow and gradual or sudden and dramatic—but not both. Today, developmental scientists agree that development includes both continuity and discontinuity (Kagan, 2008; Miller, 2009). Whether a particular developmental change appears continuous or discontinuous depends on our point of view. For example, consider human growth. We often think of increases in height as a slow and steady process of simply getting taller with time; each month, infants are taller than the prior month, illustrating continuous change. However, as shown in Figure 1.3, when researchers measured infants' height every day they discovered that infants have growth days and non-growth days, days that they show rapid change in height interspersed with days in which there is no change in height, thus illustrating discontinuous change (Lampl, Johnson, & Frongillo, 2001; Lampl, Veldhuis, & Johnson, 1992). In this example, monthly measurements of infant height suggest gradual increases, but daily measurements show spurts of growth, each lasting 24 hours or fewer. In this way, whether a given phenomenon, such as height, is described as continuous or discontinuous can vary. Most developmental scientists agree that some aspects of lifespan development are best described as continuous and others as discontinuous (Miller, 2009).

INDIVIDUALS ARE ACTIVE IN DEVELOPMENT

Do people have a role in influencing how they change over their lifetimes? That is, are people active in influencing

FIGURE 1.2: Continuous and Discontinuous Development

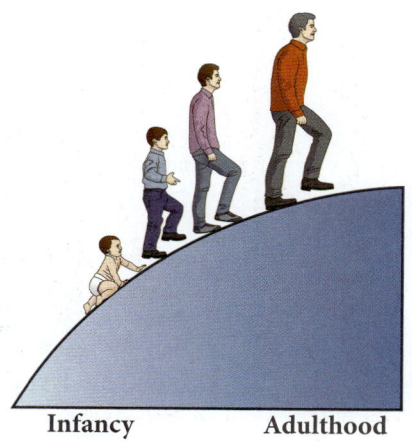

(a) Continous Development

Infancy — Adulthood

(b) Discontinous Development

Infancy — Adulthood

FIGURE 1.3: Infant Growth: A Continuous or Discontinuous Process?

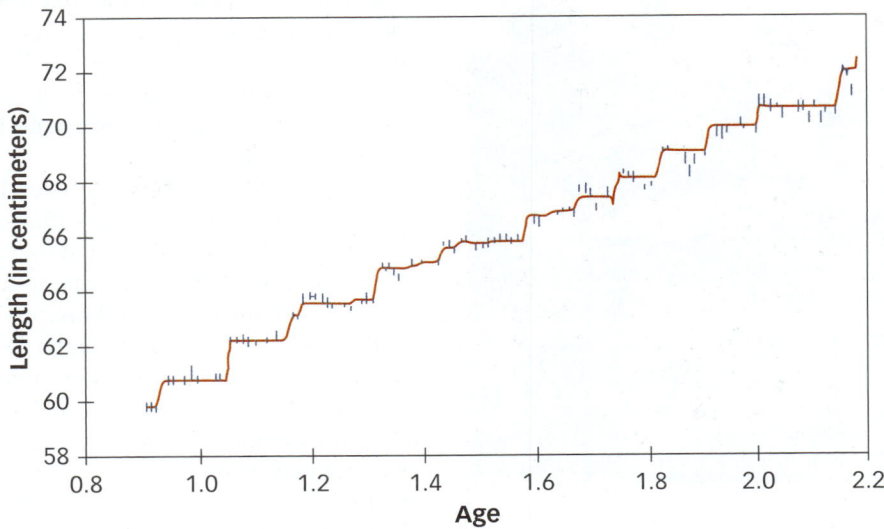

Infants' growth occurs in a random series of roughly 1-centimeter spurts in height that occur 24 hours or less. The overall pattern of growth entails increases in height, but whether the growth appears to be continuous or discontinuous depends on our point of view.

SOURCE: Lampl et al. (1992).

their own development? To say that individuals are active in their development means that they interact with and influence the world around them, create the experiences that lead to developmental change, and thereby influence how they change over the lifespan. Alternatively, if individuals take a passive role in their development, they are shaped by, but do not influence, the world around them.

The prevailing view among developmental scientists is that people are active contributors to their own development. People are influenced by the physical and social contexts in which they live, but they also play a role in influencing their development by interacting with, and changing, the contexts in which they live. For example, through their interactions, even infants influence the world around them and construct their own development. Consider an infant who smiles at each adult he sees; he influences his

Infants naturally influence people and the world around them. What reactions might these two babies elicit?

world because adults are likely to smile, use "baby talk," and play with him in response. The infant brings adults into close contact, making one-on-one interactions and creating opportunities for learning. By engaging the world around them; thinking; being curious; and interacting with people, objects, and the world around them, individuals of all ages are "manufacturers of their own development" (Flavell, 1994; Lyon & Flavell, 1993), meaning that they take an active role in shaping who they become and how they change during their lifetimes.

NATURE AND NURTURE INFLUENCE DEVELOPMENT

Perhaps the most fundamental questions about lifespan human development are as follows: What is its cause? Why do people change in predictable ways over the course of their lifetimes? The answer to these questions reflects perhaps the oldest and most heated debate within the field of human development: the **nature–nurture issue**. Is development caused by nature or nurture? Explanations that rely on nature point to inborn genetic endowments or heredity, maturational processes, and evolution as causes of developmental change. For example, most children take their first steps at about the same time as other children, suggesting a maturational trend that supports the role of nature in development. An alternative explanation for developmental change is nurture, the view that individuals are molded by the physical and social environment in which they are raised, including the home, school, workplace, neighborhood, and society. From this perspective, although most children begin to walk at about the same time, environmental conditions can speed up or slow down the process. Children who experience malnutrition may walk later than other children, and children whose parents give them daily practice making stepping movements may walk earlier (Pomerleau et al., 2005; Sigman, 1995; Vereijken & Thelen, 1997).

Although developmental scientists once attempted to determine whether nature *or* nurture influenced development, most now agree that *both* nature and nurture are important contributors to development across the lifespan (Grigorenko & Sternberg, 2003; Scarr & McCartney, 1983). As in the prior example, walking is heavily influenced by maturation (nurture), but experiences and environmental conditions can influence the timing of a child's first steps (nurture). Today, developmental scientists attempt to determine *how* nature and nurture work together to influence how people grow and change throughout life (Anastasi, 1958; Rutter, 2012).

To review, there are three basic questions regarding lifespan human development:

1. Do people remain largely the same over time, showing continuity, or do they change dramatically, illustrating discontinuity?

2. What role do people play in their own development— how much are they influenced by their surroundings and how much do they influence their surroundings? To what degree are they active or passive participants in their development?

3. To what extent is development a function of inborn genetic endowments, as compared with the environment in which individuals live?

Developmental scientists vary in their responses to these questions, as we will discover throughout this book. Different answers reflect different assumptions about the causes of development and different explanations for human development.

Thinking in Context 1.2

1. Can you identify ways you have changed very gradually over the years? Were there other times in which you showed abrupt change in aspects of your development, such as physical growth, strength and coordination, thinking abilities, or social skills? In other words, in what ways is your development characterized by continuity? Discontinuity?

2. Are people active or passive participants in their development? What role did your physical and social environment play in your growth? In what ways, if any, did you take an active role in your own development?

3. How much of who you are today is a function of nature? Nurture?

THEORETICAL PERSPECTIVES ON HUMAN DEVELOPMENT

Human development researchers offer many theoretical explanations for the changes that occur over the lifetime. Over the past century, developmental scientists have learned much about how individuals progress from infants to children to adolescents, and to adults, as well as how they change throughout adulthood. Scientists explain their observations by constructing theories of human development. A **theory** is a way of organizing a set of observations or facts into a comprehensive explanation of how something works. Theories are important tools for compiling and interpreting the growing body of research in human development as well as determining gaps in our knowledge about a given phenomenon and making predictions about what is not yet known (Crain, 1999; Green & Piel, 2002; Miller, 2009).

Effective theories generate specific **hypotheses**, or proposed explanations for a given phenomenon, that can be tested by research. It is important to note that this testing seeks to find flaws in the hypothesis—not to "prove" that it

Sigmund Freud (1856–1939), the father of the psychoanalytic perspective, believed that much of our behavior is driven by unconscious impulses.

TABLE 1.2 Freud's Psychosexual Stages

STAGE	APPROXIMATE AGE	DESCRIPTION
Oral	0 to 18 months	Basic drives focus on the mouth, tongue, and gums, whereby the infant obtains pleasure by feeding and sucking. Feeding and weaning are particularly important influences on personality development at this time. Failure to meet oral needs can be shown in behaviors that center around the mouth, such as fingernail biting, overeating, smoking, or excessive drinking.
Anal	18 months to 3 years	Basic drives are oriented toward the anus, and the infant obtains pleasure by retaining or passing of bowel and bladder movements. Toilet training is an important influence on personality development. If caregivers are too demanding, pushing the child before he or she is ready, or if caregivers are too lax, children may develop issues of control such as a need to impose extreme order and cleanliness on their environment or extreme messiness and disorder.
Phallic	3 to 6 years	Basic drives shift to the genitals. The child develops a romantic desire for the opposite-sex parent and a sense of hostility and/or fear of the same-sex parent. The conflict between the child's desires and fears arouses anxiety and discomfort. It is resolved by pushing the desires into the unconscious and spending time with the same-sex parent and adopting his or her behaviors and roles. It is through this process that children begin to become members of society by adopting societal expectations and values. Failure to resolve this conflict may result in guilt and a lack of conscience.
Latency	6 years to puberty	This is not a stage but a time of calm between stages when the child develops talents and skills and focuses on school, sports, and friendships.
Genital	Puberty to adulthood	With the physical changes of early adolescence, the basic drives again become oriented toward the genitals. The person becomes concerned with developing mature adult sexual interests and sexual satisfaction in adult relationships throughout life.

is flawless. A good theory is one that is *falsifiable*, or capable of generating hypotheses that can be tested and, potentially, refuted. As scientists conduct research and learn more about a topic, they modify their theories. Updated theories often give rise to new questions and new research studies, whose findings may further modify theories.

The great body of research findings in the field of lifespan human development has been organized into several theoretical perspectives to explain how we change throughout our lives. Given the myriad ways in which we develop, theories vary in their explanatory focus and emphasis. For example, some theories examine personality development and others address changes in how individuals reason and solve problems. As the following sections illustrate, these theoretical perspectives vary greatly in how they account for the developmental changes that occur over the lifespan.

PSYCHOANALYTIC THEORIES

Do powerful forces within us make us behave as we do? Are we pushed by inner drives? **Psychoanalytic theories** describe development and behavior as a result of the interplay of inner drives, memories, and conflicts of which we are unaware and cannot control. These inner forces influence our behavior throughout our lives. Freud and Erikson are two key psychoanalytic theorists whose theories remain influential today.

Freud's Psychosexual Theory

Sigmund Freud (1856–1939), a Viennese physician, is credited as the father of the psychoanalytic perspective. Freud believed that much of our behavior is driven by unconscious impulses that are outside of our awareness. As shown in Table 1.2, Freud believed we progress through a series of *psychosexual stages*, periods in which unconscious drives are focused on different parts of the body, making stimulation to those parts a source of pleasure. How parents direct and gratify their children's basic drives influences their personality development. Freud explained that the task for parents is to strike a balance between over- and under-gratifying a child's needs at each stage in order to help the child develop a healthy personality with the capacity for mature relationships throughout life.

Freud made many contributions to psychology, psychiatry, and Western thought. Many of his insights have stood up well to the test of time, such as the notion of unconscious processes that we are not aware of (Fonagy & Target, 2000; Westen, 1998). The idea that early experiences in the family are important contributors to development is also accepted by the general public, as is the role of emotions in development, both of which Freud espoused. However, Freud did not study children; his theory grew from his work with female psychotherapy patients. Because of its heavy emphasis on infant sexuality, Freud's psychosexual stage framework, and especially the phallic stage, is not widely accepted (Westen, 1998).

Freud's theory has declined in popularity—one reason being that it cannot be directly tested (Crews, 1996). How are we to study unconscious drives when we are not aware of them? Only about 2% of today's psychotherapists practice traditional Freudian psychoanalysis that emphasizes unconscious motivators of behavior because shorter and more behaviorally focused therapies have been found to be more effective at helping people (Leichsenring & Rabung, 2008; McDonald, 1998).

Erikson's Psychosocial Theory

Erik Erikson (1902–1994) was influenced by Freud, but he placed less emphasis on instinctual drives as motivators of development and instead focused on the role of the social world, society, and culture in shaping development. Erikson posed a lifespan theory of development in which individuals progress through eight stages of psychosocial development that include changes in how they understand and interact with others, as well as changes in how they understand themselves and their roles as members of society (Erikson, 1950; see Table 1.3). Each stage presents a unique developmental task, which Erikson referred to as a crisis or conflict that must be resolved. How well individuals address the crisis determines their ability to deal with the demands made by the next stage of development.

Regardless of their success in resolving a crisis of a given stage, individuals are driven by biological maturation and social expectations to the next psychosocial stage. No crisis is ever fully resolved, and unresolved crises are revisited throughout life. It is never too late to resolve a

Jon Erikson/Science Source

Erik Erikson (1902–1994) posited that, throughout their lives, people progress through eight stages of psychosocial development

TABLE 1.3 Erikson's Psychosocial Stages of Development

STAGE	APPROXIMATE AGE	DESCRIPTION
Trust vs. mistrust	Birth to 1 year	Infants learn to trust that others will fulfill their basic needs (nourishment, warmth, comfort) or to lack confidence that their needs will be met.
Autonomy vs. shame and doubt	1 to 3 years	Toddlers learn to be self-sufficient and independent though toilet training, feeding, walking, talking, and exploring, or to lack confidence in their own abilities and doubt themselves.
Initiative vs. guilt	3 to 6 years	Young children become inquisitive, ambitious, and eager for responsibility, or experience overwhelming guilt for their curiosity and overstepping boundaries.
Industry vs. inferiority	6 to 12 years	Children learn to be hard working, competent, and productive by mastering new skills in school, friendships and home life, or experience difficulty, leading to feelings of inadequacy and incompetence.
Identity vs. role confusion	Puberty to early adulthood	Adolescents search for a sense of self by experimenting with roles. They also look for answers to the question, "Who am I?" in terms of career, sexual, and political roles, or remain confused about who they are and their place in the world.
Intimacy vs. isolation	Early adulthood	Young adults seek companionship and close relationship with another person, or experience isolation and self-absorption through difficulty developing intimate relationships and sharing with others.
Generativity vs. stagnation	Middle adulthood	Adults contribute to, establish, and guide the next generation through work, creative activities and parenting, or stagnate, remaining emotionally impoverished and concerned about themselves.
Integrity vs. despair	Late adulthood	Older adults look back at life to make sense of it, accept mistakes, and view life as meaningful and productive, or feel despair over goals never reached and fear of death.

crisis. However, resolving a crisis from a previous stage may become more challenging over time as people focus on current demands and the current psychosocial stage.

Erikson's psychosocial theory is well regarded as one of the first lifespan views of development. He took a positive view of development and included the role of society and culture by basing his theory on a broad range of cases, including larger and more diverse samples than did Freud (Thomas, 2004). Erikson's theory is criticized as difficult to test, but it has nonetheless sparked research on specific stages, most notably on the development of identity during adolescence and the drive to guide youth and contribute to the next generation during middle adulthood (Crain, 1999; Miller, 2009). Because Erikson's lifespan theory of development holds implications for every period of life, we will revisit his theory throughout this book at each period in the lifespan: infancy, childhood, adolescence, adulthood, and old age.

BEHAVIORIST AND SOCIAL LEARNING THEORIES

In response to psychoanalytic theorists' emphasis on the psyche as an invisible influence on development and behavior, some scientists pointed to the importance of studying observable behavior rather than thoughts and emotion, which cannot be seen or objectively verified. Theorists who study **behaviorism** examine only behavior that can be observed and believe that all behavior is influenced by the physical and social environment. For example, consider this famous quote from John Watson (1925), an early founder of behaviorism:

> Give me a dozen healthy infants, well formed, and my own specified world to bring them up in and I'll guarantee to take any one at random and train him to become any type of specialist I might select—doctor, lawyer, artist, merchant, chief, and yes, even beggar-man and thief, regardless of his talents, penchants, tendencies, abilities, vocations, and race of his ancestors. (p. 82)

By controlling an infant's physical and social environment, Watson believed that he could control the child's destiny. Behaviorist theory is also known as *learning theory* because it emphasizes how people and animals learn new behaviors as a function of their environment. As discussed in the following sections, **classical conditioning** and **operant conditioning** are two forms of behaviorist learning; social learning integrates elements of behaviorist theory and information processing theories.

Classical Conditioning

Classical conditioning is a form of learning in which the person or animal comes to associate environmental stimuli with physiological responses (see Figure 1.4). Ivan Pavlov (1849–1936), a Russian physiologist, discovered classical

Ivan Pavlov (1849–1936) discovered classical conditioning when he noticed that dogs naturally salivate when they taste food, but they also salivate in response to various sights and sounds that they associate with food.

conditioning when he noticed that dogs naturally salivate when they taste food, but they also salivate in response to various sights and sounds that occur before they taste food, such as their bowl clattering or their owner opening the food cupboard. Pavlov tested his observation by pairing the sound of a tone with the dogs' food; the dogs heard the tone, then received their food. Soon the tone itself began to elicit the dogs' salivation. Through classical conditioning, a neutral stimulus (in this example, the sound of the tone) comes to elicit a response originally produced by another stimulus (food). Many fears as well as emotional associations are the result of classical conditioning. For example, some children may fear a trip to the doctor's office because they associate the doctor's office with the discomfort they felt upon receiving a vaccination shot. Classical conditioning applies to physiological and emotional responses only, yet it is a cornerstone of psychological theory. A second behaviorist theory accounts for voluntary, nonphysiological responses, as described in the following section.

Operant Conditioning

Perhaps it is human nature to notice that the consequences of our behavior influence our future behavior. A teenager who arrives home after curfew and is greeted with a severe scolding may be less likely to return home late in the future. An employer who brings coffee and bagels to her staff on Monday morning and then notices that her employees are in good spirits and productive may be more likely to bring breakfast for her employees in the future. These two examples illustrate the basic tenet of B. F. Skinner's (1905–1990) theory of operant conditioning: Behavior becomes more or less probable depending on its consequences. We repeat behaviors that have pleasant outcomes and stop behaviors with unpleasant outcomes. Behaviorist ideas about operant conditioning and the nature of human behavior are woven into the fabric of American culture and appear often in discussions of parenting (Rutherford, 2000). According to Skinner, a behavior followed by a rewarding or pleasant outcome, called

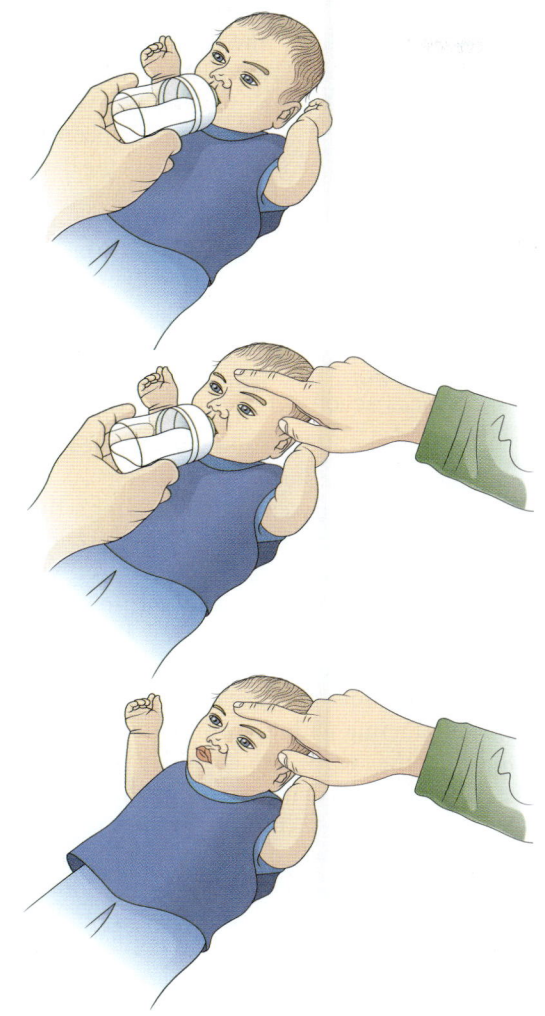

Classical conditioning has been observed in newborns, who naturally make sucking movements (unconditioned response) in response to sugar water (unconditioned stimulus). When stroking the forehead (neutral stimulus) is paired with sugar water, infants come to make sucking movements (conditioned response) in response to forehead strokes (conditioned stimulus).

SOURCE: Lampl et al. (1992).

reinforcement, will be more likely to recur, but one followed by an aversive or unpleasant outcome, called **punishment**, will be less likely to recur. Operant conditioning is a very important concept because it explains much of human behavior, including how we learn skills and habits.

Social Learning Theory

A common criticism of behaviorist theory is its overemphasis on the observable and neglect of internal influences on development and behavior (Miller, 2009). Albert Bandura (1925–) agreed that the physical and social environments are important, but he also advocated for the role of thought and emotion as contributors to development. According to Bandura's **social learning theory**, people actively process information—they think and they feel emotion—and their thoughts and feelings influence their behavior. The physical and social environment influences our behavior through their influence on our thoughts and emotions. For example, the teenager who breaks his curfew and is met by worried parents may experience remorse, feeling bad about his actions, which may then make him less likely to come home late in the future. In this example, the social environment (a discussion with worried parents) influenced the teen's thoughts and emotions (feeling bad for worrying his parents), which then influenced the teen's behavior (not breaking curfew in the future). In this way, our thoughts and emotions about the consequences of our behavior influence our future behavior. We do not need to experience punishment or reinforcement in order to change our behavior (Bandura, 2001). We can learn by thinking about the potential consequences of our actions.

One of Bandura's most enduring ideas about development is that people learn through observing and imitating models, which he referred to as **observational learning** (Bandura, 1986; Bandura, Ross, & Ross, 1963). People learn by watching others. This finding suggests that children who observe violence rewarded, such as a child successfully grabbing another child's toy, may imitate what they see and use aggressive means to take other children's toys. People also learn by observing the consequences of others' actions. A child observer might be less likely to imitate a child who takes another child's toy if the aggressor is scolded by a teacher and placed in time out. Observational learning, learning by watching and imitating others around us, is one of the most powerful ways in which we learn.

Another of Bandura's contributions that has influenced the field of lifespan human development is the concept of **reciprocal determinism**, according to which individuals and the environment interact and influence each other (Bandura, 2011, 2012). In contrast with behaviorist theorists, Bandura viewed individuals as active in their development rather than passively molded by their physical and social

Albert Bandura

In a classic study conducted by Albert Bandura, children who observed an adult playing with a bobo doll toy roughly imitated those behaviors, suggesting that children learn through observation.

FIGURE 1.5: Banduras's Model of Reciprocal Determinism

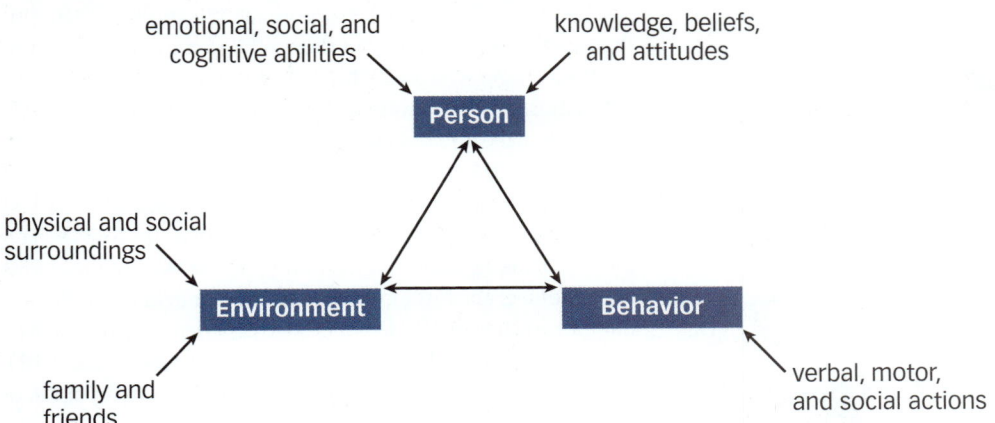

environment. Individuals can influence and change their physical and social surroundings. Specifically, development is a result of interactions between the individual's characteristics, his or her behavior, and the physical and social environment (see Figure 1.5).

As an example, let us examine how characteristics of a given person might influence that person's behavior and the surrounding social environment. Suppose Brandon is an excitable person, and his excitability makes him quick to debate with others. This behavioral tendency, in turn, stimulates others around him to engage in debate. In addition to Brandon's characteristics, behavior (being quick to debate) also is influenced by the environment (e.g., being surrounded by smart people who enjoy debating) and influences the environment (e.g., people who enjoy debating are more likely to talk to Brandon, while people who avoid debating are less likely to talk to him). This is an example of the complex interplay between person, behavior, and physical and social environment that underlies much of what we will discuss throughout this book.

Behaviorist theories make important contributions to understanding lifespan human development. Classical and operant conditioning and social learning are powerful means of explaining human behavior at all ages. Concepts such as observational learning, reinforcement, and punishment hold implications for parents, teachers, and anyone who works with people. Moreover, social learning theory and reciprocal determinism offer a more complex explanation for development and behavior than do behaviorist theories. We will revisit these concepts throughout this book.

COGNITIVE THEORIES

According to the lifespan developmental perspective, there are multiple domains of development. We grow and change in many ways over our lifetime. Whereas psychoanalytic theories examine inner influences on our personality and behavior and behaviorist and social learning theories look to the environment as an influence on development, cognitive theorists examine the role of thought on

behavior. **Cognitive-developmental theory** and information processing theorists view cognition—thought—as essential in understanding people's functioning across the lifespan.

Piaget's Cognitive-Developmental Theory

Do infants think? How do children understand physical phenomena, such as whether a ball of modeling clay changes in mass when it is rolled into the shape of a hot dog? As the first scientist to systematically examine children's thinking and reasoning, Swiss scholar Jean Piaget (1896–1980) believed that in order to understand children we must understand how they think because thinking influences all of behavior. Piaget founded the cognitive-developmental perspective on child development, which views children and adults as active explorers of their world, learning by interacting with the world around them, and organizing what they learn into cognitive **schemas**—or concepts, ideas, and ways of interacting on the world. In this way, people contribute to their own cognitive development because they are biologically driven to interact with others and through these interactions they construct and refine their own cognitive schemas. We will discuss cognitive schemas in more detail in Chapter 5.

Piaget proposed that children's drive to explore and understand the world propels them through four stages of cognitive development. With each advancing stage, people create and use more sophisticated cognitive schemas so that they think, reason, and understand their world in more complex ways. As shown in Table 1.4, individuals move from understanding the world through their senses and motor skills, to a thought-based understanding, to viewing the world in logical but concrete terms, to viewing it in complex and abstract forms. Each stage corresponds to a different period in life. We will discuss each stage in further detail in upcoming chapters.

Piaget's cognitive-developmental theory transformed the field of developmental psychology and remains one of the most widely cited developmental theories (Lourenco & Machado, 1996). It was the first to consider *how* infants and children think and to view people as active contributors to their development. Piaget's concept of cognitive stages and the suggestion that children's reasoning is limited by their stage holds implications for education—specifically the idea that effective instruction must match the child's developmental level.

Some critics of cognitive-developmental theory argue that Piaget focused too heavily on cognition and ignored

Bill Anderson / Science Source

Jean Piaget (1896–1980) believed that children's drive to explore and understand the world around them propels them through four stages of cognitive development.

emotional and social factors in development (Broughton, 1981; Winegar & Valsiuner, 1992). Others believe that Piaget neglected the influence of contextual factors by assuming that cognitive-developmental stages are universal, that all individuals everywhere progress through the stages in a sequence that does not vary (Lutz & Sternberg, 1999). Some cognitive theorists disagree with Piaget and argue that cognitive development is not a discontinuous, stagelike process and instead is a continuous process, as described in the following section.

Information Processing Theory

A developmental scientist presents a 5-year-old child with a puzzle in which a dog, cat, and mouse must find their way to a bone, piece of fish, and hunk of cheese (Klahr, 1985). To solve the puzzle, the child must move all three animals to the appropriate locations. How will the child approach this task? Which item will she move first? What steps will she take? Will the child keep all three animals in mind? Will she remember the task and show what item goes with each animal? How quickly will the child respond? What strategies will she use? What factors influence whether and how quickly a child completes this task? Finally, how does the 5-year-old child's process and performance differ from that of children older and younger than herself?

The problem described previously illustrates the questions studied by developmental scientists who favor **information processing theory**, a perspective that views thinking as information processing and posits that the mind works in ways similar to a computer because information enters, is manipulated, stored, recalled, and used to solve problems (Halford & Andrews, 2011; Klahr, 1992). Unlike the theories we have discussed thus far, information processing theory is not one theory that is attributed to an individual theorist. Instead, there are many information processing theories, and each emphasizes a different aspect of thinking. Some theories focus on how people perceive, focus on, and take in information. Others examine how people store information, create memories, and remember information. Still others examine problem solving—how people approach and solve problems in school, the workplace, and everyday life.

According to information processing theorists, we are born with the ability to process information. Our mind itself, with its processes of noticing, taking in, manipulating,

TABLE 1.4 Piaget's Stages of Cognitive Development

STAGE	APPROXIMATE AGE	DESCRIPTION
Sensorimotor	Birth to 2 years	Infants understand the world and think using only their senses and motor skills by watching, listening, touching, and tasting.
Preoperations	2 to 6 years	Preschoolers are able to explore the world using their own thoughts as guides and develop the language skills to communicate their thoughts to others. Despite these advances, their thinking is characterized by several errors in logic.
Concrete operations	7 to 11 years	School-age children become able to solve everyday logical problems. Their thinking is not yet fully mature because they are able to apply their thinking only to problems that are tangible and tied to specific substances.
Formal operations	12 years to Adulthood	Adolescents and adults can reason logically and abstractly about possibilities, imagined instances and events, and hypothetical concepts.

storing, and retrieving information does not show the radical changes that are associated with stage theories. Instead, from an information processing perspective, development is continuous and entails changes in the efficiency and speed with which we think. Maturation of the brain and nervous system contributes to changes in our information processing abilities—our tendency to become more efficient at processing information over the childhood years and to slow over the adult years (Kail, 2003; Luna, Garver, Urban, Lazar, & Sweeney, 2004). Experience and interaction with others also contribute by helping us learn new ways of managing and manipulating information. Over the childhood years we become better able to attend to and store information as well as operate on the information we have stored with a greater repertoire of strategies and greater efficiency.

Information processing theory offers a complex and detailed view of how we think, which permits scientists to make specific predictions about behavior and performance that can be tested in research studies. Information processing theory has generated a great many research studies and has garnered much empirical support (Halford & Andrews, 2011). Critics of the information processing perspective argue that a computer model cannot capture the complexity of the human mind and people's unique cognitive abilities. In addition, findings from laboratory research may not extend to the everyday contexts (those that pose great challenges to attention and require flexibility) in which people adapt to changing circumstances (Miller, 2009). Because findings from information processing research are fundamental to any discussion of cognitive development, we will explore the research in information processing as we discuss each age period throughout this book.

SOCIOCULTURAL SYSTEMS THEORY

A major tenet of lifespan development is that people play an active role in their development by interacting with the world around them. Sociocultural systems theories emphasize the role of the sociocultural context in development. People of all ages are immersed in their social contexts; they are inseparable from the cultural beliefs and societal, neighborhood, and familial contexts in which they live. The origins of sociocultural systems theory lie with two theorists, Lev Vygotsky and Urie Bronfenbrenner.

Vygotsky's Sociocultural Theory

Writing at the same time as Piaget, Russian scholar Lev Vygotsky (1896–1934) offered a different perspective on development that emphasized the importance of culture in development. As illustrated in this chapter's Cultural Influences on Development feature (p. 8), culture refers to the beliefs, values, customs, and skills of a group. Vygotsky 's (1978) **sociocultural theory** examines how culture is transmitted from one generation to the next through social interaction. Children interact with adults and more experienced peers as they talk, play, and work alongside them. It

Heritage/Corbis

Lev Vygotsky (1896–1934) emphasized the importance of culture in development. Children actively engage their social world, and the social world shapes development by transmitting culturally relevant ways of thinking and acting that guide children's thought and behavior.

is through these formal and informal contacts that children learn about their culture and what it means to be a member of their culture. In other words, cooperative dialogues and guidance from adults and more expert peers is how children adopt their culture's perspectives and practices—how they learn to think and behave as members of their society (Rogoff, 2003). As children acquire the patterns of thought and behavior that are important in their culture, they are able to apply these skills and ways of thinking to guide their own thought and behavior, thereby requiring less assistance from adults and more knowledgeable peers (Rogoff, Mosier, Mistry, & Göncü, 1993; Winsler, Carlton, & Barry, 2000). Vygotsky's sociocultural theory holds important implications for understanding cognitive development. Like Piaget, Vygotsky emphasized that children are active in their development by engaging with the world around them. Vygotsky, however, also viewed cognitive development as a social process that relies on interactions with adults, more mature peers, and other members of society. Children engage their social world, and the social world shapes development by transmitting culturally relevant ways of thinking and acting. In other words, Vygotsky emphasizes the role of the sociocultural context in influencing cognitive development. He argued that acquiring language is a particularly important milestone for children because it enables them to think in new ways and have more sophisticated dialogues with others in their culture, advancing their learning about culturally valued perspectives and activities (Vygotsky, 1934/1962). We will revisit Vygotsky's ideas about the roles of culture, language, and thought in Chapter 5.

Vygotsky's sociocultural theory is an important addition to the field of lifespan human development because it is the first theory to emphasize the role of the cultural context in influencing people's development throughout life. Critics argue that sociocultural theory overemphasizes the role of context, minimizes the role of individuals in their own development, and neglects the influence of genetic and biological factors (Wertsch, 1998). Another perspective on development, described next, refocuses attention on the individual as an actor embedded within multiple contexts.

Bronfenbrenner's Bioecological Systems Theory

Similar to other developmental theorists, Urie Bronfenbrenner (1917–2005) believed that we are active in our development and interact with the world around us. Specifically, Bronfenbrenner's **bioecological systems theory** poses that development is a result of the ongoing interactions among biological, cognitive, and psychological changes within the person and his or her changing context (Bronfenbrenner, 1979, 2005; Bronfenbrenner & Morris, 2006). Bronfenbrenner proposed that individuals are all embedded in, or surrounded by, a series of contexts: home, school, neighborhood, culture, and society. The bioecological systems theory offers a comprehensive perspective on the role of context as an influence on development. As shown in Figure 1.6, contexts are organized into a series of systems in which individuals are embedded and that interact with one another and the person to influence development.

FIGURE 1.6: Bronfenbrenner's Bioecological Model

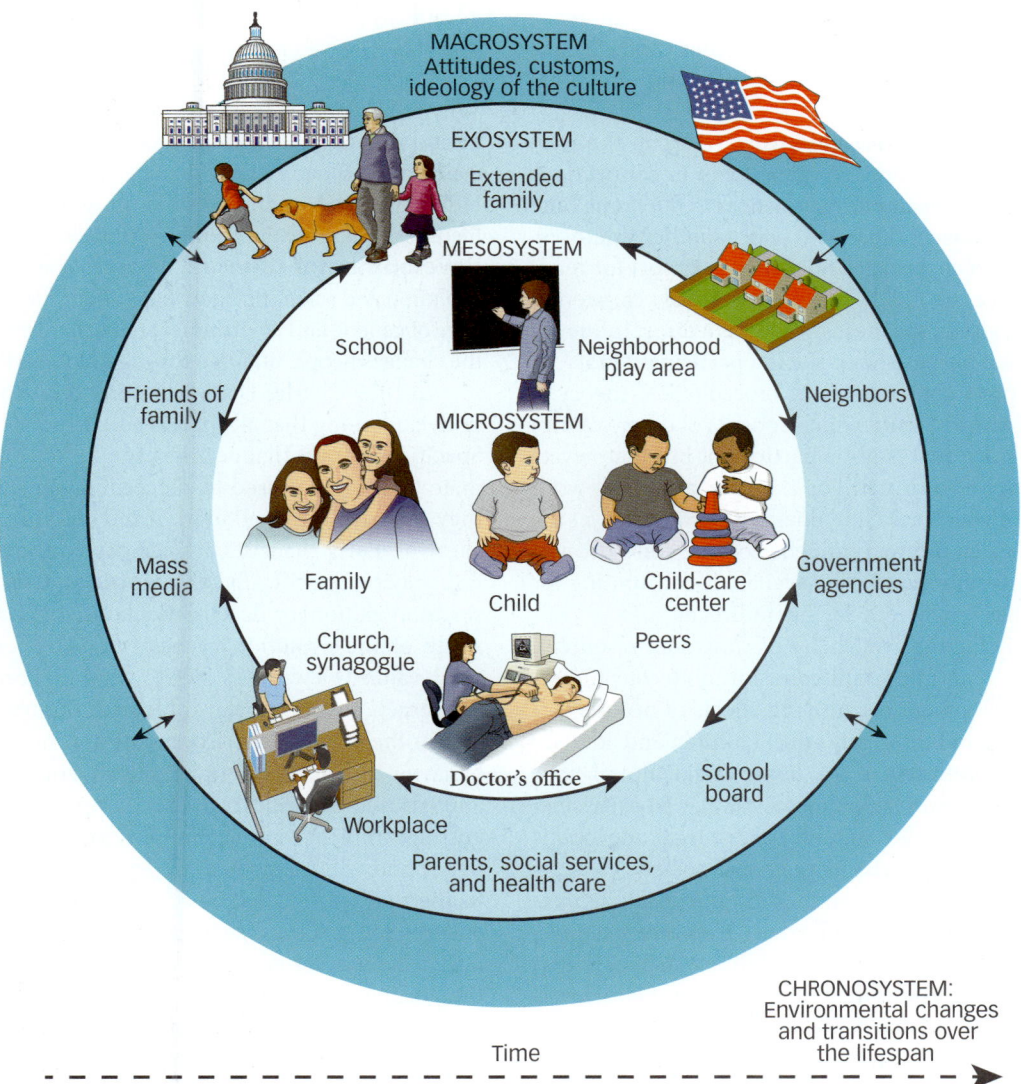

MACROSYSTEM
Attitudes, customs, ideology of the culture

EXOSYSTEM

Extended family

MESOSYSTEM

School

Neighborhood play area

Neighbors

Friends of family

MICROSYSTEM

Mass media

Family

Child

Child-care center

Government agencies

Peers

Church, synagogue

Doctor's office

School board

Workplace

Parents, social services, and health care

CHRONOSYSTEM:
Environmental changes and transitions over the lifespan

Time

SOURCE: Adapted from Bronfenbrenner and Morris (2006).

At the center of the bioecological model is the individual. The developing person's genetic, psychological, socioemotional, and personality traits interact, influencing each other. For example, biological development, such as brain maturation, may influence cognitive development, which in turn might influence social development, such as a child's understanding of friendship. Social development then may influence cognitive development, as children may learn activities or ideas from each other. In this way, the various forms of development interact. The individual interacts with the contexts in which he or she is embedded, influencing and being influenced by them (Bronfenbrenner & Ceci, 1994; Bronfenbrenner & Morris, 2006).

The individual is embedded in the innermost level of context, the **microsystem**, which includes the immediate physical and social environment surrounding the person, such as family, peers, and school. The individual interacts with elements of the microsystem by, for example, developing relationships with peers in which peers influence the person and vice versa. Because the microsystem contains the developing person, it has an immediate and direct influence on his or her development. Peer relationships can influence a person's sense of self-esteem, social skills, and emotional development.

The next level, the **mesosystem**, refers to the relations and interactions among microsystems, or connections among contexts. For example, experiences in the home (one microsystem) influence those at school (another microsystem); parents who encourage and provide support for reading will influence the child's experiences in the classroom. Like the microsystem, the mesosystem has a direct influence on the individual because he or she is a participant in it.

An important contribution of bioecological theory is the role of the **exosystem**, which consists of other settings in which the individual is not a participant but that nevertheless influence him or her. For example, a parent's work setting is one in which the child does not participate, yet the work setting has an indirect influence on the child because it affects the parent's mood. The availability of funding for schools, another exosystem factor, indirectly affects children by influencing the availability of classroom resources. The exosystem is an important contribution to our understanding of development because the effects of outside factors trickle down and indirectly affect children and adults.

The **macrosystem** is the larger sociocultural context in which the microsystem, mesosystem, and exosystem are embedded. It includes cultural values, legal and political practices, and other elements of the society at large. The macrosystem indirectly influences the child because it affects each of the other contextual levels. For example, cultural beliefs about the value of education (macrosystem) influence funding decisions made at national and local levels (exosystem), as well as what happens in the classroom and in the home (mesosystem and microsystem). Lives in Context (p. 22) illustrates how an element of the macrosystem, historical events, may influence development.

A final element of the bioecological system is the **chronosystem**, which refers to time: The bioecological system changes over time. As people grow and change, they take on and let go of various roles. For example, graduating college, getting married, and becoming a parent involve changes in roles and shifts in microsystems. These shifts in contexts, called *ecological transitions,* occur throughout life. The complexity of the bioecological model is both a strength and weakness of the theory (Dixon & Lerner, 1999). Human development is complex, and only when we consider the multiple interacting influences within the individual and context will we gain insight into the processes and outcomes of developmental change. However, we can never measure and account for all of the potential influences on development at once. Therefore, it is difficult to devise research studies to test the validity of the bioecological model. Despite this, bioecological theory remains an important contribution toward explaining developmental change across the lifespan.

ETHOLOGY AND EVOLUTIONARY DEVELOPMENTAL THEORY

Why are infants so helpless? Why is childhood such a long period in human development as compared with other species? How do nature and nurture interact to influence who individuals become and how they grow and change over their lifetimes? These are the questions addressed by **evolutionary developmental theory**, a theory that applies principles of evolution and scientific knowledge about the interactive influence of genetic and environmental mechanisms to understand the changes people undergo throughout their lifetime.

In 1859 Charles Darwin proposed his theory of evolution, explaining that all species adapt and evolve over time. Specifically, traits that permit a species to adapt, thrive, and mate tend to be passed to succeeding generations because they improve the likelihood of the individual and species' survival. Early theorists applied the concepts of evolution to behavior. Specifically, **ethological theory**, a precursor to evolutionary developmental theory, is the scientific study of the evolutionary basis of behavior and its survival value (Dewsbury, 1992). Konrad Lorenz and Kiko Tinbergen, two European zoologists, observed animal species in their natural environments and noticed patterns of behavior that appeared to be inborn, emerged early in life, and ensured their survival. For example, shortly after birth, goslings imprint to their mothers, meaning that they bond to her and will follow her, thereby ensuring they stay close to the mother, get fed, and remain protected. Imprinting ensures the goslings' survival. In order for imprinting to occur, the mother goose must be present immediately after the goslings hatch; mothers instinctively stay close to the nest so that their young may imprint and enhance their odds of surviving (Lorenz, 1952).

According to Bowlby (1969), humans also display biologically preprogrammed behaviors that have survival value

LIVES IN CONTEXT

Sociohistorical Influences on Development

Sociohistorical influences, such as the Great Depression (1929–1939), contribute, to cohort, or generational, differences in development.

Historical events, such as wars, economic and natural disasters, and periods of social unrest, are contextual influences that shape our world and our development. Glen Elder (1999) illustrated the influence of historical events by examining the progress of two generations, or cohorts, of California-born Americans from childhood to adulthood. The Oakland Growth Study consisted of individuals born in 1920 and 1921 who were adolescents during the Great Depression. The Berkeley Guidance Study consisted of individuals born in 1928 and 1929 who were young children when their families experienced the economic losses of the Great Depression. The decades-long studies of these two cohorts, who were eight years apart in age, demonstrated that they had very different experiences during their adolescent and early adult years. Influenced in part by the findings of these studies, Elder (2000) believed that the impact of historical events depends on when they occur in a person's life.

For all participants of both studies, family roles and relationships changed in response to the economic adversity wrought by the Great Depression. As fathers lost jobs and income, more work was required of children, giving them opportunities to participate in helping their families. Mothers took on an increasingly important role in the family as income earners as well as authority figures. This upheaval of traditional gender roles was accompanied by an increase in family discord and conflicts.

The older Oakland cohort were children during the affluent 1920s, a time of economic growth in California, and they experienced a prosperous and relatively stress-free childhood. But they entered adolescence during the Great Depression, a period of severe economic stress in which unemployment

skyrocketed and people's savings were depleted. As adolescents during the Great Depression, the Oakland cohort tended to behave responsibly and assist their families in coping. The boys often assumed jobs outside the home to aid financially troubled families. Their activities outside the home enhanced their social independence and reduced their exposure to family stress. Girls spent more time at home caring for siblings and completing household chores as many mothers worked outside the home; they were exposed to greater amounts of family stress and showed poorer adjustment than did the boys.

The Berkeley children, the younger cohort, experienced the Great Depression during their vulnerable early childhood years. The children experienced economic scarcity and family discord early in life, at a time when they were very dependent on family. The Berkley cohort entered adolescence during World War II, a period of additional economic and emotional stress from empty households (as both parents worked to support the war effort) and the military service and war trauma of older brothers. As adolescents, the Berkley cohort (especially the boys) experienced greater emotional difficulties, more poor attitudes toward school, and less hope, self-direction, and confidence about their future than did the Oakland cohort (who were children during the prosperous 1920s).

However, the Berkeley cohort demonstrated resilience in adulthood, largely because of the influence of military service. Seventy percent of the males in the Berkeley sample served in the military during World War II. Military service appeared to offer the men several opportunities, such as to begin again and reconsider their lives, to travel, and access to the GI Bill of Rights, which enabled them to expand their education and acquire new skills after the war. These two cohorts of young people offer striking examples of how sociohistorical context influences development. Context always plays a role in development—not only in times of social upheaval but every day and for every generation of people.

What Do You Think?

1. **Consider the sociohistorical context in which you were raised. What historical and societal events may have influenced you? What events have shaped your generation's childhood and adolescence?**

2. **Consider the societal and cultural events that your parents may have experienced in childhood and adolescence. What technology was available? What historical events did they experience? What were the popular fads of their youth? What influence do you think these sociohistorical factors may have had on your parents' development?**

3. **Compare the sociohistorical context in which you embedded today with what your parents and grandparents experienced at your age.**

---

and promote development. For example, caregivers naturally respond to infants' cues. Crying, smiling, and grasping are inborn ways that infants get attention from caregivers, obtain

physical contact, and ensure they will be safe and cared for. Many infant behaviors have adaptive significance because they meet infants' needs and promote the formation of bonds with caregivers that ensure that the caregivers will feel a strong desire and obligation to care for them (Bowlby, 1973). In this way, inborn biological drives and behaviors work together with experience to influence adaptation and ultimately an individual's survival.

Are you—your abilities, personality, and competencies—a result of your genes, which are inborn influences? Or did the physical and social environment in which you were raised—your family, friends, and school—make you who you are today? Evolutionary developmental scientists explain that these are the wrong questions to ask. From an evolutionary development perspective, genes and context interact in an ever-changing way so that it is impossible to isolate the contributions of each to development (Gottesman & Hanson, 2005; Gottlieb, 2003; Lickliter & Honeycutt, 2003). While all of our traits and characteristics are influenced by genes, contextual factors influence the expression of genetic instructions, as illustrated by Figure 1.7. Contextual factors such as gravity, light, temperature, and moisture influence how genes are expressed and therefore how individuals develop (Gilbert, 2001; Meaney, 2010; Rutter, 2010). For example, in crocodiles, sex is determined by the temperature in which the organism develops. Eggs incubated at one range of temperatures produce male crocodiles and at another temperature produce female crocodiles (Gans & Crews, 1992).

According to evolutionary developmental theory, genetic programs and biological predispositions interact with the physical and social environment to influence development and Darwinian natural selection determines what genes and traits are passed on to the next generation (Bjorklund & Pellegrini, 2000; Krebs, 2003; Lickliter & Honeycutt, 2003). People are viewed as active in their development, influencing their contexts (through their genetic characteristics and by choosing and interacting within settings), responding to the demands for adaptation posed by their contexts, and constantly interacting with and adapting

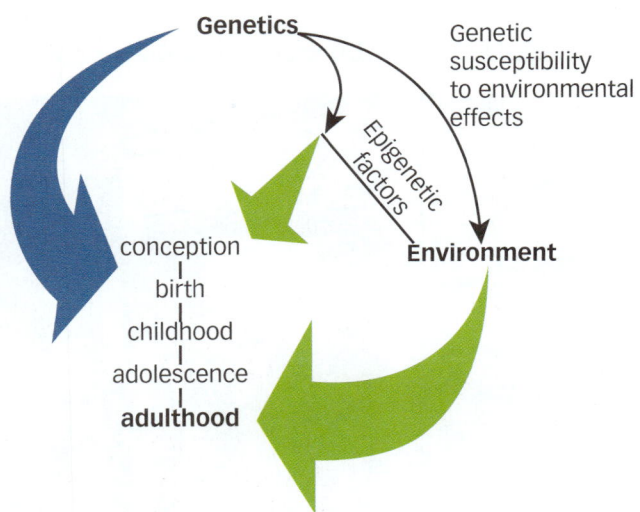

FIGURE 1.7: Interaction of Genetic and Environmental Factors

Development is influenced by the dynamic interplay of genetic and environmental factors. Genetic predispositions may influence how we experience environmental factors and environmental factors may influence how genes are expressed.

SOURCE: Picker (2005).

to the world around them. The relevance of both biological and contextual factors to human development is indisputable and most developmental scientists appreciate the contributions of evolutionary developmental theory (Frankenhuis, Panchanathan, & Clark Barrett, 2013; Gottlieb, Wahlsten, & Lickliter, 1998; Lickliter & Honeycutt, 2013). The ways in which biology and context interact and their influence on development changes over the course of the lifetime, as we will discuss throughout this book.

In summary, there are many theories of human development that offer complementary and contrasting views of how individuals change over our lifetimes. Psychoanalytic theories emphasize personality change—how unconscious forces shape people (Freud) and how sociocultural forces influence ego development (Erikson). Behaviorist and social learning theories point to the physical and social environment as a shaper of development and behavior, as well as the role of observation and imitation in learning. Other theories emphasize cognitive development. Piaget's cognitive-developmental theory explains how individuals construct their own knowledge structures through interaction with the world whereas Vygotsky emphasizes the role of sociocultural context in influencing thought. Information processing theories examine the ways in which attention, processing speed, and strategy lead to advances in thinking and problem-solving ability. Finally, Bronfenbrenner's bio-ecological theory takes a comprehensive look at the many contextual systems in which people live and how people and their contexts interact. Table 1.5 provides an at-a-glance comparison of theories of human development.

SOCIOHISTORICAL INFLUENCES ON DEVELOPMENT: DESEGREGATION

Development is influenced by sociohistorical context. In this clip, the Washington family discusses their experiences with discrimination and attending newly desegregated schools in the 1950s.

Watch the video at edge.sagepub.com/kuther

TABLE 1.5 Comparing Theories of Human Development

	CONTINUITY VS. DISCONTINUITY	ACTIVE VS. PASSIVE INDIVIDUAL	NATURE VS. NURTURE
Freud's psychosexual theory	Discontinuous: Stages are discontinuous.	Passive individuals are motivated by inborn basic drives.	Greater emphasis on nature: People are driven by inborn drives, but the extent to which the drives are satisfied influences developmental outcomes.
Erikson's psychosocial theory	Discontinuous: Stages are discontinuous.	Active individuals interact with their social world to resolve psychosocial tasks.	Both nature and nurture: Biological and social forces propel people through the stages and social and psychosocial influences determine the outcome of each stage.
Behaviorist theory	Continuous: There is a continuous process of learning new behaviors.	Passive individuals are shaped by their environment.	Nurture: Environmental influences shape behavior.
Bandura's social learning theory	Continuous: There is a continuous process of learning new behaviors.	Individuals' characteristics and behavior interact with the environment.	Both nature and nurture: Inborn characteristics and the physical and social environment influence behavior.
Piaget's cognitive-developmental theory	Discontinuous: Stages are discontinuous but there is also a continuous process of seeking equilibration.	Active individuals interact with the world to create their own schemas.	Both nature and nurture: An innate drive to learn coupled with brain development lead people to interact with the world. Opportunities provided by the physical and social environment influence development.
Vygotsky's sociocultural theory	Continuous: Interactions with others lead to developing new reasoning capacities and skills.	Active individuals interact with members of their culture.	Both nature and nurture: People learn through interactions with more skilled members of their culture; however, capacities are influenced by genes, brain development, and maturation.
Information processing theory	Continuous: There is an increase of skills and capacities.	Active individuals attend to, process, and store information.	Both nature and nurture: People are born with processing capacities that develop through maturation and environmental influences.
Bronfenbrenner's bioecological systems theory	Continuous: People constantly change through their interactions with the contexts in which they are embedded.	Active individuals interact with their contexts, being influenced by their contexts but also determining what kinds of physical and social environments are created and how they change.	Both nature and nurture: People's inborn and biological characteristics interact with an ever-changing context to influence behavior.
Ethology and evolutionary developmental theory	Both continuous and discontinuous: People gradually grow and change throughout life, but there are sensitive periods in which specific experiences and developments must occur.	Active individuals interact with their physical and social environment.	Both nature and nurture: Genetic programs and biological predispositions interact with the physical and social environment to influence development and Darwinian natural selection determines what genes and traits are passed on to the next generation

Thinking in Context 1.3

Maria and Fernando have just given birth to their first child—a healthy baby boy. Like most new parents, Maria and Fernando are nervous and overwhelmed with their new responsibilities. Of utmost importance to them is that the baby develops a strong and secure bond to them. They want their baby to feel loved and to love them.

1. What advice would a psychoanalytic theorist give Maria and Fernando? Contrast psychoanalytic with behaviorist perspectives. How might a behaviorist theorist approach this problem?

2. How might an evolutionary developmental theorist explain bonding between parents and infants? What advice might an evolutionary developmental theorist give to Maria and Fernando?

3. Considering bioecological systems theory, what microsystem and mesosystem factors influence the parent–child bond? What role might exosystem and macrosystem factors take?

RESEARCH IN HUMAN DEVELOPMENT

The many theories of lifespan human development differ in focus and explanation, but they all are the result of scientists' attempts to organize observations of people at all ages. Developmental scientists conduct research studies to gather information and answer questions about how people grow and change over their lives. They devise theories to organize what they learn from research and to suggest new hypotheses to test in research studies. In turn, research findings are used to modify theories. By conducting multiple studies over time, developmental scientists refine their theories about lifespan human development and determine new questions to ask. Developmental science also finds significant influences in contexts, as discussed in Applying Developmental Science (p. 25).

THE SCIENTIFIC METHOD

Researchers employ the **scientific method**, a process of posing and answering questions by making careful and systematic observations and gathering information. The scientific method outlines the basic steps used in formulating questions, finding answers, and communicating research discoveries.

1. Identify the research question or problem to be studied, and formulate the hypothesis, or proposed explanation, to be tested.

2. Gather information to address the research question.

3. Use statistical analysis to summarize the information gathered, and determine whether the hypothesis is refuted, or shown to be false.

4. Interpret the summarized information, consider the findings in light of prior research studies, and share findings with the scientific community and the world at large.

METHODS OF DATA COLLECTION

The basic challenge that scientists face in conducting research is determining what information is important and how to gather it. Scientists use the term *data* to refer to the information that they collect when they conduct research. How can we gather data about children, adolescents, and adults? Should we simply talk with our participants? Should we watch them as they progress through their days? Should we hook them up to machines that measure physiological activity such as heart rate or brain waves? Developmental scientists use a variety of different methods and measures to collect information.

Self-Report Measures

Interviews and **questionnaires** are known as self-report measures because the person under study answers questions about his or her experiences, attitudes, opinions, beliefs, and behavior. Interviews can take place in person, over the phone, or over the Internet.

The **open-ended interview** is very flexible because the trained interviewer uses a conversational style that encourages the participant, or the person under study, to expand his or her responses. Interviewers may vary the order of questions, probe, and ask follow-up questions based on responses. The scientist begins with a question and then follows up with prompts to obtain a better view of the person's reasoning (Ginsburg, 1997). An example of this is the Piagetian Clinical Interview, which requires specialized training to administer. Consider this dialogue between Piaget (1929) and a 5-year-old child:

Where does the dream come from?

I think you sleep so well that you dream.

Does it come from us or from outside?

From outside.

What do we dream with?

I don't know.

With the hands? With nothing?

Yes, with nothing.

When you are in bed and you dream, where is the dream?

In my bed, under the blanket. I don't really know. If it was in my stomach the bones would be in the way and I shouldn't see it.

Is the dream there when you sleep?

Yes, it is in my bed beside me.

Is the dream in your head?

It is I that am in the dream; it isn't in my head. When you dream, you don't know you are in the bed. You know you are walking. You are in the dream. You are in bed, but you don't know you are. (pp. 97–98)

Open-ended interviews permit participants to explain their thoughts thoroughly and in their own way. This method also enables researchers to gather a large amount of information quickly. However, the flexibility of open-ended interviews poses a challenge: When questions are phrased differently for each person, responses may not capture real differences in how people think about a given topic and instead may reflect differences in how the questions were posed and followed up by the interviewer.

APPLYING DEVELOPMENTAL SCIENCE

The Importance of Context in Developmental Science

In its early years, the study of human development was based in laboratory research devoted to uncovering universal aspects of development by stripping away contextual influences (Wertlieb, 2003). This basic research was designed to examine universal processes that apply to all people, such as perceptual development (e.g., what visual skills are infants born with?).

As developmental scientists began to apply their knowledge outside of laboratory settings, however, it became apparent that there are a great many individual differences in development.

Developmental scientists have since realized the importance of context. The field of **applied developmental science** has emerged, studying individuals within the contexts in which they live. This approach promotes the ability to understand the diverse range of patterns development takes throughout the life course (Lerner, 2010; Wertlieb, 2003).

Research in human development is now directed toward understanding a variety of social problems and issues of immediate social relevance, such as the capacities of preterm infants, children's ability to provide eyewitness testimony,

adolescent sexual practices, and the impact of disability on the psychological and social adjustment of older adults and their adult children (Fisher, Busch-Rossnagel, Jopp, & Brown, 2013; Lerner, 2012). Applied developmental scientists study and make contributions to social policies on issues that affect children, adolescents, adults, and their families, including environmental quality, health and health care delivery, violence, hunger and poor nutrition, school failure, and pervasive poverty (Tseng, 2012). Developmental scientists seek to enhance the life chances of diverse groups of individuals, families, and communities. Throughout this book, you will be introduced to these and more issues studied by applied developmental scientists.

What Do You Think?

1. Identify three areas that you believe are in need of study or intervention.

2. What challenges do children, adolescents, or adults face that you believe should be studied and addressed?

Structured interviews pose the same set of questions to each participant in the same way and therefore are less flexible than open-ended interviews. Because all participants receive the same set of questions, differences in responses are more likely to reflect true differences among participants and not merely differences in the manner of interviewing. For example Evans, Milanak, Medeiros, and Ross (2002) used a structured interview to examine American children's beliefs about magic. Children between the ages of 3 and 8 were asked the following set of questions:

What is magic? Who can do magic?

Is it possible to have special powers? Who has special powers?

Does someone have to learn to do magic? Where have you seen magic?

What are tricks? Who can do tricks? What is the difference between tricks and magic?

How do wishes work? What does it mean to make a wish? Do wishes come true? Who makes wishes come true?

What do you think about Santa Claus/the Tooth Fairy?

What do you think about Monsters? (p. 49)

After compiling and analyzing the children's responses as well as administering several cognitive tasks, Evans and colleagues (2002) concluded that even older children, who have the ability to think logically and perform concrete operations, may display magical beliefs.

Questionnaires, also called surveys, are sets of questions, typically multiple choice, that scientists compile and use to collect data from large samples of people. Questionnaires can be administered in person; online; or by telephone, e-mail, or postal mail. Questionnaires are popular data collection methods because they are easy to use and enable scientists to collect information from a large number of people quickly and inexpensively. Scientists who conduct research on sensitive topics, such as sexual interest and experience, often use questionnaires because they can easily be administered anonymously, protecting participants' privacy by not including any identifying information on the survey. For example, the Monitoring the Future Study is an annual survey of 50,000 8th, 10th, and 12th grade students that collects information about their behaviors, attitudes, and values concerning drug and alcohol use (Johnston, O'Malley, Miech, Bachman, & Schulenberg, 2014). In this example, the survey permits scientists to gather an enormous amount of data yet its anonymity protects the adolescents from the consequences of sharing personal information that they may not otherwise reveal.

Despite the ease of use, self-report measures are not without challenges. Sometimes people give socially desirable answers, meaning that they respond in ways they would like themselves to be perceived or believe researchers desire. A college student completing a survey about cheating, for example, might choose answers that do not truly reflect her experience as a student who sometimes looks at nearby students' papers during examinations but instead matches the person she aspires to be or the behaviors she believes the world values—that is, someone who does not cheat on exams. Self-report data may not always reflect people's true attitudes and behavior. Some argue that we are not always fully aware of our feelings and therefore cannot always provide useful insight into our own thoughts and behavior with the use of self-report measures (Westen, 1998). Whereas interviews and questionnaires measure people's self-reports of their attitudes, beliefs, and behaviors, observational measures examine people in action as they go about their daily lives.

This researcher is conducting observational research. What challenges might she experience in collecting observational data?

Observational Measures

Are you a people watcher? Have you ever sat in a coffee shop or at the student center and observed people interact, rush from place to place, laugh with others, or scowl at their laptops? If so, you have used observational skills that are similar to those used by scientists who conduct research in everyday settings. Observational measures are methods that scientists use to collect and organize information based on watching and monitoring people's behavior. Developmental scientists employ two types of observational measures: **naturalistic observation** and **structured observation**.

Scientists who use naturalistic observation observe and record behavior in natural, real-world settings. For example Ginsburg, Pappas, and Seo (2001) analyzed videotapes of 4- and 5-year-old children's everyday behavior during free play to determine the extent to which they use mathematical thinking in their play. Naturalistic observation is challenging because one must first decide on an *operational definition* of the behavior of interest. In this case, many operational definitions were required as Ginsburg and colleagues designed an elaborate coding system to categorize children's behaviors in terms of their mathematical content, location, preferred play objects, peer interaction, and play activity.

Sometimes the presence of an observer causes the person to behave in unnatural ways or ways that are not typical for him or her. This is known as *participant reactivity,* and it poses a challenge to gathering data by naturalistic observation. To minimize the effect that observation might have on the children's behaviors, Ginsburg and colleagues (2001) made video recordings and permitted the children to get used to the video recorder by exposing them to it many times before using it to collect observations. The video recorded observations revealed that children spend a surprising amount of play time (almost 50%) spontaneously engaging in mathematical activities like ordering objects; counting; comparing sizes and quantities; and exploring positions, direction, distances, and patterns. These results suggest that children naturally engage in mathematics-related play and are more competent in mathematics than many adults realize (Ginsburg et al., 2001).

Naturalistic observation permits researchers to observe behaviors in real-world settings and to observe patterns, such as whether a particular event or behavior typically precedes another. Such observations can help researchers determine which behaviors are important to study in the first place. For example, a scientist who studies bullying by observing children's play may notice that some victims act aggressively *before* a bullying encounter. The scientist may then decide to examine aggression in victims not only after a bullying incident but beforehand. Naturalistic observation is a useful way of studying events and behaviors that are common. Some behaviors and events, however, are uncommon or are difficult to observe, such as physical aggression among adults, requiring a researcher to observe for very long periods of time to obtain data on the behavior of interest. For this reason, many researchers make structured observations.

Structured observations entail observing and recording behaviors displayed in a controlled environment, a situation constructed by the experimenter. For example, children might be observed within a laboratory setting as they play with another child or complete a puzzle-solving task. The challenges of identifying and categorizing which behaviors to record are similar to those entailed by naturalistic observation. However, the laboratory environment permits researchers to exert more control on the situation than is possible in natural settings. In addition to cataloguing observable behaviors, some researchers use technology to measure biological functions such as heart rate, brain waves, and blood pressure. One challenge to conducting structured observations is that people do not always behave in laboratory settings as they do in real life. Data collection methods are summarized in Table 1.6.

RESEARCH METHODOLOGY

There are many steps in conducting research. In addition to determining the research question and deciding what information to collect, scientists must choose a research methodology, or technique, for conducting the research study. In the simplest sense, scientists have two basic choices: (1) identify correlational patterns in the data or (2) identify

TABLE 1.6 Data Collection Methods

	ADVANTAGE	DISADVANTAGE
Clinical interview	Gathers a large amount of information quickly and inexpensively	Nonstandardized questions are given. Characteristics of the interviewer may influence participant responses.
Structured interview	Gathers a large amount of information quickly and inexpensively	Characteristics of the interviewer may influence participant responses.
Questionnaire	Collects data from a large sample more quickly and inexpensively than by interview methods	Some participants may respond in socially desirable or inaccurate ways.
Naturalistic observation	Gathers data on everyday behavior in a natural environment as behaviors occur	The observer's presence may influence the participants' behavior. There is no control over the observational environment.
Structured observation	Observes in a controlled setting	It may not reflect real-life reactions and behavior.

causal processes indicating that a given event or condition caused a given outcome.

Correlational Research

Are children with high self-esteem more likely to excel at school? Are older adults with more friends happier than those with few? Are college students who work part-time less likely to graduate? All of these questions can be studied with **correlational research**, which permits researchers to examine relations among measured characteristics, behaviors, and events. For example, in one study scientists examined the relationship between children's after-school activities and their academic achievement and found that children who reported watching more television on school nights scored lower on achievement tests (Cooper, Valentine, Nye, & Lindsay, 1999). However, this correlation does not tell us *why* television viewing was associated with academic achievement. Correlational research cannot answer this question because it simply describes relationships that exist among variables; it does not enable us to make conclusions about the causes of those relationships. It is likely that other variables influence both a child's television watching and achievement (e.g., motivation) but only through **experimental research** are scientists able to determine the causes for behavior, as described next.

EXPERIMENTAL RESEARCH

Scientists who seek to test hypotheses about causal relationships, such as whether media exposure influences behavior or whether hearing particular types of music influences mood, employ experimental research to examine their research questions by conducting experiments. An experiment is a procedure that uses

control to determine causal relationships among variables or factors. Specifically, one or more variables thought to influence a behavior of interest are varied while other variables are held constant. By doing so, researchers can examine how the changing variable influences the behavior under study. If the behavior changes as the variable changes, scientists can conclude that the variable caused the change in the behavior.

For example, suppose a scientist examined the influence of exposure to aggressive media on children's aggressive behavior by choosing two cartoons: one containing many aggressive acts (e.g., hitting or punching) and another depicting few aggressive acts (e.g., including themes of sharing). Each child is asked to play with a set of toys containing cars, dolls, and stuffed animals. Researchers observe and record the number of aggressive acts the child engages in, such as hitting and throwing. Each child is tested in the same room, controlling other sounds, the temperature, and time of

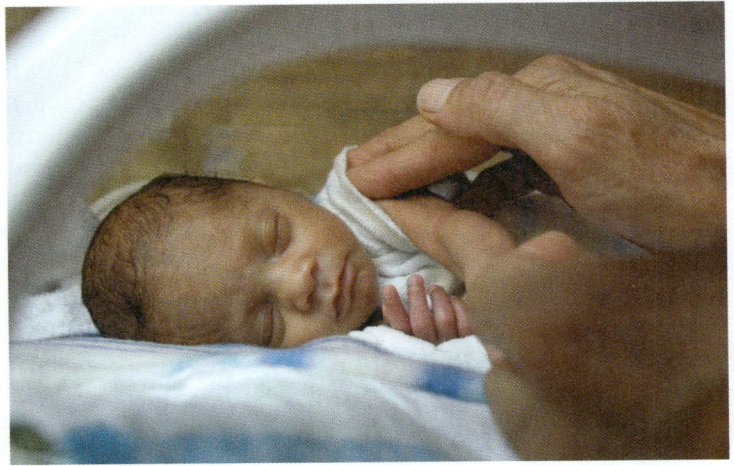

By experimentally manipulating which infants receive massage therapy, researchers determined that massage can help preterm infants gain weight, an important correlate of health.

day of testing. If researchers' ratings of children's aggression change in response to varying the type of media—showing more or less aggressive behavior—then the results suggest a causal relationship: Media exposure changed behavior.

Let us take a closer look at the components of an experiment. Conducting an experiment requires choosing at least one **dependent variable**, the behavior under study (e.g., hitting and throwing), and one **independent variable**, the factor proposed to change the behavior under study (e.g., type of cartoon). The independent variable is manipulated or varied systematically by the researcher during the experiment (e.g., varied between many aggressive acts or few aggressive acts). The dependent variable is expected to change as a result of varying the independent variable, and how it changes is thought to depend on how the independent variable is manipulated.

In an experiment, the independent variable is administered to one or more *experimental groups,* or test groups whose experiences are manipulated by varying the independent variable. The *control group* is treated in every way like the experimental group but does not receive the independent variable in order to compare the effect of the manipulation. For example, in an experiment investigating the effects of music on mood, the experimental group would experience a change in music (e.g., from "easy listening" to rock) whereas the control might hear only one type of music (e.g., "easy listening"). **Random assignment**, whereby each participant has an equal chance of being assigned to the experimental or control group, is essential for ensuring that the groups are equal in all preexisting characteristics (such as age, ethnicity, and gender). Random assignment makes it less likely that any observed differences in the outcomes of the experimental and control groups are not due to preexisting differences between the groups.

If, after the independent variable is manipulated, the experimental and control groups differ on the dependent variable, the scientist can conclude that independent variable caused the change in the dependent variable. As another example, consider a study designed to examine whether massage therapy improves weight gain in preterm infants (infants who were born well before their due date; Dieter, Field, Hernandez-Reif, Emory, & Redzepi, 2003). Infants housed in a neonatal unit were randomly assigned to a massage group (independent variable), who were touched and their arms and legs moved for three 15-minute periods per day, or a control group, which received no massage. Other than the massage/no massage periods, the two groups of infants were cared for in the same way. After five days, the preterm infants who received massage therapy gained more weight (dependent variable) than those who did not receive massage therapy. The researchers concluded that massage therapy causes improved weight gain in preterm infants.

Developmental scientists conduct studies that use both correlational and experimental research. Studying development, however, requires that scientists pay close attention to age and how people change over time, which requires the use of specialized research designs, as described in the following sections.

DEVELOPMENTAL RESEARCH DESIGNS

Does personality change over the lifespan? Do children outgrow shyness? Are infants' bonds with their parents associated with their adult relationships? These challenging questions require that developmental scientists examine relationships among variables over time. The following sections discuss the designs that researchers use to learn about human development. As you learn about each design, consider how we might employ it to learn about development. For example, how does alcohol use change from 6th grade through 12th grade?

Cross-Sectional Research Design

A common way in which developmental scientists examine questions about how variables change with age is to conduct **cross-sectional research**, comparing groups of people at different ages, at one time. For example, to examine how alcohol use changes from 6th through 12th grade, a scientist might visit a school system in 2016 and administer a survey about alcohol use to students in 6th, 8th, 10th, and 12th grades. By analyzing the survey, the scientist can describe grade differences in alcohol use—how 6th graders vary from 12th graders. Cross-sectional research permits scientists to draw conclusions about age differences—how the 6th graders differed in alcohol use from the 8th, 10th, and 12th graders. However, it is unknown whether the observed age differences in alcohol use reflect age-related or developmental change. In other words, it is unclear whether 6th graders will show the same pattern of change in alcohol use over the high school years as the 12th graders.

Cross-sectional research gathers information from people of several ages at one time, permitting age comparisons, but not conclusions about development because participants differ not only in terms of age but cohort. Recall that a cohort is a group of people of the same age who are exposed to similar historical events as well as cultural and societal influences. The 6th-grade students are a different age than the 12th-grade students, but they are also a different cohort in the school, so the two groups may differ in reported alcohol use because of development (age-related changes) or cohort (group-related changes). For example, perhaps the 6th-grade students received a new early prevention program in the school not available to the 12th-grade students back when they were in 6th grade. In this example, the difference in alcohol use between 6th graders and 12th graders may be related to the prevention program, not to age. Cross-sectional research is an important source of information about age differences, but it cannot provide information about age change.

Longitudinal Research Design

Developmental scientists who study age-related change must examine individuals over time. In **longitudinal research**, one group of participants is studied at many points in time. To examine how alcohol use changes from 6th through 12th grade, a developmental scientist who used longitudinal research might administer a survey on alcohol use to 6th graders and then follow up on them two years later when they enter 8th grade, again when they enter 10th grade, and finally in 12th grade. If a researcher began this study in 2016, the last round of data collection would not occur until 2022. Longitudinal research provides information about age change because it follows people over time, enabling scientists to describe how the 6th graders' alcohol use changed as they progressed through the school years. However, longitudinal research studies only one cohort—one generation—and is thereby prone to *cohort effects*. Do the findings indicate developmental change or are they an artifact of the cohort under study? Was the group of 6th graders that the scientist chose to follow up through 12th grade somehow different from the cohorts or groups of students who came before or after? Because only one cohort is assessed, it is not possible to determine if the observed changes are age-related changes or changes that are unique to the cohorts examined.

Sequential Research Design

Both cross-sectional and longitudinal studies provide useful information, but as we have seen, each has limitations. **Sequential research designs** combine the best features of cross-sectional and longitudinal research by assessing multiple cohorts over time, enabling scientists to make comparisons that disentangle the effects of cohort and age (see Table 1.7). Consider the alcohol use study once more. A sequential design would begin in 2016 by administering a survey to students in 6th, 8th, 10th, and 12th grades. Two years later, in 2018, the initial sample is surveyed again; the 6th graders are now 8th graders, 8th graders have become 10th graders, 10th graders have become 12th graders, and the 12th graders have graduated from the school and so are not assessed. Instead, a new group of 6th graders is surveyed. Two years later, in 2020, the participants are surveyed again and so on.

The sequential design provides information about age, cohort, and age-related change. The cross-sectional data

(comparisons of 6th, 8th, 10th, and 12th graders from a given year) permit comparisons among age groups. The longitudinal data (annual follow-up of 6th graders through 12th graders) permits age-related change. The sequential component helps scientists separate cohort effects from age-related change. Because several cohorts are studied at once, the effect of cohort can be studied. The sequential design is complex, but it permits human development researchers to disentangle the effects of age and cohort and answer questions about developmental change.

In summary, scientists use the scientific method to systematically ask and seek answers to questions about human development. Researchers' decisions about measures, such as whether to use self-report or observational measures, influence the information that they collect and the conclusions that they make. Choice of research methodology also influences conclusions researchers make about development, including statements about age differences, age change, and information about cohort effects. Researchers have responsibilities to conduct sound research and also to adhere to standards of ethical conduct in research, as the next section describes. See Table 1.8 for a comparison of research designs.

Thinking in Context 1.4

Dorothy is interested in understanding smoking in middle school students. Specifically, she believes that low self-esteem causes students to smoke.

1. How might Dorothy gather information to address her hypothesis?

2. What kind of research design should Dorothy use? What are the advantages and disadvantages of this design?

3. What are some of the challenges of measuring behaviors, such as smoking and internal characteristics such as self-esteem?

4. How can her study be improved to overcome the weaknesses you have identified?

ETHICAL ISSUES IN RESEARCH

Suppose a researcher wanted to determine the effects of an illegal drug on pregnant women or the effects of malnutrition on kindergarteners. Would it be possible to design a study in which certain pregnant women were assigned to ingest the illegal drug? Or one in which certain kindergarteners were deprived of food? If you answered no, you are correct, for U.S. and international laws regulate what kinds of research can be conducted and whether such research can expose participants to any harm,

TABLE 1.7 Sequential Research Design

	2016	2018	2020	2022	2024
6th grade	A	E	F		
8th grade	B	A	E	F	
10th grade	C	B	A	E	F
12th grade	D	C	B	A	E

A sequential design combines cross-sectional and longitudinal designs, permitting the researcher to study multiple cohorts over time.

TABLE 1.8 Comparing Research Designs

DESIGN	STRENGTHS	LIMITATIONS
General Research Design		
Correlational	Permits the analysis of relationships among variables as they exist in the real world	Cause-and-effect relations cannot be determined.
Experimental	Permits a determination of cause-and-effect relations	Data collected in artificial environments may not represent behavior in real-world environments.
Developmental Research Design		
Longitudinal	Permits the determination of age-related changes in a sample of participants assessed for a period of time	A great deal of time, resources, and expense is required. Participant attrition may limit conclusions. Only one cohort is studied, limiting the generalizability of conclusions.
Cross-sectional	Permits the determination of age differences; more efficient and less costly than the longitudinal design	It does not permit inferences regarding age change and confounds age and cohort.
Sequential	Allows for both longitudinal and cross-sectional comparisons, which reveal age differences and age change as well as cohort effects; more efficient and less costly than the longitudinal design	It is time consuming, expensive, and complicated in data collection and analysis.

or risk of harm. These kinds of questions, laws, and regulations are in the realm of *ethics*—the determination of right and wrong.

Developmental scientists' work is guided by five ethical principles: (1) beneficence and nonmaleficence, (2) responsibility, (3) integrity, (4) justice, and (5) respect for autonomy (American Psychological Association [APA], 2010). Beneficence and nonmaleficence are the dual responsibilities to do good and not to do harm. Researchers must protect and help the individuals, families, and communities with which they work by maximizing the benefits and minimizing the potential harms of their work. For example, when interviewing survivors of a natural disaster, such as an earthquake or tornado, a scientist pays attention to the participants' demeanor, and if the participant shows distress in response to a particular set of questions, the scientist might direct, even accompany, the participant to a therapist or mental health professional who can help him or her manage the distress.

Scientists act responsibly by adhering to professional standards of conduct, clarifying their obligations and roles to others, and avoiding conflicts of interest. For example, a psychologist who conducts research with children and parents must clarify her role as scientist and not therapist and help her participants understand that she is simply gathering information from them rather than conducting therapy. In this way, scientists recognize that they are responsible to people, communities, and society.

The principle of integrity requires that scientists be accurate, honest, and truthful in their work and make every effort to keep their promises to the people and communities with which they work.

Scientists have a special obligation to respect participants' autonomy—the ability to make and implement decisions. Scientists show respect for the individuals and families with whom they work by providing them with information about the research study, answering questions, helping them to make their own decisions about whether to participate in the study, and accepting their decisions. Respecting people's autonomy also means protecting those who are not capable of making judgments and asserting themselves. For example, some adults, such as those who have suffered traumatic brain injuries, may be unable to make and carry out decisions about whether to participate in research because of cognitive and social deficits. Scientists who work with patients who may be unable to make such judgments must carefully assess each patient's capacity and devise ways of protecting those who are not competent, such as by approaching the individual who is responsible for making legal decisions on the part of the patient.

Finally, the principle of justice means that the benefits and risks of participation in research must be spread equitably across individuals and groups. Scientists must take care to ensure that all people have access to and benefit from the contributions of research.

These ethical principles form the basis of professional codes of ethics for the Society for Research in Child Development (SRCD; 2007) and APA (2010), which provide guidelines for researchers who work with human participants.

RESPONSIBILITIES TO PARTICIPANTS

Sometimes researchers' desires to answer questions, learn, and solve problems by conducting research conflict with the need to protect participants in the research. For example, suppose a physician is conducting research testing the effectiveness of a drug designed to lower blood pressure. Over the course of the study, the scientist discovers that a participant has a heart defect that might someday require treatment. If the scientist discloses this information to the participant and encourages him or her to seek treatment, the scientist will have to remove the participant from the study. How should the scientist balance his or her research needs with the needs of participants? Scientists work to balance the benefits of research against the possible harm that can occur to participants—the mental, emotional, and physical risks.

In the United States and most other developed countries, the conduct of research is a regulated activity. Each college, university, hospital, and organization that conducts research has an institutional review board (IRB) that examines all plans for conducting a study before it can begin. Before a study can be conducted, the IRB examines the proposed research study in light of professional ethical codes as well as those articulated by the U.S. Department of Health and Human Services (2009). Do the study's benefits for advancing knowledge and improving conditions of life outweigh the potential costs in terms of time, money, and possible harm on the part of participants? IRBs act to protect participants by ensuring that the study has scientific merit and that risks of participating in research do not outweigh the potential benefits.

Ethical codes of conduct require that researchers obtain **informed consent** from each participant—their informed, rational, and voluntary agreement to participate. Consent must be informed, made with knowledge of the scope of the research, the potential for harm (if any), and the possible benefits of participating. Consent must be rational, meaning it must be made by a person capable of making a reasoned decision. Parents provide parental permission for their minor children to participate because researchers (and lawmakers) assume that minors are not able to meet the rational criteria of informed consent. Finally, participation must be voluntary, meaning that the decision to participate must be made freely and without coercion—individuals must understand that they are free to decide not to participate in the research study and that they will not be penalized in any way if they refuse.

Although children cannot provide informed consent, researchers respect their growing capacities for decision making in ways that are appropriate to their age by seeking *assent,* children's agreement to participate. For a young child, obtaining assent may involve simply asking if he or she wants to play with the researcher and answer some questions. With increasing cognitive and social development, children are better able to understand the nature of science and engage meaningfully in decisions about research participation (Thompson, 1990). Researchers should tailor discussions about the nature of research participation to children's capacities, provide more detailed information, and

seek more comprehensive assent as children age (Kuther, 2003). For example, a researcher about to administer early adolescents a questionnaire about their experiences with parental divorce might explain the kinds of questions that the adolescents will face; explain that in some cases a question might feel personal and might bring up memories; remind the adolescents that they are free to stop or skip any questions they choose; and finally, remind the adolescents that if they feel uncomfortable or would like to talk to someone about their feelings about the issues examined in the study, a counselor is available or the researcher can help them find someone who can help them. Moreover, seeking assent helps children learn how to make decisions and participate in decision making as they are able. Assent provides minors with opportunities to gain decision-making experience within safe contexts.

The researcher's ethical responsibilities do not end with obtaining informed consent. Most research studies are routine and uneventful because they are carried out according to plan. Sometimes, however, ethical issues arise in conducting a research study. For example, suppose that during the course of research a researcher learns that a participant is in jeopardy, whether engaging in health-compromising behaviors (such as cigarette smoking, unsafe driving, or exhibiting unhealthy behavior), contemplating suicide, or engaging in illegal or harmful activities (such as drug addiction, theft, or violence). Is a researcher responsible for helping the participant? Current ethical guidelines offer incomplete answers to questions of researchers' responsibilities to help participants in such situations.

The SRCD (2007) code of ethics suggests that researchers must help children in jeopardy by discussing the information with parents and guardians or with experts who may offer insight. Moreover, researchers may be faced with a conflict if they believe that helping the participant and dropping him or her from the research study may compromise the scientific integrity of the research, which may be especially likely if many participants are dropped. What should researchers do when they encounter participants in jeopardy? One study asked adolescents for their opinions on what researchers should do if they discover that a minor participant has a problem (Fisher, Higgins-D'Alessandro, Rau, Kuther, & Belanger, 1996). Older adolescents (e.g., age 17) tended to prefer that researchers not tell others about the problems and provide minors with self-referral information whereas young adolescents (e.g., age 13) tended to prefer that researchers report problems and potential threats to parents or trusted adults (Fisher et al., 1996). In addition, the adolescents' judgments depended on how serious they believed each problem to be. Adolescents favored reporting serious problems like abuse and threats of suicide to a parent or adult who can help. However, they preferred that the researcher not tell anyone about the problem and provide the child with self-referral information in cases of problems they rated as less serious, like smoking and nonviolent delinquent acts. Many questions remain. For example, does the age of the child matter in determining when to provide help? These are difficult decisions. Fortunately, serious ethical issues do not arise in most studies, but scientists should remain vigilant so that problems can be addressed should they arise. Table 1.9 summarizes the rights of research participants.

RESPONSIBILITIES TO SOCIETY

Researchers are responsible not only to their participants but to society at large. In reporting results, researchers should be mindful of the social and political implications of their work (SRCD, 2007). Researchers must consider how their findings will be portrayed in the media and attempt to foresee ways in which their results may be misinterpreted. This is a difficult task, but it is very important for researchers to be prepared to address questions raised as well as correct misinterpretations of research (National Academy of Sciences, 1995).

For example, one highly publicized study compiled the existing research literature examining college students who had become sexually involved with an adult prior to reaching the legal age of consent (Rind, Tromovitch, & Bauserman, 1998). After using statistics to summarize the findings of many research studies, the scientists determined that the college students' coping and development varied depending on a number of other factors within the individual, situation, and broader context. Not all appeared to be harmed, and many did well. However, some organizations, media outlets, and politicians misinterpreted the researchers' findings as suggesting that sexual involvement with minors was acceptable or even beneficial (Garrison & Kobor, 2002). Instead, the findings suggested that there are a range of outcomes to adult–minor relationships and the outcomes varied with the age of the minor and other characteristics of the situation. For example, the participants who seemed to be unharmed were more likely to be older (e.g., age 17) when the relationship began. Researchers must consider the potential social and political implications of their work, attempt to foresee the inferences that people may draw about their findings, and prepare to correct misinterpretations.

Lifespan human development is a broad field of study that integrates theory and research from many disciplines in order to describe, predict, and explain how we grow and change throughout our lifetime. Developmental scientists apply their knowledge of development to identify, prevent, and solve problems as well as improve opportunities for individuals, families, and communities. Throughout this book, you will learn the fundamentals of lifespan human development, including physical, cognitive, and socioemotional change as well the implications development science holds for social issues. We begin our journey by considering the role of genetics and environment in shaping who we become, as described in Chapter 2.

TABLE 1.9 Rights of Research Participants

RIGHT	DESCRIPTION
Protection from harm	Regardless of age, research participants have the right to be protected from physical and psychological harm. Investigators must use the least stressful research procedure in testing hypotheses and, when in doubt, consult with others. When harm is possible, researchers must determine another way to study the problem or abandon the research.
Informed consent	Participants have the right to be informed about the purpose of the research, expected duration, procedures, risks and benefits of participation, and any other aspects of the research that may influence their willingness to participate. When children are participants, a parent or guardian must provide informed consent on behalf of the child. The child should be provided information about research participation in terms appropriate to his or her development, and the investigator should seek assent from the child as a way of respecting the child's autonomy.
Voluntariness	Participants, regardless of age, have the right to choose not to participate or to discontinue participation in research at any time and without penalty.
Confidentiality	Participants have the right to conceal their identity on all information and reports obtained in the course of research.
Reporting results	Participants have the right to be informed of the results of research in language that is appropriate to their level of understanding.
Right to treatment	If an experimental treatment under investigation is believed to be beneficial, participants in control groups have the right to obtain the beneficial treatment.

SOURCES: APA (2010); SRCD (2007).

Apply Your Knowledge

1. Steven enters the school psychologist's office with a frown, grumbling to himself. His teacher, Ms. Marta, has suggested that he visit the school psychologist for help understanding and treating his academic problems. Steven is a bright fifth grader, but he has great difficulties reading and his mathematics skills lag far behind those of his peers. Ms. Marta contacts Steven's mother, reassuring her that the school has extraordinary resources for diagnosing children's learning problems and special education professionals who can intervene and help children overcome learning difficulties.

   The school psychologist interviews Steven's mother in order to compile a history of Steven's development. Through this interview he learns that Steven suffered a great deal of trauma early in life; as an infant, he was physically abused by his biological mother, then taken away and placed in foster care. At age 3, he was adopted into a middle-class, suburban family with two older, non-adopted children.

   As we have seen, each developmental theory has a unique emphasis. How might each theory address Steven's academic difficulties?

   a. What factors would psychoanalytic theories point to in order to explain Steven's functioning?

   b. How would cognitively oriented theories, such as Piaget's cognitive-developmental theory and information processing theory, account for and intervene with Steven's difficulties?

   c. Identify contextual factors that may play a role in Steven's academic problems; from Bronfenbrenner's bioecological theory, what factors may be addressed?

2. Suppose you wanted to conduct research on academic achievement during elementary and middle school.

   a. Identify a research question appropriate for a correlational research study.

   b. How would you address that question with a cross-sectional research study? Longitudinal? Sequential?

   c. What are the advantages and disadvantages of each type of study?

Chapter Summary

1.1 Outline five principles of the lifespan developmental perspective.

Development is a lifelong process. It is multidimensional, multidirectional, plastic, and influenced by the multiple contexts in which we are embedded.

1.2 Explain three theoretical controversies about human development.

Theories of human development can be compared with respect to their stance on the following questions. First, in what ways is developmental change continuous, characterized by slow and gradual change, or discontinuous, characterized by sudden and abrupt change? Second, to what extent are people active in influencing their development, interacting with and influencing the world around them? Finally, is development caused by nature or nurture, genetic endowments and heredity, or the physical and social environment?

1.3 Differentiate Freud's psychosexual theory from Erikson's psychosocial theory.

Freud's psychosexual theory explains personality development as progressing through a series of psychosexual stages during childhood. Erikson's psychosocial theory suggests that individuals move through eight stages of psychosocial development across the lifespan. Each stage presents a unique psychosocial task, or crisis. No crisis is ever fully resolved, but how well individuals address the crisis determines their ability to deal with the demands made by the next stage of development.

1.4 Distinguish operant and classical conditioning from social learning.

Behaviorist theory emphasizes the study of observable behavior; all behavior is shaped by the environment, whether through classical conditioning or operant conditioning. In classical conditioning, neutral stimuli become associated with stimuli that elicit reflex responses. Operant conditioning emphasizes the role of environmental stimuli in shaping behavior through reinforcement and punishment. Bandura's social learning theory includes cognition, explaining that people can learn through observation and do not need to experience the consequence itself. Bandura suggested that individuals and the environment interact and influence each other through reciprocal determinism.

1.5 Compare Piaget's cognitive-developmental theory and information processing theory.

Piaget's cognitive-developmental theory explains that children actively interact with the world around them and through this interaction create their own cognitive structures to organize what they have learned. Developmental change is the result of assimilation, accommodation, and equilibration. Information processing theorists study the steps entailed in cognition: perceiving and attending, representing, encoding, retrieving, and problem solving.

1.6 Contrast sociocultural systems theories and evolutionary perspectives on development.

Sociocultural systems theories look to the importance of context in shaping development. Vygotsky's sociocultural theory emphasizes interactions with members of our culture in influencing development. Bronfenbrenner's bioecological model explains development as a function of the ongoing reciprocal interaction among biological and psychological changes in the person and his or her changing context. Evolutionary developmental psychology integrates Darwinian principles of evolution and scientific knowledge about the interactive influence of genetic and environmental mechanisms to explain the changes we undergo throughout our lifetimes.

1.7 Compare self-report and observational methods of collecting information about participants.

Interviews and questionnaires are known as self-report measures because the person under study answers questions about his or her experiences, attitudes, opinions, beliefs, and behavior. In the clinical interview, or open-ended interview, the trained interviewer uses a conversational style that encourages the participant to expand his or her responses. Structured interviews pose the same set of questions to each participant in the same way. Questionnaires, or surveys, are sets of written questions that scientists compile and use to collect data from large samples of people. Observational measures are methods that scientists use to collect and organize information based on watching and monitoring people's behavior. Scientists who use naturalistic observation observe and record behavior in natural, real-world settings. Structured observations entail observing and recording behaviors displayed in the controlled environment, a situation constructed by the experimenter.

1.8 Contrast the uses of correlational and experimental research.

Correlational research describes the strength of relation between two or more variables. Scientists use correlational research to describe relations among measured characteristics, behaviors, and events. Scientists who seek to test hypotheses about causal relationships among variables employ experimental research. In an experiment, one or more independent variables thought to influence a behavior of interest are varied while other variables are held constant to examine how the changing variable influences the dependent variable, or the behavior under study.

1.9 Assess the strengths and weaknesses of cross-sectional, longitudinal, and sequential research designs.

Cross-sectional research compares groups of people at different ages, at one time, providing information about age differences; however, it is unknown whether the observed age differences reflect developmental change or cohort differences. Longitudinal research studies one group of participants at many points in time, providing information about age change. However, longitudinal research studies only one cohort; therefore, it is not possible to determine if the observed changes are age-related changes or changes that are unique to the cohort examined. Sequential designs combine the best features of cross-sectional and longitudinal designs; multiple cohorts are assessed over time, permitting comparisons that disentangle the effects of cohort and age, and answer questions about developmental change.

1.10 Discuss the responsibility of researchers to their participants and how they may protect them from harm.

Researchers must maximize the benefits to research participants and minimize the harms, safeguarding participants' welfare. They must be accurate and honest in their work and respect participants' autonomy by seeking informed consent and child assent. In addition, the benefits and risks of participation in research must be spread equitably across individuals and groups.

Key Terms

applied developmental science   25

behaviorism   24

bioecological systems theory   29

chronosystem   20

classical conditioning   24

cognitive development   4

cognitive-developmental theory   16

cohort   7

context   7

continuous development   9

correlational research   27

cross-sectional research   28

culture   7

dependent variable   28

discontinuous development   9

ethological theory   20

evolutionary developmental theory   20

exosystem   20

experimental research   27

hypotheses   11

independent variable   28

information processing theory   17

informed consent   31

lifespan human development   4

longitudinal research   28

macrosystem   20

mesosystem   20

microsystem   20

naturalistic observation   26

nature–nurture issue   10

observational learning   5

open-ended interview   24

operant conditioning   14

physical development   4

plasticity   6

psychoanalytic theories   12

punishment   15

questionnaires   24

random assignment   28

reciprocal determinism   15

reinforcement   15

schemas   16

scientific method   24

sequential research designs   29

social learning theory   15

sociocultural theory   18

socioemotional development   6

structured interview   25

structured observation   26

theory   11

CHAPTER 2

Biological and Environmental Foundations

SAGE edge™

Get the edge on your studies at edge.sagepub.com/kuther.

Master these learning objectives using key study tools in the chapter and at SAGE edge. Access original SAGE **Video Cases** to explore the lives and contexts of individuals in every stage of development, **Think Critically** and **Explore Further** with SAGE journal and reference articles, and **Watch**, **Listen**, and **Connect** with online multimedia resources.

LEARNING OBJECTIVES	KEY STUDY TOOLS
2.1. Explain how chromosomes, genes, DNA, and the genome relate to one another.	**Connect** Treating Down Syndrome
2.2. Identify and compare two processes of cell reproduction.	**Ethical and Policy Applications of Lifespan Development** Prenatal Sex Selection (p. 40) **Watch** Mitosis vs. Meiosis
2.3. Differentiate monozygotic (MZ) from dizygotic (DZ) twins.	**Video Case Twins** **Explore Further** Types of Twins
2.4. Contrast four processes of genetic inheritance.	**Connect** Interactive: Dominant Genes
2.5. Provide examples of diseases that illustrate dominant–recessive and X-linked inheritance.	**Connect** X-Linked Inheritance
2.6. Identify disorders that result from chromosomal abnormalities.	**Explore Further** Chromosomal Abnormalities
2.7. Discuss genetic counseling and prenatal testing, including common prenatal tests.	**Video Case** Genetics and Pregnancy **Think Critically** Ethics of Genetic Testing
2.8. Describe the methods and major findings of behavior genetics.	**Listen** Behavioral Genetics
2.9. Compare patterns of gene expression, including reaction range, canalization, gene–environment correlations, and epigenetic framework.	**Lives in Context** Gene-Environment Interactions and Responses to Child Maltreatment (p. 52) **Applying Developmental Science** Altering the Epigenome (p. 54)

"Roger and Ricky couldn't be more different," marveled their mother. "People are surprised to find out they are brothers." Roger is tall and athletic, with blond hair and striking blue eyes. He spends most afternoons playing ball with his friends and often invites them home to play in the yard. Ricky, two years older than Roger, is much smaller, thin and wiry. He wears thick glasses over his brown eyes that are nearly as dark as his hair. Unlike his brother, Ricky prefers solitary games and spends most afternoons at home playing video games, building model cars, and reading comic books. How can Roger and Ricky have the same parents and live in the same home yet differ markedly in appearance, personality, and preferences? In this chapter, we discuss the process of genetic inheritance and principles that can help us to understand how members of a family can share a great many similarities—and many differences.

Jasper James/Stone/Getty

GENETIC FOUNDATIONS OF DEVELOPMENT

Although Roger is quite different from his older brother, Ricky, he shares so many of his father's characteristics that most people comment on the strong physical resemblance. In other ways, however, Roger is more like his highly sociable mother. Ricky also shares similarities with each of his parents: In physical appearance, he resembles his mother and her brothers, but his quiet personality is similar to that of his father. Most of us learn early in life, and take it for granted, that children tend to resemble their parents. But to understand just how parents transmit their inborn characteristics and tendencies to their children, we must consider the human body at a cellular level.

THE GENETIC CODE

The human body is composed of trillions of units called cells. Within each cell is a nucleus that contains 23 matching pairs of rod-shaped structures called **chromosomes** (Barlow-Stewart, 2012). Each chromosome holds the basic units of heredity, known as **genes**. Genes are composed of stretches of **DNA** (or deoxyribonucleic acid), a complex molecule shaped like a twisted ladder or staircase. Genes are the blueprint for creating all of the traits that organisms carry. It is estimated that 20,000 to 25,000 genes reside within the chromosomes and influence all genetic characteristics (Barlow-Stewart, 2012; Pennisi, 2009).

The set of instructions to construct a living organism is referred to as the **genome**. Much of our genetic material is not unique to humans. Every species has a different genome, yet we share genes with all organisms, from bacteria to primates. We share 99% of our DNA with our closest genetic relative, the chimpanzee, whereas only 1% of our genes influence the characteristics that differentiate us from chimps, such as cognitive and language abilities. There is even less genetic variation among humans. People around the world share 99.7% of their genes (Watson, 2008). Although all humans share the same basic genome, every person has a slightly different code, making him or her genetically distinct from other humans.

CELL REPRODUCTION

Every cell in our body contains the same set of genes, and we retain these genes from the moment of conception until death. That is, we hold the same genetic material as adults as we did as newborns. Most cells in the human body reproduce through a process known as **mitosis** in which DNA replicates itself, permitting the duplication of chromosomes, and ultimately the formation of new cells with identical genetic material (Sadler, 2012). Specifically, in the first stage of mitosis, the rungs of the ladder-shaped DNA split, opening like a zipper. Then each half of the DNA molecule regenerates and replaces its missing parts, forming two distinct cells. It is this process that enables humans to develop from a single fertilized egg into a child, adolescent, and finally, adult.

FIGURE 2.1: Mitosis and Meiosis

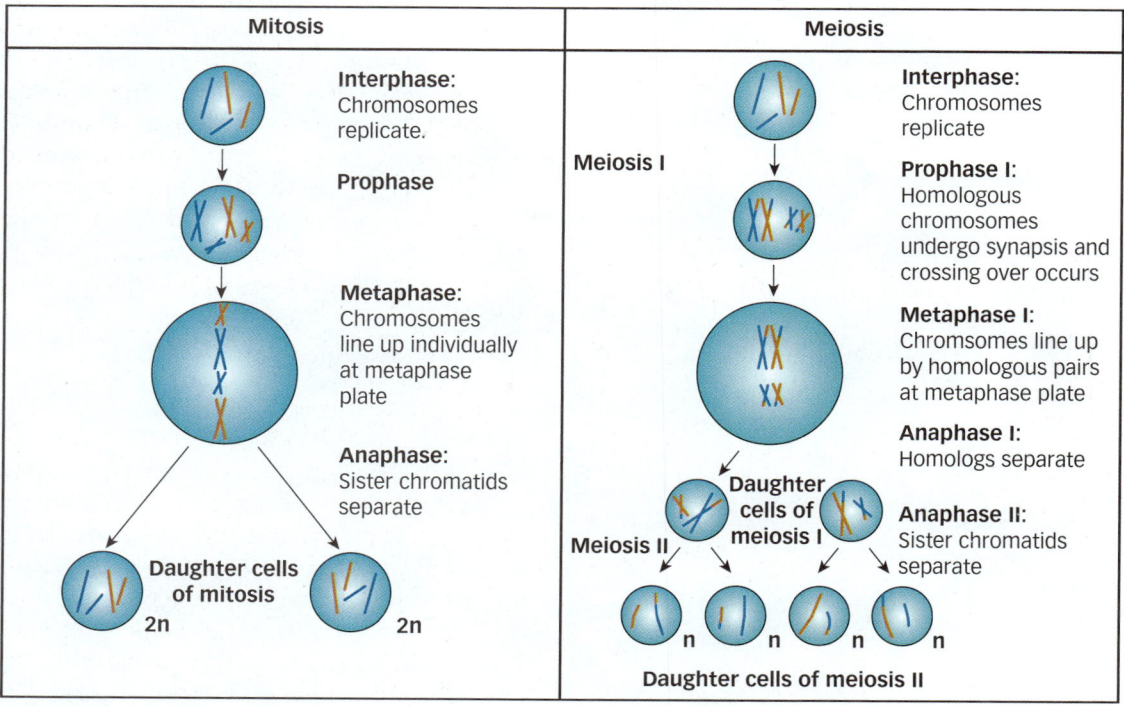

The process of mitosis accounts for the replication of all body cells. However, sex cells reproduce in a different way. Sex cells produce **gametes**, sperm in males and ova in females. The gametes are designed so that ova and sperm may combine to form a cell that will develop into a unique individual. Gametes each contain 23 chromosomes (one-half of the 46 chromosomes or 23 pairs present in body cells). Gametes reproduce through the unique process of **meiosis**.

Meiosis, the reproduction of gametes, occurs in two stages (see Figure 2.1). First, the 46 chromosomes begin to replicate as in mitosis, duplicating themselves. But before the cell completes dividing, a critical process called **crossing-over** takes place. Chromosome pairs align, and DNA segments cross over, moving from one member of the pair to the other. Crossing-over creates unique combinations of genes (Sadler, 2012). The cell then divides into two cells, each with 46 chromosomes. As the new cells replicate, they create cells containing only 23 single, unpaired chromosomes. The resulting gametes each have only one chromosome from each pair (that is, one each from the male and female). This permits the joining of sperm and ovum at fertilization to produce a fertilized egg, or **zygote**, with 46 chromosomes, forming 23 pairs with half from the biological mother and half from the biological father.

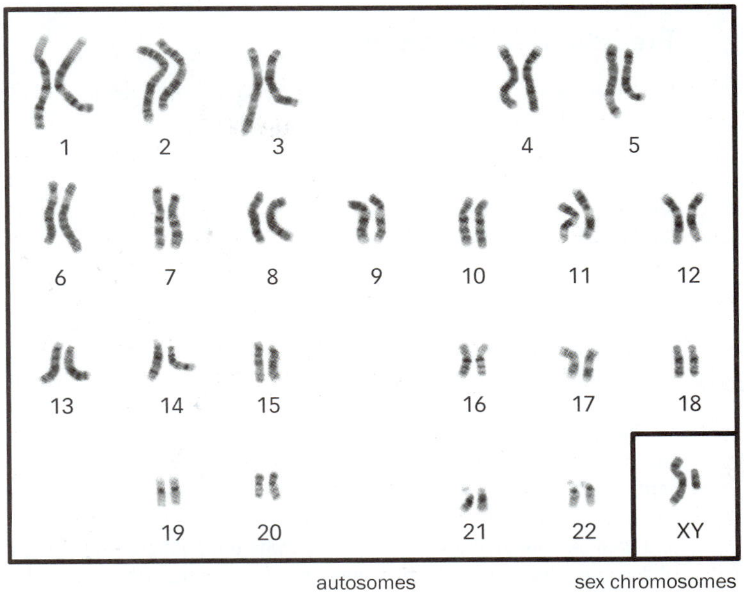

SEX DETERMINATION

As shown in Figure 2.2, 22 of the 23 pairs of chromosomes are matched containing similar genes in almost identical positions and sequence, reflecting the distinct genetic blueprint of the biological mother and father. The 23rd pair is sex chromosomes that specify the biological sex of the individual. In females, sex chromosomes consist of two large

FIGURE 2.2: Chromosomes

![Karyotype of chromosomes numbered 1 through 22 labeled autosomes, and XY labeled sex chromosomes]

autosomes   sex chromosomes

X-shaped chromosomes (XX). Males' sex chromosomes consist of one large X-shaped chromosome and one much smaller Y-shaped chromosome (XY; Barlow-Stewart, 2012; Moore & Persaud, 2013).

The sex chromosomes determine whether a zygote will develop into a male or female. Because females have two X sex chromosomes, all ova contain one X sex chromosome. A male's sex chromosome pair includes both X and Y chromosomes; therefore, one half of the sperm males produce contain an X chromosome and one half contain a Y. The Y chromosome contains genetic instructions that will cause the fetus to develop male reproductive organs. Thus, whether the fetus develops into a boy or girl is determined by which sperm fertilizes the ovum. If the ovum is fertilized by a Y sperm, a male fetus will develop, and if the ovum is fertilized by an X sperm, a female fetus will form, as shown in Figure 2.3. As discussed in Ethical and Policy Applications of Lifespan Development (p. 40), scientific advances in our ability to identify chromosomes have raised ethical questions about how to apply this knowledge, for example, by using reproductive technologies for prenatal sex selection.

GENES SHARED BY TWINS

All biological siblings share the same parents, inheriting chromosomes from each. Despite this genetic similarity, siblings are often quite different from one another. Meiosis, specifically the crossing-over process, increases genetic variability and accounts for genetic uniqueness. It is estimated that individuals can produce millions of versions of their own chromosomes (National Library of Medicine, 2013).

Twins are siblings who share the same womb. Twins occur in about 1 out of every 30 births in the United States (Martin, Hamilton, & Osterman, 2012). Are twins

FIGURE 2.3: Sex Determination

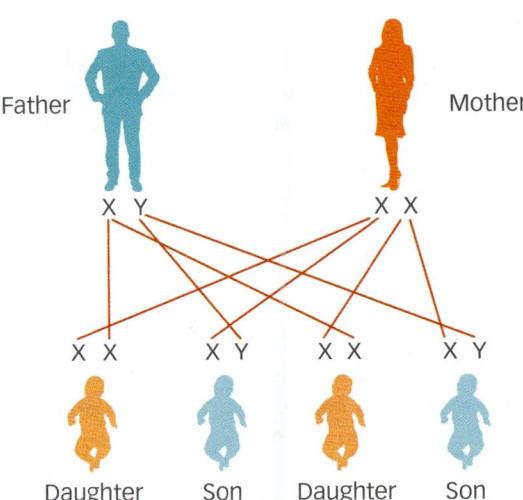

Father   Mother

X Y   X X

X X   X Y   X X   X Y

Daughter   Son   Daughter   Son

Prenatal Sex Selection

Parents have long shown a preference for giving birth to a girl or boy, depending on circumstances such as cultural or religious traditions, the availability of males or females to perform certain kinds of work important to the family or society, or the sex of the couple's other children. Yet, throughout human history until recently, the sex of an unborn child was a matter of hope, prayer, and folk rituals. It is only in the past generation that science has made it possible for parents to reliably choose the sex of their unborn child. The introduction of sex selection has been a boon to couples carrying a genetically transmitted disease (i.e., a disease carried on the sex chromosomes), enabling them to have a healthy baby of the sex unaffected by the disease they carried.

There are two methods of sex selection: preconception sperm sorting and pre-implantation genetic diagnosis (PGD; Human Fertilisation and Embryology Authority, 2003). Preconception sperm sorting involves staining the sperm with a fluorescent dye and then leading them past a laser beam where the difference in DNA content between X- and Y-bearing sperm is visible (Dondorp et al., 2013). PGD creates zygotes within the laboratory by removing eggs from the woman and fertilizing them with sperm. This is known as in vitro (literally, "in glass") fertilization because fertilization takes place in a test tube, outside of the woman's body. After three days, a cell from each blastula is extracted to examine the chromosomes and determine whether or not it contains a Y chromosome (i.e., whether it is female or male). The desired male or female embryos are then implanted into the woman's uterus. The second type of sex selection, sperm sorting, entails spinning sperm in a centrifuge to separate those that carry an X or Y chromosome. Sperm with the desired chromosomes are then used to fertilize the ovum either vaginally or through **in vitro fertilization**.

As sex selection becomes more widely available, parents may seek to choose the sex of their child because of personal desires, such as to create family balance or to conform to cultural valuing of one sex over the other, rather than to avoid transmitting genetic disorders (Robertson & Hickman, 2013). Critics argue that sex selection can lead down a "slippery slope" of selecting for other characteristics—hair color, eye color, intelligence, and more (Ethics Committee of the American Society for Reproductive Medicine, 2001). Might children born from gender selection be expected to act in certain sex-typical ways and if they do not, might that disappoint parents? Others express concerns about societal sex ratio imbalances if sex selection becomes widely practiced (Colls et al., 2009; Robertson & Hickman, 2013). Such sex ratio imbalances favoring males have occurred in India and China because of female infanticide, gender-driven abortion, and China's one-child family policy (see the Cultural Influences on Development feature in Chapter 10 for more information; Bhatia, 2010; Ethics Committee of the American Society for Reproductive Medicine, 2001).

Should selecting an embryo's sex be a matter of parental choice? A review of 36 countries, including 25 in Europe, revealed that many had no policies regarding selection; those that did, prohibited sex selection for nonmedical reasons (Darnovsky, 2009). The European Union bans socially, nontherapeutically motivated sex selection (Council of Europe, 1997). The United States does not have a formal policy regarding sex selection (Deeney, 2013). Sex selection remains hotly debated in medical journals, hospital and university ethics boards, and the public.

What Do You Think?

1. **What do you think about parents choosing the sex of their children? In your view, under what conditions is sex selection acceptable?**

2. **If you were able to selectively reproduce other characteristics, apart from sex, what might you choose? Why or why not?**

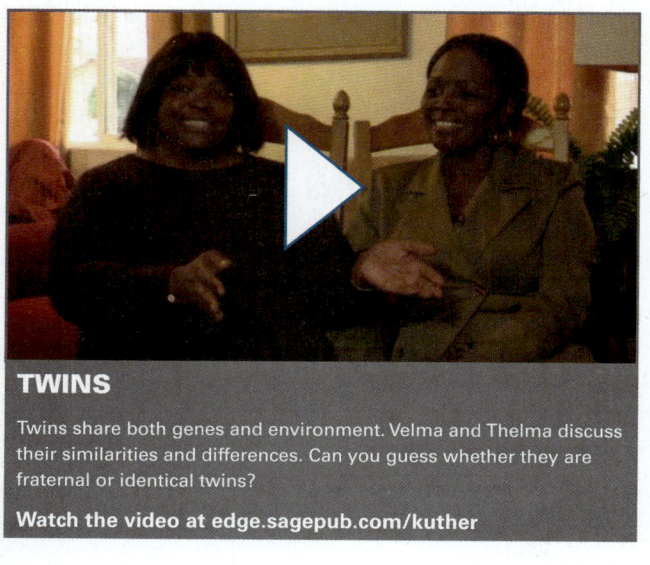

TWINS

Twins share both genes and environment. Velma and Thelma discuss their similarities and differences. Can you guess whether they are fraternal or identical twins?

Watch the video at edge.sagepub.com/kuther

more similar than other siblings? In most cases, no: About two thirds of naturally conceived twins are **dizygotic (DZ) twins**, or fraternal twins. In the United States, DZ twins occur in about 13 of every 1,000 births (Hoekstra et al., 2008). DZ twins are conceived when a woman releases more than one ovum and each is fertilized by a different sperm. Genetically, DZ twins are no more similar to each other than are other siblings that are conceived and born separately. They share about one half of their genes and can share many similarities, or like Ricky and Roger, the brothers mentioned at the beginning of this chapter, they can be very different. Like other siblings, most fraternal twins differ in appearance, such as hair color, eye color, and height. In about half of fraternal twin pairs, one twin is a boy and the other a girl. Yet sometimes same-sex DZ twins are so similar that they appear like identical twins, also known as **monozygotic (MZ) twins**. DZ twins

Monozygotic, or identical, twins share 100% of their DNA.

tend to run in families, suggesting a genetic component that controls the tendency for a woman to release more than one ovum each month. However, rates of DZ twins also increase with in vitro fertilization, maternal age, and with each subsequent birth (Fletcher, Zach, Pramanik, & Ford, 2012; Martin et al., 2012).

MZ, or identical, twins originate from the same zygote. MZ twins occur when the zygote splits into two distinct separate but identical zygotes that develop into two infants. MZ twins share the same **genotype**, with identical instructions for all physical and psychological characteristics. MZ twins are relatively rare. It is estimated that MZ twins occur in 4 of every 1,000 U.S. births (Fletcher et al., 2012). The causes of MZ twinning are not well understood. Temperature fluctuations are associated with MZ births in animals, but

it is unknown whether similar effects occur in humans (Aston, Peterson, & Carrell, 2008). In vitro fertilization and advanced maternal age (35 and older) may increase the risk of MZ twins (Aston et al., 2008; Knopman et al., 2014).

Thinking in Context 2.1

1. What is the difference between mitosis and meiosis? What purpose might each serve in transmitting genes? Why do you think they evolved?

2. In your view, why does twinning occur? From an evolutionary developmental perspective, does twinning serve an adaptive purpose for our species? Why or why not?

PATTERNS OF GENETIC INHERITANCE

Although the differences among various members of a given family may appear haphazard, they are the result of a genetic blueprint unfolding. Traits and characteristics are inherited in predictable ways. Researchers are just beginning to uncover the instructions contained in the human genome. However, we have learned a great deal about the way in which heredity influences development and behavior.

DOMINANT–RECESSIVE INHERITANCE

Lynn has red hair while her brother, Jim, does not—and neither do their parents. How did Lynn end up with red hair? These outcomes can be explained by patterns of genetic inheritance, how the sets of genes from each parent interact. As we have discussed, each person has 23 pairs of chromosomes, one pair inherited from the mother and one from the father. The genes within each chromosome can be expressed in different forms, or **alleles**, that influence a variety of physical characteristics. When alleles of the pair of chromosomes are alike with regard to a specific characteristic, such as hair color, the person is said to be **homozygous** for the characteristic and will display the inherited trait. If they are different, the person is **heterozygous**, and the trait expressed will depend on the relations among the genes (Moore & Persaud, 2013; National Center for Biotechnology Information, 2004). Some genes are passed through **dominant–recessive inheritance** in which some genes are *dominant* and are always expressed regardless of the gene they are paired with. Other genes

FIGURE 2.4: Dominant–Recessive Inheritance

Brown hair father   Brown hair mother

Parent phenotype

Parent genotype   Nr   Nr

Child genotype   NN   Nr   Nr   rr

Child phenotype

Brown hair   Brown hair   Brown hair   Red hair

are *recessive* and will be expressed only if paired with another recessive gene. Lynn and Jim's parents are heterozygous for red hair; both have dark hair, but they each carry a recessive gene for red hair.

When an individual is heterozygous for a particular trait, the dominant gene is expressed, and the person becomes a **carrier** of the recessive gene. For example, Jim has non-red hair. He may have homozygous or heterozygous genes for hair color because the gene for non-red hair (symbolized by N in Figure 2.4) is dominant over the gene for red hair (r). In other words, both a child who inherits a homozygous pair of dominant genes (NN) and one who inherits a heterozygous pair consisting of both a dominant and recessive gene (Nr) will have non-red hair, even though the two genotypes are different. If Jim is heterozygous for red hair (Nr), he is a carrier of the gene for red hair and can pass it on to his offspring. Red hair, like Lynn's, can result only from having two recessive genes (rr); both of her parents must carry the recessive gene for red hair. As shown in Table 2.1, several characteristics are passed through dominant–recessive inheritance.

INCOMPLETE DOMINANCE

In most cases, dominant–recessive inheritance is an oversimplified explanation for patterns of genetic inheritance. **Incomplete dominance** is a genetic inheritance pattern in which both genes influence the characteristic (Moore & Persaud, 2013). For example, consider blood type. Neither the alleles for blood type A and B dominate each other. A heterozygous person with the alleles for blood type A and B will express both A and B alleles and have blood type AB.

A different type of inheritance pattern is seen when a person inherits heterozygous alleles in which one allele is stronger than the other yet does not completely dominate. In this situation, the stronger allele does not mask all of

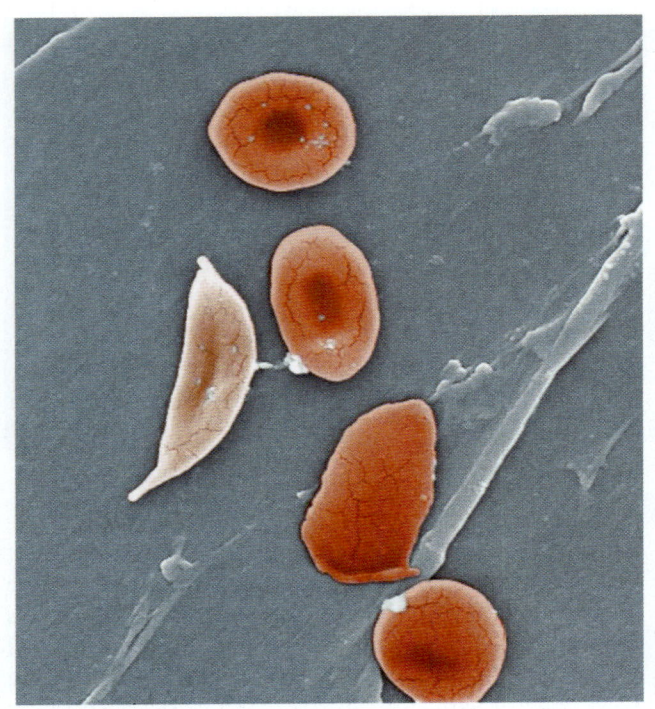

Recessive sickle cell alleles cause red blood cells to become crescent shaped and unable to distribute oxygen effectively throughout the circulatory system. Alleles for normal blood cells do not mask all of the characteristics of recessive sickle cell alleles, illustrating incomplete dominance.

the effects of the weaker allele. Therefore some, but not all, characteristics of the recessive allele appear. For example, the trait for developing normal blood cells does not completely mask the allele for developing sickle-shaped blood cells. About 8% of African Americans (and relatively few Caucasians or Asian Americans) carry the recessive sickle cell trait (Ashley-Koch, Yang, & Olney, 2000). Sickle cell alleles cause red blood cells to become crescent, or sickle, shaped. Cells that are sickle-shaped cannot distribute oxygen effectively throughout the circulatory system. However, sickle cell carriers do not develop full-blown sickle cell anemia. Carriers of the trait for sickle cell anemia may function normally but may show some symptoms such as reduced oxygen distribution throughout the body and exhaustion after exercise. Only individuals who are homozygous for the recessive sickle cell trait develop sickle cell anemia.

POLYGENIC INHERITANC\E

Whereas dominant–recessive and codominant–recessive patterns account for some genotypes, most traits are a function of the interaction of many genes, known as **polygenic inheritance**. Hereditary influences act in complex ways, and researchers cannot trace most characteristics to only one or two genes. Instead, polygenic traits are the result of interactions among many genes. Examples of polygenic

TABLE 2.1 Dominant and Recessive Characteristics

DOMINANT TRAIT	RECESSIVE TRAIT
Dark hair	Blond hair
Curly hair	Straight hair
Hair	Baldness
Non-red hair	Red hair
Facial dimples	No dimples
Brown eyes	Blue, green, hazel eyes
Second toe longer than big toe	Big toe longer than second toe
Type A blood	Type O blood
Type B blood	Type O blood
Rh-positive blood	Rh-negative blood
Normal color vision	Color blindness

SOURCES: McKusick (1998); McKusick-Nathans Institute of Genetic Medicine (2014).

traits include height, intelligence, temperament, and susceptibility to certain forms of cancer (Plomin, DeFries, McClearn, & McGuffin, 2001). As the number of genes that contribute to a trait increases, so does the range of possible traits. Genetic propensities interact with environmental influences to produce a wide range of individual differences in human traits.

GENOMIC IMPRINTING

The principles of dominant–recessive and incomplete dominance inheritance can account for over 1,000 human traits (McKusick, 2007). However, a few traits are determined by a process known as **genomic imprinting**. Genomic imprinting refers to the instance in which the expression of a gene is determined by whether it is inherited from the mother or the father (National Library of Medicine, 2013; Sadler, 2012). Genomic imprinting may influence susceptibility to illnesses such as some cancers (Das, Hampton, & Jirtle, 2009). Genes are passed on from biological parents to children and influence human characteristics in complex ways.

As an example, let us examine two conditions that illustrate genomic imprinting: Prader-Willi syndrome and Angelman syndrome. Both syndromes are caused by an abnormality in the 15th chromosome (Butler, 2011). If the abnormality occurs on chromosome 15 acquired by the father, the individual—whether a daughter or son—will develop Prader-Willi syndrome, a set of specific physical and behavioral characteristics including obesity, insatiable hunger, short stature, motor slowness, and mild to moderate intellectual impairment. If the abnormal chromosome 15 arises from the mother, the individual—again, whether it is a daughter or a son—will develop Angelman syndrome, characterized by hyperactivity, thin body frame, seizures, disturbances in gait, and severe learning disabilities including severe problems with speech. Prader-Willi and Angelman syndromes each occur in about 1 in 15,000 persons (Everman & Cassidy, 2000).

As you can see from the topics presented in this section, patterns of genetic inheritance can be complex, yet they follow predictable principles. For a summary of patterns of genetic inheritance, refer to Table 2.2.

Thinking in Context 2.2

1. Consider your own physical characteristics, such as hair and eye color. Are they indicative of recessive traits, or dominant ones?

2. Do you think that you might be a carrier of recessive traits? Why or why not?

TABLE 2.2 Summary: Patterns of Genetic Inheritance

INHERITANCE PATTERN	DESCRIPTION
Dominant–recessive inheritance	Genes that are dominant are always expressed, regardless of the gene they are paired with, and recessive genes are expressed only if paired with another recessive gene.
Incomplete dominance	Both genes influence the characteristic, and aspects of both genes appear.
Polygenic inheritance	Polygenic traits are the result of interactions among many genes.
Genomic imprinting	The expression of a gene is determined by whether it is inherited from the mother or the father.

CHROMOSOMAL AND GENETIC PROBLEMS

Fortunately, the vast majority of humans—and animals, for that matter—inherit healthy genes. However, heredity plays a role in many disorders and illnesses. Many hereditary and chromosomal abnormalities can be diagnosed prenatally, either through routine prenatal blood tests and **ultrasound** examinations or—more commonly—through specific tests recommended for couples who have a family history of such abnormalities or in which the woman is over the age of 35. Others are evident at birth, or can be detected soon after an infant begins to develop. Still others reveal themselves only over a period of many years.

GENETIC DISORDERS

Disorders and abnormalities that are inherited through the parents' genes include such well-known conditions as cystic fibrosis and sickle cell anemia, as well as others that are rare and, in some cases, never even noticed throughout the individual's life.

Dominant-Recessive Disorders

As explained earlier in this chapter, in dominant–recessive inheritance genes that are dominant are always expressed regardless of the gene they are paired with, and recessive genes are expressed only if paired with another recessive gene. Several diseases are inherited through dominant–recessive inheritance (see Table 2.3), including recessive disorders like cystic fibrosis and sickle cell anemia. Few severe disorders are inherited through dominant inheritance because individuals who inherit the allele often do not survive long enough to reproduce and pass it to the next generation. One exception is Huntington's disease, a fatal disease in which the central nervous system deteriorates (National Library of Medicine, 2013; Sadler, 2012). Individuals with the Huntington's allele develop normally in childhood, adolescence, and young adulthood. Symptoms of Huntington's disease do not appear until age 35 or later. By then, many individuals have already had children, and one half of them, on average, will inherit the dominant Huntington's gene.

One of the most common recessive disorders is **phenylketonuria (PKU)**. Diagnosed in about one 1 of every 15,000 newborns, PKU prevents the body from producing an enzyme that breaks down phenylalanine, an amino acid, from proteins (Blau, van Spronsen, & Levy, 2010). The phenylalanine builds up quickly to toxic levels that damage the central nervous system, contributing to mental retardation by 1 year of age. PKU is also an example of how genes interact with the environment to produce developmental outcomes. Intellectual disability results from the interaction of the genetic predisposition and exposure to phenylalanine from the environment. The United States and Canada require that all newborns are screened for PKU. If the disease is discovered, the infant is placed on a diet low in phenylalanine (Blau et al., 2010). Children who maintain a strict diet low in phenylalanine usually attain average or near-average levels of intelligence (Blau et al., 2010; Widaman, 2009).

Children with PKU can process only very small amounts of phenylalanine. Yet it is very difficult to remove nearly all phenylalanine from the diet. Some cognitive and motor deficits often appear in childhood and persist into adulthood, particularly in attention and planning skills (Blau et al. 2010; Enns et al., 2010). Children with PKU are at risk for behavioral and psychological problems, including sadness, depression, anxiety, and phobic reactions (Blau et al., 2010; Koch, Guttler, & Blau, 2002; Smith & Knowles, 2000). The emotional and social challenges associated with PKU, such as the pressure of a strict diet and surveillance from parents, may worsen these symptoms (Smith & Knowles, 2000).

X-Linked Disorders

A special instance of the dominant–recessive pattern occurs with genes that are located on the X chromosome. Recall that males (XY) have both an X and Y chromosome. Some recessive genetic disorders, like the gene for red-green color blindness, are carried on the X-chromosome. Males are more likely to be affected by X-linked genetic disorders because they have only one X chromosome. Females (XX) have two X chromosomes; a recessive gene located on one X chromosome will be masked

TABLE 2.3 Diseases Inherited Through Dominant–Recessive Inheritance

DISEASE	OCCURRENCE	MODE OF INHERITANCE	DESCRIPTION	TREATMENT
Huntington's disease	1 in 20,000	Dominant	Degenerative brain disorder that affects muscular coordination and cognition	No cure; death usually occurs 10 to 20 years after onset
Marfan syndrome	1 in 20,000	Dominant	A connective tissue disorder that affects the skeleton, lungs, eyes, heart and blood vessels; disease is characterized by unusually long limbs	No cure; death from complications in young adulthood is common
Cystic fibrosis	1 in 2,000–2,500	Recessive	An abnormally thick, sticky mucus clogs the lungs and digestive system, leading to respiratory infections and digestive difficulty	Bronchial drainage, diet, gene replacement therapy
Phenylketonuria (PKU)	1 in 8,000–10,000	Recessive	Inability to digest phenylalanine that, if untreated, results in neurological damage and death	Diet
Sickle cell anemia	1 in 500 African Americans	Recessive	Sickling of red blood cells leads to inefficient distribution of oxygen throughout the body that leads to organ damage and respiratory infections	No cure; blood transfusions, treat infections, bone marrow transplant; death by middle age
Tay-Sachs disease	1 in 3,600–4,000 descendants of Central and Eastern European Jews	Recessive	Degenerative brain disease	None; most die by 4 years of age
Cooley's anemia	1 in 500 people of Mediterranean descent	Recessive	Blood disorder resulting in very pale skin, retarded growth, and lethargy	No cure; frequent blood transfusions; death by complications occurs by adolescence

SOURCES: McKusick (1998); McKusick-Nathans Institute of Genetic Medicine (2014).

by a dominant gene on the other X chromosome. Females are thereby less likely to display X-linked genetic disorders because both of their X-chromosomes must carry the recessive genetic disorder for it to be displayed (Barlow-Stewart, 2012).

Hemophilia, a condition in which the blood does not clot normally, is another example of a recessive disease inherited through genes on the X chromosome. Daughters who inherit the gene for hemophilia typically do not show the disorder because the gene on their second X chromosome promotes normal blood clotting and it is a dominant gene. Females, therefore, can carry the gene for hemophilia without exhibiting the disorder. A female carrier has a 50/50 chance of transmitting the gene to each child. Sons who inherit the gene will display the disorder because the Y chromosome does not have the corresponding genetic information to counter the gene. Daughters who inherit the gene, again, will be carriers (unless their second X chromosome also carries the gene).

In contrast, fragile X syndrome is an example of a dominant recessive disorder carried on the X chromosome. Specifically, it is a structural irregularity in the chromosome consisting of a pinched site toward the end of the long arm of the X (Hagerman, 2011). Because the gene is dominant, it need appear on only one X chromosome to be displayed. That means that fragile X syndrome occurs in both males and females.

Fragile X syndrome occurs in about 1 in every 4,000 males and 1 in every 8,000 females (National Library of Medicine, 2013). Fragile X syndrome is the most common form of inherited intellectual impairment (Abrams et al., 2012), and some research suggests that it is strongly associated with autism (Cohen et al., 2005). Males with fragile X syndrome typically have a long, narrow face; large ears; and large testes. Cardiac defects are common as well as several behavioral mannerisms, including poor eye contact and repetitive behaviors such as hand flapping, hand biting, and mimicking others (Hagerman, 2011). As carriers, females may show some characteristics of the disorder but tend to display levels of intelligence within the normal or near normal range. Table 2.4 illustrates diseases acquired through X-linked inheritance.

Chris Walker/MCT/Newscom

This young man is diagnosed with Fragile X syndrome, a recessive disorder carried on the X chromosome and the most common form of inherited intellectual impairment.

CHROMOSOMAL ABNORMALITIES

As described at the beginning of this chapter, the human body is made up of cells, and within each cell are chromosomes that, in essence, provide the instructions for the growth of a human being. During both mitosis and meiosis, the cells are supposed to—and usually do—end up with the correct number of chromosomes, but occasionally an error in cell division occurs such that cells have too few or too many copies of a chromosome. In other cases, chromosomes are damaged or altered.

Down Syndrome

Occurring in about 1 of about every 700 births, the most widely known chromosome disorder is trisomy 21, more commonly called **Down syndrome** (Parker et al., 2010). Down syndrome occurs when three chromosomes, rather than two, appear in place of the 21st pair of chromosomes. The risk for Down syndrome increases markedly with maternal age and possibly with paternal age as well (see Chapter 3). Although individuals with Down syndrome vary in the severity of symptoms, Down syndrome is associated with marked physical, health, and cognitive attributes (Davis & Escobar, 2013).

TABLE 2.4 Diseases Acquired Through X-Linked Inheritance

SYNDROME/ DISEASE	OCCURRENCE	DESCRIPTION	TREATMENT
Color blindness	1 in 12 males	Difficulty distinguishing red from green; less common is difficulty distinguishing blue from green	No cure
Duchenne muscular dystrophy	1 in 3,500 males	Weakness and wasting of limb and trunk muscles; progresses slowly but will affect all voluntary muscles	Physical therapy, exercise, body braces; survival rare beyond late 20s
Fragile X syndrome	1 in 2,000 males	Symptoms include cognitive impairment; attention problems; anxiety; unstable mood; long face; large ears; flat feet; and hyperextensible joints, especially fingers	No cure
Hemophilia	1 in 3,000– 7,000 males	Blood disorder in which the blood does not clot	Blood transfusions

SOURCES: McKusick (1998); McKusick-Nathans Institute of Genetic Medicine (2014).

Digital Light Source/Universal/Getty

Down syndrome is the most common cause of intellectual disability. Children with Down syndrome show more positive developmental outcomes when adults are sensitive to their needs. Interventions that encourage children to interact with their environment can promote motor, social, and emotional development.

Physical attributes that accompany Down syndrome include a short, stocky build, and short, broad hands, often with an unusual crease in the palm. Striking facial features mark the disorder, such as a round face, almond-shaped eyes, and a flattened nose. Children with Down syndrome tend to show delays in physical and motor development relative to other children. Down syndrome children often experience health problems including congenital heart defects, vision impairments such as cataracts and poor visual acuity, and poor hearing (Hazlett, Hammer, Hooper, & Kamphaus, 2011). Many individuals with Down syndrome experience immune system deficiencies and frequent infections, especially of the respiratory tract (Ram & Chinen, 2011).

Intellectual disabilities are common in individuals with Down syndrome; in fact, it is the most common genetic cause of mental retardation (Davis & Escobar, 2013). Problems with memory and language are common (Jarrold, Nadel, & Vicari, 2009). Although children with Down syndrome tend to show slower intellectual development, abilities vary. Children with Down syndrome tend to show more positive developmental outcomes when parents are sensitive to their capacities and needs and encourage them to interact with their environment. Early intervention programs can aid children's development, especially in the motor, social, and emotion areas of functioning (Carr, 2002).

As recently as the early 1980s, individuals with Down syndrome lived to an average age of only 25. Advances in medicine have addressed many of the physical health problems associated with Down syndrome so that today many individuals with Down syndrome live well into middle age, with an average life expectancy of 60 (Carr, 2012; Davis & Escobar, 2013; Torr, Strydom, Patti, & Jokinen, 2010). Interestingly, as more adults age with Down syndrome, we have discovered a link between Down syndrome and Alzheimer's disease, a brain degenerative disease that typically strikes in older adulthood (Stancliffe et al., 2012). Individuals with Down syndrome are at risk to show signs of Alzheimer's very early relative to other adults. This is an example of how disorders and illnesses can be influenced by multiple genes and complex contextual interactions; in this case, Down syndrome and Alzheimer's disease share genetic markers.

Sex Chromosome Abnormalities

Some of the most common chromosomal abnormalities concern the 23rd pair of chromosomes: the sex chromosomes. Given their different genetic makeup, sex chromosome abnormalities yield different effects in males and females. They are summarized in Table 2.5.

One of the most common sex chromosome abnormalities, with prevalence estimates between 1 in 500 and 1 in 1,000 males, is Klinefelter syndrome, in which males are born with an extra X chromosome (XXY; Bojesen & Gravholt, 2011; National Library of Medicine, 2013). Symptoms range in severity such that some males experience symptoms that impair daily life, and others may be unaware of the disorder until they are tested for infertility (Groth, Skakkebæk, Høst, Gravholt, & Bojesen, 2013). Severe symptoms include a high-pitched voice, feminine body shape, breast enlargement, and infertility. Many boys and men with Klinefelter syndrome have short stature, a tendency to be overweight, and language and short-term memory impairments that can cause difficulties in learning (Ross, Zeger, Kushner, Zinn, & Roeltgen, 2009). As adults, men with Klinefelter syndrome are at risk for a variety of disorders that are more common in women, such as osteoporosis (Juul, Aksglaede, Bay, Grigor, & Skakkebæk, 2011).

A second type of sex chromosome abnormality experienced by men is XYY syndrome, or Jacob's syndrome, a condition that causes men to produce high levels of testosterone. In adolescence, they tend to be slender and show severe acne and poor coordination, but most men with XYY syndrome are unaware that they have a chromosomal abnormality. The prevalence of XYY syndrome is uncertain given that most men go undiagnosed.

TABLE 2.5 Sex Chromosome Abnormalities

FEMALE GENOTYPE	SYNDROME	MALE GENOTYPE	SYNDROME
XX	normal	XY	normal
XO	Turner	XXY	Klinefelter
XXX	Triple-X	XYY	XYY

Females are susceptible to a different set of sex chromosome abnormalities. About 1 in 1,000 females are born with three X chromosomes, known as triple X syndrome (Otter, Schrander-Stumpel, & Curfs, 2009). Women with triple X syndrome show an appearance within the norm. They tend to be about an inch or so taller than average with unusually long legs and slender torsos, as well as normal development of sexual characteristics and fertility. Some may show intelligence in the low range of normal with small learning difficulties. Because many cases of triple X syndrome often go unnoticed, little is known about the syndrome.

The sex chromosome abnormality known as Turner syndrome occurs when a female is born with only one X chromosome (Doswell, Visootsak, Brady, & Graham, 2006; Powell & Schulte, 2011). Girls with Turner syndrome show abnormal growth patterns. As adults, they are short in stature and often have small jaws with extra folds of skin around their necks (webbing) and lack prominent female secondary sex characteristics such as breasts. Their ovaries do not develop normally, and they do not ovulate (Knickmeyer & Davenport, 2011). About one third of females with Turner syndrome show precocious puberty (in middle to late childhood), often with spontaneous onset instead of the gradual changes that typically accompany puberty (Improda et al., 2012). They are at risk for thyroid disease, vision and hearing problems, heart defects, diabetes, and autoimmune disorders. Current estimates of its frequency range from 1 in 2,500 worldwide (National Library of Medicine, 2013). If Turner syndrome is diagnosed early, regular injections of human growth hormones can increase stature, and hormones administered at puberty can result in some breast development and menstruation (Christopoulos, Deligeoroglou, Laggari, Christogiorgos, & Creatsas, 2008).

MUTATION

Not all inborn characteristics are inherited. Some result from **mutations**—sudden changes and abnormalities in the structure of genes. A mutation may involve only one gene or many. Mutations may occur spontaneously or may be induced by exposure to environmental toxins such as radiation and agricultural chemicals in food (Burns & Bottino, 1989; Lewis, 2006). Mutations are common. It is estimated that as many as one half of all conceptions include mutated chromosomes (Plomin, DeFries, & McClearn, 1990). Most mutations are fatal—the developing organism often dies very soon after conception, often before the woman knows she is pregnant. A small number of organisms with mutations survive, often with enduring negative consequences, such as increased susceptibility to diseases (Lewis, 2006; Rimoin, Connor, & Pyeritz, 1997).

Sometimes mutations are beneficial. This is especially true if the mutation is induced by stressors in the environment and provides an adaptive advantage to the individual. For example, the sickle cell gene is a mutation that originated in areas where malaria is widespread, such as Africa. Children who inherited a single sickle cell allele were more resistant to malarial infection and more likely to survive (Allison, 2004; Williams, 2006). The sickle cell gene is not helpful in places of the world where malaria is not a risk. The frequency of the gene is decreasing in areas of the world where malaria is uncommon. For example, only 8% of African Americans are carriers, compared with as much as 30% of black Africans in some African countries (Maakaron, Taher, & Ulrich Josef Woermann, 2012). Therefore, the developmental implications of genotypes—and mutations—are context-specific, posing benefits in some contexts and risks in others.

PREDICTING AND DETECTING GENETIC DISORDERS

Deformities and disorders were once thought to be caused by witches, bad luck, or as punishment for parents' immoral deeds. Today, we recognize the role of **heritability** and chromosomal abnormalities as causes of birth defects and disorders. The likelihood of genetic disorders often can be predicted before conception. Moreover, advances in technology permit abnormalities to be detected earlier than ever before.

Genetic Counseling

The growing understanding of genetic inheritance has led many couples to wonder about their own genetic inheritance and what genes they will pass on to their children. Many couples considering having children seek **genetic counseling** to learn about the probability of conceiving a child with a genetic disorder. Genetic counseling is a medical specialty that helps prospective parents determine the risk that their children will inherit genetic defects and chromosomal abnormalities (Uhlmann, Schuette, & Yashar, 2009). This service is particularly valuable when one or both prospective parents have relatives with inborn disorders.

Upon meeting a couple, the genetic counselor constructs a family history of heritable disorders for both prospective parents in order to determine the prevalence of various disorders and diseases. If either member of the couple appears to carry a genetic disorder, genetic screening blood tests may be carried out on both parents to detect chromosomal abnormalities and the presence of dominant and recessive genes for various disorders. With the counselor's help to assess and interpret the test results, couples can use this information to make decisions about childbearing.

Candidates for genetic counseling include those whose relatives have a genetic condition, couples who have had difficulties bearing children, women over the age of 35, and couples from the same ethnic group. The results of genetic counseling can reduce the fear of the unknown and help couples to make reasoned decisions about having children Once prospective parents learn about the risk of conceiving a child with a disorder, they can determine how to proceed—whether it is to conceive a child naturally or through the use of in vitro fertilization—after screening gametes for the disorders of concern.

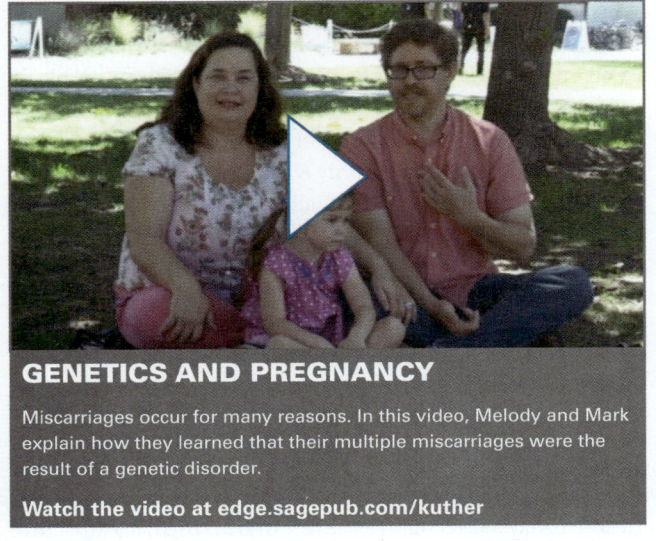

GENETICS AND PREGNANCY

Miscarriages occur for many reasons. In this video, Melody and Mark explain how they learned that their multiple miscarriages were the result of a genetic disorder.

Watch the video at edge.sagepub.com/kuther

Prenatal Diagnosis

Technology has advanced rapidly, equipping professionals with an array of tools to assess the health of the fetus (see Table 2.6). Prenatal testing is recommended when genetic counseling has determined a risk for genetic abnormalities, when the woman is older than age 35, when both parents are members of an ethnicity at risk for particular genetic disorders, or when fetal development appears abnormal (Barlow-Stewart & Saleh, 2012). Prenatal screening can detect many defects, permitting prospective parents to make informed decisions about the pregnancy. However, remember that the mother's body is designed to protect the developing person—and the vast majority of infants are born healthy.

The most widespread and routine diagnostic procedure is ultrasound, in which high-frequency sound waves directed at the mother's abdomen provide clear images of the womb represented on a video monitor. Ultrasound enables physicians to observe the fetus, measure fetal growth, judge gestational age, reveal the sex of the fetus, detect multiple pregnancies (twins, triplets, etc.), and determine physical abnormalities in the fetus. Many deformities can be observed, such as cardiac abnormalities, cleft palate, and microencephaly (small head size). At least 80% of women in the United States receive at least one prenatal ultrasound scan (Sadler, 2012). Three to four screenings over the duration of pregnancy are common in order to evaluate fetal development (Papp & Fekete, 2003). Repeated ultrasound of the fetus does not appear to affect growth and development (Stephenson, 2005).

Amniocentesis is a prenatal diagnostic procedure in which a small sample of the amniotic fluid that surrounds the fetus is extracted from the mother's uterus through a long, hollow needle that is guided by ultrasound as it is inserted into the mother's abdomen. The amniotic fluid contains fetal cells, which are grown in a laboratory dish in order to create enough cells for genetic analysis. Genetic analysis is then performed to detect genetic and chromosomal anomalies and defects.

TABLE 2.6 Methods of Prenatal Diagnosis

	EXPLANATION	ADVANTAGES	DISADVANTAGES
Ultrasound	High-frequency sound waves directed at the mother's abdomen provide clear images of the womb projected on to a video monitor.	Ultrasound enables physicians to observe the fetus, measure fetal growth, reveal the sex of the fetus, and determine physical abnormalities in the fetus.	Many abnormalities and deformities cannot be easily observed.
Amniocentesis	A small sample of the amniotic fluid that surrounds the fetus is extracted from the mother's uterus through a long, hollow needle inserted into the mother's abdomen. The amniotic fluid contains fetal cells. The fetal cells are grown in a laboratory dish in order to create enough cells for genetic analysis.	It permits a thorough analysis of the fetus's genotype. There is 100% diagnostic success rate.	It poses a greater risk to the fetus than ultrasound. If conducted before the 15th week of pregnancy, it may increase the risk of miscarriage.
Chorionic villus sampling (CVS)	CVS requires studying a small amount of tissue from the chorion, part of the membrane surrounding the fetus, for the presence of chromosomal abnormalities. The tissue sample is obtained through a long needle inserted either abdominally or vaginally, depending on the location of the fetus.	It permits a thorough analysis of the fetus's genotype. CVS is relatively painless, and there is a 100% diagnostic success rate.	It may pose a higher rate of spontaneous abortion and limb defects when conducted prior to 10 weeks' gestation.
Noninvasive prenatal testing (NIPT)	Cell-free fetal DNA are examined by drawing blood from the mother.	There is no risk to the fetus. It can diagnose several chromosomal abnormalities.	It cannot detect the full range of abnormalities. It may be less accurate than other methods.

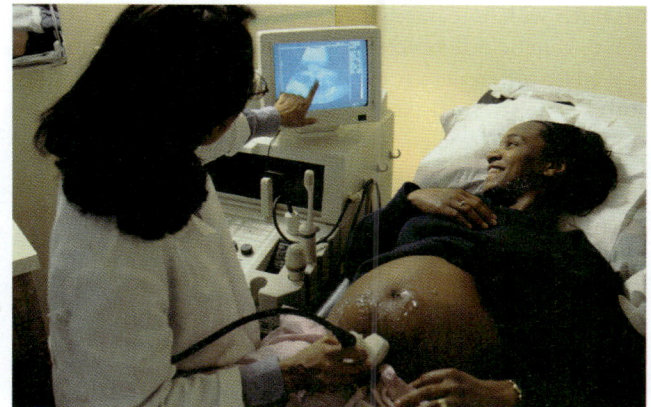

Ultrasound technology provides clear images of the womb, permitting physicians to observe the fetus, measure fetal growth, judge gestational age, reveal the sex of the fetus, detect multiple pregnancies, and determine physical abnormalities in the fetus.

Amniocentesis is less common than ultrasound, as it poses greater risk to the fetus. It is recommended for women aged 35 and over, especially if the woman and partner are both known carriers of genetic diseases (Elias, 2010). Usually amniocentesis is conducted between the 15th and 18th week of pregnancy. Conducted any earlier, an amniocentesis may increase the risk of miscarriage (Brambati & Lucia, 2005; Tabor & Alfirevic, 2010). Test results generally are available about two weeks after the procedure because it takes that long for the genetic material to grow and reproduce to the point where it can be analyzed.

A third method of prenatal monitoring, known as **chorionic villus sampling (CVS)**, can be conducted earlier than amniocentesis, between 9 and 12 weeks of pregnancy (Cunniff, 2004; Furman & Appelman, 2005; Shahbazian, Barati, Arian, & Saadati, 2012). CVS requires studying a small amount of tissue from the chorion, part of the membrane surrounding the fetus. The tissue sample is obtained through a long needle inserted either abdominally or vaginally, depending on the location of the fetus. Results are typically available about one week following the procedure. CVS is relatively painless and, like amniocentesis, has a 100% diagnostic success rate. Generally, CVS poses few risks to the fetus (Basaran, Basaran, & Topatan, 2011; Shahbazian et al., 2012; Wielgos & Wegrzyn, 2011). However, CVS should not be conducted prior to 10 weeks gestation as some studies suggest an increased risk of limb defects and miscarriages (Tabor & Alfirevic, 2010).

One of the most recent advances in prenatal testing is called **noninvasive prenatal testing (NIPT)**. As the name suggests, it is the least invasive prenatal test able to detect chromosomal abnormalities. NIPT examines cell-free fetal DNA (chromosome fragments that result in the breakdown of fetal cells; Fan et al., 2012; National Coalition for Health Professional Education in Genetics, 2012). Cell-free fetal DNA circulates in maternal blood in small concentrations that can be detected and studied by sampling the mother's blood. Testing can be done after 10 weeks, typically between 10 and 22 weeks. Given that the test involves drawing blood from the mother, there is no risk to the fetus; however, NIPT cannot detect as many chromosomal abnormalities as amniocentesis or CVS, and with less accuracy (Chan, Kwok, Choy, Leung, & Wang, 2013; National Coalition for Health Professional Education in Genetics, 2012).

Recently, researchers have identified the entire genome sequence using NIPT, suggesting that someday NIPT may be as effective as other, more invasive techniques (Tabor et al., 2012). Pregnant women and their partners, in consultation with their obstetrician, should carefully weigh the risks and benefits of any procedure designed to monitor prenatal development.

Prenatal Treatment of Genetic Disorders

Both amniocentesis and CVS can assess for some 200 different genetic and chromosomal disorders, and many of these disorders can also be detected by ultrasound and/or NIPT. What happens when problems are found? Until recently, prenatal diagnosis of a disorder confronted parents with the wrenching dilemma of whether or not to terminate the pregnancy. However, advances in genetics and in medicine have led to new therapies that can be administered prenatally to reduce the effects of many genetic abnormalities. For example, hormones and other drugs, as well as blood transfusions, can be given to the fetus by inserting a needle into the uterus (Fox & Saade, 2012; Patel, Landers, Li, Mortimer, & Richard, 2011). Most strikingly, fetal surgery can repair defects of the heart, lung, urinary tract, and other areas (Deprest et al., 2010).

Researchers believe that one day we may be able to treat many heritable disorders thorough genetic engineering, by synthesizing normal genes to replace defective ones. Theoretically, it may someday be possible to sample cells from an embryo, detect harmful genes and replace them with healthy ones, then

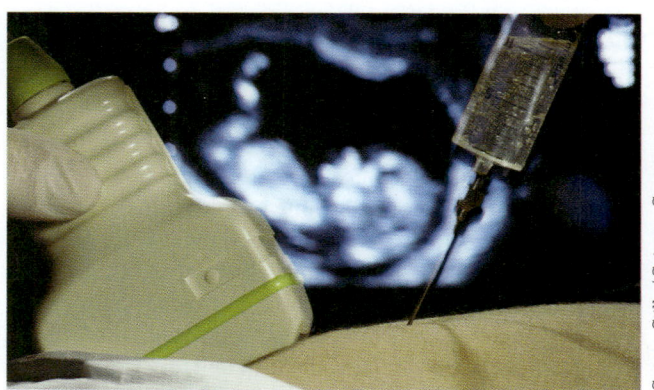

During amniocentesis, ultrasound is used to guide the insertion of a long, hollow needle into the mother's abdomen in order to extract a sample of the amniotic fluid that surrounds the fetus. The amniotic fluid contains fetal cells, which are grown in a laboratory dish and tested for genetic and chromosomal anomalies and defects.

return the healthy cells to the embryo where they reproduce and correct the genetic defect (Coutelle & Waddington, 2012). This approach has been used to correct certain heritable disorders in animals and holds promise for treating the fetus. These advances are likely in the coming years.

Thinking in Context 2.3

1. Discuss how PKU illustrates the following two themes in human development: (1) the role of nature and nurture in development and (2) interactions among domains of development.

2. Identify risk factors for genetic and chromosomal disorders. What can prospective parents do to minimize the risks? What specific advice would you give?

3. Suppose you are a 36-year-old woman pregnant with your first child. Considering the four types of prenatal diagnostic testing described in this section, what would be the advantages and disadvantages of each? What information would your health care provider need in order to recommend testing appropriate for your particular case?

HEREDITY AND ENVIRONMENT

We have learned a great deal about genetic inheritance. Most human traits, however, are influenced by a combination of genes working in concert with environmental influences. Our genetic makeup, inherited from our biological parents, consists of a complex blend of hereditary characteristics known as genotype. Our genotype is a biological influence on all of our traits, from hair and eye color to personality, health, and behavior. However, our **phenotype**, the traits we ultimately show, such as our specific eye or hair color, is not determined by genotypes alone. Phenotypes are influenced by the interaction of genotypes and our experiences.

BEHAVIORAL GENETICS

Behavioral genetics is the field of study that examines how genes and experience combine to influence the diversity of human traits, abilities, and behaviors (Lessov-Schlaggar, Agrawal, & Swan, 2013; Maxson, 2013; Plomin et al., 2001). Genotypes alone do not determine people's traits, characteristics, or personalities; instead, development is the process by which our genetic inheritance (genotype) is expressed in observable characteristics and behaviors (phenotype). Behavior geneticists recognize that even traits that have a strong genetic component, such as height, are modified by environmental influences (Lessov-Schlaggar et al., 2013).

Methods of Behavior Genetics

Behavior geneticists devise ways of estimating the heritability of specific traits and behaviors. Heritability refers to the extent to which variation among people on a given characteristic is due to genetic differences. The remaining variation not due to genetic differences is instead a result of the environment and experiences. Heritability research therefore examines the contributions of the genotype but also provides information on the role of experience in determining phenotypes (Plomin & Daniels, 2011). Behavior geneticists assess the hereditary contributions to behavior by conducting selective breeding and family studies.

Using selective breeding studies, behavior geneticists deliberately modify the genetic makeup of animals to examine the influence of heredity on attributes and behavior. For example, behavioral geneticists demonstrated that they can breed mice to be very physically active or sedentary. They selectively breed highly active mice only with each other and, in contrast, breed mice with a very low level of activity with each other. In subsequent generations, mice bred for high levels of activity were many times more active than those bred for low levels of activity (DeFries, Gervais, & Thomas, 1978). Selective breeding in rats, mice, and other animals such as chickens has revealed genetic contributions to many traits and characteristics, such as aggressiveness, emotionality, sex drive, and even maze learning (Plomin et al., 2001).

Behavior geneticists conduct family studies to compare people who live together and share varying degrees of relatedness. Two kinds of family studies are common: twin studies and adoption studies (Koenen, Amstadter, & Nugent, 2012). Twin studies compare identical and fraternal twins to estimate how much of a trait or behavior is attributable to genes. If genes affect the attribute, identical twins should be more similar than fraternal twins because identical twins share 100% of their genes whereas fraternal twins share about only 50%. Adoption studies, on the other hand, compare the degree of similarity between adopted children and their biological parents whose genes they share (50%) and their adoptive parents with whom they share no genes. If the adopted children share similarities with their biological parents, even though they were not raised by them, it suggests that the similarities are genetic.

Adoption studies also shed light on the extent to which attributes and behaviors are influenced by the environment. For example, the degree to which two genetically unrelated adopted children reared together are similar speaks to the role of environment. Comparisons of identical twins reared in the same home with those reared in different environments can also illustrate environmental contributions to phenotypes. If identical twins reared together are more similar than those reared apart, an environmental influence can be inferred.

Genetic Influences on Personal Characteristics

Research examining the contribution of genotype and environment to intellectual abilities has found a moderate role for heredity. Twin studies have shown that identical twins

TABLE 2.7 Average Correlation of Intelligence Scores From Family Studies for Related and Unrelated Kin Reared Together or Apart

	REARED TOGETHER	REARED APART
MZ twins (100% shared genes)	.86	.72
DZ twins (50% shared genes)	.60	.52
Siblings (50% shared genes)	.47	.24
Biological parent/child (50% shared genes)	.42	.22
Half-siblings (25% shared genes)	.31	—
Unrelated (adopted) siblings (0% shared genes)*	.34	—
Nonbiological parent/child (0% shared genes)*	.19	—

NOTES: *Estimated correlation for individuals sharing neither genes nor environment = .0; MZ = monozygotic; DZ = dizygotic.

SOURCE: Adapted from Bouchard and McGue (1981).

consistently have more highly correlated scores than do fraternal twins. For example, a study of intelligence in over 10,000 twin pairs showed a correlation of .86 for identical and .60 for fraternal twins (Plomin & Spinath, 2004). Table 2.7 summarizes the results of comparisons of intelligence scores from individuals who share different genetic relationships with each other. Note that correlations for all levels of kin are higher when they are reared together, supporting the role of environment. Average correlations also rise with increases in shared genes.

Genes contribute to many other traits, such as sociability, anxiety, temperament, obesity, happiness, and susceptibility to various illnesses such as heart disease and cancer, poor mental health, and a propensity to be physically aggressive (Barker et al., 2009; Chen et al., 2013; Pemment, 2013; Yoon-Mi, 2009). Yet even traits that are thought to be heavily influenced by genetics can be modified by physical and social interventions. For example, growth, body weight, and body height are largely predicted by genetics, yet environmental circumstances and opportunities influence whether genetic potentials are realized (Dubois et al., 2012). Even identical twins who share 100% of their genes are not 100% alike. Those differences are due to the influence of environmental factors, which interact with genes in a variety of ways.

GENE-ENVIRONMENT INTERACTION

"Those two boys are so different. It's hard to believe Eric and Evan are twins!" said Aunt Joan. As fraternal twins, Eric and Evan share 50% of their genes and are reared in the same home. One might expect them to be quite similar, but genes interact in complex ways to influence our characteristics, behavior, physical, cognitive, and social development as well as health (Fowler & Schreiber, 2008; Rutter, 2012). Moreover, genes do not act alone in shaping our development. Heredity and environment do not make independent contributions to our development and behavior. Several principles illustrate these interactions.

Range of Reaction

Everyone has a different genetic makeup and therefore responds to the environment in a unique way. In addition, any one genotype can be expressed in a variety of phenotypes. There is a **range of reaction** (see Figure 2.5), a wide range of potential expressions of a genetic trait, depending on environmental opportunities and constraints (Gottlieb, 2000). For example, consider height. Height is largely a function of genetics, yet an individual may show a range of sizes depending on environment and behavior. Suppose that

FIGURE 2.5: Range of Reaction

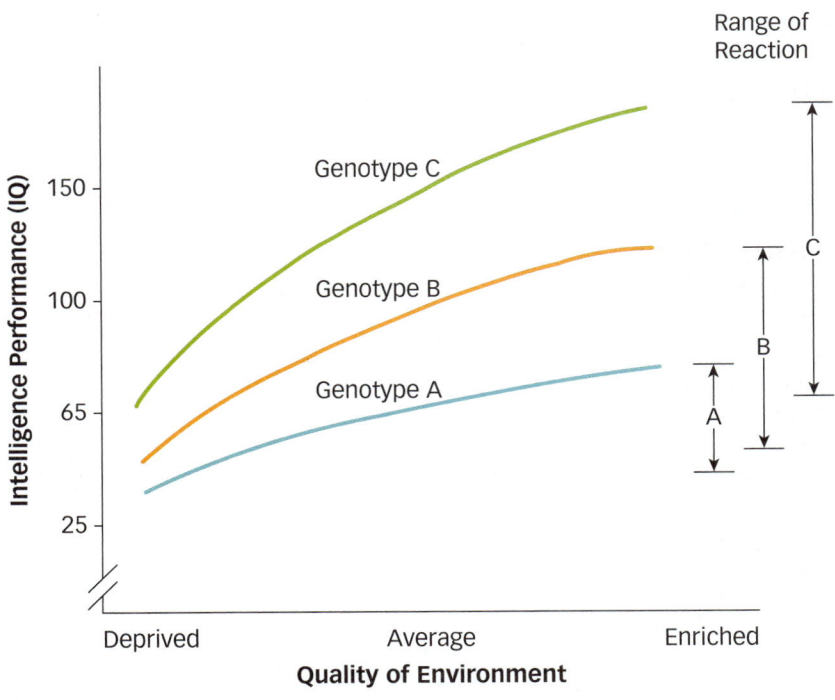

SOURCE: Gottlieb (2007).

LIVES IN CONTEXT

Gene–Environment Interactions and Responses to Child Maltreatment

Children who are maltreated or abused by their parents are at risk for developing many problems, including aggression and violent tendencies. Yet not all children who are maltreated become violent adolescents and adults. Why? A classic study examined this question.

Caspi and colleagues (2002) followed a sample of males from birth until adulthood and observed that not all maltreated boys developed problems with violence. Only boys who carried a certain type of gene were at risk for becoming violent after experiencing maltreatment. Specifically, there are two versions of a gene that controls monoamine oxidase A (MAOA), an enzyme that regulates specific chemicals in the brain; one produces high levels of the enzyme and the other produces low levels. Boys who experienced abuse and other traumatic experiences were about twice as likely to develop problems with aggression, violence, and to even be convicted of a violent crime—but only if they carried the low-MAOA gene. Maltreated boys who carried the high-MAOA gene were no more likely to become violent than non-maltreated boys. In addition, the presence of the low MAOA gene itself was not associated with violence. The low-MAOA gene predicted violence only for boys who experience abuse early in life. These findings have been replicated in another 30-year longitudinal study of boys (Fergusson, Boden, Horwood, Miller, & Kennedy, 2011).

Similar findings of a MAOA gene x environment interaction in which low-MAOA, but not high-MAOA, predicts negative outcomes in response to childhood adversity has been extended to include other mental health outcomes such as antisocial personality disorder and depression (Beach et al., 2010; Cicchetti, Rogosch, & Sturge-Apple, 2007; Kim-Cohen et al., 2006). Many of these studies have examined only males. Females show a more mixed pattern with some studies showing that girls display the MAOA gene x environment interaction but to a much lesser extent than boys whereas other studies suggest no relationship (Byrd & Manuck, 2014).

While there is no single gene that will predict general developmental outcomes, these findings suggest that some genes may increase or decrease our risk for problems in the presence of particular contexts. Just as we may adjust contextual factors to contribute to successful developmental outcomes and resilience, in the future we might learn how to "turn on" protective genes and "turn off" those that contribute to risk.

What Do You Think?

1. In your view, how important are genetic contributors to development?

2. If some genes may be protective in particular contexts, should scientists learn how to turn them on? Why or why not? What about genes that may be harmful in particular contexts?

---

a child is born to two very tall parents. She may have the genes to be tall, but unless she has adequate nutrition, she will not fulfill her genetic potential for height. In societies in which nutrition has improved dramatically over a generation, it is common for children to tower over their parents. The enhanced environmental opportunities, in this case nutrition, enabled the children to fulfill their genetic potential for height. Therefore, a genotype sets boundaries on the range of possible phenotypes, but the phenotypes ultimately displayed vary in response to different environments. In this way, genetics sets the range of development outcomes and the environment influences where, within the range, that person will fall. Lives in Context, above, provides a more complex example of gene–environment interactions.

Canalization

Some traits illustrate a wide reaction range. Others are examples of **canalization**, in which heredity narrows the range of development to only one or a few outcomes. Canalized traits are biologically programmed, and only powerful environmental forces can change their developmental path (Flatt, 2005; Waddington, 1971). For example, infants follow an age-related sequence of motor development, from crawling, to walking, to running. Around the world, most infants walk at about 12 months of age. Generally, only extreme experiences or changes in the environment can prevent this developmental sequence from occurring. For example, children reared in impoverished Romanian and Ethiopian orphanages and exposed to extreme environmental deprivation demonstrated delayed motor development, with some children not walking at 2 years of age (Miller, Tseng, Tirella, Chan, & Feig, 2008; Wilson, 2003).

At the same time, motor development is not entirely canalized because some minor changes in the environment can subtly alter its pace and timing. For example, practice facilitates stepping movements in young infants, prevents the disappearance of stepping movements in the early months of life, and leads to an earlier onset of walking (Ulrich, Lloyd, Tiernan, Looper, & Angulo-Barroso, 2008; Zelazo, Zelazo, Cohen, & Zelazo, 1993). These observations demonstrate that even highly canalized traits, such as motor development, which largely unfolds via maturation, can be subtly influenced by contextual factors.

Gene–Environment Correlations

Heredity and environment are each powerful influences on development. Not only do they interact, but heredity and environmental factors are often correlated with each other (Plomin & Asbury, 2001; Scarr & McCartney, 1983). **Gene–environment correlation** refers to the idea that

FIGURE 2.6: Gene–Environment Correlation

The availability of instruments in the home corresponds to the child's musical abilities and she begins to play guitar (passive gene-environment correlation). As she plays guitar, she evokes positive responses in others, increasing her interest in music (evocative gene-environment correlation). Over time she seeks opportunities to play, such as performing in front of an audience (niche picking).

many of our traits are supported by both our genes and environment. There are three types of gene–environment correlations—passive, reactive, and active—as shown in Figure 2.6.

Parents create homes that reflect their own genotypes. Because parents are genetically similar to their children, the homes that they create are not only in line with their own interests and preferences but they also correspond with the child's genotype—an example of a *passive gene–environment correlation*. For example, parents might provide genes that predispose a child to develop music ability and also provide a home environment that supports the development of music ability, such as by playing music in the home and owning musical instruments. This type of gene–environment correlation is seen early in life because children are reared in environments that are created by their parents, who share their genotype.

People naturally evoke responses from others and the environment, just as the environment and the actions of others evoke responses from the individual. In an *evocative gene–environment correlation*, a child's genetic traits (e.g., personality characteristics including openness to experience) influence the social and physical environment, which shape development in ways that support the genetic trait (Burt, 2009). For example, active, happy infants tend

to receive more adult attention than do passive or moody infants (Deater-Deckard & O'Connor, 2000), and even among infant twins reared in the same family, the more outgoing and happy twin receives more positive attention than does the more subdued twin (Deater-Deckard, 2001). Why? Babies who are cheerful and smile often influence their social world by evoking smiles from others, which in turn support the genetic tendency to be cheerful. In this way, genotypes influence the physical and social environment to respond in ways that support the genotype. To return to the music example, a child with a genetic trait for music talent will evoke pleasurable responses (e.g., parental approval) when she plays music; this environmental support, in turn, encourages further development of the child's musical trait.

Children also take a hands-on role in shaping their development. Recall from Chapter 1 that a major theme in understanding human development is the finding that individuals are active in their development; here we have an example of this pattern. As children grow older, they have increasing freedom in choosing their own activities and environments. An *active gene–environment correlation* occurs when the child actively creates experiences and environments that correspond to and influence his genetic predisposition. For example, the child with a genetic trait for interest and ability

Altering the Epigenome

These two mice are genetically identical. Both carry the agouti gene but in the yellow mouse the agouti gene is turned on all the time. In the brown mouse it is turned off.

One of the earliest examples of epigenetics is the case of agouti mice, which carry the agouti gene. Mice that carry the agouti gene have yellow fur, are extremely obese, shaped much like a pincushion, and prone to diabetes and cancer. When agouti mice breed, most of the offspring are identical to the parents—yellow, obese, and susceptible to life shortening disease. However, a groundbreaking study showed that yellow agouti mice can produce offspring that look very different (Waterland & Jirtle, 2003). The mice in Figure X both carry the agouti gene, yet they look very different; the brown mouse is slender, lean, and has a low risk of developing diabetes and cancer, living well into old age.

Why are these mice so different? Epigenetics. Literally, *epigenetics* means "above the gene." Whereas DNA determines your genetic profile, the epigenome stretches along the length of DNA and determines how genes are expressed, whether they are turned on or off. All cells in your body carry the same DNA—yet why are they different? Why are brain cells different from heart cells? How does the body know to produce a liver cell, for example? The epigenome carries the instructions that determine what each cell in your body will become. Those instructions are carried out by turning genes on and off.

In the case of the yellow and brown mice, the phenotype of the brown mice has been altered, but the DNA remains the same. Both carry the agouti gene, but in the yellow mouse the agouti gene

is turned on all the time. In the brown mouse, it is turned off. In 2003, Waterland and Jertle discovered that the agouti female's diet can determine her offspring's phenotype. In this study, female mice were fed foods containing chemicals that attach to a gene and turn it off. These chemical clusters are found in many foods such as onions, garlic, beets, soy, and the nutrients in prenatal vitamins. Yellow agouti mothers fed extra nutrients passed along the agouti gene to their offspring, but it was turned off. The mice looked radically different from them (brown) and were healthier (lean, not susceptible to disease) even though they carried the same genes.

Another example supports the finding that the prenatal environment can alter the epigenome and influence the lifelong characteristics of offspring. Pregnant mice were exposed to a chemical (bisphenol-A or BPA, found in certain plastics). When female mice were fed BPA two weeks prior to conception, the number of offspring with the yellow obese coat color signaling an activated agouti gene increased (Dolinoy, 2008). When the pregnant mice were exposed to BPA plus nutritional supplementation (folic acid and an ingredient found in soy products), the offspring tended to be slender and have brown coats signaling that the agouti gene was turned off. While experiences and behaviors after birth can influence the epigenome, affecting aging and disease (Brunet & Berger, 2014), these findings suggest that the prenatal environment can influence the epigenome, and thereby influence how genes are expressed—and that nutrition has the potential to buffer harm.

The most surprising finding emerging from studies of epigenetics, however, is that the epigenome can be influenced by the environment before birth and can be passed by males and females from one generation to the next without changing the DNA itself (Bernal & Jirtle, 2010; Nilsson & Skinner, 2014; Soubry, Hoyo, Jirtle, & Murphy, 2014). This means that what you eat and do today could affect the epigenome—the health and characteristics—of your children, grandchildren, and great-grandchildren (Vanhees, Vonhögen, van Schooten, & Godschalk, 2014).

What Do You Think?

1. Much of the research on epigenetics examines animals, but there is a growing body of work studying humans. In what ways, if any, might you expect research findings based on people to differ from the findings of animal research, described previously? Explain.

2. What might you do to "care for" your epigenome? Identify activities and behaviors that you think might affect the health of your genome today and tomorrow.

---

in music actively seeks experiences and environments that support that trait, such as friends with similar interests and after-school music classes. This tendency to actively seek out experiences and environments compatible and supportive of our genetic tendencies is called **niche-picking** (Scarr & McCartney, 1983).

The strength of passive, evocative, and active gene–environment correlations changes with development, as shown in Figure 2.7 (Scarr, 1992). Passive gene–environment

correlations are common at birth as caregivers determine infants' experiences. Correlations between their genotype and environment tend to occur because their environments are made by genetically similar parents. Evocative gene–environment correlations also occur from birth, as infants' inborn traits and tendencies influence others, evoking responses that support their own genetic predispositions. In contrast, active gene–environment correlations take place as children grow older and more independent. As they become

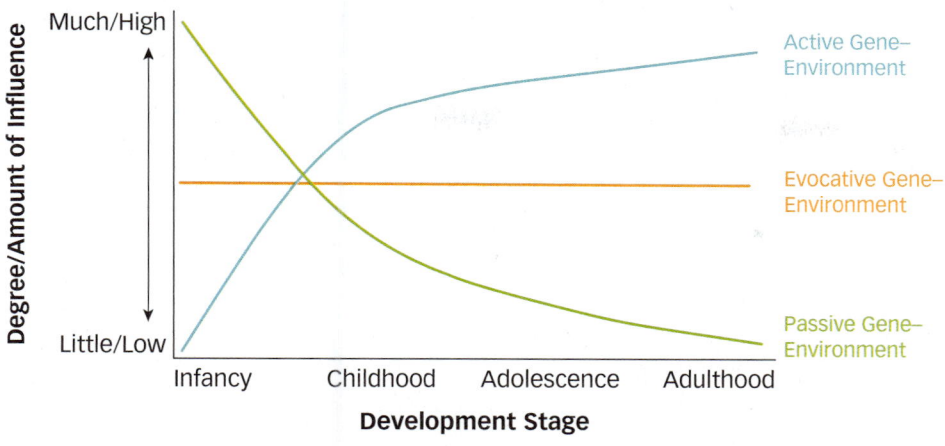

FIGURE 2.7: Development Stage and Gene–Environment Correlations

(Y-axis) Degree/Amount of Influence — Much/High ... Little/Low

Active Gene–Environment

Evocative Gene–Environment

Passive Gene–Environment

(X-axis) Development Stage — Infancy, Childhood, Adolescence, Adulthood

For example, consider brain development. Providing an infant with a healthy diet and opportunities to explore the world will support the development of brain cells, governed by genes. Brain development influences motor development, further supporting the infant's exploration of the physical and social world, thereby promoting cognitive and social development. Active engagement in the world encourages connections among brain cells. In this way, brain development, like all other aspects of development, is influenced by dynamic interactions between biological and environmental factors.

Evocative gene–environmental correlations and niche-picking point to the ways in which genetic propensities can influence the environment. Genes influence development and experience, yet gene expression is also influenced by development and experience, as illustrated in Figure 2.8 (Dodge & Rutter, 2011). These complex gene–environment interactions mean that humans are more than their genes. Interactions between heredity and environment change throughout development as does the role we play in constructing environments that support our genotypes and influence who we become. For a striking example of epigenetics, see Applying Developmental Science (p. 54).

increasingly capable of controlling parts of their environment, they engage in niche-picking by choosing their own interests and activities, actively shaping their own development. Niche-picking contributes to the differences we see in siblings, including fraternal twins, as they grow older. But identical twins tend to become more similar over time as they are increasingly able to select the environments that best fit their genetic propensities (Bouchard et al., 2004; Steves, Spector, & Jackson, 2012). As they age, identical twins—even those reared apart—become alike in attitudes, personality, and preferences as well as select similar spouses and best friends (Rushton & Bons, 2005).

In summary, human development is a function of complex interactions among genes and the contexts in which we are raised. While a few traits are canalized, most demonstrate a wide reaction range whereby the expression of genes is influenced by contextual factors.

EPIGENETIC FRAMEWORK

We have seen that every aspect of our development is the result of a dynamic interactions of heredity and environment. Without a doubt, genes provide a biological foundation for our development. However, genes never act alone in determining human characteristics. This dynamic interplay between heredity and environment is known as the **epigenetic framework** (Gottlieb, 2003; Lickliter & Honeycutt, 2013). From this perspective, development results from ongoing reciprocal interactions between genetics and environment.

Genes determine a range of reaction in which characteristics may develop depending on environmental circumstances. Not all of our genes are switched on at birth; instead, each cell in our body turns on only a fraction of its genes. Genes continue to be turned on and off over the course of development and also in response to the environment. Even traits that are highly canalized can be influenced by the environment. Environmental factors such as toxins, injuries, crowding, diet, and responsive parenting can influence the expression of genetic traits.

FIGURE 2.8: Epigenetic Framework

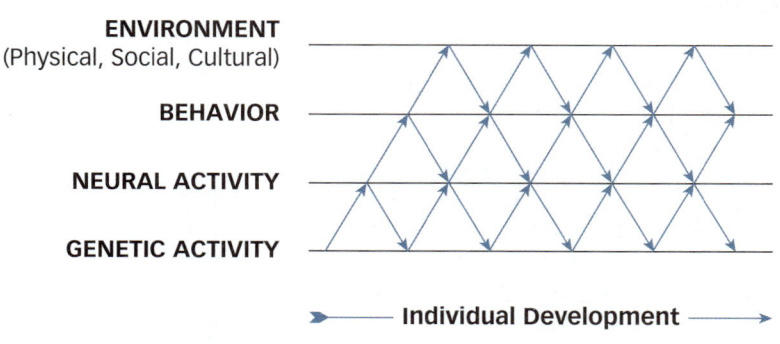

BIDIRECTIONAL INFLUENCES

ENVIRONMENT (Physical, Social, Cultural)

BEHAVIOR

NEURAL ACTIVITY

GENETIC ACTIVITY

Individual Development

SOURCE: Gottlieb (2007).

To answer the following questions, begin by thinking about how your own development reflects interactions among your genes and sociocultural context. Then, describe a skill, ability, or hobby in which you excel.

1. How might a passive genetic-environment correlation account for this ability? For example, in what ways has the context in which you were raised shaped this ability?

2. In what ways might this ability be influenced by an evocative-genetic-environment correlation?

3. Provide an example of how this ability might reflect an active genetic-environment correlation.

4. Which genetic-environment correlation do you think most accurately accounts for your skill, ability, or hobby?

5. How might you apply the epigenetic framework to account for your ability?

SAGE edge™

Want a better grade?

Get the tools you need to sharpen your study skills. Access Video Cases, multimedia resources, SAGE articles, practice quizzes, and eFlashcards at **edge.sagepub.com/kuther**

Apply Your Knowledge

Strapped in and buckled in the rear seat of her mother's bicycle, 1-year-old Jenna patted her helmet as her mother zoomed along the bike path to the beach. There she giggled and kicked her legs as her mother whooshed her through the water. As a child, Jenna loved to be outside and especially to be in the water. Jenna practiced swimming nearly every day and became quite skilled. Jenna's proud mother encouraged her daughter's athleticism by enrolling her in swim classes. Jenna decided that if she were going to become an exceptional swimmer, she would have to go to a summer swimming camp. She researched camps and asked her mother to attend. Jenna further honed her skills as a swimmer and won a college scholarship for swimming.

Many years later, Jenna was surprised to learn that she had a twin sister, Tasha. Separated at birth, Jenna and Tasha became aware of each other in their early 40s. Jenna was stunned yet couldn't wait to meet her twin sister. Upon meeting, Jenna and Tasha were surprised to find that they were not exactly the same. Whereas Jenna was athletic and lithe, Tasha was more sedentary and substantially heavier than Jenna. Unlike Jenna, Tasha grew up in a home far from the beach and with little access to outdoor activities. Instead Tasha's interest was writing. As a child, she'd write stories

and share them with others. She sought out opportunities to write and chose a college with an exceptional writing program. Both Jenna and Tasha excelled in college, as they did throughout their education, and earned nearly identical scores on the SAT.

Jenna and Tasha look very similar. Even the most casual observer could easily tell that they are sisters as both have blond hair, blue eyes, and a similar facial structure. Tasha's skin, however, is more fair and unlined. Jenna's face is sprinkled with freckles and darker spots formed after many days spent swimming outside. Jenna and Tasha both are allergic to peanuts, and they both take medication for high blood pressure. The more that Jenna and Tasha get to know each other, the more similarities they find.

1. Considering Jenna and Tasha, provide examples of three types of gene–environment correlations: passive, evocative, and active.

2. Do you think Jenna and Tasha are monozygotic or dizygotic twins? Why or why not?

3. What role might epigenetic influences play in determining Jenna and Tasha's development?

Chapter Summary

2.1 Explain how chromosomes, genes, deoxyribonucleic acid (DNA), and the genome relate to one another.

The human body is composed of cells. Within each cell is a nucleus that contains 23 matching pairs of rod-shaped structures called chromosomes. Each chromosome holds the basic units of heredity, known as genes. Genes are composed of stretches of DNA, a complex molecule shaped like a twisted ladder or staircase. Genes are the blueprint for creating all of the traits that organisms carry. The set of instructions to construct a living organism is referred to as the genome. Although all humans share the same basic genome, every person has a slightly different code, making him or her genetically distinct from other humans.

2.2 Identify and compare two processes of cell reproduction.

Most cells in the human body reproduce through mitosis in which DNA replicates itself, permitting the duplication of chromosomes, and ultimately the formation of new body cells with identical genetic material. Gametes reproduce by meiosis in which the chromosomes cross over as they replicate, creating two cells that each have 46 chromosomes; they then divide a second time, creating gametes with 23 single, unpaired chromosomes. Gametes have only one chromosome from each pair. Sperm and ovum join to produce a fertilized egg with 46 chromosomes, forming 23 pairs with half from the biological mother and half from the biological father.

2.3 Differentiate monozygotic (MZ) from dizygotic (DZ) twins.

Twins are siblings who share the same womb. Most are DZ twins who arise when a woman releases more than one ovum. Two ova are fertilized by two sperm. Genetically, DZ twins are no different from other siblings, sharing one half of their genes. Like other siblings, most differ in appearance, such as hair color, eye color, and height, but some are very similar. Unlike DZ twins, MZ twins originate from the same zygote. MZ twins arise when the zygote splits into two distinct separate yet identical zygotes that give rise to two births. MZ twins share the same genotype with identical instructions for all physical and psychological characteristics. They share phenotypes that are carried by genes.

2.4 Contrast four processes of genetic inheritance.

Some genes are passed through dominant–recessive inheritance, in which some genes are dominant and will always be expressed regardless of the gene it is paired with. Other genes are recessive and will only be expressed if paired with another recessive gene. When a person is heterozygous for a particular trait, the dominant gene is expressed and

the person remains a carrier of the recessive gene. In most cases, dominant–recessive inheritance is an oversimplified explanation for patterns of genetic inheritance. Incomplete dominance is a genetic inheritance pattern in which both genes influence the characteristic. In addition, most traits are a function of the interaction of many genes, known as polygenic inheritance. Researchers cannot trace most characteristics to only one or two genes. Instead, polygenic traits are the result of interactions among many genes. Some traits are determined by a process known as genomic imprinting. Genomic imprinting refers to the instance in which the expression of a gene is determined by whether it is inherited by the mother or the father.

2.5 Provide examples of diseases that illustrate dominant–recessive and X-linked inheritance.

PKU is a recessive disorder that occurs when both parents carry the allele. Individuals with PKU cannot produce an enzyme that breaks down phenylalanine. The phenylalanine builds up quickly to toxic levels that damage the central nervous system. Avoiding sources of phenylalanine can prevent some of the deficits. Disorders carried by dominant alleles, such as Huntington's disease on the other hand, are expressed when the individual has a single allele. Some recessive genetic disorders, like the gene for red-green color blindness, are carried on the X chromosome. Males are more likely to be affected by X-linked genetic disorders, such as hemophilia, because they have only one X chromosome. Females have two X chromosomes; a recessive gene located on one X chromosome will be masked by a dominant gene on the other X chromosome. Fragile X syndrome, on the other hand, is an example of a dominant recessive disorder carried on the X chromosome. Because the gene is dominant, it must appear on only one X chromosome to be displayed. That means that fragile X syndrome occurs in both males and females

2.6 Identify disorders that result from chromosomal abnormalities.

Klinefelter syndrome occurs in males born with an extra X chromosome (XXY). Symptoms range in severity, but most men show few symptoms that impair daily life and others may be unaware of the disorder until they are tested for infertility. A second type of sex chromosome abnormality experienced by men is XYY syndrome, also known as Jacob's syndrome, a condition that causes men to produce high levels of testosterone. Females are susceptible to a different set of sex chromosome abnormalities. Some females are born with three X chromosomes, known as triple X syndrome. Turner syndrome occurs when a female is born with only one X chromosome. The most common chromosome disorder is trisomy 21, known as Down syndrome. Down syndrome occurs when three chromosomes, rather than two, appear in place of the 21st pair of chromosomes. Although individuals with Down syndrome vary in the severity of symptoms, Down syndrome is associated with marked physical, health, and cognitive attributes.

2.7 Discuss genetic counseling and prenatal testing, including common prenatal tests.

Genetic counseling is a medical specialty that helps prospective parents determine the likelihood that their children will inherit genetic defects and chromosomal abnormalities. Prenatal testing is recommended when genetic counseling has determined a risk for genetic abnormalities or when fetal development appears abnormal. The most widespread and routine diagnostic procedure is ultrasound, in which high-frequency sound waves directed at the mother's abdomen provide clear images of the womb represented on a video monitor. Amniocentesis is a prenatal diagnostic procedure in which a small sample of the amniotic fluid that surrounds the fetus is extracted from the mother's uterus in order to conduct analyses to detect genetic and chromosomal anomalies and defects. CVS can be conducted earlier than amniocentesis, between 9 and 12 weeks of pregnancy. CVS requires studying a small amount of tissue from the chorion, part of the membrane surrounding the fetus, for the presence of chromosomal abnormalities. Advances in genetics and in medicine have led to new therapies to reduce the effects of many genetic abnormalities, such as administering drugs to the fetus and conducting fetal surgery. One day we may be able to treat many heritable disorders thorough genetic engineering.

2.8 Describe the methods and major findings of behavior genetics.

Behavior genetics is the field of study that examines how genes and experience combine to influence the diversity of human traits, abilities, and behaviors. Even traits with a strong genetic component are modified by environmental influences. Heritability refers to the extent to which variation among people on a given characteristic is due to genetic differences. Heritability research examines the contributions of the genotype in determining phenotypes but also provides information on the role of experience. In selective breeding studies, behavior geneticists deliberately modify the genetic makeup of animals to examine the influence of heredity on attributes and behavior. Family studies, such as twin and adoption studies, compare people who live together and share varying degrees of relatedness. Twin designs compare identical and fraternal twins to estimate how much of a trait or behavior is attributable to genes. Adoption studies compare the degree of similarity between adopted children and their biological parents whose genes they share and their adoptive parents with whom they share no genes. Genetics contributes to many traits, such as intellectual ability, sociability, anxiety, agreeableness, activity level, obesity, and susceptibility to various illnesses. Yet even identical twins who share 100% of their genes are not 100% alike.

2.9 Compare patterns of gene expression, including reaction range, canalization, gene–environment correlations, and epigenetic framework.

Reaction range refers to the idea that there is a wide range of potential expressions of a genetic trait, depending on environmental opportunities and constraints. Some traits illustrate canalization and require extreme changes in the environment to alter their course. Gene–environment correlations illustrate how traits often are supported by both our genes and environment. Passive gene–environment correlations occur because parents are genetically similar to their children, the homes that they create in line with their own interests and preferences also correspond with and support the child's genotype. In a reactive or evocative gene–environment correlation, a child's genetic traits, such as personality characteristics, influence the social and physical environment, which shape development in ways that support the genetic trait. An active gene–environment correlation occurs when the child actively creates experiences and environments that correspond to and influence his genetic predisposition (called niche-picking). The epigenetic framework is a model for understanding the dynamic ongoing interactions between heredity and environment. Genes influence development and experience, yet gene expression is also influenced by development and experience.

Key Terms

alleles   41

amniocentesis   48

behavioral genetics   50

canalization   52

carrier   42

chorionic villus sampling (CVS)   49

chromosomes   38

crossing-over   39

DNA   38

dominant–recessive inheritance   41

Down syndrome   45

dizygotic (DZ) twins   40

epigenetic framework   55

gametes   39

genes   38

gene–environment correlation   52

The Prenatal Period, Birth, and the Newborn

LEARNING OBJECTIVES

3.1. Describe the process of conception, identifying the roles of female and male.

3.2. Describe the three periods of prenatal development.

3.3. List six principles of teratology, and explain how they can be used to predict prenatal outcomes.

3.4. Identify drugs, illness, and environmental factors that act as teratogens.

3.5. Define *fetal alcohol spectrum disorders*, and differentiate between fetal alcohol syndrome (FAS) and fetal alcohol effects.

3.6. Discuss the contributions of maternal characteristics and behaviors on prenatal development.

3.7. Explain the process of childbirth.

3.8. Identify and explain the neonate's physical capacities.

3.9. Discuss the challenges low birth weight and small-for-date infants face as well as influences on infant adjustment.

KEY STUDY TOOLS

Ethical and Policy Applications of Lifespan Development Stem Cell Research (p. 64)

Connect Social Construction of Sex

Watch Fetal Development: Ultrasound

Think Critically Teratogens and Congenital Heart Disease

Lives in Context HIV Infection in Newborns (p. 69)

Explore Further Fetal Alcohol Syndrome

Ethical and Policy Applications of Lifespan Development Maternal Drug Use While Pregnant (p. 72)

Cultural Influences on Development Cultural Differences in Childbirth (p. 76)

Video Case The Partner's Role During Pregnancy and Birth

Video Case Labor: Preparation and Process

Watch Newborn Assessment Just After Birth

Listen Survival of Premature Babies

L ooking down at his newborn daughter's face, Remmy said admiringly, "Carla looks just like you." His wife, Darla, replied, "That's what my mother said." "I'm in awe," said Remmy. "Over a few short months, this little person popped into existence from pixie dust!" Darla laughed and protested, "My baby girl was never pixie dust!"

Remmy's silly observation describes the dramatic process of prenatal development. Over nine months, a single cell transforms and grows into a **neonate**, a newborn. Every infant is born with a unique set of characteristics that reflect the genetic makeup of both parents. In this chapter, we discuss the process of how prenatal development unfolds, how a baby is born, and what the newborn baby is like.

Education/Universal/Getty

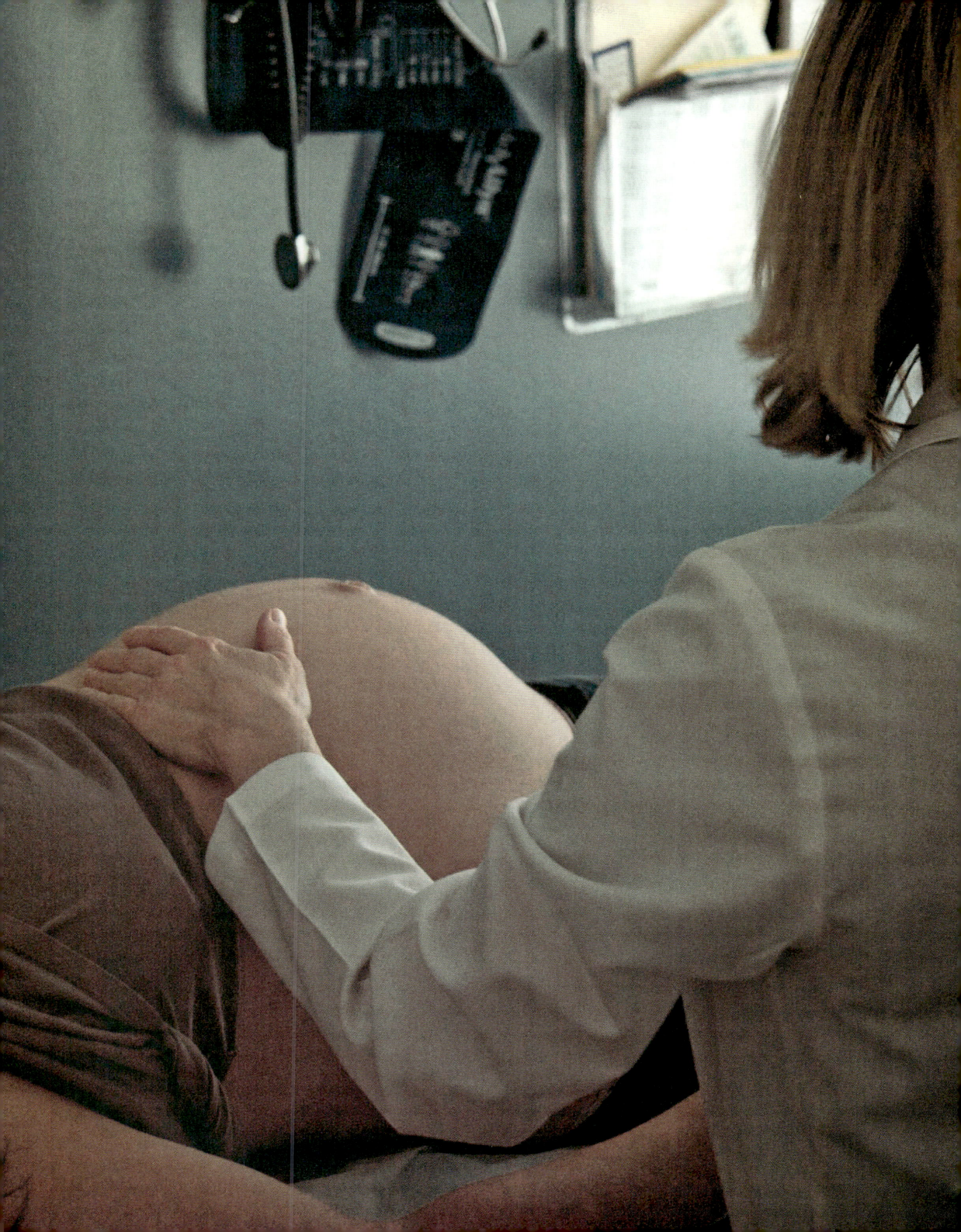

PRENATAL DEVELOPMENT

Remarkably, a human infant progresses from fertilization to birth in just 166 days, or 38 weeks. Conception, the union of **ovum** and sperm, marks the beginning of prenatal development, the transformative process in which the fertilized ovum, known as a zygote, progresses through several periods of development, finally emerging from the womb as a neonate.

CONCEPTION

A woman can conceive only during a short window of time each month. About every 28 days, an ovum bursts from one of the ovaries into the long, thin fallopian tube that leads to the uterus; this event is known as *ovulation*. The ovum is the largest cell in the human body, yet it is only 1/175th of an inch in diameter (about the size of the period at the end of this sentence). Over several days, the ovum travels down the fallopian tube while the corpus luteum, the spot on the ovary from which the ovum was released, secretes hormones that cause the lining of the uterus to thicken in preparation for the fertilized ovum (Moore & Persaud, 2013). If fertilization does not occur, the lining of the uterus is shed through menstruation about two weeks after ovulation.

Conception, of course, also involves the male. Each day, a man's testes produce millions of sperm, which are composed of a pointed head packed with 23 chromosomes' worth of genetic material and a long tail. During ejaculation, about 360 million, and as many as 500 million, sperm are released, bathed in a protective fluid called semen (Sadler, 2012). After entering the female's vagina, the sperm's tail propels it through the cervix into the uterus and onward toward the ovum. Sperm must travel for about six hours to reach the fallopian tube where an ovum may—or may not—be present. The journey is difficult: Some sperm get tangled up with other sperm, some travel up the wrong fallopian tube, others do not swim vigorously

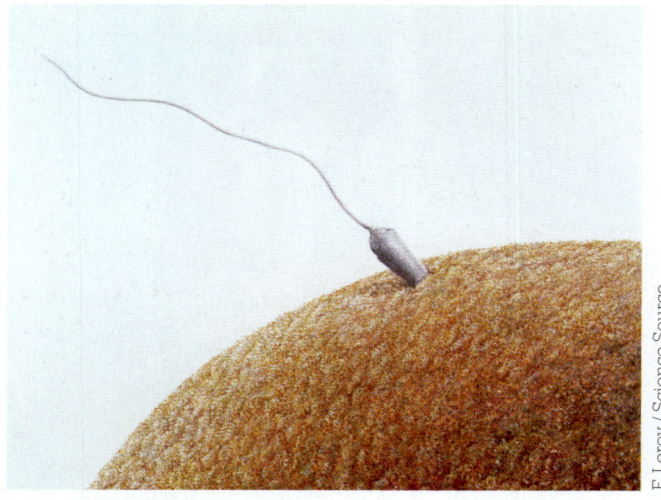

The tiny sperm is fertilizing the much larger ovum.

F. Leroy / Science Source

enough to reach the ovum. On average, about 300 sperm reach the ovum, if one is present (Moore & Persaud, 2013). Those that travel up the fallopian tube can live up to six days, able to fertilize a yet unreleased ovum. The ovum, however, remains viable for about only a day after being released into the fallopian tube.

Both sperm and ovum play a role in fertilization. The temperature gradient in the female reproductive system guides sperm toward the ovum while the sperm track the heat of an expectant ovum (Beckman, 2003). In the presence of sperm, the ovum exudes a chemical signal to draw the sperm closer. In turn, in the presence of an ovum, sperm become hyperactivated, they swim even more vigorously, and the sperm's head releases enzymes to help it penetrate the protective layers of the ovum (Krug, Riffell, & Zimmer, 2009; Primakoff & Myles, 2002). As soon as one sperm penetrates the ovum, a chemical reaction makes the ovum's membrane impermeable to other sperm. The sperm's tail falls off, and the genetic contents merge with that of the ovum.

At the moment of conception, the zygote, or fertilized egg, now contains 46 chromosomes, half from the ovum and half from the sperm. After fertilization, the zygote rapidly transforms into a multi-celled organism. Prenatal development takes place over several stages representing shifts in developmental processes.

GERMINAL PERIOD (FIRST TWO WEEKS AFTER CONCEPTION)

During the germinal period, also known as the period of the zygote, the newly created zygote begins cell

FIGURE 3.1: Female Reproductive System

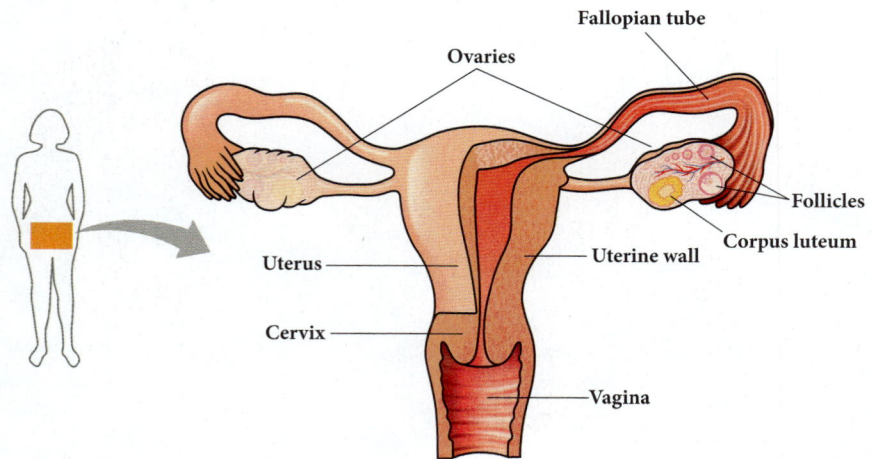

Fallopian tube
Ovaries
Follicles
Corpus luteum
Uterus
Uterine wall
Cervix
Vagina

SOURCE: Levine and Munsch (2010, p. 102).

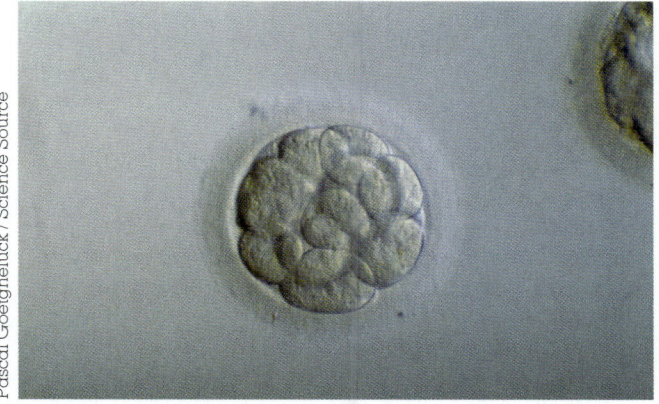

This ball of cells, known as a morula, is formed at about three days after conception. Each of these cells is identical. Differentiation has not yet begun.

division and travels down the fallopian tube toward the uterus. After a few hours, the genetic material within the zygote duplicates itself, forming two complete sets of genetic material that move to opposite sides of the cell. About 30 hours after conception, the zygote then splits down the middle, forming two identical cells (Moore & Persaud, 2013; Sadler, 2012). This process is called cleavage, and it continues at a rapid pace. As shown in Figure 3.2, the two cells each split to form four cells, then eight, and so on. Each of the resulting cells is identical until about the third set of cell divisions. Any of these cells may become a person (and sometimes do, in the case of monozygotic [MZ] or identical twins).

Cell differentiation begins roughly 72 hours after fertilization when the organism consists of about 16 to 32 cells. Differentiation means that the cells begin to specialize and are no longer identical. (Ethical and Policy Implications of Lifespan Development, p. 64, explores the use of, and ethical issues related to, undifferentiated cells known as **stem cells**.) By four days, the organism consists of about 60 to 70 cells formed into a hollow ball called a **blastocyst**, a fluid-filled sphere with cells forming a protective circle around an inner cluster of cells from which the **embryo** will develop.

Implantation, in which the blastocyst burrows into the wall of the uterus, begins at about Day 6 and is complete by about Day 11 (Moore & Persaud, 2013; Sadler, 2012). By the end of the second week, when fully implanted into the uterine wall, the outer layer of the blastocyst begins to develop into part of the **placenta**, the principal organ of exchange between the mother and developing organism. The placenta will enable the exchange of nutrients, oxygen, and wastes via the umbilical cord. Also during this stage, the developing organism is encased in amniotic fluid, providing temperature regulation, cushioning, and protection from shocks.

EMBRYONIC PERIOD (THIRD TO EIGHTH WEEK AFTER CONCEPTION)

By the third week after conception, the developing organism—now called an embryo—begins a period of structural development during which the most rapid developments of the prenatal period take place. All of the organs and major body systems form during this embryonic period. The mass of cells composing the **embryonic disk** develops into two layers: the **ectoderm**, the upper layer, will become skin, nails, hair, teeth, sensory organs, and the nervous system; the **endoderm,** the lower layer, will become the digestive system, liver, lungs, pancreas, salivary glands, and respiratory system. The middle layer, the **mesoderm**, forms later and will become muscles, skeleton, circulatory system, and internal organs.

During the third week, at about 22 days after conception, the endoderm folds to form the **neural tube**, which will develop into the central nervous system (brain and spinal cord; Moore & Persaud, 2008; Stiles & Jernigan, 2010). Now the head can be distinguished. A blood vessel that will become the heart begins to pulse, and blood begins to circulate throughout the body (Dye, 2000; Larsen, 2001). During Days 26 and 27, arm buds appear, followed by leg buds on Days 28 through 30 (Moore & Persaud, 2013; Sadler, 2012). At about this time, a tail-like appendage extends from the spine, disappearing at about 55 days after conception. The brain develops rapidly, and the head grows faster than the other parts of the body during the fifth week of development. The eyes, ears, nose, and mouth begin to form during the sixth week. Upper arms, forearms, palms, legs, and feet appear. The embryo shows reflex responses to touch.

During the seventh week, webbed fingers and toes are apparent; they separate completely by the end of the eighth week. A ridge called the **indifferent gonad** appears; it will develop into the male or female genitals, depending

FIGURE 3.2: Germinal Period

morula
fallopian tube
cell division begins
blastocyst
developing follicles
inner cell mass
corpus lutum
fertilization
ovary
implantation
ovulation

SOURCE: Levine and Munsch (2010, p. 102).

Stem Cell Research

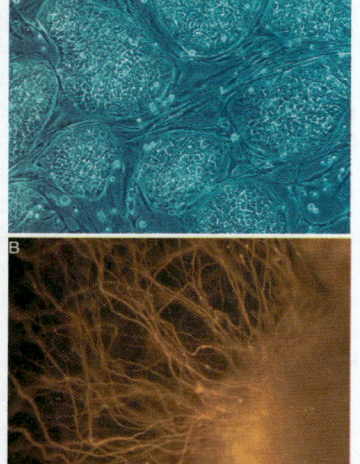

Wikimedia

Human stem cells that have not yet differentiated (top). They are identical and can develop into any kind of cell, such as a nerve cell (bottom)

Stem cells, first discovered in the late 1970s, are master cells that have the capacity to generate into any type of specialized cell in the body, such as muscle cells, blood cells, brain cells, and more (Shapiro, 2006; U.S. Department of Health and Human Services, 2010). Stem cells serve as a repair system for the body and hold promise as the basis for treatments and cures for many diseases ranging from Parkinson's disease to heart disease, and even spinal cord injury. There are several ways in which scientists derive stem cells. Each method yields a different type of stem cell, with different capacities for generating into specialized cells.

Embryonic stem cells are derived from blastocysts, about three to five days after conception, before the cells have begun to specialize into the various parts of the body. The blastocysts are created through in vitro fertilization for infertility treatments and are donated by couples when they are no longer needed or desired (Shapiro, 2006). Embryonic stem cells can become all cell types of the body because they have not differentiated (U.S. Department of Health and Human Services, 2010). Because extracting embryonic stem cells destroys the pre-implantation blastocyst, the practice has sparked ethical debates (Insoo, 2010; Robertson, 2010). Another source of stem cells relies on somatic nuclear transfer. These cells are created using cloning techniques whereby a patient's skin cell is inserted into a hollowed human egg; the resulting blastocyst is genetically identical to the patient so that any resulting therapies would not run the risk of rejection by the immune system (Tachibana et al., 2013). This process holds promise for creating stem cells without destroying embryos.

Adult stem cells, also known as somatic stem cells, are undifferentiated cells found among tissues and organs. They serve a repair function in the body, with the ability to repair the tissue in which they are found (U.S. Department of Health and Human Services, 2010). The origin of adult stem cells is unknown, although scientists have found adult stem cells in more tissues than initially thought: blood, skin, liver, and brain. Adult stem cells are thought to remain dormant for years until they are activated by disease or tissue injury, and begin replicating and repairing the tissue. A potential advantage of using adult stem cells for treating people is that the patient's own cells could be replicated and reintroduced into his or her body, eliminating the danger of immune system rejection.

Umbilical-cord stem cells are harvested from umbilical cords, without the need for human blastocysts, potentially reducing ethical concerns (Forraz & McGuckin, 2011). They are made up of blood stem cells, primarily, but also contain stem cells that may generate into bone, cartilage, heart muscle, brain, and liver (Zhong, Zhang, Asadollahi, Low, & Holzgreve, 2010). Umbilical cord cells are less plastic than embryonic stem cells; they cannot differentiate into any type of cell.

Proponents of embryonic stem cell research point out that the blastocysts are left over from in vitro fertilization treatments and would be destroyed anyway. However, advancing stem cell research would require a large supply of fresh blastocysts, more than can be supplied by fertility clinics.

There is little comprehensive or consistent regulation of stem cell research in the United States (Shapiro, 2006). In 2001, a federal ban was instituted limiting federal funding for embryonic stem cells to research conducted with the limited number of stem cells lines that currently existed. The ban led many researchers to seek funding from private sources, such as the biotech and pharmaceutical industry. This ban was revoked in 2009 by a presidential executive order freeing federal funds for work on any type of stem cell. Restoring federal funds ensures that stem cell research is conducted within similar ethical guidelines and protocols as research in other areas, perhaps addressing some of the ethical concerns regarding stem cell research. In 2009, a few weeks before the executive order restoring federal funding, the Food and Drug Administration approved the first clinical trial of a stem cell-derived therapy for spinal cord injuries. This was an important first step in moving stem cell research outside of the laboratory and into clinical practice (Robertson, 2010).

What Do You Think?

1. **What are the advantages and disadvantages of each source of stem cells?**

2. **What source, if any, do you prefer? Why?**

---

on the sex chromosomes of the **fetus** (Moore & Persaud, 2013). The Y chromosome of the male embryo instructs it to secrete testosterone, causing the indifferent gonad to create testes. In female embryos, no testosterone is released, and the indifferent gonad produces ovaries. The sex organs take

several weeks to develop. The external genital organs are not apparent until about 12 weeks.

At the end of the embryonic period, eight weeks after conception, the embryo weighs about one seventh of an ounce and is one inch long. All of the basic organs and body

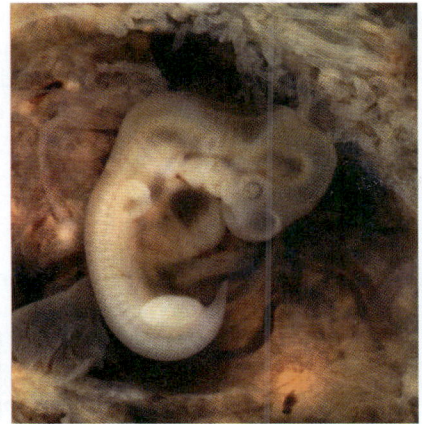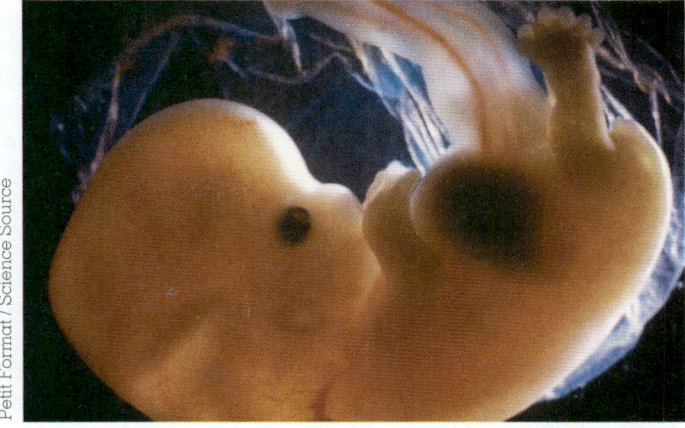

Development proceeds very quickly during the embryonic period. Note the dramatic changes from the fifth week (left) to the seventh week (right) of prenatal development.

parts have formed in a very rudimentary way. The embryo displays spontaneous reflexive movements, but it is still too small for the movements to be felt by the mother (Hepper, 2015). Serious defects that emerge during the embryonic period often cause a miscarriage, or *spontaneous abortion* (loss of the fetus); indeed, most miscarriages are the result of chromosomal abnormalities (Bainbridge, 2003). The most severely defective organisms do not survive beyond the first trimester, or third month of pregnancy. It is estimated that up to 45% of all conceptions abort spontaneously, and most occur before the pregnancy is detected (Larsen, 2001; Moore & Persaud, 2013).

FETAL PERIOD (NINTH WEEK TO BIRTH)

The fetal period is marked by the appearance of bone—at about the end of the eighth week. From 9 weeks until birth, the fetus grows rapidly, and its organs become more complex and begin to function. The end of the third month marks the close of the first trimester, at which time all parts of the fetus's body can move spontaneously, the legs kick, and the fetus can suck its thumb (an involuntary reflex). By the end of the 12th week, the upper limbs have almost reached their final relative lengths, but the lower limbs are slightly shorter than their final relative lengths (Sadler, 2012).

Second Trimester (Fourteen to Twenty-Six Weeks)

By the 14th week, at the start of the second trimester, limb movements are coordinated, but they will be too slight to be felt by the mother until about 17 to 20 weeks. The heartbeat gets stronger. Eyelids, eyebrows, fingernails, toenails, and tooth buds form. The first hair to appear is **lanugo**, a fine downlike hair that covers the fetus's body; it is gradually replaced by human hair (Dye, 2000). The skin is covered with a greasy material called the **vernix caseosa**, which protects the fetal skin from abrasions, chapping, and hardening that can occur with exposure to amniotic fluid (Moore & Persaud, 2013). At 21 weeks, rapid eye movements begin,

signifying an important time of growth and development for the fetal brain. The brain begins to become more responsive. For example, startle responses have been reported at 22 to 23 weeks in response to sudden vibrations and noises (Hepper, 2015; Sadler, 2012). During weeks 21 to 25, the fetus gains substantial weight, and its body proportions become more like those of a newborn infant. Growth of the fetal body begins to catch up to the head, yet the head remains disproportionately larger than the body at birth.

Third Trimester (Twenty-Seven to Forty Weeks; Seventh, Eighth, Ninth Months)

During the last three months of pregnancy, the fetal body grows substantially in weight and length; specifically, it typically gains over 5 pounds and grows 7 inches. At about 28 weeks after conception, brain development grows in leaps and bounds. The cerebral cortex develops convolutions and furrows, taking on the brain's characteristic wrinkly appearance (Dye, 2000). The fetal brain wave pattern shifts to include occasional bursts of activity, similar to the sleep–wake cycles of newborns. By 30 weeks, the pupils of the eyes dilate in response to light. At 35 weeks, the fetus has a firm hand grasp and spontaneously orients itself toward light.

During the third trimester, pregnant women and their caregivers are mindful that the baby may be born prematurely. Although the expected date of delivery is 166 days or 38 weeks from conception (40 weeks from the mother's last menstrual period), about one in every eight American births is premature (Centers for Disease Control and Prevention [CDC], 2014). The **age of viability**—the age at which advanced medical care permits a preterm newborn to survive outside the womb—begins at about 22 weeks after conception (Sadler, 2012). Infants born before 22 weeks rarely survive more than a few days because their brain and lungs have not begun to function. Although a 22- to 25-week fetus born prematurely may survive in intensive care, it is still at risk because its immature respiratory system may lead to death in early infancy. At about 26 weeks, the lungs become capable of breathing air and the premature infant stands a better chance of surviving if given intensive care. About 80% of infants born at 26 weeks and 87% of those born at 27 weeks survive (Stoll, Hansen, Bell, & Shankaran, 2010; Tucker & McGuire, 2004). Ninety-eight percent of 32-week premature infants survive.

Thinking in Context 3.1

1. What does it mean to say that a woman can become pregnant only during certain limited time periods but a man can impregnate a woman on any given day?

2. Petra noticed that her abdomen has not grown much since she became pregnant three months ago. She concluded that the fetus must not undergo significant development early in pregnancy. How would you respond to Petra?

ENVIRONMENTAL INFLUENCES ON PRENATAL DEVELOPMENT

The vast majority of infants are born healthy, but some are exposed before birth to environmental obstacles that hinder their development. A **teratogen** is an agent that causes damage to prenatal development, producing a birth defect. Teratogens include diseases, drugs, and other agents that influence the prenatal environment to disrupt development. The field of **teratology** attempts to find the causes of birth defects so that they may be avoided. Health care providers help pregnant women and those who intend to become pregnant to be aware of teratogens and avoid them, as much as possible, to maximize the likelihood of having a healthy baby.

PRINCIPLES OF TERATOLOGY

As we will discuss, there are many types of teratogens. It is particularly important to understand the principles according to which teratogens are likely to have an effect on the unborn baby's development. As shown in Figure 3.3, each organ of the body has a sensitive period in development during which it is most susceptible to damage from teratogens. Generally, sensitivity to teratogens begins at about three weeks after conception (Sadler, 2012). Because the embryonic period is a time of structural development, it is during this period that the organism is most vulnerable to damage from drugs, alcohol, and environmental harms. Once a body part is fully formed, it is less likely to be harmed by exposure to teratogens; however, some body parts, like the brain, remain vulnerable throughout pregnancy.

Despite what researchers have learned about sensitive periods in prenatal development, it is not always easy to predict the harm caused by teratogens. Generally, the effects of exposure to teratogens on prenatal development vary depending on the following principles (Collins, 2006; Moore & Persaud, 2013; Sadler, 2012).

FIGURE 3.3: Sensitive Periods in Prenatal Development

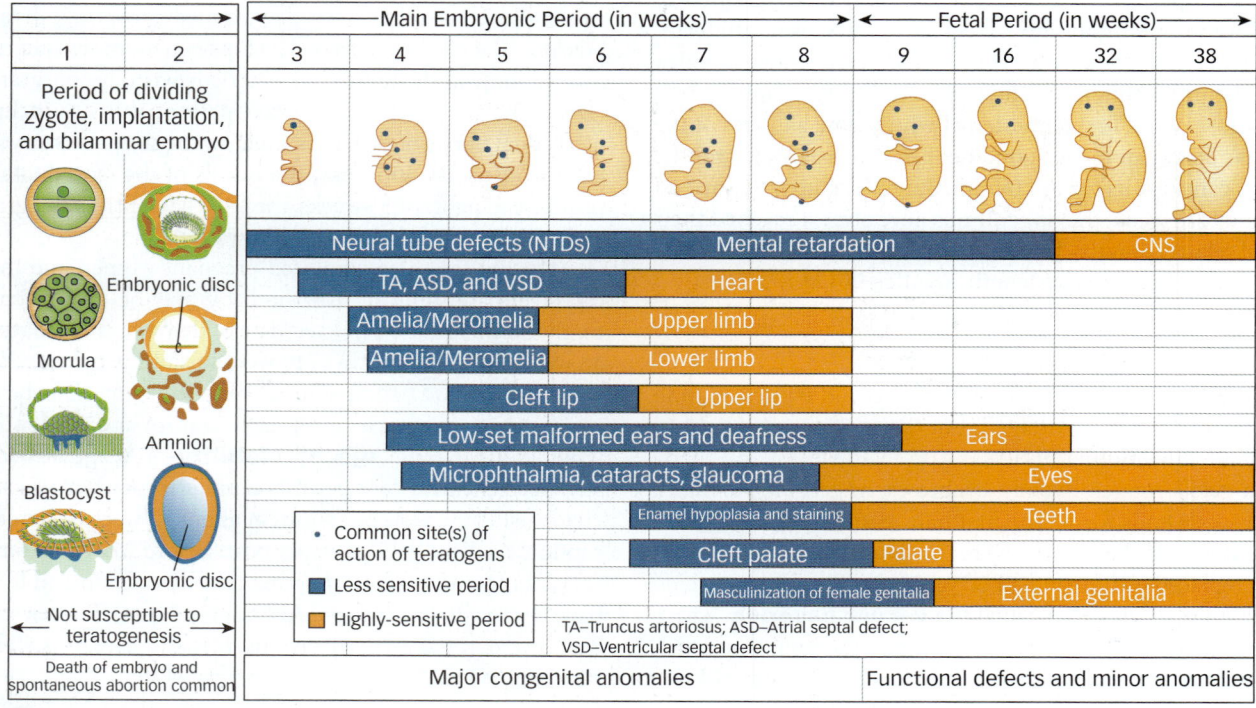

SOURCE: Levine and Munsch (2010, p. 113).

- *There are critical periods during prenatal development in which an embryo is more susceptible to damage from exposure to teratogens.* The extent to which exposure to a teratogen disrupts prenatal development depends on the stage of prenatal development when exposure occurs. Structural defects occur when the embryo is exposed to teratogen while that part of the body is developing.

- *There are individual differences in susceptibility to particular teratogens.* An organism's susceptibility to harm from exposure to a teratogen is influenced by the genetic makeup of both the organism and mother as well as the quality of the prenatal environment.

- *The amount of exposure (i.e., dose level) to a teratogen influences its effects.* Generally, the greater the dose, the more damage to development; however, teratogens also differ in their strength. Some teratogens, like alcohol, display a powerful dose–response relationship so that larger doses, heavier and more frequent drinking, result in greater damage.

- *Teratogens show complicated effects on development.* Different teratogens can cause the same birth defect, and a variety of birth defects can result from the same teratogen.

- *Some teratogens have subtle effects that result in developmental delays that are not obvious at birth.*

Infants exposed prenatally to as little as an ounce of alcohol a day usually display no obvious physical deformities but later, as children may demonstrate cognitive delays. They process information more slowly and score lower on IQ tests than children whose mothers did not drink while pregnant (Jacobson & Jacobson, 1996).

- *Some teratogens display sleeper effects—effects that are not visible until many years later.* For example, infants born to women who consumed diethylstilbestrol (DES), a hormone that was widely prescribed between 1945 and 1970 to prevent miscarriages, were born healthy but as adults were more likely to experience problems with their reproductive systems. Daughters born to mothers who took DES were more likely to develop a rare form of cervical cancer, have miscarriages, and give birth to infants who were premature or low birth weight (Barnes et al., 1980; Schrager & Potter, 2004).

TYPES OF TERATOGENS

Prenatal development can be influenced by many contextual factors, including maternal consumption of over-the-counter (OTC), prescription, and recreational drugs; illness; environmental factors; and more, as shown in Table 3.1. Although the developing organism is vulnerable to many teratogens, the mother's body is designed to protect the growing fetus.

TABLE 3.1 Hazards to Prenatal Development

TERATOGENS	POTENTIAL EFFECTS
Drugs	
Alcohol	Fetal alcohol syndrome, mental retardation; retarded fetal growth; joint abnormalities; ocular abnormalities
Amphetamines	Premature delivery; stillbirth; irritability; poor feeding among newborns
Antibiotics (tetracycline, streptomycin, terramycin)	Premature delivery; restricted skeletal growth; cataracts
Barbiturates	Lethargy in the fetus; large doses cause anoxia (oxygen starvation), restricts fetal growth
Cocaine	Retarded fetal growth; prematurity, microcephaly; neurobehavioral disturbances; genital abnormalities
Heroin	Retarded fetal growth; premature labor; newborns suffer withdrawal
Lithium	Heart and blood vessel abnormalities
Marijuana	Retarded fetal growth
Tobacco	Retarded fetal growth; miscarriage, stillbirth; infant mortality
Maternal Illness	
HIV/AIDS	Retarded fetal growth; microcephaly; mental retardation; mother-to-child transmission
Rubella	During embryonic period, causes blindness and deafness; in first and second trimesters, brain damage
Environmental Pollutants	
Lead and Mercury	Spontaneous miscarriage; preterm labor; brain damage
Radiation	Retarded growth; microcephaly; mental retardation; skeletal anomalies; cataracts

SOURCES: Moore and Persaud (2013); Sadler (2012); Weinhold (2009).

Some teratogens can be avoided by choice; for example, a woman can choose not to drink alcohol or smoke cigarettes during pregnancy. Others, however, may be involuntary, as in the case of maternal illness. Sometimes a pregnant woman and her doctor may have to make a difficult choice between forgoing a needed prescription drug and putting the fetus at risk. And, in any case, a woman may not know she is pregnant until after the first few weeks of the embryonic stage are already past. Thus, in the real world, almost no pregnancy can be entirely free of exposure to teratogens. However, each year about 97% of infants are born without defects (CDC, 2014).

Maternal Illness

Depending on the type and when it occurs, an illness experienced by the mother during pregnancy can have devastating consequences for the developing fetus. For example, rubella (German measles) prior to the 11th week of pregnancy can cause a variety of defects including blindness, deafness, heart defects, and brain damage, but after the first trimester, adverse consequences become less likely (Santis, Cavaliere, Straface, & Caruso, 2006). Other illnesses have varying effects on the fetus. For example, chicken pox can produce birth defects affecting the arms, legs, eyes, and brain; mumps can increase the risk of miscarriage (Ornoy & Tenenbaum, 2006; Tan & Koren, 2006). In addition to posing risks to development, some sexually transmitted infections (STIs), such as syphilis, can be transmitted to the fetus during pregnancy (Gomez et al., 2013; Sánchez & Wendel, 1997). Others, such as gonorrhea, genital herpes, and HIV, can be transmitted as the child passes through the birth canal during birth or through bodily fluids after birth (see Lives in Context, p. 69). Since some diseases, such as mumps and rubella, can be prevented with vaccinations, it is important for women who are considering becoming pregnant to discuss their immunization status with their health care provider.

Prescription and Nonprescription Drugs

Both prescription and nonprescription drugs can potentially harm the developing fetus. Prescription drugs that can act as teratogens include antibiotics, certain hormones, anticoagulants, anticonvulsants, and some acne drugs (Collins, 2006; Moore & Persaud, 2013; Sadler, 2012). In several cases, physicians have unwittingly prescribed drugs to ease pregnant women's discomfort that caused harm to the fetus. For example, in the late 1950s and early 1960s, many pregnant women were prescribed thalidomide to prevent morning sickness. However, taking thalidomide four to six weeks after conception (in some cases, even just one dose) caused deformities of the child's arms and legs, and, less frequently, damage to the ears, heart, kidneys, and genitals (Laughton, Cornell, Boivin, & Van Rie, 2012; Vargesson, 2009).

Nonprescription drugs, such as diet pills and cold medicine, can also cause harm, but research on OTC drugs lags far behind research on prescription drugs. We know little about the teratogenic effect of many OTC drugs (Cabbage & Neal, 2011). For example, a couple of studies have linked dextromethorphan, commonly used in cough medicine, with birth defects in animals, but little is known about its effect in humans (Black & Hill, 2003). Research on aspirin is mixed, as some research suggests that consuming aspirin increases the risk of miscarriage, poor fetal growth, poor motor control, and neurodevelopmental difficulties (Barr, Streissguth, Darby, & Sampson, 1990; Elkarmi, Abu-Samak, & Al-Qaisi, 2007; Li, Liu, & Odouli, 2003). Yet other research with **low birth weight** infants suggests no adverse long-term outcomes of prenatal exposure to aspirin (Marret et al., 2010).

Caffeine, found in coffee, tea, cola drinks, and chocolate, among other foods, is an example of a very commonly ingested nonprescription drug that has come under scrutiny for its potential effects on the fetus. Though caffeine receives media attention as a possible risk, research findings regarding teratogenic effects of caffeine consumption are mixed. Some research suggests an association between caffeine intake and low birth weight in humans (Sengpiel et al., 2013) and neural defects in chicks (Ma et al., 2012), yet other research shows no association between maternal caffeine intake and risk of premature birth and low birth weight (Jarosz, Wierzejska, & Siuba, 2012). As with all studies of teratogens in pregnancy, it is difficult to distinguish the effects of caffeine apart from other substances. Discrepancies in findings across research studies occur because researchers often use different methods of assessing caffeine intake and vary as to whether they take into account the presence of other known teratogens such as cigarette smoking and alcohol consumption. At the present time, caffeine is not known to be a human teratogen, but there is no assurance that heavy maternal caffeine consumption is safe. The American College of Obstetricians and Gynecologists (2010) and the March of Dimes (2012) suggest that pregnant women ingest no more than one cup of coffee each day.

Alcohol

An estimated 14% to nearly 30% of pregnant women report consuming alcohol during their pregnancies (Arria et al., 2006; Meschke, Holl, & Messelt, 2013; Zhao et al., 2012). Indeed, alcohol abuse during pregnancy has been identified as the leading cause of developmental disabilities (Murthy, Kudlur, George, & Mathew, 2009; Warren, Hewitt, & Thomas, 2011). **Fetal alcohol spectrum disorders** refer to the continuum of effects of exposure to alcohol, which vary with the timing and amount of exposure (Riley, Infante, & Warren, 2011). Fetal alcohol spectrum disorders are estimated to affect as many as 2% to 5% of younger schoolchildren in the United States and Western Europe (May et al., 2009). At the extreme end of the spectrum is **fetal alcohol syndrome (FAS)**, a cluster of defects appearing after heavy prenatal exposure to alcohol that is detected in two to seven infants per 1,000 births (May et al.,

HIV Infection in Newborns

Mother-to-child transmission of HIV has declined as scientists have learned more about HIV. However, it remains a worldwide problem especially in developing nations where cultural, economic, and hygienic reasons prevent mothers from seeking alternatives to breastfeeding, a primary cause of mother-to-child transmission of HIV.

The rate of mother-to-child transmission of HIV has dropped in recent years as scientists have learned more about HIV. The use of cesarean delivery as well as prescribing anti-HIV drugs to the mother during the second and third trimesters of pregnancy, and to the infant for the first six weeks of life, has reduced mother-to-child HIV transmission to less than 2% in the United States and Europe (from over 20%; Ch, 2004; Torpey, Kabaso, et al., 2010; Torpey, Kasonde, et al., 2010). Research has suggested that aggressive treatment may further reduce the transmission of

HIV to newborns. In a breakthrough case, an infant received drug therapy starting at 30 hours of age until around 18 months of age, when the child showed no detectible virus in the blood and was said to be cured (Pollack & McNeil, 2013). This case raised scientists' hopes; however, the child remained in remission for 27 months before the virus reappeared (McNeil, 2014). Based on these findings, in 2014 the National Institutes of Health began a study examining the use of aggressive drug treatment in newborns (National Institute of Allergy and infectious Diseases, 2014).

Worldwide, mother-to-child HIV transmission remains a serious issue. For example, in Zambia 40,000 infants acquire HIV each year (Torpey, Kasonde, et al., 2010). Globally, breast-feeding accounts for 30% to 50% of HIV transmission in newborns (Sullivan, 2003; World Health Organization, 2011). The World Health Organization (2010) recommends that women who test positive for HIV receive information about how HIV may be transmitted to their infants and should not breast-feed. Yet cultural, economic, and hygienic reasons often prevent mothers in developing nations from seeking alternatives to breast-feeding. For example, the widespread lack of clean water in some countries makes the use of powdered formulas dangerous. Also, in some cultures, women who do not breast-feed may be ostracized from the community (Sullivan, 2003). Balancing cultural values with medical needs is a challenge.

Treating newborns is critical, however, as worldwide, 20% to 30% of neonates with HIV develop AIDS during the first year of life and most die in infancy (United Nations Children's Fund, 2013). Between 50% and 80% of HIV-infected children show below average growth, manifested in smaller than average weight, length, and head circumference (Palmer, 2003; Venkatesh et al., 2010). In addition to chronic bacterial infections and disorders of the central nervous system, heart, gastrointestinal tract, lungs, kidneys, and skin, children with HIV tend to suffer neurodevelopmental delays, including brain atrophy, which contribute to cognitive and motor impairment, and delays in reaching developmental milestones (Blanchette, Smith, Fernandes-Penney, King, & Read, 2001; Laughton, Cornell, Boivin, & Van Rie, 2013; Sherr, Mueller, & Varrall, 2009).

What Do You Think?

Imagine that you work as an HIV educator with women in an underdeveloped country. What challenges might you face in encouraging women to take steps to reduce the potential for HIV transmission to their infants? How might you help them?

2009). FAS is associated with a distinct pattern of facial characteristics (such as small head circumference, short nose, small eye opening, and small midface); pre- and postnatal growth deficiencies; and deficits in intellectual development, school achievement, memory, visual spatial skills, attention, language, problem solving, motor coordination, and the combined abilities to plan, focus attention, problem solve, and use goal-directed behavior (Jirikowic, Gelo, & Astley, 2010; Mattson, Crocker, & Nguyen, 2011; Thomas, Warren, & Hewitt, 2010). The effects of exposure to alcohol within the womb persist throughout childhood and have been found to be associated with deficits in learning and memory in early adulthood (Coles et al., 2011; McLachlan, Roesch, Viljoen, & Douglas, 2014; Wheeler, Kenney, & Temple, 2013).

Fetal alcohol syndrome is associated with distinct facial characteristics, growth deficiencies, and deficits in intellectual development, language, motor coordination, and the combined abilities to plan, focus attention, problem solve, and use goal directed behavior that persist throughout childhood and into adulthood.

Many adults realize that heavy drinking has devastating consequences for prenatal development, but it is important to note that moderate drinking is also harmful. Pregnant women who consume alcohol in moderation place their fetuses at risk because some children are born displaying some but not all of the problems of FAS; they are said to show fetal alcohol spectrum effects known as *partial FAS* or *fetal alcohol effects* (Thomas et al., 2010). Consuming 7 to 14 drinks per week during pregnancy is associated with lower birth size; growth deficits in weight, height, and head circumference through adolescence; and lower IQ and attention and memory problems (Alati et al., 2013; Chen, 2012; O'Leary & Bower, 2012; Willford, Leech, & Day, 2006). Less than one drink per day has been associated with negative effects on fetal growth (Day & Richardson, 2004; Day et al., 2002; Mariscal et al., 2006) and with deficits in visual information processing, attention, and numerical processing at one year of age (Lu, 2005; Testa, Quigley, & Das Eiden, 2003). Scientists have yet to determine if there is a safe level of drinking; however, the research to date suggests that pregnant women be cautious. The only way to be certain of avoiding alcohol-related risks is to avoid alcohol altogether.

Cigarette Smoking

Every package of cigarettes sold in the United States includes a warning about the dangers of smoking while pregnant, yet 16% of pregnant women aged 15 to 44 years old smoke while pregnant (Bandstra, Morrow, Mansoor, & Accornero, 2010; Ebrahim & Gfroerer, 2003; Keegan, Parva, Finnegan, Gerson, & Belden, 2010). Nicotine reduces the supply of oxygen and nutrients available to the fetus, affecting growth and development. Fetal deaths, premature births, and low birth weight are associated with maternal smoking (Juárez & Merlo, 2013). Premature delivery is twice as frequent in mothers who are heavy smokers (20 cigarettes or more a day) than in mothers who do not smoke (Moore & Persaud, 2013). Infants exposed to smoke while in the womb are prone to congenital heart defects, respiratory problems, asthma, and sudden infant death syndrome (SIDS) and, as children, have more behavior problems and attention difficulties as well as score lower on intelligence and achievement tests (Kiechl-Kohlendorfer et al., 2010; Lee & Lupo, 2013). There is no safe level of smoking during pregnancy. Even babies born to light smokers (one to five cigarettes per day) show higher rates of low birth weight than do babies born to nonsmokers (Ventura, Hamilton, Mathews, & Chandra, 2003). Quitting smoking before or during pregnancy reduces the risk of adverse pregnancy outcomes.

Marijuana

The effects of marijuana on prenatal development are not well understood. Evidence suggests that that marijuana use during early pregnancy negatively affects fetal length and birth weight (Huizink, 2013; Hurd et al., 2005; Moore & Persaud, 2013). Prenatal exposure to marijuana is associated with impairments in memory, verbal skills, and quantitative skills, as well as impulsivity and depressive symptoms at ages 4 and 10 (Gray, Day, Leech, & Richardson, 2005; Huizink & Mulder, 2006; Richardson, Ryan, Willford, Day, & Goldschmidt, 2002). Other research suggests that prenatal exposure to marijuana is associated with attention problems that may influence achievement in adolescence (Goldschmidt, Richardson, Willford, Severtson, & Day, 2012; Wu, Jew, & Lu, 2011). Yet some studies find more modest effects with few consistent findings in infants (Huizink, 2013) and few cognitive difficulties later in development through adolescence (Fried & Watkinson, 2000, 2001). Some research has found that once the effects of exposure to other teratogens are controlled, marijuana does not show a teratogenic effect (Nordstrom-Klee, Delaney-Black, Covington, Ager, & Sokol, 2002; van Gelder et al., 2010). Some have thereby concluded that there is little evidence that marijuana is a human teratogen (Moore & Persaud, 2013). Given these conflicting findings, the safest course is for pregnant women to avoid marijuana.

Other Drugs

Infants exposed to drugs such as cocaine and heroin face special challenges. Prenatal exposure to cocaine is associated with reduced birth weight, length, and head circumference and impaired motor performance at birth (Frank, Augustyn, Knight, Pell, & Zuckerman, 2001). At one month after birth, babies who were exposed to cocaine have difficulty regulating their arousal states and show poor movement skills, poor reflexes, and greater excitability (Hedley et al., 2004). Children exposed to cocaine during the first three months of prenatal development displayed decreased head circumference, lower scores on memory tests, and more behavior problems at 3 years of age than children of women who never used cocaine prenatally (Richardson, Goldschmidt, & Willford, 2009). Like cocaine-exposed infants, heroin-exposed infants often show signs of addiction and withdrawal symptoms including tremors, irritability, abnormal crying, disturbed sleep, and impaired motor control. Infants exposed to heroin and methadone are less attentive to the environment and show slower motor development.

Exposure to these drugs during prenatal development influences brain development, particularly the regions associated with attention, arousal, and regulation (Behnke & Smith, 2013; Coyle, 2013; Lebel et al., 2013; Roussotte et al., 2011). Research with school children over the age of 6 has found prenatal cocaine exposure to be associated with difficulty in sustained attention and behavioral control, as well as behavioral problems in adolescence (Accornero et al., 2011; Ackerman, Riggins, & Black, 2010; Richardson, Goldschmidt, Leech, & Willford, 2011). Likewise, adolescents exposed to cocaine in utero show higher levels of substance use than do their non-exposed peers (Min et al., 2014).

Though it was once believed that cocaine- and heroin-exposed infants would suffer lifelong cognitive deficits, research suggests more mixed and subtle effects (Bandstra et al., 2010; Behnke & Smith, 2013; Lambert & Bauer, 2012). Some research has suggested that prenatal cocaine exposure is not linked with impairments in overall development, IQ, or school readiness in toddlers, elementary school-age children, or middle school-age children (Asanbe & Lockert, 2006; Behnke & Smith, 2013; Jones, 2006). Yet other research has demonstrated small but lasting effects on language skills at ages 10 and 12 (Lewis et al., 2011, 2013).

The challenge of determining the effects of prenatal exposure to cocaine and heroin is that most cocaine- and heroin-exposed infants were also exposed to other substances, including tobacco, alcohol, and marijuana (Jones, 2006), making it difficult to isolate the effect of each drug on prenatal development. We must be cautious in interpreting findings about illicit drug use and the effects on prenatal development because there are many other contextual factors that often co-occur with substance use and also pose risks for development, including poverty, malnutrition, social isolation, stress, and diminished parental responsiveness (Bandstra et al., 2010; Bendersky & Lewis, 1999; Frank et al., 2001). For example, parents who abuse drugs tend to provide poorer quality care, a home environment less conducive to cognitive development, and parent–child interaction that is less sensitive and positive than the environments provided by other parents (Hans, 2002). Children raised by substance-abusing parents are at risk for being subjected to overly harsh discipline and lack of supervision (Burlew et al., 2012) as well as disruptions in care due to factors such as parental incarceration, inability to care for a child, and even death (e.g., from a drug overdose or drug gang violence).

At the same time, quality care can lessen the long-term impact of prenatal exposure to substances (Lewis et al., 2011; Ornoy, Michailevskay, Lukashov, Barttamburger, & Harel, 1996). Some evidence suggests, for example, that developmental differences in exposed infants often disappear when medical and environmental factors are considered. Disentangling the long-term effects of prenatal exposure to substances, subsequent parenting, and contextual factors is challenging. Researchers and health care providers who construct interventions must address the contextual and parenting-related risk factors to improve the developmental outlook for children exposed to drugs prenatally (Butz et al., 2001; Kilbride, Castor, Hoffman, & Fuger, 2000). (Does maternal drug use during pregnancy constitute child abuse? See Ethical and Policy Applications of Lifespan Development, p. 72, for a discussion of this issue.)

Environmental Hazards

Prenatal development can also be harmed by factors in the environment, including chemicals, radiation, and extremes of heat and humidity. Infants exposed to heavy metals, such as lead and mercury, whether through ingestion or inhalation, score lower on tests of cognitive ability and intelligence as well as have higher rates of childhood illness (Sadler, 2012). Exposure to radiation can cause genetic mutations. For example, infants born to mothers pregnant during the atomic bomb explosions in Hiroshima and Nagasaki and after the nuclear power accident at Chernobyl displayed many physical deformities, mutations, and intellectual deficits. Prenatal exposure to radiation is associated with mental retardation, reduced head circumference, Down syndrome, and reduced intelligence scores and school performance. About 85% of the world's birth defects occur in developing countries, supporting the role of context in influencing prenatal development directly via environmental hazards, but also indirectly through the opportunities and resources for education, health, and financial support (Weinhold, 2009). Does maternal drug use during pregnancy constitute child abuse?" See Box 3.3 for a discussion of this issue.

Parental Characteristics and Behaviors

Teratogens—and the avoidance of them—are, of course, not the only determinants of how healthy a baby will be. A pregnant woman's characteristics, such as her age and her behaviors during pregnancy, including nutrition and emotional well-being, also influence prenatal outcomes.

Maternal Drug Use While Pregnant

We have seen that exposure to teratogens such as drugs and alcohol adversely affect the developing fetus. In recent years, some states have sought to penalize women for consuming illegal drugs while pregnant, characterizing such behavior as child abuse and/or neglect (Gostin, 2001). Does maternal drug use while pregnant constitute child abuse?

About one half of states require physicians to test for or report drug-exposed newborns to child protective services or other agencies (Berger & Waldfogel, 2000; Guttmacher Institute, 2014; Logan, 1999). Eighteen states classify controlled substance use during pregnancy as child abuse, which may lead to removing the infant from parental custody or even terminating parental rights. Two states, Alabama and South Carolina, actively prosecute pregnant women. And in 2014, Tennessee became the only state to specifically criminalize drug use during pregnancy, charging substance-abusing pregnant women with assault (Chokshi, 2014; Guttmacher Institute, 2014).

In many instances, however, state supreme courts have overruled the extension of child abuse laws to the fetus (Stone-Manista, 2009). Several state supreme court rulings, including those in Kentucky, Nevada, and Ohio, have held that a mother cannot be convicted of child abuse or endangerment for substance use while pregnant (Fortney, 2003).

The debate regarding policies that require drug testing and prosecutiong of pregnant women for drug use raises issues regarding women's constitutional rights (Bornstein, 2003). For example, between 1989 and 1994, pregnant women who received prenatal treatment at a public hospital operated by the Medical University of South Carolina and met one of more of these criteria—no or minimal prenatal care, birth defects or poor fetal growth, and a history of drug or alcohol abuse—were tested for substance use without their knowledge (Chande, 2001). Thirty of these women who tested positive for cocaine in urine tests given as part of their treatment were arrested. In the resulting court case on behalf of the 30 arrested women, *Ferguson v. City of Charleston*, the U.S. Supreme Court ruled that pregnant women seeking prenatal care in a public hospital could not be drug tested and have positive results turned over to police without a warrant (Gostin, 2001). It was ruled an unreasonable search without consent and unconstitutional (Flavin & Paltrow, 2010). Though this decision was controversial, many researchers and policymakers view it as important because prior to it, pregnant women who were suspected of drug use were tested without their permission. Moreover, after learning that the women tested positive, no effort was made to diagnosis their substance use

disorders, intervene, or refer the women to treatment. Women were even led away in handcuffs to face charges. Newborns were removed from their mothers and placed under the care of child services, who often directed them to foster care, where they often experienced difficulty finding suitable homes.

Both the American College of Obstetricians and Gynecologists (2011) and the American Medical Association (2014) argue that criminal sanctions for maternal drug use are ineffective as they increase the risk of harm by discouraging prenatal and postnatal care and undermining the physician–patient relationship. Such policies can cause women to develop a mistrust in medical professionals that ultimately harms their care if they become reluctant to seek medical care for themselves and their children. Others argue that these policies may be a subtle form of discrimination applied to women of color, as well as the most poor and vulnerable members of society because low income African American and Hispanic women are disproportionately tried (Flavin & Paltrow, 2010; Gostin, 2001). The criteria to determine who would be tested were those prevalent within low-income minority populations, specifically in the *Ferguson v. City of Charleston* case, including the absence of prenatal care and a previously documented history of substance abuse.

Other professionals argue that testing pregnant women for drug use could ultimately lead to permitting searches for legal drugs that are known to be harmful, such as alcohol and tobacco (Bornstein, 2003; Fortney, 2003). Pregnant women have been punished for drinking alcohol, using prescription drugs, and even driving negligently on the grounds that these behaviors harm the unborn child (Bornstein, 2003). For example, in 1987, a Michigan woman was charged with child abuse and temporarily lost custody of her infant because she had taken Valium while pregnant to relieve pain from injuries suffered in a car accident (Johnsen, 1992). Some experts have expressed concern that criminal sanctions against a pregnant woman's behavior could even be expanded to the point where the woman is considered guilty of failing to meet her duty to the fetus if she does not take enough vitamins, or uses an OTC medication (Fortney, 2003).

What Do You Think?

1. In your view, is substance use during pregnancy a form of abuse? Why or why not?

2. What do you think could be done to reduce the prevalence of substance use by pregnant women?

Nutrition Nutrition plays a role in prenatal development both before and after conception. The quality of men's and women's diets influences the health of the sperm and egg (Sinclair & Watkins, 2013). The mother's diet plays a major role in the development and health of the fetus. Most women need to consume 2,200 to 2,900 calories per day to sustain a pregnancy (Kaiser, Allen, & American Dietetic Association, 2008; Simkin, Whalley, & Keppler,

2001). Mothers who consume diets rich in nutrients tend to have fewer complications during pregnancy and give birth to healthier babies. Fetal malnutrition is associated with increased susceptibility to complex diseases in postnatal life (Chmurzynska, 2010). Unfortunately, over 1 billion people in the world are chronically hungry each year (Food and Agriculture Organization of the United Nations, 2009). Dietary supplements can reduce many

Mothers who consume nutritious diets tend to have fewer complications during pregnancy and give birth to healthier babies.

develop, resulting in death shortly after birth. As researchers have learned and disseminated the knowledge that folic acid helps prevent these defects, the frequency of neural tube defects has declined to about 1 in 1,000 births (Centers for Disease Control and Prevention, 2004; Cordero et al., 2010). However, in a national study of U.S. mothers, only 24% consumed the recommended dose of folic acid during pregnancy (Tinker, Cogswell, Devine, & Berry, 2010).

Emotional Well-Being Although stress is inherently part of almost everyone's life, exposure to chronic and severe stress during pregnancy poses risks including low birth weight, premature birth, and a longer postpartum hospital stay (Field, 2011; Kingston, Tough, & Whitfield, 2012; Marcus et al., 2011; Mulder et al., 2002). Stress may be particularly damaging to prenatal development. Pregnant women who experience one or more negative life events, such as a family member's death, in the past five months are more likely to have a spontaneous miscarriage (Nelson, Mcmahon, Joffe, & Brensinger, 2003). Maternal stress influences prenatal development because stress hormones cross the placenta, raising the fetus's heart rate and activity level. Long-term exposure to stress hormones in utero is associated with higher levels of stress hormones in newborns and may lead the newborn to become more irritable, active, and have difficulties in sleep, digestion, and self-regulation (Davis, Glynn, Waffarn, & Sandman, 2011; Kingston et al., 2012). Prenatal exposure to stress hormones is also associated with a higher risk of displaying symptoms of anxiety, attention deficit hyperactivity disorder, and aggression (Glover, 2011).

Stress also influences prenatal development in indirect ways. Stress weakens the immune system, making the mother and fetus more susceptible to disease (Christian, 2015; Coussons-Reid, Okun, & Simms, 2003; Parker & Douglas, 2010). Pregnant women who experience high levels of chronic stress are more likely to use cigarettes and marijuana during pregnancy (Nelson et al., 2003). If stress continues after birth, the mother may experience difficulty responding to the infant with sensitivity. This coupled with an irritable infant can make warm and responsive parenting a challenge (Brockington, 1996; Sameroff & Chandler, 1975). Social support from family and paternal support reduces the risk of stress on pregnancy (Feldman, Dunkel-Schetter, Sandman, & Wadhwa, 2000; Ghosh, Wilhelm, Dunkel-Schetter, Lombardi, & Ritz, 2010).

of the problems caused by maternal malnourishment (Ortolano, Mahmud, Iqbal Kabir, & Levinson, 2003), and infants who are malnourished can overcome some of the negative effects if they are raised in enriched environments. However, most children who are malnourished before birth remain malnourished; few have the opportunity to be raised in enriched environments after birth (Ricciuti, 1993).

Some deficits resulting from an inadequate diet cannot be remedied. For example, inadequate consumption of folic acid (a B vitamin) by the mother can result in the formation of neural tube defects. During the fourth week of prenatal development, the neural tube begins to close at both ends, and the brain and spinal cord begin to develop. Should either end of the neural tube fail to close, defects result. **Spina bifida** occurs when the lower part of the neural tube fails to close. Spinal nerves begin to grow outside of the vertebrae, often resulting in paralysis. Surgery must be performed before or shortly after birth, but lost capacities cannot be restored. Spina bifida is often accompanied by malformations in brain development and impaired cognitive development (Barnes et al., 2006; Dennis, Landry, Barnes, & Fletcher, 2006). Another neural tube defect, **anencephaly**, occurs when the top part of the neural tube fails to close. In an infant with anencephaly, all or part of the brain fails to

Maternal Age Maternal age at pregnancy receives a great deal of media attention. Does maternal age matter? U.S. women are becoming pregnant at later ages than ever before. The pregnancy rates for women ages 35 to 39 nearly doubled from 1985 to 2009, from 24 to 46.9 per 1,000 women; the rate more than doubled for women aged 40 to 44, from 4 to 10.1 (Ventura & Hamilton, 2011).

However, it is important to be aware that women who give birth over the age of 35, and especially over 40, are at greater risk for pregnancy and birth complications than are younger women. They are more likely to have a miscarriage or stillbirth.

FIGURE 3.4: Maternal Age and Risk of Down Syndrome

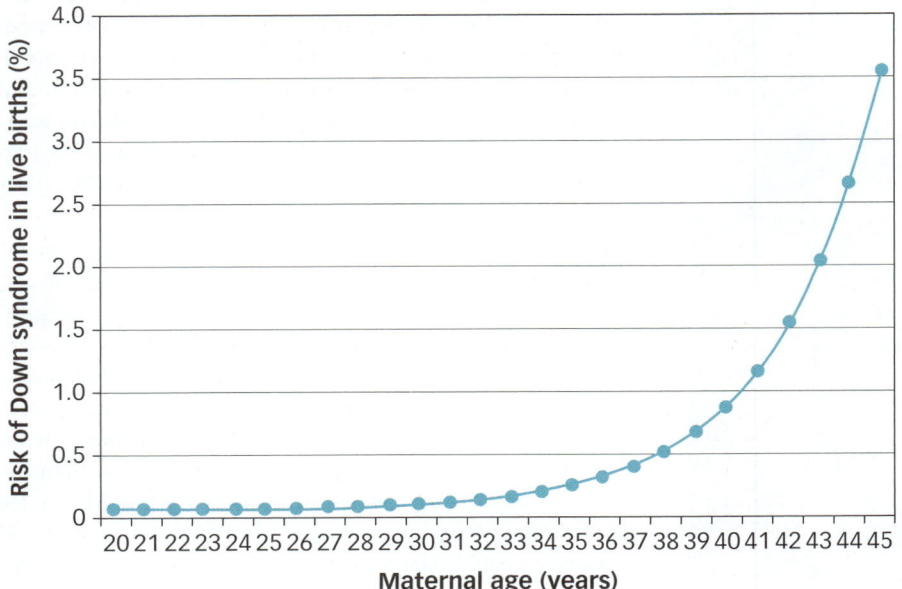

Although the risk for Down Syndrome increases dramatically with maternal age, most infants are born healthy, regardless of maternal age.

SOURCES: Data from Cuckle, Wald, and Thompson (1987); figure from Newberger (2000).

They are more vulnerable to pregnancy-related illnesses such as hypertension and diabetes, and their pregnancies involve increased risks to the newborn including low birth weight, preterm birth, respiratory problems, and related conditions requiring intensive neonatal care (Grotegut et al., 2014; Kenny et al., 2013; Khalil, Syngelaki, Maiz, Zinevich, & Nicolaides, 2013; Shrim et al., 2010). As illustrated in Figure 3.4, the risk of having a child with Down syndrome also increases sharply with maternal age, especially after age 40 (Hazlett, Hammer, Hooper, & Kamphaus, 2011). Although risks for complications rise linearly with each year (Salem Yaniv et al., 2011), it is important to note that the majority of women over age 35 give birth to healthy infants. Older mothers tend to be healthier and show lower rates of alcohol consumption and cigarette smoking than do younger mothers (Salihu, Shumpert, Slay, Kirby, & Alexander, 2003). Differences in context and behavior may compensate for some of the risks of advanced maternal age. For example, longer use of oral contraceptives is associated with a lower risk of giving birth to a child with Down syndrome (Nagy, Győrffy, Nagy, & Rigó, 2013).

Thinking in Context 3.2

1. Referring to Bronfenbrenner's bioecological model (see Chapter 1), identify factors at each bioecological level that may influence development in the womb.

2. Imagine that you are a health care provider conferring with a woman who is contemplating becoming pregnant. Give some examples of specific advice you would offer to help her promote a healthy pregnancy and baby.

BIRTH AND THE NEWBORN

At about the 166th day after conception, the placenta releases a hormone that triggers the onset of labor (Bainbridge, 2003). Hormones cause the mother's uterus to contract and relax at regular intervals, aiding delivery.

CHILDBIRTH

Childbirth, known as labor, progresses in three stages. The first stage of labor, dilation, is the longest. It typically lasts 8 to 14 hours for a woman having her first child; for later-born children, the average is 3 to 8 hours. Labor begins when the mother experiences regular uterine contractions spaced at 10- to 15-minute intervals. Initial contractions may feel like a backache or menstrual cramps, or may be extremely sharp. The amniotic sac ("water") may rupture at any time during this stage. The contractions, which gradually become stronger and closer together, cause the cervix to dilate so that the fetus's head can pass through, as shown in Figure 3.5.

The second stage of labor, delivery, begins when the cervix is fully dilated to 10 cm and the fetus's head is positioned at the opening of the cervix—known as "crowning." It ends when the baby emerges completely from the mother's body. It is during this stage that the mother typically feels an urge to push or bear down with each contraction to assist the birth process. Delivery can take from 30 minutes to an hour and a half.

THE PARTNER'S ROLE DURING PREGNANCY AND BIRTH

Pregnancy is an important event for relationships. How might it change a couple's relationship?

Watch the video at edge.sagepub.com/kuther

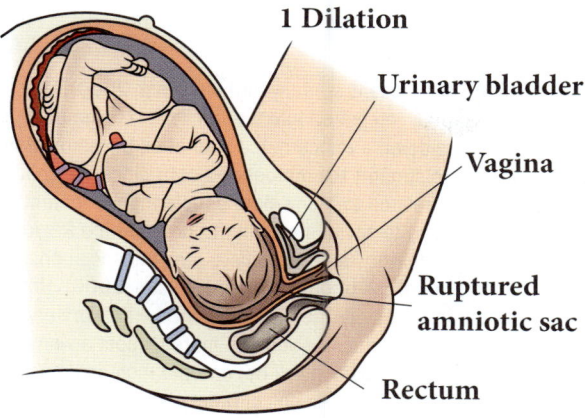

1 Dilation

Urinary bladder

Vagina

Ruptured
amniotic sac

Rectum

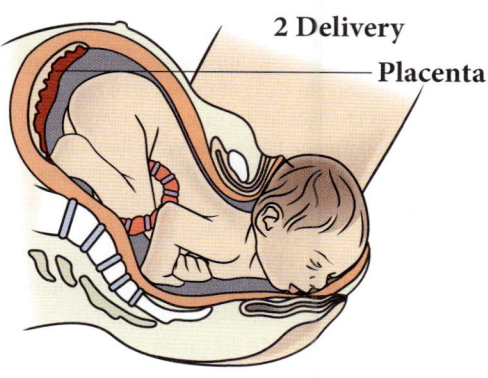

2 Delivery

Placenta

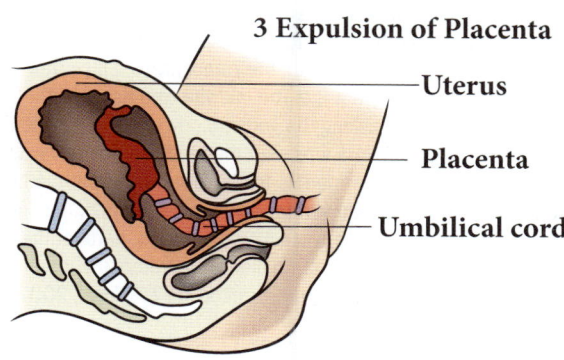

3 Expulsion of Placenta

Uterus

Placenta

Umbilical cord

In the third stage of labor, the placenta separates from the uterine wall and is expelled by uterine contractions. This typically happens about 5 to 15 minutes after the baby has emerged, and the process can take up to a half hour.

Sometimes a vaginal birth is not possible because of health or safety reasons for the mother or fetus. A **cesarean section**, or C-section, is a surgical procedure that removes the fetus from the uterus through the abdomen. About 33% of all singleton births are cesarean deliveries (Martin, Hamilton, Osterman, Curtin, & Mathews, 2013). Cesarean sections are performed when labor progresses too slowly, the fetus is in breech position (feet first) or transverse position (crosswise in the uterus), the head is too large to pass through the pelvis, or the fetus or mother is

in danger (Curtis & Schuler, 2004). Because a cesarean section is an operation, women who undergo it are at risk for infection and usually endure a longer hospital stay. Babies delivered by cesarean are exposed to more maternal medication and secrete lower levels of the stress hormones that occur with vaginal birth that are needed to facilitate respiration, enhance circulation of blood to the brain, and help the infant adapt to the world outside of the womb. Interactions between mothers and infants, however, are similar for infants delivered vaginally and by cesarean section (Durik, Hyde, & Clark, 2000).

The average newborn is about 20 inches long and weighs about 7.5 pounds. Boys tend to be slightly longer and heavier than girls. Newborns have distinctive features, including a large head (about one fourth of body length) that is often long and misshapen from passing through the birth canal. The newborn's skull bones are not yet fused— and will not be until about 18 months of age—permitting the bones to move and the head to mold to the birth canal, easing its passage. A healthy newborn is red-skinned and wrinkly at birth; skin that is bluish in color indicates that the newborn has experienced oxygen deprivation. Some babies emerge covered with lanugo, the fuzzy hair that protects the skin in the womb; for other babies, the lanugo falls off prior to birth. The newborn's body is covered with vernix caseosa, a waxy substance that protects against infection; this dries up within the first few days. Although many hospital staff wash the vernix caseosa away after birth, research suggests that it is a naturally occurring barrier to infection and should be retained at birth (Visscher et al., 2005). See Cultural Influences on Development, p. 76, for a discussion of cultural differences in childbirth.

MEDICAL AND BEHAVIORAL ASSESSMENT OF INFANTS

After birth, newborns are routinely screened with the **Apgar scale**, which provides a quick and easy overall assessment of the baby's immediate health. As shown in Table 3.2, the Apgar is composed of five subtests: appearance (color), pulse (heart rate), grimace (reflex irritability), activity (muscle tone), and respiration (breathing). The newborn is rated 0, 1, or 2 on each subscale for a maximum total score of 10. A score of 4 or lower means that the newborn is in serious condition and requires immediate medical attention. The rating is conducted twice, one minute after delivery, and again five minutes after birth; this timing ensures that hospital staff will monitor the newborn over several minutes. Over 98% of all newborns in the United States achieve a five-minute score of 7 to 10, indicating good health (Martin et al., 2013).

The **Brazelton Neonatal Behavioral Assessment Scale (NBAS)** is the most common neurobehavioral assessment administered to newborns, especially those who are judged to be at risk (Lester & Tronick, 2004). It is administered a few days after birth to assess the newborn's

CULTURAL INFLUENCES ON DEVELOPMENT

Cultural Differences in Childbirth

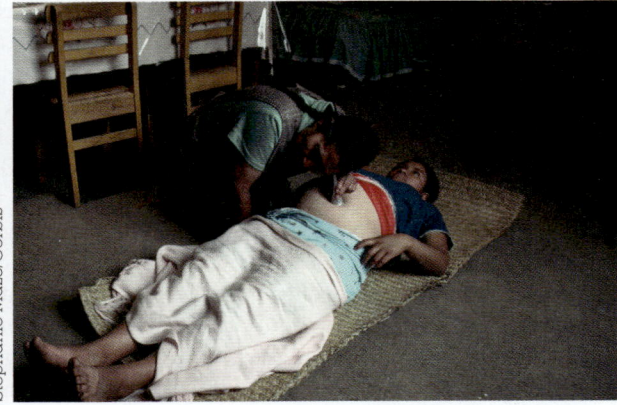

Stephanie Maze/Corbis

A midwife prepares a mother to give birth in her home. Birth practices vary by culture.

Societies vary in their customs and perceptions of childbirth, including the privacy afforded to giving birth and how newborns are integrated into the community. In the United States, birth is a private event that usually occurs in a hospital, attended by medical personnel and one or two family members. In most cases, the first-time mother has never witnessed a birth but is well educated and may have well-informed expectations. After birth, the mother and infant are often visited by family within designated hospital visiting hours; the newborn usually rooms with the mother all or part of the day.

In a small village in southern Italy, birth is a community event. It usually takes place in a hospital, attended by a midwife (Fogel, 2007; Schreiber, 1977). Just after birth, the midwife brings the mother's entire family (immediate and extended) to the mother's room, and they take turns congratulating the mother and baby, kissing them. The family provides a party including pastry and liqueurs. During labor and afterward, the mother is supported and visited by many of her friends and relatives to recognize the contribution that the mother has made to the community. The mother-in-law is an example of the social support system in place because a few days before until about one month after the birth, she brings and feeds the mother ritual foods of broth, marsala, and fresh cheeses (Fogel, 2007; Schreiber, 1977).

Other cultures see birth as a more public process. For example, the Jahara of South America give birth under a shelter in full view of everyone in the village (Fogel, 2007). On the Indonesian island of Bali, it is assumed that the husband, children, and other family will want to be present. The birth occurs in the home with the aid of a midwife and female relatives. Even when it is their first child, Balinese women know what to expect

as they have been present at many births (Diener, 2000). The baby is immediately integrated into the family and community as he or she is considered a reincarnated soul of an ancestor. Many kin are present to support the mother and baby since the child is considered to be related to many more people than its parents.

Childbirth is tied to social status in the Brong-Ahafo Region in Ghana: After a delivery, women achieve a higher social position and can then give advice to other women (Jansen, 2006). Home deliveries are highly valued. The more difficult the delivery and the less skilled assistance she receives; the more respect a woman attains, the higher her position will be; and the more influence she has on the childbirth decisions of other women, such as whether to give birth at home or in a medical setting and how to combine traditional and modern practices (Bazzano, Kirkwood, Tawiah-Agyemang, Owusu-Agyei, & Adongo, 2008).

Many cultures conduct rites that they believe protect newborns from evil and spirits. Among the Maya of the Yucatan region of Mexico, there are few changes in the expectant mother's surroundings; the Mayan woman lies in the same hammock in which she sleeps each night. The father-to-be will be present during labor and birth to take an active role but also to witness the suffering. If the child is stillborn, it is blamed on an absent father. The pregnant woman's mother is present, often in the company of other females including sisters, sisters-in-law, mothers-in-law, godmothers, and sometimes neighbors and close friends. The mother and child must remain inside the house for one week before returning to normal activity after birth because it is believed that the mother and newborn are susceptible to the influence of evil spirits from the bush (Gardiner & Kosmitzki, 2010).

A neighboring ethnic group, the Zinacanteco, place their newborns naked before a fire. The midwife who assisted the mother says prayers asking the gods to look kindly upon the infant. The infant is dressed in a long skirt made of heavy fabric extending beyond the feet; this garment is to be worn throughout the first year. The newborn is then wrapped in several layers of blankets, even covering the face, to protect against losing parts of the soul. These traditional practices are believed to protect the infant from illnesses as well as evil spirits (Brazelton, 1977; Fogel, 2007).

What Do You Think?

1. Which of these birthing customs most appeals to you? Why?

2. If you, a family member, or friend have given birth, describe the process. Where did the birth occur? Who witnessed it? What happened afterward? When did family and friends meet the baby?

---

neurological functioning, including the strength of 20 inborn reflexes, responsiveness to the physical and social environment, and changes in state. Indicators of motor organization include activity level and the ability to bring a hand to the mouth. The NBAS also assesses infants' attention and state changes, including excitability and ability to settle down after

being upset. The NBAS offers quick and early identification of infants who may have brain damage or neurological impairments. The assessment takes about 30 minutes and scores are based on an infant's best performance.

The NBAS has also been used as an intervention to help parents learn about their newborn's perceptual and

TABLE 3.2 Apgar Scale

INDICATOR	RATING (ABSENCE–PRESENCE)		
	0	1	2
Appearance (color)	Blue	Pink body, blue extremities	Pink
Pulse (heart rate)	Absent	Slow (below 100)	Rapid (over 100)
Grimace (reflex irritability)	No response	Grimace	Coughing, crying
Activity (muscle tone)	Limp	Weak and inactive	Active and strong
Respiration (breathing)	Absent	Irregular and slow	Crying, good

SOURCE: Apgar (1953).

behavioral capacities. When parents participate in their baby's NBAS screening, they learn how to interact appropriately to elicit gazes and quiet fussiness and tend to be more responsive to and involved with their infants one month later (Britt & Myers, 1994). Viewing filmed NBAS assessments and discussing the newborn's capacities with a professional also improves parent–infant interactions and sensitivity (Wendland-Carro, Piccinini, & Miller, 1999).

THE NEWBORN'S PERCEPTUAL CAPACITIES

Until recent decades, it was widely believed that the newborn was perceptually immature—blind and deaf at birth. Developmental researchers now know that the newborn is more perceptually competent than ever imagined. For example, both taste and smell are well developed at birth. Taste appears to function well before birth because research has shown that fetuses swallow sweetened amniotic fluid more quickly than bitter fluid (Sadler, 2012). Newborns can discriminate smells (Goubet et al., 2002) and calm in response

to the scent of amniotic fluid and other familiar smells (Goubet, Strasbaugh, & Chesney, 2007; Porter, Varendi, Christensson, Porter, & Winberg, 1998; Rattaz, Goubet, & Bullinger, 2005). The visual capacities of the newborn are more limited and focused primarily on the near environment. Newborn vision is blurry and best at about 18 inches away—the typical distance to a parent's face when holding the infant.

The most remarkable newborn capacities for perception and learning are auditory in nature. Pregnant women often report that they notice fetal movements in response to a loud sound like a car horn or a door slamming. The fetus responds to auditory stimulation as early as 23 to 25 weeks after conception (Hepper, 2015). By 32 to 34 weeks, the fetus responds to the mother's voice as indicated by a change in heart rate (Kisilevsky & Hains, 2011). Prior to birth, the fetus can discriminate voices and speech sounds and has auditory memory for both speech and musical sounds (Granier-Deferre, Ribeiro, Jacquet, & Bassereau, 2011). One study demonstrated that the newborn retains memory for music heard prenatally even five days after birth (James, Spencer, & Stepsis, 2002). At birth, newborns show preferences for speech sounds, their mother's voice, their native language, and even stories and music heard prenatally (Moon, Cooper, & Fifer, 1993). Moreover, from birth the newborn is an active listener, paying attention to sounds and naturally taking advantage of opportunities to learn (Philbin & Klaas, 2000; Vouloumanos, Hauser, Werker, & Martin, 2010).

NEWBORN STATES OF AROUSAL

Newborns display regular cycles of eating, elimination, and states of arousal or degrees of wakefulness. In a typical day, newborns move in and out of six infant states or levels of arousal, as shown in Table 3.3. Most newborns spend about 70% of their

TABLE 3.3 Newborn States of Arousal

STATE	DESCRIPTION	DAILY DURATION IN NEWBORNS
Regular sleep	This is being fully asleep with little or no body movement. The eyes are closed with no eye movements. The face is relaxed, and breathing is slow and regular.	8–9 hours
Irregular sleep	Facial grimaces, limb movements, occasional stirring, and eye movement behind closed lids indicate rapid eye movement (REM) sleep. Breathing is irregular.	8–9 hours
Drowsiness	Falling asleep or waking up, eyes open and close and have a glazed look. Breathing is even but faster than in regular sleep.	Varies
Quiet alertness	The eyes are open and attentive, exploring the world; the body is relatively inactive. Breathing is even.	2–3 hours
Waking activity	There are frequent bursts of uncoordinated activity. Breathing is irregular; the face may be relaxed or tense. Fussiness and crying may occur.	1–4 hours

SOURCES: Prechtl (1974); Wolff (1966).

LABOR: PREPARATION AND PROCESS

In this clip, doula Laura Erlich describes the process of labor and what women and their partners can expect.

Watch the video at edge.sagepub.com/kuther

time sleeping and wake every two to three hours. These short stretches of sleep alternate with shorter periods of wakefulness that are primarily devoted to feeding. During the first month, infants often move rapidly from one state to another, dozing off during feeding, for example. Naps are punctuated by periods of drowsiness, alert and inalert activity, and crying.

Newborn sleep cycles are brief, lasting from 45 minutes to two to three hours, but similar to those of adults in that they consist of both REM sleep, or rapid eye movement (REM) sleep, and non-REM sleep (Joseph, 2000). When a person is in REM sleep, the brain wave activity is remarkably similar to that of the waking state. Their eyes move back and forth beneath closed lids; heart rate, blood pressure and breathing are uneven; and there are slight body movements. Newborns spend about half of their sleep time in REM, but by ages 3 to 5, children spend about 15% to 20% of their sleep in REM, similar to adults (Kobayashi, Good, Mamiya, Skinner, & Garcia-Rill, 2004; Roffwarg, Muzio, & Dement, 1966).

Why do newborns spend so much time in REM sleep? REM sleep is associated with dreaming in both children and adults. Young infants appear to have a special need for REM sleep because they spend little time in the active alert state in which they get stimulation from the environment. REM is a way that the brain stimulates itself, which is important for the growth of the central nervous system. This view of REM sleep as serving a self-stimulation function is supported by findings that fetuses and preterm babies, who are even less able to take advantage of external stimulation than are newborns, spend even more time in REM sleep (DiPietro, Hodgson, Costigan, & Hilton, 1996; Sahni, Schulze, Stefanski, Myers, & Fifer, 1995). Neonates with low REM sleep activity tend to score lower on mental tests at 6 months of age (Arditi-Babchuk, Feldman, & Eidelman, 2009).

INFANTS AT RISK: LOW BIRTH WEIGHT AND SMALL-FOR-DATE BABIES

Infants who are born with low birth weight are at risk for a variety of developmental difficulties. Indeed, their very

survival is far from certain; the Centers for Disease Control and Prevention lists prematurity and low birth weight among the leading causes of infant mortality, accounting for 35% of mortality cases in infancy (Mathews & MacDorman, 2013).

There are two types of low birth weight infants: those who are **preterm**, or premature (born before their due date), and those who are **small for date**, who are full term but have experienced slow growth and are smaller than expected for their gestational age. Infants are classified as low birth weight when they weigh less than 2,500 grams (5.5 pounds) at birth; very low birth weight refers to a weight less than 1,500 grams (3.5 pounds), and extremely low birth weight refers to a weight less than 750 grams (1lb 10 oz.; Alexander & Slay, 2002). About 8% of infants born in the United States each year are low birth weight (Martin et al., 2013). Developmental outcomes vary among low birth weight infants. Infants most at risk for developmental challenges, handicaps, and difficulty surviving are those with extremely low birth weight (under 1,000 grams; Fogel, 2007). Prenatal care (see Lives in Context, p. 79) can help to prevent premature and small-for-date births.

Small-for-date babies tend to have more serious problems than preterm babies because their low birth weight is a result of stunted growth and development throughout pregnancy. Maternal illness, malnutrition, and exposure to many of the teratogens discussed earlier in this chapter can result in a baby who is small for date. Infants who are small for date show higher mortality and are more likely than preterm infants to remain small relative to other children throughout childhood, perform poorly on neurological and cognitive tests, suffer learning and behavioral problems at school, and display immature social behavior (Arcangeli, Thilaganathan, Hooper, Khan, & Bhide, 2012).

Low birth weight infants are at a disadvantage when it comes to adapting to the world outside the womb. Simply surviving is a challenge. At birth, they often experience difficulty breathing and are likely to suffer from respiratory distress syndrome, in which the newborn breathes irregularly and at times may stop breathing. Low birth

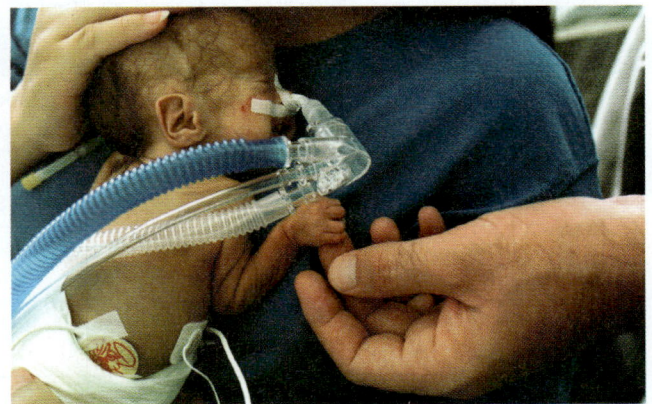

Low birthweight infants require extensive care. They are at risk for poor developmental outcomes and even death.

LIVES IN CONTEXT

Prenatal Care

Prenatal care, a set of services provided to improve pregnancy outcomes and engage the expectant mother, family members, and friends in health care decisions, is critical for the health of both mother and infant (Daniels, Noe, & Mayberry, 2006). About 26% of pregnant women in the United States do not seek prenatal care until after the first trimester; 6% seek prenatal care at the end of pregnancy or not at all (U.S. Department of Health and Human Services, 2014). Inadequate prenatal care is a risk factor for low birth weight and preterm births as well as infant mortality during the first year (Daniels et al., 2006; Handler, Rosenberg, Raube, & Lyons, 2003). In addition, use of prenatal care predicts pediatric care throughout childhood, which serves as a foundation for health and development throughout the lifespan (Handler et al., 2003).

Why do women delay or avoid seeking prenatal care? A common reason is the lack of health insurance (Maupin et al., 2004). Although government-sponsored health care is available for the poorest mothers, many low-income mothers do not qualify for care or lack information on how to take advantage of care that may be available. Other barriers to seeking prenatal care include difficulty in finding a doctor, lack of transportation, demands of caring for young children, ambivalence about the pregnancy, depression, lack of education about the importance of prenatal care, lack of social support, poor prior experiences in the health care system, and family crises (Daniels et al., 2006; Lu & Halfon, 2003).

Moreover, there are significant ethnic and socioeconomic disparities in prenatal care. Inadequate prenatal care is most likely among Native American women (23%), followed by African American (19%), Latina (17%), Asian American (14%), and white American women (13%; U.S. Department of Health and Human Services, 2013). African American women, in particular, are far more likely than all other groups to give birth to low birth weight or preterm infants, as shown in Figure 3.6 (U.S. Department of Health and Human Services, 2014). Ethnic differences are thought to be largely influenced by socioeconomic factors, as the ethnic groups least likely to seek early prenatal care are also the most economically disadvantaged members of society.

Although prenatal care predicts birth outcomes, cultural factors appear to protect some women and infants from the negative consequences of inadequate prenatal care. A phenomenon termed the *Latina paradox* (McGlade, Saha, & Dahlstrom, 2004) found that Latina mothers, despite low rates of prenatal care, experience

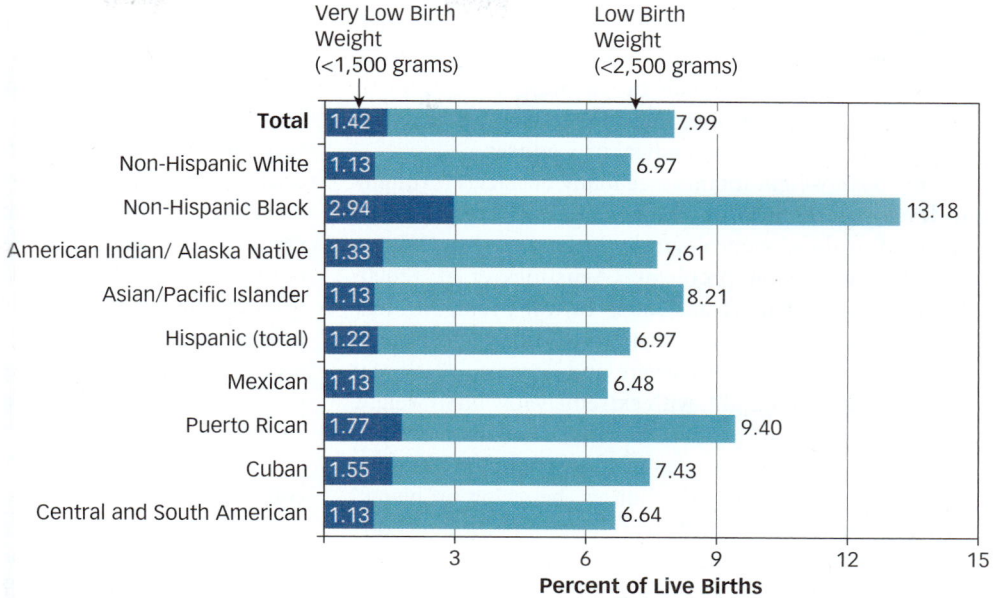

FIGURE 3.6: Very Low and Low Birth Weight Rates, by Maternal Race/Ethnicity, 2012

Very Low Birth Weight (<1,500 grams)   Low Birth Weight (<2,500 grams)

	Very Low Birth Weight	Low Birth Weight
Total	1.42	7.99
Non-Hispanic White	1.13	6.97
Non-Hispanic Black	2.94	13.18
American Indian/ Alaska Native	1.33	7.61
Asian/Pacific Islander	1.13	8.21
Hispanic (total)	1.22	6.97
Mexican	1.13	6.48
Puerto Rican	1.77	9.40
Cuban	1.55	7.43
Central and South American	1.13	6.64

Percent of Live Births

SOURCE: U.S. Department of Health and Human Services (2014).

low birth weight and mortality rates below national averages. These favorable birth outcomes are striking because of the strong and consistent association between socioeconomic status and birth outcomes as well as because Latinas as a group are among the most socioeconomically disadvantaged ethnic populations in the United States (McGlade et al., 2004).

Several factors are thought to account for the Latina paradox, including strong cultural support for maternity, healthy traditional dietary practices, and the norm of selfless devotion to the maternal role (*marianismo*; Fracasso & Busch-Rossnagel, 1992; McGlade et al., 2004). These protective cultural factors interact with strong social support networks and informal systems of health care among Latina women, in which women tend to take responsibility for the health needs of those beyond their nuclear households. Mothers benefit from the support of other family members such as sisters, aunts, and other extended family. In this way, knowledge about health is passed down from generation to generation. There is a strong tradition of women helping other women in the community, and warm interpersonal relationships, known as *personalismo*, are highly valued (Fracasso & Busch-Rossnagel, 1992; McGlade et al., 2004). These cultural factors are thought to underlie the positive birth outcomes seen in Latina women; however, these factors appear to erode as Latino women acculturate to American society and the birth advantage declines in subsequent American-born generations.

What Do You Think?

1. In your view, what are the most important contextual factors that contribute to prenatal care?

2. What is the Latina paradox with regard to prenatal care? Why do you think it declines as women acculturate to American society?

weight infants have difficulty maintaining homeostasis, a balance in their biological functioning. Their survival depends on care in neonatal hospital units, where they are confined in isolettes that separate them from the world, regulating their body temperature, aiding their breathing with the use of respirators, and protecting them from infection. Many low birth weight infants cannot yet suck from a bottle so are fed intravenously. The first few weeks and even months of life can be isolating for low birth weight infants as they live in isolettes, are fed through tubes, and undergo many medical procedures.

Low birth weight infants face many obstacles throughout development, including higher rates of cerebral palsy, seizure disorders, neurological difficulties, respiratory problems, and vision problems (Agustines et al., 2000; Aylwrad, 2005; Chan et al., 2000; Taylor, Klein, Minich, & Hack, 2001). The deficits that low birth weight infants endure range from mild to severe and correspond closely to the infant's birth weight, with extremely low birth weight infants suffering the greatest deficits. Low birth weight infants experience higher rates of sensory, motor, and language problems, learning disabilities, behavior problems, deficits in social skills, and peer rejection through adolescence (Brown, Kilbride, Turnbull, & Lemanek, 2003; Gray, Indurkhya, & McCormick, 2004; Seitz, 2006; Vohr et al., 2000; Yau et al., 2013). Very low birth weight infants are likely to experience frequent illnesses and as children have deficits in cognitive skills, academic achievement, and school performance (Talge et al., 2010; Taylor et al., 2001). Extremely low birth weight infants are at risk for particularly poor outcomes as they are less likely to catch up with peers over time (Taylor et al., 2001).

Not only are low birth weight infants at a physical disadvantage but they often begin life at an emotional disadvantage because they are at risk for experiencing difficulties in their relationships with parents. Parents of low birth weight infants tend to experience additional stress and emotional trauma because their infants are in the hospital for a great deal of time (Conner & Nelson, 1999; Singer et al., 1999). Although the causes of premature and small-for-date birth are varied and in many cases unknown, parents may feel anxiety or guilt about the baby's condition, wondering if they have "done something wrong" to cause the low birth weight. Furthermore, parenting a low birth weight infant is stressful even in the best of circumstances (Taylor et al., 2001). Premature infants tend to be easily overwhelmed by stimulation and smile less and fuss more, making parents feel unrewarded for their efforts. Low birth weight infants are slow to initiate social interactions and often do not attend to parents; they look away, fuss, or otherwise resist parental attempts to obtain their attention (Eckerman, Hsu, Molitor, Leung, & Goldstein, 1999). Because low birth weight infants often do not respond to attempts to solicit interaction, they can be frustrating to interact with and are at risk for less secure attachment to their parents (Mangelsdorf et al., 1996). Research also indicates that they experience

higher rates of child abuse (Brockington, 1996). Generally, however, parents of low birth weight infants do not differ from those of normal birth weight infants in terms of their enthusiasm and their efforts to provide the best care possible (Saigal, Hoult, Streiner, Stoskopf, & Rosenbaum, 2000).

Though low birth weight infants pose challenges to parenting, if parents have stable life circumstances and social supports, they can overcome the difficulties of caring for their babies and help them catch up in development by middle childhood (Liaw & Brooks-Gunn, 1993). For example, one study of very low birth weight infants showed that females displayed catch-up growth; by the time they were 20 years old, they were no different in size from normal birth weight infants. However, very low birth weight males remained shorter and smaller than normal birth weight males at age 20 (Hack et al., 2003). Other research suggests that the difference in intelligence between infants with low and normal birth weight grows smaller with age: At age 5, low birth weight children scored 7 IQ points lower than normal birth weight children and at age 11, it was 4 points lower (Elgen, Sommerfelt, & Ellertsen, 2003).

The long-term outcomes of low birth weight vary considerably and depend on the environment in which the children are raised. When mothers have knowledge about child development and how to foster healthy development, are involved with their children, and create a stimulating home environment, low birth weight infants tend to have good long-term outcomes (Benasich & Brooks-Gunn, 1996; Jones, Rowe, & Becker, 2009). However, low birth weight children raised in less stable and economically disadvantaged families tend to remain smaller in stature, experience more emotional problems, and show more long-term deficits in intelligence and academic performance than do those raised in more advantaged homes (Taylor et al., 2001). If parents have opportunities to engage in caregiving in the hospital setting, learn about the special needs of their infant, and understand what to expect, they can be very supportive and help their low birth weight children overcome many of the obstacles to their development (Brooks-Gunn, Klebanov, Liaw, & Spiker, 1993; McCormick, McCarton, Tonascia, & Brooks-Gunn, 1993). Synchrony in parent–infant interactions predicts positive neurodevelopmental outcomes (Treyvaud et al., 2009, 2011). Therefore, interventions to promote the development of low birth weight children often emphasize helping parents learn coping strategies for interacting with their low birth weight infants and managing parental stress (Lau & Morse, 2003; Xu & Filler, 2005). Interventions focused on teaching parents how to massage and touch their infants in therapeutic ways as well as increase skin-to-skin contact with their infants are associated with better cognitive and neurodevelopmental outcomes at age 2 (Procianoy, Mendes, & Silveira, 2010). One intervention common in developing countries where mothers may not have access to hospitals is kangaroo care. The low birth weight or premature infant is placed vertically against the parent's chest, under the shirt, providing skin-to-skin contact (Charpak et al., 2005). As the parent goes about his or her activities, the infant remains warm and close, hears her voice and heartbeat, smells her, and feels constant skin-to-skin contact. Kangaroo care is so effective that the majority of hospitals in the United States offer kangaroo care to preterm infants. Babies who receive early and consistent kangaroo care grow more quickly, sleep better, and show more cognitive gains throughout the first year of life (Jefferies, 2012).

In summary, an amazing amount of growth and development takes place between conception and birth. In nine short months, the zygote transforms into a newborn. Although there are a variety of risks to health development within the womb, most newborns are healthy. Infants are born with a surprising array of competencies, such as well-developed hearing, taste, and smell. Additional physical, cognitive, and psychosocial capacities develop shortly after birth, as we will see in upcoming chapters.

Thinking in Context 3.3

Parents' decisions about childbirth reflect their knowledge about birth options as well as cultural values.

1. Referring to Bronfenbrenner's bioecological model (see Chapter 1), identify factors at each bioecological level that may influence childbirth. For example, how might neighborhood factors influence birth options? Culture?

2. Thinking of how society and medical science have changed in recent decades, in what ways might recent cohorts of parents differ from prior cohorts? What implications might these differences hold for prenatal development and childbirth?

Apply Your Knowledge

Dr. Preemie conducted a research study of the prevalence and correlates of drug use in college students. Because of the sensitive nature of the research topic, Dr. Preemie promised her participants confidentiality. Each college student who participated completed a set of surveys and an interview about his or her lifestyle and drug use habits. One participant, Carrie, revealed that she engages in moderate to heavy drug use (i.e., drinks two to four alcoholic beverages each day and smokes marijuana several times per week). During the interview, Carrie mentioned that she's feeling nauseous. Concerned, Dr. Preemie asked, "Do you want to stop the interview and go to the campus medical center?" "No," Carrie replied, "It's just morning sickness. I'm pregnant." "Oh," said Dr. Preemie, who nodded and continued with the interview.

Afterward, in her office, Dr. Preemie was torn and wondered to herself, "I'm worried about Carrie. Drugs and alcohol disrupt prenatal development, but I promised confidentiality. I can't tell anyone about this! Should I say something to Carrie? I'm

supposed to be nonjudgmental! Intervening might keep other students from participating in my research, for fear that I'd break my promises. I don't know what to do."

1. What are the effects of teratogens, like drugs and alcohol, on prenatal development?

2. Describe the course of prenatal development. How do the effects of exposure to teratogens change during prenatal development?

3. Consider Dr. Preemie's dueling obligations. As a researcher, is she responsible to Carrie as a participant in her study who signed an informed consent form? Is Dr. Preemie responsible to the developing fetus? Why or why not? Do Dr. Preemie's actions have any ramifications for the other participants in her study? How might these responsibilities conflict?

4. What should Dr. Preemie do?

Chapter Summary

3.1 Describe the process of conception, identifying the roles of female and male.

Conception occurs in the fallopian tube. The temperature gradient in the female reproductive system guides sperm toward the ovum while the sperm track the heat of an expectant ovum. In the presence of sperm, the ovum exudes a chemical signal to draw the sperm closer. In turn, in the presence of an ovum, sperm become hyperactivated, they swim even more vigorously, and the sperm's head releases enzymes to help it penetrate the protective layers of the ovum. As soon as one sperm penetrates the ovum, a chemical reaction makes the ovum's membrane impermeable to other sperm. The sperm's tail falls off, and the genetic contents merge with that of the ovum. At the moment of conception the zygote is formed.

3.2 Describe the three periods of prenatal development.

During the germinal period, the zygote begins cell division and travels down the fallopian tube toward the uterus. During the embryonic period from weeks 2 to 8, the most rapid developments of the prenatal period take place. From 9 weeks until birth, the fetus grows rapidly, and the organs become more complex and begin to function.

3.3 List six principles of teratology, and explain how they can be used to predict prenatal outcomes.

Teratogens include diseases, drugs, and other agents that influence the prenatal environment to disrupt development. Generally, the effects of exposure to teratogens on prenatal development vary depending on the stage of prenatal development and dose. There are individual differences in effects, different teratogens can cause the same birth defect, a variety of birth defects can result from the same teratogen, and some teratogens have subtle effects that result in developmental delays that are not obvious at birth or not visible until many years later.

3.4 Identify drugs, illness, and environmental factors that act as teratogens.

There are many types of teratogens. Both prescription and nonprescription drugs can potentially harm the developing fetus. Prescription drugs that can act as teratogens include antibiotics, certain hormones, anticoagulants, anticonvulsants, some acne drugs, and thalidomide. Nonprescription drugs, such as diet pills and cold medicine, can also cause harm, but we know little about the teratogenic effect of many OTC drugs. Maternal illnesses such as rubella, chicken pox, and some STIs can also act as teratogens. Cigarette smoking and nicotine, as well as other recreational drugs, such as cocaine and heroin,

harm the fetus. Prenatal development can also be harmed by factors in the environment, including chemicals, radiation, and extremes of heat and humidity.

3.5 Define *fetal alcohol spectrum disorders*, and differentiate between fetal alcohol syndrome (FAS) and fetal alcohol effects.

Fetal alcohol spectrum disorders refer to the continuum of effects of exposure to alcohol, which vary with the timing and amount of exposure. At the extreme end of the spectrum is FAS, a cluster of defects appearing after heavy prenatal exposure to alcohol that include a distinct pattern of facial characteristics, pre- and postnatal growth deficiencies, and deficits in intellectual development as well as the combined abilities to plan, focus attention, problem solve, and use goal directed behavior. Pregnant women who consume alcohol in moderation place their fetuses at risk because some children are born displaying some but not all of the problems of FAS; they are said to show fetal alcohol effects.

3.6 Discuss the contributions of maternal characteristics and behaviors on prenatal development.

The mother's diet plays a major role in the development and health of the fetus. For example, inadequate consumption of folic acid by the mother can result in the formation of neural tube defects such as spina bifida and anencephaly. Exposure to chronic and severe stress during pregnancy poses risks including low birth weight, premature birth, and a weakened immune system. Women who give birth over the age of 35 are at greater risk for pregnancy and birth complications, more vulnerable to pregnancy-related illnesses, and are more likely to give birth to a child with Down syndrome. Although risks for complications rise, the majority of women over age 35 give birth to healthy infants.

3.7 Explain the process of childbirth.

At about the 166th day after conception, the placenta releases a hormone that triggers the onset of labor. The first stage of labor begins when the mother experiences regular uterine contractions that cause the cervix to dilate so that the fetus's head can pass through. The second stage of labor, delivery, begins when the fetus's head is positioned at the opening of the cervix and ends when the baby emerges completely from the mother's body. The placenta is expelled by uterine contractions during the third stage of labor.

3.8 Identify and explain the neonate's physical capacities.

Taste and smell are well developed at birth. Newborn vision is blurry. The most well developed sense is audition. The fetus responds to auditory stimulation as early as 23 to 25 weeks after conception. Newborns display regular cycles of eating, elimination, and states of arousal or degrees of wakefulness, spending about 50% of their sleep time in REM, thought to permit the brain to stimulate itself.

3.9 Discuss the challenges low birth weight and small-for-date infants face as well as influences on infant adjustment.

There are two types of low birth weight infants, those who are preterm and those who are small for date, who are full term but have experienced slow growth and are smaller than expected for their gestational age. At birth, low birth weight infants often experience difficulty breathing and are likely to suffer from respiratory distress syndrome. Low birth weight infants experience higher rates of sensory, motor, and language problems, learning disabilities, behavior problems, and deficits in social skills into adolescence. The long-term outcomes of low birth weight vary considerably and depend on the environment in which the children are raised.

Key Terms

age of viability   65

anencephaly   73

Apgar scale   75

blastocyst   63

Brazelton Neonatal Behavioral Assessment Scale (NBAS)   75

cesarean section   75

ectoderm   63

embryo   63

embryonic disk   63

endoderm   63

fetal alcohol spectrum disorders   68

fetal alcohol syndrome (FAS)   68

fetus   64

implantation   63

indifferent gonad   63

lanugo   65

low birth weight   68

mesoderm   63

neonate   60

neural tube   63

ovum   62

placenta   63

preterm   78

small for date   78

spina bifida   73

stem cells   63

teratogen   66

teratology   66

vernix caseosa   65

PART II

Infancy and Toddlerhood

The most dramatic developments in the lifespan occur in infancy. In addition to tripling their weight during the first year of life, infants progress through an orderly series of motor milestones that transforms them from newborns unable to lift their heads to babies able to roll over, sit up, crawl, and, at about a year of age, walk.

As infants practice their motor skills, they explore their environment, build their understanding of phenomena, and adapt to the world around them. Cognitive changes are supported by brain development. A multitude of new connections among brain cells are created and pruned in response to experience. Naturally primed to learn language, infants discriminate speech sounds from birth and progress steadily from gurgles and coos, to speech-like babbling, to first words.

Warm, sensitive, and responsive interactions with caregivers foster close and secure attachment bonds. Caregivers help infants learn to understand and regulate their emotions. In turn, infants influence their caregivers by smiling, reaching, and crawling to them. Infants' growing ability to express their thoughts and emotions advances parent-child communication and aids in sustaining a secure emotional base that supports their exploration of the world and their physical, cognitive, and socioemotional development.

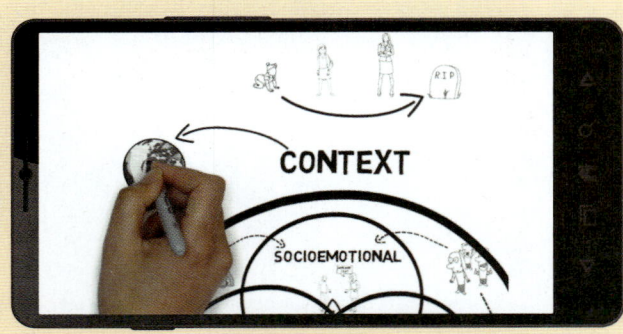

Watch at
edge.sagepub.com/kuther

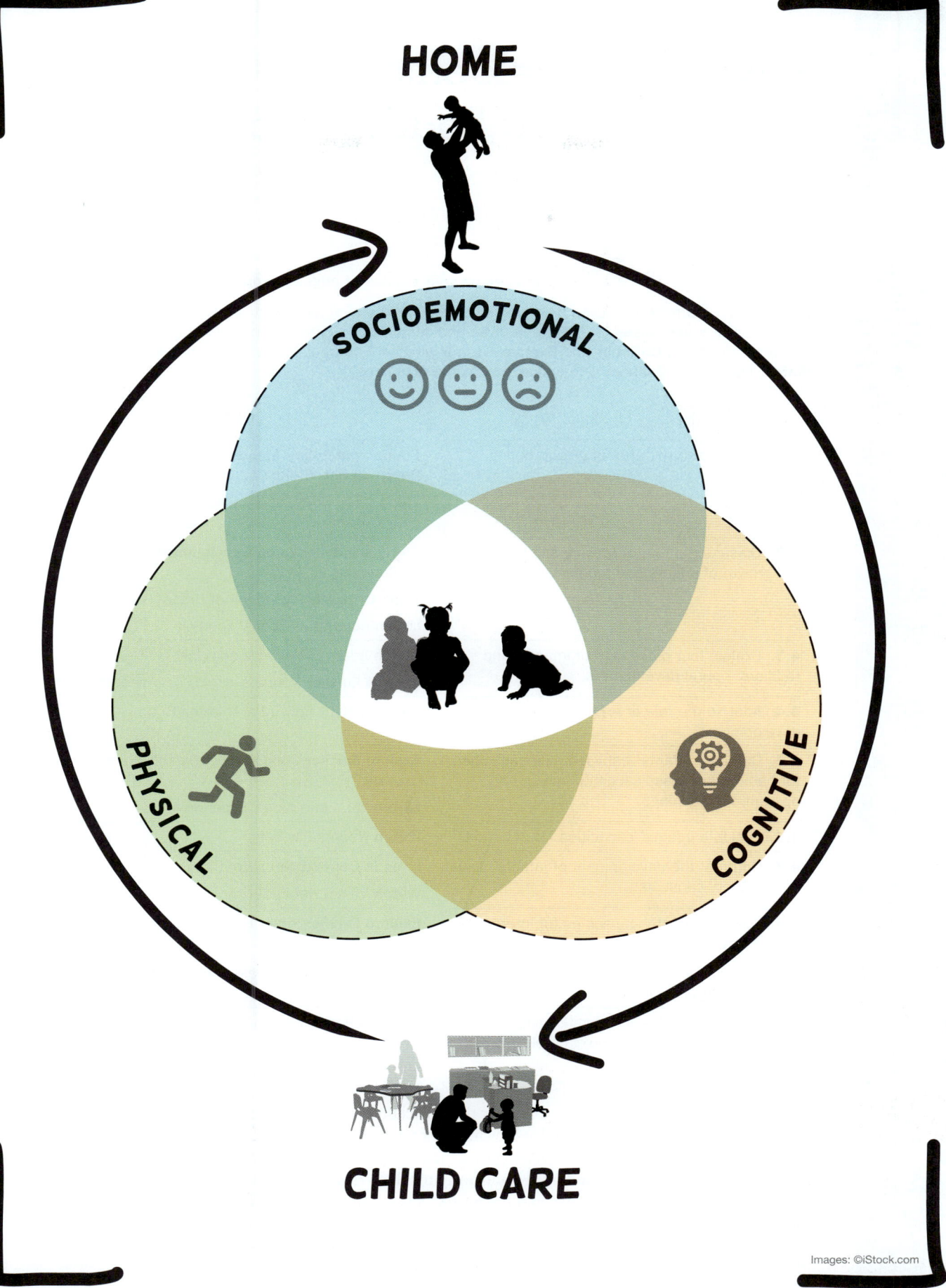

HOME

SOCIOEMOTIONAL

PHYSICAL

COGNITIVE

CHILD CARE

Images: ©iStock.com

CHAPTER 4

Physical Development in Infancy and Toddlerhood

SSAGE edge™
Get the edge on your studies at edge.sagepub.com/kuther.

Master these learning objectives using key study tools in the chapter and at SAGE edge. Access original SAGE **Video Cases** to explore the lives and contexts of individuals in every stage of development, **Think Critically** and **Explore Further** with SAGE journal and reference articles, and **Watch**, **Listen**, and **Connect** with online multimedia resources.

LEARNING OBJECTIVES	KEY STUDY TOOLS
4.1. Identify two patterns of growth during infancy.	**Ethical and Policy Applications of Lifespan Development** Childhood Vaccination (p. 89)
	Video Case Body Proportions in Infancy and Early Childhood
4.2. Discuss the role of feeding and nutrition in the growth of infants and toddlers.	**Cultural Influences on Development** Co-Sleeping (p. 91)
	Think Critically Promotion of Breast-Feeding
	Listen Benefits of Breast-Feeding
4.3. Explain four processes of infants' and toddlers' neural development.	**Watch** Infant Brain Development
	Explore Further Neuropsychological Assessment
4.4. Analyze the role of experience in neural development.	**Connect** Baby Edward's Amazing Brain
4.5. Compare infants' early learning capacities for habituation, classical conditioning, and operant conditioning.	**Explore Further** Conditioning: Classical and Operant
	Watch The Little Albert Experiment
4.6. Evaluate infants' capacities for imitation.	**Watch** Neonate Imitation
4.7. Contrast the development of infants' visual and auditory capacities.	**Lives in Context** Neonatal Circumcision (p. 102)
	Watch Visual Habituation
4.8. Discuss infants' capacities for intermodal perception.	**Explore Further** Infant Perception
4.9. Summarize milestones in infant and toddler motor development.	**Video Case** Motor Development in Infancy
4.10. Analyze the roles of maturation and contextual factors in infant and toddler motor development.	**Connect** Perceptual and Motor Development

"You're such a big girl!" the pediatric nurse exclaimed as she weighed baby Regina. Regina's mother marveled at how much her daughter had grown during the first six months of her life—she had more than doubled her weight. Over the past six months, Regina has transformed from a newborn unable to raise her head into a baby who can sit up on her own. Her mother told the nurse, "She seems to like spending time on all fours. Maybe she's practicing and getting ready to crawl." The nurse smiled and said, "Start thinking about babyproofing your home because Regina will be crawling before you know it!" In the next few months, Regina will crawl, pull herself up to stand, and eventually

walk. Babies grow and change very quickly. In this chapter, we explore the physical changes that occur in a child's first two years of life. These first years are collectively called the developmental stage of infancy and toddlerhood; the term *toddler* refers to toddling, the unsteady gait of babies who are just learning to walk. During this stage, infants and toddlers experience advances in growth, perceptual capacities, and motor skills that enable them to interact with their world and learn in new ways.

BODY GROWTH AND NUTRITION IN INFANTS AND TODDLERS

Perhaps the most obvious change that infants undergo during the first year of life is very rapid growth. Growth during the prenatal period and infancy proceeds in particular patterns, which are known as cephalocaudal and proximodistal. **Cephalocaudal development** refers to the principle that growth proceeds from the head downward. The head and upper regions of the body develop before the lower regions. For example, recall the fetus's disproportionately large head. During prenatal development, the head grows before the other body parts. Even at birth, the newborn's head is about one fourth the total body length, as shown in Figure 4.1. As the lower parts of the body develop, the head becomes more proportionate to the body. By 3 years of age, the child is less top-heavy. **Proximodistal development** refers to the principle that growth and development proceed from the center of the body outward. During prenatal development, the internal organs develop before the arms and legs. After birth, the trunk grows before the limbs and the limbs before the hands and feet.

FIGURE 4.1: Body Proportions Throughout Life

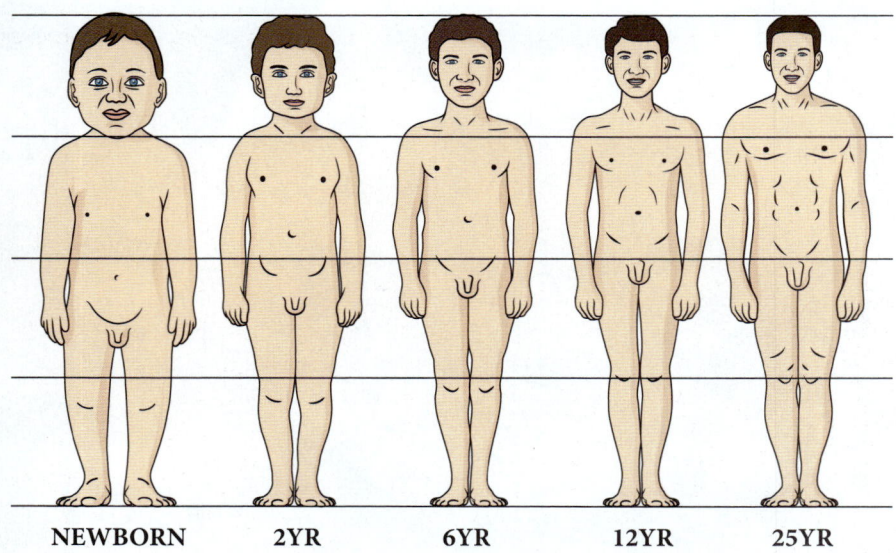

NEWBORN   2YR   6YR   12YR   25YR

SOURCE: Huelke, D. M. (1998).

BODY PROPORTIONS IN INFANCY AND EARLY CHILDHOOD

Watch 13-month-old London, 3-year-old Ella, and 4-year-old Abigail as they demonstrate changing body proportions from infancy to early childhood.

Watch the video at edge.sagepub.com/kuther

GROWTH NORMS

It is easy to observe that infants grow substantially larger and heavier over time—but there are many individual differences in growth. How can parents and caregivers tell if a child's growth is normal? By compiling information about the height and weight of large samples of children from diverse populations, researchers have determined **growth norms**. Growth norms are expectations for typical gains and variations in height and weight for children based on their chronological age and ethnic background. Genetic and environmental factors can cause some children to grow more quickly than others and fall outside of the norm.

In the first few days after birth, newborns shed excess fluid and typically lose 5% to 10% of their body weight. After this initial loss, however, infants gain weight quickly. Infants typically double their birth weight at about 5 months of age and triple it by 12 months. Most toddlers gain 5 or 6 pounds during the second year of life and another 4 to 5 pounds during the third year so that the average 3-year-old weighs about 31 pounds (Kuczmarski et al., 2000).

Gains in height of 10 to 12 inches can be expected over the first year of life, making the average 1-year-old child about 30 inches tall. Most children grow about 5 inches during their second year of life and 3 to 4 inches during their third. To parents, growth may appear slow and steady, but research has shown that it often occurs in spurts in which an infant or toddler can grow up to one quarter of an inch overnight (Lampl, Johnson, Frongillo,

ETHICAL AND POLICY APPLICATIONS OF LIFESPAN DEVELOPMENT

Childhood Vaccination

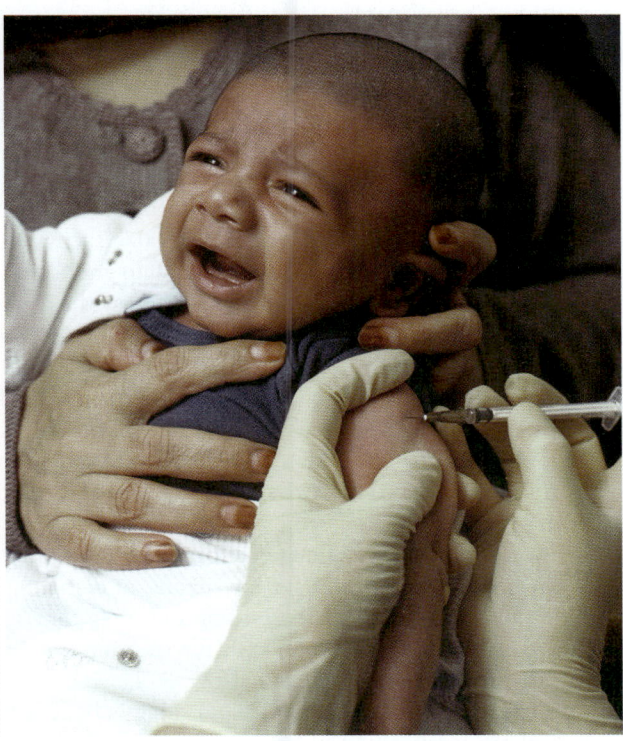

Mark Thomas / Science Source

Vaccines protect children and communities from diseases that once spread quickly and killed thousands of people.

Over the past fifty years, childhood diseases such as measles, mumps, and whooping cough have declined dramatically because of widespread immunization of infants and young children. A vaccine is a small dose of inactive virus that is injected into the body to stimulate the production of antibodies to guard against the disease. Vaccines control infectious diseases that once spread quickly and killed thousands of people.

Vaccines are administered early in life because many preventable diseases are more common in infants and young children. Vaccinations protect the child as well as those in the child's community because an immunized person is less susceptible to a disease and therefore also less likely to transmit it to others. Most public schools require that children be fully immunized before enrollment, a requirement that has increased vaccination rates and prevented many diseases (Salmon et al., 2005).

The Centers for Disease Control and Prevention (CDC) recommends that children be vaccinated against most vaccine-preventable disease by the time they are 2 years of age. Vaccination rates have increased markedly over the past 15 years. The proportion of children aged 19 to 35 months receiving the recommended series of vaccines increased from 69% to 83%

between 1994 and 2004. However, the rate has stalled since, standing at 82% in 2011 (Child Trends, 2014).

Why is the immunization rate relatively low? One reason is that many children in the United States do not have access to the health care they need. There are no ethnic differences in childhood vaccination rates, but children in families with incomes below the poverty level are less likely than are those with families with incomes at or above the poverty level to receive the combined series vaccination. Many parents are unaware that children from low-income families who do not have medical insurance can receive vaccinations through the federal Vaccines for Children Program, begun in 1994 (CDC, 1994).

Another, more troubling, reason for the stalled vaccination rate is that, based on the common misconception that vaccines are linked with autism, some parents refuse to have their children vaccinated (Gust et al., 2004). Extensive research indicates that there is no association between vaccination and autism (Gerber & Offit, 2009; Taylor, Swerdfeger, & Eslick, 2014). In fact, a U.S. court ruled against parents who sought damages from vaccine manufacturers on the basis that vaccination does not cause autism (McNeil, 2009).

One reason for the misconception is that children tend to receive vaccines at the age when some chronic illnesses and developmental disorders—such as autism—tend to emerge, but this correlation is not indicative of a cause-and-effect relationship. (Recall from Chapter 1 that correlational research documents phenomena that occur together but cannot demonstrate causation.) While specific causes of autism spectrum disorders have yet to be fully identified, we do know that autism has a strong genetic component and is also associated with both maternal and paternal age (Grether, Anderson, Croen, Smith, & Windham, 2009; Idring et al., 2014; Waltes et al., 2014).

Even when children receive the full schedule of vaccinations, many do not receive them on the timetable recommended by the National Vaccine Advisory Committee (Luman, Barker, McCauley, & Drews-Botsch, 2005). Vaccine timeliness is important because the efficacy of early and late vaccination is not always known and may vary by disease (Luman et al., 2005). *When* a child receives a vaccination may be just as important as *whether* the child receives it in promoting disease resistance.

What Do You Think?

1. What do you think about the use of vaccines?

2. In your view, what is the most important reason in favor of vaccinations?

3. Why do you think some parents object to their use? How might you respond to their objections?

& Frongillo, 2001; Lampl, Veldhuis, & Johnson, 1992). At about 2 years of age, both girls and boys have reached one half of their adult height (Huelke, 1998). During their first three years, infants and toddlers grow faster than they ever will again.

Growth is largely maturational, but it can be influenced by health and environmental factors. Today's children grow taller and faster than ever before, and the average adult is taller today than a century ago (Cole, 2003). Improved sanitation, nutrition, and access to medical care have contributed to an increase in children's growth over the past century in the United States and other industrialized countries. One significant aspect of today's medical care is the availability of **vaccinations** to prevent infectious diseases that were once an inevitable part of childhood; see Ethical and Policy Applications of Lifespan Development (p. 89).

BREAST-FEEDING

One of the best ways of meeting infants' complex nutritional needs is through breast-feeding. Recommended by the U.S. Department of Health and Human Services (2011), breast-feeding has increased in popularity in the United States from about one half of mothers ever breast-feeding in 1990 to over three quarters in 2010 (Child Trends, 2013; Li, Zhao, Mokdad, & Barker, 2003). About 49% of women continue to breast-feed after 6 months and 27% at 12 months. Breast-feeding practices vary by ethnicity, education, socioeconomic status, and maternal age (Hauck, Fenwick, Dhaliwal, & Butt, 2011).

Breast-feeding is associated with many health benefits for infants and mothers, and provides opportunities for infant–mother bonding.

Countries where women have paid maternity leave for part or all of their infants' first year of life, such as Denmark, Norway, Sweden, and Australia, show very high breast-feeding rates of 94% and more (Hauck et al., 2011; Imdad, Yakoob, & Bhutta, 2011; Roelants, Hauspie, & Hoppenbrouwers, 2010). In the United States and the United Kingdom, the lowest rates of breast-feeding are among low-income mothers, mothers who are young, and mothers with low levels of education. Researchers have observed that the employment settings of low-income mothers may offer few resources to support breast-feeding, such as private places for women to use breast pumps (Griffiths & Tate, 2007; Racine, Frick, Guthrie, & Strobino, 2009). In contrast to industrialized countries, in developing countries women with low educational levels and in the poorest social classes are usually more likely to breast-feed their children. In these countries, educated women of higher income brackets tend to shun breast-feeding; it is looked upon as an option primarily for low-income women who are unable to afford formula (Berra et al., 2003; Imdad et al., 2011; Rasheed, Frongillo, Devine, Alam, & Rasmussen, 2009).

Breast-feeding offers benefits for mothers and infants. Mothers who breast-feed have lower rates of diabetes, cardiovascular disease, and depression, and after they reach menopause they are at lower risk for ovarian and breast cancer and bone fractures (Godfrey & Lawrence, 2010; Saunders-Goldson & Edwards, 2004). Infants benefit from the unique composition of breast milk. A mother's milk is tailored to her infant and has the right amount of fat, sugar, water, and protein needed for the baby's growth and development. Most babies find it easier to digest breast milk than formula. In addition, breast milk contains immunizing agents that protect the infant against infections (Hetzner, Razza, Malone, & Brooks-Gunn, 2009; Saunders-Goldson & Edwards, 2004). Breast-feeding is associated with a reduced risk of sudden infant death syndrome (SIDS), allergies, and gastrointestinal symptoms as well as with fewer visits to physicians (Schulze & Carlisle, 2010; Stein & Kuhn, 2009). Breast-feeding for more than six months is associated with reduced risk of obesity and childhood cancer, especially lymphomas (American Academy of Pediatrics [AAP] Work Group on Breastfeeding, 1997; Savino, Fissore, Liguori, & Oggero, 2009; Schulze & Carlisle, 2010).

The effects of breast-feeding on cognitive development are less clear. In some studies, infants breast-fed for more than six months perform better on tests of cognitive ability as compared with their formula-fed counterparts (Kramer et al., 2008; Sloan, Stewart, & Dunne, 2010). Others suggest that the differences in test scores are influenced by the characteristics of mothers who breast-feed, such as higher levels of education and socioeconomic status (Der, Batty, & Deary, 2006; Schulze & Carlisle, 2010; Tanaka, Kon, Ohkawa, Yoshikawa, & Shimizu, 2009). Yet studies that control for maternal factors still support a cognitive advantage to breast-fed infants (Sloan et al., 2010). The cognitive advantages may persist throughout childhood into adolescence. The duration of breast-feeding,

Co-Sleeping

Jennie Hart/Alamy

While sharing a bedroom can enhance the infant–parent bond and make nighttime feedings easier, infants are safest in their own bassinets, such as this one, which is adapted to promote safe parent–infant contact.

The practice of co-sleeping, the infant sharing a bed with the mother or with both parents, is common in many countries, yet controversial in others. In Japan, China, Kenya, Bangladesh, and the Mayan peninsula of Mexico, co-sleeping in infancy and early childhood is the norm and is believed to enhance the child's sense of security (Morelli, Rogoff, Oppenheim, & Goldsmith, 1992; Super & Harkness, 1982; Xiao-na, Hui-shan, Li-jin, & Xi-cheng, 2010).

In Latin America and Asia, infants are not expected to go to bed and sleep alone at a regular time each night; instead, they are held until they fall asleep and then are placed in the parental bed (Lozoff, Wolf, & Davis, 1984). In contrast, in many industrialized countries, such as the United States and the United Kingdom, newborns are placed to sleep in their own bassinets, whether in their parents' room or in a separate nursery (Ball, Hooker, & Kelly, 1999; McKenna & Volpe, 2007). Parents' decisions of whether to co-sleep are influenced by their own values and beliefs, which are often shaped by the context in which they live.

Pediatricians in Western nations tend to advise separate sleeping arrangements for parents and infants. The AAP and the U.K. Department of Health have declared sharing a bed with an infant to be an unsafe practice; instead, they advise having infants sleep in a crib in the parents' room (AAP, 2005; U.K. Department

of Health, 2005). Despite these warnings, co-sleeping has become more common among Western families. When co-sleeping occurs, it is usually initiated by the mother, especially if she breast-feeds (Ball, Hooker, & Kelly, 2000; McCoy et al., 2004).

Proponents of co-sleeping argue that it best meets the physiological, psychological and developmental needs of human newborns (McKenna, 2001; McKenna & Mosko, 1993; Trevathan & McKenna, 1994; Willinger, Ko, Hoffman, Kessler, & Corwin, 2003). Infants who sleep with their mothers synchronize their sleep patterns with her, permitting more awakenings for breast-feeding yet lengthening the total time that infants sleep (Gettler & McKenna, 2011; Goldberg & Keller, 2007; Mosko, Richard, & McKenna, 1997). Both mothers and babies benefit from skin-to-skin contact, as it enhances breast milk production, stabilizes infants' heart rate, reduces apnea (gaps in the infant's breathing), increases the prevalence and duration of breast-feeding, reduces crying, and is associated with more positive mother–infant interactions (McKenna & Volpe, 2007; Taylor, Donovan, & Leavitt, 2008). Fathers report that they find co-sleeping rewarding rather than an intrusion on the marital bed (Ball et al., 2000; McCoy et al., 2004).

Some pediatricians caution that co-sleeping may become a habit that is difficult to break and that it is associated with sleep problems, like nighttime waking and bedtime protests when the child is moved to his or her own bed (Lozoff et al., 1984; McKenna & Mosko, 1993; Schachter, Fuchs, Bijur, & Stone, 1989). Most importantly, opponents of co-sleeping point to increased risk of accidental suffocation and an increased risk of SIDS, especially among mothers who smoke (Brenner et al., 2003; Mitchell, 2009). Yet other studies suggest that co-sleeping is a protective factor against SIDS (McKenna, 2001). Many experts believe that while the use of comforters and pillows is hazardous, co-sleeping can be safe if appropriate precautions are taken, such as using light bed coverings and a firm mattress (McKenna, 2001).

What Do You Think?

1. **Should infants and parents co-sleep?**

2. **In your view, what are the advantages and disadvantages of co-sleeping?**

3. **How might safety concerns be addressed?**

specifically longer than six months, is associated with higher scores in language ability at ages 5 and 10 (Whitehouse, Robinson, Li, & Oddy, 2011) and intelligence in adolescence (Isaacs et al., 2010). However, it is important to recognize that differences in cognitive development between breast-fed and formula-fed infants are small (Jenkins & Foster, 2014; Schulze & Carlisle, 2010).

Despite these benefits, many mothers do not breast-feed, either by choice or by necessity. In this case, infant formula is a safe and healthy alternative to breast milk.

Formula production is monitored by the U.S. Food and Drug Administration. Most formulas are made from cow's milk, but soy-based alternatives exist for infants with allergies or parents who choose to raise their child vegetarian. Infants subsist on milk or formula alone for the first few months of life, after which other foods begin to be integrated into their diet.

The typical newborn sleeps about 18 hours each day, waking every 2 hours to eat, and babies continue to require night-time feedings until they are 4 or 5 months old (Sola, Rogido, &

Partridge, 2002). Every 2 hours, newborns transition through several different states of sleep and wakefulness, from alert wakefulness, to fussing, to light sleep, deep sleep, and back to wakefulness, waking to eat. Infants' sleep patterns change over the first months of life, so that by 8 weeks of age they begin showing signs of day–night sleep rhythms.

Culture plays an important role in shaping how parents manage these frequent feedings. For example, parents in the United States typically look forward to the time when their infant will sleep through the night, viewing the newborn's unpredictable sleep pattern as something to fix (Harkness, 1998). In contrast, many European parents view newborn sleep as part of normal development and do not intervene to shape newborn sleep cycles. Parental behavior, in turn, can have an influence on babies' sleep patterns. Infants are more likely to continue waking overnight when their parents play with them during nighttime feedings, as stimulation and attention may reinforce nighttime waking (Bornstein, 2002). Cultures also have different beliefs and practices around sleeping arrangements for infants, toddlers, and older children—including co-sleeping—see Cultural Influences on Development, p. 91.

SOLID FOOD

Somewhere between 4 and 6 months of age, infants eat their first solid food—although "solid food" is actually a misnomer; the first food consumed is usually iron-fortified baby cereal mixed with breast milk or formula to make a very thin gruel.

FIGURE 4.2: Weight Norms for Infants and Toddlers

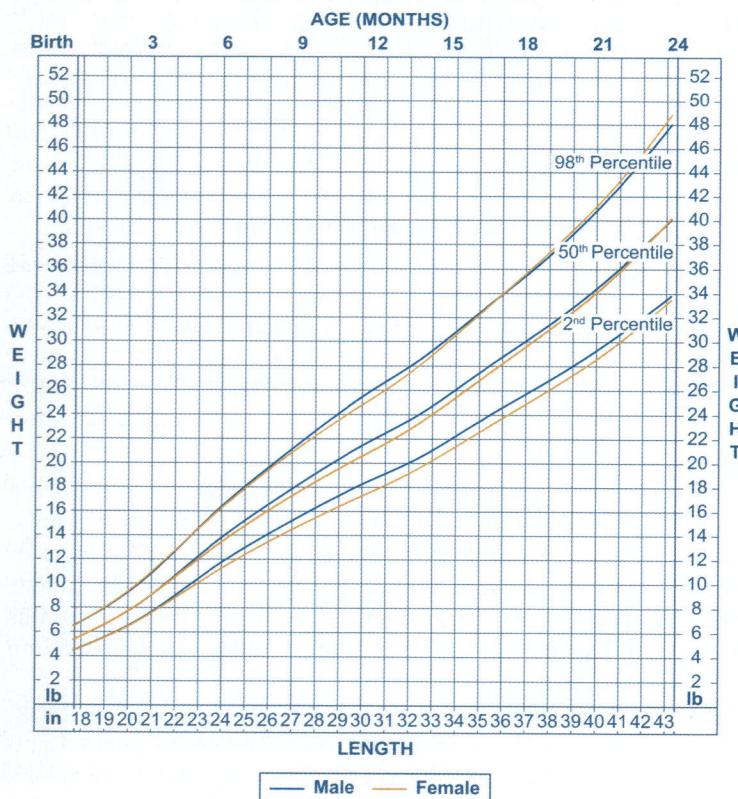

As babies get older, the amount of milk is reduced to make porridge of a thicker consistency. Now infants' diets begin to include other pureed foods, such as vegetables and fruits. The addition of pureed meats comes later. Infants do not necessarily like these new flavors and textures—many foods must be introduced over a dozen times before an infant will accept them.

As infants grow to become toddlers, their appetites decrease. They begin to feed themselves, which means meals may take more time; self-feeding might also reduce toddlers' food consumption. Toddlers' appetites tend to be less consistent than those of infants, but as long as they are offered a variety of foods and they continue to gain weight, their eating habits should not be a concern.

Although babies need adequate calories, fats, and proteins in order to grow, some babies gain more weight, even appearing chubby. Parents who feed their infants nutritious foods need not worry about increases in weight and should not restrict infants' caloric intake without consulting a pediatrician. Most chubby babies become thinner toddlers and young children as they learn to crawl, walk, run, and become more active. However, many infants are not served nutritious foods. One recent study of 4- to 24-month-olds found that many were served fattening "junk" foods such as French fries, pizza, candy, and soda (Siega-Riz et al., 2010). Many consumed 20% to 30% more calories than they needed, and up to one third consumed no vegetables regularly. Rapid, excessive weight gain in infancy is associated with childhood obesity (Botton, Heude, Maccario, Ducimetière, & Charles, 2008; Chomtho et al., 2008). Pediatricians suggest that parents consider their infants' growth in light of norms to determine whether intervention is needed. As shown in Figure 4.2, only about 5% of 12-month-old boys and girls weigh 26 pounds or more (World Health Organization, 2009).

MALNUTRITION

For many children, however, receiving adequate calories and nutrition is a challenge. Over one quarter of the world's children under age 5 are moderately or severely underweight. About one third of 3- to 5-year-old children in developing countries show growth stunting (de Onis, Blössner, & Borghi, 2012). Malnutrition has devastating effects on physical growth. A diet that is chronically insufficient in protein and calories commonly results in **marasmus**, a wasting disease in which the body's fat and muscle are depleted. Growth stops, the body wastes away, the skin becomes wrinkly and aged looking, the abdomen shrinks, and the body takes on a hollow appearance. Another malnutritive disease is **kwashiorkor**, found in children who experience a sudden deprivation of food and calories. It is characterized by lethargy; wrinkled skin; and a bloating and swelling of the stomach, face, legs and arms. Because the vital organs of the body take all of the available

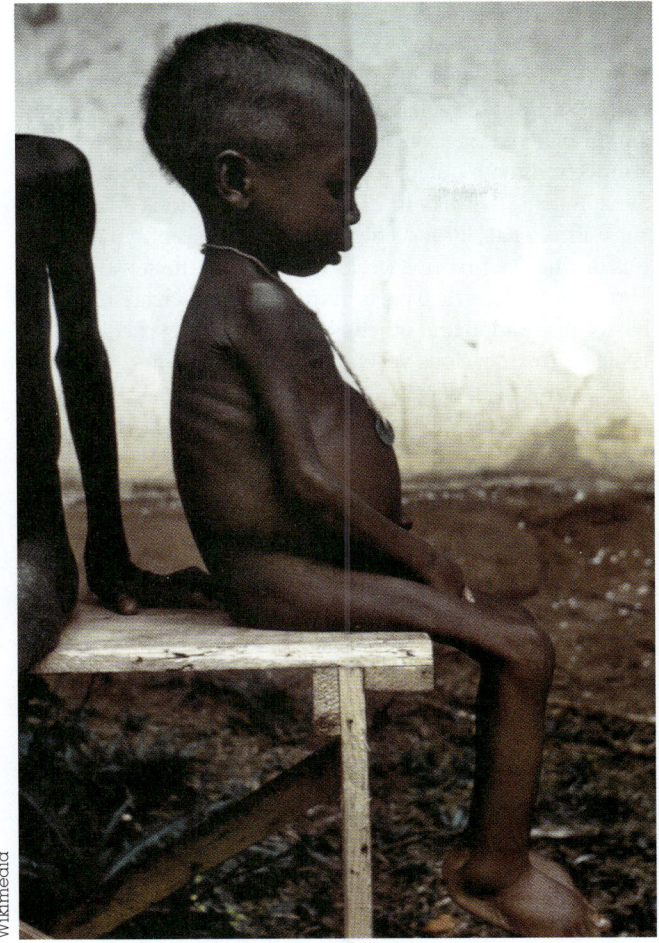
Wikimedia

This child suffers from an extreme nutritional deficiency, kwashiorkor. Early treatment can reduce the deficits associated with kwashiorkor, but most children will not reach their full potential for height and growth.

nutrients, the other parts of the body deteriorate and the hair becomes thin, brittle, and colorless.

Children who are malnourished in infancy tend to show impaired learning, concentration, and language skills throughout childhood and adolescence. For example, malnutrition in the first year of life is associated with depression in 11- to 17-year-olds (Galler et al., 2010). Some of the damage caused by malnutrition can be reversed, and motor and mental development enhanced, if nutrition is reinstated early, but long-term difficulties with attention and learning often remain (UNICEF, 2009; Victora, 2009). It is believed that growth stunting is largely irreversible after 2 years of age (UNICEF, 2009). Humanitarian relief programs often provide infants and young children with fortified foods as dietary supplements, but some researchers argue that such programs offer minimal benefits for children because they are short term and are unable to correct the underlying problems (Pérez-Expósito & Klein, 2009).

Though malnutrition is common in developing countries, it is also found in some of the world's wealthiest

countries. In 2012, 15% of American households experienced *food insecurity,* meaning that they lacked consistent access to food to support an active healthy lifestyle for all family members (Coleman-Jensen, Nord, & Singh, 2013). The most common nutrients missing from infants and toddlers' diets are iron, zinc, and calcium. Meat is an important source of iron and zinc. Dairy foods are a source of zinc and calcium, and broccoli is also rich in calcium. It is estimated that one third of toddlers fail to consume enough calcium. Few U.S. children who are malnourished will display marasmus or kwashiorkor, but their growth and cognitive development will be affected nonetheless (Gehri, Settler, & Di Paolo, 2006).

FAILURE TO THRIVE

Individual differences are the norm when it comes to growth; children grow at different rates. However, some children show significantly slower growth than other children their age. Some infants display **failure to thrive**, a condition in which their weight is less than 80% of the norm for their age without any medical reason, such as illness (Dorota, 2004). The most common cause of failure to thrive is inadequate nutrition and eating too few calories (Stephens, Gentry, Michener, & Kendall, 2008), which may be influenced by a small appetite and fussy eating. Sometimes psychosocial and contextual factors contribute to failure to thrive, such as insecure attachment to caregivers, parents who lack knowledge about parenting and child development, emotional neglect and abuse, and other stressful contexts such as living in poverty (Batchelor, 2008; Dorota, 2004).

Children with failure to thrive may be irritable and emotional, easily fatigued, lacking in age-appropriate social responses such as smiling and eye contact, and delayed in motor development. Untreated failure to thrive is accompanied by delays in cognitive, verbal, and behavioral skills that make it difficult for the child to achieve success in school, home, and peer environments (Benoit, 2009; Dykman, Casey, Ackerman, McPherson, & McPherson, 2001).

Pediatricians typically treat failure to thrive by providing the child with the nutrients necessary to grow normally. They may also work with other health professionals such as psychologists and social workers to address underlying medical and psychosocial conditions, such as abuse or neglect (Benoit, 2009). Although nutritional interventions can alleviate many of the effects of malnutrition on physical development, some children might show long-term cognitive and psychosocial deficits (Black, Dubowitz, Krishnakumar, & Starr, 2007).

We have seen that growth proceeds rapidly over the first two years of life. Consistent patterns of growth are evident and most infants' growth falls within the norm. Body growth is largely maturationally driven, but parental choices and other environmental factors influence infant growth rates. Whereas breast-feeding and introducing healthy solid foods can aid infants' growth, malnutrition and a diet of sweet and fatty foods can hinder infants' development with effects that can persist throughout childhood.

1. Why are marasmus and kwashiorkor uncommon in the United States? What contextual factors place children in developing nations at risk for these impairments?

2. What are the pros and cons of public education programs that aim to increase parents' knowledge about health topics such as breast-feeding or vaccines? If you were assigned to design such a program, what would you need to know to begin your design? How would you go about gathering information and ideas?

BRAIN DEVELOPMENT DURING INFANCY AND TODDLERHOOD

All of the developments in infants' physical and mental capacities are influenced by the dramatic changes that occur in the brain. At birth, the brain is about 25% of its adult weight and it grows rapidly throughout infancy, reaching 80% of its adult weight by 2 years of age (Nelson & Luciana, 2008). As the brain develops, it becomes larger and more complex.

PROCESSES OF NEURAL DEVELOPMENT

Just like every other part of the human body, the brain is made up of billions of cells. Brain cells are called **neurons**, and they are specialized to communicate with one another to make it possible for people to sense the world, think, move their body, and carry out their lives (Price, Jarman, Mason, & Kind, 2011; Stiles & Jernigan, 2010). Brain development begins well before birth. **Neurogenesis**, the creation of new neurons, begins in the embryo's neural tube. We are born with more than 100 billion neurons, more than we will ever need—and more than we will ever have at any other time in our lives. However, as some of our neurons die out and new ones are formed, neurogenesis continues throughout life, though at a much slower pace than during prenatal development (Stiles & Jernigan, 2010). As the brain develops, new neurons migrate along a network of **glial cells**, a second type of brain cell that outnumbers neurons 10 to 1 (Jessen, 2004; Nelson & Bloom, 1997). Glial cells nourish neurons and move throughout the brain to provide a physical structure to the brain (Klämbt, 2009). As shown in Figure 4.4, neurons travel along glial cells to the location of the brain where they will function (Nelson & Bloom, 1997; Zhang et al., 2010), such as the outer layer of the brain, known as the **cortex**, and glial cells instruct neurons to form connections with other neurons (Ullian, Sapperstein, Christopherson, & Barres, 2001).

At birth, the neural networks of axons and dendrites are simple, with few connections, or **synapses**, between neurons (DiPietro, 2000). Early in infancy, major growth takes place. Neurons and glial cells enlarge. As the dendrites grow and branch out, neurons form synapses and thereby increase connections with others, a process called **synaptogenesis**. Synaptogenesis peaks in different brain regions at different ages (Price et al., 2011). The most active areas of synaptogenesis during the first five weeks of life are in the sensorimotor cortex and subcortical parts of the brain, which are responsible for respiration and other essential survival processes. The visual cortex develops very rapidly between 3 and 4 months and reaches peak density by 12 months of age. The prefrontal cortex—responsible for planning and higher thinking—develops more slowly (Nelson & Luciana, 2008).

Throughout the lifespan, stimulation and experience are key components needed to maximize neural connections and brain development. In response to exposure to stimulation from the outside world, the number of synapses initially rises meteorically in the first year of life and the dendrites increase 500% by age 2 (Monk, Webb, & Nelson, 2001). By age 3, children have more synapses than at any other point in life, with at least 50% more synapses than in the adult brain (DiPietro, 2000; Monk et al., 2001). This explosion in connections in the early years of life has been called *transient exuberance* because the brain makes more connections than it needs, in preparation to receive any and all conceivable kinds of stimulation (Nowakowski, 1987). Those connections that are used become stronger and more efficient, while those unused eventually shrink, atrophy, and disappear. This loss of unused neural connections is a process called **synaptic pruning**. The first three years of life have been identified as a particularly important time for neural development because stimulation during infancy and early childhood influence the number of connections among neurons and, by extension, the child's cognitive potential (DiPietro, 2000).

Stimulation and experience strongly influence brain development, but maturational processes are also important. In a process called **myelination**, which begins during the

FIGURE 4.3: Image of Neurons

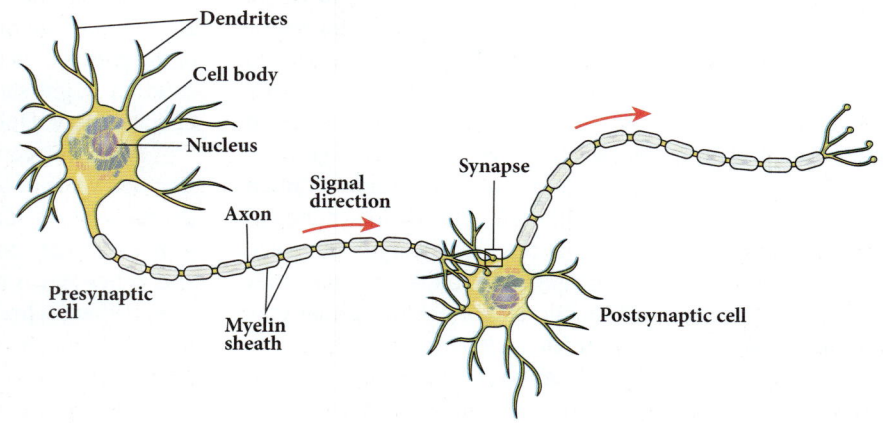

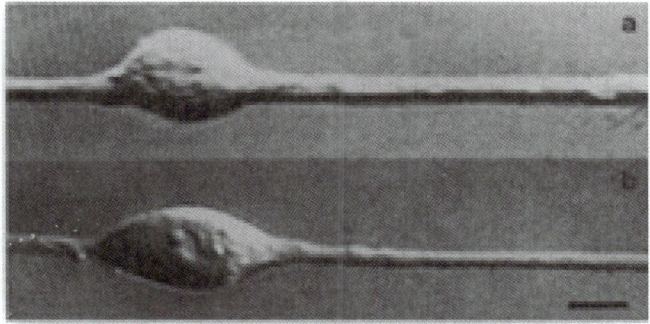

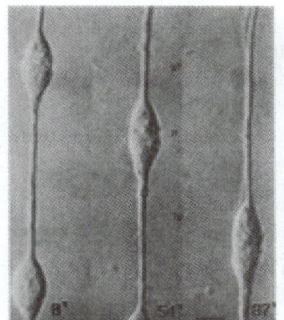

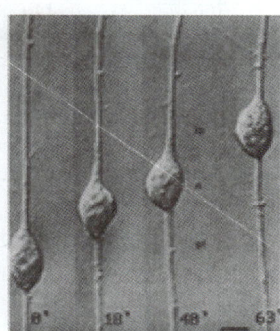

Neurons migrate along thin strands of glial cells.

SOURCE: Gasser and Hatten (1990).

first two years of life, glial cells produce and coat the axons of neurons with a fatty substance called myelin (Jessen, 2004; Nelson & Luciana, 2008; Stiles & Jernigan, 2010; Ullian et al., 2001). Myelination contributes to advances in neural communication because axons coated with myelin transmit neural impulses more quickly than unmyelinated axons. With increases in myelination, infants and children process information more quickly. Myelination proceeds most rapidly from birth to age 4 and continues through adolescence into early adulthood (Fischer & Rose, 1995; Jessen, 2004).

EXPERIENCE AND BRAIN DEVELOPMENT

Much of what we know about brain development comes from studying animals. Animals raised in stimulating environments with many toys and companions to play with develop brains that are heavier and have more synapses than do those who grow up in standard laboratory conditions (Greenough & Black, 1992; Grossman, Churchill, McKinney, Kodish, & Otte, 2003; Rosenzweig, 1984). Likewise, when animals raised in stimulating environments are moved to unstimulating standard laboratory conditions, their brains lose neural connections (Grossman et al., 2003; Thompson, 1993). This is true for humans, too. Infants who are understimulated, such as those who experience child maltreatment or who are reared in deprivation, such as in poor understaffed orphanages in foreign countries, also show cognitive and perceptual deficits (Twardosz & Lutzker, 2009; Wilson, 2003). Experience influences the physical structure of our brains throughout life. Though infancy is a particularly important time for the formation and strengthening of synapses, experience shapes brain structure at all ages of life even into adulthood (Rosenzweig, 2002; Zeanah, 2009).

The powerful role that experience plays in brain development can be categorized into two types. First, the brain depends on experiencing certain basic events and stimuli at key points in time in order to develop normally (Fox, Levitt, & Nelson, 2010); this is referred to as **experience-expectant brain development**. Experience-expectant brain development is demonstrated in sensory deprivation research with animals. If animals are blindfolded and prevented from using

their visual system for the first several weeks after birth, they never acquire normal vision because the connections among the neurons that transmit sensory information from the eyes to the visual cortex fail to develop and decay (DiPietro, 2000; Neville & Bavelier, 2001). If only one eye is prevented from seeing, the animal will be able to see well with one eye but will not develop binocular vision, the ability to focus two eyes together on a single object.

Similarly, human infants born with a congenital cataract in one eye (an opaque clouding that blocks light from reaching the retina) will lose the capacity to process visual stimuli in the affected eye if they do not receive treatment. Even with treatment, subtle differences in facial processing may remain (Fox et al., 2010). Brain organization depends on experiencing certain ordinary events, such as opportunities to hear language, see the world, touch objects, and explore the environment (Stiles & Jernigan, 2010). All infants around the world need these basic experiences in order to develop normally.

A second type of development, **experience-dependent brain development**, refers to the growth that occurs in response to learning experiences (Greenough & Black, 1992). Experiences such as learning to stack blocks or crawl on a slippery wood floor are unique to individual infants, and they influence what particular brain areas and functions are developed and reinforced. Experience-dependent development is the result of lifelong experiences that vary by individual based on contextual and cultural circumstances (Stiles & Jernigan, 2010). Exposure to enriching experiences, such as interactive play with toy cars and other objects that move; hands-on play with blocks, balls, and cups; and stimulating face-to-face play can all enhance children's development (Fox et al., 2010). Experience-expectant abilities may change and develop throughout life based on an individual's experiences (Nelson & Luciana, 2008).

Brain development is a multifaceted process that is not is a result of maturational or environmental input alone. Brains do not develop normally in the absence of a basic genetic code, nor in the absence of essential environmental input. At all points in development, intrinsic and environmental factors interact to support the increasingly complex and elaborate structures and functions of the brain.

EARLY LEARNING CAPACITIES

Can newborns learn? If we define *learning* as changing behavior in response to experience, certainly: Animals and even insects learn. Yet infants were once believed to be born incapable of sensing and understanding the physical world around them. Most new parents will quickly tell you that this is far from the truth. At birth, and even before, neonates can perceive their physical world and have powerful capacities for learning about it.

HABITUATION

Less than 1 day old, cradled next to his mother in the hospital maternity center, Tommy is already displaying the earliest form of learning: He no longer cries each time he hears the loud beep made by the machine that reads his mother's blood pressure. This type of learning is called **habituation**; it occurs when repeated exposure to a stimulus results in the gradual decline in the intensity, frequency, or duration of a response (see Figure 4.5). All animals and humans are programmed to learn. Even before birth, humans demonstrate habituation, as early as 22 to 24 weeks' gestation (Hepper, 2015). For example, 27- to 36-week-old fetuses demonstrate habituation to vibration as well as auditory stimuli, such as the sound of a tone. Initially, the fetus moves in response to the vibration, suggesting interest in a novel stimulus, but after repeated stimulation the fetus no longer responds to the stimulus, indicating that it has habituated to it (Madison, Madison, & Adubato, 1986; McCorry & Hepper, 2007; Muenssinger et al., 2013). Not only can the fetus habituate to stimuli but it can recall a stimulus, as measured by habituation, for at least 24 hours (van Heteren, Boekkooi, Jongsma, & Nijhuis, 2000).

Habituation improves with development. For example, the performance of fetuses on habituation tasks improves with gestational age (James, 2010; McCorry & Hepper, 2007). After birth, habituation is often measured by changes in an infant's heart rate and in attention, or looking at a stimulus (Colombo, 2010; Domsch, 2010). Younger infants require more time to habituate than older infants (Kavšek & Bornstein, 2010; Krafchuk, Tronick, & Clifton,

FIGURE 4.5: Habituation

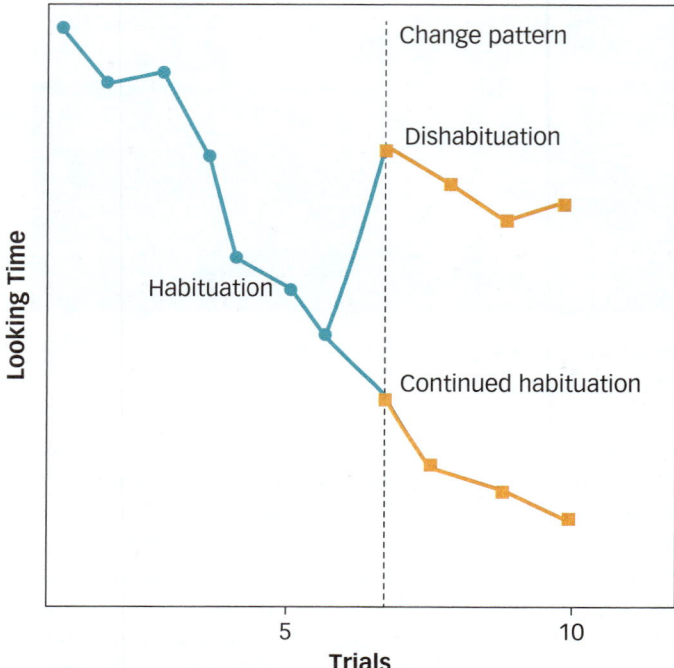

Looking time declines with each trial as the infant habituates to the pattern. Dishabituation, renewed interest, signifies that the infant detects a change in stimulus pattern.

SOURCE: Visual development by Marcela Salamanca and Donald Kline, University of Calgary (http://psych.ucalgary.ca/PACE/VA-Lab/).

1983; Rovee-Collier, 1999). Babies younger than 4 months require more exposure to a stimulus to habituate, but 5- to 12-month-old babies habituate quickly—even after just a few seconds of sustained attention—and in some cases they can recall the stimulus for weeks, such as recalling faces that they have encountered for brief periods of time (Fagan, 1984; Richards, 1997).

Neural development, specifically development of the prefrontal cortex, is thought to underlie age-related gains in habituation skill (Nakano, Watanabe, Homae, & Taga, 2009). As the brain matures, infants process information more quickly and learn more about stimuli in fewer exposures (DiPietro, 2000; Richards, 1997). Fetuses with more mature nervous systems require fewer trials to habituate than do those with less well developed nervous systems, even at the same gestational age (Morokuma et al., 2004). Fetal habituation predicts measures of information processing ability at 6 months of age (Gaultney & Gingras, 2005). Younger infants and those with low birth weight require more time to habituate than do older and more fully developed infants (Kavšek & Bornstein, 2010; Krafchuk et al., 1983; Rovee-Collier, 1987).

There are also individual differences in habituation among healthy, developmentally normal infants. Some habituate quickly and recall what they have learned for a long time. Other infants require many more exposures to habituate and quickly forget what they have learned. The speed at which infants habituate is associated with cognitive development when they grow older. Infants who habituate quickly during the first six to eight months of life tend to show more advanced capacities to learn and use language during the second year of life (Tamis-LeMonda, Song, & Bornstein, 1989). Rapid habituation is also associated with higher scores on intelligence tests in childhood (McCall & Carrigher, 1993; Rose & Feldman, 1995). The prolem-solving skills measured by intelligence tests tap information processing skills such as attention, processing speed, and memory—all of which influence the rate of habituation (McCall, 1994).

Innate learning capacities permit young infants to adapt quickly to the world, a skill essential for survival. Researchers use these capacities to study infant **perception** and cognition (Aslin, 2014). For example, to examine whether an infant can discriminate between two stimuli, a researcher presents one until the infant habituates to it. Then a second stimulus is presented. If *dishabituation*, or the recovery of attention, occurs, it indicates that the infant detects that the second stimulus is different from the first. If the infant does not react to the new stimulus by showing dishabituation, it is assumed that the infant does not perceive the difference between the two stimuli. The habituation method is very useful in studying infant perception and cognition, and underlies many of the findings discussed later in this chapter.

CLASSICAL CONDITIONING

In addition to their capacity to learn by habituation, infants are born with a second powerful tool for learning. They can learn through association. Classical conditioning entails making an association between a neutral stimulus and an unconditioned stimulus that triggers an innate reaction. Eventually the neutral stimulus (now conditioned stimulus) produces the same response as the unconditioned stimulus.

Newborns demonstrate classical conditioning. For example, when stroking the forehead was paired with tasting sugar water, 2-hour-old infants were conditioned to suck in response to having their heads stroked (Blass, Ganchrow, & Steiner, 1984). Similarly, Lipsitt and Kaye (1964) paired a tone with the presentation of a nipple to 2- and 3-day-old infants. Soon, the infants began to make sucking movements at the sound of the tone. Even premature infants can demonstrate associative learning, though at slower rates than full-term infants (Herbert, Eckerman, Goldstein, & Stanton, 2004). Research with chimpanzee fetuses has shown that they display classical conditioning before birth (Kawai, 2010). It is likely that the human fetus can as well. Although classical conditioning is innate, neurological damage can hinder infants' abilities to learn by association. Infants with fetal alcohol syndrome (FAS) require much more time than other infants to learn to associate **reflexes** such as eye blinking with external stimuli, such as sounds (Jacobson et al., 2008).

Classical conditioning is successful in newborns only for biological reflexes, such as sucking, and it requires repeated exposures because newborns process information slowly (Little, Lipsitt, & Rovee-Collier, 1984). As infants grow older, classical conditioning occurs more quickly and to a broader range of stimuli. For example, in a classic study, Watson and Raynor (1920) paired a white rat with a loud banging noise to evoke fear in an 11-month-old boy known as Little Albert. Soon Albert demonstrated fear in response to seeing the rat, indicating that emotional responses can be classically conditioned. Our capacities to learn through classical conditioning are evident at birth—and persist throughout life.

OPERANT CONDITIONING

At birth, babies are attuned to the environment and can learn from it. Infants learn to engage in behaviors based on their consequences, whether they are followed by reinforcement or punishment; this is known as operant conditioning. Behaviors increase when they are followed by reinforcement and decrease when they are followed by punishment. For example, newborns will change their rate of sucking on a pacifier, increasing or decreasing the rate of sucking, in order to hear a tape recording of their mother's voice, a reinforcer (Moon, Cooper, & Fifer, 1993). Other research shows that newborns will change their rate of sucking to see visual designs or hear human voices that they find pleasing (Floccia, Christophe, & Bertoncini, 1997). We are born with the ability to learn through operant conditioning—premature infants and even third trimester fetuses can be operantly conditioned (Dziewolska & Cautilli, 2006; Thoman & Ingersoll, 1993). For example, a 35-week-old fetus will change its rate of kicking in response to hearing the father talk against the mother's abdomen (Dziewolska & Cautilli, 2006).

As infants develop, they process information more quickly and require fewer trials pairing behavior and consequence to demonstrate operant conditioning. For example, it requires about 200 trials for 2-day-old infants to learn to turn their heads in response to a nippleful of milk, but 3-month-old infants require about 40 trials, and 5-month-olds require less than 30 trials (Papousek, 1967). Infants' early capacities for operant conditioning imply that they are active and responsive to their environments and adapt their behavior from birth.

IMITATION

Toddler Tula puts a bowl on her head and pats it just as she watched her older sister do yesterday. Imitation is an important way in which children and adults learn. Can young infants imitate others? Believe it or not, yes. Newborns have a primitive ability to learn through imitation. In a classic study (see Figure 4.6), 2-day-old infants mimicked adult facial expressions including sticking out the tongue, opening and closing the mouth, and sticking out the lower lip (Meltzoff & Moore, 1977; Nagy, 2006). The prevalence and function of neonate imitation is debated (Oostenbroek, Slaughter, Nielsen, & Suddendorf, 2013). Some studies have failed to replicate this ability and have suggested that tongue protruding is a general

FIGURE 4.6: Newborn Imitating Facial Expression

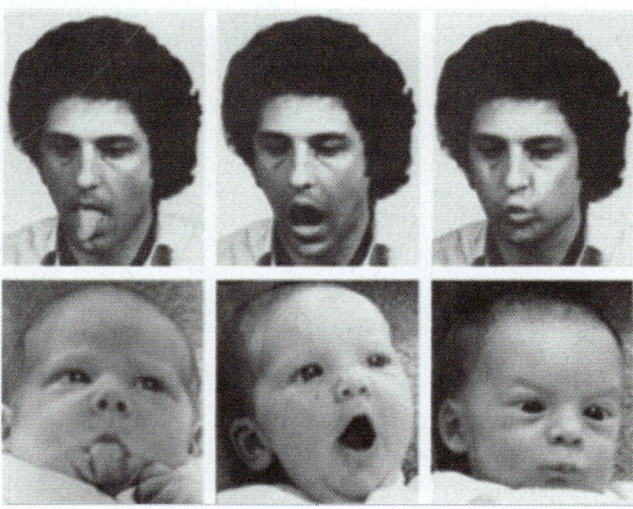

In this classic experiment Meltzoff and Moore demonstrated that neonates imitated the adults' facial expression more often than chance, suggesting that they are capable of facial imitation— a groundbreaking finding.

SOURCE: Meltzoff and Moore (1977).

newborn response to interesting stimuli (Anisfeld et al., 2001; Jones, 2006) and that neonate imitation is not developmentally similar to later social imitation (Suddendorf, Oostenbroek, Nielsen, & Slaughter, 2013). Others have confirmed that newborns from several ethnic groups and cultures display early capacities for imitation (Meltzoff & Kuhl, 1994; Nadel & Butterworth, 1999) and it is not simply an arousal response (Nagy, Pilling, Orvos, & Molnar, 2013). For example, in one study, newborns made corresponding mouth movements to both vowel and consonant vocal models; when the adult model made an *a* sound, newborns opened their mouths, and when the model made an *m* sound, newborns clutched their mouths (Chen, Striano, & Rakoczy, 2004).

Newborns mimic facial expressions, but they are simply carrying out an innate program thought to be controlled by the mirror neuron system, located in the premotor cortex (Rizzolatti, Sinigaglia, & Anderson, 2008). The mirror neuron system, an inborn capacity to make associations and respond to the actions of others by mirroring their actions in our own neural circuits, is apparent in both newborn humans and monkeys (Cook, Bird, Catmur, Press, & Heyes, 2014; Iacoboni, 2009; Keysers & Gazzola, 2010; Lepage & Théoret, 2007; Shaw & Czekóová, 2013). The ability to copy others' actions is inborn and may have fostered the evolutionary development of social communication (Nagy, 2006; Oberman, Hubbard, & McCleery, 2014; Rizzolatti et al., 2008). Neonates mimic simple facial expressions instinctively. The regulatory mechanisms to inhibit imitative responding develop during infancy (Nagy, 2006; Rizzolatti et al., 2008). Therefore, newborns do not understand imitation; rather, their facial expressions naturally mimic others (Meltzoff & Moore, 1989). But soon imitation becomes voluntary.

One important way in which infants learn is by observing and imitating others (Jones & Herbert, 2006). From 6 to 12 months of age, infants display the ability to imitate a wide range of behaviors and demonstrate deferred imitation, the ability to imitate an absent model (Meltzoff & Moore, 1999). Six- and 9-month-old infants show deferred imitation after 24 hours (Barr, Dowden, & Hayne, 1996; Collie & Hayne, 1999; Learmonth, Lamberth, & Rovee-Collier, 2004). For example, in one study, 6-month-old infants observed a model remove a mitten from a puppet's hand, shake it, and put it back on; the infants imitated the sequence of actions 24 hours later (Barr et al., 1996). Nine-month-old infants can apply actions that they have observed with one object to new objects that they have not observed 24 hours later (Lukowski, Wiebe, & Bauer, 2009). Twelve-month-old infants display deferred imitation four weeks after observing a model manipulate toys like cups, beads, and blocks (Klein & Meltzoff, 1999). Infants imitate not only adults but also peers. For example, 14-month-old infants who observed a peer playing in specific ways with toys—such as pulling, pushing, and poking them—repeated the actions in their own homes two days and then a week later (Klein & Meltzoff, 1999).

Imitation improves throughout infancy. Older infants imitate after shorter demonstration periods, display imitation after longer delays, and are more likely to generalize what they learn through imitation when they are tested with new objects in new contexts than are younger infants (Barr & Hayne, 2003; Herbert, Gross, & Hayne, 2006). By imitating others' actions on objects, older infants advance their manual skills—they observe and learn new ways of holding and manipulating objects (Fagard & Lockman, 2010). Infants not only learn from watching others but they also selectively imitate the actions of others (Kolling, Oturai, & Knopf, 2014). When 14- to 18-month-old infants observed an adult's action that was accompanied by a verbal expression indicating that the action was intentional ("There!") or accidental ("Whoops!"), the infants were more likely to imitate the intentional than the accidental actions (Carpenter, Akhtar, & Tomasello, 1998).

In summary, infants enter the world equipped with several basic learning capacities that permit them to learn even before birth. Newborns display classical and operant conditioning, imitation, and habituation, illustrating that they are wired to attend to their environment. Not only do infants display early competencies that permit them to learn quickly but they are also surprisingly adept at sensing and perceiving stimuli around them.

Thinking in Context 4.3

1. What do early learning capacities mean for parenting? What information about habituation, conditioning, or imitation should parents be aware of, if any? Why?

2. How might these learning principles be applied to address child-rearing issues, such as how to get infants to sleep through the night or how to introduce new foods?

SENSATION AND PERCEPTION DURING INFANCY AND TODDLERHOOD

Visiting the doctor's office for the first time in her young life, Kerry followed the doctor's finger with her eyes as he passed it over her face. "I think she sees it!" said her surprised mother. "She most certainly does," said the doctor. "Even as a newborn, your Kerry can sense the world. She can see, hear, and smell better than you know." Newborns can see, hear, smell, taste, and respond to touch, but it is unclear how infants perceive sensory stimuli. Developmental researchers draw a distinction between **sensation** and perception. Sensation occurs when our senses detect a stimulus. Perception refers to the sense our brain makes of the stimulus and our awareness of it. The newborn is equipped with a full range of senses, ready to experience the world.

HEARING

The capacity to hear develops in the womb, as discussed in Chapter 2; in fact, hearing is the most well-developed sense at birth. Newborns are able to hear about as well as adults (Northern, 2014). Shortly after birth, neonates can discriminate among sounds, such as tones (Hernandez-Pavon, Sosa, Lutter, Maier, & Wakai, 2008). By 3 days of age, infants can turn their head and eyes in the general direction of a sound, and this ability to localize sound improves over the first six months (Clifton, Rochat, Robin, & Berthier, 1994; Litovsky & Ashmead, 1997).

The process of learning language begins at birth, through listening. Newborns are attentive to voices and can detect their mothers' voices. Newborns only 1-day-old prefer to hear speech sounds over acoustically comparable nonspeech sounds. Newborns can perceive and discriminate nearly all sounds in human languages, but from birth, they prefer to hear their native language (Moon et al., 1993).

Infants' brain activity illustrates their preference for their native language and the developing neurological specialization for language. Neuroimaging studies have found that the areas of the brain responsible for language show greater activation when they hear speech sounds (Vouloumanos, Hauser, Werker, & Martin, 2010). Brain activity in the temporal and left frontal cortex in response to auditory stimuli indicates that newborns can discriminate speech patterns, such as differences in cadence among languages and can discriminate different speech patterns (Gervain, Macagno, Cogoi, Peña, & Mehler, 2008; Gervain & Mehler, 2010). In one study, 4-month-old Japanese infants showed increased brain activity in the left hemisphere of the brain, responsible for language in adults, in response to hearing their native language as compared with nonnative speech, emotional voices (human vocalizations with no linguistic content), monkey calls, and scrambled versions of each vocalization (Minagawa-Kawai et al., 2011).

VISION

At birth, vision is the least developed sense, but it improves rapidly. Researchers study *visual acuity*, sharpness of vision or the ability to see, in infants with the use of preferential looking tasks designed to determine whether infants prefer to look at one stimulus or another. For example, consider an array of black and white stripes. As shown in Figure 4.7, an array with more stripes (and therefore, many more narrow stripes) tends to appear gray rather than black and white because the pattern becomes more difficult to see as the stripes become more narrow. Researchers determine infants' visual acuity by comparing infants' responses to stimuli with different frequencies of stripes because infants who are unable to detect the stripes lose interest in the stimulus and look away from it. Newborn visual acuity is approximately 20/400 (Farroni & Menon, 2008). Preferential-looking studies show that infants reach adult levels of visual acuity between 6 months and 1 year of age (Courage & Adams, 1990; Gwiazda & Birch, 2001; Mercuri, Baranello, Romeo, Cesarini, & Ricci, 2007). Improvement in vision is due to the increasing maturation of the structures of the eye and the visual cortex, the part of the brain that processes visual stimuli.

Newborns are born with preferences for particular visual stimuli. Newborns prefer to look at patterns, such as a few large squares, rather than a plain stimulus such as a black or white oval shape (Fantz, 1961). Newborns also prefer to look at faces, and the preference for faces increases with age (Frank, Vul, & Johnson, 2009; Gliga, Elsabbagh, Andravizou, & Johnson, 2009). How infants explore visual stimuli changes with age. Until about 1 month of age, infants tend to scan along the outer perimeter of stimuli. For example,

FIGURE 4.7: Visual Acuity

Researchers and pediatricians use stimuli such as the Teller Acuity Cards illustrated here to determine what infants can see. Young infants attend to stimuli with wider lines and stop attending as the lines become smaller.

SOURCE: Leat, Yadev, and Irving (2009).

FIGURE 4.8: Externality Effect and Face Perception

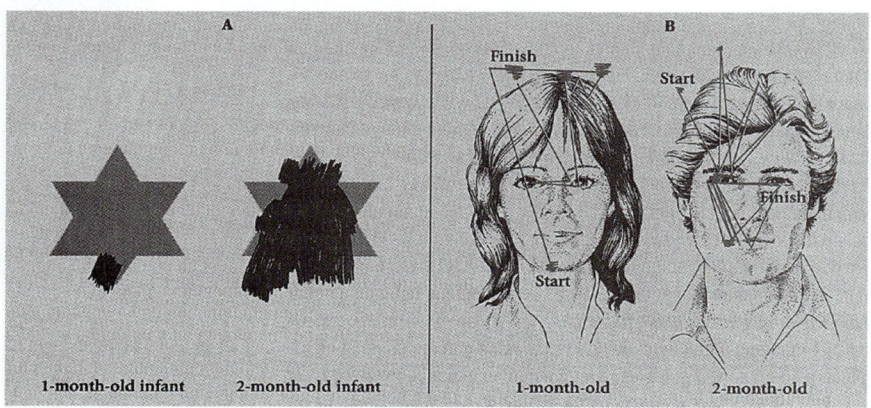

The externality effect refers to a particular pattern of infant visual processing. When presented with a complex stimulus, such as a face, infants under two months of age tend to scan along the outer contours, such as along the hairline. Older infants scan the internal features of complex images and faces, thereby processing the entire stimulus.

SOURCE: Gallotti (2011).

when presented with a face, the infant's gaze will scan along the hairline and not move to the eyes and mouth. By 6 to 7 weeks of age, infants study the eyes and mouth which hold more information than the hairline, as shown in Figure 4.8 (Hunnius & Geuze, 2004). Similarly, the ability to follow an object's movement with the eyes, known as visual tracking, is very limited at birth but improves quickly. By 2 months of age, an infant can follow a slow-moving object smoothly, and by 3 to 5 months, their eyes can dart ahead to keep pace with a fast-moving object (Richards & Holley, 1999; Teller, 1997).

Like other aspects of vision, color vision improves with age. Newborns see the world in color but have trouble discriminating colors. Early visual experience with color is necessary for normal color perception to develop (Sugita, 2004). Habituation studies show that by 1 month of age, infants can distinguish among red, green, and white (Teller, 1997). By 2 to 3 months of age, infants are as accurate as adults in discriminating the basic colors of red, yellow, and blue (Matlin & Foley, 1997; Teller, 1998). By 3 to 4 months of age, infants can distinguish many more colors as well as distinctions among closely related colors (Bornstein & Lamb, 1992; Haith, 1993). Seven-month-old infants detect color categories similar to those of adults; for example, they can group slightly different shades into the same basic color categories as adults do (e.g., see light blue as a shade of blue; Clifford, Franklin, Davies, & Holmes, 2009).

Depth perception is the ability to perceive distance—the distance of objects from each other and from ourselves. Depth perception is what permits infants to successfully reach for objects and, later, to crawl without bumping into furniture. By observing that newborns prefer to look at three-dimensional objects than two-dimensional figures, researchers have seen that we can perceive depth at birth (Slater, Rose, & Morison, 1984). Three- to 4-week-old infants blink their eyes when an object is moved toward their face, as if to hit them, suggesting that they are sensitive

to depth cues (Kayed, Farstad, & van der Meer, 2008; Náñez & Yonas, 1994). Infants learn about depth by observing and experiencing motion.

A classic series of studies using the visual cliff demonstrated that crawling influences how infants perceive depth. The visual cliff, as shown in Figure 4.9, is a Plexiglas-covered table bisected by a plank so that one side is shallow, with a checkerboard pattern right under the glass, and the other side is deep, with the checkerboard pattern a few feet below the glass (Gibson & Walk, 1960). In this classic study, crawling babies readily moved from the plank to the shallow side, but not to the deep side, even if coaxed by their mothers, suggesting that they perceive the difference in depth (Walk, 1968). The more crawling experience infants have, the more likely they are to refuse to cross the deep side of the visual cliff (Bertenthal, Campos, & Barrett, 1984).

Does this mean that babies cannot distinguish the shallow and deep sides of the visual cliff until they crawl? No, because even 3-month-old infants who are too young to crawl distinguish shallow from deep drops. When placed facedown on the glass surface of the deep side of the visual cliff, 3-month-old infants became quieter and showed a decrease in heart rate as compared with when they were placed on the shallow side of the cliff (Campos, Langer, & Krowitz, 1970; Dahl et al., 2013). The young infants can distinguish the difference between shallow and deep drops but do not yet associate fear with deep drops.

As infants gain experience crawling, their perception of depth, the meaning they associate with it, changes. Newly walking infants avoid the cliff's deep side even more consistently than do crawling infants (Dahl et al., 2013; Witherington, Campos, Anderson, Lejeune, & Seah, 2005). A new perspective on the visual cliff studies argues that infants avoid the deep side of the cliff not out of fear but simply because they perceive that they are unable to successfully navigate the drop; fear might be conditioned through later experiences, but infants are not naturally fearful of heights (Adolph, Kretch, & LoBue, 2014).

TOUCH

As compared with vision and hearing, we know much less about the sense of touch in infants. The mouth is the first part of the body to show sensitivity to touch prenatally and remains one of the most sensitive areas to touch after birth. A stroke to the newborn's cheek elicits the rooting reflex, a powerful survival mechanism for babies. In early infancy, touch, especially with the mouth, is a critical means of learning about the world (Piaget, 1936/1952).

Three month old infants show a change in heart rate when placed face down on the glass surface of the deep side of the visual cliff, suggesting that they perceive depth, but do not fear it. Crawling babies, however, show a different response. In a classic study of visual perception, crawling babies moved to the shallow side of the visual cliff, even if called by their mothers. The more crawling experience infants had, the more likely they were to refuse to cross the deep side of the visual cliff.

SOURCE: Levine and Munsch (2010).

Mark Richard/Photo Edit

Touch, specifically a caregiver's massage, can reduce stress responses in preterm and full-term neonates and is associated with weight gain in newborns (Diego et al., 2007; Hernandez-Reif, Diego, & Field, 2007). Skin-to-skin contact with a caregiver has an analgesic effect, reducing infants' pain response to the heel stick (de Sousa Freire, Santos Garcia, & Carvalho Lamy, 2008; Ferber & Makhoul, 2008). Although it was once believed that newborns were too immature to feel pain, we now know that the fetus has the capacity to feel pain by at least the 30th week of gestation (Benatar & Benatar, 2003). The neonate's capacity to feel pain has influenced debates about infant **circumcision**, as discussed in Lives in Context (p. 102).

SMELL AND TASTE

Smell and taste are well developed at birth. Classic experiments demonstrate that newborns can discriminate between smells (Goubet et al., 2002). Just hours after birth, newborns display facial expressions signifying disgust in response to odors of ammonia, fish, and other scents that adults find offensive (Steiner, 1979). Within the first days of life, newborns detect and recognize their mother's odor (Macfarlane, 1975; Porter, Varendi, Christensson, Porter, & Winberg, 1998; Russell, 1976; Schaal et al., 1980). Infants are calmed by their mother's scent. Newborns who smelled their mother's odor displayed less agitation during a heel-stick test and cried less afterward than infants presented with unfamiliar odors (Rattaz, Goubet, & Bullinger, 2005). Familiar scents reduce stress responses in infants (Goubet, Strasbaugh, & Chesney, 2007; Nishitani et al., 2009).

Infants show innate preferences for some tastes (Beauchamp & Mennella, 2011). For example, both bottle- and breast-fed newborns prefer human milk—even milk from strangers—to formula (Marlier & Schaal, 2005). Newborns prefer sugar to other substances, and a small dose of sugar can serve as an anesthetic, distracting newborns from pain (Gradin, Eriksson, Schollin, Holmqvist, & Holstein, 2002). Experience can modify taste preferences, beginning before birth: Fetuses are exposed to flavors in amniotic fluid that influence their preferences after birth (Beauchamp & Mennella, 2011). In one study, the type of formula fed to infants influenced their taste preferences at 4 to 5 years of age (Mennella & Beauchamp, 2002). Infants who were fed milk-based formulas and protein-based formulas were more likely to prefer sour flavors at 4 to 5 years of age as compared with infants who were fed soy-based formulas, who, in turn, were more likely to prefer bitter flavors. In addition, mothers reported that the infants fed protein- or soy-based formulas were more likely to prefer broccoli than those fed milk-based formulas. Touch, taste, and smell further illustrate infants' amazing capacities to sense and respond to the world around them.

INTERMODAL PERCEPTION

Though we have discussed the senses separately, when we attend to the environment we combine information from our various sensory systems to understand our world. Not only are infants able to sense in multiple modalities; they are able to coordinate their senses. **Intermodal perception** is the process of combining information from more

LIVES IN CONTEXT

Neonatal Circumcision

Neonatal circumcision, removal of the foreskin of the penis, is the oldest known planned surgery (Alanis & Lucidi, 2004). Although it is uncommon throughout much of the world, the United States leads Western nations in rates of infant circumcision (Elder, 2007). Overall, circumcision rates declined from 65% of male newborns in 1979 to 57% in 2010; however, there are regional differences, with nearly twice as many infant circumcisions in the Midwest than West (Owings, Uddin, & Williams, 2013). In recent years, circumcision has come under increasing scrutiny within the United States as some charge that it places the newborn under great distress for few medical benefits.

For decades, many scientists and physicians believed that newborns did not feel pain, leading many to perform circumcision without pain management techniques such as anesthesia or analgesia (Alanis & Lucidi, 2004). We now know that even the fetus feels pain (Benatar & Benatar, 2003). Newborns show many indicators of distress during circumcision, such as a letting out a high-pitched wail, flailing, and grimacing as well as dramatic rises in heart rate, blood pressure, palm sweating, pupil dilation, muscle tension, and cortisol levels (Paix & Peterson, 2012; Razmus, Dalton, & Wilson, 2004). Experts argue that exposure to pain early in infancy can lead to neurological changes and changes in the endocrine and immune systems that increase sensitivity to pain later in development (Bellieni et al., 2009; Razmus et al., 2004). According to the AAP Task Force on Circumcision (1999), analgesia (pain relief in which the newborn remains conscious) is safe and effective in reducing the pain associated with circumcision. Pain management, however, is not uniformly practiced; only 71% of pediatricians, 56% of family practitioners, and 25% of obstetricians report using analgesia when conducting circumcisions (Alanis & Lucidi, 2004). The American Society for Pain Management Nursing has issued a position statement that when circumcision is chosen, it must be accompanied by pain management before, during, and after the procedure (O'Conner-Von & Turner, 2013).

The medical benefits of circumcision, which are debated, include a small decrease in the rate of urinary tract infection and penile cancer and a lower risk of acquiring HIV (Benatar & Benatar, 2003). However, the American Medical Association (1999) and AAP Task Force on Circumcision (1999) noted that urinary tract infections and penile cancer show low prevalence rates. Also in the case of HIV, the research supporting this finding was conducted with adult males in Africa; whether the same effects apply to infants is uncertain (Alanis & Lucidi, 2004; Benatar & Benatar, 2003). Moreover, behavior is a more important factor in preventing infection than is circumcision. In 1999, both the American Medical

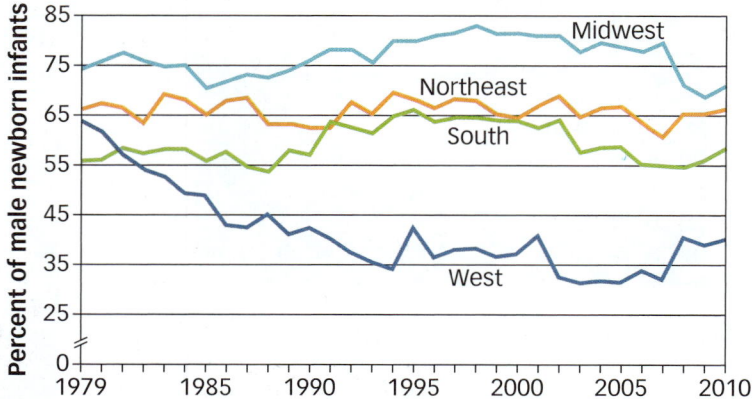

FIGURE 4.3: Rates of Circumcision Performed, 1979–2010

NOTES: Rates represent circumcisions performed during the birth hospitalization. Circumcision is identified by *International Classication of Diseases, NinthRevision, Clinical Modication* (ICD–9–CM) procedure code 64.0.

SOURCE: Owings et al. (2013).

Association and AAP Task Force on Circumcision concluded that the benefits of circumcision are not large enough to recommend routine circumcision; instead it is a parental decision. However, the AAP Task Force on Circumcision (2012) modified its view to note that the benefits of circumcision justify providing access to this procedure (by insurance companies) to families who choose it.

Education about the risks and benefits of circumcision, especially the controversy over the medical necessity of circumcision, generally does not influence parental decisions regarding circumcision (Binner, Mastrobattista, Day, Swaim, & Monga, 2003). Instead, it is tradition and culture, especially social factors such as religion, that influence parental decisions about circumcision. For example, in Jewish cultures, a boy is circumcised on the eighth day after birth in a ritual celebration known as a bris, in which the boy is welcomed as a member of the community. Parents' decisions are also influenced by social factors such as whether the father is circumcised and the desire that the child resemble his peers (Bo & Goldman, 2008; Waldeck, 2003). The decision is complicated, as parents weigh health risks and benefits with contextual factors such as religious and cultural beliefs as well as personal desires, in order to determine what is best for their child.

What Do You Think?

1. In your view, what are the most important considerations in making a decision about whether to circumcise a newborn boy?

2. Imagine that you had a newborn boy. Would you choose to circumcise your son? Why or why not?

than one sensory system. Most of the stimuli we experience are intermodal because they provide more than one type of sensory information (Slater, Quinn, Brown, & Hayes, 1999). Newborns' ability to imitate facial expressions is an example of intermodal matching, as they are able to link what they see (an adult's facial expression) with their own body and move their own facial muscles to mirror the adult's expression.

Research on intermodal perception supports the finding that infants expect vision, auditory, and tactile information to occur together (Sai, 2005). For example, newborns coordinate visual and auditory senses, turning their heads and eyes in the direction of a sound source, suggesting that they intuitively recognize that knowledge about spatial location is provided by both visual and auditory information (Clifton, Morrongiello, Kulig, & Dowd, 1981; Muir & Clifton, 1985; Newell, 2004; Wertheimer, 1961). By 6 months of age, infants who explore an object with their hands alone can recognize it by sight alone and vice versa, a finding that supports the integration of vision and touch (Pineau & Streri, 1990; Rose, Gottfried, & Bridger, 1981; Ruff & Kohler, 1978).

Infants integrate touch and vision very early in life. In one classic study, 1-month-old infants were presented with a smooth-surfaced pacifier or one with nubs on it (see Figure 4.10). After exploring it with their mouths, the infants were shown two pacifiers—one smooth and one nubbed. The infants preferred to look at the shape they had sucked, suggesting that they could match tactile and visual stimuli (Meltzoff & Borton, 1979). In another example, 8- to 31-day-old infants fitted with special goggles were presented with a virtual object created by a shadow caster (Bower, Broughton, & Moore, 1970). The virtual object was an illusory object that could be seen by the infant but not touched. When the infant reached for the object, his or her hand felt nothing and flailed through the air. Infants exposed to the virtual object attempted to reach for it and became distressed when they did not feel it, suggesting that vision and touch are integrated and infants expect to feel objects that they can see and reach. Although young infants show impressive capacities to integrate visual and tactile information, these senses are not completely integrated at birth. Newborns can visually recognize an object previously held but not seen, but they cannot tactually recognize an object previously seen and not held, suggesting that intermodal relations among senses are not bidirectional at birth (Sann & Streri, 2007).

Intermodal matching of visual and auditory stimuli shows similar patterns as visual and tactile. By 4 months of age, infants coordinate visual stimuli with expectations about auditory stimuli. For example, in one study, 4-month-old babies were presented with two films, side by side—one with a woman playing peekaboo and another with a person playing a percussion instrument. When percussion sounds were played alongside the films, infants looked more at the percussion video than the peekaboo video, preferring the film synchronized with the soundtrack (Spelke, 1976). Even neonates show evidence of linking visual and auditory stimuli. For example, 2-day-old infants shown two alternating visual stimuli, each accompanied by its own sound, demonstrated the ability to learn the arbitrary visual-auditory combinations, suggesting that we perceive and can learn intermodal relations shortly after birth (Slater, Brown, & Badenoch, 1997; Slater et al., 1999).

FIGURE 4.10: Nubbed vs. Smooth Pacifier Used to Study Intermodal Perception

Sensitivity to intermodal relations among stimuli is critical to perceptual development and learning—and this sensitivity emerges early in life (Bahrick, 2002; Gibson & Pick, 2000; Lewkowicz, 2000; Lewkowicz & Lickliter, 1994; Newell, 2004). But just how early? Newborns show a preference for viewing their mother's face at 78, 72, 12, and even just 4 hours after birth (Bushnell, Sai, & Mullin, 1989; Field, Cohen, Garcia, & Greenberg, 1984; Pascalis, Dechonen, Morton, Duruelle, & Grenet, 1995). Because 4-hour-old neonates prefer their mother's face, it was once believed that infants' preference for their mother's face was innate. However, infants are not born knowing their mother's face. Instead, they quickly learn to identify their mother. How? In one study, neonates were able to visually recognize their mother's face only if the face was paired with their mother's voice at least once after birth (Sai, 2005). Thus, intermodal perception is evident at birth because neonates can coordinate auditory and visual stimuli in order to associate their mother's face with her voice. They quickly remember the association and demonstrate a preference for her face even when it is not paired with her voice.

Newborns are equipped with remarkable capacities for sensing and perceiving stimuli. Their senses, although well developed at birth, improve rapidly over the first year of life. Moreover, capacities for intermodal perception mean that infants can combine information from various sensory modalities to construct a sophisticated and accurate picture of the world around them.

Thinking in Context 4.4

1. How might infants' powerful sensory capacities prime them to learn how to think about their world? Learn language?

2. How might parents and caregivers design caregiving environments that are tailored to infants' early learning and sensory capacities and stimulate development? What advice would you give on how to design such an environment for a newborn? For a 6-month-old infant?

MOTOR DEVELOPMENT DURING INFANCY AND TODDLERHOOD

In addition to their ability to perceive and learn, newborns also are able to respond to the stimulation they encounter in the world. The earliest ways in which infants adapt are through the use of their reflexes, involuntary and automatic responses to stimuli such as touch, light, and sound. Each reflex has its own developmental course. Some disappear early in life and others persist throughout life, as shown in Table 4.1. Infants show individual differences in how reflexes are displayed, specifically the intensity of the response. Preterm neonates, for example, show reflexes suggesting a more immature neurological system than full-term neonates (Barros, Mitsuhiro, Chalem, Laranjeira, & Guinsburg, 2011). The absence of reflexes, however, may signal neurological deficits.

MOTOR MILESTONES

Like physical development, motor skills evolve in a predictable sequence. By the end of the first month of life, most infants can reach the first milestone, or achievement, in motor development: lifting their heads while lying on their stomachs. After lifting the head, infants progress through an orderly series of motor milestones: lifting the chest, reaching for objects, rolling over, and sitting up with support (see Table 4.2). Notice that these motor achievements reflect a cephalocaudal progression of motor control, proceeding from the head downward. Researchers have long believed that all motor control proceeds from the head downward, but we now know that motor development is more variable. Instead, some infants may sit up before they roll over or not crawl at all before they walk

(Fogel, 2007). Similarly, infants reach for toys with their feet weeks before they use their hands, suggesting that early leg movements can be precisely controlled, the development of skilled reaching need not involve lengthy practice, and that early motor behavior does not necessarily follow a strict cephalocaudal pattern (Galloway & Thelen, 2004).

Gross motor development refers to the ability to control the large movements of the body—that is, to control actions that help infants move around in their environment. The first milestone in gross motor development is the ability to roll over voluntarily, which occurs at about 3 months of age. Success at initiating forward motion, or crawling (6–10 months), is particularly significant for both infants and parents. Infants vary in how they crawl. Some use their arms to pull and legs to push, some use only their arms or only their legs, and others scoot on their bottoms. Once infants can pull themselves upright while holding on to a chair or table, they begin "cruising," moving by holding on to furniture to maintain their balance while stepping sideways. At about 1 year of age, most American infants walk alone.

Once babies can walk, their entire visual field changes. Whereas crawling babies are more likely to look at the floor as they move, walking babies gaze straight ahead at caregivers, walls, and toys (Kretch, Franchak, & Adolph, 2014). Independent walking holds implications for cognitive, social, and emotional development, as it is associated not only with more attention and manipulation of objects but also with more sophisticated social interactions with caregivers, such as directing mothers' attention to particular objects and sharing, which in turn are associated with advanced language development relative to nonwalkers in both U.S. and Chinese infants (Clearfield, 2011; He, Walle, & Campos, 2015; Karasik, Tamis-LeMonda, & Adolph, 2011; Walle, 2013).

TABLE 4.1 Newborn Reflexes

NAME OF REFLEX	RESPONSE	DEVELOPMENTAL COURSE
Palmar grasp	Curling fingers around objects that touch the palm	Birth to about 4 months, when it is replaced by voluntary grasp
Rooting	Turning head and tongue toward stimulus when cheek is touched	Disappears over first few weeks of life and is replaced by voluntary head movement
Sucking	Sucking on objects placed into the mouth	Birth to about 6 months
Moro	Giving a startle response in reaction to loud noise or sudden change in the position of the head, resulting in throwing out arms, arching the back, and bringing the arms together as if to grasp something	Birth to about 5 to 7 months
Babinski	Fanning and curling the toes in response to stroking the bottom of the foot	Birth to about 8 to 12 months
Stepping	Making stepping movements as if to walk when held upright with feet touching a flat surface	Birth to about 2 to 3 months
Swimming	Holding breath and moving arms and legs, as if to swim, when placed in water	Birth to about 4 to 6 months

TABLE 4.2 Motor Milestones

AVERAGE AGE ACHIEVED	MOTOR SKILL
2 months	Lifts head Holds head steady when held upright
3 months	Pushes head and chest up with arms Rolls from stomach to back
4 months	Grasps cube
6 months	Sits without support
7 months	Rolls from back to stomach Attempts crawling Uses opposable thumb to grasp objects
8 months	Achieves sitting position alone Pulls to a stand
9 months	"Cruises" by holding on to furniture
10 months	Plays patty-cake
11 months	Stands alone
12 months	Walks alone
14 months	Builds tower of two cubes Scribbles
17 months	Walks up steps
18 months	Runs

Fine motor development refers to the ability to control small movements of the fingers such as reaching and grasping. Voluntary reaching plays an important role in cognitive development because it provides new opportunities for interacting with the world. Like other motor skills, reaching and grasping begin as gross activity and are refined with time. Newborns begin by engaging in *prereaching*, swinging their arms, and extending them toward nearby objects (Ennouri & Bloch, 1996; von Hofsten & Rönnqvist, 1993). Newborns use both arms equally and cannot control their arms and hands, so they rarely succeed in making contact with objects of interest (Lynch, Lee, Bhat, & Galloway, 2008). Prereaching stops at about 7 weeks of age.

Voluntary reaching appears at about 3 months of age and slowly improves in accuracy. At 5 months, infants can successfully reach for moving objects. By 7 months, the arms can reach independently, and infants are able to reach for an object with one arm rather than both (Spencer, Vereijken, Diedrich, & Thelen, 2000). By 10 months, infants can reach for moving objects that change direction (Fagard, Spelke, & von Hofsten, 2009). As they get experience with reaching and acquiring objects, infants develop cognitively because they learn by exploring and playing with objects—and object preferences change with experience. For example, in one study 4- to 6-month-old infants with less reaching

experience spend more time looking at and exploring larger objects whereas 5- to 6-month-old infants with more reaching experience spent more time looking at and touching smaller objects despite first looking at and touching the largest object (Libertus et al., 2013). With experience, infants' attention moves away from the motor skill (like the ability to coordinate their movement to hit a mobile), to the object (the mobile), as well as to the events that occur before and after acquiring the object (how the mobile swings and how grabbing it stops the swinging or how batting at it makes it swing faster). In this way, infants learn about cause and how to solve simple problems.

Though these motor milestones might look like isolated achievements, they are not. Motor skills develop systematically and build on each other with each new skill preparing an infant to tackle the next (Thelen, 1995; Thelen, 2000). Simple motor skills are combined in increasingly complex ways, permitting advances in movement including a wider range and more precise movements that enable babies to more effectively explore and control their environments.

DETERMINANTS OF MOTOR DEVELOPMENT

Motor development illustrates the complex interactions that take place between maturation and contextual factors. Maturation plays a very strong role in motor development. Preterm infants reach motor milestones later than do full-term infants (Gabriel et al., 2009). Cross-cultural research also supports the role of maturation because around the world, infants display roughly the same sequence of motor milestones. Among some Native Americans and other ethnic groups around the world, it is common to follow the tradition of tightly swaddling infants to cradleboards and strapping the board to the mother's back during nearly all waking hours for the first six to twelve months of the child's life. Although this might lead one to expect that swaddled babies will not learn to walk as early as babies whose movements are unrestricted,

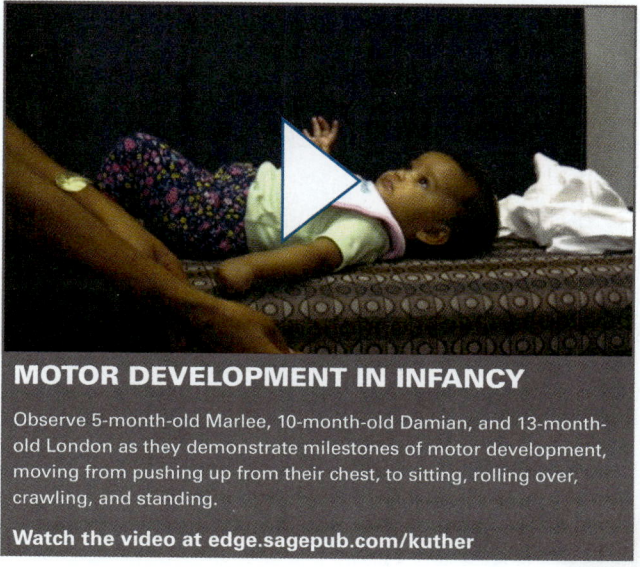

MOTOR DEVELOPMENT IN INFANCY

Observe 5-month-old Marlee, 10-month-old Damian, and 13-month-old London as they demonstrate milestones of motor development, moving from pushing up from their chest, to sitting, rolling over, crawling, and standing.

Watch the video at edge.sagepub.com/kuther

studies of Hopi Indian infants have shown that swaddling has little influence on when Hopi infants initiate walking (Dennis & Dennis, 1991; Harriman & Lukosius, 1982). Such research suggests that walking is very much maturationally programmed. Other evidence for the maturational basis of motor development comes from twin studies. Identical twins, who share the same genes, share more similarities in the timing and pace of motor development than do fraternal twins, who share half of their genes (Fogel, 2007; Wilson & Harpring, 1972).

Much of motor development is driven by maturation, yet opportunities to practice motor skills are also important. In a classic naturalistic study of institutionalized orphans in Iran who had spent their first two years of life lying on their backs in their cribs and were never placed in sitting positions or played with, none of the 1- to 2-year-old infants could walk, and less than half of them could sit up; the researchers also found that most of the 3- to 4-year-olds could not walk well alone (Dennis, 1960). While maturation is necessary for motor development, it is not sufficient; we must have opportunities to practice our motor skills.

Practice can also enhance motor development (Lobo & Galloway, 2012). For example, when infants from 1 to 7 weeks of age practice stepping reflexes each day, they retain the movements and walk earlier than infants who receive no practice (Vereijken & Thelen, 1997; Zelazo, 1983). Practice in sitting has a similar effect (Zelazo, Zelazo, Cohen, & Zelazo, 1993). Even 1-month-old infants given postural

Although this infant spends much of day tightly swaddled and carried on her mother's back, she will likely crawl at about a year of age, similar to other infants who are not regularly swaddled.

training showed more advanced control of their heads and necks than other infants (Lee & Galloway, 2012). Similarly, infants who spend supervised playtime prone on their stomachs each day reach many motor milestones, including rolling over and crawling, earlier than do infants who spend little time on their stomachs (Fetters & Hsiang-han, 2007; Kuo, Liao, Chen, Hsieh, & Hwang, 2008). In one study, over a two-week period, young infants received daily play experience with "sticky mittens"—Velcro-covered mitts that enabled them to independently pick up objects. These infants showed advances in their reaching behavior and greater visual exploration of objects, whereas a comparison group of young infants who passively watched an adult's actions on the objects showed no change (Libertus & Needham, 2010).

Practice contributes to cross-cultural differences in infant motor development. Different cultures provide infants with different experiences and opportunities for development. For example, in many cultures, including several in sub-Saharan Africa and in the West Indies, infants attain motor goals like sitting up and walking much earlier than do North American infants. Among the Kipsigi of Kenya, parents seat babies in holes dug in the ground and use rolled blankets to keep babies upright in the sitting position (Keller, 2003). The Kipsigis help their babies practice walking at 2 to 3 months of age by holding their hands, putting them on the floor, and moving them slowly forward (Keller, 2003). Infants of many sub-Saharan villages, such as the Kung San, Gusii, and Wolof, are also trained to sit using holes or containers for support and are often held upright and bounced up and down, a social interaction practice that contributes to earlier walking (Lohaus et al., 2011). Caregivers in some of these cultures further encourage walking by setting up two parallel bamboo poles that infants can hold onto with both hands, learning balance and stepping skills (Keller, 2003). Similarly, mothers in Jamaica and other parts of the West Indies use a formal handling routine to exercise their babies' muscles and help them to grow up strong and healthy (Dziewolska & Cautilli, 2006; Hopkins, 1991; Hopkins & Westra, 1989, 1990).

The social context in which infants develop influences parental behavior; parents socialize infants by fostering the skills needed for success and survival in a particular cultural and contextual setting. Sometimes survival and success requires continued dependence on caregivers and delaying motor milestone. For example, parents may not encourage crawling in potentially dangerous environments, such as environments with lots of insects, rodents, and/or reptiles on the ground. In other cases, success entails fostering early development of motor skills such as walking. An interesting contrast is found between two different nomadic cultures, the Turkana tribe of Kenya and the Ache of eastern Paraguay. While the Turkana encourage early walking in their infants (Keller, 2003), the Ache discourage their infants from crawling or moving independently. Ache infants walk at 18 to 20 months, as compared with the 12-month average of North American infants (Kaplan & Dove, 1987).

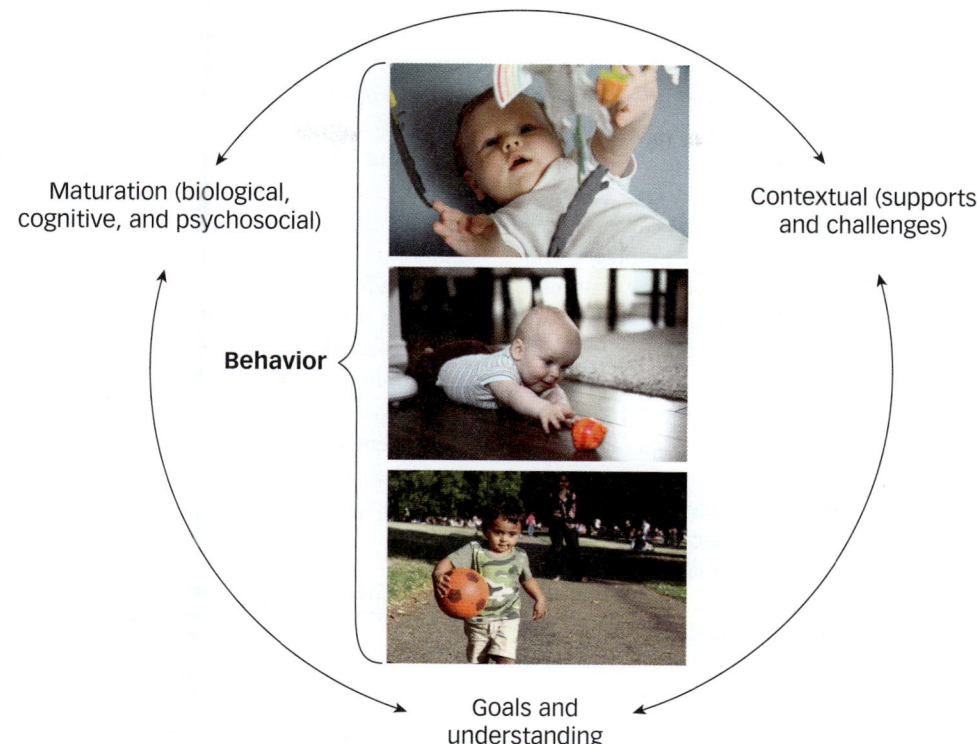

Maturation (biological, cognitive, and psychosocial)

Contextual (supports and challenges)

Behavior

Goals and understanding

The infant's abilities to reach out an arm, stretch, and grasp combine into coordinated reaching movements to obtain desired objects. Motor development progresses to sitting, crawling, walking, and eventually running, all reflections of infants' blending and coordinating abilities to achieve self-chosen goals, such as obtaining toys, and all tailored by environmental supports and challenges. (photos: istock and canstock/harishmarnad.)

Cultural differences in styles of interaction, such as a Western cultural emphasis on individualism and Eastern cultural emphasis on collectivism, influence children's motor development. In one cross-cultural study comparing infants in Germany and in the Cambodian Nso culture, the Nso infants showed overall more rapid motor development. The Nso practice of close proximity, lots of close body contact, and less object play are related to the socialization goals of fostering relationships; they also provide infants with body stimulation that fosters gross motor skills. German mothers displayed a parenting style with less body contact but more face-to-face contact and object play, socialization practices that emphasize psychological autonomy, but less gross motor exploration. However, the German infants learned how to roll from back to stomach earlier than the Nso infants, likely because Nso infants are rarely placed on their backs and instead are carried throughout the day (Lohaus et al., 2011).

Even simple aspects of the child-rearing context, such as choice of clothing, can influence motor development. In the 19th century, 40% of American infants skipped crawling, possibly because their long flowing gowns impeded movement on hands and knees (Trettien, 1990). One study of 13- and 19-month-old infants compared their gait while wearing a disposable diaper, a thicker cloth diaper, and no diaper (Cole, Lingeman, & Adolph, 2012). When naked,

infants demonstrated the most sophisticated walking with fewer missteps and falls. While wearing a diaper, infants walked as poorly as they would have done several weeks earlier had they been walking naked. Motor development is largely maturational, but subtle differences in context and cultural emphasis play a role in its timing.

MOTOR DEVELOPMENT AS A DYNAMIC SYSTEM

Motor development reflects an interaction between maturation and environment in which the infant acquires increasingly complex dynamic systems of action (Thelen, 1995; Thelen, 2000). **Dynamic systems theory** describes how separate abilities are blended together to provide more complex and effective ways of exploring and controlling the environment. For example, the abilities to sit upright, hold the head upright, match motor movements to vision, reach out an arm, and grasp are all combined into coordinated reaching movements to obtain a desired object (Corbetta & Snapp-Childs, 2009; Spencer et al., 2000). Motor development reflects goal-oriented behavior because it is initiated by an infant's desire to accomplish something, such as pick up a toy or move to the other side of the room. The infant's abilities and the immediate environment (e.g., whether he or she is being held, lying in a crib, or lying freely on the floor) determine whether and how the goal can be achieved (Spencer et al., 2000). The infant tries out behaviors and persists at those that enable him or her to move closer to the goal, practicing and refining the behavior. For example, infants learn to walk by taking lots of steps and making lots of falls, but they persist even though, at the time, crawling is a much faster and more efficient means of transportation (Adolph et al., 2012). Why? Perhaps because upright posture leads to many more interesting sights, objects, and interactions. The upright infant can see more and do more, with two hands free to grasp objects, making walking a very desirable goal (Adolph & Tamis-LeMonda, 2014).

Therefore, motor development is the result of several processes: central nervous system maturation, the infant's physical capacities, environmental supports, and the infant's desire to explore the world (see Figure 4.11). It is learned by revising and combining abilities and skills to fit the infant's goals. In this way, motor development is highly individualized as each infant has goals that are particular to his or her specific environment. For example, an infant might respond to slippery hardwood floors by crawling on her stomach rather than all fours or by shuffling her feet and hands rather than raising each. Infants attain the same motor tasks, such as climbing down stairs, at about the same age, yet differ in how they approach the task. Some, for example, might turn around and back down, others descend on their bottoms, and others slide down face first

(Berger, Theuring, & Adolph, 2007). By viewing motor development as dynamic systems of action produced by an infant's abilities, goal-directed behavior, and environmental supports and opportunities, we can account for the individual differences that we see in motor development.

Infants are born with a collection of reflexes that aid their adaptation to the world. Gross and fine motor development progress through a series of milestones that follow cephalocaudal and proximodistal patterns. Gross motor development proceeds from the head down, and fine motor development proceeds from the inner body out. Our increasing capacity to control and coordinate our body movements is the result of complex interactions between our physical maturation and the contexts in which we develop—inborn capacities are strengthened and modified by interactions with the environment and environmental experiences influence the acquisition, adaptation, and strengthening of motor behaviors.

Thinking in Context 4.5

1. Carmen is concerned because her 14-month-old baby is not walking. All of the other babies she knows have walked by 12 months of age. What would you tell Carmen?

2. How might a fine motor skill, such as learning to use a spoon, reflect the interaction of maturation and sociocultural context?

Apply Your Knowledge

Lena is 7 months old and lags behind in height and weight as compared with other infants her age. Early in life, she showed normative growth, but her growth has since slowed. Recently, Lena's parents separated, and she and her mother moved to a new home. Her mother is 19 years old, does not have a high school degree, and had few job opportunities. She took the first job that panned out, despite its long hours. Lena was placed in child care. Her mother continued to breast-feed, despite its increasing difficulty given her new work schedule. Lena's

mother insisted that Lena eat less solid food and baby food given her continued breast-feeding. Staff at the child care center approached Lena's mother to express their concern over Lena's lack of growth and development; she has not begun crawling like other infants and tends to avoid eye contact with others.

1. What are normative patterns of growth for infants? Motor skills? How does Lena's development compare with these norms?

2. What are potential causes of or influences on the developmental difficulties Lena experiences? How might contextual factors influence Lena's development?

3. What are the child care staff's responsibilities?

4. What should the mother do? What treatment do you suggest?

Chapter Summary

4.1 Identify two patterns of growth during infancy.

Growth proceeds from the head downward (cephalocaudal) and from the center of the body outward (proximodistal).

4.2 Discuss the role of feeding and nutrition in the growth of infants and toddlers.

Breast-feeding provides benefits to both mother and infant, but infant formula is also a healthy alternative. At around 4 to 6 months, gruel and progressively more solid foods can be introduced. Toddlers can be picky eaters, and many U.S. toddlers are given junk food that does not build optimal dietary habits. Malnourishment is associated with impaired learning, concentration, and language skills throughout childhood and adolescence. Severely malnourished children may suffer from diseases such as marasmus and kwashiorkor, or, more common in the United States, failure to thrive. If nutrition is reinstated early, some of the damage caused by malnutrition can be reversed, but long-term cognitive difficulties often remain.

4.3 Explain four processes of neural development.

The brain develops through several processes: neurogenesis (the creation of neurons), synaptogenesis (the creation of synapses), pruning (reducing unused neural connections), and myelination (coating the axons with myelin to increase the speed of transmission).

4.4 Analyze the role of experience in infants' and toddlers' neural development.

Experience shapes the brain structure. The brain produces an excess of connections among neurons during the first three years of life. Those connections that are used become stronger, and neural connections that are not used are pruned. Though infancy is a particularly important time for the formation and strengthening of synapses, experience shapes the brain structure at all ages of life.

4.5 Compare infants' early learning capacities for habituation, classical conditioning, and operant conditioning.

Innate learning capacities permit young infants to quickly adapt to the world. Habituation is a type of innate learning in which repeated exposure to a stimulus results in the gradual decline in the intensity, frequency, or duration of a response. In classical

conditioning, an association is formed between a neutral stimulus and one that triggers an innate reaction in an animal or person. Infants also demonstrate the ability to learn based on the consequences of the behaviors, whether they are followed by reinforcement or punishment, known as operant conditioning. Similar to habituation and classical conditioning, infants are born able learn through operant conditioning—premature infants and even third-trimester fetuses can be operantly conditioned.

4.6 Evaluate infants' capacities for imitation.

Neonates mimic simple facial and finger expressions but do so without control. The regulatory mechanisms to inhibit imitative responding develop during infancy. From 6 to 12 months of age, infants display the ability to imitate a wide range of behaviors and demonstrate deferred imitation, the ability to imitate an absent model. Imitation improves throughout infancy. Older infants imitate after shorter demonstration periods, display imitation after longer delays, and are more likely to generalize what they learn through imitation when they are tested with new objects in new contexts than are younger infants.

4.7 Contrast the development of infants' visual and auditory capacities.

Visual acuity, pattern perception, visual tracking, and color vision improve over the first few months of life. Neonates are sensitive to depth cues and young infants can distinguish depth, but crawling stimulates the perception of depth and the association of fear with sharp drops. Neonates demonstrate sound localization, which improves over the first six months. Newborns can perceive and discriminate nearly all sounds in human languages, but from birth, they prefer to hear their native language. Babies naturally notice the complex patterns of sounds around them and organize sounds into meaningful units.

4.8 Discuss infants' capacities for intermodal perception.

From birth, infants are wired to perceive the world using intermodal perception, by combining information from more than one sensory system. Infants expect vision, auditory, and tactile information to go together. Intermodal perception is evident at birth because neonates can coordinate auditory and visual stimuli to associate their mother's face with her voice—and they quickly remember the association to demonstrate a preference for her face even when it is not paired with her voice.

4.9 Summarize milestones in infant and toddler motor development.

Infants are born with reflexes; their absence signals neurological abnormalities. Each reflex has its own developmental course. After lifting the head, at about 1 month of age, infants progress through an orderly series of motor milestones: lifting the chest, reaching for objects, rolling over, sitting up, crawling, cruising, and walking alone. Gross and fine motor skills develop systematically and build on each other, with each new skill preparing the infant to tackle the next.

4.10 Analyze the roles of maturation and contextual factors in infant and toddler motor development.

Much of motor development is influenced by maturation, but infants benefit from opportunities to practice motor skills. Different cultures provide infants with different experiences and opportunities for practice, contributing to cross cultural differences in motor development. Viewing motor development as dynamic systems of action produced by an infant's abilities, goal-directed behavior, and environmental supports and opportunities accounts for the individual differences that we see in motor development.

Key Terms

cephalocaudal development   88

circumcision   101

cortex   94

deferred imitation   98

dynamic systems theory   107

experience-dependent brain development   95

experience-expectant brain development   95

failure to thrive   93

fine motor development   105

glial cells   94

gross motor development   104

growth norms   88

habituation   96

intermodal perception   101

kwashiorkor   93

marasmus   92

myelination   94

neurogenesis   94

neurons   94

perception   97

proximodistal development   88

reflexes   97

sensation   99

synapses   94

synaptic pruning   94

synaptogenesis   94

vaccinations   89

CHAPTER 5

Cognitive Development in Infancy and Toddlerhood

SAGE edge™

Get the edge on your studies at edge.sagepub.com/kuther.

Master these learning objectives using key study tools in the chapter and at SAGE edge. Access original SAGE **Video Cases** to explore the lives and contexts of individuals in every stage of development, **Think Critically** and **Explore Further** with SAGE journal and reference articles, and **Watch**, **Listen**, and **Connect** with online multimedia resources.

LEARNING OBJECTIVES	KEY STUDY TOOLS
5.1. Define *cognitive schemas*, and explain the processes by which infants and toddlers modify their cognitive schemas.	**Explore Further** Schemas **Watch** Schemas, Assimilation, and Accommodation
5.2. Summarize infants' progression through six substages of sensorimotor reasoning.	**Watch** How Babies Think
5.3. Explain the development of object permanence during the sensorimotor period.	**Video Case** Object Permanence
5.4. Discuss the core knowledge perspective as it applies to infancy and toddlerhood.	**Think Critically** Core Knowledge Perspective
5.5. Identify the parts of the information processing system and its function in infancy and toddlerhood.	**Lifespan Brain Development** The Media and Baby Geniuses (p. 123) **Connect** Information Processing Theory
5.6. Describe developmental changes in infants' capacities for attention and memory.	**Explore Further** Attention **Watch** The Still-Face Experiment
5.7. Examine how infants' categorization skills change with development.	**Connect** How Categorization is Learned
5.8. Discuss how intelligence is measured in infancy and findings regarding infant intelligence.	**Watch** Bayley Scales of Infant Development **Think Critically** Bayley-III
5.9. Explain patterns of language development from birth through infancy and toddlerhood.	**Lives in Context** Baby Signing (p. 129) **Lives in Context** Development in Internationally Adopted Children (p. 131) **Listen** 'Baby' Robot Learns Language
5.10. Contrast learning, nativist, and interactionist perspectives on language.	**Video Case** Developmental Milestones: Parent Views

Be careful with Baby Emily," Lila warned her 22-month-old son, Michael. "She's just 1 week old and very little. You were once little like her." "No," Michael said and giggled. "Big boy!" Michael picked up his teddy bear, cradled it like a baby, then held it to his chest rubbing its back, just like what he sees Mommy do with Baby Emily. In less than two years, Michael has transformed from a tiny infant, like Baby Emily, to a toddler who imitates what he sees and can verbally express his ideas. Like all newborns, Baby Emily is equipped with inborn sensory capacities and preferences that enable her

to tune in to the world around her. Baby Emily's abilities to think, reason, problem solve, and interact with objects and people will change dramatically over the next two years. In this chapter, we will explore the cognitive developments that occur during infancy and toddlerhood.

PIAGET'S COGNITIVE-DEVELOPMENTAL PERSPECTIVE

The first scientist to systematically examine children's thinking and reasoning, Swiss scholar Jean Piaget (1896–1980), believed that in order to understand children we must understand how they think because thinking influences all of behavior. Piaget formulated the cognitive-developmental perspective, which views children and adults as active explorers who learn by interacting with the world, building their own understanding of everyday phenomena, and applying it to adapt to the world around them.

SCHEMAS, ASSIMILATION, AND ACCOMMODATION

According to Piaget, children are active in their own development not simply because they engage other people but because they engage the world, adapting their ways of thinking in response to their experiences. Through these interactions, they organize what they learn to construct and refine their own schemas, or concepts, ideas, and ways of interacting on the world. Our earliest schemas are inborn motor responses, such as the reflex response that causes infants to close their fingers around an object when it touches their palm. As the infant grows and develops, these early motor schemas are transformed into cognitive schemas, or thought. At all ages, we rely on our schemas to make sense of the world, but our schemas are constantly adapting and developing in response to our experiences. According to Piaget, cognitive development is the result of two developmental processes: **assimilation** and **accommodation**.

Assimilation involves integrating a new experience into a preexisting schema. For example, suppose that 1-year-old Kelly uses the schema of "grab and shove into the mouth" to learn. He grabs and shoves his rattle into his mouth, learning about the rattle by using his preexisting schema. When Kelly comes across another object, such as Mommy's wristwatch, he transfers the schema to it—and assimilates the wristwatch by grabbing it and shoving it into his mouth. He develops an understanding of the new objects through assimilation, by fitting them into his preexisting schema.

Sometimes we encounter experiences or information that do not fit within an existing schema, so we must change the schema, adapting and modifying it in light of the new information. This process is called accommodation. For example, suppose Kelly encounters another object, a beach ball. He tries his schema of grab and shove but finds that he cannot

shove the ball into his mouth. Or perhaps he cannot even grab the ball. So he must adapt his schema, or perhaps create a new one in order to incorporate the new information—to learn about the beach ball. Kelly may squeeze and mouth the ball instead, accommodating or changing his schema to interact with the new object.

The processes of assimilation and accommodation are continually occurring and are ways that people adapt to their environment, absorbing the constant flux of information they encounter daily (see Figure 5.1). People—infants, children, and adults—constantly integrate new information into their schemas and are constantly confronted with new information that requires that they modify their schemas. Piaget proposed that people naturally strive for *cognitive equilibrium,* a balance between the processes of assimilation and accommodation. When assimilation and accommodation are balanced, individuals are neither incorporating new information into their schemas nor changing their schemas in light of new information. In other words, when we experience cognitive equilibrium, our schemas match the outside world and represent it clearly. A state of cognitive equilibrium is rare and fleeting. More frequently, people experience a mismatch or *disequilibrium* between their schemas and the world. For example, when Kelly encounters his mother's wristwatch and must learn about it by applying his grab-and-shove schema, he displays cognitive disequilibrium because he has discovered information that is new to him and therefore must be assimilated. Likewise, Kelly also displays cognitive disequilibrium when he must accommodate his schema to learn from a new experience, such as an encounter with the beach ball.

Disequilibrium leads to cognitive growth because of the mismatch between children's schemas and reality. This mismatch leads to confusion and discomfort, which in turn motivate children to modify their cognitive schemas so that

FIGURE 5.1: Assimilation and Accommodation

Bobby sees a cat that fits his schema for kitty (left). He has never seen a cat like this before (right). He must accommodate his schema for kitty to include a hairless cat.

their view of the world matches reality. It is through assimilation and accommodation that this modification takes place so that cognitive equilibrium is restored. Children's drive for cognitive equilibrium is the basis for cognitive change and propels them through the four stages of cognitive development proposed by Piaget (refer back to Table 1.4). With each advancing stage, children create and use more sophisticated cognitive schemas, enabling them to think, reason, and understand their world in more complex ways. The earliest schemas emerge during the first stage of cognitive development: the sensorimotor stage.

SUBSTAGES OF SENSORIMOTOR REASONING

During the sensorimotor stage, from birth to about 2 years old, infants learn about the world through their senses and motor skills. To think about an object, they must act on it by viewing it, listening to it, touching it, smelling it, and tasting it. Piaget believed that infants are not capable of **mental representation**—thinking about an object using mental pictures. They also lack the ability to remember and think about objects and events when they are not present. Instead, in order to think about an object, an infant must experience it through both the visual and tactile senses. The sensorimotor period of reasoning, as Piaget conceived of it, progresses through six substages in which cognition develops from reflexes to intentional action to symbolic representation.

Substage 1: Reflexes (Birth–1 Month)

In the first substage, newborns use their reflexes, such as the sucking and palmar grasp reflexes, to react to stimuli they experience. During the first month of life, infants use these reflexes to learn about their world, through the process of assimilation; they apply their sucking schema to assimilate information and learn about their environment. At about 1 month of age, newborns begin to accommodate, or modify, their sucking behaviors to specific objects, sucking differently in response to a bottle verses a pacifier. For example, they may modify their sucking schema when they encounter a pacifier, perhaps sucking less vigorously and without swallowing. During the first month of life, newborns strengthen and modify their original reflexive schemas to explore the world around them.

Substage 2: Primary Circular Reactions (1–4 Months)

During the second substage, infants begin to make accidental discoveries. Early cognitive growth in the sensorimotor period comes through engaging in **circular reactions**, the repetition of an action and its response. Infants learn to repeat pleasurable or interesting events that originally occurred by chance. Between 1 and 4 months, infants engage in behaviors called **primary circular reactions**, which consist of repeating actions involving the parts of the body that produce pleasurable or interesting results. A primary circular reaction

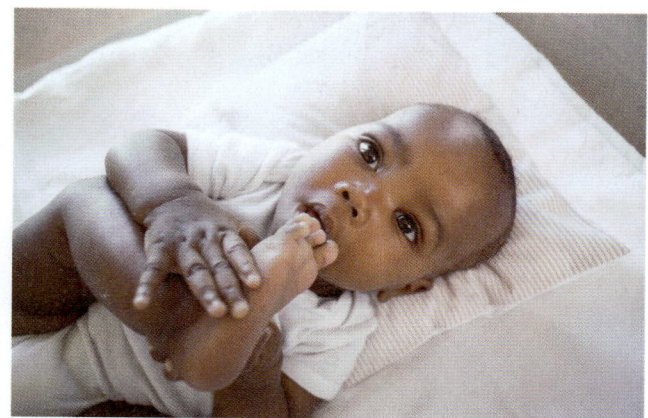

Primary circular reactions are babies' first discoveries.

begins by chance or by accident, as the infant produces a pleasurable sensation and learns to repeat the behavior to make the event happen again and experience the pleasurable effect again. For example, an infant flails her arms and accidentally puts her hand in her mouth. She is surprised at the outcome (her hand in her mouth) and tries to make it happen again. Therefore, the infant repeats the behavior to experience and explore her body.

Substage 3: Secondary Circular Reactions (4–8 Months)

During the third sensorimotor substage, infants' awareness begins to extend outside their bodies and they become interested in manipulating and learning about objects. Infants engage in **secondary circular reactions**, repetitions of actions that trigger responses in the external environment, outside of the baby's body. Now the patterns of repetition include objects and are oriented toward making interesting events occur in the infant's environment. For example, the infant shakes a rattle to hear its noise or kicks his or her legs to make a mobile hanging over the crib move. Secondary circular reactions signify that infants are beginning to understand that their actions cause results in the external environment and indicate that their **attention** has expanded to include the environment outside their bodies. As infants become more aware of objects and people, they develop new ways of interacting with their environments to continue experiencing sensations and events that they find pleasing.

Substage 4: Coordination of Secondary Schemas (8–12 Months)

While primary and secondary circular reactions are behaviors that are discovered by accident, the coordination of secondary circular reactions substage represents true means–end behaviors and signifies the beginning of intentional behavior. During this substage, infants purposefully coordinate two secondary circular reactions and apply them in new situations to achieve a goal. For example, Piaget described how his son, Laurent, combined the two activities of knocking a barrier out of his way and grasping an object. When Piaget put

This infant is showing object permanence by reaching over to uncover the toy. What does object permanence signify?

Doug Goodman / Science Source

a pillow in front of a matchbox that Laurent desired, the boy pushed the pillow aside and grabbed the box. In this way, two secondary circular reactions were integrated to achieve a goal. Now planning and goal-directed behavior have emerged.

One of the most important advances during the coordination of secondary schemas substage is **object permanence**, the understanding that objects continue to exist outside of sensory awareness (e.g., are no longer visible). According to Piaget, infants younger than 8 months of age do not yet have object permanence—out of sight is literally out of mind. An infant loses interest and stops reaching for or looking at a small toy after it is covered by a cloth. It is not until 8 to 12 months, during the coordination of secondary schemas substage, that object permanence emerges and infants will search for hidden objects. Displaying object permanence is an important cognitive advance because it signifies a capacity for mental representation, or internal thought. The ability to think about an object internally is an important step toward learning language because language uses symbols: Sounds symbolize and stand for objects (e.g., infants must understand that the sound "ball" represents an object, a ball).

Substage 5: Tertiary Circular Reactions (12–18 Months)

During the fifth substage, infants begin to experiment with new behaviors to see the results. Piaget described infants as "little scientists" during this period because they move from intentional behavior to systematic exploration. Infants now engage in active, purposeful trial-and-error exploration to search for new discoveries. They vary their actions to see how the changes affect the outcomes. Piaget referred to these mini-experiments as **tertiary circular reactions**. For example, many infants begin to experiment with gravity by dropping objects to the floor while sitting in a high chair. First an infant throws a ball and watches it bounce. Next a piece of paper floats slowly down. Then mommy's keys clatter down. And so on. This purposeful exploration is how infants search for new discoveries and learn about the world. When presented with a problem, babies in the tertiary

circular reactions substage engage in trial and error analyses, trying out behaviors until they find the best one to attain their goal.

Substage 6: Mental Representation (18–24 Months)

The sixth sensorimotor substage marks a transition between the sensorimotor and preoperational reasoning stages. Between 18 and 24 months of age, infants develop *representational thought*, the ability to use symbols such as words and mental pictures to represent objects and actions in memory. In developing this ability, infants are freed from immediate experience: They can think about objects that they no longer see directly in front of them and can engage in **deferred imitation**, imitating actions of an absent model. Now, external physical exploration of the world gives way to internal mental exploration. Children can think through potential solutions and create new solutions to problems without engaging in physical trial and error but by simply considering the potential solutions and their consequences. Table 5.1 summarizes the substages of sensorimotor reasoning.

RECENT FINDINGS ON SENSORIMOTOR REASONING

Piaget's contributions to our understanding of cognitive development are vast and invaluable. He was the first to ask what develops during childhood and how it occurs. Piaget recognized that motor action and cognition are inextricably linked, an assumption still held true by today's developmental scientists (Adolph & Berger, 2005; Beilin & Fireman, 2000; Woods & Wilcox, 2013).

Piaget's work has stimulated a great deal of research as developmental scientists have investigated the accuracy of his theory. But how is such research conducted? Measuring cognitive capabilities in infants and toddlers is

OBJECT PERMANENCE

7-month-old Nicho and 10-month-old Damian illustrate developmental changes in infants' understanding of object permanence. At 7 months of age, Nicho does not search for the hidden horse. However, Damian successfully locates the horse, even when presented with the A-not-B search task.

Watch the video at edge.sagepub.com/kuther

TABLE 5.1 Substages of Sensorimotor Reasoning

SUBSTAGE	MAJOR FEATURES	EXAMPLE
Reflexive activity (0–1 month)	Strengthens and adapts reflexes	Newborn shows a different sucking response to a nipple versus a pacifier
Primary circular reactions (1–4 months)	Repeats motor actions that produce interesting outcomes that are centered toward the body	Infant pats hand against the floor to feel sensation on palm
Secondary circular reactions (4–8 months)	Repeats motor actions that produce interesting outcomes that are directed toward the environment	Infant bats mobile with his arm and watches the mobile move
Coordination of secondary schemas (8–12 months)	Combines secondary circular reactions to achieve goals and solve problems; the beginnings of intentional behavior	Infant uses one hand to lift a bucket covering a ball and the other to grasp the ball. Infant uses both hands to pull a string attached to a ball and eventually reach the ball
Tertiary circular reactions (12–18 months)	Experiments with different actions to achieve the same goal or observe the outcome and make new discoveries	Toddler hits a pot with a wooden spoon and listens to the sound, then hits other objects in the kitchen, such as the refrigerator, stove, or plates, to hear the sound that the spoon makes against the objects
Mental representation (18–24 months)	Internal mental representation of objects and events; thinking to solve problems rather than relying on trial and error	When confronted with a problem, like a toy that is out of reach on the counter, the toddler considers possible solutions to a problem in his mind, decides on a solution, and implements it

very challenging because, unlike older children and adults, babies cannot fill out questionnaires or answer questions orally. Researchers have had to devise methods of measuring observable behavior that can provide clues to what an infant is thinking. For example, researchers measure infants' looking behavior: What does the infant look at, and for how long? Using such methods, they have found support for some of Piaget's claims and evidence that challenges others. One of the most contested aspects of Piaget's theory concerns his assumption that infants are not capable of mental representation until late in the sensorimotor period. A growing body of research conducted with object permanence and imitation tasks suggests otherwise, as described in the following sections.

Violation-of-Expectation Tasks

Piaget's method of determining whether an infant understood object permanence relied on the infant's ability to demonstrate it by uncovering a hidden object. Critics argue that many infants may understand that the object is hidden but lack the motor ability to coordinate their hands to physically demonstrate their understanding. Studying infants' looking behavior eliminates the need for infants to use motor activity to demonstrate their cognitive competence, permitting the study of object permanence in younger infants with undeveloped motor skills.

One such research design uses a **violation-of-expectation method**, a task in which a stimulus appears to violate physical laws (Baillargeon, 1994). Specifically, in a violation-of-expectation method, an infant is shown two events: one that is labeled *expected* because it follows physical laws and a second that is called *unexpected* because it violates physical laws. If the infant looks longer at the unexpected event, it suggests that he or she is surprised by it, is aware of physical properties of objects, and can mentally represent them.

In a classic study, developmental researcher Renée Baillargeon (1987) utilized the violation-of-expectation method to study the mental representation capacities of very young infants. Infants were shown a drawbridge that rotated 180 degrees. Then the infants watched as a box was placed behind the drawbridge to impede its movement. Infants watched as either the drawbridge rotated and stopped upon hitting the box or did not stop and appeared to move through the box (an "impossible" event). As shown in Figure 5.2, 4.5-month-old infants looked longer when the drawbridge appeared to move through the box (the "impossible" unexpected event) rather than when it stopped upon hitting the box. Baillargeon (1987) interpreted infants' looking longer at the unexpected event as suggesting that they maintained a mental representation of the box, even though they could not see it, and therefore understood that the drawbridge could not move through the entire box.

FIGURE 5.2: Object Permanence in Young Infants: Baillargeon's Drawbridge Study

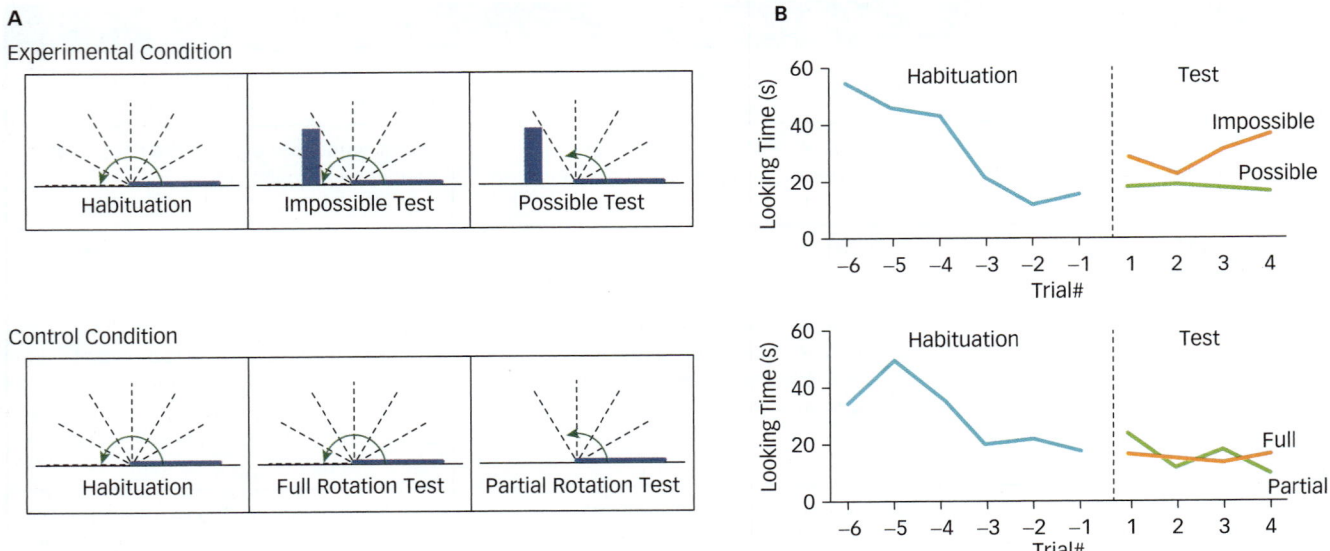

(A) Side view of habituation and test displays. Infants were habituated to a 180-degree drawbridge-like motion. (B) In the Experimental Condition, infants completed two types of test trials with a new object, a box. The Impossible Test involved the same full 180° rotation from habituation, but now the screen surprisingly passed through the box as it completed its rotation (with the box disappearing as it became obscured). The Possible Test involved a novel shorter rotation of screen up to the point where it would contact the box, where it stopped; this motion was "possible" in terms of solidity and object permanence. In the Control Condition, the screen rotations were identical, but no box was presented (such that both motions were equally possible). The results from the test phase are depicted in the right panels of (B). In the Experimental Condition, infants looked longer at the Impossible Test but not the Possible Test. However, in the Control Condition no preference was observed. They looked equally at the full and partial rotation. These results suggest a violation of infants' expectations regarding object permanence.

SOURCES: Baillargeon (1987). http://www.ncbi.nlm.nih.gov/pmc/articles/PMC2605404

Other researchers counter that these results do not demonstrate object permanence in young infants and instead illustrate infants' preference for novelty or for greater movement (Bogartz, Shinskey, & Schilling, 2000). For example, when the study was replicated without the box, 5-month-old infants looked longer at the full rotation, suggesting that infants looked at the unexpected event not because it violated physical laws but because it represented greater movement (Rivera, Wakely, & Langer, 1999). However, studies that use simpler tasks have shown support for young infants' competence. Four- and 5-month-old infants will watch a ball roll behind a barrier, gazing to where they expect it to reappear (Bertenthal, Longo, & Kenny, 2007; von Hofsten, Kochukhova, & Rosander, 2007). When 6-month-old infants are shown an object and the lights are then turned off, they will reach in the dark for the object (Goubet & Clifton, 1998; Shinskey & Munakata, 2003). They will also reach for an object hidden by being immersed in liquid (Shinskey, 2012), suggesting that they maintain a mental representation of the object and therefore have object permanence earlier than Piaget believed.

A-Not-B Tasks

Other critics of Piaget's views of infants' capacities for object permanence focus on an error that 8- to 12-month-old infants make, known as the *A-not-B error*. The A-not-B error occurs when infants are able to uncover a toy hidden behind a barrier, yet when they observe the toy moved from behind one barrier (Place A) to another (Place B), they look for the toy in the first place it was hidden, Place A, even after watching the toy be moved to Place B (see Figure 5.3). Piaget believed that the infant incorrectly, but persistently, searches for the object in Place A because he or she lacks object permanence. More recent research shows that infants look at Place B, the correct location, at the same time as they mistakenly reach for Place A (Diamond, 1985), suggesting that they understand the correct location of the object (Place B) but cannot keep themselves from reaching for Place A because of neural and motor immaturity (Diamond, 1991).

Other researchers propose that infants cannot restrain the impulse to repeat a behavior that was previously rewarded (Zelazo, Reznick, & Spinazzola, 1998). When looking time procedures are used to study the A-not-B error (Ahmed & Ruffman, 1998), infants look longer when the impossible illusory event occurs (when the toy is moved from Place A to Place B but is then found at Place A) than when the expected, possible event occurs (when the toy is moved from Place A to Place B and is found at Place B), suggesting that infants have object permanence but their motor skills prohibit them from demonstrating it in A-not-B tasks. One longitudinal study followed infants from 5 to 10 months of age and found that between 5 and 8 months infants showed better performance on an A-not-B looking task rather than a reaching task. Nine- and 10-month-old infants performed equally well on A-not-B looking and reaching tasks (Cuevas & Bell, 2010). Age-related changes in performance on A-not-B and other object permanence tasks may be due

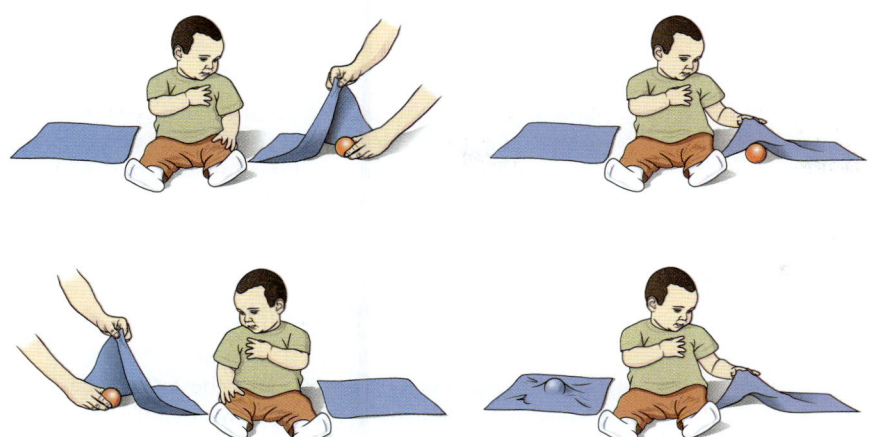

The infant continues to look for the ball under place A despite having seen the ball moved to place B.

to maturation of brain circuitry controlling motor skills and inhibition as well as advances in the ability to control attention (Cuevas & Bell, 2010; Watanabe, Forssman, Green, Bohlin, & von Hofsten, 2012).

Deferred Imitation Tasks

Another method of studying infants' capacities for mental representation relies on deferred imitation, the ability to repeat an act performed some time ago. Piaget (1962) believed that, because they lack mental representation abilities, infants under 18 months cannot engage in deferred imitation. Yet laboratory research on infant facial imitation has found that 6-week-old infants who watch an unfamiliar adult's facial expression will imitate it when they see the same adult the next day (Meltzoff & Moore, 1994). Six- and 9-month-old infants also display deferred imitation of unique actions performed with toys, such as taking a puppet's glove off, shaking it to ring a bell inside, and replacing it, over a 24-hour delay (Barr, Marrott, & Rovee-Collier, 2003).

When infants engage in deferred imitation, they act on the basis of stored representations of actions—memories—that counter Piaget's beliefs about infants' capabilities (Jones & Herbert, 2006). Many researchers now suggest that deferred imitation, along with object permanence itself, is better viewed as a continuously developing ability, rather than the stagelike shift in representational capacities that Piaget proposed (Hayne, 2004; Rovee-Collier, Hayne, & Colombo, 2002). For example, a three-year longitudinal study of infants 12, 18, and 24 months old showed that performance on deferred imitation tasks improved throughout the second year of life (Kolling, Goertz, Stefanie, & Knopf, 2010). Between 12 and 18 months, infants remember modeled behaviors for several months and imitate peers as well as adults (Hayne, Boniface, & Barr, 2000; Klein & Meltzoff, 1999). Increases in imitative capacity are observed with development up to 30 months of age as well as when shorter sequences of action are used, such as a sequence of fewer than eight unique actions (Barr, Dowden, & Hayne, 1996; Herbert & Hayne, 2000; Kressley-Mba, Lurg, & Knopf, 2005). These gradual changes suggest that infants and toddlers increase their representational capacities in a continuous developmental progression.

CORE KNOWLEDGE PERSPECTIVE AS AN ALTERNATIVE THEORY

Developmental psychologists generally agree with Piaget's description of infants as interacting with the world, actively taking in information, and constructing their own thinking. However, most researchers no longer agree with Piaget's belief that all knowledge begins with sensorimotor activity. Instead, infants are thought to have some innate, or inborn, cognitive capacities. Conservative theorists believe that infants are born with limited learning capacities such as a set of biases that cause them to attend to features of the environment that will help them to learn quickly (Kagan, 2008). Alternatively, the **core knowledge perspective** explains that infants are born with several innate knowledge systems or core domains of thought that enable early rapid learning and adaptation (Spelke & Kinzler, 2007; Spelke, Lee, & Izard, 2010).

Core knowledge theorists explain that infants learn so quickly and encounter such a great amount of sensory information that some prewired evolutionary understanding must be at work. Using the violation-of-expectation method, core knowledge researchers have found that young infants have a grasp of the physical properties of objects, including the knowledge that objects do not disappear out of existence (permanence), they cannot pass through another (solidity), and they will fall without support (gravity; Baillargeon, Li, Gertner, & Wu, 2011). Newborns are sensitive to the physical properties of objects and show preferences for causality, looking longer at stimuli that illustrate physical causality (e.g., Ball A rolling and hitting Ball B and Ball B rolling) than those that do not (e.g., Ball A rolling and Ball B rolling after a delay; Mascalzoni, Regolin, Vallortigara, & Simion, 2013). Infants are also thought to have early knowledge of numbers. Five-month-old infants can discriminate between small and large numbers of items (Cordes & Brannon, 2009; Libertus & Brannon, 2009). Even newborns are sensitive to large differences in number, distinguishing nine items from three, for example, but newborns show difficulty distinguishing small numbers from each other (two vs. three items; Coubart, Izard, Spelke, Marie, & Streri, 2014). Comparative research has shown that animals display these systems of knowledge early in life and without much experience (Vallortigara, 2012), suggesting that it is possible for infants to quickly yet naturally construct an understanding of the world (Xu & Kushnir, 2013).

Much core knowledge research employs the same looking paradigms described earlier, in which infants' visual preferences are measured as indictors of what they know. Critics argue that it is unclear whether we can interpret infants' looking in the same way as adults (Kagan, 2008). Such measures demonstrate discrimination—that young infants can tell the difference between stimuli—yet perceiving the difference between two stimuli does not necessarily mean that an infant understands how the two stimuli differ (Bremner, Slater, & Johnson, 2015). Others have suggested that infants are not detecting differences in number but differences in area (Mix, Huttenlocher, & Levine, 2002). For example, it may be that the infant attends to space rather than number and may differentiate nine items from three not because of the change in number but simply that nine items take up more space than three. More recent research has shown that 7-month-old infants can differentiate changes in number and area, are more sensitive to changes in number than area, and prefer to look at number changes over area changes (Libertus, Starr, & Brannon, 2014). Infants apply basic inferential mechanisms to quickly yet naturally construct an understanding of the world (Xu & Kushnir, 2013). Research with toddlers has suggested that they can understand, learn, and use causal principles to guide their actions (Walker & Gopnik, 2013).

Overall, Piaget's theory has had a profound influence on how we view cognitive development. However, infants and toddlers are more cognitively competent than Piaget imagined, showing signs of representational ability and conceptual thought that he believed were not possible (Flavell, 1993). Developmental scientists agree with Piaget that immature forms of cognition give way to more mature forms, that the individual is active in development, and that interaction with the environment is critical for cognitive growth. However, developmental scientists also agree that cognitive development entails increasing competence in information processing abilities. Although they represent contrasting views, both Piaget's cognitive-developmental theory and information processing theory contribute to our understanding of children's thinking.

Thinking in Context 5.1

1. Toys offer infants important opportunities to practice and hone their development, and infants play with toys in different ways at different ages. Identify a toy appropriate for an infant in the secondary circular reactions substage (e.g., a loud rattle or jingling set of toy keys).

2. Compare and contrast how infants in the secondary circular reactions substage and coordination of secondary schemas substage might play with the toy.

3. How might infants in the tertiary reactions substage play with it?

4. How might infants' play match their developing schemes?

5. Might parent–infant interactions, the home environment, and sociocultural context influence when infants develop object permanence? Why or why not?

6. Infants around the world delight in playing peekaboo. Compare and contrast how Piaget and core knowledge theorists might account for infants' attention and interest in the caregiver's disappearing and reappearing face.

INFORMATION PROCESSING

Information processing theorists describe *cognition* as a set of interrelated components that permit people to process information—to notice, take in, manipulate, store, and retrieve it. Newborns are ready to learn and adapt to their world because, like children and adults, they are born information processors.

ORGANIZATION OF THE INFORMATION PROCESSING SYSTEM

From an information processing perspective, the mind is composed of three mental stores: **sensory memory**, **working memory**, and **long-term memory**. From early infancy to mature adulthood, we use these three stores to manipulate and store information.

Sensory memory is the first step in getting information into the mind; it holds incoming sensory information in its original form. For example, look at this page, then close your eyes. Did you "see" the page for a fraction of a second after you closed your eyes? That image, or icon, represents your sensory memory. Information fades from sensory memory quickly if it is not processed, even as quickly as fractions of a second. Newborn infants display sensory memory, although it is much shorter in duration than adults' memory (Cheour et al., 2002). As a great deal of information is taken in and rapidly moves through sensory memory, much of it is discarded. When we direct our attention or awareness to information, however, it passes to the next part of the information processing system: working memory.

Working memory, sometimes called short-term memory, holds and processes information that is being "worked on" in some way: manipulated (considered, comprehended), encoded (transformed into a memory), or retrieved (recalled). Working memory is responsible for maintaining and processing information used in many complex cognitive tasks (Gathercole, 1998). All of your thoughts—that is, all conscious mental activity—occur within working memory. For example, reading this paragraph, remembering assignments, and considering how this material applies to your own experience taps your working memory. Just as your thoughts are constantly changing, so are the contents of working memory. While infants cannot tell us their thoughts, looking-time studies suggest that by 5 or 6 months of age, infants can remember and manipulate information to determine the locations of hidden objects (Reznick, Morrow, Goldman, & Snyder, 2004).

An important part of working memory is the **central executive**, a control processor that directs the flow of information and regulates cognitive activities such as attention, action, and problem solving (Daneman & Carpenter, 1980; Just & Carpenter, 1992). The central executive determines what is important to attend to, combines new information with information already in working memory, and selects and applies strategies for manipulating the information in order to understand it, make decisions, and solve problems (Andersson, 2008; Baddeley, 1986, 1996).

As information is manipulated in working memory, it becomes more likely that it will enter long-term memory, the third mental store. Long-term memory is an unlimited store that holds information indefinitely. Information is not manipulated or processed in long-term memory; it is simply stored until it is retrieved to manipulate in working memory (e.g., remembering events and thinking about them). With development, we amass a great deal of information, organize it in increasingly sophisticated ways, and encode and retrieve it more efficiently and with less effort.

We are born with the ability to take in, store, and manipulate information through our sensory, working, and long-term memory. The structure of the information processing system remains the same throughout the lifespan (see Figure 5.4). With development, we get better at moving information through our cognitive system in ways that allow us to adapt to our world. We can process more information, retain more information, and do so more quickly and efficiently. We are born with a functioning information processing system, and it develops rapidly and very early in life.

ATTENTION

Attention refers to the ability to direct one's awareness. Infant attention is often studied using preferential looking procedures (measuring the length of time infants look at two stimuli) and habituation procedures, in which researchers measure the length of time it takes infants to habituate to looking at a nonchanging stimulus, such as a geometric pattern (Oakes, 2010; Richards, 2010, 2011). Infants show more attentiveness to dynamic than static stimuli (Richards, 2010). Young infants require a long time to habituate to stimuli and will look longer at stimuli than will older infants.

By around 10 weeks of age, infants show gains in attention. They become more efficient at scanning and processing visual information and therefore require less exposure to

FIGURE 5.4: Information Processing System

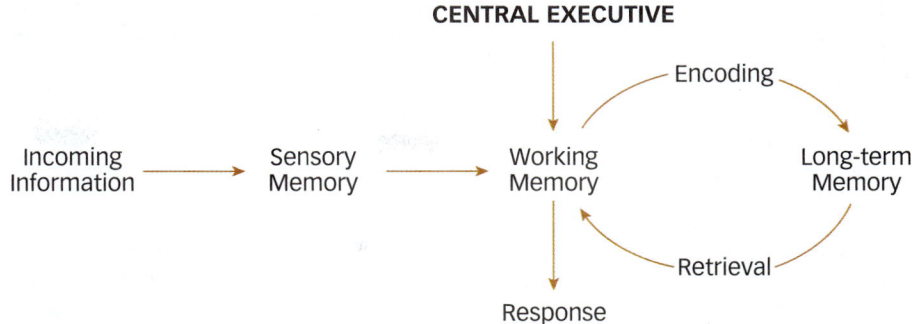

stimuli to habituate (Colombo, 2001; Colombo, McCollam, Coldren, Mitchell, & Rash, 1990). For example, in one experiment, 3- to 13-month-old infants were shown displays that included a range of static and moving stimuli (Courage, Reynolds, & Richards, 2006). Overall, looking time peaked at 14 weeks of age and dropped steadily, demonstrating infants' growing cognitive efficiency. From about 6.5 months of age, infants' looking time varied with stimulus complexity,

Burger/Phanie/Science Source

The toy keys have captured this infant's attention. How long will it take for the baby to habituate to this interesting stimulus?

decreasing for simple stimuli such as dot patterns, increasing slightly for complex stimuli such as faces, and increasing more for very complex stimuli such as video clips (Courage et al., 2006).

Most research on infant attention has studied habituation and infant looking behavior to infer attention. More recently, researchers have begun using brain imaging techniques to measure infants' brain activity because the development of infant attention is thought to be closely related to neurological development in the areas underlying attentional control (Richards, 2010). In response to tasks that challenge attention, infants show activity in the frontal cortex (used for thinking and planning) that is diffuse (widely spread) at 5.5 months of age, but more specific or localized by 7.5 months of age (Richards, 2010). Important developments in attention occur over the course of infancy and continue throughout childhood. As discussed in Lifespan Brain Development (p. 123), the changes in information processing skills like attention influence infants' ability to attend to and learn from television and video.

MEMORY

The ability to focus and switch attention is critical for selecting information to process in working memory. Even newborns have memory, as demonstrated by habituation studies (Streri, Hevia, Izard, & Coubart, 2013). When infants habituate to a stimulus and are shown the stimulus again after a delay, more rapid habituation on the second exposure indicates that they remember the stimulus (Oakes, 2010). Classic habituation studies have shown that by 3 months of age infants can remember a visual stimulus for 24 hours, and by the time they are 1 year old they can retain such memories for several days or even weeks (Fagan, 1973; Martin, 1975). In one study, 2- to 3-month-old infants were taught to kick their foot, which was tied to a mobile with a ribbon, to make the mobile move (see Figure 5.5). One week later, the infants were reattached to the mobile and kicked vigorously, indicating their memory of the first occasion. The infants would kick even four weeks later if the experimenter gave the mobile a shake to remind them of its movement (Rovee-Collier, 1999; Rovee-Collier & Bhatt, 1993). Infants have basic memory capacities common to children and adults (Rose, Feldman, Jankowski, & Van Rossem, 2011), but they are most likely to remember events when they take place in familiar contexts and when the infants are actively engaged (Learmonth, Lamberth, & Rovee-Collier, 2004).

Emotional engagement also enhances infants' memory. Infants are more likely to remember events that are associated with emotions. For example, the still-face interaction paradigm is an experimental task in which an infant interacts with an adult who first engages in normal social interaction and then suddenly becomes unresponsive (Tronick, Als, Adamson, Wise, & Brazelton, 1978). Infants usually respond to the adult's still face with brief smiles followed by negative facial expressions, crying, looking away, thumb sucking, and other responses suggesting emotional

FIGURE 5.5: Rovee-Collier Ribbon Study

Nick Alexander

Young infants were taught to kick their foot to make an attached mobile move. When tested one week later the infants remembered and kicked their legs vigorously to make the mobile move.
SOURCE: Levine and Munsch (2010).

distress (Shapiro, Fagen, Prigot, Carroll, & Shalan, 1998; Weinberg & Tronick, 1994, 1996). In one study, 5-month-old infants who were exposed to the still face demonstrated recall over a year later, at 20 months of age, by looking less at the woman who appeared in the still-face paradigm than at two other women whom the infants had never previously seen (Bornstein, Arterberry, & Mash, 2004). These lines of research suggest that memory improves over the course of infancy, but even young infants are likely to recall events in which they are actively engaged, that take place in familiar surroundings, and that are emotionally salient (Courage & Cowan, 2009; Learmonth et al., 2004).

CATEGORIZATION

In infants' eyes, the entire world is new—"one great blooming, buzzing confusion" in the famous phrase of 19th-century psychologist William James (1890). As infants are bombarded with a multitude of stimuli, encountering countless new objects, people, and events, they naturally group stimuli into classes or categories. **Categorization**, grouping different

The Media and Baby Geniuses

Most babies watch at least some television or play with electronic devices, such as their parents' mobile phones and tablets. How might viewing media influence infants' development?

Nine-month-old Derek sat in his high chair, munching cereal and watching the flickering television screen in front of him. On average, infants watch television and videos for about one to two hours each day (Rideout, 2013). In fact, 90% of parents report that their infants under the age of 2 years watch some form of electronic media, and the programming they watch is often specifically tailored to infants (AAP; Brown 2011).

Infant-directed videos are often advertised as a way to enhance babies' brain development, **intelligence**, and early learning as they offer educational content embedded in an engaging video format and focused on themes such as language and general knowledge, including, shape, color, reading, and numbers (Fenstermacher et al., 2010). Most parents believe that age-appropriate videos can have an important positive impact on early child development, providing good entertainment for babies and convenience for parents (Robb, Richert, & Wartella, 2009).

But do baby videos really aid development? Brain-building claims made by baby media manufacturers are not supported by the research literature (Christakis, 2009), and longitudinal studies suggest no evidence of long-term benefits of media use in early childhood (Courage & Howe, 2010; Ferguson & Donnellan, 2014). One study tested a popular DVD program that claims to help young infants learn to read. Ten- to 18-month-old infants

who regularly watched the program for seven months did not differ from other infants in intelligence, cognitive skills, reading skill, or word knowledge (Neuman, Kaefer, Pinkham, & Strouse, 2014). Other research has demonstrated that infants learn more readily from people than from TV, a finding known as the **video deficit effect** (Anderson & Pempek, 2005). For example, when 12- to 18-month-old infants watched a best-selling DVD that labels household objects, the infants learned very little from it as compared with what they learned though interaction with parents (DeLoache et al., 2010). Yet the video deficit is reduced when infants' memory capacities are taken into account, such as by repeating content and adding visual and auditory cues (Barr, 2013). Infants and toddlers may be capable of learning from screen media, depending on the degree to which the media content resembles infant and toddlers' real-life experiences including the use of simple stories and familiar objects or routines (Linebarger & Vaala, 2010).

Are baby videos harmful? Some studies suggest that exposure to baby media may be associated with deficits and delays in language development (Chonchaiya & Pruksananonda, 2008; Zimmerman, Christakis, & Meltzoff, 2007). The effects of media use vary with its content, quality, and context. For example, one study showed that Hispanic infants and toddlers who viewed more than two hours of television per day showed poor scores on a language measure—but the relationship was true only for infant media; those who viewed adult media showed no difference in language scores (Duch, Fisher, Ensari, & Harrington, 2013). It may not be the quantity of television viewing that is related with language outcomes but instead poor-quality viewing (e.g., television unintended for children, background television, solitary viewing, and earlier age of viewing), which were related to lower vocabulary scores overall but especially the English vocabulary scores of bilingual toddlers (Hudon, Fennell, & Hoftyzer, 2013). Age certainly matters. For example, one study showed that infants who are 17 months old and older were able to learn words from infant DVDs, as evidenced by looking measures, but not younger infants (Krcmar, 2014).

Although infant media will not turn ordinary infants into baby Einsteins, it does not seem to cause harm (Neuman et al., 2014). Parents play a role in influencing the effects of educational and interactive baby media on their infants. When parents watch videos along with their infants and talk to them about the content, infants spend more time looking at the screen, learn more from the media, and show greater knowledge of language as toddlers (Linebarger & Vaala, 2010). In today's electronically connected world, it is impossible for most families to prevent infants from coming into contact with screens, whether television, tablet, or mobile phone. Considering that nearly 40% of infants under the age of 2 have viewed a mobile device, it appears that a developmental task for today's infants and toddlers is to learn how to learn from screens (Wartella & Lauricella, 2012).

What Do You Think?

1. How might you teach infants and toddlers how to learn from screens, such as from televisions, cell phones, and tablets?

2. Imagine that you are a parent. What are some of the reasons why you might allow your young child to play with your mobile phone or tablet? In your view, what are some disadvantages to screen use by infants and toddlers?

Pictorium/Alamy

stimuli from a common class, is an adaptive mental process that allows for organized storage of information in memory, efficient retrieval of that information, and the capacity to respond with familiarity to new stimuli from a common class (Bruner, Goodnow, & Austin, 1956; Murphy, 2002). Infants naturally categorize or organize information, just as older children and adults do, for without the ability to categorize, we would have to respond anew to each novel stimulus we experience (Bornstein & Arterberry, 2010; Rosenberg & Feigenson, 2013).

Just as in studying perception and attention, developmental researchers must rely on basic learning capacities, such as habituation, to study how infants categorize objects. For example, infants are shown a series of stimuli belonging to one category (e.g., fruit: apples and oranges), and then are presented with a new stimulus of the same category (e.g., a pear or a lemon) and a stimulus of a different category (e.g., a cat or a horse). If an infant dishabituates, or shows renewed interest by looking longer at the new stimulus (e.g., cat), it suggests that he or she perceives it as belonging to a different category from that of previously encountered stimuli (Cohen & Cashon, 2006). Using this method, researchers have learned that 3-month-old infants categorize pictures of dogs as different from cats based on perceived differences in facial features (Quinn, Eimas, & Rosenkrantz, 1993).

Infants' earliest categories are based on the perceived similarity of objects (Rakison & Butterworth, 1998). By 4 months, infants can form categories based on perceptual properties, grouping objects that are similar in appearance including shape, size, and color (Colombo et al., 1990; Quinn & Eimas, 1996; Rakison & Butterworth, 1998). As early as 7 months of age, infants use conceptual categories based on perceived function and behavior (Mandler, 2000, 2004). Moreover, patterns in 6- to 7-month-old infants' brain waves correspond to their identification of novel and familiar categories (Quinn, Doran, Reiss, & Hoffman, 2010). Seven- to 12-month-old infants use many categories to organize objects, such as food, furniture, birds, animals, vehicles, kitchen utensils, and more, based on perceptual similarity and perceived function and behavior (Mandler & McDonough, 1993, 1998; Oakes, Coppage, & Dingel, 1997).

Researchers also use sequential touching tasks to study categorization in older infants (Mandler, Fivush, & Reznick, 1987). Infants are presented with a collection of objects from two categories (e.g., four animals and four vehicles), and their patterns of touching are recorded. If the infants recognize a categorical distinction among the objects, they touch those from within a category in succession more than would be expected by chance (Bornstein & Arterberry, 2010). Research using sequential touching procedures has shown that 12- to 30-month-old toddlers categorize objects first at a global level and then at more specific levels. They categorize at more inclusive levels (e.g., animals or vehicles) before less inclusive levels (e.g., types of animals or vehicles) and before even less inclusive levels (e.g., specific animals or vehicles; Bornstein & Arterberry, 2010). Infants' and toddlers' everyday experiences and exploration contribute to their growing capacity to recognize commonalities among objects and group them in meaningful ways (Mandler, 2004; Oakes & Madole, 2003). Recognizing categories is a way of organizing information that allows for more efficient storage and retrieval of information in memory. Therefore, advances in categorization are critical to cognitive development.

As shown in Table 5.2, cognition changes dramatically over the first two years of life. According to cognitive-developmental theory, infants move from basic reflexes to representational thought. Although recent research has modified the timetable of cognitive development in response to findings that infants are more competent than believed, descriptions of the cognitive advances themselves are unchanged. At the same time as infants show advances in representational thinking, the underlying information processing capacities, such as attention, memory, and categorization skill, show continuous change over the first three years of life (Rose, Feldman, & Jankowski, 2009). Infants get better at attending to the world around them, remembering what they encounter, and organizing and making sense of what they learn. Infants' emerging cognitive capacities influence all aspects of their development and functioning, including intelligence.

Thinking in Context 5.2

1. Recall from Chapter 1 that an important theme of development is that it is influenced by multiple contexts. How might contextual influences, such as family, neighborhood, sociocultural context, and even cohort or generation, influence cognitive development?

2. Identify personal examples of attention, working memory, and long-term memory. What is the earliest personal example that you can identify? How have your information processing capacities changed with development?

3. Given what we know about infants' capacities for attention, memory, and categorization, what kinds of toys and activities would you recommend to caregivers who want to entertain infants while promoting their development?

INDIVIDUAL DIFFERENCES IN INFANT INTELLIGENCE

At its simplest, intelligence refers to an individual's ability to adapt to the world. Of course, different people have different levels of intelligence—an example of the concept of individual differences or variation from one individual to another. Intelligence tests are used to measure these differences; they include questions that measure memory, pattern recognition, verbal knowledge, quantitative abilities, and logical reasoning. Measuring intelligence in infancy is challenging because, as noted earlier, infants cannot answer questions. Instead, researchers who study infant intelligence rely on an assortment of nonverbal tasks—the same kinds of methods,

TABLE 5.2 Changes in Information Processing Skills During Infancy

ABILITY	DESCRIPTION
Attention	• Attention increases steadily over infancy. • From birth, infants attend more to dynamic than static stimuli. • During the second half of their first year, infants attend more to complex stimuli such as faces and video clips. • Attention is linked with diffuse frontal lobe activity in young infants and localized frontal lobe activity by 7.5 months of age. • Individual differences appear at all ages and are stable over time. • Attention is associated with performance on visual recognition memory tasks.
Memory	• Memory improves with age. • Three-month-old infants can remember a visual stimulus for 24 hours. • By the end of the first year, infants can remember a visual stimulus for several days or even weeks. • Infants are most likely to remember events in familiar, engaging, and emotionally salient contexts.
Categorization	• Infants first categorize objects based on perceived similarity. • By 4 months, infants can form categories based on perceptual properties such as shape, size, and color. • By 6 to 7 months of age, infants' brain waves correspond to their identification of novel and familiar categories. • Seven- to 12-month-old infants can organize objects such as food, furniture, animals, and kitchen utensils, based on perceived function and behavior. • Twelve- to 30-month-old infants categorize objects first at a global level and then at more specific levels. • Infants categorize objects at more global and inclusive levels (such as motor vehicles) before more specific and less inclusive levels (such as cars, trucks, construction equipment). • The use of categories improves memory efficiency.

described earlier, that are used to study cognitive development. There are two general approaches to studying intelligence in infancy. As discussed next, the testing approach emphasizes standardized tests that compare infants with age-based norms. A second approach, the information processing approach, examines specific processing skills.

TESTING APPROACH TO INTELLIGENCE

At 3 months of age, Baby Lourdes can lift and support her upper body with her arms when on her stomach. She grabs and shakes toys with her hands and enjoys playing with other people. Lourdes's pediatrician tells her parents that her development is right on track for babies her age, and she shows typical levels of infant intelligence. Standardized tests permit the pediatrician to determine Lourdes's development relative to other infants her age.

The most often used standardized measure of infant intelligence is the Bayley Scales of Infant Development III (BSID-III), commonly called "Bayley-III" (see Figure 5.6). This test is appropriate for infants from 1 month through 42 months of age (Bayley, 1969, 2005). The Bayley-III consists of five scales: three consisting of infant responses and two of parent responses. The motor scale measures gross and fine motor skills, such as grasping objects, drinking from a cup, sitting, and climbing stairs. The cognitive scale includes items such as attending to a stimulus or searching for a hidden toy. The language scale examines comprehension and production of language, such as following

directions and naming objects. The social-emotional scale is derived from parental report regarding behaviors such as the infant's responsiveness and play behaviors. Finally, the adaptive behavior scale is based on parental reports of the infant's ability to adapt in everyday situations, including the infant's ability to communicate, regulate his or her emotions, and display certain behaviors.

The Bayley-III provides a comprehensive profile of an infant's current functioning, but infants' performance often varies considerably from one testing session to another (Bornstein, Slater, Brown, Roberts, & Barrett, 1997). Scores vary with infants' states of arousal and motivation. This

FIGURE 5.6 Bayley-III Scales (BSID-III)

Cliff Moore / Science Source

Infant assessment tests, such as the BSID-III, examine cognitive, language, social-emotional, and motor abilities, such as infants' skill in manipulating objects.

suggests that pediatricians and parents must exert great care in interpreting scores—particularly poor scores—because an infant's performance may be influenced by factors other than developmental functioning. Alternatively, some researchers have argued that perhaps the variability in Bayley-III scores from one occasion to another suggests that intelligence itself is variable in infancy (Bornstein et al., 1997). Regardless, the low test–retest reliability (recall from Chapter 1) means that infants who perform poorly on the Bayley-III should be tested more than once.

Although Bayley-III scores offer a comprehensive profile of an infant's abilities, scores do not predict performance on intelligence tests in childhood (Honzik, 1983; Luttikhuizen dos Santos, de Kieviet, Königs, van Elburg, & Oosterlaan, 2013; Rose & Feldman, 1995). Even Nancy Bayley (1949), who invented the BSID-III, noted in a longitudinal study that infant performance was not related to intelligence scores at age 18. Why is infant intelligence relatively unrelated to later intelligence? Consider what is measured by infant tests: perception and motor skills, responsiveness, and language skills. The ability to grasp an object, crawl up stairs, or search for a hidden toy—items that appear on the Bayley-III—are not measured by childhood intelligence tests (Bornstein et al., 1997). Instead, intelligence tests administered in childhood examine more complex and abstract abilities such as verbal reasoning, verbal comprehension, and problem solving.

If the Bayley-III does not predict later intelligence, why administer it? Infants whose performance is poor relative to age norms may suffer from serious developmental problems that can be addressed. The intellectual abilities measured by the Bayley-III are critical indicators of neurological health and are useful for charting developmental paths, diagnosing neurological disorders, and detecting intellectual disabilities in infants and toddlers. As such, the Bayley-III is used as a screening tool to identify infants who can benefit from medical and developmental intervention.

INFORMATION PROCESSING APPROACH TO INTELLIGENCE

The challenge in determining whether intelligence in infancy predicts performance in childhood and beyond rests in identifying measures that evaluate cognitive functioning from infancy through childhood. New approaches look to information processing as an indicator of intellectual ability (Kail, 2000). Information processing capacities, such as attention, are evident at birth and persist for a lifetime.

Individuals who process information more efficiently are thought to acquire knowledge more quickly. This is true for infants as well as for older children and adults. Information processing capacities—such as attention, memory, and processing speed—in infancy predict cognitive ability and intelligence through late adolescence (Cuevas & Bell, 2013; Luttikhuizen dos Santos et al., 2013; Rose,

Feldman, Jankowski, & Van Rossem, 2012). These information processing abilities can be measured in simple ways. For example, attention, memory, and processing speed can be measured by assessing visual reaction time (how quickly infants look when shown a stimulus) and preference for novelty (the degree to which they prefer new stimuli over familiar ones). Both of these measures have been shown to predict childhood and adolescent intelligence (Fagan, 2011; Kavšek, 2004, 2013; McCall & Carrigher, 1993).

Infants show individual differences in cognitive capacities as indexed by basic learning tasks. Habituation tasks such as those discussed earlier in this chapter are used to study what babies can perceive and how they think, but habituation tasks also provide information about the efficiency of information processing because they indicate how quickly an infant learns: Infants who learn quickly look away from an unchanging stimulus more quickly. In looking time studies assessing habituation, some infants are short-lookers, habituating quickly, and others are long-lookers, taking more time to habituate. Infants who are short-lookers require less time to process information about the stimulus and are therefore more efficient information processors. Longitudinal studies suggest that infants who are fast habituators (short-lookers) score higher on measures of intelligence measures in childhood and adolescence than do those who are slower habituators (Kavšek, 2004, 2013; Rose, Feldman, & Jankowski, 2012). For example, infant fast habituators had higher IQs and higher educational achievement when they were followed up 20 years later, in emerging adulthood (Fagan, Holland, & Wheeler, 2007).

Attention, memory, speed of thinking, and cognitive adaptability are competencies that permit individuals to make sense of and adapt to their world—qualities that constitute intelligence. Information processing skills in infancy are effective predictors of intelligence in childhood; however, these findings are generally the result of laboratory research. That is, although pediatricians might test an infant's attention and habituation as part of an examination, there is no standardized information processing test of intelligence to apply to infants, as compared with the Bayley-III. The sensory and motor skills emphasized by the Bayley-III provide information about the infant's current state and neurological functioning, which are critical to determining an infant's health.

Thinking in Context 5.3

1. Thinking back to the continuity–discontinuity theme of development, would you say that intelligence represents an example of continuous or discontinuous change? Explain your answer.

2. Why is infant intelligence a poor predictor of later intelligence?

3. How might contextual factors, such as home environment and experiences, influence the skills measured by infant intelligence tests such as the Bayley-III?

LANGUAGE DEVELOPMENT

Eleven-month-old William was wide eyed as his father handed him a ball and said, "Ball!" "Ba!" said William. Unlike the random **cooing** and **babbling** sounds he made a few months ago, William is now beginning to show evidence of understanding a few words and trying to utter them.

Developing the ability to use language is a critical step in infancy and toddlerhood; it has important implications for the child's cognitive, social, and emotional development. Gaining the ability to use words to represent objects, experience, thoughts, and feelings permits children to think and to communicate with others in increasingly flexible and adaptive ways.

We know from experiments with newborns that infants are primed to learn language from birth. Infants naturally notice the complex patterns of sounds around them and organize sounds into meaningful units. They recognize frequently heard words, like their name (Aslin, Clayards, & Bardhan, 2008). By 4.5 months of age, infants will turn their head to hear their own name but not to hear other names, even when the other names have a similar sound pattern (e.g., Annie vs. Johnny; Aslin et al., 2008; Mandel, Jusczyk, & Pisoni, 1995). Neonates prefer to listen to their native language, as well as stories that they have heard prenatally, suggesting that they are sensitive to the sound of words and the pattern of speech from birth. Newborns are able to hear all of the sounds of which the human voice is capable but by 10 to 12 months their ability to perceive nonnative sounds declines significantly (Aslin et al., 2008; Kuhl, Williams, Lacerda, Stevens, & Lindblom, 1992). The quality of mother–infant interactions plays a role in determining the timing of infants' narrowing of speech sound discrimination. Specifically, infants who experience high-quality interactions with their mothers, characterized by frequent speech, show a narrowing earlier, as early as 6 months of age (Elsabbagh et al., 2013).

PRELINGUISTIC COMMUNICATION

At birth, crying is the infant's only means of communication. Infants soon learn to make many more sounds like gurgles, grunts, squeals, and more. Between 2 and 3 months, infants begin cooing, making deliberate vowel sounds like "ahhhh," "ohhhhhh," and "eeeeeee." These vocal sounds are a form of vocal play; they are likely to be heard when the baby is awake, alert and contented. At the cooing stage, infants already use pauses that are consistent with the turn-taking pattern of spoken conversations. Babbling, repeating strings of consonants and vowels such as "ba-ba-ba-ba" and "ma-ma-ma," begins to appear at about 6 months of age. At first, babbling is universal. All babies do it, and the sounds they make are similar no matter what language their parents speak or in what part of the world they are raised. However, as mentioned earlier, infants soon become sensitive to the ambient language

around them, and it influences their vocalizations (Chen & Kent, 2010). With development and exposure to speech, babbling becomes more wordlike and sounds more like the infant's native language; by the end of the first year, infants' babbling sounds as if they are speaking (Andruski, Casielles, & Nathan, 2013; Rothgänger, 2003).

Language acquisition is a socially interactive process—babies learn by hearing others speak and by the reactions their vocalizations evoke in caregivers. Caregivers tend to recognize specific syllables and babbling repertoires, which serve as foundations for word learning (Ramsdell, Oller, Buder, Ethington, & Chorna, 2012). Infants modify their babbling in response to caregiver interactions (Tamis-LeMonda, Kuchirko, & Song, 2014).

FIRST WORDS

At about 1 year of age, the average infant speaks his or her first word. At first, infants use one-word expressions, called **holophrases**, to express a complete thought. A first word might be a complete word or a syllable. Usually the word has more than one meaning depending on the context in which it is used. For example, "Da" might mean, "I want that," "There's Daddy!" or "What's that?" Caregivers usually hear and understand first words before other adults do. The first words that infants use are those that they hear often or are meaningful for them, such as their own name, the word *no*, or the word for their caregiver.

Throughout language development, babies' receptive language (what they can understand) exceeds their productive language (what they can produce themselves). That is, infants understand more words than they can use. By 13 months of age, children begin to quickly learn the meaning of a new word, and they understand that a word corresponds to a particular thing or event (Woodward, Markman, & Fitzsimmons, 1994), but they tend to learn the names of objects more easily than the names of actions.

LEARNING WORDS

"I can't believe how quickly Matthew picks up new words. It's time for us to be more careful about what we say around him," warned Elana. Her husband agreed, "He's only 2 years old, and he has quite a vocabulary. Who would think that he'd learn so many words so quickly!" Is Matthew unusual? Most infants Matthew's age rapidly expand their vocabulary, often to the surprise of their parents. How do infants learn new words? They do it through **fast mapping**, a process of quickly acquiring and retaining a word after hearing it applied a few times. Two-year-olds are able to learn a word even after a single brief exposure under ambiguous conditions (Spiegel & Halberda, 2011). Fast mapping improves with age and accounts for the **naming explosion**, also known as the vocabulary spurt, a period of rapid vocabulary learning that occurs between 16 and 24 months of age (Dapretto & Bjork, 2000). Within weeks, a toddler may increase her vocabulary from 50 words to over 400 (Bates, Bretherton, & Snyder, 1988).

Recent research has suggested that the vocabulary spurt is not universal. Word acquisition occurs gradually for many children, rather than through a sudden spurt (Ganger & Brent, 2004; Parladé & Iverson, 2011). At 18 months, toddlers are more likely to learn a new word if both they and the speaker are attending to the new object when the speaker introduces the new word (Baldwin et al., 1996). Yet by 24 to 30 months of age, toddlers can determine the meaning of words even if they simply overhear the speaker talking to someone else (Akhtar, Jipson, & Callanan, 2001), and they can learn new words when their attention is distracted by other objects or events (Moore, Angelopoulos, & Bennett, 1999). Fast mapping helps young children learn many new words, but their own speech lags behind what they can understand, because young children have difficulty retrieving the words from memory to use (Dapretto & Bjork, 2000).

As children learn words, we see two interesting kinds of mistakes that tell us about how words are learned (Gershkoff-Stowe, 2002). **Underextension** refers to applying a word more narrowly than it is usually applied so that the word's use is restricted to a single object. For example, *cup* might refer to Daddy's cup but not to the general class of cups. Later, the opposite tendency appears. **Overextension** refers to applying a word too broadly. *Cow* might refer to cows, sheep, horses, and all farm animals. Overextension suggests that the child has learned that a word can signify a whole class of objects. As children develop a larger vocabulary and get feedback on their speech, they demonstrate fewer errors of overextension and underextension.

TWO-WORD UTTERANCES

At about 21 months of age, or usually about 8 to 12 months after they say their first word, most children compose their first simple two-word sentences, such as "Kitty come," or "Mommy milk." **Telegraphic speech**, like a telegram, only includes a few essential words. Like other milestones in language development, telegraphic speech is universal among toddlers. Children around the world use two-word phrases to express themselves.

Language development follows a predictable path, as shown in Table 5.3. By 2.5 years of age, children demonstrate an awareness of the communicative purpose of speech and the importance of being understood. For example, in one experiment, 2.5-year-old children asked an adult to hand them a toy. The child was more likely to repeat and clarify the request for the toy when the adult's verbal response indicated misunderstanding of the child's request ("Did you say to put the toy on the shelf?") than when the adult appeared to understand the request, regardless of whether the adult gave the child the toy (Shwe & Markman, 1997).

It is not until some time between 20 and 30 months that children show competence in using syntax, the rules for

TABLE 5.3 Language Milestones

AGE	LANGUAGE SKILL
2–3 months	Cooing
6 months	Babbling
1 year	First word Holophrases
16–24 months	Vocabulary spurt Learn new words by fast mapping Underextension Overextension
21 months	Telegraphic speech
21–30 months	Syntax

forming sentences in a given language. Soon they become more comfortable with using articles (such as *a*, *and*, *the*), prepositions (such as *in* or *on*), conjunctions (such as *and*, *or*, *but*), plurals, and past tense.

THEORIES OF LANGUAGE DEVELOPMENT

Over the first two years of life, children transform from wailing newborns who communicate their needs through cries to toddlers who can use words to articulate their needs, desires, and thoughts. Developmental scientists have offered several explanations for infants' rapid acquisition of language. Some explanations emphasize the role of the environment in accounting for language whereas others emphasize biological factors.

Learning Theory and Language Acquisition

Baby Howie gurgled, "Ba-ba-ba-ba!" His parents encouraged him excitedly, "Say bottle. Ba-ba!" Howie squealed, "Ba-ba-ba-ba-ba!" Parents play an important role in language development. They provide specific instruction and communicate their excitement about their infants' developing competence, encouraging infants to practice their new language skills. Learning theorist B. F. Skinner (1957) proposed that language, just like all other behaviors, is learned through operant conditioning: reinforcement and punishment.

From birth, infants make sounds at random. Caregivers respond to infants' early utterances with interest and attention, imitating and reinforcing infants' verbal behaviors (Gratier & Devouche, 2011; Pelaez, Virues-Ortega, & Gewirtz, 2011). Infants repeat the sounds. Caregivers then reward sounds that resemble adult speech with attention, smiles, and affection. Infants imitate sounds that adults make and repeat sounds that are reinforced. From this perspective, imitation and reinforcement shape children's language acquisition. The quantity and quality of the parents' verbal interactions with the child and responses to the

Baby Signing

AP/Justin Hayworth

Although signing may not accelerate language development, it offers opportunities for parent-infant interaction and play.

Few things are as frustrating for a parent as trying to decipher their baby's cry. What does she need? Is she hungry? Cold? Does she have a wet diaper? Is she hurt? Imagine that the baby could communicate her needs. The baby signing movement, teaching infants to communicate with symbolic gestures, promotes early communication between infants and parents. The assumption behind baby signing is that the gross motor skills needed for signing develop before the relatively fine motor control of the mouth, tongue, and breath needed to articulate speech (Goodwyn & Acredolo, 1998). Parents who read about the benefits of teaching signs to their infants often embrace the practice. Numerous companies have been created to promote and sell baby signing materials. Most advertise benefits such as facilitating spoken language, reducing tantrums, and increasing IQ.

The roots of baby signing lie in research conducted by Acredolo and Goodwyn. Their research has shown that babies readily acquire symbolic gestures when exposed to enhanced gestural training that they refer to as baby signs (Acredolo, Goodwyn, & Abrams, 2009). They propose that the rewards of baby signing include larger and more expressive vocabulary, advanced mental development, improved parent–child relationships, and fewer tantrums and behavior problems (Acredolo & Goodwyn, 1988; Goodwyn & Acredolo, 1998). Based on their findings, Acredolo

and Goodwyn created a signing program for infants with videos, classes, books, and cue cards (Acredolo et al., 2009).

It is generally recognized that gesture and language are linked and that babies naturally make early gestures that precede their use of language (Iverson & Goldin-Meadow, 2005). But is baby signing effective in accelerating language and other aspects of development? According to the websites promoting it, yes. However, one review of 33 websites associated with various baby signing products revealed that all claimed benefits such as faster language development and many claimed to foster higher IQs, improvements in parent–child interactions, and fewer child tantrums. Yet nearly none provided evidence to support their claims. Those that did referred to case studies (such as Acredolo & Goodwyn, 1985) and opinion articles rather than experiments (Nelson, White, & Grewe, 2012). A review of research studies examining the outcomes of baby signing programs found that although some of the studies suggest some benefits, nearly all contained methodological weaknesses like a lack of control groups or no random assignment. It was concluded that there is not enough evidence to support the claims of baby signing products (Johnston, 2005).

A recent longitudinal study tested the effects of baby signing products. Infants were followed from 8 months of age until 20 months of age (Kirk, Howlett, Pine, & Fletcher, 2013). Babies were randomly assigned to one of three conditions: baby signing training, verbal training (mothers modeled words without signs), and nonintervention. At 20 months of age, the language development was similar for all babies, regardless of intervention. Encouraging gestures did not result in higher scores on language measures, providing no support for the claims of baby signing proponents. Yet many parents report benefits of baby signing and believe that it has improved their child's ability to communicate and overall parent–infant interactions (Doherty-Sneddon, 2008; Mueller & Sepulveda, 2014). Although baby signing may not have research support for accelerating language development, it has not been shown to be harmful. If using baby signing products encourages frequent parent–infant interaction, does not rush or pressure infants, and parents feel that it is helpful, there is no reason to discourage its use.

What Do You Think?

Should we encourage parents to teach their babies how to sign? Why or why not?

---

child's communication attempts influence the child's rate of language development.

Infants and children learn by observing the world around them. Parents and caregivers offer important encouragement and reinforcement of infants' language learning. However, critics point out that learning theory cannot account for all of language development because it cannot account for the unique utterances and errors that young children make (Epstein, 1991). Word combinations are complex and varied—they cannot be acquired solely by imitation and

reinforcement. Toddlers often put words together in ways that they likely have never heard (e.g., "Mommy milk"). Young children make grammatical errors, such as "mouses" instead of "mice" or "goed" instead of "went," that cannot be the result of imitation. If language is learned through imitation, how do young children make grammatical errors that they have never heard spoken? Young children repeat things that they hear (sometimes to parents' chagrin!), but they also construct new phrases and utterances that are unique. Reinforcement from parents and caregivers is powerful encouragement for children, but language development cannot be completely explained by learning theory alone. Despite wide variations in circumstances, living situations, and contexts, infants around the world achieve language milestones at about the same time, suggesting a biological component to language development.

Nativist Theory and Language Acquisition

Nativist theorist Noam Chomsky (1959, 1965) argued that language is too complex a behavior to be learned so early and quickly from conditioning. Chomsky noted that all young children grasp the essentials of **grammar**, the rules of language, at an early age, and the languages of the world have many similarities. The human brain has an innate capacity to learn language. Specifically, Chomsky believed that infants are born with a **language acquisition device (LAD)**, an innate facilitator of language that permits infants to quickly and efficiently analyze everyday speech and determine its rules, regardless of whether their native language is English, German, Chinese, or Urdu. The LAD has an innate storehouse of rules that apply to all human languages that Chomsky (1965) referred to as **universal grammar**. When infants hear language spoken, they naturally notice its linguistic properties, and they acquire the language.

The nativist perspective can account for children's unique utterances and the unusual grammatical mistakes they make in speaking because children are biologically primed to learn language and do not rely on learning. However, like learning theory, the nativist perspective offers an incomplete account of language acquisition. Specifically, Chomsky's nativist perspective does not explain the process of language acquisition, how it occurs (Miller, 2009). Researchers have not identified the LAD or universal grammar Chomsky thought underlies all languages (Tomasello, 2009). Moreover, language does not emerge in a finished form. Instead, children learn to string words together over time based on their experiences and trial and error (Tomasello, 2012). Language learning does not occur as quickly and requires more effort on the part of children than Chomsky described. Instead, language acquisition is influenced by both nature and nurture, biology, and learning. An interactionist perspective offers the most comprehensive perspective of language development by encompassing both biology and social interaction. As described in Lives in Context (p. 131), children who are adopted from foreign countries experience particular challenges in learning language.

Interactionist Perspective on Language Acquisition

Language development is a complex process that is influenced by both maturation and context. Infants are born with the capacity to discriminate a wide variety of speech sounds including those that adults can no longer differentiate, suggesting an inborn sensitivity to language (Posner, 2001). Biological capacities interact with the social context in which children are reared to influence language development.

Biological Contributions to Language Acquisition The brain, specifically the left hemisphere, is wired for language at birth. Speech sounds produce more electrical activity in the left hemisphere of newborns' brains, while nonspeech sounds elicit more activity in the right hemisphere (Molfese, 1977). By studying individuals who have suffered brain damage, scientists have learned about two areas in the left hemisphere of the brain that are vital for language: Broca's and Wernicke's areas (Price, Jarman, Mason, & Kind, 2011). **Broca's area** controls the ability to use language for expression. Damage to this area inhibits the ability to speak fluently, leading to errors in the production of language. **Wernicke's area** is responsible for language comprehension. Damage to Wernicke's area impairs the ability to understand others' speech and sometimes the ability to speak coherently.

The brain plays a critical role in language capacities throughout life. However, biological factors, though powerful, cannot completely account for language development. For example, infants' ability to detect sounds not used in their native language declines throughout the first year of life, suggesting that contextual factors, specifically exposure to the native language influences older infants' sensitivity to speech sound (Posner, 2001; Sansavini, Bertoncini, & Giovanelli, 1997). At the same time, information processing factors largely influenced by neurological development, such as attention and memory, influence how infants comprehend and respond to social interaction and other contextual influences on language development.

Contextual Contributions to Language Acquisition Language acquisition occurs in a social context. When babies begin to engage in **canonical babbling**—a type of babbling with well-formed syllables that sounds remarkably like language— parents, regardless of socioeconomic status, ethnicity, and home environment, tune in and treat the vocalizations in a new way (Oller, Eilers, & Basinger, 2001). The utterances sound like words, and parents help infants to associate the wordlike utterances with objects and events, encouraging word learning. In this way, infants are predisposed to learn language and reside in a social context that fosters language learning (Oller et al., 2001).

Parental responsiveness to infants' vocalizations predicts the size of infants' vocabularies, the diversity of infants' communications, and the timing of language milestones (Tamis-LeMonda et al., 2014). For example, infants of highly responsive mothers achieved language milestones such as first words, vocabulary spurt, and telegraphic speech at 9 to 13 months—4 to 6 months earlier than infants of low-responsive mothers (Tamis-LeMonda, Bornstein, & Baumwell, 2001). Interactions with fathers are also important contributors to language development. Fathers' responsiveness to their 2- and 3-year-olds predicted toddlers' cognitive and language abilities (Tamis-LeMonda, Shannon, Cabrera, & Lamb, 2004). Parental responsiveness is also associated with the language skills of adopted children, supporting the contextual influence of parents (Stams, Juffer, & van IJzendoorn, 2002).

LIVES IN CONTEXT

Development in Internationally Adopted Children

AP/Elisha Page

Many internationally adopted children experience speech and language delays. Younger children tend to adapt to a new language more quickly but over time most children reach age-expected language levels.

In the three decades since the mid-1980s, international adoption has become commonplace. After the dissolution of the Soviet Union in 1990, the media drew attention to the large number of children who lived in orphanages in substandard conditions—without adequate food, clothing, or shelter and with poorly trained caregivers. Such orphanages have been found in a number of countries, including China, Ethiopia, Ukraine, Congo, and Haiti, accounting for over two thirds of internationally adopted children in 2013 (U.S. Department of State, 2014). One third of all international adoptions in 2013 included children from China. Underfunded and understaffed orphanages often provide poor, nonnurturing care for children, increasing the risks for malnutrition, infections, physical handicaps, and growth retardation.

With infant-to-caregiver ratios ranging from 10 to 60 infants per adult (Mason & Narad, 2005), children available for adoption often spend a significant amount of time deprived of consistent human contact. Observations of infants and toddlers in a Russian orphanage revealed that they experience few opportunities for interacting with caregivers. Most conversation tended to be caregiver to caregiver, even while feeding the youngest infants (Glennen, 2002). Toddlers were expected to feed themselves at the table without interaction from adults. Even while being held, children were faced outward, reducing opportunities for adult interaction.

Few internationally adopted children enter the United States healthy and at age-appropriate developmental norms. Not surprisingly, the longer the children were institutionalized, the more developmental challenges they face (Jacobs, Miller, & Tirella, 2010). Physical growth stunting is directly associated with the length of institutionalization, but catch-up growth is commonly

seen after adoption (Wilson & Weaver, 2009). As with growth, the time spent in an orphanage predicts the degree of developmental delay. Longer institutionalization is associated with delays in development of language, fine motor skills, social skills, and attention and other cognitive skills (Mason & Narad, 2005; Wiik et al., 2011).

Speech and language delays are the most consistent deficiencies among internationally adopted children (Johnson, 2000). In one study, 60% of 2.5-year-old children in a Russian orphanage had no expressive language (Glennen, 2002; Miller, 2000). One year later, only 14% used two-word utterances; at the ages of 3 to 4, the children had limited vocabulary, receptive language delays, and unintelligible speech phrases (Glennen, 2002). Other studies have demonstrated that 40% to 60% of children evaluated who were adopted from Eastern Europe and China show language delays (Albers, Johnson, Hostetter, Iverson, & Miller, 1997; Miller & Hendrie, 2000). Over half of internationally adopted children are seen by speech language pathologists (Pollack & Bechner, 2000).

The few available studies of the long-term prognosis for language development in internationally adopted children suggest that children can catch up from language delays if they are adopted at a young age (Frank, Vul, & Johnson, 2009; Mason & Narad, 2005). For example, Glennen and Masters (2002) noted an improvement in speech delay by 36 to 40 months of age; however, children adopted at older ages lagged behind in their language improvement. Generally, the younger the child is at adoption, the more quickly he or she will adapt to the new language and close any gaps in language delays (Glennan & Masters, 2002; Mason & Narad, 2005). More recent research suggests that in the presence of a high-quality parent–child relationship the age of adoption did not influence language, speech, or academic outcomes, and most children reach age-expected language levels (Glennen, 2014; Harwood, Feng, & Yu, 2013). Despite this, surveys of adoptive parents have revealed that one year following adoption, speech and language development is their top concern (Clauss & Baxter, 1997). Although there are individual differences in the degree of resilience and in functioning across developmental domains, adopted children overall show great developmental gains and resilience in physical, cognitive, and emotional development (Misca, 2014; Palacios, Román, Moreno, León, & Peñarrubia, 2014; Wilson & Weaver, 2009).

What Do You Think?

1. How might learning theory, nativist theory, and interactionist theory account for these findings?
2. In your view, what are the most important challenges adopted children and their families face? Identify sources and forms of support that might help adopted children and their parents.

The use of **infant-directed speech**, also known as "motherese," is another way in which adults attract infants' attention and influence language development.

Infant-directed speech uses shorter words and sentences, higher and more varied pitch, repetitions, a slower rate, and longer pauses (Thiessen, Hill, & Saffran, 2005). Preverbal

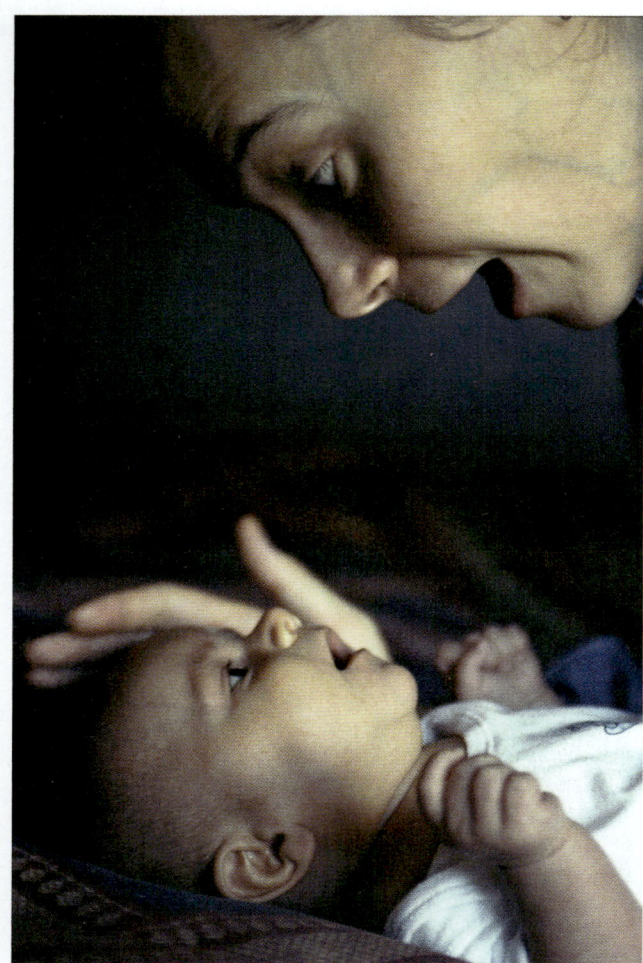

Through infant-directed speech, adults attract infants' attention by using shorter words and sentences, higher and more varied pitch, repetition, and a slower rate. Infants prefer listening to infant-directed speech, and infant-directed speech appears cross culturally.

Ali Russell/Alamy

infants prefer listening to infant-directed speech (Fernald & McRoberts, 1996), and infant-directed speech has been documented in many languages and cultures (Bryant, 2012; Kuhl et al., 1997). The pattern of infant-directed speech is similar across cultures such that adults can discriminate it from adult-directed speech even while listening to a language they do not speak. For example, when adults in the Turkana region of northwestern Kenya listened to speech produced in English by American mothers, they were able to discriminate between infant-directed and adult-directed speech, suggesting that infant-directed speech is universally recognizable (Bryant, 2012).

Infants are primed to detect infant-directed speech. Infant-directed speech influences social preferences—infants prefer adults who use it (Schachner & Hannon, 2011). Infant-directed speech appears to facilitate language development by making sounds more exaggerated, helping infants hear and distinguish the different sounds and map sounds to meanings (Burnham, Kitamura, & Vollmer-Conna, 2002;

Estes, 2013; Kitamura & Burnham, 2003; Thiessen et al., 2005). It also exaggerates lip movements, helping infants to distinguish lip movements relevant to speech (Green, Nip, Wilson, Mefferd, & Yunusova, 2010). It teaches babies how to take turns talking, models how to carry on a conversation, and helps babies learn to respond to emotional cues and link word meanings with familiar things. In one study, 7- and 8-month-old infants were more likely to learn words presented by infant-directed speech than those presented through adult-directed speech (Singh, Nestor, Parikh, & Yull, 2009). Babies learn language by interacting with more mature, expert speakers who can speak at their developmental level. Parents adjust their infant-directed speech to match infants' linguistic needs. For example, parents use longer and more complicated words and sentences as infants' comprehension increases (Englund & Behne, 2006; Sundberg, 1998). The quality of language input from parents and the number of words a child hears is related to children's vocabulary size at age 2 (Hoff, Naigles, & Nigales, 2002).

Though parents do not reliably reinforce correct grammar, they communicate in ways that tell young children when they make errors and show how to correct them (Saxton, 1997). Adults often respond to children's utterances with **expansions**, enriched versions of the child's statement. For example, if the child says, "bottle fall," the parent might respond, "Yes, the bottle fell off of the table." Adults also **recast** children's sentences into new grammatical forms. For example, "Kitty go," might be recast into, "Where is the kitty going?" When children use grammatically correct statements, parents maintain and extend the conversation (Bohannon & Stanowicz, 1988). When adults recast and expand young children's speech, the children tend to acquire grammatical rules more quickly and score higher on tests of expressive language ability than when parents rely less on these conversational techniques (Abraham, Crais, & Vernon-Feagans, 2013; Bohannon, Padgett, Nelson, & Mark, 1996).

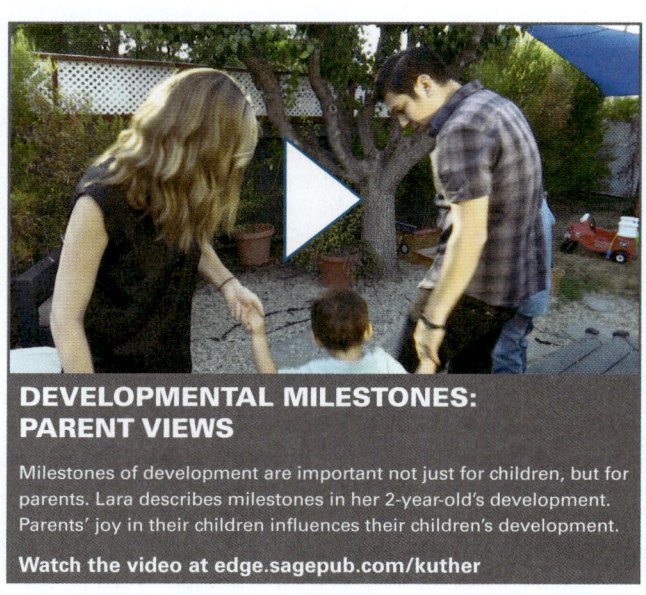

DEVELOPMENTAL MILESTONES: PARENT VIEWS

Milestones of development are important not just for children, but for parents. Lara describes milestones in her 2-year-old's development. Parents' joy in their children influences their children's development.

Watch the video at edge.sagepub.com/kuther

Culture also shapes language acquisition. Parents from different cultures may differ in how often they respond to their infants; however, parental response patterns that are warm, contingent on infant responses, and consistent are associated with positive language development in infants across cultures (Tamis-LeMonda et al., 2014). For example, in a study of six cultural communities, mothers from Berlin and Los Angeles were more likely to respond to infant nondistress vocalizations and gazes than were mothers from Beijing and Delhi and Nso mothers from various cities in Cameroon (Kärtner et al., 2008). In contrast, Nso mothers responded more often to infant touch than did mothers from other cultures. Although parental responsiveness may look different and take different forms across cultures, its benefits generalize across families from different cultural communities and socioeconomic strata (Rodriguez & Tamis-LeMonda, 2011). Culture even shapes the words that infants learn. In Asian cultures such as Japan, China, and Korea that stress interpersonal harmony, children acquire verbs and social words much more quickly than

do North American toddlers (Gopnik & Choi, 1995; Tardif et al., 2008). In another study, U.S. mothers responded to infant object play more than social play whereas Japanese mothers responded more to social play (Tamis-LeMonda, Bornstein, Cyphers, Toda, & Ogino, 1992). For example, North American infants' first words tend to include more referential language, or naming words such as *ball*, *dog*, *cup*, and so on, while Japanese infants tend to use more expressive language, or words that are used mainly in social interaction, such as *please* and *want* (Fernald & Morikawa, 1993). Italian, Spanish, French, Dutch, Hebrew, and English-speaking infants tend to display a preference for using more nouns than verbs (Bassano, 2000; Bornstein et al., 2004; Caselli et al., 1995; de Houwer & Gillis, 1998; Jackson-Maldonado, Thal, Marchman, Bates, & Gutierrez-Clellen, 1993; Maital, Dromi, Sagi, & Bornstein, 2000; Parisse & Le Normand, 2000; Tardif, Shatz, & Naigles, 1997).

The interactionist perspective on language development points to the interactive influence of biology and context (see Table 5.4). Infants are equipped with biological propensities

TABLE 5.4 Theories of Language Development

THEORY	DESCRIPTION
Learning theory	• Language is learned through reinforcement, punishment, and imitation. • Caregivers reward sounds that resemble adult speech with attention, smiles, and affection. Infants imitate sounds that adults make and repeat sounds that are reinforced. • The quantity and quality of the parents' verbal interactions with the child and responses to the child's communication attempts influence the child's rate of language development. • Learning theory cannot account for the unique utterances and errors that young children make. Young children put words together in ways that they likely have never heard and make grammatical errors that cannot be the result of imitation and reinforcement.
Nativist theory	• Despite wide variations in circumstances, living situations, and contexts, infants around the world achieve language milestones at about the same time. • Children are biologically primed to learn language and do not rely on learning. • An inborn language acquisition device (LAD) equipped with universal grammar permits infants to quickly and efficiently analyze everyday speech and determine its rules. When infants hear language spoken, they naturally notice its linguistic properties and they acquire the language. • Researchers have not identified the LAD or universal grammar Chomsky thought underlies all languages. • Language does not emerge in a finished form. Instead, children learn to string words together over time based on their experiences and trial and error.
Interactionist theory	• Language development is a complex process influenced by both maturation and context. • Infants have an inborn sensitivity to language and discriminate a wide variety of speech sounds including those that adults can no longer distinguish. • The left hemisphere of the brain, including Broca's and Wernicke's areas, is wired for language at birth. • Exposure to language influences infants' sensitivity to speech sounds and the ability to detect sounds not used in their native language declines throughout the first year of life. • Language acquisition occurs in a social context. Babies learn language by interacting with more mature, expert speakers who can speak at their developmental level. • Adults attract infants' attention with the use of infant-directed speech, which has been documented in many languages and cultures. Preverbal infants prefer listening to infant-directed speech. • Parents adjust their infant-directed speech to match infants' linguistic needs, responding to children's utterances with expansions and recasting children's sentences into new grammatical forms.

and information processing capacities that permit them to perceive and analyze speech and learn to speak. Infants are motivated to communicate with others. Interactions with others provide important learning experiences, which help infants expand their language capacities.

Thinking in Context 5.4

1. How is language development influenced by other areas of development? Specifically, what role, if any, might motor development, perception, or cognition hold in influencing a child's language development?

2. Referring to Bronfenbrenner's bioecological model (see Figure 1.6), identify contextual factors that influence language acquisition.

3. What factors at the level of Bronfenbrenner's microsystem and mesosystem play a role in language?

4. How might the exosystem influence language acquisition? Macrosystem?

Infancy represents an important time for development that illustrates the interaction of biology, maturation, and the sociocultural context. Infants are equipped with early and rapidly emerging capacities to move and control their bodies, sense the world around them, and learn and think. However, interactions with their sociocultural context strengthen and modify infants' capacities in every domain of development. In turn, babies' actions influence elements of their sociocultural context. Infants' active role in their own cognitive development cannot be denied. Infants also play an active role in their socioemotional development, as discussed in Chapter 6.

Apply Your Knowledge

Researchers use a variety of methods to study infant cognition:

- In one experiment, an infant looks longer at an expected, seemingly impossible event that occurs: a board appears to move through a box.

- An infant is shown a toy, then the overhead lights are turned off, hiding the toy from his sight. The infant successfully reaches for the toy.

- An infant watches as a researcher covers a toy with a blanket. The infant reaches for the blanket and uncovers the toy.

- An infant watches as a researcher covers a toy with a blanket several times. The infant successfully reaches for the toy every time. Next, the researcher places the toy under a different blanket, adjacent to the first hiding space. The infant reaches in the first place and is unsuccessful in finding the toy.

1. What do these tasks measure? What do the infants' responses demonstrate?

2. What Piagetian substage do each of these infants show?

3. How might changes in information processing skills contribute to these developments?

4. Are infants' responses to these tasks indicators of intelligence in infants? Why or why not?

Chapter Summary

5.1 Define *cognitive schemas*, and explain the processes by which infants and toddlers modify their cognitive schemas.

According to Piaget, cognitive development is the result of assimilation and accommodation. Assimilation involves integrating a new experience into a preexisting schema. Changing an existing schema in light of the new information is accommodation. People naturally strive for cognitive equilibrium, a state in which their schemas are matched with the outside world, clearly representing it. A state of cognitive equilibrium is rare and fleeting. Individuals' drive for cognitive equilibrium is the basis for cognitive change.

5.2 Summarize infants' progression through six substages of sensorimotor reasoning.

During the first month of life (substage 1), newborns strengthen and modify their original schemas to explore the world around them. From 1 to 4 months of age (substage 2), infants begin to engage in primary circular reactions. At 4 months of age (substage 3), infants' awareness begins to extend outside their bodies and they engage in secondary circular reactions. At 8 months (substage 4), infants purposefully coordinate two secondary circular reactions and apply them in new situations to achieve a goal.

As infants enter their second year of life, they reason at the tertiary circular reactions substage (12 to 18 months; substage 5). Infants experiment with new behaviors to see the results and search for new discoveries. Eighteen to 24 months of age marks a transition between sensorimotor and preoperational reasoning (substage 6). Infants develop representational thought and can consider potential solutions without engaging in physical trial and error.

5.3 Examine the development of object permanence during the sensorimotor period.

According to Piaget, object permanence emerges between 8 and 12 months and signifies a capacity for mental representation. Piaget's method of determining whether an infant understood object permanence relied on the infant's ability to demonstrate it by uncovering a hidden object. Violation of expectation tasks have shown that infants as young as 5.5 months maintain mental representations and show object permanence. Research examining the A-not-B error suggest that it is a result of neural immaturity and a deficit in impulse control rather than a lack of object permanence.

5.4 Discuss the core knowledge perspective as it applies to infancy and toddlerhood.

The core knowledge perspective explains that infants are born with several core domains of thought that enable early rapid learning and adaptation. Core knowledge researchers have shown that young infants have a grasp of the physical properties of objects, such as object permanence, solidity, gravity, number, and language. Critics argue that the violation of expectation method of testing infants' knowledge demonstrates discrimination, that young infants can tell the difference between stimuli, but not that infants understand how the two stimuli differ.

5.5 Identify the parts of the information processing system and its function in infancy and toddlerhood.

According to information processing theory, we are born with a functioning information processing system that is composed of three mental stores. Sensory memory holds incoming sensory information in its original form for a very brief period. When we direct our attention or awareness to information, it passes working memory, which holds and processes information that is being manipulated, encoded, or retrieved. An important part of working memory is the central executive, which directs the flow of information and regulates cognitive activities such as attention, action, and problem solving. As information is manipulated in working memory it becomes more likely that it will enter long-term memory.

5.6 Describe developmental changes in infants' capacities for attention and memory.

Young infants require a long time to habituate to stimuli and will look longer at stimuli than older infants. By around 10 weeks of age, habituation times start to decline; infants become more efficient at scanning and processing visual information and therefore require less exposure to stimuli to habituate. Individual differences in attention occur at all ages and tend to be stable over time. Classic habituation studies have shown that by 3 months of age infants can remember a visual stimulus for 24 hours and for several days or even weeks by the end of the first year of life.

5.7 Examine how infants' categorization skills change with development.

Categorization is an adaptive mental process that allows for organized storage of information in memory, efficient retrieval of that information, and the capacity to respond with familiarity to new stimuli from a common class. Infants' earliest categories are based on the perceived similarity of objects. As early as 7 months of age, infants use conceptual categories based on perceived function and behavior. Seven- to

12-month-old infants use many categories to organize objects, such as food, furniture, birds, animals, vehicles, kitchen utensils, and more. Twelve- to 30-month-old infants categorize objects first at a global level and then at more specific levels.

5.8 Discuss how intelligence is measured in infancy and findings regarding infant intelligence.

The most commonly used measure of infant intelligence is the BSID-III, or Bayley III, appropriate for infants from 2 months through 30 months of age. The intellectual abilities measured by the Bayley-III are critical indicators of neurological health and are useful for charting developmental paths, diagnosing neurological disorders, and detecting mental retardation very early in life. However, performance on infant intelligence scales tends to show little relation with intelligence and achievement in childhood. Intelligence tests administered in childhood examine more complex and abstract abilities such as verbal reasoning, verbal comprehension, and problem solving. New approaches look to information processing as an indicator of intellectual skill.

5.9 Explain patterns of language development from birth through infancy and toddlerhood.

Newborns are able to hear all of the sounds of which the human voice is capable, but by 10 to 12 months, their ability to perceive nonnative sound declines. Infants begin cooing by 3 months and babbling at about 6 months of age. At first, babbling is universal, but with exposure to speech, babbling sounds more like the infant's native language. Fast mapping helps young children learn many new words, but their own speech lags behind what they can understand, and they display underextension and overextension errors. At about 21 months of age, most children compose their first simple two-word sentences, telegraphic speech.

5.10 Contrast learning, nativist, and interactionist perspectives on language.

Learning theory poses that language is learned through operant conditioning. From this perspective, imitation and reinforcement shape children's language acquisition. Nativist theorists pose that the human brain has an innate capacity to learn language. An interactionist perspective integrates nature and nurture, noting that we have innate perceptual biases for discriminating and listening to language, and the brain is wired for language at birth. At the same time, language acquisition occurs in a social context in which adults use infant-directed speech to catch the infant's attention and facilitate language development by responding in ways that foster language learning, such as by using expansions and recasts.

Key Terms

accommodation   114

assimilation   114

attention   115

babbling   127

Broca's area   130

canonical babbling   130

categorization   122

central executive   121

circular reactions   115

cooing   127

core knowledge perspective   119

expansions   132

fast mapping   127

grammar   130

holophrases   127

infant-directed speech   131

intelligence   123

language acquisition device (LAD)   130

long-term memory   120

mental representation   115

naming explosion   127

object permanence   116

overextension   128

primary circular reactions   115

recast   132

secondary circular reactions   115

sensory memory   120

telegraphic speech   128

tertiary circular reactions   116

underextension   128

universal grammar   130

video deficit effect   123

violation-of-expectation method   117

Wernicke's area   130

working memory   120

CHAPTER 6

Socioemotional Development in Infancy and Toddlerhood

LEARNING OBJECTIVES	KEY STUDY TOOLS
6.1. Summarize the psychosocial tasks of infancy and toddlerhood.	**Explore Further** Psychosocial Development
6.2. Examine infants' developing capacities for basic and self-conscious emotions and emotional regulation.	**Explore Further** Self-Conscious Emotions
6.3. Identify contextual and cultural influences on emotional development in infants and toddlers.	**Applying Developmental Science** Postpartum Depression (p. 145) **Video Case** Parent and Infant Psychotherapy
6.4. Define *temperament* in infancy, and identify styles of temperament.	**Explore Further** Temperament
6.5. Discuss the stability of temperament and the role of goodness of fit in infant development.	**Think Critically** Goodness of Fit **Listen** Temperament Into Adulthood
6.6. Examine attachment styles.	**Explore Further** Attachment Typologies
6.7. Discuss culture and attachment as well as strategies to promote the development of attachment relationships.	**Ethical and Policy Applications of Lifespan Development** Infant Child Care (p. 153) **Lives in Context** Attachment to Fathers (p. 156) **Video Case** Transition to Parenthood
6.8. Differentiate self-concept, self-recognition, and self-control, and discuss their respective roles in infant development.	**Think Critically** Self-Recognition **Connect** Recognizing Objects, People, and Self

As a newborn, Terrence expressed distress by spreading his arms, kicking his legs, and crying. When he did this, his mother or father would scoop him up and hold him, trying to comfort him. Terrence quickly began to prefer interacting with attentive adults who cared for him. Soon, baby Terrence began to smile and gurgle when held. In turn, Terrence's parents played with him and were delighted to see his animated, excited responses. When Terrence was a toddler, his emerging language skills enabled him to express his needs in words. He quickly learned that words are powerful tools that can convey emotions ("I love you, Mommy"). He does not know it, but Terrence uses words to help him manage strong emotions and difficult situations. For example, he distracts himself from stressful stimuli,

like the scary dog in the yard next door, by singing to himself. Terrence can express his ideas and feelings to everyone around him—and that makes for new and more complicated relationships with his family, including his parents and older brothers and sisters.

As Terrence illustrates, in the first two years of life babies learn new ways of expressing their emotions. They become capable of new and more complex emotions and relationships with others and develop a greater sense of self-understanding, social awareness, and self-management. These processes collectively are referred to as socioemotional development. In addition to socioemotional development, infants are faced with two important developmental tasks. They must come to trust others and develop a sense of autonomy, or the ability to make some choices on their own and direct themselves.

PSYCHOSOCIAL DEVELOPMENT IN INFANCY

According to Erik Erikson (1950), throughout the lifespan we all proceed through a series of psychosocial crises or developmental tasks. As discussed in Chapter 1, how well each crisis is resolved, or the extent to which each developmental task is completed, influences psychological development and how the individual approaches the next crisis or developmental task. Erikson believed that infants and toddlers progress through two psychosocial stages that influence their personality development: **trust versus mistrust**, and **autonomy versus shame and doubt**.

TRUST VERSUS MISTRUST

From the day she was born, each time Erin cried, her mother or father would come to her bassinet and hold her, check her diaper, and feed her if necessary. Soon, Erin developed the basic expectation that her parents would meet her needs. According to Erikson (1950), developing a sense of trust versus mistrust is the first developmental task of life: Infants must develop a view of the world as a safe place where their basic needs will be met. Throughout the first year of life, infants depend on their caregivers for food, warmth, and affection. If parents and caregivers attend to the infant's physical and emotional needs and consistently fulfill them, the infant will develop a basic sense of trust in his or her caregivers and, by extension, in the world in general.

However, if caregivers are neglectful or inconsistent in meeting the infant's needs, he will develop a sense of mistrust toward the world and interpersonal relationships, feeling that he cannot count on others for love, affection, or the fulfillment of other basic human needs. The sense of trust or mistrust developed in infancy influences how people approach the subsequent stages of development. Specifically, when interaction with adults around them inspires trust and security, babies are more likely to feel comfortable exploring the world, which enhances their learning, social development, and emotional development.

AUTONOMY VERSUS SHAME AND DOUBT

Two-and-a-half-year-old Sarah is an active child who vigorously explores her environment, tests new toys, and attempts to learn about the world on her own. At dinnertime, she wants to feed herself and gets angry when her parents try to feed her. Each morning, she takes pleasure in attempting to dress herself and expresses frustration when her mother helps. Erin is progressing through the second stage in Erikson's scheme of psychosocial development—autonomy versus shame and doubt—which is concerned with establishing a sense of autonomy, or the feeling that one can make choices and direct oneself.

Toddlers walk on their own, talk, and express their own ideas and needs and become more independent. The developmental task for toddlers is to learn to do things for themselves and feel confident in their ability to maneuver themselves in their environment. According to Erikson (1950), if parents encourage the toddler's initiative and allow him to explore, experiment, make mistakes, and test limits, the toddler will develop autonomy, self-reliance, self-control, and confidence. If parents are overprotective or disapprove of his struggle for independence, the child may begin to doubt his abilities to do things by himself, may feel ashamed of his desire for autonomy, may passively observe, and will not develop a sense of independence and self-reliance.

Both trust and autonomy develop out of warm and sensitive parenting and developmentally appropriate expectations for exploration and behavioral control throughout infancy and toddlerhood. Without a secure sense of trust in caregivers, toddlers will struggle to establish and maintain close relationships with others and will find it challenging to develop autonomy. Adjustment difficulties are more likely when children do not develop a sense of individuality and confidence in their own abilities to meet new challenges. However, as discussed later in this chapter, the value placed on autonomy varies by culture, and parenting and child outcomes differ across cultures.

Thinking in Context 6.1

1. How do contextual factors, such as those that accompany being raised in an inner city, suburban neighborhood, rural environment, or nomadic society, influence how infants approach the psychosocial tasks of infancy—developing a sense of trust and autonomy? Would you expect infants in each of these contexts to demonstrate trust and autonomy in similar ways? Why or why not?

2. What kinds of behaviors on the part of parents promote a sense of trust in infants? Do trust-promoting activities, such as attentiveness and cuddling, also foster a sense of autonomy in infants? Why or why not?

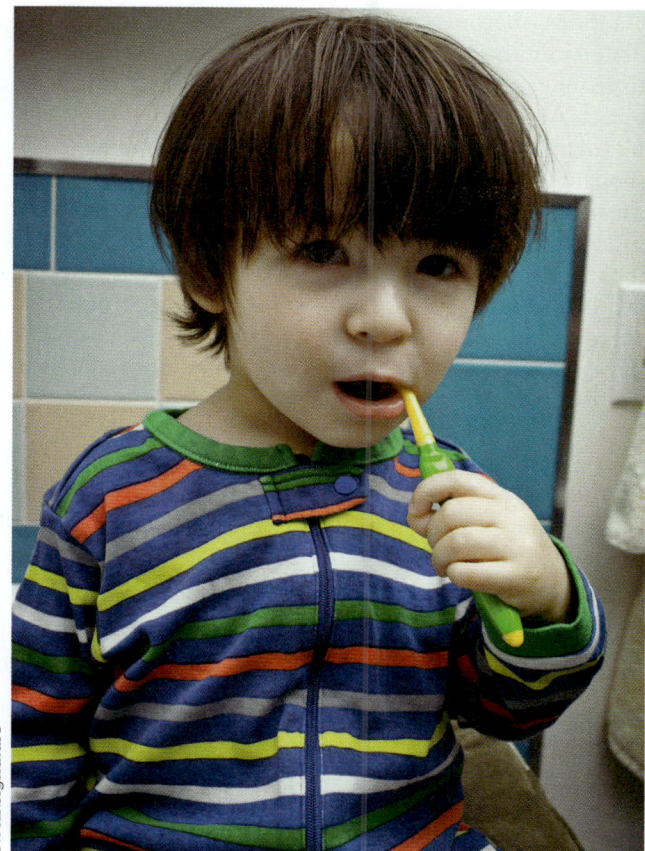

iStock/Signature

Joey takes pride in completing this task—tooth brushing—all by himself, developing a sense of autonomy.

EMOTIONAL DEVELOPMENT IN INFANCY AND TODDLERHOOD

What emotions do infants feel? Infants cannot describe their experiences and feelings, which makes studying infants' emotional development quite challenging. How do you determine what another person is feeling? Most people show their emotions on their faces, such as by smiling or frowning. If we use facial expressions as a guide to what emotions infants might feel, the first and most reliable emotion that newborns show is distress. They cry, wail, and flail their arms and bodies, alerting caregivers to their need for attention. Newborns also show interest with wide-eyed gazes when something catches their attention, and they smile when they are happy.

INFANTS' EMOTIONAL EXPERIENCE

Are we born with the ability to feel emotions? No one knows for sure because we cannot ask infants what they feel, but observation of newborn facial expressions suggests that newborns experience interest, distress, disgust, and contentment (Campos et al., 2000; Izard et al., 1995). Between 2 and 7 months of age, infants begin to display additional expressions including anger, sadness, joy, surprise, and fear (Bennett,

Bendersky, & Lewis, 2005). Of course, we do not know whether internal emotional states accompany these facial expressions, but infants' facial expressions are remarkably similar to those of adults (Sullivan & Lewis, 2003). These discrete emotional expressions, known as **basic emotions** or primary emotions, appear so early in life that researchers generally agree that they are biologically predetermined (Izard, 2007). Basic emotions emerge in all infants at about the same ages and are seen and interpreted similarly in all cultures that have been studied, suggesting that they are inborn (Camras, Oster, Campos, Miyake, & Bradshaw, 1992; Izard, 2007).

Emotions arise from interactions of richly connected structures within the brain, including the brainstem, the lower part of the brain located between the cortex and spine, and the limbic system, a collection of subcortical brain structures (Phelps & LeDoux, 2005). These structures develop prenatally and are present in animals, suggesting that emotions serve a biological purpose and are critical to survival (LeDoux & Phelps, 2008). Emotions develop in predictable ways, as shown in Table 6.1.

During the first few months of life, the form of basic emotions as well as the conditions that elicit them change. For example, consider smiling, indicative of happiness and one of the most important emotional expressions in infancy. Newborns smile. Newborn smiles are reflexive, involuntary, linked with shifts in arousal state (e.g., going from being asleep to drowsy wakefulness), and occur frequently during periods of REM sleep (Kawakami et al., 2008; Korner, 1969). At about 3 weeks old, infants smile while awake and alert and in response to familiarity—familiar sounds, voices, and tastes (Sroufe & Waters, 1976). During the second month of life, babies smile more in response to visual stimuli (Sroufe, 1997). The **social smile**, in response to seeing familiar people, emerges between 6 and 10 weeks (Lewis, Hitchcock, & Sullivan, 2004) and is indicative of social engagement (Messinger & Fogel, 2007). The social smile is an important milestone in infant development because it plays a large role in initiating and maintaining social interactions between infants and adults. The social smile enhances

TABLE 6.1 Milestones in Emotional Development

APPROXIMATE AGE	MILESTONE
Birth	Basic emotions Discriminates mother
2–3 months	Social smile Distinguishes happiness, anger, surprise, and sadness
6–8 months	Fear, stranger anxiety, and separation protest occur
7–12 months	Social referencing
18–24 months	Self-conscious emotions appear. Develops vocabulary for talking about emotions

caregiver–child bonding. Parents are enthralled when their baby shows delight in seeing them.

As infants grow, laughs begin to accompany their smiles, and they laugh more often and at more things. For example, at 6 months of age, an infant might laugh at unusual sounds or sights, such as when Mommy makes a face or hides her head under a blanket. Laughing at unusual events illustrates the baby's increasing cognitive competence as he or she knows what to expect and is surprised when something unexpected occurs. Infants may show clear expressions of joy as early as 2.5 months while playing with a parent and at 3 to 4 months of age when they laugh at stimuli that they find intensely arousing (Bornstein & Lamb, 2011).

Anger appears at about 6 months of age and develops rapidly, becoming more complex in terms of elicitors and responses (Lemerise & Dodge, 2008). Initially, physical restrictions can elicit anger, such as being restrained in a high chair or when dressing. With time, the inability to carry out a desired act, such as unsuccessfully reaching to obtain a desired toy, can provoke frustration and anger (Sullivan & Lewis, 2003, 2012). Between 8 and 20 months, the infant gradually becomes more reactive and anger is more easily elicited (Braungart-Rieker, Hill-Soderlund, & Karrass, 2010). He or she becomes aware of others' actions, and anger can be elicited by others' behaviors. For example, an infant may become upset when Mommy goes to the door to leave or when Grandma takes out the towels in preparation for bath time. During the second year of life, temper tantrums become common when the toddler's attempts at autonomy are thwarted and he or she experiences frustration or stress. The anger escalates with the child's stress level (Potegal, Robison, Anderson, Jordan, & Shapiro, 2007). Some toddlers show extreme tantrums, lie on the floor, scream, and jerk their arms and legs. Other children's tantrums are more subtle. They may whine, mope, and stick out their bottom lip.

Emotional development is an orderly process in which complex emotions build on the foundation of simple emotions. Basic emotions of contentment, interest, and distress are reflexive physiological responses to stimulation. Over the next few months, the full range of basic emotions develops to include joy, surprise, sadness, anger, and fear.

The development of **self-conscious emotions**, or secondary emotions, such as empathy, embarrassment, shame, and guilt, depends on cognitive development as well as an awareness of self and does not emerge until about 15 to 18 months (Lewis, 2008, 2011). In order to experience self-conscious emotions, the toddler must be able to observe himself and others, be aware of standards and rules, and compare his behavior with the standard (Lagattuta & Thompson, 2007).

EMOTION REGULATION

As children become aware of social standards and rules, **emotional regulation**—the ability to control their emotions—becomes more important. How do infants regulate emotions? Very young infants have been observed to manage negative emotions by sucking vigorously on objects or turning their bodies away from distressing stimuli (Mangelsdorf, Shapiro, & Marzolf, 1995). Smiling is also thought to serve a purpose in regulating emotions. It allows the infant to control aspects of the situation without losing touch with it. When an infant gets excited and smiles, she looks away briefly. This may be a way of breaking herself away from the stimulus and allowing her to regroup, preventing overstimulation. Smiling is associated with a decline in heart rate, suggesting that it is a relaxation response to decrease an infant's level of arousal.

While 6-month-old infants are more likely to use gaze aversion and fussing as primary emotional regulatory strategies, 12-month-old infants are more likely to use self-soothing (e.g., thumb sucking, rocking themselves) and distraction (chewing on objects, playing with toys), and 18-month-old toddlers use distraction and active attempts to change the situation, such as moving away from upsetting stimuli (Crockenberg & Leerkes, 2004; Mangelsdorf et al., 1995). By 18 to 24 months, toddlers try to adjust their emotional reactions to a comfortable level of intensity by distracting themselves when they are distressed, such as by playing with toys or talking (Cole, Martin, & Dennis, 2004; Feldman, Dollberg, & Nadam, 2011; Grolnick, Bridges, & Connell, 1996). Researchers have found that infants' abilities to self-regulate at 15 months predict executive functioning at 4 years (Ursache, Blair, Stifter, Voegtline, & Family Life Project Investigators, 2013).

Emotion regulation is also related to children's increasing ability to use language. After 18 months of age, toddlers' vocabulary for talking about feelings develops rapidly, presenting new opportunities for emotional regulation because toddlers can tell caregivers how they feel (Bretherton, Fritz, Zahn-Waxler, & Ridgeway, 1986). Vocabulary has been found to predict self-regulation abilities in 24-month-old infants (Vallotton & Ayoub, 2011).

SOCIAL INTERACTION AND EMOTIONAL DEVELOPMENT

Social engagement increases rapidly over the first year of life (Feldman et al., 2009). The parent–child relationship is an important context for developing emotional regulation skills. Warm and supportive interactions with parents and other caregivers can help infants understand their emotions and learn how to manage them. Responsive parenting that is attuned to infants' needs helps infants develop skills in emotional regulation, especially in managing negative emotions like anxiety as well as their physiological correlates, such as accelerated heart rate (Feldman et al., 2011; Haley & Stansbury, 2003). For example, when mothers responded promptly to their infants' cries at 2 months of age, the infants, at 4 months of the age, cried for shorter durations,

Responsive parenting helps infants learn to manage their emotions and self-regulate.

distraction and mother-oriented strategies, such as seeking help, during frustrating events (Calkins & Johnson, 1998).

Some caregivers, however, interpret some emotional displays as attempts at manipulation ("he's just trying to get attention") rather than as valid expressions of feeling, which may result in insensitive responses to children's emotional displays ("that's enough, stop it") and interfere with children's emotional development. In one study, fathers' negativity was associated with higher levels of stress hormones in infants at 7 and 24 months of age (Mills-Koonce et al., 2011).

Maladaptive social contexts, such as parental stress and family conflict, pose a risk to infants' development of emotional regulation. Specifically, exposure to anger in the family sensitizes infants to stress and increases infants' needs for aid in managing their physiological reactions. At the same time, exposure to anger places extra demands on adults' coping capacities that may interfere with their ability to provide sensitive care for their infants (Moore, 2009). In a longitudinal study following infants from 4 to 18 months of age, family factors such as maternal depression and the mother's experience of relationship stress were associated with the infant's developing strong negative emotions early in infancy which compromised infants' emotional regulation capacities (Bridgett et al., 2009). Declines in infants' regulatory control were in turn associated with negative parenting in toddlerhood because parents and children interact and influence each other reciprocally.

Changes in emotional expression and regulation are dynamic, because the changing child influences the changing parent. In particular, mothers and infants systematically influence and regulate each other's emotions and behaviors. Mothers regulate infant emotional states by interpreting their emotional signals, providing appropriate arousal, and reciprocating and reinforcing infant reactions. Infants regulate their mother's emotions through their receptivity to her initiations and stimulation and by responding to her emotions (Cole et al., 2004). By experiencing a range of emotional interactions—times when their emotions mirror those of

were better able to manage their emotions, and stopped crying more quickly than other infants (Jahromi & Stifter, 2007). Infants and young children often need outside assistance in regulating their emotions.

Parental Interaction

Parents can help their infants learn to manage their emotions with the use of many techniques, including direct intervention, modeling, selective reinforcement, control of the environment, verbal instruction, and touch (Crockenberg & Leerkes, 2004; Meléndez, 2005; Wolfe & Bell, 2007). The techniques parents use to soothe infants change with age. Touching becomes a less common regulatory strategy with age whereas vocalizing and distracting techniques increase (Jahromi & Stifter, 2007). At 7.5 months of age, infants tend to change their patterns of expression to show more positive and less negative emotions, at least partly in response to their mothers' behavior—which tends to be increasingly responsive to expressions of interest and decreasingly responsive to expressions of discomfort (Malatesta & Haviland, 1982). When mothers provide more guidance in helping infants regulate their emotions, their infants tend to engage in more

PARENT AND INFANT PSYCHOTHERAPY

Watch as therapist Kerry Taylor observes a mother and infant interact and provides advice to help them strengthen their bond.

Watch the video at edge.sagepub.com/kuther

their caregivers and times when their emotions are different from those of their caregivers—infants learn how to transform negative emotions into neutral or positive emotions and regulate their own emotional states (Cole et al., 2004; Lyons-Ruth, Bronfman, & Parsons, 1999).

Interactive Play and Test of Wills

Face-to-face social play is an important way in which infants learn how to manage their emotions. Face-to-face play involves short but intense episodes of focused interaction between an infant and adult. Each entertains the other with smiling, vocalizing, and using animated facial expressions. The goal of these interactions is to establish and maintain synchronous, or coordinated, exchanges that are pleasurable for both infant and adult. However, synchronous exchanges occur only about one third of the time mothers and infants interact with each other (Tronick, 1989; Tronick & Cohn, 1989). Instead, the typical mother–infant interaction is one that cycles from coordinated synchrony to nonmatching states and back again. For example, in studies of face-to-face interaction at 6 months of age, a loss and repair of synchrony occurs every few seconds and is influenced by the mother adjusting her interactions in light of the infant's response (Tronick, 2007). Successfully regaining synchrony and experiencing coordinated mother–infant states are associated with positive affect on the part of infants. Infants' affective experience is influenced by this dyadic regulatory process.

At 6 or 7 months of age, face-to-face play transforms into more active kinds of play that correspond to the baby's developing motor skills (Tronick & Cohn, 1989). In addition, crawling, creeping, and walking introduce new challenges to parent–infant interaction and socioemotional growth (Bertenthal & Campos, 1990; Campos et al., 2000; Campos, Kermoian, & Zumbahlen, 1992). Motor development thereby holds important implications for socioemotional development. As crawling begins, parents and caregivers respond with happiness and pride, providing the infant with an increase in emotional communication (Bertenthal, Campos, & Barrett, 1984). Crawling increases a toddler's capability to attain goals—a capability that, while often satisfying to the toddler, involves hazards such as wandering away from parents and acting in dangerous ways.

A variety of feelings are associated with these activities, and emotional outbursts become more common in infants. For example, parents report that advances in locomotion are accompanied by increased expressions of affection as well as frustration in toddlers as they attempt to move in ways that often exceed their abilities or are not permitted by parents (Campos et al., 1992; Clearfield, 2011; Karasik, Tamis-LeMonda, & Adolph, 2011). When mothers recognize the dangers that some objects, such as houseplants, vases, and electrical appliances, pose to infants, they sharply increase the anger and fear expressed to infants, which often leads to fear and frustration in infants. Toddlers, too, tend to display an increase in expressions of anger in situations that block

their goals (Pemberton Roben et al., 2012). As you might imagine, this results in a testing of wills that influences the parent–child relationship. Now, parents must actively monitor infants' whereabouts, protect them from dangerous situations, and expect infants to comply—a dynamic that is often a struggle, amounting to a test of wills between toddler and caregivers. At the same time, these struggles help the infant to begin to develop a grasp of mental states in others that are different from his or her own (Thompson, 2004). As described in Applying Developmental Science (p. 145), infants of mothers who experience **postpartum depression** are exposed to a particularly challenging emotional environment.

SOCIAL REFERENCING

The use of **social referencing** is one way that infants demonstrate that they understand that others' experience their own emotions and thoughts. Early in life, the ability to discriminate facial expressions indicating emotion emerges. For example, newborns are able to discriminate happy faces from fearful ones (Farroni, Menon, Rigato, & Johnson, 2007). Between 2 and 4 months of age, infants can distinguish other emotional expressions in others, especially happiness as opposed to anger, surprise, and sadness (Bornstein, Arterberry, & Lamb, 2013). Infants around the world develop a similar capacity to recognize the emotional signals of diverse facial expressions (Leppänen, Richmond, Vogel-Farley, Moulson, & Nelson, 2009). It is thought that infants are innately prepared to attend to facial displays of emotion as it is biologically significant and important for their survival (Leppänen, 2011). Beyond recognizing the emotional expressions of others, infants also respond to them. Between 6 and 10 months, infants begin to use social referencing, the tendency to look to the caregiver or other adults' emotional expressions to find clues for how to interpret ambiguous events (Boccia & Campos, 1989; Slaughter & McConnell, 2003; Striano, Vaish, & Benigno, 2006). For example, when a toddler grabs the sofa to pull herself up, turns and tumbles over as she takes a step, she will look to her caregiver to determine how to interpret her fall. If the caregiver has a fearful facial expression, the infant is likely to be fearful also, but if the caregiver smiles, the infant will probably remain calm and return to play.

Social referencing occurs in ambiguous situations, provides infants and toddlers with guidance in how to interpret the event, and influences their emotional responses and subsequent actions (Striano et al., 2006). The caregiver's emotional expression, whether happy, sad, or fearful, influences whether a 1-year-old will play with a new toy, be wary of strangers, or cross to the deep side of a visual cliff (Mumme, Fernald, & Herrera, 1996; Rosen, Adamson, & Bakeman, 1992; Sorce, Emde, Campos, & Klinnert, 1985; Striano et al., 2006). Older infants tend to show a negativity bias when it comes to social referencing. The effect of social

Postpartum Depression

Giving birth to a child is a monumental event that first-time mothers are often surprised to find stressful. While every mother of a newborn is likely to feel overwhelmed or sad at one time or another, about 8% to 19% of women experience clinical depression, commonly referred to as postpartum depression, following childbirth (Ko, Farr, Dietz, & Robbins, 2012; O'Hara & McCabe, 2013), Depression is not simply sadness; rather, it is characterized by a lack of emotion and a preoccupation with the self that makes it challenging for depressed mothers to care for their infants and recognize their infants' needs. Mothers are at greater risk for postpartum depression when they experience chronic stressors over the course of pregnancy across multiple domains: financial, physical, relationship, and so forth (Liu & Tronick, 2013).

Depressed mothers interact with their babies differently than do nondepressed mothers. Mothers who are depressed show more negative emotions and behaviors such as withdrawal, intrusiveness, hostility, coerciveness, and insensitivity (Jennings et al., 2008). They are more likely to lack knowledge of nurturing and sensitive parenting, be less responsive to their babies, show less affection, use more negative forms of touch, and show poor parenting practices (Jennings et al., 2008; Zajicek-Farber, 2009). Depressed mothers have difficulty paying attention to their infants and may fail to protect them from potential dangers; for example, babies might fall off their mother's lap, have access to electrical sockets, or may not be placed in a car seat (McLennan & Kotelchuck, 2000). Mothers who are depressed not only interact with their babies differently but they perceive them differently—they rate their infant's behavior more negatively than do nondepressed mothers and independent observers (Field et al., 1996; Hart, Field, & Roitfarb, 1999).

It is no surprise to observe that infants of depressed mothers show a variety of negative outcomes; these may include overall distress, withdrawn behavior, poor social engagement, problems with sleep and feeding, flat affect, and difficulty regulating emotions (Bayer, Hiscock, Hampton, & Wake, 2007; Feldman et al., 2009; Leventon & Bauer, 2013; Muscat, Obst, Cockshaw, & Thorpe, 2014; Tronick & Reck, 2009). They often show poor attentiveness, limited capacity to interact with objects and people, and difficulty reading and understanding others' emotions (Field, 2011; Lyubchik & Schlosser, 2010). In addition, they are more likely to show deficits in cognitive development, language development, and insecure **attachment** at 1 year and 18 months (Quevedo et al., 2012; Sohr-Preston & Scaramella, 2006; Speranza, Ammaniti, & Trentini, 2006). The ongoing reciprocal interactions between mothers and infants account for the long-term effects of maternal depression. For example, in one study, maternal depressive symptoms 9 months after birth predicted infants' negative reactions to maternal behavior at 18 months of age and, in turn, higher levels of depressive symptoms on the part of mothers at 27 months of age (Roben et al., 2015).

Early intervention can help foster the parent–child relationship and promote the health of both mother and infant. Mothers with postpartum depression are often prescribed antidepressant medication, and the mother along with the father—or, in some cases, the entire family—may benefit from therapy, education, and parenting support (Bobo & Yawn, 2014; Fletcher, 2009). Although postpartum depression is a risk to infants, relationships with fathers and other caregivers are an important source of support that can buffer the negative effects of poor interactions with mothers the father and other caregivers can foster the child's healthy development (Cabrera, Fitzgerald, Bradley, & Roggman, 2014).

What Do You Think?

In your view, how can we best support new mothers? If you were to create a program to help prevent postpartum depression or to help depressed mothers, what might you include?

---

referencing cues is stronger for negative cues than positive. Infants tend to attend and follow social referencing cues more closely when they indicate negative attitudes toward the object, as compared with neutral or happy (Biro, Alink, van IJzendoorn, & Bakermans-Kranenburg, 2014; Carver & Vaccaro, 2007; Leventon & Bauer, 2013; Repacholi, Meltzoff, & Olsen, 2008; Vaish, Grossmann, & Woodward, 2008). In addition, infants may be more influenced by the vocal information conveyed in emotional messages than the facial expressions themselves, especially within the context of fearful messages (Bir et al., 2014; Kim, Walden, & Knieps, 2010).

How infants employ social referencing changes with development. Ten-month-old infants show selective social referencing. They monitor the caregiver's attention and do not engage in social referencing when the adult is not attending or engaged (Striano & Rochat, 2000). At 12 months, infants use referential cues such as the caregiver's body posture, gaze, and voice direction to determine to what objects caregivers' emotional responses refer (Brooks & Meltzoff, 2008; Moses, Baldwin, Rosicky, & Tidball, 2001). Social referencing reflects infants' growing understanding of others' emotional states; it signifies that infants can observe, interpret, and use emotional information from others to form their own interpretation and response to events.

CULTURAL INFLUENCES ON EMOTIONAL DEVELOPMENT

Emotional development does not occur in a vacuum. Contextual factors, such as culture, influence how infants interpret and express emotions.

Emotional Display Rules

Every society has a set of **emotional display rules** that specify the circumstances under which various emotions should or should not be expressed (Gross & Ballif, 1991; LeVine et al., 1994; Safdar et al., 2009). We learn these emotional display rules very early in life, as every interaction between parent and infant is shaped by the culture in which they live which influences mothers' emotional behavior, infant smiles, and other emotional expressions (Bornstein et al., 2013). When North American mothers play with their 7-month-old babies, they tend to model positive emotions, restricting their own emotional displays to show joy, interest, and surprise (Malatesta & Haviland, 1982). They also are more attentive to infants' expression of positive emotions, such as interest or surprise, and respond less to negative emotions (Malatesta, Grigoryev, Lamb, Albin, & Culver, 1986). Thus, babies are socialized to respond and display their emotions in socially acceptable ways. The emotions that are considered acceptable, as well as ways of expressing them, differ by culture and context. North American parents tickle and stimulate their babies, encouraging squeals

of pleasure. The Gusii and Aka people of Central Africa prefer to keep babies calm and quiet; they engage in little face-to-face play (Hewlett, Lamb, Shannon, Leyendecker, & Scholmerich, 1998; LeVine et al., 1994). These differences in caregiving styles communicate cultural expectations about emotions. North American infants learn to express positive emotions, and Central African babies learn to restrain strong emotions.

Similarly, cultures often have particular beliefs about how much responsiveness to babies' crying and fussing is appropriate (Garcia Coll, 1990; Keller, 2003; Meléndez, 2005). The !Kung San hunter–gatherers of Botswana respond to babies' cries nearly immediately (within 10 seconds nearly all of the time), while Western mothers tend to wait a considerably longer period of time before responding to infants' cries (e.g., 10 minutes; Barr, Konner, Bakeman, & Adamson, 1991). Gusii mothers believe that constant holding, feeding, and physically caring are essential for keeping the infant fed and calm, which in turn protects the infant from harm and disease; therefore, Gusii mothers respond immediately to their babies' cries (LeVine et al., 1994). Non-Western infants are thought to cry very little because they are carried often (Bleah & Ellett, 2010). In one study, infants born to parents who were recent immigrants from Africa cried less than U.S. infants, illustrating the role of culture in influencing infant cries (Bleah & Ellett, 2010). Caregivers' responses to infant cries influence infants' capacities for self-regulation and responses to stress (Barr & Gunnar, 2000). Babies who receive more responsive and immediate caregiving when distressed show lower rates of persistent crying, spend more time in happy and calm states, and cry less overall as they approach their first birthday (Axia & Weisner, 2002; Feng, Harwood, Leyendecker, & Miller, 2001; Papoušek & Papoušek, 1990).

Stranger Wariness

Many infants around the world display **stranger wariness** (also known as stranger anxiety), a fear of unfamiliar people. Whether infants show stranger wariness depends on the infant's overall **temperament**, past experience, and the situation in which the infant meets a stranger (Thompson & Limber, 1990). In many but not all cultures, stranger wariness emerges at about 6 months and increases throughout the first year of life, beginning to decrease after about 15 months (Bornstein et al., 2013; Sroufe, 1977; Waters, Matas, & Sroufe, 1975). More recent research has suggested that the pattern of stranger wariness varies among infants, as some show rapid increases and others show slow increases in stranger wariness; once established, some infants show steady decline and others show more rapid changes. Twin studies suggest that these patterns are influenced by genetics, as monozygotic (MZ) twins show higher rates of concordance than do dizygotic (DZ) twins (Brooker et al., 2013).

Pavel Gospodinov/Design Pics/Corbis

In some cultures infants cry very little, perhaps because they are in constant contact with their mothers.

Among North American infants, stranger wariness is so common that parents and caregivers generally expect it. However, infants of the Efe people of Zaire, Africa, show little stranger wariness; this is likely related to the Efe collective caregiving system in which Efe babies are passed from one adult to another, relatives and nonrelatives alike (Tronick, Morelli, & Ivey, 1992). In contrast, babies reared in Israeli kibbutzim (cooperative agricultural settlements that tend to be isolated and have been subjected to terrorist attacks), tend to demonstrate widespread wariness of strangers. By the end of the first year, when infants look to others for cues about how to respond emotionally, kibbutz babies display far greater anxiety than babies reared in Israeli cities (Saarni, Mumme, & Campos, 1998). In this way, stranger wariness may be adaptive, modifying infants' drive to explore in light of contextual circumstances (Easterbrooks, Bartlett, Beeghly, & Thompson, 2012; Thompson & Limber, 1990).

Culture influences infants' experience of stranger wariness but so do other factors, including the infant's individual tendencies towards social interaction, past experience with strangers, the current situation, and the mother's stress reactivity and anxiety (Brooker et al., 2013; Greenberg, Hillman, & Grice, 1973; Thompson & Limber, 1990; Waters, West, & Mendes, 2014). Infants whose mothers report greater stress reactivity, who experience more anxiety and negative affect in response to stress, show higher rates of stranger wariness (Brooker et al., 2013; Waters et al., 2014). Characteristics of the stranger (e.g., his or her height), the familiarity of the setting, and how quickly the stranger approaches all influence how the infant appraises the situation. Infants are more open to strangers when the stranger approaches slowly, keeps an appropriate distance, and does not tower over them (Greenberg et al., 1973; Thompson & Limber, 1990). Infants react more positively to strangers in the presence of their mother, family, or other familiar caregivers and when the stranger is sensitive to the infant's signals and makes the child comfortable by approaching at the infant's pace (Mangelsdorf, 1992). Infants are more open to strangers in unfamiliar settings such as a laboratory as compared to a home, suggesting that infants expect to encounter unusual things and people in strange places, but not at home (Brookhart & Hock, 1976).

Over the first few months of life, young infants display the full range of basic emotions. As infants' cognitive and social capabilities develop, they are able to experience complex social emotions, such as embarrassment. The social world plays a role in emotional development. Adults interact with infants, provide opportunities to observe and practice emotional expressions, and assist in regulating emotions. Much of emotional development is the result of the interplay of infants' emerging capacities and the contexts in which they are raised. Culture influences what emotions infants experience and how they are displayed.

Thinking in Context 6.2

1. Recall from Chapter 1 that development over our lifespans is multidimensional and that various types of development interact and influence one another. Provide examples for how this might be true for physical, cognitive, and emotional development in infancy and toddlerhood.

2. Identify examples of how infants' emotional development is influenced by their interactions with elements their physical, social, and cultural context. In your view, what factors best promote healthy emotional development? Why?

3. Can you identify ways in which your own culture has influenced your development?

TEMPERAMENT

"Joshua is such an easygoing baby!" gushed his babysitter. "He eats everything, barely cries, and falls asleep without a fuss. I wish all my babies were like him." The babysitter is referring to Joshua's temperament. Temperament, the characteristic way in which an individual approaches and reacts to people and situations, is thought to be one of the basic building blocks of our emotion and personality. Temperament has strong biological determinants; it is biologically based yet influenced by reciprocal interactions among genetic predispositions, maturation, and experience (Gagne, Vendlinski, & Goldsmith, 2009; Rothbart, 2011; Thompson, 1998; Thompson, Winer, & Goodvin, 2013). Every infant behaves in a characteristic, predictable style that is influenced by his or her inborn tendencies towards arousal and stimulation and experiences with adults and contexts. In other words, every infant displays a particular temperament style.

STYLES OF TEMPERAMENT

The New York Longitudinal Study (NYLS), begun in 1956, is a pioneering study of temperament that has followed 133 infants into adulthood. Early in life, the infants in the study demonstrated differences in nine characteristics that are thought to capture the essence of temperament (Buss & Plomin, 1984; Chess & Thomas, 1991; Goldsmith et al., 1987).

- *Activity level.* Some babies wriggle, kick their legs, wave their arms, and move around a great deal while other babies tend to be more still and stay in one place.

- *Rhythmicity.* Some infants are predictable in their pattern of eating, sleeping, and defecating; other babies are not predictable.

- *Approach-withdrawal.* Some babies tend to approach new situations, people, and objects while others withdraw from novelty.

- *Adaptability.* Some babies get used to new experiences and situations quickly; others do not.

- *Intensity of reaction.* Some babies have very extreme reactions, giggling exuberantly and crying with piercing wails. Other babies show more subdued reactions, such as simple smiles and soft whimpering cries.

- *Threshold of responsiveness.* Some babies notice many stimuli—sights, sounds, and touch sensations—and react to them. Other infants notice few stimuli and seem oblivious to the changes.

- *Quality of mood.* Some babies tend toward near-constant happiness while others tend toward irritability.

- *Distractibility.* Some babies can be distracted from objects or situations easily while others cannot.

- *Attention span.* Some babies play with one toy for a long time without becoming bored while others get bored easily and change toys often.

Some aspects of infant temperament, particularly activity level, irritability, attention, and sociability or approach-withdrawal, show stability for months and years at a time—and in some cases even into adulthood (Kochanska & Knaack, 2003; Lemery, Goldsmith, Klinnert, & Mrazel, 1999; Pedlow, Sanson, Prior, & Oberklaid, 1993; Salekin & Averett, 2008; van Aken, 2009). One of the developmental tasks of infancy is to learn how to regulate attention and emotions, which may influence several components of temperament, including rhythmicity, distractibility, intensity of reaction, and attention. The components of infant temperament cluster into three profiles, as summarized in Table 6.2 (Thomas & Chess, 1977; Thomas, Chess, & Birch, 1970):

1. Babies with an **easy temperament** are often in a positive mood, even-tempered, open, adaptable, regular, and predictable in biological functioning. They establish regular feeding and sleeping schedules easily. About 40% of the NYLS sample fell into this category.

2. Babies with a **difficult temperament** are active, irritable, and irregular in biological rhythms. They are slow to adapt to changes in routine or new

situations, react vigorously to change, and have trouble adjusting to new routines. About 10% of the NYLS sample fell into this category.

3. Just as it sounds, babies with a **slow-to-warm-up temperament** tend to be inactive, moody, and slow to adapt to new situations and people. They react to new situations with mild irritability but adjust more quickly than do infants with difficult temperaments. About 15% of the NYLS sample fell into this category.

Although it may seem as if all babies were easily classifiable, about 35% of the NYLS sample did not fit squarely into any of the three categories but displayed a mix of characteristics, such as eating and sleeping regularly but being slow to warm up to new situations.

TEMPERAMENT AND DEVELOPMENT

Temperament tends to be stable over months and even years, even into adulthood. But in infancy temperament is less stable than any other time in life. Young infants' temperament can change with sensitive caregiving (e.g., helping babies regulate their negative emotions), experience, and neural development (Thompson et al., 2013). As infants gain experience and learn how to regulate their states and emotions, those who are cranky and difficult may become less so. By the second year of life, styles of responding to situations and people are better established; in early childhood, temperament is even more stable and predictive of later behavior (Caspi, 1998; Lemery et al., 1999; Thompson et al., 2013). However, there are also individual differences throughout life; some children's temperament remains the same and others' change (Rothbart & Bates, 1998; Salekin & Averett, 2008; van Aken, 2009).

Temperament as a Reciprocal Process

Temperament is part of the social exchanges that we all encounter, influenced by reciprocal reactions as one person influences the other and vice versa. An infant's temperament may be continuous over time because certain temperamental qualities evoke certain reactions from others. Easy babies

TABLE 6.2 Temperament

EASY CHILD	DIFFICULT CHILD	SLOW-TO-WARM-UP CHILD
Usually positive mood; unpleasant moods are mild	Intense and frequent unpleasant moods; cries often	Positive and unpleasant moods
Responds well to novelty in food, situations, routines, and strangers	Responds poorly to novelty in food, situations, routines, and strangers	Responds slowly to novelty in food, situations, routines, and strangers
Regular in sleep and feeding schedules	Irregular in sleep and feeding schedules	Moderately regular in sleep and feeding schedules
Accepts frustration with little fuss	Reacts to frustration with crying and tantrums	Slow to accept frustrations

usually get the most positive reactions from others, but babies with a difficult temperament receive mixed reactions (Chess & Thomas, 1991). For example, an "easy" baby tends to smile often, eliciting smiles and positive interactions from others, which reinforce those easy temperamental qualities. Conversely, a "difficult" baby may evoke more frustration and negativity from caregivers as they try unsuccessfully to soothe the baby's fussing. Researchers found that mothers who view their 6-month-old infants as difficult may be less emotionally available to them (Kim & Teti, 2014). Babies' emotionality and negative emotions predict maternal perceptions of parenting stress and poor parenting (Kiang, Moreno, & Robinson, 2004; Oddi, Murdock, Vadnais, Bridgett, & Gartstein, 2013; Paulussen-Hoogeboom, Stams, Hermanns, & Peetsma, 2007). In turn, however, research has shown that mothers who, *prior to giving birth*, believe that they are less well equipped to care for their infant are more likely to have infants who show negative aspects of temperament, such as fussiness, irritability, and difficulty being soothed, suggesting that perceptions of parenting may shape views of infant temperament—and thereby temperament (Verhage, Oosterman, & Schuengel, 2013).

Goodness of Fit

An important influence on socioemotional development is the **goodness of fit** between the child's temperament and the environment around him or her, especially the parent's temperament and child-rearing methods (Chess & Thomas, 1991). Infants with difficult temperament are more likely than others to later experience difficulties with externalizing behaviors, such as aggression and conduct problems, and internalizing behaviors, such as anxiety and depression (Rothbart & Bates, 1998; Thomas et al., 1970). Infants are at particular risk for poor outcomes when their temperaments are not well matched with the settings in which they live (Rothbart & Bates, 1998; Thomas et al., 1970). If an infant who is fussy, difficult, and slow to adapt to new situations is raised by a patient and sensitive caregiver who requires that the infant comply with rules but provides time for him or her to adapt to new routines, the infant may become less cranky and more flexible over time. The infant may adapt her temperament style to match her context so that later in childhood she may no longer be classified as difficult and no longer display behavioral problems (Bates, Pettit, Dodge, & Ridge, 1998; Chess & Thomas, 1984). If, on the other hand, a child with a difficult temperament is reared by a parent who is insensitive, coercive, and difficult in temperament, she may not learn how to regulate her emotions and may have behavioral problems and adjustment difficulties that worsen with age even into early adolescence (Pluess & Birkbeck, 2010; Thompson, 1998). Likewise, when children are placed in low-quality caregiving environments, those with difficult temperaments respond more negatively and show more behavior problems than do those with easy temperaments (Pluess & Belsky, 2009; Pluess & Birkbeck, 2010; Poehlmann et al., 2011).

As mentioned earlier, socioemotional development is a dynamic process in which infants' behavior and temperament styles influence the family processes that shape their development. Sensitive and patient caregiving is not always easy with a challenging child, and the adults' own temperamental style influences their caregiving. A poor fit between the caregiver and infant's temperament can make an infant more fussy and cranky. When a difficult infant is paired with a parent with a similar temperament, who is impatient, irritable, and forceful, behavioral problems in childhood and adolescence are likely (Chess & Thomas, 1984; Rubin, Hastings, Chen, Stewart, & McNichol, 1998).

Three months after giving birth, new mothers' feelings of competence are associated with infant temperament. Mothers' beliefs about their ability to nurture are shaped by the interaction between their infants' traits and their parenting self-efficacy and opportunities for developing successful caregiving routines (Porter & Hsu, 2003; Verhage et al., 2013). This is true across cultures as well. Both British and Pakistani mothers in the United Kingdom reported fewer problems with their infants' temperaments at 6 months of age when those mothers had a greater sense of parenting efficacy and more warm and less hostile parenting styles (Prady, Kiernan, Fairley, Wilson, & Wright, 2014). However, the most adaptive matches between infant temperament and context can sometimes be surprising. Consider the Maasai, an African agricultural society. In times of drought, when the environment becomes extremely hostile, herds of cattle and goats die, and infant mortality rises substantially. Under these challenging conditions, the infants with difficult temperaments tend to survive at higher rates than do those with easy temperaments. Infants who cry and are demanding are attended to, fed more, and are in better physical condition than do easy babies who tend to cry less and therefore are assumed to be content and not fed as much as difficult infants (Gardiner & Kosmitzki, 2010). Thus, the infants with difficult temperaments demonstrate higher rates of survival because their temperaments better fit the demands of the hostile context in which they are raised.

Cultural Differences in Temperament

There are consistent cultural differences in temperament that are rooted in cultural differences in how individuals are perceived. Japanese mothers, for example, view their infants as independent beings who must learn the importance of relationships and connections with others. Infants maintain close physical contact with their mothers, who encourage them to develop close ties and depend on their assistance. North American mothers, on the other hand, view their task as shaping babies into autonomous beings (Kojima, 1986). Japanese mothers tend to interact with their babies in soothing ways, discouraging strong emotions, whereas North American mothers are active and stimulating (Rothbaum, Weisz, Pott, Miyake, & Morelli, 2000). Differences in temperament result, such that Japanese infants tend to be more passive,

Culture plays a role in emotional development. Japanese mothers tend encourage their infants to develop close ties and depend on their assistance whereas North American mothers tend to emphasize autonomy.

less irritable and vocal, and more easily soothed when upset as compared with North American infants (Kojima, 1986; Lewis, Ramsay, & Kawakami, 1993; Rothbaum et al., 2000). Culture influences the behaviors that parents view as desirable and the means that parents use to socialize their infants. Culture, therefore, plays a role in how emotional development, in this case temperament, unfolds. The cultural context plays a similar role in the development of attachment.

Thinking in Context 6.3

1. Contrast the inborn nature of temperament with contextual factors that may promote change in temperament style. How do researchers address the question of how much of temperament is inborn? What role does goodness of fit play in determining temperament?

2. In your view, is it possible for an infant with a difficult temperament to grow into a young child with an easy temperament? Why or why not?

3. Under what conditions might a child with an easy temperament become difficult?

ATTACHMENT

Raj gurgles and cries out while lying in his crib. As his mother enters the room, he squeals excitedly. Raj's mother smiles as she reaches into the crib, and Raj giggles with delight as she picks him up. Raj and his mother have formed an important emotional bond, called an attachment. Attachment refers to a lasting emotional tie between two people who each strive to maintain closeness to the other and act to ensure that the

relationship continues. It is a strong emotional bond that endures over time. Two theorists have made particularly important contributions to our understanding about infant attachment: John Bowlby and Mary Ainsworth.

BOWLBY'S ETHOLOGICAL PERSPECTIVE ON ATTACHMENT

Bowlby, a British psychiatrist who became one of the first developmental psychologists, volunteered at a school for troubled children after he completed college in 1928. His experiences with two students changed his career: an affectionless, isolated teenager who had been expelled from his previous school for theft and who had no mother figure and an 8-year-old boy who was anxious and closely followed Bowlby as if he were his shadow (Ainsworth, 1974; Bretherton, 1992). These experiences led Bowlby to wonder about the effects of early family relationships, specifically mother–child relationships, on personality development (Bretherton, 1992). Bowlby was inspired both by psychoanalytic theory (via his undergraduate training with psychoanalytic theorist, Melanie Klein) and by ethology, particularly by Lorenz's work on the imprinting of geese (see Chapter 1) and by observations of interactions of monkeys. He was one of the first to believe that emotional disturbances are influenced by early family experiences, rather than conflicts between aggressive and libidinal drives, as the psychoanalytic theorists argued.

Bowlby (1969) developed an **ethological theory** of attachment that characterizes it as an adaptive behavior that evolved because it contributed to the survival of the human species. An attachment bond between caregivers and infants ensures that the two will remain in close proximity, thereby aiding the survival of the infant and, ultimately, the species. From this perspective, caregiving responses are inherited and are triggered by the presence of infants and young children. Infants are innately drawn to particular aspects of the caregiver. Infants use signaling behaviors, such as crying and smiling, to bring the caregiver into contact. Infants become attached to those who respond consistently and appropriately to their signaling behavior. In this way, attachment behaviors, such as crying, clinging, smiling, having stranger wariness, and having separation protest, increase infants' chances for survival and healthy development because they keep the caregiver nearby.

Magnetic resonance imaging (MRI) scans suggest that first-time mothers are innately disposed to respond to infants. Mothers' brains light up with activity when they see their own infants' faces, and areas of the brain associated with rewards are activated specifically in response to happy, but not sad, infant faces (Strathearn, Jian, Fonagy, & Montague, 2008). Bowlby proposed that attachment formation progresses through several developmental phases during infancy. With each phase, infants' behavior becomes increasingly organized, adaptable, and intentional.

Indiscriminate Social Responsiveness (Birth to 1–2 Months)

A newborn's cry is an example of a signaling behavior designed to ensure that caregivers remain near him and that he is cared for. Babies develop a repertoire of signals, such as smiling, cooing, and clinging, but crying is a particularly effective signal because it conveys negative emotion that adults can judge reliably, and it motivates adults to relieve the infant's distress (Leger, Thompson, Merritt, & Benz, 1996). Attachment behaviors provide comfort and security to infants because they bring babies close to adults who can protect them. During the first months of life, infants rely on caregivers to regulate their states and emotions—to soothe them when they are distressed and help them establish and maintain an alert state. When caregivers are sensitive and consistent in responding to babies' signals, babies learn to associate their caregivers with alertness and the relief of distress, forming the basis for an initial bond. What defines this stage as indiscriminate is that infants are satisfied with any caregiver who responds to their signals (Lamb & Lewis, 2011).

Discriminating Sociability (1–2 Months to 6–7 Months)

In this phase, babies begin to show a preference for familiar people and make discriminations among adults. Adults influence babies' states of arousal. While all adults may carry babies, help them calm themselves, and teach them about their environment, particular adults might be better able to soothe the baby, which is very rewarding to caregivers because it signifies obvious appreciation. The infant's behavior becomes more coordinated during this phase and interactions with adults involve more play. Face-to-face play teaches babies the rules of reciprocity—that social interactions entail taking turns, that they can affect the behavior of others in

TRANSITION TO PARENTHOOD

In this video, parents discuss what it's like to have an infant, their experience adjusting to parenthood, and the challenges of balancing work and child care.

Watch the video at edge.sagepub.com/kuther

consistent and reliable ways, and that caregivers can be counted on to respond when signaled (Lamb & Lewis, 2011; Thompson, 2000).

Attachments (7–24 Months)

Infants become attached to adults who attend, accurately interpret, and promptly respond to their signals (Ainsworth, 1979; Bowlby, 1969). In this phase, infants can gain proximity to caregivers through their own motor efforts, like crawling. Intentional social behavior develops as infants begin to understand reciprocity and play becomes a more important part of infant–caregiver interactions. It is the quality of interaction with caregivers that counts in forming and maintaining an attachment. Though babies tend to spend much less time with their fathers than with their mothers, they tend to become attached to both at about the same age (Lamb, 1997). Regular interaction is needed for attachments to form, but it is unclear how much or little contact is needed.

The formation of an attachment bond is crucial for infants' development because infants now begin to explore the world, using their attachment figure as a **secure base**, or foundation to return to when frightened. When infants are securely attached to their caregivers, they feel confident to explore the world and to learn by doing so. It is during the attachment phase that stranger wariness and separation protest emerge. **Separation protest** (sometimes called separation anxiety) occurs when infants respond to separations from an attachment figure with fear, distress, crying, and whining. Separation protest signals an infant's concern about the absence of an attachment figure (Lamb & Lewis, 2011). Whereas stranger wariness refers to a fear of strangers, infants who experience separation protest fear being apart from their caregiver. Separation protest tends to increase from 8 to 13 or 15 months of age and then declines (Kagan, 1983). This pattern appears across many cultures and environments as varied as the United States, Israeli kibbutzim, and !Kung San hunting and gathering groups in the Kalahari Desert in Africa (Kagan et al., 1994). It is the formation of the attachment bond that makes separation anxiety possible because infants must feel connected to their caregiver in order to feel distress in his or her absence.

Reciprocal Relationships (24–30 Months to 30 Months and Onward)

Separation protest declines during this phase as toddlers advance in cognitive development and language use. They can understand and predict parents' patterns of separation and return, reducing their confusion and distress. Toddlers now can use language to make requests of caregivers, use persuasion, and create a more sophisticated relationship.

The attachment bond developed during infancy and toddlerhood influences personality development because it becomes internally represented as an **internal working model**, or a set of expectations about one's worthiness of love and the availability of attachment figures during times of distress. The internal working model influences the development of **self-concept**, or sense of self, in infancy and becomes a guide to later relationships throughout life (Bretherton, 1992; Johnson, Dweck, & Chen, 2007; Lamb & Lewis, 2011).

AINSWORTH'S STRANGE SITUATION

Mary Salter Ainsworth, a Canadian psychologist, posed that infants must develop a dependence on parents in order to feel comfortable exploring the world (Salter, 1940). In the early 1950s she began a collaboration with John Bowlby on a project examining the effects of separation from the mother on personality development. Ainsworth's observations of children during this project formed the basis of her theory of attachment (Bretherton, 1992).

Virtually all infants are attached to their parents, but they differ in security of attachment, the extent to which the infant feels that he or she can count on the parent to be there to meet his or her needs. Mary Ainsworth developed the **Strange Situation**, a structured observational procedure that reveals the security of attachment when the child is placed under stress. As shown in Table 6.3, the Strange Situation is a heavily structured observation task consisting of eight three-minute-long episodes. In each segment, the infant is with the parent (typically the mother), with a stranger, with both, or alone. The observation begins with the child and his or her mother together in an observation room equipped with many toys and a video camera to record the observations. Every three minutes, the stranger or mother enters or leaves the room. Researchers attend to several aspects of the situation:

- *Exploration of the toys and room.* Does the infant explore and play with the toys? A secure infant happily explores the room when the mother is present.

- *Reaction during separations.* How does the infant react to the mother's departure? Securely attached infants notice the mother's departure and may or may not cry.

- *Reaction during reunions.* How does the infant react to the mother's return? Secure infants welcome the mother's return, seek comfort, and then return to play and exploration.

On the basis of responses to the Strange Situation, children are classified into one of four attachment types (Ainsworth, Blehar, Waters, & Wall, 1978).

1. About two thirds of infants in middle-class samples demonstrate **secure attachment** in the Strange Situation (Thompson, 1998). Infants who are securely attached display stranger anxiety and separation protest. The infant greets the mother enthusiastically and seeks comfort during reunion sessions. Once comforted, he or she returns to individual play. The infant uses the mother as a secure base as he or she plays and explores but returns regularly to check in with the mother (e.g., bring her a toy)

2. **Insecure–avoidant attachment** is an insecure form of attachment in which the child is minimally interested in the mother and busily explores the room. The child shows little distress during the Strange Situation and is not enthusiastic upon reuniting with the mother. The child ignores or avoids the mother on return or shows subtle signs of avoidance, like failing to greet her. Infants with avoidant attachment resist attempts to be comforted by turning away. About 20% of typical samples of infants reflect this style of attachment (Thompson, 1998).

TABLE 6.3 The Strange Situation

EPISODE	EVENT	ATTACHMENT BEHAVIOR OBSERVED
1	Experimenter introduces mother and infant to playroom and leaves	
2	Infant plays with toys and parent is seated	Mother as secure base
3	Stranger enters, talks with caregiver, and approaches infant	Reaction to unfamiliar adult
4	Mother leaves room; stranger responds to baby if upset	Reaction to separation from mother
5	Mother returns and greets infant	Reaction to reunion
6	Mother leaves room	Reaction to separation from mother
7	Stranger enters room and offers comfort to infant	Reaction to stranger and ability to be soothed by stranger
8	Mother returns and greets infant; tries to interest the infant in toys	Reaction to reunion

Infant Child Care

High-quality child care that fosters close connections with caregivers and includes stimulating activities is associated with gains in cognitive and language development and can even compensate for lower-quality home environments.

In the United States, more than half of all mothers of infants under 1 year old, and over two-thirds of mothers of children under 6, are employed (U.S. Bureau of Labor Statistics, 2015). These infants and young children are cared for in a variety of settings: in center-based care; in the home of someone other than a relative; or with a relative such as a father, grandparent, or older sibling (Federal Interagency Forum on Child and Family Statistics, 2014). What are the effects of nonparental care? Early research suggested that infants in child care are at risk for insecure attachment; however, this is not supported in more recent studies conducted with large samples of children in infancy through preschool (Belsky, 2005; Erel, Oberman, & Yirmiya, 2000).

One of the best sources of information about the effects of nonparental care is a longitudinal study of over 1,300 children, begun in 1991 and conducted by the National Institute of Child Health and Development (NICHD). This study found, perhaps

surprisingly, that infants' developmental outcomes are influenced more by characteristics of the family, such as parenting, maternal education, and maternal sensitivity, than by the type of child care (Axe, 2007; Dehaan, 2006). Maternal employment has been shown to be either unrelated to mother–infant attachment or predictive of a positive attachment bond (Barglow, Vaughn, & Molitor, 1987; Harrison & Ungerer, 2002; Hoffman, 1974).

A second critical finding of the NICHD study was not as surprising: quality of child care matters. Infants and young children exposed to poor-quality child care score lower on measures of cognitive and social competence, regardless of demographic variables such as parental education and socioeconomic status (NICHD Early Child Care Research Network, 2005). On the other hand, high-quality child care that includes specific efforts to stimulate children is associated with gains in cognitive and language development over the first three years of life and can even compensate for lower-quality home environments (Albers, Riksen-Walraven, & de Weerth, 2010; Watamura, Phillips, Morrissey, McCartney, & Bub, 2011).

Child care quality has long-term effects as well. Longitudinal research in Sweden showed that older children and adolescents who had received high-quality care as infants and toddlers scored higher on measures of cognitive, emotional, and social competence (Andersson, 1989; Andersson, Duvander, & Hank, 2004; Broberg, Wessels, Lamb, & Hwang, 1997). Other research shows that quality of child care from birth through age 4.5 predicted higher cognitive functioning and academic achievement and less problem behavior at age 15, with greater advances accompanying higher-quality care (Vandell, Belsky, Burchinal, Steinberg, & Vandergrift, 2010).

The challenge is that high-quality child care is expensive. In 2012, the annual cost of infant care in the United States ranged from about $5,700 to $15,000, and in some cities, such as Washington, DC, it was nearly $22,000 (Child Care Aware of America, 2014). In some countries, such as Sweden, Denmark, and Japan, child care is heavily subsidized by the government (Allen, 2003; Waldfogel, 2006). In the United States, however, it remains a private responsibility. The few public subsidies for child care available in the United States are tied to economic need and are mainly targeted at low-income families who receive other forms of public assistance.

What Do You Think?

1. Consider your own experience with child care, either as a child or parent. Can you identify examples of high quality care? Can you identify ways to improve the quality of care?

2. Assume that you are a parent seeking child care for your own child or that you were providing advice to a parent. What are indicators of quality care? What would you look for?

3. Initially, Ainsworth characterized this **insecure–resistant attachment** pattern as ambivalent because the infant remains preoccupied with the mother throughout the procedure, but reunions suggest that resistance and signs of anger and distress on the part of infants. They mingle proximity

seeking and contact maintaining behaviors with resistance. The infant engages in minimal exploration and is preoccupied with the mother. The child experiences difficulty settling down and simultaneously seeks and resists contact on reunion. Resistant attached infants have more difficulty feeling comfortable in the Strange Situation. At reunion, resistant attached infants are ambivalent in that they seek proximity and then push away or hit. They may show anger or be passive. About 15% of infants fall into this category (Thompson, 1998).

4. The **disorganized–disoriented attachment** category was developed more recently to account for the set of infants who show inconsistent, contradictory behaviors (Main & Solomon, 1986). The infant with disorganized–disoriented attachment may cling while crying hard with an averted glaze or may hit the parent's face or eyes while in an apparently good mood (Main & Solomon, 1986). Disorganized attachment orientation is a reliable predictor of social and emotional maladjustment from childhood into adulthood (Bernier & Meins, 2008; Wolke, Eryigit-Madzwamuse, & Gutbrod, 2014).

Attachment has lifelong consequences because it is manifested in the infant's internal working model of self and his or her feelings of worthiness of love. Early interactions with parents also influence infants' mental representations of people and relationships and create a foundation for future interactions with other people (Ranson & Urichuk, 2008). Representations of self and other act as filters to social perception, expectations, and memory that influence how children approach new social partners (Raikes & Thompson, 2008). Security of attachment is not static. However, it varies with the mother's behavior. If the mother's behavior changes over time, the infant's security of attachment and internal working model of self can change as well. As discussed in Ethical and Policy Applications of Lifespan Development (p. 153), the issue of attachment is more complex for infants and children who spend many hours in child care.

ATTACHMENT-RELATED OUTCOMES

Secure parent–child attachments are associated with a host of positive developmental outcomes. Infants who are securely attached tend to be more sociable with peers and unfamiliar adults than are those who are insecurely attached (Elicker, Englund, & Sroufe, 1992; Crugnola et al., 2011). They have more positive interactions with peers, and their attempts at friendly interactions with peers are more likely to be successful (Fagot, 1997). As preschoolers, securely attached children are better able to read others' emotions and have a more positive self-concept as compared with children with insecure attachments (Goodvin, Meyer, Thompson, & Hayes, 2008; Steele, Steele, & Croft, 2008). Likewise, preschool and school-age children who were securely attached as infants tend to be more curious, empathetic, self-confident, and socially competent as well as have more positive interactions with peers and have more close friendships (Arend, Gove, & Sroufe, 1979; Elicker et al., 1992; McElwain & Volling, 2004; NICHD Early Child

Care Research Network, 2005; Youngblade & Belsky, 1992). In multiple studies, secure attachment in infancy predicted social competence and expressive language at 3 years of age, attention at 4.5 years of age, and autonomy in adolescence (Becker-Stoll, Fremmer-Bombik, Wartner, Zimmermann, & Grossmann, 2008; Fearon & Belsky, 2004).

The advantages of secure attachment continue into adolescence and infant attachment predicts attachment in late adolescence (Weinfield, Sroufe, & Egeland, 2000). Children who were securely attached in infancy and early childhood are more socially competent; tend to be better at making and keeping friends and functioning in a social group; and demonstrate greater emotional health, self-esteem, ego resiliency, and peer competence in adolescence (Boldt, Kochanska, Yoon, & Koenig Nordling, 2014; Jaffari-Bimmel, Juffer, van IJzendoorn, Bakermans-Kranenburg, & Mooijaart, 2006; Sroufe, Carlson, & Shulman, 1993). In contrast, insecure attachment in infancy, particularly disorganized attachment, is associated with higher rates of antisocial behavior, depression, and anxiety in later childhood and adolescence (Boldt et al., 2014; Groh, Roisman, van IJzendoorn, Bakermans-Kranenburg, & Fearon, 2012). For example, insecure attachment to mother and father at 12 months of age predicted externalizing, behavior problems as rated by teachers at 6.5 years of age (Kochanska & Kim, 2013). In addition to fostering healthy development in all children, a secure attachment bond may protect children from the negative effects of being raised in disadvantaged environments.

PROMOTING SECURE ATTACHMENT

Attachment relationships serve as an important backdrop for emotional and social development. Our earliest attachments are with our primary caregivers, most often our mothers. It was once thought that feeding determined patterns of attachment. The psychoanalytic perspective, for example, emphasized feeding as a critical context for infants and caregivers to interact and for infants to have their needs met and thereby develop a sense of trust. Behaviorist theorists, on the other hand, explain attachment as a function of associating close contact with mothers with feeding, satisfying a biological need. Certainly feeding brings infants and caregivers into close contact and offers opportunities to develop attachment bonds, but feeding itself does not determine attachment. For example, in one famous study, baby rhesus monkeys were reared with two inanimate surrogate "mothers": one made of wire mesh and a second covered with terrycloth (see Figure 6.1). The baby monkeys clung to the terrycloth mother despite being fed only by the wire mother, suggesting that attachment bonds are not based in feeding but rather in contact comfort (Harlow & Zimmerman, 1959).

The most important determinant of infant attachment is the caregiver's ability to consistently and sensitively respond to the child's signals (Ainsworth et al., 1978; Behrens, Parker, & Haltigan, 2011). Infants become securely attached to mothers who are sensitive and responsive to

FIGURE 6.1: Harlow's Study: Contact Comfort and the Attachment Bond

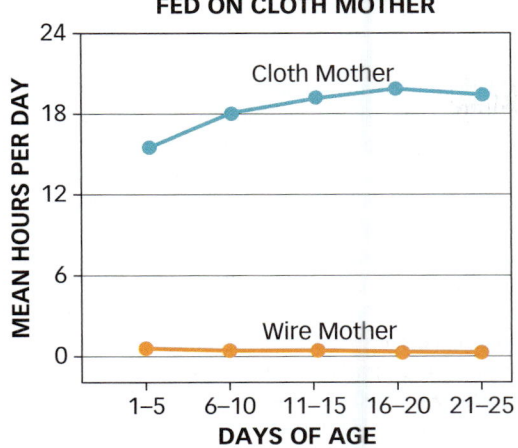

FED ON CLOTH MOTHER

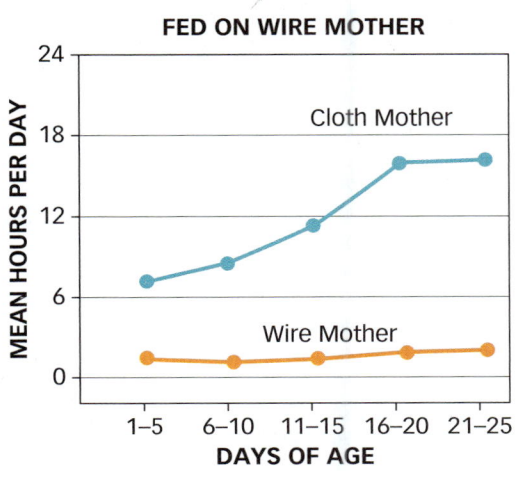

FED ON WIRE MOTHER

This infant monkey preferred to cling to the cloth-covered mother even if fed by the wire mother. Harlow concluded that attachment is based on contact comfort rather than feeding.

their signals, who accept their role as caregiver, are accessible and cooperative with infants, are not distracted by their own thoughts and needs, and feel a sense of efficacy (Belsky & Fearon, 2002; DeWolff & van IJzendoorn, 1997; Gartstein & Iverson, 2014; McElwain & Booth-LaForce, 2006; van den Boom, 1997). Mothers of securely attached infants provide stimulation and warmth and consistently synchronize or match their interactions with their infants' needs (Beebe et al., 2010; Behrens et al., 2011; Higley & Dozier, 2009).

Infants who are insecurely attached have mothers who tend to be more rigid, unresponsive, inconsistent, and demanding (Gartstein & Iverson, 2014). The insecure–avoidant attachment pattern is associated with parental rejection. Insecure–resistant attachment is associated with inconsistent and unresponsive parenting. Disorganized attachment is more common among infants who have been abused or raised in particularly poor caregiving environments and is associated with infant fear (Lamb & Lewis, 2011). Although insecure attachment responses may seem suboptimal, they may represent adaptive responses to poor caregiving environments (Weinfield, Sroufe, Egeland, & Carlson, 2008). For example, not relying on an unsupportive parent may represent a good strategy for infants (Lamb & Lewis, 2011).

Attachment patterns tend to be stable. Securely attached infants are likely to remain secure throughout development (Becker-Stoll et al., 2008; Ranson & Urichuk, 2008; Waters, Merrick, Treboux, Crowell, & Albersheim, 2000). However, negative experience can disrupt attachment. For example, the loss of a parent; parental divorce; a parent's psychiatric disorder; physical abuse; and changes in family stressors, adaptive processes, and living conditions can transform a secure attachment into an insecure attachment pattern later in childhood or adolescence (Hamilton, 2000; Lieberman & Van Horn, 2008; Thompson, 2000; Weinfield et al., 2000). Conversely, it is also the case that quality parent–child interactions can at least partially make up for poor interactions early in life. Children with insecure attachments in infancy who experience subsequent sensitive parenting show more positive social and behavioral outcomes at 54 months of age than do those who receive continuous care of poor quality (Dehaan, 2006). An insecure attachment between child and parent can be overcome by changing maladaptive interaction patterns, increasing sensitivity on the part of the parent, and fostering consistent and developmentally appropriate responses to children's behaviors. Pediatricians, counselors, and social workers can help parents identify and change

LIVES IN CONTEXT

Attachment to Fathers

Gerard Fritz/Science Source

Infants become attached to their fathers, although fathers tend to have different interaction styles than mothers. Father–infant interaction tends to be play-oriented, with high intensity stimulation and excitement, such as tickling, providing opportunities for babies to practice arousal management.

We know a great deal about the influence of mother–infant relationships on infant attachment and adjustment, but much less is known about fathers. Infants develop attachments to their fathers (Grossmann et al., 2002; van IJzendoorn & De Wolff, 1997). At birth, fathers interact with their newborns much like mothers do and provide similar levels of care by cradling the newborn and performing tasks like diaper changing, bathing, and feeding the newborn (Combs-Orme & Renkert, 2009; Lewis & Lamb, 2003). This is true of fathers in Western contexts as well as those in non-Western contexts, such as the Kadazan of Malaysia and Aka and Bofi of Central Africa (Fouts, 2008; Hossain, Roopnarine, Ismail, Hashmi, & Sombuling, 2007; Tamis-LeMonda, Kahana-Kalman, & Yoshikawa, 2009).

Early in an infant's life, fathers and mothers develop different play and communicative styles. Fathers tend to be more stimulating while mothers are more soothing (Feldman, 2003; Grossmann et al., 2002). Father–infant play is more physical in nature as compared with the social exchanges centered on mutual gaze and vocalization that is characteristic of mother–infant play (Feldman, 2003). Fathers tend to engage in more unpredictable rough-and-tumble play throughout infancy and childhood, though it becomes less prominent as children grow older (Lewis & Lamb, 2003). Paternal play styles are met with more positive reactions and arousal from infants; when young children have a choice of adult play partner, they tend to choose their fathers (Feldman, 2003; Lewis & Lamb, 2003). Overall, interactions

with fathers tend to be more play-oriented than care-oriented (Lamb, 1997). Fathers provide opportunities for babies to practice arousal management by providing high-intensity stimulation and excitement, like tickling, chasing, and laughing (Feldman, 2003).

Differences in mothers and fathers' interaction styles appear in many cultures, including France, Switzerland, Italy, and India as well as among white non-Hispanic, African American, and Hispanic American families in the United States (Best, House, Barnard, & Spicker, 1994; Hossain, Field, Pickens, Malphurs, & Del Valle, 1997; Roopnarine, Talukder, Jain, Joshi, & Srivastav, 1992). However, parent–infant interaction styles also vary by culture: German, Swedish, and Israeli kibbutzim fathers as well as fathers in the Aka ethnic group of Africa's western Congo basin are not more playful than mothers (Frodi, Lamb, Hwang, & Frodi, 1983; Hewlett et al., 1998; Hewlett, 2008; Sagi et al., 1985). Despite these findings, overall and across cultures, most of the differences between mothers and fathers are not large (Lewis & Lamb, 2003).

Father–child interaction is an important contributor to children's development and is associated with social competence, independence, and cognitive development in children (Amato, 1987; Caldera, 2004; Frascarolo, 2004). Fathers' play styles influence attachment relationships with infants. Fathers who are sensitive, supportive, and appropriately challenging during play promote father–infant attachment relationships (Grossmann et al., 2002). Rough-and-tumble play contributes to advancements in emotional and behavioral regulation in children (Flanders, Leo, Paquette, Pihl, & Séguin, 2009). When fathers are involved in the caregiving of their infants, infants are more likely to enjoy a warm relationship with their father, carry out responsibilities, follow parents' directions, and be well adjusted (Amato, 1987; Caldera, 2004). Similar to findings with mothers, sensitive parenting on the part of fathers predicts secure attachments with their children through age 3 (Brown, Mangelsdorf, & Neff, 2012; Lucassen et al., 2011). The positive social, emotional, and cognitive effects of father–child interaction continue from infancy into childhood and adolescence (Sarkadi, Kristiansson, Oberklaid, & Bremberg, 2008). Simply put, fathers serve a very important role in children's development.

What Do You Think?

1. **What are some of the challenges of studying father–child relationships? How might researchers address these challenges?**

2. **Why do you think fathers are more likely than mothers to be "playmates"?**

ineffective parenting behaviors to improve parent–child interaction patterns.

Although most research on attachment has focused on the mother–infant bond, we know that infants form multiple attachments—they become attached to fathers (see Lives in Context, above) and other caregivers too. An infant's secure attachment

relationship with a father, for example, can compensate for the negative effects of an insecure attachment to a mother (Boldt et al., 2014; Engle & Breaux, 1998; Kochanska & Kim, 2013). It is important that infants develop attachments with some caregivers, but which caregivers—whether mothers, fathers, or other responsive adults—matters less than the bond itself.

CULTURAL VARIATIONS IN ATTACHMENT CLASSIFICATIONS

Whether the Strange Situation is applicable across cultural contexts is a matter of debate. However, research has shown that infants in many countries, including Germany, Holland, Japan, and the United States approach the Strange Situation in similar ways (Sagi, van IJzendoorn, & Koren-Karie, 1991). The patterns of attachment identified by Ainsworth occur in a wide variety of cultures in North America, Europe, Asia, Africa, and the Middle East (Bornstein et al., 2013; Cassibba, Sette, Bakermans-Kranenburg, & van IJzendoorn, 2013; Gardiner & Kosmitzki, 2010; Huang, Lewin, Mitchell, & Zhang, 2012; Jin, Jacobvitz, Hazen, & Jung, 2012). Insecure–avoidant attachments are more common in Western European countries and insecure–resistant attachments are more prevalent in Japan and Israel (Van IJzendoorn & Kroonenberg, 1988). There are different cultural interpretations of infant behaviors shown in the Strange Situation. For example, while a Western sample might interpret insecure–resistant behavior as clingy, Asian parents might interpret it as successful bonding (Gardiner & Kosmitzki, 2010).

Many Japanese and Israeli infants become highly distressed during the Strange Situation and show higher rates of insecure resistance. Resistance in Japanese samples of infants can be attributed to cultural child-rearing practices that foster mother–infant closeness and physical intimacy that leaves infants unprepared for the separation episodes; the Strange Situation may be too stressful for them to the point where they resist comforting (Takahashi, 1990). Similarly, infants who are raised in small, close-knit Israeli kibbutz communities do not encounter strangers in their day-to-day lives, so the introduction of a stranger in the Strange Situation procedure can be too challenging for them. At the same time, kibbutz-reared infants spend much of their time with their peers and caregivers and see their parents infrequently, and therefore may prefer to be comforted by people other than their parents (Sagi et al., 1985).

Western cultures tend to emphasize individuality and independence whereas Eastern cultures are more likely to emphasize the importance of relationships and connections to others.

Dogon infants from Mali, West Africa, show similar rates of secure attachment to those of Western infants, but the avoidant attachment style is not observed in samples of Dogon infants (McMahan True, Pisani, & Oumar, 2001). Dogon infant care practices diminish the likelihood of avoidant attachment because the infant is in constant proximity to the mother, nurses in response to hunger and distress signals, and receives prompt responsiveness. Infant distress is answered with feeding, and infants feed on demand, so mothers cannot behave in ways that would foster avoidant attachment.

As shown in Figure 6.2, although secure attachment is most common, the prevalence of other attachment styles varies internationally. The behaviors that characterize sensitive caregiving vary with culturally specific socialization goals, values, and beliefs of the parents, family, and community

FIGURE 6.2: Cross-Cultural Variations in Attachment

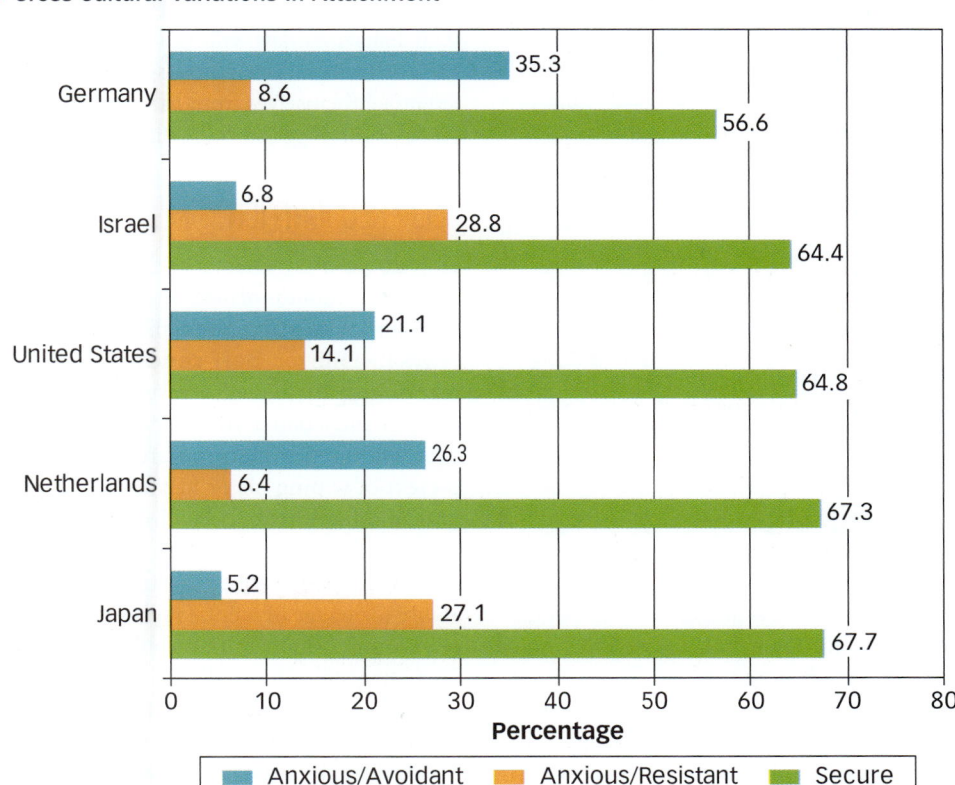

(Rothbaum et al., 2000). For example, Puerto Rican mothers often use more physical control in interactions with infants, such as picking crawling infants up and placing them in desired locations, over the first year of life than do European American mothers. They actively structure interactions in ways consistent with long-term socialization goals (oriented toward calm, attentive, and well-behaved children). Typically attachment theory conceptualizes this type of control as insensitive, yet physical control is associated with secure attachment status at 12 months in Puerto Rican infants (but not white non-Hispanic infants; Carlson & Harwood, 2003; Harwood, Scholmerich, Schulze, & Gonzalez, 1999). Similarly, German mothers operate according to the shared cultural belief that infants should become independent at an early age and learn that they cannot rely on the mother's comfort at all times. German mothers may seem unresponsive to their children's crying, yet they are demonstrating sensitive child-rearing within their context (Grossmann, Spangler, Suess, & Unzner, 1985). Therefore, the behaviors that reflect sensitive caregiving vary with culture because they are adaptations to different circumstances (Rothbaum et al., 2000).

In summary, attachment is an adaptive process in which infants and caregivers become attuned to each other and develop an enduring bond. Infants become attached to caregivers—mothers, fathers, and other adults—who are sensitive to their needs. Secure attachment in infancy is associated with emotional and social competence in infancy, early childhood, and even later childhood and adolescence. The attachment bond formed in infancy, whether secure or insecure, influences the child's developing internal working model of self and thereby his self-concept, as described in the next section.

Thinking in Context 4.4

1. Children reared in impoverished orphanages are at risk of receiving little attention from adults and experiencing few meaningful interactions with caregivers. What might this experience mean for the development of attachment? What outcomes and behaviors might you expect from children reared under such conditions? In your view, what can be done to help such children?

2. How does an infant's emotional capacities, coupled with the goodness of fit between her temperament and that of her parent, influence attachment outcomes?

SELF-CONCEPT AND SELF-RECOGNITION

What do babies know about themselves? When do they know that they have a "self"—that they are separate from the people and things that surround them? We have discussed the challenges that researchers who study infants face. Infants cannot tell us what they perceive, think, or feel. Instead, researchers must devise ways of inferring infants' states, feelings, and thoughts. As you might imagine, this makes studying infants' conceptions of self—their awareness and understanding of themselves—very difficult.

SELF-CONCEPT

Maya, 4 months of age, delights in seeing that she can make her crib mobile move by kicking her feet. Her understanding that she can influence her world suggests that she has a sense of herself as different from her environment (Rochat, 2004). This is an early sense of self-concept, or awareness of self. Before infants can take responsibility for their own actions, they must begin to see themselves as physically separate from the world around them and understand that their behavior can be described and evaluated.

Some developmental researchers believe that infants are born with a capacity to distinguish the self from the surrounding environment (Meltzoff, 1990). Newborns show distress at hearing a recording of another infant's cries but do not show distress at hearing their own cries, suggesting that they can distinguish other infants' cries from their own and thereby have a primitive notion of self (Dondi, Simion, & Caltran, 1999). Newborn facial imitation, their ability to view another person's facial expression and produce it, may suggest a primitive awareness of self and others (Meltzoff, 2007). It is unclear, however, whether these findings suggest that newborns have self-awareness or whether these are simply innate responses.

Other researchers argue that an awareness of oneself is not innate but emerges by 3 months of age (Lewis & Brooks-Gunn, 1979; Neisser, 1993) and is indicated by infants' awareness of the consequences of their own actions on others (Rochat & Striano, 1999). As infants interact with people and objects, they become aware of how their actions influence others, learn that their behaviors have effects, begin to experiment to see how their behaviors influence the world around them, begin to differentiate themselves from their environments, and develop a sense of self (Bigelow, 2001; Bigelow & Walden, 2009).

SELF-RECOGNITION

How do we know whether self-awareness is innate or develops in the early months of life? One way of studying self-awareness in infants is to examine infants' reactions to viewing themselves in a mirror. **Self-recognition**, the ability to recognize or identify the self, is assessed by the "rouge test." In this experiment, a dab of rouge or lipstick is applied to an infant's nose without the infant's awareness—for example, under the pretext of wiping his or her face. The infant is then placed in front of a mirror (Bard, Todd, Bernier, Love, & Leavens, 2006). Whether the infant recognizes himself or herself in the mirror is dependent on cognitive development, especially the ability to engage in mental representation and hold images in one's mind. Infants must be able to retain a memory of their own image in order to display self-recognition in the mirror task. If the infant has an internal representation of her face and recognizes the infant in the mirror as herself, she will notice the dab of rouge and reach for her nose.

This toddler recognizes herself in the mirror, as shown by her touching the rouge mark on her face.

Mirror self-recognition develops gradually and systematically (Courage, Edison, & Howe, 2004). From 3 months of age, infants pay attention and react positively to their mirror image, and by 8 to 9 months of age, they show awareness of the tandem movement of the mirror image with themselves and play with the image, treating it as if it is another baby (Bullock & Lutkenhaus, 1990; Lewis & Brooks-Gunn, 1979). Some 15- to 17-month-old infants show signs of self-recognition, but it is not until 18 to 24 months that a majority of infants demonstrate self-recognition by touching their nose after noticing the rouge mark in the mirror (Cicchetti, Rogosch, Toth, & Spagnola, 1997; Lewis & Brooks-Gunn, 1979).

Does experience with mirrors influence how infants respond to the rouge test? Interestingly, infants from nomadic tribes with no experience with mirrors demonstrate self-recognition at the same ages as infants reared in surroundings with mirrors (Priel & deSchonen, 1986). This suggests that extensive experience with a mirror is not needed to demonstrate self-recognition in the mirror task. In addition, research with Canadian toddlers shows that their performance on the mirror task is unrelated to their experience with mirrors in the home (Courage et al., 2004).

Mirror self-recognition is not the only indicator of a sense of self. By age 2, young children can recognize themselves in photographs. Many 18- to 24-month-old children recognize themselves in pictures and refer to themselves in the pictures as "me" or by their first names (Lewis & Brooks-Gunn, 1979). One study of 20- to 25-month-old toddlers showed that 63% could pick themselves out when they were presented with pictures of themselves and two similar children (Bullock & Lutkenhaus, 1990). By 30 months of age, nearly all of the children could pick out their own picture. In addition, 2-year-olds' speech is peppered with pronouns ("me," "mine"), suggesting self-awareness (Bates, 1990).

Self-awareness is the capability that enables toddlers to experience more complex emotions, such as self-conscious emotions, which—as mentioned earlier in this chapter—include embarrassment, shame, guilt, jealousy, and pride (Lewis & Carmody, 2008). Self-conscious emotions begin to emerge at around the second birthday; they require having an understanding of self and others (Fogel, 2007). Self-awareness is needed before children can be aware of being the focus of attention and feel embarrassment, identify with what others are feeling and feel guilt, or wish they had what someone else has and feel jealousy. In a study of 15- to 24-month-old infants, only those who recognized themselves in the mirror looked embarrassed when an adult gave them overwhelming praise. They smiled, looked away, and covered their faces with their hands. The infants who did not recognize themselves in the mirror did not show embarrassment (Lewis, 2011). A developing sense of self and the self-conscious emotions that accompany it leads toddlers to have more complex social interactions with caregivers and others.

In toddlerhood, between 18 and 30 months of age, children's sense of self-awareness expands beyond self-recognition to include a **categorical self**, a self-description based on broad categories such as sex, age, and physical characteristics (Stipek, Gralinski, & Kopp, 1990). Toddlers describe themselves as "big," "strong," "girl/boy," and "baby/big kid." Children use their categorical self as a guide to behavior. For example, once toddlers label themselves by gender, they spend more time playing with toys stereotyped for their own gender. Applying the categorical self as a guide to behavior illustrates toddlers' advancing capacities for self-control.

SELF-CONTROL

Self-awareness permits self-control, as one must be aware of oneself as separate from others to comply with requests and modify behavior in accordance with caregivers' demands. In order to engage in self-control, the infant must be able to attend to a caregiver's instructions, shift his or her attention from an attractive stimulus or task, and inhibit a behavior. Cortical development, specifically development of the frontal lobes, is responsible for this ability (Rothbart & Bates, 1998).

TABLE 6.4 The Developing Self

CONCEPT	DESCRIPTION	EMERGENCE
Self-concept	Self-description and thoughts about the self	Begins as a sense of awareness in the early months of life
Self-awareness	Awareness of the self as separate from the environment	Innate or develops in the early months of life
Self-recognition	The ability to recognize or identify the self; typically tested in mirror-recognition tasks	18–24 months
Categorical self	Self-description based on broad categories such as sex, age, and physical characteristics; indicates the emergence of self-concept	18–30 months

SOURCE: Adapted from Butterworth (1992).

Between 12 and 18 months, infants begin to demonstrate self-control by their awareness of, and compliance to, caregivers' simple requests (Kaler & Kopp, 1990).

Although toddlers are known for asserting their autonomy, such as by saying no and not complying with a caregiver's directive, compliance is much more common (Kochanska, 2000). Delay of gratification tasks suggest that between 18 and 36 months, toddlers become better able to control their impulses and wait before eating a treat or playing with a toy (Vaughn, Kopp, & Krakow, 1984). Parent–child relationships are important influences on self-control. Mother–infant affect synchrony at 3 months is related to self-control at 2 years, suggesting that regulation of affect in infancy is an important contributor to self-regulation (Feldman, Greenbaum, & Yirmiya, 1999). Similarly, warm parenting fosters self-control in toddlers. Toddlers who experience such parenting demonstrate more compliance than opposition to caregiver requests (Kochanska, Tjebkes, & Forman, 1998).

Infants make great strides in socioemotional development over the first two years of life, as summarized in Table 6.4. Infants' advances in emotional expression and regulation represent the interaction of biological predispositions, such as inborn capacities for basic emotions and temperament, and experience—particularly parent–child interactions—the contexts in which they are raised, and the goodness of fit between infants' needs and what their contexts provide. Infants' gains in emotional and social development and a growing sense of self form a socioemotional foundation for the physical and cognitive changes that they will experience in the early childhood years.

Apply Your Knowledge

A friendly lab assistant escorts 12-month-old Cassie and her mother into a research playroom containing special mirrors and hidden equipment to videotape their interactions. After providing instructions, the lab assistant leaves the mother and Cassie alone, beginning a short procedure to study the security of their attachment relationship. A female stranger enters the room to play with Cassie. Soon after, the mother leaves, and Cassie is alone with the stranger. The mother returns briefly, then leaves again; finally, the stranger leaves the room and Cassie is left alone. During each short separation from her mother, Cassie cries and wails. Surprised and disturbed to find Cassie so upset, her mother returns almost immediately.

She cannot soothe Cassie, who alternates between clinging to her mother and pushing her away angrily, crying all the time. Cassie continues to cry as they leave the laboratory.

1. What was this procedure intended to study? How? Why?

2. What might Cassie's behavior indicate about her security of attachment relationship to the mother and overall socioemotional development? Why?

3. The Strange Situation places infants under distress, the parent's behavior is the source of that distress,

and the procedure also is distressful to parents. From your perspective, what do researchers learn from such research? Should researchers use procedures that elicit distress from children and parents?

4. Is the Strange Situation an unethical research procedure, in your view? Why or why not?

5. If you were a parent to an infant, would you be willing to participate in such an experiment?

Chapter Summary

6.1 Summarize the psychosocial tasks of infancy and toddlerhood.

The psychosocial task of infancy is to develop a sense of trust. If parents and caregivers are sensitive to the infant's physical and emotional needs and consistently fulfill them, the infant will develop a basic sense of trust in his or her caregivers and the world. The task for toddlers is to learn to do things for themselves and feel confident in their ability to maneuver themselves in their environment. Psychosocial development is supported by warm and sensitive parenting and developmentally appropriate expectations for exploration and behavioral control.

6.2 Examine infants' developing capacities for basic and self-conscious emotions and emotional regulation.

Newborns display some basic emotions, such as interest, distress, and disgust. Others emerge during the early months of life. Basic emotions emerge in all infants at about the same ages and are seen and interpreted similarly in all cultures. Self-conscious emotions, such as empathy, embarrassment, shame, and guilt, depend on cognitive development, as well as an awareness of self, and do not emerge until about late infancy. With development, infants use different and more effective strategies for regulating their emotions.

6.3 Identify contextual and cultural influences on emotional development in infants and toddlers.

At about 6 months old, infants begin to use social referencing. Social referencing occurs in ambiguous situations, provides children with guidance in how to interpret the event, and influences their emotional responses and subsequent actions. Parents socialize infants to respond to and display their emotions in socially acceptable ways. The emotions that are considered acceptable, as well as ways of expressing them, differ by culture and context.

6.4 Define *temperament* in infancy, and identify styles of temperament.

Temperament is biologically based and includes inborn tendencies toward nine characteristics. Children are classified into three temperament styles: easy, slow-to-warm-up, and difficult. Temperament is influenced by the interaction of genetic predispositions, maturation, and experience.

6.5 Discuss the stability of temperament and the role of goodness of fit in infant development.

Temperament tends to be stable over months and even years, from infancy through adulthood. But there are also individual differences—some children remain the same and others change. Overall, temperament is least stable in infancy and becomes more stable with development. An important influence on socioemotional development is the goodness of fit between the child's temperament and the environment around him or her, especially the parent's temperament and child-rearing methods.

6.6 Examine attachment styles.

From an ethological perspective, attachment is seen as an adaptive behavior that evolved because it ensures that the infant and caregiver will remain in close proximity, aiding the survival of the infant. Attachment formation progresses through several developmental phases in which infants' behavior becomes increasingly organized, adaptable, and intentional. Attachments permit infants to explore the world, using their attachment figure as a secure base.

The Strange Situation is a structured observational procedure that reveals the security of attachment and classifies infants as securely attached, insecure–avoidant attached, insecure–resistant attached, or disorganized–disoriented attached. Secure attachments in infancy are associated with sociability, curiosity, empathy, self-confidence, and social competence in infancy and early childhood as well as social competence and socioemotional health in later childhood and adolescence.

6.7 Discuss culture and attachment as well as strategies to promote the development of attachment relationships.

Attachment patterns are seen in a wide variety of cultures including North America, Europe, Asia, Africa, and the Middle East, but there are different cultural interpretations of infant attachment behavior, as seen in the observational procedure of the Strange Situation. The behaviors that make up sensitive caregiving vary depending on the socialization goals, values, and beliefs of the family and community, which may vary by culture. Generally, infants become securely or insecurely attached to caregivers based on the caregiver's ability to respond sensitively to the child's signals. Mothers who consistently provide stimulation, warmth, and emotional support tend to have securely attached infants.

6.8 Differentiate self-concept, self-recognition, and self-control, and discuss their respective roles in infant development.

The earliest notion of self-concept, self-awareness, is evident in a primitive fashion at 3 months of age. Self-recognition, as indicated by mirror self-recognition, develops gradually and systematically in infants, but it is not until 18 to 24 months that a majority of infants demonstrate self-recognition in the mirror test. Once children have a sense of self, they can experience more complex emotions, such as self-conscious emotions. Self-awareness permits self-control as one must be aware of oneself as an agent apart from others to comply with requests and modify behavior in accord with caregivers' demands.

Key Terms

attachment   145

autonomy versus shame and doubt   140

basic emotions   141

categorical self   159

difficult temperament   148

disorganized–disoriented attachment   154

easy temperament   148

emotional display rules   147

emotional regulation   142

ethological theory   150

goodness of fit   149

insecure–avoidant attachment   152

insecure-resistant attachment   152

internal working model   151

postpartum depression   144

secure attachment   152

secure base   151

self-concept   152

self-conscious emotions   142

self-recognition   158

separation protest   151

slow-to-warm-up temperament   148

social referencing   144

social smile   141

Strange Situation   152

stranger wariness   146

temperament   146

trust versus mistrust   140

PART III

Early Childhood

In early childhood, advances in physical, cognitive, and socioemotional development permit young children to interact with their social world in new ways. With improvements in strength and motor skills, children engage their peers in rough and tumble play—games involving chasing, jumping, and play fighting.

Advances in cognitive development help children to become better at attending, planning, and remembering. A developing understanding of the mind helps young children become aware of other perspectives and engage in sociodramatic play—acting out roles, stories, and themes as they pretend to be mothers, astronauts, and cartoon characters.

Interactions with parents are especially important in fostering development. Children respond best to parenting that is warm and sensitive yet firm, relying on discussion and reasoning as discipline tools. Nursery school and preschool programs offer new opportunities to interact with adults and other children. Young children learn how to make and keep playmates, join groups, and manage conflict. In cooperative play children learn to work with friends to achieve a common goal, express ideas, be assertive, and regulate emotions. Through interactions within the home, school, and peer contexts, young children come to view their worlds and themselves in new ways, providing opportunities to advance physical, cognitive, and socioemotional development.

DR. KUTHER'S
CHALK TALKS

Watch at
edge.sagepub.com/kuther

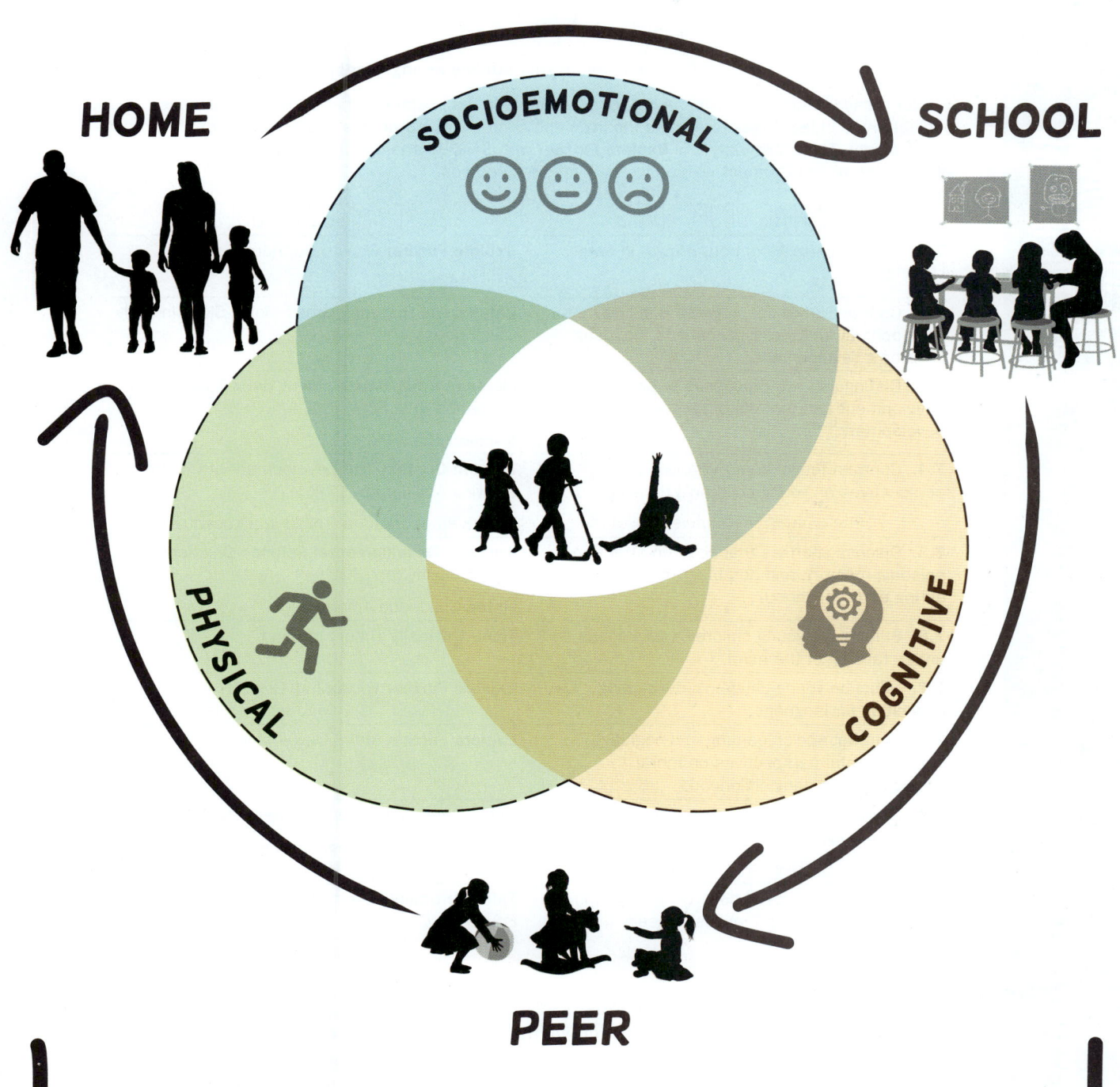

HOME

SCHOOL

SOCIOEMOTIONAL

PHYSICAL

COGNITIVE

PEER

Images: ©iStock.com

Physical and Cognitive Development in Early Childhood

⑤SAGE edge™

Get the edge on your studies at edge.sagepub.com/kuther.

Master these learning objectives using key study tools in the chapter and at SAGE edge. Access original SAGE **Video Cases** to explore the lives and contexts of individuals in every stage of development, **Think Critically** and **Explore Further** with SAGE journal and reference articles, and **Watch**, **Listen**, and **Connect** with online multimedia resources.

LEARNING OBJECTIVES	KEY STUDY TOOLS
7.1. Identify patterns of body growth in early childhood.	**Explore Further** Growth Hormone
7.2. Contrast advances in gross and fine motor development and their implications for young children's development.	**Video Case** Fostering Gross Motor Skills in Early Childhood
7.3. Distinguish two processes of brain development and the role of plasticity in development.	**Lifespan Brain Development** Brain-Based Education (p. 172) **Connect** Brain Plasticity
7.4. Contrast Piaget's and Vygotsky's perspectives on young children's thinking.	**Lives in Context** The Development of Children's Drawing Abilities (p. 178) **Watch** Preoperational Thinking: Egocentrism
7.5. Discuss changes that occur in attention, episodic memory, and autobiographic memory during early childhood.	**Applying Developmental Science** Children's Suggestibility (p. 182) **Listen** Childhood Amnesia
7.6. Summarize young children's awareness and understanding of the mind.	**Think Critically** Theory of Mind
7.7. Describe young children's developing capacities for language.	**Explore Further** Vocabulary Growth
7.8. Contrast social learning and cognitive-developmental perspectives on moral development in early childhood.	**Explore Further** Moral Development
7.9. Identify and explain two approaches to early childhood education, including their associated outcomes.	**Video Case** Child-Oriented Preschool **Ethical and Policy Applications of Lifespan Development** Project Head Start (p. 191)
7.10. Analyze effects of poverty on development and resources to help families in need.	**Think Critically** Poverty, Race, and Early Education

George's parents watched with pride as their 4-year-old son kicked the soccer ball to the other children. George has grown from a bowlegged, round-tummied, and top-heavy toddler, into a strong, well-coordinated young child. His body slimmed, grew taller, and reshaped into proportions similar to that of an adult. As a toddler, he often stumbled and fell, but George can now run, skip, and throw a ball. He has also gained better control over his fingers; he can draw recognizable pictures of objects, animals, and people. As his vocabulary and language skills have grown, George has become more adept at communicating his ideas and needs.

Zero Creatives Cultura/Newscom

How do these developments take place? In this chapter, we examine the many changes that children undergo in physical and motor development as well as how their thinking and language skills change.

GROWTH AND MOTOR DEVELOPMENT IN EARLY CHILDHOOD

George's abilities to run, skip, and manipulate his fingers to create objects with Play-Doh illustrate the many ways that children learn to control their bodies. George is also growing bigger and stronger day by day, though the speed of growth is not as dramatic as when he was younger. His pediatrician assures his parents that this is normal and counsels them about healthy dietary choices now that George has become a picky eater.

GROWTH

Although children grow very rapidly over the first two years, growth slows during early childhood. From ages 2 through 6, the average child grows 2 to 3 inches taller and gains nearly 5 pounds in weight each year. The average 6-year-old child weighs about 45 pounds and is about 46 inches tall.

Genetics plays a role in physical development (Han-Na et al., 2010). Children's height and rate of growth is closely related to that of their parents' (Malina & Bouchard, 1991). Genes influence the rate of growth by stipulating the amount of **hormones** to be released. Hormones are chemicals that are produced and secreted into the bloodstream by glands. Hormones influence cells and are a way in which genetic instructions are transformed into physical development. **Growth hormone** is secreted from birth and influences growth of nearly all parts of the body. Children with growth hormone deficiencies show slowed growth (Mayer et al., 2010), but growth hormone supplements can stimulate growth when needed (Hardin, Kemp, & Allen, 2007).

Ethnic differences in patterns of growth are apparent in England, France, Canada, Australia, and the United States. Generally, children of African descent tend to be tallest, then those of European descent, then Asian, then Latino. However, there are many individual differences. Even within a given culture, some families are much taller than others (Eveleth & Tanner, 1991).

NUTRITION

From ages 2 to 6, young children's appetites tend to decline as compared with infants and toddlers. This decline is normal and occurs as growth slows. At around age 3, it is not uncommon for children to go through a fussy eating phase where previously tolerated food is no longer accepted and it is hard to introduce new food (Fildes et al., 2014; Nicklaus, 2009). Some argue that young children's common dislike of new foods may be adaptive

PhotoPQR/La Depeche du Midi

While there is no need to rule out fast food, it should be a rare addition to a child's diet. Children require a nutritious diet filled with vegetables, fruits, whole grains, and lean protein and dairy.

from an evolutionary perspective because it encourages them to eat familiar and safe foods rather than novel and potentially dangerous foods (Birch & Fisher, 1995).

The overall incidence of picky eating declines with time, but for many children, it is chronic, lasting for several years. Picky eating appears to be a relatively stable individual trait. For example, a difficult temperament at 1.5 years predicted picky eating 2 years later (Hafstad, Abebe, Torgersen, & von Soest, 2013). This example illustrates the dynamic interaction of developmental domains, with temperament, an emotional factor, influencing diet, an influence on physical development. Parents of picky eaters report that their children consume a limited variety of foods, require foods to be prepared in specific ways, express strong likes and dislikes, and throw tantrums over feeding. Yet in most cases, picky eating does not show significant effects on growth (Mascola, Bryson, & Agras, 2010). Regardless, picky eating is an important concern for parents and may remain so through much of childhood.

Young children require a healthy diet, with the same foods that adults need. Although most children in developed nations eat enough calories, they often do not get enough vitamins or minerals (Collins et al., 2006). Foods high in iron, zinc, and calcium are often ignored in favor of other, less healthy foods. For example, for many children in the United States, juice and soda have replaced milk as naptime snacks (Jahns, Siega-Riz, & Popkin, 2001). Sweetened cereals may contain many vitamins and minerals, but the sugar increases children's risk for early tooth decay and other health problems such as obesity—a weight disorder discussed in Chapter 9—which is the most prevalent disease affecting children in developed countries (Lee et al., 2010; Lewit & Kerrebrock, 1998). One study of cereals compared those marketed to children with those marketed to adults and found that over two thirds of the cereals marketed to children did not meet U.S. nutrition standards for foods served in schools (most often because of too much sugar; Schwartz, Vartanian, Wharton, & Brownell,

2008). One study of 20 child care centers in North Carolina examined the degree to which the center-based-care diet matched federal recommendations for children 2 to 5 years of age. Only about one half to one third of center-based diets met the recommendations for milk, 13% for whole grains, and 7% for dark vegetables. Young children in full-time child care consume diets that may not meet federal guidelines for nutrition (Ball, Benjamin, & Ward, 2008). Common dietary deficiencies of the preschool years include vitamins A, B, D, and K as well as iron and calcium; these deficiencies have negative consequences for growth among children throughout the world (Kennedy, 1998; Lips, 2010; Ramakrishnan, 2002).

In developing countries, many children suffer from malnutrition either chronically or episodically (Petrou & Kupek, 2010). Inadequate nutrition is a threat to children's growth. For example, consider a three-month-long drought that took place in Kenya in 1984. During the drought, children's intake of food declined dramatically, and the elementary school children gained only half as much weight as normal (McDonald, Sigman, Espinosa, & Neumann, 1994). Malnutrition influences development in multiple ways, not simply growth. Malnourished children show cognitive deficits as well as impairments in motivation, curiosity, and the ability to interact with the environment (Arija et al., 2006; Smithers, Golley, Brazionis, & Lynch, 2011). During the drought in Kenya, the children became less active during play and less focused in class (McDonald et al., 1994). Deficits from early malnutrition last. For example, among Ghanaian children who survived a severe famine in 1983, those who were youngest at the time of the famine (under age 2) scored lower on cognitive measures throughout childhood and into adulthood than did those who were older (ages 6 to 8; Ampaabeng & Tan, 2013).

Malnutrition is not just a problem for developing countries. Many children in the United States and other

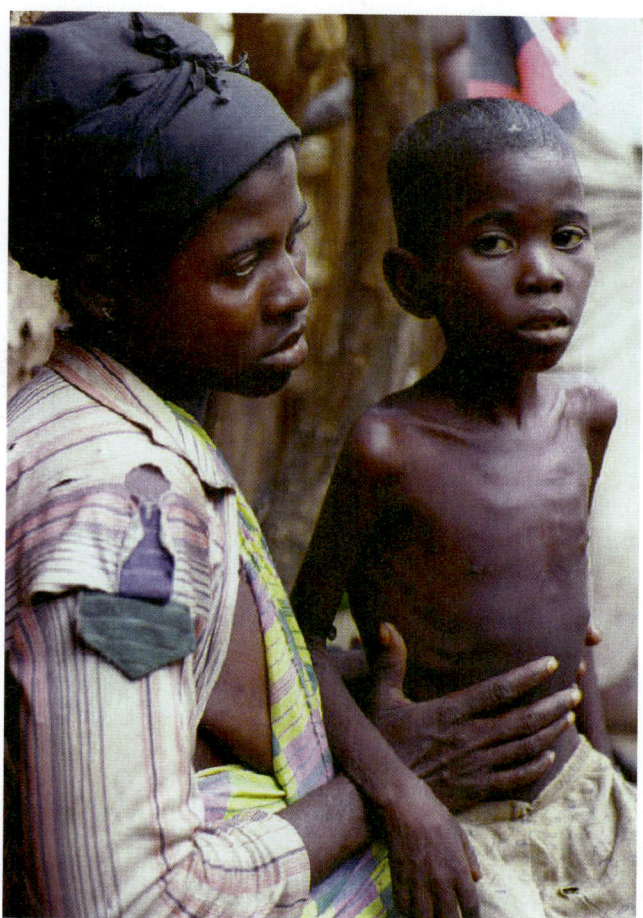

Severely malnourished children, such as this boy in Somalia, often experience cognitive deficits.

developed countries are deprived of diets that support healthy growth because of socioeconomic factors. Low-income families may have difficulty providing children with the range of foods needed for healthy development. Up to 20% of U.S. children in low-income homes, particularly Hispanic and African American children, suffer from iron deficiency (Brotanek, Gosz, Weitzman, & Flores, 2007; Killip, Bennett, & Chambers, 2007). In 2013, about 14% (or 17.5 million) households were categorized as *food insecure* (i.e., lacking the monetary or other resources to provide adequate food) at some point during the year (Coleman-Jensen, Gregory, & Singh, 2014). In the United States, we have linked inadequate nutrition with stunted growth, health problems, poor school performance and poor relationships with peers (Alaimo, Olson, & Frongillo, 2001; Galal & Hulett, 2003; Hampton, 2007).

MOTOR DEVELOPMENT

The refinement of motor skills that use the large muscles of the body—as well as those that tap hand-eye coordination and require subtle movements—is an important developmental task of early childhood.

FOSTERING GROSS MOTOR SKILLS IN EARLY CHILDHOOD

In early childhood, children make impressive gains in both gross and fine motor development. Both practice and contextual factors help advance young children's motor development. Notice how gross motor practice, as well as instruction in yoga, supports multiple domains of development—physical, cognitive, and socioemotional.

Watch the video at edge.sagepub.com/kuther

Climbing requires strength, coordination, and balance.

Gross Motor Skills

Between the ages of 3 and 6, children make great advances in **gross motor skills**—those that use the large muscles—such as running and jumping. They become physically stronger, with increases in bone and muscle strength as well as lung capacity. Children make gains in coordination as the parts of the brain responsible for sensory and motor skills develop. Now they can play harder and engage in more complicated play activities that include running, jumping, and climbing. Like other aspects of physical (and as we will see, cognitive) development, socioeconomic disadvantage is associated with poor motor skills, perhaps through inadequate nutrition and fewer environmental opportunities to practice motor skills (McPhillips & Jordan-Black, 2007). Low-income communities are more likely to lack resources that support children's play, such as parks, recreation facilities, and safe neighborhoods and streets for outside play.

Young children practice using their large motor skills to jump; run; and ride tricycles, pedal cars, and other riding toys. Coordinating complex movements, like those entailed in riding a bicycle, is challenging for young children as it requires controlling multiple limbs, balancing, and more. As they grow and gain competence in their motor skills, young children become even more coordinated and begin to show interest in skipping, balancing, and playing games that involve feats of coordination, such as throwing and catching a ball. By age 5, most North American children can throw, catch, and kick a ball; climb a ladder; and ride a tricycle. Some can even skate and ride a bicycle.

Young children's motor abilities are also influenced by their context. For example, young children of some nations can swim in rough ocean waves that many adults of other nations would not attempt. Advances in gross motor skills help children move about and develop a sense of mastery of their environment, but it is **fine motor skills** that permit young children to take responsibility for their own care.

Fine Motor Skills

Fine motor skills like the ability to button a shirt, pour milk into a glass, put puzzles together, and draw pictures involve eye–hand and small muscle coordination. As children get better at these skills, they are able to become more independent and do more for themselves. Young children become better at grasping eating utensils and become more self-sufficient at feeding. Many fine motor skills are very difficult for young children because they involve both hands and both sides of the brain. With short, stubby fingers that have not yet grown and a cerebral cortex that is not yet myelinated, a challenging task such as tying a shoelace becomes even more frustrating for young children. Tying a shoelace is a complex act requiring attention, memory for an intricate series of hand movements, and the dexterity to perform them. Though preschoolers struggle with this task, by 5 to 6 years of age most children can tie their shoes.

Table 7.1 summarizes milestones of gross and fine motor skill development in young children.

TABLE 7.1 Gross and Fine Motor Skill Development in Early Childhood

AGE	GROSS MOTOR SKILL	FINE MOTOR SKILL
2–3 years	Walks more smoothly, runs but cannot turn or stop suddenly, jumps, throws a ball with a rigid body and catches by trapping ball against chest, rides push toys using feet	Unzips large zippers, puts on and removes some clothing, uses a spoon
3–4 years	Runs, ascends stairs alternating feet, jumps 15 to 24 inches, hops, pedals and steers a tricycle	Serves food, can work large buttons, copies vertical line and circle, uses scissors
4–5 years	Runs more smoothly with control over stopping and turning, descends stairs alternating feet, jumps 24 to 33 inches, skips, throws ball by rotating the body and transferring weight to one foot, catches ball with hands, rides tricycle and steers effectively	Uses scissors to cut along a line, uses fork effectively, copies simple shapes and some letters
5–6 years	Runs more quickly, skips more effectively, throws and catches a ball like older children, makes a running jump of 28 to 36 inches, rides bicycle with training wheels	Ties shoes, uses knife to cut soft food, copies numbers and simple words

1. How would you explain to parents the influence of nature and nurture on children's growth? What advice would you give parents about fostering healthy growth in their preschooler?

2. How might contextual factors such as neighborhood, family, school, and culture influence the development of motor skills? How might these factors become more influential over the childhood years?

3. Why do motor skills matter? Consider your own development. What do you recall about the development of your motors skills, for example, when you learned to tie your shoelaces or ride a bike? How did your motor skills influence other aspects of development, such as your relationships with others or your cognitive skills?

BRAIN DEVELOPMENT IN EARLY CHILDHOOD

Continuing from infancy, early childhood is a rapid period of brain growth with an increase in synapses and connections among brain regions (Dubois et al., 2013). At age 2, the brain reaches 75% of its adult weight and 90% by age 5. Children's increasing motor and cognitive abilities are not simply due to the increase in brain matter. As discussed in Chapter 4, the neuron's dendrites are pruned in response to early experience, an important part of neurological development (Brown & Jernigan, 2012; Stiles & Jernigan, 2010). In addition, myelination contributes to many of the changes that we see in children's capacities.

As the neuron's axons become coated with fatty myelin, children's thinking becomes faster, more coordinated, and complex. Myelination aids quick complex communication between neurons and makes coordinated behaviors possible (Dubois et al., 2013; Mabbott, Noseworthy, Bouffet, Laughlin, & Rockel, 2006). Patterns of myelination correspond with the onset and refinement of cognitive functions and behaviors (Dean et al., 2014). The first areas of the brain to myelinate govern sensory and motor functions (Deoni et al., 2011). In early childhood, children process information quickly enough to complete sophisticated sequences of physical behavior, such as catching and then throwing a ball. They also become better thinkers, able to hear a question and remember it long enough to answer it appropriately. Experience also matters. As children practice activities, they become routine, which permits them to act more quickly and to multitask (Merzenich, 2001).

LATERALIZATION

In addition to the changes just described, parts of the brain become specialized for different functions. The two halves of the brain, known as hemispheres, may look alike but are not identical. Each hemisphere of the brain (and the parts of the brain that comprise each hemisphere) is specialized for particular functions and becomes more specialized with experience. This process of the hemispheres becoming specialized to carry out different functions is called **lateralization**. Lateralization ("of the side," in Latin) begins before birth and is influenced both by genes and by early experiences (Friederici, 2006; Goymer, 2007). For example, in the womb, most fetuses face toward the left, freeing the right side of the body, which permits more movement on that side and the development of greater control over the right side of the body (Previc, 1991). In this way, one hemisphere beings to dominate, known as hemispheric dominance. Most people experience hemispheric dominance, most commonly with the left hemisphere dominating over the right. Given that the left hemisphere controls the right side of the body (and the right hemisphere controls the left side of the body), most people are right-handed, which is an indicator of hemispheric dominance. About 90% of people in Western countries are right-handed. Among right-handed people, the left hemisphere plays an important role in language and the right hemisphere influences spatial skills. In left-handed people, the right hemisphere is dominant, and language is often shared over both hemispheres rather than in solely the left hemisphere (Szaflarski et al., 2002). In some cultures, left-handedness is discouraged. For example, less than 1% of adults in Tanzania are left-handed because left-handed children often are physically restrained and punished (Provins, 1997). When left-handed children are forced to use their right hands, they typically learn to write with their right hand but carry out most other activities with their left, and brain scans reveal that their brains remain right-dominant (Klöppel, Vongerichten, van Eimeren, Frackowiak, & Siebner, 2007).

Lateralization is visible prior to birth. Fetuses display lateralized mouth movements—with the right side of the mouth showing more movement over the course of gestation (Reissland, Francis, Aydin, Mason, & Exley, 2014). In newborns, the left hemisphere tends to have greater structural connectivity and efficiency than the right—more connections and pathways suggesting that they are better able to control the right side of their bodies (Ratnarajah et al., 2013). Most newborns tend to turn their heads toward the right, causing them to spend more time looking at and using their right hand (Hinojosa, Sheu, & Michel, 2003). Children display a preference for the right or left hand and their subsequent activity makes the hand more dominant because experience strengthens the hand and neural connections, and improves agility.

Despite lateralization, the two hemispheres interact in a great many complex ways to enable us to think, move, create, and exercise our senses (Efron, 1990; Springer & Deutsch, 1998). The **corpus callosum**, a collection of 250 to 800 million neural fibers, connects the left and right hemispheres of the brain, permitting them to communicate and coordinate processing (Banich & Heller, 1998). During early childhood, the corpus callosum grows and myelinates, permitting the two halves of the brain to communicate in more sophisticated and

Brain-Based Education

Effective instruction emphasizes active learning through creative play, artwork, physical activity, and social play.

The brain-based education perspective views learning as multidimensional, including more than academics. Children are encouraged to develop all aspects of their brains, tapping physical, musical, creative, cognitive, and other abilities. According to brain-based educators, the brain changes with experience and is plastic; therefore, everyday experiences such as learning an instrument, role-playing, and learning vocabulary may alter children's brains.

Some brain-based education emphasizes teaching different parts of the brain separately. For example, a common brain-based education instructional strategy is to teach for the left or right lateralized brain. The "left-brain" is said to be the "logical" hemisphere, concerned with language and analysis, while the "right-brain" is said to be the "intuitive" hemisphere concerned with spatial patterns and creativity (Sousa, 2001). Brain-based learning theorists may then encourage teachers to teach specific hemispheres during adapted lessons. To teach to the left hemisphere, teachers have students engage in reading and writing, while right hemisphere–oriented lessons have students create visual representations of concepts (Sousa, 2001).

However, some experts argue that the leap from neurological research to the classroom is large and not supported (Alferink

& Farmer-Dougan, 2010). Like most abilities, language and spatial information are processed differently but simultaneously by the two hemispheres. It is highly improbable, then, that any given lesson, regardless of analytic or spatial type, can stimulate activation of only one hemisphere. Although lateralized, the brain functions as a whole.

For many researchers, the problem of brain-based education is its reliance on the brain itself and in its oversimplification of complex theories and research (Alferink & Farmer-Dougan, 2010; Busso & Pollack, 2014). Although we have learned much, brain research is in its infancy. Researchers do not know enough about how the brain functions and learns to draw direct inferences about teaching (Bruer, 2008). For example, magnetic resonance imaging (MRI) research illuminates patterns of brain activity, but researchers do not yet conclusively know what those patterns mean or if those patterns of brain activity have implications for behavior (Willis, 2007). Using these findings to inform education is premature. Many researchers, therefore, find it problematic to state that teaching strategies should be derived from brain research—at least not yet.

On the positive side, however, brain-based education emphasizes active learning. Teachers who foster active learning encourage students to become engaged and participate in their own learning, such as being creative in artwork, physical activity, and story making (Bruer, 2008). Active learning is an important educational strategy. Active learning is in line with cognitive theory, such as Piaget's, which points to the constructive nature of knowledge, that children must interact with the world and actively construct and modify their schemes. Although many developmental researchers argue that the neurological science behind brain-based education is questionable, the active learning practices that comprise many brain-based learning activities advance children's learning.

What Do You Think?

Identify an advantage and a disadvantage to brain-based education. In your view, should preschools emphasize teaching specifically to the left or right hemisphere?

---

efficient ways and to act as one, enabling the child to execute large and fine motor activities such as catching and throwing a ball or tying shoelaces (Banich, 1998; Brown & Jernigan, 2012).

PLASTICITY

The human brain has a capacity to change its organization and function in response to experience throughout the lifespan; this is known as **plasticity** (Kolb, Gibb, & Robinson, 2003). For example, in one study, young children who were given training in music demonstrated structural brain changes over a period of 15 months that correspond with increases in music and auditory skills (Hyde et al., 2009). The brain

contains an overabundance of neurons and synapses that allow it to receive any and all kinds of sensory and motor stimulation possible (Johnston et al., 2009). However, our brains are prepared for experiences that are more diverse and varied than we actually encounter. Many of our neural connections remain unused. Active synapses, or connections among neurons that are used, continue to function, whereas unused synapses are pruned and the neurons are reserved for future use, such as compensating for brain injury or learning new skills (Huttenlocher, 1994; Johnston et al., 2009). Since the 1990s, brain-based education, deriving classroom activities and educational principles from brain research, has become popular (see Lifespan Brain Development, above; Colburn, 2009; Jensen, 2008).

Washington Post/Getty

The brain is most plastic during the first few years of life (Nelson, Thomas, & de Haan, 2006; Stiles & Jernigan, 2010). Plasticity implies that the young child's brain can reorganize itself in response to injury in ways that the adult's brain cannot. Adults who suffered brain injuries as infants and young children often have fewer cognitive difficulties than do adults who were injured later in life. The young child's brain is more flexible and less functionally committed than the adult brain, but the relative advantage of this plasticity is debated (Johnston, 2009).

The immature young brain, while offering opportunities for plasticity, is uniquely sensitive to injury (Johnston et al., 2009; Uylings, 2006). If a part of the brain is damaged at a critical point in development, functions linked to that region will be irreversibly impaired (Luciana, 2003). How well a young child's brain compensates for an injury depends on the age at the time of injury, site of injury, and brain areas and capacities compromised. Generally speaking, plasticity is greatest when neurons are forming many synapses, and it declines with pruning (Kolb et al., 2003; Nelson, 2011). However, brain injuries sustained before age 2, and in some cases 3, can result in more global and severe deficits than do those sustained later in childhood—and more long-lasting deficits (Anderson et al., 2010; Anderson et al., 2014), suggesting that a reserve of neurons is needed for the brain to show plasticity. Research with young children with brain injury showed that most experienced some cognitive deficits 18 months later and social problems at age 8, with more severe injuries associated with generalized deficits and less severe with deficits in visual memory and **executive function** (Gerrard-Morris et al., 2010; Sonnenberg, Dupuis, & Rumney, 2010).

Plasticity is not absolute. Some deficits often remain. The degree to which individuals recover depends on the injury, its nature and severity, age, experiences after the injury, and contextual factors supporting recovery, such as interventions (Anderson, Spencer-Smith, & Wood, 2011; Bryck & Fisher, 2012).

Thinking in Context 7.2

1. Children who suffer brain injuries often regain some, and sometimes all, of their capacities. How might you explain this, given what you have learned about brain development?

2. In your view, what is the most important thing about brain development that parents need to know? How might you teach them?

COGNITIVE DEVLOPMENT IN EARLY CHILDHOOD

Three-year-old Elisa can use language, plan out actions, and think of solutions to problems rather than relying on her motor skills to manipulate materials in a trial-and-error

fashion. How do these cognitive skills develop? The three major perspectives on cognition address this question in different ways. Cognitive-developmental theories emphasize the structural changes that underlie development. Sociocultural theories point to the role of context and our need to communicate in influencing thought. Information processing theories examine changes in our physical capacities and strategy use as contributors to cognitive change.

PIAGET'S COGNITIVE-DEVELOPMENTAL PERSPECTIVE: PREOPERATIONAL REASONING

Timothy stands up on his toes and releases his parachute toy, letting the action figure dangling from a parachute drift a few feet from him and collapse on the floor. "I'm going to go up high and make it faster," he says, imagining standing on the sofa and making the toy sail far into the clouds. He stands on the sofa and releases the toy, which sails a bit farther this time. "Next time he'll jump out of the plane even higher!" Timothy thinks, excitedly. His friend Martin calls out, "Let's make him land on the moon! He can meet space people!"

Timothy and Martin learn through play and by interacting with people and objects around them. From the cognitive-developmental perspective, young children's thought progresses from the sensory and motor schemes of infancy to more sophisticated representational thought. **Preoperational reasoning** appears in young children from about ages 2 to 6 and is characterized by a dramatic leap in the use of symbolic thinking that permits young children to use language, interact with others, and play using their own thoughts and imaginations to guide their behavior. It is symbolic thought that enables Timothy and Martin to use language to communicate their thoughts and desires—and it is also what allows them to send their toy on a mission to the moon to visit with pretend space people.

Young children in the preoperational stage show impressive advances in representational thinking, but they are unable to grasp logic and cannot understand complex relationships. For example, a child may not understand that her father was once her grandmother's little boy. Alternatively, a child may not understand that his brother is also his sister's brother. Understanding each of these complex relationships requires the use of cognitive operations that are beyond the preoperational child's capacities. Children who show preoperational reasoning tend to make several common errors, including **egocentrism**, **animism**, **centration**, and **irreversibility**.

Egocentrism

"See my picture?" Ricardo asks as he holds up a blank sheet of paper. Miss Jones answers, "You can see your picture, but I can't. Turn your page around so that I can see your picture. There it is! It's beautiful," she proclaims after Ricardo flips the piece of paper, permitting her to see his drawing. Ricardo did not realize that even though he could see his drawing,

Miss Jones could not. Ricardo displays egocentrism, the inability to take another person's point of view or perspective. The egocentric child views the world from his or her own perspective, assuming that other people share her feelings, knowledge, and even physical view of the world. For example, the egocentric child may present Mommy with her teddy bear when Mommy looks sad, not realizing that while the teddy bear may make *her* feel better, Mommy has different needs and preferences.

A classic task used to illustrate preoperational children's egocentrism is the *three mountain task*. As shown in Figure 7.2, the child sits at a table facing three large mountains. A doll is placed in a chair across the table from the child, facing him. The child is asked how the mountains look to the doll. Piaget found that young children in the preoperational stage described the scene from their own perspectives rather than the doll's. They could not complete the task correctly because they could not imagine that someone else could see the world differently. The children exhibited egocentrism; they were not able to take another point of view (the doll's; Piaget & Inhelder, 1967).

FIGURE 7.2: The Three Mountain Task

Children who display preoperational reasoning cannot describe the scene depicted in the three mountains task from the point of view of the teddy bear.

Animism

Egocentric thinking can also take the form of animism, the belief that inanimate objects are alive and have feelings and intentions. "It's raining because the sun is sad and it is crying," 3-year-old Melinda explains. Children accept their own explanations for phenomena as they are unable to consider another viewpoint or alternative reason. The 4-year-old child who cries after bumping her head on a table may feel better after her mother smacks the table, saying, "Bad table!" In the child's eyes, the table got what it deserved: payback!

Centration

Preoperational children exhibit centration, the tendency to focus on one part of a stimulus or situation and exclude all others. For example, a boy may believe that if he wears a dress he will become a girl. He focuses entirely on the appearance (the dress) rather than the other characteristics that make him a boy. Consider a group of children who are lined up according to height. If one child is asked, "Who is the tallest?" he or she will correctly point to the tallest child. Then, if the child is asked, "Who is the oldest?" he or she may point to the tallest child. "Who is the smartest?" Again the child points to the tallest child of the group, demonstrating centration: the child focuses on height to the exclusion of the other attributes.

Centration is illustrated by a classic task that requires the preoperational child to distinguish what something appears to be from what it really is, the **appearance–reality distinction**. In a classic study illustrating this effect, DeVries (1969) presented 3- to 6-year-old children with a cat named Maynard (see Figure 7.3). The children were permitted to pet Maynard. Then, while his head and shoulders were hidden behind a screen (and his back and tail were still visible), a dog mask was placed onto Maynard's head. The children were then asked, "What kind of animal is it now?" "Does it bark or meow?" Three-year-old children, despite Maynard's body and tail being visible during the transformation, replied that he was now a dog. Six-year-old children were able to distinguish Maynard's appearance from reality and explained that he only *looked* like a dog.

One reason that 3-year-old children fail appearance–reality tasks is because they are not yet capable of effective dual encoding, the ability to mentally represent an object in more than one way at a time (Flavell, Green, & Flavell, 1986). For example, young children are not able to understand that a scale model (like a doll house) can be both an object (something to play with) and a symbol (of an actual house; DeLoache, 2000; MacConnell & Daehler, 2004).

Irreversibility

"You ruined it!" cried Johnson after his older sister, Monique, placed a triangular block atop the tower of blocks he had just built. "No, I just put a triangle there to show it was the top and finish it," she explains. "No!" insists Johnson. "OK, I'll take it off," says Monique. "See? Now it's just how you left it." "No. It's ruined," Johnson sighs. Johnson continued to be upset after his sister removed the triangular block, not realizing that by removing the block she has restored the block structure to its original state. Young children's thinking is characterized by irreversibility, meaning that they do not understand that reversing a process can often undo it and restore the original state.

FIGURE 7.3: Appearance vs. Reality: Is It a Cat or Dog?

Young children did not understand that Maynard the cat remained a cat despite wearing a dog mask and looking like a dog.

SOURCE: DeVries (1969).

Preoperational children's irreversible thinking is illustrated by **conservation** tasks that require them to understand that the quantity of a substance is not transformed by changes in its appearance, that a change in appearance can be reversed. For example, a child is shown two identical glasses. The same amount of liquid is poured into each glass. After the child agrees that the two glasses contain the same amount of water, the liquid from one glass is poured into a taller, narrower glass, and the child is asked whether one glass contains more liquid than the other. Young children in the preoperational stage reply that the taller, narrower glass contains more liquid. Why? It has a higher liquid level relative to the shorter, wider glass. They center on the appearance of the liquid without realizing that the process can be reversed by pouring the liquid back into the shorter, wider glass. They are unable to negate the action and fail to understand that the process can be undone by pouring the liquid in the tall, narrow glass back into the shorter wider glass. They focus on the height of the water as it is poured from a short to tall glass, ignoring other aspects such as the change in width that makes the liquid appear to have changed. Young children do not understand that it is still the same water.

Figure 7.4 displays additional conservation problems. Characteristics of preoperational children's reasoning are summarized in Table 7.2.

Evaluating Piaget's Preoperational Reasoning Stage

Similar to findings that infants are more capable than Piaget envisioned (see Chapter 5), research with young children has contravened some of Piaget's conclusions. Just as Piaget's sensorimotor tasks underestimated infants' cognitive abilities, his tests of preoperational thinking underestimated young children. Success on Piaget's tasks appears to depend more on the child's language abilities than his or her actions. To be successful at the three mountain task, for example, the child must not only understand how the mounds look from the other side of the table but must be able to communicate

that understanding. Appearance–reality tasks require not simply an understanding of dual representation but the ability to express it. However, if the task is nonverbal, such as requiring reaching for an object rather than talking about it, even 3-year-old children can distinguish appearance from reality, as we will discuss in the following sections (Sapp, Lee, & Muir, 2000).

Research Findings on Egocentrism and Animism

Simple tasks demonstrate that young children are less egocentric than Piaget posited. When a 3-year-old child is shown a card with a dog on one side and a cat on another and the card is held up between the researcher who can see the cat and the child who can see the dog, the child correctly responds that the researcher can see the cat (Flavell, Everett, Croft, & Flavell, 1981). In a variation of the three mountain task, called the doll and police officer task, the child sits in front of a square board that is divided into four sections by dividers (Hughes, 1975). A toy police officer is placed at the edge of the board. A doll is placed in one section, moved to another section, and so on. With each move the child is asked whether the police officer can see the doll. Finally another police officer is placed on the board and the child is asked to hide the doll from both police officers. In this task, nearly all children ages 3.5 to 5 were able to take the police officers' perspectives and successfully complete the task. By making the task more relevant to children's everyday lives (i.e., hiding)—and less difficult—it became clear that young children are less egocentric than Piaget theorized (Hughes, 1975; Newcombe & Huttenlocher, 1992).

Likewise, although young children sometimes provide animistic answers to questions, they do not display animism as often as Piaget believed. Three-year-old children do

TABLE 7.2 Characteristics of Preoperational Children's Reasoning

CHARACTERISTIC	DESCRIPTION
Egocentrism	The inability to take another person's point of view or perspective
Animism	The belief that inanimate objects are alive and have feelings and intentions
Centration	Tendency to focus attention on one part of a stimulus or situation and exclude all others
Irreversibility	Failure to understand that reversing a process can often undo a process and restore the original state

FIGURE 7.4: Additional Conservation Problems

Conservation Task	Original Presentation	Transformation
Number	Are there the same number of pennies in each row?	Now are there the same number of pennies in each row, or does one row have more?
Mass	Is there the same amount of clay in each ball?	Now does each piece have the same amount of clay, or does one have more?
Liquid	Is there the same amount of water in each glass?	Now does each glass have the same amount of water, or does one have more?

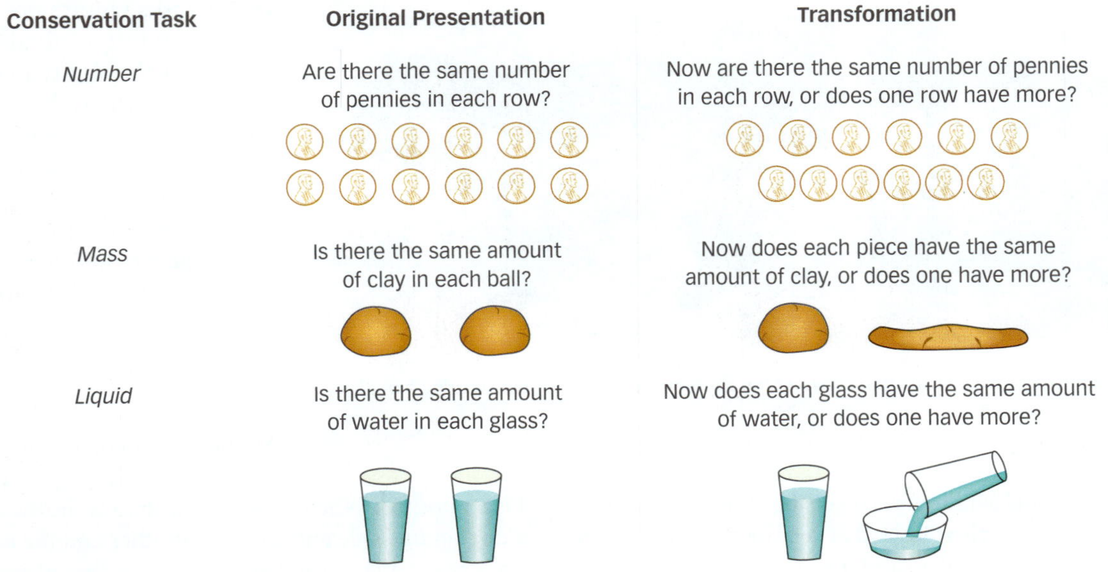

not tend to describe inanimate objects with lifelike qualities, even when the object is a robot that can move (Gelman & Gottfried, 1996). Three- and 4-year-old children recognize that living things are regulated by their own internal energy but inanimate objects are not (Gottfried & Gelman, 2005). Most 4-year-old children understand that animals grow, and even plants grow, but objects do not (Backschneider, Shatz, & Gelman, 1993). Sometimes, however, young children provide animistic responses. For example, Dolgin and Behrend (1984) found that animistic statements are not due to a belief that all objects are alive but rather that novel objects that seem to move independently are alive. Three-year-old children may display animism when considering trains and airplanes, believing that they are alive, because these objects appear to move on their own, like other living things (Massey & Gelman, 1988; Poulin-Dublis & Héroux, 1994). Finally, children show individual differences in their expressions of animism and reasoning about living things and these differences are linked with aspects of cognitive development such as memory, working memory, and inhibition (Zaitchik, Iqbal, & Carey, 2014).

Research Findings on Reversibility and the Appearance–Reality Distinction

Piaget (1970) posited that young children cannot solve or be taught to solve conservation problems because they lack the cognitive operations needed to understand reversibility and that transformations in appearance do not change a given substance. However, research has shown that 4-year-old children can be taught to conserve (Gelman, 1969; Hendler & Weisberg, 1992), suggesting that children's difficulties with reversibility and conservation tasks can be overcome (Gallagher, 2008). In addition, when a conservation of numbers task is scaled down to include only three objects instead of six, even 3-year-olds perform well without training (Gelman, 1972).

In the classic appearance–reality task, when 3-year-old children are shown a sponge that looks like a rock, they tend to say that it "really and truly is" a rock (Flavell, Flavell, & Green, 1987; Flavell, Green, & Flavell, 1989). They focus or center on the most salient feature, its rocklike appearance, displaying centration. However, if the children are told to play a trick on someone (i.e., "let's pretend that this sponge is a rock and tell Anne that it is a rock when it really is a sponge") or are asked to choose an object that can be used to clean spilled water, many choose the sponge, illustrating that they can form a dual representation of the sponge as an object that looks like a rock (Rice, Koinis, Sullivan, Tager-Flusberg, & Winner, 1997; Sapp et al., 2000). Research suggests that 3-year-old children can shift between describing the real and fake or imagined aspects of an object or situation and can flexibly describe misleading appearances and function of objects in response to natural conversational prompts, as compared with the traditional appearance–reality tasks, as depicted in Figure 7.5 (Deák, 2006; Hansen & Markman, 2005).

Some responses to appearance–reality tasks may reflect how children respond to sequences of questions rather than confusing appearance and reality (Deák, 2006). Some preschoolers will repeat their first answer to every successive question about a topic, making it hard to determine what they understand. These types of errors are related to age as 3-year-old children are especially likely to make such errors, 5-year-olds make few repetitive errors, and 4-year-old children tend to make intermediate errors, suggesting a clear developmental trend in language ability that appears on appearance–reality tests as well as other tests of cognitive ability (Deák, 2006). Preschoolers show an understanding of the appearance–reality distinction, and it develops throughout childhood (Woolley & Ghossainy, 2013).

Pura helps her grandmother grind corn for tortillas.

Researchers generally conclude that typical Piagetian tasks emphasize what young children cannot understand more than what they *can* understand (Beilin, 1992). Traditional appearance–reality tasks require that young children articulate their understanding rather than demonstrate it nonverbally. Often asking different, simplified questions enables children to demonstrate their understanding (Bullock, 1985; Deák, 2006; Hansen & Markman, 2005; Waxman & Hatch, 1992). Certainly young children are more egocentric and illogical than older, school-aged children; however, they are able to demonstrate logical reasoning about simple problems in familiar contexts. Young children can adapt their speech to their listeners, for example, using simpler language when talking to younger siblings (Gelman & Shatz, 1978), suggesting that they can understand that their sibling has a different perspective and capacity for language than they do. Young children also quickly develop increasingly sophisticated representational abilities through their symbolic play activities. Pretending that objects and people are something other than what they really are helps young children to develop capacities for dual representation, and they slowly begin to differentiate misleading appearances from reality (Golomb & Galasso, 1995). Children can also imagine what something looks like and draw a picture to represent that vision, as discussed in Lives in Context (p. 178).

VYGOTSKY'S SOCIOCULTURAL PERSPECTIVE

A second major approach to understanding cognitive development was developed by the Russian psychologist Lev Vygotsky. According to Vygotsky's sociocultural theory, we are embedded in a context that shapes how we think and who we become. Much of children's learning comes not from working alone but from collaborating with others. Children interact with more skilled partners who serve as models and provide instruction. Over time, children internalize the instruction, making it

part of their skill set, and they thereby master tasks. For example, children of the Zinacantec Maya of Chiapas, Mexico, learn by actively participating in informal tasks such as making tortillas and weaving (Maynard, 2002, 2004). Children learn by working alongside more skilled partners who provide assistance when needed (Rogoff, 1998; Rogoff, Mosier, Mistry, & Göncü, 1993). Older and more skilled members of society stimulate children's cognitive development by presenting new challenges and guiding or assisting them with particularly difficult tasks. Parents and child care providers often teach children, but anyone who is more skilled at a given task, including older siblings and peers, can promote children's cognitive development (Maynard, 2002; Rogoff, 1990).

According to the sociocultural perspective, children's social experiences teach them how to think. **Guided participation** (also known as an *apprenticeship in thinking*) is a form of sensitive teaching in which the partner is attuned to the needs of the child and helps him or her to accomplish more than the child could do alone (Rogoff, 1990). As novices, children learn from more skilled, or expert, partners by observing them and asking questions. The expert partner provides **scaffolding** that permits the child to bridge the gap between his or her current competence level and the task at hand. For example, consider a child working on a jigsaw puzzle. She is stumped, unable to complete it on her own. Suppose a more skilled partner, such as an adult, sibling, or another child who has more experience with puzzles, provides a little bit of assistance, a scaffold. The expert partner might point to an empty space on the puzzle and encourage the child to find a piece that fits that spot. If the child remains stumped, the partner might point out a piece or rotate it to help the child see the relationship. The partner acts to motivate the child and provide support to help the child finish the puzzle, emphasizing that they are working together. The child novice and expert partner interact to accomplish the goal and the expert adjusts his or her responses to meet the needs of the child. With time, the child internalizes the lesson and learns to accomplish the task on her own. In this way, cognitive development and learning occurs as the child actively internalizes elements of context, such as interactions with more skilled people (Fernyhough, 2008). Scaffolding occurs in formal educational settings, but also informally, any time a partner adjusts his or her interactional style to fit the needs of a child and guide the child to complete a task that he or she could not complete alone.

Effective scaffolding works within the **zone of proximal development**, the gap between the child's competence level, what he can do alone, and what he can do with assistance. The upper limit of this zone is what the child can accomplish with a skilled partner. Over time, the child internalizes the scaffolding, the skill becomes within his range of competence, and his zone of proximal development shifts. Adults tend to naturally provide children with scaffolds (Conner, Knight, & Cross, 1997; Rogoff, 1998).

The Development of Children's Drawing Abilities

"Very pretty! What is it?" asks Jessica as she examines the marked-up page. "A flower," answers 3-year-old Noah. "It's a beautiful flower," Jessica responds as she tries to see a flower in the messy scribbles on the page. Most parents and teachers are familiar with this scenario. What is it that children draw, and does it really have meaning? How does it change over time?

Young children's skills in drawing and writing illustrate the interaction of cognitive and motor domains of development. Drawing reflects fine motor control, planning skills, spatial understanding, and the recognition that pictures can symbolize objects, people, and events (Yamagata, 2007). Young children's drawing skills progress through a predictable sequence alongside cognitive, motor, and brain maturation (Kellogg, 1970). Drawing begins as scribbles during the second year of life (Dunst & Gorman, 2009; Toomela, 2003). At first, the physical gestures children use *are* the content, not the drawing itself. For example, an 18-month-old bounced a crayon around the page, making dots, to indicate that a rabbit jumps (Winner, 1986). One- and 2-year-olds engage in random scribbling, taking great pleasure in moving the crayon over paper and becoming interested in the paper only when they notice that their movements result in drawings. The scribbles of 2-year-olds begin to become patterns, such as vertical and zigzag lines (Dunst & Gorman, 2009). If asked to draw a human figure, 2- to 3-year-olds usually draw a tadpole-like figure with a circle for the head with eyes and sometimes a smiley mouth and then a line or two beneath to represent the rest of the body (see Figure 7.5). Tadpole-like forms are characteristic of young children's art in all cultures (Cox, 1993).

By age 3, children's scribbles become more controlled and begin to become pictures, representational forms. Often this happens by accident in that they begin drawing, notice that the shape is recognizable, and label it (Winner, 1986). Three- and 4-year-olds manipulate materials more purposefully and engage in controlled scribbling. Most 3-year-olds can draw circles, squares, rectangles, triangles, crosses, and Xs, and they begin to combine shapes into more complex designs. Some 3-year-olds create drawings that are recognizable enough for others to identify what their picture represents. Other young children begin to understand the representational function of drawings after adults show them how pictures can be used to stand for people, objects, and places (Callaghan, 1999). Even when drawings appear to be nothing more than scribbles, young children often label them as representing a particular object and remember the label. In one study, children were asked to draw a balloon and a lollipop. The drawings looked the same to adults, but the children were adamant about which was which (Bloom, 2000),

FIGURE 7.5: A Typical Two- to Three-Year-Old's Drawing of a Person

John Scofield/natgeo/Getty

suggesting that it is important to ask a child what his or her drawing is rather than guess, because children's creations reflect their perspectives.

Between ages 4 and 5, children's drawings loosely begin to depict actual objects, demonstrating the convergence of fine motor skills and the cognitive development of representational ability. By age 4, children's drawings of people consist of simple figures, mostly heads with legs and arms, and a circle is often used to represent a stomach (Cox, 1997). As cognitive and fine motor skills improve, children create more sophisticated drawings of the human form in which the head and body are differentiated. Five-year-olds include a torso, and after 5, arms and hands are included (Cox, 1997). However, even older preschoolers' drawings contain perceptual distortions. During middle childhood, the use of depth improves, and children's drawings become more perceptually realistic (Cox & Littlejohn, 1995).

The ability to copy a design and write letters predicts cognitive and academic achievement at kindergarten entry and in second grade (Cameron et al., 2012; Dinehart & Manfra, 2013).

What Do You Think?

Suppose a friend has accepted a job working with preschool-age children. What advice do you give for those times when a child asks for feedback on an unintelligible drawing?

For example, when an adult reads a picture book or storybook to a child, he or she will tend to point to items, label, and describe characters' emotional states; explain; ask questions; listen; and respond sensitively to the child helping the child understand material that they cannot on their own (Adrián, Clemente, & Villanueva, 2007; Danis, Bernard, & Leproux, 2000; Silva, Strasser, & Cain, 2014). Effective teachers take advantage of this pattern of learning by assigning children tasks that they can accomplish with some assistance, providing just enough help so that students learn to complete the tasks independently, and providing learning environments that stimulate children

Brand X/Stockbyte/Thinkstock

This mother is providing a scaffold to help her daughter learn how to complete a puzzle. Effective scaffolding occurs within the zone of proximal development, the gap between what the child can do on her own and what she can accomplish with a little bit of help.

to complete more challenging tasks on their own (Wass & Golding, 2014).

The quality of scaffolding influences children's development. In one study of preschool teachers and children, the degree to which the adult matched the child's needs for help in playing predicted more autonomous play on the part of children over a six-month period (Trawick-Smith & Dziurgot, 2011). Adults act intentionally to encourage and support children's initiative (Zuckerman, 2007). Mothers vary their scaffolding behaviors in response to children; for example, they use different behaviors depending on the child's attention skills, using more verbal engagement, strategic questions, verbal hints, and verbal prompts when children show poor attention-regulating skills (Robinson, Burns, & Davis, 2009). Adults learn as they participate in the child's zone of proximal development, and they modify their behaviors (Ferholt & Lecusay, 2010). In addition, the timing of maternal utterances helps children attend and switch tasks appropriately (Bibok, Carpendale, & Müller, 2009). Moreover, maternal reading, scaffolding, and verbal guidance is associated with 2- to 4-year-olds' capacities for cognitive control and planning (Bibok et al., 2009; Hughes & Ensor, 2009; Moriguchi, 2014).

The contextual nature of learning is illustrated by a study of two generations of Zinacantec Maya children: one generation studied in 1969 and 1970 and a second generation in 1991 and 1993 (Greenfield, Maynard, & Childs, 2003). In the intervening two decades, the community, located in Chiapas, Mexico, was involved in a transition from an economy based primarily on subsistence and agriculture to an economy based primarily on money and commerce. Researchers examined the number and quality of weaving apprenticeships as well as visual representation ability and concluded that the processes of learning and cognition changed over this period. Over time, there was a greater emphasis on independent cultural learning, abstract thinking, and creativity as well as a movement away from scaffolding, simple representation of tasks, and imitating

strategies (Greenfield et al., 2003). Changes in cultural apprenticeships were associated with shifts in the process of child cognition. The contexts in which we are embedded are always changing and evolving, as are our ways of thinking.

INFORMATION PROCESSING PERSPECTIVE

From an information processing perspective, cognitive development entails developing mental strategies to guide one's thinking and use one's cognitive resources more effectively. In early childhood, children become more efficient at attending, encoding and retrieving memories, and problem solving (see Table 7.3).

Attention

The ability to sustain one's attention improves in early childhood through the preschool years. Young children become better at planning, considering the steps needed to complete a particular act, and focusing their attention (Rueda, 2013). Preschoolers can create and abide by a plan to complete tasks that are familiar and not too complex, such as systematically searching for a lost object in a yard (Wellman, Somerville, & Haake, 1979). But they have difficulty with more complex tasks. Preschoolers do not search thoroughly when asked to compare detailed pictures and explain what's missing from one. Young children have difficulty deciding where to begin and how to proceed to complete a task in an orderly way. When they plan, young children often skip important steps (Friedman & Scholnick, 1987; Ruff & Rothbart, 1996). Preschoolers have trouble switching their attention among stimuli (Hanania & Smith, 2010). For example, young children who sort cards according to one dimension such as color may later be unable to successfully switch to a different sorting criteria (Honomichl & Zhe, 2011).

Memory

Unlike infants, young children have language skills and abilities to follow directions, which make it easier to study their memory skills. Researchers can differentiate two types of memories for experiences: **episodic memory** and **autobiographical memory**.

Episodic memory. Episodic memory refers to memory for events and information acquired during those events (Roediger & Marsh, 2003; Tulving, 2002). For example, a researcher might study episodic memory by asking a child, "Where did you go on vacation?" or "Remember the pictures I showed you yesterday?" Most laboratory studies of memory examine episodic memory, such as memory for specific information and for **scripts**.

Memory for information. Shana turns over one card and exclaims, "I've seen this one before. I know where it is!" before selecting its duplicate by turning over a second card

CHAPTER 7 || Physical and Cognitive Development in Early Childhood **179**

TABLE 7.3 Development of Information Processing Skills During Early Childhood

SKILL	DESCRIPTION
Attention	Young children are better able to focus and sustain their attention to complete tasks but have difficulty with complex tasks that require them to switch their attention among stimuli.
Memory	Young children's limited capacity to store and manipulate information in working memory influences their performance on memory and problem-solving tasks. Young children show advances in recognition memory and the ability to use scripts but recall memory lags behind because they are not able to effectively use memory strategies. They often can be taught memory strategies but do not spontaneously apply them in new situations. Episodic memory emerges in early childhood, but the extent and quality of memories increase with age.
Theory of mind	Theory of mind refers to children's awareness of their own and other people's mental processes. When researchers use vocabulary that children are familiar with, observe them in everyday activities, and use concrete examples and simple problems such as those involving belief and surprise, it is clear that young children's understanding of the mind grows and changes between the ages of 2 and 5.
Metacognition	In early childhood theory of mind, an awareness of one's own and others' minds, emerges. Young children demonstrate a growing ability for metacognition, understanding the mind. However, young children's abilities are limited and they tend to fail false belief and appearance–reality tasks, suggesting that their abilities to understand the mind and predict what other people are thinking are limited.

from an array of cards. Shana recognizes a card that she has seen before and recalls its location. Children's memory for specific information, such as the location of items, lists of words or numbers, and directions, can be studied using tasks that examine **recognition memory** and **recall memory**. Recognition memory, the ability to recognize a stimulus one has encountered before, is nearly perfect in 4- and 5-year-old children. Recall memory, the ability to generate a memory of a stimulus encountered before without seeing it again, is much poorer in young children (Myers & Perlmutter, 2014). Two-year-olds can recall one or two items whereas 4-year-olds can recall three or four items (Perlmutter, 1984).

Why do young children perform so poorly in recall tasks? Young children are not very effective at using **memory strategies**, cognitive activities that make us more likely to remember. For example, one memory strategy, *chunking*, entails grouping similar items so that they can be recalled together. Preschool children begin to use this memory strategy. When a researcher places either a piece of candy or a wooden peg in each of 12 containers and hands them to young children, asking them to remember where the candy was hidden, by age 4 the children will correctly categorize the containers, placing those that contain candy in one place and those that hold the peg in another, and will demonstrate nearly perfect recall (DeLoache & Todd, 1988).

However, when preschoolers are asked to recall items, they often do not use memory strategies. Even when they are taught to use strategies, they do not apply them in new situations (Gathercole, Adams, & Hitch, 1994; Miller & Seier, 1994). It appears that using strategies is challenging for young children because of their limited working memories. They cannot retain the material to be learned, the strategy, and apply the strategy at the same time. New information a child encounters competes with the information he or she is attempting to recall. Unlike older children and adults, preschoolers are often are unable to inhibit the new information to successfully recall older information (Aslan & Bäuml, 2010). Children do not start to apply strategies consistently and effectively until middle childhood (Kron-Sperl, Schneider, & Hasselhorn, 2008). As with other aspects of development, strategy use and memory interacts with other domains of development. For example, one study of children ages 5 to 8 found that language proficiency predicted rehearsal strategy use (Bebko, McMorris, & Metcalfe, 2014). Memory is also influenced by familiar experiences.

Memory for scripts. Young children remember familiar, repeated everyday experiences, like the process of eating dinner, taking a bath, or going to nursery school or preschool, as scripts, or descriptions, of what occurs in a particular situation. When young children begin to use scripts, they remember only the main details. A 3-year-old might describe a trip to a restaurant as follows: "You go in, eat, then pay." These early scripts include only a few acts but usually are recalled in the correct order (Bauer, 1996). As children grow older and gain cognitive competence, scripts become more elaborate. Consider a 5-year-old child's explanation of a trip to a restaurant: "You go in, you can sit at a booth or a table, then you tell the waitress what you want, you eat, if you want dessert, you can have some, then you go pay, and go home" (Hudson, Fivush, & Kuebli, 1992). Scripts help children understand repeated events, serve as an organization tool, and help children predict what to expect in the future. However, scripts may inhibit memory for new details. For example, in one laboratory study, children were presented with a script of the same series of events repeated in order multiple times as well as a single alternative event. Preschoolers were less likely than older children to spontaneously recall and provide a detailed account of the event (Brubacher, Glisic, Roberts, & Powell, 2011).

Autobiographical memory. Autobiographical memory refers to memory of personally meaningful events that took place at a specific time and place in one's past (Nelson & Fivush, 2004). Most people have no memories prior to age 3, a phenomenon known as **infantile amnesia** (Howe & Courage, 1993). Yet, as discussed in Chapter 5, infants demonstrate recall. Why, then, do we not retain memories from infancy? Just as language development yields new, more complicated ways of thinking and communicating, it also helps us learn how to use our memory (Fivush & Nelson, 2004). Autobiographical memory is thought to serve a social function. Children learn to remember through interactions with adults, and they construct autobiographical memories to share with others (Nelson & Fivush, 2004).

Leondra demonstrates a script as she explains the process of going to a restaurant and ordering from a menu.

Autobiographical memory develops steadily from 3 to 6 years of age, through adolescence, and is accompanied by increases in the length, richness and complexity of recall memory (Fivush, 2011; Pipe, Lamb, Orbach, & Esplin, 2004). Young children report fewer memories for specific events than do older children and adults (Baker-Ward, Gordon, Ornstein, Larus, & Clubb, 1993). But by age 3, they are able to retrieve and report specific memories, especially those that have personal significance, are repeated, or are highly stressful (Fivush, 1993; Nuttall, 2014). For example, in one study, children who were at least 26 months of age at the time of an accidental injury and visit to the emergency room accurately recalled the details of these experiences even after a two-year delay (Goodman, Rudy, Bottoms, & Aman, 1990). Eight-year-old children have been found to accurately remember events that occurred when they were as young as 3.5 years of age (Goodman & Aman, 1990).

Young children recall more details about events that are unique or new, such as a trip to the circus, which 3-year-old children will recall for a year or longer (Fivush, Hudson, & Nelson, 1983). Frequent events tend to blur together, and young children tend to not recall them well unless they recur several times. Young children are better at remembering things they did than things they simply watched. For example, one study examined 5-year-old children's recall of an event they either observed, were told about, or experienced. A few days later, the children were more likely to recall details in a more accurate and organized way, requiring fewer prompts, when they had experienced the event (Murachver, Pipe, Gordon, Owens, & Fivush, 1996).

The way adults talk with the child about a shared experience can influence how well the child will remember it (Haden & Fivush, 1996; Reese & Fivush, 1993). Parents with an elaborative conversational style discuss new aspects of an experience, provide more information to guide a child through a mutually rewarding conversation, and affirm the child's responses. Three-year-olds of parents who use an elaborative style engage in longer conversations about events, remember more details, and tend to remember the events better at ages 5 and 6 (Boland, Haden, & Ornstein, 2003; Fivush, 2011; Lange & Canoll, 2003; Reese, Haden, & Fivush, 1993).

Memory improves steadily between ages 4 and 10 with accelerated rates between 5 and 7 (Myers & Perlmutter, 2014; Riggins, 2014). Young children lack knowledge about how to conduct memory searches, determine what is important to recall, and structure narrative accounts of events (Leichtman & Ceci, 1995). They tend to forget information more quickly than older children, rely more on verbatim memory, and confuse different sources of event information (Ackil & Zaragoza, 1995; Levine, Stein, & Liwag, 1999; Warren & Lane, 1995). Between ages 5 and 7, children get better at linking memory and source and contextual details (Riggins, 2014). Older children can conduct internal memory searches, easily recreate images in their heads, think of information similar to the to-be-remembered event, and organize and present the recalled information in a systematic manner (Ceci, Huffman, Smith, & Loftus, 1994). In the early school years, children become more capable of providing detailed and spontaneous memory descriptions; their use of mnemonic strategies increases and they become aware of the needs of listeners.

Young children can have largely accurate memories, but they can also tell tall tales, make errors, and succumb to misleading questions. Children's ability to remember events can be influenced by information and experiences that may interfere with their memories. These can include conversations with parents and adults, exposure to media, and sometimes intentional suggestions directed at changing the child's view of what transpired. Children's vulnerability to suggestion is discussed in Applying Developmental Science (p. 192).

Children's Suggestibility

The accuracy of children's memory, especially their vulnerability to suggestion, is an important topic because children as young as 3 years of age have been called upon to relate their memories of events that they have experienced or witnessed, including abuse, maltreatment, and domestic violence (Flavell, Friedrich, & Hoyt, 1970; Kail & Park, 1992; Nelson, 1993). How suggestible are young children? Can we trust their memories?

Research suggests that repeated questioning may increase suggestibility in children (La Rooy, Lamb, & Pipe, 2011). For example, in one study preschoolers were questioned every week about events that had either happened or not happen to them; by the 11th week, nearly two thirds of the children falsely reported having experienced an event (Ceci et al., 1994). Preschool-aged children may be more vulnerable to suggestion about many topics, including those containing sexual themes, than either school-aged children or adults (Gordon, Baker-Ward, & Ornstein, 2001; Principe, Ornstein, Baker-Ward, & Gordon, 2000; Rocha, 2013). When children were asked if they could remember several events, including a fictitious instance of getting their finger caught in a mousetrap, almost none of them initially recalled these events; however, after repeated suggestive questioning, more than half of 3- and 4-year-olds and two fifths of 5- and 6-year-olds recalled these events that never happened—often vividly (Poole & White, 1991, 1993).

Young children's natural trust in others may enhance their suggestibility (Jaswal, 2010). In one study, 3-year-old children who received misleading verbal and visual information from an experimenter about a sticker's location continued to search in the wrong, suggested, location despite no success (Jaswal, 2010). In another study, 3- to 5-year-old children watched as an adult hid a toy in one location, then told the children that the toy was in a different location. When retrieving the toy, 4- and 5-year-olds relied on what they had seen and disregarded the adult's false statements, but the 3-year-olds deferred to what the adult had said, despite what they had directly observed (Ma & Ganea, 2010).

In some cases, children can resist suggestion. For example, in one study 4- and 7-year-old children either played games (e.g., dressing up in costumes, playing tickle, being photographed) with an adult confederate or merely watched the games (Ceci & Bruck, 1998). Eleven days later, each child was interviewed by an adult who included misleading questions that were often followed up with suggestions relevant to child abuse. Even the 4-year-old children resisted the false suggestions about child abuse.

Children are more vulnerable than adults, but adults are not entirely resistant to suggestion. Adults who are exposed to information that is misleading or inconsistent with their experiences are more likely to perform poorly during memory interviews—and repeated questioning has similar effects (Ceci & Friedman, 2000; Fivush, 1993; Wysman, Scoboria, Gawrylowicz, & Memon, 2014).

What Do You Think?

1. In your view, under what conditions do you think children's statements are most likely to be true?

2. Suppose you need to question a child about an event. How would you maximize your likelihood of the child's giving you an accurate account of what occurred?

THEORY OF MIND AND METACOGNITION

Theory of mind refers to children's awareness of their own and other people's mental processes. This awareness of the mind can be considered under the broader concept of **metacognition**—knowledge of how the mind works and the ability to control the mind (Lockl & Schneider, 2007). Let's explore these concepts.

Theory of Mind

Piaget (1929) was the first to probe children's understanding of the mind by asking questions like, "What are dreams? Where do they come from?" He concluded that until about 6 years of age, children do not understand the distinctions among dreams, fantasy, thoughts, and reality. However, other theorists suggest that children's developing language skills may not permit them to fully demonstrate their awareness of mental activity.

When researchers use vocabulary that children are familiar with, observe them in everyday activities, and use concrete examples and simple problems such as those involving belief and surprise, it is clear that young children's understanding of the mind grows and changes between the ages of 2 and 5 (Bower, 1993; Flavell, Green, & Flavell, 1995; Schneider, Schumann-Hengsteler, & Sodian, 2005). For example, 3-year-old children understand the difference between thinking about a cookie and having a cookie. They know that having a cookie means that one can touch, eat, or share it, while thinking about a cookie does not permit such activities (Astington, 1993). Young children also understand that a child who wants a cookie will be happy upon receiving one and sad upon not (Flavell et al., 1995; Moses, Coon, & Wusinich, 2000; Wellman, Phillips, & Rodriguez, 2000) and that a child who believes he is having hot oatmeal for breakfast will be surprised upon receiving cold spaghetti (Wellman & Banerjee, 1991). Theory of mind is commonly assessed by examining children's abilities to understand that people can hold different beliefs about an object or event.

False belief. Three-year-old children tend to perform poorly on *false belief tasks*—tasks that require them to understand that someone does not share their knowledge. For example, children who are presented with a familiar Band-Aid box that contains pencils rather than Band-Aids will show surprise but tend to believe that other children will share their knowledge and expect the Band-Aid box to hold pencils (Flavell, 1993; Flavell et al., 1995; Jenkins & Astington, 1996). In addition, the children will believe that they knew all along that the Band-Aid box contained pencils (Birch, 2005). They confuse their present knowledge with the memories for prior knowledge and have difficulty remembering ever having believed something that contradicts their current view (Bernstein, Atance, Meltzoff, & Loftus, 2007; Mitchell & Kikuno, 2000).

Three-year-old children show a pattern of false belief errors that are robust across procedures and cultures (Wellman, Cross, & Watson, 2001; Wellman & Liu, 2004). However, some researchers find that young children are much more competent than they appear because research with infants has suggested that an understanding of false belief may be evident by 15 months of age (Buttelmann, Over, Carpenter, & Tomasello, 2014; Onishi & Baillargeon, 2005). Similar to arguments regarding object permanence in infancy and egocentrism in early childhood, it may be that the task of understanding the action and communicating that understanding are overwhelming (Helming, Strickland, & Jacob, 2014). Critics counter that false belief findings with infants reflect perceptual preferences and not theory of mind (Heyes, 2014). Instead, the research to date suggests that theory of mind as evidenced by false belief tasks does not emerge until about 3 years of age. Developmental studies reveal a reliable transition in children's ability to reason about beliefs between 3 and 4 years of age (Apperly, Samson, & Humphreys, 2009). By age 3, children can understand that two people can believe different things (Rakoczy, Warneken, & Tomasello, 2007). Four-year-old children understand that people who are presented with different versions of the same event develop different beliefs (Eisbach, 2004; Pillow & Henrichon, 1996). By age 4 or 5, children become aware that they and other people can hold false beliefs (Moses et al., 2000)—representations of reality that are incorrect.

Advanced cognition is needed for children to learn abstract concepts such as belief (Carlson, Moses, & Claxton, 2004; Moses, Carlson, & Sabbagh, 2005). Performance on false belief tasks is associated with measures of executive function—that is, the set of cognitive abilities, such as attention, memory, and inhibitory control, that permit higher cognitive functions such as planning, decision-making, and goal setting (Hughes & Ensor, 2007; Perner, Lang, & Kloo, 2002; Sabbagh, Xu, Carlson, Moses, & Lee, 2006). One longitudinal study following children from ages 2 to 4 found that advances in executive functioning facilitated children's performance on theory of mind tasks (Hughes & Ensor, 2007). Reasoning about false beliefs poses heavy demands on executive functioning, requiring the capacity in working memory or other aspects of executive functioning to construct and retain complex mental representations (Apperly et al., 2009).

Children's performance on false belief tasks is closely related with language development (Bernard & Deleau, 2007; Milligan, Astington, & Dack, 2007). Everyday conversations aid children in developing a theory of mind because everyday conversations tend to center around and provide examples of mental states and their relation with behavior (Ruffman, Slade, & Crowe, 2002). When parents and other adults speak with children about mental states and emotions, connect them to behaviors and experiences, and discuss causes and consequences, children develop a more sophisticated understanding of other people's perspectives (Pavarini, Hollanda Souza, & Hawk, 2012). By interacting with others, children learn how to exchange, adjust, and even revise their beliefs about a given issue (Bernard & Deleau, 2007). The process of interacting with others helps children learn how to perspective take, become capable of taking into account other people's points of view as well as their own on a given issue at the same time (Hughes & Leekam, 2004). In one longitudinal study of French children, conversational perspective taking ability at 3.5 years of age predicted false belief scores one year later (Bernard & Deleau, 2007).

Interactions with parents offer particularly rich opportunities for children to practice perspective taking (Hughes & Leekam, 2004). Parents may encourage children to talk about mental states, such as desires, emotions, cognitions, and subjective evaluations; these early experiences facilitate children's theory of mind over the preschool years (Lu, Su, & Wang, 2008; Slaughter, Peterson, & Mackintosh, 2007; Symons, 2004). In addition, siblings provide young children with opportunities for social interaction, pretend play, and practice with deception; young children with siblings perform better on false belief tests than do those without (Jenkins & Astington, 1996; McAlister & Peterson, 2007, 2013; Perner, 2000; Ruffman, Perner, & Parkin, 1999). Success in false belief attribution tasks is most frequent in the case of children who are the most active in shared pretend play (Schwebel, Rosen, & Singer, 1999).

Context and false beliefs. The contexts in which children are embedded contribute to their developing understanding of the mind. Children in many countries, including Canada, India, Peru, Samoa, Thailand, Norway, and China, show similarity in the onset and development of theory of mind between the ages of 3 and 5 (Callaghan et al., 2005; Melinder, Endestad, & Magnussen, 2006; Wellman, Fang, & Peterson, 2011). For example, findings regarding the relation of executive functioning to performance on false belief tasks apply equally to preschoolers in the United States and in China (Sabbagh et al., 2006). Children reared in some contexts, however, show a very different pattern in understanding theory of mind (Lillard, 1998; Vinden, 1996). A study of 8-year-old children from Peru used a culturally appropriate version of the Band-Aid box task in which a sugar bowl contained tiny potatoes (Vinden, 1996). At first, the children believed the bowl contained sugar. After learning that it contained potatoes, they answered typical false belief questions incorrectly believing that others would respond that the bowl contained potatoes. Even at age 8, the children responded incorrectly, unable to explain why others might initially believe that the bowl contained sugar and be surprised to learn otherwise. One explanation is that the children in this study were raised in an isolated farming village where farmers worked from dawn to dusk and there was no reason nor time for deception (Vinden, 1996). The Peruvian children's culture did not include ideas such as false belief, as their day-to-day world was concerned more with tangible activities and things rather than considerations of people's thoughts.

Cross-cultural studies have suggested, however, that compared with European American parents, Chinese parents refer less frequently to mental states when conversing with their children about the past (Lu et al., 2008; Wang, 2001; Wang & Fivush, 2005), yet Chinese children perform just as well as their Euro-American peers on false belief tasks (Liu, Wellman, Tardif, & Sabbagh, 2008; Sabbagh et al., 2006). Whereas research with Western children has shown that mental state talk facilitates the development of theory of mind (Liu et al., 2008; Ruffman, Slade, & Crowe, 2002; Symons, Fossum, & Collins, 2006), a longitudinal study of Chinese children ages 3 to 4 found that theory of mind performance was facilitated not by mental state talk but, instead, by talking about others. In the Chinese context, where parents rarely discuss mental states with their children but often talk about information concerning other people (Wang, 2001, 2004; Wang & Fivush, 2005), children are exposed to little mental state talk and instead, they may develop theory of mind through talking about others—increases in other-references facilitated the children's success in passing the false belief tasks (Lu et al., 2008).

Children's interactions with people in their immediate contexts can also influence the development of theory of mind. Children can be trained in perspective taking. For example, when children are presented with a series of objects that look like a certain thing but are actually something else (candle and apple) and are shown the appearance and real states of the objects, along with explanation, 3-year-olds showed improvements on false belief tasks (Lohmann & Tomasello, 2003). Discussion emphasizing the existence of a variety of possible perspectives in relation to an object can improve performance in false belief tasks—dialogue can facilitate the development of theory of mind (Bernard & Deleau, 2007). Other studies have engaged North American and European children in discussion about the thoughts, beliefs, and desires of characters in stories, especially stories in which characters play tricks to surprise or deceive one another; children who receive the training improved their performance in subsequent false belief tasks (Guajardo & Watson, 2002; Liu et al., 2008; Milligan et al., 2007; Slaughter & Gopnik, 1996). Similarly, conversation about deceptive objects (e.g., a pen that looked like a flower) also improves performance on false belief tasks (Lohmann & Tomasello, 2003).

Metacognition

Between the ages of 2 and 5, children's understanding of the mind grows. They become aware that thinking takes place inside the mind. Between 3 and 5, children come to understand that they can know something that others do not, that their thoughts cannot be observed, and that there are individual differences in mental states (Flavell, Flavell, & Green, 1983; Pillow, 2008). Young children understand that someone can think of one thing while doing something else, that a person whose eyes and ears are covered can think, and that thinking is different from talking, touching, and knowing (Flavell et al., 1995). However, young children's understanding of the mind is not complete. Three- and four-year-old children do not understand that we think even when we are inactive. They look for visible indicators of thinking and assume their absence indicates the absence of thought. It is not until middle childhood that children understand that the mind is always active (Flavell et al., 1983, 1995; Flavell, 1999). Likewise, preschoolers tend to think of the mind as simply a container for items, but older children tend to see the mind as an active constructor of knowledge that receives, processes, and transforms information (Chandler & Carpendale, 1998; Flavell, 1999).

Young children show limited knowledge of memory functions. Four-year-olds recognize that increasing the number of items on a list makes recall more difficult and that longer retention intervals increase the likelihood of forgetting (Lyon & Flavell, 1993; Pillow, 2008; Wellman, 1977). But they know little about the effectiveness of deliberate memory strategies. For example, when 4-year-old children compare the effectiveness of strategies for free recall, they judged looking at the items to be recalled as more effective than naming, rehearsing, or categorizing them (Justice, 1986). Children in kindergarten showed no preference among the four strategies, but second-grade children judged rehearsal and categorization as more effective than naming or looking. However, one recent study suggests that preschoolers' poor memory performance may result less from metacognitive deficits and instead from over-optimism (Lipowski, Merriman, & Dunlosky, 2013). As we will discuss in Chapter 8, young children have a strong sense of self-confidence and tend to believe that they will be successful in all endeavors. This overconfidence may overshadow their understanding of how their minds work, leading to biased estimates of their abilities (Lipowski et al., 2013). The cognitive advances that take place during early childhood are summarized in Table 7.4.

Thinking in Context 7.3

1. In what ways might brain development account for cognitive changes that we see in early childhood such as increases in information processing capacity and changes in reasoning?

2. How are cultural and contextual factors, such as neighborhood, socioeconomic status, ethnicity and family, reflected in brain development? Cognitive development?

3. Discuss strengths and weaknesses of Piaget's cognitive developmental, Vygotsky's sociocultural, and information processing theory. How well does each account for cultural and contextual factors?

TABLE 7.4 Cognitive Advances of Early Childhood

ADVANCEMENT	DESCRIPTION
Increased use of mental representation	Uses symbols, language, categorization, and pretend play
Understanding of the nature of objects and everyday experience	Understands that magic cannot alter the nature of everyday experiences Distinguishes animate from inanimate objects Understands that superficial changes do not alter the nature of objects (e.g., number)
Perspective-taking	Takes the perspective of others
Theory of mind	Is aware of own and other's mental processes.
Increases in information processing abilities	Increases in attention on simple tasks Increases in memory, especially episodic and scripts

YOUNG CHILDREN'S LANGUAGE DEVELOPMENT

Language acquisition proceeds very rapidly in early childhood. As they enter childhood, young children use telegraphic speech. They slowly learn to use multiple elements of speech, such as plurals, adjectives, and the past tense. Toward the end of early childhood, children show much more complex vocabulary and grammar. Language development is the foundation for emergent literacy, the capacity to learn to read.

VOCABULARY

At 2 years of age, the average child knows about 500 words. Vocabulary acquisition occurs quickly. The average 3-year-old child has a vocabulary of 900 to 1,000 words. By 6 years of age, most children use about 2,600 words and can understand more than 20,000 (Owens, 2001). How is language learned so quickly? As we have discussed in Chapter 5, children use a strategy called fast mapping, which permits them to learn the meaning of a new word after hearing it once or twice. It is a contextually based understanding of a word. Generally, children fast map words for objects more easily than words for actions. However, children under 3 have been shown to fast map new verbs and apply them to other situations in which the same action occurs (Gershkoff-Stowe & Hahn, 2007; Golinkoff, Jacquet, Hirsh-Pasek, & Nandakumar, 1996). Children get better at using fast mapping with age (Brady & Goodman, 2014).

In order to fast map a word, the child must hear it. Young children can learn words simply by overhearing them

in conversation or by watching videos (O'Doherty et al., 2011). Preschoolers can learn words from watching videos with both human and robot speakers, but they learn more quickly in response to human speakers (Moriguchi, Kanda, Ishiguro, Shimada, & Itakura, 2011). Parents who wish to foster language development should have frequent conversations with their children in which they use a wide vocabulary (Hoff, Naigles,& Nigales, 2002) as well as read to children because exposure to words through storybook reading leads to increases in vocabulary (Leung, 2008). For example, one study examined the effects of adult–child interaction on 3-year-olds' vocabulary acquisition during storybook reading (Walsh & Blewitt, 2006). All children were read three storybooks repeatedly over four reading sessions. Children who were asked questions about the reading and were encouraged to talk about it showed a greater vocabulary and more novel word knowledge after the fourth session than did children who were not engaged in discussion.

Another strategy that children use to increase their vocabulary is logical extension. When learning a word, children extend it to other objects in the same category. For example, when learning that a dog with spots is called a Dalmatian, a child may refer to a Dalmatian bunny (a white bunny with black spots) or a Dalmatian horse. Children make their words their own and apply them to all the situations they want to talk about (Behrend, Scofield, & Kleinknecht, 2001). At about age 3, children demonstrate the mutual exclusivity assumption in learning new words. They tend to assume that new words are labels for unfamiliar objects (Littschwager & Markman, 1994; Markman, 1987, 1990). In one study, young children were shown one familiar object and one unfamiliar object. They were told, "Show me the X" where X is a nonsense syllable. The children reached for the unfamiliar object (Markman & Wachtel, 1988). Similarly, young children use the mutual exclusivity assumption to learn the names of parts of objects, such as the brim of a hat, cab of a truck, or bird's beak (Hansen & Markman, 2009).

By 5 years of age, many children can quickly understand and apply most words that they hear. If the word is used in context or explained with examples, most 5-year-olds can learn it. Preschoolers learn words by making inferences given the context—and inferential learning is associated with better retention than learning by direct instruction (Zosh, Brinster, & Halberda, 2013). Certain classes of words are challenging for young children. For example, words that express comparisons are relative in nature; tall and short, or high and low, are used in comparing one object to another—the context defines their meaning. Young children have difficulty understanding that to call an object tall, it is in relation to another object that is short. Children may erroneously adopt the height of tall to refer to all tall things and therefore miss the relative nature of the term (Ryalls, 2000). Children also have difficulty with words that express place and time, such as *here*, *there*, *now*, *yesterday*, and *tomorrow*. Despite these errors, young children make great advances in vocabulary, learning thousands of words each year. Interestingly, bilingual children use these same strategies

Language skills open the door to new opportunities, such as reading, which in turn is associated with advances in cognitive and language development.

Brian Summers/Newscom

in learning words (Van Horn & Kan, 2015). They also show similar rates of word learning for words learned in their first and second languages (Kan & Kohnert, 2008, 2011). Learning a second language is discussed in Chapter 9.

EARLY GRAMMAR

Young children quickly learn to combine words into sentences in increasingly sophisticated ways (Owens, 2001). Three-year-old children tend to use plurals, possessives, and past tense. They also tend to understand the use of *I, you,* and *we.* Similar to telegraphic speech, their sentences are short, leaving out words like *a* and *the.* However, their speech is more sophisticated than telegraphic speech because some pronouns, adjectives, and prepositions are included. Four- and 5-year-olds use four- to five-word sentences and can express declarative, interrogative, or imperative sentences. Context influences the acquisition of grammar. Four-year-old children will use more complex sentences with multiple clauses, such as "I'm resting because I'm tired," if their parents use such sentences (Huttenlocher, Vasilyeva, Cymerman, & Levine, 2002). Parental conversations and support for language learning are associated with faster and more correct

language use (Barrett, 1999). Children often use run-on sentences, in which ideas and sentences are strung together.

"See? I *goed* on the slide!" called out Leona. **Overregularization** errors such as Leona's are very common in young children. They occur because young children are still learning exceptions to grammatical rules. Overregularization errors are grammatical mistakes that young children make because they are applying grammatical rules too stringently. They apply the rules of grammar even when they should not. For example, to create the plural, the rule is to add *s* to the word. However, there are many exceptions to this rule. Overregularization is expressed when children refer to *foots, gooses, tooths,* and *mouses.* Overregularization illustrates that the child understands and is applying the rules. It is a sign of grammatical sophistication. Despite all of the common errors young children make, one study of 3-year-olds showed that nearly three quarters of their utterances were grammatically correct. The most common error was in making tenses (such as *is/are, fall/felled;* Eisenberg, Guo, & Germezia, 2012). At the end of the preschool years, most children use main grammar rules appropriately and confidently (Tager-Flusberg, 2001).

PRIVATE SPEECH

As Leroy played alone in the corner of the living room, he pretended to drive his toy car up a mountain and explained, "It's a high mountain. Got to push it all the way up. Oh no! Out of gas. Now they will have to stay here." Young children like Leroy often talk aloud to themselves, with no apparent intent to communicate with others. This self-talk, called **private speech**, accounts for 20% to 50% of the utterances of children ages 4 to 10 (Berk, 1986). Piaget and Vygotsky offer different views on the significance of private speech for development.

According to Piaget, private speech is a result of cognitive development and indicative of cognitive immaturity. He posited that children's self-talk, which he called *egocentric speech,* was meaningless, not addressed to anyone, not modified so that a listener can understand it, and simply reflected the egocentrism of the preoperational stage. Research, however, suggests that while children's speech is sometimes egocentric, often it is not. Children can communicate meaningfully with gestures and speech from an early age. Two-year-old children can generate speech relevant to what someone else has said but have difficulty remaining on one conversational topic (Owens, 2001). By 3 years of age, most children pay attention to how their speech affects others. If they are not understood, they attempt to explain themselves more clearly. Four-year-old children, especially girls, will use simpler language when speaking to 2-year-old children, suggesting that they can take others' perspectives (Owens, 2001; Shatz & Gelman, 1973). By 5 years of age, about half of children can stick to a conversational topic for a dozen turns. Thus, research suggests that children's speech is less egocentric than Piaget posited.

Instead, it appears that private speech serves developmental functions. Private speech is thinking; it is personal speech that guides behavior and fosters new ideas (Vygotsky & Minick, 1987). It may be useful to think of private speech as a type of scaffold that the child provides for herself, by talking out loud (Mercer, 2008). Children explain events and activities, plan, and review their knowledge to themselves. Private speech is the child's thought and eventually becomes internalized as *inner speech*, or word-based internal thought, representing the child's transition to verbal reasoning.

Private speech plays a role in **self-regulation**, the ability to control one's impulses and appropriately direct behavior—it increases during the preschool years (Berk & Garvin, 1984). Children are more likely to use private speech during challenging tasks and problem solving, especially when they encounter obstacles or do not have adult supervision(Berk, 1992; Berk & Garvin, 1984; Winsler, Fernyhough, & Montero, 2009). Private speech is used by children to problem solve, plan strategies, and regulate themselves so that they can achieve goals. Children who use private speech during a challenging activity are more attentive and involved and show better performance than children who do not (Alarcón-Rubio, Sánchez-Medina, & Prieto-García, 2014; Behrend, Rosengren, & Perlmetter, 1989; Berk & Spuhl, 1995; Winsler, Diaz, & Montero, 1997). Preschoolers who are aware of their own private speech are more likely to use expressive language skills, use more private speech, and display an understanding of deception than those who are less aware of their use of private speech (Manfra & Winsler, 2006).

As children grow older, private speech is used more effectively to accomplish tasks and it declines, becoming a whisper and eventually an entirely internal dialogue not audible or visible to others (Duncan & Pratt, 1997; Patrick & Abravanel, 2000; Winsler, Carlton, & Barry, 2000). Private speech never completely disappears. It becomes internalized as inner speech, a silent internal dialogue that we use every day to regulate and organize our behavior (Berk, 1986; Fernyhough, 2008; Kohlberg, Yaeger, & Hjertholm, 1968).

However, there is some evidence that private speech may not be as private as suggested. That is, private speech often occurs in the presence of others. When children ages 2.5 to 5 completed a challenging task either in the presence of an experimenter who sat a few feet behind the child, not interacting, or alone, the children engaged in more private speech in the presence of a listener (McGonigle-Chalmers, Slater, & Smith, 2014). This suggests that private speech may have social value and may not simply be a tool for self-regulation.

Research suggests that the pattern of change in private speech is more complicated than Vygotsky indicated. Preschool girls tend to use more mature forms of private speech than boys; the same is true of middle-income children as compared with low-income children (Berk, 1986). This pattern corresponds to the children's relative abilities in language use. Though Vygotsky considered the use of private speech a universal developmental milestone, research suggests that there are individual differences, with some children using private speech little or not at all (Berk, 1992). Talkative children use more private talk than do quiet children (McGonigle-Chalmers et al., 2014). Bright children tend to use private speech earlier, and children with learning disabilities tend to continue its use later in development (Berk, 1992). One of the educational implications of private speech is that parents and teachers must understand that talking to oneself or inaudible muttering is not misbehavior but, rather, a child's effort to complete a difficult task or regulate his or her behavior.

Thinking in Context 7.4

1. How might advances in language development influence other domains of development, such as social or cognitive development?

2. Why might some theorists point to maturation (nature, as opposed to nurture) as the main influence on language development? What do you think?

3. Given what we know about private speech, what advice do you give to parents and teachers?

MORAL DEVELOPMENT IN EARLY CHILDHOOD

Young children's cognitive capacities and skills in theory of mind influence moral reasoning, how they view and make judgments in their social world. Two-year-old children describe behaviors as good and bad. They also respond with distress when viewing or experiencing aggressive or potentially harmful actions (Kochanska, Casey, & Fukumoto, 1995). Young children's understanding of morality grows rapidly. By age 3, children can identify that a child who intentionally knocks another child off of a swing is worse than one who does so accidentally (Yuill & Perner, 1988). Four-year-old children can understand the difference between truth and lies (Bussey, 1992). By age 5, children are aware of many moral rules, such as those regarding lying and stealing. They also demonstrate conceptions of justice (e.g., "it's my turn," "hers is bigger," "it's not fair").

How does moral reasoning develop? There are many perspectives on moral development, as discussed in later chapters. Here we consider two classic views of moral development: social learning theory and cognitive-developmental theory. Both consider a young child's moral values and behavior as first externally influenced. Over time, moral values become internalized and moral behavior becomes guided by inner standards.

SOCIAL LEARNING THEORY

Social learning theory views moral behavior as being acquired through reinforcement and modeling, just like any other behavior (Bandura, 1977; Grusec, 1992). Bandura and McDonald (1963) demonstrated that the moral judgments of young children could be modified through a training procedure involving social reinforcement and modeling. Parents and others naturally dole out reinforcement and punishment that shapes the child's behavior. Modeling also plays a role in children's moral development. Adults and other children serve as models for the child, demonstrating appropriate (and sometimes not!) actions and verbalizations. When children observe a model touching a forbidden toy, they are more likely to touch the toy. Some research suggests that children who observe a model resisting temptation are less likely to do so themselves (Rosenkoetter, 1973). However, models are more effective at encouraging rather than inhibiting behavior that violates a rule or expectation. Children are more likely to follow a model's transgressions rather than appropriate behavior (Hoffman, 1970).

In order to learn by modeling, children must pay attention to the events that are modeled. Attention is influenced by many factors. Children are more likely to imitate behavior when the model is competent and powerful (Bandura, 1977). They are also more likely to imitate a model that is perceived as warm and responsive rather than cold and distant (Yarrow, Scott, & Waxler, 1973). Over the course of early childhood, children develop internalized standards of conduct based on reinforcements and punishments, and observing others and considering their explanations for behavior (Bandura, 1986; Mussen & Eisenberg-Berg, 1977). Those adopted standards are then used by children as guides for behavior. Children attempt to behave in ways that are consistent with their internalizations (Grusec & Goodnow, 1994). In this way, moral values and actions are learned and internalized, as are all behaviors. Children's behavior is shaped to conform with the rules of society.

COGNITIVE-DEVELOPMENTAL THEORY

The cognitive-developmental perspective views moral development through a cognitive lens and examines reasoning about moral issues: Is it ever right to steal even if it would help another person? Is lying ever acceptable? The resolution of moral dilemmas requires that the child consider the perspective, needs, and feelings of others—cognitive changes and related developments in perspective taking underlie moral development. Young children's reasoning about moral problems changes with development as they construct concepts about justice and fairness from their interactions in the world (Gibbs, 1991, 2003).

Piaget (1932) studied moral development by using the same methods that he used to study cognitive development: observation and the Piagetian clinical interview. He observed children playing marbles and asked them questions about the rules. What are the rules to the game? Where do the rules come from? Have they always been the same? Can they be changed? Preschool-aged children play with the marbles without attention or awareness of the rules. Their play is not

iStock/Signature

Piaget began studying morality by asking children about their understanding of the rules of marbles. Fewer children play marbles today. If you were to study children's understanding of rules today, what game would you choose?

guided by rules. They engage in solitary play for the sake of pleasure and may play with the marbles in random ways such as tossing them about without regard to the rules. By 6 years of age, children enter the first stage of Piaget's theory of morality, **morality of constraint**, in which children are aware of rules and see them as sacred and unalterable. Rules are created by adults, passed down to children, must be respected, and have always existed. Children believe that rules cannot be changed; people have always played marbles in the same way. Morality comes from outside in the sense that authority's rules are always right and their punishments are always justified. Moral behavior is behavior that is consistent with the rules that authority figures set.

Lawrence Kohlberg (1969, 1976) investigated moral development by posing hypothetical dilemmas about justice, fairness, and rights that place obedience to authority and law in conflict with helping someone. Responses to the dilemmas change with development; moral reasoning progresses through a universal order of stages representing qualitative changes in conceptions of justice. Young children who display cognitive reasoning at the preoperational stage are at the lowest level of Kohlberg's scheme: **preconventional** reasoning. Similar to Piaget, Kohlberg argued that young children's behavior is governed by self-interest, avoiding punishment and gaining rewards. Moral behavior is a response to external pressure. Young children have not internalized societal norms and their behavior is motivated by desires rather than internalized principles.

Similar to cognitive development, children are active in constructing their own moral understanding through social experiences with adults and peers (Smetana, 1995; Smetana & Braeges, 1990). This is true across cultures. Research with children from Guatemala, India, Turkey, China, and the United States suggests that children do not simply internalize what they see but instead transform and internalize the strategies used by adults by incorporating their own experience and knowledge as well as choosing when to use the strategy and what situations are appropriate (Rogoff, Mistry, Göncü, & Mosier, 1993; Wang, Bernas, & Eberhard, 2008).

As early as 3 years of age, children can differentiate between moral imperatives, which concern people's rights and welfare, and social conventions, or social customs (Smetana & Braeges, 1990). For example, they judge stealing an apple, a moral violation, more harshly than violating a social convention, such as eating with one's fingers (Nucci & Turiel, 1978; Smetana, 1995; Smetana & Braeges, 1990; Turiel, 1998). In one study, 3- and 4.5-year-old children viewed an interchange in which one puppet struggled to achieve a goal, was helped by a second puppet and violently hindered by a third puppet. When asked to distribute biscuits, the 4.5 year-olds but not 3-year-olds were more likely to give more biscuits to the helper than the hinderer puppet. Most explained the unequal distribution by referring to the helper's prosocial behavior or the hinderer's antisocial behavior (Kenward & Dahl, 2011). In addition to moral and conventional issues, between ages 3 and 5 children come to differentiate personal issues, matters of personal choice that do not violate rights, across home and school settings (Nucci, 1996; Nucci & Weber, 1995; Smetana, 1995; Weber, 1999; Yau & Smetana, 2003). Preschoolers believe that they have control over matters of personal choice, unlike moral issues whose violations are inherently wrong.

Cross-cultural research suggests that children in diverse cultures in Europe, Africa, Asia, Southeast Asia, and North and South America differentiate moral, social conventional, and personal issues (Killen, McGlothlin, & Lee-Kim, 2002; Nucci, 2001; Smetana, 1995; Turiel, 1998; Yau & Smetana, 2003). However, cultural differences in socialization contribute to children's conceptions. For example, a study of Chinese children ages 3 to 4 and 5 to 6 showed that, similar to Western samples, the children overwhelmingly considered personal issues as permissible and up to the child, rather than the adults. However, the Chinese children's justifications for moral transgressions focused overwhelmingly on the intrinsic consequences of the acts for others' welfare and fairness, as compared with the emphasis on avoiding punishment common in Western samples of preschoolers (Yau & Smetana, 2003). These differences are consistent with cultural preferences for collectivism and individualism.

Social experiences—disputes with siblings over toys, for example—help young children develop conceptions about justice and fairness (Killen & Nucci, 1995). Peers respond to moral offenses with emotion, empathy (i.e., sharing their own loss), or retaliation (Arsenio & Fleiss, 1996). In Western cultures, adults tend to emphasize the victim's rights and feelings and consequences for the individual. In contrast, Chinese children's behavior is seen as guided by their obligations to the family, and others (Chao, 1995; Yau & Smetana, 2003). One study of 4-year-old Chinese children and their mothers showed that mothers consistently drew children's attention to transgressions and emphasized the consequences for others. The children learned quickly and were able to spontaneously discuss their mothers' examples and strategies, and reenact them in their own interactions, and their explanations reflected their own understanding of rules and expectations in their own terms, rather than reflecting simple memorization (Wang et al., 2008).

How adults discuss moral issues, such as truth-telling, harm, and property rights, influences how children come to understand these issues. When adults discuss moral issues in ways that are sensitive to the child's developmental needs, children develop more sophisticated conceptions of morality and advance in their moral reasoning (Janssens & Dekovic, 1997; Walker & Taylor, 1991). As we have seen, there are cultural differences in how people think about moral and conversational issues—and these conceptualizations are communicated, internalized, and transformed by children as they construct their own concepts about morality.

Thinking in Context 7.5

1. Evaluate the social learning and cognitive-developmental perspectives on moral development. What are the strengths and weaknesses of each? In your view, is one better able to account for moral development than another? Why or why not?

2. How might cultural values influence moral development? Is moral development culture-free (i.e., is it an area in which people around the world show the same developmental progression)? Why or why not?

CONTEXTUAL INFLUENCES ON DEVELOPMENT IN EARLY CHILDHOOD

Formal education begins in early childhood, as children begin to attend preschool, prekindergarten (pre-K), and similar institutions. Many children face a particularly challenging risk for development: poverty. Even if they have access to quality education, children reared in homes and communities of pervasive poverty are at risk to develop physical, cognitive, and psychosocial deficits.

EARLY CHILDHOOD EDUCATION

Preschool programs provide educational experiences for children ages 2 to 5. Some preschools are child-centered, allowing children to choose among a variety of activities and play as vehicles for learning. The best preschool programs stimulate all aspects of development—cognitive, physical, social, and emotional—through manipulating materials and interacting with teachers and peers. Children have the opportunity to choose activities that are tailored to their interests and abilities. They learn by doing—through play—and develop confidence and self-esteem. Active play helps children learn to problem solve, get along with others, communicate, and self-regulate.

Other preschool programs emphasize academics more than play, providing children with structured learning environments through which they learn letters, numbers, shapes, and academic skills via drills and formal lessons. When academic instruction is heavily and rigidly emphasized whereby preschoolers do worksheets and passively sit through lessons, children tend to demonstrate signs of stress such as rocking, have less confidence in their skills, and avoid challenging tasks than do children who are immersed in more active forms of play-based learning (Stipek, Feiler, Daniels, & Milburn, 1995); they also achieve less in grade school (Burts et al., 1992; Hart et al., 1998). Academically oriented preschool programs that emphasize academics over self-directed exploration negatively influence motivation and learning (Stipek et al., 1995). The most effective early childhood education programs include responsive and stimulating daily interactions between teachers and children. Teachers provide educational support in the form of learning goals, instructional support, and feedback, coupled with emotional support and aid in helping children learn behavioral management skills (Hamre, 2014). Responsive teaching is attuned to children's cues and needs rather than being strictly academic.

However, effective early childhood education is defined and influenced by cultural values. In the United States, a society that emphasizes individuality, a child-centered approach in which children are given freedom of choice is associated with the most positive outcomes (Marcon, 1999). Effective early childhood education may vary for other cultures, such as Japan's collectivist culture. The most effective Japanese preschools tend to foster collectivistic values and are society centered with an emphasis on social and classroom routines, skills, and promoting group harmony (Holloway, 1999; Nagayama & Gilliard, 2005). Japanese preschools prepare children for their roles in society and provide formal instruction in academic areas as well as English, art, swordsmanship, gymnastics, tea ceremonies, and Japanese dance. Much instruction is teacher-directed and children are instructed to sit, observe, and listen. Teachers are warm, but address the group as a whole rather than individuals. This structured approach is associated with positive outcomes in Japanese children (Holloway, 1999; Nagayama & Gilliard, 2005), illustrating the role of culture in influencing outcomes of early childhood education. Even within a given country such as the United States, there exist many ethnicities and corresponding cultures, such those of Native Americans and Mexican Americans, for example. In each case, instruction that is informed by an understanding of children's home and community culture fosters a sense of academic belongingness that ultimately influences academic achievement (Gilliard & Moore, 2007).

One of the most successful early childhood education programs in the United States is known as **Project Head Start.** Created in 1965 by the federal government, Project Head Start was designed to provide economically disadvantaged children with nutritional, health, and educational services during their early childhood years, prior to entering kindergarten. In 1994, the program was expanded to serve younger children, from birth to age 3, and their families. There are more than 1,600 Head Start programs in the United States, serving over 900,000 children (see Ethical and Policy Applications of Lifespan Development, p. 191; U.S. Department of Health and Human Services, 2011).

The best evidence for the effectiveness of early childhood education interventions comes from longitudinal studies that span decades. Two major research projects, in addition to Head Start, illustrate the value of quality early childhood education: the Carolina Abecedarian Project and the Perry Preschool Project, carried out in the 1960s and 1970s. Both programs enrolled children from families with incomes below the poverty line. Both projects emphasized providing stimulating preschool experiences to promote motor, language, and social skills as well as cognitive skills including literacy and math concepts. Special emphasis was placed on rich, responsive adult–child verbal communication as well as nutrition and health services. The Abecedarian intervention began in infancy with home visits whereas the Perry Preschool Project included children at ages 3 and 4. Exposure to enriched preschool environments was associated with benefits that lasted well into adulthood. Children in these programs achieved higher reading and math scores in elementary school than their non-enrolled peers (Campbell & Ramey, 1994). As adolescents, they showed higher rates of high school graduation, higher rates of college enrollment, and lower rates of

CHILD-ORIENTED PRESCHOOL

Mark and Melody describe Ella's preschool experiences, noting characteristics of high-quality, child-oriented learning.

Watch the video at edge.sagepub.com/kuther

ETHICAL AND POLICY APPLICATIONS OF LIFESPAN DEVELOPMENT

Project Head Start

Children who attend Head Start programs have early educational experiences that improve cognitive and social skills and prepare them for kindergarten and elementary school.

The rationale for Project Head Start is that early intervention to address factors that may inhibit children's health and learning will prepare them for school and help them get a "head start" on their education. Children served by Head Start are ethnically diverse and tend to come from families with income below the poverty line.

Most Head Start programs include one to two years of preschool as well as nutrition and health services. Parents also receive assistance, such as education about child development, vocational services, and programs addressing their emotional and social needs. Parents are encouraged to be active in Head Start; they serve on committees, contribute to program planning, and act as parent aides in the classroom. Parents must occupy at least one half of the seats of each Head Start program's Policy Council (Zigler & Styfco, 2004). A large part of Head Start's success is that it reaches parents and gets them involved in their children's education. The more involved parents are, the more they learn about child development, which translates into creating a more stimulating learning environment and overall better parenting.

Over the past four decades, a great deal of research has been conducted on the effectiveness of Head Start. The most common finding is that Head Start improves cognitive performance, as illustrated in a study of young children in 18 cities (Zhai, Brooks-Gunn, & Waldfogel, 2011). The first year or two after Head Start children

begin elementary school, they perform well and show gains in IQ and achievement scores. However, over time the cognitive effects of Head Start fade such that participants' performance on cognitive measures later in childhood is similar to those who have not participated in Head Start (Duncan, Ludwig, & Magnuson, 2007; McKey et al., 1985; McLloyd, 1998). Why? Early intervention may not compensate for the pervasive and long-lasting effects of poverty-stricken neighborhoods and inadequate public schools (Schnur & Belanger, 2000).

However, there are some lasting benefits. Children who participate in Head Start are less likely to be held back a grade, less likely to be assigned to special education classes, more likely to graduate from high school, and have greater parental involvement in school (Duncan et al., 2007; Joo, 2010; Zigler & Styfco, 1993). At the same time, home environment is often a better and more consistent predictor of long-term outcomes than participation in Head Start (Joo, 2010). Head Start is associated with other long-lasting effects, such as gains in social competence and health-related outcomes including immunizations (Abbott-Shim, Lambert, & McCarty, 2003; Huston, 2008).

Effective intervention and education programs target young children very early in life to help reduce the negative effects of economic and environmental disadvantage (Ramey & Ramey, 1998). Programs must treat the whole child by providing a variety of services to promote development, including health and social services as well as transportation to ensure that children can attend. Programs should encourage parents to provide a broad range of learning experiences for their children outside of school and to become involved in their child's education. Programs that have lasting effects include continuous intervention beyond the preschool years because a two-year program cannot permanently protect a young child from the ravaging effects of economic and neighborhood disadvantage.

What Do You Think?

1. **Why do you think the gains in cognitive and achievement scores shown by children in Head Start fade over time? From your perspective, what can be done to improve such outcomes?**

2. **Consider early childhood interventions such as Head Start from the perspective of bioecological theory. Identify factors at the microsystem, mesosystem, and exosystem that programs may address to promote children's development.**

---

substance abuse and lower rates of pregnancy (Campbell, Ramey, Pungello, Sparling, & Miller-Johnson, 2002; Muennig et al.,2011). At ages 30 and 40, early intervention participants showed higher levels of education and income (Campbell et al., 2012; Schweinhart et al., 2005).

The success of the Abecedarian, Perry, and Head Start early intervention programs has influenced a movement in the United States toward comprehensive academically oriented preschool, known as pre-K. Pre-K programs are a distinct type of preschool program designed for 4-year-old children specifically to ensure that young children will be ready for kindergarten and will be successful in school by

third grade (Colker, 2009). Young children who participate in high-quality pre-K programs enter school more ready to learn than their peers and score higher on reading and math tests than their peers (Gormley, Gayer, Phillips, & Dawson, 2004). About one half of states offer some form of state-funded pre-K without income restrictions, but only 13 states offer pre-K programs in every county (Barnett, Carolan, Squires, Clarke Brown, & Horowitz, 2015). Because all children can benefit from access to quality early childhood education, states such as Oklahoma, Georgia, and Florida provide universal pre-K to all children, and many more states are moving in this direction (Williams, 2015).

EFFECTS OF EXPOSURE TO POVERTY

In 2013, children under 18 years of age represented 23% of the U.S. population but comprised 33% of all people in poverty (with poverty defined as a household income of $23,624 for a family of four or $16,057 for an adult and child; Jiang, Ekono, & Skinner, 2015). Young children under the age of 6 are at highest risk of living in poverty as 25% of all children under the age of 6 lived in poverty and an additional 23% are raised in near poverty (defined as 200% poverty level or less). Children from persistently poor families are more likely to experience malnutrition as well as growth stunting in height and weight (Eamon, 2001; Petterson & Albers, 2001). By age 7, they tend to be one inch shorter, on average, than other children (Yip, Scanlon, & Trowbridge, 1993). Children from families with low income show lower levels of cognitive and social functioning than children from more advantaged families (Hanson, McLanahan, & Thomson, 1997; Patterson, Kupersmidt, & Vaden, 1990; Petterson & Albers, 2001). By 2 years of age, children from low socioeconomic backgrounds score lower on standardized tests of cognitive ability (Duncan, Brooks-Gunn, & Klebanov, 1994; Smith, Brooks-Gunn, & Klebanov, 1997). Family income levels within the first four to five years of life predict verbal and achievement outcomes in the early school years (Klebanov, Brooks-Gunn, McCarton, & McCormick, 1998). The effects of poverty are more pronounced for children in families with the lowest income (Duncan & Brooks-Gunn, 2000). Risks to cognitive development, such as maternal education, maternal verbal comprehension, and stressful life events, are more damaging to children at the lowest levels of income than to those who are not poor (Klebanov et al., 1998).

The negative effects of persistent poverty are cumulative, increasing as children get older and have spent a greater proportion of their lives in poverty (Petterson & Albers, 2001). For example, being poor in all of the first four years of life is associated with lower cognitive scores at age 5 as compared with not being poor for all of those years. However, being poor for some, but not all, of those years produces a smaller effect on cognitive development (Duncan & Brooks-Gunn, 2000). Children reared in persistent poverty, who experience repeated instances of poverty, are more likely to have about one-half of the vocabulary of peers at age 3, have a learning disability, repeat a grade, drop out of high school, have emotional or behavior problems, and show aggressive and delinquent behavior in adolescence and adulthood (Dornfeld & Kruttschnitt, 1992; Duncan et al., 1993; Duncan et al., 2007; Najman et al., 2010; Roy, 2014). Overall, verbal ability and achievement are more affected by family income than are mental health and problem behaviors (Duncan & Brooks-Gunn, 2000). Educational resources in the home influence cognitive development of children in poverty. Compared with kindergarteners from families in the bottom fifth of the socioeconomic distribution, children from the most advantaged fifth are four times as likely to have a computer at home, have three times as many books, are read to more often, watch far less television, and are more likely to visit museums or libraries (Duncan et al., 2007).

The quality of home environment predicts children's outcomes. Children reared in low-income homes tend to experience fewer opportunities for learning and mother–child interactions that are less warm, which accounts for a large proportion of the effects of family income on young children's cognitive outcomes (Duncan & Brooks-Gunn, 2000; Duncan et al., 2007). High-quality parenting is associated with enhanced social and emotional functioning and linguistic competence in low- and middle-income children in the United States and United Kingdom (Duncan & Brooks-Gunn, 2000; Kiernan & Mensah, 2011). Low-income children are less likely to receive high-quality care outside of the home.

Not only is family income important in predicting childhood outcomes but so is the level of income in neighborhoods (Leventhal & Brooks-Gunn, 2000). The presence of affluent neighbors is associated with higher scores on cognitive tests at age 5 (Klebanov et al., 1998). Children who live in poorer neighborhoods are at a higher risk of experiencing negative developmental outcomes than children who live in more affluent neighborhoods. Families with low income often live in extremely poor neighborhoods characterized by social disorganization such as crime, unemployment, and few resources for child development such as playgrounds and parks, child care, health care, and adequate schools (Duncan & Brooks-Gunn, 2000). The salience of a neighborhood's socioeconomic conditions for either supporting or hindering development extends beyond studies conducted in the United States and has been replicated cross-nationally in other developed countries (Caspi & Taylor, 2000; Kohen, Brooks-Gunn, Leventhal, & Hertzman, 2002; Kohen, Leventhal, Dahinten, & McIntosh, 2008).

Neighborhood conditions also influence young children indirectly through effects on parents, family processes such as parenting behaviors, stimulation, and learning opportunities as well as the quality of home environment (Bradley, 1995; Klebanov et al., 1998; Kohen et al., 2008). Neighborhood context and family hardship may influence children by affecting parental mental health; increasing parental conflict; and subsequently, influencing parenting behaviors, which, in turn, influence children's outcomes (Conger et al., 2002; Elder, van Nguyen, & Caspi, 1985; Kohen et al., 2008; Linver, Brooks-Gunn, & Kohen, 2002).

Intervening in Poverty

What resources exist for low-income families, and what are the effects of these resources on child development? From the Great Depression years of the 1930s until the mid-1990s, welfare in the United States took the form of a federal program called Aid to Families with Dependent Children (AFDC), which provided financial benefits to families. Mothers who received AFDC benefits were exempt from any work requirements until their children were older than 6 years of age, although states had the option to require self-sufficiency activities, such as job training, of mothers with preschoolers or even infants (Chase-Lansdale & Vinovskis, 1995; Holland, 2004). In 1996, Congress passed the Personal Responsibility and Work Opportunity Reconciliation Act, which dismantled AFDC; created

Mario Tama/Getty

Children reared in poverty experience contextual disadvantages that place them at risk for cognitive, academic, and social problems.

another welfare program, Temporary Assistance for Needy Families (TANF); and by 2000 resulted in welfare caseloads falling dramatically in every state and by more than 50% nationwide (Administration for Children and Families, 2004).

TANF is known as a welfare-to-work program because it provides families with economic resources with mandated participation in job training and employment activities. The goal of welfare-to-work programs is to increase a mother's self-sufficiency by reducing barriers to employment like child care, enhancing education and literacy, and providing job training (Collins & Aber, 1996; Holland, 2004; Smith, Brooks-Gunn, Kohen, & McCarton, 2001). TANF is intended to transform the welfare system from one that often provided long-term support into a short-term assistance program that encourages poor mothers, including those with very young children, to work. In addition, TANF includes a five-year lifetime limit, but many states have implemented shorter time limits. Many families with children thus forgo receiving public assistance.

Transitional policies also exist, policies designed to cushion the transition to work. The earned income tax credit is a refundable tax credit for low-income workers with children. Its value increases as earnings rise for very low earners, as a reward for successful employment, making work "pay." Two-year transitional child care subsidies exist for parents who forgo welfare receipt for full-time employment. However, two years often is not enough time to ease parents' financial woes. In addition, parents' awareness and use of these transitional benefits is less than expected; aggressive outreach policies and efforts are needed (Smith et al., 2001).

How successful are welfare-to-work programs? Most studies measure success as changes in parents' welfare dependency and employment status with the emphasis on the mother as provider rather than parent (Smith et al., 2001). In terms of outcomes, there are two trajectories: (1) former recipients who have more schooling, higher cognitive abilities, and fewer mental health problems were more able to find employment and increase family income through wages but (2) former recipients who are high school dropouts or have severe mental health or cognitive impairments were more likely to experience increases in economic and food insecurity after TANF benefits end (Duncan & Brooks-Gunn, 2000; Smith et al., 2001). Less attention has been paid to the effects on mothers' emotional health and parenting behavior or on their children's development. Frequently the jobs that parents are able to obtain require off-peak working hours, such as nights and weekends, and are geographically unsuitable, creating transportation problems and child care difficulties. Children often experience stressful home environments and are left home alone, unsupervised, and are often expected to shoulder a substantial amount of responsibility (Holland, 2004). Little research has examined the effects of welfare-to-work policies on children's development.

Leaving welfare does not necessarily mean that a family is no longer poor. Many welfare-to-work programs increase employment but not income (Morris, 2002). Welfare-to-work programs that increase employment tend to have little effects on school achievement in the preschool and early school years. However, programs that increase both employment and income have beneficial effects on school achievement (Morris, 2002; Morris, Gennetian, & Duncan, 2005).

Early childhood presents opportunities for physical and cognitive growth. Young children get better at exploring and understanding their physical world. As we will see in Chapter 8, young children also get better at exploring their social and emotional world.

Thinking in Context 7.6

Social policies and programs such as early childhood education and community support programs have the potential to intervene and lessen the negative outcomes associated with poverty. In your view, which child and family needs should such programs target? What services might be provided to communities, families, and individuals?

Apply Your Knowledge

Researchers who study deception in children must find unique ways of determining when young children are capable of lying. In one study (Saarni, 1984), children were given a desirable toy and promised that they would receive another. Instead, they received an undesirable gift that was not a toy. The child's facial expressions, nonverbal behavior, and emotional displays were recorded. The researchers were interested in when children would begin to mask their feelings and lie about the desirability of the gift. In another study (Lewis, Stanger, & Sullivan, 1989), young children were left alone in a laboratory environment, told by the researcher not to peek at a toy in the researcher's absence, and later questioned about whether they had peeked at the toy. Other studies (Polak & Harris, 1999) entailed the researcher telling children not to touch the toy and later questioning them about whether they had touched the toy in the researcher's absence.

1. How does cognitive development influence children's ability to deceive?

2. What emotional capacities does lying require?

3. When would you expect young children to become capable of lying? Why?

4. What are ethical issues entailed in research on deception in children? How might considerations of children's feelings of guilt, shame, or frustration and their developing capacities for self-regulation inform this question?

Chapter Summary

7.1 Identify patterns of body growth in early childhood.

Growth slows during early childhood. Ethnic differences in patterns of growth are apparent in most Western countries, but there are many individual differences. Malnutrition poses a risk to physical development.

7.2 Contrast advances in gross and fine motor development and their implications for young children's development.

Young children make great advances in gross motor skills, becoming stronger and more coordinated, permitting them to play harder and engage in more complicated play activities. Advances in gross motor skills help children move about and develop a sense of mastery of their environment. Fine motor skills permit young children to take responsibility for their own care.

7.3 Distinguish two processes of brain development and the role of plasticity in development.

Myelination permits quick and complex communication between neurons, leading children's thinking to become faster, more coordinated, and sophisticated. Lateralization begins before birth and is influenced by genes and early experiences and increases in young childhood.

The brain is most plastic during the first few years of life. How well a young child's brain compensates for an injury depends on the age at the time of injury, site of injury, and capacities compromised.

7.4 Contrast Piaget's and Vygotsky's perspectives on young children's thinking.

Piaget explained that children in the preoperational stage of reasoning are able to think using mental symbols, but their thinking is limited because they cannot grasp logic. Simplified and nonverbal tasks demonstrate that young children are more cognitively advanced and less egocentric than Piaget posed. From Vygotsky's sociocultural perspective, children's learning occurs through guided participation, scaffolding within the zone of proximal development. With time, the child internalizes the lesson and learns to accomplish the task on her own. According to Vygotsky, cognitive development and learning entails active internalization of elements of context.

7.5 Discuss changes that occur in attention, episodic memory, and autobiographic memory during early childhood.

The ability to sustain attention improves in early childhood through the preschool years. Episodic memory improves steadily between ages 4 and 10, especially between age 5 and 7. Young children tend to lack knowledge about how to conduct memory searches, determine what is important to recall, and structure narrative accounts of events. Young children's limited working memory makes it difficult for them to use memory strategies. Autobiographical memory develops steadily from 3 to 6 years of age, through adolescence, and is accompanied by increases in the length, richness, and complexity of recall memory.

7.6 Summarize young children's awareness and understanding of the mind.

Young children's theory of mind develops rapidly. They become capable of understanding that people can believe different things, that beliefs can be inaccurate, and that sometimes people act on the basis of false beliefs. Children thereby become able to lie or use deception in play. Children's performance on false belief tasks is closely related with language development, interaction with others, and measures of executive function.

7.7 Describe young children's developing capacities for language.

Young children quickly move from telegraphic speech to combining words into sentences in increasingly sophisticated ways. Soon, young children learn to use multiple elements of speech, such as plurals, adjectives, and the past tense. Children learn new words through fast mapping and logical extension as well as the mutual exclusivity bias in learning new words. Young children make overregularization error. Parental conversations and support for language learning is associated with faster and more correct language use. At the end of the preschool years, most children use main grammar rules appropriately and confidently.

7.8 Contrast social learning and cognitive-developmental perspectives on moral development in early childhood.

Social learning theory explains that children develop internalized standards of conduct based on reinforcements and punishments as well as observing others and considering their explanations for behavior. The cognitive-developmental perspective examines reasoning about moral issues, specifically concerns of justice. Kohlberg explained that young children display preconventional moral reasoning. They have not internalized societal norms, and their behavior is motivated by desires, self-interest, and avoiding punishment rather than internalized principles. As early as 3 years of age, children in diverse cultures can differentiate between moral concerns from social conventions, or social customs. Social experiences with parents, caregivers, siblings, and peers help young children develop conceptions about justice and fairness.

7.9 Identify and explain two approaches to early childhood education, including their associated outcomes.

Child-centered preschool programs encourage children to manipulate materials; interact with teachers and peers; and learn by doing, through play. Academically oriented preschool programs provide children with structured learning environments through which they learn letters, numbers, shapes, and academic skills via drills and formal lessons. When academic instruction is heavily and rigidly emphasized, children tend to demonstrate signs of stress, have less confidence in their skills, avoid challenging tasks, and show more poor achievement than do children who are immersed in more active forms of play-based learning. However, effective early childhood education is defined and influenced by cultural values.

7.10 Analyze effects of poverty on development and resources to help families in need.

Children from persistently poor families are more likely to experience malnutrition, growth stunting, and increased vulnerability to illness. Children from families with low incomes show lower levels of cognitive, academic, social, and behavioral functioning than children from more advantaged families. The negative effects of persistent poverty are cumulative and influence the child through the quality of the home environment and neighborhood. TANF provides families with economic resources with mandated participation in job training and employment activities. Critics argue that many welfare-to-work programs increase employment but not income.

Key Terms

CHAPTER 8

Socioemotional Development in Early Childhood

$SAGE edge™   **Get the edge on your studies at edge.sagepub.com/kuther.**

Master these learning objectives using key study tools in the chapter and at SAGE edge. Access original SAGE **Video Cases** to explore the lives and contexts of individuals in every stage of development, **Think Critically** and **Explore Further** with SAGE journal and reference articles, and **Watch**, **Listen**, and **Connect** with online multimedia resources.

LEARNING OBJECTIVES

KEY STUDY TOOLS

8.1. Identify the psychosocial task of early childhood, as described by Erikson.

Lives in Context Television and Children's Development (p. 202)

Explore Further Psychosocial Stages

8.2. Discuss young children's emerging sense of self.

Explore Further Self-Concepts and Self-Esteem

8.3. Compare the development of prosocial and aggressive behavior during early childhood.

Explore Further Television and Aggression

8.4. Analyze the relation of four parenting styles and their associations with child outcomes.

Lives in Context Effects of Exposure to Community Violence (p. 211)

Video Case Parenting and Discipline

8.5. Describe the effects of discipline on children's development.

Think Critically Timeout in Early Childhood

Listen Physical Discipline

8.6. Explain the effects of child maltreatment and factors that place children at risk for experiencing maltreatment.

Explore Further Child Abuse Prevention

8.7. Summarize findings regarding gender differences during early childhood.

Applying Developmental Science Imaginary Companions (p. 217)

Connect Gender Identity Development

8.8. Compare and contrast biological, cognitive, and contextual theoretical explanations of gender role development.

Video Case Gender Schemas & Play Preferences

8.9. Discuss the function of play and the form it takes in early childhood.

Think Critically Outdoor Play Environments

"I'm not a baby anymore. I use my words to do things," four-year-old Daniel explained to his grandmother. His mother agreed. "Daniel is good at expressing his wants and needs. He doesn't cry as easily as he did when he was younger. My baby is quickly growing into a big boy." Early childhood is a time of transition from the dependence of infancy and toddlerhood to the increasing capacities for autonomy and emotional regulation characteristic of childhood. How do young children learn to understand and control their emotions? Do they experience the same complex emotions that older children and adolescents experience? What is the role of parents in children's emotional and social development? What is the function of play in development? In this chapter, we explore

children's experience and understanding of their social and emotional world and how socioemotional development changes over the early childhood years.

EMERGING SENSE OF SELF

When given a task, such as dusting off a bookcase shelf, 3-year-old Shawna called out, "I'll do it!" After completing the task, she proudly proclaimed, "I did it!" The autonomy that Shawna developed during the toddler years has prepared her to master the psychosocial task of the preschool years: developing a sense of initiative (Erikson, 1950).

PSYCHOSOCIAL DEVELOPMENT IN EARLY CHILDHOOD

During Erikson's third psychosocial stage, **initiative versus guilt**, the task is for young children to develop a sense of purposefulness and take pride in their accomplishments. Much of the work of this stage occurs through play. During play, young children learn about themselves and their social world. They can experiment and practice new skills in a safe context free of criticism. They learn to work cooperatively with other children to achieve common goals. Children also practice taking on adult roles through play: Mother, father, doctor, teacher, and police officer are common roles, and such play has been observed in all societies (Edwards, 2000). For example, Hopi Indian children pretend to be hunters and potters, and the Baka of West Africa pretend to be hut builders and spear makers (Roopnarine, Lasker, Sacks, & Stores, 1998). Through play, children also learn how to manage their emotions and develop self-regulation skills (Hoffmann & Russ, 2012).

In developing a sense of initiative, young children make plans, tackle new tasks, set goals (e.g., climbing a tree, writing their name, counting to ten), and work to achieve them, persisting enthusiastically in tasks, whether physical or social, even when frustrated. Young children's play becomes goal directed in that they want to begin and complete tasks. For example, rather than simply playing with blocks, young children want to build a tall tower, and then enjoy their success. The sense of pride that children feel from accomplishment fuels their play and fosters curiosity. Children become motivated to concentrate, persist, and try new experiences, such as climb to the top of the monkey bars, taste a new food, and learn a new dance.

During early childhood, children come to identify with their parents and internalize parental rules. Young children feel guilt when they fail to uphold rules, as well as when they fail to achieve a goal. If parents are controlling—not permitting children to carry out their sense of purpose—or are highly punitive, critical, or threatening, then children may not develop high standards and the initiative to meet them. Instead, children will be paralyzed by guilt and worry about

Children take great pleasure in completing household tasks as simple as emptying the dryer.

their inability to measure up to parental expectations. The negative outcome of this stage of Erikson's (1950) scheme is that children will develop an overly critical conscience and be enveloped in guilt, reducing their motivation to exert the effort to master new tasks.

Children who develop a sense of initiative develop a confident self-image, more self-control over their emotions, social skills, and a sense of conscience. Young children like to demonstrate that they can engage in activities by themselves. They enjoy taking on new tasks and expect others to watch them. When children demonstrate independence and act purposefully, they are primed to develop a healthy sense of **self-esteem**. Their success in taking initiative and the feeling of competence and self-esteem that accompanies it is an important basis for developing a sense of self.

SELF-CONCEPT

Children first understand themselves in concrete terms, as illustrated by Wanda: "I'm four years old. I have black hair. I'm happy, my doggy is white, and I have a television in my room. I can run really fast. Watch me!" Wanda's self-description, her self-concept, is typical of children her age.

Whereas self-esteem refers to a general emotional evaluation of one's own worth, self-concept is rather more specific. It refers to our beliefs about ourselves, our conceptions of our abilities, traits, and characteristics. Three- and 4-year-old children tend to understand and describe themselves concretely, using observable descriptors including appearance, general abilities, favorite activities, possessions, and simple psychological traits (Harter, 1999). Preschoolers often mention specific possessions when they describe themselves—they often assert their ownership and rights to toys and other objects. This is not selfishness. Rather, young children use objects as a way to set boundaries between themselves and others (Fasig, 2000). In other words, this possessiveness often indicates a strong sense of self-concept. By 3.5 years of age, children include emotions and attitudes in their self-descriptions, suggesting an emerging awareness of their own psychological characteristics, such as "I'm sad when my friends can't play" or "I like playing with doggies" (Eder, 1989). Young children's self-descriptions are stable over time (Marsh, Craven, & Debus, 1998).

When 3-year-olds describe themselves, they often focus on their abilities, demonstrate them, and tend to be unrealistically positive about their abilities. For example, "I know all my ABCs! Listen! A, B, C, D, E, F, G, H, J, L, K, O, M, P, Q, X, V!" (Harter, 1999). The preschool child typically has a very positive sense of self. Any goal is viewed as achievable, and they always view their performance favorably, even when it is not up to par (Boseovski, 2010). Young children's overoptimistic perspective on their skills can be attributed to their cognitive development, secure attachment with caregivers, as well as the overwhelmingly positive feedback that they tend to receive in response to their task-related efforts (Goodvin, Meyer, Thompson, & Hayes, 2008). Young children maintain their positive views about themselves because they do not yet engage in **social comparison**, meaning that they do not compare their performance with that of other children (Colwell & Lindsey, 2003). They also tend to underestimate the difficulty of tasks and do not recognize deficits in their abilities (Harter, 1990, 1998). Young children usually believe that they will be successful at any time. Even after failing at a task several times, they often continue to believe that the next try will bring success (Ruble, Grosovsky, Frey, & Cohen, 1992). These unrealistically positive expectations serve a developmental purpose, as they contribute to young children's developing sense of initiative and aid them in learning new skills.

As children gain life experience and develop cognitively, they begin to learn their relative strengths and weaknesses. As they grow older, their evaluations of self become more realistic (Marsh et al., 1998). With age, self-concept becomes correlated with skills, accomplishments, evaluations by others, and other external indicators of competence (Diehl, Youngblade, Hay, & Chui, 2011). For example, as children move from early childhood to middle childhood, by around age 7, self-concept becomes increasingly abstract, shifting from concrete descriptions of behavior in early childhood to trait-like psychological constructs (e.g., popular, smart, good looking; (Harter, 2006).

Children's conceptions of themselves are influenced by the cultural context in which they are raised. In one study, preschool through second grade U.S. and Chinese children were asked to recount autobiographical events and describe themselves in response to open-ended questions (Wang, 2004). The U.S. children often provided detailed accounts of their experiences. They focused on their own roles, preferences, and feelings and described their personal attributes, abstract dispositions, and inner traits in a positive tone. In contrast, Chinese children provided relatively skeletal

Cultural differences influence how children view themselves and their accomplishments.

Carlos Barria/Reuters/Corbis

accounts of past experiences that focused on social interactions and daily routines, and they often described themselves in neutral or modest tones, referring to social roles and context-specific personal characteristics. These differences are consistent with cultural values of independence in the United States and collectivism in China. In another study, U.S. preschool children reported feeling more sadness and shame in response to failure, and more pride in response to success than did Japanese preschool children (Lewis, Takai-Kawakami, Kawakami, & Sullivan, 2010). The Japanese preschool children displayed few negative emotions in response to failure but showed self-conscious embarrassment in response to success. Culture influences how children come to define and understand themselves and even the emotions with which they self-identify.

EMOTIONAL DEVELOPMENT

Young children's advances in cognitive development and growing sense of self influences the emotions they show and the contexts in which they are displayed. Moreover, young children come to understand people and social relationships in more complex ways. These changes, as well as young children's growing capacities for perspective taking, lead to advances in **empathy** and **prosocial behavior**.

Empathy and Prosocial Behavior

Young children are faced with an important task: developing a sense of empathy, the capacity to understand another person's emotions. Empathy is not simply following rules or adults' instructions to cooperate with and help others. Instead, empathy requires perspective-taking ability. The child must imagine another's perspective and imagine what might make that person feel better. The child who feels empathy for another person understands how that person feels and is primed to engage in prosocial behavior, behavior that is oriented toward others for the pure sake of helping them, without expecting a reward. Empathy, therefore, motivates prosocial behavior (Taylor, Eisenberg, Spinrad, Eggum, & Sulik, 2013).

Research on the development of prosocial behavior has indicated that from early in life children behave prosocially toward others including sharing resources with others (Svetlova, Nichols, & Brownell, 2010). Prosocial behavior appears in infants and toddlers (Paulus, 2014). For toddlers as young as 18 months, prosocial behavior includes the ability to help adults instrumentally, or offer assistance in achieving a simple action-based goal such as getting something out of reach (Warneken & Tomasello, 2006). Between 18 and 24 months of age, toddlers show increasingly prosocial responses to others' emotional and physical distress and respond with expressions of concern and comfort (Hoffman, 2007). At 3.5 years of age, children show more complex forms of instrumental assistance. Compared to 18-month-old children, 3.5-year-olds are more likely to help an adult by bringing a needed object, to do so autonomously without the adult's specific request, and to select an object appropriate to the adult's need (Svetlova et al., 2010). Between 3 and 5 years of age, young children show selectivity in prosocial behavior. They share more with children and adults who show prosocial behaviors such as sharing and helping others (Kuhlmeier, Dunfield, & O'Neill, 2014). After working together actively to obtain rewards in a collaboration task, most 3-year-old children share equally with a peer, even if they could easily monopolize those rewards (Warneken, Lohse, Melis, & Tomasello, 2011). At 5 years of age, they share more with others they expect to reciprocate by sharing with them and more with friends than with peers they dislike (Paulus & Moore, 2014). Prosocial behavior increases throughout early childhood and reflects a more advanced understanding of others' perspectives and goals (Baillargeon et al., 2011).

In early childhood, prosocial behavior becomes more complex and becomes an important way to foster friendships and other relationships. Examples of prosocial behavior are sharing a toy, giving another child candy when he or she is upset, or encouraging a shy reluctant child to play a game. Young children may engage in prosocial behavior for egocentric motives. The desire for praise and to avoid punishment and disapproval often influences their prosocial actions. Their behavior may be motivated by considerations of how they wish others to act toward them. With development, children become less egocentric and more aware of others' perspectives. Their prosocial behavior becomes motivated by empathy as well as internalized societal values for good behavior (Eisenberg & Fabes, 1998).

Preschoolers' developing cognitive and language skills permit them to become more reflective and feel empathy in more complex ways and express it with language. Empathy often yields **sympathy**—concern or sorrow for another person. Increases in emotional understanding over the early childhood years are associated with long-term advances in sympathy (Eggum et al., 2011). However, sometimes feelings of empathy for distressed others can result in personal distress, leading the child to focus on relieving his or her own distress rather than helping the person in need.

A child's temperament and personality influence how the child responds to feeling empathy for a distressed child or adult, and whether empathetic feelings result in personal distress or prosocial behavior. Empathy and prosocial responses such as sympathetic concern, helping, sharing, and comforting others are more likely in children who are sociable and successful in regulating their emotions (Eisenberg et al., 1998). Children who are unable to successfully regulate their emotions and display appropriately sympathetic and other-oriented responses tend to react to distressed others with their own physiological and emotional distress, suggesting a feeling of being overwhelmed: frowning, lip-biting, and increases in heart rate and brain activity in regions known to process negative emotions (Pickens, Field, & Nawrocki, 2001).

Influences on Empathy and Prosocial Behavior

Through their interactions with children, parents influence the development of empathy and prosocial behavior. When parents describe feelings and model the use of language to discuss feelings, toddlers are more likely to use words to describe their thoughts and emotions and attempt to understand others' emotional states (Garner, 2003). Parents who are warm and encouraging, modeling sympathetic concern, give rise to preschoolers who are more likely to display concern in response to others' distress (Taylor et al., 2013). Parents of prosocial children draw attention to models of prosocial behavior in peers and in media, such as in storybooks, movies, and television programs. They point out characters who display sharing, empathy, and cooperation, thereby modeling and encouraging prosocial behaviors in children (Singer & Singer, 1998). Other caregivers and early childhood teachers play similar roles in emotional socialization, helping children learn how to understand their own and others' emotions, express their emotions appropriately, and help others (Denham, Bassett, & Zinsser, 2012).

At the same time that parents influence children, children play a role in their own development by influencing their parents. One study that followed children from 4.5 years of age through sixth grade found that while maternal sensitivity influenced children's prosocial behavior as rated by both mothers and teachers in third and fifth grade, prosocial behavior, in turn, predicted maternal sensitivity. Children's prosocial behavior predicted mothers' subsequent sensitivity, suggesting that mothers and children influence each other (Newton, Laible, Carlo, Steele, & McGinley, 2014). Children who are more kind, compassionate, and helpful earlier in childhood may be more likely to elicit more responsive and warm parenting from their mothers later in childhood.

Siblings offer opportunities to learn and practice helping and other prosocial behaviors. Older siblings who display positive emotional responsiveness promote preschoolers' emotional and social competence (Sawyer et al., 2002). We have seen that children with siblings tend to develop a theory of mind earlier than those without siblings. Theory of mind helps children to learn how to take another person's perspective and is associated with empathetic and prosocial behavior (Walker, 2005). Children who are unable to demonstrate the perspective taking and cognitive skill that contributes to theory of mind will find it difficult to understand how others feel and help them.

The broader social world also influences the development of prosocial behavior. Collectivist cultures in which children's relationships with others are stressed, people live in extended families, and work is shared tend to promote prosocial values and behavior more so than do cultures that emphasize the individual, as is common in most Western cultures (Eisenberg et al., 1998). One study of mother–child dyads in Japan and the United States found that the Japanese mothers of 4-year-old children tended to emphasize mutuality in their interactions, stressing the relationship (e.g., "This puzzle is difficult for us. Let's see if we can solve it"), while the U.S. mothers tended to emphasize individuality (e.g., "This puzzle is hard for you, isn't it? Let's see you try again."; Dennis, Cole, Zahn-Waxler, & Mizuta, 2002). These different styles influence how children display empathy, as sharing another's emotion or simply understanding another's emotion.

Aggression

Although their capacities for empathy and prosocial responses increase, young children commonly show aggressive behavior. Over one half of a sample of 5-month-old infants followed up through 42 months of age showed some aggressive behaviors, such as hitting, biting, or kicking (Tremblay et al., 2004). Similarly, most of the children in one study who were studied from 24 months of age to third grade showed low levels of aggression that declined over time (National Institute of Child Health and Development [NICHD] Early Child Care Research, 2004). Most children learn to inhibit aggressive impulses; however, a small minority of children show high levels of aggression (e.g., repeated hitting, kicking, biting) that increase during childhood (Tremblay, 2009). Young children who show high levels of aggression are more likely to have experienced coercive parenting, family dysfunction, and low income as well as have mothers with a history of antisocial behavior and early childbearing (Tremblay, 2014; Wang, Christ, Mills-Koonce, Garrett-Peters, & Cox, 2013). Children who do not develop the impulse control and self-management skills to inhibit their aggressive responses are at risk to continue and escalate aggressive behavior over the childhood years and show poor social and academic outcomes during the school age years and beyond (Gower, Lingras, Mathieson, Kawabata, & Crick, 2014; Wang et al., 2013).

However, aggression is not always an indicator of poor adjustment. The most common form of aggression seen in early childhood is **instrumental aggression**, aggression used to achieve a goal, such as obtaining a toy. For example, a child who grabs a crayon out of another child's hand does so to obtain the crayon, not to hurt the other child. In addition to toys, preschool children often battle over space ("I was sitting there!"). All children will sometimes hit, fight, kick, and take other children's toys. Instrumental aggression typically appears in infancy, at about 1 year of age (Hay, Hurst, Waters, & Chadwick, 2011), but increases from toddlerhood into early childhood, around age 4, as children begin to play with other children and act in their own interests. Instrumental aggression usually occurs during play and is an important step in development as it is often displayed by sociable and confident preschoolers. By age 4, most children have developed the self-control to express their desires and to wait for what they want, moving from expressing aggression through physical means to using words (Coie & Dodge, 1998). A related question, often controversial, is the extent to which the media may influence children's aggressive behavior (see Lives in Context, p. 202).

Children's sense of self undergoes significant development in early childhood. Young children can describe themselves in concrete terms and their sense of self is influenced by their feelings of competence and initiative. Early childhood is accompanied by marked increases in emotional development, including the capacity for empathy and display of prosocial behavior. This is especially true for those whose parents are affectionate and model emotional competence, important components of effective parenting.

Thinking in Context 8.1

1. How might parents, child care providers, and preschool teachers promote children's developing sense of self, including self-concept, initiative, and empathy?

2. Children's prosocial and aggressive behavior occurs in context. Identify influences on children's behavior at each of the biolecological levels: microsystem, mesosystem, exosystem, and macrosystem.

PARENTING

Parents have a tremendous influence on their children's development not simply by meeting children's physical needs but through the relationship that develops between parents and children. **Parenting style** is the emotional climate of the parent–child relationship, the degree of warmth, support, and boundaries that parents provide, influences parents' efficacy, their relationship with their children, and their children's development.

PARENTING STYLES

Parenting styles are displayed as enduring sets of parenting behaviors, combinations of warmth and acceptance, and limits

LIVES IN CONTEXT

Television and Children's Development

Many children spend hours each day riveted to a screen. What effects might this have on development?

Television watching increases dramatically after 2.5 years of age, peaks at ages 10 to 12, and often remains stable for years (Anderson, Lorch, Field, Collins, & Nathan, 1986). One nationally representative sample of about 9,000 preschoolers indicated that they were exposed to about four hours of TV daily (Tandon, Zhou, Lozano, & Christakis, 2011). What effects does television watching have on children's development?

Educational television can teach children skills such as problem solving, reading, and language (Moses, 2008). *Sesame Street,* created to simultaneously entertain and teach children, especially those who may be unprepared for school, is a particularly successful educational program. Preschoolers who watch the show frequently display increases in many school readiness skills, such as knowing letters and numbers as well as writing their name. They also earn higher scores on standardized measures of vocabulary, view school and people of other ethnicities more positively, and adapt better to school (Kirkorian, Wartella, & Anderson, 2008). These changes are long lasting. Young children from low-income families who watch *Sesame Street* and other educational programs demonstrate better performance in reading, math, language ability, and overall school readiness three years later (Wright et al., 2001). Young children's learning from educational television programs is influenced by their developing social relationships with on-screen characters, such as Ernie and Elmo from *Sesame Street* (Richert, Robb, & Smith, 2011). Preschool children who watch more educational television tend to read more books, be more achievement oriented, and earn higher grades in English, math, and science as adolescents (Anderson, Huston, Schmitt, Lineberger, & Wright, 2001).

On the other hand, noneducational programs and those created for general audiences, particularly those that contain violence, have been associated with attention problems, motivation problems, and aggressive behavior in early childhood and later (Barr, Lauricella, Zack, & Calvert, 2010). About two thirds of television programs contain violence, and children's programs, particularly cartoons, contain even more (Center for Communication and Social Policy, 1998). Televised violence provides models that imply that aggression is an appropriate response to provocation and a way to obtain desired outcomes, providing models and offering messages that aggressive behaviors and attitudes are appropriate (Comstock & Scharrer, 1999; Slaby, Roedell, Arezzo, & Hendrix, 1995). Experimental studies have shown that young children exposed to media displaying aggressive models, such as adults hitting an inflated doll, are more likely to hit the doll themselves (Bandura, Ross, & Ross, 1963).

Viewing aggression on television is associated with aggressive behavior. The relation is small but long lasting and consistent over hundreds of research studies (Kirkorian et al., 2008; Moses, 2008). Preschoolers who view high amounts of violence on television tend to show higher levels of aggression and poorer school achievement in adolescence (Anderson et al., 2001). Television watching in childhood predicts aggressive behavior in early adulthood, even after controlling for parental aggression and education, intelligence, family income, and neighborhood crime (Huesmann, Moise-Titus, Podolski, & Eron, 2003). For these reasons, many professional organizations dedicated to promoting the well-being of children (including the American Psychological Association [APA], American Academy of Pediatrics [AAP], American Medical Association, American Psychiatric Association) advise parents to protect their children from violent media, including violent cartoons; the evening news; and programs designed for general audiences (Anderson & Bushman, 2002). Although exposure to aggressive and violent models on television is associated with poor developmental outcomes, moderate television watching of educatonal programs that do not contain violence is not harmful to children and can even be beneficial.

What Do You Think?

1. What guidelines might you use to determine whether a television program is appropriate for a young child?

2. What advice would you give to parents regarding their preschool-age child's television habits?

---

and **discipline** that occur across situations to form child-rearing climates. In a classic series of studies, Diana Baumrind (1971) studied 103 preschoolers and their families through interviews, home observations, and other measures. She identified several parenting styles and the typical behavior and functioning of children that accompanies each style (see Figure 8.1).

Authoritarian Parenting

Parents who use an **authoritarian parenting style** emphasize behavioral control and obedience over warmth. Children are expected to conform to parental standards without question. Violations are accompanied by forceful and often arbitrary punishment. Authoritarian parents might yell,

Parenting style is an important influence on development. Authoritarian parenting emphasizes rigid strictness over warmth. Uninvolved parenting can make children feel invisible. Extreme forms of uninvolved parenting consitute neglect.

threaten, or spank their children. Authoritarian parents tend to not accept children's involvement in decisions and do not grant much autonomy. Children are to accept their decisions without question, simply "because I say so." Parents with an authoritarian style are less supportive and warm, and more detached, even appearing cold.

Baumrind and others found that children raised by authoritarian parents tend to be withdrawn, often mistrustful, anxious, and show more behavioral problems as preschoolers and 10 years later, as adolescents (Baumrind, Larzelere, & Owens, 2010). Children reared in authoritarian homes tend to be disruptive in their interactions with peers and tend to react with hostility when they experience frustrating interactions with peers (Gagnon et al., 2013). Preschool boys raised by authoritarian parents are likely to show high rates of anger and defiance whereas girls tend to be more dependent, explore less, and be easily overwhelmed by challenging tasks.

Permissive Parenting

Permissive parents are warm and accepting, even indulgent. They emphasize self-expression and have few rules and expectations for their children. Parents with a **permissive parenting style** make few demands on children and see themselves as resources that children may choose to rely on or not. They often allow children to monitor their own behavior. A child might choose his or her own bedtime, for example. Autonomy is not granted gradually and in developmentally appropriate ways in permissive households. Instead, children are permitted to make their own decisions at any early age, often before they are able. For example, children may be allowed to play video games or watch television for as long as they want. Many children lack the self-regulation capacities to appropriately limit their activity. When rules are necessary, permissive parents may explain the reasons and consult children, but ultimately do not exert control, make demands on children's behavior, or enforce the rules.

Researchers have found that preschoolers raised by permissive parents tend to be more socioemotionally immature and show little self-control and self-regulatory capacity as compared with their peers (Piotrowski, Lapierre, & Linebarger, 2013). They often tend to be impulsive, rebellious, and bossy as well as show less task persistence, low levels of school achievement, and more behavior problems (Jewell, Krohn, Scott, Carlton, & Meinz, 2008).

Uninvolved Parenting

Parents with an **uninvolved parenting style** focus on their own needs rather than those of the child (Maccoby & Martin, 1983). They provide little support or warmth, often not noticing the child's need for affection, and also exert little control over the child, not recognizing the child's need for direction. Parents who are under stress, emotionally detached, or who are depressed often lack time or energy to devote to their children, putting them at risk for an uninvolved parenting style (Maccoby & Martin, 1983). At the extreme, uninvolved parenting is neglectful and a form of child maltreatment.

As you might imagine, uninvolved parenting—parenting with little warmth or limits—has negative consequences for all forms of children's development, including cognitive, emotional, and social development. Young children reared in neglecting homes show less knowledge about emotions than do children raised with other parenting styles (Sullivan, Carmody, & Lewis, 2010).

Authoritative Parenting

The most positive developmental outcomes are associated with the **authoritative parenting style**. Authoritative parents are warm and sensitive to children's needs but also are firm in their expectations that children conform to appropriate standards of behavior. They are receptive to the child's involvement in discussions about standards and exert firm, reasonable control but also grant children developmentally appropriate levels of autonomy permitting decision making that is appropriate to children's abilities (Hart, Newell, & Olson, 2002). Authoritative parents explain and encourage discussion about the rules so that children understand their purpose and what is expected of them. When a rule is violated, authoritative parents explain what the child did wrong and impose limited, developmentally appropriate punishments that are closely connected to the misdeed. Authoritative parents value and foster children's individuality. They encourage their children to have their own interests, opinions, and decisions, but, ultimately, they control the child's behavior.

Authoritative parenting is effective because it combines parental acceptance and involvement, limits and behavioral control, and autonomy granting. Longitudinal research shows that authoritative parenting reduces noncompliance and other negative behaviors on the part of children (Stice & Barrera, 1995). Preschoolers raised by parents with an authoritative parenting style tend to be curious, self-reliant, and assertive. Children of authoritative parents display confidence, cooperation, self-esteem, social skills, high academic achievement, and score higher on measures of executive functioning; these positive effects persist throughout childhood into adolescence (Baumrind et al., 2010; Fay-Stammbach, Hawes, & Meredith, 2014; Milevsky, Schlechter, Netter, & Keehn, 2007). Table 8.1 summarizes the four parenting styles.

DISCIPLINE

Young children's curiosity and desire to take on new tasks and master their world are crucial to healthy development but can also lead them into trouble. Young children have the cognitive ability to learn from their mistakes, and parents play an important role in helping children learn. Discipline refers to the methods a parent uses to teach and socialize children toward acceptable behavior. Learning theory can account for the effect of parents' discipline strategies on children's behavior. Specifically, the consequences of a child's behavior, whether it is reinforced or punished, influence the child's future behavior.

Children learn best when they are reinforced for good behavior. Recall from learning theory that the child must view the reinforcement as rewarding in order for it to be effective in encouraging his or her behavior. Reinforcement can be tangible, such as money or candy, or intangible, such as attention or a smile. Effective reinforcement is administered

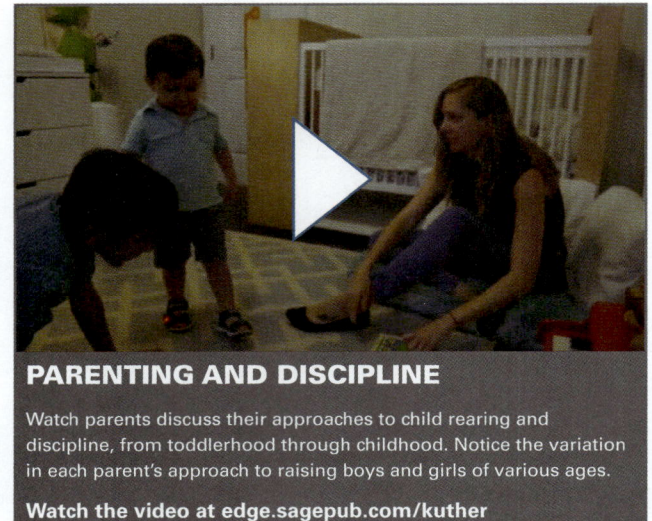

PARENTING AND DISCIPLINE

Watch parents discuss their approaches to child rearing and discipline, from toddlerhood through childhood. Notice the variation in each parent's approach to raising boys and girls of various ages.

Watch the video at edge.sagepub.com/kuther

consistently when the desired behavior occurs. Eventually the reinforcement becomes internalized by the child, and the behavior itself becomes reinforcing. The child comes to associate the behavior with pleasurable feelings, and the behavior itself eventually produces a positive feeling: sense of accomplishment.

Four-year-old Jayden throws blocks at his brother, Harlan. When Harlan cries out to their mother, Sheila, she yells at Jayden and tells him to sit down at the kitchen table while she cooks. Each day, Jayden throws blocks or hits Harlan and then is told to sit at the kitchen table. Sometimes he plays nicely with his brother, but soon he returns to his usual behavior of throwing blocks. Sheila becomes frustrated because Jayden continues to torment his brother despite being punished for his misbehavior each day. What is happening here? Frequently parents ignore good behavior but scold bad behavior, drawing attention to it and inadvertently reinforcing it. Jayden's good behavior goes unnoticed. Sheila does not reinforce his good behavior by complimenting his attempts to play nicely with Harlan. But Jayden gets attention when he misbehaves not only by having Sheila notice his behavior but also by being seated in the kitchen close to her. Sheila believes she is punishing his misbehavior, but requiring him to sit at the table while she cooks may be making Jayden more likely to misbehave.

What can parents do about their children's undesirable behavior? Is it ever permissible to use punishment? Certainly,

TABLE 8.1 Parenting Styles

PARENTING STYLE	WARMTH	CONTROL
Authoritative	High	Firm, consistent, coupled with discussion
Authoritarian	Low	High, emphasizing control and punishment without discussion or explanation
Permissive	High	Low
Uninvolved	Low	Low

Time out removes the child from overstimulating situations and stops inappropriate behaviors without humiliating him or her. Time out is effective when it is accompanied by explanation and a warm parent-child relationship.

in small doses and specific contexts. Running into the street or touching a hot stove, for example, are behaviors that are dangerous to children or to others. These behaviors must be stopped immediately to prevent injury. To be effective, punishment should occur immediately after the dangerous behavior, be applied consistently, and be clearly connected to the behavior. The purpose of such punishment is to keep the child from engaging in the dangerous behavior, to make him or her comply, but not to feel guilt. **Time out**, removing a child from the situation for a short period of time, is often effective in reducing inappropriate behavior (Morawska & Sanders, 2011). Effective punishment, such as time out, does not humiliate the child. It is administered calmly, privately, within the context of a warm parent–child relationship, and is accompanied by an explanation so that the child understands the reason for the punishment (AAP Committee on Psychosocial Aspects of Child and Family Health, 1998; Baumrind, 1996).

Physical Punishment

One form of punishment—physical punishment—can be particularly damaging to children. The use of physical

or corporal punishment, often referred to as spanking, is hotly contested around the world despite considerable research demonstrating its harm to children's development. Spanking is against the law in Sweden, yet parents in most countries of Asia, Africa, the Middle East, and both North and South America report that spanking is acceptable, appropriate, and sometimes necessary (Hicks-Pass, 2009; Oveisi et al., 2010). In the United States, the majority of adults report that they were spanked as children without harm. Why the controversy on spanking if it occurs in most cultures?

Harsh punishment is a common characteristic of the authoritarian parenting style that, as we have seen, is associated with behavioral and developmental problems in children. Children who are punished harshly show higher rates of emotional and social problems than other children (Mulvaney & Mebert, 2007). They may have difficulty accurately interpreting others' actions and words and are more likely to attribute hostile intentions and assume that others are "out to get them" (Weiss, Dodge, Bates, & Pettit, 1992). Corporal punishment is damaging to the parent–child relationship. When parents lose their self-control and yell, scream, or hit the child, the child may feel helpless, become fearful of the parent, avoid him or her, and become passive (Grusec & Goodnow, 1994). Moreover, physical punishment can foster the very behavior that parents seek to stop. Parents often punish children for aggressive behavior, yet physical punishment models the use of aggression as an effective way of resolving conflict and other problems, teaching children that might makes right (Hicks-Pass, 2009). Physical punishment is associated with behavior problems at age 3 and continued behavior problems at age 5 (Choe, Olson, & Sameroff, 2013). Sometimes parents report that spanking and physical punishment within the context of a warm parenting relationship reduce the negative effects of physical punishment. However, a study that followed children from ages 1 to 5 found that beginning as early as age 1, maternal spanking was predictive of child behavior problems, and maternal warmth did not counteract the negative consequences of the use of spanking (Lee, Altschul, & Gershoff, 2013).

Physical punishment tends to increase compliance only temporarily and is associated with anxiety, depression, rule breaking, and destructive behaviors throughout childhood and into adolescence (Bender et al., 2007; Coley, Kull, & Carrano, 2014). For example, in one study of nearly 5,000 teenagers and adults of Ontario, Canada, those who recalled being spanked or slapped sometimes or often as children were more likely to report having problems with anxiety, alcohol use, and antisocial behavior than those who reported never being spanked (MacMillan et al., 1999). Corporal punishment tends to become less effective at controlling children's behavior with repeated use and as children grow older (AAP Committee on Psychosocial Aspects of Child and Family Health, 1998). For example, the use of spanking is impractical with teenagers.

Inductive Disciplinary Methods

The strategies parents use to control children's behavior vary with the parent and child's personalities, the age of the child, the parent–child relationship, and cultural customs and expectations (Grusec & Goodnow, 1994). Parents' perceptions of their own efficacy in carrying out strategies influence which strategies they choose. Parents' strategies also vary with the situation. For example, swift enforcement of parental control may be appropriate in situations when children are in danger whereas discipline that relies on communication may be used to teach sharing (Grusec & Goodnow, 1994).

Inductive discipline methods which use reasoning, are effective alternatives to spanking in changing a child's behavior (AAP Committee on Psychosocial Aspects of Child and Family Health, 1998). Examples of inductive methods include helping children find and use words to express their feelings. Another inductive method is to provide children with choices (e.g., peas or carrots), permitting them to feel some control over the situation and be empowered. Parents who use inductive techniques model effective conflict resolution and help children to become aware of the consequences of their actions. Inductive methods are very effective in helping children to internalize rules and standards (Choe et al., 2013). One study of 54 African American kindergarten-aged children from an inner city found that those whose mothers used inductive reasoning were more likely to see that hurting other people is not just a question of breaking rules, but is wrong, as compared with children whose mothers reported taking away privileges (Jagers, Bingham, & Hans, 1996). The use of inductive discipline is part of the authoritative parent's repertoire.

The AAP recommends that parents positively reinforce good behavior and, when necessary, discourage inappropriate behavior with the use of timeout, removal of privileges, and verbal reprimands aimed at the behavior rather than the child (AAP Committee on Psychosocial Aspects of Child and Family Health, 1998). Researchers advise that punishment be used sparingly, as it often directs children's attention to themselves and their own feelings rather than to how their behavior affects others, increasing children's emphasis on themselves rather than empathetic and prosocial motives (McCord, 1996). Overall, developmental professionals agree that discipline that relies on a warm parent–child relationship, clear expectations, communication, and limit-setting is most effective in modifying children's behavior.

CULTURE, CONTEXT, AND PARENTING

One concern that researchers have regarding discussions of parenting style and discipline is that there is not just one effective way to parent. Instead, there are many cultural variations in parenting—the effectiveness of parenting style and disciplinary techniques may differ by cultural context (Cauce, 2008).

Expectations for behavior as well as methods of discipline vary with culture. North American parents permit and encourage children to express emotions, including anger, while Japanese parents encourage children to refrain from displaying strong emotions. For example, in one experiment, American preschoolers exposed to situations designed to elect stress and anger demonstrated more aggressive behaviors than did Japanese children (Zahn-Waxler, Friedman, Cole, Mizuta, & Hiruma, 1996). In comparison with North American mothers, Japanese mothers are more likely to use reasoning, empathy, and disapproval to discipline their children. Such techniques are effective for Japanese mothers because of the strong mother–child relationship and emphasis on collectivist values in Japan that emphasize the importance of relationships (Rothbaum, Pott, Azuma, Miyake, & Weisz, 2000).

Chinese parents tend to describe their parenting as more controlling without emphasizing individuality and choice (Chao, 2001). They are more directive and view exerting control as a way of teaching children self-control and encouraging high achievement (Huntsinger, Jose, & Larson, 1998). Yet most parents couple the emphasis on control with warmth (Xu et al., 2005). Such authoritative parenting is linked with cognitive and social competence. Similar to findings with American samples, authoritarian parenting is associated with depression,

JGI/Jamie Grill/Blend/Newscom

No-nonsense parenting is characterized by vigilant, strict control as well as warmth. African American children often report viewing this style as indicative of parental concern about their welfare and, unlike authoritarian parenting, this style is associated with positive outcomes—especially within challenging community contexts.

social difficulties, and poor academic achievement in Chinese children (Cheah, Leung, Tahseen, & Schultz, 2009).

In addition to the four parenting styles described earlier, researchers have identified a **no-nonsense parenting** style common in African American families that emphasizes high, even strict, parental control as well as warmth and affection (Tamis-LeMonda, Briggs, McClowry, & Snow, 2009). No-nonsense parenting is common in African American families and has been observed in Mexican American families raising children in challenging neighborhoods (White & Zeiders, 2013). In this style, mothers often stress obedience and view strict control as important in helping children develop self-control and attentiveness. African American parents who use the more controlling strategies common to no-nonsense parenting raise children who are more cognitively mature and socially competent. This is particularly true for children reared in low-income homes and communities where vigilant, strict parenting enhances children's safety (Weis & Toolis, 2010). Whereas physical discipline is associated with behavioral problems in European American children, no-nonsense parenting appears to protect some African American children from conduct problems in adolescence (Lansford, Deater-Deckard, Dodge, Bates, & Pettit, 2004). The warmth entailed in no-nonsense parenting buffers some of the negative consequences of strictness (McLoyd & Smith, 2002; Stacks, Oshio, Gerard, & Roe, 2009).

The child's perception of parenting style and intention is important in determining its effect. Children evaluate parental behavior in light of their culture and the emotional tone of the relationship. Children reared in homes with no-nonsense parents often see this parenting style as indicative of concern about their well-being (Brody & Flor, 1998).

In the United States, it is often difficult to disentangle the effects of culture and neighborhood context on parenting behaviors as African American and Latino families are disproportionately represented in disadvantaged neighborhoods. Does no-nonsense parenting embody cultural beliefs about parenting? Or is it a response to raising children in a disadvantaged environment (Murry, Brody, Simons, Cutrona, & Gibbons, 2008)? Parental perceptions of danger and their own distress influence how they parent (Cuellar, Jones, & Sterrett, 2013). Parenting behaviors must be considered within their cultural and environmental context, as parenting is not one size fits all (Sorkhabi, 2005).

CHILD MALTREATMENT

Some parenting behaviors, such as child maltreatment, are damaging to all children, regardless of culture. In 2013, there were nearly 700,000 confirmed cases of abuse or neglect in the United States (U.S. Department of Health and Human Services, 2013). Many more children experience maltreatment that is not reported. Child maltreatment resulted in over 1,500 fatalities, and nearly three quarters of all deaths were in children younger than 3 years. Over 80% of the perpetrators were parents (and nearly 90% of parent perpetrators

were biological parents), 6% relatives other than parents, and 4% were unmarried partners of parents (U.S. Department of Health and Human Services, 2015). Although these statistics are alarming, they underestimate the incidence of abuse. Many cases go unreported.

According to the Child Abuse Prevention and Treatment Act, *child abuse* is any intentional harm to a minor, an individual under 18 years of age, including actions that harm the child physically, emotionally, sexually and through neglect (U.S. Department of Health and Human Services, 2013). *Physical abuse* refers to any intentional physical injury to the child and can include striking, kicking, burning, or biting the child as well as any action that results in a physical impairment of the child; it results in pain and physical injury including cuts, burns, bruises, broken bones, and other injuries. Each year, about 18% of cases entail physical abuse. *Sexual abuse*, more common among older children, refers to inappropriate touching, comments, intercourse, and other forms of sexual activity and tends to constitute about 10% of cases. *Neglect* is defined in terms of deprivation of adequate food, clothing, shelter, or medical care; child neglect constitutes over three quarters of cases of child maltreatment (U.S. Department of Health and Human Services, 2013). The overlapping statistics reflect the fact that the various types of child maltreatment tend to concur; many children experience more than one form of abuse.

Effects of Child Maltreatment

The physical effects of maltreatment are immediate, ranging from bruises to broken bones to internal bleeding and more. Other physical effects are long lasting. Child abuse can impair brain development and functioning through physical damage, such as that caused by shaking an infant, which damages the brain (Twardosz & Lutzker, 2009). Physical harm and prolonged stress can alter the course of brain development, increasing the child's risk for post-traumatic stress disorder (PTSD), attention deficit/hyperactivity disorder, conduct disorder, and learning and memory difficulties (de Bellis, Hooper, Spratt, & Woolley, 2009).

The emotional effects of child maltreatment are especially daunting and long lasting. Infants and toddlers who are abused fail to develop secure attachments to their caregivers and instead develop anxious, insecure, or disorganized/disoriented attachments. Young children who are abused tend to have poor coping skills, low self-esteem, and difficulty regulating their emotions and impulses as well as show more negative affect, such as anger and frustration, and less positive affect than other children (Barth et al., 2007). They tend to have difficulty understanding their own and other people's emotions. Moreover, children who are abused are at risk for a range of psychological disorders, including anxiety, eating, dissociative, attention-deficit/hyperactivity disorder, PTSD, and depressive disorder (Cicchetti & Banny, 2014).

Child maltreatment, and its neurological and emotional consequences, also holds negative implications for cognitive development (Font & Berger, 2014). Preschool children who are abused score lower on measures of school readiness and problem solving. Children who are abused experience difficulty understanding and completing day-to-day schoolwork and demonstrate serious learning difficulties, often resulting in academic failure (Widom, 2014). Teachers report maltreated children as inattentive, uninvolved, passive, angry as well as lacking in creativity, initiative, persistence, and confidence.

The cognitive and emotional effects of child maltreatment contribute to the social difficulties that children who are abused face. Maltreated children have difficulty in making and maintaining friendships (Cicchetti & Banny, 2014). Children who are physically abused tend to be aggressive and active in their interactions with peers while neglected children are more likely to be passive and withdrawn. They may assume that other children are hostile and then protect themselves by being more aggressive and isolating themselves from other children (Bolger & Patterson, 2001). The quality of relationships with peers is closely associated with abuse such that the younger the child was when the abuse began and the longer it continued, the worse the relationships with peers (Bolger, Patterson, & Kupersmidt, 1998; Font & Berger, 2014). Children who are maltreated are at greater risk of being bullies or victims of bullies as they find it difficult to integrate peer groups and often remain isolated. Experiencing child abuse places children at risk for behavioral problems in adolescence, including delinquency, teen pregnancy, low academic achievement, drug use, and mental health problems (Cicchetti & Banny, 2014).

Risk Factors for Child Maltreatment

Risk factors for child abuse exist at all ecological levels: the child, parent, community, and society (McCoy & Keen, 2009). Certain child characteristics have been found to increase the risk or potential for maltreatment. Children with special needs, such as those with physical and mental disabilities, preterm birth status, or serious illness, require a great deal of care that can place them at risk of maltreatment (Bugental, 2009). Children who are temperamentally difficult, inattentive, overactive, or have other developmental problems are also at risk because they are especially taxing for parents (Crosse, Kaye, & Ratnofsky, 1993; Font & Berger, 2014).

Parents who engage in child maltreatment tend to have difficulty managing conflict and using effective disciplinary techniques, which influences their interactions with their children (Bugental, 2009). They tend to perceive their child as stubborn and noncompliant and tend to evaluate the child's misdeeds as worse than they are, leading them to use strict and physical methods of discipline (Casanueva et al., 2010). Parents who maltreat their children often lack knowledge about child development and have unrealistic expectations for their children. They often have low self-esteem, difficulty with impulse control, poor coping skills, and high levels of negative emotions (McCoy & Keen, 2009). Poor

social, problem solving, and communication skills are common among parents who maltreat their children. They often lack the ability to recognize, manage, and express their own feelings appropriately. Experiencing abuse in childhood may place a parent at risk of engaging in child maltreatment (Clarke, Stein, Sobota, Marisi, & Hanna, 1999), but this relation is not absolute. Parents who were abused as children do not necessarily repeat the cycle with their own children. It is estimated that about one third of abused children eventually victimize their own children (McCoy & Keen, 2009).

Low family income, unemployment, high levels of stress, substance use, few friends, less contact with extended family members, and overcrowded and inadequate housing contribute toward the risk that parents will engage in child maltreatment (Bishop & Leadbeater, 1999; Widom, 2014). Substance use is present in as much as three quarters of families in which children are abuse victims (Testa & Smith, 2009).

Several community factors place children at risk for abuse, such as inadequate housing, community violence, and poverty (Dodge & Coleman, 2009). Parents who abuse are more likely to be cut off from social support networks. The availability of social support within the community influences a child's likelihood of being abused; parents are less likely to engage in child maltreatment when their neighborhood has a low turnover of residents, a sense of community, and support among neighbors (McCoy & Keen, 2009). Neighborhoods with few community level support resources, such as parks, child care centers, preschool programs, recreation centers, and churches, increase the likelihood of child maltreatment (Coulton, Korbin, & Su, 1999).

At the societal level, several factors contribute toward the problem of child abuse. Legal definitions of violence and abuse and political or religious views that value independence, privacy, and noninterference in families may influence the prevalence of child abuse within a given society (Tzeng, Jackson, & Karlson, 1991). Social acceptance of violence—for example, as expressed in video games, music lyrics, and television and films—can send the message that violence is an acceptable method of managing conflict. Overall, there are many complex influences on child maltreatment. Risk factors at these various levels are represented in Figure 8.2.

Along with recognizing risk factors for parents, it is important to be aware of signs that abuse may be taking place. Table 8.2 (p. 210) provides a non-exhaustive list of signs of abuse. Not all maltreated children will show all of the signs listed. Although not all children who display one or more of the signs on this list experience maltreatment, each sign is significant enough to merit attention and treatment. All U.S. states and the District of Columbia identify **mandated reporters**, individuals who are legally obligated to report suspected child maltreatment to the appropriate agency, such as child protective services, a law enforcement agency, or a state's child abuse reporting hotline (Child Welfare Information Gateway, 2013). Individuals designated as mandatory reporters typically have frequent

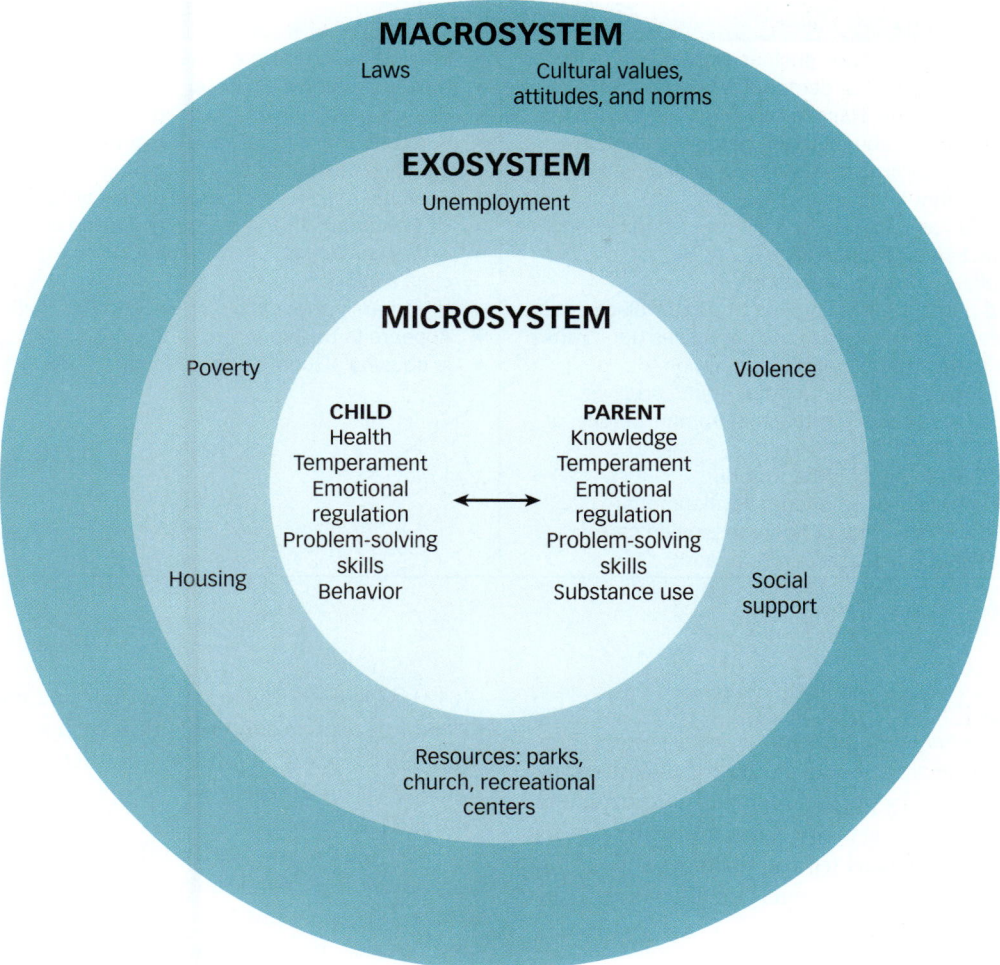

MACROSYSTEM
Laws   Cultural values,
              attitudes, and norms

EXOSYSTEM
Unemployment

MICROSYSTEM

Poverty   Violence

CHILD   **PARENT**
Health   Knowledge
Temperament   Temperament
Emotional   Emotional
regulation   regulation
Problem-solving   Problem-solving
skills   skills
Housing   Behavior   Substance use   Social
                                         support

Resources: parks,
church, recreational
centers

contact with children, such as teachers, principals, and other school personnel; child care providers; physicians, nurses, and other health care workers; counselors, therapists, and other mental health professionals; and law enforcement officers. Of course, anyone can, and is encouraged to, report suspected maltreatment of a child.

As shown in Table 8.3 (p. 212), although there are risk factors that increase a child's chances of being abused or neglected, there are also protective factors that are associated with a reduced likelihood of maltreatment—and that can be fostered by parents, teachers, pediatricians, and social workers.

The parent–child relationship is a critical context for children's development. Parents' attitudes about child-rearing, ability to show affection, and beliefs about discipline shape children's emotional development and behavior. Parenting techniques and socialization goals vary with culture and effective parenting may take different forms across contexts. However, some behaviors, such as child maltreatment, are harmful regardless of culture and context. The community in which a child lives can also play an important role in influencing development (see Lives in Context, p. 211).

Thinking in Context 8.2

1. What factors might influence whether a parent adopts an authoritative style of parenting? How might contextual factors, including family, work, community, culture, and society, along with prior experience, influence parenting style?

2. A common response to discussions of physical punishment is, "I was spanked and I turned out all right." How might you respond to this comment? Refer to what is known about the effects of physical punishment as well as the role of context and individual differences in accounting for development.

3. Child abuse is a problem with a complex set of influences at multiple bioecological levels. The most effective prevention and intervention programs target risk and protective factors in the child, parent, and community. Referring to the bioecological model, discuss factors at each bioecological level that might be incorporated into prevention and intervention programs to prevent child abuse and promote positive outcomes.

TABLE 8.2 Signs of Child Abuse and Neglect

THE CHILD	THE PARENT
• Exhibits changes in behavior, such as extremes in behavior, such as overly compliant or demanding behavior, extreme passivity, or aggression. Has not received help for physical or medical problems brought to the parents' attention. • Has difficulty concentrating or learning problems that appear to be without cause. • Is very watchful, as if waiting for something bad to happen. • Frequently lacks adult supervision. • Overly compliant, passive, or withdrawn. • Unexplained burns, bruises, broken bones, or black eyes. • Is absent often, especially with fading bruises upon return. • Is reluctant to be around a particular person • Reports injury by a parent or another adult caregiver. • Lacks needed medical or dental care, immunizations, or glasses. • Lacks sufficient clothing for the weather. • Is delayed in physical or emotional development. • States that there is no one at home to provide care. • Shrinks at the approach of a parent or adult.	• Shows little concern for the child. • Denies problems at home. • Blames problems on the child. • Suggests that the caregiver use harsh physical discipline if the child misbehaves. • Sees the child as bad or worthless, or berates the child. • Has demands that are too high for the child to achieve. • Offers conflicting, unconvincing, or no explanation for the child's injury. • Uses harsh physical discipline with the child. • Appears to be indifferent to the child. • Is abusing alcohol or other drugs.

SOURCE: Child Welfare Information Gateway (2013).

GENDER ROLE DEVELOPMENT

Three year-old Ashley called out, "I want the pink dress, just like a princess." Zachary pushed his truck and explained, "This monster truck is going to drive over the battlefield." Ask any adult, and they will likely tell you that boys and girls are very different. Are they? What accounts for differences, if they exist, between boys and girls?

GENDER DIFFERENCES

Developmental scientists have long looked for gender differences—psychological or behavioral differences between boys and girls. Despite common lay views, boys and girls are more alike than different. Reviews of thousands of research studies demonstrate few differences between boys and girls (Leaper, 2013; Martin & Ruble, 2010). The largest difference is in aggression. Among preschool-age children and up, boys tend to exhibit more physical and verbal aggression than girls, and girls show more **relational aggression**—excluding someone from social activities, withdrawing friendship, spreading rumors or humiliating the person—than do boys (Card, Stucky, Sawalani, & Little, 2008; Ostrov & Godleski, 2010). Girls show more empathy, compliance, and cooperation with adults than boys. Although intelligence tests show no differences between boys and girls, girls tend to do better at verbal and mathematical computation tasks as well as those requiring fine motor skills and boys tend to do better at spatial tasks (Ardila, Rosselli, Matute, & Inozemtseva, 2011; Miller & Halpern, 2014). These differences appear as early as they can be tested— toddlerhood and early childhood (Leaper,

2013). However, it is important to remember that there is a great deal of variability within each sex—more so than between the sexes. In other words, there is a greater number and variety of differences among boys than between boys and girls, for example.

Despite the few gender differences that exist in psychological and behavioral functioning, gender stereotypes, preconceived generalizations about the characteristics of males and females, pervade. These stereotypes are seen in most cultures and occur in children as early as 2 years of age and increase during the preschool years (Martin & Ruble, 2010). For example, young children attribute characteristics such as "strong" to boys and "helpless" to girls.

Children's perceptions and evaluations of gender are consistent with the **gender roles** that pervade society. Gender roles are the activities, attitudes, skills, and characteristics that are considered appropriate for males or females. Gender roles appear in all societies, although the specific content of gender roles may vary. Most cultures expect women to care for children and the home and men to provide for the family and protect the home. Because of these different activities, women are seen as caring and nurturing while men are seen as strong, aggressive, and competitive. As women have entered the workforce and men have taken a more active role in the home, gender roles have become more flexible in Western societies. Despite these changes, gender stereotypes persist. Children acquire gender roles early in life, a process called **gender typing**, although children vary in the degree of gender typing they display. Children's gender roles influence how they see themselves and others. For example, children tend to describe their own sex in positive terms and the other sex in more negative terms. As early as age 2, and consistently

LIVES IN CONTEXT

Effects of Exposure to Community Violence

Karl Merton Ferron/TNS/Newscom

Exposure to community violence poses risks not only to children's safety but to their emotional health, cognitive and social development, and well-being.

The neighborhoods and communities where children reside are important contextual factors that influence their development. About 38% of all children and adolescents witness violence within their communities (Kennedy & Ceballo, 2014), and the number is much higher in some inner-city neighborhoods. One study of inner-city mothers of young children enrolled in Head Start revealed that nearly three quarters reported witnessing drug transactions and violence in their neighborhood, such as people being physically assaulted, threatened with a weapon, or robbed. In addition, over two thirds of the women reported that they had been personally physically threatened or assaulted, been robbed on the street, or had their homes broken into (Farver, Xu, Eppe, Fernandez, & Schwartz, 2005).

Community violence is particularly damaging to development because it is pervasive, infiltrating all ecological levels—school, playground, neighborhood, and home. Mothers living in communities where violence is high report teaching their children to watch television lying prone and to sleep beneath window sills or in bathtubs for safety (Osofsky, 1995). The chronic and random nature of community violence presents a constant threat to children and parents' sense of safety. In such environments, children learn that the world is a dangerous and unpredictable place and that parents are unable to offer protection (Farver et al., 2005). Feeling unsafe may affect children's natural curiosity and their desire to learn by exploring the world (Balter & Tamis-LeMonda, 2006).

Children exposed to chronic community violence display anxiety and symptoms of PTSD, commonly seen in individuals exposed to the extreme trauma of war and natural disasters,

including exaggerated startle responses, difficulty eating and sleeping, and academic and cognitive problems (Fowler, Tompsett, Braciszewski, Jacques-Tiura, & Baltes, 2009; Kennedy & Ceballo, 2014). The periodic and unpredictable experience of intense emotions may interfere with children's ability to identify and regulate their emotions and can disrupt the development of empathy and prosocial responses. Children who are exposed to community violence tend to be less socially aware, less skilled, and display more aggressive and disruptive behavior than other children (McMahon et al., 2013).

Community violence targets not only children but also their parents. Parents who are exposed to community violence may feel alienated from the community with few sources of social support and may minimize associations and interactions in order to protect themselves (Shahinfar, Fox, & Leavitt, 2000). The parental distress, frustration, and sense of helplessness that accompany community violence compromise parenting (Vincent, 2009). When dealing with their own grief, fear, anxiety, and depression, parents may be less available for physical and emotional caregiving, which in turn predicts poor child adjustment (Farver et al., 2005).

Community violence is unquestionably detrimental to developmental outcomes. However, some children display more resilience to its negative effects than others. Three factors appear to protect children from the most negative effects of exposure to community violence: (1) having a supportive person in the environment; (2) having a protected place in the neighborhood that provides a safe haven from violence exposure; and (3) having personal resources such as adaptable temperament, intelligence, or coping capacities (Jain & Cohen, 2013). Unfortunately, the fear that accompanies community violence influences all members of the community, reducing supports and safe havens. Effective interventions to combat the effects of community violence include after-school community centers that allow children to interact with each other and caring adults in a safe context that permits them to develop skills in coping, conflict resolution, and emotional regulation.

What Do You Think?

1. Consider the problem of community violence from a bioecological perspective. Identify macrosystem and exosystem factors that might influence the prevalence of community violence.

2. How might community violence influence individuals through the mesosystem and microsystem?

3. Identify microsystem, mesosystem, and exosystem factors that might help children and families cope with community violence.

---

from age 3, young children will tend to choose same-sex playmates as well as toys and activities associated with their sex (Jadva, Hines, & Golombok, 2010). These predictable patterns of gender role development can be explained in a variety of ways.

THEORETICAL PERSPECTIVES ON GENDER ROLE DEVELOPMENT

How do we explain the acquisition of gender roles? Several theoretical perspectives offer explanations of gender typing.

TABLE 8.3 Risk and Protective Factors for Child Abuse and Neglect

	RISK FACTORS	PROTECTIVE FACTORS
Child	• Premature birth • Birth anomalies • Low birth weight • Temperament: Difficult or slow to warm up • Physical/cognitive/emotional disability • Chronic or serious illness • Childhood trauma • Young age • Aggression • Behavior problems • Attention deficits	• Good health • Above-average intelligence • Hobbies or interests • Easy temperament • Positive disposition • Active coping style • Positive self-esteem • Good social skills • History of adequate development • Balance between help seeking and autonomy
Parent	• Feeling a lack of control • Poor impulse control • Depression • Anxiety • Low tolerance for frustration • Feelings of insecurity • Lack of trust • Insecure attachment with own parents • Childhood history of abuse • Domestic violence • High number of children in household • Lack of social support • Psychopathology • Substance abuse • High-conflict divorce • High stress level • Poor parent–child interaction • Negative attitudes about child • Lack of knowledge about child development • Inaccurate expectations	• Secure attachment with children • Reconciliation with their own childhood history of abuse • Household rules and monitoring of the child • Extended family support • Stable relationship with parents • Family expectations of pro-social behavior • High parental education
Community	• Low socioeconomic status • Lack of access to medical care, health insurance, adequate child care, and social services unemployment • Homelessness • Poor schools • Environmental toxins • Community violence	• Middle to high socioeconomic status • Access to health care and social services • Consistent parental employment • Adequate housing • Family participation in a religious faith • Good schools • Supportive adults outside the family who serve as role models or mentors

Some lean more toward nature-oriented or biological explanations. Others use cognitive explanations and still others turn to contextual explanations. A sufficient explanation of gender development integrates aspects of each theory.

Biological Explanations

Because most cultures have similar gender roles, sex differences may be a function of biology (Whiting & Edwards, 1988). Biological explanations point to the role of evolution and look to differences in biological structures, especially the brain, as well as hormones as contributors to sex differences in psychological and behavioral functioning.

From an evolutionary perspective, males adapted to become more aggressive and competitive because these traits were advantageous in securing a mate and thereby passing along their genetic inheritance (Côté, 2009). Females became more nurturing as it was adaptive to care for the young to ensure that their genes survived to be passed along to the next generation. In support of this evolutionary perspective, most mammalian species demonstrate a preference for same-sex playmates, males are more active and aggressive, and females are more nurturing (Beatty, 1992; de Waal, 1993), suggesting that such gender differences in behavior are adaptive across species, including our own.

Gender differences begin at conception with the union of sex chromosomes, XX or XY. Genetic information on the Y chromosome leads to the formation of testes and then the production of testosterone with the sex difference in the amount of testosterone greatest between about 8 and 24 weeks of gestation and then tapering off before birth (Hines, 2011). In animals, testosterone produced prenatally influences neural survival and neural connectivity, leading to subtle sex differences in brain structure and function (Nugent & McCarthy, 2011).

Boys' and girls' behavior may also be explained by hormonal differences. Animal and human studies have demonstrated that exposure to testosterone promotes male-typical behavior development. When females are exposed to male sex hormones prenatally they show more active play and fewer caregiving activities in early childhood, as compared with their female peers (Auyeung et al., 2009). Testosterone is linked with aggression. Higher levels of testosterone, prenatally and after birth, can account for boys' tendency to be more aggressive than girls. Hormonally influenced differences in behavioral styles then influence play styles, and children choose to play with children who have similar styles, resulting in a preference for same-sex playmates (Berenbaum, Blakemore, & Beltz, 2011). In this way, biological factors influence the behaviors that are associated with gender roles. Other explanations for gender role development rely on understanding children's thinking, as described in the next section.

Cognitive-Developmental Explanations

From the cognitive-developmental perspective, children's understanding of gender is constructed in the same manner as their understanding of the world, by interacting with the world and thinking about their experiences. Infants as young as 3 to 4 months of age distinguish between female and male faces, as shown by habituation and preferential looking studies (Quinn, Yahr, Kuhn, Slater, & Pascalis, 2002). By 10 months of age, infants are able to form stereotypic associations between faces of women and men and gender-typed objects (scarf, hammer), suggesting that they have the capacity to form primitive stereotypes (Levy & Haaf, 1994). Most children develop the ability to label gender groups and to use gender labels in their speech between 18 and 24 months (Martin & Ruble, 2010).

Gender identity, awareness of whether one is a boy or a girl, occurs at about age 2 (Bussey, 2013). Once children label themselves as male or female, they classify the world around them, as well as their own behaviors, according to those labels (e.g., like me, not like me; Kohlberg, 1966). In this way, children construct their own understandings of what it means to be a boy or a girl and thereby begin to acquire gender roles (Levy & Carter, 1989). By 2 to 2.5 years of age, once children have established gender identity, children show more interest in gender-appropriate toys (e.g., dolls for girls and cars for boys), and they show a preference for playing with children of their own sex (Zosuls et al., 2009).

By about age 3, children acquire **gender stability**, the understanding that gender does not change over time. However, gender is not yet understood as a biological construct, but instead, conceptions of gender are based on external traits and behaviors. Therefore, children think it is possible for gender to change with a change in hairstyle or dress. After acquiring gender stability, children between the ages of 3 and 5 show an increase in stereotype knowledge, evaluate their own gender more positively, and tend to show more rigidly sex-typed behaviors (Halim, Ruble, Tamis-LeMonda, & Shrout, 2013). The more positively children view their own gender and the more they understood that gender categories remain stable over time, the more likely girls are to insist on wearing dresses and boys to refuse to wear anything with the hint of femininity (Halim et al., 2014).

Only toward the end of the preschool years, when children come to understand Piagetian conservation tasks, do children come to realize that a boy will always be a boy, even if he grows long hair and wears a skirt, and a girl will remain a girl no matter what she wears or activities she chooses. **Gender constancy** refers to the child's understanding that gender does not change, that he or she will always be the same regardless of appearance, activities, or attitudes (Kohlberg, 1966). Gender constancy may further gender typing as children become more aware of and pay more attention to gender norms (Arthur, Bigler, & Ruble, 2009). For example, preschool-age boys who have achieved gender constancy or are close to it tend to focus on male characters, as well as watch more sports programs on television than preschool-age boys who have not achieved gender constancy (Luecke-Aleksa, Anderson, Collins, & Schmitt, 1995). Awareness that a person's sex is a biological characteristic occurs close to eight years of age (Ruble et al., 2007).

Gender schema theory is another cognitive explanation of gender role development, which emphasizes information processing and environmental influences (Martin, Ruble, & Szkrybalo, 2002). Similar to Piaget's concept of schemes, a gender schema is a concept or a mental structure that organizes gender-related information. Once children can label their sex, they begin to form a gender schema, their understanding of what it means to be a male or female. A child's gender schema becomes an organizing principle and children notice more and more differences between males and females, such as preferred clothes, toys, activities, and more. Children also notice that their culture classifies males and females as different and encompassing different roles. Children then use their gender schemas as guides for their behavior and attitudes, and gender typing occurs. For example, when given gender-neutral toys, children first try to figure out whether they were boys' or girls' toys and then decide whether they would play with them (Martin, Eisenbud, & Rose, 1995). When told that an attractive toy is for the opposite sex, children will stop playing with it and expect same-sex peers to stop as well (Miller, Trautner, & Ruble, 2006). Young children play with peers who engage in similar levels of gender-typed activities (such as playing dress up or with tools) and, over time, engage in even more similar levels of gender-typed activities, contributing to sex segregation in children's play groups (Martin et al., 2013).

GENDER SCHEMAS & PLAY PREFERENCES

How does gender influence children's preferences? Consider 5-year-old Chace and 7-year-old Abby. Which play partners do they choose?

Watch the video at edge.sagepub.com/kuther

Gender schemas are such an important organizing principle that they can influence children's memory. For example, preschool children tend to notice and recall information that is consistent with their gender schemas (Liben, Bigler, & Hilliard, 2013). Children who see others behaving in gender inconsistent ways, such as a boy baking cookies or a girl playing with toy trucks, often will misrecall the event, distorting it in ways that are gender consistent, or they may not even recall gender inconsistent information (Signorella & Liben, 1984). It is not until around age 8 that children notice and recall information that contradicts their gender schemas. Yet even elementary school children have been shown to misrecall gender-inconsistent story information (Frawley, 2008). Clearly, children's knowledge and beliefs about gender and gender roles influence how their own gender role and behavior. However, the world around the child also holds implications for gender role development. Terms that pertain to gender role development are summarized in Table 8.4.

Contextual Explanations

A contextual approach toward understanding gender development emphasizes social learning and the influence of the sociocultural context in which children are raised. Gender typing occurs through socialization, through a child's interpretation of the world around him or her, including parents, peers, teachers, and culture. Social learning theory contributes the importance of models in acquiring gender typical behavior (Bandura & Bussey, 2004). Children observe models, typically the same-sex parent but also peers, other adults, and even characters in stories and television programs. They use models as guides to their own behavior, resulting in gender-typed behavior. Feedback from others serves as reinforcement. Sometimes parents or other adults will directly teach a child about gender-appropriate behavior or provide positive reinforcement for behaving in sex-consistent ways: boys get approval for building bridges and running fast whereas girls get approval for preparing a make-believe meal or keeping a pretty dress neat.

Parents. Gender socialization begins in infancy. Boys and girls have different social experiences from birth (Martin & Ruble, 2010). Parents perceive sons and daughters differently and have different expectations for them. For example, parents often describe competition, achievement, and activity as important for sons and closely supervised activities, warmth, and politeness as important for daughters (Turner & Gervai, 1995). Many parents encourage their children to play with gender appropriate toys. Boys tend to receive toys that emphasize action and competition, such as cars, trains, and sports equipment, and girls tend to receive toys that focus on cooperation, nurturance, and physical attractiveness, such as baby dolls, toy ovens, and play makeup (Hanish et al., 2013). In one study, 3- and 5-year-old children were asked to identify "girl toys" and "boy toys" and then asked to predict parents' reactions to their preferences about gender-specific toys and behaviors (Freeman, 2007). Children predicted that parents would approve their playing with gender-stereotyped toys and disapprove of choices to play with cross-gender toys.

Gender consistent behavior is socially regulated through approval. Parents tend to encourage boys' independent play, demands for attention, and even attempts to take toys from other children whereas parents tend to direct girls' play, provide assistance, refer to emotions, and encourage girls to participate in household tasks (Basow, 2008; Bussey, 2013). Boys tend to be reinforced for independent behavior, and girls are reinforced for behavior emphasizing closeness and dependency. Mothers even differ in how they discuss emotions with girls and boys. Mothers label emotions for girls, teaching them to identify others' feelings, and boys tend to receive explanations about emotions, emphasizing causes and consequences in order to help them understand the importance of controlling how emotions are expressed

TABLE 8.4 Gender Role Development: Terms

TERM	DEFINITION
Gender differences	Psychological or behavioral differences between males and females
Gender constancy	The understanding that gender remains the same throughout life, despite superficial changes in appearance or attitude
Gender identity	A person's awareness of being a male or female
Gender role	The behaviors and attitudes deemed appropriate for a given gender
Gender schema	A mental structure that organizes gender-related information.
Gender stability	The understanding that gender generally does not change over time; however, superficial changes in appearance might bring a change in gender
Gender typing	The process of acquiring gender roles

(Bussey, 2013). Expectations about gender-related behavior become internalized as children make gains in self-regulation. Reinforcement becomes internalized such that children feel good about themselves when their behavior is in accord with their internal standards and have negative feelings when their behavior is not. In early childhood, ages 3 to 4, children begin to self-regulate their gender-related behaviors (Bussey & Bandura, 1992).

Boys tend to be more strongly gender socialized than girls. Parents tend to give girls more freedom in choice of clothes, activities, and playmates (Miedzian, 1991). Parents, especially fathers, tend to show more discomfort with sex-atypical behavior in boys (e.g., playing with dolls) than girls (e.g., playing with trucks; Basow, 2008; Lytton & Romney, 1991). Fathers play an important role in influencing gender typing. A study of preschool children in England and Hungary revealed that children whose fathers did more housework and child care tended to demonstrate less awareness of gender stereotypes and less gender-typed play (Turner & Gervai, 1995).

Peers. The peer group also serves as a powerful influence on gender typing in young children. As early as age 3, peers

iStock/Essentials

When fathers participate in household chores children show less gender stereotyped beliefs about the division of labor in the home.

reinforce gender-typed behavior, with praise, imitation, or participation. They criticize cross-gender activities and show more disapproval of boys who engage in gender inappropriate behavior than girls who are tomboys (Hanish et al., 2013; Ruble, Martin, & Berenbaum, 2006). Girls and boys show different play styles. Boys use more commands, threats, and force; girls use more gentle tactics, such as persuasion, acceptance, and verbal requests, which are effective with other girls but ignored by boys (Leaper, Tenenbaum, & Shaffer, 1999; Leaper, 1994). Girls, therefore, may find interacting with boys unpleasant as boys pay little attention to their attempts at interaction and are generally nonresponsive. These differences in play styles influence young children's choices of play partners and contribute to sex segregation (Martin, Fabes, Hanish, Leonard, & Dinella, 2011). Peer and parental attitudes tend to be similar and reinforce each other as both are part of a larger sociocultural system of socialization agents (Bandura & Bussey, 2004; Bussey & Bandura, 1992).

Media. Children's television and G-rated movies tend to depict the world as gender stereotyped, and these media depictions can promote gender-typed behavior in children. Typical children's media displays more male than female characters, male characters in action roles such as in the military, and female characters as more likely to have domestic roles and be in romantic relationships (England, Descartes, & Collier-Meek, 2011; Smith, Pieper, Granados, & Choueiti, 2010). Television commercials advertising toys tend to illustrate only one gender or other, depending on the toy (Kahlenberg & Hein, 2010). Several Canadian towns that gained access to television for the first time demonstrated television's influence on gender typing. Children tended to have unstereotyped attitudes prior to gaining access to television and two years later demonstrate marked increases in stereotyped attitudes (Kimball, 1986).

Children's books are another influence on gender typing. Overall, there are more male characters than female characters. Female characters often need help, and male characters tend to provide it (Beal, 1994; Evans, 1998). Coloring books also display these trends with more male than female characters, and male characters as older, stronger, more powerful, and more active than female characters (e.g., as superheroes versus princesses; Fitzpatrick & McPherson, 2010). Even cereal boxes depict twice as many male as female characters (Black, Marola, Littman, Chrisler, & Neace, 2009). Children tend to expect gender stereotypes and will expect gender neutral or atypical versions of fairy tales to conform to the usual gender stereotype (Evans, 1998).

Culture. The larger culture also influences gender typing in that most cultures emphasize gender differences. Some societies closely link activities and dress with gender, such as girls and boys attend sex segregated schools and never interact (Beal, 1994). Gender typing occurs early in life and very quickly. Children learn to think and behave in the ways that are prescribed for their gender. Societies vary in what behaviors are appropriate for men and women. For example,

TABLE 8.5 Theories of Gender Role Development

	THEORETICAL EXPLANATION
Biological	Describes gender role development in evolutionary and biological terms. Males adapted to become more aggressive and competitive and females more nurturing as it ensured that their genes were passed to the next generation. Gender differences may also be explained by subtle differences in brain structure as well as differences in hormones.
Cognitive-developmental	The emergence of gender identity leads children to classify the world around them according to gender labels, and they begin to show more interest in gender appropriate toys. After acquiring gender stability, children show an increase in stereotype knowledge, evaluate their own gender more positively, and demonstrate rigidity of gender-related beliefs. Gender constancy furthers gender typing as children attend more to norms of their sex. According to gender schema theory, once children can label their sex, their gender schema forms and becomes an organizing principle. Children notice differences between males and females in preferred clothes, toys, and activities as well as how their culture classifies males and females as different and encompassing different roles. Children then use their gender schemas as guides for their behavior and attitudes, and gender typing occurs.
Contextual	Contextual explanations rely on social learning and the influence of the sociocultural context in which children are raised. Males and females have different social experiences from birth. Gender typing occurs through socialization; through a child's interpretation of the world around him or her; and modeling and reinforcement from parents, peers, and teachers.

farming is a task for women in many parts of the world, but in North America, men are traditionally in charge of farming tasks. The exact behaviors may vary across societies, but all societies have values regarding gender appropriate behavior for males and females and all societies transmit these values to young children.

From birth, children are immersed in a gender-oriented world, and they quickly learn about gender roles and gender stereotypes. Biological influences on gender role development include genes and hormones. Cognitive-developmental perspectives emphasize children's awareness and knowledge of gender as influences on their behavior. Some aspects of gender typing are influenced by modeling, reinforcement, and shaping by parents and peers. Children also learn about gender roles from various forms of media. Finally, societies generally emphasize different behaviors as appropriate for males and females—and cultures vary dramatically in how strictly gender stereotypes are applied. Theories of gender role development are summarized in Table 8.5

PLAY AND PEER RELATIONSHIPS

"Let's be pirates!" declared Ramon. "Okay. Here's my sword," Billy said as he held up the plastic wiffleball bat. Ramon and Billy ran to the playhouse at the end of the yard. "There's the boat. Let's get them!" Billy cried as he chased after his sister. Billy explained, "You're on the boat, and we're pirates coming to get you." "I'll run!" she said. Their grandmother watched from the porch as the children created stories, acted them out together, and climbed on every available surface. Clearly, play

offers important learning opportunities for young children. Play contributes to physical, cognitive, emotional, and social development. Children learn how to use their muscles, control their bodies, coordinate their senses, and learn new motor skills. Play helps children to perspective take and understand other children's viewpoints, manage challenging situations, regulate emotions, practice creativity, learn to express their thoughts and desires, and problem solve (Coplan & Arbeau, 2009; Fireman & Kose, 2010). Children may also play with imaginary "friends" (see Box 8.3).

TYPES OF PLAY

All children play, but the form that play takes varies with development (McMahon, Lytle, & Sutton-Smith, 2005). At about age 2, play takes simple forms, such as bouncing a ball and trying to catch it or rolling a toy car as far as possible. Toddlers usually play independently. Piaget (1962) explained play as an important way in which children of all ages contribute to their own knowledge by actively exploring the world around them. By 5 years of age, children develop more sophisticated ways of interacting with play partners. Their cognitive capacities (such as their growing theory of mind) and emotional capacities (their ability to regulate their emotions) enable them to join peer groups more easily, manage conflict more effectively, and select and keep playmates. Playing with other children may push them to learn to take the perspective of others and develop less egocentric ways of thinking (Piaget, 1962).

Young children's play develops over a series of steps that take place over the ages of 2 through 5 (Parten, 1932). Toddlers' play is characterized by nonsocial activity,

Imaginary Companions

Kansas City Star/Tribune/Getty

Imaginary friends are common in early childhood and are indicative of a child's creativity and imagination.

"You stay here, and I'll get the cookies," Katie told her friend, Madison. "Does Madison want cookies too?" asked Mommy. "Of course!" replied Katie as she placed two cookies at a place setting in front of an empty chair. Imaginary companions or friends are common in early childhood, as early as ages 2 to 3, and occur in about 40% of young children (Taylor, Shawber, & Mannering, 2009).

Researchers know little about imaginary companions and why they appear in a child's life. According to parents' reports, there is no clear triggering event that marks the emergence of most imaginary companions (Taylor et al., 2009). Children appear to come up with them on their own. Imaginary companions often represent extensions of real people known to the child, especially those who the child admires or characters from stories, television, or movies. Imaginary companions are usually human, although they may take the form of animals, aliens, and monsters (Gleason,

Sebanc, & Hartup, 2000). The majority of children with imaginary friends can easily describe them and draw pictures to illustrate them upon request (Taylor et al., 2009). The sense of what an invisible friend looks like is stable and can be retained for years.

Relationships with imaginary friends appear to resemble those with real friends and provide similar benefits, especially companionship (Gleason & Kalpidou, 2014). Children create realistic relationships with their imaginary companions that include pretend conflicts, feeling angry with them, and finding them unavailable to play (Taylor et al., 1999). Their similarity with real friends has sometimes caused concern in parents and professionals who fear that children create imaginary companions because they are lonely and have no playmates. However, research suggests that children with pretend friends are particularly sociable by nature and do not differ from other children in terms of the number of playmates or peer acceptance (Gleason & Hohman, 2006; Gleason & Kalpidou, 2014). In fact, children with imaginary companions score better on measures of referential communication; they are better at communicating with peers than are children without imaginary companions (Roby & Kidd, 2008). One study of 5-year-olds found that those with imaginary friends were better able to understand and talk about mental characteristics in actual friends (Davis, Meins, & Fernyhough, 2014)

In general, children with and without imaginary companions are more similar than different in terms of their peer relationships. Imaginary companions, therefore, do not indicate social problems but instead may be a marker for creativity. Children who create imaginary companions are more likely to report vivid imagery and elaborate storylines in daydreams, dreams, and in pretend games (Bouldin, 2006; Trionfi & Reese, 2009). Perhaps imaginary companions and the mental gymnastics that create and sustain them indicate psychosocial health rather than deficits.

What Do You Think?

1. **Did you, a sibling, or friend have an imaginary companion? How do your observations compare with the research on imaginary companions?**

2. **Provide advice for a parent or child care provider. What should they do if a child reports having an imaginary friend? How should they handle it?**

including inactivity, onlooker behavior, and solitary play. **Parallel play** then emerges, in which children play alongside each other but do not interact. Play shifts to include social interaction in **associative play**, in which children play alongside each other but exchange toys and talk about each other's activities. Finally, **cooperative play** represents the most advanced form of play because children play together and work toward a common goal, such as building a bridge or engaging in make-believe play. These forms of play emerge in order but are not a strict developmental sequence because later behaviors do not replace earlier ones (Yaoying & Xu, 2010). For example, nonsocial play declines with age but still occurs in preschoolers and may take up to a third of kindergarteners' playtime (Dyer & Moneta, 2006).

PLAY AND CHILDREN'S DEVELOPMENT

All children engage in **rough-and-tumble play**, which includes running, climbing, chasing, jumping, and play fighting (Pellegrini & Smith, 1998). Children's rough-and-tumble play is seen around the world and can be distinguished from aggression by the presence of a play face, smiling and laughing (Reed & Brown, 2001). Rough-and-tumble play is carefully orchestrated. It requires self-control, emotional regulation, and social skills. Children learn how to assert themselves, interact with other children, and engage in physical play without hurting the other child (Ginsburg, 2007). Rough-and-tumble play exercises children's gross motor skills and helps them to develop muscle strength and control. It first appears in early childhood, increases and peaks at about 8 to 10 years of age, and then decreases (Pellegrini & Smith, 1998). Both boys and girls engage in rough-and-tumble play, but boys do so at much higher rates. For example, in one observation of preschool children, about 80% of the instances of rough-and-tumble play occurred in boys (Tannock, 2011). Boys' **sociodramatic play** tends to involve activity and themes of danger and conflict, girls' tend to involve themes of cooperation and fostering orderly social relationships, such as pretending to enact household and school roles (e.g., parent, teacher; Nourot, 1998).

In sociodramatic play, children take on roles and engage in activities to act out stories and themes, pretending to be mothers, astronauts, cartoon characters, and more (Dunn & Hughes, 2001). Children learn from each other and from enacting roles. They learn how to explain their ideas; to regulate emotions as they pretend to be sad, angry, or afraid; and to develop a sense of self-concept as they differentiate themselves from the roles they play (Ginsburg, 2007). Sociodramatic play begins in toddlerhood, when a 2-year-old feeds or punishes a stuffed animal (Frahsek, Mack, Mack, Pfalz-Blezinger, & Knopf, 2010). It becomes more frequent and more complex with age and the cognitive, emotional, and social development that accompany age. Both boys and girls engage in sociodramatic play, with girls engaging in more sociodramatic play than boys (Benenson, 1993). As children progress through preschool, sociodramatic play becomes more complex, often entailing innovative and sophisticated storylines. Social interactions are an important context for learning as children model higher level thinking and interaction skills, scaffolding less skilled peers and helping them to reach their potential

(Vygotsky, 1978). Sociodramatic play helps children explore social rules and conventions, promotes language skills, and is associated with social competence (Gioia & Tobin, 2010; Newton & Jenvey, 2011).

Although children around the world play, peer activities take different forms by culture. Children in collectivist societies tend to play games that emphasize cooperation. For example, children in India tend to engage in sociodramatic play that involves activities in unison coupled by close physical contact—a game called *bajtto*. Bajtto entails enacting a script about going to the market, pretending to cut and share a vegetable, and touching each other's elbows and hands as their imaginations carry out this script (Roopnarine, Hossain, Gill, & Brophy, 1994). In contrast, children from Western cultures that tend to emphasize the rights of the individual tend to play competitive games such as dodgeball, follow the leader, and hide and seek. Play, like other aspects of development, is shaped by the context in which it occurs.

The early childhood years are an important time for socioemotional development. Young children develop and communicate a sense of self that influences how they interact with others. Advances in emotional development lead to increases in the experience of empathy and display of prosocial behavior. Parents play a critical role in socioemotional development though their displays of affection and acceptance and by setting and enforcing behavioral limits. Young children become very aware of gender stereotypes and gender role becomes and important influence on behavior. Peer relationships emerge in early childhood and they are based in play yet hold implications for all areas of development.

Thinking in Context 8.3

1. Thinking of the bioecological model, in what ways does gender role development reflect interactions among physical, cognitive, and social development, as well as the context in which the child is embedded?

2. Do you agree or disagree with this statement: Play styles are universal and unfold with biological development? Explain your perspective.

Apply Your Knowledge

Four-year-old Tony is an active, curious preschooler. His mother says that he "plays hard." Tony says that he wants to be the best, to climb the highest, and run the fastest. When asked how high he can jump, Tony raises his arm to his shoulder. When given the chance to show his skills, Tony is never able to jump that high, but he's certain that he will on his next try.

Tony says that his father is the best father in the whole wide world because Daddy is big and strong. He wants to be just like Daddy when he grows up. He and Daddy do all kinds of "boy things," as Mommy calls it. Mommy bought Tony a special doll for boys, named My Buddy, but Daddy said that dolls are for girls. Tony doesn't want to be a girl. He thinks Daddy is smart and fun. Tony especially likes it when they wrestle on the floor each night. He and Daddy watch TV together. Tony also watches TV most afternoons while he waits for Daddy to come home from work. Tony's favorite shows are crime fighting cartoons, but he also likes to watch wrestling.

Mommy often scolds Tony for playing too roughly with other children. She used to put Tony in time out for five minutes when he misbehaved, but that did not decrease Tony's roughhousing and misbehaving. One time, when he hurt his cousin with his roughhousing, Tony's mother gave him a spanking to show him what it feels like and stop his behavior. She was so overcome with frustration over not being able to stop Tony's roughhousing that she didn't know what else to do. Tony's father says that rough play simply is what boys do. He tells Tony to be gentler with other children.

1. Discuss Tony's developing sense of initiative and self-concept.

2. Is Tony's play style developmentally appropriate? Why or why not? When is rough play excessive?

3. Tony's father discourages him from engaging in behavior atypical for his sex whereas his mother is concerned about helping Tony avoid becoming sex typed. What would you tell Tony's parents about gender role development? What can Tony's mother do to reduce sex typing?

4. Assess Tony's risk for developing aggressive behavior. What aspects of his environment influence how likely he is to behave aggressively?

5. How does discipline factor in to Tony's developing sense of self-regulation and impulse control? How might the various forms of discipline that Tony's parents use influence his development? Offer advice to Tony's parents.

Chapter Summary

8.1 Identify the psychosocial task of early childhood, as described by Erikson.

Young children's psychosocial task is to develop a sense of initiative over guilt. Young children develop a sense of purpose and take pride in their accomplishments. Children who develop a sense of initiative develop a confident self-image, more self-control over their emotions, social skills, and a sense of conscience.

8.2 Discuss young children's emerging sense of self.

Young children tend to understand and describe themselves concretely, using observable descriptors including appearance, general abilities, favorite activities, possessions, and simple psychological traits. They tend to have unrealistically positive views about their abilities and do not yet engage in social comparison. As children gain life experience and develop cognitively, their evaluations of self become more realistic.

Self-concept becomes correlated with skills, accomplishments, evaluations by others, and other external indicators of competence.

8.3 Compare the development of prosocial and aggressive behavior during early childhood.

Young preschoolers tend to engage in prosocial behavior for egocentric motives, to gain praise and avoid punishment. With development, children become less egocentric and their prosocial behavior becomes motivated by empathy and internalized societal perspectives of good behavior. Parents of prosocial children model prosocial behavior and empathetic concern. Aggression, especially instrumental aggression, is common in early childhood. All children will sometimes hit, fight, kick, and take other children's toys. By age 4, most children have developed the self-control to express their desires and to wait for what they want, moving from using physical aggression to expressing desires with words.

8.4 Analyze the relation of four parenting styles and their associations with child outcomes.

Parenting styles are enduring sets of parenting behaviors. Authoritarian parents emphasize control and obedience over warmth and raise children who tend to be withdrawn, often mistrustful, anxious, and often tend to react to frustrating interactions with peers with hostility. Parents who are permissive are warm and accepting but have few rules and expectations for children, resulting in children with little self-control and are immature, impulsive, and rebellious. Uninvolved parents provide little support or warmth and little control, with negative consequences for all forms of development. Authoritative parents are warm and sensitive to children's needs but also are firm in their expectations that children conform to appropriate standards of behavior. They are supportive and loving but have standards that they maintain firmly. Children of authoritative parents are confident, cooperative, have self-control, self-esteem, social skills, and high academic achievement; these positive effects persist throughout childhood into adolescence.

8.5 Describe the effects of discipline on children's development.

Discipline refers to the methods a parent uses to teach and socialize children toward acceptable behavior. Appropriate punishment occurs immediately after the dangerous behavior, is applied consistently, is clearly connected to the behavior, and does not humiliate the child. Harsh punishment and spanking have negative consequences for emotional and social development. Inductive methods use reasoning. Effective discipline must be administered as part of a supportive parent–child relationship. Parenting behaviors must be considered within their cultural context as parenting is not one size fits all.

8.6 Explain the effects of child maltreatment and factors that place children at risk for experiencing maltreatment.

Children who are abused are at risk for psychological disorders, problems in brain development, cognitive difficulties, psychological disorders, poor academic achievement, and difficulty making and maintaining friendships with other children. Risk factors for child abuse exist at all ecological levels. Both child and parent characteristics increase the risk or potential for maltreatment. Low family income, unemployment, high levels of stress, substance use, little social support, and overcrowded and inadequate housing contribute toward the risk that parents will engage in child maltreatment. Community factors that place children at risk for abuse include inadequate housing, community violence, poverty, and the availability of social support.

8.7 Summarize findings regarding gender differences during early childhood.

Despite common lay views, there are few gender differences; boys and girls are more alike than different. However, among preschool-age children and up, boys tend to exhibit more physical and verbal aggression than girls, and girls show more relational aggression than do boys. Girls tend to do better at verbal, fine motor, and mathematical computation tasks, and boys tend to do better at spatial tasks.

8.8 Compare and contrast biological, cognitive, and contextual theoretical explanations of gender role development.

Gender roles appear in all societies. Young children acquire gender roles early in life. Biological explanations of gender development cite evolutionary perspectives and look to differences in biological structures, especially the brain, as well as hormones such as testosterone as contributors to sex differences in psychological and behavioral functioning. Cognitive-developmental perspectives on gender development posit that children's understanding of gender is constructed in the same manner as their understanding of the world, by interacting with the world and thinking about their experiences. Cognitive explanations of gender development focus on the gender schema as a guide for their behavior and attitudes. Contextual explanations of gender development emphasize socialization.

8.9 Discuss the function of play and the form it takes in early childhood.

Play contributes to all aspects of development. All children play, but the form that play takes varies with development. Types of play include parallel, associative, cooperative, and sociodramatic play. Although all children around the world play, peer activities take different forms in by culture.

Key Terms

PART IV

Middle Childhood

Middle childhood entails steady advances in physical, cognitive, and socioemotional functioning. With increases in body size, strength, and agility, children are better able to participate in sports and athletic activities. As children enter school, improvements in information processing abilities underlie advances in academic tasks such as reading and mathematics. Children become better able to control their attention, take in information, and use their understanding of how the mind works to retain information more effectively. Now children can incorporate feedback about their abilities from parents, teachers, and peers to view themselves in more complex and organized ways.

Relationships with parents shift over the school years as children become more independent. Parents adapt by communicating expectations, monitoring, and permitting children to make more decisions. Like younger children, school-age children respond best to warm, responsive, and firm parenting. As children transition to first grade, the school context rises in importance. Similar to parent-child relationships, high-quality, responsive, and positive interactions with teachers aid children's adjustment. Children also experience changes within the peer context. Friendships evolve to emphasize responsivity, trust, intimacy, and loyalty. Children tend to have fewer but closer friends and friendship influences their adjustment and well-being. During elementary school, the home, school, and peer contexts influence interactions among physical, cognitive, and socioemotional domains of development.

Watch at
edge.sagepub.com/kuther

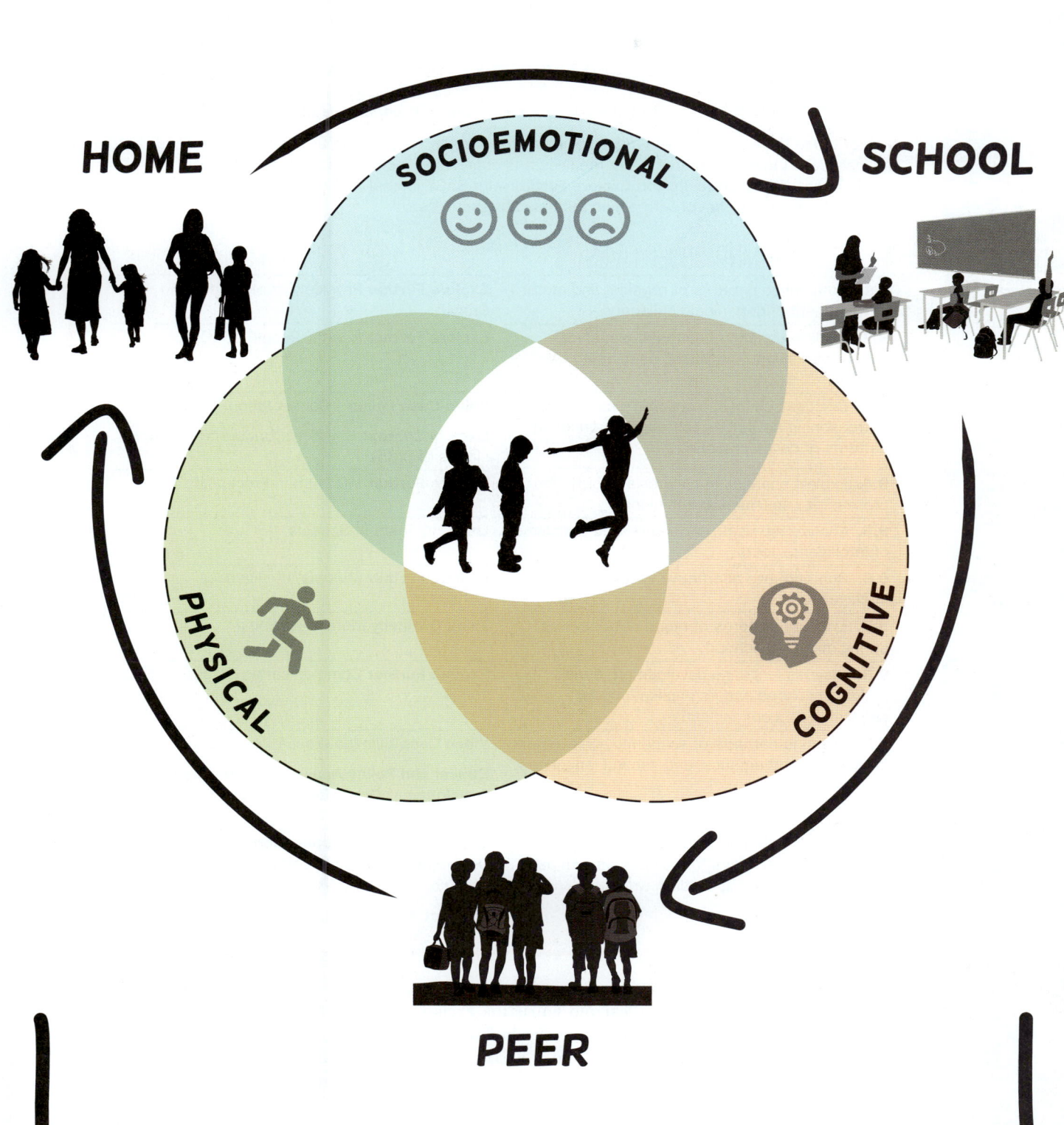

HOME

SCHOOL

SOCIOEMOTIONAL

PHYSICAL

COGNITIVE

PEER

CHAPTER 9

Physical and Cognitive Development in Middle Childhood

SAGE edge™

Get the edge on your studies at edge.sagepub.com/kuther.

Master these learning objectives using key study tools in the chapter and at SAGE edge. Access original SAGE **Video Cases** to explore the lives and contexts of individuals in every stage of development, **Think Critically** and **Explore Further** with SAGE journal and reference articles, and **Watch**, **Listen**, and **Connect** with online multimedia resources.

LEARNING OBJECTIVES

9.1. Summarize patterns of physical and motor development during middle childhood.

9.2. Analyze common health issues facing school-age children, including associated risk factors.

9.3. Discuss school-age children's capacities for reasoning as well as cultural differences in patterns of development.

9.4. Explain changes in children's information processing capacities and thinking.

9.5. Analyze the uses, correlates, and criticisms of intelligence tests.

9.6. Compare two alternative views of intelligence.

9.7. Examine patterns of moral development during middle childhood.

9.8. Discuss language development during middle childhood and its implications for capacities for communication.

9.9. Examine patterns of academic achievement in reading, mathematics, and second languages.

9.10. Identify common disabilities that pose educational challenges for children as well as methods of educating children who have special needs.

KEY STUDY TOOLS

Explore Further Physical Development and Growth

Explore Further Healthy People 2010

Video Case Piaget's Conservation Tasks

Lives in Context Children's Understanding of Illness (p. 235)

Explore Further Information Processing Theory

Listen IQ Tests in Schools

Explore Further Multiple Intelligences

Think Critically Moral Reasoning

Explore Further Communication Disorders

Video Case Bilingual Education

Ethical and Policy Applications of Lifespan Development Grade Retention and Social Promotion (p. 251)

Ethical and Policy Applications of Lifespan Development No Child Left Behind and the Common Core (p. 248)

Connect ADHD Resources

"I scored a goal today!" 8-year-old Christina exclaimed. Now that she can run faster and kick a ball farther than ever before, Christina enjoys playing on her elementary school soccer team and is becoming more skilled and interested in the sport. Christina hopes to attend soccer camp this summer. Not only does she like playing soccer but Christina spends a lot of time learning about her favorite soccer players and memorizing game-related statistics. Advances in cognition also have led Christina

to enjoy other hobbies that require concentration and planning, such as collecting soccer cards, making complex collages, and playing video games that include intricate plots. An increasingly sophisticated vocabulary, emerging social reasoning skills, and an ability to understand other people's perspectives aid Christina in expressing herself and communicating her needs. Is Christina a typical school-age child? In this chapter, we examine the physical and cognitive changes that children undergo in middle childhood, from about ages 6 to 11.

PHYSICAL AND MOTOR DEVELOPMENT

In middle childhood, physical development is more subtle and continuous than earlier in life. School-age children's bodies gradually get bigger and better coordinated, and they show advances in gross and fine motor development.

BODY GROWTH

Growth slows considerably in middle childhood as compared with infancy and early childhood. Despite a slower rate of growth, gradual day-to-day increases in height and weight add up quickly and can seemingly sneak up on a child. For example, 8 year-old Sammy stepped off of the scale, beaming at the nurse. She said, "I didn't think I grew so much!" In return, the nurse joked, "It's been six months since we've measured your height. You might be taller than your dad next time!" In middle childhood, children grow 2 to 3 inches and gain 5 to 8 pounds per year so that the average 10-year-old child weighs about 70 pounds and is about 4.5 feet tall. In late childhood, at about age 9, girls begin a period of rapid growth that will continue into adolescence. During this time girls gain about 10 pounds a year, becoming taller and heavier than same age boys. As we will discuss in Chapter 11, it is not until early adolescence, at about age 12, that boys enter a similar period of rapid growth. As children grow taller, their body proportions become more like those of adults, slimmer and with longer limbs. Physical growth is often accompanied by growing pains, intermittent aches and stiffness in the legs often experienced at night that are caused by the stretching and molding of the muscles to fit the child's growing skeleton (Pavone et al., 2011).

Genes and nutrition influence the rate of children's growth. African American children grow faster and are taller and heavier than white children of the same age. For example, 6-year-old African American girls tend to have greater muscle and bone mass than white or Mexican American girls their age (Ellis, Abrams, & Wong, 1997). Adequate nourishment is essential for growth. Children who are malnourished gain less weight and are at risk for **stunted growth**: inadequate growth in childhood as measured by low height and weight for age (World Health Organization, 2014). Children who enter middle childhood with stunted growth and nutritional deficits often do not catch up (Stein et al., 2010). Instead, stunting often continues and worsens in middle childhood, especially if children remain in the same environments that caused malnourishment (Kitsao-Wekulo et al., 2013). For example, growth stunting in children in sub-Saharan Africa tends to persist and worsen throughout the school years (Senbanjo, Oshikoya, Odusanya, & Njokanma, 2011). Children who enter middle childhood with stunted growth are likely to experience a variety of problems including cognitive deficits, aggression, behavior problems, and a greater risk of chronic illnesses and other health problems (Hoddinott, Alderman, Behrman, Haddad, & Horton, 2013).

MOTOR DEVELOPMENT

"I'll catch you! Gotcha!" Keith shouted as he pushed Craig to the ground. "Hey! It's called tag, not knock down!" Craig said and laughed. "Just wait until my turn." Vigorous play, known as rough-and-tumble play, in which chasing and play fighting among friends such as Keith and Craig, peaks in middle childhood and is an important way that children test their bodies, learn new motor skills, play with friends, and develop social skills (Pellis & Pellis, 2007; Smith, 2005). As discussed in Chapter 8, play occurs in children of all cultures and it serves a developmental purpose as it is associated with physical, cognitive, and social development (Pellegrini, Dupuis, & Smith, 2007). Like growth, children's motor development proceeds continuously, advancing gradually throughout childhood, so that motor skills from birth to age 4 predict school-age children's motor abilities (Piek, Dawson, Smith, & Gasson, 2008).

During the school years, the gross motor skills developed in early childhood, such as running and jumping, refine and combine into more complex abilities, such as running and turning to dodge a ball, walking heel to toe down the length of a balance beam and turning around, or creating elaborate jump rope routines that include twisting, turning, and hopping by quickly alternating their feet (see Figure 9.1; Gallahue & Ozmun, 2006). Increases in body size and strength contribute to advances in motor skills, which are accompanied by advances in flexibility, balance, agility, and strength (Broude, 1995; Gabbard, 2012). Now they can bend their bodies to more easily kick a ball, do a somersault, or carry out a dance routine; balance to jump rope or throw a ball; demonstrate agility to run and change speed and direction rapidly; and have the strength to jump higher and throw a ball farther than ever before (Gallahue & Ozmun, 2006; Haywood & Getchell, 2005).

Not only are older children better at running, jumping, and other physical activities than young children but they also show advances in fine motor control that allow them to develop new interests. School-age children build model cars, play with yo-yos, braid friendship bracelets, weave pot-holders, and learn to play musical instruments—all tasks that depend on fine motor control. Fine motor development

FIGURE 9.1: Gross Motor Skills

In middle childhood gross motor skills combine and become more complex, permitting faster running, higher jumping, and greater coordination, such as the ability to balance on a balance beam.

is particularly important for children's school performance, specifically penmanship. Most 6-year-old children can write the alphabet, their names, and numbers in large print, making strokes with their entire arm. With development, children learn to use their wrists and fingers to write. Uppercase letters are usually mastered first; the lowercase alphabet requires smaller movements of the hand that require much practice. By third grade, most children can write in script, or cursive writing. Girls tend to outperform boys in fine motor skills (Junaid & Fellowes, 2006; Nyiti, 1982). Success in fine motor skills, particularly writing skills, may influence academic skills as children who write with ease may be better able to express themselves in writing, for example.

Advancements in motor skill are influenced by body maturation and especially brain development. The pruning of unused synapses contributes to increases in motor speed and reaction time so that 11-year-old children tend to respond twice as quickly as 5-year-old children (Kail, 2003). Growth of the **cerebellum** (responsible for balance, coordination, and some aspects of emotion and reasoning) and myelination of its connections to the cortex contribute to advances in gross and fine motor skills and speed (Baillieux, De Smet, Paquier, De Deyn, & Mariën, 2008; Diamond, 2000; Tiemeier et al., 2010). Brain development improves children's ability to inhibit actions, which enables children to carry out more sophisticated motor activities that require the use of one hand while controlling the other, such as throwing a ball, or that require both hands to do different things, such as playing an instrument (Diamond, 2013).

Maturation, advances in physical growth and brain development, is an important influence on children's motor skills. However, contextual influences, such as nutrition, opportunities to practice motor skills, and health also matter. For example, children in different contexts have different opportunities to practice motor skills through vigorous physical play and other activities (Laukkanen, Pesola, Havu, Sääkslahti, & Finni, 2014). In addition, there are long-term implications of motor development for other domains of development. In one study, children's motor development and activity at age 8 predicted measures of cognitive development and academic achievement 8 years later, at age 16 (Kantomaa et al., 2013). The ability to explore the world and play influences opportunities to interact and play with other children and thereby social skills and, potentially, cognitive development.

COMMON HEALTH ISSUES IN MIDDLE CHILDHOOD

Middle childhood generally is a healthy time. As shown in Figure 9.2, childhood mortality declines after infancy and has declined over the past four decades (Child Trends, 2013b). However, children from low socioeconomic status homes have higher rates of mortality than do other children because of poor access to health care, poor nutrition, and stressful home and neighborhood environments (Singh & Kogan, 2007). The typical child experiences six or seven episodes of colds, flu, or viruses per year (Simasek & Blandino, 2007). In contrast to these short-term acute health issues, however, some children experience more chronic and serious health challenges. About 25% of children in the United States under age 18 are diagnosed with chronic medical conditions that require special health services (National Survey of Children's Health, 2014a). The most commonly experienced chronic illness in childhood is **asthma**.

FIGURE 9.2: Death Rates for Children Ages 1 to 19 in the United States, 1980–2013

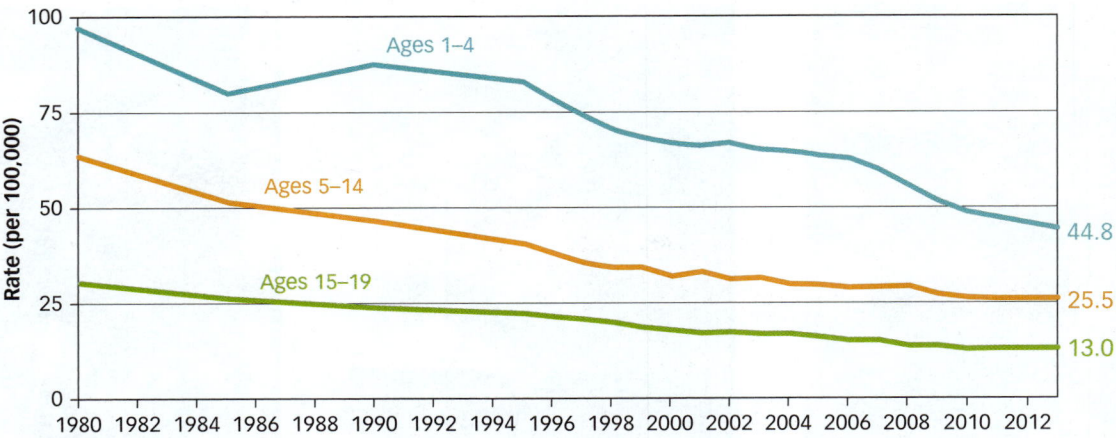

Ages 1–4

Ages 5–14

Ages 15–19

44.8

25.5

13.0

SOURCE: Child Trends (2013b).

Asthma

Diego steps off the basketball court, leaning over to catch his breath. Coach Santos asks, "Are you okay? Have you been using your inhaler?" "Not always, Coach." "Diego, you need to remember that you can't stop using your inhaler when you feel good. Asthma does not go away. You will always have to be aware and take care of yourself."

The most common chronic medical condition among children is asthma, a chronic inflammatory disorder of the airways that causes wheezing and coughing (Akinbami, Moorman, Garbe, & Sondik, 2009). Exposure to triggers such as cold weather, exercise, allergens, emotional stress, and infection cause the bronchial tubes to contract and fill with mucus, making it difficult for children to breathe. Asthma affects about 15% of children and becomes more common with age (National Survey of Children's Health, 2014a).

There has been a rapid rise in asthma diagnoses in industrialized nations in recent decades (Mitchell & McQuaid, 2008). There are genetic contributors to asthma, and African American children are at higher risk than others (see Figure 9.3). However, environmental factors also play a role (Thomsen, van der Sluis, Kyvik, Skytthe, & Backer, 2010). For example, better insulation of homes makes them more efficient at retaining heat but permits less air circulation, exposing family members to more allergens and toxins from sources such as food allergens, furry pets living in the home, and carpeting in the home (Ding, Ji, & Bao, 2014; Heinrich, 2011). Urbanization, less outdoor play, and poor access to health care (all of which tend to accompany low socioeconomic status, another correlate of asthma) increase children's risk of developing asthma (Kiechl-Kohlendorfer et al., 2007). One study of South African 6- to 7-year-old children found that those who lived in urban areas were

FIGURE 9.3: Ethnic Differences in Asthma Prevalence, 2013

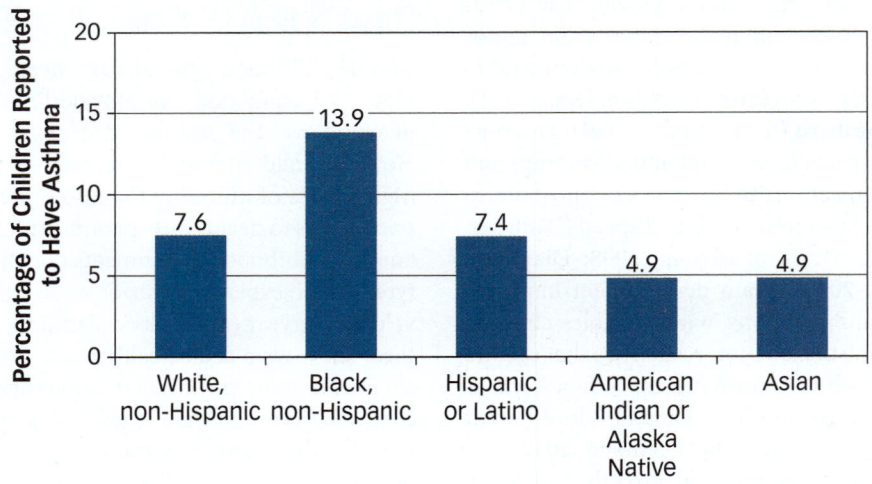

7.6

13.9

7.4

4.9

4.9

White, non-Hispanic   Black, non-Hispanic   Hispanic or Latino   American Indian or Alaska Native   Asian

SOURCE: Child Trends (2013a).

more likely to be diagnosed with asthma than those from rural areas, supporting the role of exposure to pollution and toxins in developing asthma (Wichmann, Wolvaardt, Maritz, & Voyi, 2009). Other risk factors for developing asthma include low birth weight, stress, low socioeconomic status, and exposure to secondhand smoke in the home (Ding et al., 2014; Kiechl-Kohlendorfer et al., 2007).

Asthma poses risks to children's development and functioning because children with asthma are more likely to report only fair or poor overall health and well-being and to be treated for a mental health problem than are children without asthma (Collins et al., 2008; Miller, Wood, & Smith, 2010). Asthma is the most common cause of school absence (Akinbami et al., 2009). In addition to more school absences, children with asthma tend to report more unhappiness at school and are less likely to report having a group of friends to play with (Chen, 2014; Petteway, Valerio, & Patel, 2011). Moreover, many asthmatic children report being teased or bullied (van den Bemt et al., 2010). Physical health influences, and is influenced by, socioemotional development, as demonstrated by findings on childhood **obesity**.

Obesity

Byron looked up at the menu and the pictures of each item and tried to decide what to order for lunch, "Should I have a cheeseburger? Bacon cheeseburger? Well, the one thing I'm sure I'm having is large French fries—oh, and a chocolate milkshake!" A calorie-packed junk food lunch like Byron's is a fun splurge once in a while, but for some children this is a regular everyday lunch. Children today weigh more than ever before. Health care professionals determine whether someone's weight is in the healthy range by examining **body**

mass index (BMI), calculated as weight in kilograms/ height in meters squared (k/m^2; World Health Organization, 2009). The most pressing and preventable health problem facing children today is obesity, defined as having BMI at or above the 95th percentile for height and age, as indicated by the 2000 Centers for Disease Control and Prevention (CDC) growth charts (Reilly, 2007). More than 17% of American youth are classified as obese (National Survey of Children's Health, 2014b; see Figure 9.4).

Rising rates of overweight and obesity among children are a problem in the United States, and all other developed nations, including Australia, Canada, Denmark, Finland, Germany, Great Britain, Ireland, Japan, Hong Kong, and New Zealand (de Onis, Blössner, & Borghi, 2010; Janssen et al., 2005; Wang & Lim, 2012), as shown in Figure 9.5. Obesity is also becoming more common in developing nations, such as India, Pakistan, and China, as they transition to Western-style diets higher in meats, fats, and refined foods as well as show the increased snacking and declines in physical activity linked with watching television (Poskitt, 2009; Wang & Lim, 2012).

Strides in genetic research in recent years have increased our understanding of the strong contribution of genetics to obesity (Drong, Lindgren, & McCarthy, 2012; Herrera, Keildson, & Lindgren, 2011). Contextual factors determine whether genetic predispositions to weight gain are fulfilled. In the United States, low socioeconomic status is associated with poor access to health insurance, health care, and transportation as well as unsafe neighborhoods and poor proximity to grocery stores that carry healthy foods (Vieweg, Johnston, Lanier, Fernandez, & Pandurangi, 2007), which places children in low socioeconomic status homes at higher risk for obesity as compared with their peers who live in high socioeconomic homes (Singh,

FIGURE 9.4: Prevalence of Child and Adolescent Obesity in the United States, 1963–2012

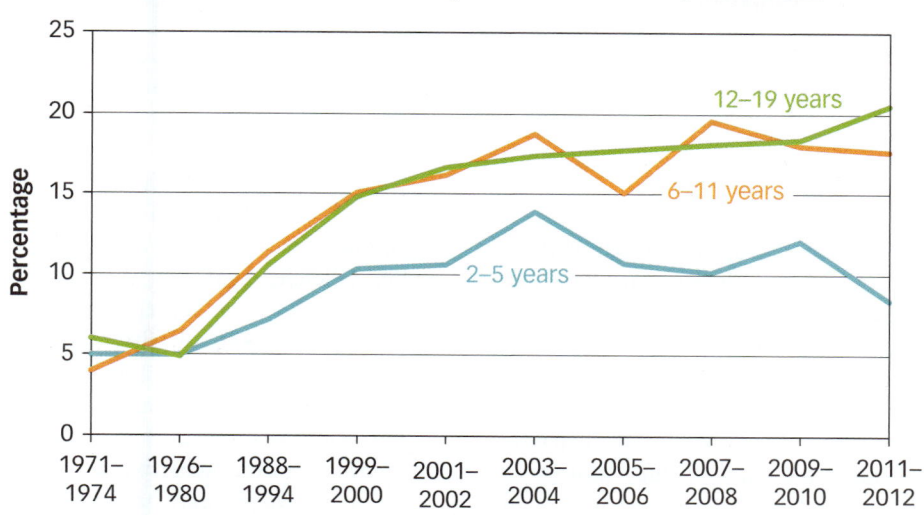

SOURCE: Fryar, Carroll, and Ogden (2014). http://www.cdc.gov/nchs/data/hestat/obesity_child_11_12/obesity_child_11_12.htm#figure1

FIGURE 9.5: Worldwide Prevalence of Overweight Children (ages 5 to 17) in 2010

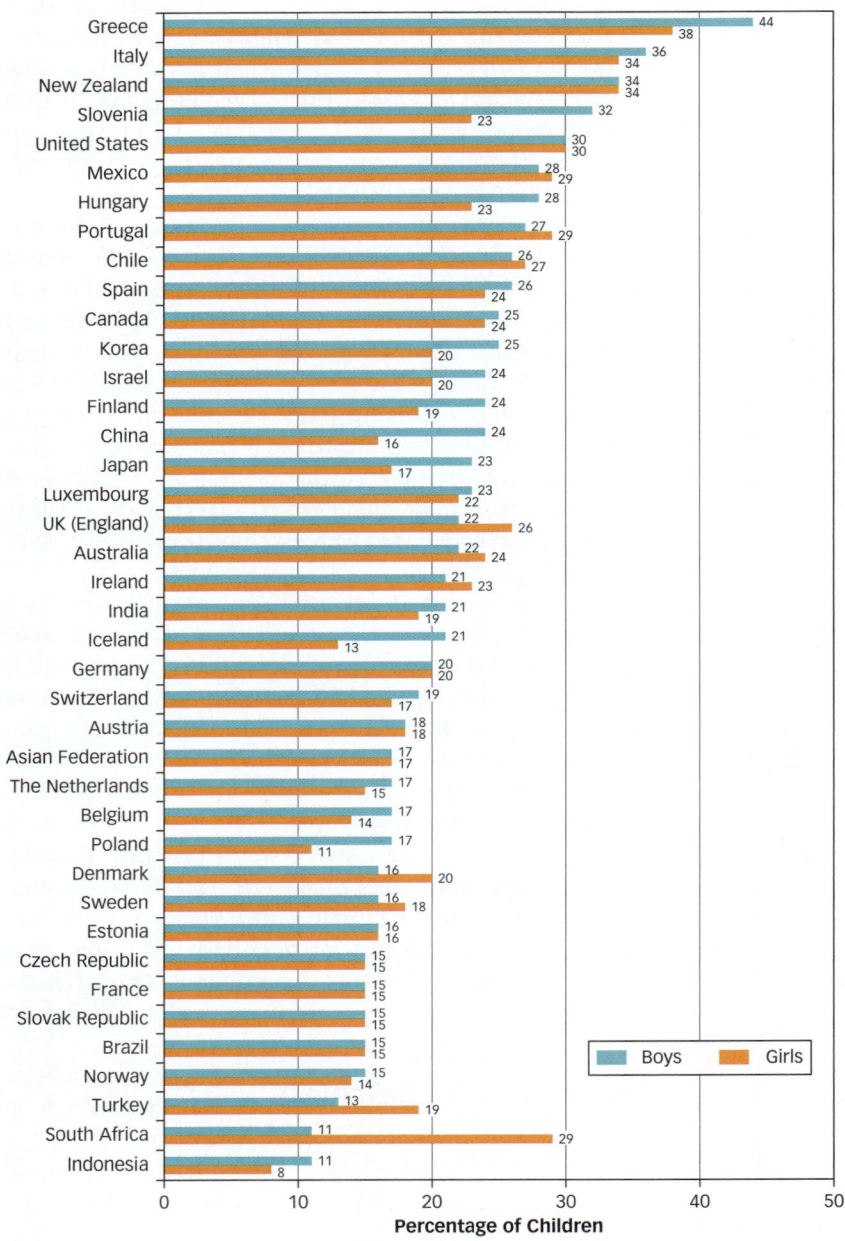

SOURCE: Organization for Economic Co-operation and Development (2014).

(Hauser et al., 2014). However, the frequency of family dinnertimes drops sharply between ages 9 and 14, and family dinners have become less common in recent decades (Rollins, Francis, & BeLue, 2007). Screen time—time spent in front of a television, computer, or electronic device screen watching television or videos, playing video games, and engaging with social media—and other sedentary activities are risk factors for a high BMI. Five- to eight-year-old children tend to average about 2.5 hours of screen time each day, about an hour of which is spent watching television (Rideout, 2013). Screen time increases with age, peaking between ages 10 and 14 at about 7 hours a day, time that is not spent on physical play and other activities (Nader, Bradley, Houts, McRitchie, & O'Brien, 2008).

Childhood obesity is associated with short- and long-term health problems, including heart disease, high blood pressure, orthopedic problems, cardiovascular disease, and diabetes (Pulgarón, 2013). Obese children are at risk for peer rejection, depression, low self-esteem, and body dissatisfaction because children and adults are more likely to report negative perceptions of obese children as sloppy, ugly, stupid, deceitful, and generally unlikable as compared with other children (Gibson et al., 2008; Puhl & Heuer, 2009). The vast majority of obese children do not outgrow obesity but instead become obese adults (Lakshman, Elks, & Ong, 2012).

Programs that effectively reduce childhood obesity target children's screen time, increase their physical activity and time spent outdoors, and teach children about nutrition, reducing their consumption of high calorie foods and increasing their consumption of fruits and vegetables (Bleich, Segal, Wu, Wilson, & Wang, 2013; Doak, Visscher, Renders, & Seidell, 2006; Nowicka & Flodmark, 2007). To prevent obesity, parents should monitor their children's activities and engage in physical activities with them such as walking, biking, and swimming. Intervention is important to reduce childhood obesity, but it must be done sensitively, as children who are pressured to lose weight may become obsessed with body size and develop a poor **body image**.

Kogan, Van Dyck, & Siahpush, 2008). In contrast, in developing nations such as India, where hunger and food insecurity are common, high BMI signifies wealth; children of high socioeconomic status are more likely to be overweight and obese than other children (Kaur, Sachdev, Dwivedi, Lakshmy, & Kapil, 2008).

U.S. children who eat an evening meal with parents tend to have more healthy diets that include more fruits and vegetables and less fried foods and soft drinks, and they are less likely to be overweight than other children

Body Image Dissatisfaction

As early as age 4, children rate thin bodies are more attractive than the average-shaped bodies they report as normal and commonly seen (Brown & Slaughter, 2011). Beginning in late childhood, body image, perception of one's body and outward appearance, becomes an important influence on self-esteem. "See how my stomach sticks out?" asked Amanda. "Sometimes it sticks out even worse, and I have to wear baggy tops. I hate that. I want to wear cropped tops like that one," Amanda said, pointing to a page in a magazine. "But I'm too fat." "Me too," said her best friend, Betsy. At 9 years of age, Amanda and Betsy display signs of body image dissatisfaction—dissatisfaction with one's physical appearance as shown by a discrepancy between one's ideal body figure and actual body figure. Many schoolchildren, like Amanda and Betsy, experience body image dissatisfaction, which is associated with poor self-esteem, depression, and unhealthy eating and exercise behaviors (Poudevigne et al., 2003; Rolland, Farnhill, & Griffiths, 1997; Tiggeman & Wilson-Barrett, 1998).

Body image dissatisfaction can be seen as early as the preschool years and rises quickly over the course of childhood (Tremblay & Limbos, 2009). For example, one study of 3- to 5-year-old children found that over two thirds of the girls of normal weight reported dissatisfaction with their bodies (Tremblay, Lovsin, Zecevic, & Larivière, 2011). Six- and seven-year-old girls in Western countries such as the United States, Britain, and Australia commonly rate their ideal figure as smaller than their current figure (Coughlin, Heinberg, Marinilli, & Guarda, 2003). About 40% to 50% of elementary schoolchildren (6–12 years) are dissatisfied with some aspect of their body and shape (Littleton & Ollendick, 2003; Smolak, 2011). Perhaps it may not be surprising, then, that dieting behaviors often begin in childhood, and about half of 8- to 10-year-old children report dieting at least some of the time (Dohnt & Tiggemann, 2005; Littleton & Ollendick, 2003; McVey, Tweed, & Blackmore, 2004). Although less well researched, boys also are vulnerable to body dissatisfaction. Studies of U.S., British, and Australian boys have shown that between one third and two thirds of boys between the ages of 5 and 10 report body dissatisfaction, desiring a thinner, larger, or broader frame (Cohane & Pope, 2001; Gustafson-Larson & Terry, 1992; Maloney, McGuire, Daniels, & Specker, 1989). Overall, body image dissatisfaction and body distortion increases with age in both boys and girls, peaking during early adolescence (Rolland et al., 1997).

Parents, peers, and media exposure are important influences on children's body image. Parents' direct comments about their child's weight, particularly mothers' comments, are most consistently associated with children's reported body concerns and behaviors (Gattario, Frisén, & Anderson-Fye, 2014; McCabe et al., 2007). Peers, however, are also important.

Like Amanda and Betsy, girls often bond over "fat talk," criticizing their own bodies (McVey, Levine, Piran, &

Body image dissatisfaction is often first seen in girls during middle childhood.

Ferguson, 2013). Many school-age girls believe that being thin would make them more likable by their peers and less likely to be teased (Dohnt & Tiggemann, 2005; McCabe, Riccardelli, & Finemore, 2002). Girls with a higher BMI report experiencing more teasing and bullying (McVey et al., 2013), which in turn is associated with body dissatisfaction (Williams et al., 2013). Even without being teased, simply having higher BMI relative to peers predicts body image concerns one year later in 9- to 12-year-old girls (Clark & Tiggemann, 2008).

Finally, greater exposure to teen media and images of thin models is associated with greater dieting awareness, more weight concerns, and greater body dissatisfaction in girls and women (Benowitz-Fredericks, Garcia, Massey, Vasagar, & Borzekowski, 2012; Evans, Tovée, Boothroyd, & Drewett, 2013; Gattario et al., 2014). The influence of the media is perhaps best illustrated by longitudinal studies of Fijian teenagers before and after the introduction of television. Disordered eating attitudes and behaviors rose after television became widely available (Dasen, 1994). With the emergence of U.S. television programming, girls from rural Fiji reported comparing their bodies to the program characters and wanting to look like them (Becker, Keel, Anderson-Fye, & Thomas, 2004). In contrast, despite increases in globalization and an accompanying heavy media exposure, girls in rural Belize rejected bodies that were too thin or without enough shape and were opposed to

Peter Dazeley/Getty

dieting, suggesting that internalized cultural values of self-care and appearance ideals influence perceptions of attractiveness and body image (Anderson-Fye, 2004). It is clear that children's perceptions of body ideals and their own bodies are influenced by multiple contextual factors.

Intervening to promote a healthy body image is challenging. School-based programs aim to educate students about body image using strategies such as lessons, group discussions, and role play as well as encourage supportive peer groups (McVey, Lieberman, Voorberg, Wardrope, & Blackmore, 2003; O'Dea & Yager, 2011). Improving media literacy is an important focus of many programs. Children are taught about media advertising and the strategies used by advertisers (Richardson, Paxton, & Thomson, 2009). Lessons might include information about the homogeneity of body shapes shown on television and magazines, airbrushing of photos, and why advertisers might want people to be unhappy with the way we look (to get them to buy the product; Neumark-Sztainer, Sherwood, Coller, & Hannan, 2000). For example, as part of a 2011 governmental initiative in British schools, Britney Spears allowed pre-airbrushed images of herself in a bikini to be shown alongside the airbrushed ones for children aged 10 to 11 to show how media might try to alter and improve images (Gattario et al., 2014). Effective programs emphasize providing children with alternative ways of thinking about beauty and body ideals (Gattario et al., 2014).

Thinking in Context 9.1

1. How might have your experiences, biological foundation, and context influenced your own physical development and health? How do your experiences compare with those of others your age? In what ways did these developments and experiences influence you as an elementary school child? Today?

2. Obesity, body image, and dieting in school-age children reflect the interaction of contextual and developmental factors. In what ways do contextual factors contribute to each of these health issues? What about genetic and developmental factors?

COGNITIVE DEVELOPMENT

We have seen that children make impressive gains in physical development, becoming bigger, stronger, and capable of a broad range of motor activities. Their leaps in cognitive development are even more impressive. Children's capacities to take in, process, and retain information all increase dramatically. They grasp the world around them in new, more adultlike ways and become capable of thinking logically, although their reasoning remains different from that of adults. Children become faster, more efficient thinkers, and they develop more sophisticated perspectives on the nature of knowledge and how the mind works.

PIAGET'S COGNITIVE-DEVELOPMENTAL PERSPECTIVE: CONCRETE OPERATIONAL REASONING

Young children in Piaget's preoperational stage of reasoning display thinking that is characterized by errors in logic, such as egocentrism. When children enter the **concrete operational stage of reasoning**, at about age 6 or 7, they gain the capacity to use logic to solve problems but still are unable to apply logic to abstract and hypothetical situations. In contrast, school-age children demonstrate a sophisticated understanding of the physical world around them, as well as the capacity to use language, as discussed in the following sections.

Classification

What hobbies did you enjoy as a child? Did you build model cars or airplanes? Collect and trade coins, stamps, rocks, or baseball cards? School-age children develop interests and hobbies that require advanced thinking skills, such as the ability to compare multiple items across several dimensions.

Peter Beck/Corbis

Stamp collecting is a hobby that relies on cognitive skills such as categorization.

The **classification** skills that accompany concrete operational reasoning permit school-age children to categorize or organize objects based on physical dimensions. Several types of classification skills emerge during the concrete operational stage: **seriation**, transitive influence, and class **inclusion**.

Seriation is the ability to order objects in a series according to a physical dimension such as height, weight, or color. For example, ask a child to arrange a handful of sticks in order by length, from shortest to longest. Four- to 5-year-old children can pick out the smallest and largest stick but cannot arrange the others in order. Instead, they arrange them haphazardly. Six- to 7-year-old children, on the other hand, arrange the sticks by picking out the smallest, and next smallest, and so on (Gardiner & Kosmitzki, 2010; Inhelder & Piaget, 1964).

The ability to infer the relationship between two objects by understanding each object's relationship to a third is called **transitive inference**. For example, present a child with three sticks: A, B, and C. She is shown that Stick A is longer than Stick B and Stick B is longer than Stick C. The concrete operational child does not need to physically compare Sticks A and C to know that Stick A is longer than the Stick C. She uses the information given about the two sticks to infer their relative lengths (Ameel, Verschueren, & Schaeken, 2007; Rogoff & Chavajay, 1995). Transitive inference emerges earlier than other concrete operational skills. By about 5 years of age, children are able to infer that A is longer than C (Goodwin & Johnson-Laird, 2008).

Classification is the ability to understand classification hierarchies, to simultaneously consider relations between a general category and more specific subcategories (Broude, 1995). For example, a child is shown a bunch of flowers (seven daisies and two roses) and is told that there are nine flowers—seven are called daisies and two are called roses. Are there more daisies or flowers? Preoperational children will answer that there are more daisies as they do not understand that daisies are a subclass of flowers (Deneault & Ricard, 2006; Inhelder & Piaget, 1964). By age 5, children have some knowledge of classification hierarchies and may grasp that daisies are flowers but do not fully understand and apply classification hierarchies (Deneault & Ricard, 2006). By about age 8, children can not only classify objects, in this case flowers, but make quantitative judgments and respond that there are more flowers than daisies (Borst, Poirel, Pineau, Cassotti, & Houdé, 2013). Children's ability and interest in hierarchical classification becomes apparent in middle childhood when they begin to collect items, such as rocks, shells, and baseball cards, and spend hours sorting their collections along various dimensions, arranging them into classes and subclasses. For example, Susan sorts her rock collection by geographic location (e.g., part of the world in which it is most commonly found), with subcategories based on hardness and color. Other times, Susan organizes her rocks based on other characteristics, such as age, composition, and more.

PIAGET'S CONSERVATION TASKS

How do children understand physical properties, such as volume and mass? Observe children as they are presented with two of Piaget's classic conservation tasks.

Watch the video at edge.sagepub.com/kuther

Conservation

In a classic conservation problem, a child is shown two identical balls of clay and watches while the experimenter rolls one ball into a long hot dog shape. When asked which piece contains more clay, a child who reasons at the preoperational stage will say that the hot dog shape contains more clay because it is longer. Eight-year-old Julio, on the other hand, knows that the two shapes contain the same amount of clay; at the concrete operational stage of reasoning, Julio grasps the principle of object identity. Object identity refers to the understanding that certain characteristics of an object do not change despite superficial changes to the object's appearance. Julio notices that the ball shape is shorter than the hot dog shape, but it is also thicker. An understanding of **reversibility**, that an object can be returned to its original state, undoing the superficial physical alterations by which it was changed, implies that Julio realizes that the hot dog–shaped clay can be reformed into its original ball shape.

Most children solve this conservation problem of substance by age 7 or 8. At about age 9 or 10, children also correctly solve conservation of weight tasks ("Which is heavier, the hot dog or the ball?"). Conservation of volume tasks (after placing the hot dog and ball-shaped clay in glasses of liquid: "Which displaces more liquid?") are solved last, at about age 12. The ability to conserve develops slowly, and children show inconsistencies in their ability to solve different types of conservation problems. Piaget posited that young school-age children's thinking is so concrete that principles often seem to be tied to particular situations. They cannot yet apply their understanding of one type of conservation to another problem even though the principles underlying all conservation problems are the same.

Alternatively, some theorists argue that children's capacities to solve conservation problems correspond to brain development and advances in information processing abilities (Morra, Gobbo, Marini, & Sheese, 2008). The earliest type of conservation, numerical conservation, is associated with development of working memory and the ability to control impulses, which permit children to manipulate numerical information to solve problems (Borst et al., 2013; Poirel et al., 2012). As compared with 5-year-old children, 9-year-old children show more activity in parts of the temporal and prefrontal cortex as well as other parts of the brain associated with working memory, inhibitory control, and executive control (Houdé et al., 2011). With practice, the abilities tested in Piagetian tasks become automatic and require less attention and fewer cognitive resources, enabling children to think in more complex ways (Case, 1998, 1999; Pascual-Leone, 2000). For example, once a child realizes that the hot dog–shaped clay was once in the shape of a ball—and thereby demonstrates an understanding of conservation of substance—the scheme becomes routine and requires less attention and mental resources than before (Siegler & Richards, 1982). Now the child can consider more challenging conservation problems. Children must practice one form of conservation in order for it to become automatic and free cognitive resources to apply that scheme to other conservation problems.

Culture and Concrete Operational Reasoning

Although the features and correlates of concrete operational reasoning are universal, cultural factors play a role in the rate of cognitive development (Siegler, 1998). Studies of children in non-Western cultures suggest that they achieve conservation and other concrete operational tasks later than children from Western cultures. However, these differences may be influenced by researchers' methodologies—specifically, the language of testing matters. When 10- and 11-year-old Canadian Micmac Indian children were tested in English on conservation problems (substance, weight, and volume), they performed worse than 10- to 11-year-old white English-speaking children. Yet when tested in their native language, by researchers from their own culture, the children performed as well as the English-speaking children (Collette & Van der Linden, 2002). Cultural differences in children's performance on tasks that measure concrete operational reasoning may be more a result of methodology and how questions are asked rather than children's abilities (D'Esposito et al., 1995).

Children around the world demonstrate concrete operational reasoning, but experience, specific cultural practices, and education play a role in how it is displayed (Manoach et al., 1997). Children are more likely to display logical reasoning when considering substances with which they are familiar. Mexican children who make pottery understand at an early age that the amount of clay remains the same when its shape is changed. They demonstrate conservation of substance earlier than other forms of conservation (Fry & Hale, 1996) and earlier than children who do not make pottery (Hitch, Towse, & Hutton, 2001; Leather & Henry, 1994). Despite having never attended school and scoring low on measures of mathematics achievement, many 6- to 15-year-old children living in the streets of Brazil demonstrate

This child in Brazil shows advanced computational skills because she sells candy and other items to earn a living. Experience and situational demands influnce cultural differences in cognitive skills.

Reuters/Ricardo Moraes

sophisticated logical and computational reasoning. Why? These children sell items such as fruit and candy to earn their living. In addition to pricing their products competitively, collecting money, making change, and giving discounts, the children adjusted prices daily to account for changes in demand, overhead, and the rate of inflation (Gathercole, Pickering, Ambridge, & Wearing, 2004). The children's competence in mathematics was influenced by experience, situational demands, and learning from others. Despite this, schooling also matters in promoting cognitive development because children with some schooling were more adept at these tasks than were unschooled children (Siegel, 1994).

Schooling influences the rate at which principles are understood. For example, children who have been in school longer tend to do better on transitive inference tasks than same age children with less schooling (Artman & Cahan, 1993). Likewise, Zimbabwean children's understanding of conservation is influenced by academic experience, age, and family socioeconomic status (Mpofu & van de Vijver, 2000). Japanese children's understanding of mathematical concepts tends to follow Piaget's theory of maturational unfolding, but other mathematical concepts are understood because of formal instruction, supportive of Vygotsky's principle of scaffolding (discussed in Chapter 7) as an influence on cognitive development (Case, Kurland, & Goldberg, 1982; Dempster, 1985). Lives in Context (p. 235) explores the development of children's capacities to understand illness.

INFORMATION PROCESSING PERSPECTIVE

"If you're finished, put your head down on your desk and rest for a moment," Mrs. McCalvert advised. She was surprised to see that three quarters of her students immediately put their heads down. "They are getting quicker and quicker! I guess next time I'll assign more challenging problems," she thought

LIVES IN CONTEXT

Children's Understanding of Illness

School-age children's emerging capacities for reasoning influence their understanding of a variety of phenomena, including their conceptions of illness (Brodie, 1974). It was once thought that children's understanding of illness was unsophisticated—for example, viewing illness as caused by misdeeds—a view referred to as *immanent justice* (Kister & Patterson, 1980; Myant & Williams, 2005).

As children advance in cognitive maturity from older childhood into adolescence, they develop more advanced conceptions of illness and distinguish specific symptoms and diseases; appreciate psychological, emotional, and social aspects of physical illness; associate illness with germs and infection; and demonstrate an understanding of contagiousness (Brewster, 1982; Kister & Patterson, 1980). For example, unlike young children, older children tend to refer to germs in their explanations of illness, but they tend to view germs as operating in an all-or-nothing fashion such that the presence of germs alone is seen as enough to make a child sick (Raman & Gelman, 2005). It is not until early adolescence or later that they understand the complexity of causal influences and interactions. These advances in children's understanding of illness are predictable and related to cognitive development rather than age.

Children in Western cultures and adults in non-Western cultures tend to rely on immanent justice and other nonbiological explanations (e.g., magic or fate) for contagious illnesses such as colds, coughs, and stomachaches (Raman & Winer, 2002). However, open-ended interviews require that the child understand not just the phenomena but be able to explain it. When researchers use less demanding tasks, such as forced choice (multiple choice) tasks, they find that Chinese and U.S. children as young as 3 years of age have an understanding that illness is not intentional, that some behaviors can prevent illness and others can make it

more likely, and that germs or contamination is responsible for the transmission of contagious illnesses (Legare, Wellman, & Gelman, 2009; Raman & Gelman, 2008; Zhu & Liu, 2007).

Overall, school-age children tend to prefer biological explanations of illness and use immanent justice reasoning only as a fallback position to explain an illness that is not within the range of their personal experience. Cultural influences also shape children's understandings of illness. For example, one study of 5- to 15-year-old children and adults from Sesotho-speaking South African communities showed that the participants, who were exposed to Western medicine, endorsed biological explanations for illness at high levels, but also often endorsed witchcraft (Legare & Gelman, 2008). Bewitchment explanations were neither the result of ignorance nor replaced by biological explanations. Instead, both natural and supernatural explanations were used to explain the same phenomena and were viewed as complementary. Although specific explanations may vary by culture, the coexistence of biological and supernatural reasoning about causes of illness is not confined to specific cultures. U.S. children and adults retain some supernatural explanations in addition to developing biological explanations (Legare, Evans, Rosengren, & Harris, 2012). Diverse, culturally constructed belief systems about illness coexist with factual understanding and explanations of illness change with development.

What Do You Think?

1. Does Piaget's theory adequately explain the changes that occur in children's understanding of illness? Why or why not?

2. Consider your own views and experience. As a child, do you remember "catching a cold"? What did that mean to you?

---

to herself. Information processing theorists would agree with Mrs. McCalvert's observation because the information processing perspective describes development as entailing changes in the efficiency of cognition rather than qualitative changes in reasoning. School-age children can take in more information, process it more accurately and quickly, and retain it more effectively than younger children. They are better able to determine what information is important, attend to it, and use their understanding of how memory works to choose among strategies to retain information more effectively. The sensory register does not appear to change much with development. Five-year-old children demonstrate similar capacities and performance as adults (Cowan, Nugent, Elliott, Ponomarev, & Saults, 1999; Kail & Reese, 2002). Working memory shows steady increases in middle childhood, especially in executive function.

Central Executive Function

Improvements in working memory are influenced by increases in storage capacity as well as advances in the ability to control and direct attention (Baddeley, 2012; Cowan, Ricker, Clark, Hinrichs, & Glass, 2015). An important part of working memory is the central executive, a control processor that regulates cognitive activities such as attention, action, and problem solving. Specifically, the central executive is responsible for (1) coordinating performance on two separate tasks or operations, such as both storing and processing information at the same time; (2) quickly switching between tasks, such as manipulating and storing information; (3) selectively attending to specific information and ignoring irrelevant information; and (4) retrieving information from long-term memory (Baddeley, 1996, 2012). Central executive function is thought to have a biological basis because the cognitive activities controlled by the central executive are associated with regions of the cortex, specifically several areas of the frontal lobe and part of the parietal lobe (Collette & Van der Linden, 2002; Petersen & Posner, 2012).

Steady increases in central executive function and working memory occur throughout childhood, from 4 years of age through adolescence, and are responsible for

Jennifer Brown/Star Ledger/Corbis

Advances in selective attention, working memory, and central executive function help older children pay attention in class, ignore distracting information, and problem solve.

the cognitive developmental changes that we see during childhood (Benes, 2001; Brocki & Bohlin, 2004). For example, during the elementary school years, working memory capacity—how much material can be held—improves substantially (Kail & Park, 1994; Schneider & Pressley, 2013b). One study demonstrated that between ages 6 and 7 children begin to use attention switching in completing memory tasks, permitting the 7-year-old children to show greater recall than the 6-year-old children (Camos & Barrouillet, 2011).

School-age children demonstrate increasingly sophisticated performance in a range of skills such language comprehension, reading, and mathematics ability (Mazzocco & Kover, 2007). Between ages 6 and 10, children become much better able to control their attention and deploy **selective attention**, focusing on the relevant information and ignoring other information, than younger children, who are easily distracted and fidget (Savage, Cornish, Manly, & Hollis, 2006). Children not only get better at attending to and manipulating information but they get better at storing it in long-term memory, which is an unlimited store that holds information indefinitely. Children amass a great deal of information, and as they get older, they organize it in more sophisticated ways and encode and retrieve it more efficiently and with less effort.

Improvements in memory, attention, and processing speed are possible because of brain development—particularly myelination and pruning. Neural systems for visiospatial working memory, auditory working memory, and response inhibition differentiate, dividing into separate parts to enable faster and more efficient processing of these critical cognitive functions (Tsujimoto, Kuwajima, & Sawaguchi, 2007). Children become quicker at matching pictures, recalling spatial information, and doing other tasks (Gathercole & Hitch, 1993). Areas of the prefrontal cortex become more specialized in late childhood. For example,

when presented with a visiospatial task in which they are shown a reference stimulus followed by test stimuli, 9-year-old children show substantial brain activity in the frontal regions of the brain, but 7-year-olds do not (Farber & Beteleva, 2011). Development of the prefrontal cortex leads to advances in *response inhibition,* the ability to withhold a behavioral response inappropriate in the current context, which increases children's capacities for self-regulation that permits them to control their thought and behavior, contributing to advances in metacognition (Tsujimoto et al., 2007).

Metamemory

Whereas young children tend to see the mind as static container for information, older children view the mind in more sophisticated terms, as an active manipulator of information (Flavell, 2004). Advances in metacognition accompany precortical development and enable schoolchildren to become mindful of their thinking and better able to consider the requirements of a task; determine how to tackle it; and monitor, evaluate, and adjust their activity to complete the task (Ardila, 2013; Kuhn, 2000).

Metamemory, an aspect of metacognition, refers to the understanding of one's memory and ability to use strategies to enhance it and improves steadily throughout the elementary school years (Cavanaugh & Perlmutter, 1982; Flavell, 2004). Kindergarten and first-grade children understand that forgetting occurs with time and studying improves memory, but by age 8 or 9, metamemory permits children to accurately evaluate what they know, such as vocabulary words, and learn more effectively. Older children perform better on cognitive tasks because metacognition permits them to be more planful. They can evaluate the task, determine how they will approach it given their cognitive resources, attention span, motivation, and knowledge, and deploy metamemory to choose and monitor the use of memory strategies that will permit them to successfully store and retrieve needed information (Camos & Barrouillet, 2011; Kuhn, 2000; Schneider & Pressley, 2013a). These abilities improve with neural maturation and experience.

Memory Strategies

As children's understanding of memory increases, they show more use of mnemonic strategies: tricks to aid memory. **Rehearsal**, organization, and elaboration are common mnemonic strategies. *Rehearsal* refers to systematically repeating information in order to retain it in working memory. For example, a child may say a phone number over and over to not forget it before writing it down. Children do not spontaneously and reliably apply rehearsal until after the first grade (Bjorklund & Douglas, 1997; Schneider & Bjorklund, 1992). Shortly after rehearsal appears, children start to use a second, very important, memory strategy. *Organization* refers to categorizing or chunking items to remember by grouping it by theme or type, such as animals, flowers, and furniture. When memorizing a list of words, a child might organize them into meaningful groups, such as foods, animals, and objects. Growth in working memory is partially attributed to an increase in the number of chunks children can retain with age (Cowan et al., 2010). Elaboration entails creating an imagined scene or story to link the material to be remembered. To remember to buy a loaf of bread, milk, and butter, for example, a child might imagine a slice of buttered bread balancing on a glass of milk. It is not until the later school years that children use elaboration without prompting and apply it to a variety of tasks (Camos & Barrouillet, 2011). As children begin to use memory strategies, their recall improves dramatically.

Throughout middle childhood, children learn more strategies and get better at selecting them, modifying them to suit the task at hand, and using them more effectively, which contributes to advances in cognitive performance (Bjorklund, 2013; Imbo & Vandierendonck, 2007). With development, children's strategy use becomes more efficient. They use more than one strategy during a given task and choose different strategies for different tasks (Justice, Baker-Ward, Gupta, & Jannings, 1997; Lehmann & Hasselhorn, 2007).

The strategies that children use to tackle cognitive tasks vary with culture. In fact, the daily tasks we face vary with our cultural context. Rehearsal, organization, and elaboration are memory strategies that help us recall bits of information. Children in Western cultures receive lots of experience with tasks that require them to recall bits of information and thereby develop considerable expertise in the use of memory strategies. On the other hand, research shows that people in non-Western cultures with no formal schooling do not use or benefit from instruction in memory strategies, such as rehearsal (Rogoff & Chavajay, 1995). Instead, they refine memory skills that are adaptive to their way of life, relying, for example, on spatial cues for memory, such as when recalling items within a three-dimensional miniature scene. Australian Aboriginal and Guatemalan Mayan children perform better at these tasks than do children from Western cultures (Rogoff & Waddell, 1982). Culture and contextual demands influence the cognitive strategies that we learn and prefer and how we use our information processing system to gather, manipulate, and store knowledge.

Knowledge

Throughout childhood, children acquire increasing amounts of information, which they naturally organize in meaningful ways. As children learn more about a topic, their knowledge structures become more elaborate and organized, the information becomes more familiar and meaningful and easier to store and recall. It is easier to recall new information about topics with which we are already familiar.

During middle childhood, children develop vast knowledge bases and organize information into elaborate hierarchical networks that enable them to apply strategies

Intelligence tests are often administered individually, one-on-one.

in more complex ways and remember more material than ever before—and more easily than ever before (Schneider & Pressley, 2013a). For example, fourth-grade students who are experts at soccer show better recall of a list of soccer-related items than do students who are soccer novices, but the groups of children do not differ on the non-soccer-related items (Schneider & Bjorklund, 1992). The soccer experts tended to organize the lists of soccer items into categories, and their knowledge helped them to organize the soccer-related information with little effort, using fewer resources on organization and permitting the use of more working memory for problem solving and reasoning. Novices did not have a knowledge base to aid their attempts at organization. Existing knowledge about a topic makes it easier to learn more about that topic (Ericsson & Moxley, 2013).

Thinking In Context 9.2

1. Physical and motor development have clear implications for cognitive development during infancy. Is the same true in middle childhood? In what ways might physical and motor development influence cognition in school-age children?

2. How might context and culture have shaped your cognition? How might your surroundings—neighborhood, home, and school— have influenced specific aspects of your thinking, such as what strategies you use and your capacities for metacognition? Provide an example of how your context influenced your cognitive development.

INTELLIGENCE

Intelligence tests (IQ tests) measure intellectual aptitude, an individual's capacity to learn, which is vital to school success. **Achievement tests** measure what one has already learned about a given topic. Schools routinely administer achievement tests to students, which measure reading, writing, arithmetic skills, and knowledge of science. Although intelligence tests are designed to measure aptitude, it is not possible to design a test that requires no prior knowledge. Many developmental researchers argue that intelligence tests overlap with achievement tests and may not accurately reflect aptitude or potential.

GROUP-ADMINISTERED AND INDIVIDUALLY ADMINISTERED INTELLIGENCE TESTS

Group-administered tests are those that are given to large numbers of people at once. The Army Alpha test was the first test that could be answered in writing by a large group (Yoakum & Yerkes, 1920). It was developed during World War I to place army recruits in positions that were appropriate to their intellectual abilities (Kaufman & Lichtenberger, 2006). Descendants of this early group-administered test are given routinely in school settings as a quick way of analyzing groups of children's intellectual abilities, their strengths and weaknesses, which aids professionals in planning educational curricula. These multiple-choice tests also identify children who are in need of further assessment with individually administered tests.

Individually administered tests are conducted in a one-on-one setting by professionally trained examiners who carefully observe and record the child's responses and behavior to determine whether the child's responses reflect environmental or behavioral factors such as noisy surroundings, fatigue, or inattention. The Wechsler tests are the most often used individually administered intelligence tests for children and are used to identify children with special needs, whether gifted or learning disabled (Kline, 2013).

The Wechsler Intelligence Scale for Children (WISC-IV), appropriate for children aged 6 through 16, is the most widely used individually administered intelligence test for children. In addition to the WISC, there are Wechsler tests for preschoolers (the Wechsler Preschool and Primary Scale of Intelligence, or WPPSI) and adults (the Wechsler Adult Intelligence Scale, or WAIS). The WISC-IV is composed of 10 subtests that comprise an overall measure of IQ as well as four indexes: verbal comprehension, perceptual reasoning, working memory, and processing speed (Wechsler, 2003). Five supplemental subtests are included to aid examiners in further assessing a child's capacities in a given area. The WISC includes verbal subtests, which tap vocabulary and knowledge, factual information that is influenced by culture, and nonverbal subtests that instead measure working memory, processing speed, and visual spatial reasoning and are thought to be less influenced by culture (DiStefano & Dombrowski, 2006). Table 9.1 presents the subtests and sample items that comprise the WISC-IV.

By carefully examining a child's pattern of subtest scores, a professional can determine whether a child has specific learning needs, whether gifted or challenged (Kaufman, Flanagan, Alfonso, & Mascolo, 2006; Mayes & Calhoun, 2007; Taylor, Reeves, & Jeffords, 2008). The WISC includes nonverbal subtests that require little language proficiency,

TABLE 9.1 Sample Items Measuring the Four Wechsler Intelligence Scale for Children Indices

WISC-IV INDEX	SAMPLE ITEM
Verbal Comprehension Index (VCI)	Vocabulary: What does *amphibian* mean?
Perceptual Reasoning Index (PRI)	Block design: In this timed task, children are shown a design composed of red-and-white bocks, are given a set of blocks, and are asked to put together the block in order to copy the design.
Working Memory Index (WMI)	Digit span: Children are read lists of numbers and asked to repeat them as heard or in reverse order.
Processing Speed Index (PSI)	Coding: In this timed task, children are shown a code that converts numbers into symbols and are asked to transcribe lists of numbers into code.

such as tasks that require the child to arrange materials such as blocks and pictures, which enables children with speech disorders and those who do not speak English to be fairly assessed (Wechsler, 2003).

The WISC is the first intelligence test to be standardized on samples of children who are geographically and ethnically representative of the total population of the United States, creating norms that permit comparisons among children who are similar in age and ethnic background (Kaufman et al., 2006; Taylor et al., 2008). In Canada, an adapted WISC, standardized with children representative of the Canadian population, is available in English and French (Sarrazin, 1999; Wechsler, 1996). The WISC has been adapted and used in many other countries, including the United Kingdom, Greece, Japan, Taiwan, Sweden, Lithuania, Slovenia, Germany, Austria, Switzerland, France, and the Netherlands (Georgas, Weiss, van de Vijver, & Saklofske, 2003).

IQ tests have been shown to have high validity in predicting school achievement, how long a child will stay in school, and career attainment in adulthood. In addition to earning higher than average grades in school (Alloway & Alloway, 2010), children with high IQ scores are more likely as adults to attain greater levels of education, work in a professional job, earn higher income, and own homes (Neisser et al., 1996; Sternberg, Grigorenko, & Bundy, 2001). Despite the advantages of intelligence testing, criticisms abound, especially concerning group differences in intelligence.

INDIVIDUAL AND GROUP DIFFERENCES IN IQ

Consistent ethnic and socioeconomic group differences exist in IQ scores, leading some to argue that IQ tests are culturally biased. Black children in America score an average of 15 IQ points below white children, but the gap is shrinking with each decade and ethnic differences are reduced and often disappear when socioeconomic differences are taken into account (Brooks-Gunn, Klebanov, & Duncan, 1996; Flynn, 2008; Ford, 2008; Rindermann & Thompson, 2013). Socioeconomic status contributes to IQ through differences in living conditions, nutrition, school resources, intellectual stimulation, culture, and life circumstances, such as the experience of discrimination, which influences cognitive and socioemotional factors related to IQ, such as self-concept, academic achievement, and motivation (Neisser et al., 1996; Nisbett et al., 2013; Turkheimer, Haley, Waldron, D'Onofrio, & Gottesman, 2003). Other contextual factors thought to contribute to the differences in IQ scores include schooling and cultural styles of communication.

Intelligence scores are closely linked with education. IQ rises with each year spent in school; improves during the school year, between October and April; and drops over the summer vacation (Ceci, 1991, 1999; Huttenlocher, Levine, & Vevea, 1998). School provides children with opportunities to be exposed to information and ways of thinking that are valued by the majority culture and reflected in IQ tests. At the same time, the results of children's IQ tests influence the schooling that they receive because IQ tests serve as gatekeepers to gifted programs (Ford, 2008).

Some experts argue that IQ tests tap the thinking style and language of the majority culture (Heath, 1989; Helms, 1992). Language difficulties also may explain some group differences. For example, Latino and Native American children tend to do better on nonverbal tasks than ones that require the use of language (Neisser et al., 1996). However, even nonverbal sorting tasks can be influenced by culture. When presented with a series of cards depicting objects and activities and told to sort the cards into meaningful categories, children from Western cultures tend to sort the cards by category, putting bird and dog in the same category of animal. Children of the Kpelle tribe in Nigeria instead sort the cards by function, placing bird with fly, for example, because birds fly (Sternberg, 1985). Learning experiences and opportunities influence children's scores on nonverbal tasks. For example, performance on spatial reasoning tasks are associated with experience with spatially oriented video games (Dirks, 1982; Subrahmanyam & Greenfield, 1996).

Most of the research that examines group differences in IQ has used an older WISC measure, the WISC-III. The WISC-IV, the most recent edition, is different from prior editions in content and structure. The WISC-IV includes an equal number of verbal and nonverbal subtests whereas the older version, WISC-III, included more verbal subtests which are thought to be more heavily influenced by culture (Kaufman et al., 2006). Ethnic differences between whites and African Americans tend to be smaller on the new WISC-IV as compared with the older WISC-III, suggesting that the structure of the test, specifically the degree to which it relies on spoken language, influences the results (Prifitera & Saklofske, 1998; Prifitera, Saklofske, & Weiss, 2005).

Finally, sociohistorical context influences intelligence. Since the 1930s, some researchers have noted that intelligence scores increase with each generation (Lynn, 2013). Over the past 60 years, intelligence scores have increased by about 9 points for measures of general knowledge and 15 points for nonverbal measures of fluid reasoning with each generation (Flynn, 1987, 1998). Referred to as the **Flynn effect**, this generational increase in IQ is thought to be a function of contextual factors—specifically, changes in education and environmental stimulation that improve children's reasoning and problem-solving skills (Flynn & Weiss, 2007). Each generation of children is exposed to more information and ideas than the generation before, and this exposure likely influences thinking itself (te Nijenhuis, 2013). More recent research suggests that the generational gains are leveling off in industrialized countries and already have flattened in Norway, Sweden, and Denmark (Flynn & Weiss, 2007; Sundet, Barlaug, & Torjussen, 2004; Teasdale & Owen, 2000). We have seen that the definition and measurement of intelligence is influenced by context. Two alternative perspectives, as described in the following section, illustrate the relevance of context in conceptualizing intelligence.

ALTERNATIVE VIEWS OF INTELLIGENCE

Arguments about the cultural bias of IQ tests have led some researchers to reconsider what it means to be intelligent. Howard Gardner and Robert Sternberg propose that intelligence entails more than academic skill. Their theories link intelligence to everyday problems and situations.

Multiple Intelligences

A skilled dancer, a champion athlete, an award-winning musician, and an excellent communicator all have talents that are not measured by traditional IQ tests. According to Howard Gardner (1993, 1995; Gardner & Moran, 2006), intelligence is the ability to solve problems or create culturally valued products. Specifically, Gardner's **multiple intelligence theory** proposes at least eight independent kinds of intelligence, as shown in Table 9.2. Multiple intelligence theory expands the use of the term *intelligence* to refer to skills not usually considered by experts as intelligence and has led to a great deal of debate among intelligence theorists and researchers (Barnett, Ceci, & Williams, 2006; Kaufman, Kaufman, & Plucker, 2013; Waterhouse, 2006)

According to multiple intelligence theory, each person has a unique pattern of intellectual strengths and weaknesses. A person may be gifted in dance (bodily kinesthetic) or communication (interpersonal), or musical intelligence yet score low on traditional measures of IQ. Each form of intelligence is thought to be biologically based and each develop on different timetables (Gardner, 1999). Assessing multiple intelligences requires observing the products of each form of intelligence (e.g., how well a child can learn a tune, navigate

TABLE 9.2 Howard Gardiner's Multiple Intelligences

INTELLIGENCE	DESCRIPTION
Verbal-linguistic intelligence	Ability to use and understand the meaning and subtleties of words ("word smarts"). People high in verbal-linguistic intelligence tend to be good at reading, writing, and explaining and often learn second languages with ease.
Logical-mathematical intelligence	Ability to manipulate logic and numbers to solve problems ("number smarts"). People high in logical-mathematic intelligence excel at mathematics, complex calculations, and scientific thinking.
Spatial intelligence	Ability to perceive the visual-spatial world accurately, to navigate an environment, and judge spatial relationships ("spatial smarts"). People high in spatial intelligence tend to be good at solving puzzles, have a good sense of direction, and are often good at drawing.
Bodily kinesthetic intelligence	Ability to move the body skillfully ("body smarts"). People high in bodily kinesthetic intelligence excel at physical activities such as sports or dance and often are good with their hands, such as building and making things.
Musical intelligence	Ability to perceive and create patterns of pitch and melody ("music smarts"). People high in musical intelligence are sensitive to sounds, rhythms, music, and pitch and usually are able to sing, play musical instruments, and compose music.
Interpersonal intelligence	Ability to understand and communicate with others ("people smarts"). People high in interpersonal intelligence are socially skilled, sensitive to others' moods, able communicate and work effectively with others, and enjoy discussion and debate.
Intrapersonal intelligence	Ability to understand the self and regulate emotions ("self-smarts"). People high in intrapersonal intelligence are highly self-aware, understand their own emotions and experience, and are often introverts and enjoy working alone.
Naturalist intelligence	Ability to distinguish and classify elements of nature: animals, minerals, and plants ("nature smarts"). People high in naturalist intelligence are sensitive to nature and are able to nurture and care for plants, animals, and the natural world around them.

an unfamiliar area, or learn dance steps), which at best is a lengthy proposition, at worst nearly impossible (Barnett et al., 2006). However, through extended observations of individuals, an examiner can identify patterns of strengths and weaknesses and help them understand and achieve their potential (Gardner, 1995; Scherer, 1985).

Educators, parents, and students tend to find the idea of multiple intelligences intuitively appealing because it is an optimistic perspective that allows everyone to be intelligent in their own way, viewing intelligence as broader than book learning and academic skills (Halpern, 2005). Currently schools tend to emphasize intelligence as defined by standardized IQ tests (i.e., verbal and logical–mathematic skills). Some educational theorists argue that if intelligence is multidimensional as Gardner suggests, then school curricula should target the many forms that intelligence may take and help students to develop a range of talents (Eisner, 2004; Gardner, 2013). Although Gardner's theory of multiple intelligences has gained a following, it is not yet grounded in research (Waterhouse, 2006). Despite criticisms, the theory of multiple intelligences draws attention to the fact that IQ tests measure a specific set of mental abilities and ignore others. Multiple intelligence theory has helped educators and parents view children's abilities in a new light.

Triarchic Theory of Intelligence

Jason Bourne, hero of the popular spy-action novel and movie series *The Bourne Trilogy,* is highly adaptive. He can quickly gather information, such as a villain's plot; process it; and devise a plan. He adapts his plan on the fly as the situation changes

AF Archive/Alamy

In *The Bourne Trilogy,* Jason Bourne (played by Matt Damon) illustrates creative, and applied intelligence, the three forms of intelligence that comprise the triarchic theory of intelligence.

and thinks creatively to get out of seemingly impossible situations—car chases, traps, and other dangerous scenarios. Certainly Jason Bourne is a fictional character, but he illustrates another view of intelligence, articulated by Robert Sternberg. According to Sternberg (1985), intelligence is a set of mental abilities that permit individuals to adapt to any context and to select and modify the contexts in which they live and behave. Sternberg's **triarchic theory of intelligence** poses three forms of intelligence: analytical, creative, and applied (Sternberg, 2005, 2011). Individuals may have strengths in any or all of them.

Analytical intelligence refers to information processing capacities, such as how efficiently people process information, acquire knowledge, engage in metacognition, and generate and apply strategies to solve problems, such as Bourne's ability to process information quickly. *Creative intelligence* taps insight and the ability to deal with novelty. People who are high in creative intelligence, like Bourne, respond to new tasks quickly and efficiently. They learn easily, compare information with what is already known, come up with new ways of organizing information, and display original thinking. *Applied intelligence* influences how people deal with their surroundings: How well they evaluate their environment, selecting and modifying it, and adapting it to fit their own needs and external demands, similar to Bourne's ability to modify his plans on the fly, using whatever resources are available. Intelligent people apply their analytical, creative, and practical abilities to suit the setting and problems at hand (Sternberg, 2011). Some situations require careful analysis, others the ability to think creatively, and others the ability to problem solve quickly in everyday settings. Many situations tap more than one form of intelligence.

Traditional IQ tests measure analytical ability, which is associated with school success. However, IQ tests do not measure creative and applied intelligence, which predict success outside of school. Some people are successful in everyday settings but less so in school settings and therefore may obtain low scores on traditional IQ tests despite being successful in career and personal life. The triarchic theory emphasizes that intelligent behavior is defined by a culture and context (see Figure 9.6). Some behaviors are more effective, and thereby more intelligent, in some contexts than others (Sternberg, 2014). People who have applied intelligence have skills that permit them to succeed in all of the contexts in which they live. For example, one study created a test that measures informal knowledge of an important aspect of adaptation to the environment in rural Kenya: knowledge of the identities and uses of natural herbal medicines used to combat illnesses. This information was a routine part of Kenyan children's lives. The children used this informal knowledge (not taught in school) on average once a week in treating themselves or suggesting treatments to other children. Children who knew what these medicines were, their use, and dosage were in better position to adapt to their environment—and therefore more intelligent (Sternberg & Grigorenko, 2008).

FIGURE 9.6: Sternberg's Triarchic Theory of Intelligence

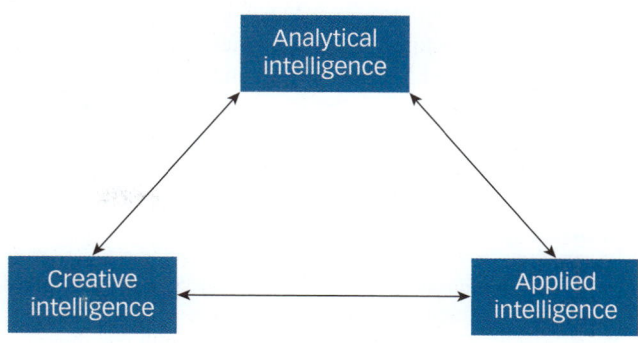

Cultures vary in the specific skills thought to constitute intelligence, but the three mental abilities that underlie intelligent behavior—analytic, creative, and applied intelligence—are the same across cultures. Still, the relative importance ascribed to each may differ (Sternberg, 2007; Sternberg & Grigorenko, 2008). In Western cultures, the intelligent person is one who spends a great deal of effort in learning, enjoys it, and enthusiastically seeks opportunities for lifelong learning. In contrast, other cultures emphasize applied intelligence. For example, the Chinese Taoist tradition emphasizes the importance of humility, freedom from conventional standards of judgment, and awareness of the self and the outside world (Yang & Sternberg, 1997). In many African cultures, conceptions of intelligence revolve around the skills that maintain harmonious interpersonal relations (Ruzgis & Grigorenko, 1994). Chewa adults in Zambia emphasize social responsibilities, cooperativeness, obedience, and respectfulness as being important to intelligence and, likewise, Kenyan parents emphasize responsible participation in family and social life (Serpell, 1974; Serpell & Jere-Folotiya, 2008; Super & Harkness, 1982).

Views of intelligence even vary within a given culture (Sternberg, 2014). For example, when parents were asked of the characteristics of an intelligent child in the first grade

The skills and abilities that are thought to comprise intelligence vary across cultures.

of elementary school, white American parents emphasized cognitive capacities. Immigrants from Cambodia, the Philippines, Vietnam, and Mexico, on the other hand, pointed to motivation, self-management, and social skills (Okagaki & Sternberg, 1993), suggesting that characteristics valued as intelligent vary across cultures but also within a given culture (Sternberg, 2014). Once again, we see that context is an important influence on development.

Thinking in Context 9.3

1. How do you define *intelligence*? From your perspective, what has influenced your own intelligence, as you have defined it? How does your view compare with the views that we have discussed?

2. How might definitions and views of intelligence differ across contexts—different levels of socioeconomic status, neighborhood, or in different cultures, such as Western and non-Western?

MORAL DEVELOPMENT

The development of moral reasoning is influenced by childhood advances in cognitive development, social experience, and opportunities to consider issues of fairness. Specifically, children's reasoning about issues of justice, of right and wrong, undergoes change in middle childhood.

MORAL REASONING: PIAGET'S PERSPECTIVE

Young children up to about age 7 display a rigid view of rules, which Piaget (1932) referred to as the morality of constraint, as discussed in Chapter 7. They submit to rules out of deference to adult authority and constraints. They see rules, even those created in play, as sacred, absolute, and unchangeable, behaviors as either right or wrong, and violations of rules as meriting punishment regardless of intent (DeVries & Zan, 2003; Nobes & Pawson, 2003). For example, young children may proclaim, without question, that there is only one way to play softball, as advocated by Coach Jones: the youngest children must be first to bat. Preschoolers will hold to this rule, explaining that it is simply the "right way" to play.

In middle childhood, at about age 7, children enter the second stage of Piaget's scheme, the **morality of cooperation** (also known as *autonomous morality*), which corresponds to the advancement to the stage of concrete operational reasoning and refers to a more flexible view of rules as self chosen rather than simply imposed on children. As children spend more time with peers and become better at taking their friends' perspectives, their understanding of rules becomes more flexible. Children begin to value fairness and equality and see rules as products of group agreement and instruments of cooperative purposes. They abandon views of absolute right or wrong for more complex and personal views of morality and take into account many factors, such as act, intent, and the situation (Piaget, 1932). Now children become interested in games with rules. They are able to see a need for agreement on rules and consequences for violations. For example, older children are likely to recognize Coach Jones' rule of softball batting order as a way to help the youngest children. Some children might agree that the rule promotes fairness while others might argue to abandon the rule as it gives younger children an unfair advantage.

Piaget did not spend a great deal of time writing and researching moral development. Instead, his career was focused on cognitive development. Despite this, Piaget's theory of moral reasoning inspired Lawrence Kohlberg, who created perhaps the most well-known theory of moral reasoning.

KOHLBERG'S THEORY OF MORAL REASONING

Similar to Piaget's ideas, Kohlberg posed that moral reasoning reflected cognitive development and was organized into stages and levels. Each level of moral reasoning is composed of two stages. Table 9.3 compares Kohlberg and Piaget's perspectives on moral development. Beginning in early childhood and persisting until about age 9, children demonstrate preconventional reasoning. Children at the preconventional stage move from concern with punishment as a motivator of moral judgments (Stage 1) to self-interest and concern about what others can do for them (Stage 2).

For example, consider the following vignette used by Kohlberg (1963) to measure moral reasoning:

> Joe's father promised he could go to camp if he earned the $50 for it, and then changed his mind and asked Joe to give him the money he had earned. Joe lied and said he had only earned $10 and went to camp using the other $40 he had made. Before he went he told his younger brother Alex about the money and about lying to their father. Should Alex tell their father? (p. 9).

The child who reasons at the preconventional stage might reply no. When asked why, he might say, "My brother would say, 'if you tell on me I'll whip you with my belt real hard'" (Kohlberg, 1963, p. 13). Young children view the correct response as the one that is associated with fewer punishments.

At about age 9 or 10, children's advances in cognitive development and perspective-taking ability enable them to demonstrate reasoning at the second level of Kohlberg's scheme, **conventional moral reasoning**. At this level, children understand and internalize the norms and standards of authority figures. They attempt to make decisions and define what is good by anticipating disapproval, viewing approval by others as the ultimate goal. At Stage 3, children uphold rules in order to please others and gain affection and sympathy. As they respond to scenarios, they often put themselves in the role of victim. In response to the question of whether Joe should tell on his brother, a child at Stage 3 might respond, "No—I wouldn't want *him* to tell on *me*." At

TABLE 9.3 Moral Development in Middle Childhood: Comparison of Piaget and Kohlberg's Theories

	PIAGET'S STAGES		KOHLBERG'S LEVELS*	
	STAGE 1: MORALITY OF CONSTRAINT	STAGE 2: MORALITY OF COOPERATION	LEVEL 1: PRECONVENTIONAL MORAL REASONING	LEVEL 2: CONVENTIONAL MORAL REASONING
Cognitive-developmental stage	Preoperational	Concrete operational	Preoperational	Concrete operational
Perspective	Individualistic. Children cannot take the perspective of others; they assume that everyone sees the world as they do.	Multiple. Children can take the perspective of others; they see that more than one point of view is possible and that others do not necessarily view issues as they do.	Individualistic. Children cannot take the perspective of others; they focus on their own needs.	Community. Children take the perspective of the community at large; there is an emphasis on societal rules and welfare.
View of justice	Absolute. Children see acts as either right or wrong, with no shades of gray. The wrongness of an act is defined by punishment.	Relative. Children see that there is often more than one point of view. Acts are seen as right or wrong regardless of punishment.	Absolute. Acts are either right or wrong, defined by punishment and rewards.	Absolute. Right or wrong acts are defined by social approval.
Understanding of rules	Rules are unalterable and sacred.	Rules are created by people and can be changed if it suits people's needs.	Rules are unalterable and imposed by authority figures.	Rules are unalterable and act to uphold the community.
Reason for compliance with rules	Rules are obeyed out of a sense of obligation to conform to authority and to avoid punishment.	Rules that are just are obeyed for their own sake rather than under threat of punishment.	Rules are followed in order to gain rewards and avoid punishment.	Rules are followed out of a sense of duty, in order to please others and gain social approval, which is more important than other rewards.

NOTE: *Each level comprises two stages. Level 3, Postconventional Moral Reasoning, is discussed in Chapter 11.
SOURCES: Adapted from Hoffman (1970); Kohlberg (1981); and Piaget (1932).

Stage 4, children buy into the rules and standards because they are concerned with maintaining social order. They seek approval from legitimate authorities and are bothered only by disapproval if it is expressed by legitimate authorities. Consider Andy, age 16: "If my father finds out later he won't trust me. My brother wouldn't either but I wouldn't have a conscience that he (my brother) didn't" (Kohlberg, 1963, p. 13). Andy's decision reflects his desire to avoid disapproval by authorities over peers. People who reason at Stage 4 view rules as reflecting rights and duties assigned by authorities as part of an organized social order. As shown by 16-year-old Andy, conventional reasoning does not always disappear—many people demonstrate conventional reasoning throughout their lives. Not everyone develops the third and final level of reasoning, postconventional reasoning. If it is achieved, it occurs in adolescence or, more typically, early adulthood.

DISTRIBUTIVE JUSTICE REASONING

An alternative perspective on moral development emphasizes how children's reasoning about distributive justice, how to divide goods fairly, develops over early and middle childhood (Damon, 1977, 1988). Every day, children are confronted with moral issues of distributive justice—for example, over how a candy bar should be divided among three siblings. Does age matter? Height? Hunger? How much the child likes chocolate as compared with other candy?

Children progress from self-serving reasons for sharing, expressed in early childhood (e.g., "I get more candy because I want it." Or "I share candy so that Mikey will play with me.") to more sophisticated and mature conceptions of distributive justice in middle childhood (Damon, 1977). Using nonverbal measures researchers have shown that

3-year-old children identify and react negatively to unfair distributions of stickers, especially when they receive less than another child (LoBue, Nishida, Chiong, DeLoache, & Haidt, 2011). Four- and 5-year-old children allocate rewards based on observable characteristics, such as age, size, or other obvious physical characteristics (e.g., "The oldest should get more candy"). Often, these decisions are based on personal desires and characteristics that adults would deem irrelevant, such as Melissa proclaiming, "Girls should get more because they're girls!" Five- and 6-year-old children think of justice as equality and emphasize equal distribution—that each child should get the same amount of candy, for example (Damon, 1977; Enright et al., 1984).

At about 7 years of age, children take merit into account and believe that extra candy should go to the child who has excelled or worked especially hard. At around 8 years of age, children can act on the basis of benevolence, believing that others at a disadvantage should get special consideration. For example, extra candy should go to the child who does not get picked to play on a sports team or a child who is excluded from an activity. Between ages 8 and 10, children come to understand that people can have different yet equally valid reasons for claiming a reward. They begin to reflect on the need to balance competing claims, such as those of merit and need. Preadolescents and young adolescents try to coordinate claims of merit, need, and equality and provide increasingly sophisticated answers that often cannot be expressed in a single sentence (Damon, 1980).

Culture influences children's ideas about distributive justice. For example, in one study Filipino and American fifth graders were presented with hypothetical scenarios that required that they distribute resources (Carson & Banuazizi, 2008). Both the Filipino and American children preferred equal division of the resources regardless of merit or need, but the children offered different explanations of their choices that are based in differences in Filipino and U.S. culture. U.S. children emphasized that the characters in the scenario preformed equally and therefore deserved equal amounts of the resources, reflecting U.S. culture's emphasis on individuality and merit. Filipino children, on the other hand, tended to be more concerned with the interpersonal and emotional consequences of an unequal distribution, in line with their culture's emphasis on the collective and the importance interpersonal relationships (Carson & Banuazizi, 2008).

Advances in perspective taking that accompany cognitive and social development influence increases in children's sensitivity to others and capacities for distributive justice reasoning. As their understanding of distributive justice improves, children are more likely to express desires to help and share with others and show advancements in social problem solving (Blotner & Bearison, 1984; McNamee & Peterson, 1986). However, with development, children also differentiate among their relationships, which may influence their distributive judgments. Older children tend to see

relationships with acquaintances as relationships of mutual exchange (e.g., you scratch my back and I'll scratch yours) whereas relationships with their best friends tend to be seen as communal and symmetrical—decisions about distributive justice are guided by concern for the other and a desire to maintain the relationship (Frederickson & Simmonds, 2008).

Children's reasoning about moral issues does not occur in a vacuum. Emotions play a role in moral judgment because emotions help children anticipate the outcomes of events and adjust their decisions and behavior accordingly (Arsenio & Gold, 2006). Prosocial emotions such as sympathy reflect an orientation toward others' welfare and influence how children think about moral issues and ultimately how they behave (Eisenberg, Fabes, & Spinrad, 2006; Malti & Latzko, 2010). For example, children may experience situations involving moral transgression as emotionally salient and associate emotions such as empathy or guilt with them, thereby viewing moral transgressions as wrong and deserving of punishment (Helwig, 2008).

DISTINGUISHING MORAL AND CONVENTIONAL RULES

As children's conceptions of justice become more sophisticated, they develop a more comprehensive understanding of the relation between moral rules and social conventions. Rather than strictly adhering to rules out of respect for authority, children begin to consider the situation and weigh a variety of variables in making decisions. Like younger children, school-age children distinguish between moral and conventional rules, judging moral rules as more absolute than conventional rules (Turiel, 2008). Moral rules are seen as less violable, contingent on authority or rules, or alterable than social conventions (Smetana, Jambon, & Ball, 2014). They anticipate feeling positive emotions after following moral rules and more likely to label violations of moral rules as disgusting (Danovitch & Bloom, 2009)

Children judge conventional rules created by adults as more legitimate than those created by children (Nobes & Pawson, 2003). In addition, children view transgressions and alterations of rules by adults as more acceptable than those by children. School-age children can distinguish among social conventions. They discriminate social conventions that have a purpose from those with no obvious purpose. For example, children distinguish among rules about not running indoors versus avoiding a section of the school yard despite no apparent danger. Social conventions that serve a purpose, such as preventing injuries (not running indoors), are evaluated as more important and more similar to moral issues than social conventions with no obvious purpose (avoiding a section of the school yard; Buchanan-Barrow & Barrett, 1998).

In considering violations of social conventions, school-age children also consider intent and the context.

As children grow older they are more likely to view relational aggression as morally wrong and comparable to physical aggression.

more harmful than did boys. As children grow older, they become better able to consider complex moral dilemmas and demonstrate more nuanced judgments. For example, 5- to 11-year-old children become increasingly tolerant of necessary harm—that is, violating moral rules in order to prevent injury to others (Jambon & Smetana, 2014). It is clear that school-age children's conceptions and reasoning about moral and conventional issues undergoes significant development.

Thinking in Context 9.4

1. Is moral development universal? Do all people progress through the same processes? Why or why not?

2. In what ways do children's decisions about right and wrong reflect maturation; cognitive change; and contextual influences such as family, friends, and school or neighborhood factors?

LANGUAGE DEVELOPMENT

While the most dramatic developments in language occur in infancy and early childhood, school-age children demonstrate important advances in their language abilities. Language is composed of a vocabulary, a mental dictionary of memorized words, an understanding of grammar, rules that permit combining words to express ideas and feelings, and an understanding of **pragmatics**, how language is used in everyday contexts. Comprehension and use of vocabulary, grammar, and pragmatics grows and becomes more sophisticated during middle childhood.

VOCABULARY AND GRAMMAR

Although school-age children's increases in vocabulary are not as noticeable to parents as compared with the changes that occurred in infancy and early childhood, 6-year-old children have large vocabularies that expand to 4 times their size by the end of the elementary school years (about 40,000 words) and 6 times by the end of formal schooling (Bloom, 2000). Older children learn words using the same strategies as younger children, such as by contextual cues (Nagy & Scott, 2000). They also learn new words by comparing complex words with simpler words (Owens, 2001). For example, they understand the meaning of the word *sadness* by considering the root word: *sad* (Anglin, 1993).

Schoolchildren learn that there are many words that can describe a given action, but the words often differ slightly in meaning (e.g., *walk, stride, hike, march, tread, strut,* and *meander*). They become more selective in their use of words, choosing the right word to meet their needs. As their vocabularies grow, children learn that some words can have more than one meaning, such as *run* (e.g., "The jogger runs down

For example, Canadian 8- to 10-year-old children understood that a flag serves as a powerful symbol of a country and its values—and that burning it purposefully is worse than accidentally burning it. The 10-year-old children also understood that flag burning is an example of freedom of expression and can be used to express disapproval of a country or its activities. They agreed that if one were in a country that is unjust, burning its flag would be acceptable (Helwig & Prencipe, 1999). Children distinguish between actions by adults and children. When adults were the agents, rules were judged to be more alterable, violable, and authority contingent than when children were the transgressors (Nobes & Pawson, 2003). Children also distinguish among moral issues. For example, although fourth- and fifth-grade students tended to adopt a moral orientation about both physical and relational aggression, they saw physical aggression as more wrong and harmful than relational aggression (Murray-Close, Crick, & Galotti, 2006). Girls, however, rated both types of aggression as more wrong and relational aggression (which they are more likely to experience) as the street," "The clock runs fast," and so on). They begin to appreciate that some words have psychological meanings as well as physical ones (e.g., a person can be smooth and a surface may be smooth). This understanding that words can be used in more than one way leads 8- to 10-year-old children to understand similes and metaphors (e.g., a person can be described as cold as ice, or sharp as a tack; Nippold, Taylor, & Baker, 1996; Winner, 1988).

Words are often acquired incidentally from uses in writing and verbal contexts rather than through explicit vocabulary instruction (Best, Dockrell, & Braisby, 2006). Some words, such as scientific terms, are conceptually complex and require acquiring deep conceptual knowledge, such as an understanding of physical processes, over repeated exposure in different contexts. For example, one study examined 4- to 10-year-old children's knowledge of two scientific terms, *eclipse* and *comet*, before and after the occurrence of a natural event, a solar eclipse. Two weeks after the solar eclipse and without instruction, the children showed improvement in their knowledge of eclipses but not comets—and older and younger children did not differ in their knowledge (Best et al., 2006). Everyday experiences shape our vocabulary, how we think, and how we speak.

In middle childhood, schoolchildren become better able to understand complex grammatical structures. They begin to use the passive voice ("The dog is being fed"), complex constructions such as the auxiliary *have* ("I have already fed the dog"), and conditional sentences ("If I had been home earlier I would have fed the dog"; Chomsky, 1969; Horgan, 1978; Pinker, Lebeaux, & Frost, 1987). Experience with language and exposure to complex constructions influence grammatical development. For example, the Inuit children of Arctic Canada are exposed to the Inuktitut language, which emphasizes full passives; they produce passive voice sentences sooner than do children from other cultures (Allen & Crago, 1996). Throughout middle childhood, sentence structure and use of grammar becomes more sophisticated and children become better at communicating their ideas.

PRAGMATICS

Pragmatics refers to the practical application of language to communicate. With age and advances in perspective-taking skill that comes with cognitive development, children are more likely to change their speech in response to the needs of listeners. They are also able to succeed at challenging tasks such as precisely describing differences among a group of similar objects, and to modify their communication in light of their audience to achieve their goals (Deutsch & Pechmann, 1982). For example, when faced with an adult who will not give the child a desired toy, 9-year-old children are more polite in restating their request than are 5-year-old children (Axia & Baroni, 1985). Children speak to adults differently than to other children. They speak differently on the playground than in class or at home. In addition, older

children begin to understand that there is often a distinction between what people say and what they mean.

One example of pragmatics that develops is the use of irony. Many contextual, linguistic, and developmental factors influence the processing and comprehension of irony, such as intonation, facial expressions, and the capacity to evaluate how well the statement matches the situation (Colston, 2002; Ivanko & Pexman, 2003; Pexman, Glenwright, Hala, Kowbel, & Jungen, 2006). Children at the ages of 5 to 6 become capable of recognizing irony when they are able to understand that a speaker believes something different from what they have said. Yet most tend to interpret irony as sincere, relying on the person's statement and disregarding other cues in the story, intonation, and gestures (Creusere, 2000; Demorest, Meyer, Phelps, Gardner, & Winner, 1984; Harris & Pexman, 2003). Cognitive development permits children to detect the discrepancy between what the speaker says and what he or she believes, and their ability to understand ironic remarks continues to develop through middle childhood, improving rapidly between ages 5 and 8 (Hancock, Dunham, & Purdy, 2000). By 9 years of age, children become able to identify and interpret inconsistencies between ironic utterances and contextual facts but they are not fully aware of the intentional use of irony (Demorest et al., 1984). However, even in adolescence the understanding of irony is still developing; children as old as 13 do not reliably distinguish irony from deception (Filippova & Astington, 2008).

Thinking in Context 9.5

1. Explain what it means to say that language development is continuous from infancy through middle childhood. Is the statement accurate?

2. In what ways does language development illustrate the interaction of developmental and contextual factors? Give some examples related to school-age children's language development.

LEARNING AND SCHOOLING

Between ages 5 and 11, children become better able to attend to stimuli, create and use strategies to manipulate information, store and retrieve information, and accumulate and apply knowledge. Schoolchildren's growing ability to think logically underlies advances in problem-solving ability, but their understanding of logic is concrete, oriented toward the tangible. It may not be surprising, then, that effective instruction for older children is straightforward and concrete in nature (Simon, 2001). Instruction that helps children see connections between new material and prior knowledge builds on what they already know, keeps pace with their growing abilities, and helps children grasp and recall complex concepts and learn to read and write.

Advances in cognitive development underlie older children's achievements in math, reading, and other academic skills.

READING AND MATHEMATICS

An important task of middle childhood is developing skills in reading and writing. From a societal perspective, the abilities to read and to understand mathematics are fundamental to advancement in science and technology, which improve economic opportunities for both individuals and societies at large. In the early school grades, math achievement and reading comprehension are supported by children's cognitive development, specifically executive functioning skills and working memory (Mazzocco & Kover, 2007; Passolunghi, Mammarella, & Altoè, 2008).

However, schooling plays a key role in enabling children to master reading and math. In past generations, most children were taught to read using the **phonics** method, based on memorizing rules and the sounds of each letter to sound out words. Phonics instruction usually involved rigorous drills and lessons to help children identify patterns of sound combinations in words (Brady, 2011; Rayner, Foorman, Perfetti, Pesetsky, & Seidenberg, 2001). In the late 1980s, the **whole-language approach** to reading instruction was introduced, in which literacy is viewed as an extension of language and children learn to read and write through trial and error discovery similar to how they learn to speak, without learning phonics or drills. The emphasis on children as active constructors of knowledge is appealing and in line with cognitive-developmental theory. As the whole-language approach is in widespread use in schools, many teachers today are not trained in phonics instruction. However, the research comparing the two approaches has offered little support for whole-language claims and overwhelming support for the efficacy of phonics training in improving children's reading skills (Brady, 2011; Jeynes, 2008; Liberman & Liberman, 1990; National Institute of Child Health and Human Development [NICHD], 2000; Stahl, McKenna, & Pagnucco, 1994).

Unfortunately, a substantial number of U.S. children are poor readers and are thereby at risk for poor academic achievement. In 2013, 32% of fourth-grade students were unable to meet basic standards for reading at their grade level (National Center for Education Statistics, 2014a). Early reading deficits influence all areas of academic competence (math, writing, science, etc.), and children who experience early difficulties in reading often remain behind (Hong & Yu, 2007; Juel, 1988). Although some research has found an overall tendency for children's attitudes, interests, and motivation in reading and writing to decline over the school years, the drop occurs more rapidly in worse readers (McKenna, Kear, & Ellsworth, 1995). Deficits in reading skill are associated with social adjustment problems, and this association increases over time (Benner, Beaudoin, Kinder, & Mooney, 2005). For example, children with poor reading skills also tend to have poor vocabularies, which may make it more difficult for them to successfully interact with peers (Benner, Nelson, & Epstein, 2002). Children with a limited knowledge of vocabulary tend to demonstrate larger academic and social deficits with time, relative to peers with a rich knowledge of vocabulary (Baker, Simmons, & Kame'enui, 1997).

Similar to reading, in past generations math was taught through rote learning, such as drills, memorization of number facts (e.g., multiplication tables), and completion of workbooks. Many children found these methods boring or restrictive; they learned to dislike math and did not perform well. In response, new methods, rooted in Vygotsky's ideas, were developed to enhance students' interest and motivation in learning mathematics (Ginsburg, 1998). In 1989, the National Council of Teachers of Mathematics modified the national mathematics curriculum to emphasize concepts and problem solving, estimating and probability; teachers were to encourage student interaction and social involvement in solving math problems. The emphasis changed from product—getting correct answers quickly—to process—learning how to understand and execute the steps in getting an answer. Teachers often use strategies that involve manipulatives, opportunities for students to interact physically with objects to learn target information rather than rely solely on abstraction. Such strategies have been shown to be effective in enhancing problem solving and retention (Carbonneau, Marley, & Selig, 2013).

In contrast with research findings about the whole-language approach to reading, changes in the mathematics curriculum are supported by student achievement as fourth-grade students' mathematical skills have improved over the past two decades. Between 1990 and 2013, the proportion of fourth-grade students performing at or above the proficient level increased from 13% to 42%, and the proportion that could not do math at their grade level fell from 50% in 1990 to 17% in 2013 (National Center for Education Statistics, 2014b). Although these represent important gains, the 17% statistic means that nearly one in five U.S. schoolchildren is still deficient in math skills, suggesting that there is more work to be done. The past decade has seen new educational initiatives with the intent to leave no children academically behind and to provide a core set of educational objectives and assessments that ensure that progress is made and children do not fall through the cracks (see Ethical and Policy Applications of Lifespan Development, p. 248).

ETHICAL AND POLICY APPLICATIONS OF LIFESPAN DEVELOPMENT

No Child Left Behind and the Common Core

Current educational policies, such as NCLB and the Common Core, are often criticized for their emphasis on frequent testing,

In an effort to remedy poor academic achievement, in 2002 a federal law known as the No Child Left Behind Act (NCLB) was enacted to ensure that all children demonstrate grade-level reading and mathematics skills. Schools were required to use frequent assessment to measure third- through eighth-grade students' achievement and determine school performance in meeting educational goals. States are held accountable for meeting their annual achievement goals and may lose funding for poor performance.

An important principle of NCLB is that parents and students must have access to quality education and must have the choice to transfer out of low-performing schools. Each year, school districts and states must release district and state report cards tracking student achievement broken down by subgroup (such as ethnicity and socioeconomic status); this information is made public for parents and taxpayers.

Although a stated goal of NCLB is to promote national standards of education, in practice wide discrepancies in achievement have persisted across states. For example, scores showing below-basic performance in math range from 7% of fourth graders in New Hampshire to about 26% in New Mexico and 34% in Washington, DC (National Center for Education Statistics, 2014b). With regard to reading, the percentage of fourth graders who are unable to read at their grade level ranges from 20% in New Hampshire to 47% in Mississippi and 50% in Washington, DC.

The law cited 2014 as the goal for all children in every state to perform at grade level in order for states to maintain full federal funding, but raising every child's academic achievement is very

challenging—so much so that many states did not meet their goals. In the years since the inception of NCLB, 43 states have been granted waivers to permit them access to federal funding as long as they set and maintain accountability standards and are able to report increases in student achievement (U.S. Department of Education, 2015).

In 2010, a new federal program known as Common Core State Standards Initiative was introduced. Developed by a group of experts designated by the governors of all states, the Common Core State Standards detail what children should know about math and language in grades K–12 to ensure that high school graduates are prepared for college and careers (Conley, 2014). A universal standard exam is proposed to assess student learning. As of 2015, there are 43 states and the District of Columbia that are participating in the Common Core State Standards.

Both NCLB and Common Core State Standards have been controversial among parents, taxpayers, educators, and policy makers. Critics point to a narrowed curriculum that devalues art and social studies; they also express concern that many schools encourage teachers to "teach to the test," overemphasizing topics that appear on the exams at the expense of providing a well-rounded education (Dee, Jacob, & Schwartz, 2012; Mathis, 2006; Sunderman & Orfield, 2007). Critics also argue that the NCLB goals are unattainable, given that failing schools often face sanctions, such as reduced federal funding, which make it even more challenging to meet educational standards (Mathis, 2006). States that adopt the Common Core Standards receive competitive advantage for federal education funding yet many have difficulty finding the state funding required to fully implement the Common Core Standards (Kober & Rentner, 2011). Perhaps the most striking criticism is that tying federal funding to performance may penalize schools attended by the neediest children because the lowest performing schools are in low socioeconomic status neighborhoods—therefore poor students are most in danger of attending schools that lose funding.

What Do You Think?

1. **Should students learn a common core of material and competencies? Why or why not?**

2. **What competencies or topics do you think are most important for students to learn?**

3. **Do you agree or disagree with the idea that making funding contingent on achievement will motivate schools to improve their students' test scores?**

ENGLISH LANGUAGE LEARNERS

Over 6,000 languages are spoken in the world, but most are not used in school settings; thus most of the world's children must learn in a foreign language (Tucker, 1998). The United States is no exception: About 22% of school-age children in

the United States speak a language other than English at home; of these, about one fourth struggle with English at school (Federal Interagency Forum on Child and Family Statistics, 2014). Although it was once thought that there was a critical period for learning a second language, we now know that people retain the capacity to acquire language throughout life

(Hakuta, Bialystok, & Wiley, 2003). School-age children are especially well equipped to learn a second language because they have reasoning and communication skills and their brains are plastic.

How should children be taught to speak English? The most common approach used in the United States is the English **immersion** approach (also known as English as a second language, or ESL), which places foreign-speaking children into English-speaking classes, requiring them to learn English and course content at the same time. Some educators believe that students should instead be taught bilingualism, two languages, learning subject matter first in their native language and then switching to English when they become competent in a given academic subject, fostering competence in both languages. A third approach is **dual language learning** (also called two-way immersion), in which English and non-English students learn together in both languages and both languages are valued equally. Advocates argue that bringing a child's native language into the classroom sends children the message that their cultural heritage is respected and strengthens their cultural identity and self-esteem. Some studies suggest that immersion brings a loss in native language (Baus, Costa, & Carreiras, 2013), and others find that dual language retains the native language while enhancing the new language (Castro, Páez, Dickinson, & Frede, 2011).

Many proponents of immersion point to its effectiveness in Canada, where both English and French are official languages. About 10% of Canadian students are enrolled in immersion programs where English-speaking children are enrolled in French classes, learning the entire curriculum in French. Canadian children in French immersion programs become proficient in both languages with no decline in their skills in English or in reading or academic achievement (Harley & Jean, 1999; Hermanto, Moreno, & Bialystok, 2012; Lipka & Siegel, 2007). However, because both English and French are official languages, Canadian children and adults are exposed to both in a great many contexts, not just in school. Researchers argue that immersion is not as effective for U.S. non-English-speaking children because the children's native languages are not official languages in the U.S. English is thus seen as a replacement for children's native language, and this may contribute to children's feelings of isolation, anxiety, and frustration (Crawford, 1997; Midobuche, 2001). Perhaps it is for this reason that longitudinal research with U.S. samples suggests that bilingual approaches, which encourage students to retain their native language while learning English, are more effective than immersion approaches at promoting successful learning of English and as well as overall academic achievement (Relji , Ferring, & Martin, 2014; Rolstad, 2005). Nevertheless, other research suggests that no one approach is best for all children in all contexts (Bialystok, 2001).

The ability to speak more than one language is associated with many cognitive skills. Individuals who have mastered two or more languages have higher scores on measures of selective attention, analytical reasoning, concept formation, cognitive flexibility, and memory (Bialystok, 2011, 2015; Bialystok, Craik, & Luk, 2008; Kormi-Nouri et al., 2008). The process of learning two languages encourages a more complex understanding of language and ability to reflect on it (Bialystok, 2001; Campbell & Sais, 1995). Other research shows that bilingual children score higher on measures of executive function, particularly the ability to control attention and ignore misleading information, suggesting that the brains of bilingual children are different than those of monolingual children (Barac & Bialystok, 2012; Barac, Bialystok, Castro, & Sanchez, 2014; Bialystok, 2015; Carlson & Meltzoff, 2008). These effects emerge slowly over years; one study of second- and fifth-grade students showed improvements over a five-year span in tasks such as verbal fluency and executive control (Bialystok, Peets, & Moreno, 2014). Moreover, when children are able to speak, read, and write in two languages, they are more cognitively and socially flexible and can take part in both cultures (Huang, 1995). At the same time, children who are bilingual show greater achievement in their native language; this is true whether their native language is Spanish or English (Sheng, Bedore, Peña, & Fiestas, 2011).

TRANSITION TO FIRST GRADE

Clarissa followed the teacher's instructions and sat at her desk. She was excited to finally be a big kid, starting first grade. She was nervous about her new surroundings and teacher, but she remembered her kindergarten teacher's advice: "Pay attention and listen to your first-grade teacher, as you did in kindergarten, and you'll be fine." Clarissa folded her hands on her desk, looked up at the teacher, and grinned to herself, "This isn't so hard. I'm a big kid now." Like Clarissa, most children go to kindergarten before entering first grade, and many go to preschool before kindergarten. Despite some experience with the educational system, children usually feel a mixture of excitement and anxiety upon entering first grade. For most

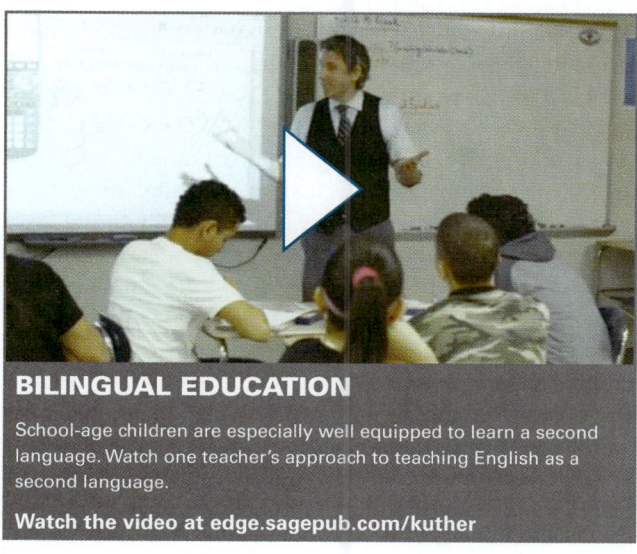

BILINGUAL EDUCATION

School-age children are especially well equipped to learn a second language. Watch one teacher's approach to teaching English as a second language.

Watch the video at edge.sagepub.com/kuther

children and parents, first grade holds symbolic value as the threshold to elementary school and older childhood.

Easing children's transition to first grade is important because adjustment and behavior during the first year of elementary school influences children's views of themselves, their academic performance, teacher perceptions, and class involvement (Zafiropoulou, Sotiriou, & Mitsiouli, 2007). Teachers play an important role in aiding children's adjustment to first grade. Instructional and emotional support provided by teachers, such as attending to students' interests, promoting initiative, providing appropriately challenging learning opportunities, and encouraging positive social relationships among children, help children develop academic and social skills such as reading and mathematics, the ability to follow directions, and self-control (Burchinal, Roberts, Zeisel, Hennon, & Hooper, 2006; Perry, Donohue, & Weinstein, 2007; Pianta, La Paro, Payne, Cox, & Bradley, 2002).

High-quality, sensitive, responsive, and positive interactions with teachers are associated with greater student motivation and academic achievement and fewer problems with anxiety and poor behavior throughout elementary school (Cadima, Leal, & Burchinal, 2010; Maldonado-Carreño & Votruba-Drzal, 2011; Pianta et al., 2002). Conversely, teacher–child conflict is associated with aggression, poor social competence, and underachievement throughout elementary school (Pianta & Stuhlman, 2004; Runions et al., 2014; Spilt, Hughes, Wu, & Kwok, 2012; White, 2013).

First grade serves as a foundation for a child's educational career because the school curriculum of each grade builds on prior grades. Starting in first grade, reading and math skills build step by step each year, so that doing well in one year helps children perform well the next year (Entwisle, Alexander, & Steffel Olson, 2005; see Box 9.3). Early school failure is harmful to students' academic functioning and intellectual development because early academic deficiencies often persist through the school years and children may fall further behind with each successive year in school (Alexander, Entwisle, & Kabbani, 2001; Ferguson, Jimerson, & Dalton, 2001; Hong & Yu, 2007). In addition, children's performance in each grade is documented into a cumulative file that follows them from year to year, influencing teachers' perceptions and expectations of them, which, in turn, influences their educational success.

CHILDREN WITH SPECIAL NEEDS

School systems must meet the needs of a diverse population of children. As we have seen, non-English-speaking children require assistance in learning English and maintaining fluency in their native language. Many other children have special educational needs and require assistance to help them overcome obstacles to learning. The most frequent needs for special education assistance are **intellectual disability**, **learning disabilities,** and **attention-deficit/hyperactivity disorder (ADHD)**.

Intellectual Disability

Formerly known as mental retardation, intellectual disability occurs when children show cognitive and social functioning that is considerably below that of other children their age. *Mental retardation* is the term used by the *Diagnostic and Statistical Manual of Mental Disorders*, 5th edition (*DSM–5*), which is the manual of diagnoses used by physicians and mental health professionals (American Psychiatric Association, 2013). In recent years, the term *mental retardation* has fallen out of favor by professionals because it is stigmatizing and potentially offensive to those with the diagnosis (American Association on Intellectual and Developmental Disabilities, 2009). The new terminology of *intellectual disability* is exemplified by organization names (e.g., American Association on Intellectual and Developmental Disabilities) and is used by U.S. federal government agencies such as the CDC.

Intellectual disability is characterized by deficits in intellectual functioning (often defined as IQ of 70 or below) and age-appropriate adaptive behavior such as social, communication, and self-care skills, that begins before 18 years of age (American Psychiatric Association, 2013). The behavioral component—the inability to appropriately adapt or modify one's behavior in light of situation demands—is essential to a diagnosis of intellectual disability. About 1% to 2% of people in the United States are diagnosed with intellectual disability (Brown et al., 2008). There are a great many causes of intellectual disability, including genetic disorders such as Down syndrome; metabolic disorders such as phenylketonuria (PKU); prenatal exposure to teratogens such as maternal use of alcohol or drugs; developmental disorders such as autism; environmental influences such as neglect, fetal malnutrition, childbirth trauma; and factors associated with poverty such as lack of access to health care and poor nutrition (Carr & O'Reilly, 2007; Ellison, Rosenfeld, & Shaffer, 2013; Vorstman & Ophoff, 2013). Genetic causes are estimated to be responsible for approximately one fourth to one half of identified cases (Srour & Shevell, 2014). Genetic counseling, prenatal care, and health care for pregnant women and infants can prevent many cases. Still other causes of intellectual disability do not happen until later in childhood; these include serious head injury, stroke, and certain infections such as meningitis (CDC, 2005). Furthermore, many cases of intellectual disability have no identifiable cause.

A supportive and engaging environment with toys, books, and warm and intellectually stimulating interactions with caregivers during infancy and early childhood coupled with help and guidance through the school years can enhance the outcomes of children with intellectual disabilities (Gorter et al., 2014). Interventions targeted to the needs of children with mild or moderate disability can help them to become independent and, as adults, live in the community with autonomy (Brown et al., 2008). Children who are profoundly intellectually disabled require greater levels of assistance and more consistent care. As adults, people with profound intellectual disabilities often reside in institutional settings that are able to meet their many needs. However,

ETHICAL AND POLICY APPLICATIONS OF LIFESPAN DEVELOPMENT

Grade Retention and Social Promotion

What should educators do when children do not meet academic standards for promotion to the next grade level? In the 1970s, **social promotion**, the practice of promoting children to the next grade when they do not meet the academic standards, became a common educational practice because grade retention, or "getting left back," became viewed as damaging to children's self-esteem (Bowman, 2005; Kelly, 1999). Social promotion, however, often did not solve the problem of school failure. As social promotion rose in popularity during the 1980s, schoolchildren's standardized test scores declined and school officials were criticized for promoting failing students to the next grade level (Shepard & Smith, 1990). By the 1990s, legislators and the general public called for an end to social promotion, and many states banned social promotion in favor of grade retention as a way to remediate poor academic performance (Frey, 2005; Jimerson, 2001; Thomas, 2000).

About 10% of U.S. youth are retained in a grade one or more times by age 19; however, retention rates vary by state and in some cases are as high as 30% (National Center for Education Statistics, 2014a; Warren & Saliba, 2012; West, 2009). Students are retained for a variety of reasons: failure to meet criteria for promotion, frequent unexcused absences, social and cognitive immaturity, and the belief that an extra year of schooling will produce successful academic outcomes. African American and Hispanic students as well as those from poor households are disproportionately likely to be retained as compared with European American students and those from middle and high socioeconomic status homes (Frey, 2005; National Association of School Psychologists, 2003).

Does grade retention work? The cumulative evidence published to date shows that students who are retained in school, even in the first two years of elementary school, later show poor performance in reading, mathematics, and language, poor school attendance,

more emotional and social difficulties, and greater dislike for school than do promoted students (Bowman, 2005; Ehmke, Drechsel, & Carstensen, 2010; Hong & Yu, 2007; Hughes, Chen, Thoemmes, & Kwok, 2010; Jimerson & Ferguson, 2007; Wu, West, & Hughes, 2010).

In some cases, retention can be a wakeup call to children and parents, but more often it is the first step on a remedial track that leads to lowered expectations, poor performance, and ultimately dropping out of school. In the United States and Canada, retained children are 2 to 11 times more likely to drop out of school than their promoted peers (Guèvremont, Roos, & Brownell, 2007; Stearns, Moller, Potochnick, & Blau, 2007). In addition, retained students are less likely to enroll in postsecondary education and are more likely to work low wage, low status jobs as compared with low-achieving, promoted students (are comparable to the general population of students; National Association of School Psychologists, 2003).

As shown in Table 9.4, the National Association of School Psychologists (2003) recommends providing students and families with a variety of academic and support resources to promote student achievement and address school failure. Promoting students to the next grade, paired with intervention, that target a student's specific needs in class and at home, can help students achieve at grade level and beyond (Jimerson & Renshaw, 2012).

What Do You Think?

1. **Under what conditions might the issue of grade retention arise?**

2. **Should students get "left back"? Why or why not?**

TABLE 9.4 National Association of School Psychologists' Recommendations to Enhance Academic Achievement and Reduce Retention and Social Promotion

TARGET	ACTION
Parental involvement	Encourage frequent contact with teachers and supervision of students' homework.
Instruction	Adopt age-appropriate and culturally sensitive instructional strategies. Systematically and continuously assess instructional strategies and effectiveness and modify instructional efforts in response. Implement effective early reading programs. Offer extended year, extended day, and summer school programs to develop and promote academic skills.
Student academic support	Use student support teams to identify students with specific learning or behavior problems, design interventions to address those problems, and evaluate the effectiveness of those interventions. Provide appropriate education services for children with educational disabilities, including collaboration between regular, remedial, and special education professionals. Implement tutoring and mentoring programs with peer, cross-age, or adult tutors.
Student psychosocial support	Create and implement school-based mental health programs that identify students in need of assistance and devise ways of aiding students. Use effective behavior management and cognitive behavior modification strategies to reduce classroom behavior problems. Establish full-service schools to organize educational, social, and health services to meet the diverse needs of at-risk students.

centers that provide care during the day and in-home-assistance services are important alternatives to institutional care as they are less costly and allow individuals with profound intellectual disabilities to remain with their families, in their homes and communities.

Learning Disabilities

Learning disabilities are diagnosed in children who demonstrate a measurable discrepancy between aptitude and achievement in a particular academic area given their age, intelligence, and amount of schooling (American Psychiatric Association, 2013). Sometimes intelligence test scores of children with learning disabilities show scattered performance, with some subtest scores very high and others very low (Fletcher, 2012). Children with learning disabilities tend to have average intelligence, normal vision, and normal hearing, yet they exhibit difficulty with sensory information and tend to be more easily distracted, less organized, and less likely to use memory strategies than other children (Loomis, 2006). Learning disabilities place children at risk for poor school performance and low self-esteem.

Dyslexia is the most commonly diagnosed learning disability. Children with dyslexia tend to be bright children yet they have difficulty reading, with reading achievement below that predicted by age or IQ. Specifically, children with dyslexia demonstrate age-inappropriate difficulty in matching letters to sounds and difficulty with word recognition and spelling despite adequate instruction and intelligence and intact sensory abilities (Peterson & Pennington, 2012; Ramus, 2014). Dyslexia is estimated to affect 5% to nearly 18% of the school population—boys and girls equally.

Dyslexia is influenced by genetics (Carrion-Castillo, Franke, & Fisher, 2013; Peterson & Pennington, 2012). Children with dyslexia have a neurologically based difficulty in processing speech sounds. They use different regions of the brain during speech tasks and are unable to recognize that words consist of small units of sound, strung together and represented visually by letters (Rosen, 2006; Schurz et al., 2014; Shaywitz et al., 1998). In one study, for example, boys with dyslexia used five times as much area in their brains to perform oral language tasks as compared with boys without dyslexia (Richards et al., 1999). Abnormalities in the brain areas responsible for reading can be seen in 11-year-olds with dyslexia but not in young children who have not been exposed to reading, suggesting that the brain abnormalities associated with dyslexia occur after reading commences (Clark et al., 2014).

Brain differences and processing defects make it difficult for children with dyslexia to decode or read words but do not affect their comprehension (Duff & Clarke, 2011). However, reading interventions can improve reading performance and can change the biological structure of the brain. Phonics instruction has been shown to help children with dyslexia learn to read (Shaywitz et al., 1998). In one study, children who were trained for eight weeks on phonics and tracing of letters, groups of letters, and words showed improvement in reading and an increase in gray matter volume in the brain areas associated with word and number recognition, memory, and integrating sensory information (Krafnick, Flowers, Napoliello, & Eden, 2011). Successful interventions include not only training in phonics but also supporting emerging skills by linking letters, sounds, and words through writing and reading from developmentally appropriate texts (Snowling, 2013).

Attention-Deficit/Hyperactivity Disorder

ADHD is the most commonly diagnosed disorder in children, diagnosed in about 10% of schoolchildren in the United States (Visser et al., 2014). Although it is commonly believed that the prevalence of ADHD is rising, research examining ADHD diagnoses in representative samples of the U.S. population suggests that levels of ADHD have remained consistent over the past three decades (Polanczyk, Willcutt, Salum, Kieling, & Rohde, 2014). ADHD is a neurodevelopmental disorder characterized by persistent difficulties with attention and/or hyperactivity/impulsivity that interferes with performance and behavior in school and daily life.

There are three different patterns ADHD may take. *ADHD Predominantly Inattentive Presentation* emphasizes difficulties with attention and distractibility, such as failing to attend to details, making careless mistakes, not appearing to listen when spoken to directly, not following through on instructions, or difficulty organizing tasks or activities. The ADHD *Predominantly Hyperactive–Impulsive Presentation* emphasizes difficulties with impulsivity, such as frequent fidgeting, squirming in seat, and leaving seat in class; often runs or climbs in situations where it is not appropriate; talks excessively often blurts out an answer before a question is completed; and has trouble waiting a turn. The *ADHD Combined* Presentation includes symptoms of both inattention and hyperactivity/impulsivity. While most children show one or two symptoms of inattention or hyperactivity at some point in their development, a diagnosis of ADHD requires consistent display of a minimum number of specific symptoms over a six-month period, and the symptoms must interfere with behavior in daily life.

Symptoms of ADHD, whether inattention or hyperactivity, make focusing on a task for more than a few minutes challenging, if not impossible. Upon sitting down to begin a task, the child might fidget, squirm in his seat, tap his legs, call out to the teacher, get up to sharpen his pencil, stop to look out the window, and so on. Children with ADHD are at risk for interpersonal difficulties because they have difficulty processing emotion-related stimuli, like faces; have poor social perspective taking skills; and act impulsively without thinking about social rules or the consequences of their actions (Da Fonseca, Seguier, Santos, Poinso, & Deruelle, 2009; DuPaul, 2007; Marton, Wiener, Rogers, Moore, & Tannock, 2009). Children with ADHD tend to enter ongoing peer activities in an abrupt manner, disrupting them, and therefore have trouble maintaining friendships, are often are not well liked and are sometimes even rejected by peers (Wiener & Mak, 2009). Girls with ADHD, particularly, show higher rates of peer victimization, being bullied by peers, as compared with other children.

ADHD has biological causes and is nearly 80% heritable (Aguiar, Eubig, & Schantz, 2010; Schachar, 2014). Environmental influences on ADHD include premature birth, maternal smoking, drug and alcohol use, lead exposure, and brain injuries (Pineda et al., 2007; Tarver, Daley, & Sayal, 2014; Thapar, Cooper, Eyre, & Langley, 2013). Contrary to popular rumors, ADHD is not associated with sugar intake or food additives (Barkley, 1998; Shaywitz et al., 1994).

Symptoms of ADHD tend to decline with age, but the disorder does not disappear and may be even be diagnosed in adults (Riddle et al., 2013). Untreated, ADHD is associated with poor academic performance, behavior problems, risky activities, and injuries (Aguiar et al., 2010; Harpin, Mazzone, Raynaud, Kahle, & Hodgkins, 2013; Tarver et al., 2014). Because children with ADHD experience academic as well as social difficulties, intervention is critical. Stimulant medication is the most common treatment for ADHD. Stimulant medication increases activity in the parts of the brain that are responsible for attention, self-control, and behavior inhibition (Rubia et al., 2013). Children who are prescribed carefully regulated dosages of medication show reductions in activity level and improvements in attention, academic performance, and social competence (Prasad et al., 2013; Rubia et al., 2013). Stimulant medication can increase children's capacity to attend, but effective interventions help children learn cognitive and behavioral strategies to help them succeed in academic and social situations, such as ways of directing their attention and ways of entering social groups and interacting with peers (Daley et al., 2014; Tarver et al., 2014).

Educating Children With Disabilities

In the United States and Canada, legislation mandates that children with learning disabilities are to be placed in the "least restrictive" environment, or classrooms that are as similar as possible to classrooms for children without learning disabilities. Whenever possible, children are to be educated in the general classroom, with their peers, for all or part of the day. This is known as **mainstreaming**. Classes that practice mainstreaming have teachers who are sensitive to the special needs of students with learning disabilities and provide additional instruction and extra time for them to complete assignments. The assumption is that when children are placed in regular classrooms with peers of all abilities, they are better prepared to function in society. The effectiveness of mainstreaming varies. Some mainstreamed

Special education classrooms that practice inclusion integrate all children into a regular classroom with additional teachers and educational support that is tailored to learning disabled students' special needs. Students with learning disabilities learn more and demonstrate more social advancement in inclusion settings.

children benefit academically and socially. Others do not. Children's responses to mainstreaming vary with the severity of their disability as well as the quality and quantity of support provided in the classroom (Klingner, Vaughn, Hughes, Schumm, & Elbaum, 1998; Waldron & McLeskey, 1998).

Mainstreaming works best when children receive instruction in a resource room that meets their specialized needs for part of the school day and the regular classroom for rest of the school day (Vaughn & Klingner, 1998). Children with learning disabilities report preferring combining time in the regular classroom with time in a resource room that is equipped with a teacher who is trained to meet their special learning needs. Mainstreaming may help children with learning disabilities to overcome difficulties with social awareness and skills that arise from their attention and processing deficits (Gresham & MacMillan, 1997; Sridhar & Vaughn, 2001). Interaction with peers and cooperative learning assignments that require children to work together to achieve academic goals help students with learning disabilities learn social skills and form friendships with peers.

A more recent approach to special education is inclusion, including children with learning disabilities in the regular classroom with a teacher or paraprofessional who is specially trained to meet their needs. Inclusion is different from mainstreaming because in mainstreaming there is only one teacher in class. Inclusion entails additional educational support within the regular classroom that is tailored to learning disabled students' special needs. Students with learning disabilities spend all of their time in the regular classroom and learn more and demonstrate more social advancement than when they are taught in a resource room for part of the day (Swenson, 2000; Waldron & McLeskey, 1998). Around the world, children learn strategies to succeed despite their limitations, but the disabilities themselves and the academic and social challenges posed by them do not disappear. Parents and teachers are most helpful when they understand the learning disabilities are not a matter of intelligence or laziness but rather a function of brain differences and when they help children to learn to monitor their behavior.

Children undergo many physical and cognitive changes in middle childhood. Their bodies and the way in which they view the world change. As they become more cognitively competent, they adapt and apply their emerging skills in new ways, to consider moral and conventional issues, to become more proficient at language, and to learn in school. In Chapter 10, we examine the psychosocial changes that occur in middle childhood—the social changes that schoolchildren experience.

Thinking in Context 9.6

1. Do you remember your experiences in first grade? Do you remember your teacher, classmates, how you spent your days? In your view, does first grade matter?

2. What are the pros and cons of mainstreaming and inclusion, in your view? How might each address the needs of intellectual disabilities or other special needs?

Apply Your Knowledge

Sally Scientist designed an experiment to examine how the feedback that children receive from adults influences their motivation and performance in academic tasks. Eight- to 10-year-old children were asked to participate in an experiment on problem solving. Each child was seated at a desk, and a piece of paper containing the following statement was distributed and then read to the child.

> My name is Sally Scientist, and I have been working on creating a short test to look at children's school smarts that will tell me how well children will do at school. Today, I'm asking that you try the test. Most children earn about 70 points on this 100-point test. Before you begin, I'd like to have an idea of how you will do on this test. What score do you think you'll get?

After estimating his or her performance, each child completed the test. At the end, the children waited in another room, and they were told that their tests were being scored and that the experimenter wanted to learn what they thought of the test. Sally Scientist did not score the test. Instead, children were provided with false feedback.

Regardless of how children scored, they were told that they scored below the score they anticipated. Sally used the child's prediction to determine the test score; each child was given a score that was 19 points below the score that he or she predicted.

Each child was asked to meet with Sally, who handed out a green sheet listing the child's name and test score; at the top of the green sheet, in bold, read the label "Poor." As Sally handed the sheet to the child, she shuffled a second pile of yellow pages with "Excellent" printed at the top. She asked the child, "Why do you think you did poorly on the test?" Afterward, the child completed a survey measuring his or her motivation to succeed in academic tasks and measures of self-esteem and depression. After receiving false feedback, children were more likely to report low academic motivation, poor self-esteem, and depressive symptoms than children who were given accurate feedback.

- Discuss influences on school achievement in middle childhood. How might the findings of Sally Scientists' study inform our understanding of children's motivation to succeed?

- Why did Sally provide the children with false information about their performance? What are the advantages of this approach?
- Providing false feedback is a type of deception. What are possible disadvantages of using deception in this study?

- How might Sally lessen the effects of the false feedback after she conducts her study?
- If you were Sally Scientist, how would you study influences on school achievement?

Chapter Summary

9.1 Summarize patterns of physical and motor development during middle childhood.

During middle childhood, growth in height and weight slows, relative to early childhood, and children demonstrate increases in strength, speed, reaction time, flexibility, balance, and coordination. Advances in growth and motor development are influenced by genetic and contextual factors.

9.2 Analyze common health issues facing school-age children, including associated risk factors.

Middle childhood is a time of health, but school-age children often face chronic health issues. Rising rates of obesity pose another problem for children. Childhood obesity is associated with short- and long-term physical and psychological health problems, and most children do not grow out of obesity but instead become obese adults. Programs that are effective at reducing childhood obesity decrease children's television and video game use, increase their physical activity, and teach children about nutrition.

9.3 Discuss school-age children's capacities for reasoning as well as cultural differences in patterns of development.

At about age 7, children enter the concrete operational state of reasoning, permitting them to use mental operations to solve problems and think logically, and then demonstrate several different kinds of classification skills and make advances in solving conservation tasks. Concrete operational reasoning is found in children around the world; however, experience, specific cultural practices, and education play a role in development.

9.4 Explain changes in children's information processing capacities and thinking.

Brain maturation leads to improvements in executive functioning and attention, memory, response inhibition, and processing speed. Mental activities that are performed often become automatic, freeing up intellectual resources, allowing more information to be remembered and for more advanced thinking. As children's understanding of their own thinking and memory increase, they get better at selecting and using mnemonic strategies and become more planful.

9.5 Analyze the uses, correlates, and criticisms of intelligence tests.

IQ tests measure intellectual aptitude and are often used to identify children with special educational needs. IQ predicts school achievement, how long a child will stay in school, and career attainment in adulthood. Persistent group differences are found in IQ scores, but contextual factors, such as socioeconomic status, living conditions, school resources, culture, and life circumstances, are thought to account for group differences.

9.6 Compare two alternative views of intelligence.

Multiple intelligence theory and the triarchic theory of intelligence conceptualize intelligence as entailing a more broad range of skills than those measured by IQ tests. Howard Gardner proposed eight forms of intelligence in which people vary; each person is thought to have a unique pattern of strengths and weaknesses. In the triarchic theory of intelligence, Robert Sternberg posed that people vary on three forms of intelligence that comprise academics, creativity, and adaptability.

9.7 Examine patterns of moral development during middle childhood.

Until about age 9, children demonstrate preconventional reasoning in Kohlberg's theory of moral development, moving from concern with punishment as a motivator of moral judgments (Stage 1) to self-interest and concern about what others can do for them (Stage 2). In late childhood, children advance to conventional moral reasoning in which they internalize the norms and standards of authority figures, becoming concerned with pleasing others (Stage 3) and maintaining social order (Stage 4). School-age children's views of fairness become more sophisticated, and they become more likely to consider the situation and weigh a variety of variables in making decisions.

9.8 Discuss language development during middle childhood and its implications for capacities for communication.

Vocabulary expands to four times its size during the elementary school years. School-age children learn words through contextual cues and by comparing complex words with simpler words. Understanding of complex grammatical structures, syntax, and pragmatics improves in middle childhood with experience with language and exposure to complex constructions and children become better communicators.

9.9 Examine patterns of academic achievement in reading, mathematics, and second languages.

Phonics methods are highly effective in teaching reading, yet most schools employ the whole-language approach to teaching reading and a substantial number of U.S. children are poor readers. U.S. students' mathematical skills have improved over the past two decades, with the introduction of a national mathematics curriculum, yet nearly one in five U.S. schoolchildren is deficient in math skills. Fluency in two languages is associated with higher scores on measures of selective attention, executive function, analytical reasoning, concept formation, and cognitive flexibility. Bilingual approaches to language learning are more effective than immersion approaches at teaching language and promoting academic achievement in children.

9.10 Identify common disabilities that pose educational challenges for children as well as methods of educating children who have special needs.

Many school-age children are diagnosed with intellectual disability, dyslexia, and ADHD. In the United States and Canada, legislation mandates that, whenever possible, children are to be mainstreamed and educated in the general classroom, with their peers, for all or part of the day. However, the effectiveness of mainstreaming varies with the severity of their disability as well as the quality and quantity of support provided in the classroom.

Key Terms

CHAPTER 10

Socioemotional Development in Middle Childhood

$SAGE edge™ **Get the edge on your studies at edge.sagepub.com/kuther.**

Master these learning objectives using key study tools in the chapter and at SAGE edge. Access original SAGE **Video Cases** to explore the lives and contexts of individuals in every stage of development, **Think Critically** and **Explore Further** with SAGE journal and reference articles, and **Watch**, **Listen**, and **Connect** with online multimedia resources.

LEARNING OBJECTIVES

LEARNING OBJECTIVES	**KEY STUDY TOOLS**
10.1. Explain three ways in which the sense of self changes in middle childhood.	**Think Critically** Sense of Self **Watch** Kids Need Structure
10.2. Analyze the typical qualities of school-age children's friendships and their developmental significance.	**Explore Further** Friendships
10.3. Explore the role of peer acceptance in children's adjustment, including popularity and rejection.	**Think Critically** Peer Acceptance
10.4. Compare the characteristics of bullies and victims, how parent and school factors contribute to bullying, and outcomes of bullying.	**Ethical and Policy Applications of Lifespan Development** Anti-Bullying Legislation (p. 268) **Connect** Stopbullying.gov
10.5. Discuss changes in family relationships during middle childhood.	**Cultural Influences on Development** China's One-Child Policy (p. 270) **Connect** Strengthening Family Relationships
10.6. Examine the adjustment of children reared in gay and lesbian families.	**Explore Further** LGBT Families and Adoption
10.7. Identify risks and protective factors that contribute to children's adjustment in single-parent and cohabiting families.	**Explore Further** Single-Parent Families
10.8. Analyze patterns of adjustment to divorce in children and factors that contribute to adjustment.	**Video Case** Blended Family **Video Case** Divorce: Parent's Perspective
10.9. Discuss common manifestations of anxiety in middle childhood.	**Lives in Context** Exposure to War and Terrorism and Children's Development (p. 282) **Connect** School Refusal
10.10. Assess risks for sexual abuse, typical outcomes, and prevention strategies.	**Explore Further** What Is Sexual Abuse?
10.11. Analyze the role of resilience in promoting adjustment, including characteristics of children and contexts that promote resilience.	**Explore Further** Family Resilience **Listen** Resilience in Millennials

Unlike his little brother, who will play with any child available, Tishaun is choosy about his friends. He meets with the same group of neighborhood boys each afternoon to play basketball in Tishaun's driveway. Tishaun especially likes playing basketball with his friends because he's much better than them. Tishaun is proud that his gym teacher suggested that he try out for the school's basketball team. He also performs well in class, is a good student, gets along with others, and is well liked by his classmates. Tishuan has successfully navigated many of the socioemotional tasks of middle childhood. He has come to understand himself in more sophisticated ways, and he has established good relationships with his parents and peers. In this chapter, we examine ways in which family and peer contexts shape school-age children's socioemotional development.

PSYCHOSOCIAL DEVELOPMENT IN MIDDLE CHILDHOOD

Middle childhood, ages 6 to 11, represents an important transition in children's conceptions of themselves and their abilities. According to Erik Erikson (1950), school-age children face the task of developing a sense of **industry over inferiority**, feeling more competent than inadequate. Children must learn and master skills that are valued in their society, such as reading, mathematics, and writing, as well as using computers. Six year-old Kia tied her shoelace and smiled to herself. "I did it again. I'm really good at tying my shoelaces—much better than my little brother." Success at culturally valued tasks as simple as shoelace tying influences children's feelings of competence and curiosity as well as their motivation to persist and succeed in all of the contexts in which they are embedded (Kowaz & Marcia, 1991). When children are unable to succeed or when they receive consistently negative feedback from parents or teachers, they may lose confidence in their ability to succeed and be productive at culturally valued tasks. Children's sense of industry influences their self-concept, self-esteem, and readiness to face the physical, cognitive, and social challenges of middle childhood.

SELF-CONCEPT

In middle childhood, children's developing cognitive capacities enable them to think about themselves in new, more complex ways and develop more sophisticated and comprehensive self-concepts (Harter, 2012). Children's perceptions of themselves, the characteristics they use to describe themselves, is known as self-concept. For example, consider this school-age child's self-description: "I'm pretty popular. . . . That's because I'm nice to people and helpful and can keep secrets. Mostly I am nice to my friends, although if I get in

a bad mood I sometimes say something that can be a little mean" (Harter, 2012, p. 59). Like most older children, this child's self-concept focuses on competencies and personality traits rather than specific behaviors (Damon & Hart, 1988). Older children include both positive and negative traits, unlike younger children who tend to describe themselves in all or none terms (Harter, 1996). Through interactions with parents, teachers, and peers children learn more about themselves (Harter, 2003; Spilt, van Lier, Leflot, Onghena, & Colpin, 2014; Verschueren, Doumen, & Buyse, 2012). For example, older children understand that their traits can vary with the context—for example, that a person can be nice or mean, depending on the situation (Heyman & Gelman, 2000). As self-concept differentiates, children develop a physical self-concept (referring to physical attributes or what they look like), academic self-concept (school performance), and social self-concept (social relationships with peers and others; Dusek & McIntyre, 2003; Harter, 2003).

Brain development plays a role in self-conceptions throughout the lifespan. The gains in executive functioning that come with neural maturation, such as self-regulation and problem solving, are associated with more sophisticated self-perceptions and the ability to take others' perspectives (Lewis & Carmody, 2008; Samson, Apperly, & Humphreys, 2007). Developmental scientists look to research with adults to understand how the brain's function changes with development (Apperly, Samson, Humphreys, & Hurnphreys, 2009). For example, parts of the temporal and parietal, and sometimes frontal cortex, are activated in self-representation tasks, such as when adults hear their own name or judge whether adjectives are relevant to themselves (Carmody & Lewis, 2006; Fossati et al., 2003; Macrae, Moran, Heatherton, Banfield, & Kelley, 2004). When processing information about the self, children use many more areas of the brain in than do adults suggesting that, with development, processing becomes more efficient and self-concept becomes more complex and differentiated (Pfeifer & Peake, 2012).

SELF-ESTEEM

If self-concept is based on a description ("what am I like?"), self-esteem is based on evaluation ("how well do I like myself?"); it refers to considering oneself worthy or valuable. Self-esteem is influenced by children's self-conceptions as well as the importance they assign to the particular ability (Hart, Atkins, & Tursi, 2006; Harter, 2006), as illustrated by a child's comment, "Even though I'm not doing well in those subjects, I still like myself as a person, because Math and Science just aren't that important to me. How I look and how popular I am are more important" (Harter, 2012, p. 95). Children tend to report feeling most interested in activities they perform well and areas that they view as their strengths (Denissen, Zarrett, & Eccles, 2007). Activities such as playing group sports can lead to increases in particular aspects of self-concept, such as physical self-concept and higher self-esteem (Slutzky & Simpkins, 2009).

Advances in cognitive development, including perspective taking and social comparison, lead children to make more complex descriptions and evaluations of themselves as they grow older. School-age children can organize their observations of their abilities, behaviors, and experiences in more complex ways than younger children, yielding more accurate and comprehensive descriptions of themselves that recognize temporal and contextual fluctuations, such as being shy in one situation and not another (Harter, 2012). Whereas preschoolers tend to have unrealistically positive self-evaluations, school-age children's sense of self-esteem becomes more realistic and connected to their abilities (Boseovski, 2010; Jacobs, Lanza, Osgood, Eccles, & Wigfield, 2002; Robins & Trzesniewski, 2005). Beliefs about the self become more closely related to behavior in late childhood through adolescence (Davis-Kean, Jager, & Andrew Collins, 2009). Social comparison, a process by which children compare their abilities and skills with other children, permits children to evaluate their own performance in relation to their peers and influences children's views of their ability and overall sense of competence (Butler, 1998). Children receive feedback about their abilities from parents, teachers, and peers, and this contributes to their growing sense of self-esteem (Hart et al., 2006). Perceived disapproval by peers, for example, is associated with concurrent declines in self-esteem (Thomaes et al., 2010).

Children's ratings of self-esteem are influenced by ethnic and cultural factors. For example, adverse contextual conditions such as poverty, unsafe neighborhoods, ongoing stressors, and the experience of racism and discrimination contributes to low scores on measures of self-esteem on the part of African American children, relative to those of white and Hispanic children (Kenny & McEachern, 2009). Despite their higher academic achievement than North American children, Chinese and Japanese children tend to score lower in self-esteem, perhaps because competition is high and Asian children experience great pressure to achieve (Chiu, 1992; Hawkins, 1994; Stevenson, Lee, & Mu, 2000). At the same time, Asian culture emphasizes collectivism and social harmony, and children are not encouraged to use social comparison to enhance their self-esteem in order to maintain relationships (Toyama, 2001). Instead, they are encouraged to praise others, including their peers, while minimizing attention to themselves (Falbo, Poston, Triscari, & Zhang, 1997; Heine & Lehman, 1995). Chinese children's relationships with peers illustrate the culture's emphasis on maintaining relationships.

Thinking in Context 10.1

1. In what ways do school children's developing self-concept influence their relationships with peers? In turn, how do peer interactions and relationships influence children's development?

PEER RELATIONSHIPS IN MIDDLE CHILDHOOD

School-age children generally become more interested in forming and nurturing relationships with peers. As children progress through the school years, they develop a more sophisticated understanding of themselves and become better able to understand and appreciate others' perspectives; peer relationships become complex and multifaceted (Selman, 1980). Older children spend more time with peers and place more importance on those relationships than do younger children (Steinberg & Morris, 2001). Friends are a source of companionship, belonging, support, validation, and opportunities to learn relationship skills such as impression management, conflict resolution, and cooperation as discussed in the following sections (Glick & Rose, 2011; Hartup, 2006; Hartup & Abecassis, 2002; Klima & Repetti, 2008).

FRIENDSHIP

Like young children, school-age children's friendships are based in similarities. Older children tend to choose friends who are like them in interests, play preferences, and demographics. One similarity that children often share is

Friends are an important source of companionship, support, and fun in middle childhood.

ethnicity. Older children are more likely to select friends of the same race and ethnicity than are younger children (Aboud, Mendelson, & Purdy, 2003, 2007). For example, in one study of 6- to 12-year-old U.S. children of Cambodian, Dominican, and Portuguese heritage, children became more proud of their heritage as they grew older and in turn showed a greater preference to form friendships within their ethnic group (Marks, Szalacha, Lamarre, Boyd, & Coll, 2007). Ethnicity often becomes an increasingly important part of children and adolescents' self-concept and therefore becomes a more salient dimension for selecting friends.

However, contextual characteristics, such as the ethnic diversity of a neighborhood or school, also influence children's choices of friends. In racially integrated schools, for example, children are more likely to report having at least one close friend of another race (DuBois & Hirsch, 1990; McGlothlin & Killen, 2006). School-age girls may be more likely to have ethnically diverse social networks and cross-race friendships than boys (Lee, Howes, & Chamberlain, 2007). Once established, cross-race friendships are similar to same-race friendships with regard to intimacy, companionship, and security (Aboud et al., 2007; McDonald et al., 2013; McGlothlin, Killen, & Edmonds, 2005). Children in cross-race friendships tend to show a lower tolerance for excluding others (Killen, Kelly, Richardson, Crystal, & Ruck, 2010), are less prone to **peer victimization** (Kawabata & Crick, 2011), and tend to feel socially and emotionally safer and less vulnerable at school (Graham, Munniksma, & Juvonen, 2014; Munniksma & Juvonen, 2012).

Friendships become more complex over the course of childhood. With advances in social cognition as children become increasingly able to take the perspective of others and consider their needs, friendship transforms into a reciprocal relationship in which children are responsive to each other's needs and trust each other (Damon, 1977; Selman, 1980). Shared values and rules become important components to friendship by 9 to 10 years of age (Rubin, Coplan, Chen, Buskirk, & Wojslawowicz, 2005). In middle to late childhood, friends are expected to be loyal and stick up for each other. Violations of trust, such as telling secrets, breaking promises, and not helping a friend in need, can break up a friendship (Rubin et al., 2005). Therefore, children perceived as trustworthy by their peers tend to have more friends and establish more friendships over time than do children perceived as less trustworthy (Rotenberg et al., 2004).

Because of their more complex perspectives on friendship, school-age children tend to name only a handful of friends, as compared with preschoolers who say that they have lots of friends. "I know a lot of kids and am inviting them all to my birthday party," explained 9-year-old Shana, "but only a few are really my friends. I don't tell them everything. I only tell everything to my best friend. Only she knows that I like Nicky." As Shana illustrates, with age, children differentiate among best friends, good friends, and casual friends, depending on how much time they spend together and how much they share with one another (Hartup & Stevens, 1999). Older children, especially girls, tend to have fewer, but closer, friends, and by age 10, most children report having a best friend (Buhrmester, 1998; Erwin, 1998).

With age, friendships are more likely to last over time. First graders tend to keep about 50% of their friendships across the school year, and fourth graders retain about 75% over the same time frame (Poulin & Chan, 2010). Friendships tend to remain stable from middle childhood into adolescence, especially among girls and among both boys and girls whose friendships are high in relationship quality, characterized by sharing, mutual perspective taking, and compromise (Berndt, 2004; Poulin & Chan, 2010). However, it is not uncommon for friendships to end during childhood. Some friendships end after only a few months or over the course of a single school year (Cairns, Leung, Buchanan, & Cairns, 1995). Friendships that lack intimacy and closeness are more likely to end, as are those high in conflict or aggression (Hektner, August, & Realmuto, 2000; Troutman & Fletcher, 2010). Ending a friendship can be a normal, inevitable, and often desirable part of friendship development. Because friendship is based largely on similar characteristics, proximity, and opportunities for interaction, friendships may come and go as individuals develop new interests, competencies, and values. They may also end as children progress into new contexts, such as a change of school or a family move to a different neighborhood (Cairns et al., 1995; Troutman & Fletcher, 2010; Wojslawowicz Bowker, Rubin, Burgess, Booth-LaForce, & Rose-Krasnor, 2006).

Older children become more upset at losing a friend and find making friends more challenging than do young children (Erwin, 1998; Hartup, 2006; Laursen & Hartup, 2002). Friendship dissolution may have serious consequences for some children, especially those who are unable to replace the friendship (Wojslawowicz Bowker et al., 2006). Some children who experience disruption and loss of close friendships experience problems with depression, loneliness, guilt, anger, anxiety, and acting out behaviors; however, it is also plausible that children with psychosocial problems are more likely to experience the loss of friendship, and, in turn, show more poor adjustment (Hektner et al., 2000; Ladd & Troop-Gordon, 2003; Rubin, Coplan, Chen, Bowker, & McDonald, 2011). Yet many children replace "lost" friendships with "new" friendships. For example, in one study of fifth graders, losing a friend was associated with adjustment difficulties only when the lost friendship was not replaced by a new friendship. For these children, the lost and new friendships were largely interchangeable (Wojslawowicz Bowker et al., 2006). For many children, the importance of stable best friendships during middle childhood may have less to do with the relationship's length and more to do with simply having a "buddy" by one's side who can provide companionship, recreation, validation, caring, help, and guidance.

PEER ACCEPTANCE, POPULARITY, AND REJECTION

Mykelle announced to her mother, "I heard from the last kid! Everyone in class is coming to my birthday party!" "Fantastic!" her mother replied with a smirk. "Now I have to figure out how to fit 25 of your friends into our house." **Peer acceptance**, the degree to which a child is viewed as a worthy social partner by his or her peers, becomes increasingly important in middle childhood. Peer evaluations become vital sources of self-validation, self-esteem, and confidence (Ladd, 1999; LaFontana & Cillessen, 2010). Some children stand out from their peers as exceptionally well liked or exceptionally disliked.

Popularity

Children who are socially skilled and valued by their peers are said to be **popular**. Popular children tend to have a variety of positive characteristics, including helpfulness, trustworthiness, and assertiveness (Robertson et al., 2010). Popularity has its roots in early childhood as young children's social skills predict peer acceptance in late childhood and adolescence (Blandon, Calkins, Grimm, Keane, & O'Brien, 2010; Rubin et al., 2011). Popular children are skilled in social information processing. That is, they are good at reading social situations, problem solving, self-disclosure, and conflict resolution (Blandon et al., 2010; Rubin et al., 2011). Their skills in emotional regulation and capacity to provide emotional support to peers makes it easy to maintain relationships (Rose & Asher, 1999). These positive social competencies and prosocial behaviors are cyclical as children who view social interaction through rose colored glasses continue to do so, their peers tend to reciprocate, and positive effects on peer relationships increase (Laible, McGinley, Carlo, Augustine, & Murphy, 2014).

A minority of popular children, however, do not show the prosocial and empathetic characteristics typical of popular children. Often labeled by peers and teachers as tough, these children are socially skilled yet show antisocial and aggressive behavior (Farmer, Hall, Leung, Estell, & Brooks, 2011; Rodkin & Roisman, 2010; Shi & Xie, 2012). Aggressive popular children show social competencies similar to prosocial popular children, yet also share many characteristics of children who are rejected by their peers.

Peer Rejection

In contrast with popular children who receive overwhelmingly positive evaluations from their peers, others are disliked and shunned by their peers, experiencing peer rejection. School-age children tend to judge rejected peers as unattractive, deviant, incompetent, and socially isolated (LaFontana & Cillessen, 2002). Children who have poor communication, language, emotional control, and social information processing skills are at risk for peer rejection (Menting, van Lier, &

Not all children have a best friend. Lacking close friendships is not indicative of maladjustment especially if children experience other close relationships.

Jeffrey Greenberg / Science Source

Can a child be happy without friends or without a best friend? An estimated 15% of children are chronically friendless or consistently without a mutual best friend (Rubin et al., 2005). Children can be well liked in school yet lack a mutual best friend (Asher, Guerry, & McDonald, 2014). Lacking a best friend itself is not necessarily harmful or indicative of problems. For example, first- through fifth-grade children who reported lacking a supportive close friendship did not show worse psychological functioning two years later than did those with such a friendship (Klima & Repetti, 2008). Likewise, other research finds that many children without friends are well adjusted, do not report loneliness, and have the social skills to interact with others when they choose (Harrist, Zaia, Bates, Dodge, & Pettit, 1997; Ladd, 1999). Lacking friends does not necessarily harm psychosocial development, especially if the children experience success that they value in another aspects of their lives, for example, by having close family relationships or demonstrating a unique talent, such as in art or music. Although lacking close friends is not associated with maladjustment, social acceptance by the peer group influences children's adjustment (Klima & Repetti, 2008).

Koot, 2011). For example, kindergarteners who had difficulty controlling their emotions were more likely than their more skilled peers to experience peer rejection through seventh grade (Bierman, Kalvin, & Heinrichs, 2014). Boys and girls with behavior problems are at risk for peer rejection—and peer rejection, in turn, is associated with increases in behavior problems throughout elementary school as well as rule breaking in adolescence (Ettekal & Ladd, 2015; Sturaro, van Lier, Cuijpers, & Koot, 2011). Rejected children show two patterns of behavior: **aggressive-rejected** and **withdrawn-rejected**.

Mrs. Connelly turned to a fellow teacher and sighed. "Poor Monica. I just don't know what to do about her. The other children just don't like her, and she doesn't help. She tries to force her way into games, like knocking Jamie out of the way to take her spot in line for jump rope. She doesn't seem to understand how her behavior affects other children and seems to act without thinking." Aggressive-rejected children like Monica are confrontational, hostile toward other children, impulsive, and hyperactive. Aggressive-rejected children tend to have difficulty taking the perspective of others, and they tend to react aggressively to slights by peers, quickly assuming hostile intentions (Fite, Hendrickson, Rubens, Gabrielli, & Evans, 2013; Laible et al., 2014). Aggressive-rejected children enter peer groups in destructive ways that disrupt the groups' interaction or activity and direct attention to them, such as Monica's strategy of pushing Jamie out of the way (Lansford, Malone, Dodge, Pettit, & Bates, 2010; Wilson, 2006). Children whose parents show little warmth and use coercive discipline and threats are likely to threaten other children, have poor social skills, show aggressive behavior, and are more likely to be rejected by other children (Bierman et al., 2014; Lansford, 2014).

Other rejected children are socially withdrawn, passive, timid, anxious, and socially awkward. Withdrawn-rejected children tend to isolate themselves from peers, rarely initiate contact with peers, and speak less frequently than their peers (Rubin, Coplan, & Bowker, 2009). They tend to spend most of their time playing alone and on the periphery of the social scene, often because of shyness or social anxiety. In turn, socially withdrawn children are more likely to experience peer rejection and be disliked by their peers than other children (Coplan et al., 2013; Oh et al., 2008). Withdrawn-rejected children often fear being scorned and attacked and often expect to be disliked by peers (Hart et al., 2000; Rabiner & Coie, 1989). As they are excluded by their peers, withdrawn children tend to become more withdrawn over time. Despite this, socially withdrawn children are just as likely to have a best friend as other children (Rubin, Wojslawowicz, Rose-Krasnor, Booth-LaForce, & Burgess, 2006).

Both rejected-aggressive and withdrawn children are similar in that they misinterpret other children's behaviors and motives, have trouble understanding and regulating their emotions, are poor listeners, and are less socially competent than other children (Ladd & Burgess, 2003). Peer rejection further hinders social development by depriving children of opportunities to learn and practice social skills such as interacting with other children, resolving conflict, and regulating emotions (Werner & Crick, 2004). Patterns of aggression and rejection tend to cycle as aggression predicts peer rejection, but elementary school children who are rejected by peers tend to show increases in physical and relational aggression one year later (Werner & Crick, 2004). Peer rejection is associated with short- and long-term problems. Children who are not well accepted by their peer group are likely to display problems with loneliness, anxiety, depression, low self-esteem, low academic achievement, and in adolescence, delinquency and school dropout (Fite et al., 2013; Menting, Koot, & van Lier, 2014; Schwartz, Lansford, Dodge, Pettit, & Bates, 2014; Zwierzynska, Wolke, & Lereya, 2013). Table 10.1 summarizes characteristics associated with popular children and those who are rejected.

BULLYING

Bullying, also known as peer victimization, refers to an ongoing interaction in which a child repeatedly attempts to inflict physical, verbal, or social harm on another child by, for example, hitting, kicking, name-calling, teasing, shunning, or humiliating them (Olweus, 1995). Bullying is a problem for school-age children in many countries. Estimated rates of bullying and victimization range from 15% to 25% of children in Australia, Austria, England, Finland, Germany, Norway and the United States (Analitis et al., 2009; Cook, Williams, Guerra, & Kim, 2010). Physical bullying is most common in childhood and verbal forms of bullying rise in childhood and remain common in adolescence (Finkelhor, Ormrod, & Turner, 2009).

Characteristics of Children Who Bully

Boys who bully tend to be above average in size, use physical aggression, and target both boys and girls. Girls who bully tend to be verbally assertive, target other girls, and use

Children who show physical forms of bullying, such as hair pulling, are often reared in homes with poor supervision, coervice control, and physical discipline.

TABLE 10.1 Characteristics of Popular and Rejected Children

	CHARACTERISTIC	OUTCOMES
Popular children	• Helpful, trustworthy, assertive • Cognitively skilled and achievement oriented • Socially skilled, able to self-disclose and provide emotional support • Good social problem-solving skills and conflict resolution skills • Prosocial orientation • Assume others have good intentions • A minority are also antisocial and aggressive. They interact with others in a hostile way, using physical or relational aggression, and are likely to bully other children.	• Positive characteristics are strengthened though experience and peer approval. • Positive peer evaluations are sources of self-validation, self-esteem, confidence, and attention from peers, and they influence adjustment. • Without intervention, the minority of popular adolescents who are aggressive are likely to continue patterns of physical or relational aggression in response to peer approval and acceptance.
Withdrawn-rejected children	• Passive, timid, and socially awkward • Social withdrawn, isolate themselves from others • Anxious • Poor social skills • Fear being disliked by peers • Misinterpret other children's behaviors and motives	• Similar outcomes for both types of rejected children • Negative characteristics are strengthened. • Few opportunities to learn and practice social skills, conflict resolution, and emotional regulation • Anxiety, depression, and low self-esteem • Behavior problems • Poor academic achievement • Increased physical and relational aggression over time • Withdrawal and loneliness
Aggressive-rejected children	• Confrontational, hostile toward other children • Impulsive and hyperactive • Difficulty with emotional regulation • Difficulty taking others' perspectives • Assume that their peers are out to get them • Poor social skills • Misinterpret other children's behaviors and motives	

verbal or psychological methods of bullying that threaten relationships, known as relational aggression, such as ridiculing, embarrassing, or spreading rumors (Veenstra et al., 2005). Boys and girls who bully tend to be impulsive, domineering, and show little anxiety or insecurity in peer contexts (Kumpulainen & Räsänen, 2000). Bullying can be motivated by the pursuit of high status and a powerful dominant position in the peer group (Rodkin, Espelage, & Hanish, 2015; Salmivalli, 2014). Relationally aggressive children, including bullies, are frequently perceived by peers as cool, powerful, and popular; bullying can be helpful in maintaining prestige (Salmivalli, 2010). Indirect forms of bullying, such as relational bullying, require social skills, which contribute to their high social status among peers (Juvonen & Graham, 2014). In support of this, many bullies report making friends easily and receive similar levels of support from their classmates as other children (Demaray, Malecki, & DeLong, 2006).

Children who show physically aggressive forms of bullying often show hyperactive behavior, poor school achievement, perceive less support from teachers than do other children, and may show higher rates of depression than other children (Turcotte Benedict, Vivier, & Gjelsvik, 2015). Bullies are more likely to experience inconsistent, hostile, and rejecting parenting. Parents of bullies are more likely to provide poor supervision, prefer coercive control and physical discipline, and tend to be permissive toward aggressive behavior, even teaching their children to strike back at perceived provocation (Holt, Kaufman Kantor, & Finkelhor, 2009; Rodkin et al., 2015; Shetgiri, Lin, & Flores, 2013).

Characteristics of Victims

"I don't know why Victor hates me. He just won't leave me alone," cried Tyler to his teacher, Mr., Johnson, after being knocked onto the ground again. Mr. Johnson thought to himself, "Tyler is the smallest kid in class, keeps to himself, and is sensitive. He cries easily. Maybe that's why he's a target." Victims of bullying, like Tyler, are more likely to be inhibited, frail in appearance, and younger than their peers (Olweus, 1995). Bullies report choosing their victims because they do not like them, often because victims are particularly weak or stand out in some way (Juvonen & Graham, 2014). Children who are bullied are often perceived by their peers as different, as more quiet and cautious than other children (DeRosier & Mercer, 2009). They often experience intrusive parenting, overprotectiveness, and criticism from parents that increases their vulnerability to bullying. Perhaps not surprisingly, children who are bullied often report feeling lonely, less happy at school, and having fewer good friends than their classmates (Reavis, Keane, & Calkins, 2010).

Many victim characteristics, such as nonassertive styles of interacting with peers, shyness, passivity, and social withdrawal, as well as anxiety, depression, and poor emotional control, are present before the child becomes a target of peer victimization and are amplified by victimization (Gini & Pozzoli, 2009; Perren, Ettekal, & Ladd, 2013). Much of the long-term stability of peer victimization and its negative effects can be explained by the dynamic interactions between risk factors for victimization and the effects of victimization (Shetgiri et al., 2013).

Although children respond in various ways to bullying, avoidance behaviors (such as not going to school and refusing to go to certain places) are common (Waasdorp & Bradshaw, 2011). Victims of bullying often tend to respond to victimization in ways that reinforce bullies, by becoming defensive, crying, and giving into bullies' demands (Champion & Clay, 2007). Not all victims of bullying are passive and withdrawn, however. Older children who experience frequent victimization may respond with more intense feelings of anger and greater desires to retaliate, making them more likely to show **reactive aggression**, an aggressive response that is preceded by an insult, confrontation, or frustration (Waasdorp & Bradshaw, 2011).

Some aggressive-rejected children become provocative victims or **bully-victims** (Veenstra et al., 2005). About one half of children who bully report also being victims of bullying (Champion & Clay, 2007). Bully-victims share characteristics of both bullies and victims but function more poorly than either. For example, bully-victims tend to show high levels of anxiety and depression and low rates of social acceptance and self-esteem common to victims, but they also show more aggression, impulsivity, and poor self-control than do other victims (Swearer & Hymel, 2015). Children who are bully-victims have difficulties managing emotions that may increase their risk for reactive aggression and acting out behaviors that invite aggressive exchanges with others (O'Brennan, Bradshaw, & Sawyer, 2009). These characteristics lead children who are both bullies and victims to have problems in peer relationships. Bully-victims often are among the most disliked members of a classroom (Dill, Vernberg, Fonagy, Twemlow, & Gamm, 2004).

Physical and relational bullying have negative emotional and academic consequences that appear as early as in kindergarten and persist over the childhood and adolescent years, often well after the bullying ends (Juvonen & Graham, 2014). For example, children who were bully-victims were more likely to experience anxiety and depression in late adolescence and in early adulthood—and even into middle adulthood (Copeland, Wolke, Angold, & Costello, 2013; Klomek et al., 2008; McDougall & Vaillancourt, 2015; Zwierzynska et al., 2013). Furthermore, the meaning and implications of bullying may vary with context. For example, relational bullying may be more emotionally damaging to children reared in collectivist cultures that heavily value relationships. For example, one comparison of Japanese and U.S. fourth graders showed more depression in Japanese victims (Kawabata, Crick, & Hamaguchi, 2010).

Intervening in Bullying

Table 10.2 summarizes interventions to combat bullying; such interventions address victims, bullies, and schools (Olweus & Limber, 2010; Nese, Horner, Dickey, Stiller, & Tomlanovich, 2014; Slee & Mohyla, 2007). By changing victims' negative perceptions of themselves, helping them to acquire the skills needed to maintain relationships with peers, and teaching them to respond to bullying in ways that do not reinforce their attackers, patterns of bullying can be broken (Olweus & Limber, 2010). Although victims' submissive behavior is reinforcing to bullies, interventions must stress that victimized children are not to blame for the abuse. Targeting victims of bullying is not enough—perpetrators of bullying also need help. Parents and teachers should help bullies learn to identify, understand, and manage their and other people's emotions as well as direct anger in safe and appropriate ways. Teacher awareness of bulling and willingness to intervene matters (Espelage, Low, & Jimerson, 2014). Bullying is more common when teachers attribute bullying to factors outside of their control. In addition, teachers' perceptions of their ability to handle bullying and their own bullying history predict student victimization rates in their classrooms. Many teachers are unaware of how serious and extensive the bullying is within their schools and are often ineffective in being able to identify bullying incidents (Espelage et al., 2014). In addition, bystanders—children who watch episodes of bullying but do not act—reinforce bullies' behaviors and increase bullying (Kärnä, Voeten, Poskiparta, & Salmivalli, 2010; Salmivalli, 2014). Class norms can influence whether bystanders intervene (Pozzoli, Gini, & Vieno, 2012). Classmates can be encouraged to support one another when bullying events occur: Rather than being bystanders or egging the bully on, tell a teacher, refuse to watch, and even, if safe, encourage bullies to stop.

Bullying is not simply a child-to-child problem, and it requires more than a child-centered solution. Stopping bullying requires awareness and change within the school by reviewing and modifying practices with an eye toward identifying how school procedures, such as grouping students by characteristics such as height, maintain and increase bullying (Nese et al., 2014). In recognition of the pervasiveness and severity of bullying, specific bully-related policies are included in public school laws in most states. Addressing the problem of bullying requires that children, teachers, and parents voice concerns about bullying, schools develop policies against bullying, teachers supervise and monitor children during lunch and recess times, and parents learn how to identify and change victims' and bullies' behaviors. Ethical and Policy Applications of Lifespan Development (p. 268) discusses anti-bullying legislation.

TABLE 10.2 Bullying Risks and Interventions

BULLYING RISK FACTOR			BULLYING INTERVENTION
Child	Victim	• Physically weak • Younger than peers • Stands out from peers • Anxious, insecure, low self-esteem, dependent • Quiet, cautious, withdrawn • Poor social support • Little prosocial behavior • Difficulty regulating moods, cries easily • Loneliness • Unhappiness at school • Poor emotional control • Fewer good friends than peers • Response to victimization in ways that increase subsequent victimization by becoming defensive, crying, and giving in to bullies' demands	• Teach assertiveness skills. • Teach children alternative responses to bullying. • Teach anxiety management as well as social and coping skills.
	Bully	• Above average in size • More physically and verbally assertive • Impulsive • Domineering, hostile toward peers • Little anxiety or insecurity in peer contexts • Makes friends easily • Hyperactive behavior • Academic difficulties • Poor emotional control	• Teach alternatives to violence. • Help children develop empathy. • Teach coping skills to reduce impulsive behavior.
Parent	Victim	• Intrusive, overprotective, and/or critical parenting	• Teach authoritative parenting skills. • Encourage parents to aid children in being independent and developing coping skills.
	Bully	• Hostile and rejecting parenting • Use of physical punishment • Models aggressive behavior • Permissive, inconsistent response to aggressive bullying behavior	• Teach authoritative parenting skills. • Parent with sensitivity and consistency. • Model nonaggressive behavior, interpersonal interactions, and conflict management strategies. • Provide positive feedback to children for appropriate social behaviors. • Use alternatives to physical punishment.
School		• Groups students by physical characteristics such as height • Policies that discourage reporting bullying incidents • Teachers and administrators who ignore bullying • Environment of negative feedback and negative attention	• Stress that victims are not to blame. • Teach social skills and conflict management. • Promote a positive school climate that encourages students to feel good about themselves. • Encourage fair discipline that is not punitive. • Train teachers to identify and respond to potentially damaging victimization. • Teachers use positive feedback and modeling to address appropriate social interactions. • School personnel never ignore bullying behaviors. • Encourage classmates to support one another and, rather than simply watch bullying events occur, tell a teacher, and refuse to watch or encourage the bully. • Review and modify school practices with an eye toward identifying how school procedures may contribute to bullying.

ETHICAL AND POLICY APPLICATIONS OF LIFESPAN DEVELOPMENT

Anti-Bullying Legislation

School policies that emphasize community, such as proclaiming school as a no-bullying zone and encouraging bystanders to intervene, are effective in reducing peer victimization.

Schools are responsible for children's physical well-being, but how far does that responsibility extend? What is the role of schools in addressing peer victimization? In a landmark case, the mother of fifth grader LaShonda Davis filed suit against the Monroe County [Georgia] Board after the school failed to intervene during the months in which her daughter was the victim of severe harassment, often sexual, by a fellow student. The 1999 decision of *Davis vs. Monroe County Board of Education* ruled that sexual harassment by peers violates Title IX of the Equal Opportunity in Education Act of 1972, which stipulates that "No person in the United States shall, on the basis of sex, be excluded from participation in, be denied the benefits of, or be subjected to discrimination under any education program or activity receiving Federal financial assistance." The court deemed that sexual harassment in the school setting violates students' rights to education. *Davis vs. Monroe* applies specifically to peer-to-peer sexual harassment, but researchers and legislators look to this ruling as an important precedent for anti-bullying legislation because bullying violates students' rights.

In recognition of the pervasiveness an d severity of bullying, 49 states in the United States include specific bully-related policies into their public school laws (Hinduja & Patchin, 2015). Anti-bullying laws do not criminalize bullying itself but stipulate that school districts take action to prevent or intervene when bullying occurs (Stuart-Cassel, Bell, & Springer, 2011). State anti-bullying laws vary enormously, but nearly all require or strongly encourage school districts to establish anti-bullying policies and usually place the responsibility for their development on school boards (Cornell & Limber, 2015).

Most developmental researchers agree that a model bullying law should include, at minimum, the following: a clear definition of bullying, explicit articulation of a bullying prohibition, implementation of prevention and treatment programs, and acknowledgment of the association between bullying and public health risks (Limber & Small, 2003; Srabstein et al., 2008). The Safe Schools Improvement Act, proposed in 2013, is an example of legislation that would require states to collect and report information on the incidence of bullying and harassment. It would also permit schools to use federal grants to prevent and respond to incidents of bullying and harassment, require schools to provide annual reports of bullying prevalence and policies, and establish grievance procedures for students and parents to register complaints regarding such conduct. Although not passed by Congress, the Safe Schools Improvement Act sets an important precedent by acknowledging the relevance of peer victimization to children's everyday lives.

What Do You Think?

What role should schools take in addressing bullying? Did your school draw attention to bullying and have rules or policies about bullying?

Thinking in Context 10.2

1. Considering Bronfenbrenner's bioecological theory from Chapter 1, what microsystem factors, such as personal characteristics, mesosystem factors, such as family and school, and exosystem factors, such as neighborhood, might lead a child to be popular or unpopular with peers? Which factors are most important, in your view?

2. As a parent, what might you to do lower the likelihood that your child might become a bully or a victim of bullying?

FAMILIES

Children are embedded in families that play an important role in their development. Children's relationships with parents and siblings are dynamic and reciprocal. Children influence and are influenced by every member of their family, and family members, in turn, interact. Families may take many forms, as described in the following sections.

PARENT–CHILD RELATIONSHIPS

"Noah is so independent," remarked his mother. "He's growing up so quickly. Once he was afraid of going on a sleepover, but now he's asked to go away to summer camp!" As school-age children become more independent, they spend less time with parents, and the parent–child relationship becomes less close than in early childhood (Hofferth & Sandberg, 2001). Parents and school-age children tend to spend their time together engaging in task-oriented activities, such as doing homework, preparing meals, cleaning, and shopping (Bryant

& Zick, 1995). Older children become more concerned with being independent and making their own decisions and often show less respect for parental authority than they did when they were younger. However, African American and Latino children whose cultures stress respect for elders, family loyalty, and the importance of relationships tend to show less of a decline in respect for parents than do European American children (Dixon, Graber, & Brooks-Gunn, 2008). Likewise, immigrants of Chinese, Korean, and Filipino descent are less likely to respond to parental attempts of control with anger than are European American youth (Chao & Aque, 2009). Sociocultural factors, specifically the one-child policy, have led most children in China to be raised as only children, with implications for parent–child relationships (see Cultural Influences on Development, p. 270).

Like many aspects of development, there tends to be continuity in parenting and parent–child relationships. Patterns of harsh verbal discipline (yelling, threatening, punishment, shaming) and insensitive parenting established in early childhood tend to persist in middle childhood and after (Bradley & Corwyn, 2008; Lansford, Staples, Bates, Pettit, & Dodge, 2013). Poor quality parent–child relationships in middle childhood tend to worsen and are associated with poor adjustment, antisocial activity, and delinquency into adolescence (Hakvoort, Bos, van Balen, & Hermanns, 2010; Keijsers, Loeber, Branje, & Meeus, 2011).

Middle childhood brings new parenting issues. Parents must adapt their parenting strategies to children's increased ability to reason and desire for independence. They tend to use less direct management and instead begin to share power—for example, by guiding and monitoring children's behavior from a distance, communicating expectations, and allowing children to be in charge of moment to moment decision making (Collins, Madsen, & Susman-Stillman, 2002). They tend to use reasoning and inductive techniques of discipline, such as pointing out the consequences of a child's behavior, explaining how a child affects others, and appealing to the child's self-esteem and sense of values. Parents who are warm and responsive, set firm and reasonable limits, and encourage open communication by engaging their children in discussions foster healthy psychological and social development. For example, in one study, third- and fourth-grade children who reported sharing information about themselves and their activities with their parents were viewed by teachers as more socially competent than other children one year later, and those who reported being more secretive were viewed as more aggressive and oppositional one year later (Bumpus & Hill, 2008). In addition to parents, siblings are an important contributor to the development of social competence during middle childhood.

SIBLINGS

Do you have a brother or sister? How large is your family? Nearly 80% of children in the United States have at least one sibling (Volling, 2012). Family size varies widely around the world. In nonindustrialized societies, like those of the rural villages of Asia, Africa, and Central and South America, families tend to be larger than in industrialized societies. The larger number of siblings helps the family to manage its work, such as maintaining a farm, and to care for young, aged, and ill family members. Girls, for example, may be responsible for caring for younger siblings by feeding, disciplining, monitoring, and comforting them. In agricultural communities, siblings work together to maintain fields, grow food, and carry out other essential tasks such as gathering firewood and transporting water. Younger siblings learn norms and values from their older brothers and sisters, including sharing, respect for elders, and the importance of maintaining social connections (Weisner, 1993).

In industrialized nations, families tend to be smaller, and siblings tend to be farther apart in age, permitting each child to receive more attention (Cicirelli, 1994). In these families, children might occasionally babysit but are not otherwise in charge of the care of their siblings. Children learn from their older siblings, but siblings play a much smaller role in socializing children as compared with nonindustrialized societies. However, in some American ethnic minority and working-class families in which the adults of the family work outside the home, sibling relationships are more similar to those in nonindustrial societies whereby siblings have family management responsibilities (McGuire & Shanahan, 2010).

Siblings spend a great deal of time together. By middle childhood, children spend more time with siblings than with parents (Dunn, 2002a). It may not be surprising that siblings exert much influence on one another. Sibling relationships are emotionally uninhibited. Children display emotions and behaviors to siblings that they would not show peers (Pike, Coldwell, & Dunn, 2005). Sibling relationships are often characterized by patterns of ambivalence and conflict, with siblings vacillating from ignoring each other to arguing (Kramer, 2010). In one study, nearly three quarters of families reported physical violence between siblings, and over 40% of children were kicked, bitten, or punched by a sibling within the past year (Feinberg, Solmeyer, & McHale, 2012).

The sibling relationship is complex as it plays a role in learning important relationship skills such as conflict resolution (McHale, Updegraff, & Whiteman, 2012). For example, 5- and 6-year-old children with at least one sibling demonstrate enhanced interpersonal skills in peer group situations, as compared with children who have no siblings (Downey & Condron, 2004; Pike et al., 2005). Through sibling interactions, children learn that relationships continue even through arguments and anger. Siblings offer each other social support and assistance with academic, family, and peer challenges (Gass, Jenkins, & Dunn, 2007). They help each other manage stressful life events and reduce the anxiety and depressive symptoms that often accompany them (Ji-Yeon, McHale, Crouter, & Osgood, 2007).

Most of us have heard the term *sibling rivalry,* which refers to a sense of competition with one's siblings, often for

China's One-Child Policy

少生优生振兴中华

David Pollack/Corbis

Posters such as this promoted the one-child policy as the key to greater resources and opportunities for families.

In 1979, the People's Republic of China implemented a policy designed to curb the nation's rapidly growing population that posed social, economic, and environmental problems. Known as the one-child policy, it restricts the number of children married couples can have to one. The one-child policy is most strictly implemented in urban areas (McLoughlin, 2005). Couples in rural areas, especially those who require assistance to manage farms, may be granted permission for two children if the first child is a girl and the couple waits four to five years between births (Yang, 2007).

The core of the one-child policy is a set of incentives, including health and education resources, but it is also enforced by means of penalties, such as out-of-plan birth fines (often two to three times that of a typical family income); child-rearing, health care, and education penalties; and possibly other penalties such as a job demotion or even job loss (McLoughlin, 2005). The official slogan of the one-child-policy is *you sheng you yu* ("give birth to fewer children, but give them better care and education"; Yang, 2007). In exchange for limiting parents' childbearing, the Chinese government provides greater opportunities and resources at the national, community, and household levels for only children who will be better off in physical and intellectual development than children with multiple siblings.

Research findings suggest that the one-child policy, insofar as it limits couples to one or two children, has led to greater

involvement by parents in child care because children of all ages are viewed as more valued and must be carefully cultivated (Short, Fengying, Siyuan, & Mingliang, 2001; Yang, 2007). Moreover, the one-child policy appears to have had an unintended effect of creating a child-centered culture with a strong belief and shared interest among the urban community in educating the only child regardless of the child's sex (Liu, 2006). This is a striking contrast with the Chinese tradition in which parents' academic expectations and investments were limited to their sons. However, like elsewhere in the world, differences in expectations for boys and girls remain.

The one-child policy was intended to impart Chinese school-age only children with advantages over those with siblings—specifically more attention and resources. Early research in the 1980s suggested that Chinese only-children score higher on measures of mathematics and verbal achievement but display more egocentrism, uncooperativeness, and difficulty managing emotions and impulses as well as less sharing, respect of elders, and prosocial than school-age children with siblings (Falbo et al., 1997; McLoughlin, 2005). Research conducted in the 21st century, however, suggests that Chinese only children score higher than those with siblings on measures of IQ but do not differ on psychosocial measures such as dependence, helping behaviors, independence, aggression, friendliness, curiosity, self-confidence, peer relationships, social competence, and academic achievement (Chen, Rubin, & Li, 1994; Guo, Yang, Liu, & Song, 2005; Wang et al., 2000).

Over three decades, the one-child policy has successfully curbed population growth, but it remains highly controversial both within and outside China because it limits individuals' autonomy and poses stiff penalties on parents who have a second child (Yang, 2007). Given Chinese culture's tradition of valuing of boys, a second concern is that the one-child policy is implicated in high rates of female infanticide and sex-selective abortions, leading to a significant gender imbalance (Mosher, 2006). A population survey of more than 4.5 million Chinese children and teens found that the male to female ratio was 126:100 overall, with several provinces showing ratios of over 130:100 (Zhu, Lu, & Hesketh, 2009). Among second births, the ratio was as high as 149:100, with ratios of over 160:100 in nine provinces (Zhu et al., 2009). Sex-selective abortion accounts for almost all the excess male children in China (Mosher, 2006).

Despite these criticisms, a survey by the Pew Research Center showed that over 75% of the Chinese population supports the policy (Pew Global Attitudes Project, 2008). Moreover, a rapidly aging population, coupled with a much smaller workforce, has recently prompted a change in the one-child policy. In 2014, the policy was relaxed in several cities to permit couples to have two children if one of the parents has no siblings (Burkitt, 2014). Couples must register and apply to have a second child. However, by 2016 it is expected that all couples will be permitted to have two children (Holliday, 2014). Despite the new relaxed guidelines, fewer couples than expected are applying for a second child. This may be because the one-child policy has changed perceived norms on family size.

What Do You Think?

Why do you think fewer Chinese couples than predicted are applying to have a second child?

In developing communities siblings often adopt the role of caregiver and play a role in socializing their younger brothers and sisters.

parental attention and favor. Sibling rivalry emerges from social comparison—siblings comparing themselves—and tends to increase in middle childhood, as children engage in a wider range of activities. Parents, teachers, peers, and other family members naturally compare siblings' characteristics, interests, and accomplishments and children naturally compare themselves to their siblings (McHale et al., 2012). The perception of parental favoritism, real or imagined, promotes negative feelings and rivalry among siblings (Dunn, 1996). Children who feel that a sibling receives more affection, approval, or resources may feel resentful, which may harm the sibling relationship (Feinberg & Hetherington, 2001). Same-sex siblings who are close in age are more often compared by parents and therefore quarrel more often and tend to have more difficulties in adjustment, especially when parents adopt an authoritarian style of parenting (Bryant, 1982). Sibling rivalry is reduced when siblings attempt to be different from one another—by selecting different activities and sports, for example. Parents can encourage and reinforce children's attempts at new activities. Although parents should refrain from making direct comparisons, children will naturally engage in social comparison with their siblings. These comparisons often motivate siblings to carve out their own uniqueness.

SAME-SEX PARENTED FAMILIES

In the early 1990s, a children's book titled *Heather Has Two Mommies* was a source of great controversy as politicians and organizations opposed to lesbian, gay, bisexual, and transgender (LGBT) rights sought to ban it from libraries and schools. Today, children like the fictional Heather are not so unusual. An estimated 37% of LGBT-identified adults have a child at some time in their lives (Gates, 2013). As shown in Figure 10.1, most LGBT parents raise biological children, although LGBT parents are more likely to adopt children than are heterosexual parents (10% and 3%, respectively). Every state permits unmarried individuals to adopt children (National

Center for Lesbian Rights, 2014). However, at the time of this writing, many states, particularly those that did not recognize same-sex marriage, did not permit same-sex partners to jointly adopt a child or for a partner to adopt his or her partner's biological child (National Center for Lesbian Rights, 2014). Federal and state policies may change in response to the U.S. Supreme Court's landmark ruling that legalized same-sex marriage nationwide (*Obergefell v. Hodges*, 2015). In January 2008, the European Court of Human Rights ruled that gay men and lesbian women have the right to adopt a child. Currently, 14 European countries, as well as Canada, Australia, and much of South America, permit gay and lesbian couples to adopt children (ABC News, 2010; Huffington Post, 2013; International Lesbian, Gay, Bisexual, Trans and Intersex Association-Europe, 2013).

More than three decades of research conducted in the United States, the United Kingdom, Belgium, and the Netherlands has failed to reveal important differences in the adjustment or development of children and adolescents reared by same-sex couples compared to those reared by other-sex couples (Acs & Nelson, 2002; Fedewa, Black, & Ahn, 2014; Patterson, 2009; Perrin & Siegel, 2013). Specifically, children and adolescents raised by lesbian mothers or gay fathers do not differ from other children on measures of emotional development, such as empathy and emotional regulation (Anderssen, Amlie, & Ytterøy, 2002; Crowl, Ahn, & Baker, 2008). Children raised by lesbian parents tend to score higher in social and academic competence and show fewer social and behavioral problems and lower levels of aggression (Gartrell & Bos, 2010; Golombok et al., 2014). Moreover, children raised by lesbian mothers and gay fathers show similar

FIGURE 10.1: Relationship of Children to Parent in Same-Sex Households in the United States, 2011

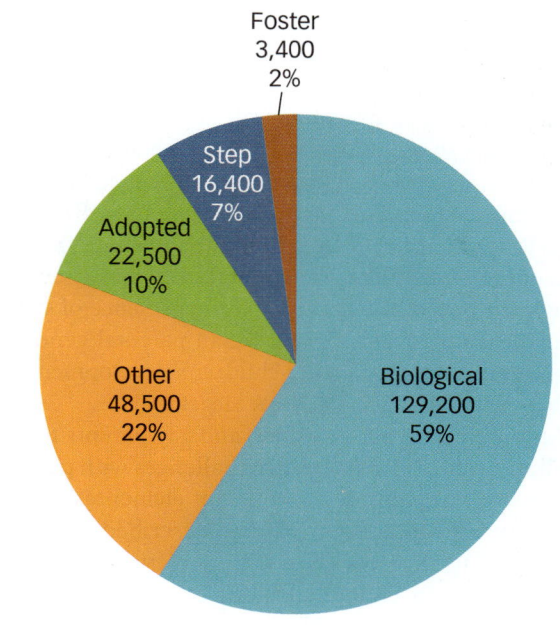

Foster
3,400
2%

Step
16,400
7%

Adopted
22,500
10%

Other
48,500
22%

Biological
129,200
59%

SOURCE: Gates (2013).

Same-sex parents show similar levels of parenting competence but often experience greater well-being as compared with heterosexual parents, often because same-sex parents tend to share household and child-rearing duties.

difficulties, with the exception that boys were more likely to report being excluded by their peers and girls gossiped about for having two mothers (Crowl et al., 2008). The degree to which children feel stigmatized and different varies with context. For example, Dutch children tend to be more open about growing up in a lesbian family, experience less homophobia, and demonstrate fewer emotional and behavioral problems than do American children (Bos, Gartrell, van Balen, Peyser, & Sandfort, 2008). However, close family relationships with lesbian mothers can counteract the effects of stigmatization (Bos & Gartrell, 2010). Contextual factors, such as attitudes and values, influence how children experience their world as well as their developmental outcomes.

patterns of gender identity and gender role development as children raised by heterosexual parents—they are not more likely to display a gay orientation in adulthood (Fedewa et al., 2014; Golombok et al., 2014; Tasker & Patterson, 2007).

The specific parenting roles and tasks that same-sex partners take vary with the way in which the family formed. Generally speaking, when the children are the result of a previous heterosexual relationship, the biological parent tends to assume most of the parenting responsibility. However, when children are a joint choice and the result of adoption or reproductive technology, partners tend to report an equal split of household and child-rearing duties, as compared with the more traditional split among heterosexual parents in which the mother is responsible for a greater proportion of household and child-rearing duties (Bos, van Balen, & van den Boom, 2007; Goldberg & Perry-Jenkins, 2007). Overall, gay fathers and lesbian mothers show similar levels of parenting competence and commitment to the parenting role as heterosexual parents and may show higher rates of well-being, especially when each take a role in coparenting (Farr & Patterson, 2013; Vanfraussen, Ponjaert-Kristoffersen, & Brewaeys, 2003). Researchers have concluded that a family's social and economic resources, the strength of the relationships among members of the family, and the presence of stigma are far more important variables than parental gender or sexual orientation in affecting children's development and well-being (Lamb, 2012; Perrin & Siegel, 2013).

Although children of lesbian and gay parents tend to be well adjusted, some encounter challenges with peers. In some studies, as many as one third of elementary school children of lesbian and gay parents described their children as having felt isolated or different from their classmates (Anderssen et al., 2002; Bos & van Balen, 2008). Other research suggests that children experience few

SINGLE-PARENT FAMILIES

In 2013, about 35% of U.S. children under age 18 lived with a single parent, most commonly with their mother (Annie E. Casey Foundation, 2014). A great deal of research over multiple decades has compared the effects of family structure, children raised in single-parent families, stepfamilies, and two-parent families. Figure 10.2 shows the various living arrangements for households with children.

Generally, children in single-parent families, whether created through divorce, death, or having never married, tend to show more physical and mental health problems, poorer academic achievement, less social competence, and more behavior problems than do children in intact two-parent families (Waldfogel, Craigie, & Brooks-Gunn, 2010). However, it is important to recognize that these effects tend to be small; the vast majority of children raised in one-parent homes are well adjusted (Lamb, 2012). Moreover, there is more variability among children in single-parent homes than there is between children of single-parent homes and two-parent homes. Many of the differences associated with family structure differences are reduced or disappear when researchers take socioeconomic status into account, suggesting that differences in child well-being across family types are largely, though not entirely, influenced by family income, access to resources, and the stresses that accompany economic difficulties (Ryan, Claessens, & Markowitz, 2015).

About one third of children raised in single-mother homes live in poverty, as compared with 16% of children in single-father homes and under 6% of children in homes headed by a married couple (DeNavas-Walt & Proctor, 2014). Regardless of family structure, children who grow up in low socioeconomic status homes experience heightened risk for academic, social, and behavioral problems

FIGURE 10.2: Family Structure: Children's Living Arrangements, 1960–2013

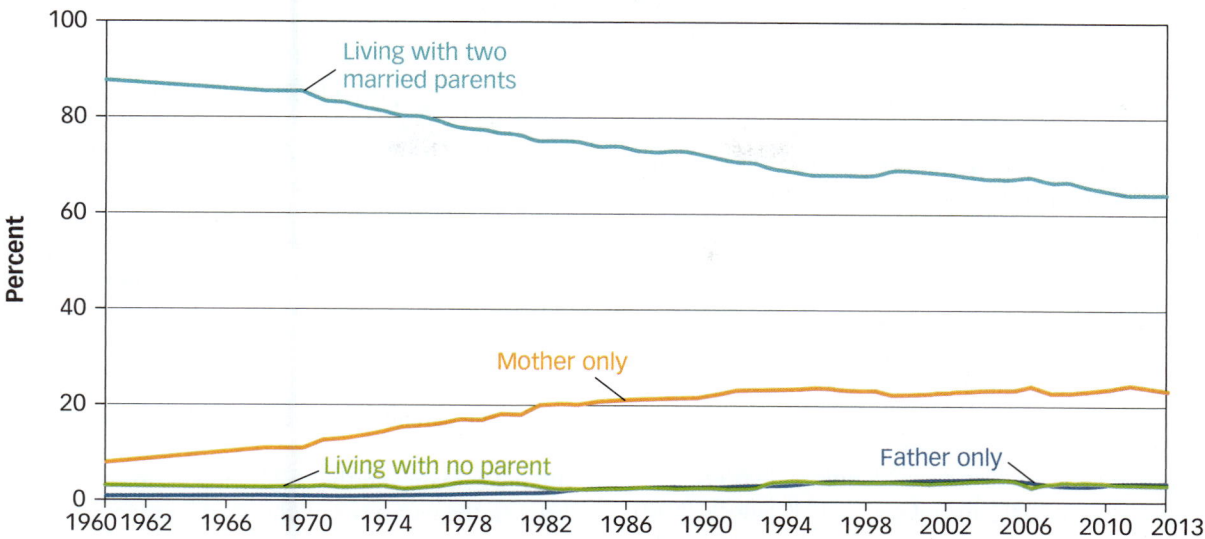

SOURCE: Child Trends Data Bank (2014).

as economic disadvantage affects children in a myriad of ways, from having less money for books, clothes, and extra-curricular activities to living in poorer school districts and neighborhoods (Lleras, 2008). For example, low-income single mothers often are in lower occupational positions with few benefits such as health insurance and sick days and with nonstandard hours. They tend to create more poor home environments with fewer educational resources and tend to spend less time with their children (Walker & Hennig, 1997). Children in single-mother families tend to receive less supervision, have more household responsibilities, experience more conflict with siblings, and have less family cohesion than do children in two-parent families (Kendig & Bianchi, 2008). In addition, families headed by single mothers often experience multiple transitions, as single mothers tend to change jobs and homes more frequently than other mothers. Each transition poses challenges to children's adjustment (Evans, Li, & Whipple, 2013). Single mothers report more depression and psychological problems than married mothers and, when depressed, undoubtedly function less well as parents (Reising et al., 2013; Waldfogel et al., 2010).

The vast majority of what we know about single-parent families comes from studying mothers; single custodial fathers are less common but are on the rise (Eggebeen, Snyder, & Manning, 1996). About one quarter of single-parent households are headed by fathers (Livingston, 2013). Single fathers are more likely than mothers to live with a cohabiting partner and tend to have higher household incomes (Livingston, 2013). Like those raised by single mothers, children reared by single fathers show mixed outcomes. While some research has suggested that children earn lower grades in single-father families as compared with single-mother and intact families (Downey, 1994), other studies suggest that children in single-father families score similarly to children in two-parent families on measures of mental health, physical health, and academic achievement (Bramlett & Blumberg, 2007; Breivik & Olweus, 2006).

The single-parent household can offer stability, continuity, and opportunities for child development, but access to economic and social resources influences the effects of single parenthood on children. The level of social support afforded single mothers influences their abilities to provide emotional support for their children and implement effective parenting strategies (Wood & Woody, 2007). In African American communities, for example, single mothers often are not isolated from the community. Instead, children have opportunities to interact with many caring adult family members and friends of the family, and children are raised as members of a larger African American community (Jayakody & Kalil, 2002). Often an adult male, such as an uncle or grandfather, takes on a fathering role, helping a child build competence and develop a relationship with a caring adult male (Hill, Bush, & Roosa, 2003). In such families, grandmothers often are highly involved, warm, and helpful, taking on important support roles. In one study of U.K. single-parent homes, grandmothers served parental roles and aided their children much as would partners (Harper & Ruicheva, 2010). When children are close to highly involved extended family members, they develop family bonds and a sense of family honor that guides them and encourages them to succeed—this is true of all children regardless of their family structure (Jaeger, 2012).

COHABITING FAMILIES

There are many kinds of families, and not all are formed through marriage. In 2013, about 8% of children lived in homes with two parents who are unmarried—cohabiting parents (Annie E. Casey Foundation, 2014). Forty percent of children will spend some time in a cohabiting-parent family before they reach age 18 (Kennedy & Bumpass, 2008). Children of unmarried cohabiting parents who have close, caring relationships with them and whose union is stable develop as well as their counterparts whose parents whose marriage is stable (Rose-Greenland & Smock, 2012).

A challenge to cohabitation is that relationships between unmarried cohabiting couples tend to be less stable than those of married couples. For example, about one third of cohabiting couples break up within 3 years (Copen, Daniels, & Mosher, 2013). In contrast, about two thirds of first marriages remain intact after 10 years (Goodwin, Mosher, & Chandra, 2010). Children living in cohabiting households are much more likely to experience their parents' separation, more conflict in the home, and more transitions in family life than are children of married parents, all of which influence adjustment (Manning, 2006; Osborne, Manning, & Smock, 2007; Rose-Greenland & Smock, 2012). Children raised in more volatile cohabiting parent families tend to show more behavior and academic problems than do those in married stepparent and intact families (Acs & Nelson, 2002; Morrison, 1998) but rates similar to children living in single-mother households (Batalova & Cohen, 2002; Kiernan, 2002).

Differences in socioeconomic status contribute to the varying outcomes in children's adjustment. Married parents tend to have considerably higher incomes and educational attainment than cohabiting parents (Manning & Lichter, 1996). On average, children raised in cohabiting-parent families experience economic situations that are better than those of children in single-parent families (e.g., higher parental education and family earnings) but more economically stressful than those reared by married parents (e.g., greater poverty and food insecurity; Manning & Brown, 2006). About 20% of children living in cohabiting families are poor, as compared with about 10% of children from two-parent married households and nearly 40% of children in single-parent households (Kennedy & Fitch, 2012).

The effect of cohabitation on children varies with contextual norms. Consensual unions and childbearing within cohabiting unions are more common among minority families (Dunifon & Kowaleski-Jones, 2002; Kennedy & Bumpass, 2008). Black and Hispanic children spend more time in cohabiting parent unions than do white children—and the difference in economic advantage between married and cohabitation is smaller for cohabiting black and Hispanic families than for white families, perhaps partially accounting for minority children's more positive outcomes (Manning & Brown, 2006; Osborne et al., 2007).

Overall, there are many kinds of families, but children's adjustment appears to be influenced by the similar factors across families, such as parent–child relationships, exposure to parental conflict, and economic resources. Exposure to parent conflict is particularly detrimental to children's adjustment yet common to divorcing families.

DIVORCE

Since 1960, divorce rates have tripled in many industrialized nations. The Russian Federation leads the world with a divorce rate of 4.7 per 1,000 people, followed by Latvia (3.6), Lithuania (3.5), and the United States (2.8; United Nations Statistics Division, 2014). Although the divorce rate in the United States is high relative to many countries, it has declined over the past three decades from its peak of 5.3 in 1981 to 3.6 in 2011 (National Center for Health Statistics, 1985, 2013). About 40% of marriages in the United States divorce within 15 years (Copen, Daniels, Vespa, & Mosher, 2012).

Divorce and Children

During the parent–teacher conference, Mrs. Rodriguez carefully explained, "Mrs. Patel, I know the divorce has been difficult for you and the children, but I'm concerned about Ryan. In the past few months, Ryan's grades have dropped; he seems to be having trouble getting along with the other children; and, most notably, I caught him taking toys from another child's book bag while the children were at recess." Is Ryan's behavior typical of children of divorced homes? For many decades, it was assumed that divorce caused significant and irreparable harm to children. Research, however, has suggested that in many cases there are no differences between children of divorced parents and those whose parents remain married (Hetherington, Bridges, & Insabella, 1998; Mensah & Fine, 2008; Oldehinkel et al., 2009). Most researchers have come to the conclusion that divorce has some negative effects on children's adjustment, such as internalizing and externalizing problems, but the effects are small, vary by particular outcome, and do not apply to all boys and girls uniformly (Amato & Anthony, 2014; Weaver & Schofield, 2015).

Augustus Butera/Getty

Children who are exposed to parental conflict tend to experience more adjustment difficulties in response to parental divorce.

Boys and girls often display different reactions to parental divorce (Davies & Lindsay, 2001; Ram & Hou, 2005). Like Ryan, boys often respond to parental divorce with increases in behavior problems and delinquent activity (Malone et al., 2004). The effect of parental divorce on boys also depends on the timing of the divorce. Boys whose parents divorced during elementary school tend to show behavior problems that persisted for years after the divorce, but boys whose parents divorced during middle school showed behavior problems that dropped over the first year after the divorce (Oldehinkel et al., 2009). Girls tend to respond to parental divorce with anxiety and depression—and this response increases with age (Amato & Sobolewski, 2001; Størksen, Røysamb, Moum, & Tambs, 2005). Variations in child, parent, and family characteristics and contexts influence children's adjustment to parental divorce, but most children show improved adjustment within two years after the divorce, suggesting that the majority of children of divorce are resilient (Amato, 2001; Lamb, 2012). As Ryan adjusts to their new homes and new family life, his behavior problems will decrease and his school performance will likely improve.

Some children of divorced homes show difficulties in adjustment that persist throughout adolescence and sometimes into adulthood (Størksen, Røysamb, Gjessing, Moum, & Tambs, 2007; VanderValk, Spruijt, de Goede, Maas, & Meeus, 2005). Children who experience divorce, especially multiple divorces, are more likely to face challenges in adolescence and early adulthood regarding sexuality and intimacy, as well as difficulties with anxiety, depression, and problem behaviors (Amato, 2006; Størksen et al., 2005; Whitton, Rhoades, Stanley, & Markman, 2008). As adolescents, they are at higher risk of pregnancy and as adults are more likely to experience divorce in their own marriages (Amato, 2010; Clarke-Stewart & Brentano, 2006).

Children show many different patterns of adjustment before and after their parents' divorce. Furthermore, what initially appear to be effects of divorce are likely to be a complex combination of parent, child, and contextual factors that precede and follow the divorce in conjunction with the divorce itself (Amato & Anthony, 2014; Bennett, 2006). For example, children reared in divorced families tend to have lower socioeconomic attainment as adults than their peers growing up in two-biological-parent families (Hetherington & Elmore, 2004), but these differences appear to be either at least partially attributable to shortages of economic and social resources in these families.

Divorce triggers a reconfiguration of family roles and parenting responsibilities shift disproportionately onto the resident parent. Over time, children tend to have less contact with noncustodial fathers (Amato & Sobolewski, 2004). After divorce, children are typically raised by their mothers and experience a drop in income that influences their access to resources and opportunities, such as after-school programs and activities (Bratberg & Tjøtta, 2008; White & Rogers, 2000). Mother-headed households often must move

DIVORCE: PARENT'S PERSPECTIVE

In this video, Peige, the mother of two boys, discusses her experience parenting during a divorce and afterward.

Watch the video at edge.sagepub.com/kuther

to more affordable housing, causing additional changes in children's school, community, and circle of friends and often reducing children's access to social support and opportunities to play with friends. Mothers who have not been in the workforce often must seek employment, and many working mothers must increase the hours that they work, leading to less contact with their children. These changes contribute to inconsistencies in family routines, activities, and parental monitoring prior to, during, and after the divorce (Kelly, 2007; Wallerstein & Lewis, 2004). High-quality family relationships, including positive interactions with the noncustodial parent and low levels of parent–parent conflict, can buffer children against these stressors (Hakvoort et al., 2011; Weaver & Schofield, 2015).

Involvement by the noncustodial parent, specifically the father, is important in lessening the negative effects of divorce. Multiple studies have found that good father–child relationships protect girls against early sexual activity and promote healthy romantic relationships, and close father-son relationships positively influence boys' psychological well-being (Amato & Sobolewski, 2004; Hakvoort et al., 2011; Oldehinkel et al., 2009). Parent–child relationships are important resources that can help children cope with difficult transitions. Secure parent–child attachments can help to buffer the negative effects of divorce and promote adjustment (Faber & Wittenborn, 2010).

Conflict and Child Adjustment

Ultimately, divorce is not a discrete event in a family's experience. It is a transition that influences living arrangements, housing, income, and family roles. The transition begins well before the divorce is announced because parental divorce tends to be preceded by a period of uncertainty and tension, often characterized by increases in conflict between parents (Amato, 2010). Harmful family processes, such as parental conflict, poor parent–child interactions, and ineffective parenting strategies, take a toll on children's emotional and psychological health and can precede parental divorce by as long as 8 to 12 years, suggesting that many children face challenges to adjustment well before their parents' divorce (Lansford, 2009; Potter, 2010). The amount of parental conflict that children are exposed to before and during parental divorce influences the emotional, psychological, and behavioral problems that may accompany parental divorce.

Parental conflict is common during the divorce, and in over one third of cases, high parental conflict continues for several years after the divorce (Bing, Nelson, & Wesolowski, 2009; Fosco & Grych, 2008). Children who are exposed to high levels of conflict between parents tend to show more poor outcomes and more adjustment difficulties with parental divorce (Drapeau, Gagne, Saint-Jacques, Lepine, & Ivers, 2009; Harold, Aitken, & Shelton, 2007). Chronic exposure to parental conflict poses challenges to children's adjustment and is associated with increased physiological arousal and an elevated stress response (Davidson, O'Hara, & Beck, 2014; Davies & Martin, 2014). Longitudinal research following children of married parents has found that children whose parents later divorce show many of the problems typical of children of divorce, such as anxiety, depression, delinquency, and poor academics, long before the divorce takes place (Strohschein, 2005, 2007).

It is not simply parental conflict that matters but how it is displayed and resolved. Unresolved hostile and aggressive interactions are particularly harmful to children as they damage children's sense of emotional security (Cummings, Goeke-Morey, & Papp, 2001; Davies & Martin, 2014). In turn, children's difficulties adapting, such as behavior problems, can increase parental conflict (Drapeau et al., 2009). However, not all parents display high levels of conflict. About one quarter show low levels of conflict post separation that remain stable years later, but about 10% of parents show low levels of conflict that later increase. Children raised in low-income homes are more likely to experience higher rates of parental conflict upon divorce and over time (Drapeau et al., 2009). The custodial parent's ability to handle stress, protect the child from exposure to conflict, provide support, monitor the child, and maintain a warm relationship with the child promotes positive adjustment and lower levels of problems including anxiety, depression, low self-esteem, and behavior problems (Mensah & Fine, 2008; Oldehinkel et al., 2009).

Divorce and Parents

Parents play an important role in their children's adjustment to divorce. As they struggle with their own adaptation, newly divorced parents may be more emotionally detached from their role as parents, less effective in monitoring and disciplining their children, and may experience more conflict and less cohesion in their relationships with their children (Wallerstein & Lewis, 2004). Parents' psychological distress and preoccupation with their own personal problems during divorce may interfere with established parenting practices and strain the parent–child relationship.

Yet research with 17,000 Canadian families suggests that mothers show little change in their parenting strategies or interactions with their children after divorce (Strohschein, 2007). Similar to findings with children, there are no set patterns of adjustment that fit all parents. Some parents show radical changes, many show some changes, and some show few changes in their parenting strategies and interactions with children (Amato, Kane, & James, 2011; Bing et al., 2009; Brenner & Hyde, 2006).

Poor parenting strategies and parents' difficulties in monitoring and interacting with their children contribute to children's adjustment in all types of families, divorced and intact. When researchers take into account the quality of parenting, the link between parental divorce and children's adjustment lessens, suggesting that parenting strategies and parent–child relationships are more important influences on children's adjustment than divorce (Bing et al., 2009; Strohschein, 2007; Whiteside & Becker, 2000; Wolchik, Wilcox, Tein, & Sandler, 2000).

Custody

Children's living arrangements change dramatically with divorce. Some parents are awarded sole legal child custody, in which they may make all decisions regarding the child and need not consult the other parent. Joint legal child custody, on the other hand, entitles both parents to make major decisions about their children, such as those regarding medical, educational, and child care issues. A distinction is made between joint legal custody and joint physical custody, which involves parents sharing daily living arrangements with the child. It is most common for parents to share joint legal custody, but one parent has physical custody; usually, this is the mother (Kelly, 2007). Although joint legal custody provides both parents with the right to participate in decisions regarding the child, in most cases the parent with physical custody usually makes daily decisions and often major decisions (Bauserman, Bos, van Balen, van den Boom, & Bauserman, 2002; Maccoby & Mnookin, 1992). In families granted joint physical custody, children spend large amounts of time with both parents but not necessarily a 50/50 share. Usually, children will spend 35% or more time with each parent (Nielsen, 2014).

How is children's adjustment related to custody arrangements? Although children in joint physical custody homes may shuffle between two homes, two sets of toys, and two sets of neighborhood friends, they typically adjust well. Children in joint physical custody arrangements tend to be better adjusted with regard to parent–child and family relationships and show higher self-esteem, lower rates of anxiety and depression, better academic achievement, and fewer behavior problems than children in sole custody homes (Bauserman, 2012; Fabricius & Luecken, 2007; Sarrazin & Cyr, 2007). We have seen that parental conflict is stressful for children and impairs their short- and long-term adjustment to divorce (Oldehinkel et al., 2009; Potter, 2010).

Parents who petition for and successfully manage joint custody of their children expose their children to lower levels of conflict before and after the divorce, thereby aiding their transition.

Stepfamilies

About 15% to 20% of U.S. children live in a stepfamily composed of a biological parent and a nonrelated adult, most commonly a mother and stepfather (Dunn, 2002a). Stepfamilies, also known as blended or reconstituted families, present children with new challenges and adjustments as the multiple transitions entailed by divorce and remarriage are stressful. It is difficult for stepfamilies to integrate and balance the many relationships among custodial and noncustodial stepparents, grandparents, and extended families (Dupuis, 2010). For example, holidays may entail visiting three or four sets of relatives. Many children and adults look back on their parents' remarriage as more stressful than the divorce itself (Ahrons, 2007; Dunn, 2002b).

Age influences adaptation to a blended family. School-age children and adolescents, both boys and girls, tend to display more difficulties in adjusting to remarriage than do younger children (Hennon, Hildenbrand, & Schedle, 2008; Ram & Hou, 2003). Some children show more difficulty than others in adjusting to a blended family (Hennon et al., 2008). Both boys and girls tend to experience psychological distress in adjusting to remarriage; however, they may direct their distress in different ways. Living with a stepparent often results in greater physical aggression, destructive behaviors, and other behavior problems among boys as well as greater indirect, passive, and not easily noticeable aggression among girls (Hetherington et al., 1998; Ram & Hou, 2005). The effects on girls tend to be more severe than boys, especially in adolescence, because much of the girls' aggression is turned inward and appears as problems with anxiety, depression, and passive aggression (Bray, 1999; Hennon et al., 2008). Girls display more challenges in adapting as stepfathers disrupt the pattern of interactions girls have with their mothers (Dunn, 2002b). Both boys and girls raised in blended families show higher rates of social and emotional problems as compared with those living in intact families (Amato & Keith, 1991b; Ram & Hou, 2003). Adjusting to a blended family may pose challenges, but frequently children reared in stepfamilies do not differ from those raised in single-parent families in a variety of developmental outcomes including cognitive skills, hyperactivity, and aggression (Ahrons, 2007). Sometimes moving to a stepfamily is even associated with improved adjustment, especially if it results in an increase in family income (Ryan et al., 2015).

Although children are more likely to live with a mother and stepfather, many report that adjusting to a father's remarriage is more stressful than their mother's, regardless of which parent has custody (Buchanan, Maccoby, & Dornbusch, 1992; Doodson & Morley, 2006). Children often

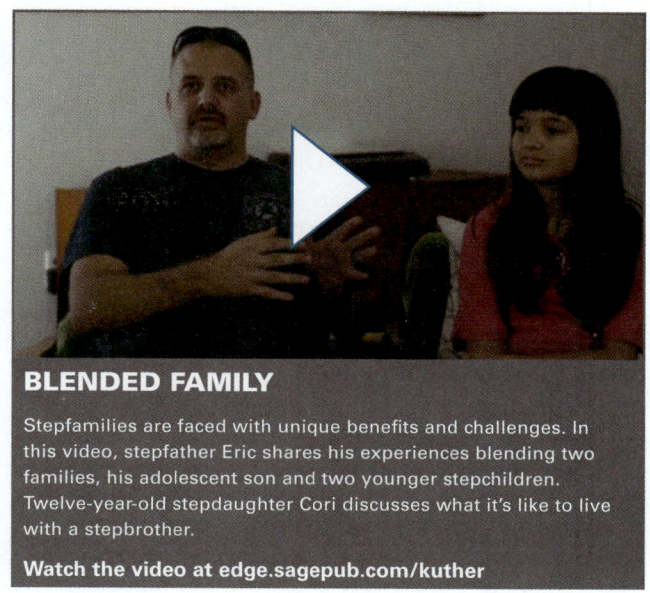

BLENDED FAMILY

Stepfamilies are faced with unique benefits and challenges. In this video, stepfather Eric shares his experiences blending two families, his adolescent son and two younger stepchildren. Twelve-year-old stepdaughter Cori discusses what it's like to live with a stepbrother.

Watch the video at edge.sagepub.com/kuther

react negatively when custodial fathers remarry, perhaps because children living with fathers may experience more difficulties to begin with (King, 2007). Often, fathers take custody of a child when he (the child in question is usually a boy) displays behavior problems and becomes too challenging for a mother to rear. If the father does not have a very close relationship with the child, remarriage may disrupt established patterns of interaction and bonds between the parent and child. Among children reared in father–stepmother homes, close relationships with both resident fathers and nonresident mothers are associated with fewer adolescent internalizing and externalizing problems, but relationships with resident stepmothers are unrelated to problems (Ganong & Coleman, 2000).

Overall, blended families adapt more easily and children show better adjustment when stepparents build a warm friendship with the child and slowly adopt their new roles (Doodson & Morley, 2006). However, stepmothers often find their role is challenging and ill defined, especially in the presence of a nonresident biological mother (Greeff & Du Toit, 2009). Stepmothers tend to report more depressive symptoms, parenting stress, and less child regard than do biological mothers (Shapiro, 2014; Shapiro & Stewart, 2011). When stepmothers seek support and clarification of their role from their spouse and approach children with honesty and acceptance, they are more likely to find success in the stepmother role (Whiting, Smith, Barnett, & Grafsky, 2007). When stepparents are warm and involved and do not exert authority too soon, children usually adjust quickly.

In middle childhood, children's social world expands to include peer, school, and community, but the home context remains an important source of nurturance, support, information, and safety. Children's growing capacities for reasoning and emerging sense of self influence their relationships with their parents and both parents and children must adjust.

Thinking in Context 10.3

1. How might children's relationships with their family influence relationships with peers? How are interactions and relationships with family members, such as siblings, similar to and different from those with peers?

2. Eight-year-old Sam's parents have announced that they plan to divorce. What are the major challenges facing Sam? What reactions and effects do you expect the divorce to have on Sam? How might those effects differ whether Sam is a girl or boy? How do you think Sam will adjust to his or her parents' remarriage?

COMMON PROBLEMS IN MIDDLE CHILDHOOD

The school years are a time of growth and change. Older children advance cognitively and socially, understanding themselves and their social worlds in new, more sophisticated ways. However, several threats to development emerge during the school years. Their more advanced conceptions of the world mean that they may experience fears and anxieties with more complex and diverse effects than earlier in development. In addition, sexual abuse, a problem throughout childhood, is most commonly reported by school-age children. Though school-age children face challenges to their development, they also display **resilience**, the capacity to adapt and bounce back.

COMMON FEARS AND ANXIETY

School-age children display many fears common to childhood, such as of the dark and thunder, harm and injury, school failure, and peer rejection. As they grow older, from late childhood to adolescence, the frequency and intensity of children's fears declines (Burnham, 2009). Children's perspectives expand to include wider contexts, such as their neighborhood, country, and world events, and their anxieties become more complex. Older children worry about parents' health, wars, and natural disasters, such as hurricanes, illnesses such as AIDS, and terrorist attacks (Burnham, Lomax, & Hooper, 2012; Gullone & King, 1997; Smith & Moyer-Gusé, 2006). Children who express many worries and anxieties tend to have a lower sense of self-confidence and perceived control than other children (Parkinson & Creswell, 2011).

Throughout childhood and adolescence, girls tend to express more worries than boys (Burnham, 2005). The social and emotional developments of middle childhood provide children with powerful resources for coping with anxiety. Most children manage anxiety by turning to others, talking with parents, friends, and trusted adults. As school-age children's capacities for emotional regulation aid them in managing anxiety, many fears decline in middle childhood.

Some children experience fear centering around school that shows itself in school refusal, refusing to attend school and finding it difficult to attend or to stay in school (Melvin & Tonge, 2012). Children who refuse school often display physical complaints such as dizziness, nausea, and stomachaches. These physical symptoms often disappear when they are allowed to stay home from school (Thambirajah, Grandison, & De-Hayes, 2008). They often miss a great deal of school and fall behind in their work (Kearney, 2001). Up to 28% of school-age children in the United States refuse school at some point in their education (Setzer, 2008). School refusal tends to be equally common across gender, racial, and income groups (Kearney, 2008). It can occur throughout the school years, but is more common from 5 to 6 years of age and 10 to 11 years of age, during transitions to elementary school, from elementary to middle or junior high school, and from childhood to adolescence (Setzer, 2008). Children who refuse school may experience many psychological problems such as excessive worrying, social anxiety, depressive symptoms, fatigue, clinginess to parents, and problems with peer relationships. They are also likely to show problem behaviors such as noncompliance, aggression, temper tantrums, and poor academic performance.

Children who display school refusal often fear a particular aspect of school, and the fears are often realistic, such as a school bully, a harsh teacher, or intense pressures to achieve from parents or teachers (Havik, Bru, & Ertesvåg, 2013; King & Bernstein, 2001). Treating school refusal requires teaching the child to cope with challenging situations and emotions, for example, by providing training in social skills, emotional regulation, and problem solving (Kearney & Roblek, 1998; Maric, Heyne, MacKinnon, van Widenfelt, & Westenberg, 2013; Melvin & Tonge, 2012). Most importantly, children must return to, and remain in, school and utilize their new strategies to manage and overcome the anxiety.

CHILD SEXUAL ABUSE

Once considered rare, **child sexual abuse** is now understood as a widespread problem around the world (Stoltenborgh, van IJzendoorn, Euser, & Bakermans-Kranenburg, 2011). Child sexual abuse is defined as engaging in any sexual activity, coerced or persuaded, with a child. It is estimated that about 27% of children under the age of 17 have experienced sexual abuse (Finkelhor, Shattuck, Turner, & Hamby, 2014). Although both boys and girls are victims of sexual abuse, girls are more often victimized. Sexual abuse may occur at any time during infancy, childhood, or adolescence, but it is most often reported in middle childhood, with about one half of cases occurring between ages 4 and 12 (U.S. Department of Health and Human Services, 2013). Typically, the most negative outcomes are seen in children who are young at the onset of abuse. Sexual abuse is associated with a range of negative outcomes, including behavioral problems in adolescence and adulthood (Kaplow & Widom, 2007; Marriott, Hamilton-Giachritsis, & Harrop, 2014). It is often difficult for children who are sexually abused to cope and heal because sexual abuse often is not a one-time event; some children experience sexual abuse that persists for years (U.S. Department of Health and Human Services, 2013).

Reported cases of child sexual abuse are more common in homes characterized by poverty, marital instability, and drug and alcohol abuse (Hilarski, 2008; Terry & Talon, 2004). Children who are raised in homes in which adults come and go—repeated marriages, separations, and revolving romantic partners—are at higher risk of sexual abuse. However, sexual abuse also occurs in intact middle-class families. In these families, children's victimization often remains undetected and unreported (Hinkelman & Bruno, 2008). Risk factors and typical outcomes for child sexual abuse appear in Table 10.3.

Perpetrators of sexual abuse are most often males whom the child knows, trusts, and has frequent contact with, such as parents, stepparents, and live-in boyfriends (Smith, 2008). About two thirds of sexual abuse cases are perpetrated by a stepfather as compared with about 11% by a biological father (Clark, Clark, & Adamec, 2007) Most sexual assaults occur in the home of the victim or the perpetrator, not—as portrayed in popular culture—in dark alleys or during abduction by a stranger. Children comply with the abuser for a variety of reasons. Some are bribed by gifts or privileges and often told that they are special and that the activity is a secret that they share (Hilarski, 2008). Others are intimidated and threatened by physical harm and reprisal for noncompliance or for telling another adult.

Children who are sexually abused display a number of problems yet not a clear, distinct set of psychological characteristics (McCoy & Keen, 2009). Both boys and girls respond in a similar way (Maikovich-Fong & Jaffee, 2010). Sexually abused children are more likely to show emotional and behavioral problems such as anxiety, depression, low self-esteem, aggression, withdrawal, sleep disturbances, acting out and risky behaviors, and low school achievement (Hilarski,

2008; Maniglio, 2011). Abusers often target children who cannot protect themselves—for example, those who are physically weak, starved for attention, and isolated, socially or emotionally, which may worsen the negative effects of abuse (Kendall-Tackett, Williams, & Finkelhor, 1993). Children who are sexually abused often are knowledgeable about sex and engage in age-inappropriate sexual activity, such as masturbating, placing objects in their genital areas, or behaving seductively (Kenny, Capri, Thakkar-Kolar, Ryan, & Runyon, 2008). Many children who are sexually abused display symptoms of **post-traumatic stress disorder (PTSD)**, an anxiety disorder that occurs after experiencing a traumatic event and includes flashbacks, nightmares, and feelings of helplessness (Maniglio, 2013; Putman, 2009).

Experiencing childhood sexual abuse is associated with long-term difficulties in adolescence and adulthood, including mental health problems, such as depression, anxiety disorder, conduct problems, antisocial behavior, substance dependence, and suicide attempts (Fergusson, Boden, & Horwood, 2008; Maniglio, 2011; Pérez-Fuentes et al., 2013). Long-term physical health issues associated with sexual victimization in childhood include gastrointestinal distress, reproductive problems, generalized pain, obesity, and overall poor health (Fergusson, McLeod, & Horwood, 2013; Herrenkohl, Hong, Klika, Herrenkohl, & Russo, 2013; Irish, Kobayashi, & Delahanty, 2010). As adolescents and adults, victims of sexual abuse are likely to show sexual problems such as risky and unprotected sexual activity, avoidance of sex, and sexual anxiety and guilt (Homma, Wang, Saewyc, & Kishor, 2012; Jones et al., 2013).

Prevention and early identification of sexual abuse is essential. When abuse is identified and stopped early, children display more positive adjustment (Fryda & Hulme, 2015). Effective prevention and early identification of sexual abuse relies on training parents and teachers to recognize the signs of abuse and report suspicions to law enforcement and child protection agencies (Wurtele & Kenny, 2010). As

TABLE 10.3 Risks and Outcomes Associated With Child Sexual Abuse

A CHILD AT RISK IS THE FOLLOWING	COMMON INDICATORS AND OUTCOMES
Female Of school age (6–11) Physically weak Seeking adult attention Emotionally or socially isolated Economically disadvantaged Homes in which adults come and go through multiple marriages, separations, and romantic partners	Withdrawal Depression Anxiety Post-traumatic stress disorder (PTSD) Conduct disorder and behavior problems Alcohol and substance dependence Social anxiety Age-inappropriate sexual knowledge and activity Early sexual activity Risky sexual activity Adolescent pregnancy Difficulty with emotional regulation and impulse control Poor sense of self and low self-esteem Poor school achievement Acting out and risk behaviors Sexual victimization in adolescence and adulthood

noted in Chapter 8, teachers and other professionals who come into contact with children are mandated reporters, legally obligated to report suspicions to authorities. Children tend to experience fewer long-term consequences of abuse if the child's account is believed; the abuse is stopped; and the home environment is structured, stable, and nurturing (Kenny et al., 2008). In addition to targeting parents, caregivers, and other adults, effective child sexual abuse prevention educates children about their bodies and their right to not be touched. When children are exposed to school-based education programs that help children learn how to recognize inappropriate touches, they are more apt to report them to teachers and other adults (Brassard & Fiorvanti, 2015; Fryda & Hulme, 2015). Table 10.4 summarizes characteristics of effective sexual abuse prevention programs.

School-based education programs increase children's knowledge about personal safety but are more likely to be successful in teaching children and adults skills and reducing rates of child sexual abuse when they engage parents (Wurtele & Kenny, 2010). The active participation of parents in self-protection programs contributes to success because many of the conditions that are necessary for abuse relate to the bond between the parent and child such as the lack of effective supervision and child desiring adult attention. The joint participation of parent and child may increase the

positive bond of their relationship and the increasing ease in which they talk about difficult anxiety-provoking things (Kenny et al., 2008). In addition, many parents lack knowledge about child sexual abuse and often adhere to common myths including underestimating the prevalence of abuse, assuming that boys cannot be sexually victimized, and not realizing that children are most commonly victimized by someone who is familiar to them (Babatsikos, 2010).

Successful prevention programs repeatedly expose children to information at school and at home, via homework and discussions with parents. In addition, successful programs explain what kinds of touches are "okay" and what are not and provide children with the vocabulary to describe their bodies (e.g., correct terms for genitals; Kenny et al., 2008). Although children as young as 3 may show benefits from such programs, children 8 years and older show substantial benefits, including having increases in vocabulary, knowledge, and skills; identifying potential abuse situations; and possessing a sense of control (Afifi & MacMillan, 2011). Yet not all children who experience traumatic events such as sexual abuse experience dire outcomes; some children show resilience to trauma and thrive despite adversity.

RESILIENCE

Best friends Jane and Margarita walk to school together every day, partly because they live next door to each other and like each other's company but also because their mothers said that they cannot walk around their neighborhood alone. One day while Jane and Margarita played in the living room at Margarita's home, they heard an argument outside, and suddenly a bullet crashed through the window, hitting the wall across the room. Since then, Jane's and Margarita's mothers don't allow them to play outside their homes and instead make them play in the kitchen, far away from the living room's windows that look out on the street. Clearly, Jane and Margarita live in a community that poses risks to their safety. They also both live with their single mothers who often leave them home alone at night as they work their part-time second jobs.

Many children like Jane and Margarita are faced with risk factors, challenges that tax their coping capacities and can evoke psychological stress, such as low socioeconomic status, exposure to poverty stricken and dangerous neighborhoods, divorce, bullying, and sexual abuse (Luthar, 2006; Masten, Best, & Garmezy, 1990). The more risks that children face, the more difficult it is for them to adjust and the more likely they are to have psychological and behavioral problems such as anxiety, depression, poor academic achievement, and delinquent activity.

Jane and Margarita attend a school with limited resources, overcrowded classrooms, outdated books, and teachers who feel overwhelmed by many students with special needs. Like many of her classmates, Jane finds it hard to stop worrying and concentrate in class, and she performs poorly in reading and math. Margarita, on the other hand, manages to earn As on many of her assignments. Margarita

TABLE 10.4 Characteristics of Effective Child Sexual Abuse Prevention Programs

CHARACTERISTIC	DESCRIPTION
Early identification	Train parents and teachers to recognize the risk factors and early signs of sexual abuse, and report suspicions to law enforcement and child protection agencies.
Educate children	Educate children in a developmentally appropriate way about their bodies and their rights to not be touched. Provide children with the vocabulary to describe their bodies. Help children learn how to recognize inappropriate touches and learn what to do if touched.
Engage parents	Educate parents and assist them in discussing sexual abuse prevention with their children. Encourage them to support school efforts by discussing school activities.
Repeat exposure	Repeatedly expose children to the material in school and at home via homework and discussions with parents.
Strengthen parenting and families	Provide parents with support, parenting education, and other resources to help them improve the bond with their child, reducing children's attention seeking behaviors.

Children's adjustment is influenced by the balance of risk and protective factors they experience. The more risks children face, such as residing in poor and dangerous communities, the more likely they are to experience difficulties with adjustment and development.

is a dynamic process involving interactions among the child's developmental capacities and his or her changing context, including relationships with other people. It is influenced by prior development, competence, risk factors, the nature of the current challenges faced, and the child's adaptive capacity and strengths, known as **protective factors** (Cicchetti, 2010; Masten & Narayan, 2012). Protective factors are influences that reduce the poor outcomes associated with adverse circumstances (Kim-Cohen, 2007; Werner, 1995).

Resilient children have strengths and powerful capacities for coping and adjustment. They benefit from multiple protective influences that help them to maintain a positive developmental trajectory despite adverse circumstances (Domhardt, Münzer, Fegert, & Goldbeck, 2014; Vanderbilt-Adriance & Shaw, 2008). For example, Margarita often attends an after-school program where she learned to play basketball and use a computer. Her uncle Pedro visits every Wednesday and Sunday, and she feels as though she can talk to him about anything. Each week, Margarita attends church with her mother, and Pedro and her mother make a big dinner. Each of these factors, school and community connections, positive and close relationships with adults, routines, and attending church promote children's adjustment and protect them against the negative outcomes associated with adversity (Masten & Monn, 2015). Resilience is not an all-or-nothing attribute that children either have or do not have (Rutter, 1985). Instead, children vary in the degree to which they are resilient based on their unique contexts, and children's capacity for resilience can vary over time (Masten, 2014).

worries about her family and her own safety, but she can put her worries aside to get back and forth from school and concentrate on her studies. Despite experiencing a variety of intense stressors, some children, like Margarita, display little trauma and are able to manage their anxiety and succeed at home and school, showing high self-esteem, low levels of depression, few behavioral problems, and positive academic achievement (Cicchetti, 2010; Kim-Cohen, 2007).

Margarita displays resilience, the ability to respond or perform positively in the face of adversity; to achieve despite the presence of disadvantages; or to significantly exceed expectations given poor home, school, and community circumstances (Masten, 2014). Adaptation to adversity

TABLE 10.5 Characteristics Associated With Resilience

INDIVIDUAL COMPETENCIES	FAMILY COMPETENCIES AND CHARACTERISTICS	SCHOOL AND COMMUNITY CHARACTERISTICS
Coping skills Easy temperament Emotional regulation abilities Good cognitive abilities Intelligence Positive outlook Positive self-concept Religiosity Self-efficacy (feeling of control over one's destiny) Talents valued by others	Close relationships with parents and caregivers Organized home Parental involvement in children's education Positive family climate Postsecondary education of parents Provision of support Religiosity and engagement with the church Socioeconomic advantage Warm but assertive parenting	Access to local churches After-school programs Availability of emergency services Mentoring programs and opportunities to form relationships with adults Health care availability Instruction in conflict management Opportunity to develop and practice leadership skills Peer programs, such as big brother/big sister programs Programs to assist developing self-management skills Public safety Support networks outside of the family, such as supportive adults and peers Ties to prosocial organizations Well-funded schools with highly qualified teachers Youth programs

SOURCE: Child Trends (2013).

LIVES IN CONTEXT

Exposure to War and Terrorism and Children's Development

Acts of war and terror are sudden, unpredictable, and dramatic as they affect the child, family, and community—and hold dire consequences for children's development (Catani et al., 2010). Living through chronic, unexpected bouts of terror and trauma, such as responding to air raids; listening to bomb blasts; fleeing a home and community in search of safety; and suddenly losing loved ones to military service, confinement, or death, evokes trauma that disrupts the contextual and social fabric of children and families' lives (Werner, 2012; Williams, 2007). Children raised in environments of war and terror may experience or witness the injury or death of family members and friends, have family members who are missing for long periods of time, and parents who are called away to the military or who are absent (Sagi-Schwartz, 2008). Victims of war are often displaced; forced to flee their homes, often with only a few belongings; and sometimes are separated from parents. Children require stability—especially in times of trauma. With sudden changes and loss of feelings of safety and tangible resources, such as the loss of the familiar environment and routines of school, social networks, and patterns of family life, children suffer multiple losses, loss of contact with community and traditional values (Cummings, Goeke-Morey, Merrilees, Taylor, & Shirlow, 2014; Morgos, Worden, & Gupta, 2007).

Healthy development requires physical resources, such as food, health care, and shelter, and socioemotional resources, such as parental and family support, love, trust, and security. Exposure to war and acts of terrorism attack all of the resources children need to grow into healthy, well-adjusted adults. School-age children are at particular risk for negative outcomes in response to exposure to the trauma of war and terrorism because they are old enough to understand the gravity of the situation but have not yet developed the emotional regulation, abstract reasoning, and socioemotional maturity to process such events (Saraiya, Garakani, & Billick, 2013). School-age children show a variety of responses as shown in Table 10.6. Children exposed to acts of terror may show a prolonged fear of being alone, safety concerns, and preoccupations with danger. They may lose interest in their favorite activities and may engage in repetitious traumatic play and retelling of trauma. Yet some children are naturally resilient. For example, one study of Palestine children exposed to the 2008–2009 war on Gaza found that about three quarters of the children showed some recovery from PTSD symptoms (Punamäki, Palosaari, Diab, Peltonen, & Qouta, 2014). Likewise, most child survivors of war who participated in long-term follow-up studies showed no enduring patterns of emotional distress or poor socioemotional outcomes (Werner, 2012).

Intervening to assist children exposed to war and terrorism is difficult because typically the trauma is ongoing, unpredictable, and dramatic. Consequences of exposure to terror damage the very factors that promote resilience in children, such as a sense of stability; supportive relationships with adults; connections with the community; and interpersonal resources such as social competence, confidence, and an easy temperament (Asarnow, 2011; Betancourt & Khan, 2008; Sagi-Schwartz, 2008). Interventions to assist children promote children's attachment with parents and caregivers by ensuring that children stay physically and emotionally close to their parents. Parents who are able to instill a sense of warmth and security are best able to support their children's needs and promote resilience (Saraiya et al., 2013). Children's physical needs must be met through adequate nutrition, health care, and opportunities to engage in physical activity. Children must also have opportunities to express ideas and feelings directly and through play, such as drawing, storytelling, drama, and games. Children who have had similar experiences can be placed together in small groups as a feeling of belonging together and having gone through similar trauma, such as bombing, displacement, or loss of family members can facilitate the healing process (Werner, 2012). School-based interventions can help children adjust (Asarnow, 2011). However, children in war zones often are displaced and lose the daily school routine. Interventions should help restore children's educational routines. When schools are closed, locally trained paraprofessionals can help families establish educational resources until children can return to their usual schools. No intervention can erase the effects of exposure to the trauma of war and terror, but interventions can help to bolster the factors that promote resilience to adversity.

What Do You Think?

Consider the problem of war or terrorism from the perspective of bioecological theory. Identify factors within the microsystem that may help children adjust to experiencing terror. What factors might make it more challenging for children to adjust? What about mesosystem factors? Exosystem? Macrosystem?

Protective factors arise from within the child, from the family or extended family, and from the community (Luthar, 2006; Lynch & Cicchetti, 1998; Werner, 2012). Resilient children tend to have personal characteristics that protect them from adversity, such as an easy temperament, sense of competence, self-control, good information processing and problem-solving skills, friendliness, and sensitivity to others that aid them in managing adversity and learning from their experiences (Afifi & MacMillan, 2011; Marriott et al., 2014; Masten, 2011). In addition, resilient individuals have a proactive orientation. They take initiative in their lives, believe in their own effectiveness, and have a positive sense of self (Alvord & Grados, 2005; Lee, Kwong, Cheung, Ungar, & Cheung, 2010). Children who are resilient tend to have strong and supportive relationships with at least one parent, caregiver, or adult who provides guidance and support (Afifi

TABLE 10.6 Children's Responses to War and Terrorism

EMOTIONAL RESPONSES	PSYCHOSOCIAL RESPONSES
Affect control	Aggression
Anger	Clinginess
Anxiety	Empathy
Depression	Interpersonal conflict
Fear	Poor interpersonal skills
Helplessness	Irritability
Numbness	Low self-esteem
Survivor guilt	Poor attachment
Trust	Regression
Posttraumatic stress	Safety
	Trust
	Withdrawal
	Defiance
	Preoccupation with danger
	School refusal
	Fear being alone
	Safety concerns

PHYSICAL RESPONSES	COGNITIVE RESPONSES
Headaches	Impaired concentration
Heightened startle response	Confusion
Insomnia	Impaired memory
Reduced appetite	Intrusive thoughts
Reduced energy	
Stomachaches	

& MacMillan, 2011; Domhardt et al., 2014). Table 10.5 and Figure 10.3 illustrate characteristics that promote resilience in children.

A fundamental characteristic of resilient children is that they are successful in regulating their emotions and behavior (Luthar, 2006; Masten, 2014). In a longitudinal study of 5-year-olds, Rydell, Berlin, and Bohlin (2003) found that children who had difficulty regulating positive emotions showed more problem behaviors and low levels of prosocial behaviors whereas those who were skilled at regulating their positive emotions showed high levels of prosocial behavior. Generally, negative life experiences and unfavorable backgrounds contribute to children's adjustment difficulties. The behavior problems common to exposure to harmful experiences at home and in the neighborhood can increase children's problems and expose them to further negative life experiences, which also increase the rate of maladjustment (Brennan, 2008). It is noteworthy, however, that some children who appear resilient may suffer from internalizing problems that are not always readily apparent, such as anxiety, depression, or low self-worth, which may have long-term negative consequences for their development and adjustment (Masten & Coatsworth, 1998). Resilient children illustrate an important finding: Exposure to adversity in childhood does not necessarily lead to maladjustment; many children thrive despite challenging experiences.

FIGURE 10.3: Characteristics of Resilient Children, as Reported by Their Parents

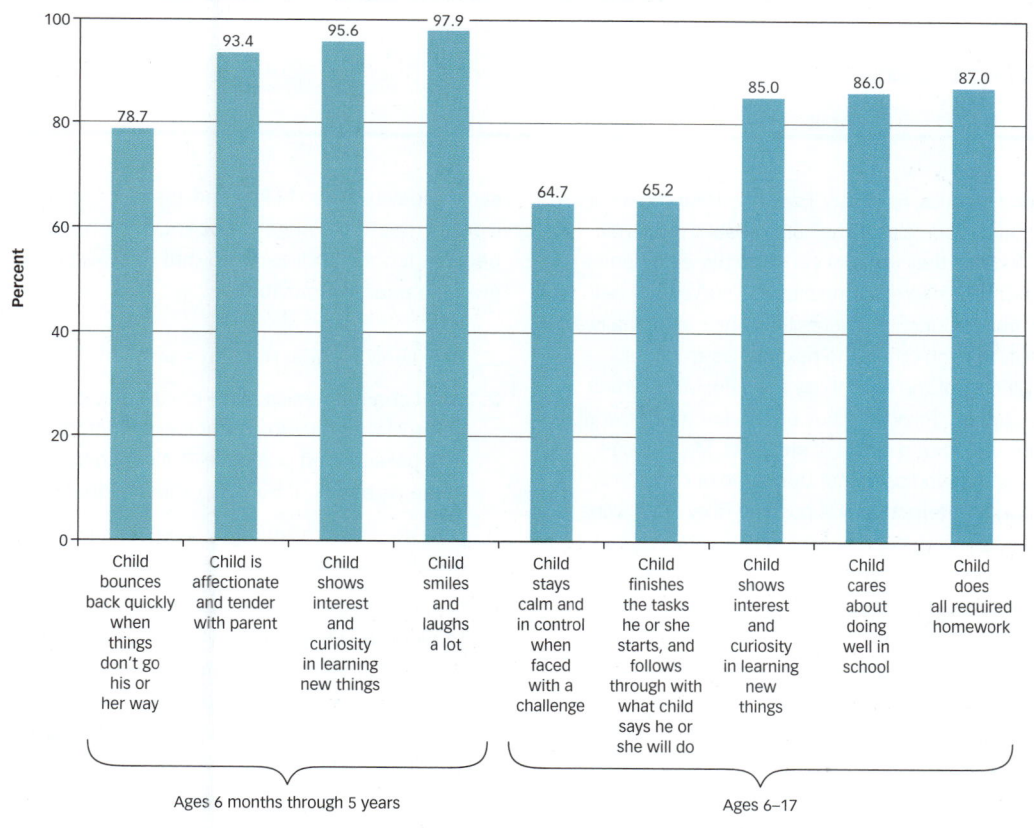

SOURCE: Child Trends (2013).

Middle childhood is an important time for socioemotional development. School-age children show dramatic changes in their self-conceptions, peer relationships, and competence. They live in diverse home environments and face common challenges to their coping skills but show a range of outcomes depending on their unique contextual conditions. The socioemotional skills developed in middle childhood prepare school-age children for the dramatic changes that they will encounter in adolescence.

Children who are exposed to violence in their communities and the violence of war are at particular risk for poor adjustment, as discussed in Lives in Context (p. 282).

Thinking in Context 10.4

Risk and protective factors illustrate the dynamic interactions among individuals and their contexts.

1. What factors within children might influence their capacity to adjust to adversity? Identify individual characteristics that may act as risk and protective factors.

2. Identify contextual factors that might influence children's capacity to adjust to adversity—that is, identify risk and protective factors within the contexts in which children are raised.

Apply Your Knowledge

Interested in peer dynamics, Professor Peer administered a survey to Ms. Holman's third-grade class. The survey asked students to list the three students they like most and the three students they like least. After the children completed the survey, the bell rang, and it was time for lunch. Students filed out into the hallway, chattering excitedly to each other. The next day as students played outside, waiting for the school day to begin, Ms. Holman noticed that one student, Riley, who has always been somewhat withdrawn, is surrounded by a crowd of students. Ms. Holman moves toward the group and sees that the crowd of children is watching two students interact: Joey is pushing Riley and calling him names. Joey has always been boisterous and physical with other students, Ms. Holman recalls. After breaking up the crowd, the students enter school and the school day begins.

In class, when Ms. Holman calls on Riley, he's slow to respond, as usual given his shyness. When he speaks, the other students make coughing noises and giggle. At lunch, Riley is again surrounded by other students, but this time Ms. Holman scolds Joey but also Mikey and Jose for teasing Riley. She worries that these negative peer experiences will make Riley become more withdrawn and that Riley will become even more prone to peer victimization.

1. How likely are Ms. Holman's worries?

2. What characteristics place children at risk for victimization by peers? What role do psychological factors and relationships with parents and peers play? What characteristics place students at risk of bullying other children?

3. How does victimization by peers influence psychological development and social relationships?

4. Consider Professor Peer's survey, which asked children to think of the students they most liked and most disliked. What role might have Professor Peer's survey played in influencing children's interactions? Do researchers have special responsibilities when they administer peer nomination measures such as this?

Chapter Summary

10.1 Explain three ways in which the sense of self changes in middle childhood.

School-age children's conceptions of themselves become more sophisticated, organized, and accurate as well as include positive and negative traits that recognize temporal and contextual fluctuations. Children incorporate feedback about their abilities from parents, teachers, and peers as well as engage in social comparison to derive a sense of self-esteem.

10.2 Analyze the typical qualities of school-age children's friendships and their developmental significance.

In middle childhood, friendship becomes a reciprocal relationship in which children like each other, are responsive to each other's needs, and trust each other. Intimacy, loyalty, and commitment become important to older children and they have fewer, closer friends; change friends less frequently; become more upset at losing a friend; and find making friends more challenging. Friendships offer opportunities for children to learn relationship skills, influence children's adjustment and psychological well-being, and protect children from the negative effects of risks and stressors.

10.3 Explore the role of peer acceptance in children's adjustment, including popularity and rejection.

Peer acceptance becomes a source of self-validation and self-esteem and influences adjustment in middle childhood. Popular children tend to be helpful, trustworthy, and bright; they are skilled in self-regulation and conflict resolution. Aggressive-rejected children show confrontational behavior, a hostile attribution bias, impulsivity, relational aggression, and poor emotional regulation skills. Withdrawn-rejected children tend to be passive, timid, anxious, and socially awkward as well as show poor emotional regulation skills. They are also at risk for peer victimization. Peer rejection is associated with short- and long-term problems such as loneliness, unhappiness, depression, low self-esteem, aggression, poor school achievement, and antisocial behavior.

10.4 Compare the characteristics of bullies and victims, how parent and school factors contribute to bullying, and outcomes of bullying.

Children who bully tend to be physically and verbally assertive and impulsive yet report making friends easily. Bullied children are more likely to be inhibited, frail, anxious, and dependent as well as have low self-esteem and poor social and emotional regulation skills. Children who bully often come from homes characterized by a lack of supervision in which parents prefer physical discipline and are permissive toward aggressive behavior. Victims of bullying often experience intrusive parenting and overprotectiveness that increases their vulnerability. School procedures, such as grouping students by physical characteristics, lack of monitoring, and little encouragement for students to report bullying, maintain and increase bullying.

10.5 Discuss changes in family relationships during middle childhood.

Older children become more concerned with independence and making their own decisions. They become less satisfied with parents' authority and often show a decline in respect for parental authority. Parents adapt by using less direct management of children's behavior and instead begin to share power with children, by guiding and monitoring their behavior from a distance, communicating expectations, using reasoning, and permitting children to be in charge of moment to moment decision making. Through their interactions with siblings, children learn important relationship skills, such as conflict resolution and intimacy, buffering the impact of stressful life events on internalizing symptoms.

10.6 Examine the adjustment of children reared in gay and lesbian families.

Over two decades of research has failed to reveal important differences in the adjustment or development of children and adolescents reared by same-sex couples compared to those reared by other-sex couples. Specifically, children and adolescents raised by same-sex parents do not differ from other children on measures of socioemotional development, such as empathy and emotional regulation, cognitive functioning, social competence, and behavior problems, and show similar patterns of gender identity and gender role development. Gay fathers and lesbian mothers show similar levels of parenting competence and commitment to the parenting role as heterosexual parents.

10.7 Identify risks and protective factors that contribute to children's adjustment in single-parent and cohabiting families.

Children in single-parent families tend to show more poor physical and mental health, academic achievement, and social competence as well as more behavior problems than do children in intact two-parent families. Single-parent households are disproportionately likely to be poor. Children raised in cohabiting-parent families tend to experience more favorable economic situations. Children in cohabiting households tend to experience transitions in family life than do children of married parents and may experience more conflict in the home, an important influence on children's adjustment. Children and adolescents living in cohabiting-parent families often show more behavior and academic problems than do those in married stepparent and intact families.

10.8 Analyze patterns of adjustment to divorce in children and factors that contribute to adjustment.

Divorce has some negative effects on children's adjustment, but the effects are small, vary by particular outcome, and do not apply to all boys and girls uniformly. Divorce influences children through changes in economic and emotional resources associated with the transition to single-parent homes, new neighborhoods, and new schools. Many of children's emotional, psychological, and behavioral problems stem from exposure to parental conflict before and after the divorce. Most children show improved adjustment within two years after the divorce.

10.9 Discuss common manifestations of anxiety in middle childhood.

The social and emotional developments of middle childhood provide children with powerful resources for coping with anxiety. Most children manage anxiety by turning to others, talking with parents, friends, and trusted adults. A common fear that develops in middle childhood concerns school and shows itself in school refusal, refusing to attend school and displaying physical complaints such as dizziness, nausea, and stomachaches that often disappear when they are allowed to stay home from school. Treating anxieties such as school refusal entails teaching the child to cope with challenging situations and emotions, for example, by providing training in social skills and emotional regulation

10.10 Assess risks for sexual abuse, typical outcomes, and prevention strategies.

Sexual abuse is most often reported in middle childhood, and girls are more often victimized than boys. Reported cases are more common in homes characterized by poverty, marital instability, and drug and alcohol abuse but are underreported in intact middle-class families. Sexually abused children display many socioemotional and behavior problems. Children tend to experience fewer long-term consequences of abuse if the child's account is believed; the abuse is stopped; and the home environment is structured, stable, and nurturing. Effective prevention and early identification of sexual abuse relies on training parents, teachers, and students to recognize the signs of abuse and report suspicions to the appropriate authority or agency.

10.11 Analyze the role of resilience in promoting adjustment, including characteristics of children and contexts that promote resilience.

Resilient children are skilled in information processing and problem solving and have a proactive orientation. They also have personal characteristics such as an easy temperament, sense of competence, and adaptability, which aid them in managing adversity and learning from their experiences. Most importantly, resilient children are able to regulate their emotions, maintaining control under trying circumstances. Resilient children benefit from multiple protective influences, such as supportive relationships with caring adults, that help them to cope and adjust to adverse circumstances.

Key Terms

aggressive-rejected   264

bully-victims   266

child sexual abuse   278

industry over inferiority   260

peer acceptance   263

peer victimization   262

popular   263

post-traumatic stress disorder (PTSD)   279

protective factors   281

reactive aggression   266

resilience   278

withdrawn-rejected   264

PART V

Adolescence

Though a hallmark of adolescence, the process of biological maturation known as puberty often begins in late childhood. Physical developments include rapid growth, changes in body shape and composition, and, most notably, the ability to reproduce. Puberty also plays a role in neurological development, including changes that increase the speed and efficiency of information processing and contribute to the development of abstract thinking. Adolescents apply these new abilities to think about themselves and begin to construct a sense of identity.

Parents foster autonomy in their children through warm and firm parenting that is accompanied by monitoring. Although adolescent-parent conflict peaks in middle adolescence, it typically consists of small arguments over mundane issues. The peer context ascends in importance as friendship cliques emerge. By mid-adolescence cliques include both boys and girls, creating opportunities for dating. The tendency to conform to peers peaks in middle adolescence, but usually pertains to day-to-day issues such as clothing choices or whether to attend a party.

Adolescents are immersed in a school context which influences them through its match to their developmental needs. Finally, many adolescents experience a part-time work context that generally does not increase responsibility, but will not cause harm. Over the adolescent years, the contexts in which young people participate grow in size and continue to interact, influencing their physical, cognitive, and socioemotional development.

Watch at
edge.sagepub.com/kuther

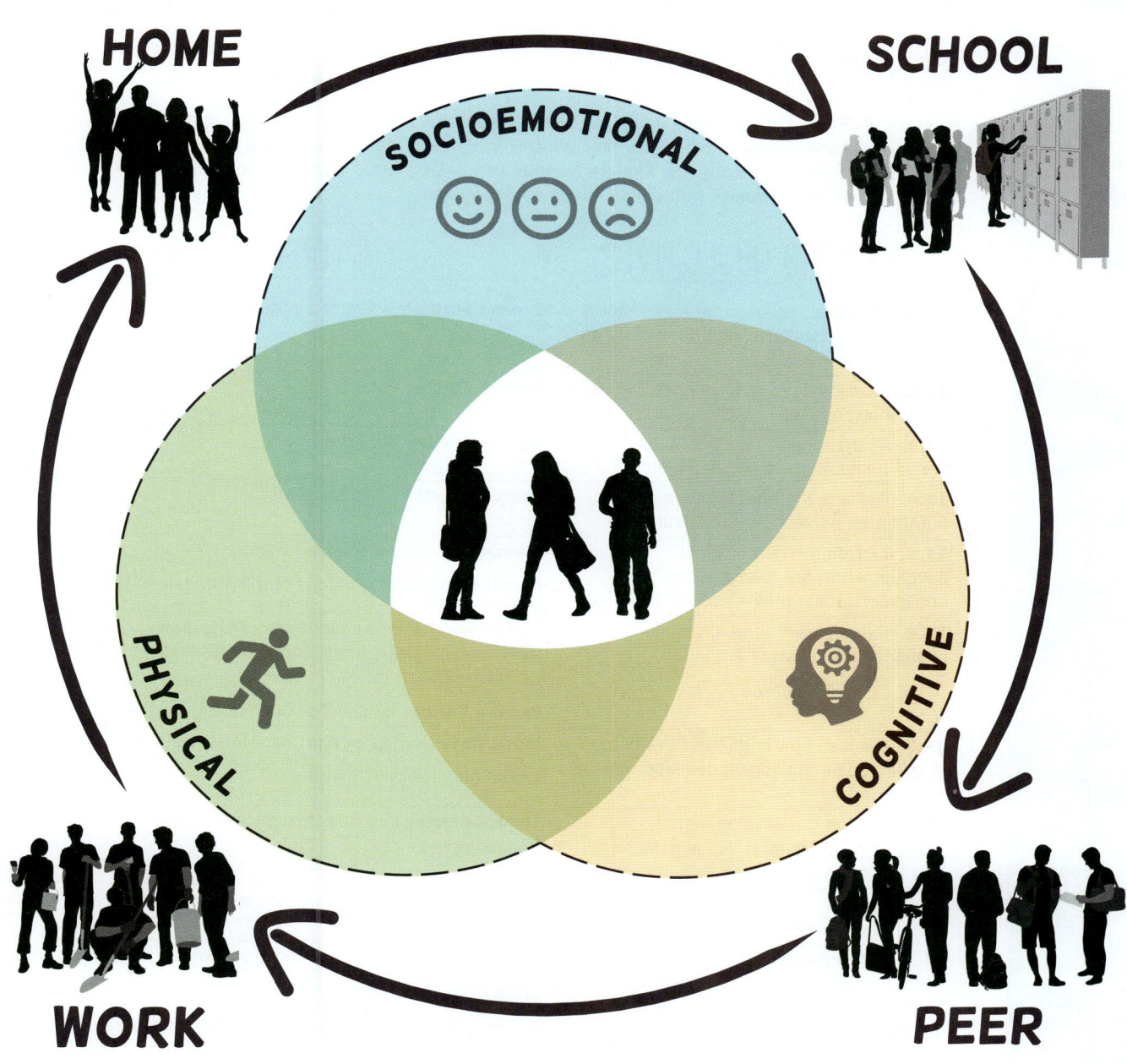

SOCIOEMOTIONAL

PHYSICAL

COGNITIVE

HOME

SCHOOL

WORK

PEER

Images: ©iStock.com

CHAPTER 11

Physical and Cognitive Development in Adolescence

LEARNING OBJECTIVES

KEY STUDY TOOLS

11.1. Compare and contrast Hall's storm and stress perspective with popular views and research evidence.

Explore Further Storm and Stress

11.2. Explain the physical changes that occur with puberty and their psychosocial effects.

Explore Further Puberty

11.3. Analyze the influence of pubertal timing on adolescent development.

Explore Further Pubertal Timing

11.4. Discuss the effects of sleep and nutrition on adolescent functioning.

Think Critically Sleep and BMI

11.5. Explain the neurological developments that take place in adolescence and their effect on behavior.

Connect Inside the Teenage Brain

Watch Mysterious Workings of the Adolescent Brain

11.6. Identify ways in which thinking changes in adolescence.

Ethical and Policy Applications of Lifespan Development Legal Implications of Adolescent Decision Making (p. 311)

Explore Further Adolescent Cognition

11.7. Discuss how cognitive development is reflected in adolescent decision making and behavior.

Video Case Coming of Age: Bat Mitzvah

Listen Impulsivity in Teens

11.8. Outline the developmental progression of moral reasoning, factors that influence it, and its link with behavior.

Think Critically Parental Discipline and Moral Reasoning

11.9. Analyze criticisms of Kohlberg's moral development theory.

Explore Further Gender and Moral Reasoning

11.10. Describe the challenges that school transitions pose for adolescents and the role of parents in academic achievement.

Video Case Transition to Middle School

Lives in Context Adolescent Employment (p. 316)

Applying Developmental Science School Dropout (p. 318)

At 16 years of age, Mark has the physique of a man, with broad shoulders, a wide back, and large arms. He excels in sports and is popular with the kids in his high school, especially the girls. Academically, Mark is less gifted as he finds schoolwork challenging. Mark sometimes feels confused by the positive feedback he receives from his coach and his friends and the more mixed messages he gets from teachers, parents, and

Myung J. Chun/L.A. Times/Getty

the outside world. He doesn't like the many rules his parents set, such as calling before getting into the car to drive to a friend's house and again after arriving, and his curfew is earlier than that of his friends. Mark feels that his parents baby him. His boss at his after school job treats Mark more like an adult by letting him run the store for a few hours each week while he runs errands. Recently Mark's older brother took him to a college party. He told Mark that if he didn't say anything no one would know that he was still in high school. Mark's brother was right. Mark was popular with the girls at the party and hooked up with Veronica, a college sophomore.

Like Mark, most young people find adolescence, the transition from childhood to adulthood, a time filled with many changes that are often confusing. In some situations, they are treated more like children, offered guidance, rules, and protection, and other times they are treated as adults, afforded autonomy, responsibility, and freedom. Adolescence poses challenges to parents and teachers who must adapt to adolescents' rapidly maturing bodies and cognitive abilities in order to balance fostering adolescents' changing needs for autonomy and protection.

Part of the challenges young people and adults face occur because adolescence spans a great many years—longer than ever before. In earlier historical periods as well as in most nonindustrialized societies today, childhood was followed nearly immediately by the assumption of adult roles, such as worker, spouse, and parent (Larson & Wilson, 2004; Schlegel, 2008). In industrialized societies, becoming an adult usually entails seeking employment, which requires increasing levels of education and vocational training. Therefore, the passage to adulthood is more gradual in industrialized societies, making it a lengthy transition with a great many changes. Because of this, adolescence in industrialized societies is best understood as entailing three phases: early adolescence (11 to 14 years), middle adolescence (14 to 16 years), and late adolescence (16 to 18 years). Some developmental scientists conceive of adolescence extending as long as 21 years (Steinberg, 2008b). Adolescents face very different developmental tasks than do children and adults—and they are treated quite different than both.

CONCEPTIONS OF ADOLESCENCE

Marissa raced into the house, threw her books on the table, and stormed off to her room, calling out, "Leave me alone!" and slamming the door. A moment later, the sounds of her stereo blasted and filled the house with a pulsing beat. Most adults are quick to dismiss Marissa's behavior as typical of moody adolescents, consistent with the common belief that the hormones of **puberty** affect adolescents' moods, leading them to experience unexpected, intense, and volatile shifts. Are adolescents naturally moody? Do you remember your own adolescence? Are moods simply to be expected?

POPULAR VIEWS OF ADOLESCENCE: STORM AND STRESS

The popular view that adolescence is a troubling time for teens and parents to endure originates with the work of G. Stanley Hall, known as the father of adolescence as he defined the field in his 1904 volume *Adolescence*. Hall theorized that adolescence is a period of "storm and stress," a universal and inevitable upheaval triggered by puberty and comprising ages 14 to 24. Hall based his theory on then-popular Lamarckian evolution, the belief that memories and acquired characteristics can be inherited from generation to generation and that the development of the individual mirrors that of the human species as a whole. Hall explained that adolescents' extreme volatility is inherited and reflects a time in human history that was very active and challenging, specifically the birth of civilization. Therefore, storm and stress and extreme turmoil, such as depression, severe troubles with parents, and delinquent activity, was to be expected and a sign of normal healthy development, triggered by puberty.

We now know that behaviors are not passed on from generation to generation; Lamarckian views have long been debunked in favor of Darwinian evolution. Despite this, Hall's storm and stress view of the nature of adolescence remains popular (Arnett, 1999). For example, teachers

G. Stanley Hall (1846–1924) believed that adolescence is a period of turmoil, or storm and stress.

and parents tend to agree with statements like the following: "Adolescence is a difficult time of life" and "Changes in behavior during early adolescence are mainly due to physical changes which are occurring." Mothers tend to agree with statements that their child will "be more concerned with friends than what I think" and "will be more difficult to get along with" (Buchanan et al., 1990). Likewise, college students tend to endorse storm and stress notions, especially about problems in parent–child relationships (Holmbeck & Hill, 1988).

IS ADOLESCENCE A PERIOD OF STORM AND STRESS?

Research is largely at odds with the storm and stress view. Instead, it appears that adolescence, though a dramatic period of change, is not as tumultuous as suggested by Hall. Instead, as we will discuss in Chapter 12, research suggests that although some conflict with parents increases in adolescence most adolescents get along with their parents, love and feel loved by them, respect them, and turn to them for advice (Steinberg, 2001). Without a doubt, adolescents engage in more risk behavior, such as delinquent activity and extreme sports, and experience more fluctuations in mood than do children and adults. However, there is wide variability and most adolescents (at least 80%) do not experience serious problems (Lerner & Israeloff, 2007; Offer & Schonert-Reichl, 1992). Overall, the rate of serious disturbance in adolescence is similar to that at other periods in life (Offer, 1989).

The contemporary perspective is that although adolescence may be stormy and/or stressful for some, it is not typically a developmental problem, nor is it inevitable or universal (Arnett, 1999; Hollenstein & Lougheed, 2013; Larson & Ham, 1993). For example, in a classic study, adolescents from 10 countries were interviewed (Australia, Bangladesh, Germany, Hungary, Israel, Italy, Japan, Taiwan, Turkey, and the United States; Offer, Ostrov, Howard, & Atkinson, 1988). Most reported that they were usually happy, felt that they got along with their parents, and felt good about their progress toward adulthood. Although every adolescent experiences puberty and biological changes undoubtedly influence behavior, contextual influences also play a role in adolescent behavior. Moreover, there are dramatic individual differences in the effects of pubertal change depending on the age of onset, duration and intensity of changes, adolescents' temperament and emotional regulation skills, and environmental supports (Hollenstein & Lougheed, 2013). This contemporary view may be best illustrated by looking at popular hallmark of adolescence: moodiness.

ADOLESCENT MOODINESS

The view that puberty is inextricably linked with adolescent moods, leading them to experience unexpected, intense, and volatile shifts in emotion, is common to portrayals of adolescence. Is 16-year-old Nate's screeching his tires of his car after storming off during an argument with his father a function of raging pubertal hormones? Probably not. The source of the changes in adolescents' mood and behavior is complex and not simply a function of puberty.

Although high and rapidly shifting levels of puberty hormones are associated with depression, irritability, and aggression in boys and girls (Buchanan, Eccles, & Becker, 1992), it is only early in puberty that hormones rapidly increase and fluctuate enough to cause such erratic and powerful shifts in adolescents' emotions and behaviors (Reiter & Lee, 2001). Researchers have found that the relationship between pubertal hormones and adolescent mood is weak and inconsistent (Balzer, Duke, Hawke, & Steinbeck, 2015; Buchanan et al., 1992; Duke, Balzer, & Steinbeck, 2014). So then what, if anything, influences adolescents' moods?

A unique method offered an important perspective on adolescents' experience. In a series of studies, adolescents and adults carried pagers; were beeped randomly throughout the day; and were asked to report what they were doing, who they were with, and how they felt (Larson & Csikszentmihalyi, 2014; Richards & Larson, 1993). This method, known as the *experience sampling method*, permits researchers a window into people's days. Similar to common views, adolescents' moods overall were less stable than those of adults. They experienced wider and quicker mood changes. Contrary to popular views, the changes were unrelated to puberty, stress, a lack of personal control, or poor psychological adjustment (Larson, Csikszentmihalyi, & Graef, 2014). Instead, adolescents' mood swings varied with the context, and adolescents reported moving from one context to another, such as from school to work to family to peers, more often than did adults (Larson & Richards, 1998; Larson & Seepersad, 2003). In addition, adolescents experienced more events that they perceived as negative and reacted to them more explosively and dramatically than did adults (Larson & Ham, 1993; Larson & Seepersad, 2003).

Adolescents' mood shifts are not simply a matter of hormones but are influenced by changes in psychological and social factors that accompany situational changes. Rather than representing turmoil, wide mood swings appear to occur naturally with the many situational changes and shifts in peer settings that occur throughout adolescents' days and weeks (Larson et al., 2014). Peers play a role in adolescents' varying mood states. In one study, fifth graders who experienced more peer problems at school showed a shift toward more negative mood and lowered self-esteem over the course of the school day (Reynolds & Repetti, 2008). Adolescents' moods are also influenced by their activities and the degree to which adolescents perceive the activity as important to them and a personal choice (Weinstein & Mermelstein, 2007). Adolescents seek independence and decision-making control. When they feel that their activities, such as reading, resting, partying, and engaging in extracurricular activities, are their own choice, they are likely to report more positive affect and greater enjoyment of the activity (Weinstein &

Adolesent moodiness corresponds more closely to changes in context and situation than hormones.

Amandine Wanert/BSIP/Corbis

Mermelstein, 2007). Mood changes do not occur in a vacuum but are influenced by adolescents' interactions with their contexts and their own perceptions.

Ultimately, developmental scientists today reject the notion that adolescence is a period of extreme storm and stress, replacing it with a more nuanced view that adolescence is a time of change characterized by individual differences in how they are experienced. Some adolescents encounter extreme turmoil, but great trauma is not the norm. Most adolescents experience some ups and downs but emerge from adolescence unscathed. The danger of the storm and stress view lies in that it may influence expectations for adolescent behavior, creating self-fulfilling prophecies that subtly influence how they are treated. For example, believing that adolescents are moody and prone to problems can lead a parent to unwittingly become more easily angered, reduce attempts to interact with the teen, or become overly restrictive or permissive, perhaps increasingly the likelihood of problems. Mothers' expectations for underage drinking have been shown to predict their teens' future underage drinking (Madon, Guyll, Spoth, & Willard, 2004). Likewise, a study of sixth and seventh graders and their mothers revealed that the students whose mothers expected high risk taking and rebelliousness during adolescence reported engaging in more

problem behavior one year later (Buchanan & Hughes, 2009). The beliefs we hold about adolescence and what we believe is normal for adolescents can have a profound effect on adolescents' development. The biological changes of adolescence are more obvious to the casual observer. We begin our discussion of normative adolescent development with puberty.

Thinking in Context 11.1

1. In your view, is adolescence best characterized by continuity or discontinuity? Compare your view with Hall as well as contemporary research findings.

2. Identify contextual factors that might make young people more or less likely to experience adolescence as a period of storm and stress.

PHYSICAL DEVELOPMENT IN ADOLESCENCE

Most people consider physical development as the hallmark of adolescence. Undoubtedly, adolescents' bodies undergo dramatic changes. Puberty is the biological transition to adulthood, in which adolescents mature physically and become capable of reproduction. The physical changes of puberty are accompanied by social changes. As adolescents appear more mature, they are treated more like adults. The physical changes serve as a signal to others of entry into a new life stage and convey personal and social meaning about new roles, expectations, and status (Graber, Nichols, & Brooks-Gunn, 2010).

PUBERTY

Although puberty is considered a biological marker of adolescence, the hormonal changes entailed by puberty begin in late childhood, by 8 or 9 years of age (DeRose & Brooks-Gunn, 2006). The hormones that drive puberty, as well as many other functions including growth, appetite, responses to stress, and sexual responses, are regulated by the **hypothalamus-pituitary-gonadal (HPG) axis**. The hypothalamus, a region at the base of the brain that is responsible for maintaining basic body functions such as eating, drinking, temperature, and the production of hormones, signals the pituitary gland, located adjacent to the hypothalamus, to produce hormones that stimulate the adrenal glands (see Figure 11.1). The adrenal glands are located above the kidneys and regulate the body's response to stress via the secretion of epinephrine (adrenaline) and norepinephrine (noradrenaline). The pituitary also releases GnRH (gonadotropin-releasing hormone), which causes the **gonads**, or sex glands (ovaries in females and testes in males) to mature, enlarge, and in turn to begin producing hormones themselves (DeRose & Brooks-Gunn,

FIGURE 11.1: Hypothalamus-Pituitary-Gonadal Axis

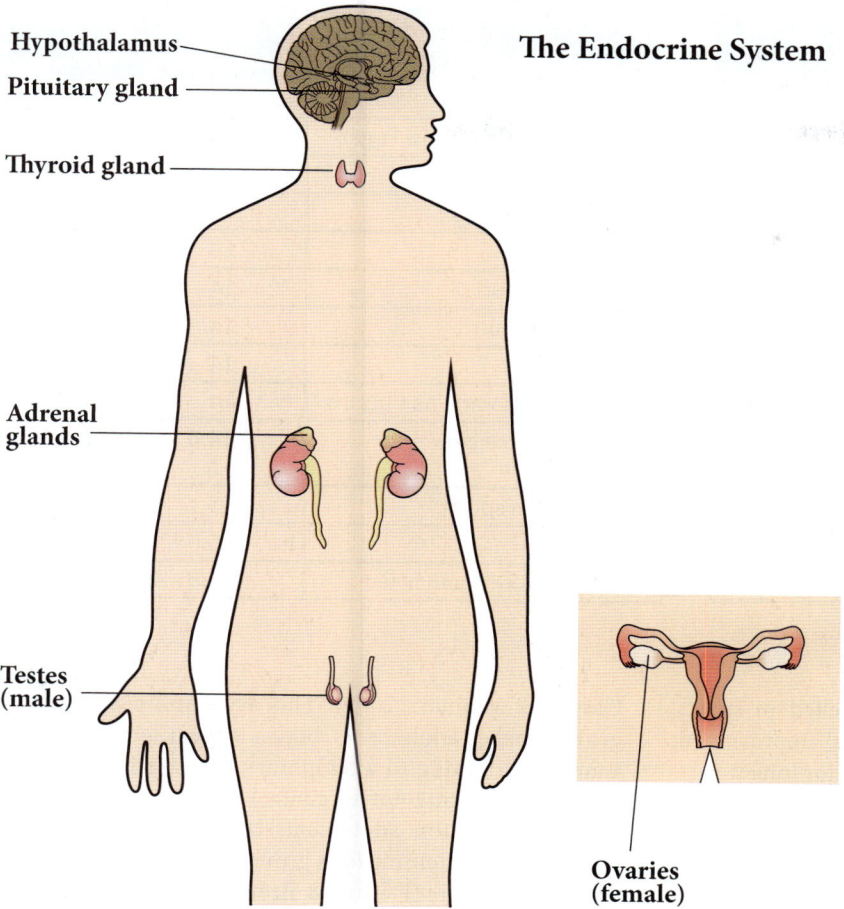

The Endocrine System

Hypothalamus
Pituitary gland
Thyroid gland
Adrenal glands
Testes (male)
Ovaries (female)

dramatically from one to seven years (Mendle, 2014). Puberty entails the development of reproductive capacity and influences a great variety of physical changes—not simply those typically associated with sexual maturity. For example, the hormones of puberty cause adolescents' bodies to grow and their internal organs to mature, as described in the next section.

Adolescent Growth Spurt

As a child, Sharene was always the same height as most of her classmates and never the tallest child in class. But when the students lined up for their fifth-grade class photograph, Sharene found herself in the very center of the portrait, as the tallest child. Surprised, Sharene wondered, "How did everyone get to be so short?" Although the hormonal changes that trigger puberty begin in late childhood, the first outward sign of puberty is the adolescent growth spurt, a rapid gain in height and weight that generally begins in girls at about age 10 (as early as 9.5 and as late as 14.5) and in boys at about age 12 (from 10.5 to16; Malina & Bouchard, 2004). Girls begin their growth spurt about two years before boys, so 10- to 13-year-old girls tend to be taller, heavier, and stronger than boys their age. It is not until boys enter their growth spurt that they become larger and stronger than girls. By starting their growth spurts two years later than girls, boys begin with an extra two years of prepubertal growth on which the adolescent growth spurt builds, leading boys to end up taller than girls (Tinggaard et al., 2012). On average, the growth spurt lasts about two years, but body growth continues at a more gradual pace. Most girls complete growth in body size by about 16 and most boys by about 18. Adolescents gain a total of about 10 inches in height (Graber, Petersen, & Brooks-Gunn, 1996). Table 11.1 lists the physical changes that boys and girls undergo with puberty.

During the growth spurt, sex differences in body shape emerge. Rapid growth and development of muscle precedes increases in bone density and is thought to influence bone strength. Although both boys and girls gain fat and muscle, they show different ratios of fat to muscle (DeRose & Brooks-Gunn, 2006). Girls gain more fat overall, particularly on their legs and hips, to comprise one fourth of their body weight—nearly twice as much as boys. Boys gain more muscle than do girls, especially in their upper bodies, doubling their arm strength between ages 13 and 18 (Seger & Thorstensson, 2000; Welsman et al., 1997).

2006; Schulz, Molenda-Figueira, & Sisk, 2009). Levels of **testosterone**, a hormone responsible for male sex characteristics, and **estrogen**, responsible for female sex characteristics, increase in both boys and girls. However, testosterone is produced at a much higher rate in boys than girls, and estrogen is produced at a much higher rate in girls than boys, leading to different patterns in reproductive development (Bogin, 2011). Hormonal changes also influence adolescents' growing sexual interests and activities, as well as psychosocial development (Berenbaum & Beltz, 2011).

On average, boys enter puberty at about 12 years of age but may begin to show pubertal changes any time between ages 9 and 16 (Tinggaard et al., 2012). Girls display signs of pubertal changes at 8 to 10 years of age, but some may show breast and pubic hair growth as early as 6 or 7 years of age (for African American or European American girls, respectively) or as late as 14 years of age. Generally, African American girls tend to be heavier and enter puberty about a year earlier than European American girls (Herman-Giddens, 2006; Wu, Mendola, & Buck, 2002). Puberty is not an event; rather, it is a process that takes about four years for boys and girls to complete (Marceau, Ram, Houts, Grimm, & Susman, 2011). Although most adolescents complete puberty in about four years, the tempo of change can vary

TABLE 11.1 Sequence of Physical Changes With Puberty

GIRLS		
CHARACTERISTIC	**MEAN AGE**	**RANGE**
Breast growth begins	10	7–13
Growth spurt begins	10	8–14
Pubic hair appears	10.5	7–14
Peak strength spurt	11.5	9.5–14
Peak height spurt	11.5	10–13.5
Peak weight spurt	12.5	10–14
Menarche	12.5	10–16
Adult stature	13	10–16
Pubic hair growth completed	14.5	14–15
Breast growth completed	15	10–18

BOYS		
CHARACTERISTIC	**MEAN AGE**	**RANGE**
Growth spurt begins	12.5	10.5–16
Testes and scrotum grow larger	11	9.5–13.5
Pubic hair appears	12	10–15
Penis growth begins	12	11–14.5
Spermarche	13	12–16
Peak height spurt	14	12.5–15.5
Peak weight spurt	14	12.5–15.5
Voice lowers	14	11.5–15.5
Facial and underarm hair begins	14	12.5–15.5
Penis and testes growth completed	14.5	12.5–16
Peak strength spurt	15	13–17
Adult stature	15.5	13.5–18
Pubic hair growth completed	15.5	14–18

SOURCES: Bundak et al. (2007); Herman-Giddens (2006); Wu et al. (2002).

Sixteen-year-old Juan has always excelled in sports. However, lately he has noticed a substantial improvement in his athletic ability. He can run faster and for longer periods than ever before, and he is not easily winded like the younger players on his team. The adolescent growth spurt has caused Juan's lungs to increase in size and capacity, permitting him to breathe more deeply than ever before. His heart has also grown, doubling in size, and the total volume of blood in his body has increased. These changes increase the overall amount of oxygen that meets with Juan's muscles, improving his physical performance and endurance.

During the adolescent growth spurt, the cephalocaudal growth trend of infancy and childhood reverses. The extremities grow first, the fingers and toes; then hands and feet; then arms and legs; and finally, the torso (Sheehy,

Peter Turnley/Corbis

Body growth often surpasses muscle strength and coordination, increasing adolescents' risk for athletic injuries.

Gasser, & Molinari, 2009). This asynchronous pattern of growth makes adolescents' bodies appear lanky and awkward, contributing to a temporary increase in clumsiness as adolescents attempt to control their quickly changing bodies. In addition, adolescents' bodies become taller and heavier before their muscles grow stronger and their internal organs mature (DeRose & Brooks-Gunn, 2006; Seger & Thorstensson, 2000). Unfortunately, adolescents, coaches, and parents often overestimate young people's capacities for athletic performance as changes in strength and endurance are not as visible as physical growth—and come after physical growth. Consequently, athletic injuries are very common during adolescence (Patel & Luckstead, 2000).

Secondary Sex Characteristics

The most noticeable signs of pubertal maturation are the **secondary sex characteristics**, the body changes that indicate physical maturation but are not directly related to fertility. Examples of changes in secondary sex characteristics include breast development, deepening of the voice, growth of body hair, and changes in the skin.

Breast development, the first clear sign of puberty in girls, follows a characteristic sequence. First is the bud stage when the nipples grow larger—fat accumulates and causes the nipples to protrude. Fat continues to gradually accumulate, and full maturation is reached toward the end of puberty (Gusterson & Stein, 2012). Levels of estrogen rise, more dramatically in girls, but many boys experience temporary breast enlargement, which may last up to 18 months and typically disappears by 16 years of age (Kirk, Bandhakavi, & Simon, 2008).

Other changes occur in the voice, skin, and hair. Testosterone causes both boys' and girls' voices to deepen, but the change is much more noticeable in boys, who occasionally lose control over their voices, emitting unpredictably high squeaks (Hodges-Simeon, Gurven, Cárdenas, & Gaulin, 2013). Most adolescents dread the changes in skin that are common during puberty. Oil and sweat glands become more active, resulting in body odor, and acne, which occurs in up to 90% of girls and boys (Cordain et al., 2002). Hair on the head, arms, and legs becomes darker, and pubic hair begins to grow, first as straight and downy, and later becomes coarse. Boys often look forward to the growth of facial and chest hair, but most girls do not welcome the small amount of hair that normally appears on the face and around the nipples.

Primary Sex Characteristics

The reproductive organs are known as **primary sex characteristics**. In females, primary sex characteristics include the ovaries, fallopian tubes, uterus, and vagina. In males, they include the penis, testes, scrotum, seminal vesicles, and prostate gland. During puberty, the reproductive organs grow larger and mature.

In girls, maturation of the primary sex characteristics entails growth of the uterus and ovaries. Sexual maturity is marked by the onset of menstruation, the monthly shedding of the uterine lining, which has thickened in preparation for the implantation of a fertilized egg. **Menarche**, the first menstruation, occurs toward the end of puberty, after the peak of the height spurt. Menarche most commonly occurs between ages 10 and 14, but as late as 16.5 (Brooks-Gunn & Ruble, 2013; Norman, 2008). In North America, the average European American girl experiences menarche shortly before turning 13 and the average African American girl shortly after turning 12 (Al-Sahab, Ardern, Hamadeh, & Tamim, 2010; Herman-Giddens, Kaplowitz, & Wasserman, 2004; Obeidallah, Brennan, Brooks-Gunn, Kindlon, & Earls, 2000). African American girls begin puberty and reach pubertal milestones such as the growth spurt and menarche earlier than do other girls (Kelly et al., 2014). In many but not all girls, during the first few months after menarche, menstruation takes place without ovulation, the ovaries' release of an ovum (Metcalf, Skidmore, Lowry, & Mackenzie, 1983). This period of temporary sterility is variable—it is unpredictable and does not apply to all girls. Menarche occurs relatively late in the process of puberty yet most children, and adults view it as a critical marker of puberty because it occurs suddenly and is memorable (Brooks-Gunn & Ruble, 2013).

What does menarche mean to girls? Generations ago, as girls received little to no information about menarche, they tended to be surprised by it and often afraid. For example, girls in the 1950s often received little information about menarche beforehand, and when information was provided, it tended to portray menstruation in a negative light as something to be endured (Costos, Ackerman, & Paradis,

2002). Today, girls are often surprised by menarche, but they are not frightened because they are informed about puberty by health education classes and parents who are more willing to talk about pubertal development than did parents in prior generations (Omar, McElderry, & Zakharia, 2003; Stidham-Hall, Moreau, & Trussell, 2012). However, the extent to which adolescents participate in discussions about menarche and sexuality varies by context and culture. For example, a study of 12- to 16-year-old Bangladeshi girls revealed that they generally were not informed about menarche, and over two thirds reacted with fear (Bosch, Hutter, & van Ginneken, 2008). However, mothers also lacked an adequate understanding of pubertal processes. How girls experience menarche is influenced by their knowledge about menstruation as well as their expectations (Brooks-Gunn & Ruble, 2013). Girls who view menstruation negatively are likely to experience menstruation negatively, with more menstrual symptoms and distress (Rembeck, Möller, & Gunnarsson, 2006). However, experience can alter girls' views on menstruation. For example, one study of Swedish girls showed that most had more positive views about menstruation before menarche than afterward (Rembeck et al., 2006).

In boys, the first primary sex characteristic to emerge is the growth of the testes, the glands that produce sperm (Tinggaard et al., 2012). About a year later, pubic hair appears, and the penis and scrotum enlarge. As the penis grows, the prostate gland and seminal vesicles begin to produce semen, the fluid that contains sperm. At about age 13, boys demonstrate a principal sign of sexual maturation: the first ejaculation, known as **spermarche** (Gaddis & Brooks-Gunn, 1985; Tomova, Lalabonova, Robeva, & Kumanov, 2011). The first ejaculations contain few living sperm. Many boys experience their first ejaculations as nocturnal emissions, or wet dreams: involuntary ejaculations that are sometimes accompanied by erotic dreams. We know little about boys' perceptions of spermarche, but some studies of small groups of adolescent boys have suggested that most boys react positively to first ejaculation, although many experience uneasiness and confusion, especially if they are uninformed about this pubertal change (Frankel, 2002; Stein & Reiser, 1994). Data on male puberty are difficult to obtain because of the absence of easily determined markers, such as menarche (Herman-Giddens et al., 2012). Boys who know about ejaculation beforehand are more likely to show positive reactions, such as feeling pleasure, happiness, and pride; unfortunately, however, many boys report that health education classes and parents generally do not discuss ejaculation (Omar et al., 2003; Stein & Reiser, 1994). Parents sometimes report discomfort talking with their sons about reproductive development, particularly ejaculation, because of the close link with sexual desire, sexuality, and masturbation (Frankel, 2002). Perhaps because of its sexual nature, boys are less likely to tell a friend about spermarche than are girls to discuss their own reproductive development (Downs & Fuller, 1991).

PUBERTAL TIMING

Casual observations of adolescents reveal that they vary in their level of physical maturation. Some 14-year-old adolescents have adultlike bodies. Many girls have fully developed breasts and hips, and many boys have broad shoulders and facial hair. Other 14-year-old adolescents have childlike bodies or are just beginning the pubertal transformation. Why do adolescents' bodies vary so much, and how do such variations influence their day-to-day behavior?

Influences on Pubertal Timing

The timing of puberty reflects the interaction of biological, contextual, and emotional influences. Without question, genes play a role in pubertal timing (Gajdos, Henderson, Hirschhorn, & Palmert, 2010; Tu et al., 2015). The age at which a mother experienced menarche is related to the timing of her daughter's menarche (Golub, 1992). Identical twins experience menarche at roughly the same time, within a month or so of each other; fraternal twins, on the other hand, can vary by a year or more (Kaprio et al., 1995). But puberty is influenced by more than genes. The onset of puberty is triggered by achieving a critical level of body weight, as an accumulation of leptin, a protein found in fat, may stimulate the HPA axis to increase the production and secretion of hormones (Elias, 2012; Maqsood et al., 2007; Sanchez-Garrido & Tena-Sempere, 2013). Leptin may play a different role in puberty for girls than boys because girls' leptin concentrations peak before the spike in other puberty hormones whereas in boys leptin levels remain somewhat constant throughout puberty (Rutters, 2009; Tinggaard et al., 2012). Girls with a greater body mass index (BMI) mature earlier than do other girls (Biro, Khoury, & Morrison, 2006; Lee, 2007) and girls who have a low percentage of body fat, whether from athletic training or severe dieting, often experience menarche late relative to other girls (Rees, 1993). Typically, a girl must weigh about 100 pounds for menarche to occur (Berkey, Gardner, Frazier, & Colditz, 2000). Similarly, weight affects the onset and tempo of puberty in boys but less so as compared with girls (Bundak et al., 2007; Tinggaard et al., 2012).

Adolescents' social contexts, especially exposure to stress, also influence pubertal timing. In fact, stress affects hormone production throughout the lifespan; it can trigger irregular ovulation and menstruation in females and reduce sperm production in males (Toufexis, Rivarola, Lara, & Viau, 2014). Exposure to severe stress such as conditions of war, extreme and enduring poverty, and trauma, delays menarche (Boynton-Jarrett et al., 2013; Ellis, 2004). Paradoxically, smaller doses of stress can speed pubertal development. For example, poor family relationships, harsh parenting, family stress and conflict, parents' marital conflict, and anxiety are associated with early menarche in North American and European girls (Graber et al., 2010; Rickard, Frankenhuis, & Nettle, 2014). In industrialized countries such as the United States, Canada, and New Zealand, girls

who are raised by single mothers experience puberty earlier than those raised in two-parent homes (Mendle et al., 2006; Posner, 2006). In addition, the absence of a biological father and the presence in the home of a biological unrelated male, such as a stepfather or mother's live-in boyfriend, is associated with earlier onset of menarche (Deardorff et al., 2011; Neberich, Penke, Lehnart, & Asendorpf, 2010; Tither & Ellis, 2008). Animal studies show a similar trend: The presence of a biologically related male delays reproductive maturation and functioning while the presence of unrelated males speeds female reproductive maturation (Neberich et al., 2010). Father absence may hold similar implications for boys' pubertal development, speeding it; however, there is much less research on boys' development (Bogaert, 2005; Sheppard & Sear, 2012).

Contextual factors outside the home also influence pubertal timing. Adolescents who live in similar contextual conditions, particularly those of socioeconomic advantage, reach menarche at about the same age, despite having different genetic backgrounds (Obeidallah, Brennan, Brooks-Gunn, & Earls, 2004). Low socioeconomic status is associated with early pubertal onset in the United States and Canada (Arim, Tramonte, Shapka, Dahinten, & Willms, 2011; Deardorff, Abrams, Ekwaru, & Rehkopf, 2014), but in regions of the world that are impoverished, malnutrition and high rates of infectious disease prevent the accumulation of adequate fat stores needed to support pubertal development so that menarche is delayed. In many parts of Africa, for example, menarche does not occur until ages 14 to 17, several years later than in Western nations (Leenstra et al., 2005; Tunau, Adamu, Hassan, Ahmed, & Ekele, 2012). In the United States, ethnic differences consistently appear in pubertal timing. African American and Latina girls tend to reach menarche before white girls. However, in some studies ethnic differences in the timing of menarche are reduced or disappear when researchers control for the influence of socioeconomic status, which is an indicator of stress and known to speed pubertal development (Obeidallah et al., 2000). These findings suggest that some of the ethnic differences in pubertal timing may be influenced instead by low socioeconomic status.

The influence of contextual conditions and physical health in triggering puberty is thought to underlie the **secular trend**, or the lowering of the average age of puberty with each generation (see Figure 11.2). Through the eighteenth century in Europe, puberty occurred as late as age 17; between 1860 and 1970, the age of menarche declined by about three to four months per decade (Tanner, 1990). Boys in the United States began puberty about a year earlier in 2000 than did boys in the 1960s (Herman-Giddens, 2006). Likewise, data gathered from Canadian boys in 2005 to 2010 suggested that the boys reached puberty 1.5 years earlier than boys four decades earlier (Herman-Giddens et al., 2012). Likewise, boys reached peak velocity of growth over one month earlier each decade between 1946 and 1991 (Bygdell, Vandenput, Ohlsson, & Kindblom, 2014). The

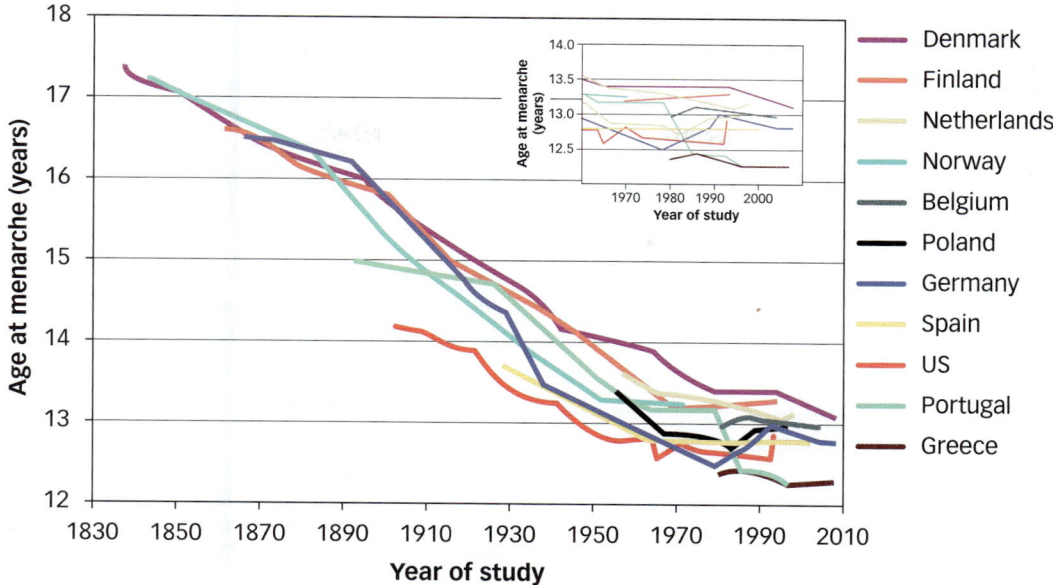

SOURCE: Sørensen et al. (2012).

secular trend continues, paralleling increases in the standard of living and average BMI among children in Western countries and is especially influenced by the growing problem of childhood obesity (Biro et al., 2006; Himes, 2006; Walvoord, 2010). It is unclear when the secular trend will stop. Girls have shown precocious puberty as early as age 5 (Scutti, 2015); however, it is unlikely that the average age of puberty will ever drop that low. The secular trend poses challenges for young people and parents because the biological entry to adolescence is lowering at the same time as the passage to adulthood is lengthening, making the period of adolescence longer than ever before. What ages mark early puberty and what does beginning the pubertal transition early or late relative to peers mean for children?

PSYCHOSOCIAL EFFECTS OF EARLY AND LATE PUBERTY

How do adolescents feel about experiencing puberty much earlier or later than their peers, and what effects does early or late puberty have on adolescents' social relationships? First, we need to define early and late puberty. Children who show signs of physical maturation before age 8 (in girls) or 9 (in boys) are considered early-maturing whereas girls who begin puberty after age 13 and boys who begin after age 14 are considered late-maturing adolescents (Dorn, Dahl, Woodward, & Biro, 2006).

Adolescents who mature early or late look different from their same-age peers, and they often are treated differently by adults and peers, with consequences for their development (Graber et al., 2010). For example, adolescents who look older than their years are more likely to be treated

in ways similar to older adolescents, which adolescents may perceive as stressful (Rudolph, Troop-Gordon, Lambert, & Natsuaki, 2014). Early maturation, in particular, poses specific challenges for girls and boys' adaptation.

Girls who mature early relative to peers tend to feel less positive about their bodies, physical appearance, and menstruation itself than do girls who mature on time or late (Cesario & Hughes, 2007; Mendle, Turkheimer, & Emery, 2007). Indeed, several studies found they are at risk for negative psychosocial outcomes such as depression, anxiety, and low self-esteem (Benoit, Lacourse, & Claes, 2013; Stojković, 2013). One reason may be that, although early-maturing girls are often popular, they are also more likely to be victims of rumor-spreading, which is associated with feelings of depression, anxiety, and poor self-esteem (Reynolds & Juvonen, 2011).

Girls' perception of their pubertal development, whether they see themselves as maturing much earlier or later than their peers, influences puberty-related outcomes (Carter, Jaccard, Silverman, & Pina, 2009; Mendle, 2014). Interestingly, though, girls' perceptions of their own development often is only loosely related to their actual development (Dorn & Biro, 2011). That is, girls are likely to hold inaccurate views of their bodies, seeing themselves are more or less developed than they are. Girls' views of their own early pubertal timing, whether they view as maturing much earlier than their peers, are often a better predictor of girls' age at first intercourse, sexual risk taking, substance use, depression, and anxiety than actual pubertal development (Mendle, 2014; Moore, Harden, & Mendle, 2014; Stojković, 2013).

In males, earlier timing of puberty historically has been viewed as advantageous because it conveys physical advantages for athletic activities. Early-maturing boys tend to be athletic, popular with peers, school leaders, and confident (Stojković, 2013). However, more recent research suggests that early and late maturation presents challenges to both boys and girls. For example, longitudinal research suggests that boys and girls who matured off-time, early or late relative to their peers, were more likely to show anxiety and depressed mood than their on-time peers in late adolescence and early adulthood (Mendle & Ferrero, 2012; Natsuaki, Biehl, Ge, & Xiaojia, 2009; Rudolph et al., 2014).

Contextual factors are thought to amplify the effects of pubertal timing on behavior (Graber et al., 2010; Skoog & Stattin, 2014). For example, early maturing girls and boys are more likely to experience depression and anxiety when they judge their peer relationships as stressful (Benoit et al., 2013; Blumenthal, Leen-Feldner, Trainor, Babson, & Bunaciu, 2009). Some of the problems that early-maturing boys and girls experience arise because they tend to seek relationships with older peers who are more similar to them in physical maturity than their classmates. Spending time with older peers makes early-maturing adolescents, especially girls, more likely to engage in age-inappropriate behaviors, such as early sexual activity and risky sexual activity relative to their same-age peers (Baams, Dubas, Overbeek, & van Aken, 2015; Moore et al., 2014). Early-maturing boys and girls around the world show higher rates of risky activity, including smoking, abusing substances, and displaying aggressive behavior than do peers their age (Mrug et al., 2014; Skoog & Stattin, 2014). Early maturers tend to show higher rates of problematic drinking, including consuming alcohol more frequently and in greater quantities, and becoming intoxicated more often than their on-time and late-maturing peers (Biehl, Natsuaki, & Ge, 2007; Schelleman-Offermans, Knibbe, & Kuntsche, 2013). Longitudinal research shows that these higher rates of alcohol use and heavy drinking behaviors persist into late adolescence and early adulthood, suggesting that early pubertal maturation may hold long term implications for young people's health (Biehl, et al., 2007).

The effects of late maturation tend to differ for boys and girls. Late maturation appears to have a protective effect on girls with regard to depression (Negriff & Susman, 2011). Findings regarding the effects of late maturation on boys are mixed and less consistent (Mendle & Ferrero, 2012). Late-maturing boys may experience more social and emotional difficulties. During early adolescence, they may be less well liked by their peers and may be more likely than their peers to experience a poor body image, overall body dissatisfaction, and depression during early adolescence, but these effects tend to decline with physical maturation (Negriff & Susman, 2011). Other research suggests that late-maturing boys do not differ in anxiety or depression from their on-time peers (Crockett, Carlo, Wolff, & Hope, 2013; Marceau et al., 2011) or that it is only late-maturing boys with poor peer relationships who experience depression (Benoit et al., 2013).

PUBERTY AND SLEEP PATTERNS

Classes begin at 7:35 a.m.—way too early for Raul—who yawns and stretches as he sits down at his desk. Raul did not go to bed until about 1:00 a.m. His mother shouted and shouted for him to get up this morning. He had barely enough time to put on clothes and brush his teeth before heading to school. Grumpy, Raul pulls out his notebook and tries to pay attention to his geometry teacher, but it is hard to focus with his headache.

Raul is not alone in feeling tired and grumpy. A less well-known effect of puberty is a change in adolescents' sleep patterns and preferred sleep schedule, known as a **delayed phase preference** (Carskadon, 2009; Crowley, Acebo, & Carskadon, 2007). Delayed phase preference is triggered by a change in the nightly release of a hormone that influences sleep, called melatonin. The rise in melatonin that accompanies the onset of sleep occurs, on average, about two hours later among adolescents who have experienced puberty as compared those who have not begun puberty (Carskadon, Acebo, & Jenni, 2004). When adolescents are permitted to regulate their own sleep schedule, they will tend to go to bed at about 1:00 a.m. and sleep until about 10:00 a.m. (Colrain & Baker, 2011). Adolescents naturally feel awake when it is time to go to sleep and groggy when it is time to wake for school in the morning. As a result, adolescents stay up later, miss out on sleep, and report sleepiness (Carskadon et al., 2004; Loessl et al., 2008). This tendency for

Rob Lewine Tetra/Newscom

Delayed phase preference leads most adolescents to feel sleepy and groggy in their early morning classes.

adolescents to go to bed later is influenced by puberty, but it also has increased over the past three decades, along with the increased availability of television and other media that compete with sleep for adolescents' time (Bartel, Gradisar, & Williamson, 2014; Carskadon & Tarokh, 2014). Most adolescents have electronic devices such as cell phones and computers in their rooms, and many report using electronic devices in bed. The more bedtime device use reported, the later most adolescents report falling asleep and the later they report waking on weekdays.

From ages 13 to 19, the average number of hours of sleep reported by adolescents in Western countries, such as the United States and Germany, decreases from about eight hours to seven hours, with greater reductions in sleep with each year (Carskadon, 2009; Loessl et al., 2008). Researchers estimate that adolescents need about nine hours of sleep each night to support healthy development. Poor sleep is associated with anxiety, irritability, and depression; increases in the probability of obesity, illnesses, and accidents; and less engagement in extracurricular school activities and declines in academic performance (Darchia & Cervena, 2014; Mitchell, Rodriguez, Schmitz, & Audrain-McGovern, 2013b; Wong, Robertson, & Dyson, 2015). Sleep problems are also associated with risk behaviors including abusing substances, risk taking, and smoking (McKnight-Eily et al., 2011; Pieters et al., 2015; Telzer, Fuligni, Lieberman, & Galván, 2013)

Most middle and high schools have earlier start times than elementary schools, often to permit adolescents time for after school sports and activities as well as, in some districts, to save on transportation costs by having the same buses and drivers make multiple runs to elementary, middle, and high schools. The transitions to earlier school start times and additional travel time that come with adolescents' move into middle school and then high school significantly decrease young people's total sleep time (Adam, Snell, & Pendry, 2007; Wolfson & Carskadon, 1998). Regardless of what time school begins, adolescents tend to go to bed at approximately the same time. One comparison of middle school students who attended an early starting school (7:15 a.m.) and a later starting school (8:37 a.m.) found that students who attended the early starting school obtained about three fourths of an hour less sleep each night, or about 3.5 hours less each week (Wolfson, Spaulding, Dandrow, & Baroni, 2007). After the students had been on their early or late school schedules for over six months, those who attended school early were tardy 4 times more often, had more absences, and worse grades than the students who attended the school with the late starting time. Similar findings were apparent in another study that examined the effects of starting school 30 minutes later (from 8:00 a.m. to 8:30 a.m.). In a similar study, after three months, students reported getting more sleep, and the change in school start time was associated with significant improvements in measures of adolescent alertness, mood, and health (Owens, Belon, & Moss, 2010). Sleep matters, and perhaps some of the moodiness characteristic of the stereotypical adolescent is related to changes in sleep patterns.

Despite consuming many calories, many adolescents have nutritional deficiencies because of poor dietary choices.

NUTRITION AND DEVELOPMENT

Adequate food consumption and good nutrition also are essential to support adolescents' physical and mental health. What are adolescents' nutritional needs? The adolescent growth spurt demands that young people increase their caloric intake to about 2,200 (for girls) and 2,700 (for boys) calories a day (Jahns, Siega-Riz, & Popkin, 2001). Good nutrition is essential to support adolescents' growth, yet young people's diets tend to worsen as they enter adolescence. Adolescents' increase their consumption of fast food, soft drinks, and salty snacks and drink less milk (Bowman, Gortmaker, Ebbeling, Pereira, & Ludwig, 2004). Fast food is high in calories, but when adolescents eat a fast-food meal they do not appear to adjust their other meals to make up for the excess calories. On days when adolescents consume high calorie fast food, which may be as much as one third of the time, they tend to consume more calories overall as compared with days when they do not consume fast food (Bowman et al., 2004; Ebbeling et al., 2004). When a fast-food restaurant is near school, students consume less fruits and vegetables, more soda, and overeat more often than students who attend schools that are not near fast-food restaurants (Davis & Carpenter, 2009). Longitudinal research shows that young people consume more fast food as they progress through adolescence (Bauer, Larson, Nelson, Story, & Neumark-Sztainer, 2009).

Poor diets leave many adolescents in industrialized nations with nutritional deficiencies. In one study of nearly 6,000 U.S. adolescents, less than 1% met the U.S. calorie specific recommendations for the consumption of fruits and vegetables (Kimmons, Gillespie, Seymour, Serdula, & Blanck, 2008). Only about 30% of males and 12% of females aged 12 to 19 drink the recommended 3 cups of milk a day; those who do not are compromising their intake of calcium, which is particularly important for the growth of bones (Cavadini, Decarli, Grin, Narring, & Michaud, 2000; U.S. Department of Agriculture, 2000). It is estimated that virtually all females aged 9 to 18 have calcium intakes below recommended levels (Suitor & Gleason, 2002). Because about one half of adult bone mass is accumulated during adolescence, reduced milk consumption contributes to insufficient bone mass in adulthood and a higher risk for osteoporosis, especially in women (Kalkwarf, 2007).

Iron deficiency is another common nutritional problem in adolescence. Unfortunately, it is during puberty that our bodies require the greatest consumption of iron, which is found in green leafy vegetables, meat, and eggs. Iron requirements are high in girls because iron is lost through menstruation; this remains true for females throughout the childbearing years. Between 10% and 20% of U.S. girls are deficient in iron (Zimmermann & Hurrell, 2007). Girls who exhibit exhaustion and irritability—which are often viewed as typical adolescent problems—should be evaluated for anemia, a reduction of red blood cells caused by insufficient levels of iron, which can cause these symptoms (Baynes & Bothwell, 1990).

Family meals are an important way of establishing healthy eating habits. Young people who participate in family meals tend to have healthier eating habits five years later, from early to middle adolescence (Burgess-Champoux, Larson, Neumark-Sztainer, Hannan, & Story, 2009). Positive interpersonal dynamics at family meals (i.e., communication, affect management, interpersonal involvement, overall family functioning) is associated with lower adolescent BMI and higher vegetable intake (Berge, Jin, Hannan, & Neumark-Sztainer, 2013). In addition, consuming higher-quality meals during adolescence becomes a pattern that tends to continue in young adulthood (Larson, Nelson, Neumark-Sztainer, Story, & Hannan, 2009).

Lack of exercise is also a contributor to overweight and obesity during adolescence. Although some teens engage in competitive sports, on average levels of physical activity decrease throughout adolescence, and many adolescents engage in no regular exercise or activity (Dumith, Gigante, Domingues, & Kohl, 2011; Duncan, Duncan, Strycker, & Chaumeton, 2007). One study of nearly 6,000 British adolescents found marked reductions in physical activity from ages 11 to 12 and 15 to 16 (Brodersen, Steptoe, Boniface, & Wardle, 2007). Moreover, it is estimated that American adolescents spend over 11 hours each day in front of a screen, viewing television and media, playing games, and participating in social media (American Academy of Pediatrics [AAP], 2013; Rideout, 2010), and screen time is associated with obesity (Mitchell, Rodriguez, Schmitz, & Audrain-McGovern, 2013a). Adolescents of low socioeconomic status are more likely to be sedentary and obese; this holds true for adolescents from a variety of countries, such as Canada, England, Finland, France, and the United States (Frederick, Snellman, & Putnam, 2014; Kantomaa, Tammelin, Näyhä, & Taanila, 2007; Lioret, Maire, Volatier, & Charles, 2007; Wang & Lim, 2012).

Research with American youth suggests a complex relation between socioeconomic status and obesity. One longitudinal study of over 4,800 U.S. children—10 and 11 years old—showed that those with the highest socioeconomic status were less likely to be obese than their peers in fifth and seventh grade (Fradkin et al., 2015). However, when ethnicity was considered, this pattern was confirmed for Latino and white adolescents, not but black adolescents. Likewise, the protective effect of daily physical activity was associated with reduced obesity only among Latino and white males in seventh grade, not fifth graders, females, or black adolescents (Fradkin, Wallander, Elliott, Cuccaro, & Schuster, 2014). Thus, the health advantage associated with higher parental education and income may not apply consistently to boys and girls across all ethnic groups. Influences on young people's health, such as socioeconomic status, must be considered within the context of the broader social and physical environments in which youth live (Schreier & Chen, 2013).

The effects of pubertal development extend far beyond changes in body shape and maturation of reproductive organs. The hormonal shifts that accompany puberty trigger a neurological growth spurt.

Thinking in Context 11.2

1. Many adults hold misconceptions about puberty and its meaning for adolescents. Consider your own views and those of your friends and family. Identify two misconceptions, explain why they are incorrect, and offer accurate alternatives.

2. In what ways might the changing sociocultural context contribute to the secular trend and the collection of psychosocial characteristics that most adults view as "typical" of adolescents?

3. How might the dramatic physical changes that adolescents undergo—and the accompanying reactions from others—influence other aspects of development, such as social or emotional development?

BRAIN DEVELOPMENT IN ADOLESCENCE

As described in earlier chapters, brain development begins before birth with a proliferation of neurons whose interconnections are pruned over the first two years of life. In early adolescence, the increase in sex hormones with puberty triggers a variety of neurological developments, including a second burst of synaptogenesis, resulting in a rapid increase of connections among neurons (Goddings, 2015; Vigil et al., 2011). The volume of the cerebral cortex increases, peaking at about 10.5 years of age in girls and 14.5 in boys, although this age difference provides no functional advantage to girls or boys (Giedd et al., 2009). Neural connections are then pruned by experience. Synaptic pruning occurs at an accelerated rate during adolescence as compared with childhood and adulthood (Zhou, Lebel, Treit, Evans, & Beaulieu, 2015). Synaptic pruning continues at a slower rate into the twenties. Synaptic pruning decreases the volume of gray matter, thins and molds the prefrontal

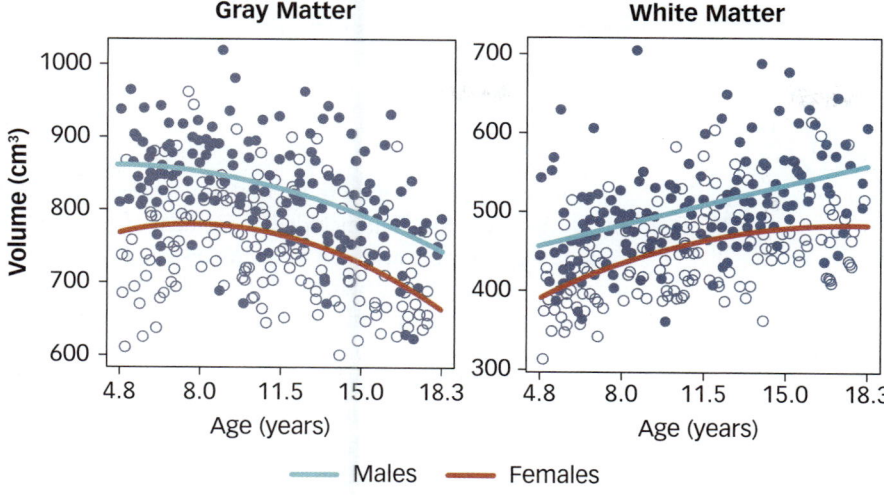

FIGURE 11.3: Developmental Changes in Gray and White Matter Across Adolescence

Gray Matter

White Matter

Males Females

SOURCE: Brain Development Cooperative Group (2012).

cortex, responsible for rational thought and executive function, and results in markedly more efficient cognition and neural functioning (Blakemore, 2012; Mills, Goddings, Clasen, Giedd, & Blakemore, 2014).

Connections between the prefrontal cortex and various brain regions strengthen, permitting rapid communication, enhanced cognitive functioning, and greater behavioral control (Jolles, van Buchem, Crone, & Rombouts, 2011; Spear, 2013). Connections strengthen especially among areas associated with higher cognitive and emotional functions.

As shown in Figure 11.3, gray matter declines, but myelination continues throughout adolescence and leads to steady increases in the brain's white matter, especially in the prefrontal cortex and the corpus callosum, which increases up to 20% in size, speeding communication between the right and left hemispheres (Barnea-Goraly et al., 2005; Luders, Thompson, & Toga, 2010). Increases in white matter are linked with improved performance on measures of working memory, executive functioning, and learning (Blakemore & Choudhury, 2006). Over the course of adolescence, young people's brains become larger, faster, and more efficient. However, different parts of the brain develop at different rates, leaving adolescents with somewhat lopsided functioning for a time. The prefrontal cortex requires the most time to develop, continuing maturation into the 20s.

According to the **dual-process model**, the **limbic system**, responsible for emotion, undergoes a burst of development well ahead of the prefrontal cortex, responsible for judgment, and this difference in development can account for many "typical" adolescent behaviors (see Figure 11.4; Mills et al., 2014; Steinberg, 2010; Strang, Chein, & Steinberg, 2013). Full development entails the prefrontal cortex catching up. These changes influence adolescents' thought

and behavior in a myriad of ways, as discussed in the following sections.

SOCIOEMOTIONAL PERCEPTION

Parents often wonder whether they are speaking in a foreign language when their teens unexpectedly break off a conversation and storm away or when conflict arises over seemingly innocuous events. However, in a way, parents *are* speaking in a foreign language because adolescents' brains do not always lead them to accurately assess situations. For example, adolescents have difficulty identifying emotions depicted in facial expressions. In studies where both adults and adolescents are shown photographs of people's faces depicting fear, adults correctly identify the emotion shown in the photograph, but many of the adolescents incorrectly identify the emotion as anger (Monk et al., 2003; Yurgelun-Todd, 2007). Performance on facial recognition tasks improves steadily during the first decade of life but dips in early adolescence, increasing in late adolescence into young adulthood (Peters, Vlamings, & Kemner, 2013; Thomas, De Bellis, Graham, & LaBar, 2007). Why? Blame the brain.

Functional magnetic imaging scans indicate that when adults view facial expressions, both their limbic system (the part of the brain known as the seat of emotion) and prefrontal cortex are active (see Figure 11.5). Scans of adolescents' brains, however, reveal a highly active limbic system but relatively inactive prefrontal cortex, suggesting that adolescents experience emotional activation with little executive processing when viewing facial stimuli as compared to adults, which often results in adolescents incorrectly labeling emotions, such as mistaking fear for anger (Monk et al., 2003; Yurgelun-Todd, 2007). Pubertal hormones cause a burst of development in the limbic system in early adolescence, well ahead of the parts of the brain responsible for executive control (Goddings et al., 2014; Strang et al., 2013). Adolescents experience heightened emotional reactivity, influencing their responses to emotionally charged stimuli. Research with people aged 7 to 37 reveals developmental changes in brain activation with facial processing with activity in parts of the frontal cortex increasing over childhood, then decreasing in early adolescence, followed by an increase in late adolescence into adulthood (Cohen Kadosh, Johnson, Dick, Cohen Kadosh, & Blakemore, 2013).

Brain structure influences affective responses and interactions with others. For example, one part of the limbic system, the **amygdala**, is implicated in aggression. When faced with emotionally arousing contexts and stimuli, adolescents tend to show exaggerated amygdala activity relative to adults and fewer functional connections between the

FIGURE 11.4: Dual Process Model: Limbic System and Prefrontal Cortex

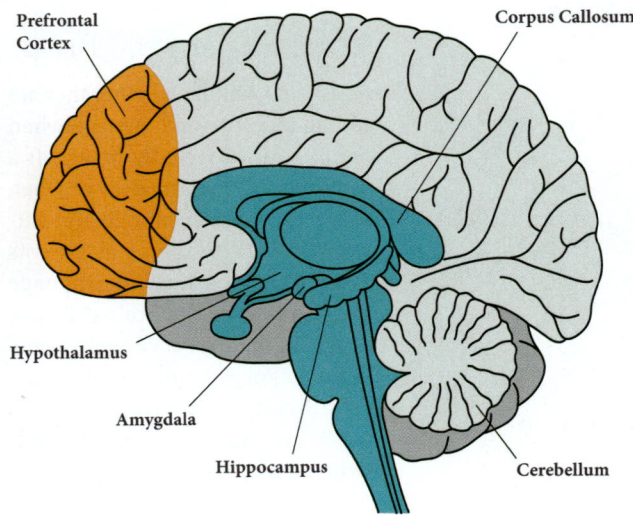

prefrontal cortex and amygdala, suggesting that adolescents experience more emotional arousal yet less cortical processing and control than adults (Blakemore & Mills, 2014; Hare et al., 2008). Amygdala volume predicts young adolescents' aggressive behavior during parent–child interactions (Whittle et al., 2008). Generally, amygdala volume increases more in adolescent males than females (Blakemore, 2012; Giedd et al., 2009). It seems that adolescents are wired to experience strong emotional reactions and to misidentify emotions in others' facial expressions, which can make communication and social interactions difficult.

RISK TAKING

Most adults look back upon their own adolescence and recall engaging in activities that included an element of risk or were even outright dangerous, such as racing bikes off of ramps to soar through the air or driving at fast speeds. Risk taking and adolescence go hand in hand, and the brain plays a large part. In early adolescence, the balance of neurotransmitters shifts. At 9 to 10 years of age, the prefrontal cortex and limbic system experience a marked shift in levels of serotonin and dopamine, neurotransmitters that are associated with impulsivity, novelty seeking, and reward salience (Padmanabhan & Luna, 2014; Smith, Chein, & Steinberg, 2013; Van Leijenhorst et al., 2010). Sensitivity to rewards peaks at the same time adolescents experience difficulty with response inhibition, behavioral control (Geier, 2013; Spear, 2013). A heightened response to motivational cues coupled with immature behavioral control biases adolescents to immediate goals over long-term consequences (Casey, Jones, & Somerville, 2011). The shift is larger for boys than girls and is thought to make potentially

FIGURE 11.5: Face Processing by Adolescents and Adults

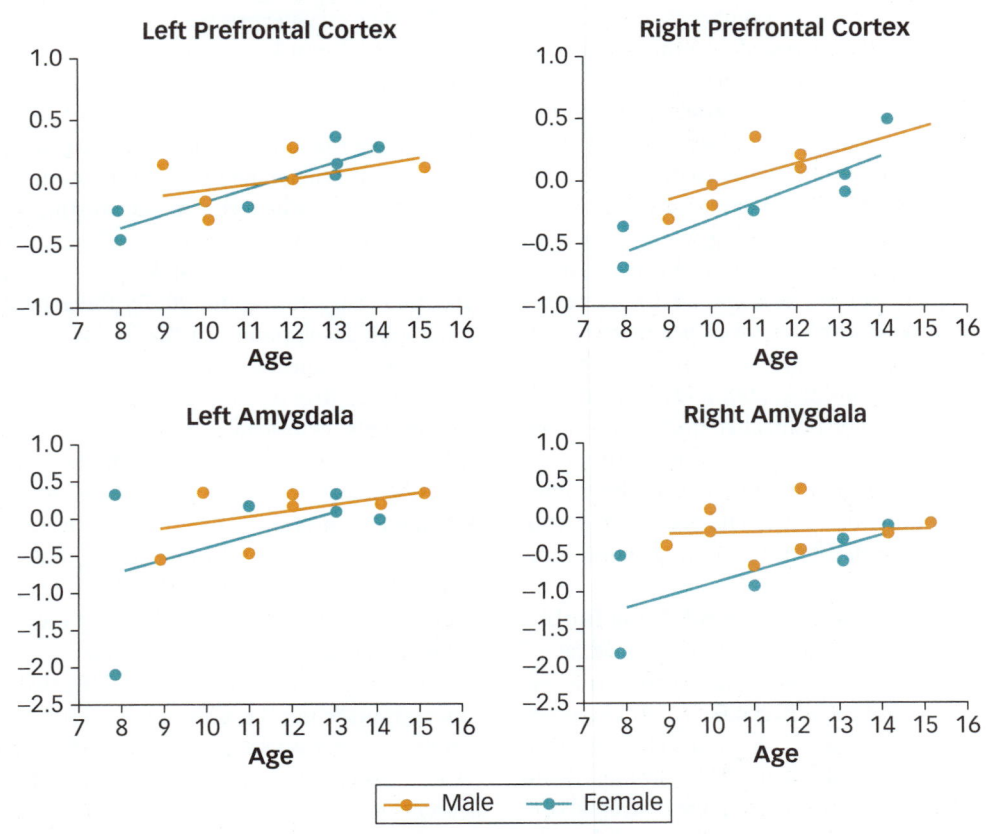

SOURCE: Yurgelun-Todd (2007).

PYMCA/Universal/Getty

Adolescents are neurologically primed to engage in risky behaviors.

rewarding stimuli even more rewarding for teens (Steinberg, 2008a). As a result, risky situations, those that entail an element of danger, become enticing. Risks become experienced as thrills (Spielberg, Olino, Forbes, & Dahl, 2014). Adolescents may find themselves drawn to extreme sports, for example, enjoying the high and element of the unknown when they direct their skateboard into the air for a daring turn.

These same mechanisms, adolescents' attraction to novelty and enhanced sensitivity to rewards, serve to increase adolescents' vulnerability to the lure of drugs and alcohol (Bava & Tapert, 2010; Van Leijenhorst et al., 2010). Neurological changes, for example in risk processing, sensitivity to novelty, and social processing, mean that all adolescents experience a heightened susceptibility to seek out and engage in risk behaviors. Yet not all adolescents engage in the same risks. Contextual factors, such as adult supervision, exposure to stressors, and impoverished communities, for example, influence the direction that adolescents' propensities for risk take (Smith et al., 2013).

Maturation and improved connectivity in the prefrontal cortex is associated with advances in many aspects of executive function such as planning ahead, weighing risks and rewards, simultaneously considering multiple sources of information, and response inhibition, or the ability to control a response. Response inhibition, in particular, is closely associated with risky activity. Adolescents who find it difficult to inhibit, or stop, a motor response in laboratory tasks show less activation of the prefrontal cortex during response inhibition tasks and are more likely

to engage in risky activity (McNamee et al., 2008). Risky activity is thought to decline in late adolescence in part because of increases in adolescents' self-regulatory capacities, or self-control, their capacities for long term planning, and inhibition of impulsive behavior (Albert, Chein, & Steinberg, 2013; Casey, 2015). Ultimately, however, risky activity is influenced by neurological developments but also the contextual demands and opportunities that adolescents face as well as their emerging cognitive capacities.

Thinking in Context 11.3

1. Most adults blame puberty for much of adolescent behavior. Researchers, however, point to the dual-process model's role in influencing adolescent behavior. Discuss.

2. How might contextual factors, such as interactions with parents and peers, and settings such as school and neighborhood, influence how brain development is manifested in adolescent behavior?

ADOLESCENT COGNITIVE DEVELOPMENT

At 14, Eric spends much of his time learning about astronomy. He wonders about the existence of dark matter—cosmological matter that cannot be observed but is inferred by its gravitational pull on objects like planets and even galaxies. Eric reads blogs written by astronomers and has started his own blog where he comments on the best websites for teenagers who are interested in learning about the galaxy. Eric's newfound ability and interest in considering complex abstract phenomena illustrates the ways in which adolescents' thinking departs from children's. As compared with childhood, cognitive development during the adolescent period receives much less attention from theorists and researchers, but adolescents show significant advances in their reasoning capacities (Kuhn, 2008). Similar to earlier periods in life, the cognitive-developmental perspective on cognition describes adolescence as entailing a transformation in thought. The information processing perspective, on the other hand, explains cognitive development in adolescence as a continuation, growth, and refinement of capacities and skills developed in childhood.

FORMAL OPERATIONAL REASONING

In early adolescence, at about 11 years of age, individuals enter the final stage of Piaget's scheme of cognitive development: formal operations. **Formal operational reasoning** entails the ability to think abstractly, logically, and systematically (Inhelder & Piaget, 1958; Piaget, 1972). Children in the concrete operational stage reason about *things*—that is, concepts that exist in reality, such as problems concerning how to equitably divide a bowl of pudding into five servings. Adolescents in the formal operational stage, however, reason about *ideas,* possibilities that do not exist in reality and that

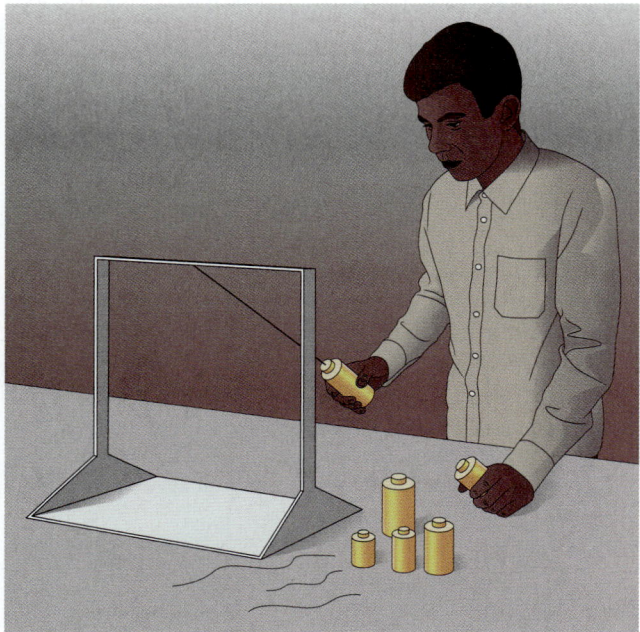

Children and adolescents are presented with a pendulum and are asked what determines the speed with which the pendulum swings. They are given materials and told that there are four variables to consider: (1) length of string (short, medium, long); (2) weight (light, medium, heavy); (3) height at which the weight is dropped; and (4) force with which the weight is dropped.

may have no tangible substance, such as whether it is possible to love equitably—to distribute love equally among several targets (Inhelder & Piaget, 1958; Piaget, 1972). The ability to think about possibilities beyond the here and now permits adolescents to plan about the future, make inferences from available information, and consider ways of solving potential but not yet real problems.

Formal operational thought enables adolescents to engage in **hypothetical–deductive reasoning**, or the ability to consider problems, generate and systematically test hypotheses, and draw conclusions. Piaget's *pendulum task* (Figure 11.6) tests children and adolescents' abilities to use scientific reasoning to solve a problem with multiple possible solutions (Inhelder & Piaget, 1958). Adolescents displaying formal operational reasoning develop hypotheses and systematically test them. For example, in the pendulum task, they change one variable while holding the others constant (e.g., trying each of the lengths of string while keeping the weight, height, and force the same). Concrete operational children, on the other hand, do not proceed systematically in a way that permits them to solve the pendulum problem; they fail to disentangle the variables and do not take into account nontangible variables such as height and force. For example, concrete operational children might test a short string with a heavy weight, then try a long string and short weight. Solving the pendulum problem requires the scientific reasoning capacities that come with formal operational reasoning.

Adolescents soon learn that hypothetical thought makes for a much more interesting, but complicated, world. Now they are primed to think about possibility and the possible becomes a reality of its own (Inhelder & Piaget, 1958). However, adolescents can get carried away with their consideration of the possible. For example, when solving a problem such as how to organize her room, an adolescent might become paralyzed by all the possibilities, ways of arranging furniture, organizing books, and classifying all that she owns, rather than simply beginning the task.

An assumption of Piaget's cognitive-developmental theory is that development is a universal process, yet the reality is that people vary in their cognitive development. For example, many adults, presumably capable of abstract reasoning, fail hypothetical–deductive tasks (Kuhn, Langer, Kohlberg, & Haan, 1977). Does this mean that they cannot think abstractly? In response to research findings suggesting variability in formal operational reasoning, Piaget (1972) explained that opportunities to use formal operational reasoning influence its development. In contrast to his position on earlier stage structures, Piaget argues that formal operations structures may vary by content area. Individuals reason at the most advanced levels when considering material with which they have the greatest experience. For example, completing college courses in math and science is associated with gains in propositional thought, while courses in social science are associated with advances in statistical reasoning skills (Lehman & Nisbett, 1990; Lehman, Lempert, & Nisbett, 1988). Experience influences the development of formal operational reasoning. In one study in the early 1990s, adolescents from 10 to 15 years of age performed better on Piagetian tasks such as the pendulum task than adolescents had done over two decades before. The researchers attributed the difference to the fact that (in France, where the studies were done) secondary education was less common in the earlier decades; therefore, adolescents had fewer opportunities to practice the reasoning measured by Piagetian tasks (Flieller, 1999).

The appearance of formal operational reasoning is not consistent across people or across intellectual domains but instead varies with situation, task, experience, context, and motivation (Kuhn, 2008; Labouvie-Vief, 2015; Piaget, 1972). Moreover, many theorists explain that formal operational reasoning does not suddenly appear in early adolescence, but instead, cognitive change occurs gradually from childhood on, with gains in knowledge, experience, and information processing capacity (Keating, 2004; Kuhn & Franklin, 2006; Moshman, 2005).

INFORMATION PROCESSING PERSPECTIVE

Adolescents' advances in the ability to think abstractly and demonstrate hypothetical–deductive reasoning are also the result of improvements in information processing capacities—such as attention, memory, knowledge base, and speed—that take place from childhood through adolescence (Kail, 2008; Luna, Garver, Urban, Lazar, & Sweeney, 2004).

Attention, Response Inhibition, and Working Memory

Greater control over attention allows adolescents to deploy it selectively, focusing on stimuli deemed important while tuning out others and remaining focused even as task demands change. Increases in attention permit material to be held in working memory while taking in and processing new material (Barrouillet, Gavens, Vergauwe, Gaillard, & Camos, 2009). For example, at age 13, Julia is able to tune out the background noise in class to listen to her teacher, determine what is important, and take notes, remembering what she's writing while listening to her teacher. She can shift her attention to take notes from movies shown in class, and remain focused even when the class format changes to discussion.

As we gain increasing control over our cognitive system, we also become better at response inhibition, not responding or not activating cognitive operations in response to a stimulus. Advances in response inhibition enable adolescents to adapt their responses to the situation by inhibiting well-learned responses when they are inappropriate to the situation and thereby speeding cognitive processing (Luna, Paulsen, Padmanabhan, & Geier, 2013; Luna et al., 2004). For example, Robin is now able to keep herself from raising her hand in response to the teacher's question, telling herself, "I need to give other students a chance, too." The ability to control and inhibit responses emerges first in infancy and advances through childhood, with substantial gains in adolescence (Geier, Terwilliger, Teslovich, Velanova, & Luna, 2010; Zhai et al., 2014). However, the neurological changes that underlie response inhibition continue to develop into the 20s, and still immature capacities for response inhibition are thought to underlie the risk taking behavior common in adolescence (Albert et al., 2013; Luna et al., 2013).

Working memory reaches adultlike levels by about age 19 (Luna et al., 2004). Combined with a growing knowledge base and increased strategy use, advances in working memory result in more sophisticated, efficient, and quick thinking and learning. Now adolescents can retain more information at once, better relate new information to what is already known, and combine information in more complex ways, underlying adolescents' increasing capacities for metacognition (Cowan et al., 2010; Gaillard, Barrouillet, Jarrold, & Camos, 2011).

Metacognition and Scientific Reasoning

Recall from Chapter 7 the concept of metacognition—knowledge of how the mind works and the ability to control the mind. As metacognition develops through middle adolescence, teenagers are better able to be planful about their cognitive system—how they take in, manipulate, and store information (Ardila, 2013; van der Stel & Veenman, 2013). They are better able to understand how they learn and remember and to choose and deploy strategies that enhance the representation,

Advanced capacities for attention make adolescents better able to concentrate and study.

storage, and retrieval of information. Eleventh grader Travis explained, "Studying for a biology exam is really different than studying for a history exam. In biology, I visualize the material, but when I study for history, I make up stories to help me remember it all." Travis illustrates the metacognitive skills that emerge in adolescence because he is able to evaluate his understanding, and he adjusts his strategies to the content what helps him learn best. Adolescents' abilities to apply metacognition in real-world settings continues to develop into late adolescence and early adulthood.

Metacognition plays an important role in scientific reasoning because it is by experimenting with and reflecting on cognitive strategies that adolescents learn about and come to appreciate logic, which they increasingly apply to situations (Kuhn, 2000; van der Stel & Veenman, 2013). Improvements in information processing capacities and metacognition enable adolescents to engage in the more sophisticated, reasoned, and efficient problem solving that underlies capacities for manipulating abstract mental representations and engaging in the hypothetical–deductive thinking that is characteristic of scientific reasoning (Bullock, Sodian, & Koerber, 2009; Demetriou, Christou, Spanoudis, & Platsidou, 2002; Kuhn, 2012). Although adolescents show advances in scientific reasoning, their reasoning tends to emphasize single solutions to problems. In one study, sixth-grade students were presented with a detailed pictorial and written information about variables that were explained to have either a causal or noncausal influence on a hypothetical problem, such as the likelihood of an avalanche occurring. The task was to apply the information in predicting outcomes. Although given information about five different variables, the students consistently chose only one factor as influential, although they chose different variables across trials. For example, a pair of students chose snow pollution as a cause of an avalanche, referring to the written materials, "Because it shows the snow pollution is high; snow is what causes an avalanche." Yet for a second prediction, the student pair turned to another single variable, slope angle, explaining "Slope angle is an important part of how snow falls." In a third prediction, they turned to yet another, different, single factor, wind speed: "We chose the wind speed because it affects how fast the snow falls" (Kuhn, Pease, & Wirkala, 2009, p. 439). Although adolescents can demonstrate scientific thinking, they tend to consistently prefer single-factor solutions. They remain unable to coordinate the effects of multiple casual influences on outcomes (Kuhn, Iordanou, Pease, & Wirkala, 2008; Kuhn et al., 2009). For many young people, the more complex reasoning required to consider multiple influences at once as well as a more sophisticated understanding of the nature of knowledge and scientific phenomena emerges in early adulthood, as discussed in Chapter 13.

Brain Development and Cognition

Changes in the brain, especially the prefrontal cortex, underlie many improvements in information processing capacities. As the structure of the prefrontal cortex changes, with decreases in gray matter and increases in white matter, cognition becomes markedly more efficient (Asato, Terwilliger, Woo, & Luna, 2010). Myelination underlies improvements in processing speed during childhood and adolescence, permitting quicker physical and cognitive responses (Silveri, Tzilos, & Yurgelun-Todd, 2008). Now not only do adolescents show faster reaction speed than children in gym class but they can connect ideas, make arguments, and draw conclusions faster than children. Processing speed increases and reaches adult levels at about age 15 and is associated with advances in working memory and cognition (Coyle, Pillow, Snyder, & Kochunov, 2011).

Development of the prefrontal cortex as well as the cerebellum leads to enhanced executive function, capacities that allow us to control and coordinate our thoughts and behavior, including attention, planning, evaluating, judging, goal directed behavior, and response inhibition (Ardila, 2013; Tiemeier et al., 2010). Connections between the prefrontal cortex and various brain regions strengthen, improving working memory and permitting rapid communication and enhanced cognitive and behavioral functioning (Tamnes et al., 2013; van den Bosch et al., 2014). With these advances in brain development, routine decisions become automatic, requiring fewer cognitive resources and therefore enabling adolescents to redirect their thinking toward more complicated problems.

IMPLICATIONS OF ADOLESCENT THINKING

Adolescents' emerging abilities to reason influence how they view the world and themselves. However, abstract thought develops gradually. Teenagers are prone to errors in reasoning and lapses in judgment, as evidenced by the emergence of **adolescent egocentrism** and changes in decision-making ability.

Adolescent Egocentrism

Adolescents' new cognitive abilities draw them to consider the intangible, such as ideas and possibilities. At the same time,

they undergo physical changes and psychological changes that lead them to direct their new abstract abilities toward themselves. Adolescents are naturally self-conscious. As 14-year-old Mayla's mother explained, "She's always in her head but also outside, paying attention to her clothes and the smallest details of her appearance as if anyone would notice anyway." Adolescents are egocentric. They have difficulty with perspective-taking, specifically with separating their own and others' perspectives (Inhelder & Piaget, 1958). Adolescent egocentrism is manifested in two phenomena: the **imaginary audience** and the **personal fable** (Elkind & Bowen, 1979).

The imaginary audience is just that: Adolescents misdirect their own preoccupation about themselves on to others and assume that they are the focus of others' attention (Elkind & Bowen, 1979). In this way, they are unable to accurately take other people's perspectives. The imaginary audience fuels adolescents' concerns with their appearance and can make the slightest criticism made in public sting painfully, as teens are convinced that all eyes are on them. The imaginary audience contributes to the heightened self-consciousness characteristic of adolescence (Albert, Elkind, & Ginsberg, 2007).

Adolescents' preoccupation with themselves also leads them to believe that they are special, unique, and invulnerable—a perspective known as the personal fable (Elkind & Bowen, 1979). A sense of self-importance underlies the personal fable belief that they will be admired, achieve fame, and be remembered. Many adolescents perceive their own experiences as unique. They believe that their emotions, the highs of happiness and depths of despair that they feel, are different and more intense than other people's emotions and that others simply do not understand. The invulnerability aspect of the personal fable, coupled with brain development that predisposes adolescents to seek risks, makes adolescents more likely to engage in risky activities, such as drug use, delinquency, and unsafe sex; they believe that they, unlike other teens, are invulnerable to the negative consequences of such behaviors (Albert et al., 2007; Greene & Krcmar, 2000). Specifically, research with 6th- through 12th graders suggests that the invulnerability aspect of the personal fable is associated with engaging in risky activities while the sense of personal uniqueness is associated with depression and suicidal ideation (Aalsma, Lapsley, & Flannery, 2006).

Both the imaginary audience and personal fable are thought to increase in early adolescence, peak in middle adolescence, and decline in late adolescence (Albert et al., 2007; Elkind & Bowen, 1979; Lapsley, Jackson, Rice, & Shadid, 1988), but some research suggests that adolescent egocentrism may persist into late adolescence and beyond (Schwartz, Maynard, & Uzelac, 2008). Even adults are susceptible to these lapses in perspective. In many instances, adolescents may be *less* likely to see themselves as invincible than are adults. Studies in which adolescents and adults evaluate the possible consequences of various behaviors, adolescents perceive more risks inherent to health behaviors show that and activities, such as substance use and risky driving, for example, than do adults (Fischhoff, 2008; Millstein &

Halpern-Felsher, 2002). Perhaps adolescent egocentrism, specifically the personal fable, may not be a feature unique to adolescence.

Decision Making

Adolescents are faced with a variety of decisions each day, ranging from the mundane, such as when to clean their rooms and how to spend an afternoon, to decisions that are important to their health, well-being, and future, such as which friendships to foster, whether to drink or smoke, what classes to take in school, and whether and where to go to college. With age and experience, adolescents take on increasing decision-making responsibility. Cognitive advances permit adolescents to engage in more sophisticated thinking than ever before and to participate meaningfully in decision making.

Researchers who study decision making from a cognitive perspective explain decision making as a rational process in which, when faced with a decision, people follow several steps. They first identify decision options, then identify the potential positive and negative consequences for each option (i.e., the pros and cons). They estimate how likely each potential outcome is, rate how desirable each outcome is, and finally combine all of this information to make a decision (Furby & Beyth-Marom, 1992). Research from this perspective has shown that, under ideal conditions, adolescents are capable of demonstrating rational decision making that is in line with their goals and is comparable to that of adults (Reyna & Farley, 2006; Reyna & Rivers, 2008). For example, comparisons of adolescents' and adults' decisions on hypothetical dilemmas, such as whether to engage in substance use, have surgery, have sex, or drink and drive, show that adults spontaneously generate more consequences to each decision option and are more likely to spontaneously mention risks and benefits of each option (Furby & Beyth-Marom, 1992; Halpern-Felsher & Cauffman, 2001). However, both adolescents

Advanced planning, decision making, and problem solving skills enable these teens to effectively collaborate on more complex tasks.

and adults show an optimistic bias wherein they view their own risks as lower than those of peers (Halpern-Felsher & Cauffman, 2001). Moreover, adolescents and adults generally do not differ in their ratings of the perceived harmfulness of risks, and in many cases, adolescents perceive greater risks than do adults (Reyna & Farley, 2006)

If adolescents are aware of the risks entailed in decisions, perhaps more so than adults, why do they often make poor decisions and engage in risk taking? While adolescents' abstract reasoning abilities permit them to consider possibilities, they often do not consider practicalities associated with each option. Adolescents are more approach oriented in response to positive feedback and less responsive to negative feedback than are adults (Cauffman et al., 2010; Javadi, Schmidt, & Smolka, 2014). Adolescents tend to place more importance on the potential benefits of decisions (e.g., social status, pleasure) than their estimation of the potential costs or risks (e.g., physical harm, short and long-term health; Rivers, Reyna, & Mills, 2008; Shulman & Cauffman, 2013). Neurological research supports these findings. For example, in the presence of rewards, adolescents show heightened activity in the brain systems that support reward processing and reduced activity in the areas responsible for inhibitory control, as compared with adults (Paulsen, Hallquist, Geier, & Luna, 2014; Smith, Steinberg, Strang, & Chein, 2015). Similarly, adolescents who engage in high-risk behavior more often show less activation of the parts of the prefrontal cortex that are associated with decision making (Luna et al., 2013; Shad et al., 2011).

Recall that executive functioning, responsible for decision making, comes with maturation of the prefrontal cortex, which lags behind the development of the limbic system, which is responsible for emotional arousal. This difference in maturational timing means that adolescents feel emotionally charged before they have corresponding self-regulation and decision-making abilities (Albert et al., 2013; Van Leijenhorst et al., 2010). Adolescents show greater activity of the reward parts of the brain than adults and are assumed to be susceptible to risk taking in situations of heightened emotional arousal (Figner, Mackinlay, Wilkening,

COMING OF AGE: BAT MITZVAH

In this video, 13-year-old Rachel describes the role of her bat mitzvah in helping to shape her sense of self and identity. Rachel and her parents discuss the roles and responsibilities that accompany coming of age within the Jewish community.

Watch the video at edge.sagepub.com/kuther

& Weber, 2009; Mills et al., 2014). Their decisions about risk taking are swayed by so-called "hot processes," emotional arousal–driven thinking that tends to interfere with "cold" rational processes of cost–benefit weighing (van Duijvenvoorde, Jansen, Visser, & Huizenga, 2010; Zelazo & Carlson, 2012). In other words, adolescents often act impulsively, seemingly without thought, and their decisions often are influenced by affective motivators such as the desire for pleasure, relaxation, stimulation, excitement (Mills et al., 2014; van Duijvenvoorde et al., 2015).

Under ideal conditions, adolescents are capable of demonstrating rational decision making that is in line with their goals and is comparable to that of adults (Reyna & Rivers, 2008). In practice, however, decision making is more complex and influenced by situational, emotional, and individual difference characteristics, such as the presence of peers, temptation of high rewards, excitement, impulsivity, and sensation seeking (Smith et al., 2013). Laboratory studies of decision making usually present adolescents with hypothetical dilemmas that are very different from the everyday decisions they face. Everyday decisions have personal relevance, require quick thinking, are emotional, and often are made in the presence and influence of others. Recall that the prefrontal cortex, responsible for executive functioning and decision making, is the last part of the brain to reach full maturity, lagging far behind the limbic system, responsible for emotion. Adolescents often feel strong emotions and impulses that they may be unable to regulate (Casey & Caudle, 2013). Therefore, laboratory studies of decision making are less useful in understanding how young people compare with adults when they must make choices that are important or occur in stressful situations in which they must rely on experience, knowledge, and intuition (Steinberg, 2013). When faced with unfamiliar emotionally charged situations, spur of the moment decisions, pressures to conform to peers, poor self-control, and risk and benefit estimates that favor good short-term and bad long-term outcomes, adolescents tend to reason more poorly than adults (Albert et al., 2013; Defoe, Dubas, Figner, & van Aken, 2012). Figure 11.7 illustrates the many influences on adolescent decision making.

When is thinking adultlike enough to treat adolescents as adults? The answer to this question holds implications for a variety of contexts. For example, when is an adolescent able to make medical decisions such as for elective surgery? In academic contexts, when is an adolescent able to drop out of school without parental permission? Perhaps the most controversial question pertains to legal contexts: When should an adolescent offender be tried or sentenced as an adult? At what age can an offender be given the death penalty or sentenced to life in prison without parole? This policy issue is discussed in Ethical and Policy Applications of Lifespan Development (p. 311).

Although many adults display faulty decision making, it is adolescents who are in need of protection from their poor decisions because the consequences of their bad decisions—such

FIGURE 11.7: Influences on Adolescent Decisions

Brain Development
Increases in cortical volume and white matter

Decreases in gray matter

Rapid limbic system development in early adolescence

Prefrontal cortex matures slowly throughout adolescence into young adulthood

Shifts in levels of neurotransmitters in early adolescence

Cognitive Development
Advances in attention, memory, processing speed, and strategy repertoire and use

Abstract thinking

Scientific Reasoning

Metacognition and metamemory

Executive functioning

Adolescent Decision-Making and Behavior
Difficulty reading other people and identifying their emotions

Emotionally charged responses before reasoning

Advances in planning abilities

Increasingly able to identify and weigh options and consider multiple sources of information

Impulsivity and novelty seeking, but over time, improvements in response inhibition

as accepting a ride from a friend who has been drinking—are potentially more serious and long lasting. Adult guidance, including discussion that aids adolescents in considering options, the pros and cons of each, the likelihood of each, and how to weigh information to come to a decision, aids adolescents in learning how to make good decisions. Experience making decisions, learning from successes and failures, coupled with developments in cognition, self-control, and emotional regulation, leads to adolescent decision making that is more reflective, confident, and successful.

Thinking in Context 11.4

1. In your view, is cognitive development, reasoning, and decision making best described as developing continuously or discontinuously? Why?

2. Compare cognitive explanations of adolescent egocentrism, risk behavior, and decision making with neurological explanations, such as the dual-process model.

3. Describe some ways in which adolescent decision making is a product of interactions among puberty, brain development, cognitive growth, and contextual influences such as parents, peers, and community.

ETHICAL AND POLICY APPLICATIONS OF LIFESPAN DEVELOPMENT

Legal Implications of Adolescent Decision Making

Developmental science has offered important insights into policy questions such as how to treat juvenile offenders.

Developmental scientists' work is often called upon to inform legal issues and influence social policy, as illustrated by a series of Supreme Court cases (Bonnie & Scott, 2013; Cohen & Casey, 2014).

Can adolescent offenders face the death penalty? In *Roper v. Simmons*, the Supreme Court considered whether the death penalty is constitutional as applied to minors. Should minors be subject to the same punishments as adults? At the time, 21 states in the United States permitted the death penalty for adolescents under the age of 18, and most of them permitted it at the age of 16 (Steinberg & Scott, 2003). As the case moved to the Supreme Court, developmental scientists collaborated with the American Psychological Association (APA) to submit an *amicus curiae* brief, a document referred to as a "friend of the court," intended to inform the justices about the developmental research relevant to the case, specifically research on adolescent judgment and decision making. The brief explained that adolescents' developmental immaturity makes them less culpable for crimes and justifies a more lenient punishment than that of adults—but still holds that they are actors who retain responsibility for the crime (Cauffman & Steinberg, 2012; Steinberg & Scott, 2003).

Recall that the lag between the development of the emotional part of the brain and the prefrontal cortex, responsible for executive functioning and decision making, contributes to adolescents' tendency to feel strong emotions and impulses that they may have difficulty controlling (Casey & Caudle, 2013). Research suggests that adolescents, especially males, react impulsively to threat cues more so than do adults or children, even when the adolescent is instructed not to respond. This response is associated with enhanced activity in the limbic regions of the brain responsible for detecting and assigning value to emotion (Dreyfuss et al., 2014).

In addition to neurological development, psychosocial development, specifically susceptibility to peer influence and future orientation, plays a prominent role in adolescent decision making and behavior (Albert et al., 2013). When adolescents make decisions in response to hypothetical dilemmas in which they must choose between engaging in an antisocial behavior suggested by friends and a prosocial one, their choices suggest that susceptibility to peer influence increases between childhood and early adolescence, peaking around age 14 and declining slowly during high school (Allen & Antonishak, 2008; Steinberg & Monahan, 2007). Not only are adolescents' decisions more likely to be influenced by peers, simply thinking about peer evaluation increases risky behavior, and the presence of peers can increase risky behavior even when the probability of a negative outcome is high (Centifanti, Modecki, MacLellan, & Gowling, 2014; Peake, Dishion, Stormshak, Moore, & Pfeifer, 2013; Smith et al., 2015).

Similarly, when adolescents and adults are compared with regard to their ability to envision themselves in the future, adults demonstrate a greater future orientation (the ability to project themselves into the future) than do adolescents (Nurmi, 1991; Steinberg et al., 2009). A poor sense of future orientation is associated with participation in risky activities (Chen & Vazsonyi, 2011, 2013). Difficulty envisioning the future coupled with the influence of strong emotions, susceptibility to peers, and poor self-control can compromise adolescents' decisions despite their neurological and cognitive advances. In all of these ways, psychosocial factors influence how adolescents weigh the costs and benefits in making decisions: to the extent that teens are less mature than adults, their decisions are likely to be more poor than those of adults, even if they are cognitively mature (Cauffman & Steinberg, 2000, 2012; Modecki, 2014).

In the case of *Roper v. Simmons*, in 2005 the Supreme Court ruled against capital punishment for minors on the basis of their lack of maturity and susceptibility to peer influence (Greenhouse, 2005; Steinberg, 2013). In 2010 and 2012, under a similar rationale, in *Florida v. Graham, Miller v. Alabama*, and *Jackson v. Hobbs*, the Supreme Court ruled that minors cannot be sentenced to life in prison without parole (APA, 2012).

What Do You Think?

1. **To what degree are adolescents culpable for their offenses? Is the death penalty or life in prison without parole appropriate penalties for adolescents? Why or why not?**

2. **What role should developmental science take in influencing policy? Should research with adolescents be used to make policy decisions such as this?**

Louie Psihoyos/Corbis

ADOLESCENT MORAL DEVELOPMENT

Adolescents' newfound abilities for abstract reasoning lead them to approach problems in different ways, consider multiple perspectives, and delight in the process of thinking itself. It is these cognitive advances that enable adolescents to demonstrate the final and most sophisticated form of reasoning described in Lawrence Kohlberg's theory of moral reasoning: **postconventional moral reasoning**.

POSTCONVENTIONAL MORAL REASONING

Much of Kohlberg's theory was based on longitudinal research with a group of boys, beginning at ages 10, 13, and 16 (Kohlberg, 1969). Over the next three decades, Kohlberg periodically interviewed the boys and discovered that their reasoning progressed through sequential stages, and in a predictable order (Colby, Kohlberg, Gibbs, & Lieberman, 1983; Kohlberg, 1981). Kohlberg measured moral reasoning by presenting individuals with hypothetical dilemmas such as the following:

> Near death, a woman with cancer learns of a drug that may save her. The woman's husband, Heinz, approaches the druggist who created the drug, but the druggist refuses to sell the drug for anything less than $2,000. After borrowing from everyone he knows, Heinz has only scraped together $1,000. Heinz asks the druggist to let him have the drug for $1,000 and he will pay him the rest later. The druggist says that it is his right to make money from the drug he developed and refuses to sell it to Heinz. Desperate for the drug, Heinz breaks into the druggist's store and steals the drug. Should Heinz have done that? Why or why not? (Kohlberg, 1969).

The Heinz dilemma is the most popular example of the hypothetical conflicts that Kohlberg used to study moral development. These problems examine how people make decisions when fairness and people's rights are pitted against obedience to authority and law. Participants' explanations of how they arrived at their decisions reveal developmental shifts through three broad levels of reasoning that correspond to cognitive development (Kohlberg, 1969, 1981).

Recall from Chapter 7 that young children reason at the preconventional level. Their decisions are influenced by self-interest, the desire to gain rewards and avoid punishments. Children who demonstrate preconventional reasoning argue that Heinz should not steal the drug because stealing is a punishable offense (Stage 1) or that he should steal the drug because his wife will be happy and be very good to him (Stage 2). Note that it is the reasoning behind the decision, and not the decision itself—that is, whether Heinz should or should not steal the drug—that indicates a person's level of moral reasoning.

As noted in Chapter 9, school-age children's moral decisions tend to be socially driven. Conventional moral reasoning entails internalizing the norms and standards of authority figures, seeking to be accepted and to maintain social order. Responses to the Heinz dilemma indicative of conventional reasoning include the following: "Heinz should steal the drug because people will think he's an awful husband if he doesn't" (Stage 3), or "Heinz should not steal the drug because stealing is against the law, which is designed to maintain social order" (Stage 4).

It is not until adolescence, according to Kohlberg, that people become capable of demonstrating the most advanced moral thinking, postconventional moral reasoning, which entails autonomous decision making from moral principles that value respect for individual rights above all else. Postconventional moral thinkers recognize that their self-chosen principles of fairness and justice may sometimes conflict with the law. When laws are unjust, they may be broken. At this level of moral reasoning, adolescents uphold individual rights over the law, and argue that Heinz should steal the drug in order to save his wife's life. At Stage 5, Social Contract Orientation, individuals view laws and rules as flexible and part of the social contract or agreement meant to further human interests. Laws and rules are to be followed as they bring good to people, but laws can be changed if they are inconsistent with the needs and rights of the majority. Sometimes, if laws are unjust—if they harm more people than they protect—they can be broken. Stage 6, Universal Ethical Principles, represents the most advanced moral reasoning, defined by abstract ethical principles that are universal, valid for all people regardless of law, such as equality and respect for human dignity. At this stage, people argue that concerns about human rights take precedence over laws and social rules, so Heinz must steal the drug because his wife's right to life trumps the druggists' rights for profit as well as laws against stealing.

A great deal of research has confirmed that individuals proceed through the first four stages of moral reasoning in a slow, gradual, and predictable fashion (Colby et al., 1983; Dawson, 2002; Walker, 1989). Specifically, reasoning at the preconventional level, Stages 1 and 2, decreases by early adolescence, Stage 3 conventional reasoning increases through middle adolescence, and Stage 4 reasoning increases in middle to late adolescence and becomes typical of most individuals by early adulthood. Few people, however, advance beyond Stage 4 moral reasoning. Postconventional reasoning is rare and appears as Stage 5 reasoning (Kohlberg, Levine, & Hewer, 1983; Kohlberg, 1981). The existence of Stage 6, the hypothesized, most advanced type of moral reasoning, is supported only by case-based anecdotal evidence. Kohlberg himself questioned the validity of Stage 6, dropped it from the stage scheme, but later included Stage 6 again because it represented an end goal state to which human development strives (Kohlberg & Ryncarz, 1990).

Kohlberg's theory of moral reasoning has led to four decades of research. Most of the research conducted has evaluated several aspects of the theory, including whether reasoning progresses through a stage sequence, the role of social interaction in promoting development, the role of gender and culture, and the link between reasoning and behavior.

SOCIAL INTERACTION AND MORAL REASONING

Moral development is not simply a function of cognitive development. Moral development occurs within parent, peer, and school contexts and is influenced by social development. High-quality parent–child relationships predict advanced moral reasoning (Malti & Latzko, 2010). Social interactions offer important opportunities for the development of moral reasoning. Reasoning advances when adolescents have opportunities to engage in discussions that are characterized by mutual perspective taking. Engaging adolescents in discussion about personal experiences, local issues, and media events—while presenting alternative points of view and asking questions—advances reasoning. For example, "Why do you think he did that? Was there something else that he could have done? How do you think other people interpret his actions?" Issue-focused discussions that present adolescents with reasoning that is slightly more advanced than their own prompts them to compare their reasoning with the new reasoning and often internalize the new reasoning, advancing their moral reasoning to a new level.

Parents who engage their children in discussion, listen with sensitivity, ask for children's input, praise them, engage them with questioning, and use humor promote the development of moral reasoning (Carlo, Mestre, Samper, Tur, & Armenta, 2011; Walker & Taylor, 1991; Wyatt & Carlo, 2002). Likewise, interactions with peers in which adolescents confront one another with differing perspectives and engage each other with in-depth discussions promote the development of moral reasoning (Power, Higgins, & Kohlberg, 1989). Adolescents who report having more close friendships in which they engage in deep conversations tend to show more advanced moral reasoning than do teens who have little social contact (Schonert-Reichl, 1999). They also report feeling positive emotions when they make unselfish moral decisions (Malti, Keller, & Buchmann, 2013). Moral reasoning is inherently social. Some have argued, however, that the social basis of morality means that men and women should reason in very different ways.

GENDER AND MORAL REASONING

A popular criticism of Kohlberg's theory of moral reasoning arises because his initial research was conducted with all male samples. Early research that studied both males and females suggested gender differences in moral reasoning, with males typically showing Stage 4 reasoning, characterized by concerns about law and order, and females showing Stage 3 reasoning, characterized by concerns about

maintaining relationships (Fishkin, Keniston, & McKinnon, 1973; Kohlberg & Kramer, 1969; Poppen, 1974). Carol Gilligan (1982) argued that Kohlberg's theory neglected a distinctively female mode of moral reasoning, a **care orientation**, which is characterized by a desire to maintain relationships and a responsibility not to cause hurt. As Gilligan explains, the care orientation contrasts with the distinctively male mode of moral reasoning, a **justice orientation**, which is based on the abstract principles of fairness and individualism captured by Kohlberg. Care and justice represent frameworks modified by experience that influence how people interpret and resolve moral problems.

Although most people are capable of raising both justice and care concerns in describing moral dilemmas, Gilligan argues that they tend to predominantly focus on either justice or care concerns. Males and females could use either a justice or a care perspective, but care reasoning was thought to be used predominantly by females and justice reasoning by males (Gilligan, 1982; Gilligan & Attanucci, 1988). In agreement with Gilligan, most researchers acknowledge that more than one mode of moral reasoning exists (Kohlberg et al., 1983), but there is considerable controversy as to whether those moral orientations are linked with gender. Early research suggested that males and females differ in moral orientation (Gilligan & Attanucci, 1988), but other studies have shown no gender differences in moral orientation (Knox, Fagley, & Miller, 2004). Male and female adolescents and adults display similar reasoning that combines concerns of justice (e.g., being fair) with those of care (e.g., being supportive and helpful), and when there are sex differences, they are very small (Jaffee & Hyde, 2000; Wark & Krebs, 1996; Weisz & Black, 2002). The most mature forms of moral reasoning incorporate both justice and care concerns.

CULTURE AND MORAL REASONING

Cross-cultural studies of Kohlberg's theory show that the sequence appears in all cultures but that people in non-Western cultures rarely score above Stage 3 (Gibbs, Basinger, Grime, & Snarey, 2007; Nisan & Kohlberg, 1982; Snarey, 1985). Similar to cognitive capacities, morality and appropriate responses to ethical dilemmas are defined by each society and its cultural perspectives. Whereas Western cultures tend to emphasize the rights of the individual (justice-based reasoning), non-Western cultures tend to value collectivism, focusing on human interdependence (care-based reasoning; Miller, 1997). Individuals in collectivist cultures tend to define moral dilemmas in terms of the responsibility to the entire community rather than simply to the individual (Miller & Bersoff, 1995). Such emphasis on the needs of others is characteristic of Stage 3 in Kohlberg's scheme. However, because moral values are relative to the cultural context, Stage 3 reasoning is an advanced form of reasoning because it embodies what is most valued in collectivist cultures, concepts such as interdependence and relationships.

Despite these cross-cultural differences, individuals in many cultures show similarities in reasoning. For example, one study examined Chinese and Canadian 12- to 19-year-old adolescents' views of the fairness of various forms of democratic and nondemocratic government (Helwig, Arnold, Tan, & Boyd, 2007). Adolescents from both China and Canada preferred democratic forms of government and appealed to fundamental democratic justice principles such as representation, voice, and majority rule to support their judgments, suggesting that adolescents in collectivist cultures are able to reason with justice principles in particular contexts. In addition, similar age-related patterns in judgments and reasoning were found across cultures and across diverse regions within China. It appears that the development of moral reasoning progresses in a similar pattern across cultures. People of different cultures are able to reason using both care and justice orientations even though cultures tend to vary in the weight they assign moral orientations, emphasizing one over another.

Engaging in volunteer work, such as caring for animals or working to improve the environment, reflects the increasing connection between moral reasoning and behavior that occurs over the course of adolescence.

MORAL REASONING AND BEHAVIOR

Moral reasoning explains how people think about issues of justice, but reasoning is only moderately related with behavior (Colby & Damon, 1992; Kupfersmid & Wonderly, 1980). People often behave in ways they know they should not. For example, an adolescent who explains that stealing and cheating are wrong may slip a pack of gum into her pocket and leave a store without paying or may peek at a classmate's paper during an exam. Like other decisions, ethical conflicts experienced in real life are complex, accompanied by intense emotions, social obligations, and practical considerations, which lead people to act in ways that contradict their judgments (Walker, 2004).

With advances in moral reasoning, adolescents often begin to behave in ways that are in line with their beliefs (Brugman, 2010; Gibbs, 2003). For example, adolescents who demonstrate higher levels of moral reasoning are more likely to share with and help others (Carlo & Eisenberg, 1996; Comunian & Gielen, 2000) and are less likely to engage in antisocial behaviors such as cheating, aggression, or delinquency (Gregg, Gibbs, & Basinger, 1994; Taylor & Walker, 1997). Although adolescents who show low levels of moral reasoning are thought to be at greater risk for delinquency, findings are mixed as some studies find low levels of reasoning predict delinquency and others show no relationship (Kuther & Higgins-D'Alessandro, 2000; Leenders & Brugman, 2005; Tarry & Emler, 2007). Perhaps the degree to which moral reasoning is associated with behavior varies with how adolescents perceive the behavior, as an issue regarding morality, social convention, or personal choice

(Berkowitz & Begun, 1994; Brugman, 2010). Adolescents' moral development influences behaviors they label as moral decisions but not those viewed as social conventions or personal issues. Adolescents who engage in delinquency are more likely than other adolescents to view delinquent behaviors as issues of social convention or personal choice rather than moral issues, suggesting that their level of moral maturity is not an influence on their delinquent behavior because they do not label the behavior as entailing a moral decision (Kuther & Higgins-D'Alessandro, 2000; Leenders & Brugman, 2005). A variety of factors influence the development of moral reasoning and how adolescents view and behave in their world.

Thinking in Context 11.5

1. Based on Kohlberg's perspective, do you think morality can be taught?

2. What, if any, might contextual factors such as socioeconomic status, community, and interactions with parents and peers play in moral development?

3. Do you think the average person can reach the highest level of Kohlberg's scheme? Why or why not?

SCHOOLS AND ACADEMIC FUNCTIONING IN ADOLESCENCE

Apart from the home context, school is the most relevant and immediate context in which adolescents live. The structure of schools has changed dramatically since the mid-29th century. In past generations, students used to make only one school transition: from elementary school (kindergarten–8th grade) to high school (9th grade–12th grade). Today's

students make more school changes, transitions, than ever before. Junior high schools, comprising 7th-, 8th-, and 9th-grade students, were created in the 1960s and modeled after high schools, serving as mini-high schools. In the late 1970s and 1980s, educators began to recognize that young adolescents have different educational needs than middle and older adolescents, and junior high schools began to be converted and organized into middle schools of 5th- or 6th-through 8th-grade students (Byrnes & Ruby, 2007). Middle schools are designed to provide more flexibility and autonomy than elementary schools while encouraging strong ties to adults, such as teachers and parents, and active learning that takes advantage of and stimulates young adolescents' emerging capacities for abstract reasoning (National Middle School Association, 2003).

SCHOOL TRANSITIONS

Change, though often exciting, can pose stress to individuals of all ages. Most students find the transition to a new school, whether middle school or high school, a challenge. Academic motivation and achievement often suffers during school transitions (Booth & Gerard, 2014). Grades tend to decline with each school transition such that students who experience more school transitions tend to perform more poorly than peers who have changed schools less often (Rudolph, Lambert, Clark, & Kurlakowsky, 2001; Seidman, Lambert, Allen, & Aber, 2003). For example, early adolescents enrolled in K–8 schools tend to score higher in academic achievement, specifically, math, and reading, than do those in middle school, who have changed schools from elementary to middle school (Byrnes & Ruby, 2007). Larger cumulative declines in academic achievement are seen when students make two school transitions before high school (elementary to middle school and middle to high school) as compared with one (K–8 elementary school to high school; Crockett, Petersen, Graber, Schulenberg, & Ebata, 1989), although some research disputes the size of this difference (Weiss & Bearman, 2007). For most students, these adjustment difficulties are temporary, and their achievement recovers within one to two years as they adapt to their new schools. However, students who perceive the school transition as more stressful tend to show greater drops in motivation and academic achievement and less connectedness to school that persists well beyond the school transition (Goldstein, Boxer, & Rudolph, 2015).

School transitions are often experienced as stressful because environments, teachers, standards, support, and, often, peers shift with each transition. With each transition, adolescents meet more stringent academic standards, yet many feel that they receive less support. Middle schools were intended to be tailored to the needs of early adolescents yet research suggests that many students view their middle school experiences less positively than their elementary school experiences (Byrnes & Ruby, 2007; Roeser, Eccles, & Sameroff, 2000; Wigfield & Eccles, 1994). Students commonly report feeling less connected to middle school

teachers than elementary school teachers and view their middle school teachers as less friendly, supportive, and fair (Anderman & Midgley, 2004; Lynch & Cicchetti, 1996; Way, Reddy, & Rhodes, 2007). High school students often report that they receive less personal attention from teachers, more class lectures, fewer hands-on demonstration activities, and fewer opportunities to participate in class discussions and group decision making than they did in middle school (Gentle-Genitty, 2009; Seidman, Aber, & French, 2004).

Although it is tempting to blame adolescents' views about school on poor perspective taking or an immature prefrontal cortex, research suggests that many teachers' views corroborate adolescents' perspectives. For example, middle and junior high school teachers hold different beliefs about students than do elementary school teachers, even when they teach students of the same chronological age (Midgley, Anderman, & Hicks, 1995). They are less likely to report trusting their students and are more likely to emphasize discipline than their peers who teach elementary school. Middle school classrooms tend to be characterized by a greater emphasis on teacher control and offer fewer opportunities for student decision making and autonomy, and evaluation becomes more frequent and formal than in elementary school (Eccles & Roeser, 2011; Eccles et al., 1992).

According to researcher Jacqueline Eccles (2004), negative effects of school transitions occur when there is little stage-environment fit. The organization and characteristics of middle school often do not fit young adolescents' needs (Eccles & Roeser, 2011). Teachers become more stringent, less personal, and more directive at the same time as young people value independence. As friendships become more important, the transition to middle school often disrupts them by dividing friends into different schools or different educational tracks. Young adolescents need more guidance and assistance with academic, social, and mental health issues just as teachers report feeling less responsibility for students' problems. The mismatch of adolescents' changing

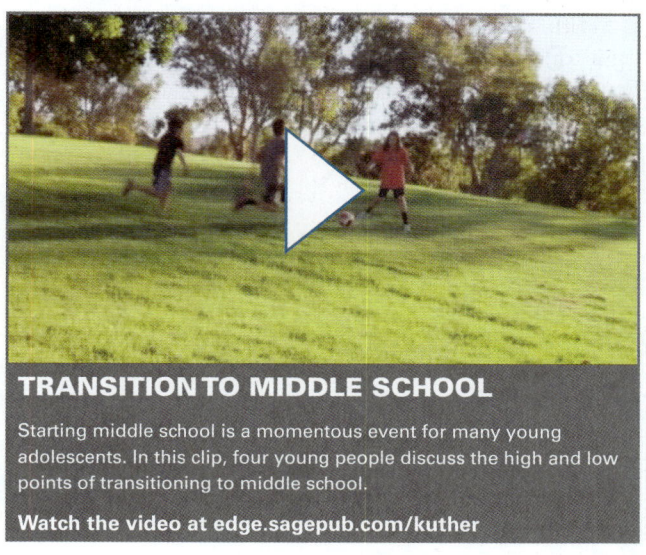

TRANSITION TO MIDDLE SCHOOL

Starting middle school is a momentous event for many young adolescents. In this clip, four young people discuss the high and low points of transitioning to middle school.

Watch the video at edge.sagepub.com/kuther

LIVES IN CONTEXT

Adolescent Employment

Working during high school is commonplace in the United States and Canada, with over one half of high school students reporting working at all during the school year (Bachman, Johnston, & O'Malley, 2014). Labor force surveys, on the other hand, report fewer employed adolescents (about 30%), but many of the jobs reported are "off the books" and unrecorded (U.S. Bureau of Labor, 2015). Regardless, adolescent employment today is at its lowest level since World War II (see Figure 11.8; Greene & Staff, 2012).

Most U.S. adolescents who work come from middle socioeconomic status families and seek part-time employment as a source of spending money (Bachman, Staff, O'Malley, & Freedman-Doan, 2013). Minority adolescents are less likely to work than white adolescents, largely because the economically depressed areas where minority teens are likely to live tend to offer few employment opportunities.

About one half of employed adolescents work 15 or fewer hours per week (Bachman et al., 2014). Working few hours (15 or less) appears to have little positive or negative effect on adolescents' academic or psychosocial functioning (Monahan, Lee, & Steinberg, 2011). One the other hand, working more than 20 hours each week, common to about one third of adolescents (Bachman et al., 2014), is associated with many poor outcomes. Although both adults and adolescents tend to view working as an opportunity to develop a sense of responsibility, research does not support the view that holding a job makes teens more personally responsible (Monahan et al., 2011). For example, one area of responsibility that working is believed to affect is money management. A job may provide opportunities to learn how to budget, save, and spend wisely. Yet most teens spend their earnings on personal expenses, such as clothes, and experience premature affluence—they get used to a luxurious standard of living before they have financial responsibilities (Bachman et al., 2013). Teens who experience premature affluence may be less satisfied with their financial situation as young adults.

More importantly, adolescents who work more than 20 hours each week tend to engage in more parent–teen conflict at home; show poor school attendance, performance, and motivation; are at higher risk of school dropout; and tend to engage in more problem behaviors such as smoking, alcohol and substance use, early sexual activity, and delinquency (Bachman et al., 2013; Dumont, Leclerc, & McKinnon, 2009; Godley, Passetti, & White, 2006; Monahan et al., 2011; Staff, Vaneseltine, Woolnough, Silver, & Burrington, 2012). Some research suggests that the negative effects of long hours of employment are most evident for white middle-class adolescents and associated with fewer disadvantages for Hispanic and African American adolescents from low income (Bachman et al., 2013). Yet other work suggests that intense adolescent employment is associated with detrimental developmental outcomes for youth regardless of neighborhood context (Kingston & Rose, 2015).

However, adolescent work can be a positive experience if it entails limited hours and if it includes educational and vocational training opportunities and contact with adults (Greene & Staff, 2012; Mortimer & Johnson, 1998). The most common jobs

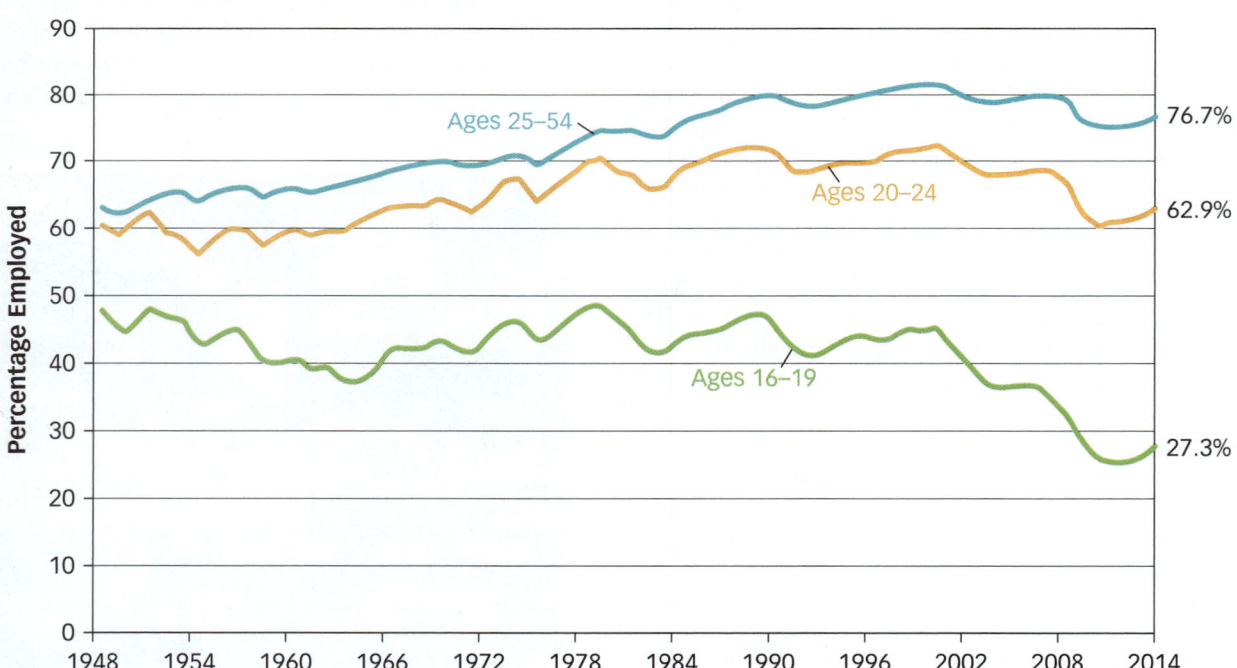

FIGURE 11.8: Employment of Adolescents and Adults in the United States, 1948–2014

SOURCE: Congressional Research Service (CRS), based on data from U.S Department of Labor, Bureau of Labor Statistics Current Population Survey.

available to adolescents often involve repetitive simple tasks such as microwaving meals at a fast-food restaurant (Steinberg, Fegley, & Dornbusch, 1993). Adolescent workers often have little contact with adults—their coworkers tend to be teens; supervisors tend to be not much older than them; and customers, if in food service and retail, tend to be adolescents (Greenberger & Steinberg, 1986). Work settings that emphasize vocational skills, such as answering phones as a receptionist, and in which adolescents interact with, and work alongside, adults, tend to promote positive attitudes towards school and work, academic motivation and achievement, and low levels of drug and alcohol use and delinquency (Staff & Uggen, 2003). The best jobs take the form of formal or informal apprenticeships whereby adolescents learn interpersonal and hands-on skills by working alongside adults (Hamilton & Hamilton, 1999; Heinz, 1999).

What Do You Think?

1. Did you hold a job during adolescence? How do your experiences compare with these findings?

2. Are you in favor of setting limits on adolescent employment, such as the number of hours they are permitted to work? Why or why not? What limits, if any, do you suggest?

developmental needs and school resources and emphases contribute to declines in academic performance, motivation, and overall functioning (Booth & Gerard, 2014). Vulnerable students, such as those from low-income families or who require special education services, tend to show a larger interruption in academic achievement (Akos, Rose, & Orthner, 2014).

Some adolescents face greater risks with school transitions. Changes in school demographics, particularly a mismatch between the ethnic composition of elementary and middle school, or middle school and high school, can pose challenges to adolescents' adjustment (Douglass, Yip, & Shelton, 2014). One study of over 900 entering high school students found that students who experienced more ethnic incongruence from middle to high school, a mismatch in demographics, reported declining feelings of connectedness to school over time and increasing worries about their academic success (Benner & Graham, 2009). Students who moved to high schools with fewer students who were ethnically similar to themselves, were most likely to experience a disconnect, as were African American male students. This is of particular concern because African American adolescents tend to experience more risk factors to academic achievement, more difficulties in school transitions, and are more likely to fall behind during school transitions than adolescents of other ethnicities (Burchinal, Roberts, Zeisel, Hennon, & Hooper, 2006). Similarly, Latino students tend to be more sensitive to changes in the school climate and experience school transitions as more challenging than do white students (Espinoza & Juvonen, 2011).

Overall, the research on stage-environment fit suggests the best student outcomes occur when schools closely match adolescents' developmental needs. While some researchers call for K–8 schools as the educational model to emulate (Juvonen, Le, Kaganoff, Augustine, & Constant, 2004), radical reorganization of school systems is largely impractical. Instead, researchers argue for small, tight-knit middle schools to help reduce the alienation that some students experience during the middle school transition (Jackson & Davis, 2000). Small schools may also foster strong teacher–student relationships through more opportunities for teachers to interact with a smaller student base (McNeely, Nonnemaker, & Blum, 2002). Close relationships may help teachers feel comfortable providing opportunities for adolescents to have autonomy in classroom interactions and assignments while providing strong support. Adolescents who report high levels of teacher support and feel connected to their schools tend to show better academic achievement and better emotional health, including lower rates of depressive and anxiety symptoms (Kidger, Araya, Donovan, & Gunnell, 2012).

Adolescents' success in navigating school transitions is also influenced by their experiences outside of school. Adolescents are most vulnerable to the negative effects of school transitions when they lack the social and emotional resources to cope with multiple stressors. Young people who report feeling supported by their families and having many friends are less bothered by day-to-day stressors and experience school transitions with few problems (Kingery, Erdley, & Marshall, 2011; Rueger, Chen, Jenkins, & Choe, 2014; Seidman et al., 2003). One influence on academic achievement is part-time employment, as noted in Lives in Context (at left and above). Finally, similar to other aspects of development, expectations matter. Adolescents who expect a positive transition to secondary school are more likely to report experiencing a positive experience (Waters, Lester, & Cross, 2014).

PARENTING AND ACADEMIC COMPETENCE

Close parent–adolescent relationships serve as an important buffer to academic motivation and performance from childhood through adolescence for young people at all levels of socioeconomic status (Dotterer, Lowe, & McHale, 2014; Schneider, Tomada, Normand, Tonci, & de Domini, 2008). Similar to other areas of development, both the overly harsh parenting characterized by the authoritarian parenting style and the lax permissive parenting style are associated with poor academic performance. Likewise, adolescents reared by uninnvolved parents tend to show the most poor school grades (Aunola & Stattin, 2000; Glasgow & Dornbusch, 1997; Gonzalez & Wolters, 2006; Heaven & Ciarrochi, 2008). Authoritative parenting, on the other hand, is associated with academic achievement in adolescents around the world, including Argentina, Australia, Canada, China, Hong Kong, Iran, Pakistan, Scotland, and the United States (Assadi et al., 2007; Garg, Levin, Urajnik, & Kauppi, 2005; Gonzalez & Wolters, 2006; Spera, 2005).

School Dropout

Who is likely to drop out of high school? It is the students who already face significant contextual risks to their development who are most likely to leave high school without a diploma. Students from low socioeconomic status are at highest risk of school dropout, and minority students are particularly vulnerable for school dropout, with rates for Latino students over 2.5 times those of non-Latino students, as shown by Figure 11.9. Dropout rates have, however, reached historic lows, with dramatic decreases for African American adolescents and especially Latino adolescents.

Students with behavior problems are more likely to drop out of high school, but many who drop out simply have academic problems, skip classes with increasing frequency, and finally completely disengage from school (Janosz, Archambault, Morizot, & Pagani, 2008; Wang & Fredricks, 2014). Research has found that dropping out of high school is not a solitary event but rather the outcome of a long gradual process of disengaging from school (Bowers & Sprott, 2012; Christenson & Thurlow, 2004; Henry, Knight, & Thornberry, 2012). Young people at risk for high school dropout show risk factors such as withdrawal (poor class participation or poor attendance) and unsuccessful school experiences (academic or behavioral problems) as early as first grade. Risks documented in first grade account for dropout almost as well as those documented in high school (Alexander, Entwisle, & Kabbani, 2001; Entwisle, Alexander, & Steffel Olson, 2005). Lack of parental involvement in children's education places students at risk for school dropout, and when parents respond to poor grades with anger and punishment, this can further reduce adolescents' academic motivation and feelings of connectedness to school (Alivernini & Lucidi, 2011).

Students who are engaged and attached to school and who participate in many school-related activities are less likely to drop out (Janosz et al., 2008; Mahoney, 2014). Conversely, feelings of anonymity at school increase the risk of dropping out. Many of the unfavorable characteristics that students report of their high schools predict dropout: large schools, unsupportive teachers, and few opportunities to form personal relationships or to speak out in class (Battin-Pearson & Newcomb, 2000; Christenson & Thurlow, 2004; Croninger & Lee, 2001; Freeman & Simonsen, 2014). Bullying and poor relationships with peers also place adolescents at risk for dropping out (Cornell, Gregory, Huang, & Fan, 2013; Frostad, Pijl, & Mjaavatn, 2014). Students who experience academic difficulties may be more vulnerable to the structural changes that are common during school transitions.

FIGURE 11.9: School Dropout Rates Among Youth Ages 16 to 24 in the United States, 1967–2013

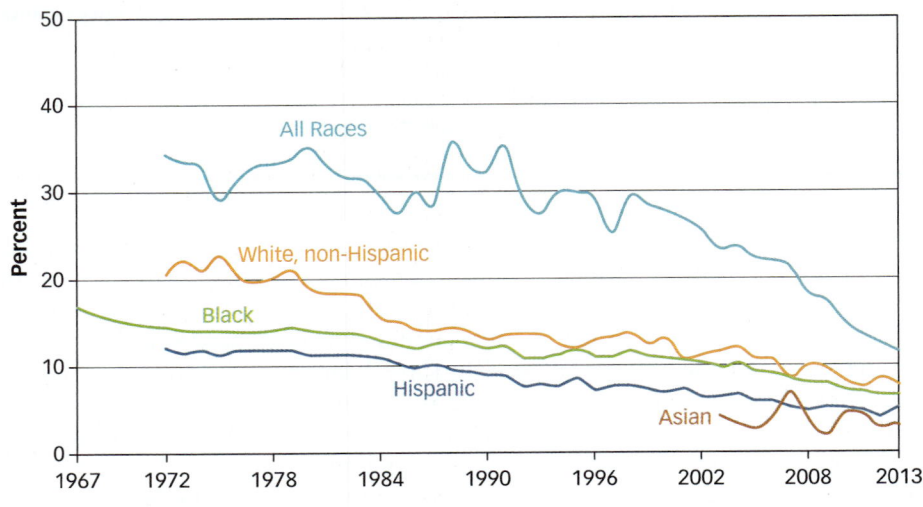

SOURCE: Child Trends (2014).

Dropping out of high school is a serious event with lifelong consequences. Adults who did not finish high school demonstrate low levels of literacy relative to high school graduates, and this has dire consequences for their employment prospects. In 2013, about 30% of high school dropouts aged 16 to 24 were unemployed (U.S. Bureau of Labor, 2014). Today's jobs require the ability to take in and manipulate information. Because young people without high school degrees lack the reading and information management skills that employers value, it is not surprising that high school dropouts in the United States and Canada experience more short- and long-term unemployment than graduates. When they are employed, they are more likely to hold low-paying jobs.

Young people who have dropped out of school have the option of taking a high school equivalency test, the General Educational Development exam, known as the GED. It was developed in the late 1940s as a way to certify that returning World War II veterans who had left their high school classrooms to serve in the war were ready for college or the labor market. Although passing the GED can signify that a young person has accumulated the knowledge entailed in earning a high school diploma, GED holders do not fare as well as regular high school graduates in the labor market, and they get much less postsecondary education (Tyler & Lofstrom, 2009).

What Do You Think?

1. What are some of the reasons why adolescents might drop out of school? Identify influences at the level of the microsystem, mesosystem, exosystem, and macrosystem.

2. What can be done to help students stay in school and graduate from high school?

Authoritative parenting, monitoring, and involvement in school homework and activities is associated with high academic achievement in middle and high school students.

When parents use the authoritative style, they will be open to discussion, involve their adolescents in joint decision making, and firmly but fairly monitor their adolescents' behavior and set limits. This style of parenting helps adolescents feel valued, respected, and encouraged to think for themselves (Dornbusch, Ritter, Mont-Reynaud, & Chen, 1990; Spera, 2005). Adolescents are in a phase when they are learning to regulate their emotions and behavior and to set, work toward, and achieve educational goals (Aunola & Stattin, 2000; Moilanen, Rasmussen, & Padilla-Walker, 2015). Authoritative parenting supports these developments.

Just as in elementary school, parents can promote high academic achievement in middle and high school students by being active and involved—for example, by knowing their teens' teachers, monitoring progress, ensuring that their teens are taking challenging and appropriate classes,

and expressing high expectations (Benner, 2011; Karbach, Gottschling, Spengler, Hegewald, & Spinath, 2013; Wang, Hill, & Hofkens, 2014). Parent–school involvement in 8th grade has been shown to predict 10th-grade students' grade point average regardless of socioeconomic status, previous academic achievement, and ethnicity, whether African American, European American, Native American, or Asian American (Keith et al., 1998). By being involved in the school, parents communicate the importance of education; they also model academic engagement and problem solving.

Ultimately over 80% of students who enter public high school as freshmen graduate on time (National Center for Education Statistics, 2014). However, about 7% of high school students drop out, meaning that they do not finish high school. Applying Developmental Science (p. 318) examines the problem of school dropout.

Overall, the physical and cognitive changes during adolescence present opportunities and challenges. As adolescents' emerging physical and cognitive capacities enable them to participate in more adult roles and decisions, the short- and long-term health, educational, and personal dangers of poor decisions require additional protections. Adolescence is clearly a balancing act for adolescents and their parents.

Thinking in Context 11.6

Discuss the ways in which the fit between a young person's needs—personal and developmental—and the opportunities and supports provided to her within the school system influence her academic adjustment and likelihood of completing high school. How might factors outside of school, in the home, peer network, community, and society contribute?

Apply Your Knowledge

At 14, Kendra had her very first alcoholic drink when her friends took her to a party hosted by Dylan, a high school senior. Soon Kendra and Dylan began dating. Kendra had always felt especially self-conscious about her body, as she had started

needing a bra at age 10, and by age 13, she had sometimes been mistaken for an adult. She thought of herself as "too big," but Dylan insisted her body was "smokin'." With Dylan, Kendra began drinking regularly at parties as she found it eased her nerves and helped her feel more comfortable interacting with the older kids. After a few drinks, she would feel comfortable enough to take off her sweatshirt and show off her tank top. Dylan also introduced Kendra to marijuana, which she preferred over alcohol because it made it easy to forget her self-consciousness. Being high on marijuana made goofing around like her friends much more fun. One night they climbed the fence surrounding the high school and spray-painted the windows black. Another time, they sneaked onto a local golf course and went skinny-dipping in the pond. However, a neighbor called the police, and Kendra, Dylan, and their friends were arrested for trespassing and possession of alcohol and drugs.

1. What might you discern about Kendra's physical development, relative to her peers? What role might physical development play in Kendra's behavior?

2. How might neurological development account for some of Kendra's behavior?

3. What role might cognitive factors, such as cognitive development, adolescent egocentrism, and decision capacities, play?

4. Does moral development have a role in Kendra's behavior? Why or why not?

Chapter Summary

11.1 Compare and contrast Hall's storm and stress perspective with popular views and research evidence.

The popular view that adolescence is a troubling time for teens and parents to endure originates with the work of G. Stanley Hall, who theorized that adolescence is a period of storm and stress, a universal and inevitable upheaval triggered by puberty. Although the basis of Hall's argument has been debunked, his storm and stress view remains popular among laypeople. Developmental scientists today reject the notion that adolescence is a period extreme storm and stress, replacing it with a more nuanced view that adolescence is a time of change characterized by individual differences in how they are experienced. Some adolescents encounter extreme turmoil, but great trauma is not the norm. Most adolescents experience some ups and downs but emerge from adolescence unscathed. The danger of the storm and stress view lies in that it may influence expectations for adolescent behavior, creating self-fulfilling prophecies that subtly influence how they are treated.

11.2 Explain the physical changes that occur with puberty and their psychosocial effects.

The most noticeable signs of pubertal maturation are the growth spurt and secondary sex characteristics. Examples of changes in secondary sex characteristics include breast development, deepening of the voice, growth of body hair, and changes in the skin. During puberty, the primary sex characteristics, the reproductive organs, grow larger and mature, and adolescents become capable of reproduction.

11.3 Analyze the influence of pubertal timing on adolescent development.

Pubertal timing is influenced by genetic and contextual factors including physical health, nutrition, body fat, exposure to stress, socioeconomic status, and the secular trend. The consequences of early and late maturation differ dramatically for girls and boys. Girls who mature early are at risk for problems with depression, anxiety, and poor body image. Both boys and girls who mature early are more likely to engage in risk behaviors and age-inappropriate behaviors such as sexual activity. Late maturation appears to have a protective effect on girls but findings regarding the effects of late maturation on boys are mixed and less consistent. Late-maturing boys may experience more social and emotional difficulties. During early adolescence, they may be less well liked by their peers and may be more likely than their peers to experience a poor body image, overall body dissatisfaction, and depression during early adolescence, but these effects tend to decline with physical maturation. Other research suggests that late-maturing boys do not differ in anxiety or depression from their on-time peers or that it is only late-maturing boys with poor peer relationships who experience depression.

11.4 Discuss the effects of sleep and nutrition on adolescent functioning.

Puberty causes a change in adolescents' sleep patterns, called delayed phase preference. Adolescents stay up later, miss out on sleep, and report sleepiness. The tendency for adolescents to go to bed later has increased over the past three decades with the availability of television and other media that compete with sleep for adolescents' time. Poor sleep is associated with internalizing and externalizing problems and increases the probability of obesity, illnesses, and accidents. Although adequate food consumption and good nutrition also are essential to support adolescents' physical and mental health and growth, young people's diets tend to worsen as they enter adolescence, leaving many adolescents in industrialized nations with nutritional deficiencies. In addition, levels of physical activity decrease throughout adolescence, and many adolescents engage in no regular exercise or activity.

11.5 Explain the neurological developments that take place in adolescence and their effect on behavior.

Changes in the volume of the cortex, interconnections among neurons, and myelination influence the speed and efficiency of thought and the capacity for executive function. According to the dual-process model, the limbic system undergoes a burst of development well ahead of the prefrontal cortex, and this difference in development can account for many "typical" adolescent behaviors. Changes in the balance of neurotransmitters that are associated with impulsivity and reward salience shift influencing adolescent engagement in risky behavior. Maturation and improved connectivity in the prefrontal cortex is associated with advances many aspects of executive function involved in planning and weighing risks and rewards as well as response inhibition and decision making.

11.6 Identify ways in which thinking changes in adolescence.

Adolescents become capable of formal operational reasoning permitting hypothetical–deductive reasoning and the use of propositional logic. Research suggests that formal operational reasoning does not suddenly appear in early adolescence, but instead, cognitive change occurs gradually from childhood on. Many adults fail hypothetical–deductive tasks. Reasoning can vary by content area. People reason at the most advanced levels when considering material with which they have the greatest experience. Adolescents' advances in cognition are the result of improvements in information processing capacities, such as attention, memory, knowledge base, response inhibition, strategy use, speed, and metacognition.

11.7 Discuss how cognitive development is reflected in adolescent decision making and behavior.

Under ideal conditions, adolescents are capable of demonstrating rational decision making that is in line with their goals and comparable to that of adults. In practice, decision making is more complex and influenced by situational, affective, and individual difference characteristics, such as the presence of peers, temptation of high rewards, excitement, impulsivity, and sensation seeking. The difference in maturational timing between the limbic system and prefrontal cortex means that adolescents feel emotionally charged before they have corresponding self-regulation and decision-making abilities, often leading to poor decisions.

11.8 Outline the developmental progression of moral reasoning, factors that influence it, and its link with behavior.

In adolescence, we become capable of demonstrating postconventional reasoning, which entails autonomous decision making from moral principles that value respect for individual rights above all else. Research has confirmed that individuals proceed through the first four stages of moral reasoning in a slow, gradual, and predictable fashion, but few people advance beyond Stage 4 moral reasoning. Social interactions offer important opportunities for the development of moral reasoning. Reasoning advances when adolescents have opportunities to engage in issue-focused discussions that are characterized by mutual perspective taking and opportunities to discuss different points of view. Moral reasoning is only moderately related with behavior because real-life conflicts are complex, accompanied by intense emotions, social obligations, and practical considerations, which lead people to act in ways that contradict their judgments. The degree to which moral reasoning is associated with behavior often varies with how adolescents perceive the behavior as an issue regarding morality, social convention, or personal choice. Adolescents' moral development influences behaviors they label as moral decisions but not those viewed as social conventions or personal issues.

11.9 Analyze criticisms of Kohlberg's moral development theory.

Early research that studied both males and females suggested gender differences in moral reasoning, with males typically scoring higher. Carol Gilligan argued that Kohlberg's theory neglected a female mode of moral reasoning, a care orientation that contrasts with the distinctively male justice orientation captured by Kohlberg. Research shows that male and female adolescents and adults display similar reasoning that combines concerns of justice and care concerns. Cross-cultural studies of Kohlberg's theory show that the sequence appears in all cultures but that cultures differ in the degree to which they value the individual or the collective.

11.10 Describe the challenges that school transitions pose for adolescents and the role of parents in academic achievement.

Academic motivation, academic achievement, and, in girls, self-esteem, often suffer during school transitions, both the transition to middle school and to high school. With each transition, adolescents meet more stringent academic standards, yet they receive less support and encounter more opportunities to fall behind in their work. Poor stage-environment fit, the mismatch of adolescents' changing developmental needs, and school resources and emphases contribute to the declines in academic performance, motivation, and overall functioning that occur during school transitions. Authoritative parenting, parent involvement in the school, and close parent-adolescent relationships are important buffers to academic motivation and performance from childhood through adolescence for young people at all levels of socioeconomic status.

Key Terms

adolescent egocentrism   308

amygdala   303

care orientation   313

delayed phase preference   300

dual-process model   303

estrogen   295

formal operational reasoning   305

gonads   294

hypothalamus-pituitary-gonadal (HPG) axis   294

hypothetical–deductive reasoning   305

imaginary audience   308

justice orientation   313

limbic system   303

menarche   297

personal fable   308

postconventional moral reasoning   313

primary sex characteristics   297

puberty   292

secondary sex characteristics   296

secular trend   298

spermarche   297

testosterone   295

CHAPTER 12

Socioemotional Development in Adolescence

$SAGE edge™

Get the edge on your studies at edge.sagepub.com/kuther.

Master these learning objectives using key study tools in the chapter and at SAGE edge. Access original SAGE **Video Cases** to explore the lives and contexts of individuals in every stage of development, **Think Critically** and **Explore Further** with SAGE journal and reference articles, and **Watch**, **Listen**, and **Connect** with online multimedia resources.

LEARNING OBJECTIVES	KEY STUDY TOOLS
12.1. Identify ways in which self-conceptions and self-esteem change during adolescence.	**Video Case** Self-Concept in Adolescence
12.2. Outline the process of identity development during adolescence, including influences and outcomes associated with identity status.	**Watch** "I Am Who I Am": Adolescent Responses **Think Critically** Male Adolescent Identity Crisis
12.3. Explore changes in adolescents' relationships with parents and the contribution of parenting style and monitoring to adolescent adjustment.	**Watch** Family Conflict and Puberty **Think Critically** Parenting Style and Delinquency
12.4. Compare and contrast the nature of friendship and dating during adolescence.	**Video Case** Friendship **Applying Developmental Science** Popularity (p. 336)
12.5. Differentiate the developmental progression of cliques and crowds.	**Lives in Context** Cyberbullying (p. 338) **Connect** Adolescent Crowds
12.6. Analyze how susceptibility to peer influence changes from early adolescence to late adolescence.	**Lives in Context** Adolescent Dating Violence (p. 340) **Connect** Teens and Peer Pressure
12.7. Compare the factors that contribute to sexual activity, contraceptive use, and the transmission of sexually transmitted infections (STIs) during adolescence.	**Watch** Benefits of Teen Sex **Watch** Abstinence-Only Education
12.8. Discuss risk factors for adolescent pregnancy and influences on the adjustment of adolescent mothers and their children.	**Explore Further** A Social Problem? **Listen** Reducing Teen Pregnancy
12.9. Compare and contrast the risk factors for and treatments for adolescent problems such as depression and suicide, eating disorders, and substance use and abuse.	**Watch** Adult vs. Teenage Depression **Applying Developmental Science** Self-Harm (p. 350)
12.10. Characterize normative delinquent activities during adolescence as compared with serious lifelong criminal activity.	**Watch** Failed Approach to Juvenile Justice **Explore Further** Serious and Violent Juvenile Offenders

"I'm a walking contradiction," declares 15-year-old Casey. "I'm shy but also outgoing, kind but sometimes I want to be mean. I don't know what I want to do with my life. I'd like to go away to college, but I don't want to leave my friends. I think protecting the environment is important, and I want to make a difference in the world. But what does that mean for me? I guess I'm still figuring myself out," Casey concludes. She has summed

up much of the socioemotional task of adolescence: figuring yourself out. Specifically, adolescents construct a sense of self and **identity**, an understanding of who they are and who they hope to be. Adolescents' attempts at self-definition and discovery are influenced by their relationships with parents and peers, relationships that become more complex during the adolescent years.

PSYCHOSOCIAL DEVELOPMENT: THE CHANGING SELF

Adolescents spend a great deal of time reflecting on themselves and engaging in introspective activities, such as writing in journals, composing poetry, and posting messages, photos, and videos about their lives on social media. Adults often view these activities as self-indulgent and egotistical, but they help adolescents work through an important developmental task: forming a sense of self. During adolescence, we undergo advances in self-concept and identity.

SELF-CONCEPT

A major developmental task of adolescence is to construct a more complex, differentiated, and organized self-concept. As discussed in Chapter 9, older children can use broad characteristics to describe their personalities (e.g., funny, smart). With cognitive advances, young adolescents use more labels to describe themselves, and the labels they choose become more abstract and complex (e.g., witty, intelligent). Adolescents learn that they can describe themselves in multiple ways that often are contradictory, such as being both silly and serious, and that they show different aspects of themselves to different people (e.g., parents, teachers, friends; Harter, 2006b; Harter, 2012). Adolescents' views of themselves influence their behavior. For example, adolescents' views of their academic competencies in early adolescence predict their academic achievement in middle adolescence (Preckel, Niepel, Schneider, & Brunner, 2013).

In middle adolescence, young people recognize that their feelings, attitudes, and behaviors may change with the situation, and they begin to use qualifiers in their self-descriptions (e.g., "I'm sort of shy"). Adolescents' awareness of the situational variability in their psychological and behavioral qualities is evident in statements such as, "I'm assertive in class, speaking out and debating my classmates, but I'm quieter with my friends. I don't want to stir up problems." Many young adolescents find these inconsistencies confusing and wonder who they really are, contributing to their challenge of forming a balanced and consistent sense of self. Adolescents identify a self that they aspire to be, the ideal self, which is characterized by traits that they value. Adjustment is influenced by the match between the actual self—the adolescents' personal characteristics—and their aspirational, ideal self. Mismatches between ideal and actual

selves are associated with depression symptoms, low self-esteem, and poor school grades (Ferguson, Hafen, & Laursen, 2010; Stevens, Lovejoy, & Pittman, 2014). Adolescents who show poor self-concept clarity, or poor stability or consistency in their self-descriptions, tend to experience higher rates of depressive and anxiety symptoms throughout adolescence (Van Dijk et al., 2014). As adolescents become increasingly concerned with how others view them, positive social characteristics such as being helpful, friendly, and kind become more important (Damon & Hart, 1988).

Self-concept is influenced by experiences in the home, school, and community. At home, the authoritative parenting style can provide support, acceptance, and give-and-take to promote the development of adolescent self-concept (Lee, Daniels, & Kissinger, 2006; Van Dijk et al., 2014). Interactions at school also influence how adolescents view themselves. African American middle school students' experiences with racial discrimination at school are associated with poor academic self-concepts, but a strong connection to their ethnic group and a feeling of affinity with African American culture can buffer the negative impact of discrimination (Eccles, Wong, & Peck, 2006). Participation in youth organizations, such as the Boys' and Girls' Clubs of America, has positive effects on the self-concept of young people reared in impoverished neighborhoods because such organizations foster competence, positive socialization, and connections with the community (Quane & Rankin, 2006). Adolescents' evaluations of their self-conceptions are the basis for self-esteem (Harter, 2006b; Marsh, Trautwein, Lüdtke, Köller, & Baumert, 2006).

SELF-ESTEEM

As self-conceptions become more differentiated, so do self-evaluations. Global self-esteem, an overall evaluation of self-worth, tends to decline at about 11 years of age, reaching its lowest point at about 12 or 13, and then rises (Harter, 2006a; Orth & Robins, 2014). Declines in global

SELF-CONCEPT IN ADOLESCENCE

In this video, four young people ranging in age from late childhood to emerging adulthood describe their views of themselves.

Watch the video at edge.sagepub.com/kuther

Close friendships and peer acceptance are important influences on self-esteem.

self-esteem are likely due to the multiple transitions that young adolescents undergo, such as body changes and the emotions that accompany those changes, as well as adolescents' self-comparisons to their peers. Although school transitions (as discussed in Chapter 11) are often associated with temporary declines in self-esteem, most adolescents view themselves more positively as they progress from early adolescence and through the high school years (Moneta, Schneider, & Csikszentmihalyi, 2001; Orth & Robins, 2014; Zeiders, Umaña-Taylor, & Derlan, 2013). For example, comparisons of adolescents in Grades 8, 10, and 12 reveal higher ratings of self-esteem with age for European American, African American, Asian American, and Latino youth (Bachman, O'Malley, Freedman-Doan, Trzesniewski, & Donnellan, 2011).

Global evaluations of self-worth give way to more complex views. Adolescents evaluate themselves with respect to multiple dimensions and relationships, such as within the context of friendships, academics, and athletic abilities (Harter, 2012). Adolescents describe and evaluate their capacities in many areas and view their abilities more positively in some and more negatively in others.

Adolescents develop a positive sense of self-esteem when they evaluate themselves favorably in the areas that they view as important. For example, sports accomplishments are more closely associated with physical self-esteem in adolescent athletes, who tend to highly value physical athleticism, than nonathletes, who tend to place less importance on athleticism (Findlay & Bowker, 2009; Wagnsson, Lindwall, & Gustafsson, 2014). Similarly, adolescents with high academic self-esteem tend to spend more time and effort on schoolwork, view academics as more important, and demonstrate high academic achievement (Preckel et al., 2013; Valentine, DuBois, & Cooper, 2004). There is also spillover as exemplary performance and self-esteem in one area, such as athletics, often is associated with positive self-evaluations in other areas, such as social, physical, and appearance (Marsh,

Trautwein, Lüdtke, Gerlach, & Brettschneider, 2007; Stein, Fisher, Berkey, & Colditz, 2007).

Whereas favorable self-evaluations are associated with positive adjustment and sociability in adolescents of all socioeconomic status and ethnic groups, low self-esteem is associated with adjustment difficulties and depression (Burwell & Shirk, 2006; McCarty, Vander Stoep, & McCauley, 2007). Low self-esteem is associated with depression during adolescence, and it also predicts depression in adulthood (Orth & Robins, 2014). For example, in one longitudinal study, researchers assessed self-esteem annually in over 1,500 12- to 16-year-old adolescents and found that both level and change in self-esteem predicted depression at ages 16 and 35 (Steiger, Allemand, Robins, & Fend, 2014). Those who entered adolescence with low self-esteem and whose self-esteem declined further during the adolescent years were more likely to show depression two decades later as adults; this pattern held for global and domain-specific self-esteem (physical appearance and academic competence).

High-quality relationships with parents, peers, and other adults (relationships characterized by many positive and few negative features) are associated with higher estimates of self-worth and better adjustment. Relationships with parents play an important role in influencing adolescents' self-evaluations. For example, a study of Dutch, Moroccan, Turkish, and Surinamese adolescents living in the Netherlands, as well as adolescents from China, Australia, Germany, and the United States, confirmed that the overall quality of the parent–adolescent relationship predicted self-esteem (Harris et al., 2015; Wang & Sheikh-Khalil, 2014; Wissink, Dekovic, & Meijer, 2006). Parents who adopt a warm, encouraging, but firm style of parenting are more likely to raise adolescents who display high self-esteem (Milevsky, Schlechter, Netter, & Keehn, 2007; Steinberg, 2001; Wouters, Doumen, Germeijs, Colpin, & Verschueren, 2013). Among Latino adolescents in the United States, high self-esteem is predicted by authoritative parenting coupled with **biculturalism**, adopting values and practices of two cultures, and **familism**, valuing the family over the individual and community (Bámaca, Umaña-Taylor, Shin, & Alfaro, 2005; Smokowski, Rose, & Bacallao, 2010; Telzer, Tsai, Gonzales, & Fuligni, 2015). In contrast, if parental feedback is critical, insulting, inconsistent, and not contingent on behavior, and parent–adolescent conflict is high, adolescents tend to develop poor self-esteem, are at risk to turn to peers for self-affirmation, and show adjustment difficulties (Milevsky et al., 2007; Wang et al., 2014).

Relationships with parents have a powerful impact on adolescents' views of themselves; however, peers also matter. Adolescents who feel supported and well-liked by peers tend to show high self-esteem (Litwack, Aikins, & Cillessen, 2010). In addition, peer acceptance has protective effects on self-esteem and can buffer the negative effects of a distant relationship with parents (Birkeland, Breivik, & Wold, 2014). Unfortunately, however, adolescents with low self-esteem are more likely to report poor relationships with peers (Laursen & Mooney, 2008; Vanhalst, Luyckx, Scholte, Engels, & Goossens, 2013).

IDENTITY

As adolescents' self-concept and self-esteem become more descriptive, comprehensive, and organized, they begin to form an identity, a coherent sense of self. In devising an identity, young people integrate all that they know about themselves, their self-conceptions, along with their evaluations of themselves, to construct a self that is coherent and consistent over time (Erikson, 1950). **Identity achievement** represents the successful resolution of this process, establishing a coherent sense of self after exploring a range of possibilities. In establishing a sense of identity, individuals must consider their past and future and come to a sense of their values, beliefs, and goals with regard to vocation, politics, religion, and sexuality.

Identity Status

"Black again?" Rose sighs. "You wear too much black." Her daughter, Stephanie, retorts, "How can anyone wear too much black?" Rose wonders where last year's preppy girl went and hopes that Stephanie will lose interest in wearing goth attire. "Maybe next year she'll try a new style and stop wearing so much black." Stephanie's changing styles of dress reflect her struggle with figuring out who she is, her identity. Researchers classify individuals' progress in identity development into four categories known as **identity status**, the degree to which individuals have explored possible selves and whether they have committed to specific beliefs and goals (Marcia, 1966).

Identity status is most commonly assessed by administering interview and survey measures (Årseth, Kroger,

Martinussen, & Marcia, 2009; Jones, Akers, & White, 1994; Schwartz, 2004). Young people typically shift among identity statuses over the adolescent years, but the specific pattern of identity development varies among adolescents (Meeus, 2011). Some adolescents remain in one identity status, such as **identity moratorium**—a state of exploration—for the bulk of adolescence, while others experience multiple transitions in identity status. The most common shifts in identity status are from **identity diffusion** (not having explored or committed to a sense of self) and **identity foreclosure** (prematurely choosing an identity) in early adolescence, to moratorium and achievement in middle and late adolescence (Al-Owidha, Green, & Kroger, 2009; Meeus, 1996; Yip, 2014). Table 12.1 depicts four identity statuses, or categories, describing a person's identity development.

Identity statuses reflect different ways of viewing and responding to the world. Having not engaged in any exploration, individuals who are in the identity-foreclosed status tend to be inflexible and view the world in black-and-white, right-and-wrong terms. Pervasive uncertainty that feels like it will never be resolved is linked with identity diffusion (Berzonsky & Kuk, 2000; Boyes & Chandler, 1992). Patterns of development vary across identity domains, such as vocation, political ideology, religious values, and sexual identity (Kroger, 2007a). For example, having chosen a career, an adolescent may demonstrate identity achievement with regard to vocation yet remain diffused with regard to political ideology, never having considered political affiliations. The overall proportion of young people in the moratorium status tends to increase during adolescence, peaking at about age 19 and declining thereafter (Kroger, Martinussen, & Marcia, 2010). Identity diffusion and foreclosure become less common in late adolescence. The identity-achieved status in each domain requires that individuals construct a sense of self through exploring or trying out new ideas and

TABLE 12.1 Identity Status

		COMMITMENT	
		PRESENT	**ABSENT**
EXPLORATION	**PRESENT**	**Identity Achievement** _Authoritative_ **Description:** Has committed to an identity after exploring multiple possibilities **Characteristics:** Active problem-solving style, high self-esteem, feelings of control, high moral reasoning, and positive views of work and school	**Identity Moratorium** _Permissive_ **Description:** Has not committed to an identity but is exploring alternatives **Characteristics:** Information-seeking, active problem-solving style, open to experience, anxiety, experimentation with alcohol or substance use
	ABSENT	**Identity Foreclosure** **Description:** Has committed to an identity without having explored multiple possibilities **Characteristics:** Avoid reflecting on their identity choice, not open to new information, especially if contracts their position, rigid and inflexible	**Identity Diffusion** _uninvolved_ **Description:** Has neither committed to an identity nor explored alternatives **Characteristics:** Avoidance; tend to not solve personal problems in favor of letting issues decide themselves, academic difficulties, apathy, and alcohol and substance use

Authoritarian

belief systems, critical examination, and reflection as well as that they have formed a commitment to a particular set of ideas, values, and beliefs. Even in early adulthood, a great many young people have not reached identity achievement (Kroger, 2007b; Kroger et al., 2010; Meeus, 2011).

Influences on Identity Development

Just as authoritative parenting fosters the development of positive self-concept and self-esteem, it also is associated with identity achievement. When parents provide a sense of stability along with autonomy, adolescents tend to explore, much as toddlers do, by using their parents as a secure base (Årseth et al., 2009; Beyers & Goossens, 2008; Meeus & de Wied, 2007). Adolescents who feel connected to their parents, supported, and accepted by them but who also feel that they are free and encouraged to develop and voice their own views, are more likely to engage in the exploration necessary to advance to the moratorium and achieved status. As adolescents become individuated from parents, they begin to make identity commitments and move toward identity achievement (Meeus, Iedema, Maassen, & Engels, 2005). Adolescents who are not encouraged or permitted to explore, who are raised in authoritarian homes, are more likely to show the foreclosed status. A lack of parental support and encouragement to develop and express ideas predicts the failure to seek out and make commitments to possible selves characteristic of identity diffusion (Hall & Brassard, 2008; Reis & Youniss, 2004; Zimmermann & Becker-Stoll, 2002).

Attachment to peers is also associated with identity exploration (Harter, 2006b; Meeus, Oosterwegel, & Vollerbergh, 2002). Peers serve as a mirror in which adolescents view their emerging identities, an audience to which they relay their self-narratives (McLean, 2005). When adolescents feel close, supported, and respected by peers, they feel more comfortable exploring identity alternatives. As with parents, conflict with peers harms identity development as adolescents often feel less free to explore identity alternatives and lack a supportive peer group to offer input on identity alternatives, which holds negative implications for identity development, such as identity foreclosure or diffusion (Hall & Brassard, 2008).

Outcomes Associated With Identity Development

Identity development is an important influence on well-being. Specifically, identity achievement and identity moratorium are both associated with positive functioning, an adaptive, mature sense of self, prosocial behavior, and the capacity for romantic attachments among high school students (Berman, Weems, Rodriguez, & Zamora, 2006). Identity achievement is also associated with high self-esteem, feelings of control, high moral reasoning, and positive views of work and school (Adams & Marshall, 1996; Kroger, 2000). In contrast, the moratorium status is associated with anxiety (Lillevoll, Kroger, & Martinussen, 2013). Young people in the moratorium status often feel puzzled by the multiple choices before them and are driven to make decisions and solve problems by using an active information-gathering style characterized by seeking, evaluating, and reflecting on information to determine their views and make decisions (Luyckx et al., 2008). Some adolescents, however, become extremely overwhelmed and anxious, which may be paralyzing and prevent identity exploration (Crocetti, Klimstra, Keijsers, Hale, & Meeus, 2009).

As noted, foreclosed and diffused identity status become less common with age, especially after 19. Foreclosure and diffusion are associated with passivity and, in late adolescence, maladaptive long-term outcomes (Archer & Waterman, 1990; Berzonsky & Kuk, 2000). Young people who show identity foreclosure have adopted an identity, often prescribed by others, without evaluation. Young people classified as identity foreclosed choose an identity without considering its implications or evaluating other options. They tend to take a rigid and inflexible stance, avoid reflecting on their identity choice, and reject information that may contradict their position (Kroger, 2007b). Individuals who display the identity-foreclosed status are not open to new experiences or considering new ways of thinking. For example, a 14-year-old adolescent in a family of doctors who has not considered any careers and comes to the decision, after prodding by her parents and grandparents, that she wants to be a doctor may be in the identity-foreclosed status. Foreclosure is common in early adolescence.

The identity-diffused status is the least mature form of identity. While it is developmentally appropriate for early adolescents to have neither explored nor committed to a sense of identity, by late adolescence identity diffusion is uncommon and has been considered indicative of maladjustment (Kroger et al., 2010). Young people who show identity diffusion tend to use a cognitive style that is characterized by avoidance; rather than dealing with personal problems and making decisions, their choices are dictated by situational pressures, not reflection. Identity-diffused individuals tend to not make independent decisions; they call upon fate, follow others, or let issues decide themselves. Academic difficulties, organization and time management problems, general apathy, and alcohol and substance abuse are associated with identity diffusion. "Bryan's again on academic probation, and it looks like he'll be expelled from the dormitory after the resident assistant found drugs in his room. And he doesn't seem to care. I just don't get it," exclaims Bryan's academic advisor. Behavior problems both precede and accompany identity diffusion. Longitudinal research suggests that behavior problems in early adolescence predict identity diffusion in late adolescence (Crocetti, Klimstra, Hale, Koot, & Meeus, 2013).

Although the task of forming an identity is first encountered during adolescence, identity development is an important task among college-age youth and remains a lifelong process for all individuals (Côté, 2006; Kroger, 2007a). Changes within the person and his or her context, such as graduating from college, changing careers, getting married, and having children, provide opportunities to reflect upon, organize, and reorganize identity.

Ethnic Identity

An important aspect of identity, especially for ethnic minority adolescents, is **ethnic identity,** or a sense of membership to an ethnic group including the attitudes, values, and culture associated with that group (Phinney, 2000; Phinney & Ong, 2007). Like other components of a sense of self, ethnic identity develops and changes over time as individuals explore, gain experience, and make choices in various contexts. Adolescents explore their ethnic identity by learning about the cultural practices associated with their ethnicity by reading, attending cultural events, and talking to members of their culture (Quintana, 2007; Romero, Edwards, Fryberg, & Orduña, 2014; Wakefield & Hudley, 2007). After developing a sense of belonging, young people may become committed to an ethnic identity. A strong sense of ethnic identity helps young people to reject negative views of their culture that are based on stereotypes (Rivas-Drake et al., 2014). For example, one study found that feelings of affirmation and belonging to ethnic heritage predicted positive psychological adjustment in Navajo youth (Jones & Galliher, 2007).

Ethnic minority adolescents often face challenges to the development of identity. With cognitive advances, adolescents can consider themselves and their worlds in more complicated ways—and become better at taking other people's perspectives. Many ethnic minority adolescents also become sensitive to negative feedback, discrimination, and inequality from the majority group. Many adolescents find it difficult to develop a feeling of cultural belonging and personal goals, especially when the standards of the larger society are different from those of the culture of origin, such as the differing emphases of collectivism and individualism. Collectivist cultures stress commitment to family, although the emphasis on family obligations often lessens the longer the family has been living in an emigrant country that emphasizes individualism (Phinney, 2000). Sometimes adolescents are restricted from participating in the larger culture out of parental fear that assimilation will undermine cultural values. One study of Vietnamese adolescent living in an ethnic enclave in southern California found that most felt that their parents encouraged them to embrace their heritage, make friends, and engage in activities within the community rather than the larger school and neighborhood community (Vo-Jutabha, Dinh, McHale, & Valsiner, 2009). As one boy explained, "My parents expect me to speak Vietnamese consistently. Every now and then they just say that I forgot it and that I don't know how to speak it anymore. . . . Of course, I understand it and my parents expect me to be in a Viet Club or something. But I mean c'mon, really c'mon" (Vo-Jutabha et al., 2009, pp. 683–684). Another girl adds, "I think living in the Asian community kinda stops me from branching out. I live in this area and all of my friends are mostly Asian and I want to have other friends" (Vo-Jutabha et al., 2009, p. 680). Adolescents who perceive excessive parental pressure and restrictions might respond with rebellion and rejection of ethnic heritage.

Discrimination against particular ethnic groups can make it difficult for youth to form a positive sense of identity. Adolescents from a variety of racial and ethnic groups, both native born and immigrant, report experiences of discrimination which are associated with lower self-esteem, depression, lower social competence behavior problems, and distress (Mrick & Mrtorell, 2011; Rivas-Drake et al., 2014; Wakefield & Hudley, 2007). For example, a study of Mexican American youth demonstrated that those who perceived and experienced more discrimination were less likely to explore their ethnicity, feel good about it, and incorporate a sense of ethnic identity (Romero & Roberts, 2003). Some ethnic minority adolescents perceive discrimination in the classroom, such as feeling like their teachers called on them less, graded them more harshly, or disciplined them more punitively. African American adolescents who face racial discrimination from teachers and peers at school show declines in grades, academic self-concept, mental health (anger, depression, self-esteem, and psychological resilience), school engagement, and ethnic identity (Dotterer, McHale, & Crouter, 2009; Wong, Eccles, & Sameroff, 2003). Likewise, in a study of Navajo 9th- and 10th-grade adolescents, those who perceived discrimination showed poorer psychosocial adjustment and higher levels of substance use over a one-year period (Galliher, Jones, & Dahl, 2011). Adolescents often must manage confusing messages to embrace their heritage while confronting discrimination, making the path to exploring and achieving ethnic identity challenging and painful for many

Adolescents explore their ethnic identity by learning about cultural practices, such as cooking. A strong sense of ethnic identity predicts healthy adjustment.

Paul Chesley/natgeo/Corbis

adolescents, leading many to remain diffused or foreclosed (Markstrom-Adams & Adams, 1995).

What fosters ethnic identity development? The exploration and commitment process key to identity achievement also underlies establishing a sense of ethnic identity (Yip, 2014). Parents can help adolescents withstand discrimination and contradictory messages and develop a positive ethnic identity by encouraging them to act prosocially and disprove stereotypes of low academic achievement or problem behavior (Phinney & Chavira, 1995; Rivas-Drake et al., 2014; Umaña-Taylor, Alfaro, Bámaca, & Guimond, 2009). Adolescents who learn about their culture, such as values, attitudes, language, and traditions, and regularly interact with parents and peers within their culture, are more likely to construct a favorable ethnic identity (Phinney, Romero, Nava, & Huang, 2001; Romero et al., 2014; Umaña-Taylor, Bhanot, & Shin, 2006). For example, ethnic identity is positively associated with an adolescent's proficiency in speaking his or her heritage language (Oh & Fuligni, 2010).

Similar to other aspects of development, perception matters. It is adolescents' perception of their ethnic socialization—their view of the degree to which they adopt the customs and values of their culture—that predicts ethnic identity rather than simply their parents' views (Hughes, Hagelskamp, Way, & Foust, 2009). Likewise, among African American adolescents, high levels of peer acceptance and popularity among African American peers and associated with a strong sense of ethnic identity (Rivas-Drake et al., 2014; Rock, Cole, Houshyar, Lythcott, & Prinstein, 2011). Adolescents' perceptions of their ethnicity and ethnic groups are influenced by multiple layers of a dynamic ecological system, including families, schools, and peers, as well as the political social and economic climate (Way, Santos, Niwa, & Kim-Gervey, 2008).

Adolescents who have achieved a positive sense of ethnic identity tend to have higher self-esteem, optimism, and a more positive view of their ethnicity (Carlson, Uppal, & Prosser, 2000; Galliher et al., 2011). A strong positive sense of ethnic identity reduces the magnitude of the negative effects of racial discrimination on academic self-concept, academic achievement, and problem behaviors among African American adolescents, as well as acts as a buffer to stress, including discrimination stress (Kiang, Gonzales-Backen, Yip, Witkow, & Fuligni, 2006; Romero et al., 2014; Seaton, 2009). Adolescents with a strong sense of ethnic identity tend to show better adjustment and coping skills and fewer emotional and behavior problems than do those who do not or only weakly identify with ethnicity (Chavous et al., 2003; Kerpelman, Eryigit, & Stephens, 2008; Mrick & Mrtorell, 2011). Ethnic identity is an important contributor to well-being and is associated with school achievement in adolescents from diverse ethnicities, such as Mexican, Chinese, Latino, African

American, and European backgrounds (Adelabu, 2008; Fuligni, Witkow, & Garcia, 2005).

Thinking in Context 12.1

1. An important theme of development is that domains or types of development interact and influence each other. How might this hold true for the development of a sense of self and identity? How might other areas of development influence how adolescents view themselves? For example, consider aspects of physical development, such as puberty, and cognitive development, such as reasoning.

2. Identify contextual influences on the development of a sense of self and identity. In what ways do interactions with contextual influences, such as parents, peers, school, community, and societal forces, shape adolescents' emerging sense of self?

ADOLESCENTS AND THEIR FAMILIES

Adolescence marks a change in parent–child relationships. As they advance cognitively and develop a more complicated sense of self, adolescents strive for autonomy, the ability to make and carry out their own decisions, and they rely on parents less (Steinberg & Silverberg, 1986). Physically, adolescents appear more mature. They also can demonstrate better self-understanding and more rational decision making and problem solving, creating a foundation for parents to treat adolescents less like children and grant them more decision-making responsibility. The parenting challenge of adolescence is to offer opportunities for adolescents to develop and practice autonomy while providing protection from danger and the consequences of poor decisions. Parents may doubt their own importance to their adolescent children, but a large body of research shows that parents play a critical role in adolescent development alongside that of peers (Steinberg, 2001; Wang, Peterson, Morphey, & Aimin, 2007).

PARENT-ADOLESCENT CONFLICT

Julio's mother orders, "Clean your room." "It's my room. I can have it my way!" Julio snaps back. This exchange between Julio and his mother reflects the type of conflict that is common during adolescence. Conflict between parents and adolescents rises in early adolescence and peaks in middle adolescence (Steinberg & Morris, 2001). Changing views of parents coupled with new capacities to reason and debate contribute to the rise in parent–child conflict in early adolescence. Adolescents begin to see their parents as people, fallible and subject to good and bad decisions, and adolescents thereby feel justified in arguing for their own autonomy (Steinberg & Silverberg, 1986).

Conflict is a normal part of adolescent–parent relationships, but the majority of adolescents and parents continue to have warm, close, communicative relationships. Most adolescents report feeling close to, and loved by, their parents, and respecting their parents (Steinberg, 2001). Parent–adolescent conflict generally takes the form of bickering over mundane matters—small arguments over the details of life, such as household responsibilities, privileges and relationships, including curfew, cleaning a room, choices of media, or music volume (Smetana, 2002; Van Doorn, Branje, & Meeus, 2011). Conflicts over religious, political, or social issues occur less frequently, as do conflicts concerning other potentially sensitive topics (e.g., substance use, dating, sexual relationships; Renk, Liljequist, Simpson, & Phares, 2005; Riesch et al., 2000).

Over the course of a typical day, adolescents report three or four conflicts or disagreements with parents, but they also report one or two conflicts with friends (Adams & Laursen, 2007). Conflict tends to be higher in homes with early-maturing girls and tends to be focused on mothers more than fathers (Caspi, Lynam, Moffitt, & Silva, 1993). Conflicts are common in early and middle adolescence and indicate adolescents' desire for increased autonomy and independence from their parents (Renk et al., 2005). Conflicts tend to decline in late adolescence, as adolescents establish autonomy from parents. One study examined adolescents and their parents over a four-year period from ages 13 to 17 and found that both parents and adolescents used conflict resolution and other positive ways of interacting and solving conflicts over time

Although parent–adolescent conflict is a natural part of development, relationships that are very high in conflict and low in acceptance are harmful to adolescent development (Demo & Acock, 1996). Moreover, in most cases of severe conflict the parent–child relationship difficulties began in childhood. One longitudinal study of parent–child conflict found that mothers' anger in conflict reactions with their 13-year-old sons predicted boys' internalizing problems two years later (Hofer et al., 2013). Severe parent–adolescent conflict is associated with internalizing problems, such as depression, externalizing problems such as aggression and delinquency, social problems, such as social withdrawal and poor conflict resolution with peers, poor school achievement, and among girls, early sexual activity (Adams & Laursen, 2007; Castellani et al., 2014; Eichelsheim et al., 2010). Fortunately, intense conflict is not the norm. One study found that conflict-filled relationships and chronic escalating conflict occurred in less than 10% of families surveyed (Collins & Laursen, 2004). Healthy parent–adolescent relationships are characterized by warmth and emotional attachments with parents in which adolescents seek and receive guidance from parents and parents provide developmentally appropriate freedom and decision-making ability (Steinberg, 2001).

Conflict exists in these relationships, but conflict is coupled with acceptance, respect, and autonomy support.

PARENTING STYLE AND MONITORING

Parenting plays a large role in the development of autonomy during adolescence. As Romana explains, "My parents have rules. I hate some of those rules. But I know that my parents will always be there for me. If I needed to, I could tell them anything. They might be mad, but they'll always help me." Romana describes the most positive form of parenting, authoritative parenting. Recall from Chapter 8 that authoritative parenting is characterized by warmth, support, and limits. Across ethnic and socioeconomic groups, and in countries around the world, multiple studies have found that authoritative parenting fosters autonomy, self-reliance, self-esteem, a positive view of the value of work, and academic competence in adolescents (Mayseless, Scharf, & Sholt, 2003; McKinney & Renk, 2011; Uji, Sakamoto, Adachi, & Kitamura, 2013; Vazsonyi, Hibbert, & Blake Snider, 2003). Parental support and acceptance, as characterized by authoritative parenting, are associated with reduced levels of depression, psychological disorders, and behavior problems (Hair, Moore, Garrett, Ling, & Cleveland, 2008). Authoritative parents' use of open discussion, joint decision-making, and firm but fair limit-setting helps adolescents feel valued, respected, and encouraged to think for themselves (Dornbusch, Ritter, Mont-Reynaud, & Chen, 1990; Spera, 2005). Parents in a given household often share a common parenting style, but when they do not, the presence of authoritative parenting in at least one parent buffers the negative outcomes associated with the other style and predicts positive adjustment (Hoeve, Dubas, Gerris, van der Laan, & Smeenk, 2011; McKinney & Renk, 2011; Simons & Conger, 2007).

In contrast, authoritarian parenting, which emphasizes control and punishment (e.g., "my way or the highway") is much less successful in promoting healthy adjustment. The authoritarian parenting style, particularly the use of psychological control, inhibits the development of autonomy and has been found to be linked with low self-esteem, depression, low academic competence, and antisocial behavior in adolescence through early adulthood in young people from Africa, Asia, Europe, the Middle East, and the Americas (Ang, 2006; Barber, Stolz, & Olsen, 2005; Griffith & Grolnick, 2013; Lansford, Laird, Pettit, Bates, & Dodge, 2014; Uji et al., 2013). Similar to findings with young children, as discussed in Chapter 8, a permissive or lax parenting style has been found to interfere with the development of self-regulatory skills that are needed to develop academic and behavioral competence (Fletcher, Darling, Steinberg, & Dornbusch, 1995; Maccoby, 2000). In other words, adolescents reared in permissive homes are more likely to show immaturity, have difficulty with self-control, and are more likely to conform to peers (Hoeve et al., 2011; Milevsky et al., 2007).

Parenting is also influenced by culture. Although many studies have shown that authoritarian parenting is associated with negative outcomes in teens reared in Western cultures, studies with adolescents reared in non-Western and collectivist cultures have shown few negative outcomes of authoritarian parenting (Dwairy & Menshar, 2006; Peterson & Bush, 2013). Non-Western cultures tend to be more collectivist, placing less emphasis on autonomy and identity and more on dependence and connection to family—characteristics that are consistent with authoritarian parenting. For example, research with Chinese, Turkish, and Arab adolescents reared in collectivist cultures has found that authoritarian parenting does not predict negative outcomes, likely because authoritarian parenting is well matched to collectivist cultures' valuing of interconnections over independence (Dwairy & Menshar, 2006). Research with Indonesian adolescents revealed that, as expected, authoritative parenting was associated with the most positive outcomes, but authoritarian parenting was not associated with either negative or positive outcomes (Abubakar, Van de Vijver, Suryani, Handayani, & Pandia, 2014). Indeed, some argue that it is inconsistency between the authoritarian parenting style and the culture that produces negative outcomes in Western cultures (Dwairy & Menshar, 2006).

Parent–child relationships develop within the context of routine family activities (Hair et al., 2008). The presence of family rituals promotes adolescents' sense of identity, self-esteem, and family cohesion as well as helps family members weather difficult times (Steinberg & Morris, 2001). Parents who encourage more regular family activities and know more about their children's friends and teachers tend to have children who are less prone to substance use through middle adolescence (Coley, Votruba-Drzal, & Schindler, 2008).

Parental monitoring, in which parents aware of their teens' whereabouts and companions, is associated with academic achievement, overall well-being, and reduced sexual activity; it has also been found to deter delinquent activity and substance use in youth of all ethnicities (Huang, Murphy, & Hser, 2011; Kiesner, Poulin, & Dishion, 2010; Racz & McMahon, 2011; Wang et al., 2014). Effective parental monitoring is accompanied by warmth and is balanced with respecting autonomy and privacy (Stattin & Kerr, 2000). On the other hand, when adolescents feel that their parents are intrusive, they are more likely to conceal their activities concurrently and over time (Rote & Smetana, 2015). Adolescents' views of the warmth and control provided by their parents is linked with their psychological adjustment, including conduct, emotional symptoms, and peer relations (Maynard & Harding, 2010). What is considered to be effective parental monitoring changes as adolescents grow older. From middle to late adolescence, parental knowledge declines as adolescents establish a private sphere and disclose less as parents exert less control (Masche, 2010; Wang, Dishion, Stormshak, & Willett, 2011).

Overall, parenting entails a delicate balance of warmth and support, monitoring, and limit-setting and enforcement—no easy task indeed.

Thinking in Context 12.2

1. In what ways might physical and cognitive development influence adolescents' interactions with their parents and, especially, parent–adolescent conflict?

2. Compare and contrast popular views of how parents should interact with their adolescent children with the research on parenting style and parental monitoring.

ADOLESCENTS AND THEIR PEERS

The most easily recognizable influence on adolescents—and that which gets the most attention from adults and the media—is the peer group. Beginning in early adolescence, the amount of time young people spend with parents declines as time spent with friends—often unsupervised—increases (Larson, 2001). Each week, adolescents spend up to one third of their waking, nonschool hours with friends (Hartup & Stevens, 1997).

After spending the school day with same-age peers, adolescents also spend most of their time out of school with friends. When relations with family are poor, adolescents often turn to friends for emotional support. Close relationships with friends can ease some of the negative effects of poor relationships with parents (Way & Greene, 2006).

FRIENDSHIPS

The typical adolescent has four to six close friends (Hartup & Stevens, 1999). The quality of friendships tends to improve with age (Poulin & Chan, 2010). With advances

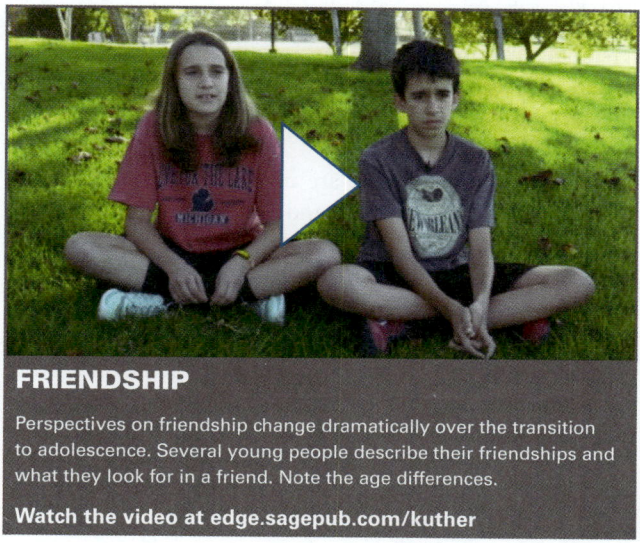

FRIENDSHIP

Perspectives on friendship change dramatically over the transition to adolescence. Several young people describe their friendships and what they look for in a friend. Note the age differences.

Watch the video at edge.sagepub.com/kuther

in cognition, adolescents view their social world in more sophisticated ways and develop more complex understandings of friendship (Buhrmester, 1996). Adolescent friendships are characterized by intimacy, self-disclosure, and trust (Bauminger, Finzi-Dottan, Chason, & Har-Even, 2008). Adolescents also expect loyalty from their friends. They expect their friends to be there for them, stand up for them, and not share their secrets or harm them. Adolescent friendships tend to include cooperation, sharing, and affirmation, which reflect their emerging capacities for perspective taking, social sensitivity, empathy, and social skills. Intimacy also increases over the course of adolescence as teens become better able to find mutually supportive and validating friendships and as they explore and achieve their own identities (Way et al., 2008).

Although both boys' and girls' friendships become more complex, girls' friendships tend to include a greater level of emotional closeness than do boys' (Markovits, Benenson, & Dolenszky, 2001). Boys get together for activities, usually sports and competitive games, and tend to be more social and vocal in groups as compared with one-on-one situations. In contrast, most girls tend to prefer one-on-one interactions over group situations and often spend their time together talking, sharing thoughts and feelings, and supporting each other (Benenson & Heath, 2006). The challenge for many adolescents is that close friendships entail a great deal of sharing, which, in the presence of conflict, can fuel relational aggression. Relational aggression, such as when a friend tells another's secrets or teases about sensitive topics, is especially common among girls and associated with more extreme negative moods in girls and increases in aggression in both girls and boys (Low, Polanin, & Espelage, 2013; Monahan & Booth-LaForce, 2015; Rusby, Westling, Crowley, & Light, 2013). However, relational aggression between best friends, such as aggressive discussions, is not always associated with maladaptive outcomes. In one longitudinal study, relational aggression among some best friend dyads was associated with higher ratings of perceived friendship quality six months later (Banny, Heilbron, Ames, & Prinstein, 2011). Adolescent friendships are complex. The intimacy that makes close friendships possible can also make adolescents feel more comfortable asserting themselves in aggressive ways.

Among early adolescents it is estimated that one third to one half of friendships are unstable, with young people regularly losing friends and making new friendships (Poulin & Chan, 2010). Early adolescent friendship instability is influenced by the many biological, cognitive, and social transitions that young people make, as well as by school transitions, which are associated with social and emotional changes, as was discussed in Chapter 11. After early adolescence, young people may retain up to 75% of their friendships over a school year (Poulin & Chan, 2010). Overall, girls' friendships tend to be shorter in duration but characterized by more closeness than are boys' (Benenson & Christakos, 2003). High-quality friendships characterized by

David Grossman/Alamy

Adolescents benefit from friendships with peers of different ethnicities. Cross-ethnic friendships are associated self-esteem, well-being, and less victimization. Why are friendships with diverse peers so beneficial?

sharing, intimacy, and open communication tend to endure over time (Hiatt, Laursen, Mooney, & Rubin, 2015). Other-sex friendships become more common in adolescence than they were in middle childhood, increasing gradually in early adolescence and continuing through high school (Poulin & Pedersen, 2007).

Similarity characterizes adolescent friendships. Friends tend to be similar in demographics, such as age, ethnicity, and socioeconomic status; they also tend to share psychological and developmental characteristics (Berndt & Murphy, 2002). Close friends tend to be similar in orientation toward risky activity, such as willingness to try drugs and engage in dangerous behaviors such as unprotected sex (Henry, Schoeny, Deptula, & Slavick, 2007; Osgood et al., 2013; Scalco, Trucco, Coffman, & Colder, 2015). For example, best friends are highly similar with one another in the onset and level of delinquent activity (Selfhout, Branje, & Meeus, 2008) and relational aggression (Dijkstra, Berger, & Lindenberg, 2011). Best friends also show similar rates of depression (Giletta et al., 2011) and body dissatisfaction (Rayner, Schniering, Rapee, Taylor, & Hutchinson, 2013). Adolescent friends tend to share interests, such as tastes in music; they are also similar in academic achievement, educational aspirations, and political beliefs; and they show similar trends in psychosocial development, such as identity status (Selfhout, Branje, ter Bogt, & Meeus, 2009; Shin & Ryan, 2014). Friends tend to select friends who are similar to themselves, but over time and through interaction, friends tend to become more similar to each other (Berndt & Murphy, 2002; Nurmi, 2004; Scalco et al., 2015).

Sometimes, however, middle and older adolescents choose friends who have different attitudes and values, which encourages them to consider new perspectives. Cross-ethnic friendships, for example, are less common than same-ethnic friendships, but are associated with unique benefits. Adolescent members of cross-ethnic friendships show decreases in racial prejudice over time

(Titzmann, Brenick, & Silbereisen, 2015). Ethnic minority adolescents with cross-ethnic friends perceive less discrimination, vulnerability, and relational victimization and show higher rates of self esteem and well-being over time (Bagci, Rutland, Kumashiro, Smith, & Blumberg, 2014; Graham, Munniksma, & Juvonen, 2014; Kawabata & Crick, 2011)

Close and stable friendships aid adolescent adjustment (Bukowski, 2001; Kingery, Erdley, & Marshall, 2011). Close friendships help adolescents explore and learn about themselves. By communicating with others and forming mutually self-disclosing supportive relationships, adolescents develop perspective taking, empathy, self-concept, and a sense of identity. Friends who are supportive and empathetic encourage prosocial behavior, promote psychological health, reduce the risk of delinquency, and help adolescents manage stress, such as the challenges of school transitions (Hiatt et al., 2015; Waldrip, Malcolm, & Jensen-Campbell, 2008; Wentzel, 2014).

CLIQUES AND CROWDS

Each day after school, Paul, Manny, and Jose go with Pete to Pete's house where they apply what they learn in their automotive class to work on each other's cars and, together, restore a classic car. During adolescence, one-on-one friendships tend to expand into tightly knit peer groups of anywhere from three to about eight but most commonly around five members who are close friends. These close-knit friendship-based groups are known as **cliques**. Paul, Manny, Jose, and Pete have formed a clique. Like most close friends, members of cliques tend to share similarities such as demographics and attitudes (Lansford et al., 2009). The norms of expected behavior and values that govern cliques derive from interactions among the group members. For example, a norm of spending time exercising together and snacking afterward as well as valuing health and avoiding smoking, alcohol, and drugs may emerge in a clique whose members are athletes. Belonging to a peer group provides adolescents with a sense of inclusion, worth, support, and companionship (Lansford et al., 2009).

Both boys and girls form cliques (Gest, Davidson, Rulison, Moody, & Welsh, 2007). In early adolescence, cliques tend to be sex segregated, with some composed of boys and others composed of girls. Girls' groups tend to be smaller than boys' groups, but both are similarly tight knit (Gest et al., 2007). By mid-adolescence, cliques become mixed and form the basis for dating. A mixed-sex group of friends provides opportunities for adolescents to learn how to interact with others of the opposite sex in a safe, nonromantic context (Connolly, Craig, Goldberg, & Pepler, 2004). By late adolescence, especially with high school graduation, mixed-sex cliques tend to split up as adolescents enter college, the workforce, and other post–high school activities (Connolly & Craig, 1999).

In contrast with cliques, which are based on intimate friendships, **crowds** are larger and looser groups based on shared characteristics, interests, and reputation. Rather than voluntarily "joining," adolescents are sorted into crowds by their peers. Common categories of peer groups found in Western nations include populars/elites (who are high in social status), athletes/jocks (who are athletically oriented), academics/brains (who are academically oriented), and partiers (who are highly social and care little about academics); other types of crowds include nonconformists (who like unconventional dress and music), deviants (who are defiant and engage in delinquent activity), and normals (who are not clearly distinct on any particular trait; Delsing, ter Bogt, Engels, & Meeus, 2007; Kinney, 1999; Stone & Brown, 1999; Sussman, Pokhrel, Ashmore, & Brown, 2007; Verkooijen, de Vries, & Nielsen, 2007).

Crowd membership is based on an adolescent's image or reputation among peers (Brown, Bank, & Steinberg, 2008; Cross & Fletcher, 2009). Members of a crowd may or may not interact with one another; however, because of similarities in appearance, activities, and perceived attitudes, they are perceived by their peers as members of the same group (Verkooijen et al., 2007). Crowds and group affiliations are crucial components of identity development because they demarcate values and lifestyles that can form the core of an individual's identity. Crowds differentiate young people on behaviors such as alcohol substance, sexual activity, academic achievement, psychiatric symptoms, and health risks. Crowds also differ on social characteristics such as social acceptance or popularity among peers, exposure to peer pressure, and the qualities or features of friendships (Brown et al., 2008; Cross & Fletcher, 2009). Crowd membership often predicts later adolescent behavior. Across a broad range of research studies, for example, adolescents within the peer classification category of deviants tend to report greater participation in drug use and other problem behaviors, longitudinally, whereas members of the academic and athlete crowds exhibit the least participation in these problem behaviors (Sussman et al., 2007). In middle adolescence, as cognitive and classification capacities increase, adolescents begin to classify their peers in more complex ways and hybrid crowds emerge, such as *popular-jocks* and *partier-jocks*. In late adolescence, and with high school graduation, crowds decline.

Some adolescents may use a particular crowd as a reference group and model their behavior and appearance accordingly, but adolescents do not always accurately perceive their own crowd status (Verkooijen et al., 2007). In one study, about one half of students placed themselves in a crowd different than that assigned by peers—generally most tended to label themselves as *normals* or as not having a crowd. Only about 20% of adolescents classified in the low-status crowds, such as *brains*, agreed with their peers on their crowd status (Brown et al., 2008). Adolescents who did not perceive themselves as part of a low-status crowd showed higher self-esteem than did adolescents who agreed with their crowd placement.

Similar to cliques, crowds tend to be apparent in high school settings. The importance of crowd affiliation declines with age, after leaving high school, and especially as young people adopt stable identities (Delsing et al., 2007). For more on affiliation and popularity, see Applying Developmental Science (p. 336).

APPLYING DEVELOPMENTAL SCIENCE

Popularity

Popular children, those who receive many peer nominations of likability and therefore experience high levels of peer acceptance, have a variety of positive characteristics, such as cooperativeness and social competence. In adolescence, popularity becomes more complicated and can be defined in more than one way. In addition to peer acceptance, in adolescence, **perceived popularity** becomes important. Perceived popularity refers to peer ratings of an adolescent's social status—that is, social dominance, influence, and prestige in the peer group (Parkhurst & Hopmeyer, 1998). Whereas adolescents who score high in peer acceptance are prosocial and low in aggression, perceived popular teens demonstrate both positive and negative qualities. Perceived popular adolescents are often viewed as powerful, arrogant, exclusionary, elitist, manipulative, controlling, and aggressive. They show behaviors of social dominance and prestige and are judged by their peers as more attractive than other peers. They are trendsetters, show high self-esteem, dress well, know how to use their social skills, and are socially visible (De Bruyn & Van den Boom, 2005). Perceived popular adolescents tend to engage in highly visible and prestigious activities like athletics and cheerleading (de Bruyn & Cillessen, 2006, 2008). Perceived popular adolescents can be some of the most aggressive members of the peer group—engaging in overt and relational bullying and aggression—and these aggressive acts actually positively predict perceived popularity (Robertson et al., 2010; Rose & Swenson, 2009). Perceived popularity is linked with risk behaviors in high school including alcohol use and sexual activity (Choukas-Bradley, Giletta, Neblett, & Prinstein, 2015; Mathys, Burk, & Cillessen, 2013).

Perceived popularity overlaps with peer nominations of likability in elementary school, but the two become less related over time, especially among girls. Relational aggression is positively related to perceived popularity but negatively related with peer nominations of likability (Cillessen & Borch, 2006;

De Bruyn, Cillessen, & Wissink, 2009). For example, girls' perceived popularity in Grade 10 predicted lower ratings of peer likability at Grade 12, as peers saw them as mean and aggressive—yet the perceived popular girls continued to engage in more aggression (Mayeux & Cillessen, 2008). It seems that for perceived popular teens, relational aggression has few repercussions (Rose & Swenson, 2009).

Teens' perceptions of their own social status predict long-term functioning so that even teens who are not broadly popular may demonstrate positive adjustment over time if they maintain a positive internal sense of their social acceptance (McElhaney, Antonishak, & Allen, 2008). Perceptions of popularity and peer acceptance are at least as critical in determining future social outcomes as is actually being liked by other teens. For example, 13- and 14-year-olds who saw themselves as socially accepted showed positive adjustment regardless of their level of popularity, and even unpopular teens became less hostile and more desirable companions when they believed that they were accepted by peers (McElhaney et al., 2008). Adolescents who feel successful will seek out social experiences and those who think they have difficulty with peers are likely to withdraw.

What Do You Think?

1. **Can you identify popular peers from middle school and high school? Describe them. What are their characteristics?**

2. **Can you distinguish between popular students and perceived popular students?**

3. **How do your experiences compare with these research findings?**

PEER CONFORMITY

"Look at these shoes. They're red. Cool, huh?" asks Jamaica's mother. "No—I want the black ones," Jamaica replies. "But honey, these are so different from what everyone else has, you'll really stand out." Jamaica shakes her head. "I don't want to stand out. The shoes need to be black. That's what everyone wears." Jamaica's insistence on wearing the black shoes that all of her friends own illustrates her desire to conform to peer norms about dressing. The pressure to conform to peers rises in early adolescence, peaks at about age 14 and declines through age 18 and after (see Figure 12.1; Berndt & Murphy, 2002; Steinberg & Monahan, 2007).

Most adults view peer pressure as a negative influence on adolescents, as pressure to behave in socially undesirable and even harmful ways. In fact, though, American youths tend to feel the greatest pressure from peers to conform to day-to-day

activities and personal choices such as appearance (clothing, hairstyle, makeup) and music (Brown, Lohr, & McClenahan, 1986; Steinberg, 2001). In laboratory experiments, adolescents were more likely to show prosocial behavior after believing that anonymous peers approve of their prosocial actions, such as sharing coins with others (van Hoorn, van Dijk, Meuwese, Rieffe, & Crone, 2014). Youths also report pressure from their friends to engage in prosocial and positive behaviors such as getting good grades, performing well athletically, getting along with parents, and avoiding smoking (Berndt & Murphy, 2002; Brown et al., 1986; Brown et al., 2008; Wentzel, 2014). For example, research with youths from Singapore demonstrates that peers exerted more pressure on one another to conform to family and academic responsibilities, values that are particularly prized in Singapore culture (Sim & Koh, 2003).

Nevertheless, peers do pressure one another to engage in risky activities and adopt an antisocial stance. Peer smoking predicts the initiation and escalation of smoking in adolescents (Bricker et al., 2006; Hoffman, Monge, Chou, & Valente, 2007). Similarly, adolescents' reports of unsafe sex are associated with their peers' sexual behavior (Choukas-Bradley, Giletta, Widman, Cohen, & Prinstein, 2014; Henry et al., 2007; van de Bongardt, Reitz, Sandfort, & Deković, 2014). Adolescents often show more deviant behavior as a group than as individuals, as teens may socialize and encourage one another to engage in activities that they would not consider alone, such as vandalizing property (Dishion, Andrews, & Crosby, 1995). It is not simply peer behavior that influences adolescent behavior, but it is adolescents' perceptions of peer behavior, beliefs about peers' activity, that predict engaging in risky activities such as smoking, alcohol use, and marijuana use (Choukas-Bradley et al., 2014; Duan, Chou, Andreeva, & Pentz, 2009).

Young people vary in how they perceive and respond to peer pressure based on a variety of factors such as age, personal characteristics, and context. Adolescents are more vulnerable to the negative effects of peer pressure during transitions, such as entering a new school and undergoing puberty, which are common in early adolescence (Brechwald & Prinstein, 2011; Bukowski, Sippola, Hoza, & Newcomb, 2000). A particular type of negative peer pressure, **cyberbullying**, is discussed in Lives in Context (p. 338).

As in other areas of adolescent development, the authoritative style of parenting, which provides support while setting limits, has been found to have positive outcomes. Adolescents with authoritative parents tend to respect them, adhere to rules, and seek advice from them, reducing teens' reliance on peers for advice (Sim, 2000). Adolescents tend to turn to peers when confronted with decisions about short-term choices such as lifestyle preferences, including hairstyles, clothing, musical tastes, and social activities (Wang et al., 2007). Parents, however, remain important influences

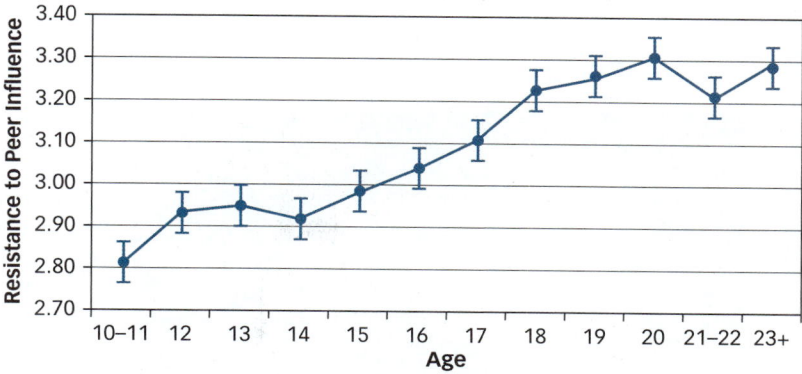

FIGURE 12.1: Age Differences in Resistance to Peer Influence

SOURCE: Obtained with permission from Steinberg and Monahan (2007, p. 1536).

on adolescents. Adolescents tend to turn to parents when making decisions with long-term future consequences, such as those regarding education and religion (Brechwald & Prinstein, 2011). Furthermore, parents tend to have more influence than peers on adolescents' long-term plans, values, and educational aspirations (Berndt & Murphy, 2002; Brown et al., 1986). Although peers' increase in importance and conformity to peers is strong in adolescence, most adolescents report feeling close to, loved by, and respected by their parents (Steinberg, 2001).

DATING

"Daryl and I are seeing each other," proclaimed 13-year-old Sharese. "Hmm. You only go out with groups of friends and are way too young to date," her mother thought to herself, but instead sighed, gave a quizzical look, and then asked, "Who's Daryl?" Establishing romantic relationships, *dating*, is part of the adolescent experience. Most young people have been involved in at least one romantic relationship by middle adolescence and by age 18 over 80% of young people have some dating experience (Carver, Joyner, & Udry, 2003). By late adolescence, the majority of adolescents are in an ongoing romantic relationship with one person (Collins & Steinberg, 2006; O'Sullivan, Cheng, Harris, & Brooks-Gunn, 2007).

Dating typically begins through the intermingling of mixed-sex peer groups, similar to that described by Sharese's mother, progresses to group dating, and then one-on-one dating and romantic relationships (Connolly et al., 2004; Connolly, Nguyen, Pepler, Craig, & Jiang, 2013; Furman, 2002). Adolescents with larger social networks and greater access to opposite-sex peers date more (Connolly & Furman, 2000). However, some research suggests that adolescents date outside of their friendship networks and that preexisting friendships are less likely to transform into romantic relationships (Kreager, Molloy, Moody, & Feinberg, 2015). Early relationships, from ages 12 to 14, tend to be brief, but by age 16 the average relationship continues for nearly two years (Carver et al., 2003).

Adolescents' beliefs about their peers' risky behavior predict their own behavior.

Cyberbullying

AP/Oliver Berg

Because adolescents can access the Internet at any time, there are few respites from cyberbullying.

Over the past decade, technology such as text messaging and the Internet has spawned a new form of bullying. Adolescents who engage in cyberbullying carry out aggressive acts against a victim by using electronic means such as text messaging, posting in chat rooms and discussion boards, and creating websites and blogs (Smith et al., 2008). Similar to traditional forms of bullying, the aggressive acts are intended to hurt the victim, are perceived as hurtful by the victim, and are conducted repeatedly against a victim who cannot easily defend himself or herself.

Several features of cyberbullying distinguish it from regular bullying. One is the difficulty of escape. Unlike school bullying, which generally ends at the end of the school day, cyberbullying is carried on 24/7. Cyberbullying can reach a reach large audience, increasing the potential for humiliation. In addition, cyberbullying is invisible. It does not occur face-to-face, making it difficult for victims to identify their attackers and easy for bullies to lack empathy for victims (Slonje & Smith, 2008). However, there is a large overlap between traditional and electronic bullying, with 85% of victims of cyberbullying also experiencing bullying at school and over 90% of cyberbullies engaging in bullying at school (Raskauskas & Stoltz, 2007). About two thirds of cyberbullying victims reported knowing their perpetrators, and most know the bully from school (Juvonen & Gross, 2008).

As Internet use has become a part of adolescents' everyday life, cyberbullying has become increasingly prevalent. Ninety-five percent of adolescents are online (Pew Research Center, 2015). Up to one quarter of adolescents engage in cyberbullying (Raskauskas & Stoltz, 2007; Slonje & Smith, 2008). Researchers estimate that between 5% and 20% of adolescents in the United States, United Kingdom, Canada, and Australia experience cyberbullying during a school year (Jones, Mitchell, & Finkelhor, 2013; Livingstone, Haddon, Görzig, & Ólafsson, 2011; Livingstone & Smith, 2014). For most adolescents, a cyberbullying episode lasts a couple of weeks, but about one third report cyberbullying that lasts over a month and in some cases a year or more (Smith et al., 2008).

Youngsters mostly react to cyberbullying by ignoring it; pretending to ignore it; and, often, bullying the bully (Dehue, Bolman, & Völlink, 2008). The majority of adolescents who experience cyberbullying do not tell adults, and only about one third report telling friends (Juvonen & Gross, 2008; Slonje & Smith, 2008). Cyberbullying has similar effects as traditional bullying, including distress, anxiety, depression, poor self-esteem, social withdrawal, and poor academic achievement (Juvonen & Graham, 2014; Mason, 2008; Wade & Beran, 2011). However, cyberbullying poses a unique threat to psychological health because it can occur 24 hours a day, not just at school. Because of this many adolescents feel hopeless and pessimistic about stopping cyberbullying, placing them at risk for suicide (Bauman, Toomey, & Walker, 2013). Cyberbullying has been linked with many cases of suicide, such as 13 year-old Megan Meier, who committed suicide after months of harassment on the social network Myspace.

School policies on bullying should include statements regarding cyberbullying. Anti-bullying strategies are also effective in reducing cyberbullying. Class-wide lessons in assertiveness, Internet safety, social skills, and strategies for standing up to bullies and cyberbullies as well as encouraging students to support each other, aids in improving class climate and reducing all forms of bullying (Mason, 2008). Education directed at parents and school personnel can increase their awareness of cyberbullying and help them learn how to assist adolescents who are victimized. Parental monitoring and restriction of Internet use serves as a protective factor against online harassment (Khurana, Bleakley, Jordan, & Romer, 2014). Monitoring can be challenging, however, given that about three quarters of adolescents access the Internet at least occasionally through a mobile device such as a cell phone or tablet, and 25% access the Internet nearly exclusively by cell phone, modes that may be challenging for parents to monitor (Madden, Lenhart, Duggan, Cortesi, & Gasser, 2013).

Cyberbullying often is hidden. By illuminating it, schools and parents can intervene effectively to reduce it and create a safe and supportive school climate.

What Do You Think?

1. What role do parents and schools have in cyberbullying?
2. From your perspective, how can they effect change?

Dating varies by culture. Youths in Western societies date earlier than those in Asian cultures. Similarly, Asian American adolescents begin dating later than African American, European American, and Latino adolescents in the United States (Regan, Durvasula, Howell, Ureño, & Rea, 2004).

Early adolescents date for fun and for popularity with peers. Often the purpose of dating is simply to have a relationship (Furman, 2002). As teens grow older, the reasons reported for dating change. In late adolescence, dating fulfills needs for intimacy, support, and affection in both boys and girls (Furman, 2002; Giordano, Longmore, & Manning, 2006). However, adolescents' capacity for romantic intimacy develops slowly and is influenced by the quality of their experiences with intimacy in friendships and their attachments to parents (Connolly & Furman, 2000; Furman, 2002; Scharf & Mayseless, 2008). Adolescents interact with their romantic partners in ways that are similar to their interactions with parents and peers (Collins, Welsh, & Furman, 2009; Furman & Shomaker, 2008). Through close friendships, adolescents learn to share of themselves, be sensitive to others' needs, and develop the capacity for intimacy. Adolescents also learn about relationships by observing their parents. For example, they may employ ineffective interactional strategies that they have observed, such as withdrawal, verbal aggression, negativity, and poor problem solving (Darling, Cohan, Burns, & Thompson, 2008).

In middle and late adolescence, dating is associated with positive self-concept, expectations for success in relationships, fewer feelings of alienation, and good health (Ciairano, Bonino, Kliewer, Miceli, & Jackson, 2006). Close romantic relationships provide opportunities to develop and practice sensitivity, cooperation, empathy, and social support as well as aid in identity development (Ciairano et al., 2006; Furman & Shaffer, 2003). Adolescents' behaviors, such as academic achievement, tend to be very similar to that of their romantic partners (Giordano, Phelps, Manning, & Longmore, 2008). Early dating, relative to peers, is associated with increases in alcohol and substance use, smoking delinquency, and low academic competence over the adolescent years as well as long-term depression, especially in early maturing girls (Connolly et al., 2013; Fidler, West, Jarvis, & Wardle, 2006; Furman & Collibee, 2014; Martin et al., 2007). Overall, romantic experiences in adolescence are continuous with romantic experiences in adulthood, suggesting that the construction of romantic relationships is an important developmental task for adolescents (Collins et al., 2009). Adolescents who date fewer partners and experience better quality dating relationships in middle adolescence tend to demonstrate smoother partner interactions and relationship processes in young adulthood (e.g., negotiating conflict, appropriate caregiving; Madsen & Collins, 2011).

Dating violence, the actual or threatened physical or sexual violence or psychological abuse directed toward a current or former boyfriend girlfriend or dating partner, is surprisingly prevalent during adolescence. Like adult domestic violence, adolescent dating violence occurs in youth of all socioeconomic, ethnic, and religious groups (Herrman, 2009). This behavior is discussed in Lives in Context (p. 340).

Thinking in Context 12.2

1. Researchers who study peer relationships in adolescence might argue that cliques get a bad rap because common lay views portray cliques as negative and harmful to adolescents. Compare the research on cliques with common views about cliques.

2. How might relationships with peers such as friends or dates vary by context? Consider an adolescent from an inner city neighborhood and another from an affluent suburban community. In what ways might their peer interactions and relationships be similar? Different? How might contextual factors influence adolescents' peer relationships?

ADOLESCENT SEXUALITY

An important dimension of socioemotional development during adolescence is sexual development, a task that entails integrating physical, cognitive, and social domains of functioning. Sexuality encompasses feelings about oneself, appraisals of the self, attitudes, and behaviors (McClelland & Tolman, 2014). With the hormonal changes of puberty, both boys and girls experience an increase in sex drive and sexual interest (Fortenberry, 2013). Social context influences how biological urges are channeled into behavior and adolescents' conceptions of sexuality.

SEXUAL ACTIVITY

Although researchers believe that sexual behaviors tend to progress from hand-holding to kissing, to touching through clothes and under clothes, to oral sex and intercourse, research on adolescent sexuality tends to focus on intercourse, leaving gaps in our knowledge about the range of sexual activity milestones young people experience (Diamond & Savin-Williams, 2009). Adolescents are about as likely to engage in oral sex as vaginal intercourse (Casey Copen, Chandra, & Martinez, 2012). The majority of one sample of over 12,000 adolescents initiated oral sex after experiencing first vaginal intercourse, with about one half initiating oral sex a year or more after the onset of vaginal sex (Haydon, Herring, Prinstein, & Halpern, 2012). Interestingly, oral sex did not appear to precede vaginal intercourse, suggesting that adolescents are not engaging in oral sex as a substitute for vaginal intercourse, contrary to popular beliefs. Overall, males and females are about as likely to indicate that they have received oral sex (47% and 42%, of 15- to 19-year-old males and females, respectively; Child Trends Data Bank, 2013).

Many adults are surprised to learn that the overall rate of sexual intercourse among U.S. high school students has declined from 54% in 1991 to 47% in 2013 (Kaiser Family Foundation, 2014). Overall, rates of sexual activity are similar internationally, with similar declines in recent years (Guttmacher Institute, 2014). About 30% of 16-year-olds have had sexual intercourse,

LIVES IN CONTEXT

Adolescent Dating Violence

Between 10% and 60% of high school students have been victimized by dating violence. Although the majority of cases are limited to psychological aggression, between 20% and 40% of adolescents report experiencing physical aggression in a dating relationship (Herrman, 2009; Raiford, Wingood, & DiClemente, 2007). The most serious dating violence—physical assault that results in serious wounds or violent sexual assault—is less frequent, with less than 2% of adolescents reporting these forms of dating violence (Wolitzky-Taylor et al., 2008).

Dating violence emerges in early adolescence, with the majority of victims experiencing their first victimization before age 15 (Leadbeater, Banister, Ellis, & Yeung, 2008). Both males and females perpetrate dating violence at roughly equal rates and within the context of relationships of mutual partner aggression in which both partners perpetrate and sustain the aggression (Sears, Sandra Byers, & Lisa Price, 2007; Williams, Connolly, Pepler, Laporte, & Craig, 2008). Girls are more likely to inflict psychological abuse and minor physical abuse (slapping, throwing objects, pinching), and boys are more likely to inflict physical abuse, including more severe types of physical abuse, such as punching, as well as sexual abuse, making girls more likely to suffer physical wounds than boys. Physical violence tends to occur alongside other problematic relationship dynamics and behaviors such as verbal conflict, jealousy, and accusations of "cheating" (Giordano, Soto, Manning, & Longmore, 2010).

Risk factors for engaging in dating violence include difficulty with anger management, poor interpersonal skills, early involvement with antisocial peers, a history of problematic relationships with parents and peers, exposure to family violence and community violence, and child maltreatment (Foshee et al., 2014, 2015; Vagi et al., 2013). Many of the risk factors for

experiencing dating victimization are also outcomes of dating violence, such as depression, anxiety, negative interactions with family and friends, unhealthy weight-control behaviors, sexually transmitted infections (STIs), poor life satisfaction, low self-esteem, substance use, and adolescent pregnancy (Exner-Cortens, Eckenrode, & Rothman, 2013; Niolon et al., 2015).

Adolescent dating violence is less likely to be reported than adult domestic violence. Only about 1 in 11 cases is reported to adults or authorities (Herrman, 2009). Common reasons for not reporting dating violence include fear of retaliation, ongoing emotional ties, denial, self-blame, hope that it will get better, and helplessness. In addition, about only one third of adolescents report that they would intervene if they became aware of a peer's involvement in dating violence, predominately believing that dating violence is the couple's own private business (Weisz & Black, 2008). Encouraging close relationships with parents is an important way of preventing dating violence because adolescents learn about romantic relationships by observing and reflecting on the behaviors of others. Adolescent girls who are close with their parents are more likely to recognize unhealthy relationships, are less likely to be victimized by dating violence, and are more likely to seek help (Leadbeater et al., 2008).

What Do You Think?

1. **From your perspective, how prevalent is dating violence in adolescence?**

2. **Why do you think it occurs?**

3. **Why is it underreported?**

4. **What can be done to reduce dating violence and help victims of dating violence?**

and most young people have sexual intercourse for the first time at about age 17 (Finer & Philbin, 2013; Guttmacher Institute, 2014). Figure 12.2 depicts rates of sexual activity by age. About 34% of high school students reported being sexually active within the last three months and, as shown in Figure 12.3, African American high school students are more likely to have had intercourse (60%) compared to white (44%) and Hispanic students (49%; Kaiser Family Foundation, 2014).

Ethnic differences in sexual activity are thought to be influenced by socioeconomic and contextual factors that are associated with ethnicity, such as an increased likelihood of growing up in a single parent home, potentially with less parental monitoring, and in poor neighborhoods with fewer community resources, all of which are associated with early sexual activity (Browning, Leventhal, & Brooks-Gunn, 2004; Carlson, McNulty, Bellair, & Watts, 2014; Santelli, Lowry,

Brener, & Robin, 2000). In addition, ethnic differences in rates of pubertal maturation, with African American girls experiencing puberty earlier than other girls, influence sexual activity as early maturation is a risk factor for early sexual activity (Carlson et al., 2014; Moore, Harden, & Mendle, 2014).

While sexual activity is normative in late adolescence, early sexual activity, prior to age 15, is associated with problem behaviors, including alcohol and substance use, poor academic achievement, and delinquent activity, as well as having a larger number of sex partners relative to peers (Armour & Haynie, 2007; McLeod & Knight, 2010; Sandfort, Orr, Hirsch, & Santelli, 2008). Risk factors for early sexual activity in U.S. teens are those that place adolescents at risk for engaging in a variety of problem behaviors, such as early pubertal maturation, poor parental monitoring, poor parent–adolescent communication, poor school performance, perceived parental attitudes as permissive toward sexual activity, and peers who are sexually active (Anaya, Cantwell, & Rotheram-Borus, 2003; Biro & Dorn, 2006; McClelland & Tolman, 2014; Negriff, Susman, & Trickett, 2011). Risks for early sexual activity begin well before adolescence. For example, early aggression and disruptive behavior during the transition to first grade is associated with school problems, antisocial behavior, and substance use in middle school, which in turn are linked with early sexual activity (Schofield, Bierman, Heinrichs, & Nix, 2008).

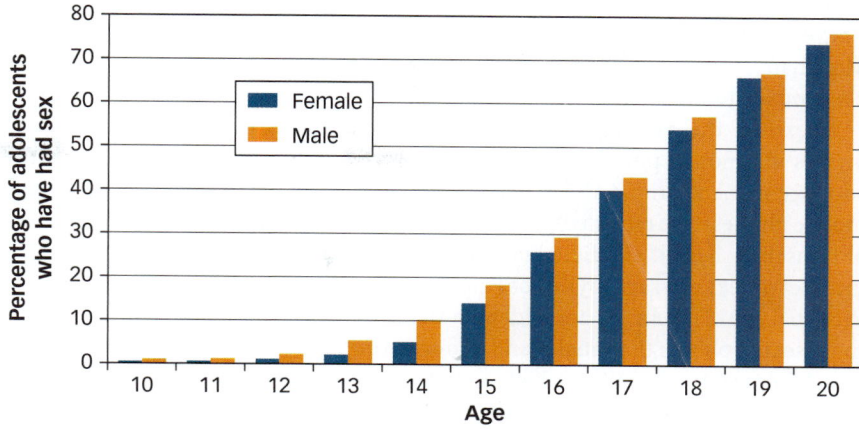

FIGURE 12.2: Sexual Initiation During Adolescence

SOURCE: Guttmacher Institute (2014).

INFLUENCES ON SEXUAL ACTIVITY

It may not be a surprise that adolescents who report many positive motivations for sexual activity show higher levels of sexual activity; these positive motivations include physical (feelings of excitement or pleasure), relationship-oriented (intimacy), social (peer approval, respect) and individual factors (gain a sense of competence, learn about the self; Manlove, Franzetta, & Ryan, 2006; Michels, Kropp, Eyre, & Halpern- Felsher, 2005; Ott, Millstein, Ofner, & Halpern-Felsher, 2006). Adolescents' beliefs about sexuality are influenced by their peers. Having sexually active peers and perceiving positive attitudes about sex among schoolmates predicts initiation and greater levels of sexual activity and a greater number of sexual partners (Coley, Kull, & Carrano, 2014; Moore et al., 2014; White & Warner, 2015). Specifically, adolescents who report having had oral sex are more likely to report that their best friend has also engaged in oral sex, believe that a greater number of friends are sexually active,

and that close friends would approve of their sexual activity (Bersamin, Walker, Fisher, & Grube, 2006; Prinstein, Meade, & Cohen, 2003). In addition, adolescents' perceptions of the sexual norms in their neighborhood, as well as siblings' sexual activity, are associated with age of initiation, casual sex, and the number of sexual partners, even after controlling for neighborhood demographic risk factors (Almy et al., 2015; Warner, Giordano, Manning, & Longmore, 2011).

Adolescents' views of normative sexual behavior are also influenced by exposure to the media. High school students who report frequent television viewing, including "sexy" prime-time programs, viewing TV for companionship, and identifying strongly with popular TV characters, tend to report greater levels of sexual experience than their peers (Cox, Shreffler, Merten, Schwerdtfeger Gallus, & Dowdy, 2014; Ward & Friedman, 2006). One study of Belgian 12- and 15-year-old boys and girls found that television viewing was associated with higher expectations for peers' sexual activity, and this relationship held regardless of the adolescents' pubertal status or own sexual experience (Eggermont, 2005). Sexually active adolescents are more likely to expose themselves to sex in the media and those exposed to sex in the media are more likely to progress in their sexual activity. These findings are consistent with others in the literature that demonstrate cross-sectional and longitudinal reciprocal links between exposure to sexual content and sexual behavior, including heightened risk for pregnancy during adolescence (Bleakley, Hennessy, Fishbein, & Jordan, 2009; Chandra et al., 2008). Recent research suggests that exposure to sexy media influences adolescents' perceptions of normative behavior. That is, those who view more sexual content tend to rate sexual behavior as more common among adolescents (Bleakley, Hennessy, Fishbein, & Jordan, 2011). However, other

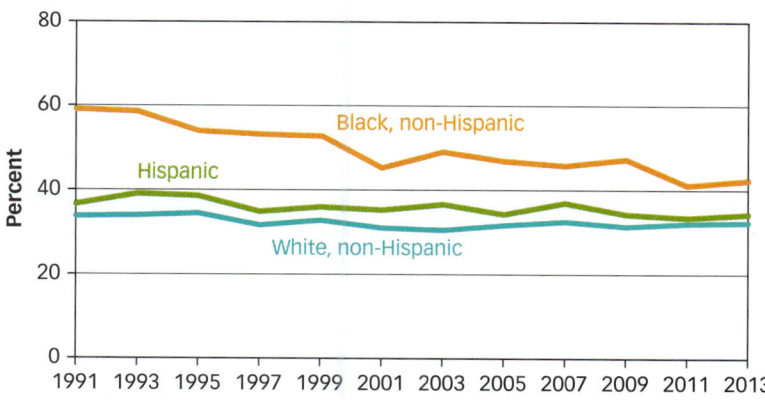

FIGURE 12.3: Percentage of High School Students Who Report They Are Sexually Active, 1991–2013

SOURCE: Kaiser Family Foundation (2014).

studies show no link between media exposure, including viewing Internet pornography and sexual behavior (Escobar-Chaves & Anderson, 2008; Luder et al., 2011; Steinberg & Monahan, 2011), suggesting that sexual behavior has multiple complex influences.

Sexting, the exchange of explicit sexual messages of images via mobile phone, is increasingly common among adolescents. An estimated 7% to 15% of adolescents with mobile phones have reported sharing a naked photo or video of himself or herself via digital communication such as the Internet or text messaging (Kaiser Family Foundation, 2014; Rice et al., 2012). Females and older youth are more likely to share sexual photos than males and younger youth.

Adolescents who themselves sexted were more likely to report being sexually active and to engage in risky sexual activity (Rice et al., 2012; Ybarra & Mitchell, 2014). Adolescents who shared sexual photos also were more likely to use substances, experience higher rates of depression, and report low self-esteem as compared with peers (Van Ouytsel, Van Gool, Ponnet, & Walrave, 2014).

What role do parents play in adolescent sexual activity? The majority of adolescents (84%) and parents (90%) report having talked with each other about sex, including topics such as intercourse and the prevention of pregnancy and STIs (Planned Parenthood Federation of America, 2012). Parent–child communication about sexuality—specifically, open conversations characterized by warmth, support, and humor—is associated with later onset of sexual activity and reductions in sexual risk taking (Lefkowitz & Stoppa, 2006; Lohman & Billings, 2008; Trejos-Castillo & Vazsonyi, 2009). However, about one half of adolescents and as many as two thirds of parents report that communicating about some aspects of sexuality is embarrassing, which may influence the quality of conversations (Jerman & Constantine, 2010; Planned Parenthood Federation of America, 2012). In addition, many parents underestimate their adolescent's sexual activity. For example, in one study, 56% of mothers of sexually active 14- to 16-year-olds, and 78% of mothers of sexually active 11- to 13-year-olds, believed that their child was not sexually active (Liddon, Michael, Dittus, & Markowitz, 2013). Authoritative parenting, regularly shared family activities (such as outings, game nights, or shared dinners), parental monitoring, and parental knowledge are associated with lower rates of sexual activity (Huang et al., 2011; McElwain & Booth-LaForce, 2006). In one study of nearly 15,000 adolescents, those who perceived that their parents made more warnings about the negative consequences of sex tended to accumulate more sexual partners (Coley et al., 2014).

Early sexual activity and greater sexual experience is more common in adolescents reared in stressful contexts, such as low socioeconomic status homes and poverty stricken and dangerous neighborhoods where community ties are weak (Carlson et al., 2014; Dupéré, Lacourse, Willms, Tremblay, & Leventhal, 2008). Positive relationships with adults can mitigate the effects of disenfranchised communities. For example, African American adolescents who reported high levels of communication and monitoring by their parents showed lower rates of sexual initiation. Similarly, religiosity acts as a protective factor—youth who perceive religion as important and are active in their religious community are less likely to engage in sexual activity than their peers (Rink, Tricker, & Harvey, 2007; Sinha, Cnaan, & Gelles, 2007).

LESBIAN, GAY, BISEXUAL, AND TRANSGENDER ADOLESCENTS

Sexual identity, one's sense of self regarding sexuality, including one's awareness and comfort regarding one's sexual attitudes, interests, and behaviors, develops in a process similar to other aspects of identity development: it entails a period of exploration and commitment. During adolescence, the identity search drives young people to consider their sexuality and determine their **sexual orientation**. Many youth enter a period of questioning in which they are uncertain of their sexuality and attempt to determine their true orientation (Saewyc, 2011). Similar to other aspects of identity, they explore and consider alternatives. For example, many preadolescents and young adolescents engage in sex play with members of the same sex yet develop a heterosexual orientation. After a period of questioning and exploration, adolescents commit to a sexual orientation and, over time, integrate their sexuality into their overall sense of identity. Eventually most lesbian, gay, and bisexual youth disclose their sexual orientation to others (Bos, Sandfort, de Bruyn, & Hakvoort, 2008; Cates, 2007). The final stage of sexual identity development, acceptance and disclosure, may occur in adolescence, but often occurs in young adulthood and afterward (Savin-Williams & Ream, 2007).

Many youth who identify as lesbian, gay, bisexual, or transgender (LGBT) report having felt "different" as children. Lesbian, gay, and bisexual youth report feeling attracted to members of the same sex whereas transgender youth report experiencing a different gender orientation that does not match their genitalia. Constructing an identity as an LGBT young person is complicated by the prejudice and discrimination that many LGBT youth experience in their schools and communities. Many middle and high school students—especially boys and younger adolescents—report that they are less willing to remain friends or want to attend schools with nonheterosexual peers (Poteat, Espelage, & Koenig, 2009). LGBT adolescents experience more harassment and victimization by peers and report a more hostile peer environment than their heterosexual peers (Robinson & Espelage, 2013). Perceived discrimination and victimization by peers contributes to LGBT adolescents' increased risk for psychological and behavioral problems, such as depression,

Ed Quinn/Corbis

Gay-straight alliances foster a culture of acceptance, help sexual minority peers connect with peers, and foster well-being in students.

self-harm, suicide, running away, poor academic performance, substance use, and risky sexual practices, (Almeida, Johnson, Corliss, Molnar, & Azrael, 2009; Collier, van Beusekom, Bos, & Sandfort, 2013; Haas et al., 2011; Plöderl et al., 2013). As sexual minority youth transition out of the school setting and experience less victimization, they tend to experience declines in distress (Birkett, Newcomb, & Mustanski, 2015).

LGBT youth tend to feel less accepted and perceive less social support and greater conflict with peers and parents, especially fathers, than do other adolescents (Bos et al., 2008; Busseri, Willoughby, Chalmers, & Bogaert, 2006). Social isolation might reflect rejection by other students or intentional withdrawal from family and other close relationships by adolescents who choose not to disclose their sexual identity from family and close relationships. Adolescents who anticipate negative responses from parents are less likely to disclose their sexual orientation; to avoid disclosure, LGBT youth may become emotionally distant from their parents and friends (Ueno, 2005). Support from parents and peers can buffer the negative effects of stigmatization and victimization (Birkett et al., 2015).

Schools can play a role in aiding LGBT students by cultivating a safe environment and climate where adolescents are able to develop a healthy sexual identity and offering protection from undue social emotional and physical harm. Certain characteristics of schools, such as a large student body, may offer a safer climate for LGBT youth. For example, students in more racially diverse schools reported greater willingness to remain friends and attend school with sexual minority peers, and adolescents with lesbian or gay friends report positive attitudes toward same-sex romantic and sexual relationships and less tolerance toward the unfair treatment of their LGBT peers (Heinze & Horn, 2009; Poteat et al., 2009). Similar to bullying, schools should develop and implement policies and procedures to promote a positive school climate and environment of acceptance and safety for all students (Fisher et al., 2008). Schools can promote acceptance for LGBT students by educating students and staff about gender identity and sexual orientation and integrating accurate information about social minority issues into the curriculum; staff development should instruct teachers and administrators on how to deal with discrimination, harassment, and bullying on the basis of sexual orientation. In addition, school-based support groups and group counseling can aid LGBT students who experience serious social, psychological, and behavioral problems (Fisher et al., 2008).

The presence of gay–straight alliances (GSAs) is an important source of support and education for students and helps sexual minority students connect with peers, reduces hopelessness, and is associated with lower suicide attempts (Davis, Royne Stafford, & Pullig, 2014). Schools that have GSAs show lower rates of student truancy, smoking, drinking, suicide attempts, and casual sex than do those in schools without GSAs, with this difference being more sizable for LGBT than heterosexual youth (Poteat, Sinclair, DiGiovanni, Koenig, & Russell, 2013). Perceived GSA support predicts greater well-being in racial and ethnic minority students, regardless of sexual orientation (Poteat et al., 2015). In addition to GSAs, LGBT adolescents often turn to the Internet as a source of information and exploration of their sexual orientation by learning about sexual orientation, communicating with other LGBT people, and finding support from others (Harper, Serrano, Bruce, & Bauermeister, 2015).

CONTRACEPTIVE USE

One of the greatest concerns to parents, teachers, health care professionals, and policy makers regarding adolescent sexuality is their sporadic use of contraceptives. About three quarters of sexually active 15- to 19-year-olds report using contraception during first intercourse (Kaiser Family Foundation, 2014; Martinez, Copen, & Abma, 2011). Two thirds of sexually active adolescents report the condom as the method used during the most recent sexual intercourse method used at first intercourse (Guttmacher Institute, 2014). However, many adolescents use contraceptives only sporadically and not consistently (Pazol et al., 2015). Common reasons given for not using contraceptives include not planning to have sex, the belief that pregnancy is unlikely, and difficulty communicating and negotiating the use of condoms (East, Jackson, O'Brien, & Peters, 2007; Johnson, Sieving, Pettingell, & McRee, 2015).

What predicts condom use, often referred to as "safe sex"? Some research indicates that authoritative parenting and open discussions about sex and contraception are key (Bersamin et al., 2008; Malcolm et al., 2013). However, parents do not always discuss sensitive topics like sexuality and sexual activity with their teens. One study of mother–adolescent communication in Latino families found that Latina mothers were more likely to discuss certain sex-related topics, such as the importance of waiting and the consequences of sexual activity, such as pregnancy, but were much less likely to discuss others, such as factual details about sexual intercourse and birth control (Guilamo-Ramos et al., 2006). At the same time, many of the adolescents expressed the desire to discuss sexual topics with their mothers, yet most did not, citing fears that their mothers would assume they were sexually active and would punish them. The influence of parental communication is complicated as other research with Scottish adolescents suggests that teens' perceptions of comfort talking about sex with their parents is not associated with sexual behavior (Wight, Williamson, & Henderson, 2006). Instead, it is adolescents' knowledge that is important. Girls with more reproductive knowledge report greater use of contraceptives and more consistent use of contraceptives (Ryan, Franzetta, & Manlove, 2007).

As with other behaviors, peers play a role in adolescents' contraceptive use. Friends' attitudes about the consequences of sexual activity and use of condoms during intercourse predict adolescents' attitudes about the potential risks of sex and condom use a year later (Henry et al., 2007). Cognitive development aids adolescents' capacities to reason about various alternatives, but recall from Chapter 11 that adolescents often pay more attention to the rewards than consequences, are swayed by emotional cognitions and situations, and often fail to apply reasoning to everyday contexts (Figner, Mackinlay, Wilkening, & Weber, 2009; Shad et al., 2011; Strang, Chein, & Steinberg, 2013).

SEXUALLY TRANSMITTED INFECTIONS

Given adolescents' overall lack of communication about sexuality and sporadic use of condoms, it may not be surprising that adolescents have higher rates of STIs than all other age groups. Teens and young adults represent only 25% of the sexually active population, but 15- to 24-year-olds account for one half of all STI diagnoses each year (Centers for Disease Control and Prevention [CDC], 2014). About one of six U.S. adolescents experiences a STI each year, three times more than do teens in Canada, which also is higher than most Western nations. Untreated STIs can result in sterility and serious, even life threatening, illness. Despite the higher risk for acquiring STIs among youth, only one third of adolescent girls and almost half (45%) of young women aged 19 to 25 report that they have discussed STIs with their health care providers (Kaiser Family Foundation, 2014).

The most serious STI is HIV, which causes AIDS. Young people aged 13 to 24 represent 21% of all new HIV/AIDS diagnoses in 2011 (Guttmacher Institute, 2014). Symptoms of AIDS, specifically a weakening of the immune system, occur about 8 to 10 years after infection with HIV.

Although it was once believed that adolescents who abuse drugs and share needles were most at risk for HIV infection, we now know that HIV is more often spread through heterosexual contact, especially from male to female (European Study Group on Heterosexual Transmission of HIV, 1992; Kelley, Borawski, Flocke, & Keen, 2003; Padian, Shiboski, & Jewell, 1991).

Although most adolescents (about 85% of high school students) receive education and demonstrate basic knowledge about HIV/AIDS (Kann et al., 2014), most underestimate their own risks, know little about other STIs, and are not knowledgeable about how to protect themselves from STIs (Boyce, Doherty, Fortin, & MacKinnon, 2003). In 2013, only 13% of high school students reported that they had ever been tested for HIV (Kann et al., 2014). Even in the Netherlands, a country with low STI rates among adolescents, most middle to late adolescents underestimate their risk of infection (Wolfers, de Zwart, & Kok, 2011). STIs are most likely among young people aged 15 to 24, and youth are especially vulnerable within the first year of initiating sexual activity (CDC, 2014; Forhan et al., 2009). The three ways to avoid STIs are to abstain from sex; to be in a long-term, mutually monogamous relationship with a partner who has been tested and does not have an STI; and to use condoms consistently and correctly. Making and carrying out decisions to abstain from sex or to engage in safe sex is challenging. With advances in cognition and executive functioning, specifically, perspective taking, decision making, and self-regulation, as well as experience, adolescents are better able to carry out their decisions in the real world, and show increase in safe sex.

ADOLESCENT PREGNANCY

In 2010, about 6% of 15- to 19-year-old girls in the United States became pregnant (Kost & Henshaw, 2014). The rate of adolescent pregnancy has dropped from its high of 117 of every 1,000 adolescent girls in 1990 to 57 of every 1,000 adolescent girls in 2010. Pregnancies are least common among girls younger than 15. In 2010, 5.4 pregnancies occurred per 1,000 teens aged 14 or younger, representing fewer than 1% of teens younger than 15 each year (Guttmacher Institute, 2014). As shown in Figure 12.4, the birth rate for U.S. adolescents has also declined substantially since 1990. The decline in adolescent birth rates can be attributed to a trend beginning in the 1990s for adolescents to initiate sexual activity later than in prior decades, as well as an increase in contraceptive use (Santelli, Lindberg, Finer, & Singh, 2007).

Despite overall declines over the past two decades, the United States continues to have one of the highest teen birth rates in the developed world (see Table 12.2; Sedgh, Finer, Bankole, Eilers, & Singh, 2015). Rates of sexual activity are similar across Western nations, but U.S. adolescents are less likely to use contraceptives than are those in other countries (Santelli et al., 2007).

One half of adolescent pregnancies in the United States occur within the first six months of the time a girl begins having sexual intercourse (Klein, 2006). More than 90% of 15- to 19-year-olds describe their pregnancies as unintended (Finer & Henshaw, 2006). The acceptability and consequences of adolescent pregnancy are influenced by social context. In places where advanced education is necessary for vocational and economic advancement, adolescent pregnancy is viewed as a handicap to success. Adolescent parenthood is a greater problem today in Western cultures, largely because adolescent girls are less likely to marry before giving birth and are less likely to receive financial or emotional support from the father than are those of prior generations. The risks for adolescent parenthood also contribute to the outcomes for adolescent parents and their children.

Because their bodies are not yet mature, girls who become pregnant shortly after menarche are at higher risk for many complications, such as spontaneous miscarriage, high blood pressure, low birth weight infants, and still birth (Phipps,

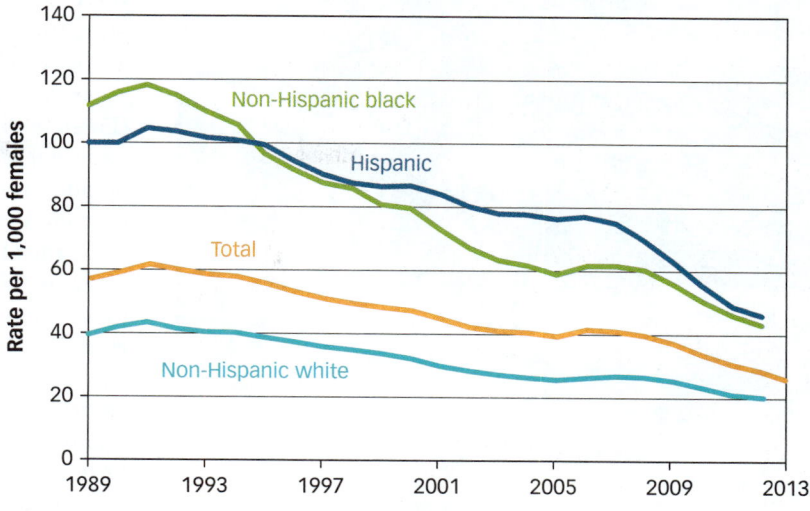

FIGURE 12.4: Birth Rates for Adolescents Aged 15 to 19, 1989–2013

SOURCE: Child Trends Data Bank (2014).

TABLE 12.2 International Adolescent Birth Rates in 2012 (per 1,000 women)

COUNTRY	RATE
Australia	12
Austria	4
Brazil	71
Canada	14
China	9
Dominican Republic	100
France	6
Germany	4
Ireland	8
Japan	5
Netherlands	6
Russian Federation	26
Switzerland	2
United Kingdom	26
United States	31

SOURCE: Adapted from World Bank (2014).

Sowers, & Demonner, 2002). Pregnancy in early adolescence interferes with girls' physical development because the hormones of pregnancy conflict with those of puberty. By age 16, in most girls the reproductive system and body growth are complete, and the complications of pregnancy and birth are no more likely than they are at age 20 (Phipps et al., 2002).

The risks for adolescent pregnancy are much the same as for early sexual activity. Low socioeconomic status homes, poor neighborhoods, and low levels of parental warmth and monitoring influence early sexual activity and the risk for adolescent pregnancy. Similarly, poor academic achievement, delinquency, substance use, depression, and affiliation with deviant peers are risk factors for early sexual activity and adolescent pregnancy (Carlson et al., 2014; Fortenberry, 2013). Girls who experience menarche early relative to peers are at risk as this early maturation predicts early sexual behavior and, in turn, pregnancy (De Genna, Larkby, & Cornelius, 2011; Dunbar, Sheeder, Lezotte, Dabelea, & Stevens-Simon, 2008). In addition, the presence of family members, especially parents and siblings, who are adolescent parents is associated with a high risk of adolescent pregnancy (East, Reyes, & Horn, 2007). Involved and firm parenting during early adolescence can buffer the effects of multiple home and community risk factors on the likelihood of early sexual activity and adolescent pregnancy (East, Khoo, Reyes, & Coughlin, 2006).

Adolescent mothers are less likely to achieve many of the typical markers of adulthood, such as completing high school, entering a stable marriage, and becoming financially and residentially independent (Casares, Lahiff, Eskenazi, & Halpern-Felsher, 2010; Taylor, 2009). Low educational attainment means that adolescent mothers often work low-paid and often unsatisfying jobs. Those who experience high levels of stress accompanied by little support

Scott Houston/Corbis

Adolescent mothers and their children face many risks to development, but educational, economic, and social supports can improve outcomes.

are at risk for maternal depression and their infants are at risk for developmental delays (Huang, Costeines, Ayala, & Kaufman, 2014). Adolescent mothers tend to spend more parenting years as single parents than do mothers who have children later in life. When they marry, adolescent mothers are more likely to divorce (Moore et al., 1993). Lack of resources, such as child care, housing, and financial support, influence poor educational outcomes; adolescents with child care and financial resources tend to show higher educational attainment (Casares et al., 2010; Mollborn, 2007). Although adolescent pregnancy is associated with negative outcomes, the risk factors for adolescent pregnancy are also those that place youth at risk for negative adult outcomes in general, such as extreme poverty, few educational and community supports, and family instability (Oxford et al., 2005). It is therefore difficult to determine the degree to which outcomes are caused by adolescent pregnancy itself or the contextual conditions that are associated with it.

It must be noted, however, that there is a great deal of variability in short- and long-term outcomes of teen pregnancy (Furstenberg, 2003; Miller, Forehand, & Kotchick, 1999). Adolescent parenthood is associated with long-term economic disadvantage. Adolescent mothers are more likely to be unemployed, have lower personal income, live in poverty, and have lower levels of education than their peers in their 30s (Assini-Meytin & Green, 2015; Gibb, Fergusson, Horwood, & Boden, 2015).

For example, a longitudinal study of adolescent mothers showed that 17 years after giving birth as adolescents, more than 70% graduated from high school, 30% received a postsecondary degree, and one half achieved income security, more positive outcomes than often reported (Furstenberg, 2003; Miller et al., 1999). In another longitudinal study of adolescent mothers, only about 15% of adolescent mothers experienced the most negative outcomes over the transition to early adulthood, such as financial dependence, low education, unemployment, unstable housing, casual sexual activity, victimization by crime, criminal activity, and illicit drug use (Oxford et al., 2005). These dire outcomes are predicted by drug and alcohol use, criminal activity, clinical depression, anxiety, and experience with violence during adolescence. The remaining 85% of adolescent mothers showed more positive outcomes including achieving markers of adulthood such as financial independence, though about one half of these young women experienced mental health issues such as anxiety or depression (Oxford et al., 2005). Figure 12.5 summarizes risk factors and outcomes for adolescent pregnancy.

Children born to adolescent mothers are at a disadvantage relative to their peers. Adolescent mothers are less likely than older mothers to seek prenatal care and are more likely to smoke and use alcohol or other drugs (Dell, 2001; Meade, Kershaw, & Ickovics, 2008). Infants born to adolescent mothers are more likely to be born preterm and low birth weight (Xi-Kuan et al., 2007). As children they tend to perform poorly in school, score lower on intelligence tests, and be disruptive. They are at risk for a variety of negative developmental outcomes such as conduct and emotional problems, lower cognitive functioning, developmental delays, and poor academic achievement (Rafferty, Griffin, & Lodise, 2011; Tang, Davis-Kean, Chen, & Sexton, 2014). Children of adolescent mothers show lower educational attainment in young adulthood (Lipman, Georgiades, & Boyle, 2011). These outcomes are influenced by the characteristics of adolescents who are likely to become mothers as well as the consequences of having a child at a young age (e.g., lower maternal education, low socioeconomic status, frequent caretaker and residence changes, poor parenting; Carothers, Borkowski, & Whitman, 2006; De Genna et al., 2011; Rafferty et al., 2011). Adolescent mothers know less about child development than do adult mothers and therefore are more likely to have unrealistically high expectations of infants, perceive their infants as difficult, and show less effective interaction skills (Moore & Florsheim, 2001; Pomerleau, Scuccimarri, & Malcuit, 2003). In one longitudinal study of infants from 14 to 36 months of age, older mothers were more supportive during play than were adolescent mothers and differences in parenting behaviors predicted cognitive and language abilities at age 3 (Rafferty et al., 2011).

Children of adolescent mothers are at risk to demonstrate increasingly deviant behavior into adolescence including

FIGURE 12.5: Influences on Adolescent Pregnancy

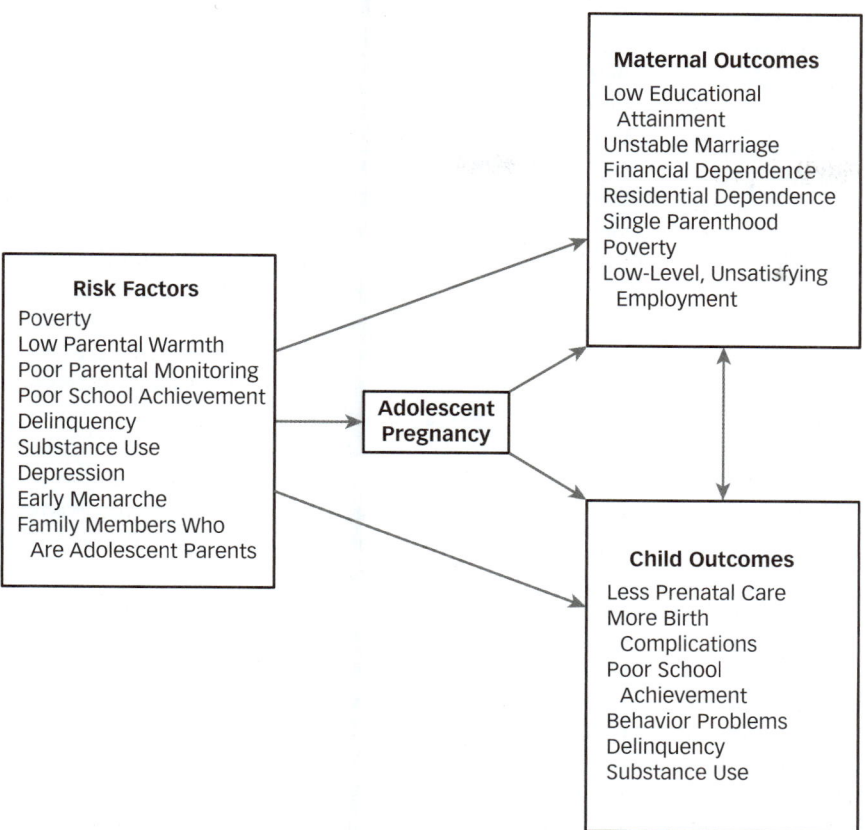

Risk factors for adolescent pregnancy also influence how adolescents adjust to parenthood, their long-term outcomes, and their children's outcomes. Protective factors—such as warm relationships with parents and other caring adults, parental monitoring, coping skills, and access to health care—promote positive adjustment in the face of risk and influence the outcomes of adolescent pregnancy for mothers and children.

delinquency, substance abuse, incarceration, school dropout, and early childbearing (Furstenberg, 2003; Jaffee, Caspi, Moffitt, Belsky, & Silva, 2001). Girls are at increased risk to themselves become adolescent parents, but after taking into account other contextual factors, the risk attributable to adolescent parenting declines (Meade et al., 2008). However, there is variability in outcomes. Many children of adolescent mothers often demonstrate resilience and adjustment in the face of these risks (Levine, Emery, & Pollack, 2007; Rhule, McMahon, Spieker, & Munson, 2006). Positive adjustment is predicted by secure attachment; low maternal depressive symptoms; and positive parenting on the part of the mother, characterized by warmth, discussion, and stimulation.

Adolescent fathers are similar to adolescent mothers in that they are more likely than their peers to have poor academic performance, higher school dropout rates, finite financial resources, and lowered income potential (Kiselica & Kiselica, 2014; Klein, 2006). Some adolescent fathers disappear from their children's lives. Many stay involved, often while struggling. In one study, about 60% of adolescent fathers maintained consistent contact over the first eight

years of the child's life (Howard, Lefever, Borkowski, & Whitman, 2006). Father contact was associated with the child's having better socioemotional and academic functioning at 8 and 10 years of age, particularly in school-related areas. Children with greater levels of father contact have fewer behavioral problems and higher scores on reading achievement (Howard et al., 2006).

Adolescent parents can be effective if provided with supports—economic, educational, and social. Effective supports for adolescent parents include health care, encouragement to stay in school, vocational training, parenting skills, coping skills, and access to affordable child care (Easterbrooks, Chaudhuri, Bartlett, & Copeman, 2011; Mollborn, 2007). Social support predicts increased parenting self-efficacy and parental satisfaction (Angley, Divney, Magriples, & Kershaw, 2015; Umaña-Taylor, Guimond, Updegraff, & Jahromi, 2013). Relationships with adults who are close, supportive, and provide guidance predict completing high school (Klaw, Rhodes, & Fitzgerald, 2003). Adolescents who share caregiving with their mothers or other adults learn as apprentices and become more competent over time (Oberlander, Black, & Starr, 2007). Adolescent parents benefit from relationships with adults who are sensitive to their needs as parents but also to their own developmental needs for autonomy and support.

Thinking in Context 12.3

1. Identify influences on adolescent sexual activity (e.g., intercourse, oral sex, contraceptive use) at each of Bronfenbrenner's ecological levels. How might interventions apply this information to reduce sexual activity and increase safe sex practices among adolescents?

2. It is a common belief that today's adolescents are more sexually active at younger ages than ever before. How would you respond to that statement, based on what you know about adolescent sexuality?

3. Given what is known about child development, specifically infant and young children's developmental needs, as well as what is known about parenting and its influence on developmental outcomes, what supports do adolescent parents need in order to become effective parents?

PROBLEMS IN ADOLESCENCE

As much as adolescence is a time of excitement, firsts, and learning about the world and the self, it can also be an emotionally challenging time. Most young people traverse the adolescent years without adversity, but about one in five teenagers experience serious problems that pose risks to their health and development (Lerner & Israeloff, 2007). Common problems during adolescence include eating disorders, substance abuse, depression, and delinquency.

DEPRESSION AND SUICIDE

When adolescents experience problems in development, they are most likely to suffer from depression. Depression is characterized by feelings of sadness, hopelessness, and frustration; changes in sleep and eating habits; problems with concentration; loss of interest in activities; and loss of energy and motivation. About 9% of adolescents experience a depressive episode, and about 2% to 8% experience chronic depression that persists over months and even years (Substance Abuse and Mental Health Services Administration, 2013). Rates of depression rise in early adolescence, and lifelong sex differences emerge, with girls reporting depression twice as often as boys (Galambos, Leadbeater, & Barker, 2004; Paxton, Valois, Watkins, Huebner, & Drane, 2007; Thapar, Collishaw, Pine, & Thapar, 2012). About one third of adolescents report feeling hopeless (Kann et al., 2014). The stereotype of the typical adolescent presents a danger when it comes to identifying depression. Parents and teachers who buy into the storm and stress myth of adolescence may assume that depressive symptoms are a normal part of adolescence and thereby ignore real problems.

There are multiple pathways to depression. Genes play a role in depression by influencing development of the brain regions responsible for emotional regulation and stress responses as well as the overall balance and production of neurotransmitters (Franić, Middeldorp, Dolan, Ligthart, & Boomsma, 2010; Maughan, Collishaw, & Stringaris, 2013). Longitudinal research suggests the role of epigenetics in depression during adolescence. For example, in one study, boys with a specific neurotransmitter allele showed severe symptoms of depression in the presence of poor family support but in the presence of high family support showed positive outcomes (Li, Berk, & Lee, 2013). The allele may increase reactivity to both negative and positive family influences, serving as a risk factor in an unsupportive family context but protective factor when coupled with family support. Genetics plays a complex role in determining depression; some alleles may serve as both risk and protective factors depending on contextual circumstances.

Many environmental factors are thought to serve as risk factors for depression (Dunn et al., 2011). Adolescents who are depressed are more likely to live in homes with depressed parents (Natsuaki et al., 2014). Depression often limits the capacity to parent effectively and with sensitivity. Feelings of alienation from parents contribute to depression (Smith, Rachel, & Catherine, 2009). Similar to adults, depression during adolescence often occurs after specific events like parental divorce, failure, or the loss of a friend (Oldehinkel, Ormel, Veenstra, De Winter, & Verholst, 2008). The longitudinal effects of stressful life events on depression are buffered by parent–child closeness and worsened by parental depression (Bouma, Ormel, Verhulst, & Oldehinkel, 2008; Ge, Natsuaki, Neiderhiser, & Reiss, 2009).

Cultural factors also play a role in influencing adolescents' susceptibility to depression. Unlike Western cultures, males and females display similar rates of depression in non-Western cultures (Culbertson, 1997). Within the United States, culturally influenced coping styles and responses to stressful life events influence sex and ethnic differences in depression. Many adolescents find the common discrepancy between their level of acculturation and that of their first-generation immigrant parents stressful. For example, Chinese immigrant parents whose level of acculturation differed from their adolescent children showed more unsupportive parenting practices and the adolescents reported greater feelings of alienation (Kim, Chen, Wang, Shen, & Orozco-Lapray, 2013). Poor parental acculturation is linked with adolescent depression when adolescent–parent relationships are poor (Kim, Qi, Jing, Xuan, & Ui Jeong, 2009). Likewise, Vietnamese fathers who are less acculturated to the United States use more authoritarian methods that fit their society, but their adolescents experience more depression (Nguyen, 2008). Latino adolescents who experience a discrepancy in acculturation as compared with their parents also are at risk for depression (Céspedes & Huey, 2008). As young people acculturate, they may challenge traditional attitudes and beliefs of their immigrant parents, leading to greater family conflict and emotional distress (Gonzales, Deardorff, Formoso, Barr, & Barrera, 2006).

Intense and long-lasting depression can lead to thoughts of suicide. Increases in depression during adolescence are accompanied by increases in the suicide rate. Suicide remains among the top three leading causes of death in the United States and Canada (Heron, 2013; Ornstein, Bowes, Shouldice, & Yanchar, 2013). For unknown reasons, rates of adolescent suicide vary widely across industrialized countries, from low in Denmark, Greece, Italy, and Spain, intermediate in Australia, Canada, Japan, and the United States, to high in Finland, New Zealand, and Singapore (Lester, 2003; McLoughlin, Gould, & Malone, 2015). Figure 12.6 illustrates the adolescent suicide rate across various countries.

Consistent ethnic differences occur in rates of suicide. Native American and Canadian Aboriginal adolescents commit suicide at very high rates relative to their peers—2 to 7 times the national averages (Joe & Marcus, 2003; Kutcher, 2008). Challenges with acculturation as well as contextual risk factors that are associated with ethnicity, like an increased likelihood of living in poverty, influence suicide rates among minority youth (Goldston et al., 2008). Gay and lesbian youth, especially males, are also at high risk with 3 to

FIGURE 12.6: Suicide Rates, Ages 15–19, 2008

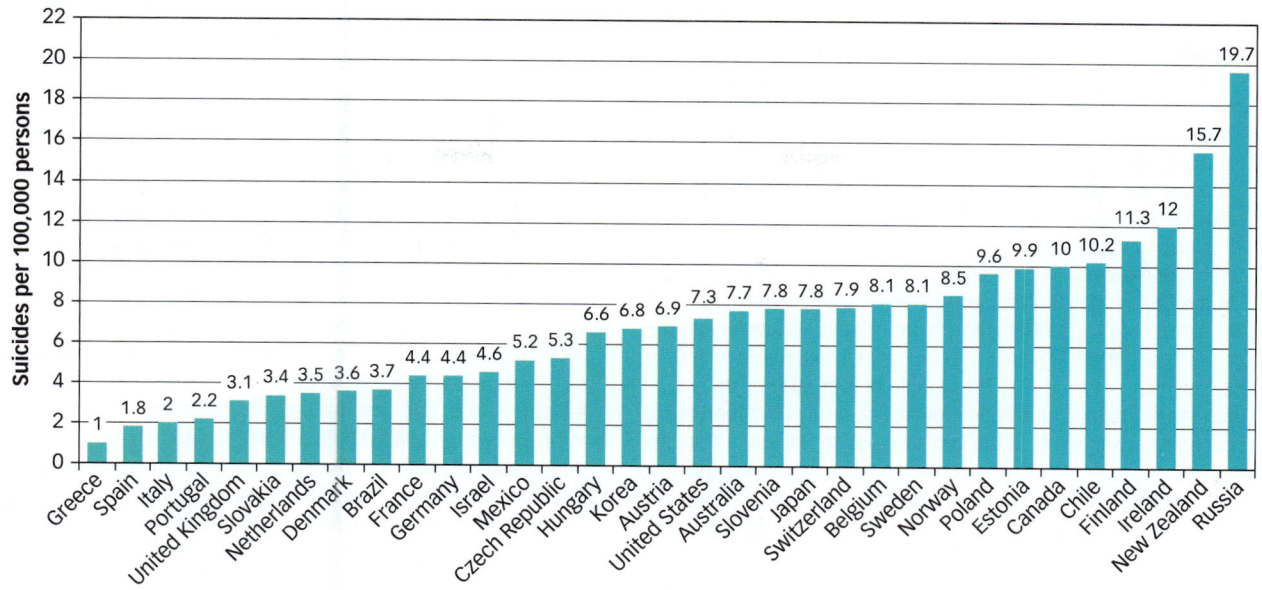

SOURCE: McLoughlin et al. (2015).

4 times as many attempts than other youths; typically, these teens report family conflict, peer rejection, and inner conflict about their sexuality as influences on their attempts (Liu & Mustanski, 2012; Mustanski & Liu, 2013).

Although females display higher rates of depression and make more suicide attempts, males are four times more likely to succeed in committing suicide (Xu, Kochanek, Murphy, & Arias, 2014). Girls tend to choose suicide methods that are more slow and passive and that they are more likely to be revived from, such as overdoses of pills. Boys tend to choose methods that are quick and irreversible, such as firearms. The methods correspond to gender roles that expect males to be active, decisive, aggressive, and less open to discussing emotions (Canetto & Sakinofsky, 1998; Hepper, Dornan, & Lynch, 2012).

Adolescents who commit suicide are more likely to have experienced multiple recent stressful events such as parental divorce; abuse and neglect; conflict with parents; family members with emotional, psychological, or antisocial problems; and economic disadvantage as well as final triggering events such as failure, loss of a friendship, or intense family arguments (Beautrais, 2003; Miranda & Shaffer, 2013) Adolescents' suicide attempts are influenced by those of their friends. Adolescents are more likely to attempt suicide following a friend's attempt (Nanayakkara, Misch, Chang, & Henry, 2013). Some adolescents who commit suicide are perfectionists who may find that they and the people around them are unable to meet their own rigidly high standards (Flett, Hewitt, & Heisel, 2014). Other adolescents who commit suicide first express their depression and frustration through antisocial activity such as bullying, fighting, stealing, abusing drugs or alcohol, and risk-taking (Fergusson, Woodward, & Horwood, 2000). Peer victimization is a risk factor for suicide attempts (Bauman et al., 2013) as is high levels of anxiety (Hill, Castellanos, & Pettit, 2011). Although 20/20 hindsight is quite clear, determining if a teen needs help is challenging. Frequently, however, adolescents who attempt suicide show warning signs beforehand, as listed in Table 12.3. The availability and advertisement of telephone

TABLE 12.3 Suicide Warning Signs

Any of the following behaviors can serve as a warning sign of increased suicide risk.

- Change in eating and sleeping habits
- Withdrawal from friends, family, and regular activities
- Violent actions, rebellious behavior, or running away
- Drug and alcohol use, especially changes in use
- Unusual neglect of personal appearance
- Marked personality change
- Persistent boredom, difficulty concentrating, or a decline in the quality of schoolwork
- Frequent complaints about physical symptoms, such as stomachaches, headaches, and fatigue
- Loss of interest in pleasurable activities
- Complaints of being a bad person or feeling rotten inside
- Verbal hints with statements such as the following: "I won't be a problem for you much longer." "Nothing matters." It's no use." "I won't see you again."
- Affairs are in order—for example, giving away favorite possessions, cleaning his or her room, and throwing away important belongings
- Suddenly cheerful after a period of depression
- Signs of psychosis (hallucinations or bizarre thoughts)

Most important: Stating "I want to kill myself," or "I'm going to commit suicide."

SOURCE: Adapted from American Academy of Child and Adolescent Psychiatry (2008).

Self-Harm

Brianna closed the door to her room, rolled up her shirtsleeve, and looked down at the scarred and healing gashes in her arm before reaching for a new razor blade. Brianna engages in self-harm, a behavior that often becomes habitual among adolescent girls. Although self-harm may indicate serious psychological disorders, it is also common among adolescents in Western countries, with lifetime prevalence rates of 13% to 23% of adolescents in the United States, Canada, Australia, Belgium, England, Hungary, Ireland, the Netherlands, and Norway (Muehlenkamp, Claes, Havertape, & Plener, 2012; Plener, Libal, Keller, Fegert, & Muehlenkamp, 2009). One sample of over 1,000 7th- and 8th-grade students in Sweden found that over 40% reported engaging in self-injury in the last six months (Bjärehed, Wångby-Lundh, & Lundh, 2012). Rates may be even higher because most self-harming adolescents never seek help or medical attention for their injuries (Hall & Place, 2010). Most adolescents who engage in self-harm behaviors do so occasionally, and most do not show recurring self-harm (Brunner et al., 2007).

Self-harm behaviors, particularly cutting, tend to emerge at around age 13, but the age of initiation ranges from 12 to 15 years (Bjärehed et al., 2012). Girls are more likely than boys to report harming themselves, most commonly by cutting behaviors, but also hitting, biting, or burning behaviors, but there are no differences on the basis of ethnicity or socioeconomic status (Laye-Gindhu & Schonert-Reichl, 2005; Nock, Prinstein, & Sterba, 2009).

Social problems and a difficulty forming close relationships are common among adolescents who self-harm (Ross, Heath, & Toste, 2009). They may view their relationships as tense, disappointing, and of poor quality and may be more likely to experience bullying (Fisher et al., 2012; Laukkanen et al., 2009). Psychological and behavioral difficulties such as anxiety, depression, antisocial behavior, poor problem-solving skills, and impulsivity are associated with self-harm (Bjärehed et al., 2012; Marshall, Tilton-Weaver, & Stattin, 2013). Adolescents who self-harm tend to report being more confused about their emotions, experiencing difficulty recognizing and responding to them and more reluctance to express their feelings and thoughts to others

(Bjärehed et al., 2012; Nock et al., 2009). Common reasons that adolescents endorse for self-harm include depression, feeling alone, anger, self-dislike, and inadequacy.

Adolescents who repeatedly engage in cutting and other acts of self-harm tend to report that the act relieves emotional pain, reducing negative emotions (Scoliers et al., 2009; Selby, Nock, & Kranzler, 2014). Interestingly, self-harming adolescents tend to show little or no pain during the harm episode (Nock, et al., 2009). Instead, the act of cutting or other self-harming behavior produces a sense of relief and satisfaction for adolescents who repeatedly self-harm. Soon, they tend to value self-harm as an effective way of relieving anxiety and negative emotions, making it a difficult habit to break (Madge et al., 2008; Selby et al., 2014). The *Diagnostic and Statistical Manual of Mental Disorders*, 5th edition, or *DSM–V* (American Psychiatric Association, 2013), includes a diagnosis for severe self-harm: nonsuicidal self-injury—self-injurious behavior that occurs with the expectation of relief from a negative feeling—to solve an interpersonal problem, or to feel better, and interpersonal difficulty and negative feelings of thoughts, premeditation, or rumination on nonsuicidal self injury. Many adolescents who self-harm receive treatment similar to other internalizing disorders, including a combination of medication, therapy, and behavioral treatment. However, repeated self-harming behaviors are difficult to treat because the relief they produce is very reinforcing to adolescents, making psychologists and other treatment providers' work very challenging (Bentley, Nock, & Barlow, 2014; Nock, 2009).

What Do You Think?

1. Why might some adolescents find that "feeling bad" makes them "feel good"?

2. What role might brain development or contextual factors such as parents and peers contribute to the increase in cutting and other self-harm behaviors that many experience in adolescence?

---

hotlines, such as the National Suicide Prevention Lifeline at (800) 273-8255 (and available at http://www .suicidepreventionlifeline.org) can help adolescents in immediate danger of suicide.

Adolescents are also at risk for self-harm: deliberate and voluntary physical self-injury that is not life-threatening and is without any conscious suicidal intent (Laye-Gindhu & Schonert-Reichl, 2005). This behavior is discussed in Applying Developmental Science (above).

Preventing and treating depression and suicide requires looking beyond myths and stereotypes about adolescent behavior to be aware of the signs of adolescents in pain. Parent and teacher education about the signs of depression is an essential first step. Although school-based suicide prevention programs tend to increase awareness and

knowledge about suicide, they are not associated with lower rates of suicide (Cusimano & Sameem, 2011). Depression is treated in a variety of ways that include therapy and the provision of antidepressant medication (Brent, 2009). Therapy that is designed to help the adolescent be more self-aware, identify harmful patterns of thinking, and change them is especially effective and can be administered in school or community settings (Shirk, Gudmundsen, Kaplinski, & McMakin, 2008). Counseling and peer support groups can be provided by schools and community centers (Corrieri et al., 2014).

After a suicide, family, friends, and schoolmates of the adolescent require immediate support and assistance in working through their grief and anger. The availability of support and counseling to all adolescents within the school and community after a suicide is important because adolescent suicides tend to occur in clusters, increasing the risk of suicide among adolescents in the community (Gould, Jamieson, & Romer, 2003; Haw, Hawton, Niedzwiedz, & Platt, 2013). Depression and suicide are challenging problems that illustrate the complex interactions between the individual and his or her context.

EATING DISORDERS

Adolescents' rapidly changing physique, coupled with media portrayals of the ideal woman as thin with few curves, leads many to become dissatisfied with their body image (Benowitz-Fredericks, Garcia, Massey, Vasagar, & Borzekowski, 2012). Girls who have a negative body image are at risk of developing a strong drive for thinness and unhealthy weight loss behaviors, such as excessive exercise and use of food supplements in place of meals (McCabe & Ricciardelli, 2006). Severe dieting can be an indicator of an eating disorder, which is defined as unhealthy and uncontrolled attitudes and patterns of weight control. Core features of eating disorders are unhealthy negative body image (overvaluing thinness, weight, or shape), obsession with weight control, extreme over or under control of eating, and extreme behavior patterns designed to control weight, such as compulsive exercise, dieting, or purging (American Psychiatric Association, 2013). Two eating disorders, **anorexia nervosa** and **bulimia nervosa**, pose serious challenges to health. About 4% of adolescents are diagnosed with anorexia nervosa and bulimia nervosa (Smink, van Hoeken, & Hoek, 2013). Table 12.4 lists symptoms of anorexia and bulimia.

Although both anorexia nervosa and bulimia nervosa entail excessive concern about body weight and attempts to lose weight, they differ by means. Young people who suffer from anorexia nervosa starve themselves in an attempt to achieve thinness, maintaining a weight that is substantially lower than expected for height and age (American Psychiatric Association, 2013). A distorted body image leads youth with anorexia to perceive themselves as "fat" despite their emaciated appearance, and they continue to lose weight (Gila, Castro, Cesena, & Toro, 2005; Skrzypek, Wehmeier, & Remschmidt, 2001). Girls with anorexia avoid eating even when hungry. For example, 16-year-old Jessica often consumed a lunch of five baby carrots and one half of an apple. In addition to avoiding eating despite hunger,

TABLE 12.4 DSM-V Criteria for the Diagnosis of Anorexia Nervosa or Bulimia Nervosa

ANOREXIA NERVOSA	BULIMIA NERVOSA

1. Persistent restriction of energy intake leading to significantly low body weight (in context of what is minimally expected for age, sex, developmental trajectory, and physical health)
 	
2. Either an intense fear of gaining weight or of becoming fat, or persistent behavior that interferes with weight gain (even though significantly low weight)
 	
3. Disturbance in the way one's body weight or shape is experienced, undue influence of body shape and weight on self-evaluation, or persistent lack of recognition of the seriousness of the current low body weight
	1. Recurrent episodes of binge eating characterized by the following:
	
	  a. Eating, in a discrete period of time (e.g., within any two-hour period) an amount of food that is definitely larger than most people would eat during a similar period of time and under similar circumstances;
	
	  b. A sense of lack of control over eating during the episode (e.g., a feeling that one cannot stop eating or control what or how much one is eating)
	
	2. Recurrent inappropriate behavior to prevent weight gain such as the following:
	
	  a. Self-induced vomiting
	  b. Misuse of laxatives, diuretics, or other medications
	  c. Fasting
	  d. Excessive exercise
	
	3. The binge eating and inappropriate compensatory behavior both occur, on average, at least once a week for three months.
	
	4. Self-evaluation unduly influenced by body shape and weight
	
	5. Disturbance does not occur exclusively during episodes of anorexia nervosa

SOURCE: American Psychiatric Association (2013).

many girls with anorexia exercise vigorously to increase their weight loss. Anorexia affects about 2% of girls 19 and under; however, many more girls show poor eating behaviors characteristic of anorexia (Smink et al., 2013; Smink, van Hoeken, Oldehinkel, & Hoek, 2014).

Bulimia nervosa is characterized by recurrent episodes of binge eating—consuming an abnormally large amount of food (thousands of calories) in a single sitting coupled with a feeling of being out of control—followed by purging, inappropriate behavior designed to compensate for the binge, such as vomiting, excessive exercise, or use of laxatives (American Psychiatric Association, 2013). Girls with bulimia nervosa experience extreme dissatisfaction with body image and attempt to lose weight, but they tend to have a body weight that is normal or high-normal (Golden et al., 2015). Bulimia is more common than anorexia, affecting between 1% and 5% of females across Western Europe and the United States (Kessler et al., 2013; Smink et al., 2014). One study estimated that many more young people in North America and Europe show symptoms of bulimia but remain undiagnosed (Keel, 2014).

Both anorexia and bulimia are dangerous to young people's health. Girls with anorexia may lose 25% to 50% of their body weight (Berkman, Lohr, & Bulik, 2007). They may not experience menarche or may stop menstruating because menstruation is dependent on maintaining at least 15% to 18% body fat (Golden et al., 2015). Starvation and malnutrition contributes to extreme sensitivity to cold, pale skin, and growth of fine hairs all over the body. The starvation characteristic of anorexia nervosa has serious health consequences, such as loss of bone mass causing brittle and easily broken bones, kidney failure, shrinkage of the heart, brain damage, and even death in as many as 16% of cases of anorexia (Golden et al., 2015; Reel, 2012). Side effects of bulimia nervosa include nutritional deficiencies, sores, ulcers, and even holes in the mouth and esophagus caused by repeated exposure to stomach acids, as well as bad breath, tooth damage and an increased likelihood of cancers of the throat and esophagus (Katzman, 2005).

What causes eating disorders? Both anorexia and bulimia occur more often in both members of identical twins than fraternal twins, indicating a genetic basis (Strober, Freeman, Lampert, Diamond, & Kaye, 2014). Eating disorders are much more prevalent in females than males, with about 1% of males diagnosed with an eating disorder as compared with about 6% of females (Raevuori, Keski-Rahkonen, & Hoek, 2014). Adolescents who develop eating disorders tend to have problems with impulse control and anxiety, as well as symptoms of depression; and these are all influenced by abnormal levels of neurotransmitters in the brain (Haleem, 2012; Kaye, Bailer, Frank, Wagner, & Henry, 2005). Girls who develop eating disorders also tend to experience body dissatisfaction and rate themselves negatively in comparison with other girls (e.g., "I am less good-looking, likable, and popular"; McCabe & Ricciardelli, 2006). Interactions with parents and especially peers influence girls' body image, dieting behaviors, and eating disorder symptoms (Blodgett Salafia & Gondoli, 2011). Girls with eating disorders often find that strictly regulating their eating is a way to exert control in their lives. Girls with anorexia, in particular, tend to set high, often unrealistic, standards for themselves. They tend to be academic achievers, perfectionists, and focused on achieving success (Halmi et al., 2000). Their perfectionist tendencies extend to their bodies, which they perceive as not meeting the societal ideal of beauty. Controlling their bodies and restricting their intake of food provides a sense of control and reduces their anxiety and negative mood states (Kaye, Wierenga, Bailer, Simmons, & Bischoff-Grethe, 2013; Tyrka, Graber, & Brooks-Gunn, 2000).

Eating disorders occur in all ethnic and socioeconomic groups in Western countries and are becoming increasingly common in Asian and Arab cultures (Isomaa, Isomaa, Marttunen, Kaltiala-Heino, & Björkqvist, 2009; Latzer, Witztum, & Stein, 2008; Pike, Hoek, & Dunne, 2014; Reel, 2012). Girls who compete in sports and activities that idealize lean figures, such as ballet, figure skating, gymnastics, and long distance running, are at higher risk for developing eating disorders than are other girls (Nordin, Harris, & Cumming, 2003; Voelker, Gould, & Reel, 2014). In the United States, white and Latina girls, especially those of higher socioeconomic status, are at higher risk for low body image and eating disorders than are black girls, who may be protected by cultural and media portrayals of African American women that value voluptuous figures (Nishina, Ammon, Bellmore, & Graham, 2006; Smink et al., 2013; Striegel-Moore & Bulik, 2007). Some researchers suggest, however, that ethnic differences in eating disorders are not as large as they appear. Instead, eating disorders may exist in Latina and black girls but remain undetected and undiagnosed because of barriers to diagnosis and treatment (Wilson, Grilo, & Vitousek, 2007).

Eating disorders are difficult to treat. In one study of over 2,500 adolescents, 82% of those diagnosed with an eating disorder showed symptoms five years later (Ackard, Fulkerson, & Neumark-Sztainer, 2011). Anorexia nervosa and bulimia nervosa are treated in similar ways but show different success rates. Standard treatment for anorexia includes hospitalization to remedy malnutrition and ensure weight gain, antianxiety or antidepressant medications, and individual and family therapy (Lock, 2011; Wilson et al., 2007). Medications are commonly prescribed, with mixed outcomes (Bulik et al., 2007). The success of therapy also varies. Therapy is designed to enhance girls' motivation to change and engage them as collaborators in treatment, providing them with a sense of control. However, the success of therapy depends on the patients' attitudes about their symptoms and illness (Bulik et al., 2007; Lock, Le Grange, & Forsberg, 2007; Lock, 2011). Unfortunately, girls with anorexia tend to deny that there is a problem as they are unable to objectively perceive their bodies. Many hold the conviction that thinness and restraint are more important and healthy than recovery, making anorexia very resistant to treatment (Berkman et al., 2007). As a result, only about 50% of girls with anorexia make a full recovery and anorexia nervosa has the highest mortality rate of all mental disorders (Smink et al., 2013).

Bulimia tends to be more amenable to treatment because girls with bulimia tend to acknowledge that their behavior is not healthy. Girls with bulimia tend to feel guilty about binging and purging and are more likely than those with anorexia to seek help. Individual therapy, support groups, nutritional education, and antianxiety or antidepressant medications are the treatments of choice for bulimia nervosa (Hay & Bacaltchuk, 2007; Le Grange & Schmidt, 2005). Medication tends to improve symptoms but, without therapy, rarely leads to the cease of purging (Shapiro et al., 2007). Individual and family-based therapy helps girls become aware of the thoughts and behaviors that cause and maintain their binging and purging behaviors, which decreases binge eating and vomiting and reduces the risk of relapse (Lock, 2011; Smink et al., 2013).

ALCOHOL AND SUBSTANCE USE

Nearly one half of U.S. teens have tried an illicit drug, and nearly three quarters have tried alcohol by the time they leave high school, as shown in Table 12.5. Experimentation with alcohol, tobacco, and marijuana use—that is, "trying

TABLE 12.5 Substance Use in U.S. Adolescents, 2014

GRADE	LIFETIME PREVALENCE (%)	30-DAY PREVALENCE (%)
Cigarettes		
8th grade	13.5	4
10th grade	22.6	7.3
12th grade	34.4	13.6
Alcohol		
8th grade	26.8	9
10th grade	49.3	23.5
12th grade	66	37.4
Been drunk		
8th grade	10.8	2.7
10th grade	30.2	11.2
12th grade	49.8	23.5
Marijuana		
8th grade	15.6	6.5
10th grade	33.7	16.6
12th grade	44.4	21.2
Illicit drugs		
8th grade	10	3.3
10th grade	15.9	5.6
12th grade	22.6	7.7

SOURCE: Johnston et al. (2015).

out" these substances—is so common that it may be considered somewhat normative for North American adolescents, especially as rates of experimentation rise during the adolescent years into young adulthood (Johnston, O'Malley, Miech, Bachman, & Schulenberg, 2007; Palmer et al., 2009; World Health Organization, 2004). Alcohol, in particular, is commonly used by adolescents around the globe; however, there are cultural differences in drinking patterns, as shown by Figure 12.7.

Most adolescents begin to use alcohol in early adolescence; show steady increases in use throughout the high school years, with a peak in the mid-20s; and then decline (Windle & Zucker, 2010). Perhaps surprising to some adults is that North American adolescents who experiment in a limited way with drugs and alcohol tend to be psychosocially healthy (Shelder & Block, 1990; Windle et al., 2008). For example, adolescents who score high on measures of subjective well-being at age 16 tend to report using alcohol at age 18, suggesting that some alcohol use in late adolescence

is common in well-adjusted middle and older adolescents (Mason & Spoth, 2011). Why? Alcohol and substance use may serve a developmental function in middle and late adolescence, such as a way of asserting independence and autonomy from parents, taking risks, forming social relationships, and learning about oneself (Englund et al., 2013). Although most adolescents experiment with alcohol, tobacco, and marijuana, without incident, there are short-term dangers of alcohol and substance use, such as overdose, accidents, and motor impairment pose serious risks as well as long-term dangers of dependence and abuse. In addition, regular intermittent use—using alcohol and substances in spurts on a regular basis (common among adolescents)—can have harmful, even catastrophic, effects on neurological and cognitive development.

Adolescents are more sensitive to neurological damage and show more cognitive impairment in response to alcohol use as compared with adults. Alcohol use, especially the regular intermittent drinking common in adolescence, is associated with damage to the brain, particularly the prefrontal cortex and hippocampus (Bava & Tapert, 2010; Feldstein Ewing, Sakhardande, & Blakemore, 2014). The resulting neurocognitive deficits reduce young people's capacities for executive function, memory, and learning. Adolescents who use alcohol heavily show smaller hippocampal and prefrontal white matter volume than other adolescents (Bava & Tapert, 2010; Jacobus et al., 2013). Adolescent heavy drinking is associated with reduced frontal cortex response during spatial working memory tasks; slower information processing; and reductions in attention, visiospatial functioning, and problem solving (Feldstein Ewing et al., 2014). Poor executive functioning, a common neurological outcome of alcohol use during adolescence, is associated with a decrease in the ability to use social information to regulate their behavior, decreased awareness of the consequences of alcohol abuse, and higher rates of drinking (Schepis, Adinoff, & Rao, 2008).

Adolescents are more vulnerable to alcohol abuse because they show reduced sensitivity to the effects of alcohol that serve as cues in adults to limit their intake, such as motor impairment, sedation, social impairment, and quietness or distress (Spear, 2011). Regular intermittent exposure to alcohol, the typical pattern of adolescent drinking, is associated with increased tolerance to the impairing effects of alcohol and reduced sensitivity to the aversive effects, such as nausea or hangover. Adolescents develop a tolerance for alcohol more quickly than do adults (Schepis et al., 2008; Spear, 2013).

Alcohol and substance use and abuse are associated with negative consequences that can interfere with adolescents' development, such as unwanted sexual encounters and risky sexual activity. Although alcohol and substance use may help adolescents feel that they are achieving social goals such as being comfortable in social situations and making friends, it may threaten their short- and long-term health and well-being. Risks and negative consequences of alcohol and substance use include academic problems, social problems,

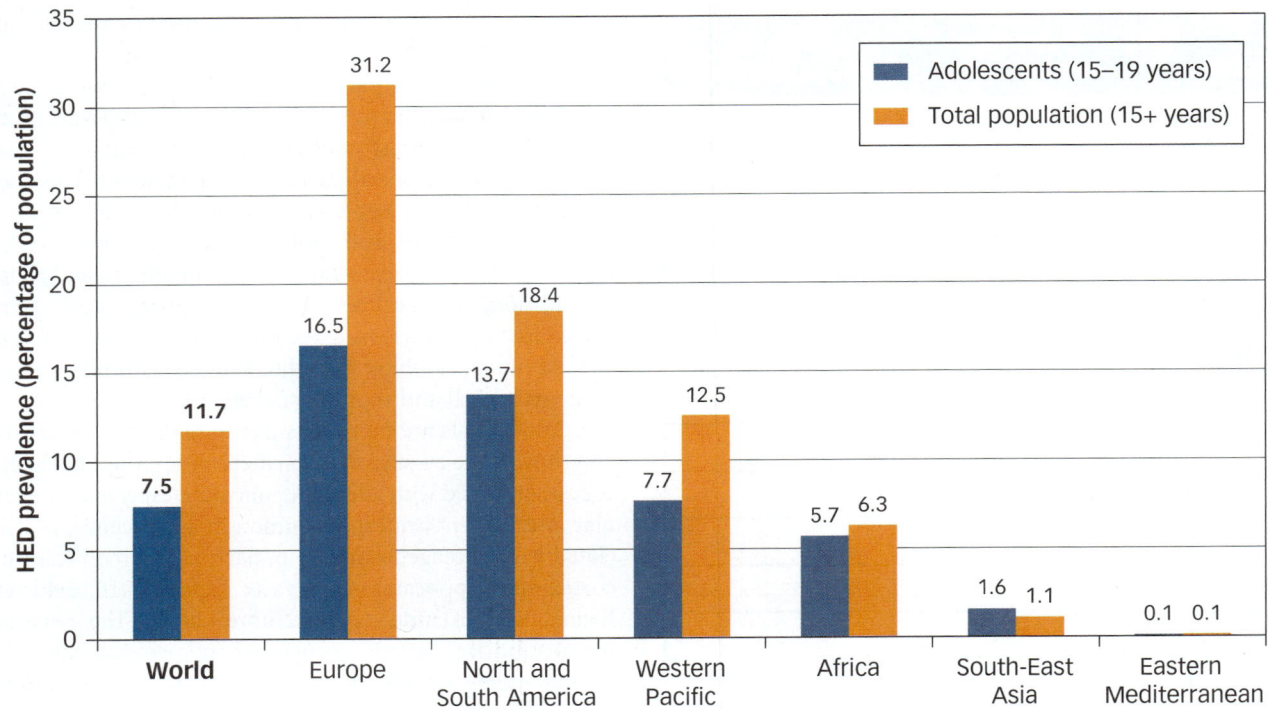

SOURCE: World Health Organization (2014).

aggression and victimization, unintentional injuries, anxiety, depression, car crashes, and suicide (Maggs & Schulenberg, 2005; Marshall, 2014). Relying on alcohol and substances to manage day-to-day stressors and hassles prevents the development of coping, self-regulatory, and decision-making skills, which in turn promotes continued drug use.

Adolescents at risk to abuse alcohol and substances tend to begin drinking earlier than their peers (Chen, Storr, & Anthony, 2009; Palmer et al., 2009). The tendency to abuse alcohol and substances has genetic roots: A family history of alcohol and substance use is a risk factor. However, contextual factors also promote use (Chassin, Ritter, Trim, & King, 2003; Silberg, Rutter, D'Onofrio, & Eaves, 2003). Adolescents are at reduced risk of developing alcohol and substance abuse problems if their parents are involved, warm, supportive, and aware of their children's whereabouts and friends. Low socioeconomic status, family members with poor mental health, drug abuse within the family and community, and disadvantaged neighborhoods increase the risk of alcohol abuse in adolescence (Chaplin et al., 2012; Trucco, Colder, Wieczorek, Lengua, & Hawk, 2014). In turn, adolescents who have mental health problems, difficulty with self-regulation, or are victims of physical or sexual abuse are at higher risk of alcohol and drug abuse than their peers. However, perhaps the most direct influences on adolescents are their peers' drinking or substance abuse behavior, their perceptions of peer support for such use, and their access to alcohol and substances (Brooks-Russell, Simons-Morton, Haynie, Farhat, & Wang, 2014).

Because adolescent alcohol and substance use is a complex problem with multiple influences, prevention and treatment programs must be multipronged. Effective prevention and intervention programs target parents by encouraging that they be warm and supportive, set rules, and be aware of their children's activities. Education is also important. Effective alcohol and substance abuse prevention and treatment programs educate adolescents about the health risks of substance use and that, contrary to depictions in the media and society, substance use is not socially acceptable. Such programs teach adolescents how to resist pressure from peers, how to refuse offers, and how to build their coping and self-regulatory skills (Poth, Greenberg, & Turrisi, 2008; Wagner, 2008; Windle & Zucker, 2010).

DELINQUENCY

"Have you got it?" asked Corey. "Here it is: Mrs. Scarcela's mailbox!" Adam announced as he dropped the stolen item on the floor in front of his friends. During adolescence, young people experiment with new ideas, activities, and limits. For many adolescents, like Adam, experimentation takes the form of delinquent activity. Nearly all young people engage in at least one delinquent, or illegal, act, such as stealing, during the adolescent years without coming into police contact (Flannery, Hussey, & Jefferis, 2005). For example, in one study boys admitted to engaging in, on average, three serious delinquent acts, and girls reported one serious delinquent act between ages 10 and 20, yet nearly none of the adolescents had been arrested (Fergusson & Horwood, 2002). Adolescents account for 9% of police arrests in the United States (Federal Bureau of Investigation, 2014). Males are about four times as likely to be arrested as females. African American youth are disproportionately likely to be arrested as compared with white and Latino youth, who are similar in their likelihood of arrest, and Asian American youth are least likely to be arrested (Andersen, 2015; Federal Bureau of Investigation, 2014).

Adolescents' own reports, however, tend to suggest few to no gender or ethnic differences in delinquent activity (Rutter, Giller, & Hagell, 1998). Differences in arrest rates may be influenced by the tendency for police to arrest and charge ethnic minority youths in low socioeconomic communities more often than European American and Asian American youths in higher socioeconomic status communities (Rutter et al., 1998).

Most adolescents tend to show an increase in delinquent activity in early adolescence that continues into middle adolescence and then declines in late adolescence into early adulthood (Farrington, 2004). Although mild delinquency is common and not necessarily cause for concern, about one quarter of violent offenses in the United States, including murder, rape, robbery, and aggravated assault, are conducted by adolescents (Office of Juvenile Justice and Delinquency Prevention, 2014). Adolescents who engage in serious crime are at risk to become repeat offenders who continue criminal activity into adulthood. Yet most young people whose delinquent activity persists and evolves into a life of crime show multiple problem behaviors that begin not in adolescence but instead in childhood (Farrington & Loeber, 2000). Chronic offenders and those who commit more serious crimes are more likely to have their first contacts with the criminal justice system by age 12 or earlier (Baglivio, Jackowski, Greenwald, & Howell, 2014).

When biological and individual risk factors are coupled with challenging home and community environments, the risk for the childhood onset of serious antisocial behavior that persists into adulthood increases. Parenting that is inconsistent, either highly controlling or negligent, accompanied by harsh punishment, and/or low in monitoring can worsen impulsive, defiant, and aggressive tendencies in children and adolescents (Bowman, Prelow, & Weaver, 2007; Chen, Voisin, & Jacobson, 2013; Harris-McKoy & Cui, 2012; Lahey, Hulle, D'Onofrio, Rodgers, & Waldman, 2008).

Communities of pervasive poverty offer limited educational, recreational, and employment activities, coupled with access to drugs and firearms, opportunities to witness and be victimized by violence, and offers of protection and companionship by gangs that engage in criminal acts, all of which contribute to the onset of antisocial behavior (Chen et al., 2013; Chung & Steinberg, 2006; Hay, Fortson, Hollist, Altheimer, & Schaible, 2007). Exposure to high levels of community violence predicts delinquent activity (Jain & Cohen, 2013; Mrug, Loosier, & Windle, 2008). Low-income communities tend to have schools that struggle to meet students' educational and developmental needs, with crowding, limited resources, and overtaxed teachers (Flannery et al., 2005). Young people who experience individual, home, community, and school risk factors for antisocial behavior tend to associate with similarly deviant peers, which tends to increase delinquent activity as well as chronic delinquency (Evans, Simons, & Simons, 2014; Lacourse, Nagin, & Tremblay, 2003).

Fortunately, for most adolescents, delinquent acts are limited to the adolescent years and do not continue into adulthood (Piquero & Moffitt, 2013). Antisocial behavior tends to increase during puberty and is sustained by affiliation with similar peers. With advances in cognition, moral reasoning, emotional regulation, social skills, and empathy, antisocial activity declines (Monahan, Steinberg, Cauffman, & Mulvey, 2013). Preventing and intervening in delinquency requires examining individual, family, and community factors. Promoting authoritative parenting and close relationships with parents by providing training in discipline, communication, and monitoring fosters healthy parent–child relationships, which buffers young people who are at risk for delinquency (Bowman et al., 2007). High-quality teachers, teacher support, resources, and economic aid foster an educational environment that protects young people from risks for antisocial behavior. A three-year longitudinal study following adolescents of low-income single mothers transitioning off welfare showed that involvement in school activities protects adolescents from some of the negative effects of low-income contexts and is associated with lower levels of delinquency over time (Mahatmya & Lohman, 2011). Economic, social, and employment resources empower communities to create environments that reduce criminal activity by all age groups and promote the development of children and adolescents.

The psychosocial developments of adolescence leave a lifelong imprint on young people. Beginning the identity search, developing more complex and autonomous relationships with parents and friends, and exploring sexuality are important tasks for adolescence that serve as a foundation for development in the next period of life: early adulthood.

Thinking in Context 12.4

1. Using Bronfenbrenner's bioecological systems theory, how do adolescents' physical, cognitive, and social characteristics interact with their context to influence their likelihood of developing an eating disorder such as anorexia nervosa or bulimia nervosa? How might context influence treatment options?

2. How might adults distinguish normative from atypical delinquent activity? For example, a rise in some delinquent activities is somewhat normative during adolescence and will decline in late adolescence, and sometimes the activity continues and increases.

3. Are there dangers in taking the perspective that some alcohol and substance use is common and simply a part of growing up? How should parents, teachers, and professionals respond to adolescent alcohol and substance use?

Apply Your Knowledge 12.1

At 16, John recently had his very first alcoholic drink while at a party hosted by his best friend. Since then, John has begun drinking at parties every few weeks, though he usually stops after a couple of beers. Afterward, he always catches a ride with a friend or a taxi. Big for his age, John is popular in school and has many opportunities to socialize. Even so, he only goes out once a week or so because his football schedule keeps him busy, and he works hard to maintain at least a B+ average.

Tim, also 16, has at least one beer nearly every day—often more than one. He explains that parents, school, work, and simply meeting expectations are overwhelming and frustrating. Drinking is calming, a refuge from the stress of everyday life. Last year, Tim's best friend brought marijuana to a party, and Tim found that it was even better than alcohol; marijuana made him feel free. Tim smokes marijuana whenever he can, which is not often given that it is much more expensive than alcohol. Lately, Tim has found that alcohol doesn't seem to

make him feel as relaxed as it once did, so he's begun trying to obtain marijuana as often as possible. Sometimes Tim steals money—from his mother, job, even teachers—to fund a fun night out.

1. What experience does the average adolescent have with substances such as alcohol and marijuana? What is normative, statistically?

2. Describe correlates of substance use in adolescence. How do John's and Tim's experience compare with that of the typical adolescent?

3. Many aspects of development offer insights into adolescent risk behavior, such as substance use, delinquency, and sexual activity. How might changing relationships with parents, including monitoring, parenting styles, and conflict, contribute to adolescent risk behavior? What role might relationships and interactions with peers take?

Chapter Summary

12.1 Identify ways in which self-conceptions and self-esteem change during adolescence.

With cognitive advances, adolescents begin to use more abstract and complex labels to describe themselves. They evaluate themselves with respect to multiple dimensions and recognize that their qualities can vary with the situation. Global self-esteem dips in early adolescence. Favorable self-evaluations are associated with positive adjustment and sociability in adolescents of all socioeconomic status and ethnic groups, while low self-esteem is associated with adjustment difficulties.

12.2 Outline the process of identity development during adolescence, including influences and outcomes associated with identity status.

Adolescents are faced with the task of constructing an identity that is coherent and consistent over time. Authoritative parenting and close relationships with peers encourage adolescents to explore identity alternatives. Identity achievement is associated with high self-esteem, feelings of control, high moral reasoning, prosocial behavior, and positive views of work and school. Foreclosed and diffused identity statuses are associated with passivity and maladaptive long-term outcomes.

12.3 Explore changes in adolescents' relationships with parents and the contribution of parenting style and monitoring to adolescent adjustment.

Conflict between parents and adolescents rises in early adolescence and peaks in middle adolescence but takes the form of small arguments over minor details. Authoritative parenting fosters autonomy, self-esteem, and academic competence in adolescents. Authoritarian parenting inhibits the development of autonomy and is linked with poor adjustment. Parental monitoring promotes well-being and is a protective factor against risky behavior.

12.4 Compare and contrast the nature of friendship and dating during adolescence.

Adolescent friendships are characterized by intimacy, loyalty, self-disclosure, and trust. Friends tend to be similar in demographics and share psychological and developmental characteristics. Over time, friends tend to become more similar. Close friendships promote positive adjustment. Dating typically begins through the intermingling of mixed-sex peer groups, progresses to group dating, and then goes to one-on-one dating and romantic relationships. Early adolescents date for fun, but in late adolescence, dating fulfills needs for intimacy and support and aids in identity development.

12.5 Differentiate the developmental progression of cliques and crowds.

During adolescence, one-on-one friendships tend to include cliques of about five to seven members who are close friends and share demographic and attitudinal similarities. In early adolescence, cliques tend to be sex segregated, but by mid-adolescence, cliques become mixed and create opportunities for dating. By late adolescence, the mixed sex clique tends to disappear. Crowds emerge in early adolescence. Crowds are reputation-based groups of adolescents who are classified by peers into groups based on perceived characteristics, interests, and reputation. Crowds decline in late adolescence.

12.6 Analyze how susceptibility to peer influence changes from early adolescence to late adolescence.

Peer conformity rises in early adolescence, peaks in middle adolescence, and declines thereafter. American youths tend to feel the greatest pressure from peers to conform to day-to-day activities and personal choices such as choice of clothes and music, appearance but also to engage in prosocial and positive behaviors and sometimes to engage in risky activities and adopt an antisocial stance.

12.7 Compare the factors that contribute to sexual activity, contraceptive use, and the transmission of sexually transmitted infections (STIs) during adolescence.

Sexual activity among U.S. adolescents has declined since 1990, and adolescents are waiting longer to have sex, yet sexual activity begins earlier in the United States than in Canada and Western Europe. Risk factors for early sexual activity include early pubertal maturation, poor parental communication and monitoring, sexually active peers, risky behaviors, and stressful homes and neighborhoods. Adolescents have higher rates of STIs than all other age groups and U.S. adolescents have higher rates of STIs than do those in nearly all Western nations. Although most adolescents receive education, most underestimate their own risks and know little about most STIs or how to protect themselves.

12.8 Discuss risk factors for adolescent pregnancy and influences on the adjustment of adolescent mothers and their children.

Despite a decline since 1990, the United States has one of the highest teen pregnancy rates in the developed world. Adolescent mothers are less likely to achieve many of the typical markers of adulthood and are more likely to work low-paid jobs, spend more years as single parents, and are more likely to divorce. However, there is variability in outcomes. Infants born to adolescent mothers are more likely to be born preterm and low birth weight and show academic and behavioral problems. Positive adjustment in children is predicted by secure attachment, low maternal depressive symptoms, and positive parenting on the part of the mother.

12.9 Compare and contrast the risk factors for and treatments for adolescent problems such as depression and suicide, eating disorders, and substance use and abuse.

Rates of depression rise in early adolescence, and lifelong sex differences emerge, with girls reporting depression twice as often as boys. Hereditary factors are coupled with environmental factors to influence susceptibility to depression. Adolescents who are depressed are more likely to live in homes with depressed parents; to have experienced significant life events such as parental divorce, failure, or the loss of a friend; and, in girls, to have matured early relative to peers.

Anorexia nervosa and bulimia nervosa become more common in adolescence. Both have a genetic basis and are influenced by problems with impulse control, anxiety, and body dissatisfaction. Treatment includes hospitalization, individual and family therapy, nutritional education, and antianxiety or antidepressant medications.

Alcohol and substance use rises during the adolescent years into young adulthood. They may serve developmental functions but are associated with short- and long-term effects, such as accidents, academic problems, risks for dependence and abuse, and impaired neurological development. Alcohol and substance abuse is influenced by genetics but also contextual factors. Effective prevention and intervention programs provide adolescents with education; teach adolescents the skills to resist pressure, refuse offers, and cope; and educate parents as well.

12.10 Characterize normative delinquent activities during adolescence as compared with serious lifelong criminal activity.

Nearly all young people engage in at least one delinquent act during adolescence without coming into police contact. Rates of delinquency rise in early adolescence and decline in late adolescence. A minority of adolescents engage in serious crime and become repeat offenders who continue criminal activity into adulthood. Most adolescents whose delinquent activity persists and evolves into a life of crime displayed antisocial behavior in childhood, engaging in delinquent acts early, relative to their peers. Preventing and intervening in delinquency entails targeting individual, family, and community factors, such as promoting authoritative parenting, parental monitoring, high quality educational environments, and close-knit communities.

Key Terms

Actual self   326

Anorexia nervosa   351

Autonomy   329

Biculturalism   327

Body image   351

Bulimia nervosa   351

Cliques   335

Crowds   335

Cyberbullying   337

Dating violence   339

Depression   326

Ethnic identity   330

Familism   327

Global self-esteem   326

Ideal self   326

Identity   326

Identity achievement   328

Identity diffusion   328

Identity foreclosure   328

Identity moratorium   328

Identity status   328

Perceived popularity   336

Parental monitoring   333

Popular   336

Self-harm   343

Sexual identity   328

Sexual orientation   342

PART VI

Early Adulthood

Early adulthood is a period of gaining and sustaining. Once physical maturity is reached, aging begins. Physical changes are gradual. Most go unnoticed. Cognitive advances continue as young adults become able to appreciate multiple viewpoints, arguments, and contradictions. Socioemotional advances help young adults integrate cognition with emotion, regulate intense emotions, and think logically about complicated everyday situations. Developing a sense of identity, a commitment to a sense of self, values, and goals, prepares young adults for establishing intimate relationships.

Cohabitation is common, and most adults marry by the end of early adulthood. Marital success is predicted by maturity, realistic expectations, joint conflict resolution, and respect. Most adults become parents and often are surprised by the wide range of emotions that accompany their new baby and set of responsibilities. As the home context ascends in salience, the number of friends and time spent with them declines. The work context becomes prominent as young adults form occupational goals, settle into careers, and monitor their progress, changing their goals in light of their experiences, abilities, and interests. The school context remains relevant for many young adults. Nontraditional students balance work, family, and school, but benefit from a more complex knowledge base, and an emphasis on applying what they learn to their lives. Overall, contexts shift in salience during early adulthood, but continue to interact and influence all domains of development.

Watch at
edge.sagepub.com/kuther

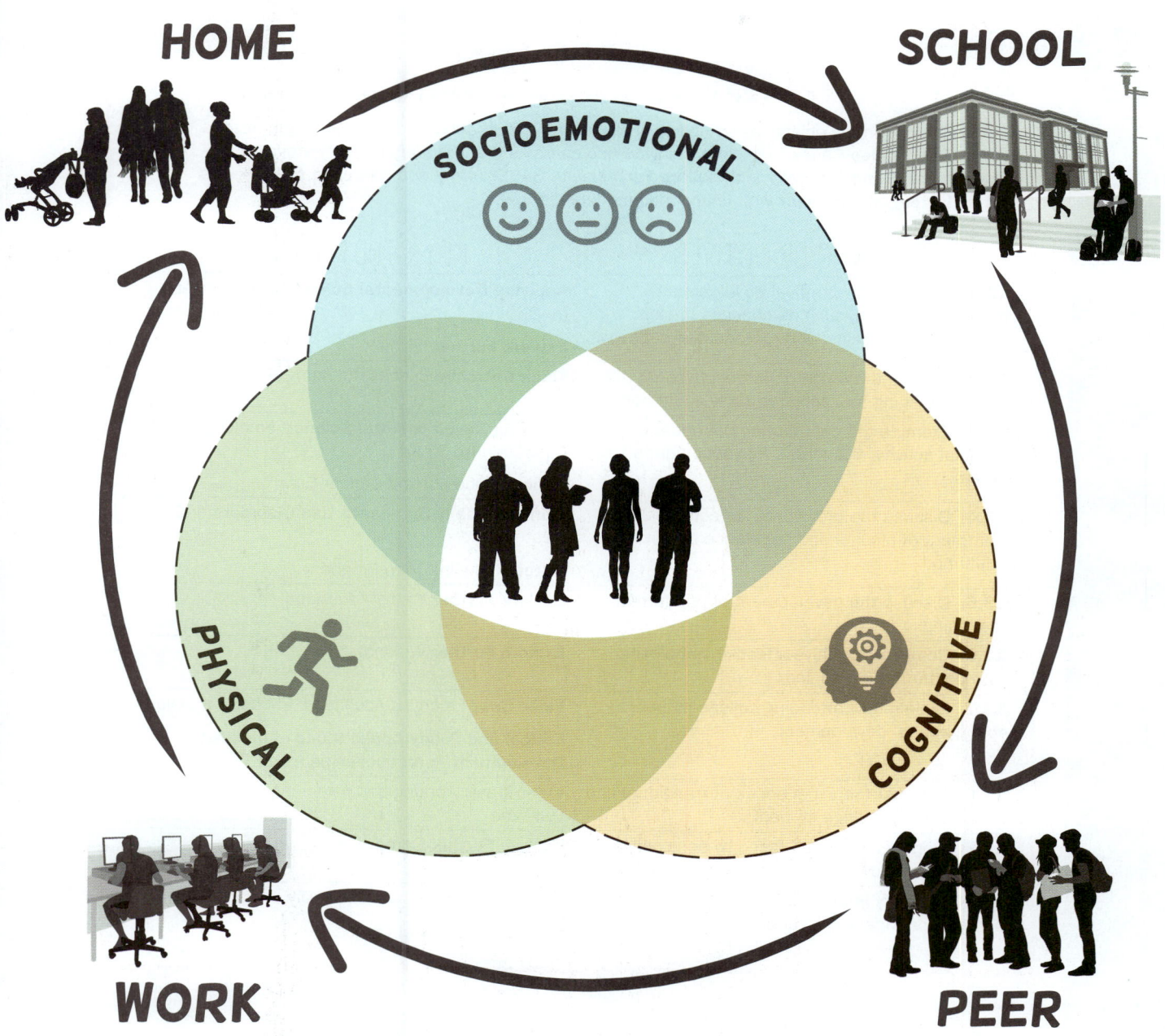

HOME

SCHOOL

SOCIOEMOTIONAL

PHYSICAL

COGNITIVE

WORK

PEER

Images: ©iStock.com

Physical and Cognitive Development in Early Adulthood

SAGE edge™   **Get the edge on your studies at edge.sagepub.com/kuther.**

Master these learning objectives using key study tools in the chapter and at SAGE edge. Access original SAGE **Video Cases** to explore the lives and contexts of individuals in every stage of development, **Think Critically** and **Explore Further** with SAGE journal and reference articles, and **Watch**, **Listen**, and **Connect** with online multimedia resources.

LEARNING OBJECTIVES

13.1. Describe the physical developments of early adulthood, such as changes in skin, muscles, motor skills, and reproductive capacity.

13.2. Analyze the range of perspectives on the causes of aging as applied to early adulthood.

13.3. Examine the contributions of obesity, physical activity, and stress for young adults' health.

13.4. Discuss the prevalence, effects, and treatment of alcohol and substance use in early adulthood.

13.5. Discuss the development of postformal reasoning.

13.6. Compare cognitive-affective complexity with postformal reasoning.

13.7. Explain how attending college influences young adults' development.

13.8. Contrast the experiences of traditional and nontraditional college students.

13.9. Identify challenges faced by non-college bound young adults.

13.10. Identify influences on vocational choice and occupational expectations in early adulthood.

KEY STUDY TOOLS

Applying Developmental Science Skin Cancer (p. 365)

Explore Further Fertility

Think Critically Successful Aging

Applying Developmental Science Smoking Cessation (p. 371)

Connect Obesity and Cancer Risk

Think Critically Substance Use Disorders and Treatment

Listen Reducing Teen Pregnancy

Explore Further Young Adulthood

Explore Further Wisdom

Video Case Emerging Adulthood: Choosing a Major

Ethical and Policy Applications of lifespan Development Apprenticeships (p. 381)

Video Case Working and Attending College Full-Time

Explore Further Career Education

Lives in Context The Gender Divide (p. 383)

Connect Vocational Choice

As he drives to school, Richard recites definitions and concepts for his biology exam. At 19 years of age, Richard has just entered his second year of college. Like many college students, Richard is not sure of his major or what career is for him. The first in his family to attend college, Richard feels a sense of responsibility to succeed, but he also finds it difficult to balance his schoolwork with his part-time job. Richard's busy schedule leaves him with little time for participating in campus activities, making friends with other students, and getting to know his professors. Many students like Richard face similar challenges that can interfere with their success in college.

Robert O'Dea/Arcaid/Corbis

As he progresses through college, Richard begins to notice that he feels more comfortable making decisions. Rather than feeling overwhelmed with many choices, he feels that he is able to consider each one, recognize its strengths and weaknesses, and weigh them in order to make decisions. Similar to his cognitive advances, as he reaches his mid-20s, Richard feels that he is physically stronger and faster than ever before. He wonders how his body will change and how his life will unfold in the coming years. Richard's developmental concerns and capacities reflect the period in life known as early adulthood. Over the next decade and one half, Richard will experience many, often subtle, physical changes as well as changes in how he thinks and views the world around him. This period in life, early adulthood, spans from about ages 18 to 40.

PHYSICAL DEVELOPMENT IN EARLY ADULTHOOD

When it comes to physical development, early adulthood is a time of becoming and of maintaining. All of the organs and body systems, including digestive, respiratory, circulatory, and reproductive systems, peak in functioning during early adulthood. We may not think of people in their 20s as aging, but the biological fact is that once individuals are physically mature with growth and physical development at adult levels, **senescence**—a pattern of gradual age-related declines in physical functioning—begins (Cristofalo, Tresini, & Francis, 1999). Aging begins at maturation, but measurable age-related changes in functioning, known as aging, are visible by about age 30, though most people do not notice these until middle adulthood. Aging entails gradual changes in strength, body proportions, sensory capacities, and fertility.

Similar to development throughout infancy, childhood, and adolescence, development in early adulthood is multidimensional and multidirectional. Different parts of the body age at different rates, and development comprises both gains and losses in capacities such as strength, endurance, and motor skill. Age and physical development are closely related in childhood, but the link is much weaker in adulthood. Young adults display a wide range of individual differences in physical functioning and aging due to differences in genetics, context, and experience, including health; socioeconomic status; and behaviors such as smoking, exercise, and diet (Bonnie, Stroud, & Breiner, 2015; Federal Interagency Forum on Child and Family Statistics, 2014). For example, lung efficiency declines with age, but it drops 5% faster per decade for smokers as compared with nonsmokers (De Martinis & Timiras, 2003). In addition, organs vary in their rate of decline (McDonald, 2014); in one individual, for example, the digestive system may show signs of aging earlier than the cardiovascular system, while it may be the other way around for another individual.

PHYSICAL DEVELOPMENT

The age-related physical changes that occur in young adulthood are so gradual that very few of us notice them. Though more apparent in middle age, by age 30 some individuals begin to notice gray hairs, as the hair follicle cells that produce pigment, or color, become less abundant. Men who are prone to hereditary baldness typically begin balding in their 30s. Age-related changes in the skin, which are predictable and virtually unavoidable, begin at about age 20. The connective tissue begins to thin by about 1% per year, resulting in less elastic skin and some visible wrinkles around the eyes by age 30 (Timiras, 2003). Most adults in their 30s notice lines developing on their foreheads, the result of a lifetime of facial expressions, and many begin to notice crow's feet at the corners of the eyes. However, the rate of skin aging is influenced by exposure to the elements, such as sun, heat, cold, and pollution. Exposure to the sun is thought to be the most dramatic contributor to skin aging, responsible for about 80% of skin changes, and—as discussed in Applying Developmental Science (p. 365)—the leading cause of skin cancer (Flament, Bazin, & Piot, 2013; Kohl, Steinbauer, Landthaler, & Szeimies, 2011). The use of sunscreen has been shown to retard skin aging (Hughes, Williams, Baker, & Green, 2013).

Muscle development increases throughout the 20s and peaks at about age 30 (Masoro & Austad, 2005). Muscle strength, as measured by the maximum force with which one can throw a ball, for example, shows a gradual decline beginning at about age 30 but is generally not noticeable to most people until middle age (Rice & Cunningham, 2002). **Isometric muscle strength**, the subtle contractions used to hold a hand grip, push off against a wall, stretch, or practice yoga, is maintained throughout adulthood (Lavender & Nosaka, 2007). Young adults' performance on activities that require body coordination and bursts of strength, such as sprinting and playing basketball, tend to peak in the early 20s whereas those that require endurance, such as distance running, peak in the early 30s (Schulz & Curnow, 1988). Although strength and motor skills show a predictable pattern of change, young adults vary in the rate of change in their performance. Research with expert athletes, for example, illustrates that practice and athletic training maintains strength and motor skills. As compared with nonathlete peers, athletes experience more subtle and gradual declines in physical abilities from the late 30s to the 60s. Their muscles and motor skills age much more slowly than their peers (Faulkner, Larkin, Claflin, & Brooks, 2007).

FERTILITY AND REPRODUCTIVE CAPACITY

Martina holds her newborn close to her while chatting with her family who has come to visit her in the maternity ward. At 32 years of age, Martina is older than the average first-time mother; most women are in their 20s when they give birth to their first child. However, as shown in Figure 13.1, births to women in their 30s have increased substantially since the early

Skin Cancer

Kevin Schaefer/Moment Mobile/Getty

The sunlamps used in tanning salons produce much more ultraviolet radiation than natural sunlight. People who use tanning beds are more than twice as likely to develop skin cancers as their peers.

In healthy skin, new skin cells push older skin cells toward the skin's surface where they die and are sloughed off. Skin cancer occurs when this process malfunctions, causing new skin cells to grow out of control and form a mass of cancer cells (National Cancer Insitute, 2010). Skin cancer is the most common type of cancer in the United States, and melanoma is the sixth most common cause of cancer deaths each year (U.S. Cancer Statistics Working Group, 2013). One in five Americans will develop skin cancer over the course of their lifetimes.

Several factors increase risk of skin cancer (National Cancer Insitute, 2010):

- A history of sunburns
- Excessive sun exposure and tanning
- Fair skin—but anyone can get skin cancer, including those with darker complexions
- Residing in sunny or high-altitude climates
- A history of moles
- A family history of skin cancer
- A weakened immune system
- Fragile skin damaged by burns, injuries, or skin conditions

- Exposure to environmental toxins
- Increasing age

Most skin cancers can be prevented by limiting or avoiding exposure to ultraviolet (UV) radiation from the sun. Many adults do not adequately protect their skin from sun damage under the mistaken belief that the majority of a person's lifetime sun exposure is acquired before age 18. Instead, only about 23% of lifetime exposure occurs by age 18 (Godar, Urbach, Gasparro, & van der Leun, 2003).

Many young adults patronize tanning salons under the belief that an indoor tan is a safe tan. However, the sunlamps used in tanning salons may produce as much as 12 times the UV radiation of natural sunlight (National Toxicology Program, 2011). People who use tanning beds are 2 to 3 times as likely to develop skin cancers as their peers. About 70% of tanning salon patrons are girls and women aged 16 to 29, and skin cancers are increasing fastest among women younger than 40 (Skin Cancer Foundation, 2009).

To protect your skin from UV rays and reduce your risk of developing skin cancer, follow these skin cancer prevention tips:

- Avoid the sun when rays are strongest, between 10:00 a.m. and 4:00 p.m.
- Wear sunscreen year-round.
- Wear protective clothing.
- Avoid tanning beds and tan-accelerating agents.
- Be aware of sun-sensitizing medications, such as some antibiotics, high blood pressure and diabetes medications, birth control pills, and acne medications.

Skin changes that could signal a cancerous or precancerous condition include new or growing moles; changes in existing moles such as irregular pigment, bleeding, or itching; and unexplained sores. An annual skin exam is recommended for everyone. The American Academy of Dermatology sponsors free "SPOT me" skin cancer screening clinics in many communities.

What Do You Think?

1. **In your view, how common is tanning among young adults? Why do you think it is popular (or not popular)?**

2. **How might you convince young people about the danger of sun tanning and skin cancer?**

1990s (Martin, Hamilton, Osterman, Curtin, & Mathews, 2015). Many young adults wait to have children until they have completed their education and established their careers. The maturity and financial stability that accompany the 30s can make for better parents. However, reproductive capacity declines with age, increasing the risk for women in their mid- to late 30s of experiencing difficulty conceiving (Schmidt, Sobotka, Bentzen, & Nyboe Andersen, 2012; Tatone, 2008).

As women's reproductive systems age, changes occur in the quality of ova and in the rate of ovulation. Women are born with about 400,000 ova (Jadav, 2004). Chromosomal anomalies accumulate as egg cells age, increasing the risk of pregnancy loss, or miscarriage (Bentov, Yavorska, Esfandiari, Jurisicova, & Casper, 2011; Tatone, 2008). A common cause of female infertility is the failure to ovulate, to release an ova into the fallopian tube. With advancing

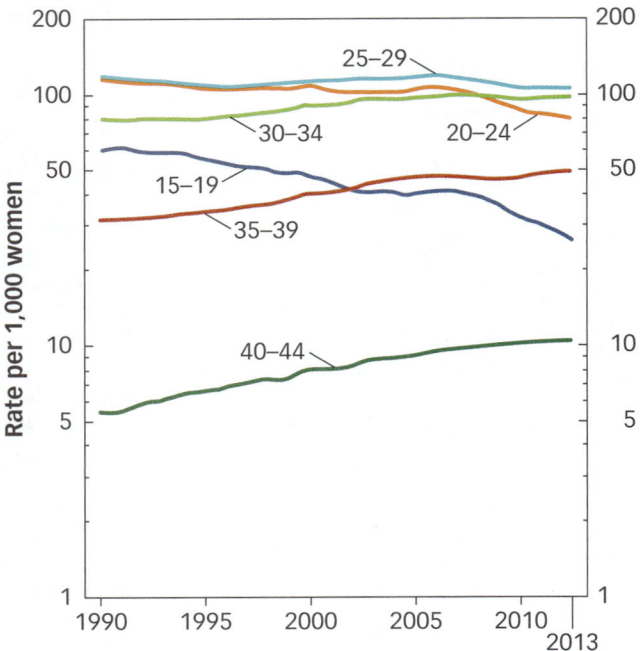

NOTE: Live births per 1,000 women. This figure illustrates the trend of increasing births among women in their thirties and forties.
SOURCE: Martin et al. (2015).

age, ovulation becomes less regular. There are also a variety of factors that can prevent ovulation; some are treatable or preventable, such as drug and alcohol abuse, environmental toxins, obesity, and being underweight (Gordon et al., 2007; Holman, O'Connor, & Wood, 2006; Malik, 2009). Illnesses that affect the reproductive system, such as ovarian cancer and ovarian cysts, can also make it difficult or impossible to conceive (Agarwal, Gupta, & Sikka, 2006; Alpay, Saed, & Diamond, 2006). In addition, dwindling reserves of ova can also prevent conception because it is thought that the body requires a minimum level of ova reserves in order to conceive (Baird et al., 2005). However, the exact minimum is unknown and, like other aspects of physical development, may vary with genetic and contextual factors (Schuh-Huerta et al., 2012).

Men's rate of change in reproductive capacity is significantly different from that of women; most men remain able to conceive into older adulthood. However, the number and quality of sperm produced does decline in middle adulthood, beginning at about age 40 (Brahem, Mehdi, Elghezal, & Saad, 2011; Ehlert & Fischbacher, 2013; Fisch, 2009; Johnson, Dunleavy, Gemmell, & Nakagawa, 2015). In young men, sperm can be affected by anything that interferes with the functioning of the body, such as fever, stress, drug abuse, alcoholism, radiation, and environmental toxins (Li, Lin, Li, & Cao, 2011). Exposure to these factors can reduce the number of sperm, or affect their physical structure, activity, and motility. The oxidative stress of exposure to **free radicals**, as discussed in the next section, may also contribute

to male infertility (Agarwal et al., 2006). In this way, lifestyle and contextual factors contribute to young men's fertility.

THEORIES OF AGING

Biological aging begins at maturity and is the result of multiple factors. There are many theoretical explanations for aging (Bengston, Gans, Pulney, & Silverstein, 2009; Cristofalo et al., 1999; Masoro & Austad, 2005). According to the **wear and tear theory of aging**, an early theory of aging, the body wears out from use and thus ages. On the contrary, research suggests that we must "use it or lose it." That is, regular exercise increases longevity in all people regardless of ethnicity or socioeconomic status (Sanchis-Gomar, Olaso-Gonzalez, Corella, Gomez-Cabrera, & Vina, 2011; Stessman, Hammerman-Rozenberg, Maaravi, Azoulai, & Cohen, 2005). Activity is a critical component of a long and healthy life.

Several other theories offer additional explanations for aging. A more recent perspective explains it as a function of programmed genetics: DNA and heredity. Recall from Chapter 2 that our genes are composed of DNA and serve as the genetic blueprint, handed down through heredity, for all of our characteristics. Parents' lifespans predict those of their children, and identical twins share more similar lifespans than do fraternal twins, suggesting a hereditary link (Hjelmborg et al., 2006; Montesanto et al., 2011). However, kin relations for markers of biological age, such as strength, respiratory capacity, blood pressure, and bone density are relatively small as health is influenced not just by genetics but by context and lifestyle. lifespans among family members often vary with context and behaviors. Aging therefore reflects the interaction of epigenetic factors (Moskalev, Aliper, Smit-McBride, Buzdin, & Zhavoronkov, 2014). It may be that it is not lifespan that we inherit but a set of genetic factors that may predict lifespan (Walter et al., 2011). Ultimately, it is the contextual factors such as the availability of health care and lifestyle factors such as health-related behaviors that matter in predicting lifespan.

Whether genetic predispositions for longevity are realized depends on environmental factors such as diet and exercise, behaviors such as alcohol use or smoking, and exposure to environmental toxins (Karasik, Demissie, Cupples, & Kiel, 2005; Tourlouki et al., 2010). Experiments with animals support the role of **caloric restriction** in longevity (Speakman & Mitchell, 2011). A nutritious diet that is extremely low in calories is associated with a longer lifespan (Anton & Leeuwenburgh, 2013; Smith, Nagy, & Allison, 2010). The immune system plays a role in aging by influencing the body's adjustment to external stressors and pathogens encountered throughout life. From this perspective, an aging immune system is less able to differentiate healthy cells from pathology, may direct the body's defenses against healthy cells, and may ignore harmful cells (Montecino-Rodriguez, Berent-Maoz, & Dorshkind, 2013; Salvioli et al., 2013).

Another account of aging relies on cellular mutation, damage to DNA and chromosomes. Research with animals shows that cell mutations increase with age (Baines, Turnbull, & Greaves, 2014; Lee, Chang, & Chi, 2010) Cellular mutations lead to a deterioration in functioning and an increase in age-related diseases and cancers. Free radicals may account for some of this damage. Free radicals are highly reactive, and corrosive substances form when cells are exposed to oxygen. As oxygen decomposes within the cell, changes occur at the level of the atom: An electron is stripped, creating a free radical. Through chemical reactions, free radicals destroy DNA, proteins, and other cellular materials in an attempt to replace the missing electrons. Free radicals are thought to contribute to many age-related diseases such as cancer, cardiovascular disorders, and arthritis (Lagouge & Larsson, 2013; Shringarpure & Davies, 2009). Genes and environment may work to defend the body from free radicals by producing material that neutralizes free radicals and reduces the harm caused by them (Miura & Endo, 2010). A diet rich in antioxidants, including vitamins C and E and beta carotene, can protect against damage from free radicals (Harman, 2006).

Reductions in the capacity for cell division, specifically the limited capacity for human cells to divide, are the basis for another explanation for aging. Human cells have the capacity to divide about 50 times in their lifespan (Hayflick, 1996). Each time the cell divides, **telomeres**, tiny caps of DNA located at both ends of the chromosomes, become shorter. Shorter telomeres may protect the cell from common mutations that occur with repeated divisions, but they also reduce the cell's capacity to reproduce itself (Sedivy, 2007; Xi, Li, Ren, Zhang, & Zhang, 2013). Telomeres that shorten past a critical length cause the cell to stop dividing all together, leading to increases in disease, cell death, and body aging (Andrews, Fujii, Goronzy, & Weyand, 2010; Campisi, 2013). In this sense, telomere length may serve as a

TABLE 13.1 Theories of Aging

THEORY	EXPLANATION
Wear and tear	The body wears out, aging from use.
Programmed genetics	The rate of aging is influenced by DNA and heredity.
Caloric restriction	A nutritious diet that is extremely low in calories is associated with a longer lifespan.
Aging immune system	With age, the immune system is less able to differentiate healthy cells from pathology and may direct the body's defenses against healthy cells instead of harmful cells.
Cellular mutation	Aging results from damage to DNA and chromosomes, leading to an increase in cellular mutations that result in age-related diseases and cancers.
Free radicals	Free radicals, highly reactive and corrosive substances that form when cells are exposed to oxygen, destroy DNA, proteins, and other cellular materials and contribute to age-related diseases and cancers.
Reduced capacity for cell division	Each time human cells divide, telomeres become shorter, protecting the cell from mutations that occur with repeated divisions but also reducing the cell's capacity to reproduce itself. Eventually, telomeres become so short that the cell stops dividing, diseases increase, and cells die.

biomarker of aging (Mather, Jorm, Parslow, & Christensen, 2011; Xu, Duc, Holcman, & Teixeira, 2013). Stress contributes to the shortening of telomeres, as well as oxidative stress such as that which results from free radicals (Epel, 2009; Shalev et al., 2013). Each of these theories of aging offers a different perspective on the causes of aging, as shown in Table 13.1. Given the complexities of development, it is likely that an adequate account of aging entails drawing from each of these theories.

Thinking in Context 13.1

1. Recall that development is characterized by continuities and discontinuities. Identify two aspects of physical development that illustrate continuity and two that illustrate discontinuity.

2. Identify factors that influence reproductive capacity and aging during early adulthood. How many might be categorized as biological in nature, and how many might be considered as contextual factors?

3. Consider theories of aging. In your view, which theory is the *least* adequate in accounting for how we change over our lifetimes? Which theory do you think best accounts for how people develop over the lifespan? Why?

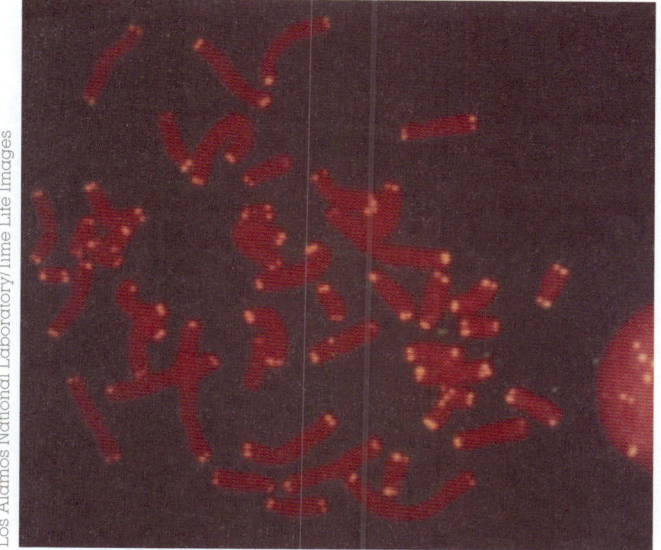

Los Alamos National Laboratory/Time Life Images

Telomeres, dyed yellow, are visible at the ends of each chromosome. Telomeres shorten with each cell division. When telomeres shorten beyond a critical length, the cell stops dividing.

HEALTH, FITNESS, AND WELLNESS IN EARLY ADULTHOOD

Generally speaking, early adulthood is a time of physical health. Few deaths among young adults are the result of illness. Instead, the leading cause of death in U.S. young adults through age 35 is unintentional injury, followed by homicide and suicide, and then cancer and heart disease (Centers for Disease Control and Prevention [CDC], 2015). Young adults who become ill or die from illness are more likely to be of low socioeconomic status. Socioeconomic indicators such as income, education, and occupation are closely related with health and illness, largely because, in the United States, health care is expensive and access is limited by socioeconomic factors (Adler & Newman, 2002; Raiz, 2006). The Affordable Care Act, signed in 2010, was implemented in 2013 with the goal of increasing the quality and affordability of health insurance in the United States, expanding public and private health insurance coverage and reducing the costs of health care. An initial estimate after the first year of operation suggests that the percentage of uninsured people may have fallen from 18% in the third quarter of 2013 to about 13% by the end of the first quarter of 2014 (Blumenthal & Collins, 2014). In Canada, universal access to health insurance has contributed to fewer economic disparities in access to health care among Canadians (Torrey & Haub, 2004).

Socioeconomic status is associated with other influences on health, such as environmental factors (e.g., exposure to crowding, stress, and pollution), health-enhancing factors (e.g., exercise, diet, and social support), and health risks (e.g., obesity and substance abuse; Cornman, Glei, Goldman, Ryff, & Weinstein, 2015; Evans & Kantrowitz, 2002). Socioeconomic differences in health status widen over the adult years. High levels of education and income are associated with better health whereas low levels of education and income are associated with deteriorating health from early adulthood through late adulthood (House, Lantz, & Herd, 2005; Schumann et al., 2011). Many of the risk and protective factors that predict health in childhood and adolescence also predict health across the adult years, as discussed in the following sections.

OVERWEIGHT AND OBESITY

During his first year of college, Byron welcomed the ability to make choices about food and plan his own meals. Without his health-conscious mother's input, he was able to munch on fried chicken wings whenever he wanted and enjoyed exercising this new freedom. By his senior year of college, Byron was 45 pounds overweight. The absence of parental controls, access to an abundance of food, and busy lives make it difficult for young adults to eat healthily. Eating habits begun in early adulthood often persist for life. Obesity, defined as a body mass index (BMI) of 30 or above, and overweight (BMI greater than 25) have increased substantially in recent decades. Over two thirds of American adults are either overweight (34%) or obese (35%; Fryar, Carroll, & Ogden, 2014; Ogden, Carroll, Kit, & Flegal, 2014). Young adult women show higher rates of weight gain than women in other age groups, perhaps because of differences in contraception, dietary behavior, physical activity, and stresses associated with life transitions (such as to college; Wane, Van Uffelen, & Brown, 2010).

Obesity is influenced by heredity, but today's obesity epidemic in Western nations has stronger ties to environmental pressures than genetic factors. Physical labor is less a part of the lifestyle in industrialized nations than ever before. Food, especially sugary, fatty, and fried foods, have become more abundant at the same time as people have become more sedentary. Sedentary lifestyles, and especially the number of hours spent viewing television, are closely associated with obesity (Heinonen et al., 2013; Pearson & Biddle, 2011). Young adults who are obese are more likely to make fewer healthy food choices and to overeat than their non-obese counterparts (Keski-Rahkonen et al., 2007). With age, it becomes more difficult to avoid overeating because caloric needs drop between the ages of 25 and 50, and the metabolic rate, the amount of energy the body uses at rest, gradually falls as muscle cells decline in number and size (Whitbourne, 2007). Low socioeconomic status in early adulthood predicts obesity in young adults, even after controlling for childhood socioeconomic status (Baum & Ruhm, 2009; Giskes, van Lenthe, Avendano-Pabon, & Brug, 2011).

Obesity is a serious health risk, associated with a range of health problems and illnesses such as high blood pressure; stroke; circulatory problems; diabetes; digestive disorders; arthritis; cancer; and, ultimately, early death (Calle, Rodriguez, Walker-Thurmond, & Thun, 2003; Drong, Lindgren, & McCarthy, 2012; Tchernof & Després, 2013). Consumption of high levels of saturated fat is associated with heightened cardiovascular reactivity (e.g., increases in heart rate), and even a single high-fat meal predicts short-term increases in cardiovascular reactivity (Jakulj et al., 2007). Obesity also holds social risks. Obese adults report more relationship difficulties with family, peers, and coworkers and have more difficulty finding mates, rental apartments, and jobs than do non-obese adults (Ambwani, Thomas, Hopwood, Moss, & Grilo, 2014; Carr & Friedman, 2005; Pachucki & Goodman, 2015).

Although young adults who have been overweight since childhood may feel it's "hopeless" to seek treatment for obesity, the fact is that health outcomes improve with even moderate weight loss (Orzano & Scott, 2004). Successful long-term weight loss, however, is challenging, as indicated by the vast array of "quick" weight loss programs advertised in the media. Only about 20% of overweight individuals are successful at long-term weight loss, defined as losing at least 10% of initial body weight and maintaining the loss for at least one year (Wing & Phelan, 2005). Successful weight loss is most often a result of lifestyle changes, such as regular moderate exercise coupled with a nutritionally balanced diet low in calories and fat (Douketis, Macie, Thabane, & Williamson, 2005; Holt, Warren, & Wallace, 2006). Effective weight loss interventions emphasize behaviors and encourage individuals to keep accurate records of what they eat and analyze eating patterns in their food choices (LeBlanc, O'Connor, Whitlock, Patnode, & Kapka, 2011; MacLean et al., 2015). Since many people overeat as a reaction to stress, training in problem-solving skills helps participants learn non-food-related ways of managing day-to-day conflicts and difficulties, as well as increasing social support to help individuals attain and sustain weight loss.

PHYSICAL ACTIVITY

Exercise is an important influence on longevity (Schnohr, Scharling, & Jensen, 2003; Schoenborn & Stommel, 2011). Regular moderate exercise enhances immunity, lowering the risk of, and speeding recovery to, illnesses (Horn et al., 2015). Other benefits of exercise include stress reduction, cardiovascular health, and cancer prevention (Sloan et al., 2009). Exercise reduces risks for obesity-related illnesses such as heart disease, cancer, and diabetes (Bassuk & Manson, 2005; Tardon et al., 2005; Wannamethee, Shaper, & Alberti, 2000). Exercise strengthens muscles, reduces blood pressure, and increases the healthy form of cholesterol (high-density lipoprotein, or HDL), which in turn helps to remove the harmful form of cholesterol (low-density lipoprotein, or LDL) from the artery walls (Mann, Beedie, & Jimenez, 2014). Regular physical activity is associated with a variety of mental health benefits such as improved mood, energy, self-esteem, working memory, and ability to cope as well as reductions in stress, anxiety, and depression (Donaghy, 2007; Hogan, Mata, & Carstensen, 2013; Penedo & Dahn, 2005; Stroth, Hille, Spitzer, & Reinhardt, 2009).

How much exercise is enough to reap health benefits? To obtain health benefits such as reduced cholesterol levels, decreased body fat, and reduced risk of developing diabetes or heart disease, national guidelines recommend engaging in at least 150 minutes of moderate activity each week (such as brisk walking, raking the lawn, or pushing a lawn mower), or 75 minutes of vigorous activity, plus muscle strengthening exercises on at least two days each week (U.S. Department of Health and Human Services, 2008). About 300 minutes of moderate or 150 minutes of vigorous exercise may be required each week to lose weight. The activity does not have to be performed in a single block of time but may be accumulated in 10-minute increments throughout the day.

Remaining active helps adults maintain motor skill competencies, such as throwing speed and jumping distance, which predict overall fitness, percentage of body fat, and strength. In addition, fitness is linked to cognitive performance throughout adulthood. Young adults who demonstrate high levels of cardiovascular fitness tend to perform better on measures of basic cognitive abilities,

Reuters/Fabian Bimmer

U.S. national guidelines recommend engaging in at least 150 minutes of moderate activity (such as brisk walking) or 75 minutes of vigorous activity (such as running), plus muscle strengthening exercises at least twice each week.

such as attention, reaction time, working memory, and processing speed than low-fitness young adults (Newson & Kemps, 2008).

It is estimated that about 31% of the world's population is physically inactive (Hallal et al., 2012). The prevalence of physical activity varies widely around the world, from 2% of women in Saudi Arabia to 81% of women in Denmark engaging in regular physical activity, and 4% of men in Brazil to 77% of men in Sweden (Sisson & Katzmarzyk, 2008). Despite the importance of physical activity in promoting health, less than one half of adults in the United States (47% of men and 43% of women) and about one half of Canadians (55% of men and 50% of women) are moderately active, with at least 30 minutes of moderate activity or its equivalent in vigorous activity daily (Gilmour, 2007; Slack, 2006). In addition to sedentary lifestyles, young adults often engage in other health-compromising behaviors such as substance use.

SUBSTANCE ABUSE

In North America, substance use, such as drug, alcohol, and tobacco use, tends to begin during adolescence, peak in the early 20s, and decline into the 30s (Chen & Jacobson, 2012; Schulenberg & Miech, 2014; Staff et al., 2010). As they transition to adulthood, young adults are typically living away from their parents for the first time in their lives and experience the drive to explore the world at the same time as they feel pressure to complete their education, establish a career, and find a mate. These circumstances, coupled with easy access to drugs and alcohol, increase the risk of using and abusing marijuana, alcohol, and other drugs in early adulthood. Substance abuse is highest in the 20s, often with dangerous consequences such as overdose, injury, accidents, and death (Chen & Jacobson, 2012). Substance use tends to decline as young adults become parents and transition into new family roles; however, substance use remains prevalent in adulthood with about 6% of middle-aged adults reporting substance use within the past month (Substance Abuse and Mental Health Services Administration, 2014).

Tobacco

About 80% of smokers have their first cigarette before age 18, but regular or daily smoking often does not begin until about age 20, and the overall risk of initiating smoking plateaus at about age 22 (Green et al., 2007). Each month, over one third of 18- to 39-year-olds in the United States report smoking tobacco cigarettes. Even low levels of tobacco use during adolescence predict smoking during young adulthood, especially among young people who initiate smoking before age 12 (Riggs, Chih-Ping, Chaoyang, & Pentz, 2007). Moreover, many smokers do not consider themselves smokers because they only engage in occasional social smoking. That is, they smoke in social groups rather than as a daily habit (Brown, Carpenter, & Sutfin, 2011). In one study, 62% of young adults who indicated they had recently smoked identified themselves as social smokers (Song & Ling, 2011). Most social smokers report no immediate desire to quit, and although they acknowledge smoking-related health risks, they minimize them as being personally irrelevant (Brown et al., 2011).

The life transitions that come with young adulthood, such as dramatic changes in social networks, living arrangements, and school and work settings, influence susceptibility to smoking and patterns of smoking behavior. During transitions to marriage, parenthood, and occupational roles, young adults may either reject tobacco use or begin smoking regularly so that it becomes an established addiction. Education acts as a protective factor: Non-college-educated adults aged 18 to 34 are more than twice as likely to smoke as their college-educated peers (CDC, 2011; Green et al., 2007; Lawrence, Fagan, Backinger, Gibson, & Hartman, 2007).

Cigarette smoking is responsible for about one of every five deaths in the United States each year (U.S. Department of Health and Human Services, 2014). Tobacco smoke harms nearly every part of the body; it is linked with cataracts, pneumonia, and lung diseases such as chronic bronchitis and emphysema and accounts for about one third of all cancer deaths. The most common cancer caused by tobacco smoke is lung cancer. Cigarette smoking is liked to about 90% of all cases of lung cancer, the top cancer killer of both men and women. Cigarette smoking is also associated with cancers of the mouth, larynx, esophagus, stomach, pancreas, cervix, kidney, and more. In addition, smoking substantially increases the risk of coronary heart disease, stroke, heart attack, vascular disease, and aneurysm (National Institute on Drug Abuse, 2009). When nonsmokers are exposed to secondhand smoke, they too experience negative health consequences, particularly lung cancer and cardiovascular disease (U.S. Department of Health and Human Services, 2014).

Why is smoking such a tenacious habit? With each cigarette, a smoker consumes 1 to 2 milligrams of nicotine in about a five-minute period. Nicotine enters the blood and reaches the brain quickly and stimulates reward pathways, making it highly addictive. Nicotine also stimulates the adrenal glands to release adrenaline, which increases blood pressure and heart rate (National Institute on Drug Abuse, 2009). Withdrawal symptoms of nicotine begin quickly, within a few hours after the last cigarette, and include irritability, craving, anxiety, and attention deficits, which often send the smoker in search of another cigarette. Other withdrawal symptoms include depression, sleep problems, and increased appetite. When a smoker quits, withdrawal symptoms often peak within the first few days of smoking cessation and usually subside within a few weeks, but some people continue to experience symptoms for months. Most smokers identify smoking as harmful and express a desire to reduce or stop using tobacco (see Applying Developmental Science, p. 371). Nearly 35 million people in the United States wish to quit smoking each year, but more than 85% of those who try to quit relapse, often within a week (National Institute on Drug Abuse, 2009).

Some smokers turn to e-cigarettes as an alternative to tobacco cigarettes, viewing e-cigarettes as safer than conventional cigarettes (Goniewicz, Lingas, & Hajek, 2013; Pearson, Richardson, Niaura, Vallone, & Abrams, 2012). E-cigarettes aerosolize nicotine and produce a vapor that emulates that of conventional cigarette (Yamin, Bitton, & Bates, 2010). As of this writing, e-cigarettes and the nicotine solutions used in e-cigarettes are not regulated by the U.S. federal government, and there is little research on their safety (Tremblay et al., 2015). Nevertheless, adolescents and young adults' use of e-cigarettes is increasing rapidly (Johnston, O'Malley, Bachman, & Schulenberg, 2015).

Marijuana

By far the most commonly used substance, after alcohol and nicotine, by young adults in the United States is marijuana, with 20%, 13%, and 6% of 18- to 20-year-olds, 21- to 25-year-olds, and 26- to 34-year-olds, respectively, reporting use in the last month (Substance Abuse and Mental Health Services Administration, 2014). For most young people, marijuana use is sporadic and limited in duration, but regular sustained use is associated with dependence and adverse health and social outcomes (Swift, Coffey, Carlin, Degenhardt, & Patton, 2008). Young people consume marijuana for different reasons; those who cite experimentation as their primary reason tend to report fewer marijuana-related problems than do those who list other common reasons, such as social enhancement, relaxation, enjoyment, and conformity to peers (Lee, Neighbors, & Woods, 2007). Weekly marijuana use in adolescence is associated with daily use and dependence at age 24 (Griffin, Bang, & Botvin, 2010; Swift et al., 2008). Sustained marijuana use is associated with self-reported cognitive difficulties and a variety of personal problems during the middle to late 20s, including

Smoking Cessation

AP/Carolyn Kaster

Quitting smoking is challenging but the health benefits are immediate and increase over time.

Quitting smoking, also known as smoking cessation, brings a variety of health benefits. Some occur nearly immediately. For example, heart rate and blood pressure begin to decline about 20 minutes after smoking a cigarette (Mahmud & Feely, 2003). In about 12 hours, levels of carbon monoxide in the blood drop to normal levels (American Cancer Society, 2009).

Circulation and lung function improve within three months after quitting (U.S. Public Health Service Office of the Surgeon General & U.S. Public Health Service Office on Smokin and Health, 1990). Within nine months, the tiny hairlike structures that move mucus out of the lungs, called cilia, begin to function normally, cleaning the lungs, reducing the risk of infection. Coughing and shortness of breath decrease. About a year after quitting, the risk of heart disease is about one half that of a smoker's. Within 10 years, cancer death rates are about one half of those of smokers, and within 5 to 15 years after quitting the stroke risk and risk of coronary disease is reduced to that of a nonsmoker (American Cancer Society, 2009; U.S. Public Health Service Office of the Surgeon General & U.S. Public Health Service Office on Smokin and Health, 1990). A 35-year-old man who quits smoking will, on average, increase his life expectancy by 5 years (National Institute on Drug Abuse, 2009).

Quitting smoking, however, is very challenging. In one study, nearly 85% of 18- to 24-year-olds and 75% of 25- to 34-year-olds reported trying to quit within the last year; less than 20% quit for 6 months, and about 40% were unable to quit for a single day (Messer, Trinidad, Al-Delaimy, & Pierce, 2008). Because nicotine is highly physiologically addictive, the most effective form of treatment to help people quit smoking is nicotine replacement in the form of nicotine gum and nicotine transdermal patches, which are available over the counter in the United States. Nicotine gum and patches provide users with lower overall nicotine levels, produce less severe physiological reactions, and do not contain the carcinogens and gasses associated with tobacco smoke.

Although nicotine replacement therapies may help alleviate the physiological effects of withdrawal, withdrawal also entails a psychological component. For example, the sight, feel, and smell of a cigarette and recalling the ritual of handling, lighting, and smoking a cigarette can intensify cravings and make withdrawal worse (National Institute on Drug Abuse, 2009).

Federal and state taxes that increase the cost of smoking are often intended as a way to reduce smoking. However, in one study, increases in cigarette taxes were associated with reductions in self-reported smoking in less than one quarter of participants and prompted quitting in only 16% of smokers (Choi, Toomey, Chen, & Forster, 2011).

Behavioral methods of smoking cessation are the most effective approach (often coupled with nicotine replacement). They help individuals to recognize high-risk smoking situations, develop alternative coping strategies, manage stress, improve problem-solving skills, and increase social support. Increasingly behavioral approaches and information are offered by telephone, Internet, and written pamphlets and other materials, permitting large numbers of people access to resources to help them quit smoking. The U.S. Department of Health and Human Services established a toll-free telephone number in 2004—800-QUIT-NOW (800-784-8669)—as a way to aid people in getting the information and assistance they need to quit smoking; the website is at www.smokefree.gov.

What Do You Think?

Consider smoking cessation from the bioecological perspective. Identify ways to help smokers quit that emphasize the microsystem, mesosystem, exosystem, and macrosystem.

---

lower levels of academic degree attainment, lower income, greater levels of unemployment and welfare dependence, lower levels of relationship satisfaction and life satisfaction, and less cohesion and more conflict with romantic partners (Conroy, Kurth, Brower, Strong, & Stein, 2015; Fergusson & Boden, 2008; Hall, 2014; Silins et al., 2014). Regular marijuana use can interfere with completing developmental tasks of young adulthood, such as reaching education and career goals, forming intimate relationships and marriage, and taking on adult roles (Blair, 2010).

Marijuana is addictive because when inhaled, the active ingredient, THC, passes from the lungs to the bloodstream to the brain and activates the brain's reward system, making the user feel euphoric. Time may seem to pass more slowly, and sensations such as color and sound may seem more intense. Sometimes, however, a user may feel anxious, fearful, or distrustful instead of euphoric. Heavy use of marijuana interferes with thinking, impairing a person's ability to shift attention from one item to another and to learn, form memories, and recall material (Bartholomew,

After alcohol, marijuana is the most commonly used substance by young adults in the United States.

Holroyd, & Heffernan, 2010; Crean, Crane, & Mason, 2011). THC binds to receptors in the cerebellum, which is responsible for balance, coordination of movement, and integration of thought, critical to executive functioning (Skosnik et al., 2008). Heavy marijuana use interferes with executive functioning—problem solving, abstract reasoning, and judgment—and the earlier the age of onset, the greater the negative effects (Crean et al., 2011; Gruber, Sagar, Dahlgren, Racine, & Lukas, 2012). For example, marijuana users tend to be less responsive to negative consequences in making decisions (Wesley, Hanlon, & Porrino, 2011). In addition, marijuana smokers experience many of the same respiratory problems common to tobacco smokers, such as cough, more frequent chest illnesses, and cancers. Marijuana smoke contains irritants and carcinogens and appears to have 50% to 79% more carcinogens than tobacco smoke (Tashkin, 2013).

Marijuana is neurologically reinforcing, making the user crave the drug and have a hard time stopping. People who try to quit report irritability, difficulty sleeping, and anxiety, similar to withdrawal from other substances such as tobacco. In psychological tests, people trying to quit show increased aggression, which peaks about a week after stopping the drug (National Institute on Drug Abuse, 2005). There has been little study of treatments for marijuana dependence because habitual marijuana abuse is very often accompanied by the abuse of alcohol and other drugs.

Alcohol

Alcohol is legal for young adults at age 21 in all U.S. states and is the drug of choice for most people throughout adulthood. Of particular concern to professionals are rates of **binge drinking**, defined as consuming five or more drinks in one sitting in men and four drinks in one sitting in women. Heavy drinking is defined as two or more instances of binge drinking within the past 30 days (Kanny, Liu, Brewer, & Lu, 2013). As shown in Figure 13.2, binge drinking and heavy drinking are highest in young adulthood, with about one third of adults aged 18 to 24 and 25 to 34 as well as one in five adults aged 35 to 44 reporting binge drinking within the past 30 days (Kanny et al., 2013). Binge and heavy drinking are concerns because they both involve intermittent but high levels of alcohol consumption, which increases the risk of developing **alcohol dependence** and abuse (Simons, Wills, & Neal, 2014). Binge drinking is associated with negative short- and long-term consequences for physical and psychological well-being including fatal and nonfatal injuries, academic failure, violence and crime, unintended pregnancies, sexually transmitted infections (STIs), and impaired driving (Brown et al., 2008; Cleveland, Mallett, White, Turrisi, & Favero, 2013; Mallett et al., 2013). Because young adults often engage in binge drinking, they are at risk of experiencing the associated negative consequences.

Research with college students has suggested that binge and heavy drinking may be part of a "stage of life phenomenon" for which the transition out of high school increases the risk (Jackson, Sher, & Park, 2005). Young people who enter college face a transition that brings many challenges and opportunities, including new roles; new friendship networks; increased autonomy and independence; separation from family and old friends; new academic choices and demands; and less parental support, guidance, and monitoring—all changes that can place them at risk for increases in alcohol use (Maggs, 1997; Schulenberg & Maggs, 2002; White, Fleming, Kim, McMorris, & Catalano, 2008). As they transition from high school to college, young people experience greater exposure to drinking and encounter higher levels of peer drinking and positive peer attitudes toward alcohol (White & Jackson, 2005). Most college students report experiencing more positive consequences of drinking (such as feeling social) than negative consequences (such as cognitive impairment), which contributes to high rates of binge and heavy drinking in this age group (Lee, Maggs, Neighbors, & Patrick, 2011).

Do young adults who attend college drink more than their peers who do not attend college? Some studies suggest that college students show higher rates of drinking than their peers (Barnes, Welte, Hoffman, & Tidwell, 2010; Carter, Brandon, & Goldman, 2010; Vergés et al., 2011), but others show no differences (Goldman, Greenbaum, Darkes, Brandon, & Del Boca, 2011). Despite these mixed findings, heavy drinking and alcohol-related problems are more common among young adults regardless of college enrollment (Barnes et al., 2010; Lanza & Collins, 2006; Vergés et al., 2011). People who report boredom and the desire to get high as the primary reasons for drinking tend to show the heaviest rates of alcohol use (Patrick, Lee, & Larimer, 2011). Overall, young people aged 18 to 29 show the highest rates of alcohol abuse and dependence, yet most young people show a spontaneous decline in drinking over the course of early adulthood. The transition to adult responsibilities such as career, marriage, and parenthood typically predicts declines in binge drinking and alcohol-related problems (Misch, 2007; Vergés et al., 2011).

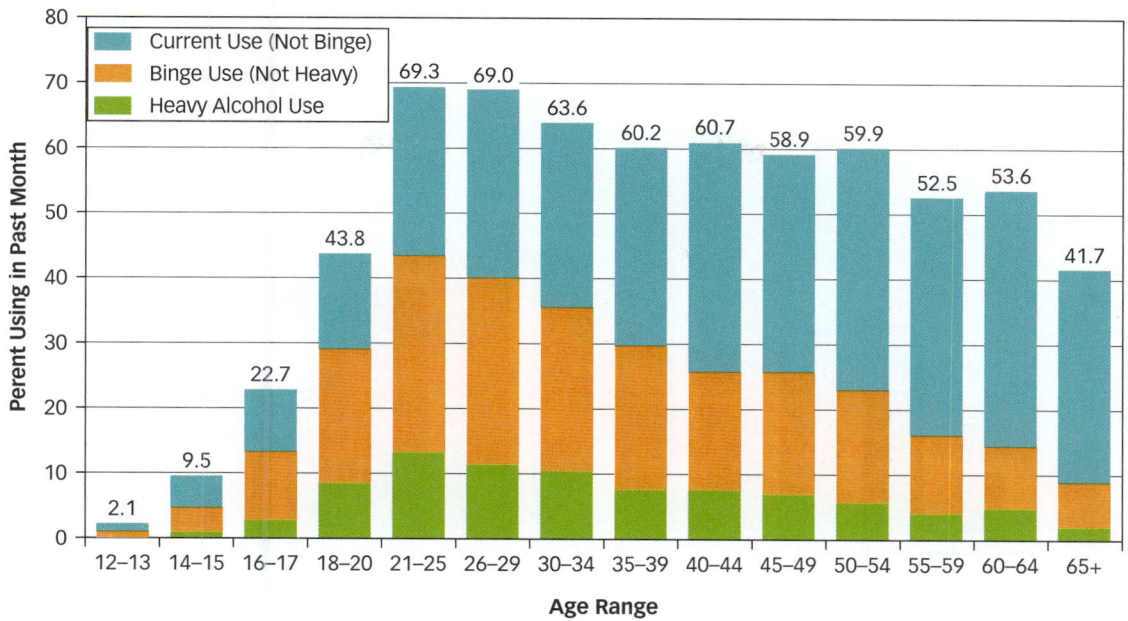

SOURCE: Substance Abuse and Mental Health Services Administration (2014).

Most young people "mature out" of drinking, moving from heavy drinking to more moderate drinking (Lee, Chassin, & Villalta, 2013).

Many young adults outgrow heavy drinking and related problems on their own and without treatment (Lee et al., 2013; Schulenberg & Maggs, 2002), but heavy drinking and binge drinking remain prevalent in adulthood, with 14% of middle-aged adults reporting binge drinking within the last month (Kanny et al., 2013). Alcohol dependence, also known as alcohol use disorder, is a maladaptive pattern of alcohol use that leads to clinically significant impairment or distress, as indicated by tolerance, withdrawal or drinking to relieve withdrawal, inability to reduce drinking, drinking more or for longer than intended, craving alcohol, recurrent alcohol use in physically hazardous situations, neglect of activities and obligations, time spent related to drinking or recovering from drinking, and continued use of alcohol despite alcohol-related psychological or physical problems (American Psychiatric Association, 2013). Although there are genetic risk factors for alcohol dependence and alcoholism, environmental factors, personal choices, and circumstances also influence whether an individual turns to alcohol as a coping mechanism (Enoch, 2013).

Alcohol dependence and chronic excessive alcohol consumption endanger health. Alcohol dependence places users at risk of developing various chronic diseases such as cardiovascular disease, intestinal problems, neurologic impairment, liver disease, and several types of cancer (Rehm, 2011). Brain damage from chronic alcohol abuse can eventually lead to memory and concentration problems, confusion, and apathy (Brun & Andersson, 2001; Stavro, Pelletier, & Potvin, 2013). Alcohol is implicated in accidents, injuries, criminal activity, and violence. For example, as shown in Figure 13.3, in 2013, about 20% of 21- to 25-year-olds and 26- to 29-year-olds and about 18% of 30- to 34-year-olds reported driving under the influence of alcohol within the past year (Substance Abuse and Mental Health Services Administration, 2014). Alcohol was implicated in one third of traffic fatalities in 2013 (National Highway Traffic Safety Administration, 2014) and implicated in 40% of all crimes (National Council on Alcoholism and Drug Dependence, 2015).

Despite experiencing alcohol-related problems and other negative consequences of drinking, people with alcohol dependence find it very difficult to stop drinking. Alcohol is physiologically addictive, and the withdrawal symptoms include anxiety, feelings of shakiness, irritability, depression, fatigue, insomnia, and confusion (Dugdale, 2009). About one half of alcoholics relapse shortly after beginning treatment (Volpicelli, 2005). Successful treatments provide individual and family counseling, group support, coping skills, and possibly aversion therapy (the use of medication that produces negative reactions to alcohol such as vomiting) to spur a distaste for alcohol (Swift, 2007; Windle & Zucker, 2010).

STRESS

"Still sick?" asked Shannon. "Yes, I just can't shake it," complained Carla. "I'm exhausted. The baby was up all night, and the babysitter was late. Traffic was awful. It looks like I'll have

FIGURE 13.3: Driving Under the Influence of Alcohol in the Past Year Among Persons Age 16 or Older, by Age, 2013

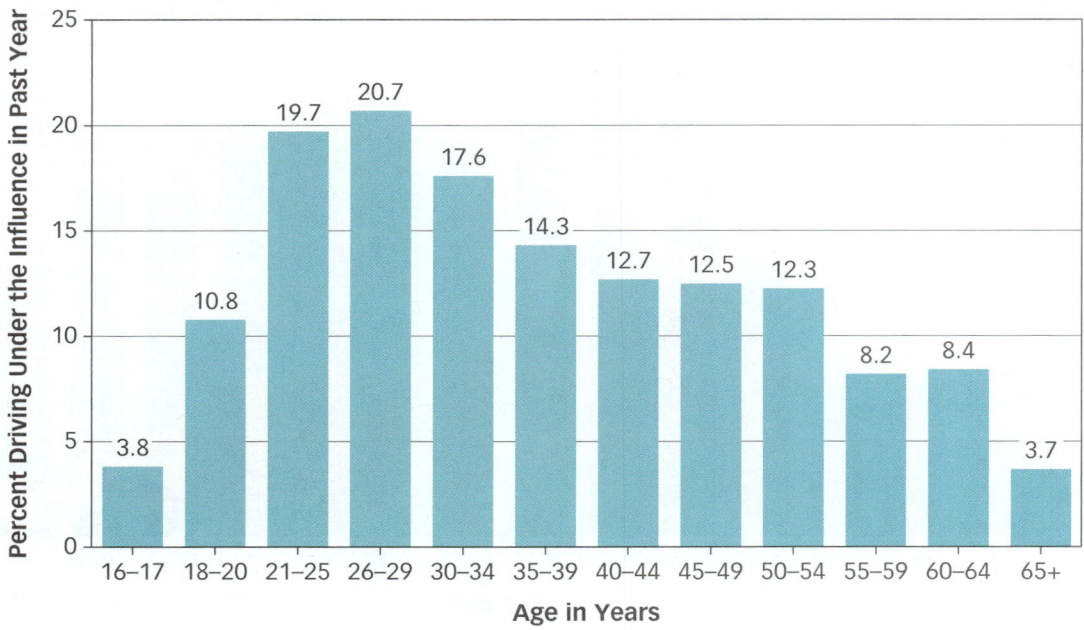

SOURCE: U.S. Department of Health and Human Services, 2012.

to work late tonight. But I need to find a way to make it to class because I have an exam." Shannon advised, "You need to carve out some time for yourself. I don't know how you do it!" "Me neither." Carla sighed. "With a job and family, I don't know how to fit in study time." Psychological stress, similar to Carla's experience, can motivate behavior or debilitate, impairing functioning. Stress is a part of every person's life. Daily hassles such as traffic, child care difficulties, work deadlines, and conflict with family and friends are small stresses that quickly accumulate to influence our mood and ability to cope (McIntyre, Korn, & Matsuo, 2008). Experiencing an overload of daily hassles, negative life events (such as serious illness in the family, death, unemployment, and divorce), and unfavorable social conditions (such as poverty, lack of resources, and unsafe communities) is associated high levels of stress and poor health.

Stress is physiologically arousing. When people experience stress, they respond with a "fight-or-flight" stress response in which cortisol is released and the body readies for action, raising blood pressure and heart rate. Individuals who experience chronic stress, such as that which accompanies living in poverty, are more likely to experience negative cardiovascular side effects of stress, such as hypertension (high blood pressure), high cholesterol, and arteriosclerosis (hardening of the arteries, which places more stress on the heart and increase the risk of heart attack and stroke; Harris et al., 2008). The stress response and negative consequences of stress tend to be higher in people of low socioeconomic status (Lantz, House, Mero, & Williams, 2005), perhaps because of the chronic stress associated with living in low-income communities and the sense that problems

are unsolvable (Almeida, Neupert, Banks, & Serido, 2005). Chronic psychological stress weakens immune functioning, triggering and increasing the severity of acute illnesses such as colds and flu, chronic illnesses such as asthma and arthritis, and serious illnesses such as cancer (Connor, 2008; Gouin, Glaser, Malarkey, Beversdorf, & Kiecolt-Glaser, 2012). Stress also influences psychological functioning. Chronic stress is associated with higher rates of anxiety and depression (Joo et al., 2009; Leonard & Myint, 2009) and can be a trigger for experiencing more serious mental illnesses that have a biological basis, such as bipolar disorder and schizophrenia (Gershon, Johnson, & Miller, 2013; Juster et al., 2011).

Early adulthood is a particularly challenging time because of the many choices available, decisions to be made, and developmental tasks. Perhaps because of these stressors, young adults are more likely to report depressive feelings than are middle-aged adults, who tend to show more career and financial stability and better coping skills (Ajdacic-Gross et al., 2006; Schiefman, Van Gundy, & Taylor, 2001). The challenges and stresses of early adulthood are not insurmountable. They can be countered by social support, which is associated with lower cortisol levels, suggesting a reduced fight-or-flight response (Ditzen et al., 2008). Social support buffers the negative emotional and health consequences that accompany psychological stress (Cropley & Steptoe, 2005). Encouraging young adults to maintain and strengthen social ties enhances their physical and psychological functioning. In addition, social support within the context of a relationship characterized by a secure attachment shows the greatest benefits for stress management (Ditzen et al., 2008).

COGNITIVE DEVELOPMENT IN EARLY ADULTHOOD: POSTFORMAL REASONING

For Alexander, a college junior majoring in biology, weighing hypotheses on evolutionary theory is easy. As he sees it, there is one account that is clearly more rational and supported by data than the others. However, like most young adults, Alexander finds personal decisions much more difficult because many are vague and have multiple options with both costs and benefits. As teenagers mature into adults, their thinking becomes increasingly flexible and practical. Adults come to expect uncertainty and ambiguity and to recognize that everyday problems are influenced by emotion and experience rather than pure reasoning. Researchers who study **postformal reasoning** examine how thinking and problem solving are restructured in adulthood to integrate abstract reasoning with practical considerations (Sinnott, 1998). Young adults who demonstrate postformal thinking recognize that most problems have multiple causes and solutions, that some solutions are better choices than others, and that all problems involve uncertainty. The development of postformal reasoning entails shifts in reasoning, as described in the following section.

EPISTEMIC COGNITION

Researchers who study postformal reasoning emphasize understanding **epistemic cognition**—the ways in which individuals understand how they arrived at ideas, beliefs, and conclusions. With maturation, young people become more likely to compare their reasoning process and justifications with others and, when their justifications fall short, seek a more adequate explanation and adjust their thinking accordingly. People's understanding of the nature of knowledge advances along a predictable path in young adulthood, especially among college students (King & Kitchener, 1994; Magolda, 2002; Perry, 1970).

When they enter college, young people tend to view knowledge as a set of facts that hold true across people and contexts (King & Kitchener, 2004; Perry, 1970). They view learning as a matter of acquiring and assessing facts. Beginning college students tend to display **dualistic thinking**, polar reasoning in which knowledge and accounts of phenomena are viewed as either right or wrong with no in-between. They tend to have difficulty grasping that several contradictory arguments can each have supporting evidence. The entering college student may sit through class lectures, wondering, "Which theory is right?" and become frustrated when the professor explains that multiple theories each have various strengths and weaknesses.

With experience in college, such as exposure to multiple viewpoints, multiple arguments, and their inherent contradictions, students show less dualistic thinking (Baxter Magolda, 2004). Instead, they move toward **relativistic thinking** in which most knowledge is viewed as relative, dependent on the situation and thinker (King & Kitchener, 2004; Perry, 1970). As students become aware of the diversity of viewpoints that exist in all realms of study, their thinking becomes more flexible. They relinquish the belief in absolute knowledge and instead embrace multiple truths, relative to individual and context. Relativistic thinkers recognize that beliefs are subjective, that there are multiple perspectives on a given issue, and that all perspectives are defensible (Magolda, 2002; Sinnott, 1998). Often students become frustrated by relativism and conclude that most topics are simply a matter of opinion and perspective, and all views are valid. For example, they may conclude that all solutions to a problem are correct as it all depends on a person's perspective. A more mature thinker, however, may acknowledge the multiple options yet carefully evaluate them to choose the most adequate solution.

As shown in Table 13.2, the most mature type of reasoning entails **reflective judgment**: reasoning that synthesizes contradictions among perspectives (King & Kitchener, 2004; Perry, 1970). Whereas a relativistic thinker may approach a problem such as deciding which theory is most adequate or which short story is best by explaining that it is simply a matter of opinion and it "depends on the person," the individual who displays reflective judgment recognizes that options and opinions can be evaluated—and generates criteria to do so (Sinnott, 2003). Although reasoning tends to advance throughout the college years, ultimately few adults demonstrate reflective judgment (Perry, 1970).

Development beyond formal operations is dependent on metacognition and experience. Exposure to situations and reasoning that challenges students' knowledge and belief systems, coupled with more explicit, powerful, and effective metacognition, permits individuals to consider the adequacy of their own thought and reasoning processes and modify them as needed (Kuhn, 2000). Advancement to postformal reasoning is associated with contextual factors—specifically, exposure to realistic but ambiguous problems and supportive guidance, such as that which is often a part of college education within Western cultures (King & Kitchener, 2002; Zeidler, Sadler, Applebaum, & Callahan, 2009).

Yet postformal reasoning is not universal across cultures. For example, Chinese college students generally do not display the typical advancement from dualism to relativism to reflective judgment (Zhang, 2004; Zhang & Watkins, 2001). When compared with their U.S. counterparts, Chinese students tend to lack opportunities for making their own

TABLE 13.2 Postformal Reasoning

	UNDERSTANDING OF KNOWLEDGE	EXAMPLES FROM INTERVIEWS WITH YOUNG ADULTS
Dualistic thinking	Knowledge is a collection of facts, and a given idea is either right or wrong.	". . . Theory might be convenient, . . . but . . . . The facts are what's there . . . and . . . should be the main thing" (Perry, 1970).
Relativistic thinking	Knowledge is relative, dependent on the situation and thinker, and a matter of opinion and perspective.	"I really can't [choose a point of view] on this issue. It depends on your beliefs since there is no way of proving either one . . . I believe they're both the same as far as accuracy" (King & Kitchener, 2004, p. 6). "People think differently and so they attack the problem differently. Other theories could be as true as my own but based on different evidence" (King & Kitchener, 2004, p. 7).
Reflective judgment	Knowledge is a synthesis of contradictory information and perspectives whose evidence can be evaluated according to certain criteria.	"[When approaching a problem] there are probably several ways to do it. What are they? Which one's most efficient? Which one will give us the most accurate results?" (Marra & Palmer, 2004, p.117). "One can judge an argument by how well thought-out the positions are, what kinds of reasoning and evidence are used to support it, and how consistent the way one argues on this topic is as compared with how one argues on other topics" (King & Kitchener, 2004, p. 7). "It is very difficult in this life to be sure. There are degrees of sureness. You come to a point at which you are sure enough for a personal stance on the issue" (King & Kitchener, 2004, p. 7).

choices and decisions in many areas such as curricula, career choices, academic majors, and residential arrangements (Zhang, 1999). Experience in decision making matters. Some theorists argue that even in Western cultures, the most advanced level of postformal reasoning (commitment within relativism) may come only with graduate study and wrestling with challenging philosophical and practical problems (King & Kitchener, 2004).

Regardless of education, culture, or age, social interaction is a critical influence on the development of postformal cognition (Kuhn, 2008). Social interaction entails discussing multiple perspectives and solutions to a problem as well as encouraging individuals to consider others' perspectives, evaluate their own reasoning, and perhaps advance to more sophisticated forms of reasoning. People's reasoning advances throughout adulthood; however, reasoning and decision making are not simply cognitive endeavors but are influenced by emotion.

PRAGMATIC THOUGHT AND COGNITIVE-AFFECTIVE COMPLEXITY

According to Gisella Labouvie-Vief (1980, 2006), development from adolescence to adulthood entails a transformation from hypothetical thought emphasizing possibilities to **pragmatic thought**, emphasizing the use of logic to address everyday problems. Similar to reflective judgment, pragmatic

thought entails acceptance of inconsistency and ambiguity (Labouvie-Vief, 2015). Managing various roles and tackling the problems of everyday life requires thinking that is flexible and accepting of contradiction. For example, young adults must come to terms with their relative power across various contexts: At home, they have autonomy and are able to carve out their own niche whereas at work they must follow the directions of their employer. Integrating dynamic roles as spouse, parent, friend, employee, and manager requires flexibility and adaptation.

Reasoning in everyday situations is not simply a matter of logic—it is fused with emotion. Advances in reasoning during the adult years entail integrating cognition with emotion. Young adults become better able to make rational decisions and are less swayed by emotion-fused thinking than are adolescents (Thornton & Dumke, 2005; Watson & Blanchard-Fields, 1998). From young adulthood through middle adulthood, individuals experience gains in **cognitive-affective complexity**, the capacity to be aware of their emotions, integrate positive and negative feelings about an issue, and regulate intense emotions to make logical decisions about complicated issues (Labouvie-Vief, 2003, 2015; Mikels et al., 2010). With gains in cognitive-affective complexity, young adults better understand others, including their perspectives, feelings, and motivations, which helps them to participate in social interactions, become more tolerant of other viewpoints, and solve day-to-day problems.

Thinking in Context 13.3

1. Can you identify examples of postformal reasoning in your own thinking? What are some challenges of evaluating one's own thinking?

2. What kinds of experiences foster the development of postformal reasoning? In your view, is higher education necessary to develop the capacity for postformal reasoning? Why or why not?

EDUCATION IN EARLY ADULTHOOD

Unlike childhood and adolescence, when education is mandated and virtually all students progress with their peers on the same schedule, early adulthood offers a wide range of educational and vocational opportunities and challenges. College represents an increasingly common transition from secondary school to the workplace.

DEVELOPMENTAL IMPACT OF ATTENDING COLLEGE

Attending college, at least for a time, has become a normative experience for emerging adults. In 2013, about 66% of high school graduates in the United States enrolled in two- or four-year colleges (National Center for Education Statistics, 2014). Students enroll in college to learn about a specific field of study, a major, and to prepare for careers, but attending college is also associated with many positive developmental outcomes.

Adults of all ages often view their college years as highly influential in shaping their thought, values, and worldview. In addition to academic learning, young people enrolled in college are presented with various perspectives and are encouraged to experiment with alternative values, behaviors, and beliefs. College students encounter a wealth of new experiences and opportunities for autonomy, ideas, and social demands. College courses often require students to construct arguments and solve complex problems, which fosters the development of postformal reasoning (Perry, 1970; Sinnott, 2003). Attending college is associated with advanced moral reasoning and the ability to synthesize the considerations of autonomy and individual rights with promoting human welfare (Kohlberg & Ryncarz, 1990). In addition to intellectual growth, college students show advances in social development (El Hassan, 2008). The expanded worldview that accompanies college attendance is displayed in young people's tolerance of diversity and interest in art, literature, and philosophy.

The positive impact of attending college is not simply a matter of the type of college one attends; research indicates that all institutions, public and private, selective and open enrollment, advance cognitive and psychological development (Montgomery & Côté, 2003). In addition, students at

Attending college has become normative for emerging adults in the United States.

Will & Deni McIntyre/Corbis

two-year community colleges show similar cognitive gains as their peers at four-year institutions (Pascarella, Bohr, & Nora, 1995). It is student involvement in campus life rather than the type of institution attended that matters in influencing developmental outcomes. Peer interaction in academic and social contexts benefits students. Students who live in residence halls have more opportunities to interact with peers and become involved in the academic and social aspects of campus life—and show the greatest cognitive gains in the college years (Reason, Terenzini, & Domingo, 2007; Terenzini, Pascarella, & Blimling, 1999). Education that challenges students and encourages them to consider perspectives other than their own; solve ambiguous, messy problems; and apply coursework to real-world problems and activities with the guidance of supportive faculty promotes cognitive-affective complexity, which underlies adaptive functioning in college as well as all the contexts in which young adults are embedded (Reason et al., 2007).

Despite these benefits, however, many students do not complete college. Only about two thirds of students who enroll in four-year institutions graduate within six years, and one third of students enrolled at two-year institutions graduate within three years (National Center for Education

EMERGING ADULTHOOD: CHOOSING A MAJOR

In this video, 19-year-old Amber discusses her experience choosing a college major. Like many students, she initially chose a field quite different from her ultimate major. Here she describes how she explored fields of study and how her interactions with family influenced her choices.

Watch the video at edge.sagepub.com/kuther

Statistics, 2014). Generally, student attrition is higher in colleges with open enrollment and less selective admission requirements. The transition to college itself predicts whether students will drop out. Most students find the transition to college challenging as it entails academic, social, and personal demands. Coursework is more difficult than in high school, and students are expected to take initiative in seeking assistance. Many students experience changes in living situation, whether a move to a dorm room or off-campus housing. College entails new psychological demands for autonomy, motivation, study skills, and self-management (Cleary, Walter, & Jackson, 2011).

Students who are the first in their families to attend college (known as first-generation college students), as well as those who are from minority or low socioeconomic homes (who also are often first-generation students), often experience the most difficulty transitioning to college and are at highest risk of dropping out of college or attending discontinuously (Aronson, 2008; Fischer, 2007; Ishitani, 2006). In 2011, about 15% of all college students enrolled in the United States were African American and 14% Hispanic (as compared with 61% white; National Center for Education Statistics, 2013). With few family and peer models of how to succeed in college, first-generation and minority students may find it difficult to understand and adjust to the college student role and expectations and may be at risk of feeling isolated (Collier & Morgan, 2008; Orbe, 2008). They may experience more difficulty choosing a major; enroll in more remedial coursework; trail in the number of credits they need in the first year of college; and be less active in campus, academic, and social activities—risk factors for college dropout (Aronson, 2008; Walpole, 2008).

Students' transition to college and success in college are also influenced by the college environment (Fischer, 2007). Institutions that are responsive to the academic, social, and cultural needs of students help them adjust to college and, ultimately, succeed. Reaching out to at-risk students during the first weeks of college can help them to feel connected to the institution. Social connection, communication skills, motivation, and study skills are associated with retention (Robbins, Allen, Casillas, Peterson, & Le, 2006). Students who live on campus, see faculty as concerned with their development, establish relationships with faculty and other students, and become involved in campus life are more likely to succeed and graduate from college (Pike & Kuh, 2005). College and universities can provide opportunities for faculty and students to interact and form connections, help students develop study skills, and assist students in getting involved on campus. When students feel that they are part of a campus community, they are more likely to persist and graduate.

NONTRADITIONAL COLLEGE STUDENTS

Virtually all of the research on the effects of college tends to focus on what most people think of as the typical college student, ages 18 through 22. However, 27% of college students are between ages 25 and 39 (National Center for Education Statistics, 2015). Why do students return to college? Nontraditional students tend to report career reasons for returning to college (Kasworm, 2003). Some seek a college degree to be eligible for higher-paying and more satisfying careers. Others enroll in college to change career paths. Employers sometimes encourage students to enroll in college to learn new skills.

Nontraditional students are more likely than traditional students to attend college part-time, work full-time, be financially independent, and have dependents—all of which pose significant challenges to success in college (Choy, 2002). They are more likely than other college students to juggle multiple life roles, such as worker, spouse, parent, and caregiver (Fairchild, 2003). Sometimes the demands of school, family, and work conflict can be overwhelming. For example, work-related travel is often disruptive to child care as well as academic demands, resulting in class absences and missed assignments.

Many nontraditional students find the practical details of college more difficult to navigate, as most colleges are oriented toward traditional students (Fairchild, 2003). For example, classes that meet two or three days each week often conflict with work schedules. Evening classes often meet once per week, permitting convenience at the expense of contact with professors. Some students may find required courses are offered only during the day. They may have difficulty accessing advisors and student support services. Nontraditional students are less likely than traditional students to earn a degree within five years (Choy, 2002).

However, nontraditional students bring several strengths to the table. They tend to show a readiness to learn and a problem-centered orientation toward learning that emphasizes acquiring the knowledge and skills needed for career advancement (Ross-Gordon, 2011). Older students tend to

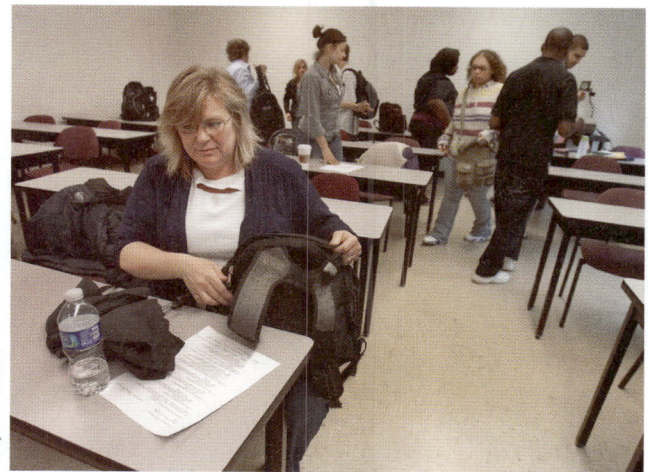

Adults return to college for many reasons, including to change career paths, obtain higher paying and more satisfying careers, learn new skills, and fulfill personal goals.

have a more complex knowledge base from which to draw and tend to emphasize seeking meaning and applying what they learn to their lives (Fairchild, 2003). Their experience and multiple roles can help nontraditional learners make meaning of theoretical concepts that may be purely abstract to younger learners (Ross-Gordon, 2011).

Adult undergraduate students typically seek colleges that are readily accessible; offer training relevant to their current life needs; and are cost-effective, flexible in course scheduling, and supportive of adult lifestyle commitments (Kasworm, 2003). Many colleges and universities are increasingly supporting the needs of nontraditional students. Colleges can support nontraditional students by extending student services beyond business hours, providing adequate and close parking for those students who rush from work to school, as well as affordable on-campus child care for part- and full-time students, including evening students (Hadfield, 2003). Some offer orientation programs for adult learners to provide information about support resources as well as help students connect with one another and begin to build a social support network of peers.

THE FORGOTTEN THIRD

It can be said that attending college is part of the American dream and has become expected of many youth. Nearly three quarters of high school students report that they expect to earn a college degree; however, by age 29, only 34% of adults hold college degrees (National Center for Education Statistics, 2014). Each year, about one third of high school graduates in the United States transition from high school to work without attending college. The population of non-college bound youth has been referred to in the literature as "forgotten" by educators, scholars, and policy makers because relatively few resources are directed toward learning about and assisting them, as compared with college-bound young adults. While

some young people cite economic barriers, such as the high cost of college or the need to support their family, as reasons for nonattendance, other academically well-prepared students report forgoing college because of a desire to work or disinterest in academics (Bozick & DeLuca, 2011).

Young adults who enter the workforce immediately after high school have fewer work opportunities than those of prior generations. In 2015, the rate of unemployment for high school graduates was twice that of bachelor's degree holders (U.S. Bureau of Labor, 2015a). In addition, many young people with high school degrees spend their first working years in jobs that are similar to those they held in high school: unskilled, with low pay and little security (Rosenbaum & Person, 2003). As illustrated in Figure 13.4, high school graduates earn less than peers with college degrees.

The curricula of most secondary schools tend to be oriented toward college-bound students, and counseling tends to be geared toward helping students gain admission to college (Krei & Rosenbaum, 2000). Many argue that secondary schools do not meet the needs of non-college bound students (Blustein, Chaves, & Diemer, 2002). Over the past three decades, secondary education has shifted toward emphasizing academics and reducing vocational training, leaving young adults who do not attend college ill-prepared for the job market (Symonds, Schwartz, & Ferguson, 2011).

Critics have argued that the one third of young adults who do not attend college are shortchanged as billions of state and federal dollars are awarded in financial aid and subsidized college tuition to aid the college-bound, yet the non-college bound receive little assistance in making the transition to adulthood (Wald, 2005). A solution proposed in the *Pathways to Prosperity* report from the Harvard Graduate School of Education is for the U.S. educational system to support multiple pathways to the transition to adulthood (Ferguson & Lamback, 2014; Symonds et al., 2011). Secondary schools can prepare individuals for a variety of

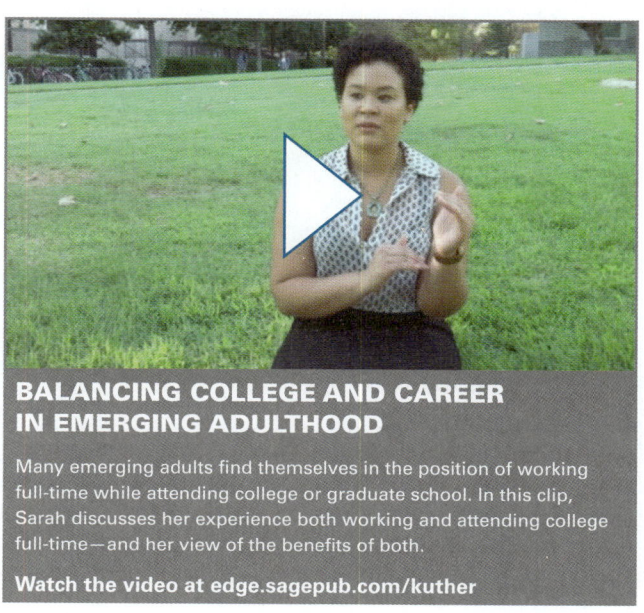

BALANCING COLLEGE AND CAREER IN EMERGING ADULTHOOD

Many emerging adults find themselves in the position of working full-time while attending college or graduate school. In this clip, Sarah discusses her experience both working and attending college full-time—and her view of the benefits of both.

Watch the video at edge.sagepub.com/kuther

FIGURE 13.4: Median Weekly Earnings by Education in 2014 (age 25 and older)

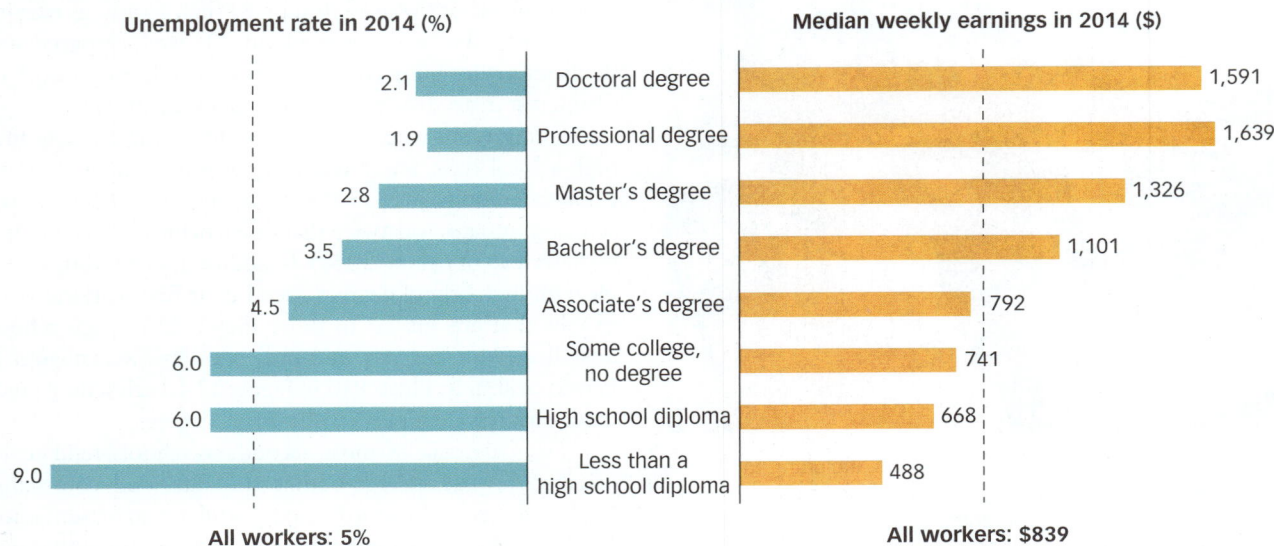

Unemployment rate in 2014 (%) | Median weekly earnings in 2014 ($)

- 2.1 Doctoral degree — 1,591
- 1.9 Professional degree — 1,639
- 2.8 Master's degree — 1,326
- 3.5 Bachelor's degree — 1,101
- 4.5 Associate's degree — 792
- 6.0 Some college, no degree — 741
- 6.0 High school diploma — 668
- 9.0 Less than a high school diploma — 488

All workers: 5% | All workers: $839

SOURCE: U.S. Bureau of Labor Statistics (2015b).

career paths, including those that do not include college attendance. Opportunities for vocational training and to obtain relevant work experience will help young people try out careers and get relevant training for specific jobs. In addition, training programs should relay specific expectations for youth with regard to their responsibility in career decision making and training and the educational and vocational support they can expect in return (Symonds et al., 2011).

VOCATIONAL DEVELOPMENT IN EARLY ADULTHOOD

Selecting an occupation is one of the most important decisions that young people make. Individuals proceed through several phases of vocational development over their lifetimes (Gottfredson, 2005; Super, 1990). Children often fantasize about careers as astronauts, actors, and rock stars—careers that bear little resemblance to the choices they ultimately make.

STAGES OF VOCATIONAL DEVELOPMENT

How do people select occupations? Developmental theorist Donald Super proposed that the development of occupational goals progresses through several stages in adolescence and early adulthood (Super, 1980, 1990; Super & Hall, 1978; Super & Jordaan, 2007).

The earliest stage of occupational development, known as *crystallization*, begins in adolescence. Adolescents from ages 14 through 18 begin to think about careers in more complex ways, considering their own interests, personality, abilities, and values as well as the requirements of each career.

Similar to the exploration entailed in identity development, career exploration is at first tentative. Adolescents seek information about careers by talking with family, friends, and teachers as well as through Internet searches. They compare what they learn with their interests.

As individuals transition into young adulthood, from ages 18 to 21, they enter the *specification* stage in which they identify specific occupational goals and pursue the education needed to achieve them. As a first-year college student, Angela knew that she wanted to do something related to business but had not yet selected among several possible majors. Once a young person has selected a general vocational area, he or she may experiment with possibilities before choosing an occupation. Angela considered several business-related majors including accounting, management, and others and also completed an internship at an investment firm before deciding to major in finance.

During *implementation*, from ages 21 to 24, young adults complete training, enter the job market, and make the transition to become an employee. The developmental task is to reconcile expectations about jobs and career goals with available jobs. Young people may take temporary jobs or change jobs as they learn about work roles and attempt to match their career goals with available jobs. For example, Yolanda majored in education but found no teaching positions available at schools near her home. She accepted a temporary position running an after-school program while she applies for jobs in other cities and states. Even young adults who attain their "dream jobs" often find that they must tailor and adapt their expectations and goals in light of their career setting.

The *stabilization* stage, from ages 25 to 35, entails becoming established in a career. Young adults settle into specific jobs, gain experience, and adapt to changes in their

ETHICAL AND POLICY APPLICATIONS OF LIFESPAN DEVELOPMENT

Apprenticeships

iStock/Signature

Through on-the-job training coupled with classroom instruction, apprenticeships help young people prepare for careers in a variety of vocational settings.

Most European countries place a much greater emphasis on vocational education than the United States. For example, non-college bound youth in European nations such as Austria, Denmark, Switzerland, and Germany have the opportunity to participate in apprenticeship programs that combine on-the-job training and classroom instruction that often is tailored to each student. Germany is particularly known for offering apprenticeships coupled with vocational schooling in hundreds of blue- and white-collar occupations (Behrens, Pilz, & Greuling, 2008). Young people who successfully complete training often are hired by their host company.

High school graduates in nations that employ apprenticeships enter the workforce with general and job-specific skills and a job whereas North American employers tend to view high school graduates as poorly prepared for the world of work. To a certain extent, this is true, as these workers often lack vocational training and experience outside of the high school curriculum. In response, the U.S. Department of Labor as well as many states have established a series of registered apprenticeships that combine on-the-job training with theoretical and practical classroom instruction to prepare young people to work in a variety of settings.

About 150,000 companies and organizations serve as program sponsors in the Apprenticeship USA registered apprenticeship program, training about 410,000 apprenticeships in over 1,000 occupations in industries such as construction, manufacturing, health care, information technology, energy, telecommunications, and more (U.S. Department of Labor, 2015). Apprentices receive on-the-job training and instruction by employers and earn wages during training. The programs must meet national standards for registration with the U.S. Department of Labor, and training results in an industry-recognized credential. Apprentices who complete the program are often hired at their apprenticeship placement, and employers benefit by hiring employees with the specific skills they need.

What Do You Think?

1. Were you aware of apprenticeship opportunities as a high school student or now as a college student? Why or why not?

2. In your view, what are the benefits of completing an apprenticeship? Are there any disadvantages to choosing an apprenticeship?

---

workplace and field. Toward the end of early adulthood, from age 35 and up, individuals progress through the final stage: *consolidation*. They accumulate experience and advance up the career ladder, moving into supervisory positions and becoming responsible for the next generation of workers.

According to Super's model, vocational maturity reflects the degree to which an individual's occupational behaviors and status match the age-appropriate occupational stage. Although a task and stage-oriented approach to understanding career development remains useful, even casual observers of adult development will notice that career development does not follow a universal pattern. Not everyone progresses through the stages in the prescribed order and at the same pace. For many adults, career development does not progress in a linear fashion because most adults do not hold the same occupation throughout adulthood. For example, adults in their 50s today have had an average of nine occupations between the ages of 18 and 40 (U.S. Bureau of Labor Statistics, 2015c). Likewise, today's young adults in their 20s are likely to have held six jobs between ages 18 and 26 (U.S. Bureau of Labor Statistics, 2014). Young adults can expect to change career paths one or more times throughout their lives.

INFLUENCES ON VOCATIONAL CHOICE

Many factors influence how young people perceive and evaluate occupational choices, but perhaps the most important factor in selecting a career is the match between young people's personality traits and abilities and their occupational interests. We are most satisfied when we select occupations that match our personalities and other individual traits, such as intelligence and skills. John Holland (1997) proposed that occupational choices can be categorized by six personality types, as shown in Table 13.3. Holland explained that each personality type is best suited to a particular type of vocation.

Although it is useful to consider careers in terms of Holland's six personality types, most people have traits that correspond to more than one personality type and are able to successfully pursue several career paths (Holland, 1997; Spokane & Cruza-Guet, 2005). Personality is an important influence on vocational choice; however, contextual influences such as family and educational opportunities also influence our choice of career.

Parents influence their children's career development in a variety of ways. Parents tend to share personality characteristics and abilities with their children and influence educational attainment, which in turn influences career choice (Ellis & Bonin, 2003; Schoon & Parsons, 2002). Parents act as role models. Socioeconomic status and parents' occupational field influence career choice (Schoon & Polek, 2011). Young people in higher socioeconomic households are more likely to receive career information from parents. For example, in one study African American mothers with at least some exposure to college were more likely than other mothers to use a variety of strategies to aid their daughters' progress on academic and career goals, such as gathering information about career options, colleges, and professionals from whom to seek advice (Kerpelman, Shoffner, & Ross-Griffin, 2002). Parental expectations and encouragement for academic success and higher-status occupations also predict vocational choice and success (Maier, 2005). Parents may also give their different types of career encouragement and guidance to their daughters than they give to their sons. The influence of gender on career choice is discussed in Lives in Context (p. 383).

OCCUPATIONAL EXPECTATIONS AND REALITY

Young people form expectations about careers from the world around them—school, parents, peers, and the media. Expectations of what they would like to become, how they will get there, and how long it will take are modified by experience. Daniel Levinson's theory of development, originally based on a sample of men and later extended to include women, discusses a range of developmental tasks for the adult years (Levinson, 1978, 1996). Young adults are faced with the first task, forming a dream, which involves defining occupational expectations. First, they attempt to achieve the dream and monitor their progress toward it. Throughout adulthood, individuals modify their occupational expectations based on their experiences. Individuals change their expectations as they realize that their interests have changed; the dream was not a good fit; or their career goal was not attainable in light of their skills, abilities, and opportunities.

Experience in the working world prompts most young people to change their occupational expectations. One longitudinal study that examined young people's occupational expectations and achievement annually during the first seven years after high school and again at age 30 found a great deal of instability during the late teens and early 20s (Rindfuss, Cooksey, & Sutterlin, 1999). At age 25, less than one half of the young people had careers that matched their expectations. Among those who did not achieve their occupational expectations at age 30, men were more likely to move into managerial positions while women were more likely to move down or leave

TABLE 13.3 Personality and Vocational Choice

PERSONALITY TYPE	VOCATIONAL INDICATIONS
Investigative	Enjoys working with ideas; likely to select a scientific career (e.g., biologist, physicist)
Social	Enjoys interacting with people; likely to select a human services career (e.g., teaching, nursing, counseling)
Realistic	Enjoys working with objects and real-world problems; likely to select a mechanical career (e.g., carpenter, mechanic, plumber)
Artistic	Enjoys individual expression; likely to select a career in the arts, including writing and performing arts
Conventional	Prefers well-structured tasks, values social status; likely to select a career in business (e.g., accounting, banking)
Enterprising	Enjoys leading and persuading others, values adventure; likely to select a career in sales, politics

The Gender Divide

John B. Carnett/Getty

Gender roles have broadened but women have been slow to reach equal representation in traditionally male-dominated careers in fields such as medicine, law, and science.

Women have entered the workforce in increasing numbers since the 1960s. As generations of women are raised by working mothers and societal perspectives on gender roles have broadened, young women have become interested in careers traditionally held by men. However, women have been slow to reach equal representation in traditionally male-dominated careers in fields such as medicine, law, and science. Careers traditionally held by females, such as nursing, administrative office support, and medical assisting, remain predominantly female—and earn less than traditionally male professions.

Why do few women enter science and other stereotypically masculine careers? We have seen in prior chapters that girls

and boys show similar cognitive capacities and that girls tend to show higher levels of achievement on reading and writing tasks. With advancing grade, and particularly entrance to high school, girls' self-esteem tends to decline and they become more uncertain of their academic abilities than do boys (Jacobs, Lanza, Osgood, Eccles, & Wigfield, 2002). During college, many women come to doubt their ability to succeed in male-dominated careers and become more likely to choose non-science majors; or, if they continue in science, they choose socially oriented fields like those in the health professions (Benbow Lubinski, Shea, & Eftekhari-Sanjani, 2000). Prior achievement in math and science is not related to gender gaps in science fields, suggesting that women who choose nonscience majors are not less skilled in these areas (Riegle-Crumb, King, Grodsky, & Muller, 2012).

Young women's ambivalence may be exacerbated by debates raised in recent years regarding whether women's professional success is incompatible with career success. Some studies suggest that parenthood had a negative effect on women's career success, especially when women give birth to their first child at around the same time they enter their careers, whereas men's career success tends to be independent of parenthood (Abele & Spurk, 2011). One study of physicians found that women with children tended to be less advanced in their specialty qualifications, less prone to choose prestigious surgical fields, less likely to have a mentor, and less often aspire to prestigious senior hospital or academic positions (Buddeberg-Fischer et al., 2010). Some conclude that successful women professionals are less likely to have children (Hewlett, 2002).

Whether high-profile traditionally male-dominated careers interfere with women's desires to have children or women who wish to remain childless enter high-power careers is questionable. Regardless, career success and child-rearing can be combined when women have adequate support (Mills, Rindfuss, McDonald, & te Velde, 2011). Experts advise that young women should consider their life plans—what they expect for their professional and personal lives—when planning their futures. There is a need for high school and college programs to help young women develop and achieve high vocational aspirations, set goals to help them achieve their aspirations, and plan ahead to integrate their professional and personal lives.

What Do You Think?

1. Compare the career and family responsibilities that men and women face.
2. From your perspective, is there a gender divide in employment opportunities and barriers? Why or why not? If so, what can be done to reduce gender differences?

the workforce. The reality that vocational expectations are not always achieved can be a shock and can influence self-concept and occupational development as young adults revise their expectations.

Overall, early adulthood is a time in which young people undergo many changes. As they complete physical development, health-promoting behaviors, such as those involving nutrition, physical activity, and ways of coping with stress, become increasingly important determinants of health in adulthood. The cognitive advancements of early adulthood mean that young people can think in increasingly abstract and flexible ways, permitting them to apply their reasoning to beyond the academic and solve practical problems. It is when young people enter careers and become financially self-sufficient that most begin to consider themselves "adults," as we will discuss in Chapter 14.

Apply Your Knowledge

Brenda dropped her bags on the floor of her dorm room and introduced herself to her new roommate, Denise. They got along easily, and after talking for some time, Denise left to go to the library. Brenda marveled at their very different lives. Whereas Denise's parents are doctors, Brenda's mother works two jobs to pay the bills. Brenda considers herself very lucky to have won a scholarship to college. She worries about leaving her mother alone with her younger siblings—there's so much work to do and the little ones need a lot of supervision if they are to stay out of trouble in the neighborhood. Brenda worries that her little brothers will grow up too quickly and make dangerous decisions like joining one of the many neighborhood gangs. She realizes that she is very fortunate to be able to leave her poor community but worries that her absence will harm her family. At the same time, Brenda is delighted to have the opportunity to learn new things, to study with bright students and professors, and to prepare for a career as a doctor. As a pre-med major, Brenda has a very busy semester ahead, and she hopes that she won't disappoint those who have given her such grand opportunities.

1. Brenda comes from an impoverished neighborhood. In the coming years as she enters early adulthood, how does the context in which she was raised and in which she lives influence her physical development and health?

2. In what ways can Brenda expect to grow cognitively over the years of early adulthood? What contributes to this change? How might cognitive advances influence her functioning and behavior on practical day-to-day level?

3. How likely is Brenda to earn a college degree? What role does attending college play in career outcomes, employment, and salary in early adulthood?

4. What challenges do first-generation students, like Brenda, face in transitioning to and succeeding in college? What contextual factors influence these risks and what might serve as protective factors and aid development?

Chapter Summary

13.1 Describe the physical developments of early adulthood, such as changes in skin, muscles, motor skills, and reproductive capacity.

Physical development continues into the 20s when all of the organs and body systems reach optimum functioning. Age-related physical changes are so gradual that most go unnoticed by young adults. Physical strength peaks at about age 30, then gradually declines but young adults vary in the rate of change in their performance. Men are capable of reproducing throughout life, but sperm production is impaired by factors that harm the body's functioning. In women, ovulation becomes less regular with age and is impaired by a variety of behavioral and environmental factors.

13.2 Analyze the range of perspectives on the causes of aging as applied to early adulthood.

Wear and tear explains aging as a function of the body wearing out from use. Aging may also be accounted for by programmed genetics; whether genetic predispositions are realized depends on environmental and behavioral factors. Caloric restriction and declines in immune system functioning may increase longevity. Increases in cellular mutation and the action of free radicals result in damage to DNA and chromosomes, contributing to many age-related diseases. Finally, human cells have a limited capacity to divide. Telomeres shorten with each division, and when they shorten past a critical length, the cell stops dividing all together, diseases increase, cell death occurs, and the body ages.

13.3 Examine the contributions of obesity, physical activity, and stress for young adults' health.

Obesity has increased substantially in recent decades and is influenced by heredity and lifestyle factors. Obesity is a serious health risk, associated with a range of health and personal problems and illnesses. Successful weight loss is a result of lifestyle changes, such as regular moderate exercise coupled with a nutritionally balanced diet, training in stress management techniques, and problem-solving skills. Regular exercise increases longevity, enhances immunity, and promotes stress reduction. Chronic stress weakens immune functioning, triggering and increasing the severity of acute illnesses and chronic illnesses. Social support buffers the negative emotional and health consequences that accompany psychological stress.

13.4 Discuss the prevalence, effects, and treatment of alcohol and substance use in early adulthood.

Alcohol and substance use tend to begin during adolescence and peak during young adulthood. Over one third of young adults smoke cigarettes. Tobacco smoke accounts for about one third of all cancer deaths. Marijuana is the most commonly used illicit substance. For most young people, marijuana use is sporadic and limited in duration, but increases in marijuana use is associated with a variety of negative cognitive and personal outcomes. Binge drinking and heavy drinking peak in young adulthood and decline by the end of early adulthood with the transition to adult responsibilities. Binge drinking is associated with negative short- and long-term consequences for physical and psychological well-being, including alcohol dependence and withdrawal symptoms.

13.5 Discuss the development of postformal reasoning.

People's understanding of the nature of knowledge advances along a predictable path in young adulthood. When they enter college, young people tend to display dualistic thinking, viewing knowledge as a set of facts that hold true across people and contexts. With experience and exposure to multiple viewpoints, arguments, and contradictions, young adults begin to display relativistic thinking. The most mature type of reasoning entails reflective judgment. Development beyond formal operations is dependent on metacognition and experience.

13.6 Compare cognitive-affective complexity with postformal reasoning.

In Lavouvie-Vief's theory, advances in reasoning during the adult years entail making gains in cognitive-affective complexity and integrating cognition with emotion, permitting individuals to utilize pragmatic thought, become more open-minded and tolerant of other viewpoints, regulate intense emotions, and think logically about complicated everyday situations.

13.7 Explain how attending college influences young adults' development.

College students encounter a wealth of opportunities to develop postformal reasoning, advanced moral reasoning, and tolerance for diversity. Student involvement in campus life more so than the type of institution attended influences developmental outcomes. One third to nearly one half of North American students drop out of college. Students who have trouble adjusting to the academic, social, and personal demands of college, especially first-generation and minority students, are at risk for dropping out.

13.8 Contrast the experiences of traditional and nontraditional college students.

Nontraditional students tend to report career reasons for returning to college. They are more likely than traditional students to attend college part-time, work full-time, be financially independent, and have dependents, all of which pose significant challenges to success in college. Many nontraditional students find the practical details of college more difficult to navigate. Older students tend to have a more complex knowledge base from which to draw and tend to emphasize seeking meaning and applying what they learn to their lives.

13.9 Identify challenges faced by non-college bound young adults.

Young people who do not attend college are more likely to be unemployed than their college-educated peers or to spend their first working years in jobs that are similar to those they held in high school, unskilled, with low pay and little security. Over the last three decades, secondary education has shifted toward emphasizing academics and reducing vocational training, leaving young adults who do not attend college ill-prepared for the job market.

13.10 Identify influences on vocational choice and occupational expectations in early adulthood.

Vocational development in early adulthood entails choosing and becoming established in a career. We select occupations that match our personalities and other individual traits. Contextual influences such as family, socioeconomic status, and educational opportunities also influence our choice of career. According to Levinson, young adults form a dream; define occupational expectations; monitor their progress; and change their expectations in light of their experiences, abilities, and changing interests.

Key Terms

alcohol dependence   372

binge drinking   372

caloric restriction   366

cognitive-affective complexity   376

dualistic thinking   375

epistemic cognition   375

free radicals   366

isometric muscle strength   364

postformal reasoning   375

pragmatic thought   376

reflective judgment   375

relativistic thinking   375

senescence   364

telomeres   367

wear and tear theory of aging   366

CHAPTER 14

Socioemotional Development in Early Adulthood

$SAGE edge™

Get the edge on your studies at edge.sagepub.com/kuther.

Master these learning objectives using key study tools in the chapter and at SAGE edge. Access original SAGE **Video Cases** to explore the lives and contexts of individuals in every stage of development, **Think Critically** and **Explore Further** with SAGE journal and reference articles, and **Watch**, **Listen**, and **Connect** with online multimedia resources.

LEARNING OBJECTIVES	KEY STUDY TOOLS
14.1. Discuss markers of emerging adulthood and the role of context in shaping this period.	**Video Case** Emerging Adulthood
14.2. Explore intimacy development and the influence of the social clock on adjustment.	**Explore Further** Intimacy
14.3. Compare and contrast influences on friendship and mate selection.	**Video Case** Romantic Relationships in Early Adulthood
	Lives in Context Internet Dating (p. 395)
	Connect Mate Selection and Genetics
14.4. Identify characteristics of intimate violence, influences on violence, and ways of addressing it.	**Watch** Why Domestic Violence Victims Don't Leave
	Think Critically Intimate Partner Violence
14.5. Contrast the correlates of singlehood and cohabitation.	**Think Critically** Cohabitation
14.6. Discuss the transition to marriage and predictors of marital success and divorce.	**Watch** The Brain in Love
	Explore Further Marital Satisfaction
14.7. Examine the effects of parenthood on young adults.	**Video Case** Planning for Parenthood and Work-Life Balance
	Listen Millennials and Parenthood
14.8. Compare and contrast the experience of stepparents, never-married parents, and same-sex parents.	**Ethical and Policy Applications of Lifespan Development** Same-Sex Marriage and the Law (p. 403)
	Listen Stepfamilies
14.9. Discuss the experience of women and minorities in the workplace.	**Ethical and Policy Applications of Lifespan Development** Family Leave Policies (p. 412)
	Watch Women in the Workplace
14.10. Examine the interaction of work and family on young adults' adjustment.	**Explore Further** Work-Family Spillover

" I guess real life begins now," Sandra remarked to her college roommate, Christiana. "Is my cap straight?" asked Christiana. Sandra adjusted Christiana's cap and stepped back to look at her friend in her graduation cap and gown, "Yep. Here we go!" Later, as she sat through her college commencement, Sandra wondered about her future. Will she like her new job? What will it be like to work full-time? What about her boyfriend, Jamal? They've dated for over a year. Will he propose? Sandra wasn't sure that

Reuters/Noah Berger

she wanted him to propose. There are many things she'd like to do before settling down. "After all, I'm just starting to figure myself out," she thought to herself. "Will I ever be ready to merge my life with someone else's? Will parenthood be right for me? Will I be able to juggle all the demands of work and family life? Do I want to?"

Most young adults have similar concerns about the transition to adult roles. In this chapter, we take a closer look at the process of becoming an adult and traversing the years of early adulthood, roughly from ages 18 to 40. Given the many changes that happen over this 22-year span, many developmental scientists have begun to differentiate between the transition to adulthood and early adulthood itself.

PSYCHOSOCIAL DEVELOPMENT IN EARLY ADULTHOOD

Sandra's ponderings about her future illustrate the developmental tasks of early adulthood: making decisions about relationships, family, career, and lifestyles, and then transitioning and committing to these roles. Some young people transition to adult roles very quickly while others take a more lengthy, windy path to adopting adult roles. Many young people find themselves in an "in-between" status in which they are not adolescents yet they have not yet assumed the roles that comprise adulthood. This extended transition to adulthood is known as **emerging adulthood** and takes place roughly from ages 18 to 25 (Arnett, 2000, 2004). The following sections discuss emerging adulthood and the psychosocial developments that occur during this transitional period.

EMERGING ADULTHOOD

Much as adolescence is believed to be a social construction, a result of societal changes that separated adolescents from adults (review Chapter 11), in recent years developmental scientists have posed that societal changes have prolonged the transition to adulthood, creating the new period of emerging adulthood (Arnett, 2000, 2004). With more high school graduates entering college than ever before, the traditional markers of adulthood, such as completing one's education, entering a career, establishing a residence, marrying, and forming a family, are delayed relative to prior generations. Increasingly, young people have extended educational experiences prior to career entry, take longer to commit to a career and settle into occupational tracks, and become financially independent more gradually and at later ages than ever before (Shanahan, 2000; Tanner, 2014). The delay of career commitment and financial independence is accompanied by delayed marriages and later family formation (Cohen, Kasen, Chen, Hartmark, & Gordon, 2003).

Emerging adulthood bridges adolescence and adulthood, extending from 18 to 25 or even into the late 20s, and is a time in which many young people who reside in

TABLE 14.1 Percentage of Individuals Aged 18 to 27 Displaying Markers of Adulthood

MARKER	YEARS OF AGE			
	18	21	24	27
In school	67%	36%	15%	16%
Employed full-time	27%	57%	76%	71%
Living with family	84%	41%	27%	15%
Ever pregnant	12%	23%	33%	48%
Biological offspring	3%	12%	20%	38%

SOURCE: Cohen et al. (2003).

Western industrialized societies have left the dependency of adolescence but have not yet assumed adult responsibilities (Arnett, 2000, 2004). Emerging adulthood is characterized by diversity in lifestyles because little is normative demographically for individuals in their late teens through mid-20s (Côté, 2006). For example, some emerging adults live with their parents, others live in college dormitories or in apartments with roommates or with spouses or alone. People aged 18 to 25 have the highest rates of residential change of any age group, shifting among residences and living situations. Some emerging adults are married; others are in long-term relationships, casual relationships, or are single. Education and vocation also varies among emerging adults. Some are in college, some are in the workforce, and some are employed while attending college. Emerging adults adopt adult roles at different times, as shown in Table 14.1.

Psychosocial Development During Emerging Adulthood

Emerging adulthood is an important time of psychosocial development. Self-esteem rises steadily from late adolescence through the mid-20s (Chung et al., 2014). Depressive symptoms decline, and well-being increases as young people make advances in emotional regulation, especially the ability to regulate intense emotions such as anger (Galambos, Barker, & Krahn, 2006; Zimmermann & Iwanski, 2014). Emerging adulthood also is a time of instability and exploration, as young people examine various life options. Emerging adults explore alternatives and make frequent changes in educational paths, romantic partners, and jobs. No longer under parental restrictions and without the full range of adult responsibilities, emerging adults are able to fully engage in the identity developmental processes described in Chapter 12, such as sampling opportunities and possible selves (Schwartz, Zamboanga, Luyckx, Meca, & Ritchie, 2013). As young people make progress toward resolving their identity, they are more likely to perceive themselves as adults (Fadjukoff, Kokko, & Pulkkinen, 2007; Nelson & Barry, 2005).

Emerging adults tend to report feeling a subjective sense of being in-between, that they are not adolescents but they also are not adults (Arnett, 1997, 2003). For example,

Emerging adulthood is an exciting time of exploration, independence, and firsts, but also one of feeling in between, neither adolescent nor adult.

less than one third of 18- to 20-year-olds tend to report they consider themselves to be adults, as compared with 50% of 21- to 24-year-olds and 70% of 25- to 28-year-olds (Arnett, 1997; Reitzle, 2006). Emerging adults tend to view becoming an adult as independent of traditional markers of adulthood, such as marriage, and instead based on acquiring a set of personal characteristics such as accepting responsibility for themselves, making independent decisions, and becoming financially independent (Arnett, 2003; Sharon, 2015). Attaining these personally important markers is associated with well-being (Sharon, 2015). However, one longitudinal study that followed 7th- to 12th-grade students into emerging adulthood (ages 18 to 24) found that emerging adults viewed both personal qualities and traditional social transition markers as contributors to self-perceived adulthood (Johnson, Berg, & Sirotzki, 2007). Although most emerging adults do not identify role transitions, such as marriage and parenthood, as necessary for people to be considered adults, young people who have experienced these role transitions are more likely to see themselves as adult than are those who have not completed similar role transitions.

Contextual Nature of Emerging Adulthood

Emerging adulthood is a response to larger societal changes, but it is not universal (Molgat, 2007). Ages for assuming adult roles are not set in stone. Young people vary with regard to when they enter careers, marriage, and parenthood (Cohen et al., 2003; Eisenberg, Spry, & Patton, 2015). One study that followed young people from 17 to 30 years of age found that the average person gained autonomy with respect to obtaining employment, establishing financial and residential independence and becoming a parent over these years; however, there was great variability in individual patterns for assuming adult roles (Cohen et al., 2003). Transitions did not occur at the same pace or order for everyone.

Young people who drop out of high school, experience early parenthood, begin working at a job immediately after high school, or who reside in low socioeconomic homes and communities may experience only a limited period of emerging adulthood or may not experience emerging adulthood at all (Hendry & Kloep, 2010; Maggs, Jager, Patrick, & Schulenberg, 2012).

In contrast, emerging adulthood may be extended into the late 20s for young people who obtain advanced training, such as attending medical school or law school, which delays entry into career, other adult roles, and financial independence. Enrollment in postsecondary education often delays residential and financial independence. College students tend to depend on parents for financial and often residential support whereas those who are employed are more likely to be financially self-supporting and to live in a residence independent of parents (Goldscheider & Goldscheider, 1999). Emerging adulthood may financially overburden families by extending children's financial dependence (Settersten & Ray, 2010). Some theorists argue that emerging adulthood is not a life stage—it does not exist everywhere and for everyone—but is simply an indicator of medium to high socioeconomic status and the educational and career opportunities that accompany such status (Côté, 2006, 2014).

Although emerging adulthood is not universal, it has been observed among young people in many cultures, including Argentinean, Austrian, Chinese, Czech, German, Israeli, Mexican, North American, Romanian, and Spanish, (Arias & Hernández, 2007; Facio & Micocci, 2003; Macek, Bejček, & Vaníčková, 2007; Mayseless & Scharf, 2003; Nelson, 2009; Nelson, Badger, & Wu, 2004; Sirsch, Dreher, Mayr, & Willinger, 2009). Each of these cultures endorses similar criteria for adulthood as well as criteria that are unique to their own culture. For example, each culture rates accepting responsibility for the consequences of one's actions as the most important criterion for adulthood, but other important criteria vary by culture. North American emerging adults

EMERGING ADULTHOOD

In this video we consider the topic of emerging adulthood from the perspective of emerging adults as well as from the perspective of parents to adult children. Compare the characteristics that young people and parents see as comprising adulthood.

Watch the video at edge.sagepub.com/kuther

also rate making independent decisions and becoming financially independent as criteria for adulthood (Arnett, 1997, 2003). In Argentina, young people rated the capacity to care for young children as the second most important criteria for women (Facio & Micocci, 2003). Israeli young adults listed being able to withstand pressure as a required attribute for adulthood (Mayseless & Scharf, 2003) whereas Romanian young people reported norm compliance as an indicator of adulthood (Nelson, 2009). Chinese emerging adults rated learning to have good control of your emotions as being necessary for adulthood (Nelson et al., 2004). Yet none of these criteria were rated as necessary for adulthood by North Americans (Arnett, 2003). In contrast, a study of 18- to 26-year-old college students and nonstudents from a rural village in India found that the majority viewed themselves as adults and believed that others viewed them as adults, contrary to predictions related to emerging adulthood; however, the college students reported higher levels of optimism characteristic of emerging adulthood than did those who did not attend college, supportive of the existence of emerging adulthood (Seiter & Nelson, 2011). It appears that emerging adulthood, the extended transition from adolescence to adulthood, often occurs in Western industrialized cultures. However, the specific features and characteristics with which young people define *adulthood* vary by culture.

INTIMACY VERSUS ISOLATION

As with earlier periods in development, psychological adjustment and health is influenced by interactions between the individual and social world. According to Erikson's (1950) lifespan theory of psychosocial development, at every phase in life, individuals encounter psychological crises that offer both opportunities and risks for psychological development. The crisis of early adulthood is the major psychosocial task of **intimacy versus isolation**: developing the capacity for intimacy and making a permanent commitment to a romantic partner.

A primary task of young adulthood is to establish intimate relationships with significant others.

Establishing an intimate relationship that is mutual and satisfying is a challenge for emerging and young adults who often continue to struggle with identity issues and are just gaining social and financial independence. Commitment to an identity, including a sense of self, values, and goals, prepares young people for establishing intimate relationships (Kroger, 2007; Zimmer-Gembeck & Petherick, 2006) and is associated with establishing intimate relationships in early adulthood (Beyers & Seiffge-Krenke, 2010). Yet, as young adults form intimate relationships, they must reshape their identity to include their role as partner and the goals, plans, and interests shared with their partner. Thus, they must resolve identity and intimacy demands that may conflict. For example, as they engage in continued identity development, they must do the work of establishing an intimate relationship, making sacrifices and compromises that may involve a temporary loss of self before expanding the sense of self to include a partner. The formation of intimate relationships is associated with well-being in young adults (Busch & Hofer, 2012). The flip side—not attaining a sense of intimacy and not making personal commitments to others—is the negative psychosocial outcome of isolation, entailing a sense of loneliness and self-absorption.

Because developing a sense of intimacy is a task of early adulthood that relies on identity development, many emerging adults who are just forming their identities are ill-prepared for this task. For example, young people who are engaging in the psychological exploration characteristic of the psychosocial moratorium are less likely to form intimate relationships whereas those who are identity achieved are more likely to engage in romantic relationships characterized by loyalty and love (Markstrom & Kalmanir, 2001). Identity achievement predicts readiness for intimate and committed romantic relationships and the capacity to actively seek and establish them (Barry, Madsen, Nelson, Carroll, & Badger, 2009; Beyers & Seiffge-Krenke, 2010; Montgomery, 2005). Emerging adults generally report feeling that they are not ready for a committed, enduring relationship (Collins & van Dulmen, 2006). Many young people do not enter into truly intimate relationships until they have traversed the transition from emerging adulthood to early adulthood.

THE SOCIAL CLOCK

"There is a time for everything," explained 14-year-old Carissa to her older sister, Erika. "At 18 you graduate high school, 22 you graduate college, 22 or 23 you get engaged, and 24 or 25 you get married." "Silly, those ages fit for some people but not everyone. It depends on your experience, career plans, and personal goals," admonished 20-year-old Erika. Yet Erika wondered to herself whether Carissa was right. Is there a "time for everything"? Developmental theorist Bernice Neugarten (1979; Neugarten & Neugarten, 1996) suggested that there is. Neugarten proposed that rather than follow simplistic age-based stages, adult development is shaped by a

The social clock marks normative age-graded events, such as graduations, marriage, and parenthood.

web of contextual influences. Throughout life, we experience a number of normative age-graded events, life events that most people encounter at specific ages, such as graduating from high school at age 18. The expected timing of normative age-graded events can be expressed as a **social clock**, age-related expectations for major life events such as occupational entry, marriage, parenthood, and retirement. Every society has a timetable for such events, and young people compare their progress on these events with that of their peers.

The degree to which individuals match their culture's social clock influences their self-esteem and psychological functioning. Most people are aware of their own timing and can describe themselves as early, late, or on time with regard to milestones such as getting married, having children, or retiring. Since the mid-20th century, Western culture's expectations for the timing of developmental milestones of adulthood have become less age conscious and rigid in that the acceptable age range for norms have widened (Peterson, 1996). Delayed parenthood is one example; today, few people blink at a 40-year-old first-time parent whereas a generation ago late parenthood was unusual. That said, many young adults experience distress and poor self-esteem when they are off-time relative to their peers.

Thinking in Context 14.1

1. In what ways is emerging adulthood socially constructed, a product of contextual factors? Did you experience, or are you currently in, emerging adulthood? Identify conditions in which emerging adulthood may not occur.

2. Identify elements of the social clock. What are events that most adolescents, emerging adults, and young adults experience? What typical ages accompany these events? Compare yourself to the social clock you have identified. How well does it match your experience?

RELATIONSHIPS IN EARLY ADULTHOOD

Young adults satisfy some of their intimacy needs through close friendships. Yet the developmental task of establishing the capacity for intimate relationships is best fulfilled by establishing a romantic relationship with a mate. The following sections discuss both types of intimate relationships: friendship and romantic relationships.

FRIENDSHIP

Like friendships in childhood and adolescence, adult friendships are based on similarity—shared interests, attitudes, and values (Hartup & Stevens, 1999). Friends tend to be similar in demographics, such as age, sex, and socioeconomic status, as these variables signal common interests and needs that may be fulfilled by friendship. In college, friendships may become more ethnically diverse among white students, less so among black students, and remain unchanged among Latino and Asian students (Stearns, Buchmann, & Bonneau, 2009). Some friendships are very intimate and marked by sharing, closeness, and support, yet other friendships are less intimate and based on a common interest, such as a favorite sport or a field of study. Some friendships are lifelong and of higher quality and are more stable than relationships with romantic partners and spouses (Hartup & Stevens, 1999). Friendship quality is associated with psychological adjustment and well-being in emerging and young adults (Buote et al., 2007; Demir, Özen, Doğan, Bilyk, & Tyrell, 2011).

Although recently married young people tend to have the greatest number of friends, single young adults tend to rely more heavily on friendships to fulfill needs for social support and acceptance than do married young adults (Carbery & Buhrmester, 1998). The more that friendships are characterized by social support and self-disclosure, the more satisfaction single young adults report and the longer the relationship lasts (Sanderson, Rahm, & Beigbeder, 2005). Women, regardless of marital and parental status, tend to have more intimate and long-lasting friendships, see their friends more often, and rely more on friends to meet social and emotional needs than do men (Carbery & Buhrmester, 1998; Radmacher & Azmitia, 2006; Sherman & de Vries, 2000). Men's friendships tend to center around sharing information and activities, such as playing sports, rather than intimate disclosure (David-Barrett et al., 2015; Radmacher & Azmitia, 2006). As male friendships endure to become long-lasting ties, self-disclosure increases and the friends become closer (Sherman & de Vries, 2000). Satisfaction with one's friendships is a better predictor of life satisfaction than is the number of friends (Gillespie, Lever, Frederick, & Royce, 2014).

Many young adults have opposite-sex friendships, which can be important sources of social support but tend not to last as long as same-sex friendships. Among men, friendships with women tend to decline after marriage, but women, especially highly educated women, tend to have more friendships with men throughout adulthood, especially in the workplace. Other-sex friendships are a source of companionship and support and offer opportunities to learn about gender differences in the expression of intimacy (Bleske-Rechek & Buss, 2001; Grover, Nangle, Serwik, & Zeff, 2007). It seems that both men and women gain from other-sex relationships. Men learn about emotional expression and intimacy, and women often report that male friends offer a different, objective point of view on problems.

Over the course of adulthood, the number of friends and time spent with them declines. Adults often turn primarily to their spouses for intimacy and social support (Carbery & Buhrmester, 1998; Kito, 2005). As young adults establish families and careers, they often have less time to spend with friends, yet friendship remains an important influence on well-being throughout life (Hartup & Stevens, 1999).

ROMANTIC RELATIONSHIPS

Romantic relationships are important sources of intimacy. They are formed in similar ways as friendships but show different patterns of progression. The developmental task of early adulthood is to form long-term intimate relationships that will endure throughout adulthood (Seiffge-Krenke, 2003). Generally speaking, there tends to be continuity in relationship quality such that quality of romantic relationships in adolescence predicts relationship quality in emerging adulthood and beyond (Shulman & Connolly, 2013). The nature of romantic relationships often does change over time, however. For example, emerging adults tend to fluctuate between relationships or to be involved in short sexual and romantic encounters (Cohen et al., 2003). Today, young adults often experience years of singlehood and dating before partnering.

Mate Selection

What do men and women look for in a mate? Men and women from many cultures show similar patterns in mate preferences. Men tend to prefer a younger mate and assign greater value to physical attractiveness and domestic skills; from an evolutionary perspective, these are attributes that signal fertility and the capacity to care for offspring (Buunk, Dijkstra, Fetchenhauer, & Kenrick, 2002; Furnham, 2009; Li et al., 2013). Women tend to assign greater importance to earning potential, intelligence, height, and moral character and seek mates who are the same age or slightly older—characteristics that may increase the likelihood that a woman's offspring will survive and thrive.

Contrary to popular belief, opposites do not make for satisfying partnerships. Differences among romantic partners may enhance their compatibility if the different traits complement one another—for example, one partner being more shy and the other outgoing. However, generally speaking, opposites might attract, but it is similarity that breeds relationship satisfaction. The more similar partners are, the more likely they are to report being satisfied with their relationship and to remain in the relationship (Blackwell & Lichter, 2004; Lutz-Zois, Bradley, Mihalik, & Moorman-Eavers, 2006). When entering a relationship, partners tend to lack information about each other and the resulting ambiguity is associated with liking (i.e., having positive feelings about) one another. As partners gain information about each other, they inevitably encounter some dissimilarities. Dissimilarities tend to reduce liking because once evidence of dissimilarity is encountered, subsequent information is more likely to be interpreted as further support of dissimilarity, further reducing liking (Norton, Frost, & Ariely, 2007).

Most intimate partners share similarities in demographics, attitudes, and values. Research has differentiated between perceived similarity (the degree to which individuals believe they are similar to their partner) and actual similarity (the measurable similarities they share). Studies have found that perceived similarity predicts attraction to potential and current mates (Montoya, Horton, & Kirchner, 2008; Taylor, Fiore, Mendelsohn, & Cheshire, 2011) and is more important in mate selection than actual similarities (Tidwell, Eastwick, & Finkel, 2013). What actual similarities do couples typically share? Common similarities shared by romantic partners include personality style, intelligence, educational aspirations, and attractiveness (Markey & Markey, 2007). Romantic partners often also share similarities in health behaviors such as smoking and tendencies toward risk taking (Smithson & Baker, 2008; Wiersma, Fischer, Harrington Cleveland, Reifman, & Harris, 2010). Young people tend to choose partners who share behavioral similarities with them, and as their relationships develop and grow, they often become more similar to each other. (This pattern resembles the one by which friends tend to become more similar to one another over time, as discussed in Chapter 12.)

Today, many adults of all ages use the Internet as a means of meeting potential romantic partners and developing relationships with them. The role of the Internet in mate selection is discussed in Lives in Context (p. 395). Mate selection is complicated and influenced by developmental, personal, social, and cultural factors.

Components of Love

Mario and Davida dated for 4 years before marrying. After 15 years of marriage and three children, Davida feels a warm sense of comfort and stability with her husband, who has become her best friend, but she sometimes misses the sparks of their dating years. Corey is planning to propose to his girlfriend of six months. "Sure, it's very soon after meeting," he thought to himself, "but I'm crazy about her, can't stop thinking about her,

LIVES IN CONTEXT

Internet Dating

With every generation come advances in technology that influence daily life, including romantic relationships. For example, in the mid-1990s, the first online dating sites were launched. Online dating, meeting, and communicating have flourished over the past two decades, enabling individuals to meet and interact with many potential dates quickly and without having to leave their homes.

In 2013 nearly 11% of adults in the United States and 38% who were currently single and seeking a partner reported having used online dating sites or mobile dating apps (Smith & Duggan, 2013). Overall, 5% of U.S. adults report having met their spouse or long-term partner online, including 11% of couples who have been together 10 years or less. Young adults are the most common users of online dating sites, with 22% of 25- to 34-year-olds and 17% of 35- to 44-year-olds reporting having dated online, roughly double the rate for those ages 18 to 24 and those ages 45 to 54 (Smith & Duggan, 2013).

Why do people choose to date online? Two thirds of online daters report that it is a good way to meet people, and nearly three quarters agree that it helps people find a better romantic match because they have access to a wide range of potential partners.

An online dating relationship usually begins with a flurry of e-mail messages. If the two decide they are interested enough to pursue the contact further, phone calls and then a face-to-face meeting follow. Unlike traditional dating, in online dating a great deal of information is shared before daters meet. The tone, or degree of emotionality, of e-mail messages influences daters' impressions of potential partners. Strong positive emotional words, such as *excited* or *wonderful*, are more likely to elicit a response from a prospective dating partner than less strong emotional words, such as *good* or *fine* (Rosen, Cheever, Cummings, & Felt, 2008). In addition, daters tend to prefer low levels of self-disclosure, a preference that also exists in traditional dating. In many ways, people using online dating and the resulting romances are very much like those that originate though friends, school, or work (Hall, Park, Hayeon, & Michael, 2010).

Online dating differs from traditional dating in that it allows daters to exert greater control over their first impressions to potential partners. Typical dating profiles include a self-description and a picture. The accuracy of photos varies. In one study, online daters, independent judges, and trained coders evaluated the accuracy of daters' photos (Hancock & Toma, 2009). While online daters rated their own photos as relatively accurate, independent judges rated approximately one third of the photographs as not accurate. Female photographs were judged as less accurate than male photographs; they were more likely to be older; to be retouched or taken by a professional photographer; and to contain inconsistencies, including changes in hair style and skin quality (Hancock & Toma, 2009). Over one half of online daters have felt that someone else misrepresented themselves in their profile (Smith & Duggan, 2013). Despite this, the degree to which online daters misrepresent themselves is low (Hall et al., 2010). Women may be more likely to fib about their weight, and men may be more prone to tell white lies on other subjects, such as their assets, relationship goals, and personal interests (Hall et al., 2010). However, differences between individuals tend to be far greater than those between the sexes.

Online daters face an ironic challenge. The increased options that dating websites provide, such as the seemingly endless supply of potential dates, may not aid them in finding a suitable partner (Finkel, Eastwick, Karney, Reis, & Sprecher, 2012). As daters face more options, they are more likely to search excessively for an ideal "Ms./Mr. Right"; they may also become distracted with details and irrelevant information, making it more difficult to screen and select partners (Southard, 2008; Wu & Chiou, 2009). With so many opportunities, online daters may find it difficult to make decisions about romantic partners, perhaps undermining their dating efforts. Indeed, about one third of online daters agree that online dating "keeps people from settling down because they always have options for people to date" (Smith & Duggan, 2013).

What Do You Think?

1. In your view, what are the advantages and disadvantages of online dating?

2. Consider friendships and the mate selection process in early adulthood. In what ways is the pursuit of romantic relationships online similar to and different from what we know about friendship formation and mate selection in early adulthood?

TABLE 14.2 Prevalence of Online Dating, by Age

AGE	KNOW SOMEONE WHO HAS USED ONLINE DATING SITES	KNOW COUPLE IN LONG-TERM RELATIONSHIP OR MARRIAGE WHO MET ONLINE
18–29	49%	31%
30–49	48%	24%
50–64	42%	26%
65+	24%	20%

SOURCE: Smith and Duggan (2013).

and can't imagine a day without seeing her." Both Davida and Corey experience love in their relationship, but they do not experience the same kind of love.

Interpersonal relationships can be categorized on the basis of different compositions of three aspects that comprise love: passion, intimacy, and commitment (Sternberg, 2004). New romantic relationships tend to be characterized by passion, excitement, and happiness that accompany intense physical attraction, physiological arousal, and cognitive preoccupation (i.e., constantly thinking about the object of

TABLE 14.3 Forms of Love

	INTIMACY	PASSION	COMMITMENT	DESCRIPTION
Liking/ friendship	X			Close friendship characterized by feelings of warmth but without commitment or a long-term commitment.
Infatuated love		X		Love characterized by passion. Many romantic relationships begin as infatuated love and later become intimate and committed. Relationships characterized by infatuated love may dissolve suddenly.
Empty love			X	Relationship characterized by commitment without love or intimacy. A more complex kind of love may dissolve into empty love. In cultures in which there are arranged marriages—in which partners are selected by their families on the basis of cultural values—relationships of empty love sometimes grow to include intimacy and/or passion.
Romantic love	X	X		Characterized by physical passion and emotional closeness. Many romantic relationships represent romantic love and later develop commitment.
Companionate love	X		X	Similar to friendships, this love is intimate and not passionate; however, it has the element of long-term commitment. It is shared by close friends who have a platonic but strong friendship. It is also characteristic of some marriages in which the passion wanes but strong feelings of emotional connection and commitment remain.
Fatuous love		X	X	Relationship where the commitment is motivated by passion. Might occur in a whirlwind, quick marriage in which the couple does not have the time to form intimacy.
Consummate love	X	X	X	Ideal relationship—passion, intimacy, commitment. The couple displaying consummate love feels close and connected passion and a long-term commitment to each other. May be difficult to maintain over time. As passion wanes may transform into companionate love.

SOURCE: Sternberg (2004).

ROMANTIC RELATIONSHIPS IN EARLY ADULTHOOD

Establishing romantic relationships is an important task for many young adults. In this clip college students Amber and Jeffrey describe the origins of their relationship and compare themselves to their peers. Emerging adult Morgan considers whether there is pressure to settle down, and parents to young adults provide their perspectives.

Watch the video at edge.sagepub.com/kuther

affection). Passion is not always accompanied by intimacy, emotional engagement, warm communication, closeness, connectedness, and caring for the other person's well-being. Commitment, the decision that partners make to stay with one another, grows as people spend more time together, create shared goals, and solve problems together. According to theorist Robert Sternberg (1988), different combinations of these three components comprise seven different types of love, as shown in Table 14.3 and Figure 14.1.

Western ideals of love, such as those depicted in movies and television programs, include all three components. However, the relative proportions of passion, intimacy, and commitment vary over the course of a relationship and with age as young adults tend to experience higher levels of passion in their relationships than older adults (and midlife and older adults tend to experience greater levels of commitment; Sumter, Valkenburg, & Peter, 2013). The euphoria of passion is influenced by novelty, spontaneity, and unfamiliarity because passion arises from physical attraction that is exciting and new. Intimacy, however, grows with familiarity. Feelings of closeness and bonding

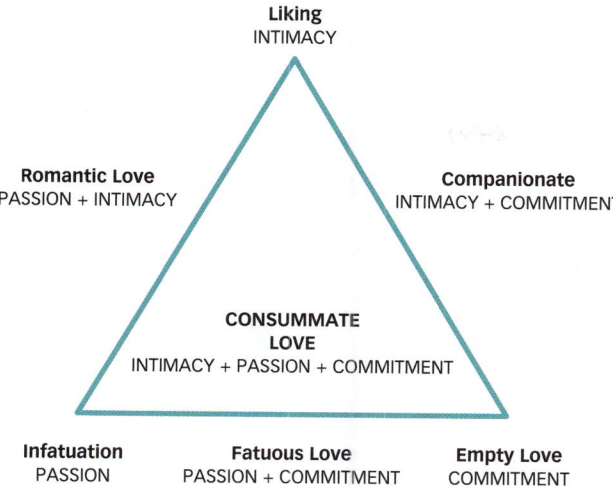

underlie the development of intimacy. It is over time that commitment strengthens. The novelty and uncertainty that fuels passion fades as the sense of security and stability that underlie intimacy and commitment grows. In turn, as intimacy and commitment increase, passion often subsides (Baumeister & Bratslavsky, 1999). Yet it is intimacy and commitment, not passion, that ultimately determine whether the romance will endure (Hendrick & Hendrick, 2004). This pattern of passion declining as intimacy and commitment increase is true of all couples, heterosexual and same-sex, married and unmarried (Kurdek, 2006). However, intimacy fluctuates from day to day, and increases in intimacy are often associated with similar increases in passion (Rubin & Campbell, 2011). Many couples show a long-term romantic love characterized by passion and intimacy, which in turn increases marital happiness and enhance their feelings of commitment (Acevedo & Aron, 2009). Successful couples acknowledge and appreciate the "ups" in intimacy and passion despite overall declines.

Eastern cultures such as those of China and Japan offer a different perspective on romantic love. Traditional collectivist views common in Eastern cultures value interdependence. The young person is defined through relationships and roles—such as the roles of daughter, son, sibling, husband, and wife—rather than as an individual. Because all relationships are important components to the young person's sense of self, affection is dispersed throughout all relationships, and romantic relationships are less intense than those experienced by Western young people. Chinese and Japanese young adults consider mate selection within the context of their other relationships and responsibilities to others. They are more likely than North American and European young adults to rate companionship, similarity in backgrounds, and career potential as important in choosing a partner and are less likely to rate physical attraction and passion as important factors (Dion & Dion, 1993). Similarly, dating couples in China report feeling less passion than do

those in the United States but report similar levels of intimacy and commitment, which in turn predict relationship satisfaction (Gao, 2001).

INTIMATE PARTNER VIOLENCE

Violence between intimate partners is a widespread health issue that is not limited by culture, ethnicity, socioeconomic status, sexual orientation, or marital status. **Intimate violence** includes physical violence, sexual abuse, and psychological harm. Victims frequently experience several forms of violence. For example, physical violence, such as throwing and breaking possessions, punching holes in walls, shaking, hitting, and kicking, tends to be accompanied by psychological abuse, including such as threats of violence and coercive tactics such as humiliation, control, and isolation from friends and family (Krebs, Breiding, Browne, & Warner, 2011). Intimate partner violence occurs at similar rates in both heterosexual and same-sex couples (Clift, Thomas, & Dutton, 2005).

Physical violence in which a male harms a female partner is the most commonly reported type of intimate violence; however, many more acts remain unreported. Research suggests that men and women report experiencing similar rates of physical assault during arguments (Archer, 2002; Próspero & Miseong, 2009). Intimate violence escalates the emotional intensity of arguments and tends to elicit retaliatory violence from the victimized partner. A particularly comprehensive form of violence is intimate terrorism, a pattern of coercive control and repeated severe battering; research has found that both males and females perpetrate intimate terrorism, at similar rates (Hamel, 2009). Partners report the main motivation for remaining in relationships characterized by intimate terrorism as fear (Leone, Lape, & Xu, 2013). Although, overall, men and women are about equally likely to instigate episodes of intimate violence, women are more likely to miss work, report depression, be injured, receive death threats, and to actually be killed by their partners (Catalano, 2007; Jasinski, Blumenstein, & Morgan, 2014; Moffitt & Caspi, 1999). Men are more likely to report partner aggression as the precipitant to their own aggression whereas women's is more precipitated by verbal aggression or something else other than physical (Fincham & Beach, 2010).

Intimate violence is not a one-time event but a process (Cattaneo, Stuewig, Goodman, Kaltman, & Dutton, 2007). A variety of factors contribute to intimate violence. Spouses who abuse often show higher rates of depression, anxiety, and low self-esteem and often display possessive, jealous, and controlling behavior toward their partner (Dixon & Browne, 2003; Johnson, Giordano, Longmore, & Manning, 2014). Many fail to see their role in the abuse and instead blame their partner for causing situations that lead to violence (Henning & Holdford, 2006). As children, those who have grown up to be abusive spouses are more likely to have observed domestic violence in the home, received

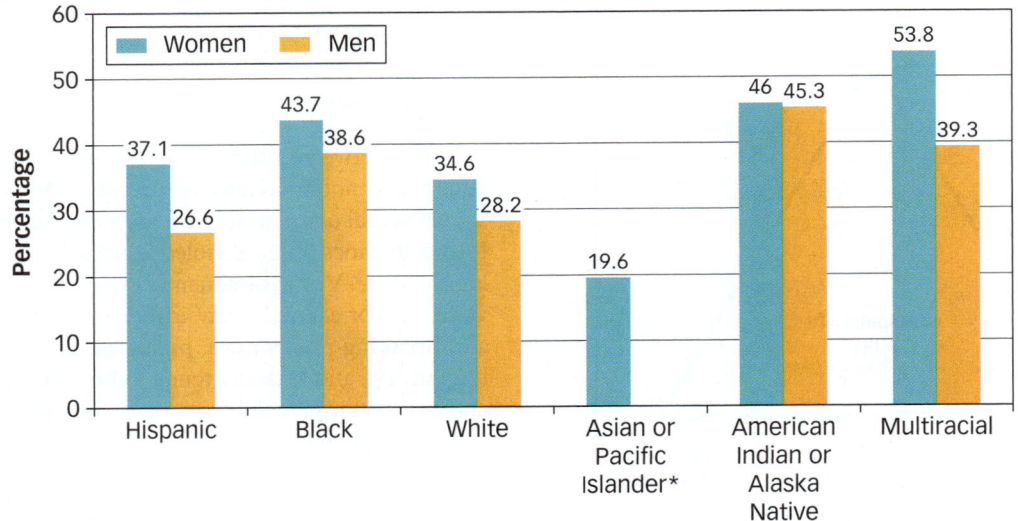

FIGURE 14.2: Lifetime Rates of Intimate Partner Violence by Sex and Ethnicity

NOTE: *No data available for Asian or Pacific Islander males.
SOURCE: Breiding et al. (2014).

physical punishment and coercive discipline as well as to have engaged in violent delinquency during adolescence (Murrell, Christoff, & Henning, 2007; Smith, Ireland, Park, Elwyn, & Thornberry, 2011). There is also overlap between perpetrator and victim roles; many victims also engage in abusive behavior (Tillyer & Wright, 2013).

About 36% of women and 29% of men experience intimate partner violence defined as rape, physical violence, or stalking at some point in their lifetime, and about 6% and 5% report experiencing intimate violence in the past year (Breiding, Chen, & Black, 2014). Although women are more likely to experience intimate partner violence, overall rates vary by ethnicity, as shown in Figure 14.2.

Contextual factors that contribute to domestic violence include stressors such as poverty, unemployment, and drug and alcohol abuse. For example, the experience of poverty and other contextual stressors may underlie the higher rates of domestic violence reported by African American women (Cho, 2012). Cultural norms and values also influence rates of partner violence.

Worldwide, about one third of women experience intimate partner violence in their lifetimes, but rates vary widely from 16% in East Asia (including China, Japan, North Korea, and South Korea) and 19% in Western Europe to 66% in Central sub-Saharan Africa (including Chad, Congo, and Rwanda) to 41% and 42% in South Asia (including Bangladesh, India, and Pakistan) and parts of Latin America, respectively (Breiding et al., 2014; Devries et al., 2013).

Around the world, the large majority of intimate abuse includes female victims. Cultural norms valuing male dominance and female submissiveness, as well as differences in women's social mobility through education and career, underlie differences in prevalence rates (and gender differences in prevalence rates) throughout the world,

including many countries in Asia, the Middle East, and Africa (Bendall, 2010; Boyle, Georgiades, Cullen, & Racine, 2009; Eng, Li, Mulsow, & Fischer, 2010; World Health Organization, 2005). In Cambodia, for example, the more contact and discussions couples have, the more likely are husbands to assert control and engage in intimate violence (Eng et al., 2010). Among women in India, education serves as a protective factor against experiencing intimate violence, but community living standards and attitudes toward maltreatment are more closely linked with partner abuse (Boyle et al., 2009).

Why do victims of intimate violence remain in these relationships? Many do so out of financial necessity, love, fear, the embarrassment of alerting authorities, and the hope that their partner will change (Dunn & Powell-Williams, 2007). Victims who remain in abusive relationships often feel that they are powerless, which is associated with increased risk for victimization and heightened symptoms of depression (Filson, Ulloa, Runfola, & Hokoda, 2010). Many communities provide services to aid victims of intimate violence, including crisis telephone lines, shelters, and clinics that provide counseling, support, and treatment. Yet victims of partner violence often return to the relationship several times before terminating it. Most victims seek help repeatedly over the course of the relationship, with more diverse and intense help-seeking accompanying more severe violence (Cattaneo et al., 2007).

Community services addressing intimate partner violence attempt to empower victims by easing their transition from dangerous homes and fostering self-help skills (Barner & Carney, 2011). Community services often include treatment for abusers, emphasizing communication, anger management, and problem solving, but many perpetrators repeat the pattern of violence despite treatment (Harway &

Hansen, 2004; Levesque, Velicer, & Castle, 2008). Finally, exposure to intimate partner violence has damaging effects on children, similar to the effects of exposure to community violence as discussed in Chapter 9, but worse because home is not a safe haven. Children reared in homes of pervasive violence are more likely to be victims of physical abuse themselves and to live in fear of experiencing or witnessing violence, risk factors for engaging in intimate partner violence as adults (Carpenter & Stacks, 2009).

Thinking in Context 14.2

1. How might developmental and contextual factors such as neighborhood, age, and life experience influence the formation and course of friendships? In what ways are romantic relationships similar and different from friendships?

2. How might culture and context influence young adults' perspectives of what characteristics to look for in seeking a romantic partner and mate? How might young people increase their odds of forming a happy and long-lasting relationship?

3. Consider the problem of intimate violence from a bioecological perspective. What microsystem, mesosystem, exosystem, and macrosystem may increase the likelihood of violence? What factors might decrease it?

MARRIAGE AND ALTERNATIVES TO MARRIAGE

Although most young people marry in early adulthood, others experience alternative living styles, whether by choice or circumstance; they may remain single or cohabit with a partner. Trends such as late marriage, divorce, and an increasing number of adults who choose not to marry mean that most adults in the United States will spend a large part of their adult lives as single; indeed, about 8% will remain single throughout life. Couples who marry are very likely to live together before marriage. Others live together in long-term **cohabitation** that does not lead to marriage.

SINGLEHOOD

Singlehood, not living with a romantic partner, is common among U.S. young adults. About one third of 25- to 39-year-old adults have never married, including 18% of 35- to 39-year olds (U.S. Bureau of the Census, 2015b). Women tend to select mates who are the same age or older, are equally or better educated, and who are professionally successful whereas men tend to marry down with regard to age, education, and professional status. Because of these tendencies, highly educated professional women who are financially independent,

and therefore lack an economic incentive to marry, may find few potential mates who are suitable; such women tend to be overrepresented among singles after age 30 (Sharp & Ganong, 2007). Overall, women are more likely than men to remain single for many years or their entire lives.

Some young people are single by deliberate choice. Many women describe themselves as single by choice when they are self-supporting, feel a sense of control over their romantic lives, and have not encountered anyone they wish to marry (Sharp & Ganong, 2007). Other young adults describe themselves as single because of circumstances that they cannot control. One study of never-married women found that some attributed singlehood to focusing more on career goals than marriage, others pointed to disappointing romantic relationships, and some reported never meeting the right person (Baumbusch, 2004). When young adults perceive themselves as single by choice, they tend to report enjoying singlehood and the freedom to take risks and experiment with lifestyle changes (Austrom & Hanel, 1985). They also tend to associate singlehood with independence, self-fulfillment, and autonomy throughout their life course, including in old age (Timonen & Doyle, 2013).

COHABITATION

Cohabitation, the practice of unmarried couples sharing a home, has increased steadily over the past three decades such that the majority of young adults in their 20s have lived with a romantic partner, and about two thirds of U.S. couples live together before marriage (Manning, 2013; Sassler & Miller, 2011). Cohabitation is even more common in Europe: Over 75% of couples in Northern and Central Europe and the United Kingdom cohabit, and about 90% do so in Sweden and Denmark (Hsueh, Morrison, & Doss, 2009; Manning, 2013; Popenoe, 2009).

Why are rates of cohabitation rising? One influence is the increasing prevalence of emerging adulthood. The trend for advanced education and delayed career entry contributes toward the tendency for each generation of young people to marry late relative to prior generations. Some young adults move in with their partners early in the relationship because of changes in employment, housing situations, or convenience, or in response to pregnancy (Sassler & Miller, 2011). Many young adults who have close romantic and sexual relationships desire stability and a shared residence, yet they report not feeling ready for marriage. Those whose parents are divorced are more likely to have attitudes supporting cohabitation and may be more wary about marriage (Cunningham & Thornton, 2007). Young adults commonly cite assessing romantic compatibility, convenience, and improving finances as reasons for cohabiting (Copen, Daniels, & Mosher, 2013; King & Scott, 2005). Many view it as a precursor to marriage or a trial marriage (Murrow & Shi, 2010). For example, in 2008, nearly 70% of high school seniors reported that living together before marriage is a good way to test compatibility (Manning, 2013), and research

Most young adults in North America and Europe cohabitate, or live together, in committed relationships.

Sacramento Bee/Tribune/Getty

suggests that cohabitation in the United States is commonly viewed as a trial marriage (Guzzo, 2009). Contextual factors, such as socioeconomic status and culture, also influence rates of cohabitation. Young adults of low socioeconomic status, as well as of African American and Puerto Rican heritage, are more likely to cohabit as an alternative to marriage (Cherlin, 2010; Seltzer, 2004). Moreover, sexually active young adults tend to report more favorable views of cohabitation (Willoughby & Carroll, 2010).

Despite its prevalence in Europe and the United States, cultures differ in the acceptability of cohabitation and policies supportive of it. In many European countries, cohabitation is viewed not as a precursor but rather as an alternative to marriage. Cohabiting couples in those cultures often hold legal rights similar to those of married couples and show similar levels of devotion as married couples (Hiekel, Liefbroer, & Poortman, 2014; Perelli-Harris & Gassen, 2012). Similarly, cohabiting couples in Canada are afforded the same rights as married couples after living together for a period of one to three years, depending on province (Le Bourdais & Lapierre-Adamcyk, 2004). Alternatively, cohabitation is nearly unheard of in some countries, such as Ireland, Italy, Japan, and the Philippines, where fewer than 10% of adults have ever lived with an unmarried partner (Batalova & Cohen, 2002; Williams, Kabamalan, & Ogena, 2007).

The stability of cohabiting unions also varies internationally. Overall, cohabiting couples in the United States tend to be less satisfied, show higher rates of intimate violence, and have less stable relationships than married couples; one third of cohabiting couples in the United States dissolve in three years (Jose, Daniel O'Leary, & Moyer, 2010; Kenneyand & McLanahan, 2006). In contrast, European cohabiting couples show much lower rates of dissolution, similar to those of married couples (Copen et al., 2013; Hiekel et al., 2014; Perelli-Harris & Gassen, 2012). Cultural views on the acceptability of cohabitation and policies that provide legal rights to cohabitants contribute to these cultural differences (Liefbroer & Dourleijn, 2006; Soons & Kalmijn, 2009).

Research suggests that cohabiting couples who go on to marry tend to have unhappier marriages with a greater likelihood of divorce (Hsueh et al., 2009; Jose et al., 2010; Rhoades, Petrella, Stanley, & Markman, 2007). For example, in one study women who cohabited before marriage reported less of a connection with their spouse, less affection, and more poor marital adjustment than did those who did not cohabit before marriage (Kulik & Havusha-Morgenstern, 2011). Yet critics argue that much of the research describing negative effects of cohabitation on marital stability in U.S. couples is based on data collected decades ago, when cohabitation was less common (Manning & Cohen, 2012). More recent research collected over the past two decades has suggested that, as cohabitation becomes more common, its association with marital instability has weakened (Reinhold, 2010). Instead, the relation of cohabitation and marital stability is complicated and influenced by other relationship factors. For example, couples who enter cohabitation with marriage plans, such as while engaged, tend to experience marriages with levels of marital quality and distress similar to those of married respondents who had not cohabited, and their unions are more stable than those who enter cohabitation with no plans of marriage (Rhoades, Stanley, & Markman, 2009; Stanley, Rhoades, Amato, Markman, & Johnson, 2010). Relationship stability is influenced by many factors, not simply whether an unmarried couple lives together.

MARRIAGE

Young people in Western countries are remaining single and cohabiting for more of their adult lives and are marrying at later ages than ever before. Yet marriage remains an important marker of the attainment of adult status for many young people. About 90% of North Americans marry at least once in their lifetimes (U.S. Bureau of the Census, 2015b). The median age of marriage in the United States is 27 and 29, for women and men respectively, an increase of more than six years since 1975 (U.S. Bureau of the Census, 2015a); see Figure 14.3. Similar increases in the median age of marriage have occurred in Canada, with the average age at first marriage being 31 for males and 30 for females—up more than six years since 1975 (Milan, 2013)—and in some European

FIGURE 14.3: U.S. Median Age at First Marriage, 1890 to 2014

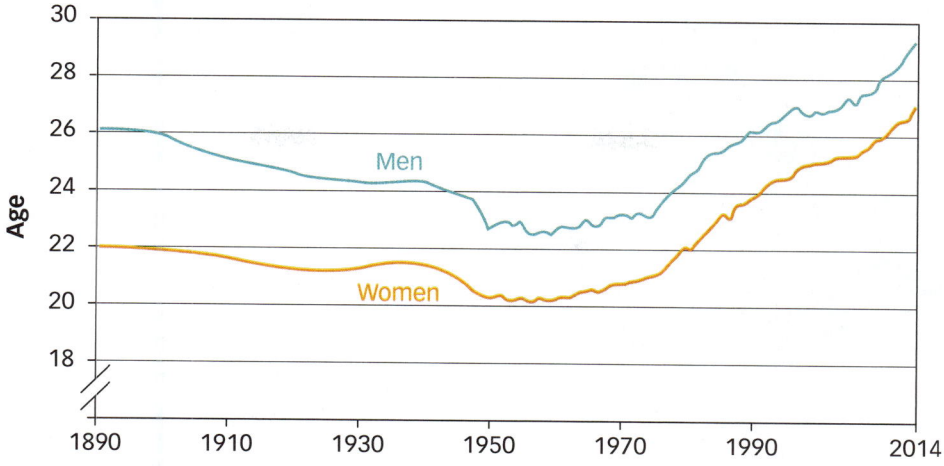

SOURCE: U.S. Bureau of the Census (2015a).

countries. In 2011 in Sweden, the median age was as high as 36 for men and 33 for women, up seven years since 1980 (United Nations Economic Commission for Europe, 2015).

Despite this trend, there remains variability in the age of first marriage. Low socioeconomic status young people tend to marry at younger ages than do those of higher socioeconomic status (Meier & Allen, 2008). In the United States, African Americans are the least likely to marry, and when they marry, they do so later and spend less time married than do European Americans (Dixon, 2009). Factors that contribute to marriage rates of African American adults include the availability of more females than males, greater employment instability among African American males, and higher rates of cohabitation as compared with other ethnic groups (Dixon, 2009).

Generally speaking, there are economic, physical, and psychological benefits to marriage. Married people around the world are happier, physically healthier, less distressed, and wealthier than nonmarried people (Koball, Moiduddin, Henderson, Goesling, & Besculides, 2010; Vanassche, Swicegood, & Matthijs, 2012). Longitudinal research over an eight-year period with a sample of nearly 2,600 African American young adults showed that rates of risky health behavior such as alcohol and drug use declined with marriage (Ali & Ajilore, 2011). Individuals who are depressed prior to marriage tend to show larger psychological gains after marriage than do those who are not depressed (Frech & Williams, 2007). The quality of the marital relationship predicts mental health and well-being in both men and women (Kurdek, 2005; Robles, 2014). Egalitarian relationships in which home and family duties are shared are associated with marital harmony and increased satisfaction in men and women (Xu & Shu-Chuan Lai, 2004). Women tend to feel most satisfied when they perceive the marital relationship as one of equal power and shared responsibility than when they feel that they alone are responsible for their spouse,

children, career, and housework (Ogolsky, Dennison, & Monk, 2014; Saginak & Saginak, 2005). This is particularly true in Western nations where egalitarian marriage roles are increasingly expected (Greenstein, 2009). Marital satisfaction is an important predictor of life satisfaction and well-being (Fincham & Beach, 2010).

Transition to Marriage

Newlyweds experience multiple changes during their first years of marriage, and these changes can be stressful. Couples must coordinate and make decisions about living arrangements, housework, eating habits, spending habits, sleeping habits, and sexual activity (Wallerstein, 1994). Newly married couples must define their relationship, including balancing autonomy and independence and negotiating conflict. Newlyweds' changing relationship influences their interactions with parents, family, and friends. They must maintain relationships with their families of origin as well as establish family traditions such as what holidays to celebrate and where to spend holidays.

Over the first year of marriage, most couples report a drop in satisfaction (Kilpatrick, Bissonnette, & Rusbult, 2002; Kurdek, 2005). This decline is influenced by a reduction in shared leisure time, including time spent talking to one another and doing things that bring each other pleasure—even seemingly minor things such as making each other laugh. Marriage also means that more time is spent on household tasks, further decreasing shared fun times. Many newlyweds struggle with rising debt, which is associated with higher levels of conflict and lower marital satisfaction (Dew, 2008). During times of conflict, newlyweds become less in tune with each others' thoughts and feelings and are less able to accurately interpret them (Kilpatrick et al., 2002). However, couples whose relationships endure the challenging first years of marriage report that they love each other more than ever before (Sprecher & Metts, 1999).

The transition to marriage poses many challenges as newlyweds must negotiate household tasks, financial obligations, and new roles.

The transition to marriage and the creation of a stable and fulfilling marital relationship entails transforming the romantic relationship from purely passionate to companionate. The growth and expression of commitment is essential to the survival of the relationship. Couples' expressions of warmth, empathy, acceptance, and respect predict long-lasting, high-quality, and satisfying relationships (Gadassi et al., 2015; Mattson, Frame, & Johnson, 2011; Phillips, Bischoff, Abbott, & Xia, 2009).

Couples who are successful at managing the transition to married life are able to address differences and resolve conflicts constructively by expressing feelings calmly, listening, clarifying the other's expressed wishes and needs, avoiding defensiveness and criticism, accepting responsibility, and compromising (Hanzal & Segrin, 2009; Johnson, Cohan, & Davila, 2005). Newlyweds with good initial relationship resources, such as supportive interactions with spouses, are better able to manage stressors and report greater marital adjustment over time (Neff & Broady, 2011). Overall, success in navigating the waters from newlywed to longtime married couple is a function of how the couple communicates and deals with conflict.

Marital Success

What predicts marital success? One strong predictor is chronological age. Generally speaking, the younger the bride and groom, the less likely they are to have a lifelong marriage (Amato & Irving, 2006; Cherlin, 2010). Psychosocial maturity also predicts marital success. Recall that Erikson proposed that a secure sense of identity is needed before intimate relationships can be forged. Emerging adults who have not attained identity achievement are more likely to refer to passion in defining love over intimacy and commitment (Aron & Westbay, 1996). It is the trust and loyalty that accompany intimacy and commitment, however, that predict marital satisfaction.

Marital success is also predicted by the degree of similarity between both members of the couple. Similarity in socioeconomic status, education, religion, and age all contribute to predicting a happy marriage (Gonzaga, Campos, & Bradbury, 2007). Most couples who marry are similar in demographics such as religion; however, heteronymous couples are increasingly common. About 15% of all new marriages in the United States in 2010 were between spouses of a different race or ethnicity from one another, more than double the share in 1980 (6.7%; Wang, 2012). Young adults tend to view successful relationships as those in which they have a partner who agrees with them on most issues (Wright, Simmons, & Campbell, 2007). They also report happier marriages when their spouse matches them in terms of behavioral choices such as substance use (Leonard & Homish, 2008).

Men generally report being happier with their marriages than women, though the difference is small (Jackson, Miller, Oka, & Henry, 2014). Women's marital satisfaction tends to vary with their marital roles (Rhoades et al., 2007). Traditional marriages entail a clear division of roles wherein the woman is responsible for nurturing and caring for the family and creating a comfortable home, and the man, as head, is responsible for the economic stability of the home. Frequently, women who have focused exclusively on parenting return to the workforce as their children grow older. Alternatively, many women continue to work while their children are young while also retaining primary responsibility for maintaining the home. Such women are said to work a "second shift" because after returning home from work they transition to their second job: homemaker.

Egalitarian marriages are those in which the man and woman share rights and responsibility. Both devote time and energy to their career, child-rearing, homemaking, and their relationship. Most professional women and college student women who plan for careers, especially in male-dominated fields, expect an egalitarian marriage and often plan for how they and their partners will integrate work and family roles (Deutsch, Kokot, & Binder, 2007; Peake & Harris, 2002). In dual-earner marriages, most men take on many more child care tasks than in prior generations but still spend less time on housework. Dual-earner couples who view themselves as equal contributors to household duties tend to divide work most equitably and report highest levels of satisfaction (Helms, Walls, Crouter, & McHale, 2010). Although many couples strive for it, true equality in marriage is rare. In determining marital satisfaction, it seems that what matters more than actual equity (how household responsibilities are distributed between partners) is the perception of equity (whether partners feel that responsibilities are distributed fairly); this holds true for both members of the couple but especially for women (Amato & Irving, 2006; Greenstein, 2009). If the division of household responsibilities feels equal, then the couple is likely to report marital satisfaction.

Successful marriages are based on realistic expectations. Happily married couples acknowledge that there are good times and bad. Most admit that there have been moments

ETHICAL AND POLICY APPLICATIONS OF LIFESPAN DEVELOPMENT

Same-Sex Marriage and the Law

Same-sex couples share many similarities with heterosexual couples, including longevity and parenting competence (Biblarz & Savci, 2010). However, until the July 2015 Supreme Court decision in *Obergefell v. Hodges*, in many states they were unable to legally marry. Marriage confers health and psychosocial benefits to all couples: same or opposite-sex. Prior to *Obergefell*, same-sex marriage was legal in 36 states and the District of Columbia, but not all states recognized same-sex unions from other states (Pew Research Center, 2015b). *Obergefell v. Hodges* combined four cases challenging states' rights to refuse to recognize or license same-sex marriages, denying couples seek legal rights and protections that come with marriage, such as the right to jointly adopt children.

The interdisciplinary nature of applied developmental science is illustrated by an amicus curiae brief for *Obergefell v. Hodges*, submitted to inform the Supreme Court justices (see http://www.apa.org/about/offices/ogc/amicus/obergefell.pdf). The brief was jointly authored and submitted by more than a dozen professional organizations in psychology, social work, and medicine, including the American Psychological Association (APA), American Medical Association, American Academy of Pediatrics (AAP), National Association of Social Workers, and Association for Marriage and Family Therapy. The amicus brief referred to scientific findings that same-sex relationships are equivalent to heterosexual relationships in essential respects and that there is no scientific basis for concluding that same-sex couples are not fit parents or

that children of same-sex couples are any less psychologically healthy and well-adjusted than children of heterosexual couples. The brief therefore argued that excluding same-sex couples from the institution of marriage denies them social, psychological, and health benefits and is stigmatizing.

With the *Obergefell* ruling, the United States joins the more than a dozen countries with national laws allowing gays and lesbians to marry, including Canada, Finland, Spain, the Netherlands, Argentina, and New Zealand (Pew Research Center, 2015a). In a 2015 survey, nearly two thirds (57%) of Americans said they supported same-sex marriage, compared with 39% who opposed it (Pew Research Center, 2015c). As shown in Figure 14.4, there are large cohort differences such that younger generations express higher levels of support for same-sex marriage, but in recent decades, older generations also have become more supportive of it.

What Do You Think?

1. **What role should developmental scientists take in advising courts and policy makers? Do you think they should participate in writing amicus curiae briefs? Why or why not?**

2. **What might be some of the reasons we see cohort differences in attitudes toward same-sex marriage? Identify contextual factors that might contribute to some of the generational differences we see.**

FIGURE 14.4: Support of Same-Sex Marriage in the United States, by Generation, 2001–2015

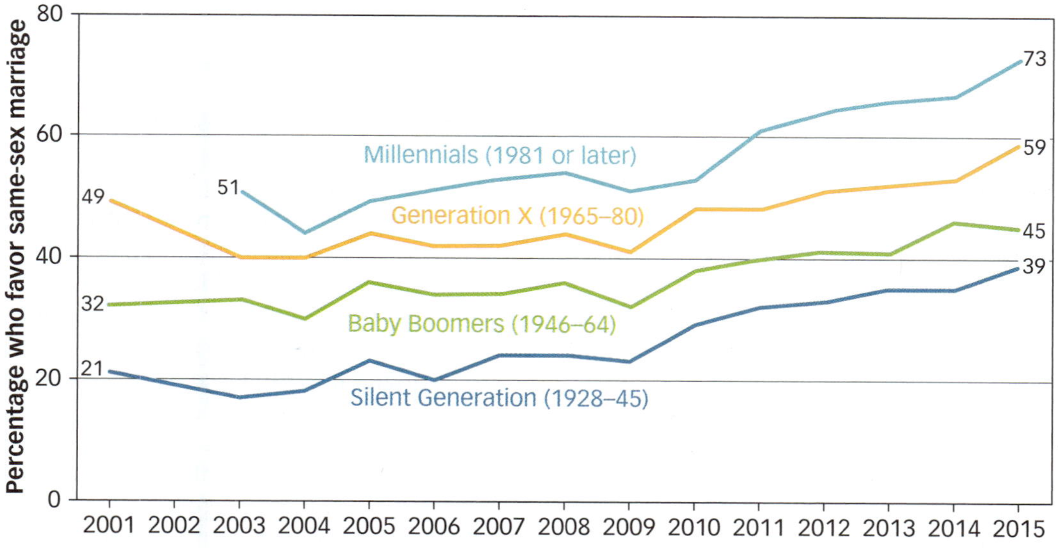

SOURCE: Pew Research Center (2015c).

when they considered calling it quits or wondered if they had made a mistake (Wallerstein, 1994). A successful marriage is an exercise in flexibility, communication, and joint conflict resolution. It takes work. Happily married couples adapt to each other's changing needs and desires as well as the changing circumstances.

The June 2015 Supreme Court ruling mandated the recognition of same-sex marriage nationwide.

Same-Sex Marriage

Like other young people, gay and lesbian adults seek love, partnership, and close intimate relationships. Intimate relationships and marriage appear to have similar meanings for gay and lesbian couples as compared with heterosexual couples (Cherlin, 2013). Until same-sex marriage began to be legal in various jurisdictions, it was very difficult to study same-sex unions. At the time of the recent Supreme Court decision mandating the recognition of same-sex marriage nationwide (*Obergefell v. Hodges*, 2015; see Ethical and Policy Applications of Lifespan Development, p. 403), over two thirds of states already permitted gay and lesbian couples to marry. Therefore, the literature comparing sexual minority and majority couples to date is sparse but growing.

Studies that have compared gay, lesbian, and heterosexual couples have found no significant differences in love, satisfaction, or the partners' evaluations of the strengths and weaknesses of their relationships (Lavner, Waterman, & Peplau, 2014; Peplau, 1991; Savin-Williams, 2000). Problems such as intimate partner violence, for example, exist in both types of relationships (Edwards, Sylaska, & Neal, 2015). Moreover, the breakup rate for same-sex couples is comparable to that for heterosexual couples; same-sex couples that have a marriage-like commitment had stable unions (Rosenfeld, 2014). The available research suggests that gay and lesbian persons experience the same psychological benefits from same-sex legal marriage and other types of legally recognized same-sex relationships such as civil unions and registered domestic partnerships (Riggle, Rostosky, & Horne, 2010; Wight, LeBlanc, de Vries, & Detels, 2012). For example, a study of over 36,000 people in the California Health Interview Survey found that same-sex married lesbian, gay, and bisexual persons in a legal relationship were significantly less distressed than lesbian, gay, and bisexual persons not in a same-sex legal relationship as well as nonmarried heterosexual persons, suggesting a mental health benefit to legal marriage (Wight, LeBlanc, & Lee Badgett, 2013).

The stressors that gay men and lesbian women face, such as the experience of stigma and prejudice, might play a role in how same-sex marriage manifests in health and psychological well-being (Hatzenbuehler, 2009). Legal recognition of same-sex relationships, legal marriage in particular, may have the potential to offset the mental health impact of these stressors at the individual level and might offset the larger macro-level effects of sanctioned discrimination (Wight et al., 2013). This is supported by research suggesting that same-sex couples living in states with legally sanctioned marriage report higher levels of self-assessed health than those living in states than bar same-sex marriage (Kail, Acosta, & Wright, 2015). Laws may represent an important contextual influence on well-being. For example, a 2009 study found that gay men and lesbian women residing in states that did *not* specifically protect sexual minorities from hate crimes or employment discrimination tended to show higher rates of mental health problems (Hatzenbuehler, Keyes, & Hasin, 2009).

As parents, gay and lesbian couples tend to coparent more equally and compatibly than heterosexual partners; however, their relationship dynamics often shift in similar ways as heterosexual parents (Biblarz & Savci, 2010). For example, lesbian couples with children tend to move from shared employment, decision making, and household work in exchange for differentiation between partners in child care and paid employment, similar to heterosexual couples (Goldberg & Perry-Jenkins, 2007; Kurdek, 2007). Less is known about gay men, but they seem to not show a domestic hierarchy that values paid work over homemaking. Instead, paid work may be seen as a compromise that takes the working partner away from spending time with their children (Kurdek, 2007).

DIVORCE

In the decades since the 1960s, divorce rates have increased substantially in many Western industrialized countries but have since stabilized and even declined (United Nations Statistics Division, 2014). In the United States, the divorce rate increased during the 1970s, peaking at 5.2 divorces per 1,000 people in 1980, and has declined since to 3.4 divorces per 1,000 people in 2012 (National Center for Health Statistics, 2015). Despite these global changes in divorce rates, there remain large international differences, as shown in Table 14.4 with the highest divorce rate in the Russian Federation and lowest in Ireland, suggesting that social contextual factors that are unique to each culture are partially responsible for international variation in divorce rates. Despite the overall decline in divorces, the United States has one of the highest divorce rates in the world.

One explanation for the rise in divorce rates is that young people's expectations for marriage have changed. Recent generations of young people tend to expect more from marriage and their spouse than did prior generations (Amato & Irving, 2006). Fifty years ago, most marriages entailed a traditional division of roles. Women raised children, cared for husbands, and tended to the home while

TABLE 14.4 Divorce Rate in Select Countries, 2012

COUNTRY	DIVORCES PER 1,000 PERSONS
Russian Federation	4.5
Denmark	2.8
United States	2.8
Australia	2.2
Germany	2.2
United Kingdom	2.1
Iran	2.0
France	2.0
China	1.8
Japan	1.8
Greece	1.2
Italy	.9
Ireland	.6

SOURCE: United Nations Statistics Division (2014).

men provided economic stability. Today's marriages often are more egalitarian, partners share roles and responsibilities, but roles are often less clearly defined than in prior generations. Both husbands and wives hold earning and caregiving responsibilities and spouses turn to each other for friendship, love, companionship, and support. Young adults may hold unrealistic expectations for their partner and their relationship, perhaps influenced by the "perfect" fictional marriages depicted on many television programs (Segrin & Nabi, 2002). Many emphasize personal fulfillment as a role for marriage, but young adults who emphasize the personal fulfillment functions of marriage are at higher risk of divorce (Campbell, Wright, & Flores, 2012). Many young adults agree with the statement that a successful marriage is one in which they and their partners agree on most issues (Wright et al., 2007). At the same time, as young adults expect more from their marriages, they spend less time with their spouses than did prior generations of young adults, and divorce itself has become more socially acceptable than in prior generations (Cherlin, 2009).

While changing expectations and increasing social acceptance influence divorce rates, the rising median age of marriage and increase in cohabitation have stabilized divorce rates over the last 25 years. Among young adults born after 1980, divorce rates have declined, perhaps due to increased selectivity (Kennedy & Ruggles, 2014). Rising rates of cohabitation among young adults mean that many domestic partnerships break up before marriage, also curtailing divorce rates (Bumpass, 2004; Heaton, 2002).

Predicting Divorce

Couples who share similarities in demographics (e.g., age, ethnicity, religion); interests (e.g., leisure activities); and personality, attitudes, and values are more likely to have successful marriages (Gonzaga et al., 2007; Hohmann-Marriott, 2006). As we have discussed, the older the bride and groom, the more likely their marriage will succeed (Lehrer, 2008). Poor education, economic disadvantage, and **role overload** as well as not attending religious services and experiencing multiple life stressors increases the risk of divorce (Brock & Lawrence, 2008; Härkönen, 2014). Parental divorce increases the risk of divorce for the two subsequent generations (Hetherington & Elmore, 2004; Storksen, Røysamb, Gjessing, Moum, & Tambs, 2007). Longitudinal research suggests that parental divorce influences children's adjustment problems and perspective of marriage as a lifelong commitment (Cunningham & Thornton, 2007). When adult children of divorced families marry, they may have poor coping and conflict resolution skills, experience more conflict in their relationships, and be less able or willing to resolve differences. More recent research suggests that the number and quality of family transitions predicts attitudes toward marriage, relationship skills, and divorce (Amato, 2010).

According to research on causes of divorce, the best predictor is the couple's communication and problem-solving style (Amato, 2010; Gottman & Driver, 2005). Troubled couples often are unable to effectively resolve differences. When one member of the couple raises a concern, the other retreats, reacting with anger, resentment, and defensiveness. Disagreements regarding financial issues are particularly strong predictors of divorce (Dew, Britt, & Huston, 2012). Negative interaction patterns and difficulty regulating discussions predict later divorce even in newlyweds reporting high marital satisfaction (Lavner & Bradbury, 2012). Negative interaction patterns in couples who later divorce are often evident even before they get married (Clements, Stanley, & Markman, 2004). The immediate precipitators of divorce are often infidelity, followed by incompatibility, alcohol abuse or drug use, and simply growing apart (Amato & Previti, 2003). Adults are more likely to blame their ex-spouses than themselves for the problems that led to the divorce. Women are more likely than men to initiate divorce, yet women tend to experience more negative consequences from divorce, as discussed in the next section.

Consequences of Divorce

The process of divorce entails a series of stressful experiences, such as conflict; physical separation; moving; distributing property; and, for some, child custody negotiations. Women are twice as likely as men to initiate the divorce, but regardless of who initiates the divorce, all family members feel stress and a confusing array of emotions, such as anger, despair, embarrassment, shame, failure, and relief (Clarke-Stewart & Brentano, 2006; Härkönen, 2014). Most couples find that the divorce is worse than expected, negatively affecting their health, financial stability, social support, happiness, and self-esteem (Andreβ & Bröckel, 2007; Forste & Heaton, 2004; Varner & Mandara, 2009). Even the partner who initiates the divorce finds the separation worse than anticipated, largely because unhappy spouses focus on the needs that are not being met in their relationship and are unaware of the needs that are fulfilled. The longer the couple is together, the more difficult the breakup because of shared property, friends, children, and intimacy. Women are more likely than men to experience loss of income and financial instability, and these problems are associated with higher rates of depression (Varner & Mandara, 2009).

People undergoing divorce often find that their social network shrinks at the same time that their needs for social support increase (Kalmijn & van Groenou, 2005). Each member of the couple loses supportive in-laws, and in-law relationships may become strained and combative. Friends and neighbors often feel that they are expected to "take sides" and consequently may avoid both members of the divorcing couple. Relocation may cause a spouse to lose contact with friends and neighbors. Recently divorced adults are prone to depression; loneliness; anxiety; an increase in risky behaviors such as drug and alcohol use; promiscuous sexual activity; and poor eating, sleeping, and working habits (Clarke-Stewart & Brentano, 2006; Kalmijn & Monden, 2006). In general, divorced people tend to be less happy than married, never-married, and widowed people (Forste & Heaton, 2004). However, for some spouses the divorce may come as a relief; many are able to adjust to a "new normal" of living without a partner. Most find that their happiness and life satisfaction improve when they find a new romantic partner and establish a relationship (Wang & Amato, 2000). Table 14.5 summarizes correlates and influences on marriage and divorce.

Thinking in Context 14.3

1. What individual, familial, neighborhood, and societal factors have influenced the rise in singlehood and cohabitation? How might extended singlehood and cohabitation influence young people's attainment of developmental tasks such as intimacy?

2. Provide advice to newlyweds. Given what is known about love, marriage, and divorce, what can they do to ensure a happy marriage and reduce the likelihood of divorce? Alternatively, what can someone who is facing divorce do to aid his or her transition?

PARENTHOOD IN EARLY ADULTHOOD

Until recently, having children was, for biological and cultural reasons, an inevitable part of adult life and not a decision. Effective methods of birth control and changing cultural views on parenthood and childlessness have made having

TABLE 14.5 Correlates and Influences on Marriage and Divorce

CORRELATES OF MARRIAGE
• Good physical health • Good mental health • Positive sense of well-being

INGREDIENTS IN MARITAL SUCCESS
• Intimacy and commitment, expressed as warmth, attentiveness, empathy, acceptance, and respect • Good communication skills including the ability to express concerns calmly and clarify the other's expressed wishes and needs • Good conflict management skills including the ability to avoid defensiveness and criticism, accept responsibility, and compromise • Effective conflict management and resolution • Degree of similarity in socioeconomic status, education, religion, and age • Perception of equity among partners

RISK FACTORS FOR DIVORCE
• Young age • Multiple life stressors • Dissimilarities in age, ethnicity, religion, attitudes, and values • Poor education • Economic disadvantage • Poor coping, communication, and conflict resolution skills

CORRELATES OF DIVORCE
• Loss of income and financial instability • Risky behaviors such as drug and alcohol use and promiscuous sexual activity • Poor self-care, including poor eating, sleeping, and working habits • Negative emotions, such as anger, despair, and shame • Poor physical and mental health • Reduced social network and support • Reduced life satisfaction

children a choice (Mills, Rindfuss, McDonald, & te Velde, 2011). Childbearing rates have declined in most industrialized nations. For example, in the 1950s the average number of children born to a woman in the United States was 3.8; today it is 2.1 (Central Intelligence Agency, 2013). The average number of children is even lower for many industrialized nations including Australia (1.8), Germany (1.4), and Japan (1.4), as compared with developing nations such as Niger (7.0), Somalia, (6.2), and Afghanistan (5.5; Central Intelligence Agency, 2013). Although families are growing smaller, the majority of married adults still become parents. As shown in Figure 14.5, the average age at which women give birth has increased over the past three decades. Emerging adults in North America tend to view delayed parenthood as normative (Koropeckyj-Cox, Romano, & Moras, 2007). Increases in the availability of effective contraception, increases in women's

FIGURE 14.5: Maternal Age at First Birth in the United States, 1970–2013

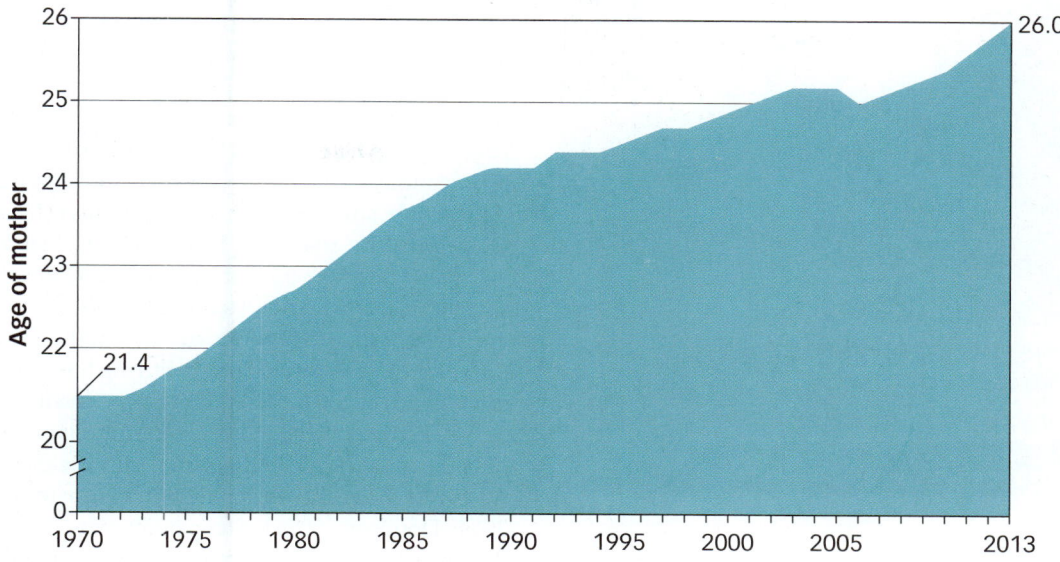

SOURCES: Matthews and Hamilton (2009); U.S. Department of Health and Human Services (2013).

education and labor market participation, and societal value changes contribute to the postponement of parenthood (Mills et al., 2011). However, as discussed in Chapter 13, women who postpone childbearing to the early 30s are at higher risk for experiencing fertility difficulties (Schmidt, Sobotka, Bentzen, & Nyboe Andersen, 2012).

BECOMING A PARENT

The decision of whether to have a child is influenced by personal and circumstantial factors, such as values, health, and financial status. Although women's employment itself does not predict parenthood, women in high-status and demanding occupations are more likely to delay or decide against childbearing than are women in less demanding occupations (Nilsen et al., 2012). North American young adults cite a variety of reasons to have children, including experiencing the parent–child bond; growth, learning, and fun experiences that come with raising a child; and the desire to help someone grow into a productive adult (O'Laughlin & Anderson, 2001). Common disadvantages of parenthood include the loss of freedom and high cost of raising a child. It is estimated that a new parent will spend about $245,340 over the course of raising a child from birth to age 18 (U.S. Department of Agriculture, 2014).

Regardless of when parenthood happens, the transition is challenging. New parents experience the exciting yet overwhelming task of getting to know their infant while meeting his or her needs for constant attention, affection, and care. New parents are greeted with a host of new responsibilities and changes: caregiving responsibilities, added housework, financial demands, loss of sleep, and less leisure time, which are associated with a reduced sense of well-being (Claxton & Perry-Jenkins, 2008; Nelson, Kushlev, & Lyubomirsky, 2014). Many new parents report not feeling prepared for the

roller coaster of emotions ranging from joy to frustration and reduced feelings of well-being that accompany parenthood (Galatzer-Levy, Mazursky, Mancini, & Bonanno, 2011; Stanca, 2012). Some research suggests that, even years after becoming parents, many people are unable to regain the reductions in happiness and life satisfaction that accompany having a child (Clark, Diener, Georgellis, & Lucas, 2008). Some theorize that parents' perceptions of the joys of parenthood may be a way of balancing the challenges, frustrations, and drops in happiness that accompany parenthood (Eibach & Mock, 2011). Regardless, parenthood is the norm rather than the exception, and new parents experience a wide range of emotions that accompany their new baby and set of responsibilities.

The transition to parenthood places stress on even the best of marriages. Parenthood is associated with sudden declines in marital satisfaction for both parents as conflict tends to rise in response to increased financial, household, and parental demands and decreased leisure time (Don & Mickelson, 2014; Trillingsgaard, Baucom, & Heyman, 2014). Mothers tend to report more stress and a higher workload with the advent of parenthood than do fathers (Krieg, 2007; Widarsson et al., 2013). In addition, most women experience a decline in physical activity and its accompanying health effects with motherhood (McIntyre & Rhodes, 2007; Perales, del Pozo-Cruz, & del Pozo-Cruz, 2015). Among dual-earner and single-parent families, finding quality child care is a major challenge, as is determining how to care for infants and children when they are sick and cannot attend child care, whether it is taking time off from work or making other arrangements. Women who work full-time often experience role burden, which is associated with poor health (Hewitt, Baxter, & Western, 2006). Lacking a sense of personal control over multiple roles associated with higher levels of distress among new parents (Keeton, Perry-Jenkins, & Sayer, 2008).

PLANNING FOR PARENTHOOD AND WORK-LIFE BALANCE

In this clip, young adults discuss their preferences regarding having children and expectations for work-life balance.

Watch the video at edge.sagepub.com/kuther

During the transition to parenthood, most American and European couples, even those in more egalitarian marriages, shift toward traditional marital roles and division of labor (Dribe & Stanfors, 2009; Katz-Wise, Priess, & Hyde, 2010; Koivunen, Rothaupt, & Wolfgram, 2009). Both parents tend to become more traditional in gender role attitudes and behaviors, but women tend to show a greater change than men (Katz-Wise et al., 2010). In dual-earner couples, the greater the degree of shared parenting responsibilities, the greater the happiness of the couple, and especially of the mother (Chong & Mickelson, 2013; Feeney, Hohaus, & Noller, 2001). Conversely, marital satisfaction drops, especially for women, if there are large disparities in caregiving responsibilities—for example, if the woman is responsible for the majority of the caregiving—and if expectations regarding shared responsibilities are violated (Biehle & Mickelson, 2012). Mothers' satisfaction with the division of child-rearing responsibilities predicts their ratings of relationship quality (Adamsons, 2013). Planning ahead for the changes that accompany a newborn as well as prepregnancy satisfaction serve protective roles for the spousal relationship (Lawrence, Rothman, Cobb, & Bradbury, 2010).

Clearly, parenting is no easy task, but most parents report that it has promoted their own development by encouraging them to become more empathetic, tolerant, and responsible (Nomaguchi & Milkie, 2003). Ultimately, the process of parenting influences parents' development, as each stage of a child's development offers tasks and challenges that shape the parents' competence and self-concept. As children enter school, parents interact with the many adults who are a part of their children's lives, such as teachers and other parents. Parents of adolescents are faced with balancing between providing teens with autonomy and setting boundaries and keeping them safe. The increase in parent–child bickering that is common during adolescence takes a toll on parents, who typically report temporary declines in marital and life satisfaction (Steinberg & Silk, 2002). Each phase of a child's life entails a different set of parenting tasks and skills, requiring flexibility on the part of adults.

STEPPARENTS

Even under ideal conditions, parenting is challenging. Stepparents face even more difficulties. Stepparents are often placed in the position of providing discipline without the warm attachment bond that characterizes most parent–child relationships. Stepmothers tend to face particularly high levels of conflict; more disliked by their stepchildren; and experience more stress, anxiety, and depression (Doodson, 2014; Gosselin, 2010; Shapiro & Stewart, 2011). Stepmothers may be expected to take on maternal roles and develop relationships quickly. However, stepparent–stepchild bonds take a great deal of time to develop, and stepmothers may feel guilty for not feeling maternal and preferring life without stepchildren (Church, 2004; Felker, Fromme, Arnaut, & Stoll, 2002).

Stepparents who do not have children of their own may hold unrealistic expectations for family life that sharply contrast with the reality they encounter (Amato & Sobolewski, 2004; Doodson, 2014). Stepparents who have children of their own have an easier time, perhaps because they are more experienced in forming warm attachments with children and tend to engage children in fun activities; this is particularly the case for stepfathers, as they experience less pressure to take on parenting roles than do stepmothers (Ganong, Coleman, Fine, & Martin, 1999; Hennon, Hildenbrand, & Schedle, 2008).

Stepparenting poses challenges for new marriages. Remarried parents tend to report high levels of tension and conflict about parenting as compared with first-married parents (Ganong & Coleman, 2000; Hetherington & Stanley-Hagan, 2002). How well adults adjust to the role of stepparent is influenced by the support of the biological parent as well as the children's perception of their relationship with the stepparent and willingness to accept the adult into the family (Jensen & Howard, 2015). Positive child communication and a high-quality marriage, as well as social support, predicts positive coping on the part of stepmothers (Whiting, Smith, Barnett, & Grafsky, 2007). Stepmothers who perceive a lack of control over parenting practices during visitations are more likely to feel powerlessness, anger, and resentment, which may be manifested in depression (Gosselin, 2010; Henry & McCue, 2009). After a challenging transition, many couples adjust to their roles as spouses and parents, and interactions with stepchildren improve (Jensen & Howard, 2015). The difficulties that stepparenting entails is one reason that the divorce rate is higher in couples with stepchildren (Teachman, 2008).

NEVER-MARRIED SINGLE PARENT

Four in 10 infants in the United States are born to never-married mothers each year, and many of these mothers remain single after giving birth (Martin, Hamilton, Osterman, Curtin, & Mathews, 2015). In 2011, about 41% of single mothers had never been married, up from 4% in 1960 (Caumont, 2013). In recent years, more single professional women in their 30s have become single parents by choice. However, these women are dissimilar to the typical never-married single parent, and we know little about the development of children born to single women with high-powered careers. Instead, similar to Britain, where the typical never-married parent is likely to be a woman of working-class status, the typical never-married parent in the United States is also of low or middle socioeconomic status, most commonly an African American young woman (Rowlingson & McKay, 2005). African American women are disproportionately likely to be never-married parents, comprising 40% of never-married mothers (as compared with 32% white non-Hispanic and 24% Hispanic; Caumont, 2013). African American women are more likely to postpone marriage after childbirth than are women of other ethnic groups. Higher rates of job loss, mortality, and persistent unemployment among many African American men influence African American young women's decisions. About one third of never-married African American mothers marry within nine years after the birth of their first child, often to a man who is not the child's biological father, and the resulting family is much like any other first-marriage family (Wu, Bumpass, & Musick, 2001).

As a group, never-married mothers often show better mental health, such as lower rates of anxiety and depression, than do married mothers (Afifi, Cox, & Enns, 2006; Taylor & Conger, 2014). Yet other research suggests that they are less happy (Baranowska-Rataj, Matysiak, & Mynarska, 2013). The experiences of never-married single mothers vary with other contextual influences such as social support. African American and Latino parents are more likely to report receiving family support, which influence maternal and child outcomes (Taylor & Conger, 2014). The primary challenge never-married mothers face is economic as they are more likely to live in poverty in the United States and European Union (Chzhen & Bradshaw, 2012; McKeever & Wolfinger, 2011). They are less likely to receive child support than divorced mothers, and about one half have at least one additional child (Wu et al., 2001). A large study of

unmarried mothers suggested that nonmarital childbearing is adversely associated with the ability to marry an economically attractive mate and maintain a long term marital union (Graefe & Lichter, 2007). As we have discussed, poverty and low socioeconomic status hold vast implications for children's development.

SAME-SEX PARENTS

Most gay and lesbian young adults in the United States plan to raise children one day (D'augelli, Rendina, Sinclair, & Grossman, 2006). It is estimated that 35% of female spousal couples and 28% of male spousal couples are raising biological, step or adopted children. For unmarried partners, the estimates are 21% and 5%, respectively (Gates, 2013). About 23% of lesbian women are parents, compared to about 68% of heterosexual women (Brewster, Tillman, & Jokinen-Gordon, 2013). Lesbian women become parents through a more diverse set of pathways than heterosexual women, including adoption and parenting a spouse or partner's child. The majority of children in same-sex parented homes are conceived through previous heterosexual marriages, but an increasing number of gay men and lesbian women become parents through adoption and reproductive technologies (Henehan, Rothblum, Solomon, & Balsam, 2007).

In the past, many state laws assumed that gay men and lesbian women were unable to be competent parents, and they often lost custody battles. Today, most U.S. states, as well as Canada, hold that sexual orientation is not related to parenting competence and, therefore, do not consider parents' sexual orientation in considering custody arrangements (Raley, Fisher, Halder, & Shanmugan, 2010; Tye, 2003). Despite this, many courts remain biased against same-sex parents in custody and adoption cases, and several states prohibit adoptions by same-sex individuals and couples (Raley et al., 2013). At least nine European countries currently permit gay and lesbian couples to adopt children: Belgium, Denmark, Germany, Iceland, Norway, the Netherlands, Spain, Sweden, and the United Kingdom. In January 2008, the European Court of Human Rights ruled that gay men and lesbian women have the right to adopt a child, suggesting that the ability of same-sex couples to adopt children will spread to include more European countries (Crumley, 2008). Research in the United States suggests that same-sex and heterosexual parents do not differ in the stresses and adaptation to adoption (Lavner et al., 2014)

As discussed in Chapter 9, children reared by lesbian and gay parents do not differ from those reared by heterosexual parents in social development, psychological adjustment, and gender orientation (Fedewa, Black, & Ahn, 2014). They also do not differ from heterosexually parented children in sexual orientation—that is, most are heterosexual (Tasker & Patterson, 2007). Same-sex parents do not differ from heterosexual parents in competence or commitment to their roles as parents (Perrin & Siegel, 2013). Instead, some research suggests that lesbian parents are more aware

Never-married mothers often experience better mental health than married mothers. However, outcomes vary with contextual factors such as social support and socioeconomic status.

of the skills necessary for effective parenting and engaging in high quality of parent–child interactions than are heterosexual parents (Bos, van Balen, & van den Boom, 2007; Vanfraussen, Ponjaert-Kristoffersen, & Brewaeys, 2003). Nonbiological social mothers establish their identities as parents through their interactions with their babies and the resulting relationship (Dahl & Malterud, 2015). Children tend to show equal preference for biological and social mothers (Goldberg, Downing, & Sauck, 2008).

The parenting role that same-sex partners take varies with the way in which the family formed. Generally speaking, the biological parent tends to assume most of the parenting responsibility when the children are the result of a previous heterosexual relationship. However, when children are a joint choice and the result of adoption or reproductive technology, partners tend to report an egalitarian split of household and child-rearing duties, as compared with the more traditional split among heterosexual parents whereby the woman is responsible for a greater proportion of household and child-rearing duties (Tasker & Patterson, 2007; Vanfraussen et al., 2003). Among lesbian parents, the child and nonbiological mother's relationship tends to be characterized by similar levels of acceptance, openness, and authority as that with the biological mother, and the two parents tend to be equally involved in the process of child-rearing (Bos et al., 2007; Goldberg & Perry-Jenkins, 2007; Vanfraussen et al., 2003).

CHILDLESSNESS

Although most adults have children, some remain childless. In 2014, 48% of women aged 15 to 44 were childless; specifically, 50% of 25- to 29-year-olds, 29% of 30- to 34-year-olds, 19% of 35- to 39-year-olds, and 15% to 17% of 40- to 50-year old women were childless (U.S. Bureau of the Census, 2015c). It is difficult to determine the rate of childlessness in men.

People remain childless for many reasons. Some are involuntarily childless after unsuccessful fertility treatments or because they have never found a suitable partner. Other adults are voluntarily childless—that is, they have chosen to not have children. Common reasons for voluntary childlessness include the desirability for flexibility and freedom from child care responsibility, pursuit of career aspirations, economic security, environmental reasons (such as not wanting to contribute to global overpopulation), and desires to preserve marital satisfaction. It is unclear how many women are childless by circumstance or by choice. One study of Italian women found that one third of those who were childless were so by choice (Koropeckyj-Cox & Pendell, 2007). Others were childless as a result of decisions to delay childbearing or the result of adverse external circumstances such as relationship dissolution. A large sample of women in the United Kingdom found that only about half of those who postponed childbearing into their 30s and who still intended to start a family managed to do so in the subsequent six years (Berrington, 2004). Some young adults decide that they do not want children, and later, often after marriage, change their minds and choose to become parents. Other adults decide against children after being married and establishing a lifestyle that suits them.

Consistent predictors of childlessness include education and career status. Adults who choose to remain childless tend to be highly educated professionals who are devoted to their careers (Kemkes-Grottenthaler, 2003). Higher levels of education predict childlessness in women from Australia, Finland, Germany, the Netherlands, the United Kingdom, and the United States (Koropeckyj-Cox & Call, 2007; Waren & Pals, 2013) Women who are voluntarily childless tend to be more assertive and self-reliant and less religious than their peers, which likely influences their adjustment throughout life (Morell, 2000; Tanturri & Mencarini, 2008).

Overall, adults who are childless by choice tend to be just as content with their lives as those who are parents. Most adults in the United States report the belief that childless adults can lead fulfilling lives. Emerging adults have few negative biases about childlessness (Koropeckyj-Cox & Pendell, 2007). Positive attitudes toward childlessness are more common among adults who are college educated, childless, and female, while negative attitudes toward childlessness are more common among adults who are male, less educated, and have conservative religious beliefs (Koropeckyj-Cox & Pendell, 2007; Koropeckyj-Cox et al., 2007).

Childlessness, however, is frequently the result of postponing parenthood rather than choosing to be childless (te Velde, Habbema, Leridon, & Eijkemans, 2012). Involuntary childlessness is associated with life dissatisfaction varying from ambivalence to deep disappointment in both men and women (Hadley & Hanley, 2011; Nichols & Pace-Nichols, 2000; Peterson, Gold, & Feingold, 2007), especially when it is accompanied by self-blame, rumination, and catastrophizing (Kraaij, Garnefski, & Vlietstra, 2008). Childlessness appears to interfere with psychosocial development and personal adjustment only when it is involuntary and a result of circumstances beyond an individual's control (Roy, Schumm, & Britt, 2014). The social context also matters, as the extent to which childlessness is associated with lower psychological well-being appears to be dependent on the societal context—specifically, the degree to which a country and culture's norms are tolerant toward childlessness (Huijts, Kraaykamp, & Subramanian, 2011).

Thinking in Context 14.4

1. What personality, developmental, and life experience factors influence whether an adult will become a parent? How might contextual factors play a role in determining whether one becomes a parent and the timing of parenthood?

2. What special challenges do stepparents, single parents, and lesbian and gay parents face? In what ways are the challenges these parents face similar? Different?

CAREERS IN EARLY ADULTHOOD

Considering that most adults spend nearly one third of their waking hours at work, it is not surprising that the career setting is an important context for psychosocial development in early adulthood. Career development does not end with selecting a vocation. Young adults must obtain a job, learn about their role and tasks, develop proficiency, work well with others, respond to direction, and develop a good working relationship with supervisors. Work life influences young people's sense of competence, independence, and financial security and often is a source of new friendships (Brooks & Everett, 2008; Schooler, 2001).

TRANSITION TO WORK

Many young people find themselves employed in careers that are not their first choice, often explaining that they simply "fell into it," without exerting much effort or a choice (Arnett, 2004). For example, one study of 1,200 Australian young adults found that over the seven years after completing their schooling, only 20% were working in a field that represented their greatest interest (Athanasou, 2002). The day-to-day work entailed by a given occupation often differs from young people's expectations. Young people often are faced with more clerical and other paperwork, longer work hours, less supportive and instructive supervisors, and lower pay than expected (Hatcher & Crook, 1988). Managing expectations in light of reality often leads young adults to resign and seek alternative jobs and careers.

Young people's jobs frequently do not match their interests and education. These mismatches are common during the early years of employment as young adults are learning about their competencies and preferences and comparing them with the reality they encounter in the workplace (Wilk, Desmarais, & Sackett, 1995). It is not uncommon for an individual to undergo as many as six job changes by age 27 (U.S. Bureau of Labor Statistics, 2014). By another estimate, the average young adult holds four jobs between the ages of 18 and 21, three between 22 to 25, three between 26 and 30, and two between ages 31 and 35 (U.S. Bureau of Labor Statistics, 2015b). In 2012, the median length of job tenure—that is, time spent in a particular position—for 25- to 34-year-olds was just over three years (Guo, 2014).

Mentoring relationships aid the transition to employment. Young people who report a mentoring relationship with someone in their chosen career have more opportunities for full-time employment, receive more advice, and become more attached to the labor force than do young people without mentors (McDonald, Erickson, Johnson, & Elder, 2007).

Career development follows a myriad of paths. Men most often are employed continuously after completing their formal education and until retirement. Women display more varied and discontinuous career trajectories, often interrupting or deferring their career in favor of child-rearing and family caretaking (Hite & McDonald, 2003); this pattern may be a reflection of maternity and family leave policies, as discussed in Ethical and Policy Applications of Lifespan Development (p. 412).

People's career goals tend to shift as they grow older and more experienced. Goal engagement is associated with increases in well-being and lower rates of depression in employed young adults but negative outcomes in young adults with unfavorable career opportunities (Haase, Heckhausen, & Silbereisen, 2012). The 20s often are a period of transitioning and settling into a career. People in their 30s often seek occupational challenge and autonomy (Raabe & Beehr, 2003). Many adults, even those established in careers, reconsider their choices throughout adulthood (Bobek & Robbins, 2005).

DIVERSITY IN THE WORKPLACE

In recent decades, the workplace has become more diverse as women and ethnic minorities have penetrated nearly all careers. Throughout Europe and North America, about half of the labor force is female (International Labour Office, 2008; U.S. Department of Labor, 2007). Fifty-nine percent of women in the United States work (U.S. Department of Labor, 2007). Ethnic diversity is also increasing in every occupation and every nation. Despite this, women and ethnic minorities are faced with many obstacles to their career success, most notably the so-called *glass ceiling*. The glass ceiling refers to the invisible barrier that prevents women and ethnic minorities from advancing to the highest levels of the career ladder. Women and ethnic minorities tend to fill lower-level positions and their numbers decline with each rung on the career ladder. For example, women hold 24% of chief executive positions, 43% of management positions, and over three quarters of office and administrative support positions (U.S. Department of Labor, 2007). Similarly, 7% of chief executive positions, 13% of management positions, and 25% of office and administrative support positions are held by African Americans and Hispanics.

Although laws guarantee equal opportunity, racial bias remains an influence on the careers of ethnic minority members. In one study, white male participants were asked to examine résumés that varied in quality (some indicated high qualifications and others low) and by the writer's race (African American, Hispanic, Asian, and white). Résumés from hypothetical Asian job seekers were rated as highly qualified for high-status jobs regardless of résumé quality. Résumés indicating high qualifications were rated higher for white and Hispanic job seekers. African American job seekers received negative evaluations regardless of résumé quality, suggesting that racial discrimination may make it hard for even highly qualified African American candidates to obtain jobs (King, Madera, Hebl, Knight, & Mendoza, 2006). Similar findings occurred when participants were to judge recommendation letters (Morgan, Elder, & King, 2013).

Family Leave Policies

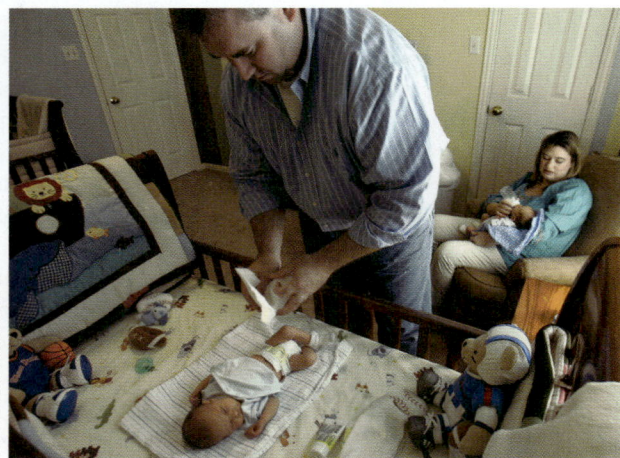

Family leave policies allow people to interrupt their employment to engage in caretaking activities, including caring for newborns and ill famiy members. The scope of family leave policies varies by state.

Most adults find managing the multiple demands of work and family challenging. There are many times in life when an adult may take on additional caretaking responsibilities, such as after the birth or adoption of a child or when a family member is seriously ill. People in most industrial nations are able to interrupt their employment to care for newborns and young children through various forms of leave.

Maternity leave is granted to mothers and is usually intended to protect the health and welfare of women and their newborns around the time of birth. Beginning in the early to mid-1950s, many countries in Europe established maternity leave policies (Moss & Deven, 2006). In 1992, the European Union introduced an international policy establishing minimum standards, including at least partial payment, for maternity leave in all of its member states. Along with Australia, the United States is one of the only developed countries that does not mandate universal paid leave for women who give birth.

Parental leave, intended to enable parents to provide care for young children, is typically taken after maternity leave. In 1998, the European Union endorsed a parental leave policy requiring all member states to permit working parents, men and women, to a minimum of three months of leave to care for children up to 8

years of age (Moss & Deven, 2006). In most of these countries, the leave is partially paid. In addition, some men are able to avail themselves of paternity leave, which is granted to fathers only around the time of birth and intended to enable fathers to provide support to their partner and to care for existing children. One survey of 19 countries, mostly in Europe, found that nearly all had paternity leave varying from 2 to 10 days and usually, but not always, paid on the same basis as maternity leave (Moss & Deven, 2006).

While the United States does not mandate maternity, paternity, or parental leave, the Family and Medical Leave Act signed in 1993 grants workers in companies of 50 or more employees up to 12 weeks of unpaid leave for the birth or adoption of a child and for the care of a sick child, spouse, or parent with a serious health condition. It also guarantees job security in that an employee is entitled to return to the same or comparable job and requires the employer to maintain health benefits as if the employee never took leave. The United States was one of the last industrialized nations to establish a family leave policy (Wisensale, 2006); however, at the time the law was signed in, about 34 states had already adopted some form of leave policy with some producing comparable or stronger legislation.

Critics of the Family and Medical Leave Act note that the policy is limited in scope. Only employers with 50 or more employees must provide leave, so it is estimated that the policy covers only about half of U.S. employees (Wisensale, 2006). Because it is unpaid, most single parents and low-income couples can't afford to take it even if given the opportunity. It was not until 2002 that a U.S. state (California) enacted a paid family leave law; it provides an employee with up to six weeks per year of paid leave to care for a new child or seriously ill family member. Rhode Island and New Jersey have since established paid family leave programs, including full or partial wage replacement for birth or adoption for up to six weeks, or to care for a family member who is suffering from a serious medical condition (National Conference of State Legislatures, 2013).

What Do You Think?

1. **Why do you think family leave policies often spark debate in the United States?**

2. **Given what you know about children and families, as well as young adults' careers, what family policies, such as the length of leave, would you suggest?**

The discontinuous nature of many women's careers contributes to their difficulty in advancing to the highest rungs of the career ladder. Many women put their careers on hold, leaving the workplace several times to raise children, often hindering their career advancement. One study of young adult women in male-dominated fields found that many had changed their career plans between ages 18 and 25 because of the desire for a flexible job, citing demands of occupations and low intrinsic value of science (Frome, Alfeld, Eccles, & Barber, 2006). Women in high-status professional

fields tend to delay childbearing or remain childless (Blair-Loy & Dehart, 2003). Moreover, negative stereotypes may hinder the career achievement of mothers. In one study, a mother or nonmother jobholder applying for a promotion in a traditionally male profession was rated by college students as well as adults in the workforce. Both students and workers tended to view the mother as showing lower job commitment, striving, dependability, and competence as compared with the nonmother (Heilman & Okimoto, 2008). Regardless of work experience, women tend to earn less than men, even in the same occupations. One year out of college, for every dollar a man earns, the same age woman earns about $.82. Across all ages, women earn $.79 for every dollar men earn (Hill, 2015).

Minority women of color are faced with multiple obstacles to their career success, such as gender and racial discrimination. Minority women who reach career success tend to display high self-efficacy, or feelings of personal control, and engage in active problem solving, confronting problems rather than avoiding them (Byars & Hackett, 1998). African American women who become leaders in their professions tend to report close supportive relationships with successful women, such as mentors, colleagues, and similarly successful friends, who help them set high expectations and provide support in achieving them. Mentoring is important for career development of all young adults. Women of color report strong desires to be mentored by a woman of their own ethnicity. However, the ethnic and gender obstacles to career success mean that women of color may find it difficult to establish a mentoring relationship with a mentor of their choice (Gonzáles-Figueroa & Young, 2005).

WORK AND FAMILY

Work–family balance is a concern to most families today, and especially to mothers. In the United States, the majority of married and unmarried mothers work, including over two thirds of mothers with a child under 6 years of age and over three quarters of mothers whose youngest child is in school (U.S. Bureau of Labor Statistics, 2015a). Nearly all married fathers work, and most share child care and household responsibilities with their wives, making work–life balance a task for both spouses. Most parents find it difficult to meet the competing demands of family and career, especially as the boundaries between today's workplace and home are often blurred as many adults are expected to bring work home or be available during nonwork hours via mobile devices.

Both men and women report feeling conflict between work and family obligations (Ammons & Kelly, 2008; Winslow, 2005). However, women are more likely than men to suffer from role overload, high levels of stress that result from attempting to balance the demands of multiple roles: employee, mother, and spouse (Cinamon & Rich, 2002; Gilbert & Kearney, 2006; Higgins, Duxbury, & Lyons, 2010). Role overload is more common in low-status occupations where workers have little control over their schedule or work, occupations that women are more likely to have than men (Devine et al., 2006). Demand overload influences one's sense of personal control, which in turn influences health (Bryson, Warner-Smith, Brown, & Fray, 2007). Role overload is associated with poor health, higher rates of depression, less effective parenting, and marital conflict in women (Hewitt et al., 2006; Pearson, 2008; Perry-Jenkins, Goldberg, Pierce, & Sayer, 2007). Control over work time predicts satisfaction with work–life balance and lower levels of work–life

Most mothers in the United States work, juggling the complex demands that accompany the often dueling roles of parent and employee.

AP/Ann Heisenfelt

conflict (Carlson et al., 2011). When hours increase, women who perceive control over their schedule show greater work–family satisfaction than do those who perceive little control (Valcour, 2007). Research comparing employees across several European countries found that poor work–life balance was associated with more health problems and poor well-being in both men and women. However, variations in reported work–life balance between countries was explained by national regulations regarding working hours, suggesting that workplace policies (often regulated by government) influence employees' sense of work–life balance and overall well-being (Lunau, Bambra, Eikemo, van der Wel, & Dragano, 2014).

Successfully managing multiple roles entails setting priorities. Women who manage multiple responsibilities while avoiding role overload tend to devote less time to maintaining the household, trading household chores and expectations for an immaculate home for more time with children (Hewitt et al., 2006). Working couples in which neither member works very long hours and each contribute to household finances and household and child-rearing tasks are happiest and are more likely to avoid either member experiencing role overload (Barnett & Gareis, 2006; Betz, 2005). In addition, research suggests that women who best manage role overload are those who seek physical and emotional support from others (Higgins et al., 2010).

Workplace policies can reduce role overload and improve employee morale and productivity. Flexible policies that permit employees to balance home and work responsibilities, such as flexible starting and stopping times, opportunities to work from home, and time off to care for sick children, are associated with better attendance, commitment to the organization, and work performance, and with fewer distress symptoms (Halpern, 2005). Workplaces with onsite child care show lower rates of employee absenteeism and higher productivity (Brandon & Temple, 2007). When adults are better able to balance work and family, they experience benefits in all of their roles. They are more productive and happy workers, more satisfied spouses, better parents; they experience greater well-being at home and work as well (Barnett & Gareis, 2006; Lunau et al., 2014; Russo, Shteigman, & Carmeli, 2015).

Early adulthood spans many years and entails many adjustments. Many people experience an extended transition to young adulthood known as emerging adulthood. Young adults traverse many career transitions, including obtaining education, seeking and changing jobs, and moving up the career ladder. They also experience changing relationships, seek mates, make lifestyle decisions, and choose whether to have children. The great many changes that occur during early adulthood give way to the middle adult years—a relatively more stable time, as discussed in Chapters 15 and 16.

Thinking in Context 14.5

1. How might we aid young adults as they transition into the work environment? What factors might improve their competence and satisfaction in their new role?

2. Diversity comes in many forms: ethnic, gender, and parental status, to name a few. What can employers do to address diversity issues in the workplace, ensure fair treatment of employees, and increase morale and productivity?

Apply Your Knowledge

In college, Kayla and Meghan were inseparable, sharing friends, majors, and even a dorm room. After college, they obtained entry-level jobs at the same firm and shared an apartment. Feeling that they were more like family than friends, Meghan would often refer to Kayla as her sister, the one who helps her get through her "20s crisis." With each promotion, Kayla and Meghan climbed up the career ladder until one day Meghan came home excitedly talking about her latest promotion, one that would require that she move across the country. Kayla and Meghan vowed to remain best friends forever.

After Meghan moved, their lives began to take different paths. Meghan's extensive business travel took her to faraway places, and her work hours grew longer. Kayla continued on her career path but began to focus more of her energy on her personal life after meeting and falling in love with Joel. Kayla and Joel married within a year, with Meghan as maid of honor. Two years later, Kayla gave birth to a son, naming Meghan as his godmother. Kayla loved her career but hated feeling torn in two directions, between home and career—for example, having to go to work when the baby was sick. After giving birth to her second child, Kayla felt even more out of control and decided to put her career on hold and focus on raising her children.

Unlike Kayla, Meghan never married. She came close, living with someone for over a year, but as time went on the passion drained from the relationship, leaving two very close friends. Meghan relished her career and rarely wondered about what could have been. On her 38th birthday, however, Meghan evaluated her life. After visiting Kayla and playing with her godchildren, she realized that she wanted a family. Meghan concluded that she may never meet the "right" man and may never marry, but she wanted a family nonetheless. Meghan called her doctor to discuss options for conceiving as a single parent.

1. Meghan and Kayla's lives have taken different paths. Describe the differences. What developmental and contextual factors contribute to them?

2. Is there such as thing as a 20s crisis? If so, what form does it take, and how do contextual factors influence it?

3. How do friendships change over the course of young adulthood?

4. Compare Kayla's and Meghan's experiences with what we know about marriage and cohabitation. What challenges do young adults face with regard to balancing the

demands of work and family? How do Kayla and Megan illustrate these themes?

5. Discuss Meghan's decision to pursue parenthood. What challenges might she experience in the coming years? How might she address them?

6. How do you think Kayla and Meghan will fare in the coming years?

Chapter Summary

14.1 Discuss markers of emerging adulthood and the role of context in shaping this period.

Advances in education have delayed the traditional markers of adulthood. Emerging adulthood is an extended transitional period between adolescence and early adulthood characterized by diversity in lifestyles, identity development, and the subjective sense of being in-between. Although emerging adulthood is observed in industrialized cultures around the world, it is not universal as it is influenced by socioeconomic status and contextual changes that have prolonged the transition into adulthood.

14.2 Explore intimacy development and the influence of the social clock on adjustment.

Erikson proposed that the psychosocial task of early adulthood is establishing an intimate relationship that is mutual and satisfying. Developing a sense of identity— commitment to a sense of self, values, and goals—prepares young people for establishing intimate relationships. Neugarten posed that it is contextual influences, rather than age-related stages, that shape adult development. Throughout life, we experience a number of normative events that represent a social clock of age-related expectations for major life events. Every society has a timetable for such events and the degree that individuals match their culture's social clock influences their adjustment.

14.3 Compare and contrast influences on friendship and mate selection.

Like friendships in childhood and adolescence, adult friendships are based on similarity. Women tend to have more intimate, long-lasting, and opposite-sex friendships than men, whose friendships tend to center around sharing information and activities rather than intimate disclosure. Men and women from many cultures seek different characteristics in mates. Despite this, most intimate partners share similarities in demographics, attitudes, and values. The more similar partners are, the more likely they are to report being satisfied with their relationship and to remain in the relationship.

14.4 Identify characteristics of intimate violence, influences on violence, and ways of addressing it.

Violence between intimate partners is not limited by culture, ethnicity, socioeconomic status, sexual orientation, or marital status. Intimate violence is not a one-time event but a process. A variety of factors contribute to intimate violence. Spouses who abuse often show higher rates of depression, anxiety, and low self-esteem as well as often display possessive, jealous, and controlling behavior toward their partner. There is also overlap between perpetrator and victim roles. Contextual factors that contribute to domestic violence include stressors such as poverty, unemployment, drug and alcohol abuse, and cultural norms. Many communities provide services to aid victims as well as perpetrators of intimate violence.

14.5 Contrast the correlates of singlehood and cohabitation.

Most North Americans spend a large part of their adult lives as single, and some remain single throughout life. The circumstances surrounding singlehood influence young adults' perceptions and reactions to being single. Cohabitation has become increasingly common in the United States and is very common in most European nations. Cohabiting couples in the United States tend to be less satisfied, less stable, and show higher rates of intimate violence than married couples. When they marry, North American cohabiting couples tend to have unhappier marriages with a greater likelihood of divorce.

14.6 Discuss the transition to marriage and predictors of marital success and divorce.

Most North Americans marry. Newlyweds experience multiple changes during their first years of marriage and often report a drop in marital satisfaction. Marital success is predicted by maturity and similarity in demographic factors. Successful marriages are based on realistic expectations, flexibility, communication, and joint conflict resolution. Couples who marry at a young age and share few similarities in demographics and interests are at higher risk of divorce. Other factors such as being at an economic disadvantage, experiencing multiple life stressors and role overload, and having poor communication and conflict resolution skills increases the risk of divorce. The process of divorce entails a series of stressful experiences. Most couples find that the divorce is worse than expected. Recently divorced adults are prone to depression, anxiety, and a variety of risky behaviors.

14.7 Examine the effects of parenthood on young adults.

New parents are greeted with a host of new responsibilities and changes. Mothers tend to report more stress and a higher workload and less physical activity with the advent of parenthood than do fathers. The transition to parenthood is associated with declines in marital satisfaction. In dual-earner couples, the greater the degree of shared parenting responsibilities, the greater the couple's happiness. Most parents report that parenthood has encouraged them to become more empathetic, tolerant, and responsible. The process of parenting influences development. Each phase of a child's life entails a different set of parenting tasks and skills, requiring flexibility on the part of adults.

14.8 Compare and contrast the experience of stepparents, never-married parents, and same-sex parents.

Stepparents are often placed in the position of providing discipline without the warm attachment bond that characterizes most parent–child relationships. Often they have unrealistic expectations for parenting skills and relationships with stepchildren and face more conflict than anticipated. Remarried parents tend to report high levels of tension and conflict about parenting as compared with first-married parents. After a challenging transition, many couples adjust to their roles as spouses and parents, and interactions with stepchildren improve, but the divorce rate is high for remarried couples with children. The typical never-married parent in the United States is of middle or low socioeconomic status and is most commonly an African American young woman. As a group, never-married mothers tend to show better mental health than do married mothers. The primary challenge never-married mothers face is economic. Same-sex parents do not differ from heterosexual parents in competence or commitment to their roles as parents. Children reared by same-sex parents do not differ from those reared by heterosexual parents in mental health, peer relationships, gender identity, and sexual orientation.

14.9 Discuss the experience of women and minorities in the workplace.

Women and ethnic minorities are faced with many obstacles to their career success, including discrimination and the glass ceiling. Although laws guarantee equal opportunity, racial discrimination can prevent even highly qualified African American candidates from obtaining jobs. The discontinuous nature of many women's careers contributes to their difficulty in advancing to the highest rungs of the career ladder. Regardless of work experience, women tend to earn less than men, even in the same occupations. Minority women are faced with multiple obstacles to their career success. Mentoring is important for career development of all young adults but especially women and ethnic minority members who may have few models for career success among family and friends.

14.10 Examine the interaction of work and family on young adults' adjustment.

Many North American adults find it difficult to balance the competing demands of family and career. Women are more likely than men to suffer from role overload. Role overload is associated with psychological distress, marital conflict, poor health, and depression. Women who manage multiple responsibilities while avoiding role overload tend to devote less time to maintaining the household and have spouses who share financial, household, and child-rearing responsibilities. Flexible workplace policies that permit employees to balance home and work responsibilities have workers who show better attendance, commitment to the organization, and work performance with fewer distress symptoms.

Key Terms

cohabitation   399

commitment   392

emerging adulthood   390

intimacy   392

intimacy versus isolation   392

intimate violence   397

role overload   405

social clock   393

PART VII

Middle Adulthood

Midlife reflects a changing balance of gains and losses. In addition to sensory changes, many middle-aged adults experience declines in strength and endurance; physical activity and life choices influence the rate and extent of change. Women's adjustment to menopause, the end of the reproductive years, is influenced by personal characteristics, circumstances, and internalized societal views about women and aging. Cognitively, midlife adults show declines in attention, working memory, and processing speed, but an expanding knowledge base and growing expertise permits them to compensate, showing few changes in functioning within everyday contexts.

In midlife, the home context takes center stage. Marital satisfaction increases as child-rearing tasks decline and couples have more time to spend with each other. Most midlife parents adjust well to the resulting empty nest as relationships with adult children tend to become closer. The grandparent role often satisfies midlife adults' emerging generative needs. Most midlife adults retain the role of adult child and provide increasing assistance to their aging parents. Adults spend much of their days within the work context and job satisfaction increases in middle adulthood, especially with career advancement. Although adults spend less time with friends than with family, friendships improve with age and continue to be important sources of social support. In short, midlife adults show positive physical, cognitive, and socioemotional adjustment, and a tendency to mellow out, as they interact in the multiple contexts in which they are embedded.

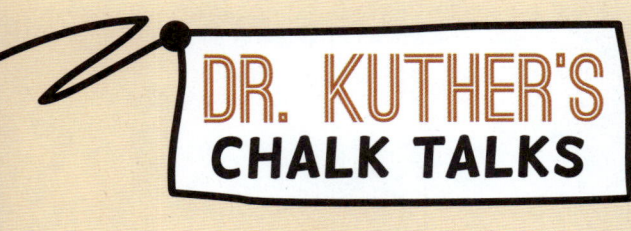

Watch at
edge.sagepub.com/kuther

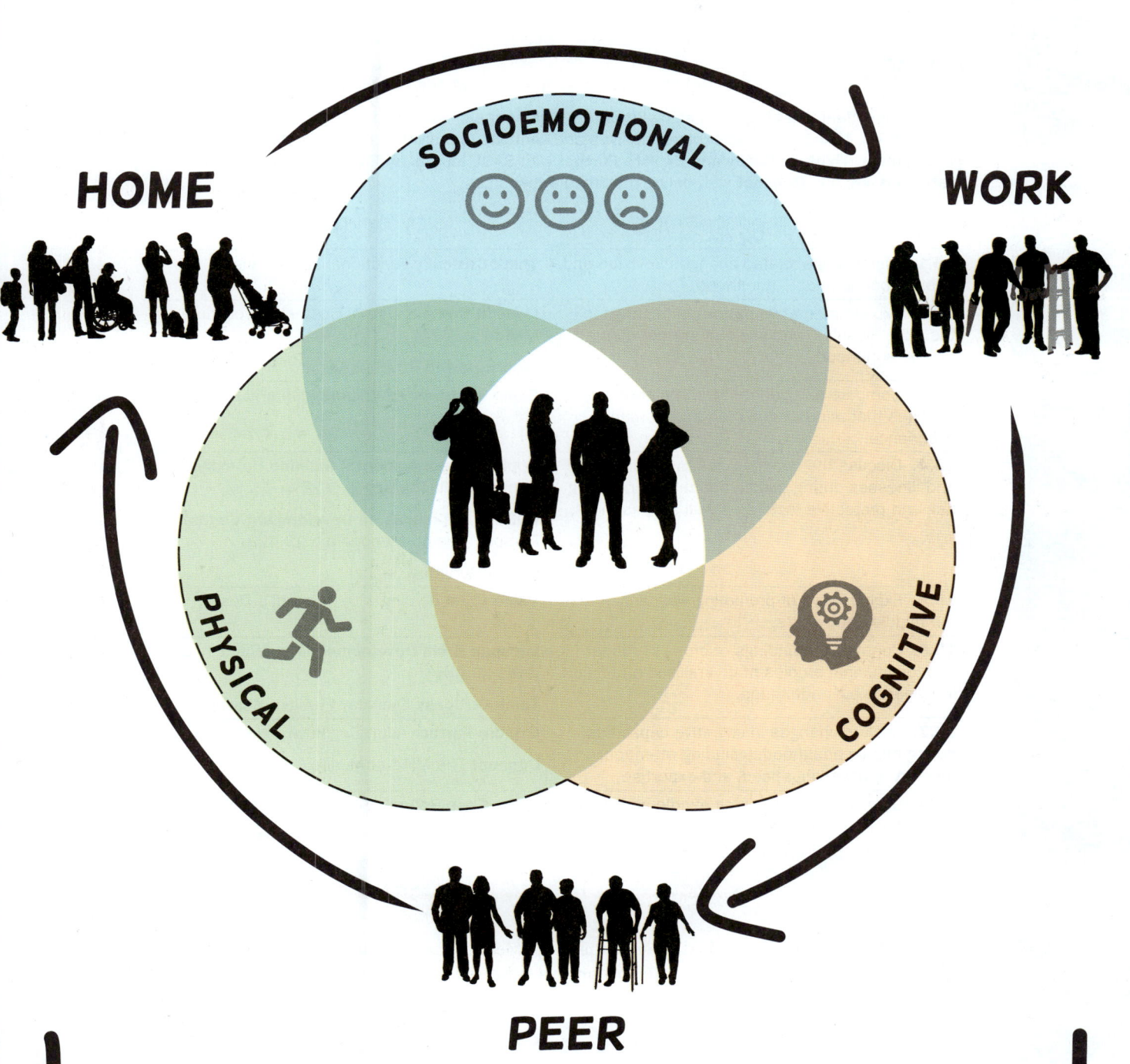

CHAPTER 15

Physical and Cognitive Development in Middle Adulthood

Get the edge on your studies at edge.sagepub.com/kuther.

Master these learning objectives using key study tools in the chapter and at SAGE edge. Access original SAGE **Video Cases** to explore the lives and contexts of individuals in every stage of development, **Think Critically** and **Explore Further** with SAGE journal and reference articles, and **Watch**, **Listen**, and **Connect** with online multimedia resources.

LEARNING OBJECTIVES	KEY STUDY TOOLS
15.1. Discuss age-related changes in vision and hearing during middle adulthood.	**Think Critically** Functional Loss in Vision
15.2. Explain normative patterns of change in the skin, muscles, and skeletal system during middle adulthood.	**Lives in Context** Use of Cosmetic Procedures in Midlife (p. 424)
	Watch How to Reverse Aging
15.3. Compare and contrast the reproductive changes that middle-aged men and women experience.	**Explore Further** Perimenopause and Menopause
15.4. Discuss the common health conditions and illnesses during middle adulthood, including risk and protective factors as well as treatment.	**Applying Developmental Science** Hormone Replacement Therapy (p. 427)
	Cultural Influences on Development Cultural Perspectives on Menopause (p. 428)
	Watch Surviving Cancer
15.5. Explain ways of promoting wellness across the middle adult years.	**Video Case** Dealing with a Parent's Death
15.6. Contrast the findings of cross-sectional and longitudinal studies of crystallized and fluid intelligence over adulthood.	**Lifespan Brain Development** The Middle-Aged Brain (p. 436)
15.7. Analyze changes in cognitive capacities during middle adulthood, including attention, memory, processing speed, and expertise.	**Think Critically** Everyday Problem Solving
	Explore Further Adult Cognitive Development
	Connect The Mind at Midlife
15.8. Discuss learning during middle adulthood, particularly for adults who return to higher education.	**Video Case** Returning to School in Midlife
	Listen Learning for the Sake of Learning

As the basketball swooshed through the hoop, Mel called out to his son, Al, "Yeah! Your dad's still got it!" Al raced toward his father, beating him for the rebound, "But I'm still faster." "You may be faster, but I'm experienced—and experience makes all the difference," Mel challenged his son.

Who is right, father or son? In many ways, both are. In this chapter, we examine the physical and cognitive changes in middle adulthood, from ages 40 to 65. Our conclusion largely will mirror this conversation: Middle-aged adults experience mild physical and cognitive declines, but experience and wisdom often permit them to compensate for any decline in capacity.

Ronnie Kaufman/Blend/Newscom

PHYSICAL DEVELOPMENT IN MIDDLE ADULTHOOD

Physical changes occur gradually throughout adulthood. Like Mel, adults often compensate for changes by modifying their behavior. Nevertheless, even active and vibrant middle-aged adults notice some changes in their body shape, strength, speed, and appearance. Most middle-aged adults begin to sense their own mortality, often in response to acute or chronic health conditions and especially after experiencing life-threatening health concerns. Many middle-aged adults begin to think of their lives in terms of years left of life rather than years lived (Neugarten, 1968). Aging itself cannot be controlled, and physical declines are inevitable. However, many middle-aged adults compensate for declines and maximize their physical capacities in order to maintain an active lifestyle.

SENSORY CHANGES

Suddenly aware that he holds the newspaper at arm's length and still squints to read, 45-year-old Dominic wondered to himself, "When did this happen? I can't see like I used to." Like much of physical development, the changes that take place in our senses represent continuous change. Over the adult years, vision and hearing capacities gradually decline. Like Dominic, most adults notice changes in vision during their 40s and changes in hearing at around age 50. The use of corrective lenses aids vision problems, and hearing aids amplify sounds, permitting better hearing.

Vision

Dominic's need to hold the newspaper at a distance in order to read is not unusual and is related to changes in the eye that occur throughout the adult years. The cornea flattens; the lens loses flexibility; and the muscle that permits the lens to change shape, or accommodate, weakens. The result is that most adults in their 40s develop **presbyopia**, also known as farsightedness—the inability to focus the lens on close objects, such as in reading small print (Hermans, Dubbelman, van der Heijde, & Heethaar, 2008; Strenk, Strenk, & Koretz, 2005). By age 50, virtually all adults are presbyopic and require reading glasses or other corrective options (Gil-Cazorla, Shah, & Naroo, 2015; Truscott, 2009). Most also require corrective lenses for distance. Bifocals that combine lenses for nearsightedness and farsightedness are helpful.

In addition to changes in the accommodative ability of the lens, the ability to see in dim light declines because, with age, the lens yellows, the size of the pupil shrinks, and over middle age, most adults have lost about one half of the rods (light receptor cells) in the retina, which reduces the ability to see in dim light and makes adults' night vision decline twice as fast as their day vision (Jackson & Owsley, 2003).

Joan experiences presbyopia, as signified by her need to hold her magazine at a distance to read.

BSIP/Science Source

As rods are lost, so too are cones (color receptive cells) because rods secrete substances that permit cones to survive (Bonnel, Mohand-Said, & Sahel, 2003). Color discrimination, thus, becomes limited with gradual declines beginning in the 30s (Kraft & Werner, 1999; Paramei & Oakley, 2014). Night vision is further reduced because the vitreous (transparent gel that fills the eyeball) becomes more opaque with age, scattering light that enters the eye (creating glare) and permitting less light to reach the retina (Scilley et al., 2002). In middle adulthood, about one third more light is needed to compensate for these changes that reduce vision (Owsley, McGwin, Jackson, Kallies, & Clark, 2007). All of these changes in vision make driving at night more challenging as headlights from other cars become blinding (Gruber, Mosimann, Müri, & Nef, 2013).

Hearing

In addition to vision, Dominic also noticed that he has difficulty hearing, at least in some situations. When he plays with his 4-year-old nephew, Dominic finds that he has to lean in close to hear the boy's speech. Sometimes he finds himself watching his teenage daughter's lips while she speaks, especially when they are having dinner in a crowded restaurant. Middle-aged adults tend to experience more difficulty hearing under conditions of background noise and perform more poorly under that condition than do young adults (Leigh-Paffenroth & Elangovan, 2011). Age-related hearing loss, **presbycusis** ("old hearing"), becomes apparent in the 50s and is caused by natural cell death that results in the deterioration of the ear structures that convert sound into neural impulses (Quaranta et al., 2015). The loss is first limited to high-pitched sounds, which enable us to distinguish between consonants such as *f* versus *s* and *p* versus *t*; as a result, the person often can hear most of a message but may misinterpret parts of it, such as names. Presbycusis hearing deficits tend to be more apparent in settings with background noise, such as a dinner party. By late adulthood, hearing loss extends to all sound frequencies. Reduced sensitivity to speech sounds influences processing as older adults show less activation of the auditory cortex in response to speech as compared with younger adults (Hwang, Li, Wu, Chen, & Liu, 2007).

Presbycusis is age-related, but contextual factors play a role in age-related hearing loss. Many middle-aged adults display hearing loss that is preventable, the result of exposure to noise in the workplace, at concerts, and through the use of headphones (Tremblay & Ross, 2007). Generally, men's hearing declines more rapidly than women's, perhaps up to twice as quickly (Gordon-Salant, 2005). Men's rapid hearing decline can be traced to exposure to intense noise (e.g., headphones and concerts); loud work environments (e.g., construction, military, and transportation work); and, in later adulthood, illnesses such as cerebrovascular disease (a disease of the blood vessels that supply the brain, often caused by atherosclerosis), which can lead to a stroke that damages the auditory cortex (Ecob et al., 2008; Helzner et al., 2005). Hearing declines are evident in some men as early as 30 years of age and also entail a genetic component (Gordon-Salant, 2005; Wingfield, Tun, & McCoy, 2005). Hearing loss can be prevented by wearing protective equipment, such as earplugs, and by lowering the volume on MP3 players. Screening to identify risk for hearing loss and early signs of hearing loss can help in delaying loss (Chou, Dana, Bougatsos, Fleming, & Beil, 2011).

SKIN, MUSCULAR, AND SKELETAL CHANGES

Karen looked at the pictures of her daughter's wedding. "What a beautiful day. Ouch! Look at this picture of me in the sunlight. When did I get so many lines around my eyes?" Age-related changes in the skin are predictable and unavoidable. Most adults in their 30s notice lines developing on their foreheads, the result of a lifetime of facial expressions. By the 40s, these lines are accompanied by crow's feet around the eyes and lines around the mouth—markers of four decades of smiles, frowns, laughter, and other emotions. During middle adulthood the skin becomes less taut as the epidermis, the outer protective layer of the skin that produces new skin cells, loosens its attachment to the thinning dermis, the middle layer of skin consisting of connective tissue that gives skin its flexibility (Quan & Fisher, 2015). The resulting loss in elasticity is accompanied by the loss of fat in the hypodermis, the innermost layer of skin composed of fat, which leads to wrinkling and loosening of the skin (Kohl, Steinbauer, Landthaler, & Szeimies, 2011).

Women tend to experience age-related changes sooner and more quickly than do men as their dermis is thinner and they experience hormonal changes, a reduction of estrogen, that exacerbate aging (Farage, Miller, Elsner, & Maibach, 2013). While age-related changes in the skin are unavoidable, there is great variability in age-related appearance (Miyamoto et al., 2011). Adults who have spent more time outdoors, especially without skin protection, tend to show signs of aging more quickly. Exposure to sun rays advances skin aging

for people of all skin types and ethnicities, as does smoking (Gragnani et al., 2014; Kohl et al., 2011; Pontius & Smith, 2011). Cosmetic procedures, as discussed in Lives in Context (p. 424), are increasingly available and popular, especially with women in middle adulthood.

As we have discussed, although most people reach their peak in muscle strength during their 20s, followed by a small gradual decline through the 30s, changes usually go unnoticed until the mid to late 40s. The rate of decline in muscle mass and strength tends to accelerate in the 40s (Keller & Engelhardt, 2013). By age 60, about 10% to 15% of maximum strength is lost. Not all parts of the body age at the same rate (Mitchell et al., 2012). Isometric strength, for example, tends to be retained (Mitchell et al., 2012). There are also individual differences. Some people experience greater losses and others fewer, depending on their level of physical activity. Loss of endurance tends to occur after age 40, but the decline is generally proportionately less than that of strength (Hayslip, Panek, & Patrick, 2007).

In addition to losses in strength and endurance, both men and women tend to experience weight gain in middle adulthood, with an increase in body fat and loss of muscle and bone. Much of the increase in fat is deposited in the torso. The abdomen increases 6% to 16% in men and 25% to 35% in women (Whitbourne, 2007). In men, fat accumulates on the back and upper abdomen, while women experience an increase in fat in the upper arms and around the waist. Over adulthood, muscle mass tends to be replaced by fat; however, good nutrition and an active lifestyle can reduce losses and even increase muscular density.

Metabolic rate slows over the course of adulthood. When adults gradually reduce their caloric intake to match their reduced need for calories, age-related weight gain is minimized. For example, a seven-year-long study of about 30,000 women aged 50 to 79 showed that a low-fat diet with lots of vegetables, fruits, and grains predicted weight loss and maintenance, regardless of socioeconomic status and ethnicity (Howard et al., 2006). Research with animals suggests that extremely low-calorie diets increase health and longevity (Bishop & Guarente, 2007; Simpson & Raubenheimer, 2007). Overall, weight in young adulthood,

Physical activity can offset midlife losses in muscle.

Use of Cosmetic Procedures in Midlife

The many physical changes that occur in middle adulthood influence adults' views of themselves as well as how they interact with, and are treated by, others. Changes in appearance are hard to deny in midlife. Most midlife adults can list how their appearance has changed, noting, for example, lines that have appeared on their face (Honigman & Castle, 2006). As people age, their concerns about their appearance increasingly focus on the face. It is not uncommon for midlife adults, especially women, to develop concerns and worries about losing their attractiveness, as judged by Western beauty standards that emphasize youth (Barrett & Robbins, 2008).

Many adults seek to improve their appearance through cosmetic procedures—both surgical and nonsurgical. As the name suggests, surgical cosmetic procedures entail surgery. Nearly 1.8 million surgical cosmetic procedures were conducted in 2014 including procedures such as liposuction, eyelid surgery, tummy tucks, and breast augmentation (American Society for Aesthetic Plastic Surgery, 2014). Nonsurgical cosmetic procedures are far more common, with 13 million conducted in 2014. The most common noninvasive procedures include Botox injections (which paralyze facial muscles, making them unable to contract and "wrinkle"), so-called injectable "fillers" (substances injected into wrinkles, temporarily filling them), and chemical peels and microdermabrasion (chemical and physical means of removing the outermost layers of skin, purporting to reveal smooth new skin).

As shown in the accompanying graph, middle-aged people are the age group most likely to obtain cosmetic procedures. At all ages, about 90% of cosmetic procedures are conducted on women.

Why do women pursue cosmetic procedures? There are multiple individual and contextual factors at play when considering how middle-aged women view themselves and their attitudes toward these procedures (Saucier, 2004; Slevec & Tiggemann, 2010). Western cultural norms equate women's aging with a decline in physical attractiveness. Television, magazines, and advertising feature the latest advances in cosmetic surgical procedures as well as prolific discussions of the latest celebrity to "go under the knife" (Sarwer & Crerand, 2004). Cosmetic surgery has also become the focus of a number of popular television

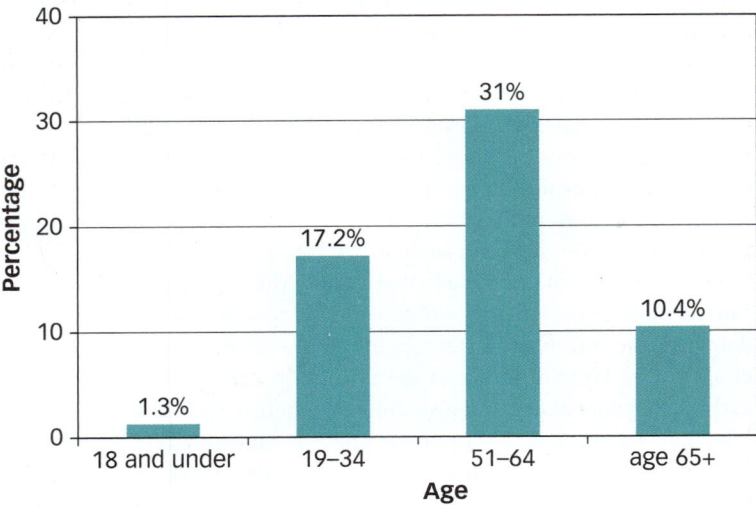

FIGURE 15.1: Cosmetic Procedures by Age in the United States, 2014

programs, such as *Botched* and *Extreme Makeover*. Continued media exposure can shape people's perceptions and normalize values and behaviors, such as those related to cosmetic procedures as a means for addressing body discontent (Slevec & Tiggemann, 2010).

Similar to other periods in life, peers are an important influence on women's attitude and behaviors. Women who perceive their friends as supportive of the use of cosmetic procedures, and especially those whose friends obtain such procedures, are likely to view cosmetic procedures positively and are more likely to obtain them (Nerini, Matera, & Stefanile, 2014; Sharp, Tiggemann, & Mattiske, 2014).

What Do You Think?

1. From your perspective, why are cosmetic procedures most popular in midlife?

2. What are some of the advantages and disadvantages or risks of such procedures?

3. How might someone make a decision about whether to pursue cosmetic procedures?

at age 25, predicts midlife weight (Waring, Eaton, Lasater, & Lapane, 2010). Moreover, activity plays a large role in maintaining weight, muscle mass, and endurance throughout adulthood (Aldwin, Spiro, & Park, 2006). Adults who remain active tend to retain their physical physique and competencies (Newell, Vaillancourt, & Sosnoff, 2006). Overweight, on the other hand, is associated with cardiovascular disease and death by cardiovascular disease (Heir, Erikssen, & Sandvik, 2011).

Many age-related changes, like those of the skin and body composition, are visible. Others, like skeletal changes, are less obvious. Bone density reaches its height in the mid- to late 30s, after which adults tend to experience gradual bone loss. Bones become thinner, more porous, and more brittle as calcium is absorbed. Bone loss increases in the 50s, especially in women, whose bones have less calcium to begin with and who lose the protective influence of estrogen on bones after **menopause**

(Chan & Duque, 2002). As the bones that make up the vertebrae in the spinal column become thin and more brittle, the disks collapse and adults lose height, about an inch or more by age 60, and more thereafter (Hannan et al., 2012). Loss of bone density causes bones to break more easily and heal more slowly, making a broken bone more serious as we age. Like other physical changes, losses in bone density can be slowed by behavior and lifestyle choices, such as avoiding smoking and excess drinking and engaging in weight-bearing exercise (Berg et al., 2008; Bleicher et al., 2011; Gass & Dawson-Hughes, 2006). Table 15.1 summarizes some of the physical changes that take place during middle adulthood.

Thinking in Context 15.1

1. How might the age-related changes that adults experience in vision and hearing influence their day-to-day functioning and interactions with others? Consider adults' roles in the workplace and at home, as employees, parents, spouses, and friends.

2. The physical changes that accompany middle adulthood can influence how adults view themselves as well as how others view and treat them. What are some of the possible implications of physical aging for adults' sense of self?

MIDDLE ADULTHOOD AND THE REPRODUCTIVE SYSTEM

In middle adulthood, the level of sex hormones in the body declines in both men and women. Women experience the end of fertility. Men retain their reproductive capacity, albeit at a diminished level. Despite these changes, sexual activity and enjoyment often continues throughout life.

REPRODUCTIVE CHANGES IN WOMEN

At about 51 years of age on average, but starting as early as age 42 and as late as 58, women experience menopause, the cessation of ovulation and menstruation (Avis & Crawford, 2006; Do et al., 1998). The timing of menopause is influenced by heredity but also by lifestyle choices and contextual influences, such as exposure to pollution (Grindler et al., 2015; Hartge, 2009). Menopause occurs earlier in women who smoke, who are malnourished, who have not given birth, and who are of lower socioeconomic status (Gold et al., 2013; Saraç, Öztekin, & Çelebi, 2011). Specifically, a woman is said to have reached menopause one year after her last menstrual period. **Perimenopause** refers to the transition to menopause, extending from three years before and after menopause. It is during perimenopause that the production of reproductive

TABLE 15.1 Physical Development During Middle Adulthood

PHYSICAL DEVELOPMENT	AGE-RELATED CHANGE
Vision	• Presbyopia affects nearly all adults by age 50. • Structural changes of the eye, including the cornea, lens, and retina, cause a decline in night vision.
Hearing	• Presbycusis is common by the 50s with the loss first limited to high-pitched sounds and settings in which there is background noise. • By late adulthood, it extends to all sound frequencies. • Contextual factors, such as exposure to noise, play a role in age-related hearing loss.
Skin	• Fine lines are apparent by the 30s, first on the forehead, and by the 40s as crow's feet around the eyes and lines around the mouth. • Skin becomes less taut as the epidermis loosens its attachment to the dermis. The resulting loss in elasticity is accompanied by the loss of fat in the hypodermis, which leads to wrinkling and loosening of the skin. • Exposure to sun rays is associated with advanced skin aging for people of all skin types and ethnicities.
Muscle	• Peak muscle strength is typically reached during the 20s, followed by a gradual decline. Changes usually are not noticeable until about age 45. • Loss of endurance tends to occur after age 40. • Good nutrition and an active lifestyle can reduce losses and even increase muscular density.
Skeleton	• Bone density peaks in the mid to late 30s, after which adults tend to experience gradual bone loss, advancing in the 50s, especially in postmenopausal women. • Losses in bone density can be slowed by behavior and lifestyle choices, such as avoiding smoking and excess drinking and engaging in weight-bearing exercise.

hormones declines and symptoms associated with menopause first appear (McNamara, Batur, & DeSapri, 2015).

The first indicator of perimenopause is a shorter menstrual cycle, followed by erratic periods (Burger, Hale, Robertson, & Dennerstein, 2007). Ovulation becomes less predictable, occurring early or late in the cycle; sometimes several ova are released and sometimes none (Nelson, 2008). This unpredictability in ovulation can sometimes lead to a "surprise" late-life pregnancy. Other women who waited to have children may find themselves frustrated by the unpredictability of their cycles, the accompanying difficulty getting pregnant, and the closing window of opportunity.

The most common symptoms of perimenopause that women experience are hot flashes, in which the expansion and contraction of blood vessels cause sudden sensations of heat throughout the body accompanied by sweating (McNamara et al., 2015). Two thirds to three quarters of U.S. women experience hot flashes (Nelson, 2008). Declining levels of estrogen slows sexual arousal and reduces vaginal lubrication, sometimes making intercourse uncomfortable (Simon, 2011); this symptom can be addressed by using a cream or gel to provide vaginal lubrication. Complaints about sexual functioning increase with age, with 35% to 40% of women reporting difficulties with sexual functioning including a reduced sex drive (Torpy, 2007; Walsh & Berman, 2004). For example, one study of women from France, Germany, Italy, the Netherlands, Switzerland, and the United Kingdom found that over one third of the women mentioned experiencing a reduced sex drive whereas over one half reported a loss of interest in sex (Nappi & Nijland, 2008). Women who report depression following menopause are more likely to report difficulties with sexual functioning (Gallicchio et al., 2007). **Hormone replacement therapy**, discussed in Applying Developmental Science (p. 427), is designed to address many of these symptoms.

The loss of estrogen increases some health risks. For example, estrogen protects against the accumulation of plaque on artery walls. The decline in estrogen is accompanied by an increase in arterial plaque, declines in cardiovascular function and metabolism, and increased risk for cardiovascular disease (Knowlton & Lee, 2012; Rosano, Vitale, Marazzi, & Volterrani, 2007). In addition, reductions in estrogen speed the loss of bone mass, increasing the risk of osteoporosis.

How women experience menopause, whether they report severe mood changes and irritability or few psychological and physical consequences, varies with their attitudes and expectations for menopause, which are influenced by personal characteristics, circumstances, and societal views about women and aging (Ayers, Forshaw, & Hunter, 2010; Delanoë et al., 2012; Lindh-Åstrand, Hoffmann, Hammar, & Kjellgren, 2007; Nosek, Kennedy, & Gudmundsdottir, 2012; Strauss, 2011). Similar to off-time physical transitions, such as girls who begin puberty early or women who experience premature menopause, experience higher rates of depression, anxiety, body dissatisfaction, sexual dysfunction, and poor self-confidence (Deeks, Gibson-Helm, Teede, & Vincent,

2011). Women who have children may view menopause as providing sexual freedom and enjoyment without worry of contraception or pregnancy. In contrast, women who desire a family but who have not given birth may view menopause as the end of fertility and the accompanying possibility of child-rearing, making menopause a difficult time indeed (Howell & Beth, 2002).

Contextual factors influence how women make sense of menopause (Delanoë et al., 2012; Strauss, 2011). When menopause is viewed as a medical event whose symptoms require treatment, women tend to view it more negatively and report more physical and emotional symptoms (Hvas & Dorte Effersøe, 2008). However, recent generations of women have objected to the notion of menopause as a disease and instead view it as a naturally occurring process. Adults of both sexes, as well as their families, tend to view menopause more positively when it is described as a life transition or symbol of aging, as compared with a medical event whose symptoms are problematic and require treatment (Dillaway, 2008; Hvas & Dorte Effersøe, 2008). In the United States, postmenopausal women tend to view menopause more positively than do younger women (Avis, Brockwell, & Colvin, 2005). They tend to report menopause as causing few difficulties and instead view it as a beginning. For example, in one study of over 2,000 postmenopausal women, about two thirds reported feeling relieved over freedom from birth control (Rossi, 2004).

Education and socioeconomic status are associated with women's views of menopause. High education and high socioeconomic status each are associated with more positive views of menopause and fewer reports of menopausal symptoms (Lawlor, Ebrahim, & Smith, 2003). Ethnicity is also related to views about menopause. African American and Mexican American women tend to hold more favorable views toward menopause than white non-Hispanic American women, often describing it as a normal and sometimes looked forward to part of life (Avis et al., 2001; Sampselle, Harris, Harlow, & Sowers, 2002). Cultural factors also influence how menopause is experienced, as discussed in Cultural Influences on Development (p. 427).

REPRODUCTIVE CHANGES IN MEN

What about men? Do they experience a sudden drop in reproductive ability similar to women? Do males experience changes similar to menopause? No. Unlike women, men's reproductive ability declines gradually and steadily over the adult years, beginning as early as age 30 in some men and continuing at a pace of about a 1% decrease per year to a total decline in testosterone of about 30% by age 70 (Federman & Walford, 2007). Men's bodies produce less testosterone and they become less fertile, but about 75% of men retain testosterone levels in the normal range with most adult males continuing to produce sperm throughout adulthood and many able to father children into their 80s (Federman & Walford, 2007).

Hormone Replacement Therapy

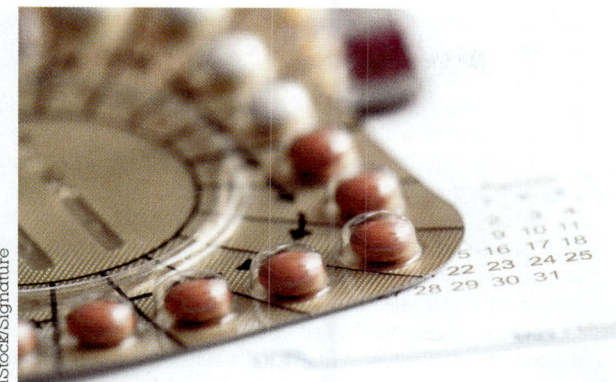

iStock/Signature

Hormone replacement therapy is commonly prescribed to manage menopausal symptoms. However, the U.S. Food and Drug Administration recommends that physicians prescribe the smallest dose to reduce menopausal symptoms and for the shortest time.

From the 1950s until recently, it was common for women to use hormone therapy to increase the levels of estrogen or progesterone in their bodies in order to reduce severe perimenopause symptoms, manage common symptoms such as hot flashes, or to attempt to retain their youth. Many postmenopausal women used hormone replacement in the belief that it reduced heart disease and improved cognitive function. The results of correlational studies supported the use of hormone therapy and it was widely prescribed (Hersh, Stefanick, & Stafford, 2004).

But in 2002, the results of the Women's Health Initiative Study, a longitudinal study of thousands of perimenopausal women, suggested that hormone replacement therapy reduces the incidence of hot flashes and decreases the risk of **osteoporosis** but does not protect against heart disease. On the contrary, it suggested that hormone replacement therapy may increase the risk of heart disease, stroke, and breast cancer (Nelson et al., 2002). These findings resulted in a dramatic worldwide decline in the use of hormone replacement therapy (Stevenson, Hodis, Pickar, & Lobo, 2009). Research with international samples suggests that the breast cancer rate declined from 2000 to

2007, as hormone replacement therapy became less common, suggesting its role (Sharpe et al., 2010).

However, like most aspects of development, the relation of hormone replacement therapy and health outcomes is much more complex than the Women's Health Initiative findings suggested as it is influenced by the dynamic interaction of genetic and contextual factors. In one study, for example, hormone replacement therapy did not lower the overall risk of heart disease across all women, but after controlling for other risk factors (such as hypertension) the risk for heart disease was lower for women taking hormone supplements (Rossouw et al., 2007). The cardiovascular risks associated with hormone replacement therapy increased with age starting only at age 60 (Stevenson et al., 2009). The breast cancer risks associated with hormone replacement therapy varies by race and ethnicity, body mass index (BMI), and breast density (Hou et al., 2013). There is no universal relationship; instead, it varies by individual.

Other research shows that hormone replacement therapy can help some postmenopausal women with selected comorbid conditions such as osteoporosis, type II diabetes, certain cardiovascular pathologies, rheumatoid arthritis, and colorectal cancer (Britto et al., 2011; Islander, Jochems, Lagerquist, Forsblad-d'Elia, & Carlsten, 2011; Panay, Hamoda, Arya, & Savvas, 2013). Findings such as these may suggest that hormone replacement therapy is a reasonable option to manage menopausal symptoms over the short term (Canderelli, Leccesse, & Miller, 2007; Hickey, Elliott, & Davison, 2012). The U.S. Food and Drug Administration recommends that physicians prescribe the smallest dose to reduce menopausal symptoms and for the shortest time (Hannon, 2010). The decision as to who should use any form of hormone replacement therapy needs to be based on the individual woman's needs, quality of life, and potential risks versus benefits (Panay et al., 2013).

What Do You Think?

1. Why might researchers' conclusions about hormone replacement therapy vary so dramatically across studies and over the past decade?

2. What factors do you think are important for women to consider when it comes to hormone replacement therapy? What advice would you give a friend?

Men experience gradual declines in testosterone over their lifetimes; however, levels can shift dramatically in response to stress and illness, creating the appearance of a "male menopause" (Shores, 2014). Stress from problems such as unemployment, illness, marital problems, children leaving home, or sexual inactivity can cause reductions in testosterone, which decreases sexual desire and responses. Low levels of testosterone may interfere with a man's ability to achieve or maintain an erection, which can influence anxiety about his sexual capacity, which can lead to further declines in testosterone (Seidman & Weiser, 2013). In this way, it might

appear as if some men go through a form of menopause, but the sudden declines in testosterone tend to be a correlate of stress and health problems rather than a biological inevitability (Donatelle, 2004). Normative declines in testosterone are gradual, and connections between testosterone levels and health-related outcomes are weak (Basaria, 2013; Simon, 2008). Regardless, media and popular views in the United States and Europe have contributed to the notion of a male menopause and a corresponding medicalization of masculinity in middle and older adulthood though the use of hormone and other treatments (Marshall, 2007; Vainionpää & Topo,

CULTURAL INFLUENCES ON DEVELOPMENT

Cultural Perspectives on Menopause

Societal and cultural views influence how menopause is perceived. In societies that value youth, women may fear the bodily changes of menopause and their perceived loss of sex appeal (Howell & Beth, 2002). On the other hand, in cultures where older women are respected and achieve social or religious power with age (e.g., powerful mother-in-law and grandmother roles), women report few complaints about menopausal symptoms (Delanoë et al., 2012).

In Japan, where women gain power and responsibility (such as monitoring household finances and caring for dependent parents) with age, women rarely report hot flashes or other menopausal symptoms (Huang, Xu, I, & Jaisamrarn, 2010; Lock & Kaufert, 2001). Middle adulthood is seen as a mature and productive time of life; menopause is not viewed as a marker of decline by Japanese women or their physicians. Research has shown that women in Asian cultures, as well as non-industrialized cultures, consistently report fewer and less severe menopausal symptoms (Gupta, Sturdee, & Hunter, 2006; Huang et al., 2010). For example, one study of Chinese women found that only one third reported experiencing hot flashes and less than one third experienced night sweats (Liu & Eden, 2007).

Similarly, Mayan women of the Yucatán achieve increased status with menopause along with freedom from child-rearing (Beyene & Martin, 2001). Mayan women marry as teenagers and by the late 30s typically have given birth to many children. Many Mayan women are eager to escape the burden of child-rearing and describe menopause in positive terms such as providing freedom, being happy, and feeling like a young girl again. Few report menopausal symptoms such as hot flashes (Beyene & Martin, 2001). In fact, there is no word in the Mayan language to describe hot flashes (Beyene, 1986). Women in rural India also report menopause as a welcomed time that is accompanied by enhanced mobility, freedom from unwanted pregnancy, and increased authority (Gupta et al., 2006).

Western women tend to have mixed feelings about menopause. They frequently describe the negatives including a loss of fertility and the physical changes that accompany it, feeling less feminine, and having a clear sign of aging (Chrisler, 2008). At the same time, menopause represents the end of dealing with menstrual periods, the end of contraceptive worries, and a sense of liberation. Older women tend to have more positive views of menopause than do younger women and are more likely to report feeling a sense of freedom and confidence (Chrisler, 2008).

What Do You Think?

1. From your perspective, how do adults in the United States view menopause? For example, how does television depict menopause or menopausal women? Identify examples in popular media to support your perspective.

2. How might individuals' perception of developments such as menopause influence what they experience (and the reverse)?

2006). For example, products designed to treat so-called "low T" are commonly advertised on television despite research suggesting that only about 6% to 10% of men experience testosterone deficiency (Araujo et al., 2004; Haring et al., 2010) Similar to the medicalization of menopause, viewing normative hormonal changes experienced by men as a disease contributes to negative views of normal aging.

Thinking in Context 15.2

1. Contextual factors, such as socioeconomic status, influence all aspects of physical aging, including the rate and form that aging takes. How might contextual factors influence the sensory changes that occur over the adult years? Reproductive changes?

2. Physical characteristics such as appearance and reproductive capacity influence adults' sense of attractiveness and desirability. How might age-related changes in physical characteristics influence and shape middle-aged adults' sense of self?

3. Compare menopause with menarche. How is the process of menopause similar and different from menarche? What is the role of context in shaping women's experience and perspective on each?

HEALTH IN MIDDLE ADULTHOOD

Although the middle adult years are generally characterized by good health, they are a time when many people begin to notice some declines in health and physical abilities. As we have discussed, changes in strength and endurance become noticeable, especially among adults who lead sedentary lifestyles. In middle adulthood, the rate of chronic illnesses increases, as do doctor's visits and hospital stays. Most midlife adults view themselves as healthy; however, self-reports of health vary by contextual condition. For example, in nearly all countries of the world, self-reports of health and death rates vary by socioeconomic status. People of high socioeconomic status report better health than those of low socioeconomic status (Mackenbach et al., 2008).

Cancer is the leading cause of death in middle adulthood, followed by cardiovascular disease and accidents (Centers for Disease Control and Prevention [CDC], 2015). Deaths by accident decrease over the adult years. Gains in life experience and declines in impulsivity reduce risk taking and novelty seeking through middle adulthood. The following sections discuss leading health concerns of middle-aged adults, including cancer, cardiovascular disease, and osteoporosis. Note that, until recently, nearly all studies of health in adulthood were conducted on men, particularly Caucasian men. Women and minorities are underrepresented in research on prevention and treatment of illness. Researchers have only recently begun to address this deficit in our understanding of illness. The following sections describe what we know about several common illnesses, discussing sex and ethnic differences when possible.

CANCER

Rates of cancer have declined 20% since the mid-1990s (Siegel, Ma, Zou, & Jemal, 2014), but cancer remains the leading cause of death in middle age, responsible for about one third of deaths between the ages of 45 and 64 (CDC, 2015; National Center for Health Statistics, 2015). It is estimated that nearly 15% of adults between the ages of 45 and 64 will develop cancer (National Cancer Institute, 2012). Adults aged 45 to 64 account for 37% of the nearly 1.7 million diagnoses of cancer each year (Siegel et al., 2014) Overall, men tend to be diagnosed with cancer at a higher rate than women (Siegel et al., 2014). Sex differences in cancer are influenced by genetics and lifestyle factors such as workplace exposure to toxins, health-related behaviors such as smoking, and fewer visits to the doctor. People of low socioeconomic status tend to experience cancer at higher rates than do other adults because of inadequate access to medical care, poor diet, high levels of stress, and occupations that may place them in contact with toxins (Jemal et al., 2008; Vona-Davis & Rose, 2009).

What is cancer? Cancerous cells are abnormal cells. Everyone has some of these abnormal cells. Cancer occurs when the genetic program that controls cell growth is disrupted. As a result, abnormal cells reproduce rapidly and spread to normal tissues and organs and the person is diagnosed with cancer. Cancer cells might undergo uncontrolled growth for three reasons. Cell mutations may cause cancer genes known as oncogenes to undergo abnormal cell division or interfere with tumor suppressor genes that keep oncogenes from multiplying (Lin et al., 2007; Vogelstein & Kinzler, 2004). Finally, cell mutations may prevent cells from repairing the DNA errors that occur as a function of cell division as well as those that occur from exposure to environmental toxins and free radicals. Whether an individual develops cancer is affected by a complex web of genetic and environmental influences.

Scientific breakthroughs have increased our knowledge of genetic risk factors for cancer. For example, women now can be tested for mutations in the genes responsible for suppressing the proliferation of breast cancer cells. Genetics, however, is not destiny. Only about 35% to 50% of women who test positive for the genetic mutation actually develop breast cancer. Those who do show more genetic mutations and tend to develop breast cancer especially early in life, often before age 30 (Stephens et al., 2012). Whether a genetic risk factor for breast cancer leads

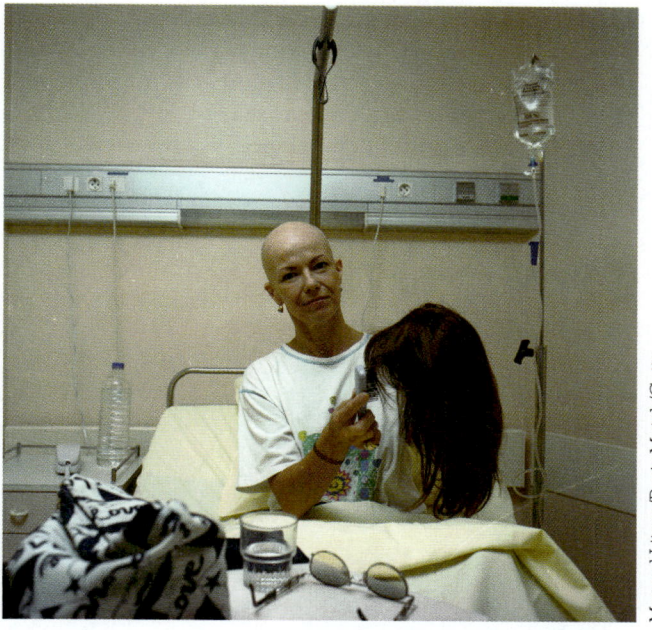

Cancer rates have declined over the last two decades and survival rates have risen to nearly three-quarters of diagnoses, but it remains the leading cause of mortality in middle age.

to developing breast cancer is influenced by the presence of environmental risk factors, such as heavy alcohol use, overweight, use of oral contraceptives, exposure to toxins, and low socioeconomic status (Khan, Afaq, & Mukhtar, 2010; Nickels et al., 2013). The biology of breast cancer is age dependent: Early-onset breast cancer is qualitatively different than late-onset breast cancer. While early-onset breast cancers are largely inherited and are often invasive, spreading quickly, late-onset breast cancers tend to grow more slowly, are less biologically aggressive, and likely follow extended exposures to environmental stimuli as well as disruptions in cell division that occur with aging (Benz, 2008). Although many people persist in the centuries-old belief that a diagnosis of cancer is a death sentence, today's medical advances permit more people to survive cancer than ever before. About 70% of adults aged 45 to 64 diagnosed with cancer survive at least five years, and many experience remission, "beating" cancer. Survival and cure rates vary by type of cancer.

CARDIOVASCULAR DISEASE

Cardiovascular disease is responsible for over one quarter of deaths of middle-aged Americans each year (National Center for Health Statistics, 2015). Markers of cardiovascular disease include high blood pressure; high blood cholesterol; plaque buildup in the arteries (arthrosclerosis; see Figure 15.2); irregular heartbeat; and, particularly serious, heart attack (blockage of blood flow to the heart caused by a blood clot occurring within a plaque-clogged coronary artery; Koh, Han, Oh, Shin, & Quon, 2010). Cardiovascular

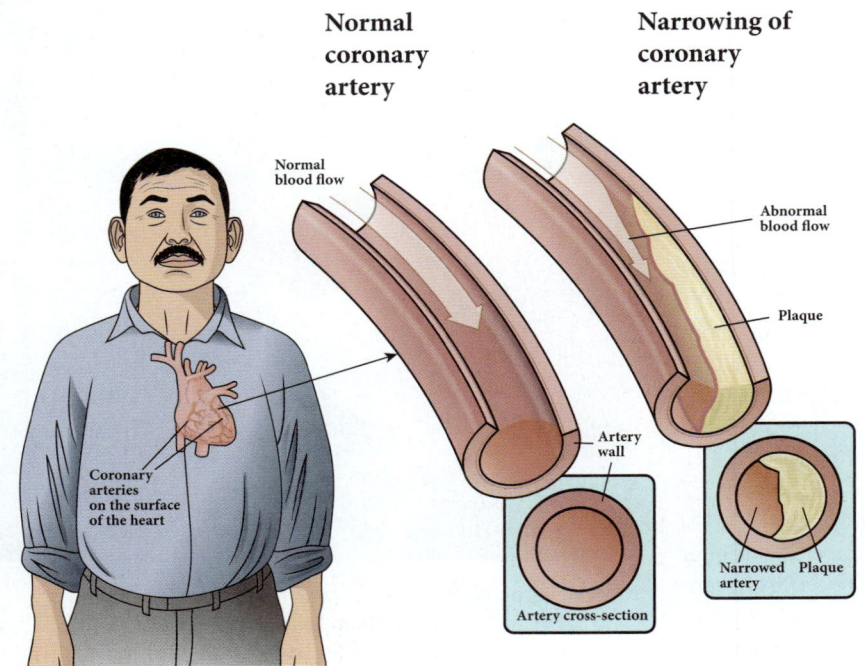

FIGURE 15.2: Cardiovascular Disease

Normal coronary artery

Narrowing of coronary artery

Normal blood flow

Abnormal blood flow

Plaque

Coronary arteries on the surface of the heart

Artery wall

Artery cross-section

Narrowed artery

Plaque

SOURCE: National Heart, Lung, and Blood Institute. (2014).

disease can also cause a stroke: After originating in the coronary arteries, a blood clot can travel to the brain, causing stroke, which can result in neurological damage, paralysis, and death.

Risk factors for cardiovascular disease include heredity, age, a diet heavy in saturated and trans fatty acids, and smoking (Go et al., 2013). One important risk factor, hypertension, has increased rapidly in the last two decades to account for over one third of U.S. adults ages 45 to 59 (Egan, Zhao, & Axon, 2010). By 2030, 40.5% of the U.S. population is projected to have some form of cardiovascular disease (Heidenreich et al., 2011). Hypertension is a global problem responsible for about 13% of all deaths in the world each year (World Health Organization, 2015). Anxiety, psychological stress, and a poor diet have negative effects on the heart and contribute to hypertension and cardiovascular disease (Backé, Seidler, Latza, Rossnagel, & Schumann, 2012; Holt et al., 2013).

Awareness of the symptoms of heart attack is critical to surviving it. About half of heart attack victims die before being admitted to a hospital (American Heart Association, 2008a). The most common symptom of heart attack is chest pain. Most heart attacks are accompanied by the sense of uncomfortable pressure, squeezing, fullness, or pain in the chest. The pain may come and go or may last. Other symptoms include discomfort or pain in other areas of the upper body, especially the left arm or both arms, but also the back, neck, jaw, or stomach. Shortness of breath can occur before or with the chest pain. Other symptoms include breaking out in a cold sweat, nausea, or light-headedness. Cardiovascular

disease has been traditionally viewed as an illness affecting men, as men are more likely to be diagnosed with cardiovascular disease. However, women are more likely to die from cardiovascular disease, especially heart attack. In addition, women tend to show different symptoms of heart attack and are more likely to report experiencing four or more symptoms than are men (Kirchberger, Heier, Kuch, Wende, & Meisinger, 2011). The most common symptom experienced by women is shortness of breath. Only about one third report chest pain, the hallmark symptom in men (McSweeney Cody, O'Sullivan, Elberson, Moser, & Garvin, 2003). When they do, they are more likely to describe it as pressure or tightness than pain. Women are more likely than men to report pain in the left shoulder or arm, pain in the throat or jaw, pain in the upper abdomen, pain between the shoulder blades, nausea, dizziness, and vomiting (Kirchberger et al., 2011).

Treatment for cardiovascular disease varies depending on the severity. Medication and behavioral changes, such as increasing physical activity, changing diet, and consuming more fish oil, may reduce hypertension and cholesterol levels (Harris et al., 2008; Koh et al., 2010). In serious cases, coronary bypass surgery may be recommended, in which damaged coronary blood vessels are replaced with those from the leg, and angioplasty, in which a needle is threaded through the arteries and a tiny balloon is inflated to flatten plaque deposits against the arterial walls and enable blood to flow unobstructed. For angioplasty, a coronary stent is often inserted to help keep the artery open. As shown in Table 15.2, various lifestyle choices can help to prevent heart disease.

OSTEOPOROSIS

The normative bone loss that occurs with reproductive aging increases the risk of osteoporosis, a disorder entailing severe bone loss that leads to brittle and easily fractured bones (Walker, 2008). About half of U.S. adults are affected by osteoporosis (10 million people) or low bone mass (Wright et al., 2014); these conditions can be identified through a routine, noninvasive bone scan. Declines in estrogen cause postmenopausal women to lose about 25% of their bone mass in the first ten years after menopause, increasing to about 50% by late adulthood (Avis et al., 2005; Vondracek, 2010). Men experience a more gradual and less extreme loss of bone, because age-related decreases in testosterone, which their bodies convert to estrogen, occur slowly; therefore, the loss of

TABLE 15.2 Prevent Heart Disease

Cardiovascular or heart disease is the second most common cause of death for middle-aged adults (and third for young adults). Lifestyle choices play a large role in the development of heart disease. Follow these guidelines to reduce your risk of heart disease.

GUIDELINE	DESCRIPTION
Don't smoke or use tobacco.	Smokers have more than twice the risk of heart disease. Chemicals in tobacco and cigarette smoke, including nicotine and carbon monoxide, make your heart work harder by narrowing your blood vessels and increasing blood pressure, leading to atherosclerosis and potentially a heart attack.
Reduce blood cholesterol levels.	Heart disease risk increases along with blood cholesterol levels. Cholesterol contributes to the formation of plaque inside the heart's arteries, leading to atherosclerosis.
Control high blood pressure.	Blood pressure is the force of blood pushing against the walls of the arteries as the heart pumps blood. High blood pressure increases the risk of heart attack and damage to the arteries and heart.
Exercise regularly.	Exercise lowers your risk of heart disease. Regular exercise will also help lower "bad" cholesterol and raise "good" cholesterol. Research has shown that getting at least 30 minutes of moderate physical activity on five or more days of the week can help lower blood pressure, lower cholesterol, and keep your weight at a healthy level.
Follow a heart-healthy diet.	Eat a diet low in fat, cholesterol, and salt and rich in fruits, vegetables, whole grains, and low-fat dairy products. Limit red meat, a source of unhealthy fat, and increase consumption of low-fat sources of protein such as beans and fish. Fish is a source of omega-3 fatty acids, a type of healthy fat, which may decrease your risk of heart attack, protect against irregular heartbeats and lower blood pressure.
Achieve and maintain a healthy weight.	Excess weight strains your heart and is associated with heart disease factors such as diabetes, high blood pressure, and high cholesterol.
Manage stress and anger.	Stress can increase the risk factors for heart disease. For example, people under stress may overeat, start smoking, or smoke more than they otherwise would.

bone mass that occurs with declines in estrogen occurs gradually over the adult years (Avis & Crawford, 2006; Walker, 2008). Most people—men and women—are diagnosed with osteoporosis only after experiencing bone fractures, but one out of every two women and one in four men over 50 will have an osteoporosis-related fracture in their lifetime (NIH Osteoporosis and Related Bone Diseases National Resource Center, 2007). Men at risk for osteoporosis are those with low body mass and the very old. Because women are more widely known to be at risk, men often go undiagnosed and untreated (Liu et al., 2008).

Heredity and lifestyle contribute to the risk of osteoporosis. For example, at least 15 genes contribute to osteoporosis susceptibility (Li et al., 2010). Identical twins are more likely to share a diagnosis of osteoporosis than are fraternal twins (Andersen, 2007). Thin, small-framed women tend to attain a lower peak bone mass than do other women and are at relatively higher risk of osteoporosis. Other risk factors include a sedentary lifestyle, calcium deficiency, cigarette smoking, and heavy alcohol consumption (Bleicher et al., 2011; Nachtigall, Nazem, Nachtigall, & Goldstein, 2013).

Osteoporosis can be prevented by encouraging young people to maximize their bone density by consuming a diet rich in calcium and vitamin D and engaging in regular exercise from childhood through adulthood (Nachtigall et al., 2013). These same diet and activity guidelines, specifically having a bone-healthy lifestyle, as well as medication that increases the absorption of calcium, can slow the bone loss associated with osteoporosis in middle adulthood (Vondracek, 2010). Consuming a diet rich in calcium and vitamin D, avoiding smoking and heavy drinking, and engaging in moderate alcohol consumption and weight-bearing exercise can offset bone loss in postmenopausal women (Berg et al., 2008; Bleicher et al., 2011; Guadalupe-Grau, Fuentes, Guerra, & Calbet, 2009).

WELLNESS

Caught in a traffic jam on the highway, Natasha used her mobile phone to call her husband. "Hi, honey, I'm running late. Can you start cooking dinner?" He replied, "Sorry, I'm not home yet. I've got a late meeting." Natasha sighed, "Okay. I'll call the babysitter and ask her to stay late. I still have to stop at Mom's house to drop off her medicine, and this traffic doesn't look like it will ease up anytime soon. I didn't expect Mom's giving up driving to take up so much of my time."

Perhaps it is not surprising that middle-aged adults experience more daily stresses than adults of any other age (Holliday, 2007). Colloquially referred to as the "sandwich generation," middle-aged adults are pressed to meet not only the multiple demands of career and family but often the demands of caring for two generations, their children and their elderly parents. As we have discussed in Chapter 12, the accumulation of daily hassles, such as traffic jams, workplace conflict, and child care difficulties, can influence our mood, ability to cope, and even our health. An overload of daily hassles, the experience of negative life events (such as job loss or illness), and disadvantageous contextual factors (such as poverty, a lack of access to medical care, and unsafe communities), contribute to poor health and illness (Almeida, Neupert, Banks, & Serido, 2005; Lantz, House, Mero, & Williams, 2005), especially when perceived as out of control (Hay & Diehl, 2010).

Change itself, whether positive or negative, is experienced as stress. Generally, the more stressful changes that take place, the more likely a person is to experience an acute illness or flare-up of a chronic illness. Stress harms health directly through physiological effects, such as increases in blood pressure, and psychological effects, such as anxiety and depression (Reagan, Grillo, & Piroli, 2008; Segerstrom & O'Connor, 2012). Exposure to stress also harms health indirectly, through behavioral responses to stress. Under stress, individuals may smoke and drink more, sleep less, get less exercise, and eat more poorly (Cropley & Steptoe, 2005). Chronic stress is associated with acute illnesses, such as cold and flu, as well as chronic illnesses, such as hypertension, arteriosclerosis, cardiovascular disease, cancer, and autoimmune diseases (e.g., lupus, Graves disease, chronic fatigue syndrome; Cass, 2006; Segerstrom & O'Connor, 2012; Stojanovich & Marisavljevich, 2008).

Stress management is an important way of reducing the negative mental and physical health effects of stress. When people learn to control their reactions to stress by using relaxation techniques, meditation, and biofeedback, they can reduce the incidence and severity of illness. An important way of reducing stress and promoting health and wellness is exercise (Gerber & Pühse, 2009; Johnson, 2007). Physically fit individuals show less psychological reactivity (e.g., spikes in blood pressure) to, and improved recovery from, psychological stressors than do unfit individuals (Forcier, Stroud, & Papandonatos, 2006).

Exercise reduces the physiological effects of stress, as it improves vascular function, reduces risk of cardiovascular disease, and protects against other health problems (Gerber & Pühse, 2009; Johnson, 2007). The health benefits of exercise persist throughout the adult years, but most middle-aged adults do not get the exercise that they need. Despite the proven benefits of physical activity, more than 50% of U.S. adults do not get enough physical activity to provide health benefits, and over one third are inactive in their leisure time (Physical Activities Council, 2015).

Many middle-aged adults face a variety of obstacles to regular exercise such as lack of time, family and work conflicts, lack of energy, and the challenges of being overweight. Middle-aged adults who begin and maintain an exercise program gain a sense of self-efficacy, the belief that they can be successful, which aids their progress in becoming more active and healthy (Blanchard et al., 2007; Purath, Miller, McCabe, & Wilbur, 2004).

Health is influenced not just by behavioral choices, such as coping effectively with stress and maintaining an exercise program, but also by attitudes and personality style. Optimism, conscientiousness, and positive emotions are associated with good health (Dainese et al., 2011; Friedman & Kern, 2014). People who score high on measures of hostility and anger, who tend to view others as having hostile intentions and are easily angered, are at risk for negative health outcomes, such as heart disease and atherosclerosis (Brydon et al., 2010; Friedman & Kern, 2014). Anger is physiologically arousing, stress hormones course through the body, increasing heart rate and blood pressure. Frequently angry displays and ruminating about events that invoke anger and other negative emotions can lead to high blood pressure that persists and, ultimately, heart disease (Brydon et al., 2010; Ohira et al., 2008).

Blend/Alamy

Middle-aged adults experience more daily hassles than adults of other ages, which pose risks to health and well-being.

Some adults are better able than others to adapt to the physical changes of midlife and the stress wrought by the changes in lifestyle that accompany midlife transitions, such as juggling career with caring for children and parents, and tend to display the personal characteristic that researchers refer to as **hardiness** (Maddi, 2007b). Individuals who display hardiness tend to have a high sense of self-efficacy, feeling a sense of control over their lives and experiences. They also view challenges as opportunities for personal growth and feel a sense of commitment to their life choices.

Hardy individuals tend to appraise stressful situations more positively, viewing them as manageable, approach problems with an active problem-focused coping style, and show fewer negative reactions to stressful situations (Bartone, 2006; Vogt, Rizvi, & Shipherd, 2008). The positive appraisals and sense of control that come with hardiness serve a protective function as they are associated with lower emotional reactivity, lower average blood pressure, slower progression of cardiovascular disease, and positive self-ratings of physical and mental health (Maddi, 2013; Sandvik et al., 2013). People who score low in hardiness tend to feel less control; experience more negative reactions to stressful situations; and are more likely to use an emotion-focused style of coping, such as avoidance or denial, which is maladaptive to health and functioning and is associated with higher stress in response to stimuli (Dolbier, Smith, & Steinhardt, 2007).

Hardiness, however, can, be learned. Training in hardy skills and attitudes, such as coping, social support, relaxation and stress reduction, nutrition, and physical activity, can increase feelings of control, challenge, and commitment that are central to hardiness (Maddi, 2007a). There is some evidence that hardy leaders can indeed increase hardy cognitions and behaviors in groups, influencing the meaning-making process so that situations are interpreted as interesting, challenging opportunities to grow and controllable (Bartone, 2006; Bartone, Roland, & Picano, 2008).

Jewel Samad/AFP/Getty

Individuals' sense of hardiness can be enhanced by learning stress management and coping techniques, such as meditation.

Fortunately, most people tend to show more adaptive responses to stress as they progress through middle adulthood. They learn to anticipate stressful events, take steps to avoid them, and approach stressful situations with more realistic attitudes about their ability to change them (Aldwin & Levenson, 2001). Overcoming stressful conditions and personal challenges contributes to a growing sense of self-efficacy over middle adulthood.

Thinking in Context 15.3

1. Genetic tests can reveal whether an individual has a gene for an illness such as cancer. What does a positive test, suggesting the presence of the gene for an illness, mean? Considering the influence of lifestyle and epigenetics (from Chapter 2), what advice would you give to a person who has the gene for an illness such as cancer?

2. Apply the bioecological framework to explain the myriad of factors that influence health and wellness in middle adulthood. Identify factors at the microsystem, mesosystem, exosystem, and macrosystem that can act as risk and protective factors to health during midlife.

3. Provide advice to a friend about what he or she can do to ensure a healthy middle age.

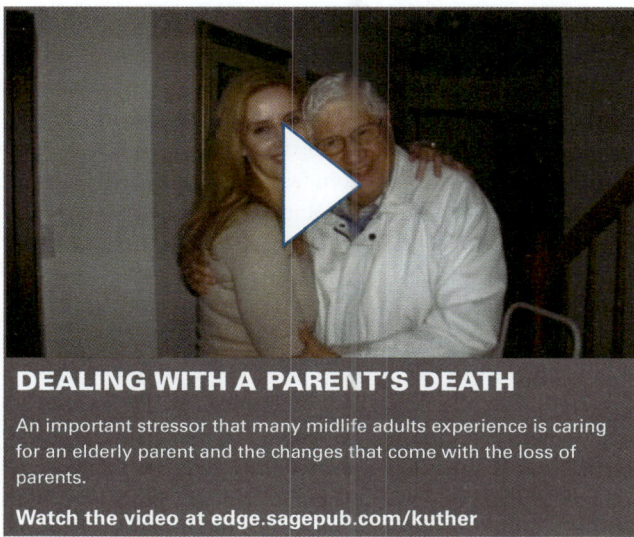

DEALING WITH A PARENT'S DEATH

An important stressor that many midlife adults experience is caring for an elderly parent and the changes that come with the loss of parents.

Watch the video at edge.sagepub.com/kuther

INTELLECTUAL ABILITIES IN MIDDLE ADULTHOOD

As we have seen, middle adulthood is a time of change in physical functioning. Are the physical changes of middle adulthood accompanied by cognitive changes? One way of assessing cognitive capacities is with the use of IQ tests. In Chapter 8, we discussed the most commonly used intelligence test, the Wechsler Adult Intelligence Scale (WAIS). The skills measured by the WAIS can be organized into two forms of intelligence: fluid and crystallized.

FLUID AND CRYSTALLIZED INTELLIGENCE

Intelligent people know a lot. They have a knowledge base acquired through experience and education. This accumulation of facts and information comprises **crystallized intelligence** (Cattell, 1963; Horn & Cattell, 1966). Examples of crystallized intelligence include memory of spelling, vocabulary, formulas, and dates in history. Although critics argue that crystallized intelligence measures examine an individual's accumulated knowledge rather than intelligence itself, people who score high on measures of crystallized intelligence not only know more but they learn more easily and remember more information than do people with lower levels of crystallized intelligence (Horn & Noll, 1997).

While crystallized intelligence refers to accumulated knowledge, **fluid intelligence** refers to a person's underlying capacity to make connections among ideas and draw inferences. Fluid intelligence permits flexible, creative, and quick thought, which enables people to solve problems quickly and adapt to complex and rapidly changing situations. Information processing abilities, such as the capacity of working memory, attention, and speed of analyzing information, influence fluid intelligence (Salthouse & Pink, 2008). Fluid and crystallized intelligence make up two separate components to intelligence (Nisbett et al., 2013), but they interact in the sense that the basic information processing capacities that embody fluid intelligence make it easier for a person to acquire knowledge and develop crystallized intelligence. That said, the relationship is not causal. Longitudinal research with midlife and older adults showed no dynamic relationship between verbal and other factors over a 16-year period, suggesting that changes in fluid abilities may not drive age changes in crystallized abilities (Christensen, Batterham, & Mackinnon, 2013; Finkel, Reynolds, McArdle, & Pedersen, 2007).

INTELLIGENCE OVER THE ADULT YEARS

How does intelligence change over the adult years? There is no simple answer to this question. Researchers using different methods have drawn different conclusions about adult intelligence. Recall from Chapter 1 that researchers learn about how people differ by age and how they change over time with the use of cross sectional, longitudinal, and cross-sequential research designs. The conclusions that researchers draw regarding intellectual change in adulthood vary with each research design.

Until recently, most researchers believed that intelligence declined with age. Early cross-sectional studies, comparing adults of various ages at once, showed clear age differences in IQ scores whereby intelligence peaked in early adulthood, declined through middle adulthood, and dropped steeply in late adulthood (Salthouse, 2014). Longitudinal studies, however, show a different picture of intellectual development in adulthood (Horn & Donaldson, 1976; Schaie, 2013). Research following children evaluated

from childhood through middle age (up to age 50) demonstrated that, contrary to prior findings from cross sectional research, intelligence scores increased into middle adulthood, especially on tests that reflect accumulated knowledge or expertise (Bayley, 1955; Deary, 2014).

How does intelligence change over the adult years? Why are the findings of cross-sectional studies very different from those of longitudinal studies? K. Warner Schaie examined this question in his groundbreaking study of intellectual change in adulthood, the Seattle Longitudinal Study. Because cross-sectional and longitudinal studies offer contradictory pictures of intellectual change in adulthood, Schaie employed a cross-sequential design that combined both research methodologies to disentangle the effects of age (change over time) and cohort (change over generations; Schaie, 1993, 2013). During the first wave of data collection, in 1956, adults ages 22 to 70 were tested. These individuals were followed up at regular intervals and new samples of adults were added. To date, the Seattle Longitudinal Study has examined over 5,000 men and women and has yielded five cross-sectional comparisons and over 60 years of longitudinal data.

The findings of the Seattle Longitudinal Study show the typical drop in intelligence scores after the mid-30s but also the typical longitudinal finding that there are modest gains through middle age that are sustained into the 60s, followed by gradual declines thereafter (Schaie, 2013; Schaie & Zanjani, 2006). As shown in Figure 15.3, crystallized and fluid intelligence show different patterns of change over the adult years. The components of crystallized intelligence, such as verbal ability and inductive reasoning, remain stable and even increase into middle adulthood, suggesting that individuals expand and retain their wealth of knowledge over their lifetimes. On the other hand, fluid intelligence, such as perceptual speed and spatial orientation, decreases beginning in the 20s, suggesting that cognitive processing slows, somewhat, with age (Horn & Masunaga, 2000; McArdle, Ferrer-Caja, Hamagami, & Woodcock, 2002; Schaie, 2013). Other samples of adults have supported these findings of gains in crystallized intelligence through middle adulthood coupled with gradual declines in fluid intelligence (Dellenbach & Zimprich, 2008; Kaufman, 2001; Singer, Verhaeghen, Ghisletta, Lindenberger, & Baltes, 2003). In late adulthood, both types of intelligence decline (Schaie, 2013).

Why does fluid intelligence decline over the adult years? Declines in performance on tasks measuring fluid intelligence may be due to the biological slowing of the central nervous system, as evident in declines in processing speed (Kaufman, 2001; Salthouse & Pink, 2008). Other research points to declines in frontal lobe functioning and reductions in interconnectivity in explaining declines in fluid intelligence (Bugg, Zook, DeLosh, Davalos, & Davis, 2006; Geerligs, Maurits, Renken, & Lorist, 2014). The ability to quickly update one's working memory is closely related to measures of fluid intelligence and some research suggests that it is the decline in working memory updating rather than speed that causes age changes in fluid intelligence (Unsworth, Fukuda,

FIGURE 15.3: Longitudinal Changes in Crystallized and Fluid Intelligence Over the Adult Years

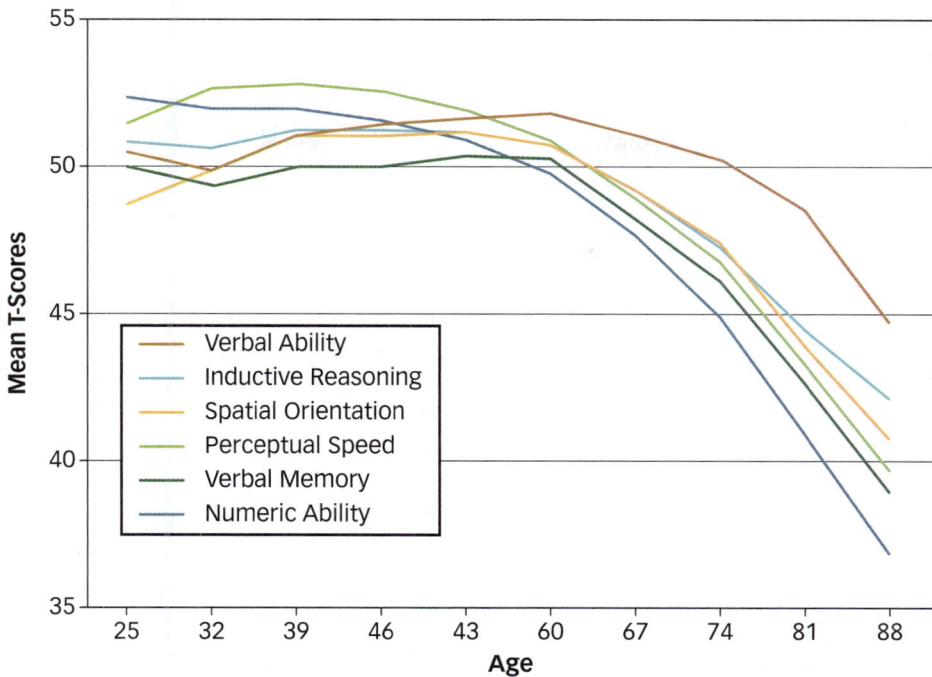

Longitudinal research shows stability over the adult years in most intellectual competencies, especially crystallized abilities, with declines occurring in late adulthood. In contrast, fluid abilities, such as perceptual speed, show steady decline throughout the adult years.

SOURCE: Schaie (2005).

Awh, & Vogel, 2014). Most notably, training in tasks that tap working memory are associated with improvements in fluid intelligence tasks (Au et al., 2015)

An important finding of the Seattle Longitudinal Study is that there are large cohort effects in intelligence. Each cohort of adults has experiences unique to their generation that influence their intellectual development. From 1889 to 1973, each cohort of adults has scored higher in verbal memory and inductive reasoning, and lower in numeric ability, than previous generations (Schaie & Zanjani, 2006). IQ gains from one generation to another have been found in many countries, typically coinciding with the advent of modernization (Nisbett et al., 2013; Williams, 2013). In addition, the drop in intelligence scores that appears after midlife happens later in more recent cohorts (Schaie, 2013). These effects can be at least partially explained by generational changes in educational attainment. With each generation, young people complete more years of education, more exposure to testing, and advanced levels of education tend to emphasize logic and self-expression, skills measured by intelligence tests (Baker et al., 2015; Williams, 2013). In addition, declines in numeric ability with each cohort may reflect each generation's increasing reliance on computers for mathematical computation.

Overall, intellectual ability increases over the adult years, especially when individuals are engaged in intellectually complex occupational and leisure activities, which are more common among recent cohorts (see Lifespan Brain Development,

p. 436; Schaie, 2013). Research suggests that the tendency to engage in mentally simulating activities such as reading is influenced by crystallized intelligence; however, engaging in stimulating activities can enhance functional intelligence in all adults (Dellenbach & Zimprich, 2008). One study of middle-aged to older adults had an experimental group engage in diverse novel and mentally stimulating activities for 10 to 12 weeks and compared them to a control group. The experimental group showed gains in fluid intelligence—gains suggesting that even brief periods of cognitive stimulation can improve problem solving and promote flexible thinking (Tranter & Koutstaal, 2008). In addition, training and practice in attention and working memory skills improves performance on tasks targeting executive control processes (Au et al., 2015; Nisbett et al., 2013).

Intellectual capacity seems to follow the "use it or lose it" principle. Adults who use their intellectual skills tend to maintain them longer than do those who are less cognitively active. Individuals who have completed higher education, hold intellectually challenging occupations, and engage in intellectual leisure pursuits show a later decline in intellectual ability as compared with adults who are less engaged (Schaie, 2013). Contextual factors also influence intellectual decline (Nisbett et al., 2013). Whereas midlife is a time of intellectual growth, individuals who live in unfavorable environments such as those of pervasive poverty, or who have experienced serious illness, may experience intellectual declines far earlier than the average adult (Schaie, 2013).

LIFESPAN BRAIN DEVELOPMENT

The Middle-Aged Brain

It is in midlife that many people hit their stride. Despite changes in some fluid abilities, midlife adults tend to be skilled at the tasks of everyday life and calmly tackle life's challenges. Middle-aged adults demonstrate selective optimization with compensation by emphasizing strengths and minimizing weaknesses. However, cognition in midlife is not simply about managing deficits. Instead, many cognitive competencies increase and peak in middle adulthood, including crystallized intelligence; problem solving; and the ability to make accurate judgments about people, jobs, and the world around us (Schaie, 2013; Thornton & Dumke, 2005).

Changes in brain organization account for many of these advances. For example, brain myelination continues to grow throughout young adulthood and peaks in middle adulthood, especially in the frontal lobes and temporal lobes—areas known for language, communication, and executive function (Giorgio et al., 2010; Sowell et al., 2004; Wang & Young, 2014). Myelination contributes to midlife adults' ability to quickly assess situations, make decisions, and problem solve.

We have seen that midlife adults often face multiple stressors, such as supporting children, caring for aging parents, and juggling career responsibilities. Though they likely face more stressors than ever before, starting in their 40s, midlife adults tend to show a happier outlook on life than do young adults. They tend to feel more competent, in control, and flexible—characteristics that are adaptive for everyday problem solving. Changes in brain activity underlie these advances in self-regulation. For example, when young and older adults view upsetting and uplifting images, the young adults tend to show activation in the amygdala for both sets of images whereas the older adults showed amygdala activation for the positive but not the disturbing images (Mather & Carstensen, 2005). Recall that the amygdala is responsible for strong emotional reactions, especially aggression. Beginning in midlife, adults become less sensitive to negative stimuli (Carstensen & Mikels, 2005; Samanez-Larkin, Robertson, Mikels, Carstensen, & Gotlib, 2009).

Other research suggests midlife adults tend to have a rosy view of the world and tend to view neutral stimuli in a positive light (van Reekum et al., 2011). This positivity bias is adaptive for everyday functioning as midlife adults are able to manage challenging situations, ignore negative stimuli, and focus on the positive (Reed & Carstensen, 2012; Reed, Chan, & Mikels, 2014). Midlife gains in emotional regulation permit them to become adaptive problem solvers and more holistic thinkers.

What Do You Think?

1. **How do these findings compare with popular stereotypes of aging?**

2. **Think about the middle-aged adults you know. How well do they fit this portrayal? Why or why not?**

Thinking in Context 15.4

1. Cross-sectional and longitudinal research designs (see Chapter 1) often result in very different conclusions. Consider this problem using research findings on adult intelligence.

2. Why do we typically find large cohort differences in intellectual abilities? Consider the contextual changes that accompany recent generations. For example, consider your own experiences with those of your parents, grandparents, and even great-grandparents. How were your worlds different, and how might this contribute to differences on intelligence measures?

COGNITIVE DEVELOPMENT IN MIDDLE ADULTHOOD

The intellectual changes and continuities that occur over midlife are influenced by adults' capacities for information processing. For example, measures of fluid intelligence tap aspects of information processing such as attention, memory, and processing speed. Crystallized intelligence is influenced by adults' memory capacities and expertise. How do information processing abilities change over the midlife years?

ATTENTION

In what ways does attention change with age? Researchers who study attention examine how much information a person can attend to at once, the ability to divide attention and change focus from one task to another in response to situational demands, and the ability to selectively attend and ignore distracters and irrelevant stimuli. With age, it becomes more difficult to divide attention—that is, to engage in two complex tasks at once and focus on relevant information (Radvansky, Zacks, & Hasher, 2005). As with other capacities, age-related declines in attention are not uniform across adults and these differences predict variations in cognitive performance. In one study, those who performed better on cognitive tasks were more attracted to and spent more time viewing novel stimuli than those who performed at average levels (Daffner, Chong, & Riis, 2007). Moreover, the magnitude of the difference between cognitively high and cognitively average performing groups grew with age from middle adulthood into old age, suggesting that the link between engagement and novelty and higher cognitive performance increases with age.

Most adults find that inhibition, the ability to resist interference from irrelevant information to stay focused on the task at hand, becomes more difficult over the adult years (Rozas, Juncos-Rabadán, & González, 2008; Sylvain-Roy, Lungu, & Belleville, 2014). For example, laboratory tasks in which participants are presented with a series of letter combinations and told to press the space bar after viewing a particular combination (such as T-L) show that adults' performance declines steadily from the 30s on; with age, adults make more errors of commission—pressing the space bar after incorrect letter combinations (Mani, Bedwell, & Miller, 2005). Errors of omission—not pressing the space bar in response to the correct sequence—increased in the presence of extraneous noise. In everyday life, these changes in attention might make adults appear more easily distracted, less able to attend, and less able to take in information with age.

However, changes in attention are not always evident in real-life functioning (Kramer & Madden, 2008). Experience and practice matters (Glisky, 2007), and this is true for all information processing capacities. People in occupations that require detecting critical stimuli and engaging in multiple complex tasks, such as air traffic controllers, develop expertise in focusing and maintaining attention and show smaller declines with age (Kennedy, Taylor, Reade, & Yesavage, 2010; Morrow et al., 2003). Experts tend to use external supports more effectively (Morrow & Schriver, 2007). Practice also improves performance and reduces

Michael Blann/DigitalVision/Thinkstock

Performance on tasks requiring attention begins to decline in middle adulthood but practice can improve performance and reduce age-related declines.

age-related decline. For example, training in how to divide attention between two tasks by using selective attention and switching back and forth between mental operations, improves the performance of older adults as much as that of younger adults, although age differences in performance remain (Kramer & Madden, 2008).

MEMORY

Memory, essential to cognitive competence, changes substantially over the adult years. The capacity of working memory declines from the 20s through the 60s and is related to changes in attention (Rowe, Hasher, & Turcotte, 2010; Sylvain-Roy et al., 2014). Middle-aged and older adults are less able to recall lists of words and numbers than are young adults; memory for prose shows similar, though less extreme, decline (Old & Naveh-Benjamin, 2008). Age differences in performance on working memory tasks can be partially explained by a decline in the use of memory strategies with age (Braver & West, 2008; Craik & Rose, 2012).

With age, adults are less likely to apply the memory strategies of organization and elaboration, which require that new information is linked with already-stored information (e.g., existing knowledge). From middle adulthood into old age, adults begin to have more difficulty retrieving information from long-term memory, which makes them less likely to spontaneously use organization and elaboration as memory strategies (Glisky, 2007). Changes in attention influence declines in working memory. As we age, it becomes more difficult to tune out irrelevant information, which then leaves less space in working memory for completing a given task (Levitt, Fugelsang, & Crossley, 2006; Radvansky et al., 2005).

Many laboratory tests of memory entail tasks that are similar to those encountered in school settings. Middle-aged and older adults may be less motivated by such tasks than younger adults who likely have more recent experience in school contexts. Laboratory findings, therefore, may not accurately illustrate the everyday memory capacity of middle-aged and older adults (Salthouse, 2012). For example, when the pace of a memory task is slowed, or participants are reminded to use organization or elaboration strategies, middle-aged and older adults show better performance (Braver & West, 2008). In addition, the type of task influences performance. For example, in one study, adults aged 19 to 68 completed memory tests under two conditions: a pressured classroom-like condition and a self-paced condition. When participants were shown a video and tested immediately (classroom-like condition), younger adults showed better recall than did the middle-aged adults. However, when participants were given a packet of information and a video to study on their own (self-paced condition), young and midlife adults did not differ on recall three days later (Ackerman & Beier, 2006; Beier & Ackerman, 2005), suggesting that with age and experience the ways in which we learn and remember

Laboratory tests of memory in middle-aged adults are influenced by factors such as motivation, task, and experience. Laboratory studies may not accurately measure the everyday memory capacity of middle-aged and older adults.

BSIP/Newscom

change. The midlife adults performed better when they could apply their own strategies and memorize the material at their own pace.

The declines in memory evident in laboratory research are less apparent in everyday settings (Salthouse, 2012). Knowledge of facts (e.g., scientific facts), procedures (e.g., how to drive a car), and information related to one's vocation either remain the same or increase over the adult years. As we have discussed, crystallized intelligence grows over the adult years (Schaie, 2013). Adults' experience and knowledge of their cognitive system (metacognition) permits them to use their memory and crystallized intelligence more effectively. For example, they use external supports and strategies to maximize their memory, such as by organizing their notes or placing their car keys in a designated spot to permit easy retrieval (Schwartz & Frazier, 2005). As with attention, memory declines vary with the individual and task. Most adults compensate for declines and show little to no differences in everyday settings; however, chronic stress impairs working memory (Lee & Goto, 2015). Midlife adults who feel overwhelmed in daily life, such as those faced with many conflicting responsibilities and stressors that demand a great deal of multitasking, are more likely to rate their memory competence as poor, likely an inaccurate portrayal of their abilities (Vestergren & Nilsson, 2011).

PROCESSING SPEED

The greatest change in information processing capacity with age is a reduction in the speed of processing. Simple reaction time tasks, such as pushing a button in response to a light, reveal a steady slowing of responses from the 20s into the 90s; see Figure 15.4 (Rozas et al., 2008; Salthouse, 1993). The more complex the task, the greater the age-related decline in reaction time. However, when reaction time tasks require a vocal response rather than a motor response, age-related declines are less dramatic (Johnson & Rybash, 1993).

In addition, adults' performance on standard tasks measuring processing speed is influenced by their capacities for attention. Adults who are highly distractible show slowed responding on standard tasks measuring processing speed, but their performance improves when tasks are designed to reduce distractions (e.g., by listing fewer items on a page). Reducing distractions improves performance, and the magnitude of improvement as a result of reducing distractions on tests of processing speed increases with age (Lustig, Hasher, & Tonev, 2006).

Processing speed is closely associated with performance on tasks measuring fluid intelligence (Salthouse, 1993; Salthouse & Pink, 2008). Declines in processing speed with age predict age-related declines in memory, reasoning, and problem-solving tasks (Levitt et al., 2006; Meijer, de Groot, van Gerven, van Boxtel, & Jolles, 2009). Moreover, the relationship between processing speed and performance on cognitive tasks becomes stronger with age (Chen & Li, 2007; Deming, Chang, Tianyong, & Guiyun, 2003; Salthouse & Pink, 2008). Changes in processing speed likely influence many of the cognitive declines associated with aging.

Why does cognitive processing slow with age? Changes in the brain underlie reductions in processing speed. The loss of white matter, myelinated connections, reduces processing speed (Bennett & Madden, 2014; Nilsson, Thomas, O'Brien, & Gallagher, 2014). In addition, the loss of neurons forces the remaining neurons to reorganize and form new, often less efficient, connections (Johnson & Rybash, 1993). Another explanation posits a loss of information with each step in cognitive processing. With age, cognitive resources decline, adults show more information loss with each step; as a result, when attempting a complex task, they perform more poorly than do young adults (Deming et al., 2003; Salthouse & Madden, 2013).

Although clearly apparent in laboratory tasks and highly reliable, the decline in the speed of processing is not as apparent in everyday situations. Middle- and older-aged adults proficiently engage in complex tasks every day, showing performance similar to, or better, than that of younger adults. For example, one study tested 19- to 72-year-olds on

FIGURE 15.4: Processing Speed Across the Lifespan

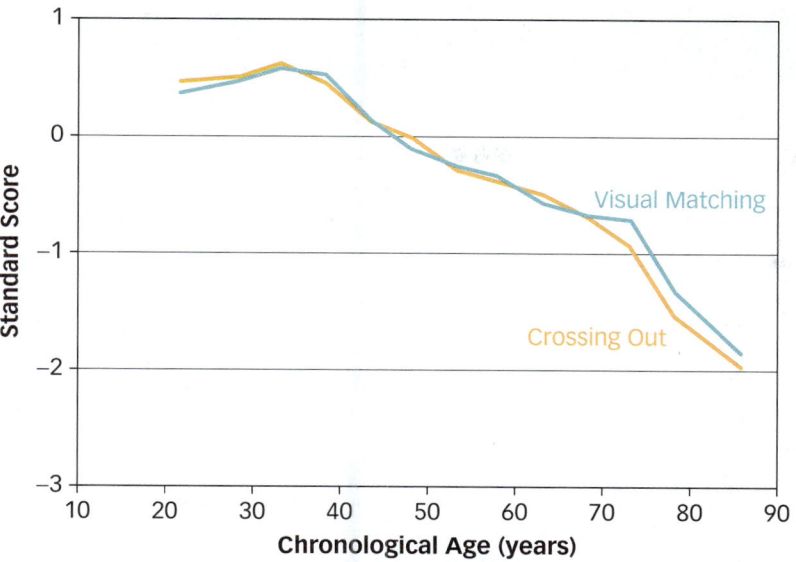

SOURCE: Salthouse (2000).

two tasks: a reaction time task and a typing task. Both tasks measured their speed and accuracy. Although the middle and older adults displayed slower reaction time as compared with young adults, their typing speed and accuracy was no different (Salthouse, 1984). With age, adults compensated for their slower reaction time by looking further ahead in the material to be typed, thereby anticipating keystrokes (Bosman, 1993; Salthouse, 1984). As they age, adults compensate for limitations in processing speed by modifying their activities to emphasize skills that rely on accumulated knowledge and thereby honing their crystallized intelligence (Bugg et al., 2006; Salthouse, 1996). Table 15.3 summarizes the changes that take place in information processing abilities over middle adulthood.

EXPERTISE

Over the course of midlife into old age, adults gain experience and knowledge, and demonstrate advances in practical problem solving in which they apply their experience and **expertise** to achieve goals and solve problems in the real world. With age, most adults develop and expand their expertise, an elaborate and integrated knowledge base that underlies extraordinary proficiency in a given task and that supports gains in practical problem solving. The development of expertise peaks in middle adulthood when experts are able to solve problems efficiently by using abstract reasoning and making intuitive judgments. Experts are not distinguished by extraordinary intellect but by knowledge and experience (Ericsson, 2014) Experts operate on hunches, intuitive judgments of how to approach a problem based on experience.

It is expertise that enables middle-aged and older adults to compensate for declines in processing speed and memory

(Ericsson & Moxley, 2013). Like the typists who compensated for declines in reaction time by looking further ahead in the material to be typed (Salthouse, 1984), one study of food service workers found that gains in expertise compensated for declines in physical performance. In this study, 20- to 60-year-old food service workers were compared on several aspects of expert performance: strength and dexterity, technical knowledge (e.g., of the menu), organizational skills (e.g., setting priorities), and social skills (e.g., providing professional service). Although middle-aged workers showed declines in physical abilities, they performed more efficiently and competently than did young adults, suggesting that expertise in other areas compensated for losses in strength and dexterity (Perlmutter, Kaplan, & Nyquest, 1990). Expert knowledge is transformative in that it permits a more sophisticated approach to problem solving than that of nonexperts. Specifically, expert thought is intuitive, automatic, strategic, and flexible (Ericsson, 2014).

Experts approach problems intuitively, relying on their past experience and evaluation of the context in determining their approach. With experience, experts' responses become automatic. As responses become automatic, information gets processed more quickly and efficiently and complex tasks become routine (Herzmann & Curran, 2011). Responses appear intuitive in that they are well rehearsed, seemingly without thought. As expertise grows experts find that their responses become so autonomic that it is hard for them to consciously explain what they do. For example, adults are better than children at tying shoelaces, yet children are far better than adults at explaining how to tie shoelaces (McLeod, Sommerville, & Reed, 2005).

In addition to operating more intuitively and automatically, expert behavior is strategic. Experts have a broader range of strategies and have better strategies than novices and can better apply them in response to unanticipated problems (Ericsson & Moxley, 2013). For example, one study presented airplane pilots with a flight simulation. They were given directions from air traffic controllers and allowed to take notes. The experienced pilots were more likely to take notes than the nonexpert pilots, and their notes tended to be more accurate and complete (Morrow et al., 2003). In actual flights comparing pilots aged 22 to 76, older pilots take more notes than do younger pilots but do not differ in their ability to repeat complex instructions regarding flight plans and conditions (Morrow et al., 2003). Similarly, expert golfers show fewer declines in performance with age as they compensate for their changing capacities (Logan & Baker, 2007). Longitudinal research with expert chess players showed that there are few age effects in chess skill (Moxley & Charness, 2013); those with greater expertise and participation in tournaments showed fewer age-related declines in chess performance but performed similarly in other areas (Roring & Charness, 2007).

TABLE 15.3 Cognitive Change During Middle Adulthood

COGNITIVE CAPACITY	AGE-RELATED CHANGE
Crystallized intelligence	Crystallized intelligence increases steadily over the adult years and declines modestly in late adulthood.
Fluid intelligence	Fluid intelligence begins to decline in the 20s and continues throughout adulthood.
Attention	With age, adults show more difficulties with divided attention and inhibition.
	Declines tend to vary with the individual and task.
	Most healthy adults compensate for declines and, until old age, show few differences in everyday settings.
Working memory	The capacity of working memory declines from the 20s through the 60s.
	Changes in working memory are influenced by declines in attention and in the use of memory strategies, such as organization and elaboration, that occur with age.
	Declines tend to vary with the individual and task.
	Most healthy adults compensate for declines and, until old age, show few differences in everyday settings.
Processing speed	Processing speed declines steadily from the 20s into the 90s.
	The more complex the task, the greater the age-related decline in reaction time.
	Declines in processing speed with age predict age-related declines in memory, reasoning, and problem-solving tasks, and the relationship between processing speed and performance on cognitive tasks becomes stronger with age.
Expertise	With age, most adults develop and expand their expertise.
	It is expertise that permits middle-aged and older adults to compensate for declines in processing speed.

Despite showing slower working memory, experts maintain their performance in their areas of expertise, often by relying on external supports, such as notes (Morrow & Schriver, 2007). Finally, intuitive and automatic application of a broad range of strategies permits experts to be more flexible than nonexperts. Experts are more open to deviating from formal procedures when they encounter problems. Experts often approach cases in an individualized way, varying their approach with contextual factors, and are sensitive to exceptions (Ormerod, 2005).

Expertise permits selective optimization with compensation, the ability to adapt to changes over time, optimize current functioning, and compensate for losses in order to preserve performance despite declines in fluid abilities (Baltes & Baltes, 1990; Baltes & Carstensen, 2003). As people age, they select aspects of functioning to optimize and improve their proficiency. Typically these are areas in which they excel. People spend effort increasing their expertise in their chosen areas, thereby optimizing their strengths (Bugg et al., 2006; Salthouse, 1984). In addition to emphasizing their strengths, people naturally devise ways of compensating for declines in physical functioning and fluid ability. Selective optimization with compensation occurs naturally—often without the individual's awareness as their expertise permits them to adapt to developmental changes. Older typists who look further ahead in their typing and experienced pilots who take more detailed notes are examples of expertise compensating for declines in working memory and processing speed. Successful aging entails selective optimization with compensation (Freund & Baltes, 2007).

LEARNING

In middle adulthood, career settings are important contexts for learning. Adults' careers provide opportunities for them to practice, maintain, and increase cognitive and problem-solving skills.

Adults who maintain their cognitive capacities tend to seek cognitive complexity and engage the world around them. In addition, experiencing cognitive challenges, such as a stimulating career, boosts cognitive skills over the adult years (Andel, Kåreholt, Parker, Thorslund, & Gatz, 2007). A growing number of midlife adults seek formal opportunities to enhance their learning. In fact, many employers and professional associations strongly encourage and often require that adults obtain continuing education to stay current in their fields. In recent years, the percentage increase in the number of students age 25 and over has been larger than the percentage increase in the number of younger students. Forty-two percent of students enrolled in American colleges and universities are adults aged 25 and up (National Center for Education Statistics, 2015).

Adults enroll in higher education for many reasons, such as to change careers, improve career opportunities, increase income, or gain personal enrichment (Sander, 2008). Over two thirds of adult learners are female (National Center for Education Statistics, 2015). Life transitions, such as divorce, unemployment, widowhood, or children entering school, often spur adults to return to formal education.

Reentering formal education is challenging. Most students, particularly women, juggle multiple and often

In 2009 Captain Sully Sullenberger successfully executed an emergency water landing of US Airways Flight 1549 in the Hudson River off Manhattan, New York City. He explained to CBS News anchor Katie Couric: "One way of looking at this might be that for 42 years, I've been making small, regular deposits in this bank of experience, education, and training. And on January 15 the balance was sufficient so that I could make a very large withdrawal."

conflicting demands of family, household, school, and work (Hostetler, Sweet, & Moen, 2007; Sweet & Moen, 2007). Divorce and responsibility for young children, more common among women, are associated with failure to complete a degree (Taniguchi & Kaufman, 2005). The multiple demands mean that most women who return to school will take fewer credits, experience more interruptions in academic progress, and will require more time to complete a degree than do returning men. Role overload often interferes with education and is the reason for failure to complete a degree (Sweet & Moen, 2007). Most returning students are aware of the challenges they face and express motivation to overcome them given the benefits of education, such as the excitement of learning, sense of personal enrichment, and value of a college degree in improving work life (Chao & Good, 2004).

Adult learners approach learning differently than traditional-age students and have unique needs. They enter learning environments with a wealth of experience on which to build. Adult learners tend to be problem-oriented in that they typically want to know why they should learn something and how it is relevant to solving problems in their jobs and personal lives (Knowles, Holton, & Swanson, 2014). They tend to value learning from experience over learning from listening to lectures considering abstract theories. Therefore, adult learners enter classroom settings with different expectations. Effective instruction for adult learners helps them discover their need to know by emphasizing experiential learning through discussion, problem-solving cases, laboratory experiments, and field experiences (Knowles, 1972). Returning students tend to show more intrinsic motivation for obtaining a college education than do traditional-age students (Bye, Pushkar, &

Conway, 2007; Knowles, 1970). Motivation is important, but returning students require support to succeed.

Returning students need support from family and friends, including emotional support and tangible assistance in making progress toward educational goals. For example, family members can help the returning student to set aside time for studying without distractions or interruptions. Colleges and universities also play a role in aiding adult learners. The availability of classes scheduled during evenings and weekends, and online, as well polices on financial aid for part time students, affects returning students' success. Opportunities to develop relationships with faculty are especially welcome by returning students, but because many take night courses and only a few credits each semester, they may be less likely to develop these close relationships. Like earlier in life, education transforms development, grants opportunities and financial rewards, and is a vehicle of self-development for midlife adults. Midlife adult students gain more than academic knowledge. They show advancements in social reasoning and self-evaluation skills (Demetriou & Bakracevic, 2009). The greater capacity to interact with others; understand social relationships; and understand themselves improve midlife adults' sense of self, their personal lives, and relationships.

Thinking in Context 15.5

1. Why are recent generations of adults maintaining their cognitive functioning longer than prior generations? What contextual factors might contribute to this change?

2. Generally speaking, cognitive declines apparent in laboratory settings are less apparent in everyday life. Discuss three examples of this. Why do adults show higher functioning in real-world settings than those in the laboratory? Given what you know about cognition and learning in adulthood, what advice would you give to a middle-aged adult who is entering college? What advice would you give instructors of adult learners?

RETURNING TO SCHOOL IN MIDLIFE

In this video, Cheryl describes the process of returning to college at age 47 in the wake of panic disorder.

Watch the video at edge.sagepub.com/kuther

Middle adulthood is a time of stability, change, and variability. Many aspects of development remain stable, such as knowledge and expertise, and others change, such as information processing skills. Variability marks midlife, especially when considering health. Most middle-aged adults report good health; however, several illnesses become more common. Lifestyle factors, such as smoking, excessive drinking, and exercising, influence heath and development throughout midlife. The degree to which adults maintain physical and cognitive capacities throughout middle adulthood influences the changes that they will experience in late adulthood, as we will discuss in Chapters 17 and 18.

Apply Your Knowledge

Over coffee, Wendy confides in her closest friends:

I sometimes wonder how I got here. I look in the mirror each day and am almost always surprised by the lines in my face and the graying of my hair. My body is changing, and I'm not sure what I think about it. Some is good, some . . . I don't know. Each time I go to aerobics class, I am quickly reminded that I am no longer 20. Yoga classes are a much better experience. I feel healthy, but my doctor still insists on administering a cardiac stress test during my annual checkup.

Her friend Latisha commiserates:

I made the mistake of scheduling my stress test before work. I didn't realize it entailed walking on a treadmill and getting sweaty! Sure, I'm no longer 20, but I'm healthy and I always remind myself that I still have my mind. Every time my son comes home from college, he's surprised that I win nearly every game of *Trivial Pursuit* we play. I keep reminding him that I have a lot of "useless" knowledge. However, sometimes I feel more forgetful and scattered than ever before. That worries me.

Violet laughs:

Try sitting in my classes. Going back to college has been a real eye-opener. Not only am I the oldest—the "mom" in the room—but it's sometimes embarrassing that I ask the most questions in class. We learned about Piaget last week, and I couldn't help but ask a ton of questions about what his theory means for my work with preschoolers. Sometimes it seems as though I'm the only one who cares.

1. What physical changes, such as sensory, strength, appearance, and reproductive, for example, can midlife adults expect? How might these physical changes influence their functioning?

2. Do you think that men and women show different patterns of physical changes and corresponding changes in functioning and how they view themselves? Why or why not?

3. Although these friends didn't discuss their health, what heath concerns are typical in midlife? What can men and women do to reduce risks and improve overall health?

4. Why might Latisha feel more scattered and forgetful? What cognitive changes occur during middle adulthood that may influence this? How do situational and contextual factors contribute to adults' feelings of forgetfulness?

5. Do you think Violet's concerns are common to returning students? Why or why not? What might Violet do to improve her experience?

6. What role does socioeconomic status play in physical and cognitive changes and how adults respond to them during middle adulthood? Is this pattern the same for men as for women?

Chapter Summary

15.1 Discuss age-related changes in vision and hearing during middle adulthood.

The eye undergoes many changes over the adult years. The cornea flattens, the lens loses flexibility, and accommodative ability declines, leading most adults in their 40s to show presbyopia. The loss of rods in middle age coupled with increases in the vitreous' opacity results in night vision declining twice as fast as day vision. In the 50s, presbycusis, becomes apparent. First limited to high-pitched sounds and more apparent in settings with background noise, by late adulthood hearing loss extends to all sound frequencies.

15.2 Explain normative patterns of change in the skin, muscles, and skeletal system during middle adulthood.

During middle adulthood, the skin becomes less taut and shows signs of aging, worsened by exposure to sun. Declines in strength and endurance become noticeable, but the rate and extent of change is influenced by physical activity. Men and women tend to gain body fat and lose muscle. Reducing caloric intake and remaining physically active helps adults retain their physical physique and competencies. Bone density reaches its height in the mid to late 30s, after which adults tend to experience gradual bone loss, making bones thinner, more porous, and more brittle and easily broken.

15.3 Compare and contrast the reproductive changes that middle-aged men and women experience.

Women experience menopause in midlife: the average age is about 51. Hot flashes are the most common symptom of perimenopause. The loss of estrogen increases some health risks, such as cardiovascular disease and osteoporosis. The timing of menopause is influenced by heredity but also by lifestyle choices. Women's experience of menopause is influenced by personal characteristics, circumstances, and societal views about women and aging. Men's reproductive ability declines gradually and steadily over the adult years, but most men continue to produce sperm throughout adulthood.

15.4 Discuss the common health conditions and illnesses during middle adulthood, including risk and protective factors as well as treatment.

Cancer and chronic health conditions are the result of a complex web of genetic and environmental influences. Advances in medicine have changed the nature of disease. More people survive cancer than ever before. Risk factors for cardiovascular disease include heredity, high blood pressure, poor diet, smoking, and psychological stress. Medication and behavioral changes may reduce hypertension and cholesterol

levels. Declines in estrogen as well as other factors place postmenopausal women at risk for osteoporosis. Intervention in the form of weight-bearing exercise, diet, and medication can prevent and slow the course of osteoporosis.

15.5 Explain ways of promoting wellness across the middle adult years.

Stress influences health directly through physiological effects, psychological effects, and behavioral responses. Chronic stress is associated with acute and chronic illnesses. Stress management as well as exercise can increase well-being. In addition, the positive appraisals and sense of control that come with hardiness serve a protective function on well-being and health. Training in hardy skills and attitudes, such as coping, social support, relaxation and stress reduction, nutrition, and physical activity, can increase feelings of control, challenge, and commitment that are central to hardiness.

15.6 Contrast the findings of cross-sectional and longitudinal studies of crystallized and fluid intelligence over adulthood.

The cross-sequential Seattle Longitudinal Study shows a cross-sectional drop in fluid intelligence after the mid-30s but also a longitudinal gain in crystallized intelligence in midlife that is sustained into the 60s. In late adulthood, both types of intelligence decline. Declines in performance on tasks measuring fluid intelligence may be due to the biological slowing of the central nervous system; however, intellectual engagement enhances crystallized intelligence as well as functional intelligence over the lifespan.

15.7 Analyze changes in cognitive capacities during middle adulthood, including attention, memory, processing speed, and expertise.

With age, it becomes more difficult to divide attention to engage in two complex tasks at once and focus on relevant information as well as to inhibit irrelevant information. The capacity of working memory declines with age because of a decline in the use of memory strategies and changes in attention. Processing speed declines from early adulthood through the middle to late adult years. An expanding knowledge base and growing expertise permits most adults to show few changes in cognitive capacity within everyday contexts and compensate for declines in processing speed.

15.8 Discuss learning during middle adulthood, particularly for adults who return to higher education.

Adults enroll in higher education for many reasons: to change careers, improve career opportunities, increase income, or gain personal enrichment. Returning students often approach learning differently than traditional-age college students. Most experience conflicting demands of family, household, school, and work. Returning students need support from family and friends—emotional support but also tangible assistance in making progress toward educational goals.

Key Terms

crystallized intelligence   434

dermis   423

epidermis   423

expertise   439

fluid intelligence   434

hardiness   433

hormone replacement therapy   426

hypodermis   423

inhibition   436

menopause   424

osteoporosis   427

perimenopause   425

presbycusis   422

presbyopia   422

selective optimization with compensation   436

CHAPTER 16

Socioemotional Development in Middle Adulthood

LEARNING OBJECTIVES

KEY STUDY TOOLS

16.1. Compare Erikson's and Levinson's perspectives of the psychosocial tasks of middle adulthood.

Watch The Psychology of Your Future Self

Explore Further Psychosocial Development

16.2. Analyze the theoretical and empirical support for the midlife crisis.

Think Critically Active Self-Acceptance

16.3. Evaluate the changes that occur in self-concept and identity during middle adulthood and their relation to well-being.

Video Case Personality in Midlife

16.4. Evaluate the stability of the Big 5 personality traits.

Explore Further Big 5 Personality Traits

16.5. Discuss the changing nature of friendship in middle adulthood.

Explore Further Friendships in Middle Adulthood

16.6. Discuss marital satisfaction, risks for divorce, and outcomes of divorce in midlife.

Explore Further Effects of Divorce

Listen Sex and Happiness

16.7. Analyze family relationships in midlife, including the parent adult–child, grandparent, and midlife child–older adult parent relationship.

Lives in Context First-Time Parenting in Midlife (p. 460)

Lives in Context Grandparents Raising Grandchildren (p. 463)

Video Case Relationships with Adult Children

16.8. Characterize job satisfaction during the midlife years.

Ethical and Policy Applications of Lifespan Development Age Discrimination (p. 467)

Connect More Than Job Satisfaction

16.9. Examine retirement planning and its effects in adjustment to retirement.

Think Critically Retirement Decisions

"I'm going to be late. I have a parent–teacher conference at John's school," Hal told the babysitter. Another midlife adult, Lena, called her assistant while catching the bus to work, "Block out the weekend of the 15th because I'm taking my daughter to college." "Mommy's going to work now. Bye-bye. I love you," Danielle said as her infant daughter clutched her tightly when Danielle dropped her off at day care. Meanwhile, Seymour worried, thinking, "I hope I have enough time to straighten the house before my grandchildren arrive," These adults have very different life experiences and occupy a variety of roles: parent to an infant, parent to an older child, parent to a college student, and grandparent—yet all are middle-aged adults.

Sonja Pacho/Corbis

We have seen that the middle adult years span a broad period of life, from roughly age 40 to 65. Over these two and one half decades, we undergo many life changes. Similar to other periods in life, concerns, priorities, and developmental tasks shift over middle adulthood (Havighurst, 1972; Hutteman, Hennecke, Orth, Reitz, & Specht, 2014). For example, parenting demands are highest when adults raise young children but typically decline in the 40s as children age and require less care. Midlife adults experience a wide range of concerns to accompany a wide range of life circumstances (Vandewater & Stewart, 2006). A 40-year-old mother of young children faces different developmental and contextual issues than a 55-year-old mother whose child has begun college and left her with an "empty nest" (Wray, 2007). Career concerns shift from achieving and maintaining professional status early in midlife to preparing for retirement in the late 50s and 60s. In this chapter, we explore socioemotional development in middle adulthood; changes in developmental tasks; and changes in middle adults' sense of self, personality, relationships, and career.

The drive for generativity often fuels middle adults' desires to give back to the community, such as by volunteering in soup kitchens.

PSYCHOSOCIAL DEVELOPMENT IN MIDDLE ADULTHOOD

Compared to childhood and old age, middle adulthood has come under study very recently and is perhaps the least-understood period of life (Graham & Lachman, 2012; Lachman, Teshale, & Agrigoroaei, 2015). One challenge of studying midlife is that it comprises several decades. Developmental concerns change over the decades, yet we know relatively little about these shifts and midlife adults' adjustment during this period. Popular views associate middle age with midlife crises, but midlife is also described as a period of psychological awakening and inner development and a time when people devote energy towards generative purposes (Erikson, 1950; Levinson, 1978, 1996). These conflicting views suggest that there are multiple paths through midlife, many factors influence midlife outcomes for better or worse, and well-being and life satisfaction vary among middle-aged adults.

ERIKSON'S GENERATIVITY VERSUS STAGNATION

Naomi spent several mornings each week coaching her daughter's softball team. Eduardo hired several high school students to work as interns at his firm and learn about his career path. Francesca volunteered her time at a child advocacy center, helping to write grant proposals to earn the funds needed for the center to remain open. Each of these adults is "giving back" to others. For Erik Erikson (1959), the developmental task of middle adulthood entails cultivating a sense of **generativity**, a concern and sense of responsibility for

future generations and society as a whole. In early midlife, generativity is often expressed through child-rearing.

Over the middle adult years, generativity expands to include a commitment to community and society at large. Personal goals become framed within the context of contributing to the social world beyond oneself and one's immediate family to future generations and even the species itself (McAdams, 2014; McAdams & Logan, 2004). Generativity fulfills adults' needs to feel needed and to make contributions that will last beyond their lifetimes, achieving a sense of immortality (Kotre, 1999). Generativity also serves a societal need for adults to guide the next generation, sharing their wisdom with youth through their roles as parents, teachers, and mentors (McAdams, Hart, & Maruna, 1998). Adults fulfill generative needs through teaching and mentoring others in the workplace and community, volunteering, and engaging in creative work. For the active and generative, middle adulthood is the prime of life even as they experience multiple conflicting demands.

In Erikson's view, adults who fail to develop a sense of generativity experience stagnation, self-absorption that interferes with personal growth and prevents them from contributing to the welfare of others (Erikson, 1959). After attaining career and family goals, some adults experience tremendous disappointment and remain self-absorbed, focusing on their own comfort and security rather than seeking challenges, being productive, and making contributions to help others and make the world a better place (McAdams & Olson, 2010).

Generativity is good for others, but it is also good for the midlife adult as it promotes personal growth (Villar, 2012). Generativity is associated with life satisfaction, self-acceptance, low rates of anxiety and depression, and overall well-being (An & Cooney, 2006; Cox, Wilt, Olson, & McAdams, 2010). The most generative adults are proactive problem solvers who approach problems by investigating multiple solutions and exploring several options before committing to any one (Beaumont & Pratt, 2011).

Generativity increases from the 30s through the 60s in adults of all ethnicities and socioeconomic backgrounds (Ackerman, Zuroff, & Moskowitz, 2000; Newton & Stewart, 2010). However, it is characterized by an interesting gender difference. Men who have children tend to score higher in measures of generativity than do childless men, although having children is not related to generativity in women (Marks, Bumpass, & Jun, 2004). Likewise, engaging in child care activities is associated with increases in generativity in men but not women (McKeering & Pakenham, 2000). Having children may draw men's attention to the need to care for the next generation while women may already be socialized to nurture young. That said, generativity is a stronger influence on well-being in women than men (An & Cooney, 2006). For both men and women, however, generativity is influenced by psychosocial issues addressed earlier in life, such as developing a sense of trust (Wilt, Cox, & McAdams, 2010). For example, the sense of trust achieved in infancy is the basis for developing autonomy in toddlerhood and both influence the growth of competence and initiative in childhood. All of these abilities come into play as adolescents and young adults establish a sense of identity and intimacy. Developing generativity in middle adulthood relies on a lifetime of psychosocial development including the ability to trust others and oneself, understand one's self, and sustain meaningful relationships.

LEVINSON'S SEASONS OF LIFE

Similar to Erikson, Daniel Levinson (1978, 1996) viewed development as consisting of qualitative shifts in challenges that result from the interplay of intrapersonal and social forces. Based on interviews with 40 men aged 35 to 45 and, later, 45 women aged 35 to 45—both the men and the women were workers in a wide variety of occupations—Levinson concluded that adults progress through a common set of phases that he called **seasons of life**.

The key element of Levinson's psychosocial theory is the **life structure**, which refers to the overall organization of a person's life, namely relationships with significant others as well as institutions, such as marriage, family, and vocation. We progress through several seasons over the course of our lives in which our life structures are constructed, then tested and modified. Each season begins with a transition period, lasting about five years when individuals conclude tasks of the prior stage and prepare for the next set of challenges. After individuals transition to the new stage, they must create and refine a life structure by integrating intrapersonal and social demands. Once adults master the developmental task of a given stage, they begin to question the resulting life structure and are spurred to progress to the next stage.

During the transition to early adulthood (17 to 22), we construct our life structure by creating a dream, an image of what we are to be in the adult world, which then guides our life choices. Young adults then work to realize their dreams and construct the resulting life structure (22 to 28).

Men tend to emphasize the occupational role and construct images of themselves as independent and successful in career settings. For example, Ben aspired to be a manager at his firm. He considered the skills he needed to develop, such as communication, leadership, and presentation skills, and focused his energy on making progress toward this goal. Women often create dual images that emphasize both marriage and career. Martha also aspired to become a manager, but she also wanted to be home early enough each day to spend time with her children and participate in their lives. Although Martha worked to develop her career skills, she chose not to spend the necessary hours at the office until the children were in elementary school. Levinson found that men who were oriented toward career spent their 20s working toward their goals by gaining professional experience and credentials. Among women and men who took on primary caregiving roles, career development tended to show a slower path and extended into middle age (Kogan & Vacha-Haase, 2002; Levinson, 1996).

During the age 30 transition (28 to 33), adults reconsider their life structure. Some adults who emphasized career over family may change their focus toward finding a partner or having children. Women who emphasized caregiver roles may become more individualistic, developing interests outside of the home, as their children grow older. Adults who do not have satisfying accomplishments at work or home may wonder if they can create and sustain a meaningful life structure and may find the age 30 transition particularly challenging or a crisis. Men tend to experience the 30s (34 to 40) as a period of settling down, focusing on some goals and relationships and giving up others based on their overall values. Many women remain unsettled as they take on new career or family commitments and balance multiple roles and aspirations. Women generally do not achieve a similar level of stability until middle age (Levinson, 1996).

Levinson observed that as adults transition to middle adulthood (40 to 45), they reexamine their dream established in early adulthood and evaluate their success in achieving it. This process of entering middle adulthood is often tumultuous. The crisis is one of identity, and it arises because of the awareness of time passing: half of life is spent. Midlife adults look back at dreams of adolescence and early adulthood and evaluate their progress, coming to terms with the fact that they will not realize many of their dreams. In those areas where they have achieved hoped-for success, they must reconcile reality with their dream and perhaps wonder whether the experience was "worth it," or whether they are missing out on some other aspects of life. Given a limited amount of time left in life, many adults reexamine the goals and values underlying their life structure. Some middle-aged adults make substantial changes, such as changing careers; divorcing; or beginning a new project, such as writing a book. Others make smaller changes while remaining in the same context, devoting more time to the family, for example.

The seasons of life are influenced by context because the process of evaluating and revising the life structure is influenced by the social opportunities and situations around us. Contexts of disadvantage, with poverty, discrimination, or limited opportunities, deplete individuals of the energy needed to examine and revise the life structure. Opportunities to advance in one's career provide avenues of growth as individuals develop satisfying life structures; achieve their modified dreams; and become able to focus on the tasks of middle adulthood, such as accepting aging and becoming generative. Although most adults find the seasons of life conceptualization of adulthood intuitively pleasing, critics note that Levinson's conclusions are based on a very small sample that overrepresents highly educated professional people of high socioeconomic status (Dare, 2011). Nevertheless, Levinson's ideas have shaped popular views of adulthood, most notably, the concept of a **midlife crisis**, as discussed in the following section.

MIDLIFE CRISIS

The 45-year-old who purchases a red convertible sports car; the middle-aged person who suddenly leaves a spouse and moves out of the home, beginning a new life in a new city; the midlifer who is suddenly gripped with anxiety over the future, the fear that half of life is over, and despair that life has not turned out as planned and little time remains to make changes— each of these people embodies aspects of the most popular stereotype about middle age, depicted in television dramas and self-help magazine articles: the midlife crisis, a stressful time in the early to middle 40s when adults are thought to evaluate their lives. The term arose in the public consciousness in the 1970s after publication of several popular books, including *Seasons of Life*, in which Daniel Levinson (1978) articulated his theory of adult development, discussed in the preceding section.

The themes of the midlife crisis are to deal with failure to achieve the dreams of youth and decide how to restructure life. Middle-aged adults evaluate their lifestyles and may question the choices that they have made. Midlife adults often seek balance between home and career, changing their focus on one over the other. Levinson proposed that successfully traversing the midlife crisis requires adults to modify their life structure, reevaluate their goals and their relations with their social context, and develop a sense of generativity.

Although the existence of a midlife crisis is widely accepted (Wethington, 2000), research is at odds with this popular view as surveys of adults over age 40 have revealed that only about 10% to 20% report having experienced a midlife crisis (Wethington, Kessler, & Pixley, 2004). Research consistently suggests that a period of crisis or psychological disturbance is not universal among middle-aged adults but instead occurs at various periods of life (Brim, Ryff, & Kessler, 2004; McCrae & Costa, 2006; Rosenberg, Rosenberg,

& Farrell, 1999). There are individual differences. Those who do experience a crisis in midlife are usually those who have upheavals at other times in their lives, and these experiences seem to be driven by personal style more than by advancing age (Freund & Ritter, 2009). Personal characteristics may determine whether a person experiences midlife, or any other point in life, as a crisis. For example, men who scored higher on measures of psychological problems in earlier adulthood were more likely to report experiencing a midlife crisis 10 years later than did men who scored lower on psychological problems (Costa et al., 1986; McCrae & Costa, 2006). Outside events that can occur at any time in adulthood, such as job loss, financial problems, or illness, may trigger responses that adults and their families may interpret as midlife crises (Beutel, Glaesmer, Wiltink, Marian, & Brähler, 2010; Wethington et al., 2004).

Most developmental scientists adopt the perspective that midlife represents a transition and, similar to the transition to adulthood, entails creating; clarifying; and evaluating values, goals, and priorities (Lachman et al., 2015). A close examination of this kind can lead to insights about oneself and decisions to revise life plans in light of conclusions (Vandewater & Stewart, 2006). Although first addressed in adolescence, identity development is a lifelong process. Going through life experiences, achieving personal milestones, and moving through life transitions often spur adults to revisit the identity development process and reassess their sense of self (Erikson, 1959). Life evaluation is common in midlife, but most people respond by making minor adjustments, creating turning points in their lives rather than dramatic changes. If they cannot revise their life paths, they try to develop a positive outlook (Wethington et al., 2004). Moreover, goals are not set in stone—they are dynamic and change over time. Adults assess and adjust goals throughout life, often without awareness.

Midlife is unquestionably a transition, given changes in middle-aged adults' bodies, families, careers, and contexts. Whether this transition takes the form of a crisis depends on individual factors and circumstances rather than age (Freund & Ritter, 2009). Despite this, the concept of a midlife crisis remains popular in our culture, perhaps because it describes exciting possibilities for making major life changes or perhaps because it is a simple explanation for the many changes that occur. Paradoxically, most adults of all ages tend to view middle adulthood as a positive time in life as shown by Figure 16.1 (Freund & Ritter, 2009). In addition, research suggests that midlife is a time of increasing life satisfaction, self-esteem, and well-being (Lachman et al., 2015; Orth, Trzesniewski, & Robins, 2010). As we will discuss later in this chapter, longitudinal studies show that personality remains stable from young adulthood, through middle adulthood, to older adulthood, suggesting that a period of upheaval and turmoil does not exist in midlife or at least is not evidenced in personality change (McCrae & Costa, 2006).

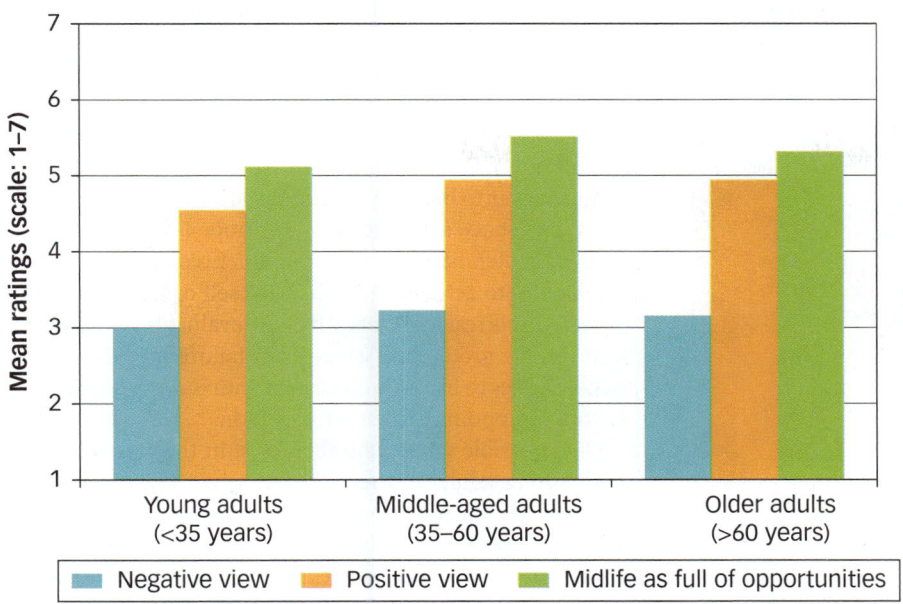

SOURCE: Freund and Ritter (2009).

Thinking in Context 16.1

1. According to Erikson's lifespan psychosocial theory, each psychosocial stage builds on the last. How does resolution of the tasks of infancy, childhood, adolescence, and young adulthood contribute to adults' capacities to address the task of midlife, developing a sense of generativity?

2. Identify instances in which a midlife crisis is depicted in popular media. In your view, how accurate are these depictions? Why?

THE SELF IN MIDDLE ADULTHOOD

It is in middle age that people often first become aware of biological aging, changes in their skin, bodies, and athletic ability. Youthfulness holds an important place in Western society. For example, analyses of women's magazines reveal that the fashion industry focuses its promotional efforts on the young and seldom includes images of women over 40 (Lewis, Medvedev, & Seponski, 2011). Television programs portray midlife women with youthful bodies and shapes and sizes of younger women. Like adolescent and young women, midlife women who report viewing these media tend to rate their body shapes more poorly (Hefner et al., 2014). Many adults deny that their bodies are aging and attempt to stop or reverse the aging process in an effort to maintain an ageless sense of self (Wray, 2007).

However, changes in body image, while salient, are not always adults' biggest concerns regarding aging. In one study of British African Caribbean, British Muslim, West Indian, and Pakistani women, all tended to perceive physical changes, but most reported that the most important body concern was maintaining physical activity and avoiding dependence on family (Wray, 2007). Less socioeconomically advantaged adults tend to have older identities, likely because of their worse health and less favorable predictions of future health as compared with their wealthier peers (Barrett, 2003). Health inequalities can shape the subjective experience of aging, including how old we feel and how we experience aging itself.

SELF-CONCEPT

As we have discussed, self-concept emerges in early childhood and, by adolescence, is refined and differentiated into an organized and comprehensive collection of traits, characteristics, and self-descriptors. Self-concept continues to develop, becoming more complex and integrated into middle adulthood (Labouvie-Vief, 2003; Lodi-Smith & Roberts, 2010). In addition to offering more complex self-descriptions, middle-aged adults are more likely to integrate autobiographical information and experiences into their self-descriptions (Pasupathi & Mansour, 2006).

Subjective evaluations of age are important parts of the sense of self (Barrett & Montepare, 2015). Adults tend to consistently identify with their younger selves, perhaps as a compensatory strategy to counteract the negative cultural messages associated with aging and to maximize their happiness. As compared with men, women tend to hold more youthful self-conceptions, perhaps because Western

PERSONALITY IN MIDLIFE

How would you describe yourself? How has that changed over the years? Four middle-aged adults answer these questions.

Watch the video at edge.sagepub.com/kuther

Middle-aged adults, especially women, may perceive a disparity between how young they feel and how they look in a mirror, which may lead to distress.

cultures tend to define aging as a more negative experience for women than men (Izard, 2007). For example, adults, especially women, with younger age identities tend to be more optimistic about their cognitive competencies and their ability to maintain memory and other aspects of cognitive abilities regardless of their actual age (Schafer & Shippee, 2010).

A typical midlife adult might look in the mirror and find that what they see does not match their sense of self. Aging is associated with a loss of youthful attractiveness and fertility in women whereas aging has some positive connotations in men such as competence, autonomy, and enhanced earnings potential. Women tend to have more youthful identities than men and may perceive a greater disparity between how they feel and what they see in the mirror, leading to distress (Barrett, 2005). Women may retain more youthful identities as a means of enhancing their self-conceptions and identifying with valued social groups. Despite this, self-concept shows remarkable stability throughout adulthood (Lachman & Bertrand, 2001; Stewart, Ostrove, & Helson, 2001). Young people who describe themselves as outgoing, nurturing, or competent, for example, are likely to hold the same view in middle and late adulthood. **Possible selves**, however, are less stable.

Possible selves, our conceptions of who we might become in the future, are self-orientations that guide and motivate choices and future-oriented behaviors (Cross & Markus, 1991). The possible self is a motivator of behavior from middle adulthood into older adulthood (Smith & Freund, 2002). People are motivated to try to become the hoped-for possible self and attempt to avoid becoming the feared self, the self we hope never to become. In middle adulthood, we compare the lives we have achieved with our hoped-for self, and the degree of match between the two influences our life satisfaction. Failure to achieve the hoped-for self or failure to avoid the feared self results in negative self-evaluations and affect. However, we protect ourselves from failure by revising our possible selves to be more consistent with our experience and to avoid disappointment and frustration.

It is possible selves who thereby shift throughout adulthood. Young adults in their 20s describe the aspirations of their possible selves as idealistic and grand—visions of fame, wealth, exceptional health and athletic prowess. By middle adulthood, most people realize that their time and life opportunities are limited, and they become motivated to balance images of their possible selves with their experiences in order to find meaning and happiness in their lives. Thus, midlife is an important time of self-growth (Lilgendahl, Helson, & John, 2013). Over their lifetimes, adults revise their possible selves to be more practical and realistic, such as to competently perform the roles of worker, spouse, and parent, and to be wealthy enough to live comfortably and meet the needs of children and aging parents (Bybee & Wells, 2003).

Older middle-aged adults tend to be more autonomous, less concerned with the evaluations and expectations of others, and more concerned with living up to self-chosen ideals and standards than are younger adults (Ryff, 1995). Middle-aged adults are more likely than young adults to acknowledge and accept both their good and bad qualities and feel positively about themselves (Ryff, 1991, 1995). Revised, more modest, possible selves influence adults' sense of well-being, permitting middle-aged and older adults to show higher self-esteem than young adults (Orth et al., 2010). Moreover, research suggests that self-esteem increases throughout middle adulthood, with longitudinal studies suggesting that self-esteem, peaks at about age 50 to 60 (Orth, Maes, & Schmitt, 2015) and cross-sectional studies suggesting a later peak in early older adulthood, as shown in Figure 16.2 (Robins, Trzesniewski, Tracy, Gosling, & Potter, 2002). Self-esteem is associated with positive emotional, social, and career outcomes throughout life, from adolescence through older adulthood (Orth, Robins, & Widaman, 2012). As discussed in the following sections, other aspects of self also change over the midlife years.

GENDER IDENTITY

Over the middle adult years, gender identity, individuals' identification with the masculine or feminine gender role, tends to become more fluid and integrated. Men and women

FIGURE 16.2: Age Differences in Self-Esteem Across the Lifespan

Males

Females

Age

SOURCE: Robins et al. (2002).

iStock/Essentials

In middle age, adults become less tied to gender stereotypes for their own behavior. Men tend to adopt more feminine characteristics, such as being warm and sensitive, and women adopt more masculine characteristics, such as becoming more assertive.

become more similar. Men adopt more traditionally feminine characteristics, such as being sensitive, considerate, and dependent, and women adopt more traditionally masculine characteristics, such as confidence, self-reliance, and boldness (Huyck, 1996). Many middle-aged adults begin to integrate masculine and feminine aspects of themselves, becoming more androgynous (James & Lewkowicz, 1995). Men may become more nurturing, enhancing their relationships at home and work. Women often become more assertive. For example, one study followed a representative sample of third-grade Finnish children for 30 years (Pulkkinen, Feldt, & Kokko, 2005). Although boys and girls adopted traditional gender characteristics in adolescence, by age 40 the men had become less aggressive and more conforming in contrast to the women, who showed a reverse pattern of becoming more assertive. Longitudinal research following adults from their 30s to 80s mirror this finding: Although there are individual differences, the average man, initially low in femininity, becomes significantly higher in femininity across the lifespan; the average woman, initially high in femininity, becomes significantly lower in femininity across the lifespan (Jones, Peskin, & Livson, 2011). This pattern of gender convergence occurs in middle-aged adults and increases through middle adulthood in Western nations as well as in non-Western cultures, such as the Mayan people of Guatemala and the Druze of the Middle East (Fry, 1985).

Androgyny, integrating masculine and feminine characteristics, provides adults with a greater repertoire of skills for meeting the demands of midlife. Middle-aged women who may be newly independent after experiencing divorce, death of a partner, or the end of child-rearing may enter the workplace, seek advancement in current careers, or enroll in college. Successfully meeting these new challenges requires self-reliance, assertiveness, and confidence. Men, on the other hand, may become more sensitive and self-reflective as they complete generative tasks of mentoring and caring for the next generation. A great deal of research has shown that androgyny predicts positive adjustment and is associated with high self-esteem, advanced moral reasoning, psychosocial maturity, and life satisfaction (Bem, 1985; Lefkowitz & Zeldow, 2006; Pilar Matud, Bethencourt, & Ibáñez, 2014). Men and women with an androgynous gender role have a greater repertoire of skills, both instrumental and expressive, which permits them to adapt to a variety of situations with greater ease than do those who adopt either a masculine or feminine gender role.

SELF AND WELL-BEING

Throughout the lifespan, the sense of self and identity are important influences on people's overall functioning and their sense of well-being (Sneed, Whitbourne, Schwartz, & Huang, 2012). In midlife, perception of, and adaptation to, age-related physical changes are important influences on the sense of self and well-being. Some midlife adults exaggerate the changes—seeing wrinkles, for example—as deeper and more pervasive than they are. Others deny changes and fail to see how their bodies have aged. Midlife adults who subjectively view themselves as younger than their chronological age (e.g., those who feel 35 years old when in fact they are 45 years old) tend to score higher on measures of well-being, mental health, and life satisfaction (Keyes & Westerhof, 2012; Ryff, 2014). At the same time, other research suggests that older subjective age predicts poor life satisfaction only when adults have negative attitudes about aging but not when aging attitudes are more favorable (Mock & Eibach, 2011). One longitudinal study showed that lower subjective age at age 50 to 75 years was associated with better episodic memory and executive function 10 years later (Stephan, Caudroit, Jaconelli, & Terracciano, 2014). Ultimately, the healthiest midlife adults are those who recognize their age but remain active and healthy, engage in prevention, and do not become stricken and paralyzed by age-related physical changes (Ryff, 2014; Vandewater & Stewart, 2006).

Despite this positive view, a lifespan perspective suggests that well-being is U-shaped, with its lowest point in early middle age, typically the early 40s (Blanchflower & Oswald, 2008; López Ulloa, Møller, & Sousa-Poza, 2013). Perhaps the overall decline in well-being in middle adulthood is related to the great many roles most midlife adults occupy. In a prior chapter, we discussed the challenge that role overload poses to well-being. Midlife well-being is influenced by the number of roles a person occupies, role quality, and adaptation to the physical changes in midlife (Vandewater & Stewart, 2006). When accompanied by a sense of control, multiple role involvement predicts positive well-being, more trusting and positive relations with others, a positive sense of life purpose, and greater overall well-being (Chrouser Ahrens & Ryff, 2006). Perceived control is associated with life satisfaction and multiple demands that midlife adults face often tests their sense of control (de Quadros-Wander, McGillivray, & Broadbent, 2013). Positive processing, a tendency to interpret events in a favorable light, is associated with high levels of well-being in midlife (Lilgendahl & McAdams, 2011). Multiple roles must be accompanied by a sense of control or mastery in that area to influence well-being, especially in women; otherwise, role strain can occur, as discussed later in this chapter.

Although most people experience midlife shifts in well-being, they typically rate their subjective overall sense of well-being in the moderate to high range. As shown in Figure 16.3, one national sample of 25- to 75-year-old adults studied over a nine-year span found that on average all ages reported feeling moderate to high levels of life satisfaction in the present as well as 10 years ago and rated their satisfaction as increasing from past to present (Röcke & Lachman, 2008). The sense of self and subjective sense of well-being tends to remain stable over midlife, even as adults experience many physical and social changes.

PERSONALITY

It is commonly believed that people change a great deal as they age, yet research suggests that self-concept and identity largely remain stable over the adult years. Extensive research on the nature of personality, conducted with multiple samples over several decades, has resulted in an empirically based theory that has collapsed the many characteristics on which people differ into five clusters of personality traits, collectively known as the **Big 5 personality traits,** shown in Table 16.1 (McCrae & Costa, 2008). The Big 5 personality factors are thought to reflect inherited predispositions that persist throughout life and a growing body of evidence supports their genetic basis (Bouchard & McGue, 2004; Penke, Denissen, & Miller, 2007).

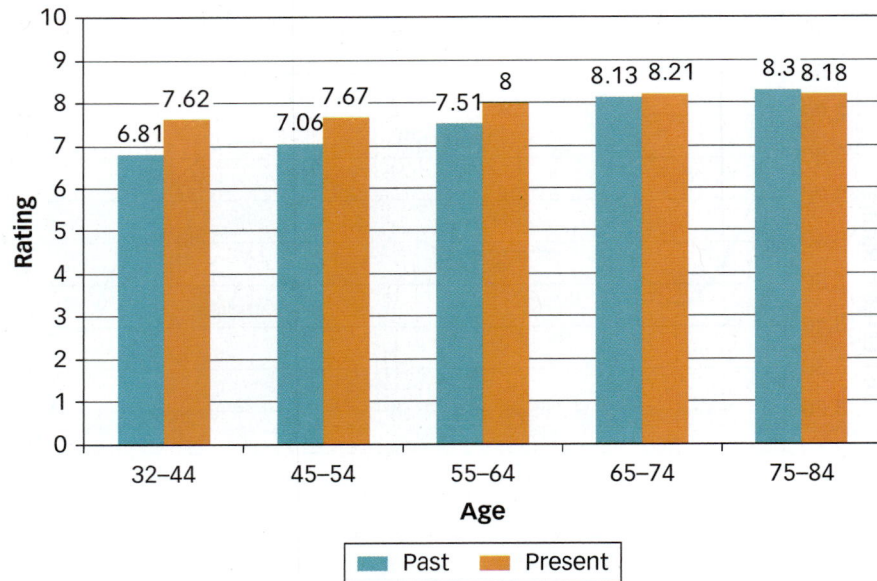

FIGURE 16.3: Adults' Mean Ratings of Their Past (10 Years Ago) and Present Life Satisfaction

NOTE: The life satisfaction scale can range from 1 (low satisfaction) to 10 (high satisfaction).
SOURCE: Röcke & Lachman (2008).

TABLE 16.1 Big 5 Personality Traits

TRAIT	DESCRIPTION
Openness	The degree to which one is open to experience, ranging from curious, explorative, and creative to disinterested, uncreative, and not open to new experiences.
Conscientiousness	The tendency to be responsible, disciplined, task oriented, and planful. This trait relates to effortful self-regulation. Individuals low in this trait tend to be irresponsible, impulsive, and inattentive.
Extroversion	Includes social outgoingness, high activity, enthusiastic interest, and assertive tendencies. This trait is related to positive emotionality. On the opposite pole, descriptors include social withdrawal and constrictedness.
Agreeableness	This trait includes descriptors such as trusting, cooperative, helpful, caring behaviors and attitudes toward others. Individuals low in agreeableness are seen as difficult, unhelpful, oppositional, and stingy.
Neuroticism	This trait relates to negative emotionality. Descriptors include moodiness, fear, worry, insecurity, and irritability. The opposite pole includes traits such as self-confidence.

Big 5 personality traits predict career, family, and personal choices in adulthood. People who are high in conscientiousness are more likely to complete college, those high in extroversion are more likely to marry, and those high in neuroticism are more likely to divorce (Hill, Turiano, Mroczek, & Roberts, 2012; Shiota & Levenson, 2007). People who are high in extroversion, agreeableness, and conscientiousness and low in neuroticism report higher levels of well-being (Cox et al., 2010). Big 5 traits even predict mortality. For example, increased mortality risk is associated with each of the following: low conscientiousness, low extroversion, and high neuroticism as well as long-term increases in neuroticism (Mroczek & Spiro, 2007). Conscientiousness has a close association with health (Friedman & Kern, 2014).

Individual differences in Big 5 personality traits are large as people show unique patterns of traits, and those patterns and individual differences in personality traits are highly stable over periods of time ranging from 3 to 30 years (McAdams & Olson, 2010). Childhood personality ratings by teachers predict personality ratings in middle adulthood (Edmonds, Goldberg, Hampson, & Barckley, 2013; Hampson & Goldberg, 2006) as do personality ratings collected during adolescence (Morizot & Le Blanc, 2003). For example, someone who is highly extroverted in young adulthood, perhaps with a very active social life, will also be highly extroverted in middle adulthood, perhaps manifested as being active in a parent–teacher organization, leading a scout troop, or participating in a book group. Although there is a great deal of continuity in personality traits at all ages, the greatest variability in traits occurs in childhood and may continue into adolescence. For example, one study of 10- to 20-year-olds found that self-ratings of personality were more inconsistent and less coherent among younger participants (Soto, John, Gosling, & Potter, 2008). Continuity in personality traits increases with age, from early adulthood, peaking in the late 30s into middle adulthood and decreasing in older adulthood (Lucas & Donnellan, 2011; McAdams & Olson, 2010).

Despite findings of within-person stability, research also shows age differences in Big 5 factors, as shown in Figure 16.4 (Soto, John, Gosling, & Potter, 2011). Cross-sectional studies of adults around the world, including those from Canada, Germany, Italy, Japan, Russia, South Korea, and the United States, have found that agreeableness and conscientiousness increase and neuroticism, extroversion, and openness decline into middle adulthood, suggesting that adults mellow out with age (McCrae & Costa, 2006; Roberts & Mroczek, 2008; Soto et al., 2011). These cross-cultural similarities in patterns of change support arguments that personality itself and age-related changes have biological origins.

How do we make sense of age trends in light of substantial data supporting stability in personality traits over the lifespan? Research with large groups of people indicates general age-related patterns of change. At the same time, individuals' relative position with regard to traits does not change (Deary, Pattie, & Starr, 2013; Roberts & Mroczek, 2008). In other words, someone who is high in openness relative to age peers will remain high in openness over time, even though as a group the adults may show a decline over the adult years.

What underlies group patterns of personality change? Recall from Chapter 1 that individuals are active in influencing their development. People's behaviors and choices shape their contexts and their personalities. Age-graded events, such as graduating from college or experiencing menopause, as well as personal transitions such as getting married or divorced, also influence age-related patterns in personality change (Mroczek, Spiro, & Griffin, 2006). Finally, normative history-graded influences, or cohort differences, contribute to personality change across generations. Exposure to events and experiences unique to a given historical period may cause some cohorts to show a greater range of personality change over their lifetime than others.

When considering the individual, personality influences a person's life choices and experiences, yet folk wisdom

FIGURE 16.4: Age Differences in Big 5 Personality Traits

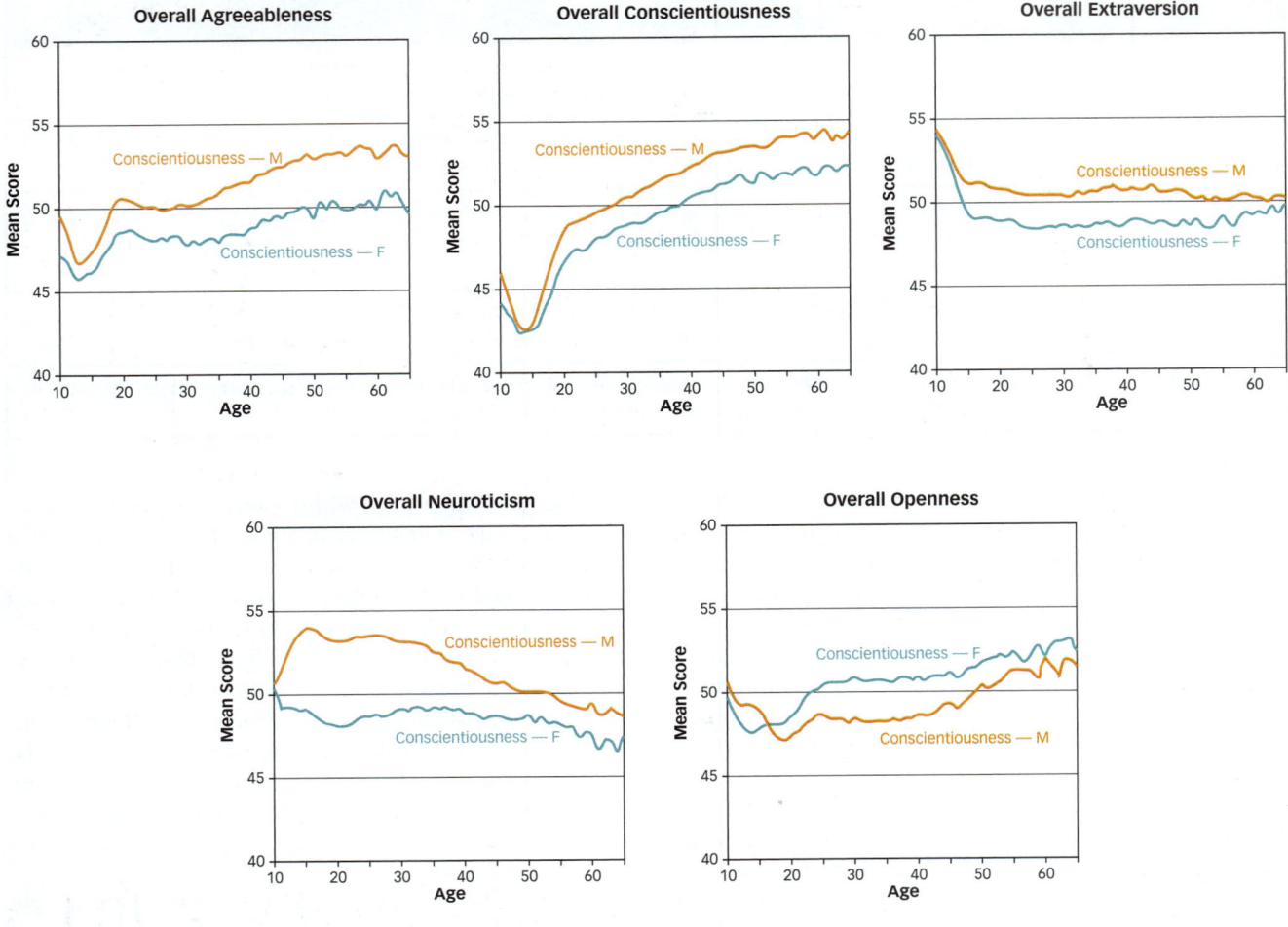

SOURCE: Soto et al. (2011).

usually adheres to the opposite: that personality in adulthood is influenced by events and experience over a lifetime. The logic goes that after a humiliating experience at a party, a person becomes more introverted and anxious about social gatherings, for example. However, research suggests that experience rarely causes large changes in personality and that instead it is our personalities that influence our choices and experiences (McCrae, 2002; McCrae & Costa, 2006). Introverted and socially anxious people may be more prone to find parties and social gatherings challenging and perhaps be more likely to have humiliating experiences. People choose behaviors, lifestyles, mates, and contexts based on their personalities, and then the outcomes of these choices and life experiences may strengthen and stabilize personality traits (Soto, 2015). For example, in one study conducted over a nine-year period, social well-being correlated positively with extroversion, agreeableness, conscientiousness, emotional stability, and openness; and changes in changes in social well-being coincided with changes on these traits (Hill et al., 2012). In this sense, stability of personality is influenced by

individuals' behaviors and choice of environments as well as by environmental factors themselves (Kandler et al., 2010). In addition, people are motivated to maintain a stable sense of personality as part of developing and maintaining a consistent sense of self (Kandler et al., 2010). Certainly, dramatic life changes, such as divorce, serious illness, or widowhood may bring about new behaviors and patterns of traits, but more commonly, such events evoke and strengthen existing patterns of traits (Mroczek et al., 2006; Roberts & Caspi, 2003). Personality traits can be expressed in many ways, depending on the situation, and personality shapes our choices, behaviors, and life course.

Overall, middle adulthood is characterized by psychosocial growth, increases in generativity, expanded self-conceptions, stability in personality, and a greater sense of well-being. Midlife adults' psychosocial functioning influences the frequency and quality of social interactions with others. Similar to other periods in life, social relationships remain important influences on midlife adults' well-being, as we discuss in the next section.

1. Consider your self-concept. Identify your possible self and feared self. In what ways do you think these have changed since your adolescent years? Consider the life tasks that you expect to engage in 15 years from now. What might your possible and feared selves look like?

2. Middle-aged adults operate within multiple contexts and roles. What factors might influence midlife adults' personality, self-concept, and sense of well-being? Identify factors at the micro, meso, and exosystem levels of context. How might these factors influence psychosocial functioning? What macrosystem factors might influence psychosocial adjustment in middle adulthood?

Friendships improve with age and are a powerful buffer against stress.

RELATIONSHIPS IN MIDDLE ADULTHOOD

Midlife adults' changing sense of self, changing family formations, and changing roles and responsibilities in the workforce and at home influence their social relationships with friends, spouses, children, and parents.

FRIENDSHIPS

Over the course of middle adulthood, most people spend more time with family than friends, but friendships continue to be important sources of social support and are associated with well-being, positive affect, and self-esteem (Huxhold, Miche, & Schüz, 2014; Ueno & Adams, 2006). Nearly 95% of middle-aged adults report having friends and, for them, most friends are old friends (Lang & Carstensen, 1994). Friendships improve with age. Whereas young adults tend to report having many friends and feel ambivalent or troubled about some, middle-aged and older adults tend to report fewer friends, but almost all are described as close and few to none are ambivalent or troubled (Fingerman, Hay, & Birditt, 2004).

As with earlier times in life, midlife adults choose friends who are similar to them in age, gender, ethnicity, and socioeconomic status (Ueno & Adams, 2006). Because of these similarities, friends tend to share experiences and values that make them useful sources of advice for dealing with serious problems such as illness, unemployment, or family troubles. Throughout the lifespan, close friendships are based in reciprocity, emotional give-and-take that entails intimacy, companionship, and support as well as behaviors such as sharing, exchanging favors, and giving advice (Hartup & Stevens, 1999). Close friends attempt to improve each other's well-being by providing emotional and social support and helping each other manage daily life, stressful transitions, and crises.

Gender differences in friendship persist throughout adulthood. Similar to earlier periods in life, women tend to have more close friends and experience more pleasure and satisfaction in their friendships than do men, perhaps because women's friendships tend to be based in intimacy and the provision of emotional support whereas men's friendships tend to center around activities (Antonucci et al., 2002; Rose, 2007). Women tend to discuss relationships and personal matters whereas men tend to not to talk about themselves, favoring discussions about sports, business, and politics. Although women have closer friendships, men have more contact with friends during middle adulthood (Adams & Ueno, 2006).

Friendships offer powerful protection against stress for both men and women. Daily hassles, such as a challenging commute and juggling the demands of career and family, and major crises, such as illness or death, are stressors that tax individuals' coping resources and contribute to illness, aging-related physical changes, and even early death (Aldwin, 2007). Adults turn to close friends for support with everyday hassles; they mobilize both high- and lower-quality friendships when managing major stressors (Birditt, Antonucci, & Tighe, 2012). Friends help one another cope with life stress by showing interest, letting each other vent, and helping each other objectively analyze situations and decide how to respond. Midlife women especially rely on social support to manage midlife challenges such as menopause as well as changes to family structure due to departure of children, divorce, changing needs of aging parents, and parental death (Krause, 2010). Increasingly women meet many of their social support needs through social networking on Internet sites such as Facebook (Dare & Green, 2011; Hogeboom, McDermott, Perrin, Osman, & Bell-Ellison, 2010). The process of seeking companionship and discussing stressful situations itself releases stress and improves adults' psychological and physical well-being.

MARRIAGE

Over the past half-century, marriage rates have declined to record lows; however, nearly all adults in the United States will marry. In 2014, over 80% of adults married by age 45,

Marital satisfaction tends to increase over the middle adult years as child-rearing tasks decline, family incomes rise, and spouses have more time to spend with each other.

Michael Keller/Corbis

satisfaction. Midlife adults have different perspectives and needs than young adults. Whereas similarity in personality predicts marital satisfaction in young adulthood, partners who are most similar in personality tend to report less marital satisfaction over a 12-year period (Shiota & Levenson, 2007). The most satisfying marriages reflect congruence in which partners' attributes complement one another (Rammstedt, Spinath, Richter, & Schupp, 2013). Successful marriage partners balance similarity and differences, such that partners have enough shared interests, goals, and interaction styles to get along but also some differences that generate and sustain interest in one another.

Marital happiness tends to be highest during the first year or so of marriage, and husbands tend to be more satisfied with marriage throughout life than are wives (Kiecolt-Glaser & Newton, 2001; Lucas & Dyrenforth, 2005). Many midlife couples have been married for 10 or 20 years and face different tasks and stressors than do younger couples. Midlife couples typically are raising a family, have more responsibility at work, and are coping with greater role strain than at any life stage (Kim & Moen, 2001). Most midlife couples find parenting to be a source of marital conflict. Child-rearing is associated with declines in marital satisfaction and intimacy (Bradbury, Fincham, & Beach, 2000; Lawrence, Rothman, Cobb, Rothman, & Bradbury, 2008). With children come financial pressures, which tend to increase marital conflict, as well as increased responsibilities and often quarrels over child-rearing and discipline techniques. Midlife couples tend to report more disagreements on finances and household responsibility than do older couples (Hatch & Bulcroft, 2004). At the same time, paradoxically, parenthood tends to be associated with increases in marital commitment (Bradbury et al., 2000; Lawrence et al., 2008).

Marital satisfaction tends to increase over the middle adult years as child-rearing tasks and stress decline, family incomes rise, and spouses get better at understanding each other and have more time to spend with each other (Fincham, Beach, & Davila, 2007). Advances in emotional regulation also improve the quality of martial interactions (Bloch, Haase, & Levenson, 2014). High-quality marital interactions predict marital satisfaction in women (Schmitt, Kliegel, & Shapiro, 2007). In one study, the most common area of desired change among married persons age 40 to 50 was to have more time together (Christensen & Miller, 2006), suggesting that the middle adult years are often very good years for marriages. By the 60s, most couples are happier. Many of their responsibilities, such as child-rearing, have subsided, and they experience less conflict and spend more time together.

DIVORCE

Most marriages that end in divorce do so within the first ten years, but about 10% of marriages break up after 20 years or longer (U.S. Bureau of the Census, 2015). By 45 years of age, over one third of men and women have ever divorced (Kreider

90% by age 60, and over 95% by age 80 (U.S. Bureau of the Census, 2015). In comparison, in 1960, only 7% of men and 6% of women had never married by age 45 (Wang & Parker, 2014). Researchers have identified several tangible health benefits to marriage. Generally speaking, married people tend to live longer and be happier and healthier than single people (Grover & Helliwell, 2014). Cross-sectional and longitudinal research has shown that married people show lower rates of depression and anxiety and fewer mental conditions (Frech & Williams, 2007; Hewitt, Baxter, & Western, 2006). Same-sex partnerships show similar benefits, although there is less research to date (Cherlin, 2013; Wight, LeBlanc, & Lee Badgett, 2013).

In Chapter 13, we discussed research on marriage in young adulthood with couples who are just beginning their life journey together. Given your knowledge of lifespan development, you may not be surprised to learn that the nature of marriage, including marital conflict and marital satisfaction, changes over the decades and with each partner's and the couple's experiences. Dating and newlywed couples must develop interest, attraction, and a feeling of similarity, which helps them to create a shared life and increase relationship

& Ellis, 2011). As we have discussed, second marriages are more than twice as likely as first marriages to end in divorce. The breakup of a second marriage tends to be more stressful for adults and children than the demise of the first marriage (Hetherington & Kelly, 2002). Overall, middle-aged adults list similar reasons for divorce as do young adults: communication problems, relationship inequality, adultery, physical and verbal abuse, and desires for autonomy (Rokach, Cohen, & Dreman, 2004; Sakraida, 2005). Women are more likely than men to initiate divorce, and women who are the initiators tend to fare better than those who do not initiate the divorce (Steiner, Suarez, Sells, & Wykes, 2011).

Divorce is associated with decreases in life satisfaction, heightened risk for a range of illnesses, and even early a 20% to 30% increase in risk for early death (Björkenstam, Hallqvist, Dalman, & Ljung, 2013; Holt-Lunstad, Smith, & Layton, 2010; Sbarra, Law, & Portley, 2011). Divorce is thought to be more harmful to women's health than men's because it tends to represent a greater economic loss for women, including often a loss of health insurance (Lavelle & Smock, 2012). However, some research suggests that, in women, illness often precedes divorce, suggesting that illness may be a contributor rather than outcome of divorce (Karraker & Latham, 2015). Economic disadvantage, perceived and real, increases stress and decreases feelings of control, which may worsen postdivorce health (Lorenz, Wickrama, Conger, & Elder, 2006; Williams & Umberson, 2004).

Although some adults show poor health outcomes of divorce (Mancini, Bonanno, & Clark, 2011; Sbarra, 2015), there are substantial individual differences in response to divorce. During and immediately after the divorce, there is often significant stress, but most people ultimately cope well and are resilient after their divorce (Amato, 2010; Sbarra, 2015). Divorce poses challenges the sense of self, as each partner must adjust his or her self-concept to that of a "single self" instead of as part of a couple. Improvement in self-concept is associated with increases in future psychological well-being (Slotter, Gardner, & Finkel, 2010). One study of more than 600 German divorcees demonstrated that nearly three quarters experienced little self-reported change in life satisfaction across a nine-year period that included the divorce (Mancini et al., 2011). Women who successfully transition through a divorce tend to show positive long-term outcomes. They tend to become more tolerant, self-reliant, and nonconforming— all characteristics that are associated with the increased autonomy and self-reliance demands that come with divorce. Men tend to remarry more quickly after divorce than do women; less is known about men's long-term adjustment to divorce. As with other life challenges, divorce represents an opportunity for growth and development (Baum, Rahav, & Sharon, 2005; Schneller & Arditti, 2004), and adaptive outcomes following divorce appear to be the norm, not the exception (Perrig-Chiello, Hutchison, & Morselli, 2014).

How can we account for these disparate findings? One answer lies in the findings that individual differences predict adjustment and the likelihood of poor or favorable

RELATIONSHIPS WITH ADULT CHILDREN

Learn what it's like to have adult children and how the parent-child relationship changes as children move through adulthood.

Watch the video at edge.sagepub.com/kuther

outcomes (Amato, 2010; Mason & Sbarra, 2012). For example, pre-divorce depression, attachment anxiety, and cognitive styles influence outcomes. During divorce, people who have a hard time distancing themselves from their psychological experiences and instead focus solely on their problems—often revisiting negative interactions blow-by-blow—tend to show excessive cardiovascular reactivity that is ultimately associated with the development of cardiovascular disease (Chida & Steptoe, 2010). Poor health outcomes are more likely when people are overly immersed in their experiences, ruminating on all that is bad and will be terrible rather than focusing on finding meaning in their experiences (Kross, Gard, Deldin, Clifton, & Ayduk, 2012; Sbarra, Smith, & Mehl, 2012). Women may find divorce more difficult as many report ruminating more about arguments, having more detailed memories of conflicts, and feeling more depressed after arguments than men (Lorenz et al., 2006; Steiner et al., 2011).

Divorce is challenging, but middle-aged persons generally show less of a decline in psychological well-being and show overall better adaptation than do young adults (Wang & Amato, 2000). It may be that increases in experience, flexibility, and problem-solving and coping skills in middle adulthood aid adaptation. In addition, adults with high levels of education and high socioeconomic status are more likely to divorce, but they are also better able to adapt than are adults who are less educated and of lower socioeconomic status (Wu & Penning, 1997).

PARENT-CHILD RELATIONSHIPS

The dynamic lifelong challenge of parenting taps adults' capacities for adaptation. Just as parents become proficient at meeting children's developmental demands at a given age, children advance, posing new challenges and requiring a transformation of skills. Middle-aged adults are parents to children ranging in age from infancy to adulthood (see Lives in Context, p. 460). However, for most parents it is in

LIVES IN CONTEXT

First-Time Parenting in Midlife

A growing number of adults are postponing parenthood into midlife. As a result, it is not uncommon for adults in their 40s and early 50s to raise young children. We have discussed the biological changes in the reproductive capacity that occur throughout young adulthood and middle adulthood. Whether through assisted reproduction, adoption, or chance, there is a growing number of new parents who are middle aged.

The transition to parenthood entails many changes for all parents. Midlife parents, however, may find the social side of their new role challenging as their daily experiences may not match those of their peers. Midlife parents of infants, for example, have different concerns and needs than their friends. A new mother may find that find that her social clock is discordant with her same-age peers who may be sending their children to college or planning for weddings and grandchildren. At the same time, a midlife mother may find herself much older than many of the other parents of infants she meets at child care, play groups, and parks. Midlife parents may find the social side of parenting a challenge.

When asked, midlife parents cite benefits to being an older parent. Many middle-aged adults have established careers with financial security, enabling flexibility in how they spend their time. Midlife parents also feel that they are better prepared for parenthood. They feel mature, competent, and generative as well as tend to be less stressed than younger parents (Mac Dougall, Beyene, & Nachtigall, 2012). Middle-aged parents tend to experience greater increases in life satisfaction with the birth of their children and are less prone to depressive symptoms (Luhmann, Hofmann, Eid, & Lucas, 2012). Middle-aged parents

tend to take a more youthful perspective, seeing middle age as extending longer and old age as starting later than do those who have children early in life (Toothman & Barrett, 2011). The most common complaints of older parents include having less energy for parenting and feeling stigmatized as older parents (Mac Dougall et al., 2012).

Children also benefit from being raised by midlife parents. The cognitive and emotional changes that take place in young and middle adulthood also contribute to midlife adults' readiness to parent. For example, in some studies mothers who were older when the first child was born tended to demonstrate more positive parenting behaviors, such as hugs, kisses, and praise, and fewer negative ones, such as threats or slaps (Barnes, Gardiner, Sutcliffe, & Melhuish, 2013; Basatemur & Sutcliffe, 2008). Finally, children raised by older mothers tend to be healthier, having fewer visits to the hospital, a greater likelihood of having had all of their immunizations by 9 months of age, and higher scores on measures of language and social development through age 5 (Sutcliffe, Barnes, Belsky, Gardiner, & Melhuish, 2012).

What Do You Think?

1. What are some of the challenges of becoming a parent in midlife? How might adults address these?

2. How might a child be influenced by parental age? How might having a parent who is older than other parents influence children? Why?

---

middle adulthood that they launch their young adult children into the world. Many parents view their children's graduation from high school in a positive light while also experiencing some regrets, especially a sense of lost time with their children that cannot be regained (DeVries, Kerrick, & Oetinger, 2007).

A son or daughter moving out of the family home is an important experience for parents and children as it marks the child's entry to adulthood and independent living. Mothers report the move as more stressful than fathers (Seiffge-Krenke, 2010), but most parents adjust well to their children's transition to independent living and the resulting empty nest (Mitchell & Lovegreen, 2009). This is especially true for parents who encouraged the development of autonomy at an early age, granting their children developmentally appropriate levels of autonomy that increased with age. In addition, parents experience less distress over the transition when communication and affection continue after the child leaves the nest, but they report poor life satisfaction when parent–child communication declines (White, 1994). Sometimes, however, parents hold higher expectations for autonomy for their emerging adult children as they enter college than their children are willing and able to fulfill, with negative consequences for parents' adjustment (Kenyon & Koerner, 2009).

Generally speaking, there is continuity in parent–child relationships throughout the lifespan. In one longitudinal study of New Zealand families, parental warmth and support in childhood and adolescence predicted contact and closeness with children in early adulthood (Belsky, Jaffee, Hsieh, & Silva, 2001). Some research suggests that relations between U.S. parents and adult children may worsen when they continue to live together, perhaps because of the adult children's dependence on parents, financial or otherwise (Ward & Spitze, 2007). Specifically, an adult child's failure to show appropriate levels of autonomy can be a source of stress for parents (Pillemer & Suitor, 2002). Parents are often concerned about their children's independence and continue to make efforts to socialize their children into adulthood (Birditt, Miller, Fingerman, & Lefkowitz, 2009). Parents and adult children tend to become closer as they mature. Parents become more generative and adult children more autonomous regardless of whether they live together (Connidis, 2001).

In all nations, families who live apart continue to provide various forms of emotional and physical support to one another, including advice, babysitting, loans, car repair, and more (Farkas & Hogan, 1995; Haberkern & Szydlik, 2010). How much support family members provide for each other depends on many factors, such as attachment, relationship quality, cultural norms, and resources. Familism is a value that mandates that the family comes before all else and that family members have a duty to care for one another, regardless of the problem or situation, whether personal, financial, or legal (Carlo, Koller, Raffaelli, & De Guzman, 2007); it is common in Hispanic cultures, among others. Financial resources also influence the level and types of support that family members provide. Poverty often leads family members to provide financial and physical assistance, including living together. For example, in most nations, low-income families, such as single parents, immigrants, and members of minority groups, are more likely to live together in three-generation households (parents, children, grandchildren; Burr & Mutchler, 1999). Generally speaking, early midlife parents continue to give children more assistance than they receive, especially when children are unmarried or facing challenging life transitions such as unemployment and career change or divorce (Zarit & Eggebeen, 2002).

Especially after the economic recession that affected much of the world in 2007 and 2008, it has become increasingly common for adult children to return home in their 20s. About one third of young adults ages 25 to 34 live with their parents, and the majority (58%) report being satisfied with their living arrangements (Parker, 2012). Over one third of young adults who return home report that living with their parents has been good for their relationship, about half say that it has had no effect on their relationship, and only 18% report that living at home has had a negative effect on their relationships. Parents report similar levels of satisfaction regardless of whether they have adult children in the home (Parker, 2012). However, other research suggests that having at least one postcollege age child living at home is associated with lower psychological well-being among mothers but not fathers (Pudrovska, 2009).

Children's success in life influences their midlife parents' sense of well-being. Both mothers and fathers show negative emotional responses to their adult children's unmet career and relationships goals (Cichy, Lefkowitz, Davis, & Fingerman, 2013). Parents are likely to feel a sense of failure if their children do not live up to expectations, one aspect of which is whether the adult son or daughter is still living at home (see Figure 16.5). Adult children's problems are associated with lower parental well-being, including more negative and less positive affect, lower levels of self-esteem, and more poor parent–child relationships (Greenfield & Marks, 2006; Greenfield, Marks, Hay, Fingerman, & Lefkowitz, 2008). For example, in one study of middle-aged adults, having an adult child with problems predicted poorer parental well-being, regardless of the presence of another successful child, and the more problems in the family, the worse parental well-being (Fingerman, Cheng, Birditt, & Zarit, 2012). Parents who perceive their grown children as needing too much support report lower life satisfaction (Fingerman, Cheng, Wesselmann, et al., 2012).

Similar to other times in life, parents who have rewarding relationships and roles apart from that of parent show the most positive adjustment to the empty nest and view it as welcomed, freeing, and rewarding, for example, rather than lonely and depressing (Dennerstein, Dudley, & Guthrie, 2002; Mitchell & Lovegreen, 2009). Most midlife parents are happy in their roles, but their satisfaction varies with parental age, health, ethnic background, parent–child relationship quality, and perception of how their children "turn out," which influence their subjective levels of happiness (Mitchell, 2010).

GRANDPARENTHOOD

Most U.S. adults become grandparents in their late 40s and early 50s (with an average of 49 for women and 52 for men; see Figure 16.6; Leopold & Skopek, 2015). Just as parenthood arrives later with each generation, so does the median age of grandparenthood. Similar to patterns of marriage and childbirth, grandparenthood occurs up to eight years later in Western European countries (such as Austria, the Netherlands, and Switzerland) and up to three years earlier in Eastern European countries (such as Bulgaria, Poland, and Ukraine) as compared with the United States (Leopold & Skopek, 2015). The role of grandparent is an important one for adults because, with increasing lifespans, many will spend one third of their lives as grandparents.

FIGURE 16.5: Proportion of Young Adults Living With Their Parents in the United States, 1968–2012

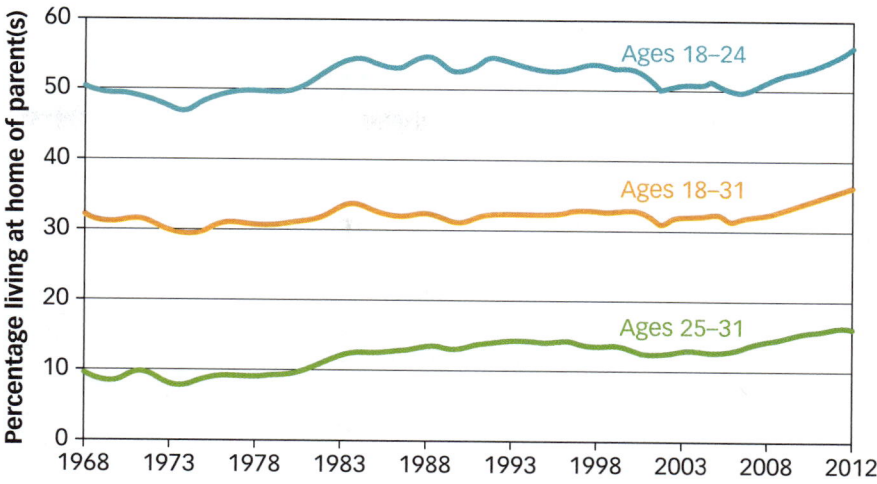

SOURCE: Parker (2012).

FIGURE 16.6: Distribution of Grandparents by Age and Gender in the United States, 2001 and 2015

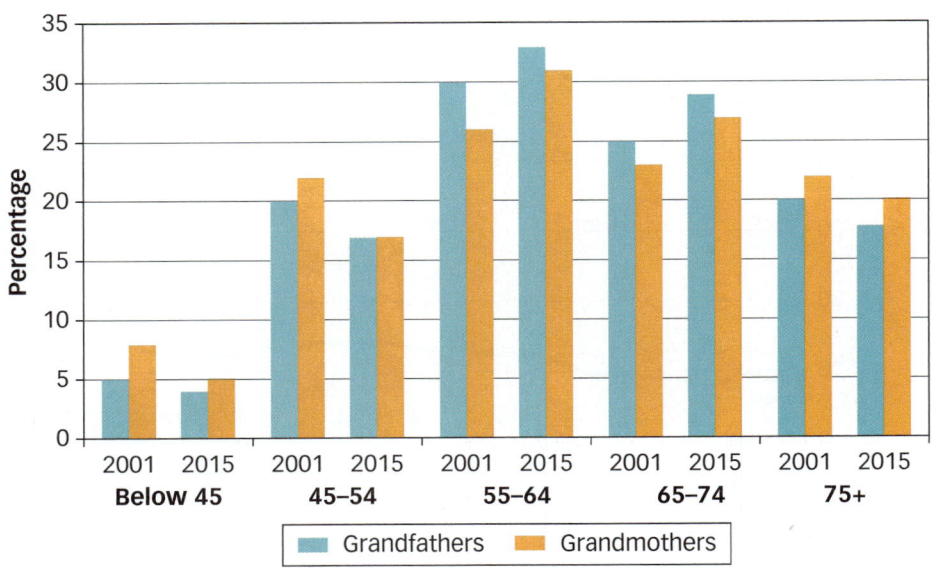

SOURCE: Tergesen (2014).

involvement is high in many minority households, such as Chinese, Korean, Mexican-American, Native American, and Canadian Aboriginal grandparents—this is especially the case for grandmothers, who take on caregiver, mentor, and disciplinarian roles (Kamo, 1998; Werner, 1991; Williams & Torrez, 1998). In particular, more regular contact, closer relationships with grandchildren, and greater parental encouragement to visit with grandchildren are associated with more grandparent involvement. Grandparents who are more engaged and spend more time with their grandchildren tend to report higher levels of life satisfaction (Moore & Rosenthal, 2015). Research with 14 European countries suggests that this is especially true for those who live in countries with high grandparent obligations, such as Italy and Greece (Neuberger & Haberkern, 2013). In some cases, grandparents step in as primary caretakers for their grandchildren, as discussed in Lives in Context (p. 463).

Relationships between grandparents and grandchildren are influenced by several factors, including grandparent and grandchild gender, geographic proximity, socioeconomic status, and culture. In most cultures grandparents and grandchildren of the same sex tend to be closer, especially grandmothers and granddaughters. Generally, grandmothers tend to have more contact with their grandchildren than do grandfathers, and they tend to report higher satisfaction with the grandparent role (Silverstein & Marenco, 2001). Grandparents who live closer to their children tend to have closer relationships with their grandchildren than do those who have contact only on special occasions like holidays and birthdays. In Western nations, most grandparents are able to visit their grandchildren regularly, and those who live far away often remain involved in their grandchildren's lives despite the distance (AARP, 2002). The farther away grandchildren and grandparents live from one another, the fewer face-to-face contacts, landline phone contacts, and mobile contacts such as text messaging (Hurme, Westerback, & Quadrello, 2010). Because parents regulate grandparent–grandchildren contact, grandparents' relationships with their own children influence their contact and relationships with their grandchildren. The parent–adult child relationship changes with the birth of a grandchild and grandparents, and their adult children set new boundaries. Grandparents balance providing support, companionship, and involvement with noninterference (Breheny, Stephens, & Spilsbury, 2014). Bonds with children's spouses are

Throughout life, the timing of developmental transitions influences adaptation. In middle adulthood, the timing of the transition to grandparenthood influences adults' experience of this role. Many middle-aged adults may find that they become grandparents at a time when they are already juggling multiple roles at work and home. Adults who become grandparents earlier than the norm may experience greater pressures between their career goals and responsibilities and their home life and expectations of their role as grandparents (Szinovacz, 1998). Some grandparents may find themselves in the position of parenting young children and adolescents while fulfilling the care and support functions of the grandparent role (Fuller-Thomson & Minkler, 2001). The grandparent role is rewarding, but for many adults, it may be accompanied by role strain as they may juggle expectations of employers, spouses, children, adult children, and grandchildren.

Adult children may expect their parents to help them with child-rearing and to share their knowledge and experience, both with their children and their grandchildren. Grandparents tend to expect frequent contact with their grandchildren at the same time as they expect their own boundaries to be respected (Thiele & Whelan, 2006). Grandparent involvement is associated with child well-being and adolescent adjustment (Griggs, Tan, Buchanan, Attar-Schwartz, & Flouri, 2010). For example, close nurturing relationships with grandparents are associated with positive adjustment and fewer problem behaviors in adolescents in divorced and single-parent homes (Attar-Schwartz, Tan, Buchanan, Flouri, & Griggs, 2009; Henderson, Hayslip, Sanders, & Louden, 2009).

In low-income families, grandparents often usually take on important financial and caregiving roles. Grandparent

Grandparents Raising Grandchildren

Najlah Feanny/Corbis Saba

Raising a grandchild is challenging yet custodial grandparents frequently mention a sense of satisfaction in parenting and in seeing grandchildren's accomplishments.

Raising a child is both challenging and rewarding. Although child-rearing is generally regarded as a one-time phase in the lifespan—reflected in such phrases as "starting a family" or "taking time off to raise a family"—some adults find themselves raising multiple cohorts of children as they take over the parenting of their children's children.

Overall, about 8% of U.S. children under the age of 18 are raised by grandparents, including about 16% of African American, 8% of Hispanic, and 4% of European American non-Hispanic and Asian American children. Large proportions of Native American children are raised by grandparents; some Indian tribes estimate that up to 60% of their children are in this living situation (Goyer, 2006). The majority of custody arrangements are informal with no involvement from child welfare agencies. Grandparents often obtain custody of their grandchildren in response to parental absence or incapacitation from substance abuse, HIV/AIDS, incarceration, abandonment, mental and physical difficulties, and death (Dolbin-MacNab & Keiley, 2006).

The transition to parenting grandchildren is not easy—partly because the reasons for parental absence, such as incarceration or illness, are stressful to both the grandparent and children.

Children often enter grandparent custodial arrangements with preexisting problems due to poor parenting and harsh contextual conditions (Smith & Hancock, 2010). Many children experience internalizing and externalizing difficulties, such as anxiety, depression, aggression, academic difficulties, behavior problems, anger, and guilt (Billing, Ehrle, & Kortenkamp, 2002; Guzell-Roe, Gerard, & Landry-Meyer, 2005). In addition, contextual factors make custodial grandparenting more difficult. Grandparent caregiver arrangements are especially common in low-income communities, as kin offer a safety net for families in crisis and nearly 20% of custodial grandparents live in poverty (Bachman & Chase-Lansdale, 2005; Goyer, 2006).

The majority of grandparents raising grandchildren are in their late 50s and early 60s, with about 70% under the age of 60 (Robinson & Wilks, 2006). As grandparent caregiving is not part of typical midlife development, the off-time nature and reduced opportunities for normative growth make the transition difficult and stressful for adults. Perhaps because of the stress, financial difficulties, feelings of grief and anger toward the parent, and feelings of social isolation, grandparent caregivers tend to suffer mental and physical health problems more than those who do not care for their grandchildren (Edwards & Benson, 2010; Letiecq, Bailey, & Kurtz, 2008). Grandparents who care for grandchildren with emotional and behavioral problems tend to experience higher rates of anxiety, stress, and depression as well as tend to report less life satisfaction (Doley, Bell, Watt, & Simpson, 2015). Research has shown that grandparents who are members of minority groups tend to experience greater risk of health problems because they are more likely to live in poverty and in disadvantaged neighborhoods; however, social support can buffer some negative outcomes (Chen, Mair, Bao, & Yang, 2014; Letiecq et al., 2008; Moore & Miller, 2007).

Despite these challenges, many grandparent caregivers adjust and report positive aspects of caregiving. Many frequently mention a sense of satisfaction in parenting, including positive feelings, such as joy, pride in influencing their grandchildren, love, and satisfaction in seeing grandchildren's accomplishments (Dolbin-MacNab, 2006). Several studies suggest that grandparent well-being is enhanced by raising grandchildren. Some grandparents report feeling fortunate to parent again and to have the opportunity to do a better job and to enjoy the love and companionship of grandchildren (Moore & Miller, 2007). Some grandparents report that raising their grandchildren is easier than parenting their own children because of greater wisdom and experience, feeling more relaxed, and having more time and attention to give to grandchildren (Dolbin-MacNab, 2006). Social support is an important influence on grandparent caregivers' sense of well-being and adjustment. Grandparents who feel that they have a social support network to turn to for emotional and physical assistance tend to show better adjustment and fewer problems (Williams, 2011).

What Do You Think?

Considering custodial grandparenting from a bioecological perspective, identify at least one factor at the microsystem, mesosystem, exosystem, and macrosystem levels that poses challenges to adults' adjustment—that is, identify risk factors. Identify at least one factor at each contextual level that acts as a protective factor, aiding adults' adjustment.

important, especially daughters-in-law, in affecting contact and ties with grandchildren (Fingerman et al., 2004). After an adult child's divorce, grandparents related to the custodial parent typically have more contact with grandchildren (Johnson, 1998).

The grandparent role provides adults opportunities to satisfy generative needs by nurturing a new generation, enjoy spending time and playing with children without the responsibility of parenthood, and gain a sense of immortality by passing along family and personal history as well as a second generation of progeny (Moore & Rosenthal, 2015). Some theorists argue that grandparental investment, the tendency for grandparents to be involved in their grandchildren's lives and transfer resources to them, stems from its provision of evolutionary benefits such as a correlation between the presence of the maternal grandmother and child survival (Coall & Hertwig, 2011). Similar to parent–child relationships, grandparent–grandchild relationships show continuity over time. Close grandparent–grandchild relationships in childhood predict close relations in adulthood (Geurts, Van Tilburg, & Poortman, 2012).

Being a grandparent provides opportunities to enjoy spending time and playing with children without the responsibility of parenthood.

Steve Mason/Photodisc/Thinkstock

CARING FOR AGING PARENTS

Although the image of the "sandwich generation"—midlife adults scrambling to meet the needs of both dependent children and frail elderly parents and thus sandwiched between the two generations (Riley & Bowen, 2005)—is popular, some experts argue that it is not very accurate (Grundy & Henretta, 2006). Rather than raise young children, most midlife parents have adult children. In Chapters 17 and 18, you will learn that most adults remain independent well into older adulthood. Only about one third of 55- to 69-year-old British and American women surveyed reported financial or everyday assistance to both their children and their parents' generations, but one fifth reported helping neither (Grundy & Henretta, 2006). In 2012, only 15% of U.S. midlife adults reported providing financial support to a parent age 65 or older while raising a minor child or supporting a grown child (Parker & Patten, 2013). It seems that the task for most midlife adults is to support still partly dependent adult children and elderly parents who require some assistance; however, middle-aged adults are more likely to provide financial support to a grown child than to an elderly parent. For example, about one third (32%) of midlife adults with a parent over the age of 65 provided some financial support in the past year, as compared with 73% of midlife adults with a child over the age of 18 who provided some financial help in the last year (Parker & Patten, 2013). Although the popular "sandwich" metaphor may exaggerate the number of midlife adults who financially support two generations, most adults do provide emotional support and assistance to multiple generations.

Adults report a range of motivations for providing care to their aging parents, including obligation, reciprocity, and the quality of the relationship (Stuifbergen, Dykstra, Lanting, & van Delden, 2010). Overall, the perceived responsibility to care for aging parents tends to decline during adulthood. Young adults tend to take an idealistic view and perceive strong obligations whereas midlife adults adopt a more realistic perspective as they anticipate the need to provide care and better appreciate the responsibilities and sacrifices (Gans & Silverstein, 2006). The level of care that adult children provide aging parents is influenced by the parent–child relationship as well as family circumstances and ethnicity. In one large sample of middle-aged adults in the Netherlands, having few siblings, a widowed parent without a new partner, and a short geographical distance between the parent and child's homes was positively associated with adult children's provision of care and support to parents (Stuifbergen, van Delden, & Dykstra, 2008). African American and Hispanic adults at all income levels are more likely than European American non-Hispanic adults to provide aging parents with financial and caregiving assistance given the cultural value of familism, a duty to care for the family (Shuey & Hardy, 2003). Chinese, Japanese, and Korean women tend to provide care for their husband's aging parents, who tend to live with them (Montgomery, Rowe, & Kosloski, 2007; Zhan, 2004). Similarly, intergenerational relations between older-age parents and their children remain close throughout life, with over 70% of older persons living with or next to a child (Knodel & Chayovan, 2009).

Generally speaking, parents and adult children who have a lifetime of close and positive relations tend to remain close and adult children tend to provide more assistance than do those whose family relations are less positive (Whitbeck & Hoyt, 1994). In middle age, many people take a close look at relationships with parents, appreciating their parents' assistance and sacrifices over the years. Relationships between mothers and daughters, usually closer than other parent–child relationships, tend to become more intimate and complex as daughters enter middle age (Fingerman, 2000, 2001; Lefkowitz & Fingerman, 2003). Daughters, especially those who live in close proximity, are most likely to be caregivers (Pillemer & Suitor, 2014). Daughters' multiple responsibilities to children and career often conflict with their ability to meet their aging mothers' increasing demands for physical and emotional care and attention. Although parent–child ties influence caregiving, adults with weak parent–child relationships often provide care to parents out of a sense of duty (Silverstein, Conroy, Wang, Giarrusso, & Bengtson, 2002).

As adults' caregiving responsibilities increase, such as when elderly parents require specialized care as is common in cases of dementia, they are more likely to experience conflicts among their many roles. Caregivers who experience role overload can feel overwhelmed by their obligations to parents, children, spouses, employers, and friends, which is associated with anxiety, exhaustion, and depression (Killian, Turner, & Cain, 2005; Savia, Almeida, Davey, & Zant, 2008). Adults of ethnic and cultural groups that emphasize familism and the duty to care for elders tend to experience more anxiety and depression with caregiving (Dilworth-Anderson, Goodwin, & Williams, 2004). As women are more likely than men to be expected to provide care, caregiving can interfere with women's employment, causing losses in hours and earnings. In one large study of U.S. women, assuming the role of caregiver was associated with worsened economic well-being eight years later. Women who provided 20 hours a week of care were 25% more likely to live in poverty, 27% more likely to receive public assistance, and 46% more likely to receive Medicaid eight years later (Killian et al., 2005). Likewise, men and women who participated in the Survey of Health, Ageing, and Retirement in Europe showed that giving informal care to one's elderly parents was associated with significant costs in terms of employment opportunities and participation (Bolin, Lindgren, & Lundborg, 2008). Caregivers who face multiple career and child-rearing demands are more likely to feel role strain, depressive symptoms, a reduced sense of personal mastery and self-efficacy as well as engage in fewer outside activities (Mausbach et al., 2012; Wang, Shyu, Chen, & Yang, 2011). Similar to adults who experience role overload in managing family and career, social support and tangible assistance in the form of caregiving assistance aids in reducing distress.

Thinking in Context 16.3

1. Consider a midlife parent, Bob. How might Bob's relationship with his adult child be influenced by parent–child interactions during childhood and adolescence? How might Bob's experiences with his own parents, in childhood through young adulthood, influence his current relationship with his adult child? Finally, how might Bob's interactions with his parents during childhood, adolescence, and young adulthood influence his current relationship with his parents?

2. What are the effects of divorce during the adult years? In your view, are young adults or midlife adults better poised to adapt to divorce? What contextual factors influence adaptation to divorce, and how might these factors change over the adult years?

CAREERS IN MIDDLE ADULTHOOD

Throughout adult life, work is usually the mainstay that structures people's days, contributes to a sense of identity and self-esteem, and provides a number of benefits aside from income. Through work, people have opportunities to interact with others; to display generativity by creating products, items, and ideas by advising and mentoring others; and to contribute to the support of their families and communities. Young adults tend to gravitate toward jobs that emphasize extrinsic rewards such as high salaries and employee benefits whereas middle-aged employees tend to place greater importance on the intrinsic rewards of work, such as friendships with coworkers, job satisfaction, self-esteem, and feeling that one is making a difference (Sterns & Huyck, 2001). As described in the following section, job satisfaction is more closely associated with the pleasures of surmounting challenges, engaging in creative pursuits, being productive, and other intrinsic rewards of work than with high pay and other extrinsic rewards.

JOB SATISFACTION

Job satisfaction tends to increase in middle adulthood—more so for professionals than blue-collar workers and men than women (Hochwarter, Ferris, Perrewé, Witt, & Kiewitz, 2001; Ng & Feldman, 2010). Blue-collar workers tend to have more highly structured jobs with fewer opportunities to control their activities than do white-collar workers, which may contribute to their relatively lower level of job satisfaction (Avolio & Sosik, 1999; Hu, Kaplan, & Dalal, 2010). As discussed in Chapter 13, women and minority members face special challenges and inequalities in the workplace, which increase with time and may influence job satisfaction.

First, women and minority members are less likely to occupy supervisory positions than are white men. One study of more than 1,300 adults in the United States found that over a 30-year career, white men were more likely to advance to managerial positions than were white women and black men, who in turn were more likely to advance than were black women (Maume, 2004). The highest and most prestigious positions in management are most likely to be held by white men. For example, women serve as CEOs of only about 5% of the top 1,000 companies in the United States (Pew Research Center, 2015). Career advancement is associated with increases in job satisfaction during middle adulthood, as midlife adults have more opportunities to participate in decision making, find workloads more manageable, and reduce their career aspirations to realistic levels given their accomplishments to date (Barnes-Farrell & Matthews, 2007). The glass ceiling that women and minority members face may translate into lower rates of job satisfaction, as fewer opportunities for career advancement contribute to a sense of inequality and dissatisfaction (Maume, 2004).

Paradoxically, however, women tend to show higher job satisfaction than men, or in some cases, similar levels of satisfaction to men (Donohue & Heywood, 2013; Zou, 2015). Research with European samples suggests that the gender-job satisfaction paradox is more apparent in countries where the job market is more challenging for women and nonexistent in countries that offer equal opportunities for women (Kaiser, 2007). Some suggest that the gender difference lies in work orientations and preferences for extrinsic versus intrinsic rewards. Specifically, for women job satisfaction is positively linked to both extrinsic and intrinsic rewards, but for men, job satisfaction tends to be positively linked to extrinsic rewards (Linz & Semykina, 2013). Women may find work intrinsically rewarding and derive satisfaction regardless of extrinsic rewards such as promotions and salaries; therefore, many experience job satisfaction in spite of the glass ceiling.

Samples of adults from China, Europe, Japan, Turkey, and the United States show that age is generally associated with increases in job satisfaction (Barnes-Farrell & Matthews, 2007). Some midlife adults, however, experience a rise in job burnout, a sense of mental exhaustion that accompanies long-term job stress, excessive workloads, and reduced feelings of control. Burnout is more frequent in professions that are interpersonally demanding and whose demands may exceed workers' coping skills, such as in the helping professions of health care, human services, and teaching (Melamed, Shirom, Toker, Berliner, & Shapira, 2006; Wu, Zhu, Li, Wang, & Wang, 2008). Males who perform physically demanding work, such as laborers and construction workers, may find that the physical changes that occur over the course of middle adulthood make them less able to perform physically demanding work (Gilbert &

Constantine, 2005). These workers are more likely to experience burnout and reduced job satisfaction.

Employee burnout is a serious problem in the workplace. Burnout is linked with impairments in attention and concentration abilities, depression, illnesses, poor job performance, workplace injuries, and high levels of employee absenteeism and turnover (Deligkaris, Panagopoulou, Montgomery, & Masoura, 2014; Shirom & Melamed, 2005). When workers receive social support, assistance in managing workloads and reducing stress, and opportunities to participate in creating an attractive workplace environment, they are less likely to experience job burnout (Warr, 2007). Middle-aged workers are sometimes the objects of age discrimination in the workplace, as discussed in Ethical and Policy Applications of Lifespan Development (p. 467)

PLANNING FOR RETIREMENT

Retirement planning is a process that often begins once the adult becomes aware that it is looming on the horizon (Kim & Moen, 2002); however, it should begin much earlier (Adams & Rau, 2011). Retirement planning is important because retirement represents a major life transition, and adults who plan ahead for the financial and lifestyle changes that accompany retirement tend to show better adjustment and greater life satisfaction (Hershey, Jacobs-Lawson, McArdle, & Hamagami, 2007; Jacobs-Lawson, Hershey, & Neukam, 2004).

In 1900, nearly 70% of men over the age of 65 were in the workforce; in 2014, about 18% of people over the age of 65 are in the workforce, with older men more likely to remain in the workforce than women (U.S. Bureau of Labor, 2015). Adults in most developed countries, including the United States and Canada, are eligible for government-sponsored retirement funds. In the United States, Social Security permits people to retire from work as early as age 62 (Chappell, Gee, McDonald, & Stones, 2003; Schultz & Shoven, 2008). An average worker today can look forward to approximately 15 years of retirement (Social Security Administration, 2015). Many may be retired for 20 or more years, or nearly one quarter of their lives.

Unfortunately, many U.S. adults are not financially prepared for retirement. It is estimated that workers should plan for retirement income of at least 70% to 80% of current pre-retirement income, yet about one third of middle-class households have no savings, including 19% of 55- to 64-year-old adults (Wells Fargo, 2014). In 2013, the median retirement account balance among all households ages 55 to 64 was only $14,500 (Wells Fargo, 2014). As of 2013, one study in 2008 found that only about half of adults reported planning for retirement, and one in four baby boomers might not ever be able to afford to stop working and retire (Korczyk, 2008). Adults with more positive beliefs about their ability to control aspects of aging are more likely to financially plan for retirement as compared with those

ETHICAL AND POLICY APPLICATIONS OF LIFESPAN DEVELOPMENT

Age Discrimination

Joe Radle/Getty

As workers approach later midlife they are more likely to experience age discrimination in the workplace.

As the baby boom generation has progressed through the lifespan, the sheer size of the cohort has influenced the contexts in which it is embedded, from the increase in elementary and secondary schools while boomers were children to the expansion of child care facilities to meet their needs for child care when they became parents. With their increased lifespan, better health, and later childbearing relative to prior generations, baby boomers are expected to spend more years in the workforce than did their parents and grandparents (Nyce, 2007)—and boomers are increasingly likely to experience age discrimination in the workplace. It is estimated that 84% of Americans over age 60 have experienced at least one instance of age discrimination (Palmore, Branch, & Harris, 2005). Examples of age discrimination include insulting jokes, disrespect, and patronizing behavior accompanying assumptions of frailty, mental incompetence, or health ailments (Palmore et al., 2005). Overall, the risk of experiencing age discrimination shows two peaks: as workers approach age 50 and as they near retirement (Roscigno, Mong, Byron, & Tester, 2007).

Older workers often encounter a mix of perceptions in the workplace. Workers over 50 are often valued for their experience, knowledge, work habits, respect for colleagues and authority, positive attitudes, commitment to quality, and ability to keep cool in crisis (Dennis & Thomas, 2007). However, older workers also encounter negative perceptions. They are sometimes stereotyped as inflexible, conservative, less engaged, less sharp, unwilling to adapt to technology, less assertive, complacent as well as having physical limitations and costing a company more for health insurance and related benefits (Gee, Pavalko, & Long, 2007).

Self-reported age discrimination is associated with tangible inequities including employment, income, and perceived status in the workplace (Mays, Cochran, & Baines, 2007). Age discrimination is stressful for adults, can undermine their sense of self, and harm psychological well-being (Jang, Chiriboga, & Small, 2008; Yuan, 2007). Perceived discrimination is associated with feelings of distress and more mental health problems. The effects of perceived discrimination and its influence on positive and negative affect vary with the person's feelings of control. One study of over 1,500 middle-aged through older adults showed that perceived discrimination was more closely associated with negative affect when the person felt little control over the situation (Jang et al., 2008). In addition, perceived discrimination was more closely associated with declines in well-being in middle-aged adults and females than older adults and males. Strategies that adults use when confronted with discrimination include identifying positive personal attributes and focusing on valued self-conceptions (Shih, Young, & Bucher, 2013).

In 1967, President Lyndon B. Johnson signed the Age Discrimination in Employment Act (ADEA), a formal acknowledgment of the existence of ageism in the workplace. The purpose of the ADEA is "to promote the employment of older persons based on ability rather than age, to prohibit arbitrary age discrimination in employment and to help employers and workers find ways to address problems arising from the impact of age on employment" (29 USC 621(b)). The original legislation protected employees between the ages of 40 and 65. In 1978, Congress passed an amendment to extend the age of the protected group from 65 to 70, and on January 1, 1987, the age cap was lifted completely (McCann, 2003). There is an exemption, however, for workers who are responsible for public safety, including firefighters, police officers, pilots, and others (Dennis & Thomas, 2007). These workers are required to retire at an earlier age, often by 55 or 60. Although the ADEA has existed for over three decades, age discrimination persists in and out of the workplace.

What Do You Think?

1. **What might be the psychological effects of experiencing age discrimination?**

2. **How might employers reduce age discrimination in the workplace?**

with an intermittent, rather than a constant, awareness of the aging process are less likely to make such financial provisions (Heraty & McCarthy, 2015).

Most adults are aware that retirement planning entails preparing for changes in income, but planning for retirement should also include recognition of impending lifestyle changes and changes in the amount of free time available and how it will be used. Work activities encompass much of adults' days, beginning in early adulthood. With retirement, most adults find that they need to determine how they will spend their time, often for the first time in their lives. With virtually unlimited possibilities, some adults may feel overwhelmed, at least temporarily; others are glad to devote themselves to endeavors they have "always wanted" to pursue, or to seek out entirely new activities and areas of interest. Some "give back" to the community or their pre-retirement careers by volunteering. Others may learn a new language, accomplish home renovations, or spend more time with family members. In contrast, retirees who do not plan how they will spend time may find themselves adrift. Just as financial planning is critical to a satisfactory retirement, planning an active life also contributes to postretirement adjustment and happiness (Noone, Stephens, & Alpass, 2009).

The two and one-half decades that span the middle adult years are a time of stability and change. Personality and many aspects of self remain consistent whereas midlife adults' closest relationships change as children grow up and parents age. Most adults adapt to changes in career and family roles with little difficulty and show positive psychosocial adjustment over middle adulthood. In Chapters 17 and 18, we will see that the older adult years entail greater demands for adjustment.

Apply Your Knowledge

"I'm so exhausted," said Marilyn. "I'm working so hard and juggling so much that I can't keep up." At 52, Marilyn held multiple roles but didn't feel a sense of control or competence in any of them. Her job was a source of stress and disappointment. Passed up for managerial work, Marilyn remained at the lower rungs of the corporate ladder despite the many new young hires each year. Sometimes she feels out of touch at meetings as she no longer keeps up with the technology and slang. For example, in a marketing meeting she was embarrassed to ask the speaker for a definition of *tweet*.

Marilyn's home life is filled with adjustments. After her youngest child moved out, Marilyn and her husband, Gene, began to feel that they no longer knew or cared deeply about each other; their connection was lost. Soon Gene moved out and began divorce proceedings. Many days, Marilyn found it hard to get out of bed and get dressed for work, feeling that the good years of her life are over and the few remaining decades will simply get worse.

Upon her daughter's arrest for drug use and subsequent stay at a long-term substance abuse treatment facility, Marilyn took on responsibility as guardian for her 7-year-old grandson, Mikey. Marilyn was furious with her daughter's irresponsibility and felt that both she and her daughter had failed as mothers.

She loved Mikey dearly but felt ill equipped to care for a child while working full-time and managing her own sadness over the divorce and her daughter's behavior. Mikey's special needs for attention as he missed his mother often led to trouble at school.

Marilyn began to experience anxiety attacks on her way to work each morning. "I never know what the day will bring, and I didn't expect my life to turn out this way," she said to her best friend, Jalna. She and Jalna had been friends for 30 years and knew everything about each other. Marilyn didn't get to see her often because the business of life got in the way, but her friendship with Jalna helped her cope with the many changes of her life.

1. Does Marilyn's experience reflect normative midlife changes? In what ways is Marilyn's experience typical of middle-aged adults? Which of her experiences are unique to her, reflecting development that is not normative?

2. Compare Marilyn's experiences with marriage, divorce, and grandparenting to research findings in this area.

3. Discuss factors that may influence Marilyn's adjustment to life changes. What contextual factors might ease her adjustment?

4. What changes can the typical midlife adult expect with regard to the sense of self, personality, career, marriage, family, and friends?

Chapter Summary

16.1 Compare Erikson's and Levinson's perspectives of the psychosocial tasks of middle adulthood.

For Erik Erikson, the psychosocial task of middle adulthood is cultivating a sense of generativity. Adults fulfill generative needs through volunteering, teaching, and mentoring others in the workplace and community. Generativity is associated with well-being. Daniel Levinson proposed that the life structure refers to the overall organization of a person's life. During the midlife transition, adults reexamine their life dream established in early adulthood, evaluate their success in achieving it, reevaluate their goals and their relations with their social context, and modify their life structures accordingly.

16.2 Analyze the theoretical and empirical support for the midlife crisis.

The most popular stereotype about middle age is the midlife crisis, a stressful time in the early to middle 40s when adults are thought to evaluate their lives. Successfully traversing the midlife crisis requires that adults modify their life structure, reevaluate their goals and their relations within their social context, and develop a sense of generativity. The midlife crisis is not universal and depends on individual factors and circumstances rather than age.

16.3 Evaluate the changes that occur in self-concept and identity during middle adulthood and their relation to well-being.

Self-concept becomes more complex and integrated into middle adulthood yet shows remarkable consistency. Midlife adults compare the lives they have achieved with their hoped-for possible selves and the degree of match between the two influences their life satisfaction. Revised possible selves permit middle-aged adults to show higher self-esteem than young adults. Over the middle adult years, many adults begin to integrate masculine and feminine aspects of themselves, becoming more androgynous. Androgyny provides adults with a greater repertoire of skills, which permits them to adapt to a variety of situations with greater ease than do those who are not androgynous.

16.4 Examine the stability of the Big 5 personality traits.

The many characteristics on which people differ can be categorized into five clusters of personality traits, collectively known as the Big 5 personality traits: openness, conscientiousness, extroversion, agreeableness, and neuroticism. The Big 5 personal factors are thought to reflect inherited predispositions that persist throughout life and predict career, family, and personal choices in adulthood. People show unique patterns of traits and individual differences in personality traits are highly stable, yet cross-sectional research suggests subtle changes, with agreeableness and conscientiousness increasing and neuroticism, extroversion, and openness declining into middle adulthood, suggesting that adults mellow out with age.

16.5 Discuss the changing nature of friendship in middle adulthood.

Midlife adults spend less time with friends than family, but friendships continue to be important sources of social support and are associated with well-being and self-esteem. Friendships improve with age. Midlife adults have fewer friends than do young adults but, unlike young adults, nearly all midlife friendships are described as close, and few to none are ambivalent or troubled. Similar to earlier periods in life, midlife friends share demographic similarities, experiences, and values that make them useful sources of advice for dealing with serious problems.

16.6 Discuss marital satisfaction, risks for divorce, and outcomes of divorce in midlife.

Many midlife couples cope with greater role strain than at any life stage. Marital satisfaction tends to increase over the middle adult years as child-rearing tasks and stress decline, family incomes rise, and spouses get better at understanding each other and have more time to spend with each other. By the 60s, most couples are happier. Divorce is challenging at all ages, but middle-aged persons show less of a decline in psychological well-being and overall better adaptation than do young adults. However, the breakup of a second marriage tends to be more stressful for adults and children than the demise of the first marriage.

16.7 Analyze family relationships in midlife, including the parent adult–child, grandparent, and midlife child–older adult parent relationship.

There is continuity in parent–child relationships throughout the lifespan. Parents and adult children tend to become closer as they mature. Grandparent involvement is associated with child well-being and adolescent adjustment. Most middle-aged adults have one or more living parents, and over the years, they provide increasing assistance to their aging parents. The level of care that adult children provide aging parents is influenced by the parent–child relationship as well as family circumstances and ethnicity. Midlife adults who care for aging parents may experience role overload.

16.8 Characterize job satisfaction during the midlife years.

Cross-culturally, job satisfaction tends to increase in middle adulthood, especially with career advancement but more so for professionals than blue-collar workers and men than women. The glass ceiling, lower rates of career advancement, that women and minority members face contribute to lower rates of job satisfaction. Some midlife adults experience a rise in job burnout, which is associated with cognitive and mental health impairments; reductions in productivity; and increases in injuries, absenteeism, and turnover.

16.9 Examine retirement planning and its effects on adjustment to retirement.

Many U.S. adults are not financially prepared for retirement. Retirement planning entails not only planning for changes in income but also changes in lifestyle and how we spend our time. Retirement planning is associated with better adjustment and satisfaction.

Key Terms

androgyny   453

Big 5 personality traits   454

generativity   448

life structure   449

midlife crisis   450

possible selves   452

seasons of life   449

PART VIII

Late Adulthood

In older adulthood the balance of gains and losses shifts. Physical losses increase; however, older adults' functioning varies widely. They compensate for losses by modifying their behaviors and environment. The benefits of regular exercise in older adulthood include increases in strength, balance, and endurance as well as improved physiological function, better mental health, and higher quality of life. Although older adults show declines in fluid intelligence, they remain adaptive problem solvers throughout adulthood, performing best on everyday problems that are relevant to the contexts they experience in their daily lives. Motivated to engage in reminiscence and life review, older adults work to find continuity, come to terms with choices, and assign meaning to their lives.

Within the home context, marital satisfaction increases in older adulthood. Parent-child relationships shift as adult children provide increasing assistance to their elderly parents. With increases in leisure time, the peer context rises in salience in older adulthood. Friendships become more important, more fulfilling, and more activity based. Most elderly Friendships are old relationships, established much earlier in life. Retirement and the loss of the work context is an important transition for many older adults and success is influenced by a sense of control over the decision. Overall, the developmental changes older adults experience in physical and cognitive domains are offset by gains in socioemotional functioning and are influenced by the multiple interacting contexts in which they are embedded.

DR. KUTHER'S
CHALK TALKS

Watch at
edge.sagepub.com/kuther

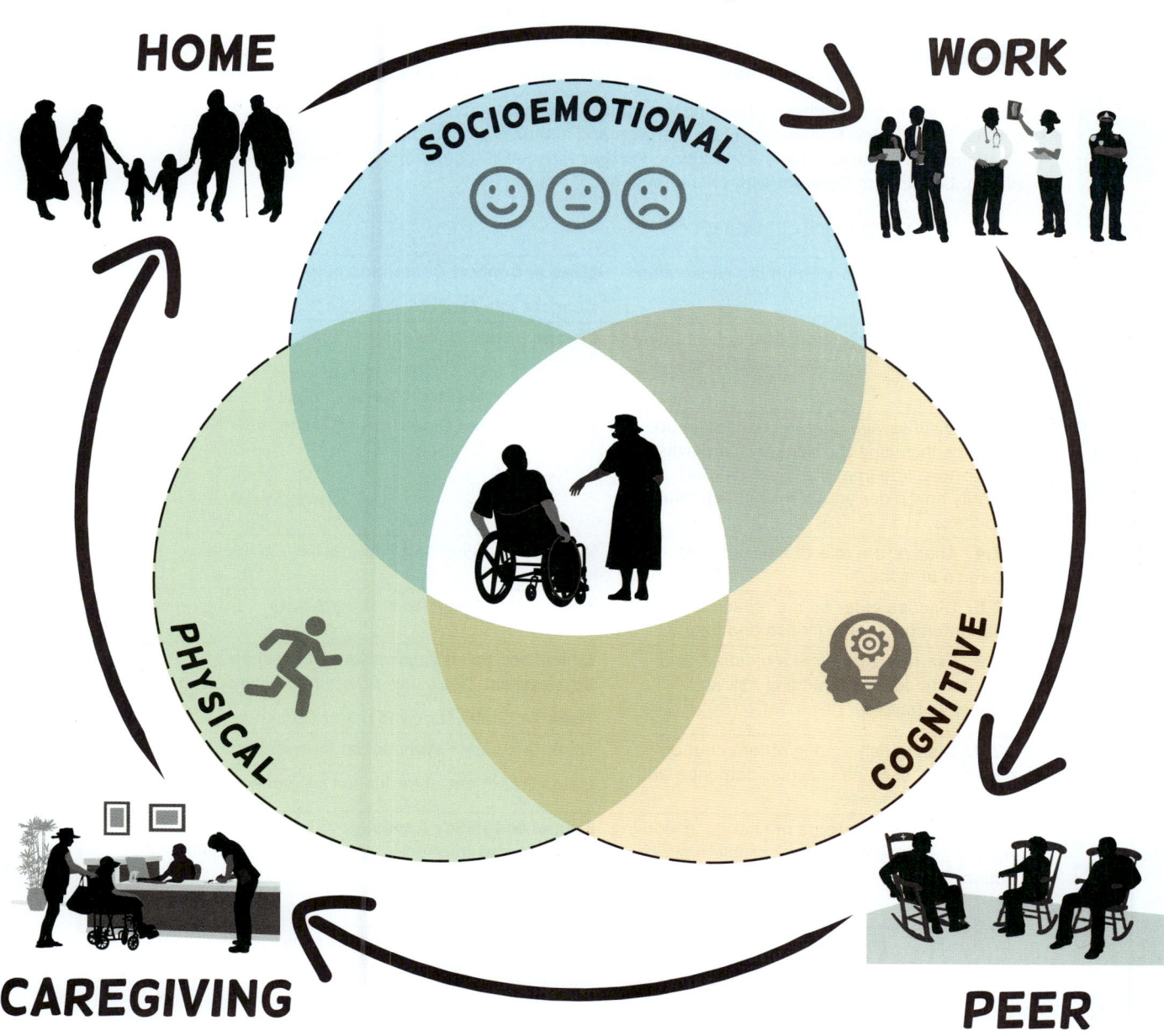

HOME

WORK

SOCIOEMOTIONAL

PHYSICAL

COGNITIVE

CAREGIVING

PEER

Images: ©iStock.com

CHAPTER 17

Physical and Cognitive Development in Late Adulthood

$SAGE edge™ **Get the edge on your studies at edge.sagepub.com/kuther.**

Master these learning objectives using key study tools in the chapter and at SAGE edge. Access original SAGE **Video Cases** to explore the lives and contexts of individuals in every stage of development, **Think Critically** and **Explore Further** with SAGE journal and reference articles, and **Watch**, **Listen**, and **Connect** with online multimedia resources.

LEARNING OBJECTIVES	KEY STUDY TOOLS
17.1. Identify influences on life expectancy.	**Lives in Context** Centenarians (p. 477)
	Connect Life Expectancy
17.2. Explain the neurological developments that take place during older adulthood.	**Lifespan Brain Development** Brain Growth in Older Adulthood (p. 480)
	Explore Further Neurobiology of Aging
17.3. Discuss age-related changes in body systems including the sensory, cardiovascular, respiratory, and immune systems, and identify how older adults may compensate for changes.	**Explore Further** Disability and Disablement
17.4. Analyze the role of nutrition and exercise in aging.	**Video Case** Aging and Physical Development
17.5. Discuss older adults' susceptibility and adaptation to chronic illness and injury.	**Video Case** Caring for Ill Older Adults
17.6. Examine Alzheimer's disease, and discuss its course, including risk and protective factors.	**Ethical and Policy Applications of Lifespan Development** Disclosing a Dementia Diagnosis (p. 493)
	Think Critically Family Risks of Dementia
17.7. Distinguish among other common dementias, such as vascular dementia and Parkinson's disease.	**Think Critically** Psychosocial Interventions
	Listen Treatment of Parkinson's Disease
17.8. Compare patterns of change in working memory, long-term memory, problem solving capacities, and wisdom.	**Ethical and Policy Applications of Lifespan Development** Informed Consent in Older Adulthood (p. 499)
	Explore Further Memory
17.9. Identify influences on cognitive change	**Explore Further** Intellectual Decline

"See you next week, Grandma!" Travis called out to his grandmother, Sylvia, as he headed toward his car. At 75 years of age, Sylvia lives alone in a condo located in a development designed for senior citizens. Thanks to a comfortable pension she inherited through her late husband's retirement plan, she is able to afford regular help around the house, including a housekeeper who does house cleaning and laundry each week and an aide who stops by a couple of days a week to help Sylvia with tasks such as grocery shopping. Sylvia no longer drives at night because of her poor vision. As Sylvia explained, "Without my hearing aid, I'm no fun at the dinner table. Physically, I'm not as quick as I used to be, but I get along just fine. The days of 5K races are over for me." Sylvia has noticed that she often

forgets new information, like people's names, so she works hard to remember names by repeating them. Overall, she feels that she is still good at making decisions. Her grandchildren—even the oldest, who recently graduated from medical school—turn to her for advice and tell her she is wise. In many ways, Sylvia is the picture of successful aging. Older adults display a range of functioning. Some, like Sylvia, remain free of physical and cognitive disabilities. All older adults experience declines in physical and cognitive areas and many experience chronic illnesses that pose demands for adaptation. In this chapter, we examine the physical and cognitive side of aging, including the challenges to physical and mental health that older adults face.

As is the case with people in other ages in life, older adults vary in their health and functioning. Many remain free of serious physical and cognitive disabilities. All older adults experience declines in physical and cognitive areas, and many experience chronic illnesses that pose demands for adaptation. In this chapter, we examine the physical and cognitive side of aging, including the challenges to physical and mental health that older adults face.

LIFE EXPECTANCY

The human lifespan has increased dramatically over the past century. A baby born in 1900 in the United States could expect to live to about 47 years of age; in 1950, 68 years of age; and in 2000, about 77 years of age (Central Intelligence Agency, 2013; National Center for Health Statistics, 2011). In 2014, infants born in the United States can expect to live to age 80. Some adults live well beyond the expected lifespan to a very old age.

The increase in life expectancy can be attributed to the influence of contextual factors such as advances in health care, nutrition, and sanitation (Hinterlong, 2008). Perhaps the most notable contributor to increases in life expectancy is the reduction in infant mortality. Death during childbirth, a common hazard to women in the early 1900s, is rare in industrialized nations. Breakthroughs in medicine and increases in the availability of health care mean that fewer people die of common ailments such as flu, pneumonia, and heart disease. A greater understanding of the role of lifestyle factors such as smoking, exercise habits, and diet also contributes to advances in longevity (Danaei et al., 2010). Although cancer remains a leading cause of death, the cancer survival rate, defined as living five years after diagnosis, is higher than ever. By 2007, over two thirds of adults diagnosed with cancer in the United States and Canada were survivors, as compared with about one half in 1977 (DeSantis et al., 2014; Siegel, Ma, Zou, & Jemal, 2014).

Centenarians, individuals who live past 100 years, are becoming more common (see Lives in Context, p. 477). There were 37,000 centenarians recorded in the United States in 1990 and nearly 54,000 in 2010 (U.S. Bureau of the Census, 2010). The longest recorded human lifespan is 122 years (Whitney, 1997). The number of centenarians is expected to rise rapidly in the coming decades.

Life expectancy varies with contextual factors such as gender, ethnicity, socioeconomic status, and nationality. For example, girls born in the United States today can expect to live about 5 years longer than boys (U.S. Bureau of the Census, 2012). In nearly all cultures, women live longer than men, although the gap is smaller in nonindustrialized countries where childbirth remains a serious threat to women's health (Central Intelligence Agency, 2013). Over the past 50 years, the gender gap in life expectancy has shrunk in Western nations because of gains in medical technology and an increasing recognition of the effects of lifestyle on health (Dodson, 2007; Phillips, 2006). In addition to gender, ethnicity is associated with life expectancy. As we have discussed, ethnicity is linked closely with socioeconomic status in the United States. Ethnic differences in life expectancy are influenced by poverty, poor access to health care, high infant mortality, injuries, high stress, and violence—all factors that accompany low socioeconomic status.

There are large international differences in lifespan, influenced by the availability of social services such as health care and housing. Estimates of life expectancy for infants born in 2014 varied among nations from a high of 89 in Monaco and 84 in Japan to a low of 49 in Chad (Central Intelligence Agency, 2013). In developing nations whose populations are more likely to be ravaged by poverty and war, most people can expect to live into their early 60s; in some countries, such as Afghanistan, Chad, and South Africa, life expectancy is only 50. Active life expectancy, defined as the number of years a person can expect to be healthy and physically and intellectually active, shows even more variation.

Advances in life expectancy have led gerontologists to categorize older adults into the **young-old**, **old-old**, and **oldest-old**. The young-old, ages 65 to 74, tend to be active, healthy, and financially and physically independent. Old-old adults (75 to 84) typically live independently but often experience some physical and mental impairment. The oldest-old, adults 85 years and older, are at highest risk for physical and mental health problems and often are unable to live independently, requiring physical and social support to carry out the tasks of daily life. Although these age categories are thought to predict physical health and dependency, some adults in their mid-60s show advanced signs of aging characteristic of the oldest-old, while others in their late 80s function similarly to old-old adults. Because of this, many developmental researchers categorize older adults not by chronological age but by functioning, using terms such as *successful aging* and *impaired aging* (Aldwin, Spiro, & Park, 2006; Baltes & Carstensen, 2003; Freund & Baltes, 2007).

Thinking in Context 17.1

Consider longevity from a bioecological perspective. What factors may help extend the lifespan? Specifically, identify factors in the microsystem, mesosystem, exosystem, and macrosystem. Which variables do you think are most important? Why?

Centenarians

Adults 90 years of age and older are the fastest growing population in Western countries. Centenarians, once an oddity, are increasingly common.

It was once thought that it was impossible to live past 100 years of age; however, medical and technological advances have led to a rise in the prevalence of centenarians. In fact, adults 90 years of age and older are the fastest growing population in Western countries (Administration on Aging, 2014). Centenarians are becoming more common in industrialized nations around the world, including the Denmark, Italy, Japan, the United Kingdom, the United States, and more (Santos-Lozano et al., 2015).

Throughout their lives, most centenarians tend to be healthier than their same-age peers, often delaying the onset of mortality-related diseases and disability until well into their 90s (Ailshire, Beltrán-Sánchez, & Crimmins, 2015; Sebastiani & Perls, 2012). Like all adults, most centenarians experience chronic age-related diseases, but nearly 25% reach age 100 with no chronic disease (Ash et al., 2015). For example, in one sample of Australian centenarians, 19% reported reaching age 100 without experiencing any of the following common diseases: osteoporosis, **dementia**, cardiovascular disease, respiratory illnesses, cancers, anxiety, and depression. An additional one third reported experiencing one or more of these ailments with an onset after age 80 (Richmond, Law, & KayLambkin, 2012). Moreover, centenarians seem to manage chronic illnesses more effectively than other older

adults, with many not experiencing disability until well into their 90s (Sebastiani & Perls, 2012).

With regard to cognitive functioning, research suggests that centenarians fall into two distinct groups. About one half to two thirds appear to reach 100 without cognitive impairment (Ailshire et al., 2015; Corrada, Brookmeyer, Paganini-Hill, Berlau, & Kawas, 2010). Other data with Japanese centenarians showed that primary memory was influenced by advanced age; specifically, the ability to store information declines but the ability to process information is maintained (Inagaki et al., 2009). In contrast, about one third to one half of centenarians show a pattern of lower cognitive performance and dementia (Davey et al., 2013).

Longevity is influenced by both genes and lifestyle factors through epigenetics. (Recall from Chapter 2 that epigenetics is the interactive process by which external or environmental factors can "switch" genes on and off.) For example, families tend to show similarities in lifespan. A particular gene known as the *APOE gene* is associated with longevity and centenarians show different patterns of APOE activation that may be linked with their lower likelihood of disease and longer lifespan (Gentilini et al., 2013; Sebastiani & Perls, 2012; Shadyab & LaCroix, 2015). Lifestyle factors, such as nutrition, stress, and smoking, may show epigenetic effects on longevity by turning particular genes on and off (Govindaraju, Atzmon, & Barzilai, 2015).

Living a long life may sound appealing, but what most people really aspire to is a long, high-quality life. What factors contribute to quality of life for those who live to an advanced age? One thing that people can choose to pursue is an engaged lifestyle, characterized by positive psychosocial functioning, such as having good relationships with children and being involved with family, friends, and community. Optimism, not feeling lonely, perceiving a sense of control over health issues, and adaptability are all associated with high ratings of perceived health among centenarians (Tigani, Artemiadis, Alexopoulos, Chrousos, & Darviri, 2012). Life satisfaction predicts future happiness and influences how centenarians frame their subjective evaluations of their own health status (Bishop, Martin, MacDonald, & Poon, 2010). Centenarians tend to attribute their longevity to lifestyle choices; social relationships and support; and to their own attitudes about life, including optimism and adaptability (Freeman, Garcia, & Marston, 2013). In addition, personality traits such as emotional stability, extraversion, openness, and conscientiousness are associated with maintaining a high level of cognitive and adaptive functioning among centenarians (Martin, Baenziger, MacDonald, Siegler, & Poon, 2009).

What Do You Think?

1. Identify some of the challenges and opportunities that come with the rapid increase of the number of centenarians in our society.

2. Provide at least two reasons why you would like to live to become a centenarian and two reasons why you would not want to become a centenarian.

PHYSICAL DEVELOPMENT IN LATE ADULTHOOD

By late adulthood, biological aging affects all body structures and systems. Although senescence began in early adulthood, the changes are gradual. Most adults show little awareness of the changes until they are faced with clear evidence of aging in their appearance, such as a full head of silver hair; decreased athletic performance, such as difficulty carrying heavy groceries up a flight of stairs; or age-related ailments, such as **cataracts** or osteoporosis.

APPEARANCE

The skin loses collagen and elasticity throughout adulthood and becomes more dry as oil glands become less active (Quan & Fisher, 2015). Pigmented marks called age spots often appear on the hands and face. The skin also thins and loses the layer of fat underneath it, making blood vessels more visible, and older adults are more sensitive to cold (Farage, Miller, Elsner, & Maibach, 2013). Exposure to sunlight exacerbates these changes (Farage, Miller, Elsner, & Maibach, 2008; Flament, Bazin, & Piot, 2013). The nose and ears grow larger and broader in older adulthood. Hair whitens, and both men and women experience hair loss as hair follicles die, while thin downy hair begins to grow from the scalp follicles of men with hereditary baldness.

Aging also brings accelerated loss of bone density, which leads both men and women to lose height in older adulthood, with women showing greater losses (Hannan et al., 2012). The condition of reduced bone density is known as *osteopenia*, and more severe bone thinning is diagnosed as osteoporosis; calcium supplements and a program of regular weight-bearing exercise are recommended to prevent, and to some extent to treat, both conditions. Body shape changes in older adulthood as fat is redistributed and accumulates in the abdomen. **Sarcopenia**, the age-related loss of muscle mass and strength, continues with average losses of 10% to 20% by 60 to 70 years of age and 30% to 50% from age 70 to 80 (Buford et al., 2010). Physical activity, especially resistance exercise, can strengthen muscles and offset losses into the 90s (Caserotti, Aagaard, Larsen, & Puggaard, 2008; Peterson, Rhea, Sen, & Gordon, 2010; Serra-Rexach et al., 2011).

NERVOUS SYSTEM

As we age, the nervous system changes in predictable ways. Brain volume shrinks as dendrites contract and are lost, accompanied by a decrease in synapses and a loss of glial cells (Schuff et al., 2012). Many neural fibers lose their coating of myelin, and communication among neurons slows accordingly. Declines are especially marked in the prefrontal cortex, responsible for executive functioning and judgment (Lu et al., 2013). Myelin losses contribute to cognitive declines with aging (Kohama, Rosene, & Sherman, 2012; Peters & Kemper, 2012). However, brain volume shrinks, on average, less than half of 1% each year (Salthouse, 2011). Also, estimates of age-related changes in brain volume vary with measurement and across research studies. For example, some cross-sectional samples that compare adults of different ages at one time show greater age differences in brain volume than do longitudinal samples, which tend to show more continuous and gradual changes in brain volume that are less tied to age (Salthouse, 2011). A program of aerobic exercise has been shown to restore brain volume, especially in the hippocampus, a brain region closely involved with memory (see Figure 17.1).

The brain compensates for structural changes such as neuronal and myelin loss throughout older adulthood. Older adults compensate for cognitive declines by showing more brain activity and using different brain areas in solving problems than do younger adults (Turner & Spreng, 2012). Older adults often show brain activity that is spread out over a larger area, including both hemispheres, compensating for neural losses, as shown in Figure 17.2 (Daselaar & Cabeza, 2005; Reuter-Lorenz & Cappell, 2008). For example, in one study older adults compensated for lower levels of parietal and occipital activity with greater activity in the frontal lobes and performed better on a working memory task than did younger adults (Osorio, Fay, Pouthas, & Ballesteros, 2010).

FIGURE 17.1: Change in Hippocampal Volume With Aerobic Exercise

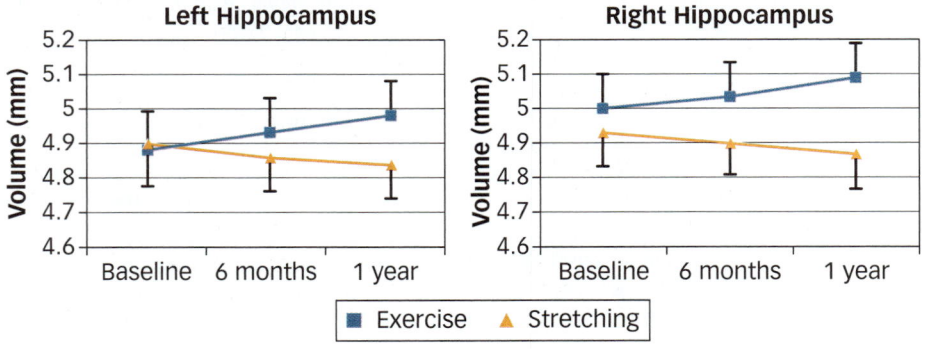

SOURCE: Erickson et al. (2011).

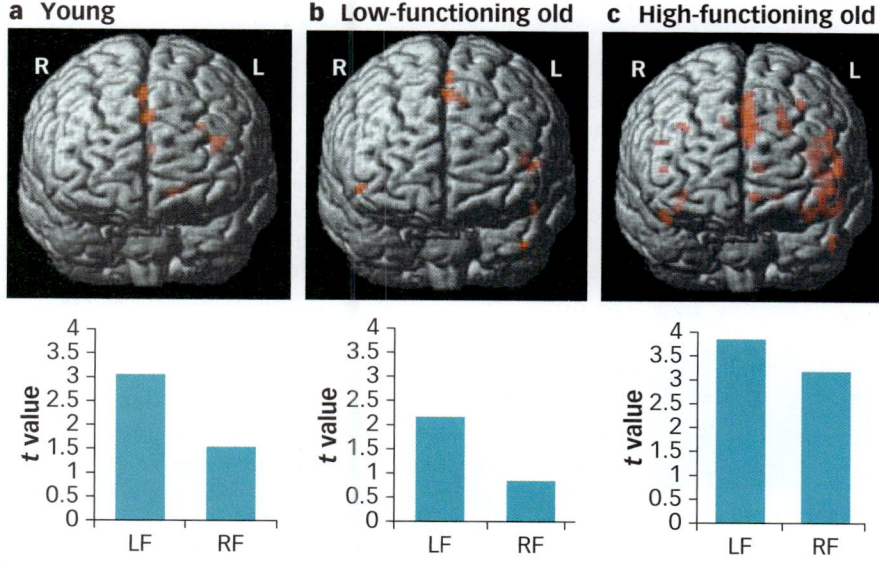

a Young   **b Low-functioning old**   **c High-functioning old**

SOURCE: Hedden and Gabrieli (2004).

Age-related brain changes are not always apparent in adults' functioning. Many adults naturally compensate for losses through **cognitive reserve**, the ability to make flexible and efficient use of available brain resources that permits cognitive, efficiency, flexibility, and adaptability (Barulli & Stern, 2013; Nair, Sabbagh, Tucker, & Stern, 2014). Cognitive reserve is cultivated throughout life from experience and environmental factors. Educational and occupational attainment and engagement in leisure activities allows some adults to cope with age-related changes better than others and show more successful aging (Barulli & Stern, 2013; Scarmeas & Stern, 2003). For example, bilingualism is associated with cognitive benefits throughout life. Adults who have daily experiences in using two languages, such as determining when to use one and inhibit another, show enhanced cognitive control abilities, more mental flexibility as well as being better able to handle tasks involving switching, inhibition, and conflict monitoring (Barac & Bialystok, 2012; Grant, Dennis, & Li, 2014).

A particularly exciting finding is that neurogenesis—the process by which new neurons are developed—continues throughout life. New neurons are created in the hippocampus and striatum (a subcortical part of the brain responsible for coordinating motivation with body movement) throughout life but at a much slower rate than prenatally (Ernst et al., 2014; Shors, 2014). Most of these neurons die off, but some survive, especially if exposed to experiences that require learning (Shors, 2014). As with neurogenesis early in life (see Chapter 4), surviving neurons migrate to the parts of the brain where they will function and create synapses with other neurons (Braun & Jessberger, 2014). It is estimated that about 2% of neurons are renewed each year (Spalding et al., 2013). Neurogenesis plays a role in cognition and in stress and emotional responses, contributing to the maintenance

of cognitive abilities and advances in psychosocial maturing in the adult years (Cameron & Glover, 2015; Ho, Hooker, Sahay, Holt, & Roffman, 2013). As described in Lifespan Brain Development (p. 480), brain growth can continue through older adulthood.

VISION

As in middle adulthood (see Chapter 15), virtually all older adults have difficulty seeing objects up close. In later adulthood, the lens yellows and the vitreous clouds, less light reaches the retina, and it becomes more difficult to see in dim light and to adapt to dramatic changes in light, such as those that accompany night driving (Owsley, 2011). Many adults develop cataracts, a clouding of the lens resulting in blurred, foggy vision that makes driving hazardous and can lead to blindness (Kline & Li, 2005). Cataracts are the result of a combination of hereditary and environmental factors associated with oxidative damage, including illnesses such as **diabetes** and behaviors such as smoking (David, Nancy, & Ying-Bo, 2010; Tan et al., 2008). By age 80, more than half of adults have cataracts (American Academy of Ophthalmology, 2011), which can be corrected through a surgical procedure in which the lens is replaced with an artificial lens.

In addition to the lens, other parts of the eye show structural changes (see Figure 17.3). Cells in the retina and

FIGURE 17.3: Age-Related Changes in the Eye

Older Eye

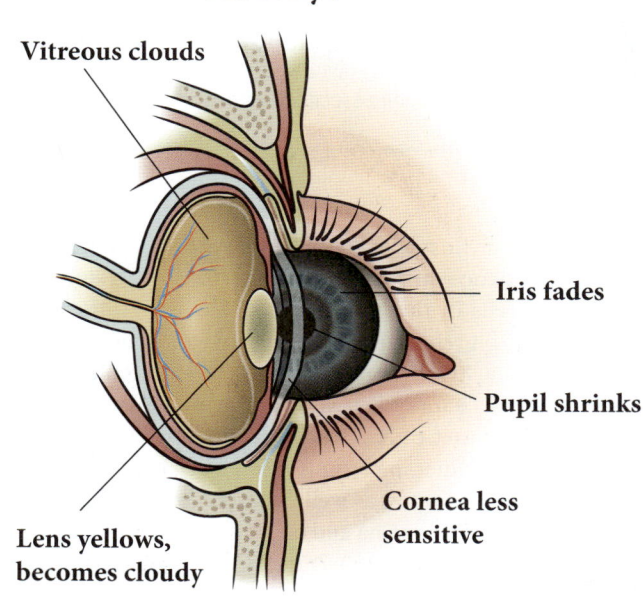

Vitreous clouds

Iris fades

Pupil shrinks

Cornea less sensitive

Lens yellows, becomes cloudy

LIFESPAN BRAIN DEVELOPMENT

Brain Growth in Older Adulthood

Melanie Stetson Freeman/Christian Science

The brain remains plastic throughout life. Aerobic exercise can reverse volume loss in the hippocampus, responsible for memory.

We have seen that children's brains are responsive to the environment. Teaching children memory strategies improves their performance on memory tasks. Does training and practice have similar effects for older adults? Can older adults learn and improve their cognitive functioning? In short, yes.

Older adults who are trained on specific strategies show large and long-lasting improvement on the trained tasks, but the skills often are not transferred to new tasks (Lustig, Shah, Seidler, & Reuter-Lorenz, 2009). However, when older adults are instead taught multiple strategies and problem-solving approaches, they show more widespread effects that generalize to everyday tasks and last over time (Dunlosky, Kubat-Silman, & Hertzog, 2003). Participants in the Seattle Longitudinal Study trained on inductive reasoning and spatial orientation showed improved performance on tasks tapping those skills for up to seven years after receiving the intervention (Schaie & Willis, 1986).

Moreover, cognitive training does not simply influence older adults' skills. It changes their brains. Expertise is associated with brain growth and changes in connectivity (Strenziok et al., 2014). Experts tend to have enlarged brain structures related to their type of expertise (Maguire et al., 2003). Cognitive training has consistently been associated with increases in volume in

the brain structures thought to be critical to the trained task (Lustig et al., 2009).

Cognitive interventions are not the only way to improve functioning and increase brain volume in older adulthood. Both cross-sectional and longitudinal studies have shown that aerobic exercise training improves cognitive function in older adults in many domains, with the largest improvement occurring on tests of executive function (Lang, Featherman, & Nesselroade, 1997). For example, one experiment examined 120 older adults without dementia and assigned one half (the treatment group) to a yearlong aerobic exercise program. The other half (the control group) participated in a program of nonaerobic stretching exercises (Erickson et al., 2011). Over a yearlong period, the older adults who received the aerobic exercise intervention showed a 2% growth in the size of the hippocampus whereas the control group showed a 1% decline consistent with the normative yearly decline in hippocampal volume. This is important because deterioration of the hippocampus has been linked to memory impairment in late adulthood (Raz et al., 2005). The aerobic exercise experiment demonstrated that the hippocampus, like other parts of the brain, remains modifiable throughout adulthood and that aerobic exercise may reverse volume loss (Erickson et al., 2011).

Likewise, other research has suggested that aerobic exercise training increases gray and white matter volume in the prefrontal context of older adults and enhances the functioning of key areas central to executive control (Colcombe et al., 2006; Rosano et al., 2010). In one study (shown in Figure 17.1), greater amounts of physical activity were associated with greater gray matter volume in several areas of the brain including the prefrontal cortex and hippocampus over a nine-year period and a reduced risk for cognitive impairment (Erickson et al., 2010).

Although the phrase "use it or lose it" is often used in reference to cognitive function, recent research suggest that the aging brain can do more than just retain its functions; plasticity means that it can also grow. Perhaps the phrase should be changed to "use it to improve it."

What Do You Think?

Identify three things that an adult of any age can do to promote positive brain development and functioning in older adulthood.

---

optical nerve are lost with aging (Owsley, 2011). Some older adults experience **macular degeneration**, a substantial loss of cells in the center area of the retina, the macula, causing blurring and eventual loss of central vision (Chakravarthy, Evans, & Rosenfeld, 2010). Hereditary and environmental factors, such as smoking and atherosclerosis, influence the onset of macular degeneration (Myers et al., 2014). A healthy diet, including green leafy vegetables high in vitamins A, C, and E, as well as carotenoids, such as carrots, may protect the retina and offset damage caused by free radicals (Rhone & Basu, 2008; Sin, Liu, & Lam, 2013). Laser

surgery, medication, and corrective eyewear can sometimes restore some vision and treat the early stages of macular degeneration; however, macular degeneration is the leading cause of blindness (Chakravarthy et al., 2010; Jager, Mieler, & Miller, 2008).

Most of these changes in vision are gradual and often go unnoticed (Owsley, 2011). Substantial vision loss, however, can have a serious effect on adults' daily lives as it interferes not only with driving but also with reading, watching television, and doing a variety of daily activities from cooking to banking. Not surprisingly, older adults with vision loss participate less than their peers in recreational and sports activities (Alma et al., 2011) and are likely to be depressed (Tabrett & Latham, 2010). In a sample of adults from 10 European countries, vision loss was associated with concentration difficulty; losing interest and enjoyment in activities; feeling fatigued, irritable, and tearful; having less hope for the future; and even wishing for death (Mojon-Azzi, Sousa-Poza, & Mojon, 2008).

HEARING

As described in Chapter 15, age-related hearing loss (known as presbycusis) typically begins in middle adulthood. It increases in older adulthood, with cell losses in the inner ear and cortex (Gates & Mills, 2005). Older adults experience difficulty distinguishing high-frequency sounds, soft sounds of all frequencies, and complex tone patterns (Gordon-Salant, 2005). As in middle adulthood, men tend to suffer hearing loss earlier and to a greater extent than do women (Cruickshanks et al., 2010; Helzner et al., 2005). About two thirds of older adults experience hearing loss (Lin, Thorpe, Gordon-Salant, & Ferrucci, 2011), which can greatly diminish quality of life and poses health risks. The inability to hear car horns and other street sounds or to hear the telephone or doorbell is a risk to safety but also to self-esteem. Turning up the volume to hear a television or radio program and then being asked by others to turn down the volume can be frustrating to older adults and their loved ones. Difficulty hearing others' speech can socially isolate older adults, reducing their social network, increasing feelings of loneliness and depression, and reducing life satisfaction (Gordon-Salant, 2005).

Many older adults compensate for their hearing loss by reducing background noise, when possible, and paying attention to nonverbal cues such as lip movements, facial expressions, and body language to optimize their ability to hear and participate in conversations. Hearing aids are widely available, but research suggests they are underused for several reasons: social attitudes that undervalue the importance of

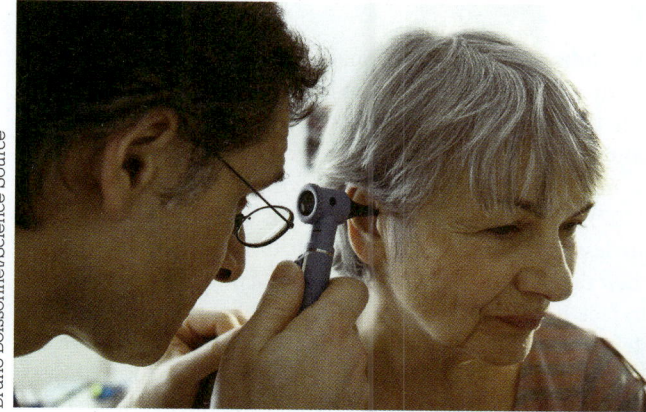

Bruno Boissonnet/Science Source

Presbycusis and other forms of hearing loss become more common in older adulthood. Hearing loss management, including examinations and communication with physicians, can improve quality of life in older adults who experience losses.

hearing; stigma associated with being seen wearing hearing aids; and their cost, which is typically not covered by health insurance (Laplante-Lévesque, Hickson, & Worrall, 2010). Quality of life for older adults can be improved with successful hearing loss management, which may include education about communication effectiveness, hearing aids, assistive listening devices, and cochlear implants for severe hearing loss. When hearing aids no longer provide benefit, cochlear implantation is the treatment of choice with excellent results even in octogenarians (Quaranta et al., 2015).

CARDIOVASCULAR, RESPIRATORY, AND IMMUNE SYSTEMS

Most adults in their 60s become aware of changes in their cardiovascular and respiratory systems, such as feeling their heart pound and taking longer to catch their breath after running to catch a train. There is a physiological reason for this: With age, the heart experiences cell loss and becomes more rigid. The heart contains pacemaker cells that signal when to initiate a contraction; over time, these cells diminish significantly, by nearly one half, and the heart becomes less responsive to their signals (Mironov, 2009). The arteries stiffen, and the walls accumulate cholesterol and fat plaques, which reduce blood flow; this condition is known as *atherosclerosis* and is a cause of heart disease (Jani & Rajkumar, 2006; Wei, 2004). As discussed in Chapter 15, cardiovascular disease may be manifested as heart valve problems, arrhythmia, heart attack, and stroke. Heart disease becomes more common with age, as shown in Figure 17.4.

Just as the heart undergoes changes with age, changes in the respiratory system also reduce the flow of oxygen to the body. Specifically, the lungs gradually lose cells and elasticity over the adult years, substantially reducing the amount of oxygen that enters the system and is absorbed by the blood (Miller, Wood, & Smith, 2010). Older adults have more trouble breathing, feel more out of breath during physical exertion, and have a harder time catching their breath than younger adults. Experience and lifestyle influence cardiovascular and respiratory system changes. Smoking and exposure to environmental toxins increases damage to the cardiovascular and repertory systems while physical activity and good nutrition can compensate for decreases in cardiovascular and reparatory function (Stanner & Denny, 2009; Visioli & Hagen, 2007).

With age, the immune system becomes less efficient and adaptive (De la Fuente & Miquel, 2009; Kusnecov, Anisman, Fenn, Corona, & Godbout, 2013). Declines in immune function place older adults at higher risk of diseases such as flu and pneumonia, cancers, and autoimmune diseases such as rheumatoid arthritis (Gomez, Nomellini, Faunce, & Kovacs, 2008; Lindstrom & Robinson, 2010). Exposure to stress reduces immune function, and the effects increase with age: Older adults often show greater immune impairment in response to stress than younger adults (Graham, Christian, &

FIGURE 17.4: Lifetime Heart Disease Prevalence in the United States, 1999–2010

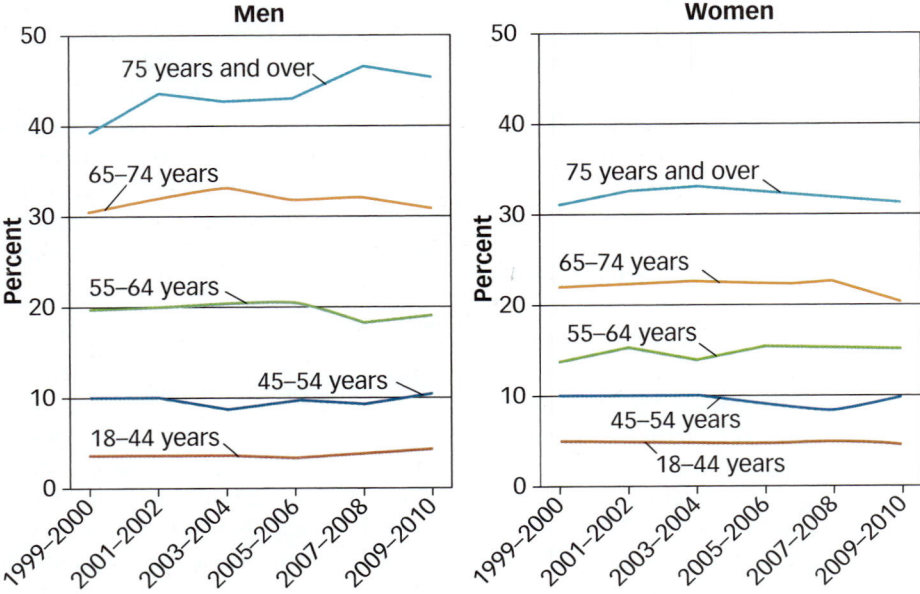

SOURCE: National Center for Health Statistics (2011).

Kiecolt-Glaser, 2006; Vitlic, Lord, & Phillips, 2014). The body's T cells become less effective at protecting the body by attacking foreign substances and the immune system becomes more likely to malfunction and display an autoimmune response by turning against body tissues. There are, however, large individual differences in immune function. Some people retain strong immune functioning into older adulthood, but most experience at least some declines (Kusnecov et al., 2013). As we will see in next section, good nutrition and exercise enhances and protects immune functioning.

Thinking in Context 17.2

1. How might the physical changes that older adults experience in vision, hearing, and body systems influence their daily activities? What are the practical implications of these developmental changes?

2. Older adults show many variations in patterns of physical change. Discuss influences on the timing and scope of physical changes during older adulthood. What are sources of variation?

HEALTH AND DISABILITY IN LATE ADULTHOOD

Older adults show a great deal of diversity in health status. As shown in Figure 17.5, even after age 75 only a portion of older adults report poor health. Over the past few decades, it has become increasingly common for older adults in industrialized nations to age well and delay disability and disease until

the final months or years of life (Fries, Bruce, & Chakravarty, 2011). This tendency is referred to as **compression of morbidity**, and it is an important public health goal, as it means that older adults enjoy more vital years and less time suffering. Research with centenarians illustrates compression of morbidity: As mentioned earlier in this chapter, many centenarians have led healthy lives; if they develop serious diseases, it is usually not until well into their 90s (Ailshire et al., 2015; Andersen, Sebastiani, Dworkis, Feldman, & Perls, 2012; Sebastiani & Perls, 2012). Advances in medicine, improvement in the standard of living, and increased recognition of the importance of lifestyle contribute to compression of morbidity (Faria, 2015).

NUTRITION

As adults age, their nutritional needs change. Losses in muscle mass contribute to weight loss and a slowed metabolism. For this reason, older adults require fewer calories than younger adults, and their diets must be more nutrient dense to meet their nutritional needs with fewer calories (Baker, 2007). Their changing dietary needs mean that older adults are less likely to get all of their nutritional needs met through their diet and are therefore at risk for a nutritional deficiency. In fact, it is estimated that two thirds of older adults in many developed countries, including Germany, Italy, Japan, the Netherlands, and the United States, are at risk for malnutrition (Kaiser et al., 2010; van Bokhorst-de van der Schueren et al., 2013). Malnutrition is associated with illness, functional disability, and mortality (Charlton et al., 2013; Payette, 2005).

Older adults typically experience a decline in the sense of taste and smell, which can influence diet for the worse as individuals seek satisfaction through added salt, sugar, and

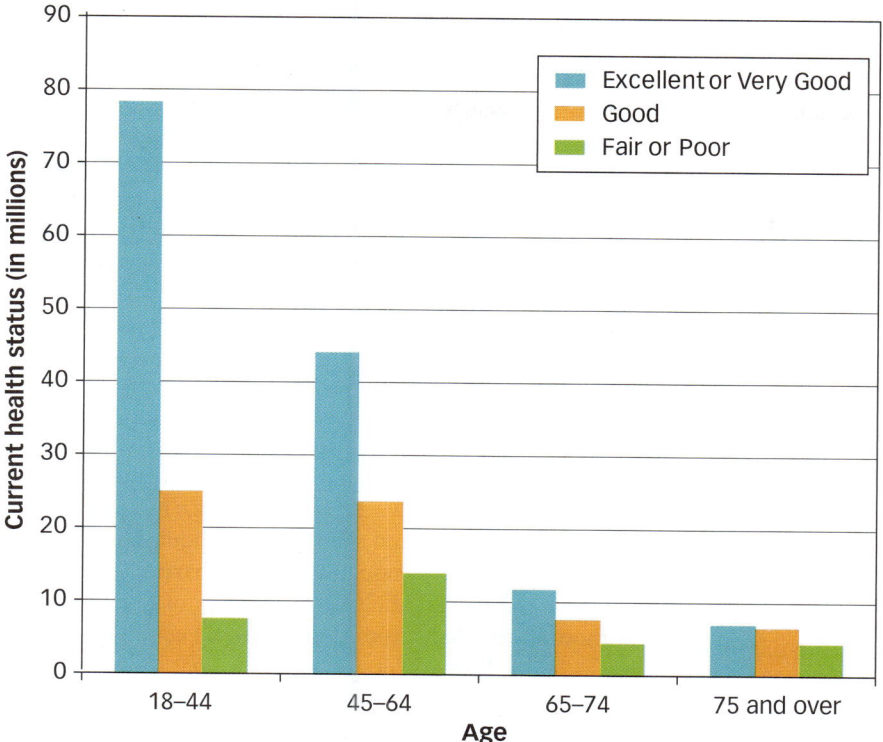

Legend:
- Excellent or Very Good
- Good
- Fair or Poor

Y-axis: Current health status (in millions)

X-axis: Age — 18–44, 45–64, 65–74, 75 and over

SOURCE: Adapted from Blackwell, Lucas, and Clarke (2012).

fat, or they may lose interest in eating altogether as favorite foods don't taste like they used to. Older adults who live alone may be reluctant to shop, cook, and eat by themselves. Illness, lengthy hospitalizations, bereavement, depression, and social isolation also contribute to malnutrition (Brownie, 2006). Older adults' nutritional needs are also influenced by medication. For example, daily use of aspirin, commonly prescribed to adults at risk of heart disease, depletes vitamin C and antibiotics interfere with the absorption of calcium, iron, and vitamin K (Meletis & Zabriskie, 2007). Vitamin deficiencies, such as in vitamin A and C, are associated with lowered resistance to infection and cancer (Amati et al., 2003).

To counteract such problems, older adults can make an effort to choose nutritious foods, including fruits; whole grains; low-fat dairy products; leafy green vegetables; and healthy sources of protein, such as fish, nuts, beans, and chicken—foods that are nutrient dense—and limit salt, sugar, and fats. However, this is easier said than done given that many older adults have a lifelong pattern of less healthy food preferences and that healthy food choices are not readily available or affordable in all local areas.

Supplements for vitamins A, B6, B12, C, and E can fill in gaps in older adults' diets and boost immunity. Specifically, antioxidant vitamins and trace elements (vitamins C, E, selenium, copper, and zinc) counteract potential damage caused by free radicals and promote an effective immune system response (Wintergerst, Maggini, & Hornig, 2007). Catechin, a

polyphenol found in green tea, has an antioxidative effect and may protect against age-related declines in cognitive functions such as those associated with learning and memory, as well as progressive neurodegenerative disorders such as Parkinson's and Alzheimer's diseases (Assuncao & Andrade, 2015; Song, Xu, Liu, & Feng, 2011). Research with aging rodents suggests that catechin protects the brain, especially spatial memory (Rodrigues et al., 2013).

Omega-3, an oil found in fish that is high in polyunsaturated fatty acids, promotes vascular health and is associated with reduced risk of cardiovascular disease (Lorente-Cebrián et al., 2013). Omega-3 is associated with reduced inflammation and degenerative diseases such as arthritis and potentially **Alzheimer's disease** (Lorente-Cebrián et al., 2015). In one double-blind study, healthy older adults aged 50 to 75 showed increases in executive function and improvements in white matter integrity and gray matter volume, suggesting that omega-3 may have important implications for neurological health and functioning (Witte et al., 2014). Moreover, consumption of omega-3 appears to have an epigenetic effect on longevity through its action on telomeres, the caps covering the tips of DNA. Recall from Chapter 13 that telomeres shorten with every cell division until they reach a critical length, stopping cell division and preceding cell death. The consumption of omega-3 is associated with slowed and even reduced telomere shortening over five- to eight-year periods (Farzaneh-Far

AGING AND PHYSICAL DEVELOPMENT

Elsie and Margaret describe the physical changes that accompany aging and how they adapt to those changes. Note the variability in experiences.

Watch the video at edge.sagepub.com/kuther

et al., 2010; Paul, 2011), suggesting that cell aging can be slowed and even extended. Improved nutrition holds the promise of protection against age-related cognitive changes, but more research is needed.

EXERCISE

As in early and middle adulthood, exercise offers powerful health benefits to older adults. Individuals as old as 80 who begin a program of cardiovascular activity, such as walking, cycling, or aerobic dancing, show gains similar to those of much younger adults. Weight-bearing exercise begun as late as 90 years of age can improve blood flow to the muscles and increase muscle size (Rice & Cunningham, 2002). The physical benefits of regular exercise influence increases in strength, balance, posture, and endurance and permit older adults to carry out everyday activities such as grocery shopping, lifting grandchildren, reaching for objects, and opening jars and bottles (Peterson et al., 2010). Throughout the adult years, moderate physical activity is associated with improved physiological function, a decreased incidence of disease, and reduced incidence of disability (Chakravarty, Hubert, Lingala, & Fries, 2008; Radak, Chung, Koltai, Taylor, & Goto, 2008).

92-year-old Harriette Thompson completed the San Diego Rock 'n' Roll Marathon in May 2015 to become the oldest woman to finish a marathon.

Jerod Harris/Getty

Exercise is not only good for the body; it is also good for the mind. Just as earlier in life, exercise offers older adults stress relief, protects against depression, and is associated with higher quality of life (Windle, Hughes, Linck, Russell, & Woods, 2010). The increased blood flow to the brain that comes with exercise is protective. Older adults who are physically active show less neural and glial cell losses throughout their cortex and less cognitive decline than do those who are sedentary (Muscari et al., 2010; Nithianantharajah & Hannan, 2009). Perhaps more significant is that exercise in older adults is associated with increased hippocampal volume (recall that new neurons are created there; Niemann, Godde, & Voelcker-Rehage, 2014). In addition, adults who get regular cardiovascular exercise, such as brisk walks, show increased brain activity in areas that control attention and perform better on tasks measuring attention than do sedentary adults. They also demonstrate improved performance on tasks examining executive function, processing speed, memory, and other cognitive processes (Erickson et al., 2011; Hindin & Zelinski, 2012).

Unfortunately, similar to younger adults, most older adults are not active enough. Common barriers to physical activity reported by adults include fears of falling, neighborhood safety, bad weather, and chronic conditions (Belza et al., 2004). Many older adults believe that the best way to manage chronic illnesses such as arthritis is to rest and that exercise will make symptoms worse. Instead, exercise offers physical and mental benefits that slow the negative effects of aging. Older adults who exercise often report feeling more energetic, experience greater life enhancement, and have a more positive psychological outlook than sedentary elders (Ruppar & Schneider, 2007). In addition, older adults who identify themselves as physical exercisers and physically fit show greater levels of life satisfaction (Strachan, Brawley, Spink, & Glazebrook, 2010).

CHRONIC ILLNESS

Chronic illnesses become more common with age. Nearly all older adults suffer from one chronic illness or another, and many have multiple diagnoses (Administration on Aging, 2014). We have discussed cardiovascular disease, a serious chronic illness that many adults face. In the following sections, we discuss the two most common chronic illnesses: arthritis and diabetes.

Arthritis

One illness that goes hand in hand with aging is arthritis, a degenerative joint disease. There are more than 100 different types of arthritis; the most common is **osteoarthritis**, which affects joints that are injured by overuse, most commonly the hips, knees, lower back, and hands. The cartilage that protects the ends of bones where they meet at joints wears away, and joints become less flexible and swell. Those who suffer from osteoarthritis experience a loss of movement and a great deal of pain. Aging is the most prominent risk factor

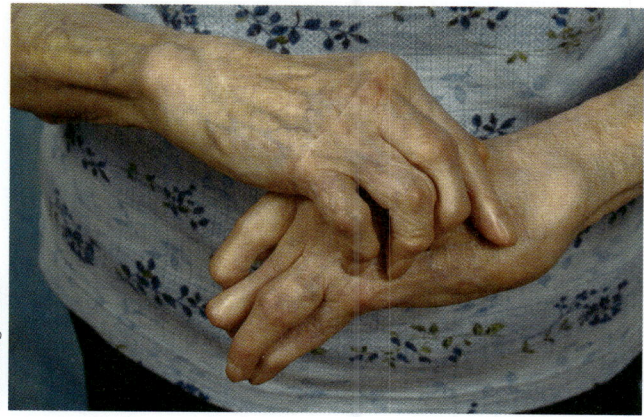
Osteoarthritis, a degenerative joint disease, often occurs in the hands, knees, and hips.

for depression (Lin, 2008; Margaretten, Katz, Schmajuk, & Yelin, 2013). In one study, over one third of a Latino sample of adults with arthritis experienced depression (Withers, Moran, Nicassio, Weisman, & Karpouzas, 2015) Although arthritis-related stressors are the predominant factors affecting well-being for European American women with arthritis, well-being in African Americans with arthritis is also closely tied to broader life contextual stressors (McIlvane, Baker, & Mingo, 2008). African American patients with rheumatoid arthritis are less likely to receive medication and seek care from a specialist (Solomon et al., 2012). Low socioeconomic status is associated with greater arthritis-related symptoms, poorer well-being, and greater use of maladaptive coping strategies among African Americans, yet socioeconomic status does not predict depressive symptoms and coping among European Americans diagnosed with arthritis (McIlvane, 2007).

for osteoarthritis; it may first appear in middle adulthood, in the 40s and 50s, but becomes more common and worsens in severity during older adulthood (Aigner, Haag, Martin, & Buckwalter, 2007). About half of adults aged 65 or older report a diagnosis of arthritis, and it is likely that many more cases remain undiagnosed (National Center for Chronic Disease Prevention and Health Promotion, 2010). Nearly all older adults show at least some signs of osteoarthritis, but there are great individual differences. People whose job or leisure activities rely on repetitive movements are most likely to experience osteoarthritis. Office workers who type every day, for example, might experience osteoarthritis in their hands. Runners might experience it in their knees. Obesity can place abnormal pressure on joints and result in osteoarthritis.

A second common type of arthritis, rheumatoid arthritis, is not age- or use-related. Rheumatoid arthritis is an autoimmune illness in which the connective tissues, the membranes that line the joints, become inflamed and stiff, thicken, and release enzymes that digest bone and cartilage, often causing the affected joint to lose its shape and alignment. Most people are diagnosed with rheumatoid arthritis between ages 20 and 50 and the prevalence increases with age (Lindstrom & Robinson, 2010). Older adults with rheumatoid arthritis have lived with a painful chronic illness for many years and likely experience multiple physical disabilities.

Arthritis is classified as a chronic disease because it is managed, not cured. When inflammation flares, more rest is needed as well as pain relief. However, instead of uninterrupted rest, it is best to deal with an arthritis flare-up with some activities or exercises to help the muscles maintain flexibility, known as range of motion. People whose osteoarthritis is related to obesity may experience some relief with weight loss. In some cases, a synthetic material can be injected into a joint to provide more cushioning and improve movement, or a severely affected joint, such as the hip or knee, can be surgically replaced. Joint replacement surgery has become increasingly common in recent decades.

Because adults with arthritis live with chronic pain and reduced ability to engage in activities, they are often at risk

Diabetes

After each meal we eat, the body digests and breaks down food, releasing glucose into the blood. Insulin, a hormone released by the pancreas, maintains a steady concentration of glucose in the blood and excess glucose is absorbed by muscle and fat. Diabetes is a disease marked by high levels of blood glucose. Diabetes occurs when the body is unable to regulate the amount of glucose in the bloodstream because there either is not enough insulin produced (type 1 diabetes) or the body shows insulin resistance and becomes less sensitive to it, failing to respond to it (type 2 diabetes; American Diabetes Association, 2014). Symptoms of diabetes include fatigue, great thirst, blurred vision, frequent infections, and slow healing. When glucose levels become too low, hypoglycemia occurs with symptoms of confusion, nervousness, and fainting. Hyperglycemia is characterized by overly high glucose levels, also resulting in serious illness. Managing diabetes entails careful monitoring of the diet and often self-injection of insulin, which permits the body to process glucose, critical to body functioning (American Diabetes Association, 2014).

About one fourth of older adults over the age of 60 have diabetes (Centers for Disease Control and Prevention [CDC], 2014), and it is the sixth leading cause of death among people age 65 and over (National Center for Health Statistics, 2015). Diabetes is influenced by heredity as well as lifestyle factors. African American, Mexican American, and Canadian Aboriginal people are diagnosed with diabetes at higher rates than European Americans because of genetic as well as contextual factors, such as the higher rates of obesity, poor health, and a sedentary lifestyle that accompanies poverty (American Diabetes Association, 2014; Best, Hayward, & Hidajat, 2005; Jeffreys et al., 2006). Diabetes has a genetic component, but lifestyle choices such as diet and exercise are important risk factors for diabetes (Scott et al., 2013). Being overweight at any point during life is associated with an increased risk of diabetes (Jeffreys et al., 2006).

People with diabetes are at risk for a variety of health problems. High levels of glucose in the bloodstream raise

About one quarter of older adults suffer from diabetes with increased risks for health and cognitive problems. Managing diabetes entails careful monitoring of the diet and often self-injection of insulin to regulate levels of glucose in the body.

brain aging, including losses of gray matter, abnormalities in white matter, and a heightened risk of dementia and Alzheimer's disease (Espeland et al., 2013; Roberts et al., 2014; Vagelatos & Eslick, 2013).

Diabetes also influences psychosocial functioning. Depression is two to three times more common among people with diabetes compared to their peers and they are more likely to experience chronic depression with up to 80% of those treated for depression experiencing a relapse of depressive symptoms within a five-year period (Park, Katon, & Wolf, 2013; Roy & Lloyd, 2012). Depression may also be underreported as it has been estimated that as many as two thirds of diabetes patients who suffer from depression do not recognize it or seek treatment (Katon, 2008). Diabetes patients' health as depressed patients are less likely to follow dietary restrictions, comply with medication, and monitor blood glucose, which are associated with worse outcomes, including increased risk of mortality (Park et al., 2013; van Dooren et al., 2013).

Maintaining a healthy weight through diet and exercise is a powerful way of preventing diabetes. After diagnosis, weight control is still beneficial, and individuals can successfully manage the disease by adopting a diet that carefully controls the amount of sugar entering the bloodstream as well as engaging in regular exercise (American Diabetes Association, 2014; Mavros et al., 2013). Frequent blood testing permits the individual to monitor his or her glucose levels and take insulin when needed to lower levels of glucose in the blood. Coping with diabetes requires a great deal of self-monitoring and self-care, but appropriate self-treatment enables adults to manage this chronic illness and live an active life.

INJURIES

Although injury-related fatalities are high in adolescence and emerging adulthood (58.6 deaths per 100,000), deaths from unintentional injuries account for 61.5 deaths per 100,000 in 65-year-old adults, and a striking 361.9 in adults aged 85 and older—about six times the rate in emerging adulthood (see Figure 17.6; U.S. Department of Health and Human Services,

the risk of heart attack, stroke, circulation problems in the legs, blindness, and reduced kidney functions (DeFronzo & Abdul-Ghani, 2011). Diabetes has serious cognitive and neurological effects: brain aging, including declines in executive function, processing speed, memory, and motor function (Palta, Schneider, Biessels, Touradji, & Hill-Briggs, 2014). Over time, diabetes is associated with accelerated

FIGURE 17.6: Fatal Injury Rate by Age in the United States, 2013

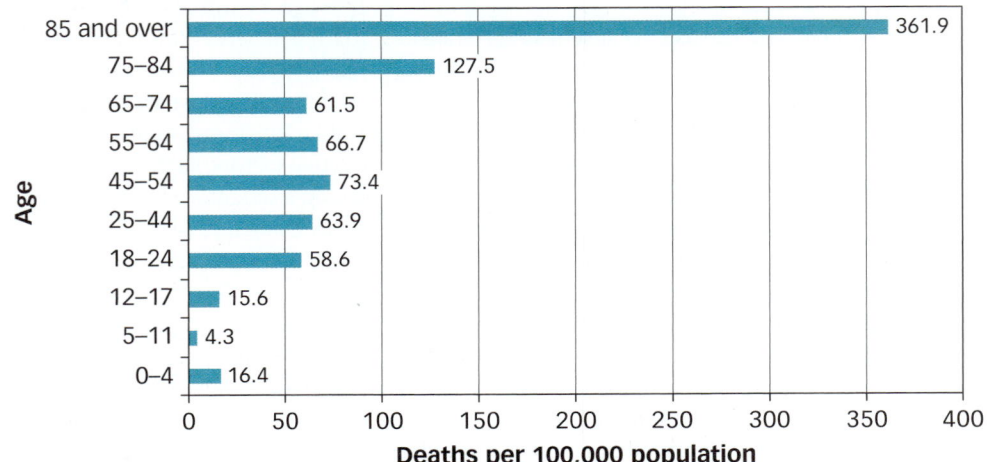

2015). Such injuries arise from a variety of causes, including motor vehicle accidents and falls.

Motor Vehicle Accidents

Driving represents autonomy. Many older adults drive as long as they are able to because driving provides a sense of control and freedom. As the baby boom generation ages, older adults are more likely to keep their driver's licenses, make up a larger proportion of the driving population, and drive more miles than ever before. The proportion of the 70-and-older drivers increased by one third between 1997 and 2012, as have the typical miles traveled (Insurance Institute for Highway Safety, 2015). Older drivers have shown a decline in nonfatal and fatal accidents over the last two decades, but there remain predictable age-related increases in accidents in older adulthood. Per mile traveled, crash rates and fatal crash rates also start increasing when the driver reaches age 70 (see Figure 17.7).

Compared with younger drivers, senior drivers are more likely to be involved in collisions in intersections, when merging into traffic, and switching lanes (Cicchino & McCartt, 2015). Although they drive more slowly and carefully than young adults, older adults are more likely to miss traffic signs, make inappropriate turns, fail to yield the right of way, and show slower reaction time—all risks to safe driving. Declines in vision account for much of the decline in older adults' driving performance (Owsley, McGwin, Jackson, Kallies, & Clark, 2007). They are likely to have difficulty with night vision and reading the dashboard. Changes in working memory and attention also account for some of the problems in older adults' driving competence. Many older adults appear to adapt to these changes and self-regulate their driving by reducing the number of trips and places they drive each week and reducing mileage, decreasing their risk for motor vehicle accidents (Festa, Ott, Manning, Davis,

& Heindel, 2013; Sandlin, McGwin, & Owsley, 2014). Many older adults voluntarily reduce their driving as they notice changes in their vision and reaction time (see Figure 17.8).

Falls

One out of three U.S. adults over the age of 65 and one half of those over the age of 80 fall each year (Hosseini & Hosseini, 2008). Many aspects of aging, such as changes in vision, hearing, motor skills, and cognition, increase the risk of falls among older adults (Dhital, Pey, & Stanford, 2010). For example, neurological and muscular changes mean that older adults are less able to regulate body sway, which increases their risk of falling on stairs (Lee & Chou, 2007). Similar age-related deficits in neuromuscular control make it more difficult for older adults to navigate and avoid obstacles, contributing to the large numbers of obstacle-related falls in the elderly population (Weerdesteyn, Nienhuis, Geurts, & Duysens, 2007). Declines in cognition, especially executive functioning and processing speed, also increase the risk of falls (Herman, Mirelman, Giladi, Schweiger, & Hausdorff, 2010; Welmerink, Longstreth, Lyles, & Fitzpatrick, 2010).

Falls are a serious hazard for older adults because the natural loss of bone and high prevalence of osteoporosis increase the risk of bone fractures; falls in older adults result in fractures about 10% to 15% of the time (Berry & Miller, 2008; Hosseini & Hosseini, 2008). Older individuals are hospitalized for fall-related injuries five times more often than they are for injuries resulting from other causes. One of the most dangerous injuries to older adults is a fractured hip, and 95% of hip fractures are the result of falls (Hosseini & Hosseini, 2008). Hip fractures immobilize an older adult, are painful, and take a great deal of time to heal. Following hip fracture, many elderly adults lose the capacity for independent living, and up to 25% die as a result of complications within a year after the fall, such as infection (Panula et al., 2011).

FIGURE 17.7: Rate of Vehicle Accidents per Million Miles Traveled in the United States, by Driver Age, 2015

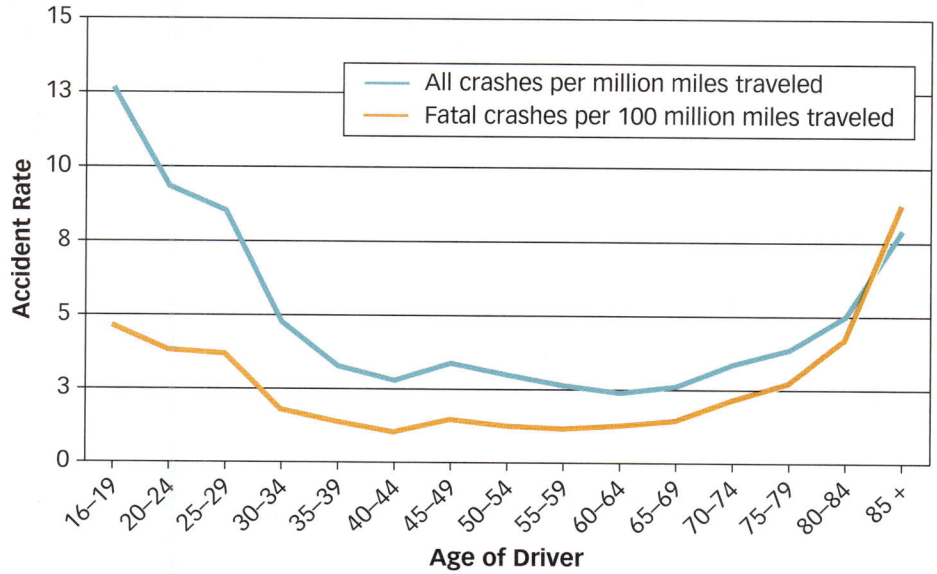

SOURCE: Insurance Institute for Highway Safety (2015).

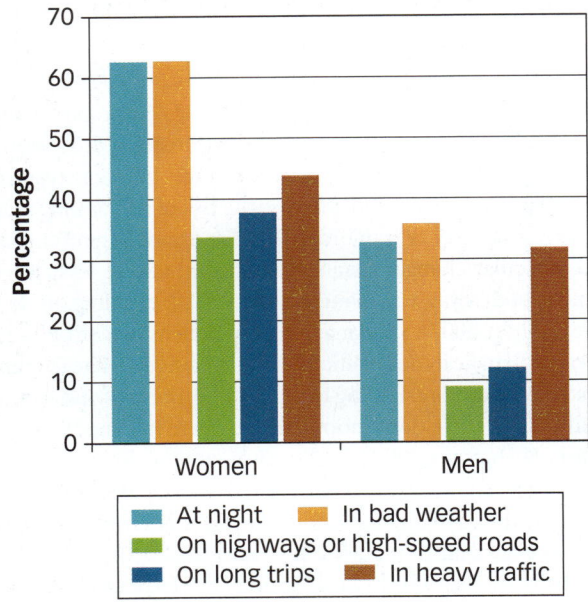

Legend:
- At night
- In bad weather
- On highways or high-speed roads
- On long trips
- In heavy traffic

SOURCE: CDC (2015).

After experiencing a fall, at least half of older adults report fear of falling (Visschedijk, Achterberg, van Balen, & Hertogh, 2010). Adults who fear falling tend to become more cautious, avoiding activities that pose a risk of falling. Avoiding activities reduces the risk of injury, but it also limits opportunities for physical activities that support physical health, retention of mobility, psychological well-being, and social connections (Visschedijk et al., 2010). There are a variety of ways to prevent falls and help older adults become more confident about their mobility. Addressing and treating risks such as poor vision and implementing environmental modifications such as slippery floors or adding handrails can prevent falls and increase older adults' autonomy. Exercise programs such as tai chi and strength and agility exercises can improve older adults' strength, balance, and confidence (Kaniewski, Stevens, Parker, & Lee, 2015).

Thinking in Context 17.3

1. Identify older adults' most important health needs. What resources do they need to maintain their health, prevent chronic illnesses, and treat already-existing illnesses?

2. What are potential barriers to older adults' meeting these needs? How might contextual influences support or challenge older adults in meeting their needs? What recommendations do you make given this analysis?

MENTAL HEALTH IN LATE ADULTHOOD

Normative age-related changes in brain structures influence aspects of cognition, such as processing speed, but do not prevent older adults from engaging in everyday activities. Some older adults, however, experience high rates of cell death and severe brain deterioration that characterize dementia. Dementia refers to a progressive deterioration in mental abilities due to changes in the brain that influence higher cortical functions such as thinking, memory, comprehension, and emotional control, and are reflected in impaired thought and behavior, interfering with the older adult's capacity to engage in everyday activities (McKhann et al., 2011; World Health Organization, 2012). Given that dementia can take many forms, with similar and different neurological features, the most recent version of the *Diagnostic and Statistical Manual of Mental Disorders* (DSM–5) has replaced the term *dementia* with *neurocognitive disorder* (American Psychiatric Association, 2013). Throughout our discussion, we will use the more commonly used term: *dementia.*

In 2013, there were 44.4 million people with dementia worldwide. This number is predicted to increase to an estimated 75.6 million in 2030, and 135.5 million in 2050 (Alzheimer's Disease International, 2015). Much of the increase will be in developing countries, as shown in Figure 17.9. Worldwide, currently 62% of people with dementia live in developing countries; by 2050, this will rise to 71%. The fastest growth in the elderly population is taking place in China, India, and their south Asian and western Pacific neighbors (Alzheimer's Disease International, 2015).

The most common cause of dementia is Alzheimer's disease, followed by **vascular dementia**. Dementia, even in its very early stages, is associated with higher rates of mortality (Andersen, Lolk, Martinussen, & Kragh-Sørensen, 2010). Most forms of dementia are progressive and irreversible. Dementias were once classified as cortical or subcortical, referring to the degree to which the disease entailed the deterioration of the cerebral cortex. Today, researchers know that brain degeneration is not neatly localized into the cortical or subcortical areas. However, the cortical-subcortical distinction describes the difference between dementias without motor features (e.g., Alzheimer's disease) and those that are characterized by motor and gait abnormalities, such as **Parkinson's disease** (Chertkow, 2008; Nation, Salmon, & Bondi, 2014). The most common forms of dementia are discussed in the following sections.

ALZHEIMER'S DISEASE

Alzheimer's disease is a progressive neurodegenerative disorder. It progresses from general cognitive decline, to include personality and behavior changes, motor complications, severe dementia, and death (Bradley-Whitman & Lovell, 2013; Finder, 2011). The risk of Alzheimer's disease grows exponentially with age, doubling approximately every five to six years in most Western countries (see Figure 17.10; Ziegler-Graham, Brookmeyer, Johnson, & Arrighi, 2008). Currently, 5.3 million Americans, including one in nine people over the age of 65, have Alzheimer's disease (Alzheimer's Association, 2015). Of those with Alzheimer's disease, an estimated 4% are under age 65, 15% are 65 to 74, 43% are 75 to 84, and 38% are 85 or older.

Projected Growth in Dementia Prevalence: Low-Income vs. High-Income Countries, 2013–2050 (projected)

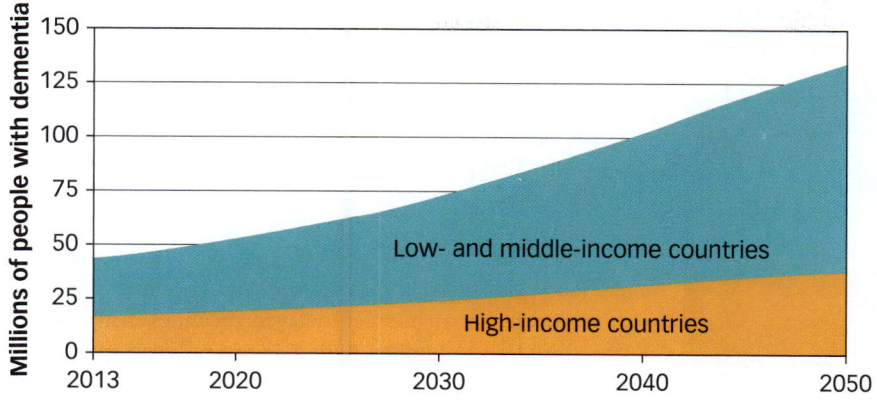

SOURCE: Alzheimer's Disease International (2015).

FIGURE 17.10: Projected Prevalence of Alzheimer's Disease in the U.S. Population, 2010–2015 (projected)

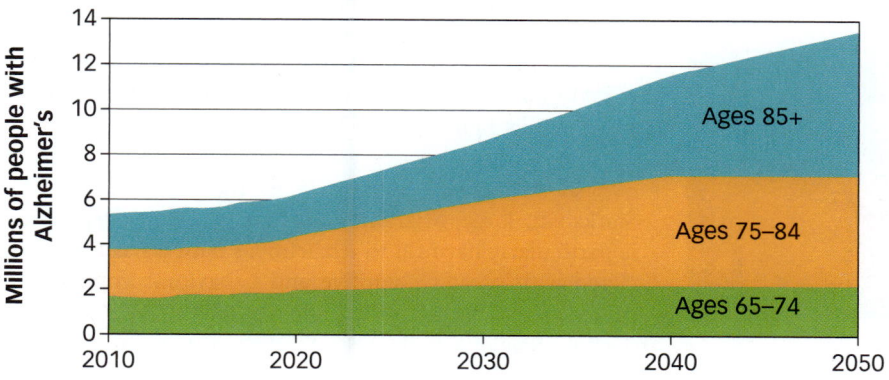

SOURCE: Alzheimer's Association (2015).

Alzheimer's disease is characterized by widespread brain deterioration and the presence of **amyloid plaques** and **neurofibrillary tangles** in the cerebral cortex (Braskie et al., 2010). Beta-amyloid is a protein present in the tissue that surrounds neurons in the healthy brain. Alzheimer's patients experience inflammation that causes the beta-amyloid to accumulate and join with clumps of dead neurons and glial cells, forming large masses called amyloid plaques (Finder, 2011; Perl, 2010). It is thought that amyloid plaques disrupt the structure and function of cell membranes (Yang, Askarova, & Lee, 2010) and contribute to the formation of neurofibrillary tangles, twisted bundles of threads of a protein called *tau* that occur when neurons collapse (Blurton-Jones & LaFerla, 2006; Perl, 2010). Even healthy brains have some tangles, but in cases of Alzheimer's there is inflammation and a proliferation of plaques and tangles, as well as a progressive loss of neurons that interfere with brain functioning (Vasto et al., 2008). Alzheimer's disease is associated with altered neurogenesis in the hippocampus, impairing the generation and development of new neurons (Grote & Hannan, 2007; Mu

& Gage, 2011). As neurons die, brain functioning declines.

Diagnosis of Alzheimer's Disease

Because the characteristic beta-amyloid plaques can only be assessed in a postmortem examination of brain tissue, Alzheimer's disease is diagnosed in living patients through exclusion: by ruling out all other causes of dementia (Rektorova, Rusina, Hort, & Matej, 2009). Symptoms, a medical history, a comprehensive set of neurological and cognitive tests, and conversations with the adult and family members can provide useful information about a person's level of functioning (Guarch, Marcos, Salamero, Gastó, & Blesa, 2008). Brain imaging can help physicians rule out other, potentially treatable, causes of dementia, such as a tumor or stoke (Hort, O'Brien, et al., 2010).

Advances in brain imaging techniques may offer opportunities in the future to diagnose Alzheimer's by studying changes in brain volume and activity. Research with animals has suggested that modified magnetic resonance imaging (MRI) scans can capture images of plaques and tangles (Marcus, 2008). Other research points to the search for biomarkers, genetic or biological traces, of the disease (Castro-Chavira, Fernandez, Nicolini, Diaz-Cintra, & Prado-Alcala, 2015; Fletcher et al., 2013). For example, cerebrospinal fluid concentrations of beta-amyloid may serve as biomarkers for Alzheimer's (Smach et al., 2009). These biomarkers are used in clinically diagnosing Alzheimer's disease in Europe; however, countries vary in the cutoff values used to diagnose Alzheimer's (Hort, Bartos, Pirttilä, & Scheltens, 2010). Searching for biomarkers is not part of a routine diagnosis in North America; researchers have concluded that such markers have promise but have not yet determined how to use them to diagnose individuals (Harvard Mental Health Letter, 2010; Rosén, Hansson, Blennow, & Zetterberg, 2013).

Progression of Alzheimer's Disease

Alzheimer's disease progresses through several predictable steps. Specific patterns of cognitive and memory loss are common in Alzheimer's dementia. The earliest symptoms of Alzheimer's disease are memory problems, likely because the neurological disruptions that comprise Alzheimer's disease usually begin in the hippocampus, which is influential in memory (Grote & Hannan, 2007). First, the older adult experiences impairments in episodic memory are soon accompanied by impairments in attentional control, which, to an outside observer, may appear as further absentmindedness and inattention, being "lost" in one's own world (Storandt, 2008). Early Alzheimer's disease can be hard to distinguish from normal aging—or at least popular views and stereotypes of aging.

Over time, the cognitive impairments broaden to include severe problems with concentration and short-term memory. Older adults may set the TV remote control down and, a moment later, be unable to find it. The person may ask the same question repeatedly, forgetting that an answer has just been given moments earlier. Alzheimer's patients show severe impairment in delayed recall, even when cues are offered and memory demands are reduced to recognition rather than recall (Salmon & Bondi, 2009), As short-term memory problems increase, the Alzheimer's patient is frequently confused (Carson, Vanderhorst, & Koenig, 2015). The older adult's vocabulary becomes more limited as he or she is likely to forget or mix up words. Speech becomes more long-winded and tangential. Personality changes are common. People who are naturally suspicious may become more so, deciding that they are not simply forgetting the location of items but that others are deceiving them (Verkaik, Nuyen, Schellevis, & Francke, 2007).

Depression and depressive symptoms occur in up to 50% of Alzheimer's patients (Chi, Yu, Tan, & Tan, 2014; Starkstein, Jorge, Mizrahi, & Robinson, 2005). Depression is particularly harmful to Alzheimer's patients as it is associated with greater cognitive and behavioral impairment, disability in activities of daily living, and a faster cognitive decline (Spalletta et al., 2012; Starkstein, Mizrahi, & Power, 2008; Van der Mussele et al., 2013). Depression can be treated with a combination of medication, counseling, and behavioral changes. A predictable routine filled with activities that are enjoyed can provide structure to aid adults who are sometimes confused about their surroundings. In addition to antidepressants, some patients' symptoms improve with the use of anti-dementia medication (Chi et al., 2014). Cognitive therapies, such as training the patient to be aware of his or her surroundings and memory training, can be effective, suggesting that perhaps increasing feelings of cognitive control can reduce depressive symptoms. In turn, a reduction in depressive symptoms is associated with improvements in cognitive function and activities of daily living (Doraiswamy et al., 2003; Lyketsos et al., 2003).

As memory and cognitive deficits increase, Alzheimer's patients become unable to care for themselves. They may forget to eat; to dress themselves properly for the weather; or how to get back inside their home after stepping outside—for example, to pick up the mail. Their communication skills deteriorate, and they sometimes become unpredictably angry or paranoid (Carson et al., 2015). Some adults may show unpredictable aggressive outbursts (Agronin, 2014). Others may become more withdrawn. Over time, the brain will fail to process information, no longer recognize objects and familiar people. Alzheimer's patients eventually become unable to

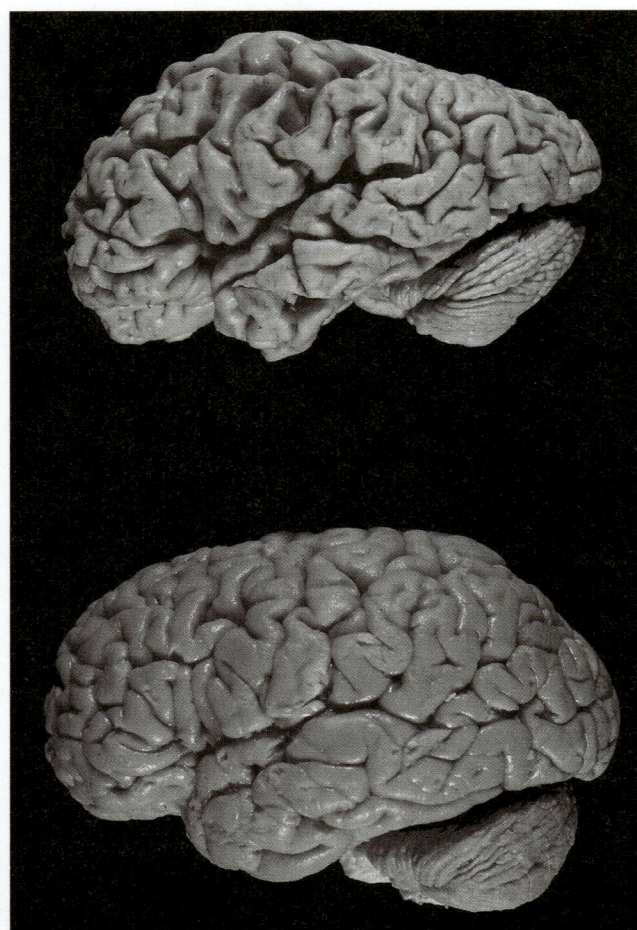

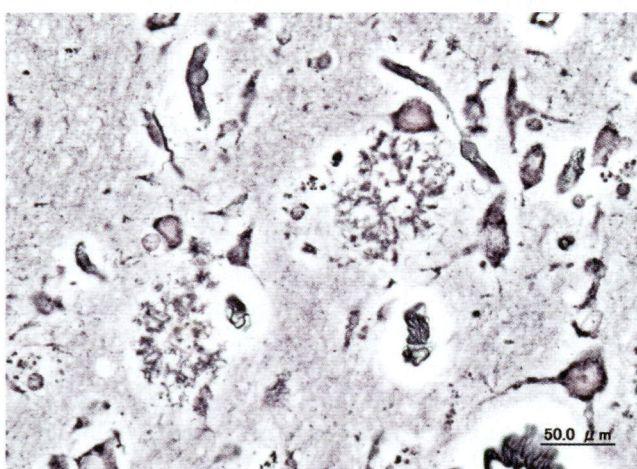

Alzheimer's disease entails a wasting of the brain, as illustrated by the decreased size in the diseased brain (top) as compared with the healthy brain (middle). Alzheimer's disease is characterized by the presence of plaques (bottom) that damage neurons and disrupt functioning.

in episodic memory that are usually attributed to absentmindedness (Bäckman, 2008). The person may forget the names of new people, recent events, appointments, and tasks such as taking a teakettle off of the stove or turning off the iron. Deficits recognize loved ones not because they have forgotten them but because the part of the brain that recognizes people has deteriorated. A woman may insist on seeing her daughter and not realize that the woman in front of her is her daughter.

In the final stages of the disease, Alzheimer's patients lose the ability to comprehend and produce speech, to control bodily functions, and to respond to stimuli (Carson et al., 2015). They show heightened vulnerability to infections and illnesses that often lead to death. Eventually brain functions deteriorate to the point where organs fail and life cannot be sustained. The average patient progresses to the final stage of Alzheimer's disease over the course of about 10 years, with a typical range of 7 to 15 years (Rektorova et al., 2009).

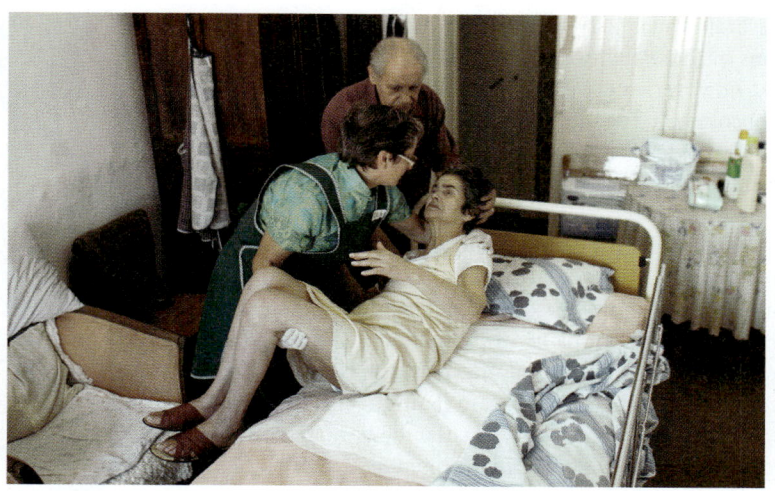

Reuters/Nacho Doce

In the final stages of Alzheimer's disease the patient loses the ability to comprehend and produce speech, to control bodily functions, and to respond to stimuli.

Risk Factors for Alzheimer's Disease

A person's risk for developing Alzheimer's disease varies with gender, age, and ethnicity. Women are at greater risk than men, perhaps because of their greater lifespans (Kirbach & Mintzer, 2008). In the United States, African Americans and Hispanic older adults are disproportionately more likely to have Alzheimer's disease and other dementias than their European American counterparts (Alzheimer's Association, 2015).

Alzheimer's disease has genetic influences and often runs in families (Bettens, Sleegers, & Van Broeckhoven, 2013; Lambert et al., 2011). Several chromosomes are implicated, including the 21st chromosome. Individuals with Down syndrome, trisomy 21, are at high risk to develop Alzheimer's disease as many show plaques and tangles in their brains as early as age 40 (Lemere, 2013).

The same factors that contribute to cardiovascular risk, such as high blood pressure and obesity, also heighten the risk for Alzheimer's disease (Knopman & Roberts, 2010). Vascular damage in the brain might lead to degeneration of neurons and the accumulation of plaques and tangles (Stampfer, 2006). People who consume a "Mediterranean diet" rich in fish and unsaturated fats such as olive oil, as well as moderate consumption of red wine, are less likely to be diagnosed with Alzheimer's disease (Sofi, Macchi, Abbate, Gensini, & Casini, 2010). Although vitamins such as vitamin B and E and folate were once thought to reduce the incidence of Alzheimer's, research is mixed (Daviglus et al., 2010; Douaud et al., 2013), and some researchers caution that there are no known nutritional recommendations for preventing Alzheimer's disease (von Arnim, Gola, & Biesalski, 2010).

Education acts as an important protective factor against Alzheimer's disease. The process of learning promotes neural activity and increases connections among neurons, thickening the cortex and boosting cognitive reserve (Liu et al., 2012; Sattler, Toro, Schönknecht, & Schröder, 2012). Cognitive reserves can protect patients from the handicapping effects of brain atrophy and synaptic loss (Stern, 2012). It is not simply education that buffers against losses. People who remain socially and physically active show a lower risk of Alzheimer's as well because such activities stimulate the brain and increase synaptic connections (Lange-Asschenfeldt & Kojda, 2008; Rolland, Abellan van Kan, & Vellas, 2008). Exercise is thought to have an important protective effect in promoting well-being and enhancing a sense of self (Cedervall, Torres, & Åberg, 2015; Frederiksen, Sobol, Beyer, Hasselbalch, & Waldemar, 2014).

VASCULAR DEMENTIA

Vascular dementia, also known as *multi-infarct dementia*, is the second most common form of dementia and loss of mental ability in older adulthood, worldwide (Jiwa, Garrard, & Hainsworth, 2010). Vascular dementia is caused by strokes, or blockages of blood vessels in the brain (Iadecola, 2013). Typically these strokes are very small and unnoticeable to the victim and those around him or her. With each small stroke, brain cells die, and an immediate loss of mental functioning occurs. For example, over the last few months, Joan had been feeling more scattered. Her daughter noticed that she had some memory lapses such as failing to pay bills and leaving the stove on. One day Joan woke from her nap to find that her arm felt heavy and weak. She called to her daughter, who noticed that Joan's speech was slurred and that she seemed especially confused. A visit to the hospital confirmed that Joan had suffered a small stroke. The doctor noted that Joan likely suffered several small strokes over the past few months and that the deficits slowly accumulated. It was only after the most recent stroke that Joan noticed the changes.

Whereas individuals with Alzheimer's disease show slow and steady decrements in mental abilities, those with vascular dementia, like Joan, tend to show sudden, but often mild, losses with each stroke (Korczyn, Vakhapova, & Grinberg, 2012; Raz, Rodrigue, Kennedy, & Acker, 2007). As time passes, individuals tend to show improvement because the brain's plasticity leads other neurons to take on functions of those that were lost. Additional strokes usually follow, however, and with each stroke, brain matter is lost and it becomes harder for the remaining neurons to compensate for losses (Troncoso et al., 2008). As vascular dementia worsens, the symptoms are similar to those of Alzheimer's disease (Korczyn et al., 2012). However, vascular dementia is neurologically different from Alzheimer's disease. Postmortem analyses of the brains of people with vascular dementia show substantial deterioration of areas of the brain and disruptions in white matter (Iadecola, 2013) but not the widespread abundance of plaques and tangles that accompany Alzheimer's disease (Salmon & Bondi, 2009).

Like many disorders, vascular dementia is influenced by both genetic and environmental factors (Schmidt, Freudenberger, Seiler, & Schmidt, 2012). Genetics may influence factors that are known to be linked with vascular dementia, such as obesity and cardiovascular disease. Obesity and overweight in middle-aged adults are strongly associated with an increased risk of vascular dementia (Knopman & Roberts, 2010; Whitmer, 2007). People who are at risk for cardiovascular disease, with high blood pressure and diabetes, for example, are also at risk for vascular dementia because both illnesses are associated with blockages of blood vessels. Cardiovascular disease significantly increases the risk of vascular dementia (Sharp, Aarsland, Day, Sønnesyn, & Ballard, 2011). Men are more likely to suffer early vascular dementia, in their 60s, than are women, because of their heightened vulnerability to cardiovascular disease. Behavioral influences on vascular dementia such as heavy alcohol use, smoking, inactivity, stress, and poor diet are more prevalent in men (Andel et al., 2012; Seshadri & Wolf, 2007).

There are also cross-cultural differences in the prevalence of vascular dementia, likely influenced by cultural and socioeconomic factors such as diet and activity patterns. In Europe and North America, vascular dementia is responsible for about 20% of dementia cases (Kalaria et al., 2008; Plassman et al., 2007), but it is the most common form of dementia in Asia (Jhoo et al., 2008; Kalaria et al., 2008). In recent decades, however, the prevalence of vascular dementia in Japan has shifted to the second most common cause of dementia, behind Alzheimer's (Catindig, Venketasubramanian, Ikram, & Chen, 2012). The shift may be attributable to changes in lifestyle, such as diet and accompanying declines in hypertension, that reduce the risk of vascular dementia. Alternatively, increased life expectancy and Westernization of lifestyle, including diet, might have contributed the increased prevalence of Alzheimer's disease, thereby making vascular dementia the second most common form of dementia (Rizzi, Rosset, & Roriz-Cruz, 2014).

Factors that prevent cardiovascular disease, such as physical activity, also prevent and slow the progression of vascular dementia (Aarsland, Sardahaee, Anderssen, & Ballard, 2010; Verdelho et al., 2012). Thus, prevention and management of vascular risks may be the best weapon in a fight against age-related cognitive decline (Chertkow, 2008;

Gary Friedman/L.A. Times/Getty

Vascular dementia shows a sudden stepwise progression. With each small stroke neurons die and individuals may suddenly lose functions, ranging from cognition to, in this woman's case, motor ability, requiring her to use a cane.

Raz et al., 2007). In addition, when symptoms of stroke arise, such as sudden vision loss, weakening or numbness in parts of the body, or problems producing or understanding speech, anti-clotting drugs can prevent the blood from clotting and forming additional strokes.

The sensitive subject of informing a patient that he or she has a dementia diagnosis is discussed in Ethical and Policy Applications of Lifespan Development (p. 493).

PARKINSON'S DISEASE

Some dementias first damage the subcortical parts of the brain, areas below the cortex. These dementias are characterized by a progressive loss of motor control. Because the damage occurs first in the subcortical areas of the brain, mental abilities, which are controlled by the cortex, are not initially affected. As the disease progresses and brain deterioration spreads to include the cortex, thought and memory deficits appear (Toulouse & Sullivan, 2008). The most common cause of subcortical dementia is Parkinson's disease.

ETHICAL AND POLICY APPLICATIONS OF LIFESPAN DEVELOPMENT

Disclosing a Dementia Diagnosis

The recognition of patients' autonomy, their right to understand and make decisions about their treatment, is a cornerstone of modern physician–patient relations. There is wide agreement that offering clear, honest information about diagnosis can improve psychological adjustment and reduce distress, providing it is done appropriately (Keightley & Mitchell, 2004). For these reasons, most ethical guidelines strongly promote disclosure of a diagnosis of dementia to the affected individual (Fisk, Beattie, Donnelly, Byszewski, & Molnar, 2007). However, the practice of nondisclosure persists in the field of dementia. It is estimated that 50% of Alzheimer's patients are not told about their diagnosis (Alzheimer's Association, 2015). People with dementia are given euphemisms ("memory loss") more often than family members (Woods & Pratt, 2005). Family members often prefer the person not to be told despite agreeing they would want to know if they were in that situation (Monaghan & Begley, 2004). The defense for withholding information is based on the duty of doctors to do no harm because the lack of certainty about the diagnosis, lack of treatment or cure, cognitive decline leading to poor retention of diagnostic information, and the possibility that receiving such a diagnosis may cause or worsen an existing depression.

However, the majority of people without cognitive impairment as well as those referred to memory clinics say that they wish to know of a diagnosis of dementia (Hort, O'Brien, et al., 2010; Iliffe et al., 2009; van den Dungen et al., 2014). Learning of a diagnosis of dementia may give people with dementia and their families time to adjust and, for people with dementia, to discuss their management and care preferences and engage in advanced decision making regarding care. Disclosure has actually been found to decrease anxiety and depression in patients and caregivers (Hort, O'Brien, et al., 2010).

It is often assumed that cognitive decline is accompanied by increasing unawareness (Woods & Pratt, 2005). However, it is becoming increasingly clear that making assessments of awareness may not be at all straightforward. For example, some people with dementia who are described as unaware by those around them may demonstrate greater levels of awareness in different contexts. In recognition of this, it may be helpful to consider disclosure of a dementia diagnosis as a process and modify disclosure practices and descriptions to the patients' level of understanding, adopting an individualized patient-centered approach that maintains the individual's personal integrity (Fisk et al., 2007).

The process of disclosure begins when cognitive impairment is first suspected and evolves over time as information is obtained. Whenever possible and appropriate, this process should involve not only the affected individual but also their family and/or other current or potential future care providers (Mastwyk, Ames, Ellis, Chiu, & Dow, 2014). Some recommend that additional time and follow-ups in order to employ a progressive disclosure process to address issues including the following: discussions of diagnostic uncertainty, treatment options, future plans, financial planning, assigning power of attorney, wills and "living wills," driving privileges and the need to eventually stop driving, available support services, and potential research participation.

What Do You Think?

1. **In your view, should older adults diagnosed with dementia be informed of their diagnosis?**

2. **Discuss the characteristics and qualities of dementia that influence your decision of whether to inform a patient.**

Parkinson's disease is a brain disorder that occurs when neurons in a part of the brain called the substantia nigra die or become impaired. Neurons in this part of the brain produce the neurotransmitter dopamine, which enables coordinated function of the body's muscles and smooth movement. Parkinson's symptoms appear when at least 50% of the nerve cells in the substantia nigra are damaged (National Parkinson Foundation, 2008). Parkinson's disease includes motor and cognitive symptoms. Motor symptoms occur first and include tremors, slowness of movement, difficulty initiating movement, rigidity, difficulty with balance, and a shuffling walk (Maetzler, Liepelt, & Berg, 2009). Typically these symptoms occur in one part of the body and slowly spread to the extremities on the same side of the body before appearing on the opposite side of the body (Truong & Wolters, 2009). Because the stiffness and rigidity are first located in one part of the body, individuals may assume that it is ordinary stiffness, perhaps the result of too much activity or simply because of aging. As the disease progresses, individuals have difficulties with balance and controlling their body movements. Neurons

Mark Wilson/Getty

Boxer Muhammad Ali and actor Michael J. Fox, both diagnosed with Parkinson's disease, pretend to spar before giving their testimony before the U.S. Senate Appropriations Subcommittee on Health and Human Services advocating that more funding be directed to finding a cure for the disease.

continue to degenerate; brain functioning declines; cognitive and speech abilities deteriorate; dementia; and, finally, death occurs (Maetzler et al., 2009).

Similar to Alzheimer's disease, among Parkinson's patients, those with larger cognitive reserves and more synaptic connections among neurons show a slower progression of neurological changes before dementia appears. People diagnosed with Parkinson's disease at advanced ages tend to develop dementia earlier into their disease than do younger people, likely because of age-related differences in cognitive capacities and neural reserves (Grossman, Bergmann, & Parker, 2006). Multiple studies support a genetic component to Parkinson's (Nalls et al., 2014; Wirdefeldt, Adami, Cole, Trichopoulos, & Mandel, 2011); however, there are some consistent findings regarding environmental and lifestyle influences (Wirdefeldt et al., 2011), suggesting that Parkinson's might be influenced by the complex gene-environment interactions characteristic of epigenetics (Cannon & Greenamyre, 2013; Feng, Jankovic, & Wu, 2014). Parkinson's disease shows no gender, ethnic, social, economic, or geographic boundaries (National Parkinson Foundation, 2008). In the United States, it is estimated that 60,000 new cases are diagnosed each year, joining the 1.5 million Americans who currently have Parkinson's disease. While the condition usually develops after the age of 65, 15% of those diagnosed are under 50 (National Parkinson Foundation, 2008).

Diagnosing Parkinson's disease is difficult because, like Alzheimer's disease, there is no test that confirms the presence of the disease. Incorrect diagnoses are common, potentially delaying treatment to Parkinson's patients (Rizzo et al., 2015). It is diagnosed by exclusion, by a thorough examination to rule out other possible causes. Parkinson's symptoms can be treated. Most medications either replace or mimic dopamine, which temporarily improves the motor symptoms of the disease; anti-inflammatory medications may also help reduce neurodegeneration (Brichta, Greengard, & Flajolet, 2013; Phani, Loike, & Przedborski, 2012). Medication can temporarily reduce symptoms and perhaps slow its path, but Parkinson's disease is not curable.

REVERSIBLE DEMENTIA

Not all dementias represent progressive and irreversible brain damage. Symptoms of dementia sometimes are caused by psychological and behavioral factors that can be reversed. For example, older adults who are socially isolated and lonely can show declines in mental functioning that reverse with the provision of social support (Fisher, Yury, & Buchanan, 2006). The challenge is that reversible dementias are often unrecognized and untreated. In one review of medical records, it was determined that 7% of the dementia cases had reversible causes (Muangpaisan, Petcharat, & Srinonprasert, 2012). Another review of over 340 medical records over a 10-year period revealed that of the 193 patients with dementia, 37 (19%) were reversible (Bello & Schultz, 2011).

Other common causes of reversible dementia are poor nutrition and dehydration (Muangpaisan et al., 2012; Panza, Solfrizzi, & Capurso, 2004; Srikanth & Nagaraja, 2005). As we have discussed, older adults require fewer calories than do younger adults, but nutritional demands remain or increase. In addition, older adults may eat less than younger adults because of depression and simply a loss of appetite that occurs with some medications. As a result, older adults are at risk for malnutrition and vitamin deficiencies, which are associated with declines in mental abilities and increases in psychological distress including depression and anxiety (Baker, 2007). Specifically, vitamin B12 deficiencies can mirror dementia symptoms, yet correcting for this deficiency restores older adults' functioning (Ringman & Varpetian, 2009).

Prescription and nonprescription drugs and drug interactions can also contribute to symptoms of dementia. Many medications impair nutrition by reducing the body's ability to absorb vitamins. Some painkillers, corticosteroid drugs, and other medications can cause confusion and erratic behavior similar to dementia (Bansal & Parle, 2014; Fisher et al., 2006). Older adults may be more easily overmedicated than younger adults because of their slower metabolism. Physical illnesses themselves can sometimes cause dementia symptoms such as memory loss and agitation, which go away as the illness is treated.

Symptoms of depression and anxiety in older adults, such as attention deficit, forgetfulness, disorientation, and other cognitive difficulties, are often mistaken for dementia (Engmann, 2011). If anxiety or depressive symptoms are misdiagnosed as dementia, the older adult may be prescribed medications that can increase dementia-like symptoms such as fatigue and slowed mental reactions to stimuli and events. Treating anxiety and depression with combinations of antianxiety and antidepressant medications as well as therapy reduces the cognitive symptoms commonly mistaken for dementia (Davies & Thorn, 2002).

CARING FOR ILL OLDER ADULTS

Elsie, a certified nurse's assistant, discusses her experiences working with older adults.

Watch the video at edge.sagepub.com/kuther

COGNITIVE DEVELOPMENT IN LATE ADULTHOOD

We have seen that sensory capacities, such as vision and hearing, decline with age. Sensory impairments mean that some information is never attended to and never makes it into the cognitive system. Thus, in most cases, older adults are never aware that they have missed it. Reductions in sensory capacities are associated with impaired cognition (Anstey, Hofer, & Luszcz, 2003; Wingfield, Tun, & McCoy, 2005). For example, in one study, 11% of the individual differences in young adults' scores on cognitive measures were associated with sensory impairment. Among older adults, sensory impairment accounted for 31% of the individual differences in cognitive scores (Lindenberger & Baltes, 1997). Reduced sensory capacities are associated with age-related declines in cognition (Baldwin & Ash, 2011). Reductions in sensory capacities mean that older adults take in information more slowly. Changes in memory capacities influence how information is processed and retained. The extent to which older adults show memory declines varies with the type of memory.

WORKING MEMORY

Working memory underlies performance on a range of tasks, including problem solving, decision making, language comprehension, abstract reasoning, and complex learning (Darowski, Helder, Zacks, Hasher, & Hambrick, 2008; McCabe, Roediger, McDaniel, Balota, & Hambrick, 2010). Age-related declines in working memory span from young through older adulthood and are supported by cross-sectional and longitudinal research (Emery, Hale, & Myerson, 2008). Problems with working memory vary with the number of tasks and task demands. The greater the number of tasks and demands, the worse the performance (Kessels, Meulenbroek, Fernandez, & Olde Rikkert, 2010; Voelcker-Rehage, Stronge, & Alberts, 2006). For example, consider an experiment that requires adults to attend and respond to two tasks at once, such as tapping a computer screen on two alternating targets whose sizes vary systematically at same time as generating a list of random numbers, spoken at two-second intervals. With age, most adults find simultaneously performing a motor and cognitive task such as this more difficult than either task along. In studies such as these, practice in the motor task makes it more automatic, reducing the demands on working memory and thereby reducing (but not eliminating) age-related deficits in cognitive performance (Voelcker-Rehage & Alberts, 2007).

Reduced sensory capacity also contributes to older adults' difficulty with working memory (Baldwin & Ash, 2011; Nettelbeck & Burns, 2010). Sensory impairments mean that information is taken in more slowly, and some information is never attended to, and never makes it into the cognitive system and thus, to working memory (Anstey et al., 2003; Wingfield et al., 2005). In addition to sensory deficits, explanations of age-related variation in working memory have focused on the role of processing speed, executive function, and especially inhibition (Bisiacchi, Borella, Bergamaschi, Carretti, & Mondini, 2008; Emery et al., 2008).

Inhibition and Working Memory

Multitasking is difficult for all adults, but it becomes more challenging in older adulthood. Managing and coordinating multiple tasks by switching attention among two sets of stimuli is associated with greater disruptions in working memory in older adults as compared with younger adults (Clapp, Rubens, Sabharwal, & Gazzaley, 2011). If, however, older adults have the opportunity to slow down to a pace with which they feel comfortable, they can show performance on working memory tasks similar to that of younger adults (Verhaeghen, Steitz, Sliwinski, & Cerella, 2003).

Older adults' poor performance in attention-demanding tasks may be attributable to a decrease in the efficiency of inhibitory mechanisms. With age, older adults become more susceptible to distraction; are less likely to discard distracting information from working memory; and, in turn, show declines in performance on working memory tasks (Darowski et al., 2008; Van Gerven, Van Boxtel, Meijer, Willems, & Jolles, 2007). Older adults are less likely to inhibit irrelevant items and more likely to retrieve them, especially in tasks that require a high memory load and include the presence of distracters (Gazzaley, Sheridan, Cooney, & D'Esposito, 2007; Rowe, Hasher, & Turcotte, 2010). On the other hand, age-related decline is less apparent in cognitive tasks that are more passive and less attentionally demanding, such as digit recall and visual pattern recall tasks (Bisiacchi et al., 2008).

Proactive interference occurs when information that has previously been remembered interferes with memory for new information (Bowles & Salthouse, 2003). Older adults are more susceptible to interference effects even when original learning is equated with that of young adults (Jacoby, Wahlheim, Rhodes, Daniels, & Rogers, 2010). Working memory span tasks present repeated trials of material to be remembered, recalled, and then forgotten. Frequently the old material interferes with older adults' ability to store new material. Thus, the role of inhibition in explaining age differences in working memory depends on task characteristics and demands (Gazzaley et al., 2007; Van Gerven et al., 2007). Simple recognition tasks show few age-related declines, but when working memory maintenance systems are taxed, older adults do not perform as well as young and middle-aged adults.

Emotion and Working Memory

Age differences in working memory are usually assessed by tasks that require older and younger adults to complete various tasks in a laboratory setting. Although standard lab tasks often show age-related declines in working memory, there are instances in which older adults show similar capacities as younger adults. Older adults score better on measures of complex thinking when the task evokes positive feelings than when the task is designed to evoke neutral or negative feelings (Carpenter, Peters, Västfjäll, & Isen, 2013). For example, one study examined age differences in working memory for emotional versus visual information. Findings demonstrate that, despite an age-related deficit for the latter, working memory for emotion was unimpaired (Mikels, Larkin, Reuter-Lorenz, & Cartensen, 2005). While young adults were better able to recall neutral words than were older adults, there were no age differences in recall of emotional words, such as peace, joy, love, or smile (Mammarella, Borella, Carretti, Leonardi, & Fairfield, 2013).

Older adults show a significant information processing bias toward positive versus negative information whereas younger adults show the opposite pattern (Reed, Chan, & Mikels, 2014). This positivity effect in older adults' memories may be due to their greater focus on emotion regulation; older adults may also use cognitive control mechanisms that enhance positive and diminish negative information (Mather & Carstensen, 2005). Affect is an important motivator of cognition (Reed & Carstensen, 2012). Affect characterizes most real-life decisions, suggesting that older adults are likely able to focus their attention and cognitive capacities on the task at hand, if it has real-world emotional relevance, such as decisions about health care, financial, and living situations (Samanez-Larkin, Robertson, Mikels, Carstensen, & Gotlib, 2009).

LONG-TERM MEMORY

Age-related changes in working memory contribute to changes in long-term memory. As cognitive processing slows, most adults show difficulties with recall. For example, while watching a television show, an older adult may retain fewer details than a young adult. However, the various types of long-term memory show different patterns of change. Semantic memory, memory for factual material, shows little age-related decline, while episodic memory, autobiographical memory, and memory for experiences tend to deteriorate with age (St-Laurent, Abdi, Burianová, & Grady, 2011).

Autobiographical memory shows predictable patterns of deterioration. When older adults are asked to discuss a personal memory or experience that comes to mind in response to cue words, such as the words *surprise* or *song*,

experiences during adolescence and early adulthood are especially common. In addition, when asked to create a timeline illustrating memorable events in their lives, older adults tend to remember events early in their lives, from adolescence through early adulthood; they also remember recent events better than midlife events (Rubin, 2000; Schroots, van Dijkum, & Assink, 2004). In addition, they are more likely to remember happy events that occurred between ages 10 and 30 than those that occurred any other time in life (Berntsen & Rubin, 2002).

Why does long-term memory follow this pattern? Perhaps we process events differently while we construct our identities, leading to lasting memories from adolescence and early adulthood. Poor recall of events from middle adulthood may be the result of proactive interference, as old memories may interfere with our recall of newer memories. Similarities among events may make it difficult to distinguish them. Throughout life, memory is malleable, and we often revise our memories in light of new experiences. However, it also appears that older adults recall fewer details from recent events (within the past five years), and different types of details, than do younger adults, suggesting that older and younger adults differ in what stimuli they attend to and select for processing (Gaesser, Sacchetti, Addis, & Schacter, 2010; Piolino et al., 2006, 2010).

Contextual factors play a role in the rate of cognitive change. Similar to findings of cohort differences in intelligence scores, there are generational differences in overall cognitive performance that are maintained throughout life with younger cohorts showing better performance on a range of cognitive measures and less steep age-related declines (Gerstorf, Ram, Hoppmann, Willis, & Schaie, 2011). Possible factors underlying cohort differences include secular trends in educational systems, disease prevalence, years of education, and quality of education (see Figure 17.12).

AGE-RELATED CHANGES IN LANGUAGE

Sensory and cognitive changes influence older adults' capacities for language. Age-related hearing loss and reductions in attention and processing speed mean that following rapid speech and understanding speech when there is background noise require more effort with age (Stine-Morrow, Shake, & Noh, 2010). Hearing loss can impair neural processing of language (Peelle, Troiani, Grossman, & Wingfield, 2011). Language comprehension itself, the ability to understand spoken or written language and retrieve the meaning of words, shows little to no change with age. In fact, older adults maintain or improve their knowledge of words and word meanings (Shafto & Tyler, 2014).

Language production, however, shows a different pattern of age-related change. Picture naming studies show that older adults name objects less accurately and more slowly than do young adults, suggesting a difficulty with language production (Feyereisen, Demaeght, & Samson, 1998; Stine-Morrow et al., 2010). In conversations, older

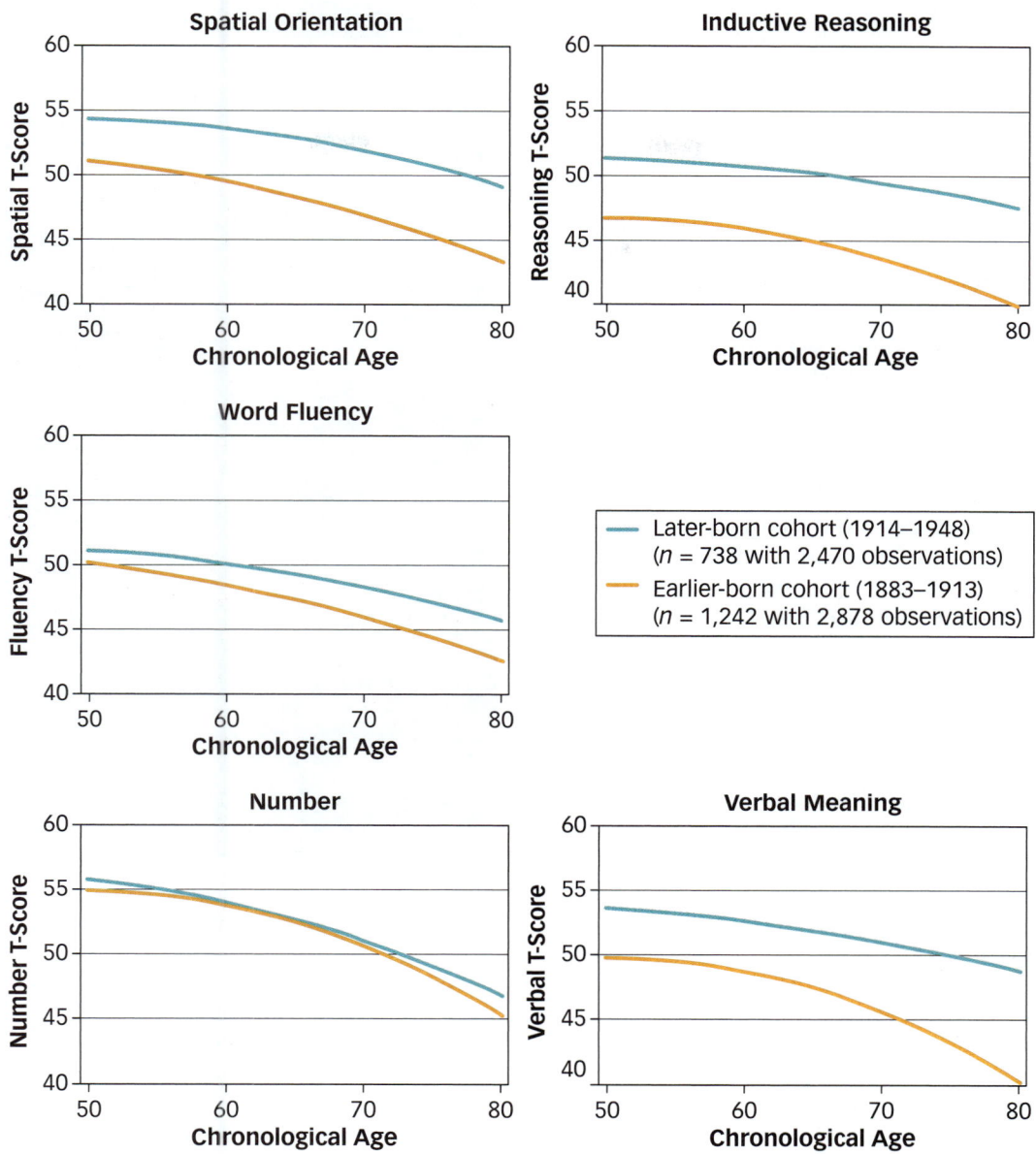

SOURCE: Gerstorf et al. (2011).

adults produce more ambiguous references and more filled pauses (e.g., saying *um* or *er*) and reformulate their words more than young adults do (Horton, Spieler, & Shriberg, 2010), suggesting that older adults have difficulty retrieving the appropriate words when speaking. They use more unclear references and speak more slowly, taking time to retrieve words. A particularly frustrating problem that becomes more common with age is the inability to produce a well-known word, known as the *tip-of-the-tongue phenomenon* (Schwartz & Frazier, 2005). Although people of all ages suffer such word-finding failures, older adults experience more tip-of-the-tongue errors than do younger adults (Mortensen, Meyer, & Humphreys, 2006; Shafto, Stamatakis, Tam, & Tyler, 2010).

Difficulties in retrieving words and producing language may diminish older adults' success in communicating and weaken their and others' views of their own language competence. Negative self-appraisals promote withdrawal from social interaction. Yet similar to managing other cognitive declines, older adults often compensate for losses. They may take more time in speaking and simplify their sentences and grammar in order to devote their cognitive resources to retrieving words and producing speech that others can comprehend.

PROBLEM SOLVING AND WISDOM

Cognitive changes in older adulthood are also reflected in problem-solving skills. Specifically, these studies have shown that problem-solving performance is influenced by cognitive functioning, including processing speed, episodic memory, executive functioning, and verbal ability, many of which decline in older adulthood (Burton, Strauss, Hultsch, & Hunter, 2006). Laboratory studies of problem solving that rely on traditional hypothetical problems show declines with age, likely because of memory changes that make it difficult for older adults to retain and manipulate the information needed to solve the problem (Sinnott, 2003). Yet when decisions tap into relevant experience or knowledge, older adults tend to be as effective at making decisions as younger adults (Denney, Pearce, & Palmer, 1982).

Despite laboratory findings of decline, examinations of problem-solving skills in everyday settings show that people remain efficient decision makers throughout adulthood. For example, older adults tend to show adaptive problem solving in response to health-related decisions and make decisions about whether they require medical attention and seeking medical care more quickly than younger adults (Artistico, Orom, Cervone, Krauss, & Houston, 2010; Löckenhoff & Carstensen, 2007; Thornton & Dumke, 2005). In one study, the quality of reasoning behind 60- to 74-year-old and 75- to 85-year-old older adults' decisions did not differ from that of college students, but older adults processed the problems more slowly (Ratcliff, Thapar, & McKoon, 2006). Generally speaking, adults perform better on everyday problems that are relevant to the contexts they experience in their daily lives (Artistico et al., 2010). Specifically, older adults outperformed young and middle-aged adults on problems set in older adult contexts, such as medical care, suggesting that age-related declines observed in laboratory settings may not be observed in everyday life. In addition, older adults are more likely to act efficiently and decisively in solving problems that they feel are under their control (Thornton & Dumke, 2005). Research suggests that older adults are better at matching their strategies to their goals than are young adults, perhaps because past experience and crystallized knowledge provides an extensive base for making real-life decisions and aligning goals with decisions (Hoppmann & Blanchard-Fields, 2010). Finally, older adults are more likely than younger people to report that they turn to spouses, children, and friends for input in making decisions (Strough, Patrick, & Swenson, 2003).

Related to everyday problem solving, it is commonly thought that older adults become wiser with age. **Wisdom** refers to "expertise in the conduct and meanings of life," characterized by emotional maturity and the ability to show insight and apply it to problems (Baltes & Kunzmann, 2003; Staudinger, Kessler, & Dörner, 2006). The belief that age brings wisdom is reflected in many societies' respect for older adults as society elders and leaders. Research, on the other hand, shows variability in the extent to which older adults display wisdom. In typical studies examining wisdom, adults aged 20 to 89 respond to hypothetical situations reflecting uncertain events, such as what to do if a friend is contemplating suicide (Staudinger,

Older adults are more likely to display insight into the meanings of life and to apply it to problems—to be wise.

Dörner, & Mickler, 2005). Researchers rate each response for the degree to which it illustrates several components of wisdom: knowledge about fundamental concerns of life, such as human nature; strategies for applying that knowledge to making life decisions; ability to consider multiple contextual demands; and awareness and management of ambiguity in that many problems have many solutions but none that are perfect. A small number of adults at all ages scored high in wisdom; they had experience in dealing with human problems, such as that which occurs in human service careers or in leadership roles (Staudinger & Baltes, 1996; Staudinger et al., 2006). When both age and experience were taken into account, older adults were indeed more likely to show wisdom than were younger adults. In another study, however, only college-educated older adults scored higher on measures of wisdom than did college students, suggesting that wisdom does not necessarily come with age but rather with the opportunity and motivation to pursue its development (Ardelt, 2010). Wisdom is rare, but it is found at all ages. However, older adults are more likely to be among the very wise.

Life experience, particularly facing and managing adversity, contributes to the development of wisdom.

ETHICAL AND POLICY APPLICATIONS OF LIFESPAN DEVELOPMENT

Informed Consent in Older Adulthood

A cornerstone of modern medicine is the recognition of patients' rights to provide informed consent to participate in research or treatment—in other words, to make decisions about whether to participate in research studies and medical procedures. Informed consent requires that the patient have knowledge and the ability to understand information about any proposed procedures, understand that participation is voluntary, and be able to make a reasoned decision of whether to engage. Many conditions common to older adults, such as dementia, slowly rob older adults of their capacities to engage in the reasoning and decision making that is essential to providing informed consent.

Basic cognitive capacities, as indicated by awareness of the date, year, and surroundings, are associated with older adults' ability to participate in decisions about whether to engage in medical decision making (Purohit & Kalairajah, 2010). In one sample of older adults in residential living facilities, the best predictors of the incapacity to provide informed consent were cognitive impairments, impairments in activities of daily living, and dementia diagnosis (Black et al., 2008). That said, only about one third of the older adults were able to meet requirements to provide informed consent (Black et al., 2008). Adults in residential facilities, however, are more likely to be ill or suffer from dementia than other older adults.

A study of older adults' abilities to consent to medical procedures showed that cognitive scores were positively related to the length of physicians' visits and length of consent discussions: Physicians spent less time discussing procedures with patients who had lower cognitive scores, presumably because these patients had less involvement in decision making (Sugarman et al., 2007). As cognitive impairment increased, patients engaged less in conversations between the physician and the patient's companion, from whom the physician was soliciting consent. When patients spoke, they primarily agreed with and approved of what was said. Although at first this might seem to signal consent, for persons with dementia, such an interpretation should be made with caution. Because affirming statements may simply be a means of engagement rather than a deliberate cognitive act, it is difficult to assess the patient's actual preference. Communicating with patients and soliciting consent is best practiced as a process rather than a one-time event (Purohit & Kalairajah, 2010). Multiple exposures to information aid ill older adults' capacities to comprehend and reason with it.

An important alternative to consent is soliciting geriatric assent, which balances the process of engaging patients in decision making with protecting them from harm. Geriatric assent takes into account older adults' remaining capacity for autonomous decision making. Physicians identify the patient's long-standing values and preferences, assess plans of care in light of the patient's values and preferences, and protect patients' remaining autonomy. Many patients with dementia can still express their values and preferences, even when they remain irreversibly below thresholds of decision-making autonomy. Geriatric assent does not encourage incompetent persons to make decisions that are beyond their capacity, thereby placing them in harm's way, but instead permits older adults to have a say in their care—as long as they are able (Molinari, McCullough, Coverdale, & Workman, 2006).

What Do You Think?

1. **What factors (noncognitive or otherwise) do you think contribute to older adults' capacities to make medical decisions?**

2. **Under what conditions should an older adult's competence be evaluated?**

One study of people who came of age during the Great Depression of the 1930s found that, 40 years later, older adults who had experienced and overcome economic adversity demonstrated higher levels of wisdom than their peers (Ardelt, 1998). Experience, particularly expertise in solving the problems of everyday life, is associated with wisdom (Baltes & Staudinger, 2000). Those who are wise are reflective; they show advanced cognition and emotional regulation skills. These qualities contribute to the development of wisdom, but they also are associated with better physical health, higher levels of education, openness to experience, positive social relationships, and overall psychological well-being, all of which aid adults in tackling the problems of everyday life (Kramer, 2003).

COGNITIVE CHANGES

We have seen that cognition changes in several ways with development. Aspects of cognition that rely on fluid intelligence decline in older adulthood, but those that rely on crystallized intelligence, accumulated knowledge, and experience remain the same or improve. A decline in processing speed, influenced by neurological changes (discussed in Chapter 14), also influences fluid intelligence and older adults' ability to take in, process, and retain information (Finkel, Reynolds, McArdle, & Pedersen, 2007; Fry & Hale, 1996). Therefore, aspects of cognition that rely on fluid intelligence decline in older adulthood, but those that rely on crystallized intelligence, accumulated knowledge, and experience remain the same or improve. Cognitive abilities tend to remain stable, relative to peers, over the lifespan. For example, high intelligence early in life (e.g., at age 11) is protective of intelligence in old age (through age 87; Gow, Corley, Starr, & Deary, 2012). However, with advancing age comes greater diversity in cognitive ability. Centenarians show greater variations in cognitive performance than do older adults aged 85 to 90 (Miller, Mitchell et al., 2010; Paúl, Ribeiro, & Santos, 2010). Differences in experience and lifestyle can account for many differences in cognitive change over adulthood.

Cross-sectional research shows that education, measured by years of formal schooling or by literacy levels on reading tests, is a strong and consistent predictor of cognitive performance and problem-solving tasks in old age (Kavé, Eyal, Shorek, & Cohen-Mansfield, 2008). In fact, findings from the Georgia Centenarian Study suggest that education accounted for the largest proportion of cognitive differences among the centenarians studied (Davey et al., 2010). Recall that cross-sectional and longitudinal studies often yield different results. Similar to research on cognitive change in older adulthood, the influence of education on cognitive change varies depending on whether the study is cross-sectional or longitudinal (Van Dijk, Van Gerven, Van Boxtel, Van Der Elst, & Jolles, 2008). Longitudinal research studies with older adults from Australia, Germany, and the United States, spanning 7 to 13 years in length with testing occurring at three to six time points, do not find a relationship between education and cognitive decline at older age (Anstey et al., 2003; Van Dijk et al., 2008). Although the effects of education are debated, it is generally recognized that throughout life, cognitive engagement, through mentally stimulating career, educational, and leisure activities, predicts the maintenance of mental abilities (Bielak, 2010; Schaie, 2013).

Physical health is a consistent predictor of cognitive performance and impairment across the lifespan (Blondell, Hammersley-Mather, & Veerman, 2014; Wang, Luo, Barnes, Sano, & Yaffe, 2014). Health conditions such as cardiovascular disease, osteoporosis, and arthritis are associated with cognitive declines (Baltes & Carstensen, 2003; Okonkwo et al., 2010). Longitudinal studies also suggest that poor mental health is associated with declines in processing speed, long-term memory, and problem solving (Lönnqvist, 2010; Margrett et al., 2010). It is difficult to disentangle the direction of effects of health and cognitive decline, however, because people who score higher on cognitive measures are more likely to engage in health promoting behaviors. Physical health and cognitive functioning intersect when it comes to the question of obtaining informed consent from elderly patients requiring various medical treatments, as discussed in Ethical and Policy Applications of Lifespan Development (p. 499).

Interventions that train older adults and encourage them to use cognitive skills can preserve and even reverse some age-related cognitive declines. One study of participants in the Seattle Longitudinal Study examined the effects of cognitive training on cognitive development in older adulthood (Schaie, 2013). Older adults were administered 51 hours'

worth of training sessions and then tested on two mental ability tests. Two thirds of adults showed gains in performance, and 40% of those who showed cognitive decline prior to the study returned to their level of functioning 14 years earlier. Training improved strategy use and performance on verbal memory, working memory, and short-term memory tasks. Most promising is that 7 years later, older adults who had received training scored higher on mental ability tests than their peers. Other research suggests that training improves measures of processing speed and fluid intelligence and these improves were retained over an eight-month period (Borella, Carretti, Riboldi, & De Beni, 2010). Older adults' improvement with intervention is often similar to that of younger adults with gains in working memory task, sustained attention, and memory complaints no different from young adults (Brehmer, Westerberg, & Bäckman, 2012).

Although older adults experience cognitive declines, there is a great deal of variability in everyday functioning. It is possible to retain and improve cognitive skills in older adulthood. The challenge is to encourage older adults to seek the experiences that will help them retain their mental abilities. Older adults who maintain a high cognitive functioning tend to engage in selective optimization with compensation: They compensate for declines in cognitive reserve or energy by narrowing their goals and selecting activities that will permit them to maximize their strengths and existing capacities (Baltes & Carstensen, 2003). In all, healthy older adults retain the capacity to engage in efficient controlled processing of information.

Thinking in Context 17.5

1. An important theme of lifespan development is that development is characterized by gains and losses. How might the cognitive changes that older adults experience illustrate this?

2. What factors might make older adults better decision makers than young adults? Worse?

3. Consider the lifespan development principle that domains of development interact. Identify examples of how specific cognitive changes might influence other areas of development, such as emotional and social development. How might the reverse be true?

Apply Your Knowledge

"Do you really think she can go back home?" Elliot asked his sister, Judith. "I don't know. The next fall might be much more serious," Judith replied. "I want to go home. I'll be fine," insisted their mother, Ruth. Hospitalized over the past two days, 85-year-old Ruth is impatient and ready to go home. Like many other older adults, she no longer drives because her vision is poor. She often finds herself not hungry so sometimes skips meals. Despite her poor eating habits, Ruth has felt that she manages her diabetes well and keeps her blood glucose levels in a healthy range. Osteoarthritis, however, makes Ruth's daily routine more challenging. She has difficulty opening pill bottles, reading newspapers, and sometimes working doorknobs. Ruth has adapted to these challenges by purchasing tools and gadgets, such as non-childproof pill bottles and nonslip grips for doorknobs. Ruth's children worry about their mother's ability to manage her daily life, and more importantly, they fear that she will injure herself in a fall or accident.

1. What developmental changes make it more difficult for older adults to live independently?

2. In your view, is Ruth capable of independent living? Why or why not? If not, what supports can help her live as independently as possible?

3. How do her illnesses complicate Ruth's ability to live independently?

4. Ruth's children worry about injuries. Is their worry founded? Discuss factors that influence injuries in older adulthood as well as the possible consequences of injuries.

Chapter Summary

17.1 Identify influences on life expectancy.

Life expectancy has increased over the last century but varies with contextual factors such as gender, ethnicity, socioeconomic status, and culture.

17.2 Explain the neurological developments that take place during older adulthood.

The loss of neurons increases from middle adulthood through older adulthood. Dendritic loss contributes to declines in synapses and an overall loss of brain volume, especially in the prefrontal cortex. Reductions in myelination contribute to slower communication among neurons.

17.3 Discuss age-related changes in body systems including the sensory, cardiovascular, respiratory, and immune systems, and identify how older adults may compensate for changes.

Structural changes in the eye make it difficult to see in dim light and to adapt to dramatic changes in light. Vision may be impaired by the presence of cataracts and macular degeneration. Hearing loss from presbycusis increases from middle into older adulthood. Older adults compensate for sensory losses by modifying their behaviors and environment as well as through surgery and medication. With age, changes in the cardiovascular and respiratory systems reduce the flow of oxygen to the body. The immune system becomes less efficient and adaptive and more likely to malfunction. Older adults are at higher risk of illnesses, cancers, and autoimmune diseases.

17.4 Analyze the role of nutrition and exercise in aging.

Older adults are the largest demographic group at risk for a nutritional deficiency. Nutrition is an important influence on immunity and overall health. The physical benefits of regular exercise in older adulthood include increases in strength, balance, posture, and endurance. Moderate physical activity is associated with improved physiological function, less disease and disability, better mental health and higher quality of life.

17.5 Discuss older adults' susceptibility and adaptation to chronic illness and injury.

Nearly all older adults show signs of osteoarthritis. It is more common among people whose job or leisure activities rely on repetitive movements. Obesity can place abnormal pressure on joints and result in osteoarthritis. Type 2 diabetes is a disease marked by high levels of blood glucose resulting from insulin resistance and the body becoming less sensitive to insulin. Diabetes raises the risk of heart attack, stroke, blindness, and more. Injury-related fatalities rise dramatically in older adulthood. In older adulthood, brittle bones means that falls result in fractures, especially hip fractures, which immobilize an older adult, are painful and take a great deal of time to heal.

17.6 Examine Alzheimer's disease, and discuss its course, including risk and protective factors.

Alzheimer's disease is characterized by widespread brain deterioration and the presence of beta-amyloid plaques and neurofibrillary tangles in the cerebral cortex. Alzheimer's disease progresses through several predicable steps, proceeding from memory problems, which broaden to severe cognitive and communication problems, personality changes, and ultimately the inability to respond to stimuli. A person's risk for developing Alzheimer's disease increases with age and varies with gender and ethnicity. Genetic factors influence susceptibility to Alzheimer's disease. Education is associated with a lower risk for Alzheimer's disease, as is social and physically activity.

17.7 Distinguish among other common dementias, such as vascular dementia and Parkinson's disease.

Vascular dementia is caused by a series of strokes, each followed by an immediate loss of mental functioning. As the losses accumulate, dementia increases and the symptoms become very similar to those of Alzheimer's disease. Parkinson's disease occurs when neurons in the substantia nigra die or become impaired and are unable to produce dopamine. Parkinson's disease includes motor and muscle symptoms, such as tremors, slowness of movement, difficulty initiating movement, rigidity, difficulty with balance, and a shuffling walk. Dementia emerges in the late stages of Parkinson's disease.

17.8 Compare patterns of change in working memory, long-term memory, problem-solving capacities, and wisdom.

Declines in working memory are influenced by reduced sensory capacity and reduced processing speed. The various types of long-term memory show different patterns of change. People remain adaptive problem solvers throughout adulthood. Adults perform best on everyday problems that are relevant to the contexts they experience in their daily lives. With age, adults are more likely to report turning to spouses, children, and friends for input in making decisions. Wisdom does not necessarily come with age but rather with the opportunity and motivation to pursue its development. Experience, particularly expertise in solving the problems of everyday life, is associated with wisdom.

17.9 Identify influences on cognitive change.

Older adults with higher levels of education, engaging careers, and leisure activities tend to retain their mental abilities. Many physical and mental conditions are associated with cognitive decline including declines in processing speed, long-term memory, and problem solving. Interventions that train older adults and encourage them to use cognitive skills can preserve and even reverse some age-related cognitive declines. Older adults who maintain a high cognitive functioning tend to engage in selective optimization with compensation. They compensate for declines in cognitive reserve or energy by narrowing their goals and selecting activities that will permit them to maximize their strengths and existing capacities.

Key Terms

Alzheimer's disease   483

amyloid plaques   489

cataracts   478

centenarians   476

cognitive reserve   478

compression of morbidity   482

dementia   477

diabetes   479

macular degeneration   480

neurofibrillary tangles   489

oldest-old   476

old-old   476

osteoarthritis   485

Parkinson's disease   488

proactive interference   495

sarcopenia   478

vascular dementia   488

wisdom   498

young-old   476

CHAPTER 18

Socioemotional Development in Late Adulthood and the End of Life

 **SAGE edge™** **Get the edge on your studies at edge.sagepub.com/kuther.**

Master these learning objectives using key study tools in the chapter and at SAGE edge. Access original SAGE **Video Cases** to explore the lives and contexts of individuals in every stage of development, **Think Critically** and **Explore Further** with SAGE journal and reference articles, and **Watch**, **Listen**, and **Connect** with online multimedia resources.

LEARNING OBJECTIVES

KEY STUDY TOOLS

18.1. Compare the roles of self-concept, reminiscence, and life review in developing a sense of ego integrity.

Watch What Is a Life Well Lived?
Think Critically Life Review

18.2. Discuss patterns of stability and change in personality traits over the adult years.

Explore Further Personality Theories

18.3. Explain the contributions of religion and social support to older adults' well-being.

Watch Social Support
Think Critically Religion, Interests, and Self-Esteem

18.4. Analyze four theories that account for changes in social interaction over the adult years.

Explore Further Disengagement Theory

18.5. Identify social contexts in which older adults live and their influence on development.

Video Case Multigenerational Family

18.6. Explain the role of relationships with friends and siblings in older adulthood.

Explore Further Family Relationships

18.7. Compare the effects of marriage, divorce, and cohabitation on older adults' functioning.

Explore Further Marital Status

18.8. Discuss features of relationships between older adults and adult children and grandchildren.

Video Case Grandparenthood

18.9. Identify types of elder maltreatment and characteristics of victims.

Connect Elder Abuse Prevention

18.10. Analyze influences on the timing of retirement and adaptation.

Lives in Context Feminization of Poverty and the Older Woman (p. 522)
Ethical and Policy Applications of Lifespan Development Social Security (p. 523)
Listen Income Inequality in Retirement

18.11. Examine the dying process and cultural views surrounding death.

Cultural Influences on Development Cultural Rituals Surrounding Death (p. 529)
Watch Cultural Views of Death

18.12. Define the concept of death with dignity, and identify ways of supporting death with dignity.

Explore Further Death, Dying, and Hospice

18.13. Discuss the grieving process.

Explore Further Types of Grief

18.14. Identify effects of widowhood in older adulthood.

Explore Further Widows and Widowers

"Hold the end, and swing it gently in time with your sister," 72-year-old Jennifer instructed her grandson as he grasped the end of the jump rope. She watched as he and his sister swung the rope and a third grandchild hopped in between them, beginning a game of jump rope. "When I was little I could jump double Dutch. Do you

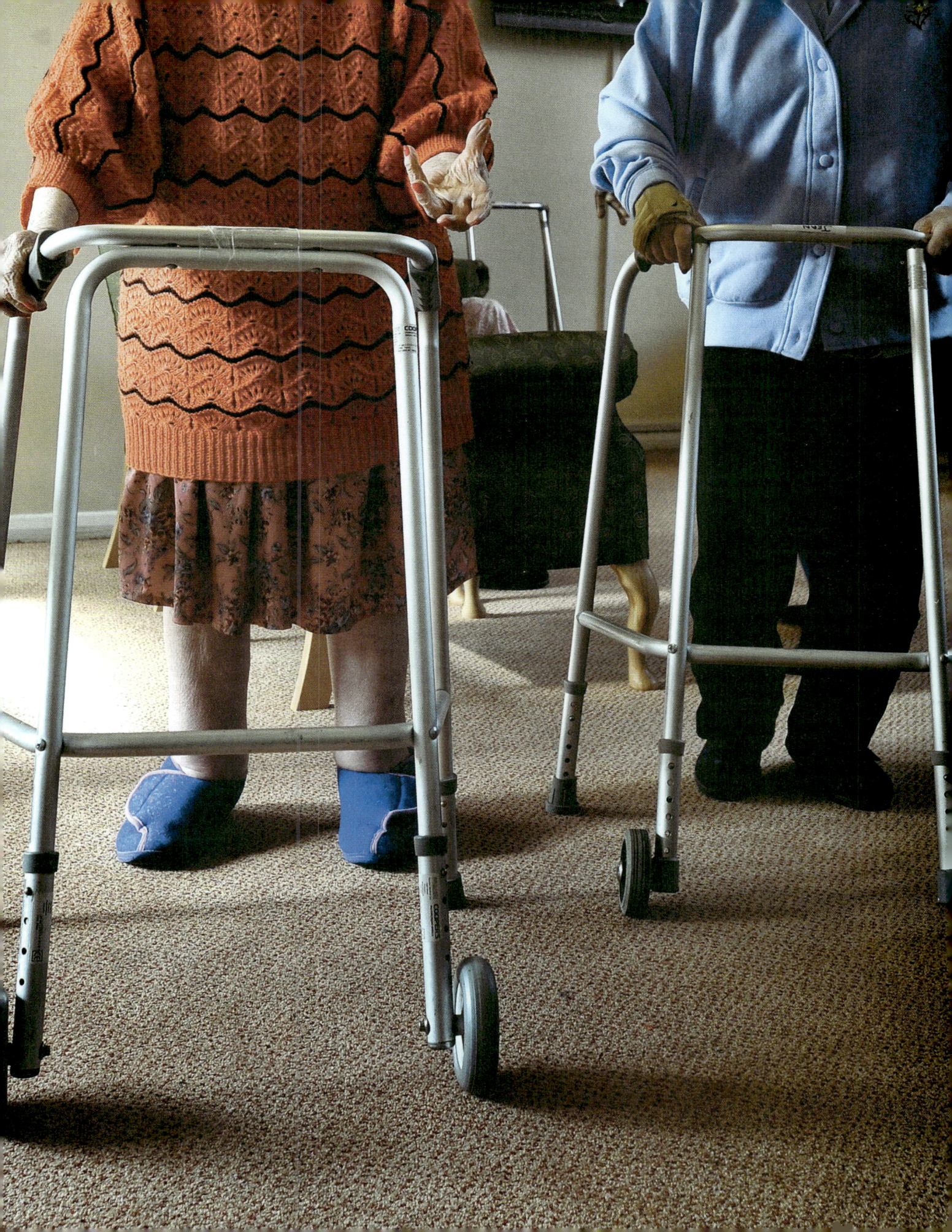

know what that is?" Jennifer asks her grandchildren. Jennifer thinks back in time, closes her eyes, and smiles before she begins her explanation.

The "terrible twos" of toddlerhood, adolescent angst, and the midlife crisis are periods of development that are accompanied by stereotypes—beliefs about commonalities shared by members of a given age group. Older adulthood is no different. Ageist attitudes abound in popular culture. Stereotypes of older adults include the belief that they are lonely; lack close friends and family; have a higher rate of mood disorders; and are rigid, unable to cope with age-related declines, one-dimensional, sick, dependent, and cognitive and psychologically impaired. Common stereotypes about elders' cognitive functioning and mental health are misguided. As shown in Figure 18.1, older adults experience fewer challenges of aging than young and middle-age adults expect.

In this chapter, we examine the socioemotional transitions of older adulthood, including changes in how elders view themselves, changes in the contexts in which they live, their evolving relationships, and changes in work habits. Again, it will be apparent that the reality of life in late adulthood does not conform to many of the stereotypes or commonly held views about older adults.

OLDER ADULTS AND THE SENSE OF SELF

With life experience, older adults' self-conceptions become more complex and stable than at any other period of life (Labouvie-Vief & Diehl, 1999). A more multifaceted and comprehensive sense of self enables older adults to accept their weaknesses and compensate by focusing on their strengths. Older adults tend to express more positive than negative self-evaluations well into old age (Meier, Orth, Denissen, & Kühnel, 2011; Rice & Pasupathi, 2010). For example, in one study, both old (70 to 84) and very old (85 to 103) adults rated themselves more positively than negatively with regard to a variety of domains including hobbies, interests, family, health, and personality, and these positive self-evaluations predicted psychological well-being (Freund & Smith, 1999). Older adults tend to compartmentalize their self-concept more so than younger and middle-age adults by categorizing the positive and negative aspects of self as separate roles whereas younger and middle-age adults tend to integrate them into one (Ready, Carvalho, & Åkerstedt, 2012). Over time, the older adults reframe their sense of self

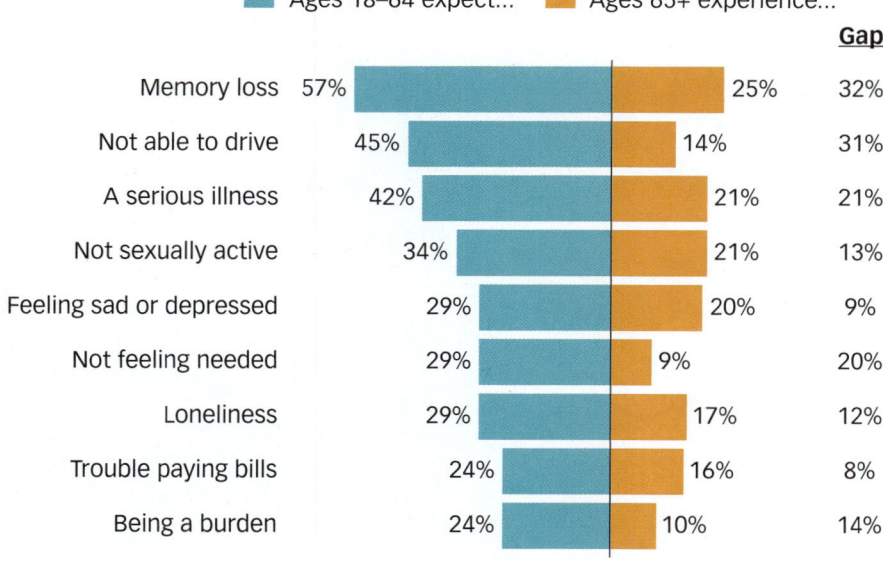

FIGURE 18.1: Challenges of Aging as Expected and Experienced by Older Adults

	Ages 18–64 expect...	Ages 65+ experience...	Gap
Memory loss	57%	25%	32%
Not able to drive	45%	14%	31%
A serious illness	42%	21%	21%
Not sexually active	34%	21%	13%
Feeling sad or depressed	29%	20%	9%
Not feeling needed	29%	9%	20%
Loneliness	29%	17%	12%
Trouble paying bills	24%	16%	8%
Being a burden	24%	10%	14%

SOURCE: Pew Research Center (2009b).

by revising their possible selves in light of experience and emphasizing goals related to the sense of self, relationships, and health (Smith & Freund, 2002).

SUBJECTIVE AGE

Throughout life, age is an important self-defining aspect. Whereas children, adolescents, and emerging adults tend to perceive themselves as older than their chronological age, adults older than 25 tend to have younger subjective ages, and the discrepancy between subjective and chronological age increases over the adult years (see Figure 18.2; Bergland, Nicolaisen, & Thorsen, 2014; Rubin & Berntsen, 2006). Longitudinal samples suggest that older adults on average feel about 13 years younger than their chronological age (Kleinspehn-Ammerlahn, Kotter-Gruhn, & Smith, 2008). Cross-cultural research in 18 countries found that the difference in subjective and chronological age is seen across cultures (Barak, 2009). People at different ages also have different ideas of when old age begins, as shown in Figure 18.3.

Why do older adults feel younger than their years? One reason may have to do with self-categorization of being old (Kornadt & Rothermund, 2012); categorizing oneself as a member of one's age group influences how individuals think about themselves, their competencies, and their future (Weiss & Lang, 2012). Given the negative stereotypes associated with aging, adults may employ strategies to avoid the negative consequences of identification with their age group, such as denying or hiding their age by excluding themselves from the "old age" category; at the same time, they may actually endorse negative stereotypes about their own age group

FIGURE 18.2: Subjective Age Across the Lifespan

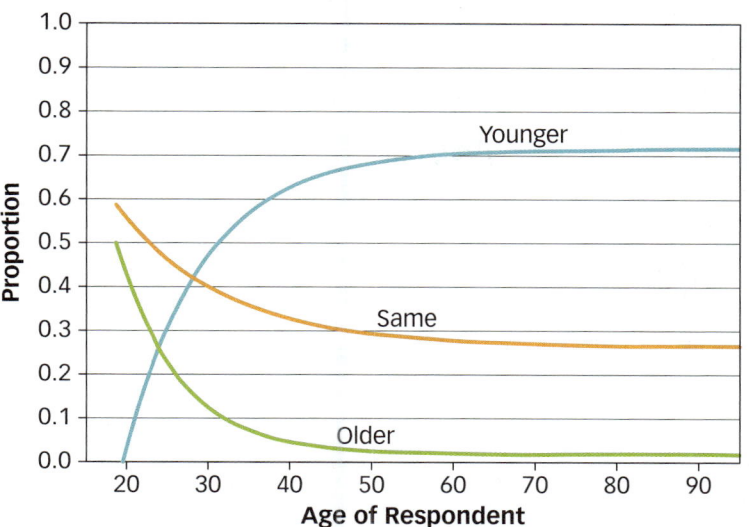

SOURCE: Rubin and Berntsen (2006).

test, but not tasks tapping crystalized intelligence, such as vocabulary. More importantly, simply expecting to take a memory test was associated with feeling subjectively older, suggesting that perception of abilities in various domains can influence perceived age (Hughes et al., 2013). Another study induced a younger subjective age in older adults: Those who received positive feedback after a measure of hand-grip performance showed a decrease in subjective age relative to their peers (Stephan, Chalabaev, Kotter-Grühn, & Jaconelli, 2013). Collectively, these findings suggest that the old adage, "You're only as old as you feel," is partially true as one's perception of age is dynamically associated with health, well-being, and cognitive performance.

REMINISCENCE AND LIFE REVIEW

After living a long life, older adults tend to reminisce and review their past experiences and achievements. They often tell stories and discuss their thoughts about people and events they have experienced. **Reminiscence**, the vocal or silent recall of events in a person's life, serves a variety of functions (Bohlmeijer, Roemer, Cuijpers, & Smit, 2007). Older adults who engage in knowledge-based reminiscence recall problems that they have encountered and problem-solving strategies they have used. Recalling past experience and acquired knowledge and sharing it with young people is rewarding, life enriching, and positively associated with well-being (O'Rourke, Cappeliez, & Claxton, 2011; Westerhof, Bohlmeijer, & Webster, 2010). Reminiscence can also help adults in managing life transitions, such as retirement or widowhood, and provide a sense of personal continuity, preserving a sense of self despite these changes (Fry, 1995; Parker, 1995). However, when adults focus and ruminate bitterly over difficult events, they sustain and even increase negative emotions, and show poor adjustment (Cully, LaVoie, & Gfeller, 2001).

(Heckhausen & Brim, 1997). Adults who do not identify with their age peers may not consider themselves as being as old as their peers, a self-related adaptation that might protect one's self-image from the perceived negative consequences of advanced chronological age (Heckhausen & Krueger, 1993).

Age stereotypes influence health and well-being, including the risk for cardiovascular disease, engagement in health behaviors, life satisfaction, and longevity (Kornadt & Rothermund, 2012; Mock & Eibach, 2011). Subjective age is associated with performance. In one longitudinal study, older adults who reported feeling younger relative to their peers tended to show better performance and slower declines in recall tasks over a 10-year period (Stephan, Caudroit, Jaconelli, & Terracciano, 2014).

Subjective age can be influenced by contextual variables. For example, one study examined older adults' subjective age and found that older adults reported feeling older after taking a memory test but not after a vocabulary test (Hughes, Geraci, & De Forrest, 2013). Recall that age-related declines are seen in tasks tapping fluid intelligence, such as a working memory

Related to reminiscence, but more comprehensive, is **life review**, reflecting on past experiences and contemplating the meaning of those experiences and their role in shaping one's life (Butler, 1963). Life review permits greater self-understanding and helps older adults assign meaning to their lives (Butler, 1974; Erikson, 1982). Specifically, life review can help elders adapt to and accept the triumphs and disappointments of their lives, become more tolerant and accepting of others, become free of the feeling that time is running out, and enhance emotional integration and life satisfaction.

Individual and group interventions can encourage and aid older adults in reminiscence and life review (Davis & Degges-White, 2008). Reminiscence is fostered by encouraging autobiographical storytelling in order to teach others, remember positive events, and enhance positive feelings. Life review interventions, often conducted by therapists and case workers at community mental health centers and senior centers, tend to focus on helping older adults to evaluate life

FIGURE 18.3: When Does Old Age Begin?

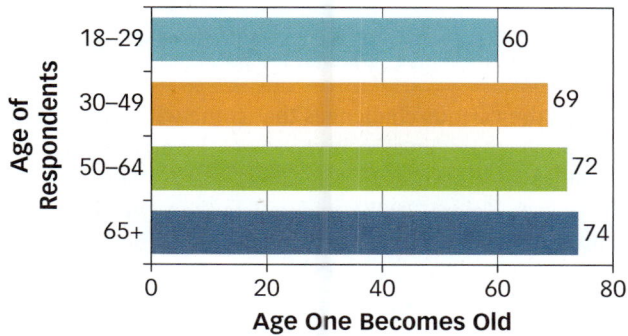

SOURCE: Pew Research Center (2009b).

iStock/Signature

Reminiscence, reviewing life stories and events, is rewarding for many older adults and can aid in life review, a task of older adulthood.

events and integrate positive and negative life events into a coherent life story (Webster, Bohlmeijer, & Westerhof, 2010). Social support may facilitate the life review process in elders, as interaction with others can help to point out blind spots and self-serving biases that arise in the process of autobiographical reconstruction (Keyes & Reitzes, 2007). Close family members and friends can provide feedback and guidance that enhances the life review process (Keyes & Reitzes, 2007). Encouraging adults to engage in reminiscence and life review is associated with increases in a sense of purpose in life, mastery, and positive mental health including the reduction of depressive symptoms, well-being, and social integration (Pinquart & Forstmeier, 2012; Westerhof & Bohlmeijer, 2014).

EGO INTEGRITY

Life review, reflecting on the cumulative choices that compose the story of the individual's life, is integral to developing a sense of **ego integrity vs. despair**, the last stage in Erikson's (1950, 1982) psychosocial theory. Older adults who are successful in establishing a sense of ego integrity are able to find a sense of coherence in life experiences and ultimately conclude

that that their lives are meaningful and valuable (Whiting & Bradley, 2007). Adults who achieve ego integrity are able to see their lives within a larger global and historical context and recognize that their own experiences, while important, are only a very small part of the big picture. Viewing one's life within the context of humanity can make death less fearsome, more a part of life, and simply the next step in one's path (Vaillant, 1994, 2004).

According to Erikson, the alternative to developing a sense of integrity is despair, the tragedy experienced if the retrospective look at one's life is evaluated as meaningless and disappointing, emphasizing faults, mistakes, and what could have been (Whiting & Bradley, 2007). The despairing older adult may ruminate over lost chances and feel overwhelmed with bitterness and defeat, becoming contemptuous toward others in order to mask self-contempt. As might be expected, elders who do not develop a sense of ego integrity are more likely to experience a poor sense of well-being and depression (Dezutter, Toussaint, & Leijssen, 2014).

How does one attain ego integrity? A sense of ego integrity relies on cognitive development, such as complexity and maturity in moral judgment and thinking style, tolerance for ambiguity, and dialectical reasoning (Hearn et al., 2011). The ability to realize that there are multiple solutions to problems and recognize that one's life path may have taken many different courses is integral to developing a sense of ego identity. Ego integrity is also predicted by social factors, including social support, generativity, and good family relationships (James & Zarrett, 2006; Sheldon & Kasser, 2001). Similar to the development of identity and generativity, ego integrity is influenced by interactions with others. When older adults relay their experiences, tell family stories from their lives, and provide advice, they have opportunities to engage in the self-evaluation that can lead to ego integrity.

Thinking in Context 18.1

1. Why do older adults tend to have a younger subjective age? Does a young subjective age serve an adaptive purpose? Why or why not?

2. How might a family member or friend help an older adult with the process of coming to a sense of ego integrity?

WELL-BEING IN OLDER ADULTHOOD

Despite the various challenges that come with aging, most older adults maintain a positive view of themselves throughout older adulthood (Diener, Suh, Lucas, & Smith, 1999; Mroczek & Kolarz, 1998), and satisfaction with life tends to increase from midlife into old age (Darbonne, Uchino, & Ong, 2012). Adults' sense of well-being typically increases into the 70s along with corresponding decreases in negative affect and sense of well-being in older adults has increased with each cohort (Carstensen et al., 2010; Jeste & Oswald,

2015). Well-being is influenced by individual factors, such as personality and religiosity, as well as social support.

PERSONALITY

As in other life periods, the Big 5 personality traits largely remain stable into late adulthood such that older adults' scores relative to peers remain stable over their lifetimes. For example, adults who scored high in extroversion relative to their peers at age 30 tend to continue to score high relative to their peers in older adulthood (Graham & Lachman, 2012). At the group level, there is a great deal of stability in personality; however, when we consider the individual, we see that there are individual differences in the pattern and magnitude of change (Graham & Lachman, 2012). Not all individuals follow the normative increase in conscientiousness scores with age, for example. Some people change more than others, and some change in ways that are contrary to general population trends (McAdams & Olson, 2010).

The stereotype of older adults becoming rigid and set in their ways is untrue. Personality traits shift subtly over the life course. Agreeableness tends to increase with age (McCrae, 2002; McCrae & Costa, 2006). For example, a longitudinal study that examined adults aged 60 through their 80s found that over one third of the sample scored highest on agreeableness in their 80s (Weiss et al., 2005). However, extroversion and openness to experience decline with age from 30 to 90, with the most pronounced drops after the mid-50s (Lucas & Donnellan, 2011; Mroczek, Spiro, & Griffin, 2006; Srivastava, John, Gosling, & Potter, 2003). Conscientiousness increases from emerging to mid-adulthood, peaks between 50 and 70 and then declines. These findings are also supported by cross-cultural research with adults from 50 countries (McCrae, Terracciano, & The Personality Profiles of Cultures Project, 2005).

Individuals' patterns of Big 5 personality traits predict physical and cognitive functioning. For example, conscientiousness is associated with health and longevity as well as better performance on cognitive tasks (Bogg & Roberts, 2013; Goodwin & Friedman, 2006; Mõttus, Luciano, Starr, Pollard, & Deary, 2013). Personality is also associated with cognitive performance (Baker & Bichsel, 2006). Neuroticism, on the other hand, is associated with worse average cognitive functioning and a steeper rate of decline over a seven-year period (Chapman et al., 2012; Luchetti, Terracciano, Stephan, & Sutin, 2015).

Big 5 personality traits show complex associations with well-being—specifically, well-being correlates with higher levels of extroversion, agreeableness, and conscientiousness and with lower levels of neuroticism. Moreover, this relationship may be bidirectional. A study of 16,000 Australian adults' traits predicted changes in well-being, yet changes in well-being in turn influenced traits; individuals who were initially extroverted, agreeable, conscientious, and emotionally stable subsequently increased in well-being and in turn became even more agreeable, conscientious, emotionally stable, and introverted (Soto, 2015). Overall, it seems that in their later years individuals become happier (more agreeable and less neurotic), more self-contented and self-centered (less extroverted and open), more laid back and satisfied with what they have, and less preoccupied with productivity (less conscientious; Marsh, Nagengast, & Morin, 2012). These personality changes aid older adults in developing a sense of acceptance, which they view as important to their well-being (Ryff, 1991) and needed to attain the Eriksonian goal of ego integrity.

RELIGIOSITY

Nearly three quarters of U.S. adults report being "absolutely certain" of the existence of God or a similar spiritual entity (Pew Forum on Religious and Public Life, 2008). British samples suggest that over a 20-year period most older adults show stability in their views of the importance of religion, with nearly all indicating that religion is very important to them (Coleman, Ivani-Chalian, & Robinson, 2004), and people tend to consider religion more important as they age (see Figures 18.4a and 18.4b; Argue, Johnson, & White, 1999; Wink & Dillon, 2002).

Religiosity, or religious involvement, can take the form of behaviors (attendance at religious services), or attitudes and orientation, such as religious affiliation and private religious practices (such as prayer; George, Ellison, & Larson, 2002). In North America, low socioeconomic ethnic minority groups, such as African American, Hispanic, Native American, and Canadian Aboriginal elders, show the highest rates of religious participation. For example, African American older adults tend to report higher levels of private religious practice and daily spiritual experiences, as well as perceptions of God as holding a great deal of control over the world, than do their European American counterparts (Krause, 2005; Lee & Sharpe, 2007); 79% report that religion is very important in their lives, as compared with 56% of the U.S. population overall (Pew Research Center, 2009b). For many older adults, the church is a place of worship that enables them to find meaning in their lives. For African American older adults, the church often provides tangible support in the form of social connections, health interventions, and activities that improve welfare. In one study, African American respondents identified God as both their primary source of social support and their personal consultant for health-related matters whereas European American respondents identified more of a variety of secular sources of help from family, friends, professionals, and clergy (Lee & Sharpe, 2007). Throughout adulthood, women show higher rates of religiosity and religious participation than men (Levin & Taylor, 1994; Simpson, Cloud, Newman, & Fuqua, 2008).

Religiosity is associated with positive socioemotional functioning, For example, a strong sense of religiosity can buffer stress in the face of disadvantages; helps older adults to find meaning in life; and is associated with higher self-esteem, slower declines in physical functioning, and lower rates of depression (Keyes & Reitzes, 2007; Park et al., 2008; Ronneberg,

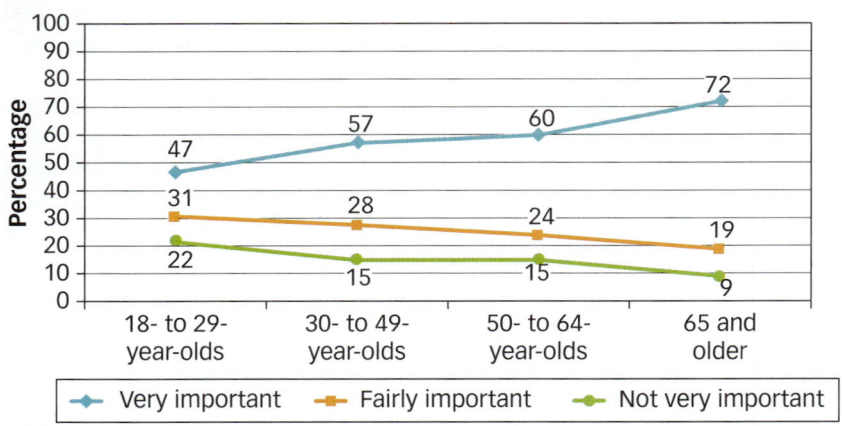

FIGURE 18.4a: Importance of Religion by Age Groups

SOURCE: Newport (2006).

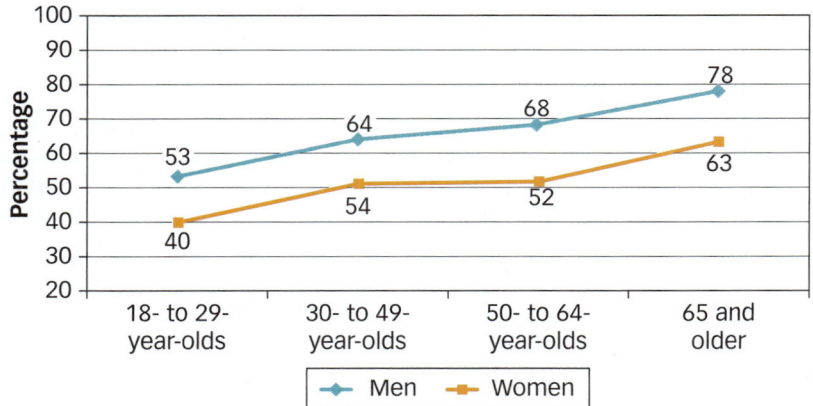

FIGURE 18.4b: Importance of Religion by Gender and Age Groups

SOURCE: Newport (2006).

Miller, Dugan, & Porell, 2014). Religiosity, specifically the perception of God-mediated control, is associated with a higher sense of self-worth, greater life satisfaction, optimism, and lower levels of death anxiety in older adults (Krause, 2005; Reed & Neville, 2014).

Religious attendance may facilitate mental health through social means, by increasing an older adults' connections with other people in the community. Church attendance is associated with larger social networks, more frequent contact, and greater perceived support (Keyes & Reitzes, 2007; Lee & Sharpe, 2007). One study of nearly 1,200 older adults found that most perceived increases in the amount of emotional support they gave and received over a seven-year period and experienced greater satisfaction, especially African American elders (Hayward & Krause, 2013).

SOCIAL SUPPORT

Older adults' physical and psychological health can benefit from social interaction and a sense of support from significant others. Spouses and children are primary sources of support,

as are siblings and other relatives. Assistance and support send the message that older adults are valued and helps them to feel a sense of belonging and see their place in the wider social order. Social support from family and friends is associated with life satisfaction and protects elders from the negative effects of stress, promotes longevity, and enhances well-being (McLaughlin, Adams, Vagenas, & Dobson, 2011; Nguyen, Chatters, Taylor, & Mouzon, 2015).

Sometimes it is not the actual level of social support that matters but rather the level that the person perceives he or she is receiving. Low levels of perceived social support are associated with higher rates of cardiovascular disease, cancer, infectious diseases, and mortality (Brummett et al., 2000; Ikeda et al., 2013; Rutledge et al., 2001; Uchino, 2006). People who perceive social support are more likely to engage in health maintenance behaviors such as exercising, eating right, and not smoking, and they are more likely to adhere to medical regimens (DiMatteo, 2004; Taylor, 2011). Social support is thought to influence health and longevity by enhancing positive feelings and a sense of control as well as buffering the negative effects of stress (Baltes & Baltes, 1986; Cohen & Wills, 1985; Uchino, 2006).

Family, neighbors, and friends often provide tangible assistance, such as help with shopping or meal preparation. As discussed in Chapters 15 and 17, successful aging entails selective optimization with compensation. An older adult might choose to focus attention and effort on writing a mystery novel or volunteering at a local child care center—asserting control over and optimizing an

Social support from family and friends promotes well-being and longevity.

activity that interests her and is within her scope of capabilities—while accepting assistance in day-to-day activities that she finds difficult, such as maintaining a tidy house and yard. For the older adult, accepting such assistance often means evaluating and sometimes modifying their feelings of competence, values, and sense of control. For example, allowing a nephew to come and do a thorough housecleaning and mow the lawn once a month might mean that he does not do these jobs the way Aunt Kathy would have done them herself, but it means the tasks get done without Aunt Kathy injuring her arthritic back and shoulders. At the same time, psychological outcomes and well-being may be influenced more by the perception of having others to turn to rather than the actual amount of help provided (Taylor & Lynch, 2004).

AGING AND THE SOCIAL WORLD

Social support is important for well-being. However, social interaction tends to decline in older adulthood as social networks become smaller (Antonucci, Akiyama, & Takahashi, 2004; Shaw, Krause, Liang, & Bennett, 2007). Several perspectives account for changes in social interaction and elders' psychological functioning.

Disengagement, Activity, and Continuity Theories

According to **disengagement theory**, older adults disengage from society as they anticipate death. At the same time, society disengages from them (Cumming & Henry, 1961). Older adults withdraw and relinquish valued social roles, reduce their social interaction, and turn inward, spending more time thinking and reflecting. Society pulls away, reducing employment obligations and social responsibilities as they are transferred to younger people. According to disengagement theory, elders' withdrawal and society's simultaneous disengagement serve to allow older adults to advance into very old age and minimize the disruptive nature of their deaths to society. In this way, they benefit both the older person and society.

In the years since disengagement theory was proposed, however, it has become apparent that most older individuals prefer to remain engaged and that they benefit from social engagement (Johnson & Mutchler, 2014). Any amount of social activity is more beneficial than a lack of involvement (Glass, Mendes De Leon, Bassuk, & Berkman, 2006; Hinterlong, Morrow-Howell, & Rozario, 2007). Many people continue rewarding aspects of their work after retirement or adopt new roles in their communities. Most older adults retain the same leisure activities from worker to retiree and many develop new hobbies (Scherger, Nazroo, & Higgs, 2011). Some have argued that disengagement does not reflect healthy development but rather a lack of opportunities for social engagement (Lang, Featherman, & Nesselroade, 1997). In contrast to disengagement theory, **activity theory** posits that declines in social interaction are not a result of elders' desires but are instead a function of social barriers to engagement. Adults attempt to remain active despite losses.

Rather than disengage, sucessful older adults remain active participants in their world. Successful elders retain a sense that they are the same person they have always been despite physical, cognitive, emotional, and social changes.

When they lose roles due to retirement or disability, they attempt to replace lost roles in an effort to stay active and busy.

Volunteer work, for example, can replace career roles and protect against decline in health and psychological well-being (Hao, 2008; Morrow-Howell, Hinterlong, Rozario, & Tang, 2003). A 13-year longitudinal study following more than 2,700 elders aged 65 and older found that civic engagement in social and productive activities reduced mortality as much as did physical fitness (Glass et al., 2006).

Yet it is not simply the quantity of activity and social relationship that influences health and well-being but the quality (Pushkar et al., 2010). The more active elders are in roles they value—such as spouse, parent, friend, and volunteer—the more likely they are to report high levels of well-being and life satisfaction and to live longer, healthier lives (Adams, Leibbrandt, & Moon, 2011; Cherry et al., 2013; Litwin, 2003).

From the perspective of **continuity theory**, successful aging entails not simply remaining active but maintaining a sense of consistency in self across their past into the future. Successful elders retain a sense that they are the same person they have always been despite physical, cognitive, emotional, and social changes. This entails acknowledging and minimizing losses, integrating them with their sense of self, and optimizing their strengths to construct a life path that maintains their sense of remaining the same person over time. Older adults tend to seek routine: familiar people, familiar activities, and familiar settings. Most of older adults' friends are old friends. Engaging in familiar activities with familiar people preserves a sense of self and offers comfort, social support, self-esteem, mastery, and identity (Pushkar et al., 2010).

Socioemotional Selectivity Theory

With advancing age, people become increasingly aware that they have little time left to live. This awareness causes them to shift their goals and priorities and accounts for continuity and change in social relationships. According to **socioemotional selectivity theory**, older adults become increasingly motivated to derive emotional meaning from life and thereby cultivate emotionally close relationships and disengage from more peripheral social ties (Carstensen, Fung, & Charles, 2003; Carstensen et al., 2010).

As perceived time left diminishes, people tend to discard peripheral relationships and focus on important ones, such as those with close family members and friends (English & Carstensen, 2014). In support of this, older adults have fewer relationships in comparison with young adults, and age is related to steeper declines in social relationships, but their relationships are particularly close, supportive, and reciprocal (Huxhold, Fiori, & Windsor, 2013; Li, Fok, & Fung, 2011). Older adults place more emphasis on the emotional quality of their social relationships and interactions. As compared with young adults, older adults tend to perceive their social network as eliciting less negative emotion and more positive emotion (English & Carstensen, 2014). Despite an overall decline in the number of relationships, this process of strengthening and pruning relationships is associated with positive well-being; it allows older adults to focus their limited time and energy on relationships that are most beneficial while avoiding those that are inconsequential or detrimental, thereby maximizing their emotional well-being. In this sense, social selectivity is an emotional regulation strategy (Sims, Hogan, & Carstensen, 2015).

According to socioemotional selectivity theory, the functions of social interactions change with age and psychological and cognitive development. Specifically, the information sharing function of friendship becomes less salient. For example, young adults often turn to friends for information, but older adults often have accumulated decades of knowledge. Instead, it is the emotion-regulating function of social relationships that become more important during older adulthood (Carstensen & Mikels, 2005).

Generally, at all ages we look to friends to affirm our sense of identity and uniqueness, we choose friends who make us feel good, and we avoid those who evoke negative feelings. According to socioemotional selectivity theory, the emotional correlates of friendship—feeling good and avoiding feeling bad—become more important over the lifespan. As we age, older adults tend to narrow their circle of friends. They are less likely to approach new people for friendship; thus, they reduce the likelihood of rejection and negative feelings. As physical frailty and psychological changes pose more challenges for adaptation, older adults tend to place a greater emphasis on having positive interactions with others, reducing negative interactions, and avoiding stress. Interacting with a handful of carefully chosen relatives and close friends increases the chances that older adults will have positive interactions. Therefore, smaller social networks are associated with greater life satisfaction in older adults than younger adults (Lang & Fingerman, 2004).

Thinking in Context 18.2

1. Identify three commonly held stereotypes or misbeliefs about well-being in adulthood. Explain research findings in these areas.

2. In what ways do personality and social relationships show both stability and change in older adulthood?

3. Considering bioecological theory, which perspective on adults' changing social world— disengagement, activity, continuous, or socioemotional selectivity theory—best incorporates a contextual perspective? Why?

LATE ADULTHOOD AND SOCIAL CONTEXTS

Social contexts are important influences on development, such as changes in physical, cognitive, and social functioning as well as adaptive functioning. The immediate contexts that influence older adults are neighborhoods and the elder's living environment, whether that is the home, a residential community, or a nursing home.

NEIGHBORHOODS

The neighborhoods and communities in which older adults reside (part of Bronfenbrenner's exosystem) influence their adaptation through the provision of physical and social resources. City, suburb, and rural communities offer different opportunities and challenges. Most older adults live in suburban communities. After retirement, they remain in the homes they have lived in for decades.

Older adults who live in the suburbs tend to be healthier and wealthier and show higher rates of life satisfaction than those who live in cities (Dandy & Bollman, 2008; DeNavas-Walt & Proctor, 2014). Research with older adults in the Netherlands, however, shows that when socioeconomic status is controlled, urban elders live longer than suburban. This finding suggests that low income may be responsible for urban elders' higher rates of mortality (van Hooijdonk, Droomers, Deerenberg, Mackenbach, & Kunst, 2008). A wide range of health conditions among older adults are clustered in the poorest neighborhoods. For example, Canadian older adults who live in poor neighborhoods are more likely than those in affluent neighborhoods to experience arthritis, diabetes, hypertension, heart disease, depression, and stroke (Menec, Shooshtari, Nowicki, & Fournier, 2010). Moreover, the effects of neighborhood poverty and disadvantage accumulate over a lifetime, with significant implications for functional decline and mortality (Clarke et al., 2014). However, urban elders have better access to transportation and health and social services than do suburban and rural elders, enhancing their opportunities for social participation (Andonian & MacRae, 2011). Older adults in

Although urban-dwelling older adults are generally poorer and less healthy than those living in suburbs, the urban environment offers better access to transportation, health services, and social participation.

more accessible and safe neighborhood contexts, including walking-friendly sidewalks and the availability of public transportation, are more likely to retain a higher degree mobility and social activity than those in less accessible contexts (Clarke & Gallagher, 2013; Friedman, Parikh, Giunta, Fahs, & Gallo, 2012).

One fourth of U.S. and one third of Canadian older adults live in rural areas where they tend to be more disadvantaged in terms of health, wealth, and availability of services, and they are less likely to live near their children (DeNavas-Walt & Proctor, 2014). Older adults who live in rural areas tend to share values and lifestyles with their neighbors and interact more with them than their urban and suburban counterparts (Shaw, 2005). Close relationships with friends and neighbors, composed of frequent interaction and high levels of social support, can make up for less interaction with far away family members.

Life satisfaction in all older adults, urban and rural, is associated with living in neighborhoods with many seniors who interact with each other. The family becomes less important as a source of support when older adults have friends who provide support (Bowling & Gabriel, 2004).

RESIDING AT HOME

Most older adults live in or near the home they have lived in most of their lives. When elders are healthy and not physically impaired, living in their own home permits them the greatest degree of control over their lives, such as choosing what and when to eat. Because of divorce, widowing, or never marrying, about one third of North American older adults live alone (see Figure 18.5), and nearly one half of women over the age of 75 live alone (Administration on Aging, 2014). Older adults who live alone are more likely to live in poverty.

As health declines, living alone poses physical and psychological risks, including social isolation and loneliness. Declines in health and widowhood often prompt older adults to relocate, but about 95% of North Americans remain in their old neighborhoods (Chappell, Gee, McDonald, & Stones, 2003). Despite the challenges, remaining in a lifelong home strengthens elders' feelings of continuity with the past, aids their sense of identity, as well as maintains connections with the community, an important source of support (Atchley, 1999). When older adults choose to move to new communities, it is often to be closer to children or to relocate to a warm climate.

African American elders are especially likely to remain in their lifelong neighborhoods and to live in poverty, but they also tend to rely on informal support systems for care, a helper network that includes spouses, children, siblings, friends, neighbors, and church members (Rasheed & Rasheed, 2003). This helper network is the basis for informal caregiving for those older persons who find themselves unable to maintain complete self-care due to illness or physical infirmities. It provides older adults with instrumental assistance, such as help in grocery shopping, transportation, and meal preparation, and expressive assistance, including emotional support, giving advice, encouragement, companionship, and prayer (Rasheed & Rasheed, 2003). Frequently, health care and transportation services are provided informally by friends and relatives in order to allow the older individual to live out his or her life within the context of

MULTIGENERATIONAL FAMILY
Margaret has recently moved into her daughter Sonia's busy multigenerational household. Watch as Margaret and Sonia describe the household and transition.

Watch the video at edge.sagepub.com/kuther

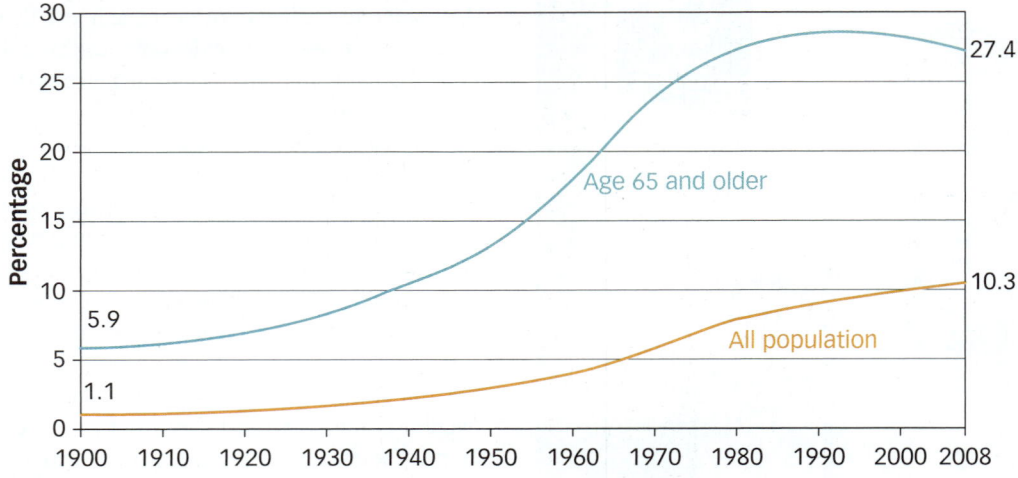

FIGURE 18.5: Percentage of Adults Who Live Alone in the United States, 1900–2008

Age 65 and older — 27.4
5.9
All population — 10.3
1.1

SOURCE: Pew Research Center (2010).

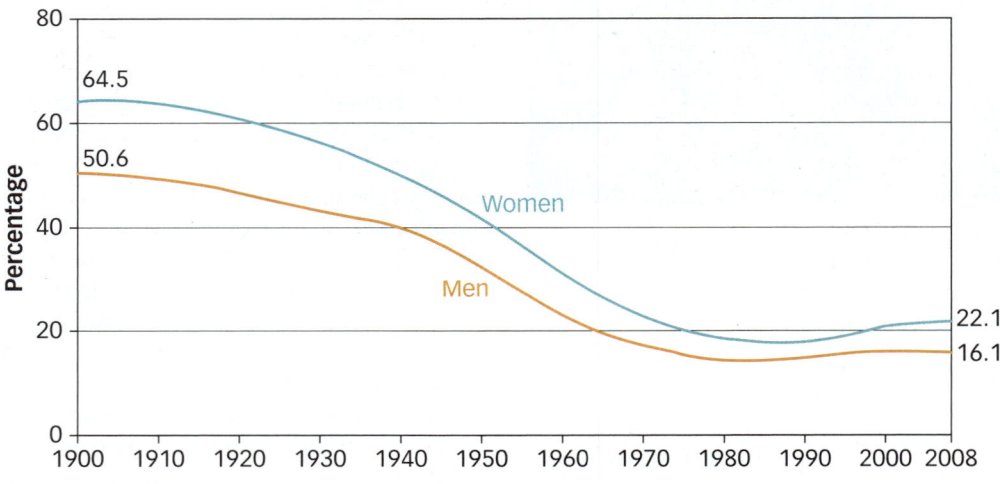

FIGURE 18.6: Older Adults Residing in Multigenerational Households in the United States, by Gender, 1900–2008

64.5
50.6
Women
Men
22.1
16.1

SOURCE: Pew Research Center (2010).

home and community. As coresidents living with kin, older adults may provide child care, shared housing, or financial assistance to younger family members in need of aid, continuing to contribute to their families (see Figure 18.6). Elder grandparents, particularly African American grandmothers, are important agents of socialization, maintaining the role of matriarch and kinkeeper (Barer, 2001).

Obligations to care for elders are not unique to African and African American cultures. Adult children of a wide variety of races and ethnicities often feel a strong responsibility to care for aging parents and grandparents (Gans & Silverstein, 2006; Gonzales, 2007). Extended families consisting of grandparents, adult children, and grandchildren are common. Most middle-aged men and women in North America perceive an obligation to assist parents, especially when the parents have serious economic and housing needs (Postigo

& Honrubia, 2010). However, when it comes to coresidence (an older family member giving up his or her own home and moving in with younger family members), an adjustment in attitude is often at issue. The older person may have concerns about not wanting to be a burden, losing autonomy, or losing privacy; younger family members may have similar concerns about an older family member disrupting the household. Unlike the multigenerational living arrangements that were common a century ago, today the typical household in the United States and other industrialized nations consists of just the nuclear family. Attitudes about coresidence are based on family obligation norms, beliefs about repaying older adults for past help, perceived relationship quality, other demands on the younger adult's resources, the older person's resources, and family members' sense of moral responsibilities to assist (Coleman & Ganong, 2008).

Residential communities offer safe housing that accommodates older adults' changing needs as well as social support and activities that permit them to remain active and engaged.

have frequent contact and communication with like-minded elders, and feel socially integrated into the community. Conversely, those who perceive a lack of social support and feel disconnected from the community are at risk for depression (Adams, Sanders, & Auth, 2004). Overall, older adults who reside in residential communities tend to show higher levels of perceived autonomy, sense of security, and quality of life as compared with elders living independently in the neighborhood (van Bilsen, Hamers, Groot, & Spreeuwenberg, 2008). Although elders in residential settings did not differ from those in regular homes with regard to their sense of well-being or feelings of loneliness, those in residential communities participate more frequently in social activities.

RESIDENTIAL COMMUNITIES

There are a variety of different types of residential communities for older adults, ranging from single houses, to small collections of condominiums, to large apartment complexes. Homes in residential communities are designed to meet older adults' physical and social needs and may include such features as grab bars in bathrooms, single level homes, and intercoms for emergency assistance. Some homes are designed for low-income elderly and are subsidized by the government. Most communities, however, are private. Older adults purchase a home in the community and entry to a community complete with recreational facilities for socializing with other elders and obtaining assistance. Other elders live in congregate housing, which permits them to live independently but provides more comprehensive support, including common areas such as a dining room, recreational facilities, meals and additional supervision and assistance with disabilities. Some older adults opt for "continuing care" communities that are designed to meet their changing needs wherein they begin with independent housing, and when needed, transfer to congregate housing, and finally nursing home care.

Residential communities hold many benefits for older adults. Environments that meet elders' changing physical abilities can help offset declines in mobility and aid elders' attempts to remain active (Fonda, Clipp, & Maddox, 2002; Jenkins, Pienta, & Horgas, 2002). Living in a community of older adults supports social activities, the formation of friendships, and provision of assistance to others, which increase a sense of competence and leadership (Ball et al., 2000; Lawrence & Schigelone, 2002).

How well elders adjust to the move from independent living to life in a residential community varies. Older adults show better adaptation to living in residential communities when they share similar backgrounds and values,

NURSING HOMES

Contrary to popular belief, only a small number of older adults reside in nursing homes. Nursing homes offer the greatest amount of care, 24 hours a day and seven days a week but also are most restrictive of elders' autonomy. Most older people prefer to avoid living in nursing homes, if possible (Rabiner, 1996). Family members often experience guilt and anguish when they see no other choice but nursing home placement for their loved one because of the constraining circumstances, particularly the lack of privacy (e.g., shared rooms and baths) and the rigidity of daily life routines (Kane, 2001; Kelley-Gillespie & Farley, 2007). Nursing homes tend to be hospital-like settings in which elders often have limited opportunities to control their schedule or interact with others and their contact with peers generally is determined by staff. Constraints on autonomy can lead to loneliness, feelings of helplessness, and depression (Anderberg & Berglund, 2010). Among older adults who are not mentally impaired, those in nursing homes tend to show higher rates of depression and anxiety than their peers in the community (Gueldner et al., 2001; Salguero, Martínez-García, Molinero, & Márquez, 2011).

Similar to other periods of life, a sense of control and social interaction with others is important to the well-being of elders who reside in nursing homes. Several factors are thought to be most influential in determining the quality of life of older adults: freedom of choice and involvement in decision making, recognition of individuality, right to privacy, continuation of normal social roles, a stimulating environment with age appropriate opportunities and activities, and a sense of connectedness between home, neighborhood, and community (Atchley, 1999). Well-being is enhanced in nursing homes that are designed to foster a sense of control over day-to-day experiences and social life. Encouraging social interaction in communal spaces, allowing residents to furnish and deinstitutionalize their spaces with some belongings, and modifying their environments to meet their changing needs while retaining as much autonomy as possible can help residents adapt to nursing home living.

Thinking in Context 18.3

1. Elders' sense of self and overall well-being is influenced by a variety of factors within the individual as well as by contextual factors. How might the social contexts in which elders reside influence their psychosocial development?

2. In what ways might contexts such as neighborhood, community, and residence influence older adults' developmental status?

Friendships improve in old age. They become more emotionally fulfilling, centered on activities, and an important source of social support.

RELATIONSHIPS IN LATE ADULTHOOD

Social and emotional connections with family and friends are essential for well-being and are important influences on adaptation and happiness. Aging places new constraints on social relationships, but most elders find that social relationships continue to be a source of support, social interaction, and fun.

FRIENDSHIPS

In older adulthood, friendships become more important and more fulfilling, partly due to the declines in family and work responsibilities. With more time to devote to leisure activities, friendships become more centered on activities, such as playing golf or card games, and older adults report having more fun with their friends than do younger adults (Larson, Mannell, & Zuzanek, 1986).

Recall from socioemotional selectivity theory that older adults tend to have fewer friends but more meaningful relationships than younger adults (Fingerman & Charles, 2010). Friends become fewer in number, but elders form new friendships throughout their lives. Older adults retain relationships with old friends who live far away, but their closest friends tend to live nearby. Similar to earlier in life, elders tend to choose friends who share similarities in age, race, ethnicity, and values. With increasing age and the death of friends, elders are more likely to report having friends of different generations (Johnson & Troll, 1994). In older adulthood, women's friendships continue to be more intimate than men's and they have more acquaintances with whom they spend time in contexts such as book clubs (Felmlee & Muraco, 2009). Men retain a few close friends, but they tend to rely on their wives for intimate and warm communication (Adams, Blieszner, & De Vries, 2000).

Older adult friends tend to provide more emotional support than instrumental support. They give and receive more affection than they offer aid with day-to-day tasks (Ikkink & van Tilburg, 1998). Older adults describe close friendships as entailing mutual interests, a sense of belonging, and opportunities to share feelings (Field, 1999). Giving and receiving support from friends is an important influence on older adults' well-being and is associated with a lower risk of depression (Bishop, 2008; Thomas, 2010). Conversely, lack of social contact and friendship is adversely related to physical health. For example, among older adults who suffered a hip fracture, those who had no social contact with friends within two weeks prior to the injury were five times more likely to die over the two subsequent years than did those who had daily contact with friends during the two weeks prior to the fracture (Mortimore et al., 2008). Friendships are also crucial in helping to manage age-related losses in health as well as **bereavement** at the death of a loved one.

SIBLING RELATIONSHIPS

The majority of older adults have a sibling, most live within 100 miles of each other, and most communicate regularly (Connidis, 1989). Older adults often report the desire to live near their siblings. Most older adults feel close to their siblings and consider them to be close friends, even if they do not live near each other and do not visit regularly (van Volkom, 2006). Unlike friends, siblings are not chosen, and usually siblings are the only living people who have known an adult over his or her entire life. The history of personal and family experiences that adult siblings share contributes to a powerful bond. Siblings grow closer with the experience of family events, hardships, and age-related issues (Myers & Kennedy-Lightsey, 2014). Typically, siblings can be relied upon like the closest of friends. The closeness that siblings share includes sharing experiences, trust, concern for the other, and enjoyment of the sibling relationship. Sisters tend to be closest, followed by cross-sex siblings (White & Riedmann, 1992). Closeness of siblings is influenced by gender roles that promote greater acceptance and expressiveness among women than men (van Volkom, 2006).

In addition to emotional support, siblings provide tangible support and are considered important sources of help in times of crisis. Older adults who have never married or who have no children rely more on siblings for support

Carlos Osorio/Toronto Star/Getty

than do those who have been married or have children (Connidis, 1989). Widowed adults show increased reliance on siblings. Close relationships with siblings influence well-being. Elders with a living sibling tend to have higher morale and a positive outlook than those who do not, perhaps because elder siblings share past experiences and reminisce (Brubaker, 1990; van Volkom, 2006). As discussed in the first section of this chapter, reminiscing is associated with higher self-esteem, fewer cases of depression, and better adjustment (Bohlmeijer et al., 2007; Coleman, 1986).

MARRIAGE AND COHABITATION

Intimate partnerships are important in late adulthood, whether in the form of a decades-long marriage, a second marriage after divorce or widowhood, or a cohabiting relationship.

Marital Satisfaction

Lifestyle changes over the course of the adult years contribute to a rise in marital satisfaction from middle adulthood to peak in late adulthood (Ko, Berg, Butner, Uchino, & Smith, 2007; Levenson, Carstensen, & Gottman, 1993). Older adult marriages are characterized by greater satisfaction, less negativity, and a higher frequency of positive marital interactions than in other developmental periods (Carstensen, Graff, Levenson, & Gottman, 1996; Story et al., 2007).

Older spouses tend to perceive more positive characteristics and fewer negative characteristics in their partners than do younger spouses (Henry, Berg, Smith, & Florsheim, 2007). As compared with middle-aged adults, older adults show greater positive sentiment override—that is, they appraise their spouse's behavior as more positive than do outside observers (Story et al., 2007). In other words, elders tend to view their spouses through rose-colored glasses. In turn, marital satisfaction influences positive sentiment override. Those who are most satisfied in their marriages have the rosiest of glasses, viewing their spouse's behavior most positively as compared with outsiders.

Age-related differences in the salience of positive and negative interpersonal behavior may be due to changes in emotional regulation (Labouvie-Vief & Medler, 2002). Older adults exhibit more emotional control and mood stability compared to middle-aged and young adults (Henry et al., 2007) and emotional regulation predicts satisfaction (Bloch, Haase, & Levenson, 2014).

Older adults describe their relationships as having less conflict and higher levels of pleasure and report greater positive affect in marital interaction than do younger adults (Carstensen et al., 1996, 2003; Waldinger & Schulz, 2010). Older couples show fewer disagreements and tend to discuss disagreements with more respect and humor and resolve arguments more quickly and constructively with less resulting anger and resentment than younger couples do (Hatch & Bulcroft, 2004). The quality of the marital relationship predicts happiness over the years (Proulx, Helms, & Buehler, 2007).

Most older adults are very satisfied in their marriages. A lifetime of shared experiences, such as raising families, navigating crises, and building memories together, brings couples closer.

As discussed in Chapters 13 and 15, people tend to select mates who are similar to them. Over the years, spouses tend to become more similar to each other in personality (Caspi, Herbener, & Ozer, 1992), cognitive functioning (Gruber-Baldini, Schaie, & Willis, 1995), and markers of aging (Ko et al., 2007). Spouses show similarity in their general well-being, including rates of depression; physical activity; and health, including risks chronic diseases, such as high blood pressure (Bookwala & Jacobs, 2004; Pettee et al., 2006; Townsend, Miller, & Guo, 2001). Marital satisfaction is associated with physical and mental health, a longer life, and life satisfaction (Carr, 2012; Liu & Waite, 2014; Manzoli, Villari, Pirone, & Boccia, 2007). Couples who share similarities tend to report greater martial satisfaction (Gonzaga, Campos, & Bradbury, 2007).

A variety of factors contribute to the rise in marital satisfaction over the adult years. The goals emphasized by couples change over the life course. In young adulthood, personal growth is a primary concern; this changes in middle adulthood to instrumental goals, such as raising children, and in late adulthood to companionship goals (Lee,

Zarit, Rovine, Birditt, & Fingerman, 2011). With grown children and the onset of retirement, adults are no longer faced with the challenges of balancing child-rearing and career. Many women perceive greater fairness in their relationships and greater equity in household tasks, as retired men often take on a greater role in completing household tasks than at earlier periods (Kulik, 2002). Retirement provides the opportunity for couples to spend more time together, which many older women report enhances feelings of closeness with their husbands (Vinick & Ekerdt, 1991). A lifetime of shared experiences, such as raising families, navigating crises, and building memories together, brings couples closer (Huston, 2000).

Cohabitation

Cohabitation is increasingly common among older adults. Cohabitation among adults over age 50 more than doubled from 1.2 million in 2000 to 2.75 million adults representing 8% of persons over age 50 (Brown, Bulanda, & Lee, 2012; U.S. Bureau of the Census, 2012).

Cohabitation is associated with more positive outcomes in older adulthood as compared with younger adulthood. Compared with younger couples, older adults who cohabit tend to be in relationships of longer duration; are more likely to have experienced the dissolution of a marriage; and tend to report fewer marriage plans, viewing the relationship as an alternative to marriage (King & Scott, 2005). Older adults may be less interested in marriage because they are past the age of childbearing. They also may be more interested in protecting the wealth they have accrued over their lifetime than they are in pooling economic resources.

Cohabitors over the age of 50 tend to report higher-quality relationships than younger cohabitors, perceiving more fairness, more time spent alone with their partner, fewer disagreements, a lower likelihood of arguing heatedly or violently than younger cohabitors, and a lower likelihood of reporting thinking their relationship might be in trouble or that they will eventually separate (King & Scott, 2005). In addition, older cohabitors report higher levels of happiness than younger cohabitors or single elders.

Older adult cohabitors do not differ from marrieds in their reports of emotional satisfaction, pleasure, openness, time spent together, criticism, and demands (Brown & Kawamura, 2010). Among older adults, cohabitation shows similar health benefits to marriage, and this finding holds true in a variety of cultures. For example, one study of Italian men showed that, similar to marriage, cohabitation was associated with reduced mortality as compared with single men who live alone (Scafato et al., 2008). A longitudinal study of over 2,500 Danish older men showed that cohabitation and marriage were both associated with reduced rates of disability over a nearly five-year period whereas, similar to findings on marriage, women did not experience similar benefits of cohabitation as compared with men (Juul Nilsson, Lund, & Avlund, 2008).

The nature of sexual expression often changes in older adulthood, but most older adults remain interested in, and satisfied by, sexual activity.

Sexuality

Media images of sexuality have traditionally portrayed only attractive young people, shaping and reinforcing societal misconceptions that sexuality disappears in older people (Bauer, McAuliffe, & Nay, 2007). Even researchers who study sexuality often overlook the views and experiences of elders by focusing on those under the age of 60 (Gott, 2005; Smith, Rissel, Richters, Grulich, & de Visser, 2003). Many assume that sexuality is irrelevant to older people, reflecting the stereotype that aging is a feared negative event marked by rapid physical and cognitive decline (Nelson, 2005). As the population of older adults increases and healthy aging becomes more common, widespread advertising of medications for sexual performance (e.g., to treat erectile dysfunction) may shift assumptions toward the view that older adults desire but are physically unable to have, sex. However, adults remain interested and capable of sexual activity well into older adulthood (see Chapter 17).

Sexuality continues and remains important well into old age and, just as in middle age, good sex in the past predicts good sex in the future. For example, five decades of research has consistently shown that older people generally maintain sexual interest and remain sexually capable well into their 80s and often 90s (DeLamater & Koepsel, 2015; Gott & Hinchliff, 2003). Research in Asia, Australia, Europe, and the United States confirms that sexual interest and activity is still viewed as important to many older people (Bauer et al., 2007; Hyde et al., 2010; Minichiello, Plummer, & Loxton, 2004; Palacios-Ceña et al., 2012). One study of older adults who have a sexual partner found that all rated sex as "important" and over one third as "very important" in their lives (Gott & Hinchliff, 2003).

The frequency of sexual activity declines with age, but sexual satisfaction often remains unchanged (Minichiello et al., 2004; Thompson et al., 2011). In one study, 54% of men and 21% of women aged 70 to 80 reported having sexual intercourse within the past year, and nearly one quarter of those men and women had intercourse more than once a week (Nicolosi et al., 2006). One third of a sample of 75- to 85-year-old men reported having at least one sexual encounter within the past year (Hyde et al., 2010). Likewise, a 30-year longitudinal study of nearly 2,800 Australian men, 40% of those aged 75 to 79, but only 11% of those aged 90 to 95, had had sex in the past year (Doskoch, 2011). Reasons for lack of sexual activity include physical problems, lack of interest, partner's lack of interest, partner's physical problems, and the loss of a partner (Palacios-Ceña et al., 2012).

The nature of sexual expression shifts with age, encompassing an array of behaviors (e.g., self-stimulation, noncoital activity with partners) as well as sexual activity in both long-term and new relationships (Hodson & Skeen, 1994; McAuliffe, Bauer, & Nay, 2007). Because of the hormonal changes that accompany menopause (see Chapter 15), women may experience lack of vaginal lubrication and therefore find intercourse uncomfortable (DeLamater & Koepsel, 2015). With increasing age, males' erections tend to take longer to achieve, are less frequent, and are more difficult to sustain; however, these normative changes should not be mistaken for erectile dysfunction (Araujo, Mohr, & McKinlay, 2004; Tan, 2011). Many factors may diminish sexual response and satisfaction, such as cigarette smoking, heavy drinking, obesity, poor health, and attitudes toward sexuality and aging (DeLamater, 2012). Many illnesses encountered in advancing age, including arthritis, heart disease, diabetes, Parkinson's disease, stroke, cancer, and depression, can negatively affect an individual's interest or participation in sexual activity (Syme, Klonoff, Macera, & Brodine, 2013; Taylor & Gosney, 2011). Likewise, prescription drugs, over-the-counter medications, and herbal supplements may have side effects that can alter or impair sexual function.

Sexual activity is a correlate of good health, as those who report good health are more likely to be sexually active (DeLamater & Koepsel, 2015; Holden, Collins, Handelsman, Jolley, & Pitts, 2014). However, just as during other phases of life, there is a bidirectional relationship: Sexual activity is likely to enhance health by reducing stress and improving well-being (Brody, 2010).

Divorce and Remarriage

As we have seen, marital satisfaction generally increases with age; couples over the age of 65 are less likely to divorce than are younger couples. Less than 1% of all divorces comprise elders. However, divorces are becoming more common because the new generation of older adults tends to be more accepting of divorce than prior generations and is more likely to have divorced and remarried, a risk factor for divorce. Similar to younger people, older adults report divorcing because of

poor communication, emotional detachment, and few shared interests (Weingarten, 1988; Wu & Schimmele, 2007).

Elders in long-term marriages find it more difficult to adjust to divorce than do younger adults. Many find it difficult to separate and feel a sense of failure after spending their lives in a relationship. Divorce poses financial challenges for couples because accumulated assets must be divided and financial security in retirement is at risk. Women face greater financial and emotional difficulties than men as they are more likely to remain single throughout the remainder of their lives (McDonald & Robb, 2004).

Social support is important for well-being throughout adulthood but is especially important in adjusting to divorce. Yet divorce changes relationships with family and friends and can reduce support and pose great challenges to adjustment. Research with U.K. elders 70 years or older, however, found that divorce itself was not related to a decline in support from adult children over a 12-year period (Glaser, Stuchbury, Tomassini, & Askham, 2008). Similarly, samples of U.S. adults show that adult children of divorced parents are just as likely as adult children of widowed parents to give care and money to their mothers but are less likely to care for their fathers after divorce (Lin, 2008). The findings suggest that divorced fathers are likely the population most in need of formal support in old age.

Rates of remarriage decline in older adulthood. Still, a substantial number of adults, particularly older men, remarry after divorce (Huyck & Gutmann, 2006). Single women, whether by divorce or widowhood, are less likely to marry than men, but women are more likely to marry after divorce than widowhood. When elders remarry, their unions tend to be more stable than those of younger people. The gains in maturity and perspective may contribute to a more realistic concept of marriage and support the longevity of late life marriages (Kemp & Kemp, 2002).

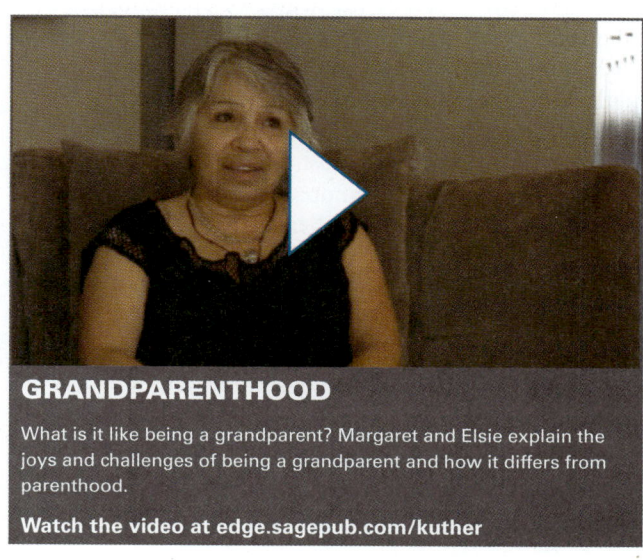

GRANDPARENTHOOD

What is it like being a grandparent? Margaret and Elsie explain the joys and challenges of being a grandparent and how it differs from parenthood.

Watch the video at edge.sagepub.com/kuther

RELATIONSHIPS WITH ADULT CHILDREN AND GRANDCHILDREN

Most North American older adults are parents, usually of middle-aged adults. The nature of the relationship and exchange of help changes over time, from predominantly parent-to-child assistance in childhood through early adulthood, to increasing assistance provided by adult children to their elderly parents. Adult child-to-parent assistance most often takes the form of emotional support and companionship, which helps elders cope with and compensate for losses such as disabilities and widowhood. Most older adults and their adult children keep in touch even when they are separated by great distance. Overall, adult daughters tend to be closer and more involved with parents than sons, speaking with and visiting more often than sons. In contrast with emotional support, fewer older adults receive instrumental assistance from adult children. Instead, many older adults, especially high socioeconomic elders, continue to assist their adult children, primarily with financial assistance (Grundy & Henretta, 2006).

Family relations may take many forms. Some parents and adult children live nearby, engage in frequent contact, and endorse family obligation norms. Support is provided either primarily from parent to adult child or adult to parent. Other families provide support at a distance where they do not live nearby, engage in frequent contact, endorse fewer family obligation norms, and provide mainly financial support—often from parents to children. Other family relationships are autonomous: not living nearby, engaging in little contact, little endorsement of family obligation norms, and few support exchanges. Each of these types of family relations are found in most European nations and likely the United States (Dykstra & Fokkema, 2010).

About one half of older adults in Western nations have an adult grandchild (AARP, 2002). Grandchildren and great-grandchildren increase elders' opportunities for emotional support. The quality of the grandparent relationship is influenced by the degree of involvement in the grandchild's life. A history of close and frequent contact, positive experiences, and affectionate ties predicts good adult child–grandparent relationships (Sheehan & Petrovic, 2008). One study of adult grandchildren in young and middle adulthood found that most adults reported that their relationships with their grandparents are close and enduring (Hodgson, 1992). Several factors were related to the strength of the grandchild–grandparent bonds: age, geographical proximity, the child–parent relationship, and the parent–grandparent relationship. Over time, contact with grandchildren tends to decline as young and middle-aged grandchildren take on time-consuming family and work roles and sometimes move far away. Regardless of distance and contact, affection between grandchildren and grandparents remains strong (Silverstein & Marenco, 2001; Thiele & Whelan, 2008).

ELDER MALTREATMENT

Most older adults maintain positive and healthy relationships with the people around them, including friends, relatives, and caregivers. In recent years, however, the media has drawn the public's attention to the problem of elder maltreatment—acts or omissions that cause harm to the older person and occur within the context of a trusting relationship (Johannesen & LoGiudice, 2013). Reports of the prevalence of elder maltreatment vary with how maltreatment is defined.

Elder maltreatment appears in several forms. Many elders fall victim to more than one form of maltreatment (Choi & Nater, 2000), which may include the following.

- Physical abuse: Intentionally inflicting physical harm or discomfort through cutting, burning, and other acts of physical force

- Sexual abuse: Inflicting unwanted sexual contact

- Psychological abuse: Intentionally inflicting emotional harm through verbal assaults, humiliation, intimidation, or withdrawal of affection

- Financial abuse: Exploiting the elder's financial resources by theft or unauthorized use (e.g., withdrawing funds from savings, selling an elder's jewelry or other possessions, charging purchases to the elder's credit card)

- Physical neglect: Providing inadequate care and failing to meet an elder's basic needs for food, medication, physical comfort, and health care; leaving an elder with special needs unattended

Elder abuse appears in all cultures. Overall about 6% to 10% of elders in industrialized countries, including Australia, Canada, China, Germany, India, Ireland, Israel, the Netherlands, Taiwan, the United Kingdom, and others, report experiencing abuse within the last month (Cooper, Selwood, & Livingston, 2008; Lowenstein & Doron, 2008; Melchiorre, Penhale, & Lamura, 2014; Podnieks, Anetzberger, Wilson, Teaster, & Wangmo, 2010). About 5% of U.S. older adults report emotional abuse, 2% physical, and 1% sexual abuse each year (Acierno et al., 2010). It is estimated that about 5% of older adults experience neglect by a caregiver and 5% experience financial abuse by a family member each year.

Similar to child abuse, elder maltreatment is underreported, and prevalence rates are likely higher than reported. Victims of maltreatment are more likely to be advanced in age and suffer from physical and mental illness, frailty, and impairments with activities of daily living (Choi & Nater, 2000; Laumann, Leitsch, & Waite, 2008). Women and minorities are more likely to be victimized, as are those who experience a lack of social support or social isolation (Choi & Nater, 2000; Johannesen & LoGiudice, 2013; Sooryanarayana, Choo, & Hairi, 2013).

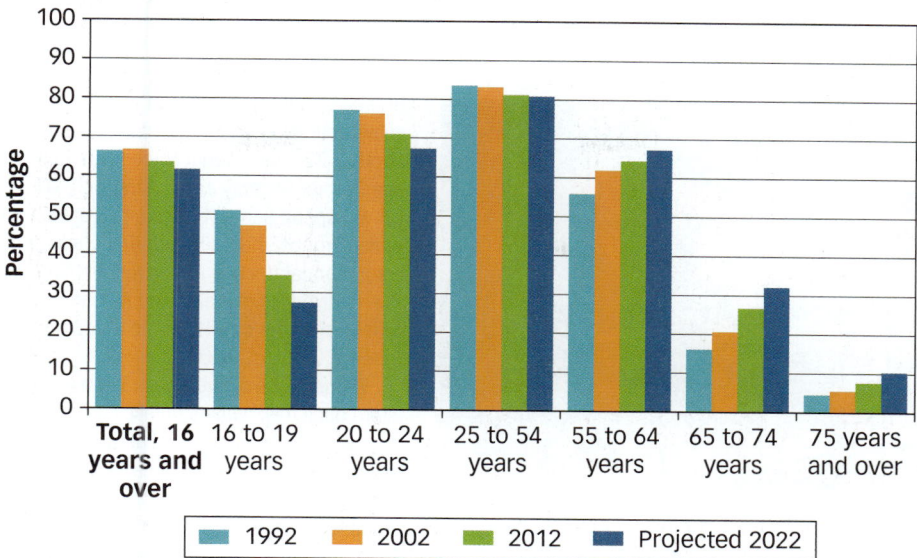

FIGURE 18.7: Labor Force Participation Rates in 1992, 2002, 2012, and Projected 2022, by Age

SOURCE: Drake (2014).

Around the world, most cases of elder maltreatment are likely to be from caregivers, most often spouses or children, who lack social support, experience psychological problems, and feel overwhelmed with the task of care giving (Choi & Nater, 2000; Dong & Simon, 2008). Within nursing homes, institutional factors such as overcrowding and understaffing contribute to caregiver stress and can increase the likelihood of elder maltreatment (Nerenberg, 2008; Thobaben, 2008; Wilber & McNeilly, 2001). Reducing the stressful working conditions for nursing home employees and increasing oversight can reduce the risk of maltreatment in institutional settings.

Providing elders and caregivers with greater social support and a feeling that they have others to turn to reduces risk of abuse, perhaps because of reduced reliance on caregivers (Dong & Simon, 2008; Lee, 2008). To the extent that elder abuse is an outgrowth of caregiver stress and burnout, aiding caregivers can lessen the likelihood of abuse. Social workers and family counselors can aid caregivers in learning how to cope with anger and manage strong emotions. Respite services such as in-home assistance or elder day care can provide physical assistance, which can reduce the stress of caregiving. The rates of elder abuse can also be reduced through education that helps vulnerable elders understand and identify maltreatment and know where to get help (Campbell Reay & Browne, 2008; Nerenberg, 2008).

Thinking in Context 18.4

1. What aspects of social relationships (e.g., friendships as well as relationships with siblings and children) are continuous over the lifespan? In what ways do these relationships change?

2. Relationships with spouses are particularly enduring and influential on adjustment and functioning. How do marital relationships form and change over the adult years? What can spouses expect in older adulthood?

3. Many older adults are single, living alone after divorce or widowhood. What challenges to adjustment does each raise? How are males and females' experience of divorce similar and different?

RETIREMENT

In most Western countries, older adults are able to work longer than ever before because of improved health and the revocation of mandatory retirement ages for most occupations (with exceptions for jobs that entail responsibility for the safety of others, such as air traffic controllers, pilots, and police officers). Despite these changes, increases in life expectancy and declines in the age of retirement mean that over the past century the period of retirement has lengthened in all Western nations. However, as indicated in Figure 18.7, not all adults retire, and it is projected that adults will increasingly postpone retirement (Drake, 2014).

DECIDING TO RETIRE

As discussed in Chapter 16, retirement is a process that begins long before the last day of employment. Typically it begins with imagining the possibility of retirement, what it might be like. Adults then assess their abilities and their resources, determine when is the best time to let go of the work role, and put plans into action (Feldman & Beehr, 2011). The decision of when to retire is influenced by job conditions,

Feminization of Poverty and the Older Woman

Elderly women are twice as likely to live in poverty than men, and the rate of poverty increases with age.

Over the past 35 years, the poverty rate among adults aged 65 and older has dropped more than one half, from about 25% in 1970 to about 10% in 2013 (Beedon & Wu, 2005; U.S. Bureau of the Census, 2014b). However, the picture is less rosy for older women, particularly older women of color, than it is for older men. Elderly women are nearly twice as likely to be poor as elderly men, and the risk of poverty increases as women age. About 12% of women over the age of 65 were poor in 2011. For African American and Hispanic women over the age of 65, rates are much higher, with 21% of African American women and 20% of Hispanic women living in poverty (U.S. Department of Health and Human Services, 2013).

Older women have fewer sources of retirement income and receive about three quarters that of men (about $15,000 and $22,000 respectively; U.S. Bureau of the Census, 2014a). The Census Bureau's poverty threshold for one person in 2014 was $11,770 (U.S. Department of Health and Human Services, 2015). In other words, the median annual income for older women is just about $4,000 above the U.S. definition of poverty.

The factors that most influence whether older women will become or stay poor during the retirement years are marital status (divorced, widowed, or never married are negatives), employment (having a job is a plus), and health (good health is a major benefit; Lee & Shaw, 2008). Because of longer life expectancy for women, they are more likely to experience the loss of their spouse, live alone in old age, and become financially vulnerable. Women who reach age 65 today are likely to live another 22 years, about three years longer than men the same age (Social Security Administration, 2015a). Most women over 65 will spend some years alone. For women of all racial and ethnic groups, marital disruption, including widowhood, results in a substantial decline in household income and assets; however, the relative loss is greater for African American and Hispanic widows than for non-Hispanic European American widows (Angel, Jiménez, & Angel, 2007).

Women have different work history patterns from men. Interrupting their careers to take care of children often reduces women's opportunities to accumulate Social Security and other retirement benefits and reduces economic well-being (Beedon & Wu, 2005; Verma, 2003; Wakabayashi & Donato, 2006). For example, average Social Security benefits for women are about $13,000 per year as compared with about $17,000 for men (U.S. Bureau of the Census, 2014a). Education, especially postsecondary education, has important effects on women's social and economic status during their preretirement years. After controlling for demographic characteristics and employment-related variables, both European American and African American women with postsecondary education were better off economically and relied less on public assistance income during their retirement (Zhan & Pandey, 2002).

Perhaps most striking is that poverty increases radically in older adulthood for all women. While poverty in old age among African American women tends to reflect continuous economic disadvantages in their earlier years, nearly two thirds of European American women who are poor in old age were not poor in the earlier years (Lee & Shaw, 2008). During their "golden years," many women find themselves living in poverty for the first time in their lives.

What Do You Think?

1. What solutions would you propose to reduce the age, gender, and ethnic gaps in poverty? For example, do you advocate changes in social policy, stronger incentives for employer retirement programs, or strategies motivating individual women to better plan for their old age?

2. What advice might you give to young or middle-aged woman who expresses concern about economic stability in her later years?

health, finances, and personal preferences. Workers tend to retire early from jobs that are stressful or hazardous and tend to delay retirement from jobs that are highly stimulating, in pleasant environments, and are a source of identity and self-esteem (AARP, 2008). Workers in professional occupations and those who are self-employed tend to stay in their jobs longer as compared with those in blue-collar or clerical positions. Women tend to retire earlier than men, often to care for an aging relative or spouse (Kim & Moen, 2001). Women in poverty, however, especially African American women, tend to work well into old age because they lack the financial resources to make retirement possible (see Lives in Context, above; Lee & Shaw, 2008; Verma, 2003).

Financial resources often are the determining factor with regard to whether and when an older adult retires. The creation of Social Security was designed to aid elders in affording retirement (see Ethical and Policy Applications of Lifespan Development, p. 523). However, changing economics influence older adults' abilities to retire as personal retirement investments such as IRAs and 401(k) plans

ETHICAL AND POLICY APPLICATIONS OF LIFESPAN DEVELOPMENT

Social Security

President Franklin D. Roosevelt signing the Social Security Act in 1935.

The Great Depression of the 1930s triggered a crisis in America's economic life. It was against this backdrop that the Social Security Act emerged, signed by President Franklin D. Roosevelt in 1935. The act created a social insurance program designed to pay retired workers aged 65 or older a continuing income. The original act provided only retirement benefits—and only to the worker. The 1939 amendments added two new categories of benefits: payments to the spouse and minor children of a retired worker (called dependents benefits) and survivors benefits paid to the family in the event of the premature death of the worker (Social Security Administration, 2007). Amendments in the 1950s and 1960s provided disabled workers and their dependents to qualify for benefits, as well as the passage of Medicare, health coverage to Social Security beneficiaries. In 1977, responsibility for Medicare moved to the newly created Health Care Financing Administration. About one in three Social Security beneficiaries is not a retiree (Shelton, 2007; Social Security Administration, 2008).

Social Security, also known as Old Age and Survivors Insurance and Disability Insurance (OASIDI), is funded by taxes paid by workers; the funds are invested in interest-bearing U.S. securities. Social Security provides older Americans with a dependable monthly income, with automatic increases tied to increases in the cost of living. Social Security has reduced poverty rates for older Americans by more than two thirds, from 35% in 1959 to less than 9% in 2012 (Dattalo, 2007; Shelton, 2013).

More than 90% of U.S. retirees now receive Social Security benefit payments each month (Social Security Administration, 2014). Social Security was never intended as a sole form of income, however. Instead, it was conceived as a supplement to income from a retirement plan, pension, and savings. However, in 2014 one half of married couples and three quarters of single adults were getting at least half of their income from Social Security; for one quarter and one half, respectively Social Security was virtually their only income (Social Security Administration, 2014). Moreover, Social Security provides critical income to older women and minorities, who are more likely than married and nonminority elders to rely on Social Security for 90% of more of their income (Social Security Administration, 2015b, 2015c).

Social Security is a pay-as-you-go retirement system. The Social Security taxes paid by today's workers and their employers are used to pay the benefits for today's retirees and other beneficiaries. There is considerable debate over whether Social Security trust funds are solvent for the long term. The main reason for Social Security's long-range financing problem is demographics. We are living longer and healthier lives than ever before. In addition, more than 80 million baby boomers started retiring in 2008. By 2050, when the surviving baby boomers will be over the age of 85, the population of older adults aged 65 and over is projected to be 83.7 million, about twice as many older Americans as in 2012 there are today (Ortman, Velkoff, & Hogan, 2014). At the same time, the number of workers paying into Social Security per beneficiary will drop from 2.8 in 2014 to about 2.1 in 2034 (Social Security Administration, 2008). These demographic changes will strain Social Security financing.

Proposed strategies to make Social Security solvent over the long term include increasing payroll taxes, decreasing benefits, and privatizing Social Security. One option that began to be phased in in the early 2000s is to increase the retirement age for full Social Security benefits. Under current law, an increase will be phased in over 23 years, reaching age 67 in 2022. Another option is to raise Social Security taxes so that all future benefits could be paid. For example, some advocate raising the income cap above which high-income earners are exempt from Social Security payroll contributions. Critics argue that payroll taxes are already very high, having been raised 20 times since the program began and that eventually Social Security taxes would have to be raised by about 50% to pay for all benefits owed. In short, there are no easy answers.

What Do You Think?

Taking a bioecological perspective, how does Social Security influence individuals? Consider the macrosystem, exosystem, mesosystem, and microsystem.

may lose value unexpectedly. In 2012, about 4 in 10 of all U.S. adults expressed concern over whether they will have enough income and assets of retirement, including 43% of 45- to 54-year-olds, 35% of 55- to 64-year-olds, and 28% of adults over age 65 (Morin & Fry, 2012). At the same time, many adults (39% of those 45 to 59 and 60 and older) report thinking about financial planning for retirement only sometimes, if at all (U.S. Federal Reserve, 2014). Furthermore, 23% of 45- to 59-year-old adults and 15% of adults age 60 and older report that they have no retirement savings.

TRANSITION TO RETIREMENT AND ADJUSTMENT

The transition to retirement begins years before leaving the workforce and continues well into retirement. Retirement is commonly thought of as a stressful experience. As we have discussed in prior chapters, the roles that adults embody influence their sense of identity, self-esteem, and overall adjustment. For most adults, the role of worker becomes an integral part of their identity (Kim & Moen, 2002). Giving up the role as worker and earner is often assumed to be stressful and associated with physical and psychological declines. However, research suggests, as with most aspects of development, the retirement transition is more complex than previously thought.

Theorists pose that the transition to retirement is a process that follows a predictable set of steps (Atchley, 1974, 1975). Prior to retirement, feelings of well-being and life satisfaction may decline as people worry and anticipate the loss of the work role. After the retirement event, retirees may experience a short honeymoon phase marked by vacations and new interests or a rest-and-relaxation phase of brief respite from the obligations of work. As retirees become accustomed to the reality of everyday life in retirement, these positive feelings may change to disenchantment. Over time, the elder develops a realistic view of the social and economic opportunities and constraints of retirement and a period of reorientation occurs in which the person attempts to replace the lost work role with new activities or become stressed if they cannot (Richardson & Kilty, 1991). Finally, stability occurs once the retirees accommodate and adjust to retirement. Therefore, it was long theorized that retirement is followed by a temporary increase in well-being and life satisfaction, followed by a marked decline, and then a smaller increase that occurs once individuals adjust to the transition (Atchley, 1993). Instead, there appear to be at least two subgroups of retirees (Pinquart & Schindler, 2007; Shultz, Morton, & Weckerle, 1998; Wang, 2007). The majority show an increase in life satisfaction and adjust well to their post retirement life whereas some show more poor adjustment and poor life satisfaction following retirement (Reitzes & Mutran, 2004).

Declines in well-being and life satisfaction may occur when the retirement transition causes an important role loss of worker that must be replaced by other social roles over time (Pinquart & Schindler, 2007; Richardson & Kilty, 1991). Work-related roles often become an important part of one's identity and source of self-esteem. The loss of a role central to an adult's identity may be especially stressful, contributing to increases in anxiety, depression, and poor well-being during the retirement transition (Kim & Moen, 2002). A review of multiple studies showed that a significant minority of retirees (estimates ranged from 10% to over 30%) reported some problems in retirement or a decline in well-being after retirement (Szinovacz, 2003). Nevertheless, on average, retirees—even those who show declines in well-being—are satisfied with their lives over time.

On the other hand, retirees with other role involvements, or those who are retiring from an unpleasant job, may be less troubled by, and even pleased with, the loss of those work roles (Adams, Prescher, Beehr, & Lepisto, 2002). For individuals who find their job stressful or burdensome, retiring could be a very positive experience, a relief from ongoing strains and conflicts, energizing and fulfilling (Fehr, 2012). Also, for individuals who would like to participate more heavily in the roles of family member and community member, retirement is an opportunity for them to enjoy the rewards and responsibilities tied to those roles. Continuity in other social roles and the ability to adapt to role changes leads to few changes in life satisfaction after retirement (Reitzes & Mutran, 2004). In addition, retirement satisfaction tends to increase for most older adults over the first half dozen years after retirement (Gall, Evans, & Howard, 1997; Wang, 2007).

INFLUENCES ON RETIREMENT ADJUSTMENT

Adjustment to retirement is influenced by a complex web of influences, including characteristics of the individual, his or her social relationships, and the job (Wang, Henkens, & van Solinge, 2011). Workers in high stress, demanding jobs, or those that provide little satisfaction tend to show positive adaptation to retirement (AARP, 2008; Adams et al., 2002). Retirement often comes as a relief. Those who are in highly satisfying, low stress, pleasant jobs tend to experience more challenges in adaptation. Generally speaking, the greater the intrinsic value of the older worker's job, the lower the levels of retirement satisfaction (van Solinge & Henkens, 2008).

The characteristics of the retirement transition also matter. Increasingly, adults are taking the route of a gradual retirement, slowly decreasing their involvement and working part time, rather than an abrupt retirement (Calvo, Haverstick, & Sass, 2009). Workers often view the idea of gradual retirement as a more attractive alternative than a "cold turkey," or abrupt, retirement. In a study of Australians, those who retired abruptly were more likely to rate their health as having deteriorated and more likely to report better adjustment to retirement (De Vaus, Wells, Kendig, & Quine, 2007). About 50% of older adults expect to work part-time during retirement; 29% of elders who work in retirement do so for enjoyment and 22% for income (AARP, 2008). Those who say work is an important component of their self-esteem and identity are more likely to work after retirement than are those who say it is less important or not important.

However, the length of the transition, whether abrupt or gradual, matters less in determining happiness after retirement than the worker's sense of control over the transition—whether the retirement is chosen or forced (Calvo et al., 2009; De Vaus et al., 2007; Quine, Wells, de Vaus, & Kendig, 2007). Having a sense of control over the decision to retire, timing, and manner of leaving work has an important positive impact on psychological and social well-being that lasts throughout the retirement transition.

Positive adjustment to retirement is associated with engagement in satisfying relationships and leisure activities (Butrica & Schaner, 2005; Morrow-Howell et al., 2003). Among married retirees, relationship satisfaction aids the transition to retirement and the increased time together can enhance marital satisfaction. Volunteer work offers elders opportunities to share their experience, mentor others, and develop and sustain social relationships, enhancing well-being (Tang, 2008; Windsor, Anstey, & Rodgers, 2008).

Volunteer work, however, often does not begin with retirement but instead is an activity that individuals take up earlier in life during their working years and preretirement engagement in volunteer work has a beneficial effect on adjustment to retirement (Hao, 2008; Wahrendorf & Siegrist, 2010). Older adults with more education are more likely to volunteer in all types of settings (religious, educational, political, senior center, etc.) and tend to devote more hours to volunteer work than adults with less education. Income, however, is found to make little difference in the extent to which elders engage in volunteer work (Reitzes & Mutran, 2004). Nonwork identities such as the volunteer role may thus provide stability and support as individuals enter retirement and act as a bridge between a pre- and posttretirement lifestyle (Reitzes & Mutran, 2004). Maintaining multiple roles in old age, through volunteering, promotes well-being (Butler & Eckart, 2007).

Thinking in Context 18.5

1. Identify individual and contextual influences on the decision to retire and adjustment to retirement.

2. In what ways might the characteristics of jobs; individuals' education and experience; and other microsystem, macrosystem, and exosystem factors influence retirement decisions and subsequent adjustment?

DEATH AND BEREAVEMENT IN OLDER ADULTHOOD

Lying in bed, 88-year-old Margaret wakes and takes in her surroundings. Her daughter and granddaughter are in the room, one reading and the other texting on her phone. Margaret is fortunate to have a private room in her nursing home, where she has been living since she suffered a stroke. Life here is better than she expected. The nurses are responsive, especially the kind night nurse who tells Margaret's daughter that she will check in often and does. The only thing Margaret doesn't like is that the nurses pressure her to socialize in the lounge each day. She'd rather sleep than be pushed out in her wheelchair to play games and watch television with the other elders. Her daughter urges her to eat, but the stroke impaired Margaret's ability to swallow so that eating is a chore, and she finds that she isn't very hungry anymore. Still, she'll happily eat a little bit of ice cream each afternoon. Margaret feels lucky to have family who live nearby and visit very often. Margaret's children notice a change in their mother. She seems less sharp and each day seems a little bit more confused. She's often too tired to talk and drifts in and out of sleep.

With time, Margaret sleeps nearly all of the time. In addition to her stroke-related impairments, she has congestive heart failure, which is not responding to treatment. A few days before her 89th birthday, the doctors tell Margaret's daughter that the time is near. Margaret's children and grandchildren gather in her room, waiting. They talk about old times and everyday life. Margaret is largely unconscious, but now and then she calls out, moans, or talks to herself, reaching her arms out in front of her. As time goes on, her breathing becomes more labored and heavy with occasional gasps. Margaret's children watch carefully and wait, attempting to talk with one another and retain a sense of normalcy. Finally, the room is quiet. Margaret's children know that she is gone. After 88 years and surrounded by family, Margaret has died.

Death is unavoidable. It comes hand in hand with life and is the end state of the Lifespan.

What is death? Simply put, death is the absence of life. Dying is the transition from being alive to being dead. However, defining *death* is much more complex than this.

THE DYING PROCESS

There are predictable changes, with variations, that occur in the dying person hours and days before death. As death is imminent, the person sleeps most of the time, may be disoriented and less able to see, and may experience visual and auditory hallucinations. The dying person shows irregular breathing, produces less urine, and may have cool hands and an overly warm trunk (Gavrin & Chapman, 1995). As the older adult is closer to death, he or she will lose interest and the ability to eat, drink, and talk. Breathing will be difficult, and the older adult may experience dry mouth and difficulty swallowing. Fluids may accumulate in the abdomen and extremities, leading to bloating. Psychological symptoms such as anxiety, depression, confusion, the inability to recognize family members, and dementia are common (Field & Cassel, 1997).

There is great variability in the dying trajectory, or rate of decline in functioning, people show prior to death (Glaser & Strauss, 1968). Dying trajectories vary by duration and descent. Some people show normal functioning and a steep decline representing a sudden death without warning or knowledge of illness, such as heart attack or accident. A second trajectory illustrates the person who typically has advance warning of a terminal illness and experiences steady losses of function. Some people show a third trajectory marked by steady declines broken by sharp drops in functioning, the final leading to a loss of life functions and death (Teno, Weitzen, Fennell, & Mor, 2001). The second

TABLE 18.1 Stages of Death

STATE	DEFINITION
1. Denial	Upon receiving the news, the dying individual denies that it is true. The dying person may not believe their diagnosis and might seek a second or third opinion.
2. Anger	As the reality sets in, the dying person often becomes angry. Dying people might ask themselves, "Why me?" Feeling cheated and robbed out of life, the dying person may feel resentment and envy toward family, friends, and caregivers, as it may feel unfair that others live while they must die.
3. Bargaining	The dying person attempts to avoid death by bargaining with God or fate in the hopes of striking a deal that would allow the person to survive. The dying person might promise to be a better person and help others if only he or she may survive. A parent might attempt to bargain a timetable, such as, "Just let me live to see my daughter give birth."
4. Depression	As the illness progresses the person eventually realizes that death cannot be escaped, prolonged, or bargained with. The dying person often experiences a sense of loss and depression. The dying person feels great loss and sorrow. The person may feel guilt over the illness and its consequences for his or her loved ones.
5. Acceptance	Sharing their feelings with others can help dying people come to an acceptance of death, the final stage. In this stage, the dying person no longer fights death. He or she accepts that death is inevitable, seems at peace, and begins to detach him- or herself from the world.

SOURCE: Kübler-Ross (1969).

and third trajectories, which imply knowledge of impending death, make it possible for older adults to cope and come to terms with their own death.

Death is universal, yet talking about death is often discouraged. Elisabeth Kübler-Ross was one of the first researchers to examine the controversial topic of the process of dying. Most people experience extreme emotional responses. After conducting more than 200 interviews with terminally ill people, Kübler-Ross categorized people's reactions into five types or ways in which people deal with death: denial, anger, bargaining, depression and acceptance, as shown in Table 18.1 (Kübler-Ross, 1969). Kübler-Ross was the first to identify commonly experienced emotional reactions in dying people. However, research suggests that the emotional reactions experienced by dying people do not progress through a sequence of stages, and not everyone experiences each emotion (Corr, Nabe, & Corr, 2009). The dying person has a myriad of emotions and must be allowed to experience and express them in order to come to terms with his or her own **grief**; complete unfinished business with loved ones; and to, ultimately, accept death (Corr et al., 2009).

DEATH WITH DIGNITY

As compared with prior generations, today in developed countries death is removed from everyday life. A century ago, death most often occurred at home. People witnessed death, and it was part of everyday life. Today most deaths occur in hospital and nursing homes, removed from the everyday world; only about one in five older adults dies at home (Span, 2012). People no longer have contact with death in everyday

TABLE 18.2 Advance Directives

ADVANCE DIRECTIVE	DEFINITION
Living will	Documents an individual's wishes regarding medical treatment and life prolonging activities. The purpose of a living will is to make one's wishes known regarding medical care in the event that the person is incapacitated by an illness or accident and is unable to speak for him or herself. The individual can identify what, if any, medical intervention should be used to prolong his or her life if he or she is unable to express a preference.
Durable power of attorney	A document in which individuals designate a trusted relative or friend (called a health care proxy) as legally authorized to make health care decisions on their behalf in the event that they are unable to do so.
Do not resuscitate (DNR) order	Instructs health care personnel to not resuscitate a patient in the event of cardiac or pulmonary arrest in which the heart and breathing stop. Without a DNR, a medical team will try to restore a normal heartbeat and respiration regardless of the patient's status, prolonging life regardless of its quality.

settings (DeSpelder & Strickland, 2002). Less exposure and experience with death has led it to become more mysterious and feared. Death anxiety refers to fear and discomfort

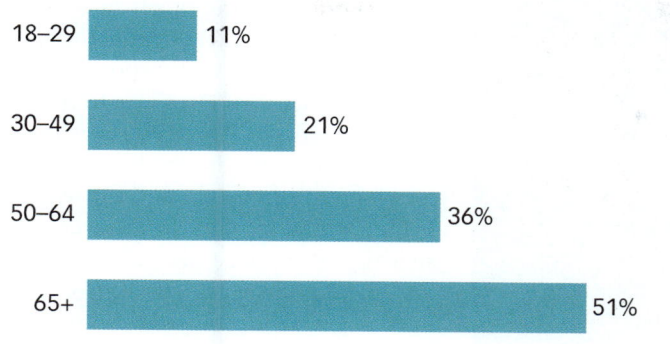

FIGURE 18.9: Communication About End-of-Life Issues

Have discussed with children. . .

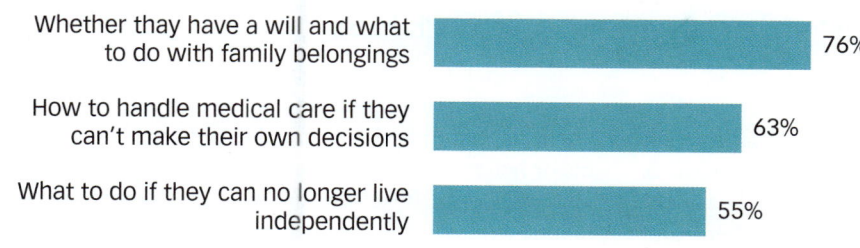

Who raised the issues?

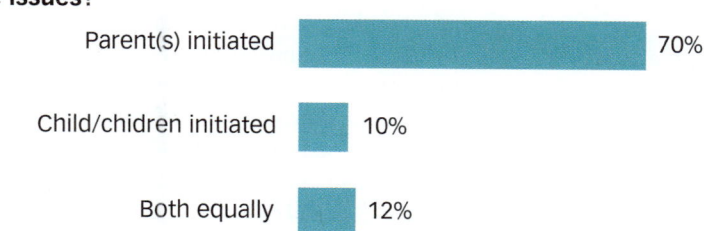

and, therefore, often are unable to participate in decisions about their own end-of-life care, such as pain management, life prolonging treatment, and memorial services. All of the persons involved—spouses, children, family members, friends, and health care workers—are likely to have different views regarding end-of-life care and postmortem decisions. **Advance directives** and health proxies, such as those in Table 18.2, are an important way that the dying can ensure that their preferences are known and respected. Determining and communicating one's final wishes in order to construct advance directives can ease the process for the dying person and his or her family. Advance directives permit patients to take control over their health care, their deaths, and what happens to their bodies and possessions after death. Advance directives foster patients' autonomy and help them to retain a sense of dignity as they die. More than half of older adults have written some form of advance directive (see Figure 18.8), and they are typically the ones to initiate conversations with family members about end-of-life issues (see Figure 18.9).

Although death occurs most often in hospitals and nursing homes, most dying people express the desire to die at home with family and friends. Dying persons have needs that set them apart from other patients; hospital settings often are not equipped to meet these needs. Rather than medical treatment, dying patients require palliative care, focusing on controlling pain and related symptoms. **Hospice** is an approach to end-of-life care that emphasizes dying patients' needs for pain management, psychological, spiritual, and social support as well as death with dignity (Ganzini et al., 2001; Russo, 2008). Hospice services are enlisted after the physician and patient believe that the illness is terminal and that no treatment or cure is possible.

Hospice services may be provided on an inpatient basis, at a formal hospice site that provides all care to patients, but they are frequently provided on an outpatient basis in a patient's home. Outpatient hospice service is becoming more common because it is cost effective and enables the patient to remain in the familiar surroundings of his or her home.

that centers around death and the process of dying. Older adults experience lower levels of death anxiety than younger and middle-aged adults (Maxfield, Pyszczynski, Greenberg, Pepin, & Davis, 2012; Thorson & Powell, 2000). Fear of dying declines in older adulthood; however, many older adults remain afraid of the circumstances of dying, as they wish to die with dignity (Cicirelli, 2008). The Yautepec of Mexico refer to death as a beautiful process when it is a good death, one with dignity (Wilches-Gutiérrez, Arenas-Monreal, Paulo-Maya, Peláez-Ballestas, & Idrovo, 2012).

Dying with dignity refers to ending life in a way that is true to one's preferences, controlling one's end-of-life care. Therefore, dying with dignity requires planning so that the individual's wishes are known ahead of time. Dying patients usually are not able to express their wishes

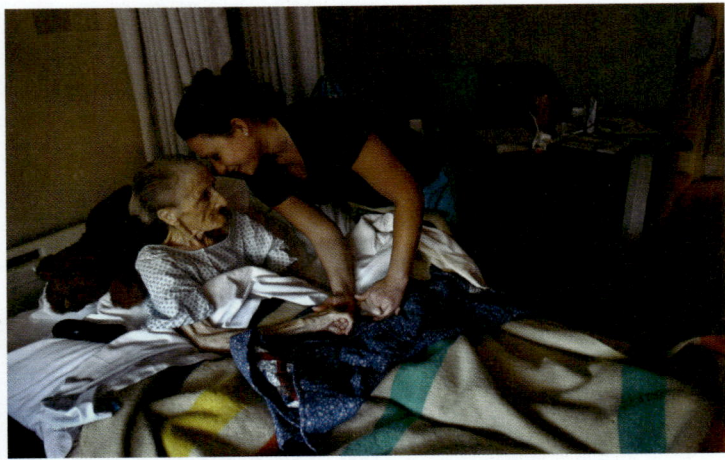

Hospice services permit dying patients to remain in their home, comfortable, and feel a sense of control in the death process. Counseling services help families assist the dying person, cope with their own needs, and strengthen connections with the dying person. Hospice services permit death with dignity that honors a loved one's wishes.

Home hospice care is associated with increased satisfaction by patients and families (Candy, Holman, Leurent, Davis, & Jones, 2011) Regardless of inpatient or outpatient, the patient care team includes physicians, nurses, social workers, and counselors who act as spiritual and bereavement counselors. Patients who receive hospice care at home receive frequent visits from members of the patient care team. The social workers and counselors help the patient and caregivers cope with the loss.

The philosophy of the hospice approach does not emphasize prolonging life but rather prolonging quality of life. The purpose is to make the person comfortable but not to delay death. Medical care is aimed at controlling pain and helping the dying person function as well as possible. The medical team seeks to reduce pain and fear and aid the patient in fulfilling his or her desires. Competence is maintained as long as possible, and social impoverishment is minimized. Counseling services help the patient's loved ones adjust and cope with their needs, strengthening relationship ties. The patients are encouraged to feel a sense of control in the death process. In this way, hospices meet the dying patients' needs for palliative care, social support, and personal control (Kastenbaum, 1999). Hospice often includes follow-up services to help loved ones after the patient's death. Although death is never an easy process, families can take comfort in knowing that their loved one's wishes were honored and he or she died with dignity.

BEREAVEMENT

The death of a loved one begins a complex transition known as bereavement, the process of coping with the sense of loss that follows death. **Mourning** and grief are aspects of bereavement. Mourning refers to culturally patterned ritualistic ways of displaying and expressing bereavement, including special clothing, food, prayers, and gatherings. Mourning rituals such as the Jewish custom of sitting *shiva*, ceasing usual activity, and instead mourning and receiving visitors at home for a week provides a sense of structure to help the bereaved manage the first days and weeks of bereavement. The process of coping with the loss of a loved one, however, is personal, complicated, and lengthy. Grief refers to the affective response to bereavement and includes an array of emotions such as hurt, anger, guilt, confusion, and other feelings. One of the first steps in the bereavement process is to organize a funeral or other ritual to mark the occasion of the loved one's death; such customs are different in various cultures around the world, as discussed in Cultural Influences on Development (p. 529).

GRIEF PROCESS

Grief is an active coping process in which the grieving person must confront the loss and come to terms with its effects on the physical world, interpersonal interactions, and his or her sense of self (Ivancovich & Wong, 2008; Worden, 1991). There are no clearly marked stages to grief, and there is no one way to grieve. Instead, grieving is an individual experience (Mallon, 2008). The person in grief must acknowledge his or her emotions, make sense of them, and learn to manage them. Most important, and most difficult, the grieving person must adjust to life without the deceased. He or she must adapt to the loss by establishing new patterns of behavior and redefining relationships with family and friends in light of the loss (Attig, 1996; Worden, 1991). The grieving person must construct a new sense of self that takes into account the loss of the deceased and how that loss has changed everyday life.

It was once believed that effective grieving entailed loosening emotional ties to the deceased, permitting the grieving person to "work through" the death (Worden, 1991). During a period of mourning, the survivor would sever attachments to the deceased and become ready for new relationships and attachments. Instead, in recent decades, theorists have come to view the bereaved continued attachment to the deceased as normative and potentially adaptive in providing a sense of continuity despite loss (Stroebe, Schut, & Boerner, 2010). Attachment is illustrated in several behaviors common among the bereaved, such as feeling that the deceased is watching over them, keeping the deceased's possessions, and talking about the deceased to keep his or her memory alive. Successful adaptation entails moving toward abstract manifestations of attachment, such as thoughts and memories, and away from concrete manifestations such as possessions (Field, Gal-Oz, & Bonanno, 2003). The deceased remains in mind, however. Grieving appears to involve learning to live with loss rather than getting over loss.

A similar view is posed by the *dual-process model of stress and coping*, which emphasizes two sets of losses that

Cultural Rituals Surrounding Death

The Cremation Ceremony held in Bali, Indonesia, is a ritual performed to send the deceased to the next life. The body is placed in a wood coffin inside a temple-like structure made of paper and wood. The structure and body are burned to release the deceased's spirit and enable reincarnation.

Every culture has its own set of rituals surrounding death that shape how individuals perceive and make sense of death (Penson, 2004). Many cultures within the South Pacific do not differentiate death as a separate category of functioning. For example, Melanesians use the term *mate* to refer to the very old, the very sick, and the dead; all other living people are referred to as *toa* (Counts & Counts, 1985). Other South Pacific cultures explain that the life force leaves the body during sleep and illness; therefore, people experience forms of death over the course of the lifetime before experiencing a final death (Counts & Counts, 1985). The Kwanga of Papua New Guinea believe that most deaths are the result of magic and

witchcraft (Brison, 1995). The social meaning of death is conveyed in a culture's funeral rituals, the degree to which death topics are taboo, the language used to describe death, the belief in an afterlife, and the treatment of the dying (Whitbourne, 2007). Culture thereby shapes the understandings people construct of death.

There is great variability in cultural views of the meaning of death and the rituals or other behaviors that express grief (Rosenblatt, 2008). Perhaps the most well-known death rituals were practiced by the ancient Egyptians. They believed that the body must be preserved through mummification in order to permanently house the spirit of the deceased in his or her new eternal life. The mummies were surrounded by valued objects and possessions and buried in elaborate tombs. Family members would regularly visit, bringing food and necessities to sustain them in the afterlife. Egyptian mummies are the most well known, but mummies have been found in other parts of the world such as the Andes mountains of Peru (Whitbourne, 2007).

In South Korea today, a small minority of people still choose to employ the services of a *mudang* (Korean "shaman") to conduct a lengthy ritual known as *Ogu Kut*, in which the *mudang* summons the deceased spirit into the ritual space; expresses the latter's feelings of unhappiness through song, dance, and the spoken word; and encourages the bereaved to express their own grievances within symbolic psychodrama. Once the emotional ties between the bereaved and the deceased have been loosened, prayers for protection are offered to various deities, and the *mudang* guides the spirit toward the Buddhist paradise. Finally, the deceased spirit's earthly possessions are cremated, and the bereaved are left better able to move on in their lives (Mills, 2012).

Death rituals vary among religions. Among Hindus, a good death is a holy death, one that is welcomed by the dying person, who rests on the ground and is surrounded by family and friends chanting prayers (Dennis, 2008). Buddhists believe that the dying person's task is to gain insight. Death is not an end, as the individual will be reincarnated in the hopes of reaching nirvana, an ultimate, perfect state of enlightenment. Among Jews, the dying person remains part of the community and is never left alone before or immediately after death. Christians generally believe that death is the entry to an eternity in heaven or hell and thereby is an event to be welcomed (generally) or feared (rarely). In Islam, death is united with life, because it is believed that the achievements and concerns of this life are fleeting and everyone should be mindful and ready for death. Muslim death rituals, such as saying prayers and washing the body, aid in the dying person's transition to the afterlife.

What Do You Think?

1. In your view, what purpose do death rituals hold?
2. **Given the ethnic and religious diversity in the United States, many people have opportunities to learn about different cultural and religious approaches to coping with death. What, if any, customs have you observed?**

occur with bereavement (Stroebe et al., 2010). The first is emotional and concerns the grief that comes with losing an attachment figure. The second set of losses are the life

changes that accompany the death, such as moving homes, experiencing social isolation, and reframing one's identity from married, for example, to single. Grieving persons may focus on the emotional losses or the life changes at any given time. Healthy adjustment is promoted by alternating focus between the two types. When the person is able, he or she confronts the emotional losses, yet at other times the person may set that task aside to instead consider the secondary consequences of the loss, the life changes (Stroebe, Schut, & Stroebe, 2005). In this way, the grieving person adaptively copes as he or she is able, gradually moving forward. Grieving is influenced by the relationship between the person and the deceased. Death of a spouse is a common type of loss in late life, yet it is experienced by most people as a profound personal loss. Spouses grieve a great deal and many grieve a very long time, with some grieving several years or more (Hansson & Stroebe, 2007).

WIDOWHOOD

About one third of U.S. older adults are widows, having lost their spouse. Women live longer than men and are less likely to remarry: 35% of women over the age of 65, as compared with 11% of men (Administration on Aging, 2014). Losing a spouse begins one of the most stressful transitions in life. Widows have lost the person closest to them, a source of companionship, support, status, and income. Widowhood poses a challenge of renegotiating a sense of identity in light of the loss of the role of spouse, often the most long-lasting intimate role held in life (Lund & Caserta, 2001; Lund, Caserta, Dimond, & Gray, 1986). The identity development task posed by the loss of a spouse is to construct a sense of self that is separate from the spouse (Cheek, 2010). As in earlier periods of life, women who have a myriad of roles apart from spouse tend to fare better in adjusting to the death of a spouse than do women who have few roles, predominantly centered around their husbands. After becoming a widow or widower, most older adults live alone, often in the same home. Those who relocate often do so for financial reasons, and they tend to move closer to children and grandchildren yet retain a separate residence.

Widowhood poses personal and social challenges to men and women. Perhaps the greatest challenge to adjustment is loneliness (Kowalski & Bondmass, 2008; Pinquart, 2003). Personal characteristics influence how elders manage the transition to widowhood. Those who are outgoing, have high self-esteem, and have a higher sense of perceived self-efficacy in managing tasks of daily living tend to fare better (Carr, 2004a; McCrae & Costa, 1988; Moore & Stratton, 2002). Maintaining close relationships with family and friends gives widows a sense of continuity, which aids in adjusting to the death of a spouse. The Changing Lives of Older Couples, a prospective study of 1,532 married individuals, suggests that close social relationships may remain stable in the course of normal aging, but widowhood brings both losses and gains in social support: It marks the loss of

Daniela White/Moment Mobile/Getty

The greatest challenge to widowhood, more common among women, is loneliness, followed by financial concerns.

a confidant but increases in support from children, friends, and relatives (Ha, 2010). Older adults maintain and even increase their social participation following spousal loss (Donnelly & Hinterlong, 2010; Isherwood, King, & Luszcz, 2012). In one sample of elders in the Netherlands, contact and support of widowed adults increased after widowhood, especially among children and sibling relationships, then started to decrease about 2.5 years after widowhood (Guiaux, van Tilburg, & van Groenou, 2007; Rosnick, Small, & Burton, 2010). Another study showed stability in the level of social support received over the two years after losing their spouse (Powers, Bisconti, & Bergeman, 2014). A prospective study of over 1,500 married individuals aged 65 and older found that spousal loss increased older adults' dependence on their children six months after the loss (Ha, Carr, Utz, & Nesse, 2006).

Compared to widowers, widows are more dependent on their children for financial and/or legal advice yet provide more emotional and instrumental support to their children. However, these gender differences are contingent on educational attainment. Education decreases widows' dependence on children for financial and legal advice yet increases widowers' provision of emotional support to their children. Positive support from children was associated with fewer depressive symptoms six months after the loss (Ha, 2010).

Bereavement is associated with increased levels of depression, anxiety, and stress as well as more poor performance on cognitive tests measuring attention, processing speed, and memory (Rosnick et al., 2010; Ward, Mathias, & Hitchings, 2007). The prevalence of anxiety and depression is especially elevated in the first year after the loss of a spouse, with about 22% meeting the diagnostic criteria for major depression (Onrust & Cuijpers, 2006). Social interaction aids in reducing depressive symptoms. Specifically, widowed adults who help others by providing instrumental support show an associated decline in depressive symptoms for 6 months to 18 months following spousal loss (Brown, Brown, House, & Smith, 2008). Men and women typically return to pre-widowhood levels of depression within 24 months of being widowed (Sasson & Umberson, 2014). Depression declines with time (Powers et al., 2014)

Widowhood also poses risks to physical health. The increased likelihood for a recently widowed person to die, often called the "widowhood effect," is one of the best documented examples of the relationship between social relations and health (Elwert & Christakis, 2008). The widowhood effect has been found among men and women of all ages throughout the world. Widowhood increases survivors' risk of dying from almost all causes (Subramanian, Elwert, & Christakis, 2008). Recent analyses put the excess mortality of widowhood (compared with marriage) among the elderly between 40% and 50% in the first six months (Moon, Kondo, Glymour, & Subramanian, 2011). However, the cause of death matters. The mortality rate for widowed adults following spouses' death from Alzheimer's disease or Parkinson's disease is lower, suggesting that anticipatory grief—that is, the ability of caregivers to prepare adequately for the death of their spouse—may provide a buffer from the widowhood effect (Elwert & Christakis, 2008). This suggests that it may be the predictability of the death rather than the duration of the spouse's terminal illness that shields the survivor from some of the adverse consequences of bereavement.

Losing a spouse poses risks to mental and physical health for both men and women, but men tend to show more health problems and higher rates of mortality (Bennett, Hughes, & Smith, 2005; Pinquart, 2003). In addition, around the world, widowers are at higher risk of suicide (Erlangsen, Jeune, Bille-Brahe, & Vaupel, 2004). Widowers tend to show less social engagement (Isherwood et al., 2012). Men often rely on their spouses for maintaining relationships with friends and family,

managing household tasks, and getting assistance in coping with stress and managing emotions—and tend to have difficulty asking for assistance (Lund & Caserta, 2001). Widowers are more likely to remarry than are widows, partly because there are far more single elderly women than men but also because men have fewer social outlets and sources of support than women (Carr, 2004b).

The degree to which a spouse adapts to widowhood is influenced by a variety of factors, such as the circumstances surrounding the spouse's death (McNamara & Rosenwax, 2010). Death of a spouse following a long illness such as cancer or Alzheimer's disease can evoke complex emotional responses because such illnesses involve drastic physical and mental deterioration and entail intense demands for caregiving (Rossi Ferrario, Cardillo, Vicario, Balzarini, & Zotti, 2004). In such cases, in addition to loss, the spouse may feel relief from watching a partner slip away and from the pressures of caregiving (Bonanno, Wortman, & Nesse, 2004). The complex intermingling of sorrow and relief may be confusing, and the widowed spouse may feel guilty. Working through the emotional issues entailed by bereavement is a complex and lengthy process that is influenced by the context of the death, the relationship between the dead and the bereaved, and other factors (Mallon, 2008). There is no one way to grieve.

There are many developments in older adulthood. Many reflect continuities from earlier periods in life. Others represent changes in response to changing social and contextual circumstances. Advances in socioemotional development and a more complex sense of self that accompanies the reminiscence and reflection common in older adulthood help elders understand their lives and prepare for death. An elder's death challenges their loved ones to cope with the loss. With time and support, the bereaved come to accept the loss, and many retain a sense of attachment to their loved one.

Thinking in Context 18.6

1. Some theorists and therapists explain that people should endeavor for a "good death." Consider the dying process, including death with dignity. In your view, what might encompass a good death?

2. Views of death and the rituals and customs to mark death offer rich examples of cultural and contextual difference. Discuss and provide examples.

3. Bereavement poses important challenges to adjustment. Discuss the mental and physical health risks that the bereaved face. Identify factors that may help bereaved persons successfully navigate this transition.

Apply Your Knowledge

On their 50th wedding anniversary, Mike and Carol celebrated with a big party, with family and friends. Their four children and 13 grandchildren attended. Nearly all of the grandchildren were married, with children of their own—some teenagers. In addition, a few very close friends attended, some from the neighborhood and a few lifelong friends they met when they were very young. "How fortunate we are," Mike remarked in a toast. His friend called out, "We hear that another congratulations is in order—you've just retired!" Carol replied, "Yes. It will be so nice to have him home with me." "Mom, don't you think he'll get underfoot?" "We'll see."

1. In what ways is Mike and Carol's social world similar to and different from those of most older adults?

2. What can the couple expect with Mike's retirement? How might it affect their marriage? What can Carol expect with regard to Mike's adjustment to retirement? How can the couple aid this adjustment?

3. What can the couple expect in the coming years? What developmental challenges will they face in their twilight?

Chapter Summary

18.1 Compare the roles of self-concept, reminiscence, and life review in developing a sense of ego integrity.

Self-conceptions are more multifaceted, complex, and stable in old age than at other periods of life. Most older adults maintain a positive view of themselves by accepting their weaknesses and compensating by focusing on their strengths. Reminiscence and life review help adults find continuity in their lives, come to term with choices, and assign meaning to their lives. Erikson posed that the task of older adulthood is to develop a sense of ego integrity, the sense that life has been well lived and the ability to see one's life within a larger global and historical context.

18.2 Discuss patterns of stability and change in personality traits over the adult years.

As in other life periods, the Big 5 personality traits largely remain stable into late adulthood; however, several subtle age-related shifts occur cross-culturally. Agreeableness and

conscientiousness tend to increase with age, and extroversion, openness, and neuroticism decline with age. Age-related declines in each of these traits are evident for most people, but older adults' scores relative to peers remain stable.

18.3 Explain the contributions of religion and social support to older adults' well-being.

Most adults become more religious as they age. The religious congregation often is a place that permits them to find meaning in their lives and can be a means of support in the form of social connections, health interventions, and activities that improve welfare. Religiosity buffers stress and is associated with higher self-esteem, fewer risky behaviors, lower rates of depression, and fewer declines in physical functioning and activities of daily living. Social support, especially interaction with significant others, protects elders from the negative effects of stress and promotes longevity, enhances well-being, and may facilitate the life review process.

18.4 Analyze four theories that account for changes in social interaction over the adult years.

Although disengagement theory posits that older adults and society mutually disengage, activity theorists explain that declines in social interaction with age are the result of social barriers to engagement. According to continuity theory, successful aging entails maintaining a sense of consistency in self despite age-related changes. Finally, socioemotional selectivity theory explains that older adults become increasingly motivated to derive emotional meaning from life and thereby strengthen and prune relationships to maximize their emotional well-being.

18.5 Identify social contexts in which older adults live and their influence on development.

Most older adults remain in the homes they have lived in for decades. There are a variety of different types of residential communities for older adults, ranging from single houses, to small collections of condominiums, to large apartment complexes. Only a small number of older adults reside in nursing homes, which offer the greatest amount of care, but also the greatest restriction of elders' autonomy. Factors that influence the quality of living environments for older adults include freedom of choice, involvement in decision making, right to privacy, stimulating environment, age appropriate opportunities and activities, and sense of connectedness.

18.6 Explain the role of relationships with friends and siblings in older adulthood.

In older adulthood, friendships become more important and more fulfilling; more activity occurs due to increased time for leisure activities. Most elderly friendships are old relationships, established much earlier in life. Similar to other times in life, elders tend to choose friends who share similarities, and women's friendships tend to be more intimate than men's. Most older adults feel close to their siblings and see them as close friends, even if they do not live near each other and do not see them regularly. In addition to emotional support, siblings tend to provide tangible support and are considered important sources of help in times of crisis.

18.7 Compare the effects of marriage, divorce, and cohabitation on older adults' functioning.

Marital satisfaction increases in older adulthood. Married couples are at increased risk for the same chronic diseases and experience similarity in their general well-being. The quality of the marital relationship predicts happiness and physical and mental health over the years. Elderly couples are less likely to divorce than younger couples, but those who do tend to experience more adjustment difficulties. Rates of remarriage decline in older adulthood, but when elders remarry, their unions tend to be more stable than those of younger people. Older adult cohabiters do not differ

from marrieds in their reports of emotional satisfaction, pleasure, openness, time spent together, criticism, and demands.

18.8 Discuss features of relationships between older adults and adult children and grandchildren.

The nature of the relationship and the exchange of help between elderly parents and their adult children changes from predominantly parent to child assistance in childhood through early adulthood to increasing assistance provided by adult children to their elderly parents. Child to parent assistance most often takes the form of emotional support. Fewer older adults receive instrumental assistance from adult children; instead, many older adults, especially high socioeconomic elders, continue to assist their adult children, primarily with financial assistance.

Grandchildren and great-grandchildren increase elders' opportunities for emotional support. Regardless of distance and contact, affection between grandchildren and grandparents remains strong.

18.9 Identify types of elder maltreatment and characteristics of victims.

Elder maltreatment appears in several forms, and many elders fall victim to more than one form of maltreatment: physical abuse, sexual abuse, psychological abuse, financial abuse, or physical neglect. Maltreated elders are more likely to be dependent on their caregivers. Advanced age, physical and mental illness, frailty, and impairments with activities of daily living are associated with increased vulnerability to maltreatment. Women and minorities are more likely to be victimized by maltreatment, as are those who experience a lack of social support or social isolation.

18.10 Identify influences on the timing of retirement and adaptation.

The period of retirement has lengthened in all Western nations. The decision of when to retire is influenced by job conditions, health, finances, and personal preferences. Financial resources often are the determining factor with regard to whether and when an older adult retires. Workers in high stress, demanding jobs, or those that provide little satisfaction tend to show positive adaptation to retirement. Research suggests the worker's sense of control influences the transition to retirement. Continuity in other social roles and the ability to adapt to role changes leads to few changes in life satisfaction after retirement. Engagement in leisure activities and volunteer work increases retirement satisfaction.

18.11 Examine the dying process and cultural views surrounding death.

Predictable changes occur in the dying person days and hours before death, but there is great variability in the dying trajectory. Every culture has its own set of rituals surrounding death that shape how individuals perceive and make sense of death. The social meaning of death is conveyed in a culture's funeral rituals, the degree to which death topics are taboo, the language used to describe death, the belief in an afterlife, and the treatment of the dying. Death rituals also vary among religions.

18.12 Define the concept of death with dignity, and identify ways of supporting death with dignity.

Dying with dignity refers to ending life in a way that is true to one's preferences and controlling one's end-of-life care. Dying patients usually are not able to express their wishes and, therefore, often are unable to participate in decisions about their own end-of-life care, such as pain management, life prolonging treatment, and memorial services. Advance directives foster patients' autonomy, that their preferences are known and respected, and help them to retain a sense of dignity as they die. Hospice is an approach to end-of-life care that emphasizes dying patients' needs for pain management as well as psychological, spiritual, and social support.

18.13 Discuss the grieving process.

Grieving is an active coping process in which the grieving person must come to terms with the loss and its effects on the physical world, interpersonal interactions, and his or her sense of self. Most importantly, the grieving person must adjust to life without the deceased by establishing new patterns of behavior and redefining relationships with family and friends in light of the loss. According to the dual-process model of stress and coping, bereaved must adjust to two sets of losses: the loss of an attachment figure and the life changes that accompany that loss.

18.14 Identify effects of widowhood in older adulthood.

About one third of U.S. older adults are widows, with women more likely to be widowed. Bereavement poses risks to physical and mental health and is associated with increased mortality. Women who have a myriad of roles apart from spouse tend to fare better in adjusting to the death of a spouse. Maintaining close relationships with family and friends gives widows a sense of continuity, which aids in adjusting to the death of a spouse. Men tend to experience more difficulty adjusting to the loss of a spouse and they are more likely to remarry.

Key Terms

accommodation – In Piaget's theory, the process by which schemas are modified or new schemas created to include with experiences.

achievement test – An assessment that measures mastery in an academic subject.

activity theory – The view that older adults want to remain active and that declines in social interaction are not a result of elders' desires but are a function of social barriers to engagement.

actual self – An adolescent's personal characteristics.

adolescent egocentrism – A characteristic of adolescents thinking in which adolescents show preoccupation with themselves and have difficulty separating others' perspectives from their own.

advance directive – A document or order that allows patients to make decisions about their health care, death, and what happens to their bodies and possessions after death.

age of viability – The age at which the fetus may survive if born prematurely; begins about 22 weeks after conception.

aggressive-rejected – A child who is rejected by peers because of hostile, antagonistic, and confrontational behavior.

alcohol dependence –a maladaptive pattern of alcohol use that leads to clinically significant impairment or distress, as indicated by tolerance, withdrawal, and inability to reduce drinking; aalso known as alcohol use disorder;

allele – A variation of a gene that can produce differences in a characteristics. Some characteristics do not vary while others have multiple alleles.

Alzheimer's disease – A neurodegenerative disorder characterized by dementia, the deterioration of memory and personality, and marked by the presence of presence of amyloid plaques and neurofibrillary tangles in the cerebral cortex.

amniocentesis – A prenatal diagnostic procedure in which a small sample of the amniotic fluid is extracted from the mother's uterus and subject to genetic analysis.

amygdala – A brain structure that is part of the limbic system and plays a role in emotion, especially fear and anger.

amyloid plaque – Found in the brains of patients with Alzheimer's disease, deposits of beta-amyloid accumulate along with clumps of dead neurons and glial cells.

androgyny – The gender identity of those who score high on both masculine and feminine characteristics.

anencephaly – A neural tube defect that results in the failure of all or part of the brain to develop, resulting in death prior or shortly after birth.

animism – The belief that inanimate objects are alive and have feelings and intentions.

anorexia nervosa – An eating disorder characterized by compulsive starvation and extreme weight loss and accompanied by a distorted body image.

Apgar scale – A quick overall assessment of a baby's immediate health at birth, including appearance, pulse, grimace, activity, and respiration.

appearance–reality distinction – The ability to distinguish between what something appears to be from what it really is.

applied developmental science – A field that studies lifespan interactions between individuals and the contexts in which they live and applies research findings to real-world settings, such as to influence social policy and create interventions.

assimilation – In Piaget's theory, the process by which new experiences are interpreted and integrated into preexisting schemas.

associative play – Social interaction in which children engage in separate activities alongside each other but interact by exchanging toys and talking about each other's activities.

asthma – A chronic disease of the respiratory system in which inflammation narrows the airways, causing wheezing, coughing, and difficulty breathing.

attachment – A lasting emotional tie between two individuals who strive to maintain closeness and act to ensure that the relationship continues.

attention – The ability to direct one's awareness.

attention-deficit/hyperactivity disorder (ADHD) – A condition characterized by persistent difficulties with attention and/or impulsivity that interfere with performance and behavior in school and daily life.

authoritarian parenting style – An approach to child-rearing that emphasizes high behavioral control and low levels of warmth and autonomy granting.

authoritative parenting style – An approach to child-rearing in which parents are warm and sensitive to children's needs, grant appropriate autonomy, and exert firm control.

autobiographical memory – The recollection of a personally meaningful event that took place at a specific time and place in one's past.

autonomy versus shame and doubt – In Erikson's theory, the psychosocial crisis of toddlerhood in which toddlers must establish of the sense that they can make choices and guide their actions and bodies.

babbling – An infant's repetition of syllables such as "ba-ba-ba-ba" and "ma-ma-ma," which begins at about 6 months of age.

basic emotion – Emotions that are universal in humans, appear early in life, and are thought to have a long evolutionary history, such as happiness, interest, surprise, fear, anger, sadness, and disgust.

behavioral genetics – The field of study that examines how genes and environment combine to influence the diversity of human traits, abilities, and behaviors.

behaviorism – A theoretical approach that studies how observable behavior is controlled by the physical and social environment through conditioning.

bereavement – The process of coping with the sense of loss that follows death.

biculturalism – The practice of adopting values and practices from two cultures.

Big 5 personality traits – Five clusters of personality traits that reflect an inhborn predisposition that is stable throughout life. The. The five traits are: openness, conscientiousness, extroversion, agreeableness, and neuroticism.

binge drinking – Heavy episodic drinking; consuming five or more alcoholic beverages in one sitting for men and four drinks in one sitting for women.

bioecological systems theory – A theory introduced by Bronfenbrenner that emphasizes the role of context in development, positing that contexts are organized into a series of systems in which individuals are embedded and that interact with one another and the person to influence development.

blastocyst – A thin-walled, fluid-filled sphere containing an inner mass of cells from which the embryo will develop; is implanted into the uterine wall during the germinal period.

body image – The perception of, and attitudes towards one's physical appearance.

body mass index (BMI) – A measure of body fat based on weight in kilograms divided by height in meters squared (k/m^2).

Brazelton Neonatal Behavioral Assessment Scale (NBAS) – The most common neurobehavioral assessment administered to newborns that is administered a few days after birth to assess neurological functioning, including the strength of 20 inborn reflexes, responsiveness to the physical and social environment, and changes in state.

Broca's area – The region in the brain that controls the ability to use language for expression; damage to the area inhibits fluent speech.

bulimia nervosa – An eating disorder characterized by recurrent episodes of binge eating and subsequent purging usually by induced vomiting and the use of laxatives.

Bully-victim – A child who attacks or inflicts harm on others and who is also attacked or harmed by others; the child is both bully and victim.

caloric restriction – The practice of restricting caloric intake for the purpose of slowing aging.

canalization – The tendency for a trait that is biologically programmed to be restricted to only a few outcomes.

canonical babbling – A type of babbling with well-formed syllables that sounds like language.

care orientation – Gilligan's feminine mode of moral reasoning, characterized by a desire to maintain relationships and a responsibility to avoid hurting others.

carrier – An individual who is heterozygous for a particular trait, in which a recessive gene is not expressed in the phenotype yet may be passed on to the carrier's offspring.

cataract – A clouding of the lens of the eye, resulting in blurred, foggy vision and can lead to blindness.

categorical self – A classification of the self based on broad ways in which people differ, such as sex, age, and physical characteristics, which children use to guide their behavior.

categorization – An adaptive mental process in which objects are grouped into conceptual categorize, allowing for organized storage of information in memory, efficient retrieval of that information, and the capacity to respond with familiarity to new stimuli from a common class.

centenarian – An individual who lives past 100 years.

central executive – In information processing, the part of our mental system that directs the flow of information and regulates cognitive activities such as attention, action, and problem solving.

centration – The tendency to focus on one part of a stimulus, situation, or idea and exclude all others; a characteristic of preoperational thought.

cephalocaudal development – The principle that growth proceeds from the head downward; the head and upper regions of the body develop before the lower regions.

cerebellum – Part of the brain at the back of the skull that is responsible for body movements, balance, and coordination.

cesarean section – Also known as a C-section; a surgical procedure that removes the fetus from the uterus through the abdomen.

child sexual abuse – Any erotic activity concerning a child.

chorionic villus sampling (CVS) – Prenatal diagnostic test that is conducted on cells sampled from the chorion to detects chromosomal abnormalities.

chromosome – One of 46 rodlike molecules that contain 23 pairs of DNA found in every body cell and collectively contain all of the genes.

chronosystem – In bioecological systems theory, refers to how the people and contexts change over time.

circular reaction – In Piaget's theory, the repetition of an action and its response in which infants try to repeat a newly discovered event caused by their own motor activity.

circumcision – The oldest known planned surgery that involves the removal of the foreskin of the penis.

classical conditioning – A form of learning in which an environmental stimulus becomes associated with stimuli that elicit reflex responses.

classification – The ability to organize things into groups based on similar characteristics.

clique – A tightly knit peer group of about three to eight close friends who share similarities such as demographics and attitudes.

cognitive development – Maturation of mental processes and tools individuals use to obtain knowledge, think, and solve problems.

cognitive reserve – The ability to make flexible and efficient use of available brain resources that permits cognitive efficiency, flexibility, and adaptability; it is cultivated throughout life from experience and environmental factors.

cognitive-affective complexity – A form of mature thinking that involves emotional awareness, the ability to integrate and regulate intense emotions, and the recognition and appreciation of individual experience.

cognitive-developmental theory – A perspective posited by Piaget that views individuals as active explorers of their world, learning by interacting with the world around them and describes cognitive development as progressing through stages.

cohabitation – An arrangement in which a committed, unmarried, couple lives together in the same home.

cohort – A generation of people born at the same time, influenced by the same historical and cultural conditions.

compression of morbidity – The tendency for older adults in industrialized nations to age well and delay disability and disease until the final months or years of life.

concrete operational stage of reasoning – Piaget's third stage of reasoning, from about 6 to 11, in which thought becomes logical and is applied to direct tangible experiences but not to abstract problems.

conservation – The principle that a physical quantity, such as number, mass, or volume, remains the same even when its appearance changes.

context – Unique conditions in which a person develops, including aspects of the physical and social environment such as family, neighborhood, culture, and historical time period.

continuity theory – The perspective that older adults strive to maintain continuity and consistency in self across the past and into the future; successful elders retain a sense that they are the same person they have always been despite physical, cognitive, emotional, and social changes.

continuous development – The view that development consists of gradual cumulative changes in existing skills and capacities.

conventional moral reasoning – The second level of Kohlberg's theory in which moral decisions are based on conforming to social rules.

cooing – An infants' repetition of , such as "ahhhh," "ohhh," and "eeee" that begins between 2 and 3 months of age months.

cooperative play – Social interaction in which children play together, working together toward a common goal.

core knowledge perspective – A framework explaining that infants are born with several innate knowledge systems or core domains of thought that enable early rapid learning and adaptation.

corpus callosum – A thick band of neurve fibers that connects the left and right hemispheres of the brain, allowing communication.

correlational research – A research design that measures relationships among participants' measured characteristics, behaviors, and development.

cortex – The outer layer of the brain containing the greatest numbers of neurons and accounting for thought and intelligence.

crossing-over – A process during meiosis in which chromosome pairs align and DNA segments cross over (moving from one member of the pair to the other), creating unique combinations of genes.

cross-sectional research– A developmental research design that compares people of different ages at a single point in time to infer age differences.

crowd – A large, loose group of individuals based on perceived characteristics, interests, stereotypes, and reputation.

crystallized intelligence – Intellectual ability that reflects accumulated knowledge acquired through experience and learning.

culture – A set of customs, knowledge, attitudes, and values shared by a group of people and learned through interactions with group members.

cyberbullying – Bullying, or repeated acts intended to hurt a victim, carried via electronic means such as text messaging, posting in chat rooms and discussion boards, and creating websites and blogs.

deferred imitation – Imitating the behavior of an absent model.

delayed phase preference – Change in hormone levels cause adolescents' preferred sleep patterns to shift such that

they tend to remain awake late at night, and are groggy early in the morning.

dementia – A progressive deterioration in mental abilities due to changes in the brain that influence higher cortical functions such as thinking, memory, comprehension, and emotional control and are reflected in impaired thought and behavior, interfering with the older adult's ability to engage in everyday activities.

dependent variable – The behavior under study in an experiment; it is expected to be affected by changes in the independent variable.

diabetes – A disease marked by high levels of blood glucose that occurs when the body is unable to regulate the amount of glucose in the bloodstream because there is not enough insulin produced (type 1 diabetes) or the body shows insulin resistance and becomes less sensitive to it, failing to respond to it (type 2 diabetes). Symptoms include fatigue, great thirst, blurred vision, frequent infections, and slow healing.

difficult temperament – A temperament characterized by irregularity in biological rhythms, slow adaptation to change, and a tendency for intense negative reactions.

discipline – The methods a parent uses to teach and socialize children.

discontinuous development – The view that growth entails abrupt transformations in abilities and capacities in which new ways of interacting with the world emerge.

disengagement theory – A perspective that declines in social interaction in older age are due to mutual withdrawal between older adults and society as they anticipate death.

disorganized–disoriented attachment – An attachment pattern in which infants show inconsistent contradictory responses to a to a caregiver's departure and return.

dizygotic (DZ) twin – Also known as a fraternal twin; occurs when two ova are released and each is fertilized by a different sperm; the resulting offspring share 50% of the genetic material.

DNA – Deoxyribonucleic acid; the chemical structure, shaped like a twisted ladder, that contains all of the genes.

dominant–recessive inheritance – A form of genetic inheritance in which the phenotype reflects only the dominant allele of a heterozygous pair.

Down syndrome – Also known as trisomy 21; a condition in which a third,

extra chromosome appears at the 21st site. Down syndrome is associated with distinctive physical characteristics accompanied by developmental disability.

dual language learning – Also known as two-way immersion; an approach in which children are taught and develop skills in two languages.

dualistic thinking – Polar reasoning in which knowledge and accounts of phenomena are viewed as absolute facts, either right or wrong with no in-between.

dual-process model – A model of the brain consisting of two systems, one emotional and the other rational, that develop on different timeframes, accounting for typical adolescent behavior.

dying with dignity – Ending one's life in a way that is true to one's preferences and controlling end-of-life care.

dynamic systems theory – A framework describing motor skills as resulting from ongoing interactions among physical, cognitive, and socioemotional influences and environmental supports in which previously mastered skills are combined to provide more complex and effective ways of exploring and controlling the environment.

dyslexia – Learning disability characterized by unusual difficulty reading.

easy temperament – A temperament characterized by regularity in biological rhythms, the tendency to adapt easily to new experiences, and a general cheerfulness.

ectoderm – The outer layer of the embryonic disk, which will develop into the skin, nails, hair, teeth, sensory organs, and the nervous system.

ego integrity vs. despair – The final stage in Erikson's psychosocial theory, in which older adults find a sense of coherence in life experiences and conclude that their lives are meaningful and valuable.

egocentrism – Piaget's term for children's inability to take another person's point of view or perspective and to assume that others share the same feelings, knowledge, and physical view of the world.

embryo – Prenatal organism between about 2 and 8 weeks after conception; a period of major structural development.

embryonic disk – A mass of cells that differentiates into three layers that will develop into the embryo.

emerging adulthood – An extended transition to adulthood that takes place from ages 18 to 25, in which a young person is no longer an adolescent yet has not assumed the roles that comprise adulthood.

emotional display rule – Unstated cultural guidelines for acceptable emotions and emotional expression that are communicated to children via parents' emotional behavior, expressions, and socialization.

emotional regulation – The ability to adjust and control our emotional state to influence how and when emotions are expressed.

empathy – The capacity to understand another person's emotions and concerns enced by many genes.

endoderm – The inner layer of an embryonic disk, which will develop into the digestive system, liver, lungs, pancreas, salivary glands, and respiratory system.

epigenetic framework – A perspective stating that development results from reciprocal interactions between genetics and the environment such that the expression of genetic inheritance is influenced by environmental forces.

episodic memory – Memory for every day experiences.

epistemic cognition – The ways in which an individual understands how he or she arrived at ideas, beliefs, and conclusions.

estrogen – The primary female sex hormone responsible for development and regulation of the female reproductive system and secondary sex characteristics.

ethnic identity – A sense of membership to an ethnic group and viewing the the attitudes and practicese associated with that group as an enduring part of the self.

ethological theory – A perspective that emphasizes the evolutionary basis of behavior and its adaptive value in ensuring survival of a species.

ethological theory – Bowlby's view characterizes the attachment between infant and parent as an adaptive behavior that evolved because it promotes survival.

evolutionary developmental theory – A perspective that applies principles of evolution and scientific knowledge about the interactive influence of genetic and environmental mechanisms to understand the adaptive value of developmental changes that are experienced with age.

executive function – The set of cognitive operations that support planning, decision-making, and goal setting abilities, such as the ability to control attention, coordinate information in working memory, and inhibit impulses.

exosystem – In bioecological systems theory, social settings in which an individual does not participate but have an indirect influence on development.

expansion – Adult responses to children's speech that elaborate and enrich its complexity.

experience-dependent brain development – Brain growth and development in response specific learning experiences.

experience-expectant brain development – Brain growth and development that is dependent on basic environmental experiences, such as visual and auditory stimulation, in order to develop normally.

experimental research – A research design that permits inferences about cause and effect by exerting control, systematically manipulating a variable, and studying the effects on measured variables.

expertise – An elaborate and integrated knowledge base that underlies extraordinary proficiency in given area.

failure to thrive – A term indicating insufficient weight gain or inappropriate weight loss such that the weight is 20% below the norm for height.

familism – The cultural belief that family members should support one another; that the family should take precedence over individuals and the community.

fast mapping – A process by which children learn new words after only a brief encounter, connecting it with their own mental categories.

fetal alcohol spectrum disorders – The continuum of physical, mental, and behavioral outcomes caused by prenatal exposure to alcohol.

fetal alcohol syndrome (FAS) – The most severe form of fetal alcohol spectrum disorder accompanying heavy prenatal exposure to alcohol, including a distinct pattern of facial characteristics, growth deficiencies, and deficits in intellectual development.

fetus – The prenatal organism from about the ninth week of pregnancy to delivery; a period of rapid growth and maturation of body structures.

fine motor development – The ability to control small movements of the fingers such as reaching and grasping.

fine motor skill – Physical abilities that small muscle coordination of the hands and fingers, such as buttoning a shirt or drawing pictures.

fluid intelligence – Intellectual ability that reflects basic information processing skills, including working memory, processing speed, and the ability to detect relations among stimuli and draw inferences. Underlies learning, is not influenced by culture, and reflects brain functioning.

Flynn effect – The rise in IQ scores that over generations in many nations.

formal operational reasoning – Piaget's fourth stage of cognitive development, characterized by abstract, logical, and systematic thinking.

free radical – A highly reactive, corrosive substance that forms when a cell is exposed to oxygen. Through chemical reactions, free radicals destroy DNA, proteins, and other cellular materials.

gamete – A reproductive cell; sperm in males and ovum in females.

gender constancy – A child's understanding of the biological permanence of gender and that it does not change regardless of appearance, activities, or attitudes.

gender identity – One's image of oneself as masculine or feminine, embodying the roles and behaviors that society associates with males and females.

gender role – The activities, attitudes, skills, and characteristics that are considered appropriate for males or females.

gender schema theory – An approach to gender typing that emphasizes information processing and environmental influences that influence the development of gender-related beliefs, which then guide children's behaviors and attitudes.

gender stability – In Kohlberg's view, young children's recognition that gender does not change over time, though it is not yet understood as a biological construct but rather based on external traits and behaviors.

gender typing – The process in which young children acquire the characteristics and attitudes that are considered appropriate for males or females.

gene – The basic unit of heredity; a small section of a chromosome that contains the string of chemicals (DNA) that provide instructions for the cell to manufacture proteins.

gene–environment correlation – The idea that many of an individual's traits are supported by his or her genes and environment; there are three types of correlations: passive, reactive, and active.

generativity – The seventh stage in Erikson's theory in which adults seek to move beyond a concern for their own personal goals and welfare in order to guide future generations and give back to society.

genetic counseling – A medical specialty that helps prospective parents determine the probability that their children will inherit genetic defects and chromosomal abnormalities.

genome – The set of DNA, genetic instructions, used to construct a living organism.

genomic imprinting – The instance when the expression of a gene is determined by whether it is inherited from the mother or father.

genotype – An individual's collection of genes that contain instructions for all physical and psychological characteristics, including hair, eye color, personality, health, and behavior.

glial cell – A type of brain cell that nourishes neurons and provides structure to the brain.

gonad – A sex gland; ovary in females and testis in males.

goodness of fit – The compatibility between a child's temperament and his or her environment, especially the parent's temperament and child-rearing methods; the greater the degree of match, the more favorable the child's adjustment.

grammar – The rules of language.

grief – The affective response to bereavement that includes distress and an intense array of emotions such as hurt, anger, and guilt.

gross motor development – The ability to control large movements of the body, such as walking and jumping.

gross motor skill – Physical abilities that involve large muscles such as walking.

growth hormone – A hormone that influences the development of nearly all parts of the body.

growth norm – The expectation for typical gains and variations in height and weight for children based on their chronological age and ethnic background.

guided participation – Also known as apprenticeship in thinking; the process by which people learn from others who guide them, providing a scaffold to help them accomplish more than the child could do alone.

habituation – The gradual decline in the intensity, frequency, or duration of a response when repeatedly exposed to a stimulus; indicates learning.

hardiness – Personal qualities, including a sense of control, orientation towards personal growth, and commitment to life choices, that influences adults' ability to adapt to changes and life circumstances.

heritability – The statistic that indicates the extent to which variation of a certain trait can be traced to genes.

heterozygous – Refers to a chromosomal pair consisting of two different alleles.

holophrase – A one-word expression used to convey a complete thought.

homozygous – Refers to a chromosomal pair consisting of two identical alleles.

hormone – A chemical that is produced and secreted into the bloodstream to affect and influence physiological functions.

hormone replacement therapy – Compensating for reductions in hormones, such as in menopause, by taking hormones.

hospice – An approach to end-of-life care that emphasizes a dying patient's need for pain management, psychological, spiritual, and social support as well as death with dignity.

hypothalamus-pituitary-gondal axis (HPG) – The collective effects of the hypothalamus, pituitary gland, and gonads behaving in cooperation in regulating the hormones that drive puberty.

hypothesis – A proposed explanation for a phenomenon that can be tested.

hypothetical–deductive reasoning – The ability to consider propositions, probabilities, generate and systematically test hypotheses, and draw conclusions.

identity – A coherent organized sense of self that includes values, attitudes, and goals to which one is committed.

identity achievement – The identity state in which after undergoing a period of exploration a person commits to self-chosen values and goals.

identity diffusion – The identity state in which an individual has not undergone exploration nor committed to self-chosen values and goals.

identity foreclosure – The identity state in which an individual has not undergone exploration but has committed to values and goals chosen by an authority figure.

identity moratorium – The identity state in which an individual is exploring but has not committed to values and goals.

identity status – The degree to which individuals have explored possible selves and whether they have committed to specific beliefs and goals, assessed by administering interview and survey measures, and categorized into four identity statuses.

imaginary audience – A manifestation of adolescent egocentrism in which assume that they are the focus of others' attention.

immersion– A strategy in which all instruction occurs in the majority language; children learn a second language, such as English, and course content simultaneously.

implantation – The process by which the blastocyst becomes attached to the uterine wall, completed by about 10 days after fertilization.

in vitro fertilization – Fertilization, the creation of zygotes, that takes place outside of a woman's body by mixing sperm with ova that have been surgically removed from the woman's body.

inclusion – The approach in which children with learning disabilities learn alongside other children in the regular classroom for all or part of the day, accompanied by additional educational support of a teacher or paraprofessional who is specially trained to meet their needs.

incomplete dominance – A genetic inheritance pattern in which both genes are expressed in the phenotype.

independent variable – The factor proposed to change the behavior under study in an experiment; it is systematically manipulated during an experiment.

indifferent gonad – A gonad in an embryo that has not yet differentiated into testes or ovaries.

inductive discipline – Strategy to control children's behavior that relies on reasoning and discussion.

industry over inferiority – Erikson's fourth stage in which children attempt new skills, developing feelings of competence in their success or feeling inferior or incompetent.

infant-directed speech – Also known as "motherese"; uses shorter words and sentences, higher and more varied pitch, repetitions, a slower rate, and longer pauses.

infantile amnesia – A phenomenon in which most children and adults are unable to recall events that happened before age 3.

information processing theory – A perspective that uses a computer analogy to describe how the mind receives information and manipulates, stores, recalls, and uses it to solve problems.

informed consent – A participant's informed (knowledge of the scope of the research and potential harm and benefits of participating), rational, and voluntary agreement to participate in a study.

initiative versus guilt – Erikson's third psychosocial stage in which young children develop a sense of purposefulness, trying new skills and activities, and take pride in their accomplishments, as well as feel guilt if they are unsuccessful.

insecure–avoidant attachment – An attachment pattern in which an infant avoids connecting with the caregiver, showing no distress when separated from a caregiver and does not seem to care about the caregiver's return.

insecure-resistant attachment – An attachment pattern in which an infant shows anxiety and uncertainty, showing great distress at separation from the caregiver and simultaneously seeks and avoids contact upon the caregiver's return.

instrumental aggression – Behavior that hurts someone else in order to achieve a goal such as gaining a possession.

intellectual disability – characterized by deficits in cognitive functioning and age-appropriate adaptive behavior, such as social, communication, and self-care skills that begin before 18 years of age; formerly known as mental retardation.

intelligence – An individual's ability to adapt to the world.

intelligence test (IQ test) – A test designed to measure the aptitude to learn at school, intellectual aptitude.

intermodal perception – The process of combining information from more than one sensory system such as visual and auditory senses.

internal working model – A set of expectations about one's worthiness of love and the availability of attachment figures during times of distress.

intimacy versus isolation – Erikson's sixth psychosocial stage in which individuals demonstrate the capacity to feel closeness and bond with another individual to make a permanent commitment to a romantic partner.

intimate violence – Physical, sexual, and psychological abuse within a romantic relationship.

irreversibility – A characteristic of preoperational thought in which a child does not understand that an action can be reversed and a thing restored to its original state.

isometric muscle strength – Subtle contractions in which the length of the muscle does not change, is maintained through adulthood.

justice orientation – A male mode of moral reasoning proposed by Gilligan that emphasizes the abstract principles of fairness and individualism.

kwashiorkor – A malnutritive disease in children caused by deprivation of protein and calories and characterized by lethargy and the bloating and swelling of the stomach.

language acquisition device (LAD) – In Chomsky's theory, an innate facilitator of language that allows infants to quickly and efficiently analyze everyday speech and determine its rules, regardless of their native language.

lanugo – A fine, down-like hair that covers the fetus's body.

lateralization – The process by which the two hemispheres of the brain become specialized to carry out different functions.

learning disability – A diagnosis for a child who demonstrates great difficulty in aspects of learning such as reading or mathematics, and shows achievement behind that expected given the child's IQ.

life review – The reflection on past experiences and one's life, permitting greater self-understanding and the assignment of meaning to their lives.

life structure – In Levenson's theory, a person's overall organization of his or her life, particularly dreams, goals, and relationships with significant others as well as institutions, such as marriage, family, and vocation.

lifespan human development – An approach to studying human development that examines ways in which individuals grow, change, and stay the same throughout their lives, from conception to death.

limbic system – A collection of brain structures responsible for emotion.

longitudinal research – A developmental study in which one group of participants is studied repeatedly to infer age changes.

long-term memory – The component of the information processing system that is an unlimited store that holds information indefinitely, until it is retrieved to manipulate working memory.

low birth weight – Classifies infants who weigh less than 2,500 grams (5.5 pounds) at birth.

macrosystem – In bioecological systems theory, the sociohistorical context—cultural values, laws, and cultural values—in which the microsystem, mesosystem, and exosystem are embedded, posing indirect influences on individuals.

macular degeneration – A substantial loss of cells in the center area of the retina (the macula), causing blurring and eventual loss of central vision; its onset is influenced by heredity and environmental factors.

mainstreaming – The approach in which children with disabilities are educated in the regular classroom with their nondisabled peers.

mandated reporter – A professional who is legally obligated to report suspected child maltreatment to law enforcement.

marasmus – A wasting disease in which the body's fat and muscle are depleted; growth stops, the body wastes away, taking on a hollow appearance.

meiosis – The process by which a gamete is formed, containing one-half of the cell's chromosomes producing creating ova and sperm with 23 single, unpaired chromosomes.

memory strategy – Deliberate cognitive activities that make an individual more likely to remember information.

metacognition – The ability to think about thinking; knowledge of how the mind works.

menarche – A girl's first menstrual period.

menopause – The end or menstruation and a woman's reproductive capacity.

mental representation – An internal depiction of an object; thinking of an object using mental pictures.

mesoderm – The middle layer of the embryonic disk; develops into the muscles, skeleton, circulatory system, and internal organs.

mesosystem – In bioecological systems theory, the relations and interactions among microsystems.

metamemory – An aspect of metacognition that refers to the understanding of memory and how to use strategies to enhance memory.

microsystem – In bioecological systems theory, the innermost level of context, which includes an individual's immediate physical and social environment.

midlife crisis – A period of self-doubt and stress attributed to entering midlife once thought to contribute to a major reorganization of personality in midlife. Now thought to occur in a small minority of adults and to be related to history more than age.

mitosis – The process of cell duplication in which DNA is replicated and the resulting cell is genetically identical to the original.

monozygotic (mz) twin – Also known as an identical twin; occurs when the zygote splits apart early in development. The resulting offspring share 100% of their genetic material.

morality of constraint – The first stage of Piaget's theory of morality in which children are aware of rules and see them as absolute and unalterable.

morality of cooperation – Also known as autonomous morality; the second stage of Piaget's approach to moral development in which chidren's understanding of rules becomes more flexible as they begin to value fairness and equality and account for factors like act, intent, and situation.

mourning – The ceremonies and rituals a culture prescribes for expressing bereavement.

multiple intelligence theory – Gardner's proposition that human intelligence is composed of a varied set of abilities.

mutation – A sudden permanent change in the structure of genes.

myelination – The process in which neurons are coated in a fatty substance, myelin, which contributes to faster neural communication.

naming explosion – Also known as a vocabulary spurt; a period of rapid vocabulary learning that begins about 16 to 18 months of age.

naturalistic observation – A research method in which a researcher views and records an individual's behavior in natural, real-world settings.

nature–nurture issue – A debate within the field of human development regarding whether development is caused by nature (genetics or heredity) or nurture (the physical and social environment).

neonate – A newborn.

neural tube – Forms during the third week after conception when the endoderm folds and will develop into the central nervous system (brain and spinal cord).

neurofibrillary tangle – A twisted bundle of threads of a protein called tau that occur in the brain when neurons collapse; found in individuals with Alzheimer's disease.

neurogenesis – The production of new neurons.

neuron – A nerve cell that stores and transmits information; billions of neurons comprise the brain.

niche-picking – An active gene-environment correlation in which individuals seek out experiences and environments that complement their genetic tendencies.

noninvasive prenatal testing (NIPT) – A prenatal diagnostic which samples cell-free fetal DNA from the mother's blood for chromosomal abnormalities.

no-nonsense parenting – A child-rearing approach that emphasizes high or strict parental control as well as warmth and affection.

obesity – In children, defined as having a body mass index at or above the 95th percentile for height and age.

object permanence – The understanding that objects continue to exist outside of sight.

observational learning – Learning that occurs by watching and imitating models, as posited by social learning theory.

oldest-old – Adults aged 85 and older, who are most likely to depend on others or physical and social support to complete daily tasks.

old-old – Adults aged 75 to 84, who typically live independently but often experience some physical and mental impairment.

open-ended interview – A research method in which a researcher asks a participant questions using a flexible, conversational style and may vary the order of questions, probe, and ask follow-up questions based on the participant's responses.

operant conditioning – A form of learning in which behavior increases or decreases based on environmental consequences.

osteoarthritis – The most common type of arthritis; it affects joints that are injured by overuse, most commonly the hips, knees, lower back, and hands, in which the cartilage protecting the ends of the bones where they meet at the joints wears away, and joints become less flexible and swell.

osteoporosis – a condition characterized by severe loss of bone mass, leading to increased risk of fractures.

overextension – A vocabulary error in which the infant applies a word too broadly to a wider class of objects than appropriate.

overregularization – Grammatical mistakes that children make because they apply grammatical rules too stringently to words that are exceptions.

ovum – The female reproductive cell or egg cell.

parallel play – A type of social interaction in which children play with similar materials near each other but do not interact or try to influence each other.

parental monitoring – Parents' awareness of their children's activities, whereabouts, and companions.

parenting style – Enduring sets of child-rearing behaviors a parent uses across situations to form a child-rearing climate.

Parkinson's disease – A chronic progressive brain disorder caused by deterioration of neurons in the substantia nigra; characterized by muscle rigidity, tremors, and sometimes dementia.

peer acceptance – Likeability or the degree to which a child is viewed as a worthy social partner by his or her peers.

peer victimization – Also known as bullying; an ongoing interaction in which a child becomes a frequent target of physical, verbal, or social harm by another child or children.

perceived popularity – The peer ratings of an adolescent's social status, his or her social dominance, influence, and prestige in the peer group.

perception – The mental processing of sensory information, which is interpreted as sight, sound, and smell, for example.

perimenopause – Transition to menopause in which the production of reproductive hormones declines and symptoms associated with menopause first appear, such as hot flashes.

permissive parenting style – A child-rearing approach characterized by high levels of warmth and low levels of control or discipline.

personal fable – A manifestation of adolescent egocentrism in which adolescents believe their thoughts, feelings, and experiences are more special and unique than anyone else's, as well as the sense that they are invulnerable.

phenotype – The observable physical or behavioral characteristics of a person, eye, hair color, or height.

phenylketonuria (PKU) – A recessive disorder that prevents the body from producing an enzyme that breaks down phenylalanine (an amino acid) from proteins, that, without treatment, leads to buildup that damages the central nervous system.

phonics – An approach to reading instruction that emphasizes teaching children to sound out words and connect sounds to written symbols.

physical development – Body maturation, including body size, proportion, appearance, health, and perceptual abilities.

placenta – The principal organ of exchange between the mother and the developing organism, enabling the exchange of nutrients, oxygen, and wastes via the umbilical cord.

plasticity – A characteristic of development refers to malleability, or openness to change in response to experience.

plasticity – The ability to change organization and function in response to experiences throughout the lifespan, especially the brain.

polygenic inheritance – Occurs when a trait is a function of the interaction of many genes, such as with height, intelligence, and temperament.

popular – A child who receives many positive ratings from peers indicating that he or she is accepted and valued by peers.

possible self – Future-oriented representations of self-concept into the future; who an individual might become, both hoped for and feared, that guides and motivates choices and behaviors.

postconventional moral reasoning – Kohlberg's third level of moral reasoning emphasizing autonomous decision-making based on principles such as valuing human dignity.

postformal reasoning – A stage of cognitive development proposed to follow Piaget's formal operational stage. Thinking and problem solving is restructured in adulthood to integrate abstract reasoning with practical considerations, recognizing that most problems have multiple causes and solutions, some solutions are better than others, and all problems involve uncertainty.

postpartum depression – Moderate to severe depression occurring in a woman after giving birth, usually within the first 3 months after delivery.

post-traumatic stress disorder (PTSD) – An anxiety disorder that occurs as a delayed reaction to experiencing a traumatic event and includes flashbacks, nightmares, and feelings of helplessness.

pragmatic thought – In Labouvie-Vief's theory, a type of thinking where logic is used as a tool to address everyday problems and contradictions are viewed as part of life.

pragmatics – The practical application of language for everyday communication.

preconventional reasoning – Kohlberg's first level of reasoning in which young children's behavior is governed by punishment and gaining rewards.

preoperational reasoning –Piaget's second stage of cognitive development, between about age 2 and 6, characterized by advances in symbolic thought, but thought is not yet logical.

presbycusis – Age-related hearing loss, first to the high frequency sounds, gradually spreading.

presbyopia – An age-related condition in which the lens becomes less able to adjust its focus on objects at a close range.

preterm – A birth that occurs 35 or fewer weeks after conception.

primary circular reaction – In Piaget's theory, repeating an action that produced a chance event involving the infant's body.

primary sex characteristic – The reproductive organs; in females, this includes the ovaries, fallopian tubes, uterus, and vagina and in males, this includes the penis, testes, scrotum, seminal vesicles, and prostate gland.

private speech – Self-directed speech that children use to guide their behavior.

Project Head Start – Early childhood intervention program education program funded by the U.S. federal government that provides low-income children with nutritional, health, and educational services, as well as helps parent become involved in their children's development.

prosocial behavior – Actions that are oriented toward others for the pure sake of helping, without a reward.

protective factor – Variable that is thought to reduce the poor outcomes associated with adverse circumstances.

proximodistal development – The principle that growth and development proceed from the center of the body outward.

psychoanalytic theory – A perspective introduced by Freud that development and behavior is stagelike and influenced by inner drives, memories, and conflicts of which an individual is unaware and cannot control.

puberty – The biological transition to adulthood, in which hormones cause the body to physically mature and permit sexual reproduction.

punishment – In operant conditioning, the process in which a behavior is followed by an aversive or unpleasant outcome that decreases the likelihood of a response.

questionnaire – A research method in which researchers use a survey or set of questions to collect data from large samples of people.

random assignment – A method of assigning participants that ensures each participant has an equal chance of being assigned to the experimental group or control group.

range of reaction – The concept that a genetic trait may be expressed in a wide range of phenotypes dependent on environmental opportunities and constraints.

reactive aggression – An impulsive, hostile response to provocation or a blocked goal.

recall memory – Remembering a stimulus that is not present.

recast – When an adult repeats a child's sentence back to him or her in a new grammatical form, helping the child to acquire grammatical rules more quickly.

reciprocal determinism – A perspective positing that individuals and the environment interact and influence each other.

recognition memory – The ability to identify a previously encountered stimulus.

reflective judgment – Mature type of reasoning that synthesizes contradictions among perspectives.

reflex – An involuntary and automatic response to a stimulus.

rehearsal – A mnemonic strategy that involves systematically repeating information to retain it in working memory.

reinforcement – In operant conditioning, the process by which a behavior is followed by a desirable outcome increases the likelihood of a response.

relational aggression – Harming someone through nonphysical acts aimed at harming a person's connections with others, such as by exclusion and rumor spreading.

relativistic thinking – Type of reasoning in which knowledge is viewed as subjective and dependent on the situation.

reminiscence – The process of telling stories from one's past, to oneself or others.

resilience – The ability to adapt to serious adversity.

reversibility – The understanding that an object that has been physically altered can be returned to its original state or a process can be done and undone.

role overload –High levels of stress resulting from balancing the demands of multiple conflicting roles.

rough-and-tumble play – Social interaction involving chasing and play fighting with no intent to harm.

sarcopenia – The age-related loss of muscle mass and strength.

scaffolding – Temporary support that permits a child to bridge the gap between his or her current competence level and the task at hand.

schema – A mental representation, such as concepts, ideas, and ways of interacting with the world.

scientific method – The process of forming and answering questions using systematic observations and gathering information.

script – Description of what occurs in a certain situation and used as guide to understand and organize daily experiences.

seasons of life – A set of life phases that Levinson concluded adults progress through in which life structures are constructed, tested, and modified, based on experiences and opportunities.

secondary circular reaction – In Piaget's theory, repeating an action that produced a chance event that triggers a response in the external environment.

secondary sex characteristic – Physical traits that indicates sexual maturity but are not directly related to fertility, such as breast development and the growth of body hair.

secular trend – The change from one generation to the next in an aspect of development, such as body size or in the timing of puberty.

secure attachment – The attachment pattern in which an infant uses the caregiver as a secure base from which to explore, seeks contact during reunions, and is easily comforted by the caregiver.

secure base – The use of a caregiver as a foundation from which to explore and return to for emotional support.

selective attention – The ability to focus on relevant stimuli and ignore others.

selective optimization with compensation – an approach by which people maintain high levels of functioning by narrowing their goals, selecting personally valued attributes to optimize, and compensating for losses.

self-concept – The set of attributes, abilities, and characteristics that a person uses to describe and define him- or herself.

self-conscious emotion – Emotions that requires cognitive development and an awareness of self, such as empathy, embarrassment, shame, and guilt.

self-esteem – The general emotional evaluation of one's own worth.

self-harm – Deliberate and voluntary physical personal injury that is not life-threatening and is without any conscious suicidal intent.

self-recognition – The ability to identify the self, typically measured as mirror recognition.

self-regulation – The ability to control one's impulses and appropriately direct behavior.

senescence – A pattern of gradual age-related declines in physical functioning.

sensation – The physical response of sensory receptors when a stimulus is detected (e.g., activity of the sensory receptors in the eye in response to light); awareness of stimuli in the senses.

sensory memory – The first step in the information processing system in which stimuli are stored for a brief moment in its original form to enable it to be processed.

separation protest – Also known as separation anxiety; occurs when infants respond to the departure of a caregiver with fear, distress, and crying.

sequential research design – A developmental design in which multiple groups of participants of different ages are followed over time, combining cross-sectional and longitudinal research.

seriation – A type of classification that involves ordering objects in a series according to a physical dimension such as height, weight, or color.

sexual identity – An individual's sense of self regarding sexuality, including the awareness and comfort regarding personal sexual attitudes, interests, and behaviors, which develops through a period of exploration and commitment.

sexual orientation – A term that refers to whether someone is sexually attracted to others of the same sex, opposite sex, or both.

slow-to-warm-up temperament – A temperament characterized by mild irregularity in biological rhythms, slow adaptation to change, mildly negative mood.

small for date – Describes an infant who is full term but who has significantly lower weight than expected for the gestational age.

social clock – A timetable based on social norms for age-related life events events events such as occupational entry, marriage, parenthood, and retirement.

social comparison – The tendency to compare and judge one's abilities, achievements, and behaviors in relation to others.

social learning theory – An approach that emphasizes the role of modeling and observational learning over people's behavior in addition to reinforcement and punishment.

social promotion – The practice of promoting children to the next grade even though they did not meet academic standards out of the belief that it will foster self-esteem.

social referencing – Seeking information from caregivers about how to interpret unfamiliar or ambiguous events by observing their emotional expressions and reactions.

social smile – A smile that emerges between 6 and 10 weeks in response to seeing familiar people.

sociocultural theory – Vygotsky's perspective that individuals acquire culturally relevant ways of thinking through social interactions with members of their culture.

sociodramatic play – Make-believe play in which children act out roles and themes.

socioemotional development – Maturation of social and emotional functioning, which includes changes in personality, emotions, personal perceptions, social skills, and interpersonal relationships.

socioemotional selectivity theory – The perspective that as the emotional regulation function of social interaction becomes increasingly important to older adults, they prefer to interact with familiar social partners, accounting for the narrowing of the social network with age.

spermarche – A boy's first ejaculation of sperm.

spina bifida – A neural tube that results in spinal nerves growing outside of the vertebrae, often resulting in paralysis and developmental disability.

stem cell – An undifferentiated master cell with the capacity to generate into any type of specialized cell in the body.

Strange Situation – A structured laboratory procedure that measures the security o attachment by observing infants' reactions to being separated from the caregiver in an unfamiliar environment.

stranger wariness – Also known as stranger anxiety; an infant's expression of fear of unfamiliar people.

structured interview – A research method in which each participant is asked the same set of questions in the same way.

structured observation – An observational measure in which an individual's behavior is viewed and recorded in a controlled environment; a situation created by the experimenter.

stunted growth – Inadequate growth as measured by low height and weight for age, typically caused by severe malnutrition.

sympathy – Concern or sorrow for another person.

synapse – The intersection or gap between the axon of one neuron and the dendrites of other neurons; the gap that neurotransmitters must cross.

synaptic pruning – The process by which synapses, neural connections, that are seldom used, disappear.

synaptogenesis – The process in which neurons form synapses and increase connections between neurons.

telegraphic speech – Two-word utterances produced by toddlers that communicates only the essential words.

telomere – A type of DNA that caps both ends of chromosomes and shortens with each cell division. Eventually telomeres shorten past a critical length and the cell to stop duplicating.

temperament – Characteristic differences among individuals in emotional reactivity, self-regulation, and activity that influences reactions to the environment and are stable, and appear early in life.

teratogen – An environmental factor that causes damage to prenatal development.

teratology – The study of abnormalities in prenatal development.

tertiary circular reaction – In Piaget's theory, repeating an action to explore and experiment in order to see the results and learn about the world.

testosterone – The primary male sex hormone responsible for development and regulation of the male reproductive system and secondary sex characteristics.

theory – An organized set of observations to describe, explain, and predict a phenomenon.

theory of mind – Children's awareness of their own and other people's mental processes and realization that other people do not share their thoughts.

time out – A discipline technique in which a child is removed from a situation for a period of time.

transitive inference – A classification skill in which a child can infer the relationship between two objects by understanding each object's relationship to a third object.

triarchic theory of intelligence – Sternberg's theory positing three independent forms of intelligence: analytical, creative, and applied.

trust versus mistrust – The first psychosocial crisis in Erikson's theory in which infants must develop a basic sense of trust of the world as a safe place where their basic needs will be met.

ultrasound – Prenatal diagnostic procedure in which high-frequency sound waves are directed at the mother's abdomen to provide clear images of the womb projected on to a video monitor.

underextension – A vocabulary error in which the infant applies a word too narrowly to a single object rather than the more appropriate, wider class of objects.

uninvolved parenting style – A child-rearing style characterized by low levels of warmth and acceptance coupled with little control or discipline.

universal grammar – In Chomsky's theory, rules that apply to all human languages.

vaccination – The administration of a small dose of inactive virus into the body to stimulate the production of antibodies to guard against a disease.

vascular dementia – Neurocognitive disorder in which sporadic and progressive losses occur, caused by small blockages of blood vessels in the brain.

vernix caseosa – Greasy material that protects the fetal skin from abrasions, chapping, and hardening that can occur from exposure to amniotic fluid.

video deficit effect – A finding that infants and toddlers perform more poorly on tasks demonstrated on video than those demonstrated live.

violation-of-expectation method – A method in which infants are shown events that appear to violate physical laws. Increased attention to the unexpected event suggests that the infant is surprised and therefore has an understanding and expectations of the physical world.

wear and tear theory of aging – An early theory of aging stating that aging is the result of the body wearing out from use.

Wernicke's area – The region of the brain that is responsible for language comprehension; damage to this area impairs the ability to understand others' speech and sometimes the ability to speak coherently.

whole-language approach – An approach to reading instruction that emphasizes meaning, not phonics. Children are exposed to reading materials without instruction and emphasis is on meaning-making.

wisdom – Expertise in the conduct and meanings of life, characterized by emotional maturity and the ability to show insight and apply it to problems.

withdrawn-rejected – A child who is rejected by peers because of a repeated pattern of passive, timid, withdrawn, or anxious behavior.

working memory – The component of the information processing system that holds and processes information that is being manipulated, encoded, or retrieved and is responsible for maintaining and processing information used in cognitive tasks.

young-old – Older adults aged 65 to 74, who tend to be active, healthy, and financially and physically independent.

zone of proximal development – Vygotsky's term for the tasks that children cannot do alone but can exercise with the aid of more skilled partners.

zygote – A fertilized ovum.

CHAPTER 1

American Psychological Association. (2010). *Ethical principles of psychologists and code of conduct*. Washington, DC: Author. Retrieved from http://www.apa.org/ethics/code/principles.pdf

Anastasi, A. (1958). Heredity, environment, and the question "how?" *Psychological Review, 65,* 197–208.

Anjos, T., Altmäe, S., Emmett, P., Tiemeier, H., Closa-Monasterolo, R., Luque, V., . . . Campoy, C. (2013). Nutrition and neurodevelopment in children: Focus on NUTRIMENTHE project. *European Journal of Nutrition, 52*(8), 1825–1842. doi:10.1007/s00394-013-0560-4

Baltes, M. M., & Carstensen, L. L. (2003). The process of successful aging: Selection, optimization and compensation. In U. M. Staudinger & U. Lindenberger (Eds.), *Understanding human development: Dialogues with lifespan psychology* (pp. 81–104). Dordrecht, Netherlands: Kluwer Academic Publishers.

Baltes, P. B. (1987). Theoretical propositions of life-span developmental psychology: On the dynamics between growth and decline. *Developmental Psychology, 23,* 611–626.

Baltes, P. B. (1997). On the incomplete architecture of human ontogeny: Selection, optimization, and compensation as foundation of developmental theory. *American Psychologist, 52,* 366–380.

Baltes, P. B., Lindenberger, U., & Staudinger, U. M. (1998). Life-span theory in developmental psychology. In R. M. Lerner (Ed.), *Handbook of child psychology: Vol. 1. Theoretical models of human development* (5th ed., pp. 1029–1143). Hoboken, NJ: John Wiley.

Bandura, A. (1986). *Social foundations of thought and action: A social cognitive theory*. Englewood Cliffs, NJ: Prentice Hall.

Bandura, A. (2001). Social cognitive theory: An agentic. *Annual Reviews of Psychology, 52,* 1–26.

Bandura, A. (2011). But what about that gigantic elephant in the room? In R. Arkin (Ed.), *Most underappreciated: 50 prominent social psychologists describe their most unloved work* (pp. 51–59). New York: Oxford University Press.

Bandura, A. (2012). Social cognitive theory. In P. A. M. Van Lange, A. W. Kruglanski, & E. T. Higgins (Eds.), *Handbook of theories of social psychology* (Vol 1, pp. 349–373). Thousand Oaks, CA: Sage.

Bandura, A., Ross, D., & Ross, S. A. (1963). Vicarious reinforcement and imitative learning. *Journal of Abnormal and Social Psychology, 67,* 601–607.

Bjorklund, D. F., & Pellegrini, A. D. (2000). Child development and evolutionary psychology. *Child Development, 71*(6), 1687–1708.

Bluck, S., & Gluck, J. (2004). Making things better and learning a lesson: Experience wisdom across the lifespan. *Journal of Personality, 72*(3), 543–572.

Boker, S. M. (2013). Selection, optimization, compensation, and equilibrium dynamics. *GeroPsych, 26*(1), 61–73. doi:10.1024/1662-9647/a000081

Bowlby, J. (1969). *Attachment and loss: Vol. 1. Attachment*. New York: Basic Books.

Bowlby, J. (1973). *Attachment and loss: Vol. 2. Separation: Anxiety and anger*. New York: Basic Books.

Bronfenbrenner, U. (1979). *The ecology of human development: Experiments by nature and design*. Cambridge, MA: Harvard University Press.

Bronfenbrenner, U. (2005). The bioecological theory of human development. In U. Bronfenbrenner (Ed.), *Making human beings human: Bioecological perspectives on human development* (pp. 3–15). Thousand Oaks, CA: Sage.

Bronfenbrenner, U., & Ceci, S. J. (1994). Nature-nurture reconceptualized in developmental perspective: A bioecological model. *Psychological Review, 101*(4), 568–586. Retrieved from http://www.ncbi.nlm.nih.gov/pubmed/7984707

Bronfenbrenner, U., & Morris, P. A. (2006). *The bioecological model of human development* (Vol. 1, pp. 793–828). Hoboken, NJ: John Wiley.

Broughton, J. (1981). Piaget's structural developmental psychology: Knowledge without a self and without history. *Human Development, 24,* 320–346.

Carstensen, L. L., & Mikels, J. A. (2005). At the intersection of emotion and cognition. Aging and the positivity effect. *Current Directions in Psychological Science, 14*(3), 117–121. doi:10.1111/j.0963-7214.2005.00348.x

Cole, M. (1999). Culture in development. In M. Bornstein & M. Lamb (Eds.), *Developmental psychology: An advanced textbook* (pp. 73–122). Mahwah, NJ: Lawrence Erlbaum.

Cooper, H., Valentine, J. C., Nye, B., & Lindsay, J. J. (1999). Relationships between five after-school activities and academic achievement. *Journal of Educational Psychology, 91*(2), 369–378.

Crain, W. C. (1999). *Theories of development* (4th ed.). Englewood Cliffs, NJ: Prentice Hall.

Crews, F. (1996). The verdict on Freud. *Psychological Science, 7*(2), 63–68.

Dewsbury, D. A. (1992). Comparative psychology and ethology: A reassessment. *American Psychologist, 47,* 208–215.

Dieter, J. N. I., Field, T., Hernandez-Reif, M., Emory, E. K., & Redzepi, M. (2003). Stable preterm infants gain more weight and sleep less after five days of massage therapy. *Journal of Pediatric Psychology, 28*(6), 403–411.

Dixon, R. A., & Lerner, R. M. (1999). History and systems in developmental psychology. In M. H. Bornstein & M. E. Lamb (Eds.), *Developmental psychology: An advanced textbook* (4th ed., pp. 3–54). Mahwah, NJ: Lawrence Erlbaum.

Elder, G. H. J. (1999). *Children of the Great Depression: Social change in life experience* (25th anniversary ed.). Boulder, CO: Westview Press.

Elder, G. H. J. (2000). Life course theory. In A. E. Kazdin (Ed.), *Encyclopedia of psychology* (Vol. 5, pp. 50–52). Washington, DC: American Psychological Association. doi:10.1037/10520-000

Erikson, E. H. (1950). *Childhood and society* (2nd ed.). New York: Norton.

Evans, D. W., Milanak, M. E., Medeiros, B., & Ross, J. L. (2002). Magical beliefs and rituals in young children. *Child Psychiatry and Human Development, 33,* 43–58.

Fawcett, L. M., & Garton, A. F. (2005). The effect of peer collaboration on children's problem-solving ability. *British Journal of Educational Psychology, 75*(2), 157–169. doi:10.1348/000709904X234ll

Fisher, C., Higgins-D'Alessandro, A., Rau, J.-M. B., Kuther, T. L., & Belanger, S. (1996). Referring and reporting research participants at risk: Views from urban adolescents. *Child Development, 67*(5), 2086–2100.

Fisher, C. B., Busch-Rossnagel, N. A., Jopp, D. S., & Brown, J. L. (2013). Applied developmental science: Contributions and challenges for the 21st century. In R. M. Lerner, M. A. Easterbrooks, & J. Mistry (Eds.), *Handbook of psychology* (Vol. 6, pp. 517–546). Hoboken, NJ: John Wiley.

Flavell, J. H. (1994). Cognitive development: Past, present, and future. In R. D. Parke, P. A. Ornstein, J. R. Rieser, & C. Zahn-Waxler (Eds.), *A century of developmental psychology*. Washington, DC: American Psychological Association.

Fonagy, P., & Target, M. (2000). The place of psychodynamic theory in developmental psychopathology. *Development & Psychopathology, 12*(3), 407–425.

Frankenhuis, W. E., Panchanathan, K., & Clark Barrett, H. (2013). Bridging developmental systems theory and evolutionary psychology using dynamic optimization. *Developmental Science, 16*(4), 584–598. doi:10.1111/desc.12053

Freund, A. M., & Baltes, P. B. (2007). Toward a theory of successful aging: Selection, optimization, and compensation. In R. Fernández-Ballesteros (Ed.), *Geropsychology: European perspectives for an aging world* (pp. 239–254). Ashland, OH: Hogrefe & Huber.

Gans, C., & Crews, D. (1992). *Hormones, brain, and behavior: Biology of the reptiles*. Chicago: University of Chicago Press.

Gardiner, H. W., & Kosmitzki, C. (2010). *Lives across cultures: Cross-cultural human development* (5th ed.). Boston: Pearson.

Garrison, E. G., & Kobor, P. C. (2002). Weathering a political storm: A contextual perspective on a psychological research controversy. *American Psychologist, 57*(3), 165–175.

Gelman, S. A., & Opfer, J. E. (2002). Development of the animate-inanimate distinction. In U. Goswami (Ed.), *Blackwell handbook of childhood cognitive development* (pp. 151–166). Malden, MA: Blackwell.

Gilbert, S. F. (2001). Ecological developmental biology: Developmental biology meets the real world. *Developmental Biology, 233,* 1–12.

Ginsburg, H. P. (1997). *Entering the child's mind: The clinical interview in psychological research & practice*. New York: Cambridge University Press.

Ginsburg, H. P., Pappas, S., & Seo, K. H. (2001). Everyday mathematical knowledge: Asking young children what is developmentally appropriate. In S. L. Golbeck (Ed.), *Psychological perspectives on early childhood education: Reframing dilemmas in research and practice* (pp. 181–219). Mahwah, NJ: Lawrence Erlbaum.

Gottesman, I. I., & Hanson, D. R. (2005). Human development: Biological and genetic processes. *Annual Review of Psychology, 56,* 263–286.

Gottlieb, G. (2003). On making behavioral genetics truly developmental. *Human Development, 46,* 337–355.

Gottlieb, G., Wahlsten, D., & Lickliter, R. (1998). The significance of biology for human development: A developmental psychobiological systems view. In R. M. Lerner (Ed.), *Handbook of child psychology: Vol. 1. Theoretical models of human development* (5th ed., pp. 233–273). Hoboken, NJ: John Wiley.

Green, M., & Piel, J. A. (2002). *Theories of human development: A comparative approach*. Boston: Allyn & Bacon.

Grigorenko, E. L., & Sternberg, R. J. (2003). The nature-nurture issue. In A. Slater & G. Bremner (Eds.), *An introduction to developmental psychology* (pp. 64–91). Malden, MA: Blackwell.

Halford, G. S., & Andrews, G. (2011). Information-processing models of cognitive development. In U. Goswami (Ed.), *The Wiley-Blackwell handbook of childhood cognitive development* (2nd ed., pp. 697–721). Malden, MA: Blackwell.

Hess, T. M., Leclerc, C. M., Swaim, E., & Weatherbee, S. R. (2009). Aging and everyday judgments: The impact of motivational and processing resource factors. *Psychology and Aging, 24*(3), 735–740. doi:10.1037/a0016340

Hofstede, G. (2001). *Culture's consequences: Comparing values, behaviors, institutions, and organizations across nations*. Thousand Oaks, CA: Sage.

Hopkins, B., & Westra, T. (1989). Maternal expectations of their infants' development: Some cultural differences. *Developmental Medicine & Child Neurology*, 31(3), 384–390.

Johnston, L. D., O'Malley, P. M., Miech, R. A., Bachman, J. G., & Schulenberg, J. E. (2014). *Monitoring the Future national survey results on drug use: 1975–2013: Overview, key findings on adolescent drug use* (p. 88). Ann Arbor: University of Michigan Institute for Social Research.

Kagan, J. (2008). In defense of qualitative changes in development. *Child Development*, 79(6), 1606–1624. doi:10.1111/j.1467-8624.2008.01211.x

Kail, R. V. (2003). Information processing and memory. In M. H. Bornstein & L. Davidson (Eds.), *Well-being: Positive development across the life course* (pp. 269–279). Mahwah, NJ: Lawrence Erlbaum.

Kim, J. S., & Böckenholt, U. (2000). Modeling stage-sequential change in ordered categorical responses. *Psychological Methods*, 5(3), 380–400. Retrieved from http://www.ncbi.nlm .nih.gov/pubmed/11004875

Klahr, D. (1985). Solving problems with ambiguous subgoal ordering: Preschoolers' performance. *Child Development*, 56, 940–952.

Klahr, D. (1992). Information-processing approaches. In R. Vasta (Ed.), *Six theories of child development: Revised formulations and current issues* (pp. 133–185). London: Jessica Kingsley.

Krebs, D. L. (2003). Fictions and facts about evolutionary approaches to human behavior: Comment on Lickliter and Honeycutt (2003). *Psychological Bulletin*, 129(6), 842–847.

Kuther, T. L. (2003). Medical decision-making and minors: Issues of consent and assent. *Adolescence*, 38(150), 343–359.

Lampl, M., Johnson, M., & Frongillo, E., Jr. (2001). Mixed distribution analysis identifies saltation and stasis growth. *Annals of Human Biology*, 28(4), 403–411.

Lampl, M., Veldhuis, J. D., & Johnson, M. L. (1992). Saltation and stasis: A model of human growth. *Science*, 258, 801–803.

Leichsenring, F., & Rabung, S. (2008). Effectiveness of long-term psychodynamic psychotherapy. *JAMA*, 300(13), 1551–1565.

Lerner, R. M. (2010). Applied developmental science: Definitions and dimensions. In V. Maholmes & C. G. Lomonaco (Eds.), *Applied research in child and adolescent development: A practical guide* (pp. 37–58). New York: Taylor & Francis.

Lerner, R. M. (2012). Developmental science: Past, present, and future. *International Journal of Developmental Science*, 6, 26–29.

Lickliter, R., & Honeycutt, H. (2003). Developmental dynamics: Toward a biologically plausible evolutionary psychology. *Psychological Bulletin*, 129(6), 819–835. doi:10.1037/0033-2909.129.6.866

Lickliter, R., & Honeycutt, H. (2013). A developmental evolutionary framework for psychology. *Review of General Psychology*, 17(2). doi:10.1037/a0032932

Lorenz, K. (1952). *King Solomon's ring*. New York: Crowell.

Lourenco, O., & Machado, A. (1996). In defense of Piaget's theory: A reply to 10 common criticisms. *Psychological Review*, 103, 143–164.

Luna, B., Garver, K. E., Urban, T. A., Lazar, N. A., & Sweeney, J. A. (2004). Maturation of cognitive processes from late childhood to adulthood. *Child Development*, 75(5), 1357–1372. doi:10.1111/j.1467-8624.2004.00745.x

Lutz, D. J., & Sternberg, R. J. (1999). Cognitive development. In M. H. Bornstein & M. E. Lamb (Eds.), *Developmental psychology: An advanced textbook* (4th ed., pp. 275–311). Mahwah, NJ: Lawrence Erlbaum.

Lyon, T. D., & Flavell, J. H. (1993). Young children's understanding of forgetting over time. *Child Development*, 64(3), 780–800.

Margrett, J. A., Allaire, J. C., Johnson, T. L., Daugherty, K. E., & Weatherbee, S. R. (2010). Everyday problem solving. In J. C. Cavanaugh, C. K. Cavanaugh, J. Berry, & R. West (Eds.), *Aging in America, Vol 1: Psychological aspects* (pp. 80–101). Santa Barbara, CA: Praeger/ABC-CLIO.

Marques, E. A., Mota, J., Viana, J. L., Tuna, D., Figueiredo, P., Guimarães, J. T., & Carvalho, J. (2013). Response of bone mineral density, inflammatory cytokines, and biochemical bone markers to a 32-week combined loading exercise programme in older men and women. *Archives of Gerontology & Geriatrics*, 57(2), 226–233. doi:10.1016/j.archger.2013.03.014

McAuley, E., Wójcicki, T. R., Gothe, N. P., Mailey, E. L., Szabo, A. N., Fanning, J., . . . Mullen, S. P. (2013). Effects of a DVD-delivered exercise intervention on physical function in older adults. *The Journals of Gerontology: Series A: Biological Sciences and Medical Sciences*, 68(9), 1076–1082.

McCrae, R. R. (2002). The maturation of personality psychology: Adult personality development and psychological well-being. *Journal of Research in Personality*, 36(4), 307–317.

McDonald, M. (1998, October 19). Burying Freud and praising him. *U.S. News & World Report*, p. 60.

Meaney, M. J. (2010). Epigenetics and the biological definition of gene-environment interactions. *Child Development*, 81(1), 41–79.

Miller, P. H. (2009). *Theories of developmental psychology* (5th ed.). New York: Worth.

Moran, R. J., Symmonds, M., Dolan, R. J., & Friston, K. J. (2014). The brain ages optimally to model its environment: Evidence from sensory learning over the adult lifespan. *PLoS Computational Biology*, 10(1), 1–8. doi:10.1371/journal.pcbi.1003422

National Academy of Sciences. (1995). *On being a scientist: Responsible conduct in research*. Washington, DC: National Academy Press.

Piaget, J. (1929). *The child's conception of the world*. London: Routledge & Kegan Paul.

Picker, J. (2005, August 1). The role of genetic and environmental factors in the development of schizophrenia. *Psychiatric Times*. Retrieved August 29, 2015, from http://www.psychiatrictimes.com/schizophrenia/role-genetic-and-environmental-factors-development-schizophrenia

Piek, J. P., Dawson, L., Smith, L. M., & Gasson, N. (2008). The role of early fine and gross motor development on later motor and cognitive ability. *Human Movement Science*, 27(5), 668–681. doi:10.1016/j.humov.2007.11.002

Pomerleau, A., Malcuit, G., Chicoine, J. F., Séguin, R., Belhumeur, C., Germain, P., . . . & Jéliu, G. (2005). Health status, cognitive and motor development of young children adopted from China, East Asia, and Russia across the first 6 months after adoption. *International Journal of Behavioral Development*, 29(5), 445-457.

Rind, B., Tromovitch, P., & Bauserman, R. (1998). A meta-analytic examination of assumed properties of child sexual abuse using college samples. *Psychological Bulletin*, 124(1), 22–53.

Roberts, B. W., & Caspi, A. (2003). The cumulative continuity model of personality development: Striking a balance between continuity and change in personality traits across the life course. In M. Ursula & U. Lindenberger (Eds.), *Understanding human development: Dialogues with lifespan psychology* (pp. 183–214). Dordrecht, Netherlands: Kluwer Academic Publishers.

Rogler, L. H. (2002). Historical generations and psychology: The case of the Great Depression and World War II. *American Psychologist*, 57, 1013–1023.

Rogoff, B. (2003). *The cultural nature of human development*. New York: Oxford University Press.

Rogoff, B., & Morelli, G. (1989). Perspectives on children's development from cultural psychology. *American Psychologist*, 44, 343–348.

Rogoff, B., Mosier, C., Mistry, J., & Göncü, A. (1993). Toddlers' guided participation with their caregivers in cultural activity. In E. A. Forman, N. Minick, & C. A. Stone (Eds.), *Contexts for learning* (pp. 230–253). New York: Oxford University Press.

Rutherford, A. (2000). Radical behaviorism and psychology's public: B. F. Skinner in the popular press, 1934–1990. *History of Psychology*, 3(4), 371–395.

Rutter, M. (2010). Gene-environment interplay. *Depression & Anxiety*, 27, 1–4.

Rutter, M. (2012). Gene–environment interdependence. *European Journal of Developmental Psychology*, 9, 391–412.

Scarr, S., & McCartney, K. (1983). How people make their own environments: A theory of genotype environment effects. *Child Development*, 54(2), 424. doi:10.1111/1467-8624.ep8877295

Schweder, R. A., Goodnow, J., Hatano, G., LeVine, R. A., Markys, H., & Miller, P. (1998). The cultural psychology of development: One mind, many mentalities. In W. Damon & R. M. Lerner (Eds.), *Handbook of child psychology: Theoretical models of human development* (Vol. 1, pp. 865–938). Hoboken, NJ: John Wiley.

Sigman, M. (1995). Nutrition and child development: More food for thought. *Current Directions in Psychological Science*, 52-55.

Singer, T., Lindenberger, U., & Baltes, P. B. (2003). Plasticity of memory for new learning in very old age: A story of major loss? *Psychology and Aging*, 18(2), 306–317.

Society for Research in Child Development. (2007). *Ethical standards in research*. Washington, DC: Author. Retrieved from http://www.srcd.org/about-us/ethical-standards-research

Staudinger, U. M., & Lindenberger, U. (2003). *Understanding human development: Dialogues with lifespan psychology*. Dordrecht, Netherlands: Kluwer Academic Publishers.

Super, C. M. (1981). Cross-cultural research on infancy. In H. C. Triandis & A. Heron (Eds.), *Handbook of cross-cultural psychology: Vol. 4. Developmental psychology*. Boston: Allyn & Bacon.

Thelen, E., Fisher, D. M., & Ridley-Johnson, R. (2002). The relationship between physical growth and a newborn reflex. *Infant Behavior & Development*, 25(1), 72–85.

Thomas, R. M. (2004). *Comparing theories of child development* (6th ed.). Belmont, CA: Wadsworth.

Thompson, R. A. (1990). Vulnerability in research: A developmental perspective on research risk. *Child Development*, 61, 1–16.

Tseng, V. (2012). The uses of research in policy and practice. *Social Policy Report of the Society for Research in Child Development*, 26(2).

Ullman, H., Almeida, R., & Klingberg, T. (2014). Structural maturation and brain activity predict future working memory capacity during childhood development. *Journal of Neuroscience*, 34(5), 1592–1598. doi:10.1523/jneurOsci.0842-13.2014

U.S. Department of Health and Human Services. (2009). *Code of Federal Regulations TITLE 45 Department of Health and Human Services PART 46*. Washington, DC: Author. Retrieved from http://www.hhs.gov/ohrp/humansubjects/guidance/45cfr46.html

Vygotsky, L. S. (1962). *Thought and language*. Cambridge, MA: MIT Press. (Original work published 1934)

Vygotsky, L. S. (1978). *Mind in society: The development of higher psychological processes.* Cambridge, MA: Harvard University Press.

Watson, J. (1925). *Behaviorism*. New York: Norton.

Wertlieb, D. (2003). Applied developmental science. In R. M. Lerner, M. A. Easterbrooks, & J. Mistry (Eds.), *Handbook of psychology: Developmental psychology* (Vol. 6, pp. 43–64). Hoboken, NJ: John Wiley.

Wertsch, J. V. (1998). *Mind as action.* New York: Oxford University Press.

Westen, D. (1998). The scientific legacy of Sigmund Freud: Toward a psychodynamically informed psychological science. *Psychological Bulletin, 124,* 333–371.

Winegar, L., & Valsiuner, J. (1992). *Children's development within the social context.* Hillsdale, NJ: Lawrence Erlbaum.

Winsler, A., Carlton, M. P., & Barry, M. J. (2000). Age-related changes in preschool children's systematic use of private speech in a natural setting. *Journal of Child Language, 27,* 665–687.

Wortman, J., Lucas, R. E., & Donnellan, M. B. (2012). Stability and change in the Big Five personality domains: Evidence from a longitudinal study of Australians. *Psychology and Aging, 27*(4), 867–874. doi:10.1037/a0029322 10.1037/a0029322.supp

CHAPTER 2

Abrams, L., Cronister, A., Brown, W. T., Tassone, F., Sherman, S. L., Finucane, B., . . . Berry-Kravis, E. (2012). Newborn, carrier, and early childhood screening recommendations for fragile X. *Pediatrics, 130*(6), 1126–1135. doi:10.1542/peds.2012-0693

Allison, A. C. (2004). Two lessons from the interface of genetics and medicine. *Genetics, 166*(4), 1591–1599.

Ashley-Koch, A., Yang, Q., & Olney, R. (2000). Sickle hemoglobin (HbS) allele and sickle cell disease: A HuGE review. *American Journal of Epidemiology, 151,* 839–845.

Aston, K. I., Peterson, C. M., & Carrell, D. T. (2008). Monozygotic twinning associated with assisted reproductive technologies: A review. *Reproduction, 136,* 377–386. Retrieved from http://www.reproduction-online.org/content/136/4/377.full?sid=0d0ae256-57c7-4146-99fe-e3866623b5d7

Barker, E. D., Larsson, H., Viding, E., Maughan, B., Rijsdijk, F., Fontaine, N., & Plomin, R. (2009). Common genetic but specific environmental influences for aggressive and deceitful behaviors in preadolescent males. *Journal of Psychopathology & Behavioral Assessment, 31*(4), 299–308. doi:10.1007/s10862-009-9132-6

Barlow-Stewart, K. (2012). *Genes and chromosomes: The genome.* Sydney, Australia: Centre for Genetics Education. Retrieved from http://www.genetics.edu.au/Information/Genetics-Fact-Sheets/Genes-and-Chromosomes-FS1

Barlow-Stewart, K., & Saleh, M. (2012). *Prenatal testing overview.* Sydney, Australia: Centre for Genetics Education. Retrieved from http://www.genetics.edu.au/Information/Genetics-Fact-Sheets/Prenatal-Testing-Overview-FS17

Basaran, A., Basaran, M., & Topatan, B. (2011). Chorionic villus sampling and the risk of preeclampsia: A systematic review and meta-analysis. *Archives of Gynecology and Obstetrics, 283*(6), 1175–1181. doi:10.1007/s00404-011-1840-y

Beach, S. R. H., Brody, G. H., Gunter, T. D., Packer, H., Wernett, P., & Philibert, R. A. (2010). Child

maltreatment moderates the association of MAOA with symptoms of depression and antisocial personality disorder. *Journal of Family Psychology, 24*(1), 12–20. doi: 10.1037/a0018074.

Bernal, A. J., & Jirtle, R. L. (2010). Epigenomic disruption: The effects of early developmental exposures. *Birth Defects Research. Part A, Clinical and Molecular Teratology, 88*(10), 938–944. doi:10.1002/bdra.20685

Bhatia, R. (2010). Constructing gender from the inside out: Sex-selection practices in the United States. *Feminist Studies, 36*(2), 260–291.

Blau, N., van Spronsen, F. J., & Levy, H. L. (2010). Phenylketonuria. *Lancet, 376*(9750), 1417–1427.

Bojesen, A., & Gravholt, C. H. (2011). Morbidity and mortality in Klinefelter syndrome (47,XXY). *Acta Paediatrica, 100*(6), 807–813. doi:10.1111/j.1651-2227.2011.02274.x

Bouchard, T. J., Jr. & McGue, M. (1981). Familial studies of intelligence: A review. *Science, 212*(4498), 1055–1059.

Bouchard, T. J., Jr., Segal, N. L., Tellegen, A., McGue, M., Keyes, M., & Krueger, R. (2004). Genetic influence on social attitudes: Another challenge to psychology from behavior genetics. In L. F. DiLalla (Ed.), *Behavior genetics principles: Perspectives in development, personality, and psychopathology* (pp. 89–104). Washington, DC: American Psychological Association. doi:10.1037/10684-006

Brambati, B., & Lucia, T. (2005). Chorionic villus sampling and amniocentesis. *Current Opinion in Obstetrics & Gynecology, 17*(2), 197–201.

Brunet, A., & Berger, S. L. (2014). Epigenetics of aging and aging-related disease. *The Journals of Gerontology: Series A: Biological Sciences and Medical Sciences, 69*(Suppl. 1), S17–S20. doi:10.1093/gerona/glu042

Burns, G. W., & Bottino, P. J. (1989). *The science of genetics* (6th ed.). New York: MacMillan.

Burt, A. (2009). A mechanistic explanation of popularity: Genes, rule breaking, and evocative gene–environment correlations. *Journal of Personality and Social Psychology, 96*(4), 783–794. doi:10.1037/a0013702

Butler, M. G. (2011). Prader-Willi syndrome: Obesity due to genomic imprinting. *Current Genomics, 12*(3), 204–215.

Byrd, A. L., & Manuck, S. B. (2014). MAOA, childhood maltreatment, and antisocial behavior: Meta-analysis of a gene-environment interaction. *Biological Psychiatry, 75*(1), 9–17. doi:10.1016/j.biopsych.2013.05.004

Carr, J. (2002). Down syndrome. In P. Howlin & O. Udwin (Eds.), *Outcomes in neurodevelopmental and genetic disorders* (pp. 169–197). New York: Cambridge University Press. doi:10.1017/cbo9780511543876.008

Carr, J. (2012). Six weeks to 45 years: A longitudinal study of a population with Down syndrome. *Journal of Applied Research in Intellectual Disabilities, 25*(5), 414–422. doi:10.1111/j.1468-3148.2011.00676.x

Caspi, A., McClay, J., Moffitt, T. E., Mill, J., Martin, J., Craig, I. W., . . . Poulton, R. (2002). Role of genotype in the cycle of violence in maltreated children. *Science, 297*(5582), 851–854. doi:10.1126/science.1072290

Chan, W., Kwok, Y., Choy, K., Leung, T., & Wang, C. (2013). Single fetal cells for non-invasive prenatal genetic diagnosis: Old myths new prospective. *Medical Journal of Obstetrics and Gynecology, 1*(1), 1004.

Chen, H., Pine, D. S., Ernst, M., Gorodetsky, E., Kasen, S., Gordon, K., . . . Cohen, P. (2013). The MAOA gene predicts happiness in women. *Progress in Neuro-Psychopharmacology & Biological Psychiatry, 40,* 122–125. doi:10.1016/j.pnpbp.2012.07.018

Christopoulos, P., Deligeoroglou, E., Laggari, V., Christogiorgos, S., & Creatsas, G. (2008).

Psychological and behavioural aspects of patients with Turner syndrome from childhood to adulthood: A review of the clinical literature. *Journal of Psychosomatic Obstetrics & Gynecology, 29*(1), 45–51. doi:10.1080/01674820701577078

Cicchetti, D., Rogosch, F. A., & Sturge-Apple, M. L. (2007). Interactions of child maltreatment and serotonin transporter and monoamine oxidase A polymorphisms: Depressive symptomatology among adolescents from low socioeconomic status backgrounds. *Development and Psychopathology, 19*(4), 1161–1180. doi:10.1017/S0954579407000600

Cohen, D., Pichard, N., Tordjman, S., Baumann, C., Burglen, L., Excoffier, E., . . . Héron, D. (2005). Specific genetic disorders and autism: Clinical contribution towards their identification. *Journal of Autism and Developmental Disorders, 35*(1), 103–116.

Colls, P., Silver, L., Olivera, G., Weier, J., Escudero, T., Goodall, N., . . . Munné, S. (2009). Preimplantation genetic diagnosis for gender selection in the USA. *Reproductive BioMedicine Online, 19*(Suppl. 2), 16–22.

Council of Europe. (1997). *Convention for the protection of human rights and dignity of the human being with regard to the application of biology and medicine: Convention on human rights and biomedicine.* Oviedo. Retrieved from http://conventions.coe.int/Treaty/en/Treaties/Html/164.htm

Coutelle, C., & Waddington, S. N. (2012). The concept of prenatal gene therapy. In C. Coutelle & S. N. Waddington (Eds.), *Methods in molecular biology* (Vol. 891, pp. 1–7). Clifton, NJ: Springer. doi:10.1007/978-1-61779-873-3_1

Cunniff, C. (2004). Prenatal screening and diagnosis for pediatricians. *Pediatrics, 114*(3), 889–893.

Darnovsky, M. (2009). *Countries with laws or policies on sex selection. Memo for the April 13 New York City sex selection meeting.* Berkeley, CA. Retrieved from http://geneticsandsociety.org/downloads/200904_sex_selection_memo.pdf

Das, R., Hampton, D. D., & Jirtle, R. L. (2009). Imprinting evolution and human health. *Mammalian Genome, 20*(9–10), 563–572. doi:10.1007/s00335-009-9229-y

Davis, A. S., & Escobar, L. F. (2013). Early childhood cognitive disorders: Down syndrome. In A. S. Davis (Ed.), *Psychopathology of childhood and adolescence: A neuropsychological approach* (pp. 569–580). New York: Springer.

Deater-Deckard, K. (2001). Nonshared environmental processes in social emotional development: An observational study of identical twin differences in the preschool period. *Developmental Science, 4*(2), 1–7.

Deater-Deckard, K., & O'Connor, T. (2000). Parent-child mutuality in early childhood: Two behavioral genetic studies. *Developmental Psychology, 36*(5), 561–571.

Deeney, M. (2013). Bioethical considerations of preimplantation genetic diagnosis for sex selection. *Washington University Jurisprudence Review, 5*(2). Retrieved from http://digitalcommons.law.wustl.edu/jurisprudence/vol5/iss2/5

DeFries, J. C., Gervais, M. C., & Thomas, E. A. (1978). Response to 30 generations of selection for open-field activity in laboratory mice. *Behavior Genetics, 8*(1), 3–13. doi:10.1007/bf01067700

Deprest, J. A., Devlieger, R., Srisupundit, K., Beck, V., Sandaite, I., Rusconi, S., . . . Lewi, L. (2010). Fetal surgery is a clinical reality. *Seminars in Fetal & Neonatal Medicine, 15*(1), 58–67. doi:10.1016/j.siny.2009.10.002

Dodge, K. A., & Rutter, M. (2011). *Gene–environment interactions in developmental psychopathology.* New York: Guilford Press.

Dolinoy, D. C. (2008). The agouti mouse model: An epigenetic biosensor for nutritional and environmental alterations on the fetal epigenome. *Nutrition Reviews, 66* (Suppl. 1), S7–S11. doi:10.1111/j.1753-4887.2008.00056.x

Dondorp, W., De Wert, G., Pennings, G., Shenfield, F., Devroey, P., Tarlatzis, B., . . . Diedrich, K. (2013). ESHRE Task Force on ethics and Law 20: Sex selection for non-medical reasons. *Human Reproduction, 28*(6), 1448–1454. doi:10.1093/humrep/det109

Doswell, B. H., Visootsak, J., Brady, A. N., & Graham, J. J. M. (2006). Turner syndrome: An update and review for the primary pediatrician. *Clinical Pediatrics, 45*(4), 301–313.

Dubois, L., Ohm Kyvik, K., Girard, M., Tatone-Tokuda, F., Pérusse, D., Hjelmborg, J., . . . Martin, N. G. (2012). Genetic and environmental contributions to weight, height, and BMI from birth to 19 years of age: An international study of over 12,000 twin pairs. *PloS One, 7*(2), e30153. doi:10.1371/journal.pone.0030153

Elias, S. (2010). Amniocentesis and fetal blood sampling. In A. Milunsky & J. M. Milunsky (Eds.), *Genetic disorders and the fetus* (6th ed., pp. 63–93). Hoboken, NJ: Wiley-Blackwell. doi:10.1002/9781444314342.ch2

Enns, G. M., Koch, R., Brumm, V., Blakely, E., Suter, R., & Jurecki, E. (2010). Suboptimal outcomes in patients with PKU treated early with diet alone: Revisiting the evidence. *Molecular Genetics & Metabolism, 101*(2–3), 99–109. doi:10.1016/j.ymgme.2010.05.017

Ethics Committee of the American Society for Reproductive Medicine. (2001). Preconception gender selection for nonmedical reasons. *Fertility and Sterility, 75*(3), 861–864.

Everman, D. B., & Cassidy, S. B. (2000). Genetics of childhood disorders: VII. Genomic imprinting: Breaking the rules. *Journal of the American Academy of Child & Adolescent Psychiatry, 39,* 386–389.

Fan, H. C., Gu, W., Wang, J., Blumenfeld, Y. J., El-Sayed, Y. Y., & Quake, S. R. (2012). Non-invasive prenatal measurement of the fetal genome. *Nature, 487*(7407), 320–324. doi:10.1038/nature11251

Fergusson, D. M., Boden, J. M., Horwood, L. J., Miller, A. L., & Kennedy, M. A. (2011). MAOA, abuse exposure and antisocial behaviour: 30-year longitudinal study. *The British Journal of Psychiatry: The Journal of Mental Science, 198*(6), 457–463. doi:10.1192/bjp.bp.110.086991

Flatt, T. (2005). The evolutionary genetics of canalization. *Quarterly Review of Biology, 80*(3), 287–316.

Fletcher, G. E., Zach, T., Pramanik, A. K., & Ford, S. P. (2012). *Multiple births.* Retrieved from http://emedicine.medscape.com/article/977234-overview#a0199

Fowler, J. H., & Schreiber, D. (2008). Biology, politics, and the emerging science of human nature. *Science, 322*(5903), 912–914.

Fox, K. A., & Saade, G. (2012). Fetal blood sampling and intrauterine transfusion. *NeoReviews, 13*(11), e661–e669. doi:10.1542/neo.13-11-e661

Furman, B., & Appelman, Z. (2005). Genetic diagnosis in multiple pregnancies: Amniocentesis versus chorionic villus sampling. *Ultrasound Review of Obstetrics & Gynecology, 5*(1), 69–74.

Gottlieb, G. (2000). Environmental and behavioral influences on gene activity. *Current Directions in Psychological Science, 9*(3), 93–97.

Gottlieb, G. (2003). On making behavioral genetics truly developmental. *Human Development, 46,* 337–355.

Gottlieb, G. (2007). Probabilistic epigenesis. *Developmental Science, 10*(1), 1–11.

Groth, K. A., Skakkebæk, A., Høst, C., Gravholt, C. H., & Bojesen, A. (2013). Klinefelter syndrome—A clinical update. *The Journal of Clinical*

Endocrinology and Metabolism, 98(1), 20–30. doi:10.1210/jc.2012-2382

Hagerman, R. J. (2011). Fragile X syndrome and Fragile X-associated disorders. In *Handbook of neurodevelopmental and genetic disorders in children* (2nd ed., pp. 261–275). New York: Guilford Press.

Hazlett, H. C., Hammer, J., Hooper, S. R., & Kamphaus, R. W. (2011). Down syndrome. In S. Goldstein & C. R. Reynolds (Eds.), *Handbook of neurodevelopmental and genetic disorders in children* (2nd ed., pp. 362–381). New York: Guilford Press.

Hoekstra, C., Zhao, Z. Z., Lambalk, C. B., Willemsen, G., Martin, N. G., Boomsma, D. I., & Montgomery, G. W. (2008). Dizygotic twinning. *Human Reproduction Update, 14*(1), 37–47. doi:10.1093/humupd/dmm036

Human Fertilization and Embryology Authority. (2003). *Sex selection: Options for regulation.* London: Author.

Improda, N., Rezzuto, M., Alfano, S., Parenti, G., Vajro, P., Pignata, C., & Salerno, M. (2012). Precocious puberty in Turner syndrome: Report of a case and review of the literature. *Italian Journal Of Pediatrics, 38,* 54. doi:10.1186/1824-7288-38-54

Jarrold, C., Nadel, L., & Vicari, S. (2009). Memory and neuropsychology in Down syndrome. *Down Syndrome: Research & Practice, 12*(3), 196–201.

Juul, A., Aksglaede, L., Bay, K., Grigor, K. M., & Skakkebæk, N. E. (2011). Klinefelter syndrome: The forgotten syndrome. *Acta Paediatrica, 100*(6) 791–792. doi:10.1111/j.1651-2227.2011.02283.x

Kim-Cohen, J., Caspi, A., Taylor, A., Williams, B., Newcombe, R., Craig, I. W., & Moffitt, T. E. (2006). MAOA, maltreatment, and gene-environment interaction predicting children's mental health: New evidence and a meta-analysis. *Molecular Psychiatry, 11*(10), 903–913. doi:10.1038/sj.mp.4001851

Knickmeyer, R. C., & Davenport, M. (2011). Turner syndrome and sexual differentiation of the brain: Implications for understanding male-biased neurodevelopmental disorders. *Journal of Neurodevelopmental Disorders, 3*(4), 293–306. doi:10.1007/s11689-011-9089-0

Knopman, J. M., Krey, L. C., Oh, C., Lee, J., McCaffrey, C., & Noyes, N. (2014). What makes them split? Identifying risk factors that lead to monozygotic twins after in vitro fertilization. *Fertility and Sterility, 102*(1), 82–89. doi:10.1016/j.fertnstert.2014.03.039

Koch, R., Guttler, F., & Blau, N. (2002). Mental illness in mild PKU responds to biopterin. *Molecular Genetics & Metabolism, 75*(3), 284–286.

Koenen, K. C., Amstadter, A. B., & Nugent, N. (2012). Genetic methods in psychology. In H. Cooper, P. M. Camic, D. L. Long, A. T. Panter, D. Rindskopf & K. J. Sher (Eds.), *APA handbook of research methods in psychology. Volume 2: Research designs: Quantitative, qualitative, neuropsychological, and biological* (pp. 663–680). Washington, DC: American Psychological Association. doi:10.1037/13620-000

Lessov-Schlaggar, C. N., Agrawal, A., & Swan, G. E. (2013). Behavior genetics. In J. A. Schinka, W. F. Velicer, & I. B. Weiner (Eds.), *Handbook of psychology: Vol. 2. Research methods in psychology* (2nd ed., pp. 342–365). Hoboken, NJ: John Wiley.

Lewis, P. D. (2006). Novel human pathological mutations. *Human Genetics, 119*(3), 359–364.

Lickliter, R., & Honeycutt, H. (2013). A developmental evolutionary framework for psychology. *Review of General Psychology, 17*(2). doi:10.1037/a0032932

Maakaron, J. E., Taher, A., & Ulrich Josef Woermann, M. D. (2012). *Sickle cell anemia.* Retrieved from http://emedicine.medscape.com/article/205926-overview#a0156

Martin, J. A., Hamilton, B. E., & Osterman, M. J. K. (2012). Three decades of twin births in the United States, 1980–2009. *NCHS Data Brief, 80.* Retrieved from http://www.cdc.gov/nchs/data/databriefs/db80.pdf

Maxson, S. C. (2013). Behavioral genetics. In R. J. Nelson, S. J. Y. Mizumori, & I. B. Weiner (Eds.), *Handbook of psychology: Vol. 3. Behavioral neuroscience* (2nd ed., pp. 1–25). Hoboken, NJ: John Wiley.

McKusick, V. A. (1998). *Mendelian inheritance in man: A catalog of human genes and genetic disorders* (12th ed.). Baltimore: Johns Hopkins University Press.

McKusick, V. A. (2007). Mendelian inheritance in man and its online version, OMIM. *American Journal of Human Genetics, 80*(4), 588–604. doi:10.1086/514346

McKusick-Nathans Institute of Genetic Medicine. (2014). *OMIM: Online Mendelian Inheritance in Man.* Washington, DC: Author. Retrieved from http://www.omim.org/about

Miller, L., Tseng, B., Tirella, L., Chan, W., & Feig, E. (2008). Health of children adopted from Ethiopia. *Maternal & Child Health Journal, 12*(5), 599–605. doi:10.1007/s10995-007-0274-4

Moore, K. L., & Persaud, T. V. N. (2013). *Before we are born: Essentials of embryology and birth defects* (8th ed.). Philadelphia: Saunders.

National Center for Biotechnology Information. (2004). *What is a genome?* Bethesda, MD: Author. Retrieved from http://www.ncbi.nlm.nih.gov/About/primer/genetics_genome.html

National Coalition for Health Professional Education in Genetics. (2012). *Non-invasive prenatal testing (NIPT) factsheet.* Lutherville, MD: Author. Retrieved from http://www.acog.org/Resources_And_Publications/Committee_Opinions/Committee_on_Genetics/Noninvasive_Prenatal_Testing_for_Fetal_Aneuploidy

National Library of Medicine. (2013). *Home reference handbook—Help me understand genetics.* Bethesda, MA: Author. Retrieved from http://ghr.nlm.nih.gov/handbook

Nilsson, E. E., & Skinner, M. K. (2014). Environmentally induced epigenetic transgenerational inheritance of disease susceptibility. *Translational Research: The Journal of Laboratory and Clinical Medicine.* doi:10.1016/j.trsl.2014.02.003

Otter, M., Schrander-Stumpel, C. T. R. M., & Curfs, L. M. G. (2009). Triple X syndrome: A review of the literature. *European Journal of Human Genetics, 18*(3), 265–271. doi:10.1038/ejhg.2009.109

Papp, Z., & Fekete, T. (2003). The evolving role of ultrasound in obstetrics/gynecology practice. *International Journal of Gynecology & Obstetrics, 82*(3), 339–347.

Parker, S. E., Mai, C. T., Canfield, M. A., Rickard, R., Wang, Y., Meyer, R. E., . . . Correa, A. (2010). Updated national birth prevalence estimates for selected birth defects in the United States, 2004–2006. *Birth Defects Research. Part A, Clinical and Molecular Teratology, 88*(12), 1008–1016. doi:10.1002/bdra.20735

Patel, J., Landers, K., Li, H., Mortimer, R. H., & Richard, K. (2011). Delivery of maternal thyroid hormones to the fetus. *Trends in Endocrinology & Metabolism, 22*(5), 164–170. doi:10.1016/j.tem.2011.02.002

Pemment, J. (2013). The neurobiology of antisocial personality disorder: The quest for rehabilitation and treatment. *Aggression & Violent Behavior, 18*(1), 79–82. doi:10.1016/j.avb.2012.10.004

Pennisi, E. (2009). No genome left behind. *Science, 326,* 794–795.

Plomin, R., & Asbury, K. (2001). Nature and nurture in the family. *Marriage & Family Review, 33*(2–3), 273–283.

Plomin, R., & Daniels, D. (2011). Why are children in the same family so different from one another?*. *International Journal of Epidemiology, 40*(3), 563–582.

Plomin, R., DeFries, J. C., & McClearn, G. E. (1990). *Behavioral genetics: A primer* (2nd ed.). New York: Freeman.

Plomin, R., DeFries, J. C., McClearn, G. E., & McGuffin, P. R. (2001). *Behavioral genetics* (4th ed.). New York: Worth.

Plomin, R., & Spinath, F. M. (2004). Intelligence: Genetics, genes, and genomics. *Journal of Personality and Social Psychology, 86*(1), 112–129. doi:10.1037/0022-3514.86.1.112

Powell, M. P., & Schulte, T. (2011). Turner syndrome. In S. Goldstein & C. R. Reynolds (Eds.), *Handbook of neurodevelopmental and genetic disorders in children* (2nd ed., pp. 261–275). New York: Guilford Press.

Ram, G., & Chinen, J. (2011). Infections and immunodeficiency in Down syndrome. *Clinical and Experimental Immunology, 164*(1), 9–16. doi:10.1111/j.1365-2249.2011.04335.x

Rimoin, D. L., Connor, J. M., & Pyeritz, R. E. (1997). Nature and frequency of genetic disease. In D. L. Rimoin, J. M. Connor, & R. E. Pyeritz (Eds.), *Emery and Rimoin's principles and practices of medical genetics: Vol. 1* (3rd ed., pp. 31–34). New York: Churchill Livingstone.

Robertson, J. A., & Hickman, T. (2013). Should PGD be used for elective gender selection? *Contemporary OB/GYN*. Retrieved from http://contemporaryobgyn.modernmedicine.com/contemporary-obgyn/news/should-pgd-be-used-elective-gender-selection

Ross, J. L., Zeger, M. P. D., Kushner, H., Zinn, A. R., & Roeltgen, D. P. (2009). An extra X or Y chromosome: Contrasting the cognitive and motor phenotypes in childhood in boys with 47,XYY syndrome or 47,XXY Klinefelter syndrome. *Developmental Disabilities Research Reviews, 15*(4), 309–317. doi:10.1002/ddrr.85

Rushton, J. P., & Bons, T. A. (2005). Mate choice and friendship in twins: Evidence for genetic similarity. *Psychological Science, 16*(7), 555–559. doi:10.1111/j.0956-7976.2005.01574.x

Rutter, M. (2012). Gene-environment interdependence. *European Journal of Development Psychology, 9*(4), 391–412.

Sadler, T. L. (2012). *Langman's medical embryology* (12th ed.). New York: Lippincott Williams & Wilkins.

Scarr, S. (1992). Developmental theories for the 1990s: Development and individual differences. *Child Development, 63*(1), 1–19. doi:10.1111/1467-8624.ep9203091721

Scarr, S., & McCartney, K. (1983). How people make their own environments: A theory of genotype environment effects. *Child Development, 54*(2), 424. doi:10.1111/1467-8624.ep8877295

Shahbazian, N., Barati, M., Arian, P., & Saadati, N. (2012). Comparison of complications of chorionic villus sampling and amniocentesis. *International Journal of Fertility & Sterility, 5*(4), 241–244.

Smith, I., & Knowles, J. (2000). Behaviour in early treated phenylketonuria: A systematic review. *European Journal of Pediatrics, 159*(14), S89–S93.

Soubry, A., Hoyo, C., Jirtle, R. L., & Murphy, S. K. (2014). A paternal environmental legacy: Evidence for epigenetic inheritance through the male germ line. *BioEssays: News and Reviews in Molecular, Cellular and Developmental Biology, 36*(4), 359–371. doi:10.1002/bies.201300113

Stancliffe, R. J., Lakin, K. C., Larson, S. A., Engler, J., Taub, S., Fortune, J., & Bershadsky, J. (2012). Demographic characteristics, health conditions, and residential service use in adults with Down syndrome in 25 U.S. states. *Intellectual & Developmental Disabilities, 50*, 92–108. doi:10.1352/1934-9556-50.2.92

Stephenson, J. (2005). Fetal ultrasound safety. *Journal of the American Medical Association, 293*(3), 286.

Steves, C. J., Spector, T. D., & Jackson, S. H. D. (2012). Ageing, genes, environment and epigenetics: What twin studies tell us now, and in the future. *Age & Ageing, 41*(5), 581–586.

Tabor, A., & Alfirevic, Z. (2010). Update on procedure-related risks for prenatal diagnosis techniques. *Fetal Diagnosis & Therapy, 27*(1), 1–7. doi:10.1159/000271995

Tabor, H. K., Murray, J. C., Gammill, H. S., Kitzman, J. O., Snyder, M. W., Ventura, M., . . . Shendure, J. (2012). Non-invasive fetal genome sequencing: Opportunities and challenges. *American Journal of Medical Genetics. Part A, 158A*(10), 2382–2384. doi:10.1002/ajmg.a.35545

Torr, J., Strydom, A., Patti, P., & Jokinen, N. (2010). Down syndrome: Morbidity and mortality. *Journal of Policy & Practice in Intellectual Disabilities, 7*, 70–81. doi:10.1111

Uhlmann, W. R., Schuette, J. L., & Yashar, B. (2009). *A guide to genetic counseling* (2nd ed.). Hoboken, NJ: Wiley-Blackwell.

Ulrich, D. A., Lloyd, M. C., Tiernan, C. W., Looper, J. E., & Angulo-Barroso, R. M. (2008). Effects of intensity of treadmill training on developmental outcomes and stepping in infants with Down syndrome: A randomized trial. *Physical Therapy, 88*(1), 114–122.

Vanhees, K., Vonhögen, I. G. C., van Schooten, F. J., & Godschalk, R. W. L. (2014). You are what you eat, and so are your children: The impact of micronutrients on the epigenetic programming of offspring. *Cellular and Molecular Life Sciences, 71*(2), 271–285. doi:10.1007/s00018-013-1427-9

Waddington, C. H. (1971). Concepts of development. In E. Tobach, L. R. Aronson, & E. Shaw (Eds.), *The biopsychology of development* (pp. 17–23). San Diego: Academic Press.

Waterland, R. A., & Jirtle, R. L. (2003). Transposable elements: Targets for early nutritional effects on epigenetic gene regulation. *Molecular and Cellular Biology, 23*(15), 5293–5300. Retrieved from http://www.pubmedcentral.nih.gov/articlerender.fcgi?artid=165709&tool=pmcentrez&rendertype=abstract

Watson, G. (2008). *Genetics and health*. Washington, DC: Genetics and Public Policy Center. Retrieved from http://www.dnapolicy.org/science.gh.php

Widaman, K. F. (2009). Phenylketonuria in children and mothers: Genes, environments, behavior. *Current Directions in Psychological Science, 18*(1), 48–52. doi:10.1111/j.1467-8721.2009.01604.x

Wielgos, M., & Wegrzyn, P. (2011). Ultrasound-guided invasive procedures in genetic prenatal diagnostics. *Donald School Journal of Ultrasound in Obstetrics & Gynecology, 5*(2/3).

Williams, T. N. (2006). Human red blood cell polymorphisms and malaria. *Current Opinion in Microbiology, 9*(4), 388–394.

Wilson, S. L. (2003). Post-institutionalization: The effects of early deprivation on development of Romanian adoptees. *Child & Adolescent Social Work Journal, 20*(6), 473–483.

Yoon-Mi, H. (2009). Genetic and environmental contributions to childhood temperament in South Korean twins. *Twin Research & Human Genetics, 12*(6), 549–554. doi:10.1375/twin.12.6.549

Zelazo, N. A., Zelazo, P. R., Cohen, K. M., & Zelazo, P. D. (1993). Specificity of practice effects on elementary neuromotor patterns. *Developmental Psychology, 29*, 686–691.

CHAPTER 3

Accornero, V. H., Anthony, J. C., Morrow, C. E., Xue, L., Mansoor, E., Johnson, A. L., . . . Bandstra, E. S. (2011). Estimated effect of prenatal cocaine exposure on examiner-rated behavior at age 7 years. *Neurotoxicology and Teratology, 33*(3), 370–378. doi:10.1016/j.ntt.2011.02.014

Ackerman, J. P., Riggins, T., & Black, M. M. (2010). A review of the effects of prenatal cocaine exposure among school-aged children. *Pediatrics, 125*(3), 554–565. doi:10.1542/peds.2009-0637

Agustines, L. A., Lin, Y. G., Rumney, P. J., Lu, M. C., Bonebrake, R., Asrat, T., & Nageotte, M. (2000). Outcomes of extremely low-birth-weight infants between 500 and 750 g. *American Journal of Obstetrics and Gynecology, 182*, 1114–1116.

Alati, R., Davey Smith, G., Lewis, S. J., Sayal, K., Draper, E. S., Golding, J., . . . Gray, R. (2013). Effect of prenatal alcohol exposure on childhood academic outcomes: Contrasting maternal and paternal associations in the ALSPAC study. *PloS One, 8*(10), e74844. doi:10.1371/journal.pone.0074844

Alexander, G. R., & Slay, M. (2002). Prematurity at birth: Trends, racial disparities, and epidemiology. *Mental Retardation and Developmental Disabilities, 8*, 215–220.

American College of Obstetricians and Gynecologists (2010). ACOG Committee Opinion No. 462: Moderate caffeine consumption during pregnancy. *Obstetrics and Gynecology, 116*(2 Pt. 1), 467–468. doi:10.1097/AOG.0b013e3181eeb2a1

American College of Obstetricians and Gynecologists. (2011). *Substance abuse reporting and pregnancy: The role of the obstetrician–gynecologist*. Washington, DC: Author. Retrieved from http://www.acog.org/~/media/Committee Opinions/Committee on Health Care for Underserved Women/co473.pdf?dmc=1&ts=20140604T1051541013

American Medical Association. (2014). Pregnant women's rights. Retrieved April 6, 2014, from http://www.ama-assn.org/ama/pub/physician-resources/legal-topics/litigation-center/case-summaries-topic/pregnant-womens-rights.page

Apgar, V. (1953). A proposal for a new method of evaluation in the newborn infant. *Current Research in Anesthesia and Analgesia, 32*, 260–267.

Arcangeli, T., Thilaganathan, B., Hooper, R., Khan, K. S., & Bhide, A. (2012). Neurodevelopmental delay in small babies at term: A systematic review. *Ultrasound in Obstetrics & Gynecology, 40*(3), 267–275. doi:10.1002/uog.11112

Arditi-Babchuk, H., Feldman, R., & Eidelman, A. I. (2009). Rapid eye movement (REM) in premature neonates and developmental outcome at 6 months. *Infant Behavior & Development, 32*(1), 27–32. doi:10.1016/j.infbeh.2008.09.001

Arria, A. M., Derauf, C., LaGasse, L. L., Grant, P, Shah, R., Smith, L., . . . Lester, B. (2006). Methamphetamine and other substance use during pregnancy: Preliminary estimates from the infant development, environment, and lifestyle (IDEAL) study. *Maternal & Child Health Journal, 10*(3), 293–302.

Asanbe, C. B., & Lockert, E. (2006). Cognitive abilities of African American children with prenatal cocaine/polydrug exposure. *Journal of Health Care for the Poor and Underserved, 17*(2), 400–412.

Aylwrad, G. P. (2005). Neurodevelopmental outcomes of infants born prematurely. *Developmental & Behavioral Pediatrics, 26*(6), 427–440.

Bainbridge, D. (2003). *Making babies: The science of pregnancy*. Cambridge, MA: Harvard University Press.

Bandstra, E. S., Morrow, C. E., Mansoor, E., & Accornero, V. H. (2010). Prenatal drug exposure: Infant and toddler outcomes. *Journal of Addictive Diseases, 29*(2), 245–258. doi:10.1080/10550881003684871

Barnes, A. B., Colton, T., Gundersen, J., Noller, K. L., Tilley, B. C., Strama, T., . . . O'Brien, P. C. (1980). Fertility and outcome of pregnancy in women exposed in utero to diethylstilbestrol. *New England Journal of Medicine*, 302(11), 609–613. doi:10.1056/NEJM198003133021105

Barnes, M. A., Wilkinson, M., Khemani, E., Boudesquie, A., Dennis, M., & Fletcher, J. M. (2006). Arithmetic processing in children with spina bifida: Calculation accuracy, strategy use, and fact retrieval fluency. *Journal of Learning Disabilities*, 39(2), 174–187.

Barr, H. M., Streissguth, A. P., Darby, B. L., & Sampson, P. D. (1990). Prenatal exposure to alcohol, caffeine, tobacco, and aspirin: Effects on fine and gross motor performance in 4-year-old children. *Developmental Psychology*, 26, 339–348.

Bazzano, A. N., Kirkwood, B., Tawiah-Agyemang, C., Owusu-Agyei, S., & Adongo, P. (2008). Social costs of skilled attendance at birth in rural Ghana. *International Journal of Gynecology & Obstetrics*, 102(1), 91–94. doi:10.1016/j.ijgo.2008.02.004

Beckman, M. (2003). Sperm like it hot. *Science Now*, 5–7.

Behnke, M., & Smith, V. C. (2013). Prenatal substance abuse: Short- and long-term effects on the exposed fetus. *Pediatrics*, 131(3), e1009–e1024. doi:10.1542/peds.2012-3931

Benasich, A. A., & Brooks-Gunn, J. (1996). Maternal attitudes and knowledge of child-rearing: Associations with family and child outcomes. *Child Development*, 67, 1186–1205.

Bendersky, M., & Lewis, M. (1999). Prenatal cocaine exposure and neonatal condition. *Infant Behavior and Development*, 22, 353–366.

Berger, L. M., & Waldfogel, J. (2000). Prenatal cocaine exposure: Long-run effects and policy implications. *Social Service Review*, 74(1), 28–54.

Black, R. A., & Hill, D. A. (2003). Over-the-counter medications in pregnancy. *American Family Physician*, 67(12), 2517–2524. Retrieved from http://www.ncbi.nlm.nih.gov/pubmed/12825840

Blanchette, N., Smith, M., Fernandes-Penney, A., King, S., & Read, S. (2001). Cognitive and motor development in children with vertically transmitted HIV infection. *Brain and Cognition*, 46(1–2), 50–53.

Bornstein, B. H. (2003). Pregnancy, drug testing, and the fourth amendment: Legal and behavioral implications. *Journal of Family Psychology*, 17(2), 220–228.

Brazelton, T. B. (1977). Implications of infant development among the Mayan Indians of Mexico. In P. H. Liederman, S. R. Tulikn, & A. Rosenfeld (Eds.), *Culture and infancy* (pp. 336–352). New York: Academic Press.

Britt, G. C., & Myers, B. J. (1994). The effects of Brazelton intervention: A review. *Infant Mental Health Journal*, 15(3), 278–292.

Brockington, I. (1996). *Motherhood and mental health*. Oxford, UK: Oxford University Press.

Brooks-Gunn, J., Klebanov, P. K., Liaw, F., & Spiker, D. (1993). Enhancing the development of low-birthweight, premature infants: Changes in cognition and behavior over the first three years. *Child Development*, 64, 736–754.

Brown, K. J., Kilbride, H. W., Turnbull, W., & Lemanek, K. (2003). Functional outcome at adolescence for infants less than 801 g birth weight: Perceptions of children and parents. *Journal of Perinatology*, 23(1), 41–47.

Burlew, A. K., Johnson, C., Smith, S., Sanders, A., Hall, R., Lampkin, B., & Schwaderer, M. (2012). Parenting and problem behaviors in children of substance abusing parents. *Child and Adolescent Mental Health*, 18(4). doi:10.1111/camh.12001

Butz, A. M., Pulsifer, M., Marano, N., Belcher, H., Lears, M. K., & Royall, R. (2001). Effectiveness of a home intervention for perceived child behavioral problems and parenting stress in children with in utero drug exposure. *Archives of Pediatrics and Adolescent Medicine*, 155, 1029–1037.

Cabbage, L. A., & Neal, J. L. (2011). Over-the-counter medications and pregnancy: An integrative review. *The Nurse Practitioner*, 36(6), 22–28. doi:10.1097/01.NPR.0000397910.59950.71

Centers for Disease Control and Prevention. (2004). Spina bifida and anencephaly before and after folic acid mandate—United States, 1995–1996 and 1999-2000. *JAMA*, 292(3), 325–327.

Centers for Disease Control and Prevention. (2014). *Birth defects: Data and statistics*. Retrieved from http://www.cdc.gov/ncbddd/birthdefects/data.html

Ch, R. (2004). Die Prävention der vertikalen HIV-Ubertragung—Eine Erfolgsgeschichte. *Therapeutische Umschau. Revue Thérapeutique*, 61, 599–602.

Chan, K., Ohlsson, A., Synnes, A., Lee, D. S. C., Chien, L.-Y., Lee, S. K., & the Canadian Neonatal Network. (2000). Survival, morbidity, and resource use of infants of 25 weeks' gestational age or less. *American Journal of Obstetrics and Gynecology*, 185, 220–226.

Chande, M. (2001). US Supreme Court overturns drug test policy for pregnant drug abusers. *Lancet*, 357(9261), 1025.

Charpak, N., Gabriel Ruiz, J., Zupan, J., Cattaneo, A., Figueroa, Z., Tessier, R., . . . Worku, B. (2005). Kangaroo Mother Care: 25 years after. *Acta Paediatrica*, 94(5), 514–522. doi:10.1111/j.1651-2227.2005.tb01930.x

Chen, J.-H. (2012). Maternal alcohol use during pregnancy, birth weight and early behavioral outcomes. *Alcohol & Alcoholism*, 47(6).

Chmurzynska, A. (2010). Fetal programming: Link between early nutrition, DNA methylation, and complex diseases. *Nutrition Reviews*, 68(2), 87–98. doi:10.1111/j.1753-4887.2009.00265.x

Chokshi, N. (2014, May 1). Criminalizing harmful substance abuse during pregnancy: Is there a problem with that? *Washington Post*. Retrieved from http://www.washingtonpost.com/blogs/govbeat/wp/2014/05/01/criminalizing-harmful-substance-abuse-during-pregnancy-is-there-a-problem-with-that

Christian, L. M. (2015). Stress and immune function during pregnancy: An emerging focus in mind-body medicine. *Current Directions in Psychological Science*, 24(1), 3–9. doi:10.1177/0963721414550704

Cochran v. Commonwealth of Kentucky. (2010). Retrieved from http://opinions.kycourts.net/sc/2008-SC-000095-DG.pdf

Coles, C. D., Goldstein, F. C., Lynch, M. E., Chen, X., Kable, J. A., Johnson, K. C., & Hu, X. (2011). Memory and brain volume in adults prenatally exposed to alcohol. *Brain & Cognition*, 75(1), 67–77. doi:10.1016/j.bandc.2010.08.013

Collins, T. F. X. (2006). History and evolution of reproductive and developmental toxicology guidelines. *Current Pharmaceutical Design*, 12(12), 1449–1465.

Conner, J. M., & Nelson, E. C. (1999). Neonatal intensive care: Satisfaction measured from a parent's perspective. *Pediatrics*, 103, 336–349.

Cordero, A., Mulinare, J., Berry, R. J., Boyle, C., Dietz, W., Johnston R., Jr. . . . Popovic, T. (2010). CDC Grand Rounds: Additional opportunities to prevent neural tube defects with folic acid fortification. *Morbidity & Mortality Weekly Report*, 59(31), 980–984.

Coussons-Reid, M., Okun, M., & Simms, S. (2003). The psychoneuroimmunology of pregnancy. *Journal of Reproductive & Infant Psychology*, 21(2), 103–112.

Coyle, J. T. (2013). Brain structural alterations induced by fetal exposure to cocaine persist into adolescence and affect behavior. *JAMA Psychiatry*, 70(10), 1113–1114. doi:10.1001/jamapsychiatry.2013.1949

Cuckle, H. S., Wald, N. J., & Thompson, S. G. Estimating a woman's risk of having a pregnancy associated with Down's syndrome using her age and serum alpha-fetoprotein level. *British Journal of Obstetrics and Gynaecology*, 94, 387–402

Curtis, G. B., & Schuler, J. (2004). *Your pregnancy: Week by week*. Cambridge, MA: De Capo Press.

Daniels, P., Noe, G. F., & Mayberry, R. (2006). Barriers to prenatal care among black women of low socioeconomic status. *American Journal of Health Behavior*, 30(2), 188–198.

Davis, E. P., Glynn, L. M., Waffarn, F., & Sandman, C. A. (2011). Prenatal maternal stress programs infant stress regulation. *Journal of Child Psychology and Psychiatry, and Allied Disciplines*, 52(2), 119–129. doi:10.1111/j.1469-7610.2010.02314.x

Day, N., Leech, S., Richardson, G., Cornelius, M., Robles, N., & Larkby, C. (2002). Prenatal alcohol exposure predicts continued deficits in offspring size at 14 years of age. *Alcoholism: Clinical and Experimental Research*, 26, 1584–1591.

Day, N., & Richardson, G. (2004). An analysis of the effects of prenatal alcohol exposure on growth: A teratologic model. *American Journal of Medical Genetics Part C: Seminars in Medical Genetics*, 127(1), 28–34.

Dennis, M., Landry, S. H., Barnes, M., & Fletcher, J. M. (2006). A model of neurocognitive function in spina bifida over the life span. *Journal of the International Neuropsychological Society*, 12(2), 285–296.

Diener, M. (2000). Gift from the Gods: A Balinese guide to early child rearing. In J. DeLoache & A. Gottlieb (Eds.), *A world of babies: Imagined childcare guides for seven societies*. Cambridge, UK: Cambridge University Press.

DiPietro, J. A., Hodgson, D. M., Costigan, K. A., & Hilton, S. C. (1996). Fetal neurobehavioral development. *Child Development*, 67, 2553–2567.

Durik, A., Hyde, J., & Clark, R. (2000). Sequelae of cesarean and vaginal deliveries: Psychosocial outcomes for mothers and infants. *Developmental Psychology*, 36, 251–260.

Dye, F. J. (2000). *Human life before birth*. Amsterdam: Harwood.

Ebrahim, S. H., & Gfroerer, J. (2003). Pregnancy-related substance use in the United States during 1996–1998. *Obstetrics & Gynecology*, 101(2), 374–379.

Eckerman, C. O., Hsu, H. C., Molitor, A., Leung, E. H. L., & Goldstein, R. F. (1999). Infant arousal as an en-face exchange with a new partner: Effects of prematurity and perinatal biological risk. *Developmental Psychology*, 35, 282–293.

Elgen, I., Sommerfelt, K., & Ellertsen, B. (2003). Cognitive performance in a low birth weight cohort at 5 and 11 years of age. *Pediatric Neurology*, 29(2), 111–116.

Elkarmi, A., Abu-Samak, M., & Al-Qaisi, K. (2007). Modeling the effects of prenatal exposure to aspirin on the postnatal development of rat brain. *Growth, Development, and Aging*, 70(1), 13–24. Retrieved from http://www.ncbi.nlm.nih.gov/pubmed/18038927

Feldman, P. J., Dunkel-Schetter, C., Sandman, C. A., & Wadhwa, P. D. (2000). Maternal social support predicts birth weight and fetal growth in human pregnancy. *Psychosomatic Medicine*, 62, 715–725.

Field, T. (2011). Prenatal depression effects on early development: A review. *Infant Behavior & Development*, 34(1), 1–14. doi:10.1016/j.infbeh.2010.09.008

Flavin, J., & Paltrow, L. M. (2010). Punishing pregnant drug-using women: Defying law, medicine, and common sense. *Journal of Addictive Diseases*, 29(2), 231–244. doi:10.1080/10550881003684830

Fogel, A. (2007). *Infancy: Infant, family, and society* (7th ed.). Cornwall-on-Hudson, NY: Sloan Educational Publishing.

Food and Agriculture Organization of the United Nations. (2009). *Summary of world food and agricultural statistics*. Rome, Italy: Author.

Forraz, N., & McGuckin, C. P. (2011). The umbilical cord: A rich and ethical stem cell source to advance regenerative medicine. *Cell Proliferation*, 44(Suppl. 1), 60–69. doi:10.1111/j.1365-2184.2010.00729.x

Fortney, S. (2003). A jurisprudential analysis of government intervention and prenatal drug abuse. *Journal of Law and Health*, 17(1), 11–35.

Fracasso, M. P., & Busch-Rossnagel, N. A. (1992). Children and parents of Hispanic origin. In M. E. P. & C. B. Fisher (Eds.), *Families: A handbook for school professionals* (pp. 83–98). New York: Teachers College Press.

Frank, D. A., Augustyn, M., Knight, W. G., Pell, T., & Zuckerman, B. (2001). Growth, development, and behavior in early childhood following prenatal cocaine exposure: A systematic review. *Journal of the American Medical Association*, 285, 1613–1625.

Fried, P. A., & Watkinson, B. (2000). Visuoperceptual functioning differs in 9- to 12-year olds prenatally exposed to cigarettes and marijuana. *Neurotoxicology and Teratology*, 22, 11–20.

Fried, P. A., & Watkinson, B. (2001). Differential effects on facets of attention in adolescents prenatally exposed to cigarettes and marijuana. *Neurotoxicology and Teratology*, 23, 421–430.

Gardiner, H. W., & Kosmitzki, C. (2010). *Lives across cultures: Cross-cultural human development* (5th ed.). Boston: Pearson.

Ghosh, J. K. C., Wilhelm, M. H., Dunkel-Schetter, C., Lombardi, C. A., & Ritz, B. R. (2010). Paternal support and preterm birth, and the moderation of effects of chronic stress: A study in Los Angeles County mothers. *Archives of Women's Mental Health*, 13(4), 327–338. doi:10.1007/s00737-009-0135-9

Glover, V. (2011). Annual research review: Prenatal stress and the origins of psychopathology: An evolutionary perspective. *Journal of Child Psychology and Psychiatry*, 52(4), 356–367. doi:10.1111/j.1469-7610.2011.02371.x

Goldschmidt, L., Richardson, G. A., Willford, J. A., Severtson, S. G., & Day, N. L. (2012). School achievement in 14-year-old youths prenatally exposed to marijuana. *Neurotoxicology and Teratology*, 34(1), 161–167. doi:10.1016/j.ntt.2011.08.009

Gomez, G. B., Kamb, M. L., Newman, L. M., Mark, J., Broutet, N., & Hawkes, S. J. (2013). Untreated maternal syphilis and adverse outcomes of pregnancy: A systematic review and meta-analysis. *Bulletin of the World Health Organization*, 91(3), 217–226. doi:10.2471/BLT.12.107623

Gostin, L. O. (2001). The rights of pregnant women: The Supreme Court and drug testing. *The Hastings Center Report*, 31, 8–9.

Goubet, N., Rattaz, C., Pierrat, V., Allémann, E., Bullinger, A., & Lequien, P. (2002). Olfactory familiarization and discrimination in preterm and full-term newborns. *Infancy*, 3(1), 53–75.

Goubet, N., Strasbaugh, K., & Chesney, J. (2007). Familiarity breeds content? Soothing effect of a familiar odor on full-term newborns. *Journal of Developmental & Behavioral Pediatrics*, 28(3), 189–194. doi:10.1097/dbp.0b013e31802d0b8d

Granier-Deferre, C., Ribeiro, A., Jacquet, A.-Y., & Bassereau, S. (2011). Near-term fetuses process temporal features of speech. *Developmental Science*, 14, 336–352. doi:10.1111/j.1467-7687.2010.00978.x

Gray, K. A., Day, N. L., Leech, S., & Richardson, G. A. (2005). Prenatal marijuana exposure: Effect on child depressive symptoms at ten years of age. *Neurotoxicology & Teratology*, 27(3), 439–448.

Gray, R., Indurkhya, A., & McCormick, M. (2004). Prevalence, stability, and predictors of clinically significant behavior problems in low birth weight children at 3, 5, and 8 years of age. *Pediatrics*, 114(3), 736–744.

Grotegut, C. A., Chisholm, C. A., Johnson, L. N. C., Brown, H. L., Heine, R. P., & James, A. H. (2014). Medical and obstetric complications among pregnant women aged 45 and older. *PloS One*, 9(4), e96237. doi:10.1371/journal.pone.0096237

Guttmacher Institute. (2014). *State policies in brief: Substance use during pregnancy*. Washington, DC: Author. Retrieved from http://www.guttmacher.org/statecenter/spibs/spib_SADP.pdf

Hack, M., Schluchter, M., Cartar, L., Rahman, M., Cuttler, L., & Borawski, E. (2003). Growth of very low birth weight infants to age 20 years. *Pediatrics*, 112(1), e30–e38.

Handler, A., Rosenberg, D., Raube, K., & Lyons, S. (2003). Satisfaction and use of prenatal care: Their relationship among African-American women in a large managed care organization. *Birth: Issues in Perinatal Care*, 30(1), 23–30.

Hans, S. L. (2002). Studies of prenatal exposure to drugs: Focusing on parental care of children. *Neurotoxicology & Teratology*, 24(3), 329–337.

Hazlett, H. C., Hammer, J., Hooper, S. R., & Kamphaus, R. W. (2011). Down syndrome. In S. Goldstein & C. R. Reynolds (Eds.), *Handbook of neurodevelopmental and genetic disorders in children* (2nd ed., pp. 362–381). New York: Guilford Press.

Hedley, A. A., Ogden, C. L., Johnson, C. L., Carroll, M. D., Curtin, L. R., & Flegal, K. M. (2004). Prevalence of overweight and obesity among US children, adolescents, and adults, 1999–2002. *JAMA*, 291(23), 2847–2850.

Hepper, P. (2015). Behavior during the prenatal period: Adaptive for development and survival. *Child Development Perspectives*, 9(1), 38–43. doi:10.1111/cdep.12104

Huizink, A., & Mulder, E. J. H. Â. (2006). Maternal smoking, drinking or cannabis use during pregnancy and neurobehavioral and cognitive functioning in human offspring. *Neuroscience & Biobehavioral Reviews*, 30(1), 24–41.

Huizink, A. C. (2013). Prenatal cannabis exposure and infant outcomes: Overview of studies. *Progress in Neuro-Psychopharmacology & Biological Psychiatry*. Advance online publication. doi:10.1016/j.pnpbp.2013.09.014

Hurd, Y., Wang, X., Anderson, V., Beck, O., Minkoff, H., & Dow-Edwards, D. (2005). Marijuana impairs growth in mid-gestation fetuses. *Neurotoxicology and Teratology*, 27(2), 221–229.

Insoo, H. (2010). The bioethics of stem cell research and therapy. *Journal of Clinical Investigation*, 120(1), 71–75. doi:10.1172/jci40435

Jacobson, J. L., & Jacobson, S. W. (1996). Methodological considerations in behavioral toxicology in infants and children. *Developmental Psychology*, 32, 390–403.

James, D. K., Spencer, C. J., & Stepsis, B. W. (2002). Fetal learning: A prospective randomized controlled trial. *Ultrasound in Obstetrics & Gynecology*, 20(5), 431–438.

Jansen, I. (2006). Decision making in childbirth: The influence of traditional structures in a Ghanaian village. *International Nursing Review*, 53(1), 41–46.

Jarosz, M., Wierzejska, R., & Siuba, M. (2012). Maternal caffeine intake and its effect on pregnancy outcomes. *European Journal of Obstetrics, Gynecology, and Reproductive Biology*, 160(2), 156–160. doi:10.1016/j.ejogrb.2011.11.021

Jefferies, A. L. (2012). Kangaroo care for the preterm infant and family. *Paediatrics & Child Health*, 17(3), 141–146. Retrieved from http://www.pubmedcentral.nih.gov/articlerender.fcgi?artid=3287094&tool=pmcentrez&rendertype=abstract

Jirikowic, T., Gelo, J., & Astley, S. (2010). Children and youth with fetal alcohol spectrum disorders: Summary of intervention recommendations after clinical diagnosis. *Enfants et Jeunes Avec Le Syndrome D'alcoolisation Fætale: Résumé Des Recommandations D'intervention Suite Au Diagnostic Clinique*, 48(5), 330–344. doi:10.1352/1934-9556-48.5.330

Johnsen, D. (1992). Shared interests: Promoting healthy births without sacrificing women's liberty. *Hastings Law Journal*, 43, 569–614.

Jones, H. E. (2006). Drug addiction during pregnancy. *Current Directions in Psychological Science*, 15(3), 126–130.

Jones, L., Rowe, J., & Becker, T. (2009). Appraisal, coping, and social support as predictors of psychological distress and parenting efficacy in parents of premature infants. *Children's Health Care*, 38(4), 245–262. doi:10.1080/02739610903235976

Joseph, R. (2000). Fetal brain behavior and cognitive development. *Developmental Review*, 20, 81–98.

Juárez, S. P., & Merlo, J. (2013). Revisiting the effect of maternal smoking during pregnancy on offspring birthweight: A quasi-experimental sibling analysis in Sweden. *PloS One*, 8(4), e61734. doi:10.1371/journal.pone.0061734

Kaiser, L., Allen, L., & American Dietetic Association. (2008). Position of the American Dietetic Association: Nutrition and lifestyle for a healthy pregnancy outcome. *Journal of the American Dietetic Association*, 108(3), 553–561. doi:10.1016/j.jada.2008.01.030

Keegan, J., Parva, M., Finnegan, M., Gerson, A., & Belden, M. (2010). Addiction in pregnancy. *Journal of Addictive Diseases*, 29(2), 175–191. doi:10.1080/10550881003684723

Kenny, L. C., Lavender, T., McNamee, R., O'Neill, S. M., Mills, T., & Khashan, A. S. (2013). Advanced maternal age and adverse pregnancy outcome: Evidence from a large contemporary cohort. *PloS One*, 8(2), e56583. doi:10.1371/journal.pone.0056583

Khalil, A., Syngelaki, A., Maiz, N., Zinevich, Y., & Nicolaides, K. H. (2013). Maternal age and adverse pregnancy outcome: A cohort study. *Ultrasound in Obstetrics & Gynecology*, 42(6), 634–643. doi:10.1002/uog.12494

Kiechl-Kohlendorfer, U., Ralser, E., Pupp Peglow, U., Reiter, G., Griesmaier, E., & Trawöger, R. (2010). Smoking in pregnancy: A risk factor for adverse neurodevelopmental outcome in preterm infants? *Acta Paediatrica*, 99(7), 1016–1019. doi:10.1111/j.1651-2227.2010.01749.x

Kilbride, H., Castor, C., Hoffman, E., & Fuger, K. L. (2000). Thirty-six-month outcome of prenatal cocaine exposure for term or near-term infants: Impact of early case management. *Journal of Developmental and Behavioral Pediatrics*, 21, 19–26.

Kingston, D., Tough, S., & Whitfield, H. (2012). Prenatal and postpartum maternal psychological distress and infant development: A systematic review. *Child Psychiatry and Human Development*, 43(5), 683–714. doi:10.1007/s10578-012-0291-4

Kisilevsky, B. S., & Hains, S. M. (2011). Onset and maturation of fetal heart rate response to the mother's voice over late gestation. *Developmental Science*, 14, 214–223. doi:10.1111/j.1467-7687.2010.00970.x

Kobayashi, T., Good, C., Mamiya, K., Skinner, R., & Garcia-Rill, E. (2004). Development of REM sleep drive and clinical implications. *Journal of Applied Physiology*, 96(2), 735–746.

Krug, P. J., Riffell, J. A., & Zimmer, R. K. (2009). Endogenous signaling pathways and chemical communication between sperm and egg. *The Journal of Experimental Biology, 212*(Pt. 8), 1092–1100.

Lambert, B. L., & Bauer, C. R. (2012). Developmental and behavioral consequences of prenatal cocaine exposure: A review. *Journal of Perinatology, 32*(11), 819–828. doi:10.1038/jp.2012.90

Larsen, W. J. (2001). *Human embryology.* New York: Churchill Livingstone.

Lau, R., & Morse, C. A. (2003). Stress experiences of parents with premature infants in a special care nursery. *Stress and Health, 19,* 69–78.

Laughton, B., Cornell, M., Boivin, M., & Van Rie, A. (2012). Thalidomide and its sequelae. *Lancet, 380*(9844).

Laughton, B., Cornell, M., Boivin, M., & Van Rie, A. (2013). Neurodevelopment in perinatally HIV-infected children: A concern for adolescence. *Journal of the International AIDS Society, 16*(1), 18603. doi:10.7448/IAS.16.1.18603

Lebel, C., Warner, T., Colby, J., Soderberg, L., Roussotte, F., Behnke, M., . . . Sowell, E. R. (2013). White matter microstructure abnormalities and executive function in adolescents with prenatal cocaine exposure. *Psychiatry Research, 213*(2), 161–168. doi:10.1016/j.pscychresns.2013.04.002

Lee, L. J., & Lupo, P. J. (2013). Maternal smoking during pregnancy and the risk of congenital heart defects in offspring: A systematic review and metaanalysis. *Pediatric Cardiology, 34*(2), 398–407. doi:10.1007/s00246-012-0470-x

Lester, B. M., & Tronick, E. Z. (2004). History and description of the neonatal intensive care unit network neurobehavioral scale. *Pediatrics, 113*(3), 634–640. Retrieved from http://pediatrics.aappublications.org/cgi/content/full/113/3/S1/634

Levine, L. E., & Munsch, J. (2010). *Child development: An active learning approach.* Thousand Oaks, CA: Sage.

Lewis, B. A., Minnes, S., Short, E. J., Min, M. O., Wu, M., Lang, A., . . . Singer, L. T. (2013). Language outcomes at 12 years for children exposed prenatally to cocaine. *Journal of Speech, Language, and Hearing Research, 56*(5), 1662–1676. doi:10.1044/1092-4388(2013/12-0119)

Lewis, B. A., Minnes, S., Short, E. J., Weishampel, P., Satayathum, S., Min, M. O., . . . Singer, L. T. (2011). The effects of prenatal cocaine on language development at 10 years of age. *Neurotoxicology and Teratology, 33*(1), 17–24. doi:10.1016/j.ntt.2010.06.006

Li, D., Liu, L., & Odouli, R. (2003). Exposure to non-steroidal anti-inflammatory drugs during pregnancy and risk of miscarriage: Population based cohort study. *British Medical Journal, 327,* 368–371.

Liaw, F., & Brooks-Gunn, J. (1993). Patterns of low-birth-weight children's cognitive development. *Developmental Psychology, 29,* 1024–1035.

Logan, E. (1999). The wrong race, committing crime, doing drugs, and maladjusted for motherhood: The nation's fury over "crack babies." *Social Justice, 26,* 115 et seq.

Lu, M. C., & Halfon, N. (2003). Racial and ethnic disparities in birth outcomes: A life-course perspective. *Maternal and Child Health Journal, 7*(1), 13–30.

Lu, S. (2005). What's wrong with just one drink? *Prevention, 57*(1), 121–122.

Ma, Z., Qin, Y., Wang, G., Li, X., He, R., Chuai, M., . . . Yang, X. (2012). Exploring the caffeine-induced teratogenicity on neurodevelopment using early chick embryo. *PloS One, 7*(3), e34278. doi:10.1371/journal.pone.0034278

Mangelsdorf, S. C., Plunkett, J. W., Dedrick, C. F., Berlin, M., Meisels, S. J., McHale, J. L., & Dichtellmiller, M. (1996). Attachment security in very low birth weight infants. *Developmental Psychology, 32,* 914–920.

March of Dimes. (2012). *Caffeine in pregnancy.* White Plains, NY. Retrieved from http://www.marchofdimes.com/pregnancy/caffeine-in-pregnancy.aspx#

Marcus, S., Lopez, J. F., McDonough, S., MacKenzie, M. J., Flynn, H., Neal, C. R., . . . Vazquez, D. M. (2011). Depressive symptoms during pregnancy: Impact on neuroendocrine and neonatal outcomes. *Infant Behavior & Development, 34*(1), 26–34. doi:10.1016/j.infbeh.2010.07.002

Mariscal, M., Palma, S., Llorca, J., Pérez–Iglesias, R., Pardo–Crespo, R., & Delgado–Rodríguez, M. (2006). Pattern of alcohol consumption during pregnancy and risk for low birth weight. *Annals of Epidemiology, 16*(6), 432–438.

Marret, S., Marchand, L., Kaminski, M., Larroque, B., Arnaud, C., Truffert, P., . . . Ancel, P-Y. (2010). Prenatal low-dose aspirin and neurobehavioral outcomes of children born very preterm. *Pediatrics, 125*(1), e29–e34. doi:10.1542/peds.2009-0994

Martin, J. A., Hamilton, B. E., Osterman, M. J. K., Curtin, S. C., & Mathews, T. J. (2013). Births: Final data for 2012. *National Vital Statistics Reports, 62*(9). Retrieved from http://www.cdc.gov/nchs/data/nvsr/nvsr62/nvsr62_09.pdf#table21

Mathews, T. J., & MacDorman, M. F. (2013). Infant mortality statistics from the 2010 period linked birth/infant death data set. *National Vital Statistics Reports, 62*(8). Retrieved from http://www.cdc.gov/nchs/data/nvsr/nvsr62/nvsr62_08.pdf

Mattson, S. N., Crocker, N., & Nguyen, T. T. (2011). Fetal alcohol spectrum disorders: Neuropsychological and behavioral features. *Neuropsychology Review, 21*(2), 81–101. doi:10.1007/s11065-011-9167-9

Maupin, R., Lyman, R., Fatsis, J., Prystowiski, E., Nguyen, A., Wright, C., . . . Miller, J. (2004). Characteristics of women who deliver with no prenatal care. *Journal of Maternal-Fetal and Neonatal Medicine, 16,* 45–50.

May, P. A., Gossage, J. P., Kalberg, W. O., Robinson, L. K., Buckley, D., Manning, M., & Hoyme, H. E. (2009). Prevalence and epidemiologic characteristics of FASD from various research methods with an emphasis on recent in-school studies. *Developmental Disabilities Research Reviews, 15*(3), 176–192. doi:10.1002/ddrr.68

McCormick, M. C., McCarton, C., Tonascia, J., & Brooks-Gunn, J. (1993). Early educational intervention for very low birth weight infants: Results from the Infant Health and Development Program. *Journal of Pediatrics, 123,* 527–533.

McGlade, M. S., Saha, S., & Dahlstrom, M. E. (2004). The Latina paradox: An opportunity for restructuring prenatal care delivery. *American Journal of Public Health, 94*(12), 2062–2065.

McLachlan, K., Roesch, R., Viljoen, J. L., & Douglas, K. S. (2014). Evaluating the psycholegal abilities of young offenders with fetal alcohol spectrum disorder. *Law and Human Behavior, 38*(1), 10–22. doi:10.1037/lhb0000037

McNeil, D. G. (2014, July 10). Evidence of H.I.V. found in a child said to be cured. *New York Times.* Retrieved from http://www.nytimes.com/2014/07/11/health/signs-of-infection-seen-in-child-believed-to-have-been-cured-of-hiv.html

Meschke, L. L., Holl, J., & Messelt, S. (2013). Older not wiser: Risk of prenatal alcohol use by maternal age. *Maternal and Child Health Journal, 17*(1), 147–155. doi:10.1007/s10995-012-0953-7

Min, M. O., Minnes, S., Lang, A., Weishampel, P., Short, E. J., Yoon, S., & Singer, L. T. (2014). Externalizing behavior and substance use related

problems at 15 years in prenatally cocaine exposed adolescents. *Journal of Adolescence, 37*(3), 269–279. doi:10.1016/j.adolescence.2014.01.004

Moon, C., Cooper, R. P., & Fifer, W. P. (1993). Two-day-old infants prefer their native language. *Infant Behavior and Development, 16,* 495–500.

Moore, K. L., & Persaud, T. V. N. (2013). *Before we are born: Essentials of embryology and birth defects* (8th ed.). Philadelphia: Saunders.

Mulder, E. J. H., Robles de Medina, P. G., Huizink, A. C., Van den Bergh, B. R. H., Buitelaar, J. K., & Visser, G. H. A. (2002). Prenatal maternal stress: Effects on pregnancy and the (unborn) child. *Early Human Development, 70*(1–2), 3–14.

Murthy, P., Kudlur, S., George, S., & Mathew, G. (2009). A clinical overview of fetal alcohol syndrome. *Addictive Disorders & Their Treatment, 8*(1), 1–12. doi:10.1097/ADT.0b013e318163b062

Nagy, G. R., Győrffy, B., Nagy, B., & Rigó, J. (2013). Lower risk for Down syndrome associated with longer oral contraceptive use: A case-control study of women of advanced maternal age presenting for prenatal diagnosis. *Contraception, 87*(4), 455–458. doi:10.1016/j.contraception.2012.08.040

National Institute of Allergy and Infectious Diseases. (2014). *NIH trial tests very early anti-HIV therapy in HIV-infected newborns.* Retrieved from http://www.niaid.nih.gov/news/newsreleases/2014/Pages/IMPAACTP1115.aspx

Nelson, D. B., Mcmahon, K., Joffe, M., & Brensinger, C. (2003). The effect of depressive symptoms and optimism on the risk of spontaneous abortion among innercity women. *Journal of Women's Health, 12*(6), 569–576.

Newberger, D. S. (2000). Down syndrome: Prenatal risk assessment and diagnosis. *American Family Physician, 62*(4), 825–832. Retrieved from http://www.aafp.org/afp/2000/0815/p825.html

Nordstrom-Klee, B., Delaney-Black, V., Covington, C., Ager, J., & Sokol, R. (2002). Growth from birth onwards of children prenatally exposed to drugs: A literature review. *Neurotoxicology & Teratology, 24*(4), 481–488.

O'Leary, C. M., & Bower, C. (2012). Guidelines for pregnancy: What's an acceptable risk, and how is the evidence (finally) shaping up? *Drug and Alcohol Review, 31*(2), 170–83. doi:10.1111/j.1465-3362.2011.00331.x

Ornoy, A., Michailevskay, V., Lukashov, I., Barttamburger, R., & Harel, S. (1996). The developmental outcome of children born to heroin-dependent mothers, raised at home or adopted. *Child Abuse & Neglect, 20,* 385–396.

Ornoy, A., & Tenenbaum, A. (2006). Pregnancy outcome following infections by coxsackie, echo, measles, mumps, hepatitis, polio and encephalitis viruses. *Reproductive Toxicology, 21*(4), 446–457. doi:10.1016/j.reprotox.2005.12.007

Ortolano, S., Mahmud, Z., Iqbal Kabir, A., & Levinson, F. (2003). Effect of targeted food supplementation and services in the Bangladesh, Integrated Nutrition Project on women and their pregnancy outcomes. *Journal of Health, Population, and Nutrition, 21*(2), 83–89.

Palmer, A. (2003). Growth failure is important factor in the survival rate of HIV infected children. *HIV Clinician, 15*(2), 1–4.

Parker, V. J., & Douglas, A. J. (2010). Stress in early pregnancy: Maternal neuro-endocrine-immune responses and effects. *Journal of Reproductive Immunology, 85*(1), 86–92. doi:10.1016/j.jri.2009.10.011

Philbin, M. K., & Klaas, P. (2000). Hearing and behavioral responses to sound in full-term newborns. *Journal of Perinatology, 20*(8, Suppl. 1), S68.

Pollack, A., & McNeil, D. G., Jr. (2013, March 4). In medical first, a baby with HIV is deemed cured. *New York Times*, p. 162. Retrieved from http://www.who.int/hiv/pub/progress_report2011/en

Porter, R., Varendi, H., Christensson, K., Porter, R. H., & Winberg, J. (1998). Soothing effect of amniotic fluid smell in newborn infants. *Early Human Development, 51*, 47–55.

Prechtl, H. F. R. (1974). The behavioural states of the newborn infant (a review). *Brain Research, 76*(2), 185–212. doi:10.1016/0006-8993(74)90454-5

Primakoff, O., & Myles, D. (2002). Penetration, adhesion, and fusion in mammalian sperm-egg interaction. *Science, 296*(5576), 2183–2186.

Procianoy, R. S., Mendes, E. W., & Silveira, R. C. (2010). Massage therapy improves neurodevelopment outcome at two years corrected age for very low birth weight infants. *Early Human Development, 86*(1), 7–11. doi:10.1016/j.earlhumdev.2009.12.001

Rattaz, C., Goubet, N., & Bullinger, A. (2005). The calming effect of a familiar odor on full-term newborns. *Journal of Developmental and Behavioral Pediatrics, 26*(2), 86–92.

Ricciuti, H. N. (1993). Nutrition and mental development. *Current Directions in Psychological Science, 2*, 43–46.

Richardson, G. A., Goldschmidt, L., Leech, S., & Willford, J. (2011). Prenatal cocaine exposure: Effects on mother- and teacher-rated behavior problems and growth in school-age children. *Neurotoxicology and Teratology, 33*(1), 69–77.

Richardson, G. A., Goldschmidt, L., & Willford, J. (2009). Continued effects of prenatal cocaine use: Preschool development. *Neurotoxicology & Teratology, 31*(6), 325–333. doi:10.1016/j.ntt.2009.08.004

Richardson, G. A., Ryan, C., Willford, J., Day, N. L., & Goldschmidt, L. (2002). Prenatal alcohol and marijuana exposure: Effects on neuropsychological outcomes at 10 years. *Neurotoxicology & Teratology, 24*(3), 309–320.

Riley, E. P., Infante, M. A., & Warren, K. R. (2011). Fetal alcohol spectrum disorders: An overview. *Neuropsychology Review, 21*(2), 73–80. doi:10.1007/s11065-011-9166-x

Robertson, J. A. (2010). Embryo stem cell research: Ten years of controversy. *Journal of Law, Medicine & Ethics, 38*(2), 191–203. doi:10.1111/j.1748-720X.2010.00479.x

Roffwarg, H. A. P., Muzio, J. N., & Dement, W. C. (1966). Ontogenetic development of the human sleep-dream cycle. *Science, 152*, 604–619.

Roussotte, F. F., Bramen, J. E., Nunez, S. C., Quandt, L. C., Smith, L., O'Connor, M. J., . . . Sowell, E. R. (2011). Abnormal brain activation during working memory in children with prenatal exposure to drugs of abuse: The effects of methamphetamine, alcohol, and polydrug exposure. *NeuroImage, 54*(4), 3067–3075.

Sadler, T. L. (2012). *Langman's medical embryology* (12th ed.). New York: Lippincott Williams & Wilkins.

Sahni, R., Schulze F., K., Stefanski, M., Myers, M. M., & Fifer, W. P. (1995). Methodological issues in coding sleep states in immature infants. *Developmental Psychobiology, 28*, 85–101.

Saigal, S., Hoult, L. A., Streiner, D. L., Stoskopf, B. L., & Rosenbaum, P. L. (2000). School difficulties at adolescence in a regional cohort of children who were extremely low birth weight. *Pediatrics, 105*, 325–331.

Salem Yaniv, S., Levy, A., Wiznitzer, A., Holcberg, G., Mazor, M., & Sheiner, E. (2011). A significant linear association exists between advanced maternal age and adverse perinatal outcome. *Archives of Gynecology and Obstetrics, 283*(4), 755–759. doi:10.1007/s00404-010-1459-4

Salihu, H. M., Shumpert, M. N., Slay, M., Kirby, R. S., & Alexander, G. R. (2003). Childbearing beyond maternal age 50 and fetal outcomes in the United States. *Obstetrics & Gynecology, 102*, 1006–1014.

Sameroff, A. J., & Chandler, P. J. (1975). Reproductive risk and the continuum of caretaking causality. In F. D. Horowitz, M. Hetherington, S. Scarr-Salapatek, & G. Siegel (Eds.), *Review of child development research* (Vol. 4, pp. 187–244). Chicago: University of Chicago Press.

Sánchez, P. J., & Wendel, G. D. (1997). Syphilis in pregnancy. *Clinics in Perinatology, 24*(1), 71–90. Retrieved from http://europepmc.org/abstract/MED/9099503

Santis, M., Cavaliere, A. F., Straface, G., & Caruso, A. (2006). Rubella infection in pregnancy. *Reproductive Toxicology, 21*(4), 390–398.

Schrager, S., & Potter, B. E. (2004). Diethylstilbestrol exposure. *American Family Physician, 69*(10), 2395–2400.

Schreiber, J. (1977). Birth, the family and the community: A southern Italian example. *Birth and the Family Journal, 4*, 153–157.

Seitz, J. (2006). Correlations between motor performance and cognitive functions in children born < 1250 g at school age. *Neuropediatrics, 37*(1), 6–12.

Sengpiel, V., Elind, E., Bacelis, J., Nilsson, S., Grove, J., Myhre, R., . . . Brantsaeter, A.-L. (2013). Maternal caffeine intake during pregnancy is associated with birth weight but not with gestational length: Results from a large prospective observational cohort study. *BMC Medicine, 11*(1), 42. doi:10.1186/1741-7015-11-42

Shapiro, R. S. (2006). Bioethics and the stem cell research debate. *Social Education, 70*(4), 203–209.

Sherr, L., Mueller, J., & Varrall, R. (2009). A systematic review of cognitive development and child human immunodeficiency virus infection. *Psychology, Health & Medicine, 14*(4), 387–404. doi:10.1080/13548500903012897

Shrim, A., Levin, I., Mallozzi, A., Brown, R., Salama, K., Gamzu, R., & Almog, B. (2010). Does very advanced maternal age, with or without egg donation, really increase obstetric risk in a large tertiary center? *Journal of Perinatal Medicine, 38*(6), 645–650. doi:10.1515/jpm.2010.084

Simkin, P., Whalley, J., & Keppler, A. (2001). *Pregnancy, childbirth, and the newborn.* New York: Simon & Schuster.

Sinclair, K. D., & Watkins, A. J. (2013). Parental diet, pregnancy outcomes and offspring health: Metabolic determinants in developing oocytes and embryos. *Reproduction, Fertility, and Development, 26*(1), 99–114. doi:10.1071/RD13290

Singer, L. T., Salvator, A., Guo, S., Collin, M., Lilien, L., & Baley, J. (1999). Maternal psychological distress and parenting after the birth of a very low-birth-weight infant. *Journal of the American Medical Association, 281*, 799–805.

Stiles, J., & Jernigan, T. L. (2010). The basics of brain development. *Neuropsychology Review, 20*(4), 327–348.

Stoll, B. J., Hansen, N. I., Bell, E. F., & Shankaran, S. (2010). Neonatal outcomes of extremely preterm infants from the NICHD Neonatal Research Network. *Pediatrics, 126*(3), 443–456. doi:10.1542/peds.2009-2959

Stone-Manista, K. (2009). Protecting pregnant women: A guide to successfully challenging criminal child abuse protections of pregnant drug addicts. *Journal of Criminal Law & Criminology, 99*(3), 823–856.

Sullivan, J. L. (2003). Prevention of mother-to-child transmission of HIV: What next? *Journal of Acquired Immune Deficiency Syndromes, 34*(Suppl. 1), S67–S72.

Tachibana, M., Amato, P., Sparman, M., Gutierrez, N. M., Tippner-Hedges, R., Ma, H., . . . Mitalipov, S. (2013). Human embryonic stem cells derived by somatic cell nuclear transfer. *Cell, 153*(6), 1228–1238. doi:10.1016/j.cell.2013.05.006

Talge, N. M., Holzman, C., Wang, J., Lucia, V., Gardiner, J., & Breslau, N. (2010). Late-preterm birth and its association with cognitive and socioemotional outcomes at 6 years of age. *Pediatrics, 126*(6), 1124–1131. doi:10.1542/peds.2010-1536

Tan, M. P., & Koren, G. (2006). Chickenpox in pregnancy: Revisited. *Reproductive Toxicology, 21*(4), 410–420. doi:10.1016/j.reprotox.2005.04.011

Taylor, H. G., Klein, N., Minich, N. M., & Hack, M. (2001). Long-term family outcomes for children with very low birth weights. *Archives of Pediatrics & Adolescent Medicine, 155.*

Testa, M., Quigley, B. M., & Das Eiden, R. (2003). The effects of prenatal alcohol exposure on infant mental development: A meta-analytical review. *Alcohol & Alcoholism, 38*(4), 295–304.

Thomas, J. D., Warren, K. R., & Hewitt, B. G. (2010). Fetal alcohol spectrum disorders. *Alcohol Research & Health, 33*(1–2), 118–126.

Tinker, S. C., Cogswell, M. E., Devine, O., & Berry, R. J. (2010). Folic acid intake among U.S. women aged 15–44 years, National Health and Nutrition Examination Survey, 2003–2006. *American Journal of Preventive Medicine, 38*(5), 534–542. doi:10.1016/j.amepre.2010.01.025

Torpey, K., Kabaso, M., Kasonde, P., Dirks, R., Bweupe, M., Thompson, C., & Mukadi, Y. D. (2010). Increasing the uptake of prevention of mother-to-child transmission of HIV services in a resource-limited setting. *BMC Health Services Research, 10*, 29–36. doi:10.1186/1472-6963-10-29

Torpey, K., Kasonde, P., Kabaso, M., Weaver, M. A., Bryan, G., Mukonka, V., . . . Colebunders, R. (2010). Reducing pediatric HIV infection: Estimating mother-to-child transmission rates in a program setting in Zambia. *Journal of Acquired Immune Deficiency Syndromes, 54*(4), 415–422.

Treyvaud, K., Anderson, V. A., Howard, K., Bear, M., Hunt, R. W., Doyle, L. W., . . . Anderson, P. J. (2009). Parenting behavior is associated with the early neurobehavioral development of very preterm children. *Pediatrics, 123*(2), 555–561. doi:10.1542/peds2008-0477

Treyvaud, K., Doyle, L. W., Lee, K. J., Roberts, G., Cheong, J. L. Y., Inder, T. E., & Anderson, P. J. (2011). Family functioning, burden and parenting stress 2 years after very preterm birth. *Early Human Development, 87*(6), 427–431.

Tucker, J., & McGuire, W. (2004). Epidemiology of preterm birth. *British Medical Journal, 329*, 675–678. Retrieved from http://bmj.bmjjournals.com/cgi/content/full/329/7467/675

United Nations Children's Fund. (2013). *Towards an AIDS-free generation: Children and AIDS sixth stocktaking report.* New York: Author. Retrieved from http://www.childinfo.org/files/str6_full_report_29-11-2013.pdf

U.S. Department of Health and Human Services. (2010). *Stem cell information.* Rockville, MD. Retrieved from http://stemcells.nih.gov/info/Pages/Default.aspx

U.S. Department of Health and Human Services. (2013). *Child health USA 2013.* Rockville, MD. Retrieved from http://mchb.hrsa.gov/chusa13/index.html

U.S. Department of Health and Human Services. (2014). *Child health USA 2014.* Rockville, MD. Retrieved from http://www.mchb.hrsa.gov/chusa14/index.html

Van Gelder, M. M. H. J., Reefhuis, J., Caton, A. R., Werler, M. M., Druschel, C. M., & Roeleveld, N. (2010). Characteristics of pregnant illicit drug users and associations between cannabis use and perinatal outcome in a population-based study. *Drug & Alcohol*

Dependence, 109(1–3), 243–247. doi:10.1016/j.drugalcdep.2010.01.007

Vargesson, N. (2009). Thalidomide-induced limb defects: Resolving a 50-year-old puzzle. BioEssays, 31(12), 1327–1336. doi:10.1002/bies.200900103

Venkatesh, K. K., Lurie, M. N., Triche, E. W., De Bruyn, G., Harwell, J. I., McGarvey, S. T., & Gray, G. E. (2010). Growth of infants born to HIV-infected women in South Africa according to maternal and infant characteristics. Tropical Medicine & International Health, 15(11), 1364–1374. doi:10.1111/j.1365-3156.2010.02634.x

Ventura, S. J., & Hamilton, B. E. (2011). Births: Preliminary data for 2010. National Vital Statistics Reports (Vol. 60). Division of Vital Statistics. Atlanta: Centers for Disease Control and Prevention. Retrieved from http://www.cdc.gov/nchs/data/nvsr/nvsr60/nvsr60_02.pdf

Ventura, S. J., Hamilton, B. E., Mathews, T. J., & Chandra, A. (2003). Trends and variations in smoking during pregnancy and low birth weight: Evidence from the birth certificate, 1990–2000. Pediatrics, 111(5), 1176–1180.

Visscher, M. O., Narendran, V., Pickens, W. L., LaRuffa, A. A., Meinzen-Derr, J., Allen, K., & Hoath, S. B. (2005). Vernix caseosa in neonatal adaptation. Journal of Perinatology, 25(7), 440–446.

Vohr, B. R., Wright, L. L., Dusick, A. M., Mele, L., Verter, J., Steichen, J. J., . . . Kaplan, M. D. (2000). Neurodevelopmental and functional outcomes of extremely low birth weight infants in the National Institute of Child Health and Human Development Neonatal Research Network, 1993–1994. Pediatrics, 105, 1216–1226.

Vouloumanos, A., Hauser, M. D., Werker, J. F., & Martin, A. (2010). The tuning of human neonates' preference for speech. Child Development, 81(2), 517–527. doi:10.1111/j.1467-8624.2009.01412.x

Warren, K. R., Hewitt, B. G., & Thomas, J. D. (2011). Fetal alcohol spectrum disorders: Research challenges and opportunities. Alcohol Research & Health, 34(1), 4–14.

Weinhold, B. (2009). Environmental factors in birth defects. Environmental Health Perspectives, 117(10), A440–A447.

Wendland-Carro, J., Piccinini, C. A., & Miller, W. S. (1999). The role of an early intervention on enhancing the quality of mother-infant interaction. Child Development, 70, 713–721.

Wheeler, J. A., Kenney, K. A., & Temple, V. (2013). Fetal alcohol spectrum disorder: Exploratory investigation of services and interventions for adults. Journal on Developmental Disabilities, 19(3).

Willford, J. A., Leech, S. L., & Day, N. L. (2006). Moderate prenatal alcohol exposure and cognitive status of children at age 10. Alcoholism: Clinical & Experimental Research, 30(6), 1051–1059.

Wolff, P. H. (1966). The causes, controls and organization of behavior in the neonate. Psychological Issues Monograph Series, 5(1).

World Health Organization. (2010). Guidelines on HIV and infant feeding 2010: Principles and recommendations for feeding in the context of HIV and a summary of evidence. Geneva, Switzerland: Author.

World Health Organization. (2011). WHO Progress report 2011: Global HIV/AIDS response. Geneva, Switzerland: Author. Retrieved from http://www.who.int/hiv/pub/progress_report2011/en

Wu, C.-S., Jew, C. P., & Lu, H.-C. (2011). Lasting impacts of prenatal cannabis exposure and the role of endogenous cannabinoids in the developing brain. Future Neurology, 6(4), 459–480. Retrieved from http://www.pubmedcentral.nih.gov/articlerender.fcgi?artid=3252200&tool=pmcentrez&rendertype=abstract

Xu, Y., & Filler, J. W. (2005). Linking assessment and intervention for developmental/functional outcomes of premature, low-birth-weight children. Early Childhood Education Journal, 32(6), 383–389.

Yau, G., Schluchter, M., Taylor, H. G., Margevicius, S., Forrest, C. B., Andreias, L., . . . Hack, M. (2013). Bullying of extremely low birth weight children: Associated risk factors during adolescence. Early Human Development, 89(5), 333–338. doi:10.1016/j.earlhumdev.2012.11.004

Zhao, G., Ford, E. S., Tsai, J., Li, C., Ahluwalia, I. B., Pearson, W. S., . . . Croft, J. B. (2012). Trends in health-related behavioral risk factors among pregnant women in the United States: 2001–2009. Journal of Women's Health, 21(3), 255–263. doi:10.1089/jwh.2011.2931

Zhong, X. Y., Zhang, B., Asadollahi, R., Low, S. H., & Holzgreve, W. (2010). Umbilical cord blood stem cells: What to expect. Annals of the New York Academy of Sciences, 1205, 17–22. doi:10.1111/j.1749-6632.2010.05659.x

CHAPTER 4

Adolph, K. E., Cole, W. G., Komati, M., Garciaguirre, J. S., Badaly, D., Lingeman, J. M., . . . Sotsky, R. B. (2012). How do you learn to walk? Thousands of steps and dozens of falls per day. Psychological Science, 23(11), 1387–1394. doi:10.1177/0956797612446346

Adolph, K. E., Kretch, K. S., & LoBue, V. (2014). Fear of heights in infants? Current Directions in Psychological Science, 23(1), 60–66. doi:10.1177/0963721413498895

Adolph, K. E., & Tamis-LeMonda, C. S. (2014). The costs and benefits of development: The transition from crawling to walking. Child Development Perspectives, 8(4), 187–192. doi:10.1111/cdep.12085

Alanis, M. C., & Lucidi, R. S. (2004). Neonatal circumcision: A review of the world's oldest and most controversial operation. Obstetrical and Gynecological Survey, 59(5), 379–395.

American Academy of Pediatrics. (2005). The changing concept of sudden infant death syndrome: Diagnostic coding shifts, controversies regarding the sleeping environment, and new variables to consider in reducing risk. Pediatrics, 116, 1245–1255.

American Academy of Pediatrics Task Force on Circumcision. (1999). Circumcision policy statement. Pediatrics, 103, 686–693.

American Academy of Pediatrics Task Force on Circumcision. (2012). Circumcision policy statement. Pediatrics, 130(3), 585–586. doi:10.1542/peds.2012-1989

American Academy of Pediatrics Work Group on Breastfeeding. (1997). Breastfeeding and the use of human milk. Pediatrics, 100, 1035–1039.

American Medical Association. (1999). Neonatal circumcision. Chicago: Author.

Anisfeld, M., Turkewitz, G., Rose, S. A., Rosenberg, F. R., Shelber, F. J., Couturier-Fagan, D. A., . . . Sommer, I. (2001). No compelling evidence that newborns imitate oral gestures. Infancy, 2, 111–122.

Aslin, R. N. (2014). Infant learning: Historical, conceptual, and methodological challenges. Infancy, 19(1), 2–27. doi:10.1111/infa.12036

Bahrick, L. E. (2002). Generalization of learning in three-and-a-half-month-old infants on the basis of amodal relations. Child Development, 73(3), 667–681.

Ball, H. L., Hooker, E., & Kelly, P. J. (1999). Where will the baby sleep? Attitudes and practices of new and experienced parents regarding co-sleeping with their new-born infants. American Anthropologist, 101, 1–9.

Ball, H. L., Hooker, E., & Kelly, P. J. (2000). Parent-infant co-sleeping: Fathers' roles and perspectives. Infant and Child Development, 9, 67–74.

Barr, R., Dowden, A., & Hayne, H. (1996). Developmental changes in deferred imitation by 6- to 24-month-old infants. Infant Behavior and Development, 19, 159–170.

Barr, R., & Hayne, H. (2003). It's not what you know, it's who you know: Older siblings facilitate imitation during infancy. International Journal of Early Years Education, 11, 7–21.

Barros, M. C. M., Mitsuhiro, S., Chalem, E., Laranjeira, R. R., & Guinsburg, R. (2011). Neurobehavior of late preterm infants of adolescent mothers. Neonatology, 99(2), 133–139. doi:10.1159/000313590

Batchelor, J. (2008). "Failure to thrive" revisited. Child Abuse Review, 17(3), 147–159.

Beauchamp, G. K., & Mennella, J. A. (2011). Flavor perception in human infants: development and functional significance. Digestion, 83(Suppl. 1), 1–6. doi:10.1159/000323397

Bellieni, C. V, Iantorno, L., Perrone, S., Rodriguez, A., Longini, M., Capitani, S., & Buonocore, G. (2009). Even routine painful procedures can be harmful for the newborn. Pain, 147(1–3), 128–131. doi:10.1016/j.pain.2009.08.025

Benatar, M., & Benatar, D. (2003). Between prophylaxis and child abuse: The ethics of neonatal male circumcision. American Journal of Bioethics, 3(2), 35–48.

Benoit, D. (2009). Feeding disorders, failure to thrive, and obesity. In C. H. Zeanah Jr. (Ed.), Handbook of infant mental health (3rd ed., pp. 377–391). New York: Guilford Press.

Berger, S. E., Theuring, C., & Adolph, K. E. (2007). How and when infants learn to climb stairs. Infant Behavior & Development, 30(1), 36–49. doi:10.1016/j.infbeh.2006.11.002

Berra, S., Sabulsky, J., Rajmil, L., Passamonte, R., Pronsato, J., & Butinof, M. (2003). Correlates of breastfeeding duration in an urban cohort from Argentina. Acta Paediatrics, 92, 952–957.

Bertenthal, B. I., Campos, J. J., & Barrett, K. (1984). Self-produced locomotion: An organizer of emotional, cognitive, and social development in infancy. In R. Emde & R. Harmon (Eds.), Continuities and discontinuities in development (pp. 174–210). New York: Plenum.

Binner, S. L., Mastrobattista, J. M., Day, M.-C., Swaim, L. S., & Monga, M. (2003). Effect of parental education on decision-making about neonatal circumcision. Southern Medical Journal, 95(4), 457–461.

Black, M. M., Dubowitz, H., Krishnakumar, A., & Starr, R. H. (2007). Early intervention and recovery among children with failure to thrive: Follow-up at age 8. Pediatrics, 120(1), 59–69. doi:10.1542/peds.2006-1657

Blass, E. M., Ganchrow, J. R., & Steiner, J. E. (1984). Classical conditioning in newborn humans 2-48 hours of age. Infant Behavior and Development, 7, 223–235.

Bo, X., & Goldman, H. (2008). Newborn circumcision in Victoria, Australia: Reasons and parental attitudes. ANZ Journal of Surgery, 78(11), 1019–1022. doi:10.1111/j.1445-2197.2008.04723.x

Bornstein, M. H. (2002). Parenting infants. In M. H. Bornstein (Ed.), Handbook of parenting: Vol. 1. Children and parenting (2nd ed., pp. 3–43). Mahwah, NJ: Lawrence Erlbaum.

Bornstein, M. H., & Lamb, M. E. (1992). Development in infancy (3rd ed.). New York: McGraw-Hill.

Botton, J., Heude, B., Maccario, J., Ducimetière, P., & Charles, M.-A. (2008). Postnatal weight and height growth velocities at different ages between birth and 5 y and body composition in adolescent boys and girls. The American Journal of Clinical Nutrition, 87(6), 1760–1768. Retrieved from http://www.ncbi.nlm.nih.gov/pubmed/18541566

Bower, T. G. R., Broughton, J. M., & Moore, M. K. (1970). The coordination of vision and tactile input in infancy. *Perception and Psychophysics, 8*, 51–53.

Brenner, R. A., Simons-Morton, B. G., Bhaskar, B., Revenis, M., Das, A., & Clemens, J. D. (2003). Infant-parent bed sharing in an inner-city population. *Archives of Pediatrics and Adolescent Medicine, 157*, 33–39.

Bushnell, I. W. R., Sai, F. Z., & Mullin, J. (1989). Neonatal recognition of the mother's face. *British Journal of Developmental Psychology, 7*, 3–15.

Campos, J. J., Langer, A., & Krowitz, A. (1970). Cardiac responses on the visual cliff in prelocomotor human infants. *Science, 170*, 196–197.

Carpenter, M., Akhtar, N., & Tomasello, M. (1998). Fourteen- through 18-month-old infants differentially imitate intentional and accidental actions. *Infant Behavior and Development, 21*, 315–330.

Centers for Disease Control and Prevention. (1994). Vaccines for children program, 1994. *Morbidity and Mortality Weekly Report, 43*(39), 705.

Chen, X., Striano, T., & Rakoczy, H. (2004). Auditory–oral matching behavior in newborns. *Developmental Science, 7*(1), 42–47.

Child Trends. (2013). *Breastfeeding: Indicators on children and youth*. Bethesda, MD. Retrieved from http://www.childtrends.org/wp-content/uploads/2012/10/90_Breastfeeding.pdf

Child Trends. (2014). *Immunization*. Bethesda, MD: Author.

Chomtho, S., Wells, J. C., Williams, J. E., Davies, P. S., Lucas, A., & Fewtrell, M. S. (2008). Infant growth and later body composition: Evidence from the 4-component model. *The American Journal of Clinical Nutrition, 87*(6), 1776–84. Retrieved from http://www.ncbi.nlm.nih.gov/pubmed/18541568

Clearfield, M. W. (2011). Learning to walk changes infants' social interactions. *Infant Behavior & Development, 34*(1), 15–25. doi:10.1016/j.infbeh.2010.04.008

Clifford, A., Franklin, A., Davies, I. R. L., & Holmes, A. (2009). Electrophysiological markers of categorical perception of color in 7-month old infants. *Brain & Cognition, 71*(2), 165–172. doi:10.1016/j.bandc.2009.05.002

Clifton, R. K., Morrongiello, B. A., Kulig, J. W., & Dowd, J. M. (1981). Newborns' orientation towards sound: Possible implications for cortical development. *Child Development, 53*, 833–838.

Clifton, R. K., Rochat, P., Robin, D. J., & Berthier, N. E. (1994). Multimodal perception in the control of infant reaching. *Journal of Experimental Psychology: Human Perception and Performance, 20*, 876–886.

Cole, T. J. (2003). The secular trend in human physical growth: A biological view. *Economics and Human Biology, 1*(2), 161–168.

Cole, W. G., Lingeman, J. M., & Adolph, K. E. (2012). Go naked: Diapers affect infant walking. *Developmental Science, 15*(6), 783–790. doi:10.1111/j.1467-7687.2012.01169.x

Coleman-Jensen, A., Nord, M., & Singh, A. (2013). *Household food security in the United States in 2012* (Vol. 2011). Economic Research Report No. (ERR-155) 41 pp, Dept. of Agriculture, Economic Research Service. Washington, DC. Retrieved from http://www.ers.usda.gov/publications/err-economic-research-report/err155.aspx#.U5B4HyisYYI

Collie, R., & Hayne, H. (1999). Deferred imitation by 6- and 9-month-old infants: More evidence for declarative memory. *Developmental Psychobiology, 35*, 83–90.

Colombo, J. D. (2010). What habituates in infant visual habituation? A psychophysiological analysis. *Infancy, 15*(2). doi: 10.1111/j.1532-7078.2009.00012

Cook, R., Bird, G., Catmur, C., Press, C., & Heyes, C. (2014). Mirror neurons: From origin to function. *The Behavioral and Brain Sciences, 37*(2), 177–192. doi:10.1017/S0140525X13000903

Corbetta, D., & Snapp-Childs, W. (2009). Seeing and touching: The role of sensory-motor experience on the development of infant reaching. *Infant Behavior & Development, 32*(1), 44–58. doi:10.1016/j.infbeh.2008.10.004

Courage, M. L., & Adams, R. J. (1990). Visual acuity assessment from birth to three years using the acuity card procedures: Cross-sectional and longitudinal samples. *Optometry and Vision Science, 67*, 713–718.

Dahl, A., Campos, J. J., Anderson, D. I., Uchiyama, I., Witherington, D. C., Ueno, M., & Barbu-roth, M. (2013). The epigenesis of wariness of heights. *Psychological Science*. Advance online publication. doi:10.1177/0956797613476047

De Onis, M., Blössner, M., & Borghi, E. (2012). Prevalence and trends of stunting among pre-school children, 1990–2020. *Public Health Nutrition, 15*(1), 142–148. doi:10.1017/S1368980011001315

De Sousa Freire, N. B., Santos Garcia, J. B., & Carvalho Lamy, Z. (2008). Evaluation of analgesic effect of skin-to-skin contact compared to oral glucose in preterm neonates. *Pain, 139*(1), 28–33. doi:10.1016/j.pain.2008.02.031

Dennis, W. (1960). Causes of retardation among institutional children: Iran. *Journal of Genetic Psychology, 96*, 47–59.

Dennis, W., & Dennis, M. G. (1991). The effect of cradling practices upon the onset of walking in Hopi children. *Journal of Genetic Psychology, 152*(4), 563–572.

Der, G., Batty, G. D., & Deary, I. J. (2006). Effect of breast feeding on intelligence in children: Prospective study, sibling pairs analysis, and meta-analysis. *BMJ, 333*(7575), 945–948.

Diego, M. A., Field, T., Hernandez-Reif, M., Deeds, O., Ascencio, A., & Begert, G. (2007). Preterm infant massage elicits consistent increases in vagal activity and gastric motility that are associated with greater weight gain. *Acta Paediatrica, 96*(11), 1588–1591. doi:10.1111/j.1651-2227.2007.00476.x

DiPietro, J. A. (2000). Baby and the brain: Advances in child development. *Annual Review of Public Health, 21*, 455–471.

Domsch, H. D. (2010). Infant attention, heart rate, and looking time during habituation/dishabituation. *Infant Behavior & Development, 33*(3). doi:10.1016/j.infbeh.2010.03.008

Dorota, I. (2004). *Children who fail to thrive: A practice guide*. Chichester, UK: John Wiley.

Dykman, R. A., Casey, P. H., Ackerman, P. T., McPherson, W. B., & McPherson, B. W. (2001). Behavioral and cognitive status in school-aged children with a history of failure to thrive during early childhood. *Clinical Pediatrics, 40*(2), 63–70.

Dziewolska, H., & Cautilli, J. (2006). The effects of a motor training package on minimally assisted standing behavior in a three-month-old infant. *The Behavior Analyst Today, 7*(1), 111–120.

Elder, J. S. (2007). Circumcision. *BJU International, 99*(6), 1553–1564. doi:10.1111/j.1464-410X.2007.06959.x

Ennouri, K., & Bloch, H. (1996). Visual control of hand approach movements in new-borns. *British Journal of Developmental Psychology, 14*(3), 327–338. doi:10.1111/j.2044-835X.1996.tb00709.x

Fagan, J. F. (1984). In M. Moscovitch (Ed.), *Infant memory: History, current trends, and relations to cognitive psychology*. New York: Plenum.

Fagard, J., & Lockman, J. J. (2010). Change in imitation for object manipulation between 10 and 12 months of age. *Developmental Psychobiology, 52*(1), 90–99. doi:10.1002/dev.20416

Fagard, J., Spelke, E., & von Hofsten, C. (2009). Reaching and grasping a moving object in 6-, 8-, and 10-month-old infants: Laterality and performance. *Infant Behavior & Development, 32*(2), 137–146. doi:10.1016/j.infbeh.2008.12.002

Fantz, R. L. (1961). The origin of form perception. *Scientific American, 204*, 66–72.

Farroni, T., & Menon, E. (2008). Visual perception and early brain development. In R. E. Tremblay, M. Boivin, & R. G. Peters (Eds.), *Encyclopedia on early childhood development* (pp. 1–6). Montreal, Quebec: Centre of Excellence for Early Childhood Development. Retrieved from http://www.child-encyclopedia.com/documents/Farroni-MenonANGxp.pdf.

Ferber, S. G., & Makhoul, I. R. (2008). Neurobehavioural assessment of skin-to-skin effects on reaction to pain in preterm infants: A randomized, controlled within-subject trial. *Acta Paediatrica, 97*(2), 171–176. doi:10.1111/j.1651-2227.2007.00607.x

Fetters, L., & Hsiang-han, H. (2007). Motor development and sleep, play, and feeding positions in very-low-birthweight infants with and without white matter disease. *Developmental Medicine & Child Neurology, 49*(11), 807–813. doi:10.1111/j.1469-8749.2007.00807.x

Field, T. M., Cohen, D., Garcia, R., & Greenberg, R. (1984). Mother-stranger face discrimination by the newborn. *Infant Behavior & Development, 7*, 19–25.

Fischer, K. W., & Rose, S. P. (1995). Concurrent cycles in the dynamic development of the brain and behavior. *SRCD Newsletter*, pp. 3–4, 15–16.

Floccia, C., Christophe, A., & Bertoncini, J. (1997). High-amplitude sucking and newborns: The quest for underlying mechanisms. *Journal of Experimental Child Psychology, 64*, 175–198.

Fogel, A. (2007). *Infancy: Infant, family, and society* (7th ed.). Cornwall-on-Hudson, NY: Sloan Educational Publishing.

Fox, S. E., Levitt, P., & Nelson III, C. A. (2010). How the timing and quality of early experiences influence the development of brain architecture. *Child Development, 81*(1), 28–40. doi:10.1111/j.1467-8624.2009.01380.x

Frank, M. C., Vul, E., & Johnson, S. P. (2009). Development of infants' attention to faces during the first year. *Cognition, 110*(2), 160–170. doi:10.1016/j.cognition.2008.11.010

Gabriel, M. A. M., Alonso, C. R. P., Bértolo, J. D. L. C., Carbonero, S. C., Maestro, M. L., Pumarega, M. M., . . . Pablos, D. L. (2009). Age of sitting unsupported and independent walking in very low birth weight preterm infants with normal motor development at 2 years. *Acta Paediatrica, 98*(11), 1815–1821. doi:10.1111/j.1651-2227.2009.01475.x

Galler, J. R., Bryce, C. P., Waber, D., Hock, R. S., Exner, N., Eaglesfield, D., . . . Harrison, R. (2010). Early childhood malnutrition predicts depressive symptoms at ages 11–17. *Journal of Child Psychology and Psychiatry, 51*(7), 789–798. doi:10.1111/j.1469-7610.2010.02208.x

Gallotti, K. M. (2011). *Cognitive development*. Thousand Oaks, CA: Sage.

Galloway, J. C., & Thelen, E. (2004). Feet first: Object exploration in young infants. *Infant Behavior & Development, 27*(1), 107–112.

Gasser, U. E., & Hatten, M. E. (1990). Central nervous system neurons migrate on astroglial fibers from heterotypic brain regions in vitro. *Proceedings of the National Academy of Sciences of the United States of America, 87*(12), 4543–4547.

Gaultney, J. F., & Gingras, J. L. (2005). Fetal rate of behavioral inhibition and preference for novelty during infancy. *Early Human Development, 81*(4), 379–386.

Gehri, M., Settler, N., & Di Paolo, E. R. (2006). Marasmus. *EMedicine*. Retrieved from http://www.emedicine.com/ped/topic164.htm

Gerber, J. S., & Offit, P. A. (2009). Vaccines and autism: A tale of shifting hypotheses. *Clinical Infectious Diseases, 48*(4), 456–461. Retrieved from 10.1086/596476

Gervain, J., Macagno, F., Cogoi, S., Peña, M., & Mehler, J. (2008). The neonate brain detects speech structure. *Proceedings of the National Academy of Sciences of the United States of America, 105*(37), 14222–14227. doi:10.1073/pnas.0806530105

Gervain, J., & Mehler, J. (2010). Speech perception and language acquisition in the first year of life. *Annual Review of Psychology, 61*, 191–218. doi:10.1146/annurev.psych.093008.100408

Gettler, L. T., & McKenna, J. J. (2011). Evolutionary perspectives on mother-infant sleep proximity and breastfeeding in a laboratory setting. *American Journal of Physical Anthropology, 144*(3), 454–462. doi:10.1002/ajpa.21426

Gibson, E. J., & Pick, A. D. (2000). *An ecological approach to perceptual learning and development.* New York: Oxford University Press.

Gibson, E. J., & Walk, R. D. (1960). The "visual cliff." *Scientific American, 202*, 64–71.

Gliga, T., Elsabbagh, M., Andravizou, A., & Johnson, M. (2009). Faces attract infants' attention in complex displays. *Infancy, 14*(5), 550–562. doi:10.1080/15250000903144199

Godfrey, J. R., & Lawrence, R. A. (2010). Toward optimal health: The maternal benefits of breastfeeding. *Journal of Women's Health, 19*(9), 1597–1602. doi:10.1089/jwh.2010.2290

Goldberg, W. A., & Keller, M. A. (2007). Parent-infant co-sleeping: Why the interest and concern? *Infant and Child Development, 16*(4), 331–339. doi:10.1002/icd.523

Goubet, N., Rattaz, C., Pierrat, V., Allémann, E., Bullinger, A., & Lequien, P. (2002). Olfactory familiarization and discrimination in preterm and full-term newborns. *Infancy, 3*(1), 53–75.

Goubet, N., Strasbaugh, K., & Chesney, J. (2007). Familiarity breeds content? Soothing effect of a familiar odor on full-term newborns. *Journal of Developmental & Behavioral Pediatrics, 28*(3), 189–194. doi:10.1097/dbp.0b013e31802d0b8d

Gradin, M., Eriksson, M., Schollin, J., Holmqvist, G., & Holstein, A. (2002). Pain reduction at venipuncture in newborns: Oral glucose compared with local anesthetic cream. *Pediatrics, 110*(6), 1053–1057.

Greenough, W. T., & Black, J. E. (1992). Induction of brain structure by experience: Substrates for cognitive development. In M. R. Gunnar & C. A. Nelson (Eds.), *Minnesota symposia on child psychology* (pp. 155–200). Hillsdale, NJ: Lawrence Erlbaum.

Grether, J. K., Anderson, M. C., Croen, L. A., Smith, D., & Windham, G. C. (2009). Risk of autism and increasing maternal and paternal age in a large North American population. *American Journal of Epidemiology, 170*(9), 1118–1126. doi:10.1093/aje/kwp247

Griffiths, L. J., & Tate, A. R. (2007). Do early infant feeding practices vary by maternal ethnic group? *Public Health Nutrition, 10*(9), 957–964.

Grossman, A. W., Churchill, J. D., McKinney, B. C., Kodish, I. M., & Otte, S. L. (2003). Experience effects on brain development: Possible contributions to psychopathology. *Journal of Child Psychology & Psychiatry & Allied Disciplines, 44*(1), 33–63.

Gust, D. A., Strine, T. W., Maurice, E., Smith, P., Yusuf, H., Wilkinson, M., . . . et al. (2004). Underimmunization among children: Effects of vaccine safety concerns on immunization status. *Pediatrics, 114*(1), e16–e22.

Gwiazda, J., & Birch, E. (2001). Perceptual development: Vision. In E. B. Goldstein (Ed.), *Blackwell's handbook of perception.* Oxford, UK: Blackwell.

Haith, M. M. (1993). Preparing for the 21st century: Some goals and challenges for studies of infant sensory and perceptual development. *Developmental Review, 13*, 354–371.

Harkness, S. (1998). Time for families. *Anthropology Newsletter, 39*(1), 4.

Harriman, A. E., & Lukosius, P. A. (1982). On why Wayne Dennis found Hopi infants retarded in age at onset of walking. *Perceptual & Motor Skills, 55*(1), 79–86.

Hauck, Y. L., Fenwick, J., Dhaliwal, S. S., & Butt, J. (2011). A Western Australian survey of breastfeeding initiation, prevalence and early cessation patterns. *Maternal & Child Health Journal, 15*(2), 260–268. doi:10.1007/s10995-009-0554-2

He, M., Walle, E. A., & Campos, J. J. (2015). A cross-national investigation of the relationship between infant walking and language development. *Infancy, 20*(3), 283–305. doi:10.1111/infa.12071

Hepper, P. (2015). Behavior during the prenatal period: Adaptive for development and survival. *Child Development Perspectives, 9*(1), 38–43. doi:10.1111/cdep.12104

Herbert, J., Eckerman, C. O., Goldstein, R. F., & Stanton, M. E. (2004). Contrasts in classical eyeblink conditioning as a function of premature birth. *Infancy, 5*(3), 367–383.

Herbert, J., Gross, J., & Hayne, H. (2006). Age-related changes in deferred imitation beween 6 and 9 months of age. *Infant Behavior & Development, 29*, 136–139.

Hernandez-Pavon, J. C., Sosa, M., Lutter, W. J., Maier, M., & Wakai, R. T. (2008). Auditory evoked responses in neonates by MEG. *AIP Conference Proceedings, 1032*(1), 114–117. doi:10.1063/1.2979244

Hernandez-Reif, M., Diego, M., & Field, T. (2007). Preterm infants show reduced stress behaviors and activity after 5 days of massage therapy. *Infant Behavior & Development, 30*(4), 557–561. doi:10.1016/j.infbeh.2007.04.002

Hetzner, N. M. P., Razza, R. A., Malone, L. M., & Brooks-Gunn, J. (2009). Associations among feeding behaviors during infancy and child illness at two years. *Maternal and Child Health Journal, 13*(6), 795–805. doi:10.1007/s10995-008-0401-x

Hopkins, B. (1991). Facilitating early motor development: An intercultural study of West Indian mothers and their infants living in Britain. In J. K. Nugent, B. M. Lester, & T. B. Brazelton (Eds.), *The cultural context of infancy: Vol. 2. Multicultural and interdisciplinary approaches to parent-infant relations.* Norwood, NJ: Ablex.

Hopkins, B., & Westra, T. (1989). Maternal expectations of their infants' development: Some cultural differences. *Developmental Medicine & Child Neurology, 31*(3), 384–390.

Hopkins, B., & Westra, T. (1990). Motor development, maternal expectations, and the role of handling. *Infant Behavior & Development, 13*(1), 117–122.

Huelke, D. F. (1998). An overview of anatomical considerations of infants and children in the adult world of automobile safety design. *Annual Proceedings/Association for the Advancement of Automotive Medicine.* Retrieved from /pmc/articles/PMC3400202/?report=abstract

Hunnius, S., & Geuze, R. H. (2004). Developmental changes in visual scanning of dynamic faces and abstract stimuli in infants: A longitudinal study. *Infancy, 6*(2), 231–255.

Iacoboni, M. (2009). Imitation, empathy, and mirror neurons. *Annual Review of Psychology, 60*(1), 653–670. doi:10.1146/annurev.psych.60.110707.163604

Idring, S., Magnusson, C., Lundberg, M., Ek, M., Rai, D., Svensson, A. C., . . . Lee, B. K. (2014). Parental age and the risk of autism spectrum disorders: Findings from a Swedish population-based cohort. *International Journal of Epidemiology, 43*(1).

Imdad, A., Yakoob, M. Y., & Bhutta, Z. A. (2011). Effect of breastfeeding promotion interventions on breastfeeding rates, with special focus on developing countries. *BMC Public Health, 11*(Suppl. 3), 1–8. doi:10.1186/1471-2458-11-s3-s24

Isaacs, E. B., Fischl, B. R., Quinn, B. T., Chong, W. K., Gadian, D. G., & Lucas, A. (2010). Impact of breast milk on intelligence quotient, brain size, and white matter development. *Pediatric Research, 67*(4), 357–362.

Jacobson, S. W., Stanton, M. E., Molteno, C. D., Burden, M. J., Fuller, D. S., Hoyme, H. E., . . . Jacobson, J. L. (2008). Impaired eyeblink conditioning in children with fetal alcohol syndrome. *Alcoholism: Clinical & Experimental Research, 32*(2), 365–372. doi:10.1111/j.1530-0277.2007.00585.x

James, D. K. (2010). Fetal learning: a critical review. *Infant & Child Development, 19*(1), 45–54. doi:10.1002/icd.653

Jenkins, J. M., & Foster, E. M. (2014). The effects of breastfeeding exclusivity on early childhood outcomes. *American Journal of Public Health, 104*(Suppl.), S128–S135. doi:10.2105/AJPH.2013.301713

Jessen, K. R. (2004). Glial cells. *International Journal of Biochemistry & Cell Biology, 36*(10), 1861–1867.

Jones, E. J. H., & Herbert, J. S. (2006). Exploring memory in infancy: Deferred imitation and the development of declarative memory. *Infant & Child Development, 15*, 195–205.

Jones, S. S. (2006). Exploration or imitation? The effect of music on 4-week-old infants' tongue protrusions. *Infant Behavior & Development, 29*(1), 126–130.

Kaplan, H., & Dove, H. (1987). Infant development among the Ache of eastern Paraguay. *Developmental Psychology, 23*(2), 190–198.

Karasik, L. B., Tamis-LeMonda, C. S., & Adolph, K. E. (2011). Transition from crawling to walking and infants' actions with objects and people. *Child Development, 82*(4), 1199–1209. doi:10.1111/j.1467-8624.2011.01595.x

Kavšek, M., & Bornstein, M. H. (2010). Visual habituation and dishabituation in preterm infants: A review and meta-analysis. *Research in Developmental Disabilities, 31*(5), 951–975. doi:10.1016/j.ridd.2010.04.016

Kawai, N. (2010). Towards a new study on associative learning in human fetuses: fetal associative learning in primates. *Infant & Child Development, 19*(1), 55–59. doi:10.1002/icd.654

Kayed, N. S., Farstad, H., & van der Meer, A. L. H. (2008). Preterm infants' timing strategies to optical collisions. *Early Human Development, 84*(6), 381–388. doi:10.1016/j.earlhumdev.2007.10.006

Keller, H. (2003). Socialization for competence: Cultural models of infancy. *Human Development, 46*(5), 288–311.

Keysers, C., & Gazzola, V. (2010). Social neuroscience: Mirror neurons recorded in humans. *Current Biology, 20*(8), R353–R354. doi:10.1016/j.cub.2010.03.013

Klämbt, C. (2009). Modes and regulation of glial migration in vertebrates and invertebrates. *Nature Reviews Neuroscience, 10*(11), 769–779. doi:10.1038/nrn2720

Klein, P. J., & Meltzoff, A. N. (1999). Long-term memory, forgetting, and deferred imitation in 12-month-old infants. *Developmental Science, 2*, 102–113.

Kolling, T., Oturai, G., & Knopf, M. (2014). Is selective attention the basis for selective imitation in infants? An eye-tracking study of deferred imitation with 12-month-olds. *Journal of Experimental Child Psychology, 124*, 18–35. doi:10.1016/j.jecp.2014.01.016

Krafchuk, E. E., Tronick, E. Z., & Clifton, R. K. (1983). Behavioral and cardiac responses to sound in preterm infants varying in risk status:

A hypothesis of their paradoxical reactivity. In T. Field & A. Sostek (Eds.), *Infants born at risk: Physiological, perceptual, and cognitive processes* (pp. 99–128). New York: Grune & Stratton.

Kramer, M. S., Fombonne, E., Igumnov, S., Vanilovich, I., Matush, L., Mironova, E., . . . Platt, R. W. (2008). Effects of prolonged and exclusive breastfeeding on child behavior and maternal adjustment: Evidence from a large, randomized trial. *Pediatrics, 121*(3), e435–e440.

Kretch, K. S., Franchak, J. M., & Adolph, K. E. (2014). Crawling and walking infants see the world differently. *Child Development, 85*(4), 1503–1518. doi:10.1111/cdev.12206

Kuczmarski, R. J., Ogden, C. L., Grummer-Strawn, L. M., Flegal, K. M., Guo, S. S., Wei, R., . . . Johnson, C. L. (2000). CDC growth charts: United States. In U.S. Department of Health and Human Services (Ed.), *Advance data from vital and health statistics from the Centers for Disease Control and Prevention/National Center of Health Statistics*. Retrieved from http://www.cdc.gov/nchs/data/ad/ad314.pdf

Kuo, Y.-L., Liao, H.-F., Chen, P.-C., Hsieh, W.-S., & Hwang, A.-W. (2008). The influence of wakeful prone positioning on motor development during the early life. *Journal of Developmental and Behavioral Pediatrics, 29*(5), 367–376. doi:10.1097/DBP.0b013e3181856d54

Lampl, M., Johnson, M. L., Frongillo, E., Jr., & Frongillo, E. A. (2001). Mixed distribution analysis identifies saltation and stasis growth. *Annals of Human Biology, 28*(4), 403–411.

Lampl, M., Veldhuis, J. D., & Johnson, M. L. (1992). Saltation and stasis: A model of human growth. *Science, 258*, 801–803.

Learmonth, A. E., Lamberth, R., & Rovee-Collier, C. (2004). Generalizations of deferred imitation during the first year of life. *Journal of Experimental Child Psychology, 88*(4), 297–318.

Leat, S. J., Yadev, N. K., & Irving, E. L. (2009). Development of visual acuity and contrast sensitivity in children. *Journal of Optometry, 2*, 19–26.

Lee, H., & Galloway, J. C. (2012). Control in very young infants. *Physical Therapy, 92*(7), 935–947.

Lepage, J.-F., & Théoret, H. (2007). The mirror neuron system: grasping others' actions from birth? *Developmental Science, 10*(5), 513–523. doi:10.1111/j.1467-7687.2007.00631.x

Levine, L. E., & Munsch, J. (2010). *Child development: An active learning approach.* Thousand Oaks, CA: Sage.

Lewkowicz, D. J. (2000). The development of intersensory temporal perception: An epigenetic systems/limitations view. *Psychological Bulletin, 126*, 281–308.

Lewkowicz, D. J., & Lickliter, R. (1994). *The development of intersensory perception: Comparative perspectives.* Hillsdale, NJ: Lawrence Erlbaum.

Li, R., Zhao, Z., Mokdad, A., & Barker, L. (2003). Prevalence of breastfeeding in the United States: The 2001 National Immunization Survey. *Pediatrics, 111*(5), 1198–1201.

Libertus, K., Gibson, J., Hidayatallah, N. Z., Hirtle, J., Adcock, R. A., & Needham, A. (2013). Size matters: How age and reaching experiences shape infants' preferences for different sized objects. *Infant Behavior & Development, 36*(2), 189–198. doi:10.1016/j.infbeh.2013.01.006

Libertus, K., & Needham, A. (2010). Teach to reach: the effects of active vs. passive reaching experiences on action and perception. *Vision Research, 50*(24), 2750–2757. doi:10.1016/j.visres.2010.09.001

Lipsitt, L. P., & Kaye, H. (1964). Conditioned sucking in the human newborn. *Psychonomic Science, 1*, 29–30.

Litovsky, R. Y., & Ashmead, D. H. (1997). Developmental of binaural and spatial hearing in infants and children. In R. H. Gilkey & T. R. Anderson (Eds.), *Binaural and special hearing in real and virtual environments* (pp. 571–592). Mahwah, NJ: Lawrence Erlbaum.

Little, A. H., Lipsitt, L. P., & Rovee-Collier, C. K. (1984). Classical conditioning and retention of the infants eyelid response: Effects of age and interstimulus interval. *Journal of Experimental Child Psychology, 37*, 512–524.

Lobo, M. A., & Galloway, J. C. (2012). Enhanced handling and positioning in early infancy advances development throughout the first year. *Child Development, 83*(4), 1290–1302. doi:10.1111/j.1467-8624.2012.01772.x

Lohaus, A., Keller, H., Lamm, B., Teubert, M., Fassbender, I., Freitag, C., . . . Schwarzer, G. (2011). Infant development in two cultural contexts: Cameroonian Nso farmer and German middle-class infants. *Journal of Reproductive and Infant Psychology, 29*(2), 148–161. doi:10.1080/02646838.2011.558074

Lozoff, B., Wolf, A. W., & Davis, N. S. (1984). Cosleeping in urban families with young children in the United States. *Pediatrics, 74*, 171–182.

Lukowski, A. F., Wiebe, S. A., & Bauer, P. J. (2009). Going beyond the specifics: Generalization of single actions, but not temporal order, at 9 months. *Infant Behavior & Development, 32*(3), 331–335. doi:10.1016/j.infbeh.2009.02.004

Luman, E. T., Barker, L. E., McCauley, M. M., & Drews-Botsch, C. (2005). Timeliness of childhood immunizations: A state-specific analysis. *American Journal of Public Health, 95*(8), 1367–1374.

Lynch, A., Lee, H. M., Bhat, A., & Galloway, J. C. (2008). No stable arm preference during the pre-reaching period: A comparison of right and left hand kinematics with and without a toy present. *Developmental Psychobiology, 50*(4), 390–398. doi:10.1002/dev.20297

Macfarlane, A. J. (1975). Olfaction in the development of social preferences in the human neonate. *Ciba Foundation Symposia, 33*, 103–117.

Madison, L. S., Madison, J. K., & Adubato, S. A. (1986). Infant behavior and development in relation to fetal movement and habituation. *Child Development, 57*, 1475–1482.

Marlier, L., & Schaal, B. (2005). Human newborns prefer human milk: Conspecific milk odor is attractive without postnatal exposure. *Child Development, 76*(1), 155–168.

Matlin, M. W., & Foley, H. J. (1997). *Sensation and perception* (4th ed.). Boston: Allyn & Bacon.

McCall, R. B. (1994). What process mediates predictions of childhood IQ from infant habituation and recognition memory? Speculations on the roles of inhibition and rate of information processing. *Intelligence, 18*(2), 107–125.

McCall, R. B., & Carrigher, M. S. (1993). A meta-analysis of infant habituation and recognition memory performance as predictors of later IQ. *Child Development, 64*, 57–79.

McCorry, N. K., & Hepper, P. G. (2007). Fetal habituation performance: Gestational age and sex effects. *British Journal of Developmental Psychology, 25*(2), 277–292.

McCoy, R. C., Hunt, C. E., Lesko, S. M., Venzina, R., Corwin, M. J., Willinger, M., . . . Mitchell, A. A. (2004). Frequency of bed sharing and its relationship to breastfeeding. *Developmental and Behavioral Pediatrics, 25*(3), 141–149.

McKenna, J. J. (2001). Why we never ask "Is it safe for infants to sleep alone?" *Academy of Breast Feeding Medicine News and Views, 7*(4), 32,38.

McKenna, J. J., & Mosko, S. (1993). Evolution and infant sleep: An experimental study of infant-parent co-sleeping and its implications for SIDS. *Acta Paediatrica Supplement, 389*, 31–36.

McKenna, J. J., & Volpe, L. E. (2007). Sleeping with baby: An Internet-based sampling of parental experiences, choices, perceptions, and interpretations in a Western industrialized context. *Infant and Child Development, 16*(4), 359–385. doi:10.1002/icd.525

McNeil, D. G. (2009). Court finds no link of vaccine and autism. *New York Times*, p. 16.

Meltzoff, A. N., & Borton, R. W. (1979). Intermodal matching by human neonates. *Nature, 282*, 403–404.

Meltzoff, A. N., & Kuhl, P. K. (1994). Faces and speech: Intermodal processing of biologically relevant signals in infants and adults. In D. J. Lewkowicz & R. Lickliter (Eds.), *The development of intersensory perception* (pp. 335–369). Hillsdale, NJ: Lawrence Erlbaum.

Meltzoff, A. N., & Moore, M. K. (1977). Imitation of facial and manual gestures by human neonates. *Science, 198*, 75–78.

Meltzoff, A. N., & Moore, M. K. (1989). Imitation in newborn infants: Exploring the range of gestures imitated and the underlying mechanisms. *Developmental Psychology, 25*(6), 954–962. doi:10.1037/0012-1649.25.6.954

Meltzoff, A. N., & Moore, M. K. (1999). Persons and representation: Why infant imitation is important for theories of human development. In J. Nadel & G. Butterworth (Eds.), *Imitation in infancy* (pp. 9–35). Cambridge, UK: Cambridge University Press.

Mennella, J. A., & Beauchamp, G. K. (2002). Flavor experiences during formula feeding are related to preferences during childhood. *Early Human Development, 68*(2), 71–82.

Mercuri, E., Baranello, G., Romeo, D. M. M., Cesarini, L., & Ricci, D. (2007). The development of vision. *Early Human Development, 83*(12), 795–800. doi:10.1016/j.earlhumdev.2007.09.014

Minagawa-Kawai, Y., van der Lely, H., Ramus, F., Sato, Y., Mazuka, R., & Dupoux, E. (2011). Optical brain imaging reveals general auditory and language-specific processing in early infant development. *Cerebral Cortex, 21*(2), 254–261. doi:10.1093/cercor/bhq082

Mitchell, E. A. (2009). Risk factors for SIDS. *BMJ, 339*, 873–874. doi:10.1136/bmj.b3466

Monk, C. S., Webb, S. J., & Nelson, C. A. (2001). Prenatal neurobiological development: Molecular mechanisms and anatomical change. *Developmental Neuropsychology, 19*(2), 211–236.

Moon, C., Cooper, R. P., & Fifer, W. P. (1993). Two-day-old infants prefer their native language. *Infant Behavior and Development, 16*, 495–500.

Morelli, G., Rogoff, B., Oppenheim, D., & Goldsmith, D. (1992). Cultural variation in infants' sleeping arrangements: Questions of independence. *Developmental Psychology, 28*, 604–613.

Morokuma, S., Fukushima, K., Kawai, N., Tomonaga, M., Satoh, S., & Nakano, H. (2004). Fetal habituation correlates with functional brain development. *Behavioural Brain Research, 153*(2), 459–463.

Mosko, S., Richard, C., & McKenna, J. (1997). Maternal sleep and arousals during bedsharing with infants. *Sleep, 201*(2), 142–150.

Muenssinger, J., Matuz, T., Schleger, F., Kiefer-Schmidt, I., Goelz, R., Wacker-Gussmann, A., . . . Preissl, H. (2013). Auditory habituation in the fetus and neonate: an fMEG study. *Developmental Science, 16*(2), 287–295. doi:10.1111/desc.12025

Muir, D., & Clifton, R. (1985). Infants' orientation to the location of sound sources. In G. Gottlieb & N. Krasnegor (Eds.), *The measurement of audition and vision during the first year of life: A methodological overview* (pp. 171–194). Norwood, NJ: Ablex.

Nadel, J., & Butterworth, G. (1999). *Imitation in infancy.* Cambridge, UK: Cambridge University Press.

Nagy, E. (2006). From imitation to conversation: The first dialogues with human neonates.

Infant & Child Development, 15(3), 223–232. doi:10.1002/icd.460

Nagy, E., Pilling, K., Orvos, H., & Molnar, P. (2013). Imitation of tongue protrusion in human neonates: Specificity of the response in a large sample. *Developmental Psychology, 49*(9), 1628–1638. doi:10.1037/a0031127

Nakano, T., Watanabe, H., Homae, F., & Taga, G. (2009). Prefrontal cortical involvement in young infants' analysis of novelty. *Cerebral Cortex, 19*(2), 455–463. doi:10.1093/cercor/bhn096

Náñez Sr., J. E., & Yonas, A. (1994). Effects of luminance and texture motion on infant defensive reactions to optical collision. *Infant Behavior & Development, 17*, 165–174.

Nelson, C. A., & Bloom, F. E. (1997). Child development and neuroscience. *Child Development, 69*, 970–987.

Nelson, C. A., & Luciana, M. (2008). *Handbook of developmental cognitive neuroscience* (2nd ed.). Cambridge, MA: MIT Press.

Neville, H. J., & Bavelier, D. (2001). Variability of developmental plasticity: Carnegie mellon symposia on cognition. In J. L. McClelland & R. S. Siegler (Eds.), *Mechanisms of cognitive development: Behavioral and neural perspectives* (pp. 271–301). Mahwah, NJ: Lawrence Erlbaum.

Newell, F. N. (2004). Cross-modal object recognition. In G. A. Calvert, C. Spence, & B. E. Stein (Eds.), *The handbook of multisensory processes* (pp. 123–139). Cambridge, MA: MIT Press.

Nishitani, S., Miyamura, T., Tagawa, M., Sumi, M., Takase, R., Doi, H., . . . Shinohara, K. (2009). The calming effect of a maternal breast milk odor on the human newborn infant. *Neuroscience Research, 63*(1), 66–71. doi:10.1016/j.neures.2008.10.007

Northern, J. L. (2014). *Hearing in children* (6th ed.). San Diego: Plural Publishing.

Nowakowski, R. S. (1987). Basic concepts of CNS development. *Child Development, 58*, 595–598.

Oberman, L. M., Hubbard, E. M., & McCleery, J. P. (2014). Associative learning alone is insufficient for the evolution and maintenance of the human mirror neuron system. *The Behavioral and Brain Sciences, 37*(2), 212–213. doi:10.1017/S0140525X13002422

O'Conner-Von, S., & Turner, H. N. (2013). American Society for Pain Management Nursing (ASPMN) position statement: Male infant circumcision pain management. *Pain Management Nursing, 14*(4), 379–382. doi:10.1016/j.pmn.2011.08.007

Oostenbroek, J., Slaughter, V., Nielsen, M., & Suddendorf, T. (2013). Why the confusion around neonatal imitation? A review. *Journal of Reproductive and Infant Psychology, 31*(4), 328–341. doi:10.1080/02646838.2013.832180

Owings, M., Uddin, S., & Williams, S. (2013). *Trends in circumcision among male newborns born in U.S. hospitals: 1979–2010.* Retrieved from http://www.cdc.gov/nchs/data/hestat/circumcision_2013/circumcision_2013.htm

Paix, B. R., & Peterson, S. E. (2012). Circumcision of neonates and children without appropriate anaesthesia is unacceptable practice. *Anaesthesia & Intensive Care, 40*(3).

Papousek, H. (1967). Conditioning during early postnatal development. In Y. Brackbill & G. G. Thompson (Eds.), *Behavior in infancy and early childhood* (pp. 268–284). New York: Free Press.

Pascalis, O., Dechonen, S., Morton, J., Duruelle, C., & Grenet, F. (1995). Mother's face recognition in neonates: A replication and an extension. *Infant Behavior and Development, 18*, 79–85.

Pérez-Expósito, A. B., & Klein, B. P. (2009). Impact of fortified blended food aid products on nutritional status of infants and young children in developing countries. *Nutrition Reviews, 67*(12), 706–718. doi:10.1111/j.1753-4887.2009.00255.x

Piaget, J. (1952). *The origins of intelligence in children.* New York: International Universities Press. (Original work published 1936).

Pineau, A., & Streri, A. (1990). Intermodal transfer of spatial arrangement of the component parts of an object in 4/5 month-old infants. *Perception, 19*, 795–804.

Porter, R., Varendi, H., Christensson, K., Porter, R. H., & Winberg, J. (1998). Soothing effect of amniotic fluid smell in newborn infants. *Early Human Development, 51*, 47–55.

Price, D., Jarman, A. P., Mason, J. O., & Kind, P. C. (2011). *Building brains: An introduction to neural development (Google eBook).* Hoboken, NJ: John Wiley. Retrieved from http://books.google.com/books?id=0PBVlxmlmAQC&pgis=1

Racine, E. F., Frick, K., Guthrie, J. F., & Strobino, D. (2009). Individual net-benefit maximization: A model for understanding breastfeeding cessation among low-income women. *Maternal & Child Health Journal, 13*(2), 241–249. doi:10.1007/s10995-008-0337-1

Rasheed, S., Frongillo, E. A., Devine, C. M., Alam, D. S., & Rasmussen, K. M. (2009). Maternal, infant, and household factors are associated with breast-feeding trajectories during infants' first 6 months of life in Matlab, Bangladesh. *Journal of Nutrition, 139*(8), 1582–1587. doi:10.3945/jn.108.102392

Rattaz, C., Goubet, N., & Bullinger, A. (2005). The calming effect of a familiar odor on full-term newborns. *Journal of Developmental and Behavioral Pediatrics, 26*(2), 86–92.

Razmus, I. S., Dalton, M. E., & Wilson, D. (2004). Pain management for newborn circumcision. *Pediatric Nursing, 30*(5), 414–427.

Richards, J. E. (1997). Effects of attention on infant's preference for briefly exposed visual stimuli in the paired-comparison recognition-memory paradigm. *Developmental Psychology, 32*, 22–31.

Richards, J. E., & Holley, F. B. (1999). Infant attention and the development of smooth pursuit tracking. *Developmental Psychology, 35*, 856–867.

Rizzolatti, G., Sinigaglia, C., & Anderson, F. (2008). *Mirrors in the brain: How our minds share actions and emotions.* New York: Oxford University Press.

Roelants, M., Hauspie, R., & Hoppenbrouwers, K. (2010). Breastfeeding, growth and growth standards: Performance of the WHO growth standards for monitoring growth of Belgian children. *Annals of Human Biology, 37*(1), 2–9. doi:10.3109/03014460903089500

Rose, S. A., & Feldman, J. F. (1995). Prediction of IQ and specific cognitive abilities from infancy measures. *Developmental Psychology, 31*, 685–696.

Rose, S. A., Gottfried, A. W., & Bridger, W. H. (1981). Cross-modal and information processing by the sense of touch in infancy. *Developmental Psychology, 17*(1), 90–98.

Rosenzweig, M. R. (1984). Experience, memory, and the brain. *American Psychologist, 39*, 365–376.

Rosenzweig, M. R. (2002). Animal research on effects of experience on brain and behavior: Implications for rehabilitation. *Infants & Young Children, 15*(2), 1–10.

Rovee-Collier, C. K. (1987). Learning and memory. In J. D. Osofsky (Ed.), *Handbook of infant development* (2nd ed., pp. 98–148). New York: John Wiley.

Rovee-Collier, C. K. (1999). The development of infant memory. *Current Directions in Psychological Science, 8*, 80–85.

Ruff, H. A., & Kohler, C. J. (1978). Tactual visual transfer in six-month-old infants. *Infant Behavior & Development, 1*, 259–264.

Russell, M. J. (1976). Human olfactory communication. *Nature, 260*, 520–522.

Sai, F. Z. (2005). The role of the mother's voice in developing mother's face preference: Evidence

for intermodal perception at birth. *Infant & Child Development, 14*, 29–50.

Salmon, D. A., Moulton, L. H., Omer, S. B., deHart, M. P., Stokley, S., & Halsey, N. A. (2005). Factors associated with refusal of childhood vaccines among parents of school-aged children: A case-control study. *Archives of Pediatrics and Adolescent Medicine, 159*, 470–476.

Sann, C., & Streri, A. (2007). Perception of object shape and texture in human newborns: Evidence from cross-modal transfer tasks. *Developmental Science, 10*(3), 399–410. doi:10.1111/j.1467-7687.2007.00593.x

Saunders-Goldson, M. S., & Edwards, Q. T. (2004). Factors associated with breastfeeding intentions of African-American women at military health care facilities. *Military Medicine, 169*, 111–116.

Savino, F., Fissore, M. F., Liguori, S. A., & Oggero, R. (2009). Can hormones contained in mothers' milk account for the beneficial effect of breast-feeding on obesity in children? *Clinical Endocrinology, 71*(6), 757–765. doi:10.1111/j.1365-2265.2009.03585.x

Schaal, B., Montagner, H., Hertling, E., Bolzoni, D., Moyse, R., & Quichon, R. (1980). Olfactory stimulations in mother-infant relationships. *Reproduction, Nutrition, Développement, 20*, 843–858.

Schachter, F. F., Fuchs, M. L., Bijur, P. E., & Stone, R. K. (1989). Cosleeping and sleep problems in Hispanic-American urban young children. *Pediatrics, 84*(3), 522–530.

Schulze, P. A., & Carlisle, S. A. (2010). What research does and doesn't say about breastfeeding: a critical review. *Early Child Development & Care, 180*(6), 703–718. doi:10.1080/03004430802263870

Shaw, D. J., & Czekóová, K. (2013). Exploring the development of the mirror neuron system: Finding the right paradigm. *Developmental Neuropsychology, 38*(4), 256–271. doi:10.1080/87565641.2013.783832

Siega-Riz, A. M., Deming, D. M., Reidy, K. C., Fox, M. K., Condon, E., & Briefel, R. R. (2010). Food consumption patterns of infants and toddlers: Where are we now? *Journal of the American Dietetic Association, 110*(Suppl. 12), S38–S51. doi:10.1016/j.jada.2010.09.001

Slater, A., Brown, E., & Badenoch, M. (1997). Intermodal perception at birth: Newborn infants' memory for arbitrary auditory-visual pairings. *Early Development and Parenting, 6*, 99–104.

Slater, A., Quinn, P. C., Brown, E., & Hayes, R. (1999). Intermodal perception at birth: Intersensory redundancy guides newborn infants' learning of arbitrary auditory-visual pairings. *Developmental Science, 2*(3), 333–338.

Slater, A., Rose, D., & Morison, V. (1984). Newborn infants' perception of similarities and differences between two- and three-dimensional stimuli. *British Journal of Developmental Psychology, 3*, 211–220.

Sloan, S., Stewart, M., & Dunne, L. (2010). The effect of breastfeeding and stimulation in the home on cognitive development in one-year-old infants. *Child Care in Practice, 16*(2), 101–110. doi:10.1080/13575270903529136

Sola, A., Rogido, M., & Partridge, J. (2002). The perinatal period. In A. Rudolph, R. Kamei, & K. Overby (Eds.), *Rudolph's fundamental of pediatrics* (pp. 125–183). New York: McGraw-Hill.

Spelke, E. S. (1976). Infants' intermodal perception of events. *Cognitive Psychology, 8*, 553–560.

Spencer, J. P., Vereijken, B., Diedrich, F. J., & Thelen, E. (2000). Posture and the emergence of manual skills. *Developmental Science, 3*(2), 216–217.

Stein, Z., & Kuhn, L. (2009). Breast feeding: A time to craft new policies. *Journal of Public Health Policy, 30*(3), 300–310. doi:10.1057/jphp.2009.23

Steiner, J. E. (1979). Human facial expressions in response to taste and smell stimulations. In L. P. Lipsitt & H. W. Reese (Eds.), *Advances in child development* (Vol. 13, pp. 257–295). New York: Academic Press.

Stephens, M. B., Gentry, B. C., Michener, M. D., & Kendall, S. K. (2008). What is the clinical workup for failure to thrive? *Journal of Family Practice, 57*(4), 264–266.

Stiles, J., & Jernigan, T. L. (2010). The basics of brain development. *Neuropsychology Review, 20*(4), 327–348. doi:10.1007/s11065-010-9148-4

Suddendorf, T., Oostenbroek, J., Nielsen, M., & Slaughter, V. (2013). Is newborn imitation developmentally homologous to later social-cognitive skills? *Developmental Psychobiology, 55*(1), 52–58. doi:10.1002/dev.21005

Sugita, Y. (2004). Experience in early infancy is indispensable for color perception. *American Journal of Ophthalmology, 138*(5), 902.

Super, C. M., & Harkness, S. (1982). The infant's niche in rural Kenya and metropolitan America. In L. L. Adler (Ed.), *Cross-cultural research at issue* (pp. 247–255). New York: Academic Press.

Tamis-LeMonda, C. S., Song, L., & Bornstein, M. H. (1989). Habituation and maternal encouragement of attention in infancy as predictors of toddler language, play, and representational competence. *Child Development, 60*, 738–751.

Tanaka, K., Kon, N., Ohkawa, N., Yoshikawa, N., & Shimizu, T. (2009). Does breastfeeding in the neonatal period influence the cognitive function of very-low-birth-weight infants at 5 years of age? *Brain & Development, 31*(4), 288–293. doi:10.1016/j.braindev.2008.05.011

Taylor, L. E., Swerdfeger, A. L., & Eslick, G. D. (2014). Vaccines are not associated with autism: An evidence-based meta-analysis of case-control and cohort studies. *Vaccine, 32*(29), 3623–3629. doi:10.1016/j.vaccine.2014.04.085

Taylor, N., Donovan, W., & Leavitt, L. (2008). Consistency in infant sleeping arrangements and mother-infant interaction. *Infant Mental Health Journal, 29*(2), 77–94. doi:10.1002/imhj.20170

Teller, D. Y. (1997). First glances: The vision of infants. *Investigative Ophthalmology & Visual Science, 38*, 2183–2203.

Teller, D. Y. (1998). Spatial and temporal aspects of infant color vision. *Vision Research, 38*, 3275–3282.

Thelen, E. (1995). Motor development: A new synthesis. *American Psychologist, 50*(2), 79–95. doi:10.1037/0003-066X.50.2.79

Thelen, E. (2000). Motor development as foundation and future of developmental psychology. *International Journal of Behavioral Development, 24*(4), 385–397.

Thoman, E. B., & Ingersoll, E. W. (1993). Learning in premature infants. *Developmental Psychology, 28*, 692–700.

Thompson, R. F. (1993). *The brain: A neuroscience primer* (3rd ed.). New York: Worth.

Trettien, A. W. (1990). Creeping and walking. *American Journal of Psychology, 12*, 1–57.

Trevathan, W. R., & McKenna, J. J. (1994). Evolutionary environments of human birth and infancy: Insights to apply to contemporary life. *Children's Environments, 11*, 88–104.

Twardosz, S., & Lutzker, J. R. (2009). Child maltreatment and the developing brain: A review of neuroscience perspectives. *Aggression and Violent Behavior, 15*(1), 59–68. doi:10.1016/j.avb.2009.08.003

U.K. Department of Health. (2005). *Reduce the risk of cot death: An easy guide.* London: Author.

Ullian, E. M., Sapperstein, S. K., Christopherson, K. S., & Barres, B. A. (2001). Control of synapse number by glia. *Science, 291*, 657–661.

UNICEF. (2009). *The state of the world's children special edition: Celebrating 20 years of the*

convention on the rights of the child. Chicago: Author.

U.S. Department of Health and Human Services. (2011). *The surgeon general's call to action to support breastfeeding.* Washington, DC: Author.

Van Heteren, C. F., Boekkooi, P. F., Jongsma, H. W., & Nijhuis, J. G. (2000). Fetal learning and memory. *Lancet*, 1169–1170.

Vereijken, B., & Thelen, E. (1997). Training infant treadmill stepping: The role of individual pattern stability. *Developmental Psychobiology, 30*, 89–102.

Victora, C. G. (2009). Nutrition in early life: A global priority. *Lancet, 374*(9696), 1123–1125.

Von Hofsten, C., & Rönnqvist, L. (1993). The structuring of neonatal arm movements. *Child Development, 64*(4), 1046–1057. Retrieved from http://www.ncbi.nlm.nih.gov/pubmed/8404256

Vouloumanos, A., Hauser, M. D., Werker, J. F., & Martin, A. (2010). The tuning of human neonates' preference for speech. *Child Development, 81*(2), 517–527. doi:10.1111/j.1467-8624.2009.01412.x

Waldeck, S. E. (2003). Social norm theory and male circumcision: Why parents circumcise. *American Journal of Bioethics, 3*(2), 56–57.

Walk, R. D. (1968). Monocular compared to binocular depth perception in human infants. *Science, 162*, 473–475.

Walle, E. A. C. J. J. (2013). Infant language development is related to the acquisition of walking. *Developmental Psychology, 50*. doi:10.1037/a0033238

Waltes, R., Duketis, E., Knapp, M., Anney, R. J. L., Huguet, G., Schlitt, S., . . . Chiocchetti, A. G. (2014). Common variants in genes of the postsynaptic FMRP signalling pathway are risk factors for autism spectrum disorders. *Human Genetics, 133*(6), 781–792. doi:10.1007/s00439-013-1416-y

Watson, J. B., & Raynor, R. (1920). Conditioned emotional reactions. *Journal of Experimental Psychology, 3*, 1–14.

Wertheimer, M. (1961). Psychomotor coordination of auditory and visual space at birth. *Science, 134*, 1692.

Whitehouse, A. J. O., Robinson, M., Li, J., & Oddy, W. H. (2011). Duration of breast feeding and language ability in middle childhood. *Paediatric & Perinatal Epidemiology, 25*(1), 44–52. doi:10.1111/j.1365-3016.2010.01161.x

Willinger, M., Ko, C.-W., Hoffman, H. J., Kessler, R. C., & Corwin, M. J. (2003). Trends in infant bed sharing in the United States, 1993–2000. *Archives of Pediatrics and Adolescent Medicine, 157*, 43–49.

Wilson, R. S., & Harpring, E. B. (1972). Mental and motor development in infant twins. *Developmental Psychology, 7*(3), 277–287.

Wilson, S. L. (2003). Post-institutionalization: The effects of early deprivation on development of Romanian adoptees. *Child & Adolescent Social Work Journal, 20*(6), 473–483.

Witherington, D. C., Campos, J. J., Anderson, D. I., Lejeune, L., & Seah, E. (2005). Avoidance of heights on the visual cliff in newly walking infants. *Infancy, 7*(3), 285–298. doi:10.1207/s15327078in0703_4

World Health Organization. (2009). *WHO child growth standards and the identification of severe acute malnutrition in infants and children: A joint statement.* Retrieved from http://www.who.int/nutrition/publications/severemalnutrition/9789241598163/en

Xiao-na, H., Hui-shan, W., Li-jin, Z., & Xi-cheng, L. (2010). Co-sleeping and children's sleep in China. *Biological Rhythm Research, 41*(3), 169–181. doi:10.1080/09291011003687940

Zeanah, C. H. (2009). The importance of early experiences: Clinical, research, and policy perspectives. *Journal of Loss & Trauma, 14*(4), 266–279. doi:10.1080/15325020903004426

Zelazo, N. A., Zelazo, P. R., Cohen, K. M., & Zelazo, P. D. (1993). Specificity of practice effects on elementary neuromotor patterns. *Developmental Psychology, 29*, 686–691.

Zelazo, P. R. (1983). The development of walking: New findings on old assumptions. *Journal of Motor Behavior, 2*, 99–137.

Zhang, Y., Niu, B., Yu, D., Cheng, X., Liu, B., & Deng, J. (2010). Radial glial cells and the lamination of the cerebellar cortex. *Brain Structure & Function, 215*(2), 115–122. doi:10.1007/s00429-010-0278-5

CHAPTER 5

Abraham, L. M., Crais, E., & Vernon-Feagans, L. (2013). Early maternal language use during book sharing in families from low-income environments. *American Journal of Speech-Language Pathology/American Speech-Language-Hearing Association, 22*(1), 71–83. doi:10.1044/1058-0360(2012/11-0153)

Acredolo, L. P., & Goodwyn, S. (1988). Symbolic gesturing in normal infants. *Child Development, 59*(2).

Acredolo, L. P., Goodwyn, S., & Abrams, D. (2009). *Baby signs: How to talk with your baby before your baby can talk* (3rd ed.). New York: McGraw-Hill. Retrieved from http://www.amazon.com/Baby-Signs-Talk-Before-Third/dp/0071615032/ref=sr_1_1?s=books&ie=UTF8&qid=1404581150&sr=1-1

Acredolo, L. P., & Goodwyn, S. W. (1985). Symbolic gesturing in language development. *Human Development, 28*(1), 40–49. doi:10.1159/10.1159/000272934

Adolph, K. E., & Berger, S. E. (2005). Physical and motor development. In M. H. Bornstein & M. E. Lamb (Eds.), *Developmental science: An advanced textbook* (5th ed., pp. 223–281). Mahwah, NJ: Lawrence Erlbaum.

Ahmed, A., & Ruffman, T. (1998). Why do infants make A not B errors in a search task, yet show memory for location of hidden objects in a non-search task? *Developmental Psychology, 34*, 441–453.

Akhtar, N., Jipson, J., & Callanan, M. A. (2001). Learning words through overhearing. *Child Development, 72*, 416–430.

Albers, L. H., Johnson, D. E., Hostetter, M. K., Iverson, S., & Miller, L. C. (1997). Health of children adopted from the former Soviet Union and Eastern Europe. Comparison with preadoptive medical records. *Journal of American Medical Association, 278*, 922–924.

Anderson, D. R., & Pempek, T. A. (2005). Television and very young children. *American Behavioral Scientist, 48*(5), 505–522. doi:10.1177/0002764204271506

Andersson, U. (2008). Working memory as a predictor of written arithmetical skills in children: The importance of central executive functions. *British Journal of Educational Psychology, 78*(2), 181–203.

Andruski, J. E., Casielles, E., & Nathan, G. (2013). Is bilingual babbling language-specific? Some evidence from a case study of Spanish–English dual acquisition. *Bilingualism: Language and Cognition, 17*(3), 660–672. doi:10.1017/S1366728913000655

Aslin, R. N., Clayards, M. A., & Bardhan, N. P. (2008). Mechanisms of auditory reorganization during development: From sounds to words. In C. A. Nelson & M. Luciana (Eds.), *Handbook of developmental cognitive neuroscience* (2nd ed., pp. 97–116). Cambridge, MA: MIT Press.

Baddeley, A. (1986). *Working memory.* London: Oxford University Press.

Baddeley, A. (1996). Exploring the central executive. *The Quarterly Journal of Experimental Psychology, 49*(a), 5–28.

Baillargeon, R. (1987). Object permanence in 3 1/2- and 4 1/2-month-old-infants. *Developmental Psychology, 23*(5), 655–664.

Baillargeon, R. (1994). How do infants learn about the physical world? *Current Directions in Psychological Science, 3*, 133–140.

Baillargeon, R., Li, J., Gertner, Y., & Wu, D. (2011). How do infants reason about physical events? In U. Goswami (Ed.), *The Wiley-Blackwell handbook of childhood cognitive development* (2nd ed., pp. 11–48). Hoboken, NJ: Wiley-Blackwell.

Baldwin, D. A., Markman, E. M., Bill, B., Desjardins, R. N., Irwin, J. M., & Tidball, G. (1996). Infants' reliance on social criteria for establishing word-object relations. *Child Development, 67*, 3135–3153.

Barr, R. (2013). Memory constraints on infant learning from picture books, television, and touchscreens. *Child Development Perspectives, 7*(4), 205–210. doi:10.1111/cdep.12041

Barr, R., Dowden, A., & Hayne, H. (1996). Developmental changes in deferred imitation by 6- to 24-month-old infants. *Infant Behavior and Development, 19*, 159–170.

Barr, R., Marrott, H., & Rovee-Collier, C. (2003). The role of sensory preconditioning in memory retrieval by preverbal infants. *Learning & Behavior, 31*(2), 111–123.

Bassano, D. (2000). Early development of nouns and verbs in French: Exploring the interface between lexicon and grammar. *Journal of Child Language, 27*, 521–559.

Bates, E., Bretherton, I., & Snyder, L. (1988). *From first words to grammar*. Cambridge, UK: Cambridge University Press.

Bayley, N. (1949). Consistency and variability in the growth of intelligence from birth to eighteen years. *The Pedagogical Seminary and Journal of Genetic Psychology, 75*(2), 165–196. doi:10.1080/08856559.1949.10533516

Bayley, N. (1969). *Manual for the Bayley Scales of Infant Development*. San Antonio, TX: Psychological Corporation.

Bayley, N. (2005). *Bayley Scales of Infant and Toddler Development* (3rd ed.). San Antonio, TX: Psychological Corporation.

Beilin, H., & Fireman, G. (2000). The foundation of Piaget's theories: Mental and physical action. In H. W. Reese (Ed.), *Advances in child development and behavior* (Vol. 27, pp. 221–246). San Diego: Academic Press.

Bertenthal, B. I., Longo, M. R., & Kenny, S. (2007). Phenomenal permanence and the development of predictive tracking in infancy. *Child Development, 78*(1), 350–363. doi:10.1111/j.1467-8624.2007.01002.x

Bogartz, R. S., Shinskey, J. L., & Schilling, T. H. (2000). Object permanence in five-and-a-half-month-old infants? *Infancy, 1*(4), 403–428. doi:10.1207/S15327078IN0104_3

Bohannon, J. N., Padgett, R. J., Nelson, K. E., & Mark, M. (1996). Useful evidence on negative evidence. *Developmental Psychology, 32*, 551–555.

Bohannon, J. N., & Stanowicz, L. (1988). The issue of negative evidence: Adult responses to children's language errors. *Developmental Psychology, 24*, 684–689.

Bornstein, M. H., & Arterberry, M. E. (2010). The development of object categorization in young children: Hierarchical inclusiveness, age, perceptual attribute, and group versus individual analyses. *Developmental Psychology, 46*(2), 350–365. doi:10.1037/a0018411

Bornstein, M. H., Arterberry, M. E., & Mash, C. (2004). Long-term memory for an emotional interpersonal interaction occurring at 5 months of age. *Infancy, 6*(4), 407–416.

Bornstein, M. H., Cote, L. R., Maital, S., Painter, K., Park, S.-Y., Pascual, L., . . . Vyt, A. (2004). Cross-linguistic analysis of vocabulary in young children: Spanish, Dutch, French, Hebrew, Italian, Korean, and American English. *Child Development, 75*(4), 1115–1139.

Bornstein, M. H., Slater, A., Brown, E., Roberts, E., & Barrett, J. (1997). Stability of mental development from infancy to later childhood: Three "waves" of research. In G. Bremner, A. Slater, & G. Butterworth (Eds.), *Infant development: Recent advances* (pp. 191–215). East Sussex, UK: Psychology Press.

Bremner, J. G., Slater, A. M., & Johnson, S. P. (2015). Perception of object persistence: The origins of object permanence in infancy. *Child Development Perspectives, 9*(1), 7–13. doi:10.1111/cdep.12098

Brown, A. (2011). Media use by children younger than 2 years. *Pediatrics, 128*(5), 1040–1045. doi:10.1542/peds.2011-1753

Bruner, J. S., Goodnow, J. J., & Austin, G. A. (1956). *A study of thinking*. Hoboken, NJ: John Wiley.

Bryant, G. A. (2012). Recognizing infant-directed speech across distant cultures: Evidence from Africa. *Journal of Evolutionary Psychology, 10*(2). doi:10.1556/JEP.10.2012.2.1

Burnham, D., Kitamura, C., & Vollmer-Conna, U. (2002). What's new pussycat? On talking to babies and animals. *Science, 296*, 1435.

Caselli, M. C., Bates, E., Casadio, P., Fenson, J., Fenson, L., Sanderl, L., & Weir, J. (1995). A cross-linguistic study of early lexical development. *Cognitive Development, 10*, 159–199.

Chen, L.-M., & Kent, R. D. (2010). Segmental production in Mandarin-learning infants. *Journal of Child Language, 37*(2), 341–371. doi:10.1017/s0305000909009581

Cheour, M., Ceponiene, R., Leppanen, P., Alho, K., Kujala, T., Renlund, M., . . . Naatanen, R. (2002). The auditory sensory memory trace decays rapidly in newborns. *Scandinavian Journal of Psychology, 43*(1), 33–39. doi:10.1111/1467-9450.00266

Chomsky, N. (1959). Review of B. F. Skinner's *Verbal Behavior. Language, 35*, 26–58.

Chomsky, N. (1965). *Aspects of the theory of syntax*. Cambridge, MA: MIT Press.

Chonchaiya, W., & Pruksananonda, C. (2008). Television viewing associates with delayed language development. *Acta Paediatrica, 97*(7), 977–982. doi:10.1111/j.1651-2227.2008.00831.x

Christakis, D. A. (2009). The effects of infant media usage: What do we know and what should we learn? *Acta Paediatrica, 98*(1), 8–16. doi:10.1111/j.1651-2227.2008.01027.x

Clauss, D., & Baxter, S. (1997). Post adoption survey of Russian and Eastern European children. *Roots and Wings Adoption Magazine, 6*, 6–9.

Cohen, L. B., & Cashon, C. H. (2006). Infant cognition. In D. Kuhn, R. S. Siegler, W. Damon, & R. M. Lerner (Eds.), *Handbook of child psychology: Vol. 2, Cognition, perception, and language* (6th ed., pp. 214–251). Hoboken, NJ: John Wiley.

Colombo, J. (2001). The development of visual attention in infancy. *Annual Review of Psychology, 52*, 337–367.

Colombo, J., McCollam, K., Coldren, J. T., Mitchell, D. W., & Rash, S. J. (1990). Form categorization in 10-month-olds. *Journal of Experimental Child Psychology, 49*, 173–188.

Cordes, S., & Brannon, E. M. (2009). Crossing the divide: Infants discriminate small from large numerosities. *Developmental Psychology, 45*(6), 1583–1594. doi:10.1037/a0015666

Coubart, A., Izard, V., Spelke, E. S., Marie, J., & Streri, A. (2014). Dissociation between small and large numerosities in newborn infants. *Developmental Science, 17*(1), 11–22. doi:10.1111/desc.12108

Courage, M. L., & Cowan, N. (2009). *The development of memory in infancy and childhood* (2nd ed.). New York: Psychology Press.

Courage, M. L., & Howe, M. L. (2010). To watch or not to watch: Infants and toddlers in a brave new electronic world. *Developmental Review, 30*(2), 101–115. doi:10.1016/j.dr.2010.03.002

Courage, M. L., Reynolds, G. D., & Richards, J. E. (2006). Infants' attention to patterned stimuli: Developmental change from 3 to 12 months of age. *Child Development, 77*(3), 680–695. doi:10.1111/j.1467-8624.2006.00897.x

Cuevas, K., & Bell, M. A. (2010). Developmental progression of looking and reaching performance on the A-not-B task. *Developmental Psychology, 46*(5), 1363–1371. doi:10.1037/a0020185

Cuevas, K., & Bell, M. A. (2013). Infant attention and early childhood executive function. *Child Development, 85*(2), 397–404. doi:10.1111/cdev.12126

Daneman, M., & Carpenter, P. A. (1980). Individual differences in working memory and reading. *Journal of Verbal Learning and Verbal Behavior, 19*, 450–466.

Dapretto, M., & Bjork, E. L. (2000). The development of word retrieval abilities in the second year and it's relation to early vocabulary growth. *Child Development, 71*, 635–648.

De Houwer, A., & Gillis, S. (1998). *The acquisition of Dutch*. Amsterdam: Benjamins.

DeLoache, J. S., Chiong, C., Sherman, K., Islam, N., Vanderborght, M., Troseth, G. L., . . . O'Doherty, K. (2010). Do babies learn from baby media? *Psychological Science, 21*(11), 1570–1574. doi:10.1177/0956797610384145

Diamond, A. (1985). The development of the ability to use recall to guide action as indicated by infants' performance on A-B. *Child Development, 56*, 868–883.

Diamond, A. (1991). Neuropsychological insights into the meaning of object concept development. In S. Carey & R. Gelman (Eds.), *The epigenesis of mind: Essays on biology and cognition* (pp. 67–110). Hillsdale, NJ: Lawrence Erlbaum.

Doherty-Sneddon, G. (2008). The great baby signing debate: Academia meets public interest. *British Psychological Society*. Retrieved from https://dspace.stir.ac.uk/handle/1893/385

Duch, H., Fisher, E. M., Ensari, I., & Harrington, A. (2013). Screen time use in children under 3 years old: A systematic review of correlates. *The International Journal of Behavioral Nutrition and Physical Activity, 10*(1), 102. doi:10.1186/1479-5868-10-102

Elsabbagh, M., Hohenberger, A., Campos, R., Van Herwegen, J., Serres, J., de Schonen, S., . . . Karmiloff-Smith, A. (2013). Narrowing perceptual sensitivity to the native language in infancy: Exogenous influences on developmental timing. *Behavioral Sciences, 3*(1), 120–132. doi:10.3390/bs3010120

Englund, K., & Behne, D. (2006). Changes in infant directed speech in the first six months. *Infant & Child Development, 15*, 139–160.

Epstein, R. (1991). Skinner, creativity, and the problem of spontaneous behavior. *Psychological Science, 2*(6), 362–370.

Estes, K. G. (2013). Infant-directed prosody helps infants map sounds to meanings. *Infancy, 18*(5). doi:10.1111/infa.12006

Fagan, J. F. (1973). Infants' delayed recognition memory and forgetting. *Journal of Experimental Child Psychology, 16*, 424–450.

Fagan, J. F. (2011). Intelligence in infancy. In R. J. Sternberg & S. B. Kaufman (Eds.), *The Cambridge handbook of intelligence* (pp. 130–142). New York: Cambridge University Press. Retrieved from http://books.google.com/books?hl=en&lr=&id=FtYeTcNwzQ4C&pgis=1

Fagan, J. F., Holland, C. R., & Wheeler, K. (2007). The prediction, from infancy, of adult IQ and achievement. *Intelligence, 35*(3), 225–231. doi:10.1016/j.intell.2006.07.007

Fenstermacher, S. K., Barr, R., Salerno, K., Garcia, A., Shwery, C. E., Calvert, S. L., & Linebarger, D. L. (2010). Infant-directed media: An analysis of product information and claims. *Infant & Child Development, 19*(6), 556–557. doi:10.1002/icd.718

Ferguson, C. J., & Donnellan, M. B. (2014). Is the association between children's baby video viewing and poor language development robust? A reanalysis of Zimmerman, Christakis, and Meltzoff (2007). *Developmental Psychology, 50*(1), 129–137. doi:10.1037/a0033628

Fernald, A., & McRoberts, G. (1996). Prosaic bootstrapping: A critical analysis of the argument and the evidence. In J. L. Morgan & K. Demuth (Eds.), *Signal to syntax.* Hillsdale, NJ: Lawrence Erlbaum.

Fernald, A., & Morikawa, H. (1993). Common themes and cultural variations in Japanese and American mothers' speech to infants. *Child Development, 64*, 657–674.

Flavell, J. H. (1993). The development of children's understanding of false belief and the appearance-reality distinction. *International Journal of Psychology, 28*, 595–604.

Frank, M. C., Vul, E., & Johnson, S. P. (2009). Development of infants' attention to faces during the first year. *Cognition, 110*(2), 160–170. doi:10.1016/j.cognition.2008.11.010

Ganger, J., & Brent, M. R. (2004). Reexamining the vocabulary spurt. *Developmental Psychology, 40*(4), 621–632.

Gathercole, S. E. (1998). The development of memory. *Journal of Child Psychology and Psychiatry and Allied Disciplines, 39*, 3–27.

Gershkoff-Stowe, L. (2002). Object naming, vocabulary growth, and the development of word retrieval abilities. *Journal of Memory & Language, 46*(4), 665.

Glennen, S. (2002). Language development and delay in internationally adopted infants and toddlers: A review. *American Journal of Speech-Language Pathology, 11*, 333–339.

Glennen, S. (2014). A longitudinal study of language and speech in children who were internationally adopted at different ages. *Language, Speech, and Hearing Services in Schools, 45*(3), 185–203. doi:10.1044/2014_LSHSS-13-0035

Glennen, S., & Masters, M. (2002). Typical and atypical language development in infants and toddlers adopted from Eastern Europe. *American Journal of Speech-Language Pathology, 11*, 417–433.

Goodwyn, S. W., & Acredolo, L. P. (1998). Encouraging symbolic gestures: A new perspective on the relationship between gesture and speech. *New Directions for Child and Adolescent Development, 1998*(79), 61–73. doi:10.1002/cd.23219987905

Gopnik, A., & Choi, S. (1995). *Beyond names for things: Children's acquisition of verbs.* Hillsdale, NJ: Lawrence Erlbaum.

Goubet, N., & Clifton, R. K. (1998). Object and event representation in 6½-month-old infants. *Developmental Psychology, 34*, 63–76.

Gratier, M., & Devouche, E. (2011). Imitation and repetition of prosodic contour in vocal interaction at 3 months. *Developmental Psychology, 47*, 67–76.

Green, J. R., Nip, I. S. B., Wilson, E. M., Mefferd, A. S., & Yunusova, Y. (2010). Lip movement exaggerations during infant-directed speech. *Journal of Speech, Language & Hearing Research, 53*(6), 1529–1542. doi:10.1044/1092-4388(2010/09-0005)

Harwood, R., Feng, X., & Yu, S. (2013). Preadoption adversities and postadoption mediators of mental health and school outcomes among international, foster, and private adoptees

in the United States. *Journal of Family Psychology, 27*(3), 409–420. doi:10.1037/a0032908

Hayne, H. (2004). Infant memory development: Implications for childhood amnesia. *Developmental Review, 24*, 33–73.

Hayne, H., Boniface, J., & Barr, R. (2000). The development of declarative memory in human infants: Age-related changes in deferred imitation. *Behavioral Neuroscience, 114*(1), 77–83. doi:10.1037/0735-7044.114.1.77

Herbert, J., & Hayne, H. (2000). Memory retrieval by 18-30 month olds: Age related changes in representational flexibility. *Developmental Psychology, 36*, 473–484.

Hoff, E., Naigles, L., & Nigales, L. (2002). How children use input to acquire a lexicon. *Child Development, 73*(2), 418–433.

Honzik, M. P. (1983). Measuring mental abilities in infancy: The value and limitations. In M. Lewis (Ed.), *Origins of Intelligence* (2nd ed.). New York: Plenum.

Hudon, T. M., Fennell, C. T., & Hoftyzer, M. (2013). Quality not quantity of television viewing is associated with bilingual toddlers' vocabulary scores. *Infant Behavior & Development, 36*(2), 245–254. doi:10.1016/j.infbeh.2013.01.010

Iverson, J. M., & Goldin-Meadow, S. (2005). Gesture paves the way for language development. *Psychological Science, 16*(5), 367–371. doi:10.1111/j.0956-7976.2005.01542.x

Jackson-Maldonado, D., Thal, D., Marchman, V., Bates, E., & Gutierrez-Clellen, V. (1993). Early lexical development in Spanish-speaking infants and toddlers. *Journal of Child Language, 20*, 523–549.

Jacobs, E., Miller, L. C., & Tirella, L. G. (2010). Developmental and behavioral performance of internationally adopted preschoolers: A pilot study. *Child Psychiatry & Human Development, 41*(1), 15–29. doi:10.1007/s10578-009-0149-6

James, W. (1890). *Principles of psychology.* New York: Henry Holt.

Johnson, D. E. (2000). Medical and developmental sequelae of early childhood institutionalization in Eastern European adoptees. *Minnesota Symposium on Child Psychology: Vol. 31. The Effects of Adversity on Neurobehavioral Development, 31*, 113–162.

Johnston, J. C. (2005). Teaching gestural signs to infants to advance child development: A review of the evidence. *First Language, 25*(2), 235–251. doi:10.1177/0142723705050340

Jones, E. J. H., & Herbert, J. S. (2006). Exploring memory in infancy: Deferred imitation and the development of declarative memory. *Infant & Child Development, 15*, 195–205.

Just, M. A., & Carpenter, P. A. (1992). A capacity theory of comprehension: Individual differences in working memory. *Psychological Review, 99*, 122–149.

Kagan, J. (2008). In defense of qualitative changes in development. *Child Development, 79*(6), 1606–1624. doi:10.1111/j.1467-8624.2008.01211.x

Kail, R. (2000). Speed of information processing: Developmental change and links to intelligence. *Journal of School Psychology, 38*, 51–61.

Kärtner, J., Keller, H., Lamm, B., Abels, M., Yovsi, R. D., Chaudhary, N., & Su, Y. (2008). Similarities and differences in contingency experiences of 3-month-olds across sociocultural contexts. *Infant Behavior & Development, 31*(3), 488–500. doi:10.1016/j.infbeh.2008.01.001

Kavšek, M. (2004). Predicting later IQ from infant visual habituation and dishabituation: A meta-analysis. *Journal of Applied Developmental Psychology, 25*(3), 369–393. doi:10.1016/j.appdev.2004.04.006

Kavšek, M. (2013). The comparator model of infant visual habituation and dishabituation:

Recent insights. *Developmental Psychobiology, 55*(8), 793–808. doi:10.1002/dev.21081

Kirk, E., Howlett, N., Pine, K. J., & Fletcher, B. C. (2013). To sign or not to sign? The impact of encouraging infants to gesture on infant language and maternal mind-mindedness. *Child Development, 84*(2), 574–590. doi:10.1111/j.1467-8624.2012.01874.x

Kitamura, C., & Burnham, D. (2003). Pitch and communicative intent in mother's speech: Adjustments for age and sex in the first year. *Infancy, 4*(1), 85–110.

Klein, P. J., & Meltzoff, A. N. (1999). Long-term memory, forgetting, and deferred imitation in 12-month-old infants. *Developmental Science, 2*, 102–113.

Kolling, T., Goertz, C., Stefanie, F., & Knopf, M. (2010). Memory development throughout the second year: Overall developmental pattern, individual differences, and developmental trajectories. *Infant Behavior & Development, 33*(2), 159–167. doi:10.1016/j.infbeh.2009.12.007

Krcmar, M. (2014). Can infants and toddlers learn words from repeat exposure to an infant directed DVD? *Journal of Broadcasting & Electronic Media, 58*(2), 196–214. doi:10.1080/08838151.2014.906429

Kressley-Mba, R. A., Lurg, S., & Knopf, M. (2005). Testing for deferred imitation of 2- and 3-step action sequences with 6-month-olds. *Infant Behavior & Development, 28*(1), 82–86.

Kuhl, P. K., Andruski, J. E., Christovich, I. A., Christovich, L. A., Kozhevnikova, E. V., Ryskina, V. L., . . . Lacerda, F. (1997). Cross-language analysis of phonetic units in language addressed to infants. *Science, 277*, 684–686.

Kuhl, P. K., Williams, K. A., Lacerda, F., Stevens, K. N., & Lindblom, B. (1992). Linguistic experience alters phonetic perception in infants by 6 months of age. *Science, 255*, 606–608.

Learmonth, A. E., Lamberth, R., & Rovee-Collier, C. (2004). Generalizations of deferred imitation during the first year of life. *Journal of Experimental Child Psychology, 88*(4), 297–318.

Levine, L. E., & Munsch, J. (2010). *Child development: An active learning approach.* Thousand Oaks, CA: Sage.

Libertus, M. E., & Brannon, E. M. (2009). Behavioral and neural basis of number sense in infancy. *Current Directions in Psychological Science, 18*(6), 346–351. doi:10.1111/j.1467-8721.2009.01665.x

Libertus, M. E., Starr, A., & Brannon, E. M. (2014). Number trumps area for 7-month-old infants. *Developmental Psychology, 50.* doi:10.1037/a0032986

Linebarger, D. L., & Vaala, S. E. (2010). Screen media and language development in infants and toddlers: An ecological perspective. *Developmental Review, 30*(2), 176–202. doi:10.1016/j.dr.2010.03.006

Luttikhuizen dos Santos, E. S., de Kieviet, J. F., Königs, M., van Elburg, R. M., & Oosterlaan, J. (2013). Predictive value of the Bayley Scales of Infant Development on development of very preterm/very low birth weight children: A meta-analysis. *Early Human Development, 89*(7), 487–496. doi:10.1016/j.earlhumdev.2013.03.008

Maital, S. L., Dromi, E., Sagi, A., & Bornstein, M. H. (2000). The Hebrew Communicative Development Inventory: Language specific properties and cross-linguistic generalizations. *Journal of Child Language, 27*, 43–67.

Mandel, D. R., Jusczyk, P. W., & Pisoni, D. B. (1995). Infants' recognition of the sound patterns of their own names. *Psychological Science, 6*(5), 314–317.

Mandler, J. M. (2000). What global-before-basic trend? Comment on perceptually based approaches to early categorizations. *Infancy, 1*, 99–110.

Mandler, J. M. (2004). *The foundations of mind: Origins of conceptual thought*. New York: Oxford University Press.

Mandler, J. M., Fivush, R., & Reznick, J. S. (1987). The development of contextual categories. *Cognitive Development, 2*(4), 339–354. doi:10.1016/s0885-2014(87)80012-6

Mandler, J. M., & McDonough, L. (1993). Concept formation in infancy. *Cognitive Development, 8*, 291–318.

Mandler, J. M., & McDonough, L. (1998). On developing a knowledge base in infancy. *Developmental Psychology, 34*, 1274–1288.

Martin, R. M. (1975). Effects of familiar and complex stimuli on infant attention. *Developmental Psychology, 11*, 178–185.

Mascalzoni, E., Regolin, L., Vallortigara, G., & Simion, F. (2013). The cradle of causal reasoning: Newborns' preference for physical causality. *Developmental Science, 16*(3), 327–335. doi:10.1111/desc.12018

Mason, P., & Narad, C. (2005). International adoption: A health and developmental perspective. *Seminars in Speech and Language, 26*(1), 1–9.

McCall, R. B., & Carriger, M. S. (1993). A meta-analysis of infant habituation and recognition memory performance as predictors of later IQ. *Child Development, 64*, 57–79.

Meltzoff, A. N., & Moore, M. K. (1994). Imitation, memory, and the representation of persons. *Infant Behavior & Development, 17*(1), 83–99. doi:10.1016/0163-6383(94)90024-8

Miller, L. C. (2000). Initial assessment of growth, development, and the effects of institutionalization in internationally adopted children. *Pediatrics Annals, 69*, 1092–1106.

Miller, L. C., & Hendrie, N. W. (2000). Health of children adopted from China. *Pediatrics, 105*, 1–6.

Miller, P. H. (2009). *Theories of developmental psychology* (5th ed.). New York: Worth.

Misca, G. (2014). The "quiet migration": Is intercountry adoption a successful intervention in the lives of vulnerable children? *Family Court Review, 52*(1), 60–68. doi:10.1111/fcre.12070

Mix, K. S., Huttenlocher, J., & Levine, S. C. (2002). Multiple cues for quantification in infancy: Is number one of them? *Psychological Bulletin, 128*(2), 278–294. Retrieved from http://www.ncbi.nlm.nih.gov/pubmed/11931520

Molfese, D. L. (1977). Infant cerebral asymmetry. In S. J. Segalowitz & F. A. Gruber (Eds.), *Language development and neurological theory* (pp. 21–35). Orlando, FL: Academic Press.

Moore, C., Angelopoulos, M., & Bennett, P. (1999). Word learning in the context of referential and salience cues. *Developmental Psychology, 35*, 60–68.

Mueller, V., & Sepulveda, A. (2014). Parental perception of a baby sign workshop on stress and parent–child interaction. *Early Child Development and Care, 184*(3), 450–468. doi:10.1080/03004430.2013.797899

Murphy, G. L. (2002). *The big book of concepts*. Cambridge, MA: MIT Press.

Nelson, L. H., White, K. R., & Grewe, J. (2012). Evidence for website claims about the benefits of teaching sign language to infants and toddlers with normal hearing. *Infant and Child Development, 21*(5), 474–502. doi:10.1002/icd.1748

Neuman, S. B., Kaefer, T., Pinkham, A., & Strouse, G. (2014). Can babies learn to read? A randomized trial of baby media. *Journal of Educational Psychology, 106*(3), 815–830.

Oakes, L. M. (2010). Using habituation of looking time to assess mental processes in infancy. *Journal of Cognition & Development, 11*(3), 255–268. doi:10.1080/15248371003699977

Oakes, L. M., Coppage, D. J., & Dingel, A. (1997). By land or by sea: The role of perceptual similarity in infants' categorization of animals. *Developmental Psychology, 33*, 396–407.

Oakes, L. M., & Madole, K. L. (2003). Principles of developmental change in infants' category formation. In D. H. Rakison & L. M. Oakes (Eds.), *Early category and concept development: Making sense of the blooming, buzzing confusion* (pp. 132–158). New York: Oxford University Press.

Oller, D. K., Eilers, R. E., & Basinger, D. (2001). Intuitive identification of infant vocal sounds by parents. *Developmental Science, 4*(1), 49–60.

Palacios, J., Román, M., Moreno, C., León, E., & Peñarrubia, M.-G. (2014). Differential plasticity in the recovery of adopted children after early adversity. *Child Development Perspectives, 8*(3), 169–174. doi:10.1111/cdep.12083

Parisse, C., & Le Normand, M. (2000). How children build their morphosyntax: The case of French. *Journal of Child Language, 27*, 267–292.

Parladé, M. V, & Iverson, J. M. (2011). The interplay between language, gesture, and affect during communicative transition: A dynamic systems approach. *Developmental Psychology*. doi:10.1037/a0021811

Pelaez, M., Virues-Ortega, J., & Gewirtz, J. L. (2011). Reinforcement of vocalizations through contingent vocal imitation. *Journal of Applied Behavior Analysis, 44*(1), 33–40. doi:10.1901/jaba.2011.44-33

Piaget, J. (1962). *Play, dreams, and imitation in childhood*. New York: Norton.

Pollack, S., & Bechner, A. (2000). *Wisconsin international adoption research project: A study of our children's development*. Unpublished manuscript, University of Wisconsin–Madison.

Posner, M. I. (2001). The developing human brain. *Developmental Science, 4*(3), 253–387.

Price, D., Jarman, A. P., Mason, J. O., & Kind, P. C. (2011). *Building brains: An introduction to neural development (Google eBook)*. Hoboken, NJ: John Wiley. Retrieved from http://books.google.com/books?id=0PBVlxmImAQC&pgis=1

Quinn, P. C., Doran, M. M., Reiss, J. E., & Hoffman, J. E. (2010). Neural markers of subordinate-level categorization in 6- to 7-month-old infants. *Developmental Science, 13*(3), 499–507. doi:10.1111/j.1467-7687.2009.00903.x

Quinn, P. C., & Eimas, P. D. (1996). Perceptual organization and categorization in young infants. In C. Rovee-Collier & L. P. Lipsitt (Eds.), *Advances in infancy research* (Vol. 10, pp. 1–36). Norwood, NJ: Ablex.

Quinn, P. C., Eimas, P. D., & Rosenkrantz, S. L. (1993). Evidence for representations of perceptual similar natural categories by 3 and 4 month old infants. *Perception, 22*, 463–475.

Rakison, D. H., & Butterworth, G. E. (1998). Infants' use of object parts in early categorization. *Developmental Psychology, 34*, 49–62.

Ramsdell, H. L., Oller, D. K., Buder, E. H., Ethington, C. A., & Chorna, L. (2012). Identification of prelinguistic phonological categories. *Journal of Speech, Language, and Hearing Research, 55*(6), 1626–1639. doi:10.1044/1092-4388(2012/11-0250)

Reznick, J. S., Morrow, J. D., Goldman, B. D., & Snyder, J. (2004). The onset of working memory in infants. *Infancy, 6*(1), 145–154. doi:10.1207/s15327078in0601_7

Richards, J. E. (2010). The development of attention to simple and complex visual stimuli in infants: Behavioral and psychophysiological measures. *Developmental Review, 30*(2), 203–219. doi:10.1016/j.dr.2010.03.005

Richards, J. E. (2011). Infant attention, arousal, and the brain. In L. M. Oakes, C. H. Cashon, M. Casasola, & D. H. Rakison (Eds.), *Infant perception and cognition: Recent advances, emerging theories, and future directions* (pp. 27–49). New York: Oxford University Press.

Rideout, V. J. (2013). *Zero to eight: Children's media use in America 2013*. New York. Retrieved from https://www.commonsensemedia.org/research/zero-to-eight-childrens-media-use-in-america-2013

Rivera, S. M., Wakely, A., & Langer, J. (1999). The drawbridge phenomenon: Representational reasoning or perceptual preference? *Developmental Psychology, 35*(2), 427–435.

Robb, M. B., Richert, R. A., & Wartella, E. A. (2009). Just a talking book? Word learning from watching baby videos. *British Journal of Developmental Psychology, 27*(1), 27–45. doi:10.1348/026151008X320156

Rodriguez, E. T., & Tamis-LeMonda, C. S. (2011). Trajectories of the home learning environment across the first 5 years: Associations with children's vocabulary and literacy skills at prekindergarten. *Child Development, 82*(4), 1058–1075. doi:10.1111/j.1467-8624.2011.01614.x

Rose, S. A., & Feldman, J. F. (1995). Prediction of IQ and specific cognitive abilities from infancy measures. *Developmental Psychology, 31*, 685–696.

Rose, S. A., Feldman, J. F., & Jankowski, J. J. (2009). Information processing in toddlers: Continuity from infancy and persistence of preterm deficits. *Intelligence, 37*(3), 311–320. doi:10.1016/j.intell.2009.02.002

Rose, S. A., Feldman, J. F., & Jankowski, J. J. (2012). Implications of infant cognition for executive functions at age 11. *Psychological Science, 23*(11), 1345–1355. doi:10.1177/0956797612444902

Rose, S. A., Feldman, J. F., Jankowski, J. J., & Van Rossem, R. (2011). The structure of memory in infants and toddlers: An SEM study with full-terms and preterms. *Developmental Science, 14*(1), 83–91. doi:10.1111/j.1467-7687.2010.00959.x

Rose, S. A., Feldman, J. F., Jankowski, J. J., & Van Rossem, R. (2012). Information processing from infancy to 11 years: Continuities and prediction of IQ. *Intelligence, 40*(5), 445–457. doi:10.1016/j.intell.2012.05.007

Rosenberg, R. D., & Feigenson, L. (2013). Infants hierarchically organize memory representations. *Developmental Science, 16*(4), 610–621. doi:10.1111/desc.12055

Rothgänger, H. (2003). Analysis of the sounds of the child in the first year of age and a comparison to the language. *Early Human Development, 75*(1–2), 55–69.

Rovee-Collier, C., Hayne, H., & Colombo, J. (2002). *The development of implicit and explicit memory*. Amsterdam, Netherlands: John Benjamins Publishing Company.

Rovee-Collier, C. K. (1999). The development of infant memory. *Current Directions in Psychological Science, 8*, 80–85.

Rovee-Collier, C. K., & Bhatt, R. S. (1993). Evidence of long-term memory in infancy. *Annals of Child Development, 9*, 1–45.

Sansavini, A., Bertoncini, J., & Giovanelli, G. (1997). Newborns discriminate the rhythm of multisyllabic stressed words. *Developmental Psychology, 33*(1), 3–11.

Saxton, M. (1997). The contrast theory of negative input. *Journal of Child Language, 24*, 139–161.

Schachner, A., & Hannon, E. E. (2011). Infant-directed speech drives social preferences in 5-month-old infants. *Developmental Psychology, 47*(1), 19–25. doi:10.1037/a0020740

Shapiro, B., Fagen, J., Prigot, J., Carroll, M., & Shalan, J. (1998). Infants' emotional and regulatory behaviors in response to violations of expectancies. *Infant Behavior and Development, 27*, 299–313.

Shinskey, J. L. (2012). Disappearing décalage: Object search in light and dark at 6 months. *Infancy*, 17(3), 272–294. doi:10.1111/j.1532-7078.2011.00078.x

Shinskey, J. L., & Munakata, Y. (2003). Are infants in the dark about hidden objects? *Developmental Science*, 6, 273–282.

Shwe, H. I., & Markman, E. M. (1997). Young children's appreciation of the mental impact of their communicative signals. *Developmental Psychology*, 33, 630–636.

Singh, L., Nestor, S., Parikh, C., & Yull, A. (2009). Influences of infant-directed speech on early word recognition. *Infancy*, 14(6), 654–666. doi:10.1080/15250000903263973

Skinner, B. F. (1957). *Verbal behavior*. New York: Appleton-Century-Crofts.

Spelke, E., Lee, S. A., & Izard, V. (2010). Beyond core knowledge: Natural geometry. *Cognitive Science: A Multidisciplinary Journal*, 34(5), 863–884. doi:10.1111/j.1551-6709.2010.01110.x

Spelke, E. S., & Kinzler, K. D. (2007). Core knowledge. *Developmental Science*, 10(1), 89–96. doi:10.1111/j.1467-7687.2007.00569.x

Spiegel, C., & Halberda, J. (2011). Rapid fast-mapping abilities in 2-year-olds. *Journal of Experimental Child Psychology*, 109(1), 132–140. doi:10.1016/j.jecp.2010.10.013

Stams, G. J., Juffer, F., & Van IJzendoorn, M. H. (2002). Maternal sensitivity, infant attachment, and temperament in early childhood predict adjustment in middle childhood: The case of adopted children and their biologically unrelated parents. *Developmental Psychology*, 38(5), 806–821.

Streri, A., Hevia, M., Izard, V., & Coubart, A. (2013). What do we know about neonatal cognition? *Behavioral Sciences*, 3(1), 154–169. doi:10.3390/bs3010154

Sundberg, U. (1998). *Mother tongue-phonetic aspects of infant-directed speech* (Doctoral dissertation). Stockholm, Sweden: PERILUS.

Tamis-LeMonda, C. S., Bornstein, M. H., & Baumwell, L. (2001). Maternal responsiveness and children's achievement of language milestones. *Child Development*, 72(3), 748–767. Retrieved from http://www.ncbi.nlm.nih.gov/pubmed/11405580

Tamis-LeMonda, C. S., Bornstein, M. H., Cyphers, L., Toda, S., & Ogino, M. (1992). Language and play at one year: A comparison of toddlers and mothers in the United States and Japan. *International Journal of Behavioral Development*, 15(1), 19–42. doi:10.1177/016502549201500102

Tamis-LeMonda, C. S., Kuchirko, Y., & Song, L. (2014). Why is infant language learning facilitated by parental responsiveness? *Current Directions in Psychological Science*, 23(2), 121–126. doi:10.1177/0963721414522813

Tamis-LeMonda, C. S., Shannon, J. D., Cabrera, N. J., & Lamb, M. E. (2004). Fathers and mothers at play with their 2- and 3-year-olds: Contributions to language and cognitive development. *Child Development*, 75(6), 1806–1820. doi:10.1111/j.1467-8624.2004.00818.x

Tardif, T., Fletcher, P., Liang, W., Zhang, Z., Kaciroti, N., & Marchman, V. A. (2008). Baby's first 10 words. *Developmental Psychology*, 44(4), 929–938. doi:10.1037/0012-1649.44.4.929

Tardif, T., Shatz, M., & Naigles, L. (1997). Caregiver speech and children's use of nouns versus verbs: A comparison of English, Italian, and Mandarin. *Journal of Child Language*, 24, 535–565.

Thiessen, E. D., Hill, E. A., & Saffran, J. R. (2005). Infant-directed speech facilitates word segmentation. *Infancy*, 7(1), 53–71.

Tomasello, M. (2009). *Constructing a language: A usage-based theory of language acquisition*.

Camridge, MA: Harvard University Press. Retrieved from http://books.google.com/books?hl=en&lr=&id=7M_ISEfzTQoC&pgis=1

Tomasello, M. (2012). A usage-based approach to child language acquisition. *Proceedings of the Annual Meeting of the Berkeley Linguistics Society*, 26(1).

Tronick, E. Z., Als, H., Adamson, L., Wise, S., & Brazelton, B. (1978). The infants' response to entrapment between contradictory messages in face-to-face interaction. *American Academy of Child Psychiatry*, 1, 1–13.

U.S. Department of State. (2014). *FY 2013 annual report on intercountry adoption*. Washington, DC. Author. Retrieved from http://adoption.state.gov/content/pdf/fy2013_annual_report.pdf

Vallortigara, G. (2012). Core knowledge of object, number, and geometry: A comparative and neural approach. *Cognitive Neuropsychology*, 29(1–2), 213–236. doi:10.1080/02643294.2012.654772

Von Hofsten, C., Kochukhova, O., & Rosander, K. (2007). Predictive tracking over occlusions by 4-month-old infants. *Developmental Science*, 10(5), 625–640. doi:10.1111/j.1467-7687.2006.00604.x

Walker, C. M., & Gopnik, A. (2013). Toddlers infer higher-order relational principles in causal learning. *Psychological Science*, 25(1), 161–169. doi:10.1177/0956797613502983

Wartella, E. A., & Lauricella, A. R. (2012). Should babies be watching television and DVDs? *Pediatric Clinics of North America*, 59(3), 613–621, vii. doi:10.1016/j.pcl.2012.03.027

Watanabe, H., Forssman, L., Green, D., Bohlin, G., & von Hofsten, C. (2012). Attention demands influence 10- and 12-month-old infants' perseverative behavior. *Developmental Psychology*, 48(1), 46–55. doi:10.1037/a0025412

Weinberg, M. K., & Tronick, E. Z. (1994). Beyond the face: An empirical study of infant affective configurations of facial, vocal, gestural, and regulatory behaviors. *Child Development*, 65, 1503–1515.

Weinberg, M. K., & Tronick, E. Z. (1996). Infants' affective reactions to the resumption of maternal interaction after the still-face. *Child Development*, 67, 905–914.

Wiik, K. L., Loman, M. M., Van Ryzin, M. J., Armstrong, J. M., Essex, M. J., Pollak, S. D., & Gunnar, M. R. (2011). Behavioral and emotional symptoms of post-institutionalized children in middle childhood. *Journal of Child Psychology and Psychiatry*, 52(1), 56–63. doi:10.1111/j.1469-7610.2010.02294.x

Wilson, S. L., & Weaver, T. L. (2009). Follow-up of developmental attainment and behavioral adjustment for toddlers adopted internationally into the USA. *International Social Work*, 52(5), 679–684. doi:10.1177/0020872809337684

Woods, R. J., & Wilcox, T. (2013). Posture support improves object individuation in infants. *Developmental Psychology*, 49(8), 1413–1424. doi:10.1037/a0030344

Woodward, A. L., Markman, E. M., & Fitzsimmons, C. M. (1994). Rapid word learning in 13- and 18-month-olds. *Developmental Psychology*, 30, 553–566.

Xu, F., & Kushnir, T. (2013). Infants are rational constructivist learners. *Current Directions in Psychological Science*, 22(1).

Zelazo, P. D., Reznick, J. S., & Spinazzola, J. (1998). Representational flexibility and response control in a multistep, multilocation search task. *Developmental Psychology*, 34, 203–214.

Zimmerman, F. J., Christakis, D. A., & Meltzoff, A. N. (2007). Associations between media viewing and language development in children under age 2 years. *The Journal of Pediatrics*, 151(4), 364–368. doi:10.1016/j.jpeds.2007.04.071

CHAPTER 6

Ainsworth, M. D. S. (1974). *Citation for the G. Stanley Hall Award to John Bowlby*. Unpublished manuscript.

Ainsworth, M. D. S. (1979). Attachment as related to mother-infant interaction. In J. S. Rosenblatt, R. A. Hinde, C. Beer, & M. Busnel (Eds.), *Advances in the study of behavior* (Vol. 9). Orlando, FL: Academic Press.

Ainsworth, M. D. S., Blehar, M. C., Waters, E., & Wall, S. (1978). *Patterns of attachment*. Hillsdale, NJ: Lawrence Erlbaum.

Albers, E. M., Riksen-Walraven, J. M., & de Weerth, C. (2010). Developmental stimulation in child care centers contributes to young infants' cognitive development. *Infant Behavior & Development*, 33(4), 401–408. doi:10.1016/j.infbeh.2010.04.004

Allen, S. F. (2003). Working parents with young children: Cross-national comparisons of policies and programmes in three countries. *International Journal of Social Welfare*, 12(4), 261. doi:10.1111/1467-9671.00281

Amato, P. R. (1987). Family processes in one-parent, stepparent, and intact families: The child's point of view. *Journal of Marriage and Family*, 49, 327–337.

Andersson, B.-E. (1989). Effects of public day-care: A longitudinal study. *Child Development*, 60(4), 857. doi:10.1111/1467-8624.ep9676141

Andersson, G., Duvander, A.-Z., & Hank, K. (2004). Do child-care characteristics influence continued child bearing in Sweden? An investigation of the quantity, quality, and price dimension. *Journal of European Social Policy*, 14(4), 407–418. doi:10.1177/0958928704046881

Arend, R., Gove, F., & Sroufe, L. A. (1979). Continuity of individual adaptation from infancy to kindergarten: A predictive study of ego-resiliency and curiosity in preschoolers. *Child Development*, 50, 950–959.

Axe, J. B. (2007). Child care and child development: Results from the NICHD Study of Early Child Care and Youth Development. *Education & Treatment of Children*, 30(3), 129–136.

Axia, V. D., & Weisner, T. S. (2002). Infant stress reactivity and Home Cultural Ecology of Italian infants and families. *Infant Behavior & Development*, 25(3), 255.

Bard, K. A., Todd, B. K., Bernier, C., Love, J., & Leavens, D. A. (2006). Self-awareness in human and chimpanzee infants: What is measured and what is meant by the mark and mirror test? *Infancy*, 9(2), 191–219. doi:10.1207/s15327078in0902_6

Barglow, P., Vaughn, B. E., & Molitor, N. (1987). Effects of maternal absence due to employment on the quality of infant-mother attachment in a low-risk sample. *Child Development*, 58(4), 945–954. Retrieved from http://www.ncbi.nlm.nih.gov/pubmed/3608664

Barr, R. G., & Gunnar, M. (2000). Colic: The "transient responsivity" hypothesis. In R. G. Barr, B. Hopkins, & J. A. Green (Eds.), *Crying as a sign, a symptom, & a signal: Clinical emotional and developmental aspects of infant and toddler crying* (pp. 41–66). New York: Cambridge University Press.

Barr, R. G., Konner, M., Bakeman, R., & Adamson, L. (1991). Crying in !Kung San infants: A test of the cultural specificity hypothesis. *Developmental Medicine & Child Neurology*, 33(7), 601–610.

Bates, E. (1990). Language about me and you: Pronominal reference and the emerging concept of self. In D. Cicchetti & M. Beeghly (Eds.), *The self in transition: Infancy to childhood* (pp. 165–182). Chicago: University of Chicago Press.

Bates, J., Pettit, G., Dodge, K., & Ridge, B. (1998). Interaction of temperamental resistance to control and restrictive parenting in the development of externalizing behavior. *Developmental Psychology, 34,* 982–995.

Bayer, J. K., Hiscock, H., Hampton, A., & Wake, M. (2007). Sleep problems in young infants and maternal mental and physical health. *Journal of Paediatrics & Child Health, 43*(1–2), 66–73. doi:10.1111/j.1440-1754.2007.01005.x

Becker-Stoll, F., Fremmer-Bombik, E., Wartner, U., Zimmermann, P., & Grossmann, K. E. (2008). Is attachment at ages 1, 6 and 16 related to autonomy and relatedness behavior of adolescents in interaction towards their mothers? *International Journal of Behavioral Development, 32*(5), 372–380. doi:10.1177/0165025408093654

Beebe, B., Jaffe, J., Markese, S., Buck, K., Chen, H., Cohen, P., . . . Feldstein, S. (2010). The origins of 12-month attachment: A microanalysis of 4-month mother-infant interaction. *Attachment & Human Development, 12*(1–2), 3–141. doi:10.1080/14616730903338985

Behrens, K. Y., Parker, A. C., & Haltigan, J. D. (2011). Maternal sensitivity assessed during the Strange Situation Procedure predicts child's attachment quality and reunion behaviors. *Infant Behavior & Development, 34*(2), 378–381. doi:10.1016/j.infbeh.2011.02.007

Belsky, J. (2005). Attachment theory and research in ecological perspective: Insights from the Pennsylvania Infant and Family Development Project and the NICHD Study of Early Child Care. In K. E. Grossmann, K. Grossmann, & E. Waters (Eds.), *Attachment from infancy to adulthood: The major longitudinal studies* (pp. 71–97). New York: Guilford Press.

Belsky, J., & Fearon, R. M. P. (2002). Infant-mother attachment security, contextual risk, and early development: A moderational analyses. *Development and Psychopathology, 14,* 293–310.

Bennett, D. S., Bendersky, M., & Lewis, M. (2005). Does the organization of emotional expression change over time? Facial expressivity from 4 to 12 months. *Infancy, 8*(2), 167–187. doi:10.1207/s15327078in0802_4

Bernier, A., & Meins, E. (2008). A threshold approach to understanding the origins of attachment disorganization. *Developmental Psychology, 44*(4), 969–982. doi:10.1037/0012-1649.444.969

Bertenthal, B. I., & Campos, J. J. (1990). A systems approach to the organizing effects of self-produced locomotion during infancy. In C. Rovee-Collier & L. P. Lipsitt (Eds.), *Advances in infancy research* (pp. 1–60). Norwood, NJ: Ablex.

Bertenthal, B. I., Campos, J. J., & Barrett, K. (1984). Self-produced locomotion: An organizer of emotional, cognitive, and social development in infancy. In R. Emde & R. Harmon (Eds.), *Continuities and discontinuities in development* (pp. 174–210). New York: Plenum Press.

Best, D. L., House, A. S., Barnard, A. E., & Spicker, B. S. (1994). Parent-child interactions in France, Germany, and Italy: The effects of gender and culture. *Journal of Cross-Cultural Psychology, 25*(2), 181–193. doi:10.1177/0022022194252002

Bigelow, A. E. (2001). Discovering self through other: Infants' preference for social contingency. *Bulletin of the Menninger Clinic, 65*(3), 335.

Bigelow, A. E., & Walden, L. M. (2009). Infants' response to maternal mirroring in the still face and replay tasks. *Infancy, 14*(5), 526–549. doi:10.1080/15250000903144181

Biro, S., Alink, L. R. A., van IJzendoorn, M. H., & Bakermans-Kranenburg, M. J. (2014). Infants' monitoring of social interactions: The effect of emotional cues. *Emotion, 14*(2), 263–271.

Bleah, D. A., & Ellett, M. L. (2010). Infant crying among recent African immigrants. *Health Care for Women International, 31*(7), 652–663. doi:10.1080/07399331003628446

Bobo, W. V, & Yawn, B. P. (2014). Concise review for physicians and other clinicians: Postpartum depression. *Mayo Clinic Proceedings, 89*(6), 835–844. doi:10.1016/j.mayocp.2014.01.027

Boccia, M., & Campos, J. J. (1989). Maternal emotional signals, social referencing, and infants' reactions to strangers. *New Directions for Child and Adolescent Development, 44,* 25–49.

Boldt, L. J., Kochanska, G., Yoon, J. E., & Koenig Nordling, J. (2014). Children's attachment to both parents from toddler age to middle childhood: Links to adaptive and maladaptive outcomes. *Attachment & Human Development, 16*(3), 211–229. doi:10.1080/14616734.2014.889181

Bornstein, M. H., Arterberry, M. E., & Lamb, M. E. (2013). *Development in infancy: A contemporary introduction.* New York: Psychology Press. Retrieved from http://books .google.com/books?id=7UYdAAAAQBAJ&pgis=1

Bornstein, M. H., & Lamb, M. E. (2011). *Developmental science: An advanced textbook* (6th ed.). New York: Psychology Press. Retrieved from http://books.google.com/ books?id=3pN5AgAAQBAJ&pgis=1

Bowlby, J. (1969). *Attachment and loss.* In *Attachment* (Vol. 1). New York: Basic Books.

Braungart-Rieker, J. M., Hill-Soderlund, A. L., & Karrass, J. (2010). Fear and anger reactivity trajectories from 4 to 16 months: The roles of temperament, regulation, and maternal sensitivity. *Developmental Psychology, 46*(4), 791–804. doi:10.1037/a0019673

Bretherton, I. (1992). The origins of attachment theory: John Bowlby and Mary Ainsworth. *Developmental Psychology, 28,* 759–775.

Bretherton, I., Fritz, J., Zahn-Waxler, C., & Ridgeway, D. (1986). Learning to talk about emotions: A functionalist perspective. *Child Development, 57,* 529–548.

Bridgett, D. J., Gartstein, M. A., Putnam, S. P., McKay, T., Iddins, E., Robertson, C., . . . Rittmueller, A. (2009). Maternal and contextual influences and the effect of temperament development during infancy on parenting in toddlerhood. *Infant Behavior & Development, 32*(1), 103–116. doi:10.1016/j.infbeh.2008.10.007

Broberg, A. G., Wessels, H., Lamb, M. E., & Hwang, C. P. (1997). Effects of day care on the development of cognitive abilities in 8-year-olds: A longitudinal study. *Developmental Psychology, 33*(1), 62–69. doi:10.1037/0012-1649.33.1.62

Brooker, R. J., Buss, K. A., Lemery-Chalfant, K., Aksan, N., Davidson, R. J., & Goldsmith, H. H. (2013). The development of stranger fear in infancy and toddlerhood: Normative development, individual differences, antecedents, and outcomes. *Developmental Science, 16*(6), 864–878. doi:10.1111/desc.12058

Brookhart, J., & Hock, E. (1976). The effects of experimental context and experiential background on infants' behavior toward their mothers and a stranger. *Child Development, 47*(2), 333–340. doi:10.1111/1467-8624.ep12189679

Brooks, R., & Meltzoff, A. N. (2008). Infant gaze following and pointing predict accelerated vocabulary growth through two years of age: A longitudinal, growth curve modeling study. *Journal of Child Language, 35*(1), 207–220. doi:10.1017/ s030500090700829x

Brown, G. L., Mangelsdorf, S. C., & Neff, C. (2012). Father involvement, paternal sensitivity, and father-child attachment security in the first 3 years. *Journal of Family Psychology, 26*(3), 421–430. doi:10.1037/a0027836

Bullock, M., & Lutkenhaus, P. (1990). Who am I? Self-understanding in toddlers. *Merrill-Palmer Quarterly, 36,* 217–238.

Buss, A. H., & Plomin, R. (1984). *Temperament: Early developing personality traits.* Hillsdale, NJ: Lawrence Erlbaum.

Butterworth, G. (1992). Origins of self-perception in infancy. *Psychological Inquiry, 3*(2), 103–111. doi:10.1207/s15327965pli0302_1

Cabrera, N. J., Fitzgerald, H. E., Bradley, R. H., & Roggman, L. (2014). The ecology of father-child relationships: An expanded model. *Journal of Family Theory & Review, 6*(4), 336–354. doi:10.1111/jftr.12054

Caldera, Y. M. (2004). Paternal involvement and infant-father attachment: A q-set study. *Fathering: A Journal of Theory, Research, & Practice About Men as Fathers, 2*(2), 191–210.

Calkins, S. D., & Johnson, M. C. (1998). Toddler regulation of distress to frustrating events: Temperamental and maternal correlates. *Infant Behavior & Development, 21,* 379–395.

Campos, J. J., Anderson, D. I., Barbu-Roth, M. A., Hubbard, E. M., Hertenstein, J. J., & Witherington, D. (2000). Travel broadens the mind. *Infancy, 1,* 149–219.

Campos, J. J., Kermoian, R., & Zumbahlen, M. R. (1992). Socioemotional transformation in the family system following infant crawling onset. In N. Eisenberg & R. A. Fabes (Eds.), *New directions for child development* (Vol. 55, pp. 25–40). San Francisco: Jossey-Bass.

Camras, L. A., Oster, H., Campos, J. J., Miyake, K., & Bradshaw, D. (1992). Japanese and American infants' responses to arm restraint. *Developmental Psychology, 28,* 578–583.

Carlson, V. J., & Harwood, R. L. (2003). Attachment, culture, and the caregiving system: The cultural patterning of everyday experiences among Anglo and Puerto Rican mother-infant pairs. *Infant Mental Health Journal, 24,* 53–73.

Carver, L. J., & Vaccaro, B. G. (2007). 12-month-old infants allocate increased neural resources to stimuli associated with negative adult emotion. *Developmental Psychology, 43*(1), 54–69. doi:10.1037/0012-1649.43.1.54

Caspi, A. (1998). Personality development across the life course. In N. Eisenberg (Ed.), *Handbook of child psychology: Vol. 3. Social, emotional, and personality development* (5th ed., pp. 311–388). Hoboken, NJ: John Wiley.

Cassibba, R. D., Sette, G., Bakermans-Kranenburg, M. J., & van IJzendoorn, M. H. (2013). Attachment the Italian way: In search of specific patterns of infant and adult attachments in Italian typical and atypical samples. *European Psychologist, 18*(1). doi:10.10271016-9040a000128

Chess, S., & Thomas, A. (1984). *Origins and evolution of behavior disorders.* New York: Brunner/Mazel.

Chess, S., & Thomas, A. (1991). Temperament and the concept of goodness of fit. In J. Strelau & A. Angleitner (Eds.), *Explorations in temperament: International perspectives on theory and measurement* (pp. 15–28). New York: Plenum Press.

Child Care Aware of America. (2014). *Parents and the high cost of child care 2013 report.* Retrieved from http://usa.childcareaware.org/sites/ default/files/cost_of_care_2013_103113_0.pdf

Cicchetti, D., Rogosch, F. A., Toth, S. L., & Spagnola, M. (1997). Affect, cognition, and the emergence of self-knowledge in the toddler offspring of. *Journal of Experimental Child Psychology, 67*(3), 338.

Clearfield, M. W. (2011). Learning to walk changes infants' social interactions. *Infant Behavior & Development, 34*(1), 15–25. doi:10.1016/j.infbeh.2010.04.008

Cole, P. M., Martin, S. E., & Dennis, T. A. (2004). Emotion regulation as a scientific construct: Methodological challenges and directions for child development research. *Child Development, 75*(2), 317–333.

Combs-Orme, T., & Renkert, L. E. (2009). Fathers and their infants: Caregiving and affection in the modern family. *Journal of Human Behavior in the Social Environment, 19*(4), 394–418. doi:10.1080/10911350902790753

Courage, M. L., Edison, S. C., & Howe, M. L. (2004). Variability in the early development of visual self-recognition. *Infant Behavior & Development, 27*(4), 509–532. doi:10.1016/j. infbeh.2004.06.001

Crockenberg, S. C., & Leerkes, E. M. (2004). Infant and maternal behaviors regulate infant reactivity to novelty at 6 months. *Developmental Psychology, 40*(6), 1123–1132.

Crugnola, C. R., Tambelli, R., Spinelli, M., Gazzotti, S., Caprin, C., & Albizzati, A. (2011). Attachment patterns and emotion regulation strategies in the second year. *Infant Behavior & Development*, 34(1), 136–151. doi:10.1016/j.infbeh.2010.11.002

Dehaan, L. (2006). Child care and development: Results from the NICHD Study of Early Child Care and Youth Development. The NICHD Early Child Care Research Network. *Journal of Marriage and Family*, 68(1), 252–253. doi:10.1111/j.1741-3737.2006.00245.x

DeWolff, M. S., & van IJzendoorn, M. H. (1997). Sensitivity and attachment: A meta-analysis on parental antecedents of infant attachment. *Child Development*, 68, 571–591.

Dondi, M., Simion, F., & Caltran, G. (1999). Can newborns discriminate between their own cry and the cry of another newborn infant? *Developmental Psychology*, 35, 418–426.

Easterbrooks, M. A., Bartlett, J. D., Beeghly, M., & Thompson, R. A. (2012). Social and emotional development in infancy. In I. B. Weiner, R. M. Lerner, M. A. Easterbrooks, & J. Mistry (Eds.), *Handbook of psychology, developmental psychology* (p. 752). Hoboken, NJ: John Wiley. Retrieved from http://books.google.com/books?id=JM5Uo3Aok0YC&pgis=1

Elicker, J., Englund, M., & Sroufe, L. A. (1992). Predicting peer competence and peer relationships in childhood from early parent-child relationships. In R. D. Parke & G. W. Ladd (Eds.), *Family-peer relationships: Modes of linkage* (pp. 77–106). Hillsdale, NJ: Lawrence Erlbaum.

Engle, P. L., & Breaux, C. (1998). Fathers' involvement with children: Perspectives from developing countries. *Social Policy Report*, 12(1), 1–21.

Erel, O., Oberman, Y., & Yirmiya, N. (2000). Maternal versus nonmaternal care and seven domains of children's development. *Psychological Bulletin*, 126(5), 727–747. doi:10.1037/0033-2909.126.5.727

Erikson, E. H. (1950). *Childhood and society* (2nd ed.). New York: Norton.

Fagot, B. I. (1997). Attachment, parenting, and peer interactions of toddler children. *Developmental Psychology*, 33, 489–499.

Farroni, T., Menon, E., Rigato, S., & Johnson, M. H. (2007). The perception of facial expressions in newborns. *European Journal of Developmental Psychology*, 4(1), 2–13. doi:10.1080/17405620601046832

Fearon, R. M. P., & Belsky, J. (2004). Attachment and attention: Protection in relation to gender and cumulative social-contextual adversity. *Child Development*, 75(6), 1677–1693. doi:10.1111/j.1467-8624.2004.00809.x

Federal Interagency Forum on Child and Family Statistics. (2014). *America's children: Key national indicators of well-being, 2013*. Washington, DC: Author. Retrieved from http://www.childstats.gov/americaschildren

Feldman, R. (2003). Infant–mother and infant–father synchrony: The coregulation of positive arousal. *Infant Mental Health Journal*, 24(1), 1–23. doi:10.1002/imhj.10041

Feldman, R., Dollberg, D., & Nadam, R. (2011). The expression and regulation of anger in toddlers: Relations to maternal behavior and mental representations. *Infant Behavior & Development*, 34(2), 310–320. doi:10.1016/j.infbeh.2011.02.001

Feldman, R., Granat, A., Pariente, C., Kanety, H., Kuint, J., & Gilboa-Schechtman, E. (2009). Maternal depression and anxiety across the postpartum year and infant social engagement, fear regulation, and stress reactivity. *Journal of the American Academy of Child & Adolescent Psychiatry*, 48(9), 919–927. doi:10.1097/CHI.0b013e3181b21651

Feldman, R., Greenbaum, C. W., & Yirmiya, N. (1999). Mother–infant affect synchrony as an antecedent of the emergence of self-control.

Developmental Psychology, 35(1), 223–231. doi:10.1037/0012-1649.35.1.223

Feng, X., Harwood, R. L., Leyendecker, B., & Miller, A. M. (2001). Changes across the first year of life in infants' daily activities and social contacts among middle-class Anglo and Puerto Rican families. *Infant Behavior & Development*, 24(3), 317–339. doi:10.1016/s0163-6383(01)00080-7

Field, T. (2011). Prenatal depression effects on early development: A review. *Infant Behavior & Development*, 34(1), 1–14. doi:10.1016/j.infbeh.2010.09.008

Field, T., Grizzle, N., Scafidi, F., Abrams, S., Richardson, S., Kuhn, C., & Schanberg, S. (1996). Massage therapy for infants of depressed mothers. *Infant Behavior & Development*, 19(1), 107–112. doi:10.1016/s0163-6383(96)90048-x

Flanders, J. L., Leo, V., Paquette, D., Pihl, R. O., & Séguin, J. R. (2009). Rough-and-tumble play and the regulation of aggression: An observational study of father–child play dyads. *Aggressive Behavior*, 35(4), 285–295. doi:10.1002/ab.20309

Fletcher, R. (2009). Promoting infant well-being in the context of maternal depression by supporting the father. *Infant Mental Health Journal*, 30(1), 95–102. doi:10.1002/imhj.20205

Fogel, A. (2007). *Infancy: Infant, family, and society* (7th ed.). Cornwall-on-Hudson, NY: Sloan Educational Publishing.

Fouts, H. N. (2008). Father involvement with young children among the Aka and Bofi foragers. *Cross-Cultural Research: The Journal of Comparative Social Science*, 42(3), 290–312. doi:10.1177/1069397108317484

Frascarolo, F. (2004). Paternal involvement in child caregiving and infant sociability. *Infant Mental Health Journal*, 25(6), 509–521. doi:10.1002/imhj.20023

Frodi, A. M., Lamb, M. E., Hwang, C.-P., & Frodi, M. (1983). Father-mother infant interaction in traditional and nontraditional Swedish families: A longitudinal study. *Alternative Lifestyles*, 5(3), 142–163. doi:10.1007/bf01091325

Gagne, J. R., Vendlinski, M. K., & Goldsmith, H. H. (2009). The genetics of childhood temperament. In Y.-K. Kim (Ed.), *Handbook of behavior genetics* (pp. 251–267). New York: Springer Science + Business Media.

Garcia Coll, C. T. (1990). Developmental outcome of minority infants: A process-oriented look into our beginnings. *Child Development*, 61(2), 270. doi:10.1111/1467-8624.ep5878982

Gardiner, H. W., & Kosmitzki, C. (2010). *Lives across cultures: Cross-cultural human development* (5th ed.). Boston: Pearson.

Gartstein, M. A., & Iverson, S. (2014). Attachment security: The role of infant, maternal, and contextual factors. *International Journal of Psychology and Psychological Therapy*, 14(2).

Goldsmith, H. H., Buss, A. H., Plomin, R., Rothbart, M. K., Thomas, A., Chess, S., . . . McCall, R. B. (1987). Roundtable: What is temperament? Four approaches. *Child Development*, 58, 505–529.

Goodvin, R., Meyer, S., Thompson, R. A., & Hayes, R. (2008). Self-understanding in early childhood: Associations with child attachment security and maternal negative affect. *Attachment & Human Development*, 10(4), 433–450. doi:10.1080/14616730802461466

Greenberg, D. J., Hillman, D., & Grice, D. (1973). Infant and stranger variables related to stranger anxiety in the first year of life. *Developmental Psychology*, 9(2), 207–212. doi:10.1037/h0035084

Groh, A. M., Roisman, G. I., van IJzendoorn, M. H., Bakermans-Kranenburg, M. J., & Fearon, R. P. (2012). The significance of insecure and disorganized attachment for children's internalizing symptoms: A meta-analytic study. *Child Development*, 83(2), 591–610. doi:10.1111/j.1467-8624.2011.01711.x

Grolnick, W. S., Bridges, L. J., & Connell, J. P. (1996). Emotion regulation in two-year-olds: Strategies and emotional expression in four contexts. *Child Development*, 67, 928–941.

Gross, A. L., & Ballif, B. (1991). Children's understanding of emotion from facial expressions and situations: A review. *Developmental Review*, 11, 368–398.

Grossman, K., Grossman, K. E., Fremmer-Bombik, E., Kindler, H., Scheuerer-Englisch, H., & Zimmermann, P. (2002). The uniqueness of the child–father attachment relationship: Fathers' sensitive and challenging play as a pivotal variable in a 16-year longitudinal study. *Social Development*, 11(3), 301–337.

Grossmann, K. E., Spangler, G., Suess, G., & Unzner, L. (1985). Maternal sensitivity and newborns' orientation responses as related to quality of attachment in Northern Germany. In I. Bretherton & E. Waters (Eds.), Growing points of attachment theory and research. *Monographs of the Society for Research in Child Development*, 50(1-2, Serial No. 209), 233–256.

Haley, D. W., & Stansbury, K. (2003). Infant stress and parent responsiveness: Regulation of physiology and behavior during still-face and reunion. *Child Development*, 74(5), 1534–1546. doi:10.1111/1467-8624.00621

Hamilton, C. E. (2000). Continuity and discontinuity of attachment from infancy through adolescence. *Child Development*, 71, 690–694.

Harlow, H. F. (1958). The nature of love. *American Psychologist*, 13(12).

Harlow, H. F., & Zimmerman, R. (1959). Affectional responses in the infant monkey. *Science*, 130, 421–432.

Harrison, L. J., & Ungerer, J. A. (2002). Maternal employment and infant-mother attachment security at 12 months postpartum. *Developmental Psychology*, 38(5), 758–773. Retrieved from http://www.ncbi.nlm.nih.gov/pubmed/12220053

Hart, S., Field, T., & Roitfarb, M. (1999). Depressed mothers' assessments of their neonates' behaviors. *Infant Mental Health Journal*, 20(2), 200–210.

Harwood, R. L., Scholmerich, A., Schulze, P. A., & Gonzalez, Z. (1999). Cultural differences in maternal beliefs and behaviors: A study of middle class Anglo and Puerto Rican mother-infant pairs in four everyday situations. *Child Development*, 70, 1005–1016.

Hewlett, B. S. (2008). Fathers and infants among Aka pygmies. In R. A. LeVine & R. S. New (Eds.), *Anthropology and child development: A cross-cultural reader* (pp. 84–99). Malden, MA: Blackwell.

Hewlett, B. S., Lamb, M. E., Shannon, D., Leyendecker, B., & Scholmerich, A. (1998). Culture and early infancy among central African foragers and farmers. *Developmental Psychology*, 34, 653–661.

Higley, E., & Dozier, M. (2009). Nighttime maternal responsiveness and infant attachment at one year. *Attachment & Human Development*, 11(4), 347–363. doi:10.1080/14616730903016979

Hoffman, L. W. (1974). Effects of maternal employment on the child: A review of the research. *Developmental Psychology*, 10(2), 204–228. Retrieved from http://www.childstats.gov/americaschildren13/index.asp

Hossain, Z., Field, T., Pickens, J., Malphurs, J., & Del Valle, C. (1997). Fathers' caregiving in low-income African-American and Hispanic-American families. *Early Development & Parenting*, 6(2), 73–82. doi:10.1002/(sici)1099-0917(199706)6:2<73::aid-edp145>3.0.co;2-o

Hossain, Z., Roopnarine, J. L., Ismail, R., Hashmi, S. I., & Sombuling, A. (2007). Fathers' and mothers' reports of involvement in caring for infants in Kadazan families in Sabah, Malaysia. *Fathering: A Journal of Theory, Research, & Practice about Men as Fathers*, 5(1), 58–72. doi:10.3149/fth.0501.58

Huang, Z. J., Lewin, A., Mitchell, S. J., & Zhang, J. (2012). Variations in the relationship between maternal depression, maternal sensitivity, and child attachment by race/ethnicity and nativity: Findings from a nationally representative cohort study. *Maternal and Child Health Journal*, 16(1), 40–50. doi:10.1007/s10995-010-0716-2

Izard, C. E. (2007). Basic emotions, natural kinds, emotion schemas, and a new paradigm. *Perspectives on Psychological Science*, 2(3), 260–280. doi:10.1111/j.1745-6916.2007.00044.x

Izard, C. E., Fantauzzo, C. A., Castle, J. M., Haynes, O. M., Rayias, M. F., & Putnam, P. H. (1995). The ontogeny and significance of infants' facial expressions in the first 9 months of life. *Developmental Psychology*, 31, 997–1013.

Jaffari-Bimmel, N., Juffer, F., van IJzendoorn, M. H., Bakermans-Kranenburg, M. J., & Mooijaart, A. (2006). Social development from infancy to adolescence: Longitudinal and concurrent factors in an adoption sample. *Developmental Psychology*, 42(6), 1143–1153. doi:10.1037/0012-1649.42.6.1143

Jahromi, L. B., & Stifter, C. A. (2007). Individual differences in the contribution of maternal soothing to infant distress reduction. *Infancy*, 11(3), 255–269. doi:10.1080/15250000701310371

Jennings, K. D., Sandberg, I., Kelley, S. A., Valdes, L., Yaggi, K., Abrew, A., & Macey-Kalcevic, M. (2008). Understanding of self and maternal warmth predict later self-regulation in toddlers. *International Journal of Behavioral Development*, 32(2), 108–118. doi:10.1177/0165025407087209

Jin, M. K., Jacobvitz, D., Hazen, N., & Jung, S. H. (2012). Maternal sensitivity and infant attachment security in Korea: Cross-cultural validation of the Strange Situation. *Attachment & Human Development*, 14(1), 33–44. doi:10.1080/14616734.2012.636656

Johnson, S. C., Dweck, C. S., & Chen, F. S. (2007). Evidence for infants' internal working models of attachment. *Psychological Science*, 18(6), 501–502. doi:10.1111/j.1467-9280.2007.01929.x

Kagan, J. (1983). Stress and coping in early development. In N. Garmezy & M. Rutter (Eds.), *Stress, coping, and development in children* (pp. 191–216). Baltimore: Johns Hopkins University Press.

Kagan, J., Arcus, D., Snidman, N., Feng, W., Handler, J., & Greene, S. (1994). Reactivity in infants: A cross national comparison. *Developmental Psychology*, 30, 342–345.

Kaler, S. B., & Kopp, C. B. (1990). Compliance and comprehension in very young toddlers. *Child Development*, 61, 1997–2003.

Karasik, L. B., Tamis-LeMonda, C. S., & Adolph, K. E. (2011). Transition from crawling to walking and infants' actions with objects and people. *Child Development*, 82(4), 1199–1209. doi:10.1111/j.1467-8624.2011.01595.x

Kawakami, K., Takai-Kawakami, K., Kawakami, F., Tomonaga, M., Suzuki, M., & Shimizu, Y. (2008). Roots of smile: A preterm neonates' study. *Infant Behavior & Development*, 31(3), 518–522. doi:10.1016/j.infbeh.2008.03.002

Keller, H. (2003). Socialization for competence: Cultural models of infancy. *Human Development*, 46(5), 288–311.

Kiang, L., Moreno, A. J., & Robinson, J. L. (2004). Maternal preconceptions about parenting predict child temperament, maternal sensitivity, and children's empathy. *Developmental Psychology*, 40(6), 1081–1092. doi:10.1037/0012-1649.40.6.1081

Kim, B.-R., & Teti, D. M. (2014). Maternal emotional availability during infant bedtime: An ecological framework. *Journal of Family Psychology*, 28(1), 1–11. doi:10.1037/a0035157

Kim, G., Walden, T. A., & Knieps, L. J. (2010). Impact and characteristics of positive and fearful emotional messages during infant social referencing. *Infant Behavior & Development*, 33(2), 189–195. doi:10.1016/j.infbeh.2009.12.009

Ko, J. Y., Farr, S. L., Dietz, P. M., & Robbins, C. L. (2012). Depression and treatment among U.S. pregnant and nonpregnant women of reproductive age, 2005–2009. *Journal of Women's Health*, 21(8), 830–836. doi:10.1089/jwh.2011.3466

Kochanska, G. (2000). Mother-child mutually responsive orientation and conscience development: From toddler to early school age. *Child Development*, 71(2), 417.

Kochanska, G., & Kim, S. (2013). Early attachment organization with both parents and future behavior problems: From infancy to middle childhood. *Child Development*, 84(1), 283–296. doi:10.1111/j.1467-8624.2012.01852.x

Kochanska, G., & Knaack, A. (2003). Effortful control as a personality characteristic of young children: Antecedents, correlates, and consequences. *Journal of Personality*, 71(6), 1087. doi:10.1111/1467-6494.7106008

Kochanska, G., Tjebkes, T. L., & Forman, D. R. (1998). Children's emerging regulation of conduct: Restraint, compliance, and internalization from infancy to the second year. *Child Development*, 69, 1378–1389.

Kojima, H. (1986). Becoming nurturant in Japan: Past and present. In A. Fogel & G. F. Melson (Eds.), *Origins of nurturance: Developmental, biological, and cultural perspectives on caregiving* (pp. 359–376). Hillsdale, NJ: Lawrence Erlbaum.

Korner, A. F. (1969). Neonatal startles, smiles, erections, and reflex sucks as related to state, sex and individuality. *Child Development*, 40(4), 1039.

Lagattuta, K. H., & Thompson, R. A. (2007). The development of self-conscious emotions: Cognitive processes and social influences. In J. L. Tracy, R. W. Robins, & J. P. Tangney (Eds.), *The self-conscious emotions: Theory and research* (pp. 91–113). New York: Guilford Press.

Lamb, M. E. (1997). The development of father-infant relationships. In M. E. Lamb (Ed.), *The role of the father in child development*. Hoboken, NJ: John Wiley.

Lamb, M. E., & Lewis, C. (2011). The role of parent-child relationships in child development. In M. H. Bornstein & M. E. Lamb (Eds.), *Developmental science: An advanced textbook* (6th ed., pp. 469–517). New York: Psychology Press.

LeDoux, J. E., & Phelps, E. A. (2008). Emotional networks in the brain. In M. Lewis, J. M. Haviland-Jones, & L. F. Barrett (Eds.), *Handbook of emotions* (3rd ed., pp. 159–179). New York: Guilford Press.

Leger, D. W., Thompson, R. A., Merritt, J. A., & Benz, J. J. (1996). Adult perception of emotion intensity in human infant cries: Effects of infant age and cry acoustics. *Child Development*, 67, 3238–3249.

Lemerise, E. A., & Dodge, K. A. (2008). The development of anger and hostile interactions. In M. Lewis, J. M. Haviland-Jones, & L. F. Barrett (Eds.), *Handbook of emotions* (3rd ed., pp. 730–741). New York: Guilford Press.

Lemery, K. S., Goldsmith, H. H., Klinnert, M. D., & Mrazel, D. A. (1999). Developmental models of infant and childhood temperament. *Developmental Psychology*, 35, 189–204.

Leppänen, J. M. (2011). Neural and developmental bases of the ability to recognize social signals of emotions. *Emotion Review*, 3(2), 179–188. doi:10.1177/1754073910387942

Leppänen, J. M., Richmond, J., Vogel-Farley, V. K., Moulson, M. C., & Nelson, C. A. (2009). Categorical representation of facial expressions in the infant brain. *Infancy*, 14(3), 346–362. doi:10.1080/15250000902839393

Leventon, J. S., & Bauer, P. J. (2013). The sustained effect of emotional signals on neural processing in 12-month-olds. *Developmental Science*, 16(4), 485–498. doi:10.1111/desc.12041

LeVine, R. A., Dixon, S., LeVine, S., Richman, A., Leiderman, P. H., Keefer, C. H., & Brazelton, T. B. (1994). *Child care and culture: Lessons from Africa*. New York: Cambridge University Press.

Lewis, C., & Lamb, M. E. (2003). Fathers' influences on children's development: The evidence from two-parent families. *European Journal of Psychology of Education*, 18(2), 212–228.

Lewis, M. (2008). Self-conscious emotions: Embarrassment, pride, shame, and guilt. In M. Lewis, J. M. Haviland-Jones, & L. F. Barrett (Eds.), *Handbook of emotions* (3rd ed., pp. 742–756). New York: Guilford Press.

Lewis, M. (2011). Inside and outside: The relation between emotional states and expressions. *Emotion Review*, 3(2), 189–196. doi:10.1177/1754073910387947

Lewis, M., & Brooks-Gunn, J. (1979). *Social cognition and the acquisition of self*. New York: Plenum Press.

Lewis, M., & Carmody, D. P. (2008). Self-representation and brain development. *Developmental Psychology*, 44(5), 1329–1334. doi:10.1037/a0012681

Lewis, M., Hitchcock, D. F. A., & Sullivan, M. W. (2004). Physiological and emotional reactivity to learning and frustration. *Infancy*, 6(1), 121–143.

Lewis, M., Ramsay, D. S., & Kawakami, K. (1993). Differences between Japanese infants and Caucasian American infants in behavioral and cortisol response to inoculation. *Child Development*, 64, 1722–1731.

Lieberman, A. F., & Van Horn, P. (2008). *Psychotherapy with infants and young children: Repairing the effects of stress and trauma on early attachment*. New York: Guilford Press.

Liu, C. H., & Tronick, E. (2013). Re-conceptualising prenatal life stressors in predicting post-partum depression: Cumulative-, specific-, and domain-specific approaches to calculating risk. *Paediatric and Perinatal Epidemiology*, 27(5), 481–490. doi:10.1111/ppe.12072

Lucassen, N., Tharner, A., van IJzendoorn, M. H., Bakermans-Kranenburg, M. J., Volling, B. L., Verhulst, F. C., . . . Tiemeier, H. (2011). The association between paternal sensitivity and infant-father attachment security: A meta-analysis of three decades of research. *Journal of Family Psychology*, 25(6), 986–992. doi:10.1037/a0025855

Lyons-Ruth, K., Bronfman, E., & Parsons, E. (1999). Maternal frightened, frightening, or atypical behavior and disorganized infant attachment patterns. *Monographs of the Society for Research in Child Development*, 64(3, Serial No. 258), 67–96.

Lyubchik, A. C., & Schlosser, L. (2010). Empathic and aversive responses to others among 16-month-olds: Associations with maternal depressive and relational variables. *Journal of Reproductive & Infant Psychology*, 28(4), 372–383. doi:10.1080/02646830903487318

Main, M., & Solomon, J. (1986). Discovery of an insecure, disorganized/disoriented attachment pattern: Procedures, findings, and implications for the classification of behavior. In M. Yogman & T. B. Brazelton (Eds.), *Affective development in infancy*. Norwood, NJ: Ablex.

Malatesta, C. Z., Grigoryev, P., Lamb, C., Albin, M., & Culver, C. (1986). Emotion socialization and expressive development in preterm and full-term infants. *Child Development*, 57, 316–330.

Malatesta, C. Z., & Haviland, J. M. (1982). Learning display rules: The socialization of emotion expression in infancy. *Child Development*, 53(4), 991–1003. Retrieved from http://www.ncbi.nlm.nih.gov/pubmed/7128264

Mangelsdorf, S. C. (1992). Developmental changes in infant-stranger interaction. *Infant Behavior & Development*, 15(2), 191–208. doi:10.1016/0163-6383(92)80023-n

Mangelsdorf, S. C., Shapiro, J. R., & Marzolf, D. (1995). Developmental and temperamental differences in emotion regulation in infancy. *Child Development*, 66, 1817–1828.

McElwain, N. L., & Booth-LaForce, C. (2006). Maternal sensitivity to infant distress and nondistress as predictors of infant-mother attachment security. *Journal of Family Psychology*, 20(2), 247–255. doi:10.1037/0893-3200.20.2.247

McElwain, N. L., & Volling, B. (2004). Attachment security and parental sensitivity during infancy: Associations with friendship quality and false-belief understanding at age 4. *Journal of Social and Personal Relationships, 21*(5), 639–667.

McLennan, J. D., & Kotelchuck, M. (2000). Parental prevention practices for young children in the context of maternal depression. *Pediatrics, 105*(5), 1090–1095.

McMahan True, M., Pisani, L., & Oumar, F. (2001). Infant–mother attachment among the Dogon of Mali. *Child Development, 72*(5), 1451.

Meléndez, L. (2005). Parental beliefs and practices around early self-regulation: The impact of culture and immigration. *Infants & Young Children, 18*(2), 136–146.

Meltzoff, A. N. (1990). Towards a developmental cognitive science. *Annals of the New York Academy of Sciences, 608*, 1–37.

Meltzoff, A. N. (2007). "Like me": A foundation for social cognition. *Developmental Science, 10*(1), 126–134. doi:10.1111/j.1467-7687.2007.00574.x

Messinger, D., & Fogel, A. (2007). The interactive development of social smiling. In R. V Kail (Ed.), *Advances in child development and behavior* (Vol. 35, pp. 327–366). San Diego: Elsevier Academic Press.

Mills-Koonce, W. R., Garrett-Peters, P., Barnett, M., Granger, D. A., Blair, C., & Cox, M. J. (2011). Father contributions to cortisol responses in infancy and toddlerhood. *Developmental Psychology, 47*(2), 388–395. doi:10.1037/a0021066

Moore, G. A. (2009). Infants' and mothers' vagal reactivity in response to anger. *Journal of Child Psychology and Psychiatry, 50*(11), 1392–1400. doi:10.1111/j.1469-7610.2009.02171.x

Moses, L. J., Baldwin, D. A., Rosicky, J. G., & Tidball, G. (2001). Evidence for referential understanding in the emotions domain at twelve and eighteen months. *Child Development, 72*, 718–735.

Mumme, D. L., Fernald, A., & Herrera, C. (1996). Infants' responses to facial and vocal emotional signals in a social referencing paradigm. *Child Development, 67*, 3219–3237.

Muscat, T., Obst, P., Cockshaw, W., & Thorpe, K. (2014). Beliefs about infant regulation, early infant behaviors and maternal postnatal depressive symptoms. *Birth, 41*(2), 206–213. doi:10.1111/birt.12107

Neisser, U. (1993). *The perceived self: Ecological and interpersonal sources of self-knowledge.* New York: Cambridge University Press.

NICHD Early Child Care Research Network. (2005). Early child care and children's development in the primary grades: Follow-up results from the NICHD study of early child care. *American Educational Research Journal, 42*(3), 537–570. doi:10.3102/00028312042003537

Oddi, K. B., Murdock, K. W., Vadnais, S., Bridgett, D. J., & Gartstein, M. A. (2013). Maternal and infant temperament characteristics as contributors to parenting stress in the first year postpartum. *Infant and Child Development, 22*(6), 553–579. doi:10.1002/icd.1813

O'Hara, M. W., & McCabe, J. E. (2013). Postpartum depression: Current status and future directions. *Annual Review of Clinical Psychology, 9*, 379–407. doi:10.1146/annurev-clinpsy-050212-185612

Papoušek, M., & Papoušek, H. (1990). Excessive infant crying and intuitive parental care: Buffering support and its failures in parent-infant interaction. *Early Child Development and Care, 65*, 117–126. doi:10.1080/0300443900650114

Paulussen-Hoogeboom, M. C., Stams, G. J. J. M., Hermanns, J. M. A., & Peetsma, T. T. D. (2007). Child negative emotionality and parenting from infancy to preschool: A meta-analytic review. *Developmental Psychology, 43*(2), 438–453. doi:10.1037/0012-1649.43.2.438

Pedlow, R., Sanson, A., Prior, M., & Oberklaid, F. (1993). Stability of maternally reported temperament from infancy to 8 years. *Developmental Psychology, 29*, 998–1007.

Pemberton Roben, C. K., Bass, A. J., Moore, G. A., Murray-Kolb, L., Tan, P. Z., Gilmore, R. O., . . . Teti, L. O. (2012). Let me go: The influences of crawling experience and temperament on the development of anger expression. *Infancy, 17*(5), 558–577. doi:10.1111/j.1532-7078.2011.00092.x

Phelps, E. A., & LeDoux, J. E. (2005). Contributions of the amygdala to emotion processing: From animal models to human behavior. *Neuron, 48*(2), 175–187. doi:10.1016/j.neuron.2005.09.025

Pluess, M., & Belsky, J. (2009). Differential susceptibility to rearing experience: The case of childcare. *Journal of Child Psychology and Psychiatry, 50*(4), 396–404. doi:10.1111/j.1469-7610.2008.01992.x

Pluess, M., & Birkbeck, J. B. (2010). Differential susceptibility to parenting and quality child care. *Developmental Psychology, 46*(2), 379–390.

Poehlmann, J., Schwichtenberg, A. J. M., Shlafer, R. J., Hahn, E., Bianchi, J.-P., & Warner, R. (2011). Emerging self-regulation in toddlers born preterm or low birth weight: Differential susceptibility to parenting? *Development & Psychopathology, 23*(1), 177–193. doi:10.1017/s0954579410000726

Porter, C. L., & Hsu, H.-C. (2003). First-time mothers' perceptions of efficacy during the transition to motherhood: Links to infant temperament. *Journal of Family Psychology, 17*(1), 54–64. doi:10.1037/0893-3200.17.1.54

Potegal, M., Robison, S., Anderson, F., Jordan, C., & Shapiro, E. (2007). Sequence and priming in 15 month-olds' reactions to brief arm restraint: Evidence for a hierarchy of anger responses. *Aggressive Behavior, 33*(6), 508–518. doi:10.1002/ab.20207

Prady, S. L., Kiernan, K., Fairley, L., Wilson, S., & Wright, J. (2014). Self-reported maternal parenting style and confidence and infant temperament in a multi-ethnic community: Results from the Born in Bradford cohort. *Journal of Child Health Care, 18*(1), 31–46. doi:10.1177/1367493512473855

Priel, B., & deSchonen, S. (1986). Self-recognition: A study of a population without mirrors. *Journal of Experimental Child Psychology, 41*, 237–250.

Quevedo, L. A., Silva, R. A., Godoy, R., Jansen, K., Matos, M. B., Tavares Pinheiro, K. A., & Pinheiro, R. T. (2012). The impact of maternal post-partum depression on the language development of children at 12 months. *Child: Care, Health and Development, 38*(3), 420–424. doi:10.1111/j.1365-2214.2011.01251.x

Raikes, H. A., & Thompson, R. A. (2008). Attachment security and parenting quality predict children's problem-solving, attributions, and loneliness with peers. *Attachment & Human Development, 10*(3), 319–344. doi:10.1080/14616730802113620

Ranson, K. E., & Urichuk, L. J. (2008). The effect of parent-child attachment relationships on child biopsychosocial outcomes: A review. *Early Child Development and Care, 178*(2), 129–152. doi:10.1080/03004430600685282

Repacholi, B. M., Meltzoff, A. N., & Olsen, B. (2008). Infants' understanding of the link between visual perception and emotion: "If she can't see me doing it, she won't get angry" *Developmental Psychology, 44*(2), 561–574. doi:10.1037/0012-1649.44.2.561

Roben, C. K. P., Moore, G. A., Cole, P. M., Molenaar, P., Leve, L. D., Shaw, D. S., . . . Neiderhiser, J. M. (2015). Transactional patterns of maternal depressive symptoms and mother-child mutual negativity in an adoption sample. *Infant and Child Development, 24*(3), 322–342. doi:10.1002/icd.1906

Rochat, P. (2004). *The infant's world.* Cambridge, MA: Harvard University Press.

Rochat, P., & Striano, T. (1999). Social–cognitive development in the first year. In P. Rochat (Ed.), *Early social cognition: Understanding others in the first months of life* (pp. 3–34). Mahwah, NJ: Lawrence Erlbaum.

Roopnarine, J. L., Talukder, E., Jain, D., Joshi, P., & Srivastav, P. (1992). Personal well-being, kinship tie, and mother-infant and father-infant interactions in single-wage and dual-wage families in New Delhi, India. *Journal of Marriage and Family, 54*(2), 293–301.

Rosen, W. D., Adamson, L. B., & Bakeman, R. (1992). An experimental investigation of infant social referencing: Mothers' messages and gender differences. *Developmental Psychology, 28*, 1172–1178.

Rothbart, M. K. (2011). *Becoming who we are: Temperament and personality in development.* New York: Guilford Press. Retrieved from http://books.google.com/books?hl=en&lr=&id=StR9ernDY-kC&pgis=1

Rothbart, M. K., & Bates, J. E. (1998). Temperament. In N. Eisenberg (Ed.), *Handbook of child psychology: Vol. 3. Social, emotional, and personality development* (5th ed., pp. 105–176). Hoboken, NJ: John Wiley.

Rothbaum, F., Weisz, J., Pott, M., Miyake, K., & Morelli, G. (2000). Attachment and culture: Security in the United States and Japan. *American Psychologist, 55*, 1093–1104.

Rubin, K. H., Hastings, P., Chen, X., Stewart, S., & McNichol, K. (1998). Interpersonal and maternal correlates of aggression, conflict, and externalizing problems in toddlers. *Child Development, 69*, 1614–1629.

Saarni, C., Mumme, D. L., & Campos, J. J. (1998). Emotional development: Action, communication, and understanding. In N. Eisenberg & W. Damon (Eds.), *Handbook of child psychology: Vol 3. Social, emotional, and personality development* (5th ed., pp. 237–309). Hoboken, NJ: John Wiley.

Safdar, S., Friedlmeier, W., Matsumoto, D., Yoo, S. H., Kwantes, C. T., Kakai, H., & Shigemasu, E. (2009). Variations of emotional display rules within and across cultures: A comparison between Canada, USA, and Japan. *Canadian Journal of Behavioural Science/Revue Canadienne Des Sciences Du Comportement, 41*(1), 1–10. doi:10.1037/a0014387

Sagi, A., Lamb, M. E., Lewkowicz, K. S., Shoham, R., Dvir, R., & Estes, D. (1985). Security of infant-mother, -father, and -metapelet attachments among kibbutz-reared Israeli children. *Monographs of the Society for Research in Child Development, 50*(1–2), 257–275. doi:10.1111/1540-5834.ep11890146

Sagi, A., van IJzendoorn, M. H., & Koren-Karie, N. (1991). Primary appraisal of the Strange Situation: A cross-cultural analysis of preseparation episodes. *Developmental Psychology, 27*(4), 587–596.

Salekin, R. T., & Averett, C. A. (2008). Personality in childhood and adolescence. In M. Hersen & A. M. Gross (Eds.), *Handbook of clinical psychology: Vol 2. Children and adolescents* (pp. 351–385). Hoboken, NJ: John Wiley.

Salter, M. D. (1940). *An evaluation of adjustment based upon the concept of security.* Toronto: University of Toronto Press. Retrieved from http://books.google.com/books/about/An_Evaluation_of_Adjustment_Based_Upon_t.html?id=hbCLAAAACAAJ&pgis=1

Sarkadi, A., Kristiansson, R., Oberklaid, F., & Bremberg, S. (2008). Fathers' involvement and children's developmental outcomes: A systematic review of longitudinal studies. *Acta Paediatrica, 97*(2), 153–158. doi:10.1111/j.1651-2227.2007.00572.x

Slaughter, V., & McConnell, D. (2003). Emergence of joint attention: Relationships between gaze following, social referencing, imitation, and naming in infancy. *Journal of Genetic Psychology, 164*(1), 54.

Sohr-Preston, S. L., & Scaramella, L. V. (2006). Implications of timing of maternal depressive symptoms for early cognitive and language development. *Clinical Child & Family Psychology Review, 9*(1), 65–83. doi:10.1007/s10567-006-0004-2

Sorce, J. F., Emde, R. N., Campos, J., & Klinnert, M. D. (1985). Maternal emotional signaling: Its effect on the visual cliff behavior of 1-year-olds. *Developmental Psychology, 21*, 195–200.

Speranza, A. M., Ammaniti, M., & Trentini, C. (2006). An overview of maternal depression, infant reactions and intervention programmes. *Clinical Neuropsychiatry: Journal of Treatment Evaluation*, 3(1), 57–68.

Sroufe, L. A. (1977). Wariness of strangers and the study of infant development. *Child Development*, 48(3), 731–746.

Sroufe, L. A. (1997). Psychopathology as an outcome of development. *Development and Psychopathology*, 7, 323–336.

Sroufe, L. A., Carlson, E., & Shulman, S. (1993). Individuals in relationships: Development from infancy through adolescence. In D. C. Funder, R. D. Parke, C. Tomlinson-Keasey, & K. Widaman (Eds.), *Studying lives through time: Personality and development* (pp. 315–342). Washington, DC: American Psychological Association.

Sroufe, L. A., & Waters, E. (1976). The ontogenesis of smiling and laughter: A perspective on the organization of development in infancy. *Psychological Review*, 83(3), 173–189. doi:10.1037/0033-295x.83.3.173

Steele, H., Steele, M., & Croft, C. (2008). Early attachment predicts emotion recognition at 6 and 11 years old. *Attachment & Human Development*, 10(4), 379–393. doi:10.1080/14616730802461409

Stipek, D. J., Gralinski, J. H., & Kopp, C. B. (1990). Self-concept development in the toddler years. *Developmental Psychology*, 26(6), 972–977. doi:10.1037/0012-1649.26.6.972

Strathearn, L., Jian, L., Fonagy, P., & Montague, P. R. (2008). What's in a smile? Maternal brain responses to infant facial cues. *Pediatrics*, 122(1), 40–51. doi:10.1542/peds.2007-1566

Striano, T., & Rochat, P. (2000). Emergence of selective social referencing in infancy. *Infancy*, 1, 253–264.

Striano, T., Vaish, A., & Benigno, J. P. (2006). The meaning of infants' looks: Information seeking and comfort seeking? *British Journal of Developmental Psychology*, 24(3), 615–630. doi:10.1348/026151005x67566

Sullivan, M. W., & Lewis, M. (2003). Contextual determinants of anger and other negative expressions in young infants. *Developmental Psychology*, 39(4), 693–705. doi:10.1037/0012-1649.39.4.693

Sullivan, M. W., & Lewis, M. (2012). Relations of early goal blockage response and gender to subsequent tantrum behavior. *Infancy: The Official Journal of the International Society on Infant Studies*, 17(2), 159–178. doi:10.1111/j.1532-7078.2011.00077.x

Takahashi, K. (1990). Are the key assumptions of the "Strange Situation" procedure universal? A view from Japanese research. *Human Development*, 33, 23–30.

Tamis-LeMonda, C. S., Kahana-Kalman, R., & Yoshikawa, H. (2009). Father involvement in immigrant and ethnically diverse families from the prenatal period to the second year: Prediction and mediating mechanisms. *Sex Roles*, 60(7), 496–509. doi:10.1007/s11199-009-9593-9

Thomas, A., & Chess, S. (1977). *Temperament and development*. New York: Brunner/Mazel.

Thomas, A., Chess, S., & Birch, H. G. (1970). The origin of personality. *Scientific American*, 223, 102–109.

Thompson, R. A. (1998). Early sociopersonality development. In W. Damon, D. Kuhn, & R. S. Siegler (Eds.), *Handbook of child psychology: Social, emotional, and personality development*. Hoboken, NJ: John Wiley.

Thompson, R. A. (2000). The legacy of early attachments. *Child Development*, 71(1), 145–152.

Thompson, R. A. (2004). Development in the first years of life. In E. F. Zigler, D. G. Singer, & S. J. Bishop-Josef (Eds.), *Children's play: The roots of reading* (pp. 15–31). Washington, DC: ZERO TO THREE/National Center for Infants, Toddlers and Families.

Thompson, R. A., & Limber, S. P. (1990). "Social anxiety" in infancy: Stranger and separation reactions. In H. Leitenberg (Ed.), *Handbook of social and evaluation anxiety* (pp. 85–137). New York: Plenum Press.

Thompson, R. A., Winer, A. C., & Goodvin, R. (2013). The individual child: Temperament, emotion, self, and personality. In M. H. Bornstein & M. E. Lamb (Eds.), *Developmental science: An advanced textbook* (5th ed.). New York: Psychology Press.

Tronick, E. (2007). *The neurobehavioral and social-emotional development of infants and children*. New York: W. W. Norton & Company.

Tronick, E., & Reck, C. (2009). Infants of depressed mothers. *Harvard Review of Psychiatry*, 17(2), 147–156. doi:10.1080/10673220902899714

Tronick, E. Z. (1989). Emotions and emotional communication in infants. *American Psychologist*, 44, 112–119.

Tronick, E. Z., & Cohn, J. F. (1989). Infant-mother face-to-face interaction: Age and gender differences in coordination and the occurrence of miscoordination. *Child Development*, 60, 85–92.

Tronick, E. Z., Morelli, G. A., & Ivey, P. K. (1992). The Efe forager infant and toddler's pattern of social relationships: Multiple and simultaneous. *Developmental Psychology*, 28, 568–577.

Ursache, A., Blair, C., Stifter, C., Voegtline, K., & Family Life Project Investigators. (2013). Emotional reactivity and regulation in infancy interact to predict executive functioning in early childhood. *Developmental Psychology*, 40(1), 760.

U.S. Bureau of Labor Statistics. (2015). *Employment characteristics of families—2014*. Retrieved from http://www.bls.gov/news.release/famee.nr0.htm

Vaish, A., Grossmann, T., & Woodward, A. (2008). Not all emotions are created equal: The negativity bias in social-emotional development. *Psychological Bulletin*, 134(3), 383–403. doi:10.1037/0033-2909.134.3.383

Vallotton, C., & Ayoub, C. (2011). Use your words: The role of language in the development of toddlers' self-regulation. *Early Childhood Research Quarterly*, 26(2), 169–181.

Van Aken, M. A. G. (2009). Personality in children and adolescents: Development and consequences. In R. E. Tremblay, M. A. G. van Aken, & W. Koops (Eds.), *Development and prevention of behaviour problems: From genes to social policy* (pp. 131–142). New York: Psychology Press.

Van den Boom, D. C. (1997). Sensitivity and attachment: Next steps for developmentalists. *Child Development*, 68(4), 592. doi:10.1111/1467-8624.ep9710021673

Van IJzendoorn, M. H., & De Wolff, M. S. (1997). In search of the absent father—Meta-analyses of infant-father attachment: A rejoinder. *Child Development*, 68(4), 604. doi:10.1111/1467-8624.ep9710021677

Van IJzendoorn, M. H., & Kroonenberg, P. M. (1988). Cross-cultural patterns of attachment: A meta-analysis of the strange situation. *Child Development*, 59, 147–156.

Vandell, D. L., Belsky, J., Burchinal, M., Steinberg, L., & Vandergrift, N. (2010). Do effects of early child care extend to age 15 years? Results from the NICHD Study of Early Child Care and Youth Development. *Child Development*, 81(3), 737–756. doi:10.1111/j.1467-8624.2010.01431.x

Vaughn, B. E., Kopp, C. B., & Krakow, J. B. (1984). The emergence and consolidation of self-control from eighteen to thirty months of age: Normative trends and individual differences. *Child Development*, 55(3), 990–1004. doi:10.1111/1467-8624.ep12427046

Verhage, M. L., Oosterman, M., & Schuengel, C. (2013). Parenting self-efficacy predicts perceptions of infant negative temperament characteristics, not vice versa. *Journal of Family Psychology*, 27(5), 844–849. doi:10.1037/a0034263

Waldfogel, J. (2006). Early childhood policy: A comparative perspective. In K. McCartney & D. Phillips (Eds.), *Blackwell handbook of early childhood development* (pp. 576–594). Malden, MA: Blackwell.

Watamura, S. E., Phillips, D. A., Morrissey, T. W., McCartney, K., & Bub, K. (2011). Double jeopardy: Poorer social-emotional outcomes for children in the NICHD SECCYD experiencing home and child-care environments that confer risk. *Child Development*, 82(1), 48–65. doi:10.1111/j.1467-8624.2010.01540.x

Waters, E., Matas, L., & Sroufe, L. A. (1975). Infants' reactions to an approaching stranger: Description, validation, and functional significance of wariness. *Child Development*, 46(2), 348–356. Retrieved from http://www.ncbi.nlm.nih.gov/pubmed/1183268

Waters, E., Merrick, S., Treboux, D., Crowell, J., & Albersheim, L. (2000). Attachment security in infancy and early adulthood: A twenty-year longitudinal study. *Child Development*, 71, 684–689.

Waters, S. F., West, T. V., & Mendes, W. B. (2014). Stress contagion: Physiological covariation between mothers and infants. *Psychological Science*, 25(4), 934–942. doi:10.1177/0956797613518352

Weinfield, N. S., Sroufe, L. A., & Egeland, B. (2000). Attachment from infancy to early adulthood in a high-risk sample: Continuity, discontinuity, and their correlates. *Child Development*, 71, 695–702.

Weinfield, N. S., Sroufe, L. A., Egeland, B., & Carlson, E. (2008). Individual differences in infant-caregiver attachment: Conceptual and empirical aspects of security. In J. Cassidy & P. R. Shaver (Eds.), *Handbook of attachment: Theory, research, and clinical applications*. New York: Guilford Press.

Wolfe, C. D., & Bell, M. A. (2007). The integration of cognition and emotion during infancy and early childhood: Regulatory processes associated with the development of working memory. *Brain and Cognition*, 65(1), 3–13. doi:10.1016/j.bandc.2006.01.009

Wolke, D., Eryigit-Madzwamuse, S., & Gutbrod, T. (2014). Very preterm/very low birthweight infants' attachment: Infant and maternal characteristics. *Archives of Disease in Childhood. Fetal and Neonatal Edition*, 99(1), F70–F75. doi:10.1136/archdischild-2013-303788

Youngblade, L. M., & Belsky, J. (1992). Parent-child antecedents of 5-year-olds' close friendships: A longitudinal analysis. *Developmental Psychology*, 28, 700–713.

Zajicek-Farber, M. (2009). Postnatal depression and infant health practices among high-risk women. *Journal of Child & Family Studies*, 18(2), 236–245. doi:10.1007/s10826-008-9224-z

CHAPTER 7

Abbott-Shim, M., Lambert, R., & McCarty, F. (2003). A comparison of school readiness outcomes for children randomly assigned to a Head Start program and the program's wait list. *Journal of Education for Students Placed at Risk*, 8(2), 191–214.

Ackil, J. K., & Zaragoza, M. (1995). Developmental differences in eyewitness suggestibility and memory for source. *Journal of Experimental Child Psychology*, 60, 57–83.

Administration for Children and Families. (Ed.). (2004). *Aid to Families with Dependent Children/Temporary Assistance for Needy Families: Average monthly number of families and recipients, 1997*. Washington, DC: Author. Retrieved from http://www.acf.hhs.gov/programs/ofa/data-reports/caseload/1997/FYCY97.htm

Adrián, J. E., Clemente, R. A., & Villanueva, L. (2007). Mothers' use of cognitive state verbs in picture-book reading and the development of children's understanding of mind: A longitudinal study. *Child Development, 78*(4), 1052–1067.

Alaimo, K., Olson, C. M., & Frongillo Jr., E. A. (2001). Food insufficiency and American school-aged children's cognitive, academic, and psychosocial development. *Pediatrics, 108,* 44–53.

Alarcón-Rubio, D., Sánchez-Medina, J. A., & Prieto-García, J. R. (2014). Executive function and verbal self-regulation in childhood: Developmental linkages between partially internalized private speech and cognitive flexibility. *Early Childhood Research Quarterly, 29*(2), 95–105. doi:10.1016/j.ecresq.2013.11.002

Alferink, L. A., & Farmer-Dougan, V. (2010). Brain-(not) based education: Dangers of misunderstanding and misapplication of neuroscience research. *Exceptionality, 18*(1), 42–52. doi:10.1080/09362830903462573

Ampaabeng, S. K., & Tan, C. M. (2013). The long-term cognitive consequences of early childhood malnutrition: The case of famine in Ghana. *Journal of Health Economics, 32*(6), 1013–1027. doi:10.1016/j.jhealeco.2013.08.001

Anderson, V., Jacobs, R., Spencer-Smith, M., Coleman, L., Anderson, P., Williams, J., . . . Leventer, R. (2010). Does early age at brain insult predict worse outcome? Neuropsychological implications. *Journal of Pediatric Psychology, 35*(7), 716–727. doi:10.1093/jpepsy/jsp100

Anderson, V., Spencer-Smith, M., & Wood, A. (2011). Do children really recover better? Neurobehavioural plasticity after early brain insult. *Brain, 134*(Pt. 8), 2197–2221. doi:10.1093/brain/awr103

Anderson, V. A., Spencer-Smith, M. M., Coleman, L., Anderson, P. J., Greenham, M., Jacobs, R., . . . Leventer, R. J. (2014). Predicting neurocognitive and behavioural outcome after early brain insult. *Developmental Medicine and Child Neurology, 56*(4), 329–336. doi:10.1111/dmcn.12387

Apperly, I. A., Samson, D., & Humphreys, G. W. (2009). Studies of adults can inform accounts of theory of mind development. *Developmental Psychology, 45*(1), 190–201. doi:10.1037/a0014098

Arija, V., Esparó, G., Fernández-Ballart, J., Murphy, M. M., Biarnés, E., & Canals, J. (2006). Nutritional status and performance in test of verbal and non-verbal intelligence in 6 year old children. *Intelligence, 34*(2), 141–149.

Arsenio, W., & Fleiss, K. (1996). Typical and behaviourally disruptive children's understanding of the emotional consequences of socio-moral events. *British Journal of Developmental Psychology, 14,* 173–186.

Aslan, A., & Bäuml, K.-H. (2010). Retrieval-induced forgetting in young children. *Psychonomic Bulletin & Review, 17*(5), 704–709. doi:10.3758/pbr.17.5.704

Astington, J. W. (1993). *The child's discovery of the mind.* Cambridge, MA: Harvard University Press.

Backschneider, A. G., Shatz, M., & Gelman, S. A. (1993). Preschoolers' ability to distinguish living kinds as a function of regrowth. *Child Development, 64,* 1242–1257.

Baker-Ward, L., Gordon, B. N., Ornstein, P. A., Larus, D. M., & Clubb, P. A. (1993). Young children's long-term retention of a pediatric examination. *Child Development, 64,* 1519–1533.

Ball, S. C., Benjamin, S. E., & Ward, D. S. (2008). Dietary intakes in North Carolina child-care centers: Are children meeting current recommendations? *Journal of the American Dietetic Association, 108*(4), 718–721. doi:10.1016/j.jada.2008.01.014

Bandura, A. (1977). *Social learning theory.* Englewood Cliffs, NJ: Prentice Hall.

Bandura, A. (1986). *Social foundations of thought and action: A social cognitive theory.* Englewood Cliffs, NJ: Prentice Hall.

Bandura, A., & McDonald, F. J. (1963). The influence of social reinforcement and the behavior of models in shaping children's moral judgments. *Journal of Abnormal and Social Psychology, 67,* 274–281.

Banich, M. T. (1998). Integration of information between the cerebral hemispheres. *Current Directions in Psychological Science, 7,* 32–37.

Banich, M. T., & Heller, W. (1998). Evolving perspectives on lateralization of function. *Current Directions in Psychological Science, 7,* 1–2.

Barnett, W. S., Carolan, M. E., Squires, J. H., Clarke Brown, K., & Horowitz, M. (2015). *The state of preschool 2014: State preschool yearbook.* New Brunswick, NJ: National Institute for Early Education Research.

Barrett, M. (1999). *The development of language.* Hove, UK: Psychology Press.

Bauer, P. J. (1996). Development of memory in early childhood. In N. Cowan (Ed.), *The development of memory in childhood* (pp. 83–112). Hove, UK: Psychology Press.

Bebko, J. M., McMorris, C. A., & Metcalfe, A. (2014). Language proficiency and metacognition as predictors of spontaneous rehearsal in children. *Canadian Journal of Experimental Psychology, 68*(1). doi:10.1037/cep0000013

Behrend, D. A., Rosengren, K., & Perlmetter, M. (1989). A new look at children's private speech: The effects of age, task difficulty, and parent presence. *International Journal of Behavioral Development, 12,* 305–320.

Behrend, D. A., Scofield, J., & Kleinknecht, E. E. (2001). Beyond fast mapping: Young children's extensions of novel words and novel facts. *Developmental Psychology, 37,* 698–705.

Beilin, H. (1992). Piaget's enduring contribution to developmental psychology. *Developmental Psychology, 28,* 191–204.

Berk, L. E. (1986). Development of private speech among preschool children. *Early Child Development and Care, 24,* 113–136.

Berk, L. E. (1992). The extracurriculum. In P. W. Jackson (Ed.), *Handbook of research on curriculum* (pp. 1003–1043). New York: Macmillan.

Berk, L. E., & Garvin, R. A. (1984). Development of private speech among low-income Appalachian children. *Developmental Psychology, 20,* 271–286.

Berk, L. E., & Spuhl, S. (1995). Maternal interaction, private speech, and task performance in preschool children. *Early Childhood Research Quarterly, 10,* 145–169.

Bernard, S., & Deleau, M. (2007). Conversational perspective-taking and false belief attribution: A longitudinal study. *British Journal of Developmental Psychology, 25*(3), 443–460. doi:10.1348/026151006X171451

Bernstein, D. M., Atance, C., Meltzoff, A. N., & Loftus, G. R. (2007). Hindsight bias and developing theories of mind. *Child Development, 78*(4), 1374–1394. doi:10.1111/j.1467-8624.2007.01071.x

Bibok, M. B., Carpendale, J. I. M., & Müller, U. (2009). Parental scaffolding and the development of executive function. *New Directions for Child & Adolescent Development, 2009*(123), 17–34. doi:10.1002/cd.233

Birch, L. L., & Fisher, J. A. (1995). Appetite and eating behavior in children. *Pediatric Clinics of North America, 42,* 931–953.

Birch, S. A. J. (2005). When knowledge is a curse: Biases in mental state attribution. *Current Directions in Psychological Science, 14,* 25–29.

Bloom, L. (2000). Commentary: Breaking the language barrier: An emergentist coalition model for the origins of word learning. *Monographs of the Society for Research in Child Development, 65*(3, Serial No. 262), 124–135.

Boland, A. M., Haden, C. A., & Ornstein, P. A. (2003). Boosting children's memory by training mothers in the use of an elaborative conversational style as an event unfolds. *Journal of Cognition and Development, 4*(1), 39–65.

Bower, B. (1993). A child's theory of mind. *Science News, 144,* 40–42.

Bradley, R. H. (1995). Environment and parenting. In M. H. Bornstein (Ed.), *Handbook of parenting, Vol. 2: Biology and ecology of parenting* (pp. 235–261). Hillsdale, NJ: Lawrence Erlbaum.

Brady, K. W., & Goodman, J. C. (2014). The type, but not the amount, of information available influences toddlers' fast mapping and retention of new words. *American Journal of Speech-Language Pathology, 23*(2), 120–133. doi:10.1044/2013_AJSLP-13-0013

Brotanek, J. M., Gosz, J., Weitzman, M., & Flores, G. (2007). Iron deficiency in early childhood in the United States: Risk factors and racial/ethnic disparities. *Pediatrics, 120*(3), 568–575.

Brown, T. T., & Jernigan, T. L. (2012). Brain development during the preschool years. *Neuropsychology Review, 22*(4), 313–333. doi:10.1007/s11065-012-9214-1

Brubacher, S. P., Glisic, U. N. A., Roberts, K. P., & Powell, M. (2011). Children's ability to recall unique aspects of one occurrence of a repeated event. *Applied Cognitive Psychology, 25*(3), 351–358. doi:10.1002/acp.1696

Bruer, J. T. (2008). In search of...brain-based education. In M. H. Immordino-Yang (Ed.), *The Jossey-Bass reader on the brain and learning* (pp. 51–69). San Francisco: Jossey-Bass.

Bryck, R. L., & Fisher, P. A. (2012). Training the brain: Practical applications of neural plasticity from the intersection of cognitive neuroscience, developmental psychology, and prevention science. *American Psychologist, 67*(2), 87–100.

Bullock, M. (1985). Animism in childhood thinking: A new look at an old question. *Developmental Psychology, 21,* 217–225.

Burts, D. C., Hart, C. H., Charlesworth, R., Fleege, P. O., Mosely, J., & Thomasson, R. H. (1992). Observed activities and stress behaviors of children in developmentally appropriate and inappropriate kindergarten classrooms. *Early Childhood Research Quarterly, 7,* 297–318.

Bussey, K. (1992). Lying and truthfulness: Children's definitions, standards, and evaluative reactions. *Child Development, 63,* 129–137.

Busso, D. S., & Pollack, C. (2014). No brain left behind: Consequences of neuroscience discourse for education. *Learning, Media and Technology,* 1–19. doi:10.1080/17439884.2014.908908

Buttelmann, D., Over, H., Carpenter, M., & Tomasello, M. (2014). Eighteen-month-olds understand false beliefs in an unexpected-contents task. *Journal of Experimental Child Psychology, 119,* 120–126. doi:10.1016/j.jecp.2013.10.002

Callaghan, T., Rochat, P., Lillard, A., Claux, M. L., Odden, H., Itakura, S., . . . Singh, S. (2005). Synchrony in the onset of mental-state reasoning. *Psychological Science, 16*(5), 378–384. doi:10.1111/j.0956-7976.2005.01544.x

Callaghan, T. C. (1999). Early understanding and production of graphic symbols. *Child Development, 70,* 1314–1324.

Cameron, C. E., Brock, L. L., Murrah, W. M., Bell, L. H., Worzalla, S. L., Grissmer, D., & Morrison, F. J. (2012). Fine motor skills and executive function both contribute to kindergarten achievement. *Child Development, 83*(4), 1229–1244. doi:10.1111/j.1467-8624.2012.01768.x

Campbell, F. A., Pungello, E. P., Burchinal, M., Kainz, K., Pan, Y., Wasik, B. H., . . . Ramey, C. T. (2012). Adult outcomes as a function of an early childhood educational program: An Abecedarian Project follow-up. *Developmental Psychology, 48*(4), 1033–1043. doi:10.1037/a0026644

Campbell, F. A., & Ramey, C. T. (1994). Effects of early intervention on intellectual and academic achievement: A follow-up study of children from low-income families. *Child Development*, 65(2), 684–698. doi:10.1111/j.1467-8624.1994.tb00777.x

Campbell, F. A., Ramey, C. T., Pungello, E., Sparling, J., & Miller-Johnson, S. (2002). Early childhood education: Young adult outcomes from the Abecedarian Project. *Applied Developmental Science*, 6(1), 42–57. Retrieved from http://www.safetylit.org/citations/index.php?fuseaction=citations.viewdetails&citationIds%5B%5D=citjournalarticle_416815_38

Carlson, S. M., Moses, L. J., & Claxton, L. J. (2004). Individual differences in executive functioning and theory of mind: An investigation of inhibitory control and planning ability. *Journal of Experimental Child Psychology*, 87(4), 299. doi:10.1016/j.jecp.2004.01.002

Caspi, A., & Taylor, A. (2000). Neighborhood deprivation affects children's mental health: Environmental risks identified in a genetic design. *Psychological Science*, 11(4), 338.

Ceci, S. J., & Bruck, M. (1998). The ontogeny and durability of true and false memories: A fuzzy trace account. *Journal of Experimental Child Psychology*, 71, 165–169.

Ceci, S. J., & Friedman, R. D. (2000). The suggestibility of children: Scientific research and legal implications. *Cornell Law Review*, 86, 34–108.

Ceci, S. J., Huffman, M. L., Smith, E., & Loftus, E. F. (1994). Repeatedly thinking about a non-event: Source misattributions among preschoolers. *Consciousness and Cognition*, 3, 388–407.

Chandler, M. J., & Carpendale, J. I. (1998). Inching toward a mature theory of mind. In M. Ferrari & R. J. Sternberg (Eds.), *Self-awareness: Its nature and development* (pp. 148–190). New York: Guilford Press.

Chao, R. K. (1995). Chinese and European American cultural models of the self related in mothers' child rearing beliefs. *Ethos*, 23(3), 328–354.

Chase-Lansdale, P. L., & Vinovskis, M. (1995). Whose responsibility? An historical analysis of the changing roles of mothers, fathers, and society. In P. L. Chase-Lansdale & J. Brooks-Gunn (Eds.), *Escape from poverty: What makes a difference for children?* (pp. 11–37). New York: Cambridge University Press.

Colburn, A. (2009). Brain-based education. *Science Teacher*, 76(2), 10–11.

Coleman-Jensen, A., Gregory, C., & Singh, A. (2014). *Report summary: Household food security in the United States in 2013*. Washington, DC: U.S. Department of Agriculture. Retrieved from http://www.ers.usda.gov/media/1565410/err173_summary.pdf

Colker, L. J. (2009). Pre-K (What is it?). *Teaching Young Chidlren*, 2(1). Retrieved from https://www.naeyc.org/files/tyc/file/PreK-WhatExactlyIsIt.pdf

Collins, A., & Aber, J. L. (1996). *State welfare waiver evaluations: Will they increase our understanding of the impact of welfare reform on children?* New York: National Center for Children in Poverty Columbia University School of Public Health.

Collins, S., Dent, N., Binns, P., Bahwere, P., Sadler, K., & Hallam, A. (2006). Management of severe acute malnutrition in children. *Lancet*, 368(9551), 1992–2000.

Conger, R. D., Wallace, L. E., Sun, Y., Simons, R. L., McLoyd, V. C., & Brody, G. H. (2002). Economic pressure in African American families: A replication and extension of the family stress model. *Developmental Psychology*, 38(2), 179–193.

Conner, D. B., Knight, D. K., & Cross, D. R. (1997). Mothers' and fathers' scaffolding of their 2-year-olds during problem-solving and literacy interactions. *British Journal of Developmental Psychology*, 15, 323–338.

Cox, M., & Littlejohn, K. (1995). Children's use of converging obliques in their perspective drawings. *Educational Psychology*, 15, 127–139.

Cox, M. V. (1993). *Children's drawings of the human figure*. Hillsdale, NJ: Lawrence Erlbaum.

Cox, M. V. (1997). *Drawings of people by the under-5s*. London: Falmer Press.

Danis, A., Bernard, J.-M., & Leproux, C. (2000). Shared picture-book reading: A sequential analysis of adult-child verbal interactions. *British Journal of Developmental Psychology*, 18, 369–388.

Deák, G. O. (2006). Do children really confuse appearance and reality? *Trends in Cognitive Sciences*, 10(12), 546–550.

Dean, D. C., O'Muircheartaigh, J., Dirks, H., Waskiewicz, N., Walker, L., Doernberg, E., . . . Deoni, S. C. L. (2014). Characterizing longitudinal white matter development during early childhood. *Brain Structure & Function*, 220(4), 1921–1933. doi:10.1007/s00429-014-0763-3

DeLoache, J. S. (2000). Dual representation and young children's use of scale models. *Child Development*, 71, 329–338.

DeLoache, J. S., & Todd, C. M. (1988). Young children's use of spatial categorization as a mnemonic strategy. *Journal of Experimental Child Psychology*, 46, 1–20.

Deoni, S. C. L., Mercure, E., Blasi, A., Gasston, D., Thomson, A., Johnson, M., . . . Murphy, D. G. M. (2011). Mapping infant brain myelination with magnetic resonance imaging. *The Journal of Neuroscience*, 31(2), 784–791. doi:10.1523/JNEUROSCI.2106-10.2011

DeVries, R. (1969). Constancy of generic identity in the years three to six. *Monographs of the Society for Research in Child Development*, 34(Serial No. 127).

Dinehart, L., & Manfra, L. (2013). Associations between low-income children's fine motor skills in preschool and academic performance in second grade. *Early Education & Development*, 24(2), 138–161. doi:10.1080/10409289.2011.636729

Dolgin, K. G., & Behrend, D. A. (1984). Children's knowledge about animates and inanimates. *Child Development*, 55, 1646–1650.

Dornfeld, M., & Kruttschnitt, C. (1992). Do the stereotypes fit? Mapping gender-specific outcomes and risk factors. *Criminology*, 30, 397–419.

Dubois, J., Dehaene-Lambertz, G., Kulikova, S., Poupon, C., Hüppi, P. S., & Hertz-Pannier, L. (2013). The early development of brain white matter: A review of imaging studies in fetuses, newborns and infants. *Neuroscience*, 276, 48–71. doi:10.1016/j.neuroscience.2013.12.044

Duncan, G. J., & Brooks-Gunn, J. (2000). Family poverty, welfare reform, and child development. *Child Development*, 71(1), 188–196.

Duncan, G. J., Brooks-Gunn, J., & Klebanov, P. K. (1994). Economic deprivation and early childhood development. *Child Development*, 65(2), 296–318.

Duncan, G. J., Gustafson, B., Hauser, R., Schmauss, G., Messinger, H., Muffels, R., . . . Ray, J.-C. (1993). Poverty dynamics in eight countries. *Journal of Population Economics*, 6(3), 215–234.

Duncan, G. J., Ludwig, J., & Magnuson, K. A. (2007). Reducing poverty through preschool interventions. *The Future of Children*, 17(2), 143–160.

Duncan, R. M., & Pratt, M. W. (1997). Microgenetic change in the quantity and quality of preschoolers' private speech. *International Journal of Behavioral Development*, 20, 367–383.

Dunst, C. J., & Gorman, E. (2009). Development of infant and toddler mark making and scribbling. *CELLReviews*, 2(2), 1–16.

Eamon, M. K. (2001). The effects of poverty on children's socioemotional development: An ecological systems analysis. *Social Work*, 46(3), 256–266.

Efron, R. (1990). *The decline and fall of hemispheric specialization*. Hillsdale, NJ: Lawrence Erlbaum.

Eisbach, A. O. (2004). Children's developing awareness of diversity in people's trains of thoughts. *Child Development*, 75(6), 1694–1707.

Eisenberg, S. L., Guo, L.-Y., & Germezia, M. (2012). How grammatical are 3-year-olds? *Language, Speech, and Hearing Services in Schools*, 43(1), 36–52. doi:10.1044/0161-1461(2011/10-0093)

Elder Jr., G. H., van Nguyen, T., & Caspi, A. (1985). Linking family hardship to children's lives. *Child Development*, 56(2), 361. doi:10.1111/1467-8624.ep7251622

Eveleth, P. B., & Tanner, J. M. (1991). *Worldwide variation in human growth* (2nd ed.). Cambridge, UK: Cambridge University Press.

Ferholt, B., & Lecusay, R. (2010). Adult and child development in the zone of proximal development: Socratic dialogue in a playworld. *Mind, Culture & Activity*, 17(1), 59–83. doi:10.1080/10749030903342246

Fernyhough, C. (2008). Getting Vygotskian about theory of mind: Mediation, dialogue, and the development of social understanding. *Developmental Review*, 28(2), 225–262. doi:10.1016/j.dr.2007.03.001

Fildes, A., Llewellyn, C., Van Jaarsveld, C. H. M., Fisher, A., Cooke, L., & Wardle, J. (2014). Common genetic architecture underlying food fussiness in children, and preference for fruits and vegetables. *Appetite*, 76, 200. doi:10.1016/j.appet.2014.01.023

Fivush, R. (1993). Developmental perspectives on autobiographical recall. In G. S. Goodman & B. L. Bottoms (Eds.), *Child victims, child witnesses* (pp. 1–24). New York: Guilford Press.

Fivush, R. (2011). The development of autobiographical memory. *Annual Review of Psychology*, 62, 559–582. doi:10.1146/annurev.psych.121208.131702

Fivush, R., Hudson, J., & Nelson, K. (1983). Children's long-term memory for a novel event: An exploratory study. *Merrill-Palmer Quarterly*, 30, 303–316.

Fivush, R., & Nelson, K. (2004). Culture and language in the emergence of autobiographical memory. *Psychological Science*, 15(9), 573–577. doi:10.1111/j.0956-7976.2004.00722.x

Flavell, J. H. (1993). The development of children's understanding of false belief and the appearance-reality distinction. *International Journal of Psychology*, 28, 595–604.

Flavell, J. H. (1999). Cognitive development: Children's knowledge about the mind. *Annual Review of Psychology*, 50, 21–45.

Flavell, J. H., Everett, B. H., Croft, K., & Flavell, E. R. (1981). Young children's knowledge about visual perception: Further evidence for the level 1-level 2 distinction. *Developmental Psychology*, 17, 99–103.

Flavell, J. H., Flavell, E. R., & Green, F. L. (1983). Development of the appearance-reality distinction. *Cognitive Psychology*, 15, 95–120.

Flavell, J. H., Flavell, E. R., & Green, F. L. (1987). Young children's knowledge about apparent-real and pretend-real distinctions. *Developmental Psychology*, 23, 816–822.

Flavell, J. H., Friedrich, A. G., & Hoyt, J. D. (1970). Developmental changes in memorization processes. *Cognitive Psychology*, 1, 324–340.

Flavell, J. H., Green, F. L., & Flavell, E. R. (1986). Development of knowledge about the appearance-reality distinction. *Monographs of the Society for Research in Child Development*, 51(1, Serial No. 212).

Flavell, J. H., Green, F. L., & Flavell, E. R. (1989). Young children's ability to differentiate appearance-reality and level 2 perspectives in the tactile modality. *Child Development*, 60, 201–213.

Flavell, J. H., Green, F. L., & Flavell, E. R. (1995). Young children's knowledge about thinking. *Monographs of the Society for Research in Child Development*, 60(1, Serial No. 243).

Friederici, A. D. (2006). The neural basis of language development and its impairment. *Neuron*, 52(6), 941–952.

Friedman, S. L., & Scholnick, E. K. (1987). Setting the stage: An integrative framework for understanding research on planning. In S. L. Friedman & E. K. Scholnick (Eds.), *The developmental psychology of planning: Why, how, and when do we plan?* (pp. 3–22). Mahwah, NJ: Lawrence Erlbaum.

Galal, O., & Hulett, J. (2003). The relationship between nutrition and children's educational performance: A focus on the United Arab Emirates. *Nutrition Bulletin*, 28(1), 11–20.

Gallagher, A. (2008). *Developing thinking with four and five year old pupils: The impact of a cognitive acceleration programme through early science skill development*. Education Department and School of Chemical Sciences, Dublin City University, Dublin, Ireland.

Gathercole, S. E., Adams, A.-M. M., & Hitch, G. (1994). Do young children rehearse? An individual-differences analysis. *Memory and Cognition*, 22, 201–207.

Gelman, R. (1969). Conservation acquisition: A problem of learning to attend to relevant attributes. *Journal of Experimental Child Psychology*, 7, 167–187.

Gelman, R. (1972). Logical capacity of very young children: Number invariance rules. *Child Development*, 43, 75–90.

Gelman, R., & Shatz, M. (1978). Appropriate speech adjustments: The operation of conversational constraints on talk to two-year-olds. In M. Lewis & L. A. Rosenblum (Eds.), *Interaction, conversation, and the development of language* (pp. 27–61). New York: Wiley.

Gelman, S. H., & Gottfried, G. M. (1996). Children's causal explanations of animate and inanimate motion. *Child Development*, 67, 1970–1987.

Gerrard-Morris, A., Taylor, H. G., Yeates, K. O., Walz, N. C., Stancin, T., Minich, N., & Wade, S. L. (2010). Cognitive development after traumatic brain injury in young children. *Journal of the International Neuropsychological Society*, 16(1), 157–168. doi:10.1017/s1355617709991135

Gershkoff-Stowe, L., & Hahn, E. R. (2007). Fast mapping skills in the developing lexicon. *Journal of Speech, Language & Hearing Research*, 50(3), 682–697.

Gibbs, J. C. (1991). Sociomoral developmental delay and cognitive distortion: Implications for the treatment of antisocial youth. In W. M. Kurtines & J. L. Gewirtz (Eds.), *Handbook of moral behavior and development, Volume 3: Application* (pp. 95–110). Hillsdale, NJ: Lawrence Erlbaum.

Gibbs, J. C. (2003). *Moral development and reality: Beyond the theories of Kohlberg and Hoffman*. Thousand Oaks, CA: Sage.

Gilliard, J. L., & Moore, R. A. (2007). An investigation of how culture shapes curriculum in early care and education programs on a Native American Indian reservation. *Early Childhood Education Journal*, 34(4), 251–258. doi:10.1007/s10643-006-0136-5

Golinkoff, R. M., Jacquet, R. C., Hirsh-Pasek, K., & Nandakumar, R. (1996). Lexical principles may underlie the learning of verbs. *Child Development*, 67, 3101–3119.

Golomb, C., & Galasso, L. (1995). Make believe and reality: Explorations of the imaginary realm. *Developmental Psychology*, 31, 800–810.

Goodman, G. S., & Aman, C. J. (1990). Children's use of anatomically detailed dolls to recount an event. *Child Development*, 61, 1859–1871.

Goodman, G. S., Rudy, L., Bottoms, B. L., & Aman, C. (1990). Children's concerns and memory: Issues of ecological validity in the study of children's eyewitness testimony. In R. Fivush & J. A. Hudson (Eds.), *Knowing and remembering in young children* (pp. 249–284). New York: Cambridge University Press.

Gordon, B. N., Baker-Ward, L., & Ornstein, P. A. (2001). Children's testimony: A review of research on memory for past experiences. *Clinical Child and Family Psychology Review*, 4(2), 157–181.

Gormley, W., Gayer, T., Phillips, D., & Dawson, B. (2004). *The effects of Oklahoma's universal pre-K program on school readiness: An executive summary*. Retrieved from http://fcd-us.org/sites/default/files/EffectsOfOKsPKProgram-ExecutiveSummary.pdf

Gottfried, G. M., & Gelman, S. A. (2005). Developing domain-specific causal-explanatory frameworks: The role of insides and immanence. *Cognitive Development*, 20(1), 137–158.

Goymer, P. (2007). Genes know their left from their right. *Nature Reviews Genetics*, 8(9), 652. doi:10.1038/nrg2194

Greenfield, P. M., Maynard, A. E., & Childs, C. P. (2003). Historical change, cultural learning, and cognitive representation in Zinacantec Maya children. *Cognitive Development*, 18(4), 455.

Grusec, J. E. (1992). Social learning theory and developmental psychology: The legacies of Robert Sears and Albert Bandura. *Developmental Psychology*, 28(5), 776–786.

Grusec, J. E., & Goodnow, J. J. (1994). Impact of parental discipline methods on the child's internalization of values: A reconceptualization of current points of view. *Developmental Psychology*, 30, 4–19.

Guajardo, N. R., & Watson, A. C. (2002). Narrative discourse and theory of mind development. *Journal of Genetic Psychology*, 163(3), 305.

Haden, C. A., & Fivush, F. (1996). Contextual variation in maternal conversational styles. *Merrill-Palmer Quarterly*, 42, 200–227.

Hafstad, G. S., Abebe, D. S., Torgersen, L., & von Soest, T. (2013). Picky eating in preschool children: The predictive role of the child's temperament and mother's negative affectivity. *Eating Behaviors*, 14(3), 274–277. doi:10.1016/j.eatbeh.2013.04.001

Hampton, T. (2007). Food insecurity harms health, well-being of millions in the United States. *JAMA*, 298, 1851–1853.

Hamre, B. K. (2014). Teachers' daily interactions with children: An essential ingredient in effective early childhood programs. *Child Development Perspectives*, 8(4), 223–230. doi:10.1111/cdep.12090

Hanania, R., & Smith, L. B. (2010). Selective attention and attention switching: Towards a unified developmental approach. *Developmental Science*, 13(4), 622–635. doi:10.1111/j.1467-7687.2009.00921.x

Han-Na, K., Eun-Ju, L., Sung-Chul, J., Jong-Young, L., Hye Won, C., & Hyung-Lae, K. (2010). Genetic variants that affect length/height in infancy/early childhood in Vietnamese-Korean families. *Journal of Human Genetics*, 55(10), 681–690. doi:10.1038/jhg.2010.88

Hansen, M. B., & Markman, E. M. (2005). Appearance questions can be misleading: A discourse-based account of the appearance-reality problem. *Cognitive Psychology*, 50(3), 233–263. doi:10.1016/j.cogpsych.2004.09.001

Hansen, M. B., & Markman, E. M. (2009). Children's use of mutual exclusivity to learn labels for parts of objects. *Developmental Psychology*, 45(2), 592–596. doi:10.1037/a0014838

Hanson, T. L., McLanahan, S., & Thomson, E. (1997). Economic resources, parental practices, and children's well-being. In G. J. Duncan & J. Brooks-Gunn (Eds.), *Consequences of growing up poor* (pp. 190–238). New York: Russell Sage Foundation.

Hardin, D. S., Kemp, S. F., & Allen, D. B. (2007). Twenty years of recombinant human growth hormone in children: Relevance to pediatric care providers. *Clinical Pediatrics*, 46(4), 279–286.

Hart, C. H., Burts, D. C., Durland, M. A., Charlesworth, R., DeWolf, M., & Fleege, P. O. (1998). Stress behaviors and activity type participation of preschoolers in more and less developmentally appropriate classrooms: SES and sex differences. *Journal of Research in Childhood Education*, 13, 176–196.

Helming, K. A., Strickland, B., & Jacob, P. (2014). Making sense of early false-belief understanding. *Trends in Cognitive Sciences*, 18(4), 167–170. doi:10.1016/j.tics.2014.01.005

Hendler, M., & Weisberg, P. (1992). Conservation acquisition, maintenance, and generalization of mentally retarded children using quality-rule training. *Journal of Experimental Child Psychology*, 53, 258–276.

Heyes, C. (2014). False belief in infancy: A fresh look. *Developmental Science,* 17(5), 647–659. doi:10.1111/desc.12148

Hinojosa, T., Sheu, C.-F., & Michel, G. F. (2003). Infant hand-use preferences for grasping objects contributes to the development of a hand-use preference for manipulating objects. *Developmental Psychobiology*, 43(4), 328–334. doi:10.1002/dev.10142

Hoff, E., Naigles, L., & Nigales, L. (2002). How children use input to acquire a lexicon. *Child Development*, 73(2), 418–433.

Hoffman, M. L. (1970). Conscience, personality, and socialization technique. *Human Development*, 13, 90–126.

Holland, E. (2004). From welfare to work: What the 1996 Welfare Reform Initiative has meant for children. *Georgetown Journal on Poverty Law and Policy*, 115, 115.

Holloway, S. D. (1999). Divergent cultural models of child rearing and pedagogy in Japanese preschools. *New Directions for Child and Adolescent Development*, 83, 61–75.

Honomichl, R. D., & Zhe, C. (2011). Relations as rules: The role of attention in the dimensional change card sort task. *Developmental Psychology*, 47(1), 50–60. doi:10.1037/a0021025

Howe, M. L., & Courage, M. L. (1993). On resolving the enigma of infantile amnesia. *Psychological Bulletin*, 113(2), 305–326. Retrieved from http://www.ncbi.nlm.nih.gov/pubmed/8451337

Hudson, J. A., Fivush, R., & Kuebli, J. (1992). Scripts and episodes: The development of event memory. *Applied Cognitive Psychology*, 6, 483–505.

Hughes, C. H., & Ensor, R. (2007). Executive function and theory of mind: Predictive relations from ages 2 to 4. *Developmental Psychology*, 43(6), 1447–1459. doi:10.1037/0012-l 649.43.6.1447

Hughes, C. H., & Ensor, R. A. (2009). How do families help or hinder the emergence of early executive function? *New Directions for Child & Adolescent Development*, 2009(123), 35–50. doi:10.1002/cd.234

Hughes, C. H., & Leekam, S. (2004). What are the links between theory of mind and social relations? Review, reflections and new directions for studies of typical and atypical developmen. *Social Development*, 13, 590–619.

Hughes, M. (1975). *Egocentrism in preschool children. Unpublished doctoral dissertation.* Edinburgh, Scotland: Edinburgh University.

Huston, A. C. (2008). From research to policy and back. *Child Development, 79*(1), 1–12. doi:10.1111/j.1467-8624.2007.01107.x

Huttenlocher, J., Vasilyeva, M., Cymerman, E., & Levine, S. (2002). Language input and child syntax. *Cognitive Psychology, 45*(3), 337.

Huttenlocher, P. R. (1994). Synaptogenesis in the human cerebral cortex. In G. Dawson & K. W. Fischer (Eds.), *Human behavior and the developing brain* (pp. 137–152). New York: Guilford Press.

Hyde, K. L., Lerch, J., Norton, A., Forgeard, M., Winner, E., Evans, A. C., & Schlaug, G. (2009). Musical training shapes structural brain development. *Journal of Neuroscience, 29*(10), 3019–3025. doi:10.1523/JNEUROSCI.5118-08.2009

Jahns, L., Siega-Riz, A. M., & Popkin, B. M. (2001). The increasing prevalence of snacking among U.S. children from 1977 to 1996. *Journal of Pediatrics, 138*, 493–498.

Janssens, J. M. A. M., & Dekovic, M. (1997). Child rearing, prosocial moral reasoning, and prosocial behaviour. *International Journal of Behavioral Development, 20*, 509–527.

Jaswal, V. K. (2010). Believing what you're told: Young children's trust in unexpected testimony about the physical world. *Cognitive Psychology, 61*(3), 248–272. doi:10.1016/j.cogpsych.2010.06.002

Jenkins, J. M., & Astington, J. W. (1996). Cognitive factors and family structure associated with theory of mind development in young children. *Developmental Psychology, 32*, 70–78.

Jensen, E. P. (2008). A fresh look at brain-based education (Cover story). *Phi Delta Kappan, 89*(6), 408–417.

Jiang, Y., Ekono, M., & Skinner, C. (2015). *Basic facts about low-income children: Children under 6 years, 2013.* New York. Retrieved from http://www.nccp.org/publications/pub_1097.html

Johnston, M. V. (2009). Plasticity in the developing brain: Implications for rehabilitation. *Developmental Disabilities Research Reviews, 15*(2), 94–101. doi:10.1002/ddr.64

Johnston, M. V, Ishida, A., Ishida, W. N., Matsushita, H. B., Nishimura, A., & Tsuji, M. (2009). Plasticity and injury in the developing brain. *Brain & Development, 31*(1), 1–10. doi:10.1016/j.braindev.2008.03.014

Joo, M. (2010). Long-term effects of Head Start on academic and school outcomes of children in persistent poverty: Girls vs. boys. *Children & Youth Services Review, 32*(6), 807–814. doi:10.1016/j.childyouth.2010.01.018

Justice, E. M. (1986). Developmental changes in judgments of relative strategy effectiveness. *British Journal of Developmental Psychology, 4*(1), 75–81.

Kail, R., & Park, Y. (1992). Global developmental change in processing time. *Merrill-Palmer Quarterly, 38*, 525–541.

Kan, P. F., & Kohnert, K. (2008). Fast mapping by bilingual preschool children. *Journal of Child Language, 35*(3), 495–514. doi:10.1017/S0305000907008604

Kan, P. F., & Kohnert, K. (2011). A growth curve analysis of novel word learning by sequential bilingual preschool children. *Bilingualism: Language and Cognition, 15*(03), 452–469. doi:10.1017/S1366728911000356

Kellogg, R. (1970). Understanding children's art. In P. Cramer (Ed.), *Readings in developmental psychology today.* Delmar, CA: CRM.

Kennedy, C. M. (1998). Childhood nutrition. *Annual Review of Nursing Research, 16*, 3–38.

Kenward, B., & Dahl, M. (2011). Preschoolers distribute scarce resources according to the moral valence of recipients' previous actions. *Developmental Psychology, 47*(4), 1054–1064. doi:10.1037/a0023869

Kiernan, K. E., & Mensah, F. K. (2011). Poverty, family resources and children's early educational attainment: The mediating role of parenting. *British Educational Research Journal, 37*(2), 317–336. doi:10.1080/01411921003596911

Killen, M., McGlothlin, H., & Lee-Kim, J. (2002). Between individuals and culture: Individuals' evaluations of exclusion from social groups. In H. Keller, Y. Poortinga, & A. Schoelmerich (Eds.), *Between biology and culture: Perspectives on ontogenetic development.* Cambridge, UK: Cambridge University Press.

Killen, M., & Nucci, L. P. (1995). Morality, autonomy, and social conflict. In M. Killen & D. Hart (Eds.), *Morality in everyday life: Developmental perspectives* (pp. 52–86). Cambridge, UK: Cambridge University Press.

Killip, S., Bennett, J. M., & Chambers, M. D. (2007). Iron deficiency anemia. *American Family Physician, 75*(5), 671–678.

Klebanov, P. K., Brooks-Gunn, J., McCarton, C., & McCormick, M. C. (1998). The contribution of neighborhood and family income to developmental test scores over the first three years of life. *Child Development, 69*(5), 1420–1436.

Klöppel, S., Vongerichten, A., van Eimeren, T., Frackowiak, R. S. J., & Siebner, H. R. (2007). Can left-handedness be switched? Insights from an early switch of handwriting. *The Journal of Neuroscience, 27*(29), 7847–7853. doi:10.1523/jneurosci.1299-07.2007

Kochanska, G., Casey, R. J., & Fukumoto, A. (1995). Toddlers' sensitivity to standard violations. *Child Development, 66*, 643–656.

Kohen, D. E., Brooks-Gunn, J., Leventhal, T., & Hertzman, C. (2002). Neighborhood income and physical and social disorder in Canada: Associations with young children's competencies. *Child Development, 73*(6), 1844–1860. doi:10.1111/1467-8624.t01-1-00510

Kohen, D. E., Leventhal, T., Dahinten, V. S., & McIntosh, C. N. (2008). Neighborhood disadvantage: Pathways of effects for young children. *Child Development, 79*(1), 156–169. doi:10.1111/j.1467-8624.2007.01117.x

Kohlberg, L. (1969). Stage and sequence: The cognitive-developmental approach to socialization. In D. A. Goslin (Ed.), *Handbook of socialization* (pp. 347–480). Chicago: Rand McNally.

Kohlberg, L. (1976). Moral stages and moralization: The cognitive developmental approach. In T. Lickona (Ed.), *Moral development and moral behavior: Theory, research, and social issues* (pp. 31–53). New York: Holt, Rinehart & Winston.

Kohlberg, L., Yaeger, J., & Hjertholm, E. (1968). Private speech: Four studies and a review of theories. *Child Development, 39*, 691–736.

Kolb, B., Gibb, R., & Robinson, T. E. (2003). Brain plasticity and behavior. *Current Directions in Psychological Science, 12*(1), 1–5. doi:10.1111/1467-8721.01210

Kron-Sperl, V., Schneider, W., & Hasselhorn, M. (2008). The development and effectiveness of memory strategies in kindergarten and elementary school: Findings from the Würzburg and Göttingen longitudinal memory studies. *Cognitive Development, 23*(1), 79–104. doi:10.1016/j.cogdev.2007.08.011

La Rooy, D., Lamb, M. E., & Pipe, M. (2011). Repeated interviewing: A critical evaluation of the risks and potential benefits. In K. Kuehnle & M. Connell (Eds.), *The evaluation of child sexual abuse allegations: A comprehensive guide to assessment and testimony* (pp. 327–361). Chichester, UK: Wiley-Blackwell.

Lange, G., & Canoll, D. E. (2003). Mother-child conversation styles and children's laboratory memory for narrative and nonnarrative materials. *Journal of Cognition & Development, 4*(4), 435–457.

Lee, J. M., Pilli, S., Gebremariam, A., Keirns, C. C., Davis, M. M., Vijan, S., . . . Gurney, J. G. (2010). Getting heavier, younger: Trajectories of obesity over the life course. *International Journal of Obesity, 34*(4), 614–623. doi:10.1038/ijo.2009.235

Leichtman, M. D., & Ceci, S. J. (1995). The effects of stereotypes and suggestions on preschoolers' reports. *Developmental Psychology, 31*, 568–578.

Leung, C. B. (2008). Preschoolers' acquisition of scientific vocabulary through repeated read-aloud events, retellings, and hands-on dcience activities. *Reading Psychology, 29*(2), 165–193. doi:10.1080/02702710801964090

Leventhal, T., & Brooks-Gunn, J. (2000). The neighborhoods they live in: The effects of neighborhood residence on child and adolescent. *Psychological Bulletin, 126*(2), 309.

Levine, L. J., Stein, N. L., & Liwag, M. D. (1999). Remembering children's emotions: Sources of concordance and discordance between parents and children. *Developmental Psychology, 35*, 790–801.

Lewis, M., Stanger, C., & Sullivan, M. W. (1989). Deception in 3-year-olds. *Developmental Psychology, 25*(3), 439–443. doi:10.1037/0012-1649.25.3.439

Lewit, E. M., & Kerrebrock, N. (1998). Child indicators: Dental health. *The Future of Children: Protecting Children from Abuse and Neglect, 8*(1), 133–142.

Lillard, A. (1998). Ethnopsychologies: Cultural variations in theories of mind. *Psychological Bulletin, 123*, 3–32.

Linver, M. R., Brooks-Gunn, J., & Kohen, D. (2002). Family processes as pathways from income to young children's development. *Developmental Psychology, 38*(5), 719–734.

Lipowski, S. L., Merriman, W. E., & Dunlosky, J. (2013). Preschoolers can make highly accurate judgments of learning. *Developmental Psychology, 49*(8), 1505–1516.

Lips, P. (2010). Worldwide status of vitamin D nutrition. *Journal of Steroid Biochemistry & Molecular Biology, 121*(1–2), 297–300. doi:10.1016/j.jsbmb.2010.02.021

Littschwager, J. C., & Markman, E. M. (1994). Sixteen- and 24-month-olds' use of mutual exclusivity as a default assumption in second-label learning. *Developmental Psychology, 30*, 955–968.

Liu, D., Wellman, H. M., Tardif, T., & Sabbagh, M. A. (2008). Theory of mind development in Chinese children: A meta-analysis of false-belief understanding across cultures and languages. *Developmental Psychology, 44*(2), 523–531. doi:10.1037/0012-1649.44.2.523

Lockl, K., & Schneider, W. (2007). Knowledge about the mind: Links between theory of mind and later metamemory. *Child Development, 78*(1), 148–167. doi:10.1111/j.1467-8624.2007.00990.x

Lohmann, H., & Tomasello, M. (2003). The role of language in the development of false belief understanding: A training study. *Child Development, 74*(4), 1130–1144. doi:10.1111/1467-8624.00597

Lu, H., Su, Y., & Wang., Q. (2008). Talking about others facilitates theory of mind in Chinese preschoolers. *Developmental Psychology, 44*(6), 1726–1736. doi:10.1037/a0013074

Luciana, M. (2003). Cognitive development in children born preterm: Implications for theories of brain plasticity following early injury. *Development and Psychopathology, 15*(4), 1017–1047. doi:10.1017/s095457940300049x

Lyon, T. D., & Flavell, J. H. (1993). Young children's understanding of forgetting over time. *Child Development, 64*(3), 789–800.

Ma, L., & Ganea, P. A. (2010). Dealing with conflicting information: Young children's reliance on what they see versus what they are told. *Developmental Science, 13*(1), 151–160. doi:10.1111/j.1467-7687.2009.00878.x

Mabbott, D. J., Noseworthy, M., Bouffet, E., Laughlin, S., & Rockel, C. (2006). White matter growth as a mechanism of cognitive development in children. *NeuroImage, 33*(3), 936–946.

MacConnell, A., & Daehler, M. W. (2004). The development of representational insight: Beyond the model/room paradigm. *Cognitive Development, 19*(3), 345–362.

Malina, R. M., & Bouchard, C. (1991). *Growth, maturation, and physical activity.* Champaign, IL: Human Kinetics Books.

Manfra, L., & Winsler, A. (2006). Preschool children's awareness of private speech. *International Journal of Behavioral Development, 30*(6), 537–549.

Marcon, R. A. (1999). Positive relationships between parent-school involvement and public school inner-city preschoolers' development and academic performance. *School Psychology Review, 28*, 395–412.

Markman, E. M. (1987). How children constrain the possible meaning of words. In U. Neisser (Ed.), *Congress and conceptual development: Ecological and intellectual factors in categorization* (pp. 255–287). Cambridge, UK: Cambridge University Press.

Markman, E. M. (1990). Constraints children place on word meanings. *Cognitive Science, 14*, 57–77.

Markman, E. M., & Wachtel, G. F. (1988). Children's use of mutual exclusivity to constrain the meaning of words. *Cognitive Psychology, 20*(2), 121–157. doi:10.1016/0010-0285(88)90017-5

Mascola, A. J., Bryson, S. W., & Agras, W. S. (2010). Picky eating during childhood: A longitudinal study to age 11 years. *Eating Behaviors, 11*(4), 253–257. doi:10.1016/j.eatbeh.2010.05.006

Massey, C., & Gelman, R. (1988). Preschoolers' ability to decide whether a photographed unfamiliar object can move itself. *Developmental Psychology, 24*(3), 307–317.

Mayer, M., Schmitt, K., Kapelari, K., Frisch, H., Köstl, G., & Voigt, M. (2010). Spontaneous growth in growth hormone deficiency from birth until 7 years of age: Development of disease-specific growth curves. *Hormone Research in Paediatrics, 74*(2), 136–144. doi:10.1159/000281020

Maynard, A. E. (2002). Cultural teaching: The development of teaching skills in Maya sibling interactions. *Child Development, 73*, 969–982.

Maynard, A. E. (2004). Cultures of teaching in childhood: Formal schooling and Maya sibling teaching at home. *Cognitive Development, 19*(4), 517–535.

McAlister, A., & Peterson, C. (2007). A longitudinal study of child siblings and theory of mind development. *Cognitive Development, 22*(2), 258–270.

McAlister, A. R., & Peterson, C. C. (2013). Siblings, theory of mind, and executive functioning in children aged 3-6 years: New longitudinal evidence. *Child Development, 84*(4), 1442–1458. doi:10.1111/cdev.12043

McDonald, M. A., Sigman, M., Espinosa, M. P., & Neumann, C. G. (1994). Impact of a temporary food shortage on children and their mothers. *Child Development, 65*, 404–415.

McGonigle-Chalmers, M., Slater, H., & Smith, A. (2014). Rethinking private speech in preschoolers: The effects of social presence. *Developmental Psychology, 50*(3), 829–836. doi:10.1037/a0033909

McKey, R. H., Condelli, L., Ganson, H., Barrett, B. J., McConkey, C., & Plantz, M. C. (1985). *The impact of Head Start on children, families, and communities (Final report of the Head Start Evaluation Synthesis, and Utilization Project).* Washington DC: U.S. Department of Health and Human Services, Administration on Children, Youth, and Families.

McLloyd, V. C. (1998). Children in poverty, development, public policy, and practice. In I. E. Siegel & K. A. Renninger (Eds.), *Handbook of child psychology* (4th ed.). New York: Wiley.

McPhillips, M., & Jordan-Black, J.-A. (2007). The effect of social disadvantage on motor development in young children: A comparative study. *Journal of Child Psychology & Psychiatry, 48*(12), 1214–1222.

Melinder, A., Endestad, T. O. R., & Magnussen, S. (2006). Relations between episodic memory, suggestibility, theory of mind, and cognitive inhibition in the preschool child. *Scandinavian Journal of Psychology, 47*(6), 485–495.

Mercer, N. (2008). Talk and the development of reasoning and understanding. *Human Development (0018716X), 51*(1), 90–100. doi:10.1159/000113158

Merzenich, M. M. (2001). Cortical plasticity contributing to child development. In J. L. McClelland & R. S. Siegler (Eds.), *Mechanisms of cognitive development: Behavioral and neural perspectives* (pp. 67–95). Mahwah, NJ: Lawrence Erlbaum.

Miller, P. H., & Seier, W. L. (1994). Strategy utilization deficiencies in children: When, where, and why. In H. W. Reese (Ed.), *Advances in child development and behavior* (Vol. 24, pp. 107–156). New York: Academic Press.

Milligan, K., Astington, J. W., & Dack, L. A. (2007). Language and theory of mind: Meta-analysis of the relation between language ability and false-belief understanding. *Child Development, 78*(2), 622–646.

Mitchell, P., & Kikuno, H. (2000). Belief as construction: Inference and processing bias. In P. Mitchell & K. J. Riggs (Eds.), *Children's reasoning and the mind* (pp. 281–299). Hove, UK: Psychology Press.

Moriguchi, Y. (2014). The early development of executive function and its relation to social interaction: A brief review. *Frontiers in Psychology, 5*, 388. doi:10.3389/fpsyg.2014.00388

Moriguchi, Y., Kanda, T., Ishiguro, H., Shimada, Y., & Itakura, S. (2011). Can young children learn words from a robot? *Interaction Studies: Social Behaviour and Communication in Biological and Artificial Systems, 12*(1), 107–118.

Morris, P. A. (2002). The effects of welfare reform policies on children. *Social Policy Report, Society for Research in Child Development, 16*(1), 4–18.

Morris, P. A., Gennetian, L. A., & Duncan, G. J. (2005). Effects of welfare and employment policies on young children: New findings on policy experiments conducted in the early 1990s. *Social Policy Report, Society for Research in Child Development, 19*(2), 3–17.

Moses, L. J., Carlson, S. M., & Sabbagh, M. A. (2005). On the specificity of the relation between executive function and children's theories of mind. In W. Schneider, R. Schumann-Hengsteler, & B. Sodian (Eds.), *Young children's cognitive development: Interrelationships among executive functioning, working memory, verbal ability, and theory of mind* (pp. 131–145). Mahwah, NJ: Lawrence Erlbaum.

Moses, L. J., Coon, J. A., & Wusinich, N. (2000). Young children's understanding of desire information. *Developmental Psychology, 36*, 77–90.

Muennig, P., Robertson, D., Johnson, G., Campbell, F., Pungello, E. P., & Neidell, M. (2011). The effect of an early education program on adult health: The Carolina Abecedarian Project randomized controlled trial. *American Journal of Public Health, 101*(3), 512–516. doi:10.2105/AJPH.2010.200063

Murachver, T., Pipe, M., Gordon, R., Owens, J. L., & Fivush, R. (1996). Do, show, and tell: Children's event memories acquired through direct experience, observation, and stories. *Child Development, 67*, 3029–3044.

Mussen, P., & Eisenberg-Berg, N. (1977). *Roots of caring, sharing, and helping.* San Francisco: Freeman.

Myers, N. A., & Perlmutter, M. (2014). Memory in the years from two to five. In P. A. Ornstein (Ed.), *Memory development in children* (pp. 191–218). New York: Psychology Press.

Nagayama, M., & Gilliard, J. L. (2005). An Investigation of Japanese and American Early Care and Education. *Early Childhood Education Journal, 33*(3), 137–143.

Najman, J. M., Clavarino, A., McGee, T. R., Bor, W., Williams, G. M., & Hayatbakhsh, M. R. (2010). Timing and chronicity of family poverty and development of unhealthy behaviors in children: A longitudinal study. *Journal of Adolescent Health, 46*(6), 538–544. doi:10.1016/j.jadohealth.2009.12.001

Nelson, C. A. (2011). Neural development and lifelong plasticity. In D. P. Keating (Ed.), *Nature and nurture in early child development* (pp. 45–69). New York: Cambridge University Press.

Nelson, C. A., Thomas, K. M., & de Haan, M. (2006). *Neuroscience of cognitive development: The role of experience and the developing brain.* Hoboken, NJ: Wiley.

Nelson, K. (1993). The psychological and social origins of autobiographical memory. *Psychological Science, 4*, 1–8.

Nelson, K., & Fivush, R. (2004). The emergence of autobiographical memory: A social cultural developmental theory. *Psychological Review, 111*(2), 486–511. doi:10.1037/0033-295X.111.2.486

Newcombe, N., & Huttenlocher, J. (1992). Children's early ability to solve perspective-taking problems. *Developmental Psychology, 28*, 635–643.

Nicklaus, S. (2009). Development of food variety in children. *Appetite, 52*(1), 253–255. doi:10.1016/j.appet.2008.09.018

Nucci, L. P. (1996). Morality and the personal sphere of action. In E. Reed, E. Turiel, & T. Brown (Eds.), *Values and knowledge* (pp. 41–60). Hillsdale, NJ: Lawrence Erlbaum.

Nucci, L. P. (2001). *Education in the moral domain.* Cambridge, UK: Cambridge University Press.

Nucci, L. P., & Turiel, E. (1978). Social interactions and the development of social concepts in preschool children. *Child Development, 49*(2), 400–407.

Nucci, L. P., & Weber, E. K. (1995). Social interactions in the home and the development of young children's conceptions of the personal. *Child Development, 66*(5), 1438–1452.

Nuttall, A. K. (2014). Autobiographical memory specificity among preschool-aged children. *Developmental Psychology, 50.* doi:10.1037/a0036988

O'Doherty, K., Troseth, G. L., Shimpi, P. M., Goldenberg, E., Akhtar, N., & Saylor, M. M. (2011). Third-party social interaction and word learning from video. *Child Development, 82*(3), 902–915. doi:10.1111/j.1467-8624.2011.01579.x

Onishi, K. H., & Baillargeon, R. (2005). Do 15-month-old infants understand false beliefs? *Science, 308*(5719), 255–258. doi:10.1126/science.1107621

Owens, R. E. (2001). *Language development: An introduction* (5th ed.). Needham Heights, MA: Allyn & Bacon.

Patrick, E., & Abravanel, E. (2000). The self-regulatory nature of preschool children's private speech in a naturalistic setting. *Applied Psycholinguistics, 21*, 45–61.

Patterson, C. J., Kupersmidt, J. B., & Vaden, N. A. (1990). Income levels, gender, ethnicity, and household composition as predictors of children's school-based competence. *Child Development, 61,* 485–494.

Pavarini, G., Hollanda Souza, D., & Hawk, C. K. (2012). Parental practices and theory of mind development. *Journal of Child and Family Studies, 22*(6), 844–853. doi:10.1007/s10826-012-9643-8

Perlmutter, M. (1984). Continuities and discontinuities in early human memory: Paradigms, processes, and performances. In J. R. V. Kail & N. R. Spear (Eds.), *Comparative perspectives on the development of memory* (pp. 253–287). Hillsdale, NJ: Lawrence Erlbaum.

Perner, J. (2000). About + belief + counterfactual. In P. Mitchell & K. Riggs (Eds.), *Children's reasoning and the mind* (pp. 367–397). Hove, UK: Psychology Press.

Perner, J., Lang, B., & Kloo, D. (2002). Theory of mind and self-control: More than a common problem of inhibition. *Child Development, 73,* 752–767.

Petrou, S., & Kupek, E. (2010). Poverty and childhood undernutrition in developing countries: A multi-national cohort study. *Social Science & Medicine, 71*(7), 1366–1373. doi:10.1016/j.socscimed.2010.06.038

Petterson, S. M., & Albers, A. B. (2001). Effects of poverty and maternal depression on early child development. *Child Development, 72*(6), 1794–1813.

Piaget, J. (1929). *The child's conception of the world.* London: Routledge & Kegan Paul.

Piaget, J. (1932). *The moral judgment of the child.* New York: Harcourt Brace.

Piaget, J. (1970). Piaget's theory. In P. H. Mussen (Ed.), *Carmichael's manual of child psychology* (Vol. 1). New York: Wiley.

Piaget, J., & Inhelder, B. (1967). *The child's conception of space.* New York: Norton.

Pillow, B. H. (2008). Development of children's understanding of cognitive activities. *Journal of Genetic Psychology, 169*(4), 297–321.

Pillow, B. H., & Henrichon, A. J. (1996). There's more to the picture than meets the eye: Young children's difficulty understanding biased interpretation. *Child Development, 67,* 803–819.

Pipe, M. E., Lamb, M. E., Orbach, Y., & Esplin, E. (2004). Recent research on children's testimony about experienced and witnessed events. *Developmental Review, 24,* 440–468.

Polak, A., & Harris, P. L. (1999). Deception by young children following noncompliance. *Developmental Psychology, 35*(2), 561–568. doi:10.1037/0012-1649.35.2.561

Poole, D. A., & White, L. T. (1991). Effects of question repetition on the eyewitness testimony of children and adults. *Developmental Psychology, 27,* 975–986.

Poole, D. A., & White, L. T. (1993). Two years later: Effects of question repetition and retention interval on the eyewitness testimony of children and adults. *Developmental Psychology, 29,* 844–853.

Poulin-Dublis, D., & Héroux, G. (1994). Movement and children's attributions of life properties. *International Journal of Behavioral Development, 17,* 329–347.

Previc, F. H. (1991). A general theory concerning the prenatal origins of cerebral lateralization in humans. *Psychological Review, 98*(3), 299–334. doi:10.1037/0033-295x.98.3.299

Principe, G. F., Ornstein, P. A., Baker-Ward, L., & Gordon, B. N. (2000). The effects of intervening experiences on children's memory for a physical examination. *Applied Cognitive Psychology, 14,* 59–80.

Provins, K. A. (1997). Handedness and speech: A critical reappraisal of the role of genetic and environmental factors in the cerebral lateralization

of function. *Psychological Review, 104*(3), 554–571. doi:10.1037/0033-295x.104.3.554

Rakoczy, H., Warneken, F., & Tomasello, M. (2007). "This way!", "No! That way!"—3-year olds know that two people can have mutually incompatible desires. *Cognitive Development, 22*(1), 47–68.

Ramakrishnan, U. (2002). Prevalence of micronutrient malnutrition worldwide. *Nutrition Reviews, 60*(Suppl. 5), i–S52. doi:10.1301/00296640260130731

Ramey, C. T., & Ramey, S. L. (1998). Prevention of intellectual disabilities: Early interventions to improve cognitive development. *Preventive Medicine, 27,* 224–232.

Ratnarajah, N., Rifkin-Graboi, A., Fortier, M. V., Chong, Y. S., Kwek, K., Saw, S.-M., . . . Qiu, A. (2013). Structural connectivity asymmetry in the neonatal brain. *NeuroImage, 75,* 187–194. doi:10.1016/j.neuroimage.2013.02.052

Reese, E., & Fivush, R. (1993). Parental styles for talking about the past. *Developmental Psychology, 29,* 596–606.

Reese, E., Haden, C. A., & Fivush, R. (1993). Mother-child conversations about the past: Relationships of style and memory over time. *Cognitive Development, 8,* 403–430.

Reissland, N., Francis, B., Aydin, E., Mason, J., & Exley, K. (2014). Development of prenatal lateralization: Evidence from fetal mouth movements. *Physiology & Behavior, 131,* 160–163. doi:10.1016/j.physbeh.2014.04.035

Rice, C., Koinis, D., Sullivan, K., Tager-Flusberg, H., & Winner, E. (1997). When 3-year-olds pass the appearance-reality test. *Developmental Psychology, 33,* 54–61.

Riggins, T. (2014). Longitudinal investigation of source memory reveals different developmental trajectories for item memory and binding. *Developmental Psychology, 50*(2), 449–459. doi:10.1037/a0033622

Robinson, J. B., Burns, B. M., & Davis, D. W. (2009). Maternal scaffolding and attention regulation in children living in poverty. *Journal of Applied Developmental Psychology, 30*(2), 82–91. doi:10.1016/j.appdev.2008.10.013

Rocha, E. M. (2013). The effect of forced-choice questions on children's suggestibility: A comparison of multiple-choice and yes/no questions. *Canadian Journal of Behavioural Science/Revue Canadienne Des Sciences Du Comportement, 45*(1). doi:10.1037/a0028507

Roediger, H. L., & Marsh, E. J. (2003). Episodic and autobiographical memory. In I. B. Weiner (Ed.), *Handbook of psychology, Part six. Complex learning and memory processes.* Hoboken, NJ: John Wiley & Sons.

Rogoff, B. (1990). *Apprenticeship in thinking: Cognitive development in social context.* New York: Oxford University Press.

Rogoff, B. (1998). Cognition as a collaborative process. In D. Kuhn & R. S. Siegler (Eds.), *Handbook of child psychology: Vol. 2. Cognition, perception, and language* (5th ed., pp. 679–744). New York: Wiley.

Rogoff, B., Mistry, J., Göncü, A., & Mosier, C. (1993). Guided participation in cultural activity by toddlers and caregivers. *Monographs of the Society for Research in Child Development, 58*(8), v–vi, 1–174; discussion 175–179. Retrieved from http://www.ncbi.nlm.nih.gov/pubmed/8284000

Rogoff, B., Mosier, C., Mistry, J., & Göncü, A. (1993). Toddlers' guided participation with their caregivers in cultural activity. In E. A. Forman, N. Minick, & C. A. Stone (Eds.), *Contexts for learning* (pp. 230–253). New York: Oxford University Press.

Rosenkoetter, L. I. (1973). Resistance to temptation: Inhibitory and disinhibitory effects of models. *Developmental Psychology, 8,* 80–84.

Roy, A. L. (2014). Are all risks equal? Early experiences of poverty-related risk and children's

functioning. *Journal of Family Psychology, 28.* doi:10.1037/a0036683

Rueda, M. R. (2013). Developement of attention. In K. N. Ochsner & S. Kosslyn (Eds.), *The Oxford handbook of cognitive neuroscience, Volume 1: Core topics* (p. 656). New York: Oxford University Press. Retrieved from http://books.google.com/books?hl=en&lr=&id=CtlBAgAAQBAJ&pgis=1

Ruff, H. A., & Rothbart, M. K. (1996). *Attention in early development.* New York: Oxford University Press.

Ruffman, T., Perner, J., & Parkin, L. (1999). How parenting style affects false belief development. *Social Development, 8,* 395–411.

Ruffman, T., Slade, L., & Crowe, E. (2002). The relation between children's and mothers' mental state language and theory-of-mind understanding. *Child Development, 73,* 734–751.

Ryalls, B. O. (2000). Dimensional adjectives: Factors affecting children's ability to compare objects using novel words. *Journal of Experimental Child Psychology, 76*(1), 26–49.

Saarni, C. (1984). An observational study of children's attempts to monitor their expressive behavior. *Child Development, 55*(4), 1504. doi:10.1111/1467-8624.ep7303036

Sabbagh, M. A., Xu, F., Carlson, S. M., Moses, L. J., & Lee., K. (2006). The development of executive functioning and theory of mind. *Psychological Science, 17*(1), 74–81.

Sapp, F., Lee, K., & Muir, D. (2000). Three-year-olds' difficulty with the appearance-reality distinction: Is it real or is it apparent? *Developmental Psychology, 36,* 547–560.

Schneider, W., Schumann-Hengsteler, R., & Sodian, B. (2005). *Young children's cognitive development: Interrelationships among executive functioning, working memory, verbal ability, and theory of mind.* Mahwah, NJ: Lawrence Erlbaum.

Schnur, E., & Belanger, S. (2000). What works in Head Start. In M. P. Kluger, G. Alexander, & P. A. Curtis (Eds.), *What works in child welfare* (pp. 277–284). Washington, DC: Child Welfare League of America.

Schwartz, M. B., Vartanian, L. R., Wharton, C. M., & Brownell, K. D. (2008). Examining the nutritional quality of breakfast cereals marketed to children. *Journal of the American Dietetic Association, 108*(4), 702–705. doi:10.1016/j.jada.2008.01.003

Schwebel, D. C., Rosen, C. S., & Singer, J. L. (1999). Preschoolers' pretend play and theory of mind: The role of jointly constructed pretence. *British Journal of Developmental Psychology, 17*(3), 333–348. doi:10.1348/026151099165320

Schweinhart, L. J., Montie, J., Iang, Z., Barnett, W. S., Belfield, C. R., & Nores, M. (2005). *Lifetime effects: The High/Scope Perry Preschool Study through age 40.* Ypsilanti, MI: High/Scope Press.

Shatz, M., & Gelman, R. (1973). The development of communication skills: Modifications in the speech of young children as a function of listener. *Monographs of the Society for Research in Child Development, 38*(5, Serial No. 152).

Silva, M., Strasser, K., & Cain, K. (2014). Early narrative skills in Chilean preschool: Questions scaffold the production of coherent narratives. *Early Childhood Research Quarterly, 29*(2), 205–213. doi:10.1016/j.ecresq.2014.02.002

Slaughter, V., & Gopnik, A. (1996). Conceptual coherence in the child's theory of mind: Training children to understand belief. *Child Development, 67*(6), 2967–2988.

Slaughter, V., Peterson, C. C., & Mackintosh, E. (2007). Mind what mother says: Narrative input and theory of mind in typical children and those on the autism spectrum. *Child Development, 78*(3), 839–858.

Smetana, J. G. (1995). Morality in context: Abstractions, ambiguities, and applications. In R.

Vasta (Ed.), *Annals of Child Development* (Vol. 10, pp. 83–130). London: Jessica Kingsley.

Smetana, J. G., & Braeges, J. L. (1990). The development of toddler's moral and conventional judgments. *Merrill-Palmer Quarterly, 36*, 329–346.

Smith, J. R., Brooks-Gunn, J., & Klebanov, P. (1997). The consequences of living in poverty for young children's cognitive and verbal ability and early school achievement. In G. J. Duncan & J. Brooks-Gunn (Eds.), *Consequences of growing up poor* (pp. 132–189). New York: Russell Sage Foundation.

Smith, J. R., Brooks-Gunn, J., Kohen, D., & McCarton, C. (2001). Transitions on and off AFDC: Implications for parenting and children's cognitive development. *Child Development, 72*(5), 1512–1533.

Smithers, L. G., Golley, R. K., Brazionis, L., & Lynch, J. W. (2011). Characterizing whole diets of young children from developed countries and the association between diet and health: A systematic review. *Nutrition Reviews, 69*(8), 449–467. doi:10.1111/j.1753-4887.2011.00407.x

Sonnenberg, L. K., Dupuis, A., & Rumney, P. G. (2010). Pre-school traumatic brain injury and its impact on social development at 8 years of age. *Brain Injury, 24*(7–8), 1003–1007. doi:10.3109/02699052.2010.489033

Sousa, D. A. (2001). *How the brain learns: A classroom teacher's guide.* Thousand Oaks, CA: Corwin. Retrieved from http://books.google.com/books/about/How_the_brain_learns.html?id=gW_uAAAAMAAJ&pgis=1

Springer, S. P., & Deutsch, G. (1998). *Left brain, right brain: Perspectives from cognitive neuroscience* (5th ed.). New York: Freeman.

Stiles, J., & Jernigan, T. L. (2010). The basics of brain development. *Neuropsychology Review, 20*(4), 327–348. doi:10.1007/s11065-010-9148-4

Stipek, D. J., Feiler, R., Daniels, D., & Milburn, S. (1995). Effects of different instructional approaches on young children's achievement and motivation. *Child Development, 66*, 209–223.

Symons, D. (2004). Mental state discourse and theory of mind: Internalisation of self–other understanding within a social–cognitive framework. *Developmental Review, 24*, 159–188.

Symons, D. K., Fossum, K.-L. M., & Collins, T. B. K. (2006). A longitudinal study of belief and desire state discourse during mother–child play and later false belief understanding. *Social Development, 15*(4), 676–691. doi:10.1111/j.1467-9507.2006.00364.x

Szaflarski, J. P., Binder, J. R., Possing, E. T., McKiernan, K. A., Ward, B. D., & Hammeke, T. A. (2002). Language lateralization in left-handed and ambidextrous people: fMRI data. *Neurology, 59*(2), 238–244.

Tager-Flusberg, H. (2001). A re-examination of the theory of mind hypothesis of autism. In J. Burack, T. Charman, N. Yirmiya, & P. Zelazo (Eds.), *The development of autism: Perspectives from theory and research* (pp. 173–193). Mahwah, NJ: Lawrence Erlbaum.

Toomela, A. (2003). Developmental stages in children's drawings of a cube and a doll. *TRAMES: A Journal of the Humanities & Social Sciences, 7*(3), 164–182.

Trawick-Smith, J., & Dziurgot, T. (2011). "Good-fit" teacher–child play interactions and the subsequent autonomous play of preschool children. *Early Childhood Research Quarterly, 26*(1), 110–123. doi:10.1016/j.ecresq.2010.04.005

Tulving, E. (2002). Episodic memory: From mind to brain. *Annual Review of Psychology, 53*, 1–25.

Turiel, E. (1998). The development of morality. In N. Eisenberg (Ed.), *Handbook of child psychology, Vol. 3: Social, emotional, and personality development* (5th ed., pp. 863–932). New York: Wiley.

U.S. Department of Health and Human Services. (2011). *Head Start program fact sheet.* Retrieved from http://www.acf.hhs.gov/programs/ohs/about/fy2010.html

Uylings, H. B. M. (2006). Development of the human cortex and the concept of "critical" or "sensitive" periods. *Language Learning, 56*, 59–90.

Van Horn, D., & Kan, P. F. (2015). Fast mapping by bilingual children: Storybooks and cartoons. *Child Language Teaching and Therapy.* doi:10.1177/0265659015584975

Vinden, P. (1996). Junín Quechua children's understanding of mind. *Child Development, 67*, 1707–1716.

Vygotsky, L. S., & Minick, N. (1987). In T. N. Minick (Ed.), *Thinking and speech.* New York: Plenum Press.

Walker, L. J., & Taylor, J. H. (1991). Family interactions and the development of moral reasoning. *Child Development, 62*, 264–283.

Walsh, B. A., & Blewitt, P. (2006). The effect of questioning style during storybook reading on novel vocabulary acquisition of preschoolers. *Early Childhood Education Journal, 33*(4), 273–278. doi:10.1007/s10643-005-0052-0

Wang, Q. (2001). "Did you have fun?" American and Chinese mother-child conversations about shared emotional experiences. *Cognitive Development, 16*(2), 693–715.

Wang, Q. (2004). The emergence of cultural self-constructs: Autobiographical memory and self-description in European American and Chinese children. *Developmental Psychology, 40*(1), 3–15.

Wang, Q., & Fivush, R. (2005). Mother–child conversations of emotionally salient events: Exploring the functions of emotional reminiscing in European-American and Chinese families. *Social Development, 14*(3), 473–495. doi:10.1111/j.1467-9507.2005.00312.x

Wang, X., Bernas, R., & Eberhard, P. (2008). Responding to children's everyday transgressions in Chinese working-class families. *Journal of Moral Education, 37*(1), 55–79. doi:10.1080/03057240701803684

Warren, A. R., & Lane, P. (1995). Effects of timing and type of questioning on eyewitness accuracy and suggestibility. In M. S. Zaragoza, J. R. Graham, G. C. N. Hall, R. Hirschman, & Y. S. Ben-Porath (Eds.), *Memory and testimony in the child witness* (pp. 44–60). Thousand Oaks, CA: Sage.

Wass, R., & Golding, C. (2014). Sharpening a tool for teaching: The zone of proximal development. *Teaching in Higher Education, 19*(6), 671–684. doi:10.1080/13562517.2014.901958

Waxman, S. R., & Hatch, T. (1992). Beyond the basics: Preschool children label objects flexibly at multiple hierarchical level. *Journal of Child Language, 19*, 153–166.

Weber, E. K. (1999). Children's personal prerogative in home and school contexts. *Early Education and Development, 10*(4), 499–515.

Wellman, H. M. (1977). Tip of the tongue and feeling of knowing experience: A developmental study of memory monitoring. *Child Development, 48*(1), 13–21.

Wellman, H. M., & Banerjee, M. (1991). Mind and emotion: Children's understanding of the emotional consequences of beliefs and desires. *British Journal of Developmental Psychology, 9*, 191–214.

Wellman, H. M., Cross, D., & Watson, J. (2001). Meta-analysis of theory-of-mind development: The truth about false belief. *Child Development, 72*(3), 655.

Wellman, H. M., Fang, F., & Peterson, C. C. (2011). Sequential progressions in a theory-of-mind scale: Longitudinal perspectives. *Child Development, 82*(3), 780–792. doi:10.1111/j.1467-8624.2011.01583.x

Wellman, H. M., & Liu, D. (2004). Scaling of theory-of-mind tasks. *Child Development, 75*(2), 523–541.

Wellman, H. M., Phillips, A. T., & Rodriguez, T. (2000). Young children's understanding of perception, desire, and emotion. *Child Development, 71*, 895–912.

Wellman, H. M., Somerville, S. C., & Haake, R. J. (1979). Development of search procedures in real-life spatial environments. *Developmental Psychology, 15*, 530–542.

Williams, E. (2015). Pre-kindergarten across states. *New America Ed Central.* Retrieved from http://www.edcentral.org/prekstatefunding

Willis, J. (2007). Which brain research can educators trust? *Phi Delta Kappan, 88*(9), 697–699.

Winner, E. (1986). Where pelicans kiss seals. *Psychology Today, 20*(8), 25–35.

Winsler, A., Carlton, M. P., & Barry, M. J. (2000). Age-related changes in preschool children's systematic use of private speech in a natural setting. *Journal of Child Language, 27*, 665–687.

Winsler, A., Diaz, R. M., & Montero, I. (1997). The role of private speech in the transition from collaborative to independent task performance in young children. *Early Childhood Research Quarterly, 12*, 59–79.

Winsler, A., Fernyhough, C., & Montero, I. (2009). *Private speech, executive functioning, and the development of verbal self-regulation.* Cambridge, UK: Cambridge University Press.

Woolley, J. D., & E Ghossainy, M. (2013). Revisiting the fantasy-reality distinction: Children as naïve skeptics. *Child Development, 84*(5), 1496–1510. doi:10.1111/cdev.12081

Wysman, L., Scoboria, A., Gawrylowicz, J., & Memon, A. (2014). The cognitive interview buffers the effects of subsequent repeated questioning in the absence of negative feedback. *Behavioral Sciences & the Law, 32*(2), 207–219. doi:10.1002/bsl.2115

Yamagata, K. (2007). Differential emergence of representational systems: Drawings, letters, and numerals. *Cognitive Development, 22*(2), 244–257.

Yarrow, M. R., Scott, P. M., & Waxler, C. Z. (1973). Learning concern for others. *Developmental Psychology, 8*, 240–260.

Yau, J., & Smetana, J. G. (2003). Conceptions of moral, social-conventional, and personal events among Chinese preschoolers in Hong Kong. *Child Development, 74*(3), 647–658.

Yip, R., Scanlon, K., & Trowbridge, F. (1993). Trends and patterns in height and weight status of low-income U.S. children. *Critical Reviews in Food Science and Nutrition, 33*, 409–421.

Yuill, N., & Perner, J. (1988). Intentionality and knowledge in children's judgments of actor's responsibility and recipient's emotional reaction. *Developmental Psychology, 24*, 358–365.

Zaitchik, D., Iqbal, Y., & Carey, S. (2014). The effect of executive function on biological reasoning in young children: An individual differences study. *Child Development, 85*(1), 160–175. doi:10.1111/cdev.12145

Zhai, F., Brooks-Gunn, J., & Waldfogel, J. (2011). Head Start and urban children's school readiness: A birth cohort study in 18 cities. *Developmental Psychology, 47*(1), 134–152. doi:10.1037/a0020784

Zigler, E., & Styfco, S. J. (1993). *Head Start and beyond.* New Haven, CT: Yale University Press.

Zigler, E., & Styfco, S. J. (2004). Moving Head Start to the states: One experiment too many. *Applied Developmental Science, 8*(1), 51–55.

Zosh, J. M., Brinster, M., & Halberda, J. (2013). Optimal contrast: Competition between two referents improves word learning. *Applied Developmental Science, 17*(1), 20–28. doi:10.1080/10888691.2013.748420

Zuckerman, G. (2007). Child-adult interaction that creates a zone of proximal development. *Journal of Russian & East European Psychology, 45*(3), 43–69. doi:10.2753/RPO1061-0405450302

CHAPTER 8

American Academy of Pediatrics Committee on Psychosocial Aspects of Child and Family Health. (1998). Guidance for effective discipline. *Pediatrics, 101,* 723–728.

Anderson, C. A., & Bushman, B. J. (2002). Human aggression. *Annual Review of Psychology, 53,* 27–51.

Anderson, D. R., Huston, A. C., Schmitt, K. L., Lineberger, D. L., & Wright, J. C. (2001). Early childhood television viewing and adolescent behavior: The recontact study. *Monographs of the Society for Research in Child Development, 66*(Serial No. 264).

Anderson, D. R., Lorch, E. P., Field, D. E., Collins, P. A., & Nathan, J. G. (1986). Television viewing at home: Age trends in visual attention and time with TV. *Child Development, 57,* 1024–1033.

Ardila, A., Rosselli, M., Matute, E., & Inozemtseva, O. (2011). Gender differences in cognitive development. *Developmental Psychology, 47*(4), 984–990. doi:10.1037/a0023819 10.1037/a0023819.supp

Arthur, A. E., Bigler, R. S., & Ruble, D. N. (2009). An experimental test of the effects of gender constancy on sex typing. *Journal of Experimental Child Psychology, 104*(4), 427–446. doi:10.1016/j.jecp.2009.08.002

Auyeung, B., Baron-Cohen, S., Ashwin, E., Knickmeyer, R., Taylor, K., Hackett, G., & Hines, M. (2009). Fetal testosterone predicts sexually differentiated childhood behavior in girls and in boys. *Psychological Science, 20*(2), 144–148. doi:10.1111/j.1467-9280.2009.02279.x

Baillargeon, R. H., Morisset, A., Keenan, K., Normand, C. L., Jeyaganth, S., Boivin, M., & Tremblay, R. E. (2011). The development of prosocial behaviors in young children: A prospective population-based cohort study. *Journal of Genetic Psychology, 172*(3), 221–251. doi:10.1080/00221325.2010.533719

Balter, L., & Tamis-LeMonda, C. S. (2006). *The impact of community violence on preschool development. Child psychology: A handbook of contemporary issues* (2nd ed.). New York: Psychology Press.

Bandura, A., & Bussey, K. (2004). On broadening the cognitive, motivational, and sociostructural scope of theorizing about gender development and functioning: Comment on Martin, Ruble, and Szkrybalo (2002). *Psychological Bulletin, 130*(5), 691–701.

Bandura, A., Ross, D., & Ross, S. A. (1963). Imitation of film-mediated aggressive models. *Journal of Abnormal and Social Psychology, 66,* 3–11.

Barr, R., Lauricella, A., Zack, E., & Calvert, S. L. (2010). Infant and early childhood exposure to adult-directed and child-directed television programming. *Merrill-Palmer Quarterly, 56*(1), 21–48.

Barth, R. P., Scarborough, A., Lloyd, E. C., Losby, J., Casanueva, C., & Mann, T. (2007). In Office of the Assistant Secretary for Planning and Evaluation, US. Department of Health and Human Services (Ed.), *Developmental status and early intervention service needs of maltreated children.* Washington, DC: Office of the Assistant Secretary for Planning and Evaluation, U.S. Department of Health and Human Services.

Basow, S. (2008). Gender socialization, or how long a way has baby come? In J. C. Chrisler, C. Golden, & P. D. Rozee (Eds.), *Lectures on the psychology of women* (4th ed., pp. 81–95). New York: McGraw-Hill.

Baumrind, D. (1971). Current patterns of parental authority. *Developmental Psychology, 4*(Monograph 1), 1–103.

Baumrind, D. (1996). A blanket injunction against disciplinary use of spanking is not warranted by the data. *Pediatrics, 88,* 828–831.

Baumrind, D., Larzelere, R. E., & Owens, E. B. (2010). Effects of preschool parents' power assertive patterns and practices on adolescent development. *Parenting: Science & Practice, 10*(3), 157–201. doi:10.1080/15295190903290790

Beal, C. R. (1994). *Boys and girls: The development of gender roles.* New York: McGraw-Hill.

Beatty, W. W. (1992). Gonadal hormones and sex differences in nonreproductive behaviors. In A. A. Gerall, H. Moltz, & I. L. Ward (Eds.), *Handbook of behavioral neurobiology: Vol. 11. Sexual differentiation* (pp. 85–128). New York: Plenum.

Bender, H. L., Allen, J. P., McElhaney, K. B., Antonishak, J., Moore, C. M., Kelly, H. O., & Davis, S. M. (2007). Use of harsh physical discipline and developmental outcomes in adolescence. *Development and Psychopathology, 19*(1), 227–242. doi:10.1017/s0954579407070125

Benenson, J. F. (1993). Greater preference among females than males for dyadic interaction in early childhood. *Child Development, 64,* 544–555.

Berenbaum, S. A., Blakemore, J. E. O., & Beltz, A. M. (2011). A role for biology in gender-related behavior. *Sex Roles, 64*(11–12), 804–825. doi:10.1007/s11199-011-9990-8

Bishop, S., & Leadbeater, B. (1999). Maternal social support patterns and child maltreatment: Comparison of maltreating and nonmaltreating mothers. *American Journal of Orthopsychiatry, 69,* 172–181.

Black, K., Marola, J., Littman, A., Chrisler, J., & Neace, W. (2009). Gender and form of cereal box characters: Different medium, same disparity. *Sex Roles, 60*(11–12), 882–889. doi:10.1007/s11199-008-9579-z

Bolger, K. E., & Patterson, C. J. (2001). Developmental pathways from child maltreatment to peer rejection. *Child Development, 72,* 549–568.

Bolger, K. E., Patterson, C. J., & Kupersmidt, J. B. (1998). Peer relationships and self-esteem among children who have been maltreated. *Child Development, 69,* 1171–1197.

Boseovski, J. J. (2010). Evidence for "rose-colored glasses": An examination of the positivity bias in young children's personality judgments. *Child Development Perspectives, 4*(3), 212–218. doi:10.1111/j.1750-8606.2010.00149.x

Bouldin, P. (2006). An investigation of the fantasy predisposition and fantasy style of children with imaginary companions. *Journal of Genetic Psychology, 167,* 17–29.

Brody, G. H., & Flor, D. L. (1998). Maternal resources, parenting practices, and child competence in rural, single-parent African American families. *Child Development, 69,* 803–816.

Bugental, D. (2009). Predicting and preventing child maltreatment: A biocognitive transactional approach. In A. Sameroff (Ed.), *The transactional model of development: How children and contexts shape each other* (pp. 97–115). Washington, DC: American Psychological Association. doi:10.1037/11877-006

Bussey, K. (2013). Gender development. In M. K. Ryan & N. R. Branscombe (Eds.), *The SAGE handbook of gender and psychology.* Thousand Oaks, CA: Sage.

Bussey, K., & Bandura, A. (1992). Self-regulatory mechanisms governing gender development. *Child Development, 63,* 1236–1250.

Card, N. A., Stucky, B. D., Sawalani, G. M., & Little, T. D. (2008). Direct and indirect aggression during childhood and adolescence: A meta-analytic review of gender differences, intercorrelations, and relations to maladjustment. *Child Development, 79*(5), 1185–1229. doi:10.1111/j.1467-8624.2008.01184.x

Casanueva, C., Goldman-Fraser, J., Ringeisen, H., Lederman, C., Katz, L., & Osofsky, J. (2010). Maternal perceptions of temperament among infants and toddlers investigated for maltreatment: Implications for services need and referral. *Journal of Family Violence, 25*(6), 557–574. doi:10.1007/s10896-010-9316-6

Cauce, A. M. (2008). Parenting, culture, and context: Reflections on excavating culture. *Applied Developmental Science, 12*(4), 227–229. doi:10.1080/10888690802388177

Center for Communication and Social Policy. (1998). *National television violence study* (Vol. 2). Newbury Park, CA: Sage.

Chao, R. K. (2001). Extending research on the consequences of parenting style for Chinese Americans and European Americans. *Child Development, 72,* 1832–1843.

Cheah, C. S. L., Leung, C. Y. Y., Tahseen, M., & Schultz, D. (2009). Authoritative parenting among immigrant Chinese mothers of preschoolers. *Journal of Family Psychology, 23*(3), 311–320. doi:10.1037/a0015076

Child Welfare Information Gateway. (2013). *What is child abuse and neglect? Recognizing the signs and symptoms.* Washington DC: Author. Retrieved from https://www.childwelfare.gov/pubpdfs/whatiscan.pdf

Choe, D. E., Olson, S. L., & Sameroff, A. J. (2013). The interplay of externalizing problems and physical and inductive discipline during childhood. *Developmental Psychology, 49*(11), 2029–2039. doi:10.1037/a0032054

Cicchetti, D., & Banny, A. (2014). A developmental psychopathology perspective on child maltreatment. In M. Lewis & K. D. Rudolph (Eds.), *Handbook of developmental psychopathology* (pp. 723–741). New York: Springer. doi:10.1007/978-1-4614-9608-3

Clarke, J., Stein, M., Sobota, M., Marisi, M., & Hanna, L. (1999). Victims as victimizers: Physical aggression by persons with a history of childhood abuse. *Archives of Internal Medicine, 159,* 1920–1924.

Coie, J. D., & Dodge, K. A. (1998). Aggression and antisocial behavior. In N. Eisenberg (Ed.), *Handbook of child psychology: Vol. 3. Social, emotional, and personality development* (5th ed., pp. 786–788). Hoboken, NJ: John Wiley.

Coley, R. L., Kull, M. A., & Carrano, J. (2014). Parental endorsement of spanking and children's internalizing and externalizing problems in African American and Hispanic families. *Journal of Family Psychology, 28*(1), 22–31. doi:10.1037/a0035272

Colwell, M. J., & Lindsey, E. W. (2003). Teacher-child interactions and preschoolers perceptions of self and peers. *Early Child Development and Care, 173,* 249–258.

Comstock, G., & Scharrer, E. (1999). *Television: What's on, who's watching, and what it means.* San Diego: Academic Press.

Coplan, R. J., & Arbeau, K. A. (2009). Peer interactions and play in early childhood. In K. H. Rubin, W. M. Bukowski, & B. Laursen (Eds.), *Handbook of peer interactions, relationships, and groups* (pp. 143–161). New York: Guilford Press.

Côté, S. M. (2009). A developmental perspective on sex differences in aggressive behaviours. In R. E. Tremblay, M. A. G. van Aken, & W. Koops (Eds.), *Development and prevention of behaviour problems: From genes to social policy* (pp. 143–163). New York: Psychology Press.

Coulton, C. J., Korbin, J. E., & Su, M. (1999). Neighborhoods and child maltreatment: A multi-level study. *Child Abuse and Neglect, 23,* 1019–1040.

Crosse, S., Kaye, E., & Ratnofsky, A. (1993). *A report on the maltreatment of children with disabilities.* Washington, DC: National Clearinghouse on Child Abuse and Neglect Information.

Cuellar, J., Jones, D. J., & Sterrett, E. (2013). Examining parenting in the neighborhood context: A review. *Journal of Child and Family Studies, 24*(1), 195–219. doi:10.1007/s10826-013-9826-y

Davis, P. E., Meins, E., & Fernyhough, C. (2014). Children with imaginary companions focus on mental characteristics when describing their real-life friends. *Infant and Child Development, 23*(6), 622–633. doi:10.1002/icd.1869

De Bellis, M. D., Hooper, S. R., Spratt, E. G., & Woolley, D. P. (2009). Neuropsychological findings in childhood neglect and their relationships to pediatric PTSD. *Journal of the International Neuropsychological Society, 15*(6), 868–878. doi:10.1017/s1355617709990464

De Waal, F. B. M. (1993). Sex differences in chimpanzee (and human) behavior: A matter of social values? In M. Hechter, L. Nadel, & R. E. Michod (Eds.), *The origin of values* (pp. 285–303). New York: Aldine de Gruyter.

Denham, S. A., Bassett, H. H., & Zinsser, K. (2012). Early childhood teachers as socializers of young children's emotional competence. *Early Childhood Education Journal, 40*(3), 137–143. doi:10.1007/s10643-012-0504-2

Dennis, T. A., Cole, P. M., Zahn-Waxler, C., & Mizuta, I. (2002). Self in context: Autonomy and relatedness in Japanese and U. S. mother-preschooler dyads. *Child Development, 73,* 1803–1817.

Diehl, M., Youngblade, L. M., Hay, E. L., & Chui, H. (2011). The development of self-representations across the life span. In K. L. Fingerman, C. A. Berg, J. Smith, & T. C. Antonucci (Eds.), *Handbook of life-span development* (pp. 611–646). New York: Springer.

Dodge, K. A., & Coleman, D. L. (2009). *Preventing child maltreatment: Community approaches.* New York: Guilford Press.

Dunn, J., & Hughes, C. (2001). "I got some swords and you're dead": Violent fantasy, antisocial behavior, friendship, and moral sensibility in young children. *Child Development, 72,* 491–505.

Dyer, S., & Moneta, G. B. (2006). Frequency of parallel, associative, and cooperative play in British children of difference socioeconomic status. *Social Behavior & Personality, 34*(5), 587–592.

Eder, R. A. (1989). The emergent personologist: The structure and content of 3 ½, 5 ½, and 7 ½ year-olds' concepts of themselves and other persons. *Child Development, 60,* 1218–1228.

Edwards, C. P. (2000). Children's play in cross-cultural perspective: A new look at the six cultures study. *Cross-Cultural Research, 34*(4), 318.

Eggum, N. D., Eisenberg, N., Kao, K., Spinrad, T. L., Bolnick, R., Hofer, C., . . . Fabricius, W. V. (2011). Emotion understanding, theory of mind, and prosocial orientation: Relations over time in early childhood. *The Journal of Positive Psychology, 6*(1), 4–16. doi:10.1080/17439760.2010.53 6776

Eisenberg, N., & Fabes, R. A. (1998). Prosocial development. In N. Eisenberg (Ed.), *Handbook of child psychology: Vol. 3. Social, emotional, and personality development* (5th ed., pp. 701–778). Hoboken, NJ: John Wiley.

Eisenberg, N., Fabes, R. A., Shepard, S. A., Murphy, B. C., Jones, S., & Guthrie, I. K. (1998). Contemporaneous and longitudinal prediction of children's sympathy from dispositional regulation and emotionality. *Developmental Psychology, 34,* 910–924.

England, D. E., Descartes, L., & Collier-Meek, M. A. (2011). Gender role portrayal and the Disney princesses. *Sex Roles, 64*(7–8), 555–567. doi:10.1007/s11199-011-9930-7

Erikson, E. H. (1950). *Childhood and society* (2nd ed.). New York: Norton.

Evans, J. (1998). "Princesses are not into war 'n things, they always scream and run off": Exploring gender stereotypes in picture books." *Reading,* 5–11.

Farver, J. A. M., Xu, Y., Eppe, S., Fernandez, A., & Schwartz, D. (2005). Community violence, family conflict, and preschoolers' socioemotional functioning. *Developmental Psychology, 41,* 160–170.

Fasig, L. G. (2000). Toddlers' understanding of ownership: Implications for self-concept development. *Social Development, 9*(3), 370–382.

Fay-Stammbach, T., Hawes, D. J., & Meredith, P. (2014). Parenting influences on executive function in early childhood: A review. *Child Development Perspectives, 8*(4), 258–264. doi:10.1111/cdep.12095

Fireman, G. D., & Kose, G. (2010). Perspective taking. In E. H. Sandberg & B. L. Spritz (Eds.), *A clinician's guide to normal cognitive development in childhood* (pp. 85–100). New York: Routledge.

Fitzpatrick, M., & McPherson, B. (2010). Coloring within the lines: Gender stereotypes in contemporary coloring books. *Sex Roles, 62*(1–2), 127–137. doi:10.1007/s11199-009-9703-8

Font, S. A., & Berger, L. M. (2014). Child maltreatment and children's developmental trajectories in early to middle childhood. *Child Development, 86*(2), 536–556. doi:10.1111/cdev.12322

Fowler, P. J., Tompsett, C. J., Braciszewski, J. M., Jacques-Tiura, A. J., & Baltes, B. B. (2009). Community violence: A meta-analysis on the effect of exposure and mental health outcomes of children and adolescents. *Development and Psychopathology, 21*(1), 227–259. doi:10.1017/s0954579409000145

Frahsek, S., Mack, W., Mack, C., Pfalz-Blezinger, C., & Knopf, M. (2010). Assessing different aspects of pretend play within a play setting: Towards a standardized assessment of pretend play in young children. *British Journal of Developmental Psychology, 28*(2), 331–345. doi:10.1348/026151009x413666

Frawley, T. J. (2008). Gender schema and prejudicial recall: How children misremember, fabricate, and distort gendered picture book information. *Journal of Research in Childhood Education, 22*(3), 291–303.

Freeman, N. (2007). Preschoolers' perceptions of gender appropriate toys and their parents' beliefs about genderized behaviors: Miscommunication, mixed messages, or hidden truths? *Early Childhood Education Journal, 34*(5), 357–366. doi:10.1007/s10643-006-0123-x

Gagnon, S. G., Huelsman, T. J., Reichard, A. E., Kidder-Ashley, P., Griggs, M. S., Struby, J., & Bollinger, J. (2013). Help me play! Parental behaviors, child temperament, and preschool peer play. *Journal of Child and Family Studies, 23*(5), 872–884. doi:10.1007/s10826-013-9743-0

Garner, P. W. (2003). Child and family correlates of toddlers' emotional and behavioral responses to a mishap. *Infant Mental Health Journal, 24*(6), 580.

Ginsburg, K. R. (2007). The importance of play in promoting healthy child development and maintaining strong parent-child bonds. *Pediatrics, 119*(1), 182–191.

Gioia, K. A., & Tobin, R. M. (2010). Role of sociodramatic play in promoting self-regulation. In C. E. Schaefer (Ed.), *Play therapy for preschool children* (pp. 181–198). Washington, DC: American Psychological Association. doi:10.1037/12060-009

Gleason, T. R., & Hohman, L. M. (2006). Concepts of real and imaginary friendships in early childhood. *Social Development, 15*(1), 128–144.

Gleason, T. R., & Kalpidou, M. (2014). Imaginary companions and young children's coping and competence. *Social Development, 23*(4), 820–839. doi:10.1111/sode.12078

Gleason, T. R., Sebanc, A. M., & Hartup, W. W. (2000). Imaginary companions of preschool children. *Developmental Psychology,* 419–428.

Goodvin, R., Meyer, S., Thompson, R. A., & Hayes, R. (2008). Self-understanding in early childhood: Associations with child attachment security and maternal negative affect. *Attachment & Human Development, 10*(4), 433–450. doi:10.1080/14616730802461466

Gower, A. L., Lingras, K. A., Mathieson, L. C., Kawabata, Y., & Crick, N. R. (2014). The role of preschool relational and physical aggression in the transition to kindergarten: Links with social-psychological adjustment. *Early Education and Development, 25*(5), 619–640. doi:10.1080/104 09289.2014.844058

Grusec, J. E., & Goodnow, J. J. (1994). Impact of parental discipline methods on the child's internalization of values: A reconceptualization of current points of view. *Developmental Psychology, 30,* 4–19.

Halim, M. L., Ruble, D., Tamis-LeMonda, C., & Shrout, P. E. (2013). Rigidity in gender-typed behaviors in early childhood: A longitudinal study of ethnic minority children. *Child Development, 84*(4), 1269–1284. doi:10.1111/cdev.12057

Halim, M. L., Ruble, D. N., Tamis-LeMonda, C. S., Zosuls, K. M., Lurye, L. E., & Greulich, F. K. (2014). Pink frilly dresses and the avoidance of all things "girly": Children's appearance rigidity and cognitive theories of gender development. *Developmental Psychology, 50*(4), 1091–1101. doi:10.1037/a0034906

Hanish, L. D., Fabes, R. A., Leaper, C., Bigler, R., Hayes, A. R., Hamilton, V., & Beltz, A. M. (2013). Gender: Early socialization. In E. T. Gershoff, R. S. Mistry, & D. A. Crosby (Eds.), *Societal contexts of child development: Pathways of influence and implications for practice and policy.* New York: Oxford University Press.

Hart, C. H., Newell, L. D., & Olson, S. F. (2002). Parenting skills and social/communicative competence in childhood. In J. O. Greene & B. R. Burleson (Eds.), *Handbook of communication and social interaction skill.* Hillsdale, NJ: Lawrence Erlbaum.

Harter, S. (1990). Issues in the assessment of the self-concept of children and adolescents. In A. LaGreca (Ed.), *Through the eyes of a child* (pp. 292–325). Boston: Allyn & Bacon.

Harter, S. (1998). The development of self-representations. In N. Eisenberg (Ed.), *Handbook of child psychology: Vol. 3. Social, emotional, and personality development* (5th ed., pp. 553–618). Hoboken, NJ: John Wiley.

Harter, S. (1999). *The construction of the self: A developmental perspective.* New York: Guilford Press.

Harter, S. (2006). The self. In N. Eisenberg, W. Damon, & R. M. Lerner (Eds.), *Handbook of child psychology: Vol. 3. Social, emotional, and personality development* (6th ed., pp. 505–570). Hoboken, NJ: John Wiley.

Hay, D. F., Hurst, S.-L., Waters, C. S., & Chadwick, A. (2011). Infants' use of force to defend toys: The origins of instrumental aggression. *Infancy, 16*(5), 471–489. doi:10.1111/j.1532-7078.2011.00069.x

Hicks-Pass, S. (2009). Corporal punishment in America today: Spare the rod, spoil the child? A systematic review of the literature. *Best Practice in Mental Health, 5*(2), 71–88.

Hines, M. (2011). Gender development and the human brain. *Annual Review of Neuroscience, 34*(1), 69–88. doi:10.1146/annurev-neuro-061010-113654

Hoffman, M. L. (2007). The origins of empathic morality in toddlerhood. In C. A. Brownell & C. B. Kopp (Eds.), *Socioemotional development in the toddler years: Transitions and transformations* (pp. 132–145). New York: Guilford Press.

Hoffmann, J., & Russ, S. (2012). Pretend play, creativity, and emotion regulation in children. *Psychology of Aesthetics, Creativity, and the Arts*, 6(2), 175–184 doi:10.1037/a0026299

Huesmann, L. R., Moise-Titus, J., Podolski, C.-L. L., & Eron, L. D. (2003). Longitudinal relations between children's exposure to TV violence and their aggressive and violent behavior in young adulthood: 1977–1992. *Developmental Psychology*, 39, 201–221.

Huntsinger, C. S., Jose, P. E., & Larson, S. L. (1998). Do parent practices to encourage academic competence influence the social adjustment of young European American and Chinese American children? *Developmental Psychology*, 34, 747–756.

Jadva, V., Hines, M., & Golombok, S. (2010). Infants' preferences for toys, colors, and shapes: Sex differences and similarities. *Archives of Sexual Behavior*, 39(6), 1261–1273. doi:10.1007/s10508-010-9618-z

Jagers, R. J., Bingham, K., & Hans, S. L. (1996). Socialization and social judgments among inner-city African-American kindergartners. *Child Development*, 67, 140–150.

Jain, S., & Cohen, A. K. (2013). Behavioral adaptation among youth exposed to community violence: A longitudinal multidisciplinary study of family, peer and neighborhood-level protective factors. *Prevention Science: The Official Journal of the Society for Prevention Research*, 14(6), 606–617. doi:10.1007/s11121-012-0344-8

Jewell, J. D., Krohn, E. J., Scott, V. G., Carlton, M., & Meinz, E. (2008). The differential impact of mothers' and fathers' discipline on preschool children's home and classroom behavior. *North American Journal of Psychology*, 10(1), 173–188.

Kahlenberg, S. G., & Hein, M. M. (2010). Progression on Nickelodeon? Gender-role stereotypes in toy commercials. *Sex Roles*, 62(11–12), 830–847. doi:10.1007/s11199-009-9653-1

Kennedy, T. M., & Ceballo, R. (2014). Who, what, when, and where? Toward a dimensional conceptualization of community violence exposure. *Review of General Psychology*, 18(2), 69–81. doi:10.1037/gpr0000005

Kimball, M. M. (1986). Television and sex-role attitudes. In T. M. Williams (Ed.), *The impact of television: A natural experiment in three communities* (pp. 265–301). Orlando, FL: Academic Press.

Kirkorian, H. L., Wartella, E. A., & Anderson, D. R. (2008). Media and young children's learning. *The Future of Children*, 18(1), 39–61. doi:10.1353/foc.0.0002

Kohlberg, L. (1966). A cognitive-developmental analysis of children's sex-role concepts and attitudes. In E. E. Maccoby (Ed.), *The development of sex differences* (pp. 82–173). Stanford, CA: Stanford University Press.

Kuhlmeier, V., Dunfield, K., & O'Neill, A. (2014). Selectivity in early prosocial behavior. *Frontiers in Psychology*, 5(00836). doi:10.3389/fpsyg.2014.00836

Lansford, J. E., Deater-Deckard, K., Dodge, K. A., Bates, J. E., & Pettit, G. S. (2004). Ethnic differences in the link between physical discipline and later adolescent externalizing behaviors. *Journal of Child Psychology and Psychiatry*, 45(4), 801–812. doi:10.1111/j.1469-7610.2004.00273.x

Leaper, C. (1994). Exploring the correlates and consequences of gender segregation: Social relationships in childhood, adolescence, and adulthood. In C. Leaper (Ed.), *New directions for child development* (pp. 67–86, No. 65). San Francisco: Jossey-Bass.

Leaper, C. (2013). Gender development during childhood. In P. D. Zelaz (Ed.), *The Oxford handbook of developmental psychology: Vol. 2. Self and other* (pp. 326–377). New York: Oxford University Press.

Leaper, C., Tenenbaum, H. R., & Shaffer, T. G. (1999). Communication patterns of African-American girls and boys from low-income, urban backgrounds. *Child Development*, 70, 1489–1503.

Lee, S. J., Altschul, I., & Gershoff, E. T. (2013). Does warmth moderate longitudinal associations between maternal spanking and child aggression in early childhood? *Developmental Psychology*, 49(11), 2017–2028. doi:10.1037/a0031630

Levy, G. D., & Carter, D. B. (1989). Gender schema, gender constancy, and gender-role knowledge: The roles of cognitive factors in preschoolers' gender-role stereotype attributions. *Developmental Psychology*, 25, 444–449.

Levy, G. D., & Haaf, R. A. (1994). Detection of gender-related categories by 10-month-old infants. *Infant Behavior & Development*, 17(4), 457–459. doi:10.1016/0163-6383(94)90037-x

Lewis, M., Takai-Kawakami, K., Kawakami, K., & Sullivan, M. W. (2010). Cultural differences in emotional responses to success and failure. *International Journal of Behavioral Development*, 34(1), 53–61. doi:10.1177/0165025409348559

Liben, L. S., Bigler, R. S., & Hilliard, L. J. (2013). Gender development. In E. T. Gershoff, R. S. Mistry, & D. A. Crosby (Eds.), *Societal contexts of child development: Pathways of influence and implications for practice and policy*. New York: Oxford University Press.

Luecke-Aleksa, D., Anderson, D. R., Collins, P. A., & Schmitt, K. L. (1995). Gender constancy and television viewing. *Developmental Psychology*, 31, 773–780.

Lytton, H., & Romney, D. M. (1991). Parents' differential socialization of boys and girls: A meta-analysis. *Psychological Bulletin*, 109(2), 267–296.

Maccoby, E. E., & Martin, J. A. (1983). Socialization in the context of the family: Parent-child interaction. In E. M. Hetherington (Ed.), *Handbook of child psychology: Vol. 4. Socialization, personality, and social development* (4th ed., pp. 1–101). Hoboken, NJ: John Wiley.

MacMillan, H. L., Boyle, M. H., Wong, M. Y.-Y. Y., Duku, E. K., Fleming, J. E., & Walsh, C. A. (1999). Slapping and spanking in childhood and its association with lifetime prevalence of psychiatric disorders in a general population sample. *Canadian Medical Association Journal*, 161(7), 805–809.

Marsh, H. W., Craven, R., & Debus, R. (1998). Structure, stability, and development of young children's self-concepts: A multicohort-multioccasion study. *Child Development*, 69, 1030–1053.

Martin, C., Fabes, R., Hanish, L., Leonard, S., & Dinella, L. (2011). Experienced and expected similarity to same-gender peers: Moving toward a comprehensive model of gender segregation. *Sex Roles*, 65(5–6), 421–434. doi:10.1007/s11199-011-0029-y

Martin, C. L., Eisenbud, L., & Rose, H. (1995). Children's gender-based reasoning about toys. *Child Development*, 66, 1453–1471.

Martin, C. L., Kornienko, O., Schaefer, D. R., Hanish, L. D., Fabes, R. A., & Goble, P. (2013). The role of sex of peers and gender-typed activities in young children's peer affiliative networks: A longitudinal analysis of selection and influence. *Child Development*, 84(3), 921–937. doi:10.1111/cdev.12032

Martin, C. L., & Ruble, D. N. (2010). Patterns of gender development. *Annual Review of Psychology*, 61, 353–381. doi:10.1146/annurev.psych.093008.100511

Martin, C. L., Ruble, D. N., & Szkrybalo, J. (2002). Cognitive theories of early gender development. *Psychological Bulletin*, 128, 903–933.

McCord, J. (1996). Unintended consequences of punishment. *Pediatrics*, 88, 832–834.

McCoy, M. L., & Keen, S. M. (2009). *Child abuse and neglect*. New York: Psychology Press.

McLoyd, V. C., & Smith, J. (2002). Physical discipline and behavior problems in African American, European American, and Hispanic children: Emotional support as a moderator. *Journal of Marriage and Family*, 64, 40–53.

McMahon, F. F., Lytle, D. E., & Sutton-Smith, B. (2005). *Play: An interdisciplinary synthesis*. Lanham, MD: University Press of America.

McMahon, S. D., Todd, N. R., Martinez, A., Coker, C., Sheu, C.-F., Washburn, J., & Shah, S. (2013). Aggressive and prosocial behavior: Community violence, cognitive, and behavioral predictors among urban African American youth. *American Journal of Community Psychology*, 51(3–4), 407–421. doi:10.1007/s10464-012-9560-4

Miedzian, M. (1991). *Boys will be boys: Breaking the link between masculinity and violence*. New York: Doubleday.

Milevsky, A., Schlechter, M., Netter, S., & Keehn, D. (2007). Maternal and paternal parenting styles in adolescents: Associations with self-esteem, depression and life-satisfaction. *Journal of Child and Family Studies*, 16(1), 39–47. doi:10.1007/s10826-006-9066-5

Miller, C. F., Trautner, H. M., & Ruble, D. N. (2006). The role of gender stereotypes in children's preferences and behavior. In L. Balter & C. S. Tamis-LeMonda (Eds.), *Child psychology: A handbook of contemporary issues* (2nd ed., pp. 293–323). New York: Psychology Press.

Miller, D. I., & Halpern, D. F. (2014). The new science of cognitive sex differences. *Trends in Cognitive Sciences*, 18(1), 37–45. doi:10.1016/j.tics.2013.10.011

Morawska, A., & Sanders, M. (2011). Parental use of time out revisited: A useful or harmful parenting strategy? *Journal of Child and Family Studies*, 20(1), 1–8. doi:10.1007/s10826-010-9371-x

Moses, A. M. (2008). Impacts of television viewing on young children's literacy development in the USA: A review of the literature. *Journal of Early Childhood Literacy*, 8(1), 67–102. doi:10.1177/1468798407087162

Mulvaney, M. K., & Mebert, C. J. (2007). Parental corporal punishment predicts behavior problems in early childhood. *Journal of Family Psychology*, 21(3), 389–397. doi:10.1037/0893-3200.21.3.389

Murry, V. M., Brody, G. H., Simons, R. L., Cutrona, C. E., & Gibbons, F. X. (2008). Disentangling ethnicity and context as predictors of parenting within rural African American families. *Applied Developmental Science*, 12(4), 202–210. doi:10.1080/10888690802388144

National Institute of Child Health and Development Early Child Care Research. (2004). Trajectories of physical aggression from toddlerhood to middle childhood predictors, correlates, and outcomes. *Monographs of the Society for Research in Child Development*, 69(4), vii–146.

Newton, E., & Jenvey, V. (2011). Play and theory of mind: Associations with social competence in young children. *Early Child Development & Care*, 181(6), 761–773. doi:10.1080/03004430.2010.486898

Newton, E. K., Laible, D., Carlo, G., Steele, J. S., & McGinley, M. (2014). Do sensitive parents foster kind children, or vice versa? Bidirectional influences between children's prosocial behavior and parental sensitivity. *Developmental Psychology*, 50(6), 1808–1816. doi:10.1037/a0036495

Nourot, P. M. (1998). Sociodramatic play: Pretending together. In D. P. Fromberg & D. Bergen (Eds.), *Play from birth to twelve and beyond: Contexts, perspectives, and meanings* (pp. 378–391). New York: Garland.

Nugent, B. M., & McCarthy, M. M. (2011). Epigenetic underpinnings of developmental sex differences in the brain. *Neuroendocrinology*, 93(3), 150–158. doi:10.1159/000325264

Osofsky, J. D. (1995). The effects of exposure to violence on young children. *American Psychologist*, 50, 781–788.

Ostrov, J. M., & Godleski, S. A. (2010). Toward an integrated gender-linked model of aggression subtypes in early and middle childhood. *Psychological Review*, 117(1), 233–242. doi:10.1037/a0018070

Oveisi, S., Eftekhare Ardabili, H., Majzadeh, R., Mohammadkhani, P., Alaqband Rad, J., & Loo, J. (2010). Mothers' attitudes toward corporal punishment of children in Qazvin-Iran. *Journal of Family Violence*, 25(2), 159–164. doi:10.1007/s10896-009-9279-7

Parten, M. (1932). Social participation among preschool children. *Journal of Abnormal and Social Psychology*, 27, 243–269.

Paulus, M. (2014). The emergence of prosocial behavior: Why do infants and toddlers help, comfort, and share? *Child Development Perspectives*, 8(2), 77–81. doi:10.1111/cdep.12066

Paulus, M., & Moore, C. (2014). The development of recipient-dependent sharing behavior and sharing expectations in preschool children. *Developmental Psychology*, 50(3), 914–921. doi:10.1037/a0034169

Pellegrini, A. D., & Smith, P. K. (1998). Physical activity play: The nature and function of a neglected aspect of play. *Child Development*, 69, 577–598.

Piaget, J. (1962). *Play, dreams, and imitation in childhood*. New York: Norton.

Pickens, J., Field, T., & Nawrocki, T. (2001). Frontal EEG asymmetry in response to emotional vignettes in preschool age children. *International Journal of Behavioral Development*, 25, 105–112.

Piotrowski, J. T., Lapierre, M. A., & Linebarger, D. L. (2013). Investigating correlates of self-regulation in early childhood with a representative sample of English-speaking American families. *Journal of Child and Family Studies*, 22(3), 423–436. doi:10.1007/s10826-012-9595-z

Quinn, P. C., Yahr, J., Kuhn, A., Slater, A. M., & Pascalis, O. (2002). Representation of the gender of human faces by infants: A preference for female. *Perception*, 31(9), 1109–1121. doi:10.1068/p3331

Reed, T., & Brown, M. (2001). The expression of care in the rough and tumble play of boys. *Journal of Research in Childhood Education*, 15(1), 104–116.

Richert, R. A., Robb, M. B., & Smith, E. I. (2011). Media as social partners: The social nature of young children's learning from screen media. *Child Development*, 82(1), 82–95. doi:10.1111/j.1467-8624.2010.01542.x

Roby, A. C., & Kidd, E. (2008). The referential communication skills of children with imaginary companions. *Developmental Science*, 11(4), 531–540. doi:10.1111/j.1467-7687.2008.00699.x

Roopnarine, J. L., Hossain, Z., Gill, P., & Brophy, H. (1994). Play in the East Indian context. In J. L. Roopnarine, J. E. Johnson, & F. H. Hooper (Eds.), *Children's play in diverse cultures* (pp. 9–30). Albany: State University of New York Press.

Roopnarine, J. L., Lasker, J., Sacks, M., & Stores, M. (1998). The cultural contexts of children's play. In O. N. Saracho & B. Spodek (Eds.), *Multiple perspectives on play in early childhood education* (pp. 194–219). Albany: State University of New York Press.

Rothbaum, F., Pott, M., Azuma, H., Miyake, K., & Weisz, J. (2000). The development of close relationships in Japan and the United States: Paths of symbiotic harmony and generative tension. *Child Development*, 71, 1121–1142.

Ruble, D. N., Grosovsky, E. H., Frey, K. S., & Cohen, R. (1992). Developmental changes in competence assessment. In A. K. Boggiano & T. S. Pittman (Eds.), *Achievement and motivation: A social developmental perspective* (pp. 138–164). New York: Cambridge University Press.

Ruble, D. N., Martin, C. L., & Berenbaum, S. A. (2006). Gender development. In N. Eisenberg, W. Damon, & R. M. Lerner (Eds.), *Handbook of child psychology: Vol. 3. Social, emotional, and personality development* (6th ed., pp. 858–932). Hoboken, NJ: John Wiley.

Ruble, D. N., Taylor, L. J., Cyphers, L., Greulich, F. K., Lurye, L. E., & Shrout, P. E. (2007). The role of gender constancy in early gender development. *Child Development*, 78(4), 1121–1136.

Sawyer, K. S., Denham, S., DeMulder, E., Blair, K., Auerbach-Major, S., & Levitas, J. (2002). The contribution of older siblings' reaction to emotions to preschoolers' emotional and social competence. *Marriage & Family Review*, 34(3–4), 183.

Shahinfar, A., Fox, N. A., & Leavitt, L. A. (2000). Preschool children's exposure to violence: Relation of behavior problems to parent and child reports. *American Journal of Orthopsychiatry*, 70(1), 115–125.

Signorella, M., & Liben, L. S. (1984). Recall and reconstruction of gender-related pictures: Effects of attitude, task difficulty, and age. *Child Development*, 55, 393–405.

Singer, J. L., & Singer, D. G. (1998). *Barney & Friends* as entertainment and education: Evaluating the quality and effectiveness of a television series for preschool children. In J. K. Asamen & G. L. Berry (Eds.), *Research paradigms, television, and social behavior* (pp. 305–367). Thousand Oaks, CA: Sage.

Slaby, R. G., Roedell, W. C., Arezzo, D., & Hendrix, K. (1995). *Early violence prevention*. Washington, DC: National Association for the Education of Young Children.

Smith, S., Pieper, K., Granados, A., & Choueiti, M. (2010). Assessing gender-related portrayals in top-grossing G-rated films. *Sex Roles*, 62(11–12), 774–786. doi:10.1007/s11199-009-9736-z

Sorkhabi, N. (2005). Applicability of Baumrind's parent typology to collective cultures: Analysis of cultural explanations of parent socialization effects. *International Journal of Behavioral Development*, 29(6), 552–563.

Stacks, A. M., Oshio, T., Gerard, J., & Roe, J. (2009). The moderating effect of parental warmth on the association between spanking and child aggression: A longitudinal approach. *Infant & Child Development*, 18(2), 178–194. doi:10.1002/icd.596

Stice, E., & Barrera, M. (1995). A longitudinal examination of the reciprocal relations between perceived parenting and adolescents' substance use and externalizing behaviors. *Developmental Psychology*, 31, 322–334.

Sullivan, M. W., Carmody, D. P., & Lewis, M. (2010). How neglect and punitiveness influence emotion knowledge. *Child Psychiatry and Human Development*, 41(3), 285–298. doi:10.1007/s10578-009-0168-3

Svetlova, M., Nichols, S. R., & Brownell, C. A. (2010). Toddlers prosocial behavior: From instrumental to empathic to altruistic helping. *Child Development*, 81(6), 1814–1827. doi:10.1111/j.1467-8624.2010.01512.x

Tamis-LeMonda, C. S., Briggs, R. D., McClowry, S. G., & Snow, D. L. (2009). Maternal control and sensitivity, child gender, and maternal education in relation to children's behavioral outcomes in African American families. *Journal of Applied Developmental Psychology*, 30(3), 321–331. doi:10.1016/j.appdev.2008.12.018

Tandon, P. S., Zhou, C., Lozano, P., & Christakis, D. A. (2011). Preschoolers' total daily screen time at home and by type of child care. *The Journal of Pediatrics*, 158(2), 297–300. doi:10.1016/j.jpeds.2010.08.005

Tannock, M. (2011). Observing young children's rough-and-tumble play. *Australasian Journal of Early Childhood*, 36(2), 13–20.

Taylor, M., Shawber, A. B., & Mannering, A. M. (2009). Children's imaginary companions: What is it like to have an invisible friend? In K. D. Markman, W. M. P. Klein, & J. A. Suhr (Eds.), *Handbook of imagination and mental simulation* (pp. 211–224). New York: Psychology Press.

Taylor, Z. E., Eisenberg, N., Spinrad, T. L., Eggum, N. D., & Sulik, M. J. (2013). The relations of ego-resiliency and emotion socialization to the development of empathy and prosocial behavior across early childhood. *Emotion*, 13(5). doi:10.1037/a0032894

Testa, M. F., & Smith, B. (2009). Prevention and drug treatment. *The Future of Children/Center for the Future of Children, the David and Lucile Packard Foundation*, 19(2), 147–168. Retrieved from http://www.ncbi.nlm.nih.gov/pubmed/19719026

Tremblay, R. E. (2009). The development of chronic physical aggression: Genes and environments matter from the beginning. In R. E. Tremblay, M. A. G. van Aken, & W. Koops (Eds.), *Development and prevention of behaviour problems: From genes to social policy* (pp. 113–130). New York: Psychology Press.

Tremblay, R. E. (2014). Early development of physical aggression and early risk factors for chronic physical aggression in humans. *Current Topics in Behavioral Neurosciences*, 17, 315–327. doi:10.1007/7854_2013_262

Tremblay, R. E., Nagin, D. S., Séguin, J. R., Zoccolillo, M., Zelazo, P. D., Boivin, M., . . . Japel, C. (2004). Physical aggression during early childhood: Trajectories and predictors. *Pediatrics*, 114(1), e43–e50.

Trionfi, G., & Reese, E. (2009). A good story: Children with imaginary companions create richer narratives. *Child Development*, 80(4), 1301–1313. doi:10.1111/j.1467-8624.2009.01333.x

Turner, P. J., & Gervai, J. (1995). A multidimensional study of gender typing in preschool children and their parents: Personality, attitudes, preferences, behavior, and cultural differences. *British Journal of Developmental Psychology*, 11, 323–342.

Twardosz, S., & Lutzker, J. R. (2009). Child maltreatment and the developing brain: A review of neuroscience perspectives. *Aggression and Violent Behavior*, 15(1), 59–68. doi:10.1016/j.avb.2009.08.003

Tzeng, O., Jackson, J., & Karlson, H. (1991). *Theories of child abuse and neglect: Differential perspectives, summaries, and evaluations*. New York: Praeger Publishers.

U.S. Department of Health and Human Services. (2013). *Child maltreatment, 2012*. Washington DC: Author. Retrieved from http://www.acf.hhs.gov/programs/cb/resource/child-maltreatment-2012

U.S. Department of Health and Human Services. (2015). *Child maltreatment, 2013*. Washington, DC: Author. Retrieved from http://www.acf.hhs.gov/sites/default/files/cb/cm2013.pdf

Vincent, N. J. (2009). Exposure to community violence and the family: Disruptions in functioning and relationships. *Families in Society*, 90(2), 137–143.

Vygotsky, L. S. (1978). *Mind in society: The development of higher psychological processes*. Cambridge, MA: Harvard University Press.

Walker, S. (2005). Gender differences in the relationship between young children's peer-related social competence and individual differences in theory of mind. *Journal of Genetic Psychology*, 166(3), 297–312.

Wang, F., Christ, S. L., Mills-Koonce, W. R., Garrett-Peters, P., & Cox, M. J. (2013). Association between maternal sensitivity and externalizing behavior from preschool to preadolescence. *Journal of Applied Developmental Psychology, 34*(2), 89–100. doi:10.1016/j.appdev.2012.11.003

Wang, Q. (2004). The emergence of cultural self-constructs: Autobiographical memory and self-description in European American and Chinese children. *Developmental Psychology, 40*(1), 3–15.

Warneken, F., Lohse, K., Melis, A. P., & Tomasello, M. (2011). Young children share the spoils after collaboration. *Psychological Science, 22*(2), 267–273. doi:10.1177/0956797610395392

Warneken, F., & Tomasello, M. (2006). Altruistic helping in human infants and young chimpanzees. *Science, 311*(5765), 1301–1303.

Weis, R., & Toolis, E. E. (2010). Parenting across cultural contexts in the USA: Assessing parenting behaviour in an ethnically and socioeconomically diverse sample. *Early Child Development & Care, 180*(7), 849–867. doi:10.1080/03004430802472083

Weiss, B., Dodge, K. A., Bates, J. E., & Pettit, G. S. (1992). Some consequences of early harsh discipline: Child aggression and a maladaptive social information processing style. *Child Development, 63*, 1321–1335.

White, R. M. B., & Zeiders, K. H. (2013). Cultural values, U.S. neighborhood danger, and Mexican American parents' parenting. *Journal of Family Psychology, 27*(3).

Whiting, B., & Edwards, C. P. (1988). A cross-cultural analysis of sex differences in the behavior of children aged 3 through 11. In G. Handel (Ed.), *Childhood socialization* (pp. 281–297). New York: Aldine de Gruyter.

Widom, C. S. (2014). Longterm consequences of child maltreatment. In J. E. Korbin & R. D. Krugman (Eds.), *Handbook of child maltreatment* (Vol. 2, pp. 225–247). Dordrecht, Netherlands: Springer. doi:10.1007/978-94-007-7208-3

Wright, J. C., Huston, A. C., Murphy, K. C., St. Peters, M., Piñon, M., Scantlin, R., & Kotler, J. (2001). The relations of early television viewing to school readiness and vocabulary of children from low-income families: The Early Window Project. *Child Development, 72*, 1347–1366.

Xu, Y., Farver, J. A. M., Zhang, Z., Zeng, Q., Yu, L., & Cai, B. (2005). Mainland Chinese parenting styles and parent-child interaction. *International Journal of Behavioral Development, 29*(6), 524–531.

Yaoying, X., & Xu, Y. (2010). Children's social play sequence: Parten's classic theory revisited. *Early Child Development and Care, 180*(4), 489–498. doi:10.1080/03004430802090430

Zahn-Waxler, C., Friedman, R. J., Cole, P. M., Mizuta, I., & Hiruma, N. (1996). Japanese and United States preschool children's responses to conflict and distress. *Child Development, 67*, 2462–2477.

Zosuls, K. M., Ruble, D. N., Tamis-LeMonda, C. S., Shrout, P. E., Bornstein, M. H., & Greulich, F. K. (2009). The acquisition of gender labels in infancy: Implications for gender-typed play. *Developmental Psychology, 45*(3), 688–701. doi:10.1037/a0014053

CHAPTER 9

Aguiar, A., Eubig, P. A., & Schantz, S. L. (2010). Attention deficit/hyperactivity disorder: A focused overview for children's environmental health researchers. *Environmental Health Perspectives, 118*(12), 1646–1653. doi:10.1289/ehp.1002326

Akinbami, L. J., Moorman, J. E., Garbe, P. L., & Sondik, E. J. (2009). Status of childhood asthma in the United States, 1980–2007. *Pediatrics, 123* (Suppl. 3), S131–S145. doi:10.1542/peds.2008-2233C

Alexander, K. L., Entwisle, D. R., & Kabbani, N. S. (2001). The dropout process in life course perspective: Early risk factors at home and school. *Teachers College Record, 103*, 760–822.

Allen, S. E. M., & Crago, M. B. (1996). Early passive acquisition in Inukitut. *Journal of Child Language, 23*, 129–156.

Alloway, T. P., & Alloway, R. G. (2010). Investigating the predictive roles of working memory and IQ in academic attainment. *Journal of Experimental Child Psychology, 106*(1), 20–29. doi:10.1016/j.jecp.2009.11.003

Ameel, E., Verschueren, N., & Schaeken, W. (2007). The relevance of selecting what's relevant: A dual process approach to transitive reasoning with spatial relations. *Thinking & Reasoning, 13*(2), 164–167.

American Association on Intellectual and Developmental Disabilities. (2009). FAQ on intellectual disability. Washington, DC: Author. Retrieved from http://www.aamr.org/content_104.cfm?navID=22

American Psychiatric Association. (2013). *Diagnostic and statistical manual of mental disorders* (5th ed.). Washington, DC: Author.

Anderson-Fye, E. P. (2004). A "Coca-Cola" shape: Cultural change, body image, and eating disorders in San Andrés, Belize. *Culture, Medicine and Psychiatry, 28*(4), 561–595. Retrieved from http://www.ncbi.nlm.nih.gov/pubmed/15847054

Anglin, J. M. (1993). Vocabulary development: A morphological analysis. *Monographs of the Society for Research in Child Development, 59*(5, Serial No. 242).

Ardila, A. (2013). Development of metacognitive and emotional executive functions in children. *Applied Neuropsychology. Child, 2*(2), 82–87. doi:10.1080/21622965.2013.748388

Arsenio, W. F., & Gold, J. (2006). The effects of social injustice and inequality on children's moral judgments and behavior: Towards a theoretical model. *Cognitive Development, 21*(4), 388–400. doi:10.1016/j.cogdev.2006.06.005

Artman, L., & Cahan, S. (1993). Schooling and the development of transitive inference. *Developmental Psychology, 29*(4), 753–759.

Axia, G., & Baroni, R. (1985). Linguistic politeness at different age levels. *Child Development, 56*, 918–927.

Baddeley, A. (1996). Exploring the central executive. *The Quarterly Journal of Experimental Psychology, 49*(a), 5–28.

Baddeley, A. (2012). Working memory: Theories, models, and controversies. *Annual Review of Psychology, 63*, 1–29. doi:10.1146/annurev-psych-120710-100422

Baillieux, H., De Smet, H. J., Paquier, P. F., De Deyn, P. P., & Mariën, P. (2008). Cerebellar neurocognition: Insights into the bottom of the brain. *Clinical Neurology & Neurosurgery, 110*(8), 763–773. Retrieved from 10.1016/j.clineuro.2008.05.013

Baker, S. K., Simmons, D. C., & Kame'enui, E. J. (1997). Vocabulary acquisition: Research bases. In D. C. Simmons & E. J. Kame'enui (Eds.), *What reading research tells us about children with diverse learning needs: Bases and basics* (pp. 183–217). Mahwah, NJ: Lawrence Erlbaum.

Barac, R., & Bialystok, E. (2012). Bilingual effects on cognitive and linguistic development: Role of language, cultural background, and education. *Child Development, 83*(2), 413–422. doi:10.1111/j.1467-8624.2011.01707.x

Barac, R., Bialystok, E., Castro, D. C., & Sanchez, M. (2014). The cognitive development of young dual language learners: A critical review. *Early Childhood Research Quarterly, 29*(4), 699–714. doi:10.1016/j.ecresq.2014.02.003

Barkley, R. A. (1998). Attention-deficit hyperactivity disorder. *Scientific American*, pp. 66–71.

Barnett, S. M., Ceci, S. J., & Williams, W. M. (2006). Is the ability to make a bacon sandwich a mark of intelligence? and other issues: Some reflections on Gardner's theory of multiple intelligences. In J. A. Schaler (Ed.), *Howard Gardner under fire: The rebel psychologist faces his critics* (pp. 95–114). Chicago: Open Court.

Baus, C., Costa, A., & Carreiras, M. (2013). On the effects of second language immersion on first language production. *Acta Psychologica, 142*(3), 402–409. doi:10.1016/j.actpsy.2013.01.010

Becker, A. E., Keel, P., Anderson-Fye, E. P., & Thomas, J. J. (2004). Genes and/or jeans?: Genetic and socio-cultural contributions to risk for eating disorders. *Journal of Addictive Diseases, 23*(3), 81–103. doi:10.1300/J069v23n03_07

Benes, F. M. (2001). The development of prefrontal cortex: The maturation of neurotransmitter systems and their interactions. In C. A. Nelson & M. Luciana (Eds.), *Handbook of developmental cognitive neuroscience* (pp. 79–92). Cambridge, MA: MIT Press.

Benner, G. J., Beaudoin, K., Kinder, D., & Mooney, P. (2005). The relationship between the beginning reading skills and social adjustment of a general sample of elementary aged children. *Education & Treatment of Children, 28*(3), 250–264.

Benner, G. J., Nelson, J. R., & Epstein, M. H. (2002). The language skills of students with emotional and behavioral disorders: A literature review. *Journal of Emotional and Behavioral Disorders, 10*, 43–59.

Benowitz-Fredericks, C. A., Garcia, K., Massey, M., Vasagar, B., & Borzekowski, D. L. G. (2012). Body image, eating disorders, and the relationship to adolescent media use. *Pediatric Clinics of North America, 59*(3), 693–704, ix. doi:10.1016/j.pcl.2012.03.017

Best, R. M., Dockrell, J. E., & Braisby, N. R. (2006). Real-world word learning: Exploring children's developing semantic representations of a science term. *British Journal of Developmental Psychology, 24*(2), 265–282.

Bialystok, E. (2001). *Bilingualism in development: Language, literacy, and cognition*. Cambridge, UK: Cambridge University Press.

Bialystok, E. (2011). Coordination of executive functions in monolingual and bilingual children. *Journal of Experimental Child Psychology, 110*(3), 461–468. doi:10.1016/j.jecp.2011.05.005

Bialystok, E. (2015). Bilingualism and the development of executive function: The role of attention. *Child Development Perspectives, 9*(2), 117–121. doi:10.1111/cdep.12116

Bialystok, E., Craik, F., & Luk, G. (2008). Cognitive control and lexical access in younger and older bilinguals. *Journal of Experimental Psychology: Learning, Memory, and Cognition, 34*(4), 859–873.

Bialystok, E., Peets, K. F., & Moreno, S. (2014). Producing bilinguals through immersion education: Development of metalinguistic awareness. *Applied Psycholinguistics, 35*(1), 177–191. doi:10.1017/S0142716412000288

Bjorklund, D. F. (2013). *Children's strategies: Contemporary views of cognitive development*. Hove, UK: Psychology Press.

Bjorklund, D. F., & Douglas, R. N. (1997). The development of memory strategies. In N. Cowan (Ed.), *The development of memory in childhood* (pp. 83–111). Hove, UK: Psychology Press.

Bleich, S. N., Segal, J., Wu, Y., Wilson, R., & Wang, Y. (2013). Systematic review of community-based childhood obesity prevention studies. *Pediatrics, 132*(1), e201–e210. doi:10.1542/peds.2013-0886

Bloom, L. (2000). Commentary: Breaking the language barrier: An emergentist coalition model for the origins of word learning. *Monographs of the Society for Research in Child Development, 65*(3, Serial No. 262), 124–135.

Blotner, R., & Bearison, D. J. (1984). Developmental consistencies in socio-moral knowledge: Justice reasoning and altruistic behavior. *Merrill-Palmer Quarterly, 30,* 349–367.

Borst, G., Poirel, N., Pineau, A., Cassotti, M., & Houdé, O. (2013). Inhibitory control efficiency in a Piaget-like class-inclusion task in school-age children and adults: A developmental negative priming study. *Developmental Psychology, 49*(7), 1366–1374. doi:10.1037/a0029622

Bowman, L. J. (2005). Grade retention: Is it a help or hindrance to student academic success? *Preventing School Failure, 49*(3), 42–46.

Brady, S. A. (2011). Efficacy of phonics teaching for reading outcomes: Indications from Post-NRP Research. In S. A. Brady, D. Braze, & C. A. Fowler (Eds.), *Explaining individual differences in reading: Theory and evidence.* Hove, UK: Psychology Press.

Brewster, A. B. (1982). Chronically ill hospitalized children's concepts of their illness. *Pediatrics, 69,* 355–362.

Brocki, K. C., & Bohlin, G. (2004). Executive functions in children aged 6 to 13: A dimensional and developmental study. *Developmental Neuropsychology, 26*(2), 571–593.

Brodie, B. (1974). Views of healthy children towards illness. *American Journal of Public Health, 64,* 1156–1159.

Brooks-Gunn, J., Klebanov, P. K., & Duncan, G. J. (1996). Ethnic differences in children's intelligence test scores: Role of economic deprivation, home environment, and maternal characteristics. *Child Development, 67,* 396–408.

Broude, G. J. (1995). *Growing up: A cross-cultural encyclopedia.* Santa Barbara, CA: ABC-CLIO.

Brown, F. L., & Slaughter, V. (2011). Normal body, beautiful body: Discrepant perceptions reveal a pervasive "thin ideal" from childhood to adulthood. *Body Image, 8*(2), 119–125. doi:10.1016/j.bodyim.2011.02.002

Brown, R. T., Antonuccio, D. O., DuPaul, G. J., Fristad, M. A., King, C. A., Leslie, L. K., . . . Vitiello, B. (2008). Autism spectrum disorders and mental retardation. In R. T. Brown et al. (Eds.), *Childhood mental health disorders: Evidence base and contextual factors for psychosocial, psychopharmacological, and combined interventions* (pp. 105–112). Washington, DC: American Psychological Association.

Buchanan-Barrow, E., & Barrett, M. (1998). Children's rule discrimination within the context of the school. *British Journal of Developmental Psychology, 16,* 539–551.

Burchinal, M., Roberts, J. E., Zeisel, S. A., Hennon, E. A., & Hooper, S. (2006). Social risk and protective child, parenting, and child care factors in early elementary school years. *Parenting: Science & Practice, 6*(1), 79–113.

Cadima, J., Leal, T., & Burchinal, M. (2010). The quality of teacher–student interactions: Associations with first graders' academic and behavioral outcomes. *Journal of School Psychology, 48*(6), 457–482. doi:10.1016/j.jsp.2010.09.001

Camos, V., & Barrouillet, P. (2011). Developmental change in working memory strategies: From passive maintenance to active refreshing. *Developmental Psychology, 47*(3), 898–904. doi:10.1037/a0023193

Campbell, R., & Sais, E. (1995). Accelerated metalinguistic (phonological) awareness in bilingual children. *British Journal of Developmental Psychology, 13,* 61–68.

Carbonneau, K. J., Marley, S. C., & Selig, J. P. (2013). A meta-analysis of the efficacy of teaching mathematics with concrete manipulatives. *Journal of Educational Psychology, 105*(2), 380–400. doi:10.1037/a0031084

Carlson, S. M., & Meltzoff, A. N. (2008). Bilingual experience and executive functioning in young children. *Developmental Science, 11*(2),

282–298. Retrieved from 10.1111/j.1467-7687.2008.00675.x

Carr, A., & O'Reilly, G. (2007). Diagnsis, classification and epidemiology. In A. Carr, G. O'Reilly, P. N. Walsk, & J. McEvoy (Eds.), *The handbook of intellectual disability and clinical psychology practice.* New York: Routledge.

Carrion-Castillo, A., Franke, B., & Fisher, S. E. (2013). Molecular genetics of dyslexia: An overview. *Dyslexia, 19*(4), 214–240. doi:10.1002/dys.1464

Carson, A. S., & Banuazizi, A. (2008). "That's not fair": Similarities and differences in distributive justice reasoning between American and Filipino children. *Journal of Cross-Cultural Psychology, 39*(4), 493–514.

Case, R. (1998). The development of conceptual structures. In D. K. & R. S. Siegler (Eds.), *Handbook of child psychology: Vol. 2. Cognition, perception, and language* (5th ed., pp. 745–800). Hoboken, NJ: John Wiley.

Case, R. (1999). Cognitive development. In M. Bennett (Ed.), *Developmental psychology: Achievements and prospects* (pp. 36–54). Philadelphia: Taylor & Francis.

Case, R., Kurland, D. M., & Goldberg, J. (1982). Operational efficiency and the growth of short term memory span. *Journal of Experimental Child Psychology, 33,* 386–404.

Castro, D. C., Páez, M. M., Dickinson, D. K., & Frede, E. (2011). Promoting language and literacy in young dual language learners: Research, practice, and policy. *Child Development Perspectives, 5*(1), 15–21. doi:10.1111/j.1750-8606.2010.00142.x

Cavanaugh, J. C., & Perlmutter, M. (1982). Metamemory: A critical examination. *Child Development, 53*(1), 11–28. Retrieved from http://eric.ed.gov/?id=EJ260166

Ceci, S. J. (1991). How much does schooling influence general intelligence and its cognitive components? A reassessment of the evidence. *Developmental Psychology, 27,* 703–722.

Ceci, S. J. (1999). Schooling and intelligence. In S. J. Ceci & W. M. Williams (Eds.), *The nature-nurture debate: The essential readings* (pp. 168–175). Oxford, UK: Blackwell.

Centers for Disease Control and Prevention. (2005). *Intellectual disability.* Washington, DC: Author. Retrieved from http://www.cdc.gov/ncbddd/dd/mr3.htm

Chen, J.-H. (2014). Asthma and child behavioral skills: Does family socioeconomic status matter? *Social Science & Medicine, 115,* 38–48. doi:10.1016/j.socscimed.2014.05.048

Child Trends. (2013a). *Asthma.* Bethesda, MD: Author. Retrieved from http://www.childtrends.org/?indicators=asthma

Child Trends. (2013b). *Infant, child, and teen mortality.* Bethesda, MD: Author. Retrieved from http://www.childtrends.org/?indicators=infant-child-and-teen-mortality

Chomsky, C. S. (1969). *The acquisition of syntax in children from five to ten.* Cambridge, MA: MIT Press.

Clark, K. A., Helland, T., Specht, K., Narr, K. L., Manis, F. R., Toga, A. W., & Hugdahl, K. (2014). Neuroanatomical precursors of dyslexia identified from pre-reading through to age 11. *Brain, 137*(12), 3136–3141. doi:10.1093/brain/awu229

Clark, L., & Tiggemann, M. (2008). Sociocultural and individual psychological predictors of body image in young girls: A prospective study. *Developmental Psychology, 44*(4), 1124–1134. Retrieved from 10.1037/0012-1649.44.4.1124

Cohane, G. H., & Pope, H. G. (2001). Body image in boys: A review of the literature. *The International Journal of Eating Disorders, 29*(4), 373–379. Retrieved from http://www.ncbi.nlm.nih.gov/pubmed/11285574

Collette, F., & Van der Linden, M. (2002). Brain imaging of the central executive component of working memory. *Neuroscience & Biobehavioral Reviews, 26*(2), 105–125.

Collins, J. E., Gill, T. K., Chittleborough, C. R., Martin, A. J., Taylor, A. W., & Winefield, H. (2008). Mental, emotional, and social problems among school children with asthma. *Journal of Asthma, 45*(6), 489–493. Retrieved from 10.1080/02770900802074802

Colston, H. L. (2002). Contrast and assimilation in verbal irony. *Journal of Pragmatics, 34,* 111–142.

Conley, D. T. (2014). *The Common Core State Standards: Insight into their development and purpose.* Washington, DC: Council of Chief State School Officers. Retrieved from http://www.ccsso.org/Documents/2014/CCSS_Insight_Into_Development_2014.pdf

Coughlin, J. W., Heinberg, L. J., Marinilli, A., & Guarda, A. S. (2003). Body image dissatisfaction in children: Prevalence and parental influence. *Healthy Weight Journal, 17,* 56–59.

Cowan, N., Hismjatullina, A., AuBuchon, A. M., Saults, J. S., Horton, N., Leadbitter, K., & Towse, J. (2010). With development, list recall includes more chunks, not just larger ones. *Developmental Psychology, 46*(5), 1119–1131. doi:10.1037/a0020618

Cowan, N., Nugent, L. D., Elliott, E. M., Ponomarev, I., & Saults, J. S. (1999). The role of attention in the development of short-term memory: Age differences in the verbal span of apprehension. *Child Development, 70,* 1082–1097.

Cowan, N., Ricker, T. J., Clark, K. M., Hinrichs, G. A., & Glass, B. A. (2015). Knowledge cannot explain the developmental growth of working memory capacity. *Developmental Science, 18*(1), 132–145. doi:10.1111/desc.12197

Crawford, J. (1997). *Best evidence: Research foundations of the bilingual education act.* Washington, DC: National Clearinghouse for Bilingual Education.

Creusere, M. A. (2000). A developmental test of theoretical perspectives on the understanding of verbal irony: Children's recognition of allusion and pragmatic insincerity. *Metaphor and Symbol, 15,* 29–45.

D'Esposito, M., Detre, J. A., Alsop, D. C., Shin, R. K., Atlas, S., & Grossman, M. (1995). The neural basis of the central executive system of working memory. *Nature, 378,* 279–281.

Da Fonseca, D., Seguier, V., Santos, A., Poinso, F., & Deruelle, C. (2009). Emotion understanding in children with ADHD. *Child Psychiatry & Human Development, 40*(1), 111–121. Retrieved from 10.1007/s10578-008-0114-9

Daley, D., Van der Oord, S., Ferrin, M., Danckaerts, M., Doepfner, M., Cortese, S., & Sonuga-Barke, E. J. S. (2014, June 26). Behavioral interventions for children and adolescents with attention deficit hyperactivity disorder: A meta-analysis of randomized controlled trials across multiple outcome domains. *Journal of the American Academy of Child and Adolescent Psychiatry.* Advance online publication.

Damon, W. (1977). *The social world of the child.* San Francisco: Jossey-Bass.

Damon, W. (1980). Patterns of change in children's social reasoning: A two-year longitudinal study. *Child Development, 51*(4), 1010–1017.

Damon, W. (1988). *The moral child.* New York: Free Press.

Danovitch, J., & Bloom, P. (2009). Children's extension of disgust to physical and moral events. *Emotion, 9*(1), 107–112. doi:10.1037/a0014113

Dasen, P. R. (1994). Culture and cognitive development from a Piagetian perspective. In W. J. Lonner & R. Malpass (Eds.), *Psychology and culture.* Boston: Allyn & Bacon.

De Onis, M., Blössner, M., & Borghi, E. (2010). Global prevalence and trends of overweight and obesity among preschool children. *The American Journal of Clinical Nutrition, 92*(5), 1257–1264. doi:10.3945/ajcn.2010.29786

Dee, T. S., Jacob, B., & Schwartz, N. L. (2012). The effects of NCLB on school resources and practices. *Educational Evaluation and Policy Analysis, 35*(2), 252–279. doi:10.3102/0162373712467080

Demorest, A., Meyer, C., Phelps, E., Gardner, H., & Winner, E. (1984). Words speak louder than actions: Understanding deliberately false remarks. *Child Development, 55*, 1527–1534.

Dempster, F. N. (1985). Short-term memory development. In C. J. Brainerd & M. Pressley (Eds.), *Basic processes in memory development* (pp. 208–248). New York: Springer-Verlag.

Deneault, J., & Ricard, M. (2006). The assessment of children's understanding of inclusion relations: Transitivity, asymmetry, and quantification. *Journal of Cognition & Development, 7*(4), 551–570.

Deutsch, W., & Pechmann, T. (1982). Social interaction and the development of definite descriptions. *Cognition, 11*, 159–184.

DeVries, R., & Zan, B. (2003). When children make rules. *Educational Leadership, 61*(1), 64–67.

Diamond, A. (2000). Close interrelation of motor development and cognitive development and of the cerebellum and prefrontal cortex. *Child Development, 71*(1), 44.

Diamond, A. (2013). Executive functions. *Annual Review of Psychology, 64*, 135–168. doi:10.1146/annurev-psych-113011-143750

Ding, G., Ji, R., & Bao, Y. (2014). Risk and protective factors for the development of childhood asthma. *Paediatric Respiratory Reviews, 116*(2), 133–139. doi:10.1016/j.prrv.2014.07.004

Dirks, J. (1982). The effect of a commercial game on children's Block Design scores on the WISC-R test. *Intelligence, 6*, 109–123.

DiStefano, C., & Dombrowski, S. C. (2006). Investigating the theoretical structure of the Stanford-Binet-Fifth Edition. *Journal of Psychoeducational Assessment, 24*(2), 123–136.

Doak, C. M., Visscher, T. L. S., Renders, C. M., & Seidell, J. C. (2006). The prevention of overweight and obesity in children and adolescents: a review of interventions and programmes. *Obesity Reviews*. Oxford, UK: Blackwell Publishing Limited.

Dohnt, H. K., & Tiggemann, M. (2005). Peer influences on body dissatisfaction and dieting awareness in young girls. *British Journal of Developmental Psychology, 23*, 103–116.

Drong, A. W., Lindgren, C. M., & McCarthy, M. I. (2012). The genetic and epigenetic basis of type 2 diabetes and obesity. *Clinical Pharmacology and Therapeutics, 92*(6), 707–715. doi:10.1038/clpt.2012.149

Duff, F. J., & Clarke, P. J. (2011). Practitioner Review: Reading disorders: What are the effective interventions and how should they be implemented and evaluated? *Journal of Child Psychology and Psychiatry, and Allied Disciplines, 52*(1), 3–12. doi:10.1111/j.1469-7610.2010.02310.x

DuPaul, G. J. (2007). School-based interventions for students with attention deficit hyperactivity disorder: Current status and future directions. *School Psychology Review, 36*(2), 183–194.

Ehmke, T., Drechsel, B., & Carstensen, C. H. (2010). Effects of grade retention on achievement and self-concept in science and mathematics. *Studies in Educational Evaluation, 36*(1–2), 27–35. doi:10.1016/j.stueduc.2010.10.003

Eisenberg, N., Fabes, R. A., & Spinrad, T. L. (2006). Prosocial development. In N. Eisenberg, W. Damon, & R. M. Lerner (Eds.), *Handbook of child psychology: Vol. 3. Social, emotional, and personality development* (6th ed., pp. 646–718). Hoboken, NJ: John Wiley.

Eisner, E. (2004). Multiple intelligences: Its tensions and possibilities. *Teachers College Record, 106*(1), 31–39.

Ellis, K. J., Abrams, S. A., & Wong, W. W. (1997). Body composition of a young, multiethnic female population. *American Journal of Clinical Nutrition, 65*, 724–731.

Ellison, J. W., Rosenfeld, J. A., & Shaffer, L. G. (2013). Genetic basis of intellectual disability. *Annual Review of Medicine, 64*, 441–450. doi:10.1146/annurev-med-042711-140053

Enright, R. D., Bjerstedt, Å., Enright, W. F., Levy, V. M., Jr., Lapsley, D. K., Buss, R. R., . . . Zindler, M. (1984). Distributive justice development: Cross-cultural, contextual, and longitudinal evaluations. *Child Development, 55*(5), 1737. Retrieved from 10.1111/1467-8624.ep7304494

Entwisle, D. R., Alexander, K. L., & Steffel Olson, L. (2005). First grade and educational attainment by age 22: A new story. *American Journal of Sociology, 110*(5), 1458–1502.

Ericsson, K. A., & Moxley, J. H. (2013). Experts' superior memory: From accumulation of chunks to building memory skills that mediate improved performance and learning. In T. J. Perfect & D. Stephen Lindsay (Ed.), *The SAGE handbook of applied memory*. Thousand Oaks, CA: Sage.

Evans, E. H., Tovée, M. J., Boothroyd, L. G., & Drewett, R. F. (2013). Body dissatisfaction and disordered eating attitudes in 7- to 11-year-old girls: Testing a sociocultural model. *Body Image, 10*(1), 8–15. doi:10.1016/j.bodyim.2012.10.001

Farber, D. A., & Beteleva, T. G. (2011). Development of the brain's organization of working memory in young schoolchildren. *Human Physiology, 37*(1), 1–13. doi:10.1134/s0362119710061015

Federal Interagency Forum on Child and Family Statistics. (2014). *America's children: Key national indicators of well-being, 2013.* Washington, DC: Author. Retrieved from http://www.childstats.gov/americaschildren

Ferguson, P., Jimerson, S., & Dalton, M. (2001). Sorting out successful failures: Exploratory analyses of factors associated with academic and behavioral outcomes of retained students. *Psychology in the Schools, 38*, 327–342.

Filippova, E., & Astington, J. W. (2008). Further development in social reasoning revealed in discourse irony understanding. *Child Development, 79*(1), 126–138.

Flavell, J. H. (2004). Theory-of-mind development: Retrospect and prospect. *Merrill-Palmer Quarterly: Journal of Developmental Psychology, 50*(3), 274–290. Retrieved from http://eric.ed.gov/?id=EJ683875

Fletcher, J. M. (2012). Classification and identification of learning disabilities. Learning about learning disabilities. In B. Wong & D. L. Butler (Eds.), *Learning about learning disabilities*. Waltham, MA: Academic Press.

Flynn, J. (2008). Still a question of black vs. white? *New Scientist, 199*, 48–50.

Flynn, J. R. (1987). Massive IQ gains in 14 nations: What IQ tests really measure. *Psychological Bulletin of the World Health Organization, 101*, 171–191.

Flynn, J. R. (1998). IQ gains over time: Toward finding the causes. In I. U. Neisser (Ed.), *The rising curve: Long-term gains in IQ and related measures* (pp. 25–66). Washington, DC: American Psychological Association.

Flynn, J. R., & Weiss, L. G. (2007). American IQ gains from 1932 to 2002: The WISC subtests and educational progress. *International Journal of Testing, 7*(2), 209–224.

Ford, D. Y. (2008). Intelligence testing and cultural diversity: The need for alternative instruments, policies, and procedures. In J. L. VanTassel-Baska (Ed.), *Alternative assessments with gifted and talented students* (pp. 107–128). Waco, TX: Prufrock Press.

Frederickson, N. L., & Simmonds, E. A. (2008). Special needs, relationship type and distributive justice norms in early and later years of middle childhood. *Social Development, 17*(4), 1056–1073. doi:10.1111/j.1467-9507.2008.00477.x

Frey, A. J., Mandlawitz, M., & Alvarez, M. E. (2012). Leaving NCLB behind. *Children & Schools, 34*(2), 67–69. doi:10.1093/cs/cds021

Frey, N. (2005). Retention, social promotion, and academic redshirting: What do we know and need to know? *Remedial and Special Education, 26*(6), 332–346.

Fry, A. F., & Hale, S. (1996). Processing speed, working memory, and fluid intelligence: Evidence for a developmental cascade. *Psychological Science, 7*, 237–241.

Fryar, C. D., Carroll, M. D., & Ogden, C. L. (2014). *Prevalence of overweight and obesity among children and adolescents: United States, 1963–1965 through 2011–2012.* Atlanta: Centers for Disease Control and Prevention. Retrieved from http://www.cdc.gov/nchs/data/hestat/obesity_child_11_12/obesity_child_11_12.htm#figure1

Gabbard, C. P. (2012). *Lifelong motor development* (6th ed.). San Francisco: Pearson.

Gallahue, D. L., & Ozmun, J. C. (2006). *Understanding motor development: Infants, children, adolescents, adults* (6th ed.). Boston: McGraw-Hill.

Gardiner, H. W., & Kosmitzki, C. (2010). *Lives across cultures: Cross-cultural human development* (5th ed.). Boston: Pearson.

Gardner, H. (1993). *Frames of mind: The theory of multiple intelligences.* New York: Basic Books. (Original Work Published in 1983).

Gardner, H. (1995). Reflections on multiple intelligences: Myths and messages. *Phi Delta Kappan*, pp. 200–209.

Gardner, H. (1999). *Intelligence reframed: Multiple intelligences for the 21st century.* New York: Basic Books.

Gardner, H. (2013). *The unschooled mind: How children think and how schools should teach* (Vol. 25). New York: Basic Books. Retrieved from http://books.google.com/books?id=4YqtMUVSsEEC&pgis=1

Gardner, H., & Moran, S. (2006). The science of multiple intelligences theory: A response to Lynn Waterhouse. *Educational Psychologist, 41*(4), 227–232. doi:10.1207/s15326985ep4104_2

Gathercole, S. E., & Hitch, G. J. (1993). Developmental changes in short-term memory: A revised working memory perspective. In A. Collins, S. E. Gathercole, M. A. Conway, & P. E. Morris (Eds.), *Theories of memory* (pp. 189–210). Hove, UK: Lawrence Erlbaum.

Gathercole, S. E., Pickering, S. J., Ambridge, B., & Wearing, H. (2004). A structural analysis of working memory from 4 to 15 years of age. *Developmental Psychology, 40*, 177–190.

Gattario, K. H., Frisén, A., & Anderson-Fye, E. (2014). Body image and child well-being. In A. Ben-Arieh, F. Casas, I. Frones, & J. E. Korbin (Eds.), *Handbook of child well-being* (pp. 2409–2436). Netherlands: Springer.

Georgas, J., Weiss, L. G., van de Vijver, F. J. R., & Saklofske, D. H. (2003). Cross-cultural psychology, intelligence, and cognitive processes. In *Culture and children's intelligence: Cross-cultural analysis of the WISC-III* (pp. 23–37). San Diego: Academic Press.

Gibson, L. Y., Byrne, S. M., Blair, E., Davis, E. A., Jacoby, P., & Zubrick, S. R. (2008). Clustering of psychosocial symptoms in overweight children. *Australian & New Zealand Journal of Psychiatry, 42*(2), 118–125. doi:10.1080/00048670701787560

Ginsburg, H. P. (1998). Mathematics learning disabilities: A view from developmental psychology. In D. P. Rivera (Ed.), *Mathematics education for students with learning disabilities* (pp. 33–58). Austin, TX: Pro-Ed.

Goodwin, G. P., & Johnson-Laird, P. N. (2008). Transitive and pseudo-transitive inferences. *Cognition*, 108(2), 320–352. doi:10.1016/j.cognition.2008.02.010

Gorter, J. W., Stewart, D., Smith, M. W., King, G., Wright, M., Nguyen, T., . . . Swinton, M. (2014). Pathways toward positive psychosocial outcomes and mental health for youth with disabilities: A knowledge synthesis of developmental trajectories. *Canadian Journal of Community Mental Health*, 33(1), 45–61. doi:10.7870/cjcmh-2014-005

Gresham, F. M., & MacMillan, D. L. (1997). Social competence and affective characteristics of students with mild disabilities. *Review of Educational Research*, 67, 377–415.

Guèvremont, A., Roos, N. P., & Brownell, M. (2007). Predictors and consequences of grade retention: Examining data from Manitoba, Canada. *Canadian Journal of School Psychology*, 22(1), 50–67.

Gustafson-Larson, A., & Terry, R. D. (1992). Weight-related behaviors and concerns of fourth-grade children. *Journal of the American Dietetic Association*, 92, 818–822.

Hakuta, K., Bialystok, E., & Wiley, E. (2003). Critical evidence: A test of the critical-period hypothesis for second-language acquisitions. *Psychological Science*, 14, 31–38.

Halpern, D. F. (2005). An anniversary celebration for multiple intelligences. *PsycCritiques*, 20(12), Art. 9.

Hancock, J. T., Dunham, P. J., & Purdy, K. (2000). Children's comprehension of critical and complimentary forms of verbal irony. *Journal of Cognition and Development, 1*, 227–248.

Harley, B., & Jean, G. (1999). Vocabulary skills of French immersion students in their second language. *Zeitschrift Für Interkulturellen Fremdsprachenunterricht*. Retrieved from http://www.ualberta.ca

Harpin, V., Mazzone, L., Raynaud, J.-P., Kahle, J., & Hodgkins, P. (2013). Long-term outcomes of ADHD: A systematic review of self-esteem and social function. *Journal of Attention Disorders*. Advance online publication. doi:10.1177/1087054713486516

Harris, M., & Pexman, P. M. (2003). Children's perceptions of the social functions of verbal irony. *Discourse Processes*, 36, 147–165.

Hauser, S. I., Economos, C. D., Nelson, M. E., Goldberg, J. P., Hyatt, R. R., Naumova, E. N., . . . Must, A. (2014). Household and family factors related to weight status in first through third graders: A cross-sectional study in Eastern Massachusetts. *BMC Pediatrics*, 14(1), 167. doi:10.1186/1471-2431-14-167

Haywood, K. M., & Getchell, N. (2005). *Life span motor development* (4th ed.). Champaign, IL: Human Kinetics.

Heath, S. B. (1989). Oral and literate tradition among black Americans living in poverty. *American Psychologist*, 44, 367–373.

Heinrich, J. (2011). Influence of indoor factors in dwellings on the development of childhood asthma. *International Journal of Hygiene & Environmental Health*, 214(1), 1–25. doi:10.1016/j.ijheh.2010.08.009

Helms, J. E. (1992). Why is there no study of cultural equivalence in standardized cognitive ability testing? *American Psychologist*, 47, 1083–1101.

Helwig, C. C. (2008). The moral judgment of the child reevaluated. In J. G. C. Wainryb & & E. T. Smetana (Eds.), *Social development, social inequalities, and social justice* (pp. 27, 52). New York: Lawrence Erlbaum.

Helwig, C. C., & Prencipe, A. (1999). Children's judgments of flags and flag-burning. *Child Development*, 70, 132–143.

Hermanto, N., Moreno, S., & Bialystok, E. (2012). Linguistic and metalinguistic outcomes of intense immersion education: How bilingual? *International Journal of Bilingual Education and Bilingualism*, 15(2), 131–145. doi:10.1080/13670050.2011.652591

Herrera, B. M., Keildson, S., & Lindgren, C. M. (2011). Genetics and epigenetics of obesity. *Maturitas*, 69(1), 41–49. doi:10.1016/j.maturitas.2011.02.018

Hitch, G. J., Towse, J. N., & Hutton, U. (2001). What limits children's working memory span? Theoretical accounts and applications for scholastic development. *Journal of Experimental Psychology*, 130(2), 184–198.

Hoddinott, J., Alderman, H., Behrman, J. R., Haddad, L., & Horton, S. (2013). The economic rationale for investing in stunting reduction. *Maternal & Child Nutrition*, 9(Suppl. 2), 69–82. doi:10.1111/mcn.12080

Hoffman, M. L. (1970). Conscience, personality, and socialization technique. *Human Development*, 13, 90–126.

Hong, G., & Yu, B. (2007). Early-grade retention and children's reading and math learning in elementary years. *Educational Evaluation and Policy Analysis*, 29(4), 239–261.

Horgan, D. (1978). The development of the full passive. *Journal of Child Language*, 5, 65–80.

Houdé, O., Pineau, A., Leroux, G., Poirel, N., Perchey, G., Lanoë, C., . . . Mazoyer, B. (2011). Functional magnetic resonance imaging study of Piaget's conservation-of-number task in preschool and school-age children: A neo-Piagetian approach. *Journal of Experimental Child Psychology*, 110(3), 332–346. doi:10.1016/j.jecp.2011.04.008

Huang, G. G. (1995). Self-reported biliteracy and self-esteem: A study of Mexican American 8th graders. *Applied Psycholinguistics*, 16, 271–291.

Hughes, J. N., Chen, Q., Thoemmes, F., & Kwok, O. (2010). An investigation of the relationship between retention in first grade and performance on high stakes tests in third grade. *Educational Evaluation and Policy Analysis*, 32(2), 166–182. doi:10.3102/0162373710367682

Huttenlocher, J., Levine, S., & Vevea, J. (1998). Environmental input and cognitive growth: A study using time-period comparisons. *Child Development*, 69, 1012–1029.

Imbo, I., & Vandierendonck, A. (2007). The development of strategy use in elementary school children: Working memory and individual differences. *Journal of Experimental Child Psychology*, 96(4), 284–309.

Inhelder, B., & Piaget, J. (1964). *The early growth of logic in the child: Classification and seriation*. New York: Harper & Row. Retrieved from http://books.google.com/books?id=9xKrQ34CXOcC&pgis=1

Ivanko, S. L., & Pexman, P. M. (2003). Context incongruity and irony processing. *Discourse Processes*, 35, 241–279.

Jambon, M., & Smetana, J. G. (2014). Moral complexity in middle childhood: Children's evaluations of necessary harm. *Developmental Psychology*, 50(1), 22–33.

Janssen, I., Katzmarzyk, P. T., Boyce, W. F., Vereecken, C., Mulvihill, C., Roberts, C., . . . Health Behaviour in School-Aged Children Obesity Working Group. (2005). Comparison of overweight and obesity prevalence in school-aged youth from 34 countries and their relationships with physical activity and dietary patterns. *Obesity Reviews*, 6, 123–132.

Jeynes, W. H. (2008). A meta-analysis of the relationship between phonics instruction and minority elementary school student academic achievement. *Education & Urban Society*, 40(2), 151–166.

Jimerson, S. R. (2001). Meta-analysis of grade retention research: Implications for practice in the 21st century. *School Psychology Review*, 30(3), 420–437.

Jimerson, S. R., & Ferguson, P. (2007). A longitudinal study of grade retention: Academic and behavioral outcomes of retained students through adolescence. *School Psychology Quarterly*, 22(3), 314–339.

Jimerson, S. R., & Renshaw, T. L. (2012). Retention and social promotion. Principal Leadership. *Retention and Social Promotion. Principal Leadership*, 13(1), 12–16.

Juel, C. (1988). Learning to read and write: A longitudinal study of 54 children from first through fourth grades. *Journal of Educational Psychology*, 80, 417–447.

Junaid, K. A., & Fellowes, S. (2006). Gender differences in the attainment of motor skills on the Movement Assessment Battery for Children. *Physical & Occupational Therapy in Pediatrics*, 26(1–2), 5–11.

Justice, E. M., Baker-Ward, L., Gupta, S., & Jannings, L. R. (1997). Means to the goal of remembering: Developmental changes in awareness of strategy use-performance relations. *Journal of Experimental Child Psychology*, 65, 293–314.

Kail, R., & Park, Y. (1994). Processing time, articulation time, and memory span. *Journal of Experimental Child Psychology*, 57, 281–291.

Kail, R. V. (2003). Information processing and memory. In M. H. Bornstein & L. Davidson (Eds.), *Well-being: Positive development across the life course* (pp. 269–279). Mahwah, NJ: Lawrence Erlbaum.

Kail, R. V, & Reese, H. W. (2002). *Advances in child development and behavior* (Vol. 29). San Diego: Academic Press.

Kantomaa, M. T., Stamatakis, E., Kankaanpää, A., Kaakinen, M., Rodriguez, A., Taanila, A., . . . Tammelin, T. (2013). Physical activity and obesity mediate the association between childhood motor function and adolescents' academic achievement. *Proceedings of the National Academy of Sciences of the United States of America*, 110(5), 1917–1922. doi:10.1073/pnas.1214574110

Kaufman, A. S., Flanagan, D. P., Alfonso, V. C., & Mascolo, J. T. (2006). Review of Wechsler Intelligence Scale for Children, Fourth Edition (WISC-IV). *Journal of Psychoeducational Assessment*, 24(3), 278–295.

Kaufman, A. S., & Lichtenberger, E. O. (2006). *Assessing adolescent and adult intelligence* (3rd ed.). Hoboken, NJ: John Wiley.

Kaufman, J. C., Kaufman, S. B., & Plucker., J. A. (2013). Contemporary theories of intelligence. In *Oxford Handbook of Cognitive Psychology*. Advance online publication.

Kaur, S., Sachdev, H. P. S., Dwivedi, S. N., Lakshmy, R., & Kapil, U. (2008). Prevalence of overweight and obesity amongst school children in Delhi, India. *Asia Pacific Journal of Clinical Nutrition*, 17(4), 592–596.

Kelly, K. (1999). Retention vs. promotion: Schools search for alternatives. Harvard Education Letter Research Online. *Harvard Education Letter Research Online*. Retrieved from http://www.edletter.org/past/issues/1999-jf/retention.shtml

Kiechl-Kohlendorfer, U., Horak, E., Mueller, W., Strobl, R., Haberland, C., Fink, F.-M., . . . Kiechl, S. (2007). Neonatal characteristics and risk of atopic asthma in schoolchildren: Results from a large prospective birth-cohort study. *Acta Paediatrica*, 96(11), 1606–1610.

Kister, M. C., & Patterson, C. J. (1980). Children's conceptions of the causes of illness. Understanding contagion and the use of immanent justice. *Child Development*, 51, 839–846.

Kitsao-Wekulo, P. K., Holding, P., Taylor, H. G., Abubakar, A., Kvalsvig, J., & Connolly, K. (2013).

Nutrition as an important mediator of the impact of background variables on outcome in middle childhood. *Frontiers in Human Neuroscience, 7*, 713. doi:10.3389/fnhum.2013.00713

Kline, P. (2013). *Handbook of psychological testing*. New York: Routledge.

Klingner, J. K., Vaughn, S., Hughes, M. T., Schumm, J. S., & Elbaum, B. (1998). Outcomes for students with and without learning disabilities in inclusive classrooms. *Learning Disabilities Research and Practice, 13*, 153–161.

Kober, N., & Rentner, D. S. (2011). Year two of implementing the Common Core State Standards: States' progress and challenges. *Center on Education Policy*. Retrieved from http://eric.ed.gov/?id=ED528907

Kohlberg, L. (1963). The development of children's orientations toward a moral order. *Human Development, 51*(1), 8–20. doi:10.1159/000112530

Kohlberg, L. (1981). *Essays on moral development*. San Francisco: Harper & Row.

Kormi-Nouri, R., Shojaei, R.-S., Moniri, S., Gholami, A.-R., Moradi, A.-R., Akbari-Zardkhaneh, S., & Nilsson, L.-G. (2008). The effect of childhood bilingualism on episodic and semantic memory tasks. *Scandinavian Journal of Psychology, 49*(2), 93–109.

Krafnick, A. J., Flowers, D. L., Napoliello, E. M., & Eden, G. F. (2011). Gray matter volume changes following reading intervention in dyslexic children. *NeuroImage, 57*(3), 733–741. doi:10.1016/j.neuroimage.2010.10.062

Kuhn, D. (2000). Metacognitive development. *Current Directions in Psychological Science, 9*, 178–181.

Laitsch, D. (2006). *Assessment, high stakes, and alternative visions: Appropriate use of the right tools to leverage improvement*. Tempe: Arizona State University.

Lakshman, R., Elks, C. E., & Ong, K. K. (2012). Childhood obesity. *Circulation, 126*(14), 1770–1779. doi:10.1161/CIRCULATIONAHA.111.047738

Laukkanen, A., Pesola, A., Havu, M., Sääkslahti, A., & Finni, T. (2014). Relationship between habitual physical activity and gross motor skills is multifaceted in 5- to 8-year-old children. *Scandinavian Journal of Medicine & Science in Sports, 24*(2), e102–e110. doi:10.1111/sms.12116

Leather, C. V, & Henry, L. A. (1994). Working memory span and phonological awareness tasks as predictors of early reading ability. *Journal of Experimental Child Psychology, 58*, 88–111.

Legare, C. H., Evans, E. M., Rosengren, K. S., & Harris, P. L. (2012). The coexistence of natural and supernatural explanations across cultures and development. *Child Development, 83*(3), 779–793. doi:10.1111/j.1467-8624.2012.01743.x

Legare, C. H., & Gelman, S. A. (2008). Bewitchment, biology, or both: The co-existence of natural and supernatural explanatory frameworks across development. *Cognitive Science, 32*(4), 607–642. doi:10.1080/03640210802066766

Legare, C. H., Wellman, H. M., & Gelman, S. A. (2009). Evidence for an explanation advantage in naive biological reasoning. *Cognitive Psychology, 58*(2), 177–194. doi:10.1016/j.cogpsych.2008.06.002

Lehmann, M., & Hasselhorn, M. (2007). Variable memory strategy use in children's adaptive intratask learning behavior: Developmental changes and working memory influences in free recall. *Child Development, 78*(4), 1068–1082.

Liberman, I. Y., & Liberman, A. M. (1990). Whole language vs. code emphasis: Underlying assumptions and their implications for reading instruction. *Annals of Dyslexia, 40*, 51–76.

Lipka, O., & Siegel, L. S. (2007). The development of reading skills in children with English as a second language. *Scientific Studies of Reading, 11*(2), 105–131. doi:10.1080/10888430701343597

Littleton, H. L., & Ollendick, T. (2003). Negative body image and disordered eating behavior in children and adolescents: What places youth at risk and how can these problems be prevented? *Clinical Child and Family Psychology Review, 6*(1), 51–66.

LoBue, V., Nishida, T., Chiong, C., DeLoache, J. S., & Haidt, J. (2011). When getting something good is bad: Even three-year-olds react to inequality. *Social Development, 20*(1), 154–170. doi:10.1111/j.1467-9507.2009.00560.x

Loomis, J. W. (2006). Learning disabilities. In R. T. Ammerman (Ed.), *Comprehensive handbook of personality and psychopathology* (Vol. 3, pp. 272–284). Hoboken, NJ: John Wiley.

Lynn, R. (2013). Who discovered the Flynn effect? A review of early studies of the secular increase of intelligence. *Intelligence, 41*(6), 765–769. doi:10.1016/j.intell.2013.03.008

Maldonado-Carreño, C., & Votruba-Drzal, E. Teacher-child relationships and the development of academic and behavioral skills during elementary school: A within- and between-child analysis. *Child Development, 82*(2), 601–616. doi:10.1111/j.1467-8624.2010.01533.x

Maleyko, G., & Gawlik, M. A. (2011). No Child Left Behind: What we know and what we need to know. *Education, 131*(3), 600–624.

Maloney, M. J., McGuire, J. B., Daniels, S. R., & Specker, B. (1989). Dieting behavior and eating attitudes in children. *Pediatrics, 84*, 482–489.

Malti, T., & Latzko, B. (2010). Children's moral emotions and moral cognition: Towards an integrative perspective. *New Directions for Child and Adolescent Development, 2010*(129), 1–10. doi:10.1002/cd.272

Manoach, D. S., Schlaug, G., Siewert, B., Darby, D. G., Bly, B. M., Benfield, A., . . . Warach, S. (1997). Prefrontal cortex fMRI signal changes are correlated with working memory load. *NeuroReport, 8*, 545–549.

Marton, I., Wiener, J., Rogers, M., Moore, C., & Tannock, R. (2009). Empathy and social perspective taking in children with attention-deficit/hyperactivity disorder. *Journal of Abnormal Child Psychology, 37*(1), 107–118. doi:10.1007/s10802-008-9262-4

Mathis, W. J. (2006). *The accuracy and effectiveness of adequate yearly progress, NCLB's school evaluation system*. Tempe: Arizona State University Education Policy Research Unit.

Mayes, S. D., & Calhoun, S. L. (2007). Wechsler Intelligence Scale for Children—Third and fourth edition predictors of academic achievement in children with attention-deficit/hyperactivity disorder. *School Psychology Quarterly, 22*(2), 234–249.

Mazzocco, M. M. M., & Kover, S. T. (2007). A longitudinal assessment of executive function skills and their association with math performance. *Child Neuropsychology, 13*(1), 18–45.

McCabe, M. P., Riccardelli, L. A., & Finemore, J. (2002). The role of puberty, media and popularity with peers on strategies to increase weight, decrease weight and increase muscle tone among adolescent boys and girls. *Journal of Psychosomatic Research, 52*, 145–153.

McCabe, M. P., Ricciardelli, L. A., Stanford, J., Holt, K., Keegan, S., & Miller, L. (2007). Where is all the pressure coming from? Messages from mothers and teachers about preschool children's appearance, diet and exercise. *European Eating Disorders Review, 15*(3), 221–230.

McKenna, M. C., Kear, D. J., & Ellsworth, R. A. (1995). Children's attitudes toward reading: A national survey. *Reading Research Quarterly, 30*, 934–956.

McNamee, S., & Peterson, J. (1986). Young children's distributive justice reasoning, behavior, and role taking: Their consistency and relationship. *Journal of Genetic Psychology, 146*, 399–404.

McVey, G. L., Levine, M., Piran, N., & Ferguson, H. B. (2013). *Preventing eating-related and weight-related disorders: Collaborative research, advocacy, and policy change: Collaborative research, advocacy, and policy change*. Waterloo, Ontario: Wilfrid Laurier University Press. Retrieved from http://books.google.com/books?id=JlvZAgAAQBAJ&pgis=1

McVey, G. L., Lieberman, M., Voorberg, N., Wardrope, D., & Blackmore, E. (2003). School-based peer support groups: A new approach to the prevention of disordered eating. *Eating Disorders, 11*(3), 169–185. doi:10.1080/10640260390218297

McVey, G. L., Tweed, S., & Blackmore, E. (2004). Dieting among preadolescent and young adolescent females. *Canadian Medical Association Journal, 170*(10), 1559–1561.

Midobuche, E. (2001). More than empty footprints in the sand: Educating immigrant children. *Harvard Educational Review, 71*, 529–535.

Miller, B. D., Wood, B. L., & Smith, B. A. (2010). Respiratory illness. In R. J. Shaw & D. R. DeMaso (Eds.), *Textbook of pediatric psychosomatic medicine* (pp. 303–317). Arlington, VA: American Psychiatric Publishing.

Mitchell, D. K., & McQuaid, E. (2008). Asthma. In B. A. Boyer & M. I. Paharia (Eds.), *Comprehensive handbook of clinical health psychology* (pp. 251–276). Hoboken, NJ: John Wiley.

Morra, S., Gobbo, C., Marini, Z., & Sheese, R. (2008). *Cognitive development: Neo-Piagetian perspectives*. New York: Taylor & Francis.

Mpofu, E., & van de Vijver, F. J. R. (2000). Taxonomic structure in early to middle childhood: A longitudinal study with Zimbabwean schoolchildren. *International Journal of Behavioral Development, 24*(2), 204–212.

Murray-Close, D., Crick, N. R., & Galotti, K. M. (2006). Children's moral reasoning regarding physical and relational aggression. *Social Development, 15*(3), 345–372.

Myant, K. A., & Williams, J. M. (2005). Children's concepts of health and illness: Understanding of contagious illnesses, non-contagious illnesses and injuries. *Journal of Health Psychology, 10*(6), 805–819.

Nader, P. R., Bradley, R. H., Houts, R. M., McRitchie, S. L., & O'Brien, M. (2008). Moderate-to-vigorous physical activity from ages 9 to 15 years. *JAMA, 300*(3), 295–305.

Nagy, W. E., & Scott, J. A. (2000). Vocabulary processes. In M. L. Kamil & P. B. Mosenthal (Eds.), *Handbook of reading research* (Vol. 3, pp. 269–284). Mahwah, NJ: Lawrence Erlbaum.

National Association of School Psychologists. (2003). *Position statement on student grade retention and social promotion*. Retrieved from http://www.nasponline.org/about_nasp/pospaper_graderetent.aspx

National Center for Education Statistics. (2014a). *The condition of education—2014*. Washington, DC: Author. Retrieved from http://nces.ed.gov/pubsearch/pubsinfo.asp?pubid=2014083

National Center for Education Statistics. (2014b). *The Nation's Report Card 2014*. Retrieved from http://www.nationsreportcard.gov/reading_math_2013/#/

National Institute of Child Health and Human Development. (2000). *Teaching children to read: An evidence-based assessment of the scientific research literature on reading and its implications for reading instruction*. Washington, DC: Author. doi:NIH Pub. No. 00-4769

National Survey of Children's Health. (2014a). *Asthma: Chronic health conditions—Data* query from the Child and Adolescent Health Measurement Initiative NSCH 2011/12, Data Resource Center for Child and Adolescent Health website. Retrieved from http://www.childhealthdata.org/browse/survey/results?q=2401&r=1

National Survey of Children's Health. (2014b). Weight status: Data query from the Child and Adolescent Health Measurement Initiative NSCH 2007 Resource Center for Child and Adolescent Health website. Retrieved from http://www.childhealthdata.org/browse/survey/results?q=226

Neisser, U., Boodoo, G., Bouchard, T. J., Jr., Boykin, A. W., Brody, N., Ceci, S. J., . . . Urbina, S. (1996). Intelligence: Knowns and unknowns. American Psychologist, 51(2), 77–101.

Neumark-Sztainer, D., Sherwood, N. E., Coller, T., & Hannan, P. J. (2000). Primary prevention of disordered eating among preadolescent girls: Feasibility and short-term effect of a community-based intervention. Journal of the American Dietetic Association, 100(12), 1466–1473. doi:10.1016/S0002-8223(00)00410-7

Nippold, M. A., Taylor, C. L., & Baker, J. M. (1996). Idiom understanding in Australian youth: A cross-cultural comparison. Journal of Speech and Hearing Research, 39, 442–447.

Nisbett, R. E., Aronson, J., Blair, C., Dickens, W., Flynn, J., Halpern, D. F., & Turkheimer, E. (2013). Intelligence: New findings and theoretical developments. American Psychologist, 67(2), 130–159.

Nobes, G., & Pawson, C. (2003). Children's understanding of social rules and social status. Merrill-Palmer Quarterly, 49, 77–99.

Nowicka, P., & Flodmark, C.-E. (2007). Physical activity: Key issues in treatment of childhood obesity. Acta Paediatrica, 96, 39–45.

Nyiti, R. M. (1982). The validity of "cultural differences explanations" for cross-cultural variation in the rate of Piagetian cognitive development. In H. W. Stevenson & D. A. Wagner (Eds.), Cultural perspectives on child development (pp. 146–166). San Francisco: W. H. Freeman.

O'Dea, J. A., & Yager, Z. (2011). School-based psychoeducational approaches to prevention. In I. T. F. Cash & L. Smolak (Eds.), Body image: A handbook of science, practice, and prevention. New York: Guilford Press.

Okagaki, L., & Sternberg, R. J. (1993). Parental beliefs and children's school performance. Child Development, 64, 36–56.

Organization for Economic Co-operation and Development. (2014). Obesity update. Retrieved from http://www.oecd.org/health/Obesity-Update-2014.pdf

Owens, R. E. (2001). Language development: An introduction (5th ed.). Needham Heights, MA: Allyn & Bacon.

Pascual-Leone, L. (2000). Reflections on working memory: Are the two models complementary? Journal of Experimental Child Psychology, 77, 138–154.

Passolunghi, M. C., Mammarella, I. C., & Altoè, G. (2008). Cognitive abilities as precursors of the early acquisition of mathematical skills during first through second grades. Developmental Neuropsychology, 33(3), 229–250. doi:10.1080/87565640801982320

Pavone, V., Lionetti, E., Gargano, V., Evola, F. R., Costarella, L., & Sessa, G. (2011). Growing pains: A study of 30 cases and a review of the literature. Journal of Pediatric Orthopedics, 31(5), 606–609. doi:10.1097/BPO.0b013e318220ba5e

Pellegrini, A. D., Dupuis, D., & Smith, P. K. (2007). Play in evolution and development. Developmental Review, 27(2), 261–276.

Pellis, S. M., & Pellis, V. C. (2007). Rough-and-tumble play and the development of the social brain. Current Directions in Psychological Science, 16(2), 95–98. doi:10.1111/j.1467-8721.2007.00483.x

Perry, K. E., Donohue, K. M., & Weinstein, R. S. (2007). Teaching practices and the promotion of achievement and adjustment in first grade. Journal of School Psychology, 45(3), 269–292.

Petersen, S. E., & Posner, M. I. (2012). The attention system of the human brain: 20 years after. Annual Review of Neuroscience, 35, 73–89. doi:10.1146/annurev-neuro-062111-150525

Peterson, R. L., & Pennington, B. F. (2012). Developmental dyslexia. Lancet, 379(9830), 1997–2007. doi:10.1016/S0140-6736(12)60198-6

Petteway, R. J., Valerio, M. A., & Patel, M. R. (2011). What about your friends? Exploring asthma-related peer interactions. Journal of Asthma, 48(4), 393–399. doi:10.3109/02770903.2011.563807

Pexman, P. M., Glenwright, M., Hala, S., Kowbel, S. L., & Jungen, S. (2006). Children's use of trait information in understanding verbal irony. Metaphor & Symbol, 21(1), 39–60.

Piaget, J. (1932). The moral judgment of the child. New York: Harcourt Brace.

Pianta, R. C., La Paro, K. M., Payne, C., Cox, M. J., & Bradley, R. (2002). The relation of kindergarten classroom environment to teacher, family, and school characteristics and child outcomes. The Elementary School Journal, 102(3), 225–238.

Pianta, R. C., & Stuhlman, M. W. (2004). Teacher-child relationships and children's success in the first years of school. School Psychology Review, 33(3). Retrieved from http://eric.ed.gov/?id=EJ683606

Piek, J. P., Dawson, L., Smith, L. M., & Gasson, N. (2008). The role of early fine and gross motor development on later motor and cognitive ability. Human Movement Science, 27(5), 668–681. doi:10.1016/j.humov.2007.11.002

Pineda, D. A., Palacio, L. G., Puerta, I. C., Merchán, V., Arango, C. P., Galvis, A. Y., . . . Arcos-Burgos, M. (2007). Environmental influences that affect attention deficit/hyperactivity disorder. European Child & Adolescent Psychiatry, 16(5), 337–346.

Pinker, S., Lebeaux, D. S., & Frost, L. A. (1987). Productivity and constraints in the acquisition of the passive. Cognition, 26, 195–267.

Poirel, N., Borst, G., Simon, G., Rossi, S., Cassotti, M., Pineau, A., & Houdé, O. (2012). Number conservation is related to children's prefrontal inhibitory control: An fMRI study of a Piagetian task. PLoS ONE, 7(7), e40802. Retrieved from https://hal.archives-ouvertes.fr/hal-00839858/

Polanczyk, G. V, Willcutt, E. G., Salum, G. A., Kieling, C., & Rohde, L. A. (2014). ADHD prevalence estimates across three decades: An updated systematic review and meta-regression analysis. International Journal of Epidemiology, 43(2), 434–442. doi:10.1093/ije/dyt261

Poskitt, E. M. E. (2009). Countries in transition: Underweight to obesity non-stop? Annals of Tropical Paediatrics, 29(1), 1–11. doi:10.1179/146532809X401971

Poudevigne, M. S., O'Connor, P. J., Laing, E. M., Wilson, A. M. R., Modlesky, C. M., & Lewis, R. D. (2003). Body images of 4-8-year-old girls at the outset of their first artistic gymnastics class. International Journal of Eating Disorders, 34, 244–250.

Prasad, V., Brogan, E., Mulvaney, C., Grainge, M., Stanton, W., & Sayal, K. (2013). How effective are drug treatments for children with ADHD at improving on-task behaviour and academic achievement in the school classroom? A systematic review and meta-analysis. European Child & Adolescent Psychiatry, 22(4), 203–216. doi:10.1007/s00787-012-0346-x

Prifitera, A., & Saklofske, D. H. (1998). WISC-III clinical use and interpretation: Scientist-practitioner perspectives. San Diego: Elsevier Academic Press.

Prifitera, A., Saklofske, D. H., & Weiss, L. G. (2005). WISC-IV clinical use and interpretation: Scientist-practitioner perspectives. San Diego: Elsevier Academic Press.

Puhl, R. M., & Heuer, C. A. (2009). The stigma of obesity: A review and update. Obesity, 17(5), 941–964. doi:10.1038/oby.2008.636

Pulgarón, E. R. (2013). Childhood obesity: A review of increased risk for physical and psychological comorbidities. Clinical Therapeutics, 35(1), A18–A32. doi:10.1016/j.clinthera.2012.12.014

Raman, L., & Gelman, S. A. (2005). Children's understanding of the transmission of genetic disorders and contagious illnesses. Developmental Psychology, 41(1), 171–182.

Raman, L., & Gelman, S. A. (2008). Do children endorse psychosocial factors in the transmission of illness and disgust? Developmental Psychology, 44(3), 801–813.

Raman, L., & Winer, G. A. (2002). Children's and adults' understanding of illness: Evidence in support of a coexistence model. Genetic, Social, and General Psychology Monographs, 128(4), 325–355.

Ramus, F. (2014). Neuroimaging sheds new light on the phonological deficit in dyslexia. Trends in Cognitive Sciences, 18(6), 274–275. doi:10.1016/j.tics.2014.01.009

Rayner, K., Foorman, B. R., Perfetti, C. A., Pesetsky, D., & Seidenberg, M. S. (2001). How psychological science informs the teaching of reading. Psychological Science in the Public Interest, 2, 31–74.

Reilly, J. J. (2007). Childhood obesity: An overview. Children & Society, 21(5), 390–396.

Relji , G., Ferring, D., & Martin, R. (2014). A meta-analysis on the effectiveness of bilingual programs in Europe. Review of Educational Research. Advance online publication. doi:10.3102/0034654314548514

Richards, T. L., Dager, S. R., Corina, D., Serafini, S., Heide, A. C., Steury, K., . . . Berninger, V. W. (1999). Dyslexic children have abnormal brain lactate response to reading-related language tasks. American Journal of Neuroradiology, 20, 1393–1398.

Richardson, S. M., Paxton, S. J., & Thomson, J. S. (2009). Is BodyThink an efficacious body image and self-esteem program? A controlled evaluation with adolescents. Body Image, 6(2), 75–82. doi:10.1016/j.bodyim.2008.11.001

Riddle, M. A., Yershova, K., Lazzaretto, D., Paykina, N., Yenokyan, G., Greenhill, L., . . . Posner, K. (2013). The Preschool Attention-Deficit/Hyperactivity Disorder Treatment Study (PATS) 6-year follow-up. Journal of the American Academy of Child and Adolescent Psychiatry, 52(3), 264–278. doi:10.1016/j.jaac.2012.12.007

Rideout, V. J. (2013). Zero to eight: Children's media use in America 2013. New York: Common Sense Media. Retrieved from https://www.commonsensemedia.org/research/zero-to-eight-childrens-media-use-in-america-2013

Rindermann, H., & Thompson, J. (2013). Ability rise in NAEP and narrowing ethnic gaps? Intelligence, 41(6), 821–831. doi:10.1016/j.intell.2013.06.016

Rogoff, B., & Chavajay, P. (1995). What's become of research on the cultural basis of cognitive development? American Psychologist, 50, 859–877.

Rogoff, B., & Waddell, K. J. (1982). Memory for information organized in a scene by children from two cultures. Child Development, 53(5), 1224–1228. Retrieved from http://www.ncbi.nlm.nih.gov/pubmed/7140428

Rolland, K., Farnhill, D., & Griffiths, R. A. (1997). Body figure perceptions and eating attitudes among Australian schoolchildren aged 8 to 12 years. *International Journal of Eating Disorders*, *21*, 273–278.

Rollins, B., Francis, L., & BeLue, R. (2007). Family meal frequency and weight status in young children. *Annals of Epidemiology*, *17*(9), 745.

Rolstad, K. (2005). The big picture: A meta-analysis of program effectiveness research on English language learners. *Educational Policy*, *19*(4), 572–594. doi:10.1177/0895904805278067

Rosen, G. D. (2006). *The dyslexic brain: New pathways in neuroscience discovery*. Mahwah, NJ: Lawrence Erlbaum.

Rubia, K., Alegria, A. A., Cubillo, A. I., Smith, A. B., Brammer, M. J., & Radua, J. (2013). Effects of stimulants on brain function in attention-deficit/hyperactivity disorder: A systematic review and meta-analysis. *Biological Psychiatry*, *76*(8), 616–628. doi:10.1016/j.biopsych.2013.10.016

Runions, K. C., Vitaro, F., Cross, D., Shaw, T., Hall, M., & Boivin, M. (2014). Teacher–child relationship, parenting, and growth in likelihood and severity of physical aggression in the early school years. *Merrill-Palmer Quarterly*, *60*(3), 274–301. Retrieved from http://muse.jhu.edu/journals/merrill-palmer_quarterly/v060/60.3.runions.html

Ruzgis, P., & Grigorenko, E. L. (1994). Cultural meaning systems, intelligence, and personality. In R. J. Sternberg & P. Ruzgis (Eds.), *Personality and intelligence* (pp. 248–270). New York: Cambridge University Press.

Sarrazin, G. (1999). *WISC-III, Échelle d'intelligence de Wechsler pour Enfants troisième Édition, adaptation canadienne-française, Manuel d'administration*. Toronto: Psychological Corporation.

Savage, R., Cornish, K., Manly, T., & Hollis, C. (2006). Cognitive processes in children's reading and attention: The role of working memory, divided attention, and response inhibition. *British Journal of Psychology*, *97*(3), 365–385.

Schachar, R. (2014). Genetics of attention deficit hyperactivity disorder (ADHD): Recent updates and future prospects. *Current Developmental Disorders Reports*, *1*(1), 41–49. doi:10.1007/s40474-013-0004-0

Scherer, M. (1985). How many ways is a child intelligent? *Instructor*, pp. 32–35.

Schneider, W., & Bjorklund, D. F. (1992). Expertise, aptitude, and strategic remembering. *Child Development*, *63*(2), 461–473. doi:10.1111/j.1467-8624.1992.tb01640.x

Schneider, W., & Pressley, M. (2013a). *Memory development between 2 and 20*. New York: Springer-Verlag.

Schneider, W., & Pressley, M. (2013b). *Memory development between two and twenty* (3rd ed.). Mahwah, NJ: Lawrence Erlbaum.

Schurz, M., Wimmer, H., Richlan, F., Ludersdorfer, P., Klackl, J., & Kronbichler, M. (2014). Resting-state and task-based functional brain connectivity in developmental dyslexia. *Cerebral Cortex*. Advance online publication. doi:10.1093/cercor/bhu184

Senbanjo, I. O., Oshikoya, K. A., Odusanya, O. O., & Njokanma, O. F. (2011). Prevalence of and risk factors for stunting among school children and adolescents in Abeokuta, southwest Nigeria. *Journal of Health, Population, and Nutrition*, *29*(4), 364–370. Retrieved from http://www.pubmedcentral.nih.gov/articlerender.fcgi?artid=3190367&tool=pmcentrez&rendertype=abstract

Serpell, R. (1974). Aspects of intelligence in a developing country. *African Social Research*, *17*, 578–596.

Serpell, R., & Jere-Folotiya, J. (2008). Developmental assessment, cultural context, gender, and schooling in Zambia. *International Journal of Psychology*, *43*(2), 88–96.

Shaywitz, B. A., Sullivan, C. M., Anderson, G. M., Gillespie, S. M., Sullivan, B., & Shaywitz, S. E. (1994). Aspartame, behavior, and cognitive function in children with attention deficit disorder. *Pediatrics*, *93*, 70–75.

Shaywitz, S. E., Shaywitz, B. A., Pugh, K. A., Fulbright, R. K., Constable, R. T., Mencl, W. E., . . . Gore, J. C. (1998). Functional disruption of the organization of the brain for reading in dyslexia. *Proceedings of the National Academy of Sciences of the United States of America*, *95*, 2636–2641.

Sheng, L., Bedore, L. M., Peña, E. D., & Fiestas, C. (2011). Semantic development in Spanish-English bilingual children: Effects of age and language experience. *Child Development*, *84*(3), 1034–1045. doi:10.1111/cdev.12015

Shepard, L. S., & Smith, M. L. (1990). Synthesis of research on grade retention. *Educational Leadership*, *47*(8), 84–88.

Siegel, L. S. (1994). Working memory and reading: A life-span perspective. *International Journal of Behavioural Development*, *17*, 109–124.

Siegler, R. S. (1998). *Emerging minds: The process of change in children's thinking*. New York: Oxford University Press.

Siegler, R. S., & Richards, D. (1982). The development of intelligence. In R. Sternberg (Ed.), *Handbook of human intelligence*. London: Cambridge University Press.

Simasek, M., & Blandino, D. A. (2007). Treatment of the common cold. *American Family Physician*, *75*(4), 515–520. Retrieved from http://www.ncbi.nlm.nih.gov/pubmed/17323712

Simon, H. A. (2001). Learning to research about learning. In S. M. Carver & D. Klahr (Eds.), *Cognition and instruction* (pp. 205–226). Mahwah, NJ: Lawrence Erlbaum.

Singh, G. K., & Kogan, M. D. (2007). Widening socioeconomic disparities in US childhood mortality, 1969–2000. *American Journal of Public Health*, *97*(9), 1658–1665.

Singh, G. K., Kogan, M. D., Van Dyck, P. C., & Siahpush, M. (2008). Racial/ethnic, socioeconomic, and behavioral determinants of childhood and adolescent obesity in the United States: Analyzing independent and joint associations. *Annals of Epidemiology*, *18*(9), 682–695. doi:10.1016/j.annepidem.2008.05.001

Smetana, J. G., Jambon, M., & Ball., C. (2013). The social domain approach to children's moral and social judgments. In M. Killen & J. G. Smetana (Eds.), *Handbook of Moral Development*. New York: Psychology Press.

Smith, P. K. (2005). Play: Types and functions in human development. In B. J. Ellis & D. F. Bjorklund (Eds.), *Origins of the social mind: Evolutionary psychology and child development* (pp. 271–291). New York: Guilford Press.

Smolak, L. (2011). Body image development in childhood. In T. F. Cash & L. Smolak (Eds.), *Body image: A handbook of science, practice, and prevention* (pp. 67–75). New York: Guilford Press.

Snowling, M. J. (2013). Early identification and interventions for dyslexia: A contemporary view. *Journal of Research in Special Educational Needs*, *13*(1), 7–14. doi:10.1111/j.1471-3802.2012.01262.x

Spilt, J. L., Hughes, J. N., Wu, J.-Y., & Kwok, O.-M. (2012). Dynamics of teacher-student relationships: Stability and change across elementary school and the influence on children's academic success. *Child Development*, *83*(4), 1180–1195. doi:10.1111/j.1467-8624.2012.01761.x

Sridhar, D., & Vaughn, S. (2001). Social functioning of students with learning disabilities. In D. P. Hallahan & B. K. Keogh (Eds.), *Research and global perspectives in learning disabilities* (pp. 65–91). Mahwah, NJ: Lawrence Erlbaum.

Srour, M., & Shevell, M. (2014). Genetics and the investigation of developmental delay/intellectual disability. *Archives of Disease in Childhood*, *99*(4), 386–389. doi:10.1136/archdischild-2013-304063

Stahl, S. A., McKenna, M. C., & Pagnucco, J. R. (1994). The effects of whole-language instruction: An update and a reappraisal. *Educational Psychologist*, *29*, 175–185.

Stearns, E., Moller, S., Potochnick, S., & Blau, J. (2007). Staying back and dropping out: The relationship between grade retention and school dropout. *Sociology of Education*, *80*(3), 210–240.

Stein, A. D., Wang, M., Martorell, R., Norris, S. A., Adair, L. S., Bas, I., . . . Victora, C. G. (2010). Growth patterns in early childhood and final attained stature: Data from five birth cohorts from low- and middle-income countries. *American Journal of Human Biology*, *22*(3), 353–359. doi:10.1002/ajhb.20998

Sternberg, R. J. (1985). *Beyond IQ: A triarchic theory of human intelligence*. Cambridge, UK: Cambridge University Press.

Sternberg, R. J. (2005). The triarchic theory of successful intelligence. In D. P. Flanagan & P. L. Harrison (Eds.), *Contemporary intellectual assessment: Theories, tests, and issues* (pp. 103–119). New York: Guilford Press.

Sternberg, R. J. (2007). Intelligence and culture. In S. Kitayama & D. Cohen (Eds.), *Handbook of cultural psychology* (pp. 547–568). New York: Guilford Press.

Sternberg, R. J. (2011). The theory of successful intelligence. In R. J. Sternberg & S. B. Kaufman (Eds.), *The Cambridge handbook of intelligence* (pp. 504–527). New York: Cambridge University Press.

Sternberg, R. J. (2014). The development of adaptive competence: Why cultural psychology is necessary and not just nice. *Developmental Review*, *34*(3), 208–224. doi:10.1016/j.dr.2014.05.004

Sternberg, R. J., & Grigorenko, E. L. (2008). Ability testing across cultures. In L. A. Suzuki & J. G. Ponterotto (Eds.), *Handbook of multicultural assessment: Clinical, psychological, and educational applications* (pp. 449–470). San Francisco: Jossey-Bass.

Sternberg, R. J., Grigorenko, E. L., & Bundy, D. A. (2001). The predictive value of IQ. *Merrill-Palmer Quarterly*, *47*, 1–41.

Subrahmanyam, K., & Greenfield, P. M. (1996). Effect of video game practice on spatial skills in girls and boys. In P. M. Greenfield & R. R. Cocking (Eds.), *Interacting with video* (pp. 95–114). Norwood, NJ: Ablex.

Sunderman, G. L., & Orfield, G. (2007). Do states have the capacity to meet the NCLB mandates? *Phi Delta Kappan*, *89*(2), 137–139.

Sundet, J. M., Barlaug, D. G., & Torjussen, T. M. (2004). The end of the Flynn effect? A study of secular trends in mean intelligence test scores of Norwegian conscripts during half a century. *Intelligence*, *32*, 349–362.

Super, C. M., & Harkness, S. (1982). The infant's niche in rural Kenya and metropolitan America. In L. L. Adler (Ed.), *Cross-cultural research at issue* (pp. 247–255). New York: Academic Press.

Swenson, N. C. (2000). Comparing traditional and collaborative settings for language intervention. *Communication Disorders Quarterly*, *22*, 12–18.

Tarver, J., Daley, D., & Sayal, K. (2014). Attention-deficit hyperactivity disorder (ADHD): An updated review of the essential facts. *Child: Care, Health and Development*, *40*(6), 762–774. doi:10.1111/cch.12139

Taylor, L. A., Reeves, C. B., & Jeffords, E. (2008). Intellectual assessment. In M. Hersen & A. M. Gross (Eds.), *Handbook of clinical psychology: Vol. 2. Children and adolescents* (pp. 480–496). Hoboken, NJ: John Wiley.

Te Nijenhuis, J. (2013). The Flynn effect, group differences, and g loadings. *Personality and Individual Differences*, 55(3), 224–228. doi:10.1016/j.paid.2011.12.023

Teasdale, T. W., & Owen, D. R. (2000). Forty-year secular trends in cognitive abilities. *Intelligence*, 28, 115–120.

Thapar, A., Cooper, M., Eyre, O., & Langley, K. (2013). What have we learnt about the causes of ADHD? *Journal of Child Psychology and Psychiatry, and Allied Disciplines*, 54(1), 3–16. doi:10.1111/j.1469-7610.2012.02611.x

Thomas, V. G. (2000). Ending social promotion: Help or hindrance? *Kappa Delta Pi Record*, 37(1), 30–32.

Thomsen, S. F., van der Sluis, S., Kyvik, K. O., Skytthe, A., & Backer, V. (2010). Estimates of asthma heritability in a large twin sample. *Clinical & Experimental Allergy*, 40(7), 1054–1061. doi:10.1111/j.1365-2222.2010.03525.x

Tiemeier, H., Lenroot, R. K., Greenstein, D. K., Tran, L., Pierson, R., & Giedd, J. N. (2010). Cerebellum development during childhood and adolescence: A longitudinal morphometric MRI study. *NeuroImage*, 49(1), 63–70. doi:10.1016/j.neuroimage.2009.08.016

Tiggeman, M., & Wilson-Barrett, E. (1998). Children's figure ratings: Relationship to self-esteem and negative stereotyping. *International Journal of Eating Disorders*, 23, 83–88.

Tremblay, L., & Limbos, M. (2009). Body image disturbance and psychopathology in children: Research evidence and implications for prevention and treatment. *Current Psychiatry Reviews*, 5(1), 62–72. doi:10.2174/157340009787315307

Tremblay, L., Lovsin, T., Zecevic, C., & Larivière, M. (2011). Perceptions of self in 3-5-year-old children: A preliminary investigation into the early emergence of body dissatisfaction. *Body Image*, 8(3), 287–292. doi:10.1016/j.bodyim.2011.04.004

Tsujimoto, S., Kuwajima, M., & Sawaguchi, T. (2007). Developmental fractionation of working memory and response inhibition during childhood. *Experimental Psychology*, 54(1), 30–37.

Tucker, G. R. (1998). A global perspective on multilingualism and multilingual education. In J. Cenoz & F. Genesee (Eds.), *Beyond bilingualism: Multilingualism and multilingual education*. Clevedon, UK: Multilingual Matters.

Turiel, E. (2008). Thought about actions in social domains: Morality, social conventions, and social interactions. *Cognitive Development*, 23(1), 136–154. doi:10.1016/j.cogdev.2007.04.001

Turkheimer, E., Haley, A., Waldron, M., D'Onofrio, B., & Gottesman, I. I. (2003). Socioeconomic status modifies heritability of IQ in young children. *Psychological Science*, 14(6), 623–628.

U.S. Department of Education. (2015). *ESEA flexibility*. Retrieved from http://www2.ed.gov/policy/elsec/guid/esea-flexibility/index.html

Van den Bemt, L., Kooijman, S., Linssen, V., Lucassen, P., Muris, J., Slabbers, G., & Schermer, T. (2010). How does asthma influence the daily life of children? Results of focus group interviews. *Health & Quality of Life Outcomes*, 8, 1–10. doi:10.1186/1477-7525-8-5

Vaughn, S., & Klingner, J. K. (1998). Students' perceptions of inclusion and resource room settings. *Journal of Special Education*, 32, 79–88.

Vieweg, V. R., Johnston, C. H., Lanier, J. O., Fernandez, A., & Pandurangi, A. K. (2007). Correlation between high risk obesity groups and low socioeconomic status in school children. *Southern Medical Journal*, 100(1), 8–13.

Visser, S. N., Danielson, M. L., Bitsko, R. H., Holbrook, J. R., Kogan, M. D., Ghandour, R. M., . . . Blumberg, S. J. (2014). Trends in the parent-report of health care provider-diagnosed and medicated attention-deficit/hyperactivity disorder: United States, 2003–2011. *Journal of the American Academy of Child and Adolescent Psychiatry*, 53(1), 34–46. doi:10.1016/j.jaac.2013.09.001

Vorstman, J. A. S., & Ophoff, R. A. (2013). Genetic causes of developmental disorders. *Current Opinion in Neurology*, 26(2), 128–136. doi:10.1097/WCO.0b013e32835f1a30

Waldron, N. L., & McLeskey, J. (1998). The effects of an inclusive school program on students with mild and severe learning disabilities. *Exceptional Children*, 64, 395–405.

Wang, Y., & Lim, H. (2012). The global childhood obesity epidemic and the association between socio-economic status and childhood obesity. *International Review of Psychiatry*, 24(3), 176–188. doi:10.3109/09540261.2012.688195

Warren, J. R., & Saliba, J. (2012). First through eighth grade retention rates for all 50 states: A new method and initial results. *Educational Researcher*, 41(8), 320–329. doi:10.3102/0013189X12457813

Waterhouse, L. (2006). Multiple intelligences, the Mozart effect, and emotional intelligence: A critical review. *Educational Psychologist*, 41(4), 207–225. doi:10.1207/s15326985ep4104_1

Wechsler, D. (1996). *Canadian supplement manual for the WISC-III*. Toronto: Psychological Corporation.

Wechsler, D. (2003). *Wechsler Intelligence Scale for Children* (4th ed.). San Antonio, TX: Psychological Corporation.

West, T. C. (2009). *Still a freshman: Examining the prevalence and characteristics of ninth-grade retention across six states*. Baltimore: Everyone Graduates CEnter, Johns Hopkins University.

White, K. M. (2013). Associations between teacher–child relationships and children's writing in kindergarten and first grade. *Early Childhood Research Quarterly*, 28(1), 166–176. doi:10.1016/j.ecresq.2012.05.004

Wichmann, J., Wolvaardt, J. E., Maritz, C., & Voyi, K. V. V. (2009). Household conditions, eczema symptoms and rhinitis symptoms: Relationship with wheeze and severe wheeze in children living in the Polokwane area, South Africa. *Maternal & Child Health Journal*, 13(1), 107–118. doi:10.1007/s10995-007-0309-x

Wiener, J., & Mak, M. (2009). Peer victimization in children with attention-deficit/hyperactivity disorder. *Psychology in the Schools*, 46(2), 116–131.

Williams, N. A., Fournier, J., Coday, M., Richey, P. A., Tylavsky, F. A., & Hare, M. E. (2013). Body esteem, peer difficulties and perceptions of physical health in overweight and obese urban children aged 5 to 7 years. *Child: Care, Health and Development*, 39(6), 825–834. doi:10.1111/j.1365-2214.2012.01401.x

Winner, E. (1988). *The point of words: Children's understanding of metaphor and irony*. Cambridge, MA: Harvard University Press.

World Health Organization. (2009). *BMI classification*. Retrieved from http://apps.who.int/bmi/index.jsp?introPage=intro_3.html

World Health Organization. (2014). *WHO global nutrition target: Stunting policy brief*. Geneva, Switzerland: Author. Retrieved from http://www.who.int/nutrition/topics/globaltargets_stunting_policybrief.pdf?ua=1

Wu, W., West, S. G., & Hughes, J. N. (2010). Effect of grade retention in first grade on psychosocial outcomes. *Journal of Educational Psychology*, 102(1), 135–152. doi:10.1037/a0016664

Yang, S., & Sternberg, R. J. (1997). Conceptions of intelligence in ancient Chinese philosophy. *Journal of Theoretical and Philosophical Psychology*, 17(2), 101–119.

Yoakum, C. S., & Yerkes, R. M. (1920). *Army mental tests*. New York: Holt.

Zafiropoulou, M., Sotiriou, A., & Mitsiouli, V. (2007). Relation of self-concept in kindergarten and first grade to school adjustment. *Perceptual & Motor Skills*, 104(3), 1313–1327. doi:10.2466/PMS.104.4.1313-1327

Zhu, L., & Liu, G. (2007). Preschool children's understanding of illness. *Acta Psychologica Sinica*, 39(1), 96–103.

CHAPTER 10

ABC News. (2010, September 9). Same-sex adoption bill passes NSW Parliament. *ABC News*. Retrieved from http://www.abc.net.au/news/2010-09-09/same-sex-adoption-bill-passes-nsw-parliament/2255290

Aboud, F. E., Mendelson, M. J., & Purdy, K. T. (2003). Cross-race peer relations and friendship quality. *International Journal of Behavioral Development*, 27(2), 165.

Aboud, F. E., Mendelson, M. J., & Purdy, K. T. (2007). Ethnic heterogeneity of social networks and cross-ethnic friendships of elementary school boys and girls. *Merrill-Palmer Quarterly*, 53(3), 325–346.

Acs, G., & Nelson, S. (2002). *The kids alright? Children's well-being and the rise in cohabitation (New Federalism National Survey of America's Families)*. Washington, DC: Urban Institute.

Afifi, T. O., & MacMillan, H. L. (2011). Resilience following child maltreatment: A review of protective factors. *La Résilience Après La Maltraitance Clans L'enfance : Une Revue Des Facteurs Protecteurs*, 56(5), 266–272.

Ahrons, C. R. (2007). Family ties after divorce: Long-term implications for children. *Family Process*, 46(1), 53–65. doi:10.1111/j.1545-5300.2006.00191.x

Alvord, M. K., & Grados, J. J. (2005). Enhancing resilience in children: A proactive approach. *Professional Psychology: Research and Practice*, 36(3), 238–245.

Amato, P. R. (2001). Children of divorce in the 1990s: An update of the Amato and Keith (1991) meta-analysis. *Journal of Family Psychology*, 15(3), 355–370. Retrieved from http://www.ncbi.nlm.nih.gov/pubmed/11584788

Amato, P. R. (2006). Marital discord, divorce, and children's well-being: Results from a 20-year longitudinal study of two generations. In A. Clarke-Stewart & J. Dunn (Eds.), *Families count: Effects on child and adolescent development* (pp. 179–202). New York: Cambridge University Press.

Amato, P. R. (2010). Research on divorce: Continuing trends and new developments. *Journal of Marriage and Family*, 72(3), 650–666. doi:10.1111/j.1741-3737.2010.00723.x

Amato, P. R., & Anthony, C. J. (2014). Estimating the effects of parental divorce and death with fixed effects models. *Journal of Marriage and Family*, 76(2), 370–386. doi:10.1111/jomf.12100

Amato, P. R., Kane, J. B., & James, S. (2011). Reconsidering the "Good Divorce." *Family Relations*, 60(5), 511–524. doi:10.1111/j.1741-3729.2011.00666.x

Amato, P. R., & Sobolewski, J. M. (2001). The effects of divorce and marital discord on adult children's psychological well-being. *American Sociological Review*, 66, 900–921.

Amato, P. R., & Sobolewski, J. M. (2004). The effects of divorce on fathers and children: Nonresidential fathers and stepfathers. In M. E. Lamb (Ed.), *The role of the father in child development* (4th ed., pp. 341–367). Hoboken, NJ: John Wiley.

Analitis, F., Velderman, M. K., Ravens-Sieberer, U., Detmar, S., Erhart, M., Herdman, M., . . . Rajmil, L. (2009). Being bullied: Associated factors in children and adolescents 8 to 18 years old in 11 European countries. *Pediatrics, 123*(2), 569–577. doi:10.1542/peds.2008-0323

Anderssen, N., Amlie, C., & Ytterøy, E. A. (2002). Outcomes for children with lesbian or gay parents. A review of studies from 1978 to 2000. *Scandinavian Journal of Psychology, 43*(4), 335–351.

Annie E. Casey Foundation. (2014). *The 2014 kids count data book.* Baltimore: Author. Retrieved from http://www.aecf.org/resources/the-2014-kids-count-data-book/

Apperly, I. A., Samson, D., Humphreys, G. W., & Humphreys, G. W. (2009). Studies of adults can inform accounts of theory of mind development. *Developmental Psychology, 45*(1), 190–201. doi:10.1037/a0014098

Asarnow, J. R. (2011). Promoting stress resistance in war-exposed children. *Journal of the American Academy of Child & Adolescent Psychiatry, 50*(4), 320–322. doi:10.1016/j.jaac.2011.01.010

Asher, S. R., Guerry, W. B., & McDonald, K. L. (2014). Children as friends. In G. B. Melton, A. Ben-Arieh, J. Cashmore, G. S. Goodman, & N. K. Worley (Eds.), *The SAGE Handbook of Child Research* (pp. 169–194). Thousand Oaks, CA: Sage.

Babatsikos, G. (2010). Parents' knowledge, attitudes and practices about preventing child sexual abuse: A literature review. *Child Abuse Review, 19*(2), 107–129. doi:10.1002/car.1102

Batalova, J. A., & Cohen, P. N. (2002). Premarital cohabitation and housework: Couples in cross-national perspective. *Journal of Marriage and Family, 64*(3), 743–755.

Bauserman, R. (2012). A Meta-analysis of parental satisfaction, adjustment, and conflict in joint custody and sole custody following divorce. *Journal of Divorce & Remarriage, 53*(6), 464–488. doi:10.1080/10502556.2012.682901

Bauserman, R., Bos, H. M. W., van Balen, F., van den Boom, D. C., & Bauserman, R. (2002). Child adjustment in joint-custody versus sole-custody arrangements: A meta-analytic review. *Journal of Family Psychology, 16*(1), 91–102. doi:10.1037//0893-3200.16.1.91

Bennett, K. M. (2006). Does marital status and marital status change predict physical health in older adults? *Psychological Medicine, 36*(9), 1313–1320.

Berndt, T. J. (2004). Children's friendships: Shifts over a half-century in perspectives on their development and their effects. *Merrill-Palmer Quarterly, 50*(3), 138–155.

Betancourt, T. S., & Khan, K. T. (2008). The mental health of children affected by armed conflict: Protective processes and pathways to resilience. *International Review of Psychiatry, 20*(3), 317–328. doi:10.1080/09540260802090363

Bierman, K. L., Kalvin, C. B., & Heinrichs, B. S. (2014). Early childhood precursors and adolescent sequelae of grade school peer rejection and victimization. *Journal of Clinical Child & Adolescent Psychology, 44*(3), 367–379. doi:10.1080/15374416.2013.873983

Bing, N. M., Nelson, W. M., & Wesolowski, K. L. (2009). Comparing the effects of amount of conflict on children's adjustment following parental divorce. *Journal of Divorce & Remarriage, 50*(3), 159–171. doi:10.1080/10502550902717699

Blandon, A. Y., Calkins, S. D., Grimm, K. J., Keane, S. P., & O'Brien, M. (2010). Testing a developmental cascade model of emotional and social competence and early peer acceptance. *Development and Psychopathology, 22*(4), 737–748. doi:10.1017/S0954579410000428

Bos, H. M. W., & Gartrell, N. (2010). Adolescents of the USA national longitudinal lesbian family study: Can family characteristics counteract the negative effects of stigmatization? *Family Process, 49*(4), 559–572. doi:10.1111/j.1545-5300.2010.01340.x

Bos, H. M. W., Gartrell, N. K., van Balen, F., Peyser, H., & Sandfort, T. G. M. (2008). Children in planned lesbian families: A cross-cultural comparison between the United States and the Netherlands. *American Journal of Orthopsychiatry, 78*(2), 211–219. doi:10.1037/a0012711

Bos, H. M. W., & van Balen, F. (2008). Children in planned lesbian families: Stigmatisation, psychological adjustment and protective factors. *Culture, Health & Sexuality, 10*(3), 221–236. doi:10.1080/13691050701601702

Bos, H. M. W., van Balen, F., & van den Boom, D. C. (2007). Child adjustment and parenting in planned lesbian-parent families. *American Journal of Orthopsychiatry, 77*(1), 38–48.

Boseovski, J. J. (2010). Evidence for "rose-colored glasses": An examination of the positivity bias in young children's personality judgments. *Child Development Perspectives, 4*(3), 212–218. doi:10.1111/j.1750-8606.2010.00149.x

Bradley, R. H., & Corwyn, R. F. (2008). Infant temperament, parenting, and externalizing behavior in first grade: A test of the differential susceptibility hypothesis. *Journal of Child Psychology and Psychiatry, 49*(2), 124–131. doi:10.1111/j.1469-7610.2007.01829.x

Bramlett, M. D., & Blumberg, S. J. (2007). Family structure and children's physical and mental health. *Health Affairs, 26*(2), 549–558. doi:10.1377/hlthaff.26.2.549

Brassard, M. R., & Fiorvanti, C. M. (2015). School-based child abuse prevention programs. *Psychology in the Schools, 52*(1), 40–60. doi:10.1002/pits.21811

Bratberg, E., & Tjøtta, S. (2008). Income effects of divorce in families with dependent children. *Journal of Population Economics, 21*(2), 439–461. doi:10.1007/s00148-005-0029-8

Bray, J. H. (1999). From marriage to remarriage and beyond: Findings from the Developmental Issues in Stepfamilies Research Project. In E. M. Hetherington (Ed.), *Coping with divorce, single parenting, and remarriage: A risk and resiliency perspective* (pp. 295–319). Mahwah, NJ: Lawrence Erlbaum.

Breivik, K., & Olweus, D. (2006). Adolescent's adjustment in four post-divorce family structures. *Journal of Divorce & Remarriage, 44*(3–4), 99–124. doi:10.1300/J087v44n03_07

Brennan, M. A. (2008). Conceptualizing resiliency: An interactional perspective for community and youth development. *Child Care in Practice, 14*(1), 55–64. doi:10.1080/13575270701733732

Brenner, J. R., & Hyde, J. S. (2006). Parental divorce and mother-child interaction. *Journal of Divorce & Remarriage, 45*(3–4), 93–108. doi:10.1300/J087v45n03-05

Bryant, B. K. (1982). Sibling relationships in middle childhood. In M. E. Lamb & B. Sutton-Smith (Eds.), *Sibling relationships: Their nature and significance across the lifespan* (pp. 87–121). New York: Psychology Press.

Bryant, W. K., & Zick, C. D. (1995). An examination of parent-child shared time. *Journal of Marriage and Family, 58*(1), 227–237. Retrieved from http://eric.ed.gov/?id=EJ529055

Buchanan, C. M., Maccoby, E. E., & Dornbusch, S. (1992). Adolescents and their families after divorce: Three residential arrangements compared. *Journal of Research on Adolescence, 2*, 261–291.

Buhrmester, D. (1998). Need fulfillment, interpersonal competence, and the developmental contexts of early adolescent friendship. In W. M. Bukowski, A. F. Newcomb, & W. W. Hartup (Eds.), *The company they keep: Friendship in childhood and adolescence* (pp. 158–185). New York: Cambridge University Press.

Bumpus, M. F., & Hill, L. G. (2008). Secrecy and parent-child communication during middle childhood: Associations with parental knowledge and child adjustment. *Parenting: Science & Practice, 8*(2), 93–116. doi:10.1080/15295190802058868

Burkitt, L. (2014, November 7). China's changed one-child policy doesn't give baby boost. *Wall Street Journal.* Retrieved from http://www.wsj.com/articles/chinas-changed-one-child-policy-doesnt-give-baby-boost-1415359577

Burnham, J. J. (2005). Fears of children in the United States: An examination of the American fear survey schedule with 20 new contemporary fear items. *Measurement and Evaluation in Counseling and Development, 38*(2), 78. Retrieved from http://eric.ed.gov/?id=EJ750115

Burnham, J. J. (2009). Contemporary fears of children and adolescents: Coping and resiliency in the 21st century. *Journal of Counseling & Development, 87*(1), 28–35.

Burnham, J. J., Lomax, R. G., & Hooper, L. M. (2012). Gender, age, and racial differences in self-reported fears among school-aged youth. *Journal of Child and Family Studies, 22*(2), 268–278. doi:10.1007/s10826-012-9576-2

Butler, R. (1998). Age trends in the use of social and temporal comparison for self-evaluation: Examination of a novel developmental hypothesis. *Child Development, 69*, 1054–1073.

Cairns, R. B., Leung, M.-C., Buchanan, L., & Cairns, B. D. (1995). Friendships and social networks in childhood and adolescence: Fluidity, reliability, and interrelations. *Child Development, 66*, 1330–1345.

Carmody, D. P., & Lewis, M. (2006). Brain activation when hearing one's own and others' names. *Brain Research, 1116*(1), 153–158. doi:10.1016/j.brainres.2006.07.121

Catani, C., Gewirtz, A. H., Wieling, E., Schauer, E., Elbert, T., & Neuner, F. (2010). Tsunami, war, and cumulative risk in the lives of Sri Lankan schoolchildren. *Child Development, 81*(4), 1176–1191. doi:10.1111/j.1467-8624.2010.01461.x

Champion, K. M., & Clay, D. L. (2007). Individual differences in responses to provocation and frequent victimization by peers. *Child Psychiatry & Human Development, 37*(3), 205–220. doi:10.1007/s10578-006-0030-9

Chao, R. K., & Aque, C. (2009). Interpretations of parental control by Asian immigrant and European American youth. *Journal of Family Psychology, 23*(3), 342–354. doi:10.1037/a0015828

Chen, X., Rubin, K. H., & Li, B. (1994). Only children and sibling children in urban China: A re-examination. *International Journal of Behavioral Development, 17*(3), 413–421.

Child Trends. (2013). *Measures of flourishing.* Retrieved from http://www.childtrends.org/?indicators=measures-of-flourishing#sthash.ODuubJhm.dpuf

Child Trends Data Bank. (2014). *Family structure.* Bethesda, MD: Author. Retrieved from http://www.childtrends.org/?indicators=family-structure

Chiu, L.-H. H. (1992). Self-esteem in American and Chinese (Taiwanese) children. *Current Psychology: Research and Reviews, 11*, 309–313.

Cicchetti, D. (2010). Resilience under conditions of extreme stress: A multilevel perspective. *World Psychiatry, 9*(3), 145–154. doi:10.1002/j.2051-5545.2010.tb00297.x

Cicirelli, V. G. (1994). Sibling relationships in cross-cultural perspective. *Journal of Marriage and Family, 56*, 7–20.

Clark, R. E., Clark, J. F., & Adamec, C. A. (2007). *The encyclopedia of child abuse.* New York: Infobase Publishing. Retrieved from https://books.google.com/books?id=Dl4Qm54Km7YC&pgis=1

Clarke-Stewart, A., & Brentano, C. (2006). *Divorce: Causes and consequences.* New Haven, CT: Yale University Press.

Collins, W. A., Madsen, S. D., & Susman-Stillman, A. (2002). Parenting during middle childhood. In M. H. Bornstein (Ed.), *Handbook of parenting: Vol. 1* (2nd ed., pp. 73–101). Mahwah, NJ: Lawrence Erlbaum.

Cook, C. R., Williams, K. R., Guerra, N. G., & Kim, T. (2010). Variability in the prevalence of bullying and victimization: A cross-national and methodological analysis. In S. M. S. S. R. Jimerson & & D. L. Espelage (Eds.), *Handbook of bullying in schools: An international perspective* (pp. 347– 362). New York: Routledge.

Copeland, W. E., Wolke, D., Angold, A., & Costello, E. J. (2013). Adult psychiatric outcomes of bullying and being bullied by peers in childhood and adolescence. *JAMA Psychiatry, 70*(4), 419–426. doi:10.1001/jamapsychiatry.2013.504

Copen, C. E., Daniels, K., & Mosher, W. D. (2013). First premarital cohabitation in the United States: 2006–2010 National Survey of Family Growth. *National Health Statistics Reports, 64.*

Copen, C. E., Daniels, K., Vespa, J., & Mosher, W. D. (2012). First marriages in the United States: Data from the 2006–2010 National Survey of Family Growth. *National Health Statistics Reports, 49.* Retrieved from http://www.cdc.gov/nchs/data/nhsr/nhsr049.pdf#x2013

Coplan, R. J., Rose-Krasnor, L., Weeks, M., Kingsbury, A., Kingsbury, M., & Bullock, A. (2013). Alone is a crowd: Social motivations, social withdrawal, and socioemotional functioning in later childhood. *Developmental Psychology, 49*(5), 861–875.

Cornell, D., & Limber, S. P. (2015). Law and policy on the concept of bullying at school. *The American Psychologist, 70*(4), 333–343. doi:10.1037/a0038558

Crowl, A., Ahn, S., & Baker, J. (2008). A meta-analysis of developmental outcomes for children of same-sex and heterosexual parents. *Journal of GLBT Family Studies, 4*(3), 385–407.

Cummings, E. M., Goeke-Morey, M. C., Merrilees, C. E., Taylor, L. K., & Shirlow, P. (2014). A social-ecological, process-oriented perspective on political violence and child development. *Child Development Perspectives, 8*(2), 82–89. doi:10.1111/cdep.12067

Cummings, E. M., Goeke-Morey, M. C., & Papp, L. M. (2001). Couple conflict, children, and families: It's not just you and me, babe. In A. Booth, A. C. Crouter, & M. L. Clements (Eds.), *Couples in conflict* (pp. 117–147). Mahwah, NJ: Lawrence Erlbaum.

Damon, W. (1977). *The social world of the child.* San Francisco: Jossey-Bass.

Damon, W., & Hart, D. (1988). *Self-understanding in childhood and adolescence.* New York: Cambridge University Press.

Davidson, R. D., O'Hara, K. L., & Beck, C. J. A. (2014). Psychological and biological processes in children associated with high conflict parental divorce. *Juvenile and Family Court Journal, 65*(1), 29–44. doi:10.1111/jfcj.12015

Davies, P., & Martin, M. (2014). Children's coping and adjustment in high-conflict homes: The reformulation of emotional security theory. *Child Development Perspectives, 8*(4), 242–249. doi:10.1111/cdep.12094

Davies, P. T., & Lindsay, L. L. (2001). Does gender moderate the effects of marital conflict on children? In J. H. Gruch & F. D. Fincham (Eds.), *Interparental conflict and child development* (pp. 64–97). New York: Cambridge University Press.

Davis-Kean, P. E., Jager, J., & Andrew Collins, W. (2009). The self in action: An emerging link between self-beliefs and behaviors in middle childhood. *Child Development Perspectives, 3*(3), 184–188. doi:10.1111/j.1750-8606.2009.00104.x

Demaray, M. K., Malecki, C. K., & DeLong, L. K. (2006). Support in the lives of aggressive students, their victims, and their peers. In S. R. Jimerson & M. Furlong (Eds.), *Handbook of school violence and school safety: From research to practice* (pp. 21–29). Mahwah, NJ: Lawrence Erlbaum.

DeNavas-Walt, C., & Proctor, B. D. (2014). *Income and poverty in the United States: 2013.* Washington, DC. Retrieved from http://www.census.gov/hhes/www/poverty/data/incpovhlth/2013/

Denissen, J. J. A., Zarrett, N. R., & Eccles, J. S. (2007). I like to do it, I'm able, and I know I am: Longitudinal couplings between domain-specific achievement, self-concept, and interest. *Child Development, 78*(2), 430–447.

DeRosier, M. E., & Mercer, S. H. (2009). Perceived behavioral atypicality as a predictor of social rejection and peer victimization: Implications for emotional adjustment and academic achievement. *Psychology in the Schools, 46*(4), 375–387.

Dill, E. J., Vernberg, E. M., Fonagy, P., Twemlow, S. W., & Gamm, B. K. (2004). Negative affect in victimized children: The roles of social withdrawal, peer rejection, and attitudes towards bullying. *Journal of Abnormal Child Psychology, 32*(2), 159–173.

Dixon, S. V., Graber, J. A., & Brooks-Gunn, J. (2008). The roles of respect for parental authority and parenting practices in parent-child conflict among African American, Latino, and European American families. *Journal of Family Psychology, 22*(1), 1–10. doi:10.1037/0893-3200.22.1.1

Domhardt, M., Münzer, A., Fegert, J. M., & Goldbeck, L. (2014). Resilience in survivors of child sexual abuse: A systematic review of the literature. *Trauma, Violence & Abuse, 16,* 476–493. doi:10.1177/1524838014557288

Doodson, L., & Morley, D. (2006). Understanding the roles of non-residential stepmothers. *Journal of Divorce & Remarriage, 45*(3–4), 109–130. doi:10.1300/J087v45n03-06

Downey, D. B. (1994). The school performance of children from single-mother and single-father families: Economic or interpersonal deprivation? *Journal of Family Issues, 15*(1), 129–147. doi:10.1177/019251394015001006

Downey, D. B., & Condron, D. J. (2004). Playing well with others in kindergarten: The benefit of siblings at home. *Journal of Marriage and Family, 66,* 333–350.

Drapeau, S., Gagne, M.-H., Saint-Jacques, M.-C., Lepine, R., & Ivers, H. (2009). Post-separation conflict trajectories: A longitudinal study. *Marriage & Family Review, 45*(4), 353–373. doi:10.1080/01494920902821529

DuBois, D. L., & Hirsch, B. J. (1990). School and neighborhood friendship patterns of blacks and whites in early adolescence. *Child Development, 61,* 524–536.

Dunifon, R., & Kowaleski-Jones, L. (2002). Who's in the house? Race differences in cohabitation, single parenthood, and child development. *Child Development, 73,* 1249–1264.

Dunn, J. (1996). Sibling relationships and perceived self-competence: Patterns of stability between childhood and early adolescence. In A. J. Sameroff & M. M. Haith (Eds.), *The five to seven year shift* (pp. 253–270). Chicago: University of Chicago Press.

Dunn, J. (2002a). Sibling relationships. In P. K. Smith & C. H. Hart (Eds.), *Blackwell handbook of childhood social development* (pp. 223–237). Oxford, UK: Blackwell.

Dunn, J. (2002b). The adjustment of children in stepfamilies: Lessons from community studies. *Child & Adolescent Mental Health, 7*(4), 154–161.

Dupuis, S. (2010). Examining the blended family: The application of systems theory toward an understanding of the blended family system.

Journal of Couple & Relationship Therapy, 9(3), 239–251. doi:10.1080/15332691.2010.491784

Dusek, J. B., & McIntyre, J. G. (2003). Self-concept and self-esteem development. In G. R. Adams & M. D. Berzonsky (Eds.), *Blackwell handbooks of developmental psychology* (pp. 290–309). Malden, MA: Blackwell Publishing.

Eggebeen, D. J., Snyder, A. R., & Manning, W. D. (1996). Children in single-father families in demographic perspective. *Journal of Family Issues, 17*(4), 441–465. doi:10.1177/019251396017004002

Erikson, E. H. (1950). *Childhood and society* (2nd ed.). New York: Norton.

Erwin, P. (1998). *Friendship in childhood and adolescence.* London: Routledge.

Espelage, D. L., Low, S. K., & Jimerson, S. R. (2014). Understanding school climate, aggression, peer victimization, and bully perpetration: Contemporary science, practice, and policy. *School Psychology Quarterly, 29*(3), 233–237.

Ettekal, I., & Ladd, G. W. (2015). Developmental pathways from childhood aggression-disruptiveness, chronic peer rejection, and deviant friendships to early-adolescent rule breaking. *Child Development, 86*(2), 614–631. doi:10.1111/cdev.12321

Evans, G. W., Li, D., & Whipple, S. S. (2013). Cumulative risk and child development. *Psychological Bulletin, 139*(6), 1342–1396. doi:10.1037/a0031808

Faber, A. J., & Wittenborn, A. K. (2010). The role of attachment in children's adjustment to divorce and remarriage. *Journal of Family Psychotherapy, 21*(2), 89–104. doi:10.1080/08975353.2010.483625

Fabricius, W. V, & Luecken, L. J. (2007). Postdivorce living arrangements, parent conflict, and long-term physical health correlates for children of divorce. *Journal of Family Psychology, 21*(2), 195–205.

Falbo, T., Poston, D. L. Jr., Triscari, R. S., & Zhang, X. (1997). Self-enhancing illusions among Chinese schoolchildren. *Journal of Cross-Cultural Psychology, 28,* 172–191.

Farmer, T. W., Hall, C. M., Leung, M.-C., Estell, D. B., & Brooks, D. (2011). Social prominence and the heterogeneity of rejected status in late elementary school. *School Psychology Quarterly, 26*(4), 260–274.

Farr, R. H., & Patterson, C. J. (2013). Coparenting among lesbian, gay, and heterosexual couples: Associations with adopted children's outcomes. *Child Development, 84*(4), 1226–1240. doi:10.1111/cdev.12046

Fedewa, A. L., Black, W. W., & Ahn, S. (2014). Children and adolescents with same-gender parents: A meta-analytic approach in assessing outcomes. *Journal of GLBT Family Studies, 11*(1), 1–34. doi:10.1080/1550428X.2013.869486

Feinberg, M. E., & Hetherington, E. M. (2001). Differential parenting as a within-family variable. *Journal of Family Psychology, 51,* 22–37.

Feinberg, M. E., Solmeyer, A. R., & McHale, S. M. (2012). The third rail of family systems: Sibling relationships, mental and behavioral health, and preventive intervention in childhood and adolescence. *Clinical Child and Family Psychology Review, 15*(1), 43–57. doi:10.1007/s10567-011-0104-5

Fergusson, D. M., Boden, J. M., & Horwood, L. J. (2008). Exposure to childhood sexual and physical abuse and adjustment in early adulthood. *Child Abuse & Neglect, 32*(6), 607–619. doi:10.1016/j.chiabu.2006.12.018

Fergusson, D. M., McLeod, G. F. H., & Horwood, L. J. (2013). Childhood sexual abuse and adult developmental outcomes: Findings from a 30-year longitudinal study in New Zealand. *Child Abuse & Neglect, 37*(9), 664–674. doi:10.1016/j.chiabu.2013.03.013

Finkelhor, D., Ormrod, R. K., & Turner, H. A. (2009). The developmental epidemiology of childhood victimization. *Journal of Interpersonal Violence*, 24(5), 711–731.

Finkelhor, D., Shattuck, A., Turner, H. A., & Hamby, S. L. (2014). The lifetime prevalence of child sexual abuse and sexual assault assessed in late adolescence. *The Journal of Adolescent Health*, 55(3), 329–333. doi:10.1016/j.jadohealth.2013.12.026

Fite, P. J., Hendrickson, M., Rubens, S. L., Gabrielli, J., & Evans, S. (2013). The role of peer rejection in the link between reactive aggression and academic performance. *Child & Youth Care Forum*, 42(3), 193–205. doi:10.1007/s10566-013-9199-9

Fosco, G. M., & Grych, J. H. (2008). Emotional, cognitive, and family systems mediators of children's adjustment to interparental conflict. *Journal of Family Psychology*, 22(6), 843–854. doi:10.1037/a0013809

Fossati, P., Hevenor, S. J., Graham, S. J., Grady, C., Keightley, M. L., Craik, F., & Mayberg, H. (2003). In search of the emotional self: An fMRI study using positive and negative emotional words. *American Journal of Psychiatry*, 160(11), 1938–1945.

Fryda, C. M., & Hulme, P. A. (2015). School-based childhood sexual abuse prevention programs: An integrative review. *The Journal of School Nursing*, 31(3), 167–182. doi:10.1177/1059840514544125

Ganong, L. H., & Coleman, M. (2000). Remarried families. In C. Hendrick & S. S. Hendrick (Eds.), *Close relationships* (pp. 155–168). Thousand Oaks, CA: Sage.

Gartrell, N., & Bos, H. (2010). US national longitudinal lesbian family study: Psychological adjustment of 17-year-old adolescents. *Pediatrics*, 126(1), 28–36. doi:10.1542/peds2009-3153

Gass, K., Jenkins, J., & Dunn, J. (2007). Are sibling relationships protective? A longitudinal study. *Journal of Child Psychology and Psychiatry*, 48(2), 167–175.

Gates, G. J. (2013). *LGBT parenting in the United States*. Los Angeles, CA. Retrieved from http://williamsinstitute.law.ucla.edu/wp-content/uploads/LGBT-Parenting.pdf

Gini, G., & Pozzoli, T. (2009). Association between bullying and psychosomatic problems: A meta-analysis. *Pediatrics*, 123(3), 1059–1065. doi:10.1542/peds.2008-1215

Glick, G. C., & Rose, A. J. (2011). Prospective associations between friendship adjustment and social strategies: Friendship as a context for building social skills. *Developmental Psychology*, 47(4), 1117–1132.

Goldberg, A. E., & Perry-Jenkins, M. (2007). The division of labor and perceptions of parental roles: Lesbian couples across the transition to parenthood. *Journal of Social and Personal Relationships*, 24(2), 297–318. doi:10.1177/0265407507075415

Golombok, S., Mellish, L., Jennings, S., Casey, P., Tasker, F., & Lamb, M. E. (2014). Adoptive gay father families: Parent-child relationships and children's psychological adjustment. *Child Development*, 85(2), 456–468. doi:10.1111/cdev.12155

Goodwin, P., Mosher, W., & Chandra, A. (2010). Marriage and cohabitation In the United States: A statistical portrait based on Cycle 6 (2002) of the National Survey of Family Growth. *Vital and Health Statistics*, 23(28).

Graham, S., Munniksma, A., & Juvonen, J. (2014). Psychosocial benefits of cross-ethnic friendships in urban middle schools. *Child Development*, 85(2), 469–483. doi:10.1111/cdev.12159

Greeff, A. P., & Du Toit, C. (2009). Resilience in remarried families. *American Journal of Family Therapy*, 37(2), 114–126. doi:10.1080/01926180802151919

Gullone, E., & King, N. J. (1997). Three-year follow-up of normal fear in children and adolescents aged 7 to 18 years. *British Journal of Developmental Psychology*, 15, 97–111.

Guo, L., Yang, L., Liu, Z., & Song, T. (2005). An experimental research on the formation of primary school pupils' self-confidence. *Psychological Science*, 28(5), 1068–1071.

Hakvoort, E. M., Bos, H. M. W., van Balen, F., & Hermanns, J. M. A. (2010). Family relationships and the psychosocial adjustment of school-aged children in intact families. *Journal of Genetic Psychology*, 171(2), 182–201.

Hakvoort, E. M., Bos, H. M. W., Van Balen, F., & Hermanns, J. M. A. (2011). Postdivorce relationships in families and children's psychosocial adjustment. *Journal of Divorce & Remarriage*, 52(2), 125–146. doi:10.1080/10502556.2011.546243

Harold, G. T., Aitken, J. J., & Shelton, K. H. (2007). Inter-parental conflict and children's academic attainment: A longitudinal analysis. *Journal of Child Psychology and Psychiatry and Allied Disciplines*, 48, 1223–1232.

Harper, S., & Ruicheva, I. (2010). Grandmothers as replacement parents and partners: The role of grandmotherhood in single parent families. *Journal of Intergenerational Relationships*, 8(3), 219–233. doi:10.1080/15350770.2010.498779

Harrist, A. W., Zaia, A. F., Bates, J. E., Dodge, K. A., & Pettit, G. S. (1997). Subtypes of social withdrawal in early childhood: Sociometric status and social-cognitive differences across four years. *Child Development*, 68, 278–294.

Hart, C. H., Yang, C., Nelson, L. J., Robinson, C. C., Olsen, J. A., Nelson, D. A., . . . Wu, P. (2000). Peer acceptance in early childhood and subtypes of socially withdrawn behavior in China, Russia, and the Unites States. *International Journal of Behavioral Development*, 24, 73–81.

Hart, D., Atkins, R., & Tursi, N. (2006). Origins and developmental influences on self-esteem. In M. H. Kernis (Ed.), *Self-esteem issues and answers: A sourcebook of current perspectives* (pp. 157–162). New York: Psychology Press.

Harter, S. (1996). Developmental changes in self-understanding across the 5 to 7 shift. In A. J. Sameroff & M. M. Haith (Eds.), *The five to seven year shift* (pp. 207–236). Chicago: University of Chicago Press.

Harter, S. (2003). The development of self-representations during childhood and adolescence. In M. R. Leary & J. P. Tangney (Eds.), *Handbook of self and identity* (pp. 610–642). New York: Guilford Press.

Harter, S. (2006). Developmental and individual difference perspectives on self-esteem. In D. K. Mroczek & T. D. Little (Eds.), *Handbook of personality development* (pp. 311–334). Mahwah, NJ: Lawrence Erlbaum.

Harter, S. (2012). *The construction of the self: Developmental and sociocultural foundations* (2nd ed.). New York: Guilford Press.

Hartup, W. W. (2006). Relationships in early and middle childhood. In A. L. Vangelisti & D. Perlman (Eds.), *The Cambridge handbook of personal relationships* (pp. 177–190). New York: Cambridge University Press.

Hartup, W. W., & Abecassis, M. (2002). Friends and enemies. In P. K. Smith & C. H. Hart (Eds.), *Blackwell handbook of childhood social development* (pp. 286–306). Malden, MA: Blackwell Publishing.

Hartup, W. W., & Stevens, N. (1999). Friendships and adaptation across the life span. *Current Directions in Psychological Science*, 8, 76–79.

Havik, T., Bru, E., & Ertesvåg, S. K. (2013). Parental perspectives of the role of school factors in school refusal. *Emotional and Behavioural Difficulties*, 19(2), 131–153. doi:10.1080/13632752.2013.816199

Hawkins, J. N. (1994). Issues of motivation in Asian education. In H. F. O'Neil Jr. & M. Drillings (Eds.), *Motivation: Theory and research* (pp. 101–115). Hillsdale, NJ: Lawrence Erlbaum.

Heine, S. J., & Lehman, D. R. (1995). Cultural variation in unrealistic optimism: Does the West feel more invulnerable than the East? *Journal of Personality and Social Psychology*, 68, 595–607.

Hektner, J. M., August, G. J., & Realmuto, G. M. (2000). Patterns and temporal changes in peer affiliation among aggressive and nonaggressive children participating in a summer school program. *Journal of Clinical Child Psychology*, 29, 603–614.

Hennon, C. B., Hildenbrand, B., & Schedle, A. (2008). Stepfamilies and children. In T. P. Gullotta & G. M. Blau (Eds.), *Family influences on childhood behavior and development: Evidence-based prevention and treatment approaches* (pp. 161–185). New York: Routledge/Taylor & Francis Group.

Herrenkohl, T. I., Hong, S., Klika, J. B., Herrenkohl, R. C., & Russo, M. J. (2013). Developmental impacts of child abuse and neglect related to adult mental health, substance use, and physical health. *Journal of Family Violence*, 28(2). doi:10.1007/s10896-012-9474-9

Hetherington, E. M., Bridges, M., & Insabella, G. M. (1998). What matters? What does not? Five perspectives on the association between marital transitions and children's adjustment. *American Psychologist*, 53, 167–184.

Hetherington, E. M., & Elmore, A. M. (2004). The intergenerational transmission of couple instability. In P. L. Chase-Lansdale, K. Kiernan, & R. J. Friedman (Eds.), *Human development across lives and generations: The potential for change* (pp. 171–203). New York: Cambridge University Press.

Heyman, G. D., & Gelman, S. A. (2000). Beliefs about the origins of human psychological traits. *Developmental Psychology*, 36, 663–678.

Hilarski, C. (2008). Child and adolescent sexual abuse. In C. Hilarski, J. S. Wodarski, & M. D. Feit (Eds.), *Handbook of social work in child and adolescent sexual abuse* (pp. 29–50). New York: Haworth Press/Taylor & Francis Group.

Hill, N. E., Bush, K. R., & Roosa, M. W. (2003). Parenting and socialization strategies and children's mental health: Low-income Mexican-American and Euro-American mothers and children. *Child Development*, 74, 189–204.

Hinduja, S., & Patchin, J. (2015). *State cyberbullying laws: A brief review of state cyberbullying laws and policies*. Retrieved from http://www.cyberbullying.us/Bullying-and-Cyberbullying-Laws.pdf

Hinkelman, L., & Bruno, M. (2008). Identification and reporting of child sexual abuse: The role of elementary school professionals. *Elementary School Journal*, 108(5), 376–391.

Hofferth, S. L., & Sandberg, J. F. (2001). How American children spend their time. *Journal of Marriage and Family*, 63(2), 295–308. doi:10.1111/j.1741-3737.2001.00295.x

Holliday, K. (2014, October 21). China to ease 1-child rule further, but do people care? *CNBC News*. Retrieved from http://www.cnbc.com/id/102104640#

Holt, M. K., Kaufman Kantor, G., & Finkelhor, D. (2009). Parent/child concordance about bullying involvement and family characteristics related to bullying and peer victimization. *Journal of School Violence*, 8(1), 42–63. doi:10.1080/15388220802067813

Homma, Y., Wang, N., Saewyc, E., & Kishor, N. (2012). The relationship between sexual abuse and risky sexual behavior among adolescent boys: A meta-analysis. *The Journal of Adolescent Health*, 51(1), 18–24. doi:10.1016/j.jadohealth.2011.12.032

Huffington Post. (2013, June 3). *6 Most LGBT-Friendly Countries In Latin America.* Retrieved from http://www.huffingtonpost.com/2013/06/03/lgbt-friendly-latin-america_n_3378373.html

International Lesbian, Gay, Bisexual, Trans and Intersex Association-Europe. (2013). *Austria becomes the 14th European country to allow same-sex second-parent adoption.* Retrieved from http://www.ilga-europe.org/home/guide_europe/country_by_country/austria/austria_second_parent_adoption_13th

Irish, L., Kobayashi, I., & Delahanty, D. L. (2010). Long-term physical health consequences of childhood sexual abuse: A meta-analytic review. *Journal of Pediatric Psychology, 35*(5), 450–461. doi:10.1093/jpepsy/jsp118

Jacobs, J. E., Lanza, S., Osgood, D. W., Eccles, J. S., & Wigfield, A. (2002). Changes in children's self-competence and values: Gender and domain differences across grades one through twelve. *Child Development, 73,* 509–527.

Jaeger, M. M. (2012). The extended family and children's educational success. *American Sociological Review, 77*(6), 903–922. doi:10.1177/0003122412464040

Jayakody, R., & Kalil, A. (2002). Social fathering in low-income, African American families with preschool children. *Journal of Marriage and Family, 64,* 504–516.

Ji-Yeon, K., McHale, S. M., Crouter, A. C., & Osgood, D. W. (2007). Longitudinal linkages between sibling relationships and adjustment from middle childhood through adolescence. *Developmental Psychology, 43*(4), 960–973.

Jones, D. J., Lewis, T., Litrownik, A., Thompson, R., Proctor, L. J., Isbell, P., . . . Runyan, D. (2013). Linking childhood sexual abuse and early adolescent risk behavior: The intervening role of internalizing and externalizing problems. *Journal of Abnormal Child Psychology, 41*(1), 139–150. doi:10.1007/s10802-012-9656-1

Juvonen, J., & Graham, S. (2014). Bullying in schools: The power of bullies and the plight of victims. *Annual Review of Psychology, 65,* 159–185. doi:10.1146/annurev-psych-010213-115030

Kaplow, J. B., & Widom, C. S. (2007). Age of onset of child maltreatment predicts long-term mental health outcomes. *Journal of Abnormal Psychology, 116,* 176–187.

Kärnä, A., Voeten, M., Poskiparta, E., & Salmivalli, C. (2010). Vulnerable children in varying classroom contexts: Bystanders' behaviors moderate the effects of risk factors on victimization. *Merrill-Palmer Quarterly, 56*(3), 261–282.

Kawabata, Y., & Crick, N. R. (2011). The significance of cross-racial/ethnic friendships: Associations with peer victimization, peer support, sociometric status, and classroom diversity. *Developmental Psychology, 47*(6), 1763–1775. doi:10.1037/a0025399

Kawabata, Y., Crick, N. R., & Hamaguchi, Y. (2010). The role of culture in relational aggression: Associations with social-psychological adjustment problems in Japanese and U.S. school-aged children. *International Journal of Behavioral Development, 34*(4), 354–362. doi:10.1177/0165025409339151

Kearney, C. A. (2001). *School refusal behavior in youth: A functional approach to assessment and treatment.* Washington, DC: American Psychological Association.

Kearney, C. A. (2008). School absenteeism and school refusal behavior in youth: A contemporary review. *Clinical Psychology Review, 28*(3), 451–471. doi:10.1016/j.cpr.2007.07.012

Kearney, C. A., & Roblek, T. L. (1998). Parent training in the treatment of school refusal behavior. In J. M. Briesmeister & C. E. Schaefer (Eds.), *Handbook of parent training: Parents as co-therapists for children's behavior problems* (2nd ed., pp. 225–256). Hoboken, NJ: John Wiley.

Keijsers, L., Loeber, R., Branje, S., & Meeus, W. H. J. (2011). Bidirectional links and concurrent development of parent-child relationships and boys' offending behavior. *Journal of Abnormal Psychology, 120,* 878–889. doi:10.1037/a0024588

Kelly, J. B. (2007). Children's living arrangements following separation and divorce: Insights from empirical and clinical research. *Family Process, 46*(1), 35–52.

Kendall-Tackett, K. A., Williams, L. M., & Finkelhor, D. (1993). The impact of sexual abuse on children: A review and synthesis of recent empirical studies. *Psychological Bulletin, 113*(1), 164–180.

Kendig, S. M., & Bianchi, S. M. (2008). Single, cohabitating, and married mothers' time with children. *Journal of Marriage & Family, 70*(5), 1228–1240. doi:10.1111/j.1741-3737.2008.00562.x

Kennedy, S., & Bumpass, L. (2008). Cohabitation and children's living arrangements: New estimates from the United States. *Demographic Research, 19,* 1663–1692.

Kennedy, S., & Fitch, C. A. (2012). Measuring cohabitation and family structure in the United States: Assessing the impact of new data from the Current Population Survey. *Demography, 49*(4), 1479–1498. doi:10.1007/s13524-012-0126-8

Kenny, M. C., Capri, V., Thakkar-Kolar, R. R., Ryan, E. E., & Runyon, M. (2008). Child sexual abuse: From prevention to self-protection. *Child Abuse Review, 17*(1), 36–54.

Kenny, M. C., & McEachern, A. (2009). Children's self-concept: A multicultural comparison. *Professional School Counseling, 12*(3), 207–212.

Kiernan, K. (2002). Cohabitation in Western Europe: Trends, issues, and implications. In A. Booth & A. C. Crouter (Eds.), *Just living together: Implications of cohabitation on families, children, and social policy* (pp. 3–31). Mahwah, NJ: Lawrence Erlbaum.

Killen, M., Kelly, M., Richardson, C., Crystal, D., & Ruck, M. (2010). European-American children's and adolescents' evaluations of interracial exclusion. *Group Processes & Intergroup Relations, 13*(3), 283–300. doi:10.1177/1368430209346700

Kim-Cohen, J. (2007). Resilience and developmental psychopathology. *Child and Adolescent Psychiatric Clinics of North America, 16*(2), 271–283.

King, N. J., & Bernstein, G. A. (2001). School refusal in children and adolescents: A review of the past 10 years. *Journal of the American Academy of Child and Adolescent Psychiatry, 40*(2), 197–205.

King, V. (2007). When children have two mothers: Relationships with nonresident mothers, stepmothers, and fathers. *Journal of Marriage & Family, 69*(5), 1178–1193.

Klima, T., & Repetti, R. L. (2008). Children's peer relations and their psychological adjustment: Differences between close friendships and the larger peer group. *Merrill-Palmer Quarterly, 54*(2), 151–178.

Klomek, A. B., Sourander, A., Kumpulainen, K., Piha, J., Tamminen, T., Moilanen, I., . . . Gould, M. S. (2008). Childhood bullying as a risk for later depression and suicidal ideation among Finnish males. *Journal of Affective Disorders, 109*(1–2), 47–55. doi:10.1016/j.jad.2007.12.226

Kowaz, A. M., & Marcia, J. E. (1991). Development and validation of a measure of Eriksonian industry. *Journal of Personality and Social Psychology, 60*(3), 390–397. doi:10.1037/0022-3514.60.3.390

Kramer, L. (2010). The essential ingredients of successful sibling relationships: An emerging framework for advancing theory and practice. *Child Development Perspectives, 4*(2), 80–86. doi:10.1111/j.1750-8606.2010.00122.x

Kumpulainen, K., & Räsänen, E. (2000). Children involved in bullying at elementary school age: Their psychiatric symptoms and deviance in adolescence: An epidemiological sample. *Child Abuse & Neglect, 24*(12), 1567–1577.

Ladd, G. W. (1999). Peer relationships and social competence during early and middle childhood. *Annual Review of Psychology, 50,* 333–359. doi:10.1146/annurev.psych.50.1.333

Ladd, G. W., & Burgess, K. B. (2003). Charting the relationship trajectories of aggressive, withdrawn, and aggressive/withdrawn children during early grade school. In M. E. Hertzig & E. A. Farber (Eds.), *Annual progress in child psychiatry and child development: 2000-2001* (pp. 535–570). New York: Brunner-Routledge.

Ladd, G. W., & Troop-Gordon, W. (2003). The role of chronic peer difficulties in the development of children's psychological adjustment problems. *Child Development, 74*(5), 1344–1367.

LaFontana, K. M., & Cillessen, A. H. N. (2002). Children's perceptions of popular and unpopular peers: A multimethod assessment. *Developmental Psychology, 38*(5), 635–647.

LaFontana, K. M., & Cillessen, A. H. N. (2010). Developmental changes in the priority of perceived status in childhood and adolescence. *Social Development, 19*(1), 130–147. doi:10.1111/j.1467-9507.2008.00522.x

Laible, D., McGinley, M., Carlo, G., Augustine, M., & Murphy, T. (2014). Does engaging in prosocial behavior make children see the world through rose-colored glasses? *Developmental Psychology, 50*(3), 872–880.

Lamb, M. E. (2012). Mothers, fathers, families, and circumstances: Factors affecting children's adjustment. *Applied Developmental Science, 16*(2), 98–111. doi:10.1080/10888691.2012.667344

Lansford, J. E. (2009). Parental divorce and children's adjustment. *Perspectives on Psychological Science, 4*(2), 140–152. doi:10.1111/j.1745-6924.2009.01114.x

Lansford, J. E. (2014). Parenting across cultures. In H. Selin (Ed.), *Parenting across cultures* (Vol. 7, pp. 445–458). Dordrecht: Springer Netherlands. doi:10.1007/978-94-007-7503-9

Lansford, J. E., Malone, P. S., Dodge, K. A., Pettit, G. S., & Bates, J. E. (2010). Developmental cascades of peer rejection, social information processing biases, and aggression during middle childhood. *Development & Psychopathology, 22*(3), 593–602. doi:10.1017/S0954579410000301

Lansford, J. E., Staples, A. D., Bates, J. E., Pettit, G. S., & Dodge, K. A. (2013). Trajectories of mothers' discipline strategies and interparental conflict: Interrelated change during middle childhood. *Journal of Family Communication, 13*(3), 178–195. doi:10.1080/15267431.2013.796947

Laursen, B., & Hartup, W. W. (2002). The origins of reciprocity and social exchange in friendships. *New Directions for Child and Adolescent Development, 2002*(95), 27–40.

Lee, L., Howes, C., & Chamberlain, B. (2007). Ethnic heterogeneity of social networks and cross-ethnic friendships of elementary school boys and girls. *Merrill-Palmer Quarterly, 53*(3), 325–346.

Lee, T., Kwong, W., Cheung, C., Ungar, M., & Cheung, M. (2010). Children's resilience-related beliefs as a predictor of positive child development in the face of adversities: Implications for interventions to enhance children's quality of life. *Social Indicators Research, 95*(3), 437–453. doi:10.1007/s11205-009-9530-x

Lewis, M., & Carmody, D. P. (2008). Self-representation and brain development. *Developmental Psychology, 44*(5), 1329–1334. doi:10.1037/a0012681

Limber, S. P., & Small, M. A. (2003). State laws and policies to address bullying in schools. *School Psychology Review, 32*(3), 445–455.

Liu, F. (2006). Boys as only-children and girls as only-children—Parental gendered expectations of the only-child in the nuclear Chinese family in present-day China. *Gender & Education*, 18(5), 491–505.

Livingston, G. (2013). *The rise of single fathers*. Washington, DC. Retrieved from http://www.pewsocialtrends.org/2013/07/02/the-rise-of-single-fathers

Lleras, C. (2008). Employment, work conditions, and the home environment in single-mother families. *Journal of Family Issues*, 29(10), 1268–1297.

Luthar, S. S. (2006). Resilience in development: A synthesis of research across five decades. In D. Cicchetti & D. J. Cohen (Eds.), *Developmental psychopathology, Vol 3: Risk, disorder, and adaptation* (2nd ed., pp. 739–795). Hoboken, NJ: John Wiley.

Lynch, M., & Cicchetti, D. (1998). An ecological-transactional analysis of children and contexts: The longitudinal interplay among child maltreatment, community violence, and children's symptomatology. *Development and Psychopathology*, 10, 235–257.

Maccoby, E. E., & Mnookin, R. H. (1992). *Dividing the child: Social and legal dilemmas of custody*. Cambridge, MA: Harvard University Press.

Macrae, C. N., Moran, J. M., Heatherton, T. F., Banfield, J. F., & Kelley, W. M. (2004). Medial prefrontal activity predicts memory for self. *Cerebral Cortex*, 14(6), 647–654. doi:10.1093/cercor/bhh025

Maikovich-Fong, A. K., & Jaffee, S. R. (2010). Sex differences in childhood sexual abuse characteristics and victims' emotional and behavioral problems: Findings from a national sample of youth. *Child Abuse & Neglect*, 34(6), 429–437. doi:10.1016/j.chiabu.2009.10.006

Malone, P. S., Lansford, J. E., Castellino, D. R., Berlin, L. J., Dodge, K. A., Bates, J. E., & Pettit, G. S. (2004). Divorce and child behavior problems: Applying latent change score models to life event data. *Structural Equation Modeling: A Multidisciplinary Journal*, 11(3), 401–423. doi:10.1207/s15328007sem1103_6

Maniglio, R. (2011). The role of child sexual abuse in the etiology of substance-related disorders. *Journal of Addictive Diseases*, 30(3), 216–228. doi:10.1080/10550887.2011.581987

Maniglio, R. (2013). Child sexual abuse in the etiology of anxiety disorders: A systematic review of reviews. *Trauma, Violence & Abuse*, 14(2), 96–112. doi:10.1177/1524838012470032

Manning, W. D. (2006). Cohabitation and child well-being. *Gender Issues*, 23(3), 21–34.

Manning, W. D., & Brown, S. (2006). Children's economic well-being in married and cohabiting parent families. *Journal of Marriage & Family*, 68(2), 345–362.

Manning, W. D., & Lichter, D. (1996). Parental cohabitation and children's economic well-being. *Journal of Marriage and the Family*, 58, 998–1010.

Maric, M., Heyne, D. A., MacKinnon, D. P., van Widenfelt, B. M., & Westenberg, P. M. (2013). Cognitive mediation of cognitive-behavioural therapy outcomes for anxiety-based school refusal. *Behavioural and Cognitive Psychotherapy*, 41(5), 549–564. doi:10.1017/S1352465812000756

Marks, A. K., Szalacha, L. A., Lamarre, M., Boyd, M. J., & Coll, C. G. (2007). Emerging ethnic identity and interethnic group social preferences in middle childhood: Findings from the Children of Immigrants Development in Context (CIDC) study. *International Journal of Behavioral Development*, 31(5), 501–513.

Marriott, C., Hamilton-Giachritsis, C., & Harrop, C. (2014). Factors promoting resilience following childhood sexual abuse: A structured, narrative review of the literature. *Child Abuse Review*, 23(1), 17–34. doi:10.1002/car.2258

Masten, A. S. (2011). Resilience in children threatened by extreme adversity: Frameworks for research, practice, and translational synergy. *Development and Psychopathology*, 23(2), 493–506. doi:10.1017/s0954579411000198

Masten, A. S. (2014). Global perspectives on resilience in children and youth. *Child Development*, 85(1), 6–20. doi:10.1111/cdev.12205

Masten, A. S., Best, K., & Garmezy, N. (1990). Resilience and development: Contributions from the study of children who overcome adversity. *Development and Psychopathology*, 2, 425–444.

Masten, A. S., & Coatsworth, J. D. (1998). The development of competence in favorable and unfavorable environments: Lessons from research on successful children. *American Psychologist*, 53, 205–220.

Masten, A. S., & Monn, A. R. (2015). Child and family resilience: A call for integrated science, practice, and professional training. *Family Relations*, 64(1), 5–21. doi:10.1111/fare.12103

Masten, A. S., & Narayan, A. J. (2012). Child development in the context of disaster, war, and terrorism: Pathways of risk and resilience. *Annual Review of Psychology*, 63, 227–257. doi:10.1146/annurev-psych-120710-100356

McCoy, M. L., & Keen, S. M. (2009). *Child abuse and neglect*. New York: Psychology Press.

McDonald, K. L., Dashiell-Aje, E., Menzer, M. M., Rubin, K. H., Oh, W., & Bowker, J. C. (2013). Contributions of racial and sociobehavioral homophily to friendship stability and quality among same-race and cross-race friends. *The Journal of Early Adolescence*, 33(7), 897–919. doi:10.1177/0272431612472259

McDougall, P., & Vaillancourt, T. (2015). Long-term adult outcomes of peer victimization in childhood and adolescence: Pathways to adjustment and maladjustment. *American Psychologist*, 70(4), 300–310. doi:10.1037/a0039174

McGlothlin, H., & Killen, M. (2006). Intergroup attitudes of European American children attending ethnically homogeneous schools. *Child Development*, 77(5), 1375–1386.

McGlothlin, H., Killen, M., & Edmonds, C. (2005). European-American children's intergroup attitudes about peer relationships. *British Journal of Developmental Psychology*, 23(2), 227–249. doi:10.1348/026151005x26101

McGuire, S., & Shanahan, L. (2010). Sibling experiences in diverse family contexts. *Child Development Perspectives*, 4(2), 72–79. doi:10.1111/j.1750-8606.2010.00121.x

McHale, S. M., Updegraff, K. A., & Whiteman, S. D. (2012). Sibling relationships and influences in childhood and adolescence. *Journal of Marriage and the Family*, 74(5), 913–930. Retrieved from http://www.pubmedcentral.nih.gov/articlerender.fcgi?artid=3956653&tool=pmcentrez&rendertype=abstract

McLoughlin, C. S. (2005). The coming-of-age of China's single-child policy. *Psychology in the Schools*, 42(3), 305–313. doi:10.1002/pits.20081

Melvin, G. A., & Tonge, B. J. (2012). School refusal. In P. Sturmey & M. Hersen (Eds.), *Handbook of evidence-based practice in clinical psychology*. Hoboken, NJ: John Wiley.

Mensah, K., & Fine, M. (2008). Divorce and children. In T. P. Gullotta & G. M. Blau (Eds.), *Family influences on childhood behavior and development: Evidence-based prevention and treatment approaches* (pp. 143–160). New York: Routledge/Taylor & Francis Group.

Menting, B., Koot, H., & van Lier, P. (2014). Peer acceptance and the development of emotional and behavioural problems: Results from a preventive intervention study. *International Journal of Behavioral Development*. Advance online publication. doi:10.1177/0165025414558853

Menting, B., van Lier, P. A. C., & Koot, H. M. (2011). Language skills, peer rejection, and the development of externalizing behavior from kindergarten to fourth grade. *Journal of Child Psychology and Psychiatry*, 52(1), 72–79. doi:10.1111/j.1469-7610.2010.02279.x

Morgos, D., Worden, J. W., & Gupta, L. (2007). Psychosocial effects of war experiences among displaced children in Southern Darfur. *Omega: Journal of Death & Dying*, 56(3), 229–253. doi:10.2190/OM.56.3.b

Morrison, D. R. (1998). The costs of economic uncertainty: Child well-being in cohabitating and remarried unions following parental divorce. In *Annual Meeting of the Population Association of America*. Los Angeles, CA.

Mosher, S. W. (2006). China's one-child policy: Twenty-five years later. *Human Life Review*, 32(1), 76–101.

Munniksma, A., & Juvonen, J. (2012). Cross-ethnic friendships and sense of social-emotional safety in a multiethnic middle school: An exploratory study. *Merrill-Palmer Quarterly*, 58(4), 489–506. doi:10.1353/mpq.2012.0023

National Center for Health Statistics. (1985). Advance report of final divorce statistics, 1982. *Monthly Vital Statistics Report*, 33(11). Retrieved from http://www.cdc.gov/nchs/data/mvsr/supp/mv33_11s.pdf

National Center for Health Statistics. (2013). Provisional number of marriages and marriage rate: United States, 2000–2011. *National Vital Statistics System*. Retrieved January 2, 2015, from http://www.cdc.gov/nchs/nvss/marriage_divorce_tables.htm

National Center for Lesbian Rights. (2014). *Adoption by lesbian, gay, and bisexual parents: An overview of current law*. San Francisco: Author. Retrieved from http://www.nclrights.org/wp-content/uploads/2013/07/adptn0204.pdf

Nese, R. N. T., Horner, R. H., Dickey, C. R., Stiller, B., & Tomlanovich, A. (2014). Decreasing bullying behaviors in middle school: Expect respect. *School Psychology Quarterly*, 29(3), 272–286.

Nielsen, L. (2014). Shared physical custody: Summary of 40 studies on outcomes for children. *Journal of Divorce & Remarriage*, 55(8), 613–635. doi:10.1080/10502556.2014.965578

Obergefell v. Hodges, No. 14-556 at 23 (U.S. June 26, 2015). Retrieved from https://supreme.justia.com/cases/federal/us/576/14-556/dissent7.html

O'Brennan, L. M., Bradshaw, C. P., & Sawyer, A. L. (2009). Examining developmental differences in the social-emotional problems among frequent bullies, victims, and bully/victims. *Psychology in the Schools*, 46(2), 100–115.

Oh, W., Rubin, K. H., Bowker, J. C., Booth-LaForce, C., Rose-Krasno, L., & Laursen, B. (2008). Trajectories of social withdrawal from middle childhood to early adolescence. *Journal of Abnormal Child Psychology*, 36(4), 553–566. doi:10.1007/s10802-007-9199-z

Oldehinkel, A. J., Ormel, J., Veenstra, R., De Winter, A. F., Verholst, F. C., & Lansford, J. E. (2009). Parental divorce and children's adjustment. *Perspectives on Psychological Science*, 4(2), 140–152. doi:10.1111/j.1745-6924.2009.01114.x

Oldenburg, B., van Duijn, M., Sentse, M., Huitsing, G., van der Ploeg, R., Salmivalli, C., & Veenstra, R. (2015). Teacher characteristics and peer victimization in elementary schools: A classroom-level perspective. *Journal of Abnormal Child Psychology*, 43(1), 33–44. doi:10.1007/s10802-013-9847-4

Olweus, D. (1995). Bullying or peer abuse at school: Facts and intervention. *Current Directions in Psychological Science*, 4, 196–200.

Olweus, D., & Limber, S. P. (2010). Bullying in school: Evaluation and dissemination of the Olweus Bullying Prevention Program. *American Journal of Orthopsychiatry, 80*(1), 124–134. doi:10.1111/j.1939-0025.2010.01015.x

Osborne, C., Manning, W. D., & Smock, P. J. (2007). Married and cohabiting parents' relationship stability: A focus on race and ethnicity. *Journal of Marriage & Family, 69*(5), 1345–1366.

Parkinson, M., & Creswell, C. (2011). Worry and problem-solving skills and beliefs in primary school children. *British Journal of Clinical Psychology, 50*(1), 106–112. doi:10.1348/014466510x523887

Patterson, C. J. (2009). Children of lesbian and gay parents: Psychology, law, and policy. *American Psychologist, 64*(8), 727–736. doi:10.1037/0003-066x.64.8.727

Pérez-Fuentes, G., Olfson, M., Villegas, L., Morcillo, C., Wang, S., & Blanco, C. (2013). Prevalence and correlates of child sexual abuse: A national study. *Comprehensive Psychiatry, 54*(1), 16–27. doi:10.1016/j.comppsych.2012.05.010

Perren, S., Ettekal, I., & Ladd, G. (2013). The impact of peer victimization on later maladjustment: Mediating and moderating effects of hostile and self-blaming attributions. *Journal of Child Psychology and Psychiatry and Allied Disciplines, 54*(1), 46–55. doi:10.1111/j.1469-7610.2012.02618.x

Perrin, E. C., & Siegel, B. S. (2013). Promoting the well-being of children whose parents are gay or lesbian. *Pediatrics, 131*(4), e1374–e1383. doi:10.1542/peds.2013-0377

Pew Global Attitudes Project. (2008). *The Chinese celebrate their roaring economy, as they struggle with its costs.* Washington, DC: Pew Research Center. Retrieved from http://pewglobal.org/reports/display.php?ReportID=261.

Pfeifer, J. H., & Peake, S. J. (2012). Self-development: Integrating cognitive, socioemotional, and neuroimaging perspectives. *Developmental Cognitive Neuroscience, 2*(1), 55–69. doi:10.1016/j.dcn.2011.07.012

Pike, A., Coldwell, J., & Dunn, J. F. (2005). Sibling relationships in early/middle childhood: Links with individual adjustment. *Journal of Family Psychology, 19*(4), 523–532.

Potter, D. (2010). Psychosocial well-being and the relationship between divorce and children's academic achievement. *Journal of Marriage and Family, 72*(4), 933–946. doi:10.1111/j.1741-3737.2010.00740.x

Poulin, F., & Chan, A. (2010). Friendship stability and change in childhood and adolescence. *Developmental Review, 30*(3), 257–272. doi:10.1016/j.dr.2009.01.001

Pozzoli, T., Gini, G., & Vieno, A. (2012). The role of individual correlates and class norms in defending and passive bystanding behavior in bullying: A multilevel analysis. *Child Development, 83*(6), 1917–1931. doi:10.1111/j.1467-8624.2012.01831.x

Punamäki, R.-L., Palosaari, E., Diab, M., Peltonen, K., & Qouta, S. R. (2014). Trajectories of posttraumatic stress symptoms (PTSS) after major war among Palestinian children: Trauma, family- and child-related predictors. *Journal of Affective Disorders, 172C*, 133–140. doi:10.1016/j.jad.2014.09.021

Putman, S. E. (2009). The monsters in my head: Posttraumatic stress disorder and the child survivor of sexual abuse. *Journal of Counseling & Development, 87*(1), 80–89.

Rabiner, D., & Coie, J. (1989). Effect of expectancy induction on rejected peers' acceptance by unfamiliar peers. *Developmental Psychology, 25*, 450–457.

Ram, B., & Hou, F. (2003). Changes in family structure and child outcomes: Roles of economic and familial resources. *Policy Studies Journal, 31*(3), 309–330.

Ram, B., & Hou, F. (2005). Sex differences in the effects of family structure on children's aggressive behavior. *Journal of Comparative Family Studies, 36*(2), 329–341.

Reavis, R. D., Keane, S. P., & Calkins, S. D. (2010). Trajectories of peer victimization: The role of multiple relationships. *Merrill-Palmer Quarterly, 56*(3), 303–332.

Reising, M. M., Watson, K. H., Hardcastle, E. J., Merchant, M. J., Roberts, L., Forehand, R., & Compas, B. E. (2013). Parental depression and economic disadvantage: The role of parenting in associations with internalizing and externalizing symptoms in children and adolescents. *Journal of Child and Family Studies, 22*(3). doi:10.1007/s10826-012-9582-4

Robertson, D. L., Farmer, T. W., Fraser, M. W., Day, S. H., Duncan, T., Crowther, A., & Dadisman, K. A. (2010). Interpersonal competence configurations and peer relations in early elementary classrooms: Perceived popular and unpopular aggressive subtypes. *International Journal of Behavioral Development, 34*(1), 73–87. doi:10.1177/0165025409345074

Robins, R. W., & Trzesniewski, K. H. (2005). Self-esteem development across the lifespan. *Current Directions in Psychological Science, 14*(3), 158–162. doi:10.1111/j.0963-7214.2005.00353.x

Rodkin, P. C., Espelage, D. L., & Hanish, L. D. (2015). A relational framework for understanding bullying: Developmental antecedents and outcomes. *The American Psychologist, 70*(4), 311–321. doi:10.1037/a0038658

Rodkin, P. C., & Roisman, G. I. (2010). Antecedents and correlates of the popular-aggressive phenomenon in elementary school. *Child Development, 81*(3), 837–850. doi:10.1111/j.1467-8624.2010.01437.x

Rose, A. J., & Asher, S. R. (1999). Children's goals and strategies in response to conflicts within a friendship. *Developmental Psychology, 35*, 69–79.

Rose-Greenland, F., & Smock, P. J. (2012). Living together unmarried: What do we know about cohabiting families? In G. W. Peterson & K. R. Bush (Eds.), *Handbook of Marriage and the Family.* New York: Springer.

Rotenberg, K. J., McDougall, P., Boulton, M. J., Vaillancourt, T., Fox, C., & Hymel, S. (2004). Cross-sectional and longitudinal relations among peer-reported trustworthiness, social relationships, and psychological adjustment in children and early adolescents from the United Kingdom and Canada. *Journal of Experimental Child Psychology, 88*(1), 46. doi:10.1016/j.jecp.2004.01.005

Rubin, K. H., Coplan, R., Chen, X., Bowker, J., & McDonald, K. L. (2011). Peer relationships in childhood. In M. H. Bornstein & M. E. Lamb (Eds.), *Developmental science: An advanced textbook* (6th ed., pp. 519–570). New York: Psychology Press.

Rubin, K. H., Coplan, R., Chen, X., Buskirk, A. A., & Wojslawowicz, J. C. (2005). Peer relationships in childhood. In M. H. Bornstein & M. E. Lamb (Eds.), *Developmental science: An advanced textbook* (5th ed., pp. 469–512). Mahwah, NJ: Lawrence Erlbaum.

Rubin, K. H., Coplan, R. J., & Bowker, J. C. (2009). Social Withdrawal in Childhood. *Annual Review of Psychology, 60*(1), 141–171. doi: 10.1146/annurev.psych.60110707.163642

Rubin, K. H., Wojslawowicz, J. C., Rose-Krasnor, L., Booth-LaForce, C., & Burgess, K. B. (2006). The best friendships of shy/withdrawn children: Prevalence, stability, and relationship quality. *Journal of Abnormal Child Psychology, 34*(2), 143–157. doi:10.1007/s10802-005-9017-4

Rutter, M. (1985). Resilience in the face of adversity: Protective factors and resistance to psychiatric disorder. *British Journal of Psychiatry, 147*, 598–611.

Ryan, R. M., Claessens, A., & Markowitz, A. J. (2015). Associations between family structure

change and child behavior problems: The moderating effect of family income. *Child Development, 86*(1), 112–127. doi:10.1111/cdev.12283

Rydell, A., Berlin, L., & Bohlin, G. (2003). Emotionality, emotion regulation, and adaptation among 5- to 8-year-old children. *Emotion, 3*, 30–47.

Sagi-Schwartz, A. (2008). The well being of children living in chronic war zones: The Palestinian-Israeli case. *International Journal of Behavioral Development, 32*(4), 322–336. doi:10.1177/0165025408090974

Salmivalli, C. (2010). Bullying and the peer group: A review. *Aggression and Violent Behavior, 15*(2), 112–120. doi:10.1016/j.avb.2009.08.007

Salmivalli, C. (2014). Participant roles in bullying: How can peer bystanders be utilized in interventions? *Theory Into Practice, 53*(4), 286–292. doi:10.1080/00405841.2014.947222

Samson, D., Apperly, I. A., & Humphreys, G. W. (2007). Error analyses reveal contrasting deficits in "theory of mind": Neuropsychological evidence from a 3-option false belief task. *Neuropsychologia, 45*(11), 2561–2569.

Saraiya, A., Garakani, A., & Billick, S. B. (2013). Mental health approaches to child victims of acts of terrorism. *The Psychiatric Quarterly, 84*(1), 115–124. doi:10.1007/s11126-012-9232-4

Sarrazin, J., & Cyr, F. (2007). Parental conflicts and their damaging effects on children. *Journal of Divorce & Remarriage, 47*(1–2), 77–93.

Schwartz, D., Lansford, J. E., Dodge, K. A., Pettit, G. S., & Bates, J. E. (2014). Peer victimization during middle childhood as a lead indicator of internalizing problems and diagnostic outcomes in late adolescence. *Journal of Clinical Child and Adolescent Psychology, 44*(3), 393–404. doi:10.1080/15374416.2014.881293

Selman, R. L. (1980). *The growth of interpersonal understanding.* New York: Academic Press.

Setzer, N. (2008). Understanding why your kids refuse school: Prevalence and defining characteristics. *Brown University Child & Adolescent Behavior Letter, 24*(10), 8.

Shapiro, D. (2014). Stepparents and parenting stress: The roles of gender, marital quality, and views about gender roles. *Family Process, 53*(1), 97–108. doi:10.1111/famp.12062

Shapiro, D. N., & Stewart, A. J. (2011). Parenting stress, perceived child regard, and depressive symptoms among stepmothers and biological mothers. *Family Relations, 60*(5), 533–544. doi:10.1111/j.1741-3729.2011.00665.x

Shetgiri, R., Lin, H., & Flores, G. (2013). Trends in risk and protective factors for child bullying perpetration in the United States. *Child Psychiatry and Human Development, 44*(1), 89–104. doi:10.1007/s10578-012-0312-3

Shi, B., & Xie, H. (2012). Popular and nonpopular subtypes of physically aggressive preadolescents: Continuity of aggression and peer mechanisms during the transition to middle school. *Merrill-Palmer Quarterly, 58*(4), 530–553. doi:10.1353/mpq.2012.0025

Short, S. E., Fengying, Z., Siyuan, X., & Mingliang, Y. (2001). China's one-child policy and the care of children: An analysis of qualitative and quantitative data. *Social Forces, 79*(3), 913–943.

Slee, P. T., & Mohyla, J. (2007). The PEACE Pack: An evaluation of interventions to reduce bullying in four Australian primary schools. *Educational Research, 49*(2), 103–114.

Slutzky, C. B., & Simpkins, S. D. (2009). The link between children's sport participation and self-esteem: Exploring the mediating role of sport self-concept. *Psychology of Sport & Exercise, 10*(3), 381–389. doi:10.1016/j.psychsport.2008.09.006

Smith, M. J. (2008). *Child sexual abuse: Issues and challenges.* Hauppauge, NY: Nova Science Publishers.

Smith, S. L., & Moyer-Gusé, E. (2006). Children and the war on Iraq: Developmental differences in fear responses to television news coverage. *Media Psychology, 8*(3), 213–237. doi:10.1207/s1532785xmep0803_2

Spilt, J. L., van Lier, P. A. C., Leflot, G., Onghena, P., & Colpin, H. (2014). Children's social self-concept and internalizing problems: The influence of peers and teachers. *Child Development, 85*(3), 1248–1256. doi:10.1111/cdev.12181

Srabstein, J., Joshi, P. T., Due, P., Wright, J., Leventhal, B., Merrick, J., . . . Riibner, K. (2008). Antibullying legislation: A public health perspective. *Journal of Adolescent Health, 42*(1), 11–20. doi:10.1016/j.jadohealth.2007.10.007

Steinberg, L., & Morris, A. S. (2001). Adolescent development. *Annual Review of Psychology, 52*, 83–112.

Stevenson, H. W., Lee, S., & Mu, X. (2000). Successful achievement in mathematics: China and the United States. In C. F. M. van Lieshout & P. G. Heymans (Eds.), *Developing talent across the life span* (pp. 167–183). New York: Psychology Press.

Stoltenborgh, M., van Ijzendoorn, M. H., Euser, E. M., & Bakermans-Kranenburg, M. J. (2011). A global perspective on child sexual abuse: Meta-analysis of prevalence around the world. *Child Maltreatment, 16*(2), 79–101. doi:10.1177/1077559511403920

Størksen, I., Røysamb, E., Gjessing, H. K., Moum, T., & Tambs, K. (2007). Marriages and psychological distress among adult offspring of divorce: A Norwegian study. *Scandinavian Journal of Psychology, 48*(6), 467–476.

Størksen, I., Røysamb, E., Moum, T., & Tambs, K. (2005). Adolescents with a childhood experience of parental divorce: A longitudinal study of mental health and adjustment. *Journal of Adolescence, 28*(6), 725–739. doi:10.1016/j.adolescence.2005.01.001

Strohschein, L. (2005). Parental divorce and child mental health trajectories. *Journal of Marriage and Family, 67*(5), 1286–1300.

Strohschein, L. (2007). Challenging the presumption of diminished capacity to parent: Does divorce really change parenting practices? *Family Relations, 56*(4), 358–368.

Stuart-Cassel, V., Bell, A., & Springer, J. F. (2011). *Analysis of state bullying laws and policies.* Retrieved from http://www2.ed.gov/rschstat/eval/bullying/state-bullying-laws/state-bullying-laws.pdf

Sturaro, C., van Lier, P. A. C., Cuijpers, P., & Koot, H. M. (2011). The role of peer relationships in the development of early school-age externalizing problems. *Child Development, 82*(3), 758–765. doi:10.1111/j.1467-8624.2010.01532.x

Swearer, S. M., & Hymel, S. (2015). Understanding the psychology of bullying: Moving toward a social-ecological diathesis-stress model. *The American Psychologist, 70*(4), 344–353. doi:10.1037/a0038929

Tasker, F., & Patterson, C. J. (2007). Research on gay and lesbian parenting: Retrospect and prospect. *Journal of GLBT Family Studies, 3*(2–3), 9–34.

Terry, K. J., & Talon, J. (2004). *Child sexual abuse: A review of the literature.* New York: John Jay College. Retrieved from www.usccb.org/nrb/johnjaystudy/litreview.pdf

Thambirajah, M. S., Grandison, K. J., & De-Hayes, L. (2008). *Understanding school refusal: A handbook for professionals in education, health and social care.* London: Jessica Kingsley Publishers.

Thomaes, S., Reijntjes, A., Orobio de Castro, B., Bushman, B. J., Poorthuis, A., & Telch, M. J. (2010). I like me if you like me: On the interpersonal modulation and regulation of preadolescents' state self-esteem. *Child Development, 81*(3), 811–825. doi:10.1111/j.1467-8624.2010.01435.x

Toyama, M. (2001). Developmental changes in social comparison in pre-school and elementary school children: Perceptions, feelings, and behavior. *Japanese Journal of Educational Psychology, 49*, 500–507.

Troutman, D. R., & Fletcher, A. C. (2010). Context and companionship in children's short-term versus long-term friendships. *Journal of Social and Personal Relationships, 27*(8), 1060–1074. doi:10.1177/0265407510381253

Turcotte Benedict, F., Vivier, P. M., & Gjelsvik, A. (2015). Mental health and bullying in the United States among children aged 6 to 17 years. *Journal of Interpersonal Violence, 30*(5), 782–795. doi:10.1177/0886260514536279

U.S. Department of Health and Human Services. (2013). *Child Maltreatment 2012.* Washington DC: Author. Retrieved from http://www.acf.hhs.gov/programs/cb/resource/child-maltreatment-2012

United Nations Statistics Division. (2014). *Demographic yearbook: 2013.* Retrieved from http://unstats.un.org/unsd/demographic/products/dyb/dyb2.htm

Vanderbilt-Adriance, E., & Shaw, D. (2008). Protective factors and the development of resilience in the context of neighborhood disadvantage. *Journal of Abnormal Child Psychology, 36*(6), 887–901. doi:10.1007/s10802-008-9220-1

VanderValk, I., Spruijt, E., de Goede, M., Maas, C., & Meeus, W. H. J. (2005). Family structure and problem behavior of adolescents and young adults: A growth-curve study. *Journal of Youth and Adolescence, 34*(6), 533–546.

Vanfraussen, K., Ponjaert-Kristoffersen, I., & Brewaeys, A. (2003). Family functioning in lesbian families created by donor insemination. *American Journal of Orthopsychiatry, 73*(1), 78–90.

Veenstra, R., Lindenberg, S., Oldehinkel, A. J., De Winter, A. F., Verhulst, F. C., & Ormel, J. (2005). Bullying and victimization in elementary schools: A comparison of bullies, victims, bully/victims, and uninvolved preadolescents. *Developmental Psychology, 41*(4), 672–682. doi:10.1037/0012-1649.41.4.672

Verschueren, K., Doumen, S., & Buyse, E. (2012). Relationships with mother, teacher, and peers: Unique and joint effects on young children's self-concept. *Attachment & Human Development, 14*(3), 233–248. doi:10.1080/14616734.2012.672263

Volling, B. L. (2012). Family transitions following the birth of a sibling: An empirical review of changes in the firstborn's adjustment. *Psychological Bulletin, 138*(3), 497–528. doi:10.1037/a0026921

Waasdorp, T. E., & Bradshaw, C. P. (2011). Examining student responses to frequent bullying: A latent class approach. *Journal of Educational Psychology, 103*(2), 336–352. doi:10.1037/a0022747

Waldfogel, J., Craigie, T.-A., & Brooks-Gunn, J. (2010). Fragile families and child wellbeing. *The Future of Children, 20*(2), 87–112. Retrieved from http://www.pubmedcentral.nih.gov/articlerender.fcgi?artid=3074431&tool=pmcentrez&rendertype=abstract

Walker, L. J., & Hennig, K. H. (1997). Parent/child relationships in single-parent families. *Canadian Journal of Behavioral Science, 29*, 63–75.

Wallerstein, J. S., & Lewis, J. M. (2004). The unexpected legacy of divorce: Report of a 25-year study. *Psychoanalytic Psychology, 21*(3), 353–370.

Wang, D., Kato, N., Inaba, Y., Tango, T., Yoshida, Y., Kusaka, Y., . . . Zhang, Q. (2000). Physical and personality traits of preschool children in Fuzhou, China: Only child vs sibling. *Child: Care, Health & Development, 26*(1), 49–60.

Weaver, J. M., & Schofield, T. J. (2015). Mediation and moderation of divorce effects on children's behavior problems. *Journal of Family Psychology,* 29(1), 39–48 Retrieved from http://dx.doi.org/10.1037/fam0000043

Weisner, T. S. (1993). Ethnographic and ecocultural perspectives on sibling relationships. In Z. Stoneman & P. W. Berman (Eds.), *The effects of mental retardation, disability, and illness on sibling relationships* (pp. 51–83). Baltimore: Paul H. Brookes.

Werner, E. E. (1995). Resilience in development. *Current Directions in Psychological Science, 4*(3), 81–85.

Werner, E. E. (2012). Children and war: Risk, resilience, and recovery. *Development and Psychopathology, 24*(2), 553–558. Retrieved from http://journals.cambridge.org/abstract_S0954579412000156

Werner, N. E., & Crick, N. R. (2004). Maladaptive peer relationships and the development of relational and physical aggression during middle childhood. *Social Development, 13*(4), 495–514.

White, L., & Rogers, S. J. (2000). Economic circumstances and family outcomes: A review of the 1990s. *Journal of Marriage and Family, 62*, 1035–1051.

Whiteside, M. F., & Becker, B. J. (2000). Parental factors and the young child's postdivorce adjustment: A meta-analysis with implications for parenting arrangements. *Journal of Family Psychology, 14*, 5–26.

Whiting, J. B., Smith, D. R., Barnett, T., & Grafsky, E. L. (2007). Overcoming the Cinderella myth: A mixed methods study of successful stepmothers. *Journal of Divorce & Remarriage, 47*(1–2), 95–109.

Whitton, S. W., Rhoades, G. K., Stanley, S. M., & Markman, H. J. (2008). Effects of parental divorce on marital commitment and confidence. *Journal of Family Psychology, 22*(5), 789–793.

Williams, R. (2007). The psychosocial consequences for children of mass violence, terrorism and disasters. *International Review of Psychiatry, 19*(3), 263–277. doi:10.1080/09540260701349480

Wilson, B. J. (2006). The entry behavior of aggressive/rejected children: The contributions of status and temperament. *Social Development, 15*(3), 463–479.

Wojslawowicz Bowker, J. C., Rubin, K. H., Burgess, K. B., Booth-LaForce, C., & Rose-Krasnor, L. (2006). Behavioral characteristics associated with stable and fluid best friendship patterns in middle childhood. *Merrill-Palmer Quarterly, 52*(4), 671–693.

Wolchik, S. A., Wilcox, K. L., Tein, J.-Y. Y., & Sandler, I. N. (2000). Maternal acceptance and consistency of discipline as buffers of divorce stressors on children's psychological adjustment problems. *Journal of Abnormal Child Psychology, 28*, 87–102.

Wood, D., & Woody, D. J. (2007). The significance of social support on parenting among a group of single, low-income, African American mothers. *Journal of Human Behavior in the Social Environment, 15*(2–3), 183–198.

Wurtele, S. K., & Kenny, M. C. (2010). Partnering with parents to prevent childhood sexual abuse. *Child Abuse Review, 19*(2), 130–152. doi:10.1002/car.1112

Yang, J. (2007). The one-child policy and school attendance in China. *Comparative Education Review, 51*(4), 471–495.

Zhu, W. X., Lu, L., & Hesketh, T. (2009). China's excess males, sex selective abortion, and one child policy: Analysis of data from 2005 national intercensus survey. *BMJ, 338*(7700), 920–923.

Zwierzynska, K., Wolke, D., & Lereya, T. S. (2013). Peer victimization in childhood and internalizing problems in adolescence: A prospective longitudinal study. *Journal of Abnormal Child Psychology, 41*(2), 309–323. doi:10.1007/s10802-012-9678-8

CHAPTER 11

Aalsma, M. C., Lapsley, D. K., & Flannery, D. J. (2006). Personal fables, narcissism, and adolescent adjustment. *Psychology in the Schools*, *43*(4), 481–491.

Adam, E. K., Snell, E. K., & Pendry, P. (2007). Sleep timing and quantity in ecological and family context: A nationally representative time-diary study. *Journal of Family Psychology*, *21*(1), 4–19. doi:10.1037/0893-3200.21.1.4

Akos, P., Rose, R. A., & Orthner, D. (2014). Sociodemographic moderators of middle school transition effects on academic achievement. *The Journal of Early Adolescence*, *35*(2), 170–198. doi:10.1177/0272431614529367

Albert, D., Chein, J., & Steinberg, L. (2013). The teenage brain: Peer influences on adolescent decision making. *Current Directions in Psychological Science*, *22*, 114–120. doi:10.1177/0963721412471347

Alberts, A., Elkind, D., & Ginsberg, S. (2007). The personal fable and risk-taking in early adolescence. *Journal of Youth and Adolescence*, *36*(1), 71–76.

Alexander, K. L., Entwisle, D. R., & Kabbani, N. S. (2001). The dropout process in life course perspective: Early risk factors at home and school. *Teachers College Record*, *103*, 760–822.

Alivernini, F., & Lucidi, F. (2011). Relationship between social context, self-efficacy, motivation, academic achievement, and intention to drop out of high school: A longitudinal study. *The Journal of Educational Research*, *104*(4), 241–252. doi:10.1080/00220671003728062

Allen, J. P., & Antonishak, J. (2008). Adolescent peer influences: Beyond the dark side. In M. J. Prinstein & K. A. Dodge (Eds.), *Understanding peer influence in children and adolescents* (pp. 141–160). New York: Guilford Press.

Al-Sahab, B., Ardern, C. I., Hamadeh, M. J., & Tamim, H. (2010). Age at menarche in Canada: Results from the National Longitudinal Survey of Children and Youth. *BMC Public Health*, *10*(1), 736. doi:10.1186/1471-2458-10-736

American Academy of Pediatrics. (2013). Children, adolescents, and the media. *Pediatrics*, *132*(5), 958–961. doi:10.1542/peds.2013-2656

American Psychological Association. (2012). *Miller v. Alabama* and *Jackson v. Hobbs*. Retrieved from http://www.apa.org/about/offices/ogc/amicus/miller-hobbs.aspx

Anderman, E. M., & Midgley, C. (2004). Changes in self-reported academic cheating across the transition from middle school to high school. *Contemporary Educational Psychology*, *29*(4), 499–517.

Ardila, A. (2013). Development of metacognitive and emotional executive functions in children. *Applied Neuropsychology Child*, *2*(2), 82–87. doi:10.1080/21622965.2013.748388

Arim, R. G., Tramonte, L., Shapka, J. D., Dahinten, V. S., & Willms, J. D. (2011). The family antecedents and the subsequent outcomes of early puberty. *Journal of Youth and Adolescence*, *40*(11), 1423–1435. doi:10.1007/s10964-011-9638-6

Arnett, J. J. (1999). Adolescent storm and stress, reconsidered. *American Psychologist*, *54*(5), 317–326. Retrieved from http://www.ncbi.nlm.nih.gov/pubmed/10354802

Asato, M. R., Terwilliger, R., Woo, J., & Luna, B. (2010). White matter development in adolescence: A DTI study. *Cerebral Cortex*, *20*(9), 2122–2131. doi:10.1093/cercor/bhp282

Assadi, S. M., Zokaei, N., Kaviani, H., Mohammadi, M. R., Ghaeli, P., Gohari, M. R., & van de Vijver, F. J. R. (2007). Effect of sociocultural context and parenting style on scholastic achievement among Iranian adolescents. *Social Development*, *16*, 169–180.

Aunola, K., & Stattin, H. (2000). Parenting styles and adolescents' achievement strategies. *Journal of Adolescence*, *23*(2), 205–223.

Baams, L., Dubas, J. S., Overbeek, G., & van Aken, M. A. G. (2015). Transitions in body and behavior: A meta-analytic study on the relationship between pubertal development and adolescent sexual behavior. *The Journal of Adolescent Health*. Advance online publication. doi:10.1016/j.jadohealth.2014.11.019

Bachman, J. G., Johnston, L. D., & O'Malley, P. M. (2014). *Monitoring the future: Questionnaire responses from the nation's high school seniors, 2012*. Ann Arbor, MI. Retrieved from http://monitoringthefuture.org/datavolumes/2012/2012dv.pdf

Bachman, J. G., Staff, J., O'Malley, P. M., & Freedman-Doan, P. (2013). Adolescent work intensity, school performance, and substance use: Links vary by race/ethnicity and socioeconomic status. *Developmental Psychology*, *49*(11), 2125–2134. doi:10.1037/a0031464

Balzer, B. W. R., Duke, S.-A., Hawke, C. I., & Steinbeck, K. S. (2015). The effects of estradiol on mood and behavior in human female adolescents: A systematic review. *European Journal of Pediatrics*. Advance online publication. doi:10.1007/s00431-014-2475-3

Barnea-Goraly, N., Menon, V., Eckert, M., Tamm, L., Bammer, R., Karchemskiy, A., . . . Reiss, A. L. (2005). White matter development during childhood and adolescence: A cross-sectional diffusion tensor imaging study. *Cerebral Cortex*, *15*.

Barrouillet, P., Gavens, N., Vergauwe, E., Gaillard, V., & Camos, V. (2009). Working memory span development: A time-based resource-sharing model account. *Developmental Psychology*, *45*(2), 477–490. doi:10.1037/a0014615

Bartel, K. A., Gradisar, M., & Williamson, P. (2014). Protective and risk factors for adolescent sleep: A meta-analytic review. *Sleep Medicine Reviews*. doi:10.1016/j.smrv.2014.08.002

Battin-Pearson, S., & Newcomb, M. D. (2000). Predictors of early high school dropout: A test of five theories. *Journal of Educational Psychology*, *92*(3), 15.

Bauer, K. W., Larson, N. I., Nelson, M. C., Story, M., & Neumark-Sztainer, D. (2009). Fast food intake among adolescents: Secular and longitudinal trends from 1999 to 2004. *Preventive Medicine*, *48*(3), 284–287. doi:10.1016/j.ypmed.2008.12.021

Bava, S., & Tapert, S. F. (2010). Adolescent brain development and the risk for alcohol and other drug problems. *Neuropsychology Review*, *20*(4), 398–413. doi:10.1007/s11065-010-9146-6

Baynes, R. D., & Bothwell, T. H. (1990). Iron deficiency. *Annual Review of Nutrition*, *10*, 133–148.

Benner, A. D. (2011). The transition to high school: Current knowledge, future directions. *Educational Psychology Review*, *23*(3), 299–328. doi:10.1007/s10648-011-9152-0

Benner, A. D., & Graham, S. (2009). The transition to high school as a developmental process among multiethnic urban youth. *Child Development*, *80*(2), 356–376. doi:10.1111/j.1467-8624.2009.01265.x

Benoit, A., Lacourse, E., & Claes, M. (2013). Pubertal timing and depressive symptoms in late adolescence: The moderating role of individual, peer, and parental factors. *Development and Psychopathology*, *25*(2), 455–471. doi:10.1017/S0954579412001174

Berenbaum, S. A., & Beltz, A. M. (2011). Sexual differentiation of human behavior: Effects of prenatal and pubertal organizational hormones. *Frontiers in Neuroendocrinology*, *32*(2), 183–200. doi:10.1016/j.yfrne.2011.03.001

Berge, J. M., Jin, S. W., Hannan, P., & Neumark-Sztainer, D. (2013). Structural and interpersonal characteristics of family meals: Associations with adolescent body mass index and dietary patterns. *Journal of the Academy of Nutrition and Dietetics*, *113*(6), 816–822. doi:10.1016/j.jand.2013.02.004

Berkey, C. S., Gardner, J. D., Frazier, A. L., & Colditz, G. A. (2000). Relation of childhood diet and body size to menarche and adolescent growth in girls. *American Journal of Epidemiology*, *152*, 446–452.

Berkowitz, M. W., & Begun, A. L. (1994). Assessing how adolescents think about the morality of substance use. *Drugs & Society*, *8*(3–4), 111.

Biehl, M., Natsuaki, M., & Ge, X. (2007). The influence of pubertal timing on alcohol use and heavy drinking trajectories. *Journal of Youth and Adolescence*, *36*(2), 153–167.

Biro, F. M., Khoury, P., & Morrison, J. A. (2006). Influence of obesity on timing of puberty. *International Journal of Andrology*, *29*(1), 272–277.

Blakemore, S.-J. (2012). Imaging brain development: The adolescent brain. *NeuroImage*, *61*(2), 397–406. doi:10.1016/j.neuroimage.2011.11.080

Blakemore, S.-J., & Choudhury, S. S. (2006). Development of the adolescent brain: Implications for executive function and social cognition. *Journal of Child Psychology and Psychiatry*, *47*(3–4), 296–312.

Blakemore, S.-J., & Mills, K. L. (2014). Is adolescence a sensitive period for sociocultural processing? *Annual Review of Psychology*, *65*, 187–207. doi:10.1146/annurev-psych-010213-115202

Blumenthal, H., Leen-Feldner, E. W., Trainor, C. D., Babson, K. A., & Bunaciu, L. (2009). Interactive roles of pubertal timing and peer relations in predicting social anxiety symptoms among youth. *Journal of Adolescent Health*, *44*(4), 401–403. doi:10.1016/j.jadohealth.2008.08.023

Bogaert, A. F. (2005). Age at puberty and father absence in a national probability sample. *Journal of Adolescence*, *28*(4), 541–546.

Bogin, B. (2011). Puberty and adolescence: An evolutionary perspective. In *Encyclopedia of Adolescence* (pp. 275–286). New York: Elsevier. doi:10.1016/B978-0-12-373951-3.00033-8

Bonnie, R. J., & Scott, E. S. (2013). The teenage brain: Adolescent brain research and the law. *Current Directions in Psychological Science*, *22*(2), 158–161. doi:10.1177/0963721412471678

Booth, M. Z., & Gerard, J. M. (2014). Adolescents' stage-environment fit in middle and high school: The relationship between students' perceptions of their schools and themselves. *Youth & Society*, *46*(6), 735–755. doi:10.1177/0044118X12451276

Bosch, A. M., Hutter, I., & van Ginneken, J. K. (2008). Perceptions of adolescents and their mothers on reproductive and sexual development in Matlab, Bangladesh. *International Journal of Adolescent Medicine and Health*, *20*(3), 329–342.

Bowers, A. J., & Sprott, R. (2012). Examining the multiple trajectories associated with dropping out of high school: A growth mixture model analysis. *The Journal of Educational Research*, *105*(3), 176–195. doi:10.1080/00220671.2011.552075

Bowman, S. A., Gortmaker, S. L., Ebbeling, C. B., Pereira, M. A., & Ludwig, D. S. (2004). Effects of fast-food consumption on energy intake and diet quality among children in a national household survey. *Pediatrics*, *113*(1), 112–118.

Boynton-Jarrett, R., Wright, R. J., Putnam, F. W., Lividoti Hibert, E., Michels, K. B., Forman, M. R., & Rich-Edwards, J. (2013). Childhood abuse and age at menarche. *The Journal of Adolescent Health*, *52*(2), 241–247. doi:10.1016/j.jadohealth.2012.06.006

Brain Development Cooperative Group. (2012). Total and regional brain volumes in a population-based normative sample from 4 to 18 years: The NIH MRI Study of Normal Brain Development. *Cerebral Cortex, 22*(1), 1–12. Retrieved from http://doi.org/10.1093/cercor/bhr018

Brodersen, N. H., Steptoe, A., Boniface, D. R., & Wardle, J. (2007). Trends in physical activity and sedentary behaviour in adolescence: Ethnic and socioeconomic differences. *British Journal of Sports Medicine, 41*(3), 140–144.

Brooks-Gunn, J., & Ruble, D. N. (2013). Developmental processes in the experience of menarche. In A. Baum & J. E. Singer (Ed.), *Issues in child health and adolescent health: Handbook of psychology and health* (pp. 117–148). New York: Psychology Press.

Brugman, D. (2010). Moral reasoning competence and the moral judgment-action discrepancy in young adolescents. In W. Koops, D. Brugman, T. J. Ferguson, & A. F. Sanders (Ed.), *The development and structure of conscience* (pp. 119–133). New York: Psychology Press.

Buchanan, C. M., Eccles, J. S., & Becker, J. B. (1992). Are adolescents the victims of raging hormones? Evidence for activational effects of hormones on moods and behavior at adolescence. *Psychological Bulletin, 111*, 62–107.

Buchanan, C. M., Eccles, J. S., Flanagan, C., Midgley, C., Feldlaufer, H., & Harold, R. D. (1990). Parents' and teachers' beliefs about adolescents: Effects of sex and experience. *Journal of Youth and Adolescence, 19*(4), 363–394. doi:10.1007/BF01537078

Buchanan, C. M., & Hughes, J. L. (2009). Construction of social reality during early adolescence: Can expecting storm and stress increase real or perceived storm and stress? *Journal of Research on Adolescence, 19*(2), 261–285. doi:10.1111/j.1532-7795.2009.00596.x

Bullock, M., Sodian, B., & Koerber, S. (2009). Doing experiments and understanding science: Development of scientific reasoning from childhood to adulthood. In W. Schneider & M. Bullock (Eds.), *Human development from early childhood to early adulthood: Findings from a 20 year longitudinal study* (pp. 173–197). New York: Psychology Press.

Bundak, R., Darendeliler, F., Gunoz, H., Bas, F., Saka, N., & Neyzi, O. (2007). Analysis of puberty and pubertal growth in healthy boys. *European Journal of Pediatrics, 166*(6), 595–600.

Burchinal, M., Roberts, J. E., Zeisel, S. A., Hennon, E. A., & Hooper, S. (2006). Social risk and protective child, parenting, and child care factors in early elementary school years. *Parenting: Science & Practice, 6*(1), 79–113.

Burgess-Champoux, T. L., Larson, N., Neumark-Sztainer, D., Hannan, P. J., & Story, M. (2009). Are family meal patterns associated with overall diet quality during the transition from early to middle adolescence? *Journal of Nutrition Education and Behavior, 41*(2), 79–86.

Bygdell, M., Vandenput, L., Ohlsson, C., & Kindblom, J. M. (2014). A secular trend for pubertal timing in Swedish men born 1946–1991—The best cohort : Puberty: From bench to bedside. *ENDO Meetings*. Retrieved from http://press.endocrine.org/doi/abs/10.1210/endo-meetings.2014.PE.10.0R11-3

Byrnes, V., & Ruby, A. (2007). Comparing achievement between K–8 and middle schools: A large-scale empirical study. *American Journal of Education, 114*(1), 101–135.

Carlo, G., & Eisenberg, N. (1996). A cross-national study on the relations among prosocial moral. *Developmental Psychology, 32*(2), 231–241.

Carlo, G., Mestre, M. V., Samper, P., Tur, A., & Armenta, B. E. (2011). The longitudinal relations among dimensions of parenting styles, sympathy, prosocial moral reasoning, and prosocial behaviors. *International Journal of Behavioral Development, 35*(2), 116–124. doi:10.1177/0165025410375921

Carskadon, M. A. (2009). Adolescents and sleep: Why teens can't get enough of a good thing. *Brown University Child & Adolescent Behavior Letter, 25*(4), 1–6.

Carskadon, M. A., Acebo, C., & Jenni, O. G. (2004). Regulation of adolescent sleep: Implications for behavior. *Annals of the New York Academy of Sciences, 1021*, 276–291.

Carskadon, M. A., & Tarokh, L. (2014). Developmental changes in sleep biology and potential effects on adolescent behavior and caffeine use. *Nutrition Reviews, 72*(Suppl. 1), 60–64. doi:10.1111/nure.12147

Carter, R., Jaccard, J., Silverman, W. K., & Pina, A. A. (2009). Pubertal timing and its link to behavioral and emotional problems among "at-risk" African American adolescent girls. *Journal of Adolescence, 32*(3), 467–481. doi:10.1016/j.adolescence.2008.07.005

Casey, B., & Caudle, K. (2013). The teenage brain: Self control. *Current Directions in Psychological Science, 22*(2), 82–87. doi:10.1177/0963721413480170

Casey, B. J. (2015). Beyond simple models of self-control to circuit-based accounts of adolescent behavior. *Annual Review of Psychology, 66*, 295–319. doi:10.1146/annurev-psych-010814-015156

Casey, B., Jones, R. M., & Somerville, L. H. (2011). Braking and accelerating of the adolescent brain. *Journal of Research on Adolescence, 21*(1), 21–33. doi:10.1111/j.1532-7795.2010.00712.x

Cauffman, E., Shulman, E. P., Steinberg, L., Claus, E., Banich, M. T., Graham, S., & Woolard, J. (2010). Age differences in affective decision making as indexed by performance on the Iowa Gambling Task. *Developmental Psychology, 46*(1), 193–207. doi:10.1037/a0016128

Cauffman, E., & Steinberg, L. (2000). (Im)maturity of judgment in adolescence: Why adolescents may be less culpable than adults*. *Behavioral Sciences & the Law, 18*(6), 741–760.

Cauffman, E., & Steinberg, L. (2012). Emerging findings from research on adolescent justice, 428–449. doi:10.1080/15564886.2012.713901

Cavadini, C., Decarli, B., Grin, J., Narring, F., & Michaud, P. A. (2000). Food habits and sport activity during adolescence: Differences between athletic and non-athletic teenagers in Switzerland. *European Journal of Clinical Nutrition, 54*(3), S16.

Centifanti, L. C. M., Modecki, K. L., MacLellan, S., & Gowling, H. (2014). Driving under the influence of risky peers: An experimental study of adolescent risk taking. *Journal of Research on Adolescence*. Advance online publication. doi:10.1111/jora.12187

Cesario, S. K., & Hughes, L. A. (2007). Precocious puberty: A comprehensive review of literature. *Journal of Obstetric, Gynecologic, & Neonatal Nursing, 36*(3), 263–274.

Chen, P., & Vazsonyi, A. T. (2011). Future orientation, impulsivity, and problem behaviors: A longitudinal moderation model. *Developmental Psychology, 47*(6), 1633–1645.

Chen, P., & Vazsonyi, A. T. (2013). Future orientation, school contexts, and problem behaviors: A multilevel study. *Journal of Youth and Adolescence, 42*(1), 67–81. doi:10.1007/s10964-012-9785-4

Child Trends. (2014). *High school dropout rates*. Bethesda, MD: Author. Retrieved from http://www.childtrends.org/?indicators=high-school-dropout-rates

Christenson, S. L., & Thurlow, M. L. (2004). School dropouts: Prevention considerations, interventions, and challenges. *Current Directions in Psychological Science, 13*(1), 36–39. doi:10.1111/j.0963-7214.2004.01301010.x

Cohen, A. O., & Casey, B. J. (2014). Rewiring juvenile justice: The intersection of developmental neuroscience and legal policy. *Trends in Cognitive Sciences, 18*(2), 63–65. doi:10.1016/j.tics.2013.11.002

Cohen Kadosh, K., Johnson, M. H., Dick, F., Cohen Kadosh, R., & Blakemore, S.-J. (2013). Effects of age, task performance, and structural brain development on face processing. *Cerebral Cortex, 23*(7), 1630–1642. doi:10.1093/cercor/bhs150

Colby, A., & Damon, W. (1992). *Some do care: Contemporary lives of moral commitment*. New York: Free Press.

Colby, A., Kohlberg, L., Gibbs, J., & Lieberman, M. (1983). A longitudinal study of moral judgment. *Monographs of the Society for Research in Child Development, 48*(1).

Colrain, I. M., & Baker, F. C. (2011). Changes in sleep as a function of adolescent development. *Neuropsychology Review, 21*(1), 5–21. doi:10.1007/s11065-010-9155-5

Comunian, A. L., & Gielen, U. P. (2000). Sociomoral reflection and prosocial and antisocial behavior: Two Italian studies. *Psychological Reports, 87*(1), 161–176.

Cordain, L., Lindeberg, S., Hurtado, M., Hill, K., Eaton, S. B., & Brand-Miller, J. (2002). Acne vulgaris: A disease of western civilization. *Archives of Dermatology, 138*, 1584–1590.

Cornell, D., Gregory, A., Huang, F., & Fan, X. (2013). Perceived prevalence of teasing and bullying predicts high school dropout rates. *Journal of Educational Psychology, 105*(1), 138–149.

Costos, D., Ackerman, R., & Paradis, L. (2002). Recollections of menarche: Communication between mothers and daughters regarding menstruation. *Sex Roles, 46*(1-2), 49–59. doi:10.1023/A:1016037618567

Cowan, N., Hismjatullina, A., AuBuchon, A. M., Saults, J. S., Horton, N., Leadbitter, K., & Towse, J. (2010). With development, list recall includes more chunks, not just larger ones. *Developmental Psychology, 46*(5), 1119–1131. doi:10.1037/a0020618

Coyle, T. R., Pillow, D. R., Snyder, A. C., & Kochunov, P. (2011). Processing speed mediates the development of general intelligence (g) in adolescence. *Psychological Science, 22*(10), 1265–1269. doi:10.1177/0956797611418243

Crockett, L. J., Carlo, G., Wolff, J. M., & Hope, M. O. (2013). The role of pubertal timing and temperamental vulnerability in adolescents' internalizing symptoms. *Development and Psychopathology, 25*(2), 377–389. doi:10.1017/S0954579412001125

Crockett, L. J., Petersen, A. C., Graber, J. A., Schulenberg, J. E., & Ebata, A. (1989). School transitions and adjustment during early adolescence. *The Journal of Early Adolescence, 9*(3), 181–210. doi:10.1177/0272431689093002

Croninger, R. G., & Lee, V. E. (2001). Social capital and dropping out of high school: Benefits to at-risk students of teachers' support and guidance. *Teachers College Record, 103*(4), 548–582.

Crowley, S. J., Acebo, C., & Carskadon, M. A. (2007). Sleep, circadian rhythms, and delayed phase in adolescence. *Sleep Medicine, 8*(6), 602–612. doi:10.1016/j.sleep.2006.12.002

Darchia, N., & Cervena, K. (2014). The journey through the world of adolescent sleep. *Reviews in the Neurosciences, 25*(4). doi:10.1515/revneuro-2013-0065

Davis, B., & Carpenter, C. (2009). Proximity of fast-food restaurants to schools and adolescent obesity. *American Journal of Public Health, 99*(3), 505–510. doi:10.2105/ajph.2008.137638

Dawson, T. L. (2002). New tools, new insights: Kohlberg's moral judgement stages revisited.

International Journal of Behavioral Development, 26(2), 154–166.

Deardorff, J., Abrams, B., Ekwaru, J. P., & Rehkopf, D. H. (2014). Socioeconomic status and age at menarche: An examination of multiple indicators in an ethnically diverse cohort. *Annals of Epidemiology*, 24(10), 727–733. doi:10.1016/j.annepidem.2014.07.002

Deardorff, J., Ekwaru, J. P., Kushi, L. H., Ellis, B. J., Greenspan, L. C., Mirabedi, A., . . . Hiatt, R. A. (2011). Father absence, body mass index, and pubertal timing in girls: Differential effects by family income and ethnicity. *The Journal of Adolescent Health*, 48(5), 441–447. doi:10.1016/j.jadohealth.2010.07.032

Defoe, I. N., Dubas, J. S., Figner, B., & van Aken, M. A. (2012). A meta-analysis on age differences in risky decision making: Adolescents versus children and adults. *Psychology Bulletin*, 141(1), 29. doi:10.1037/a0038088

Demetriou, A., Christou, C., Spanoudis, G., & Platsidou, M. (2002). The development of mental processing: Efficiency, working memory and thinking. *Monographs of the Society for Research in Child Development*, 67(1, Serial No. 268), 1–154.

DeRose, L. M., & Brooks-Gunn, J. (2006). Transition into adolescence: The role of pubertal processes. In L. Balter & C. S. Tamis-LeMonda (Eds.), *Child psychology: A handbook of contemporary issues* (2nd ed., pp. 385–414). New York: Psychology Press.

Dorn, L. D., & Biro, F. M. (2011). Puberty and its measurement: A decade in review. *Journal of Research on Adolescence*, 21(1), 180–195. doi:10.1111/j.1532-7795.2010.00722.x

Dorn, L. D., Dahl, R. E., Woodward, H. R., & Biro, F. (2006). Defining the boundaries of early adolescence: A user's guide to assessing pubertal status and pubertal timing in research with adolescents. *Applied Developmental Science*, 10(1), 30–56.

Dornbusch, S. M., Ritter, P. L., Mont-Reynaud, R., & Chen, Z. (1990). Family decision making and academic performance in a diverse high school population. *Journal of Adolescent Research*, 5(2), 143–160.

Dotterer, A. M., Lowe, K., & McHale, S. M. (2014). Academic growth trajectories and family relationships among African American youth. *Journal of Research on Adolescence*, 24(4), 734–747. doi:10.1111/jora.12080

Douglass, S., Yip, T., & Shelton, J. N. (2014). Intragroup contact and anxiety among ethnic minority adolescents: Considering ethnic identity and school diversity transitions. *Journal of Youth and Adolescence*, 43(10), 1628–1641. doi:10.1007/s10964-014-0144-5

Downs, A. C., & Fuller, M. J. (1991). Recollections of spermarche: An exploratory investigation. *Current Psychology*, 10(1–2), 93–102.

Dreyfuss, M., Caudle, K., Drysdale, A. T., Johnston, N. E., Cohen, A. O., Somerville, L. H., . . . Casey, B. J. (2014). Teens impulsively react rather than retreat from threat. *Developmental Neuroscience*, 36(3–4), 220–227. doi:10.1159/000357755

Duke, S. A., Balzer, B. W. R., & Steinbeck, K. S. (2014). Testosterone and its effects on human male adolescent mood and behavior: A systematic review. *The Journal of Adolescent Health*, 55(3), 315–322. doi:10.1016/j.jadohealth.2014.05.007

Dumith, S. C., Gigante, D. P., Domingues, M. R., & Kohl, H. W. (2011). Physical activity change during adolescence: A systematic review and a pooled analysis. *International Journal of Epidemiology*, 40(3), 685–698. doi:10.1093/ije/dyq272

Dumont, M., Leclerc, D., & McKinnon, S. (2009). Consequences of part-time work on the academic and psychosocial adaptation of adolescents. *Canadian Journal of School Psychology*, 24(1), 58–75. doi:10.1177/0829573509333197

Duncan, S. C., Duncan, T. E., Strycker, L. A., & Chaumeton, N. R. (2007). A cohort-sequential latent growth model of physical activity from ages 12 to 17 years. *Annals of Behavioral Medicine*, 33(1), 80–89.

Ebbeling, C. B., Sinclair, K. B., Pereira, M. A., Garcia-Lago, E., Feldman, H. A., & Ludwig, D. S. (2004). Compensation for energy intake from fast food among overweight and lean adolescents. *JAMA*, 291(23), 2828–2833.

Eccles, J. S. (2004). Schools, academic motivation, and stage-environment fit. In R. M. Lerner & L. Steinberg (Eds.), *Handbook of adolescent psychology* (2nd ed., pp. 125–153). Hoboken, NJ: John Wiley.

Eccles, J. S., & Roeser, R. W. (2011). Schools as developmental contexts during adolescence. *Journal of Research on Adolescence*, 21(1), 225–241. doi:10.1111/j.1532-7795.2010.00725.x

Eccles, J. S., Wigfield, A., Midgley, C., Reuman, D., Mac Iver, D., & Feldlaufer, H. (1992). Negative effects of traditional middle schools on students' motivation. *Elementary School Journal*, 93(5), 553–574. Retrieved from http://eric.ed.gov/?id=ej464543

Elias, C. F. (2012). Leptin action in pubertal development: Recent advances and unanswered questions. *Trends in Endocrinology and Metabolism*, 23(1), 9–15. doi:10.1016/j.tem.2011.09.002

Elkind, D., & Bowen, R. (1979). Imaginary audience behavior in children and adolescents. *Developmental Psychology*, 15(1), 38–44.

Ellis, B. J. (2004). Timing of pubertal maturation in girls: An integrated life history approach. *Psychological Bulletin*, 130, 920–958.

Entwisle, D. R., Alexander, K. L., & Steffel Olson, L. (2005). First grade and educational attainment by age 22: A new story. *American Journal of Sociology*, 110(5), 1458–1502.

Espinoza, G., & Juvonen, J. (2011). Perceptions of the school social context across the transition to middle school: Heightened sensitivity among Latino students? *Journal of Educational Psychology*, 103(3), 749–758. doi:10.1037/a0023811

Figner, B., Mackinlay, R. J., Wilkening, F., & Weber, E. U. (2009). Affective and deliberative processes in risky choice: Age differences in risk taking in the Columbia Card Task. *Journal of Experimental Psychology: Learning, Memory, and Cognition*, 35(3), 709–730. doi:10.1037/a0014983

Fischhoff, B. (2008). Assessing adolescent decision-making competence. *Developmental Review*, 28(1), 12–28. doi:10.1016/j.dr.2007.08.001

Fishkin, J., Keniston, K., & McKinnon, C. (1973). Moral reasoning and political ideology. *Journal of Personality and Social Psychology*, 27(1), 109–119. doi:10.1037/h0034434

Flieller, A. (1999). Comparison of the development of formal thought in adolescent cohorts aged 10 to 15 (1967–1996). *Developmental Psychology*, 35(4), 1048.

Fradkin, C., Wallander, J. L., Elliott, M. N., Cuccaro, P., & Schuster, M. A. (2014). Regular physical activity has differential association with reduced obesity among diverse youth in the United States. *Journal of Health Psychology*. Advance online publication. doi:10.1177/1359105314559622

Fradkin, C., Wallander, J. L., Elliott, M. N., Tortolero, S., Cuccaro, P., & Schuster, M. A. (2015). Associations between socioeconomic status and obesity in diverse, young adolescents: Variation across race/ethnicity and gender. *Health Psychology*, 34(1), 1–9. doi:10.1037/hea0000099

Frankel, L. L. (2002). "I've never thought about it": Contradictions and taboos surrounding American males' experiences of first ejaculation (semenarche). *Journal of Men's Studies*, 11(1), 37–54.

Frederick, C. B., Snellman, K., & Putnam, R. D. (2014). Increasing socioeconomic disparities in adolescent obesity. *Proceedings of the National Academy of Sciences of the United States of America*, 111(4), 1338–1342. doi:10.1073/pnas.1321355110

Freeman, J., & Simonsen, B. (2014). Examining the impact of policy and practice interventions on high school dropout and school completion rates: A systematic review of the literature. *Review of Educational Research*. Advance online publication. doi:10.3102/0034654314554431

Frostad, P., Pijl, S. J., & Mjaavatn, P. E. (2014). Losing all interest in school: Social participation as a predictor of the intention to leave upper secondary school early. *Scandinavian Journal of Educational Research*, 59(1), 110–122. doi:10.1080/00313831.2014.904420

Furby, L., & Beyth-Marom, R. (1992). Risk taking in adolescence: A decision-making perspective. *Developmental Review*, 12(1), 1–44.

Gaddis, A., & Brooks-Gunn, J. (1985). The male experience of pubertal change. *Journal of Youth and Adolescence*, 14(1), 61–69.

Gaillard, V., Barrouillet, P., Jarrold, C., & Camos, V. (2011). Developmental differences in working memory: Where do they come from? *Journal of Experimental Child Psychology*, 110(3), 469–479. doi:10.1016/j.jecp.2011.05.004

Gajdos, Z. K. Z., Henderson, K. D., Hirschhorn, J. N., & Palmert, M. R. (2010). Genetic determinants of pubertal timing in the general population. *Molecular and Cellular Endocrinology*, 324(1–2), 21–29. doi:10.1016/j.mce.2010.01.038

Garg, R., Levin, E., Urajnik, D., & Kauppi, C. (2005). Parenting style and academic achievement for East Indian and Canadian adolescents. *Journal of Comparative Family Studies*, 36(4), 653–661.

Geier, C. F. (2013). Adolescent cognitive control and reward processing: Implications for risk taking and substance use. *Hormones and Behavior*, 64(2), 333–342. doi:10.1016/j.yhbeh.2013.02.008

Geier, C. F., Terwilliger, R., Teslovich, T., Velanova, K., & Luna, B. (2010). Immaturities in reward processing and its influence on inhibitory control in adolescence. *Cerebral Cortex*, 20(7), 1613–1629. doi:10.1093/cercor/bhp225

Gentle-Genitty, C. (2009). Best practice program for low-income African American students transitioning from middle to high school. *Children & Schools*, 31(2), 109–117.

Gibbs, J. C. (2003). *Moral development and reality: Beyond the theories of Kohlberg and Hoffman*. Thousand Oaks, CA: Sage.

Gibbs, J. C., Basinger, K. S., Grime, R. L., & Snarey, J. R. (2007). Moral judgment development across cultures: Revisiting Kohlberg's universality claims. *Developmental Review*, 27(4), 443–500. doi:10.1016/j.dr.2007.04.001

Giedd, J. N., Lalonde, F. M., Celano, M. J., White, S. L., Wallace, G. L., Lee, N. R., & Lenroot, R. K. (2009). Anatomical brain magnetic resonance imaging of typically developing children and adolescents. *Journal of the American Academy of Child & Adolescent Psychiatry*, 48(5), 465–470. doi:10.1097/CHI.0b013e31819f215

Gilligan, C. (1982). *In a different voice: Psychological theory and women's development*. Cambridge, MA: Harvard University Press.

Gilligan, C., & Attanucci, J. (1988). Two moral orientations: Gender differences and similarities. *Merrill-Palmer Quarterly*, 34(3), 223–237.

Glasgow, K. L., & Dornbusch, S. M. (1997). Parenting styles, adolescents' attributions, and educational outcomes in nine heterogeneous high. *Child Development*, 68(3), 507–529.

Goddings, A.-L. (2015). The role of puberty in human adolescent brain development. In J.-P. Bourguignon, J.-C. Carel, & Y. Christen (Eds.), *Brain crosstalk in puberty and adolescence* (Vol.

13, pp. 75–83). Cham, Switzerland: Springer International Publishing. doi:10.1007/978-3-319-09168-6

Goddings, A.-L., Mills, K. L., Clasen, L. S., Giedd, J. N., Viner, R. M., & Blakemore, S.-J. (2014). The influence of puberty on subcortical brain development. NeuroImage, 88, 242–251. doi:10.1016/j.neuroimage.2013.09.073

Godley, S. H., Passetti, L. L., & White, M. K. (2006). Employment and adolescent alcohol and drug treatment and recovery: An exploratory study. American Journal on Addictions, 15, 137–143.

Goldstein, S. E., Boxer, P., & Rudolph, E. (2015). Middle school transition stress: Links with academic performance, motivation, and school experiences. Contemporary School Psychology, 19(1), 21–29. doi:10.1007/s40688-014-0044-4

Golub, S. (1992). Periods: From menarche to menopause. Newbury Park, CA: Sage.

Gonzalez, A.-L., & Wolters, C. A. (2006). The relation between perceived parenting practices and achievement motivation in mathematics. Journal of Research in Childhood Education, 21(2), 203–217.

Graber, J. A., Nichols, T. R., & Brooks-Gunn, J. (2010). Putting pubertal timing in developmental context: Implications for prevention. Developmental Psychobiology, 52(3), 254–262. doi:10.1002/dev.20438

Graber, J. A., Petersen, A. C., & Brooks-Gunn, J. (1996). Pubertal processes: Methods, measures, and models. In J. A. Graber, J. Brooks-Gunn, & A. C. Petersen (Eds.), Transitions through adolescence: Interpersonal domains and context (pp. 23–53). Hoboken, NJ: Lawrence Erlbaum.

Greenberger, E., & Steinberg, L. (1986). When teenagers work: The psychological and social costs of adolescent employment. New York: Basic Books.

Greene, K., & Krcmar, M. (2000). Targeting adolescent risk-taking behaviors: The contributions of egocentrism and sensation-seeking. Journal of Adolescence, 23, 439–462.

Greene, K. M., & Staff, J. (2012). Teenage employment and career readiness. New Directions for Youth Development, 2012(134), 23–31. doi:10.1002/yd.20012

Greenhouse, L. (2005). Supreme court, 5–4, forbids execution in juvenile crime [Cover story]. New York Times, pp. A1–A14.

Gregg, V., Gibbs, J. C., & Basinger, K. S. (1994). Patterns of developmental delay in moral judgment by male and female delinquents. Merrill-Palmer Quarterly, 40(4), 538–553.

Gusterson, B. A., & Stein, T. (2012). Human breast development. Seminars in Cell & Developmental Biology, 23(5), 567–573. doi:10.1016/j.semcdb.2012.03.013

Hall, G. S. (1904). Adolescence. New York: Appleton.

Halpern-Felsher, B. L., & Cauffman, E. (2001). Costs and benefits of a decision. Decision-making competence in adolescents and adults. Journal of Applied Developmental Psychology, 22(3), 257–273.

Hamilton, S. F., & Hamilton, M. A. (1999). Creating new pathways to adulthood by adapting German apprenticeship in the United States. In W. R. Heinz (Ed.), From education to work: Cross-national perspectives (pp. 194–213). New York: Cambridge University Press.

Hare, T. A., Tottenham, N., Galvan, A., Voss, H. U., Glover, G. H., & Casey, B. J. (2008). Biological substrates of emotional reactivity and regulation in adolescence during an emotional go-nogo task. Biological Psychiatry, 63(10), 927–934. doi:10.1016/j.biopsych.2008.03.015

Heaven, P. C. L., & Ciarrochi, J. (2008). Parental styles, conscientiousness, and academic performance in high school: A three-wave longitudinal study. Personality and Social Psychology Bulletin, 34(4), 451–461. doi:10.1177/0146167207311909

Heinz, W. R. (1999). From education to work: Cross-national perspectives. New York: Cambridge University Press.

Helwig, C. C., Arnold, M. L., Tan, D., & Boyd, D. (2007). Mainland Chinese and Canadian adolescents' judgments and reasoning about the fairness of democratic and other forms of government. Cognitive Development, 22(1), 96–109.

Henry, K. L., Knight, K. E., & Thornberry, T. P. (2012). School disengagement as a predictor of dropout, delinquency, and problem substance use during adolescence and early adulthood. Journal of Youth and Adolescence, 41(2), 156–166. doi:10.1007/s10964-011-9665-3

Herman-Giddens, M. E. (2006). Recent data on pubertal milestones in United States children: The secular trend toward earlier development. International Journal of Andrology, 29(1), 241–246.

Herman-Giddens, M. E., Kaplowitz, P. B., & Wasserman, R. (2004). Navigating the recent articles on girls' puberty in pediatrics: What do we know and where do we go from here? Pediatrics, 113(4), 911–917.

Herman-Giddens, M. E., Steffes, J., Harris, D., Slora, E., Hussey, M., Dowshen, S. A., . . . Reiter, E. O. (2012). Secondary sexual characteristics in boys: Data from the Pediatric Research in Office Settings Network. Pediatrics, 130(5), e1058–e1068. doi:10.1542/peds.2011-3291

Himes, J. H. (2006). Examining the evidence for recent secular changes in the timing of puberty in US children in light of increases in the prevalence of obesity. Molecular & Cellular Endocrinology, 254–255, 13–21.

Hodges-Simeon, C. R., Gurven, M., Cárdenas, R. A., & Gaulin, S. J. C. (2013). Voice change as a new measure of male pubertal timing: A study among Bolivian adolescents. Annals of Human Biology, 40(3), 209–219. doi:10.3109/03014460.2012.759622

Hollenstein, T., & Lougheed, J. P. (2013). Beyond storm and stress: Typicality, transactions, timing, and temperament to account for adolescent change. The American Psychologist, 68(6), 444–454. doi:10.1037/a0033586

Holmbeck, G. N., & Hill, J. P. (1988). Storm and stress beliefs about adolescence: Prevalence, self-reported antecedents, and effects of an undergraduate course. Journal of Youth and Adolescence, 17(4), 285–306. doi:10.1007/BF01537671

Inhelder, B., & Piaget, J. (1958). The growth of logical thinking: From childhood to adolescence. New York: Basic Books.

Jackson, A. W., & Davis, G. A. (2000). Turning points 2000: Educating adolescents in the 21st century. Williston, VT: Teachers College Press. Retrieved from http://eric.ed.gov/?id=ED448910

Jaffee, S., & Hyde, J. S. (2000). Gender differences in moral orientation: A meta-analysis. Psychological Bulletin, 126(5), 703.

Jahns, L., Siega-Riz, A. M., & Popkin, B. M. (2001). The increasing prevalence of snacking among US children from 1977 to 1996. Journal of Pediatrics, 138, 493–498.

Janosz, M., Archambault, I., Morizot, J., & Pagani, L. S. (2008). School engagement trajectories and their differential predictive relations to dropout. Journal of Social Issues, 64(1), 21–40. doi:10.1111/j.1540-4560.2008.00546.x

Javadi, A. H., Schmidt, D. H. K., & Smolka, M. N. (2014). Differential representation of feedback and decision in adolescents and adults. Neuropsychologia, 56, 280–288. doi:10.1016/j.neuropsychologia.2014.01.021

Jolles, D. D., van Buchem, M. A., Crone, E. A., & Rombouts, S. A. (2011). A comprehensive study of whole-brain functional connectivity in children and young adults. Cerebral Cortex, 21(2), 385–391. doi:10.1093/cercor/bhq104

Juvonen, J., Le, V.-N., Kaganoff, T., Augustine, C. H., & Constant, L. (2004). Focus on the wonder years: Challenges facing the American middle school. Santa Monica, CA: Rand Corporation. Retrieved from https://books.google.com/books?id=LX7nSC1vdggC&pgis=1

Kail, R. V. (2008). Speed of processing in childhood and adolescence: Nature, consequences, and implications for understanding atypical development. In J. DeLuca & J. H. Kalmar (Eds.), Information processing speed in clinical populations (pp. 101–123). Philadelphia: Taylor & Francis.

Kalkwarf, H. J. (2007). Childhood and adolescent milk intake and adult bone health. International Congress Series, 1297, 39–49.

Kantomaa, M. T., Tammelin, T. H., Näyhä, S., & Taanila, A. M. (2007). Adolescents' physical activity in relation to family income and parents' education. Preventive Medicine, 44(5), 410–415.

Kaprio, J., Rimpela, A., Rimpelä, A., Winter, T., Viken, R. J., Rimpelä, M., & Rose, R. J. (1995). Common genetic influences on BMI and age at menarche. Human Biology, 67(5), 739. Retrieved from http://www.ncbi.nlm.nih.gov/pubmed/8543288

Karbach, J., Gottschling, J., Spengler, M., Hegewald, K., & Spinath, F. M. (2013). Parental involvement and general cognitive ability as predictors of domain-specific academic achievement in early adolescence. Learning and Instruction, 23, 43–51. doi:10.1016/j.learninstruc.2012.09.004

Keating, D. P. (2004). Cognitive and brain development. In R. M. Lerner & L. Steinberg (Eds.), Handbook of adolescent psychology (2nd ed., pp. 45–84). Hoboken, NJ: John Wiley.

Keith, T. Z., Keith, P. B., Quirk, K. J., Sperduto, J., Santillo, S., & Killings, S. (1998). Longitudinal effects of parent involvement on high school grades: Similarities and differences. Journal of School Psychology, 35(3), 335–364.

Kelly, A., Winer, K. K., Kalkwarf, H., Oberfield, S. E., Lappe, J., Gilsanz, V., & Zemel, B. S. (2014). Age-based reference ranges for annual height velocity in US children. The Journal of Clinical Endocrinology and Metabolism, 99(6), 2104–2112. doi:10.1210/jc.2013-4455

Kidger, J., Araya, R., Donovan, J., & Gunnell, D. (2012). The effect of the school environment on the emotional health of adolescents: A systematic review. Pediatrics, 129(5), 925–949. doi:10.1542/peds.2011-2248

Kimmons, J. E., Gillespie, C., Seymour, J., Serdula, M., & Blanck, H. M. (2008). Fruit and vegetable intake among adolescents and adults in the United States: Percentage meeting individualized recommendations. Medscape Journal of Medicine, 11(1). Retrieved from http://www.pubmedcentral.nih.gov/articlerender.fcgi?artid=2654704

Kingery, J. N., Erdley, C. A., & Marshall, K. C. (2011). Peer acceptance and friendship as predictors of early adolescents' adjustment across the middle school transition. Merrill-Palmer Quarterly, 57(3), 215–243. doi:10.1353/mpq.2011.0012

Kingston, S., & Rose, A. (2015). Do the effects of adolescent employment differ by employment intensity and neighborhood context? American Journal of Community Psychology, 55(1–2), 37–47. doi:10.1007/s10464-014-9690-y

Kirk, J., Bandhakavi, M., & Simon, C. (2008). Disorders of puberty. InnovAiT, 1(11), 722–728. doi:10.1093/innovait/inn157

Knox, P. L., Fagley, N. S., & Miller, P. M. (2004). Care and justice moral orientation among African American college students. Journal of Adult Development, 11(1), 41–45.

Kohlberg, L. (1969). Stage and sequence: The cognitive-developmental approach to socialization. In D. A. Goslin (Ed.), *Handbook of socialization* (pp. 347–480). Chicago: Rand McNally.

Kohlberg, L. (1981). *Essays on moral development*. San Francisco: Harper & Row.

Kohlberg, L., & Kramer, R. (1969). Continuities and discontinuities in childhood and adult moral development. *Human Development*, 12(2), 3–120.

Kohlberg, L., Levine, C., & Hewer, A. (1983). *Moral stages: A current formulation and a response to critics*. New York: Karger.

Kohlberg, L., & Ryncarz, R. A. (1990). Beyond justice reasoning: Moral development and consideration of a seventh stage. In C. N. Alexander & E. J. Langer (Eds.), *Higher stages of human development: Perspectives on adult growth* (pp. 191–207). New York: Oxford University Press.

Kuhn, D. (2000). Metacognitive development. *Current Directions in Psychological Science*, 9, 178–181.

Kuhn, D. (2008). Formal operations from a twenty-first century perspective. *Human Development*, 51(1), 48–55. doi:10.1159/000113155

Kuhn, D. (2012). The development of causal reasoning. *Wiley Interdisciplinary Reviews: Cognitive Science*, 3(3), 327–335. doi:10.1002/wcs.1160

Kuhn, D., & Franklin, S. (2006). The second decade: What develops (and how). In D. Kuhn, R. S. Siegler, W. Damon, & R. M. Lerner (Eds.), *Handbook of child psychology: Vol 2. Cognition, perception, and language* (6th ed., pp. 953–993). Hoboken, NJ: John Wiley.

Kuhn, D., Iordanou, K., Pease, M., & Wirkala, C. (2008). Beyond control of variables: What needs to develop to achieve skilled scientific thinking? *Cognitive Development*, 23(4), 435–451. doi:10.1016/j.cogdev.2008.09.006

Kuhn, D., Langer, J., Kohlberg, L., & Haan, N. S. (1977). The development of formal operations in logical and moral judgment. *Genetic Psychology Monographs*, 95(1), 97–188.

Kuhn, D., Pease, M., & Wirkala, C. (2009). Coordinating the effects of multiple variables: A skill fundamental to scientific thinking. *Journal of Experimental Child Psychology*, 103(3), 268–284. doi:10.1016/j.jecp.2009.01.009

Kupfersmid, J. H., & Wonderly, D. M. (1980). Moral maturity and behavior: Failure to find a link. *Journal of Youth and Adolescence*, 9(3), 249–261.

Kuther, T. L., & Higgins-D'Alessandro, A. (2000). Bridging the gap between moral reasoning and adolescent engagement in risky behavior. *Journal of Adolescence*, 23(4), 409–423.

Labouvie-Vief, G. (2015). *Integrating emotions and cognition throughout the lifespan*. New York: Springer.

Lapsley, D. K., Jackson, S., Rice, K., & Shadid, G. E. (1988). Self-monitoring and the "new look" at the imaginary audience and personal fable: An ego-developmental analysis. *Journal of Adolescent Research*, 3(1), 17–31.

Larson, N. I., Nelson, M. C., Neumark-Sztainer, D., Story, M., & Hannan, P. J. (2009). Making time for meals: Meal structure and associations with dietary intake in young adults. *Journal of the American Dietetic Association*, 109(1), 72–79. doi:10.1016/j.jada.2008.10.017

Larson, R., & Csikszentmihalyi, M. (2014). The experience sampling method. In M. Csikszentmihalyi. (Ed.), *Flow and the foundations of positive psychology* (pp. 21–34). Dordrecht: Springer Netherlands. Retrieved from http://link.springer.com/chapter/10.1007/978-94-017-9088-8_3

Larson, R., Csikszentmihalyi, M., & Graef, R. (2014). Mood variability and the psycho-social adjustment of adolescents. In M. Csikszentmihalyi (Ed.), *Applications of flow in human development and education* (pp.

285–304). Dordrecht: Springer Netherlands. Retrieved from http://link.springer.com/chapter/10.1007/978-94-017-9094-9_15

Larson, R., & Ham, M. (1993). Stress and "storm and stress" in early adolescence: The relationship of negative events with. *Developmental Psychology*, 29(1), 130.

Larson, R., & Richards, M. (1998). Waiting for the weekend: Friday and Saturday night as the emotional climax of the week. *New Directions for Child and Adolescent Development*, 1998(82), 37–51.

Larson, R., & Seepersad, S. (2003). Adolescents' leisure time in the United States: Partying, sports, and the American experiment. *New Directions for Child and Adolescent Development*, 2003(99), 53–64.

Larson, R., & Wilson, S. (2004). Adolescence across place and time. In R. M. Lerner & L. Steinberg (Eds.), *Handbook of adolescent psychology*. Hoboken, NJ: John Wiley.

Lee, J. M. (2007). Weight status in young girls and the onset of puberty. *Pediatrics*, 119.

Leenders, I., & Brugman, D. D. (2005). Moral/non-moral domain shift in young adolescents in relation to delinquent behaviour. *British Journal of Developmental Psychology*, 23(1), 65–79.

Leenstra, T., Petersen, L. T., Kariuki, S. K., Oloo, A. J., Kager, P. A., & ter Kuile, F. O. (2005). Prevalence and severity of malnutrition and age at menarche; cross-sectional studies in adolescent schoolgirls in western Kenya. *European Journal of Clinical Nutrition*, 59(1), 41–48. doi:10.1038/sj.ejcn.1602031

Lehman, D. R., Lempert, R. O., & Nisbett, R. E. (1988). The effects of graduate training on reasoning: Formal discipline and thinking about everyday life events. *American Psychologist*, 43, 431–443. Retrieved from http://deepblue.lib.umich.edu/handle/2027.42/92173

Lehman, D. R., & Nisbett, R. E. (1990). A longitudinal study of the effects of undergraduate training on reasoning. *Developmental Psychology*, 26, 952–960.

Lerner, R. M., & Israeloff., R. (2007). *The good teen: Rescuing adolescence from the myths of the storm and stress years*. New York: Crown.

Lioret, S., Maire, B., Volatier, J. L., & Charles, M. A. (2007). Child overweight in France and its relationship with physical activity, sedentary behaviour and socioeconomic status. *European Journal of Clinical Nutrition*, 61(4), 509–516.

Loessl, B., Valerius, G., Kopasz, M., Hornyak, M., Riemann, D., & Voderholzer, U. (2008). Are adolescents chronically sleep-deprived? An investigation of sleep habits of adolescents in the Southwest of Germany. *Child: Care, Health & Development*, 34(5), 549–556. doi:10.1111/j.1365-2214.2008.00845.x

Luders, E., Thompson, P. M., & Toga, A. W. (2010). The development of the corpus callosum in the healthy human brain. *The Journal of Neuroscience*, 30(33), 10985–10990. doi:10.1523/JNEUROSCI.5122-09.2010

Luna, B., Garver, K. E., Urban, T. A., Lazar, N. A., & Sweeney, J. A. (2004). Maturation of cognitive processes from late childhood to adulthood. *Child Development*, 75(5), 1357–1372. doi:10.1111/j.1467-8624.2004.00745.x

Luna, B., Paulsen, D. J., Padmanabhan, A., & Geier, C. (2013). The teenage brain: Cognitive control and motivation. *Current Directions in Psychological Science*, 22(2), 94–100. doi:10.1177/0963721413478416

Lynch, M., & Cicchetti, D. (1996). Children's relationships with adults and peers: An examination of elementary and junior high school students. *Journal of School Psychology*, 35(1), 81–99. Retrieved from http://eric.ed.gov/?id=EJ551717

Madon, S., Guyll, M., Spoth, R., & Willard, J. (2004). Self-fulfilling prophecies: The synergistic accumulative effect of parents' beliefs on children's drinking behavior. *Psychological Science*, 15(12), 837–845. doi:10.1111/j.0956-7976.2004.00764.x

Mahoney, J. L. (2014). School extracurricular activity participation and early school dropout: A mixed-method study of the role of peer social networks. *Journal of Educational and Developmental Psychology*, 4(1), 143. doi:10.5539/jedp.v4n1p143

Malina, R. M., & Bouchard, C. (2004). *Growth, maturation, and physical activity*. Champaign, IL: Human Kinetics Academic.

Malti, T., Keller, M., & Buchmann, M. (2013). Do moral choices make us feel good? The development of adolescents' emotions following moral decision making. *Journal of Research on Adolescence*, 23(2), 389–397. doi:10.1111/jora.12005

Malti, T., & Latzko, B. (2010). Children's moral emotions and moral cognition: Towards an integrative perspective. *New Directions for Child & Adolescent Development*, 2010(129), 1–10. doi:10.1002/cd.272

Maqsood, A. R., Trueman, J. A., Whatmore, A. J., Westwood, M., Price, D. A., Hall, C. M., & Clayton, P. E. (2007). The relationship between nocturnal urinary leptin and gonadotrophins as children progress towards puberty. *Hormone Research*, 68(5), 225–230.

Marceau, K., Ram, N., Houts, R. M., Grimm, K. J., & Susman, E. J. (2011). Individual differences in boys' and girls' timing and tempo of puberty: Modeling development with nonlinear growth models. *Developmental Psychology*, 47(5), 1389–1409. doi:10.1037/a0023838

McKnight-Eily, L. R., Eaton, D. K., Lowry, R., Croft, J. B., Presley-Cantrell, L., & Perry, G. S. (2011). Relationships between hours of sleep and health-risk behaviors in US adolescent students. *Preventive Medicine*, 53(4–5), 271–273. doi:10.1016/j.ypmed.2011.06.020

McNamee, R. L., Dunfee, K. L., Luna, B., Clark, D. B., Eddy, W. F., & Tarter, R. E. (2008). Brain activation, response inhibition, and increased risk for substance use disorder. *Alcoholism: Clinical & Experimental Research*, 32(3), 405–413. doi:10.1111/j.1530-0277.2007.00604.x

McNeely, C. A., Nonnemaker, J. M., & Blum, R. W. (2002). Promoting school connectedness: Evidence from the National Longitudinal Study of Adolescent Health. *Journal of School Health*, 72(4), 138–147.

Mendle, J. (2014). Beyond pubertal timing: New directions for studying individual differences in development. *Current Directions in Psychological Science*, 23(3), 215–219. doi:10.1177/0963721414530144

Mendle, J., & Ferrero, J. (2012). Detrimental psychological outcomes associated with pubertal timing in adolescent boys. *Developmental Review*, 32(1), 49–66. doi:10.1016/j.dr.2011.11.001

Mendle, J., Turkheimer, E., & Emery, R. E. (2007). Detrimental psychological outcomes associated with early pubertal timing in adolescent girls. *Developmental Review*, 27(2), 151–171.

Mendle, J., Turkheimer, E., D'Onofrio, B. M., Lynch, S. K., Emery, R. E., Slutske, W. S., & Martin, N. G. (2006). Family structure and age at menarche: A children-of-twins approach. *Developmental Psychology*, 42, 533–542.

Metcalf, M. G., Skidmore, D. S., Lowry, G. F., & Mackenzie, J. A. (1983). Incidence of ovulation in the years after the menarche. *Journal of Endocrinology*, 97(2), 213–219. doi:10.1677/joe.0.0970213

Midgley, C., Anderman, E., & Hicks, L. (1995). Differences between elementary and middle school teachers and students: A goal theory approach. *The Journal of Early Adolescence, 15*(1), 90–113. doi:10.1177/0272431695015001006

Miller, J. G. (1997). Culture and self: Uncovering the cultural grounding of psychological theory. In J. G. Snodgrass & R. L. Thompson (Eds.), *Self across psychology: Self-recognition, self-awareness, and the self concept* (pp. 217–231). New York: New York Academy of Sciences.

Miller, J. G., & Bersoff, D. M. (1995). Development in the context of everyday family relationships: Culture, interpersonal morality, and adaptation. In M. Killen & D. Hart (Eds.), *Morality in everyday life: Developmental perspectives* (pp. 259–282). New York: Cambridge University Press.

Mills, K. L., Goddings, A.-L., Clasen, L. S., Giedd, J. N., & Blakemore, S.-J. (2014). The developmental mismatch in structural brain maturation during adolescence. *Developmental Neuroscience, 36*(3–4), 147–160. doi:10.1159/000362328

Millstein, S. G., & Halpern-Felsher, B. L. (2002). Perceptions of risk and vulnerability. *Journal of Adolescent Health, 31,* 10–27.

Mitchell, J. A., Rodriguez, D., Schmitz, K. H., & Audrain-McGovern, J. (2013a). Greater screen time is associated with adolescent obesity: A longitudinal study of the BMI distribution from Ages 14 to 18. *Obesity, 21*(3), 572–575. doi:10.1002/oby.20157

Mitchell, J. A., Rodriguez, D., Schmitz, K. H., & Audrain-McGovern, J. (2013b). Sleep duration and adolescent obesity. *Pediatrics, 131*(5), e1428–e1434. doi:10.1542/peds.2012-2368

Modecki, K. L. (2014). Maturity of judgment. In R J. R. Levesque, *Encyclopedia of adolescence* (pp. 1660–1665). New York: Springer. Retrieved from http://link.springer.com/referenceworkentry/10.1007/978-1-4419-1695-2_213

Moilanen, K. L., Rasmussen, K. E., & Padilla-Walker, L. M. (2015). Bidirectional associations between self-regulation and parenting styles in early adolescence. *Journal of Research on Adolescence, 25*(2). doi:10.1111/jora.12125

Monahan, K. C., Lee, J. M., & Steinberg, L. (2011). Revisiting the impact of part-time work on adolescent adjustment: Distinguishing between selection and socialization using propensity score matching. *Child Development, 82*(1), 96–112. doi:10.1111/j.1467-8624.2010.01543.x

Monk, C. S., McClure, E. B., Nelson, E. E., Zarahn, E., Bilder, R. M., Leibenluft, E., . . . Pine, D. S. (2003). Adolescent immaturity in attention-related brain engagement to emotional facial expressions. *NeuroImage, 20*(1), 420–429.

Moore, S. R., Harden, K. P., & Mendle, J. (2014). Pubertal timing and adolescent sexual behavior in girls. *Developmental Psychology, 50*(6), 1734–1745. doi:10.1037/a0036027

Mortimer, J. T., & Johnson, M. K. (1998). New perspectives on adolescent work and the transition to adulthood. In R. Jessor (Ed.), *New perspectives on adolescent risk behavior* (pp. 425–496). New York: Cambridge University Press.

Moshman, D. (2005). *Adolescent psychological development: Rationality, morality, and identity* (2nd ed). Mahwah, NJ: Lawrence Erlbaum.

Mrug, S., Elliott, M. N., Davies, S., Tortolero, S. R., Cuccaro, P., & Schuster, M. A. (2014). Early puberty, negative peer influence, and problem behaviors in adolescent girls. *Pediatrics, 133*(1), 7–14. doi:10.1542/peds.2013-0628

National Center for Education Statistics. (2014). *The condition of education—2014.* Washington, DC: Author. Retrieved from http://nces.ed.gov/pubsearch/pubsinfo.asp?pubid=2014083

National Middle School Association. (2003). *This we believe: Successful schools for young adolescents.* Westerville, OH: Author.

Natsuaki, M. N., Biehl, M. C., Ge, X., & Xiaojia, G. (2009). Trajectories of depressed mood from early adolescence to young adulthood: The effects of pubertal timing and adolescent dating. *Journal of Research on Adolescence, 19*(1), 47–74. doi:10.1111/j.1532-7795.2009.00581.x

Neberich, W., Penke, L., Lehnart, J., & Asendorpf, J. B. (2010). Family of origin, age at menarche, and reproductive strategies: A test of four evolutionary-developmental models. *European Journal of Developmental Psychology, 7*(2), 153–177. doi:10.1080/17405620801928029

Negriff, S., & Susman, E. J. (2011). Pubertal timing, depression, and externalizing problems: A framework, review, and examination of gender differences. *Journal of Research on Adolescence, 21*(3), 717–746. doi:10.1111/j.1532-7795.2010.00708.x

Nisan, M., & Kohlberg, L. (1982). Universality and variation in moral judgment: A longitudinal and cross-sectional study in Turkey. *Child Development, 53*(4), 865–877.

Norman, R. (2008). Reproductive changes in the female lifespan. In J. J. Robert-McComb, R. Norman, & M. Zumwalt (Eds.), *The active female: Health issues throughout the lifespan* (pp. 17–24). Totowa, NJ: Humana Press.

Nurmi, J.-E. (1991). How do adolescents see their future? A review of the development of future orientation and planning. *Developmental Review, 11*(1), 1–59.

Obeidallah, D., Brennan, R. T., Brooks-Gunn, J., & Earls, F. (2004). Links between pubertal timing and neighborhood contexts: Implications for girls' violent behavior. *Journal of the American Academy of Child & Adolescent Psychiatry, 43*(12), 1460–1468.

Obeidallah, D. A., Brennan, R. T., Brooks-Gunn, J., Kindlon, D., & Earls, F. (2000). Socioeconomic status, race, and girls' pubertal maturation: Results from the project on human development in Chicago neighborhoods. *Journal of Research on Adolescence, 10*(4), 443–464.

Offer, D. (1989). Adolescence. *American Journal of Diseases of Children, 143*(6), 731. doi:10.1001/archpedi.1989.02150180113031

Offer, D., Ostrov, E., Howard, K. I., & Atkinson, R. (1988). *The teenage world: Adolescents' self-image in ten countries* (Vol. 11). New York: Springer Science + Business Media. Retrieved from https://books.google.com/books?id=yQuGBwAAQBAJ&pgis=1

Offer, D., & Schonert-Reichl, K. A. (1992). Debunking the myths of adolescence: Findings from recent research. *Journal of the American Academy of Child and Adolescent Psychiatry, 31*(6), 1003–1014. doi:10.1097/00004583-199211000-00001

Omar, H., McElderry, D., & Zakharia, R. (2003). Educating adolescents about puberty: What are we missing? *International Journal of Adolescent Medicine and Health, 15,* 79–83.

Owens, J. A., Belon, K., & Moss, P. (2010). Impact of delaying school start time on adolescent sleep, mood, and behavior. *Archives of Pediatrics & Adolescent Medicine, 164*(7), 608–614. doi:10.1001/archpediatrics.2010.96

Padmanabhan, A., & Luna, B. (2014). Developmental imaging genetics: Linking dopamine function to adolescent behavior. *Brain and Cognition, 89,* 27–38. doi:10.1016/j.bandc.2013.09.011

Patel, D. R., & Luckstead, E. F. (2000). Sport participation, risk taking, and health risk behaviors. *Adolescent Medicine, 11,* 141–155.

Paulsen, D. J., Hallquist, M. N., Geier, C. F., & Luna, B. (2014). Effects of incentives, age, and behavior on brain activation during inhibitory control: A longitudinal fMRI study. *Developmental Cognitive Neuroscience, 11,* 105–115. doi:10.1016/j.dcn.2014.09.003

Peake, S. J., Dishion, T. J., Stormshak, E. A., Moore, W. E., & Pfeifer, J. H. (2013). Risk-taking and social exclusion in adolescence: Neural mechanisms underlying peer influences on decision-making. *NeuroImage, 82,* 23–34. doi:10.1016/j.neuroimage.2013.05.061

Peters, J. C., Vlamings, P., & Kemner, C. (2013). Neural processing of high and low spatial frequency information in faces changes across development: Qualitative changes in face processing during adolescence. *The European Journal of Neuroscience, 37*(9), 1448–1457. doi:10.1111/ejn.12172

Piaget, J. (1972). Intellectual evolution from adolescence to adulthood. *Human Development, 51*(1), 40–47. doi:10.1159/000112531

Pieters, S., Burk, W. J., Van der Vorst, H., Dahl, R. E., Wiers, R. W., & Engels, R. C. M. E. (2015). Prospective relationships between sleep problems and substance use, internalizing and externalizing problems. *Journal of Youth and Adolescence, 44*(2), 379–388.doi:10.1007/s10964-014-0213-9

Poppen, P. (1974). Sex differences in moral judgment. *Personality and Social Psychology Bulletin, 1*(1), 313–315. doi:10.1177/014616727400100106

Posner, R. B. (2006). Early menarche: A review of research on trends in timing, racial differences, etiology and psychosocial consequences. *Sex Roles, 54*(5–6), 315–322.

Power, F. C., Higgins, A., & Kohlberg, L. (1989). *Lawrence Kohlberg's approach to moral education.* New York: Columbia University Press.

Rees, M. (1993). Menarche when and why? *Lancet, 342,* 1375–1377.

Reiter, E. O., & Lee, P. A. (2001). Have the onset and tempo of puberty changed? *Archives of Pediatrics & Adolescent Medicine, 155*(9), 988–989.

Rembeck, G., Möller, M., & Gunnarsson, R. (2006). Attitudes and feelings towards menstruation and womanhood in girls at menarche. *Acta Paediatrica, 95*(6), 707–714.

Reyna, V. F., & Farley, F. (2006). Risk and rationality in adolescent decision making: Implications for theory, practice, and public policy. *Psychological Science in the Public Interest, 7*(1), 1–44.

Reyna, V. F., & Rivers, S. E. (2008). Current theories of risk and rational decision making. *Developmental Review, 28*(1), 1–11. doi:10.1016/j.dr.2008.01.002

Reynolds, B. M., & Juvonen, J. (2011). The role of early maturation, perceived popularity, and rumors in the emergence of internalizing symptoms among adolescent girls. *Journal of Youth and Adolescence, 40*(11), 1407–1422. doi:10.1007/s10964-010-9619-1

Reynolds, B. M., & Repetti, R. L. (2008). Contextual variations in negative mood and state self-esteem: What role do peers play? *The Journal of Early Adolescence, 28*(3), 405–427.

Richards, M. H., & Larson, R. (1993). Pubertal development and the daily subjective states of young adolescents. *Journal of Research on Adolescence, 3*(2), 145–169.

Rickard, I. J., Frankenhuis, W. E., & Nettle, D. (2014). Why are childhood family factors associated with timing of maturation? A role for internal prediction. *Perspectives on Psychological Science, 9*(1), 3–15. doi:10.1177/1745691613513467

Rideout, V. J. (2010). *Generation M2: Media in the lives of 8- to 18-year-olds.* Menlo Park, CA. Retrieved from http://kff.org/other/event/generation-m2-media-in-the-lives-of/

Rivers, S. E., Reyna, V. F., & Mills, B. (2008). Risk taking under the influence: A fuzzy-trace theory of emotion in adolescence. *Developmental Review, 28*(1), 107–144. doi:10.1016/j.dr.2007.11.002

Roeser, R. W., Eccles, J. S., & Sameroff, A. J. (2000). School as a context of early adolescents' academic and social-emotional development: A summary of research findings. *Elementary School Journal, 100*(5), 443–471.

Rudolph, K. D., Lambert, S. F., Clark, A. G., & Kurlakowsky, K. D. (2001). Negotiating the transition to middle school: The role of self-regulatory processes. *Child Development*, 72(3), 929–947.

Rudolph, K. D., Troop-Gordon, W., Lambert, S. F., & Natsuaki, M. N. (2014). Long-term consequences of pubertal timing for youth depression: Identifying personal and contextual pathways of risk. *Development and Psychopathology*, 26(4 Pt. 2), 1423–1444. Retrieved from http://journals.cambridge.org/abstract_S0954579414001126

Rueger, S. Y., Chen, P., Jenkins, L. N., & Choe, H. J. (2014). Effects of perceived support from mothers, fathers, and teachers on depressive symptoms during the transition to middle school. *Journal of Youth and Adolescence*, 43(4), 655–670. doi:10.1007/s10964-013-0039-x

Rutters., F. (2009). The relationship between leptin, gonadotropic hormones, and body composition during puberty in a Dutch children cohort. *European Journal of Endocrinology*, 160(6), 973–978.

Sanchez-Garrido, M. A., & Tena-Sempere, M. (2013). Metabolic control of puberty: Roles of leptin and kisspeptins. *Hormones and Behavior*, 64(2), 187–194. doi:10.1016/j.yhbeh.2013.01.014

Schelleman-Offermans, K., Knibbe, R. A., & Kuntsche, E. (2013). Are the effects of early pubertal timing on the initiation of weekly alcohol use mediated by peers and/or parents? A longitudinal study. *Developmental Psychology*, 49(7), 1277–1285.

Schlegel, A. (2008). A cross-cultural approach to adolescence. In D. L. Browning (Ed.), *Adolescent identities: A collection of readings* (pp. 31–44). New York: The Analytic Press.

Schneider, B. H., Tomada, G., Normand, S., Tonci, E., & de Domini, P. (2008). Social support as a predictor of school bonding and academic motivation following the transition to Italian middle school. *Journal of Social and Personal Relationships*, 25(2), 287–310. doi:10.1177/0265407507087960

Schonert-Reichl, K. A. (1999). Relations of peer acceptance, friendship adjustment, and social behavior to moral reasoning during early adolescence. *The Journal of Early Adolescence*, 19(2), 31.

Schreier, H. M. C., & Chen, E. (2013). Socioeconomic status and the health of youth: A multilevel, multidomain approach to conceptualizing pathways. *Psychological Bulletin*, 139(3), 606–654. doi:10.1037/a0029416

Schulz, K. M., Molenda-Figueira, H. A., & Sisk, C. L. (2009). Back to the future: The organizational–activational hypothesis adapted to puberty and adolescence. *Hormones & Behavior*, 55(5), 597–604. doi:10.1016/j.yhbeh.2009.03.010

Schwartz, P. D., Maynard, A. M., & Uzelac, S. M. (2008). Adolescent egocentrism: A contemporary view. *Adolescence*, 43(171), 441–448.

Scutti, S. (2015). Puberty comes earlier and earlier for girls. *Newsweek*. Retrieved February 7, 2015, from http://www.newsweek.com/2015/02/06/puberty-comes-earlier-and-earlier-girls-301920.html

Seger, J. Y., & Thorstensson, A. (2000). Muscle strength and electromyogram in boys and girls followed through puberty. *European Journal of Applied Physiology*, 81(1–2), 54–61. doi:10.1007/PL00013797

Seidman, E., Aber, J. L., & French, S. E. (2004). The organization of schooling and adolescent development. In K. I. Maton, C. J. Schellenbach, B. J. Leadbeater, & A. L. Solarz (Eds.), *Investing in children, youth, families, and communities: Strengths-based research and policy* (pp. 233–250). Washington, DC: American Psychological Association.

Seidman, E., Lambert, L. E., Allen, L., & Aber, J. L. (2003). Urban adolescents' transition to junior high school and protective family transactions. *The Journal of Early Adolescence*, 23(2), 166–194.

Shad, M. U., Bidesi, A. S., Chen, L.-A., Thomas, B. P., Ernst, M., & Rao, U. (2011). Neurobiology of decision-making in adolescents. *Behavioural Brain Research*, 217(1), 67–76. doi:10.1016/j.bbr.2010.09.033

Sheehy, A., Gasser, T., & Molinari, L. (2009). *An analysis of variance of the pubertal and midgrowth spurts for length and width*. Retrieved from http://informahealthcare.com/doi/abs/10.1080/030144699282642

Sheppard, P., & Sear, R. (2012). Father absence predicts age at sexual maturity and reproductive timing in British men. *Biology Letters*, 8(2), 237–240. doi:10.1098/rsbl.2011.0747

Shulman, E. P., & Cauffman, E. (2013). Reward-biased risk appraisal and its relation to juvenile versus adult crime. *Law and Human Behavior*, 37(6), 412–423. doi:10.1037/lhb0000033

Silveri, M. M., Tzilos, G. K., & Yurgelun-Todd, D. A. (2008). Relationship between white matter volume and cognitive performance during adolescence: Effects of age, sex and risk for drug use. *Addiction*, 103(9), 1509–1520. doi:10.1111/j.1360-0443.2008.02272.x

Skoog, T., & Stattin, H. (2014). Why and under what contextual conditions do early-maturing girls develop problem behaviors? *Child Development Perspectives*, 8(3), 158–162. doi:10.1111/cdep.12076

Smith, A. R., Chein, J., & Steinberg, L. (2013). Impact of socio-emotional context, brain development, and pubertal maturation on adolescent risk-taking. *Hormones and Behavior*, 64(2), 323–332. doi:10.1016/j.yhbeh.2013.03.006

Smith, A. R., Steinberg, L., Strang, N., & Chein, J. (2015). Age differences in the impact of peers on adolescents' and adults' neural response to reward. *Developmental Cognitive Neuroscience*, 11, 75–82. doi:10.1016/j.dcn.2014.08.010

Snarey, J. R. (1985). Cross-cultural universality of social-moral development: A critical review of Kohlbergian research. *Psychological Bulletin*, 97(2), 202–232.

Sørensen, K., Mouritsen, A., Aksglaede, L., Hagen, C. P., Mogensen, S. S., & Juul, A. (2012). Recent secular trends in pubertal timing: Implications for evaluation and diagnosis of precocious puberty. *Hormone Research in Pædiatrics*, 77(3), 137–145. doi:10.1159/000336325

Spear, L. P. (2013). Adolescent neurodevelopment. *The Journal of Adolescent Health*, 52(2 Suppl. 2), S7–13. doi:10.1016/j.jadohealth.2012.05.006

Spera, C. (2005). A review of the relationship among parenting practices, parenting styles, and adolescent school achievement. *Educational Psychology Review*, 17(2), 125–146.

Spielberg, J. M., Olino, T. M., Forbes, E. E., & Dahl, R. E. (2014). Exciting fear in adolescence: Does pubertal development alter threat processing? *Developmental Cognitive Neuroscience*, 8, 86–95. doi:10.1016/j.dcn.2014.01.004

Staff, J., & Uggen, C. (2003). The fruits of good work: Early work experiences and adolescent deviance. *Journal of Research in Crime & Delinquency*, 40(3), 263–290.

Staff, J., Vaneseltine, M., Woolnough, A., Silver, E., & Burrington, L. (2012). Adolescent work experiences and family formation behavior. *Journal of Research on Adolescence*, 22(1), 150–164. doi:10.1111/j.1532-7795.2011.00755.x

Stein, J. H., & Reiser, L. W. (1994). A study of white middle-class adolescent boys' responses to "semenarche" (the first ejaculation). *Journal of Youth and Adolescence*, 23(3), 373–384. doi:10.1007/BF01536725

Steinberg, L. (2001). We know some things: Parent-adolescent relationships in retrospect and prospect. *Journal of Research on Adolescence*, 11(1), 1–19.

Steinberg, L. (2008a). A social neuroscience perspective on adolescent risk-taking. *Developmental Review*, 28(1), 78–106. doi:10.1016/j.dr.2007.08.002

Steinberg, L. (2008b). *Adolescence* (8th ed.). New York: McGraw-Hill.

Steinberg, L. (2010). A dual systems model of adolescent risk-taking. *Developmental Psychobiology*, 52(3), 216–224. doi:10.1002/dev.20445

Steinberg, L. (2013). Does recent research on adolescent brain development inform the mature minor doctrine? *Journal of Medicine and Philosophy*, 38, 256–267. doi:10.1093/jmp/jht017

Steinberg, L., Fegley, S., & Dornbusch, S. M. (1993). Negative impact of part-time work on adolescent adjustment: Evidence from a longitudinal study. *Developmental Psychology*, 29(2), 171–180.

Steinberg, L., Graham, S., O'Brien, L., Woolard, J., Cauffman, E., & Banich, M. (2009). Age differences in future orientation and delay discounting. *Child Development*, 80(1), 28–44. doi:10.1111/j.1467-8624.2008.01244.x

Steinberg, L., & Monahan, K. C. (2007). Age differences in resistance to peer influence. *Developmental Psychology*, 43(6), 1531–1543. doi:10.1037/0012-1649.43.6.1531

Steinberg, L., & Scott, E. S. (2003). Less guilty by reason of adolescence: Developmental immaturity, diminished responsibility, and the juvenile death penalty. *American Psychologist*, 58(12), 1009–1018.

Stidham-Hall, K., Moreau, C., & Trussell, J. (2012). Patterns and correlates of parental and formal sexual and reproductive health communication for adolescent women in the United States, 2002-2008. *The Journal of Adolescent Health*, 50(4), 410–413. doi:10.1016/j.jadohealth.2011.06.007

Stojković, I. (2013). Pubertal timing and self-esteem in adolescents: The mediating role of body-image and social relations. *European Journal of Developmental Psychology*, 10(3), 359–377. doi:10.1080/17405629.2012.682145

Strang, N. M., Chein, J. M., & Steinberg, L. (2013). The value of the dual systems model of adolescent risk-taking. *Frontiers in Human Neuroscience*, 7, 223. doi:10.3389/fnhum.2013.00223

Suitor, C. W., & Gleason, P. M. (2002). Using dietary reference intake-based methods to estimate the prevalence of inadequate nutrient intake among school-aged children. *Journal of the American Dietetic Association*, 102(4), 530–536. doi:10.1016/s0002-8223(02)90121-5

Tamnes, C. K., Walhovd, K. B., Grydeland, H., Holland, D., Østby, Y., Dale, A. M., & Fjell, A. M. (2013). Longitudinal working memory development is related to structural maturation of frontal and parietal cortices. *Journal of Cognitive Neuroscience*, 25(10), 1611–1623. doi:10.1162/jocn_a_00434

Tanner, J. M. (1990). *Foetus into man: Physical growth from conception to maturity*. Harvard, MA: Harvard University Press.

Tarry, H., & Emler, N. (2007). Attitude, values and moral reasoning as predictors of delinquency. *British Journal of Developmental Psychology*, 25(2), 169–183. doi:10.1348/026151006x113671

Taylor, J. H., & Walker, L. J. (1997). Moral climate and the development of moral reasoning: The effects of dyadic discussions between. *Journal of Moral Education*, 26(1), 21–45.

Telzer, E. H., Fuligni, A. J., Lieberman, M. D., & Galván, A. (2013). The effects of poor quality sleep on brain function and risk taking in adolescence. *NeuroImage*, 71, 275–283. doi:10.1016/j.neuroimage.2013.01.025

Thomas, L. A., De Bellis, M. D., Graham, R., & LaBar, K. S. (2007). Development of emotional facial recognition in late childhood and adolescence. *Developmental Science, 10*(5), 547–558. doi:10.1111/j.1467-7687.2007.00614.x

Tiemeier, H., Lenroot, R. K., Greenstein, D. K., Tran, L., Pierson, R., & Giedd, J. N. (2010). Cerebellum development during childhood and adolescence: A longitudinal morphometric MRI study. *NeuroImage, 49*(1), 63–70. doi:10.1016/j.neuroimage.2009.08.016

Tinggaard, J., Mieritz, M. G., Sørensen, K., Mouritsen, A., Hagen, C. P., Aksglaede, L., . . . Juul, A. (2012). The physiology and timing of male puberty. *Current Opinion in Endocrinology, Diabetes, and Obesity, 19*(3), 197–203. doi:10.1097/MED.0b013e3283535614

Tither, J. M., & Ellis, B. J. (2008). Impact of fathers on daughters' age at menarche: A genetically and environmentally controlled sibling study. *Developmental Psychology, 44*(5), 1409–1420. doi:10.1037/a0013065

Tomova, A., Lalabonova, C., Robeva, R. N., & Kumanov, P. T. (2011). Timing of pubertal maturation according to the age at first conscious ejaculation. *Andrologia, 43*(3), 163–166. doi:10.1111/j.1439-0272.2009.01037.x

Toufexis, D., Rivarola, M. A., Lara, H., & Viau, V. (2014). Stress and the reproductive axis. *Journal of Neuroendocrinology, 26*(9), 573–586. http://doi.org/10.1111/jne.12179

Tu, W., Wagner, E. K., Eckert, G. J., Yu, Z., Hannon, T., Pratt, J. H., & He, C. (2015). Associations between menarche-related genetic variants and pubertal growth in male and female adolescents. *The Journal of Adolescent Health, 56*(1), 66–72. doi:10.1016/j.jadohealth.2014.07.020

Tunau, K., Adamu, A., Hassan, M., Ahmed, Y., & Ekele, B. (2012). Age at menarche among school girls in Sokoto, Northern Nigeria. *Annals of African Medicine.* Usmanu Danfodiyo University Teaching Hospital. Retrieved from http://www.ajol.info/index.php/aam/article/view/75230

Tyler, J. H., & Lofstrom, M. (2009). Finishing high school: Alternative pathways and dropout recovery. *The Future of Children/Center for the Future of Children, the David and Lucile Packard Foundation, 19*(1), 77–103. Retrieved from http://europepmc.org/abstract/med/21141706

U.S. Bureau of Labor. (2014). *College enrollment and work activity of 2013 high school graduates.* Washington, DC: Author. Retrieved from http://www.bls.gov/news.release/hsgec.nr0.htm

U.S. Bureau of Labor. (2015). *Labor force statistics from the current population survey: Employment status of the civilian noninstitutional population by age, sex, and race.* Washington, DC: Author. Retrieved from http://www.bls.gov/cps/cpsaat03.htm

U.S. Department of Agriculture. (2000). *Pyramid servings intake by U.S. children and adults: 1994–96, 1998.* Retrieved from http://www.barc.usda.gov/bhnrc/cnrg

Van den Bosch, G. E., El Marroun, H., Schmidt, M. N., Tibboel, D., Manoach, D. S., Calhoun, V. D., & White, T. J. H. (2014). Brain connectivity during verbal working memory in children and adolescents. *Human Brain Mapping, 35*(2), 698–711. doi:10.1002/hbm.22193

Van der Stel, M., & Veenman, M. V. J. (2013). Metacognitive skills and intellectual ability of young adolescents: A longitudinal study from a developmental perspective. *European Journal of Psychology of Education, 29*(1), 117–137. doi:10.1007/s10212-013-0190-5

Van Duijvenvoorde, A. C. K., Huizenga, H. M., Somerville, L. H., Delgado, M. R., Powers, A., Weeda, W. D., . . . Figner, B. (2015). Neural correlates of expected risks and returns in risky choice across development. *The Journal of Neuroscience, 35*(4), 1549–1560. doi:10.1523/JNEUROSCI.1924-14.2015

Van Duijvenvoorde, A. C. K., Jansen, B. R. J., Visser, I., & Huizenga, H. M. (2010). Affective and cognitive decision-making in adolescents. *Developmental Neuropsychology, 35*(5), 539–554. doi:10.1080/87565641.2010.494749

Van Leijenhorst, L., Zanolie, K., Van Meel, C. S., Westenberg, P. M., Rombouts, S. A. R. B., & Crone, E. A. (2010). What motivates the adolescent? Brain regions mediating reward sensitivity across adolescence. *Cerebral Cortex, 20*(1), 61–69. doi:10.1093/cercor/bhp078

Vigil, P., Orellana, R. F., Cortés, M. E., Molina, C. T., Switzer, B. E., & Klaus, H. (2011). Endocrine modulation of the adolescent brain: A review. *Journal of Pediatric and Adolescent Gynecology, 24*(6), 330–337. doi:10.1016/j.jpag.2011.01.061

Walker, L. J. (1989). A longitudinal study of moral reasoning. *Child Development, 60*(1), 157.

Walker, L. J. (2004). Progress and prospects in the psychology of moral development. *Merrill-Palmer Quarterly, 50*(4), 546–557.

Walker, L. J., & Taylor, J. H. (1991). Family interactions and the development of moral reasoning. *Child Development, 62*, 264–283.

Walvoord, E. C. (2010). The timing of puberty: Is it changing? Does it matter? *The Journal of Adolescent Health, 47*(5), 433–439. doi:10.1016/j.jadohealth.2010.05.018

Wang, M.-T., & Fredricks, J. A. (2014). The reciprocal links between school engagement, youth problem behaviors, and school dropout during adolescence. *Child Development, 85*(2), 722–737. doi:10.1111/cdev.12138

Wang, M.-T., Hill, N. E., & Hofkens, T. (2014). Parental involvement and African American and European American adolescents' academic, behavioral, and emotional development in secondary school. *Child Development, 85*(6), 2151–2168. doi:10.1111/cdev.12284

Wang, Y., & Lim, H. (2012). The global childhood obesity epidemic and the association between socio-economic status and childhood obesity. *International Review of Psychiatry, 24*(3), 176–188. doi:10.3109/09540261.2012.688195

Wark, G. R., & Krebs, D. L. (1996). Gender and dilemma differences in real-life moral judgment. *Developmental Psychology, 32*, 220–231.

Waters, S. K., Lester, L., & Cross, D. (2014). Transition to secondary school: Expectation versus experience. *Australian Journal of Education, 58*(2), 153–166. doi:10.1177/0004944114523371

Way, N., Reddy, R., & Rhodes, J. (2007). Students' perceptions of school climate during the middle school years: Associations with trajectories of psychological and behavioral adjustment. *American Journal of Community Psychology, 40*(3–4), 194–213. doi:10.1007/s10464-007-9143-y

Weinstein, S. M., & Mermelstein, R. (2007). Relations between daily activities and adolescent mood: The role of autonomy. *Journal of Clinical Child & Adolescent Psychology, 36*(2), 182–194. doi:10.1080/15374410701274967

Weiss, C. C., & Bearman, P. S. (2007). Fresh starts: Reinvestigating the effects of the transition to high school on student outcomes. *American Journal of Education, 113*(3), 395–421.

Weisz, A. N., & Black, B. M. (2002). Gender and moral reasoning: African American youth respond to dating dilemmas. *Journal of Human Behavior in the Social Environment, 5*(1), 35–52.

Welsman, J. R., Armstrong, N., Kirby, B. J., Winsley, R. J., Parsons, G., & Sharpe, P. (1997). Exercise performance and magnetic resonance imaging-determined thigh muscle volume in children. *European Journal of Applied Physiology and Occupational Physiology, 76*(1), 92–97. doi:10.1007/s004210050218

Whittle, S., Yap, M. B. H., Yücel, M., Fornito, A., Simmons, J. G., Barrett, A., . . . Allen, N. B. (2008). Prefrontal and amygdala volumes are related to adolescents' affective behaviors during parent-adolescent interactions. *Proceedings of the National Academy of Sciences of the United States of America, 105*(9), 3652–3657. doi:10.1073/pnas.0709815105

Wigfield, A., & Eccles, J. S. (1994). Children's competence beliefs, achievement values, and general self-esteem. *The Journal of Early Adolescence, 14*(2), 107–139.

Wolfson, A. R., & Carskadon, M. A. (1998). Sleep schedules and daytime functioning in adolescents. *Child Development, 69*(4), 875–888.

Wolfson, A. R., Spaulding, N. L., Dandrow, C., & Baroni, E. M. (2007). Middle school start times: The importance of a good night's sleep for young adolescents. *Behavioral Sleep Medicine, 5*(3), 194–209. doi:10.1080/15402000701263809

Wong, M. M., Robertson, G. C., & Dyson, R. B. (2015). Prospective relationship between poor sleep and substance-related problems in a national sample of adolescents. *Alcoholism, Clinical and Experimental Research.* Advance online publication. doi:10.1111/acer.12618

Wu, T., Mendola, P., & Buck, G. M. (2002). Ethnic differences in the presence of secondary sex characteristics and menarche among US girls: The Third National Health and Nutrition Examination Survey, 1988–1994. *Pediatrics, 110*(4), 752.

Wyatt, J. M., & Carlo, G. (2002). What will my parents think? Relations among adolescents' expected parental reactions, prosocial moral reasoning, and prosocial and antisocial behaviors. *Journal of Adolescent Research, 17*, 646–667.

Yurgelun-Todd, D. (2007). Emotional and cognitive changes during adolescence. *Current Opinion in Neurobiology, 17*(2), 251–257.

Zelazo, P. D., & Carlson, S. M. (2012). Hot and cool executive function in childhood and adolescence: Development and plasticity. *Child Development Perspectives.* Advance online publication. doi:10.1111/j.1750-8606.2012.00246.x

Zhai, Z. W., Pajtek, S., Luna, B., Geier, C. F., Ridenour, T. A., & Clark, D. B. (2014). Reward-modulated response inhibition, cognitive shifting, and the orbital frontal cortex in early adolescence. *Journal of Research on Adolescence.* Advance online publication. doi:10.1111/jora.12168

Zhou, D., Lebel, C., Treit, S., Evans, A., & Beaulieu, C. (2015). Accelerated longitudinal cortical thinning in adolescence. *NeuroImage, 104*, 138–145. doi:10.1016/j.neuroimage.2014.10.005

Zimmermann, M. B., & Hurrell, R. F. (2007). Nutritional iron deficiency. *Lancet, 370*, 511–520.

CHAPTER 12

Abubakar, A., Van de Vijver, F. J. R., Suryani, A. O., Handayani, P., & Pandia, W. S. (2014). Perceptions of parenting styles and their associations with mental health and life satisfaction among urban Indonesian adolescents. *Journal of Child and Family Studies, 24*(9), 2680–2692. doi:10.1007/s10826-014-0070-x

Ackard, D. M., Fulkerson, J. A., & Neumark-Sztainer, D. (2011). Stability of eating disorder diagnostic classifications in adolescents: Five-year longitudinal findings from a population-based study. *Eating Disorders, 19*(4), 308–322. doi:10.1080/10640266.2011.584804

Adams, G. R., & Marshall, S. K. (1996). A developmental social psychology of identity: Understanding the person-in-context. *Journal of Adolescence, 19*, 429–443.

Adams, R. E., & Laursen, B. (2007). The correlates of conflict: Disagreement is not necessarily detrimental. *Journal of Family Psychology, 21*(3), 445–458.

Adelabu, D. H. (2008). Future time perspective, hope, and ethnic identity among African American adolescents. *Urban Education, 43*(3), 347–360.

Almeida, J., Johnson, R. M., Corliss, H. L., Molnar, B. E., & Azrael, D. (2009). Emotional distress among LGBT youth: The influence of perceived discrimination based on sexual orientation. *Journal of Youth and Adolescence*, 38(7), 1001–1014. doi:10.1007/s10964-009-9397-9

Almy, B., Long, K., Lobato, D., Plante, W., Kao, B., & Houck, C. (2015). Perceptions of siblings' sexual activity predict sexual attitudes among at-risk adolescents. *Journal of Developmental and Behavioral Pediatrics*, 36(4), 258–266.

Al-Owidha, A., Green, K. E., & Kroger, J. (2009). On the question of an identity status category order: Rasch model step and scale statistics used to identify category order. *International Journal of Behavioral Development*, 33(1), 88–96. doi:10.1177/0165025408100110

American Academy of Child and Adolescent Psychiatry. (2008). *Teen suicide. Facts for families.* Retrieved from http://www.aacap.org/galleries/FactsForFamilies/10_teen_suicide.pdf

American Psychiatric Association. (2013). *Diagnostic and statistical manual of mental disorders* (5th ed.). Washington, DC: Author.

Anaya, H. D., Cantwell, S. M., & Rotheram-Borus, M. J. (2003). Sexual risk behaviors among adolescents. In A. Biglan, M. C. Wang, & H. J. Walberg (Eds.), *Preventing youth problems* (pp. 113–143). New York: Kluwer Academic/Plenum Publishers.

Andersen, T. S. (2015). Race, ethnicity, and structural variations in youth risk of arrest: Evidence from a national longitudinal sample. *Criminal Justice and Behavior*, 42(9), 900–916. doi:10.1177/0093854815570963

Ang, R. P. (2006). Effects of parenting style on personal and social variables for Asian adolescents. *American Journal of Orthopsychiatry*, 76, 503–511.

Angley, M., Divney, A., Magriples, U., & Kershaw, T. (2015). Social support, family functioning and parenting competence in adolescent parents. *Maternal and Child Health Journal*, 19(1), 67–73. doi:10.1007/s10995-014-1496-x

Archer, S. L., & Waterman, A. S. (1990). Varieties of identity diffusions and foreclosures: An exploration of subcategories of the identity statuses. *Journal of Adolescent Research*, 5(1), 96–111.

Armour, S., & Haynie, D. (2007). Adolescent sexual debut and later delinquency. *Journal of Youth and Adolescence*, 36(2), 141–152. doi:10.1007/s10964-006-9128-4

Årseth, A. K., Kroger, J., Martinussen, M., & Marcia, J. E. (2009). Meta-analytic studies of identity status and the relational issues of attachment and intimacy. *Identity*, 9(1), 1–32. doi:10.1080/15283480802579532

Assini-Meytin, L. C., & Green, K. M. (2015). Long-term consequences of adolescent parenthood among African-American urban youth: A propensity score matching approach. *The Journal of Adolescent Health*, 56(5), 529–535. doi:10.1016/j.jadohealth.2015.01.005

Bachman, J. G., O'Malley, P. M., Freedman-Doan, P., Trzesniewski, K. H., & Donnellan, M. B. (2011). Adolescent self-esteem: Differences by race/ethnicity, gender, and age. *Self and Identity*, 10(4), 445–473. doi:10.1080/15298861003794538

Bagci, S. C., Rutland, A., Kumashiro, M., Smith, P. K., & Blumberg, H. (2014). Are minority status children's cross-ethnic friendships beneficial in a multiethnic context? *The British Journal of Developmental Psychology*, 32(1), 107–115. doi:10.1111/bjdp.12028

Baglivio, M. T., Jackowski, K., Greenwald, M. A., & Howell, J. C. (2014). Serious, Violent, and Chronic Juvenile Offenders. *Criminology & Public Policy*, 13(1), 83–116. doi:10.1111/1745-9133.12064

Bámaca, M. Y., Umaña-Taylor, A. J., Shin, N., & Alfaro, E. C. (2005). Latino adolescents' perception of parenting behaviors and self-esteem: Examining the role of neighborhood risk. *Family Relations*, 54(5), 621–632.

Banny, A. M., Heilbron, N., Ames, A., & Prinstein, M. J. (2011). Relational benefits of relational aggression: Adaptive and maladaptive associations with adolescent friendship quality. *Developmental Psychology*, 47(4), 1153–1166. doi:10.1037/a0022546

Barber, B. K., Stolz, H. E., & Olsen, J. A. (2005). Parental support, psychological control, and behavioral control: Assessing relevance across time, culture, and method. *Monographs of the Society for Research in Child Development*, 70(4), 1–137.

Bauman, S., Toomey, R. B., & Walker, J. L. (2013). Associations among bullying, cyberbullying, and suicide in high school students. *Journal of Adolescence*, 36(2), 341–350. doi:10.1016/j.adolescence.2012.12.001

Bauminger, N., Finzi-Dottan, R., Chason, S., & Har-Even, D. (2008). Intimacy in adolescent friendship: The roles of attachment, coherence, and self-disclosure. *Journal of Social & Personal Relationships*, 25(3), 409–428. doi:10.1177/0265407508090866

Bava, S., & Tapert, S. F. (2010). Adolescent brain development and the risk for alcohol and other drug problems. *Neuropsychology Review*, 20(4), 398–413. doi:10.1007/s11065-010-9146-6

Beautrais, A. L. (2003). Suicide and serious suicide attempts in youth: A multiple-group comparison study. *American Journal of Psychiatry*, 160, 1093–1100.

Benenson, J. F., & Christakos, A. (2003). The greater fragility of females' versus males' closest same-sex friendships. *Child Development*, 74, 1123–1129.

Benenson, J. F., & Heath, A. (2006). Boys withdraw more in one-on-one interactions, whereas girls withdraw more in groups. *Developmental Psychology*, 42, 272–282.

Benowitz-Fredericks, C. A., Garcia, K., Massey, M., Vasagar, B., & Borzekowski, D. L. G. (2012). Body image, eating disorders, and the relationship to adolescent media use. *Pediatric Clinics of North America*, 59(3), 693–704, ix. doi:10.1016/j.pcl.2012.03.017

Bentley, K. H., Nock, M. K., & Barlow, D. H. (2014). The four-function model of nonsuicidal self-injury: Key directions for future research. *Clinical Psychological Science*, 2(5), 638–656. doi:10.1177/2167702613514563

Berkman, N. D., Lohr, K. N., & Bulik, C. M. (2007). Outcomes of eating disorders: A systematic review of the literature. *International Journal of Eating Disorders*, 40(4), 293–309.

Berman, S. L., Weems, C. F., Rodriguez, E. T., & Zamora, I. J. (2006). The relation between identity status and romantic attachment style in middle and late adolescence. *Journal of Adolescence*, 29(5), 737–748.

Berndt, T. J., & Murphy, L. M. (2002). Influences of friends and friendships: Myths, truths, and research recommendations. In R. V. Kail (Ed.), *Advances in child development and behavior* (Vol. 30, pp. 275–310). San Diego: Academic Press.

Bersamin, M. M., Walker, S., Fisher, D. A., & Grube, J. W. (2006). Correlates of oral sex and vaginal intercourse in early and middle adolescence. *Journal of Research on Adolescence*, 16, 59–68.

Bersamin, M., Todd, M., Fisher, D. A., Hill, D. L., Grube, J. W., & Walker, S. (2008). Parenting practices and adolescent sexual behavior: A longitudinal study. *Journal of Marriage & Family*, 70(1), 97–112. doi:10.1111/j.1741-3737.2007.00464.x

Berzonsky, M. D., & Kuk, L. S. (2000). Identity status, identity processing style, and the transition to university. *Journal of Adolescent Research*, 15, 81–99.

Beyers, W., & Goossens, L. (2008). Dynamics of perceived parenting and identity formation in late adolescence. *Journal of Adolescence*, 31(2), 165–184. doi:10.1016/j.adolescence.2007.04.003

Birkeland, M. S., Breivik, K., & Wold, B. (2014). Peer acceptance protects global self-esteem from negative effects of low closeness to parents during adolescence and early adulthood. *Journal of Youth and Adolescence*, 43(1), 70–80. doi:10.1007/s10964-013-9929-1

Birkett, M., Newcomb, M. E., & Mustanski, B. (2015). Does it get better? A longitudinal analysis of psychological distress and victimization in lesbian, gay, bisexual, transgender, and questioning youth. *Journal of Adolescent Health*, 56(3), 280–285. doi:10.1016/j.jadohealth.2014.10.275

Biro, F. M., & Dorn, L. D. (2006). Puberty and adolescent sexuality. *Psychiatric Annals*, 36, 685–690.

Bjärehed, J., Wångby-Lundh, M., & Lundh, L.-G. (2012). Nonsuicidal self-injury in a community sample of adolescents: Subgroups, stability, and associations with psychological difficulties. *Journal of Research on Adolescence*, 22(4), 678–693. doi:10.1111/j.1532-7795.2012.00817.x

Bleakley, A., Hennessy, M., Fishbein, M., & Jordan, A. (2009). How sources of sexual information relate to adolescents' beliefs about sex. *American Journal of Health Behavior*, 33(1), 37–48.

Bleakley, A., Hennessy, M., Fishbein, M., & Jordan, A. (2011). Using the integrative model to explain how exposure to sexual media content influences adolescent sexual behavior. *Health Education & Behavior*, 38(5), 530–540. doi:10.1177/1090198110385775

Blodgett Salafia, E. H., & Gondoli, D. M. (2011). A 4-year longitudinal investigation of the processes by which parents and peers influence the development of early adolescent girls' bulimic symptoms. *Journal of Early Adolescence*, 31(3), 390–414. doi:10.1177/0272431610366248

Bos, H. M. W., Sandfort, T. G. M., de Bruyn, E. H., & Hakvoort, E. M. (2008). Same-sex attraction, social relationships, psychosocial functioning, and school performance in early adolescence. *Developmental Psychology*, 44(1), 59–68. doi:10.1037/0012-164944.1.59

Bouma, E. M. C., Ormel, J., Verhulst, F. C., & Oldehinkel, A. J. (2008). Stressful life events and depressive problems in early adolescent boys and girls: The influence of parental depression, temperament and family environment. *Journal of Affective Disorders*, 105(1–3), 185–193. doi:10.1016/j.jad.2007.05.007

Bowman, M. A., Prelow, H. M., & Weaver, S. R. (2007). Parenting behaviors, association with deviant peers, and delinquency in African American adolescents: A mediated-moderation model. *Journal of Youth and Adolescence*, 36, 517–527.

Boyce, W., Doherty, M., Fortin, C., & MacKinnon, D. (2003). *Canadian youth, sexual health, and HIV/AIDS study*. Toronto, Ontario: Council of Ministers of Education, Canada. Retrieved from http://www.cmec.ca/publications/aids

Boyes, M. C., & Chandler, M. (1992). Cognitive development, epistemic doubt, and identity formation in adolescence. *Journal of Youth and Adolescence*, 21(3), 277–304.

Brechwald, W. A., & Prinstein, M. J. (2011). Beyond homophily: A decade of advances in understanding peer influence processes. *Journal of Research on Adolescence*, 21(1), 166–179. doi:10.1111/j.1532-7795.2010.00721.x

Brent, D. A. (2009). Youth depression and suicide: Selective serotonin reuptake inhibitors treat the former and prevent the latter. *Canadian Journal of Psychiatry*, 54(2), 76–77.

Bricker, J. B., Peterson, A. V, Andersen, M. R., Rajan, K. B., Leroux, B. G., & Sarason, I. G. (2006). Childhood friends who smoke: Do they influence adolescents to make smoking transitions? *Addictive Behaviors*, 31, 889–900.

Brooks-Russell, A., Simons-Morton, B., Haynie, D., Farhat, T., & Wang, J. (2014). Longitudinal relationship between drinking with peers, descriptive norms, and adolescent alcohol use. *Prevention Science*, 15(4), 497–505. doi:10.1007/s11121-013-0391-9

Brown, B., Bank, H., & Steinberg, L. (2008). Smoke in the looking glass: Effects of discordance between self- and peer rated crowd affiliation on adolescent anxiety, depression and self-feelings. *Journal of Youth and Adolescence*, 37(10), 1163–1177. doi:10.1007/s10964-007-9198-y

Brown, B. B., Lohr, M. J., & McClenahan, E. L. (1986). Early adolescents' perceptions of peer pressure. *Journal of Early Adolescence*, 6(2), 139–154.

Browning, C. R., Leventhal, T., & Brooks-Gunn, J. (2004). Neighborhood context and racial differences in early adolescent sexual activity. *Demography*, 41(4), 697–720. doi:10.1353/dem.2004.0029

Brunner, R., Parzer, P., Haffner, J., Steen, R., Roos, J., Klett, M., & Resch, F. (2007). Prevalence and psychological correlates of occasional and repetitive deliberate self-harm in adolescents. *Archives of Pediatrics & Adolescent Medicine*, 161(7), 641–649. doi:10.1001/archpedi.161.7.641

Buhrmester, D. (1996). Need fulfillment, interpersonal competence, and the developmental contexts of early adolescent friendship. In W. M. Bukowski, A. F. Newcomb, & W. W. Hartup (Eds.), *The company they keep: Friendship during childhood and adolescence* (pp. 158–185). New York: Cambridge University Press.

Bukowski, W. M. (2001). Friendship and the worlds of childhood. *New Directions for Child & Adolescent Development*, 2001, 93–106.

Bukowski, W. M., Sippola, L., Hoza, B., & Newcomb, A. F. (2000). Pages from a sociometric notebook: An analysis of nomination and rating scale measures of acceptance, rejection, and social preference. *New Directions for Child & Adolescent Development*, 88, 11–26.

Bulik, C. M., Berkman, N. D., Brownley, K. A., Sedway, J. A., Lohr, K. N., & Shapiro, J. R. (2007). Anorexia nervosa treatment: A systematic review of randomized controlled trials. *International Journal of Eating Disorders*, 40(4), 321–336.

Burwell, R. A., & Shirk, S. R. (2006). Self processes in adolescent depression: The role of self-worth contingencies. *Journal of Research on Adolescence*, 16(3), 479–490. doi:10.1111/j.1532-7795.2006.00503.x

Busseri, M. A., Willoughby, T., Chalmers, H., & Bogaert, A. R. (2006). Same-sex attraction and successful adolescent development. *Journal of Youth and Adolescence*, 35(4), 561–573. doi:10.1007/s10964-006-9071-4

Canetto, S. S., & Sakinofsky, I. (1998). The gender paradox in suicide. *Suicide and Life-Threatening Behavior*, 28, 1–23.

Carlson, C., Uppal, S., & Prosser, E. C. (2000). Ethnic differences in processes contributing to the self-esteem of early adolescent girls. *Journal of Early Adolescence*, 20(1), 44–67.

Carlson, D. L., McNulty, T. L., Bellair, P. E., & Watts, S. (2014). Neighborhoods and racial/ethnic disparities in adolescent sexual risk behavior. *Journal of Youth and Adolescence*, 43(9), 1536–1549. doi:10.1007/s10964-013-0052-0

Carothers, S. S., Borkowski, J. G., & Whitman, T. L. (2006). Children of adolescent mothers: Exposure to negative life events and the role of social supports on their socioemotional adjustment. *Journal of Youth and Adolescence*, 35(5), 822–832. doi:10.1007/s10964-006-9096-8

Carver, K., Joyner, K., & Udry, J. R. (2003). *National estimates of adolescent romantic relationships.* Mahwah, NJ: Lawrence Erlbaum.

Casares, W. N., Lahiff, M., Eskenazi, B., & Halpern-Felsher, B. L. (2010). Unpredicted trajectories: The relationship between race/ethnicity, pregnancy during adolescence, and young women's outcomes. *Journal of Adolescent Health*, 47(2), 143–150. doi:10.1016/j.jadohealth.2010.01.013

Casey Copen, E., Chandra, A., & Martinez, G. (2012). Prevalence and timing of oral sex with opposite-sex partners among females and males aged 15–24 years: United States, 2007–2010. *National Health Statistics Reports*, 56. Retrieved from http://web.csulb.edu/~nmatza/powerpoint/HSc411BAssign/Course Docs/HSC 411b Docs/oral.sex.teens2012.pdf

Caspi, A., Lynam, D., Moffitt, T. E., & Silva, P. A. (1993). Unraveling girls' delinquency: Biological, dispositional, and contextual contributions to adolescent misbehavior. *Developmental Psychology*, 29(1), 19–30.

Castellani, V., Pastorelli, C., Eisenberg, N., Caffo, E., Forresi, B., & Gerbino, M. (2014). The development of perceived maternal hostile, aggressive conflict from adolescence to early adulthood: Antecedents and outcomes. *Journal of Adolescence*, 37(8), 1517–1527. doi:10.1016/j.adolescence.2014.07.001

Cates, J. (2007). Identity in crisis: Spirituality and homosexuality in adolescence. *Child & Adolescent Social Work Journal*, 24(4), 369–383. doi:10.1007/s10560-007-0089-6

Centers for Disease Control and Prevention. (2014). *Sexually transmitted disease surveillance 2013.* Atlanta: Author. Retrieved from http://www.cdc.gov/std/stats13/default.htm

Céspedes, Y. M., & Huey Jr, S. J. (2008). Depression in Latino adolescents: A cultural discrepancy perspective. *Cultural Diversity & Ethnic Minority Psychology*, 14(2), 168–172. doi:10.1037/1099-9809.14.2.168

Chandra, A., Martino, S. C., Collins, R. L., Elliott, M. N., Berry, S. H., Kanouse, D. E., & Miu, A. (2008). Does watching sex on television predict teen pregnancy? Findings from a national longitudinal survey of youth. *Pediatrics*, 122(5), 1047–1054. doi:10.1542/peds.2007-3066

Chaplin, T. M., Sinha, R., Simmons, J. A., Healy, S. M., Mayes, L. C., Hommer, R. E., & Crowley, M. J. (2012). Parent-adolescent conflict interactions and adolescent alcohol use. *Addictive Behaviors*, 37(5), 605–612. doi:10.1016/j.addbeh.2012.01.004

Chassin, L., Ritter, J., Trim, R. S., & King, K. M. (2003). Adolescent substance use disorders. In E. J. Mash & R. A. Barkley (Eds.), *Child psychopathology* (2nd ed., pp. 199–230). New York: Guilford Press.

Chavous, T. M., Bernat, D. H., Schmeelk-Cone, K., Caldwell, C. H., Kohn-Wood, L., & Zimmerman, M. A. (2003). Racial identity and academic attainment among African American adolescents. *Child Development*, 74(4), 1076–1090.

Chen, C.-Y., Storr, C. L., & Anthony, J. C. (2009). Early-onset drug use and risk for drug dependence problems. *Addictive Behaviors*, 34(3), 319–322. doi:10.1016/j.addbeh.2008.10.021

Chen, P., Voisin, D. R., & Jacobson, K. C. (2013). Community violence exposure and adolescent delinquency: Examining a spectrum of promotive factors. *Youth & Society*. Advance online publication. doi:10.1177/0044118X13475827

Child Trends Data Bank. (2013). *Oral sex behaviors among teens.* Retrieved May 4, 2015, from http://www.childtrends.org/?indicators=oral-sex-behaviors-among-teens

Child Trends Data Bank. (2014). *Teen Births: Indicators on children and youth.* Bethesda, MD. Retrieved from http://www.childtrends.org/?indicators=teen-births

Choukas-Bradley, S., Giletta, M., Neblett, E. W., & Prinstein, M. J. (2015). Ethnic differences in associations among popularity, likability, and trajectories of adolescents' alcohol use and frequency. *Child Development*, 86(2), 519–535. doi:10.1111/cdev.12333

Choukas-Bradley, S., Giletta, M., Widman, L., Cohen, G. L., & Prinstein, M. J. (2014). Experimentally measured susceptibility to peer influence and adolescent sexual behavior trajectories: A preliminary study. *Developmental Psychology*, 50(9), 2221–2227. doi:10.1037/a0037300

Chung, H. L., & Steinberg, L. (2006). Relations between neighborhood factors, parenting behaviors, peer deviance, and delinquency among serious juvenile offenders. *Developmental Psychology*, 42(2), 319–331.

Ciairano, S., Bonino, S., Kliewer, W., Miceli, R., & Jackson, S. (2006). Dating, sexual activity, and well-being in Italian adolescents. *Journal of Clinical Child & Adolescent Psychology*, 35(2), 275–282.

Cillessen, A. H. N., & Borch, C. (2006). Developmental trajectories of adolescent popularity: A growth curve modelling analysis. *Journal of Adolescence*, 29(6), 935–959. doi:10.1016/j.adolescence.2006.05.005

Coley, R. L., Kull, M. A., & Carrano, J. (2014). Parental endorsement of spanking and children's internalizing and externalizing problems in African American and Hispanic families. *Journal of Family Psychology*, 28(1), 22–31. doi:10.1037/a0035272

Coley, R. L., Votruba-Drzal, E., & Schindler, H. S. (2008). Trajectories of parenting processes and adolescent substance use: Reciprocal effects. *Journal of Abnormal Child Psychology*, 36(4), 613–625. doi:10.1007/s10802-007-9205-5

Collier, K. L., van Beusekom, G., Bos, H. M. W., & Sandfort, T. G. M. (2013). Sexual orientation and gender identity/expression related peer victimization in adolescence: A systematic review of associated psychosocial and health outcomes. *Journal of Sex Research*, 50(3–4), 299–317. doi:10.1080/00224499.2012.750639

Collins, W. A., & Laursen, B. (2004). Changing relationships, changing youth: Interpersonal contexts of adolescent development. *Journal of Early Adolescence*, 24(1), 55–62.

Collins, W. A., & Steinberg, L. (2006). Adolescent development in interpersonal context. In N. Eisenberg, W. Damon, & R. M. Lerner (Eds.), *Handbook of child psychology: Vol. 3, Social, emotional, and personality development* (6th ed., pp. 1003–1067). Hoboken, NJ: John Wiley & Sons.

Collins, W. A., Welsh, D. P., & Furman, W. (2009). Adolescent romantic relationships. *Annual Review of Psychology*, 60, 631–652. doi:10.1146/annurev.psych.60.110707.163459

Connolly, J., & Craig, W. (1999). Conceptions of cross-sex friendships and romantic relationships in early adolescence. *Journal of Youth and Adolescence*, 481–509, 14p.

Connolly, J., Craig, W., Goldberg, A., & Pepler, D. (2004). Mixed-gender groups, dating, and romantic relationships in early adolescence. *Journal of Research on Adolescence*, 14, 185–207.

Connolly, J., & Furman, W. (2000). The role of peers in the emergence of heterosexual romantic relationships in adolescence. *Child Development*, 71, 1395–1409.

Connolly, J., Nguyen, H. N. T., Pepler, D., Craig, W., & Jiang, D. (2013). Developmental trajectories of romantic stages and associations with problem behaviours during adolescence. *Journal of Adolescence*, 36(6), 1013–1024. doi:10.1016/j.adolescence.2013.08.006

Corrieri, S., Heider, D., Conrad, I., Blume, A., König, H.-H., & Riedel-Heller, S. G. (2014). School-based prevention programs for depression and anxiety in adolescence: A systematic review. *Health Promotion International*, 29(3), 427–441. doi:10.1093/heapro/dat001

Côté, J. E. (2006). Emerging adulthood as an institutionalized moratorium: Risks and benefits to identity formation. In J. J. Arnett & J. L. Tanner (Eds.), *Emerging adults in America: Coming of age in the 21st century* (pp. 85–116). Washington, DC: American Psychological Association.

Cox, R. B., Shreffler, K. M., Merten, M. J., Schwerdtfeger Gallus, K. L., & Dowdy, J. L. (2014). Parenting, peers, and perceived norms: What predicts attitudes toward sex among early adolescents? *The Journal of Early Adolescence*, 35(1), 30–53. doi:10.1177/0272431614523131

Crocetti, E., Klimstra, T., Keijsers, L., Hale III, W. W., & Meeus, W. H. J. (2009). Anxiety trajectories and identity development in adolescence: A five-wave longitudinal study. *Journal of Youth and Adolescence*, 38(6), 839–849. doi:10.1007/s10964-008-9302-y

Crocetti, E., Klimstra, T. A., Hale, W. W., Koot, H. M., & Meeus, W. H. J. (2013). Impact of early adolescent externalizing problem behaviors on identity development in middle to late adolescence: A prospective 7-year longitudinal study. *Journal of Youth and Adolescence*, 42(11), 1745–1758. doi:10.1007/s10964-013-9924-6

Cross, J. R., & Fletcher, K. L. (2009). The challenge of adolescent crowd research: Defining the crowd. *Journal of Youth and Adolescence*, 38(6), 747–764. doi:10.1007/s10964-008-9307-6

Culbertson, F. M. (1997). Depression and gender: An international review. *American Psychologist*, 52(1).

Cusimano, M. D., & Sameem, M. (2011). The effectiveness of middle and high school-based suicide prevention programmes for adolescents: A systematic review. *Injury Prevention*, 17(1), 43–49. doi:10.1136/ip.2009.025502

Damon, W., & Hart, D. (1988). *Self-understanding in childhood and adolescence*. New York: Cambridge University Press.

Darling, N., Cohan, C. L., Burns, A., & Thompson, L. (2008). Within-family conflict behaviors as predictors of conflict in adolescent romantic relations. *Journal of Adolescence*, 31(6), 671–690. doi:10.1016/j.adolescence.2008.10.003

Davis, B., Royne Stafford, M. B., & Pullig, C. (2014). How gay-straight alliance groups mitigate the relationship between gay-bias victimization and adolescent suicide attempts. *Journal of the American Academy of Child and Adolescent Psychiatry*, 53(12), 1271–1278. doi:10.1016/j.jaac.2014.09.010

De Bruyn, E. H., & Cillessen, A. H. N. (2006). Popularity in early adolescence: Prosocial and antisocial subtypes. *Journal of Adolescent Research*, 21(6), 607–627. doi:10.1177/0743558406293966

De Bruyn, E. H., & Cillessen, A. H. N. (2008). Leisure activity preferences and perceived popularity in early adolescence. *Journal of Leisure Research*, 40(3), 442–457.

De Bruyn, E. H., Cillessen, A. H. N., & Wissink, I. B. (2009). Associations of peer acceptance and perceived popularity with bullying and victimization in early adolescence. *The Journal of Early Adolescence*, 30(4), 543–566. doi:10.1177/0272431609340517

De Bruyn, E. H., & Van den Boom, D. C. (2005). Interpersonal behavior, peer popularity, and self-esteem in early adolescence. *Social Development*, 14(4), 555–573. doi:10.1111/j.1467-9507.2005.00317.x

De Genna, N., Larkby, C., & Cornelius, M. (2011). Pubertal timing and early sexual intercourse in the offspring of teenage mothers. *Journal of Youth and Adolescence*, 40(10), 1315–1328. doi:10.1007/s10964-010-9609-3

Dehue, F., Bolman, C., & Völlink, T. (2008). Cyberbullying: Youngsters' experiences and parental perception. *CyberPsychology & Behavior*, 11(2), 217–223. doi:10.1089/cpb.2007.0008

Dell, D. L. (2001). Adolescent pregnancy. In N. L. Stotland & D. E. Stewart (Eds.), *Psychological aspects of women's health care: The interface between psychiatry and obstetrics and gynecology* (pp. 95–116). Washington, DC: American Psychiatric Publishing.

Delsing, M. J. M. H., ter Bogt, T. F. M., Engels, R. C. M. E., & Meeus, W. H. J. (2007). Adolescents' peer crowd identification in the Netherlands: Structure and associations with problem behaviors. *Journal of Research on Adolescence*, 17(2), 467–480. doi:10.1111/j.1532-7795.2007.00530.x

Demo, D. H., & Acock, A. C. (1996). Family structure, family process, and adolescent well-being. *Journal of Research on Adolescence*, 6, 457–488.

Diamond, L. M., & Savin-Williams, R. C. (2009). Adolescent sexuality. In R. M. Lerner & L. Steinberg (Eds.), *Handbook of adolescent psychology* (p. 479). Hoboken, NJ: John Wiley & Sons.

Dijkstra, J. K., Berger, C., & Lindenberg, S. (2011). Do physical and relational aggression explain adolescents' friendship selection? The competing roles of network characteristics, gender, and social status. *Aggressive Behavior*, 37(5), 417–429. doi:10.1002/ab.20402

Dishion, T. J., Andrews, D. W., & Crosby, L. (1995). Antisocial boys and their friends in early adolescence: Relationship characteristics, quality, and interactional processes. *Child Development*, 66, 139–151.

Dornbusch, S. M., Ritter, P. L., Mont-Reynaud, R., & Chen, Z. (1990). Family decision making and academic performance in a diverse high school population. *Journal of Adolescent Research*, 5(2), 143–160.

Dotterer, A. M., McHale, S. M., & Crouter, A. C. (2009). Sociocultural factors and school engagement among African American youth: The roles of racial discrimination, racial socialization, and ethnic identity. *Applied Developmental Science*, 13(2), 61–73. doi:10.1080/10888690902801442

Duan, L., Chou, C.-P., Andreeva, V., & Pentz, M. (2009). Trajectories of peer social influences as long-term predictors of drug use from early through late adolescence. *Journal of Youth and Adolescence*, 38(3), 454–465. doi:10.1007/s10964-008-9310-y

Dunbar, J., Sheeder, J., Lezotte, D., Dabelea, D., & Stevens-Simon, C. (2008). Age at menarche and first pregnancy among psychosocially at-risk adolescents. *American Journal of Public Health*, 98, 1822–1824.

Dunn, E. C., Uddin, M., Subramanian, S. V, Smoller, J. W., Galea, S., & Koenen, K. C. (2011). Research review: Gene-environment interaction research in youth depression—a systematic review with recommendations for future research. *Journal of Child Psychology & Psychiatry*, 52(12), 1223–1238. doi:10.1111/j.1469-7610.2011.02466.x

Dupéré, V., Lacourse, É., Willms, J. D., Tremblay, R. E., & Leventhal, T. (2008). Neighborhood poverty and early transition to sexual activity in young adolescents: A developmental ecological approach. *Child Development*, 79(5), 1463–1476. doi:10.1111/j.1467-8624.2008.01199.x

Dwairy, M., & Menshar, K. E. (2006). Parenting style, individuation, and mental health of Egyptian adolescents. *Journal of Adolescence*, 29(1), 103–117. doi:10.1016/j.adolescence.2005.03.002

East, L., Jackson, D., O'Brien, L., & Peters, K. (2007). Use of the male condom by heterosexual adolescents and young people: Literature review. *Journal of Advanced Nursing*, 59(2), 103–110.

East, P. L., Khoo, S. T., Reyes, B. T., & Coughlin, L. (2006). AAP report on pregnancy in adolescents. *Perspectives on Sexual & Reproductive Health*, 10, 12p.

East, P. L., Reyes, B. T., & Horn, E. J. (2007). Association between adolescent pregnancy and a family history of teenage births. *Perspectives on Sexual & Reproductive Health*, 39, 108–115.

Easterbrooks, M. A., Chaudhuri, J. H., Bartlett, J. D., & Copeman, A. (2011). Resilience in parenting among young mothers: Family and ecological risks and opportunities. *Children and Youth Services Review*, 33(1), 42–50. doi:10.1016/j.childyouth.2010.08.010

Eccles, J. S., Wong, C. A., & Peck, S. C. (2006). Ethnicity as a social context for the development of African-American adolescents. *Journal of School Psychology*, 44(5), 407–426.

Eggermont, S. (2005). Young adolescents' perceptions of peer sexual behaviours: The role of television viewing. *Child: Care, Health & Development*, 31, 459–468.

Eichelsheim, V. I., Buist, K. L., Deković, M., Wissink, I. B., Frijns, T., van Lier, P. A. C., . . . Meeus, W. H. J. (2010). Associations among the parent-adolescent relationship, aggression and delinquency in different ethnic groups: A replication across two Dutch samples. *Social Psychiatry and Psychiatric Epidemiology*, 45(3), 293–300. doi:10.1007/s00127-009-0071-z

Englund, M. M., Siebenbruner, J., Oliva, E. M., Egeland, B., Chung, C.-T., & Long, J. D. (2013). The developmental significance of late adolescent substance use for early adult functioning. *Developmental Psychology*, 49(8), 1554–1564. doi:10.1037/a0030229

Erikson, E. H. (1950). *Childhood and society* (2nd ed.). New York: Norton.

Escobar-Chaves, S. L., & Anderson, C. A. (2008). Media and risky behaviors. *Future of Children*, 18(1), 147–180.

European Study Group on Heterosexual Transmission of HIV. (1992). Comparison of female to male and male to female transmission of HIV in 563 stable couples. *British Medical Journal*, 304, 809–813.

Evans, S. Z., Simons, L. G., & Simons, R. L. (2014). Factors that influence trajectories of delinquency throughout adolescence. *Journal of Youth and Adolescence*. Advance online publication. doi:10.1007/s10964-014-0197-5

Exner-Cortens, D., Eckenrode, J., & Rothman, E. (2013). Longitudinal associations between teen dating violence victimization and adverse health outcomes. *Pediatrics*, 131(1), 71–78. doi:10.1542/peds.2012-1029

Farrington, D. P. (2004). Conduct disorder, aggression, and delinquency. In R. M. Lerner & L. Steinberg (Eds.), *Handbook of adolescent psychology* (2nd ed., pp. 627–664). Hoboken, NJ: John Wiley & Sons.

Farrington, D. P., & Loeber, R. (2000). Epidemiology of juvenile violence. *Juvenile Violence*, 9, 733–748.

Federal Bureau of Investigation. (2014). *Crime in the United States, 2013*. Washington, DC: Author. Retrieved from http://www.fbi.gov/about-us/cjis/ucr/crime-in-the-u.s/2013/crime-in-the-u.s.-2013

Feldstein Ewing, S. W., Sakhardande, A., & Blakemore, S.-J. (2014). The effect of alcohol consumption on the adolescent brain: A systematic review of MRI and fMRI studies of alcohol-using youth. *NeuroImage: Clinical*, 5, 420–437. doi:10.1016/j.nicl.2014.06.011

Ferguson, G. M., Hafen, C. A., & Laursen, B. (2010). Adolescent psychological and academic adjustment as a function of discrepancies between actual and ideal self-perceptions. *Journal of Youth and Adolescence*, 39(12), 1485–1497. doi:10.1007/s10964-009-9461-5

Fergusson, D. M., & Horwood, L. J. (2002). Male and female offending trajectories. *Development and Psychopathology*, 14(1), 159–177.

Fergusson, D. M., Woodward, L. J., & Horwood, L. J. (2000). Risk factors and life processes associated with the onset of suicidal behaviour during adolescence and early adulthood. *Psychological Medicine*, 30, 23–39.

Fidler, J. A., West, R., Jarvis, M. J., & Wardle, J. (2006). Early dating predicts smoking during adolescence: A prospective study. *Addiction*, *101*(12), 1805–1813. doi:10.1111/j.1360-0443.2006.01613.x

Figner, B., Mackinlay, R. J., Wilkening, F., & Weber, E. U. (2009). Affective and deliberative processes in risky choice: Age differences in risk taking in the Columbia Card Task. *Journal of Experimental Psychology: Learning, Memory, and Cognition*, *35*(3), 709–730. doi:10.1037/a0014983

Findlay, L. C., & Bowker, A. (2009). The link between competitive sport participation and self-concept in early adolescence: A consideration of gender and sport orientation. *Journal of Youth and Adolescence*, *38*(1), 29–40. doi:10.1007/s10964-007-9244-9

Finer, L. B., & Henshaw, S. K. (2006). Disparities in rates of unintended pregnancy in the United States, 1994 and 2001. *Perspectives on Sexual and Reproductive Health, 2004, 36*(1), 6–10.

Finer, L. B., & Philbin, J. M. (2013). Sexual initiation, contraceptive use, and pregnancy among young adolescents. *Pediatrics*, *131*(5), 886–91. doi:10.1542/peds.2012-3495

Fisher, E. S., Komosa-Hawkins, K., Saldaña, E., Hsiao, C., Miller, D., Rauld, M., & Thomas, G. M. (2008). Promoting school success for lesbian, gay, bisexual, transgendered, and questioning students: Primary, secondary, and tertiary prevention and intervention strategies. *California School Psychologist*, *13*, 79–91.

Fisher, H. L., Moffitt, T. E., Houts, R. M., Belsky, D. W., Arseneault, L., & Caspi, A. (2012). Bullying victimisation and risk of self harm in early adolescence: longitudinal cohort study. *BMJ*, *344*, e2683. doi:10.1136/bmj.e2683

Flannery, D. J., Hussey, D., & Jefferis, E. (2005). Adolescent delinquency and violent behavior. In T. P. Gullotta & G. R. Adams (Eds.), *Handbook of adolescent behavioral problems: Evidence-based approaches to prevention and treatment* (pp. 415–438). New York: Springer Science + Business Media.

Fletcher, A. C., Darling, N. E., Steinberg, L., & Dornbusch, S. (1995). The company they keep: Relation of adolescents' adjustment and behavior to their friends' perceptions of authoritative parenting in the social network. *Developmental Psychology*, *31*, 300–310.

Flett, G. L., Hewitt, P. L., & Heisel, M. J. (2014). The destructiveness of perfectionism revisited: Implications for the assessment of suicide risk and the prevention of suicide. *Review of General Psychology*, *18*(3), 156–172. doi:10.1037/gpr0000011

Forhan, S. E., Gottlieb, S. L., Sternberg, M. R., Xu, F., Datta, S. D., McQuillan, G. M., . . . Markowitz, L. E. (2009). Prevalence of sexually transmitted infections among female adolescents aged 14 to 19 in the United States. *Pediatrics*, *124*(6), 1505–1512. doi:10.1542/peds.2009-0674

Fortenberry, J. D. (2013). Puberty and adolescent sexuality. *Hormones and Behavior*, *64*(2), 280–287. doi:10.1016/j.yhbeh.2013.03.007

Foshee, V. A., McNaughton Reyes, H. L., Vivolo-Kantor, A. M., Basile, K. C., Chang, L.-Y., Faris, R., & Ennett, S. T. (2014). Bullying as a longitudinal predictor of adolescent dating violence. *The Journal of Adolescent Health*, *55*(3), 439–444. doi:10.1016/j.jadohealth.2014.03.004

Foshee, V. A., McNaughton Reyes, L., Tharp, A. T., Chang, L.-Y., Ennett, S. T., Simon, T. R., . . . Suchindran, C. (2015). Shared longitudinal predictors of physical peer and dating violence. *The Journal of Adolescent Health*, *56*(1), 106–112. doi:10.1016/j.jadohealth.2014.08.003

Franic, S., Middeldorp, C. M., Dolan, C. V, Ligthart, L., & Boomsma, D. I. (2010). Childhood and adolescent anxiety and depression: Beyond heritability. *Journal of the American Academy of Child & Adolescent Psychiatry*, *49*(8), 820–829.

Fuligni, A. J., Witkow, M., & Garcia, C. (2005). Ethnic identity and the academic adjustment of adolescents from Mexican, Chinese, and European backgrounds. *Developmental Psychology*, *41*(5), 799–811.

Furman, W. (2002). The emerging field of adolescent romantic relationships. *Current Directions in Psychological Science*, *11*(5), 177–180.

Furman, W., & Collibee, C. (2014). A matter of timing: Developmental theories of romantic involvement and psychosocial adjustment. *Development and Psychopathology*, *26*(4 Pt. 1), 1149–1160. doi:10.1017/S0954579414000182

Furman, W., & Shaffer, L. (2003). The role of romantic relationships in adolescent development. In P. Florsheim (Ed.), *Adolescent romantic relations and sexual behavior: Theory, research, and practical implications* (pp. 3–22). Mahwah, NJ: Lawrence Erlbaum.

Furman, W., & Shomaker, L. B. (2008). Patterns of interaction in adolescent romantic relationships: Distinct features and links to other close relationships. *Journal of Adolescence*, *31*(6), 771–788. doi:10.1016/j.adolescence.2007.10.007

Furstenberg, F. (2003). Teenage childbearing as a public issue and private concern. *Annual Review of Psychology*, *29*, 23–39.

Galambos, N. L., Leadbeater, B. J., & Barker, E. T. (2004). Gender differences in and risk factors for depression in adolescence: A 4-year longitudinal study. *International Journal of Behavioral Development*, *28*, 16–26.

Galliher, R. V, Jones, M. D., & Dahl, A. (2011). Concurrent and longitudinal effects of ethnic identity and experiences of discrimination on psychosocial adjustment of Navajo adolescents. *Developmental Psychology*, *47*(2), 509–526. doi:10.1037/a0021061

Ge, X., Natsuaki, M. N., Neiderhiser, J. M., & Reiss, D. (2009). The longitudinal effects of stressful life events on adolescent depression are buffered by parent-child closeness. *Development & Psychopathology*, *21*(2), 621–635. doi:10.1017/s0954579409000339

Gest, S. D., Davidson, A. J., Rulison, K. L., Moody, J., & Welsh, J. A. (2007). Features of groups and status hierarchies in girls' and boys' early adolescent peer networks. *New Directions for Child & Adolescent Development*, *2007*(118), 43–60.

Gibb, S. J., Fergusson, D. M., Horwood, L. J., & Boden, J. M. (2015). Early motherhood and long-term economic outcomes: Findings from a 30-year longitudinal study. *Journal of Research on Adolescence*, *25*(1), 163–172. doi:10.1111/jora.12122

Gila, A., Castro, J., Cesena, J., & Toro, J. (2005). Anorexia nervosa in male adolescents: Body image, eating attitudes and psychological traits. *Journal of Adolescent Health*, *36*, 221–226.

Giletta, M., Scholte, R. H. J., Burk, W. J., Engels, R. C. M. E., Larsen, J. K., Prinstein, M. J., & Ciairano, S. (2011). Similarity in depressive symptoms in adolescents' friendship dyads: Selection or socialization? *Developmental Psychology*, *47*(6), 1804–1814. doi:10.1037/a0023872

Giordano, P. C., Longmore, M. A., & Manning, W. D. (2006). Gender and the meanings of adolescent romantic relationships: A focus on boys. *American Sociological Review*, *71*(2), 260–287.

Giordano, P. C., Phelps, K. D., Manning, W. D., & Longmore, M. A. (2008). Adolescent academic achievement and romantic relationships. *Social Science Research*, *37*(1), 37–54. doi:10.1016/j.ssresearch.2007.06.004

Giordano, P. C., Soto, D. A., Manning, W. D., & Longmore, M. A. (2010). The characteristics of romantic relationships associated with teen dating violence. *Social Science Research*, *39*(6), 863–874. doi:10.1016/j.ssresearch.2010.03.009

Golden, N. H., Katzman, D. K., Sawyer, S. M., Ornstein, R. M., Rome, E. S., Garber, A. K., . . . Kreipe, R. E. (2015). Update on the medical management of eating disorders in adolescents. *The Journal of Adolescent Health*, *56*(4), 370–375. doi:10.1016/j.jadohealth.2014.11.020

Goldston, D. B., Molock, S. D., Whitbeck, L. B., Murakami, J. L., Zayas, L. H., Nagayama Hall, G. C., . . . Murakami, J. L. (2008). Cultural considerations in adolescent suicide prevention and psychosocial treatment. *American Psychologist*, *63*(1), 14–31. doi:10.1037/0003-066x.63.1.14

Gonzales, N. A., Deardorff, J., Formoso, D., Barr, A., & Barrera, M. (2006). Family mediators of the relation between acculturation and adolescent mental health. *Family Relations*, *55*(3), 318–330. doi:10.1111/j.1741-3729.2006.00405.x

Gould, M., Jamieson, P., & Romer, D. (2003). Media contagion and suicide among the young. *American Behavioral Scientist*, *46*(9), 1269.

Graham, S., Munniksma, A., & Juvonen, J. (2014). Psychosocial benefits of cross-ethnic friendships in urban middle schools. *Child Development*, *85*(2), 469–483. doi:10.1111/cdev.12159

Griffith, S. F., & Grolnick, W. S. (2013). Parenting in Caribbean families: A look at parental control, structure, and autonomy support. *Journal of Black Psychology*, *40*(2), 166–190. doi:10.1177/0095798412475085

Guilamo-Ramos, V., Dittus, P., Jaccard, J., Goldberg, V., Casillas, E., & Bouris, A. (2006). The content and process of mother–adolescent communication about sex in Latino families. *Social Work Research*, *30*, 169–181.

Guttmacher Institute. (2014). *American teens' sexual and reproductive health*. Washington, DC: Author. Retrieved from http://www.guttmacher.org/pubs/fb_ATSRH.html

Haas, A. P., Eliason, M., Mays, V. M., Mathy, R. M., Cochran, S. D., D'Augelli, A. R., . . . Clayton, P. J. (2011). Suicide and suicide risk in lesbian, gay, bisexual, and transgender populations: Review and recommendations. *Journal of Homosexuality*, *58*(1), 10–51. doi:10.1080/00918369.2011.534038

Hair, E. C., Moore, K. A., Garrett, S. B., Ling, T., & Cleveland, K. (2008). The continued importance of quality parent–adolescent relationships during late adolescence. *Journal of Research on Adolescence*, *18*(1), 187–200. doi:10.1111/j.1532-7795.2008.00556.x

Haleem, D. J. (2012). Serotonin neurotransmission in anorexia nervosa. *Behavioural Pharmacology*, *23*(5–6), 478–495. doi:10.1097/FBP.0b013e328357440d

Hall, B., & Place, M. (2010). Cutting to cope—a modern adolescent phenomenon. *Child: Care, Health & Development*, *36*(5), 623–629. doi:10.1111/j.1365-2214.2010.01095.x

Hall, S. P., & Brassard, M. R. (2008). Relational support as a predictor of identity status in an ethnically diverse early adolescent sample. *Journal of Early Adolescence*, *28*(1), 92–114. doi:10.1177/0272431607308668

Halmi, K. A., Sunday, S. R., Strober, M., Kaplan, A., Woodside, D. B., Fichter, M., . . . Kaye, W. H. (2000). Perfectionism in anorexia nervosa: Variation by clinical subtype, obsessionality, and pathological eating behavior. *American Journal of Psychiatry*, *157*(11), 1799–1805. doi:10.1176/appi.ajp.157.11.1799

Harper, G. W., Serrano, P. A., Bruce, D., & Bauermeister, J. A. (2015). The Internet's multiple roles in facilitating the sexual orientation identity development of gay and bisexual male adolescents. Advance online publication. *American Journal of Men's Health*. doi:10.1177/1557988314566227

Harris, M. A., Gruenenfelder-Steiger, A. E., Ferrer, E., Donnellan, M. B., Allemand, M., Fend, H., . . . Trzesniewski, K. H. (2015). Do parents foster self-esteem? Testing the prospective impact of parent closeness on adolescent self-esteem. *Child Development*, *86*(4), 995–1013. doi:10.1111/cdev.12356

Harris-McKoy, D., & Cui, M. (2012). Parental control, adolescent delinquency, and young adult criminal behavior. *Journal of Child and Family Studies*, *22*(6), 836–843. doi:10.1007/s10826-012-9641-x

Harter, S. (2006a). The Development of Self-Esteem. In M. H. Kernis (Ed.), *Self-esteem issues and answers: A sourcebook of current perspectives* (pp. 144–150). New York: Psychology Press.

Harter, S. (2006b). The self. In N. Eisenberg, W. Damon, & R. M. Lerner (Eds.), *Handbook of child psychology: Vol. 3, Social, emotional, and personality development* (6th ed., pp. 505–570). Hoboken, NJ: John Wiley & Sons.

Harter, S. (2012). *The construction of the self: Developmental and sociocultural foundations* (2nd ed.). New York: Guilford Press.

Hartup, W. W., & Stevens, N. (1997). Friendships and adaptation in the life course. *Psychological Bulletin*, *121*, 355–370.

Hartup, W. W., & Stevens, N. (1999). Friendships and adaptation across the life span. *Current Directions in Psychological Science*, *8*, 76–79.

Haw, C., Hawton, K., Niedzwiedz, C., & Platt, S. (2013). Suicide clusters: A review of risk factors and mechanisms. *Suicide & Life-Threatening Behavior*, *43*(1), 97–108. doi:10.1111/j.1943-278X.2012.00130.x

Hay, C., Fortson, E. N., Hollist, D. R., Altheimer, I., & Schaible, L. M. (2007). Compounded risk: The implications for delinquency of coming from a poor family that lives in a poor community. *Journal of Youth and Adolescence*, *36*, 593–605.

Hay, P. J., & Bacaltchuk, J. (2007). Bulimia nervosa. *American Family Physician*, *75*, 1699–1702.

Haydon, A. A., Herring, A. H., Prinstein, M. J., & Halpern, C. T. (2012). Beyond age at first sex: Patterns of emerging sexual behavior in adolescence and young adulthood. *The Journal of Adolescent Health*, *50*(5), 456–463. doi:10.1016/j.jadohealth.2011.09.006

Heinze, J. E., & Horn, S. S. (2009). Intergroup contact and beliefs about homosexuality in adolescence. *Journal of Youth and Adolescence*, *38*(7), 937–951. doi:10.1007/s10964-009-9408-x

Henry, D. B., Schoeny, M. E., Deptula, D. P., & Slavick, J. T. (2007). Peer selection and socialization effects on adolescent intercourse without a condom and attitudes about the costs of sex. *Child Development*, *78*, 825–838.

Hepper, P. G., Dornan, J. C., & Lynch, C. (2012). Sex differences in fetal habituation. *Developmental Science*, *15*(3), 373–383. doi:10.1111/j.1467-7687.2011.01132.x

Heron, M. (2013). *Deaths: Leading causes for 2010. National vital statistics reports* (Vol. 62). Retrieved from http://www.cdc.gov/nchs/data/nvsr/nvsr62/nvsr62_06.pdf

Herrman, J. W. (2009). There's a fine line. . . Adolescent dating violence and prevention. *Pediatric Nursing*, *35*(3), 164–170.

Hiatt, C., Laursen, B., Mooney, K. S., & Rubin, K. H. (2015). Forms of friendship: A person-centered assessment of the quality, stability, and outcomes of different types of adolescent friends. *Personality and Individual Differences*, *77*, 149–155. doi:10.1016/j.paid.2014.12.051

Hill, R. M., Castellanos, D., & Pettit, J. W. (2011). Suicide-related behaviors and anxiety in children and adolescents: A review. *Clinical Psychology Review*, *31*(7), 1133–1144. doi:10.1016/j.cpr.2011.07.008

Hoeve, M., Dubas, J. S., Gerris, J. R. M., van der Laan, P. H., & Smeenk, W. (2011). Maternal and paternal parenting styles: Unique and combined links to adolescent and early adult delinquency. *Journal of Adolescence*, *34*(5), 813–827. doi:10.1016/j.adolescence.2011.02.004

Hofer, C., Eisenberg, N., Spinrad, T. L., Morris, A. S., Gershoff, E., Valiente, C., . . . Eggum, N. D. (2013). Mother-adolescent conflict: Stability, change, and relations with externalizing and internalizing behavior problems. *Social Development*, *22*(2), 259–279. doi:10.1111/sode.12012

Hoffman, B. R., Monge, P. R., Chou, C.-P., & Valente, T. W. (2007). Perceived peer influence and peer selection on adolescent smoking. *Addictive Behaviors*, *32*, 1546–1554.

Howard, K. S., Lefever, J. E. B., Borkowski, J. G., & Whitman, T. L. (2006). Fathers' influence in the lives of children with adolescent mothers. *Journal of Family Psychology*, *20*(3).

Huang, C. Y., Costeines, J., Ayala, C., & Kaufman, J. S. (2014). Parenting stress, social support, and depression for ethnic minority adolescent mothers: Impact on child development. *Journal of Child and Family Studies*, *23*(2), 255–262. doi:10.1007/s10826-013-9807-1

Huang, D. Y. C., Murphy, D. A., & Hser, Y.-I. (2011). Parental monitoring during early adolescence deters adolescent sexual initiation: Discrete-time survival mixture analysis. *Journal of Child and Family Studies*, *20*(4), 511–520. doi:10.1007/s10826-010-9418-z

Hughes, D., Hagelskamp, C., Way, N., & Foust, M. D. (2009). The role of mothers' and adolescents' perceptions of ethnic-racial socialization in shaping ethnic-racial identity among early adolescent boys and girls. *Journal of Youth and Adolescence*, *38*(5), 605–626. doi:10.1007/s10964-009-9399-7

Isomaa, R., Isomaa, A.-L., Marttunen, M., Kaltiala-Heino, R., & Björkqvist, K. (2009). The prevalence, incidence and development of eating disorders in finnish adolescents—a two-step 3-year follow-up study. *European Eating Disorders Review*, *17*(3), 199–207. doi:10.1002/erv.919

Jacobus, J., Thayer, R. E., Trim, R. S., Bava, S., Frank, L. R., & Tapert, S. F. (2013). White matter integrity, substance use, and risk taking in adolescence. *Psychology of Addictive Behaviors*, *27*(2), 431–442. doi:10.1037/a0028235

Jaffee, S., Caspi, A., Moffitt, T. E., Belsky, J., & Silva, P. (2001). Why are children born to teen mothers at risk for adverse outcomes in young adulthood? Results from a 20-year longitudinal study. *Development and Psychopathology*, *13*, 377–397.

Jain, S., & Cohen, A. K. (2013). Behavioral adaptation among youth exposed to community violence: A longitudinal multidisciplinary study of family, peer and neighborhood-level protective factors. *Prevention Science*, *14*(6), 606–617. doi:10.1007/s11121-012-0344-8

Jerman, P., & Constantine, N. A. (2010). Demographic and psychological predictors of parent-adolescent communication about sex: A representative statewide analysis. *Journal of Youth and Adolescence*, *39*(10), 1164–1174. doi:10.1007/s10964-010-9546-1

Joe, S., & Marcus, S. C. (2003). Datapoints: Trends by race and gender in suicide attempts among U.S. adolescents, 1991-2001. *Hospital & Community Psychiatry*, *54*, 454.

Johnson, A. Z., Sieving, R. E., Pettingell, S. L., & McRee, A.-L. (2015). The roles of partner communication and relationship status in adolescent contraceptive use. *Journal of Pediatric Health Care*, *29*(1), 61–69. doi:10.1016/j.pedhc.2014.06.008

Johnston, L. D., O'Malley, P. M., Miech, R. A., Bachman, J. G., & Schulenberg, J. E. (2015). *Monitoring the future national survey results on drug use: 1975–2014: Overview, key findings on adolescent drug use.* Ann Arbor: Institute for Social Research, University of Michigan.

Jones, L. M., Mitchell, K. J., & Finkelhor, D. (2013). Online harassment in context: Trends from three youth Internet safety surveys (2000, 2005, 2010). *Psychology of Violence*, *31*(1), 53–69.

Jones, M. D., & Galliher, R. V. (2007). Ethnic identity and psychosocial functioning in Navajo adolescents. *Journal of Research on Adolescence*, *17*(4), 683–696. doi:10.1111/j.1532-7795.2007.00541.x

Jones, R. M., Akers, J. F., & White, J. M. (1994). Revised classification criteria for the Extended Objective Measure of Ego Identity Status (EOMEIS). *Journal of Adolescence*, *17*(6).

Juvonen, J., & Graham, S. (2014). Bullying in schools: The power of bullies and the plight of victims. *Annual Review of Psychology*, *65*, 159–185. doi:10.1146/annurev-psych-010213-115030

Juvonen, J., & Gross, E. F. (2008). Extending the school grounds?—Bullying experiences in cyberspace. *Journal of School Health*, *78*(9), 496–505. doi:10.1111/j.1746-1561.2008.00335.x

Kaiser Family Foundation. (2014). Sexual health of adolescents and young adults in the United States. Menlo Park, CA: Author. Retrieved May 4, 2015, from http://kff.org/womens-health-policy/fact-sheet/sexual-health-of-adolescents-and-young-adults-in-the-united-states

Kann, L., Kinchen, S., Shanklin, S. L., Flint, K. H., Kawkins, J., Harris, W. A., . . . Zaza, S. (2014). Youth risk behavior surveillance—United States, 2013. *Morbidity and Mortality Weekly Report. Surveillance Summaries (Washington, DC: 2002)*, *63*(Suppl. 4), 1–168. Retrieved from http://www.ncbi.nlm.nih.gov/pubmed/24918634

Katzman, D. K. (2005). Medical complications in adolescents with anorexia nervosa: A review of the literature. *International Journal of Eating Disorders*, *37*, 52–59.

Kawabata, Y., & Crick, N. R. (2011). The significance of cross-racial/ethnic friendships: Associations with peer victimization, peer support, sociometric status, and classroom diversity. *Developmental Psychology*, *47*(6), 1763–1775. doi:10.1037/a0025399

Kaye, W. H., Bailer, U. F., Frank, G. K., Wagner, A., & Henry, S. E. (2005). Brain imaging of serotonin after recovery from anorexia and bulimia nervosa. *Physiology & Behavior*, *86*, 15–17.

Kaye, W. H., Wierenga, C. E., Bailer, U. F., Simmons, A. N., & Bischoff-Grethe, A. (2013). Nothing tastes as good as skinny feels: The neurobiology of anorexia nervosa. *Trends in Neurosciences*, *36*(2), 110–120. doi:10.1016/j.tins.2013.01.003

Keel, P. K. (2014). Bulimia nervosa. In R. L. Cautin & S. O. Lilienfeld (Eds.), *The encyclopedia of clinical psychology*. Hoboken, NJ: John Wiley & Sons. Retrieved from http://onlinelibrary.wiley.com/doi/10.1002/9781118625392.wbecp251/abstract?deniedAccessCustomisedMessage=&userIsAuthenticated=false

Kelley, S. S., Borawski, E. A., Flocke, S. A., & Keen, K. J. (2003). The role of sequential and concurrent sexual relationships in the risk of sexually transmitted diseases among adolescents. *Journal of Adolescent Health*, *32*(4), 296–305.

Kerpelman, J. L., Eryigit, S., & Stephens, C. J. (2008). African American adolescents' future education orientation: Associations with self-efficacy, ethnic identity, and perceived parental support. *Journal of Youth and Adolescence*, *37*(8), 997–1008. doi:10.1007/s10964-007-9201-7

Kessler, R. C., Berglund, P. A., Chiu, W. T., Deitz, A. C., Hudson, J. I., Shahly, V., . . . Xavier, M. (2013). The prevalence and correlates of binge eating disorder in the World Health Organization World Mental Health Surveys. *Biological Psychiatry*, *73*(9), 904–914. doi:10.1016/j.biopsych.2012.11.020

Khurana, A., Bleakley, A., Jordan, A. B., & Romer, D. (2014). The protective effects of parental monitoring and Internet restriction on adolescents' risk of online harassment. *Journal of Youth and Adolescence, 44*(5), 1039–1047. doi:10.1007/s10964-014-0242-4

Kiang, L., Gonzales-Backen, M., Yip, T., Witkow, M., & Fuligni, A. J. (2006). Ethnic identity and the daily psychological well-being of adolescents from Mexican and Chinese backgrounds. *Child Development, 77*(5), 1338–1350.

Kiesner, J., Poulin, F., & Dishion, T. J. (2010). Adolescent substance use with friends: Moderating and mediating effects of parental monitoring and peer activity contexts. *Merrill-Palmer Quarterly, 56*(4), 529–556. Retrieved from http://www.pubmedcentral.nih.gov/articlerender.fcgi?artid=3002110&tool=pmcentrez&rendertype=abstract

Kim, S. Y., Chen, Q., Wang, Y., Shen, Y., & Orozco-Lapray, D. (2013). Longitudinal linkages among parent-child acculturation discrepancy, parenting, parent-child sense of alienation, and adolescent adjustment in Chinese immigrant families. *Developmental Psychology, 49*(5), 900–912. doi:10.1037/a0029169

Kim, S. Y., Qi, C., Jing, L., Xuan, H., & Ui Jeong, M. (2009). Parent-child acculturation, parenting, and adolescent depressive symptoms in Chinese immigrant families. *Journal of Family Psychology, 23*(3), 426–437. doi:10.1037/a0016019

Kingery, J. N., Erdley, C. A., & Marshall, K. C. (2011). Peer acceptance and friendship as predictors of early adolescents' adjustment across the middle school transition. *Merrill-Palmer Quarterly, 57*(3), 215–243. doi:10.1353/mpq.2011.0012

Kinney, D. A. (1999). From "headbangers" to "hippies": Delineating adolescents' active attempts to form an alternative peer culture. *New Directions for Child & Adolescent Development, 1999*, 21–35.

Kiselica, M. S., & Kiselica, A. M. (2014). The complicated worlds of adolescent fathers: Implications for clinical practice, public policy, and research. *Psychology of Men & Masculinity, 15*(3), 260. doi: 10.1037/a0037043

Klaw, E. L., Rhodes, J. E., & Fitzgerald, L. F. (2003). Natural mentors in the lives of African American adolescent mothers: Tracking relationships over time. *Journal of Youth and Adolescence, 32*(3), 223.

Klein, J. D. (2006). Adolescent pregnancy: Current trends and issues. *Journal of the American Academy of Child & Adolescent Psychiatry, 45*(1), 68.

Kost, K., & Henshaw, S. (2014). *U.S. teenage pregnancies, births and abortions, 2010: National and state trends by age, race and ethnicity.* Washington, DC: Guttmacher Institute. Retrieved from http://www.guttmacher.org/pubs/USTPtrends10.pdf

Kreager, D. A., Molloy, L. E., Moody, J., & Feinberg, M. E. (2015). Friends first? The peer network origins of adolescent dating. *Journal of Research on Adolescence.* Advance online publication. doi:10.1111/jora.12189

Kroger, J. (2000). Ego identity status research in the new millennium. *International Journal of Behavioral Development, 24*(2), 145–148.

Kroger, J. (2007a). *Identity development: Adolescence through adulthood* (2nd ed.). Thousand Oaks, CA: Sage.

Kroger, J. (2007b). Why is identity achievement so elusive? *Identity, 7*(4), 331–348. doi:10.1080/15283480701600793

Kroger, J., Martinussen, M., & Marcia, J. E. (2010). Identity status change during adolescence and young adulthood: A meta-analysis. *Journal of Adolescence, 33*(5), 683–698. doi:10.1016/j.adolescence.2009.11.002

Kutcher, S. P. (2008). Youth suicide prevention. *Canadian Medical Association Journal, 178*(3), 282–285. doi:10.1503/cmaj.071315

Lacourse, E., Nagin, D., & Tremblay, R. E. (2003). Developmental trajectories of boys' delinquent group membership and facilitation of violent behaviors during adolescence. *Development and Psychopathology, 15*(1), 183–197.

Lahey, B., Hulle, C., D'Onofrio, B., Rodgers, J., & Waldman, I. (2008). Is parental knowledge of their adolescent offspring's whereabouts and peer associations spuriously associated with offspring delinquency? *Journal of Abnormal Child Psychology, 36*(6), 807–823. doi:10.1007/s10802-008-9214-z

Lansford, J. E., Costanzo, P. R., Grimes, C., Putallaz, M., Miller, S., & Malone, P. S. (2009). Social network centrality and leadership status: Links with problem behaviors and tests of gender differences. *Merrill-Palmer Quarterly, 55*(1), 1–25.

Lansford, J. E., Laird, R. D., Pettit, G. S., Bates, J. E., & Dodge, K. A. (2014). Mothers' and fathers' autonomy-relevant parenting: Longitudinal links with adolescents' externalizing and internalizing behavior. *Journal of Youth and Adolescence, 43*(11), 1877–1889. doi:10.1007/s10964-013-0079-2

Larson, R. W. (2001). How U.S. children and adolescents spend time: What it does (and doesn't) tell us about their development. *Current Directions in Psychological Science, 10*, 160–165.

Latzer, Y., Witztum, E., & Stein, D. (2008). Eating disorders and disordered eating in Israel: An updated review. *European Eating Disorders Review, 16*(5), 361–374. doi:10.1002/erv.875

Laukkanen, E., Rissanen, M.-L., Honkalampi, K., Kylmä, J., Tolmunen, T., & Hintikka, J. (2009). The prevalence of self-cutting and other self-harm among 13- to 18-year-old Finnish adolescents. *Social Psychiatry & Psychiatric Epidemiology, 44*(1), 23–28. doi:10.1007/s00127-008-0398-x

Laursen, B., & Mooney, K. S. (2008). Relationship network quality: Adolescent adjustment and perceptions of relationships with parents and friends. *American Journal of Orthopsychiatry, 78*(1), 47–53. doi:10.1037/0002-9432.78.1.47

Laye-Gindhu, A., & Schonert-Reichl, K. A. (2005). Nonsuicidal self-harm among community adolescents: Understanding the "whats" and "whys" of self-harm. *Journal of Youth and Adolescence, 34*(5), 447–457.

Le Grange, D., & Schmidt, U. (2005). The treatment of adolescents with bulimia nervosa. *Journal of Mental Health, 14*(6), 587–597.

Leadbeater, B., Banister, E., Ellis, W., & Yeung, R. (2008). Victimization and relational aggression in adolescent romantic relationships: The influence of parental and peer behaviors, and individual adjustment. *Journal of Youth and Adolescence, 37*(3), 359–372. doi:10.1007/s10964-007-9269-0

Lee, S. M., Daniels, M. H., & Kissinger, D. B. (2006). Parental influences on adolescent adjustment: Parenting styles versus parenting practices. *Family Journal, 14*, 253–259.

Lefkowitz, E. S., & Stoppa, T. M. (2006). Positive sexual communication and socialization in the parent-adolescent context. *New Directions for Child & Adolescent Development, 112*, 39–55.

Lerner, R. M., & Israeloff., R. (2007). *The good teen: Rescuing adolescence from the myths of the storm and stress years.* New York: Crown.

Lester, D. (2003). Adolescent suicide from an international perspective. *American Behavioral Scientist, 46*(9), 1157.

Levine, J. A., Emery, C. R., & Pollack, H. (2007). The well-being of children born to teen mothers. *Journal of Marriage and Family, 69*(1), 105–122. doi:10.1111/j.1741-3737.2006.00348.x

Li, J. J., Berk, M. S., & Lee, S. S. (2013). Differential susceptibility in longitudinal models of gene-environment interaction for adolescent depression. *Development and Psychopathology, 25*(4 Pt. 1), 991–1003. doi:10.1017/S0954579413000321

Liddon, N., Michael, S. L., Dittus, P., & Markowitz, L. E. (2013). Maternal underestimation of child's sexual experience: Suggested implications for HPV vaccine uptake at recommended ages. *The Journal of Adolescent Health, 53*(5), 674–676. doi:10.1016/j.jadohealth.2013.07.026

Lillevoll, K. R., Kroger, J., & Martinussen, M. (2013). Identity status and anxiety: A meta-analysis. *Identity, 13*(3), 214–227. doi:10.1080/15283488.2013.799432

Lipman, E. L., Georgiades, K., & Boyle, M. H. (2011). Young adult outcomes of children born to teen mothers: Effects of being born during their teen or later years. *Journal of the American Academy of Child & Adolescent Psychiatry, 50*(3), 232–241. doi:10.1016/j.jaac.2010.12.007

Litwack, S. D., Aikins, J. W., & Cillessen, A. H. N. (2010). The distinct roles of sociometric and perceived popularity in friendship: Implications for adolescent depressive affect and self-esteem. *The Journal of Early Adolescence, 32*(2), 226–251. doi:10.1177/0272431610387142

Liu, R. T., & Mustanski, B. (2012). Suicidal ideation and self-harm in lesbian, gay, bisexual, and transgender youth. *American Journal of Preventive Medicine, 42*(3), 221–228. doi:10.1016/j.amepre.2011.10.023

Livingstone, S., & Smith, P. K. (2014). Annual research review: Harms experienced by child users of online and mobile technologies: The nature, prevalence and management of sexual and aggressive risks in the digital age. *Journal of Child Psychology and Psychiatry, and Allied Disciplines, 55*(6), 635–654. doi:10.1111/jcpp.12197

Livingstone, S., Haddon, L., Görzig, A., & Ólafsson, K. (2011). *EU Kids Online II: Final Report.* London: LSE.

Lock, J. (2011). Evaluation of family treatment models for eating disorders. *Current Opinion in Psychiatry, 24*(4), 274–279. doi:10.1097/YCO.0b013e328346f71e

Lock, J., Le Grange, D., & Forsberg, S. (2007). Is family therapy effective in children with anorexia nervosa? *Brown University Child & Adolescent Behavior Letter, 23*(1), 3.

Lohman, B. J., & Billings, A. (2008). Protective and risk factors associated with adolescent boys' early sexual debut and risky sexual behaviors. *Journal of Youth and Adolescence, 37*(6), 723–735. doi:10.1007/s10964-008-9283-x

Low, S., Polanin, J. R., & Espelage, D. L. (2013). The role of social networks in physical and relational aggression among young adolescents. *Journal of Youth and Adolescence, 42*(7), 1078–1089. doi:10.1007/s10964-013-9933-5

Luder, M.-T., Pittet, I., Berchtold, A., Akré, C., Michaud, P.-A., & Surís, J.-C. (2011). Associations between online pornography and sexual behavior among adolescents: Myth or reality? *Archives of Sexual Behavior, 40*(5), 1027–1035. doi:10.1007/s10508-010-9714-0

Luyckx, K., Schwartz, S. J., Berzonsky, M. D., Soenens, B., Vansteenkiste, M., Smits, I., & Goossens, L. (2008). Capturing ruminative exploration: Extending the four-dimensional model of identity formation in late adolescence. *Journal of Research in Personality, 42*(1), 58–82. doi:10.1016/j.jrp.2007.04.004

Maccoby, E. E. (2000). Parenting and its effects on children: On reading and misreading behavior genetics. *Annual Review of Psychology, 51.*

Madden, M., Lenhart, A., Duggan, M., Cortesi, S., & Gasser, U. (2013). *Teens and Technology, 2013.* Retrieved from http://www.pewinternet.org/files/old-media//Files/Reports/2013/PIP_TeensandTechnology2013.pdf

Madge, N., Hewitt, A., Hawton, K., De Wilde, E. J., Corcoran, P., Fekete, S., . . . Ystgaard, M. (2008). Deliberate self-harm within an international community sample of young people: Comparative findings from the Child & Adolescent Self-harm in Europe (CASE) Study. *Journal of Child Psychology & Psychiatry, 49*(6), 667–677. doi:10.1111/j.1469-7610.2008.01879.x

Madsen, S. D., & Collins, W. A. (2011). The salience of adolescent romantic experiences for romantic relationship qualities in young adulthood. *Journal of Research on Adolescence, 21*(4), 789–801. doi:10.1111/j.1532-7795.2011.00737.x

Maggs, J. L., & Schulenberg, J. E. (2005). Trajectories of alcohol use during the transition to adulthood. *Alcohol Research & Health, 28*(4), 195–201.

Mahatmya, D., & Lohman, B. (2011). Predictors of late adolescent delinquency: The protective role of after-school activities in low-income families. *Children and Youth Services Review, 33*(7), 1309–1317. doi:10.1016/j.childyouth.2011.03.005

Malcolm, S., Huang, S., Cordova, D., Freitas, D., Arzon, M., Jimenez, G. L., . . . Prado, G. (2013). Predicting condom use attitudes, norms, and control beliefs in Hispanic problem behavior youth: The effects of family functioning and parent-adolescent communication about sex on condom use. *Health Education & Behavior, 40*(4), 384–391. doi:10.1177/1090198112440010

Manlove, J., Franzetta, K., & Ryan, S. (2006). Adolescent sexual relationships, contraceptive consistency, and pregnancy prevention approaches. In A. C. Crouter & A. Booth (Eds.), *Romance and sex in adolescence and emerging adulthood: Risks and opportunities.* Mahwah, NJ: Lawrence Erlbaum.

Marcia, J. E. (1966). Development and validation of ego-identity status. *Journal of Personality and Social Psychology, 3*(5), 551–558.

Markovits, H., Benenson, J., & Dolenszky, E. (2001). Evidence that children and adolescents have internal models of peer interactions that are gender differentiated. *Child Development, 72,* 879–886.

Markstrom-Adams, C., & Adams, G. R. (1995). Gender, ethnic group, and grade differences in psychosocial functioning during middle adolescence? *Journal of Youth and Adolescence, 24*(4), 397–417.

Marsh, H. W., Trautwein, U., Lüdtke, O., Gerlach, E., & Brettschneider, W.-D. (2007). Longitudinal study of preadolescent sport self-concept and performance: Reciprocal effects and causal ordering. *Child Development, 78*(6), 1640–1656. doi:10.1111/j.1467-8624.2007.01094.x

Marsh, H. W., Trautwein, U., Lüdtke, O., Köller, O., & Baumert, J. (2006). Integration of multidimensional self-concept and core personality constructs: Construct validation and relations to well-being and achievement. *Journal of Personality, 74,* 403–456.

Marshall, E. J. (2014). Adolescent alcohol use: Risks and consequences. *Alcohol and Alcoholism, 49*(2), 160–164. doi:10.1093/alcalc/agt180

Marshall, S. K., Tilton-Weaver, L. C., & Stattin, H. (2013). Non-suicidal self-injury and depressive symptoms during middle adolescence: A longitudinal analysis. *Journal of Youth and Adolescence, 42*(8), 1234–1242. doi:10.1007/s10964-013-9919-3

Martin, C. A., Lommel, K., Cox, J., Kelly, T., Rayens, M. K., Woodring, J. H., & Omar, H. (2007). Kiss and tell: What do we know about pre- and early adolescent females who report dating? A pilot study. *Journal of Pediatric & Adolescent Gynecology, 20,* 45–49.

Martinez, G., Copen, C. E., & Abma, J. C. (2011). Teenagers in the United States: Sexual activity, contraceptive use, and childbearing, 2006–2010 national survey of family growth. *Vital and Health Statistics. Series 23, Data from the National Survey of Family Growth, 31,* 1–35. Retrieved from http://www.ncbi.nlm.nih.gov/pubmed/22256688

Masche, J. G. (2010). Explanation of normative declines in parents' knowledge about their adolescent children. *Journal of Adolescence, 33*(2), 271–284. doi:10.1016/j.adolescence.2009.08.002

Mason, K. L. (2008). Cyberbullying: A preliminary assessment for school personnel. *Psychology in the Schools, 45*(4), 323–348. doi:10.1002/pits.20301

Mason, W. A., & Spoth, R. L. (2011). Longitudinal associations of alcohol involvement with subjective well-being in adolescence and prediction to alcohol problems in early adulthood. *Journal of Youth and Adolescence, 40*(9), 1215–1224. doi:10.1007/s10964-011-9632-z

Mathys, C., Burk, W. J., & Cillessen, A. H. N. (2013). Popularity as a moderator of peer selection and socialization of adolescent alcohol, marijuana, and tobacco use. *Journal of Research on Adolescence, 23*(3), 513–523. doi:10.1111/jora.12031

Maughan, B., Collishaw, S., & Stringaris, A. (2013). Depression in childhood and adolescence. *Journal of the Canadian Academy of Child and Adolescent Psychiatry, 22*(1), 35–40. Retrieved from http://www.pubmedcentral.nih.gov/articlerender.fcgi?artid=3565713&tool=pmcentrez&rendertype=abstract

Mayeux, L., & Cillessen, A. H. N. (2008). It's not just being popular, it's knowing it, too: The role of self-perceptions of status in the associations between peer status and aggression. *Social Development, 17*(4), 871–888. doi:10.1111/j.1467-9507.2008.00474.x

Maynard, M. J., & Harding, S. (2010). Perceived parenting and psychological well-being in UK ethnic minority adolescents. *Child: Care, Health and Development, 36*(5), 630–638. doi:10.1111/j.1365-2214.2010.01115.x

Mayseless, O., Scharf, M., & Sholt, M. (2003). From authoritative parenting practices to an authoritarian context: Exploring the person–environment fit. *Journal of Research on Adolescence, 13,* 427–457.

McCabe, M. P., & Ricciardelli, L. A. (2006). A prospective study of extreme weight change behaviors among adolescent boys and girls. *Journal of Youth and Adolescence, 35*(3), 425–434.

McCarty, C. A., Vander Stoep, A., & McCauley, E. (2007). Cognitive features associated with depressive symptoms in adolescence: Directionality and specificity. *Journal of Clinical Child & Adolescent Psychology, 36*(2), 147–158. doi:10.1080/15374410701274926

McClelland, S. I., & Tolman, D. L. (2014). Adolescent sexuality. In T. Tio (Ed.), *Encyclopedia of critical psychology* (pp. 40–47). New York: Springer.

McElhaney, K. B., Antonishak, J., & Allen, J. P. (2008). "They like me, they like me not": Popularity and adolescents' perceptions of acceptance predicting social functioning over time. *Child Development, 79*(3), 720–731. doi:10.1111/j.1467-8624.2008.01153.x

McElwain, N. L., & Booth-LaForce, C. (2006). Maternal sensitivity to infant distress and nondistress as predictors of infant-mother attachment security. *Journal of Family Psychology, 20*(2), 247–255. doi:10.1037/0893-3200.20.2.247

McKinney, C., & Renk, K. (2011). A multivariate model of parent-adolescent relationship variables in early adolescence. *Child Psychiatry and Human Development, 42*(4), 442–462. doi:10.1007/s10578-011-0228-3

McLean, K. C. (2005). Late adolescent identity development: Narrative meaning making and memory telling. *Developmental Psychology, 41*(4), 683–691.

McLeod, J. D., & Knight, S. (2010). The association of socioemotional problems with early sexual initiation. *Perspectives on Sexual and Reproductive Health, 42*(2), 93–101. doi:10.1363/4209310

McLoughlin, A. B., Gould, M. S., & Malone, K. M. (2015). Global trends in teenage suicide: 2003–2014. *QJM: An International Journal of Medicine.* Advance online publication. doi:10.1093/qjmed/hcv026

Meade, C. S., Kershaw, T. S., & Ickovics, J. R. (2008). The intergenerational cycle of teenage motherhood: An ecological approach. *Health Psychology, 27*(4), 419–429. doi:10.1037/0278-6133.27.4.419

Meeus, W. H. J. (1996). Studies on identity development in adolescence: An overview of research and some new data. *Journal of Youth and Adolescence, 25,* 569–599.

Meeus, W. H. J. (2011). The study of adolescent identity formation 2000–2010: A review of longitudinal research. *Journal of Research on Adolescence, 21*(1), 75–94. doi:10.1111/j.1532-7795.2010.00716.x

Meeus, W. H. J., & de Wied, M. (2007). Relationships with parents and identity in adolescence: A review of 25 years of research. In M. Watzlawik & A. Born (Eds.), *Capturing identity: Quantitative and qualitative methods* (pp. 131–147). Lanham, MD: University Press of America.

Meeus, W. H. J., Iedema, J., Maassen, G., & Engels, R. (2005). Separation—individuation revisited: On the interplay of parent—adolescent relations, identity and emotional adjustment in adolescence. *Journal of Adolescence, 28*(1), 89–106.

Meeus, W. H. J., Oosterwegel, A., & Vollebergh, W. (2002). Parental and peer attachment and identity development in adolescence. *Journal of Adolescence, 25,* 93–107.

Michels, T. M., Kropp, R. Y., Eyre, S. L., & Halpern-Felsher, B. L. (2005). Initiating sexual experiences: How do young adolescents make decisions regarding early sexual activity? *Journal of Research on Adolescence, 15*(4), 583–607.

Milevsky, A., Schlechter, M., Netter, S., & Keehn, D. (2007). Maternal and paternal parenting styles in adolescents: Associations with self-esteem, depression and life-satisfaction. *Journal of Child & Family Studies, 16*(1), 39–47. doi:10.1007/s10826-006-9066-5

Miller, K. S., Forehand, R., & Kotchick, B. A. (1999). Adolescent sexual behavior in two ethnic minority samples: The role of family variables. *Journal of Marriage & Family, 61,* 85–98.

Miranda, R., & Shaffer, D. (2013). Understanding the suicidal moment in adolescence. *Annals of the New York Academy of Sciences, 1304,* 14–21. doi:10.1111/nyas.12291

Mollborn, S. (2007). Making the best of a bad situation: Material resources and teenage parenthood. *Journal of Marriage & Family, 69*(1), 92–104. doi:10.1111/j.1741-3737.2006.00347.x

Monahan, K. C., & Booth-LaForce, C. (2015). Deflected pathways: Becoming aggressive, socially withdrawn, or prosocial with peers during the transition to adolescence. *Journal of Research on Adolescence, 25.* doi:10.1111/jora.12190

Monahan, K. C., Steinberg, L., Cauffman, E., & Mulvey, E. P. (2013). Psychosocial (im)maturity from adolescence to early adulthood: distinguishing between adolescence-limited and persisting antisocial behavior. *Development and Psychopathology, 25*(4 Pt. 1), 1093–1105. doi:10.1017/S0954579413000394

Moneta, G. B., Schneider, B., & Csikszentmihalyi, M. (2001). A longitudinal study of the self-concept and experiential components of self-worth and affect across adolescence. *Applied Developmental Science, 5*(3), 125–142.

Moore, D. R., & Florsheim, P. (2001). Interpersonal processes and psychopathology among expectant and nonexpectant adolescent couples. *Journal of Consulting and Clinical Psychology, 69*, 101–113.

Moore, K. A., Myers, D. E., Morrison, D. R., Nord, C. W., Brown, B., & Edmonston, B. (1993). Age at first childbirth and later poverty. *Journal of Research on Adolescence, 3*, 393–422.

Moore, S. R., Harden, K. P., & Mendle, J. (2014). Pubertal timing and adolescent sexual behavior in girls. *Developmental Psychology, 50*(6), 1734–1745. doi:10.1037/a0036027

Mrick, S. E., & Mrtorell, G. A. (2011). Sticks and stones may break my bones: Protective factors for the effects of perceived discrimination on social competence in adolescence. *Personal Relationships, 18*(3), 487–501. doi:10.1111/j.1475-6811.2010.01320.x

Mrug, S., Loosier, P. S., & Windle, M. (2008). Violence exposure across multiple contexts: Individual and joint effects on adjustment. *American Journal of Orthopsychiatry, 78*(1), 70–84. doi:10.1037/0002-9432.78.1.70

Muehlenkamp, J. J., Claes, L., Havertape, L., & Plener, P. L. (2012). International prevalence of adolescent non-suicidal self-injury and deliberate self-harm. *Child and Adolescent Psychiatry and Mental Health, 6*, 10. doi:10.1186/1753-2000-6-10

Mustanski, B., & Liu, R. T. (2013). A longitudinal study of predictors of suicide attempts among lesbian, gay, bisexual, and transgender youth. *Archives of Sexual Behavior, 42*(3), 437–448. doi:10.1007/s10508-012-0013-9

Nanayakkara, S., Misch, D., Chang, L., & Henry, D. (2013). Depression and exposure to suicide predict suicide attempt. *Depression and Anxiety, 30*(10), 991–996. doi:10.1002/da.22143

Natsuaki, M. N., Shaw, D. S., Neiderhiser, J. M., Ganiban, J. M., Harold, G. T., Reiss, D., & Leve, L. D. (2014). Raised by depressed parents: Is it an environmental risk? *Clinical Child and Family Psychology Review, 17*(4), 357–367. doi:10.1007/s10567-014-0169-z

Negriff, S., Susman, E. J., & Trickett, P. K. (2011). The developmental pathway from pubertal timing to delinquency and sexual activity from early to late adolescence. *Journal of Youth and Adolescence, 40*(10), 1343–1356. doi:10.1007/s10964-010-9621-7

Nguyen, P. V. (2008). Perceptions of Vietnamese fathers' acculturation levels, parenting styles, and mental health outcomes in Vietnamese American adolescent immigrants. *Social Work, 53*(4), 337–346.

Niolon, P. H., Vivolo-Kantor, A. M., Latzman, N. E., Valle, L. A., Kuoh, H., Burton, T., . . . Tharp, A. T. (2015). Prevalence of teen dating violence and co-occurring risk factors among middle school youth in high-risk urban communities. *Journal of Adolescent Health, 56*(2), S5–S13. doi:10.1016/j.jadohealth.2014.07.019

Nishina, A., Ammon, N. Y., Bellmore, A. D., & Graham, S. (2006). Body dissatisfaction and physical development among ethnic minority adolescents. *Journal of Youth and Adolescence, 35*(2), 189–201. doi:10.1007/s10964-005-9012-7

Nock, M. K. (2009). Why do people hurt themselves?: New insights into the nature and functions of self-injury. *Current Directions in Psychological Science, 18*(2), 78–83. doi:10.1111/j.1467-8721.2009.01613.x

Nock, M. K., Prinstein, M. J., & Sterba, S. K. (2009). Revealing the Form and Function of Self-Injurious Thoughts and Behaviors: A Real-Time Ecological Assessment Study Among Adolescents and Young Adults. *Journal of Abnormal Psychology, 118*(4), 816–827. doi:10.1037/a0016948

Nordin, S. M., Harris, G., & Cumming, J. (2003). Disturbed eating in young, competitive gymnasts: Differences between three gymnastics disciplines. *European Journal of Sport Science, 3*(5), 1–14.

Nurmi, J.-E. (2004). Socialization and self-development: Channeling, selection, adjustment, and reflection. In R. M. Lerner & L. Steinberg (Eds.), *Handbook of adolescent psychology* (2nd ed., pp. 85–124). Hoboken, NJ: John Wiley & Sons.

O'Sullivan, L. F., Cheng, M. M., Harris, K. M., & Brooks-Gunn, J. (2007). I wanna hold your hand: The progression of social, romantic and sexual events in adolescent relationships. *Perspectives on Sexual & Reproductive Health, 39*(2), 100–107. doi:10.1363/3910007

Oberlander, S. E., Black, M. M., & Starr, J. R. H. (2007). African American adolescent mothers and grandmothers: A multigenerational approach to parenting. *American Journal of Community Psychology, 39*(1–2), 37–46. doi:10.1007/s10464-007-9087-2

Office of Juvenile Justice and Delinquency Prevention. (2014). *Statistical briefing book.* Retrieved from http://www.ojjdp.gov/ojstatbb

Oh, J. S., & Fuligni, A. J. (2010). The role of heritage language development in the ethnic identity and family relationships of adolescents from immigrant backgrounds. *Social Development, 19*(1), 202–220. doi:10.1111/j.1467-9507.2008.00530.x

Oldehinkel, A. J., Ormel, J., Veenstra, R., De Winter, A. F., & Verholst, F. C. (2008). Parental divorce and offspring depressive symptoms: Dutch developmental trends during early adolescence. *Journal of Marriage & Family, 70*(2), 284–293. doi:10.1111/j.1741-3737.2008.00481.x

Ornstein, A., Bowes, M., Shouldice, Y., & Yanchar, N. (2013, October 1). The importance of child and youth death review. *Paediatrics & Child Health.* Retrieved from http://europepmc.org/articles/PMC3887082

Orth, U., & Robins, R. W. (2014). The development of self-esteem. *Current Directions in Psychological Science, 23*(5), 381–387. doi:10.1177/0963721414547414

Osgood, D. W., Ragan, D. T., Wallace, L., Gest, S. D., Feinberg, M. E., & Moody, J. (2013). Peers and the emergence of alcohol use: Influence and selection processes in adolescent friendship networks. *Journal of Research on Adolescence, 23*(3). doi:10.1111/jora.12059

Ott, M. A., Millstein, S. G., Ofner, S., & Halpern-Felsher, B. L. (2006). Greater expectations: Adolescents' positive motivations for sex. *Perspectives on Sexual & Reproductive Health, 38*(2), 84–89.

Oxford, M. L., Gilchrist, L. D., Lohr, M. J., Gillmore, M. R., Morrison, D. M., & Spieker, S. J. (2005). Life course heterogeneity in the transition from adolescence to adulthood among adolescent mothers. *Journal of Research on Adolescence, 15*(4), 479–504.

Padian, N. S., Shiboski, S. C., & Jewell, N. P. (1991). Female-to-male transmission of human immunodeficiency virus. *Journal of the American Medical Association, 266*, 1664–1667.

Palmer, R. H. C., Young, S. E., Hopfer, C. J., Corley, R. P., Stallings, M. C., Crowley, T. J., & Hewitt, J. K. (2009). Developmental epidemiology of drug use and abuse in adolescence and young adulthood: Evidence of generalized risk. *Drug & Alcohol Dependence, 102*(1–3), 78–87. doi:10.1016/j.drugalcdep.2009.01.012

Parkhurst, J. T., & Hopmeyer, A. (1998). Sociometric popularity and peer-perceived popularity: Two distinct dimensions of peer dtatus. *The Journal of Early Adolescence, 18*(2), 125–144. doi:10.1177/0272431698018002001

Paxton, R. J., Valois, O. F., Watkins, K. W., Huebner, E. S., & Drane, J. W. (2007). Sociodemographic differences in depressed mood: Results from a nationally representative sample of high school adolescents. *Journal of School Health, 77*, 180–186.

Pazol, K., Whiteman, M. K., Folger, S. G., Kourtis, A. P., Marchbanks, P. A., & Jamieson, D. J.

(2015). Sporadic contraceptive use and nonuse: Age-specific prevalence and associated factors. *American Journal of Obstetrics and Gynecology, 212*(3), 324. doi:10.1016/j.ajog.2014.10.004

Peterson, G. W., & Bush, K. R. (2013). Conceptualizing cultural influences on socialization: Comparing parent–adolescent relationships in the United States and Mexico. In G. W. Peterson & K. R. Bush (Eds.), *Handbook of marriage and the family* (pp. 177–208). New York: Springer.

Pew Research Center. (2015). *Teens fact sheet.* Retrieved April 4, 2015, from http://www.pewinternet.org/fact-sheets/teens-fact-sheet

Phinney, J. S. (2000). Identity formation across cultures: The interaction of personal, societal, and historical change. *Human Development, 43*(1), 27–31.

Phinney, J. S., & Chavira, V. (1995). Parental ethnic socialization and adolescent coping with problems related to ethnicity. *Journal of Research on Adolescence, 5*(1), 31–53.

Phinney, J. S., & Ong, A. D. (2007). Conceptualization and measurement of ethnic identity: Current status and future directions. *Journal of Counseling Psychology, 54*(3), 271–281. doi:10.1037/0022-067.54.3.271

Phinney, J. S., Romero, I., Nava, M., & Huang, D. (2001). The role of language, parents, and peers in ethnic identity among adolescents in immigrant families. *Journal of Youth and Adolescence, 30*(2), 135–153.

Phipps, M. C., Sowers, M., & Demonner, S. M. (2002). The risk for infant mortality among adolescent childbearing groups. *Journal of Women's Health, 11*, 889–898.

Pike, K. M., Hoek, H. W., & Dunne, P. E. (2014). Cultural trends and eating disorders. *Current Opinion in Psychiatry, 27*(6), 436–442. doi:10.1097/YCO.0000000000000100

Piquero, A. R., & Moffitt, T. E. (2013). Moffitt's developmental taxonomy of antisocial behavior. In G. Bruinsma & D. Weisburd (Eds.), *Encyclopedia of Criminology and Criminal Justice* (pp. 3121–3127). New York: Springer.

Planned Parenthood Federation of America. (2012). *Half of all teens feel uncomfortable talking to their parents about sex while only 19 percent of parents feel the same, new survey shows.* Retrieved May 4, 2015, from http://www.plannedparenthood.org/about-us/newsroom/press-releases/half-all-teens-feel-uncomfortable-talking-their-parents-about-sex-while-only-19-percent-parents

Plener, P. L., Libal, G., Keller, F., Fegert, J. M., & Muehlenkamp, J. J. (2009). An international comparison of adolescent non-suicidal self-injury (NSSI) and suicide attempts: Germany and the USA. *Psychological Medicine, 39*(9), 1549–1558. doi:10.1017/s0033291708005114

Plöderl, M., Wagenmakers, E.-J., Tremblay, P., Ramsay, R., Kralovec, K., Fartacek, C., & Fartacek, R. (2013). Suicide risk and sexual orientation: A critical review. *Archives of Sexual Behavior, 42*(5), 715–727. doi:10.1007/s10508-012-0056-y

Pomerleau, A., Scuccimarri, C., & Malcuit, G. (2003). Mother-infant behavioral interactions in teenage and adult mothers during the first six months postpartum: Relations with infant development. *Infant Mental Health Journal, 24*(5), 495–509.

Poteat, V. P., Espelage, D. L., & Koenig, B. W. (2009). Willingness to remain friends and attend school with lesbian and gay peers: Relational expressions of prejudice among heterosexual youth. *Journal of Youth and Adolescence, 38*(7), 952–962. doi:10.1007/s10964-009-9416-x

Poteat, V. P., Sinclair, K. O., DiGiovanni, C. D., Koenig, B. W., & Russell, S. T. (2013). Gay-straight alliances are associated with student health: A multischool comparison of LGBTQ and heterosexual youth. *Journal of Research on Adolescence, 23*(2), 319–330. doi:10.1111/j.1532-7795.2012.00832.x

Poteat, V. P., Yoshikawa, H., Calzo, J. P., Gray, M. L., DiGiovanni, C. D., Lipkin, A., . . . Shaw, M. P. (2015). Contextualizing gay-straight alliances: Student, advisor, and structural factors related to positive youth development among members. *Child Development, 86*(1), 176–193. doi:10.1111/cdev.12289

Poth, R., Greenberg, M., & Turrisi, R. (2008). Preventive interventions addressing underage drinking: State of the evidence and steps toward public health impact. *Pediatrics, 121*, S311–S336. doi:10.1542/peds.2007-2243E

Poulin, F., & Chan, A. (2010). Friendship stability and change in childhood and adolescence. *Developmental Review, 30*(3), 257–272. doi:10.1016/j.dr.2009.01.001

Poulin, F., & Pedersen, S. (2007). Developmental changes in gender composition of friendship networks in adolescent girls and boys. *Developmental Psychology, 43*(6), 1484–1496. doi:10.1037/0012-1649.43.6.1484

Preckel, F., Niepel, C., Schneider, M., & Brunner, M. (2013). Self-concept in adolescence: A longitudinal study on reciprocal effects of self-perceptions in academic and social domains. *Journal of Adolescence, 36*(6), 1165–1175. doi:10.1016/j.adolescence.2013.09.001

Prinstein, M. J., Meade, C. S., & Cohen, G. L. (2003). Adolescent oral sex, peer popularity, and perceptions of best friends's sexual behavior. *Journal of Pediatric Psychology, 28*(4), 243–249.

Quane, J. M., & Rankin, B. H. (2006). Does it pay to participate? Neighborhood-based organizations and the social development of urban adolescents. *Children & Youth Services Review, 28*, 1229–1250.

Quintana, S. M. (2007). Racial and ethnic identity: Developmental perspectives and research. *Journal of Counseling Psychology, 54*(3), 259–270.

Racz, S. J., & McMahon, R. J. (2011). The relationship between parental knowledge and monitoring and child and adolescent conduct problems: A 10-year update. *Clinical Child and Family Psychology Review, 14*(4), 377–398. doi:10.1007/s10567-011-0099-y

Raevuori, A., Keski-Rahkonen, A., & Hoek, H. W. (2014). A review of eating disorders in males. *Current Opinion in Psychiatry, 27*(6), 426–430. doi:10.1097/YCO.0000000000000113

Rafferty, Y., Griffin, K. W., & Lodise, M. (2011). Adolescent motherhood and developmental outcomes of children in early Head Start: The influence of maternal parenting behaviors, well-being, and risk factors within the family setting. *American Journal of Orthopsychiatry, 81*(2), 228–245. doi:10.1111/j.1939-0025.2011.01092.x

Raiford, J. L., Wingood, G. M., & DiClemente, R. J. (2007). Prevalence, incidence, and predictors of dating violence: A longitudinal study of African American female adolescents. *Journal of Women's Health, 16*(6), 822–832. doi:10.1089/jwh.2006.0002

Raskauskas, J., & Stoltz, A. D. (2007). Involvement in traditional and electronic bullying among adolescents. *Developmental Psychology, 43*(3), 564–575. doi:10.1037/0012-1649.43.3.564

Rayner, K. E., Schniering, C. A., Rapee, R. M., Taylor, A., & Hutchinson, D. M. (2013). Adolescent girls' friendship networks, body dissatisfaction, and disordered eating: Examining selection and socialization processes. *Journal of Abnormal Psychology, 122*(1), 93–104. doi:10.1037/a0029304

Reel, J. J. (2012). *Eating disorders: An encyclopedia of causes, treatment, and prevention.* Santa Barbara, CA: ABC-CLIO.

Regan, P. C., Durvasula, R., Howell, L., Ureño, O., & Rea, M. (2004). Gender, ethnicity, and the developmental timing of first sexual and romantic experiences. *Social Behavior & Personality, 32*(7), 667–676.

Reis, O., & Youniss, J. (2004). Patterns in identity change and development in relationships with mothers and friends. *Journal of Adolescent Research, 19*(1), 31–44.

Renk, K., Liljequist, L., Simpson, J. E., & Phares, V. (2005). Gender and age differences in the topics of parent-adolescent conflict. *Family Journal, 13*(2), 139–149. doi:10.1177/1066480704271190

Rhule, D. M., McMahon, R. J., Spieker, S. J., & Munson, J. A. (2006). Positive adjustment and associated protective factors in children of adolescent mothers. *Journal of Child & Family Studies, 15*(2), 224–244.

Rice, E., Rhoades, H., Winetrobe, H., Sanchez, M., Montoya, J., Plant, A., & Kordic, T. (2012). Sexually explicit cell phone messaging associated with sexual risk among adolescents. *Pediatrics, 130*(4), 667–673. doi:10.1542/peds.2012-0021

Riesch, S. K., Bush, L., Nelson, C. J., Ohm, B. J., Portz, P. A., Abell, B., . . . Jenkins, P. (2000). Topics of conflict between parents and young adolescents. *Journal of the Society of Pediatric Nurses, 5*(1), 27.

Rink, E., Tricker, R., & Harvey, S. M. (2007). Onset of sexual intercourse among female adolescents: The influence of perceptions, depression, and ecological factors. *Journal of Adolescent Health, 41*(4), 398–406.

Rivas-Drake, D., Seaton, E. K., Markstrom, C., Quintana, S., Syed, M., Lee, R. M., . . . Yip, T. (2014). Ethnic and racial identity in adolescence: Implications for psychosocial, academic, and health outcomes. *Child Development, 85*(1), 40–57. doi:10.1111/cdev.12200

Robertson, D. L., Farmer, T. W., Fraser, M. W., Day, S. H., Duncan, T., Crowther, A., & Dadisman, K. A. (2010). Interpersonal competence configurations and peer relations in early elementary classrooms: Perceived popular and unpopular aggressive subtypes. *International Journal of Behavioral Development, 34*(1), 73–87. doi:10.1177/0165025409345074

Robinson, J. P., & Espelage, D. L. (2013). Peer victimization and sexual risk differences between lesbian, gay, bisexual, transgender, or questioning and nontransgender heterosexual youths in grades 7–12. *American Journal of Public Health, 103*(10), 1810–1819. doi:10.2105/AJPH.2013.301387

Rock, P. F., Cole, D. J., Houshyar, S., Lythcott, M., & Prinstein, M. J. (2011). Peer status in an ethnic context: Associations with African American adolescents' ethnic identity. *Journal of Applied Developmental Psychology, 32*(4), 163–169. doi:10.1016/j.appdev.2011.03.002

Romero, A. J., Edwards, L. M., Fryberg, S. A., & Orduña, M. (2014). Resilience to discrimination stress across ethnic identity stages of development. *Journal of Applied Social Psychology, 44*(1), 1–11. doi:10.1111/jasp.12192

Romero, A. J., & Roberts, R. E. (2003). The impact of multiple dimensions of ethnic identity on discrimination and adolescents' self-esteem. *Journal of Applied Social Psychology, 33*(11), 2288–2305.

Rose, A. J., & Swenson, L. P. (2009). Do perceived popular adolescents who aggress against others experience emotional adjustment problems themselves? *Developmental Psychology, 45*(3), 868–872. doi:10.1037/a0015408

Ross, S., Heath, N. L., & Toste, J. R. (2009). Non-suicidal self-injury and eating pathology in high school students. *American Journal of Orthopsychiatry, 79*(1), 83–92. doi:10.1037/a0014826

Rote, W. M., & Smetana, J. G. (2015). Beliefs about parents' right to know: Domain differences

and associations with change in concealment. *Journal of Research on Adolescence, 25.* doi:10.1111/jora.12194

Rusby, J. C., Westling, E., Crowley, R., & Light, J. M. (2013). Concurrent and predictive associations between early adolescent perceptions of peer affiliates and mood states collected in real time via ecological momentary assessment methodology. *Psychological Assessment, 25*(1), 47–60. doi:10.1037/a0030393

Rutter, M., Giller, H., & Hagell, A. (1998). *Antisocial behavior by young people.* New York: Cambridge University Press.

Ryan, S., Franzetta, K., & Manlove, J. (2007). Knowledge, perceptions, and motivations for contraception. *Youth & Society, 39*(2), 182–208.

Saewyc, E. M. (2011). Research on adolescent sexual orientation: Development, health disparities, stigma, and resilience. *Journal of Research on Adolescence, 21*(1), 256–272. doi:10.1111/j.1532-7795.2010.00727.x

Sandfort, T. G. M., Orr, M., Hirsch, J. S., & Santelli, J. (2008). Long-term health correlates of timing of sexual debut: Results from a national US study. *American Journal of Public Health, 98*(1), 155–161.

Santelli, J. S., Lindberg, L. D., Finer, L. B., & Singh, S. (2007). Explaining recent declines in adolescent pregnancy in the United States: The contribution of abstinence and improved contraceptive use. *American Journal of Public Health, 97*, 150–156.

Santelli, J. S., Lowry, R., Brener, N. D., & Robin, L. (2000). The Association of Sexual Behaviors With Socioeconomic Status, Family Structure, and Race/Ethnicity Among US Adolescents. *American Journal of Public Health, 90*(10), 1582–1588.

Savin-Williams, R. C., & Ream, G. L. (2007). Prevalence and stability of sexual orientation components during adolescence and young adulthood. *Archives of Sexual Behavior, 36*(3), 385–394. doi:10.1007/s10508-006-9088-5

Scalco, M. D., Trucco, E. M., Coffman, D. L., & Colder, C. R. (2015). Selection and socialization effects in early adolescent alcohol use: A propensity score analysis. *Journal of Abnormal Child Psychology, 43*(6), 1131–1143. doi:10.1007/s10802-014-9969-3

Scharf, M., & Mayseless, O. (2008). Late adolescent girls' relationships with parents and romantic partner: The distinct role of mothers and fathers. *Journal of Adolescence, 31*(6), 837–855. doi:10.1016/j.adolescence.2008.06.012

Schepis, T. S., Adinoff, B., & Rao, U. (2008). Neurobiological processes in adolescent addictive disorders. *American Journal on Addictions, 17*(1), 6–23. doi:10.1080/10550490701756146

Schofield, H.-L. T., Bierman, K. L., Heinrichs, B., & Nix, R. L. (2008). Predicting early sexual activity with behavior problems exhibited at school entry and in early adolescence. *Journal of Abnormal Child Psychology, 36*(8), 1175–1188. doi:10.1007/s10802-008-9252-6

Schwartz, S. J. (2004). Brief report: Construct validity of two identity status measures: The EIPQ and the EOM-EIS-II. *Journal of Adolescence, 27*, 477–483.

Scoliers, G., Portzky, G., Madge, N., Hewitt, A., Hawton, K., de Wilde, E. J., . . . Van Heeringen, K. (2009). Reasons for adolescent deliberate self-harm: A cry of pain and/or a cry for help? *Social Psychiatry & Psychiatric Epidemiology, 44*(8), 601–607. doi:10.1007/s00127-008-0469-z

Sears, H. A., Sandra Byers, E., & Lisa Price, E. (2007). The co-occurrence of adolescent boys' and girls' use of psychologically, physically, and sexually abusive behaviours in their dating relationships. *Journal of Adolescence, 30*(3), 487–504. doi:10.1016/j.adolescence.2006.05.002

Seaton, E. K. (2009). Perceived racial discrimination and racial identity profiles among

African American adolescents. *Cultural Diversity and Ethnic Minority Psychology, 15*(2), 137–144. doi:10.1037/a0015506

Sedgh, G., Finer, L. B., Bankole, A., Eilers, M. A., & Singh, S. (2015). Adolescent pregnancy, birth, and abortion rates across countries: Levels and recent trends. *The Journal of Adolescent Health, 56*(2), 223–230. doi:10.1016/j.jadohealth.2014.09.007

Selby, E. A., Nock, M. K., & Kranzler, A. (2014). How does self-injury feel? Examining automatic positive reinforcement in adolescent self-injurers with experience sampling. *Psychiatry Research, 215*(2), 417–423. doi:10.1016/j.psychres.2013.12.005

Selfhout, M. H. W., Branje, S. J. T., & Meeus, W. H. J. (2008). The development of delinquency and perceived friendship quality in adolescent best friendship dyads. *Journal of Abnormal Child Psychology, 36*(4), 471–485. doi:10.1007/s10802-007-9193-5

Selfhout, M. H. W., Branje, S. J. T., ter Bogt, T. F. M., & Meeus, W. H. J. (2009). The role of music preferences in early adolescents' friendship formation and stability. *Journal of Adolescence, 32*(1), 95–107. doi:10.1016/j.adolescence.2007.11.004

Shad, M. U., Bidesi, A. S., Chen, L.-A., Thomas, B. P., Ernst, M., & Rao, U. (2011). Neurobiology of decision-making in adolescents. *Behavioural Brain Research, 217*(1), 67–76. doi:10.1016/j.bbr.2010.09.033

Shapiro, J. R., Berkman, N. D., Brownley, K. A., Sedway, J. A., Lohr, K. N., & Bulik, C. M. (2007). Bulimia nervosa treatment: A systematic review of randomized controlled trials. *The International Journal of Eating Disorders, 40*(4), 321–336. doi:10.1002/eat.20372

Shelder, J., & Block, J. (1990). Adolescent drug use and psychological health: A longitudinal inquiry. *American Psychologist, 45*(5), 612–630.

Shin, H., & Ryan, A. M. (2014). Early adolescent friendships and academic adjustment: Examining selection and influence processes with longitudinal social network analysis. *Developmental Psychology, 50*(11), 2462–2472. doi:10.1037/a0037922

Shirk, S. R., Gudmundsen, G., Kaplinski, H. C., & McMakin, D. L. (2008). Alliance and outcome in cognitive-behavioral therapy for adolescent depression. *Journal of Clinical Child & Adolescent Psychology, 37*(3), 631–639. doi:10.1080/15374410802148061

Silberg, J., Rutter, M., D'Onofrio, B., & Eaves, L. (2003). Genetic and environmental risk factors in adolescent substance use. *Journal of Child Psychology & Psychiatry & Allied Disciplines, 44*(5), 664–676.

Sim, T. N. (2000). Adolescent psychosocial competence: The importance and role of regard for parents. *Journal of Research on Adolescence, 10*, 49–64.

Sim, T. N., & Koh, S. F. (2003). A domain conceptualization of adolescent susceptibility to peer pressure. *Journal of Research on Adolescence, 13*, 58–80.

Simons, L. G., & Conger, R. D. (2007). Linking mother–father differences in parenting to a typology of family parenting styles and adolescent outcomes. *Journal of Family Issues, 28*, 212–241.

Sinha, J. W., Cnaan, R. A., & Gelles, R. J. (2007). Adolescent risk behaviors and religion: Findings from a national study. *Journal of Adolescence, 30*(2), 231–249.

Skrzypek, S., Wehmeier, P. M., & Remschmidt, H. (2001). Body image assessment using body size estimation in recent studies on anorexia nervosa: A brief review. *European Child & Adolescent Psychiatry, 10*(4), 215–222.

Slonje, R., & Smith, P. K. (2008). Cyberbullying: Another main type of bullying? *Scandinavian Journal of Psychology, 49*(2), 147–154. doi:10.1111/j.1467-9450.2007.00611.x

Smetana, J. G. (2002). Culture, autonomy, and personal jurisdiction in adolescent-parent relationships. In R. V Kail & H. W. Reese (Eds.), *Advances in child development and behavior* (pp. 51–87). San Diego: Academic Press.

Smink, F. R. E., van Hoeken, D., & Hoek, H. W. (2013). Epidemiology, course, and outcome of eating disorders. *Current Opinion in Psychiatry, 26*(6), 543–548. doi:10.1097/YCO.0b013e328365a24f

Smink, F. R. E., van Hoeken, D., Oldehinkel, A. J., & Hoek, H. W. (2014). Prevalence and severity of DSM-5 eating disorders in a community cohort of adolescents. *The International Journal of Eating Disorders, 47*(6), 610–619. doi:10.1002/eat.22316

Smith, M., Rachel, C., & Catherine, B. (2009). Psychological factors linked to self-reported depression symptoms in late adolescence. *Behavioural & Cognitive Psychotherapy, 37*(1), 73–85.

Smith, P. K., Mahdavi, J., Carvalho, M., Fisher, S., Russell, S., & Tippett, N. (2008). Cyberbullying: Its nature and impact in secondary school pupils. *Journal of Child Psychology & Psychiatry, 49*(4), 376–385. doi:10.1111/j.1469-7610.2007.01846.x

Smokowski, P. R., Rose, R. A., & Bacallao, M. (2010). Influence of risk factors and cultural assets on Latino adolescents' trajectories of self-esteem and internalizing symptoms. *Child Psychiatry and Human Development, 41*(2), 133–155. doi:10.1007/s10578-009-0157-6

Spear, L. (2013). The teenage brain: Adolescents and alcohol. *Current Directions in Psychological Science, 22*(2), 152–157. doi:10.1177/0963721412472192

Spear, L. P. (2011). Adolescent neurobehavioral characteristics, alcohol sensitivities, and intake: Setting the stage for alcohol use disorders? *Child Development Perspectives, 5*(4), 231–238. doi:10.1111/j.1750-8606.2011.00182.x

Spera, C. (2005). A review of the relationship among parenting practices, parenting styles, and adolescent school achievement. *Educational Psychology Review, 17*(2), 125–146.

Stattin, H., & Kerr, M. (2000). Parental monitoring: A reinterpretation. *Child Development, 71*, 1072–1086.

Steiger, A. E., Allemand, M., Robins, R. W., & Fend, H. A. (2014). Low and decreasing self-esteem during adolescence predict adult depression two decades later. *Journal of Personality and Social Psychology, 106*(2), 325–338. doi:10.1037/a0035133

Stein, C., Fisher, L., Berkey, C., & Colditz, G. (2007). Adolescent physical activity and perceived competence: Does change in activity level impact self-perception? *Journal of Adolescent Health, 40*(5), 462.

Steinberg, L. (2001). We know some things: parent-adolescent relationships in retrospect and prospect. *Journal of Research on Adolescence, 11*(1), 1–19.

Steinberg, L., & Monahan, K. C. (2007). Age differences in resistance to peer influence. *Developmental Psychology, 43*(6), 1531–1543. doi:10.1037/0012-1649.43.6.1531

Steinberg, L., & Monahan, K. C. (2011). Adolescents' exposure to sexy media does not hasten the initiation of sexual intercourse. *Developmental Psychology, 47*(2), 562–576. doi:10.1037/a0020613

Steinberg, L., & Morris, A. S. (2001). Adolescent development. *Annual Review of Psychology, 52*, 83–112.

Steinberg, L., & Silverberg, S. B. (1986). The vicissitudes of autonomy in early adolescence. *Child Development, 57*(4), 841.

Stevens, E. N., Lovejoy, M. C., & Pittman, L. D. (2014). Understanding the relationship between actual: Ideal discrepancies and depressive symptoms: A developmental examination. *Journal of Adolescence, 37*(5), 612–621. doi:10.1016/j.adolescence.2014.04.013

Stone, M. R., & Brown, B. B. (1999). Identity claims and projections: Descriptions of self and crowds in secondary school. *New Directions for Child & Adolescent Development, 84*, 7–20.

Strang, N. M., Chein, J. M., & Steinberg, L. (2013). The value of the dual systems model of adolescent risk-taking. *Frontiers in Human Neuroscience, 7*, 223. doi:10.3389/fnhum.2013.00223

Striegel-Moore, R. H., & Bulik, C. M. (2007). Risk factors for eating disorders. *American Psychologist, 62*(3), 181–198.

Strober, M., Freeman, R., Lampert, C., Diamond, J., & Kaye, W. (2014). Controlled family study of anorexia nervosa and bulimia nervosa: Evidence of shared liability and transmission of partial syndromes. *American Journal of Psychiatry, 157*(3), 393–401. Retrieved from http://ajp.psychiatryonline.org/doi/10.1176/appi.ajp.157.3.393

Substance Abuse and Mental Health Services Administration. (2013). *Results from the 2012 National Survey on Drug Use and Health: Mental health findings*. Rockville, MD: Author.

Sussman, S., Pokhrel, P., Ashmore, R. D., & Brown, B. B. (2007). Adolescent peer group identification and characteristics: A review of the literature. *Addictive Behaviors, 32*, 1602–1627.

Tang, S., Davis-Kean, P. E., Chen, M., & Sexton, H. R. (2014). Adolescent pregnancy's intergenerational effects: Does an adolescent mother's education have consequences for her children's achievement? *Journal of Research on Adolescence*. Advance online publication. doi:10.1111/jora.12182

Taylor, J. L. (2009). Midlife impacts of adolescent parenthood. *Journal of Family Issues, 30*(4), 484–510.

Telzer, E. H., Tsai, K. M., Gonzales, N., & Fuligni, A. J. (2015). Mexican American adolescents' family obligation values and behaviors: Links to internalizing symptoms across time and context. *Developmental Psychology, 51*(1), 75–86. doi:10.1037/a0038434

Thapar, A., Collishaw, S., Pine, D. S., & Thapar, A. K. (2012). Depression in adolescence. *Lancet, 379*(9820), 1056–1067. doi:10.1016/S0140-6736(11)60871-4

Titzmann, P. F., Brenick, A., & Silbereisen, R. K. (2015). Friendships fighting prejudice: A longitudinal perspective on adolescents' cross-group friendships with immigrants. *Journal of Youth and Adolescence, 44*(6), 1318–1331. doi:10.1007/s10964-015-0256-6

Trejos-Castillo, E., & Vazsonyi, A. T. (2009). Risky sexual behaviors in first and second generation Hispanic immigrant youth. *Journal of Youth and Adolescence, 38*(5), 719–731. doi:10.1007/s10964-008-9369-5

Trucco, E. M., Colder, C. R., Wieczorek, W. F., Lengua, L. J., & Hawk, L. W. (2014). Early adolescent alcohol use in context: How neighborhoods, parents, and peers impact youth. *Development and Psychopathology, 26*(2), 425–436. doi:10.1017/S0954579414000042

Tyrka, A. R., Graber, J. A., & Brooks-Gunn, J. (2000). The development of disordered eating: Correlates and predictors of eating problems in the context of adolescence. In A. J. Sameroff, M. Lewis, & S. M. Miller (Eds.), *Handbook of developmental psychopathology* (2nd ed., pp. 607–624). Dordrecht, Netherlands: Kluwer Academic Publishers.

Ueno, K. (2005). Sexual orientation and psychological distress in adolescence: Examining interpersonal stressors and social support processes. *Social Psychology Quarterly, 68*(3), 258–277.

Uji, M., Sakamoto, A., Adachi, K., & Kitamura, T. (2013). The impact of authoritative, authoritarian, and permissive parenting styles on children's later mental health in Japan: Focusing on parent and child gender. *Journal of Child and Family Studies, 23*(2), 293–302. doi:10.1007/s10826-013-9740-3

Umaña-Taylor, A. J., Alfaro, E. C., Bámaca, M. Y., & Guimond, A. B. (2009). The central role of familial ethnic socialization in Latino adolescents' cultural orientation. *Journal of Marriage & Family, 71*(1), 46–60. doi:10.1111/j.1741-3737.2008.00579.x

Umaña-Taylor, A. J., Bhanot, R., & Shin, N. (2006). Ethnic identity formation during adolescence: The critical role of families. *Journal of Family Issues, 27*(3), 390–414. doi:10.1177/0192513x05282960

Umaña-Taylor, A. J., Guimond, A. B., Updegraff, K. A., & Jahromi, L. (2013). A longitudinal examination of support, self-esteem, and Mexican-origin adolescent mothers' parenting efficacy. *Journal of Marriage and the Family, 75*(3). doi:10.1111/jomf.12019

Vagi, K. J., Rothman, E. F., Latzman, N. E., Tharp, A. T., Hall, D. M., & Breiding, M. J. (2013). Beyond correlates: A review of risk and protective factors for adolescent dating violence perpetration. *Journal of Youth and Adolescence, 42*(4), 633–649. doi:10.1007/s10964-013-9907-7

Valentine, J. C., DuBois, D. L., & Cooper, H. (2004). The relation between self-beliefs and academic achievement: A meta-analytic review. *Educational Psychologist, 39*, 111–133.

Van de Bongardt, D., Reitz, E., Sandfort, T., & Deković, M. (2014). A meta-analysis of the relations between three types of peer norms and adolescent sexual behavior. *Personality and Social Psychology Review, 19*(3), 203–234. doi:10.1177/1088868314544223

Van Dijk, M. P. A., Branje, S., Keijsers, L., Hawk, S. T., Hale, W. W., & Meeus, W. H. J. (2014). Self-concept clarity across adolescence: Longitudinal associations with open communication with parents and internalizing symptoms. *Journal of Youth and Adolescence, 43*(11), 1861–1876. doi:10.1007/s10964-013-0055-x

Van Doorn, M. D., Branje, S. J. T., & Meeus, W. H. J. (2011). Developmental changes in conflict resolution styles in parent-adolescent relationships: A four-wave longitudinal study. *Journal of Youth and Adolescence, 40*(1), 97–107. doi:10.1007/s10964-010-9516-7

Van Hoorn, J., van Dijk, E., Meuwese, R., Rieffe, C., & Crone, E. A. (2015). Peer influence on prosocial behavior in adolescence. *Journal of Research on Adolescence, 25*. doi:10.1111/jora.12173

Van Ouytsel, J., Van Gool, E., Ponnet, K., & Walrave, M. (2014). Brief report: The association between adolescents' characteristics and engagement in sexting. *Journal of Adolescence, 37*(8), 1387–1391. doi:10.1016/j.adolescence.2014.10.004

Vanhalst, J., Luyckx, K., Scholte, R. H., Engels, R. C., & Goossens, L. (2013). Low self-esteem as a risk factor for loneliness in adolescence: Perceived—but not actual—social acceptance as an underlying mechanism. *Journal of Abnormal Child Psychology, 41*(7), 1067–1081. doi:10.1007/s10802-013-9751-y

Vazsonyi, A. T., Hibbert, J. R., & Blake Snider, J. (2003). Exotic enterprise no more? Adolescent reports of family and parenting processes from youth in four countries. *Journal of Adolescent Research, 13*(2), 135–174.

Verkooijen, K. T., de Vries, N. K., & Nielsen, G. A. (2007). Youth crowds and substance use: The impact of perceived group norm and multiple group identification. *Psychology of Addictive Behaviors, 21*(1), 55–61. doi:10.1037/0893-164x.21.1.55

Voelker, D. K., Gould, D., & Reel, J. J. (2014). Prevalence and correlates of disordered eating in female figure skaters. *Psychology of Sport and Exercise, 15*(6), 696–704. doi:10.1016/j.psychsport.2013.12.002

Vo-Jutabha, E. D., Dinh, K. T., McHale, J. P., & Valsiner, J. (2009). A qualitative analysis of Vietnamese adolescent identity exploration within and outside an ethnic enclave. *Journal of Youth and Adolescence, 38*(5), 672–690. doi:10.1007/s10964-008-9365-9

Wade, A., & Beran, T. (2011). Cyberbullying: The new era of bullying. *Canadian Journal of School Psychology, 26*(1), 44–61. doi:10.1177/0829573510396318

Wagner, E. F. (2008). Developmentally informed research on the effectiveness of clinical trials: A primer for assessing how developmental issues may influence treatment responses among adolescents with alcohol use problems. *Pediatrics, 121*, S337–S347. doi:10.1542/peds.2007-2243F

Wagnsson, S., Lindwall, M., & Gustafsson, H. (2014). Participation in organized sport and self-esteem across adolescence: The mediating role of perceived sport competence. *Journal of Sport & Exercise Psychology, 36*(6), 584–594. doi:10.1123/jsep.2013-0137

Wakefield, W. D., & Hudley, C. (2007). Ethnic and racial identity and adolescent well-being. *Theory Into Practice, 46*(2), 147–154. doi:10.1080/00405840701233099

Waldrip, A. M., Malcolm, K. T., & Jensen-Campbell, L. A. (2008). With a little help from your friends: The importance of high-quality friendships on early adolescent adjustment. *Social Development, 17*(4), 832–852. doi:10.1111/j.1467-9507.2008.00476.x

Wang, A., Peterson, G. W., Morphey, L. K., & Aimin, W. (2007). Who is more important for early adolescents' developmental choices? Peers or parents? *Marriage & Family Review, 42*(2), 95–122. doi:10.1300/J002v42n02_06

Wang, C., Xia, Y., Li, W., Wilson, S. M., Bush, K., & Peterson, G. (2014). Parenting behaviors, adolescent depressive symptoms, and problem behavior: The role of self-esteem and school adjustment difficulties among Chinese adolescents. *Journal of Family Issues, 23*. doi:10.1177/0192513X14542433

Wang, M.-T., Dishion, T. J., Stormshak, E. A., & Willett, J. B. (2011). Trajectories of family management practices and early adolescent behavioral outcomes. *Developmental Psychology, 47*(5), 1324–1341. doi:10.1037/a0024026

Wang, M.-T., & Sheikh-Khalil, S. (2014). Does parental involvement matter for student achievement and mental health in high school? *Child Development, 85*(2), 610–625. doi:10.1111/cdev.12153

Ward, L. M., & Friedman, K. (2006). Using TV as a guide: Associations between television viewing and adolescents' sexual attitudes and behavior. *Journal of Research on Adolescence, 16*, 133–156.

Warner, T. D., Giordano, P. C., Manning, W. D., & Longmore, M. A. (2011). Everybody's doin' it (right?): Neighborhood norms and sexual activity in adolescence. *Social Science Research, 40*(6), 1676–1690. doi:10.1016/j.ssresearch.2011.06.009

Way, N., & Greene, M. L. (2006). Trajectories of perceived friendship quality during adolescence: The patterns and contextual predictors. *Journal of Research on Adolescence, 16*(2), 293–320. doi:10.1111/j.1532-7795.2006.00133.x

Way, N., Santos, C., Niwa, E. Y., & Kim-Gervey, C. (2008). To be or not to be: An exploration of ethnic identity development in context. *New Directions for Child & Adolescent Development, 2008*(120), 61–79.

Weisz, A. N., & Black, B. M. (2008). Peer intervention in dating violence: Beliefs of African-American middle school adolescents. *Journal of Ethnic & Cultural Diversity in Social Work, 17*(2), 177–196. doi:10.1080/15313200801947223

Wentzel, K. R. (2014). Prosocial behavior and peer relations in adolescence. In G. C. Laura M. Padilla-Walker (Ed.), *Prosocial development: A multidimensional approach* (pp. 178–200). New York: Oxford University Press.

White, C. N., & Warner, L. A. (2015). Influence of family and school-level factors on age of sexual initiation. *The Journal of Adolescent Health, 56*(2), 231–237. doi:10.1016/j.jadohealth.2014.09.017

Wight, D., Williamson, L., & Henderson, M. (2006). Parental influences on young people's sexual behaviour: A longitudinal analysis. *Journal of Adolescence, 29*, 473–494.

Williams, T. S., Connolly, J., Pepler, D., Laporte, L., & Craig, W. (2008). Risk models of dating aggression across different adolescent relationships: A developmental psychopathology approach. *Journal of Consulting and Clinical Psychology, 76*(4), 622–632. doi:10.1037/0022-006x.76.4.622

Wilson, G. T., Grilo, C. M., & Vitousek, K. M. (2007). Psychological treatment of eating disorders. *American Psychologist, 62*(3), 199–216.

Windle, M., Spear, L. P., Fuligni, A. J., Angold, A., Brown, J. D., Pine, D., . . . Dahl, R. E. (2008). Transitions into underage and problem drinking: Developmental processes and mechanisms between 10 and 15 years of age. *Pediatrics, 121*, S273–S289. doi:10.1542/peds.2007-2243C

Windle, M., & Zucker, R. A. (2010). Reducing underage and young adult drinking: How to address critical drinking problems during this developmental period. *Alcohol Research & Health, 33*(1–2), 29–44.

Wissink, I. B., Dekovic, M., & Meijer, A. M. (2006). Parenting behavior, quality of the parent-adolescent relationship, and adolescent functioning in four ethnic groups. *Journal of Early Adolescence, 26*(2), 133–159.

Wolfers, M., de Zwart, O., & Kok, G. (2011). Adolescents in the Netherlands underestimate risk for sexually transmitted infections and deny the need for sexually transmitted infection testing. *AIDS Patient Care and STDs, 25*(5), 311–319. doi:10.1089/apc.2010.0186

Wolitzky-Taylor, K. B., Ruggiero, K. J., Danielson, C. K., Resnick, H. S., Hanson, R. F., Smith, D. W., . . . Kilpatrick, D. G. (2008). Prevalence and correlates of dating violence in a national sample of adolescents. *Journal of the American Academy of Child & Adolescent Psychiatry, 47*(7), 755–762. doi:10.1097/CHI.0b013e318172ef5f

Wong, C. A., Eccles, J. S., & Sameroff, A. (2003). The influence of ethnic discrimination and ethnic identification on African American adolescents' school and socioemotional adjustment. *Journal of Personality, 71*(6), 1197–1232.

World Bank. (2014). Adolescent fertility rate (birhts to 1,000 women ages 15–19). Retrieved from http://data.worldbank.org/indicator/SPADO.TFRT

World Health Organization. (2004). *Young people's health in context. Health Behaviour in School-aged Children (HBSC) study: International report from the 2001/2002 survey.* Retrieved from http://www.euro.who.int/eprise/main/who/informationsources/publications/catalogue/20040518_1

World Health Organization. (2014). Global status report on alcohol and health 2014. Retrieved form http://apps.who.int/iris/bitstream/10665/112736/1/9789240692763_eng.pdf?ua=1

Wouters, S., Doumen, S., Germeijs, V., Colpin, H., & Verschueren, K. (2013). Contingencies of self-worth in early adolescence: The antecedent role of perceived parenting. *Social Development, 22*(2), 242–258. doi:10.1111/sode.12010

Xi-Kuan, C., Shi Wu, W., Nathalie, F., Kitaw, D., George, G. R., & Mark, W. (2007). Teenage pregnancy and adverse birth outcomes: A large population based retrospective cohort study. *International Journal of Epidemiology, 36,* 368.

Xu, J., Kochanek, K. D., Murphy, S. L., & Arias, E. (2014). Mortality in the United States, 2012. *NCHS Data Brief, 168,* 1–8. Retrieved from http://europepmc.org/abstract/med/25296181

Ybarra, M. L., & Mitchell, K. J. (2014). "Sexting" and its relation to sexual activity and sexual risk behavior in a national survey of adolescents. *The Journal of Adolescent Health, 55*(6), 757–764. doi:10.1016/j.jadohealth.2014.07.012

Yip, T. (2014). Ethnic identity in everyday life: The influence of identity development status. *Child Development, 85*(1), 205–219. doi:10.1111/cdev.12107

Zeiders, K. H., Umaña-Taylor, A. J., & Derlan, C. L. (2013). Trajectories of depressive symptoms and self-esteem in Latino youths: Examining the role of gender and perceived discrimination. *Developmental Psychology, 49*(5), 951–963. doi:10.1037/a0028866

Zimmermann, P., & Becker-Stoll, F. (2002). Stability attachment representations during adolescence: The influence of ego-identity status. *Journal of Adolescence, 25,* 107–135.

CHAPTER 13

Abele, A. E., & Spurk, D. (2011). The dual impact of gender and the influence of timing of parenthood on men's and women's career development: Longitudinal findings. *International Journal of Behavioral Development, 35*(3), 225–232. doi:10.1177/0165025411398181

Adler, N. E., & Newman, K. (2002). Socioeconomic disparities in health: Pathways and policies. *Health Affairs, 21*(2), 60.

Agarwal, A., Gupta, S., & Sikka, S. (2006). The role of free radicals and antioxidants in reproduction. *Current Opinion in Obstetrics & Gynecology, 18,* 325–332.

Ajdacic-Gross, V., Horvath, S., Canjuga, M., Gamma, A., Angst, J., Rössler, W., & Eich, D. (2006). How ubiquitous are physical and psychological complaints in young and middle adulthood? *Social Psychiatry & Psychiatric Epidemiology, 41*(11), 881–888.

Almeida, D. M., Neupert, S. D., Banks, S. R., & Serido, J. (2005). Do daily stress processes account for socioeconomic health disparities? *The Journals of Gerontology: Series B: Psychological Sciences and Social Sciences, 60B,* 34–39.

Alpay, Z., Saed, G. M., & Diamond, M. P. (2006). Female infertility and free radicals: Potential role in adhesions and endometriosis. *Journal of the Society for Gynecologic Investigation, 13,* 390–398.

Ambwani, S., Thomas, K. M., Hopwood, C. J., Moss, S. A., & Grilo, C. M. (2014). Obesity stigmatization as the status quo: Structural considerations and prevalence among young adults in the U.S. *Eating Behaviors, 15*(3), 366–370. doi:10.1016/j.eatbeh.2014.04.005

American Cancer Society. (2009). *Guide to quitting smoking.* Atlanta: Author. Retrieved from http://www.cancer.org/docroot/PED/content/PED_10_13X_Guide_for_Quitting_Smoking.asp?sitearea=&amp

American Psychiatric Association. (2013). *Diagnostic and statistical manual of mental disorders* (5th ed.). Washington, DC: Author.

Andrews, N. P., Fujii, H., Goronzy, J. J., & Weyand, C. M. (2010). Telomeres and immunological diseases of aging. *Gerontology, 56*(4), 390–403. doi:10.1159/000268620

Anton, S., & Leeuwenburgh, C. (2013). Fasting or caloric restriction for healthy aging. *Experimental Gerontology, 48*(10), 1003–1005. doi:10.1016/j.exger.2013.04.011

Aronson, P. (2008). Breaking barriers or locked out? Class-based perceptions and experiences of postsecondary education. *New Directions for Child and Adolescent Development, 2008*(119), 41–54. doi:10.1002/cd.208

Baines, H. L., Turnbull, D. M., & Greaves, L. C. (2014). Human stem cell aging: Do mitochondrial DNA mutations have a causal role? *Aging Cell, 13*(2), 201–205. doi:10.1111/acel.12199

Baird, D. T., Collins, J., Egozcue, J., Evers, L. H., Gianaroli, L., & Leridon, H. (2005). Fertility and ageing. *Human Reproduction Update, 11,* 261–276.

Barnes, G. M., Welte, J. W., Hoffman, J. H., & Tidwell, M.-C. O. (2010). Comparisons of gambling and alcohol use among college students and noncollege young people in the United States. *Journal of American College Health, 58*(5), 443–452.

Bartholomew, J., Holroyd, S., & Heffernan, T. M. (2010). Does cannabis use affect prospective memory in young adults? *Journal of Psychopharmacology, 24*(2), 241–246. doi:10.1177/0269881109106909

Bassuk, S. S., & Manson, J. E. (2005). Epidemiological evidence for the role of physical activity in reducing risk of type 2 diabetes and cardiovascular disease. *Journal of Applied Physiology, 99*(3), 1193–1204.

Baum, C. L., & Ruhm, C. J. (2009). Age, socioeconomic status and obesity growth. *Journal of Health Economics, 28*(3), 635–648. doi:10.1016/j.jhealeco.2009.01.004

Baxter Magolda, M. B. (2004). Evolution of a constructivist conceptualization of epistemological reflection. *Educational Psychologist, 39*(1), 31–42. doi:10.1207/s15326985ep3901_4

Behrens, M., Pilz, M., & Greuling, O. (2008). Taking a straightforward detour: Learning and labour market participation in the German apprenticeship system. *Journal of Vocational Education & Training, 60*(1), 93–104. doi:10.1080/13636820701837730

Benbow Lubinski, D., Shea, D. L., & Eftekhari-Sanjani, H., C. P. (2000). Sex differences in mathematical reasoning ability: Their status 20 years later. *Psychological Science, 11,* 474–480.

Bengston, V. L., Gans, D., Pulney, N. M., & Silverstein, M. (2009). *Handbook of theories of aging* (2nd ed.). New York: Springer.

Bentov, Y., Yavorska, T., Esfandiari, N., Jurisicova, A., & Casper, R. (2011). The contribution of mitochondrial function to reproductive aging. *Journal of Assisted Reproduction & Genetics, 28*(9), 773–783. doi:10.1007/s10815-011-9588-7

Blair, S. L. (2010). The influence of risk-taking behaviors on the transition into marriage: An examination of the long-term consequences of adolescent behavior. *Marriage & Family Review, 46*(1–2), 126–146. doi:10.1080/01494921003685169

Blumenthal, D., & Collins, S. R. (2014). Health care coverage under the Affordable Care Act—A progress report. *The New England Journal of Medicine, 371*(3), 275–281. doi:10.1056/NEJMhpr1405667

Blustein, D. L., Chaves, A. P., & Diemer, M. A. (2002). Voices of the forgotten half: The role of social class in the school-to-work transition. *Journal of Counseling Psychology, 49*(3), 311. Bonnie, R. J., Stroud, C., & Breiner, H. (2015). *Investing in the health and well-being of young adults.* Washington DC: National Academies Press.

Bozick, R., & DeLuca, S. (2011). Not making the transition to college: School, work, and opportunities in the lives of American youth. *Social Science Research, 40*(4), 1249–1262. doi:10.1016/j.ssresearch.2011.02.003

Brahem, S., Mehdi, M., Elghezal, H., & Saad, A. (2011). The effects of male aging on semen quality, sperm DNA fragmentation and chromosomal abnormalities in an infertile population. *Journal of Assisted Reproduction & Genetics, 28*(5), 425–432. doi:10.1007/s10815-011-9537-5

Brown, A. E., Carpenter, M. J., & Sutfin, E. L. (2011). Occasional smoking in college: Who, what, when and why? *Addictive Behaviors, 36*(12), 1199–1204. doi:10.1016/j.addbeh.2011.07.024

Brown, S. A., McGue, M., Maggs, J., Schulenberg, J., Hingson, R., Swartzwelder, S., . . . Murphy, S. (2008). A developmental perspective on alcohol and youths 16 to 20 years of age. *Pediatrics, 121,* S290–S310. doi:10.1542/peds.2007-2243D

Brun, A., & Andersson, J. (2001). Frontal dysfunction and frontal cortical synapse loss in alcoholism—The main cause of alcohol dementia? *Dementia And Geriatric Cognitive Disorders, 12*(4), 289–294.

Buddeberg-Fischer, B., Stamm, M., Buddeberg, C., Bauer, G., Häemmig, O., Knecht, M., & Klaghofer, R. (2010). The impact of gender and parenthood on physicians' careers—Professional and personal situation seven years after graduation. *BMC Health Services Research, 10*(1), 40. doi:10.1186/1472-6963-10-40

Calle, E. E., Rodriguez, C., Walker-Thurmond, K., & Thun, M. J. (2003). Overweight, obesity, and mortality from cancer in a prospectively studied cohort of U.S. adults. *New England Journal of Medicine, 348*(17), 1625–1638.

Campisi, J. (2013). Aging, cellular senescence, and cancer. *Annual Review of Physiology, 75,* 685–705. doi:10.1146/annurev-physiol-030212-183653

Carr, D., & Friedman, M. A. (2005). Is obesity stigmatizing? Body weight, perceived discrimination, and psychological well-being in the United States. *Journal of Health & Social Behavior, 46*(3), 244–259.

Carter, A. C., Brandon, K. O., & Goldman, M. S. (2010). The college and noncollege experience: A review of the factors that influence drinking behavior in young adulthood. *Journal of Studies on Alcohol & Drugs, 71*(5), 742–750.

Centers for Disease Control and Prevention. (2011). Current cigarette smoking prevalence among working adults—United States, 2004–2010. *Morbidity and Mortality Weekly Report, 60*(38), 1305–1309. Retrieved from http://www.ncbi.nlm.nih.gov/pubmed/21956406

Centers for Disease Control and Prevention. (2015). 10 leading causes of death—by age group—2013. *Vital and Health Statistics.* Atlanta: Author. Retrieved from ftp://ftp.cdc.gov/pub/ncipc/10LC-2003/JPEG/10lc-2003.jpg

Chen, P., & Jacobson, K. C. (2012). Developmental trajectories of substance use from early adolescence to young adulthood: Gender and racial/ethnic differences. *Journal of Adolescent Health, 50*(2), 154–163. doi:10.1016/j.jadohealth.2011.05.013

Choi, K., Toomey, T. L., Chen, V., & Forster, J. L. (2011). Awareness and reported consequences of a cigarette tax increase among older adolescents and young adults. *American Journal of Health Promotion, 25*(6), 379–386.

Choy, S. (2002). *Nontraditional undergraduates, NCES 2002–012.* Washington, DC. Retrieved from https://nces.ed.gov/pubs2002/2002012.pdf

Cleary, M., Walter, G., & Jackson, D. (2011). "Not always smooth sailing": Mental health issues associated with the transition from high school to college. *Issues in Mental Health Nursing, 32*(4), 250–254. doi:10.3109/01612840.2010.548906

Cleveland, M. J., Mallett, K. A., White, H. R., Turrisi, R., & Favero, S. (2013). Patterns of alcohol use and related consequences in non-college-attending emerging adults. *Journal of Studies on Alcohol and Drugs, 74*(1), 84–93. Retrieved from http://www.pubmedcentral.nih .gov/articlerender.fcgi?artid=3517266&tool=p mcentrez&rendertype=abstract

Collier, P., & Morgan, D. (2008). "Is that paper really due today?": Differences in first-generation and traditional college students' understandings of faculty expectations. *Higher Education, 55*(4), 425–446. doi:10.1007/s10734-007-9065-5

Connor, T. J. (2008). Don't stress out your immune system—Just relax. *Brain, Behavior, and Immunity, 22*(8), 1128–1129. doi:10.1016/j. bbi.2008.07.009

Conroy, D. A., Kurth, M. E., Brower, K. J., Strong, D. R., & Stein, M. D. (2015). Impact of marijuana use on self-rated cognition in young adult men and women. *The American Journal on Addictions, 24*(2), 160–165. doi:10.1111/j.1521-0391.2014.12157.x

Cornman, J. C., Glei, D. A., Goldman, N., Ryff, C. D., & Weinstein, M. (2015). Socioeconomic status and biological markers of health: An examination of adults in the United States and Taiwan. *Journal of Aging and Health, 27*(1), 75–102. doi:10.1177/0898264314538661

Crean, R. D., Crane, N. A., & Mason, B. J. (2011). An evidence-based review of acute and long-term effects of cannabis use on executive cognitive functions. *Journal of Addiction Medicine, 5*(1), 1–8. doi:10.1097/ADM.0b013e31820c23fa

Cristofalo, V. J., Tresini, M., & Francis, M. K. (1999). Biological theories of senescence. In V. L. Bengtson & K. W. Schaie (Eds.), *Handbook of theories of aging* (pp. 98–112). New York: Springer.

Cropley, M., & Steptoe, A. (2005). Social support, life events and physical symptoms: A prospective study of chronic and recent life stress in men and women. *Psychology, Health & Medicine, 10*(4), 317–325.

De Martinis, M., & Timiras, P. S. (2003). The pulmonary respiration, hemotopoiesis and erythrocytes. In P. S. Timiras (Ed.), *Physiological basis of aging ad geriatrics* (3rd ed., pp. 319–336). Boca Raton, FL: CRC Press.

Ditzen, B., Schmidt, S., Strauss, B., Nater, U. M., Ehlert, U., & Heinrichs, M. (2008). Adult attachment and social support interact to reduce psychological but not cortisol responses to stress. *Journal of Psychosomatic Research, 64*(5), 479–486. doi:10.1016/j. jpsychores.2007.11.011

Donaghy, M. E. (2007). Exercise can seriously improve your mental health: Fact or fiction? *Advances in Physiotherapy, 9*(2), 76–88.

Douketis, J. D., Macie, C., Thabane, L., & Williamson, D. F. (2005). Systematic review of long-term weight loss studies in obese adults: Clinical significance and applicability to clinical practice. *International Journal of Obesity, 29*(10), 1153–1167.

Drong, A. W., Lindgren, C. M., & McCarthy, M. I. (2012). The genetic and epigenetic basis of type 2 diabetes and obesity. *Clinical Pharmacology and Therapeutics, 92*(6), 707–715. doi:10.1038/ clpt.2012.149

Dugdale, D. C. (2009). Alcohol withdrawal. In U.S. National Library of Medicine (Ed.), *Medline plus*. Bethesda, MD: U.S. National Library of Medicine. Retrieved from http://www.nlm.nih .gov/medlineplus/ency/article/000764.htm

Ehlert, U., & Fischbacher, S. (2013). Reproductive health. In M. D. Gellman & J. R. Turner (Eds.), *Encyclopedia of behavioral medicine* (pp. 1658–1665). New York: Springer. doi:10.1007/978-1-4419-1005-9

El Hassan, K. (2008). Identifying indicators of student development in college. *College Student Journal, 42*(2), 517–530.

Ellis, L., & Bonin, S. L. (2003). Genetics and occupation-related preferences. Evidence from adoptive and non-adoptive families. *Personality & Individual Differences, 35*(4), 929.

Enoch, M.-A. (2013). Genetic influences on the development of alcoholism. *Current Psychiatry Reports, 15*(11), 412. doi:10.1007/s11920-013-0412-1

Epel, E. S. (2009). Telomeres in a life-span perspective: A new "psychobiomarker"? *Current Directions in Psychological Science, 18*(1), 6–10. doi:10.1111/j.1467-8721.2009.01596.x

Evans, G. W., & Kantrowitz, E. (2002). Socioeconomic status and health: The potential role of environmental risk exposure. *Annual Review of Public Health, 23*(1), 303.

Fairchild, E. E. (2003). Multiple roles of adult learners. *New Directions for Student Services, 2003*(102), 11–16. http://doi.org/10.1002/ss.84

Faulkner, J. A., Larkin, L. M., Claflin, D. R., & Brooks, S. V. (2007). Age-related changes in the structure and function of skeletal muscles. *Clinical & Experimental Pharmacology & Physiology, 34*(11), 1091–1096. doi:10.1111/ j.1440-1681.2007.04752.x

Federal Interagency Forum on Child and Family Statistics. (2014). *America's young adults: Special issue, 2014*. Washington, DC: Author. Retrieved from http://www.childstats.gov/pdf/ac2014/ YA_14.pdf

Ferguson, R. F., & Lamback, S. (2014). *Creating pathways to prosperity: A blueprint for action*. Report issued by the Pathways to Prosperity Project at the Harvard Graduate School of Education and the Achievement Gap Initiative at Harvard University. Retrieved from http://www.agi.harvard.edu/pathways/ CreatingPathwaystoProsperityReport2014.pdf

Fergusson, D. M., & Boden, J. M. (2008). Cannabis use and later life outcomes. *Addiction, 103*(6), 969–976. doi:10.1111/j.1360-0443.2008.02221.x

Fisch, H. (2009). The aging male and his biological clock. *Geriatrics, 64*(1), 14–17.

Fischer, M. J. (2007). Settling into campus life: Differences by race/ethnicity in college involvement and outcomes. *Journal of Higher Education, 78*, 125–161.

Flament, F., Bazin, R., & Piot, B. (2013). Effect of the sun on visible clinical signs of aging in Caucasian skin. *Clinical, Cosmetic and Investigational Dermatology, 6*, 221. doi:10.2147/ CCID.S44686

Fryar, C. D., Carroll, M. D., & Ogden, C. L. (2014). Prevalence of overweight, obesity, and extreme obesity among adults: United States, 1960–1962 through 2011–2012. *NCES-Health Stat*. Retrieved from http://www.cdc.gov/nchs/data/hestat/ obesity_adult_11_12/obesity_adult_11_12.htm

Gershon, A., Johnson, S. L., & Miller, I. (2013). Chronic stressors and trauma: Prospective influences on the course of bipolar disorder. *Psychological Medicine, 43*(12), 2583–2592. doi:10.1017/S0033291713000147

Gilmour, H. (2007). Physically active Canadians. *Health Reports, 18*(3), 45–65.

Giskes, K., van Lenthe, F., Avendano-Pabon, M., & Brug, J. (2011). A systematic review of environmental factors and obesogenic dietary intakes among adults: Are we getting closer to understanding obesogenic environments? *Obesity Reviews, 12*, e95–e106. doi:10.1111/j.1467-789X.2010.00769.x

Godar, D. E., Urbach, F., Gasparro, F. P., & van der Leun, J. C. (2003). UV doses of young adults. *Photochemistry and Photobiology, 77*(4), 453–457.

Goldman, M. S., Greenbaum, P. E., Darkes, J., Brandon, K. O., & Del Boca, F. K. (2011). How many versus how much: 52 weeks of alcohol consumption in emerging adults. *Psychology of Addictive Behaviors, 25*(1), 16–27. doi:10.1037/ a0021744

Goniewicz, M. L., Lingas, E. O., & Hajek, P. (2013). Patterns of electronic cigarette use and user beliefs about their safety and benefits: An internet survey. *Drug and Alcohol Review, 32*(2), 133–140. doi:10.1111/j.1465-3362.2012.00512.x

Gordon, J. D., Rydfors, J. T., Druzin, M. L., Tadir, Y., El-Sayed, Y., Chan, J., . . . Fuh, K. (2007). *Obstetrics, gynecology and infertility: Handbook for clinicians*. New York: Scrub Hill Press.

Gottfredson, L. S. (2005). Applying Gottfredson's theory of circumscription and compromise in career guidance and counseling. In S. D. Brown & R. W. Lent (Eds.), *Career development and counseling: Putting theory and research to work* (pp. 71–100). Hoboken, NJ: John Wiley.

Gouin, J.-P., Glaser, R., Malarkey, W. B., Beversdorf, D., & Kiecolt-Glaser, J. (2012). Chronic stress, daily stressors, and circulating inflammatory markers. *Health Psychology, 31*(2), 264–268. doi:10.1037/a0025536

Green, M. P., McCausland, K. L., Xiao, H., Duke, J. C., Vallone, D. M., & Healton, C. G. (2007). A closer look at smoking among young adults: Where tobacco control should focus its attention. *American Journal of Public Health, 97*(8), 1427–1433.

Griffin, K. W., Bang, H., & Botvin, G. J. (2010). Age of alcohol and marijuana use onset predicts weekly substance use and related psychosocial problems during young adulthood. *Journal of Substance Use, 15*(3), 174–183. doi:10.3109/14659890903013109

Gruber, S. A., Sagar, K. A., Dahlgren, M. K., Racine, M., & Lukas, S. E. (2012). Age of onset of marijuana use and executive function. *Psychology of Addictive Behaviors, 26*(3), 496–506. doi:10.1037/a0026269

Hadfield, J. (2003). Recruiting and retaining adult students. *New Directions for Student Services, 2003*(102), 17–26. http://doi.org/10.1002/ ss.85

Hall, W. (2014). What has research over the past two decades revealed about the adverse health effects of recreational cannabis use? *Addiction, 110*(1). doi:10.1111/add.12703

Hallal, P. C., Andersen, L. B., Bull, F. C., Guthold, R., Haskell, W., & Ekelund, U. (2012). Global physical activity levels: Surveillance progress, pitfalls, and prospects. *Lancet, 380*(9838), 247–257. doi:10.1016/S0140-6736(12) 60646-1

Harman, D. (2006). Free radical theory of aging: An update: Increasing the functional life span. *Annals of the New York Academy of Sciences, 1067*, 10–21.

Harris, W. S., Miller, M., Tighe, A. P., Davidson, M. H., Schaefer, E. J., & Dimsdale, J. E. (2008). Psychological stress and cardiovascular disease. *Journal of the American College of Cardiology, 51*(13), 1237–1246. Retrieved from 10.1016/j. jacc.2007.12.024

Hayflick, L. (1996). *How and why we age*. New York: Ballantine Books.

Heinonen, I., Helajärvi, H., Pahkala, K., Heinonen, O. J., Hirvensalo, M., Pälve, K., . . . Raitakari, O. T. (2013). Sedentary behaviours and obesity in adults: The cardiovascular risk in Young Finns Study. *BMJ Open, 3*(6). doi:10.1136/ bmjopen-2013-002901

Hewlett, S. (2002). *Creating a life: Professional women and the quest for children*. New York: Miramax.

Hjelmborg, J., Iachine, I., Skytthe, A., Vaupel, J. W., McGue, M., Koskenvuo, M., . . . Christensen, K. (2006). Genetic influence on human lifespan and longevity. *Human Genetics, 119*(3), 312–321.

Hogan, C. L., Mata, J., & Carstensen, L. L. (2013). Exercise holds immediate benefits for affect and cognition in younger and older adults. *Psychology and Aging, 28*(2), 587–594. doi:10.1037/a0032634

Holland, J. L. (1997). *Making vocational choices: A theory of vocational personalities and work environments* (3rd ed.). Odessa, FL: Psychological Assessment Resources.

Holman, D. J., O'Connor, K. A., & Wood, J. W. (2006). Age and female reproductive function: Identifying the most important biological determinants. In C. Sauvin-Dugerdil, H. Leridon, & N. Mascie-Taylor (Eds.), *Human clocks: The bio-cultural meanings of age* (pp. 171–199). New York: Peter Lang Publishing.

Holt, J., Warren, L., & Wallace, R. (2006). What behavioral interventions are safe and effective for treating obesity? *Journal of Family Practice, 55*(6), 536–538.

Horn, P. L., West, N. P., Pyne, D. B., Koerbin, G., Lehtinen, S. J., Fricker, P. A., & Cripps, A. W. (2015). Routine exercise alters measures of immunity and the acute phase reaction. *European Journal of Applied Physiology, 115*(2), 407–415. doi:10.1007/s00421-014-3028-1

House, J. S., Lantz, P. M., & Herd, P. (2005). Continuity and change in the social stratification of aging and health over the life course: Evidence from a nationally representative longitudinal study from 1986 to 2001/2002 (Americans' Changing Lives Study). *The Journals of Gerontology: Series B: Psychological Sciences and Social Sciences, 60B*, 15–26.

Hughes, M. C. B., Williams, G. M., Baker, P., & Green, A. C. (2013). Sunscreen and prevention of skin aging: A randomized trial. *Annals of Internal Medicine, 158*(11), 781–790. doi:10.7326/0003-4819-158-11-201306040-00002

Ishitani, T. T. (2006). Studying attrition and degree completion behavior among first-generation college students in the United States. *Journal of Higher Education, 77*, 861–885.

Jackson, K. M., Sher, K. J., & Park, A. (2005). Drinking among college students: Consumption and consequences. In M. Galanter (Ed.), *Recent developments in alcoholism: Alcohol problems in adolescents and young adults* (Vol. 17, pp. 85–117). New York: Springer.

Jacobs, J. E., Lanza, S., Osgood, D. W., Eccles, J. S., & Wigfield, A. (2002). Changes in children's self-competence and values: Gender and domain differences across grades one through twelve. *Child Development, 73*, 509–527.

Jadav, S. D. (2004). Occupational female reproductive hazards. *Journal of Health Management, 6*(2), 201–210. doi:10.1177/097206340400600210

Jakulj, F., Zernicke, K., Bacon, S. L., van Wielingen, L. E., Key, B. L., West, S. G., & Campbell, T. S. (2007). A high-fat meal increases cardiovascular reactivity to psychological stress in healthy young adults. *Journal of Nutrition, 137*(4), 935–939.

Johnson, S. L., Dunleavy, J., Gemmell, N. J., & Nakagawa, S. (2015). Consistent age-dependent declines in human semen quality: A systematic review and meta-analysis. *Ageing Research Reviews, 19C*, 22–33. doi:10.1016/j.arr.2014.10.007

Johnston, L. D., O'Malley, P. M., Bachman, J. G., & Schulenberg, J. E. (2015). *Monitoring the Future national survey results on drug use, 1975–2014: Volume I, Secondary school students.* Ann Arbor: Institute for Social Research, the University of Michigan. Retrieved from http://monitoringthefuture.org/pubs.html#monograp hs

Joo, Y., Choi, K. M., Lee, Y. H., Kim, G., Lee, D. H., Roh, G. S., . . . Kim, H. J. (2009). Chronic immobilization stress induces anxiety- and depression-like behaviors and decreases transthyretin in the mouse cortex. *Neuroscience Letters, 461*(2), 121–125. doi:10.1016/j.neulet.2009.06.025

Juster, R.-P., Bizik, G., Picard, M., Arsenault-Lapierre, G., Sindi, S., Trepanier, L., . . . Lupien, S. J. (2011). A transdisciplinary perspective of chronic stress in relation to psychopathology throughout life span development. *Development and Psychopathology, 23*(3), 725–776. doi:10.1017/S0954579411000289

Kanny, D., Liu, Y., Brewer, R. D., & Lu, H. (2013). Binge drinking—United States, 2011. *MMWR Surveillance Summaries, 62*(3), 77–80.

Karasik, D., Demissie, S., Cupples, L. A., & Kiel, D. P. (2005). Disentangling the genetic determinants of human aging: Biological age as an alternative to the use of survival measures. *The Journals of Gerontology: Series A: Biological Sciences and Medical Sciences, 60A*(5), 574–587. Retrieved from www.cinahl.com/cgi-bin/refsvc?jid=1022&accno=2005123450

Kasworm, C. E. (2003). Setting the stage: Adults in higher education. *New Directions for Student Services, 2003*(102), 3–10. http://doi.org/10.1002/ss.83

Kerpelman, J. L., Shoffner, M. F., & Ross-Griffin, S. (2002). African American mothers' and daughters' beliefs about possible selves and their strategies for reaching the adolescents' future academic and career goals. *Journal of Youth and Adolescence, 31*(4), 289.

Keski-Rahkonen, A., Bulik, C. M., Pietiläinen, K. H., Rose, R. J., Kaprio, J., & Rissanen, A. (2007). Eating styles, overweight and obesity in young adult twins. *European Journal of Clinical Nutrition, 61*(7), 822–829. doi:10.1038/sj.ejcn.1602601

King, P. M., & Kitchener, K. S. (1994). *Developing reflective judgment: Understanding and promoting intellectual growth and critical thinking in adolescence and adults.* San Francisco: Jossey-Bass.

King, P. M., & Kitchener, K. S. (2002). The reflective judgment model: Twenty years of research on epistemic cognition. In B. K. Hofer & P. R. Pintrich (Eds.), *Personal epistemology: The psychological beliefs about knowledge and knowing* (pp. 37–61). Mahwah, NJ: Lawrence Erlbaum.

King, P. M., & Kitchener, K. S. (2004). Reflective judgment: Theory and research on the development of epistemic assumptions through adulthood. *Educational Psychologist, 39*, 5–18.

Kohl, E., Steinbauer, J., Landthaler, M., & Szeimies, R.-M. (2011). Skin ageing. *Journal of the European Academy of Dermatology and Venereology, 25*(8), 873–884. doi:10.1111/j.1468-3083.2010.03963.x

Kohlberg, L., & Ryncarz, R. A. (1990). Beyond justice reasoning: Moral development and consideration of a seventh stage. In C. N. Alexander & E. J. Langer (Eds.), *Higher stages of human development: Perspectives on adult growth* (pp. 191–207). New York: Oxford University Press.

Krei, M. S., & Rosenbaum, J. E. (2000). Career and college advice to the forgotten half: What do counselors and vocational teachers advise? *Teachers College Record, 103*(5), 823–842. Retrieved from http://eric.ed.gov/?id=EJ638357

Kuhn, D. (2000). Theory of mind, metacognition, and reasoning: A life-span perspective. In P. Mitchell & K. J. Riggs (Eds.), *Children's reasoning and the mind* (pp. 301–326). Hove, UK: Psychology Press.

Kuhn, D. (2008). Formal operations from a twenty-first century perspective. *Human Development, 51*(1), 48–55. doi:10.1159/000113155

Labouvie-Vief, G. (1980). Beyond formal operations: Uses and limits of pure logic in life-span development. *Human Development, 23*(3), 141–161.

Labouvie-Vief, G. (2003). Dynamic integration: Affect, cognition, and the self in adulthood. *Current Directions in Psychological Science, 12*(6), 201–206.

Labouvie-Vief, G. (2006). Emerging structures of adult thought. In J. J. Arnett & J. L. Tanner (Eds.), *Emerging adults in America: Coming of age in the 21st century* (pp. 59–84). Washington, DC: American Psychological Association.

Labouvie-Vief, G. (2015). *Integrating emotions and cognition throughout the lifespan.* New York: Springer.

Lagouge, M., & Larsson, N.-G. (2013). The role of mitochondrial DNA mutations and free radicals in disease and ageing. *Journal of Internal Medicine, 273*(6), 529–543. doi:10.1111/joim.12055

Lantz, P. M., House, J. S., Mero, R. P., & Williams, D. R. (2005). Stress, life events, and socioeconomic disparities in health: Results from the Americans' Changing Lives Study. *Journal of Health & Social Behavior, 46*(3), 274–288.

Lanza, S. T., & Collins, L. M. (2006). A mixture model of discontinuous development in heavy drinking from ages 18 to 30: The role of college enrollment. *Journal of Studies on Alcohol, 67*(4), 552–561.

Lavender, A. P., & Nosaka, K. (2007). Fluctuations of isometric force after eccentric exercise of the elbow flexors of young, middle-aged, and old men. *European Journal of Applied Physiology, 100*(2), 161–167. doi:10.1007/s00421-007-0418-7

Lawrence, D., Fagan, P., Backinger, C. L., Gibson, J. T., & Hartman, A. (2007). Cigarette smoking patterns among young adults aged 18–24 years in the United States. *Nicotine & Tobacco Research, 9*(6), 687–697. doi:10.1080/14622200701365319

LeBlanc, E. S., O'Connor, E., Whitlock, E. P., Patnode, C. D., & Kapka, T. (2011). Effectiveness of primary care-relevant treatments for obesity in adults: A systematic evidence review for the U.S. Preventive Services Task Force. *Annals of Internal Medicine, 155*(7), 434–W.131.

Lee, C. M., Maggs, J. L., Neighbors, C., & Patrick, M. E. (2011). Positive and negative alcohol-related consequences: Associations with past drinking. *Journal of Adolescence, 34*(1), 87–94. doi:10.1016/j.adolescence.2010.01.009

Lee, C. M., Neighbors, C., & Woods, B. A. (2007). Marijuana motives: Young adults' reasons for using marijuana. *Addictive Behaviors, 32*(7), 1384–1394. doi:10.1016/j.addbeh.2006.09.010

Lee, H.-C., Chang, C.-M., & Chi, C.-W. (2010). Somatic mutations of mitochondrial DNA in aging and cancer progression. *Ageing Research Reviews, 9*, S47–S58. doi:10.1016/j.arr.2010.08.009

Lee, M. R., Chassin, L., & Villalta, I. K. (2013). Maturing out of alcohol involvement: transitions in latent drinking statuses from late adolescence to adulthood. *Development and Psychopathology, 25*(4 Pt. 1), 1137–1153. doi:10.1017/S0954579413000424

Leonard, B. E., & Myint, A. (2009). The psychoneuroimmunology of depression. *Human Psychopharmacology: Clinical & Experimental, 24*(3), 165–175. doi:10.1002/hup.1011

Levinson, D. J. (1978). *The seasons of a man's life.* New York: Knopf.

Levinson, D. J. (1996). *The seasons of a woman's life.* New York: Knopf.

Li, Y., Lin, H., Li, Y., & Cao, J. (2011). Association between socio-psycho-behavioral factors and male semen quality: Systematic review and meta-analyses. *Fertility & Sterility, 95*(1), 116–123. doi:10.1016/j.fertnstert.2010.06.031

MacLean, P. S., Wing, R. R., Davidson, T., Epstein, L., Goodpaster, B., Hall, K. D., . . . Ryan, D. (2015). NIH working group report: Innovative research to improve maintenance of weight loss. *Obesity, 23*(1), 7–15. doi:10.1002/oby.20967

Maggs, J. L. (1997). Alcohol use and binge drinking as goal-directed action during the transition to postsecondary education. In J. Schulenberg, J. L. Maggs, & K. Horrelmann (Eds.), *Health risks and developmental transitions during adolescence* (pp. 345–371). New York: Cambridge University Press.

Magolda, M. B. B. (2002). Epistemological reflection: The evolution of epistemological assumptions from 10 to 30. In B. K. Hofer & P. R. Pintrich (Eds.), Personal epistemology (pp. 89–102). Mahwah, NJ: Lawrence Erlbaum.

Mahmud, A., & Feely, J. (2003). Effect of smoking on arterial stiffness and pulse pressure amplification. Hypertension, 41, 183.

Maier, K. S. (2005). Transmitting educational values: Parent occupation and adolescent development. In B. Schneider & L. J. Waite (Eds.), Being together, working apart: Dual-career families and the work-life balance (pp. 396–418). New York: Cambridge University Press.

Malik, S. (2009). Impact of obesity on female fertility and fertility treatment. British Journal of Midwifery, 17(7), 452–454.

Mallet, K. A., Varvil-Weld, L., Borsari, B., Read, J. P., Neighbors, C., & White, H. R. (2013). An update of research examining college student alcohol-related consequences: New perspectives and implications for interventions. Alcoholism, Clinical and Experimental Research, 37(5), 709–716. doi:10.1111/acer.12031

Mann, S., Beedie, C., & Jimenez, A. (2014). Differential effects of aerobic exercise, resistance training and combined exercise modalities on cholesterol and the lipid profile: Review, synthesis and recommendations. Sports Medicine, 44(2), 211–221. doi:10.1007/s40279-013-0110-5

Martin, J. A., Hamilton, B. E., Osterman, M., Curtin, S. C., & Mathews, T. J. (2015). Births: Final data for 2013. National Vital Statistics Reports, 64(1). Retrieved from http://www.cdc.gov/nchs/data/nvsr/nvsr64/nvsr64_01.pdf

Masoro, E. J., & Austad, S. N. (2005). Handbook of the biology of aging (6th ed.). New York: Academic Press.

Mather, K. A., Jorm, A. F., Parslow, R. A., & Christensen, H. (2011). Is telomere length a biomarker of aging? A review. The Journals of Gerontology: Series A: Biological Sciences and Medical Sciences, 66(2), 202–213. doi:10.1093/gerona/glq180

McDonald, R. B. (2014). Biology of aging. New York: Garland Science.

McIntyre, K., Korn, J. H., & Matsuo, H. (2008). Sweating the small stuff: how different types of hassles result in the experience of stress. Stress & Health, 24(5), 383–392. doi:10.1002/smi.1190

Messer, K., Trinidad, D. R., Al-Delaimy, W. K., & Pierce, J. P (2008). Smoking cessation rates in the United States: A comparison of young adult and older smokers. American Journal of Public Health, 98(2), 317–322.

Mikels, J. A., Löckenhoff, C. E., Maglio, S. J., Goldstein, M. K., Garber, A., & Carstensen, L. L. (2010). Following your heart or your head: Focusing on emotions versus information differentially influences the decisions of younger and older adults. Journal of Experimental Psychology: Applied, 16(1), 87–95. doi:10.1037/a0018500

Mills, M., Rindfuss, R. R., McDonald, P, & te Velde, E. (2011). Why do people postpone parenthood? Reasons and social policy incentives. Human Reproduction Update, 17(6), 848–860.

Misch, D. A. (2007). "Natural recovery" from alcohol abuse among college students. Journal of American College Health, 55(4), 215–218.

Miura, Y., & Endo, T. (2010). Survival responses to oxidative stress and aging. Geriatrics & Gerontology International, 10, 51–59. doi:10.1111/j.1447-0594.2010.00597.x

Montecino-Rodriguez, E., Berent-Maoz, B., & Dorshkind, K. (2013). Causes, consequences, and reversal of immune system aging. The Journal of Clinical Investigation, 123(3), 958–965. doi:10.1172/JCI64096

Montesanto, A., Latorre, V., Giordano, M., Martino, C., Domma, F., & Passarino, G. (2011). The genetic component of human longevity: Analysis of the survival advantage of parents and siblings of Italian nonagenarians. European Journal of Human Genetics, 19(8), 882–886. http://doi.org/10.1038/ejhg.2011.40

Montgomery, M. J., & Côté, J. E. (2003). College as a transition to adulthood. In G. R. Adams & M. D. Berzonsky (Eds.), Blackwell handbook of adolescence (pp. 149–172). Malden, MA: Blackwell Publishing.

Moskalev, A. A., Aliper, A. M., Smit-McBride, Z., Buzdin, A., & Zhavoronkov, A. (2014). Genetics and epigenetics of aging and longevity. Cell Cycle, 13(7), 1063–1077. doi:10.4161/cc.28433

National Cancer Institute. (2010). What you need to know about melanoma and other skin cancers— NIH Publication No.10-7625. Washington, DC: U.S. Department of Health and Human Services. Retrieved from http://www.cancer.gov/publications/patient-education/skin.pdf

National Center for Education Statistics. (2013). Digest of education statistics. Washington, DC: Author.

National Center for Education Statistics. (2014). The condition of education—2014. Washington, DC: Author. Retrieved from http://nces.ed.gov/pubsearch/pubsinfo.asp?pubid=2014083

National Center for Education Statistics. (2015). Digest of Education Statistics, 2013. Washington, DC: Author. Retrieved from https://nces.ed.gov/programs/digest/d13/index.asp

National Council on Alcoholism and Drug Dependence. (2015). Alcohol and crime. Retrieved from https://ncadd.org/learn-about-alcohol/alcohol-and-crime

National Highway Traffic Safety Administration. (2014). alcohol impaired driving, 2013 data. Traffic Safety Facts. Retrieved from http://www-nrd.nhtsa.dot.gov/Pubs/812102.pdf

National Institute on Drug Abuse. (2005). Research report series—Marijuana abuse. Bethesda, MD: Author. Retrieved from http://www.drugabuse.gov/ResearchReports/Marijuana/default.html

National Institute on Drug Abuse. (2009). Are there effective treatments for tobacco addiction? Bethesda, MD: National Institutes of Health. Retrieved from http://www.nida.nih.gov/ResearchReports/Nicotine/treatment.html

National Toxicology Program. (2011). Report on carcinogens (12th ed.). Washington, DC: Author. Retrieved from http://ntp.niehs.nih.gov/ntp/roc/twelfth/profiles/UltravioletRadiationRelatedExposures.pdf

Newson, R. S., & Kemps, E. B. (2008). Relationship between fitness and cognitive performance in younger and older adults. Psychology & Health, 23(3), 369–386. doi:10.1080/08870440701421545

Ogden, C. L., Carroll, M. D., Kit, B. K., & Flegal, K. M. (2014). Prevalence of childhood and adult obesity in the United States, 2011–2012. JAMA, 311(8), 806–814. doi:10.1001/jama.2014.732

Orbe, M. P (2008). Theorizing multidimensional identity negotiation: Reflections on the lived experiences of first-generation college students. New Directions for Child and Adolescent Development, 2008(120), 81–95.

Orzano, A. J., & Scott, J. G. (2004). Diagnosis and treatment of obesity in adults: An applied evidence-based review. The Journal of the American Board of Family Practice, 17(5), 359–369.

Pacchucki, M. C., & Goodman, E. (2015). Social relationships and obesity: Benefits of incorporating a lifecourse perspective. Current Obesity Reports. Advance online publication. doi:10.1007/s13679-015-0145-z

Pascarella, E., Bohr, L., & Nora, A. (1995). Cognitive effects of 2-year and 4-year colleges: New evidence. Educational Evaluation and Policy Analysis, 17(1), 83–96.

Patrick, M. E., Lee, C. M., & Larimer, M. E. (2011). Drinking motives, protective behavioral strategies, and experienced behavioral consequences: Identifying students at risk. Addictive Behaviors, 36(3), 270–273. doi:10.1016/j.addbeh.2010.11.007

Pearson, J. L., Richardson, A., Niaura, R. S., Vallone, D. M., & Abrams, D. B. (2012). e-Cigarette awareness, use, and harm perceptions in US adults. American Journal of Public Health, 102(9), 1758–1766. doi:10.2105/AJPH.2011.300526

Pearson, N., & Biddle, S. J. H. (2011). Sedentary behavior and dietary intake in children, adolescents, and adults: A systematic review. American Journal of Preventive Medicine, 41(2), 178–188. doi:10.1016/j.amepre.2011.05.002

Penedo, F. J., & Dahn, J. R. (2005). Exercise and well-being: A review of mental and physical health benefits associated with physical activity. Current Opinion in Psychiatry, 18(2), 189–193.

Perry, W. G. (1970). Forms of intellectual and ethical development in the college years: A scheme. San Francisco: Jossey-Bass.

Pike, G. R., & Kuh, G. D. (2005). First- and second-generation college students: A comparison of their engagement and intellectual development. Journal of Higher Education, 76(3), 276–300.

Raiz, L. (2006). Health care poverty. Journal of Sociology & Social Welfare, 33(4), 87–104.

Reason, R. D., Terenzini, P. T., & Domingo, R. J. (2007). Developing social and personal competence in the first year of college. Review of Higher Education, 30(3), 271–299.

Rehm, J. (2011). The risks associated with alcohol use and alcoholism. Alcohol Research & Health, 34(2), 135–143. doi:Fea-AR&H-65

Rice, C., & Cunningham, D. A. (2002). Aging of the neuromuscular system: Influences of gender and physical activity. In R. J. Spehard (Ed.), Gender, physical activity, and aging (pp. 121–150). Boca Raton, FL: CRC Press.

Riegle-Crumb, C., King, B., Grodsky, E., & Muller, C. (2012). The more things change, the more they stay the same? Examining gender equality in prior achievement and entry into STEM college majors over time. American Educational Research Journal, 49(6), 1048–1073. doi:10.3102/0002831211435229

Riggs, N. R., Chih-Ping, C., Chaoyang, L., & Pentz, M. A. (2007). Adolescent to emerging adulthood smoking trajectories: When do smoking trajectories diverge, and do they predict early adulthood nicotine dependence? Nicotine & Tobacco Research, 9(11), 1147–1154. doi:10.1080/14622200701485359

Robbins, S. B., Allen, J., Casillas, A., Peterson, C. H., & Le, H. (2006). Unraveling the differential effects of motivational and skills, social, and self-management measures from traditional predictors of college outcomes. Journal of Educational Psychology, 98(3), 598–616.

Rosenbaum, J. E., & Person, A. E. (2003). Beyond college for all: Policies and practices to improve transitions into college and jobs. Professional School Counseling, 6(4), 252.

Ross-Gordon, J. M. (2011). Research on adult learners: Supporting the needs of a student population that is no longer nontraditional. Peer Review, 3(1), 26–29. Retrieved from http://www.aacu.org/publications-research/periodicals/

research-adult-learners-supporting-needs-student-population-no

Salvioli, S., Monti, D., Lanzarini, C., Conte, M., Pirazzini, C., Giulia Bacalini, M., ... Franceschi, C. (2013). Immune system, cell senescence, aging and longevity—Inflamm-aging reappraised. Current Pharmaceutical Design, 19(9), 1675-1679. Retrieved from http://www.ingentaconnect.com/content/ben/cpd/2013/00000019/00000009/art00015

Sanchis-Gomar, F., Olaso-Gonzalez, G., Corella, D., Gomez-Cabrera, M. C., & Vina, J. (2011). Increased average longevity among the "Tour de France" cyclists. International Journal of Sports Medicine, 32(8), 644-647. doi:10.1055/s-0031-1271711

Schiffman, S., Van Gundy, K., & Taylor, J. (2001). Status, role, and resource explanations for age patterns in psychological distress. Journal of Health & Social Behavior, 42(1), 80-96.

Schmidt, L., Sobotka, T., Bentzen, J. G., & Nyboe Andersen, A. (2012). Demographic and medical consequences of the postponement of parenthood. Human Reproduction Update, 18(1), 29-43. doi:10.1093/humupd/dmr040

Schnohr, P., Scharling, H., & Jensen, J. S. (2003). Changes in leisure-time physical activity and risk of death: An observational study of 7,000 men and women. American Journal of Epidemiology, 158(7), 639-644.

Schoenborn, C. A., & Stommel, M. (2011). Adherence to the 2008 adult physical activity guidelines and mortality risk. American Journal of Preventive Medicine, 40(5), 514-521. doi:10.1016/j.amepre.2010.12.029

Schoon, I., & Parsons, S. (2002). Competence in the face of adversity: The influence of early family environment and long-term consequences. Children & Society, 16(4), 260-272.

Schoon, I., & Polek, E. (2011). Teenage career aspirations and adult career attainment: The role of gender, social background and general cognitive ability. International Journal of Behavioral Development, 35(3), 210-217. doi:10.1177/0165025411398183

Schuh-Huerta, S. M., Johnson, N. A., Rosen, M. P., Sternfeld, B., Cedars, M. I., & Reijo Pera, R. A. (2012). Genetic variants and environmental factors associated with hormonal markers of ovarian reserve in Caucasian and African American women. Human Reproduction, 27(2), 594-608. doi:10.1093/humrep/der391

Schulenberg, J. E., & Maggs, J. L. (2002). A developmental perspective on alcohol use and heavy drinking during adolescence and the transition to young adulthood [Supplemental material]. Journal of Studies on Alcohol, 54-70.

Schulenberg, J. E., & Miech, R. A. (2014). Monitoring the Future national survey results on drug use, 1975-2013: College students and adults ages 19-55 (Vol. 2). Ann Arbor: Institute for Social Research, the University of Michigan. Retrieved from http://www.monitoringthefuture.org//pubs/monographs/mtf-vol2_2013.pdf

Schulz, R., & Curnow, C. (1988). Peak performance and age among superathletes: Track and field, swimming, baseball, tennis, and golf. Journal of Gerontology, 43, 113-120.

Schumann, B., Küttig, A., Tiller, D., Werdan, K., Haerting, J., & Greiser, K. H. (2011). Association of childhood and adult socioeconomic indicators with cardiovascular risk factors and its modification by age: The CARLA Study 2002-2006. BMC Public Health, 11(1), 289-298. doi:10.1186/1471-2458-11-289

Sedivy, J. M. (2007). Telomeres limit cancer growth by inducing senescence: Long-sought in vivo evidence obtained. Cancer Cell, 11(5), 389-391.

Shalev, I., Entringer, S., Wadhwa, P. D., Wolkowitz, O. M., Puterman, E., Lin, J., & Epel, E. S. (2013). Stress and telomere biology: A lifespan perspective. Psychoneuroendocrinology, 38(9), 1835-1842. doi:10.1016/j.psyneuen.2013.03.010

Shringarpure, R., & Davies, K. J. A. (2009). Free radicals and oxidative stress in aging. In V. L. Bengtson, D. Gans, N. M. Putney, & M. Silverstein (Eds.), Handbook of theories of aging (2nd ed., pp. 229-243). New York: Springer.

Sillins, E., Horwood, L. J., Patton, G. C., Fergusson, D. M., Olsson, C. A., Hutchinson, D. M., ... Mattick, R. P. (2014). Young adult sequelae of adolescent cannabis use: An integrative analysis. The Lancet Psychiatry, 1(4), 286-293. doi:10.1016/S2215-0366(14)70307-4

Simons, J. S., Wills, T. A., & Neal, D. J. (2014). The many faces of affect: A multilevel model of drinking frequency/quantity and alcohol dependence symptoms among young adults. Journal of Abnormal Psychology, 123(3), 676-694. doi:10.1037/a0036926

Sinnott, J. D. (1998). The development of logic in adulthood: Postformal thought and its applications. New York: Plenum.

Sinnott, J. D. (2003). Postformal thought and adult development: Living in balance. In J. Demick & C. Andreoletti (Eds.), Handbook of adult development (pp. 221-238). New York: Kluwer.

Sisson, S. B., & Katzmarzyk, P. T. (2008). International prevalence of physical activity in youth and adults. Obesity Reviews, 9(6), 606-614. doi:10.1111/j.1467-789X.2008.00506.x

Skin Cancer Foundation. (2009). Skin cancer facts. New York: Author.

Skosnik, P. D., Edwards, C. R., O'Donnell, B. F., Steffen, A., Steinmetz, J. E., & Hetrick, W. P. (2008). Cannabis use disrupts eyeblink conditioning: Evidence for cannabinoid modulation of cerebellar-dependent learning. Neuropsychopharmacology, 33(7), 1432-1440. doi:10.1038/sj.npp.1301506

Slack, M. K. (2006). Interpreting current physical activity guidelines and incorporating them into practice for health promotion and disease prevention. American Journal of Health-System Pharmacy, 63(17), 1647-1653.

Sloan, R. P., Shapiro, P. A., DeMeersman, R. E., Bagiella, E., Brondolo, E. N., McKinley, P. S., ... Myers, M. M. (2009). The effect of aerobic training and cardiac autonomic regulation in young adults. American Journal of Public Health, 99(6), 921-928.

Smith, J. D., Nagy, T. R., & Allison, D. B. (2010). Calorie restriction: What recent results suggest for the future of ageing research. European Journal of Clinical Investigation, 40(5), 440-450. doi:10.1111/j.1365-2362.2010.02276.x

Song, A. V., & Ling, P. M. (2011). Social smoking among young adults: Investigation of intentions and attempts to quit. American Journal of Public Health, 101(7), 1291-1296. doi:10.2105/alph.2010.300012

Speakman, J. R., & Mitchell, S. E. (2011). Caloric restriction. Molecular Aspects of Medicine, 32(3), 159-221. doi:10.1016/j.mam.2011.07.001

Spokane, A. R., & Cruza-Guet, M. C. (2005). Holland's theory of vocational personalities in work environments. In S. D. Brown & R. W. Lent (Eds.), Career development and counseling: Putting theory and research to work (pp. 24-41). Hoboken, NJ: John Wiley.

Staff, J., Schulenberg, J. E., Maslowsky, J., Bachman, J. G., O'Malley, P. M., Maggs, J. L., & Johnston, L. D. (2010). Substance use changes and social role transitions: Proximal developmental effects on ongoing trajectories from late adolescence through early adulthood. Development and Psychopathology, 22(4), 917-932. doi:10.1017/S0954579410000544

Stavro, K., Pelletier, J., & Potvin, S. (2013). Widespread and sustained cognitive deficits in alcoholism: A meta-analysis. Addiction Biology, 18(2), 203-213. doi:10.1111/j.1369-1600.2011.00418.x

Stessman, J., Hammerman-Rozenberg, R., Maaravi, Y., Azoulai, D., & Cohen, A. (2005). Strategies to enhance longevity and independent function: The Jerusalem longitudinal study. Mechanisms Of Ageing And Development, 126(2), 327-331.

Stroth, S., Hille, K., Spitzer, M., & Reinhardt, R. (2009). Aerobic endurance exercise benefits memory and affect in young adults. Neuropsychological Rehabilitation, 19(2), 223-243. doi:10.1080/09602010802091183

Substance Abuse and Mental Health Services Administration. (2014). Results from the 2013 National Survey on Drug Use and Health: Summary of national findings. Rockville, MD: Author. Retrieved from http://www.samhsa.gov/data/sites/default/files/NSDUHresultsPDFWHTML2013/Web/NSDUHresults2013.pdf

Super, D. E. (1980). A life-span, life-space approach to career development. Journal of Vocational Behavior, 16(3), 282-298. doi:10.1016/0001-8791(80)90056-1

Super, D. E. (1990). A life-span, life-space approach to career development. In D. Brown & L. Brooks (Eds.), Career choice and development: Applying contemporary theories to practice (2nd ed., pp. 197-261). San Francisco: Jossey-Bass.

Super, D. E., & Hall, D. T. (1978). Career development: Exploration and planning. Annual Review of Psychology, 29, 333-372. doi:10.1146/annurev.ps.29.020178.002001

Super, D. E., & Jordaan, J. P. (2007). Career development theory. British Journal of Guidance and Counselling. Retrieved from http://www.tandfonline.com/doi/abs/10.1080/03069887308259333#.ValqHrlojxE

Swift, R. (2007). Emerging approaches to managing alcohol dependence. American Journal of Health-System Pharmacy, 64, S12-S22.

Swift, W., Coffey, C., Carlin, J. B., Degenhardt, L., & Patton, G. C. (2008). Adolescent cannabis users at 24 years: Trajectories to regular weekly use and dependence in young adulthood. Addiction, 103(8), 1361-1370. doi:10.1111/j.1360-0443.2008.02246.x

Symonds, W. C., Schwartz, R., & Ferguson, R. F. (2011). Pathways to prosperity: Meeting the challenge of preparing young Americans. Cambridge, MA: Pathways to Prosperity Project, Harvard University Graduate School of Education.

Tardon, A., Lee, W. J., Delgado-Rodriguez, M., Dosemeci, M., Albanes, D., Hoover, R., & Blair, A. (2005). Leisure-time physical activity and lung cancer: A meta-analysis. Cancer Causes & Control, 16(4), 389-397.

Taskin, D. P. (2013). Effects of marijuana smoking on the lung. Annals of the American Thoracic Society, 10(3), 239-247. Retrieved from http://www.atsjournals.org/doi/abs/10.1513/annalsats.201212-127fr#.ValqHrlojxE

Tatone, C. (2008). Oocyte senescence: A firm link to age-related female subfertility. Gynecological Endocrinology, 24(2), 59-63. doi:10.1080/09513590701733504

Tchernof, A., & Despres, J.-P. (2013). Pathophysiology of human visceral obesity: An update. Physiological Reviews, 93(1), 359-404. doi:10.1152/physrev.00033.2011

Terenzini, P. T., Pascarella, E. T., & Blimling, G. S. (1999). Students' out-of-class experiences and their influence on learning and cognitive development: A literature review. Journal of College Student Development, 40(5), 610-623.

Thornton, W. J. L., & Dumke, H. A. (2005). Age differences in everyday problem-solving and decision-making effectiveness: A meta-analytic review. Psychology and Aging, 20(1), 85-99.

Timiras, P. S. (2003). Physiological basis of aging and geriatrics (3rd ed.). Boca Raton, FL: CRC Press.

Torrey, B. B., & Haub, C. (2004). A comparison of US and Canadian mortality in 1998. *Population & Development Review*, 30(3), 519–530.

Tourlouki, E., Polychronopoulos, E., Zeimbekis, A., Tsakountakis, N., Bountziouka, V., Lioliou, E., . . . Panagiotakos, D. B. (2010). The "secrets" of the long livers in Mediterranean islands: The MEDIS study. *European Journal of Public Health*, 20(6), 659–664.

Tremblay, M.-C., Pluye, P., Gore, G., Granikov, V., Filion, K. B., & Eisenberg, M. J. (2015). Regulation profiles of e-cigarettes in the United States: A critical review with qualitative synthesis. *BMC Medicine*, 13(1), 130. doi:10.1186/s12916-015-0370-z

U.S. Bureau of Labor Statistics. (2014). *America's young adults at 27: Labor market activity, education, and household composition: Results from a longitudinal survey summary*. Retrieved from http://www.bls.gov/news.release/nlsyth.nr0.htm

U.S. Bureau of Labor Statistics. (2015a). *Labor force statistics from the current population survey: Employment status of the civilian noninstitutional population by age, sex, and race*. Washington, DC: Author. Retrieved from http://www.bls.gov/cps/cpsaat03.htm

U.S. Bureau of Labor Statistics. (2015b). *Employment projections*. Retrieved from http://www.bls.gov/emp/ep_chart_001.htm

U.S. Bureau of Labor Statistics. (2015b). *Number of jobs held, labor market activity, and earnings growth among the youngest baby boomers: Results from a longitudinal survey summary*. Retrieved from http://www.bls.gov/news.release/nlsoy.nr0.htm

U.S. Cancer Statistics Working Group. (2013). *United States cancer statistics: 1999–2010 incidence and mortality web-based report*. Atlanta: Centers for Disease Control and Prevention. Retrieved from http://www.cdc.gov/uscs.

U.S. Department of Health and Human Services. (2008). *2008 physical activity guidelines for Americans*. Retrieved from http://www.health.gov/PAGuidelines.

U.S. Department of Health and Human Services. (2012). *Results from the 2011 National Survey on Drug Use and Health: Summary of National Findings*, NSDUH Series H-44, HHS Publication No. (SMA) 12-4713. Rockville, MD: Substance Abuse and Mental Health Services Administration, 2012.

U.S. Department of Health and Human Services. (2014). *The health consequences of smoking—50 years of progress. A report of the surgeon general*. Atlanta: Author. Retrieved from http://www.surgeongeneral.gov/library/reports/50-years-of-progress

U.S. Department of Labor. (2015). *Registered apprenticeship national results fiscal year 2014*. Retrieved from http://doleta.gov/oa/data_statistics.cfm

Vergés, A., Jackson, K. M., Bucholz, K. K., Grant, J. D., Trull, T. J., Wood, P. K., & Sher, K. J. (2011). Deconstructing the age-prevalence curve of alcohol dependence: Why "maturing out" is only a small piece of the puzzle. *Journal of Abnormal Psychology*, 121(2), 511–523. doi:10.1037/a0026027

Volpicelli, J. R. (2005). New options for the treatment of alcohol dependence. *Psychiatric Annals*, 35(6), 484–491.

Wald, M. (2005). Foreword. In D. W. Osgood, M. Foster, C. Flanagan, & G. Ruth (Eds.), *On your own without a net: The transition to adulthood for vulnerable populations* (pp. vii–xi). Chicago: University of Chicago Press.

Walpole, M. (2008). Emerging from the pipeline: African American students, socioeconomic status, and college experiences and outcomes. *Research in Higher Education*, 49(3), 237–255. doi:10.1007/s11162-007-9079-y

Walter, S., Atzmon, G., Demerath, E. W., Garcia, M. E., Kaplan, R. C., Kumari, M., . . . Evans,

D. A. (2011). A genome-wide association study of aging. *Neurobiology of Aging*, 32(11), 2109.e15–2109.e28. doi:10.1016/j.neurobiolaging.2011.05.026

Wane, S., Van Uffelen, J. G. Z., & Brown, W. (2010). Determinants of weight gain in young women: A review of the literature. *Journal of Women's Health*, 19(7), 1327–1340. doi:10.1089/jwh.2009.1738

Wannamethee, S. G., Shaper, A. G., & Alberti, K. G. (2000). Physical activity, metabolic factors, and the incidence of coronary heart disease and type 2 diabetes. *Archives of Internal Medicine*, 160(14), 2108–2116.

Watson, T. L., & Blanchard-Fields, F. (1998). Thinking with your head and your heart: Age differences in everyday problem-solving strategy preferences. *Aging, Neuropsychology, and Cognition*, 5(3), 225–240.

Wesley, M. J., Hanlon, C. A., & Porrino, L. J. (2011). Poor decision-making by chronic marijuana users is associated with decreased functional responsiveness to negative consequences. *Psychiatry Research: Neuroimaging Section*, 191(1), 51–59. doi:10.1016/j.pscychresns.2010.10.002

Whitbourne, S. K. (2007). *Adult development and aging: Biopsychosocial perspectives*. Hoboken, NJ: John Wiley.

White, H. R., Fleming, C. B., Kim, M. J., McMorris, B. J., & Catalano, R. F. (2008). Identifying two potential mechanisms for changes in alcohol use among college-attending and non-college-attending emerging adults. *Developmental Psychology*, 44(6), 1625–1639. doi:10.1037/a0013855

White, H.-R., & Jackson, K. (2005). Social and psychological influences on emerging adult drinking behavior. *Alcohol Research & Health*, 28(4), 182–190.

Windle, M., & Zucker, R. A. (2010). Reducing underage and young adult drinking: How to address critical drinking problems during this developmental period. *Alcohol Research & Health*, 33(1–2), 29–44.

Wing, R. R., & Phelan, S. (2005). Long-term weight loss maintenance. *American Journal of Clinical Nutrition*, 82(1), 222S–225S. Retrieved from http://ajcn.nutrition.org/content/82/1/222S.long

Xi, H., Li, C., Ren, F., Zhang, H., & Zhang, L. (2013). Telomere, aging and age-related diseases. *Aging Clinical and Experimental Research*, 25(2), 139–146. doi:10.1007/s40520-013-0021-1

Xu, Z., Duc, K. D., Holcman, D., & Teixeira, M. T. (2013). The length of the shortest telomere as the major determinant of the onset of replicative senescence. *Genetics*, 194(4), 847–857. doi:10.1534/genetics.113.152322

Yamin, C. K., Bitton, A., & Bates, D. W. (2010). E-cigarettes: A rapidly growing Internet phenomenon. *Annals of Internal Medicine*, 153(9), 607–609. doi:10.7326/0003-4819-153-9-201011020-00011

Zeidler, D. L., Sadler, T. D., Applebaum, S., & Callahan, B. E. (2009). Advancing reflective judgment through socioscientific issues. *Journal of Research in Science Teaching*, 46(1), 74–101. doi:10.1002/tea.20281

Zhang, L. (1999). A comparison of U.S. and Chinese university students' cognitive development: The cross-cultural applicability of Perry's theory. *Journal of Psychology*, 133(4), 425–440.

Zhang, L. (2004). The Perry scheme: Across cultures, across approaches to the study of human psychology. *Journal of Adult Development*, 11(2), 123–138.

Zhang, L., & Watkins, D. (2001). Cognitive development and student approaches to learning: An investigation of Perry's theory with Chinese and U.S. university students. *Higher Education*, 41(3), 239–261.

CHAPTER 14

Acevedo, B. P., & Aron, A. (2009). Does a long-term relationship kill romantic love? *Review of General Psychology*, 13(1), 59–65. doi:10.1037/a0014226

Adamsons, K. (2013). Predictors of relationship quality during the transition to parenthood. *Journal of Reproductive and Infant Psychology*, 31(2), 160–171. doi:10.1080/02646838.2013.791919

Afifi, T. O., Cox, B. J., & Enns, M. W. (2006). Mental health profiles among married, never-married, and separated/divorced mothers in a nationally representative sample. *Social Psychiatry & Psychiatric Epidemiology*, 41(2), 122–129. doi:10.1007/s00127-005-0005-3

Ali, M. M., & Ajilore, O. (2011). Can marriage reduce risky health behavior for African-Americans? *Journal of Family and Economic Issues*, 32(2), 191–203. doi:10.1007/s10834-010-9242-z

Amato, P. R. (2010). Research on divorce: Continuing trends and new developments. *Journal of Marriage and Family*, 72(3), 650–666. doi:10.1111/j.1741-3737.2010.00723.x

Amato, P. R., & Irving, S. (2006). Historical trends in divorce in the United States. In M. A. Fine & J. H. Harvey (Eds.), *Handbook of divorce and relationship dissolution* (pp. 41–57). Mahwah, NJ: Lawrence Erlbaum.

Amato, P. R., & Previti, D. (2003). People's reasons for divorcing: Gender, social class, the life course, and adjustment. *Journal of Family Issues*, 24(5), 602–626. doi:10.1177/0192513X03254507

Amato, P. R., & Sobolewski, J. M. (2004). The effects of divorce on fathers and children: Nonresidential fathers and stepfathers. In M. E. Lamb (Ed.), *The role of the father in child development* (4th ed., pp. 341–367). Hoboken, NJ: John Wiley.

Ammons, S. K., & Kelly, E. L. (2008). Social class and the experience of work-family conflict during the transition to adulthood. *New Directions for Child and Adolescent Development*, 2008(119), 71–84. doi:10.1002/cd.210

Andreß, H.-J., & Bröckel, M. (2007). Income and life satisfaction after marital disruption in Germany. *Journal of Marriage and Family*, 69(2), 500–512. doi:10.1111/j.1741-3737.2007.00379.x

Archer, J. (2002). Sex differences in physically aggressive acts between heterosexual partners: A meta-analytic review. *Aggression and Violent Behavior*, 7(4), 313–351.

Arias, D. F., & Hernández, A. M. (2007). Emerging adulthood in Mexican and Spanish youth: Theories and realities. *Journal of Adolescent Research*, 22(5), 476–503.

Arnett, J. J. (1997). Young people's conceptions of the transition to adulthood. *Youth & Society*, 29(1), 3.

Arnett, J. J. (2000). Emerging adulthood: A theory of development from the late teens through the twenties. *American Psychologist*, 55(5), 469–480. doi:10.1037/0003-066X.55.5.469

Arnett, J. J. (2003). Conceptions of the transition to adulthood among emerging adults in American ethnic groups. *New Directions for Child and Adolescent Development*, 2003(100), 63–76.

Arnett, J. J. (2004). *Emerging adulthood: The winding road from the late teens through the twenties*. New York: Oxford University Press.

Aron, A., & Westbay, L. (1996). Dimensions of the prototype of love. *Journal of Personality and Social Psychology*, 70(3), 535–551. doi:10.1037/0022-3514.70.3.535

Athanasou, J. A. (2002). Vocational pathways in the early part of a career: An Australian study. *Career Development Quarterly*, 51(1), 78–86.

Austrom, D., & Hanel, K. (1985). Psychological issues of single life in Canada: An exploratory study. *International Journal of Women's Studies, 8*(1), 12–23.

Baranowska-Rataj, A., Matysiak, A., & Mynarska, M. (2013). Does lone motherhood decrease women's happiness? Evidence from qualitative and quantitative research. *Journal of Happiness Studies, 15*(6), 1457–1477. doi:10.1007/s10902-013-9486-z

Barner, J. R., & Carney, M. M. (2011). Interventions for intimate partner violence: A historical review. *Journal of Family Violence, 26*(3), 235–244. doi:10.1007/s10896-011-9359-3

Barnett, R. C., & Gareis, K. C. (2006). Role theory perspectives on work and family. In M. Pitt-Catsouphes, E. E. Kossek, & S. Sweet (Eds.), *The work and family handbook: Multi-disciplinary perspectives, methods, and approaches* (pp. 209–221). Mahwah, NJ: Lawrence Erlbaum.

Barry, C. M., Madsen, S. D., Nelson, L. J., Carroll, J. S., & Badger, S. (2009). Friendship and romantic relationship qualities in emerging adulthood: Differential associations with identity development and achieved adulthood criteria. *Journal of Adult Development, 16*(4), 209–222. doi:10.1007/s10804-009-9067-x

Batalova, J. A., & Cohen, P. N. (2002). Premarital cohabitation and housework: Couples in cross-national perspective. *Journal of Marriage and Family, 64*(3), 743–755.

Baumbusch, J. L. (2004). Unclaimed treasures: Older women's reflections on lifelong singlehood. *Journal of Women & Aging, 16*(1–2), 105–121.

Baumeister, R. F., & Bratslavsky, E. (1999). Passion, intimacy, and time: Passionate love as a function of change in intimacy. *Personality and Social Psychology Review, 3*, 49–68.

Bendall, C. (2010). The domestic violence epidemic in South Africa: Legal and practical remedies. *Women's Studies, 39*(2), 100–118. doi:10.1080/00497870903459275

Berrington, A. (2004). Perpetual postponers? Women's, men's and couple's fertility intentions and subsequent fertility behaviour. *Population Trends, 117*, 9–19. Retrieved from http://eprints.soton.ac.uk/34148/1/BerringtonPopTrends2004.pdf

Betz, N. E. (2005). Women's career development. In S. D. Brown & R. W. Lent (Eds.), *Career development and counseling: Putting theory and research to work* (pp. 253–277). Hoboken, NJ: John Wiley.

Beyers, W., & Seiffge-Krenke, I. (2010). Does identity precede intimacy? Testing Erikson's theory on romantic development in emerging adults of the 21st century. *Journal of Adolescent Research, 25*(3), 387–415. doi:10.1177/0743558410361370

Biblarz, T. J., & Savci, E. (2010). Lesbian, gay, bisexual, and transgender families. *Journal of Marriage and Family, 72*(3), 480–497. doi:10.1111/j.1741-3737.2010.00714.x

Biehle, S. N., & Mickelson, K. D. (2012). First-time parents' expectations about the division of childcare and play. *Journal of Family Psychology, 26*(1), 36–45. doi:10.1037/a0026608

Blackwell, D. L., & Lichter, D. T. (2004). Homogamy among dating, cohabiting, and married couples. *Sociological Quarterly, 45*(4), 719–737.

Blair-Loy, M., & Dehart, G. (2003). Family and career trajectories among African American female attorneys. *Journal of Family Issues, 24*(7), 908–933. doi:10.1177/0192513X03255455

Bleske-Rechek, A. L., & Buss, D. M. (2001). Opposite-sex friendship: Sex differences and similarities in initiation, selection, and dissolution. *Personality and Social Psychology Bulletin, 27*(10), 1310–1323.

Bobek, B. L., & Robbins, S. B. (2005). Counseling for career transition: Career pathing, job loss, and reentry. In S. D. Brown & R. W. Lent (Eds.), *Career development and counseling: Putting theory and research to work* (pp. 625–650). Hoboken, NJ: John Wiley.

Bos, H. M. W., van Balen, F., & van den Boom, D. C. (2007). Child adjustment and parenting in planned lesbian-parent families. *American Journal of Orthopsychiatry, 77*(1), 38–48.

Boyle, M. H., Georgiades, K., Cullen, J., & Racine, Y. (2009). Community influences on intimate partner violence in India: Women's education, attitudes towards mistreatment and standards of living. *Social Science & Medicine, 69*(5), 691–697. doi:10.1016/j.socscimed.2009.06.039

Brandon, P. D., & Temple, J. B. (2007). Family provisions at the workplace and their relationship to absenteeism, retention, and productivity of workers: Timely evidence from prior data. *Australian Journal of Social Issues, 42*(4), 447–460.

Breiding, M. J., Chen, J., & Black, M. C. (2014). Intimate partner violence in the United States—2010. Retrieved from https://www.ncjrs.gov/App/Publications/abstract.aspx?ID=267363

Brewster, K. L., Tillman, K. H., & Jokinen-Gordon, H. (2013). Demographic characteristics of lesbian parents in the United States. *Population Research and Policy Review, 33*(4), 503–526. doi:10.1007/s11113-013-9296-3

Brock, R. L., & Lawrence, E. (2008). A longitudinal investigation of stress spillover in marriage: Does spousal support adequacy buffer the effects? *Journal of Family Psychology, 22*(1), 11–20.

Brooks, R., & Everett, G. (2008). The predominance of work-based training in young graduates' learning. *Journal of Education and Work, 21*(1), 61–73. doi:10.1080/13639080801956966

Bryson, L., Warner-Smith, P., Brown, P., & Fray, L. (2007). Managing the work–life roller-coaster: Private stress or public health issue? *Social Science & Medicine, 65*(6), 1142–1153. doi10.1016/j.socscimed.2007.04.027

Bumpass, L. L. (2004). Social change and the American family. In S. G. Kaler & O. M. Rennert (Eds.), *Understanding and optimizing human development: From cells to patients to populations* (pp. 213–219). New York: New York Academy of Sciences.

Buote, V. M., Pancer, S. M., Pratt, M. W., Adams, G., Birnie-Lefcovitch, S., Polivy, J., & Wintre, M. G. (2007). The importance of friends: Friendship and adjustment among 1st-year university students. *Journal of Adolescent Research, 22*(6), 665–689.

Busch, H., & Hofer, J. (2012). Self-regulation and milestones of adult development: Intimacy and generativity. *Developmental Psychology, 48*(1), 282–293. doi:10.1037/a0025521

Buunk, B. P., Dijkstra, P., Fetchenhauer, D., & Kenrick, D. T. (2002). Age and gender differences in mate selection criteria for various involvement levels. *Personal Relationships, 9*(3), 271–278.

Byars, A. M., & Hackett, G. (1998). Applications of social cognitive theory to the career development of women of color. *Applied & Preventive Psychology, 7*(4), 255–267. doi:10.1016/S0962-1849(98)80029-2

Campbell, K., Wright, D. W., & Flores, C. G. (2012). Newlywed women's marital expectations: Lifelong monogamy? *Journal of Divorce & Remarriage, 53*(2), 108–125. doi:10.1080/10502556.2012.651966

Carbery, J., & Buhrmester, D. (1998). Friendship and need fulfillment during three phases of young adulthood. *Journal of Social and Personal Relationships, 15*(3), 393.

Carlson, D. S., Grzywacz, J. G., Ferguson, M., Hunter, E. M., Clinch, C. R., & Arcury, T. A. (2011). Health and turnover of working mothers after childbirth via the work-family interface: An analysis across time. *The Journal of Applied Psychology, 96*(5), 1045–1054. doi:10.1037/a0023964

Carpenter, G. L., & Stacks, A. M. (2009). Developmental effects of exposure to intimate partner violence in early childhood: A review of the literature. *Children and Youth Services Review, 31*(8), 831–839. doi:10.1016/j.childyouth.2009.03.005

Catalano, S. (2007). *Intimate partner violence in the United States.* Washington, DC: Bureau of Justice Statistics. Retrieved from http://www.ojp.usdoj.gov/bjs/intimate/ipv.htm

Cattaneo, L. B., Stuewig, J., Goodman, L. A., Kaltman, S., & Dutton, M. A. (2007). Longitudinal helpseeking patterns among victims of intimate partner violence: The relationship between legal and extralegal services. *American Journal of Orthopsychiatry, 77*(3), 467–477. doi:10.1037/0002-9432.77.3.467

Caumont, A. (2013). *More of today's single mothers have never been married.* Washington, DC. Retrieved from http://www.pewresearch.org/fact-tank/2013/08/16/more-of-todays-single-mothers-have-never-been-married

Central Intelligence Agency. (2013). *World Fact Book, 2013–14.* Washington, DC: Author. Retrieved from https://www.cia.gov/library/publications/the-world-factbook/index.html

Cherlin, A. J. (2009). The origins of the ambivalent acceptance of divorce. *Journal of Marriage and Family, 71*(2), 226–229. doi:10.1111/j.1741-3737.2009.00593.x

Cherlin, A. J. (2010). Demographic trends in the United States: A review of research in the 2000s. *Journal of Marriage and Family, 72*(3), 403–419. doi:10.1111/j.1741-3737.2010.00710.x

Cherlin, A. J. (2013). Health, marriage, and same-sex partnerships. *Journal of Health and Social Behavior, 54*(1), 64–66. doi:10.1177/0022146512474430

Cho, H. (2012). Racial differences in the prevalence of intimate partner violence against women and associated factors. *Journal of Interpersonal Violence, 27*(2), 344–363. doi:10.1177/0886260511416469

Chong, A., & Mickelson, K. D. (2013). Perceived fairness and relationship satisfaction during the transition to parenthood: The mediating role of spousal support. *Journal of Family Issues.* Advance online publication. doi:10.1177/0192513X13516764

Chung, J. M., Robins, R. W., Trzesniewski, K. H., Noftle, E. E., Roberts, B. W., & Widaman, K. F. (2014). Continuity and change in self-esteem during emerging adulthood. *Journal of Personality and Social Psychology, 106*(3), 469–483. doi:10.1037/a0035135

Church, E. (2004). *Understanding stepmothers: Women share their struggles, successes, and insights.* Toronto: HarperCollins.

Chzhen, Y., & Bradshaw, J. (2012). Lone parents, poverty and policy in the European Union. *Journal of European Social Policy, 22*(5), 487–506. doi:10.1177/0958928712456578

Cinamon, R. G., & Rich, Y. (2002). Gender differences in the importance of work and family roles: Implications for work-family conflict. *Sex Roles, 47*(11–12), 531–541.

Clark, A. E., Diener, E., Georgellis, Y., & Lucas, R. E. (2008). Lags and leads in life satisfaction: A test of the baseline hypothesis*. *The Economic Journal, 118*(529), F222–F243. doi:10.1111/j.1468-0297.2008.02150.x

Clarke-Stewart, A., & Brentano, C. (2006). *Divorce: Causes and consequences.* New Haven, CT: Yale University Press.

Claxton, A., & Perry-Jenkins, M. (2008). No fun anymore: Leisure and marital quality across the transition to parenthood. *Journal of Marriage and Family, 70*(1), 28–43. doi:10.1111/j.1741-3737.2007.00459.x

Clements, M. L., Stanley, S. M., & Markman, H. J. (2004). Before they said "I do": Discriminating

among marital outcomes over 13 years. *Journal of Marriage and Family, 66*(3), 613–626.

Clift, R. J. W., Thomas, L. A., & Dutton, D. G. (2005). Two-year reliability of the propensity for abusiveness scale. *Journal of Family Violence, 20*(4), 231–234. Retrieved from 10.1007/s10896-005-5986-x

Cohen, P., Kasen, S., Chen, H., Hartmark, C., & Gordon, K. (2003). Variations in patterns of developmental transitions in the emerging adulthood period. *Developmental Psychology, 39*(4), 657. Retrieved from http://www.ncbi.nlm.nih.gov/pubmed/12859120

Collins, A., & van Dulmen, M. (2006). Friendships and romance in emerging adulthood: Assessing distinctiveness in close relationships. In J. J. Arnett & J. L. Tanner (Eds.), *Emerging adults in America: Coming of age in the 21st century* (pp. 219–234). Washington, DC: American Psychological Association.

Copen, C. E., Daniels, K., & Mosher, W. D. (2013). First premarital cohabitation in the United States: 2006–2010 National Survey of Family Growth. *National Health Statistics Reports, 64*.

Côté, J. E. (2006). Emerging adulthood as an institutionalized moratorium: Risks and benefits to identity formation. In J. J. Arnett & J. L. Tanner (Eds.), *Emerging adults in America: Coming of age in the 21st century* (pp. 85–116). Washington, DC: American Psychological Association.

Côté, J. E. (2014). The dangerous myth of emerging adulthood: An evidence-based critique of a flawed developmental theory. *Applied Developmental Science, 18*(4), 177–188. Retrieved from http://www.tandfonline.com/doi/abs/10.1080/10888691.2014.954451#.VTOQ7JMug8Q

Crumley, B. (2008). France overruled on gay adoption. *Time*. Retrieved from http://www.time.com/time/world/article/0,8599,1706514,00.html

Cunningham, M., & Thornton, A. (2007). Direct and indirect influences of parents' marital instability on children's attitudes toward cohabitation in young adulthood. *Journal of Divorce & Remarriage, 46*(3–4), 125–143.

D'augelli, A. R., Rendina, J. H., Sinclair, K. O., & Grossman, A. H. (2006). Lesbian and gay youth's aspirations for marriage and raising children. *Journal of LGBT Issues in Counseling, 1*(4), 77–98.

Dahl, B., & Malterud, K. (2015). Neither father nor biological mother. A qualitative study about lesbian co-mothers' maternity care experiences. *Sexual & Reproductive Healthcare*. Advance online publication. doi:10.1016/j.srhc.2015.02.002

David-Barrett, T., Rotkirch, A., Carney, J., Behncke Izquierdo, I., Krems, J. A., Townley, D., . . . Dunbar, R. I. M. (2015). Women favour dyadic relationships, but men prefer clubs: Cross-cultural evidence from social networking. *PLOS ONE, 10*(3), e0118329. doi:10.1371/journal.pone.0118329

Demir, M., Özen, A., Doğan, A., Bilyk, N. A., & Tyrell, F. A. (2011). I matter to my friend, therefore I am happy: Friendship, mattering, and happiness. *Journal of Happiness Studies, 12*(6), 983–1005. doi:10.1007/s10902-010-9240-8

Deutsch, F. M., Kokot, A. P., & Binder, K. S. (2007). College women's plans for different types of egalitarian marriages. *Journal of Marriage and Family, 69*(4), 916–929.

Devine, C. M., Jastran, M., Jabs, J., Wethington, E., Farell, T. J., & Bisogni, C. A. (2006). A lot of sacrifices: Work–family spillover and the food choice coping strategies of low-wage employed parents. *Social Science & Medicine, 63*(10), 2591–2603.

Devries, K. M., Mak, J. Y. T., García-Moreno, C., Petzold, M., Child, J. C., Falder, G., . . . Watts, C. H. (2013). Global health. The global prevalence of intimate partner violence against women. *Science, 340*(6140), 1527–1528. doi:10.1126/science.1240937

Dew, J. (2008). Debt change and marital satisfaction change in recently married couples. *Family Relations, 57*(1), 60–71. doi:10.1111/j.1741-3729.2007.00483.x

Dew, J., Britt, S., & Huston, S. (2012). Examining the relationship between financial issues and divorce. *Family Relations, 61*(4), 615–628. doi:10.1111/j.1741-3729.2012.00715.x

Dion, K. L., & Dion, K. K. (1993). Gender and ethnocultural comparisons in styles of love. *Psychology of Women Quarterly, 17*(4), 463–473.

Dixon, L., & Browne, K. (2003). The heterogeneity of spouse abuse: A review. *Aggression & Violent Behavior, 8*(1), 107.

Dixon, P. (2009). Marriage among African Americans: What does the research reveal? *Journal of African American Studies, 13*(1), 29–46. doi:10.1007/s12111-008-9062-5

Don, B. P., & Mickelson, K. D. (2014). Relationship satisfaction trajectories across the transition to parenthood among low-risk parents. *Journal of Marriage and Family, 76*(3), 677–692. doi:10.1111/jomf.12111

Doodson, L. J. (2014). Understanding the factors related to stepmother anxiety: A qualitative approach. *Journal of Divorce & Remarriage, 55*(8), 645–667. doi:10.1080/10502556.2014.959111

Dribe, M., & Stanfors, M. (2009). Does parenthood strengthen a traditional household division of labor? Evidence from Sweden. *Journal of Marriage and Family, 71*(1), 33–45. doi:10.1111/j.1741-3737.2008.00578.x

Dunn, J. L., & Powell-Williams, M. (2007). "Everybody makes choices": Victim advocates and the social construction of battered women's victimization and agency. *Violence Against Women, 13*(10), 977–1001. doi:10.1177/1077801207305932

Edwards, K. M., Sylaska, K. M., & Neal, A. M. (2015). Intimate partner violence among sexual minority populations: A critical review of the literature and agenda for future research. *Psychology of Violence, 5*(2), 112–121.

Eibach, R. P., & Mock, S. E. (2011). Idealizing parenthood to rationalize parental investments. *Psychological Science, 22*(2), 203–208. doi:10.1177/0956797610397057

Eisenberg, M. E., Spry, E., & Patton, G. C. (2015). From emerging to established: Longitudinal patterns in the timing of transition events among Australian emerging adults. *Emerging Adulthood*. Advance online publication. doi:10.1177/2167696815574639

Eng, S., Li, Y., Mulsow, M., & Fischer, J. (2010). Domestic violence against women in Cambodia: Husband's control, frequency of spousal discussion, and domestic violence reported by Cambodian women. *Journal of Family Violence, 25*(3), 237–246. doi:10.1007/s10896-009-9287-7

Erikson, E. H. (1950). *Childhood and society* (2nd ed.). New York: Norton.

Facio, A., & Micocci, F. (2003). Emerging adulthood in Argentina. In J. J. Arnett & N. L. Galambos (Eds.), *Exploring cultural conceptions of the transition to adulthood: New directions for child and adolescent development, Number 100* (pp. 21–31). San Francisco: Jossey-Bass.

Fadjukoff, P., Kokko, K., & Pulkkinen, L. (2007). Implications of timing of entering adulthood for identity achievement. *Journal of Adolescent Research, 22*(5), 504–530.

Fedewa, A. L., Black, W. W., & Ahn, S. (2014). Children and adolescents with same-gender parents: A meta-analytic approach in assessing outcomes. *Journal of GLBT Family Studies, 11*(1), 1–34. doi:10.1080/1550428X.2013.869486

Feeney, J. A., Hohaus, L., & Noller, P. (2001). *Becoming parents: Exploring the bonds between mothers, fathers, and their infants*. New York: Cambridge University Press.

Felker, J. A., Fromme, D. K., Arnaut, G. L., & Stoll, B. M. (2002). A qualitative analysis of stepfamilies: The stepparent. *Journal of Divorce & Remarriage, 38*(1–2), 125.

Filson, J., Ulloa, E., Runfola, C., & Hokoda, A. (2010). Does powerlessness explain the relationship between intimate partner violence and depression? *Journal of Interpersonal Violence, 25*(3), 400–415.

Fincham, F. D., & Beach, S. R. H. (2010). Marriage in the new millennium: A decade in review. *Journal of Marriage and Family, 72*(3), 630–649. doi:10.1111/j.1741-3737.2010.00722.x

Finkel, E. J., Eastwick, P. W., Karney, B. R., Reis, H. T., & Sprecher, S. (2012). Online dating: A critical analysis from the perspective of psychological science. *Psychological Science in the Public Interest, 13*(1), 3–66. doi:10.1177/1529100612436522

Forste, R., & Heaton, T. B. (2004). The divorce generation: Well-being, family attitudes, and socioeconomic consequences of marital disruption. *Journal of Divorce & Remarriage, 41*(1–2), 95–114.

Frech, A., & Williams, K. (2007). Depression and the psychological benefits of entering marriage. *Journal of Health & Social Behavior, 48*(2), 149–163.

Frome, P. M., Alfeld, C. J., Eccles, J. S., & Barber, B. L. (2006). Why don't they want a male-dominated job? An investigation of young women who changed their occupational aspirations. *Educational Research & Evaluation, 12*(4), 359–372.

Furnham, A. (2009). Sex differences in mate selection preferences. *Personality & Individual Differences, 47*(4), 262–267. doi:10.1016/j.paid.2009.03.013

Gadassi, R., Bar-Nahum, L. E., Newhouse, S., Anderson, R., Heiman, J. R., Rafaeli, E., & Janssen, E. (2015). Perceived partner responsiveness mediates the association between sexual and marital satisfaction: A daily diary study in newlywed couples. *Archives of Sexual Behavior*. Advance online publication. doi:10.1007/s10508-014-0448-2

Galambos, N. L., Barker, E. T., & Krahn, H. J. (2006). Depression, self-esteem, and anger in emerging adulthood: Seven-year trajectories. *Developmental Psychology, 42*(2), 350–365.

Galatzer-Levy, I. R., Mazursky, H., Mancini, A. D., & Bonanno, G. A. (2011). What we don't expect when expecting: Evidence for heterogeneity in subjective well-being in response to parenthood. *Journal of Family Psychology, 25*(3), 384–392. doi:10.1037/a0023759

Ganong, L., Coleman, M., Fine, M., & Martin, P. (1999). Stepparents' affinity-seeking and affinity-maintaining strategies with stepchildren. *Journal of Family Issues, 20*(3), 299–327.

Ganong, L. H., & Coleman, M. (2000). Remarried families. In C. Hendrick & S. S. Hendrick (Eds.), *Close relationships* (pp. 155–168). Thousand Oaks, CA: Sage.

Gao, G. (2001). Intimacy, passion and commitment in Chinese and US American romantic relationships. *International Journal of Intercultural Relations, 25*(3), 329–342.

Gates, G. J. (2013). *LGBT parenting in the United States*. Los Angeles: Williams Institute, University of California Law School. Retrieved from http://williamsinstitute.law.ucla.edu/wp-content/uploads/LGBT-Parenting.pdf

Gilbert, L. A., & Kearney, L. K. (2006). Sex, gender, and dual-earner families: Implications and applications for career counseling for women. In W. B. Walsh & M. J. Heppner (Eds.), *Handbook of career counseling for women* (2nd ed., pp. 193–217). Mahwah, NJ: Lawrence Erlbaum.

Gillespie, B. J., Lever, J., Frederick, D., & Royce, T. (2014). Close adult friendships, gender, and the life cycle. *Journal of Social and Personal Relationships*. Advance online publication. doi:10.1177/0265407514546977

Goldberg, A. E., Downing, J. B., & Sauck, C. C. (2008). Perceptions of children's parental preferences in lesbian two-mother households. *Journal of Marriage and Family, 70*(2), 419–434. Retrieved from 10.1111/j.1741-3737.2008.00491.x

Goldberg, A. E., & Perry-Jenkins, M. (2007). The division of labor and perceptions of parental roles: Lesbian couples across the transition to parenthood. *Journal of Social and Personal Relationships, 24*(2), 297–318. doi:10.1177/0265407507075415

Goldscheider, F., & Goldscheider, C. (1999). The changing transition to adulthood: Leaving and returning home. In F. Goldscheider & C. Goldscheider, *Understanding families* (Vol. 17). Thousand Oaks, CA: Sage.

Gonzaga, G. C., Campos, B., & Bradbury, T. (2007). Similarity, convergence, and relationship satisfaction in dating and married couples. *Journal of Personality and Social Psychology, 93*(1), 34–48.

Gonzáles-Figueroa, E., & Young, A. M. (2005). Ethnic identity and mentoring among Latinas in professional roles. *Cultural Diversity and Ethnic Minority Psychology, 11*(3), 213–226.

Gosselin, J. (2010). Individual and family factors related to psychosocial adjustment in stepmother families with adolescents. *Journal of Divorce & Remarriage, 51*(2), 108–123. doi:10.1080/10502550903455174

Gottman, J. M., & Driver, J. L. (2005). Dysfunctional marital conflict and everyday marital interaction. *Journal of Divorce & Remarriage, 43*(3–4), 63–77. doi:10.1300/J087v43n03_04

Graefe, D. R., & Lichter, D. T. (2007). When unwed mothers marry. *Journal of Family Issues, 28*(5), 595–622.

Greenstein, T. N. (2009). National context, family satisfaction, and fairness in the division of household labor. *Journal of Marriage and Family, 71*(4), 1039–1051. doi:10.1111/j.1741-3737.2009.00651.x

Grover, R. L., Nangle, D. W., Serwik, A., & Zeff, K. R. (2007). Girl friend, boy friend, girlfriend, boyfriend: Broadening our understanding of heterosocial competence. *Journal of Clinical Child & Adolescent Psychology, 36*(4), 491–502.

Guo, J. (2014, September 4). Millennials aren't changing jobs as much. That's a big problem for the economy. *Washington Post*. Retrieved from http://www.washingtonpost.com/news/storyline/wp/2014/09/04/millennials-arent-changing-jobs-as-much-thats-a-big-problem-for-the-economy

Guzzo, K. B. (2009). Marital intentions and the stability of first cohabitations. *Journal of Family Issues, 30*(2), 179–205.

Haase, C. M., Heckhausen, J., & Silbereisen, R. K. (2012). The interplay of occupational motivation and well-being during the transition from university to work. *Developmental Psychology, 48*(6), 1739–1751. doi:10.1037/a0026641

Hadley, R., & Hanley, T. (2011). Involuntarily childless men and the desire for fatherhood. *Journal of Reproductive and Infant Psychology, 29*(1), 56–68. doi:10.1080/02646838.2010.544294

Hall, J. A., Park, N., Hayeon, S., & Michael, J. C. (2010). Strategic misrepresentation in online dating: The effects of gender, self-monitoring, and personality traits. *Journal of Social and Personal Relationships, 27*(1), 117–135. doi:10.1177/0265407509349633

Halpern, D. F. (2005). How time-flexible work policies can reduce stress, improve health, and save money. *Stress & Health, 21*(3), 157–168. doi:10.1002/smi.1049

Hamel, J. (2009). Toward a gender-inclusive conception of intimate partner violence research and theory: Part 2—New directions.

International Journal of Men's Health, 8(1), 41–59. doi:10.3149/jmh.0801.41

Hancock, J. T., & Toma, C. L. (2009). Putting your best face forward: The accuracy of online dating photographs. *Journal of Communication, 59*(2), 367–386. doi:10.1111/j.1460-2466.2009.01420.x

Hanzal, A., & Segrin, C. (2009). The role of conflict resolution styles in mediating the relationship between enduring vulnerabilities and marital quality. *Journal of Family Communication, 9*(3), 150–169. doi:10.1080/15267430902945612

Härkönen, J. (2014). Divorce. In J. Treas, J. Scott, & M. Richards (Eds.), *The Wiley Blackwell companion to the sociology of families* (pp. 303–322). Hoboken, NJ: John Wiley.

Hartup, W. W., & Stevens, N. (1999). Friendships and adaptation across the life span. *Current Directions in Psychological Science, 8*, 76–79.

Harway, M., & Hansen, M. (2004). *Spouse abuse: Assessing & treating battered women, batterers, & their children* (2nd ed.). Sarasota, FL: Professional Resource Press/Professional Resource Exchange.

Hatcher, L., & Crook, J. C. (1988). First-job surprises for college graduates: An exploratory investigation. *Journal of College Student Development, 29*(5), 441–448.

Hatzenbuehler, M. L. (2009). How does sexual minority stigma "get under the skin"? A psychological mediation framework. *Psychological Bulletin, 135*(5), 707–730. doi:10.1037/a0016441

Hatzenbuehler, M. L., Keyes, K. M., & Hasin, D. S. (2009). State-level policies and psychiatric morbidity in lesbian, gay, and bisexual populations. *American Journal of Public Health, 99*(12), 2275–2281. doi:10.2105/AJPH.2008.153510

Heaton, T. B. (2002). Factors contributing to increasing marital stability in the United States. *Journal of Family Issues, 23*(3), 392–409.

Heilman, M. E., & Okimoto, T. G. (2008). Motherhood: A potential source of bias in employment decisions. *Journal of Applied Psychology, 93*(1), 189–198.

Helms, H. M., Walls, J. K., Crouter, A. C., & McHale, S. M. (2010). Provider role attitudes, marital satisfaction, role overload, and housework: A dyadic approach. *Journal of Family Psychology, 24*(5), 568–577. doi:10.1037/a0020637

Hendrick, C., & Hendrick, S. S. (2004). Sex and romantic love: Connects and disconnects. In J. H. Harvey, A. Wenzel, & S. Sprecher (Eds.), *The handbook of sexuality in close relationships* (pp. 159–182). Mahwah, NJ: Lawrence Erlbaum.

Hendry, L. B., & Kloep, M. (2010). How universal is emerging adulthood? An empirical example. *Journal of Youth Studies, 13*(2), 169–179. doi:10.1080/13676260903295067

Henehan, D., Rothblum, E. D., Solomon, S. E., & Balsam, K. F. (2007). Social and demographic characteristics of gay, lesbian, and heterosexual adults with and without children. *Journal of GLBT Family Studies, 3*(2–3), 35–79.

Henning, K., & Holdford, R. (2006). Minimization, denial, and victim blaming by batterers: How much does the truth matter? *Criminal Justice and Behavior, 33*(1), 110–130.

Hennon, C. B., Hildenbrand, B., & Schedle, A. (2008). Stepfamilies and children. In T. P. Gullotta & G. M. Blau (Eds.), *Family influences on childhood behavior and development: Evidence-based prevention and treatment approaches* (pp. 161–185). New York: Routledge/Taylor & Francis Group.

Henry, P. J., & McCue, J. (2009). The experience of nonresidential stepmothers. *Journal of Divorce & Remarriage, 50*(3), 185–205. doi:10.1080/10502550902717780

Hetherington, E. M., & Elmore, A. M. (2004). The intergenerational transmission of couple instability. In P. L. Chase-Lansdale, K. Kiernan, & R. J. Friedman (Eds.), *Human development across lives and generations: The potential for change* (pp. 171–203). New York: Cambridge University Press.

Hetherington, E. M., & Stanley-Hagan, M. (2002). Parenting in divorced and remarried families. In M. H. Bornstein (Ed.), *Handbook of parenting: Vol. 3.* (2nd ed., pp. 287–315). Mahwah, NJ: Lawrence Erlbaum.

Hewitt, B., Baxter, J., & Western, M. (2006). Family, work and health: The impact of marriage, parenthood and employment on self-reported health of Australian men and women. *Journal of Sociology, 42*(1), 61–78.

Hiekel, N., Liefbroer, A. C., & Poortman, A.-R. (2014). Understanding diversity in the meaning of cohabitation across Europe. *European Journal of Population, 30*(4), 391–410. doi:10.1007/s10680-014-9321-1

Higgins, C. A., Duxbury, L. E., & Lyons, S. T. (2010). Coping with overload and stress: Men and women in dual-earner families. *Journal of Marriage and Family, 72*(4), 847–859. doi:10.1111/j.1741-3737.2010.00734.x

Hill, C. (2015). *The simple truth about the gender pay gap*. Washington, DC: AAUW. Retrieved from http://www.aauw.org/research/the-simple-truth-about-the-gender-pay-gap

Hite, L. M., & McDonald, K. S. (2003). Career aspirations of non-managerial women: Adjustment and adaptation. *Journal of Career Development, 29*(4), 221–235.

Hohmann-Marriott, B. E. (2006). Shared beliefs and the union stability of married and cohabiting couples. *Journal of Marriage and Family, 68*(4), 1015–1028.

Hsueh, A. C., Morrison, K. R., & Doss, B. D. (2009). Qualitative reports of problems in cohabiting relationships: Comparisons to married and dating relationships. *Journal of Family Psychology, 23*(2), 236–246. doi:10.1037/a0015364

Huijts, T., Kraaykamp, G., & Subramanian, S. V. (2011). Childlessness and psychological well-being in context: A multilevel study on 24 European countries. *European Sociological Review, 29*(1), 32–47. doi:10.1093/esr/jcr037

International Labour Office. (2008). *Global employment trends for women*. Geneva, Switzerland: International Labour Organization.

Jackson, J. B., Miller, R. B., Oka, M., & Henry, R. G. (2014). Gender differences in marital satisfaction: A meta-analysis. *Journal of Marriage and Family, 76*(1), 105–129. doi:10.1111/jomf.12077

Jasinski, J., Blumenstein, L., & Morgan, R. (2014). Testing Johnson's typology: Is there gender symmetry in intimate terrorism? *Violence and Victims, 29*(1), 73–88. doi:10.1891/0886-6708.VV-D-12-00146

Jensen, T. M., & Howard, M. O. (2015). Perceived stepparent–child relationship quality: A systematic review of stepchildren's perspectives. *Marriage & Family Review*, 1–55. doi:10.1080/01494929.2015.1006717

Johnson, M. D., Cohan, C. L., & Davila, J. (2005). Problem-solving skills and affective expressions as predictors of change in marital satisfaction. *Journal of Consulting and Clinical Psychology, 73*(1), 15–27.

Johnson, M. K., Berg, J. A., & Sirotzki, T. (2007). Differentiation in self-perceived adulthood: Extending the confluence model of subjective age identity. *Social Psychology Quarterly, 70*(3), 243–261.

Johnson, W. L., Giordano, P. C., Longmore, M. A., & Manning, W. D. (2014). Intimate partner violence and depressive symptoms during adolescence and young adulthood. *Journal* of Health and Social Behavior, 55(1), 39–55. doi:10.1177/0022146513520430

Jose, A., Daniel O'Leary, K., & Moyer, A. (2010). Does premarital cohabitation predict subsequent marital stability and marital quality? A meta-analysis. Journal of Marriage and Family, 72(1), 105–116. doi:10.1111/j.1741-3737.2009.00686.x

Kail, B. L., Acosta, K. L., & Wright, E. R. (2015). State-level marriage equality and the health of same-sex couples. American Journal of Public Health, 105(6), 1101–1105. doi:10.2105/AJPH.2015.302589

Kalmijn, M., & Monden, C. W. S. (2006). Are the negative effects of divorce on well-being dependent on marital quality? Journal of Marriage and Family, 68(5), 1197–1213.

Kalmijn, M., & van Groenou, M. B. (2005). Differential effects of divorce on social integration. Journal of Social and Personal Relationships, 22(4), 455–476. doi:10.1177/0265407505054516

Katz-Wise, S. L., Priess, H. A., & Hyde, J. S. (2010). Gender-role attitudes and behavior across the transition to parenthood. Developmental Psychology, 46(1), 18–28. doi:10.1037/a0017820

Keeton, C. P., Perry-Jenkins, M., & Sayer, A. G. (2008). Sense of control predicts depressive and anxious symptoms across the transition to parenthood. Journal of Family Psychology, 22(2), 212–221.

Kemkes-Grottenthaler, A. (2003). Postponing or rejecting parenthood? Results of a survey among female academic professionals. Journal of Biosocial Science, 35(2), 213–226. Retrieved from 10.1017/S002193200300213X

Kennedy, S., & Ruggles, S. (2014). Breaking up is hard to count: The rise of divorce in the United States, 1980–2010. Demography, 51(2), 587–598. doi:10.1007/s13524-013-0270-9

Kenneyand, C. T., & McLanahan, S. S. (2006). Why are cohabiting relationships more violent than marriages? Demography, 43(1), 127–140.

Kilpatrick, S. D., Bissonnette, V. L., & Rusbult, C. E. (2002). Empathic accuracy and accommodative behavior among newly married couples. Personal Relationships, 9(4), 369–393.

King, E. B., Madera, J. M., Hebl, M. R., Knight, J. L., & Mendoza, S. A. (2006). What's in a name? A multiracial investigation of the role of occupational stereotypes in selection decisions. Journal of Applied Social Psychology, 36(5), 1145–1159.

King, V., & Scott, M. E. (2005). A comparison of cohabiting relationships among older and younger adults. Journal of Marriage and Family, 67(2), 271–285.

Kito, M. (2005). Self-disclosure in romantic relationships and friendships among American and Japanese college students. Journal of Social Psychology, 145(2), 127–140.

Koball, H. L., Moiduddin, E., Henderson, J., Goesling, B., & Besculides, M. (2010). What do we know about the link between marriage and health? Journal of Family Issues, 31(8), 1019–1040. doi:10.1177/0192513X10365834

Koivunen, J. M., Rothaupt, J. W., & Wolfgram, S. M. (2009). Gender dynamics and role adjustment during the transition to parenthood: Current perspectives. Family Journal, 17(4), 323–328. doi:10.1177/1066480709347360

Koropeckyj-Cox, T., & Call, V. R. A. (2007). Characteristics of older childless persons and parents. Journal of Family Issues, 28(10), 1362–1414.

Koropeckyj-Cox, T., & Pendell, G. (2007). Attitudes about childlessness in the United States. Journal of Family Issues, 28(8), 1054–1082.

Koropeckyj-Cox, T., Romano, V. R., & Moras, A. (2007). Through the lenses of gender, race, and class: Students' perceptions of childless/childfree individuals and couples. Sex Roles, 56(7–8), 415–428.

Kraaij, V., Garnefski, N., & Vlietstra, A. (2008). Cognitive coping and depressive symptoms in definitive infertility: A prospective study. Journal of Psychosomatic Obstetrics & Gynecology, 29(1), 9–16. doi:10.1080/01674820701505889

Krebs, C., Breiding, M. J., Browne, A., & Warner, T. (2011). The association between different types of intimate partner violence experienced by women. Journal of Family Violence, 26(6), 487–500. doi:10.1007/s10896-011-9383-3

Krieg, D. B. (2007). Does motherhood get easier the second-time around? Examining parenting stress and marital quality among mothers having their first or second child. Parenting: Science and Practice, 7(2), 149–175.

Kroger, J. (2007). Identity development: Adolescence through adulthood (2nd ed.). Thousand Oaks, CA: Sage.

Kulik, L., & Havusha-Morgenstern, H. (2011). Does cohabitation matter? Differences in initial marital adjustment among women who cohabited and those who did not. Families in Society, 92(1), 120–127.

Kurdek, L. A. (2005). Gender and marital satisfaction early in marriage: A growth curve approach. Journal of Marriage and Family, 67(1), 68–84.

Kurdek, L. A. (2006). Differences between partners from heterosexual, gay, and lesbian cohabiting couples. Journal of Marriage and Family, 68(2), 509–528.

Kurdek, L. A. (2007). The allocation of household labor by partners in gay and lesbian couples. Journal of Family Issues, 28(1), 132–148. doi:10.1177/0192513X06292019

Lavner, J. A., & Bradbury, T. N. (2012). Why do even satisfied newlyweds eventually go on to divorce? Journal of Family Psychology, 26(1), 1–10. doi:10.1037/a0025966

Lavner, J. A., Waterman, J., & Peplau, L. A. (2014). Parent adjustment over time in gay, lesbian, and heterosexual parent families adopting from foster care. The American Journal of Orthopsychiatry, 84(1), 46–53. doi:10.1037/h0098853

Lawrence, E., Rothman, A. D., Cobb, R. J., & Bradbury, T. N. (2010). Marital satisfaction across the transition to parenthood: Three eras of research. In M. S. Schulz, M. K. Pruett, P. K. Kerig, & R. D. Parke (Eds.), Strengthening couple relationships for optimal child development: Lessons from research and intervention (pp. 97–114). Washington, DC: American Psychological Association. doi:10.1037/12058-007

Le Bourdais, C., & Lapierre-Adamcyk, É. (2004). Changes in conjugal life in Canada: Is cohabitation progressively replacing marriage? Journal of Marriage and Family, 66(4), 929–942.

Lehrer, E. L. (2008). Age at marriage and marital instability: Revisiting the Becker–Landes–Michael hypothesis. Journal of Population Economics, 21(2), 463–484. doi:10.1007/s00148-006-0092-9

Leonard, K. E., & Homish, G. G. (2008). Predictors of heavy drinking and drinking problems over the first 4 years of marriage. Psychology of Addictive Behaviors, 22(1), 25–35.

Leone, J. M., Lape, M. E., & Xu, Y. (2013). Women's decisions to not seek formal help for partner violence: A comparison of intimate terrorism and situational couple violence. Journal of Interpersonal Violence, 29(10), 1850–1876. doi:10.1177/0886260513511701

Levesque, D. A., Velicer, W. F., & Castle, P. H. (2008). Resistance among domestic violence offenders: Measurement development and initial validation. Violence Against Women, 14(2), 158–184. doi:10.1177/1077801207312397

Li, N. P., Yong, J. C., Tov, W., Sng, O., Fletcher, G. J. O., Valentine, K. A., . . . Balliet, D. (2013). Mate preferences do predict attraction and choices in the early stages of mate selection. Journal of Personality and Social Psychology, 105(5), 757–776. doi:10.1037/a0033777

Liefbroer, A. C., & Dourleijn, E. (2006). Unmarried cohabitation and union stability: Testing the role of diffusion using data from 16 European countries. Demography, 43(2), 203–221.

Lunau, T., Bambra, C., Eikemo, T. A., van der Wel, K. A., & Dragano, N. (2014). A balancing act? Work-life balance, health and well-being in European welfare states. European Journal of Public Health, 24(3), 422–427. doi:10.1093/eurpub/cku010

Lutz-Zois, C. J., Bradley, A. C., Mihalik, J. L., & Moorman-Eavers, E. R. (2006). Perceived similarity and relationship success among dating couples: An idiographic approach. Journal of Social and Personal Relationships, 23(6), 865–880.

Macek, P., Bejček, J., & Vaníčková, J. (2007). Contemporary Czech emerging adults: Generation growing up in the period of social changes. Journal of Adolescent Research, 22(5), 444–475.

Maggs, J. L., Jager, J., Patrick, M. E., & Schulenberg, J. (2012). Social role patterning in early adulthood in the USA: Adolescent predictors and concurrent wellbeing across four distinct configurations. Longitudinal and Life Course Studies, 3(2), 190–210. Retrieved from http://www.pubmedcentral.nih.gov/articlerender.fcgi?artid=3495328&tool=pmcentrez&rendertype=abstract

Manning, W. D. (2013). Trends in cohabitation: Over twenty years of change, 1987–2010. Bowling Green, OH: Bowling Green State University. Retrieved from https://www.bgsu.edu/content/dam/BGSU/college-of-arts-and-sciences/NCFMR/documents/FP/FP-13-12.pdf

Manning, W. D., & Cohen, J. A. (2012). Premarital cohabitation and marital dissolution: An examination of recent marriages. Journal of Marriage and the Family, 74(2), 377–387. doi:10.1111/j.1741-3737.2012.00960.x

Markey, P. M., & Markey, C. N. (2007). Romantic ideals, romantic obtainment, and relationship experiences: The complementarity of interpersonal traits among romantic partners. Journal of Social and Personal Relationships, 24(4), 517–533.

Markstrom, C. A., & Kalmanir, H. M. (2001). Linkages between the psychosocial stages of identity and intimacy and the ego strengths of fidelity and love. Identity, 1(2), 179–196.

Martin, J. A., Hamilton, B. E., Osterman, M., Curtin, S. C., & Mathews, T. J. (2015). Births: Final data for 2013. National Vital Statistics Reports Statistics Reports, 64(1). Retrieved from http://www.cdc.gov/nchs/data/nvsr/nvsr64/nvsr64_01.pdf

Mattson, R. E., Frame, L. E., & Johnson, M. D. (2011). Premarital affect as a predictor of postnuptial marital satisfaction. Personal Relationships, 18(4), 532–546. doi:10.1111/j.1475-6811.2010.01315.x

Mayseless, O., & Scharf, M. (2003). What does it mean to be an adult? The Israeli experience. New Directions for Child and Adolescent Development, 2003(100), 5–20.

McDonald, S., Erickson, L. D., Johnson, M. K., & Elder, G. H. (2007). Informal mentoring and young adult employment. Social Science Research, 36(4), 1328–1347.

McIntyre, C. A., & Rhodes, R. E. (2007). Transitions to motherhood and its effect on physical activity. JSEP, 29, S186–S187.

McKeever, M., & Wolfinger, N. H. (2011). Thanks for nothing: Income and labor force participation for never-married mothers since 1982. Social Science Research, 40(1), 63–76. doi:10.1016/j.ssresearch.2010.06.008

Meier, A., & Allen, G. (2008). Intimate relationship development during the transition to adulthood: Differences by social class. *New Directions for Child and Adolescent Development*, 2008(119), 25–39.

Milan, A. (2013). *Marital status: Overview, 2011: Report on the Demographic Situation in Canada (91-209-X)*. Retrieved from http://www.statcan.gc.ca/pub/91-209-x/2013001/article/11788-eng.htm

Mills, M., Rindfuss, R. R., McDonald, P., & te Velde, E. (2011). Why do people postpone parenthood? Reasons and social policy incentives. *Human Reproduction Update*, 17(6), 848–860.

Moffitt, T. E., & Caspi, A. (1999). Findings about partner violence from the Dunedin multidisciplinary health and development study. *National Institute of Justice: Research in Brief*. Washington, DC: U.S. Department of Justice.

Molgat, M. (2007). Do transitions and social structures matter? How "emerging adults" define themselves as adults. *Journal of Youth Studies*, 10(5), 495–516. doi:10.1080/13676260701580769

Montgomery, M. J. (2005). Psychosocial intimacy and identity: From early adolescence to emerging adulthood. *Journal of Adolescent Research*, 20(3), 346–374.

Montoya, R. M., Horton, R. S., & Kirchner, J. (2008). Is actual similarity necessary for attraction? A meta-analysis of actual and perceived similarity. *Journal of Social and Personal Relationships*, 25(6), 889–922. doi:10.1177/0265407508096700

Morell, C. (2000). Saying no: Women's experiences with reproductive refusal. *Feminism & Psychology*, 10(3), 313.

Morgan, W. B., Elder, K. B., & King, E. B. (2013). The emergence and reduction of bias in letters of recommendation. *Journal of Applied Social Psychology*, 43(11), 2297–2306. doi:10.1111/jasp.12179

Moss, P., & Deven, F. (2006). Leave policies and research: A cross-national overview. *Marriage & Family Review*, 39(3–4), 255–285.

Murrell, A., Christoff, K., & Henning, K. (2007). Characteristics of domestic violence offenders: Associations with childhood exposure to violence. *Journal of Family Violence*, 22(7), 523–532.

Murrow, C., & Shi, L. (2010). The Influence of cohabitation purposes on relationship quality: An examination in dimensions. *The American Journal of Family Therapy*, 38(5), 397–412. doi:10.1080/01926187.2010.513916

National Center for Health Statistics. (2015). Provisional number of divorces and annulments and rate: United States, 2000–2011. *National Marriage and Divorce Rate Trends*. Retrieved June 5, 2015, from http://www.cdc.gov/nchs/nvss/marriage_divorce_tables.htm

National Conference of State Legislatures. (2013). *State family and medical leave laws*. Washington, DC. Retrieved from http://www.ncsl.org/research/labor-and-employment/state-family-and-medical-leave-laws.aspx#2

Neff, L. A., & Broady, E. F. (2011). Stress resilience in early marriage: Can practice make perfect? *Journal of Personality and Social Psychology*, 101(5), 1050–1067. doi:10.1037/a0023809

Nelson, L. J. (2009). An examination of emerging adulthood in Romanian college students. *International Journal of Behavioral Development*, 33(5), 402–411. doi:10.1177/0165025409340093

Nelson, L. J., Badger, S., & Wu, B. (2004). The influence of culture in emerging adulthood: Perspectives of Chinese college students. *International Journal of Behavioral Development*, 28, 26–36.

Nelson, L. J., & Barry, C. M. (2005). Distinguishing features of emerging adulthood: The role of self-classification as an adult. *Journal of Adolescent Research*, 90, 242–262.

Nelson, S. K., Kushlev, K., & Lyubomirsky, S. (2014). The pains and pleasures of parenting: When, why, and how is parenthood associated with more or less well-being? *Psychological Bulletin*, 140(3), 846–895. doi:10.1037/a0035444

Neugarten, B. L. (1979). Time, age, and the life cycle. *American Journal of Psychiatry*, 136(7), 887–894.

Neugarten, B. L., & Neugarten, D. A. (1996). *The meanings of age: Selected papers of Bernice L. Neugarten*. Chicago: University of Chicago Press.

Nichols, W. C., & Pace-Nichols, M. A. (2000). Childless married couples. In W. C. Nichols, M. A. Pace-Nichols, D. S. Becvar, & A. Y. Napier (Eds.), *Handbook of family development and intervention* (pp. 171–188). Hoboken, NJ: John Wiley.

Nilsen, A. B. V., Waldenström, U., Hjelmstedt, A., Hjelmsted, A., Rasmussen, S., & Schytt, E. (2012). Characteristics of women who are pregnant with their first baby at an advanced age. *Acta Obstetricia et Gynecologica Scandinavica*, 91(3), 353–362x. doi:10.1111/j.1600-0412.2011.01335.x

Nomaguchi, K. M., & Milkie, M. A. (2003). Costs and rewards of children: The effects of becoming a parent on adults' lives. *Journal of Marriage and Family*, 65(2), 356–374.

Norton, M. I., Frost, J. H., & Ariely, D. (2007). Less is more: The lure of ambiguity, or why familiarity breeds contempt. *Journal of Personality and Social Psychology*, 92(1), 97–105.

Obergefell v. Hodges, No. 14-556 at 23 (U.S. June 26, 2015). Retrieved from

https://supreme.justia.com/cases/federal/us/576/14-556/dissent7.html

O'Laughlin, E. M., & Anderson, V. N. (2001). Perceptions of parenthood among young adults: Implications for career and family planning. *American Journal of Family Therapy*, 29(2), 95–108.

Ogolsky, B. G., Dennison, R. P., & Monk, J. K. (2014). The role of couple discrepancies in cognitive and behavioral egalitarianism in marital quality. *Sex Roles*, 70(7–8), 329–342. doi:10.1007/s11199-014-0365-9

Peake, A., & Harris, K. L. (2002). Young adults' attitudes toward multiple role planning: The influence of gender, career traditionality and marriage plans. *Journal of Vocational Behavior*, 60(3), 405–421.

Pearson, Q. M. (2008). Role overload, job satisfaction, leisure satisfaction, and psychological health among employed women. *Journal of Counseling & Development*, 86(1), 57–63.

Peplau, L. A. (1991). Lesbian and gay relationships. In J. C. Gonsiorek & J. D. Weinrich (Eds.), *Homosexuality: Research implications for public policy* (pp. 177–196). Newbury Park, CA: Sage.

Perales, F., del Pozo-Cruz, J., & del Pozo-Cruz, B. (2015). Long-term dynamics in physical activity behaviour across the transition to parenthood. *International Journal of Public Health*, 60(3), 301–308. doi:10.1007/s00038-015-0653-3

Perelli-Harris, B., & Gassen, N. S. (2012). How similar are cohabitation and marriage? Legal approaches to cohabitation across Western Europe. *Population and Development Review*, 38(3), 435–467. doi:10.1111/j.1728-4457.2012.00511.x

Perrin, E. C., & Siegel, B. S. (2013). Promoting the well-being of children whose parents are gay or lesbian. *Pediatrics*, 131(4), e1374–e1383. doi:10.1542/peds.2013-0377

Perry-Jenkins, M., Goldberg, A. E., Pierce, C. P., & Sayer, A. G. (2007). Shift work, role overload, and the transition to parenthood. *Journal of Marriage and Family*, 69(1), 123–138.

Peterson, B. D., Gold, L., & Feingold, T. (2007). The experience and influence of infertility: Considerations for couple counselors. *Family Journal*, 251–257.

Peterson, C. C. (1996). The ticking of the social clock: Adults' beliefs about the timing of transition events. *International Journal of Aging and Human Development*, 42(3), 189.

Pew Research Center. (2015a). *Gay marriage around the world*. Retrieved from http://www.pewforum.org/2013/12/19/gay-marriage-around-the-world-2013

Pew Research Center. (2015b). *Same-sex marriage state-by-state*. Retrieved from http://www.pewforum.org/2015/04/21/same-sex-marriage-state-by-state

Pew Research Center. (2015c). *Support for same-sex marriage at record high, but key segments remain opposed*. Washington, DC: Author. Retrieved from http://www.people-press.org/2015/06/08/support-for-same-sex-marriage-at-record-high-but-key-segments-remain-opposed

Phillips, E. E., Bischoff, R. J., Abbott, D. A., & Xia, Y. (2009). Connecting behaviors and newlyweds' sense of shared-meaning and relationship satisfaction. *Journal of Couple & Relationship Therapy*, 8(3), 247–263. doi:10.1080/15332690903049257

Popenoe, D. (2009). Cohabitation, marriage, and child wellbeing: A cross-national perspective. *Society*, 46(5), 429–436. doi:10.1007/s12115-009-9242-5

Próspero, M., & Miseong, K. (2009). Mutual partner violence. *Journal of Interpersonal Violence*, 24(12), 2039–2056.

Raabe, B., & Beehr, T. A. (2003). Formal mentoring, versus supervisor and coworker relationships: Differences in perceptions and impact. *Journal of Organizational Behavior*, 24(3), 271–293.

Radmacher, K., & Azmitia, M. (2006). Are there gendered pathways to intimacy in early adolescents' and emerging adults' friendships? *Journal of Adolescent Research*, 21(4), 415–448.

Raley, J. A., Fisher, W. M., Halder, R., & Shanmugan, K. (2013). Child custody and homosexual/bisexual parents: A survey of judges. *Journal of Child Custody*, 10(1), 54–67. doi:10.1080/15379418.2013.781843

Reinhold, S. (2010). Reassessing the link between premarital cohabitation and marital instability. *Demography*, 47(3), 719–733. doi:10.1353/dem.0.0122

Reitzle, M. (2006). The connections between adulthood transitions and the self-perception of being adult in the changing contexts of East and West Germany. *European Psychologist*, 11(1), 25–38.

Rhoades, G. K., Petrella, J. N., Stanley, S. M., & Markman, H. J. (2007). Premarital cohabitation, husbands' commitment, and wives' satisfaction with the division of household contributions. *Marriage & Family Review*, 40(4), 5–22.

Rhoades, G. K., Stanley, S. M., & Markman, H. J. (2009). The pre-engagement cohabitation effect: A replication and extension of previous findings. *Journal of Family Psychology*, 23(1), 107–111. doi:10.1037/a0014358

Riggle, E. D. B., Rostosky, S. S., & Horne, S. G. (2010). Psychological distress, well-being, and legal recognition in same-sex couple relationships. *Journal of Family Psychology*, 24(1), 82–86. doi:10.1037/a0017942

Robles, T. F. (2014). Marital quality and health: Implications for marriage in the 21st century. *Current Directions in Psychological Science*, 23(6), 427–432. doi:10.1177/0963721414549043

Rosen, L. D., Cheever, N. A., Cummings, C., & Felt, J. (2008). The impact of emotionality and self-disclosure on online dating versus traditional dating. *Computers in Human Behavior*, 24(5), 2124–2157. doi:10.1016/j.chb.2007.10.003

Rosenfeld, M. J. (2014). Couple longevity in the era of same-sex marriage in the United States. *Journal of Marriage and Family*, 76(5), 905–918. doi:10.1111/jomf.12141

Rowlingson, K., & McKay, S. (2005). Lone motherhood and socio-economic disadvantage: Insights from quantitative and qualitative evidence. *Sociological Review*, 53(1), 30–49. doi:10.1111/j.1467-954X.2005.00502.x

Roy, R. N., Schumm, W. R., & Britt., S. L. (2014). Voluntary versus involuntary childlessness. In *Transition to parenthood*. New York: Springer.

Rubin, H., & Campbell, L. (2011). Day-to-day changes in intimacy predict heightened relationship passion, sexual occurrence, and sexual satisfaction: A dyadic diary analysis. *Social Psychological and Personality Science*, 3(2), 224–231. doi:10.1177/1948550611416520

Russo, M., Shteigman, A., & Carmeli, A. (2015). Workplace and family support and work–life balance: Implications for individual psychological availability and energy at work. *The Journal of Positive Psychology*, 1–16. doi:10.1080/17439760.2015.1025424

Saginak, K. A., & Saginak, M. A. (2005). Balancing work and family: Equity, gender, and marital satisfaction. *The Family Journal*, 13(2), 162–166.

Sanderson, C. A., Rahm, K. B., & Beigbeder, S. A. (2005). The link between the pursuit of intimacy goals and satisfaction in close same-sex friendships: An examination of the underlying processes. *Journal of Social and Personal Relationships*, 22(1), 75–98.

Sassler, S., & Miller, A. J. (2011). Class differences in cohabitation processes. *Family Relations*, 60(2), 163–177. doi:10.1111/j.1741-3729.2010.00640.x

Savin-Williams, R. C. (2000). Lesbian, gay, and bisexual families. In *Handbook of family diversity* (pp. 197– 215). New York: Oxford University Press.

Schmidt, L., Sobotka, T., Bentzen, J. G., & Nyboe Andersen, A. (2012). Demographic and medical consequences of the postponement of parenthood. *Human Reproduction Update*, 18(1), 29–43. doi:10.1093/humupd/dmr040

Schooler, C. (2001). The intellectual effects of the demands of the work environment. In R. J. Sternberg & E. L. Grigorenko (Eds.), *Environmental effects on cognitive abilities* (pp. 363–380). Mahwah, NJ: Lawrence Erlbaum.

Schwartz, S. J., Zamboanga, B. L., Luyckx, K., Meca, A., & Ritchie, R. A. (2013). Identity in emerging adulthood: Reviewing the field and looking forward. *Emerging Adulthood*, 1(2), 96–113. doi:10.1177/2167696813479781

Segrin, C., & Nabi, R. L. (2002). Does television viewing cultivate unrealistic expectations about marriage? *Journal of Communication*, 52(2), 247.

Seiffge-Krenke, I. (2003). Testing theories of romantic development from adolescence to young adulthood: Evidence of a developmental sequence. *International Journal of Behavioral Development*, 27(6), 519–531. doi:10.1080/01650250344000145

Seiter, L. N., & Nelson, L. J. (2011). An examination of emerging adulthood in college students and nonstudents in India. *Journal of Adolescent Research*, 26(4), 506–536. doi:10.1177/0743558410391262

Seltzer, J. A. (2004). Cohabitation in the United States and Britain: Demography, kinship, and the future. *Journal of Marriage and Family*, 66(4), 921–928.

Settersten, R. A., & Ray, B. (2010). What's going on with young people today? The long and twisting path to adulthood. *The Future of Children*, 20(1), 19–41. doi:10.1353/foc.0.0044

Shanahan, M. J. (2000). Pathways to adulthood in changing societies: Variability and mechanisms in life course perspective. *Annual Review of Sociology*, 26(1), 667.

Shapiro, D. N., & Stewart, A. J. (2011). Parenting stress, perceived child regard, and depressive symptoms among stepmothers and biological mothers. *Family Relations*, 60(5), 533–544. doi:10.1111/j.1741-3729.2011.00665.x

Sharon, T. (2015). Constructing adulthood: Markers of adulthood and well-being among emerging adults. *Emerging Adulthood*. Advance online publication. doi:10.1177/2167696815579826

Sharp, E. A., & Ganong, L. (2007). Living in the gray: Women's experiences of missing the marital transition. *Journal of Marriage and Family*, 69(3), 831–844. doi:10.1111/j.1741-3737.2007.00408.x

Sherman, A. M., & de Vries, B. (2000). Friendship in childhood and adulthood: Lessons across the life span. *International Journal of Aging and Human Development*, 51(1), 31.

Shulman, S., & Connolly, J. (2013). The challenge of romantic relationships in emerging adulthood: Reconceptualization of the field. *Emerging Adulthood*, 1(1), 27–39. doi:10.1177/2167696812467330

Sirsch, U., Dreher, E., Mayr, E., & Willinger, U. (2009). What does it take to be an adult in Austria?: Views of adulthood in Austrian adolescents, emerging adults, and adults. *Journal of Adolescent Research*, 24(3), 275–292.

Smith, A., & Duggan, M. (2013). Online dating & relationships. Washington, DC: Pew Research Center. Retrieved from http://www.pewinternet.org/2013/10/21/online-dating-relationships

Smith, C. A., Ireland, T. O., Park, A., Elwyn, L., & Thornberry, T. P. (2011). Intergenerational continuities and discontinuities in intimate partner violence: A two-generational prospective study. *Journal of Interpersonal Violence*, 26(18), 3720–3752. doi:10.1177/0886260511403751

Smithson, M., & Baker, C. (2008). Risk orientation, loving, and liking in long-term romantic relationships. *Journal of Social and Personal Relationships*, 25(1), 87–103. doi:10.1177/0265407507086807

Soons, J. P. M., & Kalmijn, M. (2009). Is marriage more than cohabitation? Well-being differences in 30 European countries. *Journal of Marriage and Family*, 71(5), 1141–1157. doi:10.1111/j.1741-3737.2009.00660.x

Southard, S. (2008). "Shopping" for a mate: Expected versus experienced preferences in online mate choice. *Technical Communication*, 55(4), 454.

Sprecher, S., & Metts, S. (1999). Romantic beliefs: Their influence on relationships and patterns of change over time. *Journal of Social and Personal Relationships*, 16(6), 834.

Stanca, L. (2012). Suffer the little children: Measuring the effects of parenthood on well-being worldwide. *Journal of Economic Behavior & Organization*, 81(3), 742–750. doi:10.1016/j.jebo.2010.12.019

Stanley, S. M., Rhoades, G. K., Amato, P. R., Markman, H. J., & Johnson, C. A. (2010). The timing of cohabitation and engagement: Impact on first and second marriages. *Journal of Marriage and the Family*, 72(4), 906–918. doi:10.1111/j.1741-3737.2010.00738.x

Stearns, E., Buchmann, C., & Bonneau, K. (2009). Interracial friendships in the transition to college: Do birds of a feather flock together once they leave the nest? *Sociology of Education*, 82(2), 173–195.

Steinberg, L., & Silk, J. S. (2002). Parenting adolescents. In M. H. Bornstein (Ed.), *Handbook of parenting: Vol. 1. Children and parenting* (pp. 103–133). Mahwah, NJ: Lawrence Erlbaum.

Sternberg, R. J. (1988). Triangulating love. In R. J. Sternberg & M. L. Barnes (Eds.), *The psychology of love* (pp. 119–138). New Haven, CT: Yale University Press.

Sternberg, R. J. (2004). A triangular theory of love. In H. T. Reis & C. E. Rusbult (Eds.), *Close relationships: Key readings* (pp. 213–227). Philadelphia: Taylor & Francis.

Storksen, I., Røysamb, E., Gjessing, H. K., Moum, T., & Tambs, K. (2007). Marriages and psychological distress among adult offspring of divorce: A Norwegian study. *Scandinavian Journal of Psychology*, 48(6), 467–476.

Sumter, S. R., Valkenburg, P. M., & Peter, J. (2013). Perceptions of love across the lifespan: Differences in passion, intimacy, and commitment. *International Journal of Behavioral Development*, 37(5), 417–427. doi:10.1177/0165025413492486

Tanner, J. L. (2014). Emerging adulthood. In R. J. R. Levesque (Ed.), *Encyclopedia of adolescence* (pp. 818–825). New York: Springer. doi:10.1007/978-1-4419-1695-2

Tanturri, M. L., & Mencarini, L. (2008). Childless or childfree? Paths to voluntary childlessness in Italy. *Population & Development Review*, 34(1), 51–77. doi:10.1111/j.1728-4457.2008.00205.x

Tasker, F., & Patterson, C. J. (2007). Research on gay and lesbian parenting: Retrospect and prospect. *Journal of GLBT Family Studies*, 3(2–3), 9–34.

Taylor, L. S., Fiore, A. T., Mendelsohn, G. A., & Cheshire, C. (2011). "Out of my league": A real-world test of the matching hypothesis. *Personality and Social Psychology Bulletin*, 37(7), 942–954. doi:10.1177/0146167211409947

Taylor, Z. E., & Conger, R. D. (2014). Risk and resilience processes in single-mother families: An interactionist perspective. In Z. Sloboda & H. Petras (Eds.), *Defining prevention science* (pp. 195–217). New York: Springer. doi:10.1007/978-1-4899-7424-2

Te Velde, E., Habbema, D., Leridon, H., & Eijkemans, M. (2012). The effect of postponement of first motherhood on permanent involuntary childlessness and total fertility rate in six European countries since the 1970s. *Human Reproduction*, 27(4), 1179–1183. doi:10.1093/humrep/der455

Teachman, J. (2008). Complex life course patterns and the risk of divorce in second marriages. *Journal of Marriage and Family*, 70(2), 294–305. doi:10.1111/j.1741-3737.2008.00482.x

Tidwell, N. D., Eastwick, P. W., & Finkel, E. J. (2013). Perceived, not actual, similarity predicts initial attraction in a live romantic context: Evidence from the speed-dating paradigm. *Personal Relationships*, 20(2), 199–215. doi:10.1111/j.1475-6811.2012.01405.x

Tillyer, M. S., & Wright, E. M. (2013). Intimate partner violence and the victim-offender overlap. *Journal of Research in Crime and Delinquency*, 51(1), 29–55. doi:10.1177/0022427813484315

Timonen, V., & Doyle, M. (2013). Life-long singlehood: Intersections of the past and the present. *Ageing and Society*, 34(10), 1749–1770. doi:10.1017/S0144686X13000500

Trillingsgaard, T., Baucom, K. J. W., & Heyman, R. E. (2014). Predictors of change in relationship satisfaction during the transition to parenthood. *Family Relations*, 63(5), 667–679. doi:10.1111/fare.12089

Tye, M. C. (2003). Lesbian, gay, bisexual, and transgender parents: Special considerations for the custody and adoption evaluator. *Family Court Review*, 41(1), 92–103.

United Nations Economic Commission for Europe. (2015). *Statistical database*. Retrieved May 5, 2015, from http://w3.unece.org/pxweb/QuickStatistics/IndicatorsList.asp?lang=1#17

United Nations Statistics Division. (2014). *Demographic yearbook: 2013*. Retrieved from http://unstats.un.org/unsd/demographic/products/dyb/dyb2.htm

U.S. Bureau of the Census. (2015a). *Estimated median age at first marriage, by sex: 1890 to the present; current population survey*. Washington, DC: Author. Retrieved from http://www.census.gov/hhes/families/data/marital.html

U.S. Bureau of the Census. (2015b). *Marital status of people 15 years and over, by age, sex, personal earnings, race, and Hispanic origin: 2014; current population survey*. Washington, DC: Author. Retrieved from https://www.census.gov/hhes/families/data/cps2014A.html

U.S. Bureau of the Census. (2015c). *Women's number of children ever born by age and marital status: June 2014*. Retrieved from http://www.census.gov/hhes/fertility/data/cps/2014.html

U.S. Bureau of Labor Statistics. (2014). *America's young adults at 27: Labor market activity, education, and household composition: Results from a longitudinal survey summary*. Retrieved from http://www.bls.gov/news.release/nlsyth.nr0.htm

U.S. Bureau of Labor Statistics. (2015a). *Employment characteristics of families—2014*. Retrieved from http://www.bls.gov/news.release/famee.nr0.htm

U.S. Bureau of Labor Statistics. (2015b). *Number of jobs held, labor market activity, and earnings growth among the youngest baby boomers: Results from a longitudinal survey summary*. Retrieved from http://www.bls.gov/news.release/nlsoy.nr0.htm

U.S. Department of Agriculture. (2014). *Expenditures on children by families, 2013*. Retrieved from http://www.cnpp.usda.gov/sites/default/files/expenditures_on_children_by_families/crc2013.pdf

U.S. Department of Health and Human Services. (2013). *Child Health USA 2012*. Rockville, MD: Author.

U.S. Department of Labor. (2007). *Women in the workforce: A databook*. Washington, DC: U.S. Bureau of Labor Statistics. Retrieved from http://www.bls.gov/cps/wlf-databook2007.htm

Valcour, M. (2007). Work-based resources as moderators of the relationship between work hours and satisfaction with work-family balance. *Journal of Applied Psychology*, 92(6), 1512–1523.

Vanassche, S., Swicegood, G., & Matthijs, K. (2012). Marriage and children as a key to happiness? Cross-national differences in the effects of marital status and children on well-being. *Journal of Happiness Studies*, 14(2), 501–524. doi:10.1007/s10902-012-9340-8

Vanfraussen, K., Ponjaert-Kristoffersen, I., & Brewaeys, A. (2003). Family functioning in lesbian families created by donor insemination. *American Journal of Orthopsychiatry*, 73(1), 78–90.

Varner, F., & Mandara, J. (2009). Marital transitions and changes in African American mothers' depressive symptoms: The buffering role of financial resources. *Journal of Family Psychology*, 23(6), 839–847. doi:10.1037/a0017007

Wallerstein, J. S. (1994). The early psychological tasks of marriage: Part I. American *Journal of Orthopsychiatry*, 64(4), 640–650.

Wang, H., & Amato, P. R. (2000). Predictors of divorce adjustment: Stressors, resources, and definitions. *Journal of Marriage and Family*, 62(3), 655–668.

Wang, W. (2012). The rise of intermarriage: Rates, characteristics vary by race and gender. Washington, DC: Pew Research Center

Retrieved from http://www.pewsocialtrends.org/2012/02/16/the-rise-of-intermarriage

Waren, W., & Pals, H. (2013). Comparing characteristics of voluntarily childless men and women. *Journal of Population Research*, 30(2), 151–170. doi:10.1007/s12546-012-9103-8

Whiting, J. B., Smith, D. R., Barnett, T., & Grafsky, E. L. (2007). Overcoming the Cinderella myth: A mixed methods study of successful stepmothers. *Journal of Divorce & Remarriage*, 47(1–2), 95–109.

Widarsson, M., Engström, G., Rosenblad, A., Kerstis, B., Edlund, B., & Lundberg, P. (2013). Parental stress in early parenthood among mothers and fathers in Sweden. *Scandinavian Journal of Caring Sciences*, 27(4), 839–847. doi:10.1111/j.1471-6712.2012.01088.x

Wiersma, J. D., Fischer, J. L., Harrington Cleveland, H., Reifman, A., & Harris, K. S. (2010). Selection and socialization of drinking among young adult dating, cohabiting, and married partners. *Journal of Social and Personal Relationships*, 28(2), 182–200. doi:10.1177/0265407510380083

Wight, R. G., LeBlanc, A. J., de Vries, B., & Detels, R. (2012). Stress and mental health among midlife and older gay-identified men. *American Journal of Public Health*, 102(3), 503–510. doi:10.2105/AJPH.2011.300384

Wight, R. G., LeBlanc, A. J., & Lee Badgett, M. V. (2013). Same-sex legal marriage and psychological well-being: Findings from the California Health Interview Survey. *American Journal of Public Health*, 103(2), 339–346. doi:10.2105/AJPH.2012.301113

Wilk, S. L., Desmarais, L. B., & Sackett, P. R. (1995). Gravitation to jobs commensurate with ability: Longitudinal and cross-sectional tests. *Journal of Applied Psychology*, 80(1), 79–85.

Williams, L., Kabamalan, M., & Ogena, N. (2007). Cohabitation in the Philippines: Attitudes and behaviors among young women and men. *Journal of Marriage and Family*, 69(5), 1244–1256.

Willoughby, B. J., & Carroll, J. S. (2010). Sexual experience and couple formation attitudes among emerging adults. *Journal of Adult Development*, 17(1), 1–11. doi:10.1007/s10804-009-9073-z

Winslow, S. (2005). Work-family conflict, gender, and parenthood, 1977–1997. *Journal of Family Issues*, 26(6), 727–755. doi:10.1177/0192513X05227522

Wisensale, S. K. (2006). Commentary: What role for the Family and Medical Leave Act in long-term care policy? *Journal of Aging & Social Policy*, 18(3–4), 79–93.

World Health Organization. (2005). *World Health Organization multi-country study on women's health and domestic violence against women*. Geneva, Switzerland: Author. Retrieved from http://www.who.int/gender/violence/who_multicountry_study/en/index.html

Wright, D. W., Simmons, L. A., & Campbell, K. (2007). Does a marriage ideal exist? Using Q-Sort methodology to compare young adults' and professional educators' views on healthy marriages. *Contemporary Family Therapy*, 29(4), 223–236.

Wu, L. L., Bumpass, L. L., & Musick, K. (2001). Historical and life course trajectories of nonmarital childbearing. In L. L. Wu & B. Wolfe (Eds.), *Out of wedlock: Causes and consequences of nonmarital fertility* (pp. 3–48). New York: Russell Sage Foundation.

Wu, P.-L., & Chiou, W.-B. (2009). More options lead to more searching and worse choices in finding partners for romantic relationships online: An experimental study. *CyberPsychology & Behavior*, 12(3), 315–318. doi:10.1089/cpb.2008.0182

Xu, X., & Shu-Chuan Lai, C. (2004). Gender ideologies, marital roles, and marital quality in Taiwan. *Journal of Family Issues*, 25(3), 318–355.

Zimmer-Gembeck, M. J., & Petherick, J. (2006). Intimacy dating goals and relationship satisfaction during adolescence and emerging adulthood: Identity formation, age and sex as moderators. *International Journal of Behavioral Development*, 30(2), 167–177.

Zimmermann, P., & Iwanski, A. (2014). Emotion regulation from early adolescence to emerging adulthood and middle adulthood: Age differences, gender differences, and emotion-specific developmental variations. *International Journal of Behavioral Development*, 38(2), 182–194. doi:10.1177/0165025413515405

CHAPTER 15

Ackerman, P. L., & Beier, M. E. (2006). Determinants of domain knowledge and independent study learning in an adult sample. *Journal of Educational Psychology*, 98(2), 366–381.

Aldwin, C. M., & Levenson, M. R. (2001). Stress, coping, and health at midlife: A developmental perspective. In M. E. Lachman (Ed.), *Handbook of midlife development* (pp. 188–214). Hoboken, NJ: John Wiley.

Aldwin, C. M., Spiro, A. I. I. I., & Park, C. (2006). Health, behavior, and optimal aging: A life span developmental perspective. In J. E. Birren & K. W. Schaire (Eds.), *Handbook of the psychology of aging* (6th ed., pp. 85–104). Amsterdam, Netherlands: Elsevier.

Almeida, D. M., Neupert, S. D., Banks, S. R., & Serido, J. (2005). Do daily stress processes account for socioeconomic health disparities? *The Journals of Gerontology: Series B: Psychological Sciences & Social Sciences*, 60B, 34–39.

American Heart Association. (2008). *Sudden cardiac death*. Retrieved from http://www.americanheart.org/presenter.jhtml?identifier=4741).

American Society for Aesthetic Plastic Surgery. (2014). *Cosmetic Surgery National Data Bank statistics*. Retrieved from http://www.surgery.org/sites/default/files/2014-Stats.pdf

Andel, R., Kåreholt, I., Parker, M. G., Thorslund, M., & Gatz, M. (2007). Complexity of primary lifetime occupation and cognition in advanced old age. *Journal of Aging & Health*, 19(3), 397–415.

Andersen, S. J. (2007). Osteoporosis in the older woman. *Clinical Obstetrics & Gynecology*, 50(3), 752–766.

Araujo, A. B., O'Donnell, A. B., Brambilla, D. J., Simpson, W. B., Longcope, C., Matsumoto, A. M., & McKinlay, J. B. (2004). Prevalence and incidence of androgen deficiency in middle-aged and older men: Estimates from the Massachusetts Male Aging Study. *The Journal of Clinical Endocrinology and Metabolism*, 89(12), 5920–5926. doi:10.1210/jc.2003-031719

Au, J., Sheehan, E., Tsai, N., Duncan, G. J., Buschkuehl, M., & Jaeggi, S. M. (2015). Improving fluid intelligence with training on working memory: A meta-analysis. *Psychonomic Bulletin & Review*, 22(2), 366–377. doi:10.3758/s13423-014-0699-x

Avis, N. E., Brockwell, S., & Colvin, A. (2005). A universal menopausal syndrome? *American Journal of Medicine*, 118(12), 1406. doi:10.1016/j.amjmed.2005.10.010

Avis, N. E., & Crawford, S. (2006). Menopause: Recent research findings. In S. K. Whitbourne & S. L. Willis (Eds.), *The baby boomers grow up: Contemporary perspectives on midlife* (pp. 75–109). Mahwah, NJ: Lawrence Erlbaum.

Avis, N. E., Stellato, R., Crawford, S., Bromberger, J., Ganz, P., Cain, V., & Kagawa-Singer, M. (2001). Is there a menopausal syndrome? Menopausal status and symptoms across racial/ethnic groups. *Social Science & Medicine*, 52(3), 345.

Ayers, B., Forshaw, M., & Hunter, M. S. (2010). The impact of attitudes towards the menopause on women's symptom experience: A systematic review. *Maturitas*, 65(1), 28–36. doi:10.1016/j.maturitas.2009.10.016

Backé, E.-M., Seidler, A., Latza, U., Rossnagel, K., & Schumann, B. (2012). The role of psychosocial stress at work for the development of cardiovascular diseases: A systematic review. *International Archives of Occupational and Environmental Health*, 85(1), 67–79. doi:10.1007/s00420-011-0643-6

Baker, D. P., Eslinger, P. J., Benavides, M., Peters, E., Dieckmann, N. F., & Leon, J. (2015). The cognitive impact of the education revolution: A possible cause of the Flynn Effect on population IQ. *Intelligence*, 49, 144–158. doi:10.1016/j.intell.2015.01.003

Baltes, M. M., & Carstensen, L. L. (2003). The process of successful aging: Selection, optimization and compensation. In U. M. Staudinger & U. Lindenberger (Eds.), *Understanding human development: Dialogues with lifespan psychology* (pp. 81–104). Dordrecht, Netherlands: Kluwer Academic Publishers.

Baltes, P. B., & Baltes, M. M. (1990). Psychological perspectives on successful aging: The model of selective optimization with compensation. In P. B. Baltes & M. M. Baltes (Eds.), *Successful aging: Perspectives from the behavioral sciences* (pp. 1–34). New York: Cambridge University Press.

Barrett, A. E., & Robbins, C. (2008). The multiple sources of women's aging anxiety and their relationship with psychological distress. *Journal of Aging and Health*, 20(1), 32–65. doi:10.1177/0898264307309932

Bartone, P. T. (2006). Resilience under military operational stress: Can leaders influence hardiness? *Military Psychology*, 18, S131–S148.

Bartone, P. T., Roland, R. R., & Picano, J. J. (2008). Psychological hardiness predicts success in U.S. Army Special Forces candidates. *International Journal of Selection and Assessment*, 16(1), 78–81.

Basaria, S. (2013). Reproductive aging in men. *Endocrinology and Metabolism Clinics of North America*, 42(2), 255–270. doi:10.1016/j.ecl.2013.02.012

Bayley, N. (1955). On the growth of intelligence. *American Psychologist*, 10(12), 805–818. doi:10.1037/h0043803

Beier, M. E., & Ackerman, P. L. (2005). Age, ability, and the role of prior knowledge on the acquisition of new domain knowledge: Promising results in a real-world learning environment. *Psychology and Aging*, 20(2), 341–355.

Bennett, I. J., & Madden, D. J. (2014). Disconnected aging: Cerebral white matter integrity and age-related differences in cognition. *Neuroscience*, 276, 187–205. doi:10.1016/j.neuroscience.2013.11.026

Benz, C. C. (2008). Impact of aging on the biology of breast cancer. *Critical Reviews in Oncology/Hematology*, 66(1), 65–74. doi:10.1016/j.critrevonc.2007.09.001

Berg, K. M., Kunins, H. V, Jackson, J. L., Nahvi, S., Chaudhry, A., Harris, K. A., . . . Arnsten, J. H. (2008). Association between alcohol consumption and both osteoporotic fracture and bone density. *American Journal of Medicine*, 121(5), 406–418. doi:10.1016/j.amjmed.2007.12.012

Beyene, Y. (1986). Cultural significance and physiological manifestations of menopause a biocultural analysis. *Culture, Medicine and Psychiatry*, 10(1), 47–71. doi:10.1007/BF00053262

Beyene, Y., & Martin, M. C. (2001). Menopausal experiences and bone density of Mayan women in Yucatan, Mexico. *American Journal of Human Biology*, 13(4), 505–511.

Bishop, N. A., & Guarente, L. (2007). Genetic links between diet and lifespan: Shared mechanisms from yeast to humans. *Nature Reviews Genetics*, 8(11), 835–844. doi:10.1038/nrg2188

Blanchard, C. M., Fortier, M., Sweet, S., O'Sullivan, T., Hogg, W., Reid, R. D., & Sigal, R. J. (2007). Explaining physical activity levels from a self-efficacy perspective: The physical activity counseling trial. *Annals of Behavioral Medicine*, 34(3), 323–328.

Bleicher, K., Cumming, R. G., Naganathan, V., Seibel, M. J., Sambrook, P. N., Blyth, F. M., . . . Waite, L. M. (2011). Lifestyle factors, medications, and disease influence bone mineral density in older men: Findings from the CHAMP study. *Osteoporosis International*, 22(9), 2421–2437. doi:10.1007/s00198-010-1478-9

Bonnel, S., Mohand-Said, S., & Sahel, J.-A. (2003). The aging of the retina. *Experimental Gerontology*, 38(8), 825. doi:10.1016/S0531-5565(03)00093-7

Bosman, E. A. (1993). Age-related differences in the motoric aspects of transcription typing skill. *Psychology and Aging*, 8, 87–102.

Braver, T. S., & West, R. (2008). Working memory, executive control, and aging. In F. I. M. Craik & T. A. Salthouse (Eds.), *The handbook of aging and cognition* (3rd ed., pp. 311–372). New York: Psychology Press.

Britto, R., Araújo, L., Barbosa, I., Silva, L., Rocha, S., & Valente, A. P. (2011). Hormonal therapy with estradiol and testosterone implants: Bone protection? *Gynecological Endocrinology*, 27(2), 96–100. doi:10.3109/09513590.2010.489131

Brydon, L., Strike, P. C., Bhattacharyya, M. R., Whitehead, D. L., McEwan, J., Zachary, I., & Steptoe, A. (2010). Hostility and physiological responses to laboratory stress in acute coronary syndrome patients. *Journal of Psychosomatic Research*, 68(2), 109–116. doi:10.1016/j.jpsychores.2009.06.007

Bugg, J. M., Zook, N. A., DeLosh, E. L., Davalos, D. B., & Davis, H. P. (2006). Age differences in fluid intelligence: Contributions of general slowing and frontal decline. *Brain & Cognition*, 62(1), 9–16. doi:10.1016/j.bandc.2006.02.006

Burger, H. G., Hale, G. E., Robertson, D. M., & Dennerstein, L. (2007). A review of hormonal changes during the menopausal transition: Focus on findings from the Melbourne Womens Midlife Health Project. *Human Reproduction Update*, 13(6), 559.

Bye, D., Pushkar, D., & Conway, M. (2007). Motivation, interest, and positive affect in traditional and nontraditional undergraduate students. *Adult Education Quarterly*, 57(2), 141–158.

Canderelli, R., Leccesse, L. A., & Miller, N. L. (2007). Benefits of hormone replacement therapy in postmenopausal women. *Journal of the American Academy of Nurse Practitioners*, 19(12), 635–641.

Carstensen, L. L., & Mikels, J. A. (2005). At the intersection of emotion and cognition. Aging and the positivity effect. *Current Directions in Psychological Science*, 14(3), 117–121. doi:10.1111/j.0963-7214.2005.00348.x

Cass, H. (2006). Stress and the immune system. *Total Health*, 27(6), 24–25.

Cattell, R. B. (1963). Theory of fluid and crystallized intelligence: A critical experiment. *Journal of Educational Psychology*, 54(1), 1–22. doi:10.1037/h0046743

Centers for Disease Control and Prevention. (2015). *10 leading causes of death—by age group—2013. Vital and health statistics*. Atlanta: Author. Retrieved from ftp://ftp.cdc.gov/pub/ncipc/10LC-2003/JPEG/10lc-2003.jpg

Chan, G. K., & Duque, G. (2002). Age-related bone loss: Old bone, new facts. *Gerontology*, 48(2), 62–71.

Chao, R., & Good, G. E. (2004). Non-traditional students' perspectives on college education. *Journal of College Counseling*, 7, 5–12.

Chen, T., & Li, D. (2007). The roles of working memory updating and processing speed in mediating age-related differences in fluid intelligence. *Aging, Neuropsychology & Cognition*, 14(6), 631–646.

Chou, R., Dana, T., Bougatsos, C., Fleming, C., & Beil, T. (2011). Screening adults aged 50 years or older for hearing loss: A review of the evidence for the U.S. preventive services task force. *Annals of Internal Medicine*, 154(5), 347–355. doi:10.7326/0003-4819-154-5-201103010-00009

Chrisler, J. C. (2008). The menstrual cycle in a biopsychosocial context. In F. L. Denmark & M. A. Paludi (Eds.), *Psychology of women: A handbook of issues and theories* (2nd ed., pp. 400–439). Westport, CT: Praeger.

Christensen, H., Batterham, P. J., & Mackinnon, A. J. (2013). The getting of wisdom: Fluid intelligence does not drive knowledge acquisition. *Journal of Cognition and Development*, 14(2), 321–331. doi:10.1080/15248372.2012.664590

Craik, F. I. M., & Rose, N. S. (2012). Memory encoding and aging: A neurocognitive perspective. *Neuroscience and Biobehavioral Reviews*, 36(7), 1729–1739. doi:10.1016/j.neubiorev.2011.11.007

Cropley, M., & Steptoe, A. (2005). Social support, life events and physical symptoms: A prospective study of chronic and recent life stress in men and women. *Psychology, Health & Medicine*, 10(4), 317–325.

Daffner, K. R., Chong, H., & Riis, J. (2007). Cognitive status impacts age-related changes in attention to novel and target events in normal adults. *Neuropsychology*, 21(3), 291–300.

Dainese, S. M., Allemand, M., Ribeiro, N., Bayram, S., Martin, M., & Ehlert, U. (2011). Protective factors in midlife: How do people stay healthy? *GeroPsych*, 24(1), 19–29.

Deary, I. J. (2014). The stability of intelligence from childhood to old age. *Current Directions in Psychological Science*, 23(4), 239–245. doi:10.1177/0963721414536905

Deeks, A. A., Gibson-Helm, M., Teede, H., & Vincent, A. (2011). Premature menopause: A comprehensive understanding of psychosocial aspects. *Climacteric*, 14(5), 565–572. doi:10.3109/13697137.2011.566390

Delanoë, D., Hajri, S., Bachelot, A., Mahfoudh Draoui, D., Hassoun, D., Marsicano, E., & Ringa, V. (2012). Class, gender and culture in the experience of menopause. A comparative survey in Tunisia and France. *Social Science & Medicine*, 75(2), 401–409. doi:10.1016/j.socscimed.2012.02.051

Dellenbach, M., & Zimprich, D. (2008). Typical intellectual engagement and cognition in old age. *Aging, Neuropsychology & Cognition*, 15(2), 208–231. doi: 10.1080/13825580701338094

Demetriou, A., & Bakracevic, K. (2009). Reasoning and self-awareness from adolescence to middle age: Organization and development as a function of education. *Learning and Individual Differences*, 19(2), 181–194. doi:10.1016/j.lindif.2008.10.007

Deming, L., Chang, L., Tianyong, C., & Guiyun, L. (2003). The roles of processing speed and working memory in cognitive aging. *Acta Psychologica Sinica*, 35(4), 471–475.

Dillaway, H. E. (2008). "Why can't you control this?" How women's interactions with intimate partners define menopause and family. *Journal of Women & Aging*, 20(1–2), 47–64.

Do, K.-A., Treloar, S., Pandeya, N., Purdie, D., Green, A., Heath, A., & Martin, N. (1998). Predictive factors of age at menopause in a large Australian twin study. *Human Biology*, 70(6), 1073–1091. Retrieved from http://digitalcommons.wayne.edu/humbiol/vol70/iss6/8

Dolbier, C. L., Smith, S. E., & Steinhardt, M. A. (2007). Relationships of protective factors to stress and symptoms of illness. *American Journal of Health Behavior*, 31(4), 423–433.

Donatelle, R. (2004). *Health: The basics*. San Francisco: Benjamin Cummings.

Ecob, R., Sutton, G., Rudnicka, A., Smith, P., Power, C., Strachan, D., & Davis, A. (2008). Is the relation of social class to change in hearing threshold levels from childhood to middle age explained by noise, smoking, and drinking behaviour? *International Journal of Audiology*, 47(3), 100–108. doi:10.1080/14992020701647942

Egan, B. M., Zhao, Y., & Axon, R. N. (2010). US trends in prevalence, awareness, treatment, and control of hypertension, 1988–2008. *JAMA*, 303(20), 2043–2050. doi:10.1001/jama.2010.650

Ericsson, K. A. (2014). Expertise. *Current Biology*, 24(11), R508–R510. doi:10.1016/j.cub.2014.04.013

Ericsson, K. A., & Moxley, J. H. (2013). Experts' superior memory: From accumulation of chunks to building memory skills that mediate improved performance and learning. In T. J. Perfect (Ed.), *The SAGE handbook of applied memory*. Thousand Oaks, CA: Sage.

Farage, M. A., Miller, K. W., Elsner, P., & Maibach, H. I. (2013). Characteristics of the aging skin. *Advances in Wound Care*, 2(1), 5–10. doi:10.1089/wound.2011.0356

Federman, D. D., & Walford, G. A. (2007). Is male menopause real? [Cover story]. *Newsweek*, 149(3), 58–60.

Finkel, D., Reynolds, C. A., McArdle, J. J., & Pedersen, N. L. (2007). Age changes in processing speed as a leading indicator of cognitive aging. *Psychology and Aging*, 22(3), 558–568.

Forcier, K., Stroud, L. R., & Papandonatos, G. D. (2006). Links between physical fitness and cardiovascular reactivity and recovery to psychological stressors: A meta-analysis. *Health Psychology*, 25(6), 723–739.

Freund, A. M., & Baltes, P. B. (2007). Toward a theory of successful aging: Selection, optimization, and compensation. In R. Fernández-Ballesteros (Ed.), *Geropsychology: European perspectives for an aging world* (pp. 239–254). Ashland, OH: Hogrefe & Huber Publishers.

Friedman, H. S., & Kern, M. L. (2014). Personality, well-being, and health. *Annual Review of Psychology*, 65(1), 719–742. doi:10.1146/annurev-psych-010213-115123

Gallicchio, L., Schilling, C., Tomic, D., Miller, S. R., Zacur, H., & Flaws, J. A. (2007). Correlates of sexual functioning among mid-life women. *Climacteric*, 10(2), 132–142.

Gass, M., & Dawson-Hughes, B. (2006). Preventing osteoporosis-related fractures: An overview. *American Journal of Medicine*, 119, S3–S11.

Geerligs, L., Maurits, N. M., Renken, R. J., & Lorist, M. M. (2014). Reduced specificity of functional connectivity in the aging brain during task performance. *Human Brain Mapping*, 35(1), 319–330. doi:10.1002/hbm.22175

Gerber, M., & Pühse, U. (2009). Do exercise and fitness protect against stress-induced health complaints? A review of the literature. *Scandinavian Journal of Public Health*, 37(8), 801–819. doi:10.1177/1403494809350522

Gil-Cazorla, R., Shah, S., & Naroo, S. A. (2015). A review of the surgical options for the correction of presbyopia. *The British Journal of Ophthalmology*. Advance online publication. doi:10.1136/bjophthalmol-2015-306663

Giorgio, A., Santelli, L., Tomassini, V., Bosnell, R., Smith, S., De Stefano, N., & Johansen-Berg, H. (2010). Age-related changes in grey and white matter structure throughout adulthood. *NeuroImage*, 51(3), 943–951. doi:10.1016/j.neuroimage.2010.03.004

Glisky, E. L. (2007). Changes in cognitive function in human aging. In D. R. Riddle (Ed.), *Brain aging: Models, methods, and mechanisms* (pp. 3–20). Boca Raton, FL: CRC Press.

Go, A. S., Mozaffarian, D., Roger, V. L., Benjamin, E. J., Berry, J. D., Borden, W. B., . . . Turner, M. B. (2013). Heart disease and stroke statistics—2013 update: A report from the American Heart Association. *Circulation*, 127(1), e6–e245. doi:10.1161/CIR.0b013e31828124ad

Gold, E. B., Crawford, S. L., Avis, N. E., Crandall, C. J., Matthews, K. A., Waetjen, L. E., . . . Harlow, S. D. (2013). Factors related to age at natural menopause: Longitudinal analyses from SWAN. *American Journal of Epidemiology*, 178(1), 70–83. doi:10.1093/aje/kws421

Gordon-Salant, S. J. (2005). Hearing loss and aging: New research findings and clinical implications. *Journal of Rehabilitation Research & Development*, 42, 9–23. doi:101682/JRRD.2005.01.0006

Gragnani, A., Cornick, S. Mac, Chominski, V., Ribeiro de Noronha, S. M., Alves Corrêa de Noronha, S. A., & Ferreira, L. M. (2014). Review of major theories of skin aging. *Advances in Aging Research*, 03(04), 265–284. doi:10.4236/aar.2014.34036

Grindler, N. M., Allsworth, J. E., Macones, G. A., Kannan, K., Roehl, K. A., & Cooper, A. R. (2015). Persistent organic pollutants and early menopause in U.S. women. *PloS One*, 10(1). doi:10.1371/journal.pone.0116057

Gruber, N., Mosimann, U. P., Müri, R. M., & Nef, T. (2013). Vision and night driving abilities of elderly drivers. *Traffic Injury Prevention*, 14(5), 477–485. doi:10.1080/15389588.2012.727510

Guadalupe-Grau, A., Fuentes, T., Guerra, B., & Calbet, J. A. L. (2009). Exercise and bone mass in adults. *Sports Medicine*, 39(6), 439–468.

Gupta, P., Sturdee, D. W., & Hunter, M. S. (2006). Mid-age health in women from the Indian subcontinent (MAHWIS): General health and the experience of menopause in women. *Climacteric*, 9(1), 13–22.

Hannan, M. T., Broe, K. E., Cupples, L. A., Dufour, A. B., Rockwell, M., & Kiel, D. P. (2012). Height loss predicts subsequent hip fracture in men and women of the Framingham Study. *Journal of Bone and Mineral Research*, 27(1), 146–152. doi:10.1002/jbmr.557

Hannon, K. (2010). Dealing with the hormone dilemma. *U.S. News & World Report*, 147(2), 51–52.

Haring, R., Ittermann, T., Völzke, H., Krebs, A., Zygmunt, M., Felix, S. B., . . . Wallaschofski, H. (2010). Prevalence, incidence and risk factors of testosterone deficiency in a population-based cohort of men: Results from the study of health in Pomerania. *The Aging Male*, 13(4), 247–257. doi:10.3109/13685538.2010.487553

Harris, W. S., Miller, M., Tighe, A. P., Davidson, M. H., Schaefer, E. J., & Dimsdale, J. E. (2008). Psychological stress and cardiovascular disease. *Journal of the American College of Cardiology*, 51(13), 1237–1246. doi:10.1016/j.jacc.2007.12.024

Hartge, P. (2009). Genetics of reproductive lifespan. *Nature Genetics*, 41(6), 637–638. doi:10.1038/ng0609-637

Hay, E. L., & Diehl, M. (2010). Reactivity to daily stressors in adulthood: The importance of stressor type in characterizing risk factors. *Psychology and Aging*, 25(1), 118–131. doi:10.1037/a0018747

Hayslip, B. J., Panek, P. E., & Patrick, J. H. (2007). *Adult development and aging* (4th ed.). Malabar, FL: Krieger Publishing Company.

Heidenreich, P. A., Trogdon, J. G., Khavjou, O. A., Butler, J., Dracup, K., Ezekowitz, M. D., . . . Woo, Y. J. (2011). Forecasting the future of cardiovascular disease in the United States: A policy statement from the American Heart Association. *Circulation*, 123(8), 933–944. doi:10.1161/CIR.0b013e31820a55f5

Heir, T., Erikssen, J., & Sandvik, L. (2011). Overweight as predictor of long-term mortality among healthy, middle-aged men: A prospective cohort study. *Preventive Medicine*, 52(3–4), 223–226. doi:10.1016/j.ypmed.2011.01.010

Helzner, E. P., Cauley, J. A., Pratt, S. R., Wisniewski, S. R., Zmuda, J. M., Talbott, E. O., . . . al, et. (2005). Race and sex differences in age-related hearing loss: The health, aging and body composition study. *Journal of the American Geriatrics Society*, 53(12), 2119–2127. Retrieved from www.cinahl.com/cgi-bin/refsvc?jid=748&accno=2009083727

Hermans, E. A., Dubbelman, M., van der Heijde, G. L., & Heethaar, R. M. (2008). Change in the accommodative force on the lens of the human eye with age. *Vision Research*, 48(1), 119–126. doi:10.1016/j.visres.2007.10.017

Hersh, A. L., Stefanick, M. L., & Stafford, R. S. (2004). National use of postmenopausal hormone therapy: Annual trends and response to recent evidence. *JAMA*, 291, 47–53.

Herzmann, G., & Curran, T. (2011). Experts' memory: An ERP study of perceptual expertise effects on encoding and recognition. *Memory & Cognition*, 39(3), 412–432. doi:10.3758/s13421-010-0036-1

Hickey, M., Elliott, J., & Davison, S. L. (2012). Hormone replacement therapy. *BMJ*, 344, e763. doi:10.1136/bmj.e763

Holliday, R. (2007). *Aging: The paradox of life*. New York: Springer.

Holt, R. I. G., Phillips, D. I. W., Jameson, K. A., Cooper, C., Dennison, E. M., & Peveler, R. C. (2013). The relationship between depression, anxiety and cardiovascular disease: Findings from the Hertfordshire Cohort Study. *Journal of Affective Disorders*, 150(1), 84–90. doi:10.1016/j.jad.2013.02.026

Honigman, R., & Castle, D. J. (2006). Aging and cosmetic enhancement. *Clinical Interventions in Aging*, 1(2), 115–119. Retrieved from http://www.pubmedcentral.nih.gov/articlerender.fcgi?artid=2695163&tool=pmcentrez&rendertype=abstract

Horn, J. L., & Cattell, R. B. (1966). Refinement and test of the theory of fluid and crystallized general intelligences. *Journal of Educational Psychology*, 57(5), 253–270.

Horn, J. L., & Donaldson, G. (1976). On the myth of intellectual decline in adulthood. *American Psychologist*, 31(10), 701–719.

Horn, J. L., & Masunaga, H. (2000). New directions for research into aging and intelligence: The development of expertise. In T. J. Perfect & E. A. Maylor (Eds.), *Models of cognitive aging* (pp. 125–159). New York: Oxford University Press.

Horn, J. L., & Noll, J. (1997). Human cognitive capabilities: Gf-Gc theory. In D. P. Flanagan, J. L. Genshaft, & P. L. Harrison (Eds.), *Contemporary intellectual assessment: Theories, tests, and issues* (pp. 53–91). New York: Guilford Press.

Hostetler, A. J., Sweet, S., & Moen, P. (2007). Gendered career paths: A life course perspective on returning to school. *Sex Roles*, 56(1), 85–103.

Hou, N., Hong, S., Wang, W., Olopade, O. I., Dignam, J. J., & Huo, D. (2013). Hormone replacement therapy and breast cancer: Heterogeneous risks by race, weight, and breast density. *Journal of the National Cancer Institute*, 105(18), 1365–1372. doi:10.1093/jnci/djt207

Howard, B. V, Van Horn, L., Hsia, J., Manson, J. E., Stefanick, M. L., Wassertheil-Smoller, S., . . . Robbins, J. (2006). Low-fat diet and weight change in postmenopausal women. *JAMA*, 295(6), 655–666.

Howell, L. C., & Beth, A. (2002). Midlife myths and realities: Women reflect on their experiences. *Journal of Women & Aging*, 14(3–4), 189.

Huang, K.-E., Xu, L., I, N. N., & Jaisamrarn, U. (2010). The Asian menopause survey: Knowledge, perceptions, hormone treatment and sexual function. *Maturitas, 65*(3), 276–283. doi:10.1016/j.maturitas.2009.11.015

Hvas, L., & Dorte Effersøe, G. (2008). Discourses on menopause—Part II: How do women talk about menopause? *Health: An Interdisciplinary Journal for the Social Study of Health, Illness & Medicine, 12*(2), 177–192. doi:10.1177/1363459307086842

Hwang, J.-H., Li, C.-W., Wu, C.-W., Chen, J.-H., & Liu, T.-C. (2007). Aging effects on the activation of the auditory cortex during binaural speech listening in white noise: An fMRI study. *Audiology & Neuro-Otology, 12*(5), 285–294.

Islander, U., Jochems, C., Lagerquist, M. K., Forsblad-d'Elia, H., & Carlsten, H. (2011). Estrogens in rheumatoid arthritis; the immune system and bone. *Molecular & Cellular Endocrinology, 335*(1), 14–29. doi:10.1016/j.mce.2010.05.018

Jackson, G. R., & Owsley, C. (2003). Visual dysfunction, neurodegenerative diseases, and aging. *Neurologic Clinics, 21*(3), 709–728.

Jemal, A., Thun, M. J., Ward, E. E., Henley, S. J., Cokkinides, V. E., & Murray, T. E. (2008). Mortality from leading causes by education and race in the United States, 2001. *American Journal of Preventive Medicine, 34*(1), 1–8.

Johnson, S. H., & Rybash, J. M. (1993). A cognitive neuroscience perspective on age-related slowing: Developmental changes in the functional architecture. In J. Cerella, J. M. Rybash, W. Hoyer, & M. L. Commons (Eds.), *Adult information processing: Limits on loss* (pp. 143–173). San Diego: Academic Press.

Johnson, T. D. (2007). Exercising your way to better health. *Nation's Health, 37*(4), 17.

Kaufman, A. S. (2001). WAIS-III IQs, Horn's theory, and generational changes from young adulthood to old age. *Intelligence, 29*(2), 131.

Keller, K., & Engelhardt, M. (2013). Strength and muscle mass loss with aging process. Age and strength loss. *Muscles, Ligaments and Tendons Journal, 3*(4), 346–350. Retrieved from http://europepmc.org/articles/PMC3940510/?report=abstract

Kennedy, Q., Taylor, J. L., Reade, G., & Yesavage, J. A. (2010). Age and expertise effects in aviation decision making and flight control in a flight simulator. *Aviation, Space, and Environmental Medicine, 81*(5), 489–497. Retrieved from http://www.pubmedcentral.nih.gov/articlerender.fcgi?artid=2905035&tool=pmcentrez&rendertype=abstract

Khan, N., Afaq, F., & Mukhtar, H. (2010). Lifestyle as risk factor for cancer: Evidence from human studies. *Cancer Letters, 293*(2), 133–143. doi:10.1016/j.canlet.2009.12.013

Kirchberger, I., Heier, M., Kuch, B., Wende, R., & Meisinger, C. (2011). Sex differences in patient-reported symptoms associated with myocardial infarction (from the population-based MONICA/KORA Myocardial Infarction Registry). *The American Journal of Cardiology, 107*(11), 1585–1589. http://doi.org/10.1016/j.amjcard.2011.01.040

Knowles, M. S. (1970). *The modern practice of adult education.* New York: New York Association Press.

Knowles, M. S. (1972). Innovations in teaching styles and approaches based upon adult learning. *Journal of Education for Social Work, 8*(2), 32–39. doi:10.1080/00220612.1972.10671913

Knowles, M. S., Holton, E. F., & Swanson, R. A. (2014). *The adult learner: The definitive classic in adult education and human resource development* (8th ed.). Abingdon, UK: Routledge.

Knowlton, A. A., & Lee, A. R. (2012). Estrogen and the cardiovascular system. *Pharmacology & Therapeutics, 135*(1), 54–70. doi:10.1016/j.pharmthera.2012.03.007

Koh, K. K., Han, S. H., Oh, P. C., Shin, E. K., & Quon, M. J. (2010). Combination therapy

for treatment or prevention of atherosclerosis: Focus on the lipid-RAAS interaction. *Atherosclerosis, 209*(2), 307–313. doi:10.1016/j.atherosclerosis.2009.09.007

Kohl, E., Steinbauer, J., Landthaler, M., & Szeimies, R.-M. (2011). Skin ageing. *Journal of the European Academy of Dermatology and Venereology, 25*(8), 873–884. doi:10.1111/j.1468-3083.2010.03963.x

Kraft, J. M., & Werner, J. S. (1999). Aging and the saturation of colors: 1. Colorimetric purity discrimination. *Journal of the Optical Society of America, A, Optics, Image Science & Vision, 16*(2), 223–230.

Kramer, A. F., & Madden, D. J. (2008). Attention. In F. I. M. Craik & T. A. Salthouse (Eds.), *The handbook of aging and cognition* (3rd ed., pp. 189–249). New York: Psychology Press.

Lantz, P. M., House, J. S., Mero, R. P., & Williams, D. R. (2005). Stress, life events, and socioeconomic disparities in health: Results from the Americans' Changing Lives study. *Journal of Health & Social Behavior, 46*(3), 274–288.

Lawlor, D. A., Ebrahim, S., & Smith, G. D. (2003). The association of socio-economic position across the life course and age at menopause: The British Women's Heart and Health Study. *BJOG: An International Journal of Obstetrics & Gynaecology, 110*(12), 1078.

Lee, Y.-A., & Goto, Y. (2015). Chronic stress effects on working memory: Association with prefrontal cortical tyrosine hydroxylase. *Behavioural Brain Research, 286*, 122–127. doi:10.1016/j.bbr.2015.03.007

Leigh-Paffenroth, E. D., & Elangovan, S. (2011). Temporal processing in low-frequency channels: Effects of age and hearing loss in middle-aged listeners. *Journal of the American Academy of Audiology, 22*(7), 393–404. doi:10.3766/jaaa.22.7.2

Levitt, T., Fugelsang, J., & Crossley, M. (2006). Processing speed, attentional capacity, and age-related memory change. *Experimental Aging Research, 32*(3), 263–295.

Li, W.-F., Hou, S.-X., Yu, B., Li, M.-M., Férec, C., & Chen, J.-M. (2010). Genetics of osteoporosis: Accelerating pace in gene identification and validation. *Human Genetics, 127*(3), 249–285. doi:10.1007/s00439-009-0773-z

Lin, J., Gan, C. M., Zhang, X., Jones, S., Sjöblom, T., Wood, L. D., . . . Velculescu, V. E. (2007). A multidimensional analysis of genes mutated in breast and colorectal cancers. *Genome Research, 17*(9), 7.

Lindh-Åstrand, L., Hoffmann, M., Hammar, M., & Kjellgren, K. (2007). Women's conception of the menopausal transition—A qualitative study. *Journal of Clinical Nursing, 16*(3), 509–517.

Liu, H., Paige, N. M., Goldzweig, C. L., Wong, E., Zhou, A., Suttorp, M. J., . . . Shekelle, P. (2008). Screening for osteoporosis in men: A systematic review for an American College of Physicians Guideline. *Annals of Internal Medicine, 148*(9), 685–W138.

Liu, J., & Eden, J. (2007). Experience and attitudes toward menopause in Chinese women living in Sydney—A cross sectional survey. *Maturitas, 58*(4), 359–365.

Lock, M., & Kaufert, P. (2001). Menopause, local biologies, and cultures of aging. *American Journal of Human Biology, 13*(4), 494–504.

Logan, A. J., & Baker, J. (2007). Cross-sectional and longitudinal profiles of age related decline in golf performance. *JSEP, 29*, S15.

Lustig, C., Hasher, L., & Tonev, S. T. (2006). Distraction as a determinant of processing speed. *Psychonomic Bulletin & Review, 13*(4), 619–625.

Mackenbach, J. P., Stirbu, I., Roskam, A.-J. R., Schaap, M. M., Menvielle, G., Leinsalu, M., & Kunst, A. E. (2008). Socioeconomic inequalities in health in 22 European countries. *New England*

Journal of Medicine, 358(23), 2468–2481. doi:10.1056/NEJMsa0707519

Maddi, S. R. (2007a). Relevance of hardiness assessment and training to the military context. *Military Psychology, 19*(1), 61–70. doi:10.1080/08995600701323301

Maddi, S. R. (2007b). The story of hardiness: Twenty years of theorizing, research, and practice. In A. Monat, R. S. Lazarus, & G. Reevy (Eds.), *The Praeger handbook on stress and coping* (Vol. 2, pp. 327–340). Westport, CT: Praeger.

Maddi, S. R. (2013). Personal hardiness as the basis for resilience. In *Hardiness: Turning stressful circumstances into resilient growth* (pp. 7–17). Dordrecht: Springer Netherlands. doi:10.1007/978-94-007-5222-1

Mani, T. M., Bedwell, J. S., & Miller, L. S. (2005). Age-related decrements in performance on a brief continuous performance test. *Archives of Clinical Neuropsychology, 20*(5), 575–586.

Marshall, B. L. (2007). Climacteric redux? *Men & Masculinities, 9*(4), 509–529.

Mather, M., & Carstensen, L. L. (2005). Aging and motivated cognition: The positivity effect in attention and memory. *Trends in Cognitive Sciences, 9*(10), 496–502. doi:10.1016/j.tics.2005.08.005

McArdle, J. J., Ferrer-Caja, E., Hamagami, F., & Woodcock, R. W. (2002). Comparative longitudinal structural analyses of the growth and decline of multiple intellectual abilities over the life span. *Developmental Psychology, 38*(1), 115–142.

McLeod, P., Sommerville, P., & Reed, N. (2005). Are automated actions beyond conscious access? In J. Duncan, P. McLeod, & L. Phillips (Eds.), *Measuring the mind* (pp. 359–371). New York: Oxford University Press.

McNamara, M., Batur, P., & DeSapri, K. T. (2015). In the clinic. Perimenopause. *Annals of Internal Medicine, 162*(3), ITC1–15. doi:10.7326/AITC201502030

McSweeney Cody, M., O'Sullivan, P., Elberson, K., Moser, D. K., & Garvin, B. J., J. C. (2003). Women's early warning symptoms of acute myocardial infarction. *Circulation, 108*, 2619–2623.

Meijer, W. A., de Groot, R. H. M., van Gerven, P. W. M., van Boxtel, M. P. J., & Jolles, J. (2009). Level of processing and reaction time in young and middle-aged adults and the effect of education. *European Journal of Cognitive Psychology, 21*(2–3), 216–234. doi:10.1080/09541440802091780

Mitchell, W. K., Williams, J., Atherton, P., Larvin, M., Lund, J., & Narici, M. (2012). Sarcopenia, dynapenia, and the impact of advancing age on human skeletal muscle size and strength; a quantitative review. *Frontiers in Physiology, 3*, 260. doi:10.3389/fphys.2012.00260

Miyamoto, K., Inoue, Y., Hsueh, K., Liang, Z., Yan, X., Yoshii, T., & Furue, M. (2011). Characterization of comprehensive appearances of skin ageing: An 11-year longitudinal study on facial skin ageing in Japanese females at Akita. *Journal of Dermatological Science, 64*(3), 229–236. doi:10.1016/j.jdermsci.2011.09.009

Morrow, D. G., Menard, W. E., Ridolfo, H. E., Stine-Morrow, E. A. L., Teller, T., & Bryant, D. (2003). Expertise, cognitive ability, and age effects on pilot communication. *International Journal of Aviation Psychology, 13*(4), 345.

Morrow, D. G., & Schriver, A. (2007). External support for pilot communication: Implications for age-related design. *International Journal of Cognitive Technology, 12*(1), 21–30.

Moxley, J. H., & Charness, N. (2013). Meta-analysis of age and skill effects on recalling chess positions and selecting the best move. *Psychonomic Bulletin & Review, 20*(5), 1017–1022. doi:10.3758/s13423-013-0420-5

Nachtigall, M. J., Nazem, T. G., Nachtigall, R. H., & Goldstein, S. R. (2013). Osteoporosis risk factors and early life-style modifications to decrease disease burden in women. *Clinical Obstetrics and Gynecology*, *56*(4), 650–653. doi:10.1097/GRF.0b013e3182aa1daf

Nappi, R. E., & Nijland, E. A. (2008). Women's perception of sexuality around the menopause: Outcomes of a European telephone survey. *European Journal of Obstetrics & Gynecology & Reproductive Biology*, *137*(1), 10–16. doi:10.1016/j.ejogrb.2006.10.036

National Cancer Institute. (2012). *Surveillance, Epidemiology, and End Results (SEER) program (www.seer.cancer.gov) DevCan database: "SEER 18 Incidence and Mortality, 2000–2010, with Kaposi Sarcoma and Mesothelioma."* Retrieved from http://canques.seer.cancer.gov/cgi-bin/cq_submit?dir=devcan2012&db=1&rpt=TAB&sel=1^5^1^1^59^8^13&dec=2&template=null

National Center for Education Statistics. (2015). *Digest of education statistics, 2013*. Washington, DC: Author. Retrieved from https://nces.ed.gov/programs/digest/d13/index.asp

National Center for Health Statistics. (2015). *Deaths: Final data for 2013. National Vital Statistics Reports*. Retrieved from http://www.cdc.gov/nchs/data/nvsr/nvsr64/nvsr64_02.pdf

National Heart, Lung, and Blood Institute. (2014). What is coronary heart disease? Bethesda, MD: National Institutes of Health, Department of Health and Human Services. Retrieved from http://www.nhlbi.nih.gov/health/health-topics/topics/cad

Nelson, H. D. (2008). Menopause. *Lancet*, *371*(9614), 760–770.

Nelson, H. D., Humphrey, L. L., LeBlanc, E., Miller, J., Takano, L., Chan, B. K. S., . . . Teutsch, S. M. (2002). Postmenopausal hormone replacement therapy for primary prevention of chronic conditions. Summary of the evidence for the U.S. Preventive Services Task Force. Rockville, MD: Agency for Healthcare Research and Quality. Retrieved from http://www.ahrq.gov/clinic/3rduspstf/hrt/hrtsum1.htm

Nerini, A., Matera, C., & Stefanile, C. (2014). Psychosocial predictors in consideration of cosmetic surgery among women. *Aesthetic Plastic Surgery*, *38*(2), 461–466. doi:10.1007/s00266-014-0294-6

Neugarten, B. L. (1968). The awareness of middle aging. In B. L. Neugarten (Ed.), *Middle age and aging* (pp. 137–147). Chicago: University of Chicago Press.

Newell, K. M., Vaillancourt, D. E., & Sosnoff, J. (2006). Aging, complexity, and motorp. In J. E. Birren & K. W. Schaire (Eds.), *Handbook of the psychology of aging* (6th ed., pp. 163–182). Amsterdam, Netherlands: Elsevier.

Nickels, S., Truong, T., Hein, R., Stevens, K., Buck, K., Behrens, S., . . . Chang-Claude, J. (2013). Evidence of gene-environment interactions between common breast cancer susceptibility loci and established environmental risk factors. *PLoS Genetics*, *9*(3). doi:10.1371/journal.pgen.1003284

NIH Osteoporosis and Related Bone Diseases National Resource Center. (2007). *Osteoporosis*. Retrieved from http://www.niams.nih.gov/Health_Info/Bone/Osteoporosis/default.asp

Nilsson, J., Thomas, A. J., O'Brien, J. T., & Gallagher, P. (2014). White matter and cognitive decline in aging: A focus on processing speed and variability. *Journal of the International Neuropsychological Society*, *20*(3), 262–267. doi:10.1017/S1355617713001458

Nisbett, R. E., Aronson, J., Blair, C., Dickens, W., Flynn, J., Halpern, D. F., & Turkheimer, E. (2013). Intelligence: New findings and theoretical developments. *American Psychologist*, *67*(2), 130–159.

Nosek, M., Kennedy, H. P., & Gudmundsdottir, M. (2012). Distress during the menopause transition: A rich contextual analysis of midlife women's narratives. *SAGE Open*, *2*(3). doi:10.1177/2158244012455178

Ohira, T., Hozawa, A., Iribarren, C., Daviglus, M. L., Matthews, K. A., Gross, M. D., & Jacobs, D. R. (2008). Longitudinal association of serum carotenoids and tocopherols with hostility: The CARDIA study. *American Journal of Epidemiology*, *167*(1), 42.

Old, S. R., & Naveh-Benjamin, M. (2008). Differential effects of age on item and associative measures of memory: A meta-analysis. *Psychology and Aging*, *23*(1), 104–118.

Ormerod, T. C. (2005). Planning and ill-defined problems. In R. Morris & G. Ward (Eds.), *The cognitive psychology of planning*. London: Psychology Press.

Owsley, C., McGwin, G., Jackson, G. R., Kallies, K., & Clark, M. (2007). Cone- and rod-mediated dark adaptation impairment in age-related maculopathy. *Ophthalmology*, *114*(9), 1728–1735.

Panay, N., Hamoda, H., Arya, R., & Savvas, M. (2013). The 2013 British Menopause Society & Women's Health Concern recommendations on hormone replacement therapy. *Menopause International*, *19*(2), 59–68. doi:10.1177/1754045313489645

Paramei, G. V, & Oakley, B. (2014). Variation of color discrimination across the life span. *Journal of the Optical Society of America. A, Optics, Image Science, and Vision*, *31*(4), A375–A384. doi:10.1364/JOSAA.31.00A375

Perlmutter, M., Kaplan, M., & Nyquest, L. (1990). Development of adaptive competence in adulthood. *Human Development*, *33*, 185–197.

Physical Activities Council. (2015). *2015 participation report*. Retrieved from http://www.physicalactivitycouncil.com/PDFs/current.pdf

Pontius, A. T., & Smith, P. W. (2011). An antiaging and regenerative medicine approach to optimal skin health. *Facial Plastic Surgery*, *27*(1), 29–34.

Purath, J., Miller, A. M., McCabe, G., & Wilbur, J. (2004). A brief intervention to increase physical activity in sedentary working women. *The Canadian Journal of Nursing Research*, *36*(1), 76–91.

Quan, T., & Fisher, G. J. (2015). Role of age-associated alterations of the dermal extracellular matrix microenvironment in human skin aging: A mini-review. *Gerontology*, *61*, 427–434. doi:10.1159/000371708

Quaranta, N., Coppola, F., Casulli, M., Barulli, M. R., Panza, F., Tortelli, R., . . . Logroscino, G. (2015). Epidemiology of age related hearing loss: A review. *Hearing, Balance and Communication*, *13*(2), 1–5. doi:10.3109/21695717.2014.994869

Radvansky, G. A., Zacks, R. T., & Hasher, L. (2005). Age and inhibition: The retrieval of situation models. *The Journals of Gerontology: Series B: Psychological Sciences & Social Sciences*, *60B*(5), P276–P278.

Reagan, L. P., Grillo, C. A., & Piroli, G. G. (2008). The As and Ds of stress: Metabolic, morphological and behavioral consequences. *European Journal of Pharmacology*, *585*(1), 64–75. doi:10.1016/j.ejphar.2008.02.050

Reed, A. E., & Carstensen, L. L. (2012). The theory behind the age-related positivity effect. *Frontiers in Psychology*, *3*, 339. doi:10.3389/fpsyg.2012.00339

Reed, A. E., Chan, L., & Mikels, J. A. (2014). Meta-analysis of the age-related positivity effect: Age differences in preferences for positive over negative information. *Psychology and Aging*, *29*(1), 1–15. doi:10.1037/a0035194

Roring, R. W., & Charness, N. (2007). A multilevel model analysis of expertise in chess across the life span. *Psychology and Aging*, *22*(2), 291–299.

Rosano, G. M. C., Vitale, C., Marazzi, G., & Volterrani, M. (2007). Menopause and cardiovascular disease: The evidence. *Climacteric*, *10*, 19–24.

Rossi, A. S. (2004). The menopausal transition and aging processes. In O. G. Brim, C. D. Ryff, & R. C. Kessler (Eds.), *How healthy are we?: A national study of well-being at midlife* (pp. 153–201). Chicago: University of Chicago Press.

Rossouw, J. E., Prentice, R. L., Manson, J. E., Wu, L., David Barad, M. D., Barnabei, V. M., . . . Stefanick, M. L. (2007). Postmenopausal hormone therapy and risk of cardiovascular disease by age and years since menopause. *JAMA*, *297*, 1465–1477.

Rowe, G., Hasher, L., & Turcotte, J. (2010). Interference, aging, and visuospatial working memory: The role of similarity. *Neuropsychology*, *24*(6), 804–807. doi:10.1037/a0020244

Rozas, A. X. P., Juncos-Rabadán, O., & González, M. S. R. (2008). Processing speed, inhibitory control, and working memory: Three important factors to account for age-related cognitive decline. *International Journal of Aging and Human Development*, *66*(2), 115–130.

Salthouse, T. A. (1984). Effects of age and skill in typing. *Journal of Experimental Psychology: General*, *113*, 345–371.

Salthouse, T. A. (1993). Speed mediation of adult age differences in cognition. *Developmental Psychology*, *29*(4), 722–738.

Salthouse, T. A. (1996). Constraints on theories of cognitive aging. *Psychonomic Bulletin & Review*, *3*(3), 287–299.

Salthouse, T. A. (2000). Aging and measures of processing speed. *Biological Psychology*, *54*(1–3), 35–54. http://doi.org/10.1016/S0301-0511(00)00052-1

Salthouse, T. A. (2012). Consequences of age-related cognitive declines. *Annual Review of Psychology*, *63*, 201–226. doi:10.1146/annurev-psych-120710-100328

Salthouse, T. A. (2014). Why are there different age relations in cross-sectional and longitudinal comparisons of cognitive functioning? *Current Directions in Psychological Science*, *23*(4), 252–256. doi:10.1177/0963721414535212

Salthouse, T. A., & Madden, D. J. (2013). Information processing speed and aging. In J. DeLuca & J. H. Kalmar (Eds.), *Information processing speed in clinical populations* (pp. 221–239). New York: Psychology Press.

Salthouse, T. A., & Pink, J. E. (2008). Why is working memory related to fluid intelligence? *Psychonomic Bulletin & Review*, *15*(2), 364–371. Retrieved from http://www.pubmedcentral.nih.gov/articlerender.fcgi?artid=2485208&tool=pmcentrez&rendertype=abstract

Samanez-Larkin, G. R., Robertson, E. R., Mikels, J. A., Carstensen, L. L., & Gotlib, I. H. (2009). Selective attention to emotion in the aging brain. *Psychology and Aging*, *24*(3), 519–529. doi:10.1037/a0016952

Sampselle, C. M., Harris, V., Harlow, S. D., & Sowers, M. (2002). Midlife development and menopause in African American and Caucasian women. *Health Care for Women International*, *23*(4), 351–363. Sander, L. (2008). Blue-collar boomers take work ethic to college [Cover story]. *Chronicle of Higher Education*, *54*(19), A1–A22.

Sandvik, A. M., Bartone, P. T., Hystad, S. W., Phillips, T. M., Thayer, J. F., & Johnsen, B. H. (2013). Psychological hardiness predicts neuroimmunological responses to stress. *Psychology, Health & Medicine*, *18*(6), 705–713. doi:10.1080/13548506.2013.772304

Saraç, F., Öztekin, K., & Çelebi, G. (2011). Early menopause association with employment, smoking, divorced marital status and low leptin levels. *Gynecological Endocrinology*, *27*(4), 273–278. doi:10.3109/09513590.2010.491165

Sarwer, D. B., & Crerand, C. E. (2004). Body image and cosmetic medical treatments. *Body Image*, *1*(1), 99–111. doi:10.1016/S1740-1445(03)00003-2

Saucier, M. G. (2004). Midlife and beyond: Issues for aging women. *Journal of Counseling & Development*, 82(4), 420–425. doi:10.1002/j.1556-6678.2004.tb00329.x

Schaie, K. W. (1993). The Seattle Longitudinal Studies of Adult Intelligence. *Current Directions in Psychological Science*, 2(6), 171–175.

Schaie, K. W. (2005). *Developmental influences on adult intelligence: The Seattle Longitudinal Study* (p. 127). New York: Oxford University Press. Retrieved from http://www.ncbi.nlm.nih.gov/pmc/articles/PMC1350981

Schaie, K. W. (2013). *Developmental influences on adult intelligence: The Seattle Longitudinal Study*. New York: Oxford University Press.

Schaie, K. W., & Zanjani, F. A. K. (2006). Intellectual development across adulthood. In C. Hoare (Ed.), *Handbook of adult development and learning* (pp. 99–122). New York: Oxford University Press.

Schwartz, B. L., & Frazier, L. D. (2005). Tip-of-the-tongue states and aging: Contrasting psycholinguistic and metacognitive perspectives. *Journal of General Psychology*, 132(4), 377–391.

Scilley, K., Jackson, G. R., Cideciyan, A. V, Maguire, M. G., Jacobson, S. G., & Owsley, C. (2002). Early age-related maculopathy and self-reported visual difficulty in daily life. *Ophthalmology*, 109(7), 1235.

Segerstrom, S. C., & O'Connor, D. B. (2012). Stress, health and illness: Four challenges for the future. *Psychology & Health*, 27(2), 128–140. doi:10.1080/08870446.2012.659516

Seidman, S. N., & Weiser, M. (2013). Testosterone and mood in aging men. *The Psychiatric Clinics of North America*, 36(1), 177–182. doi:10.1016/j.psc.2013.01.007

Sharp, G., Tiggemann, M., & Mattiske, J. (2014). The role of media and peer influences in Australian women's attitudes towards cosmetic surgery. *Body Image*, 11(4), 482–487. doi:10.1016/j.bodyim.2014.07.009

Sharpe, K. H., McClements, P., Clark, D. I., Collins, J., Springbett, A., & Brewster, D. H. (2010). Reduced risk of oestrogen receptor positive breast cancer among peri- and post-menopausal women in Scotland following a striking decrease in use of hormone replacement therapy. *European Journal of Cancer*, 46(5), 937–943. doi:10.1016/j.ejca.2010.01.003

Shores, M. M. (2014). The implications of low testosterone on mortality in men. *Current Sexual Health Reports*, 6(4), 235–243. doi:10.1007/s11930-014-0030-x

Siegel, R., Ma, J., Zou, Z., & Jemal, A. (2014). Cancer statistics, 2014. *CA: A Cancer Journal for Clinicians*, 64(1), 9–29. doi:10.3322/caac.21208

Simon, C. (2008). Testosterone deficiency—The male menopause? *InnovAiT*, 1(9), 625–630. doi:10.1093/innovait/inn103

Simon, J. A. (2011). Identifying and treating sexual dysfunction in postmenopausal women: The role of estrogen. *Journal of Women's Health*, 20(10), 1453–1465. doi:10.1089/jwh.2010.2151

Simpson, S. J., & Raubenheimer, D. (2007). Caloric restriction and aging revisited: The need for a geometric analysis of the nutritional bases of aging. *The Journals of Gerontology: Series A: Biological Sciences & Medical Sciences*, 62A(7), 707–713.

Singer, T., Verhaeghen, P., Ghisletta, P., Lindenberger, U., & Baltes, P. B. (2003). The fate of cognition in very old age: Six-year longitudinal findings in the Berlin Aging Study (BASE). *Psychology and Aging*, 18(2), 318–331.

Slevec, J., & Tiggemann, M. (2010). Attitudes toward cosmetic surgery in middle-aged women: Body image, aging anxiety, and the media. *Psychology of Women Quarterly*, 34(1), 65–74. doi:10.1111/j.1471-6402.2009.01542.x

Stephens, P. J., Tarpey, P. S., Davies, H., Van Loo, P., Greenman, C., Wedge, D. C., . . . Stratton, M. R. (2012). The landscape of cancer genes and mutational processes in breast cancer. *Nature*, 486(7403), 400–404. doi:10.1038/nature11017

Stevenson, J. C., Hodis, H. N., Pickar, J. H., & Lobo, R. A. (2009). Coronary heart disease and menopause management: The swinging pendulum of HRT. *Atherosclerosis*, 207(2), 336–340. doi:10.1016/j.atherosclerosis.2009.05.033

Stojanovich, L., & Marisavljevich, D. (2008). Stress as a trigger of autoimmune disease. *Autoimmunity Reviews*, 7(3), 209–213. doi:10.1016/j.autrev.2007.11.007

Strauss, J. R. (2011). Contextual influences on women's health concerns and attitudes toward menopause. *Health & Social Work*, 36(2), 121–127. doi:10.1093/hsw/36.2.121

Strenk, S. A., Strenk, L. M., & Koretz, J. F. (2005). The mechanism of presbyopia. *Progress in Retinal & Eye Research*, 24(3), 379–393. doi:10.1016/j.preteyeres.2004.11.001

Sweet, S., & Moen, P. (2007). Integrating educational careers in work and family: Women's return to school and family life quality. *Community, Work & Family*, 10(2), 231–250.

Sylvain-Roy, S., Lungu, O., & Belleville, S. (2014). Normal aging of the attentional control functions that underlie working memory. *The Journals of Gerontology: Series B: Psychological Sciences and Social Sciences*, 70(5), 698–708. doi:10.1093/geronb/gbt166

Taniguchi, H., & Kaufman, G. (2005). Degree completion among nontraditional college students. *Social Science Quarterly*, 86(4), 912–927. doi:10.1111/j.0038-4941.2005.00363.x

Thornton, W. J. L., & Dumke, H. A. (2005). Age differences in everyday problem-solving and decision-making effectiveness: A meta-analytic review. *Psychology and Aging*, 20(1), 85–99.

Torpy, J. M. (2007). Women's sexual concerns after menopause. *JAMA*, 297(6), 664.

Tranter, L. J., & Koutstaal, W. (2008). Age and flexible thinking: An experimental demonstration of the beneficial effects of increased cognitively stimulating activity on fluid intelligence in healthy older adults. *Aging, Neuropsychology & Cognition*, 15(2), 184–207. doi:10.1080/13825580701322163

Tremblay, K., & Ross, B. (2007). Auditory rehabilitation and the aging brain. *ASHA Leader*, 12(16), 12–13.

Truscott, R. J. (2009). Presbyopia. Emerging from a blur towards an understanding of the molecular basis for this most common eye condition. *Experimental Eye Research*, 88(2), 241–247. doi:10.1016/j.exer.2008.07.003

Unsworth, N., Fukuda, K., Awh, E., & Vogel, E. K. (2014). Working memory and fluid intelligence: Capacity, attention control, and secondary memory retrieval. *Cognitive Psychology*, 71, 1–26. doi:10.1016/j.cogpsych.2014.01.003

Vainionpää, K., & Topo, P. (2006). The construction of male menopause in Finnish popular magazines. *Critical Public Health*, 16(1), 19–34.

Van Reekum, C. M., Schaefer, S. M., Lapate, R. C., Norris, C. J., Greischar, L. L., & Davidson, R. J. (2011). Aging is associated with positive responding to neutral information but reduced recovery from negative information. *Social Cognitive and Affective Neuroscience*, 6(2), 177–185. doi:10.1093/scan/nsq031

Vestergren, P., & Nilsson, L.-G. (2011). Perceived causes of everyday memory problems in a population-based sample aged 39-99. *Applied Cognitive Psychology*, 25(4), 641–646. doi:10.1002/acp.1734

Vogelstein, B., & Kinzler, K. W. (2004). Cancer genes and the pathways they control. *Nature Medicine*, 10(8), 789–799.

Vogt, D. S., Rizvi, S. L., & Shipherd, J. C. (2008). Longitudinal investigation of reciprocal relationship between stress reactions and hardiness. *Personality and Social Psychology Bulletin*, 34(1), 61–73.

Vona-Davis, L., & Rose, D. P. (2009). The influence of socioeconomic disparities on breast cancer tumor biology and prognosis: A review. *Journal of Women's Health*, 18(6), 883–893. doi:10.1089/jwh.2008.1127

Vondracek, S. F. (2010). Managing osteoporosis in postmenopausal women. *American Journal of Health-System Pharmacy*, 67, S9–S19. doi:10.2146/ajhp100076

Walker, J. (2008). Osteoporosis: Pathogenesis, diagnosis and management. *Nursing Standard*, 22(17), 48–56.

Walsh, K. E., & Berman, J. R. (2004). Sexual dysfunction in the older woman. *Drugs & Aging*, 21(10), 655–675.

Wang, S., & Young, K. M. (2014). White matter plasticity in adulthood. *Neuroscience*, 276, 148–160. doi:10.1016/j.neuroscience.2013.10.018

Waring, M. E., Eaton, C. B., Lasater, T. M., & Lapane, K. L. (2010). Correlates of weight patterns during middle age characterized by functional principal components analysis. *Annals of Epidemiology*, 20(3), 201–209. doi:10.1016/j.annepidem.2009.11.013

Whitbourne, S. K. (2007). *Adult development and aging: Biopsychosocial perspectives*. Hoboken, NJ: John Wiley.

Williams, R. L. (2013). Overview of the Flynn effect. *Intelligence*, 41(6), 753–764. doi:10.1016/j.intell.2013.04.010

Wingfield, A., Tun, P. A., & McCoy, S. L. (2005). Hearing loss in older adulthood. *Current Directions in Psychological Science*, 14(3), 144–148. doi:10.1111/j.0963-7214.2005.00356.x

World Health Organization. (2015). World health statistics 2015. Retrieved from http://www.who.int/gho/publications/world_health_statistics/2015/en

Wright, N. C., Looker, A. C., Saag, K. G., Curtis, J. R., Delzell, E. S., Randall, S., & Dawson-Hughes, B. (2014). The recent prevalence of osteoporosis and low bone mass in the United States based on bone mineral density at the femoral neck or lumbar spine. *Journal of Bone and Mineral Research*, 29(11), 2520–2526. doi:10.1002/jbmr.2269

CHAPTER 16

AARP. (2002). *The grandparent study: 2002 report.* Washington, DC: Author.

Ackerman, S., Zuroff, D. C., & Moskowitz, D. S. (2000). Generativity in midlife and young adults: Links to agency, communion, and subjective well-being. *International Journal of Aging and Human Development*, 50(1), 17–41. Retrieved from 10.2190/9F51-LR6T-JHRJ-2QW6

Adams, G. A., & Rau, B. L. (2011). Putting off tomorrow to do what you want today: Planning for retirement. *American Psychologist*, 66(3), 180–192. doi:10.1037/a0022131

Adams, R. G., & Ueno, K. (2006). Middle-aged and older adult men's friendships. In V. H. Bedford & B. Formaniak Turner (Eds.), *Men in relationships: A new look from a life course perspective* (pp. 103–124). New York: Springer.

Aldwin, C. M. (2007). *Stress, coping, and development: An integrative perspective* (2nd ed.). New York: Guilford Press.

Amato, P. R. (2010). Research on divorce: Continuing trends and new developments. *Journal of Marriage and Family*, 72(3), 650–666. doi:10.1111/j.1741-3737.2010.00723.x

An, J. S., & Cooney, T. M. (2006). Psychological well-being in mid to late life: The role of generativity development and parent–child relationships across the lifespan. *International Journal of Behavioral Development*, 30(5), 410–421.

Antonucci, T. C., Lansford, J. E., Akiyama, H., Smith, J., Baltes, M. M., Takahashi, K., . . . Dartigues, J. (2002). Differences between men and women in social relations, resource deficits, and depressive symptomatology during later life in four nations. *Journal of Social Issues*, 58(4), 767–783.

Attar-Schwartz, S., Tan, J.-P., Buchanan, A., Flouri, E., & Griggs, J. (2009). Grandparenting and adolescent adjustment in two-parent biological, lone-parent, and step-families. *Journal of Family Psychology*, 23(1), 67–75. doi:10.1037/a0014383

Avolio, B. J., & Sosik, J. J. (1999). A life-span framework for assessing the impact of work on white-collar workers. In S. L. Willis & J. D. Reid (Eds.), *Life in the middle: Psychological and social development in middle age* (pp. 249–274). San Diego: Academic Press.

Bachman, H. J., & Chase-Lansdale, P. L. (2005). Custodial grandmothers' physical, mental, and economic well-being: Comparisons of primary caregivers from low-income neighborhoods. *Family Relations*, 54(4), 475–487.

Barnes, J., Gardiner, J., Sutcliffe, A., & Melhuish, E. (2013). The parenting of preschool children by older mothers in the United Kingdom. *European Journal of Developmental Psychology*, 11(4), 397–419. doi:10.1080/17405629.2013.863728

Barnes-Farrell, J. L., & Matthews, R. A. (2007). Age and work attitudes. In K. S. Shultz & G. A. Adams (Eds.), *Aging and work in the 21st century* (pp. 139–162). Mahwah, NJ: Lawrence Erlbaum.

Barrett, A. E. (2003). Socioeconomic status and age identity: The role of dimensions of health in the subjective construction of age. *The Journals of Gerontology: Series B: Psychological Sciences & Social Sciences*, 58B(2), S101.

Barrett, A. E. (2005). Gendered experiences in midlife: Implications for age identity. *Journal of Aging Studies*, 19(2), 163–183.

Barrett, A. E., & Montepare, J. M. (2015). "It's about time": Applying life span and life course perspectives to the study of subjective age. *Annual Review of Gerontology and Geriatrics*, 35(1), 55–77. doi:10.1891/0198-8794.35.55

Basatemur, E., & Sutcliffe, A. (2008). Follow-up of children born after ART. *Placenta*, 29(Suppl. B), 135–140. doi:10.1016/j.placenta.2008.08.013

Baum, N., Rahav, G., & Sharon, D. (2005). Changes in the self-concepts of divorced women. *Journal of Divorce & Remarriage*, 43(1), 47–67.

Beaumont, S. L., & Pratt, M. M. (2011). Identity processing styles and psychosocial balance during early and middle adulthood: The role of identity in intimacy and generativity. *Journal of Adult Development*, 18(4), 172–183. doi:10.1007/s10804-011-9125-z

Belsky, J., Jaffee, S., Hsieh, K.-H., & Silva, P. A. (2001). Child-rearing antecedents of intergenerational relations in young adulthood: A prospective study. *Developmental Psychology*, 37(6), 801–813.

Bem, S. L. (1985). Androgyny and gender schema theory: A conceptual and empirical integration. In T. B. Sondregger (Ed.), *Nebraska Symposium on Motivation, 1984: Psychology and gender* (pp. 76–103). Lincoln: University of Nebraska Press.

Beutel, M. E., Glaesmer, H., Wiltink, J., Marian, H., & Brähler, E. (2010). *Life satisfaction, anxiety, depression and resilience across the life span of men.* Retrieved from http://informahealthcare.com/doi/abs/10.3109/13685530903296698

Billing, A., Ehrle, J., & Kortenkamp, K. (2002). *Children cared for by relatives: What do we know about their well-being?* Washington, DC: The Urban Institute.

Birditt, K. S., Antonucci, T. C., & Tighe, L. (2012). Enacted support during stressful life events in middle and older adulthood: An examination of the interpersonal context. *Psychology and Aging*, 27(3), 728–741. doi:10.1037/a0026967

Birditt, K. S., Miller, L. M., Fingerman, K. L., & Lefkowitz, E. S. (2009). Tensions in the parent and adult child relationship: Links to solidarity and ambivalence. *Psychology and Aging*, 24(2), 287–295. doi:10.1037/a0015196

Björkenstam, E., Hallqvist, J., Dalman, C., & Ljung, R. (2013). Risk of new psychiatric episodes in the year following divorce in midlife: Cause or selection? A nationwide register-based study of 703,960 individuals. *International Journal of Social Psychiatry*, 59(8), 801–804. doi:10.1177/0020764012461213

Blanchflower, D. G., & Oswald, A. J. (2008). Is well-being U-shaped over the life cycle? *Social Science & Medicine*, 66(8), 1733–1749. Retrieved from 10.1016/j.socscimed.2008.01.030

Bloch, L., Haase, C. M., & Levenson, R. W. (2014). Emotion regulation predicts marital satisfaction: More than a wives' tale. *Emotion*, 14(1), 130–144. doi:10.1037/a0034272

Bolin, K., Lindgren, B., & Lundborg, P. (2008). Your next of kin or your own career?: Caring and working among the 50+ of Europe. *Journal of Health Economics*, 27(3), 718–738. doi:10.1016/j.jhealeco.2007.10.004

Bouchard, T. J., Jr., & McGue, M. (2004). Genetic influence on human psychological traits. *Current Directions in Psychological Science*, 13(4), 148–151. doi:10.1111/j.0963-7214.2004.00295.x

Bradbury, T. N., Fincham, F. D., & Beach, S. R. H. (2000). Research on the nature and determinants of marital satisfaction: A decade in review. *Journal of Marriage and Family*, 62(4), 964–980.

Breheny, M., Stephens, C., & Spilsbury, L. (2014). Involvement without interference: How grandparents negotiate intergenerational expectations in relationships with grandchildren. *Journal of Family Studies*, 19(2), 174–184. doi:10.5172/jfs.2013.19.2.174

Brim, O. G., Ryff, C. D., & Kessler, R. C. (2004). *How healthy are we?: A national study of well-being at midlife. The John D. and Catherine T. MacArthur foundation series on mental health and development. Studies on successful midlife development.* Chicago: University of Chicago Press.

Burr, J. A., & Mutchler, J. E. (1999). Race and ethnic variation in norms of filial responsibility among older persons. *Journal of Marriage and Family*, 61(3), 674–687. doi:10.2307/353569

Bybee, J. A., & Wells, Y. V. (2003). The development of possible selves during adulthood. In J. Demick & C. Andreoletti (Eds.), *Handbook of adult development* (pp. 257–270). New York: Kluwer Academic/Plenum Publishers.

Carlo, G., Koller, S., Raffaelli, M., & De Guzman, M. R. T. (2007). Culture-related strengths among Latin American families: A case study of Brazil. *Marriage & Family Review*, 42(3), 335–360.

Chappell, N., Gee, E., McDonald, L., & Stones, M. (2003). *Aging in contemporary Canada*. Toronto: Pearson Education Canada.

Chen, F., Mair, C. A., Bao, L., & Yang, Y. C. (2014). Race/ethnic dfferentials in the health consequences of caring for grandchildren for grandparents. *The Journals of Gerontology: Series B: Psychological Sciences and Social Sciences*. Advance online publication. doi:10.1093/geronb/gbu160

Cherlin, A. J. (2013). Health, marriage, and same-sex partnerships. *Journal of Health and Social Behavior*, 54(1), 64–66. doi:10.1177/0022146512474430

Chida, Y., & Steptoe, A. (2010). Greater cardiovascular responses to laboratory mental stress are associated with poor subsequent cardiovascular risk status: A meta-analysis of prospective evidence. *Hypertension*, 55(4), 1026–1032. doi:10.1161/HYPERTENSIONAHA.109.146621

Christensen, S. A., & Miller, R. B. (2006). Areas of desired change among married midlife individuals. *Journal of Couple & Relationship Therapy*, 5(3), 35–57.

Chrouser Ahrens, C. J., & Ryff, C. D. (2006). Multiple roles and well-being: Sociodemographic and psychological moderators. *Sex Roles*, 55(11–12), 801–815.

Cichy, K. E., Lefkowitz, E. S., Davis, E. M., & Fingerman, K. L. (2013). "You are such a disappointment!": Negative emotions and parents' perceptions of adult children's lack of success. *The Journals of Gerontology: Series B: Psychological Sciences and Social Sciences*, 68(6), 893–901. doi:10.1093/geronb/gbt053

Coall, D. A., & Hertwig, R. (2011). Grandparental investment: A relic of the past or a resource for the future? *Current Directions in Psychological Science*, 20(2), 93–98. doi:10.1177/0963721411403269

Connidis, I. A. (2001). *Family ties and aging*. Thousand Oaks, CA: Sage.

Costa, P. T. J., McCrae, R. R., Zonderman, A. B., Barbano, H. E., Lebowitz, B., & Larson, D. M. (1986). Cross-sectional studies of personality in a national sample: II. Stability in neuroticism, extraversion, and openness. *Psychology and Aging*, 1(2), 144–149.

Cox, K. S., Wilt, J., Olson, B., & McAdams, D. P. (2010). Generativity, the big five, and psychosocial adaptation in midlife adults. *Journal of Personality*, 78(4), 1185–1208. doi:10.1111/j.1467-6494.2010.00647.x

Cross, S., & Markus, H. (1991). Possible selves across the life span. *Human Development*, 34(4), 230–255.

Dare, J., & Green, L. (2011). Rethinking social support in women's midlife years: Women's experiences of social support in online environments. *European Journal of Cultural Studies*, 14(5), 473–490. doi:10.1177/1367549411412203

Dare, J. S. (2011). Transitions in midlife women's lives: Contemporary experiences. *Health Care for Women International*, 32(2), 111–133. doi:10.1080/07399332.2010.500753

De Quadros-Wander, S., McGillivray, J., & Broadbent, J. (2013). The influence of perceived control on subjective wellbeing in later life. *Social Indicators Research*, 115(3), 999–1010. doi:10.1007/s11205-013-0243-9

Deary, I. J., Pattie, A., & Starr, J. M. (2013). The stability of intelligence from age 11 to age 90 years. *The Lothian Birth Cohort of 1921*, 1–8. doi:10.1177/0956797613486487

Deligkaris, P., Panagopoulou, E., Montgomery, A. J., & Masoura, E. (2014). *Job burnout and cognitive functioning: A systematic review.* Retrieved from http://www.tandfonline.com/doi/abs/10.1080/02678373.2014.909545

Dennerstein, L., Dudley, E., & Guthrie, J. (2002). Empty nest or revolving door? A prospective study of women's quality of life in midlife during the phase of children leaving and re-entering the home. *Psychological Medicine*, 32(3), 545–550.

Dennis, H., & Thomas, K. (2007). Ageism in the workplace. *Generations*, 31(1), 84–89.

DeVries, H. M., Kerrick, S., & Oetinger, M. (2007). Satisfactions and regrets of midlife parents: A qualitative analysis. *Journal of Adult Development*, 14(1), 6–15.

Dilworth-Anderson, P., Goodwin, P. Y., & Williams, S. W. (2004). Can culture help explain the physical health effects of caregiving over time among African American caregivers? *The Journals of Gerontology: Series B: Psychological Sciences and Social Sciences*, 59B(3), S138–S145.

Dolbin-MacNab, M. L. (2006). Just like raising your own? Grandmothers' perceptions of parenting a second time around. *Family Relations*, 55(5), 564–575.

Dolbin-MacNab, M. L., & Keiley, M. K. (2006). A systemic examination of grandparents' emotional closeness with their custodial grandchildren. *Research in Human Development*, 3(1), 59–71.

Doley, R., Bell, R., Watt, B., & Simpson, H. (2015). Grandparents raising grandchildren: Investigating factors associated with distress among custodial grandparent. *Journal of Family Studies*, 1–19. doi:10.1080/13229400.2015.1015215

Donohue, S. M., & Heywood, J. S. (2013). Job satisfaction and gender: An expanded specification from the NLSY. *International Journal of Manpower*. Advance online publication. Retrieved from http://www.emeraldinsight.com/doi/abs/10.1108/01437720410536007

Edmonds, G. W., Goldberg, L. R., Hampson, S. E., & Barckley, M. (2013). Personality stability from childhood to midlife: Relating teachers' assessments in elementary school to observer- and self-ratings 40 years later. *Journal of Research in Personality*, 47(5), 505–513. doi:10.1016/j.jrp.2013.05.003

Edwards, O. W., & Benson, N. F. (2010). A four-factor social support model to mediate stressors experienced by children raised by grandparents. *Journal of Applied School Psychology*, 26(1), 54–69. doi:10.1080/15377900903368862

Erikson, E. H. (1950). *Childhood and society* (2nd ed.). New York: Norton.

Erikson, E. H. (1959). *Identity and the life cycle*. New York: Norton.

Farkas, J. I., & Hogan, D. P. (1995). The demography of changing intergenerational relationships. In V. L. Bengtson, K. W. Schaie, & L. M. Burton (Eds.), *Adult intergenerational relations: Effects of societal change* (pp. 1–29). New York: Springer.

Fincham, F. D., Beach, S. R. H., & Davila, J. (2007). Longitudinal relations between forgiveness and conflict resolution in marriage. *Journal of Family Psychology*, 21(3), 542–545.

Fingerman, K. L. (2000). 'We had a nice little chat': Age and generational differences in mothers' and daughters'. *The Journals of Gerontology: Series B: Psychological Sciences & Social Sciences*, 55B(2), P95.

Fingerman, K. L. (2001). A distant closeness: Intimacy between parents and their children in later life. *Generations*, 25(2), 26.

Fingerman, K. L., Cheng, Y.-P., Birditt, K., & Zarit, S. (2012). Only as happy as the least happy child: Multiple grown children's problems and successes and middle-aged parents' well-being. *The Journals of Gerontology: Series B: Psychological Sciences and Social Sciences*, 67(2), 184–193. doi:10.1093/geronb/gbr086

Fingerman, K. L., Cheng, Y.-P., Wesselmann, E. D., Zarit, S., Furstenberg, F., & Birditt, K. S. (2012). Helicopter parents and landing pad kids: Intense parental support of grown children. *Journal of Marriage and Family*, 74(4), 880–896. doi:10.1111/j.1741-3737.2012.00987.x

Fingerman, K. L., Hay, E. L., & Birditt, K. S. (2004). The best of ties, the worst of ties: Close, problematic, and ambivalent social relationships. *Journal of Marriage and Family*, 66(3), 792–808.

Frech, A., & Williams, K. (2007). Depression and the psychological benefits of entering marriage. *Journal of Health & Social Behavior*, 48(2), 149–163.

Freund, A. M., & Ritter, J. O. (2009). Midlife crisis: A debate. *Gerontology*, 55(5), 582–591. doi:10.1159/000227322

Friedman, H. S., & Kern, M. L. (2014). Personality, well-being, and health. *Annual Review of Psychology*, 65(1), 719–742. doi:10.1146/annurev-psych-010213-115123

Fry, C. L. (1985). Culture, behavior, and aging in the comparative perspective. In J. E. Birren &

K. W. Schaie (Eds.), *Handbook of the psychology of aging* (2nd ed., pp. 216–244). New York: Van Nostrand Reinhold Co.

Fuller-Thomson, E., & Minkler, M. (2001). American grandparents providing extensive child care to their grandchildren: Prevalence and profile. *The Gerontologist*, 41(2), 201–209. doi:10.1093/geront/41.2.201

Gans, D., & Silverstein, M. (2006). Norms of filial responsibility for aging parents across time and generations. *Journal of Marriage and Family*, 68(4), 961–976.

Gee, G. C., Pavalko, E. K., & Long, J. S. (2007). Age, cohort and perceived age discrimination: Using the life course to assess self-reported age discrimination. *Social Forces*, 86(1), 265–290.

Geurts, T., Van Tilburg, T. G., & Poortman, A.-R. (2012). The grandparent-grandchild relationship in childhood and adulthood: A matter of continuation? *Personal Relationships*, 19(2), 267–278. doi:10.1111/j.1475-6811.2011.01354.x

Gilbert, R., & Constantine, K. (2005). When strength can't last a lifetime: Vocational challenges of male workers in early and middle adulthood. *Men and Masculinities*, 7(4), 424–433. doi:10.1177/1097184X03257582

Goyer, A. (2006). *Intergenerational relationships: Grandparents raising grandchildren*. Washington, DC: AARP.

Graham, E. K., & Lachman, M. E. (2012). Personality stability is associated with better cognitive performance in adulthood: Are the stable more able? *The Journals of Gerontology: Series B: Psychological Sciences and Social Sciences*, 67(5), 545–554. doi:10.1093/geronb/gbr149

Greenfield, E. A., & Marks, N. F. (2006). Linked lives: Adult children's problems and their parents' psychological and relational well-being. *Journal of Marriage and Family*, 68(2), 442–454.

Greenfield, E. A., Marks, N. F., Hay, E. L., Fingerman, K. L., & Lefkowitz, E. S. (2008). The worries adult children and their parents experience for one another. *International Journal of Aging and Human Development*, 67(2), 101–127.

Griggs, J., Tan, J.-P., Buchanan, A., Attar-Schwartz, S., & Flouri, E. (2010). "They've always been there for me": Grandparental involvement and child well-being. *Children & Society*, 24(3), 200–214. doi:10.1111/j.1099-0860.2009.00215.x

Grover, S., & Helliwell, J. F. (2014). *How's life at home? New evidence on marriage and the set point for happiness*. Retrieved from http://www.nber.org/papers/w20794

Grundy, E., & Henretta, J. C. (2006). Between elderly parents and adult children: A new look at the intergenerational care provided by the "sandwich generation." *Ageing & Society*, 26(5), 707–722.

Guzell-Roe, J. R., Gerard, J. M., & Landry-Meyer, L. (2005). Custodial grandparents' perceived control over caregiving outcomes: Raising children the second Time Around. *Journal of Intergenerational Relationships*, 3(2), 43–61. doi: 10.1300/J194v03n02_04

Haberkern, K., & Szydlik, M. (2010). State care provision, societal opinion and children's care of older parents in 11 European countries. *Ageing & Society*, 30(2), 299–323.

Hampson, S. E., & Goldberg, L. R. (2006). A first large cohort study of personality trait stability over the 40 years between elementary school and midlife. *Journal of Personality and Social Psychology*, 91(4), 763–779.

Hartup, W. W., & Stevens, N. (1999). Friendships and adaptation across the life span. *Current Directions in Psychological Science*, 8, 76–79.

Hatch, L. R., & Bulcroft, K. (2004). Does long-term marriage bring less frequent disagreements? Five explanatory frameworks. *Journal of Family Issues*, 25(4), 465–495. doi:10.1177/0192513X03257766

Havighurst, R. J. (1972). *Developmental tasks and education*. New York: McKay Company.

Hefner, V., Woodward, K., Figge, L., Bevan, J. L., Santora, N., & Baloch, S. (2014). The influence of television and film viewing on midlife women's body image, disordered eating, and food choice. *Media Psychology*, 17(2), 185–207. doi:10.1080/15213269.2013.838903

Henderson, C. E., Hayslip, J. B., Sanders, L. M., & Louden, L. (2009). Grandmother–grandchild relationship quality predicts psychological adjustment among youth from divorced families. *Journal of Family Issues*, 30(9), 1245–1264.

Heraty, N., & McCarthy, J. (2015). Unearthing psychological predictors of financial planning for retirement among late career older workers: Do self-perceptions of aging matter? *Work, Aging and Retirement*. Advance online publication. doi:10.1093/workar/wav008

Hershey, D. A., Jacobs-Lawson, J. M., McArdle, J. J., & Hamagami, F. (2007). Psychological foundations of financial planning for retirement. *Journal of Adult Development*, 14(1–2), 26–36. doi:10.1007/s10804-007-9028-1

Hetherington, E. M., & Kelly, J. (2002). *For better or for worse: Divorce reconsidered*. New York: Norton.

Hewitt, B., Baxter, J., & Western, M. (2006). Family, work and health: The impact of marriage, parenthood and employment on self-reported health of Australian men and women. *Journal of Sociology*, 42(1), 61–78.

Hill, P. L., Turiano, N. A., Mroczek, D. K., & Roberts, B. W. (2012). Examining concurrent and longitudinal relations between personality traits and social well-being in adulthood. *Social Psychological and Personality Science*, 3(6), 698–705. doi:10.1177/1948550611433888

Hochwarter, W. A., Ferris, G. R., Perrewé, P. L., Witt, L. A., & Kiewitz, C. (2001). A note on the nonlinearity of the age-job-satisfaction relationship. *Journal of Applied Social Psychology*, 31(6), 1223–1237.

Hogeboom, D. L., McDermott, R. J., Perrin, K. M., Osman, H., & Bell-Ellison, B. A. (2010). Internet use and social networking among middle aged and older adults. *Educational Gerontology*, 36(2), 93–111. doi:10.1080/03601270903058507

Holt-Lunstad, J., Smith, T. B., & Layton, J. B. (2010). Social relationships and mortality risk: A meta-analytic review. *PLoS Medicine*, 7(7). doi:10.1371/journal.pmed.1000316

Hu, X., Kaplan, S., & Dalal, R. S. (2010). An examination of blue- versus white-collar workers' conceptualizations of job satisfaction facets. *Journal of Vocational Behavior*, 76(2), 317–325. doi:10.1016/j.jvb.2009.10.014

Hurme, H., Westerback, S., & Quadrello, T. (2010). Traditional and new forms of contact between grandparents and grandchildren. *Journal of Intergenerational Relationships*, 8(3), 264–280. doi:10.1080/15350770.2010.498739

Hutteman, R., Hennecke, M., Orth, U., Reitz, A. K., & Specht, J. (2014). Developmental tasks as a framework to study personality development in adulthood and old age. *European Journal of Personality*, 28(3), 267–278.

Huxhold, O., Miche, M., & Schüz, B. (2014). Benefits of having friends in older ages: Differential effects of informal social activities on well-being in middle-aged and older adults. *The Journals of Gerontology: Series B: Psychological Sciences and Social Sciences*, 69(3), 366–375. doi:10.1093/geronb/gbt029

Huyck, M. H. (1996). Continuities and discontinuities in gender identity. In V. L. Bengtson (Ed.), *Adulthood and aging: Research on continuities and discontinuities* (pp. 98–121). New York: Springer.

Izard, C. E. (2007). Basic emotions, natural kinds, emotion schemas, and a new paradigm.

Perspectives on Psychological Science, 2(3), 260–280. doi:10.1111/j.1745-6916.2007.00044.x

Jacobs-Lawson, J. M., Hershey, D. A., & Neukam, K. A. (2004). Gender differences in factors that influence time spent planning for retirement. *Journal of Women & Aging, 16*(3–4), 55–69.

James, J. B., & Lewkowicz, C. (1995). Rethinking the gender identity crossover hypothesis: A test of a new model. *Sex Roles, 32*(3), 185–207.

Jang, Y., Chiriboga, D. A., & Small, B. J. (2008). Perceived discrimination and psychological well-being: The mediating and moderating role of sense of control. *International Journal of Aging and Human Development, 66*(3), 213–227.

Johnson, C. L. (1998). Effects of adult children's divorce on grandparenthood. In M. E. Szinovacz (Ed.), *Handbook on grandparenthood* (pp. 184–199). Westport, CT: Greenwood Press.

Jones, C. J., Peskin, H., & Livson, N. (2011). Men's and women's change and individual differences in change in femininity from age 33 to 85: Results from the intergenerational studies. *Journal of Adult Development, 18*(4), 155–163. doi:10.1007/s10804-010-9108-5

Kaiser, L. C. (2007). Gender-job satisfaction differences across Europe. *International Journal of Manpower, 28*(1), 75–94. doi:10.1108/01437720710733483

Kamo, Y. (1998). Asian grandparents. In M. E. Szinovacz (Ed.), *Handbook on grandparenthood* (pp. 97–112). Westport, CT: Greenwood Press.

Kandler, C., Bleidorn, W., Riemann, R., Spinath, F. M., Thiel, W., & Angleitner, A. (2010). Sources of cumulative continuity in personality: A longitudinal multiple-rater twin study. *Journal of Personality and Social Psychology, 98*(6), 995–1008. doi:10.1037/a0019558

Karraker, A., & Latham, K. (2015). In sickness and in health? Physical illness as a risk factor for marital dissolution in later life. *Journal of Health and Social Behavior, 56*(1), 59–73. doi:10.1177/0022146514568351

Kenyon, D. B., & Koerner, S. S. (2009). Examining emerging-adults' and parents' expectations about autonomy during the transition to college. *Journal of Adolescent Research, 24*(3), 293–320.

Keyes, C. L. M., & Westerhof, G. J. (2012). Chronological and subjective age differences in flourishing mental health and major depressive episode. *Aging & Mental Health, 16*(1), 67–74. doi:10.1080/13607863.2011.596811

Kiecolt-Glaser, J. K., & Newton, T. L. (2001). Marriage and health: His and hers. *Psychological Bulletin, 127*(4), 472–503.

Killian, T., Turner, J., & Cain, R. (2005). Depressive symptoms of caregiving women in midlife: The role of physical health. *Journal of Women & Aging, 17*(1–2), 115–127. doi:10.1300/J074v17n01_09

Kim, J. E., & Moen, P. (2001). Is retirement good or bad for subjective well-being? *Current Directions in Psychological Science, 10*(3), 83–86. doi:10.1111/1467-8721.00121

Kim, J. E., & Moen, P. (2002). Retirement transitions, gender, and psychological well-being: A life-course, ecological model. *The Journals of Gerontology: Series B: Psychological Sciences and Social Sciences,* (3), 212–222.

Knodel, J., & Chayovan, N. (2009). Intergenerational relationships and family care and support for Thai elderly. *Ageing International, 33*(1–4), 15–27. doi:10.1007/s12126-009-9026-7

Kogan, L. R., & Vacha-Haase, T. (2002). Supporting adaptation to new family roles in middle age. In C. L. Juntunen & D. R. Atkinson (Eds.), *Counseling across the lifespan: Prevention and treatment* (pp. 299–327). Thousand Oaks, CA: Sage.

Korczyk, S. (2008). *Who's ready for retirement, how ready, and how can we know?* Washington, DC: AARP.

Kotre, J. N. (1999). *Make it count: How to generate a legacy that gives meaning to your life.* New York: Free Press.

Krause, N. (2010). Close companion friends, self-expression, and psychological well-being in late life. *Social Indicators Research, 95*(2), 199–213. doi:10.1007/s11205-008-9358-9

Kreider, R. M., & Ellis, R. (2011). *Number, timing, and duration of marriages and divorces: 2009. Current population reports.* Retrieved from https://www.census.gov/prod/2011pubs/p70-125.pdf

Kross, E., Gard, D., Deldin, P., Clifton, J., & Ayduk, O. (2012). "Asking why" from a distance: Its cognitive and emotional consequences for people with major depressive disorder. *Journal of Abnormal Psychology, 121*(3), 559–569. doi:10.1037/a0028808

Labouvie-Vief, G. (2003). Dynamic integration: Affect, cognition, and the self in adulthood. *Current Directions in Psychological Science, 12*(6), 201–206.

Lachman, M. E., & Bertrand, R. M. (2001). Personality and the self in midlife. In M. E. Lachman (Ed.), *Handbook of midlife development* (pp. 279–309). Hoboken, NJ: John Wiley.

Lachman, M. E., Teshale, S., & Agrigoroaei, S. (2015). Midlife as a pivotal period in the life course: Balancing growth and decline at the crossroads of youth and old age. *International Journal of Behavioral Development, 39*(1), 20–31. doi:10.1177/0165025414533223

Lang, F. R., & Carstensen, L. L. (1994). Close emotional relationships in late life: Further support for proactive aging in the social domain. *Psychology and Aging, 9*(2), 315–324.

Lavelle, B., & Smock, P. J. (2012). Divorce and women's risk of health insurance loss. *Journal of Health and Social Behavior, 53*(4), 413–431. doi:10.1177/0022146512465758

Lawrence, E., Rothman, A. D., Cobb, R. J., Rothman, M. T., & Bradbury, T. N. (2008). Marital satisfaction across the transition to parenthood. *Journal of Family Psychology, 22*(1), 41–50.

Lefkowitz, E. S., & Fingerman, K. L. (2003). Positive and negative emotional feelings and behaviors in mother-daughter ties in late life. *Journal of Family Psychology, 17*(4), 607–617.

Lefkowitz, E. S., & Zeldow, P. B. (2006). Masculinity and femininity predict optimal mental health: A belated test of the androgyny hypothesis. *Journal of Personality Assessment, 87*(1), 95–101.

Leopold, T., & Skopek, J. (2015). The demography of grandparenthood: An international profile. *Social Forces.* Advance online publication. doi:10.1093/sf/sov066

Letiecq, B. L., Bailey, S. J., & Kurtz, M. A. (2008). Depression among rural native American and European American grandparents rearing their grandchildren. *Journal of Family Issues, 29*(3), 334–356.

Levinson, D. J. (1978). *The seasons of a man's life.* New York: Knopf.

Levinson, D. J. (1996). *The seasons of a woman's life.* New York: Knopf.

Lewis, D. C., Medvedev, K., & Seponski, D. M. (2011). Awakening to the desires of older women: Deconstructing ageism within fashion magazines. *Journal of Aging Studies, 25*(2), 101–109. doi:10.1016/j.jaging.2010.08.016

Lilgendahl, J. P., Helson, R., & John, O. P. (2013). Does ego development increase during midlife? The effects of openness and accommodative processing of difficult events. *Journal of Personality, 81*(4), 403–416. doi:10.1111/jopy.12009

Lilgendahl, J. P., & McAdams, D. P. (2011). Constructing stories of self-growth: How individual differences in patterns of autobiographical

reasoning relate to well-being in midlife. *Journal of Personality, 79*(2), 391–428. doi:10.1111/j.1467-6494.2010.00688.x

Linz, S., & Semykina, A. (2013). Job satisfaction, expectations, and gender: beyond the European Union. *International Journal of Manpower, 34*(6), 584–615. doi:10.1108/IJM-06-2013-0149

Lodi-Smith, J., & Roberts, B. W. (2010). Getting to know me: Social role experiences and age differences in self-concept clarity during adulthood. *Journal of Personality, 78*(5), 1383–1410. doi:10.1111/j.1467-6494.2010.00655.x

López Ulloa, B. F., Møller, V., & Sousa-Poza, A. (2013). How does subjective well-being evolve with age? A literature review. *Journal of Population Ageing, 6*(3), 227–246. doi:10.1007/s12062-013-9085-0

Lorenz, F. O., Wickrama, K. A. S., Conger, R. D., & Elder, G. H. J. (2006). The short-term and decade-long effects of divorce on women's midlife health. *Journal of Health and Social Behavior, 47*(2), 111–125.

Lucas, R. E., & Donnellan, M. B. (2011). Personality development across the life span: Longitudinal analyses with a national sample from Germany. *Journal of Personality and Social Psychology, 101*(4), 847–861. doi:10.1037/a0024298

Lucas, R. E., & Dyrenforth, P. S. (2005). The myth of marital bliss? *Psychological Inquiry, 16*(2), 111–115.

Luhmann, M., Hofmann, W., Eid, M., & Lucas, R. E. (2012). Subjective well-being and adaptation to life events: A meta-analysis. *Journal of Personality and Social Psychology, 102*(3), 592–615. doi:10.1037/a0025948

Mac Dougall, K., Beyene, Y., & Nachtigall, R. D. (2012). "Inconvenient biology:" advantages and disadvantages of first-time parenting after age 40 using in vitro fertilization. *Human Reproduction, 27*(4), 1058–1065. doi:10.1093/humrep/des007

Mancini, A. D., Bonanno, G. A., & Clark, A. E. (2011). Stepping off the hedonic treadmill. *Journal of Individual Differences, 32*(3), 144–152. doi:10.1027/1614-0001/a000047

Marks, N. F., Bumpass, L. L., & Jun, H. (2004). Family roles and well-being during the middle life course. In O. G. Brim, C. D. Ryff, & R. C. Kessler (Eds.), *How healthy are we?: A national study of well-being at midlife* (pp. 514–549). Chicago: University of Chicago Press.

Mason, A., & Sbarra, D. A. (2012). Romantic separation, loss, and health: A review of moderators. In M. Newman & N. Robters (Eds.), *Handbook of health and social relationships* (pp. 95–120). Washington, DC: American Psychological Association.

Maume, D. J. (2004). Is the glass ceiling a unique form of inequality? Evidence from a random-effects model of managerial attainment. *Work & Occupations, 31*(2), 250–274.

Mausbach, B. T., Roepke, S. K., Chattillion, E. A., Harmell, A. L., Moore, R., Romero-Moreno, R., . . . Grant, I. (2012). Multiple mediators of the relations between caregiving stress and depressive symptoms. *Aging & Mental Health, 16*(1), 27–38. doi:10.1080/13607863.2011.615738

Mays, V. M., Cochran, S., & Baines, N. W. (2007). Race, race-based discrimination and health outcomes among African Americans. *Annual Review of Psychology, 68*, 201–225.

McAdams, D. P. (2014). The life narrative at midlife. *New Directions for Child and Adolescent Development, 2014*(145), 57–69. doi:10.1002/cad.20067

McAdams, D. P., Hart, H. M., & Maruna, S. (1998). The anatomy of generativity. In D. P. McAdams & E. de St. Aubin (Eds.), *Generativity and adult development: How and why we care for the next generation* (pp. 7–43). Washington, DC: American Psychological Association. doi:10.1037/10288-001

McAdams, D. P., & Logan, R. L. (2004). What is generativity? In E. de St. Aubin, D. P. McAdams, & T.-C. Kim (Eds.), *The generative society: Caring for future generations* (pp. 15–31). Washington, DC: American Psychological Association. doi:10.1037/10622-002

McAdams, D. P., & Olson, B. D. (2010). Personality development: Continuity and change over the life course. *Annual Review of Psychology*, 61, 517–542. doi:10.1146/annurev.psych.093008.100507

McCann, I. (2003). *Age discrimination in employment legislation in the United States experience.* Washington, DC: AARP Foundation Litigation.

McCrae, R. R. (2002). The maturation of personality psychology: Adult personality development and psychological well-being. *Journal of Research in Personality*, 36(4), 307–317.

McCrae, R. R., & Costa, P. T., Jr. (2006). Cross-cultural perspectives on adult personality trait development. In D. K. Mroczek & T. D. Little (Eds.), *Handbook of personality development* (pp. 129–145). Mahwah, NJ: Lawrence Erlbaum.

McCrae, R. R., & Costa, P. T., Jr. (2008). The five-factor theory of personality. In O. P. John, R. W. Robins, & L. A. Pervin (Eds.), *Handbook of personality psychology: Theory and research* (3rd ed., pp. 159–181). New York: Guilford Press.

McKeering, H., & Pakenham, K. I. (2000). Gender and generativity issues in parenting: Do fathers benefit more than mothers from involvement in child care activities? *Sex Roles*, 43(7), 459–480.

Melamed, S., Shirom, A., Toker, S., Berliner, S., & Shapira, I. (2006). Burnout and risk of cardiovascular disease: Evidence, possible causal paths, and promising research directions. *Psychological Bulletin*, 132(3), 327–353.

Mitchell, B. A. (2010). Happiness in midlife parental roles: A contextual mixed methods analysis. *Family Relations*, 59(3), 326–339. Retrieved from http://cat.inist.fr/?aModele=afficheN&cpsidt=23030811

Mitchell, B. A., & Lovegreen, L. D. (2009). The empty nest syndrome in midlife families: A multimethod exploration of parental gender differences and cultural dynamics. *Journal of Family Issues*, 30(12), 1651–1670.

Mock, S. E., & Eibach, R. P. (2011). Aging attitudes moderate the effect of subjective age on psychological well-being: Evidence from a 10-year longitudinal study. *Psychology and Aging*, 26(4), 979–986. Retrieved from http://cat.inist.fr/?aModele=afficheN&cpsidt=25229491

Montgomery, R. J. V., Rowe, J. M., & Kosloski, K. (2007). Family caregiving. In J. A. Blackburn & C. N. Dulmus (Eds.), *Handbook of gerontology: Evidence-based approaches to theory, practice, and policy* (pp. 426–454). Hoboken, NJ: John Wiley.

Moore, S. M., & Rosenthal, D. A. (2015). Personal growth, grandmother engagement and satisfaction among non-custodial grandmothers. *Aging & Mental Health*, 19(2), 136–143. doi:10.1080/13607863.2014.920302

Moore, V. R., & Miller, S. D. (2007). Coping resources: Effects on the psychological Well-being of African American grandparents raising grandchildren. *Journal of Health & Social Policy*, 22(3–4), 137–148.

Morizot, J., & Le Blanc, M. (2003). Continuity and change in personality traits from adolescence to midlife: A 25-year longitudinal study comparing representative and adjudicated men. *Journal of Personality*, 71(5), 705.

Mroczek, D. K., & Spiro, A. (2007). Personality change influences mortality in older men. *Psychological Science*, 18(5), 371–376. Retrieved from 10.1111/j.1467-9280.2007.01907.x

Mroczek, D. K., Spiro, A. I. I. I., & Griffin, P. W. (2006). Personality and aging. In J. E. Birren & K. W. Schaire (Eds.), *Handbook of the psychology of aging* (6th ed., pp. 363–377). Amsterdam, Netherlands: Elsevier.

Neuberger, F. S., & Haberkern, K. (2013). Structured ambivalence in grandchild care and the quality of life among European grandparents. *European Journal of Ageing*, 11(2), 171–181. doi:10.1007/s10433-013-0294-4

Newton, N., & Stewart, A. J. (2010). The middle ages: Change in women's personalities and social roles. *Psychology of Women Quarterly*, 34(1), 75–84. doi:10.1111/j.1471-6402.2009.01543.x

Ng, T. W. H., & Feldman, D. C. (2010). The relationships of age with job attitudes: A meta-analysis. *Personnel Psychology*, 63(3), 677–718. doi:10.1111/j.1744-6570.2010.01184.x

Noone, J. H., Stephens, C., & Alpass, F. M. (2009). Preretirement planning and well-Bbeing in later life: A prospective study. *Research on Aging*, 31(3), 295–317.

Nyce, S. A. (2007). The aging workforce: Is demography destiny? *Generations*, 31(1), 9–15.

Orth, U., Maes, J., & Schmitt, M. (2015). Self-esteem development across the life span: A longitudinal study with a large sample from Germany. *Developmental Psychology*, 51(2), 248–259.

Orth, U., Robins, R. W., & Widaman, K. F. (2012). Life-span development of self-esteem and its effects on important life outcomes. *Journal of Personality and Social Psychology*, 102(6), 1271–1288. doi:10.1037/a0025558

Orth, U., Trzesniewski, K. H., & Robins, R. W. (2010). Self-esteem development from young adulthood to old age: A cohort-sequential longitudinal study. *Journal of Personality and Social Psychology*, 98(4), 645–658. doi:10.1037/a0018769

Palmore, E. B., Branch, L., & Harris, D. K. (2005). *Encyclopedia of ageism.* Binghamton, NY: Haworth Pastoral Press.

Parker, K. (2012). *The boomerang generation feeling OK about living with mom and dad.* Retrieved from http://www.pewsocialtrends.org/2012/03/15/the-boomerang-generation

Parker, K., & Patten, E. (2013). *The sandwich generation rising financial burdens for middle-aged Americans.* Retrieved from http://www.pewsocialtrends.org/2013/01/30/the-sandwich-generation

Pasupathi, M., & Mansour, E. (2006). Adult age differences in autobiographical reasoning in narratives. *Developmental Psychology*, 42(5), 798–808.

Penke, L., Denissen, J. J. A., & Miller, G. F. (2007). The evolutionary genetics of personality. *European Journal of Personality*, 21(5), 549–587. doi:10.1002/per.629

Perrig-Chiello, P., Hutchison, S., & Morselli, D. (2014). Patterns of psychological adaptation to divorce after a long-term marriage. *Journal of Social and Personal Relationships*, 32(3), 386–405. doi:10.1177/0265407514533769

Pew Research Center. (2015). *Women and leadership: Public says women are equally qualified, but barriers persist.* Retrieved from http://www.pewsocialtrends.org/2015/01/14/women-and-leadership

Pilar Matud, M., Bethencourt, J. M., & Ibáñez, I. (2014). Relevance of gender roles in life satisfaction in adult people. *Personality and Individual Differences*, 70, 206–211. doi:10.1016/j.paid.2014.06.046

Pillemer, K., & Suitor, J. J. (2002). Explaining mothers' ambivalence toward their adult children. *Journal of Marriage and Family*, 64(3), 602–613.

Pillemer, K., & Suitor, J. J. (2014). Who provides care? A prospective study of caregiving among adult siblings. *The Gerontologist*, 54(4), 589–598. doi:10.1093/geront/gnt066

Pudrovska, T. (2009). Parenthood, stress, and mental health in late midlife and early old age. *International Journal of Aging and Human Development*, 68(2), 127–147. doi:10.2190/AG.68.2.b

Pulkkinen, L., Feldt, T., & Kokko, K. (2005). Personality in young adulthood and functioning in middle age. In S. L. Willis & M. Martin (Eds.), *Middle adulthood: A lifespan perspective* (pp. 99–141). Thousand Oaks: CA: Sage.

Rammstedt, B., Spinath, F. M., Richter, D., & Schupp, J. (2013). Partnership longevity and personality congruence in couples. *Personality and Individual Differences*, 54(7), 832–835. doi:10.1016/j.paid.2012.12.007

Riley, L. D., & Bowen, C. (2005). The sandwich generation: Challenges and coping strategies of multigenerational families. *Family Journal*, 13(1), 52–58. doi:10.1177/1066480704270099

Roberts, B. W., & Caspi, A. (2003). The cumulative continuity model of personality development: Striking a balance between continuity and change in personality traits across the life course. In M. Ursula & U. Lindenberger (Eds.), *Understanding human development: Dialogues with lifespan psychology* (pp. 183–214). Dordrecht, Netherlands: Kluwer Academic Publishers.

Roberts, B. W., & Mroczek, D. (2008). Personality trait change in adulthood. *Current Directions in Psychological Science*, 17(1), 31–35. doi:10.1111/j.1467-8721.2008.00543.x

Robins, R. W., Trzesniewski, K. H., Tracy, J. L., Gosling, S. D., & Potter, J. (2002). Global self-esteem across the life span. *Psychology and Aging*, 17(3), 423–434. Retrieved from http://www.ncbi.nlm.nih.gov/pubmed/12243384

Robinson, M. M., & Wilks, S. E. (2006). "Older but not wiser": What custodial grandparents want to tell social workers about raising grandchildren. *Social Work & Christianity*, 33(2), 164–177.

Röcke, C., & Lachman, M. E. (2008). Perceived trajectories of life satisfaction across past, present, and future: Profiles and correlates of subjective change in young, middle-aged, and older adults. *Psychology and Aging*, 23(4), 833–847. doi:10.1037/a0013680

Rokach, R., Cohen, O., & Dreman, S. J. (2004). Who pulls the trigger? Who initiates divorce among over 45-year-olds. *Journal of Divorce & Remarriage*, 42(1–2), 61–83. doi:10.1300/J087v42n01_03

Roscigno, V. J., Mong, S., Byron, R., & Tester, G. (2007). Age discrimination, social closure and employment. *Social Forces*, 86(1), 313–334.

Rose, S. M. (2007). Enjoying the returns: Women's friendships after 50. In V. Muhlbauer & J. C. Chrisler (Eds.), *Women over 50: Psychological perspectives* (pp. 112–130). New York: Springer Science + Business Media.

Rosenberg, S. D., Rosenberg, H. J., & Farrell, M. P. (1999). The midlife crisis revisited. In S. L. Willis & J. D. Reid (Eds.), *Life in the middle: Psychological and social development in middle age* (pp. 47–73). San Diego: Academic Press.

Ryff, C. D. (1991). Possible selves in adulthood and old age: A tale of shifting horizons. *Psychology and Aging*, 6(2), 286–295.

Ryff, C. D. (1995). Psychological well-being in adult life. *Current Directions in Psychological Science*, 4(4), 99–104. doi:10.1111/1467-8721.ep10772395

Ryff, C. D. (2014). Psychological well-being revisited: Advances in the science and practice of eudaimonia. *Psychotherapy and Psychosomatics*, 83(1), 10–28. doi:10.1159/000353263

Sakraida, T. J. (2005). Common themes in the divorce transition experience of midlife women. *Journal of Divorce & Remarriage*, 43(1–2), 69–88. doi:10.1300/J087v43n01_04

Savia, J., Almeida, D. M., Davey, A., & Zant, S. H. (2008). Routine assistance to parents: Effects on daily mood and other stressors. *The Journals of Gerontology: Series B: Psychological Sciences & Social Sciences, 36B*(3), S154–S161.

Sbarra, D. A. (2015). Divorce and health: Current trends and future directions. *Psychosomatic Medicine, 77*(3), 227–236.

Sbarra, D. A., Law, R. W., & Portley, R. M. (2011). Divorce and death: A meta-analysis and research agenda for clinical, social, and health psychology. *Perspectives on Psychological Science, 6*(5), 454–474. doi:10.1177/1745691611414724

Sbarra, D. A., Smith, H. L., & Mehl, M. R. (2012). When leaving your ex, love yourself: Observational ratings of self-compassion predict the course of emotional recovery following marital separation. *Psychological Science, 23*(3), 261–269. doi:10.1177/0956797611429466

Schafer, M. H., & Shippee, T. P. (2010). Age identity, gender, and perceptions of decline: Does feeling older lead to pessimistic dispositions about cognitive aging? *The Journals of Gerontology: Series B: Psychological Sciences & Social Sciences, 65B*(1), 91–96.

Schmitt, M., Kliegel, M., & Shapiro, A. (2007). Marital interaction in middle and old age: A predictor of marital satisfaction? *International Journal of Aging and Human Development, 65*(4), 283–300.

Schneller, D. P., & Arditti, J. A. (2004). After the breakup: Interpreting divorce and rethinking intimacy. *Journal of Divorce & Remarriage, 42*(1), 1–37.

Schultz, G. P., & Shoven, J. B. (2008). *Putting our house in order: A guide to Social Security and health care reform.* New York: W. W. Norton.

Seiffge-Krenke, I. (2010). Predicting the timing of leaving home and related developmental tasks: Parents' and children's perspectives. *Journal of Social and Personal Relationships, 27*(4), 495–518. doi:10.1177/0265407510363426

Shih, M., Young, M. J., & Bucher, A. (2013). Working to reduce the effects of discrimination: Identity management strategies in organizations. *American Psychologist, 68*(3), 145–157. doi:10.1037/a0032250

Shiota, M. N., & Levenson, R. W. (2007). Birds of a feather don't always fly farthest: Similarity in Big Five personality predicts more negative marital satisfaction trajectories in long-term marriages. *Psychology and Aging, 22*(4), 666–675.

Shirom, A., & Melamed, S. (2005). Does burnout affect physical health? A review of the evidence. In A.-S. G. Antoniou & C. L. Cooper (Eds.), *Research companion to organizational health psychology* (pp. 599–622). Northampton, MA: Edward Elgar.

Shuey, K., & Hardy, M. A. (2003). Assistance to aging parents and parents-in-law: Does lineage affect family allocation decisions? *Journal of Marriage and Family, 65*(2), 418–431.

Silverstein, M., Conroy, S. J., Wang, H., Giarrusso, R., & Bengtson, V. L. (2002). Reciprocity in parent-child relations over the adult life course. *The Journals of Gerontology: Series B: Psychological Sciences & Social Sciences, 57B*(1), 3.

Silverstein, M., & Marenco, A. (2001). How Americans enact the grandparent role across the family life course. *Journal of Family Issues, 22*(4), 493–522.

Slotter, E. B., Gardner, W. L., & Finkel, E. J. (2010). Who am I without you? The influence of romantic breakup on the self-concept. *Personality and Social Psychology Bulletin, 36*(2), 147–160. doi:10.1177/0146167209352250

Smith, G. C., & Hancock, G. R. (2010). Custodial grandmother-grandfather dyads: Pathways among marital distress, grandparent dysphoria, parenting practice, and grandchild adjustment. *Family Relations, 59*(1), 45–59. doi:10.1111/j.1741-3729.2009.00585.x

Smith, J., & Freund, A. M. (2002). The dynamics of possible selves in old age. *The Journals of Gerontology: Series B: Psychological Sciences & Social Sciences, 57B*(6), P492.

Sneed, J. R., Whitbourne, S. K., Schwartz, S. J., & Huang, S. (2012). The relationship between identity, intimacy, and midlife well-being: Findings from the Rochester Adult Longitudinal Study. *Psychology and Aging, 27*(2), 318–323. doi:10.1037/a0026378

Social Security Administration. (2015). *Life expectancy.* Retrieved from http://www.ssa.gov/planners/lifeexpectancy.html

Soto, C. J. (2015). Is happiness good for your personality? Concurrent and prospective relations of the big five with subjective well-being. *Journal of Personality, 83*(1), 45–55. doi:10.1111/jopy.12081

Soto, C. J., John, O. P., Gosling, S. D., & Potter, J. (2008). The developmental psychometrics of big five self-reports: Acquiescence, factor structure, coherence, and differentiation from ages 10 to 20. *Journal of Personality and Social Psychology, 94*(4), 718–737. doi:10.1037/0022-3514.94.4.718

Soto, C. J., John, O. P., Gosling, S. D., & Potter, J. (2011). Age differences in personality traits from 10 to 65: Big Five domains and facets in a large cross-sectional sample. *Journal of Personality and Social Psychology, 100*(2), 330–348. doi:10.1037/a0021717

Steiner, L. M., Suarez, E. C., Sells, J. N., & Wykes, S. D. (2011). Effect of age, initiator status, and infidelity on women's divorce adjustment. *Journal of Divorce & Remarriage, 52*(1), 33–47. doi:10.1080/10502556.2011.534394

Stephan, Y., Caudroit, J., Jaconelli, A., & Terracciano, A. (2014). Subjective age and cognitive functioning: A 10-year prospective study. *The American Journal of Geriatric Psychiatry, 22*(11), 1180–1187. doi:10.1016/j.jagp.2013.03.007

Sterns, H. L., & Huyck, M. H. (2001). The role of work in midlife. In M. E. Lachman (Ed.), *Handbook of midlife development* (pp. 447–486). Hoboken, NJ: John Wiley.

Stewart, A. J., Ostrove, J. M., & Helson, R. (2001). Middle aging in women: Patterns of personality change from the 30s to the 50s. *Journal of Adult Development, 8*(1), 23–37. doi:10.1023/A:1026445704288

Stuifbergen, M. C., Dykstra, P. A., Lanting, K. N., & van Delden, J. J. M. (2010). Autonomy in an ascribed relationship: The case of adult children and elderly parents. *Journal of Aging Studies, 24*(4), 257–265. doi:10.1016/j.jaging.2010.05.006

Stuifbergen, M. C., van Delden, J. J. M., & Dykstra, P. A. (2008). The implications of today's family structures for support giving to older parents. *Ageing & Society, 28*(3), 413–434. doi:10.1017/S0144686X07006666

Sutcliffe, A. G., Barnes, J., Belsky, J., Gardiner, J., & Melhuish, E. (2012). The health and development of children born to older mothers in the United Kingdom: Observational study using longitudinal cohort data. *BMJ, 345*, e5116. doi:10.1136/bmj.e5116

Szinovacz, M. E. (1998). Grandparents today: A demographic profile. *The Gerontologist, 38*(1), 37–52. doi:10.1093/geront/38.1.37

Tergesen, A. (2014, March 30). The long (long) wait to be a grandparent as more couples delay having children, ties between generations are feeling the strain. *Wall Street Journal.* Retrieved from http://www.wsj.com/articles/SB10001424052702303775504579395501172676002

Thiele, D. M., & Whelan, T. A. (2006). The nature and dimensions of the grandparent role. *Marriage & Family Review, 40*(1), 93–108.

Toothman, E. L., & Barrett, A. E. (2011). Mapping midlife: An examination of social factors shaping conceptions of the timing of middle age. *Advances in Life Course Research, 16*(3), 99–111. doi:10.1016/j.alcr.2011.08.003

Ueno, K., & Adams, R. G. (2006). Adult friendship: A decade review. In P. Noller & J. A. Feeney (Eds.), *Close relationships: Functions, forms and processes* (pp. 151–169). Hove, UK: Psychology Press.

U.S. Bureau of the Census. (2015). *Table A1. Marital status of people 15 years and over, by age, sex, personal earnings, race, and hispanic origin: 2014. America's families and living arrangements: 2014.* Washington, DC: Author. Retrieved from http://www.census.gov/hhes/families/data/cps2014A.html

U.S. Bureau of Labor. (2015). *Labor force statistics from the Current Population Survey: Employment status of the civilian noninstitutional population by age, sex, and race.* Washington, DC: Author. Retrieved from http://www.bls.gov/cps/cpsaat03.htm

Vandewater, E., & Stewart, A. (2006). Paths to late midlife well-being for women and men: The importance of identity development and social role quality. *Journal of Adult Development, 13*(2), 76–83.

Villar, F. (2012). Successful ageing and development: The contribution of generativity in older age. *Ageing and Society, 32*(07), 1087–1105. doi:10.1017/S0144686X11000973

Wang, H., & Amato, P. R. (2000). Predictors of divorce adjustment: Stressors, resources, and definitions. *Journal of Marriage and Family, 62*(3), 655–668.

Wang, W., & Parker, K. (2014). *Record share of Americans have never married.* Retrieved from http://www.pewsocialtrends.org/2014/09/24/record-share-of-americans-have-never-married

Wang, Y.-N., Shyu, Y.-I. L., Chen, M.-C., & Yang, P.-S. (2011). Reconciling work and family caregiving among adult-child family caregivers of older people with dementia: Effects on role strain and depressive symptoms. *Journal of Advanced Nursing, 67*(4), 829–840. doi:10.1111/j.1365-2648.2010.05505.x

Ward, R. A., & Spitze, G. D. (2007). Nestleaving and coresidence by young adult children: The role of family relations. *Research on Aging, 29*(3), 257–277.

Warr, P. (2007). *Work, happiness, and unhappiness.* Mahwah, NJ: Lawrence Erlbaum.

Wells Fargo. (2014). *2014 Wells Fargo middle class retirement study.* Retrieved from https://www08.wellsfargomedia.com/downloads/pdf/com/retirement-employee-benefits/insights/2014-retirement-study.pdf

Werner, E. E. (1991). Grandparent-grandchild relationships amongst US ethnic groups. In P. K. Smith (Ed.), *The psychology of grandparenthood: An international perspective* (pp. 68–82). Florence, KY: Taylor & Francis.

Wethington, E. (2000). Expecting stress: Americans and the "midlife crisis." *Motivation and Emotion, 24*(2), 85–103.

Wethington, E., Kessler, R. C., & Pixley, J. E. (2004). Turning points in adulthood. In O. G. Brim, C. D. Ryff, & R. C. Kessler (Eds.), *How healthy are we?: A national study of well-being at midlife* (pp. 586–613). Chicago: University of Chicago Press.

Whitbeck, L., & Hoyt, D. R. (1994). Early family relationships, intergenerational solidarity, and support provided to parents by. *Journal of Gerontology, 49*(2), S85.

White, L. (1994). Coresidence and leaving home: Young adults and their parents. *Annual Review of Sociology, 20*(1), 81–102.

Wight, R. G., LeBlanc, A. J., & Lee Badgett, M. V. (2013). Same-sex legal marriage and psychological well-being: Findings from the California Health Interview Survey. *American Journal of Public Health, 103*(2), 339–346. doi:10.2105/AJPH.2012.301113

Williams, K., & Umberson, D. (2004). Marital status, marital transitions, and health: A gendered life course perspective. *Journal of Health and Social Behavior, 45*(1), 81–98.

Williams, M. N. (2011). The changing roles of grandparents raising grandchildren. *Journal of Human Behavior in the Social Environment, 21*(8), 948–962. doi:10.1080/10911359.2011.588 535

Williams, N., & Torrez, D. J. (1998). Grandparenthood among Hispanics. In M. E. Szinovacz (Ed.), *Handbook on grandparenthood* (pp. 87–96). Westport, CT: Greenwood Press.

Wilt, J., Cox, K., & McAdams, D. P. (2010). The Eriksonian life story: Developmental scripts and psychosocial adaptation. *Journal of Adult Development, 17*(3), 156–161. doi:10.1007/s10804-010-9093-8

Wray, S. (2007). Women making sense of midlife: Ethnic and cultural diversity. *Journal of Aging Studies, 21*(1), 31–42. doi:10.1016/j.jaging.2006.03.001

Wu, S., Zhu, W., Li, H., Wang, Z., & Wang, M. (2008). Relationship between job burnout and occupational stress among doctors in China. *Stress and Health, 24*(2), 143–149.

Wu, Z., & Penning, M. J. (1997). Marital instability after midlife. *Journal of Family Issues, 18*(5), 459–478.

Yuan, A. S. V. (2007). Perceived age discrimination and mental health. *Social Forces, 86*(1), 291–311.

Zarit, S. H., & Eggebeen, D. J. (2002). Parent-child relationships in adulthood and later years. In M. H. Bornstein (Ed.), *Handbook of parenting: Vol. 1. Children and parenting* (2nd ed., pp. 135–161). Mahwah, NJ: Lawrence Erlbaum.

Zhan, H. J. (2004). Willingness and expectations: Intergenerational differences in attitudes toward filial responsibility in China. *Marriage & Family Review, 36*(1–2), 175–200. doi:10.1300/J002v36n01_08

Zou, M. (2015). Gender, work orientations and job satisfaction. *Work, Employment & Society, 29*(1), 3–22. doi:10.1177/0950017014559267

CHAPTER 17

Aarsland, D., Sardahaee, F. S., Anderssen, S., & Ballard, C. (2010). Is physical activity a potential preventive factor for vascular dementia? A systematic review. *Aging & Mental Health, 14*(4), 386–395. doi:10.1080/13607860903586136

Administration on Aging. (2014). *A profile of older Americans: 2014.* Retrieved from http://www.aoa.acl.gov/Aging_Statistics/Profile/index.aspx

Agronin, M. E. (2014). *Alzheimer's disease and other dementias: A practical guide.* New York: Routledge. Retrieved from https://books.google.com/books?id=sbsTAwAAQBAJ&pgis=1

Aigner, T., Haag, J., Martin, J., & Buckwalter, J. (2007). Osteoarthritis: Aging of matrix and cells—Going for a remedy. *Current Drug Targets, 8*(2), 325–331. doi:10.2174/138945007779940070

Ailshire, J. A., Beltrán-Sánchez, H., & Crimmins, E. M. (2015). Becoming centenarians: Disease and functioning trajectories of older US adults as they survive to 100. *The Journals of Gerontology: Series A: Biological Sciences and Medical Sciences, 70*(2), 193–201. doi:10.1093/gerona/glu124

Aldwin, C. M., Spiro, A. I. I. I., & Park, C. (2006). Health, behavior, and optimal aging: A life span developmental perspective. In J. E. Birren & K. W. Schaire (Eds.), *Handbook of the psychology of aging* (6th ed., pp. 85–104). Amsterdam, Netherlands: Elsevier.

Alma, M. A., van der Mei, S. F., Melis-Dankers, B. J. M., van Tilburg, T. G., Groothoff, J. W., & Suurmeijer, T. P. B. M. (2011). Participation of the elderly after vision loss. *Disability and Rehabilitation, 33*(1), 63–72. doi:10.3109/09638288.2010.488711

Alzheimer's Association. (2015). *2015 Alzheimer's disease facts and figures.* Retrieved from http://www.alz.org/facts/downloads/facts_figures_2015.pdf

Alzheimer's Disease International. (2015). *World Alzheimer report 2014: Dementia and risk reduction.* Retrieved from http://www.alz.co.uk/research/world-report-2014

Amati, L., Cirimele, D., Pugliese, V., Covelli, V., Resta, F., & Jirillo, E. (2003). Nutrition and immunity: Laboratory and clinical aspects. *Current Pharmaceutical Design, 9*(24), 1924.

American Academy of Ophthalmology. (2011). *Eye health statistics at a glance.* Retrieved from http://www.aao.org/newsroom/upload/Eye-Health-Statistics-April-2011.pdf

American Diabetes Association. (2014). Standards of medical care in diabetes—2014. *Diabetes Care, 37*(Suppl. 1), S11–S66. doi:10.2337/dc13-S011

American Psychiatric Association. (2013). *Diagnostic and statistical manual of mental disorders* (5th ed.). Washington, DC: Author.

Andel, R., Crowe, M., Hahn, E. A., Mortimer, J. A., Pedersen, N. L., Fratiglioni, L., . . . Gatz, M. (2012). Work-related stress may increase the risk of vascular dementia. *Journal of the American Geriatrics Society, 60*(1), 60–67. doi:10.1111/j.1532-5415.2011.03777.x

Andersen, K., Lolk, A., Martinussen, T., & Kragh-Sørensen, P. (2010). Very mild to severe dementia and mortality: A 14-year follow-up—The Odense study. *Dementia & Geriatric Cognitive Disorders, 29*(1), 61–67. doi:10.1159/000265553

Andersen, S. L., Sebastiani, P., Dworkis, D. A., Feldman, L., & Perls, T. T. (2012). Health span approximates life span among many supercentenarians: Compression of morbidity at the approximate limit of life span. *The Journals of Gerontology: Series A: Biological Sciences and Medical Sciences, 67A*(4), 395–405. doi:10.1093/gerona/glr223

Anstey, K. J., Hofer, S. M., & Luszcz, M. A. (2003). A latent growth curve analysis of late-life sensory and cognitive function over 8 years: Evidence for specific and common factors underlying change. *Psychology and Aging, 18*(4), 714–726.

Ardelt, M. (1998). Social crisis and individual growth: The long-term effects of the great depression. *Journal of Aging Studies, 12*(3), 291.

Ardelt, M. (2010). Are older adults wiser than college students? A comparison of two age cohorts. *Journal of Adult Development, 17*(4), 193–207. doi:10.1007/s10804-009-9088-5

Artistico, D., Orom, H., Cervone, D., Krauss, S., & Houston, E. (2010). Everyday challenges in context: The influence of contextual factors on everyday problem solving among young, middle-aged, and older adults. *Experimental Aging Research, 36*(2), 230–247. doi:10.1080/03610731003613938

Ash, A. S., Kroll-Desrosiers, A. R., Hoaglin, D. C., Christensen, K., Fang, H., & Perls, T. T. (2015). Are members of long-lived families healthier than their equally long-lived peers? Evidence from the long life family study. *The Journals of Gerontology: Series A: Biological Sciences and Medical Sciences.* Advance online publication. doi:10.1093/gerona/glv015

Assuncao, M., & Andrade, J. P. (2015). Protective action of green tea catechins in neuronal mitochondria during aging. *Frontiers in Bioscience, 20*, 247–262. Retrieved from http://europepmc.org/abstract/med/25553449

Bäckman, L. (2008). Memory and cognition in preclinical dementia: What we know and what we do not know. *Canadian Journal of Psychiatry, 53*(6), 354–360.

Baker, H. (2007). Nutrition in the elderly: An overview [Cover story]. *Geriatrics, 62*(7), 28–31.

Baldwin, C. L., & Ash, I. K. (2011). Impact of sensory acuity on auditory working memory span in young and older adults. *Psychology and Aging, 26*(1), 85–91. doi:10.1037/a0020360

Baltes, M. M., & Carstensen, L. L. (2003). The process of successful aging: Selection, optimization and compensation. In U. M. Staudinger & U. Lindenberger (Eds.), *Understanding human development: Dialogues with lifespan psychology* (pp. 81–104). Dordrecht, Netherlands: Kluwer Academic Publishers.

Baltes, P. B., & Kunzmann, U. (2003). Wisdom. *The Psychologist, 16*(3), 131–133.

Baltes, P. B., & Staudinger, U. M. (2000). Wisdom: A metaheuristic (pragmatic) to orchestrate mind and virtue toward excellence. *American Psychologist, 55*(1), 122–136. doi:10.1037/0003-066X.55.1.122

Bansal, N., & Parle, M. (2014). Dementia: An overview. *Management, 1*(1), 281–297.

Barac, R., & Bialystok, E. (2012). Bilingual effects on cognitive and linguistic development: Role of language, cultural background, and education. *Child Development, 83*(2), 413–422. doi:10.1111/j.1467-8624.2011.01707.x

Barulli, D., & Stern, Y. (2013). Efficiency, capacity, compensation, maintenance, plasticity: Emerging concepts in cognitive reserve. *Trends in Cognitive Sciences, 17*(10), 502–509. doi:10.1016/j.tics.2013.08.012

Bello, V. M. E., & Schultz, R. R. (2011). Prevalence of treatable and reversible dementias. A study in a dementia outpatient clinic. *Dementia & Neuropsychologia, 5*(1), 44–47. Retrieved from http://www.redalyc.org/resumen.oa?id=339529026008

Belza, B., Walwick, J., Shiu-Thornton, S., Schwartz, S., Taylor, M., & LoGerfo, J. (2004). Older adult perspectives on physical activity and exercise: Voices from multiple cultures. *Preventing Chronic Disease, 1*(4), A09. Retrieved from http://www.pubmedcentral.nih.gov/articlerender.fcgi?artid=1277949&tool=pmcentrez&rendertype=abstract

Berntsen, D., & Rubin, D. C. (2002). Emotionally charged autobiographical memories across the life span: The recall of happy, sad, traumatic and involuntary memories. *Psychology and Aging, 17*(4), 636–652.

Berry, S. D., & Miller, R. R. (2008). Falls: Epidemiology, pathophysiology, and relationship to fracture. *Current Osteoporosis Reports, 6*(4), 149–154. Retrieved from http://www.pubmedcentral.nih.gov/articlerender.fcgi?artid=2793090&tool=pmcentrez&rendertype=abstract

Best, L. E., Hayward, M. D., & Hidajat, M. M. (2005). Life course pathways to adult-onset diabetes. *Social Biology, 52*(3–4), 94–111.

Bettens, K., Sleegers, K., & Van Broeckhoven, C. (2013). Genetic insights in Alzheimer's disease. *The Lancet Neurology, 12*(1), 92–104. doi:10.1016/S1474-4422(12)70259-4

Bishop, A. J., Martin, P., MacDonald, M., & Poon, L. (2010). Predicting happiness among centenarians. *Gerontology, 56*(1), 88–92. doi:10.1159/000272017

Bisiacchi, P. S., Borella, E., Bergamaschi, S., Carretti, B., & Mondini, S. (2008). Interplay between memory and executive functions in normal and pathological aging. *Journal of Clinical & Experimental Neuropsychology, 30*(6), 723–733. doi:10.1080/13803390701689587

Black, B. S., Brandt, J., Rabins, P. V., Samus, Q. M., Steele, C. D., Lyketsos, C. G., & Rosenblatt, A. (2008). Participation in dementia research: Rates and correlates of capacity to give informed consent. *Journal of Medical Ethics, 34*(3), 167–170. doi: 10.1136/jme.2006.019786

Blackwell, D., Lucas, J., & Clarke, T. (2012). Summary health statistics for U.S. adults: National Health Interview Survey, 2012. *Vital Health Statistics, 10*(260). Retrieved from http://www.cdc.gov/nchs/data/series/sr_10/sr10_260.pdf

Blondell, S. J., Hammersley-Mather, R., & Veerman, J. L. (2014). Does physical activity prevent cognitive decline and dementia?: A systematic review and meta-analysis of longitudinal studies. *BMC Public Health, 14*(1), 510. doi:10.1186/1471-2458-14-510

Blurton-Jones, M., & LaFerla, F. M. (2006). Pathways by which Abeta facilitates tau pathology. *Current Alzheimer Research, 3*(5), 437–448. doi:10.2174/156720506779025242

Borella, E., Carretti, B., Riboldi, F., & De Beni, R. (2010). Working memory training in older adults: Evidence of transfer and maintenance effects. *Psychology and Aging, 25*(4), 767–778. doi:10.1037/a0020683

Bowles, R. P., & Salthouse, T. A. (2003). Assessing the age-related effects of proactive interference on working memory tasks using the Rasch model. *Psychology and Aging, 18*(3), 608–615.

Bradley-Whitman, M. A., & Lovell, M. A. (2013). Epigenetic changes in the progression of Alzheimer's disease. *Mechanisms of Ageing and Development, 134*(10), 486–495. doi:10.1016/j.mad.2013.08.005

Braskie, M. N., Klunder, A. D., Hayashi, K. M., Protas, H., Kepe, V., Miller, K. J., . . . Thompson, P. M. (2010). Plaque and tangle imaging and cognition in normal aging and Alzheimer's disease. *Neurobiology of Aging, 31*(10), 1669–1678. doi:10.1016/j.neurobiolaging.2008.09.012

Braun, S. M. G., & Jessberger, S. (2014). Adult neurogenesis: Mechanisms and functional significance. *Development, 141*(10), 1983–1986. doi:10.1242/dev.104596

Brehmer, Y., Westerberg, H., & Bäckman, L. (2012). Working-memory training in younger and older adults: Training gains, transfer, and maintenance. *Frontiers in Human Neuroscience, 6*, 63. doi:10.3389/fnhum.2012.00063

Brichta, L., Greengard, P., & Flajolet, M. (2013). Advances in the pharmacological treatment of Parkinson's disease: Targeting neurotransmitter systems. *Trends in Neurosciences, 36*(9), 543–554. doi:10.1016/j.tins.2013.06.003

Brownie, S. (2006). Why are elderly individuals at risk of nutritional deficiency? *International Journal of Nursing Practice, 12*(2), 110–118. doi:10.1111/j.1440-172X.2006.00557.x

Buford, T. W., Anton, S. D., Judge, A. R., Marzetti, E., Wohlgemuth, S. E., Carter, C. S., . . . Manini, T. M. (2010). Models of accelerated sarcopenia: Critical pieces for solving the puzzle of age-related muscle atrophy. *Ageing Research Reviews, 9*(4), 369–383. doi:10.1016/j.arr.2010.04.004

Burton, C. L., Strauss, E., Hultsch, D. F., & Hunter, M. A. (2006). Cognitive functioning and everyday problem solving in older adults. *Clinical Neuropsychologist, 20*(3), 432–452. doi:10.1080/13854040590967063

Cameron, H. A., & Glover, L. R. (2015). Adult neurogenesis: Beyond learning and memory. *Annual Review of Psychology, 66*, 53–81. doi:10.1146/annurev-psych-010814-015006

Cannon, J. R., & Greenamyre, J. T. (2013). Gene-environment interactions in Parkinson's disease: Specific evidence in humans and mammalian models. *Neurobiology of Disease, 57*, 38–46. doi:10.1016/j.nbd.2012.06.025

Carpenter, S. M., Peters, E., Västfjäll, D., & Isen, A. M. (2013). Positive feelings facilitate working memory and complex decision making among older adults. *Cognition & Emotion, 27*(1), 184–192. doi:10.1080/02699931.2012.698251

Carson, V. B., Vanderhorst, K., & Koenig, H. G. (2015). *Care giving for Alzheimer's disease: A compassionate guide for clinicians and loved ones.* New York: Springer-Verlag. Retrieved from https://books.google.com/books?id=vjyDBwAAQBAJ&pgis=1

Caserotti, P., Aagaard, P., Larsen, J. B., & Puggaard, L. (2008). Explosive heavy-resistance training in old and very old adults: Changes in rapid muscle force, strength and power. *Scandinavian Journal of Medicine & Science in Sports, 18*(6), 773–782. doi:10.1111/j.1600-0838.2007.00732.x

Castro-Chavira, S. A., Fernandez, T., Nicolini, H., Diaz-Cintra, S., & Prado-Alcala, R. A. (2015). Genetic markers in biological fluids for aging-related major neurocognitive disorder. *Current Alzheimer Research, 12*(3), 200–209. Retrieved from http://www.ingentaconnect.com/content/ben/car/2015/00000012/00000003/art00002

Catindig, J.-A. S., Venketasubramanian, N., Ikram, M. K., & Chen, C. (2012). Epidemiology of dementia in Asia: Insights on prevalence, trends and novel risk factors. *Journal of the Neurological Sciences, 321*(1–2), 11–16. doi:10.1016/j.jns.2012.07.023

Cedervall, Y., Torres, S., & Åberg, A. C. (2015). Maintaining well-being and selfhood through physical activity: Experiences of people with mild Alzheimer's disease. *Aging & Mental Health, 19*(8), 679–688. doi:10.1080/13607863.2014.962004

Centers for Disease Control and Prevention. (2014). *National Diabetes Statistics Report: Estimates of diabetes and its burden in the United States, 2014.* Atlanta: Author.

Centers for Disease Control and Prevention. (2015). *New data on older drivers.* Retrieved from http://www.cdc.gov/Features/dsOlderDrivers

Central Intelligence Agency. (2013). *World fact book, 2013–14.* Washington, DC: Author. Retrieved from https://www.cia.gov/library/publications/the-world-factbook/index.html

Chakravarthy, U., Evans, J., & Rosenfeld, P. J. (2010). Age related macular degeneration. *BMJ, 340*(7745), 526–530. doi:10.1136/bmj.c981

Chakravarty, E. F., Hubert, H. B., Lingala, V. B., & Fries, J. F. (2008). Reduced disability and mortality among aging runners. *Archives of Internal Medicine, 168*(15), 1638–1646.

Charlton, K. E., Batterham, M. J., Bowden, S., Ghosh, A., Caldwell, K., Barone, L., . . . Milosavljevic, M. (2013). A high prevalence of malnutrition in acute geriatric patients predicts adverse clinical outcomes and mortality within 12 months. *E-SPEN Journal, 8*(3), e120–e125. doi:10.1016/j.clnme.2013.03.004

Chertkow, H. (2008). Diagnosis and treatment of dementia: Introduction. *CMAJ*, 316–321. doi:10.1503/cmaj.070795

Chi, S., Yu, J.-T., Tan, M.-S., & Tan, L. (2014). Depression in Alzheimer's disease: Epidemiology, mechanisms, and management. *Journal of Alzheimer's Disease, 42*(3), 739–755. doi:10.3233/JAD-140324

Cicchino, J. B., & McCartt, A. T. (2015). *Critical older driver errors in a sample of serious U.S. crashes. Accident Analysis & Prevention, 80*, 211–219.

Clapp, W. C., Rubens, M. T., Sabharwal, J., & Gazzaley, A. (2011). Deficit in switching between functional brain networks underlies the impact of multitasking on working memory in older adults. *Proceedings of the National Academy of Sciences of the United States of America, 108*(17), 7212–7217. doi:10.1073/pnas.1015297108

Colcombe, S. J., Erickson, K. I., Scalf, P. E., Kim, J. S., Prakash, R., McAuley, E., . . . Kramer, A. F. (2006). Aerobic exercise training increases brain volume in aging humans. *The Journals of Gerontology: Series A: Biological Sciences and Medical Sciences, 61A*(11), 1166–1170.

Corrada, M. M., Brookmeyer, R., Paganini-Hill, A., Berlau, D., & Kawas, C. H. (2010). Dementia incidence continues to increase with age in the oldest old: The 90+ study. *Annals of Neurology, 67*(1), 114–121. doi:10.1002/ana.21915

Cruickshanks, K. J., Nondahl, D. M., Tweed, T. S., Wiley, T. L., Klein, B. E. K., Klein, R., . . . Nash, S. D. (2010). Education, occupation, noise exposure history and the 10-yr cumulative incidence of hearing impairment in older adults. *Hearing Research, 264*(1–2), 3–9. doi:10.1016/j.heares.2009.10.008

Danaei, G., Rimm, E. B., Oza, S., Kulkarni, S. C., Murray, C. J. L., & Ezzati, M. (2010). The promise of prevention: The effects of four preventable risk factors on national life expectancy and life expectancy disparities by race and county in the United States. *PLoS Medicine, 7*(3), 1–13. doi:10.1371/journal.pmed.1000248

Darowski, E. S., Helder, E., Zacks, R. T., Hasher, L., & Hambrick, D. Z. (2008). Age-related differences in cognition: The role of distraction control. *Neuropsychology, 22*(5), 638–644.

Daselaar, S., & Cabeza, R. (2005). Age-related changes in hemispheric organization. In R. Cabeza, L. Nyberg, & D. C. Park (Eds.), *Cognitive neuroscience of aging: Linking cognitive and cerebral aging* (pp. 325–353). New York: Oxford University Press.

Davey, A., Dai, T., Woodard, J. L., Miller, L. S., Gondo, Y., Johnson, M. A., . . . Poon, L. W. (2013). Profiles of cognitive functioning in a population-based sample of centenarians using factor mixture analysis. *Experimental Aging Research, 39*(2), 125–144. doi:10.1080/0361073X.2013.761869

Davey, A., Elias, M. F., Siegler, I. C., Lele, U., Martin, P., Johnson, M. A., . . . Poon, L. W. (2010). Cognitive function, physical performance, health, and disease: Norms from the Georgia Centenarian Study. *Experimental Aging Research, 36*(4), 394–425. doi:10.1080/0361073x.2010.509010

David, C. B., Nancy, M. H., & Ying-Bo, S. (2010). Oxidative damage and the prevention of age-related cataracts. *Ophthalmic Research, 44*(3), 155–165.

Davies, C. G., & Thorn, B. L. (2002). Psychopharmacology with older adults in residential care. In R. D. Hill, B. L. Thorn, J. Bowling, & A. Morrison (Eds.), *Geriatric residential care* (pp. 161–181). Mahwah, NJ: Lawrence Erlbaum.

Daviglus, M. L., Bell, C. C., Berrettini, W., Bowen, P. E., Connolly, E. S., Cox, N. J., . . . Trevisan, M. (2010). National Institutes of Health State-of-the-Science Conference Statement: Preventing Alzheimer disease and cognitive decline. *Annals of Internal Medicine.* doi:10.1059/0003-4819-153-3-201008030-00260

De la Fuente, M., & Miquel, J. (2009). An update of the oxidation-inflammation theory of aging: The involvement of the immune system in oxi-inflamm-aging. *Current Pharmaceutical Design, 15*(26), 3003–3026.

DeFronzo, R. A., & Abdul-Ghani, M. (2011). Assessment and treatment of cardiovascular risk in prediabetes: Impaired glucose tolerance and impaired fasting glucose. *The American Journal of Cardiology, 108*(3), 3B–24B. doi:10.1016/j.amjcard.2011.03.013

Denney, N. W., Pearce, K. A., & Palmer, A. M. (1982). A developmental study of adults' performance on traditional and practical problem-solving tasks. *Experimental Aging Research, 8*(2), 115–118. doi:10.1080/03610738208258407

DeSantis, C. E., Lin, C. C., Mariotto, A. B., Siegel, R. L., Stein, K. D., Kramer, J. L., . . . Jemal, A. (2014). Cancer treatment and survivorship statistics, 2014. *CA: A Cancer Journal for Clinicians, 64*(4), 252–271. doi:10.3322/caac.21235

Dhital, A., Pey, T., & Stanford, M. R. (2010). Visual loss and falls: A review. *Eye, 24*(9), 1437–1446. doi:10.1038/eye.2010.60

Dodson, D. C. (2007). Men's health compared with women's health in the 21st century USA. *Journal of Men's Health & Gender, 4*(2), 121–123.

Doraiswamy, P. M., Krishnan, K. R. R., Oxman, T., Jenkyn, L. R., Coffey, D. J., Burt, T., & Clary, C. M. (2003). Does antidepressant therapy improve cognition in elderly depressed patients? *The Journals of Gerontology: Series A: Biological Sciences and Medical Sciences, 58*(12), M1137–M1144. doi:10.1093/gerona/58.12.M1137

Douaud, G., Refsum, H., de Jager, C. A., Jacoby, R., Nichols, T. E., Smith, S. M., & Smith, A. D. (2013). Preventing Alzheimer's disease-related gray matter atrophy by B-vitamin treatment. *Proceedings of the National Academy of Sciences of the United States of America, 110*(23), 9523–9528. doi:10.1073/pnas.1301816110

Dunlosky, J., Kubat-Silman, A. K., & Hertzog, C. (2003). Training monitoring skills improves older adults' self-paced associative learning. *Psychology and Aging, 18*(2), 340–345. doi:10.1037/0882-7974.18.2.340

Emery, L., Hale, S., & Myerson, J. (2008). Age differences in proactive interference, working memory, and abstract reasoning. *Psychology and Aging, 23*(3), 634–645.

Engmann, B. (2011). Mild cognitive impairment in the elderly: A review of the influence of depression, possible other core symptoms, and diagnostic findings. *GeroPsych: The Journal of Gerontopsychology and Geriatric Psychiatry, 24*(2), 71–76.

Erickson, K. I., Raji, C. A., Lopez, O. L., Becker, J. T., Rosano, C., Newman, A. B., . . . Kuller, L. H. (2010). Physical activity predicts gray matter volume in late adulthood: The Cardiovascular Health Study. *Neurology, 75*(16), 1415–1422. doi:10.1212/WNL.0b013e3181f88359

Erickson, K. I., Voss, M. W., Prakash, R. S., Basak, C., Szabo, A., Chaddock, L., . . . Kramer, A. F. (2011). Exercise training increases size of hippocampus and improves memory. *Proceedings of the National Academy of Sciences of the United States of America, 108*(7), 3017–3022. doi:10.1073/pnas.1015950108

Ernst, A., Alkass, K., Bernard, S., Salehpour, M., Perl, S., Tisdale, J., . . . Frisén, J. (2014). Neurogenesis in the striatum of the adult human brain. *Cell, 156*(5), 1072–1083. doi:10.1016/j.cell.2014.01.044

Espeland, M. A., Bryan, R. N., Goveas, J. S., Robinson, J. G., Siddiqui, M. S., Liu, S., . . . Resnick, S. M. (2013). Influence of type 2 diabetes on brain volumes and changes in brain volumes: Results from the Women's Health Initiative Magnetic Resonance Imaging studies. *Diabetes Care, 36*(1), 90–97. doi:10.2337/dc12-0555

Farage, M. A., Miller, K. W., Elsner, P., & Maibach, H. I. (2008). Intrinsic and extrinsic factors in skin ageing: A review. *International Journal of Cosmetic Science, 30*(2), 87–95. doi:10.1111/j.1468-2494.2007.00415.x

Farage, M. A., Miller, K. W., Elsner, P., & Maibach, H. I. (2013). Characteristics of the aging skin. *Advances in Wound Care, 2*(1), 5–10. doi:10.1089/wound.2011.0356

Faria, M. A. (2015). Longevity and compression of morbidity from a neuroscience perspective: Do we have a duty to die by a certain age? *Surgical Neurology International, 6*, 49. doi:10.4103/2152-7806.154273

Farzaneh-Far, R., Lin, J., Epel, E. S., Harris, W. S., Blackburn, E. H., & Whooley, M. A. (2010). Association of marine omega-3 fatty acid levels with telomeric aging in patients with coronary heart disease. *JAMA, 303*(3), 250–257.

Feng, Y., Jankovic, J., & Wu, Y.-C. (2014). Epigenetic mechanisms in Parkinson's disease. *Journal of the Neurological Sciences, 349*(1), 3–9. doi:10.1016/j.jns.2014.12.017

Festa, E. K., Ott, B. R., Manning, K. J., Davis, J. D., & Heindel, W. C. (2013). Effect of cognitive status on self-regulatory driving behavior in older adults: An assessment of naturalistic driving using in-car video recordings. *Journal of Geriatric Psychiatry and Neurology, 26*(1), 10–18. doi:10.1177/0891988712473801

Feyereisen, P., Demaeght, N., & Samson, D. (1998). Why do picture naming latencies increase with age: General. *Experimental Aging Research, 24*(1), 21.

Finder, V. H. (2011). Alzheimer's disease: A general introduction and pathomechanism. *Journal of Alzheimer's Disease, 22*, 5–19. doi:10.3233/jad-2010-100975

Finkel, D., Reynolds, C. A., McArdle, J. J., & Pedersen, N. L. (2007). Age changes in processing speed as a leading indicator of cognitive aging. *Psychology and Aging, 22*(3), 558–568.

Fisher, J. E., Yury, C., & Buchanan, J. A. (2006). Dementia. In J. E. Fisher & W. T. O'Donohue (Eds.), *Practitioner's guide to evidence-based psychotherapy* (pp. 214–229). New York: Springer Science + Business Media.

Fisk, J. D., Beattie, B. L., Donnelly, M., Byszewski, A., & Molnar, F. J. (2007). Disclosure of the diagnosis of dementia. *Alzheimer's & Dementia, 3*(4), 404–410.

Flament, F., Bazin, R., & Piot, B. (2013). Effect of the sun on visible clinical signs of aging in Caucasian skin. *Clinical, Cosmetic and Investigational Dermatology, 6*, 221. doi:10.2147/CCID.S44686

Fletcher, L. C. B., Burke, K. E., Caine, P. L., Rinne, N. L., Braniff, C. A., Davis, H. R., . . . Packer, C. (2013). Diagnosing Alzheimer's disease: Are we any nearer to useful biomarker-based, non-invasive tests? *GMS Health Technology Assessment, 9*, Doc01. doi:10.3205/hta000107

Frederiksen, K. S., Sobol, N., Beyer, N., Hasselbalch, S., & Waldemar, G. (2014). Moderate-to-high intensity aerobic exercise in patients with mild to moderate Alzheimer's disease: A pilot study. *International Journal of Geriatric Psychiatry, 29*(12), 1242–1248. doi:10.1002/gps.4096

Freeman, S., Garcia, J., & Marston, H. R. (2013). Centenarian self-perceptions of factors responsible for attainment of extended health and longevity. *Educational Gerontology, 39*(10), 717–728. doi:10.1080/03601277.2012.750981

Freund, A. M., & Baltes, P. B. (2007). Toward a theory of successful aging: Selection, optimization, and compensation. In R. Fernández-Ballesteros (Ed.), *Geropsychology: European perspectives for an aging world* (pp. 239–254). Ashland, OH: Hogrefe & Huber.

Fries, J. F., Bruce, B., & Chakravarty, E. (2011). Compression of morbidity 1980-2011: A focused review of paradigms and progress. *Journal of Aging Research, 2011*, 261702. doi:10.4061/2011/261702

Fry, A. F., & Hale, S. (1996). Processing speed, working memory, and fluid intelligence: Evidence for a developmental cascade. *Psychological Science, 7*, 237–241.

Gaesser, B., Sacchetti, D. C., Addis, D. R., & Schacter, D. L. (2010). Characterizing age-related changes in remembering the past and imagining the future. *Psychology and Aging, 26*(1), 80–84. doi:10.1037/a0021054

Gates, G. A., & Mills, J. H. (2005). Presbycusis. *Lancet, 366*(9491), 1111–1120. doi:10.1016/S0140-6736(05)67423-5

Gazzaley, A., Sheridan, M. A., Cooney, J. W., & D'Esposito, M. (2007). Age-related deficits in component processes of working memory. *Neuropsychology, 21*(5), 532–539.

Gentilini, D., Mari, D., Castaldi, D., Remondini, D., Ogliari, G., Ostan, R., . . . Vitale, G. (2013). Role of epigenetics in human aging and longevity: Genome-wide DNA methylation profile in centenarians and centenarians' offspring. *Age, 35*(5), 1961–1973. doi:10.1007/s11357-012-9463-1

Gerstorf, D., Ram, N., Hoppmann, C., Willis, S. L., & Schaie, K. W. (2011). Cohort differences in cognitive aging and terminal decline in the Seattle Longitudinal Study. *Developmental Psychology, 47*(4), 1026–1041. doi:10.1037/a0023426

Gomez, C. R., Nomellini, V., Faunce, D. E., & Kovacs, E. J. (2008). Innate immunity and aging. *Experimental Gerontology, 43*(8), 718–728. doi:10.1016/j.exger.2008.05.016

Gordon-Salant, S. J. (2005). Hearing loss and aging: New research findings and clinical implications. *Journal of Rehabilitation Research & Development, 42*, 9–23. doi:101682/JRRD.2005.01.0006

Govindaraju, D., Atzmon, G., & Barzilai, N. (2015). Genetics, lifestyle and longevity: Lessons from centenarians. *Applied & Translational Genomics, 4*, 23–32. doi:10.1016/j.atg.2015.01.001

Gow, A. J., Corley, J., Starr, J. M., & Deary, I. J. (2012). Reverse causation in activity-cognitive ability associations: The Lothian Birth Cohort 1936. *Psychology and Aging, 27*(1), 250–255. doi:10.1037/a0024144

Graham, J. E., Christian, L. M., & Kiecolt-Glaser, J. K. (2006). Stress, age, and immune function: Toward a lifespan approach. *Journal of Behavioral Medicine, 29*(4), 389–400.

Grant, A., Dennis, N. A., & Li, P. (2014). Cognitive control, cognitive reserve, and memory in the aging bilingual brain. *Frontiers in Psychology, 5*, 1401. doi:10.3389/fpsyg.2014.01401

Grossman, H., Bergmann, C., & Parker, S. (2006). Dementia: A brief review. *Mount Sinai Journal of Medicine, 73*(7), 985–992.

Grote, H. E., & Hannan, A. J. (2007). Regulators of adult neurogenesis in the healthy and diseased brain. *Clinical & Experimental Pharmacology & Physiology, 34*(5–6), 533–545.

Guarch, J., Marcos, T., Salamero, M., Gastó, C., & Blesa, R. (2008). Mild cognitive impairment: A risk indicator of later dementia, or a preclinical phase of the disease? *International Journal of Geriatric Psychiatry, 23*(3), 257–265. doi:10.1002/gps.1871

Hannan, M. T., Broe, K. E., Cupples, L. A., Dufour, A. B., Rockwell, M., & Kiel, D. P. (2012). Height loss predicts subsequent hip fracture in men and women of the Framingham Study. *Journal of Bone and Mineral Research, 27*(1), 146–152. doi:10.1002/jbmr.557

Harvard Mental Health Letter. (2010). Biomarkers for Alzheimer's disease: The research advances incrementally, but clinical use is still years away. *Harvard Mental Health Letter, 27*(5), 1–3.

Hedden, T., & Gabrieli, J. D. E. (2004). Insights into the ageing mind: A view from cognitive neuroscience. *Nature Reviews. Neuroscience, 5*(2), 87–96. doi:10.1038/nrn1323

Helzner, E. P., Cauley, J. A., Pratt, S. R., Wisniewski, S. R., Zmuda, J. M., Talbott, E. O., . . . Newman, A. B. (2005). Race and sex differences in age-related hearing loss: The health, aging and body composition study. *Journal of the American Geriatrics Society, 53*(12), 2119–2127. Retrieved from www.cinahl.com/cgi-bin/refsvc?jid=748&accno=2009083727

Herman, T., Mirelman, A., Giladi, N., Schweiger, A., & Hausdorff, J. M. (2010). Executive control deficits as a prodrome to falls in healthy older adults: A prospective study linking thinking, walking, and falling. *The Journals of Gerontology: Series A: Biological Sciences and Medical Sciences, 65A*(10), 1086–1092.

Hindin, S. B., & Zelinski, E. M. (2012). Extended practice and aerobic exercise interventions benefit untrained cognitive outcomes in older adults: A meta-analysis. *Journal of the American Geriatrics Society, 60*(1), 136–141. doi:10.1111/j.1532-5415.2011.03761.x

Hinterlong, J. E. (2008). Productive engagement among older Americans: Prevalence, patterns, and implications for public policy. *Journal of Aging & Social Policy*, 20(2), 141–164.

Ho, N. F., Hooker, J. M., Sahay, A., Holt, D. J., & Roffman, J. L. (2013). In vivo imaging of adult human hippocampal neurogenesis: Progress, pitfalls and promise. *Molecular Psychiatry*, 18(4), 404–416. doi:10.1038/mp.2013.8

Hoppmann, C. A., & Blanchard-Fields, F. (2010). Goals and everyday problem solving: Manipulating goal preferences in young and older adults. *Developmental Psychology*, 46(6), 1433–1443. doi:10.1037/a0020676

Hort, J., Bartos, A., Pirttilä, T., & Scheltens, P. (2010). Use of cerebrospinal fluid biomarkers in diagnosis of dementia across Europe. *European Journal of Neurology*, 17(1), 90–96. doi:10.1111/j.1468-1331.2009.02753.x

Hort, J., O'Brien, J. T., Gainotti, G., Pirttila, T., Popescu, B. O., Rektorova, I., . . . Scheltens, P. (2010). EFNS guidelines for the diagnosis and management of Alzheimer's disease. *European Journal of Neurology*, 17(10), 1236–1248. doi:10.1111/j.1468-1331.2010.03040.x

Horton, W. S., Spieler, D. H., & Shriberg, E. (2010). A corpus analysis of patterns of age-related change in conversational speech. *Psychology and Aging*, 25(3). doi:10.1037/a0019424

Hosseini, H., & Hosseini, N. (2008). Epidemiology and prevention of fall injuries among the elderly. *Hospital Topics*, 86(3), 15–20.

Iadecola, C. (2013). The pathobiology of vascular dementia. *Neuron*, 80(4), 844–866. doi:10.1016/j.neuron.2013.10.008

Iliffe, S., Robinson, L., Brayne, C., Goodman, C., Rait, G., Manthorpe, J., & Ashley, P. (2009). Primary care and dementia: 1. diagnosis, screening and disclosure. *International Journal of Geriatric Psychiatry*, 24(9), 895–901. doi:10.1002/gps.2204

Inagaki, H., Gondo, Y., Hirose, N., Masui, Y., Kitagawa, K., Arai, Y., . . . Homma, A. (2009). Cognitive function in Japanese centenarians according to the Mini-Mental State Examination. *Dementia & Geriatric Cognitive Disorders*, 28(1), 6–12. doi:10.1159/000228713

Insurance Institute for Highway Safety. (2015). *Older drivers*. Retrieved from http://www.iihs.org/iihs/topics/t/older-drivers/qanda

Jacoby, L. L., Wahlheim, C. N., Rhodes, M. G., Daniels, K. A., & Rogers, C. S. (2010). Learning to diminish the effects of proactive interference: Reducing false memory for young and older adults. *Memory & Cognition*, 38(6), 820–829. doi:10.3758/mc.38.6.820

Jager, R. D., Mieler, W. F., & Miller, J. W. (2008). Age-related macular degeneration. *New England Journal of Medicine*, 358(24), 2606–2617. doi:10.1056/NEJMra0801537

Jani, B., & Rajkumar, C. (2006). Ageing and vascular ageing. *Postgraduate Medical Journal*, 82(968), 357–362.

Jeffreys, M., Lawlor, D. A., Galobardes, B., McCarron, P., Kinra, S., Ebrahim, S., & Smith, G. D. (2006). Lifecourse weight patterns and adult-onset diabetes: The Glasgow Alumni and British Women's Heart and Health studies. *International Journal of Obesity*, 30(3), 507–512.

Jhoo, J. H., Kim, K. W., Huh, Y., Lee, S. B., Park, J. H., Lee, J. J., . . . Woo, J. I. (2008). Prevalence of dementia and its subtypes in an elderly urban Korean population: Results from the Korean Longitudinal Study on Health and Aging (KLoSHA). *Dementia & Geriatric Cognitive Disorders*, 26(3), 270–276. doi:10.1159/000160960

Jiwa, N. S., Garrard, P., & Hainsworth, A. H. (2010). Experimental models of vascular dementia and vascular cognitive impairment: A systematic review. *Journal of Neurochemistry*, 115(4), 814–828. doi:10.1111/j.1471-4159.2010.06958.x

Kaiser, M. J., Bauer, J. M., Rämsch, C., Uter, W., Guigoz, Y., Cederholm, T., . . . Sieber, C. C. (2010). Frequency of malnutrition in older adults: A multinational perspective using the mini nutritional assessment. *Journal of the American Geriatrics Society*, 58(9), 1734–1738. doi:10.1111/j.1532-5415.2010.03016.x

Kalaria, R. N., Maestre, G. E., Arizaga, R., Friedland, R. P., Galasko, D., Hall, K., . . . Antuono, P. (2008). Alzheimer's disease and vascular dementia in developing countries: Prevalence, management, and risk factors. *The Lancet Neurology*, 7(9), 812–826. doi:10.1016/S1474-4422(08)70169-8

Kaniewski, M., Stevens, J. A., Parker, E. M., & Lee, R. (2015). An introduction to the Centers for Disease Control and Prevention's efforts to prevent older adult falls. *Frontiers in Public Health*, 2, e119. doi:10.3389/fpubh.2014.00119

Katon, W. J. (2008). The comorbidity of diabetes mellitus and depression. *American Journal of Medicine*, 121(11), S8–S15. doi:10.1016/j.amjmed.2008.09.008

Kavé, G., Eyal, N., Shorek, A., & Cohen-Mansfield, J. (2008). Multilingualism and cognitive state in the oldest old. *Psychology and Aging*, 23(1), 70–78.

Keightley, J., & Mitchell, A. (2004). What factors influence mental health professionals when deciding whether or not to share a diagnosis of dementia with the person? *Aging & Mental Health*, 8(1), 13–20.

Kessels, R. P. C., Meulenbroek, O., Fernandez, G., & Olde Rikkert, M. G. M. (2010). Spatial working memory in aging and mild cognitive impairment: Effects of task load and contextual cueing. *Aging, Neuropsychology & Cognition*, 17(5), 556–574. doi:10.1080/13825585.2010.481354

Kirbach, S. E., & Mintzer, J. (2008). Alzheimer's disease burdens African-Americans: A review of epidemiological risk factors and implications for prevention and treatment. *Current Psychiatry Reviews*, 4(1), 58–62.

Kline, D. W., & Li, W. (2005). Cataracts and the aging driver. *Ageing International*, 30(2), 105–121.

Knopman, D. S., & Roberts, R. (2010). Vascular risk factors: Imaging and neuropathologic correlates. *Journal of Alzheimer's Disease*, 20(3), 699–709. doi:10.3233/jad-2010-091555

Kohama, S. G., Rosene, D. L., & Sherman, L. S. (2012). Age-related changes in human and non-human primate white matter: From myelination disturbances to cognitive decline. *Age*, 34(5), 1093–1110. doi:10.1007/s11357-011-9357-7

Korczyn, A. D., Vakhapova, V., & Grinberg, L. T. (2012). Vascular dementia. *Journal of the Neurological Sciences*, 322(1–2), 2–10. doi:10.1016/j.jns.2012.03.027

Kramer, D. (2003). The ontogeny of wisdom in its variations. In J. Demick & C. Andreoletti (Eds.), *Handbook of adult development* (pp. 131–151). New York: Kluwer Academic/Plenum Publishers.

Kusnecov, A. W., Anisman, H., Fenn, A. M., Corona, A. W., & Godbout, J. P. (2013). In A. W. Kusnecov & H. Anisman (Eds.), *The Wiley-Blackwell handbook of psychoneuroimmunology*. Chichester, UK: John Wiley . doi:10.1002/9781118314814

Lambert, J.-C., Sleegers, K., González-Pérez, A., Ingelsson, M., Beecham, G. W., Hiltunen, M., . . . Tzourio, C. (2011). The CALHM1 P86L polymorphism is a genetic modifier of age at onset in Alzheimer's disease: A meta-analysis study. *Journal of Alzheimer's Disease*, 22(1), 247–255. doi:10.3233/jad-2010-100933

Lang, F. R., Featherman, D. L., & Nesselroade, J. R. (1997). Social self-efficacy and short-term variability in social relationships: The MacArthur Successful Aging Studies. *Psychology and Aging*, 12(4), 657–666.

Lange-Asschenfeldt, C., & Kojda, G. (2008). Alzheimer's disease, cerebrovascular dysfunction and the benefits of exercise: From vessels to neurons. *Experimental Gerontology*, 43(6), 499–504. doi:10.1016/j.exger.2008.04.002

Laplante-Lévesque, A., Hickson, L., & Worrall, L. (2010). Rehabilitation of older adults with hearing impairment: A critical review. *Journal of Aging & Health*, 22(2), 143–153. doi:10.1177/0898264309352731

Lee, H.-J., & Chou, L.-S. (2007). Balance control during stair negotiation in older adults. *Journal of Biomechanics*, 40(11), 2530–2536.

Lemere, C. (2013). Alzheimer's disease and Down syndrome. *Alzheimer's & Dementia*, 9(4), P513. doi:10.1016/j.jalz.2013.04.223

Lin, E. H. B. (2008). Depression and osteoarthritis. *American Journal of Medicine*, 121(11), S16–S19. doi:10.1016/j.amjmed.2008.09.009

Lin, F. R., Thorpe, R., Gordon-Salant, S., & Ferrucci, L. (2011). Hearing loss prevalence and risk factors among older adults in the United States. *The Journals of Gerontology: Series A: Biological Sciences and Medical Sciences*, 66A(5), 582–590. doi:10.1093/gerona/glr002

Lindenberger, U., & Baltes, P. B. (1997). Intellectual functioning in old and very old age: Cross-sectional results from the Berlin Aging Study. *Psychology and Aging*, 12(3), 410–432. doi:10.1037/0882-7974.12.3.410

Lindstrom, T. M., & Robinson, W. H. (2010). Rheumatoid arthritis: A role for immunosenescence? *Journal of the American Geriatrics Society*, 58(8), 1565–1575. doi:10.1111/j.1532-5415.2010.02965.x

Liu, Y., Julkunen, V., Paajanen, T., Westman, E., Wahlund, L.-O., Aitken, A., . . . Soininen, H. (2012). Education increases reserve against Alzheimer's disease—Evidence from structural MRI analysis. *Neuroradiology*, 54(9), 929–938. doi:10.1007/s00234-012-1005-0

Löckenhoff, C. E., & Carstensen, L. L. (2007). Aging, emotion, and health-related decision strategies: Motivational manipulations can reduce age differences. *Psychology and Aging*, 22(1), 134–146.

Lönnqvist, J. (2010). Cognition and mental ill-health. *European Psychiatry*, 25(5), 297–299. doi:10.1016/j.eurpsy.2010.01.006

Lorente-Cebrián, S., Costa, A. G. V, Navas-Carretero, S., Zabala, M., Laiglesia, L. M., Martínez, J. A., & Moreno-Aliaga, M. J. (2015). An update on the role of omega-3 fatty acids on inflammatory and degenerative diseases. *Journal of Physiology and Biochemistry*, 71(2), 341–349. doi:10.1007/s13105-015-0395-y

Lorente-Cebrián, S., Costa, A. G. V, Navas-Carretero, S., Zabala, M., Martínez, J. A., & Moreno-Aliaga, M. J. (2013). Role of omega-3 fatty acids in obesity, metabolic syndrome, and cardiovascular diseases: A review of the evidence. *Journal of Physiology and Biochemistry*, 69(3), 633–651. doi:10.1007/s13105-013-0265-4

Lu, P. H., Lee, G. J., Tishler, T. A., Meghpara, M., Thompson, P. M., & Bartzokis, G. (2013). Myelin breakdown mediates age-related slowing in cognitive processing speed in healthy elderly men. *Brain and Cognition*, 81(1), 131–138. doi:10.1016/j.bandc.2012.09.006

Lustig, C., Shah, P., Seidler, R., & Reuter-Lorenz, P. A. (2009). Aging, training, and the brain: A review and future directions. *Neuropsychology Review*, 19(4), 504–522. doi:10.1007/s11065-009-9119-9

Lyketsos, C. G., DelCampo, L., Steinberg, M., Miles, Q., Steele, C. D., Munro, C., . . . Rabins, P. V. (2003). Treating depression in Alzheimer disease: Efficacy and safety of sertraline therapy, and the benefits of depression reduction: The DIADS. *Archives of General Psychiatry*, 60(7), 737–746. doi:10.1001/archpsyc.60.7.737

Maetzler, W., Liepelt, I., & Berg, D. (2009). Progression of Parkinson's disease in the clinical phase: Potential markers. *The Lancet Neurology*, 8(12), 1158–1171. doi:10.1016/s1474-4422(09)70291-1

Maguire, E. A., Spiers, H. J., Good, C. D., Hartley, T., Frackowiak, R. S. J., & Burgess, N. (2003). Navigation expertise and the human hippocampus: A structural brain imaging analysis. *Hippocampus*, 13(2), 250–259. doi:10.1002/hipo.10087

Mammarella, N., Borella, E., Carretti, B., Leonardi, G., & Fairfield, B. (2013). Examining an emotion enhancement effect in working memory: Evidence from age-related differences. *Neuropsychological Rehabilitation*, 23(3), 416–428. doi:10.1080/09602011.2013.775065

Marcus, M. B. (2008). MRI could be key in Alzheimer's fight. *USA Today*.

Margaretten, M. E., Katz, P., Schmajuk, G., & Yelin, E. (2013). Missed opportunities for depression screening in patients with arthritis in the United States. *Journal of General Internal Medicine*, 28(12), 1637–1642. doi:10.1007/s11606-013-2541-y

Margrett, J., Martin, P., Woodard, J. L., Miller, L. S., MacDonald, M., Baenziger, J., . . . Poon, L. (2010). Depression among centenarians and the oldest old: Contributions of cognition and personality. *Gerontology*, 56(1), 93–99. doi:10.1159/000272018

Martin, P., Baenziger, J., MacDonald, M., Siegler, I. C., & Poon, L. W. (2009). Engaged lifestyle, personality, and mental status among centenarians. *Journal of Adult Development*, 16(4), 199–208. doi:10.1007/s10804-009-9066-y

Mastwyk, M., Ames, D., Ellis, K. A., Chiu, E., & Dow, B. (2014). Disclosing a dementia diagnosis: What do patients and family consider important? *International Psychogeriatrics*, 26(8), 1263–1272. doi:10.1017/S1041610214000751

Mather, M., & Carstensen, L. L. (2005). Aging and motivated cognition: The positivity effect in attention and memory. *Trends in Cognitive Sciences*, 9(10), 496–502. doi:10.1016/j.tics.2005.08.005

Mavros, Y., Kay, S., Anderberg, K. A., Baker, M. K., Wang, Y., Zhao, R., . . . Fiatarone Singh, M. A. (2013). Changes in insulin resistance and HbA1c are related to exercise-mediated changes in body composition in older adults with type 2 diabetes: Interim outcomes from the GREAT2DO trial. *Diabetes Care*, 36(8), 2372–2379. doi:10.2337/dc12-2196

McCabe, D. P., Roediger III, H. L., McDaniel, M. A., Balota, D. A., & Hambrick, D. Z. (2010). The relationship between working memory capacity and executive functioning: Evidence for a common executive attention construct. *Neuropsychology*, 24(2), 222–243. doi:10.1037/a0017619

McIlvane, J. M. (2007). Disentangling the effects of race and SES on arthritis-related symptoms, coping, and well-being in African American and White women. *Aging & Mental Health*, 11(5), 556–569. doi:10.1080/13607860601086520

McIlvane, J. M., Baker, T. A., & Mingo, C. A. (2008). Racial differences in arthritis-related stress, chronic life stress, and depressive symptoms among women with arthritis: A contextual perspective. *The Journals of Gerontology: Series B: Psychological Sciences and Social Sciences*, 63B(5), S320–S327.

McKhann, G. M., Knopman, D. S., Chertkow, H., Hyman, B. T., Jack, C. R., Kawas, C. H., . . . Phelps, C. H. (2011). The diagnosis of dementia due to Alzheimer's disease: Recommendations from the National Institute on Aging–Alzheimer's Association workgroups on diagnostic guidelines for Alzheimer's disease. *Alzheimer's & Dementia*, 7(3), 263–269. doi:10.1016/j.jalz.2011.03.005

Meletis, C. D., & Zabriskie, N. (2007). Common nutrient depletions caused by pharmaceuticals. *Alternative and Complementary Therapies*, 13, 10–17.

Mikels, J. A., Larkin, G. R., Reuter-Lorenz, P. A., & Cartensen, L. L. (2005). Divergent trajectories in the aging mind: Changes in working memory for affective versus visual information with age. *Psychology and Aging*, 20(4), 542–553. doi:10.1037/0882-7974.20.4.542

Miller, B. D., Wood, B. L., & Smith, B. A. (2010). Respiratory illness. In R. J. Shaw & D. R. DeMaso (Eds.), *Textbook of pediatric psychosomatic medicine* (pp. 303–317). Arlington, VA: American Psychiatric Publishing.

Miller, L. S., Mitchell, M. B., Woodard, J. L., Davey, A., Martin, P., & Poon, L. W. (2010). Cognitive performance in centenarians and the oldest old: Norms from the Georgia Centenarian Study. *Aging, Neuropsychology & Cognition*, 17(5), 575–590. doi:10.1080/13825585.2010.481355

Mironov, S. (2009). Respiratory circuits: Function, mechanisms, topology, and pathology. *Neuroscientist*, 15(2), 194–208.

Mojon-Azzi, S. M., Sousa-Poza, & Mojon, D. S. (2008). Impact of low vision on well-being in 10 European countries. *Ophthalmologica*, 222(3), 205–212.

Molinari, V., McCullough, L. B., Coverdale, J. H., & Workman, R. (2006). Principles and practice of geriatric assent. *Aging & Mental Health*, 10(1), 48–54. doi:10.1080/13607860500307829

Monaghan, C., & Begley, A. (2004). ORIGINAL ARTICLE Dementia diagnosis and disclosure: A dilemma in practice. *Journal of Clinical Nursing*, 13, 22–29. doi:10.1111/j.1365-2702.2004.00922.x

Mortensen, L., Meyer, A. S., & Humphreys, G. W. (2006). Age-related effects on speech production: A review. *Language & Cognitive Processes*, 21(1–3), 238–290.

Mu, Y., & Gage, F. H. (2011). Adult hippocampal neurogenesis and its role in Alzheimer's disease. *Molecular Neurodegeneration*, 6, 85. doi:10.1186/1750-1326-6-85

Muangpaisan, W., Petcharat, C., & Srinonprasert, V. (2012). Prevalence of potentially reversible conditions in dementia and mild cognitive impairment in a geriatric clinic. *Geriatrics & Gerontology International*, 12(1), 59–64. doi:10.1111/j.1447-0594.2011.00728.x

Muscari, A., Giannoni, C., Pierpaoli, L., Berzigotti, A., Maietta, P., Foschi, E., . . . Zoli, M. (2010). Chronic endurance exercise training prevents aging-related cognitive decline in healthy older adults: A randomized controlled trial. *International Journal of Geriatric Psychiatry*, 25(10), 1055–1064.

Myers, C. E., Klein, B. E. K., Gangnon, R., Sivakumaran, T. A., Iyengar, S. K., & Klein, R. (2014). Cigarette smoking and the natural history of age-related macular degeneration: The Beaver Dam Eye Study. *Ophthalmology*, 121(10), 1949–1955. doi:10.1016/j.ophtha.2014.04.040

Nair, A. K., Sabbagh, M. N., Tucker, A. M., & Stern, Y. (2014). Cognitive reserve and the aging brain. In A. K. Nair & M. N. Sabbagh (Eds.), *Geriatric neurology*. Chichester, UK: John Wiley. doi:10.1002/9781118730676

Nalls, M. A., Pankratz, N., Lill, C. M., Do, C. B., Hernandez, D. G., Saad, M., . . . Singleton, A. B. (2014). Large-scale meta-analysis of genome-wide association data identifies six new risk loci for Parkinson's disease. *Nature Genetics*, 46(9), 989–993. doi:10.1038/ng.3043

Nation, D. A., Salmon, D. P., & Bondi, M. W. (2014). The neuroscience of cortical dementias: Linking neuroanatomy, neurophysiology, and neuropsychology. In C. Noggle (Ed.), *The neuropsychology of cortical dementias* (pp. 3–34). New York: Springer. Retrieved from https://books.google.com/books?id=D-OfBQAAQBAJ&pgis=1

National Center for Chronic Disease Prevention and Health Promotion. (2010). Prevalence of doctor-diagnosed arthritis and arthritis-attributable activity limitation—United States, 2007–2009. *Morbidity and Mortality Weekly Report*, 59(39), 1261–1265.

National Center for Health Statistics. (2011). *Health United States, 2011*. Retrieved from http://www.cdc.gov/nchs/data/hus/2011/022.pdf

National Center for Health Statistics. (2015). Deaths: Final data for 2013. *National Vital Statistics Reports*. Retrieved from http://www.cdc.gov/nchs/data/nvsr/nvsr64/nvsr64_02.pdf

National Parkinson Foundation. (2008). *About Parkinson's disease*. Retrieved from http://www.parkinson.org/NETCOMMUNITY/Page.aspx?pid=225&srcid=201

Nettelbeck, T., & Burns, N. R. (2010). Processing speed, working memory and reasoning ability from childhood to old age. *Personality and Individual Differences*, 48(4), 379–384. doi:10.1016/j.paid.2009.10.032

Niemann, C., Godde, B., & Voelcker-Rehage, C. (2014). Not only cardiovascular, but also coordinative exercise increases hippocampal volume in older adults. *Frontiers in Aging Neuroscience*, 6, 170. doi:10.3389/fnagi.2014.00170

Nithiananthanrajah, J., & Hannan, A. J. (2009). The neurobiology of brain and cognitive reserve: Mental and physical activity as modulators of brain disorders. *Progress in Neurobiology*, 89(4), 369–382. doi:10.1016/j.pneurobio.2009.10.001

Okonkwo, O. C., Cohen, R. A., Gunstad, J., Tremont, G., Alosco, M. L., & Poppas, A. (2010). Longitudinal trajectories of cognitive decline among older adults with cardiovascular disease. *Cerebrovascular Diseases*, 30(4), 362–373. doi:10.1159/000319564

Osorio, A., Fay, S., Pouthas, V., & Ballesteros, S. (2010). Ageing affects brain activity in highly educated older adults: An ERP study using a word-stem priming task. *Cortex*, 46(4), 522–534. doi:10.1016/j.cortex.2009.09.003

Owsley, C. (2011). Aging and vision. *Vision Research*, 51(13), 1610–1622. doi:10.1016/j.visres.2010.10.020

Owsley, C., McGwin, G., Jackson, G. R., Kallies, K., & Clark, M. (2007). Cone- and rod-mediated dark adaptation impairment in age-related maculopathy. *Ophthalmology*, 114(9), 1728–1735.

Palta, P., Schneider, A. L. C., Biessels, G. J., Touradji, P., & Hill-Briggs, F. (2014). Magnitude of cognitive dysfunction in adults with type 2 diabetes: A meta-analysis of six cognitive domains and the most frequently reported neuropsychological tests within domains. *Journal of the International Neuropsychological Society*, 20(3), 278–291. doi:10.1017/S1355617713001483

Panula, J., Pihlajamäki, H., Mattila, V. M., Jaatinen, P., Vahlberg, T., Aarnio, P., & Kivelä, S. L. (2011). Mortality and cause of death in hip fracture patients aged 65 or older-a population-based study. *BMC Musculoskeletal Disorders*, 12(1).

Panza, F., Solfrizzi, V., & Capurso, A. (2004). *Diet and cognitive decline*. Hauppauge, NY: Nova Science Publishers.

Park, M., Katon, W. J., & Wolf, F. M. (2013). Depression and risk of mortality in individuals with diabetes: A meta-analysis and systematic review. *General Hospital Psychiatry*, 35(3), 217–225. doi:10.1016/j.genhosppsych.2013.01.006

Paúl, C., Ribeiro, O., & Santos, P. (2010). Cognitive impairment in old people living in the community. *Archives of Gerontology & Geriatrics*, 51(2), 121–124. doi:10.1016/j.archger.2009.09.037

Paul, L. (2011). Diet, nutrition and telomere length. *The Journal of Nutritional Biochemistry*, 22(10), 895–901. doi:10.1016/j.jnutbio.2010.12.001

Payette, H. (2005). Nutrition as a determinant of functional autonomy and quality of life in aging: A research program. *Canadian Journal of Physiology & Pharmacology*, 83(11), 1061–1070. doi:10.1139/Y05-086

Peelle, J. E., Troiani, V., Grossman, M., & Wingfield, A. (2011). Hearing loss in older adults affects neural systems supporting speech comprehension. *The Journal of Neuroscience 31*(35), 12638–12643. doi:10.1523/JNEUROSCI.2559-11.2011

Perl, D. P. (2010). Neuropathology of Alzheimer's disease. *Mount Sinai Journal of Medicine, 77*(1), 32–42. doi:10.1002/msj.20157

Peters, A., & Kemper, T. (2012). A review of the structural alterations in the cerebral hemispheres of the aging rhesus monkey. *Neurobiology of Aging, 33*(10), 2357–2372. doi:10.1016/j.neurobiolaging.2011.11.015

Peterson, M. D., Rhea, M. R., Sen, A., & Gordon, P. M. (2010). Resistance exercise for muscular strength in older adults: A meta-analysis. *Ageing Research Reviews, 9*(3), 226–237. doi:10.1016/j.arr.2010.03.004

Phani, S., Loike, J. D., & Przedborski, S. (2012). Neurodegeneration and inflammation in Parkinson's disease. *Parkinsonism & Related Disorders, 18*(Suppl. 1), S207–S209. doi:10.1016/S1353-8020(11)70064-5

Phillips, S. P. (2006). Risky business: Explaining the gender gap in longevity. *Journal of Men's Health & Gender, 3*(1), 43–46.

Piolino, P., Coste, C., Martinelli, P., Macé, A.-L., Quinette, P., Guillery-Girard, B., & Belleville, S. (2010). Reduced specificity of autobiographical memory and aging: Do the executive and feature binding functions of working memory have a role? *Neuropsychologia, 48*(2), 429–440. doi:10.1016/j.neuropsychologia.2009.09.035

Piolino, P., Desgranges, B., Clarys, D., Guillery-Girard, B., Taconnat, L., Isingrini, M., & Eustache, F. (2006). Autobiographical memory, autonoetic consciousness, and self-perspective in aging. *Psychology and Aging, 21*(3), 510–525.

Plassman, B. L., Langa, K. M., Fisher, G. G., Heeringa, S. G., Weir, D. R., Ofstedal, M. B., . . . Wallace, R. B. (2007). Prevalence of dementia in the United States: The aging, demographics, and memory study. *Neuroepidemiology, 29*(1), 125–132.

Purohit, N., & Kalairajah, Y. (2010). Are patients with fractured hips giving valid consent for surgery? *International Journal of Risk & Safety in Medicine, 22*(2), 71–76.

Quan, T., & Fisher, G. J. (2015). Role of age-associated alterations of the dermal extracellular matrix microenvironment in human skin aging: A mini-review. *Gerontology.* Advance online publication. doi:10.1159/000371708

Quaranta, N., Coppola, F., Casulli, M., Barulli, M. R., Panza, F., Tortelli, R., . . . Logroscino, G. (2015). Epidemiology of age related hearing loss: A review. *Hearing, Balance and Communication*, 1–5. doi:10.3109/21695717.2014.994869

Radak, Z., Chung, H. Y., Koltai, E., Taylor, A. W., & Goto, S. (2008). Exercise, oxidative stress and hormesis. *Ageing Research Reviews, 7*(1), 34–42. doi:10.1016/j.arr.2007.04.004

Ratcliff, R., Thapar, A., & McKoon, G. (2006). Aging and individual differences in rapid two-choice decisions. *Psychonomic Bulletin & Review, 13*(4), 626–635.

Raz, N., Lindenberger, U., Rodrigue, K. M., Kennedy, K. M., Head, D., Williamson, A., . . . Acker, J. D. (2005). Regional brain changes in aging healthy adults: General trends, individual differences and modifiers. *Cerebral Cortex, 15*(11), 1676–1689.

Raz, N., Rodrigue, K. M., Kennedy, K. M., & Acker, J. D. (2007). Vascular health and longitudinal changes in brain and cognition in middle-aged and older adults. *Neuropsychology, 21*(2), 149–157.

Reed, A. E., & Carstensen, L. L. (2012). The theory behind the age-related positivity effect. *Frontiers in Psychology, 3*, 339. doi:10.3389/fpsyg.2012.00339

Reed, A. E., Chan, L., & Mikels, J. A. (2014). Meta-analysis of the age-related positivity effect: Age differences in preferences for positive over negative information. *Psychology and Aging, 29*(1), 1–15. doi:10.1037/a0035194

Rektorova, I., Rusina, R., Hort, J., & Matej, R. (2009). The degenerative dementias. In R. P. Lisak, D. D. Truong, W. M. Carroll, & R. Bhidayasiri (Eds.), *International neurology: A clinical approach.* Hoboken, NJ: John Wiley.

Reuter-Lorenz, P. A., & Cappell, K. A. (2008). Neurocognitive aging and the compensation hypothesis. *Current Directions in Psychological Science, 17*(3), 177–182. doi:10.1111/j.1467-8721.2008.00570.x

Rhone, M., & Basu, A. (2008). Phytochemicals and age-related eye diseases. *Nutrition Reviews, 66*(8), 465–472. doi:10.1111/j.1753-4887.2008.00078.x

Rice, C., & Cunningham, D. A. (2002). Aging of the neuromuscular system: Influences of gender and physical activity. In R. J. Scephard (Ed.), *Gender, physical ativity, and aging* (pp. 121–150). Boca Raton, FL: CBC Press.

Richmond, R. L., Law, J., & KayLambkin, F. (2012). Morbidity profiles and lifetime health of Australian centenarians. *Australasian Journal on Ageing, 31*(4), 227–232. doi:10.1111/j.1741-6612.2011.00570.x

Ringman, J. M., & Varpetian, A. (2009). Other dementias. In R. P. Lisak, D. D. Truong, W. M. Carroll, & R. Bhidayasiri (Eds.), *International neurology: A clinical approach* (pp. 137–143). Hoboken, NJ: John Wiley.

Rizzi, L., Rosset, I., & Roriz-Cruz, M. (2014). Global epidemiology of dementia: Alzheimer's and vascular types. *BioMed Research International, 2014*, 908915. doi:10.1155/2014/908915

Rizzo, G., Arcuti, S., Martino, D., Copetti, M., Fontana, A., & Logroscino, G. (2015). Accuracy of clinical diagnosis of Parkinson's disease: A systematic review and Bayesian meta-analysis (S36.001). *Neurology, 84*(Suppl. 14). Retrieved from http://www.neurology.org/content/84/14_Supplement/S36.001.short

Roberts, R. O., Knopman, D. S., Przybelski, S. A., Mielke, M. M., Kantarci, K., Preboske, G. M., . . . Jack, C. R. (2014). Association of type 2 diabetes with brain atrophy and cognitive impairment. *Neurology, 82*(13), 1132–1141. doi:10.1212/WNL.0000000000000269

Rodrigues, J., Assunção, M., Lukoyanov, N., Cardoso, A., Carvalho, F., & Andrade, J. P. (2013). Protective effects of a catechin-rich extract on the hippocampal formation and spatial memory in aging rats. *Behavioural Brain Research, 246*, 94–102. doi:10.1016/j.bbr.2013.02.040

Rolland, Y., Abellan van Kan, G., & Vellas, B. (2008). Physical activity and Alzheimer's disease: From prevention to therapeutic perspectives. *Journal of the American Medical Directors Association, 9*(6), 390–405. doi:10.1016/j.jamda.2008.02.007

Rosano, C., Venkatraman, V. K., Guralnik, J., Newman, A. B., Glynn, N. W., Launer, L., . . . Aizenstein, H. (2010). Psychomotor speed and functional brain MRI 2 years after completing a physical activity treatment. *The Journals of Gerontology: Series A: Biological Sciences and Medical Sciences, 65A*(6), 639–647.

Rosén, C., Hansson, O., Blennow, K., & Zetterberg, H. (2013). Fluid biomarkers in Alzheimer's disease—Current concepts. *Molecular Neurodegeneration, 8*, 20. doi:10.1186/1750-1326-8-20

Rowe, G., Hasher, L., & Turcotte, J. (2010). Interference, aging, and visuospatial working memory: The role of similarity. *Neuropsychology, 24*(6), 804–807. doi:10.1037/a0020244

Roy, T., & Lloyd, C. E. (2012). Epidemiology of depression and diabetes: A systematic review. *Journal of Affective Disorders, 142*(Suppl.), S8–S21. doi:10.1016/S0165-0327(12)70004-6

Rubin, D. C. (2000). Autobiographical memory and aging. In D. C. Park & N. Schwarz (Eds.), *Cognitive aging: A primer* (pp. 131–149). New York: Psychology Press.

Ruppar, T. M., & Schneider, J. K. (2007). Self-reported exercise behavior and interpretations of exercise in older adults. *Western Journal of Nursing Research, 29*(2), 140–157.

Salmon, D. P., & Bondi, M. W. (2009). Neuropsychological assessment of dementia. *Annual Review Psychology, 60*, 257–282.

Salthouse, T. A. (2011). Neuroanatomical substrates of age-related cognitive decline. *Psychological Bulletin, 137*(5), 753–784. doi:10.1037/a0023262

Samanez-Larkin, G. R., Robertson, E. R., Mikels, J. A., Carstensen, L. L., & Gotlib, I. H. (2009). Selective attention to emotion in the aging brain. *Psychology and Aging, 24*(3), 519–529. doi:10.1037/a0016952

Sandlin, D., McGwin, G., & Owsley, C. (2014). Association between vision impairment and driving exposure in older adults aged 70 years and over: A population-based examination. *Acta Ophthalmologica, 92*(3), e207–e212. doi:10.1111/aos.12050

Santos-Lozano, A., Sanchis-Gomar, F., Pareja-Galeano, H., Fiuza-Luces, C., Emanuele, E., Lucia, A., & Garatachea, N. (2015). Where are supercentenarians located? A worldwide demographic study. *Rejuvenation Research.* Advance online publication. Retrieved from http://online.liebertpub.com/doi/abs/10.1089/rej.2014.1609

Sattler, C., Toro, P., Schönknecht, P., & Schröder, J. (2012). Cognitive activity, education and socioeconomic status as preventive factors for mild cognitive impairment and Alzheimer's disease. *Psychiatry Research, 196*(1), 90–95. doi:10.1016/j.psychres.2011.11.012

Scarmeas, N., & Stern, Y. (2003). Cognitive reserve and lifestyle. *Journal of Clinical and Experimental Neuropsychology, 25*(5), 625–633. doi:10.1076/jcen.25.5.625.14576

Schaie, K. W. (2013). *Developmental influences on adult intelligence: The Seattle Longitudinal Study.* New York: Oxford University Press.

Schaie, K. W., & Willis, S. L. (1986). Can decline in adult intellectual functioning be reversed? *Developmental Psychology, 22*(2), 223–232. doi:10.1037/0012-1649.22.2.223

Schmidt, H., Freudenberger, P., Seiler, S., & Schmidt, R. (2012). Genetics of subcortical vascular dementia. *Experimental Gerontology, 47*(11), 873–877. doi:10.1016/j.exger.2012.06.003

Schroots, J. J. F., van Dijkum, C., & Assink, M. H. J. (2004). Autobiographical memory from a life span perspective. *International Journal of Aging and Human Development, 58*(1), 69–85.

Schuff, N., Tosun, D., Insel, P. S., Chiang, G. C., Truran, D., Aisen, P. S., . . . Weiner, M. W. (2012). Nonlinear time course of brain volume loss in cognitively normal and impaired elders. *Neurobiology of Aging, 33*(5), 845–855. doi:10.1016/j.neurobiolaging.2010.07.012

Schwartz, B. L., & Frazier, L. D. (2005). Tip-of-the-tongue states and aging: Contrasting psycholinguistic and metacognitive perspectives. *Journal of General Psychology, 132*(4), 377–391.

Scott, R. A., Langenberg, C., Sharp, S. J., Franks, P. W., Rolandsson, O., Drogan, D., . . . Wareham, N. J. (2013). The link between family history and risk of type 2 diabetes is not explained by anthropometric, lifestyle or genetic risk factors: The EPIC-InterAct study. *Diabetologia, 56*(1), 60–69. doi:10.1007/s00125-012-2715-x

Sebastiani, P., & Perls, T. T. (2012). The genetics of extreme longevity: Lessons from the new

England centenarian study. *Frontiers in Genetics*, *3*, 277. doi:10.3389/fgene.2012.00277

Serra-Rexach, J. A., Bustamante-Ara, N., Hierro Villarán, P., González Gil, P., Sanz Ibáñez, M. J., Blanco Sanz, N., . . . Lucia, A. (2011). Short-term, light- to moderate-intensity exercise training improves leg muscle strength in the oldest old: A randomized controlled trial. *Journal of the American Geriatrics Society*, *59*(4), 594–602. doi:10.1111/j.1532-5415.2011.03356.x

Seshadri, S., & Wolf, P. A. (2007). Lifetime risk of stroke and dementia: Current concepts, and estimates from the Framingham Study. *The Lancet Neurology*, *6*(12), 1106–1114.

Shadyab, A. H., & LaCroix, A. Z. (2015). Genetic factors associated with longevity: A review of recent findings. *Ageing Research Reviews*, *19*, 1–7. doi:10.1016/j.arr.2014.10.005

Shafto, M. A., Stamatakis, E. A., Tam, P. P., & Tyler, L. K. (2010). Word retrieval failures in old age: The relationship between structure and function. *Journal of Cognitive Neuroscience*, *22*(7), 1530–1540. doi:10.1162/jocn.2009.21321

Shafto, M. A., & Tyler, L. K. (2014). Language in the aging brain: The network dynamics of cognitive decline and preservation. *Science*, *346*(6209), 583–587. doi:10.1126/science.1254404

Sharp, S. I., Aarsland, D., Day, S., Sønnesyn, H., & Ballard, C. (2011). Hypertension is a potential risk factor for vascular dementia: Systematic review. *International Journal of Geriatric Psychiatry*, *26*(7), 661–669. doi:10.1002/gps.2572

Shors, T. J. (2014). The adult brain makes new neurons, and effortful learning keeps them alive. *Current Directions in Psychological Science*, *23*(5), 311–318. doi:10.1177/0963721414540167

Siegel, R., Ma, J., Zou, Z., & Jemal, A. (2014). Cancer statistics, 2014. *CA: A Cancer Journal for Clinicians*, *64*(1), 9–29. doi:10.3322/caac.21208

Sin, H. P. Y., Liu, D. T. L., & Lam, D. S. C. (2013). Lifestyle modification, nutritional and vitamins supplements for age-related macular degeneration. *Acta Ophthalmologica*, *91*(1), 6–11. doi:10.1111/j.1755-3768.2011.02357.x

Sinnott, J. D. (2003). Postformal thought adn adult development: Living in balance. In J. Demick & C. Andreoletti (Eds.), *Handbook of adult development* (pp. 221–238). New York: Kluwer.

Smach, M. A., Charfeddine, B., Ben Othman, L., Lammouchi, T., Dridi, H., Nafati, S., . . . Limem, K. (2009). Evaluation of cerebrospinal fluid tau/beta-amyloid(42) ratio as diagnostic markers for Alzheimer disease. *European Neurology*, *62*(6), 349–355. doi:10.1159/000241881

Sofi, F., Macchi, C., Abbate, R., Gensini, G. F., & Casini, A. (2010). Effectiveness of the Mediterranean diet: Can it help delay or prevent Alzheimer's disease? *Journal of Alzheimer's Disease*, *20*(3), 795–801. doi:10.3233/jad-2010-1418

Solomon, D. H., Ayanian, J. Z., Yelin, E., Shaykevich, T., Brookhart, M. A., & Katz, J. N. (2012). Use of disease-modifying medications for rheumatoid arthritis by race and ethnicity in the National Ambulatory Medical Care Survey. *Arthritis Care & Research*, *64*(2), 184–189. doi:10.1002/acr.20674

Song, J., Xu, H., Liu, F., & Feng, L. (2011). Tea and cognitive health in late life: Current evidence and future directions. *The Journal of Nutrition, Health & Aging*, *16*(1), 31–34. doi:10.1007/s12603-011-0139-9

Spalding, K. L., Bergmann, O., Alkass, K., Bernard, S., Salehpour, M., Huttner, H. B., . . . Frisén, J. (2013). Dynamics of hippocampal neurogenesis in adult humans. *Cell*, *153*(6), 1219–1227. doi:10.1016/j.cell.2013.05.002

Spalletta, G., Caltagirone, C., Girardi, P., Gianni, W., Casini, A. R., & Palmer, K. (2012). The role of persistent and incident major depression on rate of cognitive deterioration in newly diagnosed Alzheimer's disease patients. *Psychiatry*

Research, *198*(2), 263–268. doi:10.1016/j.psychres.2011.11.018

Srikanth, S., & Nagaraja, A. V. (2005). A prospective study of reversible dementias: Frequency, causes, clinical profile and results of treatment. *Neurology India*, *53*(3), 291–294.

Stampfer, M. J. (2006). Cardiovascular disease and Alzheimer's disease: Common links. *Journal of Internal Medicine*, *260*(3), 211–223. doi:10.1111/j.1365-2796.2006.01687.x

Stanner, S., & Denny, A. (2009). Healthy ageing: The role of nutrition and lifestyle—A new British Nutrition Foundation Task Force Report. *Nutrition Bulletin*, *34*(1), 58–63. doi:10.1111/j.1467-3010.2008.01734.x

Starkstein, S. E., Jorge, R., Mizrahi, R., & Robinson, R. G. (2005). The construct of minor and major depression in Alzheimer's disease. *The American Journal of Psychiatry*, *162*(11), 2086–2093. doi:10.1176/appi.ajp.162.11.2086

Starkstein, S. E., Mizrahi, R., & Power, B. D. (2008). Depression in Alzheimer's disease: Phenomenology, clinical correlates and treatment. *International Review of Psychiatry*, *20*(4), 382–388. doi:10.1080/09540260802094480

Staudinger, U. M., & Baltes, P. B. (1996). Interactive minds: A facilitative setting of wisdom-related performance? *Journal of Personality and Social Psychology*, *71*(4), 746–762.

Staudinger, U. M., Dörner, J., & Mickler, C. (2005). Wisdom and personality. In R. J. Sternberg & J. Jordan (Eds.), *A handbook of wisdom: Psychological perspectives* (pp. 191–219). New York: Cambridge University Press.

Staudinger, U. M., Kessler, E.-M., & Dörner, J. (2006). Wisdom in social context. In K. W. Schaie & L. L. Carstensen (Eds.), *Social structures, aging, and self-regulation in the elderly* (pp. 33–67). New York: Springer.

Stern, Y. (2012). Cognitive reserve in ageing and Alzheimer's disease. *The Lancet Neurology*, *11*(11), 1006–1012. doi:10.1016/S1474-4422(12)70191-6

Stine-Morrow, E. A. L., Shake, M. C., & Noh, S. R. (2010). Language and communication. In J. C. Cavanaugh, C. K. Cavanaugh, J. Berry, & R. West (Eds.), *Aging in America, Vol 1: Psychological aspects* (pp. 56–78). Santa Barbara, CA: Praeger/ABC-CLIO.

St-Laurent, M., Abdi, H., Burianová, H., & Grady, C. L. (2011). Influence of aging on the neural correlates of autobiographical, episodic, and semantic memory retrieval. *Journal of Cognitive Neuroscience*, *23*(12), 4150–4163. doi:10.1162/jocn_a_00079

Storandt, M. (2008). Cognitive deficits in the early stages of Alzheimer's disease. *Current Directions in Psychological Science*, *17*(3), 198–202. doi:10.1111/j.1467-8721.2008.00574.x

Strachan, S. M., Brawley, L. R., Spink, K., & Glazebrook, K. (2010). Older adults' physically-active identity: Relationships between social cognitions, physical activity and satisfaction with life. *Psychology of Sport and Exercise*, *11*(2), 114–121. doi:10.1016/j.psychsport.2009.09.002

Strenziok, M., Parasuraman, R., Clarke, E., Cisler, D. S., Thompson, J. C., & Greenwood, P. M. (2014). Neurocognitive enhancement in older adults: Comparison of three cognitive training tasks to test a hypothesis of training transfer in brain connectivity. *NeuroImage*, *85* (Pt. 3), 1027–1039. doi:10.1016/j.neuroimage.2013.07.069

Strough, J., Patrick, J. H., & Swenson, L. M. (2003). Strategies for solving everyday problems faced by grandparents: The role of experience. In B. Hayslip Jr. & J. H. Patrick (Eds.), *Working with custodial grandparents* (pp. 257–275). New York: Springer.

Sugarman, J., Roter, D., Cain, C., Wallace, R., Schmechel, D., & Welsh-Bohmer, K. A. (2007). Proxies and consent discussions for dementia research. *Journal of the American Geriatrics*

Society, *55*(4), 556–561. doi:10.1111/j.1532-5415.2007.01101.x

Tabrett, D. R., & Latham, K. (2010). Depression and vision loss. *Optician*, *240*(6274), 22–29.

Tan, J. S. L., Wang, J. J., Younan, C., Cumming, R. G., Rochtchina, E., & Mitchell, P. (2008). Smoking and the long-term incidence of cataract: The Blue Mountains Eye Study. *Ophthalmic Epidemiology*, *15*(3), 155–161. doi:10.1080/09286580701840362

Thornton, W. J. L., & Dumke, H. A. (2005). Age differences in everyday problem-solving and decision-making effectiveness: A meta-analytic review. *Psychology and Aging*, *20*(1), 85–99.

Tigani, X., Artemiadis, A. K., Alexopoulos, E. C., Chrousos, G. P., & Darviri, C. (2012). Self-rated health in centenarians: A nation-wide cross-sectional Greek study. *Archives of Gerontology and Geriatrics*, *54*(3), e342–e348. doi:10.1016/j.archger.2012.01.012

Toulouse, A., & Sullivan, A. M. (2008). Progress in Parkinson's disease: Where do we stand? *Progress in Neurobiology*, *85*(4), 376–392. doi:10.1016/j.pneurobio.2008.05.003

Troncoso, J. C., Zonderman, A. B., Resnick, S. M., Crain, B., Pletnikova, O., & O'Brien, R. J. (2008). Effect of infarcts on dementia in the Baltimore Longitudinal Study of Aging. *Annals of Neurology*, *64*(2), 168–176.

Truong, D. D., & Wolters, E. C. (2009). Recognition and management of Parkinson's disease during the premotor (prodromal) phase. *Expert Review of Neurotherapeutics*, *9*(6), 847–857. doi:10.1586/ern.09.50

Turner, G. R., & Spreng, R. N. (2012). Executive functions and neurocognitive aging: Dissociable patterns of brain activity. *Neurobiology of Aging*, *33*(4), 826.e1–13. doi:10.1016/j.neurobiolaging.2011.06.005

U.S. Bureau of the Census. (2012). *Current Population Survey*. Washington, DC: Author. Retrieved from http://www.bls.gov/emp/ep_chart_001.htm

U.S. Bureau of the Census. (2010). *Statistical abstract of the United States—2010*. Washington, DC: Author.

U.S. Department of Health and Human Services. (2015). Leading health indicators: Injury and violence. *Healthy People 2020*. Retrieved from https://www.healthypeople.gov/2020/leading-health-indicators/2020-lhi-topics/Injury-and-Violence/data

Vagelatos, N. T., & Eslick, G. D. (2013). Type 2 diabetes as a risk factor for Alzheimer's disease: The confounders, interactions, and neuropathology associated with this relationship. *Epidemiologic Reviews*, *35*, 152–160. doi:10.1093/epirev/mxs012

Van Bokhorst-de van der Schueren, M. A. E., Lonterman-Monasch, S., de Vries, O. J., Danner, S. A., Kramer, M. H. H., & Muller, M. (2013). Prevalence and determinants for malnutrition in geriatric outpatients. *Clinical Nutrition*, *32*(6), 1007–1011. doi:10.1016/j.clnu.2013.05.007

Van den Dungen, P., van Kuijk, L., van Marwijk, H., van der Wouden, J., Moll van Charante, E., van der Horst, H., & van Hout, H. (2014). Preferences regarding disclosure of a diagnosis of dementia: A systematic review. *International Psychogeriatrics*, *26*(10), 1603–1618. Retrieved from http://journals.cambridge.org/abstract_S1041610214000969

Van der Mussele, S., Bekelaar, K., Le Bastard, N., Vermeiren, Y., Saerens, J., Somers, N., . . . Engelborghs, S. (2013). Prevalence and associated behavioral symptoms of depression in mild cognitive impairment and dementia due to Alzheimer's disease. *International Journal of Geriatric Psychiatry*, *28*(9), 947–958. doi:10.1002/gps.3909

Van Dijk, K. R. A., Van Gerven, P. W. M., Van Boxtel, M. P. J., Van Der Elst, W., & Jolles, J.

(2008). No protective effects of education during normal cognitive aging: Results from the 6-year follow-up of the Maastricht Aging Study. *Psychology & Aging*, 23(1), 119–130. doi:10.1037/0882-7974.23.1.119

Van Dooren, F. E. P., Nefs, G., Schram, M. T., Verhey, F. R. J., Denollet, J., & Pouwer, F. (2013). Depression and risk of mortality in people with diabetes mellitus: A systematic review and meta-analysis. *PloS One*, 8(3), e57058. doi:10.1371/journal.pone.0057058

Van Gerven, P. W. M., Van Boxtel, M. P. J., Meijer, W. A., Willems, D., & Jolles, J. (2007). On the relative role of inhibition in age-related working memory decline. *Aging, Neuropsychology & Cognition*, 14(1), 95–107.

Vasto, S., Candore, G., Listì, F., Balistreri, C. R., Colonna-Romano, G., Malavolta, M., . . . Caruso, C. (2008). Inflammation, genes and zinc in Alzheimer's disease. *Brain Research Reviews*, 58(1), 96–105. doi:10.1016/j.brainresrev.2007.12.001

Verdelho, A., Madureira, S., Ferro, J. M., Baezner, H., Blahak, C., Poggesi, A., . . . Inzitari, D. (2012). Physical activity prevents progression for cognitive impairment and vascular dementia: Results from the LADIS (leukoaraiosis and disability) study. *Stroke*, 43(12), 3331–3335. doi:10.1161/STROKEAHA.112.661793

Verhaeghen, P., Steitz, D. W., Sliwinski, M. J., & Cerella, J. (2003). Aging and dual-task performance: A meta-analysis. *Psychology and Aging*, 18(3), 443–460.

Verkaik, R., Nuyen, J., Schellevis, F., & Francke, A. (2007). The relationship between severity of Alzheimer's disease and prevalence of comorbid depressive symptoms and depression: A systematic review. *International Journal of Geriatric Psychiatry*, 22(11), 1063–1086.

Visioli, F., & Hagen, T. M. (2007). Nutritional strategies for healthy cardiovascular aging: Focus on micronutrients. *Pharmacological Research*, 55(3), 199–206. doi:10.1016/j.phrs.2007.01.008

Visschedijk, J., Achterberg, W., van Balen, R., & Hertogh, C. (2010). Fear of falling after hip fracture: A systematic review of measurement instruments, prevalence, interventions, and related factors. *Journal of the American Geriatrics Society*, 58(9), 1739–1748. doi:10.1111/j.1532-5415.2010.03036.x

Vitlic, A., Lord, J. M., & Phillips, A. C. (2014). Stress, ageing and their influence on functional, cellular and molecular aspects of the immune system. *Age* 36(3), 9631. doi:10.1007/s11357-014-9631-6

Voelcker-Rehage, C., & Alberts, J. L. (2007). Effect of motor practice on dual-task performance in older adult. *The Journals of Gerontology: Series B: Psychological Sciences and Social Sciences*, (3), P141–P148.

Voelcker-Rehage, C., Stronge, A. J., & Alberts, J. L. (2006). Age-related differences in working memory and force control under dual-task conditions. *Aging, Neuropsychology, and Cognition*, 13(3), 366–384.

Von Arnim, C. A. F., Gola, U., & Biesalski, H. K. (2010). More than the sum of its parts? Nutrition in Alzheimer's disease. *Nutrition*, 26(7–8), 694–700. doi:10.1016/j.nut.2009.11.009

Wang, S., Luo, X., Barnes, D., Sano, M., & Yaffe, K. (2014). Physical activity and risk of cognitive impairment among oldest-old women. *The American Journal of Geriatric Psychiatry*, 22(11), 1149–1157. doi:10.1016/j.jagp.2013.03.002

Weerdesteyn, V., Nienhuis, B., Geurts, A. C. H., & Duysens, J. (2007). Age-related deficits in early response characteristics of obstacle avoidance under time pressure. *The Journals of Gerontology: Series A: Biological Sciences and Medical Sciences*, 62A(9), 1042–1047.

Wei, J. Y. (2004). Understanding the aging cardiovascular system. *Geriatrics & Gerontology International*, 4, S298–S303.

Welmerink, D. B., Longstreth, W. T., Lyles, M. F., & Fitzpatrick, A. L. (2010). Cognition and the risk of hospitalization for serious falls in the elderly: Results from the Cardiovascular Health Study. *The Journals of Gerontology: Series A: Biological Sciences and Medical Sciences*, 65A(11), 1242–1249.

Whitmer, R. A. (2007). The epidemiology of adiposity and dementia. *Current Alzheimer Research*, 4(2), 117–122.

Whitney, C. R. (1997). Jeanne Calment, world's elder, dies at 122. *New York Times*. Retrieved from http://www.nytimes.com/1997/08/05/world/jeanne-calment-world-s-elder-dies-at-122.html

Windle, G., Hughes, D., Linck, P., Russell, I., & Woods, B. (2010). Is exercise effective in promoting mental well-being in older age? A systematic review. *Aging & Mental Health*, 14(6), 652–669. doi:10.1080/13607861003713232

Wingfield, A., Tun, P. A., & McCoy, S. L. (2005). Hearing loss in older adulthood. *Current Directions in Psychological Science*, 14(3), 144–148. doi:10.1111/j.0963-7214.2005.00356.x

Wintergerst, E. S., Maggini, S., & Hornig, D. H. (2007). Contribution of selected vitamins and trace elements to immune function. *Annals of Nutrition & Metabolism*, 51(4), 301–323.

Wirdefeldt, K., Adami, H.-O., Cole, P., Trichopoulos, D., & Mandel, J. (2011). Epidemiology and etiology of Parkinson's disease: A review of the evidence. *European Journal of Epidemiology*, 26(Suppl. 1), S1–58. doi:10.1007/s10654-011-9581-6

Withers, M., Moran, R., Nicassio, P., Weisman, M. H., & Karpouzas, G. A. (2015). Perspectives of vulnerable US Hispanics with rheumatoid arthritis on depression: Awareness, barriers to disclosure, and treatment options. *Arthritis Care & Research*, 67(4), 484–492. doi:10.1002/acr.22462

Witte, A. V., Kerti, L., Hermannstädter, H. M., Fiebach, J. B., Schreiber, S. J., Schuchardt, J. P., . . . Flöel, A. (2014). Long-chain omega-3 fatty acids improve brain function and structure in older adults. *Cerebral Cortex*, 24(11), 3059–3068. doi:10.1093/cercor/bht163

Woods, B., & Pratt, R. (2005). Awareness in dementia: Ethical and legal issues in relation to people with dementia. *Aging & Mental Health*, 9(5), 423–429.

World Health Organization. (2012). *Dementia: A public health priority*. Retrieved from http://www.alzheimer.ca/en/sk/Get-involved/Raise-your-voice/~/media/WHO_ADI_dementia_report_final.ashx

Yang, X., Askarova, S., & Lee, J. C. M. (2010). Membrane biophysics and mechanics in Alzheimer's disease. *Molecular Neurobiology*, 41(2–3), 138–148. doi:10.1007/s12035-010-8121-9

Ziegler-Graham, K., Brookmeyer, R., Johnson, E., & Arrighi, H. M. (2008). Worldwide variation in the doubling time of Alzheimer's disease incidence rates. *Alzheimer's & Dementia*, 4(5), 316–323.

CHAPTER 18

AARP. (2002). *The Grandparent Study 2002 Report*. Washington, DC: Author.

AARP. (2008). *Update on the aged 55+ worker: 2007*. Washington, DC: Author.

Acierno, R., Hernandez, M. A., Amstadter, A. B., Resnick, H. S., Steve, K., Muzzy, W., & Kilpatrick, D. G. (2010). Prevalence and correlates of emotional, physical, sexual, and financial abuse and potential neglect in the United States: The National Elder Mistreatment Study. *American Journal of Public Health*, 100(2), 292–297. doi:10.2105/ajph.2009.163089

Adams, G. A., Prescher, J., Beehr, T. A., & Lepisto, L. (2002). Applying work-role attachment theory to retirement decision-making. *International Journal of Aging and Human Development*, 54(2), 125–137. doi:10.2190/JRUQ-XQ2N-UP0A-M432

Adams, K. B., Leibbrandt, S., & Moon, H. (2011). A critical review of the literature on social and leisure activity and wellbeing in later life. *Ageing & Society*, 31(4), 683–712. doi:10.1017/s0144686x10001091

Adams, K. B., Sanders, S., & Auth, E. A. (2004). Loneliness and depression in independent living retirement communities: Risk and resilience factors. *Aging & Mental Health*, 8(6), 475–485. doi:10.1080/13607860410001725054

Adams, R. G., Blieszner, R., & De Vries, B. (2000). Definitions of friendship in the third age: Age, gender, and study location effects. *Journal of Aging Studies*, 14(1), 117.

Adminstration on Aging. (2014). *A profile of older Americans: 2014*. Retrieved from http://www.aoa.acl.gov/Aging_Statistics/Profile/index.aspx

Anderberg, P., & Berglund, A.-L. (2010). Elderly persons' experiences of striving to receive care on their own terms in nursing homes. *International Journal of Nursing Practice*, 16(1), 64–68. doi:10.1111/j.1440-172X.2009.01808.x

Andonian, L., & MacRae, A. (2011). Well older adults within an urban context: Strategies to create and maintain social participation. *The British Journal of Occupational Therapy*, 74(1), 2–11. doi:10.4276/03080221 1X12947686093486

Angel, J. L., Jiménez, M. A., & Angel, R. J. (2007). The economic consequences of widowhood for older minority women. *Gerontologist*, 47(2), 224–234.

Antonucci, T. C., Akiyama, H., & Takahashi, K. (2004). Attachment and close relationships across the life span. *Attachment & Human Development*, 6(4), 353–370. Retrieved from 10.1080/1461673042000303136

Araujo, A. B., Mohr, B. A., & McKinlay, J. B. (2004). Changes in sexual function in middle-aged and older men: Longitudinal data from the Massachusetts Male Aging Study. *Journal of the American Geriatrics Society*, 52(9), 1502–1509. doi:10.1111/j.0002-8614.2004.52413.x

Argue, A., Johnson, D. R., & White, L. K. (1999). Age and religiosity: Evidence from a three-wave panel analysis. *Journal for the Scientific Study of Religion*, 38(3), 423.

Atchley, R. C. (1974). The meaning of retirement. *Journal of Communication*, 24(4), 97–100. Retrieved from 10.1111/j.1460-2466.1974.tb00414.x

Atchley, R. C. (1975). Adjustment to loss of job at retirement. *International Journal of Aging and Human Development*, 6(1), 17–27.

Atchley, R. C. (1993). Critical perspectives on retirement. In T. R. Cole, W. A. Achenbaum, P. L. Jakobi, & R. Kastenbaum (Eds.), *Voices and visions of aging: Toward a critical gerontology* (pp. 3–19). New York: Springer.

Atchley, R. C. (1999). Continuity and adaptation in aging: Creating positive experiences. Baltimore: Johns Hopkins University Press.

Attig, T. (1996). *How we grieve: Relearning the world*. New York: Oxford University Press.

Baker, T. J., & Bichsel, J. (2006). Personality predictors of intelligence: Differences between young and cognitively healthy older adults. *Personality and Individual Differences*, 41(5), 861–871. doi:10.1016/j.paid.2006.02.017

Ball, M. M., Whittington, F. J., Perkins, M. M., Patterson, V. L., Hollingworth, C., King, S. V, & Combs, B. L. (2000). Quality of life in assisted living facilities: Viewpoints of residents. *Journal of Applied Gerontology*, 19(3), 304–325.

Baltes, M. M., & Baltes, P. B. (1986). The psychology of control and aging (psychology revivals). New York: Psychology Press. Retrieved from https://books.google.com/books?hl=en&lr=&id=P1ItBAAAQBAJ&pgis=1

Barak, B. (2009). Age identity: A cross-cultural global approach. International Journal of Behavioral Development, 33(1), 2–11. doi:10.1177/0165025408099485

Barer, B. M. (2001). The "grands and greats" of very old black grandmothers. Journal of Aging Studies, 15(1), 1.

Bauer, M., McAuliffe, L., & Nay, R. (2007). Sexuality, health care and the older person: An overview of the literature. International Journal of Older People Nursing, 2(1), 63–68.

Beedon, L., & Wu, K. (2005). Women age 65 and older: Their sources of income. Washington, DC: AARP.

Bennett, K. M., Hughes, G. M., & Smith, P. T. O. (2005). Psychological response to later life widowhood: Coping and the effects of gender. Omega, 51(1), 33–52.

Bergland, A., Nicolaisen, M., & Thorsen, K. (2014). Predictors of subjective age in people aged 40-79 years: A five-year follow-up study. The impact of mastery, mental and physical health. Aging & Mental Health, 18(5), 653–661. doi:10.1080/13607863.2013.869545

Bishop, B. J. (2008). Stress and depression among older residents in religious monasteries: Do friends and God matter? International Journal of Aging and Human Development, 67(1), 1–23.

Bloch, L., Haase, C. M., & Levenson, R. W. (2014). Emotion regulation predicts marital satisfaction: More than a wives' tale. Emotion, 14(1), 130–144. doi:10.1037/a0034272

Bogg, T., & Roberts, B. W. (2013). The case for conscientiousness: Evidence and implications for a personality trait marker of health and longevity. Annals of Behavioral Medicine, 45(3), 278–288. doi:10.1007/s12160-012-9454-6

Bohlmeijer, E., Roemer, M., Cuijpers, P., & Smit, F. (2007). The effects of reminiscence on psychological well-being in older adults: A meta-analysis. Aging & Mental Health, 11(3), 291–300. doi:10.1080/13607860600963547

Bonanno, G. A., Wortman, C. B., & Nesse, R. M. (2004). Prospective patterns of resilience and maladjustment during widowhood. Psychology and Aging, 19(2), 260–271. doi:10.1037/0882-7974.19.2.260

Bookwala, J., & Jacobs, J. (2004). Age, marital processes, and depressed affect. Gerontologist, 44(3), 328–338.

Bowling, A., & Gabriel, Z. (2004). An integrational model of quality of life in older age: Results from the ESRC/MRC HSRC Quality of Life Survey in Britain. Social Indicators Research, 69(1), 1–36. doi:10.1023/B:SOCI.0000032656.01524.07

Brison, K. J. (1995). You will never forget: Narrative, bereavement, and worldview among Kwanga women. Ethos, 23(4), 474–488. doi:10.1525/eth.1995.23.4.02a00060

Brody, S. (2010). The relative health benefits of different sexual activities. The Journal of Sexual Medicine, 7(4 Pt. 1), 1336–1361. doi:10.1111/j.1743-6109.2009.01677.x

Brown, S. L., Bulanda, J. R., & Lee, G. R. (2012). Transitions into and out of cohabitation in later life. Journal of Marriage and Family, 74(4), 774–793. doi:10.1111/j.1741-3737.2012.00994.x

Brown, S. L., Brown, R. M., House, J. S., & Smith, D. M. (2008). Coping with spousal loss: Potential buffering effects of self-reported helping behavior. Personality and Social Psychology Bulletin, 34(6), 849–861.

Brown, S. L., & Kawamura, S. (2010). Relationship quality among cohabitors and marrieds in older adulthood. Social Science Research, 39(5), 777–786. doi:10.1016/j.ssresearch.2010.04.010

Brubaker, T. H. (1990). Families in later life: A burgeoning research area. Journal of Marriage and Family, 52(4), 959–981.

Brummett, B. H., Barefoot, J. C., Siegler, I. C., Clapp-Channing, N. E., Lytle, B. L., Bosworth, H. B., . . . Mark, D. B. (2000). Characteristics of socially isolated patients with coronary artery disease who are at elevated risk for mortality. Psychosomatic Medicine, 63(2), 267–272. Retrieved from http://www.ncbi.nlm.nih.gov/pubmed/11292274

Butler, R. N. (1963). The life review: An interpretation of reminiscence in the aged. Psychiatry: Interpersonal and Biological Processes, 26(1), 65–76. Retrieved from http://www.tandfonline.com/doi/abs/10.1521/00332747.1963.11023339?journalCode=upsy20

Butler, R. N. (1974). Succesful aging and the role of the life review. Journal of the American Geriatrics Society, 22(12), 529–535. Retrieved from http://www.ncbi.nlm.nih.gov/pubmed/4420325

Butler, S. S., & Eckart, D. (2007). Civic engagement among older adults in a rural community: A case study of the Senior Companion Program. Journal of Community Practice, 15(3), 77. doi:10.1300/J125v15n03_05

Butrica, B. A., & Schaner, S. G. (2005). Satisfaction and engagement in retirement. Washington, DC: Urban Institute.

Calvo, E., Haverstick, K., & Sass, S. A. (2009). Gradual retirement, sense of control, and retirees' happiness. Research on Aging, 31(1), 112–135.

Campbell Reay, A., & Browne, K. D. (2008). Elder abuse and neglect. In R. Woods & L. Clare (Eds.), Handbook of the clinical psychology of ageing (2nd ed., pp. 311–322). Hoboken, NJ: John Wiley.

Candy, B., Holman, A., Leurent, B., Davis, S., & Jones, L. (2011). Hospice care delivered at home, in nursing homes and in dedicated hospice facilities: A systematic review of quantitative and qualitative evidence. International Journal of Nursing Studies, 48(1), 121–133. doi:10.1016/j.ijnurstu.2010.08.003

Carr, D. (2004a). Gender, preloss marital dependence, and older adults' adjustment to widowhood. Journal of Marriage and Family, 66(1), 220–235.

Carr, D. (2004b). The desire to date and remarry among older widows and widowers. Journal of Marriage and Family, 66(4), 1051–1068.

Carr, J. (2012). Six weeks to 45 years: A longitudinal study of a population with Down syndrome. Journal of Applied Research in Intellectual Disabilities, 25(5), 414–422. doi:10.1111/j.1468-3148.2011.00676.x

Carstensen, L. L., Fung, H. H., & Charles, S. T. (2003). Socioemotional selectivity theory and the regulation of emotion in the second half of life. Motivation and Emotion, 27(2), 103–123. doi:10.1023/A:1024569803230

Carstensen, L. L., Graff, J., Levenson, R. W., & Gottman, J. M. (1996). Affect in intimate relationships: The developmental course of marriage. In C. Magai & S. H. McFadden (Eds.), Handbook of emotion, adult development, and aging (pp. 227–247). San Diego: Academic Press.

Carstensen, L. L., & Mikels, J. A. (2005). At the intersection of emotion and cognition. Aging and the positivity effect. Current Directions in Psychological Science, 14(3), 117–121. doi:10.1111/j.0963-7214.2005.00348.x

Carstensen, L. L., Turan, B., Scheibe, S., Ram, N., Ersner-Hershfield, H., Samanez-Larkin, G. R., . . . Nesselroade, J. R. (2010). Emotional experience improves with age: Evidence based on over 10 years of experience sampling. Psychology and Aging. Advance online publication. doi:10.1037/a0021285

Caspi, A., Herbener, E. S., & Ozer, D. J. (1992). Shared experiences and the similarity of personalities: A longitudinal study of married couples. Journal of Personality and Social Psychology, 62(2), 281–291. doi:10.1037/0022-3514.62.2.281

Chapman, B., Duberstein, P., Tindle, H. A., Sink, K. M., Robbins, J., Tancredi, D. J., & Franks, P. (2012). Personality predicts cognitive function over 7 years in older persons. The American Journal of Geriatric Psychiatry, 20(7), 612–621. doi:10.1097/JGP.0b013e31822cc9cb

Chappell, N., Gee, E., McDonald, L., & Stones, M. (2003). Aging in contemporary Canada. Toronto: Pearson Education Canada.

Cheek, C. (2010). Passing over: Identity transition in widows. International Journal of Aging and Human Development, 70(4), 345–364. doi:10.2190/AG.70.4.d

Cherry, K. E., Walker, E. J., Brown, J. S., Volaufova, J., LaMotte, L. R., Welsh, D. A., . . . Frisard, M. I. (2013). Social engagement and health in younger, older, and oldest-old adults in the Louisiana Healthy Aging Study. Journal of Applied Gerontology, 32(1), 51–75. doi:10.1177/0733464811409034

Choi, N. G., & Nater, J. (2000). Elder abuse, neglect, and exploitation: Risk factors and prevention strategies. Journal of Gerontological Social Work, 33(2), 5–25.

Cicirelli, V. G. (2008). End-of-life decisions: Research findings and implications. In A. Tomer, G. T. Eliason, & P. T. P. Wong (Eds.), Existential and spiritual issues in death attitudes (pp. 115–138). Mahwah, NJ: Lawrence Erlbaum.

Clarke, P., & Gallagher, N. A. (2013). Optimizing mobility in later life: The role of the urban built environment for older adults aging in place. Journal of Urban Health, 90(6), 997–1009. doi:10.1007/s11524-013-9800-4

Clarke, P., Morenoff, J., Debbink, M., Golberstein, E., Elliott, M. R., & Lantz, P. M. (2014). Cumulative exposure to neighborhood context: Consequences for health transitions over the adult life course. Research on Aging, 36(1), 115–142. doi:10.1177/0164027512470702

Cohen, S., & Wills, T. A. (1985). Stress, social support, and the buffering hypothesis. Psychological Bulletin, 98(2), 310–357. Retrieved from http://europepmc.org/abstract/med/3901065

Coleman, M., & Ganong, L. (2008). Normative beliefs about sharing housing with an older family member. International Journal of Aging and Human Development, 66(1), 49–72.

Coleman, P. (1986). Issues in the therapeutic use of reminiscence with elderly people. In I. Hanley & M. Gilhooly (Eds.), Psychological therapies for the elderly (pp. 41–64). London: Croom Helm.

Coleman, P. G., Ivani-Chalian, C., & Robinson, M. (2004). Religious attitudes among British older people: Stability and change in a 20-year longitudinal study. Ageing & Society, 24(2), 167–188.

Connidis, I. A. (1989). Siblings as friends in later life. American Behavioral Scientist, 33(1), 81.

Cooper, C., Selwood, A., & Livingston, G. (2008). The prevalence of elder abuse and neglect: A systematic review. Age & Ageing, 37(2), 151–160. doi:10.1093/ageing/afm194

Corr, C. A., Nabe, C. M., & Corr, D. M. (2009). Death and dying, life and living. Boston: Cengage.

Counts, D. A., & Counts, D. R. (1985). I'm not dead yet? Aging and death: Processes and experiences in Kalia. In D. A. Counts & D. R. Counts (Eds.), Aging and its transformations (pp. 131–156). Langham, MD: University of America Press.

Cully, J. A., LaVoie, D., & Gfeller, J. D. (2001). Reminiscence, personality, and psychological functioning in older adults. The Gerontologist, 41(1), 89–95.

Cumming, E. M., & Henry, W. E. (1961). *Growing old: The process of disengagement*. New York: Basic Books.

Dandy, K., & Bollman, R. D. (2008). Seniors in rural Canada. *Rural and Small Town Canada Analysis Bulletin, 7*(8).

Darbonne, A., Uchino, B. N., & Ong, A. D. (2012). What mediates links between age and well-being? A test of social support and interpersonal conflict as potential interpersonal pathways. *Journal of Happiness Studies, 14*(3), 951–963. doi:10.1007/s10902-012-9363-1

Dattalo, P. (2007). Borrowing to save: A critique of recent proposals to partially privatize Social Security. *Social Work, 52*(3), 233–242.

Davis, N. L., & Degges-White, S. (2008). Catalysts for developing productive life reviews: A multiple case study. *Adultspan: Theory Research & Practice, 7*(2), 69–79.

De Vaus, D., Wells, Y., Kendig, H., & Quine, S. (2007). Does gradual retirement have better outcomes than abrupt retirement? Results from an Australian panel study. *Ageing & Society, 27*(5), 667–682.

DeLamater, J. (2012). Sexual expression in later life: A review and synthesis. *Journal of Sex Research, 49*(2–3), 125–141. doi:10.1080/0022 4499.2011.603168

DeLamater, J., & Koepsel, E. (2015). Relationships and sexual expression in later life: A biopsychosocial perspective. *Sexual and Relationship Therapy, 30*(1), 37–59. doi:10.1080/ 14681994.2014.939506

DeNavas-Walt, C., & Proctor, B. D. (2014). Income and poverty in the United States: 2013. Washington, DC. US Census Bureau. Retrieved from http://www.census.gov/hhes/www/poverty/ data/incpovhlth/2013/

Dennis, D. (2008). *Living, dying, grieving*. Sudbury, MA: Jones & Bartlett.

DeSpelder, L. A., & Strickland, A. L. (2002). *The last dance: Encountering death and dying* (6th ed.). New York: McGraw-Hill.

Dezutter, J., Toussaint, L., & Leijssen, M. (2014). Forgiveness, ego-integrity, and depressive symptoms in community-dwelling and residential elderly adults. *The Journals of Gerontology: Series B: Psychological Sciences and Social Sciences.* Advance online publication. Advance online publication. doi:10.1093/geronb/gbu146

Diener, E., Suh, E. M., Lucas, R. E., & Smith, H. L. (1999). Subjective well-being: Three decades of progress. *Psychological Bulletin, 125*(2), 276–302. doi:10.1037/0033-2909.125.2.276

DiMatteo, M. R. (2004). Social support and patient adherence to medical treatment: A meta-analysis. *Health Psychology, 23*(2), 207–218. Retrieved from http://cat.inist. fr/?aModele=afficheN&cpsidt=15748159

Dong, X., & Simon, M. A. (2008). Is greater social support a protective factor against elder mistreatment? *Gerontology, 54*(6), 381–388. doi:10.1159/000143228

Donnelly, E. A., & Hinterlong, J. E. (2010). Changes in social participation and volunteer activity among recently widowed older adults. *Gerontologist, 50*(2), 158–169.

Doskoch, P. (2011). Many men 75 and older consider sex important and remain sexually active. *Perspectives on Sexual and Reproductive Health, 43*(1), 67–68. doi:10.1363/4306711

Drake, B. (2014). *Number of older Americans in the workforce is on the rise*. Washington, DC: Pew Research Center Retrieved from http://www. pewresearch.org/fact-tank/2014/01/07/number- of-older-americans-in-the-workforce-is-on-the-rise

Dykstra, P. A., & Fokkema, T. (2010). Relationships between parents and their adult children: A West European typology of late-life families. *Ageing and Society, 31*(04), 37–59. doi:10.1017/ S0144686X10001108

Elwert, F., & Christakis, N. A. (2008). The effect of widowhood on mortality by the causes of death of both spouses. *American Journal of Public Health, 98*(11), 2092–2098.

English, T., & Carstensen, L. L. (2014). Selective narrowing of social networks across adulthood is associated with improved emotional experience in daily life. *International Journal of Behavioral Development, 38*(2), 195–202. doi:10.1177/0165025413515404

Erikson, E. H. (1950). *Childhood and society* (2nd ed.). New York: Norton.

Erikson, E. H. (1982). *The life cycle completed*. New York: Norton.

Erlangsen, A., Jeune, B., Bille-Brahe, U., & Vaupel, J. W. (2004). Loss of partner and suicide risks among oldest old: A population-based register study. *Age & Ageing, 33*(4), 378–383. doi:10.1093/ageing/afh128

Fehr, R. (2012). Is retirement always stressful? The potential impact of creativity. *American Psychologist, 67*(1), 76–77. doi:10.1037/ a0026574

Feldman, D. C., & Beehr, T. A. (2011). A three-phase model of retirement decision making. *The American Psychologist, 66*(3), 193–203. doi:10.1037/a0022153

Felmlee, D., & Muraco, A. (2009). Gender and friendship norms among older adults. *Research on Aging, 31*(3), 318–344.

Field, D. (1999). Stability of older women's friendships: A commentary on Roberto. *International Journal of Aging and Human Development, 48*(1), 81.

Field, M. J., & Cassel, C. K. (1997). *Approaching death: Improving care at the end of life*. Washington, DC: National Academy Press.

Field, N. P., Gal-Oz, E., & Bonanno, G. A. (2003). Continuing bonds and adjustment at 5 years after the death of a spouse. *Journal of Consulting and Clinical Psychology, 71*(1), 110–117. doi:10.1037/0022-006x.71.1.110

Fingerman, K. L., & Charles, S. T. (2010). It takes two to tango: Why older people have the best relationships. *Current Directions in Psychological Science, 19*(3), 172–176. doi:10.1177/0963721410370297

Fonda, S. J., Clipp, E. C., & Maddox, G. L. (2002). Patterns in functioning among residents of an affordable assisted living housing facility. *Gerontologist, 42*(2), 178.

Freund, A. M., & Smith, J. (1999). Methodological comment: Temporal stability of older person's spontaneous self-definition. *Experimental Aging Research, 25*(1), 95.

Friedman, D., Parikh, N. S., Giunta, N., Fahs, M. C., & Gallo, W. T. (2012). The influence of neighborhood factors on the quality of life of older adults attending New York City senior centers: Results from the Health Indicators Project. *Quality of Life Research, 21*(1), 123–131. doi:10.1007/ s11136-011-9923-6

Fry, P. S. (1995). A conceptual model of socialization and agentic trait factors that mediate the development of reminiscence styles and their health outcomes. In B. K. Haight & J. D. Webster (Eds.), *The art and science of reminiscing: Theory, research, methods, and applications* (pp. 49–60). Philadelphia: Taylor & Francis.

Gall, T. L., Evans, D. R., & Howard, J. (1997). The retirement adjustment process: Changes in the well-being of male retirees across time. *The Journals of Gerontology: Series B: Psychological Sciences and Social Sciences* (3), P110–P117.

Gans, D., & Silverstein, M. (2006). Norms of filial responsibility for aging parents across time and generations. *Journal of Marriage and Family, 68*(4), 961–976.

Ganzini, L., Nelson, H. D., Lee, M. A., Kraemer, D. F., Schmidt, T. A., & Delorit, M. A. (2001). Oregon physicians' attitudes about and experiences with end-of-life care since passage of the Oregon Death with Dignity Act. *JAMA, 285*(18), 2363.

Gavrin, J., & Chapman, C. R. (1995). Clinical management of dying patients. *Western Journal of Medicine, 163*, 268–277.

George, L. K., Ellison, C. G., & Larson, D. B. (2002). Target article: Explaining the relationships between religious involvement and health. *Psychological Inquiry, 13*(3), 190–200. doi:10.1207/S15327965PLI1303_04

Glaser, B., & Strauss, A. (1968). *Time for dying*. Chicago: Aldine.

Glaser, K., Stuchbury, R., Tomassini, C., & Askham, J. (2008). The long-term consequences of partnership dissolution for support in later life in the United Kingdom. *Ageing & Society, 28*(3), 329–351. doi:10.1017/S0144686X07006642

Glass, T. A., Mendes De Leon, C. F., Bassuk, S. S., & Berkman, L. F. (2006). Social engagement and depressive symptoms in late life. *Journal of Aging & Health, 16*(4), 604–628.

Gonzaga, G. C., Campos, B., & Bradbury, T. (2007). Similarity, convergence, and relationship satisfaction in dating and married couples. *Journal of Personality and Social Psychology, 93*(1), 34–48.

Gonzales, A. M. (2007). Determinants of parent–child coresidence among older Mexican parents: The salience of cultural values. *Sociological Perspectives, 50*(4), 561–577.

Goodwin, R. D., & Friedman, H. S. (2006). Health status and the five-factor personality traits in a nationally representative sample. *Journal of Health Psychology, 11*(5), 643–654. doi:10.1177/1359105306066610

Gott, M. (2005). *Sexuality, sexual health and ageing*. Maidenhead, Berkshire: Open University Press.

Gott, M., & Hinchliff, S. (2003). How important is sex in later life? The views of older people. *Social Science & Medicine, 56*, 1617–1628.

Graham, E. K., & Lachman, M. E. (2012). Personality stability is associated with better cognitive performance in adulthood: Are the stable more able? *The Journals of Gerontology: Series B: Psychological Sciences and Social Sciences, 67*(5), 545–554. doi:10.1093/geronb/ gbr149

Gruber-Baldini, A. L., Schaie, K. W., & Willis, S. L. (1995). Similarity in married couples: A longitudinal study of mental abilities and rigidity-flexibility. *Journal of Personality and Social Psychology, 69*(1), 191–203. doi:10.1037/0022-3514.69.1.191

Grundy, E., & Henretta, J. C. (2006). Between elderly parents and adult children: A new look at the intergenerational care provided by the "sandwich generation." *Ageing & Society, 26*(5), 707–722.

Gueldner, S. H., Loeb, S., Morris, D., Penrod, J., Bramlett, M., Johnston, L., & Schlotzhauer, P. (2001). A comparison of life satisfaction and mood in nursing home residents and community- dwelling elders. *Archives of Psychiatric Nursing, 15*(5), 232–240. doi:10.1053/apnu.2001.27020

Guiaux, M., van Tilburg, T., & van Groenou, M. B. (2007). Changes in contact and support exchange in personal networks after widowhood. *Personal Relationships, 14*(3), 457–473.

Ha, J., Carr, D., Utz, R. L., & Nesse, R. (2006). Older adults' perceptions of intergenerational support after widowhood: How do men and women differ? *Journal of Family Issues, 27*(1), 3–30.

Ha, J.-H. (2010). The effects of positive and negative support from children on widowed older adults' psychological adjustment: A longitudinal analysis. *Gerontologist, 50*(4), 471–481.

Hansson, R. O., & Stroebe, M. S. (2007). *Bereavement in late life: Coping, adaptation, and developmental influences*. Washington,

DC: American Psychological Association. doi:10.1037/11502-000

Hao, Y. (2008). Productive activities and psychological well-being among older adults. *The Journals of Gerontology: Series B: Psychological Sciences and Social Sciences, 63*(2), S65–S72.

Hatch, L. R., & Bulcroft, K. (2004). Does long-term marriage bring less frequent disagreements? Five explanatory frameworks. *Journal of Family Issues, 25*(4), 465–495. doi:10.1177/0192513X03257766

Hayward, R. D., & Krause, N. (2013). Changes in church-based social support relationships during older adulthood. *The Journals of Gerontology: Series B: Psychological Sciences and Social Sciences, 68*(1), 85–96. doi:10.1093/geronb/gbs100

Hearn, S., Saulnier, G., Strayer, J., Glenham, M., Koopman, R., & Marcia, J. E. (2011). Between integrity and despair: Toward construct validation of Erikson's eighth stage. *Journal of Adult Development, 19*(1), 1–20. doi:10.1007/s10804-011-9126-y

Heckhausen, J., & Brim, O. G. (1997). Perceived problems for self and others: Self-protection by social downgrading throughout adulthood. *Psychology and Aging, 12*(4), 610–619. Retrieved from http://www.ncbi.nlm.nih.gov/pubmed/9416630

Heckhausen, J., & Krueger, J. (1993). Developmental expectations for the self and most other people: Age grading in three functions of social comparison. *Developmental Psychology, 29*(3), 539–548. Retrieved from http://eric.ed.gov/?id=EJ464520

Henry, N. J. M., Berg, C. A., Smith, T. W., & Florsheim, P. (2007). Positive and negative characteristics of marital interaction and their association with marital satisfaction in middle-aged and older couples. *Psychology and Aging, 22*(3), 428–441.

Hinterlong, J. E., Morrow-Howell, N., & Rozario, P. A. (2007). Productive engagement and late life physical and mental health: Findings from a nationally representative panel study. *Research on Aging, 29*(4), 348–370. doi:10.1177/0164027507300806

Hodgson, L. G. (1992). Adult grandchildren and their grandparents: Their enduring bond. *International Journal of Aging and Human Development, 34*(3), 209–225. doi:10.2190/PU9M-96XD-CFYQ-A8UK

Hodson, D. S., & Skeen, P. (1994). Sexuality and aging: The hammerlock of myths. *Journal of Applied Gerontology, 13*(3), 219–235. doi:10.1177/073346489401300301

Holden, C. A., Collins, V. R., Handelsman, D. J., Jolley, D., & Pitts, M. (2014). Healthy aging in a cross-sectional study of Australian men: What has sex got to do with it? *The Aging Male, 17*(1), 25–29. doi:10.3109/13685538.2013.843167

Van Hooijdonk, C., Droomers, M., Deerenberg, I. M., Mackenbach, J. P., & Kunst, A. E. (2008). Higher mortality in urban neighbourhoods in the Netherlands: Who is at risk? *Journal of Epidemiology & Community Health, 62*(6), 499–505. doi:10.1136/jech.2007.060145

Hughes, M. L., Geraci, L., & De Forrest, R. L. (2013). Aging 5 years in 5 minutes: The effect of taking a memory test on older adults' subjective age. *Psychological Science, 24*(12), 2481–2488. doi:10.1177/0956797613494853

Huston, T. L. (2000). The social ecology of marriage and other intimate unions. *Journal of Marriage and Family, 62*(2), 298–320.

Huxhold, O., Fiori, K. L., & Windsor, T. D. (2013). The dynamic interplay of social network characteristics, subjective well-being, and health: The costs and benefits of socio-emotional selectivity. *Psychology and Aging, 28*(1), 3–16. doi:10.1037/a0030170

Huyck, M. H., & Gutmann, D. L. (2006). Men and their wives: Why are some married men

vulnerable at midlife? In V. H. Bedford & B. Formaniak Turner (Eds.), *Men in relationships: A new look from a life course perspective* (pp. 27–50). New York: Springer.

Hyde, Z., Flicker, L., Hankey, G. J., Almeida, O. P., McCaul, K. A., Chubb, S. A. P., & Yeap, B. B. (2010). Prevalence of sexual activity and associated factors in men aged 75 to 95 years. *Annals of Internal Medicine, 153*(11), 693–702.

Ikeda, A., Kawachi, I., Iso, H., Iwasaki, M., Inoue, M., & Tsugane, S. (2013). Social support and cancer incidence and mortality: The JPHC study cohort II. *Cancer Causes & Control, 24*(5), 847–860. doi:10.1007/s10552-013-0147-7

Ikkink, K. K., & van Tilburg, T. (1998). Do older adults' network members continue to provide instrumental support in unbalanced relationships? *Journal of Social and Personal Relationships, 15*(1), 59.

Isherwood, L. M., King, D. S., & Luszcz, M. A. (2012). A longitudinal analysis of social engagement in late-life widowhood. *International Journal of Aging and Human Development, 74*(3), 211–229.

Ivancovich, D. A., & Wong, P. T. P. (2008). The role of existential and spiritual coping in anticipatory grief. In A. Tomer, G. T. Eliason, & P. T. P. Wong (Eds.), *Existential and spiritual issues in death attitudes* (pp. 209–233). Mahwah, NJ: Lawrence Erlbaum.

James, J. B., & Zarrett, N. (2006). Ego integrity in the lives of older women. *Journal of Adult Development, 13*(2), 61–75. doi:10.1007/s10804-006-9003-2

Jenkins, K. R., Pienta, A. M., & Horgas, A. L. (2002). Activity and health-related quality of life in continuing care retirement communities. *Research on Aging, 24*(1), 124.

Jeste, D. V., & Oswald, A. J. (2015). *Individual and societal wisdom: Explaining the paradox of human aging and high well-being.* Retrieved from http://www.tandfonline.com/doi/abs/10.1521/psyc.2014.77.4.317

Johannesen, M., & LoGiudice, D. (2013). Elder abuse: A systematic review of risk factors in community-dwelling elders. *Age and Ageing, 42*(3), 292–298. doi:10.1093/ageing/afs195

Johnson, C. L., & Troll, L. E. (1994). Constraints and facilitators to friendships in late late life. *The Gerontologist, 34*(1), 79–87.

Johnson, K. J., & Mutchler, J. E. (2014). The emergence of a positive gerontology: from disengagement to social involvement. *The Gerontologist, 54*(1), 93–100. doi:10.1093/geront/gnt099

Juul Nilsson, C., Lund, R., & Avlund, K. (2008). Cohabitation status and onset of disability among older Danes. *Journal of Aging & Health, 20*(2), 235–253.

Kane, R. A. (2001). Long-term care and a good quality of life: Bringing them closer together. *The Gerontologist, 41*(3), 293–304.

Kastenbaum, R. (1999). Dying and bereavement. In J. C. Cavanaugh & S. K. Whitbourne (Eds.), *Gerontology: An interdisciplinary perspective* (pp. 155–185). New York: Oxford University Press.

Kelley-Gillespie, N., & Farley, O. W. (2007). The effect of housing on perceptions of quality of life of older adults participating in a Medicaid long-term care demonstration project. *Journal of Gerontological Social Work, 49*(3), 205–228.

Kemp, E. A., & Kemp, J. E. (2002). *Older couples: New romances: Finding & keeping love in later life.* Berkeley, CA: Celestial Arts.

Keyes, C. L. M., & Reitzes, D. C. (2007). The role of religious identity in the mental health of older working and retired adults. *Aging & Mental Health, 11*(4), 434–443. Retrieved from 10.1080/13607860601086371

Kim, J. E., & Moen, P. (2001). Is retirement good or bad for subjective well-being? *Current*

Directions in Psychological Science, 10(3), 83–86. doi:10.1111/1467-8721.00121

Kim, J. E., & Moen, P. (2002). Retirement transitions, gender, and psychological well-being: A life-course, ecological model. *The Journals of Gerontology: Series B: Psychological Sciences and Social Sciences, 57*(3), P212–P222.

King, V., & Scott, M. E. (2005). A comparison of cohabiting relationships among older and younger adults. *Journal of Marriage and Family, 67*(2), 271–285.

Kleinspehn-Ammerlahn, A., Kotter-Gruhn, D., & Smith, J. (2008). Self-perceptions of aging: Do subjective age and satisfaction with aging change during old age? *The Journals of Gerontology: Series B: Psychological Sciences and Social Sciences, 63*(6), P377–P385. doi:10.1093/geronb/63.6.P377

Ko, K. J., Berg, C. A., Butner, J., Uchino, B. N., & Smith, T. W. (2007). Profiles of successful aging in middle-aged and older adult married couples. *Psychology and Aging, 22*(4), 705–718.

Kornadt, A. E., & Rothermund, K. (2012). Internalization of age stereotypes into the self-concept via future self-views: A general model and domain-specific differences. *Psychology and Aging, 27*(1), 164–172. doi:10.1037/a0025110

Kowalski, S. D., & Bondmass, M. D. (2008). Physiological and psychological symptoms of grief in widows. *Research in Nursing & Health, 31*(1), 23–30. doi:10.1002/nur.20228

Krause, N. (2005). God-mediated control and psychological well-being in late life. *Research on Aging, 27*(2), 136–164. doi:10.1177/0164027504270475

Kübler-Ross, E. (1969). *On death and dying.* New York: Collier Books.

Kulik, L. (2002). Marital equality and the quality of long-term marriage in later life. *Ageing & Society, 22*(4), 459.

Labouvie-Vief, G., & Diehl, M. (1999). Self and personality development. In J. C. Cavanaugh & S. K. Whitbourne (Eds.), *Gerontology: An interdisciplinary perspective* (pp. 238–268). New York: Oxford University Press.

Labouvie-Vief, G., & Medler, M. (2002). Affect optimization and affect complexity: Modes and styles of regulation in adulthood. *Psychology and Aging, 17*(4), 571–587.

Lang, F. R., Featherman, D. L., & Nesselroade, J. R. (1997). Social self-efficacy and short-term variability in social relationships: The MacArthur Successful Aging Studies. *Psychology and Aging, 12*(4), 657–666.

Lang, F. R., & Fingerman, K. L. (2004). *Growing together: Personal relationships across the lifespan.* New York: Cambridge University Press.

Larson, R., Mannell, R., & Zuzanek, J. (1986). Daily well-being of older adults with friends and family. *Psychology and Aging, 1*(2), 117–126. doi:10.1037/0882-7974.1.2.117

Laumann, E. O., Leitsch, S. A., & Waite, L. J. (2008). Elder mistreatment in the United States: Prevalence estimates from a nationally representative study. *The Journals of Gerontology: Series B: Psychological Sciences and Social Sciences,* (4), S248–s254.

Lawrence, A. R., & Schigelone, A. R. S. (2002). Reciprocity beyond dyadic relationships: Aging-related communal coping. *Research on Aging, 24*(6), 684–704. doi:10.1177/016402702237187

Lee, E.-K. O., & Sharpe, T. (2007). Understanding religious/spiritual coping and support resources among African American older adults: A mixed-method approach. *Journal of Religion, Spirituality & Aging, 19*(3), 55–75.

Lee, J. E., Zarit, S. H., Rovine, M. J., Birditt, K. S., & Fingerman, K. L. (2011). Middle-aged couples' exchanges of support with aging parents: Patterns and association with marital satisfaction. *Gerontology, 58*(1), 88–96. doi:10.1159/000324512

Lee, M. (2008). Caregiver stress and elder abuse among Korean family caregivers of older adults with disabilities. *Journal of Family Violence, 23*(8), 707–712. doi:10.1007/s10896-008-9195-2

Lee, S., & Shaw, L. (2008). *From work to retirement: Tracking changes in women's poverty status.* Washington, DC: AARP. Retrieved from http://www.aarp.org/research/assistance/lowincome/inb156_poverty.html

Levenson, R. W., Carstensen, L. L., & Gottman, J. M. (1993). Long-term marriage: Age, gender, and satisfaction. *Psychology and Aging, 8*(2), 301–313. doi:10.1037/0882-7974.8.2.301

Levin, J. S., & Taylor, R. J. (1994). Race and gender differences in religiosity among older adults: Findings from four national surveys. *Journal of Gerontology, 49*(3), S137.

Li, T., Fok, H. K., & Fung, H. H. (2011). Is reciprocity always beneficial? Age differences in the association between support balance and life satisfaction. *Aging & Mental Health, 15*(5), 541–547. doi:10.1080/13607863.2010.551340

Lin, I.-F. (2008). Consequences of parental divorce for adult children's support of their frail parents. *Journal of Marriage and Family, 70*(1), 113–128. doi:10.1111/j.1741-3737.2007.00465.x

Litwin, H. (2003). Social predictors of physical activity in later life: The contribution of social-network type. *Journal of Aging and Physical Activity, 11*(3), 389–406.

Liu, H., & Waite, L. (2014). Bad marriage, broken heart? Age and gender differences in the link between marital quality and cardiovascular risks among older adults. *Journal of Health and Social Behavior, 55*(4), 403–423. doi:10.1177/0022146514556893

Lowenstein, A., & Doron, I. (2008). Times of transition: Elder abuse and neglect in Israel. *Journal of Elder Abuse & Neglect, 20*(2), 181–206.

Lucas, R. E., & Donnellan, M. B. (2011). Personality development across the life span: Longitudinal analyses with a national sample from Germany. *Journal of Personality and Social Psychology, 101*(4), 847–861. doi:10.1037/a0024298

Luchetti, M., Terracciano, A., Stephan, Y., & Sutin, A. R. (2015). Personality and cognitive decline in older adults: Data from a longitudinal sample and meta-analysis. *The Journals of Gerontology: Series B: Psychological Sciences and Social Sciences.* Advance online publication. doi:10.1093/geronb/gbu184

Lund, D. A., & Caserta, M. S. (2001). When the unexpected happens: Husbands coping with the deaths of their wives. In D. A. Lund (Ed.), *Men coping with grief* (pp. 147–167). Amityville, NY: Baywood Publishing.

Lund, D. A., Caserta, M. S., Dimond, M. F., & Gray, R. M. (1986). Impact of bereavement on the self-conceptions of older surviving spouses. *Symbolic Interaction, 9*(2), 235–244. doi:10.1525/si.1986.9.2.235

Mallon, B. (2008). *Death, dying and grief: Working with adult bereavement.* Thousand Oaks, CA: Sage.

Manzoli, L., Villari, P., M, Pirone, G., & Boccia, A. (2007). Marital status and mortality in the elderly: A systematic review and meta-analysis. *Social Science & Medicine, 64*(1), 77–94.

Marsh, H. W., Nagengast, B., & Morin, A. J. S. (2012). Measurement invariance of Big-Five factors over the life span: ESEM tests of gender, age, plasticity, maturity, and La Dolce Vita effects. *Developmental Psychology, 49,* 1194–1218 doi:10.1037/a0026913 10.1037/a0026913.supp

Maxfield, M., Pyszczynski, T., Greenberg, J., Pepin, R., & Davis, H. P. (2012). The moderating role of executive functioning in older adults' responses to a reminder of mortality. *Psychology and Aging, 27*(1), 256–263. doi:10.1037/a0023902

McAdams, D. P., & Olson, B. D. (2010). Personality development: Continuity and change over the life course. *Annual Review of Psychology, 61,* 517–542. doi:10.1146/annurev.psych.093008.100507

McAuliffe, L., Bauer, M., & Nay, R. (2007). Barriers to the expression of sexuality in the older person: The role of the health professional. *International Journal of Older People Nursing, 2*(1), 69–75.

McCrae, R. R. (2002). The maturation of personality psychology: Adult personality development and psychological well-being. *Journal of Research in Personality, 36*(4), 307–317.

McCrae, R. R., & Costa, P. T. (1988). Psychological resilience among widowed men and women: A 10-year follow-up of a national sample. *Journal of Social Issues, 44*(3), 129–142.

McCrae, R. R., & Costa, P. T. J. (2006). Cross-cultural perspectives on adult personality trait development. In D. K. Mroczek & T. D. Little (Eds.), *Handbook of personality development* (pp. 129–145). Mahwah, NJ: Lawrence Erlbaum.

McCrae, R. R., Terracciano, A., & The Personality Profiles of Cultures Project. (2005). Universal features of personality traits from the observer's perspective: Data from 50 cultures. *Journal of Personality and Social Psychology, 88,* 547–561.

McDonald, L., & Robb, A. L. (2004). The economic legacy of divorce and separation for women in old age. *Canadian Journal on Aging, 23,* S83–S97.

McLaughlin, D., Adams, J. O. N., Vagenas, D., & Dobson, A. (2011). Factors which enhance or inhibit social support: A mixed-methods analysis of social networks in older women. *Ageing & Society, 31*(1), 18–33. doi:10.1017/s0144686x10000668

McNamara, B., & Rosenwax, L. (2010). Which careers of family members at the end of life need more support from health services and why? *Social Science & Medicine, 70*(7), 1035–1041. doi:10.1016/j.socscimed.2009.11.029

Meier, L. L., Orth, U., Denissen, J. J. A., & Kühnel, A. (2011). Age differences in instability, contingency, and level of self-esteem across the life span. *Journal of Research in Personality, 45*(6), 604–612. doi:10.1016/j.jrp.2011.08.008

Melchiorre, M. G., Penhale, B., & Lamura, G. (2014). Understanding elder abuse in Italy: Perception and prevalence, types and risk factors from a review of the literature. *Educational Gerontology, 40*(12), 909–931. doi:10.1080/0360 1277.2014.912839

Menec, V. H., Shooshtari, S., Nowicki, S., & Fournier, S. (2010). Does the relationship between neighborhood socioeconomic status and health outcomes persist into very old age? A population-based study. *Journal of Aging & Health, 22*(1), 27–47. doi:10.1177/0898264309349029

Mills, S. (2012). Sounds to soothe the soul: Music and bereavement in a traditional South Korean death ritual. *Mortality, 17*(2), 145–157. doi:10.1080/13576275.2012.675231

Minichiello, V., Plummer, D., & Loxton, D. (2004). Factors predicting sexual relationships in older people: An Australian study. *Australasian Journal on Ageing, 23,* 125–130.

Mock, S. E., & Eibach, R. P. (2011). Aging attitudes moderate the effect of subjective age on psychological well-being: Evidence from a 10-year longitudinal study. *Psychology and Aging, 26*(4), 979–986. Retrieved from http://cat.inist.fr/?aModele=afficheN&cpsidt=25229491

Moon, J. R., Kondo, N., Glymour, M. M., & Subramanian, S. V. (2011). Widowhood and mortality: A meta-analysis. *PloS One, 6*(8), e23465. doi:10.1371/journal.pone.0023465

Moore, A. J., & Stratton, D. C. (2002). *Resilient widowers: Older men speak for themselves.* New York: Springer.

Morin, R., & Fry, R. (2012). More Americans worry about financing retirement. Washington, DC: Pew Research Center. Retrieved from http://www.pewsocialtrends.org/2012/10/22/more-americans-worry-about-financing-retirement

Morrow-Howell, N., Hinterlong, J., Rozario, P. A., & Tang., F. (2003). Effects of volunteering on the well-being of older adults. *The Journals of Gerontology: Series B: Psychological Sciences & Social Sciences, 58B*(3), S137.

Mortimore, E., Haselow, D., Dolan, M., Hawkes, W. G., Langenberg, P., Zimmerman, S., & Magaziner, J. (2008). Amount of social contact and hip fracture mortality. *Journal of the American Geriatrics Society, 56*(6), 1069–1074. doi:10.1111/j.1532-5415.2008.01706.x

Mõttus, R., Luciano, M., Starr, J. M., Pollard, M. C., & Deary, I. J. (2013). Personality traits and inflammation in men and women in their early 70s: The Lothian Birth Cohort 1936 study of healthy aging. *Psychosomatic Medicine, 75*(1), 11–19. doi:10.1097/PSY.0b013e31827576cc

Mroczek, D. K., & Kolarz, C. M. (1998). The effect of age on positive and negative affect: A developmental perspective on happiness. *Journal of Personality and Social Psychology, 75*(5), 1333–1349. Retrieved from 10.1037/0022-3514.75.5.1333

Mroczek, D. K., Spiro, A. I. I. I., & Griffin, P. W. (2006). Personality and aging. In J. E. Birren & K. W. Schaire (Eds.), *Handbook of the psychology of aging* (6th ed., pp. 363–377). Amsterdam, Netherlands: Elsevier.

Myers, S. A., & Kennedy-Lightsey, C. D. (2014). Communication in adult sibling relationships. In L. H. Turner & R. West (Eds.), *The SAGE handbook of family communication* (p. 504). Thousand Oaks, CA: Sage. Retrieved from https://books.google.com/books?hl=en&lr=&id=Y-4XBAAAQBAJ&pgis=1

Nelson, T. D. (2005). Ageism: prejudice against our feared future self. *Journal of Social Issues, 61,* 207–221.

Nerenberg, L. (2008). *Elder abuse prevention: Emerging trends and promising strategies.* New York: Springer.

Newport, F. (2006). *Religion most important to blacks, women, and older Americans: Gallup Poll.* Retrieved from http://www.gallup.com/poll/25585/Religion-Most-Important-Blacks-Women-Older-Americans.aspx

Nguyen, A. W., Chatters, L. M., Taylor, R. J., & Mouzon, D. M. (2015). Social support from family and friends and subjective well-being of older African Americans. *Journal of Happiness Studies.* Advance online publication. doi:10.1007/s10902-015-9626-8

Nicolosi, A., Buvat, J., Glasser, D. B., Hartmann, U., Laumann, E. O., Gingell, C., & GSSAB Investigator's Group. (2006). Sexual behaviour, sexual dysfunctions and related help seeking patterns in middle-aged and elderly Europeans: The global study of sexual attitudes and behaviors. *World Journal of Urology, 24,* 423–428.

O'Rourke, N., Cappeliez, P., & Claxton, A. (2011). Functions of reminiscence and the psychological well-being of young-old and older adults over time. *Aging & Mental Health, 15*(2), 272–281. doi:10.1080/13607861003713281

Onrust, S. A., & Cuijpers, P. (2006). Mood and anxiety disorders in widowhood: A systematic review. *Aging & Mental Health, 10*(4), 327–334. doi:10.1080/13607860600638529

Ortman, J. M., Velkoff, V. A., & Hogan, H. (2014). An aging nation: The older population in the United States. *Current Population Reports.* PS25-1140 U.S. Bureau of the Census. Retrieved from http://beta.census.gov/content/dam/Census/library/publications/2014/demo/p25-1140.pdf

Palacios-Ceña, D., Carrasco-Garrido, P., Hernández-Barrera, V., Alonso-Blanco, C., Jiménez-García, R., & Fernández-de-las-Peñas, C. (2012). Sexual behaviors among older adults in Spain: Results from a population-based national sexual health survey. *The Journal of Sexual Medicine, 9*(1), 121–129. doi:10.1111/j.1743-6109.2011.02511.x

Park, N. S., Klemmack, D. L., Roff, L. L., Parker, M. W., Koenig, H. G., Sawyer, P., & Allman, R. M. (2008). Religiousness and longitudinal trajectories in elders' functional status. *Research on Aging, 30*(3), 279–298.

Parker, R. G. (1995). Reminiscence: A community theory framework. *The Gerontologist, 35*(4), 515–525.

Penson, R. T. (2004). Bereavement across cultures. In R. J. Moore & D. Spiegel (Eds.), *Cancer, culture, and communication* (pp. 241–279).

New York: Kluwer Academic/Plenum Publishers. doi:10.1007/0-306-48007-7_11

Pettee, K. K., Brach, J. S., Kriska, A. M., Boudreau, R., Richardson, C. R., Colbert, L. H., . . . Newman, A. B. (2006). Influence of marital status on physical activity levels among older adults. *Medicine & Science in Sports & Exercise*, 38(3), 541–546.

Pew Forum on Religious and Public Life. (2008). *U.S. Religious Landscape Survey. Religious affiliation: Diverse and dynamic*. Washington, DC: Author.

Pew Research Center. (2009a). *End-of-life decisions: How Americans cope*. Retrieved from http://www.pewsocialtrends.org/2009/08/20/end-of-life-decisions-how-americans-cope

Pew Research Center. (2009b). *Growing old in America: Expectations vs. reality*. Retrieved from http://www.pewsocialtrends.org/2009/06/29/growing-old-in-america-expectations-vs-reality

Pew Research Center. (2010). *The return of the multi-generational family household*. Retrieved from http://www.pewsocialtrends.org/2010/03/18/the-return-of-the-multi-generational-family-household

Pinquart, M. (2003). Loneliness in married, widowed, divorced, and never-married older adults. *Journal of Social and Personal Relationships*, 20(1), 31.

Pinquart, M., & Forstmeier, S. (2012). Effects of reminiscence interventions on psychosocial outcomes: A meta-analysis. *Aging & Mental Health*, 16(5), 541–558. doi:10.1080/13607863.2011.651434

Pinquart, M., & Schindler, I. (2007). Changes of life satisfaction in the transition to retirement: A latent-class approach. *Psychology & Aging*, 22(3), 442–455. doi:10.1037/0882-7974.22.3.442

Podnieks, E., Anetzberger, G. J., Wilson, S. J., Teaster, P. B., & Wangmo, T. (2010). WorldView environmental scan on elder abuse. *Journal of Elder Abuse & Neglect*, 22(1–2), 164–179. doi:10.1080/08946560903445974

Postigo, J. M. L., & Honrubia, R. L. (2010). The co-residence of elderly people with their children and grandchildren. *Educational Gerontology*, 36(4), 330–349. doi:10.1080/03601270903212351

Powers, S. M., Bisconti, T. L., & Bergeman, C. S. (2014). Trajectories of social support and well-being across the first two years of widowhood. *Death Studies*, 38(8), 499–509. doi:10.1080/07481187.2013.846436

Proulx, C. M., Helms, H. M., & Buehler, C. (2007). Marital quality and personal well-being: A meta-analysis. *Journal of Marriage and Family*, 69(3), 576–593. doi:10.1111/j.1741-3737.2007.00393.x

Pushkar, D., Chaikelson, J., Conway, M., Etezadi, J., Giannopoulus, C., Li, K., & Wrosch, C. (2010). Testing continuity and activity variables as predictors of positive and negative affect in retirement. *The Journals of Gerontology: Series B: Psychological Sciences and Social Sciences*, 65B(1), 42–49. doi:10.1093/geronb/gbp079

Quine, S., Wells, Y., de Vaus, D., & Kendig, H. (2007). When choice in retirement decisions is missing: Qualitative and quantitative findings of impact on well-being. *Australasian Journal on Ageing*, 26(4), 173–179.

Rabiner, D. J. (1996). Attitudes toward and use of subsequent nursing home services among a national sample of older adults. *Journal of Aging and Health*, 8(3), 417–443. doi:10.1177/089826439600800306

Rasheed, M. N., & Rasheed, J. M. (2003). Rural African American older adults and the black helping tradition. *Journal of Gerontological Social Work*, 41(1–2), 137–150.

Ready, R. E., Carvalho, J. O., & Åkerstedt, A. M. (2012). Evaluative organization of the self-concept in younger, midlife, and older adults. *Research on Aging*, 34(1), 56–79. doi:10.1177/0164027511415244

Reed, T. D., & Neville, H. A. (2014). The influence of religiosity and spirituality on psychological well-being among black women.

Journal of Black Psychology, 40(4), 384–401. doi:10.1177/0095798413490956

Reitzes, D. C., & Mutran, E. J. (2004). The transition to retirement: Stages and factors that influence retirement adjustment. *International Journal of Aging and Human Development*, 59(1), 63–84.

Rice, C., & Pasupathi, M. (2010). Reflecting on self-relevant experiences: Adult age differences. *Developmental Psychology*, 46(2), 479–490. doi:10.1037/a0018098

Richardson, V., & Kilty, K. M. (1991). Adjustment to retirement: Continuity vs. discontinuity. *International Journal of Aging and Human Development*, 33(2), 151–169. doi:10.2190/6RPT-U8GN-VUCV-P0TU

Ronneberg, C. R., Miller, E. A., Dugan, E., & Porell, F. (2014). The protective effects of religiosity on depression: A 2-year prospective study. *The Gerontologist*. Advance online publication. doi:10.1093/geront/gnu073

Rosenblatt, P. C. (2008). Grief across cultures: A review and research agenda. In M. S. Stroebe, R. O. Hansson, H. Schut, W. Stroebe, & E. Van den Blink (Eds.), *Handbook of bereavement research and practice: Advances in theory and intervention* (pp. 207–222). Washington, DC: American Psychological Association.

Rosnick, C. B., Small, B. J., & Burton, A. M. (2010). The effect of spousal bereavement on cognitive functioning in a sample of older adults. *Aging, Neuropsychology & Cognition*, 17(3), 257–269. doi:10.1080/13825580903042692

Rossi Ferrario, S., Cardillo, V., Vicario, F., Balzarini, E., & Zotti, A. M. (2004). Advanced cancer at home: Caregiving and bereavement. *Palliative Medicine*, 18(2), 129–136. doi:10.1191/0269216304pm870oa

Rubin, D. C., & Berntsen, D. (2006). People over forty feel 20% younger than their age: Subjective age across the lifespan. *Psychonomic Bulletin & Review*, 13(5), 776–780. doi:10.3758/BF03193996

Russo, R. (2008). *A healing touch: True stories of life, death, and hospice*. Camden, MI: Down East Books.

Rutledge, T., Reis, S. E., Olson, M., Owens, J., Kelsey, S. F., Pepine, C. J., . . . Matthews, K. A. (2001). Social networks are associated with lower mortality rates among women with suspected coronary disease: The National Heart, Lung, and Blood Institute-Sponsored Women's Ischemia Syndrome Evaluation study. *Psychosomatic Medicine*, 66(6), 882–888. doi:10.1097/01.psy.0000145819.94041.52

Ryff, C. D. (1991). Possible selves in adulthood and old age: A tale of shifting horizons. *Psychology and Aging*, 6(2), 286–295.

Salguero, A., Martínez-García, R., Molinero, O., & Márquez, S. (2011). Physical activity, quality of life and symptoms of depression in community-dwelling and institutionalized older adults. *Archives of Gerontology and Geriatrics*, 53(2), 152–157. doi:10.1016/j.archger.2010.10.005

Sasson, I., & Umberson, D. J. (2014). Widowhood and depression: New light on gender differences, selection, and psychological adjustment. *The Journals of Gerontology: Series B: Psychological Sciences and Social Sciences*, 69(1), 135–145. doi:10.1093/geronb/gbt058

Scafato, E., Galluzzo, L., Gandin, C., Ghirini, S., Baldereschi, M., Capurso, A., . . . Farchi, G. (2008). Marital and cohabitation status as predictors of mortality: A 10-year follow-up of an Italian elderly cohort. *Social Science & Medicine*, 67(9), 1456–1464. doi:10.1016/j.socscimed.2008.06.026

Scherger, S., Nazroo, J., & Higgs, P. (2011). Leisure activities and retirement: do structures of inequality change in old age? *Ageing & Society*, 31(1), 146–172. doi:10.1017/s0144686x10000577

Shaw, B. A. (2005). Anticipated support from neighbors and physical functioning during later life. *Research on Aging*, 27(5), 503–525. doi:10.1177/0164027505277884

Shaw, B. A., Krause, N., Liang, J., & Bennett, J. (2007). Tracking changes in social relations throughout late life. *The Journals of Gerontology:*

Series B: Psychological Sciences & Social Sciences, 62B(2), S90–S99.

Sheehan, N. W., & Petrovic, K. (2008). Grandparents and their adult grandchildren: Recurring themes from the literature. *Marriage & Family Review*, 44(1), 99–124.

Sheldon, K. M., & Kasser, T. (2001). Getting older, getting better? Personal strivings and psychological maturity across the life span. *Developmental Psychology*, 37(4), 491–501.

Shelton, A. (2007). *Social Security: Basic data*. Washington, DC: AARP.

Shelton, A. (2013). Social Security: Still lifting many older Americans out of poverty. Retrieved from http://blog.aarp.org/2013/07/01/social-security-still-lifting-many-older-americans-out-of-poverty

Shultz, K. S., Morton, K. R., & Weckerle, J. R. (1998). The influence of push and pull factors on voluntary and involuntary early retirees' retirement decision and adjustment. *Journal of Vocational Behavior*, 53(1), 45–57. doi:10.1006/jvbe.1997.1610

Silverstein, M., & Marenco, A. (2001). How Americans enact the grandparent role across the family life course. *Journal of Family Issues*, 22(4), 493–522.

Simpson, D. B., Cloud, D. S., Newman, J. L., & Fuqua, D. R. (2008). Sex and gender differences in religiousness and spirituality. *Journal of Psychology & Theology*, 36(1), 42–52.

Sims, T., Hogan, C. L., & Carstensen, L. L. (2015). Selectivity as an emotion regulation strategy: Lessons from older adults. *Current Opinion in Psychology*, 3, 80–84. doi:10.1016/j.copsyc.2015.02.012

Smith, A. M. A., Rissel, C. E., Richters, J., Grulich, A. E., & de Visser, R. O. (2003). Sex in Australia: Reflections and recommendations for future research. *Australian & New Zealand Journal of Public Health*, 27, 251–256.

Smith, J., & Freund, A. M. (2002). The dynamics of possible selves in old age. *The Journals of Gerontology: Series B: Psychological Sciences & Social Sciences*, 57B(6), P492.

Social Security Administration. (2007). *Social Security: A brief history*. Washington, DC: Author. Retrieved from http://www.ssa.gov/history/pdf/2007historybooklet.pdf

Social Security Administration. (2008). *The future of Social Security*. Washington, DC: Author.

Social Security Administration. (2014). *Social Security basic facts*. Retrieved from http://www.ssa.gov/news/press/basicfact.html

Social Security Administration. (2015a). *Life expectancy*. Retrieved from http://www.ssa.gov/planners/lifeexpectancy.html

Social Security Administration. (2015b). *Social Security is important to African Americans*. Retrieved from http://www.ssa.gov/news/press/factsheets/africanamer.htm

Social Security Administration. (2015c). *Social Security is important to women*. Retrieved from http://www.ssa.gov/news/press/factsheets/women.htm

Sooryanarayana, R., Choo, W.-Y., & Hairi, N. N. (2013). A review on the prevalence and measurement of elder abuse in the community. *Trauma, Violence & Abuse*, 14(4), 316–325. doi:10.1177/1524838013495963

Soto, C. J. (2015). Is happiness good for your personality? Concurrent and prospective relations of the big five with subjective well-being. *Journal of Personality*, 83(1), 45–55. doi:10.1111/jopy.12081

Span, P. (2012, April 18). Where the oldest die now. *New York Times*. Retrieved from http://newoldage.blogs.nytimes.com/2012/04/18/where-the-oldest-die-now

Srivastava, S., John, O. P., Gosling, S. D., & Potter, J. (2003). Development of personality in early and middle adulthood: Set like plaster or persistent change? *Journal of Personality and Social Psychology*, 84, 1041–1053.

Stephan, Y., Caudroit, J., Jaconelli, A., & Terracciano, A. (2014). Subjective age and cognitive functioning: A 10-year prospective study. *The American Journal of Geriatric Psychiatry*, 22(11), 1180–1187. doi:10.1016/j.jagp.2013.03.007

Stephan, Y., Chalabaev, A., Kotter-Grühn, D., & Jaconelli, A. (2013). "Feeling younger, being stronger": An experimental study of subjective age and physical functioning among older adults. *The Journals of Gerontology: Series B: Psychological Sciences and Social Sciences*, 68(1), 1–7. doi:10.1093/geronb/gbs037

Story, T. N., Berg, C. A., Smith, T. W., Beveridge, R., Henry, N. J. M., & Pearce, G. (2007). Age, marital satisfaction, and optimism as predictors of positive sentiment override in middle-aged and older married couples. *Psychology and Aging*, 22(4), 719–727.

Stroebe, M., Schut, H., & Boerner, K. (2010). Continuing bonds in adaptation to bereavement: Toward theoretical integration. *Clinical Psychology Review*, 30(2), 259–268. doi:10.1016/j.cpr.2009.11.007

Stroebe, M., Schut, H., & Stroebe, W. (2005). Attachment in coping with bereavement: A theoretical integration. *Review of General Psychology*, 9(1), 48–66. doi:10.1037/1089-2680.9.1.48

Subramanian, S. V, Elwert, F., & Christakis, N. (2008). Widowhood and mortality among the elderly: The modifying role of neighborhood concentration of widowed individuals. *Social Science & Medicine*, 66(4), 873–884.

Syme, M. L., Klonoff, E. A., Macera, C. A., & Brodine, S. K. (2013). Predicting sexual decline and dissatisfaction among older adults: The role of partnered and individual physical and mental health factors. *The Journals of Gerontology: Series B: Psychological Sciences and Social Sciences*, 68(3), 323–332. doi:10.1093/geronb/gbs087

Szinovacz, M. E. (2003). Contexts and pathways: Retirement as institution, process, and experience. In G. A. Adams & T. A. Beehr (Eds.), *Retirement: Reasons, processes, and results* (pp. 6–52). New York: Springer.

Tan, R. S. (2011). *Aging men's health: A case-based approach*. New York: Thieme.

Tang, F. (2008). Socioeconomic disparities in voluntary organization involvement among older adults. *Nonprofit & Voluntary Sector Quarterly*, 37(1), 57–75.

Taylor, A., & Gosney, M. A. (2011). Sexuality in older age: Essential considerations for healthcare professionals. *Age and Ageing*, 40(5), 538–543. doi:10.1093/ageing/afr049

Taylor, M. G., & Lynch, S. M. (2004). Trajectories of impairment, social support, and depressive symptoms in later life. *The Journals of Gerontology: Series B: Psychological Sciences and Social Sciences*, (4), S238–S246.

Taylor, S. E. (2011). Social support: A review. In H. S. Friedman (Ed.), *The Oxford Handbook of Health Psychology* (p. 936). New York: Oxford University Press. Retrieved from https://books.google.com/books?hl=en&lr=&id=apBoAgAAQBAJ&pgis=1

Teno, J. M., Weitzen, S., Fennell, M. L., & Mor, V. (2001). Dying trajectory in the last year of life: Does cancer trajectory fit other diseases? *Journal of Palliative Medicine*, 4(4), 457–464. doi:10.1089/109662101753381593

Thiele, D. M., & Whelan, T. A. (2008). The relationship between grandparent satisfaction, meaning, and generativity. *International Journal of Aging and Human Development*, 66(1), 21–48.

Thobaben, M. (2008). Elder abuse prevention. *Home Health Care Management & Practice*, 20(2), 194–196.

Thomas, P. A. (2010). Is it better to give or to receive? Social support and the well-being of older adults. *The Journals of Gerontology: Series B: Psychological Sciences and Social Sciences*, 65B(3), 351–357. doi:10.1093/geronb/gbp113

Thompson, W. K., Charo, L., Vahia, I. V, Depp, C., Allison, M., & Jeste, D. V. (2011). Association

between higher levels of sexual function, activity, and satisfaction and self-rated successful aging in older postmenopausal women. *Journal of the American Geriatrics Society*, 59(8), 1503–1508. doi:10.1111/j.1532-5415.2011.03495.x

Thorson, J. A., & Powell, F. C. (2000). Death anxiety in younger and older adults. In A. Tomer (Ed.), *Death attitudes and the older adult: Theories, concepts, and applications* (pp. 123–136). New York: Brunner-Routledge.

Townsend, A. J., Miller, B., & Guo., S. (2001). Depressive symptomatology in middle-aged and older married couples: A dyadic analysis. *The Journals of Gerontology: Series B: Psychological Sciences & Social Sciences*, 56B(6), S352.

Uchino, B. N. (2006). Social support and health: A review of physiological processes potentially underlying links to disease outcomes. *Journal of Behavioral Medicine*, 29(4), 377–387. doi:10.1007/s10865-006-9056-5

U.S. Bureau of the Census. (2012). *Current Population Survey*. Washington, DC: Author. Retrieved from http://www.bls.gov/emp/ep_chart_001.htm

U.S. Bureau of the Census. (2014a). 2013 person income. *CPS 2014 Annual Social and Economic Supplement*. Retrieved from https://www.census.gov/hhes/www/cpstables/032014/perinc/pinc09_000.htm

U.S. Bureau of the Census. (2014b). 2013 poverty. *CPS 2014 Annual Social and Economic Supplement*.

U.S. Department of Health and Human Services. (2013). *Women's health USA: 2013*. Washington, DC: Author. Retrieved from http://mchb.hrsa.gov/whusa13

U.S. Department of Health and Human Services. (2015). *2015 poverty guidelines*. Retrieved from http://aspe.hhs.gov/poverty/15poverty.cfm

U.S. Federal Reserve. (2014). Report on the economic well-being of U.S. households in 2013. Washington, DC: Author. Retrieved from http://www.federalreserve.gov/econresdata/2013-report-economic-well-being-us-households-201407.pdf

Vaillant, G. E. (1994). "Successful aging" and psychosocial well-being: Evidence from a 45-year study. In E. H. Thompson Jr. (Ed.), *Older men's lives* (pp. 22–41). Thousand Oaks, CA: Sage.

Vaillant, G. E. (2004). Positive aging. In P. A. Linley & S. Joseph (Eds.), *Positive psychology in practice* (pp. 561–578). Hoboken, NJ: John Wiley.

Van Bilsen, P. M. A., Hamers, J. P. H., Groot, W., & Spreeuwenberg, C. (2008). Sheltered housing compared to independent housing in the community. *Scandinavian Journal of Caring Sciences*, 22(2), 265–274. doi:10.1111/j.1471-6712.2007.00529.x

Van Solinge, H., & Henkens, K. (2008). Adjustment to and satisfaction with retirement: Two of a kind? *Psychology and Aging*, 23(2), 422–434.

Van Volkom, M. (2006). Sibling relationships in middle and older adulthood: A review of the literature. *Marriage & Family Review*, 40(2–3), 151–170. doi:10.1300/J002v40n02-08

Verma, S. (2003). Retirement coverage of women and minorities: Analysis from SIPP 1998 Data. Washington, DC: AARP. Retrieved from http://www.aarp.org/research/financial/pensions/aresearch-import-350-DD92.html

Vinick, B. H., & Ekerdt, D. J. (1991). The transition to retirement: Responses of husbands and wives. In B. B. Hess & E. W. Markson (Eds.), *Growing old in America* (4th ed., pp. 305–317). New Brunswick, NJ: Transaction Publishers.

Wahrendorf, M., & Siegrist, J. (2010). Are changes in productive activities of older people associated with changes in their well-being? Results of a longitudinal European study. *European Journal of Ageing*, 7(2), 59–68. doi:10.1007/s10433-010-0154-4

Wakabayashi, C., & Donato, K. M. (2006). Does caregiving increase poverty among women in later life? Evidence from the Health and Retirement Survey. *Journal of Health & Social Behavior*, 47(3), 258–274.

Waldinger, R. J., & Schulz, M. S. (2010). What's love got to do with it? Social functioning, perceived health, and daily happiness in married octogenarians. *Psychology and Aging*, 25(2), 422–431. doi:10.1037/a0019087

Wang, M. (2007). Profiling retirees in the retirement transition and adjustment process: Examining the longitudinal change patterns of retirees' psychological well-being. *Journal of Applied Psychology*, 92(2), 455–474.

Wang, M., Henkens, K., & van Solinge, H. (2011). A review of theoretical and empirical advancements. *The American Psychologist*, 66(3), 204–213. doi:10.1037/a0022414

Ward, L., Mathias, J. L., & Hitchings, S. E. (2007). Relationships between bereavement and cognitive functioning in older adults. *Gerontology*, 53(6), 362–372. doi:10.1159/000104787

Webster, J. D., Bohlmeijer, E. T., & Westerhof, G. J. (2010). Mapping the future of reminiscence: A conceptual guide for research and practice. *Research on Aging*, 32(4), 527–564. doi:10.1177/0164027510364122

Weingarten, H. R. (1988). The impact of late life divorce: A conceptual and empirical study. *Journal of Divorce*, 12(1), 21–39.

Weiss, A., Costa, P. T., Jr., Karuza, J., Duberstein, P. R., Friedman, B., & McCrae, R. R. (2005). Cross-sectional age differences in personality among Medicare patients aged 65 to 100. *Psychology and Aging*, 20(1), 182–185. doi:10.1037/0882-7974.20.1.182

Weiss, D., & Lang, F. R. (2012). "They" are old but "I" feel younger: age-group dissociation as a self-protective strategy in old age. *Psychology and Aging*, 27(1), 153–163. doi:10.1037/a0024887

Westerhof, G. J., & Bohlmeijer, E. T. (2014). Celebrating fifty years of research and applications in reminiscence and life review: State of the art and new directions. *Journal of Aging Studies*, 29, 107–114. doi:10.1016/j.jaging.2014.02.003

Westerhof, G. J., Bohlmeijer, E., & Webster, J. D. (2010). Reminiscence and mental health: A review of recent progress in theory, research and interventions. *Ageing & Society*, 30(4), 697–721.

Whitbourne, S. K. (2007). *Adult development and aging: Biopsychosocial perspectives*. Hoboken, NJ: John Wiley.

White, L. K., & Riedmann, A. (1992). When the Brady Bunch grows up: Step/half- and fullsibling relationships in adulthood. *Journal of Marriage and Family*, 54(1), 197–208.

Whiting, P., & Bradley, L. J. (2007). Artful witnessing of the story: Loss in aging adults. *Adultspan: Theory Research & Practice*, 6(2), 119–128.

Wilber, K. H., & McNeilly, D. P. (2001). Elder abuse and victimization. In J. E. Birren & K. W. Schaie (Eds.), *Handbook of the psychology of aging* (5th ed., pp. 569–591). San Diego: Academic Press.

Wilches-Gutiérrez, J. L., Arenas-Monreal, L., Paulo-Maya, A., Peláez-Ballestas, I., & Idrovo, A. J. (2012). A "beautiful death": Mortality, death, and holidays in a Mexican municipality. *Social Science & Medicine*, 74(5), 775–782. doi:10.1016/j.socscimed.2011.11.018

Windsor, T. D., Anstey, K. J., & Rodgers, B. (2008). Volunteering and psychological well-being among young-old adults: How much is too much? *Gerontologist*, 48(1), 59–70.

Wink, P., & Dillon, M. (2002). Spiritual development across the adult life course: Findings from a longitudinal study. *Journal of Adult Development*, 9(1), 79–94.

Worden, J. W. (1991). *Grief counseling and grief therapy: A handbook for the mental health practitioner* (2nd ed.). New York: Springer.

Wu, Z., & Schimmele, C. M. (2007). Uncoupling in late life. *Generations*, 31(3), 41–46.

Zhan, M., & Pandey, S. (2002). Postsecondary education and the well-being of women in retirement. *Social Work Research*, 26(3), 171.

Crumley, B., 409
Cruza-Guet, M. C., 382
Crystal, D., 262
Csikszentmihalyi, M., 293, 327
Cuccaro, P., 302
Cuellar, J., 207
Cuevas, K., 119, 126
Cui, M., 355
Cuijpers, P., 264, 507, 531
Culbertson, F. M., 348
Cullen, J., 398
Cully, J. A., 507
Culver, C., 146
Cumming, E. M., 511
Cumming, J., 352
Cummings, C., 395
Cummings, E. M., 276, 282
Cunniff, C., 49
Cunningham, D. A., 364, 484
Cunningham, M., 399, 405
Cupples, L. A., 366
Curfs, L. M. G., 47
Curnow, C., 364
Curran, T., 439
Curtin, S. C., 75, 365, 408
Cusimano, M. D., 350
Cutrona. C. E., 207
Cymerman, E., 186
Cyphers, L., 133
Cyr, F., 276
Czekóová, K., 98

D'augelli, A. R., 409
D'Esposito, M., 234, 495
D'Onofrio, B., 239, 354, 355
Da Fonseca, D., 252
Dabelea, D., 345
Dack, L. A., 183
Daeher, M. W., 174
Daffner, K. R., 436
Dahinten, V. S., 192, 298
Dahl, A., 100, 330
Dahl, B., 410
Dahl, M., 189
Dahl, R. E., 299, 304
Dahlgren, M. K., 372
Dahlstrom, M. E., 79
Dahn, J. R., 369
Dainese, S. M., 432
Dalal, R. S., 465
Daley, D., 253
Dalman, C., 459
Dalton, M., 250
Dalton, M. E., 102
Damon, M., 240
Damon, W., 243–244, 260, 262, 314, 326
Dana, T., 423
Danaei, G., 476
Dandrow, C., 301
Dandy, K., 512
Daneman, M., 121
Daniels, D., 50, 190
Daniels, K., 274, 399
Daniels, K. A., 495
Daniels, M. H., 326
Daniels, P., 79
Daniels, S. R., 231
Danis, A., 178
Danovitch, J., 244
Dapretto, M., 127
Darbonne, A., 508
Darby, B. L., 68
Darchia, N., 301
Dare, J., 457
Dare. J. S., 450
Darkes, J., 372
Darling, N., 332, 339
Darowski, E. S., 495
Darviri, C., 477
Darwin, Charles, 20, 22
Das Eiden, R., 70
Das, R., 43
Daselaar, S., 478
Dasen, P. R., 231
Dattalo, P., 523
Daugherty, K. E., 6
Davalos, D. B., 434
Davenport, 47
Davey, A., 465, 477, 500
David-Barret, T., 393
David, C. B., 479
Davidson A. J., 335

Davidson, R. D., 276
Davies, C. G., 494
Davies, I. R. L., 100
Davies, K. J. A., 367
Davies, P., 276
Davies, P. T., 275
Daviglus, M. L., 491
Davila, J., 402, 458
Davis-Kean, P. E., 261, 346
Davis, A. S., 45–46
Davis, B., 301, 343
Davis, D. W., 179
Davis, E. M., 461
Davis, E. P., 73
Davis, H. P., 434, 527
Davis, J. D., 487
Davis, LaShonda, 268
Davis, N. L., 507
Davis, N. S., 91
Davis, P. E., 217
Davis, S., 528
Davis. B., 317
Davison, S. L., 427
Dawson-Hughes, B., 425
Dawson, B., 191
Dawson, L., 9, 226
Dawson, T. L., 312
Day, M.-C., 102
Day, N. L., 70
Day, S., 492
de Bellis, M. D., 207, 303
De Beni, R., 500
de Bruyn, E. H., 336, 342
De Deyn, P P., 227
de Domini, P., 317
De Forrest, R. L., 507
De Genna, N., 345, 346
de Goede, M., 275
de Groot, R. H. M., 438
De Guzman, M. R. T., 461
de Haan, M., 173
de Houwer, A., 133
de Kieviet, J. F., 126
De la Fuente, M., 481
De Martinis, M., 364
de Onis, M., 92, 229
de Quadros-Wander, S., 454
De Smet, H. J., 227
de Sousa Freire, N. B., 101
De Vaus, D., 524
de Visser, R. O., 518
de Vries, B., 393, 404
De Vries, B., 516
de Vries, N. K., 335
de Waal, F. B. M., 212
de Weerth, C., 153
de Wied, M., 329
De Winter, A. F., 348
De Wolff, M. S., 156
de Zwart, O., 344
De-Hayes, L., 278
Deák, G. O., 176–177
Dean, D. C., 171
Deardorff, J., 298, 348
Deary, I. J., 434, 455, 499, 509
Deater-Deckard, K., 53, 207
Decarli, B., 301
Dechonen, S., 103
Dee, T. S., 248
Deeks, A. A., 426
Deeney, M., 40
Deerenberg, I. M., 512
Defoe, I. N., 310
DeFries, J. C., 43, 47, 50
DeFronzo, R. A., 486
Degenhardt, L., 370
Degges-White, S., 507
Dehaan, L., 153, 155
Dehart, G., 412
Dehue, F., 338
Dekovic, M., 189, 327
Dekovi⊠, M., 337
Del Boca, F. K., 372
del Pozo-Cruz, 407
Del Valle, C., 156
Delahanty, D. L., 279
DeLamater, J., 518–519
Delaney-Black, V., 70
Delanoë, D., 426, 428
Deldin, P., 459
Deleau, M., 183, 184
Deligeoroglou, E., 47

Deligkaris, P., 466
Dell, D. L., 346
Dellenbach, M., 434
DeLoache, J., 244
DeLoache, J. S., 123, 174, 180
DeLong, L. K., 265
DeLosh, E. L., 434
Delsing, M. J. M., 335
DeLuca, 379
Demaeght, N., 496
Demaray, M. K., 265
Dement, W. C., 78
Demetriou, A., 307, 441
Deming, L., 438
Demir, M., 393
Demissie, S., 366
Demo, D. H., 332
Demonner, S. M., 345
Demorest, A., 246
Dempster, F. N., 234
DeNavas-Walt, C., 272, 512–513
Deneault, J., 233
Denham, S. A., 200
Denissen, J. J. A., 260, 454, 506
Dennerstein, L., 426, 461
Denney, N. W., 498
Dennis, D., 529
Dennis, H., 467
Dennis, M., 73
Dennis, N. A., 479
Dennis, T. A., 142, 201
Dennis, W., 106
Dennison, R. P., 401
Denny, A., 481
Deoni, S. C. L., 171
Deprest, J. A., 49
Deptula, D. P., 334
Derlan, C. L., 327
DeRose, L. M., 294, 295–296
DeRosier, M. E., 265
Deruelle, C., 252
DeSantis, C. E., 476
DeSapri, K. T., 426
Descartes, L., 215
deSchonen, S., 159
Desmarais, L. B., 411
DeSpelder, L. A., 525
Després, J.-P., 368
Detels, R., 404
Deutsch, F. M., 402
Deutsch, G., 171
Deutsch, W., 246
Deven, F., 412
Devine, C. M., 90, 413
Devine, O., 73
Devouche, E., 128
DeVries, H. M., 398, 460
DeVries, R., 174, 242
Dew, J., 401, 405
DeWolff, M. S., 154
Dewsbury, D., 20
Dezutter, J., 508
Dhaliwal, S. S., 90
Dhital, A., 487
Di Paolo, E. R., 93
Diab, M., 282
Diamond, A., 118, 227
Diamond, J., 352
Diamond, L. M., 339
Diamond, M. P., 366
Diaz-Cintra, S., 489
Diaz, R. M., 187
Dick, F., 303
Dickey, C. R., 266
Dickinson, D. K., 249
DiClemente, R. J., 340
Diego, M. A., 101
Diehl, M., 199, 432, 506
Diemer, M. A., 379
Diener, E., 407, 508
Diener, M., 76
Dieter, J. N. I., 28
Dietz, P. M., 145
DiGiovanni, C. D., 343
DiiMatteo, M. R., 510
Dijkstra, J. K., 334
Dijkstra, P., 394
Dill, E. J., 266
Dillaway, H. E., 426
Dillon, M., 509
Dilworth-Anderson, P., 465
Dimond, M. F., 530

Endestad, T. O. R., 183
Endo, T., 367
Eng, S., 398
Engelhardt, M., 423
Engels, R., 329
Engels, R. C., 328
Engels, R. C. M. E., 335
England, D. E., 215
Engle, P. L., 156
English, T., 512
Englund, K., 132
Englund, M., 154
Englund, M. M., 353
Engmann, B., 494
Ennouri, K., 105
Enns, G. M., 44
Enns, M. W., 409
Enoch, M.-A., 373
Enright, R. D., 244
Ensari, I., 123
Ensor, R., 179, 183
Entwhistle, D. R., 250
Entwisle, D. R., 318
Eppe, S., 211
Epstein, M. H., 247
Epstein, R., 129
Erdley, C. A., 317, 335
Erel, O., 153
Erickson, K. I., 480, 484
Erickson, L. D., 411
Ericsson, K. A., 237, 439
Erikson, E. H., 328, 448–449, 450, 507, 508
Erikson, Erik, 13–14, 22–23, 140, 198, 260, 392
Erikssen, J., 424
Eriksson, M., 101
Erlangsen, A., 531
Ernst, A., 479
Eron, L. D., 202
Ertesvåg, S. K., 278
Erwin, P., 262
Eryigit-Madzwamuse, S., 154
Eryigit, S., 331
Escobar-Chaves, S. L., 342
Escobar, L. F., 45–46
Esfandiari, N., 365
Eskenazi, B., 345
Eslick, G. D., 89
Espelage, D. L., 265, 266, 334, 342
Espinosa, M. P., 169
Espinoza, G., 317
Esplin, E., 181
Estell, D. B., 263
Estes, K. G., 132
Ethington, C. A., 127
Ettekal, I., 264, 266
Eubig, P. A., 253
Euser, E. M., 278
Evans, A., 302
Evans, D. R., 524
Evans, D. W., 25
Evans, E. H., 231
Evans, E. M., 235
Evans, G. W., 368
Evans, J., 215, 480
Evans, S., 264
Evans, S. Z., 355
Evans, G. W., 273
Eveleth, P. B., 168
Everett, B. H., 175
Everett, G., 411
Everman, D. B., 43
Exley, K., 171
Exner-Cortens, D., 340
Eyal, N., 500
Eyre, O., 253
Eyre, S. L., 341

Faber, A. J., 275
Fabes, R. A., 200, 215, 244
Fabricius, W. V., 276
Facio, A., 391–392
Fadjukoff, P., 390
Fagan, J. F., 96, 122, 126
Fagan, P., 370
Fagard, J., 98
Fagen, J., 122
Fagley, N. S., 313
Fagot, B. I., 154
Fahs, M. C., 513
Fairchild, E. E., 378–379
Fairfield, B., 496
Fairley, L., 149

Falbo, T., 261, 270
Family Life Project Investigators, 142
Fan, H. C., 49
Fan, X., 318
Fang, F., 183
Fantz, R. L., 99
Farage, M. A., 423, 478
Farber, D. A., 236
Faria, M. A., 482
Farkas, J. I., 460
Farley, F., 309
Farley, O. W., 515
Farmer-Dougan, V., 172
Farmer, T. W., 263
Farnhill, D., 231
Farr, R. H., 272
Farr, S. L., 145
Farrell, M. P., 450
Farrington, D. P., 355
Farroni, T., 99, 144
Farstad, H., 100
Farver, J. A. M., 211
Farzaneh-Far, R., 483
Fasig, L. G., 198
Faulkner, J. A., 364
Faunce, D. E., 481
Favero, S., 372
Fawcett, L. M., 7
Fay-Stammbach, T., 203
Fay, S., 478
Fearon, R. M. P., 154
Featherman, D. L., 480, 511
Federman, D. D., 426
Fedewa, A. L., 271–272, 409
Feely, J., 371
Feeney, J. A., 408
Fegert, J. M., 281, 350
Fegley, S., 317
Fehr, R., 524
Feig, E., 52
Feigenson, L., 124
Feiler, R., 190
Feinberg, M. E., 269, 271, 337
Feingold, T., 410
Feketem T., 48
Feldman, D. C., 465, 521
Feldman, J. F., 97, 122, 124, 126
Feldman, P. J., 73
Feldman, R., 78, 142, 145, 156, 160
Feldman. L., 482
Feldstein Ewing, S. W., 353
Felker, J. A., 408
Fellowes, S., 227
Felmlee, D., 516
Felt, J., 395
Fend, H., 327
Feng, L., 483
Feng, X., 146
Feng, Y., 494
Feng. X., 131
Fengying, Z., 270
Fenn, A. M., 481
Fennell, C. T., 123
Fennell, M. L., 525
Fenstermacher, S. K., 123
Fenwick, J., 90
Ferber, S. G., 101
Ferguson, C. J., 123
Ferguson, G. M., 326
Ferguson, H. B., 231
Ferguson, P., 231, 250
Ferguson, R. F., 379
Fergusson, D. M., 52, 279, 346, 349, 355, 371
Ferholt, B., 179
Fernald, A., 132, 133, 144
Fernandes-Penney, A., 69
Fernandez, A., 211, 230
Fernandez, G., 495
Fernandez, Z., 489
Fernyhough, 187
Fernyhough, C., 177, 217
Ferrer-Caja, E., 434
Ferrero, J., 300
Ferring, D., 249
Ferris, G. R., 465
Ferrucci, L., 481
Festa, E. K., 487
Fetchenhauer, D., 394
Fetters, L., 106
Feyereisen, P., 496
Fidler, B., 339

Field, D., 516
Field, D. E., 202
Field, M. J., 525
Field, N. P., 529
Field, T., 28, 73, 101, 145, 156, 200
Field, T. M., 103
Fiestas, C., 249
Fifer, W. P., 77, 78, 97
Figner, B., 309, 310, 344
Fildes, A., 168
Filippova, E., 246
Filson, J., 398
Fincham, F. D., 397, 401, 458
Finder, V. H., 488–489
Findlay, L. C., 327
Fine, M., 274, 276, 408
Finemore, J., 231
Finer, L. B., 340, 344–345
Fingerman, K. L., 457, 460, 461, 464–465, 512, 516, 518
Finkel, D., 434, 499
Finkel, E. J., 394, 395, 459
Finkelhor, D., 264, 265, 278, 279, 338
Finnegan, M., 70
Finni, T., 227
Finzi-Dottan, R., 334
Fiore, A. T., 394
Fiori, K. L., 512
Fiorvanti, C. M., 280
Fireman, G., 116
Fireman, G. D., 216
Fisch, H., 366
Fischbacher, S., 366
Fischer, J., 398
Fischer, J. L., 394
Fischer, K. W., 95
Fischer, M. J., 378
Fischhoff, B., 308
Fishbein, M., 341–342
Fisher, C., 31
Fisher, C. B., 6, 25
Fisher, D. A., 343
Fisher, E. M., 123
Fisher, G. J., 478
Fisher, H. L., 350
Fisher, J. A., 168
Fisher, J. E., 494
Fisher, L., 327
Fisher, P. A., 173
Fisher, S. E., 252
Fisher, W. M., 409
Fishkin, J., 313
Fisk, J. D., 493
Fissore, M. F., 90
Fitch, C. A., 274
Fite, P. J., 264
Fitzgerald, H. E., 145
Fitzgerald, L. F., 347
Fitzpatrick, A. L., 487
Fitzpatrick, M., 215
Fitzsimmons, C. M., 127
Fivush, R., 124, 181, 182, 184
Flajolet, M., 494
Flament, F., 364
Flanagan, D. P., 238
Flanders, J. L., 156
Flannery, D., 355
Flannery, D. J., 308, 354
Flatt, T., 52
Flavell, E. R., 174–176, 182, 184
Flavell, J. H., 10, 120, 174–176, 182–184, 236
Flavin, J., 72
Flegal, K. M., 368
Fleiss, K., 189
Fleming, C. B., 372
Fleming. C., 423
Fletcher K. L., 335
Fletcher, A. C., 262, 332
Fletcher, B. C., 129
Fletcher, G. E., 41
Fletcher, J. M., 73, 252
Fletcher, L. C. B., 489
Fletcher, R., 145
Flett, G. L., 349
Flieller, A., 306
Floccia, C., 97
Flocke, S. A., 344
Flodmark, C.-E., 230
Flor, D. L., 207
Flores, C., 405
Flores, G., 169, 265
Florsheim, P., 346, 517

Flouri, E., 462
Flowers, D. L., 252
Flynn, J., 239
Fogel, A., 76, 104, 106, 141, 159
Fok, H. K., 512
Fokkema, T., 520
Foley, H. J., 100
Fonagy, P., 12, 150, 266
Fonda, S. J., 515
Font, S. A., 208
Foorman, B. R., 247
Forbes, E. E., 304
Forcier, K., 432
Ford, D. Y., 239
Ford, S. P., 41
Forehand, R., 346
Forhan, S. E., 344
Forman, D., 160
Formoso, D., 348
Forraz, N., 64
Forsberg, S., 352
Forsblad-d'Elia, H., 427
Forshaw, M., 426
Forssman, L., 119
Forste, R., 406
Forster, J. L., 371
Forstmeier, S., 508
Fortenberry, J. D., 339, 345
Fortin, C., 344
Fortney, S., 72
Fortson, E. N., 355
Fosco, G. M., 276
Foshee, V. A., 340
Fossati, P., 260
Fossum, K.-L., 184
Foster, E. M., 90
Fournier, S., 512
Foust, M. D., 331
Fouts, H. N., 156
Fowler, J. H., 51
Fowler, P. J., 211
Fox, K. A., 49
Fox, Michael J., 493
Fox, N. A., 211
Fox, S. E., 95
Fracasso, M. P., 79
Frackowiak, R. S. J., 171
Fradkin, C., 302
Frahsek, S., 218
Frame, L. E., 402
Franchak, J. M., 104
Francis, B., 171
Francis, L., 230
Francis, M. K., 364
Francke, A., 490
FranⓍ, S., 348
Frank, D. A., 71
Frank, G. K., 352
Franke, B., 252
Frankel, L. L., 297
Frankenhuis, W. E., 22, 298
Franklin, A., 100
Franklin, S., 306
Franzetta, K., 341, 344
Frawley, T. J., 214
Fray, L., 413
Frazier, A. L., 298
Frazier, L. D., 338, 497
Frech, A., 401, 458
Frede, E., 249
Frederick, C. B., 302
Frederick, D., 393
Frederickson, N. L., 244
Frederiksen, K. S., 491
Fredricks, J. A., 318
Freedman-Doan, P., 316, 327
Freeman, J., 318
Freeman, R., 352
Freeman, S., 477
Fremmer-Bombik, E., 154
French, S. E., 315
Freud, Sigmund, 11–13, 22–23
Freudenberger, P., 492
Freund, A. M., 6, 440, 450, 476, 506
Frey, K. S., 199
Frey, N., 251
Frick, K., 90
Fried, P. A., 70
Friederici, A. D., 171
Friedman, D., 513
Friedman, H. S., 432, 455, 509

Friedman, K., 341
Friedman, M. A., 368
Friedman, R. J., 206
Friedman, S. L., 179, 182
Fries, J. F., 482, 484
Frisén, A., 231
Friston, K. J., 6
Fritz, J., 142
Frodi, A. M., 156
Frodi, M., 156
Frome, P. M., 412
Fromme, D. K., 408
Frongillo, E. A., 88, 90, 169
Frongillo, E., Jr., 9, 88
Frost, J. H., 394
Frost, L. A., 246
Frostad, P., 318
Fry, A. F., 234, 499
Fry, C. L., 452
Fry, P. S., 507
Fry, R., 523
Fryar, C. D., 368
Fryberg, S. A., 330
Fryda, C. M., 279–280
Fuchs, M. L., 91
Fuentes, T., 431
Fugelsang, J., 437
Fuger, K. L., 71
Fujii, H., 367
Fukuda, K., 434
Fukumoto, A., 187
Fuligni, A. J., 301, 327, 331
Fulkerson, J. A., 352
Fuller-Thomson, E., 462
Fuller, M. J., 297
Fung, H. H., 512
Fuqua, D. R., 509
Furby, L., 309
Furman, B., 49
Furman, W., 337, 339
Furnham, A., 394
Furstenberg, F., 346–347

Gabbard, C. P., 226
Gabriel, M. A. M., 105
Gabriel, Z., 513
Gabrielli, J., 264
Gadassi, R., 402
Gaddis, A., 297
Gage, F. H., 489
Gagne, J. R., 147
Gagne, M.-H., 276
Gagnon, S. G., 203
Gaillard, V., 306–307
Gajdos, Z. K. Z., 298
Gal-Oz, E., 529
Galal, O., 169
Galambos N. L., 348
Galambos, N. L., 390
Galasso, L., 177
Galatzer-Levy, I. R., 407
Gall, T. L., 524
Gallagher, A., 176
Gallagher, N. A., 513
Gallagher, P., 438
Gallahue, D. L., 226
Galler, J. R., 93
Gallicchio, L., 426
Galliher, R. V., 330, 331
Gallo, W. T., 513
Galloway, J. C., 104–106
Galotti, K. M., 245
Galván, A., 301
Gamm, B. K., 266
Ganchrow, J. R., 97
Ganea, P. A., 182
Ganger, J., 128
Ganong, 399
Ganong, L., 408, 515
Ganong, L. H., 277
Gans, C., 22
Gans, D., 366, 464, 514
Ganzini, L., 528
Gao, G., 397
Garakani, A., 282
Garbe, P. L., 228
Garcia Coll, C. T., 146
Garcia-Rill, E., 78
Garcia, C., 331
Garcia, J., 477
Garcia, K., 231, 351
Garcia, R., 103

Gard, D., 459
Gardiner, J., 460
Gardner, H. W., 8, 76, 150, 157, 233, 239–240, 246
Gardner, J. D., 298
Gardner, W. L., 459
Gareis, K. C., 413, 414
Garg, R., 317
Garmezy, N., 280
Garnefski, N., 410
Garner, P. W., 200
Garrard, P., 491
Garrett-Peters, P., 201
Garrett, S. B., 332
Garrision, E. G., 32
Garton, A. F., 7
Gartrell, N., 272
Gartstein, M. A., 149, 154–155
Garver, K. E., 18, 306
Garvin, B. J., 430
Garvin, R. A., 187
Gasparro, F. P., 365
Gass, K., 269
Gass, M., 425
Gassen, N. S., 400
Gasser, T., 296
Gasser, U., 338
Gasson, N., 9, 226
Gastó, C., 489
Gates, G. A., 481
Gates, G. J., 271, 409
Gathercole, S. E., 120, 180, 234, 236
Gattario, K. H., 231–232
Gaulin, S. J. C., 297
Gavens, N., 306
Gavrin, J., 525
Gawrylowicz, J., 182
Gayer, T., 191
Gazzaley, A., 495
Gazzola, V., 98
Ge, X., 300, 348
Gee, E., 466, 467, 513
Geerligs, L., 434
Gehri, M., 93
Geier, C. F., 304, 307, 309
Gelles, R. J., 342
Gelman, R., 177, 186
Gelman, S. A., 9, 235, 260
Gelman, S. H., 176
Gelo, J., 69
Gemmell, N. J., 366
Gennetian, L. A., 193
Gensini, G., 491
Gentilini, D., 477
Gentle-Genitty, C., 315
Gentry, B. C., 93
Georgas, J., 238
George, L. K., 509
Georgellis, Y., 407
Georgiades, K., 346, 398
Geraci, L., 507
Gerard, J., 207
Gerard, J. M., 315, 317, 463
Gerber, J. S., 89
Gerber, M., 432
Gerlach, E., 327
Germeijs, V., 327
Germezia, M., 186
Gerrard-Morris, A., 173
Gerris, J. R. M., 332
Gershkoff-Stowe, L., 128, 185
Gershoff, E. T., 205
Gershon, A., 374
Gerson, A., 70
Gerstorf, D., 496
Gertner, Y., 119
Gervai, J., 215
Gervain, J., 99
Gervais, M. C., 50
Gest, S.D., 335
Getchell, N., 226
Gettler, L. T., 91
Geurts, A. C., 487
Geurts, T., 464
Geuze, R. H., 100
Gewirtz, J. L., 128
Gfeller, J. D., 507
Gfroerer, J., 70
Ghisletta, P., 434
Ghosh, J. K. C., 73
Ghossainy, M., 176
Giarrusso, R., 465

Larkin, L. M., 364
Larsen, J. B., 478
Larsen, W. J., 63
Larson, C. G., 509
Larson, N., 302
Larson, N. I., 301
Larson, R., 292, 293, 516
Larson, R. W., 333
Larson, S. L., 206
Larsson, N.-G., 367
Larus, D. M., 181
Larzelere, R. E., 203
Lasater, T. M., 424
Lasker, J., 198
Latham, K., 459, 481
Latza, U., 430
Latzer, Y., 352
Latzko, B., 244, 313
Laughton, B., 68, 69
Laukkanan, A., 227
Laukkanen, A., 350
Lauman, E. O., 520
Lauricella, A. R., 123
Laursen, B., 262, 326, 328, 332, 334
Lavelle, B., 459
Lavender, A. P., 364
Lavner, J. A., 404, 405, 409
LaVoie, D., 507
Law, J., 477
Law, R. W., 459
Lawlor, D. A., 426
Lawrence, A. R., 515
Lawrence, D., 370
Lawrence, E., 405, 408, 458
Lawrence, R. A., 90
Laye-Gindhu, A., 350
Layton, J. B., 459
Lazar, N. A., 18, 306
Le Blanc, M., 455
Le Bourdais, C., 400
Le Grange, D., 352
Le Normand, M., 133
Le, H., 378
Le, V.-N., 317
Leadbeater, B., 208, 340
Leadbeater, B. J., 348
Leal, T., 250
Leaper, C., 210, 215
Learmonth, A. E., 98, 122
Leather, C. V., 234
Leavens, D. A., 158
Leavitt, L., 91
Leavitt, L. A., 211
Lebeaux, D. S., 246
Lebel, C., 71, 302
LeBlanc, A. J., 369, 404, 458
Leccesse, L. A., 427
Leclerc, C. M., 6
Leclerc, D., 316
Lecusay, R., 179
LeDoux, J. E., 141
Lee Badgett, M. V., 458
Lee, A. R., 426
Lee, C. M., 370, 372–373
Lee, G. R., 518
Lee, H., 106
Lee, H. M., 105
Lee, H.-C., 367
Lee, H.-J., 487
Lee, J. C. M., 489
Lee, J. E., 518
Lee, J. M., 168, 183, 298, 316
Lee, K., 175
Lee, L., 262
Lee, L. J., 70
Lee, L.-K. O, 509–510
Lee, P. A., 293
Lee, R., 488
Lee, S., 261, 522
Lee, S. A., 119
Lee, S. J., 205
Lee, S. M., 326
Lee, S. S., 348
Lee, T., 282
Lee, V. E., 318
Lee, Y.-A., 438
Leech, S., 70, 71
Leekam, S., 183
Leen-Feldner, E. W., 300
Leenders, I., 314
Leenstra, T., 298
Leerkes, E. M., 142

Leeuwenburgh, C., 366
Lefever, J. E. B., 347
Lefkowitz, E. S., 342, 452, 460, 461, 465
Leflot, G., 260
Legare, C. H., 235
Leger, D. W., 151
Lehman, D. R., 261, 306
Lehmann, R., 237
Lehnart, J., 298
Lehrer, E. L., 405
Leibbrandt, S., 511
Leichsenring, F., 13
Leichtman, M. D., 181
Leigh-Paffenroth, E. D., 422
Leijssen, M., 508
Leitsch, S. A., 520
Lejeune, L., 100
Lemanek, K., 80
Lemerise, E. A., 142
Lemery, K. S., 148
Lempert, R. O., 306
Lengua, L. J., 354
Lenhart, A., 338
Leo, V., 156
León, E., 131
Leonard, B. E., 374
Leonard, K. E., 402
Leonard, S., 215
Leonardi, G., 496
Leone, J. M., 397
Leopold, T., 461
Lepage, J.-F., 98
Lepine, R., 276
Lepisto, L., 524
Leppänen, J. M., 144
Leproux, C., 178
Lereya, T. S., 264
Leridon, H., 410
Lerner, R. M., 20, 25, 293, 348
Lessov-Schlaggar, 50, C. N.
Lester, B. M., 75
Lester, D., 348
Lester, L., 317
Letiecq. B. L, 463
Leung, C. B., 185
Leung, C. Y. Y., 207
Leung, E., 80
Leung, M.-C., 262, 263
Leung, T., 49
Leurent, B., 528
Levenson, M. R., 433
Levenson, R. W., 455, 458, 517
Leventhal, T., 192, 340, 342
Leventon, J. S., 145
Lever, J., 393
Levesque, D. A., 399
Levin, E., 317
Levin, J. S., 509
Levine, C., 312
Levine, J. A., 347
Levine, L. E., 62
Levine, L. J., 181, 186
Levine, M., 231
LeVine, R. A., 146
Levine, S. C., 120
Levinson, D., 382
Levinson, D. J., 449–450
Levinson, F., 73
Levitt, P., 95
Levitt, T., 437, 438
Levy, G. D., 213
Levy, H. L., 44
Lewin, A., 157
Lewis, C., 142
Lewis, D.C., 451
Lewis, M., 71, 141–142, 150–151, 155–156, 158–159, 199, 203, 260, 275–276
Lewis, P. D., 47
Lewit, E. M., 168
Lewkowicz, D. J., 103
Lewkowicz, E. S., 452
Leyendecker, B., 146
Lezotte, D., 345
Li-jin, Z., 91
Li, B., 270
Li, C., 367
Li, C.-W., 423
Li, D., 68, 273, 438
Li, H., 49, 466
Li, J., 90, 119
Li, J. J., 348
Li, N. P., 394

Li, P., 479
Li, R., 90
Li, T., 512
Li, W.-F., 431
Li, Y., 366, 398
Li, Y. (2), 366
Liang, J., 511
Liao, H.-F., 106
Liaw, F., 80
Libal, G., 350
Liben, L. S., 214
Liberman, A. M., 247
Liberman, I. Y., 247
Libertus, K., 105
Libertus, M. E., 119, 120
Lichtenberger, E. O., 238
Lichter, D., 274
Lichter, D. T., 394, 409
Lickliter, R., 22, 55, 103
Liddon, N., 342
Lieberman, A. F., 155
Lieberman, M., 232, 312
Lieberman, M. D., 301
Liefbroer, A. C., 400
Liepelt, I., 493
Light, J. M., 334
Lighthart, L., 348
Liguori, S. A., 90
Lilgendahl, J. P., 452, 454
Liljequist, L., 332
Lillard, A., 183
Lillevoll, K. R., 329
Lim, H., 229, 302
Limber, S. P., 146, 147, 266, 268
Limbos, M., 231
Lin, E. H. B., 485
Lin, F. R., 481
Lin, H., 265, 366
Lin, I.-F., 519
Linck, P., 484
Lindberg, L. D., 344
Lindblom, B., 127
Lindenberg, S., 334
Lindenberger, U., 4, 6–7, 434, 495
Lindgren, B., 465
Lindgren, C. M., 229
Lindh-Åstrand, L., 426
Lindsay, J. J., 27
Lindsay, L. L., 275
Lindsey, E. W., 199
Lindstrom, T. M., 481, 485
Lindwall, M., 327
Linebarger, D. L., 123
Lineberger, D. L., 202, 203
Ling, P. M., 370
Ling, T., 332
Lingala, V. B., 484
Lingas, E. O., 370
Lingeman, J., 107
Lingras, K. A., 201
Linver, M. R., 192
Linz, S., 466
Lioret, S., 302
Llpka, 249
Lipman, E. L., 346
Lips, P., 169
Lipsitt, L. P., 97
Litovsky, R. Y., 99
Little, A. H., 97
Little, T. D., 210
Littlejohn, K., 178
Littleton, H. L., 231
Littman, A., 215
Littschwager, J. C., 185
Litwack, S. D., 327
Litwin, H., 511
Liu, D., 183, 184
Liu, D. T. L., 480
Liu, F., 483
Liu, G., 235
Liu, H., 431, 517
Liu, J., 428
Liu, R. T., 349
Liu, T.-C., 423
Liu, Y., 372, 491
Liu, Z., 270
Livingston, G., 273, 520
Livingstone, S., 338
Livson, N., 452
Liwag, M. D., 181
Ljung, R., 459
Lleras, C., 273

Mercuri, E., 99
Meredith, P., 203
Mermelstein, R., 293–294
Mero, R. P., 374, 432
Merrick, S., 155
Merrilees, C. E., 282
Merritt, J. A., 151
Merten, M. J., 341
Merzenich, M. M., 171
Meschke, L. L., 68
Messelt, S., 68
Messer, K., 371
Messinger, D., 141
Mestre, M. V., 313
Metcalf, M. G., 297
Metcalfe, A., 180
Metts, S., 402
Meulenbroek, O., 495
Meuwese R., 336
Meyer, A. S., 497
Meyer, C., 246
Meyer, S., 154, 199
MGonigle-Chalmers, M., 187
Miceli, R., 339
Michael, J. C., 395
Michael, S. L., 342
Michailevskay, V., 71
Michaud, P. A., 301
Miche, M., 457
Michel, G. F., 171
Michels, T. M., 341
Michener, M. D, 93
Mickelson, K. D., 407, 408
Mickler, C., 498
Micocci, F., 391–392
Middeldorp, C. M., 348
Midgley, C., 315
Midobuche, E., 249
Miech, R. A., 25, 353, 369
Miedzian, M., 215
Mieler, W. F., 480
Mihalik, J. L., 394
Mikels, J. A., 6, 376, 436, 496, 512
Milan, A., 401
Milanak, M. E., 25
Milburn, S., 190
Milevsky, A., 203, 327, 332
Milkie, M. A., 408
Miller-Johnson, S., 191
Miller, A. J., 399
Miller, A. M., 146, 432
Miller, B. D., 229, 481
Miller, C. F., 213
Miller, D. L., 210
Miller, E. A., 509, 517
Miller, G. F., 454
Miller, I., 374
Miller, J. G., 313
Miller, J. W., 480
Miller, K. S., 346
Miller, K. W., 437, 478
Miller, L., 52
Miller, L. C., 130, 131
Miller, L. M., 460
Miller, L. S., 499
Miller, N. L., 427
Miller, P. H., 9, 14–15, 18, 180
Miller, P. M., 313
Miller, R. B., 402, 458
Miller, R. R., 487
Miller, S. D., 463
Miller, W. S., 77
Milligan, K., 183, 184
Milller, K. W., 423
Mills-Koonce, W. R., 143, 201
Mills, J. H., 481
Mills, K. L., 303–304, 309
Mills, M., 383, 406–407
Mills, S., 529
Millstein, S. G., 308, 341
Min, M. O., 71
Minagawa-Kawai, Y., 99
Mingliang, Y., 270
Mingo, C. A., 485
Minich, N. M., 80
Minichiello, V., 518–519
Minick, N., 187
Minkler, M., 462
Mintzer, J., 491
Miquel, J., 481
Miranda, R., 349
Mirelman, A., 487

Mironov, S., 481
Misca, G., 131
Misch, D., 349
Misch, D. A., 372
Miseong, K., 397
Mistry, J., 18, 177, 189
Mitchell, A., 493
Mitchell, B. A., 460, 461
Mitchell, D. K., 228
Mitchell, D. W., 121
Mitchell, E. A., 91
Mitchell, J. A., 301, 302
Mitchell, K., 342
Mitchell, K. J., 338
Mitchell, M. B., 499
Mitchell, P., 183
Mitchell, S. E., 366
Mitchell, S. J., 157
Mitchell, W. K., 423
Mitsiouli, V., 250
Mitsuhiro, S., 104
Miura, Y., 367
Mix, K. S., 120
Miyake, K., 141, 150, 206
Miyamoto, K., 423
Mizrahi, R., 490
Mizuta, I., 201, 206
Mjaavatn, P. E., 318
Mnookin, R. H., 276
Mock, S. E., 407, 454, 507
Modecki, K. L., 301
Moen, P., 441, 458, 466, 522, 524
Moffitt, T. E., 332, 347, 355, 397
Mohand-Said, S., 422
Mohr, B. A., 519
Mohyla, J., 266
Moiduddin, E., 401
Moilanen, K. L., 319
Moise-Titus, J., 202
Mojon-Azzi, S. M., 481
Mojon, D. S., 481
Mokdad, A., 90
Molborn, S., 347
Molenda-Figueira, H. A., 295
Molgat, M., 391
Molinari, L., 296
Molinari, V., 499
Molinero, O., 515
Molitor, A., 80
Molitor, N., 153
Mollborn, S., 346
Möller, M., 297
Moller, S., 251
Møller, V., 454
Molloy, L. E., 337
Molnar, B.E., 343
Molnar, F. J., 493
Molnar, P., 98
Monaghan, C., 493
Monahan, K. C., 311, 316, 334, 336, 342, 355
Monden, C. W. S., 406
Mondini, S., 495
Moneta, G. B., 217, 327
Mong, S., 467
Monga, M., 102
Monge, P. R., 337
Monk, C. S., 94, 303
Monk, J. K., 401
Monn, A. R., 281
Mont-Reynaud, R., 319, 332
Montague, P. R., 150
Montecino-Rodriguez, E., 366
Montepare, J.M., 451
Montero, I., 187
Montesanto, A., 366
Montgomery, A. J., 466
Montgomery, M. J., 377, 392
Montgomery, R. J. V., 464
Montoya, R. M., 394
Moody, J., 335, 337
Mooijaart, A., 154
Moon, C., 77, 97, 99
Moon, H., 511
Moon, J. R., 531
Mooney, K. S., 328, 334
Mooney, P., 247
Moore, C., 128, 252
Moore, G. A., 143
Moore, K. A., 332
Moore, K. L., 39, 41–42, 62–64, 66–68, 70, 97–98, 119, 200, 341, 346, 462, 530

Moore, M. K., 103
Moore, R. A., 190
Moore, S. M., 464
Moore, S. R., 299, 300, 340
Moore, V. R., 463
Moore, W. E., 311
Moorman-Eavers, E. R., 394
Moorman, J. E., 228
Mor, V., 525
Moran, J. M., 260
Moran, R., 6, 485
Moran, S., 239
Moras, A., 406
Moreau, C., 297
Morell, C., 410
Morelli, G., 8, 91, 150
Morelli, G. A., 147
Moreno, A. J., 149
Moreno, C., 131
Moreno, S., 249
Morgan, D., 378
Morgan, R., 397
Morgan, W. B., 411
Morgos, D., 282
Moriguchi, Y., 179, 185
Morikawa, H., 133
Morin, A. J. S., 509
Morin, R., 523
Morison, V., 100
Morizot, J., 318, 455
Morley, D., 277
Morokuma, S., 96
Morphey, L, K., 331
Morra, S., 233
Morris, A. S., 261, 331, 333
Morris, P. A., 19–20, 193
Morrison, D. R., 274
Morrison, J. A., 298
Morrison, K. R., 399
Morrissey, T., 153
Morrongiello, B. A., 103
Morrow-Howell, N., 511, 525
Morrow, C. E., 70
Morrow, D. G., 437, 439–440
Morrow, J. D., 121
Morselli, D., 459
Mortensen, L., 497
Mortimer, J. T., 316
Mortimer, R. H., 49
Mortimore, E., 516
Morton, J., 103
Morton, K. R., 524
Moser, D. K., 430
Moses, A. M., 202
Moses, L. J., 145, 182, 183
Mosher, S. W., 270
Mosher, W., 274
Mosher, W. D., 399
Moshman, D., 306
Mosier, C., 18, 177, 189
Mosimann, U. P., 422
Moskalev, A. A., 366
Mosko, S., 91
Moskowitz, D. S., 449
Moss, P., 301, 412
Moss, S. A., 368
Mõttus, R., 509
Moulson, M. C., 144
Moum, T., 275, 405
Mouzon, D. M., 510
Moxley, J. H., 237, 439
Moyer-Gusé, E., 278
Moyer, A., 400
Mpofu, E., 234
Mrazel, D. A., 148
Mrick, S. E., 330, 331
Mroczek, D. K., 455–456, 508, 509
Mrtorell, G. A., 331
Mrtoroell, G. A., 330
Mrug, S., 300, 355
Mu, X., 261
Mu, Y., 489
Muangpaisan, W., 494
Muehlenkamp, J. J., 350
Mueller, J., 69
Mueller, V., 129
Muennig, P., 191
Muenssinger, J., 96
Muir, D., 103, 175
Mukhtar, H., 429
Mulder, E. J. H. A., 73

Ross, J. L., 25, 46
Ross, S., 350
Ross, S. A., 15, 202
Rosselli, M., 210
Rosset, I., 492
Rossi Ferrario, S., 531
Rossi, A. S., 426
Rossnagel, K., 430
Rossouw, J. E., 427
Rostosky, S. S., 404
Rote, W. M., 333
Rotenberg, K. J., 262
Rothaupt, J. W., 408
Rothbart, M. K., 147, 148, 159, 179
Rothbaum, F., 150, 158, 206
Rothblum, E. D., 409
Rotheram-Borus, M. J., 341
Rothermund, K., 506–507
Rothgänger, H., 127
Rothman, A. D., 408, 458
Rothman, E., 340
Rothman, M. T., 458
Roussotte, F., 71
Rovee-Collier, C., 98, 119
Rovee-Collier, C. K., 96, 97, 122
Rovine, M. J., 518
Rowe, G., 437, 495
Rowe, J., 80
Rowe, J. M., 464
Rowlingson, K., 409
Roy, A. L., 192
Roy, R. N., 410
Roy, T., 486
Royce, T., 393
Royne Stafford, M. B., 343
Røysamb, E., 275, 405
Rozario, P. A., 511
Rozas, A. X. P., 436, 438
Rubens, M. T., 495
Rubens, S. L., 264
Rubia, K., 253
Rubin, D. C., 496, 506
Rubin, H., 397
Rubin, K. H., 149, 262, 263, 264, 270, 334
Ruble, D. N., 199, 210, 213, 215, 297
Ruby, A., 315
Ruck, M., 262
Rudolph, E., 315
Rudolph, K. D., 299, 300, 315
Rudy, L., 181
Rueda, M. R., 179
Rueger, S. Y., 317
Ruff, H. A., 179
Ruffman, T., 183, 184
Ruggles, S., 405
Ruhn, C. J., 368
Ruicheva, I., 273
Rulison, K. L., 335
Rumney, P. G., 173
Runfola, C., 398
Runions, K. C., 250
Runyon, M., 279
Ruppar, T. M., 484
Rusbult, C. E., 401
Rusby, J. C., 334
Rushton, J. P., 55
Rusina, R., 489
Russ, S., 198
Russell, I., 484
Russell, M. J., 101
Russell, S. T., 343
Russo, M., 414
Russo, M. J., 279
Russo, R., 528
Rutherford, A., 15
Rutland, A., 335
Rutledge, T., 510
Rutter, M., 11, 22, 51, 55, 281, 298, 354, 355
Ruzgis, P., 241
Ryalls, B. O., 185
Ryan, A. M., 334
Ryan, C., 70
Ryan, E. E., 279
Ryan, R. M., 272, 277
Ryan, S., 341, 344
Rybash, J. M., 438
Rydell, A., 283
Ryff, C. D., 368, 450, 452, 454, 509
Ryncarz, R. A., 312, 377

Saad, A., 366
Saadati, N., 49

Saade, G., 49
Sääkslashti, A., 227
Saarni, C., 147
Sabbagh, M. A., 183, 184
Sabbagh, M. N., 478
Sabharwal, J., 495
Sachdev, H. P. S., 230
Sackett, P. R., 411
Sacks, M., 198
Sadler, T. L., 38–39, 43, 48, 62–63, 65, 67, 68, 71, 77, 375
Saed, G. M., 366
Saewyc, E., 279
Saewyc, E. M., 342
Safdar, S., 146
Saffran, J. R., 131
Sagar, K. A., 372
Sagi-Schwartz, A., 282
Sagi, A., 133, 156, 157
Saginak, K. A., 401
Saginak, M. A., 401
Saha, S., 79
Sahay, A., 479
Sahel, J.-A., 422
Sahni, R., 78
Sai, F. Z., 102, 103
Saigal, S., 80
Saint-Jacques, M.-C., 276
Sais, E., 249
Sakamoto, A., 332
Sakhardande, A., 353
Sakinofsky, I., 349
Saklofske, D. H., 238, 239
Sakraida, T. J., 459
Salamero, M., 489
Salekin, R. T., 148
Salem Yaniv, S., 74
Salguero, A., 515
Saliba, J., 251
Salihu, H. M., 74
Salmivalli, C., 265, 266
Salmon, D. A., 89
Salmon, D. P., 488, 490, 492
Salter, M. D., 152
Salthouse, T. A., 434, 437–438, 438–439, 440, 478, 495
Salum, G., 252
Salvioli, S., 366
Samanez-Larkin, G. R., 436, 496
Sameem, M., 350
Sameroff, A. J., 73, 205, 315, 330
Samper, P., 313
Sampselle, C. M., 426
Sampson, P. D., 68
Samson, D., 183, 260, 496
Sanchez-Garrido, M. A., 298
Sánchez-Medina, J. A., 187
Sanchez, M., 249
Sánchez, P. J., 68
Sanchis-Gomar, F., 366
Sandberg, J. F., 268
Sander, L., 440
Sanders, L. M., 462
Sanders, M., 205
Sanders, S., 515
Sanderson, C. A., 393
Sandfort, T. G. M., 272, 337, 340, 342, 343
Sandler, I. N., 276
Sandlin, D., 461
Sandman, C. A., 73
Sandvik, A. M., 433
Sandvik, L., 424
Sann, C., 103
Sano, M., 500
Sansavini, A., 130
Sanson, A., 148
Santelli, J. S., 340, 344
Santis, M., 68
Santos Garcia, J. B., 101
Santos-Lozano, A., 476
Santos, A., 252
Santos, C., 331
Santos, E. S., 101
Santos, P., 499
Sapp, F., 175, 176
Sapperstein, S. K., 94
Saraç, F., 425
Saralya, A., 282
Sardahaee, F. S., 492
Sarkadi, A., 156
Sarrazin, G., 238
Sarrazin, J., 276

Sass, S. A., 524
Sassler, S., 399
Sasson, I., 531
Sattler, C., 491
Saucier, M. G., 424
Sauck, C. C., 410
Saults, J. S., 235
Saunder-Goldson, M. S., 90
Savage, R., 236
Savci, E., 403, 404
Savia, J., 465
Savin-Williams, R. C., 339, 342, 404
Savino, F., 90
Savvas, M., 427
Sawaguchi, T., 236
Sawalani, G. M., 210
Sawyer, A. L., 266
Sawyer, K. S., 201
Saxton, M., 132
Sayal, K., 253
Sayer, A. G., 407, 413
Sbarra, D. A., 459
Scafato, E., 518
Scalo, M. D., 334
Scanlon, K., 192
Scaramella, L. V., 145
Scarmeas, N., 479
Scarr, S., 11, 52, 54
Schaal, B., 101
Schachar, R., 253
Schachner, A., 132
Schachter, F. F., 91
Schacter, D. L., 496
Schaeken, W., 233
Schafer, M. H., 452
Schaible, L. M., 355
Schaie, F. W., 438
Schaie, K. W., 434–436, 480, 496, 500, 517
Schaner, S. G., 525
Schantz, S. L., 253
Scharf, M., 332, 339, 391–392
Scharling, H., 369
Scharrer, E., 202
Schedle, A., 277, 408
Schelleman-Offermans, K., 300
Schellevis, F., 490
Scheltens, P., 489
Schepis, T. S., 353
Scherer, M., 240
Scherger, S., 511
Schiefman, S., 374
Schigelone, A. R. S., 515
Schimmele, C. M., 519
Schindler, H. S., 333
Schindler, I., 524
Schlechter, M., 203, 327
Schlegel, A., 292
Schlosser, L., 145
Schmajuk, G., 485
Schmidt, D. H. K., 309
Schmidt, H., 492
Schmidt, L., 365, 407
Schmidt, R., 492
Schmidt, U., 352
Schmitt, K. L., 202, 213
Schmitt, M., 452, 458
Schmitz, K. H., 301, 302
Schneider, A. L. C., 486
Schneider, B., 327
Schneider, B. H., 317
Schneider, J. K., 484
Schneider, M., 326
Schneider, W., 180, 182, 236, 237
Schneller, D. P., 459
Schniering, C. A., 334
Schnohr, P., 369
Schnur, E., 191
Schoenborn, 369
Schoeny, M. E., 334
Schofield, H.-L. T., 341
Schofield, T. J., 274, 275
Schollin, J., 101
Scholmerich, A., 146, 158
Scholnick, E. K., 179
Scholte, R. H., 328
Schonert-Reichl, K. A., 293, 313, 350
Schönknecht, P., 491
Schooler, C., 411
Schoon, I., 382
Schrager, S., 67
Schrander-Stumpel, C. T. R. M., 47
Schreiber, D., 51